Commentary
on the
OLD TESTAMENT

Commentary
on the
OLD TESTAMENT
IN TEN VOLUMES

by

C. F. KEIL and F. DELITZSCH

VOLUME I

The Pentateuch
Three Volumes in One

WILLIAM B. EERDMANS PUBLISHING COMPANY
Grand Rapids, Michigan

COMMENTARY ON THE OLD TESTAMENT
by C. F. Keil and F. Delitzsch
Translated from the German

Volumes translated by James Martin
THE PENTATEUCH
JOSHUA, JUDGES, RUTH
THE BOOKS OF SAMUEL
THE BOOKS OF THE KINGS
THE PROPHECIES OF ISAIAH
THE PROPHECIES OF EZEKIEL
THE TWELVE MINOR PROPHETS

Volumes translated by Andrew Harper
THE BOOKS OF THE CHRONICLES

Volumes translated by Sophia Taylor
THE BOOKS OF EZRA, NEHEMIAH, ESTHER

Volumes translated by Francis Bolton
THE BOOK OF JOB
THE PSALMS

Volumes translated by M. G. Easton
PROVERBS OF SOLOMON
THE SONG OF SONG AND ECCLESIASTES
THE BOOK OF DANIEL

Volumes translated by David Patrick
THE PROPHECIES OF JEREMIAH, VOL. I

Volumes translated by James Kennedy
THE PROPHECIES OF JEREMIAH, VOL. II

ISBN 0-8028-8035-5
Reprinted, January 1980

TABLE OF CONTENTS

THE SECOND BOOK OF MOSES (EXODUS).

INTRODUCTION.

PREFACE

THE Old Testament is the basis of the New. "God, who at sundry times and in divers manners spake unto the fathers by the prophets, hath spoken unto us by His only-begotten Son." The Church of Christ is built upon the foundation of the apostles and prophets. For Christ came not to destroy the law or the prophets, but to fulfil. As He said to the Jews, "Search the Scriptures, for in them ye think ye have eternal life, and they are they which testify of Me ;" so also, a short time before His ascension, He opened the understanding of His disciples, that they might understand the Scriptures, and beginning at Moses and all the prophets, expounded unto them in all the Scriptures the things concerning Himself. With firm faith in the truth of this testimony of our Lord, the fathers and teachers of the Church in all ages have studied the Old Testament Scriptures, and have expounded the revelations of God under the Old Covenant in learned and edifying works, unfolding to the Christian community the riches of the wisdom and knowledge of God which they contain, and impressing them upon the heart, for doctrine, for reproof, for improvement, for instruction in righteousness. It was reserved for the Deism, Naturalism, and Rationalism which became so prevalent in the closing quarter of the eighteenth century, to be the first to undermine the belief in the inspiration of the first covenant, and more and more to choke up this well of saving truth ; so that at the present day depreciation of the Holy Scriptures of the Old Testament is as widely spread as ignorance of what they really contain. At the same time, very much has been done during the last thirty years on the part of believers in divine revelation, to bring about a just appreciation and correct understanding of the Old Testament Scriptures.

May the Lord grant His blessing upon our labours, and assist with His own Spirit and power a work designed to promote the knowledge of His holy Word.

C. F. KEIL.

GENERAL INTRODUCTION

TO

THE FIVE BOOKS OF MOSES

———————

§ 1. PROLEGOMENA ON THE OLD TESTAMENT AND ITS LEADING DIVISIONS.

THE Holy Scriptures of the Old Testament contain the divine revelations which prepared the way for the redemption of fallen man by Christ. The revelation of God commenced with the creation of the heaven and the earth, when the triune God called into existence a world teeming with organized and living creatures, whose life and movements proclaimed the glory of their Creator; whilst, in the person of man, who was formed in the image of God, they were created to participate in the blessedness of the divine life. But when the human race, having yielded in its progenitors to the temptation of the wicked one, and forsaken the path appointed by its Creator, had fallen a prey to sin and death, and involved the whole terrestrial creation in the effects of its fall; the mercy of God commenced the work of restoration and redemption, which had been planned in the counsel of the triune love before the foundation of the world. Hence, from the very beginning, God not only manifested His eternal power and godhead in the creation, preservation, and government of the world and its inhabitants, but also revealed through His Spirit His purpose and desire for the well-being of man. This manifesta-

tion of the personal God upon and in the world assumed, in
consequence of the fall, the form of a plan of *salvation*, rising
above the general providence and government of the world, and
filling the order of nature with higher powers of spiritual life, in
order that the evil, which had entered through sin into the
nature of man and passed from man into the whole world,
might be overcome and exterminated, the world be transformed
into a kingdom of God in which all creatures should follow
His holy will, and humanity glorified into the likeness of God
by the complete transfiguration of its nature. These manifestations of divine grace, which made the history of the world
" a development of humanity into a kingdom of God under the
educational and judicial superintendence of the living God,"
culminated in the incarnation of God in Christ to reconcile the
world unto Himself.

This act of unfathomable love divides the whole course of
the world's history into two periods—the times of preparation,
and the times of accomplishment and completion. The former
extend from the fall of Adam to the coming of Christ, and have
their culminating point in the economy of the first covenant.
The latter commence with the appearance of the Son of God on
earth in human form and human nature, and will last till His
return in glory, when He will change the kingdom of grace
into the kingdom of glory through the last judgment and the
creation of a new heaven and new earth out of the elements of
the old world, " the heavens and the earth which are now."
The course of the universe will then be completed and closed,
and time exalted into eternity (1 Cor. xv. 23–28; Rev. xx.
and xxi.).

If we examine the revelations of the first covenant, as they
have been handed down to us in the sacred scriptures of the
Old Testament, we can distinguish three stages of progressive
development : preparation for the kingdom of God in its Old
Testament form; its establishment through the mediatorial
office of Moses; and its development and extension through
the prophets. In all these periods God revealed Himself and
His salvation to the human race by words and deeds. As the
Gospel of the New Covenant is not limited to the truths and
moral precepts taught by Christ and His apostles, but the fact
of the incarnation of God in Christ Jesus, and the work of re-

demption completed by the God-man through deeds and sufferings, death and resurrection, constitute the quintessence of the
Christian religion; so also the divine revelations of the Old
Covenant are not restricted to the truths proclaimed by Moses,
and by the patriarchs before him and prophets after him, as to
the real nature of God, His relation to the world, and the divine
destiny of man, but consist even more of the historical events
by which the personal and living God manifested Himself to
men in His infinite love, in acts of judgment and righteousness,
of mercy and grace, that He might lead them back to Himself
as the only source of life. Hence all the acts of God in history,
by which the rising tides of iniquity have been stemmed, and
piety and morality promoted, including not only the judgments
of God which have fallen upon the earth and its inhabitants,
but the calling of individuals to be the upholders of His salvation and the miraculous guidance afforded them, are to be regarded as essential elements of the religion of the Old Testament,
quite as much as the verbal revelations, by which God made
known His will and saving counsel through precepts and
promises to holy men, sometimes by means of higher and
supernatural light within them, at other times, and still more
frequently, through supernatural dreams, and visions, and theophanies in which the outward senses apprehended the sounds
and words of human language. Revealed religion has not only
been introduced into the world by the special interposition of
God, but is essentially a history of what God has done to
establish His kingdom upon the earth; in other words, to restore
a real personal fellowship between God whose omnipresence
fills the world, and man who was created in His image, in order
that God might renew and sanctify humanity by filling it with
His Spirit, and raise it to the glory of living and moving in
His fulness of life.

The way was opened for the establishment of this kingdom
in its Old Testament form by the call of Abraham, and his
election to be the father of that nation, with which the Lord
was about to make a covenant of grace as the source of blessing
to all the families of the earth. The *first stage* in the sacred
history commences with the departure of Abraham, in obedience
to the call of God, from his native country and his father's
house, and reaches to the time when the posterity promised to

the patriarch had expanded in Egypt into the twelve tribes of
Israel. The divine revelations during this period consisted of
promises, which laid the foundation for the whole future development of the kingdom of God on earth, and of that special
guidance, by which God proved Himself, in accordance with
these promises, to be the God of Abraham, Isaac, and Jacob.

The *second stage* commences with the call of Moses and the
deliverance of Israel from the bondage of Egypt, and embraces
the establishment of the Old Testament kingdom of God, not
only through the covenant which God made at Sinai with the
people of Israel, whom He had redeemed with mighty deeds out
of Egypt, but also through the national constitution, which He
gave in the Mosaic law to the people whom He had chosen as
His inheritance, and which regulated the conditions of their
covenant relation. In this constitution the eternal truths and
essential characteristics of the real, spiritual kingdom are set
forth in earthly forms and popular institutions, and are so far
incorporated in them, that the visible forms shadow forth
spiritual truths, and contain the germs of that spiritual and
glorified kingdom in which God will be all in all. In consequence of the design of this kingdom being merely to prepare
and typify the full revelation of God in His kingdom, its predominant character was that of law, in order that, whilst producing a deep and clear insight into human sinfulness and
divine holiness, it might excite an earnest craving for deliverance from sin and death, and for the blessedness of living
in the peace of God. But the laws and institutions of this
kingdom not only impressed upon the people the importance of
consecrating their whole life to the Lord God, they also opened
up to them the way of holiness and access to the grace of God,
whence power might be derived to walk in righteousness before
God, through the institution of a sanctuary which the Lord of
heaven and earth filled with His gracious presence, and of a
sacrificial altar which Israel might approach, and there in the
blood of the sacrifice receive the forgiveness of its sins and rejoice in the gracious fellowship of its God.

The *third stage* in the Old Testament history embraces the
progressive development of the kingdom of God established upon
Sinai, from the death of Moses, the lawgiver, till the extinction
of prophecy at the close of the Babylonian captivity. During

this lengthened period God revealed Himself as the covenant God and the monarch in His kingdom, partly by the special protection which He afforded to His people, so long as they were faithful to Him, or when they returned to Him after a time of apostasy and sought His aid, either by raising up warlike heroes to combat the powers of the world, or by miraculous displays of His own omnipotence, and partly by the mission of prophets endowed with the might of His own Spirit, who kept His law and testimony before the minds of the people, denounced judgment upon an apostate race, and foretold to the righteous the Messiah's salvation, attesting their divine mission, wherever it was necessary, by the performance of miraculous deeds. In the first centuries after Moses there was a predominance of the direct acts of God to establish His kingdom in Canaan, and exalt it to power and distinction in comparison with the nations round about. But after it had attained its highest earthly power, and when the separation of the ten tribes from the house of David had been followed by the apostasy of the nation from the Lord, and the kingdom of God was hurrying rapidly to destruction, God increased the number of prophets, and thus prepared the way by the word of prophecy for the full revelation of His salvation in the establishment of a new covenant.

Thus did the works of God go hand in hand with His revelation in the words of promise, of law, and of prophecy, in the economy of the Old Covenant, not merely as preparing the way for the introduction of the salvation announced in the law and in prophecy, but as essential factors of the plan of God for the redemption of man, as acts which regulated and determined the whole course of the world, and contained in the germ the consummation of all things;—the law, as a "schoolmaster to bring to Christ," by training Israel to welcome the Saviour; and prophecy, as proclaiming His advent with growing clearness, and even shedding upon the dark and deadly shades of a world at enmity against God, the first rays of the dawn of that coming day of salvation, in which the Sun of Righteousness would rise upon the nations with healing beneath His wings.

As the revelation of the first covenant may be thus divided into three progressive stages, so the documents containing this revelation, the sacred books of the Old Testament, have also been divided into three classes—the *Law*, the *Prophets*, and the *Hagio-*

grapha or holy writings. But although this triple classification of the Old Testament canon has reference not merely to three stages of canonization, but also to three degrees of divine inspiration, the three parts of the Old Testament do not answer to the three historical stages in the development of the first covenant. The only division sustained by the historical facts is that of *Law* and *Prophets*. These two contain all that was objective in the Old Testament revelation, and so distributed that the *Thorah*, as the five books of Moses are designated even in the Scriptures themselves, contains the groundwork of the Old Covenant, or that revelation of God in words and deeds which laid the foundation of the kingdom of God in its Old Testament form, and also those revelations of the primitive ages and the early history of Israel which prepared the way for this kingdom; whilst the *Prophets*, on the other hand, contain the revelations which helped to preserve and develop the Israelitish kingdom of God, from the death of Moses till its ultimate dissolution. The Prophets are also subdivided into two classes. The first of these embraces the so-called *earlier prophets* (*prophetæ priores*), *i.e.* the prophetical books of history (Joshua, Judges, Samuel, and the Kings), which contain the revelation of God as fulfilled in the historical guidance of Israel by judges, kings, high priests, and prophets; the second, the *later prophets* (*prophetæ posteriores*), *i.e.* the prophetical books of prediction (Isaiah, Jeremiah, Ezekiel, and the twelve minor prophets), which contain the progressive testimony to the counsel of God, delivered in connection with the acts of God during the period of the gradual decay of the Old Testament kingdom. The former, or historical books, are placed among the Prophets in the Old Testament canon, not merely because they narrate the acts of prophets in Israel, but still more, because they exhibit the development of the Israelitish kingdom of God from a prophet's point of view, and, in connection with the historical development of the nation and kingdom, set forth the progressive development of the revelation of God. The predictions of the later prophets, which were not composed till some centuries after the division of the kingdom, were placed in the same class with these, as being " the national records, which contained the pledge of the heavenly King, that the fall of His people and kingdom in the world had not taken place in opposition to His will, but expressly in accordance with it, and that He had not therefore given up His people and kingdom, but at some future time, when its inward condition allowed, would restore it again in new and more exalted power and glory" (*Auberlen*).

The other writings of the Old Covenant are all grouped together in the third part of the Old Testament canon under the title of γραφεῖα, *Scripta*, or *Hagiographa*, as being also composed under the influence of the Holy Ghost. The *Hagiographa* differ from the prophetical books both of history and prediction in their peculiarly subjective character, and the individuality of their representations of the facts and truths of divine revelation; a feature common to all the writings in this class, notwithstanding their diversities in form and subject-matter. They include, (1) the *poetical books*: Psalms, Job, Proverbs, Song of Solomon, Ecclesiastes, and the Lamentations of Jeremiah,—which bear witness of the spiritual fruits already brought to maturity in the faith, the thinking, and the life of the righteous by the revealed religion of the Old Covenant;—(2) the *book of Daniel*, who lived and laboured at the Chaldean and Persian court, with its rich store of divinely inspired dreams and visions, prophetic of the future history of the kingdom of God;—(3) the *historical books* of Ruth, Chronicles, Ezra, Nehemiah, and Esther, which depict the history of the government of David and his dynasty, with special reference to the relation in which the kings stood to the Levitical worship in the temple, and the fate of the remnant of the covenant nation, which was preserved in the downfall of the kingdom of Judah, from the time of its captivity until its return from Babylon, and its re-establishment in Jerusalem and Judah.

---

§ 2. TITLE, CONTENTS, AND PLAN OF THE BOOKS OF MOSES.

The five books of Moses (ἡ Πεντάτευχος sc. βίβλος, *Penta-teuchus sc. liber*, the book in five parts) are called in the Old Testament *Sepher hattorah, the Law-book* (Deut. xxxi. 26; Josh. i. 8, etc.), or, more concisely still, *Hattorah*, ὁ νόμος, *the Law* (Neh. viii. 2, 7, 13, etc.),—a name descriptive both of the contents of the work and of its importance in relation to the economy of the Old Covenant. The word תּוֹרָה, a Hiphil noun from הוֹרָה, *demonstrare, docere*, denotes instruction. The *Thorah* is the book of instruction, which Jehovah gave through Moses to the people of Israel, and is therefore called *Torath Jehovah* (2 Chron. xvii. 9, xxxiv. 14; Neh. ix. 3) and *Torath Mosheh* (Josh. viii. 31; 2 Kings xiv. 6; Neh. viii. 1), or *Sepher Mosheh,* the book of Moses (2 Chron. xxv. 4, xxxv. 12; Ezra vi. 18; Neh. xiii. 1). Its contents are a divine revelation in words and deeds, or rather *the* fundamental revelation, through which Jehovah selected Israel to be His people, and gave to them their rule of life (νομός), or theocratical constitution as a people and kingdom.

The entire work, though divided into five parts, forms both in plan and execution one complete and carefully constructed whole, commencing with the creation, and reaching to the death of Moses, the mediator of the Old Covenant. The foundation for the divine revelation was really laid in and along with the creation of the world. The world which God created is the scene of a history embracing both God and man, the site for the kingdom of God in its earthly and temporal form. All that the *first* book contains with reference to the early history of the human race, from Adam to the patriarchs of Israel, stands in a more or less immediate relation to the kingdom of God in Israel, of which the other books describe the actual establishment. The *second* depicts the inauguration of this kingdom at Sinai. Of the *third* and *fourth,* the former narrates the spiritual, the latter the political, organization of the kingdom by facts and legal precepts. The *fifth* recapitulates the whole in a hortatory strain, embracing both history and legislation, and impresses it upon the hearts of the people, for the purpose of arousing true fidelity to the covenant, and securing its lasting duration. The economy of the Old Covenant having been thus established, the revelation of the law closes with the death of its mediator.

The division of the work into five books was, therefore, the most simple and natural that could be adopted, according to the contents and plan which we have thus generally described. The three middle books contain the history of the establishment of the Old Testament kingdom; the first sketches the preliminary history, by which the way was prepared for its introduction; and the fifth recapitulates and confirms it. This fivefold division was not made by some later editor, but is founded in the entire plan of the law, and is therefore to be regarded as original. For even the three central books, which contain a continuous history of the establishment of the theocracy, are divided into three by the fact, that the middle portion, the third book of the Pentateuch, is separated from the other two, not only by its contents, but also by its introduction, chap. i. 1, and its concluding formula, chap. xxvii. 34.

---

§ 3. ORIGIN AND DATE OF THE BOOKS OF MOSES.

The five books of Moses occupy the first place in the canon of the Old Testament, not merely on account of their peculiar character as the foundation and norm of all the rest, but also because of their actual date, as being the oldest writings in the canon, and the groundwork of the whole of the Old Testament literature; all the historical, prophetic, and poetical works of the Israelites subsequent to the Mosaic era pointing back to the law of Moses as their primary source and type, and assuming the existence not merely of the law itself, but also of a book of the law, of precisely the character and form of the five books of Moses. In all the other historical books of the Old Testament not a single trace is to be found of any progressive expansion of, or subsequent additions to, the statutes and laws of Israel; for the account contained in 2 Kings xxii. and 2 Chron. xxxiv. of the discovery of the book of the law, *i.e.* of the copy placed by the side of the ark, cannot be construed, without a wilful perversion of the words, into a historical proof, that the Pentateuch or the book of Deuteronomy was composed at that time, or that it was then brought to light for the first time.[1] On

[1] *Vaihinger* seeks to give probability to *Ewald's* idea of the progressive growth of the Mosaic legislation, and also of the Pentateuch, during a period of nine or ten centuries, by the following argument :—" We observe in the law-books of the ancient Parsees, in the Zendavesta, and in the historical writings of India and Arabia, that it was a custom in the East to *supplement* the earlier works, and after a lapse of time to reconstruct them, so that whilst the root remained, the old stock was pruned and supplanted by a new one. Later editors constantly brought new streams to the old, until eventually the circle of legends and histories was closed, refined, and transfigured. Now, as the Israelites belonged to the same great family as

the contrary, we find that, from the time of Joshua to the age of Ezra and Nehemiah, the law of Moses and his book of the law were the only valid and unalterable code by which the national life was regulated, either in its civil or its religious institutions. Numerous cases undoubtedly occur, in which different commands contained in the law were broken, and particular ordinances were neglected; but even in the anarchical and troubled times of the Judges, public worship was performed in the tabernacle at Shiloh by priests of the tribe of Levi according to the directions of the *Thorah*, and the devout made their periodical pilgrimages to the house of God at the appointed feasts to worship and sacrifice before Jehovah at Shiloh (Judg. xviii. 31, cf Josh. xviii. 1; 1 Sam. i. 1–iv. 4). On the establishment of the monarchy (1 Sam. viii.–x.), the course adopted was in complete accordance with the laws contained in Deut. xvii. 14 sqq. The priesthood and the place of worship were reorganized by David and Solomon in perfect harmony with the law of Moses. Jehoshaphat made provision for the instruction of the people in the book of the law, and reformed the jurisdiction of the land according to its precepts (2 Chron. xvii. 7 sqq., xix. 4 sqq.). Hezekiah and Josiah not only abolished the idolatry introduced by their predecessors, as Asa had done, but restored the worship of Jehovah, and kept the Passover as a national feast, according to the regulations of the Mosaic law (2 Chron. xxix.–xxxi.; 2 Kings xxiii.; and 2 Chron. xxxiv. and xxxv.). Even in the kingdom of the ten tribes, which separated from the Davidic kingdom, the law of Moses retained its force not merely in questions of civil law, but also in connection with the religious life of the devout, in spite of

the rest of the Oriental nations (*sic!* so that the Parsees and Hindoos are Semitic!), and had almost everything in common with them so far as dress, manners, and customs were concerned, there is ground for the supposition, that their literature followed the same course" (*Herzog's Cycl.*). But to this we reply, that the literature of a nation is not an outward thing to be put on and worn like a dress, or adopted like some particular custom or habit, until something more convenient or acceptable induces a change; and that there is a considerable difference between Polytheism and heathen mythology on the one hand, and Monotheism and revealed religion on the other, which forbids us to determine the origin of the religious writings of the Israelites by the standard of the Indian Veda and Purana, or the different portions of the Zendavesta.

the worship established by Jeroboam in opposition to the law, as we may clearly see from the labours of Elijah and Elisha, of Hosea and Amos, within that kingdom. Moreover, all the historical books are richly stored with unmistakeable allusions and references to the law, which furnish a stronger proof than the actual mention of the book of the law, how deeply the *Thorah* of Moses had penetrated into the religious, civil, and political life of Israel. (For proofs, see my Introduction to the Old Test. § 34, i.)

In precisely the same way *prophecy* derived its authority and influence throughout from the law of Moses; for all the prophets, from the first to the last, invariably kept the precepts and prohibitions of the law before the minds of the people. They judged, reproved, and punished the conduct, the sins, the crimes of the people according to its rules; they resumed and expanded its threats and promises, proclaiming their certain fulfilment; and finally, they employed the historical events of the books of Moses for the purpose of reproof or consolation, frequently citing the very words of the *Thorah*, especially the threats and promises of Lev. xxvi. and Deut. xxviii., to give force and emphasis to their warnings, exhortations, and prophecies. And, lastly, the *poetry*, that flourished under David and Solomon, had also its roots in the law, which not only scans, illumines, and consecrates all the emotions and changes of a righteous life in the Psalms, and all the relations of civil life in the Proverbs, but makes itself heard in various ways in the book of Job and the Song of Solomon, and is even commended in Ecclesiastes (chap. xii. 13) as the sum and substance of true wisdom.

Again, the internal character of the book is in perfect harmony with this indisputable fact, that the Thorah, as *Delitzsch* says, "is as certainly presupposed by the whole of the post-Mosaic history and literature, as the root is by the tree." For it cannot be shown to bear any traces of post-Mosaic times and circumstances; on the contrary, it has the evident stamp of Mosaic origin both in substance and in style. All that has been adduced in proof of the contrary by the so-called modern criticism is founded either upon misunderstanding and misinterpretation, or upon a misapprehension of the peculiarities of the Semitic style of historical writing, or lastly upon doctrinal prejudices, in other words, upon a repudiation of all the super-

natural characteristics of divine revelation, whether in the form
of miracle or prophecy. The evidence of this will be given in
the Commentary itself, in the exposition of the passages which
have been supposed to contain either allusions to historical circumstances and institutions of a later age, or contradictions and
repetitions that are irreconcilable with the Mosaic origin of
the work. The Thorah "answers all the expectations which
a study of the personal character of Moses could lead us justly
to form of any work composed by him. He was one of those
master-spirits, in whose life the rich maturity of one historical
period is associated with the creative commencement of another,
in whom a long past culminates, and a far-reaching future
strikes its roots. In him the patriarchal age terminated, and
the period of the law began; consequently we expect to find
him, as a sacred historian, linking the existing revelation with
its patriarchal and primitive antecedents. As the mediator of
the law, he was a prophet, and, indeed, the greatest of all prophets: we expect from him, therefore, an incomparable, prophetic insight into the ways of God in both past and future.
He was learned in all the wisdom of the Egyptians; a work
from his hand, therefore, would show, in various intelligent
allusions to Egyptian customs, laws, and incidents, the well-
educated native of that land" (*Delitzsch*). In all these respects,
not only does the *Thorah* satisfy in a general manner the demands which a modest and unprejudiced criticism makes upon
a work of Moses; but on a closer investigation of its contents, it
presents so many marks of the Mosaic age and Mosaic spirit,
that it is *a priori* probable that Moses was its author. How
admirably, for example, was the way prepared for the revelation of God at Sinai, by the revelations recorded in Genesis
of the primitive and patriarchal times! The same God who,
when making a covenant with Abram, revealed Himself to him
in a vision as JEHOVAH who had brought him out of Ur of the
Chaldees (Gen. xv. 7), and who afterwards, in His character
of EL SHADDAI, *i.e.* the omnipotent God, maintained the covenant which He had made with him (Gen. xvii. 1 sqq.), giving
him in Isaac the heir of the promise, and leading and preserving
both Isaac and Jacob in their way, appeared to Moses at Horeb,
to manifest Himself to the seed of Abraham, Isaac, and Jacob
in the full significance of His name JEHOVAH, by redeeming

the children of Israel from the bondage of Egypt, and by ac-
cepting them as the people of His possession (Ex. vi. 2 sqq.).
How magnificent are the prophetic revelations contained in the
Thorah, embracing the whole future history of the kingdom of
God till its glorious consummation at the end of the world!
Apart from such promises as Gen. xii. 1–3, Ex. xix. 5, 6, and
others, which point to the goal and termination of the ways of
God from the very commencement of His work of salvation;
not only does Moses in the ode sung at the Red Sea behold his
people brought safely to Canaan, and Jehovah enthroned as the
everlasting King in the sanctuary established by Himself (Ex.
xv. 13, 17, 18), but from Sinai and in the plains of Moab he
surveys the future history of his people, and the land to which
they are about to march, and sees the whole so clearly in the
light of the revelation received in the law, as to foretell to a
people just delivered from the power of the heathen, that they
will again be scattered among the heathen for their apostasy
from the Lord, and the beautiful land, which they are about
for the first time to take possession of, be once more laid waste
(Lev. xxvi.; Deut. xxviii.–xxx., but especially xxxii.). And with
such exactness does he foretell this, that all the other prophets, in
their predictions of the captivity, base their prophecies upon the
words of Moses, simply extending the latter in the light thrown
upon them by the historical circumstances of their own times.[1]
How richly stored, again, are all five books with delicate and
casual allusions to Egypt, its historical events, its manners,
customs, and natural history! *Hengstenberg* has accumulated
a great mass of proofs, in his "Egypt and the Books of Moses,"
of the most accurate acquaintance on the part of the author of
the *Thorah*, with Egypt and its institutions. To select only a
few—and those such as are apparently trivial, and introduced
quite incidentally into either the history or the laws, but which
are as characteristic as they are conclusive,—we would mention
the thoroughly Egyptian custom of men carrying baskets upon
their heads, in the dream of Pharaoh's chief baker (Gen. xl. 16);
the shaving of the beard (xli. 14); prophesying with the cup

---

[1] Yet we never find in these words of Moses, or in the Pentateuch
generally, the name JEHOVAH SABAOTH, which was unknown in the Mosaic
age, but was current as early as the time of Samuel and David, and so
favourite a name with all the prophets.

(xliv. 5); the custom of embalming dead bodies and placing them in sarcophagi (l. 2, 3, and 26); the basket made of the papyrus and covered with asphalt and pitch (Ex. ii. 3), the prohibition against lying with cattle (Ex. xxii. 19; Lev. xviii. 23, xx. 15, 16), and against other unnatural crimes which were common in Egypt; the remark that Hebron was built seven years before Zoan in Egypt (Num. xiii. 22); the allusion in Num. xi. 5 to the ordinary and favourite food of Egypt; the Egyptian mode of watering (Deut. xi. 10, 11); the reference to the Egyptian mode of whipping (Deut. xxv. 2, 3); the express mention of the eruptions and diseases of Egypt (Deut. vii. 15, xxviii. 27, 35, 60), and many other things, especially in the account of the plagues, which tally so closely with the natural history of that country (Ex. vii. 8–x. 23).

In its general form, too, the *Thorah* answers the expectations which we are warranted in entertaining of a work of Moses. In such a work we should expect to find "the unity of a magnificent plan, comparative indifference to the mere details, but a comprehensive and spirited grasp of the whole and of salient points; depth and elevation combined with the greatest simplicity. In the magnificent unity of plan, we shall detect the mighty leader and ruler of a people numbering tens of thousands; in the childlike simplicity, the shepherd of Midian, who fed the sheep of Jethro far away from the varied scenes of Egypt in the fertile clefts of the mountains of Sinai" (*Delitzsch*). The unity of the magnificent plan of the *Thorah* we have already shown in its most general outlines, and shall point out still more minutely in our commentary upon the separate books. The childlike *naiveté* of the shepherd of Midian is seen most distinctly in those figures and similes drawn from the immediate contemplation of nature, which we find in the more rhetorical portions of the work. To this class belong such poetical expressions as "covering the eye of the earth" (Ex. x. 5, 15; Num. xxii. 5, 11); such similes as these: "as a nursing father beareth the suckling" (Num. xi. 12); "as a man doth bear his son" (Deut. i. 31); "as the ox licketh up the grass of the field" (Num. xxii. 4); "as sheep which have no shepherd" (Num. xxvii. 17); "as bees do" (Deut. i. 44); "as the eagle flieth" (Deut. xxviii. 49);—and again the figurative expressions "borne on eagles' wings" (Ex. xix. 4, cf. Deut. xxxii. 11); "de-

vouring fire" (Ex. xxiv. 17 ; Deut. iv. 24, ix. 3) ; "head and tail"
(Deut. xxviii. 13, 44) ; "a root that beareth gall and wormwood"
(Deut. xxix. 18); "wet to dry" (Deut. xxix. 19), and many others.

To this we may add the antiquated character of the style,
which is common to all five books, and distinguishes them essentially from all the other writings of the Old Testament. This
appears sometimes in the use of words, of forms, or of phrases,
which subsequently disappeared from the spoken language, and
which either do not occur again, or are only used here and
there by the writers of the time of the captivity and afterwards,
and then are taken from the Pentateuch itself ; at other times,
in the fact that words and phrases are employed in the books
of Moses in simple prose, which were afterwards restricted to
poetry alone ; or else have entirely changed their meaning.
For example, the pronoun הוּא and the noun נַעַר are used in the
Pentateuch for both genders, whereas the forms הִיא and נַעֲרָה
were afterwards employed for the feminine ; whilst the former
of these occurs only eleven times in the Pentateuch, the latter
only once. The demonstrative pronoun is spelt הָאֵל, afterwards
הָאֵלֶּה ; the infinitive construct of the verbs ל"ה is often written ה
or י without ת, as עֲשׂוֹ Gen. xxxi. 38, עֲשֹׂהוּ Ex. xviii. 18, רְאֹה Gen.
xlviii. 11 ; the third person plural of verbs is still for the most
part the full form ן, not merely in the imperfect, but also here
and there in the perfect, whereas afterwards it was softened into
י. Such words, too, as אָבִיב an ear of corn ; אַמְתַּחַת a sack ; בָּתַר
dissecuit hostias ; בֶּתֶר a piece ; גּוֹזָל a young bird ; זֶבֶד a present ;
זָבַד to present ; חֶרְמֵשׁ a sickle ; טֶנֶא a basket ; הַיְקוּם an existing,
living thing ; מַסְוֶה a veil, covering ; עֶקֶר a sprout (applied to
men) ; שְׁאֵר a blood-relation ; such forms as זָכוּר for זָכָר *mas,*
כֶּבֶשׂ for כֶּבֶשׂ a lamb ; phrases like נֶאֱסַף אֶל־עַמָּיו, "gathered to his
people ;" and many others which I have given in my Introduc-
tion,—you seek in vain in the other writings of the Old Testament, whilst the words and phrases, which are used there instead,
are not found in the books of Moses.

And whilst the contents and form of the *Thorah* bear witness that it belongs to the Mosaic age, there are express statements to the effect that it was written by Moses himself. Even
in the central books, certain events and laws are said to have
been written down. After the defeat of the Amalekites, for
example, Moses received orders from God to write the command

to exterminate Amalek, for a memorial, *in the book* (*i.e.* a book appointed for a record of the acts of the Lord in Israel : Ex. xvii. 14). According to Ex. xxiv. 3, 4, 7, Moses wrote the words of the covenant (Ex. xx. 2–17) and the laws of Israel (Ex. xxi.-xxiii.) in the book of the covenant, and read them to the people. Again, in Ex. xxxiv. 27, Moses is commanded to write the words of the renewed covenant, which he no doubt did. And lastly, it is stated in Num. xxxiii. 2, that he wrote an account of the different encampments of the Israelites in the desert, according to the commandment of God. It is true that these statements furnish no direct evidence of the Mosaic authorship of the whole Thorah ; but from the fact that the covenant of Sinai was to be concluded, and actually was concluded, on the basis of a written record of the laws and privileges of the covenant, it may be inferred with tolerable certainty, that Moses committed all those laws to writing, which were to serve the people as an inviolable rule of conduct towards God. And from the record, which God commanded to be made, of the two historical events already mentioned, it follows unquestionably, that it was the intention of God, that all the more important manifestations of the covenant fidelity of Jehovah should be handed down in writing, in order that the people in all time to come might study and lay them to heart, and their fidelity be thus preserved towards their covenant God. That Moses recognised this divine intention, and for the purpose of upholding the work already accomplished through his mediatorial office, committed to writing not merely the whole of the law, but the entire work of the Lord in and for Israel,—in other words, that he wrote out the whole *Thorah* in the form in which it has come down to us, and handed over the work to the nation before his departure from this life, that it might be preserved and obeyed,—is distinctly stated at the conclusion of the *Thorah*, in Deut. xxxi. 9, 24. When he had delivered his last address to the people, and appointed Joshua to lead them into their promised inheritance, " he wrote *this Thorah*, and delivered it unto the priests, the sons of Levi, and unto all the elders of Israel" (Deut. xxxi. 9), with a command that it was to be read to the people every seven years at the feast of Tabernacles, when they came to appear before the Lord at the sanctuary. Thereupon, it is stated (vers. 24 sqq.) that " it came to pass, when Moses had made an end of writing the words of this law in a book, to the very close, that Moses commanded the Levites, which bare the ark of the covenant of the Lord, saying : Take this book of the law, and put it by the side of the ark of the covenant of Jehovah your God, that it may be there for a witness against thee," etc.   This double testimony to the Mosaic authorship of the Thorah is confirmed still further by the command in Deut. xvii. 18, that the king to be afterwards chosen should cause a copy of this law to be written in a book by the Levitical priests, and should read therein all the days of his life, and by the repeated allusions to "the words of this law, which are written in this book," or "in the book of the law" (Deut. xxviii. 58, 61, xxix. 21, xxx. 10, xxxi. 26); for the former command and the latter allusions are not intelligible on any other supposition, than that Moses was engaged in writing the book of the law, and intended to hand it over to the nation in a complete form previous to his death ; though it may not have been finished when the command itself was written down and the words in question were uttered, but, as Deut. xxxi. 9 and 24 distinctly affirm, may have been completed after his address to the people, a short time before his death, by the arrangement and revision of the earlier portions, and the addition of the fifth and closing book.

The validity of this evidence must not be restricted, however, to the fifth book of the Thorah, viz. Deuteronomy, alone ; it extends to all five books, that is to say, to the whole connected work. For it cannot be exegetically proved from Deuteronomy, that the expression, "this law," in every passage of the book from chap. i. 5 to xxxi. 24 relates to the so-called *Deuterosis* of the law, *i.e.* to the fifth book alone, or that Deuteronomy was written before the other four books, the contents of which it invariably presupposes. Nor can it be historically proved that the command respecting the copy of the law to be made for the future king, and the regulations for the reading of the law at the feast of Tabernacles, were understood by the Jews as referring to Deuteronomy only. *Josephus* says nothing about any such limitation, but speaks, on the contrary, of the reading of the law generally (ὁ ἀρχιερεὺς . . . ἀναγινωσκέτω τοὺς νόμους πᾶσι, Ant. iv. 8, 12). The Rabbins, too, understand the words "this law," in Deut. xxxi. 9 and 24, as relating to the whole Thorah from Gen. i. to Deut. xxxiv., and only differ in opinion

as to the question whether Moses wrote the whole work at once
after his last address, or whether he composed the earlier books
gradually, after the different events and the publication of the
law, and then completed the whole by writing Deuteronomy and
appending it to the four books in existence already.[1]

[1] Cf. *Hävernick's* Introduction, and the opinions of the Rabbins on
Deut. xxxi. 9 and 24 in *Meyer's adnotatt. ad Seder Olam.* But as *Delitzsch*
still maintains that Deut. xxxi. 9 sqq. merely proves that the book of
Deuteronomy was written by Moses, and observes in support of this, that
at the time of the second temple it was an undoubted custom to read that
book alone at the feast of Tabernacles in the year of release, as is evident
from *Sota*, c. 7, and a passage of *Sifri* (one of the earliest *Midrashim* of the
school of Rab, born *c.* 165, .d. 247), quoted by *Rashi* on Sota 41, we will
give a literal translation of the two passages for the benefit of those who
may not possess the books themselves, that they may judge for themselves
what ground there is for this opinion. The passage from the *Sota* is headed,
*sectio regis quomodo, i.e. sectio a Rege prælegenda, quibus ritibus recitata
est,* and runs thus:—" Transacta festivitatis tabernaculorum prima die,
completo jam septimo anno et octavo ineunte, parabant Regi suggestum
ligneum in Atrio, huic insidebat juxta illud : a fine septem annorum, etc.
(Deut. xxxi. 10). Tum Ædituus (more correctly, diaconus Synagogæ)
sumto libro legis tradidit eum Primario cœtus (synagogæ), hic porrigebat
eum Antistiti, Antistes Summo Sacerdoti, Summus Sacerdos denique exhi-
bebat ipsum regi. Rex autem stans eum accipiebat, verum prælegens con-
sedit." Then follows a Haggada on a reading of King Agrippa's, and it
proceeds :—" Prælegit vero (rex) ab initio Deuteronomii usque ad illa :
Audi Israel (c. 4, 4), quæ et ipse prælegit. Tum subjecit (ex. c. 11, 13) :
Eritque si serio auscultaveritis, etc. Dehinc (ex. c. 14, 22) : Fideliter
decimato, etc. Postea (ex. c. 26, 22) : Cum absolveritis dare omnes deci-
mas, etc. Deinde sectionem de Rege (quæ habetur, c. 17, 14 sqq.). Denique benedictiones et exsecrationes (ex. cc. 27 et 28) usque dum totam
illam sectionem finiret." But how can a mere tradition of the Talmud like
this, respecting the formalities with which the king was to read certain
sections of the Thorah on the second day of the feast of Tabernacles, be
adduced as a proof that in the year of release the book of Deuteronomy
alone, or certain extracts from it, were read to the assembled people? Even
if this rule was connected with the Mosaic command in Deut. xxxi. 10, or
derived from it, it does not follow in the remotest degree, that either by
ancient or modern Judaism the public reading of the Thorah appointed by
Moses was restricted to this one reading of the king's. And even if the
precept in the Talmud was so understood or interpreted by certain Rabbins,
the other passage quoted by *Delitzsch* from *Sifri* in support of his opinion,
proves that this was not the prevailing view of the Jewish synagogue, or
of modern Judaism. The passage runs thus: " He (the king) shall write
אֶת מִשְׁנֵה הַתּוֹרָה הַזֹּאת. He shall do this himself, for he is not to use his
ancestor's copy. *Mishneh* in itself means nothing more than *Thorah Mishneh*

Still less can this evidence be set aside or rendered doubtful by the objection, offered by *Vaihinger*, that " Moses cannot have related his own death and burial (Deut. xxxiv.); and yet the account of these forms an essential part of the work as we possess it now, and in language and style bears a close resemblance to Num. xxvii. 12–23." The words in chap. xxxi. 24, " When Moses had finished writing the words of this law in a book to the end," are a sufficient proof of themselves that the account of his death was added by a different hand, without its needing to be distinctly stated.[1] The argument, moreover, re-

(Deuteronomy). How do I know that the other words of the *Thorah* were to be written also? This is evident from the Scriptures, which add, ' to do all the words of this law.' But if this be the case, why is it called *Mishneh Thorah?* Because there would be a transformation of the law. Others say that on the day of assembly Deuteronomy alone was read." From this passage of the ancient Midrash we learn, indeed, that many of the Rabbins were of opinion, that at the feast of Tabernacles in the sabbatical year, the book of Deuteronomy only was to be read, but that the author himself was of a different opinion; and, notwithstanding the fact that he thought the expression *Mishneh Thorah* must be understood as applying to the Deuterosis of the law, still maintained that the law, of which the king was to have a copy taken, was not only Deuteronomy, but the whole of the Pentateuch, and that he endeavoured to establish this opinion by a strange but truly rabbinical interpretation of the word *Mishneh* as denoting a transformation of the law.

[1] The weakness of the argument against the Mosaic authorship of the Thorah, founded upon the account of the death and burial of Moses, may be seen from the analogous case cited by *Hengstenberg in his Dissertation* on the Pentateuch. In the last book of the *Commentarii de statu religionis et reipublicæ Carolo V. Cæsare, by J. Sleidanus,* the account of Charles having abdicated and sailed to Spain is followed, without any break, by the words: " *Octobris die ultimo Joannes Sleidanus, J. U. L., vir et propter eximias animi dotes et singularem doctrinam omni laude dignus, Argentorati e vita decedit, atque ibidem honorifice sepelitur.*" This account of the death and burial of Sleidan is given in every edition of his *Commentarii,* containing the 26th book, which the author added to the 25 books of the first edition of April 1555, for the purpose of bringing down the life of Charles V. to his abdication in September 1556. Even in the very first edition, *Argentorati* 1558, it is added without a break, and inserted in the table of contents as an integral part of the book, without the least intimation that it is by a different hand. " No doubt the writer thought that it was quite unnecessary to distinguish himself from the author of the work, as everybody would know that a man could not possibly write an account of his own death and burial." Yet any one who should appeal to this as a proof that *Sleidan* was not the author of the *Commentarii,* would make himself ridiculous in the eyes of every student of history.

tains all its force, even if not only chap. xxxiv., the blessing of
Moses in chap. xxxiii., whose title proves it to be an appendix
to the Thorah, and the song in chap. xxxii., are included in the
supplement added by a different hand, but if the supplement
commences at chap. xxxi. 24, or, as *Delitzsch* supposes, at chap.
xxxi. 9. For even in the latter case, the precepts of Moses on
the reading of the Thorah at the feast of Tabernacles of the
year of release, and on the preservation of the copy by the side
of the ark, would have been inserted in the original prepared by
Moses himself before it was deposited in the place appointed;
and the work of Moses would have been concluded, after his
death, with the notice of his death and burial. The supplement
itself was undoubtedly added, not merely by a contemporary,
but by a man who was intimately associated with Moses, and
occupied a prominent position in the Israelitish community, so
that his testimony ranks with that of Moses.

Other objections to the Mosaic authorship we shall notice,
so far as they need any special refutation, in our commentary
upon the passages in question. At the close of our exposition
of the whole five books, we will review the modern hypotheses,
which regard the work as the resultant of frequent revisions.

------

§ 4. HISTORICAL CHARACTER OF THE BOOKS OF MOSES.

Acknowledgment of the historical credibility of the facts
recorded in the books of Moses requires a previous admission of
the reality of a supernatural revelation from God. The wide-
spread naturalism of modern theologians, which deduces the
origin and development of the religious ideas and truths of the
Old Testament from the nature of the human mind, must of
necessity remit all that is said in the Pentateuch about direct or
supernatural manifestations or acts of God, to the region of fictitious sagas and myths, and refuse to admit the historical truth
and reality of miracles and prophecies. But such an opinion
must be condemned as neither springing from the truth nor
leading to the truth, on the simple ground that it is directly at
variance with what Christ and His apostles have taught in the
New Testament with reference to the Old, and also as leading
either to an unspiritual Deism or to a comfortless Pantheism,

which ignores the working of God on the one hand, and the
inmost nature of the human mind on the other.   Of the reality
of the divine revelations, accompanied by miracles and prophecies, the Christian, *i.e.* the believing Christian, has already a
pledge in the miracle of regeneration and the working of the
Holy Spirit within his own heart.   He who has experienced in
himself this spiritual miracle of divine grace, will also recognise
as historical facts the natural miracles, by which the true and
living God established His kingdom of grace in Israel, wherever
the testimony of eye-witnesses ensures their credibility.   Now
we have this testimony in the case of all the events of Moses'
own time, from his call downwards, or rather from his birth till
his death; that is to say, of all the events which are narrated
in the last four books of Moses.   The legal code contained in
these books is now acknowledged by the most naturalistic opponents of biblical revelation to have proceeded from Moses, so far
as its most essential elements are concerned; and this is in itself
a simple confession that the Mosaic age is not a dark and mythical one, but falls within the clear light of history.   The events
of such an age might, indeed, by possibility be transmuted into
legends in the course of centuries; but only in cases where they
had been handed down from generation to generation by simple
word of mouth.   Now this cannot apply to the events of the
Mosaic age; for even the opponents of the Mosaic origin of the
Pentateuch admit, that the art of writing had been learned by
the Israelites from the Egyptians long before that time, and
that not merely separate laws, but also memorable events, were
committed to writing.   To this we must add, that the historical
events of the books of Moses contain no traces of legendary
transmutation, or mythical adornment of the actual facts.   Cases
of discrepancy, which some critics have adduced as containing
proofs of this, have been pronounced by others of the same theological school to be quite unfounded.   Thus *Bertheau* says, with
regard to the supposed contradictions in the different laws: " It
always appears to me rash, to assume that there are contradictions in the laws, and to adduce these as evidence that the contradictory passages must belong to different periods.   The state
of the case is really this: even if the Pentateuch did gradually
receive the form in which it has come down to us, whoever made
additions must have known what the existing contents were, and

would therefore not only admit nothing that was contradictory, but would erase anything contradictory that might have found its way in before. The liberty to make additions does not appear to me to be either greater, or more involved in difficulties, than that to make particular erasures." And on the supposed discrepancies in the historical accounts, *C. v. Lengerke* himself says: " The discrepancies which some critics have discovered in the historical portions of Deuteronomy, as compared with the earlier books, have really no existence." Throughout, in fact, the pretended contradictions have for the most part been introduced into the biblical text by the critics themselves, and have so little to sustain them in the narrative itself, that on closer research they resolve themselves into mere appearance, and the differences can for the most part be easily explained.—The result is just the same in the case of the repetitions of the same historical events, which have been regarded as legendary reduplications of things that occurred but once. There are only two miraculous occurrences mentioned in the Mosaic era which are said to have been repeated; only two cases, therefore, in which it is possible to place the repetition to the account of legendary fiction: viz. the feeding with quails, and bringing of water from a rock. But both of these are of such a character that the appearance of identity vanishes entirely before the distinctness of the historical accounts, and the differences in the attendant circumstances. The first feeding with quails took place in the desert of Sin, before the arrival of the Israelites at Sinai, in the second month of the first year; the second occurred after their departure from Sinai, in the second month of the second year, at the so-called graves of lust. The latter was sent as a judgment or plague, which brought the murmurers into the graves of their lust; the former merely supplied the deficiency of animal food. The water was brought from the rock the first time in Rephidim, during the first year of their journey, at a spot which was called in consequence *Massah and Meribah;* the second time, at Kadesh, in the fortieth year,—and on this occasion Moses and Aaron sinned so grievously that they were not allowed to enter Canaan.

It is apparently different with the historical contents of the book of Genesis. If Genesis was written by Moses, even between the history of the patriarchs and the time of Moses there is an interval of four or five centuries, in which the tradition might possibly have been corrupted or obscured. But to infer the reality from the bare possibility would be a very unscientific proceeding, and at variance with the simplest rules of logic. Now, if we look at the history which has been handed down to us in the book of Genesis from the primitive times of the human race and the patriarchal days of Israel, the traditions from the primitive times are restricted to a few simple incidents naturally described, and to genealogies which exhibit the development of the earliest families, and the origin of the different nations, in the plainest possible style. These transmitted accounts have such a genuine historical stamp, that no well-founded question can be raised concerning their credibility; but, on the contrary, all thorough historical research into the origin of different nations only tends to their confirmation. This also applies to the patriarchal history, in which, with the exception of the divine manifestations, nothing whatever occurs that could in the most remote degree call to mind the myths and fables of the heathen nations, as to the lives and deeds of their heroes and progenitors. There are three separate accounts, indeed, in the lives of Abraham and Isaac of an abduction of their wives; and modern critics can see nothing more in these, than three different mythical embellishments of one single event. But on a close and unprejudiced examination of the three accounts, the attendant circumstances in all three cases are so peculiar, and correspond so exactly to the respective positions, that the appearance of a legendary multiplication vanishes, and all three events must rest upon a good historical foundation. "As the history of the world, and of the plan of salvation, abounds not only in repetitions of wonderful events, but also in wonderful repetitions, critics had need act modestly, lest in excess of wisdom they become foolish and ridiculous" (*Delitzsch*). Again, we find that in the guidance of the human race, from the earliest ages downwards, more especially in the lives of the three patriarchs, God prepared the way by revelations for the covenant which He made at Sinai with the people of Israel. But in these preparations we can discover no sign of any legendary and unhistorical transference of later circumstances and institutions, either Mosaic or post-Mosaic, to the patriarchal age; and they are sufficiently justified by the facts themselves, since the Mosaic economy cannot possibly have been brought into the world, like a *deus ex machina*, without the slightest previous preparation. The natural simplicity of the patriarchal life, which shines out in every narrative, is another thing that produces on every unprejudiced reader the impression of a genuine historical tradition. This tradition, therefore, even though for the most part transmitted from generation to generation by word of mouth alone, has every title to credibility, since it was perpetuated within the patriarchal family, " in which, according to divine command (Gen. xviii. 19), the manifestations of God in the lives of the fathers were handed down as an heirloom, and that with all the greater ease, in proportion to the longevity of the patriarchs, the simplicity of their life, and the closeness of their seclusion from foreign and discordant influences. Such a tradition would undoubtedly be guarded with the greatest care. It was the foundation of the very existence of the chosen family, the bond of its unity, the mirror of its duties, the pledge of its future history, and therefore its dearest inheritance" (*Delitzsch*). But we are by no means to suppose that all the accounts and incidents in the book of Genesis were dependent upon oral tradition ; on the contrary, there is much which was simply copied from written documents handed down from the earliest times. Not only the ancient genealogies, which may be distinguished at once from the historical narratives by their antique style, with its repetitions of almost stereotyped formularies, and by the peculiar forms of the names which they contain, but certain historical sections—such, for example, as the account of the war in Gen. xiv., with its superabundance of genuine and exact accounts of a primitive age, both historical and geographical, and its old words, which had disappeared from the living language before the time of Moses, as well as many others—were unquestionably copied by Moses from ancient documents. (See *Hävernick's* Introduction.)

To all this must be added the fact, that the historical contents, not of Genesis only, but of all the five books of Moses, are pervaded and sustained by the spirit of true religion. This spirit has impressed a seal of truth upon the historical writings of the Old Testament, which distinguishes them from all merely human historical compositions, and may be recognised in the fact, that to all who yield themselves up to the influence of the Spirit which lives and moves in them, it points the way to the knowledge of that salvation which God Himself has revealed.

THE FIRST BOOK OF MOSES

(GENESIS.)

INTRODUCTION

CONTENTS, DESIGN, AND PLAN OF THE BOOK OF GENESIS.

THE first book of Moses, which has the superscription בראשית in the original, Γένεσις Κόσμου in the *Cod. Alex.* of the LXX., and is called *liber creationis* by the Rabbins, has received the name of GENESIS from its entire contents. Commencing with the creation of the heaven and the earth, and concluding with the death of the patriarchs Jacob and Joseph, this book supplies us with information with regard not only to the first beginnings and earlier stages of the world and of the human race, but also to those of the divine institutions which laid the foundation for the kingdom of God. Genesis commences with the creation of the world, because the heavens and the earth form the appointed sphere, so far as time and space are concerned, for the kingdom of God; because God, according to His eternal counsel, appointed the world to be the scene both for the revelation of His invisible essence, and also for the operations of His eternal love within and among His creatures; and because in the beginning He created the world to be and to become the kingdom of God. The creation of the heaven and the earth, therefore, receives as its centre, paradise; and in paradise, man, created in the image of God, is the head and crown of all created beings. The history of the world and of the kingdom of God begins with him. His fall from God brought death and corruption into the whole creation (Gen. iii. 17 sqq.; Rom. viii. 19 sqq.); his redemp-

tion from the fall will be completed in and with the glorification of the heavens and the earth (Isa. lxv. 17, lxvi. 22 ; 2
Pet. iii. 13 ; Rev. xxi. 1). By sin, men have departed and
separated themselves from God; but God, in His infinite mercy,
has not cut Himself off from men, His creatures. Not only
did He announce redemption along with punishment immediately after the fall, but from that time forward He continued
to reveal Himself to them, that He might draw them back to
Himself, and lead them from the path of destruction to the way
of salvation. And through these operations of God upon the
world in theophanies, or revelations by word and deed, the historical development of the human race became a history of the
plan of salvation. The book of Genesis narrates that history in
broad, deep, comprehensive sketches, from its first beginning to
the time of the patriarchs, whom God chose from among the
nations of the earth to be the bearers of salvation for the entire
world. This long space of 2300 years (from Adam to the
flood, 1656 ; to the entrance of Abram into Canaan, 365 ; to
Joseph's death, 285 ; in all, 2306 years) is divisible into two
periods. The *first period* embraces the development of the
human race from its first creation and fall to its dispersion over
the earth, and the division of the one race into many nations,
with different languages (chap. ii. 4–xi. 26) ; and is divided by
the flood into two distinct ages, which we may call the primeval
age and the preparatory age. All that is related of the *primeval
age*, from Adam to Noah, is the history of the fall ; the mode of
life, and longevity of the two families which descended from the
two sons of Adam ; and the universal spread of sinful corruption
in consequence of the intermarriage of these two families, who
differed so essentially in their relation to God (chap. ii. 4–vi. 8).
The primeval history closes with the flood, in which the old
world perished (chap. vi. 9–viii. 19). Of the *preparatory age*,
from Noah to Terah the father of Abraham, we have an account
of the covenant which God made with Noah, and of Noah's
blessing and curse ; the genealogies of the families and tribes
which descended from his three sons ; an account of the confusion of tongues, and the dispersion of the people ; and the
genealogical table from Shem to Terah (chap. viii. 20–xi. 26).—
The *second period* consists of the patriarchal era. From this we
have an elaborate description cf the lives of the three patriarchs

of Israel, the family chosen to be the people of God, from the call of Abraham to the death of Joseph (chap. xi. 27–l.).   Thus the history of humanity is gathered up into the history of the one family, which received the promise, that God would multiply it into a great people, or rather into a multitude of peoples, would make it a blessing to all the families of the earth, and would give it the land of Canaan for an everlasting possession.

This general survey will suffice to bring out the *design* of the book of Genesis, viz., to relate the early history of the Old Testament kingdom of God.   By a simple and unvarnished description of the development of the world under the guidance and discipline of God, it shows how God, as the preserver and governor of the world, dealt with the human race which He had created in His own image, and how, notwithstanding their fall and through the misery which ensued, He prepared the way for the fulfilment of His original design, and the establishment of the kingdom which should bring salvation to the world. Whilst by virtue of the blessing bestowed in their creation, the human race was increasing from a single pair to families and nations, and peopling the earth; God stemmed the evil, which sin had introduced, by words and deeds, by the announcement of His will in commandments, promises, and threats, and by the infliction of punishments and judgments upon the despisers of His mercy.   Side by side with the law of expansion from the unity of a family to the plurality of nations, there was carried on from the very first a law of separation between the ungodly and those that feared God, for the purpose of preparing and preserving a holy seed for the rescue and salvation of the whole human race.   This double law is the organic principle which lies at the root of all the separations, connections, and disposi- tions which constitute the history of the book of Genesis.   In accordance with the law of reproduction, which prevails in the preservation and increase of the human race, the genealogies show the historical bounds within which the persons and events that marked the various epochs are confined; whilst the law of selection determines the arrangement and subdivision of such historical materials as are employed.

So far as the *plan* of the book is concerned, the historical contents are divided into ten groups, with the uniform heading, " *These are the generations* " (with the exception of chap. v. 1 :

" This is the book of the generations "); the account of the
creation forming the substratum of the whole. These groups
consist of the *Tholedoth* : 1. of the heavens and the earth (chap.
ii. 4–iv. 26); 2. of Adam (v. 1–vi. 8); 3. of Noah (vi. 9–ix.
29); 4. of Noah's sons (x. 1–xi. 9); 5. of Shem (xi. 10–26);
6. of Terah (xi. 27–xxv. 11); 7. of Ishmael (xxv. 12–18); 8.
of Isaac (xxv. 19–xxxv. 29); 9. of Esau (xxxvi.); and 10. of
Jacob (xxxvii.–l.). There are five groups in the first period,
and five in the second. Although, therefore, the two periods
differ considerably with regard to their scope and contents, in
their historical importance to the book of Genesis they are upon
a par ; and the number *ten* stamps upon the entire book, or
rather upon the early history of Israel recorded in the book, the
character of completeness. This arrangement flowed quite
naturally from the contents and purport of the book. The two
periods, of which the early history of the kingdom of God in
Israel consists, evidently constitute two great divisions, so far as
their internal character is concerned. All that is related of
the first period, from Adam to Terah, is obviously connected, no
doubt, with the establishment of the kingdom of God in Israel,
but only in a remote degree. The account of paradise exhibits
the primary relation of man to God and his position in the
world. In the fall, the necessity is shown for the interposition
of God to rescue the fallen. In the promise which followed the
curse of transgression, the first glimpse of redemption is seen.
The division of the descendants of Adam into a God-fearing and
an ungodly race exhibits the relation of the whole human race
to God. The flood prefigures the judgment of God upon the
ungodly; and the preservation and blessing of Noah, the protection of the godly from destruction. And lastly, in the
genealogy and division of the different nations on the one hand,
and the genealogical table of Shem on the other, the selection of
one nation is anticipated to be the recipient and custodian of
the divine revelation. The special preparations for the training
of this nation commence with the call of Abraham, and consist
of the care bestowed upon Abraham, Isaac, and Jacob, and their
posterity, and of the promises which they received. The leading
events in the first period, and the prominent individuals in the
second, also furnished, in a simple and natural way, the requisite
points of view for grouping the historical materials of each under

a fivefold division. The proof of this will be found in the exposition. Within the different groups themselves the arrangement adopted is this: the materials are arranged and distributed according to the law of divine selection; the families which branched off from the main line are noticed first of all; and when they have been removed from the general scope of the history, the course of the main line is more elaborately described, and the history itself is carried forward. According to this plan, which is strictly adhered to, the history of Cain and his family precedes that of Seth and his posterity; the genealogy of Japhet and Ham stands before that of Shem; the history of Ishmael and Esau, before that of Isaac and Jacob; and the death of Terah, before the call and migration of Abraham to Canaan. In this regularity of composition, according to a settled plan, the book of Genesis may clearly be seen to be the careful production of one single author, who looked at the historical development of the human race in the light of divine revelation, and thus exhibited it as a complete and well arranged introduction to the history of the Old Testament kingdom of God.

THE CREATION OF THE WORLD.

CHAP. I. 1–II. 3.

The account of the creation, its commencement, progress, and completion, bears the marks, both in form and substance, of a historical document in which it is intended that we should accept as actual truth, not only the assertion that God created the heavens, and the earth, and all that lives and moves in the world, but also the description of the creation itself in all its several stages. If we look merely at the *form* of this document, its place at the beginning of the book of Genesis is sufficient to warrant the expectation that it will give us history, and not fiction, or human speculation. As the development of the human family has been from the first a historical fact, and as man really occupies that place in the world which this record assigns him, the creation of man, as well as that of the earth on which, and the heaven for which, he is to live, must also be a work of God, *i.e.* a fact of objective truth and reality. The grand simplicity of the account is in perfect harmony with the fact. " The whole narrative is sober, definite, clear, and concrete. The historical events described contain a rich treasury of speculative thoughts and poetical glory; but they themselves are free from the influence of human invention and human philosophizing" (*Delitzsch*). This is also true of the arrangement of the whole. The work of creation does not fall, as *Herder* and others maintain, into two triads of days, with the work of the second answering to that of the first. For although the creation of the light on the first day seems to correspond to that of the light-bearing stars on the fourth, there is no reality in the parallelism which some discover between the second and third days on the one hand, and the third and fourth on the other. On the second day the firmament or atmosphere is formed ; on the fifth, the fish and fowl. On the third, after the sea and land are separated, the plants are formed ; on the sixth, the animals of the dry land and man. Now, if the creation of the fowls which fill the air answers to that of the firmament, the formation of the fish as the inhabitants of the waters ought to be assigned to the sixth day, and not to the fifth, as being parallel to the creation of the seas. The creation of the fish and fowl on the same day is an evident proof that a parallelism between the first three days of creation and the last three is not intended, and does not exist. Moreover, if the division of the work of creation into so many days had been the result of human reflection ; the creation of man, who was appointed lord of the earth, would certainly not have been assigned to the same day as that of the beasts and reptiles, but would have been kept distinct from the creation of the beasts, and allotted to the seventh day, in which the creation was completed,—a meaning which *Richers* and *Keerl* have actually tried to force upon the text of the Bible. In the different acts of creation we perceive indeed an evident progress from the general to the particular, from the lower to the higher orders of creatures, or rather a steady advance towards more and more concrete forms. But on the fourth day this progress is interrupted in a way which we cannot explain. In the transition from the creation of the plants to that of sun, moon, and stars, it is impossible to discover either a " well-arranged and constant progress," or " a genetic advance," since the stars are not intermediate links between plants and animals, and, in fact, have no place at all in the scale of earthly creatures. —If we pass on to the *contents* of our account of the creation, they differ as widely from all other cosmogonies as truth from fiction. Those of heathen nations are either hylozoistical, deducing the origin of life and living beings from some primeval matter; or pantheistical, regarding the whole world as emanating from a common divine substance; or mythological, tracing both gods and men to a chaos or world-egg. They do not even rise to the notion of a creation, much less to the knowledge of an almighty God, as the Creator of all things.[1] Even in the Etruscan and Persian myths, which correspond so remarkably to the biblical account that they must have been derived from it, the successive acts of creation are arranged according to the suggestions of human probability and adaptation.[2] In contrast

[1] According to *Berosus* and *Syncellus*, the Chaldean myth represents the "All" as consisting of darkness and water, filled with monstrous creatures, and ruled by a woman, *Markaya*, or Ὁμόρωκα (? Ocean). Bel divided the darkness, and cut the woman into two halves, of which he formed the heaven and the earth; he then cut off his own head, and from the drops of blood men were formed.—According to the Phœnician myth of *Sanchuniathon*, the beginning of the All was a movement of dark air, and a dark, turbid chaos. By the union of the spirit with the All, Μώτ, *i.e.* slime, was formed, from which every seed of creation and the universe was developed; and the heavens were made in the form of an egg, from which the sun and moon, the stars and constellations, sprang. By the heating of the earth and sea there arose winds, clouds and rain, lightning and thunder, the roaring of which wakened up sensitive beings, so that living creatures of both sexes moved in the waters and upon the earth. In another passage Sanchuniathon represents Κολπία (probably קוֹל פִּיחַ, the moaning of the wind) and his wife Βάαυ (*bohu*) as producing Αἰών and πρωτόγονος, two mortal men, from whom sprang Γένος and Γενεά, the inhabitants of Phœnicia.—It is well known from *Hesiod's theogony* how the Grecian myth represents the gods as coming into existence at the same time as the world. The numerous inventions of the Indians, again, all agree in this, that they picture the origin of the world as an emanation from the absolute, through Brahma's thinking, or through the contemplation of a primeval being called *Tad* (it).—Buddhism also acknowledges no God as creator of the world, teaches no creation, but simply describes the origin of the world and the beings that inhabit it as the necessary consequence of former acts performed by these beings themselves.

[2] According to the Etruscan saga, which *Suidas* quotes from a historian, who was a " παρ αὐτοῖς (the Tyrrhenians) ἔμπειρος ἀνήρ (therefore

with all these mythical inventions, the biblical account shines out in the clear light of truth, and proves itself by its contents to be an integral part of the revealed history, of which it is accepted as the pedestal throughout the whole of the sacred Scriptures. This is not the case with the Old Testament only; but in the New Testament also it is accepted and taught by Christ and the apostles as the basis of the divine revelation. To select only a few from the many passages of the Old and New Testaments, in which God is referred to as the Creator of the heavens and the earth, and the almighty operations of the living God in the world are based upon the fact of its creation: in Ex. xx. 9–11, xxxi. 12–17, the command to keep the Sabbath is founded upon the fact that God rested on the seventh day, when the work of creation was complete; and in Ps. viii. and civ., the creation is depicted as a work of divine omnipotence in close adherence to the narrative before us. From the creation of man, as described in Gen. i. 27 and ii. 24, Christ demonstrates the indissoluble character of marriage as a divine ordinance (Matt. xix. 4–6); Peter speaks of the earth as standing out of the water and in the water by the word of God (2 Pet. iii. 5); and the author of the Epistle to the Hebrews, "starting from Gen. ii. 2, describes it as the motive principle of all history, that the Sabbath of God is to become the Sabbath of the creature" (*Delitzsch*).

The biblical account of the creation can also vindicate its claim to be true and actual history, in the presence of the doctrines of philosophy and the established results of natural science. So long, indeed, as philosophy undertakes to construct the universe from general ideas, it will be utterly unable to comprehend the creation; but ideas will never explain the exist-

not a native)," God created the world in six periods of one thousand years each: in the first, the heavens and the earth; in the second, the firmament; in the third, the sea and other waters of the earth; in the fourth, sun, moon, and stars; in the fifth, the beasts of the air, the water, and the land; in the sixth, men. The world will last twelve thousand years, the human race six thousand.—According to the saga of the Zend in Avesta, the supreme Being Ormuzd created the visible world by his word in six periods or thousands of years: (1) the heaven, with the stars; (2) the water on the earth, with the clouds; (3) the earth, with the mountain Alborj and the other mountains; (4) the trees; (5) the beasts, which sprang from the primeval beast; (6) men, the first of whom was Kajomorts. Every one of these separate creations is celebrated by a festival. The world will last twelve thousand years.

ence of things. Creation is an act of the personal God, not a
process of nature, the development of which can be traced to
the laws of birth and decay that prevail in the created world.
But the work of God, as described in the history of creation, is
in perfect harmony with the correct notions of divine omnipotence, wisdom, and goodness. The assertion, so frequently made,
that the course of the creation takes its form from the Hebrew
week, which was already in existence, and the idea of God's resting on the seventh day, from the institution of the Hebrew Sabbath, is entirely without foundation. There is no allusion in
Gen. ii. 2, 3 to the Sabbath of the Israelites; and the week of
seven days is older than the Sabbath of the Jewish covenant.
Natural research, again, will never explain the origin of the
universe, or even of the earth; for the creation lies beyond the
limits of the territory within its reach. By all modest naturalists, therefore, it is assumed that the origin of matter, or of the
original material of the world, was due to an act of divine creation. But there is no firm ground for the conclusion which they
draw, on the basis of this assumption, with regard to the formation or development of the world from its first chaotic condition
into a fit abode for man. All the theories which have been
adopted, from *Descartes* to the present day, are not the simple
and well-established inductions of natural science founded upon
careful observation, but combinations of partial discoveries empirically made, with speculative ideas of very questionable worth.
The periods of creation, which modern geology maintains with
such confidence, that not a few theologians have accepted them
as undoubted and sought to bring them into harmony with the
scriptural account of the creation, if not to deduce them from
the Bible itself, are inferences partly from the successive strata
which compose the crust of the earth, and partly from the
various fossil remains of plants and animals to be found in
those strata. The former are regarded as proofs of successive
formation; and from the difference between the plants and
animals found in a fossil state and those in existence now, the
conclusion is drawn, that their creation must have preceded the
present formation, which either accompanied or was closed by
the advent of man. But it is not difficult to see that the former
of these conclusions could only be regarded as fully established,
if the process by which the different strata were formed were

clearly and fully known, or if the different formations were
always found lying in the same order, and could be readily distinguished from one another. But with regard to the origin of
the different species of rock, geologists, as is well known, are
divided into two contending schools : the Neptunists, who attribute all the mountain formations to deposit in water; and the
Plutonists, who trace all the non-fossiliferous rocks to the action
of heat. According to the Neptunists, the crystalline rocks are
the earliest or primary formations; according to the Plutonists,
the granite burst through the transition and stratified rocks, and
were driven up from within the earth, so that they are of later
date. But neither theory is sufficient to account in this mechanical way for all the phenomena connected with the relative
position of the rocks ; consequently, a third theory, which supposes the rocks to be the result of chemical processes, is steadily
gaining ground. Now if the rocks, both crystalline and stratified, were formed, not in any mechanical way, but by chemical
processes, in which, besides fire and water, electricity, galvanism,
magnetism, and possibly other forces at present unknown to
physical science were at work ; the different formations may
have been produced contemporaneously and laid one upon
another. Till natural science has advanced beyond mere opinion and conjecture, with regard to the mode in which the rocks
were formed and their positions determined ; there can be no
ground for assuming that conclusions drawn from the successive
order of the various strata, with regard to the periods of their
formation, must of necessity be true. This is the more apparent,
when we consider, on the one hand, that even the principal formations (the primary, transitional, stratified, and tertiary), not to
mention the subdivisions of which each of these is composed, do
not always occur in the order laid down in the system, but in
not a few instances the order is reversed, crystalline primary
rocks lying upon transitional, stratified, and tertiary formations
(granite, syenite, gneiss, etc., above both Jura-limestone and
chalk) ; and, on the other hand, that not only do the different
leading formations and their various subdivisions frequently
shade off into one another so imperceptibly, that no boundary
line can be drawn between them and the species distinguished
by *oryctognosis* are not sharply and clearly defined in nature,
but that, instead of surrounding the entire globe, they are all

met with in certain localities only, whilst whole series of intermediate links are frequently missing, the tertiary formations
especially being universally admitted to be only partial.—The
second of these conclusions also stands or falls with the assumptions on which they are founded, viz. with the three proposi-
tions : (1) that each of the fossiliferous formations contains an
order of plants and animals peculiar to itself ; (2) that these are
so totally different from the existing plants and animals, that
the latter could not have sprung from them ; (3) that no fossil
remains of man exist of the same antiquity as the fossil remains
of animals.   Not one of these can be regarded as an established
truth, or as the unanimously accepted result of geognosis.   The
assertion so often made as an established fact, that the transition
rocks contain none but fossils of the lower orders of plants and
animals, that mammalia are first met with in the Trias, Jura,
and chalk formations, and warm-blooded animals in the tertiary
rocks, has not been confirmed by continued geognostic researches, but is more and more regarded as untenable.   Even
the frequently expressed opinion, that in the different forms of
plants and animals of the successive rocks there is a gradual and
to a certain extent progressive development of the animal and
vegetable world, has not commanded universal acceptance.
Numerous instances are known, in which the remains of one
and the same species occur not only in two, but in several successive formations, and there are some types that occur in nearly
all.   And the widely spread notion, that the fossil types are altogether different from the existing families of plants and animals,
is one of the unscientific exaggerations of actual facts.   All the
fossil plants and animals can be arranged in the orders and
classes of the existing flora and fauna.   Even with regard to the
genera there is no essential difference, although many of the
existing types are far inferior in size to the forms of the old
world.   It is only the species that can be shown to differ, either
entirely or in the vast majority of cases, from species in existence now.   But even if all the species differed, which can by
no means be proved, this would be no valid evidence that the
existing plants and animals had not sprung from those that
have passed away, so long as natural science is unable to obtain
any clear insight into the origin and formation of species, and
the question as to the extinction of a species or its transition into

another has met with no satisfactory solution. Lastly, even now the occurrence of fossil human bones among those of animals that perished at least before the historic age, can no longer be disputed, although Central Asia, the cradle of the human race, has not yet been thoroughly explored by palæontologists. —If then the premises from which the geological periods have been deduced are of such a nature that not one of them is firmly established, the different theories as to the formation of the earth also rest upon two questionable assumptions, viz. (1) that the immediate working of God in the creation was restricted to the production of the chaotic matter, and that the formation of this primary matter into a world peopled by innumerable organisms and living beings proceeded according to the laws of nature, which have been discovered by science as in force in the existing world ; and (2) that all the changes, which the world and its inhabitants have undergone since the creation was finished, may be measured by the standard of changes observed in modern times, and still occurring from time to time. But the Bible actually mentions two events of the primeval age, whose effect upon the form of the earth and the animal and vegetable world no natural science can explain. We refer to the curse pronounced upon the earth in consequence of the fall of the progenitors of our race, by which even the animal world was made subject to φθορά (Gen. iii. 17, and Rom. viii. 20); and the flood, by which the earth was submerged even to the tops of the highest mountains, and all the living beings on the dry land perished, with the exception of those preserved by Noah in the ark. Hence, even if geological doctrines do contradict the account of the creation contained in Genesis, they cannot shake the credibility of the Scriptures.

But if the biblical account of the creation has full claim to be regarded as historical truth, the question arises, whence it was obtained. The opinion that the Israelites drew it from the cosmogony of this or the other ancient people, and altered it according to their own religious ideas, will need no further refutation, after what we have said respecting the cosmogonies of other nations. Whence then did Israel obtain a pure knowledge of God, such as we cannot find in any heathen nation, or in the most celebrated of the wise men of antiquity, if not from divine revelation ? This is the source from which the biblical account of the creation springs. God revealed it to men,—not first to Moses or Abraham, but undoubtedly to the first men, since without this revelation they could not have understood either their relation to God or their true position in the world. The account contained in Genesis does not lie, as *Hofmann* says, " within that sphere which was open to man through his historical nature, so that it may be regarded as the utterance of the knowledge possessed by the first man cf things which preceded his own existence, and which he might possess, without needing any special revelation, if only the present condition of the world lay clear and transparent before him." By simple intuition the first man might discern what nature had effected, viz. the existing condition of the world, and possibly also its causality, but not the fact that it was created in six days, or the successive acts of creation, and the sanctification of the seventh day. Our record contains not merely religious truth transformed into history, but the true and actual history of a work of God, which preceded the existence of man, and to which he owes his existence. Of this work he could only have obtained his knowledge through divine revelation, by the direct instruction of God. Nor could he have obtained it by means of a vision. The seven days' works are not so many " prophetico-historical tableaux," which were spread before the mental eye of the seer, whether of the historian or the first man. The account before us does not contain the slightest marks of a vision, is no picture of creation, in which every line betrays the pencil of a painter rather than the pen of a historian, but is obviously a historical narrative, which we could no more transform into a vision than the account of paradise or of the fall. As God revealed Himself to the first man not in visions, but by coming to him in a visible form, teaching him His will, and then after his fall announcing the punishment (ii. 16, 17, iii. 9 sqq.); as He talked with Moses " face to face, as a man with his friend," " mouth to mouth," not in vision or dream : so does the written account of the Old Testament revelation commence, not with visions, but with actual history. The manner in which God instructed the first men with reference to the creation must be judged according to the intercourse carried on by Him, as Creator and Father, with these His creatures and children. What God revealed to them upon this subject, they transmitted

to their children and descendants, together with everything of
significance and worth that they had experienced and discovered for themselves. This tradition was kept in faithful
remembrance by the family of the godly; and even in the confusion of tongues it was not changed in its substance, but
simply transferred into the new form of the language spoken by
the Semitic tribes, and thus handed down from generation to
generation along with the knowledge and worship of the true
God, until it became through Abraham the spiritual inheritance
of the chosen race. Nothing certain can be decided as to the
period when it was committed to writing; probably some time
before Moses, who inserted it as a written record in the Thorah
of Israel.

Chap. i. 1. " *In the beginning God created the heaven and the
earth.*"—Heaven and earth have not existed from all eternity,
but had a beginning; nor did they arise by emanation from an
absolute substance, but were created by God. This sentence,
which stands at the head of the records of revelation, is not a
mere heading, nor a summary of the history of the creation, but
a declaration of the primeval act of God, by which the universe
was called into being. That this verse is not a heading merely,
is evident from the fact that the following account of the course
of the creation commences with ו (*and*), which connects the
different acts of creation with the fact expressed in ver. 1, as
the primary foundation upon which they rest. בְּרֵאשִׁית (in the
beginning) is used absolutely, like ἐν ἀρχῇ in John i. 1, and
מֵרֵאשִׁית in Isa. xlvi. 10. The following clause cannot be treated
as subordinate, either by rendering it, " in the beginning when
God created . . , the earth was," etc., or " in the beginning
when God created . . (but the earth was then a chaos, etc.),
God said, Let there be light " (*Ewald* and *Bunsen*). The first is
opposed to the grammar of the language, which would require
ver. 2 to commence with וַתְּהִי הָאָרֶץ; the second to the simplicity
of style which pervades the whole chapter, and to which so
involved a sentence would be intolerable, apart altogether from
the fact that this construction is invented for the simple purpose
of getting rid of the doctrine of a *creatio ex nihilo*, which is so
repulsive to modern Pantheism. רֵאשִׁית in itself is a relative
notion, indicating the commencement of a series of things or
events; but here the context gives it the meaning of the very

first beginning, the commencement of the world, when time itself began. The statement, that in the beginning God created the heaven and the earth, not only precludes the idea of the eternity of the world *a parte ante*, but shows that the creation of the heaven and the earth was the actual beginning of all things. The verb בָּרָא, indeed, to judge from its use in Josh. xvii. 15, 18, where it occurs in the *Piel* (to hew out), means literally "to cut, or hew," but in *Kal* it always means *to create*, and is only applied to a divine creation, the production of that which had no existence before. It is never joined with an accusative of the material, although it does not exclude a pre-existent material unconditionally, but is used for the creation of man (ver. 27, ch. v. 1, 2), and of everything new that God creates, whether in the kingdom of nature (Num. xvi. 30) or of that of grace (Ex. xxxiv. 10; Ps. li. 10, etc.). In this verse, however, the existence of any primeval material is precluded by the object created: "the heaven and the earth." This expression is frequently employed to denote the world, or universe, for which there was no single word in the Hebrew language; the universe consisting of a twofold whole, and the distinction between heaven and earth being essentially connected with the notion of the world, the fundamental condition of its historical development (*vid.* ch. xiv. 19, 22; Ex. xxxi. 17). In the earthly creation this division is repeated in the distinction between spirit and nature; and in man, as the microcosm, in that between spirit and body. Through sin this distinction was changed into an actual opposition between heaven and earth, flesh and spirit; but with the complete removal of sin, this opposition will cease again, though the distinction between heaven and earth, spirit and body, will remain, in such a way, however, that the earthly and corporeal will be completely pervaded by the heavenly and spiritual, the new Jerusalem coming down from heaven to earth, and the earthly body being transfigured into a spiritual body (Rev. xxi. 1, 2; 1 Cor. xv. 35 sqq.). Hence, if in the beginning God created the heaven and the earth, "there is nothing belonging to the composition of the universe, either in material or form, which had an existence out of God prior to this divine act in the beginning" (*Delitzsch*). This is also shown in the connection between our verse and the one which follows: "*and the earth was without form and void*," not before, but when, or

after God created it. From this it is evident that the void and
formless state of the earth was not uncreated, or without beginning. At the same time it is obvious from the creative acts
which follow (vers. 3–18), that the heaven and earth, as God
created them in the beginning, were not the well-ordered universe, but the world in its elementary form; just as *Euripides*
applies the expression οὐρανὸς καὶ γαῖα to the undivided mass
(μορφὴ μία), which was afterwards formed into heaven and
earth.

Vers. 2–5. THE FIRST DAY.—Though treating of the creation of the heaven and the earth, the writer, both here and in
what follows, describes with minuteness the original condition
and progressive formation of the earth alone, and says nothing
more respecting the heaven than is actually requisite in order to
show its connection with the earth. He is writing for inhabitants
of the earth, and for religious ends; not to gratify curiosity,
but to strengthen faith in God, the Creator of the universe.
What is said in ver. 2 of the chaotic condition of the earth, is
equally applicable to the heaven, " for the heaven proceeds from
the same chaos as the earth."—" *And the earth was* (not became)
waste and void." The alliterative nouns *tohu vabohu*, the etymology of which is lost, signify waste and empty (barren), but
not laying waste and desolating. Whenever they are used
together in other places (Isa. xxxiv. 11; Jer. iv. 23), they are
taken from this passage; but *tohu* alone is frequently employed
as synonymous with אַיִן, non-existence, and הֶבֶל, nothingness
(Isa. xl. 17, 23, xlix. 4). The coming earth was at first waste
and desolate, a formless, lifeless mass, *rudis indigestaque moles,*
ὕλη ἄμορφος (Wisdom xi. 17) or χάος.—" *And darkness was
upon the face of the deep.*" תְּהוֹם, from הוּם, to roar, to rage,
denotes the raging waters, the roaring waves (Ps. xlii. 7) or
flood (Ex. xv. 5; Deut. viii. 7); and hence the depths of the
sea (Job xxviii. 14, xxxviii. 16), and even the abyss of the
earth (Ps. lxxi. 20). As an old traditional word, it is construed
like a proper name without an article (*Ewald*, Gramm.). The
chaotic mass in which the earth and the firmament were still
undistinguished, unformed, and as it were unborn, was a heaving deep, an abyss of waters (ἄβυσσος, LXX.), and this deep
was wrapped in darkness. But it was in process of formation,

for the Spirit of God moved upon the waters. רוּחַ (breath) denotes wind and spirit, like πνεῦμα from πνέω. *Ruach Elohim* is
not a breath of wind caused by God (*Theodoret*, etc.), for the verb
does not suit this meaning, but the creative Spirit of God, the
principle of all life (Ps. xxxiii. 6, civ. 30), which worked upon
the formless, lifeless mass, separating, quickening, and preparing
the living forms, which were called into being by the creative
words that followed. רחף in the *Piel* is applied to the hovering
and brooding of a bird over its young, to warm them, and develop
their vital powers (Deut. xxxii. 11). In such a way as this the
Spirit of God moved upon the deep, which had received at its
creation the germs of all life, to fill them with vital energy by
His breath of life. The three statements in our verse are
parallel; the substantive and participial construction of the second
and third clauses rests upon the וְהָיְתָה of the first. All three
describe the condition of the earth immediately after the creation
of the universe. This suffices to prove that the theosophic speculation of those who " make a gap between the first two verses,
and fill it with a wild horde of evil spirits and their demoniacal
works, is an arbitrary interpolation" (*Ziegler*).—Ver. 3. The
word of God then went forth to the primary material of the
world, now filled with creative powers of vitality, to call into
being, out of the germs of organization and life which it contained, and in the order pre-ordained by His wisdom, those creatures of the world, which proclaim, as they live and move, the
glory of their Creator (Ps. viii.). The work of creation commences
with the words, " *and God said.*" The words which God speaks
are existing things. " He speaks, and it is done; He commands,
and it stands fast." These words are deeds of the essential Word,
the λόγος, by which " all things were made." Speaking is the
revelation of thought; the creation, the realization of the thoughts
of God, a freely accomplished act of the absolute Spirit, and not
an emanation of creatures from the divine essence. The first
thing created by the divine Word was " *light,*" the elementary
light, or light-material, in distinction from the " *lights,*" or light-
bearers, bodies of light, as the sun, moon, and stars, created
on the fourth day, are called. It is now a generally accepted
truth of natural science, that the light does not spring from the
sun and stars, but that the sun itself is a dark body, and the
light proceeds from an atmosphere which surrounds it. Light

was the first thing called forth, and separated from the dark
chaos by the creative mandate, " *Let there be*,"—the first radiation
of the life breathed into it by the Spirit of God, inasmuch as it
is the fundamental condition of all organic life in the world, and
without light and the warmth which flows from it no plant or
animal could thrive.   The expression in ver. 4, " *God saw the
light that it was good*," for " God saw that the light was good,"
according to a frequently recurring *antiptosis* (cf. ch. vi. 2, xii.
14, xiii. 10), is not an anthropomorphism at variance with enlightened thoughts of God ; for man's seeing has its type in God's,
and God's seeing is not a mere expression of the delight of the
eye or of pleasure in His work, but is of the deepest significance
to every created thing, being the seal of the perfection which
God has impressed upon it, and by which its continuance before
God and through God is determined.   The creation of light,
however, was no annihilation of darkness, no transformation
of the dark material of the world into pure light, but a separation of the light from the primary matter, a separation which
established and determined that interchange of light and darkness, which produces the distinction between day and night.
Hence it is said in ver. 5, " *God called the light Day, and the
darkness Night ;* " for, as *Augustine* observes, " all light is not
day, nor all darkness night ; but light and darkness alternating
in a regular order constitute day and night."   None but superficial thinkers can take offence at the idea of created things
receiving names from God.   The name of a thing is the expression of its nature.   If the name be given by man, it fixes in a word
the impression which it makes upon the human mind ; but when
given by God, it expresses the reality, what the thing is in God's
creation, and the place assigned it there by the side of other
things.—" *Thus evening was and morning was one day.*"   אֶחָד
(*one*), like εἶς and *unus*, is used at the commencement of a
numerical series for the ordinal *primus* (cf. ch. ii. 11, iv. 19, viii.
5, 15).   Like the numbers of the days which follow, it is without
the article, to show that the different days arose from the constant recurrence of evening and morning.   It is not till the sixth
and last day that the article is employed (ver. 31), to indicate
the termination of the work of creation upon that day.   It is to
be observed, that the days of creation are bounded by the coming
of evening and morning.   The first day did not consist of the

primeval darkness and the origination of light, but was formed
after the creation of the light by the first interchange of evening and morning. The first evening was not the gloom, which
possibly preceded the full burst of light as it came forth from
the primary darkness, and intervened between the darkness
and full, broad daylight. It was not till after the light had been
created, and the separation of the light from the darkness had
taken place, that evening came, and after the evening the morning; and this coming of evening (*lit.* the obscure) and morning
(the breaking) formed one, or the first day. It follows from
this, that the days of creation are not reckoned from evening to
evening, but from morning to morning. The first day does not
fully terminate till the light returns after the darkness of night;
it is not till the break of the new morning that the first interchange of light and darkness is completed, and a ἡμερονύκτιον
has passed. The rendering, " out of evening and morning there
came one day," is at variance with grammar, as well as with the
actual fact. With grammar, because such a thought would
require לְיוֹם אֶחָד; and with fact, because the time from evening
to morning does not constitute a day, but the close of a day.
The first day commenced at the moment when God caused the
light to break forth from the darkness; but this light did not
become a day, until the evening had come, and the darkness
which set in with the evening had given place the next morning to the break of day. Again, neither the words ויהי ערב ויהי
בקר, nor the expression ערב בקר, evening-morning (= day), in
Dan. viii. 14, corresponds to the Greek νυχθήμερον, for morning is not equivalent to day, nor evening to night. The reckoning of days from evening to evening in the Mosaic law (Lev.
xxiii. 32), and by many ancient tribes (the pre-Mohammedan
Arabs, the Athenians, Gauls, and Germans), arose not from the
days of creation, but from the custom of regulating seasons by
the changes of the moon. But if the days of creation are regulated by the recurring interchange of light and darkness, they
must be regarded not as periods of time of incalculable duration, of years or thousands of years, but as simple earthly days.
It is true the morning and evening of the first three days were
not produced by the rising and setting of the sun, since the sun
was not yet created; but the constantly recurring interchange
of light and darkness, which produced day and night upon the

earth, cannot for a moment be understood as denoting that the light called forth from the darkness of chaos returned to that darkness again, and thus periodically burst forth and disappeared. The only way in which we can represent it to ourselves, is by supposing that the light called forth by the creative mandate, "Let there be," was separated from the dark mass of the earth, and concentrated outside or above the globe, so that the interchange of light and darkness took place as soon as the dark chaotic mass began to rotate, and to assume in the process of creation the form of a spherical body. The time occupied in the first rotations of the earth upon its axis cannot, indeed, be measured by our hour-glass; but even if they were slower at first, and did not attain their present velocity till the completion of our solar system, this would make no essential difference between the first three days and the last three, which were regulated by the rising and setting of the sun.[1]

Vers. 6-8. THE SECOND DAY.—When the light had been separated from the darkness, and day and night had been created, there followed upon a second fiat of the Creator, the division of the chaotic mass of waters through the formation of the firmament, which was placed as a wall of separation (מַבְדִּיל) in the midst of the waters, and divided them into upper and lower waters. רָקִיעַ, from רָקַע to stretch, spread out, then beat or tread out, means *expansum*, the spreading out of the air, which surrounds the earth as an atmosphere. According to optical appearance, it is described as a carpet spread out above the earth (Ps. civ. 2), a curtain (Isa. xl. 22), a transparent work of sapphire (Ex. xxiv. 10), or a molten looking-glass (Job xxxvii. 18); but there is nothing in these poetical similes to warrant the

[1] Exegesis must insist upon this, and not allow itself to alter the plain sense of the words of the Bible, from irrelevant and untimely regard to the so-called certain inductions of natural science. Irrelevant we call such considerations, as make interpretation dependent upon natural science, because the creation lies outside the limits of empirical and speculative research, and, as an act of the omnipotent God, belongs rather to the sphere of miracles and mysteries, which can only be received by faith (Heb. xi. 3); and untimely, because natural science has supplied no certain conclusions as to the origin of the earth, and geology especially, even at the present time, is in a chaotic state of fermentation, the issue of which it is impossible to foresee.

idea that the heavens were regarded as a solid mass, a σιδήρεον, or χάλκεον or πολύχαλκον, such as Greek poets describe. The רָקִיעַ (rendered *Veste* by *Luther*, after the στερέωμα of the LXX. and *firmamentum* of the Vulgate) is called *heaven* in ver. 8, *i.e.* the vault of heaven, which stretches out above the earth. The waters *under* the firmament are the waters upon the globe itself; those *above* are not ethereal waters[1] beyond the limits of the

[1] There is no proof of the existence of such " ethereal waters" to be found in such passages as Rev. iv. 6, xv. 2, xxii. 1; for what the holy seer there beholds before the throne as " a sea of glass like unto crystal mingled with fire," and " a river of living water, clear as crystal," flowing from the throne of God into the streets of the heavenly Jerusalem, are wide as the poles from any fluid or material substance from which the stars were made upon the fourth day. Of such a fluid the Scriptures know quite as little, as of the nebular theory of *La Place*, which, notwithstanding the bright spots in Mars and the inferior density of Jupiter, Saturn, and other planets, is still enveloped in a mist which no astronomy will ever disperse. If the waters above the firmament were the elementary matter of which the stars were made, the waters beneath must be the elementary matter of which the earth was formed; for the waters were one and the same before the creation of the firmament. But the earth was not formed from the waters beneath; on the contrary, these waters were merely spread upon the earth and then gathered together into one place, and this place is called Sea. The earth, which appeared as dry land after the accumulation of the waters in the sea, was created in the beginning along with the heavens; but until the separation of land and water on the third day, it was so completely enveloped in water, that nothing could be seen but " the deep," or " the waters" (ver. 2). If, therefore, in the course of the work of creation, the heaven with its stars, and the earth with its vegetation and living creatures, came forth from this deep, or, to speak more correctly, if they appeared as well-ordered, and in a certain sense as finished worlds; it would be a complete misunderstanding of the account of the creation to suppose it to teach, that the water formed the elementary matter, out of which the heaven and the earth were made with all their hosts. Had this been the meaning of the writer, he would have mentioned *water* as the first creation, and not the heaven and the earth. How irreconcilable the idea of the waters above the firmament being ethereal waters is with the biblical representation of the opening of the windows of heaven when it rains, is evident from the way in which *Keerl*, the latest supporter of this theory, sets aside this difficulty, viz. by the bold assertion, that the mass of water which came through the windows of heaven at the flood was different from the rain which falls from the clouds; in direct opposition to the text of the Scriptures, which speaks of it not merely as rain (vii. 12), but as the water of the clouds. *Vid.* ch. ix. 12 sqq., where it is said that when God brings a cloud over the earth, He will set the rainbow in the cloud, as a sign that the water (of the clouds collected above the earth) shall not become a flood to destroy the earth again.

terrestrial atmosphere, but the waters which float in the atmosphere, and are separated by it from those upon the earth, the waters which accumulate in clouds, and then bursting these their bottles, pour down as rain upon the earth. For, according to the Old Testament representation, whenever it rains heavily, the doors or windows of heaven are opened (ch. vii. 11, 12; Ps. lxxviii. 23, cf. 2 Kings vii. 2, 19; Isa. xxiv. 18). It is in (or with) the upper waters that God layeth the beams of His chambers, from which He watereth the hills (Ps. civ. 3, 13), and the clouds are His tabernacle (Job xxxvi. 29). If, therefore, according to this conception, looking from an earthly point of view, the mass of water which flows upon the earth in showers of rain is shut up in heaven (cf. viii. 2), it is evident that it must be regarded as above the vault which spans the earth, or, according to the words of Ps. cxlviii. 4, "above the heavens."[1]

Vers. 9–13. THE THIRD DAY.—The work of this day was twofold, yet closely connected. At first the waters beneath the heavens, *i.e.* those upon the surface of the earth, were gathered together, so that the dry (הַיַּבָּשָׁה, the solid ground) appeared. In what way the gathering of the earthly waters in the sea and the appearance of the dry land were effected, whether by the sinking or deepening of places in the body of the globe, into which the water was drawn off, or by the elevation of the solid ground, the record does not inform us, since it never describes the process by which effects are produced. It is probable, however, that the separation was caused both by depression and elevation. With the dry land the mountains naturally arose as the headlands of the mainland. But of this we have no physical explanations, either in the account before us, or in the poetical description of the creation in Ps. civ. Even if we render Ps. civ. 8, "the mountains arise, and they (the waters)

---

[1] In ver. 8 the LXX. interpolate καὶ εἶδεν ὁ Θεὸς ὅτι καλόν (and God saw that it was good), and transfer the words "and it was so" from the end of ver. 7 to the close of ver. 6. Two apparent improvements, but in reality two arbitrary changes. The transposition is copied from vers. 9, 15, 24; and in making the interpolation, the author of the gloss has not observed that the division of the waters was not complete till the separation of the dry land from the water had taken place, and therefore the proper place for the expression of approval is at the close of the work of the third day.

descend into the valleys, to the place which Thou (Jehovah) hast founded for them," we have no proof, in this poetical account, of the elevation-theory of geology, since the psalmist is not speaking as a naturalist, but as a sacred poet describing the creation on the basis of Gen. i. " *The dry*" God called *Earth*, and " *the gathering of the waters*," *i.e.* the place into which the waters were collected, He called *Sea*. יַמִּים, an intensive rather than a numerical plural, is the great ocean, which surrounds the mainland on all sides, so that the earth appears to be founded upon seas (Ps. xxiv. 2). Earth and sea are the two constituents of the globe, by the separation of which its formation was completed. The " seas " include the rivers which flow into the ocean, and the lakes which are as it were "detached fragments" of the ocean, though they are not specially mentioned here. By the divine act of naming the two constituents of the globe, and the divine approval which follows, this work is stamped with permanency; and the second act of the third day, the clothing of the earth with vegetation, is immediately connected with it. At the command of God " *the earth brought forth green* (דֶּשֶׁא), *seed yielding herb* (עֵשֶׂב), *and fruit-bearing fruit-trees* (עֵץ פְּרִי)." These three classes embrace all the productions of the vegetable kingdom. דֶּשֶׁא, *lit.* the young, tender green, which shoots up after rain and covers the meadows and downs (2 Sam. xxiii. 4; Job xxxviii. 27; Joel ii. 22; Ps. xxiii. 2), is a generic name for all grasses and cryptogamous plants. עֵשֶׂב, with the epithet מַזְרִיעַ זֶרַע, yielding or forming seed, is used as a generic term for all herbaceous plants, corn, vegetables, and other plants by which seed-pods are formed. עֵץ פְּרִי : not only fruit-trees, but all trees and shrubs, bearing fruit in which there is a seed according to its kind, *i.e.* fruit with kernels. עַל הָאָרֶץ (upon the earth) is not to be joined to "fruit-tree," as though indicating the superior size of the trees which bear seed above the earth, in distinction from vegetables which propagate their species upon or in the ground; for even the latter bear their seed above the earth. It is appended to תַּדְשֵׁא, as a more minute explanation: the earth is to bring forth grass, herb, and trees, upon or above the ground, as an ornament or covering for it. לְמִינוֹ (after its kind), from מִין *species*, which is not only repeated in ver. 12 in its old form לְמִינֵהוּ in the case of the fruit-tree, but is also appended to the herb. It indicates that the herbs and trees sprang out of the earth according to their kinds, and received, together with power to bear seed and fruit, the capacity to propagate and multiply their own kind. In the case of the grass there is no reference either to different kinds, or to the production of seed, inasmuch as in the young green grass neither the one nor the other is apparent to the eye. Moreover, we must not picture the work of creation as consisting of the production of the first tender germs which were gradually developed into herbs, shrubs, and trees ; on the contrary, we must regard it as one element in the miracle of creation itself, that at the word of God not only tender grasses, but herbs, shrubs, and trees, sprang out of the earth, each ripe for the formation of blossom and the bearing of seed and fruit, without the necessity of waiting for years before the vegetation created was ready to blossom and bear fruit. Even if the earth was employed as a medium in the creation of the plants, since it was God who caused it to bring them forth, they were not the product of the powers of nature, *generatio æquivoca* in the ordinary sense of the word, but a work of divine omnipotence, by which the trees came into existence before their seed, and their fruit was produced in full development, without expanding gradually under the influence of sunshine and rain.

Vers. 14–19. THE FOURTH DAY.—After the earth had been clothed with vegetation, and fitted to be the abode of living beings, there were created on the fourth day the sun, moon, and stars, heavenly bodies in which the elementary light was concentrated, in order that its influence upon the earthly globe might be sufficiently modified and regulated for living beings to exist and thrive beneath its rays, in the water, in the air, and upon the dry land. At the creative word of God the bodies of light came into existence in the firmament, as lamps. On יְהִי, the singular of the predicate before the plural of the subject, in ver. 14, v. 23, ix. 29, etc., *vid. Gesenius*, Heb. Gr. § 147. מְאֹרֹת, bodies of light, light-bearers, then *lamps*. These bodies of light received a threefold appointment : (1) They were " *to divide between the day and the night*," or, according to ver. 18, between the light and the darkness, in other words, to regulate from that time forward the difference, which had existed ever since the creation of light, between the night and the day.

(2) *They were to be* (or serve : וְהָיוּ after an imperative has the force of a command),—(*a*) *for signs* (*sc.* for the earth), partly as portents of extraordinary events (Matt. ii. 2 ; Luke xxi. 25) and divine judgments (Joel ii. 30 ; Jer. x. 2 ; Matt. xxiv. 29), partly as showing the different quarters of the heavens, and as prognosticating the changes in the weather ;—(*b*) *for seasons*, or for fixed, definite times (מוֹעֲדִים, from יעד to fix, establish),—not for festal seasons merely, but "to regulate definite points and periods of time, by virtue of their periodical influence upon agriculture, navigation, and other human occupations, as well as upon the course of human, animal, and vegetable life (*e.g.* the breeding time of animals, and the migrations of birds, Jer. viii. 7, etc.) ;— (*c*) *for days and years, i.e.* for the division and calculation of days and years. The grammatical construction will not allow the clause to be rendered as a *Hendiadys*, viz. "as signs for definite times and for days and years," or as signs both for the times and also for days and years. (3.) They were to serve as lamps upon the earth, *i.e.* to pour out their light, which is indispensable to the growth and health of every creature. That this, the primary object of the lights, should be mentioned last, is correctly explained by *Delitzsch :* "From the astrological and chronological utility of the heavenly bodies, the record ascends to their universal utility which arises from the necessity of light for the growth and continuance of everything earthly." This applies especially to the two great lights which were created by God and placed in the firmament ; the greater to rule the day, the lesser to rule the night. "*The great*" and "*the small*" in correlative clauses are to be understood as used comparatively (cf. *Gesenius,* § 119, 1). That the sun and moon were intended, was too obvious to need to be specially mentioned. It might appear strange, however, that these lights should not receive names from God, like the works of the first three days. This cannot be attributed to forgetfulness on the part of the author, as *Tuch* supposes. As a rule, the names were given by God only to the greater sections into which the universe was divided, and not to individual bodies (either plants or animals). The man and the woman are the only exceptions (chap. v. 2). The sun and moon are called great, not in comparison with the earth, but in contrast with the stars, according to the amount of light which shines from them upon the earth and determines their

rule over the day and night ; not so much with reference to the fact, that the stronger light of the sun produces the daylight, and the weaker light of the moon illumines the night, as to the influence which their light exerts by day and night upon all nature, both organic and inorganic—an influence generally admitted, but by no means fully understood. In this respect the sun and moon are the two great lights, the stars small bodies of light ; the former exerting great, the latter but little, influence upon the earth and its inhabitants.

This truth, which arises from the relative magnitude of the heavenly bodies, or rather their apparent size as seen from the earth, is not affected by the fact that from the standpoint of natural science many of the stars far surpass both sun and moon in magnitude. Nor does the fact, that in our account, which was written for inhabitants of the earth and for religious purposes, it is only the utility of the sun, moon, and stars to the inhabitants of the earth that is mentioned, preclude the possibility of each by itself, and all combined, fulfilling other purposes in the universe of God. And not only is our record silent, but God Himself made no direct revelation to man on this subject ; because astronomy and physical science, generally, neither lead to godliness, nor promise peace and salvation to the soul. Belief in the truth of this account as a divine revelation could only be shaken, if the facts which science has discovered as indisputably true, with regard to the number, size, and movements of the heavenly bodies, were irreconcilable with the biblical account of the creation. But neither the innumerable host nor the immeasurable size of many of the heavenly bodies, nor the almost infinite distance of the fixed stars from our earth and the solar system, warrants any such assumption. Who can set bounds to the divine omnipotence, and determine what and how much it can create in a moment ? The objection, that the creation of the innumerable and immeasurably great and distant heavenly bodies in one day, is so disproportioned to the creation of this one little globe in six days, as to be irreconcilable with our notions of divine omnipotence and wisdom, does not affect the Bible, but shows that the account of the creation has been misunderstood. We are not taught here that on *one* day, viz. the fourth, God created all the heavenly bodies out of nothing, and in a perfect condition ; on the contrary, we are told that in the beginning God created the *heaven* and the earth, and on the fourth day that He made the sun, the moon, and the stars (planets, comets, and fixed stars) in the firmament, to be lights for the earth. According to these distinct words, the primary material, not only of the earth, but also of the heaven and the heavenly bodies, was created in the beginning. If, therefore, the heavenly bodies were first made or created on the fourth day, as lights for the earth, in the firmament of heaven; the words can have no other meaning than that their creation was completed on the fourth day, just as the creative formation of our globe was finished on the third; that the creation of the heavenly bodies therefore proceeded side by side, and probably by similar stages, with that of the earth, so that the heaven with its stars was completed on the fourth day. Is this representation of the work of creation, which follows in the simplest way from the word of God, at variance with correct ideas of the omnipotence and wisdom of God? Could not the Almighty create the innumerable host of heaven at the same time as the earthly globe? Or would Omnipotence require more time for the creation of the moon, the planets, and the sun, or of Orion, Sirius, the Pleiades, and other heavenly bodies whose magnitude has not yet been ascertained, than for the creation of the earth itself? Let us beware of measuring the works of Divine Omnipotence by the standard of human power. The fact, that in our account the gradual formation of the heavenly bodies is not described with the same minuteness as that of the earth; but that, after the general statement in ver. 1 as to the creation of the heavens, all that is mentioned is their completion on the fourth day, when for the first time they assumed, or were placed in, such a position with regard to the earth as to influence its development; may be explained on the simple ground that it was the intention of the sacred historian to describe the work of creation from the standpoint of the globe: in other words, as it would have appeared to an observer from the earth, if there had been one in existence at the time. For only from such a standpoint could this work of God be made intelligible to all men, uneducated as well as learned, and the account of it be made subservient to the religious wants of all.[1]

[1] Most of the objections to the historical character of our account, which have been founded upon the work of the fourth day, rest upon a miscon-

Vers. 20–23. THE FIFTH DAY.—"*God said : Let the waters swarm with swarms, with living beings, and let birds fly above the earth in the face* (the front, *i.e.* the side turned towards the earth) *of the firmament*." יִשְׁרְצוּ and יְעוֹפֵף are imperative. Earlier translators, on the contrary, have rendered the latter as a relative clause, after the πετεινὰ πετόμενα of the LXX., " and with birds that fly;" thus making the birds to spring out of the water, in opposition to chap. ii. 19. Even with regard to the element out of which the water animals were created the text is silent; for the assertion that שׁרץ is to be understood " with a causative colouring" is erroneous, and is not sustained by Ex. viii. 3 or Ps. cv. 30. The construction with the accusative is common to all verbs of multitude. שֶׁרֶץ, from שָׁרַץ, to creep and swarm, is applied, " without regard to size, to those animals which congregate together in great numbers, and move about among one another." נֶפֶשׁ חַיָּה, *anima viva*, living soul, animated beings (*vid.* ii. 7), is in apposition to שֶׁרֶץ, " swarms consisting of living beings." The expression applies not only to fishes, but to all water animals from the greatest to the least, including reptiles, etc. In carrying out His word, God created (ver. 21) *the great "tanninim,"*—*lit.* the long-stretched, from תָּנַן, to stretch,—whales, crocodiles, and other sea-monsters; and " *all moving living beings with which the waters swarm after their kind, and all (every) winged fowl after its kind*." That the water animals and birds of every kind were created on the same day, and before the land animals, cannot be explained on the ground assigned by early writers, that there is a similarity between the air and the water, and a consequent correspondence between the two classes of animals. For in the light of natural history the birds are at all events quite as near to the mammalia as to the fishes; and the supposed resemblance between the fins of fishes and the wings of birds, is counterbalanced by the no less striking resemblance between birds and land animals, viz. that both have feet. The

ception of the proper point of view from which it should be studied. And. in addition to that, the conjectures of astronomers as to the immeasurable distance of most of the fixed stars, and the time which a ray of light would require to reach the earth, are accepted as indisputable mathematical proof; whereas these approximative estimates of distance rest upon the unsubstantiated supposition, that everything which has been ascertained with regard to the nature and motion of light in our solar system, must be equally true of the light of the fixed stars.

real reason is rather this, that the creation proceeds throughout
from the lower to the higher; and in this ascending scale the fishes
occupy to a great extent a lower place in the animal economy
than birds, and both water animals and birds a lower place than
land animals, more especially the mammalia. Again, it is not
stated that only a single pair was created of each kind; on the
contrary, the words, "let the waters swarm with living beings,"
seem rather to indicate that the animals were created, not only
in a rich variety of genera and species, but in large numbers of
individuals. The fact that but one human being was created at
first, by no means warrants the conclusion that the animals were
created singly also; for the unity of the human race has a very
different signification from that of the so-called animal species.
—(Ver. 22). As animated beings, the water animals and fowls
are endowed, through the divine blessing, with the power *to be
fruitful and multiply*. The word of blessing was the actual communication of the capacity to propagate and increase in numbers.

Vers. 24–31. THE SIXTH DAY.—Sea and air are filled
with living creatures; and the word of God now goes forth to
the earth, to produce living beings after their kind. These are
divided into three classes. בְּהֵמָה, *cattle*, from בהם, *mutum, brutum
esse*, generally denotes the larger domesticated quadrupeds (*e.g.*
chap. xlvii. 18; Ex. xiii. 12, etc.), but occasionally the larger
land animals as a whole. רֶמֶשׂ (*the creeping*) embraces the smaller
land animals, which move either without feet, or with feet that
are scarcely perceptible, viz. reptiles, insects, and worms. In
ver. 25 they are distinguished from the race of water reptiles by
the term הָאֲדָמָה. חַיְתוֹ אֶרֶץ (the old form of the construct state,
for חַיַּת הָאָרֶץ), *the beast of the earth, i.e.* the freely roving wild animals.—"*After its kind:*" this refers to all three classes of living
creatures, each of which had its peculiar species; consequently
in ver. 25, where the word of God is fulfilled, it is repeated with
every class. This act of creation, too, like all that precede it, is
shown by the divine word "good" to be in accordance with the
will of God. But the blessing pronounced is omitted, the author
hastening to the account of the creation of man, in which the
work of creation culminated. The creation of man does not
take place through a word addressed by God to the earth, but as
the result of the divine decree, "*We will make man in Our*

image, after our likeness," which proclaims at the very outset the
distinction and pre-eminence of man above all the other creatures of the earth. The plural " *We*" was regarded by the
fathers and earlier theologians almost unanimously as indicative
of the Trinity : modern commentators, on the contrary, regard it
either as *pluralis majestatis* ; or as an address by God to Himself,
the subject and object being identical; or as *communicative*, an
address to the spirits or angels who stand around the Deity and
constitute His council. The last is *Philo's* explanation : διαλέ-
γεται ὁ τῶν ὅλων πατὴρ ταῖς ἑαυτοῦ δυνάμεσιν (δυνάμεις=angels).
But although such passages as 1 Kings xxii. 19 sqq., Ps. lxxxix.
8, and Dan. x., show that God, as King and Judge of the world,
is surrounded by heavenly hosts, who stand around His throne
and execute His commands, the last interpretation founders
upon this rock : either it assumes without sufficient scriptural
authority, and in fact in opposition to such distinct passages as
chap. ii. 7, 22, Isa. xl. 13 seq., xliv. 24, that the spirits took part
in the creation of man; or it reduces the plural to an empty
phrase, inasmuch as God is made to summon the angels to co-
operate in the creation of man, and then, instead of employing
them, is represented as carrying out the work alone. Moreover,
this view is irreconcilable with the words " in our image, after
our likeness;" since man was created in the image of God alone
(ver. 27, chap. v. 1), and not in the image of either the angels,
or God and the angels. A likeness to the angels cannot be inferred from Heb. ii. 7, or from Luke xx. 36. Just as little
ground is there for regarding the plural here and in other passages (iii. 22, xi. 7 ; Isa. vi. 8, xli. 22) as reflective, an appeal to
self ; since the singular is employed in such cases as these, even
where God Himself is preparing for any particular work (cf. ii.
18 ; Ps. xii. 5 ; Isa. xxxiii. 10). No other explanation is left,
therefore, than to regard it as *pluralis majestatis*,—an interpretation which comprehends in its deepest and most intensive form
(God speaking of Himself and with Himself in the plural number, not *reverentiæ causa*, but with reference to the fulness of the
divine powers and essences which He possesses) the truth that
lies at the foundation of the trinitarian view, viz. that the potencies concentrated in the absolute Divine Being are something
more than powers and attributes of God; that they are *hypo-
stases*, which in the further course of the revelation of God in

His kingdom appeared with more and more distinctness as persons of the Divine Being. On the words *" in our image, after our likeness"* modern commentators have correctly observed, that there is no foundation for the distinction drawn by the Greek, and after them by many of the Latin Fathers, betwen εἰκών (*imago*) and ὁμοίωσις (*similitudo*), the former of which they supposed to represent the physical aspect of the likeness to God, the latter the ethical; but that, on the contrary, the older Lutheran theologians were correct in stating that the two words are synonymous, and are merely combined to add intensity to the thought: " an image which is like Us" (*Luther*); since it is no more possible to discover a sharp or well-defined distinction in the ordinary use of the words between צֶלֶם and דְּמוּת, than between בְּ and כְּ. צֶלֶם, from צֵל, *lit.* a shadow, hence sketch, outline, differs no more from דְּמוּת, likeness, portrait, copy, than the German words *Umriss* or *Abriss* (outline or sketch) from *Bild* or *Abbild* (likeness, copy). בְּ and כְּ are also equally interchangeable, as we may see from a comparison of this verse with chap. v. 1 and 3. (Compare also Lev. vi. 4 with Lev. xxvii. 12, and for the use of בְּ to denote a norm, or sample, Ex. xxv. 40, xxx. 32, 37, etc.). There is more difficulty in deciding in what the likeness to God consisted. Certainly not in the bodily form, the upright position, or commanding aspect of the man, since God has no bodily form, and the man's body was formed from the dust of the ground; nor in the dominion of man over nature, for this is unquestionably ascribed to man simply as the consequence or effluence of his likeness to God. Man is the image of God by virtue of his spiritual nature, of the breath of God by which the being, formed from the dust of the earth, became a living soul.[1] The image of God consists, therefore, in the spiritual personality of man, though not merely in unity of self-consciousness and self-determination, or in the fact that man was created a consciously free *Ego ;* for personality

[1] " The breath of God became the soul of man ; the soul of man therefore is nothing but the breath of God. The rest of the world exists through the word of God ; man through His own peculiar breath. This breath is the seal and pledge of our relation to God, of our godlike dignity; whereas the breath breathed into the animals is nothing but the common breath, the life-wind of nature, which is moving everywhere, and only appears in the animal fixed and bound into a certain independence and individuality, so that the animal soul is nothing but a nature-soul individualized into certain, though still material spirituality."—*Ziegler.*

is merely the basis and form of the divine likeness, not its real
essence.   This consists rather in the fact, that the man endowed
with free self-conscious personality possesses, in his spiritual as
well as corporeal nature, a creaturely copy of the holiness and
blessedness of the divine life.   This concrete essence of the
divine likeness was shattered by sin; and it is only through
Christ, the brightness of the glory of God and the expression
of His essence (Heb. i. 3), that our nature is transformed into
the image of God again (Col. iii. 10; Eph. iv. 24).—" *And they*
(אָדָם, a generic term for *men*) *shall have dominion over the fish*,"
etc.   There is something striking in the introduction of the expression " *and over all the earth*," after the different races of
animals have been mentioned, especially as the list of races
appears to be proceeded with afterwards.   If this appearance
were actually the fact, it would be impossible to escape the conclusion that the text is faulty, and that חַיַּת has fallen out; so
that the reading should be, " *and over all the wild beasts of the
earth*," as the Syriac has it.   But as the identity of " every
creeping thing that creepeth upon the *earth*" (הָאָרֶץ) with " every
thing that creepeth upon the *ground*" (הָאֲדָמָה) in ver. 25 is not
absolutely certain; on the contrary, the change in expression
indicates a difference of meaning; and as the Masoretic text is
supported by the oldest critical authorities (*LXX., Sam., Onk.*),
the Syriac rendering must be dismissed as nothing more than a
conjecture, and the Masoretic text be understood in the following manner.   The author passes on from the cattle to the entire
earth, and embraces all the animal creation in the expression,
" every moving thing (כָּל־הָרֶמֶשׂ) that moveth upon the earth,"
just as in ver. 28, " every living thing הָרֹמֶשֶׂת upon the earth."
According to this, God determined to give to the man about to be
created in His likeness the supremacy, not only over the animal
world, but over the earth itself; and this agrees with the blessing
in ver. 28, where the newly created man is exhorted to replenish
the earth and subdue it; whereas, according to the conjecture
of the Syriac, the subjugation of the earth by man would be
omitted from the divine decree.—Ver. 27. In the account of the
accomplishment of the divine purpose the words swell into a
jubilant song, so that we meet here for the first time with a
parallelismus membrorum, the creation of man being celebrated
in three parallel clauses.   The distinction drawn between אֹתוֹ (in

the image of God created He *him*) and אֹתָם (as man and woman created He *them*) must not be overlooked. The word אֹתָם, which indicates that God created the man and woman as two human beings, completely overthrows the idea that man was at first androgynous (cf. chap. ii. 18 sqq.). By the blessing in ver. 28, God not only confers upon man the power to multiply and fill the earth, as upon the beasts in ver. 22, but also gives him dominion over the earth and every beast. In conclusion, the food of both man and beast is pointed out in vers. 29, 30, exclusively from the vegetable kingdom. Man is to eat of *" every seed-bearing herb on the face of all the earth, and every tree on which there are fruits containing seed,"* consequently of the productions of both field and tree, in other words, of corn and fruit ; the animals are to eat of *" every green herb,"* *i.e.* of vegetables or green plants, and grass.

From this it follows, that, according to the creative will of God, men were not to slaughter animals for food, nor were animals to prey upon one another ; consequently, that the fact which now prevails universally in nature and the order of the world, the violent and often painful destruction of life, is not a primary law of nature, nor a divine institution founded in the creation itself, but entered the world along with death at the fall of man, and became a necessity of nature through the curse of sin. It was not till after the flood, that men received authority from God to employ the flesh of animals as well as the green herb as food (ix. 3) ; and the fact that, according to the biblical view, no carnivorous animals existed at the first, may be inferred from the prophetic announcements in Isa. xi. 6–8, lxv. 25, where the cessation of sin and the complete transformation of the world into the kingdom of God are described as being accompanied by the cessation of slaughter and the eating of flesh, even in the case of the animal kingdom. With this the legends of the heathen world respecting the golden age of the past, and its return at the end of time, also correspond (cf. *Gesenius* on Isa. xi. 6–8). It is true that objections have been raised by natural historians to this testimony of Scripture, but without scientific ground. For although at the present time man is fitted by his teeth and alimentary canal for the combination of vegetable and animal food ; and although the law of mutual destruction so thoroughly pervades the whole

animal kingdom, that not only is the life of one sustained by
the death of another, but " as the graminivorous animals check
the overgrowth of the vegetable kingdom, so the excessive increase of the former is restricted by the beasts of prey, and of
these again by the destructive implements of man;" and although, again, not only beasts of prey, but evident symptoms of
disease are met with among the fossil remains of the aboriginal
animals : all these facts furnish no proof that the human and
animal races were originally constituted for death and destruction, or that disease and slaughter are older than the fall. For,
to reply to the last objection first, geology has offered no conclusive evidence of its doctrine, that the fossil remains of beasts
of prey and bones with marks of disease belong to a pre-Adamite
period, but has merely inferred it from the hypothesis already
mentioned (pp. 41, 42) of successive periods of creation. Again,
as even in the present order of nature the excessive increase of
the vegetable kingdom is restrained, not merely by the graminivorous animals, but also by the death of the plants themselves
through the exhaustion of their vital powers; so the wisdom of
the Creator could easily have set bounds to the excessive increase of the animal world, without requiring the help of huntsmen and beasts of prey, since many animals even now lose their
lives by natural means, without being slain by men or eaten by
beasts of prey. The teaching of Scripture, that death entered
the world through sin, merely proves that the human race was
created for eternal life, but by no means necessitates the assumption that the animals were also created for endless existence. As the earth produced them at the creative word of God,
the different individuals and generations would also have passed
away and returned to the bosom of the earth, without violent
destruction by the claws of animals or the hand of man, as soon
as they had fulfilled the purpose of their existence. The decay
of animals is a law of nature established in the creation itself,
and not a consequence of sin, or an effect of the death brought
into the world by the sin of man. At the same time, it was so
far involved in the effects of the fall, that the natural decay of
the different animals was changed into a painful death or violent
end. Although in the animal kingdom, as it at present exists,
many varieties are so organized that they live exclusively upon
the flesh of other animals, which they kill and devour; this by

no means necessitates the conclusion, that the carnivorous beasts of prey were created after the fall, or the assumption that they were originally intended to feed upon flesh, and organized accordingly. If, in consequence of the curse pronounced upon the earth after the sin of man, who was appointed head and lord of nature, the whole creation was subjected to vanity and the bondage of corruption (Rom. viii. 20 sqq.) ; this subjection might have been accompanied by a change in the organization of the animals, though natural science, which is based upon the observation and combination of things empirically discovered, could neither demonstrate the fact nor explain the process. And if natural science cannot boast that in any one of its many branches it has discovered all the phenomena connected with the animal and human organism of the existing world, how could it pretend to determine or limit the changes through which this organism may have passed in the course of thousands of years?

The creation of man and his installation as ruler on the earth brought the creation of all earthly beings to a close (ver. 31). God saw His work, and *behold it was all very good; i.e.* everything perfect in its kind, so that every creature might reach the goal appointed by the Creator, and accomplish the purpose of its existence. By the application of the term "good" to everything that God made, and the repetition of the word with the emphasis "very" at the close of the whole creation, the existence of anything evil in the creation of God is absolutely denied, and the hypothesis entirely refuted, that the six days' work merely subdued and fettered an ungodly, evil principle, which had already forced its way into it. The sixth day, as being the last, is distinguished above all the rest by the article— יוֹם הַשִּׁשִׁי "*a day, the sixth*" (*Gesenius*, § 111, 2a).

Chap. ii. 1–3. THE SABBATH OF CREATION.—"*Thus the heavens and the earth were finished, and all the host of them.*" צָבָא here denotes the totality of the beings that fill the heaven and the earth: in other places (see especially Neh. ix. 6) it is applied to the host of heaven, *i.e.* the stars (Deut. iv. 19, xvii. 3), and according to a still later representation, to the angels also (1 Kings xxii. 19; Isa. xxiv. 21; Neh. ix. 6; Ps. cxlviii. 2). These words of ver. 1 introduce the completion of the work of crea-

tion, and give a greater definiteness to the announcement in
vers. 2, 3, that on the seventh day God ended the work which
He had made, by ceasing to create, and blessing the day and
sanctifying it.   The completion or finishing (כִּלָּה) of the work
of creation on the seventh day (not on the sixth, as the LXX.,
Sam., and *Syr.* erroneously render it) can only be understood
by regarding the clauses vers. 2b and 3, which are connected
with וַיְכַל by וַ *consec.* as containing the actual completion, *i.e.* by
supposing the completion to consist, negatively in the cessation
of the work of creation, and positively in the blessing and sanctifying of the seventh day.   The *cessation* itself formed part of
the completion of the work (for this meaning of שָׁבַת *vid.* chap.
viii. 22, Job xxxii. 1, etc.).   As a human artificer completes his
work just when he has brought it up to his ideal and ceases to
work upon it, so in an infinitely higher sense, God completed
the creation of the world with all its inhabitants by ceasing to
produce anything new, and entering into the rest of His all-
sufficient eternal Being, from which He had come forth, as it
were, at and in the creation of a world distinct from His own
essence.   Hence ceasing to create is called resting (נוח) in Ex.
xx. 11, and being refreshed (יִנָּפֵשׁ) in Ex. xxxi. 17.   The rest
into which God entered after the creation was complete, had its
own reality " in the reality of the work of creation, in contrast
with which the preservation of the world, when once created,
had the appearance of rest, though really a continuous creation " (*Ziegler*, p. 27).   This rest of the Creator was indeed
" the consequence of His self-satisfaction in the now united and
harmonious, though manifold whole;" but this self-satisfaction
of God in His creation, which we call His pleasure in His work,
was also a spiritual power, which streamed forth as a blessing
upon the creation itself, bringing it into the blessedness of the
rest of God and filling it with His peace.   This constitutes the
positive element in the completion which God gave to the work
of creation, by blessing and sanctifying the seventh day, because on it He found rest from the work which He by making
(לַעֲשׂוֹת *faciendo :* cf. *Ewald*, § 280d) had created.   The divine
act of blessing was a real communication of powers of salvation,
grace, and peace ; and sanctifying was not merely declaring
holy, but " communicating the attribute of holy," " placing in a
living relation to God, the Holy One, raising to a participation

in the pure clear light of the holiness of God." On קָדֹשׁ see
Ex. xix. 6. The blessing and sanctifying of the seventh day had
regard, no doubt, to the Sabbath, which Israel as the people of
God was afterwards to keep; but we are not to suppose that the
theocratic Sabbath was instituted here, or that the institution of
that Sabbath was transferred to the history of the creation. On
the contrary, the Sabbath of the Israelites had a deeper meaning, founded in the nature and development of the created
world, not for Israel only, but for all mankind, or rather for the
whole creation. As the whole earthly creation is subject to the
changes of time and the law of temporal motion and development; so all creatures not only stand in need of definite recurring periods of rest, for the sake of recruiting their strength
and gaining new power for further development, but they also
look forward to a time when all restlessness shall give place to
the blessed rest of the perfect consummation. To this rest the
resting of God (ἡ κατάπαυσις) points forward; and to this rest,
this divine σαββατισμός (Heb. iv. 9), shall the whole world,
especially man, the head of the earthly creation, eventually come.
For this God ended His work by blessing and sanctifying the
day when the whole creation was complete. In connection with
Heb. iv., some of the fathers have called attention to the fact,
that the account of the seventh day is not summed up, like the
others, with the formula "evening was and morning was;" thus,
e.g., *Augustine* writes at the close of his confessions: *dies septimus
sine vespera est nec habet occasum, quia sanctificasti eum ad per-
mansionem sempiternam.* But true as it is that the Sabbath of
God has no evening, and that the σαββατισμός, to which the
creature is to attain at the end of his course, will be bounded by
no evening, but last for ever; we must not, without further
ground, introduce this true and profound idea into the seventh
creation-day. We could only be warranted in adopting such
an interpretation, and understanding by the concluding day
of the work of creation a period of endless duration, on the
supposition that the six preceding days were so many periods in
the world's history, which embraced the time from the beginning of the creation to the final completion of its development.
But as the six creation-days, according to the words of the text,
were earthly days of ordinary duration, we must understand the
seventh in the same way; and that all the more, because in every

passage, in which it is mentioned as the foundation of the theocratic Sabbath, it is regarded as an ordinary day (Ex. xx. 11,
xxxi. 17). We must conclude, therefore, that on the seventh
day, on which God rested from His work, the world also, with
all its inhabitants, attained to the sacred rest of God; that the
κατάπαυσις and σαββατισμός of God were made a rest and
sabbatic festival for His creatures, especially for man; and that
this day of rest of the new created world, which the forefathers
of our race observed in paradise, as long as they continued in a
state of innocence and lived in blessed peace with their God
and Creator, was the beginning and type of the rest to which
the creation, after it had fallen from fellowship with God
through the sin of man, received a promise that it should once
more be restored through redemption, at its final consummation.

I. HISTORY OF THE HEAVENS AND THE EARTH.

CHAP. II. 4–IV. 26.

Contents and Heading.

The historical account of the world, which commences at the
completion of the work of creation, is introduced as the "*History of the heavens and the earth*," and treats in three sections,
(*a*) of the original condition of man in paradise (chap. ii. 5–
25); (*b*) of the fall (chap. iii.); (*c*) of the division of the human
race into two widely different families, so far as concerns their
relation to God (chap. iv.).—The words, "*these are the tholedoth
of the heavens and the earth when they were created*," form the
heading to what follows. This would never have been disputed,
had not preconceived opinions as to the composition of Genesis
obscured the vision of commentators. The fact that in every
other passage, in which the formula "these (and these) are the
tholedoth" occurs (viz. ten times in Genesis; also in Num. iii. 1,
Ruth iv. 18, 1 Chron. i. 29), it is used as a heading, and that in
this passage the true meaning of תולדות precludes the possibility
of its being an appendix to what precedes, fully decides the
question. The word תולדות, which is only used in the plural,

and never occurs except in the construct state or with suffixes, is a *Hiphil* noun from הוֹלִיד, and signifies literally the generation or posterity of any one, then the development of these generations or of his descendants; in other words, the history of those who are begotten, or the account of what happened to them and what they performed. In no instance whatever is it the history of the birth or origin of the person named in the genitive, but always the account of his family and life. According to this use of the word, we cannot understand by the *tholedoth* of the heavens and the earth the account of the *origin* of the universe, since according to the biblical view the different things which make up the heavens and the earth can neither be regarded as generations or products of cosmogonic and geogonic evolutions, nor be classed together as the posterity of the heavens and the earth. All the creatures in the heavens and on earth were made by God, and called into being by His word, notwithstanding the fact that He caused some of them to come forth from the earth. Again, as the completion of the heavens and the earth with all their host has already been described in chap. ii. 1–3, we cannot understand by "the heavens and the earth," in ver. 4, the primary material of the universe in its elementary condition (in which case the literal meaning of הוֹלִיד would be completely relinquished, and the "*tholedoth* of the heavens and the earth" be regarded as indicating this chaotic beginning as the first stage in a series of productions), but the universe itself after the completion of the creation, at the commencement of the historical development which is subsequently described. This places its resemblance to the other sections, commencing with "these are the generations," beyond dispute. Just as the *tholedoth* of Noah, for example, do not mention his birth, but contain his history and the birth of his sons; so the *tholedoth* of the heavens and the earth do not describe the origin of the universe, but what happened to the heavens and the earth after their creation. בְּהִבָּרְאָם does not preclude this, though we cannot render it " after they were created." For even if it were grammatically allowable to resolve the participle into a pluperfect, the parallel expressions in chap. v. 1, 2, would prevent our doing so. As "the day of their creation" mentioned *there*, is not a day after the creation of Adam, but the day on which he was created; the same words, when occurring *here*, must also refer to a time when the heavens and the earth were already created: and just as in chap. v. 1 the creation of the universe forms the starting-point to the account of the development of the human race through the generations of Adam, and is recapitulated for that reason; so here the creation of the universe is mentioned as the starting-point to the account of its historical development, because this account looks back to particular points in the creation itself, and describes them more minutely as the preliminaries to the subsequent course of the world. הבראם is explained by the clause, "*in the day that Jehovah God created the earth and the heavens.*" Although this clause is closely related to what follows, the simplicity of the account prevents our regarding it as the *protasis* of a period, the apodosis of which does not follow till ver. 5 or even ver. 7. The former is grammatically impossible, because in ver. 5 the noun stands first, and not the verb, as we should expect in such a case (cf. iii. 5). The latter is grammatically tenable indeed, since vers. 5, 6, might be introduced into the main sentence as conditional clauses; but it is not probable, inasmuch as we should then have a parenthesis of most unnatural length. The clause must therefore be regarded as forming part of the heading. There are two points here that are worthy of notice: first, the unusual combination, "earth and heaven," which only occurs in Ps. cxlviii. 13, and shows that the *earth* is the scene of the history about to commence, which was of such momentous importance to the whole world; and secondly, the introduction of the name JEHOVAH in connection with ELOHIM. That the hypothesis, which traces the interchange in the two names in Genesis to different documents, does not suffice to explain the occurrence of Jehovah Elohim in chap. ii. 4–iii. 24, even the supporters of this hypothesis cannot possibly deny. Not only is God called Elohim alone in the middle of this section, viz. in the address to the serpent, a clear proof that the interchange of the names has reference to their different significations; but the use of the double name, which occurs here twenty times though rarely met with elsewhere, is always significant. In the Pentateuch we only find it in Ex. ix. 30; in the other books of the Old Testament, in 2 Sam. vii. 22, 25; 1 Chron. xvii. 16, 17; 2 Chron. vi. 41, 42; Ps. lxxxiv. 8, 11; and Ps. l. 1, where the order is reversed; and in every instance it is used with peculiar emphasis, to give prominence to the fact that *Jehovah* is truly Elohim, whilst in Ps. l. 1 the Psalmist advances from the general name *El* and *Elohim* to *Jehovah*, as the personal name of the God of Israel. In this section the combination *Jehovah Elohim* is expressive of the fact, that Jehovah is God, or one with Elohim. Hence Elohim is placed after Jehovah. For the constant use of the double name is not intended to teach that Elohim who created the world was Jehovah, but that Jehovah, who visited man in paradise, who punished him for the transgression of His command, but gave him a promise of victory over the tempter, was Elohim, the same God, who created the heavens and the earth.

The two names may be distinguished thus : *Elohim*, the plural of אֱלוֹהַּ, which is only used in the loftier style of poetry, is an infinitive noun from אָלַהּ to fear, and signifies awe, fear, then the object of fear, the highest Being to be feared, like פַּחַד, which is used interchangeably with it in chap. xxxi. 42, 53, and מוֹרָא in Ps. lxxvi. 12 (cf. Isa. viii. 12, 13). The plural is not used for the abstract, in the sense of divinity, but to express the notion of God in the fulness and multiplicity of the divine powers. It is employed both in a numerical, and also in an intensive sense, so that Elohim is applied to the (many) gods of the heathen as well as to the one true God, in whom the highest and absolute fulness of the divine essence is contained. In this intensive sense Elohim depicts the one true God as the infinitely great and exalted One, who created the heavens and the earth, and who preserves and governs every creature. According to its derivation, however, it is object rather than subject, so that in the plural form the concrete unity of the personal God falls back behind the wealth of the divine potencies which His being contains. In this sense, indeed, both in Genesis and the later, poetical, books, Elohim is used without the article, as a proper name for the true God, even in the mouth of heathen (1 Sam. iv. 7); but in other places, and here and there in Genesis, it occurs as an appellative *with* the article, by which prominence is given to the absoluteness or personality of God (chap. v. 22, vi. 9, etc.).—The name JEHOVAH, on the other hand, was originally a proper name, and according to the explanation given by God Himself to Moses (Ex. iii. 14, 15), was formed from the imperfect of the verb הָיָה = הָוָה. God calls Himself אֶהְיֶה אֲשֶׁר אֶהְיֶה, then more briefly

אֶהְיֶה, and then again, by changing the first person into the third, יהוה. From the derivation of this name from the imperfect, it follows that it was either pronounced יַהְוֶה or יֲהֶוֶה, and had come down from the pre-Mosaic age; for the form הָוָה had been forced out of the spoken language by הָיָה even in Moses' time. The Masoretic pointing יְהֹוָה belongs to a time when the Jews had long been afraid to utter this name at all, and substituted אֲדֹנָי, the vowels of which therefore were placed as *Keri*, the word to be read, under the *Kethib* יהוה, unless יהוה stood in apposition to אֲדֹנָי, in which case the word was read אֱלֹהִים and pointed יֱהֹוִה (a pure monstrosity).[1] This custom, which sprang from a mis-interpretation of Lev. xxiv. 16, appears to have originated shortly after the captivity. Even in the canonical writings of this age the name Jehovah was less and less employed, and in the Apocrypha and the Septuagint version ὁ Κύριος (the Lord) is invariably substituted, a custom in which the New Testament writers follow the LXX. (*vid. Oehler*).—If we seek for the meaning of יהוה, the expression אֶהְיֶה אֲשֶׁר אֶהְיֶה, in Ex. iii. 14, is neither to be rendered ἔσομαι ὃς ἔσομαι (*Aq., Theodt.*), " I shall be that I shall be " (*Luther*), nor " I shall be that which I will or am to be " (*M. Baumgarten*). Nor does it mean, " He who will be because He is Himself, the God of the future " (*Hofmann*). For in names formed from the third person im-perfect, the imperfect is not a future, but an aorist. According to the fundamental signification of the imperfect, names so formed point out a person as distinguished by a frequently or constantly manifested quality, in other words, they express a dis-tinctive characteristic (*vid. Ewald*, § 136; chap. xxv. 26, xxvii. 36, also xvi. 11 and xxi. 6). The Vulgate gives it correctly: *ego sum qui sum*, "I am who I am." "The repetition of the verb in the same form, and connected only by the relative, signifies that the being or act of the subject expressed in the verb is de-

---

[1] For a fuller discussion of the meaning and pronunciation of the name JEHOVAH vid. *Hengstenberg*, Dissertations on the Pentateuch i. p. 213 sqq.; *Oehler* in *Herzog's* Cyclopædia; and *Hölemann* in his Bibelstudien. The last, in common with *Stier* and others, decides in favour of the Masoretic pointing יְהֹוָה as giving the original pronunciation, chiefly on the ground of Rev. i. 4 and 5, 8; but the *theological* expansion ὁ ὢν καὶ ὁ ἦν καὶ ὁ ἐρχόμενος cannot be regarded as a *philological* proof of the formation of יהוה by the fusion of יְהִי, הֹוֶה, הָוָה into one word.

termined only by the subject itself" (*Hofmann*). The verb הָיָה
signifies "to be, to happen, to become;" but as neither happen-
ing nor becoming is applicable to God, the unchangeable, since
the pantheistic idea of a becoming God is altogether foreign
to the Scriptures, we must retain the meaning "*to be;*" not
forgetting, however, that as the Divine Being is not a resting,
or, so to speak, a dead being, but is essentially living, displaying
itself as living, working upon creation, and moving in the world,
the formation of יהוה from the imperfect precludes the idea of
abstract existence, and points out the Divine Being as moving,
pervading history, and manifesting Himself in the world. So
far then as the words אהיה אשר אהיה are condensed into a proper
name in יהוה, and God, therefore, " is He who is," inasmuch as
in His being, as historically manifested, He is the self-deter-
mining one, the name JEHOVAH, which we have retained as
being naturalized in the ecclesiastical phraseology, though we
are quite in ignorance of its correct pronunciation, " includes
both the absolute independence of God in His historical movements," and " the absolute constancy of God, or the fact that
in everything, in both words and deeds, He is essentially in
harmony with Himself, remaining always consistent" (*Oehler*).
The " I am who am," therefore, is the absolute *I*, the absolute
personality, moving with unlimited freedom ; and in distinction
from ELOHIM (the Being to be feared), He is the personal God
in His historical manifestation, in which the fulness of the
Divine Being unfolds itself to the world. This movement of
the personal God in history, however, has reference to the realization of the great purpose of the creation, viz. the salvation
of man. Jehovah therefore is the God of the history of salvation. This is not shown in the etymology of the name, but
in its historical expansion. It was as JEHOVAH that God manifested Himself to Abram (xv. 7), when He made the covenant
with him ; and as this name was neither derived from an attribute
of God, nor from a divine manifestation, we must trace its origin
to a revelation from God, and seek it in the declaration to Abram,
" I am Jehovah." Just as Jehovah here revealed Himself to
Abram as the God who led him out of Ur of the Chaldees, to
give him the land of Canaan for a possession, and thereby described Himself as the author of all the promises which Abram
received at his call, and which were renewed to him and to his

descendants, Isaac and Jacob; so did He reveal Himself to Moses (Ex. iii.) as the God of his fathers, to fulfil His promise to their seed, the people of Israel. Through these revelations Jehovah became a proper name for the God, who was working out the salvation of fallen humanity; and in this sense, not only is it used proleptically at the call of Abram (chap. xii.), but transferred to the primeval times, and applied to all the manifestations and acts of God which had for their object the rescue of the human race from its fall, as well as to the special plan inaugurated in the call of Abram. The preparation commenced in paradise. To show this, Moses has introduced the name *Jehovah* into the history in the present chapter, and has indicated the identity of Jehovah with Elohim, not only by the constant association of the two names, but also by the fact that in the heading (ver. 4*b*) he speaks of the creation described in chap. i. as the work of JEHOVAH ELOHIM.

PARADISE.—CHAP. II. 5–25.

The account in vers. 5–25 is not a second, complete and independent history of the creation, nor does it contain mere appendices to the account in chap. i.; but it describes the commencement of the history of the human race. This commencement includes not only a complete account of the creation of the first human pair, but a description of the place which God prepared for their abode, the latter being of the highest importance in relation to the self-determination of man, with its momentous consequences to both earth and heaven. Even in the history of the creation man takes precedence of all other creatures, as being created in the image of God and appointed lord of all the earth, though he is simply mentioned there as the last and highest link in the creation. To this our present account is attached, describing with greater minuteness the position of man in the creation, and explaining the circumstances which exerted the greatest influence upon his subsequent career. These circumstances were—the formation of man from the dust of the earth and the divine breath of life; the tree of knowledge in paradise; the formation of the woman, and the relation of the woman to the man. Of these three elements, the first forms the substratum to the other two. Hence the more exact

account of the creation of Adam is subordinated to, and inserted in, the description of paradise (ver. 7). In vers. 5 and 6,
with which the narrative commences, there is an evident allusion
to paradise: "*And as yet there was* (arose, grew) *no shrub of
the field upon the earth, and no herb of the field sprouted; for
Jehovah El had not caused it to rain upon the earth, and there
was no man to till the ground; and a mist arose from the earth
and watered the whole surface of the ground.*" הָיָה in parallelism
with צָמַח means to become, to arise, to proceed. Although the
growth of the shrubs and sprouting of the herbs are represented here as dependent upon the rain and the cultivation of
the earth by man, we must not understand the words as meaning that there was neither shrub nor herb before the rain and
dew, or before the creation of man, and so draw the conclusion
that the creation of the plants occurred either after or contemporaneously with the creation of man, in direct contradiction to chap. i. 11, 12. The creation of the plants is not alluded
to here at all, but simply the planting of the garden in Eden.
The growing of the shrubs and sprouting of the herbs is
different from the creation or first production of the vegetable
kingdom, and relates to the growing and sprouting of the plants
and germs which were called into existence by the creation, the
natural development of the plants as it had steadily proceeded
ever since the creation. This was dependent upon rain and
human culture; their creation was not. Moreover, *the shrub
and herb of the field* do not embrace the whole of the vegetable
productions of the earth. It is not a fact that "*the field* is
used in the second section in the same sense as *the earth* in the
first." שָׂדֶה is not "the widespread plain of the earth, the broad
expanse of land," but a field of arable land, soil fit for cultivation, which forms only a part of the "earth" or "ground."
Even the "beast of the field" in ver. 19 and iii. 1 is not
synonymous with the "beast of the earth" in chap. i. 24, 25,
but is a more restricted term, denoting only such animals as
live upon the field and are supported by its produce, whereas
the "beast of the earth" denotes all wild beasts as distinguished
from tame cattle and reptiles. In the same way, the "shrub of
the field" consists of such shrubs and tree-like productions of
the cultivated land as man raises for the sake of their fruit, and
the "herb of the field," all seed-producing plants, both corn

and vegetables, which serve as food for man and beast.—The mist (אֵד, vapour, which falls as rain, Job xxxvi. 27) is correctly regarded by *Delitzsch* as the creative beginning of the rain (הִמְטִיר) itself, from which we may infer, therefore, that it rained before the flood.

Ver. 7. " *Then Jehovah God formed man from dust of the ground.*" עָפָר is the accusative of the material employed (*Ewald* and *Gesenius*). The *Vav consec. imperf.* in vers. 7, 8, 9, does not indicate the order of time, or of thought; so that the meaning is not that God planted the garden in Eden after He had created Adam, nor that He caused the trees to grow after He had planted the garden and placed the man there. The latter is opposed to ver. 15; the former is utterly improbable. The process of man's creation is described minutely here, because it serves to explain his relation to God and to the surrounding world. He was formed from dust (not *de limo terræ*, from a clod of the earth, for עָפָר is not a solid mass, but the finest part of the material of the earth), and into his nostril a breath of life was breathed, by which he became an animated being. Hence the nature of man consists of a material substance and an immaterial principle of life. " *The breath of life*," *i.e.* breath producing life, does not denote the spirit by which man is distinguished from the animals, or the soul of man from that of the beasts, but only the life-breath (*vid.* 1 Kings xvii. 17). It is true, נְשָׁמָה generally signifies the human soul, but in chap. vii. 22 נִשְׁמַת־רוּחַ חַיִּים is used of men and animals both; and should any one explain this, on the ground that the allusion is chiefly to men, and the animals are connected *per zeugma*, or should he press the *ruach* attached, and deduce from this the use of *neshamah* in relation to men and animals, there are several passages in which *neshamah* is synonymous with *ruach* (*e.g.* Isa. xlii. 5; Job xxxii. 8, xxxiii. 4), or רוּח חַיִּים applied to animals (chap. vi. 17, vii. 15), or again *neshamah* used as equivalent to *nephesh* (*e.g.* Josh. x. 40, cf. vers. 28, 30, 32). For *neshamah*, the breathing, πνοή, is " the *ruach* in action" (*Auberlen*). Beside this, the man formed from the dust became, through the breathing of the " breath of life," a נֶפֶשׁ חַיָּה, an animated, and as such a living being; an expression which is also applied to fishes, birds, and land animals (i. 20, 21, 24, 30), and there is no proof of pre-eminence on the part of man. As

נֶפֶשׁ חַיָּה, ψυχη ζῶσα, does not refer to the soul merely, but to the whole man as an animated being, so נְשָׁמָה does not denote the spirit of man as distinguished from body and soul. On the relation of the soul to the spirit of man nothing can be gathered from this passage; the words, correctly interpreted, neither show that the soul is an emanation, an exhalation of the human spirit, nor that the soul was created before the spirit and merely received its life from the latter. The formation of man from dust and the breathing of the breath of life we must not understand in a mechanical sense, as if God first of all constructed a human figure from dust, and then, by breathing His breath of life into the clod of earth which he had shaped into the form of a man, made it into a living being. The words are to be understood θεοπρεπῶς. By an act of divine omnipotence man arose from the dust; and in the same moment in which the dust, by virtue of creative omnipotence, shaped itself into a human form, it was pervaded by the divine breath of life, and created a living being, so that we cannot say the body was earlier than the soul. The dust of the earth is merely the earthly substratum, which was formed by the breath of life from God into an animated, living, self-existent being. When it is said, "God breathed into his nostril the breath of life," it is evident that this description merely gives prominence to the peculiar sign of life, viz. breathing; since it is obvious, that what God breathed into man could not be the air which man breathes; for it is not that which breathes, but simply that which is breathed. Consequently, breathing into the nostril can only mean, that "God, through His own breath, produced and combined with the bodily form that principle of life, which was the origin of all human life, and which constantly manifests its existence in the breath inhaled and exhaled through the nose" (*Delitzsch*, Psychol. p. 62). Breathing, however, is common both to man and beast; so that this cannot be the sensuous analogon of the supersensuous spiritual life, but simply the principle of the physical life of the soul. Nevertheless the vital principle in man is different from that in the animal, and the human soul from the soul of the beast. This difference is indicated by the way in which man received the breath of life from God, and so became a living soul. "The beasts arose at the creative word of God, and no communication of the spirit is mentioned even in ch. ii. 19; the origin of their soul was coincident with that of their corporeality, and their life was merely the individualization of the universal life, with which all matter was filled in the beginning by the Spirit of God. On the other hand, the human spirit is not a mere individualization of the divine breath which breathed upon the material of the world, or of the universal spirit of nature; nor is his body merely a production of the earth when stimulated by the creative word of God. The earth does not bring forth his body, but God Himself puts His hand to the work and forms him; nor does the life already imparted to the world by the Spirit of God individualize itself in him, but God breathes directly into the nostrils of the one man, in the whole fulness of His personality, the breath of life, that in a manner corresponding to the personality of God he may become a living soul" (*Delitzsch*). This was the foundation of the pre-eminence of man, of his likeness to God and his immortality; for by this he was formed into a personal being, whose immaterial part was not merely soul, but a soul breathed entirely by God, since spirit and soul were created together through the inspiration of God. As the spiritual nature of man is described simply by the act of breathing, which is discernible by the senses, so the name which God gives him (chap. v. 2) is founded upon the earthly side of his being: ADAM, from אדמה (*adamah*), earth, the earthly element, like *homo* from *humus*, or from χαμα, χαμαί, χαμάθεν, to guard him from self-exaltation, not from the red colour of his body, since this is not a distinctive characteristic of man, but common to him and to many other creatures. The name man (*Mensch*), on the other hand, from the Sanskrit *mânuscha, manuschja*, from *man* to think, manas = mens, expresses the spiritual inwardness of our nature.

Ver. 8. The abode, which God prepared for the first man, was a "*garden in Eden*," also called "the garden of Eden" (ver. 15, chap. iii. 23, 24; Joel ii. 3), or Eden (Isa. li. 3; Ezek. xxviii. 13, xxxi. 9). EDEN (עֵדֶן, *i.e.* delight) is the proper name of a particular district, the situation of which is described in vers. 10 sqq.; but it must not be confounded with the Eden of Assyria (2 Kings xix. 12, etc.) and Cœlesyria (Amos i. 5), which is written with double seghol. The garden (*lit.* a place hedged round) was to the east, *i.e.* in the eastern portion, and is generally called Paradise from the Septuagint version, in which the word is ren-

dered παράδεισος. This word, according to *Spiegel*, was derived
from the Zendic *pairi-daêza*, a hedging round, and passed into
the Hebrew in the form פַּרְדֵּס (Cant. iv. 13; Eccl. ii. 5; Neh.
ii. 8), a park, probably through the commercial relations which
Solomon established with distant countries. In the garden itself
God caused all kinds of trees to grow out of the earth; and
among them were two, which were called "the tree of life" and
"the tree of knowledge of good and evil," on account of their
peculiar significance in relation to man (see ver. 16 and chap. iii.
22). הַדַּעַת, an infinitive, as Jer. xxii. 16 shows, has the article
here because the phrase דַעַת טוֹב וָרָע is regarded as one word, and
in Jeremiah from the nature of the predicate.—Ver. 10. "*And
there was a river going out of Eden, to water the garden; and from
thence it divided itself, and became four heads;*" *i.e.* the stream
took its rise in Eden, flowed through the garden to water it, and
on leaving the garden was divided into four heads or beginnings
of rivers, that is, into four arms or separate streams. For this
meaning of רָאשִׁים see Ezek. xvi. 25, Lam. ii. 19. Of the four
rivers whose names are given to show the geographical situation of paradise, the last two are unquestionably Tigris and
Euphrates. *Hiddekel* occurs in Dan. x. 4 as the Hebrew name
for Tigris; in the inscriptions of Darius it is called *Tigrâ* (or the
arrow, according to *Strabo, Pliny,* and *Curtius*), from the Zendic
tighra, pointed, sharp, from which probably the meaning stormy
(*rapidus Tigris, Hor. Carm.* 4, 14, 46) was derived. It flows
before (קִדְמַת), in front of, Assyria, not to the east of Assyria;
for the province of Assyria, which must be intended here, was
on the eastern side of the Tigris: moreover, neither the meaning, "to the east of," nor the identity of קִדְמַת and מִקֶּדֶם has
been, or can be, established from chap. iv. 16, 1 Sam. xiii. 5,
or Ezek. xxxix. 11, which are the only other passages in which
the word occurs, as *Ewald* himself acknowledges. *P'rath,* which
was not more minutely described because it was so generally
known, is the Euphrates; in old Persian, *Ufrâta,* according to
Delitzsch, or the good and fertile stream; *Ufrâtu,* according to
Spiegler, or the well-progressing stream. According to the
present condition of the soil, the sources of the Euphrates and
Tigris are not so closely connected that they could be regarded
as the commencements of a common stream which has ceased to
exist. The main sources of the Tigris, it is true, are only 2000

paces from the Euphrates, but they are to the north of Diar-
bekr, in a range of mountains which is skirted on three sides by
the upper course of the Euphrates, and separates them from
this river.   We must also look in the same country, the highlands of Armenia, for the other two rivers, if the description of
paradise actually rests upon an ancient tradition, and is to be
regarded as something more than a mythical invention of the
fancy.   The name *Phishon* sounds like the *Phasis* of the ancients, with which *Reland* supposed it to be identical; and *Chavilah* like *Colchis*, the well-known gold country of the ancients.
But the Φάσις ὁ Κόλχος (*Herod.* 4, 37, 45) takes its rise in the
Caucasus, and not in Armenia.   A more probable conjecture,
therefore, points to the *Cyrus* of the ancients, which rises in
Armenia, flows northwards to a point not far from the eastern
border of Colchis, and then turns eastward in Iberia, from which
it flows in a south-easterly direction to the Caspian Sea.   The
expression, "*which compasseth the whole land of Chavilah*," would
apply very well to the course of this river from the eastern border of Colchis; for סבב does not necessarily signify to surround,
but to pass through with different turns, or to skirt in a semi-
circular form, and *Chavilah* may have been larger than modern
Colchis.   It is not a valid objection to this explanation, that in
every other place Chavilah is a district of Southern Arabia.
The identity of this Chavilah with the Chavilah of the Jok-
tanites (chap. x. 29, xxv. 18 ; 1 Sam. xv. 7) or of the Cushites
(chap. x. 7 ; 1 Chron. i. 9) is disproved not only by the article
used here, which distinguishes it from the other, but also by the
description of it as land where gold, bdolach, and the shoham-
stone are found; a description neither requisite nor suitable in
the case of the Arabian Chavilah, since these productions are
not to be met with there.   This characteristic evidently shows
that the Chavilah mentioned here was entirely distinct from the
other, and a land altogether unknown to the Israelites.—What
we are to understand by הַבְּדֹלַח is uncertain.   There is no certain
ground for the meaning "*pearls*," given in *Saad.* and the later
Rabbins, and adopted by *Bochart* and others.   The rendering
βδέλλα or βδέλλιον, *bdellium*, a vegetable gum, of which *Dioscorus* says, οἱ δὲ μάδελκον οἱ δὲ βολχὸν καλοῦσι, and *Pliny*, " *alii
brochon appellant, alii malacham, alii maldacon*," is favoured by
the similarity in the name ; but, on the other side, there is the

fact that *Pliny* describes this gum as *nigrum* and *hadrobolon*,
and *Dioscorus* as ὑποπέλιον (blackish), which does not agree
with Num. xi. 7, where the appearance of the *white* grains of
the manna is compared to that of *bdolach*.—The stone *shoham*,
according to most of the early versions, is probably the *beryl*,
which is most likely the stone intended by the LXX. (ὁ λίθος
ὁ πράσινος, the leek-green stone), as *Pliny*, when speaking of
beryls, describes those as *probatissimi, qui viriditatem puri maris
imitantur;* but according to others it is the *onyx* or *sardonyx*
(*vid. Ges. s. v.*).[1] The *Gihon* (from גיח to break forth) is the
Araxes, which rises in the neighbourhood of the Euphrates,
flows from west to east, joins the Cyrus, and falls with it into
the Caspian Sea. The name corresponds to the Arabic *Jaihun*,
a name given by the Arabians and Persians to several large
rivers. The land of *Cush* cannot, of course, be the later Cush,
or Ethiopia, but must be connected with the Asiatic Κοσσαία,
which reached to the Caucasus, and to which the Jews (of Shir-
wan) still give this name. But even though these four streams
do not now spring from one source, but on the contrary their
sources are separated by mountain ranges, this fact does not
prove that the narrative before us is a myth. Along with or
since the disappearance of paradise, that part of the earth may
have undergone such changes that the precise locality can no
longer be determined with certainty.[2]

[1] The two productions furnish no proof that the Phishon is to be sought
for in India. The assertion that the name *bdolach* is Indian, is quite unfounded, for it cannot be proved that *madâlaka* in Sanscrit is a vegetable
gum; nor has this been proved of *madâra*, which is possibly related to it
(cf. *Lassen's indische Althk.* 1, 290 note). Moreover, *Pliny* speaks of *Bac-
triana* as the land " *in qua Bdellium est nominatissimum,*" although he adds,
"*nascitur et in Arabia Indiaque, et Media ac Babylone ;*" and *Isidorus* says
of the *Bdella* which comes from India, " *Sordida est et nigra et majori
gleba,*" which, again, does not agree with Num. xi. 7.—The *shoham-stone*
also is not necessarily associated with India ; for although *Pliny* says of the
beryls, "*India eos gignit, raro alibi repertos,*" he also observes, " *in nostro
orbe aliquando circa Pontum inveniri putantur.*"

[2] That the continents of our globe have undergone great changes since
the creation of the human race, is a truth sustained by the facts of natural
history and the earliest national traditions, and admitted by the most celebrated naturalists. (See the collection of proofs made by *Keerl.*) These
changes must not be all attributed to the flood ; many may have occurred
before and many after, like the catastrophe in which the Dead Sea origin-

Vers. 15–17. After the preparation of the garden in Eden God placed the man there, to dress it and to keep it. יַנִּיחֵהוּ not merely expresses removal thither, but the fact that the man was placed there to lead a life of repose, not indeed in inactivity, but in fulfilment of the course assigned him, which was very different from the trouble and restlessness of the weary toil into which he was plunged by sin. In paradise he was to dress (*colere*) the garden; for the earth was meant to be tended and cultivated by man, so that without human culture, plants and even the different varieties of corn degenerate and grow wild. Cultivation therefore preserved (שמר to keep) the divine plantation, not merely from injury on the part of any evil power, either penetrating into, or already existing in the creation, but also from running wild through natural degeneracy. As nature was created for man, it was his vocation not only to ennoble it by his work, to make it subservient to himself, but also to raise it into the sphere of the spirit and further its glorification. This applied not merely to the soil beyond the limits of paradise, but to the garden itself, which, although the most perfect portion of the terrestrial creation, was nevertheless susceptible of development, and which was allotted to man, in order that by his care and culture he might make it into a transparent mirror of the glory of the Creator.—Here too the man was to commence his own spiritual development. To this end God had planted two trees in the midst of the garden of Eden; the one to train his spirit through the exercise of obedience to the word of God, the other to transform his earthly nature into the spiritual essence of eternal life. These trees received their names from their relation to man, that is to say, from the effect which the eating of their fruit was destined to produce upon human life and its development. The fruit of the tree of life conferred the power of eternal, immortal life; and the tree of knowledge was planted, to lead men to the knowledge of good and evil. The knowledge of good and evil was no mere experience of good and ill, but a moral element in that spiritual development, through

ated, without being recorded in history as this has been. Still less must we interpret chap. xi. 1 (compared with x. 25), as *Fabri* and *Keerl* have done, as indicating a complete revolution of the globe, or a geogonic process, by which the continents of the old world were divided, and assumed their present physiognomy.

which the man created in the image of God was to attain to the
filling out of that nature, which had already been planned in the
likeness of God. For not to know what good and evil are, is a
sign of either the immaturity of infancy (Deut. i. 39), or the
imbecility of age (2 Sam. xix. 35); whereas the power to distinguish good and evil is commended as the gift of a king (1
Kings iii. 9) and the wisdom of angels (2 Sam. xiv. 17), and in
the highest sense is ascribed to God Himself (chap. iii. 5, 22).
Why then did God prohibit man from eating of the tree of the
knowledge of good and evil, with the threat that, as soon as he
ate thereof, he would surely die? (The inf. abs. before the
finite verb intensifies the latter: vid. *Ewald*, § 312*a*). Are we
to regard the tree as poisonous, and suppose that some fatal property resided in the fruit? A supposition which so completely
ignores the ethical nature of sin is neither warranted by the
antithesis, nor by what is said in chap. iii. 22 of the tree of
life, nor by the fact that the eating of the forbidden fruit was
actually the cause of death. Even in the case of the tree of
life, the power is not to be sought in the physical character of
the fruit. No earthly fruit possesses the power to give immortality to the life which it helps to sustain. Life is not rooted
in man's corporeal nature; it was in his spiritual nature that it
had its origin, and from this it derives its stability and permanence also. It may, indeed, be brought to an end through
the destruction of the body; but it cannot be exalted to perpetual duration, *i.e.* to immortality, through its preservation and
sustenance. And this applies quite as much to the original
nature of man, as to man after the fall. A body formed from
earthly materials could not be essentially immortal: it would of
necessity either be turned to earth, and fall into dust again, or
be transformed by the spirit into the immortality of the soul.
The power which transforms corporeality into immortality is
spiritual in its nature, and could only be imparted to the earthly
tree or its fruit through the word of God, through a special
operation of the Spirit of God, an operation which we can only
picture to ourselves as sacramental in its character, rendering
earthly elements the receptacles and vehicles of celestial powers.
God had given such a sacramental nature and significance to the
two trees in the midst of the garden, that their fruit could and
would produce supersensual, mental, and spiritual effects upon

the nature of the first human pair. The tree of life was to impart the power of transformation into eternal life. The tree of knowledge was to lead man to the knowledge of good and evil; and, according to the divine intention, this was to be attained through his not eating of its fruit. This end was to be accomplished, not only by his discerning in the limit imposed by the prohibition the difference between that which accorded with the will of God and that which opposed it, but also by his coming eventually, through obedience to the prohibition, to recognise the fact that all that is opposed to the will of God is an evil to be avoided, and, through voluntary resistance to such evil, to the full development of the freedom of choice originally imparted to him into the actual freedom of a deliberate and self-conscious choice of good. By obedience to the divine will he would have attained to a godlike knowledge of good and evil, *i.e.* to one in accordance with his own likeness to God. He would have detected the evil in the approaching tempter; but instead of yielding to it, he would have resisted it, and thus have made good his own property acquired with consciousness and of his own free-will, and in this way by proper self-determination would gradually have advanced to the possession of the truest liberty. But as he failed to keep this divinely appointed way, and ate the forbidden fruit in opposition to the command of God, the power imparted by God to the fruit was manifested in a different way. He learned the difference between good and evil from his own guilty experience, and by receiving the evil into his own soul, fell a victim to the threatened death. Thus through his own fault the tree, which should have helped him to attain true freedom, brought nothing but the sham liberty of sin, and with it death, and that without any demoniacal power of destruction being conjured into the tree itself, or any fatal poison being hidden in its fruit.

Vers. 18-25. CREATION OF THE WOMAN.—As the creation of man is introduced in chap. i. 26, 27, with a divine decree, so here that of the woman is preceded by the divine declaration, *It is not good that the man should be alone; I will make him* עֵזֶר כְּנֶגְדּוֹ, *a help of his like:* " *i.e.* a helping being, in which, as soon as he sees it, he may recognise himself" (*Delitzsch*). Of such a help the man stood in need, in order that he might fulfil his calling, not only to perpetuate and multiply his race, but to cultivate and govern the earth. To indicate this, the general word עזר כנגדו is chosen, in which there is an allusion to the relation of the sexes. To call out this want, God brought the larger quadrupeds and birds to the man, " *to see what he would call them* (לו *lit.* each one); *and whatsoever the man might call every living being should be its name.*" The time when this took place must have been the sixth day, on which, according to chap. i. 27, the man and woman were created: and there is no difficulty in this, since it would not have required much time to bring the animals to Adam to see what he would call them, as the animals of paradise are all we have to think of; and the deep sleep into which God caused the man to fall, till he had formed the woman from his rib, need not have continued long. In chap. i. 27 the creation of the woman is linked with that of the man; but here the order of sequence is given, because the creation of the woman formed a chronological incident in the history of the human race, which commences with the creation of Adam. The circumstance that in ver. 19 the formation of the beasts and birds is connected with the creation of Adam by the *imperf. c.* ו *consec.*, constitutes no objection to the plan of creation given in chap. i. The arrangement may be explained on the supposition, that the writer, who was about to describe the relation of man to the beasts, went back to their creation, in the simple method of the early Semitic historians, and placed this first instead of making it subordinate; so that our modern style of expressing the same thought would be simply this: " God brought to Adam the beasts which He had formed."[1] Moreover, the allusion is not

---

[1] A striking example of this style of narrative we find in 1 Kings vii. 13. First of all, the building and completion of the temple are noticed several times in chap. vi., and the last time in connection with the year and month (chap. vi. 9, 14, 37, 38); after that, the fact is stated, that the royal palace was thirteen years in building; and then the writer proceeds thus: " And king Solomon sent and fetched Hiram from Tyre . . . . and he came to king Solomon, and did all his work; and made the two pillars," etc. Now, if we were to understand the historical preterite with *consec.*, here, as giving the order of sequence, Solomon would be made to send for the Tyrian artist, thirteen years after the temple was finished, to come and prepare the pillars for the porch, and all the vessels needed for the temple. But the writer merely expresses in Semitic style the simple thought, that " Hiram, whom Solomon fetched from Tyre, made the vessels," etc. Another instance we find in Judg. ii. 6.

to the creation of all the beasts, but simply to that of the beasts living in the field (game and tame cattle), and of the fowls of the air,—to beasts, therefore, which had been formed like man from the earth, and thus stood in a closer relation to him than water animals or reptiles. For God brought the animals to Adam, to show him the creatures which were formed to serve him, that He might see what he would call them. Calling or naming presupposes acquaintance. Adam is to become acquainted with the creatures, to learn their relation to him, and by giving them names to prove himself their lord. God does not order him to name them; but by bringing the beasts He gives him an opportunity of developing that intellectual capacity which constitutes his superiority to the animal world. "The man sees the animals, and thinks of what they are and how they look; and these thoughts, in themselves already inward words, take the form involuntarily of audible names, which he utters to the beasts, and by which he places the impersonal creatures in the first spiritual relation to himself, the personal being" (*Delitzsch*). Language, as *W. v. Humboldt* says, is "the organ of the inner being, or rather the inner being itself as it gradually attains to inward knowledge and expression." It is merely thought cast into articulate sounds or words. The thoughts of Adam with regard to the animals, to which he gave expression in the names that he gave them, we are not to regard as the mere results of reflection, or of abstraction from merely outward peculiarities which affected the senses; but as a deep and direct mental insight into the nature of the animals, which penetrated far deeper than such knowledge as is the simple result of reflecting and abstracting thought. The naming of the animals, therefore, led to this result, that there was not found a help meet for man. Before the creation of the woman we must regard the man (Adam) as being " neither male, in the sense of complete sexual distinction, nor androgynous as though both sexes were combined in the one individual created at the first, but as created in anticipation of the future, with a preponderant tendency, a male in simple potentiality, out of which state he passed, the moment the woman stood by his side, when the mere *potentia* became an actual antithesis" (*Ziegler*).—Then God caused a deep sleep to fall upon the man (ver. 21). תַּרְדֵּמָה, a deep sleep, in which all consciousness of the outer world and of one's own existence vanishes. Sleep is an essential element in the nature of man as ordained by God, and is quite as necessary for man as the interchange of day and night for all nature besides. But this deep sleep was different from natural sleep, and God caused it to fall upon the man by day, that He might create the woman out of him. " Everything out of which something new is to spring, sinks first of all into such a sleep " (*Ziegler*). צֵלָע means the side, and, as a portion of the human body, the rib. The correctness of this meaning, which is given by all the ancient versions, is evident from the words, " *God took one of his* צַלְעֹתָיו," which show that the man had several of them. " *And closed up flesh in the place thereof ;*" *i.e.* closed the gap which had been made, with flesh which He put in the place of the rib. The woman was created, not of dust of the earth, but from a rib of Adam, because she was formed for an inseparable unity and fellowship of life with the man, and the mode of her creation was to lay the actual foundation for the moral ordinance of marriage. As the moral idea of the unity of the human race required that man should not be created as a genus or plurality,[1] so the moral relation of the two persons establishing the unity of the race required that man should be created first, and then the woman from the body of the man. By this the priority and superiority of the man, and the dependence of the woman upon the man, are established as an ordinance of divine creation. This ordinance of God forms the root of that tender

---

[1] Natural science can only demonstrate the unity of the human race, not the descent of all men from one pair, though many naturalists question and deny even the former, but without any warrant from anthropological facts. For every thorough investigation leads to the conclusion arrived at by the latest inquirer in this department, *Th. Waitz*, that not only are there no facts in natural history which preclude the unity of the various races of men, and fewer difficulties in the way of this assumption than in that of the opposite theory of specific diversities ; but even in mental respects there are no specific differences within the limits of the race. *Delitzsch* has given an admirable summary of the proofs of unity. " That the races of men," he says, " are not species of one genus, but varieties of one species, is confirmed by the agreement in the physiological and pathological phenomena in them all, by the similarity in the anatomical structure, in the fundamental powers and traits of the mind, in the limits to the duration of life, in the normal temperature of the body and the average rate of pulsation, in the duration of pregnancy, and in the unrestricted fruitfulness of marriages between the various races."

love with which the man loves the woman as himself, and by which marriage becomes a type of the fellowship of love and life, which exists between the Lord and His Church (Eph. vi. 32). If the fact that the woman was formed from a rib, and not from any other part of the man, is significant ; all that we can find in this is, that the woman was made to stand as a helpmate by the side of the man, not that there was any allusion to conjugal love as founded in the heart ; for the text does not speak of the rib as one which was next the heart. The word בָּנָה is worthy of note : from the rib of the man God *builds* the female, through whom the human race is to be *built up* by the male (chap. xvi. 2, xxx. 3).—Vers. 23, 24. The design of God in the creation of the woman is perceived by Adam, as soon as he awakes, when the woman is brought to him by God. Without a revelation from God, he discovers in the woman *bone of his bones and flesh of his flesh.*" The words, " *this is now* (הַפַּעַם *lit. this time*) *bone of my bones,*" etc., are expressive of joyous astonishment at the suitable helpmate, whose relation to himself he describes in the words, " *she shall be called Woman, for she is taken out of man.*" אִשָּׁה is well rendered by *Luther*, " *Männin*" (a female man), like the old Latin *vira* from *vir*. The words which follow, " *therefore shall a man leave his father and his mother, and shall cleave unto his wife, and they shall become one flesh,*" are not to be regarded as Adam's, first on account of the עַל־כֵּן, which is always used in Genesis, with the exception of chap. xx. 6, xlii. 21, to introduce remarks of the writer, either of an archæological or of a historical character, and secondly, because, even if Adam on seeing the woman had given prophetic utterance to his perception of the mystery of marriage, he could not with propriety have spoken of father and mother. They are the words of Moses, written to bring out the truth embodied in the fact recorded as a divinely appointed result, to exhibit marriage as the deepest corporeal and spiritual unity of man and woman, and to hold up monogamy before the eyes of the people of Israel as the form of marriage ordained by God. But as the words of Moses, they are the utterance of divine revelation ; and Christ could quote them, therefore, as the word of God (Matt. xix. 5). By the leaving of father and mother, which applies to the woman as well as to the man, the conjugal union is shown to be a spiritual oneness, a vital communion of heart as well as of body, in which it finds its consummation. This union is of a totally different nature from that of parents and children ; hence marriage between parents and children is entirely opposed to the ordinance of God. Marriage itself, notwithstanding the fact that it demands the leaving of father and mother, is a holy appointment of God ; hence celibacy is not a higher or holier state, and the relation of the sexes for a pure and holy man is a pure and holy relation. This is shown in ver. 25: " *They were both naked* (עֲרוּמִּים, with *dagesh* in the מ, is an abbreviated form of עֲרֵמִּים iii. 7, from עוּר to strip), *the man and his wife, and were not ashamed.*" Their bodies were sanctified by the spirit, which animated them. Shame entered first with sin, which destroyed the normal relation of the spirit to the body, exciting tendencies and lusts which warred against the soul, and turning the sacred ordinance of God into sensual impulses and the lust of the flesh.

THE FALL.—CHAP. III.

The man, whom God had appointed lord of the earth and its inhabitants, was endowed with everything requisite for the development of his nature and the fulfilment of his destiny. In the fruit of the trees of the garden he had food for the sustenance of his life; in the care of the garden itself, a field of labour for the exercise of his physical strength ; in the animal and vegetable kingdom, a capacious region for the expansion of his intellect; in the tree of knowledge, a positive law for the training of his moral nature; and in the woman associated with him, a suitable companion and help. In such circumstances as these he might have developed both his physical and spiritual nature in accordance with the will of God. But a tempter approached him from the midst of the animal world, and he yielded to the temptation to break the command of God. The *serpent* is said to have been the tempter. But to any one who reads the narrative carefully in connection with the previous history of the creation, and bears in mind that man is there described as exalted far above all the rest of the animal world, not only by the fact of his having been created in the image of God and invested with dominion over all the creatures of the earth, but also because God breathed into him the breath of life, and no help meet for

him was found among the beasts of the field, and also that this
superiority was manifest in the gift of speech, which enabled
him to give names to all the rest—a thing which they, as speechless, were unable to perform,—it must be at once apparent that
it was not from the serpent, as a sagacious and crafty animal,
that the temptation proceeded, but that the serpent was simply
the tool of that evil spirit, who is met with in the further course
of the world's history under the name of SATAN (the opponent),
or the DEVIL (ὁ διάβολος, the slanderer or accuser).[1] When
the serpent, therefore, is introduced as speaking, and that just as
if it had been entrusted with the thoughts of God Himself, the
speaking must have emanated, not from the serpent, but from a
superior spirit, which had taken possession of the serpent for the
sake of seducing man.   This fact, indeed, is not distinctly stated
in the canonical books of the Old Testament; but that is simply
for the same educational reason which led Moses to transcribe
the account exactly as it had been handed down, in the pure
objective form of an outward and visible occurrence, and without any allusion to the causality which underlay the external
phenomenon, viz. not so much to oppose the tendency of contemporaries to heathen superstition and habits of intercourse
with the kingdom of demons, as to avoid encouraging the disposition to transfer the blame to the evil spirit which tempted man,
and thus reduce sin to a mere act of weakness.   But we find the
fact distinctly alluded to in the book of Wisdom ii. 24; and not
only is it constantly noticed in the rabbinical writings, where
the prince of the evil spirits is called the old serpent, or the serpent, with evident reference to this account, but it was introduced
at a very early period into Parsism also.   It is also attested by
Christ and His apostles (John viii. 44; 2 Cor. xi. 3 and 14;
Rom. xvi. 20; Rev. xii. 9, xx. 2), and confirmed by the tempta-

---

[1] There was a fall, therefore, in the higher spiritual world before the fall
of man; and this is not only plainly taught in 2 Pet. ii. 4 and Jude 6, but
assumed in everything that the Scriptures say of Satan.   But this event in
the world of spirits neither compels us to place the fall of Satan before the
six days' work of creation, nor to assume that the days represent long periods.
For as man did not continue long in communion with God, so the angel-
prince may have rebelled against God shortly after his creation, and not only
have involved a host of angels in his apostasy and fall, but have proceeded
immediately to tempt the men, who were created in the image of God, to
abuse their liberty by transgressing the divine command.

tion of our Lord.   The temptation of Christ is the counterpart of that of Adam.   Christ was tempted by the devil, not only like Adam, but because Adam had been tempted and overcome, in order that by overcoming the tempter He might wrest from the devil that dominion over the whole race which he had secured by his victory over the first human pair.   The tempter approached the Saviour openly ; to the first man he came in disguise.   The serpent is not a merely symbolical term applied to Satan ; nor was it only the form which Satan assumed ; but it was a real serpent, perverted by Satan to be the instrument of his temptation (vers. 1 and 14).   The possibility of such a perversion, or of the evil spirit using an animal for his own purposes, is not to be explained merely on the ground of the supremacy of spirit over nature, but also from the connection established in the creation itself between heaven and earth ; and still more, from the position originally assigned by the Creator to the spirits of heaven in relation to the creatures of earth.   The origin, force, and limits of this relation it is impossible to determine *a priori*, or in any other way than from such hints as are given in the Scriptures ; so that there is no reasonable ground for disputing the possibility of such an influence.   Notwithstanding his self-willed opposition to God, Satan is still a creature of God, and was created a good spirit ; although, in proud self-exaltation, he abused the freedom essential to the nature of a superior spirit to purposes of rebellion against his Maker.   He cannot therefore entirely shake off his dependence upon God.   And this dependence may possibly explain the reason, why he did not come " disguised as an angel of light" to tempt our first parents to disobedience, but was obliged to seek the instrument of his wickedness among the beasts of the field.   The trial of our first progenitors was ordained by God, because probation was essential to their spiritual development and self-determination.   But as He did not desire that they should be tempted to their fall, He would not suffer Satan to tempt them in a way which should surpass their human capacity. The tempted might therefore have resisted the tempter.   If, instead of approaching them in the form of a celestial being, in the likeness of God, he came in that of a creature, not only far inferior to God, but far below themselves, they could have no excuse for allowing a mere animal to persuade them to break the commandment of God.   For they had been made to have do-

minion over the beasts, and not to take their own law from them.
Moreover, the fact that an evil spirit was approaching them in
the serpent, could hardly be concealed from them. Its speaking
alone must have suggested that; for Adam had already become
acquainted with the nature of the beasts, and had not found one
among them resembling himself—not one, therefore, endowed
with reason and speech. The substance of the address, too, was
enough to prove that it was no good spirit which spake through
the serpent, but one at enmity with God. Hence, when they
paid attention to what he said, they were altogether without
excuse.

Vers. 1–8. *" The serpent was more subtle than all the beasts
of the field, which Jehovah God had made."*—The serpent is here
described not only as a beast, but also as a creature of God; it
must therefore have been good, like everything else that He
had made. Subtilty was a natural characteristic of the serpent
(Matt. x. 16), which led the evil one to select it as his instrument. Nevertheless the predicate עָרוּם is not used here in the
good sense of φρόνιμος (LXX.), *prudens*, but in the bad sense of
πανοῦργος, *callidus*. For its *subtilty* was manifested as the craft
of a tempter to evil, in the simple fact that it was to the weaker
woman that it turned; and *cunning* was also displayed in what
it said: *" Hath God indeed said, Ye shall not eat of all the trees of
the garden?"* אַף כִּי is an interrogative expressing surprise (as in
1 Sam. xxiii. 3, 2 Sam. iv. 11): "Is it really the fact that God
has prohibited you from eating of *all* the trees of the garden?"
The Hebrew may, indeed, bear the meaning, "hath God said,
ye shall not eat of *every* tree?" but from the context, and especially the conjunction, it is obvious that the meaning is, "ye
shall not eat of *any* tree." The serpent calls God by the name
of Elohim alone, and the woman does the same. In this more
general and indefinite name the personality of the living God
is obscured. To attain his end, the tempter felt it necessary to
change the living personal God into a merely general *numen
divinum*, and to exaggerate the prohibition, in the hope of excit
ing in the woman's mind partly distrust of God Himself, and
partly a doubt as to the truth of His word. And his words
were listened to. Instead of turning away, the woman replied,
*" We may eat of the fruit of the trees of the garden; but of the
fruit of the tree which is in the midst of the garden, God hath said,*

Ye shall not eat of it, neither shall ye touch it, lest ye die." She was aware of the prohibition, therefore, and fully understood its meaning; but she added, " *neither shall ye touch it,*" and proved by this very exaggeration that it appeared too stringent even to her, and therefore that her love and confidence towards God were already beginning to waver. Here was the beginning of her fall: " for doubt is the father of sin, and *skepsis* the mother of all transgression; and in this father and this mother, all our present knowledge has a common origin with sin" (*Ziegler*). From doubt, the tempter advances to a direct denial of the truth of the divine threat, and to a malicious suspicion of the divine love (vers. 4, 5). " *Ye will by no means die* " (לֹא is placed before the infinitive absolute, as in Ps. xlix. 8 and Amos ix. 8; for the meaning is not, " ye will not *die;*" but, ye will positively *not* die). " *But[1] God doth know that in the day ye eat thereof, your eyes will be opened,[2] and ye will be like God, knowing good and evil.*" That is to say, it is not because the fruit of the tree will injure you that God has forbidden you to eat it, but from ill-will and envy, because He does not wish you to be like Himself. "A truly satanic *double entendre*, in which a certain agreement between truth and untruth is secured!" By eating the fruit, man did obtain the knowledge of good and evil, and in this respect became like God (vers. 7 and 22). This was the truth which covered the falsehood " ye shall not die," and turned the whole statement into a lie, exhibiting its author as the father of lies, who abides not in the truth (John viii. 44). For the knowledge of good and evil, which man obtains by going into evil, is as far removed from the true likeness of God, which he would have attained by avoiding it, as the imaginary liberty of a sinner, which leads into bondage to sin and ends in death, is from the true liberty of a life of fellowship with God.—Ver. 6. The illusive hope of being like God excited a longing for the forbidden fruit. " *The woman saw that the tree was good for food, and that it was a pleasure to the eyes, and to be desired to make one wise* (הַשְׂכִּיל signifies to gain or show discernment or insight); *and she took of its fruit and ate, and gave to her husband by her* (who was present), *and he did eat.*" As distrust of God's com-

---

[1] כִּי used to establish a denial.

[2] וְנִפְקְחוּ perfect *c.* ו *consec.* See *Gesenius*, § 126, Note 1.

mand leads to a disregard of it, so the longing for a false independence excites a desire for the seeming good that has been
prohibited ; and this desire is fostered by the senses, until it
brings forth sin.   Doubt, unbelief, and pride were the roots of
the sin of our first parents, as they have been of all the sins of
their posterity.   The more trifling the object of their sin seems
to have been, the greater and more difficult does the sin itself
appear ; especially when we consider that the first men " stood
in a more direct relation to God, their Creator, than any other
man has ever done, that their hearts were pure, their discernment clear, their intercourse with God direct, that they were
surrounded by gifts just bestowed by Him, and could not excuse
themselves on the ground of any misunderstanding of the divine
prohibition, which threatened them with the loss of life in the
event of disobedience" (*Delitzsch*).   Yet not only did the woman
yield to the seductive wiles of the serpent, but even the man
allowed himself to be tempted by the woman.—Vers. 7, 8.
" *Then the eyes of them both were opened* " (as the serpent had
foretold : but what did they see ?), " *and they knew that they were
naked.*"   They had lost " that blessed blindness, the ignorance
of innocence, which knows nothing of nakedness" (*Ziegler*).
The discovery of their nakedness excited shame, which they
sought to conceal by an outward covering.   " *They sewed fig-
leaves together, and made themselves aprons.*"   The word תְּאֵנָה
always denotes the fig-tree, not the pisang (*Musa paradisiaca*),
nor the Indian banana, whose leaves are twelve feet long and two
feet broad, for there would have been no necessity to sew them
together at all.   חֲגֹרֹת, περιζώματα, are aprons, worn round the
hips.   It was here that the consciousness of nakedness first
suggested the need of covering, not because the fruit had poi-
soned the fountain of human life, and through some inherent
quality had immediately corrupted the reproductive powers of
the body (as *Hoffmann* and *Baumgarten* suppose), nor because
any physical change ensued in consequence of the fall ; but
because, with the destruction of the normal connection between
soul and body through sin, the body ceased to be the pure abode
of a spirit in fellowship with God, and in the purely natural
state of the body the consciousness was produced not merely of
the distinction of the sexes, but still more of the worthlessness
of the flesh ; so that the man and woman stood ashamed in each

other's presence, and endeavoured to hide the disgrace of their spiritual nakedness, by covering those parts of the body through which the impurities of nature are removed. That the natural feeling of shame, the origin of which is recorded here, had its root, not in sensuality or any physical corruption, but in the consciousness of guilt or shame before God, and consequently that it was the conscience which was really at work, is evident from the fact that the man and his wife hid themselves from Jehovah God among the trees of the garden, as soon as they heard the sound of His footsteps. קוֹל יְהוָֹה (the voice of Jehovah, ver. 8) is not the voice of God speaking or calling, but the sound of God walking, as in 2 Sam. v. 24, 1 Kings xiv. 6, etc.—*In the cool of the day* (lit. in the wind of the day), *i.e.* towards the evening, when a cooling wind generally blows. The men have broken away from God, but God will not and cannot leave them alone. He comes to them as one man to another. This was the earliest form of divine revelation. God conversed with the first man in a visible shape, as the Father and Instructor of His children. He did not adopt this mode for the first time after the fall, but employed it as far back as the period when He brought the beasts to Adam, and gave him the woman to be his wife (chap. ii. 19, 22). This human mode of intercourse between man and God is not a mere figure of speech, but a reality, having its foundation in the nature of humanity, or rather in the fact that man was created in the image of God, but not in the sense supposed by *Jakobi,* that "God *theomorphised* when creating man, and man therefore necessarily *anthropomorphises* when he thinks of God." The anthropomorphies of God have their real foundation in the divine condescension which culminated in the incarnation of God in Christ. They are to be understood, however, as implying, not that corporeality, or a bodily shape, is an essential characteristic of God, but that God having given man a bodily shape, when He created him in His own image, revealed Himself in a manner suited to his bodily senses, that He might thus preserve him in living communion with Himself.

Vers. 9–15. The man could not hide himself from God. "*Jehovah God called unto Adam, and said unto him, Where art thou?*" Not that He was ignorant of his hiding-place, but to bring him to a confession of his sin. And when Adam said that he had

hidden himself through fear of his nakedness, and thus sought
to hide the sin behind its consequences, his disobedience behind
the feeling of shame; this is not to be regarded as a sign of peculiar obduracy, but easily admits of a psychological explanation,
viz. that at the time he actually thought more of his nakedness
and shame than of his transgression of the divine command, and
his consciousness of the effects of his sin was keener than his
sense of the sin itself. To awaken the latter God said, " *Who
told thee that thou wast naked?*" and asked him whether he had
broken His command. He could not deny that he had, but
sought to excuse himself by saying, that the woman whom God
gave to be with him had given him of the tree. When the
woman was questioned, she pleaded as her excuse, that *the serpent had beguiled her* (or rather deceived her, ἐξαπάτησεν, 2 Cor.
xi. 3). In offering these excuses, neither of them denied the
fact. But the fault in both was, that they did not at once smite
upon their breasts. " It is so still; the sinner first of all endeavours to throw the blame upon others as tempters, and then upon
circumstances which God has ordained."—Vers. 14, 15. The sentence follows the examination, and is pronounced first of all upon
the serpent as the tempter : " *Because thou hast done this, thou art
cursed before all cattle, and before every beast of the field.*" מִן, literally *out of* the beasts, separate from them (Deut. xiv. 2 ; Judg. v.
24), is not a comparative signifying *more than*, nor does it mean
by ; for the curse did not proceed from the beasts, but from God,
and was not pronounced upon all the beasts, but upon the serpent
alone. The κτίσις, it is true, including the whole animal creation, has been " made subject to vanity" and " the bondage of
corruption," in consequence of the sin of man (Rom. viii. 20, 21);
yet this subjection is not to be regarded as the effect of the
curse, which was pronounced upon the serpent, having fallen
upon the whole animal world, but as the consequence of death
passing from man into the rest of the creation, and thoroughly
pervading the whole. The creation was drawn into the fall of
man, and compelled to share its consequences, because the whole
of the irrational creation was made for man, and made subject
to him as its head; consequently the ground was cursed for
man's sake, but not the animal world for the serpent's sake, or
even along with the serpent. The curse fell upon the serpent
for having tempted the woman, according to the same law by

which not only a beast which had injured a man was ordered to be put to death (chap. ix. 5; Ex. xxi. 28, 29), but any beast which had been the instrument of an unnatural crime was to be slain along with the man (Lev. xx. 15, 16); not as though the beast were an accountable creature, but in consequence of its having been made subject to man, not to injure his body or his life, or to be the instrument of his sin, but to subserve the great purpose of his life. "Just as a loving father," as *Chrysostom* says, "when punishing the murderer of his son, might snap in two the sword or dagger with which the murder had been committed." The proof, therefore, that the serpent was merely the instrument of an evil spirit, does not lie in the punishment itself, but in the manner in which the sentence was pronounced. When God addressed the animal, and pronounced a curse upon it, this presupposed that the curse had regard not so much to the irrational beast as to the spiritual tempter, and that the punishment which fell upon the serpent was merely a symbol of his own. The punishment of the serpent corresponded to the crime. It had exalted itself above the man; therefore upon its belly it should go, and dust it should eat all the days of its life. If these words are not to be robbed of their entire meaning, they cannot be understood in any other way than as denoting that the form and movements of the serpent were altered, and that its present repulsive shape is the effect of the curse pronounced upon it, though we cannot form any accurate idea of its original appearance. Going upon the belly (= creeping, Lev. xi. 42) was a mark of the deepest degradation; also the eating of dust, which is not to be understood as meaning that dust was to be its only food, but that while crawling in the dust it would also swallow dust (cf. Micah vii. 17; Isa. xlix. 23). Although this punishment fell literally upon the serpent, it also affected the tempter in a figurative or symbolical sense. He became the object of the utmost contempt and abhorrence; and the serpent still keeps the revolting image of Satan perpetually before the eye. This degradation was to be perpetual. "While all the rest of creation shall be delivered from the fate into which the fall has plunged it, according to Isa. lxv. 25, the instrument of man's temptation is to remain sentenced to perpetual degradation in fulfilment of the sentence, 'all the days of thy life,' and thus to prefigure the fate of the real tempter, for whom there is no deliverance" (*Hengstenberg*, Christology i. 15).—The presumption of the tempter was punished with the deepest degradation; and in like manner his sympathy with the woman was to be turned into eternal hostility (ver. 15) God established perpetual enmity, not only between the serpent and the woman, but also between the serpent's and the woman's seed, *i.e.* between the human and the serpent race. The seed of the woman would crush the serpent's head, and the serpent crush the heel of the woman's seed. The meaning, *terere, conterere*, is thoroughly established by the Chald., Syr., and Rabb. authorities, and we have therefore retained it, in harmony with the word συντρίβειν in Rom. xvi. 20, and because it accords better and more easily with all the other passages in which the word occurs, than the rendering *inhiare*, to regard with enmity, which is obtained from the combination of שׁוּף with שָׁאַף. The verb is construed with a double accusative, the second giving greater precision to the first (*vid. Ges.* § 139, note, and *Ewald,* § 281). The same word is used in connection with both head and heel, to show that on both sides the intention is to destroy the opponent; at the same time, the expressions head and heel denote a *majus* and *minus,* or, as *Calvin* says, *superius et inferius.* This contrast arises from the nature of the foes. The serpent can only seize the heel of the man, who walks upright; whereas the man can crush the head of the serpent, that crawls in the dust. But this difference is itself the result of the curse pronounced upon the serpent, and its crawling in the dust is a sign that it will be defeated in its conflict with man. However pernicious may be the bite of a serpent in the heel when the poison circulates throughout the body (chap. xlix. 17), it is not immediately fatal and utterly incurable, like the crushing of a serpent's head.

But even in this sentence there is an unmistakeable allusion to the evil and hostile being concealed behind the serpent. That the human race should triumph over the serpent, was a necessary consequence of the original subjection of the animals to man. When, therefore, God not merely confines the serpent within the limits assigned to the animals, but puts enmity between it and the woman, this in itself points to a higher, spiritual power, which may oppose and attack the human race through the serpent, but will eventually be overcome. Observe, too, that although in the first clause the seed of the serpent is opposed to the seed of the woman, in the second it is not over the seed of the serpent but over the serpent itself that the victory is said to be gained. *It*, *i.e.* the seed of the woman will crush *thy* head, and *thou* (not thy seed) wilt crush its heel. Thus the seed of the serpent is hidden behind the unity of the serpent, or rather of the foe who, through the serpent, has done such injury to man. This foe is Satan, who incessantly opposes the seed of the woman and bruises its heel, but is eventually to be trodden under its feet. It does not follow from this, however, apart from other considerations, that by the seed of the woman we are to understand *one* solitary person, one individual only. As the woman is the mother of all living (ver. 20), her seed, to which the victory over the serpent and its seed is promised, must be the human race. But if a direct and exclusive reference to Christ appears to be exegetically untenable, the allusion in the word to Christ is by no means precluded in consequence. In itself the idea of זֶרַע, the seed, is an indefinite one, since the posterity of a man may consist of a whole tribe or of one son only (iv. 25, xxi. 12, 13), and on the other hand, an entire tribe may be reduced to one single descendant and become extinct in him. The question, therefore, who is to be understood by the "seed" which is to crush the serpent's head, can only be answered from the history of the human race. But a point of much greater importance comes into consideration here. Against the natural serpent the conflict may be carried on by the whole human race, by all who are born of woman, but not against Satan. As he is a foe who can only be met with spiritual weapons, none can encounter him successfully but such as possess and make use of spiritual arms. Hence the idea of the "seed" is modified by the nature of the foe. If we look at the natural development of the human race, Eve bore three sons, but only one of them, viz. *Seth*, was really the seed by whom the human family was preserved through the flood and perpetuated in Noah: so, again, of the three sons of Noah, *Shem*, the blessed of Jehovah, from whom Abraham descended, was the only one in whose seed all nations were to be blessed, and that not through Ishmael, but through Isaac alone. Through these constantly repeated acts of divine selection, which were not arbitrary exclusions, but were rendered necessary by differences in the spiritual condition of the individuals concerned, the

"seed," to which the victory over Satan was promised, was
spiritually or ethically determined, and ceased to be co-extensive
with physical descent. This spiritual seed culminated in Christ,
in whom the Adamitic family terminated, henceforward to be
renewed by Christ as the second Adam, and restored by Him
to its original exaltation and likeness to God. In this sense
Christ is the seed of the woman, who tramples Satan under His
feet, not as an individual, but as the head both of the posterity
of the woman which kept the promise and maintained the conflict with the old serpent before His advent, and also of all those
who are gathered out of all nations, are united to Him by faith,
and formed into one body of which He is the head (Rom. xvi.
20). On the other hand, all who have not regarded and preserved the promise, have fallen into the power of the old serpent,
and are to be regarded as the seed of the serpent, whose head
will be trodden under foot (Matt. xxiii. 33; John viii. 44; 1
John iii. 8). If then the promise culminates in Christ, the fact
that the victory over the serpent is promised to the posterity of
the woman, not of the man, acquires this deeper significance,
that as it was through the woman that the craft of the devil
brought sin and death into the world, so it is also through the
woman that the grace of God will give to the fallen human race
the conqueror of sin, of death, and of the devil. And even if
the words had reference first of all to the fact that the woman
had been led astray by the serpent, yet in the fact that the
destroyer of the serpent was born of a woman (without a human
father) they were fulfilled in a way which showed that the promise must have proceeded from that Being, who secured its
fulfilment not only in its essential force, but even in its apparently casual form.

Vers. 16–19. It was not till the prospect of victory had been
presented, that a sentence of punishment was pronounced upon
both the man and the woman on account of their sin. The
woman, who had broken the divine command for the sake of
earthly enjoyment, was punished in consequence with the
sorrows and pains of pregnancy and childbirth. *" I will greatly
multiply* (הַרְבָּה is the *inf. abs.* for הִרְבָּה, which had become an
adverb: vid. Ewald, § 240c, as in chap. xvi. 10 and xxii. 17)
*thy sorrow and thy pregnancy: in sorrow thou shalt bring forth
children."* As the increase of conceptions, regarded as the ful-

filment of the blessing to "be fruitful and multiply" (i. 28), could be no punishment, וְהֵרֹנֵךְ must be understood as in apposition to עִצְּבוֹנֵךְ *thy sorrow* (*i.e.* the sorrows peculiar to a woman's life), *and indeed* (or more especially) thy pregnancy (*i.e.* the sorrows attendant upon that condition). The sentence is not rendered more lucid by the assumption of a *hendiadys*. "That the woman should bear children was the original will of God; but it was a punishment that henceforth she was to bear them in sorrow, *i.e.* with pains which threatened her own life as well as that of the child" (*Delitzsch*). The punishment consisted in an enfeebling of nature, in consequence of sin, which disturbed the normal relation between body and soul.—The woman had also broken through her divinely appointed subordination to the man; she had not only emancipated herself from the man to listen to the serpent, but had led the man into sin. For that, she was punished with a *desire* bordering upon disease (תְּשׁוּקָה from שׁוּק to run, to have a violent craving for a thing), and with *subjection* to the man. "*And he shall rule over thee.*" Created for the man, the woman was made subordinate to him from the very first; but the supremacy of the man was not intended to become a despotic rule, crushing the woman into a slave, which has been the rule in ancient and modern Heathenism, and even in Mahometanism also,—a rule which was first softened by the sin-destroying grace of the Gospel, and changed into a form more in harmony with the original relation, viz. that of a rule on the one hand, and subordination on the other, which have their roots in mutual esteem and love.

Vers. 17–19. "*And unto Adam:*" the noun is here used for the first time as a *proper name* without the article. In chap. i. 26 and ii. 5, 20, the noun is appellative, and there are substantial reasons for the omission of the article. The sentence upon Adam includes a twofold punishment: first the cursing of the ground, and secondly death, which affects the woman as well, on account of their common guilt. By listening to his wife, when deceived by the serpent, Adam had repudiated his superiority to the rest of creation. As a punishment, therefore, nature would henceforth offer resistance to his will. By breaking the divine command, he had set himself above his Maker, death would therefore show him the worthlessness of his own nature. "*Cursed be the ground for thy sake; in sorrow shalt thou eat it* (the ground by *synecdoche* for its produce, as in Isa. i. 7) *all the days of thy life : thorns and thistles shall it bring forth to thee, and thou shalt eat the herb of the field.*" The curse pronounced on man's account upon the soil created for him, consisted in the fact, that the earth no longer yielded spontaneously the fruits requisite for his maintenance, but the man was obliged to force out the necessaries of life by labour and strenuous exertion. The herb of the field is in contrast with the trees of the garden, and sorrow with the easy dressing of the garden. We are not to understand, however, that because man failed to guard the good creation of God from the invasion of the evil one, a host of demoniacal powers forced their way into the material world to lay it waste and offer resistance to man ; but because man himself had fallen into the power of the evil one, therefore God cursed the earth, not merely withdrawing the divine powers of life which pervaded Eden, but changing its relation to man. As *Luther* says, " *primum in eo, quod illa bona non fert quæ tulisset, si homo non esset lapsus, deinde in eo quoque, quod multa noxia fert quæ non tulisset, sicut sunt infelix lolium, steriles avenæ, zizania, urticæ, spinæ, tribuli, adde venena, noxias bestiolas, et si qua sunt alia hujus generis.*" But the curse reached much further, and the writer has merely noticed the most obvious aspect.[1] The disturbance and distortion of the original harmony of body and soul, which sin introduced into the nature of man, and by which the flesh gained the mastery over the spirit, and the body, instead of being more and more transformed into the life of the spirit, became a prey

---

[1] "*Non omnia incommoda enumerat Moses, quibus se homo per peccatum implicuit : constat enim ex eodem prodiisse fonte omnes præsentis vitæ ærumnas, quas experientia innumeras esse ostendit. Aëris intemperies, gelu, tonitrua, pluviæ intempestivæ, uredo, grandines et quicquid inordinatum est in mundo, peccati sunt fructus. Nec alia morborum prima est causa : idque poeticis fabulis celebratum fuit : haud dubie quod per manus a patribus traditum esset. Unde illud Horatii :*

> *Post ignem ætherea domo*
> *Subductum, macies et nova febrium*
> *Terris incubuit cohors :*
> *Semotique prius tarda necessitas*
> *Lethi corripuit gradum.*

Sed Moses qui brevitati studet, suo more pro communi vulgi captu attingere contentus fuit quod magis apparuit : ut sub exemplo uno discamus, hominis vitio inversum fuisse totum naturæ ordinem."—Calvin.

to death, spread over the whole material world; so that everywhere on earth there were to be seen wild and rugged wastes,
desolation and ruin, death and corruption, or ματαιότης and
φθορά (Rom. viii. 20, 21). Everything injurious to man in the
organic, vegetable and animal creation, is the effect of the curse
pronounced upon the earth for Adam's sin, however little we
may be able to explain the manner in which the curse was
carried into effect; since our view of the causal connection
between sin and evil even in human life is very imperfect, and
the connection between spirit and matter in nature generally is
altogether unknown. In this causal link between sin and the
evils in the world, the wrath of God on account of sin was
revealed; since, as soon as the creation (πᾶσα ἡ κτίσις, Rom. viii.
22) had been wrested through man from its vital connection
with its Maker, He gave it up to its own ungodly nature, so
that whilst, on the one hand, it has been abused by man for the
gratification of his own sinful lusts and desires, on the other, it
has turned against man, and consequently many things in the
world and nature, which in themselves and without sin would
have been good for him, or at all events harmless, have become
poisonous and destructive since his fall. For in the sweat of
his face man is to eat his bread (לֶחֶם the bread-corn which
springs from the earth, as in Job xxviii. 5; Psa. civ. 14) until
he return to the ground. Formed out of the dust, he shall return to dust again. This was the fulfilment of the threat, "In
the day thou eatest thereof thou shalt surely die," which began
to take effect immediately after the breach of the divine command; for not only did man then become mortal, but he also
actually came under the power of death, received into his nature
the germ of death, the maturity of which produced its eventual
dissolution into dust. The reason why the life of the man did
not come to an end immediately after the eating of the forbidden fruit, was not that "the woman had been created between the threat and the fall, and consequently the fountain
of human life had been divided, the life originally concentrated
in one Adam shared between man and woman, by which the
destructive influence of the fruit was modified or weakened"
(v. Hoffmann), but that the mercy and long-suffering of God
afforded space for repentance, and so controlled and ordered the
sin of men and the punishment of sin, as to render them sub-

servient to the accomplishment of His original purpose and the glorification of His name.

Vers. 20-24. As justice and mercy were combined in the divine sentence ; justice in the fact that God cursed the tempter alone, and only punished the tempted with labour and mortality, mercy in the promise of eventual triumph over the serpent : so God also displayed His mercy to the fallen, before carrying the sentence into effect. It was through the power of divine grace that Adam believed the promise with regard to the woman's seed, and manifested his faith in the name which he gave to his wife. חַוָּה *Eve*, an old form of חָיָה, signifying life (ζωή, LXX.), or life-spring, is a substantive, and not a feminine adjective meaning "the living one," nor an abbreviated form of מְחַוָּה, from חַוָּה = חָיָה (xix. 32, 34), the life-receiving one. This name was given by Adam to his wife, "*because*," as the writer explains with the historical fulfilment before his mind, "*she became the mother of all living*," *i.e.* because the continuance and life of his race were guaranteed to the man through the woman. God also displayed His mercy by clothing the two with coats of skin, *i.e.* the skins of beasts. The words, "God made coats," are not to be interpreted with such bare literality, as that God sewed the coats with His own fingers ; they merely affirm "that man's first clothing was the work of God, who gave the necessary directions and ability" (*Delitzsch*). By this clothing, God imparted to the feeling of shame the visible sign of an awakened conscience, and to the consequent necessity for a covering to the bodily nakedness, the higher work of a suitable discipline for the sinner. By selecting the skins of beasts for the clothing of the first men, and therefore causing the death or slaughter of beasts for that purpose, He showed them how they might use the sovereignty they possessed over the animals for their own good, and even sacrifice animal life for the preservation of human ; so that this act of God laid the foundation for the sacrifices, even if the first clothing did not prefigure our ultimate "clothing upon" (2 Cor. v. 4), nor the coats of skins the robe of righteousness.—Vers. 22, 23. Clothed in this sign of mercy, the man was driven out of paradise, to bear the punishment of his sin. The words of Jehovah, "*The man is become as one of Us, to know good and evil*," contain no irony, as though man had exalted himself to a position of autonomy resembling

that of God ; for "irony at the expense of a wretched tempted
soul might well befit Satan, but not the Lord." Likeness to
God is predicated only with regard to the knowledge of good and
evil, in which the man really had become like God. In order
that, after the germ of death had penetrated into his nature
along with sin, he might not "*take also of the tree of life, and eat
and live for ever* (יַ֫ח contracted from חָיֵי = חָיָה, as in chap. v. 5 ;
1 Sam. xx. 31), *God sent him forth from the garden of Eden.*"
With וַיְשַׁלְּחֵהוּ (sent him forth) the narrative passes over from the
words to the actions of God. From the גַם (*also*) it follows that
the man had not yet eaten of the tree of life. Had he continued in fellowship with God by obedience to the command
of God, he might have eaten of it, for he was created for
eternal life. But after he had fallen through sin into the power
of death, the fruit which produced immortality could only do
him harm. For immortality in a state of sin is not the ζωὴ
αἰώνιος, which God designed for man, but endless misery, which
the Scriptures call " the second death" (Rev. ii. 11, xx. 6, 14,
xxi. 8). The expulsion from paradise, therefore, was a punishment inflicted for man's good, intended, while exposing him to
temporal death, to preserve him from eternal death. To keep
the approach to the tree of life, " *God caused cherubim to dwell*
(to encamp) *at the east* (on the eastern side) *of the garden, and
the* (*i.e.* with the) *flame of the sword turning to and fro*" (מִתְהַפֶּ֫כֶת,
moving rapidly). The word כְּרוּב *cherub* has no suitable etymology in the Semitic, but is unquestionably derived from the same
root as the Greek γρύψ or γρυπές, and has been handed down
from the forefathers of our race, though the primary meaning
can no longer be discovered. The *cherubim*, however, are creatures of a higher world, which are represented as surrounding
the throne of God, both in the visions of Ezekiel (i. 22 sqq.,
x. 1) and the Revelation of John (chap. iv. 6) ; not, however, as
throne-bearers or throne-holders, or as forming the chariot of
the throne, but as occupying the highest place as living beings
(חַיּוֹת, ζῶα) in the realm of spirits, standing by the side of God
as the heavenly King when He comes to judgment, and proclaiming the majesty of the Judge of the world. In this character
God stationed them on the eastern side of paradise, not " to inhabit the garden as the temporary representatives of man," but
" to keep the way of the tree of life," *i.e.* to render it impossible

for man to return to paradise, and eat of the tree of life. Hence there appeared by their side the flame of a sword, apparently in constant motion, cutting hither and thither, representing the devouring fire of the divine wrath, and showing the cherubim to be ministers of judgment. With the expulsion of man from the garden of Eden, paradise itself vanished from the earth. God did not withdraw from the tree of life its supernatural power, nor did He destroy the garden before their eyes, but simply prevented their return, to show that it should be preserved until the time of the end, when sin should be rooted out by the judgment, and death abolished by the Conqueror of the serpent (1 Cor. xv. 26), and when upon the new earth the tree of life should flourish again in the heavenly Jerusalem, and bear fruit for the redeemed (Rev. xx. and xxi.).

THE SONS OF THE FIRST MAN.—CHAP. IV.

Vers. 1–8. The propagation of the human race did not commence till after the expulsion from paradise. Generation in man is an act of personal free-will, not a blind impulse of nature, and rests upon a moral self-determination. It flows from the divine institution of marriage, and is therefore knowing (יָדַע) the wife. —At the birth of the first son Eve exclaimed with joy, "*I have gotten* (קָנִיתִי) *a man with Jehovah ;*" wherefore the child received the name *Cain* (קַיִן from קוּן=קָנָה, κτᾶσθαι). So far as the grammar is concerned, the expression אֶת־יְהוָֹה might be rendered, as in apposition to אִישׁ, "*a man, the Lord*" (*Luther*), but the sense would not allow it. For even if we could suppose the faith of Eve in the promised conqueror of the serpent to have been sufficiently alive for this, the promise of God had not given her the slightest reason to expect that the promised seed would be of divine nature, and might be Jehovah, so as to lead her to believe that she had given birth to Jehovah now. אֶת is a preposition in the sense of helpful association, as in chap. xxi. 20, xxxix. 2, 21, etc. That she sees in the birth of this son the commencement of the fulfilment of the promise, and thankfully acknowledges the divine help in this display of mercy, is evident from the name *Jehovah*, the God of salvation. The use of this name is significant. Although it cannot be supposed that Eve herself knew and uttered this name, since it was not till a later period that it was made known to man, and it really belongs to the Hebrew, which was not formed till after the division of tongues, yet it expresses the feeling of Eve on receiving this proof of the gracious help of God.—Ver. 2. But her joy was soon overcome by the discovery of the vanity of this earthly life. This is expressed in the name *Abel*, which was given to the second son (הֶבֶל, in pause הָבֶל, *i.e.* nothingness, vanity), whether it indicated generally a feeling of sorrow on account of his weakness, or was a prophetic presentiment of his untimely death. The occupation of the sons is noticed on account of what follows. "*Abel was a keeper of sheep, but Cain was a tiller of the ground.*" Adam had, no doubt, already commenced both occupations, and the sons selected each a different department. God Himself had pointed out both to Adam,—the tilling of the ground by the employment assigned him in Eden, which had to be changed into agriculture after his expulsion; and the keeping of cattle in the clothing that He gave him (iii. 21). Moreover, agriculture can never be entirely separated from the rearing of cattle; for a man not only requires food, but clothing, which is procured directly from the hides and wool of tame animals. In addition to this, sheep do not thrive without human protection and care, and therefore were probably associated with man from the very first. The different occupations of the brothers, therefore, are not to be regarded as a proof of the difference in their dispositions. This comes out first in the sacrifice, which they offered after a time to God, each one from the produce of his vocation.—"*In process of time*" (*lit.* at the end of days, *i.e.* after a considerable lapse of time: for this use of יָמִים cf. chap. xl. 4; Num. ix. 2) *Cain brought of the fruit of the ground a gift* (מִנְחָה) *to the Lord; and Abel, he also brought of the firstlings of his flock, and indeed* (*vav* in an explanatory sense, *vid. Ges.* § 155, 1) *of their fat,*" *i.e.* the fattest of the firstlings, and not merely the first good one that came to hand. חֲלָבִים are not the *fat portions* of the animals, as in the Levitical law of sacrifice. This is evident from the fact, that the sacrifice was not connected with a sacrificial meal, and animal food was not eaten at this time. That the usage of the Mosaic law cannot determine the meaning of this passage, is evident from the word *minchah*, which is applied in Leviticus to bloodless sacrifices only, whereas it is used here in connection with Abel's sacrifice. "*And Jehovah looked upon Abel and his gift; and upon Cain and his gift He did not look."* The look of Jehovah was in any case a visible sign of satisfaction. It is a common and ancient opinion that fire consumed Abel's sacrifice, and thus showed that it was graciously accepted. *Theodotion* explains the words by καὶ ἐνεπύρισεν ὁ Θεός. But whilst this explanation has the analogy of Lev. ix. 24 and Judg. vi. 21 in its favour, it does not suit the words, " upon Abel and his gift." The reason for the different reception of the two offerings was the state of mind towards God with which they were brought, and which manifested itself in the selection of the gifts. Not, indeed, in the fact that Abel brought a bleeding sacrifice and Cain a bloodless one; for this difference arose from the difference in their callings, and each necessarily took his gift from the produce of his own occupation. It was rather in the fact that Abel offered the fattest firstlings of his flock, the best that he could bring; whilst Cain only brought a portion of the fruit of the ground, but not the first-fruits. By this choice Abel brought πλείονα θυσίαν παρὰ Κάϊν, and manifested that disposition which is designated faith (πίστις) in Heb. xi. 4. The nature of this disposition, however, can only be determined from the meaning of the offering itself.

The sacrifices offered by Adam's sons, and that not in consequence of a divine command, but from the free impulse of their nature as determined by God, were the first sacrifices of the human race. The origin of sacrifice, therefore, is neither to be traced to a positive command, nor to be regarded as a human invention. To form an accurate conception of the idea which lies at the foundation of all sacrificial worship, we must bear in mind that the first sacrifices were offered after the fall, and therefore presupposed the spiritual separation of man from God, and were designed to satisfy the need of the heart for fellowship with God. This need existed in the case of Cain, as well as in that of Abel; otherwise he would have offered no sacrifice at all, since there was no command to render it compulsory. Yet it was not the wish for forgiveness of sin which led Adam's sons to offer sacrifice; for there is no mention of expiation, and the notion that Abel, by slaughtering the animal, confessed that he deserved death on account of sin, is transferred to this passage from the expiatory sacrifices of the Mosaic law. The offerings were expressive of gratitude to God, to whom they owed

all that they had ; and were associated also with the desire to
secure the divine favour and blessing, so that they are to be
regarded not merely as thank-offerings, but as supplicatory sacrifices, and as propitiatory also, in the wider sense of the word. In
this the two offerings are alike. The reason why they were not
equally acceptable to God is not to be sought, as *Hofmann* thinks,
in the fact that Cain merely offered thanks " for the preservation
of this present life," whereas Abel offered thanks " for the forgiveness of sins," or " for the sin-forgiving clothing received by
man from the hand of God." To take the nourishment of the
body literally and the clothing symbolically in this manner, is an
arbitrary procedure, by which the Scriptures might be made to
mean anything we chose. The reason is to be found rather in
the fact, that Abel's thanks came from the depth of his heart,
whilst Cain merely offered his to keep on good terms with God,—
a difference that was manifested in the choice of the gifts, which
each one brought from the produce of his occupation. This
choice shows clearly " that it was the pious feeling, through
which the worshipper put his heart as it were into the gift, which
made the offering acceptable to God" (*Oehler*) ; that the essence
of the sacrifice was not the presentation of a gift to God, but
that the offering was intended to shadow forth the dedication of
the heart to God. At the same time, the desire of the worshipper, by the dedication of the best of his possessions to secure
afresh the favour of God, contained the germ of that substitutionary meaning of sacrifice, which was afterwards expanded in
connection with the deepening and heightening of the feeling of
sin into a desire for forgiveness, and led to the development of
the idea of expiatory sacrifice.—On account of the preference
shown to Abel, " *it burned Cain sore* (the subject, ' wrath,' is
wanting, as it frequently is in the case of חָרָה, cf. chap. xviii. 30,
32, xxxi. 36, etc.), *and his countenance fell*" (an indication of his
discontent and anger: cf. Jer. iii. 12 ; Job xxix. 24). God
warned him of giving way to this, and directed his attention
to the cause and consequences of his wrath. " *Why art thou
wroth, and why is thy countenance fallen?*" The answer to this
is given in the further question, " *Is there not, if thou art good,
a lifting up*" (*sc.* of the countenance)? It is evident from the
context, and the antithesis of falling and lifting up (נפל and נשׂא),
that פָּנִים must be supplied after שְׂאֵת. By this God gave him to

understand that his look was indicative of evil thoughts and intentions; for the lifting up of the countenance, *i.e.* a free, open
look, is the mark of a good conscience (Job xi. 15). *" But if
thou art not good, sin lieth before the door, and its desire is to thee*
(directed towards thee); *but thou shouldst rule over it."* The
fem. חַטָּאת is construed as a masculine, because, with evident
allusion to the serpent, sin is personified as a wild beast, lurking
at the door of the human heart, and eagerly desiring to devour
his soul (1 Pet. v. 8). הֵיטִיב, to make good, signifies here not
good action, the performance of good in work and deed, but
making the disposition good, *i.e.* directing the heart to what is
good. Cain is to rule over the sin which is greedily desiring
him, by giving up his wrath, not indeed that sin may cease to
lurk for him, but that the lurking evil foe may obtain no entrance
into his heart. There is no need to regard the sentence as interrogative, "Wilt thou, indeed, be able to rule over it?" (*Ewald*),
nor to deny the allusion in בּוֹ to the lurking sin, as *Delitzsch*
does. The words do not command the suppression of an inward
temptation, but resistance to the power of evil as pressing from
without, by hearkening to the word which God addressed to Cain
in person, and addresses to us through the Scriptures. There is
nothing said here about God appearing visibly; but this does not
warrant us in interpreting either this or the following conversation as a simple process that took place in the heart and conscience of Cain. It is evident from vers. 14 and 16 that God
did not withdraw His personal presence and visible intercourse
from men, as soon as He had expelled them from the garden of
Eden. " God talks to Cain as to a wilful child, and draws out
of him what is sleeping in his heart, and lurking like a wild
beast before his door. And what He did to Cain He does to
every one who will but observe his own heart, and listen to the
voice of God" (*Herder*). But Cain paid no heed to the divine
warning. Ver. 8. He *" said to his brother Abel."* What he said
is not stated. We may either supply *" it,"* viz. what God had
just said to him, which would be grammatically admissible, since
אָמַר is sometimes followed by a simple accusative (xxii. 3, xliv.
16), and this accusative has to be supplied from the context (as in
Ex. xix. 25); or we may supply from what follows some such
expressions as *" let us go into the field,"* as the LXX., *Sam.*,
Jonathan, and others have done. This is also allowable, so that

we need not imagine a gap in the text, but may explain the construction as in chap. iii. 22, 23, by supposing that the writer hastened on to describe the carrying out of what was said, without stopping to set down the words themselves. This supposition is preferable to the former, since it is psychologically most improbable that Cain should have related a warning to his brother which produced so little impression upon his own mind. In the field " *Cain rose up against Abel his brother, and slew him.*" Thus the sin of Adam had grown into fratricide in his son. The writer intentionally repeats again and again the words " *his brother,*" to bring clearly out the horror of the sin. Cain was the first man who let sin reign in him; he was " of the wicked one" (1 John iii. 12). In him the seed of the woman had already become the seed of the serpent; and in his deed the real nature of the wicked one, as " a murderer from the beginning," had come openly to light: so that already there had sprung up that contrast of two distinct seeds within the human race, which runs through the entire history of humanity.

Vers. 9–15. Defiance grows with sin, and punishment keeps pace with guilt. Adam and Eve fear before God, and acknowledge their sin; Cain boldly denies it, and in reply to the question, " *Where is Abel thy brother?*" declares, " *I know not, am I my brother's keeper?*" God therefore charges him with his crime: " *What hast thou done! voice of thy brother's blood crying to Me from the earth.*" The verb "*crying*" refers to the "*blood*," since this is the principal word, and the *voice* merely expresses the adverbial idea of "*aloud,*" or "*listen*" (*Ewald*, § 317*d*). דָּמִים (drops of blood) is sometimes used to denote natural hemorrhage (Lev. xii. 4, 5, xx. 18); but is chiefly applied to blood shed unnaturally, *i.e.* to murder. "Innocent blood has no voice, it may be, that is discernible by human ears, but it has one that reaches God, as the cry of a wicked deed demanding vengeance" (*Delitzsch*). Murder is one of the sins that cry to heaven. " *Primum ostendit Deus se de factis hominum cognoscere utcunque nullus queratur vel accuset; deinde sibi magis charam esse hominum vitam quam ut sanguinem innoxium impune effundi sinat; tertio curam sibi piorum esse non solum quamdiu vivunt sed etiam post mortem*" (Calvin). Abel was the first of the saints, whose blood is precious in the sight of God (Ps. cxvi. 15); and by virtue of his faith, he being dead yet speaketh through his blood which cried unto God (Heb. xi. 4).—Vers. 11, 12. "*And now* (*sc.* because thou hast done this) *be cursed from the earth.*" *From*: *i.e.* either *away from the earth*, driven forth so that it shall no longer afford a quiet resting-place (*Gerlach, Delitzsch,* etc.), or *out of the earth*, through its withdrawing its strength, and thus securing the fulfilment of perpetual wandering (*Baumgarten*, etc.). It is difficult to choose between the two; but the clause, "*which hath opened her mouth,*" etc., seems rather to favour the latter. Because the earth has been compelled to drink innocent blood, it rebels against the murderer, and when he tills it, withdraws its strength, so that the soil yields no produce; just as the land of Canaan is said to have spued out the Canaanites, on account of their abominations (Lev. xviii. 28). In any case, the idea that "the soil, through drinking innocent blood, became an accomplice in the sin of murder," has no biblical support, and is not confirmed by Isa. xxvi. 21 or Num. xxxv. 33. The suffering of irrational creatures through the sin of man is very different from their participating in his sin. "*A fugitive and vagabond* (נָע וָנָד, *i.e.* banished and homeless) *shalt thou be in the earth.*" Cain is so affected by this curse, that his obduracy is turned into despair. "*My sin,*" he says in ver. 13, "*is greater than can be borne.*" נָשָׂא עָוֹן signifies to take away and bear sin or guilt, and is used with reference both to God and man. God takes guilt away by forgiving it (Ex. xxxiv. 7); man carries it away and bears it, by enduring its punishment (cf. Num. v. 31). *Luther,* following the ancient versions, has adopted the first meaning; but the context sustains the second: for Cain afterwards complains, not of the greatness of the sin, but only of the severity of the punishment. "*Behold, Thou hast driven me out this day from the face of the earth, and from Thy face shall I be hid; . . . and it shall come to pass that every one that findeth me shall slay me.*" The *adamah,* from the face of which the curse of Jehovah had driven Cain, was Eden (cf. ver. 16), where he had carried on his agricultural pursuits, and where God had revealed His face, *i.e.* His presence, to the men after their expulsion from the garden; so that henceforth Cain had to wander about upon the wide world, homeless and far from the presence of God, and was afraid lest any one who found him might slay him. By "*every one that findeth me*" we are not to understand *omnis creatura,* as though Cain had excited the hostility of all creatures, but every man; not in the sense, however, of such as existed apart from the family of Adam, but such as were aware of his crime, and knew him to be a murderer. For Cain is evidently afraid of revenge on the part of relatives of the slain, that is to say, of descendants of Adam, who were either already in existence, or yet to be born. Though Adam might not at this time have had "many grandsons and great-grandsons," yet according to ver. 17 and chap. v. 4, he had un-doubtedly other children, who might increase in number, and sooner or later might avenge Abel's death. For, that blood shed demands blood in return, " is a principle of equity written in the heart of every man ; and that Cain should see the earth full of avengers is just like a murderer, who sees avenging spirits ('Eρινύες) ready to torture him on every hand."—Ver. 15. Although Cain expressed not penitence, but fear of punishment, God displayed His long-suffering and gave him the promise, "*Therefore* (לָכֵן not in the sense of לֹא כֵן, but because it was the case, and there was reason for his complaint) *whosoever slayeth Cain, vengeance shall be taken on him sevenfold.*" כָּל־הֹרֵג קַיִן is cas. *absolut.* as in chap. ix. 6; and הֻקַּם avenged, *i.e.* resented, punished, as Ex. xxi. 20, 21. The mark which God put upon Cain is not to be regarded as a mark upon his body, as the Rabbins and others supposed, but as a certain sign which protected him from vengeance, though of what kind it is impossible to deter-mine. God granted him continuance of life, not because banishment from the place of God's presence was the greatest possible punishment, or because the preservation of the human race required at that time that the lives of individuals should be spared,—for God afterwards destroyed the whole human race, with the exception of one family,—but partly because the tares were to grow with the wheat, and sin develop itself to its utmost extent, partly also because from the very first God determined to take punishment into His own hands, and protect human life from the passion and wilfulness of human vengeance.

Vers. 16–24. *The family of the Cainites.*—Ver. 16. The geographical situation of the land of *Nod*, in the front of Eden (קִדְמַת, see chap. ii. 14), where Cain settled after his departure from the place or the land of the revealed presence of God (cf. Jonah i. 3), cannot be determined. The name *Nod* denotes a land of flight and banishment, in contrast with Eden, the land of delight, where Jehovah walked with men. There Cain knew his wife. The text assumes it as self-evident that she accompanied him in his exile; also, that she was a daughter of Adam, and consequently a sister of Cain. The marriage of brothers and sisters was inevitable in the case of the children of the first men, if the human race was actually to descend from a single pair, and may therefore be justified in the face of the Mosaic prohibition of such marriages, on the ground that the sons and daughters of Adam represented not merely the family but the genus, and that it was not till after the rise of several families that the bands of fraternal and conjugal love became distinct from one another, and assumed fixed and mutually exclusive forms, the violation of which is sin. (Comp. Lev. xviii.) His son he named *Hanoch* (consecration), because he regarded his birth as a pledge of the renovation of his life. For this reason he also gave the same name to the city which he built, inasmuch as its erection was another phase in the development of his family. The construction of a city by Cain will cease to surprise us, if we consider that at the commencement of its erection, centuries had already passed since the creation of man, and Cain's descendants may by this time have increased considerably in numbers; also, that עִיר does not necessarily presuppose a large town, but simply an enclosed space with fortified dwellings, in contradistinction to the isolated tents of shepherds; and lastly, that the words וַיְהִי בֹּנֶה, "he was building," merely indicate the commencement and progress of the building, but not its termination. It appears more surprising that Cain, who was to be a fugitive and a vagabond upon the earth, should have established himself in the land of Nod. This cannot be fully explained, either on the ground that he carried on the pursuits of agriculture, which lead to settled abodes, or that he strove against the curse. In addition to both the facts referred to, there is also the circumstance, that the curse, "the ground shall not yield to thee her strength," was so mollified by the grace of God, that Cain and his descendants were enabled to obtain sufficient food in the land of his settlement, though it was by dint of hard work and strenuous effort; unless, indeed, we follow *Luther* and understand the curse, that he should be a fugitive upon the earth, as relating to his expulsion from Eden, and his removal *ad incertum locum et opus, non addita ulla vel promissione vel mandato, sicut avis quæ in libero cælo incerta vagatur.* The fact that Cain undertook the erection of a city, is also significant. Even if we do not regard this city as "the first foundation-stone of the kingdom of the world, in which the spirit of the beast bears sway," we cannot fail to detect the desire to neutralize the curse of banishment, and create for his family a point of unity, as a compensation for the loss of unity in fellowship with God, as well as the inclination of the family of Cain for that which was earthly. The powerful development of the worldly mind and of ungodliness among the Cainites was openly displayed in Lamech, in the sixth generation. Of the intermediate links, the names only are given. (On the use of the passive with the accusative of the object in the clause "*to Hanoch was born* (they bore) *Irad,*" see Ges. § 143, 1.) Some of these names resemble those of the Sethite genealogy, viz. Irad and Jared, Mehujael and Mahalaleel, Methusael and Methuselah, also Cain and Cainan; and the names Enoch and Lamech occur in both families. But neither the recurrence of similar names, nor even of the same names, warrants the conclusion that the two genealogical tables are simply different forms of one primary legend. For the names, though similar in sound, are very different in meaning. *Irad* probably signifies the townsman, *Jered,* descent, or that which has descended; *Mehujael,* smitten of God, and *Mahalaleel,* praise of God; *Methusael,* man of prayer, and Methuselah, man of the sword or of increase. The repetition of the two names Enoch and Lamech even loses all significance, when we consider the different places which they occupy in the respective lines, and observe also that in the case of these very names, the more precise descriptions which are given so thoroughly establish the difference of character in the two individuals, as to preclude the possibility of their being the same, not to mention the fact, that in the later history the same names frequently occur in totally different families; *e.g. Korah* in the families of Levi (Ex. vi. 21) and Esau (chap. xxxvi. 5); *Hanoch* in those of Reuben (chap. xlvi. 9) and Midian (chap. xxv. 4); *Kenaz* in those of Judah (Num. xxxii. 12) and Esau (chap. xxxvi. 11). The identity and similarity of names can prove nothing more than that the two branches of the human race did not keep entirely apart from each other; a fact established by their subsequently intermarrying.—Lamech took two wives, and thus was the first to prepare the way for polygamy, by which the ethical aspect of marriage, as ordained by God, was turned into the lust of the eye and lust of the flesh. The names of the women are indicative of sensual attractions: *Adah*, the adorned; and *Zillah*, either the shady or the tinkling. His three sons are the authors of inventions which show how the mind and efforts of the Cainites were directed towards the beautifying and perfecting of the earthly life. *Jabal* (probably = *jebul*, produce) became *the father of such as dwelt in tents, i.e.* of nomads who lived in tents and with their flocks, getting their living by a pastoral occupation, and possibly also introducing the use of animal food, in disregard of the divine command (Gen. i. 29). *Jubal* (sound), the father of all such as handle the harp and pipe, *i.e.* the inventors of stringed and wind instruments. כִּנּוֹר a guitar or harp; עוּגָב the shepherd's reed or bagpipe. *Tubal-Cain*, "*hammering all kinds of cutting things* (the verb is to be construed as neuter) *in brass and iron;*" the inventor therefore of all kinds of edge-tools for working in metals: so that Cain, from קין to forge, is probably to be regarded as the surname which Tubal received on account of his inventions. The meaning of Tubal is obscure; for the Persian *Tupal*, iron-*scoria*, can throw no light upon it, as it must be a much later word. The allusion to the sister of Tubal-Cain is evidently to be attributed to her name, *Naamah*, the lovely, or graceful, since it reflects the worldly mind of the Cainites. In the arts, which owed their origin to Lamech's sons, this disposition reached its culminating point; and it appears in the form of pride and defiant arrogance in the song in which Lamech celebrates the inventions of Tubal-Cain (vers. 23, 24): "*Adah and Zillah, hear my voice; ye wives of Lamech, hearken unto my speech: Men I slay for my wound, and young men for my stripes. For sevenfold is Cain avenged, and Lamech seven and seventy-fold.*" The perfect הָרַגְתִּי is expressive not of a deed accomplished, but of confident assurance (Ges. § 126, 4; Ewald, § 135c); and the suffixes in חַבֻּרָתִי and פִּצְעִי are to be taken in a passive sense. The idea is this: whoever inflicts a wound or stripe on me, whether man or youth, I will put to death; and for every injury done to my person, I will take ten times more vengeance than that with which God promised to avenge the murder of my ancestor Cain. In this song, which contains in its rhythm, its strophic arrangement of the thoughts, and its poetic diction, the germ of the later poetry, we may detect " that Titanic arrogance, of which the Bible says that its power is its god (Hab. i. 11), and that it carries its god, viz. its sword, in its hand (Job xii. 6) " (*Delitzsch*).—According to these accounts, the principal arts and manufactures were invented by the Cainites, and carried out in an ungodly spirit; but they are not therefore to be attributed to the curse which rested upon the family. They have their roots rather in the mental powers with which man was endowed for the sovereignty and subjugation of the earth, but which, like all the other powers and tendencies of his nature, were pervaded by sin, and desecrated in its service. Hence these inventions have become the common property of humanity, because they not only may promote its intended development, but are to be applied and consecrated to this purpose for the glory of God.

Vers. 25, 26. The character of the ungodly family of Cainites was now fully developed in Lamech and his children. The history, therefore, turns from them, to indicate briefly the origin of the godly race. After Abel's death a third son was born to Adam, to whom his mother gave the name of *Seth* (שֵׁת, from שִׁית, a present participle, the appointed one, the compensation); "*for*," she said, "*God hath appointed me another seed* (descendant) *for Abel, because Cain slew him.*" The words "because Cain slew him" are not to be regarded as an explanatory supplement, but as the words of Eve; and כִּי by virtue of the previous תַּחַת is to be understood in the sense of תַּחַת כִּי. What Cain (*human* wickedness) took from her, that has Elohim (*divine* omnipotence) restored. Because of this antithesis she calls the giver *Elohim* instead of *Jehovah*, and not because her hopes had been sadly depressed by her painful experience in connection with the first-born.—Ver. 26. " *To Seth, to him also* (גַּם הוּא, intensive, *vid. Ges.* § 121, 3) *there was born a son, and he called his name Enosh.*" אֱנוֹשׁ, from אָנַשׁ to be weak, faint, frail, designates man from his frail and mortal condition (Ps. viii. 4, xc. 3, ciii. 15, etc.). In this name, therefore, the feeling and knowledge of human weakness and frailty were expressed (the opposite of the pride and arrogance displayed by the Canaanitish family); and this feeling led to God, to that invocation of the name of Jehovah which commenced under Enos. קָרָא בְּשֵׁם יְהוָֹה, literally *to call in* (or by) *the name of Jehovah*, is

used for a solemn calling of the name of God. When applied
to men, it denotes invocation (here and chap. xii. 8, xiii. 4, etc.);
to God, calling out or proclaiming His name (Ex. xxxiii. 19,
xxxiv. 5). The *name of God* signifies in general " the whole
nature of God, by which He attests His personal presence in
the relation into which He has entered with man, the divine
self-manifestation, or the whole of that revealed side of the
divine nature, which is turned towards man" *(Oehler)*. We
have here an account of the commencement of that worship of
God which consists in prayer, praise, and thanksgiving, or in
the acknowledgment and celebration of the mercy and help of
Jehovah. While the family of Cainites, by the erection of a city,
and the invention and development of worldly arts and business,
were laying the foundation for the kingdom of this world; the
family of the Sethites began, by united invocation of the name of
the God of grace, to found and to erect the kingdom of God.

II. THE HISTORY OF ADAM.

CHAP. V.–VI. 8.

GENERATIONS FROM ADAM TO NOAH.—CHAP. V.

The origin of the human race and the general character of
its development having been thus described, all that remained
of importance to universal or sacred history, in connection with
the progress of our race in the primeval age, was to record the
order of the families (chap. v.) and the ultimate result of the
course which they pursued (chap. vi. 1–8).—First of all, we
have the genealogical table of Adam with the names of the first
ten patriarchs, who were at the head of that seed of the woman
by which the promise was preserved, viz. the posterity of the
first pair through Seth, from Adam to the flood. We have also
an account of the ages of these patriarchs before and after the
birth of those sons in whom the line was continued; so that the
genealogy, which indicates the line of development, furnishes
at the same time a chronology of the primeval age. In the
genealogy of the Cainites no ages are given, since this family,
as being accursed by God, had no future history. On the other
hand, the family of Sethites, which acknowledged God, began
from the time of Enos to call upon the name of the Lord, and

was therefore preserved and sustained by God, in order that under the training of mercy and judgment the human race might eventually attain to the great purpose of its creation. The genealogies of the primeval age, to quote the apt words of *M. Baumgarten*, are "memorials, which bear testimony quite as much to the faithfulness of God in fulfilling His promise, as to the faith and patience of the fathers themselves." This testimony is first placed in its true light by the numbers of the years. The historian gives not merely the age of each patriarch at the time of the birth of the first-born, by whom the line of succession was continued, but the number of years that he lived after that, and then the entire length of his life. Now if we add together the ages at the birth of the several first-born sons, and the hundred years between the birth of Shem and the flood, we find that the duration of the first period in the world's history was 1656 years. We obtain a different result, however, from the numbers given by the LXX. and the Samaritan version, which differ in almost every instance from the Hebrew text, both in chap. v. and chap. xi. (from Shem to Terah), as will appear from the following table:—

The Fathers before the Flood.—Chap. v.

Names.	Hebrew Text.			Samaritan Text.			Septuagint.			Year of birth (from creation), Hebrew Text.	Year of death (from creation), Hebrew Text.
	Age at birth of first-born.	Rest of life.	Whole life.	Age at birth of first-born.	Rest of life.	Whole life.	Age at birth of first-born.	Rest of life.	Whole life.		
Adam, . . .	130	800	930	130	800	930	230	700	930	1	930
Seth, ...	105	807	912	105	807	912	205	707	912	130	1042
Enos, . . .	90	815	905	90	815	905	190	715	905	235	1140
Cainan, . .	70	840	910	70	840	910	170	740	910	325	1235
Mahalaleel,	65	830	895	65	830	895	165	730	895	395	1290
Jared, . . .	162	800	962	62	785	847	162	800	962	460	1422
Enoch, . . .	65	300	365	65	300	365	165	200	365	622	987
Methuselah,	187	782	969	67	653	720	167 (187)	802 (782)[1]	969	687	1656
Lamech, . .	182	595	777	53	600	653	188	565	753	874	1651
Noah, . . .	500	450	950	500	450	950	500	450	950	1056	2066
To the flood,	100			100			100				
Total, . . .	1656			1307			2242				

[1] The numbers in brackets are the reading of the *Cod. Alexandrinus* of the LXX. In the genealogical table, chap. xi. 10 sqq., the Samaritan text is the only one which gives the whole duration of life.

The Fathers from the Flood to the call of Abram.—Chap. xi. 10–26.

Names.	Hebrew Text.			Samaritan Text.			Septuagint.			Year of birth (from creation), Hebrew Text.	Year of death (from creation), Hebrew Text.
	Age at birth of first-born.	Rest of life.	Whole life.	Age at birth of first-born.	Rest of life.	Whole life.	Age at birth of first-born.	Rest of life.	Whole life.		
Shem, . . .	100	500	600	100	500	600	100	500	600	1556	2156
Arphaxad, .	35	403	438	135	303	438	135	400	535	1656	2094
								(430)	(565)		
(Καϊνάν),	...	...	...	...	...	...	130	330	460		
Salah, . . .	30	403	433	130	303	433	130	330	460	1691	2124
Eber, . . .	34	430	464	134	270	404	134	270	404	1721	2185
								(370)	(504)		
Peleg, . . .	30	209	239	130	109	239	130	209	339	1755	1994
Regu, . . .	32	207	239	132	107	239	132	207	339	1785	2024
Serug, . . .	30	200	230	130	100	230	130	200	330	1817	2047
Nahor, . . .	29	119	148	79	69	148	179	125	304	1847	1995
							(79)	(129)	(208)		
Terah, . . .	70	135	205	70	75	145	70	135	205	1876	2081
Abram, . .	...	...	...	...	...	...	...	...	...	1946	2121
His call, . .	75			75			75				
Total, . . .	365			1015			1245			2021	

The principal deviations from the Hebrew in the case of the
other two texts are these : in chap. v. the Samaritan places the
birth of the first-born of Jared, Methuselah, and Lamech 100
years earlier, whilst the Septuagint places the birth of the first-
born of all the other fathers (except Noah) 100 years later than
the Hebrew ; in chap. xi. the latter course is adopted in both
texts in the case of all the fathers except Shem and Terah. In
consequence of this, the interval from Adam to the flood is
shortened in the Samaritan text by 349 years as compared with
the Hebrew, and in the Septuagint is lengthened by 586 (*Cod.
Alex.* 606). The interval from the flood to Abram is lengthened
in both texts ; in the *Sam.* by 650 years, in the *Sept.* by 880
(*Cod. Alex.* 780). In the latter, Cainan is interpolated between
Arphaxad and Salah, which adds 130 years, and the age of the
first-born of Nahor is placed 150 years later than in the Hebrew,
whereas in the former the difference is only 50 years. With
regard to the other differences, the reason for reducing the lives
of Jared, Methuselah, and Lamech in the Samaritan text after
the birth of their sons, was evidently to bring their deaths within

the time before the flood. The age of Methuselah, as given in the *Cod. Alex.* of the LXX., is evidently to be accounted for on the same ground, since, according to the numbers of the Vatican text, Methuselah must have lived 14 years after the flood. In the other divergences of these two texts from the Hebrew, no definite purpose can be detected; at the same time they are sufficient to show a twofold tendency, viz. to lengthen the interval from the flood to Abram, and to reduce the ages of the fathers at the birth of their first-born to greater uniformity, and to take care that the age of Adam at the birth of Seth should not be exceeded by that of any other of the patriarchs, especially in the time before the flood. To effect this, the *Sept.* adds 100 years to the ages of all the fathers, before and after the flood, whose sons were born before their 100th year; the *Sam.*, on the other hand, simply does this in the case of the fathers who lived after the flood, whilst it deducts 100 years from the ages of all the fathers before the flood who begot their first-born at a later period of their life than Adam and Seth. The age of Noah alone is left unaltered, because there were other data connected with the flood which prevented any arbitrary alteration of the text. That the principal divergences of both texts from the Hebrew are intentional changes, based upon chronological theories or cycles, is sufficiently evident from their internal character, viz. from the improbability of the statement, that whereas the average duration of life after the flood was about half the length that it was before, the time of life at which the fathers begot their first-born after the flood was as late, and, according to the Samaritan text, generally later than it had been before. No such intention is discernible in the numbers of the Hebrew text; consequently every attack upon the historical character of its numerical statements has entirely failed, and no tenable argument can be adduced against their correctness. The objection, that such longevity as that recorded in our chapter is inconceivable according to the existing condition of human nature, loses all its force if we consider "that all the memorials of the old world contain evidence of gigantic power; that the climate, the weather, and other natural conditions, were different from those after the flood; that life was much more simple and uniform; and that the after-effects of the condition of man in paradise would not be immediately exhausted" (*Delitzsch*). This longevity, moreover, necessarily contributed greatly to the increase of the human race; and the circumstance that the children were not born till a comparatively advanced period of life,—that is, until the corporeal and mental development of the parent was perfectly complete,—necessarily favoured the generation of a powerful race. From both these circumstances, however, the development of the race was sure to be characterized by peculiar energy in evil as well as in good; so that whilst in the godly portion of the race, not only were the traditions of the fathers transmitted faithfully and without adulteration from father to son, but family characteristics, piety, discipline, and morals took deep root, whilst in the ungodly portion time was given for sin to develop itself with mighty power in its innumerable forms.

The heading in ver. 1 runs thus : "This is the book (*sepher*) of the generations (*tholedoth*) of Adam." On *tholedoth*, see chap. ii. 4. *Sepher* is a writing complete in itself, whether it consist of one sheet or several, as for instance the "bill of divorcement" in Deut. xxiv. 1, 3. The addition of the clause, " *in the day that God created man*," etc., is analogous to chap. ii. 4 ; the creation being mentioned again as the starting point, because all the development and history of humanity was rooted there.— Ver. 3. As Adam was created in the image of God, so did he beget " *in his own likeness, after his image ;* " that is to say, he transmitted the image of God in which he was created, not in the purity in which it came direct from God, but in the form given to it by his own self-determination, modified and corrupted by sin. The begetting of the son by whom the line was perpetuated (no doubt in every case the first-born), is followed by an account of the number of years that Adam and the other fathers lived after that, by the statement that each one begat (other) sons and daughters, by the number of years that he lived altogether, and lastly, by the assertion וַיָּמֹת " *and he died.*" This apparently superfluous announcement is "intended to indicate by its constant recurrence that death reigned from Adam downwards as an unchangeable law (*vid.* Rom. v. 14). But against this background of universal death, the power of life was still more conspicuous. For the man did not die till he had propagated life, so that in the midst of the death of individuals the life of the race was preserved, and the hope of the seed sustained, by which the author of death should be overcome." In g] so that he did not see (experience) death] so that he did not see (experience) death] so that he did not see (experience) death] so that he did not see (experience) death] so that he did not see (experience) death] so that he did not see (experience) death not see (experience) death not see (experience) death] so that he did not see (experience) death] so that he did not see (experience) death] so that he did not see (experience) death] so that he did not see (experience) death] so that he did not see (experience) death] so that he did not see (experience) death] so that he did not see (experience) death] so that he did not see (experience) death] so that he did not see (experience) death] so that he did not see (experience) death] so that he did not see (experience) death] so that he did not see (experience) death

the case of one of the fathers indeed, viz. Enoch (vers. 21 sqq.), life had not only a different issue, but also a different form. Instead of the expression " *and he lived*," which introduces in every other instance the length of life after the birth of the first-born, we find in the case of Enoch this statement, " *he walked with God (Elohim)* ; " and instead of the expression " *and he died*," the announcement, "*and he was not, for God (Elohim) took him*." The phrase "walked with God," which is only applied to Enoch and Noah (chap. vi. 9), denotes the most confidential intercourse, the closest communion with the personal God, a walking as it were by the side of God, who still continued His visible intercourse with men (*vid.* iii. 8). It must be distinguished from "walking before God" (chap. xvii. 1, xxiv. 40, etc.), and "walking after God" (Deut. xiii. 4), both which phrases are used to indicate a pious, moral, blameless life under the law according to the directions of the divine commands. The only other passage in which this expression " walk with God " occurs is Mal. ii. 6, where it denotes not the piety of the godly Israelites generally, but the conduct of the priests, who stood in a closer relation to Jehovah under the Old Testament than the rest of the faithful, being permitted to enter the Holy Place, and hold direct intercourse with Him there, which the rest of the people could not do. The article in האלהים gives prominence to the personality of Elohim, and shows that the expression cannot refer to inter course with the spiritual world.—In Enoch, the seventh from Adam through Seth, godliness attained its highest point; whilst ungodliness culminated in Lamech, the seventh from Adam through Cain, who made his sword his god. Enoch, therefore, like Elijah, was taken away by God, and carried into the heavenly paradise, so that he did not see (experience) death (Heb. xi. 5); *i.e.* he was taken up from this temporal life and transfigured into life eternal, being exempted by God from the law of death and of return to the dust, as those of the faithful will be, who shall be alive at the coming of Christ to judgment, and who in like manner shall not taste of death and corruption, but be changed in a moment. There is no foundation for the opinion, that Enoch did not participate at his translation in the glorification which awaits the righteous at the resurrection. For, according to 1 Cor. xv. 20, 23, it is not in glorification, but in the resurrection, that Christ is the first-fruits. Now the

latter presupposes death.   Whoever, therefore, through the grace
of God is exempted from death, cannot rise from the dead, but
reaches ἀφθαρσία, or the glorified state of perfection, through
being "changed" or "clothed upon" (2 Cor. v. 4).   This does
not at all affect the truth of the statement in Rom. v. 12, 14.
For the same God who has appointed death as the wages of sin,
and given us, through Christ, the victory over death, possesses
the power to glorify into eternal life an Enoch and an Elijah,
and all who shall be alive at the coming of the Lord without
chaining their glorification to death and resurrection.   Enoch
and Elijah were translated into eternal life with God without
passing through disease, death, and corruption, for the consolation of believers, and to awaken the hope of a life after death.
Enoch's translation stands about half way between Adam and
the flood, in the 987th year after the creation of Adam.   Seth,
Enos, Cainan, Mahalaleel, and Jared were still alive.   His son
Methuselah and his grandson Lamech were also living, the latter
being 113 years old.   Noah was not yet born, and Adam was
dead.   His translation, in consequence of his walking with God,
was " an example of repentance to all generations," as the son of
Sirach says (Ecclus. xliv. 16) ; and the apocryphal legend in the
book of Enoch i. 9 represents him as prophesying of the coming
of the Lord, to execute judgment upon the ungodly (Jude 14,
15).   In comparison with the longevity of the other fathers,
Enoch was taken away young, before he had reached half the
ordinary age, as a sign that whilst long life, viewed as a time for
repentance and grace, is indeed a blessing from God, when the
ills which have entered the world through sin are considered, it
is also a burden and trouble which God shortens for His chosen.
That the patriarchs of the old world felt the ills of this earthly
life in all their severity, was attested by Lamech (vers. 28, 29),
when he gave his son, who was born 69 years after Enoch's
translation, the name of *Noah,* saying, " *This same shall comfort
us concerning our work and the toil of our hands, because of the
ground which the Lord hath cursed.*"   *Noah,* נֹחַ from נוּחַ to rest
and הֵנִיחַ to bring rest, is explained by נָחַם to comfort, in the
sense of helpful and remedial consolation.   Lamech not only
felt the burden of his work upon the ground which God had
cursed, but looked forward with a prophetic presentiment to the
time when the existing misery and corruption would terminate,

and a change for the better, a redemption from the curse, would come. This presentiment assumed the form of hope when his son was born; he therefore gave expression to it in his name. But his hope was not realized, at least not in the way that he desired. A change did indeed take place in the lifetime of Noah. By the judgment of the flood the corrupt race was exterminated, and in Noah, who was preserved because of his blameless walk with God, the restoration of the human race was secured; but the effects of the curse, though mitigated, were not removed; whilst a covenant sign guaranteed the preservation of the human race, and therewith, by implication, his hope of the eventual removal of the curse (ix. 8–17).—The genealogical table breaks off with Noah; all that is mentioned with reference to him being the birth of his three sons, when he was 500 years old (ver. 32; see chap. xi. 10), without any allusion to the remaining years of his life,—an indication of a later hand. "The mention of three sons leads to the expectation, that whereas hitherto the line has been perpetuated through one member alone, in the future each of the three sons will form a new beginning (*vid.* ix. 18, 19, x. 1)."—*M. Baumgarten.*

MARRIAGE OF THE SONS OF GOD AND THE DAUGHTERS OF MEN.—CHAP. VI. 1–8.

The genealogies in chap. iv. and v., which trace the development of the human race through two fundamentally different lines, headed by Cain and Seth, are accompanied by a description of their moral development, and the statement that through marriages between the "*sons of God*" (*Elohim*) and the "*daughters of men,*" the wickedness became so great, that God determined to destroy the men whom He had created. This description applies to the whole human race, and presupposes the intercourse or marriage of the Cainites with the Sethites.—Ver. 1 relates to the increase of men generally (הָאָדָם, without any restriction), *i.e.* of the whole human race; and whilst the moral corruption is represented as universal, the whole human race, with the exception of Noah, who found grace before God (ver. 8), is described as ripe for destruction (vers. 3 and 5–8). To understand this section, and appreciate the causes of this complete degeneracy of the race, we must first obtain a correct interpretation of the expressions

" sons of God" (בני האלהים) and " daughters of men" (בנות האדם).
Three different views have been entertained from the very earliest times: the " sons of God" being regarded as (a) the sons
of princes, (b) angels, (c) the Sethites or godly men ; and the
" daughters of men," as the daughters (a) of people of the lower
orders, (b) of mankind generally, (c) of the Cainites, or of the rest
of mankind as contrasted with the godly or the children of God.
Of these three views, the first, although it has become the traditional one in orthodox rabbinical Judaism, may be dismissed at
once as not warranted by the usages of the language, and as
altogether unscriptural. The second, on the contrary, may be
defended on two plausible grounds : first, the fact that the " sons
of God," in Job i. 6; ii. 1, and xxxviii. 7, and in Dan. iii. 25, are
unquestionably angels (also בְּנֵי אֵלִים in Ps. xxix. 1 and lxxxix. 7) ;
and secondly, the antithesis, " sons of God" and " daughters
of men." Apart from the context and tenor of the passage,
these two points would lead us most naturally to regard the
" sons of God" as angels, in distinction from men and the
daughters of men. But this explanation, though the first to
suggest itself, can only lay claim to be received as the correct
one, provided the language itself admits of no other. Now that
is not the case. For it is not to angels only that the term " sons
of Elohim," or " sons of Elim," is applied ; but in Ps. lxxiii. 15,
in an address to Elohim, the godly are called " the generation of
Thy sons," i.e. sons of Elohim ; in Deut. xxxii. 5 the Israelites
are called His (God's) sons, and in Hos. i. 10, " sons of the living
God ;" and in Ps. lxxx. 17, Israel is spoken of as the son, whom
Elohim has made strong. These passages show that the expression " sons of God" cannot be elucidated by philological means,
but must be interpreted by theology alone. Moreover, even
when it is applied to the angels, it is questionable whether it is
to be understood in a physical or ethical sense. The notion that
" it is employed in a physical sense as *nomen naturæ*, instead of
angels as *nomen officii*, and presupposes generation of a physical
kind," we must reject as an unscriptural and gnostic error. According to the scriptural view, the heavenly spirits are creatures of
God, and not begotten from the divine essence. Moreover, all the
other terms applied to the angels are ethical in their character.
But if the title " sons of God" cannot involve the notion of physical generation, it cannot be restricted to celestial spirits, but is

applicable to all beings which bear the image of God, or by virtue of their likeness to God participate in the glory, power, and blessedness of the divine life,—to men therefore as well as angels, since God has caused man to " want but little of Elohim," or to stand but a little behind Elohim (Ps. viii. 5), so that even magistrates are designated " Elohim, and sons of the Most High" (Ps. lxxxii. 6). When *Delitzsch* objects to the application of the expression " sons of Elohim" to pious men, because, " although the idea of a child of God may indeed have pointed, even in the O. T., beyond its theocratic limitation to Israel (Ex. iv. 22 ; Deut. xiv. 1) towards a wider ethical signification (Ps. lxxiii. 15 ; Prov. xiv. 26), yet this extension and expansion were not so completed, that in historical prose the terms ' sons of God' (for which ' sons of Jehovah' should have been used to prevent mistake), and ' sons (or daughters) of men,' could be used to distinguish the children of God and the children of the world,"— this argument rests upon the erroneous supposition, that the expression " sons of God" was introduced by Jehovah for the first time when He selected Israel to be the covenant nation. So much is true, indeed, that before the adoption of Israel as the first-born son of Jehovah (Ex. iv. 22), it would have been out of place to speak of sons of Jehovah ; but the notion is false, or at least incapable of proof, that there were not children of God in the olden time, long before Abraham's call, and that, if there were, they could not have been called " sons of Elohim." The idea was not first introduced in connection with the theocracy, and extended thence to a more universal signification. It had its roots in the divine image, and therefore was general in its application from the very first; and it was not till God in the character of Jehovah chose Abraham and his seed to be the vehicles of salvation, and left the heathen nations to go their own way, that the expression received the specifically theocratic signification of " son of Jehovah," to be again liberated and expanded into the more comprehensive idea of υἱοθεσία τοῦ Θεοῦ (*i.e. Elohim*, not τοῦ κυρίου = *Jehovah*), at the coming of Christ, the Saviour of all nations. If in the olden time there were pious men who, like Enoch and Noah, walked with Elohim, or who, even if they did not stand in this close priestly relation to God, made the divine image a reality through their piety and fear of God, then there were sons (children) of God, for whom the only correct appellation was " sons of Elohim," since sonship to Jehovah was introduced with the call of Israel, so that it could only have been proleptically that the children of God in the old world could be called " sons of Jehovah." But if it be still argued, that in mere prose the term " sons of God" could not have been applied to children of God, or pious men, this would be equally applicable to " sons of Jehovah." On the other hand, there is this objection to our applying it to angels, that the pious, who walked with God and called upon the name of the Lord, had been mentioned just before, whereas no allusion had been made to angels, not even to their creation.

Again, the antithesis " sons of God" and " daughters of men" does not prove that the former were angels. It by no means follows, that because in ver. 1 האדם denotes man as a genus, i.e. the whole human race, it must do the same in ver. 2, where the expression " daughters of men" is determined by the antithesis " sons of God." And with reasons existing for understanding by the sons of God and the daughters of men two species of the genus האדם, mentioned in ver. 1, no valid objection can be offered to the restriction of האדם, through the antithesis Elohim, to all men with the exception of the sons of God; since this mode of expression is by no means unusual in Hebrew. "From the expression ' daughters of men,'" as Dettinger observes, " it by no means follows that the sons of God were not men; any more than it follows from Jer. xxxii. 20, where it is said that God had done miracles ' in Israel, and among men,' or from Isa. xliii. 4, where God says He will give men for the Israelites, or from Judg. xvi. 7, where Samson says, that if he is bound with seven green withs he shall be as weak as a man, or from Ps. lxxiii. 5, where it is said of the ungodly they are not in trouble as men, that the Israelites, or Samson, or the ungodly, were not men at all. In all these passages אדם (men) denotes the remainder of mankind in distinction from those who are especially named." Cases occur, too, even in simple prose, in which the same term is used, first in a general, and then directly afterwards in a more restricted sense. We need cite only one, which occurs in Judg. xix.–xxi. In chap. xix. 30 reference is made to the coming of the children of Israel (i.e. of the twelve tribes) out of Egypt; and directly afterwards (chap. xx. 1, 2) it is related that " all the children of Israel," " all the tribes of Israel," assembled together

(to make war, as we learn from vers. 3 sqq., upon Benjamin);
and in the whole account of the war, chap. xx. and xxi., the
tribes of Israel are distinguished from the tribe of Benjamin :
so that the expression " tribes of Israel" really means the rest of
the tribes with the exception of Benjamin.   And yet the Benjamites were Israelites.   Why then should the fact that the
sons of God are distinguished from the daughters of men prove
that the former could not be men ?   There is not force enough
in these two objections to compel us to adopt the conclusion that
the sons of God were angels.

The question whether the " sons of Elohim " were celestial
or terrestrial sons of God (angels or pious men of the family of
Seth) can only be determined from the context, and from the
substance of the passage itself, that is to say, from what is related respecting the conduct of the sons of God and its results.
That the *connection* does not favour the idea of their being
angels, is acknowledged even by those who adopt this view.
" It cannot be denied," says *Delitzsch*, " that the connection of
chap. vi. 1-8 with chap. iv. necessitates the assumption, that
such intermarriages (of the Sethite and Cainite families) did
take place about the time of the flood (cf. Matt. xxiv. 38 ; Luke
xvii. 27) ; and the prohibition of mixed marriages under the law
(Ex. xxxiv. 16 ; cf. Gen. xxvii. 46, xxviii. 1 sqq.) also favours the
same idea."   But this " assumption " is placed beyond all doubt,
by what is here related of the sons of God.   In ver. 2 it is
stated that " the sons of God saw the daughters of men, that
they were fair; and they took them wives of all which they
chose," *i.e.* of any with whose beauty they were charmed ; and
these wives bare children to them (ver. 4).   Now לָקַח אִשָּׁה (to
take a wife) is a standing expression throughout the whole of
the Old Testament for the marriage relation established by God
at the creation, and is never applied to πορνεία, or the simple
act of physical connection.   This is quite sufficient of itself to
exclude any reference to angels.   For Christ Himself distinctly
states that the angels cannot marry (Matt. xxii. 30 ; Mark xii.
25 ; cf. Luke xx. 34 sqq.).   And when *Kurtz* endeavours to
weaken the force of these words of Christ, by arguing that they
do not prove that it is impossible for angels so to fall from their
original holiness as to sink into an unnatural state ; this phrase
has no meaning, unless by conclusive analogies, or the clear

testimony of Scripture,[1] it can be proved that the angels either possess by nature a material corporeality adequate to the contraction of a human marriage, or that by rebellion against their Creator they can acquire it, or that there are some creatures in heaven and on earth which, through sinful degeneracy, or by sinking into an unnatural state, can become possessed of the

---

[1] We cannot admit that there is any force in *Hofmann's* argument in his *Schriftbeweis* 1, p. 426, that "the begetting of children on the part of angels is not more irreconcilable with a nature that is not organized, like that of man, on the basis of sexual distinctions, than partaking of food is with a nature that is altogether spiritual; and yet food was eaten by the angels who visited Abraham." For, in the first place, the eating in this case was a miracle wrought through the condescending grace of the omnipotent God, and furnishes no standard for judging what angels can do by their own power in rebellion against God. And in the second place, there is a considerable difference between the act of eating on the part of the angels of God who appeared in human shape, and the taking of wives and begetting of children on the part of sinning angels. We are quite unable also to accept as historical testimony, the myths of the heathen respecting demigods, sons of gods, and the begetting of children on the part of their gods, or the fables of the book of Enoch (chap. vi. sqq.) about the 200 angels, with their leaders, who lusted after the beautiful and delicate daughters of men, and who came down from heaven and took to themselves wives, with whom they begat giants of 3000 (or according to one MS. 300) cubits in height. Nor do 2 Pet. ii. 4 and Jude 6 furnish any evidence of angel marriages. Peter is merely speaking of sinning angels in general (ἀγγέλων ἁμαρτησάντων) whom God did not spare, and not of any particular sin on the part of a small number of angels; and Jude describes these angels as τοὺς μὴ τηρήσαντας τὴν ἑαυτῶν ἀρχήν, ἀλλὰ ἀπολιπόντας τὸ ἴδιον οἰκητήριον, those who kept not their princedom, their position as rulers, but left their own habitation. There is nothing here about marriages with the daughters of men or the begetting of children, even if we refer the word τούτοις in the clause τὸν ὅμοιον τούτοις τρόπον ἐκπορνεύσασαι in ver. 7 to the angels mentioned in ver. 6 ; for ἐκπορνεύειν, the commission of fornication, would be altogether different from marriage, that is to say, from a conjugal bond that was permanent even though unnatural. But it is neither certain nor probable that this is the connection of τούτοις. *Huther*, the latest commentator upon this Epistle, who gives the preference to this explanation of τούτοις, and therefore cannot be accused of being biassed by doctrinal prejudices, says distinctly in the 2d Ed. of his commentary, "τούτοις may be grammatically construed as referring to Sodom and Gomorrah, or *per synesin* to the inhabitants of these cities; but in that case the sin of Sodom and Gomorrah would only be mentioned indirectly." There is nothing in the rules of syntax, therefore, to prevent our connecting the word with Sodom and Gomorrah ; and it is not a fact, that " *grammaticæ et logicæ præcepta* compel us to refer this word to the angels," as *G. v. Zeschwitz* says. But

power, which they have not by nature, of generating and pro-
pagating their species. As man could indeed destroy by sin
the nature which he had received from his Creator, but could
not by his own power restore it when destroyed, to say nothing
of implanting an organ or a power that was wanting before; so
we cannot believe that angels, through apostasy from God, could

the very same reason which *Huther* assigns for not connecting it with
Sodom and Gomorrah, may be also assigned for not connecting it with the
angels, namely, that in that case the sin of the angels would only be mentioned indirectly. We regard *Philippi's* explanation (in his *Glaubenslehre*
iii. p. 303) as a possible one, viz. that the word τούτοις refers back to the
ἄνθρωποι ἀσελγεῖς mentioned in ver. 4, and as by no means set aside by
De Wette's objection, that the thought of ver. 8 would be anticipated in that
case; for this objection is fully met by the circumstance, that not only does
the word οὗτοι, which is repeated five times from ver. 8 onwards, refer back
to these men, but even the word τούτοις in ver. 14 also. On the other hand,
the reference of τούτοις to the angels is altogether precluded by the clause
καὶ ἀπελθοῦσαι ὀπίσω σαρκὸς ἑτέρας, which follows the word ἐκπορνεύσασαι.
For fornication on the part of the angels could only consist in their going
after flesh, or, as *Hofmann* expresses it, " having to do with flesh, for which
they were not created," but not in their going after *other*, or foreign flesh.
There would be no sense in the word ἑτέρας unless those who were ἐκπορ-
νεύσαντες were themselves possessed of σάρξ; so that this is the only alternative, either we must attribute to the angels a σάρξ or fleshly body, or the
idea of referring τούτοις to the angels must be given up. When *Kurtz*
replies to this by saying that " to angels human bodies are quite as much a
ἑτέρα σάρξ, *i.e.* a means of sensual gratification opposed to their nature and
calling, as man can be to human man," he hides the difficulty, but does not
remove it, by the ambiguous expression " opposed to their nature and calling." The ἑτέρα σάρξ must necessarily presuppose an ἰδία σάρξ.—But it is
thought by some, that even if τούτοις in ver. 7 do not refer to the angels
in ver. 6, the words of Jude agree so thoroughly with the tradition of the
book of Enoch respecting the fall of the angels, that we must admit the
allusion to the Enoch legend, and so indirectly to Gen. vi., since Jude could
not have expressed himself more clearly to persons who possessed the book
of Enoch, or were acquainted with the tradition it contained. Now this
conclusion would certainly be irresistible, if the only sin of the angels
mentioned in the book of Enoch, as that for which they were kept in chains
of darkness still the judgment-day, had been their intercourse with human
wives. For the fact that Jude was acquainted with the legend of Enoch,
and took for granted that the readers of his Epistle were so too, is evident
from his introducing a prediction of Enoch in vers. 14, 15, which is to be
found in chap. i. 9 of Dillmann's edition of the book of Enoch. But it is
admitted by all critical writers upon this book, that in the book of Enoch
which has been edited by *Dillmann*, and is only to be found in an Ethiopic
version, there are contradictory legends concerning the fall and judgment

acquire sexual power of which they had previously been destitute.

Ver. 3. The sentence of God upon the " sons of God" is also appropriate to men only. *"Jehovah said : My spirit shall not rule in men for ever ; in their wandering they are flesh."* The verb דּוּן = דִּין. signifies to rule (hence אָדוֹן the ruler), and to judge, of the angels ; that the book itself is composed of earlier and later materials ; and that those very sections (chap. vi.–xvi. 106, etc.) in which the legend of the angel marriages is given without ambiguity, belong to the so-called book of *Noah*, *i.e.* to a later portion of the Enoch legend, which is opposed in many passages to the earlier legend. The *fall* of the angels is certainly often referred to in the earlier portions of the work ; but among all the passages adduced by Dillmann in proof of this, there is only one (chap. xix. 1) which mentions the angels who had taken wives. In the others, the only thing mentioned as the sin of the angels or of the hosts of Azazel, is the fact that they were subject to Satan, and seduced those who dwelt on the earth (chap. liv. 3–6), or that they came down from heaven to earth, and revealed to the children of men what was hidden from them, and then led them astray to the commission of sin (chap. lxiv. 2). There is nothing at all here about their taking wives. Moreover, in the earlier portions of the book, besides the fall of the angels, there is frequent reference made to a fall, *i.e.* an act of sin, on the part of the stars of heaven and the army of heaven, which transgressed the commandment of God before they rose, by not appearing at their appointed time (*vid.* chap. xviii. 14, 15, xxi. 3, xc. 21, 24, etc.) ; and their punishment and place of punishment are described, in just the same manner as in the case of the wicked angels, as a prison, a lofty and horrible place in which the seven stars of heaven lie bound like great mountains and flaming with fire (chap. xxi. 2, 3), as an abyss, narrow and deep, dreadful and dark, in which the star which fell first from heaven is lying, bound hand and foot (chap. lxxxviii. 1, cf. xc. 24). From these passages it is quite evident, that the legend concerning the fall of the angels and stars sprang out of Isa. xxiv. 21, 22 (" And it shall come to pass in that day, that the Lord shall visit the host of the height (צְבָא הַמָּרוֹם, the host of heaven, by which stars and angels are to be understood) on high (*i.e.* the spiritual powers of the heavens) and the kings of the earth upon the earth, and they shall be gathered together, bound in the dungeon, and shut up in prison, and after many days they shall be punished"), along with Isa. xiv. 12 (" How art thou fallen from heaven, thou beautiful morning star!"), and that the account of the sons of God in Gen. vi., as interpreted by those who refer it to the angels, was afterwards combined and amalgamated with it. Now if these different legends, describing the judgment upon the stars that fell from heaven, and the angels that followed Satan in seducing man, in just the same manner as the judgment upon the angels who begot giants from women, were in circulation at the time when the Epistle of Jude was written ; we must not interpret the sin of the angels, referred to by Peter and as the consequence of ruling. רוּחַ is the divine spirit of life bestowed upon man, the principle of physical and ethical, natural and spiritual life. This His spirit God will withdraw from man, and thereby put an end to their life and conduct. בְּשַׁגַּם is regarded by many as a particle, compounded of בְּ, שֶׁ a contraction

Jude, in a one-sided manner, and arbitrarily connect it with only such passages of the book of Enoch as speak of angel marriages, to the entire disregard of all the other passages, which mention totally different sins as committed by the angels, that are punished with bands of darkness ; but we must interpret it from what Jude himself has said concerning this sin, as Peter gives no further explanation of what he means by ἁμαρτῆσαι. Now the only sins that Jude mentions are μὴ τηρῆσαι τὴν ἑαυτῶν ἀρχήν and ἀπολιπεῖν τὸ ἴδιον οἰκητήριον. The two are closely connected. Through not keeping the ἀρχή (i.e. the position as rulers in heaven) which belonged to them, and was assigned them at their creation, the angels left " their own habitation " (ἴδιον οἰκητήριον) ; just as man, when he broke the commandment of God and failed to keep his position as ruler on earth, also lost " his own habitation " (ἴδιον οἰκητήριον), that is to say, not paradise alone, but the holy body of innocence also, so that he needed a covering for his nakedness, and will continue to need it, until we are " clothed upon with our house which is from heaven " (οἰκητήριον ἡμῶν ἐξ οὐρανοῦ). In this description of the angels' sin, there is not the slightest allusion to their leaving heaven to woo the beautiful daughters of men. The words may be very well interpreted, as they were by the earlier Christian theologians, as relating to the fall of Satan and his angels, to whom all that is said concerning their punishment fully applies. If Jude had had the πορνεία of the angels, mentioned in the Enoch legends, in his mind, he would have stated this distinctly, just as he does in ver. 9 in the case of the legend concerning Michael and the devil, and in ver. 11 in that of Enoch's prophecy. There was all the more reason for his doing this, because not only do contradictory accounts of the sin of the angels occur in the Enoch legends, but a comparison of the parallels cited from the book of Enoch proves that he deviated from the Enoch legend in points of no little importance. Thus, for example, according to Enoch liv. 3, " *iron* chains of immense weight " are prepared for the hosts of Azazel, to put them into the lowest hell, and cast them on that great day into the furnace with flaming fire. Now Jude and Peter say nothing about *iron* chains, and merely mention "everlasting chains under darkness " and "chains of darkness." Again, according to Enoch x. 12, the angel sinners are " bound fast under the earth *for seventy generations*, till the day of judgment and their completion, till the last judgment shall be held for all eternity." Peter and Jude make no allusion to this point of time, and the supporters of the angel marriages, therefore, have thought well to leave it out when quoting this parallel to Jude 6. Under these circumstances, the silence of the apostles as to either marriages or fornication on the part of the sinful angels, is a sure sign that they gave no credence to these fables of a Jewish gnosticizing tradition.

of אֲשֶׁר, and גַּם (also), used in the sense of *quoniam*, because, (בְּשַׁ = בַּאֲשֶׁר, as שַׁ or שֶׁ = אֲשֶׁר Judg. v. 7, vi. 17; Song of Sol. i. 7). But the objection to this explanation is, that the גַּם, "because he *also* is flesh," introduces an incongruous emphasis into the clause. We therefore prefer to regard שַׁגַּם as the *inf.* of שָׁגַג = שָׁגָה with the suffix: "*in their erring* (that of men) *he* (man as a genus) *is flesh;*" an explanation to which, to our mind, the extremely harsh change of number (*they, he*), is no objection, since many examples might be adduced of a similar change (*vid. Hupfeld* on Ps. v. 10). Men, says God, have proved themselves by their erring and straying to be flesh, *i.e.* given up to the flesh, and incapable of being ruled by the Spirit of God and led back to the divine goal of their life. בָּשָׂר is used already in its ethical signification, like σάρξ in the New Testament, denoting not merely the natural corporeality of man, but his materiality as rendered ungodly by sin. "*Therefore his days shall be* 120 *years:*" this means, not that human life should in future never attain a greater age than 120 years, but that a respite of 120 years should still be granted to the human race. This sentence, as we may gather from the context, was made known to Noah in his 480th year, to be published by him as "preacher of righteousness" (2 Pet. ii. 5) to the degenerate race. The reason why men had gone so far astray, that God determined to withdraw His spirit and give them up to destruction, was that the sons of God had taken wives of such of the daughters of men as they chose. Can this mean, because angels had formed marriages with the daughters of men? Even granting that such marriages, as being unnatural connections, would have led to the complete corruption of human nature; the men would in that case have been the tempted, and the real authors of the corruption would have been the angels. Why then should judgment fall upon the tempted alone? The judgments of God in the world are not executed with such partiality as this. And the supposition that nothing is said about the punishment of the angels, because the narrative has to do with the history of man, and the spiritual world is intentionally veiled as much as possible, does not meet the difficulty. If the sons of God were angels, the narrative is concerned not only with men, but with angels also; and it is not the custom of the Scriptures merely to relate the judgments which fall upon the tempted, and say nothing at all about the tempters. For the contrary, see chap. iii. 14 sqq. If the "sons of God" were not men, so as to be included in the term אָדָם, the punishment would need to be specially pointed out in their case, and no deep revelations of the spiritual world would be required, since these celestial tempters would be living with men upon the earth, when they had taken wives from among their daughters. The judgments of God are not only free from all unrighteousness, but avoid every kind of partiality.

Ver. 4. " *The Nephilim were on the earth in those days, and also after that, when the sons of God came in unto the daughters of men, and they bare children to them: these are the heroes* (הַגִּבֹּרִים) *who from the olden time* (מֵעוֹלָם, as in Ps. xxv. 6 ; 1 Sam. xxvii. 8) *are the men of name*" (*i.e.* noted, renowned or notorious men). נְפִילִים, from נָפַל to fall upon (Job i. 15 ; Josh. xi. 7), signifies the invaders (ἐπιπίπτοντες Aq., βιαῖοι Sym.). *Luther* gives the correct meaning, "tyrants :" they were called *Nephilim* because they fell upon the people and oppressed them.[1] The meaning of the verse is a subject of dispute. To an unprejudiced mind, the words, as they stand, represent the *Nephilim*, who were on the earth in those days, as existing before the sons of God began to marry the daughters of men, and clearly distinguish them from the fruits of these marriages. הָיוּ can no more be rendered "they became, or arose," in this connection, than הָיָה in chap. i. 2. וַיִּהְיוּ would have been the proper word. The expression "in those days" refers most naturally to the

---

[1] The notion that the *Nephilim* were giants, to which the Sept. rendering γίγαντες has given rise, was rejected even by *Luther* as fabulous. He bases his view upon Josh. xi. 7 : " *Nephilim non dictos a magnitudine corporum, sicut Rabbini putant, sed a tyrannide et oppressione quod vi grassati sint, nulla habita ratione legum aut honestatis, sed simpliciter indulgentes suis voluptatibus et cupiditatibus.*" The opinion that giants are intended derives no support from Num. xiii. 32, 33. When the spies describe the land of Canaan as " a land that eateth up the inhabitants thereof," and then add (ver. 33), " and there we saw the *Nephilim*, the sons of Anak among (מִן *lit.* from, out of, in a partitive sense) the Nephilim," by the side of whom they were as grasshoppers ; the term *Nephilim* cannot signify giants, since the spies not only mention them especially along with the inhabitants of the land, who are described as people of great stature, but single out only a portion of the *Nephilim* as "sons of Anak" (בְּנֵי עֲנָק), *i.e.* long-necked people or giants. The explanation " fallen from heaven" needs no refutation ; inasmuch as the main element, " from heaven," is a purely arbitrary addition.

time when God pronounced the sentence upon the degenerate
race; but it is so general and comprehensive a term, that it
must not be confined exclusively to that time, not merely because the divine sentence was first pronounced after these marriages were contracted, and the marriages, if they did not
produce the corruption, raised it to that fulness of iniquity
which was ripe for the judgment, but still more because the
words "after that" represent the marriages which drew down
the judgment as an event that followed the appearance of the
Nephilim. "*The same were mighty men :*" this might point back
to the *Nephilim ;* but it is a more natural supposition, that it
refers to the children born to the sons of God. "*These,*"
i.e. the sons sprung from those marriages, "*are the heroes, those
renowned heroes of old.*" Now if, according to the simple
meaning of the passage, the *Nephilim* were in existence at the
very time when the sons of God came in to the daughters of
men, the appearance of the *Nephilim* cannot afford the slightest
evidence that the "sons of God" were angels, by whom a family
of monsters were begotten, whether demigods, dæmons, or angel-
men.[1]

[1] How thoroughly irreconcilable the contents of this verse are with the
angel-hypothesis is evident from the strenuous efforts of its supporters to
bring them into harmony with it. Thus, in *Reuter's Repert.*, p. 7, *Del.*
observes that the verse cannot be rendered in any but the following manner: "The giants *were* on the earth in those days, and also afterwards, when
the sons of God went in to the daughters of men, these they bare to them,
or rather, and these bare to them ;" but, for all that, he gives this as the
meaning of the words, "At the time of the divine determination to inflict
punishment the giants *arose*, and also afterwards, when this unnatural connection between super-terrestrial and human beings continued, there arose
such giants ;" not only substituting "arose" for "were," but changing
"when they connected themselves with them" into "when this connection
continued." Nevertheless he is obliged to confess that "it is strange that
this unnatural connection, which I also suppose to be the intermediate cause
of the origin of the giants, should not be mentioned in the first clause of
ver. 4." This is an admission that the text says nothing about the origin
of the giants being traceable to the marriages of the sons of God, but that
the commentators have been obliged to insert it in the text to save their
angel marriages. *Kurtz* has tried three different explanations of this verse,
but they are all opposed to the rules of the language. (1) In the History of
the Old Covenant he gives this rendering: "Nephilim were on earth in these
days, and that even after the sons of God had formed connections with the
daughters of men ;" in which he not only gives to הַ the unsupportable

Vers. 5–8. Now when the wickedness of man became great, and "*every imagination of the thoughts of his heart was only evil the whole day*," *i.e.* continually and altogether evil, it repented God that He had made man, and He determined to destroy them. This determination and the motive assigned are also irreconcilable with the angel-theory. "Had the godless race, which God destroyed by the flood, sprung either entirely or in part from the marriage of angels to the daughters of men, it would no longer have been the race first created by God in Adam, but a grotesque product of the Adamitic factor created by God, and an entirely foreign and angelic factor" (*Phil.*).[1] The force of יִנָּחֶם, "it *repented* the Lord,"

meaning, "even, just," but takes the imperfect יָבֹא in the sense of the perfect בָּא. (2) In his *Ehen der Söhne Gottes* (p. 80) he gives the choice of this and the following rendering: "The Nephilim were on earth in those days, and also after this had happened, that the sons of God came to the daughters of men and begat children," where the ungrammatical rendering of the imperfect as the perfect is artfully concealed by the interpolation of "after this had happened." (3) In "*die Söhne Gottes*," p. 85: "In these days and also afterwards, when the sons of God came (continued to come) to the daughters of men, they bare to them (*sc.* Nephilim)," where יָבֹאוּ, they came, is arbitrarily altered into יֹסִיפוּ לָבוֹא, they continued to come. But when he observes in defence of this *quid pro quo*, that "the imperfect denotes here, as *Hengstenberg* has correctly affirmed, and as so often is the case, an action frequently repeated in past times," this remark only shows that he has neither understood the nature of the usage to which H. refers, nor what *Ewald* has said (§ 136) concerning the force and use of the imperfect.

[1] When, on the other hand, the supporters of the angel marriages maintain that it is only on this interpretation that the necessity for the flood, *i.e.* for the complete destruction of the whole human race with the exception of righteous Noah, can be understood, not only is there no scriptural foundation for this argument, but it is decidedly at variance with those statements of the Scriptures, which speak of the corruption of *the men whom God had created*, and not of a race that had arisen through an unnatural connection of angels and men and forced their way into God's creation. If it were really the case, that it would otherwise be impossible to understand where the necessity could lie, for all the rest of the human race to be destroyed and a new beginning to be made, whereas afterwards, when Abraham was chosen, the rest of the human race was not only spared, but preserved for subsequent participation in the blessings of salvation: we should only need to call Job to mind, who also could not comprehend the necessity for the fearful sufferings which overwhelmed him, and was unable to discover the justice of God, but who was afterwards taught a better

may be gathered from the explanatory יִתְעַצֵּב, "it grieved Him at His heart." This shows that the repentance of God does not presuppose any variableness in His nature or His purposes. In this sense God never repents of anything (1 Sam. xv. 29), "*quia nihil illi inopinatum vel non prævisum accidit*" (*Calvin*). The repentance of God is an anthropomorphic expression for the pain of the divine love at the sin of man, and signifies that "God is hurt no less by the atrocious sins of men than if they pierced His heart with mortal anguish" (*Calvin*). The destruction of all, "from man unto beast," etc., is to be explained on the ground of the sovereignty of man upon the earth, the irrational creatures being created for him, and therefore involved in his fall. This destruction, however, was not to bring the human race to an end. "Noah found grace in the eyes of the Lord." In these words mercy is seen in the midst of wrath, pledging the preservation and restoration of humanity.

III. THE HISTORY OF NOAH.

CHAP. VI. 9–IX. 29.

The important relation in which Noah stands both to sacred and universal history, arises from the fact, that he found mercy on account of his blameless walk with God; that in him the human race was kept from total destruction, and he was preserved from the all-destroying flood, to found in his sons a new

lesson by God Himself, and reproved for his rash conclusions, as a sufficient proof of the deceptive and futile character of all such human reasoning. But this is not the true state of the case. The Scriptures expressly affirm, that after the flood the moral corruption of man was the same as before the flood; for they describe it in chap. viii. 21 in the very same words as in chap. vi. 5: and the reason they assign for the same judgment not being repeated, is simply the promise that God would no more smite and destroy all living, as He had done before—an evident proof that God expected no change in human nature, and out of pure mercy and long-suffering would never send a second flood. "Now, if the race destroyed had been one that sprang from angel-fathers, it is difficult to understand why no improvement was to be looked for after the flood; for the repetition of any such unnatural angel-tragedy was certainly not probable, and still less inevitable" (*Philippi*).

beginning to the history of the world. The piety of Noah, his preservation, and the covenant through which God appointed him the head of the human race, are the three main points in this section. The first of these is dismissed in a very few words. The second, on the contrary, viz. the destruction of the old world by the flood, and the preservation of Noah, together with the animals enclosed in the ark, is circumstantially and elaborately described, " because this event included, on the one hand, a work of judgment and mercy of the greatest significance to the history of the kingdom of God"—a judgment of such universality and violence as will only be seen again in the judgment at the end of the world ; and, on the other hand, an act of mercy which made the flood itself a flood of grace, and in that respect a type of baptism (1 Pet. iii. 21), and of life rising out of death. " Destruction ministers to preservation, immersion to purification, death to new birth ; the old corrupt earth is buried in the flood, that out of this grave a new world may arise" (*Delitzsch*).

PREPARATION FOR THE FLOOD.—CHAP. VI. 9–22.

Vers. 9–12 contain a description of Noah and his contemporaries ; vers. 13–22, the announcement of the purpose of God with reference to the flood.—Ver. 9. " *Noah, a righteous man, was blameless among his generations :*" *righteous* in his moral relation to God ; *blameless* (τέλειος, *integer*) in his character and conduct. דֹּרֹת, γενεαί, were the *generations* or families " which passed by Noah, the Nestor of his time." His righteousness and integrity were manifested in his walking with God, in which he resembled Enoch (chap. v. 22).—In vers. 10–12, the account of the birth of his three sons, and of the corruption of all flesh, is repeated. This corruption is represented as corrupting the whole earth and filling it with wickedness ; and thus the judgment of the flood is for the first time fully accounted for. " *The earth was corrupt before God* (*Elohim* points back to the previous *Elohim* in ver. 9)," it became so conspicuous to God, that He could not refrain from punishment. The corruption proceeded from the fact, that " *all flesh*"—*i.e.* the whole human race which had resisted the influence of the Spirit of God and become flesh (see ver. 3)—" *had corrupted its way.*" The term " flesh " in ver. 12 cannot include the animal world, since the

expression, " corrupted its way," is applicable to man alone. The
fact that in vers. 13 and 17 this term embraces both men and
animals is no proof to the contrary, for the simple reason, that
in ver. 19 " all flesh " denotes the animal world only, an evident
proof that the precise meaning of the word must always be determined from the context.—Ver. 13. " *The end of all flesh is
come before Me.*" אֶל בּוֹא, when applied to rumours, invariably
signifies " to reach the ear" (*vid.* chap. xviii. 21 ; Ex. iii. 9 ;
Esth. ix. 11) ; hence לְפָנַי בָּא in this case cannot mean *a me con-
stitutus est* (*Ges.*).   קֵץ, therefore, is not the end in the sense of
destruction, but the end (extremity) of depravity or corruption,
which leads to destruction.   " *For the earth has become full of
wickedness* מִפְּנֵיהֶם," *i.e.* proceeding from them, " *and I destroy
them along with the earth.*"   Because all flesh had *destroyed* its
way, it should be *destroyed* with the earth by God.   The *lex
talionis* is obvious here.—Vers. 14 sqq. Noah was exempted
from the extermination.   He was to build an ark, in order that
he himself, his family, and the animals might be preserved.
תֵּבָה, which is only used here and in Ex. ii. 3, 5, where it is
applied to the ark in which Moses was placed, is probably an
Egyptian word : the LXX. render it κίβωτος here, and θίβη in
Exodus ; the Vulgate *arca*, from which our word *ark* is derived.
Gopher-wood (*ligna bituminata ; Jerome*) is most likely *cypress*.
The ἀπ. λεγ. *gopher* is related to כֹּפֶר, resin, and κυπάρισσος ; it
is no proof to the contrary that in later Hebrew the cypress is
called *berosh*, for *gopher* belongs to the pre-Hebraic times.   The
ark was to be made cells, *i.e.* divided into cells, קִנִּים (*lit.* nests,
niduli, mansiunculæ), and pitched (כָּפַר *denom.* from כֹּפֶר) within
and without with *copher*, or asphalte (LXX. ἄσφαλτος, *Vulg.
bitumen*).   On the supposition, which is a very probable one,
that the ark was built in the form not of a ship, but of a chest,
with flat bottom, like a floating house, as it was not meant for
sailing, but merely to float upon the water, the dimensions,
300 cubits long, 50 broad, and 30 high, give a superficial area
of 15,000 square cubits, and a cubic measurement of 450,000
cubits, probably of the ordinary standard, " after the elbow
of a man " (Deut. iii. 11), *i.e.* measured from the elbow to
the end of the middle finger.—Ver. 16.   " *Light shalt thou
make to the ark, and in a cubit from above shalt thou finish
it.*"   As the meaning *light* for צֹהַר is established by the word

צָהֳרִים, "double-light" or mid-day, the passage can only signify that a hole or opening for light and air was to be so constructed as to reach within a cubit of the edge of the roof. A window only a cubit square could not possibly be intended; for צֹהַר is not synonymous with חַלּוֹן (chap. viii. 6), but signifies, generally, a space for light, or by which light could be admitted into the ark, and in which the window, or lattice for opening and shutting, could be fixed; though we can form no distinct idea of what the arrangement was. The door he was to place in the side; and to make "*lower, second, and third* (*sc.* cells)," *i.e.* three distinct stories.[1]—Vers. 17 sqq. Noah was to build this ark, because God was about to bring a flood upon the earth, and would save him, with his family, and one pair of every kind of animal. מַבּוּל, (the flood), is an archaic word, coined expressly for the waters of Noah (Isa. liv. 9), and is used nowhere else except Ps. xxix. 10. מַיִם עַל הָאָרֶץ is in apposition to *mabbul*: "*I bring the flood, waters upon the earth, to destroy all flesh, wherein is a living breath*" (*i.e.* man and beast). With Noah, God made a covenant. On בְּרִית see chap. xv. 18. As not only the human race, but the animal world also was to be preserved through Noah, he was to take with him into the ark his wife, his sons and their wives, and of every living thing, of all flesh, two of every sort, a male and a female, to keep them alive; also all kinds of food for himself and family, and for the sustenance of the beasts.—Ver. 22. "*Thus did Noah, according to all that God commanded him*" (with regard to the building of the ark). Cf. Heb. xi. 7.

[1] As the height of the ark was thirty cubits, the three stories of cells can hardly have filled the entire space, since a room ten cubits high, or nine cubits if we deduct the thickness of the floors, would have been a prodigality of space beyond what the necessities required. It has been conjectured that above or below these stories there was space provided for the necessary supplies of food and fodder. At the same time, this is pure conjecture, like every other calculation, not only as to the number and size of the cells, but also as to the number of animals to be collected and the fodder they would require. Hence every objection that has been raised to the suitability of the structure, and the possibility of collecting all the animals in the ark and providing them with food, is based upon arbitrary assumptions, and should be treated as a perfectly groundless fancy. As natural science is still in the dark as to the formation of species, and therefore not in a condition to determine the number of pairs from which all existing species are descended, it is ridiculous to talk, as *Pfaff* and others do, of 2000 species of mammalia, and 6500 species of birds, which Noah would have had to feed every day.

HISTORY OF THE FLOOD.—CHAP. VII.–VIII. 19.

The account of the commencement, course, and termination of the flood abounds in repetitions; but although it progresses somewhat heavily, the connection is well sustained, and no link could be erased without producing a gap.—Vers. 1–16. When the ark was built, and the period of grace (vi. 3) had passed, Noah received instructions from Jehovah to enter the ark with his family, and with the animals, viz. seven of every kind of clean animals, and two of the unclean; and was informed that within seven days God would cause it to rain upon the earth forty days and forty nights. The date of the flood is then given (ver. 6): " *Noah was six hundred years old, and the flood was* (namely) *water upon the earth;*" and the execution of the divine command is recorded in vers. 7–9. There follows next the account of the bursting forth of the flood, the date being given with still greater minuteness; and the entrance of the men and animals into the ark is again described as being fully accomplished (vers. 10–16).—The fact that in the command to enter the ark a distinction is now made between clean and unclean animals, seven of the former being ordered to be taken,—*i.e.* three pair and a single one, probably a male for sacrifice,—is no more a proof of different authorship, or of the fusion of two accounts, than the interchange of the names Jehovah and Elohim. For the distinction between clean and unclean animals did not originate with Moses, but was confirmed by him as a long established custom, in harmony with the law. It reached back to the very earliest times, and arose from a certain innate feeling of the human mind, when undisturbed by unnatural and ungodly influences, which detects types of sin and corruption in many animals, and instinctively recoils from them (see my *biblische Archäologie* ii. p. 20). That the variations in the names of God furnish no criterion by which to detect different documents, is evident enough from the fact, that in chap. vii. 1 it is *Jehovah* who commands Noah to enter the ark, and in ver. 4 Noah does as *Elohim* had commanded, whilst in ver. 16, in two successive clauses, Elohim alternates with Jehovah—the animals entering the ark at the command of Elohim, and Jehovah shutting Noah in. With regard to the entrance of the animals into the ark, it is worthy of notice, that in vers. 9 and 15 it is stated that "*they came two and two,*" and in ver. 16 that "*the coming ones came male and female of all flesh.*" In this expression "they came" it is clearly intimated, that the animals collected about Noah and were taken into the ark, without his having to exert himself to collect them, and that they did so in consequence of an instinct produced by God, like that which frequently leads animals to scent and try to flee from dangers, of which man has no presentiment. The time when the flood commenced is said to have been the 600th year of Noah's life, on the 17th day of the second month (ver. 11). The months must be reckoned, not according to the Mosaic ecclesiastical year, which commenced in the spring, but according to the natural or civil year, which commenced in the autumn at the beginning of sowing time, or the autumnal equinox; so that the flood would be pouring upon the earth in October and November. "*The same day were all the fountains of the great deep* (תְּהוֹם the unfathomable ocean) *broken up, and the sluices* (windows, lattices) *of heaven opened, and there was* (happened, came) *pouring rain* (גֶּשֶׁם in distinction from מָטָר) *upon the earth* 40 *days and* 40 *nights.*" Thus the flood was produced by the bursting forth of fountains hidden within the earth, which drove seas and rivers above their banks, and by rain which continued incessantly for 40 days and 40 nights.—Ver. 13. "*In the self-same day had Noah . . . entered into the ark:*" בָּא, pluperfect "*had come,*" not *came,* which would require יָבֹא. The idea is not that Noah, with his family and all the animals, entered the ark on the very day on which the rain began, but that on that day he had entered, had completed the entering, which occupied the seven days between the giving of the command (ver. 4) and the commencement of the flood (ver. 10).

Vers. 17–24 contain a description of the flood: how the water increased more and more, till it was 15 cubits above all the lofty mountains of the earth, and how, on the one hand, it raised the ark above the earth and above the mountains, and, on the other, destroyed every living being upon the dry land, from man to cattle, creeping things, and birds. "The description is simple and majestic; the almighty judgment of God, and the love manifest in the midst of the wrath, hold the historian fast. The tautologies depict the fearful monotony of the immeasurable expanse of water: *omnia pontus erant et deerant litera ponto.*" The words of ver. 17, " *and the flood was* (came) *upon the earth for forty days,*" relate to the 40 days' rain combined with the bursting forth of the fountains beneath the earth. By these the water was eventually raised to the height given, at which it remained 150 days (ver. 24). But if the water covered " *all the high hills under the whole heaven,*" this clearly indicates the universality of the flood. The statement, indeed, that it rose 15 cubits above the mountains, is probably founded upon the fact, that the ark drew 15 feet of water, and that when the waters subsided, it rested upon the top of Ararat, from which the conclusion would very naturally be drawn as to the greatest height attained. Now as Ararat, according to the measurements of *Perrot,* is only 16,254 feet high, whereas the loftiest peaks of the Himalaya and Cordilleras are as much as 26,843, the submersion of these mountains has been thought impossible, and the statement in ver. 19 has been regarded as a rhetorical expression, like Deut. ii. 25 and iv. 19, which is not of universal application. But even if those peaks, which are higher than Ararat, were not covered by water, we cannot therefore pronounce the flood merely partial in its extent, but must regard it as universal, as extending over every part of the world, since the few peaks uncovered would not only sink into vanishing points in comparison with the surface covered, but would form an exception not worth mentioning, for the simple reason that no living beings could exist upon these mountains, covered with perpetual snow and ice ; so that *everything that lived upon the dry land, in whose nostrils there was a breath of life,* would inevitably die, and, with the exception of those shut up in the ark, neither man nor beast would be able to rescue itself, and escape destruction. A flood which rose 15 cubits above the top of Ararat could not remain partial, if it only continued a few days, to say nothing of the fact that the water was rising for 40 days, and remained at the highest elevation for 150 days. To speak of such a flood as partial is absurd , even if it broke out at only one spot, it would spread over the earth from one end to the other, and reach everywhere to the same elevation. However impossible, therefore, scientific men may declare it to be for them to conceive of a universal flood of such a height and duration in accordance with the known laws of nature, this inability on their part does not justify any one in questioning the possibility of such an event being produced by the omnipotence of God. It has been justly remarked, too, that the proportion of such a quantity of water to the entire mass of the earth, in relation to which the mountains are but like the scratches of a needle on a globe, is no greater than that of a profuse perspiration to the body of a man. And to this must be added, that, apart from the legend of a flood, which is found in nearly every nation, the earth presents unquestionable traces of submersion in the fossil remains of animals and plants, which are found upon the Cordilleras and Himalaya even beyond the limit of perpetual snow.[1] In ver. 23, instead of וַיִּמַח (*imperf. Niphal*) read וַיִּמַח (*imperf. Kal*): "*and He* (Jehovah) *destroyed every existing thing*," as He had said in ver. 4.

Chap. viii. 1–5. With the words, "*then God remembered Noah and all the animals . . . in the ark*," the narrative turns to the description of the gradual decrease of the water until the ground was perfectly dry. The fall of the water is described in the same pictorial style as its rapid rise. God's "remembering" was a manifestation of Himself, an effective restraint of the force of the raging element. He caused a wind to blow over the earth, so that the waters sank, and shut up the fountains of the deep, and the sluices of heaven, so that the rain from heaven was restrained. "*Then the waters turned* (יָשֻׁבוּ *i.e.* flowed off) *from the earth, flowing continuously* (the inf. absol. הָלוֹךְ וָשׁוֹב expresses continuation), *and decreased at the end of* 150 *days*." The decrease first became perceptible when the ark rested upon the

[1] The geological facts which testify to the submersion of the entire globe are collected in *Buckland's reliquiæ diluv.*, *Schubert's Gesch. der Natur*, and *C. v. Raumer's Geography*, and are of such importance that even *Cuvier* acknowledged "Je pense donc, avec MM. Deluc et Dolomieu, que s'il y a quelque chose de constaté en géologie ; c'est que la surface de notre globe a été victime d'une grande et subite révolution, dont la date ne peut remonter beaucoup au delà de cinq ou six mille ans " (Discours sur les *révol. de la surface du globe*, p. 290, ed. 6). The latest phase of geology, however, denies that these facts furnish any testimony to the historical character of the flood, and substitutes the hypothesis of a submersion of the entire globe before the creation of man : 1. because the animals found are very different from those at present in existence ; and 2. because no certain traces have hitherto been found of fossil human bones. We have already shown that there is no force in these arguments. *Vid. Keerl*, pp. 489 sqq.

mountains of Ararat on the 17th day of the seventh month; *i.e.*, reckoning 30 days to a month, exactly 150 days after the flood commenced. From that time forth it continued without inter-mission, so that on the first day of the tenth month, probably 73 days after the resting of the ark, the tops of the mountains were seen, viz. the tops of the Armenian highlands, by which the ark was surrounded. *Ararat* was the name of a province (2 Kings xix. 37), which is mentioned along with *Minni* (Armenia) as a kingdom in Jer. li. 27, probably the central province of the country of Armenia, which *Moses v. Chorene* calls *Arairad, Araratia.* The mountains of Ararat are, no doubt, the group of mountains which rise from the plain of the Araxes in two lofty peaks, the greater and lesser Ararat, the former 16,254 feet above the level of the sea, the latter about 12,000. This land-ing-place of the ark is extremely interesting in connection with the development of the human race as renewed after the flood. Armenia, the source of the rivers of paradise, has been called " a cool, airy, well-watered mountain-island in the midst of the old continent;" but Mount Ararat especially is situated almost in the middle, not only of the great desert route of Africa and Asia, but also of the range of inland waters from Gibraltar to the Baikal Sea—in the centre, too, of the longest line that can be drawn through the settlements of the Caucasian race and the Indo-Germanic tribes; and, as the central point of the longest land-line of the ancient world, from the Cape of Good Hope to the Behring Straits, it was the most suitable spot in the world, for the tribes and nations that sprang from the sons of Noah to descend from its heights and spread into every land (*vid. K. v. Raumer,* Paläst. pp. 456 sqq.).

Vers. 6–12. Forty days after the appearance of the mountain tops, Noah opened the window of the ark and let a raven fly out (*lit. the* raven, *i.e.* the particular raven known from that circum-stance), for the purpose of ascertaining the drying up of the waters. The raven went out and returned until the earth was dry, but without being taken back into the ark, as the mountain tops and the carcases floating upon the water afforded both rest-ing-places and food. After that, Noah let a dove fly out three times, at intervals of seven days. It is not distinctly stated that he sent it out the first time seven days after the raven, but this is implied in the statement that he stayed yet *other* seven days before sending it out the second time, and the same again before sending it the third time (vers. 10 and 12). The dove, when first sent out, *"found no rest for the sole of its foot;"* for a dove will only settle upon such places and objects as are dry and clean. It returned to the ark and let Noah take it in again (vers. 8, 9). The second time it returned in the evening, having remained out longer than before, and brought a fresh (מָרָף freshly plucked) olive-leaf in its mouth. Noah perceived from this that the water must be almost gone, had "abated from off the earth," though the ground might not be perfectly dry, as the olive-tree will put out leaves even under water. The fresh olive-leaf was the first sign of the resurrection of the earth to new life after the flood, and the dove with the olive-leaf a herald of salvation. The third time it did not return; a sign that the waters had completely receded from the earth. The fact that Noah waited 40 days before sending the raven, and after that always left an interval of seven days, is not to be accounted for on the supposition that these numbers were already regarded as significant. The 40 days correspond to the 40 days during which the rain fell and the waters rose; and Noah might assume that they would require the same time to recede as to rise. The seven days constituted the week established at the creation, and God had already conformed to it in arranging their entrance into the ark (chap. vii. 4, 10). The selection which Noah made of the birds may also be explained quite simply from the difference in their nature, with which Noah must have been acquainted; that is to say, from the fact that the raven in seeking its food settles upon every carcase that it sees, whereas the dove will only settle upon what is dry and clean.

Vers. 13–19. Noah waited some time, and then, on the first day of the first month, in the 601st year of his life, removed the covering from the ark, that he might obtain a freer prospect over the earth. He could see that the surface of the earth was dry; but it was not till the 27th day of the second month, 57 days, therefore, after the removal of the roof, that the earth was completely dried up. Then God commanded him to leave the ark with his family and all the animals; and so far as the latter were concerned, He renewed the blessing of the creation (ver. 17 cf. i. 22). As the flood commenced on the 17th of the second month of the 600th year of Noah's life, and ended on the 27th of the second month of the 601st year, it lasted a year and ten days; but whether a solar year of 360 or 365 days, or a lunar year of 352, is doubtful. The former is the more probable, as the first five months are said to have consisted of 150 days, which suits the solar year better than the lunar. The question cannot be decided with certainty, because we neither know the number of days between the 17th of the seventh month and the 1st of the tenth month, nor the interval between the sending out of the dove and the 1st day of the first month of the 601st year.

NOAH'S SACRIFICE, CURSE, AND BLESSING.—CHAP. VIII. 20–IX. 29.

Two events of Noah's life, of world-wide importance, are recorded as having occurred after the flood: his sacrifice, with the divine promise which followed it (chap. viii. 20–ix. 17); and the prophetic curse and blessing pronounced upon his sons (ix. 18–29).—Vers. 20–22. The first thing which Noah did, was to build an altar for burnt sacrifice, to thank the Lord for gracious protection, and pray for His mercy in time to come. This altar—מִזְבֵּחַ, *lit.* a place for the offering of slain animals, from זָבַח, like θυσιαστήριον from θύειν—is the first altar mentioned in history. The sons of Adam had built no altar for their offerings, because God was still present on the earth in paradise, so that they could turn their offerings and hearts towards that abode. But with the flood God had swept paradise away, withdrawn the place of His presence, and set up His throne in heaven, from which He would henceforth reveal Himself to man (cf. chap. xi. 5, 7). In future, therefore, the hearts of the pious had to be turned towards heaven, and their offerings and prayers needed to ascend on high if they were to reach the throne of God. To give this direction to their offerings, heights or elevated places were erected, from which they ascended towards heaven in fire. From this the offerings received the name of עֹלָה from עָלָה, the ascending, not so much because the sacrificial animals ascended or were raised upon the altar, as because they rose from the altar to heaven (cf. Judg. xx. 40; Jer. xlviii. 15; Amos iv. 10). Noah took his offerings from every clean beast and every clean fowl—from those animals, therefore, which were destined for man's food; probably the seventh of every kind, which he had taken into the ark. "*And Jehovah smelled the smell of satisfaction*," *i.e.* He graciously accepted the feelings of the offerer which rose to Him in the odour of the sacrificial flame. In the sacrificial flame the essence of the animal was resolved into vapour; so that when man presented a sacrifice in his own stead, his inmost being, his spirit, and his heart ascended to God in the vapour, and the sacrifice brought the feeling of his heart before God. This feeling of gratitude for gracious protection, and of desire for further communications of grace, was well-pleasing to God. He "*said to His heart*" (to, or in Himself; *i.e.* He resolved), "*I will not again curse the ground any more for man's sake, because the image* (*i.e.* the thought and desire) *of man's heart is evil from his youth up* (*i.e.* from the very time when he begins to act with consciousness)." This hardly seems an appropriate reason. As Luther says: "Hic inconstantiæ videtur Deus accusari posse. Supra puniturus hominem causam consilii dicit, quia figmentum cordis humani malum est. Hic promissurus homini gratiam, quod posthac tali ira uti nolit, eandem causam allegat." Both *Luther* and *Calvin* express the same thought, though without really solving the apparent discrepancy. It was not because the thoughts and desires of the human heart are *evil* that God would not smite any more every living thing, that is to say, would not exterminate it judicially; but because they are evil *from his youth up*, because evil is innate in man, and for that reason he needs the forbearance of God; and also (and here lies the principal motive for the divine resolution) because in the offering of the righteous Noah, not only were thanks presented for past protection, and entreaty for further care, but the desire of man was expressed, to remain in fellowship with God, and to procure the divine favour. "*All the days of the earth;*" *i.e.* so long as the earth shall continue, the regular alternation of day and night and of the seasons of the year, so indispensable to the continuance of the human race, would never be interrupted again.

Chap. ix. 1–7. These divine purposes of peace, which were communicated to Noah while sacrificing, were solemnly confirmed by the renewal of the blessing pronounced at the creation and the establishment of a covenant through a visible sign, which would be a pledge for all time that there should never be a flood again. In the words by which the first blessing was transferred to Noah and his sons (ver. 2), the supremacy granted to man over the animal world was expressed still more forcibly than in chap. i. 26 and 28; because, inasmuch as sin with its consequences had loosened the bond of voluntary subjection on the part of the animals to the will of man,—man, on the one hand, having lost the power of the spirit over nature, and nature, on the other hand, having become estranged from man, or rather having rebelled against him, through the curse pronounced upon the earth,—henceforth it was only by force that he could rule over it, by that "fear and dread" which God instilled into the animal creation. Whilst the animals were thus placed in the hand (power) of man, permission was also given to him to slaughter them for food, the eating of the blood being the only thing forbidden. Vers. 3, 4. "*Every moving thing that liveth shall be food for you; even as the green of the herb have I given you all* (הַכֹּל = אֶת־כֹּל)." These words do not affirm that man then first began to eat animal food, but only that God then for the first time authorized, or allowed him to do, what probably he had previously done in opposition to His will. "*Only flesh in its soul, its blood* (דָּמוֹ in apposition to בְּנַפְשׁוֹ), *shall ye not eat;*" i.e. flesh in which there is still blood, because the soul of the animal is in the blood. The prohibition applies to the eating of flesh with blood in it, whether of living animals, as is the barbarous custom in Abyssinia, or of slaughtered animals from which the blood has not been properly drained at death. This prohibition presented, on the one hand, a safeguard against harshness and cruelty; and contained, on the other, "an undoubted reference to the sacrifice of animals, which was afterwards made the subject of command, and in which it was the blood especially that was offered, as the seat and soul of life (see note on Lev. xvii. 11, 14); so that from this point of view sacrifice denotes the surrender of one's own inmost life, of the very essence of life, to God" (*Ziegler*). Allusion is made to the first again in the still further limitation given in ver. 5: "*and only* (וְאַךְ) *your blood, with regard to your souls* (? indicative of reference to an individual object, *Ewald*, § 310a), *will I seek* (demand or avenge, cf. Ps. ix. 13) *from the hand of every beast, and from the hand of man, from the hand of every one, his brother;*" i.e. from every man, whoever he may be, because he is his (the slain man's) brother, inasmuch as all men are brethren. The life of man was thus made secure against animals as well as men. God would avenge or inflict punishment for every murder,—not directly, however, as He promised to do in the case of Cain, but indirectly by giving the command, "*Whoso sheddeth man's blood, by man shall his blood be shed,*" and thus placing in the hand of man His own judicial power. "This was the first command," says *Luther,* "having reference to the temporal sword. By these words temporal government was established, and the sword placed in its hand by God." It is true the punishment of the murderer is enjoined upon "man" universally; but as all the judicial relations and ordinances of the increasing race were rooted in those of the family, and grew by a natural process out of that, the family relations furnished of themselves the norm for the closer definition of the expression "man." Hence the command does not sanction revenge, but lays the foundation for the judicial rights of the divinely appointed "powers that be" (Rom. xiii. 1). This is evident from the reason appended: "*for in the image of God made He man.*" If murder was to be punished with death because it destroyed the image of God in man, it is evident that the infliction of the punishment was not to be left to the caprice of individuals, but belonged to those alone who represent the authority and majesty of God, *i.e.* the divinely appointed rulers, who for that very reason are called *Elohim* in Ps. lxxxii. 6. This command then laid the foundation for all civil government,[1] and formed a necessary complement to that unalterable continuance of the order of nature which had been promised to the human race for its further development. If God on account of the innate sinfulness of man would no more bring an exterminating judgment upon the earthly creation, it was necessary that by commands and authorities He should erect a barrier against the supremacy of evil, and thus lay the foundation for a well-ordered civil development of humanity, in accordance with the words of the blessing, which are repeated in ver. 7, as showing the intention and goal of this new historical beginning.

---

[1] "Hic igitur fons est, ex quo manat totum jus civile et jus gentium. Nam si Deus concedit homini potestatem super vitam et mortem, profecto etiam concedit potestatem super id, quod minus est, ut sunt fortunæ, familia, uxor, liberi, servi, agri ; Hæc omnia vult certorum hominum potestati esse obnoxia Deus, ut reos puniant."—*Luther.*

Vers. 8–17. To give Noah and his sons a firm assurance of the prosperous continuance of the human race, God condescended to establish a covenant with them and their descendants, and to confirm this covenant by a visible sign for all generations. הֵקִים בְּרִית is not equivalent to כָּרַת בְּרִית; it does not denote the formal conclusion of an actual covenant, but the " setting up of a covenant," or the giving of a promise possessing the nature of a covenant. In summing up the animals in ver. 10, the prepositions are accumulated: first בְּ embracing the whole, then the partitive מִן restricting the enumeration to those which went out of the ark, and lastly לְ, " with regard to," extending it again to every individual. There was a correspondence between the covenant (ver. 11) and the sign which was to keep it before the sight of men (ver. 12): " I give (set) My bow in the cloud" (ver. 13). When God gathers (עָנַן ver. 14, lit. clouds) clouds over the earth, " the bow shall be seen in the cloud," and that not for man only, but for God also, who will look at the bow, " to remember His everlasting covenant." An "everlasting covenant" is a covenant " for perpetual generations," i.e. one which shall extend to all ages, even to the end of the world. The fact that God Himself would look at the bow and remember His covenant, was " a glorious and living expression of the great truth, that God's covenant signs, in which He has put His promises, are real vehicles of His grace, that they have power and essential worth not only with men, but also before God" (O. v. Gerlach). The establishment of the rainbow as a covenant sign of the promise that there should be no flood again, presupposes that it appeared then for the first time in the vault and clouds of heaven. From this it may be inferred, not that it did not rain before the flood, which could hardly be reconciled with chap. ii. 5, but that the atmosphere was differently constituted ; a supposition in perfect harmony with the facts of natural history, which point to differences in the climate of the earth's surface before and after the flood. The fact that the rainbow, that " coloured splendour thrown by the bursting forth of the sun upon the departing clouds," is the result of the reciprocal action of light, and air, and water, is no disproof of the origin and design recorded here. For the laws of nature are ordained by God, and have their ultimate ground and purpose in the divine plan of the universe which links together both nature and grace. " Springing as it does from the effect of the sun upon the dark mass of clouds, it typifies the readiness of the heavenly to pervade the earthly; spread out as it is between heaven and earth, it proclaims peace between God and man; and whilst spanning the whole horizon, it teaches the all-embracing universality of the covenant of grace" (*Delitzsch*).

Vers. 18—29. The *second* occurrence in the life of Noah after the flood exhibited the germs of the future development of the human race in a threefold direction, as manifested in the characters of his three sons. As all the families and races of man descend from them, their names are repeated in ver. 18; and in prospective allusion to what follows, it is added that "*Ham was the father of Canaan.*" From these three " *the earth* (the earth's population) *spread itself out.*" " *The earth*" is used for the population of the earth, as in chap. x. 25 and xi. 1, and just as lands or cities are frequently substituted for their inhabitants. נָפְצָה : probably *Niphal* for נָפְצָה, from פּוּץ to scatter (xi. 4), to spread out. "*And Noah the husbandman began, and planted a vineyard.*" As אִישׁ הָאֲדָמָה cannot be the predicate of the sentence, on account of the article, but must be in apposition to Noah, וַיִּטַּע and וַיָּחֶל must be combined in the sense of " began to plant" (*Ges.* § 142, 3). The writer does not mean to affirm that Noah resumed his agricultural operations after the flood, but that as a husbandman he began to cultivate the vine; because it was this which furnished the occasion for the manifestation of that diversity in the character of his sons, which was so eventful in its consequences in relation to the future history of their descendants. In ignorance of the fiery nature of wine, Noah drank and was drunken, and uncovered himself in his tent (ver. 21). Although excuse may be made for this drunkenness, the words of *Luther* are still true: " *Qui excusant patriarcham, volentes hanc consolationem, quam Spiritus S. ecclesiis necessariam judicavit, abjiciunt, quod scilicet etiam summi sancti aliquando labuntur.*" This trifling fall served to display the hearts of his sons. Ham saw the nakedness of his father, and told his two brethren without. Not content with finding pleasure himself in his father's shame, " *nunquam enim vino victum patrem filius risisset, nisi prius ejecisset animo illam reverentiam et opinionem, quœ in liberis de parentibus ex mandato Dei existere debet*" (*Luther*), he must proclaim his disgraceful pleasure to his brethren, and thus exhibit his shameless sensuality. The brothers, on the contrary, with reverential modesty covered their father with a garment (הַשִּׂמְלָה the garment, which was at hand), walking backwards that they might not see his nakedness (ver. 23), and thus manifesting their childlike reverence as truly as their refined purity and modesty. For this they receive their father's blessing, whereas Ham reaped for his son Canaan the patriarch's curse. In ver. 24 Ham is called בְּנוֹ הַקָּטָן "his (Noah's) little son," and it is questionable whether the adjective is to be taken as comparative in the sense of "the younger," or as superlative, meaning "the youngest." Neither grammar nor the usage of the language will enable us to decide. For in 1 Sam. xvii. 14, where David is contrasted with his brothers, the word means not the youngest of the four, but the younger by the side of the three elder, just as in chap. i. 16 the sun is called "the *great*" light, and the moon "the *little*" light, not to show that the sun is the greatest and the moon the least of all lights, but that the moon is the smaller of the two. If, on the other hand, on the ground of 1 Sam. xvi. 11, where "the little one" undoubtedly means the youngest of all, any one would press the superlative force here, he must be prepared, in order to be consistent, to do the same with *haggadol*, "the great one," in chap. x. 21, which would lead to this discrepancy, that in the verse before us Ham is called Noah's youngest son, and in chap. x. 21 Shem is called Japhet's oldest brother, and thus *implicite* Ham is described as older than Japhet. If we do not wish lightly to introduce a discrepancy into the text of these two chapters, no other course is open than to follow the LXX., *Vulg.* and others, and take "the little" here and "the great" in chap. x. 21 as used in a comparative sense, Ham being represented here as Noah's younger son, and Shem in chap. x. 21 as Japhet's elder brother. Consequently the order in which the three names stand is also an indication of their relative ages. And this is not only the simplest and readiest assumption, but is even confirmed by chap. x., though the order is inverted there, Japhet being mentioned first, then Ham, and Shem last; and it is also in harmony with the chronological datum in chap. xi. 10, as compared with chap. v. 32 (*vid.* chap. xi. 10).

To understand the words of Noah with reference to his sons (vers. 25—27), we must bear in mind, on the one hand, that as the moral nature of the patriarch was transmitted by generation to his descendants, so the diversities of character in the sons of Noah foreshadowed diversities in the moral inclinations of the tribes of which they were the head; and on the other hand, that Noah, through the Spirit and power of that God with whom he walked, discerned in the moral nature of his sons, and the different tendencies which they already displayed, the germinal commencement of the future course of their posterity, and uttered words of blessing and of curse, which were prophetic of the history of the tribes that descended from them. In the sin of Ham "there lies the great stain of the whole Hamitic race, whose chief characteristic is sexual sin" (*Ziegler*); and the curse which Noah pronounced upon this sin still rests upon the race. It was not Ham who was cursed, however, but his son Canaan. Ham had sinned against his father, and he was punished in his son. But the reason why Canaan was the only son named, is not to be found in the fact that Canaan was the youngest son of Ham, and Ham the youngest son of Noah, as *Hofmann* supposes. The latter is not an established fact; and the purely external circumstance, that Canaan had the misfortune to be the youngest son, could not be a just reason for cursing him alone. The real reason must either lie in the fact that Canaan was already walking in the steps of his father's impiety and sin, or else be sought in the name *Canaan*, in which Noah discerned, through the gift of prophecy, a significant *omen ;* a supposition decidedly favoured by the analogy of the blessing pronounced upon Japhet, which is also founded upon the name. *Canaan* does not signify lowland, nor was it transferred, as many maintain, from the land to its inhabitants; it was first of all the name of the father of the tribe, from whom it was transferred to his descendants, and eventually to the land of which they took possession. The meaning of *Canaan* is "the submissive one," from כָּנַע to stoop or submit, *Hiphil*, to bend or subjugate (Deut. ix. 3; Judg. iv. 23, etc.). "Ham gave his son the name from the obedience which he required, though he did not render it himself. The son was to be the servant (for the name points to servile obedience) of a father who was as tyrannical towards those beneath him, as he was refractory towards those above. The father, when he gave him the name, thought only of submission to his own commands. But the secret providence of God, which rules in all such things, had a different submission

in view" (Hengstenberg, *Christol.* i. 28, transl.). "Servant of
servants (*i.e.* the lowest of slaves, *vid.* Ewald, § 313) let him
become to his brethren." Although this curse was expressly
pronounced upon Canaan alone, the fact that Ham had no share
in Noah's blessing, either for himself or his other sons, was a
sufficient proof that his whole family was included by implication in the curse, even if it was to fall chiefly upon Canaan.
And history confirms the supposition. The Canaanites were
partly exterminated, and partly subjected to the lowest form of
slavery, by the Israelites, who belonged to the family of Shem;
and those who still remained were reduced by Solomon to the
same condition (1 Kings ix. 20, 21). The Phœnicians, along
with the Carthaginians and the Egyptians, who all belonged to
the family of Canaan, were subjected by the Japhetic Persians,
Macedonians, and Romans; and the remainder of the Hamitic
tribes either shared the same fate, or still sigh, like the negroes,
for example, and other African tribes, beneath the yoke of the
most crushing slavery.—Ver. 26. In contrast with the curse,
the blessings upon Shem and Japhet are introduced with a fresh
" *and he said,*" whilst Canaan's servitude comes in like a *refrain*
and is mentioned in connection with both his brethren : " *Blessed
be Jehovah, the God of Shem, and let Canaan be servant to them.*"
Instead of wishing good to Shem, Noah praises the God of
Shem, just as Moses in Deut. xxxiii. 20, instead of blessing Gad,
blesses Him " that enlargeth Gad," and points out the nature of
the good which he is to receive, by using the name *Jehovah*.
This is done "*propter excellentem benedictionem. Non enim
loquitur de corporali benedictione, sed de benedictione futura per
semen promissum. Eam tantam videt esse ut explicari verbis non
possit, ideo se vertit ad gratiarum actionem*" (*Luther*). Because
Jehovah is the God of Shem, Shem will be the recipient and
heir of all the blessings of salvation, which God as Jehovah bestows upon mankind. לָמוֹ = לָהֶם neither stands for the singular
לוֹ (*Ges.* § 103, 2), nor refers to Shem and Japhet. It serves to
show that the announcement does not refer to the personal relation
of Canaan to Shem, but applies to their descendants.—Ver. 27.
" *Wide let God make it to Japhet, and let him dwell in the tents
of Shem.*" Starting from the meaning of the name, Noah
sums up his blessing in the word יַפְתְּ (*japht*), from פָּתָה to be wide
(Prov. xx. 19), in the *Hiphil* with לְ, to procure a wide space for

any one, used either of extension over a wide territory, or of removal to a free, unfettered position; analogous to הִרְחִיב לְ, chap. xxvi. 22 ; Ps. iv. 1, etc. Both allusions must be retained here, so that the promise to the family of Japhet embraced not only a wide extension, but also prosperity on every hand. This blessing was desired by Noah, not from *Jehovah*, the God of Shem, who bestows saving spiritual good upon man, but from *Elohim*, God as Creator and Governor of the world ; for it had respect primarily to the blessings of the earth, not to spiritual blessings; although Japhet would participate in these as well, for he should come and dwell in the tents of Shem. The dis puted question, whether God or Japhet is to be regarded as the subject of the verb " shall dwell," is already decided by the use of the word *Elohim*. If it were God whom Noah described as dwelling in the tents of Shem, so that the expression denoted the gracious presence of God in Israel, we should expect to find the name Jehovah, since it was as Jehovah that God took up His abode among Shem in Israel. It is much more natural to regard the expression as applying to Japhet, (*a*) because the *refrain*, "Canaan shall be his servant," requires that we should understand ver. 27 as applying to Japhet, like ver. 26 to Shem; (*b*) because the plural, *tents*, is not applicable to the abode of Jehovah in Israel, inasmuch as in the parallel passages " we read of God dwelling in His tent, on His holy hill, in Zion, in the midst of the children of Israel, and also of the faithful dwelling in the tabernacle or temple of God, but never of God dwelling in the tents of Israel" (*Hengstenberg*) ; and (*c*) be- cause we should expect the act of affection, which the two sons so delicately performed in concert, to have its corresponding blessing in the relation established between the two (*Delitzsch*). Japhet's dwelling in the tents of Shem is supposed by *Bochart* and others to refer to the fact, that Japhet's descendants would one day take the land of the Shemites, and subjugate the inhabitants; but even the fathers almost unanimously under- stand the words in a spiritual sense, as denoting the participation of the Japhetites in the saving blessings of the Shemites. There is truth in both views. Dwelling presupposes possession; but the idea of taking by force is precluded by the fact, that it would be altogether at variance with the blessing pronounced upon Shem. If history shows that the tents of Shem were conquered and taken by the Japhetites, the dwelling predicted here still relates not to the forcible conquest, but to the fact that the conquerors entered into the possessions of the conquered; that along with them they were admitted to the blessings of salvation; and that, yielding to the spiritual power of the vanquished, they lived henceforth in their tents as brethren (Ps. cxxxiii. 1). And if the dwelling of .Japhet in the tents of Shem presupposes the conquest of the land of Shem by Japhet, it is a blessing not only to Japhet, but to Shem also, since, whilst Japhet enters into the spiritual inheritance of Shem, he brings to Shem all the good of this world (Isa. lx.). " The fulfilment," as *Delitzsch* says, "is plain enough, for we are all Japhetites dwelling in the tents of Shem; and the language of the New Testament is the language of Javan entered into the tents of Shem." To this we may add, that by the Gospel preached in this language, Israel, though subdued by the imperial power of Rome, became the spiritual conqueror of the *orbis terrarum Romanus,* and received it into his tents. Moreover it is true of the blessing and curse of Noah, as of all prophetic utterances, that they are fulfilled with regard to the nations and families in question as a whole, but do not predict, like an irresistible fate, the unalterable destiny of every individual; on the contrary, they leave room for freedom of personal decision, and no more cut off the individuals in the accursed race from the possibility of conversion, or close the way of salvation against the penitent, than they secure the individuals of the family blessed against the possibility of falling from a state of grace, and actually losing the blessing. Hence, whilst a Rahab and an Araunah were received into the fellowship of Jehovah, and the Canaanitish woman was relieved by the Lord because of her faith, the hardened Pharisees and scribes had woes pronounced upon them, and Israel was rejected because of its unbelief. In vers. 28, 29, the history of Noah is brought to a close, with the account of his age, and of his death.

IV. HISTORY OF THE SONS OF NOAH.

CHAP. X.–XI. 9.

PEDIGREE OF THE NATIONS.—CHAP. X.

Of the sons of Noah, all that is handed down is the pedigree of the nations, or the list of the tribes which sprang from them (chap. x.), and the account of the confusion of tongues, together with the dispersion of men over the face of the earth (chap. xi. 1–9); two events that were closely related to one another, and of the greatest importance to the history of the human race and of the kingdom of God. The genealogy traces the origin of the tribes which were scattered over the earth; the confusion of tongues shows the cause of the division of the one human race into many different tribes with peculiar languages.

The genealogy of the tribes is not an ethnographical myth, nor the attempt of an ancient Hebrew to trace the connection of his own people with the other nations of the earth by means of uncertain traditions and subjective combinations, but a historical record of the genesis of the nations, founded upon a tradition handed down from the fathers, which, to judge from its contents, belongs to the time of Abraham (cf. Hävernick's Introduction to Pentateuch, p. 118 sqq. transl.), and was inserted by Moses in the early history of the kingdom of God on account of its universal importance in connection with sacred history. For it not only indicates the place of the family which was chosen as the recipient of divine revelation among the rest of the nations, but traces the origin of the entire world, with the prophetical intention of showing that the nations, although they were quickly suffered to walk in their own ways (Acts xiv. 16), were not intended to be for ever excluded from the counsels of eternal love. In this respect the genealogies prepare the way for the promise of the blessing, which was one day to spread from the chosen family to all the families of the earth (chap. xii. 2, 3).— The historical character of the genealogy is best attested by the contents themselves, since no trace can be detected, either of any pre-eminence given to the Shemites, or of an intention to fill up gaps by conjecture or invention. It gives just as much as had been handed down with regard to the origin of the different tribes. Hence the great diversity in the lists of the descendants of the different sons of Noah. Some are brought down only to the second, others to the third or fourth generation, and some even further; and whilst in several instances the founder of a tribe is named, in others we have only the tribes themselves; and in some cases we are unable to determine whether the names given denote the founder or the tribe. In many instances, too, on account of the defects and the unreliable character of the accounts handed down to us from different ancient sources with regard to the origin of the tribes, there are names which cannot be identified with absolute certainty.[1]

Vers. 1-5. DESCENDANTS OF JAPHET. — In ver. 1 the names of the three sons are introduced according to their relative ages, to give completeness and finish to the *Tholedoth;* but in the genealogy itself Japhet is mentioned first and Shem last, according to the plan of the book of Genesis as already explained at p. 37. In ver. 2 seven sons of Japhet are given. The names, indeed, afterwards occur as those of tribes; but here undoubtedly they are intended to denote the tribe-fathers, and may without hesitation be so regarded. For even if in later times many nations received their names from the lands of which they took possession, this cannot be regarded as a universal rule, since unquestionably the natural rule in the derivation of the names would be for the tribe to be called after its ancestor, and for the countries to receive their names from their earliest inhabitants. *Gomer* is most probably the tribe of the *Cimmerians,* who dwelt, according to *Herodotus,* on the Maeotis, in the Taurian Chersonesus, and from whom are descended the *Cumri* or *Cymry* in

---

[1] *Sam. Bochart* has brought great learning to the explanation of the table of nations in *Phaleg,* the first part of his *geographia sacra,* to which *Michaelis* and *Rosenmüller* made valuable additions,—the former in his *spicil. geogr. Hebr. ext.* 1769 and 1780, the latter in his Biblical Antiquities. *Knobel* has made use of all the modern ethnographical discoveries in his " Völkertafel der Genesis" (1850), but many of his combinations are very speculative. *Kiepert,* in his article *über d. geograph. Stellung der nördlichen Länder in der phönikisch-hebräischen Erdkunde* (in the *Monatsberichte d. Berliner Akad.* 1859), denies entirely the ethnographical character of the table of nations, and reduces it to a mere attempt on the part of the Phœnicians to account for the geographical position of the nations with which they were acquainted.

Wales and Brittany, whose relation to the Germanic *Cimbri* is still in obscurity. *Magog* is connected by *Josephus* with the *Scythians* on the Sea of Asof and in the Caucasus; but *Kiepert* associates the name with *Macija* or *Maka*, and applies it to Scythian nomad tribes which forced themselves in between the Arian or Arianized Medes, Kurds, and Armenians. *Madai* are the Medes, called *Mada* on the arrow-headed inscriptions. *Javan* corresponds to the Greek 'Ιάων, from whom the Ionians ('Ιάονες) are derived, the parent tribe of the Greeks (in Sanskrit *Javana*, old Persian *Junâ*). *Tubal* and *Meshech* are undoubtedly the *Tibareni* and *Moschi*, the former of whom are placed by Herodotus upon the east of the *Thermodon*, the latter between the sources of the Phasis and Cyrus. *Tiras* : according to *Josephus*, the *Thracians*, whom *Herodotus* calls the most numerous tribe next to the Indian. As they are here placed by the side of Meshech, so we also find on the old Egyptian monuments *Mashuash* and *Tuirash*, and upon the Assyrian *Tubal* and *Misek* (*Rawlinson*).—Ver. 3. *Descendants of Gomer*. *Ashkenaz*: according to the old Jewish explanation, the *Germani;* according to *Knobel*, the family of *Asi*, which is favoured by the German legend of *Mannus*, and his three sons, *Iscus* (*Ask*, 'Ασκάνιος), *Ingus*, and *Hermino*. *Kiepert*, however, and *Bochart* decide, on geographical grounds, in favour of the *Ascanians* in Northern Phrygia. *Riphath :* in *Knobel's* opinion the Celts, part of whom, according to Plutarch, crossed the ὄρη 'Ρίπαια, *Montes Rhipaei*, towards the Northern Ocean to the furthest limits of Europe; but *Josephus*, whom *Kiepert* follows, supposed 'Ριβάθης to be Paphlagonia. Both of these are very uncertain. *Togarmah* is the name of the Armenians, who are still called the house of *Thorgom* or *Torkomatsi*.—Ver. 4. *Descendants of Javan*. *Elishah* suggests *Elis*, and is said by *Josephus* to denote the *Æolians*, the oldest of the Thessalian tribes, whose culture was Ionian in its origin; *Kiepert*, however, thinks of Sicily. *Tarshish* (in the Old Testament the name of the colony of *Tartessus* in Spain) is referred by *Knobel* to the *Etruscans* or *Tyrsenians*, a Pelasgic tribe of Greek derivation; but *Delitzsch* objects, that the Etruscans were most probably of Lydian descent, and, like the Lydians of Asia Minor, who were related to the Assyrians, belonged to the Shemites. Others connect the name with *Tarsus* in Cilicia. But the connection with the Spanish Tartessus must be retained, although, so long as the origin of this colony remains in obscurity, nothing further can be determined with regard to the name. *Kittim* embraces not only the *Citiæi, Citienses* in Cyprus, with the town *Cition,* but, according to *Knobel* and *Delitzsch,* probably "the *Carians,* who settled in the lands at the eastern end of the Mediterranean Sea; for which reason *Ezekiel* (xxvii. 6) speaks of the "isles of Chittim." *Dodanim (Dardani)*: according to *Delitzsch,* "the tribe related to the Ionians and dwelling with them from the very first, which the legend has associated with them in the two brothers Jasion and Dardanos;" according to *Knobel,* "the whole of the Illyrian or north Grecian tribe."— Ver. 5. "*From these have the islands of the nations divided themselves in their lands;*" *i.e.* from the Japhetites already named, the tribes on the Mediterranean descended and separated from one another as they dwell in their lands, "*every one after his tongue, after their families, in their nations.*" The *islands* in the Old Testament are the islands and coastlands of the Mediterranean, on the European shore. from Asia Minor to Spain.

Vers. 6–20. DESCENDANTS OF HAM.—*Cush:* the *Ethiopians* of the ancients, who not only dwelt in Africa, but were scattered over the whole of Southern Asia, and originally, in all probability, settled in Arabia, where the tribes that still remained, mingled with Shemites, and adopted a Shemitic language. *Mizraim* is *Egypt:* the dual form was probably transferred from the land to the people, referring, however, not to the *double strip, i.e.* the two strips of land into which the country is divided by the Nile, but to the two Egypts, Upper and Lower, two portions of the country which differ considerably in their climate and general condition. The name is obscure, and not traceable to any Semitic derivation; for the term מָצוֹר in Isa. xix. 6, etc., is not to be regarded as an etymological interpretation, but as a significant play upon the word. The old Egyptian name is *Kemi* (Copt. Chêmi, Kême), which, *Plutarch* says, is derived from the dark ash-grey colour of the soil covered by the slime of the Nile, but which it is much more correct to trace to *Ham,* and to regard as indicative of the Hamitic descent of its first inhabitants. *Put* denotes the *Libyans* in the wider sense of the term (old Egypt. *Phet;* Copt. *Phaiat*), who were spread over Northern Africa as far as Mauritania, where even in the time of Jerome a river with the neighbouring district still bore the name of *Phut;* cf. *Bochart,* Phal. iv. 33. On *Canaan,* see chap. ix. 25.— Ver. 7. *Descendants of Cush.* *Seba :* the inhabitants of *Meroë;* according to *Knobel,* the northern Ethiopians, the ancient *Blemmyer,* and modern *Bisharin.* *Havilah :* the Αὐαλῖται or Ἀβαλῖται of the ancients, the Macrobian Ethiopians in modern Habesh. *Sabtah :* the Ethiopians inhabiting Hadhramaut, whose chief city was called *Sabatha* or *Sabota.* *Raamah :* Ῥεγμά, the inhabitants of a city and bay of that name in south-eastern Arabia (*Oman*). *Sabtecah :* the Ethiopians of Caramania, dwelling to the east of the Persian Gulf, where the ancients mention a seaport town and a river Σαμυδάκη. The descendants of Raamah, *Sheba* and *Dedan,* are to be sought in the neighbourhood of the Persian Gulf, "from which the Sabæan and Dedanitic Cushites spread to the north-west, where they formed mixed tribes with descendants of Joktan and Abraham." See notes on ver. 28 and chap. xxv. 3.

Vers. 8–12. Besides the tribes already named, there sprang from Cush *Nimrod,* the founder of the first imperial kingdom, the origin of which is introduced as a memorable event into the genealogy of the tribes, just as on other occasions memorable events are interwoven with the genealogical tables (cf. 1 Chron. ii. 7, 23, iv. 22, 23, 39–41).[1] Nimrod "*began to be a mighty one in the earth.*" גִּבֹּר is used here, as in chap. vi. 4, to denote a man who makes himself renowned for bold and daring deeds. Nimrod was mighty in hunting, and that in opposition to Jehovah (ἐναντίον κυρίου, LXX.) ; not before Jehovah in the sense of, according to the purpose and will of Jehovah, still less, like לֵאלֹהִים in Jonah iii. 3, or τῷ Θεῷ in Acts vii. 20, in a simply superlative sense. The last explanation is not allowed by the usage of the language, the second is irreconcilable with the context. The name itself, *Nimrod* from מָרַד, "we will revolt," points to some violent resistance to God. It is so characteristic that it can only have been given by his contemporaries, and thus have become a proper name.[2] In addition to this, Nimrod

---

[1] These analogies overthrow the assertion that the verses before us have been interpolated by the Jehovist into the Elohistic document; since the use of the name Jehovah is no proof of difference of authorship, nor the use of יָלַד for הוֹלִיד, as the former also occurs in vers. 13, 15, 24, and 26.

[2] This was seen even by *Perizonius* (*Origg. Babyl.* p. 183), who says,

as a mighty hunter founded a powerful kingdom ; and the founding of this kingdom is shown by the verb וַיְהִי with ו consec. to have been the consequence or result of his strength in hunting, so that the hunting was most intimately connected with the establishment of the kingdom.   Hence, if the expression " a mighty hunter " relates primarily to hunting in the literal sense, we must add to the literal meaning the figurative signification of a "hunter of men " ("a trapper of men by stratagem and force," Herder) ; Nimrod the hunter became a tyrant, a powerful hunter of men.   This course of life gave occasion to the proverb, " like Nimrod, a mighty hunter against the Lord," which immortalized not his skill in hunting beasts, but the success of his hunting of men in the establishment of an imperial kingdom by tyranny and power.   But if this be the meaning of the proverb, לִפְנֵי יְהוָֹה " in the face of Jehovah " can only mean in defiance of Jehovah, as Josephus and the Targums understand it.   And the proverb must have arisen when other daring and rebellious men followed in Nimrod's footsteps, and must have originated with those who saw in such conduct an act of rebellion against the God of salvation, in other words, with the possessors of the divine promises of grace.[1]—Ver. 10.   " And the beginning of his kingdom was Babel," the well-known city of Babylon on the Euphrates, which from the time of Nimrod downwards has been the symbol of the power of the world in its hostility to God ;—"and Erech" ('Ορέχ, LXX.), one of the seats of the Cutheans (Samaritans), Ezra iv. 9, no doubt Orchoë, situated, according to Rawlinson, on the site of the present ruins of Warka, thirty hours' journey to the south-east of Babel ;—and Accad ('Αρχάδ, LXX.), a place not yet determined, though, judging from its situation between Erech and Calneh, it was not

" Crediderim hominem hunc utpote venatorem ferocem et sodalium comitatu succinctum semper in ore habuisse et ingeminasse, ad reliquos in rebellionem excitandos, illud nimrod, nimrod, h.e. rebellemus, rebellemus, atque inde postea ab aliis, etiam ab ipso Mose, hoc vocabalo tanquam proprio nomine designatum," and who supports his opinion by other similar instances in history.

[1] This view of Nimrod and his deeds is favoured by the Eastern legend, which not only makes him the builder of the tower of Babel, which was to reach to heaven, but has also placed him among the constellations of heaven as a heaven-storming giant, who was chained by God in consequence.   Vid. Herzog's Real-Encycl. Art. Nimrod.

far from either, and *Pressel* is probably right in identifying it with the ruins of *Niffer*, to the south of Hillah;—"*and Calneh:*" this is found by early writers on the site of *Ctesiphon*, now a great heap of ruins, twenty hours north-east of Babel. These four cities were in the land of *Shinar*, i.e. of the province of Babylon, on the Lower Euphrates and Tigris.—Vers. 11, 12. From Shinar Nimrod went to *Assyria* (אַשּׁוּר is the accusative of direction), the country on the east of the Tigris, and there built four cities, or probably a large imperial city composed of the four cities named. As three of these cities—*Rehoboth-Ir*, i.e. city markets (not " street-city," as *Bunsen* interprets it), *Chelach*, and *Resen*—are not met with again, whereas *Nineveh* was renowned in antiquity for its remarkable size (*vid.* Jonah iii. 3), the words " *this is the great city* " must apply not to Resen, but to Nineveh. This is grammatically admissible, if we regard the last three names as subordinate to the first, taking as the sign of subordination (*Ewald*, § 339*a*), and render the passage thus : " he built Nineveh, with Rehoboth-Ir, Cheloch, and Resen between Nineveh and Chelach, this is the great city." From this it follows that the four places formed a large composite city, a large range of towns, to which the name of the (well-known) great city of *Nineveh* was applied, in distinction from Nineveh in the more restricted sense, with which Nimrod probably connected the other three places so as to form one great capital, possibly also the chief fortress of his kingdom on the Tigris. These four cities most likely correspond to the ruins on the east of the Tigris, which *Layard* has so fully explored, viz. *Nebbi Yûnus* and *Kouyunjik* opposite to Mosul, *Khorsabad* five hours to the north, and *Nimrud* eight hours to the south of Mosul.[1]

Vers. 13, 14. From Mizraim descended *Ludim:* not the Semitic Ludim (ver. 22), but, according to *Movers*, the old tribe of the *Lewâtah* dwelling on the Syrtes, according to others, the Moorish tribes collectively. Whether the name is connected with the *Laud flumen* (*Plin.* v. 1) is uncertain; in any case *Knobel* is wrong in thinking of Ludian Shemites, whether Hyksos, who forced their way to Egypt, or Egyptianized Arabians. *Anamim:* inhabitants of the Delta, according to *Knobel*. He associates the 'Ενεμετιείμ of the LXX. with

---

[1] This supposition of *Rawlinson, Grote, M. v. Niebuhr, Knobel, Delitzsch*, and others, has recently been adopted by *Ewald* also.

Sanemhit, or Northern Egypt: "*tsanemhit, i.e. pars, regio septentrionis.*" *Lehabim* (= *Lubim*, Nahum iii. 9) are, according to Josephus, the Λίβυες or Λύβιες, not the great Libyan tribe (*Phut*, ver. 6), which Nahum distinguishes from them, but the *Libyaegyptii* of the ancients. *Naphtuchim:* in *Knobel's* opinion, the Middle Egyptians, as the nation of *Pthah*, the god of Memphis: but *Bochart* is more probably correct in associating the name with Νέφθυς, in *Plut. de Is.*, the northern coast line of Egypt. *Pathrusim :* inhabitants of *Pathros*, Παθούρης, Egypt. *Petrês*, land of the south ; *i.e.* Upper Egypt, the *Thebais* of the ancients. *Casluchim:* according to general admission the *Colchians*, who descended from the Egyptians (Herod. ii. 104), though the connection of the name with *Cassiotis* is uncertain. "*From thence (i.e.* from *Casluchim*, which is the name of both people and country) *proceeded the Philistines.*" *Philistim*, LXX. Φυλιστιείμ or Ἀλλόφυλοι, lit. emigrants or immigrants from the Ethiopic *fallâsa*. This is not at variance with Amos ix. 7 and Jer. xlvii. 4, according to which the Philistines came from *Caphtor*, so that there is no necessity to transpose the relative clause after Philistim. The two statements may be reconciled on the simple supposition that the Philistian nation was primarily a Casluchian colony, which settled on the south-eastern coast line of the Mediterranean between Gaza (ver. 19) and Pelusium, but was afterwards strengthened by immigrants from *Caphtor*, and extended its territory by pressing out the Avim (Deut. ii. 23, cf. Josh. xiii. 3). *Caphtorim :* according to the old Jewish explanation, the *Cappadocians ;* but according to Lakemacher's opinion, which has been revived by *Ewald*, etc., the *Cretans.* This is not decisively proved, however, either by the name *Cherethites*, given to the Philistines in 1 Sam. xxx. 14, Zeph. ii. 5, and Ezek. xxv. 16, or by the expression " isle of Caphtor " in Jer. xlvii. 4.—Vers. 15 sqq. From Canaan descended "*Zidon his first-born, and Heth.*" Although *Zidon* occurs in ver. 19 and throughout the Old Testament as the name of the oldest capital of the Phœnicians, here it must be regarded as the name of a person, not only because of the apposition " *his first-born*," and the verb יָלַד, "*begat*," but also because the name of a city does not harmonize with the names of the other descendants of Canaan, the analogy of which would lead us to expect the *nomen gentile* " *Sidonian*" (Judg. iii. 3, etc.);

and lastly, because the word Zidon, from צוּד to hunt, to catch, is not directly applicable to a sea-port and commercial town, and there are serious objections upon philological grounds to *Justin's* derivation, " *quam a piscium ubertate Sidona appellave-runt, nam piscem Phœnices Sidon vocant*" (*var. hist.* 18, 3). *Heth* is also the name of a person, from which the term *Hittite* (xxv. 9 ; Num. xiii. 29), equivalent to " *sons of Heth*" (chap. xxiii. 5), is derived. " *The Jebusite :*" inhabitants of Jebus, afterwards called Jerusalem. " *The Amorite :*" not the inhabitants of the mountain or heights, for the derivation from אָמִיר, " *summit*," is not established, but a branch of the Canaanites, descended from Emor (Amor), which was spread far and wide over the moun-tains of Judah and beyond the Jordan in the time of Moses, so that in chap. xv. 16, xlviii. 22, all the Canaanites are compre-hended by the name. " *The Girgashites*," Γεργεσαῖος (LXX.), are also mentioned in chap. xv. 21, Deut. vii. 1, and Josh. xxiv. 11 ; but their dwelling-place is unknown, as the reading Γεργε-σηνοί in Matt. viii. 28 is critically suspicious. " *The Hivites*" dwelt in Sichem (xxxiv. 2), at Gibeon (Josh. ix. 7), and at the foot of Hermon (Josh xi. 3) ; the meaning of the word is un-certain. " *The Arkites :*" inhabitants of Ἀρκή, to the north of Tripolis at the foot of Lebanon, the ruins of which still exist (*vid. Robinson*). " *The Sinite :*" the inhabitants of *Sin* or *Sinna*, a place in Lebanon not yet discovered. " *The Arvadite*," or *Aradians*, occupied from the eighth century before Christ, the small rocky island of *Arados* to the north of Tripolis. " *The Zemarite :*" the inhabitants of Simyra in Eleutherus. " *The Hamathite :*" the inhabitants or rather founders of *Hamath* on the most northerly border of Palestine (Num. xiii. 21, xxxiv. 8), afterwards called *Epiphania*, on the river Orontes, the present *Hamâh*, with 100,000 inhabitants. The words in ver. 18, " *and afterward were the families of the Canaanites spread abroad*," mean that they all proceeded from one local centre as branches of the same tribe, and spread themselves over the country, the limits of which are given in two directions, with evident refer-ence to the fact that it was afterwards promised to the seed of Abraham for its inheritance, viz. from north to south,—" *from Sidon, in the direction (lit.* as thou comest) *towards Gerar* (see chap. xx. 1), *unto Gaza*," the primitive Avvite city of the Philis-tines (Deut. ii. 23), now called *Guzzeh*, at the S.W. corner of

Palestine,—and thence from west to east, "*in the direction towards Sodom, Gomorrah, Admah, and Zeboim* (see xix. 24) *to Lesha,*" *i.e. Calirrhoe,* a place with sulphur baths, on the eastern side of the Dead Sea, in Wady *Serka Maein* (*Seetzen* and *Ritter*).

Vers. 21–32. Descendants of Shem.—Ver. 21. For the construction, *vid.* chap. iv. 26. *Shem* is called the father of all the sons of *Eber,* because two tribes sprang from Eber through Peleg and Joktan, viz. the Abrahamides, and also the Arabian tribe of the Joktanides (vers. 26 sqq.).—On the expression, " *the brother of Japhet* הַגָּדוֹל," see chap. ix. 24. The names of the five sons of Shem occur elsewhere as the names of tribes and countries; at the same time, as there is no proof that in any single instance the name was transferred from the country to its earliest inhabitants, no well-grounded objection can be offered to the assumption, which the analogy of the other descendants of Shem renders probable, that they were originally the names of individuals. As the name of a people, *Elam* denotes the *Elymæans,* who stretched from the Persian Gulf to the Caspian Sea, but who are first met with as Persians no longer speaking a Semitic language. *Asshur:* the *Assyrians* who settled in the country of *Assyria,* 'Ατουρία, to the east of the Tigris, but who afterwards spread in the direction of Asia Minor. *Arphaxad:* the inhabitants of 'Αῤῥαπαχῖτις in northern Assyria. The explanation given of the name, viz. " fortress of the Chaldeans" (*Ewald*), "highland of the Chaldeans" (*Knobel*), " territory of the Chaldeans" (*Dietrich*), are very questionable. *Lud:* the *Lydians* of Asia Minor, whose connection with the Assyrians is confirmed by the names of the ancestors of their kings. *Aram:* the ancestor of the *Aramæans* of Syria and Mesopotamia.—Ver 23. *Descendants of Aram. Uz:* a name which occurs among the *Nahorides* (chap. xxii. 21) and Horites (xxxvi. 28), and which is associated with the *Αἰσῖται* of Ptolemy, in *Arabia deserta* towards Babylon; this is favoured by the fact that *Uz,* the country of Job, is called by the LXX. χώρα Αὐσῖτις, although the notion that these *Aesites* were an Aramæan tribe, afterwards mixed up with Nahorides and Horites, is mere conjecture. *Hul: Delitzsch* associates this with *Cheli* (*Cheri*), the old Egyptian name for the Syrians, and the *Hylatæ* who dwelt near the Emesenes (Plin. 5, 19). *Gether* he

connects with the name given in the Arabian legends to the
ancestor of the tribes *Themûd* and *Ghadis*. *Mash:* for which we
find *Meshech* in 1 Chron. i. 17, a tribe mentioned in Ps. cxx. 5
along with Kedar, and since the time of *Bochart* generally associated with the ὄρος Μάσιον above *Nisibis*.—Ver. 25. Among
the descendants of Arphaxad, Eber's eldest son received the
name of *Peleg*, because in his days the earth, *i.e.* the population
of the earth, was divided, in consequence of the building of the
tower of Babel (xi. 8). His brother *Joktan* is called Kachtan
by the Arabians, and is regarded as the father of all the primitive tribes of Arabia. The names of his sons are given in vers.
26–29. There are thirteen of them, some of which are still
retained in places and districts of Arabia, whilst others are not
yet discovered, or are entirely extinct. Nothing certain has
been ascertained about *Almodad, Jerah, Diklah, Obal, Abimael,*
and *Jobab*. Of the rest, *Sheleph* is identical with *Salif* or
Sulaf (in Ptol. 6, 7, Σαλαπηνοί), an old Arabian tribe, also a
district of *Yemen*. *Hazarmaveth* (*i.e.* forecourt of death) is
the Arabian *Hadhramaut* in South-eastern Arabia on the
Indian Ocean, whose name *Jauhari* is derived from the un-
healthiness of the climate. *Hadoram:* the Ἀδραμῖται of Ptol.
6, 7, *Atramitæ* of Plin. 6, 28, on the southern coast of Arabia.
Uzal: one of the most important towns of *Yemen*, south-west of
Mareb. *Sheba:* the *Sabæans*, with the capital *Saba* or *Mareb*,
Mariaba regia (Plin.), whose connection with the Cushite (ver.
7) and *Abrahamite* Sabæans (chap. xxv. 3) is quite in obscurity.
Ophir has not yet been discovered in Arabia; it is probably to
be sought on the Persian Gulf, even if the Ophir of Solomon
was not situated there. *Havilah* appears to answer to *Chaulaw*
of *Edrisi*, a district between Sanaa and Mecca. But this district, which lies in the heart of Yemen, does not fit the account
in 1 Sam. xv. 7, nor the statement in chap. xxv. 18, that
Havilah formed the boundary of the territory of the Ishmaelites.
These two passages point rather to Χαυλοταῖοι, a place on the
border of Arabia Petræa towards Yemen, between the Nabatæans and Hagrites, which *Strabo* describes as habitable.—Ver.
30. The settlements of these Joktanides lay "*from Mesha
towards Sephar the mountain of the East.*" *Mesha* is still unknown: according to *Gesenius*, it is *Mesene* on the Persian Gulf,
and in *Knobel's* opinion, it is the valley of *Bisha* or *Beishe* in the

north of Yemen; but both are very improbable. *Sephar* is supposed by *Mesnel* to be the ancient Himyaritish capital, *Shafâr*, on the Indian Ocean; and the *mountain of the East*, the mountain of incense, which is situated still farther to the east.—The genealogy of the Shemites closes with ver. 31, and the entire genealogy of the nations with ver. 32. According to the Jewish Midrash, there are seventy tribes, with as many different languages; but this number can only be arrived at by reckoning Nimrod among the Hamites, and not only placing Peleg among the Shemites, but taking his ancestors Salah and Eber to be names of separate tribes. By this we obtain for Japhet 14, for Ham 31, and for Shem 25,—in all 70 names. The Rabbins, on the other hand, reckon 14 Japhetic, 30 Hamitic, and 26 Semitic nations; whilst the fathers make 72 in all. But as these calculations are perfectly arbitrary, and the number 70 is nowhere given or hinted at, we can neither regard it as intended, nor discover in it "the number of the divinely appointed varieties of the human race," or "of the cosmical development," even if the seventy disciples (Luke x. 1) were meant to answer to the seventy nations whom the Jews supposed to exist upon the earth. —Ver. 32. The words, "*And by these were the nations of the earth divided in the earth after the flood,*" prepare the way for the description of that event which led to the division of the one race into many nations with different languages.

THE CONFUSION OF TONGUES.—CHAP. XI. 1–9.

Ver. 1. "*And the whole earth (i.e.* the population of the earth, *vid.* chap. ii. 19) *was one lip and one kind of words:*" *unius labii eorundemque verborum.* The unity of language of the whole human race follows from the unity of its descent from one human pair (*vid.* ii. 22). But as the origin and formation of the races of mankind are beyond the limits of empirical research, so no philology will ever be able to prove or deduce the original unity of human speech from the languages which have been historically preserved, however far comparative grammar may proceed in establishing the genealogical relation of the languages of different nations.—Vers. 2 sqq. As men multiplied they moved from the land of Ararat "*eastward,*" or more strictly to the *south-east,* and settled in a plain. בִּקְעָה does not denote a valley between mountain ranges, but a broad plain, πεδίον μέγα, as *Herodotus* calls the neighbourhood of Babylon. There they resolved to build an immense tower; and for this purpose they made bricks and burned them thoroughly (לִשְׂרֵפָה) " to burning " serves to intensify the verb like the *inf. absol.*), so that they became stone; whereas in the East ordinary buildings are constructed of bricks of clay, simply dried in the sun. For mortar they used asphalt, in which the neighbourhood of Babylon abounds. From this material, which may still be seen in the ruins of Babylon, they intended to build a city and a tower, whose top should be in heaven, *i.e.* reach to the sky, to make to themselves a name, that they might not be scattered over the whole earth. עָשָׂה לּוֹ שֵׁם denotes, here and everywhere else, to establish a name, or reputation, to set up a memorial (Isa. lxiii. 12, 14; Jer. xxxii. 20, etc.). The real motive therefore was the desire for renown, and the object was to establish a noted central point, which might serve to maintain their unity. The one was just as ungodly as the other. For, according to the divine purpose, men were to fill the earth, *i.e.* to spread over the whole earth, not indeed to separate, but to maintain their inward unity notwithstanding their dispersion. But the fact that they were afraid of dispersion is a proof that the inward spiritual bond of unity and fellowship, not only "the oneness of their God and their worship," but also the unity of brotherly love, was already broken by sin. Consequently the undertaking, dictated by pride, to preserve and consolidate by outward means the unity which was inwardly lost, could not be successful, but could only bring down the judgment of dispersion.—Vers. 5 sqq. " *Jehovah came down to see the city and the tower, which the children of men had built*" (the perfect בָּנוּ refers to the building as one finished up to a certain point). Jehovah's "coming down" is not the same here as in Ex. xix. 20, xxxiv. 5, Num. xi. 25, xii. 5, viz. the descent from heaven of some visible symbol of His presence, but is an anthropomorphic description of God's interposition in the actions of men, primarily a "judicial cognizance of the actual fact," and then, ver. 7, a judicial infliction of punishment. The reason for the judgment is given in the word, *i.e.* the sentence, which Jehovah pronounces upon the undertaking (ver. 6) : " *Behold one people* (עַם *lit.* union, connected whole, from עָמַם to bind) *and one language have they all, and this* (the building of this city and tower) *is* (only) *the beginning of their deeds; and now* (*sc.* when they have finished this) *nothing will be impossible to them* (לֹא יִבָּצֵר מֵהֶם *lit.* cut off from them, prevented) *which they purpose to do*" (יָזְמוּ for יִזְמוּ from זָמַם, see chap. ix. 19). By the firm establishment of an ungodly unity, the wickedness and audacity of men would have led to fearful enterprises. But God determined, by confusing their language, to prevent the heightening of sin through ungodly association, and to frustrate their design. "*Up*" (הָבָה "go to," in ironical imitation of the same expression in vers. 3 and 4), "*We will go down, and there confound their language* (on the plural, see chap. i. 26; נָבְלָה for נִבְלָה, *Kal* from בָּלַל, like יָזְמוּ in ver. 6), *that they may not understand one another's speech.*" The execution of this divine purpose is given in ver. 8, in a description of its consequences: "*Jehovah scattered them abroad from thence upon the face of all the earth, and they left off building the city.*" We must not conclude from this, however, that the differences in language were simply the result of the separation of the various tribes, and that the latter arose from discord and strife; in which case the confusion of tongues would be nothing more than "*dissensio animorum, per quam factum sit, ut qui turrem struebant distracti sint in contraria studia et consilia*" (*Vitringa*). Such a view not only does violence to the words "*that one may not discern* (understand) *the lip* (language) *of the other,*" but is also at variance with the object of the narrative. When it is stated, first of all, that God resolved to destroy the unity of lips and words by a confusion of the lips, and then that He scattered the men abroad, this act of divine judgment cannot be understood in any other way, than that God deprived them of the ability to comprehend one another, and thus effected their dispersion. The event itself cannot have consisted merely in a change of the organs of speech, produced by the omnipotence of God, whereby speakers were turned into stammerers who were unintelligible to one another. This opinion, which is held by *Vitringa* and *Hofmann*, is neither reconcilable with the text, nor tenable as a matter of fact. The differences, to which this event gave rise, consisted not merely in variations of sound, such as might be attributed to differences in the formation in the organs of speech (the lip or tongue), but had a much deeper foundation in the human mind. If language is the audible expression of emotions, conceptions, and thoughts of the mind, the cause of the confusion or division of the one human language into different national dialects must be sought in an effect produced upon the human mind, by which the original unity of emotion, conception, thought, and will was broken up. This inward unity had no doubt been already disturbed by sin, but the disturbance had not yet amounted to a perfect breach. This happened first of all in the event recorded here, through a direct manifestation of divine power, which caused the disturbance produced by sin in the unity of emotion, thought, and will to issue in a diversity of language, and thus by a miraculous suspension of mutual understanding frustrated the enterprise by which men hoped to render dispersion and estrangement impossible. More we cannot say in explanation of this miracle, which lies before us in the great multiplicity and variety of tongues, since even those languages which are genealogically related—for example, the Semitic and Indo-Germanic—were no longer intelligible to the same people even in the dim primeval age, whilst others are so fundamentally different from one another, that hardly a trace remains of their original unity. With the disappearance of unity the one original language was also lost, so that neither in the Hebrew nor in any other language of history has enough been preserved to enable us to form the least conception of its character.[1] The primitive language is extinct, buried in the materials of the languages of the nations, to rise again one day to eternal life in the glorified form of the καιναὶ γλῶσσαι intelligible to all the redeemed, when sin with its consequences is overcome and extinguished by the power of grace. A type and pledge of this hope was given in the gift of tongues on the outpouring of the Holy Spirit upon the Church

---

[1] The opinion of the Rabbins and earlier theologians, that the Hebrew was the primitive language, has been generally abandoned in consequence of modern philological researches. The fact that the biblical names handed down from the earliest times are of Hebrew extraction proves nothing. With the gradual development and change of language, the traditions with their names were cast into the mould of existing dialects, without thereby affecting the truth of the tradition. For as *Drechster* has said, " it makes no difference whether I say that Adam's eldest son had a name corresponding to the name *Cain* from קָיִן, or to the name *Ctesias* from κτᾶσθαι ; the truth of the Thorah, which presents us with the tradition handed down from the sons of Noah through Shem to Abraham and Israel, is not a verbal, but a living tradition—is not in the letter, but in the spirit."

on the first Christian day of Pentecost, when the apostles, filled with the Holy Ghost, spoke with other or new tongues of "the wonderful works of God," so that the people of every nation under heaven understood in their own language (Acts ii. 1–11).

From the confusion of tongues the city received the name *Babel* (בָּבֶל i.e. confusion, contracted from בַּלְבֵּל from בָּלַל to confuse), according to divine direction, though without any such intention on the part of those who first gave the name, as a standing memorial of the judgment of God which follows all the ungodly enterprises of the power of the world.[1] Of this city considerable ruins still remain, including the remains of an enormous tower, *Birs Nimrud,* which is regarded by the Arabs as the tower of Babel that was destroyed by fire from heaven. Whether these ruins have any historical connection with the tower of the confusion of tongues, must remain, at least for the present, a matter of uncertainty. With regard to the date of the event, we find from ver. 10 that the division of the human race occurred in the days of Peleg, who was born 100 years after the flood. In 150 or 180 years, with a rapid succession of births, the descendants of the three sons of Noah, who were already 100 years old and married at the time of the flood, might have become quite numerous enough to proceed to the erection of such a building. If we reckon, for example, only four male and four female births as the average number to each marriage, since it is evident from chap. xi. 12 sqq. that children were born as early as the 30th or 35th year of their parent's age, the sixth generation would be born by 150 years after the flood, and the human race would number 12,288 males and as many females. Consequently there would be at least about 30,000 people in the world at this time.

[1] Such explanations of the name as " gate, or house, or fortress of Bel," are all the less worthy of notice, because the derivation ἀπὸ τοῦ Βήλου in the *Etymol. magn.,* and in Persian and Nabatean works, is founded upon the myth, that *Bel* was the founder of the city. And as this myth is destitute of historical worth, so is also the legend that the city was built by Semiramis, which may possibly have so much of history as its basis, that this half-mythical queen extended and beautified the city, just as Nebuchadnezzar added a new quarter, and a second fortress, and strongly fortified it.

V. HISTORY OF SHEM.

CHAP. XI. 10–26.

After describing the division of the one family which sprang
from the three sons of Noah, into many nations scattered over
the earth and speaking different languages, the narrative returns
to Shem, and traces his descendants in a direct line to Terah the
father of Abraham. The first five members of this pedigree have
already been given in the genealogy of the Shemites; and in that
case the object was to point out the connection in which all the
descendants of Eber stood to one another. They are repeated
here to show the direct descent of the Terahites through Peleg
from Shem, but more especially to follow the chronological
thread of the family line, which could not be given in the genealogical tree without disturbing the uniformity of its plan. By
the statement in ver. 10, that " *Shem, a hundred years old, begat
Arphaxad two years after the flood,*" the chronological *data*
already given of Noah's age at the birth of his sons (chap. v. 32)
and at the commencement of the flood (vii. 11) are made still
more definite. As the expression "after the flood" refers to the
commencement of the flood (chap. ix. 28), and according to chap.
vii. 11 the flood began in the second month, or near the beginning of the six hundredth year of Noah's life, though the year
600 is given in chap. vii. 6 in round numbers, it is not *necessary*
to assume, as some do, in order to reconcile the difference between
our verse and chap. v. 32, that the number 500 in chap. v. 32
stands as a round number for 502. On the other hand, there
can be no objection to such an assumption. The different statements may be easily reconciled by placing the birth of Shem at
the end of the five hundredth year of Noah's life, and the birth
of Arphaxad at the end of the hundredth year of that of Shem;
in which case Shem would be just 99 years old when the flood
began, and would be fully 100 years old "two years after the
flood," that is to say, in the second year from the commencement
of the flood, when he begat Arphaxad. In this case the "two
years after the flood" are not to be added to the sum-total of the
chronological *data*, but are included in it. The table given here
forms in a chronological and material respect the direct con-

tinuation of the one in chap. v., and differs from it only in form,
viz. by giving merely the length of life of the different fathers
before and after the birth of their sons, without also summing
up the whole number of their years as is the case there, since
this is superfluous for chronological purposes. But on comparing
the chronological *data* of the two tables, we find this very important difference in the duration of life before and after the
flood, that the patriarchs after the flood lived upon an average
only half the number of years of those before it, and that with
Peleg the average duration of life was again reduced by one
half. Whilst Noah with his 950 years belonged entirely to the
old world, and Shem, who was born before the flood, reached
the age of 600, Arphaxad lived only 438 years, Salah 433, and
Eber 464; and again, with Peleg the duration of life fell to 239
years, Reu also lived only 239 years, Serug 230, and Nahor not
more than 148. Here, then, we see that the two catastrophes,
the flood and the separation of the human race into nations,
exerted a powerful influence in shortening the duration of life;
the former by altering the climate of the earth, the latter by
changing the habits of men. But while the length of life
diminished, the children were born proportionally earlier. Shem
begat his first-born in his hundredth year, Arphaxad in the thirty-
fifth, Salah in the thirtieth, and so on to Terah, who had no
children till his seventieth year; consequently the human race,
notwithstanding the shortening of life, increased with sufficient
rapidity to people the earth very soon after their dispersion.
There is nothing astonishing, therefore, in the circumstance, that
wherever Abraham went he found tribes, towns, and kingdoms,
though only 365 years had elapsed since the flood, when we consider that eleven generations would have followed one another
in that time, and that, supposing every marriage to have been
blessed with eight children on an average (four male and four
female), the eleventh generation would contain 12,582,912
couples, or 25,165,824 individuals. And if we reckon ten children as the average number, the eleventh generation would contain 146,484,375 pairs, or 292,968,750 individuals. In neither
of these cases have we included such of the earlier generations
as would be still living, although their number would be by no
means inconsiderable, since nearly all the patriarchs from Shem
to Terah were alive at the time of Abram's migration. In ver.

26 the genealogy closes, like that in chap. v. 32, with the names of three sons of Terah, all of whom sustained an important relation to the subsequent history, viz. *Abram* as the father of the chosen family, *Nahor* as the ancestor of Rebekah (cf. ver. 29 with chap. xxii. 20–23), and *Haran* as the father of Lot (ver. 27).

VI. HISTORY OF TERAH.

CHAP. XI. 27–XXV. 11.

FAMILY OF TERAH.—CHAP. XI. 27–32.

The genealogical *data* in vers. 27–32 prepare the way for the history of the patriarchs. The heading, " *These are the generations of Terah*," belongs not merely to vers. 27–32, but to the whole of the following account of Abram, since it corresponds to " the generations" of Ishmael and of Isaac in chap. xxv. 12 and 19. Of the three sons of Terah, who are mentioned again in ver. 27 to complete the plan of the different *Toledoth*, such genealogical notices are given as are of importance to the history of Abram and his family. According to the regular plan of Genesis, the fact that Haran the youngest son of Terah begat Lot, is mentioned first of all, because the latter went with Abram to Canaan; and then the fact that he died before his father Terah, because the link which would have connected Lot with his native land was broken in consequence. " *Before his father*," עַל פְּנֵי *lit.* upon the face of his father, so that he saw and survived his death. *Ur of the Chaldees* is to be sought either in the " *Ur nomine persicum castellum*" of *Ammian* (25, 8), between Hatra and Nisibis, near Arrapachitis, or in *Orhoi*, Armenian *Urrhai*, the old name for *Edessa*, the modern *Urfa*.—Ver. 29. Abram and Nahor took wives from their kindred. Abram married Sarai, his half-sister (xx. 12), of whom it is already related, in anticipation of what follows, that she was barren. Nahor married Milcah, the daughter of his brother Haran, who bore to him Bethuel, the father of Rebekah (xxii. 22, 23). The reason why Iscah is mentioned is doubtful. For the rabbinical notion, that Iscah is another name for Sarai, is irreconcilable with chap. xx. 12, where Abram calls Sarai his sister, daughter of his father, though not of his mother; on the other hand, the circumstance that Sarai is introduced in ver 31 merely as the daughter-in-law of Terah, may be explained on the ground that she left Ur, not as his daughter, but as the wife of his son Abram. A better hypothesis is that of *Ewald*, that Iscah is mentioned because she was the wife of Lot; but this is pure conjecture. According to ver. 31, Terah already prepared to leave Ur of the Chaldees with Abram and Lot, and to remove to Canaan. In the phrase " *they went forth with them*," the subject cannot be the unmentioned members of the family, such as Nahor and his children; though Nahor must also have gone to Haran, since it is called in chap. xxiv. 10 the city of Nahor. For if he accompanied them at this time, there is no perceptible reason why he should not have been mentioned along with the rest. The nominative to the verb must be Lot and Sarai, who went with Terah and Abram; so that although Terah is placed at the head, Abram must have taken an active part in the removal, or the resolution to remove. This does not, however, necessitate the conclusion, that he had already been called by God in Ur. Nor does chap. xv. 7 require any such assumption. For it is not stated there that God called Abram in Ur, but only that He *brought him out.* But the simple fact of removing from Ur might also be called a leading out, as a work of divine superintendence and guidance, without a special call from God. It was in Haran that Abram first received the divine call to go to Canaan (xii. 1–4), when he left not only his country and kindred, but also his father's house. Terah did not carry out his intention to proceed to Canaan, but remained in Haran, in his native country Mesopotamia, probably because he found there what he was going to look for in the land of Canaan. Haran, more properly *Charan*, חָרָן, is a place in north-western Mesopotamia, the ruins of which may still be seen, a full day's journey to the south of Edessa (Gr. Κάρραι, Lat. *Carræ*), where Crassus fell when defeated by the Parthians. It was a leading settlement of the Ssabians, who had a temple there dedicated to the moon, which they traced back to Abraham. There Terah died at the age of 205, or sixty years after the departure of Abram for Canaan; for, according to ver. 26, Terah was seventy years old when Abram was born, and Abram was seventy-five years old when he arrived in Canaan. When Stephen, therefore, placed the removal of Abram from Haran to Canaan after the death of his father, he merely inferred this from the fact, that the call of Abram (chap. xii.) was not mentioned till after the death of Terah had been noticed, taking the order of the narrative as the order of events; whereas, according to the plan of Genesis, the death of Terah is introduced here, because Abram never met with his father again after leaving Haran, and there was consequently nothing more to be related concerning him.

CHARACTER OF THE PATRIARCHAL HISTORY.

The dispersion of the descendants of the sons of Noah, who had now grown into numerous families, was necessarily followed on the one hand by the rise of a variety of nations, differing in language, manners, and customs, and more and more estranged from one another; and on the other by the expansion of the germs of idolatry, contained in the different attitudes of these nations towards God, into the polytheistic religions of heathenism, in which the glory of the immortal God was changed into an image made like to mortal man, and to birds, and four-footed beasts, and creeping things (Rom. i. 23 cf. Wisdom xiii.–xv.). If God therefore would fulfil His promise, no more to smite the earth with the curse of the destruction of every living thing because of the sin of man (chap. viii. 21, 22), and yet would prevent the moral corruption which worketh death from sweeping all before it; it was necessary that by the side of these self-formed nations He should form a nation for Himself, to be the recipient and preserver of His salvation, and that in opposition to the rising kingdoms of the world He should establish a kingdom for the living, saving fellowship of man with Himself. The foundation for this was laid by God in the call and separation of Abram from his people and his country, to make him, by special guidance, the father of a nation from which the salvation of the world should come. With the choice of Abram the revelation of God to man assumed a select character, inasmuch as God manifested Himself henceforth to Abram and his posterity alone as the author of salvation and the guide to true life; whilst other nations were left to follow their own course according to the powers conferred upon them, in order that they might learn that in their way, and without fellowship with the living God, it was impossible to find peace to the soul, and the true blessedness of life (cf. Acts xvii. 27).

But this exclusiveness contained from the very first the germ of universalism. Abram was called, that through him all the families of the earth might be blessed (chap. xii. 1-3). Hence the new form which the divine guidance of the human race assumed in the call of Abram was connected with the general development of the world,—on the one hand, by the fact that Abram belonged to the family of Shem, which Jehovah had blessed, and on the other, by his not being called alone, but as a married man with his wife. But whilst, regarded in this light, the continuity of the divine revelation was guaranteed, as well as the plan of human development established in the creation itself, the call of Abram introduced so far the commencement of a new period, that to carry out the designs of God their very foundations required to be renewed. Although, for example, the knowledge and worship of the true God had been preserved in the families of Shem in a purer form than among the remaining descendants of Noah, even in the house of Terah the worship of God was corrupted by idolatry (Josh. xxiv. 2, 3); and although Abram was to become the father of the nation which God was about to form, yet his wife was barren, and therefore, in the way of nature, a new family could not be expected to spring from him.

As a perfectly new beginning, therefore, the patriarchal history assumed the form of a family history, in which the grace of God prepared the ground for the coming Israel. For the nation was to grow out of the family, and in the lives of the patriarchs its character was to be determined and its development foreshadowed. The early history consists of three stages, which are indicated by the three patriarchs, peculiarly so called, Abraham, Isaac, and Jacob; and in the sons of Jacob the unity of the chosen family was expanded into the twelve immediate fathers of the nation. In the triple number of the patriarchs, the divine election of the nation on the one hand, and the entire formation of the character and guidance of the life of Israel on the other, were to attain to their fullest typical manifestation. These two were the pivots, upon which all the divine revelations made to the patriarchs, and all the guidance they received, were made to turn. The revelations consisted almost exclusively of promises; and so far as these promises were fulfilled in the lives of the patriarchs, the fulfilments themselves were predictions and pledges of the ultimate and complete fulfilment, reserved for a distant, or for the most remote futurity. And the guidance vouchsafed had for its object the calling forth of faith in response to the promise, which should maintain itself amidst all the changes of this earthly life. " A faith, which laid hold of the word of promise, and on the strength of that word gave up the visible and present for the invisible and future, was the fundamental characteristic of the patriarchs" (*Delitzsch*). This faith Abram manifested and sustained by great sacrifices, by enduring patience, and by self-denying obedience of such a kind, that he thereby became the father of believers (πατὴρ πάντων τῶν πιστευόντων, Rom. iv. 11). Isaac also was strong in patience and hope; and Jacob wrestled in faith amidst painful circumstances of various kinds, until he had secured the blessing of the promise. " Abraham was a man of faith that works; Isaac, of faith that endures; Jacob, of faith that wrestles" (*Baumgarten*).—Thus, walking in faith, the patriarchs were types of faith for all the families that should spring from them, and be blessed through them, and ancestors of a nation which God had resolved to form according to the election of His grace. For the election of God was not restricted to the separation of Abram from the family of Shem, to be the father of the nation which was destined to be the vehicle of salvation ; it was also manifest in the exclusion of Ishmael, whom Abram had begotten by the will of man, through Hagar the handmaid of his wife, for the purpose of securing the promised seed, and in the new life imparted to the womb of the barren Sarai, and her consequent conception and birth of Isaac, the son of promise. And lastly, it appeared still more manifestly in the twin sons born by Rebekah to Isaac, of whom the first-born, Esau, was rejected, and the younger, Jacob, chosen to be the heir of the promise; and this choice, which was announced before their birth, was maintained in spite of Isaac's plans, so that Jacob, and not Esau, received the blessing of the promise. —All this occurred as a type for the future, that Israel might know and lay to heart the fact, that bodily descent from Abraham did not make a man a child of God, but that they alone were children of God who laid hold of the divine promise in faith, and walked in the steps of their forefather's faith (cf. Rom. ix. 6–13).

If we fix our eyes upon the method of the divine revelation, we find a new beginning in this respect, that as soon as Abram is called, we read of the *appearing* of God. It is true that from the very beginning God had manifested Himself visibly to men; but in the olden time we read nothing of appearances, because before the flood God had not withdrawn His presence from the earth. Even to Noah He revealed Himself before the flood as one who was present on the earth. But when He had established a covenant with him after the flood, and thereby had assured the continuance of the earth and of the human race, the direct manifestations ceased, for God withdrew His visible presence from the world; so that it was from heaven that the judgment fell upon the tower of Babel, and even the call to Abram in his home in Haran was issued through His word, that is to say, no doubt, through an inward monition. But as soon as Abram had gone to Canaan, in obedience to the call of God, Jehovah *appeared* to him there (chap. xii. 7). These appearances, which were constantly repeated from that time forward, must have taken place from heaven; for we read that Jehovah, after speaking with Abram and the other patriarchs, " went away" (chap. xviii. 33), or " went up" (chap. xvii. 22, xxxv. 13); and the patriarchs saw them, sometimes while in a waking condition, in a form discernible to the bodily senses, sometimes in visions, in a state of mental ecstasy, and at other times in the form of a dream (chap. xxviii. 12 sqq.). On the form in which God appeared, in most instances, nothing is related. But in chap. xviii. 1 sqq. it is stated that three men came to Abram, one of whom is introduced as Jehovah, whilst the other two are called angels (chap. xix. 1). Beside this, we frequently read of appearances of the " angel of Jehovah" (xvi. 7, xxii. 11, etc.), or of " Elohim," and the " angel of Elohim" (chap. xxi. 17, xxxi. 11, etc.), which were repeated throughout the whole of the Old Testament, and even occurred, though only in vision, in the case of the prophet Zechariah. The appearances of the angel of Jehovah (or Elohim) cannot have been essentially different from those of Jehovah (or Elohim) Himself; for Jacob describes the appearance of Jehovah at Bethel (chap. xxviii. 13 sqq.) as an appearance of " the angel of Elohim," and of " the God of Bethel" (chap. xxxi. 11, 13); and in his blessing on the sons of Joseph (chap. xlviii. 15, 16), " The God (*Elohim*) before whom my fathers Abraham and Isaac did walk, the God (*Elohim*) which fed me all my life long unto this day, the *angel* which redeemed me from all evil, bless the lads," he places the angel of God on a perfect equality with God, not only regarding Him as the Being to whom he has been indebted for protection all his life long, but entreating from Him a blessing upon his descendants.

The question arises, therefore, whether the *angel of Jehovah,* or *of God,* was God Himself in one particular phase of His self-manifestation, or a created angel of whom God made use as the organ of His self-revelation.[1] The former appears to us to be the only scriptural view. For the essential unity of the Angel of Jehovah with Jehovah Himself follows indisputably from the following facts. In the first place, the Angel of God identifies Himself with Jehovah and Elohim, by attributing to Himself divine attributes and performing divine works : *e.g.,* chap. xxii. 12, "Now *I* know that thou fearest God, seeing thou hast·not withheld thy son, thine only son, from *me*" (*i.e.* hast been willing to offer him up as a burnt sacrifice to God) ; again (to Hagar) chap. xvi. 10, "*I* will multiply thy seed exceedingly, that it shall not be numbered for multitude;" chap. xxi., '*I* will make him a great nation,"—the very words used by Elohim in chap. xvii. 20 with reference to Ishmael, and by Jehovah in chap. xiii. 16, xv. 4, 5, with regard to Isaac; also Ex. iii. 6 sqq., "*I* am the God of thy father, the God of Abraham, the God of Isaac, and the God of Jacob : *I* have surely seen the affliction of *My* people which are in Egypt, and have heard their cry, and *I* am come down to deliver them" (cf. Judg. ii. 1). In addition to this, He performs miracles, consuming with fire the offering placed before Him by Gideon, and the sacrifice prepared by Manoah, and ascending to heaven in the flame of the burnt-offering (Judg. vi. 21, xiii. 19, 20). *Secondly,* the Angel of God was recognised as God by those to whom He appeared,

[1] In the old Jewish synagogue the Angel of Jehovah was regarded as the *Shechinah,* the indwelling of God in the world, *i.e.* the only Mediator between God and the world, who bears in the Jewish theology the name *Metatron.* The early Church regarded Him as the *Logos,* the second person of the Deity ; and only a few of the fathers, such as *Augustine* and *Jerome,* thought of a created angel (*vid. Hengstenberg,* Christol. vol. 3, app.). This view was adopted by many Romish theologians, by the Socinians, Arminians, and others, and has been defended recently by *Hofmann,* whom *Delitzsch, Kurtz,* and others follow. But the opinion of the early Church has been vindicated most thoroughly by *Hengstenberg* in his Christology.

on the one hand by their addressing Him as *Adonai* (*i.e.* the Lord God; Judg. vi. 15), declaring that they had seen God, and fearing that they should die (chap. xvi. 13; Ex. iii. 6; Judg. vi. 22, 23, xiii. 22), and on the other hand by their paying Him divine honour, offering sacrifices which He accepted, and worshipping Him (Judg. vi. 20, xiii. 19, 20, cf. ii. 5). The force of these facts has been met by the assertion, that the ambassador perfectly represents the person of the sender; and evidence of this is adduced not only from Grecian literature, but from the Old Testament also, where the addresses of the prophets often glide imperceptibly into the words of Jehovah, whose instrument they are. But even if the address in chap. xxii. 16, where the oath of the Angel of Jehovah is accompanied by the words, "saith the Lord," and the words and deeds of the Angel of God in certain other cases, might be explained in this way, a created angel sent by God could never say, "*I* am the God of Abraham, Isaac, and Jacob," or by the acceptance of sacrifices and adoration, encourage the presentation of divine honours to himself. How utterly irreconcilable this fact is with the opinion that the Angel of Jehovah was a created angel, is conclusively proved by Rev. xxii. 9, which is generally regarded as perfectly corresponding to the account of the "Angel of Jehovah" of the Old Testament. The angel of God, who shows the sacred seer the heavenly Jerusalem, and who is supposed to say, "Behold, I come quickly" (ver. 7), and "I am Alpha and Omega" (ver. 13), refuses in the most decided way the worship which John is about to present, and exclaims, "See I am thy fellow-servant: worship God." *Thirdly*, the Angel of Jehovah is also identified with Jehovah by the sacred writers themselves, who call the Angel Jehovah without the least reserve (cf. Ex. iii. 2 and 4, Judg. vi. 12 and 14–16, but especially Ex. xiv. 19, where the Angel of Jehovah goes before the host of the Israelites, just as Jehovah is said to do in Ex. xiii. 21).— On the other hand, the objection is raised, that ἄγγελος κυρίου in the New Testament, which is confessedly the Greek rendering of מלאך יהוה, is always a created angel, and for that reason cannot be the uncreated Logos or Son of God, since the latter could not possibly have announced His own birth to the shepherds at Bethlehem. But this important difference has been overlooked, that according to Greek usage, ἄγγελος κυρίου denotes an (any) angel of the Lord, whereas according to the rules of the Hebrew language מַלְאַךְ יְהוָֹה means *the* angel of the Lord ; that in the New Testament the angel who appears is always described as ἄγγελος κυρίου without the article, and the definite article is only introduced in the further course of the narrative to denote the angel whose appearance has been already mentioned, whereas in the Old Testament it is always "*the* Angel of Jehovah" who appears, and whenever the appearance of a created angel is referred to, he is introduced first of all as "an angel" (*vid.* 1 Kings xix. 5 and 7).[1] At the same time, it does not follow from this use of the expression *Maleach Jehovah*, that the (particular) angel of Jehovah was essentially one with God, or that *Maleach Jehovah* always has the same signification ; for in Mal. ii. 7 the priest is called *Maleach Jehovah*, *i.e.* the messenger of the Lord. Who the messenger or angel of Jehovah was, must be determined in each particular instance from the connection of the passage ; and where the context furnishes no criterion, it must remain undecided. Consequently such passages as Ps. xxxiv. 7, xxxv. 5, 6, etc., where the angel of Jehovah is not more particularly described, or Num. xx. 16, where the general term *angel* is intentionally employed, or Acts vii. 30, Gal. iii. 19, and Heb. ii. 2, where the words are general and indefinite, furnish no evidence that *the* Angel of Jehovah, who proclaimed Himself in His appearances as one with God, was not in reality equal with God, unless we are to adopt as the rule for interpreting Scripture the inverted principle, that clear and definite statements are to be explained by those that are indefinite and obscure.

In attempting now to determine the connection between the appearance of the Angel of Jehovah (or Elohim) and the appearance of Jehovah or Elohim Himself, and to fix the precise meaning of the expression *Maleach Jehovah*, we cannot make

---

[1] The force of this difference cannot be set aside by the objection that the New Testament writers follow the usage of the Septuagint, where מלאך יהוה is rendered ἄγγελος κυρίου. For neither in the New Testament nor in the Alex. version of the Old is ἄγγελος κυρίου used as a proper name ; it is a simple appellative, as is apparent from the fact that in every instance, in which further reference is made to an angel who has appeared, he is called ὁ ἄγγελος, with or without κυρίου. All that the Septuagint rendering proves, is that the translators supposed "the angel of the Lord" to be a created angel ; but it by no means follows that their supposition is correct.

use, as recent opponents of the old Church view have done, of the manifestation of God in Gen. xviii. and xix., and the allusion to the great prince *Michael* in Dan. x. 13, 21, xii. 1; just because neither the appearance of Jehovah in the former instance, nor that of the archangel Michael in the latter, is represented as an appearance of the Angel of Jehovah. We must confine ourselves to the passages in which "the Angel of Jehovah" is actually referred to. We will examine these, first of all, for the purpose of obtaining a clear conception of the form in which the Angel of Jehovah appeared. Gen. xvi., where He is mentioned for the first time, contains no distinct statement as to His shape, but produces on the whole the impression that He appeared to Hagar in a human form, or one resembling that of man; since it was not till after His departure that she drew the inference from His words, that Jehovah had spoken with her. He came in the same form to Gideon, and sat under the terebinth at Ophrah with a staff in His hand (Judg. vi. 11 and 21); also to Manoah's wife, for she took Him to be a man of God, *i.e.* a prophet, whose appearance was like that of the Angel of Jehovah (Judg. xiii. 6); and lastly, to Manoah himself, who did not recognise Him at first, but discovered afterwards, from the miracle which He wrought before his eyes, and from His miraculous ascent in the flame of the altar, that He was the Angel of Jehovah (vers. 9–20). In other cases He revealed Himself merely by calling and speaking from heaven, without those who heard His voice perceiving any form at all: *e.g.*, to Hagar, in Gen. xxi. 17 sqq., and to Abraham, chap. xxii. 11 sqq. On the other hand, He appeared to Moses (Ex. iii. 2) in a flame of fire, speaking to him from the burning bush, and to the people of Israel in a pillar of cloud and fire (Ex. xiv. 19, cf. xiii. 21 sq.), without any angelic form being visible in either case. Balaam He met in a human or angelic form, with a drawn sword in His hand (Num. xxii. 22, 23). David saw Him by the threshing-floor of Araunah, standing between heaven and earth, with the sword drawn in His hand and stretched out over Jerusalem (1 Chron. xxi. 16); and He appeared to Zechariah in a vision as a rider upon a red horse (Zech. i. 9 sqq.).—From these varying forms of appearance it is evident that the opinion that the Angel of the Lord was a real angel, a divine manifestation, "not in the disguise of angel, but through the actual

appearance of an angel," is not in harmony with all the statements of the Bible. The form of the Angel of Jehovah, which
was discernible by the senses, varied according to the purpose of
the appearance; and, apart from Gen. xxi. 17 and xxii. 11, we
have a sufficient proof that it was not a real angelic appearance,
or the appearance of a created angel, in the fact that in two
instances it was not really an angel at all, but a flame of fire
and a shining cloud which formed the earthly substratum of the
revelation of God in the Angel of Jehovah (Ex. iii. 2, xiv. 19),
unless indeed we are to regard natural phenomena as angels,
without any scriptural warrant for doing so.[1] These earthly
substrata of the manifestation of the "Angel of Jehovah" perfectly suffice to establish the conclusion, that the Angel of
Jehovah was only a peculiar form in which Jehovah Himself
appeared, and which differed from the manifestations of God
described as appearances of Jehovah simply in this, that in "the
Angel of Jehovah," God or Jehovah revealed Himself in a mode
which was more easily discernible by human senses, and exhibited in a guise of symbolical significance the design of each
particular manifestation. In the appearances of Jehovah no
reference is made to any form visible to the bodily eye, unless
they were through the medium of a vision or a dream, excepting
in one instance (Gen. xviii.), where Jehovah and two angels
come to Abraham in the form of three men, and are entertained

---

[1] The only passage that could be adduced in support of this, viz. Ps.
civ. 4, does not prove that God makes natural objects, winds and flaming
fire, into forms in which heavenly spirits appear, or that He creates spirits
out of them. Even if we render this passage, with *Delitzsch*, "making His
messengers of winds, His servants of flaming fire," the allusion, as *Delitzsch*
himself observes, is not to the creation of angels; nor can the meaning be,
that God gives wind and fire to His angels as the material of their appearance, and as it were of their self-incorporation. For עָשָׂה, constructed with
two accusatives, the second of which expresses the *materia ex qua*, is never
met with in this sense, not even in 2 Chron. iv. 18–22. For the greater
part of the temple furniture summed up in this passage, of which it is stated
that Solomon made them of gold, was composed of pure gold; and if some
of the things were merely covered with gold, the writer might easily apply
the same expression to this, because he had already given a more minute
account of their construction (*e.g.* chap. iii. 7). But we neither regard
this rendering of the psalm as in harmony with the context, nor assent to
the assertion that עָשָׂה with a double accusative, in the sense of making
into anything, is ungrammatical

by him,—a form of appearance perfectly resembling the appearances of the Angel of Jehovah, but which is not so described by the author, because in this case Jehovah does not appear alone, but in the company of two angels, that "the Angel of Jehovah" might not be regarded as a created angel.

But although there was no essential difference, but only a formal one, between the appearing of Jehovah and the appearing of the Angel of Jehovah, the distinction between Jehovah and the Angel of Jehovah points to a distinction in the divine nature, to which even the Old Testament contains several obvious allusions. The very name indicates such a difference. מַלְאַךְ יְהֹוָה (from לָאַךְ to work, from which come מְלָאכָה the work, *opus*, and מַלְאָךְ, *lit.* he through whom a work is executed, but in ordinary usage restricted to the idea of a messenger) denotes the person through whom God works and appears. Beside these passages which represent "the Angel of Jehovah" as one with Jehovah, there are others in which the Angel distinguishes Himself from Jehovah; *e.g.* when He gives emphasis to the oath by Himself as an oath by Jehovah, by adding "saith Jehovah" (Gen. xxii. 16); when He greets Gideon with the words, "Jehovah with thee, thou brave hero" (Judg. vi. 12); when He says to Manoah, "Though thou constrainedst me, I would not eat of thy food; but if thou wilt offer a burnt-offering to Jehovah, thou mayest offer it" (Judg. xiii. 16); or when He prays, in Zech. i. 12, "Jehovah Sabaoth, how long wilt Thou not have mercy on Jerusalem?" (Compare also Gen. xix. 24, where Jehovah is distinguished from Jehovah.) Just as in these passages the Angel of Jehovah distinguishes Himself personally from Jehovah, there are others in which a distinction is drawn between a self-revealing side of the divine nature, visible to men, and a hidden side, invisible to men, *i.e.* between the self-revealing and the hidden God. Thus, for example, not only does Jehovah say of the Angel, whom He sends before Israel in the pillar of cloud and fire, "My name is in Him," *i.e.* he reveals My nature (Ex. xxiii. 21), but He also calls Him פָּנַי, "My face" (xxxiii. 14); and in reply to Moses' request to see His glory, He says "Thou canst not see My face, for there shall no man see Me and live," and then causes His glory to pass by Moses in such a way that he only sees His back, but not His face (xxxiii. 18–23). On the strength of these expressions, He in whom Jehovah manifested Himself to His people as a Saviour is called in Isa. lxiii. 9, "the Angel of His face," and all the guidance and protection of Israel are ascribed to Him. In accordance with this, Malachi, the last prophet of the Old Testament, proclaims to the people waiting for the manifestation of Jehovah, that is to say, for the appearance of the Messiah predicted by former prophets, that the Lord (הָאָדוֹן, *i.e.* God), the Angel of the covenant, will come to His temple (iii. 1). This "Angel of the covenant," or "Angel of the face," has appeared in Christ. The Angel of Jehovah, therefore, was no other than the Logos, which not only "was with God," but "was God," and in Jesus Christ "was made flesh" and "came unto His own" (John i. 1, 2, 11); the only-begotten Son of God, who was *sent* by the Father into the world, who, though one with the Father, prayed to the Father (John xvii.), and who is even called "the Apostle," ὁ ἀπόστολος, in Heb. iii. 1. From all this it is sufficiently obvious, that neither the title Angel or Messenger of Jehovah, nor the fact that the Angel of Jehovah prayed to Jehovah Sabaoth, furnishes any evidence against His essential unity with Jehovah. That which is unfolded in perfect clearness in the New Testament through the incarnation of the Son of God, was still veiled in the Old Testment according to the wisdom apparent in the divine training. The difference between Jehovah and the Angel of Jehovah is generally hidden behind the unity of the two, and for the most part Jehovah is referred to as He who chose Israel as His nation and kingdom, and who would reveal Himself at some future time to His people in all His glory; so that in the New Testament nearly all the manifestations of Jehovah under the Old Covenant are referred to Christ, and regarded as fulfilled through Him.[1]

[1] This is not a mere accommodation of Scripture, but the correct interpretation of the obscure hints of the Old Testament by the light of the fulfilment in the New. For not only is the Maleach Jehovah the revealer of God, but Jehovah Himself is the revealed God and Saviour. Just as in the history of the Old Testament there are not only revelations of the Maleach Jehovah, but revelations of Jehovah also; so in the prophecies the announcement of the Messiah, the sprout of David and servant of Jehovah, is intermingled with the announcement of the coming of Jehovah to glorify His people and perfect His kingdom.

CALL OF ABRAM.   HIS REMOVAL TO CANAAN, AND JOURNEY
INTO EGYPT.—CHAP. XII.

The life of Abraham, from his call to his death, consists of
four stages, the commencement of each of which is marked by a
divine revelation of sufficient importance to constitute a distinct
epoch.   The first stage (chap. xii.–xiv.) commences with his call
and removal to Canaan ; the second (chap. xv. xvi.), with the
promise of a lineal heir and the conclusion of a covenant; the
third (chap. xvii.–xxi.), with the establishment of the covenant,
accompanied by a change in his name, and the appointment of
the covenant sign of circumcision ; the fourth (chap. xxii.–xxv.
11), with the temptation of Abraham to attest and perfect his life
of faith.   All the revelations made to him proceed from Jehovah ;
and the name Jehovah is employed throughout the whole life of
the father of the faithful, Elohim being used only where Jehovah,
from its meaning, would be either entirely inapplicable, or at any
rate less appropriate.[1]

Vers. 1–3. THE CALL.—The word of Jehovah, by which
Abram was called, contained a command and a promise.   Abram
was to leave all—his country, his kindred (see chap. xliii. 7), and
his father's house—and to follow the Lord into the land which He
would show him.   Thus he was to trust entirely to the guidance
of God, and to follow wherever He might lead him.   But as he
went in consequence of this divine summons into the land of
Canaan (ver. 5), we must assume that God gave him at the very
first a distinct intimation, if not of the land itself, at least of the
direction he was to take.   That Canaan was to be his destination,
was no doubt made known as a matter of certainty in the revelation which he received after his arrival there (ver. 7).—For thus
renouncing and denying all natural ties, the Lord gave him the
inconceivably great promise, " *I will make of thee a great nation ;
and I will bless thee, and make thy name great ; and thou shalt be a
blessing.*"   The four members of this promise are not to be divided

---

[1] The hypothesis, that the history is compounded of Jehovistic and Elohistic documents, can only be maintained by those who misunderstand the
distinctive meaning of these two names, and arbitrarily set aside the *Jehovah*
in chap. xvii. 1, on account of an erroneous determination of the relation in
which אֵל שַׁדַּי stands to יהוה.

into two parallel members, in which case the *athnach* would stand in the wrong place ; but are to be regarded as an ascending climax, expressing four elements of the salvation promised to Abram, the last of which is still further expanded in ver. 3. By placing the *athnach* under שְׁמֶךָ the fourth member is marked as a new and independent feature added to the other three. The four distinct elements are—1. increase into a numerous people 2. a blessing, that is to say, material and spiritual prosperity ; 3. the exaltation of his name, *i.e.* the elevation of Abram to honour and glory ; 4. his appointment to be the possessor and dispenser of the blessing. Abram was not only to *receive* blessing, but to *be* a blessing ; not only to be blessed by God, but to become a blessing, or the medium of blessing, to others. The blessing, as the more minute definition of the expression " *be a blessing*" in ver. 3 clearly shows, was henceforth to keep pace as it were with Abram himself, so that (1) the blessing and cursing of men were to depend entirely upon their attitude towards him, and (2) all the families of the earth were to be blessed in him. קָלַל, *lit.* to treat as light or little, to despise, denotes " blasphemous cursing on the part of a man ;" אָרַר " judicial cursing on the part of God." It appears significant, however, " that the plural is used in relation to the blessing, and the singular only in relation to the cursing ; grace expects that there will be many to bless, and that only an individual here and there will render not blessing for blessing, but curse for curse."—In ver. 3 *b*, Abram, the one, is made a blessing for all. In the word בְּךָ the primary meaning of בְ, *in*, is not to be given up, though the instrumental sense, *through*, is not to be excluded. Abram was not merely to become a mediator, but the source of blessing for all. The expression " *all the families of the ground*" points to the division of the one family into many (chap. x. 5, 20, 31), and the word הָאֲדָמָה to the curse pronounced upon the ground (chap. iii. 17). The blessing of Abraham was once more to unite the divided families, and change the curse, pronounced upon the ground on account of sin, into a blessing for the whole human race. This concluding word comprehends all nations and times, and condenses, as *Baumgarten* has said, the whole fulness of the divine counsel for the salvation of men into the call of Abram. All further promises, therefore, not only to the patriarchs, but also to Israel, were merely expansions and closer definitions of the salvation held out to the whole human race in the first promise. Even the assurance, which Abram received after his entrance into Canaan (ver. 6), was implicitly contained in this first promise; since a great nation could not be conceived of, without a country of its own. This promise was renewed to Abram on several occasions: first after his separation from Lot (xiii. 14–16), on which occasion, however, the "blessing" was not mentioned, because not required by the connection, and the two elements only, viz. the numerous increase of his seed, and the possession of the land of Canaan, were assured to him and to his seed, and that "for ever;" secondly, in chap. xviii. 18 somewhat more casually, as a reason for the confidential manner in which Jehovah explained to him the secret of His government; and lastly, at the two principal turning points of his life, where the whole promise was confirmed with the greatest solemnity, viz. in chap. xvii. at the commencement of the establishment of the covenant made with him, where "I will make of thee a great nation" was heightened into "I will make nations of thee, and kings shall come out of thee," and his being a blessing was more fully defined as the establishment of a covenant, inasmuch as Jehovah would be God to him and to his posterity (vers. 3 sqq.), and in chap. xxii. after the attestation of his faith and obedience, even to the sacrifice of his only son, where the innumerable increase of his seed and the blessing to pass from him to all nations were guaranteed by an oath. The same promise was afterwards renewed to Isaac, with a distinct allusion to the oath (chap. xxvi. 3, 4), and again to Jacob, both on his flight from Canaan for fear of Esau (chap. xxviii. 13, 14), and on his return thither (chap. xxxv. 11, 12). In the case of these renewals, it is only in chap. xxviii. 14 that the last expression, "all the families of the Adamah," is repeated *verbatim*, though with the additional clause "and in thy seed;" in the other passages "all the nations of the earth" are mentioned, the family connection being left out of sight, and the national character of the blessing being brought into especial prominence. In two instances also, instead of the *Niphal* נִבְרְכוּ we find the *Hithpael* הִתְבָּרֲכוּ. This change of conjugation by no means proves that the *Niphal* is to be taken in its original reflective sense. The *Hithpael* has no doubt the meaning "to wish one's self blessed" (Deut. xxix. 19), with בְּ of the person from whom the blessing is sought (Isa. lxv. 16; Jer. iv. 2), or whose blessing is desired

(Gen. xlviii. 20). But the *Niphal* נִבְרַךְ has only the passive signification " to be blessed." And the promise not only meant that all families of the earth would wish for the blessing which Abram possessed, but that they would really receive this blessing in Abram and his seed. By the explanation " wish themselves blessed" the point of the promise is broken off ; and not only is its connection with the prophecy of Noah respecting Japhet's dwelling in the tents of Shem overlooked, and the parallel between the blessing on all the families of the earth, and the curse pronounced upon the earth after the flood, destroyed, but the actual participation of all the nations of the earth in this blessing is rendered doubtful, and the application of this promise by Peter (Acts iii. 25) and Paul (Gal. iii. 8) to all nations, is left without any firm scriptural basis. At the same time, we must not attribute a passive signification on that account to the *Hithpael* in chap. xxii. 18 and xxvi. 4. In these passages prominence is given to the subjective attitude of the nations towards the blessing of Abraham,—in other words, to the fact that the nations would desire the blessing promised to them in Abraham and his seed.

Vers. 4—9. REMOVAL TO CANAAN.—Abram cheerfully followed the call of the Lord, and " departed as the Lord had spoken to him." He was then 75 years old. His age is given, because a new period in the history of mankind commenced with his exodus. After this brief notice there follows a more circumstantial account, in ver. 5, of the fact that he left Haran with his wife, with Lot, and with all that they possessed of servants and cattle, whereas Terah remained in Haran (cf. chap. xi. 31). הַנֶּפֶשׁ אֲשֶׁר עָשׂוּ are not the souls which they had begotten, but the male and female slaves that Abram and Lot had acquired.— Ver. 6. On his arival in Canaan, " *Abram passed through the land to the place of Sichem :* " *i.e.* the place where Sichem, the present Nablus, afterwards stood, between Ebal and Gerizim, in the heart of the land. " *To the terebinth* (or, according to Deut. xi. 30, the terebinths) *of Moreh :* " אֵלוֹן, אֵיל (chap. xiv. 6) and אֵילָה are the terebinth, אַלּוֹן and אַלָּה the oak; though in many MSS. and editions אַלּוֹן and אֵלוֹן are interchanged in Josh. xix. 33 and Judg. iv. 11, either because the pointing in one of these passages is inaccurate, or because the word itself was uncertain, as the ever-green oaks and terebinths resemble one another in the colour of their foliage and their fissured bark of sombre grey.—The notice that "*the Canaanites were then in the land*" does not point to a post-Mosaic date, when the Canaanites were extinct. For it does not mean that the Canaanites were then still in the land, but refers to the promise which follows, that God would give this land to the seed of Abram (ver. 7), and merely states that the land into which Abram had come was not uninhabited and without a possessor ; so that Abram could not regard it at once as his own and proceed to take possession of it, but could only wander in it in faith as in a foreign land (Heb. xi. 9).—Ver. 7. Here in Sichem Jehovah appeared to him, and assured him of the possession of the land of Canaan for his descendants. The assurance was made by means of an appearance of Jehovah, as a sign that this land was henceforth to be the scene of the manifestation of Jehovah. Abram understood this, "*and there builded he an altar to Jehovah, who appeared to him*," to make the soil which was hallowed by the appearance of God a place for the worship of the God who appeared to him.—Ver. 8. He did this also in the mountains, to which he probably removed to secure the necessary pasture for his flocks, after he had pitched his tent there "*Bethel westwards and Ai eastwards,*" *i.e.* in a spot with Ai to the east and Bethel to the west. The name *Bethel* occurs here proleptically : at the time referred to, it was still called *Luz* (chap. xxviii. 19); its present name is *Beitin* (*Robinson's* Palestine). At a distance of about five miles to the east was *Ai*, ruins of which are still to be seen, bearing the name of *Medinet Gai* (*Ritter's Erdkunde*). On the words "*called upon the name of the Lord,*" see chap. iv. 26. From this point Abram proceeded slowly to the *Negeb*, *i.e.* to the southern district of Canaan towards the Arabian desert (*vid.* chap. xx. 1).

Vers. 10-20. ABRAM IN EGYPT.—Abram had scarcely passed through the land promised to his seed, when a famine compelled him to leave it, and take refuge in Egypt, which abounded in corn ; just as the Bedouins in the neighbourhood are accustomed to do now. Whilst the famine in Canaan was to teach Abram, that even in the promised land food and clothing come from the Lord and His blessing, he was to discover in

Egypt that earthly craft is soon put to shame when dealing with the possessor of the power of this world, and that help and deliverance are to be found with the Lord alone, who can so smite the mightiest kings, that they cannot touch His chosen or do them harm (Ps. cv. 14, 15).—When trembling for his life in Egypt on account of the beauty of Sarai his wife, he arranged with her, as he approached that land, that she should give herself out as his sister, since she really was his half-sister (chap. xi. 29). He had already made an arrangement with her, that she should do this in certain possible contingencies, when they first removed to Canaan (chap. xx. 13). The conduct of the Sodomites (chap. xix.) was a proof that he had reason for his anxiety; and it was not without cause even so far as Egypt was concerned. But his precaution did not spring from faith. He might possibly hope, that by means of the plan concerted, he should escape the danger of being put to death on account of his wife, if any one should wish to take her; but how he expected to save the honour and retain possession of his wife, we cannot understand, though we must assume, that he thought he should be able to protect and keep her as his sister more easily, than if he acknowledged her as his wife. But the very thing he feared and hoped to avoid actually occurred.—Vers. 15 sqq. The princes of Pharaoh finding her very beautiful, extolled her beauty to the king, and she was taken to Pharaoh's house. As Sarah was then 65 years old (cf. chap. xvii. 17 and xii. 4), her beauty at such an age has been made a difficulty by some. But as she lived to the age of 127 (chap. xxiii. 1), she was then middle-aged; and as her vigour and bloom had not been tried by bearing children, she might easily appear very beautiful in the eyes of the Egyptians, whose wives, according to both ancient and modern testimony, were generally ugly, and faded early. *Pharaoh* (the Egyptian *ouro*, king, with the article *Pi*) is the Hebrew name for all the Egyptian kings in the Old Testament; their proper names being only occasionally mentioned, as, for example, Necho in 2 Kings xxiii. 29, or Hophra in Jer. xliv. 30. For Sarai's sake Pharaoh treated Abram well, presenting him with cattle and slaves, possessions which constitute the wealth of nomads. These presents Abram could not refuse, though by accepting them he increased his sin. God then interfered (ver. 17), and smote Pharaoh and his house with great plagues. What the nature of these plagues was, cannot be determined; they were certainly of such a kind, however, that whilst Sarah was preserved by them from dishonour, Pharaoh saw at once that they were sent as punishment by the Deity on account of his relation to Sarai; he may also have learned, on inquiry from Sarai herself, that she was Abram's wife. He gave her back to him, therefore, with a reproof for his untruthfulness, and told him to depart, appointing men to conduct him out of the land together with his wife and all his possessions. שָׁלַח, to dismiss, to give an escort (xviii. 16, xxxi. 27), does not necessarily denote an involuntary dismissal here. For as Pharaoh had discovered in the plague the wrath of the God of Abraham, he did not venture to treat him harshly, but rather sought to mitigate the anger of his God, by the safe-conduct which he granted him on his departure. But Abram was not justified by this result, as was very apparent from the fact, that he was mute under Pharaoh's reproofs, and did not venture to utter a single word in vindication of his conduct, as he did in the similar circumstances described in chap. xx. 11, 12. The saving mercy of God had so humbled him, that he silently acknowledged his guilt in concealing his relation to Sarah from the Egyptian king.

ABRAM'S SEPARATION FROM LOT.—CHAP. XIII.

Vers. 1–4. Abram, having returned from Egypt to the south of Canaan with his wife and property uninjured, through the gracious protection of God, proceeded with Lot לְמַסָּעָיו " *according to his journeys*" (*lit.* with the repeated breaking up of his camp, required by a nomad life; on נָסַע to break up a tent, to remove, see Ex. xii. 37) into the neighbourhood of Bethel and Ai, where he had previously encamped and built an altar (chap. xii. 8), that he might there call upon the name of the Lord again. That וַיִּקְרָא (ver. 4) is not a continuation of the relative clause, but a resumption of the main sentence, and therefore corresponds with וַיֵּלֶךְ (ver. 3), "*he went . . . and called upon the name of the Lord there*," has been correctly concluded by *Delitzsch* from the repetition of the subject *Abram.*—Vers. 5–7. But as Abram was very rich (כָּבֵד, *lit. weighty*) in possessions (מִקְנֶה, *cattle and slaves*), and Lot also had flocks, and herds, and tents (אֹהָלִים for אֳהָלִים, *Ges.* § 93, 6, 3) for his men, of whom there must have been many therefore, the land *did not bear them when dwelling together* (נָשָׂא, masculine at the commencement of the sentence, as is often the case when the verb precedes the subject, *vid. Ges.* § 147), *i.e.* the land did not furnish space enough for the numerous herd to graze. Consequently disputes arose between the two parties of herdsmen. The difficulty was increased by the fact that the Canaanites and Perizzites were then dwelling in the land, so that the space was very contracted. The *Perizzites,* who are mentioned here and in chap. xxxiv. 30, Judg. i. 4, along with the Canaanites, and who are placed in the other lists of the inhabitants of Canaan among the different Canaanitish tribes (chap. xv. 20 ; Ex. iii. 8, 17, etc.), are not mentioned among the descendants of Canaan (chap. x. 15–17), and may therefore, like the Kenites, Kenizzites, Kadmonites, and Rephaim (xv. 19–21), not have been descendants of Ham at all. The common explanation of the name Perizzite as equivalent to יֹשֵׁב אֶרֶץ פְּרָזוֹת "inhabitant of the level ground" (Ezek. xxxviii. 11), is at variance not only with the form of the word, the inhabitant of the level ground being called הַפְּרָזִי (Deut. iii. 5), but with the fact of their combination sometimes with the Canaanites, sometimes with the other tribes of Canaan, whose names were derived from their founders. Moreover, to explain the term " Canaanite," as denoting " the civilised inhabitants of towns," or " the trading Phœnicians," is just as arbitrary as if we were to regard the Kenites, Kenizzites, and the other tribes mentioned chap. xv. 19 sqq. along with the Canaanites, as all alike traders or inhabitants of towns. The origin of the name Perizzite is involved in obscurity, like that of the Kenites and other tribes settled in Canaan that were not descended from Ham. But we may infer from the frequency with which they are mentioned in connection with the Hamitic inhabitants of Canaan, that they were widely dispersed among the latter. *Vid.* chap. xv. 19–21.—Vers. 8, 9. To put an end to the strife between their herdsmen, Abram proposed to Lot that they should separate, as strife was unseemly between אֲנָשִׁים אַחִים, men who stood in the relation of brethren, and left him to choose his ground. *" If thou to the left, I will turn to the right ; and if thou to the right, I will turn to the left."* Although Abram was the older, and the leader of the company, he was magnanimous enough to leave the choice to his nephew, who was the younger, in the confident assurance that the Lord would so direct the decision, that His promise would be fulfilled.—Vers. 10–13. Lot chose what was apparently the best portion of the land, the whole district of the Jordan, or the valley on both sides of the Jordan from the Lake of Gennesareth to what was then the vale of Siddim. For previous to the destruction of Sodom and Gomorrah, this whole country was well watered, " *as the garden of Jehovah*," the garden planted by Jehovah in paradise, and " *as Egypt*," the land rendered so fertile by the overflowing of the Nile, " *in the direction of Zoar.*" Abram therefore remained in the land of Canaan, whilst Lot settled in the cities of the plain of the Jordan, and tented (pitched his tents) as far as Sodom. In anticipation of the succeeding history (chap. xix.), it is mentioned here (ver. 13), that the inhabitants of Sodom were very wicked, and sinful before Jehovah.—Vers. 14–18. After Lot's departure, Jehovah repeated to Abram (by a mental, inward assurance, as we may infer from the fact that אָמַר " said " is not accompanied by וַיֵּרָא " he appeared") His promise that He would give the land to him and to his seed in its whole extent, northward, and southward, and eastward, and westward, and would make his seed innumerable like the dust of the earth. From this we may see that the separation of Lot was in accordance with the will of God, as Lot had no share in the promise of God; though God afterwards saved him from destruction for Abram's sake. The possession of the land is promised עַד עוֹלָם " *for ever.*" The promise of God is unchangeable. As the seed of Abraham was to exist before God for ever, so Canaan was to be its everlasting possession. But this applied not to the lineal posterity of Abram, to his seed according to the flesh, but to the true spiritual seed, which embraced the promise in faith, and held it in a pure believing heart. The promise, therefore, neither precluded the expulsion of the unbelieving seed from the land of Canaan, nor guarantees to existing Jews a return to the earthly Palestine after their conversion to Christ. For as *Calvin* justly says, " *quum terra in sæculum promittitur, non simpliciter notatur perpetuitas; sed quæ finem accepit in Christo.*" Through Christ the promise has been exalted from its temporal form to its true essence; through Him the whole earth becomes Canaan (*vid.* chap. xvii. 8). That Abram might appropriate this renewed and now more fully expanded promise, Jehovah directed him to walk through the land in the length of it and the breadth of it. In doing this he came in his "*tenting*," *i.e.* his wandering through the land, to Hebron, where he settled by the terebinth of the Amorite Mamre (chap. xiv. 13), and built an altar to Jehovah. The term ישֶׁב (set himself, settled down, sat, dwelt) denotes that Abram made this place the central point of his subsequent stay in Canaan (cf. chap. xiv. 13, xviii. 1, and chap. xxiii.). On Hebron, see chap. xxiii. 2.

ABRAM'S MILITARY EXPEDITION; AND HIS SUBSEQUENT
MEETING WITH MELCHIZEDEK.—CHAP. XIV.

Vers. 1–12. The war, which furnished Abram with an opportunity, while in the promised land of which as yet he could not really call a single rood his own, to prove himself a valiant warrior, and not only to smite the existing chiefs of the imperial power of Asia, but to bring back to the kings of Canaan the booty that had been carried off, is circumstantially described, not so much in the interests of secular history as on account of its significance in relation to the kingdom of God. It is of importance, however, as a simple historical fact, to see that in the statement in ver. 1, the king of Shinar occupies the first place, although the king of Edom, Chedorlaomer, not only took the lead in the expedition, and had allied himself for that purpose with the other kings, but had previously subjugated the cities of the valley of Siddim, and therefore had extended his dominion very widely over hither Asia. If, notwithstanding this, the time of the war related here is connected with "*the days of Amraphel, king of Shinar*," this is done, no doubt, with reference to the fact that the first worldly kingdom was founded in Shinar by Nimrod (chap. x. 10), a kingdom which still existed under Amraphel, though it was now confined to Shinar itself, whilst Elam possessed the supremacy in inner Asia. There is no ground whatever for regarding the four kings mentioned in ver. 1 as four Assyrian generals or viceroys, as Josephus has done in direct contradiction to the biblical text; for, according to the more careful historical researches, the commencement of the Assyrian kingdom belongs to a later period; and *Berosus* speaks of an earlier Median rule in Babylon, which reaches as far back as the

age of the patriarchs (cf. *M. v. Niebuhr, Gesch. Assurs,* p. 271).
It appears significant also, that the imperial power of Asia had
already extended as far as Canaan, and had subdued the valley of
the Jordan, no doubt with the intention of holding the Jordan
valley as the high-road to Egypt. We have here a prelude of
the future assault of the worldly power upon the kingdom of
God established in Canaan; and the importance of this event to
sacred history consists in the fact, that the kings of the valley of
the Jordan and the surrounding country submitted to the worldly
power, whilst Abram, on the contrary, with his home-born servants, smote the conquerors and rescued their booty,—a prophetic sign that in the conflict with the power of the world the
seed of Abram would not only not be subdued, but would be
able to rescue from destruction those who appealed to it for aid.

In vers. 1–3 the account is introduced by a list of the parties
eugaged in war. The kings named here are not mentioned
again. On *Shinar,* see chap. x. 10; and on *Elam,* chap. x. 22.
It cannot be determined with certainty where *Ellasar* was.
Knobel supposes it to be *Artemita,* which was also called Χαλάσαρ,
in southern Assyria, to the north of Babylon. *Goyim* is not
used here for nations generally, but is the name of one particular nation or country. In *Delitzsch's* opinion it is an older
name for Galilee, though probably with different boundaries (cf.
Josh. xii. 23; Judg. iv. 2; and Isa. ix. 1).—The verb עָשׂוּ (*made*),
in ver. 2, is governed by the kings mentioned in ver. 1. To
Bela, whose king is not mentioned by name, the later name *Zoar*
(*vid.* xix. 22) is added as being better known.—Ver. 3. "*All
these* (five kings) *allied themselves together,* (and came with their
forces) *into the vale of Siddim* (הַשִּׂדִּים, prob. fields or plains),
which is the Salt Sea;" that is to say, which was changed into the
Salt Sea on the destruction of its cities (chap. xix. 24, 25). That
there should be five kings in the five cities (πεντάπολις, Wisdom
x. 6) of this valley, was quite in harmony with the condition of
Canaan, where even at a later period every city had its king.—
Vers. 4 sqq. The occasion of the war was the revolt of the kings
of the vale of Siddim from Chedorlaomer. They had been
subject to him for twelve years, "*and the thirteenth year they rebelled.*" In the fourteenth year Chedorlaomer came with his
allies to punish them for their rebellion, and attacked on his way
several other cities to the east of the Arabah, as far as the

Elanitic Gulf, no doubt because they also had withdrawn from his dominion. The army moved along the great military road from inner Asia, past Damascus, through Peræa, where they smote the Rephaims, Zuzims, Emims, and Horites. " *The Rephaim in Ashteroth Karnaim:* " all that is known with certainty of the Rephaim is, that they were a tribe of gigantic stature, and in the time of Abram had spread over the whole of Peræa, and held not only Bashan, but the country afterwards possessed by the Moabites; from which possessions they were subsequently expelled by the descendants of Lot and the Amorites, and so nearly exterminated, that Og, king of Bashan, is described as the remnant of the Rephaim (Deut. ii. 20, iii. 11, 13; Josh. xii. 4, xiii. 12). Beside this, there were Rephaim on this side of the Jordan among the Canaanitish tribes (chap. xv. 20), some to the west of Jerusalem, in the valley which was called after them the valley of the Rephaim (Josh. xv. 8, xviii. 16; 2 Sam. v. 18, etc.), others on the mountains of Ephraim (Josh. xvii. 15); while the last remains of them were also to be found among the Philistines (2 Sam. xxi. 16 sqq.; 1 Chron. xx. 4 sqq.). The current explanation of the name, viz. " the long-stretched," or giants (*Ewald*), does not prevent our regarding רָפָא as the personal name of their forefather, though no intimation is given of their origin. That they were not Canaanites may be inferred from the fact, that on the eastern side of the Jordan they were subjugated and exterminated by the Canaanitish branch of the Amorites. Notwithstanding this, they may have been descendants of Ham, though the fact that the Canaanites spoke a Semitic tongue rather favours the conclusion that the oldest population of Canaan, and therefore the Rephaim, were of Semitic descent. At any rate, the opinion of *J. G. Müller,* that they belonged to the aborigines, who were not related to Shem, Ham, and Japhet, is perfectly arbitrary.—*Ashteroth Karnaim,* or briefly *Ashtaroth,* the capital afterwards of Og of Bashan, was situated in Hauran; and ruins of it are said to be still seen in *Tell Ashtereh,* two hours and a half from *Nowah,* and one and three-quarters from the ancient *Edrei,* somewhere between Nowah and Mezareib (see *Ritter, Erdkunde*).[1]—" *The Zuzims in Ham*"

---

[1] *J. G. Wetztein,* however, has lately denied the identity of Ashteroth Karnaim, which he interprets as meaning Ashtaroth near Karnaim, with Ashtaroth the capital of Og (See *Reiseber. üb. Hauran,* etc. 1860, p. 107).

were probably the people whom the Ammonites called *Zam zummim*, and who were also reckoned among the Rephaim (Deut. ii. 20). *Ham* was possibly the ancient name of *Rabba* of the Ammonites (Deut. iii. 11), the remains being still preserved in the ruins of *Ammân*.—" *The Emim in the plain of Kiryathaim :*" the אֵימִים or אֵמִים (*i.e.* fearful, terrible), were the earlier inhabitants of the country of the Moabites, who gave them the name; and, like the Anakim, they were also reckoned among the Rephaim (Deut. ii. 11). *Kiryathaim* is certainly not to be found where *Eusebius* and *Jerome* supposed, viz. in Καριάδα, *Coraiatha,* the modern *Koerriath* or *Kereyat,* ten miles to the west of Medabah; for this is not situated in the plain, and corresponds to *Kerioth* (Jer. xlviii. 24), with which *Eusebius* and *Jerome* have confounded *Kiryathaim.* It is probably still to be seen in the ruins of *el Teym* or *et Tueme,* about a mile to the west of Medabah. " *The Horites* (from חֹרִי, dwellers in caves), *in the mountains of Seir,*" were the earlier inhabitants of the land between the Dead Sea and the Elanitic Gulf, who were conquered and exterminated by the Edomites (xxxvi. 20 sqq.).— " *To El-Paran, which is by the wilderness :*" *i.e.* on the eastern side of the desert of Paran (see chap. xxi. 21), probably the same as *Elath* (Deut. ii. 8) or *Eloth* (1 Kings ix. 26), the important harbour of *Aila* on the northern extremity of the so-called Elanitic Gulf, near the modern fortress of *Akaba,* where extensive heaps of rubbish show the site of the former town, which received its name *El* or *Elath* (*terebinth,* or rather *wood*) probably from the palm-groves in the vicinity.—Ver. 7. From *Aila* the conquerors turned round, and marched (not through the Arabah, but on the desert plateau which they ascended from

But he does so without sufficient reason. He disputes most strongly the fact that Ashtaroth was situated on the hill Ashtere, because the Arabs now in Hauran assured him, that the ruins of this Tell (or hill) suggested rather a monastery or watch-tower than a large city, and associates it with the *Bostra* of the Greeks and Romans, the modern *Bozra,* partly on account of the central situation of this town, and its consequent importance to Hauran and Peræa generally, and partly also on account of the similarity in the name, as *Bostra* is the latinized form of *Beeshterah,* which we find in Josh. xxi. 27 in the place of the Ashtaroth of 1 Chron. vi. 56; and that form is composed of *Beth Ashtaroth,* to which there are as many analogies as there are instances of the omission of *Beth* before the names of towns, which is a sufficient explanation of Ashtaroth (cf. *Ges. thes.,* p. 175 and 193).

Aila) to *En-mishpat* (*well of judgment*), the older name of *Kadesh,* the situation of which, indeed, cannot be proved with certainty, but which is most probably to be sought for in the neighbourhood of the spring *Ain Kades,* discovered by *Rowland,* to the south of *Bir Seba* and *Khalasa* (*Elusa*), twelve miles E.S.E. of *Moyle,* the halting-place for caravans, near Hagar's well (xvi. 14), on the heights of *Jebel Halal* (see *Ritter, Erdkunde,* and Num. xiii.). " *And they smote all the country of the Amalekites,*" *i.e.* the country afterwards possessed by the Amalekites (*vid.* chap. xxxvi. 12),[1] to the west of Edomitis on the southern border of the mountains of Judah (Num. xiii. 29), " *and also the Amorites, who dwelt in Hazazon-Thamar,*" *i.e. Engedi,* on the western side of the Dead Sea (2 Chron. xx. 2).—Vers. 8 sqq. After conquering all these tribes to the east and west of the Arabah, they gave battle to the kings of the Pentapolis in the vale of Siddim, and put them to flight. The kings of Sodom and Gomorrah fell there, the valley being full of asphalt-pits, and the ground therefore unfavourable for flight; but the others escaped to the mountains (הֶרָה for הָהָרָה), that is, to the Moabitish highlands with their numerous defiles. The conquerors thereupon plundered the cities of Sodom and Gomorrah, and carried off Lot, who dwelt in Sodom, and all his possessions, along with the rest of the captives, probably taking the route through the valley of the Jordan up to Damascus.

Vers. 13–16. A fugitive (lit. *the* fugitive; the article denotes the genus, Ewald, § 277) brought intelligence of this to Abram the *Hebrew* (הָעִבְרִי, an immigrant from beyond the Euphrates). Abram is so called in distinction from Mamre and his two brothers, who were Amorites, and had made a defensive treaty with him. To rescue Lot, Abram *ordered his trained slaves* (חֲנִיכָיו, *i.e.* practised in arms) *born in the house* (cf. xvii. 12), 318 *men, to turn out* (*lit.* to pour themselves out); and with these, and (as the supplementary remark in ver. 24 shows) with his allies, he pursued the enemy as far as *Dan,* where " *he divided*

---

[1] The circumstance that in the midst of a list of tribes who were defeated, we find not the tribe but only the *fields* (שָׂדֵה) of the Amalekites mentioned, can only be explained on the supposition that the nation of the Amalekites was not then in existence, and the country was designated proleptically by the name of its future and well-known inhabitants (*Hengstenberg,* Diss. ii. p. 249, translation).

himself against them, he and his servants, by night,"—*i.e.* he divided his men into companies, who fell upon the enemy by night from different sides,—" *smote them, and pursued them to Hobah, to the left* (or north) *of Damascus."* Hobah has probably been preserved in the village of *Hoba,* mentioned by *Troilo,* a quarter of a mile to the north of Damascus. So far as the situation of *Dan* is concerned, this passage proves that it cannot have been identical with *Leshem* or *Laish* in the valley of Beth Rehob, which the Danites conquered and named Dan (Judg. xviii. 28, 29; Josh. xix. 47); for this Laish-Dan was on the central source of the Jordan, *el Leddan* in *Tell el Kady,* which does not lie in either of the two roads, leading from the vale of Siddim or of the Jordan to Damascus.[1] This Dan belonged to Gilead (Deut. xxxiv. 1), and is no doubt the same as the *Dan-Jaan* mentioned in 2 Sam. xxiv. 6 in connection with Gilead, and to be sought for in northern Peræa to the south-west of Damascus.

Vers. 17–24.—As Abram returned with the booty which he had taken from the enemy, the king of Sodom (of course, the successor to the one who fell in the battle) and Melchizedek, king of Salem, came to meet him to congratulate him on his victory; the former probably also with the intention of asking for the prisoners who had been rescued. They met him in *" the valley of Shaveh, which is* (what was afterwards called) *the King's dale."* This valley, in which Absalom erected a monument for himself (2 Sam. xviii. 18), was, according to *Josephus,* two *stadia* from Jerusalem, probably by the brook Kidron therefore, although Absalom's pillar, which tradition places there, was of the Grecian style rather than the early Hebrew. The name *King's dale* was given to it undoubtedly with reference to the event referred to here, which points to the neighbourhood of Jerusalem. For the *Salem* of Melchizedek cannot have been the Salem near to which John baptized (John iii. 23), or Ænon, which was eight Roman miles south of Scythopolis, as a march

---

[1] One runs below the Sea of Galilee past Fik and Nowa, almost in a straight line to Damascus; the other from Jacob's Bridge, below Lake Merom. But if the enemy, instead of returning with their booty to Thapsacus, on the Euphrates, by one of the direct roads leading from the Jordan past Damascus and Palmyra, had gone through the land of Canaan to the sources of the Jordan, they would undoubtedly, when defeated at Laish-Dan, have fled through the *Wady et Teim* and the *Bekaa* to Hamath, and not by Damascus at all (*vid. Robinson,* Bibl. Researches.

of about forty hours for the purpose of meeting Abraham, if not romantic, would at least be at variance with the text of Scripture, where the kings are said to have gone out to Abram after his return. It must be Jerusalem, therefore, which is called by the old name *Salem* in Ps. lxxvi. 2, out of which the name Jerusalem (founding of peace, or possession of peace) was formed by the addition of the prefix יְרוּ = יְרוּ "founding," or יְרֹשׁ "possession." Melchizedek brings bread and wine from Salem " to supply the exhausted warriors with food and drink, but more especially as a mark of gratitude to Abram, who had conquered for them peace, freedom, and prosperity" (*Delitzsch*). This gratitude he expresses, as a priest of the supreme God, in the words, " *Blessed be Abram of the Most High God, the founder of heaven and earth; and blessed be God, the Most High, who hath delivered thine enemies into thy hand.*" The form of the blessing is poetical, two parallel members with words peculiar to poetry, צָרֶיךָ for אֹיְבֶיךָ, and מִגֵּן.—אֵל עֶלְיוֹן without the article is a proper name for the supreme God, the God over all (cf. Ex. xviii. 11), who is pointed out as the only true God by the additional clause, " founder of the heaven and the earth." On the construction of בָּרוּךְ with לְ, *vid.* chap. xxxi. 15, Ex. xii. 16, and *Ges.* § 143, 2. קֹנֵה, founder and possessor : קָנָה combines the meanings of κτίζειν and κτᾶσθαι. This priestly reception Abram reciprocated by giving him the tenth of all, *i.e.* of the whole of the booty taken from the enemy. Giving the tenth was a practical acknowledgment of the divine priesthood of Melchizedek ; for the tenth was, according to the general custom, the offering presented to the Deity. Abram also acknowledged the God of Melchizedek as the true God ; for when the king of Sodom asked for his people only, and would have left the rest of the booty to Abram, he lifted up his hand as a solemn oath " *to Jehovah, the Most High God, the founder of heaven and earth,*"— acknowledging himself as the servant of this God by calling Him by the name Jehovah,—and swore that he would not take " *from a thread to a shoe-string,*" *i.e.* the smallest or most worthless thing belonging to the king of Sodom, that he might not be able to say, he had made Abram rich. אִם, as the sign of an oath, is negative, and in an earnest address is repeated before the verb. " *Except* (בִּלְעָדַי, *lit.* not to me, nothing for me) *only what the young men* (Abram's men) *have eaten, and the portion*

of my allies . . . . *let them take their portion:*" *i.e.* his followers
should receive what had been consumed as their share, and the
allies should have the remainder of the booty.

Of the property belonging to the king of Sodom, which he
had taken from the enemy, Abram would not keep the smallest
part, because he would not have anything in common with
Sodom. On the other hand, he accepted from Salem's priest
and king, Melchizedek, not only bread and wine for the invigoration of the exhausted warriors, but a priestly blessing also,
and gave him in return the tenth of all his booty, as a sign that
he acknowledged this king as a priest of the living God, and
submitted to his royal priesthood. In this self-subordination of
Abram to Melchizedek there was the practical prediction of a
royal priesthood which is higher than the priesthood entrusted to
Abram's descendants, the sons of Levi, and foreshadowed in the
noble form of Melchizedek, who blessed as king and priest the
patriarch whom God had called to be a blessing to all the families of the earth. The name of this royal priest is full of meaning: *Melchizedek, i.e.* King of Righteousness. Even though,
judging from Josh. x. 1, 3, where a much later king is called
Adonizedek, i.e. Lord of Righteousness, this name may have
been a standing title of the ancient kings of Salem, it no doubt
originated with a king who ruled his people in righteousness,
and was perfectly appropriate in the case of the Melchizedek
mentioned here. There is no less significance in the name of
the seat of his government, *Salem,* the peaceful or peace, since
it shows that the capital of its kings was a citadel of peace, not
only as a natural stronghold, but through the righteousness of
its sovereign; for which reason David chose it as the seat of
royalty in Israel; and Moriah, which formed part of it, was
pointed out to Abraham by Jehovah as the place of sacrifice for
the kingdom of God which was afterwards to be established.
And, lastly, there was something very significant in the appearance in the midst of the degenerate tribes of Canaan of this
king of righteousness, and priest of the true God of heaven and
earth, without any account of his descent, or of the beginning
and end of his life; so that he stands forth in the Scriptures,
" without father, without mother, without descent, having neither
beginning of days nor end of life." Although it by no means
follows from this, however, that Melchizedek was a celestial

being (the Logos, or an angel), or one of the primeval patriarchs
(Enoch or Shem), as Church fathers, Rabbins, and others have
conjectured, and we can see in him nothing more than one, perhaps the last, of the witnesses and confessors of the early revelation of God, coming out into the light of history from the dark
night of heathenism; yet this appearance does point to a priesthood of universal significance, and to a higher order of things,
which existed at the commencement of the world, and is one day
to be restored again. In all these respects, the noble form of
this king of Salem and priest of the Most High God was a
type of the God-King and eternal High Priest Jesus Christ;
a thought which is expanded in Heb. vii. on the basis of this
account, and of the divine utterance revealed to David in the
Spirit, that the King of Zion sitting at the right hand of Jehovah should be a priest for ever after the order of Melchizedek
(Ps. cx. 4).

THE COVENANT.—CHAP. XV

With the formula "*after these things*" there is introduced a
new revelation of the Lord to Abram, which differs from the
previous ones in form and substance, and constitutes a new
turning point in his life. The "*word of Jehovah*" came to him
"*in a vision;*" *i.e.* neither by a direct internal address, nor by such
a manifestation of Himself as fell upon the outward senses, nor
in a dream of the night, but in a state of ecstasy by an inward
spiritual intuition, and that not in a nocturnal vision, as in chap.
xlvi. 2, but in the day-time. The expression "in a vision" applies to the whole chapter. There is no pause anywhere, nor
any sign that the vision ceased, or that the action was transferred to the sphere of the senses and of external reality. Consequently the whole process is to be regarded as an internal
one. The vision embraces not only vers. 1–4 or 8, but the
entire chapter, with this difference merely, that from ver. 12
onwards the ecstasy assumed the form of a prophetic sleep produced by God. It is true that the bringing Abram out, his
seeing the stars (ver. 5), and still more especially his taking the
sacrificial animals and dividing them (vers. 9, 10), have been
supposed by some to belong to the sphere of external reality,
on the ground that these purely external acts would not neces-

sarily presuppose a cessation of the ecstasy, since the vision was no catalepsy, and did not preclude the full (?) use of the outward senses. But however true this may be, not only is every mark wanting, which would warrant us in assuming a transition from the purely inward and spiritual sphere, to the outward sphere of the senses, but the entire revelation culminates in a prophetic sleep, which also bears the character of a vision. As it was in a deep sleep that Abram saw the passing of the divine appearance through the carefully arranged portions of the sacrifice, and no reference is made either to the burning of them, as in Judg. vi. 21, or to any other removal, the arrangement of the sacrificial animals must also have been a purely internal process. To regard this as an outward act, we must break up the continuity of the narrative in a most arbitrary way, and not only transfer the commencement of the vision into the night, and suppose it to have lasted from twelve to eighteen hours, but we must interpolate the burning of the sacrifices, etc., in a still more arbitrary manner, merely for the sake of supporting the erroneous assumption, that visionary procedures had no objective reality, or, at all events, less evidence of reality than outward acts, and things perceived by the senses. A vision wrought by God was not a mere fancy, or a subjective play of the thoughts, but a spiritual fact, which was not only in all respects as real as things discernible by the senses, but which surpassed in its lasting significance the acts and events that strike the eye. The covenant which Jehovah made with Abram was not intended to give force to a mere agreement respecting mutual rights and obligations,—a thing which could have been accomplished by an external sacrificial transaction, and by God passing through the divided animals in an assumed human form,— but it was designed to establish the purely spiritual relation of a living fellowship between God and Abram, of the deep inward meaning of which, nothing but a spiritual intuition and experience could give to Abram an effective and permanent hold.

Vers. 1-6. The words of Jehovah run thus: "*Fear not, Abram: I am a shield to thee, thy reward very much.*" הַרְבֵּה an *inf. absol.*, generally used adverbially, but here as an adjective, equivalent to "*thy very great reward.*" The divine promise to be a *shield* to him, that is to say, a protection against all enemies, and a *reward, i.e.* richly to reward his confidence, his ready obedience, stands here, as the opening words "after these things" indicate, in close connection with the previous guidance of Abram. Whilst the protection of his wife in Egypt was a practical pledge of the possibility of his having a posterity, and the separation of Lot, followed by the conquest of the kings of the East, was also a pledge of the possibility of his one day possessing the promised land, there was as yet no prospect whatever of the promise being realized, that he should become a great nation, and possess an innumerable posterity. In these circumstances, anxiety about the future might naturally arise in his mind. To meet this, the word of the Lord came to him with the comforting assurance, "Fear not, I am thy shield." But when the Lord added, "and thy very great reward," Abram could only reply, as he thought of his childless condition: "*Lord Jehovah, what wilt Thou give me, seeing I go childless?*" Of what avail are all my possessions, wealth, and power, since I have no child, and the heir of my house is Eliezer the Damascene? מֶשֶׁק, synonymous with מִמְשָׁק (Zeph. ii. 9), possession, or the seizure of possession, is chosen on account of its assonance with דַּמֶּשֶׂק. בֶּן־מֶשֶׁק, son of the seizing of possession = seizer of possession, or heir. *Eliezer of Damascus* (lit. Damascus viz. Eliezer): Eliezer is an explanatory apposition to Damascus, in the sense of the Damascene Eliezer; though דַּמֶּשֶׂק, on account of its position before אֱלִיעֶזֶר, cannot be taken grammatically as equivalent to דַּמַּשְׂקִי.[1]—To give still more distinct utterance to his grief, Abram adds (ver. 3): "*Behold, to me Thou hast given no seed; and lo, an inmate of my house* (בֶּן־בֵּיתִי in distinction from יְלִיד־בַּיִת, home-born, chap. xiv. 14) *will be my heir.*" The word of the Lord then came to him: "*Not he, but one who shall come forth from thy body, he will be thine heir.*" God then took him into the open air, told him to look up to heaven, and promised him a posterity as numerous as the innumerable host of stars (cf. chap. xxii. 17, xxvi. 4; Ex. xxxii. 13, etc). Whether Abram at this time was "in the body or out of the body," is a matter of no moment. The reality of the occurrence is the same in either case. This is evident from the remark made by Moses (the historian) as to the conduct of Abram in relation to

[1] The legend of Abram having been king in Damascus appears to have originated in this, though the passage before us does not so much as show that Abram obtained possession of Eliezer on his way through Damascus.

the promise of God: "*And he believed in Jehovah, and He counted it to him for righteousness.*" In the strictly objective character of the account in Genesis, in accordance with which the simple facts are related throughout without any introduction of subjective opinions, this remark appears so striking, that the question naturally arises, What led Moses to introduce it? In what way did Abram make known his faith in Jehovah? And in what way did Jehovah count it to him as righteousness? The reply to both questions must not be sought in the New Testament, but must be given or indicated in the context. What reply did Abram make on receiving the promise, or what did he do in consequence? When God, to confirm the promise, declared Himself to be Jehovah, who brought him out of Ur of the Chaldees to give him that land as a possession, Abram replied, "Lord, whereby shall I know that I shall possess it?" God then directed him to "fetch a heifer of three years old," etc.; and Abram fetched the animals required, and arranged them (as we may certainly suppose, though it is not expressly stated) as God had commanded him. By this readiness to perform what God commanded him, Abram gave a practical proof that he believed Jehovah; and what God did with the animals so arranged was a practical declaration on the part of Jehovah, that He reckoned this faith to Abram as righteousness. The significance of the divine act is, finally, summed up in ver. 18, in the words, "*On that day Jehovah made a covenant with Abram.*" Consequently Jehovah reckoned Abram's faith to him as righteousness, by making a covenant with him, by taking Abram into covenant fellowship with Himself. הֶאֱמִן, from אָמַן to continue and to preserve, to be firm and to confirm, in *Hiphil* to trust, believe (πιστεύειν), expresses "that state of mind which is sure of its object, and relies firmly upon it;" and as denoting conduct towards God, as "a firm, inward, personal, self-surrendering reliance upon a personal being, especially upon the source of all being," it is construed sometimes with לְ (*e.g.* Deut. ix. 23), but more frequently with בְּ (Num. xiv. 11, xx. 12; Deut. i. 32), "to believe the Lord," and "to believe on the Lord," to trust in Him,—πιστεύειν ἐπὶ τὸν Θεόν, as the apostle has more correctly rendered the ἐπίστευσεν—τῷ Θεῷ of the LXX. (*vid.* Rom. iv. 5). Faith therefore is not merely *assensus*, but *fiducia* also, unconditional trust in the Lord and His word, even where the natural course of events furnishes no ground for hope or expectation. This faith Abram manifested, as the apostle has shown in Rom. iv. ; and this faith God reckoned to him as righteousness by the actual conclusion of a covenant with him. צְדָקָה, righteousness, as a human characteristic, is correspondence to the will of God both in character and conduct, or a state answering to the divine purpose of a man's being. This was the state in which man was first created in the image of God ; but it was lost by sin, through which he placed himself in opposition to the will of God and to his own divinely appointed destiny, and could only be restored by God. When the human race had universally corrupted its way, Noah alone was found righteous before God (vii. 1), because he was blameless and walked with God (vi. 9). This righteousness Abram acquired through his unconditional trust in the Lord, his undoubting faith in His promise, and his ready obedience to His word. This state of mind, which is expressed in the words הֶאֱמִן בַּיהוָֹה, was reckoned to him as righteousness, so that God treated him as a righteous man, and formed such a relationship with him, that he was placed in living fellowship with God. The foundation of this relationship was laid in the manner described in vers. 7–11.

Vers. 7–11. Abram's question, " *Whereby shall I know that I shall take possession of it* (the land) ?" was not an expression of doubt, but of desire for the confirmation or sealing of a promise, which transcended human thought and conception. To gratify this desire, God commanded him to make preparation for the conclusion of a covenant. " *Take Me, He said, a heifer of three years old, and a she-goat of three years old, and a ram of three years old, and a turtle-dove, and a young pigeon ;*" one of every species of the animals suitable for sacrifice. Abram took these, and " *divided them in the midst,*" *i.e.* in half, " *and placed one half of each opposite to the other* (אִישׁ בִּתְרוֹ, every one its half, cf. xlii. 25 ; Num. xvii. 17) ; *only the birds divided he not,*" just as in sacrifice the doves were not divided into pieces, but placed upon the fire whole (Lev. i. 17). The animals chosen, as well as the fact that the doves were left whole, corresponded exactly to the ritual of sacrifice. Yet the transaction itself was not a real sacrifice, since there was neither sprinkling of blood nor offering upon an altar (*oblatio*), and no mention is made of the pieces being burned. The proceeding corresponded rather to the custom, prevalent in many ancient nations, of slaughtering animals when concluding a covenant, and after dividing them into pieces, of laying the pieces opposite to one another, that the persons making the covenant might pass between them. Thus *Ephraem Syrus* (1, 161) observes, that God condescended to follow the custom of the Chaldeans, that He might in the most solemn manner confirm His oath to Abram the Chaldean. The wide extension of this custom is evident from the expression used to denote the conclusion of a covenant, כָּרַת בְּרִית to hew, or cut a covenant, *Aram.* גְּזַר קְיָם, Greek ὅρκια τέμνειν, *fœdus ferire*, *i.e. ferienda hostia facere fœdus*; cf. *Bochart* (*Hieroz.* 1, 332); whilst it is evident from Jer. xxxiv. 18, that this was still customary among the Israelites of later times. The choice of sacrificial animals for a transaction which was not strictly a sacrifice, was founded upon the symbolical significance of the sacrificial animals, *i.e.* upon the fact that they represented and took the place of those who offered them. In the case before us, they were meant to typify the promised seed of Abram. This would not hold good, indeed, if the cutting of the animals had been merely intended to signify, that any who broke the covenant would be treated like the animals that were there cut in pieces. But there is no sure ground in Jer. xxxiv. 18 sqq. for thus interpreting the ancient custom. The meaning which the prophet there assigns to the symbolical usage, may be simply a different application of it, which does not preclude an earlier and different intention in the symbol. The division of the animals probably denoted originally the two parties to the covenant, and the passing of the latter through the pieces laid opposite to one another, their formation into one : a signification to which the other might easily have been attacned as a further consequence and explanation. And if in such a case the sacrificial animals represented the parties to the covenant, so also even in the present instance the sacrificial animals were fitted for that purpose, since, although originally representing only the owner or offerer of the sacrifice, by their consecration as sacrifices they were also brought into connection with Jehovah. But in the case before us the animals represented Abram and his seed, not in the fact of their being slaughtered, as significant of the slaying of that seed, but only in what happened to and in

connection with the slaughtered animals : birds of prey attempted
to eat them, and when extreme darkness came on, the glory of
God passed through them.   As all the seed of Abram was concerned, one of every kind of animal suitable for sacrifice was
taken, *ut ex toto populo et singulis partibus sacrificium unum
fieret* (*Calvin*).   The age of the animals, three years old, was
supposed by *Theodoret* to refer to the three generations of
Israel which were to remain in Egypt, or the three centuries
of captivity in a foreign land ; and this is rendered very probable
by the fact, that in Judg. vi. 25 the bullock of seven years old
undoubtedly refers to the seven years of Midianitish oppression.
On the other hand, we cannot find in the six halves of the three
animals and the undivided birds, either 7 things or the sacred
number 7, for two undivided birds cannot represent one whole,
but two ; nor can we attribute to the eight pieces any symbolical
meaning, for these numbers necessarily followed from the choice
of one specimen of every kind of animal that was fit for sacrifice, and from the division of the larger animals into two.—Ver.
11. " *Then birds of prey* (הָעַיִט with the article, as chap. xiv. 13)
came down upon the carcases, and Abram frightened them away."
The birds of prey represented the foes of Israel, who would
seek to eat up, *i.e.* exterminate it.   And the fact that Abram
frightened them away was a sign, that Abram's faith and his
relation to the Lord would preserve the whole of his posterity
from destruction, that Israel would be saved for Abram's sake
(Ps. cv. 42).

Vers. 12–17. " *And when the sun was just about to go down*
(on the construction, see Ges. § 132), *and deep sleep* (תַּרְדֵּמָה, as
in chap. ii. 21, a deep sleep produced by God) *had fallen upon
Abram, behold there fell upon him terror, great darkness.*"   The
vision here passes into a prophetic sleep produced by God.   In
this sleep there fell upon Abram dread and darkness ; this is
shown by the interchange of the perfect נפלה and the participle
נֹפֶלֶת.   The reference to the time is intended to show " the
supernatural character of the darkness and sleep, and the distinction between the vision and a dream" (*O. v. Gerlach*).   It
also possesses a symbolical meaning.   The setting of the sun
prefigured to Abram the departure of the sun of grace, which
shone upon Israel, and the commencement of a dark and dreadful period of suffering for his posterity, the very anticipation of

which involved Abram in darkness. For the words which he
heard in the darkness were these (vers. 13 sqq.) : *" Know of a
surety, that thy seed shall be a stranger in a land that is not theirs,
and shall serve them* (the lords of the strange land), *and they* (the
foreigners) *shall oppress them* 400 *years."* That these words
had reference to the sojourn of the children of Israel in Egypt,
is placed beyond all doubt by the fulfilment. The 400 years
were, according to prophetic language, a round number for the
430 years that Israel spent in Egypt (Ex. xii. 40). *" Also
that nation whom they shall serve will I judge* (see the fulfilment,
Ex. vi. 11) ; *and afterward shall they come out with great substance* (the actual fact according to Ex. xii. 31–36). *And thou
shalt go to thy fathers in peace, and be buried in a good old age*
(cf. chap. xxv. 7, 8) ; *and in the fourth generation they shall come
hither again."* The calculations are made here on the basis of a
hundred years to a generation : not too much for those times,
when the average duration of life was above 150 years, and
Isaac was born in the hundredth year of Abraham's life. *" For
the iniquity of the Amorites is not yet full."* *Amorite*, the name
of the most powerful tribe of the Canaanites, is used here as the
common name of all the inhabitants of Canaan, just as in Josh.
xxiv. 15 (cf. x. 5), Judg. vi. 10, etc.).—By this revelation
Abram had the future history of his seed pointed out to him in
general outlines, and was informed at the same time why
neither he nor his descendants could obtain immediate possession of the promised land, viz. because the Canaanites were not
yet ripe for the sentence of extermination.—Ver. 17. When
the sun had gone down, and thick darkness had come on (הָיָה
impersonal), *" behold a smoking furnace, and* (with) *a fiery
torch, which passed between those pieces,"*—a description of what
Abram saw in his deep prophetic sleep, corresponding to the
mysterious character of the whole proceeding. תַּנּוּר, a stove, is
a cylindrical fire-pot, such as is used in the dwelling-houses of
the East. The phenomenon, which passed through the pieces
as they lay opposite to one another, resembled such a smoking
stove, from which a fiery torch, *i.e.* a brilliant flame, was
streaming forth. In this symbol Jehovah manifested Himself
to Abram, just as He afterwards did to the people of Israel in
the pillar of cloud and fire. Passing through the pieces, He
ratified the covenant which He made with Abram. His glory

was enveloped in fire and smoke, the product of the consuming fire,—both symbols of the wrath of God (cf. Ps. xviii. 9, and *Hengstenberg in loc.*), whose fiery zeal consumes whatever opposes it (*vid.* Ex. iii. 2).—To establish and give reality to the covenant to be concluded with Abram, Jehovah would have to pass through the seed of Abram when oppressed by the Egyptians and threatened with destruction, and to execute judgment upon their oppressors (Ex. vii. 4, xii. 12). In this symbol, the passing of the Lord between the pieces meant something altogether different from the oath of the Lord by Himself in chap. xxii. 16, or by His life in Deut. xxxii. 40, or by His soul in Amos vi. 8 and Jer. li. 14. It set before Abram the condescension of the Lord to his seed, in the fearful glory of His majesty as the judge of their foes. Hence the pieces were not consumed by the fire; for the transaction had reference not to a sacrifice, which God accepted, and in which the soul of the offerer was to ascend in the smoke to God, but to a covenant in which God came down to man. From the nature of this covenant, it followed, however, that God alone went through the pieces in a symbolical representation of Himself, and not Abram also. For although a covenant always establishes a reciprocal relation between two individuals, yet in that covenant which God concluded with a man, the man did not stand on an equality with God, but God established the relation of fellowship by His promise and His gracious condescension to the man, who was at first purely a recipient, and was only qualified and bound to fulfil the obligations consequent upon the covenant by the reception of gifts of grace.

In vers. 18–21 this divine revelation is described as the making of a covenant (בְּרִית, from בָּרָה to cut, *lit.* the bond concluded by cutting up the sacrificial animals), and the substance of this covenant is embraced in the promise, that God would give that land to the seed of Abram, from the river of Egypt to the great river Euphrates. The river (נְהַר) of Egypt is the Nile, and not the brook (נַחַל) of Egypt (Num. xxxiv. 5), *i.e.* the boundary stream *Rhinocorura*, Wady *el Arish*. According to the oratorical character of the promise, the two large rivers, the Nile and the Euphrates, are mentioned as the boundaries within which the seed of Abram would possess the promised land, the exact limits of which are more minutely described in the list of the tribes who were then in possession.   Ten tribes are mentioned between the southern border of the land and the extreme north, " to convey the impression of universality without exception, of unqualified completeness, the symbol of which is the number ten" (*Delitzsch*).   In other passages we find sometimes seven tribes mentioned (Deut. vii. 1 ; Josh. iii. 10), at other times six (Ex. iii. 8, 17, xxiii. 23 ; Deut. xx. 17), at others five (Ex. xiii. 5), at others again only two (chap. xiii. 7) ; whilst occasionally they are all included in the common name of Canaanites (chap. xii. 6).   The absence of the Hivites is striking here, since they are not omitted from any other list where as many as five or seven tribes are mentioned.   Out of the eleven descendants of Canaan (chap. x. 15–18) the names of four only are given here ; the others are included in the common name of Canaanites.   On the other hand, four tribes are given, whose descent from Canaan is very improbable.   The origin of the *Kenites* cannot be determined.   According to Judg. i. 16, iv. 11, Hobab, the brother-in-law of Moses, was a Kenite.   His being called a Midianite (Num. x. 29) does not prove that he was descended from Midian (Gen. xxv. 2), but is to be accounted for from the fact that he dwelt in the land of Midian, or among the Midianites (Ex. ii. 15). This branch of the Kenites went with the Israelites to Canaan, into the wilderness of Judah (Judg. i. 16), and dwelt even in Saul's time among the Amalekites on the southern border of Judah (1 Sam. xv. 6), and in the same towns with members of the tribe of Judah (1 Sam. xxx. 29).   There is nothing either in this passage, or in Num. xxiv. 21, 22, to compel us to distinguish these Midianitish Kenites from those of Canaan.   The *Philistines* also were not Canaanites, and yet their territory was assigned to the Israelites.   And just as the Philistines had forced their way into the land, so the Kenites may have taken possession of certain tracts of the country.   All that can be inferred from the two passages is, that there were Kenites outside Midian, who were to be exterminated by the Israelites.   On the *Kenizzites*, all that can be affirmed with certainty is, that the name is neither to be traced to the Edomitish *Kenaz* (chap. xxxvi. 15, 42), nor to be identified with the Kenezite Jephunneh, the father of Caleb of Judah (Num. xxxii. 12 ; Josh. xiv. 6 : see my Comm. on Joshua, p. 356, Eng. tr.).—The *Kadmonites* are never mentioned again, and their origin cannot be determined.   On the

Perizzites see chap. xiii. 7 ; on the *Rephaims,* chap. xiv. 5 ; and on the other names, chap. x. 15, 16.

BIRTH OF ISHMAEL.—CHAP. XVI.

Vers. 1–6. As the promise of a lineal heir (chap. xv. 4) did not seem likely to be fulfilled, even after the covenant had been made, Sarai resolved, ten years after their entrance into Canaan, to give her Egyptian maid Hagar to her husband, that if possible she might " *be built up by her,*" *i.e.* obtain children, who might found a house or family (chap. xxx. 3). The resolution seemed a judicious one, and according to the customs of the East, there would be nothing wrong in carrying it out. Hence Abraham consented without opposition, because, as Malachi (ii. 15) says, he sought the seed promised by God. But they were both of them soon to learn, that their thoughts were the thoughts of man and not of God, and that their wishes and actions were not in accordance with the divine promise. Sarai, the originator of the plan, was the first to experience its evil consequences. When the maid was with child by Abram, " *her mistress became little in her eyes.*" When Sarai complained to Abram of the contempt she received from her maid (saying, " *My wrong,*" the wrong done to me, " *come upon thee,*" cf. Jer. li. 35; Gen. xxvii. 13), and called upon Jehovah to judge between her and her husband,[1] Abram gave her full power to act as mistress towards her maid, without raising the slave who was made a concubine above her position. But as soon as Sarai made her feel her power, Hagar fled. Thus, instead of securing the fulfilment of their wishes, Sarai and Abram had reaped nothing but grief and vexation, and apparently had lost the maid through their self-concerted scheme. But the faithful covenant God turned the whole into a blessing.

Vers. 7–14. Hagar no doubt intended to escape to Egypt by a road used from time immemorial, that ran from Hebron past Beersheba, " *by the way of Shur.*"—*Shur,* the present *Jifar,* is the name given to the north-western portion of the desert of Arabia (cf. Ex. xv. 22). There the angel of the Lord found

[1] בֵּינֶיךָ, with a point over the second Jod, to show that it is irregular and suspicious; since בֵּין with the singular suffix is always treated as a singular, and only with a plural suffix as plural.

her by a well, and directed her to return to her mistress, and submit to her; at the same time he promised her the birth of a son, and an innumerable multiplication of her descendants. As the fruit of her womb was the seed of Abram, she was to return to his house and there bear him a son, who, though not the seed promised by God, would be honoured for Abram's sake with the blessing of an innumerable posterity.   For this reason also Jehovah appeared to her in the form of the Angel of Jehovah (cf. p. 129).   הָרָה is *adj. verb.* as in chap. xxxviii. 24, etc. : " *thou art with child and wilt bear;*" יֹלַדְתְּ for יֹלֶדֶת (chap. xvii. 19) is found again in Judg. xiii. 5, 7. This son she was to call *Ishmael* ("*God hears*"), "*for Jehovah hath hearkened to thy distress.*" עֳנִי *afflictionem sine dubio vocat, quam Hagar afflictionem sentiebat esse, nempe conditionem servitem et quod castigata esset a Sara* (*Luther*).   It was *Jehovah,* not *Elohim,* who had heard, although the latter name was most naturally suggested as the explanation of *Ishmael,* because the hearing, *i.e.* the multiplication of Ishmael's descendants, was the result of the covenant grace of Jehovah.   Moreover, in contrast with the oppression which she had endured and still would endure, she received the promise that her son would endure no such oppression.   "*He will be a wild ass of a man.*" The figure of a פֶּרֶא, *onager,* that wild and untameable animal, roaming at its will in the desert, of which so highly poetic a description is given in Job xxxix. 5–8, depicts most aptly "the Bedouin's boundless love of freedom as he rides about in the desert, spear in hand, upon his camel or his horse, hardy, frugal, revelling in the varied beauty of nature, and despising town life in every form;" and the words, "*his hand will be against every man, and every man's hand against him,*" describe most truly the incessant state of feud, in which the Ishmaelites live with one another or with their neighbours.   "*He will dwell before the face of all his brethren.*"   עַל פְּנֵי denotes, it is true, to the east of (cf. chap. xxv. 18), and this meaning is to be retained here; but the geographical notice of the dwelling-place of the Ishmaelites hardly exhausts the force of the expression, which also indicated that Ishmael would maintain an independent standing before (in the presence of) all the descendants of Abraham.   History has confirmed this promise.   The Ishmaelites have continued to this day in free and undiminished possession of the extensive peninsula between the Euphrates, the

Straits of Suez, and the Red Sea, from which they have overspread both Northern Africa and Southern Asia.—Ver. 13.
In the angel, Hagar recognised God manifesting Himself to her,
the presence of Jehovah, and called Him, " *Thou art a God of
seeing; for she said, Have I also seen here after seeing?*" Believing that a man must die if he saw God (Ex. xx. 19, xxxiii. 20),
Hagar was astonished that she had seen God and remained
alive, and called Jehovah, who had spoken to her, "God of
seeing," *i.e.* who allows Himself to be seen, because here, on the
spot where this sight was granted her, after seeing she still saw,
i.e. remained alive.   From this occurrence the well received
the name of "*well of the seeing alive,*" *i.e.* at which a man saw
God and remained alive.   *Beer-lahai-roi:* according to *Ewald*,
חַי רֹאִי is to be regarded as a composite noun, and לְ as a sign of
the genitive; but this explanation, in which רֹאִי is treated as a
pausal form of רְאִי, does not suit the form רֹאִי with the accent
upon the last syllable, which points rather to the participle רֹאֶה
with the first pers. suffix.   On this ground *Delitzsch* and others
have decided in favour of the interpretation given in the Chaldee
version, "Thou art a God of seeing, *i.e.* the all-seeing, from
whose all-seeing eye the helpless and forsaken is not hidden even
in the farthest corner of the desert."   "*Have I not even here* (in
the barren land of solitude) *looked after Him, who saw me?*" and
Beer-lahai-roi, "the well of the Living One who sees me, *i.e.* of
the omnipresent Providence."   But still greater difficulties lie in
the way of this view.   It not only overthrows the close connection
between this and the similar passages chap. xxxii. 31, Ex. xxxiii.
20, Judg. xiii. 22, where the sight of God excites a fear of death,
but it renders the name, which the well received from this appearance of God, an inexplicable riddle.   If Hagar called the
God who appeared to her אֵל רֹאִי because she looked after Him
whom she saw, *i.e.* as we must necessarily understand the word,
saw not His face, but only His back; how could it ever occur
to her or to any one else, to call the well Beer-lahai-roi, "well
of the Living One, who sees me," instead of Beer-el-roi?   Moreover, what completely overthrows this explanation, is the fact
that neither in Genesis nor anywhere in the Pentateuch is God
called "the Living One;" and throughout the Old Testament it
is only in contrast with the dead gods or idols of the heathen, a
contrast never thought of here, that the expressions אֱלֹהִים חַי and

אֵל חַי occur, whilst הֵחַי is never used in the Old Testament as a name of God. For these reasons we must abide by the first explanation, and change the reading רֹאִי into רֳאִי.[1] With regard to the well, it is still further added that it was between Kadesh (xiv. 7) and Bered. Though *Bered* has not been discovered, *Rowland* believes, with good reason, that he has found the well of Hagar, which is mentioned again in chap. xxiv. 62, xxv. 11, in the spring *Ain Kades*, to the south of Beersheba, at the leading place of encampment of the caravans passing from Syria to Sinai, *viz. Moyle*, or *Moilahi*, or *Muweilih* (Robinson, Pal. i. p. 280), which the Arabs call *Moilahi Hagar*, and in the neighbourhood of which they point out a rock *Beit Hagar*. Bered must lie to the west of this.

Vers. 15–16. Having returned to Abram's house, Hagar bare him a son in his 86th year. He gave it the name *Ishmael*, and regarded it probably as the promised seed, until, thirteen years afterwards, the counsel of God was more clearly unfolded to him.

SEALING OF THE COVENANT BY THE GIVING OF NEW NAMES AND BY THE RITE OF CIRCUMCISION.—CHAP. XVII.

Vers. 1–14. The covenant had been made with Abram for at least fourteen years, and yet Abram remained without any visible sign of its accomplishment, and was merely pointed in faith to the inviolable character of the promise of God. Jehovah now appeared to Him again, when he was ninety-nine years old, twenty-four years after his migration, and thirteen after the birth of Ishmael, to give effect to the covenant and prepare for its execution. Having come down to Abram in a visible form (ver 22), He said to him, "*I am* EL SHADDAI (almighty God): *walk before Me and be blameless.*" At the establishment of the

---

[1] The objections to this change in the accentuation are entirely counterbalanced by the grammatical difficulty connected with the second explanation. If, for example, רֹאִי is a participle with the 1st pers. suff., it should be written רֹאֵנִי (Isa. xxix. 15) or רֹאֵנִי (Isa. xlvii. 10). רֹאִי cannot mean, "who sees me," but "my seer," an expression utterly inapplicable to God, which cannot be supported by a reference to Job vii. 8, for the accentuation varies there ; and the derivation of רֹאִי from רְאִי " eye of the seeing," for the eye which looks after me, is apparently fully warranted by the analogous expression אֵשֶׁת לֵדָה in Jer. xiii. 21.

covenant, God had manifested Himself to him as Jehovah (xv. 7); here Jehovah describes Himself as El Shaddai, God the Mighty One. שַׁדַּי: from שָׁדַד to be strong, with the substantive termination *ai*, like חַגַּי the festal, יְשִׁישִׁי the old man, סִינַי the thorn-grown, etc. This name is not to be regarded as identical with *Elohim*, that is to say, with God as Creator and Preserver of the world, although in simple narrative *Elohim* is used for *El Shaddai*, which is only employed in the more elevated and solemn style of writing. It belonged to the sphere of salvation, forming one element in the manifestation of Jehovah, and describing Jehovah, the covenant God, as possessing the power to realize His promises, even when the order of nature presented no prospect of their fulfilment, and the powers of nature were insufficient to secure it. The name which Jehovah thus gave to Himself was to be a pledge, that in spite of "his own body now dead," and "the deadness of Sarah's womb" (Rom. iv. 19), God could and would give him the promised innumerable posterity. On the other hand, God required this of Abram, " *Walk before Me* (cf. chap.v. 22) *and be blameless*" (vi. 9). "Just as righteousness received in faith was necessary for the establishment of the covenant, so a blameless walk before God was required for the maintenance and confirmation of the covenant." This introduction is followed by a more definite account of the new revelation; first of the promise involved in the new name of God (vers. 2–8), and then of the obligation imposed upon Abram (vers. 9–14). " *I will give My covenant*," says the Almighty, " *between Me and thee, and multiply thee exceedingly*." נָתַן בְּרִית signifies, not to make a covenant, but to give, to put, *i.e.* to realize, to set in operation the things promised in the covenant—equivalent to setting up the covenant (cf. ver. 7 and ix. 12 with ix. 9). This promise Abram appropriated to himself by falling upon his face in worship, upon which God still further expounded the nature of the covenant about to be executed.—Ver. 4. On the part of God (אֲנִי placed at the beginning absolutely: so far as I am concerned, for my part) it was to consist of this: (1) that God would make Abram the father (אַב instead of אֲבִי chosen with reference to the name Abram) of a multitude of nations, the ancestor of nations and kings; (2) that He would be God, show Himself to be God, in an eternal covenant relation, to him and to his posterity, according to their families, according to all their successive generations; and (3) that He would give them the land in which he had wandered as a foreigner, viz. all Canaan, for an everlasting possession. As a pledge of this promise God changed his name אַבְרָם, *i.e.* high father, into אַבְרָהָם, *i.e.* father of the multitude, from אב and רָהָם, *Arab. ruhâm* = multitude. In this name God gave him a tangible pledge of the fulfilment of His covenant, inasmuch as a name which God gives cannot be a mere empty sound, but must be the expression of something real, or eventually acquire reality.—Vers. 9 sqq. On the part of Abraham (וְאַתָּה *thou*, the antithesis to אֲנִי, *as for me*, ver. 4) God required that he and his descendants in all generations should keep the covenant, and that as a sign he should circumcise himself and every male in his house. הִמּוֹל *Niph.* of מוּל, and נִמְלְתֶּם *perf. Niph.* for נִמְלַתֶּם, from מוּל=מָלַל. As the sign of the covenant, circumcision is called in ver. 13, "*the covenant in the flesh*," so far as the nature of the covenant was manifested in the flesh. It was to be extended not only to the seed, the lineal descendants of Abraham, but to all the males in his house, even to every foreign slave not belonging to the seed of Abram, whether born in the house or acquired (*i.e.* bought) with money, and to the "*son of eight days*," *i.e.* the male child eight days old; with the threat that the uncircumcised should be exterminated from his people, because by neglecting circumcision he had broken the covenant with God. The form of speech נִכְרְתָה הַנֶּפֶשׁ הַהִיא, by which many of the laws are enforced (cf. Ex. xii. 15, 19; Lev. vii. 20, 21, 25, etc.), denotes not rejection from the nation, or banishment, but death, whether by a direct judgment from God, an untimely death at the hand of God, or by the punishment of death inflicted by the congregation or the magistrates, and that whether מוֹת יוּמַת is added, as in Ex. xxxi. 14, etc., or not. This is very evident from Lev. xvii. 9, 10, where the extermination to be effected by the authorities is distinguished from that to be executed by God Himself (see my *biblische Archäologie* ii. § 153, 1). In this sense we sometimes find, in the place of the earlier expression "*from his people*," *i.e.* his nation, such expressions as "from among his people" (Lev. xvii. 4, 10; Num. xv. 30), "from Israel" (Ex. xii. 15; Num. xix. 13), "from the congregation of Israel" (Ex. xii. 19); and instead of "that soul," in Lev. xvii. 4, 9 (cf. Ex. xxx. 33, 38), we find "that man."

Vers. 15–21. The appointment of the sign of the covenant

was followed by this further revelation as to the promised seed,
that Abram would receive it through his wife Sarai. In confirmation of this her exalted destiny, she was no longer to be called
Sarai (שָׂרַי, probably from שָׂרַר with the termination *ai*, the
princely), but שָׂרָה, the princess; for she was to become nations,
the mother of kings of nations. Abraham then fell upon his face
and laughed, saying in himself (*i.e.* thinking), " *Shall a child be
born to him that is a hundred years old, or shall Sarah, that is
ninety years old, bear?*" " The promise was so immensely great,
that he sank in adoration to the ground, and so immensely paradoxical, that he could not help laughing" (*Del.*). " Not that he
either ridiculed the promise of God, or treated it as a fable, or
rejected it altogether; but, as often happens when things occur
which are least expected, partly lifted up with joy, partly carried
out of himself with wonder, he burst out into laughter" (*Calvin*).
In this joyous amazement he said to God (ver. 18), " *O that
Ishmael might live before Thee!*" To regard these words, with
Calvin and others, as intimating that he should be satisfied with
the prosperity of Ishmael, as though he durst not hope for anything higher, is hardly sufficient. The prayer implies anxiety,
lest Ishmael should have no part in the blessings of the covenant.
God answers, " *Yes* (אֲבָל *imo*), *Sarah thy wife bears thee a son,
and thou wilt call his name Isaac* (according to the Greek form
Ἰσαάκ, for the Hebrew יִצְחָק, *i.e. laugher*, with reference to
Abraham's laughing; ver. 17, cf. xxi. 6), *and I will establish My
covenant with him,*" *i.e.* make him the recipient of the covenant
grace. And the prayer for Ishmael God would also grant: He
would make him very fruitful, so that he should beget twelve
princes and become a great nation. But the covenant, God
repeated (ver. 21), should be established with Isaac, whom
Sarah was to bear to him at that very time in the following
year.—Since Ishmael therefore was excluded from participating
in the covenant grace, which was ensured to Isaac alone; and
yet Abraham was to become a multitude of nations, and that
through Sarah, who was to become "nations" through the son
she was to bear (ver. 16); the "multitude of nations" could
not include either the Ishmaelites or the tribes descended from
the sons of Keturah (chap. xxv. 2 sqq.), but the descendants of
Isaac alone; and as one of Isaac's two sons received no part of
the covenant promise, the descendants of Jacob alone. But the

whole of the twelve sons of Jacob founded only the *one* nation
of Israel, with which Jehovah established the covenant made
with Abraham (Ex. vi. and xx.–xxiv.), so that Abraham
became through Israel the lineal father of *one* nation only.
From this it necessarily follows, that the posterity of Abraham,
which was to expand into a multitude of nations, extends beyond this one lineal posterity, and embraces the spiritual
posterity also, *i.e.* all nations who are grafted ἐκ πίστεως
Ἀβραάμ into the seed of Abraham (Rom. iv. 11, 12, and
16, 17). Moreover, the fact that the seed of Abraham was
not to be restricted to his lineal descendants, is evident from
the fact, that circumcision as the covenant sign was not confined to them, but extended to all the inmates of his house, so
that these strangers were received into the fellowship of the
covenant, and reckoned as part of the promised seed. Now, if
the whole land of Canaan was promised to this posterity, which
was to increase into a multitude of nations (ver. 8), it is perfectly evident, from what has just been said, that the sum and
substance of the promise was not exhausted by the gift of the
land, whose boundaries are described in chap. xv. 18–21, as a
possession to the nation of Israel, but that the extension of the
idea of the lineal posterity, "Israel after the flesh," to the spiritual posterity, "Israel after the spirit," requires the expansion
of the idea and extent of the earthly Canaan to the full extent
of the spiritual Canaan, whose boundaries reach as widely as the
multitude of nations having Abraham as father; and, therefore,
that in reality Abraham received the promise "that he should
be the heir of the *world*" (Rom. iv. 13).[1]

And what is true of the seed of Abraham and the land of
Canaan must also hold good of the covenant and the covenant sign.

[1] What stands out clearly in this promise—viz. the fact that the expressions "*seed of Abraham*" (people of Israel) and "*land of Canaan*" are not
exhausted in the physical Israel and earthly Canaan, but are to be understood spiritually, Israel and Canaan acquiring the typical significance of the
people of God and land of the Lord—is still further expanded by the prophets, and most distinctly expressed in the New Testament by Christ and
the apostles. This scriptural and spiritual interpretation of the Old Testament is entirely overlooked by those who, like *Auberlen*, restrict all the
promises of God and the prophetic proclamations of salvation to the physical Israel, and reduce the application of them to the "Israel after the
spirit," *i.e.* to believing Christendom, to a mere accommodation.

Eternal duration was promised only to the covenant established by God with the seed of Abraham, which was to grow into a multitude of nations, but not to the covenant institution which God established in connection with the lineal posterity of Abraham, the twelve tribes of Israel. Everything in this institution which was of a local and limited character, and only befitted the physical Israel and the earthly Canaan, existed only so long as was necessary for the seed of Abraham to expand into a multitude of nations. So again it was only in its essence that circumcision could be a sign of the eternal covenant. Circumcision, whether it passed from Abraham to other nations, or sprang up among other nations independently of Abraham and his descendants (see my Archäologie, § 63, 1), was based upon the religious view, that the sin and moral impurity which the fall of Adam had introduced into the nature of man had concentrated itself in the sexual organs, because it is in sexual life that it generally manifests itself with peculiar force ; and, consequently, that for the sanctification of life, a purification or sanctification of the organ of generation, by which life is propagated, is especially required. In this way circumcision in the flesh became a symbol of the circumcision, i.e. the purification, of the heart (Deut. x. 16, xxx. 6, cf. Lev. xxvi. 41, Jer. iv. 4, ix. 25, Ezek. xliv. 7), and a covenant sign to those who received it, inasmuch as they were received into the fellowship of the holy nation (Ex. xix. 6), and required to sanctify their lives, in other words, to fulfil all that the covenant demanded. It was to be performed on every boy on the eighth day after its birth, not because the child, like its mother, remains so long in a state of impurity, but because, as the analogous rule with regard to the fitness of young animals for sacrifice would lead us to conclude, this was regarded as the first day of independent existence (Lev. xxii. 27; Ex. xxii. 29; see my Archäologie, § 63).

Vers. 22–27. When God had finished His address and ascended again, Abraham immediately fulfilled the covenant duty enjoined upon him, by circumcising himself on that very day, along with all the male members of his house. Because Ishmael was 13 years old when he was circumcised, the Arabs even now defer circumcision to a much later period than the Jews, generally till between the ages of 5 and 13, and frequently even till the 13th year.

VISIT OF JEHOVAH, WITH TWO ANGELS, TO ABRAHAM'S TENT.
—CHAP. XVIII.

Having been received into the covenant with God through
the rite of circumcision, Abraham was shortly afterwards honoured by being allowed to receive and entertain the Lord and
two angels in his tent. This fresh manifestation of God had a
double purpose, viz. to establish Sarah's faith in the promise
that she should bear a son in her old age (vers. 1–15), and to
announce the judgment on Sodom and Gomorrah (vers. 16–33).
Vers. 1–15. When sitting, about mid-day, in the grove of
Mamre, in front of his tent, Abraham looked up and unexpect-
edly saw three men standing at some distance from him (עָלָיו
above him, looking down upon him as he sat), viz. *Jehovah* (ver.
13) and *two angels* (xix. 1); all three in human form. Perceiving at once that one of them was the Lord (אֲדֹנָי, *i.e.* God),
he prostrated himself reverentially before them, and entreated
them not to pass him by, but to suffer him to entertain them as
his guests : " *Let a little water be fetched, and wash your feet, and
recline yourselves* (הִשָּׁעֲנוּ to recline, leaning upon the arm) *under
the tree.*"—" *Comfort your hearts :*" lit. " strengthen the heart,"
i.e. refresh yourselves by eating and drinking (Judg. xix. 5 ;
1 Kings xxi. 7). "*For therefore* (sc. to give me an opportunity to
entertain you hospitably) *have ye come over to your servant :*" כִּי
עַל כֵּן does not stand for עַל כֵּן כִּי (*Ges. thes.* p. 682), but means
" because for this purpose" (*vid. Ewald*, § 353).—Vers. 6 sqq.
When the three men had accepted the hospitable invitation,
Abraham, just like a Bedouin sheikh of the present day, directed
his wife to take three seahs (374 cubic inches each) of fine meal,
and bake cakes of it as quickly as possible (עֻגּוֹת round unleavened cakes baked upon hot stones); he also had a tender
calf killed, and sent for milk and butter, or curdled milk, and
thus prepared a bountiful and savoury meal, of which the guests
partook. The eating of material food on the part of these
heavenly beings was not in appearance only, but was really
eating ; an act which may be attributed to the corporeality
assumed, and is to be regarded as analogous to the eating on the
part of the risen and glorified Christ (Luke xxiv. 41 sqq.),
although the miracle still remains physiologically incomprehensible.—Vers. 9–15. During the meal, at which Abraham stood,

and waited upon them as the host, they asked for Sarah, for whom the visit was chiefly intended. On being told that she was in the tent, where she could hear, therefore, all that passed under the tree in front of the tent, the one whom Abraham addressed as *Adonai* (my Lord), and who is called Jehovah in ver. 13, said, "*I will return to thee* (כָּעֵת חַיָּה) *at this time, when it lives again*" (חַיָּה, *reviviscens*, without the article, *Ges.* § 111, 2*b*), *i.e.* at this time next year; "*and, behold, Sarah, thy wife, will* (then) *have a son.*" Sarah heard this at the door of the tent; "*and it was behind Him*" (Jehovah), so that she could not be seen by Him as she stood at the door. But as the fulfilment of this promise seemed impossible to her, on account of Abraham's extreme age, and the fact that her own womb had lost the power of conception, she laughed within herself, thinking that she was not observed. But that she might know that the promise was made by the omniscient and omnipotent God, He reproved her for laughing, saying, "*Is anything too wonderful* (*i.e.* impossible) *for Jehovah? at the time appointed I will return unto thee,*" etc.; and when her perplexity led her to deny it, He convicted her of falsehood. Abraham also had laughed at this promise (chap. xvii. 17), and without receiving any reproof. For his laughing was the joyous outburst of astonishment; Sarah's, on the contrary, the result of doubt and unbelief, which had to be broken down by reproof, and, as the result showed, really was broken down, inasmuch as she conceived and bore a son, whom she could only have conceived in faith (Heb. xi. 11).

Vers. 16–33. After this conversation with Sarah, the heavenly guests rose up and turned their faces towards the plain of Sodom (עַל פְּנֵי, as in chap. xix. 28; Num. xxi. 20, xxiii. 28). Abraham accompanied them some distance on the road; according to tradition, he went as far as the site of the later *Caphar barucha*, from which you can see the Dead Sea through a ravine, —*solitudinem ac terras Sodomæ.* And Jehovah said, "Shall I hide from Abraham what I propose to do? Abraham is destined to be a great nation and a blessing to all nations (xii. 2, 3); for I have known, *i.e.* acknowledged him (chosen him in anticipative love, יָדַע as in Amos iii. 2; Hos. xiii. 4), that he may command his whole posterity to keep the way of Jehovah, to practise justice and righteousness, that all the promises may be fulfilled in them." God then disclosed to Abraham what he was about

to do to Sodom and Gomorrah, not, as *Kurtz* supposes, because
Abraham had been constituted the hereditary possessor of the
land, and Jehovah, being mindful of His covenant, would not
do anything to it without his knowledge and assent (a thought
quite foreign to the context), but because Jehovah had chosen
him to be the father of the people of God, in order that, by instructing his descendants in the fear of God, he might lead them
in the paths of righteousness, so that they might become partakers of the promised salvation, and not be overtaken by judgment.   The destruction of Sodom and the surrounding cities
was to be a permanent memorial of the punitive righteousness
of God, and to keep the fate of the ungodly constantly before
the mind of Israel.   To this end Jehovah explained to Abraham
the cause of their destruction in the clearest manner possible,
that he might not only be convinced of the justice of the divine
government, but might learn that when the measure of iniquity
was full, no intercession could avert the judgment,—a lesson
and a warning to his descendants also.—Ver. 20. *" The cry of
Sodom and Gomorrah, yea it is great; and their sin, yea it is
very grievous."*   The cry is the appeal for vengeance or punishment, which ascends to heaven (chap. iv. 10).   The כִּי serves to
give emphasis to the assertion, and is placed in the middle of the
sentence to give the greater prominence to the leading thought
(cf. *Ewald,* § 330).—Ver. 21. God was about to go down, and
convince Himself whether they had done entirely according to
the cry which had reached Him, or not.   עָשׂוּ כָלָה, *lit.* to make
completeness, here referring to the extremity of iniquity, generally to the extremity of punishment (Nahum i. 8, 9; Jer. iv.
27, v. 10) : כָּלָה is a noun, as Isa. x. 23 shows, not an adverb, as
in Ex. xi. 1.   After this explanation, the men (according to
chap. xix. 1, the two angels) turned from thence to go to Sodom
(ver. 22) ; but Abraham continued standing before Jehovah,
who had been talking with him, and approached Him with earnestness and boldness of faith to intercede for Sodom.   He was
urged to this, not by any special interest in Lot, for in that case
he would have prayed for his deliverance ; nor by the circumstance that, as he had just before felt himself called upon to
become the protector, avenger, and deliverer of the land from
its foes, so he now thought himself called upon to act as mediator, and to appeal from Jehovah's judicial wrath to Jehovah's

covenant grace (*Kurtz*), for he had not delivered the land from the foe, but merely rescued his nephew Lot and all the booty that remained after the enemy had withdrawn ; nor did he appeal to the covenant grace of Jehovah, but to His justice alone; and on the principle that the Judge of all the earth could not possibly destroy the righteous with the wicked, he founded his entreaty that God would forgive the city if there were but fifty righteous in it, or even if there were only ten. He was led to intercede in this way, not by "*communis erga quinque populos miseri-cordia*" (*Calvin*), but by the love which springs from the con-sciousness that one's own preservation and rescue are due to compassionate grace alone; love, too, which cannot conceive of the guilt of others as too great for salvation to be possible. This sympathetic love, springing from the faith which was counted for righteousness, impelled him to the intercession which *Luther* thus describes: "*sexies petiit, et cum tanto ardore ac affectu sic urgente, ut præ nimia angustia, qua cupit consultum miseris civi-tatibus, videatur quasi stulte loqui.*" There may be apparent folly in the words, "*Wilt Thou also destroy the righteous with the wicked ?*" but they were only "*violenta oratio et impetuosa, quasi cogens Deum ad ignoscendum.*" For Abraham added, "*perad-venture there be fifty righteous within the city ; wilt Thou also destroy and not forgive* (נָשָׂא, to take away and bear the guilt, *i.e.* forgive) *the place for the fifty righteous that are therein ?*" and described the slaying of the righteous with the wicked as irreconcilable with the justice of God. He knew that he was speaking to the Judge of all the earth, and that before Him he was "*but dust and ashes*"—"dust in his origin, and ashes in the end ;" and yet he made bold to appeal still further, and even as low as ten righteous, to pray that for their sake He would spare the city.—אַךְ הַפַּעַם (ver. 32) signifies "*only this* (one) *time more,*" as in Ex. x. 17. This "seemingly commercial kind of entreaty is," as Delitzsch observes, "the essence of true prayer. It is the holy ἀναίδεια, of which our Lord speaks in Luke xi. 8, the shamelessness of faith, which bridges over the infinite distance of the creature from the Creator, appeals with importunity to the heart of God, and ceases not till its point is gained. This would indeed be neither permissible nor possible, had not God, by virtue of the mysterious interlacing of necessity and freedom in His nature and operations, granted a power to the prayer of faith, to which He consents to yield; had He not, by virtue of His absoluteness, which is anything but blind necessity, placed Himself in such a relation to men, that He not merely works upon them by means of His grace, but allows them to work upon Him by means of their faith; had He not interwoven the life of the free creature into His own absolute life, and accorded to a created personality the right to assert itself in faith, in distinction from His own." With the promise, that even for the sake of ten righteous He would not destroy the city, Jehovah "went His way," that is to say, vanished; and Abraham returned to his place, viz. to the grove of Mamre. The judgment which fell upon the wicked cities immediately afterwards, proves that there were not ten "*righteous persons*" in Sodom; by which we understand, not merely ten sinless or holy men, but ten who through the fear of God and conscientiousness had kept themselves free from the prevailing sin and iniquity of these cities.

INIQUITY AND DESTRUCTION OF SODOM. ESCAPE OF LOT, AND HIS SUBSEQUENT HISTORY.—CHAP. XIX.

Vers. 1–11. The messengers (angels) sent by Jehovah to Sodom, arrived there in the evening, when Lot, who was sitting at the gate, pressed them to pass the night in his house. The gate, generally an arched entrance with deep recesses and seats on either side, was a place of meeting in the ancient towns of the East, where the inhabitants assembled either for social intercourse or to transact public business (vid. chap. xxxiv. 20; Deut. xxi. 19, xxii. 15, etc.). The two travellers, however (for such Lot supposed them to be, and only recognised them as angels when they had smitten the Sodomites miraculously with blindness), said that they would spend the night in the street—בָּרְחוֹב the broad open space within the gate—as they had been sent to inquire into the state of the town. But they yielded to Lot's entreaty to enter his house; for the deliverance of Lot, after having ascertained his state of mind, formed part of their commission, and entering into his house might only serve to manifest the sin of Sodom in all its heinousness. While Lot was entertaining his guests with the greatest hospitality, the people of Sodom gathered round his house, "*both old and young, all people from every quarter*" (of the town, as in Jer. li. 31), and

demanded. with the basest violation of the sacred rite of hospitality and the most shameless proclamation of their sin (Isa.
iii. 9), that the strangers should be brought out, that they
might know them. יָדַע is applied, as in Judg. xix. 22, to the
carnal sin of *poederastia*, a crime very prevalent among the
Canaanites (Lev. xviii. 22 sqq., xx. 23), and according to
Rom. i. 27, a curse of heathenism generally.—Vers. 6 sqq.
Lot went out to them, shut the door behind him to protect
his guests, and offered to give his virgin daughters up to
them. " *Only to these men* (הָאֵל, an archaism for הָאֵלֶּה, occurs
also in ver. 25, chap. xxvi. 3, 4, Lev. xviii. 27, and Deut.
iv. 42, vii. 22, xix. 11; and אֵל for אֵלֶּה in 1 Chron. xx. 8) *do
nothing, for therefore* (viz. to be protected from injury) *have
they come under the shadow of my roof.*" In his anxiety, Lot
was willing to sacrifice to the sanctity of hospitality his duty as
a father, which ought to have been still more sacred, " and committed the sin of seeking to avert sin by sin." Even if he expected that his daughters would suffer no harm, as they were
betrothed to Sodomites (ver. 14), the offer was a grievous violation of his paternal duty. But this offer only heightened the
brutality of the mob. " *Stand back* " (make way, Isa. xlix. 20),
they said; " *the man, who came as a foreigner, is always wanting
to play the judge*" (probably because Lot had frequently reproved
them for their licentious conduct, 2 Pet. ii. 7, 8) : " *now will we
deal worse with thee than with them.*" With these words they
pressed upon him, and approached the door to break it in. The
men inside, that is to say, the angels, then pulled Lot into the
house, shut the door, and by miraculous power smote the people
without with blindness (סַנְוֵרִים here and 2 Kings vi. 18 for
mental blindness, in which the eye sees, but does not see the
right object), as a punishment for their utter moral blindness,
and an omen of the coming judgment.

Vers. 12–22. The sin of Sodom had now become manifest.
The men, Lot's guests, made themselves known to him as the
messengers of judgment sent by Jehovah, and ordered him to
remove any one that belonged to him out of the city. " *Son-
in-law* (the singular without the article, because it is only
assumed as a possible circumstance that he may have sons-in-
law), *and thy sons, and thy daughters, and all that belongs to thee* "
(*sc.* of persons, not of things). *Sons* Lot does not appear to

have had, as we read nothing more about them, but only " *sons in-law* (לְקֹחֵי בְנֹתָיו) *who were about to take his daughters*," as *Josephus*, the *Vulgate*, *Ewald*, and many others correctly render it.   The *LXX.*, *Targums*, *Knobel*, and *Delitzsch* adopt the rendering "who had taken his daughters," in proof of which the last two adduce הַנִּמְצָאֹת in ver. 15 as decisive.   But without reason; for this refers not to the daughters who were still in the father's house, as distinguished from those who were married, but to his wife and two daughters who were to be found with him in the house, in distinction from the bridegrooms, who also belonged to him, but were not yet living with him, and who had received his summons in scorn, because in their carnal security they did not believe in any judgment of God (Luke xvii. 28, 29).   If Lot had had married daughters, he would undoubtedly have called upon them to escape along with their husbands, his sons-in-law.—Ver. 15. As soon as it was dawn, the angels urged Lot to hasten away with his family ; and when he still delayed, his heart evidently clinging to the earthly home and possessions which he was obliged to leave, they laid hold of him, with his wife and his two daughters, בְּחֶמְלַת יְהֹוָה עָלָיו, " *by virtue of the sparing mercy of Jehovah* (which operated) *upon him*," and led him out of the city.—Ver. 17. When they left him here (הִנִּיחַ, to let loose, and leave, to leave to one's self), the Lord commanded him, for the sake of his life, not to look behind him, and not to stand still in all the plain (כִּכָּר, xiii. 10), but to flee to the mountains (afterwards called the mountains of Moab).   In ver. 17 we are struck by the change from the plural to the singular : " when *they* brought them forth, *he* said."   To think of one of the two angels—the one, for example, who led the conversation—seems out of place, not only because Lot addressed him by the name of God, "*Adonai*" (ver. 18), but also because the speaker attributed to himself the judgment upon the cities (vers. 21, 22), which is described in ver. 24 as executed by Jehovah.   Yet there is nothing to indicate that Jehovah suddenly joined the angels.   The only supposition that remains, therefore, is that Lot recognised in the two angels a manifestation of God, and so addressed *them* (ver. 18) as *Adonai* (my Lord), and that the angel who spoke addressed him as the messenger of Jehovah in the name of God, without its following from this, that Jehovah was present in the two angels.

Lot, instead of cheerfully obeying the commandment of the Lord, appealed to the great mercy shown to him in the preservation of his life, and to the impossibility of his escaping to the mountains, without the evil overtaking him, and entreated therefore that he might be allowed to take refuge in the small and neighbouring city, *i.e.* in *Bela,* which received the name of *Zoar* (chap. xiv. 2) on account of Lot's calling it little. *Zoar,* the Σηγώρ of the LXX., and *Segor* of the Crusaders, is hardly to be sought for on the peninsula which projects a long way into the southern half of the Dead Sea, in the Ghor of *el Mezraa,* as *Irby* and *Robinson* (Pal. iii. p. 481) suppose; it is much more probably to be found on the south-eastern point of the Dead Sea, in the Ghor of *el Szaphia,* at the opening of the Wady *el Ahsa* (*vid. v. Raumer,* Pal. p. 273, Anm. 14).

Vers. 23–28. " *When the sun had risen and Lot had come towards Zoar* (*i.e.* was on the way thither, but had not yet arrived), *Jehovah caused it to rain brimstone and fire from Jehovah out of heaven, and overthrew those cities, and the whole plain, and all the inhabitants of the cities, and the produce of the earth.*" In the words "Jehovah caused it to rain from Jehovah" there is no distinction implied between the hidden and the manifested God, between the Jehovah present upon earth in His angels who called down the judgment, and the Jehovah enthroned in heaven who sent it down; but the expression "from Jehovah" is *emphatica repetitio, quod non usitato naturæ ordine tunc Deus pluerit, sed tanquam exerta manu palam fulminaverit præter solitum morem : ut satis constaret nullis causis naturalibus conflatam fuisse pluviam illam ex igne et sulphure* (*Calvin*). The rain of fire and brimstone was not a mere storm with lightning, which set on fire the soil already overcharged with naphtha and sulphur. The two passages, Ps. xi. 6 and Ezek. xxxviii. 22, cannot be adduced as proofs that lightning is ever called fire and brimstone in the Scriptures, for in both passages there is an allusion to the event recorded here. The words are to be understood quite literally, as meaning that brimstone and fire, *i.e.* burning brimstone, fell from the sky, even though the examples of burning bituminous matter falling upon the earth which are given in *Oedmann's vermischte Sammlungen* (iii. 120) may be called in question by historical criticism. By this rain of fire and brimstone not only were the cities and their inhabi-

tants consumed, but even the soil, which abounded in asphalt,
was set on fire, so that the entire valley was burned out and
sank, or was overthrown (הָפַךְ) *i.e.* utterly destroyed, and the
Dead Sea took its place.[1] In addition to Sodom, which was
probably the chief city of the valley of Siddim, Gomorrah and
the whole valley (*i.e.* the valley of Siddim, chap. xiv. 3) are
mentioned ; and along with these the cities of Admah and Zeboim, which were situated in the valley (Deut. xxix. 23, cf. Hos.
xi. 8), also perished, Zoar alone, which is at the south-eastern end
of the valley, being spared for Lot's sake.   Even to the present
day the Dead Sea, with the sulphureous vapour which hangs
about it, the great blocks of saltpetre and sulphur which lie
on every hand, and the utter absence of the slightest trace of
animal and vegetable life in its waters, are a striking testimony
to this catastrophe, which is held up in both the Old and New
Testaments as a fearfully solemn judgment of God for the
warning of self-secure and presumptuous sinners.—Ver. 26. On
the way, Lot's wife, notwithstanding the divine command, looked
" *behind him away*,"—*i.e.* went behind her husband and looked
backwards, probably from a longing for the house and the
earthly possessions she had left with reluctance (cf. Luke xvii
31, 32),—and " *became a pillar of salt.*"   We are not to suppose
that she was actually turned into one, but having been killed by
the fiery and sulphureous vapour with which the air was filled,
and afterwards encrusted with salt, she resembled an actual
statue of salt ; just as even now, from the saline exhalation of
the Dead Sea, objects near it are quickly covered with a crust
of salt, so that the fact, to which Christ refers in Luke xvii. 32,
may be understood without supposing a miracle.[2]—In vers. 27,

[1] Whether the Dead Sea originated in this catastrophe, or whether there
was previously a lake, possibly a fresh water lake, at the north of the valley
of Siddim, which was enlarged to the dimensions of the existing sea by the
destruction of the valley with its cities, and received its present character
at the same time, is a question which has been raised, since Capt. *Lynch* has
discovered by actual measurement the remarkable fact, that the bottom of the
lake consists of two totally different levels, which are separated by a peninsula that stretches to a very great distance into the lake from the eastern
shore ; so that whilst the lake to the north of this peninsula is, on an
average, from 1000 to 1200 feet deep, the southern portion is at the most
16 feet deep, and generally much less, the bottom being covered with salt
mud, and heated by hot springs from below.

[2] But when this pillar of salt is mentioned in Wisdom xi. 7 and *Clemens*

28, the account closes with a remark which points back to chap. xviii. 17 sqq., viz. that Abraham went in the morning to the place where he had stood the day before, interceding with the Lord for Sodom, and saw how the judgment had fallen upon the entire plain, since the smoke of the country went up like the smoke of a furnace. Yet his intercession had not been in vain.

Vers. 29-38. For on the destruction of these cities, God had thought of Abraham, and rescued Lot. This rescue is attributed to Elohim, as being the work of the Judge of the whole earth (chap. xviii. 25), and not to Jehovah the covenant God, because Lot was severed from His guidance and care on his separation from Abraham. The fact, however, is repeated here, for the purpose of connecting with it an event in the life of Lot of great significance to the future history of Abraham's seed.—Vers. 30 sqq. From Zoar Lot removed with his two daughters to the (Moabitish) mountains, for fear that Zoar might after all be destroyed, and dwelt in one of the caves (מְעָרָה with the generic article), in which the limestone rocks abound (*vid. Lynch*), and so became a dweller in a cave. While there, his daughters resolved to procure children through their father; and to that end on two successive evenings they made him intoxicated with wine, and then lay with him in the night, one after the other, that they might conceive seed. To this accursed crime they were impelled by the desire to preserve their family, because they thought there was no man on the earth to come in unto them, *i.e.* to marry them, "after the manner of all the earth." Not that they imagined the whole human race to have perished in the destruction of the valley of Siddim, but because they were afraid that no man would link himself with them, the only survivors of a country smitten by the curse of God. If it was not lust, therefore, which impelled them to this shameful deed, their conduct was worthy of Sodom, and shows quite as much as their previous betrothal to men of Sodom, that they were deeply imbued with the sinful character of that city. The words of vers. 33 and 35, "And he knew not of her lying down and of her

ad Cor. xi. as still in existence, and *Josephus* professes to have seen it, *this* legend is probably based upon the pillar-like lumps of salt, which are still to be seen at Mount *Usdum* (Sodom), on the south-western side of the Dead Sea.

rising up," do not affirm that he was in an unconscious state, as
the Rabbins are said by *Jerome* to have indicated by the point
over בְּקוּמָהּ : " *quasi incredibile et quod natura rerum non capiat,
coire quempiam nescientem.*" They merely mean, that in his intoxicated state, though not entirely unconscious, yet he lay with
his daughters without clearly knowing what he was doing.—
Vers. 36 sqq. But Lot's daughters had so little feeling of shame
in connection with their conduct, that they gave names to the
sons they bore, which have immortalized their paternity. *Moab*,
another form of מֵאָב " from the father," as is indicated in the
clause appended in the LXX.: λέγουσα ἐκ τοῦ πατρός μου, and
also rendered probable by the reiteration of the words " of our
father" and " by their father" (vers. 32, 34, and 36), as well
as by the analogy of the name *Ben-Ammi* = *Ammon*, Ἀμμάν,
λέγουσα Υἰὸς γένους μου (LXX.). For עַמּוֹן, the sprout of the
nation, bears the same relation to עַם, as אַגְמוֹן, the rush or sprout
of the marsh, to אֲגַם (*Delitzsch*).—This account was neither the
invention of national hatred to the Moabites and Ammonites,
nor was it placed here as a brand upon those tribes. These
discoveries of a criticism imbued with hostility to the Bible are
overthrown by the fact, that, according to Deut. ii. 9, 19, Israel
was ordered not to touch the territory of either of these tribes
because of their descent from Lot; and it was their unbrotherly
conduct towards Israel alone which first prevented their reception into the congregation of the Lord, Deut. xxiii. 4, 5.—Lot
is never mentioned again. Separated both outwardly and inwardly from Abraham, he was of no further importance in
relation to the history of salvation, so that even his death is not
referred to. His descendants, however, frequently came into
contact with the Israelites; and the history of their descent is
given here to facilitate a correct appreciation of their conduct
towards Israel.

ABRAHAM'S SOJOURN AT GERAR.—CHAP. XX.

Vers. 1-7. After the destruction of Sodom and Gomorrah,
Abraham removed from the grove of Mamre at Hebron to the
south country, hardly from the same fear as that which led Lot
from Zoar, but probably to seek for better pasture. Here he
dwelt between Kadesh (xiv. 7) and Shur (xvi. 7), and remained

for some time in *Gerar*, a place the name of which has been preserved in the deep and broad Wady *Jurf el Gerâr* (*i.e.* torrent of Gerar) about eight miles S.S.E. of Gaza, near to which *Row land* discovered the ruins of an ancient town bearing the name of *Khirbet el Gerâr*. Here Abimelech, the Philistine king of Gerar, like Pharaoh in Egypt, took Sarah, whom Abraham had again announced to be his sister, into his harem,—not indeed because he was charmed with the beauty of the woman of 90, which was either renovated, or had not yet faded (*Kurtz*), but in all probability " to ally himself with Abraham, the rich nomad prince" (*Delitzsch*). From this danger, into which the untruthful statement of both her husband and herself had brought her, she was once more rescued by the faithfulness of the covenant God. In a dream by night God appeared to Abimelech, and threatened him with death (הִנְּךָ מֵת *en te moriturum*) on account of the woman, whom he had taken, because she was married to a husband.—Vers. 4 sqq. Abimelech, who had not yet come near her, because God had hindered him by illness (vers. 6 and 17), excused himself on the ground that he had done no wrong, since he had supposed Sarah to be Abraham's sister, according to both her husband's statement and her own. This plea was admitted by God, who told him that He had kept him from sinning through touching Sarah, and commanded him to restore the woman immediately to her husband, who was a prophet, that he might pray for him and save his life, and threatened him with certain death to himself and all belonging to him in case he should refuse. That Abimelech, when taking the supposed sister of Abraham into his harem, should have thought that he was acting " in innocence of heart and purity of hands," *i.e.* in perfect innocence, is to be fully accounted for, from his undeveloped moral and religious standpoint, by considering the customs of that day. But that God should have admitted that he had acted " in innocence of heart," and yet should have proceeded at once to tell him that he could only remain alive through the intercession of Abraham, that is to say, through his obtaining forgiveness of a sin that was deserving of death, is a proof that God treated him as capable of deeper moral discernment and piety. The history itself indicates this in the very characteristic variation in the names of God. First of all (ver. 3), *Elohim* (without the article, *i.e.* Deity generally) appears to him in a dream; but Abimelech recognises the Lord, *Adonai, i.e.* God (ver. 4); whereupon the historian represents האלהים (Elohim with the article), the personal and true God, as speaking to him. The address of God, too, also shows his susceptibility of divine truth. Without further pointing out to him the wrong which he had done in simplicity of heart, in taking the sister of the stranger who had come into his land, for the purpose of increasing his own harem, since he must have been conscious of this himself, God described Abraham as a prophet, whose intercession alone could remove his guilt, to show him the way of salvation. *A prophet: lit.* the God-addressed or inspired, since the " inward speaking " (*Ein-sprache*) or inspiration of God constitutes the essence of prophecy. Abraham was προφήτης as the recipient of divine revelation, and was thereby placed in so confidential a relation to God, that he could intercede for sinners, and atone for sins of infirmity through his intercession.

Vers. 8–15. Abimelech carried out the divine instructions. The next morning he collected his servants together and related what had occurred, at which the men were greatly alarmed. He then sent for Abraham, and complained most bitterly of his conduct, by which he had brought a great sin upon him and his kingdom.—Ver. 10. " *What sawest thou,*" *i.e.* what hadst thou in thine eye, with thine act (thy false statement)? Abimelech did this publicly in the presence of his servants, partly for his own justification in the sight of his dependants, and partly to put Abraham to shame. The latter had but two weak excuses: (1) that he supposed there was no fear of God at all in the land, and trembled for his life because of his wife; and (2) that when he left his father's house, he had arranged with his wife that in every foreign place she was to call herself his sister, as she really was his half-sister. On the subject of his emigration, he expressed himself indefinitely and with reserve, accommodating himself to the polytheistic standpoint of the Philistine king : " *when God* (or the gods, Elohim) *caused me to wander,*" *i.e.* led me to commence an unsettled life in a foreign land ; and saying nothing about Jehovah, and the object of his wandering as revealed by Him.— Vers. 14 sqq. Abimelech then gave him back his wife with a liberal present of cattle and slaves, and gave him leave to dwell wherever he pleased in his land. To Sarah he said, " *Behold, I have given a thousand shekele of silver to thy brother; behold, it is to thee a covering of the eyes* (*i.e.* an expiatory gift) *with regard to all that are with thee* ("because in a mistress the whole family is disgraced," *Del.*), *and with all—so art thou justified.*" The thousand shekels (about £131) were not a special present made to Sarah, but indicate the value of the present made to Abraham, the amount of which may be estimated by this standard, that at a later date (Ex. xxi. 32) a slave was reckoned at 30 shekels. By the "covering of the eyes" we are not to understand a veil, which Sarah was to procure for 1000 shekels; but it is a figurative expression for an atoning gift, and is to be explained by the analogy of the phrase פ׳ פְּנֵי כִּפֶּר "to cover any one's face," so that he may forget a wrong done (cf. chap. xxxii. 21 ; and Job ix. 24, "he covereth the faces of the judges," *i.e.* he bribes them). וְנֹכָחַת can only be the 2 pers. fem. sing. perf. Niphal, although the *Dagesh lene* is wanting in the ח ; for the rules of syntax will hardly allow us to regard this form as a participle, unless we imagine the extremely harsh ellipsis of נוֹכַחַת for אַתְּ נוֹכַחַת. The literal meaning is "so thou art judged," *i.e.* justice has been done thee.—Vers. 17, 18. After this reparation, God healed Abimelech at Abraham's intercession ; also his wife and maids, so that they could bear again, for Jehovah had closed up every womb in Abimelech's house on Sarah's account. אֲמָהוֹת, maids whom the king kept as concubines, are to be distinguished from שְׁפָחוֹת female slaves (ver. 14). That there was a material difference between them, is proved by 1 Sam. xxv. 41. עָצַר כָּל־רֶחֶם does not mean, as is frequently supposed, to prevent actual childbirth, but to prevent conception, *i.e.* to produce barrenness (1 Sam. i. 5, 6). This is evident from the expression "He hath restrained me from bearing" in chap. xvi. 2 (cf. Isa. lxvi. 9, and 1 Sam. xxi. 6), and from the opposite phrase, "open the womb," so as to facilitate conception (chap. xxix. 31, and xxx. 22). The plague brought upon Abimelech's house, therefore, consisted of some disease which rendered the begetting of children (the *coitus*) impossible. This might have occurred as soon as Sarah was taken into the royal harem, and therefore need not presuppose any lengthened stay there. There is no necessity, therefore, to restrict וַיֵּלֵדוּ to the women and regard it as equivalent to וַתֵּלַדְנָה, which would be grammatically inadmissible ; for it may refer to Abimelech also, since יָלַד signifies to beget as well as to bear. We may adopt *Knobel's* explanation, therefore, though without approving of the inference that ver. 18 was an appendix of the Jehovist, and arose from a misunderstanding of the word וַיֵּלְדוּ in ver. 17. A later addition ver. 18 cannot be; for the simple reason, that without the explanation given there, the previous verse would be unintelligible, so that it cannot have been wanting in any of the accounts. The name Jehovah, in contrast with *Elohim* and *Ha-Elohim* in ver. 17, is obviously significant. The cure of Abimelech and his wives belonged to the Deity (*Elohim*). Abraham directed his intercession not to *Elohim*, an indefinite and unknown God, but to הָאֱלֹהִים; for the God, whose prophet he was, was the personal and true God. It was He too who had brought the disease upon Abimelech and his house, not as *Elohim* or *Ha-Elohim*, but as *Jehovah*, the God of salvation; for His design therein was to prevent the disturbance or frustration of His saving design, and the birth of the promised son from Sarah.

But if the divine names *Elohim* and *Ha-Elohim* indicate the true relation of God to Abimelech, and here also it was Jehovah who interposed for Abraham and preserved the mother of the promised seed, our narrative cannot be merely an Elohistic side-piece appended to the Jehovistic account in chap. xii. 14 sqq., and founded upon a fictitious legend. The thoroughly distinctive character of this event is a decisive proof of the fallacy of any such critical conjecture. Apart from the one point of agreement—the taking of Abraham's wife into the royal harem, because he said she was his sister in the hope of thereby saving his own life (an event, the repetition of which in the space of 24 years is by no means startling, when we consider the customs of the age)—all the more minute details are entirely different in the two cases. In king Abimelech we meet with a totally different character from that of Pharaoh. We see in him a heathen imbued with a moral consciousness of right, and open to receive divine revelation, of which there is not the slightest trace in the king of Egypt. And Abraham, in spite of his natural weakness, and the consequent confusion which he manifested in the presence of the pious heathen, was exalted by the compassionate grace of God to the position of His own friend, so that even the heathen king, who seems to have been in the right in this instance, was compelled to bend before him and to seek the removal of the divine punishment, which had fallen upon him and his house, through the medium of his intercession. In this way God proved to the Philistine king, on the one hand, that He suffers no harm to befall His prophets (Ps. cv. 15), and to Abraham, on the other, that He can maintain His covenant and secure the realization of His promise against all opposition from the sinful desires of earthly potentates. It was in this respect that the event possessed a typical significance in relation to the future attitude of Israel towards surrounding nations.

BIRTH OF ISAAC. EXPULSION OF ISHMAEL. ABIMELECH'S TREATY WITH ABRAHAM.—CHAP. XXI.

Vers. 1–7. BIRTH OF ISAAC.—Jehovah did for Sarah what God had promised in chap. xvii. 6 (cf. xviii. 14) : she conceived, and at the time appointed bore a son to Abraham, when he was 100 years old. Abraham gave it the name of *Jizchak* (or Isaac), and circumcised it on the eighth day. The name for the promised son had been selected by God, in connection with Abraham's laughing (chap. xvii. 17 and 19), to indicate the nature of his birth and existence. For as his laughing sprang from the contrast between the idea and the reality ; so through a miracle of grace the birth of Isaac gave effect to this contrast between the promise of God and the pledge of its fulfilment on the one hand, and the incapacity of Abraham for begetting children, and of Sarah for bearing them, on the other ; and through this name, Isaac was designated as the fruit of omnipotent grace working against and above the forces of nature. Sarah also, who had previously laughed with unbelief at the divine promise (xviii. 12), found a reason in the now accomplished birth of the promised son for laughing with joyous amazement ; so that she exclaimed, with evident allusion to his name, "*A laughing hath God prepared for me ; every one who hears it will laugh to me*" (*i.e.* will rejoice with me, in amazement at the blessing of God which has come upon me even in my old age), and gave a fitting expression to the joy of her heart, in this inspired *tristich* (ver. 7): "*Who would have said unto Abraham : Sarah is giving suck ; for I have born a son to his old age.*" מִלֵּל is the poetic word for דִּבֶּר, and מִי before the perfect has the sense of—whoever has said, which we should express as a subjunctive ; cf. 2 Kings xx. 9 ; Ps. xi. 3, etc.

Vers. 8–21. EXPULSION OF ISHMAEL.—The weaning of the child, which was celebrated with a feast, furnished the outward occasion for this.   Sarah saw Ishmael mocking, making ridicule on the occasion.   " Isaac, the object of holy laughter, was made the butt of unholy wit or profane sport.   He did not laugh (צָחַק), but he made fun (מְצַחֵק).   The little helpless Isaac a father of nations !   Unbelief, envy, pride of carnal superiority, were the causes of his conduct.   Because he did not understand the sentiment, ' Is anything too wonderful for the Lord?' it seemed to him absurd to link so great a thing to one so small" (*Hengstenberg*).   Paul calls this the persecution of him that was after the Spirit by him that was begotten after the flesh (Gal. iv. 29), and discerns in this a prediction of the persecution, which the Church of those who are born after the spirit of faith endures from those who are in bondage to the righteousness of the law.—Ver. 9. Sarah therefore asked that the maid and her son might be sent away, saying, the latter " shall not be heir with Isaac."   The demand, which apparently proceeded from maternal jealousy, displeased Abraham greatly " *because of his son,*"—partly because in Ishmael he loved his own flesh and blood, and partly on account of the promise received for him (chap. xvii. 18 and 20).   But God (*Elohim*, since there is no appearance mentioned, but the divine will was made known to him inwardly) commanded him to comply with Sarah's demand : " *for in Isaac shall seed* (posterity) *be called to thee.*"   This expression cannot mean " thy descendants will call themselves after Isaac," for in that case, at all events, זַרְעֶךָ would be used ; nor " in (through) Isaac shall seed be called into existence to thee," for קָרָא does not mean to call into existence ; but, " in the person of Isaac shall there be posterity to thee, which shall pass as such," for נִקְרָא includes existence and the recognition of existence.   Though the noun is not defined by any article, the seed intended must be that to which all the promises of God referred, and with which God would establish His covenant (chap. xvii. 21, cf. Rom. ix. 7, 8 ; Heb. xi. 18).   To make the dismissal of Ishmael easier to the paternal heart, God repeated to Abraham (ver. 13) the promise already given him with regard to this son (chap. xvii. 20).—Vers. 14 sqq. The next morning Abraham sent Hagar away with Ishmael.   The words, " *he took bread and a bottle of water and gave it to Hagar, putting it* (שָׂם participle, not perfect) *upon her shoulder, and the boy, and sent her away,*" do not state that Abraham gave her Ishmael also to carry. For וְאֶת־הַיֶּלֶד does not depend upon שָׂם and וַיִּתֵּן because of the copula ו, but upon יִקַּח, the leading verb of the sentence, although it is separated from it by the parenthesis "putting it upon her shoulder." It does not follow from these words, therefore, that Ishmael is represented as a little child. Nor is this implied in the statement which follows, that Hagar, when wandering about in the desert, "cast the boy under one of the shrubs," because the water in the bottle was gone. For יֶלֶד like נַעַר does not mean an infant, but a boy, and also a young man (iv. 23);— Ishmael must have been 15 or 16 years old, as he was 14 before Isaac was born (cf. ver. 5, and xvi. 16);—and הִשְׁלִיךְ, "to throw," signifies that she suddenly left hold of the boy, when he fell exhausted from thirst, just as in Matt. xv. 30 ῥίπτειν is used for laying hastily down. Though despairing of his life, the mother took care that at least he should breathe out his life in the shade, and she sat over against him weeping, "in the distance as archers," *i.e.* according to a concise simile very common in Hebrew, as far off as archers are accustomed to place the target. Her maternal love could not bear to see him die, and yet she would not lose sight of him.—Vers. 17 sqq. Then God heard the voice (the weeping and crying) of the boy, and the angel of God called to Hagar from heaven, "*What aileth thee, Hagar? Fear not, for God hath heard the voice of the boy, where he is*" (בַּאֲשֶׁר for בְּמָקוֹם אֲשֶׁר, 2 Sam. xv. 21), *i.e.* in his helpless condition : "*arise, lift up the lad,*" etc. It was Elohim, not Jehovah, who heard the voice of the boy, and appeared as the angel of Elohim, not of Jehovah (as in chap. xvi. 7), because, when Ishmael and Hagar had been dismissed from Abraham's house, they were removed from the superintendence and care of the covenant God to the guidance and providence of God the ruler of all nations. God then opened her eyes, and she saw what she had not seen before, a well of water, from which she filled the bottle and gave her son to drink.—Ver. 20. Having been miraculously saved from perishing by the angel of God, Ishmael grew up under the protection of God, settled in the wilderness of Paran, and "*became as he grew up an archer.*" Although preceded by וַיִּגְדַּל, the רֹבֶה is not tautological ; and there is no reason for attributing to it the meaning of "archer," in which sense רָבַב alone occurs in the one passage Gen. xlix. 23. The desert of *Paran* is the present large desert of *et-Tih,* which stretches along the southern border of Canaan, from the western fringe of the Arabah, towards the east to the desert of Shur (*Jifar*), on the frontier of Egypt, and extends southwards to the promontories of the mountains of Horeb (*vid.* Num. x. 12). On the northern edge of this desert was *Beersheba* (proleptically so called in ver. 14), to which Abraham had removed from Gerar; so that in all probability Hagar and Ishmael were sent away from his abode there, and wandered about in the surrounding desert, till Hagar was afraid that they should perish with thirst. Lastly, in preparation for chap. xxv. 12–18, it is mentioned in ver. 21 that Ishmael married a wife out of Egypt.

Vers. 22–34. ABIMELECH'S TREATY WITH ABRAHAM.— Through the divine blessing which visibly attended Abraham, the Philistine king *Abimelech* was induced to secure for himself and his descendants the friendship of a man so blessed; and for that purpose he went to Beersheba, with his captain *Phicol,* to conclude a treaty with him. Abraham was perfectly ready to agree to this; but first of all he complained to him about a well which Abimelech's men had stolen, *i.e.* had unjustly appropriated to themselves. Abimelech replied that this act of violence had never been made known to him till that day, and as a matter of course commanded the well to be returned. After the settlement of this dispute the treaty was concluded, and Abraham presented the king with sheep and oxen, as a material pledge that he would reciprocate the kindness shown, and live in friendship with the king and his descendants. Out of this present he selected seven lambs and set them by themselves; and when Abimelech inquired what they were, he told him to take them from his hand, that they might be to him (Abraham) for a witness that he had digged the well. It was not to redeem the well, but to secure the well as his property against any fresh claims on the part of the Philistines, that the present was given; and by the acceptance of it, Abraham's right of possession was practically and solemnly acknowledged.— Ver. 31. From this circumstance, the place where it occurred received the name בְּאֵר שֶׁבַע, *i.e.* seven-well, "because there they sware both of them." It does not follow from this note, that the writer interpreted the name "oath-well," and took שֶׁבַע in the sense of שִׁבְעָה. The idea is rather the following : the place received its name from the seven lambs, by which Abraham secured to himself possession of the well, because the treaty was sworn to on the basis of the agreement confirmed by the seven lambs. There is no mention of sacrifice, however, in connection with the treaty (see chap. xxvi. 33). נִשְׁבַּע to swear, *lit.* to seven one's self, not because in the oath the divine number 3 is combined with the world-number 4, but because, from the sacredness of the number 7, the real origin and ground of which are to be sought in the number 7 of the work of creation, seven things were generally chosen to give validity to an oath, as was the case, according to *Herodotus* (3, 8), with the Arabians among others. *Beersheba* was in the Wady *es-Seba*, the broad channel of a winter-torrent, 12 hours' journey to the south of Hebron on the road to Egypt and the Dead Sea, where there are still stones to be found, the relics of an ancient town, and two deep wells with excellent water, called *Bir es Seba, i.e.* seven-well (not lion-well, as the Bedouins erroneously interpret it) : cf. *Robinson's* Pal. i. pp. 300 sqq.—Ver. 33. Here Abraham planted a tamarisk and called upon the name of the Lord (*vid.* chap. iv. 26), the everlasting God. Jehovah is called the everlasting God, as the eternally true, with respect to the eternal covenant, which He established with Abraham (chap. xvii. 7). The planting of this long-lived tree, with its hard wood, and its long, narrow, thickly clustered, evergreen leaves, was to be a type of the ever-enduring grace of the faithful covenant God.— Ver. 34. Abraham sojourned a long time there in the Philistines' land. There Isaac was probably born, and grew up to be a young man (xxii. 6), capable of carrying the wood for a sacrifice; cf. xxii. 19. The expression " in the land of the Philistines " appears to be at variance with ver. 32, where Abimelech and Phicol are said to have returned to the land of the Philistines. But the discrepancy is easily reconciled, on the supposition that at that time the land of the Philistines had no fixed boundary, at all events, towards the desert. Beersheba did not belong to Gerar, the kingdom of Abimelech in the stricter sense; but the Philistines extended their wanderings so far, and claimed the district as their own, as is evident from the fact that Abimelech's people had taken the well from Abraham. On the other hand, Abraham with his numerous flocks would not confine himself to the Wady *es Seba*, but must have sought for pasture-ground in the whole surrounding country; and as Abimelech had given him full permission to dwell in his land (xx. 15), he would still, as heretofore, frequently come as far as Gerar, so that his dwelling at Beersheba (xxii. 19) might be correctly described as sojourning (nomadizing) in the land of the Philistines.

OFFERING UP OF ISAAC UPON MORIAH.   FAMILY OF NAHOR.—
CHAP. XXII.

Vers. 1-19. OFFERING UP OF ISAAC.—For many years had Abraham waited for the promised seed, in which the divine promise was to be fulfilled. At length the Lord had given him the desired heir of his body by his wife Sarah, and directed him to send away the son of the maid. And now that this son had grown into a young man, the word of God came to Abraham, to offer up this very son, who had been given to him as the heir of the promise, for a burnt-offering, upon one of the mountains which should be shown him. This word did not come from his own heart,—was not a thought suggested by the sight of the human sacrifices of the Canaanites, that he would offer a similar sacrifice to his God; nor did it originate with the tempter to evil. The word came from *Ha-Elohim*, the personal, true God, who tried him (נִסָּה), *i.e.* demanded the sacrifice of the only, beloved son, as a proof and attestation of his faith. The issue shows, that God did not desire the sacrifice of Isaac by slaying and burning him upon the altar, but his complete surrender, and a willingness to offer him up to God even by death. Nevertheless the divine command was given in such a form, that Abraham could not understand it in any other way than as requiring an outward burnt-offering, because there was no other way in which Abraham could accomplish the complete surrender of Isaac, than by an actual preparation for really offering the desired sacrifice. This constituted the trial, which necessarily produced a severe internal conflict in his mind. *Ratio humana simpliciter concluderet aut mentiri promissionem aut mandatum non esse Dei sed Diaboli; est enim contradictio manifesta. Si enim debet occidi Isaac, irrita est promissio; sin rata est promissio, impossibile est hoc esse Dei mandatum* (*Luther*). But Abraham brought his reason into captivity to the obedience of faith. He did not question the truth of the word of God, which had been addressed to him in a mode that was to his mind perfectly infallible (not in a vision of the night, however, of which there is not a syllable in the text), but he stood firm in his faith, "accounting that God was able to raise him up, even from the dead" Heb. xi. 19). Without taking counsel with flesh and blood, Abraham started early in the morning (vers. 3, 4), with his son Isaac and two servants, to obey the divine command; and on the third day (for the distance from Beersheba to Jerusalem is about $20\frac{1}{2}$ hours; Rob. Pal. iii. App. 66, 67) he saw in the distance the place mentioned by God, the land of Moriah, *i.e.* the mountainous country round about Jerusalem. The name מֹרִיָּה, composed of the Hophal partic. of רָאָה and the divine name יה, an abbreviation of יְהֹוָה (*lit.* "the shown of Jehovah," equivalent to the manifestation of Jehovah), is no doubt used proleptically in ver. 2, and given to the mountain upon which the sacrifice was to be made, with direct reference to this event and the appearance of Jehovah to Abraham there. This is confirmed by ver. 14, where the name is connected with the event, and explained in the fuller expression *Jehovah-jireh*. On the ground of this passage the mountain upon which Solomon built the temple is called הַמּוֹרִיָּה with reference to the appearance of the angel of the Lord to David on that mountain at the threshing-floor of Araunah (2 Sam. xxiv. 16, 17), the old name being revived by this appearance.

Ver. 5. When in sight of the distant mountain, Abraham left the servants behind with the ass, that he might perform the last and hardest part of the journey alone with Isaac, and, as he said to the servants, "*worship yonder and then return.*" The servants were not to see what would take place there; for they could not understand this "worship," and the issue even to him, notwithstanding his saying "we will come again to you," was still involved in the deepest obscurity. This last part of the journey is circumstantially described in vers. 6–8, to show how strong a conflict every step produced in the paternal heart of the patriarch. They go both together, he with the fire and the knife in his hand, and his son with the wood for the sacrifice upon his shoulder. Isaac asks his father, where is the lamb for the burnt-offering; and the father replies, not "Thou wilt be it, my son,"

but " God (Elohim without the article—God as the all-pervading
supreme power) will provide it;" for he will not and cannot
yet communicate the divine command to his son. *Non vult
filium macerare longa cruce et tentatione (Luther).*—Vers. 9, 10.
Having arrived at the appointed place, Abraham built an altar,
arranged the wood upon it, bound his son and laid him upon the
wood of the altar, and then stretched out his hand and took the
knife to slay his son.—Vers. 11 sqq. In this eventful moment,
when Isaac lay bound like a lamb upon the altar, about to receive
the fatal stroke, the angel of the Lord called down from heaven
to Abraham to stop, and do his son no harm. For the Lord now
knew that Abraham was יְרֵא אֱלֹהִים God-fearing, and that his obedience of faith did extend even to the sacrifice of his own beloved
son. The sacrifice was already accomplished in his heart, and
he had fully satisfied the requirements of God. He was not to
slay his son: therefore God prevented the outward fulfilment of
the sacrifice by an immediate interposition, and showed him a
ram, which he saw, probably being led to look round through a
rustling behind him, with its horns fast in a thicket (אַחַר *adv.*
behind, in the background) ; and as an offering provided by God
Himself, he sacrificed it instead of his son.—Ver. 14. From this
interposition of God, Abraham called the place *Jehovah-jireh,*
" Jehovah sees," *i.e.* according to ver. 8, provides, *providet ;* so
that (אֲשֶׁר, as in chap. xiii. 16, is equivalent to עַל כֵּן, x. 9) men are
still accustomed to say, " *On the mountain where Jehovah appears*"
(יֵרָאֶה), from which the name *Moriah* arose. The rendering " on
the mount of Jehovah it is provided" is not allowable, for the
Niphal of the verb does not mean *provideri,* but " appear."
Moreover, in this case the medium of God's seeing or interposition was His appearing.—Vers. 15–19. After Abraham had offered
the ram, the angel of the Lord called to him a second time from
heaven, and with a solemn oath renewed the former promises, as
a reward for this proof of his obedience of faith (cf. xii. 2, 3).
To confirm their unchangeableness, Jehovah swore by Himself
(cf. Heb. vi. 13 sqq.), a thing which never occurs again in His
intercourse with the patriarchs ; so that subsequently not only do
we find repeated references to this oath (chap. xxiv. 7, xxvi. 3,
l. 24 ; Ex. xiii. 5, 1x, xxxii. 1, etc.), but, as *Luther* observes, all
that is said in Ps. lxxxix. 36, cxxxii. 11, cx. 4 respecting the oath
given to David, is founded upon this. *Sicut enim promissio*

seminis Abrahæ derivata est in semen Davidis, ita Scriptura S. jus-jurandum Abrahæ datum in personam Davidis transfert. For in the promise upon which these psalms are based nothing is said about an oath (cf. 2 Sam. vii.; 1 Chron. xvii.). The declaration on oath is still further confirmed by the addition of נְאֻם יְהֹוָה " *edict (Ausspruch) of Jehovah,*" which, frequently as it occurs in the prophets, is met with in the Pentateuch only in Num. xiv. 28, and (without Jehovah) in the oracles of Balaam, Num. xxiv. 3, 15, 16. As the promise was intensified in form, so was it also in substance. To express the innumerable multiplication of the seed in the strongest possible way, a comparison with the sand of the sea-shore is added to the previous simile of the stars. And this seed is also promised the possession of the gate of its enemies, *i.e.* the conquest of the enemy and the capture of his cities (cf. xxiv. 60).

This glorious result of the test so victoriously stood by Abraham, not only sustains the historical character of the event itself, but shows in the clearest manner that the trial was necessary to the patriarch's life of faith, and of fundamental importance to his position in relation to the history of salvation. The question, whether the true God could demand a human sacrifice, was settled by the fact that God Himself prevented the completion of the sacrifice; and the difficulty, that at any rate God contradicted Himself, if He first of all demanded a sacrifice and then prevented it from being offered, is met by the significant interchange of the names of God, since God, who commanded Abraham to offer up Isaac, is called *Ha-Elohim*, whilst the actual completion of the sacrifice is prevented by "the angel of Jehovah," who is identical with *Jehovah* Himself. The sacrifice of the heir, who had been both promised and bestowed, was demanded neither by *Jehovah*, the God of salvation or covenant God, who had given Abraham this only son as the heir of the promise, nor by *Elohim*, God as creator, who has the power to give life and take it away, but by *Ha-Elohim*, the true God, whom Abraham had acknowledged and adored as his personal God, and with whom he had entered into a personal relation. Coming from the true God whom Abraham served, the demand could have no other object than to purify and sanctify the feelings of the patriarch's heart towards his son and towards his God, in accordance with the great purpose of his call. It

was designed to purify his love to the son of his body from all
the dross of carnal self-love and natural selfishness which might
still adhere to it, and so to transform it into love to God, from
whom he had received him, that he should no longer love the
beloved son as his flesh and blood, but simply and solely as a
gift of grace, as belonging to his God,—a trust committed to
him, which he should be ready at any moment to give back to
God.   As he had left his country, kindred, and father's house
at the call of God (xii. 1), so was he in his walk with God
cheerfully to offer up even his only son, the object of all his
longing, the hope of his life, the joy of his old age.   And still
more than this, not only did he possess and love in Isaac the heir
of his possessions (xv. 2), but it was upon him that all the promises
of God rested : in Isaac should his seed be called (xxi. 12).   By
the demand that he should sacrifice to God this only son of his
wife Sarah, in whom his seed was to grow into a multitude of
nations (xvii. 4, 6, 16), the divine promise itself seemed to be
cancelled, and the fulfilment not only of the desires of his heart,
but also of the repeated promises of his God, to be frustrated.
And by this demand his faith was to be perfected into unconditional trust in God, into the firm assurance that God could even
raise him up from the dead.—But this trial was not only one of
significance to Abraham, by perfecting him, through the conquest
of flesh and blood, to be the father of the faithful, the progenitor
of the Church of God ; Isaac also was to be prepared and sancti
fied by it for his vocation in connection with the history of
salvation.   In permitting himself to be bound and laid upon the
altar without resistance, he gave up his natural life to death, to
rise to a new life through the grace of God.   On the altar he
was sanctified to God, dedicated as the first beginning of the
holy Church of God, and thus " the dedication of the first-born,
which was afterwards enjoined in the law, was perfectly fulfilled
in him."   If therefore the divine command exhibits in the most
impressive way the earnestness of the demand of God upon His
people to sacrifice all to Him, not excepting the dearest of their
possessions (cf. Matt. x. 37, and Luke xiv. 26) ; the issue of the
trial teaches that the true God does not demand a literal human
sacrifice from His worshippers, but the spiritual sacrifice of an
unconditional denial of the natural life, even to submission to
death itself.   By the sacrifice of a ram as a burnt-offering in the

place of his son, under divine direction, not only was animal sacrifice substituted for human, and sanctioned as an acceptable symbol of spiritual self-sacrifice, but the offering of human sacrifices by the heathen was condemned and rejected as an ungodly ἐθελοθρησκεία. And this was done by Jehovah, the God of salvation, who prevented the outward completion of the sacrifice. By this the event acquires prophetic importance for the Church of the Lord, to which the place of sacrifice points with peculiar clearness, viz. Mount Moriah, upon which under the legal economy all the typical sacrifices were offered to Jehovah; upon which also, in the fulness of time, God the Father gave up His only-begotten Son as an atoning sacrifice for the sins of the whole world, that by this one true sacrifice the shadows of the typical sacrifices might be rendered both real and true. If therefore the appointment of Moriah as the scene of the sacrifice of Isaac, and the offering of a ram in his stead, were primarily only typical in relation to the significance and intent of the Old Testament institution of sacrifice; this type already pointed to the antitype to appear in the future, when the eternal love of the heavenly Father would perform what it had demanded of Abraham; that is to say, when God would not spare His only Son, but give Him up to the real death, which Isaac suffered only in spirit, that we also might die with Christ spiritually, and rise with Him to everlasting life (Rom. viii. 32, vi. 5, etc.).

Vers. 20-24. DESCENDANTS OF NAHOR.—With the sacrifice of Isaac the test of Abraham's faith was now complete, and the purpose of his divine calling answered: the history of his life, therefore, now hastens to its termination. But first of all there is introduced quite appropriately an account of the family of his brother Nahor, which is so far in place immediately after the story of the sacrifice of Isaac, that it prepares the way for the history of the marriage of the heir of the promise. The connection is pointed out in ver. 20, as compared with chap. xi. 29, in the expression, "she also." Nahor, like Ishmael and Jacob, had twelve sons, eight by his wife Milcah and four by his concubine; whereas Jacob had his by two wives and two maids, and Ishmael apparently all by one wife. This difference with regard to the mothers proves that the agreement as to the number twelve rests upon a good historical tradition, and is no product of a later

myth, which traced to Nahor the same number of tribes as to
Ishmael and Jacob. For it is a perfectly groundless assertion
or assumption, that Nahor's twelve sons were the fathers of as
many tribes. There are only a few names, of which it is probable that their bearers were the founders of tribes of the same
name. On *Uz*, see chap. x. 23. *Buz* is mentioned in Jer. xxv.
23 along with Dedan and Tema as an Arabian tribe; and
Elihu was a Buzite of the family of *Ram* (Job xxxii. 2).
Kemuel, the father of Aram, was not the founder of the Aramæans, but the forefather of the family of *Ram*, to which the
Buzite Elihu belonged,—Aram being written for Ram, like
Arammim in 2 Kings viii. 29 for Rammim in 2 Chron. xxii. 5.
Chesed again was not the father of the Chasdim (Chaldeans),
for they were older than Chesed; at the most he was only
the founder of one branch of the *Chasdim*, possibly those who
stole Job's camels *(Knobel; vid.* Job i. 17). Of the remaining
names, *Bethuel* was not the founder of a tribe, but the father of
Laban and Rebekah (chap. xxv. 20). The others are never met
with again, with the exception of *Maachah*, from whom probably the Maachites (Deut. iii. 14; Josh. xii. 5) in the land of
Maacah, a small Arabian kingdom in the time of David (2 Sam.
x. 6, 8; 1 Chron. xix. 6), derived their origin and name; though
Maachah frequently occurs as the name of a person (1 Kings
ii. 39; 1 Chron. xi. 43, xxvii. 16).

DEATH OF SARAH; AND PURCHASE OF THE CAVE AT
MACHPELAH.—CHAP. XXIII.

Vers. 1, 2. Sarah is the only woman whose age is mentioned in the Scriptures, because as the mother of the promised seed she became the mother of all believers (1 Pet. iii. 6).
She died at the age of 127, thirty-seven years after the birth of
Isaac, at Hebron, or rather in the grove of Mamre near that
city (xiii. 18), whither Abraham had once more returned after a
lengthened stay at Beersheba (xxii. 19). The name Kirjath
Arba, *i.e.* the city of Arba, which Hebron bears here and also
in chap. xxxv. 27, and other passages, and which it still bore at
the time of the conquest of Canaan by the Israelites (Josh. xiv.
15), was not the original name of the city, but was first given to
it by Arba the Anakite and his family, who had not yet arrived

there in the time of the patriarchs. It was probably given by them when they took possession of the city, and remained until the Israelites captured it and restored the original name. The place still exists, as a small town on the road from Jerusalem to Beersheba, in a valley surrounded by several mountains, and is called by the Arabs, with allusion to Abraham's stay there, *el Khalil, i.e.* the friend (of God), which is the title given to Abraham by the Mohammedans. The clause "*in the land of Canaan*" denotes, that not only did Sarah die in the land of promise, but Abraham as a foreigner acquired a burial-place by purchase there. "*And Abraham came*" (not from Beersheba, but from the field where he may have been with the flocks), "*to mourn for Sarah and to weep for her,*" *i.e.* to arrange for the customary mourning ceremony.

Vers. 3–16. He then went to the Hittites, the lords and possessors of the city and its vicinity at that time, to procure from them "a possession of a burying-place." The negotiations were carried on in the most formal style, in a public assembly "of the people of the land," *i.e.* of natives (ver. 7), in the gate of the city (ver. 10). As a foreigner and sojourner, Abraham presented his request in the most courteous manner to all the citizens ("all that went in at the gate," vers. 10, 18; a phrase interchangeable with "all that went out at the gate," chap. xxxiv. 24, and those who "go out and in," Jer. xvii. 19). The citizens with the greatest readiness and respect offered "the prince of God," *i.e.* the man exalted by God to the rank of a prince, "the choice" (מִבְחַר, *i.e.* the most select) of their graves for his use (ver. 6). But Abraham asked them to request Ephron, who, to judge from the expression "his city" in ver. 10, was then ruler of the city, to give him for a possession the cave of *Machpelah*, at the end of his field, of which he was the owner, "for full silver," *i.e.* for its full worth. Ephron thereupon offered to make him a present of both field and cave. This was a turn in the affair which is still customary in the East; the design, so far as it is seriously meant at all, being either to obtain a present in return which will abundantly compensate for the value of the gift, or, what is still more frequently the case, to preclude any abatement in the price to be asked. The same design is evident in the peculiar form in which Ephron stated the price, in reply to Abraham's repeated declaration that he was determined to buy the piece of land: "a piece of land of 400 shekels of silver, what is that between me and thee" (ver. 15)? Abraham understood it so (יִשְׁמַע ver. 16), and weighed him the price demanded. The shekel of silver "current with the merchant," *i.e.* the shekel which passed in trade as of standard weight, was 274 Parisian grains, so that the price of the piece of land was £52, 10s.; a very considerable amount for that time.

Vers. 17–20. "*Thus arose* (וַיָּקָם) *the field . . . to Abraham for a possession;*" *i.e.* it was conveyed to him in all due legal form. The expression "the field of Ephron which is at Machpelah" may be explained, according to ver. 9, from the fact that the cave of Machpelah was at the end of the field, the field, therefore, belonged to it. In ver. 19 the shorter form, "cave of Machpelah," occurs; and in ver. 20 the field is distinguished from the cave. The name *Machpelah* is translated by the LXX. as a common noun, τὸ σπήλαιον τὸ διπλοῦν, from מַכְפֵּלָה doubling; but it had evidently grown into a proper name, since it is used not only of the cave, but of the adjoining field also (chap. xlix. 30, l. 13), though it undoubtedly originated in the form of the cave. The cave was before, *i.e.* probably to the east of, the grove of Mamre, which was in the district of Hebron. This description cannot be reconciled with the tradition, which identifies Mamre and the cave with *Ramet el Khalil*, where the strong foundation-walls of an ancient heathen temple (according to Rosenmüller's conjecture, an Idumæan one) are still pointed out as Abraham's house, and where a very old terebinth stood in the early Christian times; for this is an hour's journey to the north of modern Hebron, and even the ancient Hebron cannot have stretched so far over the mountains which separate the modern city from *Rameh*, but must also, according to chap. xxxvii. 14, have been situated in the valley (see Robinson's later Biblical Researches, pp. 365 sqq.). There is far greater probability in the Mohammedan tradition, that the Harem, built of colossal blocks with grooved edges, which stands on the western slope of the *Geabireh* mountain, in the north-western portion of the present town, contains hidden within it the cave of Machpelah with the tomb of the patriarchs (cf. *Robinson*, Pal. ii. 435 sqq.); and *Rosen.* is induced to look for Mamre on the eastern slope of

the *Rumeidi* hill, near to the remarkable well *Ain el Jedid.*—
Ver. 20. The repetition of the statement, that the field with the
cave in it was conveyed to Abraham by the Hittites for a burial-
place, which gives the result of the negotiation that has been
described with, so to speak, legal accuracy, shows the great importance of the event to the patriarch. The fact that Abraham
purchased a burying-place in strictly legal form as an hereditary
possession in the promised land, was a proof of his strong faith
in the promises of God and their eventual fulfilment. In this
grave Abraham and Sarah, Isaac and Rebekah, were buried ;
there Jacob buried Leah ; and there Jacob himself requested
that he might be buried, thus declaring his faith in the promises,
even in the hour of his death.

ISAAC'S MARRIAGE.—CHAP. XXIV.

Vers. 1–9. After the death of Sarah, Abraham had still to
arrange for the marriage of Isaac. He was induced to provide
for this in a mode in harmony with the promise of God, quite
as much by his increasing age as by the blessing of God in
everything, which necessarily instilled the wish to transmit that
blessing to a distant posterity. He entrusted this commission to
his servant, "the eldest of his house,"—*i.e.* his upper servant,
who had the management of all his house (according to general
opinion, to Eliezer, whom he had previously thought of as the
heir of his property, but who would now, like Abraham, be extremely old, as more than sixty years had passed since the occurrence related in chap. xv. 2),—and made him swear that he would
not take a wife for his son from the daughters of the Canaanites,
but would fetch one from his (Abraham's) native country, and
his kindred. Abraham made the servant take an oath in order
that his wishes might be inviolably fulfilled, even if he himself
should die in the interim. In swearing, the servant put his
hand under Abraham's hip. This custom, which is only mentioned here and in chap. xlvii. 29, the so-called bodily oath,
was no doubt connected with the significance of the hip as the
part from which the posterity issued (xlvi. 26), and the seat of
vital power ; but the early Jewish commentators supposed it to
be especially connected with the rite of circumcision. The oath
was by "*Jehovah,* God of heaven and earth," as the God who

rules in heaven and on earth, not by *Elohim* ; for it had respect
not to an ordinary oath, but to a question of great importance in
relation to the kingdom of God. "Isaac was not regarded as
a merely pious candidate for matrimony, but as the heir of the
promise, who must therefore be kept from any alliance with the
race whose possessions were to come to his descendants, and which
was ripening for the judgment to be executed by those descendants" (*Hengstenberg*, Dissertations i. 350). For this reason the rest
of the negotiation was all conducted in the name of Jehovah.—
Vers. 5 sqq. Before taking the oath, the servant asks whether,
in case no woman of their kindred would follow him to Canaan,
Isaac was to be conducted to the land of his fathers. But Abraham rejected the proposal, because Jehovah took him from his
father's house, and had promised him the land of Canaan for a
possession. He also discharged the servant, if that should be the
case, from the oath which he had taken, in the assurance that
the Lord through His angel would bring a wife to his son from
thence.

Vers. 10–28. The servant then went, with ten camels and
things of every description belonging to his master, into Mesopotamia to the city of Nahor, *i.e.* Haran, where Nahor dwelt
(xi. 31, and xii. 4). On his arrival there, he made the camels
kneel down, or rest, without the city by the well, "*at the time of
evening, the time at which the women come out to draw water*," and
at which, now as then, women and girls are in the habit of fetching the water required for the house (*vid. Robinson's* Palestine ii. 368 sqq.). He then prayed to Jehovah, the God of
Abraham, "*Let there come to meet me to-day*," *sc.* the person desired, the object of my mission. He then fixed upon a sign connected with the custom of the country, by the occurrence of which
he might decide upon the maiden (הַנַּעַר *puella*, used in the Pentateuch for both sexes, except in Deut. xxii. 19, where נַעֲרָה occurs)
whom Jehovah had indicated as the wife appointed for His servant Isaac. הוֹכִיחַ (ver. 14) to set right, then to point out as
right; not merely to appoint. He had scarcely ended his prayer
when his request was granted. Rebekah did just what he had
fixed upon as a token, not only giving him to drink, but offering to water his camels, and with youthful vivacity carrying
out her promise. *Niebuhr* met with similar kindness in those
regions (see also *Robinson*, Pal. ii. 351, etc.). The servant did

not give himself blindly up to first impressions, however, but tested the circumstances.—Ver. 21. "*The man, wondering at her, stood silent, to know whether Jehovah had made his journey prosperous or not.*" מִשְׁתָּאֵה, from שָׁאָה to be desert, inwardly laid waste, *i.e.* confused. Others derive it from שָׁאָה = שָׁעָה to see; but in the *Hithpael* this verb signifies to look restlessly about, which is not applicable here.—Vers. 22 sqq. After the watering of the camels was over, the man took a golden nose-ring of the weight of a beka, *i.e.* half a shekel (Ex. xxxviii. 26), and two golden armlets of 10 shekels weight, and (as we find from vers. 30 and 47) placed these ornaments upon her, not as a bridal gift, but in return for her kindness. He then asked her about her family, and whether there was room in her father's house for him and his attendants to pass the night there; and it was not till after Rebekah had told him that she was the daughter of Bethuel, the nephew of Abraham, and had given a most cheerful assent to his second question, that he felt sure that this was the wife appointed by Jehovah for Isaac. He then fell down and thanked Jehovah for His grace and truth, whilst Rebekah in the meantime had hastened home to relate all that had occurred to "*her mother's house,*" *i.e.* to the female portion of her family. חֶסֶד the condescending love, אֱמֶת the truth which God had displayed in the fulfilment of His promise, and here especially manifested to him in bringing him to the home of his master's relations.

Vers. 29–54. As soon as Laban her brother had seen the splendid presents and heard her account, he hurried out to the stranger at the well, to bring him to the house with his attendants and animals, and to show to him the customary hospitality of the East. The fact that Laban addressed him as the blessed of Jehovah (ver. 31), may be explained from the words of the servant, who had called his master's God Jehovah. The servant discharged his commission before he partook of the food set before him (the Kethibh וַיִּישֶׂם in ver. 33 is the *imperf. Kal* of שׂוּם = יָשֶׂם); and commencing with his master's possessions and family affairs, he described with the greatest minuteness his search for a wife, and the success which he had thus far met with, and then (in ver. 49) pressed his suit thus: "*And now, if ye will show kindness and truth to my lord, tell me; and if not, tell me; that I may turn to the right hand or to the left,*" *sc.* to seek in other families a wife for Isaac.—Ver. 50. Laban and Bethuel recognised in this the guidance of God, and said, "*From Jehovah* (the God of Abraham) *the thing proceedeth; we cannot speak unto thee bad or good,*" *i.e.* cannot add a word, cannot alter anything (Num. xxiv. 13 ; 2 Sam. xiii. 22). That Rebekah's brother Laban should have taken part with her father in deciding, was in accordance with the usual custom (cf. xxxiv. 5, 11, 25, Judg. xxi. 22, 2 Sam. xiii. 22), which may have arisen from the prevalence of polygamy, and the readiness of the father to neglect the children (daughters) of the wife he cared for least.—Ver. 52. After receiving their assent, the servant first of all offered thanks to Jehovah with the deepest reverence; he then gave the remaining presents to the bride, and to her relations (brother and mother) ; and after everything was finished, partook of the food provided.

Vers. 54-60. The next morning he desired at once to set off on the journey home; but her brother and mother wished to keep her with them יָמִים אוֹ עָשׂוֹר, "*some days, or rather ten;*" but when she was consulted, she decided to go, *sc.* without delay. "*Then they sent away Rebekah their sister* (Laban being chiefly considered, as the leading person in the affair) *and her nurse*" (Deborah; Ch. xxxv. 8), with the parting wish that she might become the mother of an exceedingly numerous and victorious posterity. "*Become thousands of myriads*" is a hyperbolical expression for an innumerable host of children. The second portion of the blessing (ver. 60*b*) is almost *verbatim* the same as chap. xxii. 17, but is hardly borrowed thence, as the thought does not contain anything specifically connected with the history of salvation.

Vers. 61-67. When the caravan arrived in Canaan with Rebekah and her maidens, Isaac had just come from going to the well Lahai-Roi (xvi. 14), as he was then living in the south country ; and he went towards evening (לִפְנוֹת עֶרֶב, at the turning, coming on, of the evening, Deut. xxiii. 12) to the field "to meditate." It is impossible to determine whether Isaac had been to the well of Hagar which called to mind the omnipresence of God, and there, in accordance with his contemplative character, had laid the question of his marriage before the Lord (*Delitzsch*), or whether he had merely travelled thither to look after his flocks and herds (*Knobel*). But the object of his going *to the field to meditate,* was undoubtedly to lay the question of his marriage before God in solitude. שׂיח, *meditari*, is rendered " *to pray* " in the *Chaldee*, and by *Luther* and others, with substantial correctness. The caravan arrived at the time ; and Rebekah, as soon as she saw the man in the field coming to meet them, sprang (נָפַל signifying a hasty descent, 2 Kings v. 21) from the camel to receive him, according to Oriental custom, in the most respectful manner. She then inquired the name of the man ; and as soon as she heard that it was Isaac, she enveloped herself in her veil, as became a bride when meeting the bridegroom. צָעִיף, θέριστρον, the cloak-like veil of Arabia (see my *Archäologie*, § 103, 5). The servant then related to Isaac the result of his journey ; and Isaac conducted the maiden, who had been brought to him by God, into the tent of Sarah his mother, and she became his wife, and he loved her, and was consoled after his mother, *i.e.* for his mother's death. הָאֹהֱלָה with ה local, in the construct state, as in chap. xx. 1, xxviii. 2, etc. ; and in addition to that, with the article prefixed (cf. *Ges. Gram.* § 110, 2*bc*).

ABRAHAM'S MARRIAGE TO KETURAH—HIS DEATH AND BURIAL.—CHAP. XXV.

Vers. 1–4. ABRAHAM'S MARRIAGE TO KETURAH is generally supposed to have taken place after Sarah's death, and his power to beget six sons at so advanced an age is attributed to the fact, that the Almighty had endowed him with new vital and reproductive energy for begetting the son of the promise. But there is no firm ground for this assumption; as it is not stated anywhere, that Abraham did not take Keturah as his wife till after Sarah's death. It is merely an inference drawn from the fact, that it is not mentioned till afterwards; and it is taken for granted that the history is written in strictly chronological order. But this supposition is precarious, and is not in harmony with the statement, that Abraham sent away the sons of the concubines with gifts during his own lifetime ; for in the case supposed, the youngest of Keturah's sons would not have been more than twenty-five or thirty years old at Abraham's death ; and in those days, when marriages were not generally contracted before the fortieth year, this seems too young for them to have been sent away from their father's house. This difficulty, however, is not decisive. Nor does the fact that Keturah is called a concubine in ver. 6, and 1 Chron. i. 32, necessarily show that she was cotemporary with Sarah, but may be explained on the ground that Abraham did not place her on the same footing as Sarah, his sole wife, the mother of the promised seed. Of the sons and grandsons of Keturah, who are mentioned in 1 Chron. i. 32 as well as here, a few of the names may still be found among the Arabian tribes, but in most instances the attempt to trace them is very questionable. This remark applies to the identification of *Zimran* with *Zaβράμ* (Ptol. vi. 7, 5), the royal city of the *Kιναιδοκολπῖται* to the west of Mecca, on the Red Sea ; of *Jokshan* with the *Kασσανῖται*, on the Red Sea (Ptol. vi. 7, 6), or with the Himyaritish tribe of *Jakish* in Southern Arabia ; of *Ishbak* with the name *Shobek*, a place in the Edomitish country first mentioned by *Abulfeda ;* of *Shuah* with the tribe *Syayhe* to the east of Aila, or with *Szyhhan* in Northern Edom (*Burck-hardt*, Syr. 692, 693, and 945), although the epithet the Shuhite, applied to Bildad, points to a place in Northern Idumæa. There is more plausibility in the comparison of *Medan* and *Midian* with *Moδιάνα* on the eastern coast of the Elanitic Gulf, and *Mαδιάνα*, a tract to the north of this (Ptol. vi. 7, 2, 27 ; called by Arabian geographers *Madyan*, a city five days' journey to the south of Aila). The relationship of these two tribes will explain the fact, that the *Midianim*, chap. xxxvii. 28, are called *Medanim* in ver. 36.—Ver. 3. Of the sons of Jokshan, *Sheba* was probably connected with the Sabæans, who are associated in Job vi. 19 with *Tema*, are mentioned in Job i. 15 as having stolen Job's oxen and asses, and, according to *Strabo* (xvi. 779), were neighbours of the Nabatæans in the vicinity of Syria. *Dedan* was probably the trading people mentioned in Jer. xxv. 23 along with Tema and Bus (Isa. xxi. 13 ; Jer. xlix. 8), in the neighbourhood of Edom (Ezek. xxv. 13), with whom the tribe of *Banu Dudan*, in Hejas, has been compared. On their relation to the Cushites of the same name, *vid.* chap. x. 7 and 28.—Of the sons of Dedan, the *Asshurim* have been associated with the warlike tribe of the *Asır* to the south of Hejas, the *Letushim* with the *Banu Leits* in Hejas, and the *Leummim* with the tribe of the *Banu Lâm*, which extended even to Babylon and Mesopotamia. Of the descendants of Midian, *Ephah* is mentioned in Isa. lx. 6, in connection with Midian, as a people trading in gold and incense. *Epher* has been compared with the

Banu Gifar in Hejas ; *Hanoch,* with the place called *Hanakye,* three days' journey to the north of Medinah ; *Abidah* and *El-daah,* with the tribes of *Abide* and *Vadaa* in the neighbourhood of Asir. But all this is very uncertain.

Vers. 5–11. Before his death, Abraham made a final disposition of his property. Isaac, the only son of his marriage with Sarah, received all his possessions. The sons of the concubines (Hagar and Keturah) were sent away with presents from their father's house into the east country, *i.e.* Arabia in the widest sense, to the east and south-east of Palestine.—Vers. 7, 8. Abraham died at the good old age of 175, and was "*gathered to his people.*" This expression, which is synonymous with "going to his fathers" (xv. 15), or "being gathered to his fathers" (Judg. ii. 10), but is constantly distinguished from departing this life and being buried, denotes the reunion in Sheol with friends who have gone before, and therefore presupposes faith in the personal continuance of a man after death, as a presentiment which the promises of God had exalted in the case of the patriarchs into a firm assurance of faith (Heb. xi. 13).—Vers. 9, 10. The burial of the patriarch in the cave of Machpelah was attended to by Isaac and Ishmael ; since the latter, although excluded from the blessings of the covenant, was acknowledged by God as the son of Abraham by a distinct blessing (xvii. 20), and was thus elevated above the sons of Keturah.—Ver. 11. After Abraham's death the blessing was transferred to Isaac, who took up his abode by Hagar's well, because he had already been there, and had dwelt in the south country (xxiv. 62). The blessing of Isaac is traced to *Elohim,* not to Jehovah ; because it referred neither exclusively nor pre-eminently to the gifts of grace connected with the promises of salvation, but quite gene: lly to the inheritance of earthly possessions, which Isaac had received from his father.

VII. HISTORY OF ISHMAEL.

CHAP. XXV. 12–18.

(Compare 1 Chron. i. 28–31.)

To show that the promises of God, which had been made to
Ishmael (chap. xvi. 10 sqq. and xvii. 20), were fulfilled, a short
account is given of his descendants; and according to the settled
plan of Genesis, this account precedes the history of Isaac.
This is evidently the intention of the list which follows of the
twelve sons of Ishmael, who are given as princes of the tribes
which sprang from them. *Nebajoth* and *Kedar* are mentioned
in Isa. lx. 7 as rich possessors of flocks, and, according to the
current opinion which *Wetzstein* disputes, are the *Nabatæi et
Cedrei* of *Pliny* (h. n. 5, 12). The *Nabatæans* held possession
of *Arabia Petræa*, with *Petra* as their capital, and subsequently
extended toward the south and north-east, probably as far as
Babylon; so that the name was afterwards transferred to all
the tribes to the east of the Jordan, and in the Nabatæan
writings became a common name for Chaldeans (ancient Babylonians), Syrians, Canaanites, and others. The *Kedarenes* are
mentioned in Isa. xxi. 17 as good bowmen. They dwelt in the
desert between Arabia Petræa and Babylon (Isa. xlii. 11; Ps.
cxx. 5). According to *Wetzstein*, they are to be found in the
nomad tribes of Arabia Petræa up to *Harra*. The name *Dumah*,
Δούμεθα, Δουμαίθα (Ptol. v. 19, 7, *Steph. Byz.*), *Domata* (Plin.
6, 32), has been retained in the modern *Dumat el Jendel* in
Nejd, the Arabian highland, four days' journey to the north of
Taima.—*Tema*: a trading people (Job vi. 19; Isa. xxi. 14;
mentioned in Jer. xxv. 23, between Dedan and Bus) in the
land of *Taima*, on the border of Nejd and the Syrian desert.
According to *Wetzstein*, *Dûma* and *Têma* are still two important
places in Eastern Hauran, three-quarters of an hour apart.
Jetur and *Naphish* were neighbours of the tribes of Israel to
the east of the Jordan (1 Chron. v. 19), who made war upon
them along with the Hagrites, the Ἀγραῖοι of Ptol. and Strabo.
From *Jetur* sprang the *Ituræans*, who lived, according to *Strabo*,
near the Trachonians in an almost inaccessible, mountainous,

and cavernous country; according to *Wetsztein*, in the mountains of the Druses in the centre of the Hauran, possibly the forefathers of the modern Druses. The other names are not yet satisfactorily determined. For *Adbeel, Mibsam,* and *Kedma,* the Arabian legends give no corresponding names. *Mishma* is associated by *Knobel* with the Μαισαιμανεῖς of Ptol. vi. 7, 21, to the N.E. of Medina; *Massa* with the Μασανοί on the N.E. of Duma; *Hadad* (the proper reading for *Hadar,* according to 1 Chron. i. 30, the LXX., Sam., Masor., and most MSS.) with the Arabian coast land, *Chathth,* between Oman and Bahrein, a district renowned for its lancers (Χαττηνία, *Polyb.; Attene, Plin.*).—Ver. 16. These are the Ishmaelites "*in their villages and encampments, twelve princes according to their tribes.*" חָצֵר : premises hedged round, then a village without a wall in contrast with a walled town (Lev. xxv. 31). טִירָה : a circular encampment of tents, the tent village of the *Duâr* of the Bedouins. אֻמּוֹת, here and Num. xxv. 15, is not used of nations, but of the tribe-divisions or single tribes of the Ishmaelites and Midianites, for which the word had apparently become a technical term among them.—Vers. 17, 18. Ishmael died at the age of 137, and his descendants dwelt in Havilah—*i.e.* according to chap. x. 29, the country of the *Chaulotæans,* on the borders of Arabia Petræa and Felix—as far as *Shur* (the desert of *Jifar,* xvi. 7) to the east of Egypt, "in the direction of Assyria." Havilah and Shur therefore formed the south-eastern and south-western boundaries of the territories of the Ishmaelites, from which they extended their nomadic excursions towards the N.E. as far as the districts under Assyrian rule, *i.e.* to the lands of the Euphrates, traversing the whole of the desert of Arabia, or (as *Josephus* says, Ant. i. 12, 4) dwelling from the Euphrates to the Red Sea. Thus, according to the announcement of the angel, Ishmael "encamped in the presence of all his brethren." נָפַל, to throw one's self, to settle down, with the subordinate idea of keeping by force the place you have taken (Judg. vii. 12). *Luther* wavers between *corruit, vel cecidit, vel fixit tabernaculum.*

VIII. HISTORY OF ISAAC.

Chap. xxv. 19–xxxv.

ISAAC'S TWIN SONS.—CHAP. XXV. 19-34.

According to the plan of Genesis, the history (*tholedoth*) of Isaac commences with the birth of his sons. But to give it the character of completeness in itself, Isaac's birth and marriage are mentioned again in vers. 19, 20, as well as his age at the time of his marriage. The name given to the country of Rebekah (ver. 20) and the abode of Laban in chap. xxviii. 2, 6, 7, xxxi. 18, xxxiii. 18, xxxv. 9, 26, xlvi. 15, viz. *Padan-Aram*, or more concisely *Padan* (chap. xlviii. 7), "the flat, or flat land of Aram," for which Hosea uses " the field of Aram" (Hos. xii. 12), is not a peculiar expression employed by the Elohist, or in the so-called foundation-work, for *Aram Naharaim*, Mesopotamia (chap. xxiv. 10), but a more exact description of one particular district of Mesopotamia, viz. of the large plain, surrounded by mountains, in which the town of *Haran* was situated. The name was apparently transferred to the town itself afterwards. The history of Isaac consists of two stages: (1) the period of his active life, from his marriage and the birth of his sons till the departure of Jacob for Mesopotamia (xxv. 20–xxviii. 9); and (2) the time of his suffering endurance in the growing infirmity of age, when the events of Jacob's life form the leading feature of the still further expanded history of salvation (chap. xxviii. 10–xxxv. 29). This suffering condition, which lasted more than 40 years, reflected in a certain way the historical position which Isaac held in the patriarchal triad, as a passive rather than active link between Abraham and Jacob; and even in the active period of his life many of the events of Abraham's history were repeated in a modified form.

The name *Jehovah* prevails in the historical development of the *tholedoth* of Isaac, in the same manner as in that of Terah; although, on closer examination of the two, we find, *first*, that in this portion of Genesis the references to God are less frequent than in the earlier one; and *secondly*, that instead of the name *Jehovah* occurring more frequently than *Elohim*, the name *Elohim* predominates in this second stage of the history.

The first difference arises from the fact, that the historical matter
furnishes less occasion for the introduction of the name of God,
just because the revelations of God are more rare, since the appearances of Jehovah to Isaac and Jacob together are not so
numerous as those to Abraham alone.   The second may be explained partly from the fact, that Isaac and Jacob did not perpetually stand in such close and living faith in Jehovah as Abraham,
and partly also from the fact, that the previous revelations of God
gave rise to other titles for the covenant God, such as " God of
Abraham," " God of my father," etc., which could be used in the
place of the name *Jehovah* (cf. chap. xxvi. 24, xxxi. 5, 42, xxxv.
1, 3, and the remarks on chap. xxxv. 9).

Vers. 21–26. Isaac's marriage, like Abraham's, was for a long
time unfruitful; not to extreme old age, however, but only for 20
years.   The seed of the promise was to be prayed for from the
Lord, that it might not be regarded merely as a fruit of nature,
but be received and recognised as a gift of grace.   At the same
time Isaac was to be exercised in the patience of faith in the
promise of God.   After this lengthened test, Jehovah heard
his prayer in relation to his wife.   לְנֹכַח, ver. 21 and chap. xxx.
38, *lit.* opposite to, so that the object is before the eyes, has been
well explained by *Luther* thus : *quod toto pectore et intentus in
calamitatem uxoris oraverit.   Sicut quando oro pro aliquo, pro-
pono illum mihi in conspectum cordis mei, et nihil aliud video
aut cogito; in eum solum animo intueor.*—Vers. 22, 23. When
Rebekah conceived, the children struggled together in her
womb.   In this she saw an evil omen, that the pregnancy
so long desired and entreated of Jehovah would bring misfortune, and that the fruit of her womb might not after all secure
the blessing of the divine promise; so that in intense excitement
she cried out, *"If it be so, wherefore am I?"* i.e. why am I alive?
cf. chap. xxvii. 46.   But she sought counsel from God : she
went to inquire of Jehovah.   Where and how she looked for
a divine revelation in the matter, is not recorded, and therefore cannot be determined with certainty.   Some suppose
that it was by prayer and sacrifice at a place dedicated to
Jehovah.   Others imagine that she applied to a prophet—to
Abraham, Melchizedek, or Shem (*Luther*); a frequent custom
in Israel afterwards (1 Sam. ix. 9), but not probable in the patriarchal age.   The divine answer, couched in the form of a

prophetic oracle, assured her that she carried two nations in her womb, one stronger than the other; and that the greater (elder or first-born) should serve the less (younger). מִמֵּעַיִךְ הִפָּרֵד : "*proceeding from thy womb, are separated.*"—Vers. 24 sqq. When she was delivered, there were twins; the first-born was reddish, *i.e.* of a reddish-brown colour (1 Sam. xvi. 12, xvii. 42), and "all over like a hairy cloak," *i.e.* his whole body as if covered with a fur, with an unusual quantity of hair (*hypertrichosis*), which is sometimes the case with new-born infants, but was a sign in this instance of excessive sensual vigour and wildness. The second had laid hold of the heel of the first, *i.e.* he came into the world with his hand projected and holding the heel of the first-born, a sign of his future attitude towards his brother. From these accidental circumstances the children received their names. The elder they called *Esau*, the hairy one; the younger *Jacob*, heel-holder: יַעֲקֹב from עָקֵב (*denom.* of עָקֵב heel, Hos. xii. 3), to hold the heel, then to outwit (xxvii. 36), just as in wrestling an attempt may be made to throw the opponent by grasping the heel.

Vers. 27–34. Esau became "*a cunning hunter, a man of the field,*" *i.e.* a man wandering about in the fields. He was his father's favourite, for "*venison was in his mouth,*" *i.e.* he was fond of it. But Jacob was אִישׁ תָּם, "a pious man" (*Luther*); תָּם, *integer*, denotes here a disposition that finds pleasure in the quiet life of home. יֹשֵׁב אֹהָלִים, not dwelling in tents, but sitting in the tents, in contrast with the wild hunter's life led by his brother; hence he was his mother's favourite.—Vers. 29 sqq. The difference in the characters of the two brothers was soon shown in a singular circumstance, which was the turning-point in their lives. Esau returned home one day from the field quite exhausted, and seeing Jacob with a dish of lentils, still a favourite dish in Syria and Egypt, he asked with passionate eagerness for some to eat: "*Let me swallow some of that red, that red there;*" אָדֹם, the brown-red lentil pottage. From this he received the name *Edom*, just as among the ancient Arabians persons received names from quite accidental circumstances, which entirely obscured their proper names. Jacob made use of his brother's hunger to get him to sell his birthright. The birthright consisted afterwards in a double portion of the father's inheritance (Deut. xxi. 17); but with the patri-

archs it embraced the chieftainship, the rule over the brethren
and the entire family (xxvii. 29), and the title to the blessing of
the promise (xxvii. 4, 27–29), which included the future possession of Canaan and of covenant fellowship with Jehovah (xxviii.
4). Jacob knew this, and it led him to anticipate the purposes
of God. Esau also knew it, but attached no value to it. There
is proof enough that he knew he was giving away, along with
the birthright, blessings which, because they were not of a material but of a spiritual nature, had no particular value in his
estimation, in the words he made use of: " *Behold I am going to
die* (to meet death), *and what is the birthright to me?*" The only
thing of value to him was the sensual enjoyment of the present;
the spiritual blessings of the future his carnal mind was unable
to estimate. In this he showed himself to be βέβηλος (Heb.
xii. 16), a profane man, who cared for nothing but the momentary gratification of sensual desires, who " *did eat and drink, and
rose up, and went his way, and so despised his birthright*" (ver.
34). With these words the Scriptures judge and condemn the
conduct of Esau. Just as Ishmael was excluded from the promised blessing because he was begotten " according to the
flesh," so Esau lost it because his disposition was according to
the flesh. The frivolity with which he sold his birthright to his
brother for a dish of lentils, rendered him unfit to be the heir
and possessor of the promised grace. But this did not justify
Jacob's conduct in the matter. Though not condemned here,
yet in the further course of the history it is shown to have been
wrong, by the simple fact that he did not venture to make this
transaction the basis of a claim.

ISAAC'S JOYS AND SORROWS.—CHAP. XXVI.

The incidents of Isaac's life which are collected together in
this chapter, from the time of his sojourn in the south country,
resemble in many respects certain events in the life of Abraham; but the distinctive peculiarities are such as to form a true
picture of the dealings of God, which were in perfect accordance with the character of the patriarch.

Vers. 1–5. RENEWAL OF THE PROMISE.—A famine " *in the
land* " (*i.e.* Canaan, to which he had therefore returned from

Hagar's well; xxv. 11), compelled Isaac to leave Canaan, as it
had done Abraham before.   Abraham went to Egypt, where
his wife was exposed to danger, from which she could only be
rescued by the direct interposition of God.   Isaac also intended
to go there, but on the way, viz. in Gerar, he received instruction through a divine manifestation that he was to remain there.
As he was the seed to whom the land of Canaan was promised,
he was directed not to leave it.   To this end Jehovah assured
him of the fulfilment of all the promises made to Abraham on
oath, with express reference to His oath (xxii. 16) to him
and to his posterity, and on account of Abraham's obedience of
faith.   The only peculiarity in the words is the plural, " *all these
lands.*"   This plural refers to all the lands or territories of the
different Canaanitish tribes, mentioned in chap. xv. 19–21, like
the different divisions of the kingdom of Israel or Judah in 1
Chron. xiii. 2, 2 Chron. xi. 23.   הָאֵל ; an antique form of הָאֵלֶּה
occurring only in the Pentateuch.   The piety of Abraham is
described in words that indicate a perfect obedience to all the
commands of God, and therefore frequently recur among the
legal expressions of a later date.   שָׁמַר מִשְׁמֶרֶת יְהוָֹה " to take care
of Jehovah's care," *i.e.* to observe Jehovah, His person, and His
will.   *Mishmereth,* reverence, observance, care, is more closely
defined by " *commandments, statutes, laws,*" to denote constant
obedience to all the revelations and instructions of God.

Vers. 6–11. PROTECTION OF REBEKAH AT GERAR.—As
Abraham had declared his wife to be his sister both in Egypt
and at Gerar, so did Isaac also in the latter place.   But the
manner in which God protected Rebekah was very different from
that in which Sarah was preserved in both instances.   Before
any one had touched Rebekah, the Philistine king discovered
the untruthfulness of Isaac's statement, having seen Isaac "sport-
ing with Rebekah," *sc.* in a manner to show that she was his
wife; whereupon he reproved Isaac for what he had said, and
forbade any of his people to touch Rebekah on pain of death.
Whether this was the same Abimelech as the one mentioned in
chap. xx. cannot be decided with certainty.   The name proves
nothing, for it was the standing official name of the kings of
Gerar (cf. 1 Sam. xxi. 11 and Ps. xxxiv.), as Pharaoh was of
the kings of Egypt.   The identity is favoured by the pious con-

duct of Abimelech in both instances ; and no difficulty is caused either by the circumstance that 80 years had elapsed between the two events (for Abraham had only been dead five years, and the age of 150 was no rarity then), or by the fact, that whereas the first Abimelech had Sarah taken into his harem, the second not only had no intention of doing this, but was anxious to protect her from his people, inasmuch as it would be all the easier to conceive of this in the case of the same king, on the ground of his advanced age.

Vers. 12—17. ISAAC'S INCREASING WEALTH.—As Isaac had experienced the promised protection (" I will be with thee," ver. 3) in the safety of his wife, so did he receive while in Gerar the promised blessing. He sowed and received in that year " *a hundred measures*," *i.e.* a hundred-fold return. This was an unusual blessing, as the yield even in very fertile regions is not generally greater than from twenty-five to fifty-fold (*Niebuhr* and *Burckhardt*), and it is only in the *Ruhbe*, that small and most fruitful plain of Syria, that wheat yields on an average eighty, and barley a hundred-fold. Agriculture is still practised by the Bedouins, as well as grazing (*Robinson*, Pal. i. 77, and *Seetzen*) ; so that Isaac's sowing was no proof that he had been stimulated by the promise of Jehovah to take up a settled abode in the promised land.—Vers. 13 sqq. Being thus blessed of Jehovah, Isaac became increasingly (הָלוֹךְ, *vid.* chap. viii. 3) greater (*i.e.* stronger), until he was very powerful and his wealth very great; so that the Philistines envied him, and endeavoured to do him injury by stopping up and filling with rubbish all the wells that had been dug in his father's time ; and even Abimelech requested him to depart, because he was afraid of his power. Isaac then encamped in the valley of Gerar, *i.e.* in the " undulating land of Gerar," through which the torrent (*Jurf*) from Gerar flows from the south-east (*Ritter*, Erdk. 14, pp. 1084–5).

Vers. 18–22. REOPENING AND DISCOVERY OF WELLS.—In this valley Isaac dug open the old wells which had existed from Abraham's time, and gave them the old names. His people also dug three new wells. But Abimelech's people raised a contest about two of these ; and for this reason Isaac called them *Esek* and *Sitnah*, strife and opposition. The third there was no dis-

pute about ; and it received in consequence the name *Rehoboth*,
" breadths," for Isaac said, " *Yea now* (כִּי־עַתָּה, as in chap. xxix.
32, etc.) *Jehovah has provided for us a broad space, that we may
be fruitful* (multiply) *in the land.*" This well was probably not
in the land of Gerar, as Isaac had removed thence, but in the
Wady *Ruhaibeh*, the name of which is suggestive of Rehoboth,
which stands at the point where the two roads from Gaza and
Hebron meet, about 3 hours to the south of *Elusa*, 8⅓ to the south
of Beersheba, and where there are extensive ruins of the city of
the same name upon the heights, also the remains of wells
(*Robinson*, Pal. i. 289 sqq.; *Strauss*, Sinai and Golgotha); where
too the name *Sitnah* seems to have been retained in the Wady
Shutein, with ruins on the northern hills between *Ruhaibeh* and
Khulasa (*Elusa*).

Vers. 23–25. ISAAC'S JOURNEY TO BEERSHEBA.—Here,
where Abraham had spent a long time (xxi. 33 sqq.), Jehovah
appeared to him during the night and renewed the promises already given ; upon which, Isaac built an altar and performed a
solemn service. Here his servants also dug a well near to the tents.

Vers. 26–33. ABIMELECH'S TREATY WITH ISAAC. — The
conclusion of this alliance was substantially only a repetition
or renewal of the alliance entered into with Abraham; but the
renewal itself arose so completely out of the circumstances, that
there is no ground whatever for denying that it occurred, or for
the hypothesis that our account is merely another form of the
earlier alliance; to say nothing of the fact, that besides the
agreement in the leading event itself, the attendant circumstances are altogether peculiar, and correspond to the events
which preceded. Abimelech not only brought his chief captain
Phicol (supposed to be the same as in chap. xxi. 22, if *Phicol* is
not also an official name), but his מֵרֵעַ "*friend*," *i.e.* his privy
councillor, *Ahuzzath*. Isaac referred to the hostility they had
shown; to which Abimelech replied, that they (he and his people)
did not smite him (נֶגַע), *i.e.* drive him away by force, but let
him depart in peace, and expressed a wish that there might be
an oath between them. אָלָה the oath, as an act of self-impreca-
tion, was to form the basis of the covenant to be made. From
this אָלָה came also to be used for a covenant sanctioned by an

oath (Deut. xxix. 11, 13). אִם תַּעֲשֶׂה "that thou do not: " אִם a
particle of negation used in an oath (xiv. 23, etc.). (On the verb
with *zere*, see Ges. § 75, Anm. 17; Ewald, § 224.)—The same
day Isaac's servants informed him of the well which they had
dug; and Isaac gave it the name *Shebah* (שִׁבְעָה, oath), in commemoration of the treaty made on oath. "*Therefore the city
was called Beersheba.*" This derivation of the name does not
shut the other (xxi. 31) out, but seems to confirm it. As the
treaty made on oath between Abimelech and Isaac was only a
renewal of his covenant concluded before with Abraham, so the
name *Beersheba* was also renewed by the well *Shebah*. The
reality of the occurrence is supported by the fact that the two
wells are in existence still (*vid.* chap. xxi. 31).

Vers. 34, 35. ESAU'S MARRIAGE.—To the various troubles
which the Philistines prepared for Isaac, but which, through
the blessing of God, only contributed to the increase of his
wealth and importance, a domestic cross was added, which
caused him great and lasting sorrow. Esau married two wives
in the 40th year of his age, the 100th of Isaac's life (xxv. 26);
and that not from his own relations in Mesopotamia, but from
among the Canaanites whom God had cast off. On their names,
see chap. xxxvi. 2, 3. They became "*bitterness of spirit*," the
cause of deep trouble, to his parents, viz. on account of their
Canaanitish character, which was so opposed to the vocation of
the patriarchs; whilst Esau by these marriages furnished another
proof, how thoroughly his heart was set upon earthly things.

ISAAC'S BLESSING.—CHAP. XXVII.

Vers. 1-4. When Isaac had grown old, and his eyes were
dim, so that he could no longer see (מֵרְאֹת from seeing, with the
neg. מִן as in chap. xvi. 2, etc.), he wished, in the consciousness of
approaching death, to give his blessing to his elder son. Isaac
was then in his 137th year, at which age his half-brother
Ishmael had died fourteen years before;[1] and this, with the
increasing infirmities of age, may have suggested the thought

[1] Cf. *Lightfoot, opp.* 1, p. 19. This correct estimate of *Luther's* is based
upon the following calculation:—When Joseph was introduced to Pharaoh
he was thirty years old (xli. 46), and when Jacob went into Egypt, thirty-

of death, though he did not die till forty-three years afterwards
(xxxv. 28). Without regard to the words which were spoken
by God with reference to the children before their birth, and
without taking any notice of Esau's frivolous barter of his
birthright and his ungodly connection with Canaanites, Isaac
maintained his preference for Esau, and directed him therefore
to take his things (בֵּלִים, hunting gear), his quiver and bow, to
hunt game and prepare a savoury dish, that he might eat, and
his soul might bless him. As his preference for Esau was fostered and strengthened by, if it did not spring from, his liking
for game (xxv. 28), so now he wished to raise his spirits for
imparting the blessing by a dish of venison prepared to his
taste. In this the infirmity of his flesh is evident. At the
same time, it was not merely because of his partiality for Esau,
but unquestionably on account of the natural rights of the first-
born, that he wished to impart the blessing to him, just as the
desire to do this before his death arose from the consciousness
of his patriarchal call.

Vers. 5–17. Rebekah, who heard what he said, sought to
frustrate this intention, and to secure the blessing for her
(favourite) son Jacob. Whilst Esau was away hunting, she
told Jacob to take his father a dish, which she would prepare
from two kids according to his taste; and, having introduced
himself as Esau, to ask for the blessing "*before Jehovah.*"
Jacob's objection, that the father would know him by his smooth
skin, and so, instead of blessing him, might pronounce a curse
upon him as a mocker, *i.e.* one who was trifling with his blind
father, she silenced by saying, that she would take the curse
upon herself. She evidently relied upon the word of promise,
and thought that she ought to do her part to secure its fulfilment by directing the father's blessing to Jacob; and to this
end she thought any means allowable. Consequently she was
so assured of the success of her stratagem as to have no fear of
the possibility of a curse. Jacob then acceded to her plan, and

nine, as the seven years of abundance and two of famine had then passed
by (xlv. 6). But Jacob was at that time 130 years old (xlvii. 9). Consequently Joseph was born before Jacob was ninety-one; and as his birth
took place in the fourteenth year of Jacob's sojourn in Mesopotamia (cf.
xxx. 25, and xxix. 18, 21, and 27), Jacob's flight to Laban occurred in
the seventy-seventh year of his own life, and the 137th of Isaac's.

fetched the goats. Rebekah prepared them according to her husband's taste; and having told Jacob to put on Esau's best clothes which were with her in the dwelling (the tent, not the house), she covered his hands and the smooth (*i.e.* the smooth parts) of his neck with the skins of the kids of the goats,[1] and sent him with the savoury dish to his father.

Vers. 18–29. But Jacob had no easy task to perform before his father. As soon as he had spoken on entering, his father asked him, "*Who art thou, my son?*" On his replying, "*I am Esau, thy first-born,*" the father expressed his surprise at the rapid success of his hunting; and when he was satisfied with the reply, "*Jehovah thy God sent it* (the thing desired) *to meet me,*" he became suspicious about the voice, and bade him come nearer, that he might feel him. But as his hands appeared hairy like Esau's, he did not recognise him; and "*so he blessed him.*" In this remark (ver. 23) the writer gives the result of Jacob's attempt; so that the blessing is merely mentioned proleptically here, and refers to the formal blessing described afterwards, and not to the first greeting and salutation.—Vers. 24 sqq. After his father, in order to get rid of his suspicion about the voice, had asked him once more, "*Art thou really my son Esau?*" and Jacob had replied, "*I am*" (אָנִי = yes), he told him to hand him the savoury dish that he might eat. After eating, he kissed his son as a sign of his paternal affection, and in doing so he smelt the odour of his clothes, *i.e.* the clothes of Esau, which were thoroughly scented with the odour of the fields, and then imparted his blessing (vers. 27–29). The blessing itself is thrown, as the sign of an elevated state of mind, into the poetic style of parallel clauses, and contains the peculiar forms of poetry, such as רָאָה for הִנֵּה, הֲוֶה for חָיָה, etc. The smell of the clothes with the scent of the field suggested to the patriarch's mind the image of his son's future prosperity, so that he saw him in possession of the promised land and the full enjoyment of its valuable blessings, having the smell of the field which Jehovah blessed, *i.e.* the garden of paradise, and broke out into the wish, "*God* (*Ha-Elohim*, the personal God, not *Jehovah*, the

---

[1] We must not think of our European goats, whose skins would be quite unsuitable for any such deception. "It is the camel-goat of the East, whose black, silk-like hair was used even by the Romans as a substitute for human hair. *Martial* xii. 46."—*Tuch* on ver. 16.

covenant God) *give thee from the dew of heaven, and the fat
fields of the earth, and plenty of corn and wine,*" *i.e.* a land
blessed with the dew of heaven and a fruitful soil. In Eastern
countries, where there is so little rain, the dew is the most important prerequisite for the growth of the fruits of the earth,
and is often mentioned therefore as a source of blessing (Deut.
xxxiii. 13, 28; Hos. xiv. 6; Zech. viii. 12). In מִשְׁמַנֵּי, notwithstanding the absence of the Dagesh from the שׁ, the מ is the
prep. מִן, as the parallel מִטַּל proves; and שְׁמַנִּים both here and in
ver. 39 are the fat (fertile) districts of a country. The rest of
the blessing had reference to the future pre-eminence of his
son. He was to be lord not only over his brethren (*i.e.* over
kindred tribes), but over (foreign) peoples and nations also.
The blessing rises here to the idea of universal dominion, which
was to be realized in the fact that, according to the attitude
assumed by the people towards him as their lord, it would
secure to them either a blessing or a curse. If we compare this
blessing with the promises which Abraham received, there are
two elements of the latter which are very apparent; viz. the
possession of the land, in the promise of the rich enjoyment of
its produce, and the numerous increase of posterity, in the promised dominion over the nations. The third element, however,
the blessing of the nations in and through the seed of Abraham, is so generalized in the expression, which is moulded
according to chap. xii. 3, "Cursed be every one that curseth
thee, and blessed be he that blesseth thee," that the person
blessed is not thereby declared to be the medium of salvation to
the nations. Since the intention to give the blessing to Esau
the first-born did not spring from proper feelings towards
Jehovah and His promises, the blessing itself, as the use of the
word *Elohim* instead of *Jehovah* or *El Shaddai* (cf. xxviii. 3)
clearly shows, could not rise to the full height of the divine
blessings of salvation, but referred chiefly to the relation in
which the two brothers and their descendants would stand to
one another, the theme with which Isaac's soul was entirely
filled. It was only the painful discovery that, in blessing
against his will, he had been compelled to follow the saving
counsel of God, which awakened in him the consciousness of
his patriarchal vocation, and gave him the spiritual power to
impart the " blessing of Abraham " to the son whom he had

kept back, but whom Jehovah had chosen, when he was about to send him away to Haran (xxviii. 3, 4).

Vers. 30–40. Jacob had hardly left his father, after receiving the blessing (אַךְ יָצֹא יָצָא, was only gone out), when Esau returned and came to Isaac, with the game prepared, to receive the blessing. The shock was inconceivable which Isaac received, when he found that he had blessed another, and not Esau—that, in fact, he had blessed Jacob. At the same time he neither could nor would, either curse him on account of the deception which he had practised, or withdraw the blessing imparted. For he could not help confessing to himself that he had sinned and brought the deception upon himself by his carnal preference for Esau. Moreover, the blessing was not a matter of subjective human affection, but a right entrusted by the grace of God to paternal supremacy and authority, in the exercise of which the person blessing, being impelled and guided by a higher authority, imparted to the person to be blest spiritual possessions and powers, which the will of man could not capriciously withdraw. Regarding this as the meaning of the blessing, Isaac necessarily saw in what had taken place the will of God, which had directed to Jacob the blessing that he had intended for Esau. He therefore said, "*I have blessed him; yea, he will be* (remain) *blessed*" (cf. Heb. xii. 17). Even the great and bitter lamentation into which Esau broke out could not change his father's mind. To his entreaty in ver. 34, "*Bless me, even me also, O my father!*" he replied, "*Thy brother came with subtilty, and hath taken away thy blessing.*" Esau answered, "*Is it that* (הֲכִי) *they have named him Jacob* (overreacher), *and he has overreached me twice?*" *i.e.* has he received the name Jacob from the fact that he has twice outwitted me? הֲכִי is used "when the cause is not rightly known" (cf. chap. xxix. 15). To his further entreaty, "*Hast thou not reserved a blessing for me?*" (אָצַל, *lit.* to lay aside), Isaac repeated the substance of the blessing given to Jacob, and added, "*and to thee* (לְכָה for לְךָ as in chap. iii. 9), *now, what can I do, my son?*" When Esau again repeated, with tears, the entreaty that Isaac would bless him also, the father gave him a blessing (vers. 39, 40), but one which, when compared with the blessing of Jacob, was to be regarded rather as "a modified curse," and which is not even described as a blessing, but "introduced a disturbing element into Jacob's blessing, a retribution for the impure means by which he had obtained it." "*Behold*," it states, "*from the fat fields of the earth will thy dwelling be, and from the dew of heaven from above.*" By a play upon the words Isaac uses the same expression as in ver. 28, "from the fat fields of the earth, and from the dew," but in the opposite sense, מִן being partitive there, and privative here, "from=away from." The context requires that the words should be taken thus, and not in the sense of "thy dwelling shall partake of the fat of the earth and the dew of heaven" (*Vulg., Luth.*, etc.).[1] Since Isaac said (ver. 37) he had given Jacob the blessing of the super-abundance of corn and wine, he could not possibly promise Esau also fat fields and the dew of heaven. Nor would this agree with the words which follow, "*By thy sword wilt thou live.*" Moreover, the privative sense of מִן is thoroughly poetical (cf. 2 Sam. i. 22; Job xi. 15, etc.). The idea expressed in the words, therefore, was that the dwelling-place of Esau would be the very opposite of the land of Canaan, viz. an unfruitful land. This is generally the condition of the mountainous country of Edom, which, although not without its fertile slopes and valleys, especially in the eastern portion (cf. Robinson, Pal. ii. p. 552), is thoroughly waste and barren in the western; so that *Seetzen* says it consists of "the most desolate and barren mountains probably in the world." The mode of life and occupation of the inhabit-ants were adapted to the country. "*By* (*lit.* on) *thy sword thou wilt live;*" *i.e.* thy maintenance will depend on the sword (עַל as in Deut. viii. 3 cf. Isa. xxxviii. 16), "live by war, rapine, and freebooting" (*Knobel*). "*And thy brother thou wilt serve; yet it will come to pass, as* (כַּאֲשֶׁר, *lit.* in proportion as, cf. Num. xxvii. 14) *thou shakest* (tossest), *thou wilt break his yoke from thy neck.*" רוּד, "to rove about" (Jer. ii. 31; Hos. xii. 1), *Hiphil* "to cause (the thoughts) to rove about" (Ps. lv. 3); but *Hengstenberg's* rendering is the best here, viz. "to shake, *sc.* the yoke." In the wild, sport-loving Esau there was aptly prefigured the character of his posterity. *Josephus* describes the Idumæan people as "a tumultuous and disorderly nation, always on the watch on every

---

[1] I cannot discover, however, in Mal. i. 3 an authentic proof of the privative meaning, as *Kurtz* and *Delitzsch* do, since the prophet's words, " I have hated Esau, and laid his mountains and his heritage waste," are not descriptive of the natural condition of Idumæa, but of the desolation to which the land was given up.

motion, delighting in mutations" (*Whiston's tr.: de bell* Jud. 4, 4, 1). The mental eye of the patriarch discerned in the son his whole future family in its attitude to its brother-nation, and he promised Edom, not freedom from the dominion of Israel (for Esau was to serve his brother, as Jehovah had predicted before their birth), but only a repeated and not unsuccessful struggle for freedom. And so it was; the historical relation of Edom to Israel assumed the form of a constant reiteration of servitude, revolt, and reconquest. After a long period of independence at the first, the Edomites were defeated by Saul (1 Sam. xiv. 47) and subjugated by David (2 Sam. viii. 14); and, in spite of an attempt at revolt under Solomon (1 Kings xi. 14 sqq.), they remained subject to the kingdom of Judah until the time of Joram, when they rebelled. They were subdued again by Amaziah (2 Kings xiv. 7; 2 Chron. xxv. 11 sqq.), and remained in subjection under Uzziah and Jotham (2 Kings xiv. 22; 2 Chron. xxvi. 2). It was not till the reign of Ahaz that they shook the yoke of Judah entirely off (2 Kings xvi. 6; 2 Chron. xxviii. 17), without Judah being ever able to reduce them again. At length, however, they were completely conquered by John Hyrcanus about B.C. 129, compelled to submit to circumcision, and incorporated in the Jewish state (*Josephus*, Ant. xiii. 9, 1, xv. 7, 9). At a still later period, through Antipater and Herod, they established an Idumæan dynasty over Judea, which lasted till the complete dissolution of the Jewish state.

Thus the words of Isaac to his two sons were fulfilled,— words which are justly said to have been spoken "in faith concerning things to come" (Heb. xi. 20). For the blessing was a prophecy, and that not merely in the case of Esau, but in that of Jacob also; although Isaac was deceived with regard to the person of the latter. Jacob remained blessed, therefore, because, according to the predetermination of God, the elder was to serve the younger; but the deceit by which his mother prompted him to secure the blessing was never approved. On the contrary, the sin was followed by immediate punishment. Rebekah was obliged to send her pet son into a foreign land, away from his father's house, and in an utterly destitute condition. She did not see him for twenty years, even if she lived till his return, and possibly never saw again. Jacob had to atone for his sin against both brother and father by a long and painful exile, in the

midst of privation, anxiety, fraud, and want. Isaac was punished
for retaining his preference for Esau, in opposition to the revealed
will of Jehovah, by the success of Jacob's stratagem; and Esau
for his contempt of the birthright, by the loss of the blessing of
the first-born. In this way a higher hand prevailed above the
acts of sinful men, bringing the counsel and will of Jehovah to
eventual triumph, in opposition to human thought and will.

Vers. 41-46. Esau's complaining and weeping were now
changed into mortal hatred of his brother. "*The days of mourning,*" he said to himself, "*for my father are at hand, and I will
kill my brother Jacob.*" אֲבֶל אָבִי: *genit. obj.* as in Amos viii. 10;
Jer. vi. 26. He would put off his intended fratricide that he
might not hurt his father's mind.—Ver. 42. When Rebekah
was informed by some one of Esau's intention, she advised Jacob
to protect himself from his revenge (הִתְנַחֵם to procure comfort
by retaliation, equivalent to "avenge himself," הִתְנַקֵּם, Isa. i. 24[1]),
by fleeing to her brother Laban in Haran, and remaining there
"*some days,*" as she mildly puts it, until his brother's wrath was
subdued. "*For why should I lose you both in one day?*" viz.
Jacob through Esau's vengeance, and Esau as a murderer by
the avenger of blood (chap. ix. 6, cf. 2 Sam. xiv. 6, 7). In
order to obtain Isaac's consent to this plan, without hurting his
feelings by telling him of Esau's murderous intentions, she spoke
to him of her troubles on account of the Hittite wives of Esau,
and the weariness of life that she should feel if Jacob also were
to marry one of the daughters of the land, and so introduced the
idea of sending Jacob to her relations in Mesopotamia, with a
view to his marriage there.

JACOB'S FLIGHT TO HARAN AND DREAM IN BETHEL.—CHAP.
XXVIII.

Vers. 1-9. JACOB'S DEPARTURE FROM HIS PARENTS' HOUSE.
—Rebekah's complaint reminded Isaac of his own call, and his
consequent duty to provide for Jacob's marriage in a manner
corresponding to the divine counsels of salvation.—Vers. 1-5.
He called Jacob, therefore, and sent him to Padan-Aram to his
mother's relations, with instructions to seek a wife there, and not

---

[1] This reference is incorrect; the *Niphal* is used in Isa. i. 24, the
Hithpael in Jer. v. 9-29. Tr.

among the daughters of Canaan, giving him at the same time the "*blessing of Abraham*," *i.e.* the blessing of promise, which Abraham had repeatedly received from the Lord, but which is more especially recorded in chap. xvii. 2 sqq., and xxii. 16–18.— Vers. 6–9. When Esau heard of this blessing and the sending away of Jacob, and saw therein the displeasure of his parents at his Hittite wives, he went to Ishmael—*i.e.* to the family of Ishmael, for Ishmael himself had been dead fourteen years (p. 273)— and took as a third wife Mahalath, a daughter of Ishmael (called Bashemath in chap. xxxvi. 3, a descendant of Abraham therefore), a step by which he might no doubt ensure the approval of his parents, but in which he failed to consider that Ishmael had been separated from the house of Abraham and family of promise by the appointment of God; so that it only furnished another proof that he had no thought of the religious interests of the chosen family, and was unfit to be the recipient of divine revelation.

Vers. 10–22. JACOB'S DREAM AT BETHEL.—As he was travelling from Beersheba, where Isaac was then staying (xxvi. 25), to Haran, Jacob came to a place where he was obliged to stop all night, because the sun had set. The words "*he hit* (lighted) *upon the place*," indicate the apparently accidental, yet really divinely appointed choice of this place for his night-quarters; and the definite article points it out as having become well known through the revelation of God that ensued. After making a pillow with the stones (מְרַאֲשֹׁת, head-place, pillow), he fell asleep and had a dream, in which he saw a ladder resting upon the earth, with the top reaching to heaven; and upon it angels of God going up and down, and Jehovah Himself standing above it. The ladder was a visible symbol of the real and uninterrupted fellowship between God in heaven and His people upon earth. The angels upon it carry up the wants of men to God, and bring down the assistance and protection of God to men. The ladder stood there upon the earth, just where Jacob was lying in solitude, poor, helpless, and forsaken by men. Above in heaven stood Jehovah, and explained in words the symbol which he saw. Proclaiming Himself to Jacob as the God of his fathers, He not only confirmed to him all the promises of the fathers in their fullest extent, but promised him protection on his journey and a safe return to his home (vers. 13–15). But as the fulfilment of this promise to Jacob was still far off, God added the firm assurance, " *I will not leave thee till I have done* (carried out) *what I have told thee.*"—Vers. 16 sqq. Jacob gave utterance to the impression made by this vision as soon as he awoke from sleep, in the words, " *Surely Jehovah is in this place, and I knew it not.*" Not that the omnipresence of God was unknown to him; but that Jehovah in His condescending mercy should be near to him even here, far away from his father's house and from the places consecrated to His worship,— it was this which he did not know or imagine. The revelation was intended not only to stamp the blessing, with which Isaac had dismissed him from his home, with the seal of divine approval, but also to impress upon Jacob's mind the fact, that although Jehovah would be near to protect and guide him even in a foreign land, the land of promise was the holy ground on which the God of his fathers would set up the covenant of His grace. On his departure from that land, he was to carry with him a sacred awe of the gracious presence of Jehovah there. To that end the Lord proved to him that He was near, in such a way that the place appeared " *dreadful,*" inasmuch as the nearness of the holy God makes an alarming impression upon unholy man, and the consciousness of sin grows into the fear of death. But in spite of this alarm, the place was none other than " *the house of God and the gate of heaven,*" *i.e.* a place where God dwelt, and a way that opened to Him in heaven.—Ver. 18. In the morning Jacob set up the stone at his head, as a monument (מַצֵּבָה) to commemorate the revelation he had received from God; and poured oil upon the top, to consecrate it as a memorial of the mercy that had been shown him there (*visionis insigne μνημόσυνον, Calvin*), not as an idol or an object of divine worship (*vid.* Ex. xxx. 26 sqq.).—He then gave the place the name of *Bethel, i.e.* House of God, whereas (וְאוּלָם) the town had been called *Luz* before. This antithesis shows that Jacob gave the name, not to the place where the pillar was set up, but to the town, in the neighbourhood of which he had received the divine revelation. He renewed it on his return from Mesopotamia (xxxv. 15). This is confirmed by chap. xlviii. 3, where Jacob, like the historian in chap. xxxv. 6, 7, speaks of Luz as the place of this revelation. There is nothing at variance with this in

Josh. xvi. 2, xviii. 13 ; for it is not Bethel as a city, but the mountains of Bethel, that are there distinguished from Luz (see my Commentary on Josh. xvi. 2).[1]—Ver. 20, Lastly, Jacob made a vow : that if God would give him the promised protection on his journey, and bring him back in safety to his father's house, Jehovah should be his God (וְהָיָה in ver. 21 commences the apodosis), the stone which he had set up should be a house of God, and Jehovah should receive a tenth of all that He gave to him. It is to be noticed here, that *Elohim* is used in the protasis instead of *Jehovah*, as constituting the essence of the vow : if Jehovah, who had appeared to him, proved Himself to be GOD by fulfilling His promise, then he would acknowledge and worship Him as his God, by making the stone thus set up into a house of God, *i.e.* a place of sacrifice, and by tithing all his possessions. With regard to the fulfilment of this vow, we learn from chap. xxxv. 7 that Jacob built an altar, and probably also dedicated the tenth to God, *i.e.* offered it to Jehovah ; or, as some have supposed, applied it partly to the erection and preservation of the altar, and partly to burnt and thank-offerings combined with sacrificial meals, according to the analogy of Deut. xiv. 28, 29 (cf. chap. xxxi. 54, xlvi. 1).

JACOB'S STAY IN HARAN. HIS DOUBLE MARRIAGE AND CHILDREN.—CHAP. XXIX. AND XXX.

Vers. 1–14. ARRIVAL IN HARAN, AND RECEPTION BY LABAN.—Being strengthened in spirit by the nocturnal vision, Jacob proceeded on his journey into "the land of the sons of the East ;" by which we are to understand, not so much the

---

[1] The fact mentioned here has often been cited as the origin of the anointed stones (βαίτυλοι) of the heathen, and this heathen custom has been regarded as a degeneration of the patriarchal. But apart from this essential difference, that the Baetulian worship was chiefly connected with meteoric stones (cf. *F. von Dalberg, üb. d. Meteor-cultus d. Alten*), which were supposed to have come down from some god, and were looked upon as deified, this opinion is at variance with the circumstance, that Jacob himself, in consecrating the stone by pouring oil upon it, only followed a custom already established, and still more with the fact, that the name βαίτυλοι, βαιτύλια, notwithstanding its sounding like *Bethel*, can hardly have arisen from the name *Beth-El*, Gr. Βαιθήλ, since the τ for θ would be perfectly inexplicable. *Dietrich* derives βαιτύλιον from בָּטֵל, to render inoperative, and interprets it amulet.

Arabian desert, that reaches to the Euphrates, as Mesopotamia, which lies on the other side of that river. For there he saw the well in the field (ver. 2), by which three flocks were lying, waiting for the arrival of the other flocks of the place, before they could be watered. The remark in ver. 2, that the stone upon the well's mouth was large (גְּדֹלָה without the article is a predicate), does not mean that the united strength of all the shepherds was required to roll it away, whereas Jacob rolled it away alone (ver. 10); but only that it was not in the power of every shepherd, much less of a shepherdess like Rachel, to roll it away. Hence in all probability the agreement that had been formed among them, that they would water the flocks together. The scene is so thoroughly in harmony with the customs of the East, both ancient and modern, that the similarity to the one described in chap. xxiv. 11 sqq. is by no means strange (vid. Rob. Pal. i. 301, 304, ii. 351, 357, 371). Moreover the well was very differently constructed from that at which Abraham's servant met with Rebekah. There the water was drawn at once from the (open) well and poured into troughs placed ready for the cattle, as is the case now at most of the wells in the East; whereas here the well was closed up with a stone, and there is no mention of pitchers and troughs. The well, therefore, was probably a cistern dug in the ground, which was covered up or closed with a large stone, and probably so constructed, that after the stone had been rolled away the flocks could be driven to the edge to drink.[1]—Vers. 5, 6. Jacob asked the shepherds where they lived; from which it is probable that the well was not situated, like that in chap. xxiv. 11, in the immediate neighbourhood of the town of Haran; and when they said they were from Haran, he inquired after Laban, the son, i.e. the descendant, of Nahor, and how he was (הֲשָׁלוֹם לוֹ: is he well?); and received the reply, " Well; and behold Rachel, his daughter, is just coming (בָּאָה particip.) with the flock." When Jacob thereupon told the shepherds to water the flocks and feed them again, for

---

[1] Like the cistern Bir Beshat, described by Rosen., in the valley of Hebron, or those which Robinson found in the desert of Judah (Pal. ii. 165), hollowed out in the great mass of rock, and covered with a large, thick, flat stone, in the middle of which a round hole had been left, which formed the opening of the cistern, and in many cases was closed up with a heavy stone, which it would take two or three men to roll away.

the day was still "great,"—*i.e.* it wanted a long while to the evening, and was not yet time to drive them in (to the folds to rest for the night),—he certainly only wanted to get the shepherds away from the well, that he might meet with his cousin alone. But as Rachel came up in the meantime, he was so carried away by the feelings of relationship, possibly by a certain love at first sight, that he rolled the stone away from the well, watered her flock, and after kissing her, introduced himself with tears of joyous emotion as her cousin (אֲחִי אָבִיהָ, brother, *i.e.* relation of her father) and Rebekah's son. What the other shepherds thought of all this, is passed over as indifferent to the purpose of the narrative, and the friendly reception of Jacob by Laban is related immediately afterwards. When Jacob had told Laban "*all these things*,"—*i.e.* hardly "the cause of his journey, and the things which had happened to him in relation to the birthright" (*Rosenmüller*), but simply the things mentioned in vers. 2–12,—Laban acknowledged him as his relative : "*Yes, thou art my bone and my flesh*" (cf. ii. 23 and Judg. ix. 2) ; and thereby *eo ipso* ensured him an abode in his house.

Vers. 15–30. JACOB'S DOUBLE MARRIAGE.—After a full month ("a month of days," chap. xli. 1 ; Num. xi. 20, etc.), during which time Laban had discovered that he was a good and useful shepherd, he said to him, "*Shouldst thou, because thou art my relative, serve me for nothing? fix me thy wages.*" Laban's selfishness comes out here under the appearance of justice and kindness. To preclude all claim on the part of his sister's son to gratitude or affection in return for his services, he proposes to pay him like an ordinary servant. Jacob offered to serve him seven years for *Rachel*, the younger of his two daughters, whom he loved because of her beauty ; *i.e.* just as many years as the week has days, that he might bind himself to a complete and sufficient number of years of service. For the elder daughter, *Leah*, had weak eyes, and consequently was not so good-looking ; since bright eyes, with fire in them, are regarded as the height of beauty in Oriental women. Laban agreed. He would rather give his daughter to him than to a stranger.[1] Jacob's proposal may be explained, partly on the

---

[1] This is the case still with the Bedouins, the Druses, and other Eastern tribes. (*Burckhardt, Volney, Layard,* and *Lane.*)

ground that he was not then in a condition to give the customary dowry, or the usual presents to relations, and partly also
from the fact that his situation with regard to Esau compelled
him to remain some time with Laban. The assent on the part
of Laban cannot be accounted for from the custom of selling
daughters to husbands, for it cannot be shown that the purchase of wives was a general custom at that time; but is to be
explained solely on the ground of Laban's selfishness and avarice,
which came out still more plainly afterwards. To Jacob, however, the seven years seemed but "*a few days, because he loved
Rachel.*" This is to be understood, as *C. a Lapide* observes,
"not *affective*, but *appretiative*," *i.e.* in comparison with the reward to be obtained for his service.—Vers. 21 sqq. But when
Jacob asked for his reward at the expiration of this period, and
according to the usual custom a great marriage feast had been
prepared, instead of Rachel, Laban took his elder daughter
Leah into the bride-chamber, and Jacob went in unto her,
without discovering in the dark the deception that had been
practised. Thus the overreacher of Esau was overreached himself, and sin was punished by sin.—Vers. 25 sqq. But when
Jacob complained to Laban the next morning of his deception,
he pleaded the custom of the country: בֵן יֵעָשֶׂה לֹא, "*it is not
accustomed to be so in our place, to give the younger before the
first-born.*" A perfectly worthless excuse; for if this had really
been the custom in Haran as in ancient India and elsewhere,
he ought to have told Jacob of it before. But to satisfy Jacob,
he promised him that in a week he would give him the younger
also, if he would serve him seven years longer for her.—Ver.
27. "*Fulfil her week;*" *i.e.* let Leah's marriage-week pass over.
The wedding feast generally lasted a week (cf. Judg. xiv. 12;
Job xi. 19). After this week had passed, he received Rachel
also: two wives in eight days. To each of these Laban gave
one maid-servant to wait upon her; less, therefore, than Bethuel
gave to his daughter (xxiv. 61).—This bigamy of Jacob must
not be judged directly by the Mosaic law, which prohibits marriage with two sisters at the same time (Lev. xviii. 18), or set
down as incest (*Calvin*, etc.), since there was no positive law on
the point in existence then. At the same time, it is not to be
justified on the ground, that the blessing of God made it the
means of the fulfilment of His promise, viz. the multiplication

of the seed of Abraham into a great nation. Just as it had arisen from Laban's deception and Jacob's love, which regarded outward beauty alone, and therefore from sinful infirmities, so did it become in its results a true school of affliction to Jacob, in which God showed to him, by many a humiliation, that such conduct as his was quite unfitted to accomplish the divine counsels, and thus condemned the ungodliness of such a marriage, and prepared the way for the subsequent prohibition in the law.

Vers. 31–35. LEAH'S FIRST SONS.—Jacob's sinful weakness showed itself even after his marriage, in the fact that he loved Rachel more than Leah; and the chastisement of God, in the fact that the hated wife was blessed with children, whilst Rachel for a long time remained unfruitful. By this it was made apparent once more, that the origin of Israel was to be a work not of nature, but of grace. Leah had four sons in rapid succession, and gave them names which indicated her state of mind: (1) *Reuben*, " see, a son!" because she regarded his birth as a pledge that Jehovah had graciously looked upon her misery, for now her husband would love her; (2) *Simeon, i.e.* " hearing," for Jehovah had heard, *i.e.* observed that she was hated; (3) *Levi, i.e.* attachment, for she hoped that this time, at least, after she had born three sons, her husband would become attached to her, *i.e.* show her some affection; (4) *Judah* (יְהוּדָה, verbal, of the *fut. hoph.* of יָדָה), *i.e.* praise, not merely the praised one, but the one for whom Jehovah is praised. After this fourth birth there was a pause (ver. 31), that she might not be unduly lifted up by her good fortune, or attribute to the fruitfulness of her own womb what the faithfulness of Jehovah, the covenant God, had bestowed upon her.

Chap. xxx. 1–8. BILHAH'S SONS.—When Rachel thought of her own barrenness, she became more and more envious of her sister, who was blessed with sons. But instead of praying, either directly or through her husband, as Rebekah had done, to Jehovah, who had promised His favour to Jacob (xxviii. 13 sqq.), she said to Jacob, in passionate displeasure, " *Get me children, or I shall die;*" to which he angrily replied, " *Am I in God's stead* (*i.e.* equal to God, or God), *who hath withheld from thee the fruit of the womb?*" *i.e.*, Can I, a powerless man, give thee what

the Almighty God has withheld? Almighty like God Jacob
certainly was not ; but he also wanted the power which he might
have possessed, the power of prayer, in firm reliance upon the
promise of the Lord.   Hence he could neither help nor advise
his beloved wife, but only assent to her proposal, that he should
beget children for her through her maid Bilhah (cf. xvi. 2),
through whom two sons were born to her.   The first she named
Dan, i.e. judge, because God had judged her, *i.e.* procured her
justice, hearkened to her voice (prayer), and removed the reproach of childlessness ; the second *Naphtali, i.e.* my conflict, or
my fought one, for " *fightings of God, she said, have I fought
with my sister, and also prevailed.*"   נַפְתּוּלֵי אֱלֹהִים are neither
luctationes quam maximæ, nor " a conflict in the cause of God,
because Rachel did not wish to leave the founding of the nation
of God to Leah alone" (*Knobel*), but " fightings for God and
His mercy" (*Hengstenberg*), or, what comes to the same thing,
" wrestlings of prayer she had wrestled with Leah ; in reality,
however, with God Himself, who seemed to have restricted His
mercy to Leah alone" (*Delitzsch*).   It is to be noticed, that
Rachel speaks of *Elohim* only, whereas Leah regarded her first
four sons as the gift of Jehovah.   In this variation of the names,
the attitude of the two women, not only to one another, but also
to the cause they served, is made apparent.   It makes no difference whether the historian has given us the very words of the
women on the birth of their children, or, what appears more
probable, since the name of God is not introduced into the names
of the children, merely his own view of the matter as related by
him (chap. xxix. 31, xxx. 17, 22).   Leah, who had been forced
upon Jacob against his inclination, and was put by him in the
background, was not only proved by the four sons, whom she
bore to him in the first years of her marriage, to be the wife
provided for Jacob by Elohim, the ruler of human destiny ; but
by the fact that these four sons formed the real stem of the
promised numerous seed, she was proved still more to be the wife
selected by Jehovah, in realization of His promise, to be the
tribe-mother of the greater part of the covenant nation.   But
this required that Leah herself should be fitted for it in heart and
mind, that she should feel herself to be the handmaid of Jehovah, and give glory to the covenant God for the blessing of children, or see in her children actual proofs that Jehovah had

accepted her and would bring to her the affection of her husband. It was different with Rachel, the favourite and therefore high-minded wife. Jacob should give her, what God alone could give. The faithfulness and blessing of the covenant God were still hidden from her. Hence she resorted to such earthly means as procuring children through her maid, and regarded the desired result as the answer of God, and a victory in her contest with her sister. For such a state of mind the term *Elohim*, God the sovereign ruler, was the only fitting expression.

Vers. 9–13. ZILPAH's SONS.—But Leah also was not content with the divine blessing bestowed upon her by Jehovah. The means employed by Rachel to retain the favour of her husband made her jealous; and jealousy drove her to the employment of the same means. Jacob begat two sons by Zilpah her maid. The one Leah named *Gad, i.e.* " good fortune," saying, בָּגָד, " with good fortune," according to the *Chethib*, for which the Masoretic reading is בָּא גָד, " good fortune has come,"—not, however, from any ancient tradition, for the *Sept.* reads ἐν τύχῃ, but simply from a subjective and really unnecessary conjecture, since בְּגָד = " to my good fortune," *sc.* a son is born, gives a very suitable meaning. The second she named *Asher, i.e.* the happy one, or bringer of happiness; for she said, בְּאָשְׁרִי, " to my happiness, for daughters call me happy," *i.e.* as a mother with children. The *perfect* אִשְּׁרוּנִי relates to " what she had now certainly reached " (*Del.*). Leah did not think of God in connection with these two births. They were nothing more than the successful and welcome result of the means she had employed.

Vers. 14–21. THE OTHER CHILDREN OF LEAH.—How thoroughly henceforth the two wives were carried away by constant jealousy of the love and attachment of their husband, is evident from the affair of the love-apples, which Leah's son Reuben, who was then four years old, found in the field and brought to his mother. דוּדָאִים, μῆλα μανδραγορῶν (LXX.), the yellow apples of the *alraun* (*Mandragora vernalis*), a mandrake very common in Palestine. They are about the size of a nutmeg, with a strong and agreeable odour, and were used by the ancients, as they still are by the Arabs, as a means of promoting child-bearing. To Rachel's request that she would give her some, Leah replied (ver. 15): " *Is it too little, that thou hast taken* (drawn away from me) *my husband, to take also*" (לָקַחַת *infin.*), *i.e.* that thou wouldst also take, "*my son's mandrakes?*"   At length she parted with them, on condition that Rachel would let Jacob sleep with her the next night.   After relating how Leah conceived again, and Rachel continued barren in spite of the mandrakes, the writer justly observes (ver. 17), "*Elohim hearkened unto Leah*," to show that it was not from such natural means as love-apples, but from God the author of life, that she had received such fruitfulness.   Leah saw in the birth of her fifth son a divine reward for having given her maid to her husband—a recompense, that is, for her self-denial; and she named him on that account *Issaschar*, יִשָּׂשׁכָר, a strange form, to be understood either according to the Chethib יֵשׁ שָׂכָר "there is reward," or according to the *Keri* יִשָּׂא שָׂכָר "he bears (brings) reward."   At length she bore her sixth son, and named him *Zebulun*, *i.e.* "dwelling;" for she hoped that now, after God had endowed her with a good portion, her husband, to whom she had born six sons, would dwell with her, *i.e.* become more warmly attached to her.   The name is from זָבַל to dwell, with *acc. constr.* "to inhabit," formed with a play upon the alliteration in the word זָבַד to present—two ἅπαξ λεγόμενα.   In connection with these two births, Leah mentions Elohim alone, the supernatural giver, and not Jehovah, the covenant God, whose grace had been forced out of her heart by jealousy.   She afterwards bore a daughter, *Dinah*, who is mentioned simply because of the account in chap. xxxiv.; for, according to chap. xxxvii. 35 and xlvi. 7, Jacob had several daughters, though they are nowhere mentioned by name.

Vers. 22–24. BIRTH OF JOSEPH.—At length God gave Rachel also a son, whom she named *Joseph*, יוֹסֵף, *i.e.* taking away (= אָסַף, cf. 1 Sam. xv. 6; 2 Sam. vi. 1; Ps. civ. 29) and adding (from יָסַף), because his birth not only furnished an actual proof that God had *removed* the reproach of her childlessness, but also excited the wish, that Jehovah might *add* another son. The fulfilment of this wish is recorded in chap. xxxv. 16 sqq. The double derivation of the name, and the exchange of *Elohim* for *Jehovah*, may be explained, without the hypothesis of a double source, on the simple ground, that Rachel first of all looked back at the past, and, thinking of the earthly means that had been applied in vain for the purpose of obtaining a child, regarded the son as a gift of God. At the same time, the good fortune which had now come to her banished from her heart her envy of her sister (ver. 1), and aroused belief in that God, who, as she had no doubt heard from her husband, had given Jacob such great promises; so that in giving the name, probably at the circumcision, she remembered Jehovah and prayed for another son from His covenant faithfulness.

After the birth of Joseph, Jacob asked Laban to send him away, with the wives and children for whom he had served him (ver. 25). According to this, Joseph was born at the end of the 14 years of service that had been agreed upon, *or* seven years after Jacob had taken Leah and (a week later) Rachel as his wives (xxix. 21-28). Now if all the children, whose births are given in chap. xxix. 32–xxx. 24, had been born one after another during the period mentioned, not only would Leah have had seven children in 7, or literally $6\frac{1}{4}$ years, but there would have been a considerable interval also, during which Rachel's maid and her own gave birth to children. But this would have been impossible; and the text does not really state it. When we bear in mind that the *imperf. c.* ן *consec.* expresses not only the order of time, but the order of thought as well, it becomes apparent that in the history of the births, the intention to arrange them according to the mothers prevails over the chronological order, so that it by no means follows, that because the passage, "when Rachel saw that she bare Jacob no children," occurs after Leah is said to have had four sons, therefore it was not till after the birth of Leah's fourth child that Rachel became aware of her own barrenness. There is nothing on the part of the grammar to prevent our arranging the course of events thus. Leah's first four births followed as rapidly as possible one after the other, so that four sons were born in the first four years of the second period of Jacob's service. In the meantime, not necessarily after the birth of Leah's fourth child, Rachel, having discovered her own barrenness, had given her maid to Jacob; so that not only may Dan have been born *before* Judah, but Naphtali also not long after him. The rapidity and regularity with which Leah had born her first four sons, would make her notice all the more quickly the cessation that took place; and jealousy of Rachel, as well as the success of the means she had adopted, would impel her to attempt in the same way to increase the number of her children. Moreover, Leah herself may have conceived again before the birth of her maid's second son, and may have given birth to her last two sons in the sixth and seventh years of their marriage. And contemporaneously with the birth of Leah's last son, or immediately afterwards, Rachel may have given birth to Joseph. In this way Jacob may easily have had eleven sons within seven years of his marriage. But with regard to the birth of Dinah, the expression "afterwards" (ver. 21) seems to indicate, that she was not born during Jacob's years of service, but during the remaining six years of his stay with Laban.

Vers. 25—43. NEW CONTRACT OF SERVICE BETWEEN JACOB AND LABAN.—As the second period of seven years terminated about the time of Joseph's birth, Jacob requested Laban to let him return to his own place and country, *i.e.* to Canaan. Laban, however, entreated him to remain, for he had perceived that Jehovah, Jacob's God, had blessed him for his sake; and told him to fix his wages for further service. The words, "*if I have found favour in thine eyes*" (ver. 27), contain an *aposiopesis, sc.* then remain. נִחַשְׁתִּי "a heathen expression, like *augurando cognovi*" (*Delitzsch*). שְׂכָרְךָ עָלַי *thy wages*, which it will be binding *upon me* to give. Jacob reminded him, on the other hand, what service he had rendered him, how Jehovah's blessing had followed "*at his foot*," and asked when he should begin to provide for his own house. But when Laban repeated the question, what should he give him, Jacob offered to feed and keep his flock still, upon one condition, which was founded upon the fact, that in the East the goats, as a rule, are black or dark-brown, rarely white or spotted with white, and that the sheep for the most part are white, very seldom black or speckled. Jacob required as wages, namely, all the speckled, spotted, and black among the sheep, and all the speckled, spotted, and white among the goats; and offered "*even to-day*" to commence separating them, so that "*to-morrow*" Laban might convince himself of the uprightness of his proceedings. הָסֵר (ver. 32) cannot be *imperative*, because of the preceding אֶעֱבֹר, but must be infinitive: "I will go through the whole flock to-day to remove from thence all . . ;" and הָיָה שְׂכָרִי signifies "what is removed shall be my wages," but not everything of an abnormal colour that shall hereafter be found in the flock. This was no doubt intended by Jacob, as the further course of the narrative shows, but it is not involved in the words of ver. 32. Either the writer has restricted himself to the main fact, and omitted to mention that it was also agreed at the same time that the separation should be repeated at certain regular periods, and that all the sheep of an abnormal colour in Laban's flock should also be set aside as part of Jacob's wages; or this point was probably not mentioned at first, but taken for granted by both parties, since Jacob took measures with that idea to his own advantage, and even Laban, notwithstanding the frequent alteration of the contract with which Jacob charged him (xxxi. 7, 8, and 41), does not appear to have disputed this right.—Vers. 34 sqq. Laban cheerfully accepted the proposal, but did not leave Jacob to make the selection. He undertook that himself, probably to make more sure, and then gave those which were set apart as Jacob's wages to his own sons to tend, since it was Jacob's duty to take care of Laban's flock, and "*set three days' journey betwixt himself and Jacob,*" *i.e.* between the flock to be tended by himself through his sons, and that to be tended by Jacob, for the purpose of preventing any copulation between the animals of the two flocks. Nevertheless he was overreached by Jacob, who adopted a double method of increasing the wages agreed upon. In the first place (vers. 37–39), he took fresh rods of storax, maple, and walnut-trees, all of which have a dazzling white wood under their dark outside, and peeled white stripes upon them, מַחְשֹׂף הַלָּבָן (the verbal noun instead of the inf. abs. חָשֹׂף), "*peeling the white naked in the rods.*" These partially peeled, and therefore mottled rods, he placed in the drinking-troughs (רְהָטִים *lit.* gutters, from רוּץ=רָהַט to run, is explained by שִׁקֲתוֹת הַמַּיִם water-troughs), to which the flock came to drink, in front of the animals, in order that, if copulation took place at the drinking time, it might occur near the mottled sticks, and the young be speckled and spotted in consequence. וַתֵּחַמְנָה a rare, antiquated form for וַתֶּחֱמַנָה from חָמַם, and וַיֵּחַמּוּ for וַיֵּחַמּוּ *imperf. Kal* of חָמַם=יָחַם. This artifice was founded upon a fact frequently noticed, particularly in the case of sheep, that whatever fixes their attention in copulation is marked upon the young (see the proofs in *Bochart, Hieroz.* 1, 618, and *Friedreich zur Bibel* 1, 37 sqq.).—*Secondly* (ver. 40), Jacob separated the speckled animals thus obtained from those of a normal colour, and caused the latter to feed so that the others would be constantly in sight, in order that he might in this way obtain a constant accession of mottled sheep. As soon as these had multiplied sufficiently, he formed separate flocks (viz. of the speckled additions), *"and put them not unto Laban's cattle;"* *i.e.* he kept them apart in order that a still larger number of speckled ones might be procured, through Laban's one-coloured flock having this mottled group constantly in view.—Vers. 41, 42. He did not adopt the trick with the rods, however, on every occasion of copulation, for the sheep in those countries lamb twice a year, but only at the copulation of the strong sheep (הַמְקֻשָּׁרוֹת the bound ones, *i.e.* firm and compact),—*Luther,* "the spring flock;" לְיַחֵמְנָה *inf. Pi.* "to conceive it (the young);"—but not "in the weakening of the sheep," *i.e.* when they were weak, and would produce weak lambs. The meaning is probably this: he only adopted this plan at the summer copulation, not the autumn; for, in the opinion of the ancients (*Pliny, Columella*), lambs that were conceived in the spring and born in the autumn were stronger than those born in the spring (cf. *Bochart l.c.* p. 582). Jacob did this, possibly, less to spare Laban, than to avoid exciting suspicion, and so leading to the discovery of his trick.—In ver. 43 the account closes with the remark, that the man increased exceedingly, and became rich in cattle (צֹאן רַבּוֹת many head of sheep and goats) and slaves, without expressing approbation of Jacob's conduct, or describing his increasing wealth as a blessing from God.   The verdict is contained in what follows.

JACOB'S FLIGHT, AND FAREWELL OF LABAN.—CHAP. XXXI.

Vers. 1–21. The flight.—Through some angry remarks of Laban's sons with reference to his growing wealth, and the evident change in the feelings of Laban himself towards him (vers. 1, 2), Jacob was inwardly prepared for the termination of his present connection with Laban; and at the same time he received instructions from Jehovah, to return to his home, together with a promise of divine protection. In consequence of this, he sent for Rachel and Leah to come to him in the field, and explained to them (vers. 4–13), how their father's disposition had changed towards him, and how he had deceived him in spite of the service he had forced out of him, and had altered his wages ten times ; but that the God of his father had stood by him, and had transferred to him their father's cattle, and now at length had directed him to return to his home.—Ver. 6. אֶתְנָה : the original form of the abbreviated אֵת, which is merely copied from the Pentateuch in Ez. xiii. 11, 20, xxxiv. 17. Ver. 9. אֲבִיכֶם : for אֲבִיכֶן as in chap. xxxii. 16, etc.—" *Ten times :*" *i.e.* as often as possible, the ten as a round number expressing the idea of completeness. From the statement that Laban had changed his wages ten times, it is evident that when Laban observed, that among his sheep and goats, of one colour only, a large number of mottled young were born, he made repeated attempts to limit the original stipulation by changing the rule as to the colours of the young, and so diminishing Jacob's wages. But when Jacob passes over his own stratagem in silence, and represents all that he aimed at and secured by crafty means as the fruit of God's blessing, this differs no doubt from the account in chap. xxx. It is not a contradiction, however, pointing to a difference in the sources of the two chapters, but merely a difference founded upon actual fact, viz. the fact that Jacob did not tell the whole truth to his wives. Moreover self-help and divine help do not exclude one another. Hence his account of the dream, in which he saw that the rams that leaped upon the cattle were all of various colours, and heard the voice of the angel of God calling his attention to what had been seen, in the words, " *I have seen all that Laban hath done to thee,*" may contain actual truth ; and the dream may be regarded as a divine revelation, which was either sent to explain to him now, at the end of the sixth year, " that it was not his stratagem, but the providence of God which had prevented him from falling a victim to Laban's avarice, and had brought him such wealth" (*Delitzsch*) ; or, if the dream occurred at an earlier period, was meant to teach him, that " the help of God, without any such self-help, could procure him justice and safety in spite of Laban's selfish covetousness" (*Kurtz*). It is very difficult to decide between these two interpretations. As Jehovah's instructions to him to return were not given till the end of his period of service, and Jacob connects them so closely with the vision of the rams that they seem contemporaneous, *Delitzsch's* view appears to deserve the preference. But the עֹשֶׂה in ver. 12, " all that Laban *is doing* to thee," does not exactly suit this meaning ; and we should rather expect to find עָשָׂה used at the end of the time of

service.   The participle rather favours *Kurtz's* view, that Jacob
had the vision of the rams and the explanation from the angel
at the beginning of the last six years of service, but that in his
communication to his wives, in which there was no necessity to
preserve a strict continuity or distinction of time, he connected
it with the divine instructions to return to his home, which he
received at the end of his time of service.   But if we decide in
favour of this view, we have no further guarantee for the objective reality of the vision of the rams, since nothing is said
about it in the historical account, and it is nowhere stated that
the wealth obtained by Jacob's craftiness was the result of the
divine blessing.   The attempt so unmistakeably apparent in
Jacob's whole conversation with his wives, to place his dealings
with Laban in the most favourable light for himself, excites the
suspicion, that the vision of which he spoke was nothing more
than a natural dream, the materials being supplied by the three
thoughts that were most frequently in his mind, by night as well
as by day, viz. (1) his own schemes and their success; (2) the
promise received at Bethel; (3) the wish to justify his actions
to his own conscience; and that these were wrought up by an
excited imagination into a visionary dream, of the divine origin
of which Jacob himself may not have had the slightest doubt.—
In ver. 13 הָאֵל has the article in the construct state, contrary to
the ordinary rule; cf. Ges. § 110, 2*b*; Ewald, § 290.

Vers. 14 sqq. The two wives naturally agreed with their
husband, and declared that they had no longer any part or inheritance in their father's house.   For he had not treated them
as daughters, but sold them like strangers, *i.e.* servants.   "*And
he has even constantly eaten our money,*" *i.e.* consumed the property brought to him by our service.   The *inf. abs.* אָכוֹל after
the finite verb expresses the continuation of the act, and is intensified by נם "*yes, even.*"   כִּי in ver. 16 signifies "so that,"
as in Deut. xiv. 24, Job x. 6.—Vers. 17–19. Jacob then set
out with his children and wives, and all the property that he had
acquired in Padan-Aram, to return to his father in Canaan;
whilst Laban had gone to the sheep-shearing, which kept him
some time from his home on account of the size of his flock.
Rachel took advantage of her father's absence to rob him of his
teraphim (*penates*), probably small images of household gods in
human form, which were worshipped as givers of earthly pros-

perity, and also consulted as oracles (see my *Archäologie*, § 90).—
Ver. 20. " *Thus Jacob deceived Laban the Syrian, in that he told
him not that he fled;*"—גְּנֵב לֵב to steal the heart (as the seat of the
understanding), like κλέπτειν νόον, and גְּנֵב with the simple *accus.
pers.*, ver. 27, like κλέπτειν τινα, signifies to take the knowledge of anything away from a person, to deceive him ;—" *and
passed over the river* (Euphrates), *and took the direction to the
mountains of Gilead.*"

Vers. 22–54. LABAN'S PURSUIT, RECONCILIATION, AND
COVENANT WITH JACOB.—As Laban was not told till the third
day after the flight, though he pursued the fugitives with his
brethren, *i.e.* his nearest relations, he did not overtake Jacob for
seven days, by which time he had reached the mountains of
Gilead (vers. 22–24). The night before he overtook them, he
was warned by God in a dream, " *not to speak to Jacob from
good to bad,*" *i.e.* not to say anything decisive and emphatic for
the purpose of altering what had already occurred (*vid.* ver. 29,
and the note on xxiv. 50). Hence he confined himself, when they
met, " to bitter reproaches combining paternal feeling on the one
hand with hypocrisy on the other;" in which he told them that
he had the power to do them harm, if God had not forbidden
him, and charged them with stealing his gods (the teraphim).—
Ver. 26. " *Like sword-booty;*" *i.e.* like prisoners of war (2 Kings
vi. 22) carried away unwillingly and by force.—Ver. 27. " *So I
might have conducted thee with mirth and songs, with tabret and
harp,*" *i.e.* have sent thee away with a parting feast. Ver. 28.
עֲשׂוֹ: an old form of the infinitive for עֲשׂוֹת as in chap. xlviii.
11, l. 20.—Ver. 29. יֶשׁ לְאֵל יָדִי : " *there is to God my hand*"
(Mic. ii. 1 ; cf. Deut. xxviii. 32 ; Neh. v. 5), *i.e.* my hand
serves me as God (Hab. i. 11 ; Job xii. 6), a proverbial expression for " the power lies in my hand."—Ver. 30. " *And now
thou art gone* (for, if thou art gone), *because thou longedst after
thy father's house, why hast thou stolen my gods?*" The meaning is this : even if thy secret departure can be explained, thy
stealing of my gods cannot.—Vers. 31, 32. The first, Jacob met
by pleading his fear lest Laban should take away his daughters
(keep them back by force). " *For I said:*" equivalent to " for
I thought." But Jacob knew nothing of the theft; hence he
declared, that with whomsoever he might find the gods he should

be put to death, and told Laban to make the strictest search among all the things that he had with him. *"Before our brethren,"* *i.e.* the relations who had come with Laban, as being impartial witnesses (cf. ver. 37); not, as *Knobel* thinks, before Jacob's horde of male and female slaves, of women and of children.— Vers. 33 sqq. Laban looked through all the tents, but did not find his teraphim; for Rachel had put them in the saddle of her camel and was sitting upon them, and excused herself to her lord (*Adonai,* ver. 35), on the ground that the custom of women was upon her. *" The camel's furniture,"* *i.e.* the saddle (not " the camel's litter :" *Luther*), here the woman's riding saddle, which had a comfortable seat formed of carpets on the top of the packsaddle. The fact that Laban passed over Rachel's seat because of her pretended condition, does not presuppose the Levitical law in Lev. xv. 19 sqq., according to which, any one who touched the couch or seat of such a woman was rendered unclean. For, in the first place, the view which lies at the foundation of this law was much older than the laws of Moses, and is met with among many other nations (cf. *Bähr*, Symbolik ii. 466, etc.); consequently Laban might refrain from making further examination, less from fear of defilement, than because he regarded it as impossible that any one with the custom of women upon her should sit upon his gods.—Vers. 36 sqq. As Laban found nothing, Jacob grew angry, and pointed out the injustice of his hot pursuit and his search among all his things, but more especially the harsh treatment he had received from him in return for the unselfish and self-denying services that he had rendered him for twenty years. Acute sensibility and elevated self-consciousness give to Jacob's words a rhythmical movement and a poetical form. Hence such expressions as דָּלַק אַחֲרֵי *" hotly pursued,"* which is only met with in 1 Sam. xvii. 53 ; אֲחַטֶּנָּה for אֲחַטְּאֶנָּה *" I had to atone for it,"* *i.e.* to *bear* the loss ; " *the Fear of Isaac,"* used as a name for God, פַּחַד, σέβας = σέβασμα, the object of Isaac's fear or sacred awe.—Ver. 40. " *I have been ; by day* (*i.e.* I have been in this condition, that by day) *heat has consumed* (prostrated) *me, and cold by night"*—for it is well known, that in the East the cold by night corresponds to the heat by day; the hotter the day the colder the night, as a rule.—Ver. 42. " *Except the God of my father . . . had been for me, surely thou wouldst now have sent me away empty. God has seen mine affliction and the labour of my hands, and last night He judged it.*" By the warning given to Laban, God pronounced sentence upon the matter between Jacob and Laban, condemning the course which Laban had pursued, and still intended to pursue, towards Jacob; but not on that account sanctioning all that Jacob had done to increase his own possessions, still less confirming Jacob's assertion that the vision mentioned by Jacob (vers. 11, 12) was a revelation from God. But as Jacob had only met cunning with cunning, deceit with deceit, Laban had no right to punish him for what he had done. Some excuse may indeed be found for Jacob's conduct in the heartless treatment he received from Laban, but the fact that God defended him from Laban's revenge did not prove it to be right. He had not acted upon the rule laid down in Prov. xx. 22 (cf. Rom. xii. 17; 1 Thess. v. 15).

Vers. 43–54. These words of Jacob " cut Laban to the heart with their truth, so that he turned round, offered his hand, and proposed a covenant." Jacob proceeded at once to give a practical proof of his assent to this proposal of his father-in-law, by erecting a stone as a memorial, and calling upon his relations also (" his brethren," as in ver. 23, by whom Laban and the relations who came with him are intended, as ver. 54 shows) to gather stones into a heap, which formed a table, as is briefly observed in ver. 46b, for the covenant meal (ver. 54). This stone-heap was called *Jegar-Sahadutha* by Laban, and *Galeed* by Jacob (the former is the Chaldee, the latter the Hebrew; they have both the same meaning, viz. " heaps of witness" [1]), because, as Laban, who spoke first, as being the elder, explained, the heap was to be a " witness between him and Jacob." The historian then adds this explanation : " *therefore they called his name Gal'ed*," and immediately afterwards introduces a second name, which the heap received from words that were spoken by Laban at the conclusion of the covenant (ver. 49) : " *And Mizpah*," i.e. watch, watch-place (*sc.* he called it), "*for he* (Laban) *said, Jehovah watch between me and thee ; for we are hidden from one another* (from the face of one another), *if thou*

---

[1] These words are the oldest proof, that in the native country of the patriarchs, Mesopotamia, Aramæan or Chaldæan was spoken, and Hebrew in Jacob's native country, Canaan; from which we may conclude that Abraham's family first acquired the Hebrew in Canaan from the Canaanites (Phœnicians).

shalt oppress my daughters, and if thou shalt take wives to my daughters! No man is with us, behold God is witness between me and thee!" (vers. 49, 50). After these words of Laban, which are introduced parenthetically,[1] and in which he enjoined upon Jacob fidelity to his daughters, the formation of the covenant of reconciliation and peace between them is first described, according to which, neither of them (*sive ego sive tu*, as in Ex. xix. 13) was to pass the stone-heap and memorial-stone with a hostile intention towards the other. Of this the memorial was to serve as a witness, and the God of Abraham and the God of Nahor, the God of their father (Terah), would be umpire between them. To this covenant, in which Laban, according to his polytheistic views, placed the God of Abraham upon the same level with the God of Nahor and Terah, Jacob swore by "the Fear of Isaac" (ver. 42), the God who was worshipped by his father with sacred awe. He then offered sacrifices upon the mountain, and invited his relations to eat, *i.e.* to partake of a sacrificial meal, and seal the covenant by a feast of love.

The geographical names *Gilead* and *Ramath-Mizpeh* (Josh. xiii. 26), also *Mizpeh-Gilead* (Judg ii. 29), sound so obviously like *Gal'ed* and *Mizpah*, that they are no doubt connected, and owe their origin to the monument erected by Jacob and Laban; so that it was by prolepsis that the scene of this occurrence was called "the mountains of Gilead" in vers. 21, 23, 25. By the *mount* or *mountains of Gilead* we are not to understand the mountain range to the south of the Jabbok (Zerka), the present *Jebel Jelaad*, or *Jebel es Salt*. The name *Gilead* has a much more comprehensive signification in the Old Testament; and the mountains to the south of the Jabbok are called in Deut. iii. 12 the half of Mount Gilead; the mountains to the

---

[1] There can be no doubt that vers. 49 and 50 bear the marks of a subsequent insertion. But there is nothing in the nature of this interpolation to indicate a compilation of the history from different sources. That Laban, when making this covenant, should have spoken of the future treatment of his daughters, is a thing so natural, that there would have been something strange in the omission. And it is not less suitable to the circumstances, that he calls upon the God of Jacob, *i.e.* Jehovah, to watch in this affair. And apart from the use of the name *Jehovah*, which is perfectly suitable here, there is nothing whatever to point to a different source; to say nothing of the fact that the critics themselves cannot agree as to the nature of the source supposed.

north of the Jabbok, the *Jebel-Ajlun*, forming the other half. In this chapter the name is used in the broader sense, and refers primarily to the northern half of the mountains (above the Jabbok); for Jacob did not cross the Jabbok till afterwards (xxxii. 23, 24). There is nothing in the names Ramath-Mizpeh, which *Ramoth* in Gilead bears in Josh. xiii. 26, and *Mizpeh-Gilead*, which it bears in Judg. xi. 29, to compel us to place Laban's meeting with Jacob in the southern portion of the mountains of Gilead. For even if this city is to be found in the modern *Salt*, and was called Ramath-Mizpeh from the event recorded here, all that can be inferred from that is, that the tradition of Laban's covenant with Jacob was associated in later ages with Ramoth in Gilead, without the correctness of the association being thereby established.

THE CAMP OF GOD AND JACOB'S WRESTLING.—CHAP. XXXII.

Vers. 1–3. THE HOST OF GOD.—When Laban had taken his departure peaceably, Jacob pursued his journey to Canaan. He was then met by some angels of God, in whom he discerned an encampment of God; and he called the place where they appeared *Mahanaim, i.e.* double camp or double host, because the host of God joined his host as a safeguard. This appearance of angels necessarily reminded him of the vision of the ladder, on his flight from Canaan. Just as the angels ascending and descending had then represented to him the divine protection and assistance during his journey and sojourn in a foreign land, so now the angelic host was a signal of the help of God for the approaching conflict with Esau of which he was in fear, and a fresh pledge of the promise (chap. xxviii. 15), "I will bring thee back to the land," etc. Jacob saw it during his journey; in a waking condition, therefore, not internally, but out of or above himself: but whether with the eyes of the body or of the mind (cf. 2 Kings vi. 17), cannot be determined. *Mahanaim* was afterwards a distinguished city, which is frequently mentioned, situated to the north of the Jabbok; and the name and remains are still preserved in the place called *Mahneh* (*Robinson*, Pal. Appendix, p. 166), the site of which, however, has not yet been minutely examined (see my Comm. on Joshua, p. 259).

Vers. 4–13. From this point Jacob sent messengers forward to his brother Esau, to make known his return in such a style of humility ("thy servant," "my lord") as was adapted to conciliate him. אֵחַר (ver. 5) is the first pers. imperf. Kal for אֶאֱחַר, from אָחַר to delay, to pass a time; cf. Prov. viii. 17, and Ges. § 68, 2. The statement that Esau was already in the land of Seir (ver. 4), or, as it is afterwards called, the field of Edom, is not at variance with chap. xxxvi. 6, and may be very naturally explained on the supposition, that with the increase of his family and possessions, he severed himself more and more from his father's house, becoming increasingly convinced, as time went on, that he could hope for no change in the blessings pronounced by his father upon Jacob and himself, which excluded him from the inheritance of the promise, viz. the future possession of Canaan. Now, even if his malicious feelings towards Jacob had gradually softened down, he had probably never said anything to his parents on the subject, so that Rebekah had been unable to fulfil her promise (chap. xxvii. 45); and Jacob, being quite uncertain as to his brother's state of mind, was thrown into the greatest alarm and anxiety by the report of the messengers, that Esau was coming to meet him with 400 men. The simplest explanation of the fact that Esau should have had so many men about him as a standing army, is that given by *Delitzsch*; namely, that he had to subjugate the Horite population in Seir, for which purpose he might easily have formed such an army, partly from the Canaanitish and Ishmaelitish relations of his wives, and partly from his own servants. His reason for going to meet Jacob with such a company may have been, either to show how mighty a prince he was, or with the intention of making his brother sensible of his superior power, and assuming a hostile attitude if the circumstances favoured it, even though the lapse of years had so far mitigated his anger, that he no longer seriously thought of executing the vengeance he had threatened twenty years before. For we are warranted in regarding Jacob's fear as no vain, subjective fancy, but as having an objective foundation, by the fact that God endowed him with courage and strength for his meeting with Esau, through the medium of the angelic host and the wrestling at the Jabbok; whilst, on the other hand, the brotherly affection and openness with which Esau met him, are to be attributed partly to Jacob's humble demeanour, and still more to the fact, that by the influence of God, the still remaining malice had been rooted out from his heart.—Vers. 8 sqq. Jacob, fearing the worst, divided his people and flocks into two camps, that if Esau smote the one, the other might escape. He then turned to the Great Helper in every time of need, and with an earnest prayer besought the God of his fathers, Abraham and Isaac, who had directed him to return, that, on the ground of the abundant mercies and truth (cf. xxiv. 27) He had shown him thus far, He would deliver him out of the hand of his brother, and from the threatening destruction, and so fulfil His promises. —Ver. 12. "*For I am in fear of him, that* (פֶּן *ne*) *he come and smite me, mother with children.*" אֵם עַל בָּנִים is a proverbial expression for unsparing cruelty, taken from the bird which covers its young to protect them (Deut. xxii. 6, cf. Hos. x. 14). עַל *super, una cum,* as in Ex. xxxv. 22.

Vers. 14–22. Although hoping for aid and safety from the Lord alone, Jacob neglected no means of doing what might help to appease his brother. Having taken up his quarters for the night in the place where he received the tidings of Esau's approach, he selected from his flocks ("*of that which came to his hand,*" *i.e.* which he had acquired) a very respectable present of 550 head of cattle, and sent them in different detachments to meet Esau, "*as a present from his servant Jacob,*" who was coming behind. The selection was in harmony with the general possessions of nomads (cf. Job i. 3, xliii. 12), and the proportion of male to female animals was arranged according to the agricultural rule of *Varro* (*de re rustica* 2, 3). The division of the present, "*drove and drove separately,*" *i.e.* into several separate droves which followed one another at certain intervals, was to serve the purpose of gradually mitigating the wrath of Esau. כִּפֶּר פָּנִים, ver 21, to appease the countenance; נָשָׂא פָנִים to raise any one's countenance, *i.e.* to receive him in a friendly manner. This present he sent forward; and he himself remained the same night (mentioned in ver. 14) in the camp.

Vers. 23–33. THE WRESTLING WITH GOD.—The same night, he conveyed his family with all his possessions across the ford of the Jabbok. *Jabbok* is the present Wady *es Zerka* (*i.e.* the blue), which flows from the east towards the Jordan, and

with its deep rocky valley formed at that time the boundary between the kingdoms of Sihon at Heshbon and Og of Bashan.
It now separates the countries of *Moerad* or *Ajlun* and *Belka*.
The ford by which Jacob crossed was hardly the one which he
took on his outward journey, upon the Syrian caravan-road by
Kalaat-Zerka, but one much farther to the west, between *Jebel
Ajlun* and *Jebel Jelaad*, through which *Buckingham, Burckhardt*,
and *Seetzen* passed; and where there are still traces of walls and
buildings to be seen, and other marks of cultivation.—Ver. 25.
When Jacob was left alone on the northern side of the Jabbok,
after sending all the rest across, "*there wrestled a man with him
until the breaking of the day.*" נֵאָבֵק, an old word, which only occurs here (vers. 25, 26), signifying to wrestle, is either derived
from אָבַק to wind, or related to חָבַק to contract one's self, to
plant limb and limb firmly together. From this wrestling the
river evidently received its name of *Jabbok* (יַבֹּק = יֵאָבֵק).—Ver.
26. "*And when He* (the unknown) *saw that He did not overcome
him, He touched his hip-socket; and his hip-socket was put out o,
joint* (תֵּקַע from יָקַע) *as He wrestled with him.*" Still Jacob
would not let Him go until He blessed him. He then said to
Jacob, "*Thy name shall be called no more Jacob, but Israel* (יִשְׂרָאֵל,
God's fighter, from שָׂרָה to fight, and אֵל God); *for thou hast
fought with God and with men, and hast prevailed.*" When
Jacob asked Him His name, He declined giving any definite
answer, and "*blessed him there.*" He did not tell him His
name; not merely, as the angel stated to Manoah in reply to a
similar question (Judg. xiii. 18), because it was פֶּלִא wonder, *i.e.*
incomprehensible to mortal man, but still more to fill Jacob's
soul with awe at the mysterious character of the whole event,
and to lead him to take it to heart. What Jacob wanted to
know, with regard to the person of the wonderful Wrestler,
and the meaning and intention of the struggle, he must
already have suspected, when he would not let Him go until
He blessed him; and it was put before him still more plainly
in the new name that was given to him with this explanation, "*Thou hast fought with Elohim and with men, and hast
conquered.*" God had met him in the form of a man:
God in the angel, according to Hos. xii. 4, 5, *i.e.* not in a
created angel, but in the Angel of Jehovah, the visible manifestation of the invisible God. Our history does not speak of

Jehovah, or the Angel of Jehovah, but of *Elohim*, for the purpose of bringing out the contrast between God and the creature. This remarkable occurrence is not to be regarded as a dream or an internal vision, but fell within the sphere of sensuous perception. At the same time, it was not a natural or corporeal wrestling, but a "real conflict of both mind and body, a work of the spirit with intense effort of the body" (*Delitzsch*), in which Jacob was lifted up into a highly elevated condition of body and mind resembling that of ecstasy, through the medium of the manifestation of God. In a merely outward conflict, it is impossible to conquer through prayers and tears. As the idea of a dream or vision has no point of contact in the history; so the notion, that the outward conflict of bodily wrestling, and the spiritual conflict with prayer and tears, are two features opposed to one another and spiritually distinct, is evidently at variance with the meaning of the narrative and the interpretation of the prophet Hosea. Since Jacob still continued his resistance, even after his hip had been put out of joint, and would not let Him go till He had blessed him, it cannot be said that it was not till all hope of maintaining the conflict by bodily strength was taken from him, that he had recourse to the weapon of prayer. And when Hosea (xii. 4, 5) points his contemporaries to their wrestling forefather as an example for their imitation, in these words, "He took his brother by the heel in the womb, and in his human strength he fought with God; and he fought with the Angel and prevailed; he wept and made supplication unto Him," the turn by which the explanatory periphrasis of Jacob's words, "I will not let Thee go except Thou bless me," is linked on to the previous clause by בָּכָה without a copula or *vav consec.*, is a proof that the prophet did not regard the weeping and supplication as occurring after the wrestling, or as only a second element, which was subsequently added to the corporeal struggle. Hosea evidently looked upon the weeping and supplication as the distinguishing feature in the conflict, without thereby excluding the corporeal wrestling. At the same time, by connecting this event with what took place at the birth of the twins (xxv. 26), the prophet teaches that Jacob merely completed, by his wrestling with God, what he had already been engaged in even from his mother's womb, viz. his striving for the birthright; in other words, for the possession of the covenant promise and the covenant blessing. This meaning is also indicated by the circumstances under which the event took place. Jacob had wrested the blessing of the birthright from his brother Esau; but it was by cunning and deceit, and he had been obliged to flee from his wrath in consequence. And now that he desired to return to the land of promise and his father's house, and to enter upon the inheritance promised him in his father's blessing; Esau was coming to meet him with 400 men, which filled him with great alarm. As he felt too weak to enter upon a conflict with him, he prayed to the covenant God for deliverance from the hand of his brother, and the fulfilment of the covenant promises. The answer of God to this prayer was the present wrestling with God, in which he was victorious indeed, but not without carrying the marks of it all his life long in the dislocation of his thigh. Jacob's great fear of Esau's wrath and vengeance, which he could not suppress notwithstanding the divine revelations at Bethel and Mahanaim, had its foundation in his evil conscience, in the consciousness of the sin connected with his wilful and treacherous appropriation of the blessing of the first-born. To save him from the hand of his brother, it was necessary that God should first meet him as an enemy, and show him that his real opponent was God Himself, and that he must first of all overcome Him before he could hope to overcome his brother. And Jacob overcame God; not with the power of the flesh however, with which he had hitherto wrestled for God against man (God convinced him of that by touching his hip, so that it was put out of joint), but by the power of faith and prayer, reaching by firm hold of God even to the point of being blessed, by which he proved himself to be a true wrestler of God, who fought with God and with men, *i.e.* who by his wrestling with God overcame men as well. And whilst by the dislocation of his hip the carnal nature of his previous wrestling was declared to be powerless and wrong, he received in the new name of *Israel* the prize of victory, and at the same time directions from God how he was henceforth to strive for the cause of the Lord.—By his wrestling with God, Jacob entered upon a new stage in his life. As a sign of this, he received a new name, which indicated, as the result of this conflict, the nature of his new relation to God. But whilst Abram and Sarai, from the time when God changed their names (xvii. 5 and 15), are always called by their new names; in the history of Jacob we find the old name used interchangeably with the new. "For the first two names denoted a change into a new and permanent position, effected and intended by the will and promise of God; consequently the old names were entirely abolished. But the name Israel denoted a spiritual state determined by faith; and in Jacob's life the natural state, determined by flesh and blood, still continued to stand side by side with this. Jacob's new name was transmitted to his descendants, however, who were called *Israel* as the covenant nation. For as the blessing of their forefather's conflict came down to them as a spiritual inheritance, so did they also enter upon the duty of preserving this inheritance by continuing in a similar conflict.

Ver. 31. The remembrance of this wonderful conflict Jacob perpetuated in the name which he gave to the place where it had occurred, viz. *Pniel* or *Pnuel* (with the connecting sound ו or '), because there he had seen Elohim face to face, and his soul had been delivered (from death, xvi. 13).—Vers. 32, 33. With the rising of the sun after the night of his conflict, the night of anguish and fear also passed away from Jacob's mind, so that he was able to leave Pnuel in comfort, and go forward on his journey. The dislocation of the thigh alone remained. For this reason the children of Israel are accustomed to avoid eating the *nervus ischiadicus*, the principal nerve in the neighbourhood of the hip, which is easily injured by any violent strain in wrestling. " *Unto this day:*" the remark is applicable still.

JACOB'S RECONCILIATION WITH ESAU AND RETURN TO CANAAN.—CHAP. XXXIII.

Vers. 1–17. MEETING WITH ESAU.—Vers. 1 sqq. As Jacob went forward, he saw Esau coming to meet him with his 400 men. He then arranged his wives and children in such a manner, that the maids with their children went first, Leah with hers in the middle, and Rachel with Joseph behind, thus forming a long procession. But he himself went in front, and met Esau with sevenfold obeisance. יִשְׁתַּחוּ אַרְצָה does not denote complete prostration, like אַפַּיִם אַרְצָה in chap. xix. 1, but a deep Oriental bow, in which the head approaches the ground, but does not touch it. By this manifestation of deep reverence, Jacob hoped to win his brother's heart. He humbled himself before him as the elder, with the feeling that he had formerly sinned against him. Esau, on the other hand, " had a comparatively better, but not so tender a conscience." At the sight of Jacob he was carried away by the natural feelings of brotherly affection, and running up to him, embraced him, fell on his neck, and kissed him ; and they both wept. The *puncta extraordinaria* above יִשָּׁקֵהוּ are probably intended to mark the word as suspicious. They " are like a note of interrogation, questioning the genuineness of this kiss ; but without any reason " (*Del.*). Even if there was still some malice in Esau's heart, it was overcome by the humility with which his brother met him, so that he allowed free course to the generous emotions of his heart ; all the more, because the " roving life " which suited his nature had procured him such wealth and power, that he was quite equal to his brother in earthly possessions.—Vers. 5–7. When his eyes fell upon the women and children, he inquired respecting them, " *Whom hast thou here ?* " And Jacob replied, " *The children with whom Elohim hath favoured me.*" Upon this, the mothers and their children approached in order, making reverential obeisance. חָנַן with double acc. " graciously to present." *Elohim :* " to avoid reminding Esau of the blessing of *Jehovah,* which had occasioned his absence " (*Del.*).—Vers. 8–11. Esau then inquired about the *camp* that had met him, *i.e.* the presents of cattle that were sent to meet him, and refused to accept them, until Jacob's urgent persuasion eventually induced him to do so. —Ver. 10. " *For therefore,*" *sc.* to be able to offer thee this present, " *have I come to see thy face, as man seeth the face of God, and thou hast received me favourably.*" The thought is this : In thy countenance I have been met with divine (heavenly) friendliness (cf. 1 Sam. xxix. 9, 2 Sam. xiv. 17). Jacob might say this without cringing, since he " must have discerned the work of God in the unexpected change in his brother's disposition towards him, and in his brother's friendliness a reflection of the divine."—Ver. 11. *Blessing :* i.e. the present, expressive of his desire to bless, as in 1 Sam. xxv. 27, xxx. 26. הֻבָאת : for הֵבֵאָה, as in Deut. xxxi. 29, Isa. vii. 14, etc. ; sometimes also in verbs ל"ה, Lev. xxv. 21, xxvi. 34. יֶשׁ־לִי כֹל : "*I have all*" (not all kinds of things) ; viz. as the heir of the divine promise.

Vers. 12–15. Lastly, Esau proposed to accompany Jacob on his journey. But Jacob politely declined not only his own company, but also the escort, which Esau afterwards offered him, of a portion of his attendants; the latter as being unnecessary, the former as likely to be injurious to his flocks. This did not spring from any feeling of distrust; and the ground assigned was no mere pretext. He needed no military guard, " for he knew that he was defended by the hosts of God;" and the reason given was a very good one: " *My lord knoweth that the children are tender, and the flocks and herds that are milking* (עָלוֹת from עָל, giving milk or suckling) *are upon me*" (עָלַי): *i.e.* because they are giving milk they are an object of especial anxiety to me; " *and if one should overdrive them a single day, all the sheep would die.*" A caravan, with delicate children and cattle that required care, could not possibly keep pace with Esau and his horsemen, without taking harm. And Jacob could not expect his brother to accommodate himself to the rate at which he was travelling. For this reason he wished Esau to go on first; and he would drive gently behind, " *according to the foot of the cattle* (מְלָאכָה possessions = cattle), *and according to the foot of the children,*" i.e. " according to the pace at which the cattle and the children could go" (*Luther*). " *Till I come to my lord to Seir:*" these words are not to be understood as meaning that he intended to go direct to Seir; consequently they were not a wilful deception for the purpose of getting rid of Esau. Jacob's destination was Canaan, and in Canaan probably Hebron. where his father Isaac still lived. From thence he may have thought of paying a visit to Esau in Seir. Whether he carried out this intention or not, we cannot tell; for we have not a record of all that Jacob did, but only of the principal events of his life. We afterwards find them both meeting together as friends at their father's funeral (xxxv. 29). Again, the attitude of inferiority which Jacob assumed in his conversation with Esau, addressing him as lord, and speaking of himself as servant, was simply an act of courtesy suited to the circumstances, in which he paid to Esau the respect due to the head of a powerful band; since he could not conscientiously have maintained the attitude of a brother, when inwardly and spiritually, in spite of Esau's friendly meeting, they were so completely separated the one from the other.—Vers. 16, 17. Esau set off the same day for Mount Seir, whilst Jacob proceeded to *Succoth*, where he built himself a house and made *succoth* for his flocks, *i.e.* probably not huts of branches and shrubs, but hurdles or folds made of twigs woven together. According to Josh. xiii. 27, *Succoth* was in the valley of the Jordan, and was allotted to the tribe of Gad, as part of the district of the Jordan, " on the other side Jordan eastward ;" and this is confirmed by Judg. viii. 4, 5, and by *Jerome* (*quæst. ad h. l.*) : *Sochoth usque hodie civitas trans Jordanem in parte Scythopoleos.* Consequently it cannot be identified with the *Sâcut* on the western side of the Jordan, to the south of Beisan, above the Wady *el Mâlih.*—How long Jacob remained in Succoth cannot be determined ; but we may conclude that he stayed there some years from the circumstance, that by erecting a house and huts he prepared for a lengthened stay. The motives which induced him to remain there are also unknown to us. But when *Knobel* adduces the fact, that Jacob came to Canaan for the purpose of visiting Isaac (xxxi. 18), as a reason why it is improbable that he continued long at Succoth, he forgets that Jacob could visit his father from Succoth just as well as from Shechem, and that, with the number of people and cattle that he had about him, it was impossible that he should join and subordinate himself to Isaac's household, after having attained through his past life and the promises of God a position of patriarchal independence.

Vers. 18-20. From Succoth, Jacob crossed a ford of the Jordan, and " *came in safety to the city of Sichem in the land of Canaan.*" שָׁלֵם is not a proper name meaning " to Shalem," as it is rendered by *Luther* (and Eng. Vers., *Tr.*) after the LXX., Vulg., etc. ; but an adjective, safe, peaceful, equivalent to בְּשָׁלוֹם, " in peace," in chap. xxviii. 21, to which there is an evident allusion. What Jacob had asked for in his vow at Bethel, before his departure from Canaan, was now fulfilled. He had returned in safety " to the land of Canaan ;" Succoth, therefore, did not belong to the land of Canaan, but must have been on the eastern side of the Jordan. עִיר שְׁכֶם, *lit.* city of Shechem ; so called from Shechem the son of the Hivite prince Hamor [1] (ver. 19, xxxiv. 2 sqq.), who founded it and called it by the name of his son, since it was not in existence in Abraham's time (*vid.* xii. 6). Jacob pitched his tent before the town, and then bought the piece of ground upon which he encamped from the sons of Hamor for 100

---

[1] *Mamortha*, which according to *Plin.* (h. n. v. 14) was the earlier name of *Neapolis* (Nablus), appears to have been a corruption of Chamor.

Kesita. קְשִׂיטָה is not a piece of silver of the value of a lamb (according to the ancient versions), but a quantity of silver weighed out, of considerable, though not exactly determinable value : cf. *Ges. thes. s. v.* This purchase showed that Jacob, in reliance upon the promise of God, regarded Canaan as his own home and the home of his seed. This piece of field, which fell to the lot of the sons of Joseph, and where Joseph's bones were buried (Josh. xxiv. 32), was, according to tradition, the plain which stretches out at the south-eastern opening of the valley of Shechem, where Jacob's well is still pointed out (John iv. 6), also Joseph's grave, a Mahometan wely (grave) two or three hundred paces to the north (Rob. Pal. iii. 95 sqq.). Jacob also erected an altar, as Abraham had previously done after his entrance into Canaan (xii. 7), and called it *El-elohe-Israel,* " *God* (the mighty) *is the God of Israel,*" to set forth in this name the spiritual acquisition of his previous life, and according to his vow (xxviii. 21) to give glory to the " God of Israel" (as he called Jehovah, with reference to the name given to him at chap. xxxii. 29), for having proved Himself to be EL, a mighty God, during his long absence, and that it might serve as a memorial for his descendants.

VIOLATION OF DINAH; REVENGE OF SIMEON AND LEVI.—
CHAP. XXXIV.

Vers. 1–4. During their stay at Shechem, *Dinah,* Jacob's daughter by Leah, went out one day to see, *i.e.* to make the acquaintance of the daughters of the land; when Shechem the Hivite, the son of the prince, took her with him and seduced her. Dinah was probably between 13 and 15 at the time, and had attained perfect maturity; for this is often the case in the East at the age of 12, and sometimes earlier. There is no ground for supposing her to have been younger. Even if she was born after Joseph, and not till the end of Jacob's 14 years' service with Laban, and therefore was only five years old when they left Mesopotamia, eight or ten years may have passed since then, as Jacob may easily have spent from eight to eleven years in Succoth, where he had built a house, and Shechem, where he had bought " a parcel of a field." But she cannot have been older; for, according to chap. xxxvii. 2, Joseph was sold by his brethren when he was 17 years old, *i.e.* in the 11th year after

Jacob's return from Mesopotamia, as he was born in the 14th year of Jacob's service with Laban[1] (cf. xxx. 24). In the interim between Dinah's seduction and the sale of Joseph there occurred nothing but Jacob's journey from Shechem to Bethel and thence to Ephratah, in the neighbourhood of which Benjamin was born and Rachel died, and his arrival in Hebron (chap. xxxv.). This may all have taken place within a single year. Jacob was still at Hebron, when Joseph was sent to Shechem and sold by his brethren (xxxvii. 14); and Isaac's death did not happen for 12 years afterwards, although it is mentioned in connection with the account of Jacob's arrival at Hebron (chap. xxxv. 27 sqq.). —Ver. 3. Shechem "*loved the girl, and spoke to her heart;*" *i.e.* he sought to comfort her by the promise of a happy marriage, and asked his father to obtain her for him as a wife.

Vers. 5–12. When Jacob heard of the seduction of his daughter, "*he was silent,*" *i.e.* he remained quiet, without taking any active proceedings (Ex. xiv. 14; 2 Sam. xix. 11) until his sons came from the field. When they heard of it, they were grieved and burned with wrath at the disgrace. טִמֵּא to defile = to dishonour, disgrace, because it was an uncircumcised man who had seduced her. "*Because he had wrought folly in Israel, by lying with Jacob's daughter.*" "To work folly" was a standing phrase for crimes against the honour and calling of Israel as the people of God, especially for shameful sins of the flesh (Deut. xxii. 21; Judg. xx. 10; 2 Sam. xiii. 2, etc.); but it was also applied to other great sins (Josh. vii. 15). As Jacob had become Israel, the seduction of his daughter was a crime against Israel, which is called folly, inasmuch as the relation of Israel to God was thereby ignored (Ps. xiv. 1). "*And this ought not to be done:*" יֵעָשֶׂה *potentialis* as in chap. xx. 9.—Hamor went to Jacob to ask for his daughter (ver. 6); but Jacob's sons reached home at the same time (ver. 7), so that Hamor spoke to them (Jacob and his sons). To attain his object Hamor proposed a further intermarriage, unrestricted movement on their part in the land, and that they should dwell there, trade (ἐμπορεύεσθαι), and secure possessions (נֶאֱחָזוּ settle down securely, as in xlvii. 27). Shechem also offered (vers. 11, 12) to give anything

[1] This view is generally supported by the earlier writers, such as *Demetrius, Petavius* (Hengst. Diss.), etc.; only they reckon Dinah's age at 16, placing her birth in the 14th year of Jacob's service.

they might ask in the form of dowry (מֹהַר not purchase-money, but the usual gift made to the bride, *vid.* xxiv. 53) and presents (for the brothers and mother), if they would only give him the damsel.

Vers. 13–17. Attractive as these offers of the Hivite prince and his son were, they were declined by Jacob's sons, who had the chief voice in the question of their sister's marriage (*vid.* xxiv. 50). And they were quite right; for, by accepting them, they would have violated the sacred call of Israel and his seed, and sacrificed the promises of Jehovah to Mammon. But they did it in a wrong way; for "*they answered with deceit and acted from behind*" (דִּבֵּר : בְּמִרְמָה וַיְדַבְּרוּ is to be rendered *dolos struxit;* דִּבֵּר דְּבָרִים would be the expression for "giving mere words," Hos. x. 4; vid. *Ges. thes.*), "*because he had defiled Dinah their sister.*" They told him that they could not give their sister to an uncircumcised man, because this would be a reproach to them; and the only condition upon which they would consent (נֵאוֹת *imperf. Niph.* of אוּת) was, that the Shechemites should all be circumcised; otherwise they would take their sister and go.

Vers. 18–24. The condition seemed reasonable to the two suitors, and by way of setting a good example, "*the young man did not delay to do this word,*" *i.e.* to submit to circumcision, "*as he was honoured before all his father's house.*" This is stated by anticipation in ver. 19; but before submitting to the operation, he went with his father to the gate, the place of public assembly, to lay the matter before the citizens of the town. They knew so well how to make the condition palatable, by a graphic description of the wealth of Jacob and his family, and by expatiating upon the advantages of being united with them, that the Shechemites consented to the proposal. שְׁלֵמִים: *integri,* people whose bearing is unexceptionable. "*And the land, behold broad on both sides it is before them,*" *i.e.* it offers space enough in every direction for them to wander about with their flocks. And then the gain : "*Their cattle, and their possessions, and their beasts of burden . . . shall they not be ours?*" מִקְנֶה is used here for flocks and herds, בְּהֵמָה for beasts of burden, viz. camels and asses (cf. Num. xxxii. 26). But notwithstanding the advantages here pointed out, the readiness of all the citizens of Shechem (*vid.* chap. xxiii. 10) to consent to be circumcised, could only be satisfactorily explained from the fact that this religious rite was already customary in different nations (according to *Herod.* 2, 104, among the Egyptians and Colchians), as an act of religious or priestly consecration.

Vers. 25–31. But on the third day, when the Shechemites were thoroughly prostrated by the painful effects of the opera- tion, Simeon and Levi (with their servants of course) fell upon the town בֶּטַח (*i.e.* while the people were off their guard, as in Ezek. xxx. 9), slew all the males, including Hamor and Shechem, with the edge of the sword, *i.e.* without quarter (Num. xxi. 24; Josh. x. 28, etc.), and brought back their sister. The sons of Jacob then plundered the town, and carried off all the cattle in the town and in the fields, and all their possessions, including the women and the children in their houses. By the sons of Jacob (ver. 27) we are not to understand the rest of his sons to the exclusion of Simeon, Levi, and even Reuben, as *Delitzsch* supposes, but all his sons. For the supposition, that Simeon and Levi were content with taking their murderous revenge, and had no share in the plunder, is neither probable in itself nor reconcilable with what Jacob said on his death-bed (chap. xlix. 5–7, observe עָקְרוּ שׁוֹר) about this very crime; nor can it be inferred from וַיֵּצְאוּ in ver. 26, for this relates merely to their going away from the house of the two princes, not to their leaving Shechem altogether. The abrupt way in which the plundering is linked on to the slaughter of all the males, without any copulative *Vav*, gives to the account the character of indignation at so revolting a crime; and this is also shown in the verbosity of the descrip- tion. The absence of the copula is not be accounted for by the hypothesis that vers. 27–29 are interpolated; for an interpolator might have supplied the missing link by a *vav*, just as well as the LXX. and other ancient translators.—Vers. 30, 31. Jacob re- proved the originators of this act most severely for their wicked- ness: " *Ye have brought me into trouble* (*conturbare*), *to make me stink* (an abomination) *among the inhabitants of the land; . . . and yet I* (with my attendants) *am a company that can be numbered* (*lit.* people of number, easily numbered, a small band, Deut. iv. 27, cf. Isa. x. 19); *and if they gather together against me, they will slay me*," etc. If Jacob laid stress simply upon the consequences which this crime was likely to bring upon himself and his house, the reason was, that this was the view most adapted to make an impression upon his sons. For his last words concerning Simeon and Levi (xlix. 5–7) are a sufficient proof that the wickedness of their conduct was also an object of deep abhorrence. And his fear was not groundless. Only God in His mercy averted all the evil consequences from Jacob and his house (chap. xxxv. 5, 6). But his sons answered, *"Are they to treat our sister like a harlot?"* הַכְזוֹנָה: as in Lev. xvi. 15, etc. Their indignation was justifiable enough; and their seeking revenge, as Absalom avenged the violation of his sister on Amnon (2 Sam. xiii. 22 sqq.), was in accordance with the habits of nomadic tribes. In this way, for example, seduction is still punished by death among the Arabs, and the punishment is generally inflicted by the brothers (cf. *Niebuhr*, Arab. p. 39; *Burckhardt*, Syr. p. 361, and Beduinen, p. 89, 224–5). In addition to this, Jacob's sons looked upon the matter not merely as a violation of their sister's chastity, but as a crime against the peculiar vocation of their tribe. But for all that, the deception they practised, the abuse of the covenant sign of circumcision as a means of gratifying their revenge, and the extension of that revenge to the whole town, together with the plundering of the slain, were crimes deserving of the strongest reprobation. The crafty character of Jacob degenerated into malicious cunning in Simeon and Levi; and jealousy for the exalted vocation of their family, into actual sin. This event "shows us in type all the errors into which the belief in the pre-eminence of Israel was sure to lead in the course of history, whenever that belief was rudely held by men of carnal minds" (*O. v. Gerlach*).

JACOB'S RETURN TO BETHEL AND HEBRON. DEATH OF ISAAC.—CHAP. XXXV.

Vers. 1–8. *Journey to Bethel.*—Jacob had allowed ten years to pass since his return from Mesopotamia, without performing the vow which he made at Bethel when fleeing from Esau (xxviii. 20 sqq.), although he had recalled it to mind when resolving to return (xxxi. 13), and had also erected an altar in Shechem to the "God of Israel" (xxxiii. 20). He was now directed by God (ver. 1) to go to Bethel, and there build an altar to the God who had appeared to him on his flight from Esau. This command stirred him up to perform what had been neglected, viz. to put away from his house the strange gods, which he had tolerated in weak consideration for his wives, and which had no doubt occasioned the long neglect, and to pay to God the vow that he had made in the day of his trouble. He therefore commanded his house (vers. 2, 3), *i.e.* his wives and children, and "*all that were with him*," *i.e.* his men and maid-servants, to put away the strange gods, to purify themselves, and wash their clothes. He also buried "all the strange gods," *i.e.* Rachel's teraphim (xxxi. 19), and whatever other idols there were, with the earrings which were worn as amulets and charms, "*under the terebinth at Shechem*," probably the very tree under which Abraham once pitched his tent (xii. 6), and which was regarded as a sacred place in Joshua's time (*vid.* Josh. xxiv. 26, though the pointing is אַלָּה there). The burial of the idols was followed by purification through the washing of the body, as a sign of the purification of the heart from the defilement of idolatry, and by the putting on of clean and festal clothes, as a symbol of the sanctification and elevation of the heart to the Lord (Josh. xxiv. 23). This decided turning to the Lord was immediately followed by the blessing of God. When they left Shechem a "*terror of God*," *i.e.* a supernatural terror, "*came upon the cities round about*," so that they did not venture to pursue the sons of Jacob on account of the cruelty of Simeon and Levi (ver. 5). Having safely arrived in Bethel, Jacob built an altar, which he called *El Bethel* (God of Bethel) in remembrance of the manifestation of God on His flight from Esau.—Ver. 8. There *Deborah*, Rebekah's nurse, died, and was buried below Bethel under an oak, which was henceforth called the "oak of weeping," a mourning oak, from the grief of Jacob's house on account of her death. Deborah had either been sent by Rebekah to take care of her daughters-in-law and grandsons, or had gone of her own accord into Jacob's household after the death of her mistress. The mourning at her death, and the perpetuation of her memory, are proofs that she must have been a faithful and highly esteemed servant in Jacob's house.

Vers. 9–15. THE FRESH REVELATION AT BETHEL.—After Jacob had performed his vow by erecting the altar at Bethel, God appeared to him again there ("*again*," referring to chap. xxviii.), "*on his coming out of Padan-Aram*," as He had appeared to him 30 years before on his journey thither,—though it was then in a dream, now by daylight in a visible form (cf. ver. 13, " *God went up from him* "). The gloom of that day of fear had now brightened into the clear daylight of salvation. This appearance was the answer, which God gave to Jacob on his acknowledgment of Him; and its reality is thereby established, in opposition to the conjecture that it is merely a legendary repetition of the previous vision.[1] The former theophany had promised to Jacob divine protection in a foreign land and restoration to his home, on the ground of his call to be the bearer of the blessings of salvation. This promise God had fulfilled, and Jacob therefore performed his vow. On the strength of this, God now confirmed to him the name of Israel, which He had already given him in chap. xxxii. 28, and with it the promise of a numerous seed and the possession of Canaan, which, so far as the form and substance are concerned, points back rather to chap. xvii. 6 and 8 than to chap. xxviii. 13, 14, and for the fulfilment of which, commencing with the birth of his sons and his return to Canaan, and stretching forward to the most remote future, the name of *Israel* was to furnish him with a pledge.—Jacob alluded to this second manifestation of God at Bethel towards the close of his life (chap. xlviii. 3, 4); and Hosea (xii. 4) represents it as the result of his wrestling with God. The remembrance of this appearance Jacob transmitted to his descendants by erecting a memorial stone, which he not only anointed with oil like the former one in chap. xxviii. 18, but consecrated by a drink-offering and by the renewal of the name Bethel.

[1] This conjecture derives no support from the fact that the manifestations of God are ascribed to *Elohim* in vers. 1 and 9 sqq., although the whole chapter treats of the display of mercy by the covenant God, *i.e.* *Jehovah*. For the occurrence of *Elohim* instead of *Jehovah* in ver. 1 may be explained, partly from the antithesis of God and man (because *Jacob*, the man, had neglected to redeem his vow, it was necessary that he should be reminded of it by God), and partly from the fact that there is no allusion to any *appearance* of God, but the words " God said " are to be understood, no doubt, as relating to an inward communication. The use of *Elohim* in vers. 9 sqq. follows naturally from the injunction of Elohim in ver. 1; and there was the less necessity for an express designation of the God appearing as *Jehovah*, because, on the one hand, the object of this appearance was simply to renew and confirm the former appearance of *Jehovah* (xxviii. 12 sqq.), and on the other hand, the title assumed in ver. 11, *El Shaddai*, refers to chap. xvii. 1, where Jehovah announces Himself to Abram as *El Shaddai*.

Vers. 16–20. Birth of Benjamin and death of Rachel. —Jacob's departure from Bethel was not in opposition to the divine command, " dwell there " (ver. 1). For the word שֵׁב does not enjoin a permanent abode; but, when taken in connection with what follows, "make there an altar," it merely directs him to stay there and perform his vow. As they were travelling forward, Rachel was taken in labour not far from Ephratah. כִּבְרַת הָאָרֶץ is a space, answering probably to the Persian parasang, though the real meaning of כִּבְרָה is unknown. The birth was a difficult one. תְּקַשׁ בְּלִדְתָּהּ: she had difficulty in her labour (instead of *Piel* we find *Hiphil* in ver. 17 with the same signification). The midwife comforted her by saying: " *Fear not, for this also is to thee a son,*"—a wish expressed by her when Joseph was born (xxx. 24). But she expired ; and as she was dying, she called him *Ben-oni*, " son of my pain." Jacob, however, called him *Ben-jamin*, probably son of good fortune, according to the meaning of the word *jamin* sustained by the Arabic, to indicate that his pain at the loss of his favourite wife was compensated by the birth of this son, who now completed the number twelve. Other explanations are less simple. He buried Rachel on the road to Ephratah, or Ephrath (probably the fertile, from פָּרָה), *i.e.* Bethlehem (bread-house), by which name it is better known, though the origin of it is obscure. He also erected a monument over her grave (מַצֵּבָה, στήλη), on which the historian observes, " *This is the pillar of Rachel's grave unto this day :*" a remark which does not necessarily point to a post-Mosaic period, but which could easily have been made even 10 or 20 years after its erection. For the fact that a grave-stone had been preserved upon the high road in a foreign land, the inhabitants of which had no interest whatever in it, might appear worthy of notice even though only a single decennary had passed away.[1]

---

[1] But even if this *Mazzebah* was really preserved till the conquest of Canaan by the Israelites, *i.e.* more than 450 years, and the remark referred to that time, it might be an interpolation by a later hand. The grave was certainly a well-known spot in Samuel's time (1 Sam. x. 2) ; but a *monumentum ubi Rachel posita est uxor Jacob* is first mentioned again by the Bordeaux pilgrims of A.D. 333 and *Jerome*. The *Kubbet Rahil* (Rachel's grave), which is now shown about half an hour's journey to the north of Bethlehem, to the right of the road from Jerusalem to Hebron, is merely " an ordinary Muslim wely, or tomb of a holy person, a small square build-

Vers. 21, 22*a*. REUBEN'S INCEST.—As they travelled on-ward, Jacob pitched his tent on the other side of *Migdal Eder*, where Reuben committed incest with Bilhah, his father's con-cubine. It is merely alluded to here in the passing remark that Israel heard it, by way of preparation for chap. xlix. 4. *Migdal Eder* (flock-tower) was a watch-tower built for the protection of flocks against robbers (cf. 2 Kings xviii. 8 ; 2 Chron. xxvi. 10, xxvii. 4) on the other side of Bethlehem, but hardly within 1000 paces of the town, where it has been placed by tradition since the time of Jerome. The *piska* in the middle of ver. 22 does not indicate a gap in the text, but the conclusion of a *parashah*, a division of the text of greater antiquity and greater correctness than the Masoretic division.

Vers. 22*b*–29. JACOB'S RETURN TO HIS FATHER'S HOUSE, AND DEATH OF ISAAC.—Jacob had left his father's house with no other possession than a staff, and now he returned with 12 sons. Thus had he been blessed by the faithful covenant God. To show this, the account of his arrival in his father's tent at Hebron is preceded by a list of his 12 sons, arranged according to their respective mothers; and this list is closed with the re-mark, " *These are the sons of Jacob, which were born to him in Padan-Aram*" (יֻלַּד for יֻלְּדוּ ; *Ges.* § 143, 1), although Benjamin, the twelfth, was not born *in* Padan-Aram, but on the journey back.—Vers. 27, 28. Jacob's arrival in " *Mamre Kirjath-Arbah*," *i.e.* in the terebinth-grove of Mamre (xiii. 18) by Kirjath-Arbah or Hebron (*vid.* xxiii. 2), constituted his entrance into his father's house, to remain there as Isaac's heir. He had probably visited his father during the ten years that had elapsed since his return from Mesopotamia, though no allusion is made to this, since such visits would have no importance, either in themselves or their consequences, in connection with the sacred history. This was not the case, however, with his return to enter upon the family

ing of stone with a dome, and within it a tomb in the ordinary Mohammedan form" (*Rob.* Pal. 1, p. 322). It has been recently enlarged by a square court with high walls and arches on the eastern side (Rob. Bibl. Researches, p. 357). Now although this grave is not ancient, the correctness of the tradition, which fixes upon this as the site of Rachel's grave, cannot on the whole be disputed. At any rate, the reasons assigned to the contrary by *Thenius, Kurtz,* and others are not conclusive.

inheritance. With this, therefore, the history of Isaac's life is brought to a close. Isaac died at the age of 180, and was buried by his two sons in the cave of Machpelah (chap. xlix. 31), Abraham's family grave, Esau having come from Seir to Hebron to attend the funeral of his father. But Isaac's death did not actually take place for 12 years after Jacob's return to Hebron. For as Joseph was 17 years old when he was sold by his brethren (xxxvii. 2), and Jacob was then living at Hebron (xxxvii. 14), it cannot have been more than 31 years after his flight from Esau when Jacob returned home (cf. chap. xxxiv. 1). Now since, according to our calculation at chap. xxvii. 1, he was 77 years old when he fled, he must have been 108 when he returned home; and Isaac would only have reached his 168th year, as he was 60 years old when Jacob was born (xxv. 26). Consequently Isaac lived to witness the grief of Jacob at the loss of Joseph, and died but a short time before his promotion in Egypt, which occurred 13 years after he was sold (xli. 46), and only 10 years before Jacob's removal with his family to Egypt, as Jacob was 130 years old when he was presented to Pharaoh (xlvii. 9). But the historical significance of his life was at an end, when Jacob returned home with his twelve sons.

IX. HISTORY OF ESAU.

CHAP. XXXVI.

" Esau and Jacob shook hands once more over the corpse of their father. Henceforth their paths diverged, to meet no more" (*Del.*). As Esau had also received a divine promise (xxv. 23), and the history of his tribe was already interwoven in the paternal blessing with that of Israel (xxvii. 29 and 40), an account is given in the book of Genesis of his growth into a nation; and a separate section is devoted to this, which, according to the invariable plan of the book, precedes the *tholedoth* of Jacob. The account is subdivided into the following sections, which are distinctly indicated by their respective headings. (Compare with these the parallel list in 1 Chron. i. 35-54.)

Vers. 1–8. ESAU'S WIVES AND CHILDREN. HIS SETTLE-MENT IN THE MOUNTAINS OF SEIR.—In the heading (ver. 1) the surname *Edom* is added to the name Esau, which he received at his birth, because the former became the national designation of his descendants.—Vers. 2, 3. The names of Esau's three wives differ from those given in the previous accounts (chap. xxvi. 34 and xxviii. 9), and in one instance the father's name as well. The daughter of Elon the Hittite is called *Adah* (the ornament), and in chap. xxvi. 34 *Basmath* (the fragrant); the second is called *Aholibamah* (probably tent-height), the daughter of Anah, daughter, *i.e.* grand-daughter of Zibeon the Hivite, and in xxvi. 34, *Jehudith* (the praised or praiseworthy), daughter of Beeri the Hittite; the third, the daughter of Ishmael, is called *Basmath* here and *Mahalath* in chap. xxviii. 9. This difference arose from the fact, that Moses availed himself of genealogical documents for Esau's family and tribe, and inserted them without alteration. It presents no irreconcilable discrepancy, therefore, but may be explained from the ancient custom in the East, of giving surnames, as the Arabs frequently do still, founded upon some important or memorable event in a man's life, which gradually superseded the other name (*e.g.* the name Edom, as explained in chap. xxv. 30); whilst as a rule the women received new names when they were married (cf. *Chardin, Hengstenberg, Dissertations,* vol. ii. p. 223–6). The different names given for the father of Aholibamah or Judith, *Hengstenberg* explains by referring to the statement in ver. 24, that Anah, the son of Zibeon, while watching the asses of his father in the desert, discovered the warm springs (of Calirrhoe), on which he founds the acute conjecture, that from this discovery Anah received the surname *Beeri, i.e.* spring-man, which so threw his original name into the shade, as to be the only name given in the genealogical table. There is no force in the objection, that according to ver. 25 Aholibamah was not a daughter of the discoverer of the springs, but of his uncle of the same name. For where is it stated that the Aholibamah mentioned in ver. 25 was Esau's wife? And is it a thing unheard of that aunt and niece should have the same name? If Zibeon gave his second son the name of his brother Anah (cf. vers. 24 and 20), why could not his son Anah have named his daughter after his cousin, the daughter of his father's brother? The reception of Aholibamah into the list of the Seirite princes is no proof that she was Esau's wife, but may be much more naturally supposed to have arisen from the same (unknown) circumstance as that which caused one of the seats of the Edomitish *Alluphim* to be called by her name (ver. 41).—Lastly, the remaining diversity, viz. that Anah is called a Hivite in ver. 2 and a Hittite in chap. xxvi. 34, is not to be explained by the conjecture, that for Hivite we should read Horite, according to ver. 20, but by the simple assumption that Hittite is used in chap. xxvi. 34 *sensu latiori* for Canaanite, according to the analogy of Josh. i. 4, 1 Kings x. 29, 2 Kings vii. 6 ; just as the two Hittite wives of Esau are called daughters of Canaan in chap. xxviii. 8.   For the historical account, the ge neral name Hittite sufficed ; but the genealogical list required the special name of the particular branch of the Canaanitish tribes, viz. the Hivites.   In just as simple a manner may the introduc. tion of the Hivite Zibeon among the Horites of Seir (vers. 20 and 24) be explained, viz. on the supposition that he removed to the mountains of Seir, and there became a Horite, *i.e.* a troglodyte, or dweller in a cave.—The names of Esau's sons occur again in 1 Chron. i. 35.   The statement in vers. 6, 7, that Esau went with his family and possessions, which he had acquired in Canaan, into the land of Seir, from before his brother Jacob, does not imply (in contradiction to chap. xxxii. 4, xxxiii. 14–16) that he did not leave the land of Canaan till after Jacob's return. The words may be understood without difficulty as meaning, that after founding a house of his own, when his family and flocks increased, Esau sought a home in Seir, because he knew that Jacob, as the heir, would enter upon the family possessions, but without waiting till he returned and actually took possession. In the clause " *went into the country*" (ver. 6), the name *Seir* or *Edom* (cf. ver. 16) must have dropt out, as the words " into the country" convey no sense when standing by themselves.

Vers. 9–14 (cf. 1 Chron. i. 36, 37). ESAU'S SONS AND GRANDSONS AS FATHERS OF TRIBES.—Through them he be came the *father of Edom, i.e.* the founder of the Edomitish nation on the mountains of Seir.   *Mount Seir* is the mountain- ous region between the Dead Sea and the Elanitic Gulf, the northern half of which is called *Jebâl* (Γεβαλήνη) by the Arabs, the southern half, *Sherah* (Rob. Pal. ii. 552).—In the case of two of the wives of Esau, who bore only one son each, the tribes were founded not by the sons, but by the grandsons; but in that of Aholibamah the three sons were the founders. Among the sons of Eliphaz we find *Amalek*, whose mother was Timna, the concubine of Eliphaz. He was the ancestor of the Amalekites, who attacked the Israelites at Horeb as they came out of Egypt under Moses (Ex. xvii. 8 sqq.), and not merely of a mixed tribe of Amalekites and Edomites, belonging to the supposed aboriginal Amalekite nation. For the Arabic legend of *Amlik* as an aboriginal tribe of Arabia is far too recent, confused, and contradictory to counterbalance the clear testimony of the record before us. The allusion to the fields of the Amalekites in chap. xiv. 7 does not imply that the tribe was in existence in Abraham's time, nor does the expression "first of the nations," in the saying of Balaam (Num. xxiv. 20), represent Amalek as the aboriginal or oldest tribe, but simply as the first heathen tribe by which Israel was attacked. The Old Testament says nothing of any fusion of Edomites or Horites with Amalekites, nor does it mention a double Amalek (cf. *Hengstenberg*, Dessertations 2, 247 sqq., and *Kurtz*, History i. 122, 3, ii. 240 sqq.).[1] If there had been an Amalek previous to Edom, with the important part which they took in opposition to Israel even in the time of Moses, the book of Genesis would not have omitted to give their pedigree in the list of the nations. At a very early period the Amalekites separated from the other tribes of Edom and formed an independent people, having their headquarters in the southern part of the mountains of Judah, as far as Kadesh (xiv. 7; Num. xiii. 29, xiv. 43, 45), but, like the Bedouins, spreading themselves as a nomad tribe over the whole of the northern portion of Arabia Petræa, from Havilah to Shur on the border of Egypt (1 Sam. xv. 3, 7, xxvii. 8); whilst one branch penetrated into the heart of Canaan, so that a range of hills, in what was afterwards the inheritance of Ephraim, bore the name of mountains of the Amalekites (Judg. xii. 15, cf. v. 14). Those who settled in Arabia seem also to have separated in the course of time into several branches, so that Amalekite hordes invaded the land of

[1] The occurrence of "Timna and Amalek" in 1 Chron. i. 36, as co-ordinate with the sons of Eliphaz, is simply a more concise form of saying "and from Timna, Amalek."

Israel in connection sometimes with the Midianites and the sons of the East (the Arabs, Judg. vi. 3, vii. 12), and at other times with the Ammonites (Judg. iii. 13). After they had been defeated by Saul (1 Sam. xiv. 48, xv. 2 sqq.), and frequently chastised by David (1 Sam. xxvii. 8, xxx. 1 sqq.; 2 Sam. viii. 12), the remnant of them was exterminated under Hezekiah by the Simeonites on the mountains of Seir (1 Chron. iv. 42, 43).

Vers. 15–19. THE TRIBE-PRINCES WHO DESCENDED FROM ESAU.—אַלּוּפִים was the distinguishing title of the Edomite and Horite phylarchs; and it is only incidentally that it is applied to Jewish heads of tribes in Zech. ix. 7, and xii. 5. It is probably derived from אֶלֶף or אֲלָפִים, equivalent to מִשְׁפָּחוֹת, families (1 Sam. x. 19; Mic. v. 2),—the heads of the families, *i.e.* of the principal divisions, of the tribe. The names of these *Alluphim* are not names of places, but of persons—of the three sons and ten grandsons of Esau mentioned in vers. 9–14; though *Knobel* would reverse the process and interpret the whole geographically.—In ver. 16 *Korah* has probably been copied by mistake from ver. 18, and should therefore be erased, as it really is in the *Samar.* Codex.

Vers. 20–30 (parallel, 1 Chron. i. 38–42). DESCENDANTS OF SEIR THE HORITE;—the inhabitants of the land, or pre-Edomitish population of the country.—"*The Horite:*" ὁ Τρωγλοδύτης, the dweller in caves, which abound in the mountains of Edom (*vid.* Rob. Pal. ii. p. 424). The Horites, who had previously been an independent people (xiv. 6), were partly exterminated and partly subjugated by the descendants of Esau (Deut. ii. 12, 22). Seven sons of Seir are given as tribe-princes of the Horites, who are afterwards mentioned as *Alluphim* (vers. 29, 30), also their sons, as well as two daughters, *Timna* (ver. 22) and *Aholibamah* (ver. 25), who obtained notoriety from the fact that two of the headquarters of Edomitish tribe-princes bore their names (vers. 40 and 41). *Timna* was probably the same as the concubine of Eliphaz (ver. 12); but *Aholibamah* was not the wife of Esau (cf. ver. 2).—There are a few instances in which the names in this list differ from those in the Chronicles. But they are differences which either consist of variations in form, or have arisen from mistakes in copying.[1] Of *Anah*, the son of Zibeon, it is related (ver. 24), that as he fed the asses of his father in the desert, he "found הַיֵּמִם;"—not "he invented mules," as the Talmud, Luther, etc., render it, for mules are פְּרָדִים, and מָצָא does not mean to invent; but he discovered *aquæ calidæ* (*Vulg.*), either the hot sulphur springs of *Calirrhoe* in the Wady *Zerka Maein* (*vid.* x. 19), or those in the Wady *el Ahsa* to the S.E. of the Dead Sea, or those in the Wady *Hamad* between Kerek and the Dead Sea.[2]— Ver. 30. "*These are the princes of the Horites according to their princes*," *i.e.* as their princes were individually named in the land of Seir. לְ in enumerations indicates the relation of the individual to the whole, and of the whole to the individual.

Vers. 31–39 (parallel, 1 Chron. i. 43–50). THE KINGS IN THE LAND OF EDOM : before the children of Israel had a king. It is to be observed in connection with the eight kings mentioned here, that whilst they follow one another, that is to say,

[1] *Knobel* also undertakes to explain these names geographically, and to point them out in tribes and places of Arabia, assuming, quite arbitrarily and in opposition to the text, that the names refer to tribes, not to persons, although an incident is related of Zibeon's son, which proves at once that the list relates to persons and not to tribes ; and expecting his readers to believe that not only are the descendants of these troglodytes, who were exterminated before the time of Moses, still to be found, but even their names may be traced in certain Bedouin tribes, though more than 3000 years have passed away ! The utter groundlessness of such explanations, which rest upon nothing more than similarity of names, may be seen in the association of *Shobal* with *Syria Sobal* (Judith iii. 1), the name used by the Crusaders for *Arabia iertia*, *i.e.* the southernmost district below the Dead Sea, which was conquered by them. For notwithstanding the resemblance of the name *Shobal* to *Sobal*, no one could seriously think of connecting *Syria Sobal* with the Horite prince *Shobal*, unless he was altogether ignorant of the apocryphal origin of the former name, which first of all arose from the Greek or Latin version of the Old Testament, and in fact from a misunderstanding of Ps. lx. 2, where, instead אֲרַם צוֹבָה, *Aram Zobah*, we find in the LXX. Συρία Σοβάλ, and in the *Vulg.* *Syria et Sobal.*

[2] It is possible that there may be something significant in the fact that it was "as he was feeding his father's asses," and that the asses may have contributed to the discovery ; just as the whirlpool of Karlsbad is said to have been discovered through a hound of Charles IV., which pursued a stag into a hot spring, and attracted the huntsmen to the spot by its howling.

one never comes to the throne till his predecessor is dead, yet
the son never succeeds the father, but they all belong to different
families and places, and in the case of the last the statement that
" he died" is wanting.   From this it is unquestionably obvious,
that the sovereignty was elective ; that the kings were chosen
by the phylarchs ; and, as Isa. xxxiv. 12 also shows, that they
lived or reigned contemporaneously with these.   The contemporaneous existence of the *Alluphim* and the kings may also be
inferred from Ex. xv. 15 as compared with Num. xx. 14 sqq.
Whilst it was with the king of Edom that Moses treated respecting the passage through the land, in the song of Moses it
is the princes who tremble with fear on account of the miraculous passage through the Red Sea (cf. Ezek. xxxii. 29).   Lastly,
this is also supported by the fact, that the account of the seats
of the phylarchs (vers. 40–43) follows the list of the kings.
This arrangement would have been thoroughly unsuitable if the
monarchy had been founded upon the ruins of the phylarchs
(*vid. Hengstenberg, ut sup.* pp. 238 sqq.).   Of all the kings of
Edom, not one is named elsewhere.   It is true, the attempt has
been made to identify the fourth, *Hadad* (ver. 35), with the
Edomite Hadad who rose up against Solomon (1 Kings xi. 14) ;
but without foundation.   The contemporary of Solomon was of
royal blood, but neither a king nor a pretender ; our Hadad, on
the contrary, was a king, but he was the son of an unknown
Hadad of the town of *Avith,* and no relation to his predecessor
Husham of the country of the Temanites.   It is related of him
that he smote Midian in the fields of Moab (ver. 35) ; from which
Hengstenberg (pp. 235–6) justly infers that this event cannot
have been very remote from the Mosaic age, since we find the
Midianites allied to the Moabites in Num. xxii. ; whereas afterwards, viz. in the time of Gideon, the Midianites vanished from
history, and in Solomon's days the fields of Moab, being Israelitish territory, cannot have served as a field of battle for the
Midianites and Moabites.—Of the tribe-cities of these kings
only a few can be identified now.   *Bozrah,* a noted city of the
Edomites (Isa. xxxiv. 6, lxiii. 1, etc.), is still to be traced in *el
Buseireh,* a village with ruins in *Jebal* (Rob. Pal. ii. 571).—The
land of the *Temanite* (ver. 34) is a province in northern Idumæa,
with a city, *Teman,* which has not yet been discovered ; according to *Jerome, quinque millibus* from Petra.—*Rehoboth* of the

river (ver. 37) can neither be the Idumæan *Robotha,* nor *er Ruheibeh* in the wady running towards *el Arish,* but must be sought for on the Euphrates, say in *Errachabi* or *Rachabeh,* near the mouth of the Chaboras. Consequently Saul, who sprang from Rehoboth, was a foreigner.—Of the last king, *Hadar* (ver. 39 ; not Hadad, as it is written in 1 Chron. i. 50), the wife, the mother-in-law, and the mother are mentioned : his death is not mentioned here, but is added by the later chronicler (1 Chron. i. 51). This can be explained easily enough from the simple fact, that at the time when the table was first drawn up, Hadad was still alive and seated upon the throne. In all probability, therefore, Hadad was the king of Edom, to whom Moses applied for permission to pass through the land (Num. xx. 14 sqq.).[1] At any rate the list is evidently a record relating to the Edomitish kings of a pre-Mosaic age. But if this is the case, the heading, " *These are the kings that reigned in the land of Edom, before there reigned any king over the children of Israel,*" does not refer to the time when the monarchy was introduced into Israel under Saul, but was written with the promise in mind, that kings should come out of the loins of Jacob (xxxv. 11, cf. xvii. 4 sqq.), and merely expresses the thought, that Edom became a kingdom at an earlier period than Israel. Such a thought was by no means inappropriate to the Mosaic age. For the idea, " that

[1] If this be admitted ; then, on the supposition that this list of kings contains all the previous kings of Edom, the introduction of monarchy among the Edomites can hardly have taken place more than 200 years before the exodus ; and, in that case, none of the phylarchs named in vers. 15–18 can have lived to see its establishment. For the list only reaches to the grandsons of Esau, none of whom are likely to have lived more than 100 or 150 years after Esau's death. It is true we do not know when Esau died ; but 413 years elapsed between the death of Jacob and the exodus, and Joseph, who was born in the 91st year of Jacob's life, died 54 years afterwards, *i.e.* 359 years before the exodus. But Esau was married in his 40th year, 37 years before Jacob (xxvi. 34), and had sons and daughters before his removal to Seir (ver. 6). Unless, therefore, his sons and grandsons attained a most unusual age, or were married remarkably late in life, his grandsons can hardly have outlived Joseph more than 100 years. Now, if we fix their death at about 250 years before the exodus of Israel from Egypt, there remains from that point to the arrival of the Israelites at the land of Edom (Num. xx. 14) a period of 290 years ; amply sufficient for the reigns of eight kings, even if the monarchy was not introduced till after the death of the last of the phylarchs mentioned in vers. 15–18.

Israel was destined to grow into a kingdom with monarchs of his own family, was a hope handed down to the age of Moses, which the long residence in Egypt was well adapted to foster" (*Del.*).

Vers. 40–43 (parallel, 1 Chron. i. 51–54). SEATS OF THE TRIBE-PRINCES OF ESAU ACCORDING TO THEIR FAMILIES.— That the names which follow are not a second list of Edomitish tribe-princes (viz. of those who continued the ancient constitution, with its hereditary aristocracy, after Hadar's death), but merely relate to the capital cities of the old phylarchs, is evident from the expression in the heading, "*After their places, by their names,*" as compared with ver. 43, "*According to their habitations in the land of their possession.*" This being the substance and intention of the list, there is nothing surprising in the fact, that out of the eleven names only two correspond to those given in vers. 15–19. This proves nothing more than that only two of the capitals received their names from the princes who captured or founded them, viz. *Timnah* and *Kenaz.* Neither of these has been discovered yet. The name *Aholibamah* is derived from the Horite princess (ver. 25); its site is unknown. *Elah* is the port *Aila* (*vid.* xiv. 6). *Pinon* is the same as *Phunon*, an encampment of the Israelites (Num. xxxiii. 42–3), celebrated for its mines, in which many Christians were condemned to labour under Diocletian, between Petra and Zoar, to the northeast of Wady Musa. *Teman* is the capital of the land of the Temanites (ver. 34). *Mibzar* is supposed by *Knobel* to be Petra; but this is called *Selah* elsewhere (2 Kings xiv. 7). *Magdiel* and *Iram* cannot be identified. The concluding sentence, "*This is Esau, the father* (founder) *of Edom*" (*i.e.* from him sprang the great nation of the Edomites, with its princes and kings, upon the mountains of Seir), not only terminates this section, but prepares the way for the history of Jacob, which commences with the following chapter.

X. HISTORY OF JACOB.

CHAP. XXXVII.–L.

ITS SUBSTANCE AND CHARACTER.

The history (*tholedoth*) of Isaac commenced with the founding of his house by the birth of his sons (p. 266); but Jacob was abroad when his sons were born, and had not yet entered into undisputed possession of his inheritance. Hence his *tholedoth* only commence with his return to his father's tent and his entrance upon the family possessions, and merely embrace the history of his life as patriarch of the house which he founded. In this period of his life, indeed, his sons, especially Joseph and Judah, stand in the foreground, so that "Joseph might be described as the moving principle of the following history." But for all that, Jacob remains the head of the house, and the centre around whom the whole revolves. This section is divided by the removal of Jacob to Egypt, into the period of his residence in Canaan (chap. xxxvii.–xlv.), and the close of his life in Goshen (chap. xlvi.–l.). The first period is occupied with the events which prepared the way for, and eventually occasioned, his migration into Egypt. The way was prepared, directly by the sale of Joseph (chap. xxxvii.), indirectly by the alliance of Judah with the Canaanites (chap. xxxviii.), which endangered the divine call of Israel, inasmuch as this showed the necessity for a temporary removal of the sons of Israel from Canaan. The way was opened by the wonderful career of Joseph in Egypt, his elevation from slavery and imprisonment to be the ruler over the whole of Egypt (xxxix.–xli.). And lastly, the migration was occasioned by the famine in Canaan, which rendered it necessary for Jacob's sons to travel into Egypt to buy corn, and, whilst it led to Jacob's recovery of the son he had mourned for as dead, furnished an opportunity for Joseph to welcome his family into Egypt (chap. xlii.–xlv.). The *second* period commences with the migration of Jacob into Egypt, and his settlement in the land of Goshen (chap. xlvi.–xlvii. 27). It embraces the patriarch's closing years, his last instructions respecting his burial in Canaan (chap. xlvii. 28–31), his adoption of Joseph's sons, and the blessing given to his twelve sons (chap. xlix.), and extends to his burial and Joseph's death (chap. l.).

Now if we compare this period of the patriarchal history with the previous ones, viz. those of Isaac and Abraham, it differs from them most in the absence of divine revelations—in the fact, that from the time of the patriarch's entrance upon the family inheritance to the day of his death, there was only one other occasion on which God appeared to him in a dream, viz. in Beersheba, on the border of the promised land, when he had prepared to go with his whole house into Egypt: the God of his father then promised him the increase of his seed in Egypt into a great nation, and their return to Canaan (xlvi. 2–4). This fact may be easily explained on the ground, that the end of the divine manifestations had been already attained ; that in Jacob's house with his twelve sons the foundation was laid for the development of the promised nation ; and that the time had come, in which the chosen family was to grow into a nation,—a process for which they needed, indeed, the blessing and protection of God, but no special revelations, so long at least as this growth into a nation took its natural course. That course was not interrupted, but rather facilitated by the removal into Egypt. But as Canaan had been assigned to the patriarchs as the land of their pilgrimage, and promised to their seed for a possession after it had become a nation ; when Jacob was compelled to leave this land, his faith in the promise of God might have been shaken, if God had not appeared to him as he departed, to promise him His protection in the foreign land, and assure him of the fulfilment of His promises. More than this the house of Israel did not need to know, as to the way by which God would lead them, especially as Abraham had already received a revelation from the Lord (xv. 13–16).

In perfect harmony with the character of the time thus commencing for Jacob-Israel, is the use of the names of God in this last section of Genesis : viz. the fact, that whilst in chap. xxxvii. (the sale of Joseph) the name of God is not met with at all, in chap. xxxviii. and xxxix. we find the name of *Jehovah* nine times and *Elohim* only once (xxxix. 9), and that in circumstances in which *Jehovah* would have been inadmissible ; and after chap. xl. 1, the name *Jehovah* almost entirely disappears, occurring only once in chap. xl.–l. (chap. xlix. 18, where Jacob uses it), whereas *Elohim* is used eighteen times and *Ha-Elohim* seven, not to mention such expressions as "your God" (xliii. 23), or "the God of his, or your father" (xlvi. 1, 3). So long as the attention is confined to this numerical proportion of Jehovah, and Elohim or Ha-Elohim, it must remain " a difficult enigma." But when we look at the way in which these names are employed, we find the actual fact to be, that in chap. xxxviii. and xxxix. the writer mentions God nine times, and calls Him *Jehovah*, and that in chap. xl.–l. he only mentions God twice, and then calls Him *Elohim* (xlvi. 1, 2), although the God of salvation, *i.e.* Jehovah, is intended. In every other instance in which God is referred to in chap. xl.–l., it is always by the persons concerned : either Pharaoh (xli. 38, 39), or Joseph and his brethren (xl. 8, xli. 16, 51, 52, etc., *Elohim ;* and xli. 25, 28, 32, etc., *Ha-Elohim*), or by Jacob (xlviii. 11, 20, 21, *Elohim*). Now the circumstance that the historian speaks of God nine times in chap. xxxviii. xxxix. and only twice in chap. xl.–l. is explained by the substance of the history, which furnished no particular occasion for this in the last eleven chapters. But the reason why he does not name *Jehovah* in chap. xl.–l. as in chap. xxxviii.–xxxix., but speaks of the " God of his (Jacob's) father Isaac," in chap. xlvi. 1, and directly afterwards of *Elohim* (ver. 2), could hardly be that the periphrasis "the God of his father" seemed more appropriate than the simple name *Jehovah*, since Jacob offered sacrifice at Beersheba to the God who appeared to his father, and to whom Isaac built an altar there, and this God (*Elohim*) then appeared to him in a dream and renewed the promise of his fathers. As the historian uses a periphrasis of the name *Jehovah*, to point out the internal connection between what Jacob did and experienced at Beersheba and what his father experienced there ; so Jacob also, both in the blessing with which he sends his sons the second time to Egypt (xliii. 14) and at the adoption of Joseph's sons (xlviii. 3), uses the name *El Shaddai*, and in his blessings on Joseph's sons (xlviii. 15) and on Joseph himself (xlix. 24, 25) employs rhetorical periphrases for the name *Jehovah*, because Jehovah had manifested Himself not only to him (xxxv. 11, 12), but also to his fathers Abraham and Isaac (xvii. 1 and xxviii. 3) as *El Shaddai*, and had proved Himself to be the Almighty, " the God who fed him," " the Mighty One of Jacob," "the Shepherd and Rock of Israel." In these set

discourses the titles of God here mentioned were unquestionably
more significant and impressive than the simple name *Jehovah.*
And when Jacob speaks of *Elohim* only, not of *Jehovah*, in chap.
xlviii. 11, 20, 21, the *Elohim* in vers. 11 and 21 may be easily
explained from the antithesis of Jacob to both man and God,
and in ver. 20 from the words themselves, which contain a common and, so to speak, a stereotyped saying.   Wherever the
thought required the name Jehovah as the only appropriate one,
there Jacob used this name, as chap. xlix. 18 will prove.   But
that name would have been quite unsuitable in the mouth of
Pharaoh in chap. xli. 38, 39, in the address of Joseph to the
prisoners (xl. 8) and to Pharaoh (xli. 16, 25, 28, 32), and in his
conversation with his brethren before he made himself known
(xlii. 18, xliii. 29), and also in the appeal of Judah to Joseph as
an unknown Egyptian officer of state (xliv. 16).   In the meantime the brethren of Joseph also speak to one another of *Elohim*
(xlii. 28) ; and Joseph not only sees in the birth of his sons merely
a gift of Elohim (xli. 51, 52, xlviii. 9), but in the solemn moment in which he makes himself known to his brethren (xlv. 5–9)
he speaks of *Elohim* alone : " *Elohim* did send me before you
to preserve life " (ver. 5) ; and even upon his death-bed he says,
" I die, and *Elohim* will surely visit you and bring you out of
this land " (l. 24, 25).   But the reason of this is not difficult to
discover, and is no other than the following : Joseph, like his
brethren, did not clearly discern the ways of the Lord in the
wonderful changes of his life ; and his brethren, though they
felt that the trouble into which they were brought before the
unknown ruler of Egypt was a just punishment from God for
their crime against Joseph, did not perceive that by the sale of
their brother they had sinned not only against Elohim (God the
Creator and Judge of men), but against Jehovah the covenant
God of their father.   They had not only sold their brother, but
in their brother they had cast out a member of the seed promised
and given to Abraham, Isaac, and Jacob, from the fellowship of
the chosen family, and sinned against the God of salvation and
His promises.   But this aspect of their crime was still hidden
from them, so that they could not speak of Jehovah.   In the
same way, Joseph regarded the wonderful course of his life as a
divine arrangement for the preservation or rescue of his family ,
and he was so far acquainted with the promises of God, that he

regarded it as a certainty, that Israel would be led out of Egypt, especially after the last wish expressed by Jacob. But this did not involve so full and clear an insight into the ways of Jehovah, as to lead Joseph to recognise in his own career a special appointment of the covenant God, and to describe it as a gracious work of Jehovah.[1]

The disappearance of the name Jehovah, therefore, is to be explained, partly from the fact that previous revelations and acts of grace had given rise to other phrases expressive of the idea of Jehovah, which not only served as substitutes for this name of the covenant God, but in certain circumstances were much more appropriate ; and partly from the fact that the sons of Jacob, including Joseph, did not so distinctly recognise in their course the saving guidance of the covenant God, as to be able to describe it as the work of *Jehovah.* This imperfect insight, however, is intimately connected with the fact that the direct revelations of God had ceased ; and that Joseph, although chosen by God to be the preserver of the house of Israel and the instrument in accomplishing His plans of salvation, was separated at a very early period from the fellowship of his father's house, and formally naturalized in Egypt, and though endowed with the supernatural power to interpret dreams, was not favoured, as Daniel afterwards was in the Chaldæan court, with visions or revelations of God. Consequently we cannot place Joseph on a level with the three patriarchs, nor assent to the statement, that " as the noblest blossom of the patriarchal life is seen in Joseph, as in him the whole meaning of the patriarchal life is summed up and fulfilled, so in Christ we see the perfect blossom and sole fulfilment of the whole of the Old Testament dispensation" (*Kurtz,* Old Covenant ii. 95), as being

[1] The very fact that the author of Genesis, who wrote in the light of the further development and fuller revelation of the ways of the Lord with Joseph and the whole house of Jacob, represents the career of Joseph as a gracious interposition of *Jehovah* (chap. xxxix.), and yet makes Joseph himself speak of *Elohim* as arranging the whole, is by no means an unimportant testimony to the historical fidelity and truth of the narrative ; of which further proofs are to be found in the faithful and exact representation of the circumstances, manners, and customs of Egypt, as *Hengstenberg* has proved in his Egypt and the Books of Moses, from a comparison of these accounts of Joseph's life with ancient documents and monuments connected with this land.

either correct or scriptural, so far as the first portion is concerned.
For Joseph was not a medium of salvation in the same way as
Abraham, Isaac, and Jacob. He was indeed a benefactor, not
only to his brethren and the whole house of Israel, but also to
the Egyptians; but salvation, *i.e.* spiritual help and culture, he
neither brought to the Gentiles nor to the house of Israel. In
Jacob's blessing he is endowed with the richest inheritance of
the first-born in earthly things; but salvation is to reach the
nations through Judah. We may therefore without hesitation
look upon the history of Joseph as a "type of the pathway of
the Church, not of Jehovah only, but also of Christ, from low-
liness to exaltation, from slavery to liberty, from suffering to
glory" (*Delitzsch*); we may also, so far as the history of Israel
is a type of the history of Christ and His Church, regard the
life of Joseph, as believing commentators of all centuries have
done, as a type of the life of Christ, and use these typical traits
as aids to progress in the knowledge of salvation; but that we
may not be seduced into typological trifling, we must not overlook the fact, that neither Joseph nor his career is represented,
either by the prophets or by Christ and His apostles, as typical
of Christ,—in anything like the same way, for example, as the
guidance of Israel into and out of Egypt (Hos. xi. 1 cf. Matt. ii.
15), and other events and persons in the history of Israel.

SALE OF JOSEPH INTO EGYPT.—CHAP. XXXVII.

Vers. 1–4. The statement in ver. 1, which introduces the
tholedoth of Jacob, "*And Jacob dwelt in the land of his father's
pilgrimage, in the land of Canaan,*" implies that Jacob had now
entered upon his father's inheritance, and carries on the patriarchal pilgrim-life in Canaan, the further development of which
was determined by the wonderful career of Joseph. This strange
and eventful career of Joseph commenced when he was 17 years
old. The notice of his age at the commencement of the narrative which follows, is introduced with reference to the principal
topic in it, viz. the sale of Joseph, which was to prepare the way,
according to the wonderful counsel of God, for the fulfilment
of the divine revelation to Abraham respecting the future history of his seed (xv. 13 sqq.). While feeding the flock with his
brethren, and, as he was young, with the sons of Bilhah and

Zilpah, who were nearer his age than the sons of Leah, he brought an evil report of them to his father (רָעָה intentionally indefinite, connected with דִּבָּתָם without an article). The words וְהוּא נַעַר, "*and he a lad*," are subordinate to the main clause: they are not to be rendered, however, "he was a lad with the sons," but, "as he was young, he fed the flock with the sons of Bilhah and Zilpah."—Ver. 3. "*Israel* (Jacob) *loved Joseph more than all his* (other) *sons, because he was born in his old age*," as the first-fruits of the beloved Rachel (Benjamin was hardly a year old at this time). *And he made him* כְּתֹנֶת פַּסִּים : a long coat with sleeves ($\chi\iota\tau\grave{\omega}\nu$ $\dot{\alpha}\sigma\tau\rho\alpha\gamma\acute{\alpha}\lambda\epsilon\iota\sigma$, *Aqu.*, or $\dot{\alpha}\sigma\tau\rho\alpha\gamma\alpha\lambda\omega\tau\acute{\sigma}$, LXX. at 2 Sam. xiii. 18, *tunica talaris*, *Vulg.* ad Sam.), *i.e.* an upper coat reaching to the wrists and ankles, such as noblemen and kings' daughters wore, not "a coat of many colours" ("*bunter Rock*," as *Luther* renders it, from the $\chi\iota\tau\hat{\omega}\nu\alpha$ $\pi\sigma\iota\kappa\acute{\iota}\lambda\sigma\nu$, *tunicam polymitam*, of the LXX. and Vulgate). This partiality made Joseph hated by his brethren ; so that they could not "*speak peaceably unto him*," *i.e.* ask him how he was, offer him the usual salutation, "Peace be with thee."

Vers. 5-11. This hatred was increased when Joseph told them of two dreams that he had had : viz. that as they were binding sheaves in the field, his sheaf "stood and remained standing," but their sheaves placed themselves round it and bowed down to it ; and that the sun (his father), and the moon (his mother, "not Leah, but Rachel, who was neither forgotten nor lost"), and eleven stars (his eleven brethren) bowed down before him. These dreams pointed in an unmistakeable way to the supremacy of Joseph ; the first to supremacy over his brethren, the second over the whole house of Israel. The repetition seemed to establish the thing as certain (cf. xli. 32); so that not only did his brethren hate him still more "*on account of his dreams and words*" (ver. 8), *i.e.* the substance of the dreams and the open interpretation of them, and become jealous and envious, but his father gave him a sharp reproof for the second, though he preserved the matter, *i.e.* retained it in his memory (שָׁמַר LXX. $\delta\iota\epsilon\tau\acute{\eta}\rho\eta\sigma\epsilon$, cf. $\sigma\upsilon\nu\epsilon\tau\acute{\eta}\rho\epsilon\iota$, Luke ii. 19). The brothers with their ill-will could not see anything in the dreams but the suggestions of his own ambition and pride of heart ; and even the father, notwithstanding his partiality, was grieved by the second dream. The dreams are not represented as divine revelations; yet they are not to be regarded as pure flights of fancy from an ambitious heart, but as the presentiments of deep inward feelings, which were not produced without some divine influence being exerted upon Joseph's mind, and therefore were of prophetic significance, though they were not inspired directly by God, inasmuch as the purposes of God were still to remain hidden from the eyes of men for the saving good of all concerned.

Vers. 12–24. In a short time the hatred of Joseph's brethren grew into a crime. On one occasion, when they were feeding their flock at a distance from Hebron, in the neighbourhood of Shechem (Nablus, in the plain of Mukhnah), and Joseph who was sent thither by Jacob to inquire as to the welfare (*shalom, valetudo*) of the brethren and their flocks, followed them to *Dothain* or *Dothan*, a place 12 Roman miles to the north of Samaria (*Sebaste*), towards the plain of Jezreel, they formed the malicious resolution to put him, "this dreamer," to death, and throw him into one of the pits, *i.e.* cisterns, and then to tell (his father) that a wild beast had slain him, and so to bring his dreams to nought.—Vers. 21 sqq. *Reuben,* who was the eldest son, and therefore specially responsible for his younger brother, opposed this murderous proposal. He dissuaded his brethren from killing Joseph (נֶפֶשׁ פ׳ הִכָּה), and advised them to throw him "*into this pit in the desert,*" *i.e.* into a dry pit that was near. As Joseph would inevitably perish even in that pit, their malice was satisfied; but Reuben intended to take Joseph out again, and restore him to his father. As soon, therefore, as Joseph arrived, they took off his coat with sleeves and threw him into the pit, which happened to be dry.

Vers. 25–36. Reuben had saved Joseph's life indeed by his proposal; but his intention to send him back to his father was frustrated. For as soon as the brethren sat down to eat, after the deed was performed, they saw a company of Ishmaelites from Gilead coming along the road which leads from Beisan past Jenin (Rob. Pal. iii. 155) and through the plain of Dothan to the great caravan road that runs from Damascus by Lejun (*Legio, Megiddo*), Ramleh, and Gaza to Egypt (Rob. iii. 27, 178). The caravan drew near, laden with spices: viz. נְכֹאת, gum-tragacanth; צְרִי, balsam, for which Gilead was celebrated (xliii. 11; Jer. viii. 22, xlvi. 11); and לֹט, *ladanum,* the fragrant resin of the cistus-rose. Judah seized the opportunity to propose to his brethren to sell Joseph to the Ishmaelites. *" What profit have we,"* he said, *" that we slay our brother and conceal his blood? Come, let us sell him to the Ishmaelites; and our hand, let it not lay hold of him* (sc. to slay him), *for he is our brother, our flesh."* Reuben wished to deliver Joseph entirely from his brothers' malice. Judah also wished to save his life, though not from brotherly love so much as from the feeling of horror, which was not quite extinct within him, at incurring the guilt of fratricide; but he would still like to get rid of him, that his dreams might not come true. Judah, like his brethren, was probably afraid that their father might confer upon Joseph the rights of the first-born, and so make him lord over them. His proposal was a welcome one. When the Arabs passed by, the brethren fetched Joseph out of the pit and sold him to the Ishmaelites, who took him into Egypt. The different names given to the traders—viz. *Ishmaelites* (vers. 25, 27, and 28*b*), *Midianites* (ver. 28*a*), and *Medanites* (ver. 36)—do not show that the account has been drawn from different legends, but that these tribes were often confounded, from the fact that they resembled one another so closely, not only in their common descent from Abraham (xvi. 15 and xxv. 2), but also in the similarity of their mode of life and their constant change of abode, that strangers could hardly distinguish them, especially when they appeared not as tribes but as Arabian merchants, such as they are here described as being: *" Midianitish men, merchants."* That descendants of Abraham should already be met with in this capacity is by no means strange, if we consider that 150 years had passed by since Ishmael's dismissal from his father's house,—a period amply sufficient for his descendants to have grown through marriage into a respectable tribe. The price, *" twenty* (sc. shekels) *of silver,"* was the price which Moses afterwards fixed as the value of a boy between 5 and 20 (Lev. xxvii. 5), the average price of a slave being 30 shekels (Ex. xxi. 32). But the Ishmaelites naturally wanted to make money by the transaction.—Vers. 29 sqq. The business was settled in Reuben's absence; probably because his brethren suspected that he intended to rescue Joseph. When he came to the pit and found Joseph gone, he rent his clothes (a sign of intense grief on the part of the natural man) and exclaimed: *" The boy is no more, and I, whither shall I go!"* —how shall I account to his father for his disappearance! But the brothers were at no loss; they dipped Joseph's coat in the blood of a goat and sent it to his father, with the message, "*We have found this; see whether it is thy son's coat or not.*" Jacob recognised the coat at once, and mourned bitterly in mourning clothes (שַׂק) for his son, whom he supposed to have been devoured and destroyed by a wild beast (טָרֹף טֹרַף *inf. abs.* of *Kal* before *Pual*, as an indication of undoubted certainty), and refused all comfort from his children, saying, "*No* (כִּי *immo*, elliptical: Do not attempt to comfort me, for) *I will go down mourning into Sheol to my son.*" *Sheol* denotes the place where departed souls are gathered after death; it is an infinitive form from שָׁאַל to demand, the demanding, applied to the place which inexorably summons all men into its shade (cf. Prov. xxx. 15, 16; Isa. v. 14; Hab. ii. 5). How should his sons comfort him, when they were obliged to cover their wickedness with the sin of lying and hypocrisy, and when even Reuben, although at first beside himself at the failure of his plan, had not courage enough to disclose his brothers' crime?—Ver. 36. But Joseph, while his father was mourning, was sold by the Midianites to Potiphar, the chief of Pharaoh's *trabantes*, to be first of all brought low, according to the wonderful counsel of God, and then to be exalted as ruler in Egypt, before whom his brethren would bow down, and as the saviour of the house of Israel. The name *Potiphar* is a contraction of *Poti Pherah* (xli. 50); the LXX. render both Πετεφρής or Πετεφρῆ (*vid.* xli. 50). סָרִים (eunuch) is used here, as in 1 Sam. viii. 15 and in most of the passages of the Old Testament, for courtier or chamberlain, without regard to the primary meaning, as Potiphar was married. "*Captain of the guard*" (*lit.* captain of the slaughterers, *i.e.* the executioners), commanding officer of the royal body-guard, who executed the capital sentences ordered by the king, as was also the case with the Chaldeans (2 Kings xxv. 8; Jer. xxxix. 9, lii. 12. See my Commentary on the Books of Kings, vol. i. pp. 35, 36, Eng. Tr.).

JUDAH'S MARRIAGE AND CHILDREN. HIS INCEST WITH
THAMAR.—CHAP. XXXVIII.

The following sketch from the life of Judah is intended to point out the origin of the three leading families of the future princely tribe in Israel, and at the same time to show in what danger the sons of Jacob would have been of forgetting the sacred vocation of their race, through marriages with Canaanitish women, and of perishing in the sin of Canaan, if the mercy of God had not interposed, and by leading Joseph into Egypt prepared the way for the removal of the whole house of Jacob into that land, and thus protected the family, just as it was expanding into a nation, from the corrupting influence of the manners and customs of Canaan. This being the intention of the narrative, it is no episode or interpolation, but an integral part of the early history of Israel, which is woven here into the history of Jacob, because the events occurred subsequently to the sale of Joseph.

Vers. 1–11. About this time, *i.e.* after the sale of Joseph, while still feeding the flocks of Jacob along with his brethren (xxxvii. 26),[1] Judah separated from them, and went down (from Hebron, xxxvii. 14, or the mountains) to Adullam, in the lowland (Josh. xv. 35), into the neighbourhood of a man named Hirah. "*He pitched* (his tent, xxvi. 25) *up to a man of Adullam*," *i.e.* in his neighbourhood, so as to enter into friendly intercourse with him.—Vers. 2 sqq. There Judah married the daughter of Shuah, a Canaanite, and had three sons by her: Ger (עֵר), Onan, and Shelah. The name of the place is mentioned when the last is born, viz. Chezib or Achzib (Josh. xv. 44; Micah i. 14),

[1] As the expression "at that time" does not compel us to place Judah's marriage after the sale of Joseph, many have followed *Augustine* (quæst. 123), and placed it some years earlier. But this assumption is rendered extremely improbable, if not impossible, by the fact that Judah was not merely accidentally present when Joseph was sold, but was evidently living with his brethren, and had not yet set up an establishment of his own; whereas he had settled at Adullam previous to his marriage, and seems to have lived there up to the time of the birth of the twins by Thamar. Moreover, the 23 years which intervened between the taking of Joseph into Egypt and the migration of Jacob thither, furnish space enough for all the events recorded in this chapter. If we suppose that Judah, who was 20 years old when Joseph was sold, went to Adullam soon afterwards and married there, his three sons might have been born four or five years after Joseph's captivity. And if his eldest son was born about a year and a half after the sale of Joseph, and he married him to Thamar when he was 15 years old, and gave her to his second son a year after that, Onan's death would occur at least five years before Jacob's removal to Egypt; time enough, therefore, both for the generation and birth of the twin-sons of Judah by Thamar, and for Judah's two journeys into Egypt with his brethren to buy corn. (See chap. xlvi. 8 sqq.)

in the southern portion of the lowland of Judah, that the descendants of Shelah might know the birth-place of their ancestor. This was unnecessary in the case of the others, who died childless.—Vers. 6 sqq. When Ger was grown up, according to ancient custom (cf. xxi. 21, xxxiv. 4) his father gave him a wife, named Thamar, probably a Canaanite, of unknown parentage. But Ger was soon put to death by Jehovah on account of his wickedness. Judah then wished Onan, as the brother-in-law, to marry the childless widow of his deceased brother, and raise up seed, *i.e.* a family, for him. But as he knew that the first-born son would not be the founder of his own family, but would perpetuate the family of the deceased and receive his inheritance, he prevented conception when consummating the marriage by spilling the semen. שִׁחֵת אַרְצָה, "destroyed to the ground (*i.e.* let it fall upon the ground), so as not to give seed to his brother" (נְתֹן for תֵּת only here and Num. xx. 21). This act not only betrayed a want of affection to his brother, combined with a despicable covetousness for his possession and inheritance, but was also a sin against the divine institution of marriage and its object, and was therefore punished by Jehovah with sudden death. The custom of levirate marriage, which is first mentioned here, and is found in different forms among Indians, Persians, and other nations of Asia and Africa, was not founded upon a divine command, but upon an ancient tradition, originating probably in Chaldea. It was not abolished, however, by the Mosaic law (Deut. xxv. 5 sqq.), but only so far restricted as not to allow it to interfere with the sanctity of marriage; and with this limitation it was enjoined as a duty of affection to build up the brother's house, and to preserve his family and name (see my Bibl. Archäologie, § 108).—Ver. 11. The sudden death of his two sons so soon after their marriage with Thamar made Judah hesitate to give her the third as a husband also, thinking, very likely, according to a superstition which we find in Tobit iii. 7 sqq., that either she herself, or marriage with her, had been the cause of her husbands' deaths. He therefore sent her away to her father's house, with the promise that he would give her his youngest son as soon as he had grown up; though he never intended it seriously, "*for he thought lest* (אָמַר פֶּן, *i.e.* he was afraid that) *he also might die like his brethren.*"

Vers. 12–30. But when Thamar, after waiting a long time,

saw that Shelah had grown up and yet was not given to her as a husband, she determined to procure children from Judah himself, who had become a widower in the meantime; and his going to Timnath to the sheep-shearing afforded her a good opportunity. The time mentioned ("the days multiplied," *i.e.* a long time passed by) refers not to the statement which follows, that Judah's wife died, but rather to the leading thought of the verse, viz. Judah's going to the sheep-shearing. וַיִּנָּחֶם: *he comforted himself, i.e.* he ceased to mourn. *Timnath* is not the border town of Dan and Judah between Beth-shemesh and Ekron in the plain (Josh. xv. 10, xix. 43), but *Timnah* on the mountains of Judah (Josh. xv. 57, cf. Rob. Pal. ii. 343, note), as the expression "*went up*" shows. The sheep-shearing was a fête with shepherds, and was kept with great feasting. Judah therefore took his friend Hirah with him; a fact noticed in ver. 12 in relation to what follows.—Vers. 13, 14. As soon as Thamar heard of Judah's going to this feast, she took off her widow's clothes, put on a veil, and sat down, disguised as a harlot, by the gate of Enayim, where Judah would be sure to pass on his return from Timnath. *Enayim* was no doubt the same as *Enam* in the lowland of Judah (Josh. xv. 34).—Vers. 15 sqq. When Judah saw her here and took her for a harlot, he made her an offer, and gave her his signet-ring, with the band (פְּתִיל) by which it was hung round his neck, and his staff, as a pledge of the young buck-goat which he offered her. They were both objects of value, and were regarded as ornaments in the East, as *Herodotus* (i. 195) has shown with regard to the Babylonians (see my *Bibl. Arch.* 2, 48). He then lay with her, and she became pregnant by him.—Vers. 19 sqq. After this had occurred, Thamar laid aside her veil, put on her widow's dress again, and returned home. When Judah, therefore, sent the kid by his friend Hirah to the supposed harlot for the purpose of redeeming his pledges, he could not find her, and was told, on inquiring of the inhabitants of Enayim, that there was no קְדֵשָׁה there. הַקְּדֵשָׁה: lit. "the consecrated," *i.e.* the *hierodule,* a woman sacred to Astarte, a goddess of the Canaanites, the deification of the generative and productive principle of nature; one who served this goddess by prostitution (*vid.* Deut. xxiii. 18). This was no doubt regarded as the most respectable designation for public prostitutes in Canaan.—Vers. 22, 23. When his friend returned with the kid and reported his want of success, Judah resolved to leave his pledges with the girl, that he might not expose himself to the ridicule of the people by any further inquiries, since he had done his part towards keeping his promise. " *Let her take them (i.e.* keep the signet-ring and staff) *for herself, that we may not become a* (an object of) *ridicule.*" The pledges were unquestionably of more value than a young he-goat.

Vers. 24–26. About three months afterwards (מִשָּׁלֹשׁ prob. for מִשָּׁלֹשׁ with the prefix מ) Judah was informed that Thamar had played the harlot and was certainly (הִנֵּה) with child. He immediately ordered, by virtue of his authority as head of the tribe, that she should be brought out and burned. Thamar was regarded as the affianced bride of Shelah, and was to be punished as a bride convicted of a breach of chastity. But the Mosaic law enjoined stoning in the case of those who were affianced and broke their promise, or of newly married women who were found to have been dishonoured (Deut. xxii. 20, 21, 23, 24) ; and it was only in the case of the whoredom of a priest's daughter, or of carnal intercourse with a mother or a daughter, that the punishment of burning was enjoined (Lev. xxi. 9 and xx. 14). Judah's sentence, therefore, was more harsh than the subsequent law ; whether according to patriarchal custom, or on other grounds, cannot be determined. When Thamar was brought out, she sent to Judah the things which she had kept as a pledge, with this message : " *By a man to whom these belong am I with child : look carefully therefore to whom this signet-ring, and band, and stick belong.*" Judah recognised the things as his own, and was obliged to confess, " *She is more in the right than I; for therefore* (sc. that this might happen to me, or that it might turn out so; on כִּי־עַל־כֵּן see chap. xviii. 5) *have I not given her to my son Shelah.*" In passing sentence upon Thamar, Judah had condemned himself. His sin, however, did not consist merely in his having given way to his lusts so far as to lie with a supposed public prostitute of Canaan, but still more in the fact, that by breaking his promise to give her his son Shelah as her husband, he had caused his daughter-in-law to practise this deception upon him, just because in his heart he blamed her for the early and sudden deaths of his elder sons, whereas the real cause of the deaths which had so grieved his paternal

heart was the wickedness of the sons themselves, the main-
spring of which was to be found in his own marriage with a
Canaanite in violation of the patriarchal call. And even if the
sons of Jacob were not unconditionally prohibited from marrying the daughters of Canaanites, Judah's marriage at any rate
had borne such fruit in his sons Ger and Onan, as Jehovah the
covenant God was compelled to reject. But if Judah, instead
of recognising the hand of the Lord in the sudden death of his
sons, traced the cause to Thamar, and determined to keep her
as a childless widow all her life long, not only in opposition to
the traditional custom, but also in opposition to the will of God
as expressed in His promises of a numerous increase of the seed
of Abraham, Isaac, and Jacob ; Thamar had by no means acted
rightly in the stratagem by which she frustrated his plan, and
sought to procure from Judah himself the seed of which he was
unjustly depriving her, though her act might be less criminal
than Judah's. For it is evident from the whole account, that
she was not driven to her sin by lust, but by the innate desire
for children (ὅτι δὲ παιδοποιίας χάριν, καὶ οὐ φιληδονίας τοῦτο
ὁ Θάμαρ ἐμηχανήσατο,—Theodoret) ; and for that reason she
was more in the right than Judah. Judah himself, however,
not only saw his guilt, but he confessed it also ; and showed both
by this confession, and also by the fact that he had no further
conjugal intercourse with Thamar, an earnest endeavour to
conquer the lusts of the flesh, and to guard against the sin into
which he had fallen. And because he thus humbled himself,
God gave him grace, and not only exalted him to be the chief
of the house of Israel, but blessed the children that were begotten in sin.

Vers. 27–30. Thamar brought forth twins ; and a circumstance occurred at the birth, which does occasionally happen
when the children lie in an abnormal position, and always im-
pedes the delivery, and which was regarded in this instance as
so significant that the names of the children were founded upon
the fact. At the birth וַיִּתֶּן־יָד "there was a hand," i.e. a hand
came out (יִתֵּן as in Job xxxvii. 10, Prov. xiii. 10), round which
the midwife tied a scarlet thread, to mark this as the first-born.
—Ver. 29. " And it came to pass, when it (the child) drew back
its hand (כְּמֵשִׁיב for בְּהִיוֹת מֵשִׁיב as in chap. xl. 10), behold its
brother came out. Then she (the midwife) said, What a breach

hast thou made for thy part? Upon thee the breach;" i.e. thou
bearest the blame of the breach. פֶּרֶץ signifies not *rupturam
perinoei*, but breaking through by pressing forward. From that
he received the name of *Perez* (breach, breaker through). Then
the other one with the scarlet thread came into the world, and
was named *Zerah* (זֶרַח exit, rising), because he sought to appear
first, whereas in fact Perez was the first-born, and is even placed
before Zerah in the lists in chap. xlvi. 12, Num. xxvi. 20.
Perez was the ancestor of the tribe-prince Nahshon (Num. ii.
3), and of king David also (Ruth iv. 18 sqq.; 1 Chron. ii. 5
sqq.). Through him, therefore, Thamar has a place as one of
the female ancestors in the genealogy of Jesus Christ.

JOSEPH IN POTIPHAR'S HOUSE, AND IN PRISON.—CHAP. XXXIX.

Vers. 1–18. IN POTIPHAR'S HOUSE.—Potiphar had bought
him of the Ishmaelites, as is repeated in ver. 1 for the purpose
of resuming the thread of the narrative; and Jehovah was
with him, so that he prospered in the house of his Egyptian
master. אִישׁ מַצְלִיחַ: a man who has prosperity, to whom God
causes all that he undertakes and does to prosper. When
Potiphar perceived this, Joseph found favour in his eyes, and
became his servant, whom he placed over his house (made
manager of his household affairs), and to whom he entrusted
all his property (כָּל־יֶשׁ־לּוֹ ver. 4 = כָּל־אֲשֶׁר יֶשׁ־לוֹ vers. 5, 6). This
confidence in Joseph increased, when he perceived how the
blessing of Jehovah (Joseph's God) rested upon his property
in the house and in the field; so that now "*he left to Joseph
everything that he had, and did not trouble himself* אִתּוֹ (with or
near him) *about anything but his own eating.*"—Vers. 6*b* sqq.
Joseph was handsome in form and feature; and Potiphar's
wife set her eyes upon the handsome young man, and tried
to persuade him to lie with her. But Joseph resisted the adulterous proposal, referring to the unlimited confidence which
his master had placed in him. He (Potiphar) was not greater
in that house than he, and had given everything over to
him except her, because she was his wife. "How could he so
abuse this confidence, as to do this great wickedness and sin
against God!"—Vers. 10 sqq. But after she had repeated her
enticements day after day without success, "*it came to pass at*

that time (כְּהַיּוֹם הַזֶּה for the more usual כַּיּוֹם הַזֶּה (chap. l. 20), *lit.* about this day, *i.e.* the day in the writer's mind, on which the thing to be narrated occurred) *that Joseph came into his house to attend to his duties, and there were none of the house-servants within."* And she laid hold of him by his garment and entreated him to lie with her; but he left his garment in her hand and fled from the house.—Vers. 13–18. When this daring assault upon Joseph's chastity had failed, on account of his faithfulness and fear of God, the adulterous woman reversed the whole affair, and charged him with an attack upon her modesty, in order that she might have her revenge upon him and avert suspicion from herself. She called her house-servants and said, " *See, he* (her husband, whom she does not think worth naming) *has brought us a Hebrew man* ("no *epitheton ornans* to Egyptian ears: xliii. 32") *to mock us* (צְחֹק to show his wantonness; *us*, the wife and servants, especially the female portion): *he came in unto me to lie with me; and I cried with a loud voice . . . and he left his garment by me."* She said אֶצְלִי "by my side," not "in my hand," as that would have shown the true state of the case. She then left the garment lying by her side till the return of Joseph's master, to whom she repeated her tale.

Vers. 19–23. JOSEPH IN PRISON.—Potiphar was enraged at what he heard, and put Joseph into the prison where (אֲשֶׁר for אֲשֶׁר שָׁם, xl. 3 like xxxv. 13) the king's prisoners (state-prisoners) were confined. בֵּית הַסֹּהַר: *lit.* the house of enclosure, from סהר, to surround or enclose (ὀχύρωμα, LXX.); the state-prison surrounded by a wall. This was a very moderate punishment. For according to *Diod. Sic.* (i. 78) the laws of the Egyptians were πικροὶ περὶ τῶν γυναικῶν νόμοι. An attempt at adultery was to be punished with 1000 blows, and rape upon a free woman still more severely. It is possible that Potiphar was not fully convinced of his wife's chastity, and therefore did not place unlimited credence in what she said.[1] But even in that

---

[1] *Credibile est aliquod fuisse indicium, quo Josephum innocentem esse Potiphari constiteret; neque enim servi vita tanti erat ut ei parceretur in tam gravi delicto. Sed licet innocuum, in carcere tamen detinebat, ut uxoris honori et suo consuleret* (*Clericus*). The chastity of Egyptian women has been in bad repute from time immemorial (Diod. Sic. i. 59 ; Herod. ii. 111). Even in the middle ages the Fatimite *Hakim* thought it necessary to adopt

case it was the mercy of the faithful covenant God, which now as before (xxxvii. 20 sqq.) rescued Joseph's life.

Vers. 21–23. In the prison itself Jehovah was with Joseph, procuring him favour in the eyes of the governor of the prison, so that he entrusted all the prisoners to his care, leaving everything that they had to do, to be done through him, and not troubling himself about anything that was in his hand, *i.e.* was committed to him, because Jehovah made all that he did to prosper. "*The keeper*" was the governor of the prison, or superintendent of the gaolers, and was under Potiphar, the captain of the *trabantes* and chief of the executioners (chap. xxxvii. 36).

THE PRISONERS' DREAMS AND JOSEPH'S INTERPRETATION.— CHAP. XL.

Vers. 1–8. The head cup-bearer and head baker had committed crimes against the king of Egypt, and were imprisoned in "*the prison of the house of the captain of the trabantes, the prison where Joseph himself was confined;*" the state-prison, according to Eastern custom, forming part of the same building as the dwelling-house of the chief of the executioners. From a regard to the exalted position of these two prisoners, Potiphar ordered Joseph to wait upon them, not to keep watch over them; for פָּקַד אֶת does not mean to appoint as guard, but to place by the side of a person.—Ver. 5. After some time ("days," ver. 4, as in iv. 3), and on the same night, these two prisoners had each a peculiar dream, "*each one according to the interpretation of his dream;*" *i.e.* each one had a dream corresponding to the interpretation which specially applied to him. On account of these dreams, which seemed to them to have some bearing upon their fate, and, as the issue proved, were really true omens of it, Joseph found them the next morning looking anxious, and asked them the reason of the trouble which was depicted upon their countenances.—Ver. 8. On their replying that they had dreamed, and there was no one to interpret the dream, Joseph reminded them first of all that "interpretations are God's," come from

severe measures against their immorality (*Bar-Hebræi*, chron. p. 217), and at the present day, according to *Burckhardt* (arab. Sprichwörter, pp. 222, 227), chastity is "a great rarity" among women of every rank in Cairo.

God, are His gift; at the same time he bade them tell him their dreams, from a consciousness, no doubt, that he was endowed with this divine gift.

Vers. 9–15. The cup-bearer gave this account: "*In my dream, behold there was a vine before me, and on the vine three branches; and it was as though blossoming, it shot forth its blossom* (נִצָּהּ either from the *hapax l.* נֵץ=נִצָּה, or from נִצָּה with the fem. termination resolved into the 3 pers. suff.: *Ewald*, § 257d), *its clusters ripened into grapes. And Pharaoh's cup was in my hand; and I took the grapes and pressed them into Pharaoh's cup, and gave the cup into Pharaoh's hand.*" In this dream the office and duty of the royal cup-bearer were represented in an unmistakeable manner, though the particular details must not be so forced as to lead to the conclusion, that the kings of ancient Egypt drank only the fresh juice of the grape, and not fermented wine as well. The cultivation of the vine, and the making and drinking of wine, among the Egyptians, are established beyond question by ancient testimony and the earliest monuments, notwithstanding the statement of Herodotus (2, 77) to the contrary (see *Hengstenberg*, Egypt and the Books of Moses, pp. 13 sqq.).— Vers. 12 sqq. Joseph then gave this interpretation: The three branches were three days, in which time Pharaoh would restore him to his post again ("lift up his head," *i.e.* raise him from his degradation, send and fetch him from prison, 2 Kings xxv. 27). And he added this request (ver. 14): "*Only think of me, as it goes well with thee, and show favour to me . . . for I was stolen* (*i.e.* carried away secretly and by force; I did not abscond because of any crime) *out of the land of the Hebrews* (the land where the *Ibrim* live); *and here also I have done nothing* (committed no crime) *for which they should put me into the hole.*" בּוֹר: the cell, applied to a prison as a miserable hole, because often dry cesspools were used as prisons.

Vers. 16–19. Encouraged by this favourable interpretation, the chief baker also told his dream: "*I too, . . . in my dream: behold, baskets of white bread upon my head, and in the top basket all kinds of food for Pharaoh, pastry; and the birds ate it out of the basket from my head.*" In this dream, the carrying of the baskets upon the head is thoroughly Egyptian; for, according to *Herod.* 2, 35, the men in Egypt carry burdens upon the head, the women upon the shoulders. And, according to the

monuments, the variety of confectionary was very extensive (cf.
Hengst. p. 27). In the opening words, " *I too,*" the baker points
to the resemblance between his dream and the cup-bearer's.
The resemblance was not confined to the sameness of the numbers—three baskets of white bread, and three branches of the
vine,—but was also seen in the fact that his official duty at the
court was represented in the dream. But instead of Pharaoh
taking the bread from his hand, the birds of heaven ate it out of
the basket upon his head. And Joseph gave this interpretation :
" *The three baskets signify three days : within that time Pharaoh
will take away thy head from thee* (" lift up thy head," as in
ver. 13, but with מֵעָלֶיךָ " away from thee," *i.e.* behead thee), *and
hang thee on the stake* (thy body after execution ; *vid.* Deut. xxi.
22, 23), *and the birds will eat thy flesh from off thee.*" However
simple and close this interpretation of the two dreams may appear, the exact accordance with the fulfilment was a miracle
wrought by God, and showed that as the dreams originated in
the instigation of God, the interpretation was His inspiration also.

Vers. 20–23. Joseph's interpretations were fulfilled three
days afterwards, on the king's birth-day. יוֹם הֻלֶּדֶת : the day of
being born ; the *inf. Hoph.* is construed as a passive with the
accus. obj., as in chap. iv. 18, etc. Pharaoh gave his servants
a feast, and lifted up the heads of both the prisoners, but in very
different ways. The cup-bearer was pardoned, and reinstated
in his office ; the baker, on the other hand, was executed.—Ver.
23. But the former forgot Joseph in his prosperity, and did
nothing to procure his liberation.

PHARAOH'S DREAMS AND JOSEPH'S EXALTATION.—CHAP. XLI.

Vers. 1–36. PHARAOH'S DREAMS AND THEIR INTERPRETA-
TION.—Two full years afterwards (יָמִים *accus.* " in days," as in
chap. xxix. 14) Pharaoh had a dream. He was standing by the
Nile, and saw seven fine fat cows ascend from the Nile and feed
in the Nile-grass (אָחוּ an Egyptian word); and behind them seven
others, ugly (according to ver. 19, unparalleled in their ugliness),
lean (דַּקּוֹת בָּשָׂר " thin in flesh," for which we find in ver. 19 דַּלּוֹת
" fallen away," and רַקּוֹת בָּשָׂר withered in flesh, fleshless), which
placed themselves beside those fat ones on the brink of the Nile
and devoured them, without there being any effect to show that

they had eaten them. He then awoke, but fell asleep again and had a second, similar dream : seven fat (ver. 22, full) and fine ears grew upon one blade, and were swallowed up by seven thin (ver. 23, " and hardened") ones, which were blasted by the east wind (קָדִים *i.e.* the S.E. wind, Chamsin, from the desert of Arabia).—Ver. 7. *" Then Pharaoh awoke, and behold it was a dream."* The dream was so like reality, that it was only when he woke that he perceived it was a dream.—Ver. 8. Being troubled about this double dream, Pharaoh sent the next morning for all the scribes and wise men of Egypt, to have it interpreted. חַרְטֻמִּים, from חֶרֶט a stylus (pencil), are the ἱερογραμματεῖς, men of the priestly caste, who occupied themselves with the sacred arts and sciences of the Egyptians, the hieroglyphic writings, astrology, the interpretation of dreams, the foretelling of events, magic, and conjuring, and who were regarded as the possessors of secret arts (*vid.* Ex. vii. 11) and the *wise men* of the nation. But not one of these could interpret it, although the clue to the interpretation was to be found in the religious symbols of Egypt. For the cow was the symbol of Isis, the goddess of the all-sustaining earth, and in the hieroglyphics it represented the earth, agriculture, and food; and the Nile, by its overflowing, was the source of the fertility of the land. But however simple the explanation of the fat and lean cows ascending out of the Nile appears to be, it is "the fate of the wisdom of this world, that where it suffices it is compelled to be silent. For it belongs to the government of God to close the lips of the eloquent, and take away the understanding of the aged (Job xii. 20)." *Baumgarten.*

Vers. 9 sqq. In this dilemma the head cup-bearer thought of Joseph ; and calling to mind his offence against the king (xl. 1), and his ingratitude to Joseph (xl. 23), he related to the king how Joseph had explained their dreams to him and the chief baker in the prison, and how entirely the interpretation had come true.—Vers. 14 sqq. Pharaoh immediately sent for Joseph. As quickly as possible he was fetched from the prison ; and after shaving the hair of his head and beard, and changing his clothes, as the customs of Egypt required (see Hengst. Egypt and the Books of Moses, p. 30), he went in to the king. On the king's saying to him, *" I have heard of thee* (עָלֶיךָ *de te*), *thou hearest a dream to interpret it,"*—*i.e.* thou only needest to hear a dream, and thou canst at once interpret it, –Joseph replied, *" Not I* (בִּלְעָדָי,

lit. "not so far as me," this is not in my power, *vid.* xiv. 24), *God will answer Pharaoh's good*," *i.e.* what shall profit Pharaoh; just as in chap. xl. 8 he had pointed the two prisoners away from himself to God. Pharaoh then related his double dream (vers. 17-24), and Joseph gave the interpretation (vers. 25-32): "*The dream of Pharaoh is one* (*i.e.* the two dreams have the same meaning); *God hath showed Pharaoh what He is about to do.*" The seven cows and seven ears of corn were seven years, the fat ones very fertile years of superabundance, the lean ones very barren years of famine; the latter would follow the former over the whole land of Egypt, so that the years of famine would leave no trace of the seven fruitful years; and, "*for that the dream was doubled unto Pharaoh twice*" (*i.e.* so far as this fact is concerned, it signifies) "*that the thing is firmly resolved by God, and God will quickly carry it out.*" In the confidence of this interpretation which looked forward over fourteen years, the divinely enlightened seer's glance was clearly manifested, and could not fail to make an impression upon the king, when contrasted with the perplexity of the Egyptian augurs and wise men. Joseph followed up his interpretation by the advice (vers. 33-36), that Pharaoh should "*look out* (יֵרֶא) *a man discreet and wise, and set him over the land of Egypt;*" and cause (יַעֲשֶׂה) that in the seven years of superabundance he should raise fifths (חִמֵּשׁ), *i.e.* the fifth part of the harvest, through overseers, and have the corn, or the stores of food (אֹכֶל), laid up in the cities "under the hand of the king," *i.e.* by royal authority and direction, as food for the land for the seven years of famine, that it might not perish through famine.

Vers. 37-57. JOSEPH'S PROMOTION.—This counsel pleased Pharaoh and all his servants, so that he said to them, "*Shall we find a man like this one, in whom the Spirit of God is?*" "*The Spirit of Elohim;*" *i.e.* the spirit of supernatural insight and wisdom. He then placed Joseph over his house, and over all Egypt; in other words, he chose him as his grand vizier, saying to him, "*After God hath showed thee all this, there is none discreet and wise as thou.*" עַל־פִּיךָ יִשַּׁק, "*according to thy mouth* (*i.e.* command, chap. xlv. 21) *shall my whole people arrange itself.*" נָשַׁק does not mean to kiss (*Rabb., Ges.*, etc.), for נָשַׁק עַל is not Hebrew, and kissing the mouth was not customary as an act of

homage, but "to dispose, arrange one's self" (*ordine disposuit*).
"*Only in the throne will I be greater than thou.*"—Vers. 42 sqq.
As an installation in this post of honour, the king handed him
his signet-ring, the seal which the grand vizier or prime minister
wore, to give authority to the royal edicts (Esth. iii. 10), clothed
him in a byssus dress (שֵׁשׁ, fine muslin or white cotton fabric),[1]
and put upon his neck the golden chain, which was usually worn
in Egypt as a mark of distinction, as the Egyptian monuments
show (Hgst. pp. 30, 31).—Ver. 43. He then had him driven in
the second chariot, the chariot which followed immediately upon
the king's state-carriage; that is to say, he directed a solemn
procession to be made through the city, in which they (heralds)
cried before him אַבְרֵךְ (*i.e.* bow down),—an Egyptian word, which
has been pointed by the Masorites according to the *Hiphil* or *Aphel*
of בָּרַךְ. In Coptic it is *abork, projicere*, with the signs of the
imperative and the second person. Thus he placed him over all
Egypt. וְנָתוֹן *inf. absol.* as a continuation of the finite verb (*vid.*
Ex. viii. 11; Lev. xxv. 14, etc.).—Ver. 44. "*I am Pharaoh*," he
said to him, "*and without thee shall no man lift his hand or foot
in all the land of Egypt;*" *i.e.* I am the actual king, and thou, the
next to me, shalt rule over all my people.—Ver. 45. But in order
that Joseph might be perfectly naturalized, the king gave him
an Egyptian name, *Zaphnath-Paaneah*, and married him to
Asenath, the daughter of *Potipherah*, the priest at *On*. The
name *Zaphnath-Paaneah* (a form adapted to the Hebrew, for
Ψονθομφανήχ (LXX.); according to a Greek scholium, σωτήρ
κόσμου, "salvator mundi" (*Jerome*)), answers to the Coptic
P-sote-m-ph-eneh,—*P* the article, *sote* salvation, *m* the sign of the
genitive, *ph* the article, and *eneh* the world (*lit. œtas, seculum*); or
perhaps more correctly, according to *Rosellini* and more recent
Egyptologists, to the Coptic *P-sōnt-em-ph-anh*, *i.e. sustentator
vitœ*, support or sustainer of life, with reference to the call entrusted to him by God.[2] *Asenath,* Ἀσενέθ (LXX.), possibly

---

[1] See my Bibl. Antiquities, § 17, 5. The reference, no doubt, is to the
ἐσθῆτα λινέην, worn by the Egyptian priests, which was not made of linen,
but of the *frutex quem aliqui gossipion vocant, plures xylon et ideo* LINA *inde
facta xylina. Nec ulla sunt eis candore mollitiave præferenda.*—Vestes inde
sacerdotibus Ægypti gratissimæ. Plin. h. n. xix. 1.

[2] *Luther* in his version, "privy councillor," follows the rabbinical explanation, which was already to be found in *Josephus* (Ant. ii. 6, 1): κρυπτῶν
εὑρετής, from צְפֻנוֹת == צָפַן *occulta*, and פַּעֲנַח *revelator*.

connected with the name *Neith*, the Egyptian *Pallas*. *Poti-Phera*, Πετεφρῆ (LXX.), a Coptic name signifying *ille qui solis est*, consecrated to the sun (φρη with the aspirated article signifies the sun in Memphitic). *On* was the popular name for *Heliopolis* ('Ηλιούπολις, LXX.), and according to *Cyrill. Alex.* ad Hos. v. 8 signifies *the sun*; whilst the name upon the monuments is *ta-Râ* or *pa-Râ*, house of the sun (*Brugsch*, Reisebericht, p. 50). From a very early date there was a celebrated temple of the sun here, with a learned priesthood, which held the first place among the priests' colleges of Egypt (*Herod.* 2, 3; *Hengst.* pp. 32 sqq.). This promotion of Joseph, from the position of a Hebrew slave pining in prison to the highest post of honour in the Egyptian kingdom, is perfectly conceivable, on the one hand, from the great importance attached in ancient times to the interpretation of dreams and to all occult science, especially among the Egyptians, and on the other hand, from the despotic form of government in the East; but the miraculous power of God is to be seen in the fact, that God endowed Joseph with the gift of infallible interpretation, and so ordered the circumstances that this gift opened the way for him to occupy that position in which he became the preserver, not of Egypt alone, but of his own family also. And the same hand of God, by which he had been so highly exalted after deep degradation, preserved him in his lofty post of honour from sinking into the heathenism of Egypt; although, by his alliance with the daughter of a priest of the sun, the most distinguished caste in the land, he had fully entered into the national associations and customs of the land.— Ver. 46. Joseph was 30 years old when he stood before Pharaoh, and went out from him and passed through all the land of Egypt, *i.e.* when he took possession of his office; consequently he had been in Egypt for 13 years as a slave, and at least three years in prison.

Vers. 47 sqq. For the seven years of superabundance the land bore לִקְמָצִים, in full hands or bundles; and Joseph gathered all the provisional store of these years (*i.e.* the fifth part of the produce, which was levied) into the cities. "The food of the field of the city, which was round about it, he brought into the midst of it;" *i.e.* he provided granaries in the towns, in which the corn of the whole surrounding country was stored. In this manner he collected as much corn " as the sand of the sea," until he left off reckoning the quantity, or calculating the number of bushels, which the monuments prove to have been the usual mode adopted (*vid. Hengst.* p. 36).—Vers. 50–52. During the fruitful years two sons were born to Joseph. The first-born he named *Manasseh, i.e.* causing to forget; "*for, he said, God hath made me forget all my toil and all my father's house* (נַשַּׁנִי, an Aram. Piel form, for נִשַּׁנִי, on account of the resemblance in sound to מְנַשֶּׁה)." *Hæc pia est, ac sancta gratiarum actio, quod Deus oblivisci eum fecit pristinas omnes ærumnas : sed nullus honor tanti esse debuit, ut desiderium et memoriam paternæ domus ex animo deponeret (Calvin).* But the true answer to the question, whether it was a Christian boast for him to make, that he had forgotten father and mother, is given by *Luther :* "I see that God would take away the reliance which I placed upon my father ; for God is a jealous God, and will not suffer the heart to have any other foundation to rely upon, but Him alone." This also meets the objection raised by *Theodoret,* why Joseph did not inform his father of his life and promotion, but allowed so many years to pass away, until he was led to do so at last in consequence of the arrival of his brothers. The reason of this forgetfulness and silence can only be found in the fact, that through the wondrous alteration in his condition he had been led to see, that he was brought to Egypt according to the counsel of God, and was redeemed by God from slavery and prison, and had been exalted by Him to be lord over Egypt ; so that, knowing he was in the hand of God, the firmness of his faith led him to renounce all wilful interference with the purposes of God, which pointed to a still broader and more glorious goal (*Baumgarten, Delitzsch*).—Ver. 52. The second son he named *Ephraim, i.e.* double-fruitfulness ; "*for God hath made me fruitful in the land of my affliction.*" Even after his elevation Egypt still continued the land of affliction, so that in this word we may see one trace of a longing for the promised land.—Vers. 53–57. When the years of scarcity commenced, at the close of the years of plenty, the famine spread over all (the neighbouring) lands ; only in Egypt was there bread. As the famine increased in the land, and the people cried to Pharaoh for bread, he directed them to Joseph, who "opened all in which was" (bread), *i.e.* all the granaries, and sold corn (שָׁבַר, *denom.* from שֶׁבֶר, signifies to trade in corn, to buy and sell corn) to the Egyptians, and (as the writer adds, with a view to what follows) to all the world (כָּל־הָאָרֶץ, ver. 57), that came thither to buy corn, because the famine was great on every hand.—Years of famine have frequently fallen, like this one, upon Egypt, and the neighbouring countries to the north. The cause of this is to be seen in the fact, that the overflowing of the Nile, to which Egypt is indebted for its fertility, is produced by torrents of rain falling in the alpine regions of Abyssinia, which proceed from clouds formed in the Mediterranean and carried thither by the wind; consequently it has a common origin with the rains of Palestine (see the proofs in *Hengst.* pp. 37 sqq.).

FIRST JOURNEY MADE TO EGYPT BY JOSEPH'S BRETHREN, WITHOUT BENJAMIN.—CHAP. XLII.

Vers. 1–6. With the words " *Why do ye look at one another?*" viz. in such a helpless and undecided manner, Jacob exhorted his sons to fetch corn from Egypt, to preserve his family from starvation. Joseph's ten brothers went, as their aged father would not allow his youngest son Benjamin to go with them, for fear that some calamity might befall him (קָרָה = קָרָא, xliv. 29 as in ver. 38 and xlix. 1); and they came " *in the midst of the comers,*" *i.e.* among others who came from the same necessity, and bowed down before Joseph with their faces to the earth. For he was "the ruler over the land," and had the supreme control of the sale of the corn, so that they were obliged to apply to him. הַשַּׁלִּיט seems to have been the standing title which the Shemites gave to Joseph as ruler in Egypt; and from this the later legend of Σάλατις the first king of the Hyksos arose (*Josephus* c. Ap. i. 14). The only other passages in which the word occurs in the Old Testament are in writings of the captivity or a still later date, and there it is taken from the Chaldee; it belongs, however, not merely to the Aramæan thesaurus, but to the Arabic also, from which it was introduced into the passage before us.

Vers. 7–17. Joseph recognised his brothers at once; but they could not recognise a brother who had not been seen for 20 years, and who, moreover, had not only become thoroughly Egyptianized, but had risen to be a great lord. And he acted as a foreigner (יִתְנַכֵּר) towards them, speaking harshly, and asking them whence they had come. In ver. 7, according to a truly Semitic style of narrative, we have a condensation of what is more circumstantially related in vers. 8–17.—Vers. 9 sqq. As the sight of his brethren bowing before him with the deepest reverence reminded Joseph of his early dreams of the sheaves and stars, which had so increased the hatred of his brethren towards him as to lead to a proposal to kill him, and an actual sale, he said to them, " *Ye are spies; to see the nakedness of the land* (*i.e.* the unfortified parts of the kingdom which would be easily accessible to a foe) *ye are come;*" and persisted in this charge notwithstanding their reply, " *Nay, my lord, but* (וְ see Ges. § 155, 1*b*) *to buy food are thy servants come. We are all one man's sons* (נַחְנוּ for אֲנַחְנוּ, only in Ex. xvi. 7, 8; Num. xxxii. 32; 2 Sam. xvii. 12; Lam. iii. 42): *honest* (כֵּנִים) *are we; thy servants are no spies.*" *Cum exploratio sit delictum capitale, non est verisimile; quod pater tot filios uno tempore vitæ periculo expositurus sit* (*J. Gerhard*). But as their assertion failed to make any impression upon the Egyptian lord, they told him still more particularly about their family (vers. 13 sqq.): " *Twelve are thy servants, brothers are we, sons of a man in the land of Canaan; and behold the youngest is now with our father, and one is no more* (אֵינֶנּוּ as in chap. v. 24). Joseph then replied, " *That is it* (הוּא neut. like xx. 16) *that I spake unto you, saying ye are spies. By this shall ye be proved: By the life of Pharaoh! ye shall not* (אִם, like xiv. 23) *go hence, unless your youngest brother come hither. Send one of you, and let him fetch your brother; but ye shall be in bonds, and your words shall be proved, whether there be truth in you or not. By the life of Pharaoh! ye are truly spies!*" He then had them put into custody for three days. By the coming of the youngest brother, Joseph wanted to test their assertion, not because he thought it possible that he might not be living with them, and they might have treated him as they did Joseph (*Kn.*), but because he wished to discover their feelings towards Benjamin, and see what affection they had for this son of Rachel, who had taken Joseph's place as his father's favourite. And with his harsh mode of addressing them, Joseph had no intention whatever to administer to his brethren " a just punishment for their wickedness towards him," for his heart could not have stooped to such mean revenge; but he wanted to probe thoroughly the feelings of their hearts, " whether they felt that they deserved the pun-

ishment of God for the sin they had committed," and how they
felt towards their aged father and their youngest brother.[1]
Even in the fact that he did not send the one away directly to
fetch Benjamin, and merely detain the rest, but put the whole
ten in prison, and afterwards modified his threat (vers. 18 sqq.),
there was no indecision as to the manner in which he should
behave towards them—no "wavering between thoughts of
wrath and revenge on the one hand, and forgiving love and
meekness on the other;" but he hoped by imprisoning them to
make his brethren feel the earnestness of his words, and to give
them time for reflection, as the curt "is no more" with which
they had alluded to Joseph's removal was a sufficient proof that
they had not yet truly repented of the deed.

Vers. 18–25. On the third day Joseph modified his severity.
"This do and live," i.e. then ye shall live: "I fear God."
One shall remain in prison, but let the rest of you take home
"corn for the famine of your families," and fetch your youngest
brother, that your words may be verified, and ye may not die,
i.e. may not suffer the death that spies deserve. That he might
not present the appearance of despotic caprice and tyranny by
too great severity, and so render his brethren obdurate, Joseph
stated as the reason for his new decision, that he feared God.
From the fear of God, he, the lord of Egypt, would not punish
or slay these strangers upon mere suspicion, but would judge
them justly. How differently had they acted towards their
brother! The ruler of all Egypt had compassion on their families who were in Canaan suffering from hunger; but they had

---

[1] Joseph nihil aliud agit quam ut revelet peccatum fratrum hoc duris-
simo opere et sermone. Descendunt enim in Ægyptum una cum aliis em-
tum frumentum, securi et negligentes tam atrocis delicti, cujus sibi erant
conscii, quasi nihil unquam deliquissent contra patrem decrepitum aut
fratrem innocentem, cogitant Joseph jam diu exemtum esse rebus humanis,
patrem vero rerum omnium ignarum esse. Quid ad nos? Non agunt pœnitentiam. Hi silices et adamantes frangendi et conterendi sunt ac aperiendi
oculi eorum, ut videant atrocitatem sceleris sui, idque ubi perfecit Joseph
statim verbis et gestibus humaniorem se præbet eosque honorifice tractat.—
Hæc igitur atrocitas scelerum movit Joseph ad explorandos animos fratrum
accuratius, ita ut non solum priorum delictorum sed et cogitationum pra-
varum memoriam renovaret, ac fuit sane inquisitio satis ingrata et acerba
et tamen ab animo placidissimo profecta. Ego durius eos tractassem. Sed
hæc acerbitas, quam præ se fert, non pertinet ad vindicandum injuriam sed
ad salutarem eorum pœnitentiam, ut humilientur.—Luther.

intended to leave their brother in the pit to starve! These and similar thoughts could hardly fail to pass involuntarily through their minds at Joseph's words, and to lead them to a penitential acknowledgment of their sin and unrighteousness. The notion that Joseph altered his first intention merely from regard to his much afflicted father, appears improbable, for the simple reason, that he can only have given utterance to the threat that he would keep them all in prison till one of them had gone and fetched Benjamin, for the purpose of giving the greater force to his accusation, that they were spies. But as he was not serious in making this charge, he could not for a moment have thought of actually carrying out the threat. *"And they did so:"* in these words the writer anticipates the result of the colloquy which ensued, and which is more fully narrated afterwards. Joseph's intention was fulfilled. The brothers now saw in what had happened to them a divine retribution: *"Surely we atone because of our brother, whose anguish of soul we saw, when he entreated us and we would not hear; therefore is this distress come upon us."* And Reuben reminded them how he had warned them to no purpose, not to sin against the boy—*"and even his blood . . . behold it is required"* (cf. ix. 5); *i.e.* not merely the sin of casting him into the pit and then selling him, but his death also, of which we have been guilty through that sale. Thus they accused themselves in Joseph's presence, not knowing that he could understand; *"for the interpreter was between them."* Joseph had conversed with them through an interpreter, as an Egyptian who was ignorant of their language. *"The* interpreter," viz. the one appointed for that purpose; בֵּינוֹת like xxvi. 28. But Joseph understood their words, and *"turned away and wept"* (ver. 24), with inward emotion at the wonderful leadings of divine grace, and at the change in his brothers' feelings. He then turned to them again, and, continuing the conversation with them, had Simeon bound before their eyes, to be detained as a hostage (not Reuben, who had dissuaded them from killing Joseph, and had taken no part in the sale, but Simeon, the next in age). He then ordered his men to fill their sacks with corn, to give every one (אִישׁ as in chap. xv. 10) his money back in his sack, and to provide them with food for the journey.

Vers. 26—38. Thus they started with their asses laden with the corn. On the way, when they had reached their halting-place for the night, one of them opened his sack to feed the ass, and found his money in it. מָלוֹן, camping-place for the night, is merely a resting-place, not an inn, both here and in Ex. iv. 24; for there can hardly have been caravanserais at that time, either in the desert or by the desert road. אַמְתַּחַת: an antiquated word for a corn-sack, occurring only in these chapters, and used even here interchangeably with שַׂק.—Ver 28. When this discovery was made known to the brethren, their hearts sank within them. They turned trembling to one another, and said, "*What is this that God hath done to us!*" Joseph had no doubt had the money returned, "merely because it was against his nature to trade with his father and brethren for bread;" just as he had caused them to be supplied with food for the journey, for no other reason than to give them a proof of his good-will. And even if he may have thought it possible that the brothers would be alarmed when they found the money, and thrown into a state of much greater anxiety from the fear of being still further accused by the stern lord of Egypt of cheating or of theft, there was no reason why he should spare them this anxiety, since it could only help to break their hard hearts still more At any rate, this salutary effect was really produced, even if Joseph had no such intention. The brothers looked upon this incomprehensible affair as a punishment from God, and neglected in their alarm to examine the rest of the sacks.—Vers. 29-34. On their arrival at home, they told their father all that had occurred.—Vers. 35 sqq. But when they emptied their sacks, and, to their own and their father's terror, found their bundles of money in their separate sacks, Jacob burst out with the complaint, "*Ye are making me childless! Joseph is gone, and Simeon is gone, and will ye take Benjamin! All this falls upon me*" (כֻּלָּנָה for כֻּלָּן as in Prov. xxxi. 29).—Vers. 37, 38. Reuben then offered his two sons to Jacob as pledges for Benjamin, if Jacob would entrust him to his care: Jacob might slay them, if he did not bring Benjamin back—the greatest and dearest offer that a son could make to a father. But Jacob refused to let him go. "*If mischief befell him by the way, ye would bring down my grey hairs with sorrow into Sheol*" (cf. xxxvii. 35).

THE SECOND VISIT OF JOSEPH'S BRETHREN TO EGYPT, ALONG WITH BENJAMIN.—CHAP. XLIII.

Vers. 1–15. When the corn brought from Egypt was all consumed, as the famine still continued, Jacob called upon his sons to go down and fetch a little corn (little in proportion to their need).—Vers. 3 sqq. Judah then declared, that they would not go there again unless their father sent Benjamin with them ; for the man (Joseph) had solemnly protested (הָעֵד הֵעִד) that they should not see his face without their youngest brother. Judah undertook the consultation with his father about Benjamin's going, because Reuben, the eldest son, had already been refused, and Levi, who followed Reuben and Simeon, had forfeited his father's confidence through his treachery to the Shechemites (chap. xxxiv.).—Vers. 6 sqq. To the father's reproachful question, why they had dealt so ill with him, as to tell the man that they had a brother, Judah replied : *"The man asked after us and our kinsmen: Is your father yet alive? have ye a brother? And we answered him in conformity* (עַל פִּי as in Ex. xxxiv. 27, etc.) *with these words (i.e.* with his questions). *Could we know, then, that he would say, Bring your brother down?"* Joseph had not made direct inquiries, indeed, about their father and their brother; but by his accusation that they were spies, he had compelled them to give an exact account of their family relationships. So that Judah, when repeating the main points of the interview, could very justly give them in the form just mentioned.—Ver. 8. He then repeated the only condition on which they would go to Egypt again, referring to the death by famine which threatened them, their father, and their children, and promising that he would himself be surety for the youth (הַנַּעַר, Benjamin was twenty-three years old), and saying, that if he did not restore him, he would bear the blame (חָטָא to be guilty of a sin and atone for it, as in 1 Kings i. 21) his whole life long. He then concluded with the deciding words, *" for if we had not delayed, surely we should already have returned a second time."*— Ver. 11. After this, the old man gave way to what could not be avoided, and let Benjamin go. But that nothing might be wanting on his part, which could contribute to the success of the journey, he suggested that they should take a present for the man, and that they should also take the money which was brought back in their sacks, in addition to what was necessary for the corn they were to purchase; and he then commended them to the mercy of Almighty God. " *If it must be so, yet do this* (אֵפוֹא belongs to the imperative, although it precedes it here, cf. xxvii. 37) : *take of the prize* (the most choice productions) *of the land* —*a little balm and a little honey* (דְּבַשׁ the Arabian *dibs*, either new honey from bees, or more probably honey from grapes,—a thick syrup boiled from sweet grapes, which is still carried every year from Hebron to Egypt), *gum-dragon and myrrh* (*vid.* xxxvii. 25), *pistachio nuts and almonds.*" בָּטְנִים, which are not mentioned anywhere else, are, according to the *Samar. vers.*, the fruit of the *pistacia vera*, a tree resembling the terebinth,—long angular nuts of the size of hazel-nuts, with an oily kernel of a pleasant flavour; it does not thrive in Palestine now, but the nuts are imported from Aleppo.—Ver. 12. " *And take second* (*i.e.* more) *money* (כֶּסֶף מִשְׁנֶה is different from מִשְׁנֵה־כֶּסֶף doubling of the money = double money, ver. 15) *in your hand; and the money that returned in your sacks take with you again; perhaps it is a mistake,*" *i.e.* was put in your sacks by mistake.—Ver. 14. Thus Israel let his sons go with the blessing, " *God Almighty give you mercy before the man, that he may liberate to you your other brother (Simeon) and Benjamin;*" and with this resigned submission to the will of God, " *And I, if I am bereaved, I am bereaved,*" *i.e.* if I am to lose my children, let it be so ! For this mode of expression, cf. Esth. iv. 16 and 2 Kings vii. 4. שָׁכֹלְתִּי with the pausal *â*, answering to the feelings of the speaker, which is frequently used for *o*; *e.g.* יִטְרֹף for יִטְרָף, chap. xlix. 27.

Vers. 16-25. When the brethren appeared before Joseph, he ordered his steward to take them into the house, and prepare a dinner for them and for him. טְבֹחַ the original form of the *imperative* for טְבַח. But the brethren were alarmed, thinking that they were taken into the house because of the money which returned the first time (הַשָּׁב which came back, they could not imagine how), that he might take them unawares (*lit.* roll upon them), and fall upon them, and keep them as slaves, along with their asses. For the purpose of averting what they dreaded, they approached (ver. 19) the steward and told him, "at the door of the house," before they entered therefore, how, at the first purchase of corn, on opening their sacks, they found the money that had been paid, " *every one's money in the mouth of his sack,*

our money according to its weight," *i.e.* in full, and had now
brought it back, together with some more money to buy corn,
and they did not know who had put their money in their sacks
(vers. 20–22). The steward, who was initiated into Joseph's
plans, replied in a pacifying tone, *" Peace be to you* (שָׁלוֹם לָכֶם
is not a form of salutation here, but of encouragement, as in
Judg. vi. 23): *fear not; your God and the God of your father has
given you a treasure in your sacks; your money came to me;"* and
at the same time, to banish all their fear, he brought Simeon
out to them. He then conducted them into Joseph's house, and
received them in Oriental fashion as the guests of his lord.
But, previous to Joseph's arrival, they arranged the present
which they had brought with them, as they heard that they were
to dine with him.

Vers. 26–34. When Joseph came home, they handed him the
present with the most reverential obeisance.—Ver. 27. Joseph first
of all inquired after their own and their father's health (שָׁלוֹם first
as substantive, then as adjective = שָׁלֵם xxxiii. 18), whether he was
still living; which they answered with thanks in the affirmative,
making the deepest bow. His eyes then fell upon Benjamin,
the brother by his own mother, and he asked whether this was
their youngest brother; but without waiting for their reply, he
exclaimed, *" God be gracious to thee, my son!"* יָחְנְךָ for יְחָנְךָ as in
Isa. xxx. 19 (cf. Ewald, § 251*d*). He addressed him as " my
son," in tender and, as it were, paternal affection, and with special regard to his youth. Benjamin was 16 years younger than
Joseph, and was quite an infant when Joseph was sold.—Vers.
30, 31. And "his (Joseph's) bowels did yearn" (נִכְמְרוּ *lit.* were
compressed, from the force of love to his brother), so that he
was obliged to seek (a place) as quickly as possible to weep, and
went into the chamber, that he might give vent to his feelings
in tears; after which, he washed his face and came out again,
and, putting constraint upon himself, ordered the dinner to be
brought in.—Vers. 32, 33. Separate tables were prepared for
him, for his brethren, and for the Egyptians who dined with
them. This was required by the Egyptian spirit of caste, which
neither allowed Joseph, as minister of state and a member of the
priestly order, to eat along with Egyptians who were below him,
nor the latter along with the Hebrews as foreigners. *" They cannot* (*i.e.* may not) *eat* (cf. Deut. xii. 17, xvi. 5, xvii. 15). *For*

this was an abomination to the Egyptians." The Hebrews and others, for example, slaughtered and ate animals, even female animals, which were regarded by the Egyptians as sacred; so that, according to Herod. ii. 41, no Egyptian would use the knife, or fork, or saucepan of a Greek, nor would any eat of the flesh of a clean animal which had been cut up with a Grecian knife (cf. Ex. viii. 22).—Vers. 33, 34. The brothers sat in front of Joseph, "*the first-born according to his birthright, and the smallest (youngest) according to his smallness* (youth);" *i.e.* the places were arranged for them according to their ages, so that they looked at one another with astonishment, since this arrangement necessarily impressed them with the idea that this great man had been supernaturally enlightened as to their family affairs. To do them honour, they brought (יִשָּׂא, Ges. § 137, 3) them dishes from Joseph, *i.e.* from his table; and to show especial honour to Benjamin, his portion was five times larger than that of any of the others (יָדוֹת *lit.* hands, grasps, as in chap. xlvii. 24; 2 Kings xi. 7). The custom is met with elsewhere of showing respect to distinguished guests by giving them the largest and best pieces (1 Sam. ix. 23, 24; *Homer*, Il. 7, 321; 8, 162, etc.), by double portions (*e.g.* the kings among the Spartans, Herod. 6, 57), and even by fourfold portions in the case of the Archons among the Cretans (*Heraclid. polit.* 3). But among the Egyptians the number 5 appears to have been preferred to any other (cf. chap. xli. 34, xlv. 22, xlvii. 2, 24; Isa. xix. 18). By this partiality Joseph intended, with a view to his further plans, to draw out his brethren to show their real feelings towards Benjamin, that he might see whether they would envy and hate him on account of this distinction, as they had formerly envied him his long coat with sleeves, and hated him because he was his father's favourite (xxxvii. 3, 4). This honourable treatment and entertainment banished all their anxiety and fear. "*They drank, and drank largely with him,*" *i.e.* they were perfectly satisfied with what they ate and drank; not, they were intoxicated (cf. *Hag.* i. 9).

THE LAST TEST AND ITS RESULTS.—CHAP. XLIV.

Vers. 1–13. THE TEST.—Vers. 1, 2. After the dinner Joseph had his brothers' sacks filled by his steward with corn, as much as they could hold, and every one's money placed inside; and in addition to that, had his own silver goblet put into Benjamin's sack.—Vers. 3–6. Then as soon as it was light (אוֹר, 3d pers. perf. in *o: Ges.* § 72, 1), they were sent away with their asses. But they were hardly outside the town, "not far off," when he directed his steward to follow the men, and as soon as he overtook them, to say, " *Wherefore have ye rewarded evil for good? Is it not this from which my lord drinketh, and he is accustomed to prophesy from it? Ye have done an evil deed!*" By these words they were accused of theft; the thing was taken for granted as well known to them all, and the goblet purloined was simply described as a very valuable possession of Joseph's. נָחֵשׁ: *lit.* to whisper, to mumble out formularies, incantations, then to prophesy, *divinare.* According to this, the Egyptians at that time practised λεκανοσκοπίη or λεκανομαντεία and ὑδρομαντεία, the plate and water incantations, of which *Jamblichus* speaks (*de myst.* iii. 14), and which consisted in pouring clean water into a goblet, and then looking into the water for representations of future events ; or in pouring water into a goblet or dish, dropping in pieces of gold and silver, also precious stones, and then observing and interpreting the appearances in the water (cf. *Varro apud August. civ. Dei* 7, 35; *Plin. h. n.* 37, 73; *Strabo,* xvi. p. 762). Traces of this have been continued even to our own day (see *Norden's* Journey through Egypt and Nubia). But we cannot infer with certainty from this, that Joseph actually adopted this superstitious practice. The intention of the statement may simply have been to represent the goblet as a sacred vessel, and Joseph as acquainted with the most secret things (ver. 15).—Vers. 7–9. In the consciousness of their innocence the brethren repelled this charge with indignation, and appealed to the fact that they brought back the gold which was found in their sacks, and therefore could not possibly have stolen gold or silver; and declared that whoever should be found in possession of the goblet, should be put to death, and the rest become slaves.—Ver. 10. The man replied, "*Now let it be even* (גַּם placed first for the sake of emphasis) *according to your words: with whom it is found, he shall be my slave, and ye* (the rest) *shall remain blameless.*" Thus he modified the sentence, to assume the appearance of justice.—Vers. 11–13. They then took down their sacks as quickly as possible ; and he examined them, beginning with the eldest and finishing with the youngest; and the goblet was found in Benjamin's sack. With anguish and alarm at this new calamity they rent their clothes (*vid.* xxxvii. 34), loaded their asses again, and returned to the city. It would now be seen how they felt in their inmost hearts towards their father's favourite, who had been so distinguished by the great man of Egypt: whether now as formerly they were capable of giving up their brother, and bringing their aged father with sorrow to the grave; or whether they were ready, with unenvying, self-sacrificing love, to give up their own liberty and lives for him. And they stood this test.

Vers. 14–34. RESULT OF THE TEST.—Vers. 14–17. With Judah leading the way, they came into the house to Joseph, and fell down before him begging for mercy. Joseph spoke to them harshly: "*What kind of deed is this that ye have done? Did ye not know that such a man as I* (a man initiated into the most secret things) *would certainly divine this?*" נִחֵשׁ *augurari.* Judah made no attempt at a defence. "*What shall we say to my lord? how speak, how clear ourselves? God (Ha-Elohim,* the personal God) *has found out the wickedness of thy servants (i.e.* He is now punishing the crime committed against our brother, cf. xlii. 21). *Behold, we are my lord's slaves, both we, and he in whose hand the cup was found.*" But Joseph would punish mildly and justly. The guilty one alone should be his slave; the others might go in peace, *i.e.* uninjured, to their father.— Vers. 18 sqq. But that the brothers could not do. Judah, who had pledged himself to his father for Benjamin, ventured in the anguish of his heart to approach Joseph, and implore him to liberate his brother. "I would give very much," says *Luther,* " to be able to pray to our Lord God as well as Judah prays to Joseph here; for it is a perfect specimen of prayer, the true feeling that there ought to be in prayer." Beginning with the request for a gracious hearing, as he was speaking to the ears of one who was equal to Pharaoh (who could condemn or pardon like the king), Judah depicted in natural, affecting, powerful, and irresistible words the love of their aged father to this son of his old age, and his grief when they told him that they were not to come into the presence of the lord of Egypt again without Benjamin; the intense anxiety with which, after a severe struggle, their father had allowed him to come, after he

(Judah) had offered to be answerable for his life; and the grievous fact, that if they returned without the youth, they must bring down the grey hairs of their father with sorrow to the grave.—Ver. 21. To "*set eyes upon him*" signifies, with a gracious intention, to show him good-will (as in Jer. xxxix. 12, xl. 4).—Ver. 27. "*That my wife bore me two* (sons):" Jacob regards Rachel alone as his actual wife (cf. xlvi. 19).— Ver. 28 וָאֹמַר, preceded by a preterite, is to be rendered "*and I was obliged to say, Only* (nothing but) *torn in pieces has he become.*"—Ver. 30. "*His soul is bound to his soul:*" equivalent to, "he clings to him with all his soul."—Vers. 33, 34. Judah closed his appeal with the entreaty, "*Now let thy servant* (me) *remain instead of the lad as slave to my lord, but let the lad go up with his brethren; for how could I go to my father without the lad being with me!* (I cannot,) *that I may not see the calamity which will befall my father!*"

THE RECOGNITION. INVITATION TO JACOB TO COME DOWN TO EGYPT.—CHAP. XLV.

Vers. 1–15. THE RECOGNITION.—Ver. 1. After this appeal, in which Judah, speaking for his brethren, had shown the tenderest affection for the old man who had been bowed down by their sin, and the most devoted fraternal love and fidelity to the only remaining son of his beloved Rachel, and had given a sufficient proof of the change of mind, the true conversion, that had taken place in themselves, Joseph could not restrain himself any longer in relation to all those who stood round him. He was obliged to relinquish the part which he had hitherto acted for the purpose of testing his brothers' hearts, and to give full vent to his feelings. "*He called out: Cause every man to go out from me. And there stood no man* (of his Egyptian attendants) *with him, while Joseph made himself known to his brethren,*" *quia effusio illa affectuum et στοργῆς erga fratres et parentem tanta fuit, ut non posset ferre alienorum praesentiam et aspectum* (*Luther*).— Vers. 2, 3. As soon as all the rest were gone, he broke out into such loud weeping, that the Egyptians outside could hear it; and the house of Pharaoh, *i.e.* the royal family, was told of it (cf. vers. 2 and 16). He then said to his brethren: "*I am Joseph. Is my father still alive?*" That his father was still living, he

had not only been informed before (xliii. 27), but had just been
told again; but his filial heart impels him to make sure of it once
more. *"But his brethren could not answer him, for they were
terrified before him:"* they were so smitten in their consciences,
that from astonishment and terror they could not utter a word.
—Vers. 4, 5. Joseph then bade his brethren approach nearer,
and said: *"I am Joseph, your brother, whom ye sold into Egypt.
But now be not grieved nor angry with yourselves* (אַל־יִחַר בְּעֵינֵיכֶם
as in chap. xxxi. 35) *that ye sold me hither; for God hath sent
me before you to preserve life."* Sic enim Joseph interpretatur
venditionem. *Vos quidem me vendidistis, sed Deus emit, asseruit et
vindicavit me sibi pastorem, principem et salvatorem populorum
eodem consilio, quo videbar amissus et perditus* (Luther). *"For,"*
he continues in explanation, *"now there are two years of famine
in the land, and there are five years more, in which there will be
no ploughing and reaping. And God hath sent me before you to
establish you a remnant* (cf. 2 Sam. xiv. 7) *upon the earth* (*i.e.* to
secure to you the preservation of the tribe and of posterity during
this famine), *and to preserve your lives to a great deliverance,"*
i.e. to a great nation delivered from destruction, cf. l. 20. פְּלֵיטָה
that which has escaped, the band of men or multitude escaped
from death and destruction (2 Kings xix. 30, 31). Joseph
announced prophetically here, that God had brought him into
Egypt to preserve through him the family which He had chosen
for His own nation, and to deliver them out of the danger of
starvation which threatened them now, as a very great nation.—
Ver. 8. *"And now* (this was truly the case) *it was not you that
sent me hither; but God* (*Ha-Elohim*, the personal God, in contrast with his brethren) *hath made me a father to Pharaoh* (*i.e.* his
most confidential counsellor and friend; cf. 1 Macc. xi. 32, Ges.
thes. 7), *and lord of all his house, and a ruler throughout all the
land of Egypt;"* cf. xli. 40, 41.

Vers. 9 sqq. Joseph then directed his brethren to go up to
their father with all speed, and invite him in his name to
come without delay, with all his family and possessions, into
Egypt, where he would keep him near himself, in the land of
Goshen (see xlvii. 11), that he might not perish in the still
remaining five years of famine. הִוָּרֵשׁ: ver. 11, *lit.* to be
robbed of one's possessions, to be taken possession of by another,
from יָרַשׁ to take possession.—Vers. 12, 13. But the brethren

were so taken by surprise and overpowered by this unexpected discovery, that to convince them of the reality of the whole affair, Joseph was obliged to add, " Behold, your eyes see, and the eyes of my brother Benjamin, that it is my mouth that speaketh unto you. And tell my father all my glory in Egypt, and all that ye have seen, and bring my father quickly hither."—Vers. 14, 15. He then fell upon Benjamin's neck and wept, and kissed all his brethren and wept on them, *i.e.* whilst embracing them ; " *and after that, his brethren talked with him.*" אַחֲרֵי כֵן : after Joseph by a triple assurance, that what they had done was the leading of God for their own good, had dispelled their fear of retribution, and, by embracing and kissing them with tears, had sealed the truth and sincerity of his words.

Vers. 16–28. INVITATION TO JACOB TO COME INTO EGYPT. —Vers. 16 sqq. The report of the arrival of Joseph's brethren soon found its way into the palace, and made so favourable an impression upon Pharaoh and his courtiers, that the king sent a message through Joseph to his brethren to come with their father and their families ("*your houses*") into Egypt, saying that he would give them " *the good of the land of Egypt,*" and they should eat " *the fat of the land.*" טוֹב, " the good," is not the best part, but the good things (produce) of the land, as in vers. 20, 23, xxiv. 10, 2 Kings viii. 9.   חֵלֶב fat, *i.e.* the finest productions.—Vers. 19, 20. At the same time Pharaoh empowered Joseph (" thou art commanded ") to give his brethren carriages to take with them, in which to convey their children and wives and their aged father, and recommended them to leave their goods behind them in Canaan, for the good of all Egypt was at their service.   From time immemorial Egypt was rich in small, two-wheeled carriages, which could be used even where there were no roads (cf. chap. l. 9, Ex. xiv. 6 sqq. with Isa. xxxvi. 9) " *Let not your eye look with mourning* (תָּחֹס) *at your goods ;* " *i.e.* do not trouble about the house-furniture which you are obliged to leave behind.   The good-will manifested in this invitation of Pharaoh towards Jacob's family was to be attributed to the feeling of gratitude to Joseph, and " is related circumstantially, because this free and honourable invitation involved the right of Israel to leave Egypt again without obstruction " (*Delitzsch*).

Vers. 21 sqq. The sons of Israel carried out the instructions

of Joseph and the invitation of Pharaoh (vers. 25–27). But
Joseph not only sent carriages according to Pharaoh's directions,
and food for the journey, he also gave them presents, changes of
raiment, a suit for every one, and five suits for Benjamin, as
well as 300 shekels of silver. חֲלִפוֹת שְׂמָלוֹת: change of clothes,
clothes to change ; i.e. dress clothes which were worn on special
occasions and frequently changed (Judg. xiv. 12, 13, 19; 2
Kings v. 5). "And to his father he sent like these;" i.e. not
changes of clothes, but presents also, viz. ten asses "carrying
of the good of Egypt," and ten she-asses with corn and provisions for the journey; and sent them off with the injunction :
אַל־תִּרְגְּזוּ, μὴ ὀργίζεσθε (LXX.), "do not get angry by the way."
*Placatus erat Joseph fratribus, simul eos admonet, ne quid tur-
barum moveant. Timendum enim erat, ne quisque se purgando
crimen transferre in alios studeret atque ita surgeret contentio*
(*Calvin*).—Vers. 25–28. When they got back, and brought
word to their father, "Joseph is still living, yea (וְכִי an emphatic assurance, *Ewald*, § 3306) he is ruler in all the land of
Egypt, his heart stopped, for he believed them not;" i.e. his heart
did not beat at this joyful news, for he put no faith in what
they said. It was not till they told him all that Joseph had said,
and he saw the carriages that Joseph had sent, that "*the spirit
of their father Jacob revived; and Israel said: It is enough!
Joseph my son is yet alive: I will go and see him before I die.*"
Observe the significant interchange of *Jacob* and *Israel*. When
once the crushed spirit of the old man was revived by the certainty that his son Joseph was still alive, Jacob was changed
into Israel, the "conqueror overcoming his grief at the previous
misconduct of his sons " (*Fr. v. Meyer*).

REMOVAL OF ISRAEL TO GOSHEN IN EGYPT.—CHAP. XLVI.

Vers. 1–7. "*So Israel took his journey* (from Hebron, chap.
xxxvii. 14) *with all who belonged to him, and came to Beersheba.*"
There, on the border of Canaan, where Abraham and Isaac had
called upon the name of the Lord (xxi. 33, xxvi. 25), he offered
sacrifices to the God of his father Isaac, *ut sibi firmum et ratum
esse testetur fœdus, quod Deus ipse cum Patribus pepigerat* (*Calvin*). Even though Jacob might see the ways of God in the
wonderful course of his son Joseph, and discern in the friendly

invitation of Joseph and Pharaoh, combined with the famine prevailing in Canaan, a divine direction to go into Egypt; yet this departure from the land of promise, in which his fathers had lived as pilgrims, was a step which necessarily excited serious thoughts in his mind as to his own future and that of his family, and led him to commend himself and his followers to the care of the faithful covenant God, whether in so doing he thought of the revelation which Abram had received (chap. xv. 13–16), or not.—Ver. 2. Here God appeared to him in a vision of the night (מַרְאֹת, an intensive plural), and gave him, as once before on his flight from Canaan (xxviii. 12 sqq.), the comforting promise, " *I am* הָאֵל (the Mighty One), *the God of thy father: fear not to go down into Egypt* (מֵרְדָה for מֵרֶדֶת, as in Ex. ii. 4 דֵעָה for דַעַת, cf. *Ges.* § 69, 3, Anm. 1); *for I will there make thee a great nation. I will go down with thee into Egypt, and I—bring thee up again also will I, and Joseph shall close thine eyes.*" נַם־עָלֹה an *inf. abs.* appended emphatically (as in chap. xxxi. 15); according to Ges. *inf. Kal.*—Vers. 5–7. Strengthened by this promise, Jacob went into Egypt with children and children's children, his sons driving their aged father together with their wives and children in the carriages sent by Pharaoh, and taking their flocks with all the possessions that they had acquired in Canaan.[1]

Vers. 8–27. The size of Jacob's family, which was to grow into a great nation, is given here, with evident allusion to the fulfilment of the divine promise with which he went into Egypt. The list of names includes not merely the " sons of Israel" in the stricter sense; but, as is added immediately afterwards, "*Jacob and his sons,*" or, as the closing formula expresses it (ver. 27), "*all the souls of the house of Jacob, who came into Egypt*" (הַבָּאָה for אֲשֶׁר בָּאָה, *Ges.* § 109), including the patriarch himself, and Joseph with his two sons, who were born before Jacob's arrival in Egypt. If we reckon these, the house of Jacob consisted of 70 souls; and apart from these, of 66, besides his sons' wives. The sons are arranged according to the four mothers. Of *Leah*

---

[1] Such a scene as this, with the emigrants taking their goods laden upon asses, and even two children in panniers upon an ass's back, may be seen depicted upon a tomb at *Beni Hassan*, which might represent the immigration of Israel, although it cannot be directly connected with it. (See the particulars in *Hengstenberg*, Egypt and the Books of Moses.)

there are given 6 sons, 23 grandsons, 2 great-grandsons (sons of Pharez, whereas Er and Onan, the sons of Judah who died in Canaan, are not reckoned), and 1 daughter, Dinah, who remained unmarried, and was therefore an independent member of the house of Jacob; in all, therefore, $6+23+2+1=32$, or with Jacob, 33 souls. Of *Zilpah*, Leah's maid, there are mentioned 2 sons, 11 grandsons, 2 great-grandsons, and 1 daughter (who is reckoned like Dinah, both here and Num. xxvi. 46, for some special reason, which is not particularly described); in all, $2+11+2+1=16$ souls. Of *Rachel*, "Jacob's (favourite) wife," 2 sons and 12 grandsons are named, of whom, according to Num. xxvi. 40, two were great-grandsons, $=14$ souls; and of Rachel's maid *Bilhah*, 2 sons and 5 grandsons $=$ 7 souls. The whole number therefore was $33+16+14+7=$ 70.[1] The wives of Jacob's sons are neither mentioned by name nor reckoned, because the families of Israel were not founded by them, but by their husbands alone. Nor is their parentage given either here or anywhere else. It is merely casually that one of the sons of Simeon is called the son of a Canaanitish woman (ver. 10); from which it may be inferred that it was quite an exceptional thing for the sons of Jacob to take their wives from among the Canaanites, and that as a rule they were chosen from their paternal relations in Mesopotamia; besides whom, there were also their other relations, the families of Ishmael, Keturah, and Edom. Of the "daughters of Jacob" also, and the "daughters of his sons," none are mentioned except Dinah and Serah the daughter of Asher, because they were not the founders of separate houses.

If we look more closely into the list itself, the first thing which strikes us is that Pharez, one of the twin-sons of Judah, who were not born till after the sale of Joseph, should already have had two sons. Supposing that Judah's marriage to the

---

[1] Instead of the number 70 given here, Ex. i. 5, and Deut. x. 22, Stephen speaks of 75 (Acts vii. 14), according to the LXX., which has the number 75 both here and Ex. i. 5, on account of the words which follow the names of Manasseh and Ephraim in ver. 20: ἐγένοντο δὲ υἱοὶ Μανασσῆ, οὓς ἔτεκεν αὐτῷ ἡ παλλακὴ ἡ Σύρα, τὸν Μαχίρ· Μαχὶο δὲ ἐγέννησε τὸν Γαλαάδ. υἱοὶ δὲ Ἐφραὶμ ἀδελφοῦ Μανασσῆ· Σουταλαὰμ καὶ Τάαμ. υἱοὶ δὲ Σουταλαάμ· Ἐδώμ: and which are interpolated by conjecture from chap. 1. 23, and Num. xxvi. 29, 35, and 36 (33, 39, and 40), these three grandsons and two great-grandsons of Joseph being reckoned in.

daughter of Shuah the Canaanite occurred, notwithstanding
the reasons advanced to the contrary in chap. xxxviii., before the
sale of Joseph, and shortly after the return of Jacob to Canaan,
during the time of his sojourn at Shechem (xxxiii. 18), it cannot have taken place more than five, or at the most six, years
before Joseph was sold; for Judah was only three years older
than Joseph, and was not more than 20 years old, therefore, at
the time of his sale. But even then there would not be more
than 28 years between Judah's marriage and Jacob's removal to
Egypt; so that Pharez would only be about 11 years old, since
he could not have been born till about 17 years after Judah's
marriage, and at that age he could not have had two sons.
Judah, again, could not have taken four sons with him into
Egypt, since he had at the most only two sons a year before
their removal (xlii. 37); unless indeed we adopt the extremely
improbable hypothesis, that two other sons were born within
the space of 11 or 12 months, either as twins, or one after the
other. Still less could Benjamin, who was only 23 or 24 years
old at the time (*vid*. pp. 311 and 319), have had 10 sons already,
or, as Num. xxvi. 38–40 shows, eight sons and two grandsons.
From all this it necessarily follows, that in the list before us
grandsons and great-grandsons of Jacob are named who were
born afterwards in Egypt, and who, therefore, according to a
view which we frequently meet with in the Old Testament,
though strange to our modes of thought, came into Egypt *in
lumbis patrum*. That the list is really intended to be so understood, is undoubtedly evident from a comparison of the "sons
of Israel" (ver. 8), whose names it gives, with the description
given in Num. xxvi. of the whole community of the sons of
Israel according to their fathers' houses, or their tribes and
families. In the account of the families of Israel at the time
of Moses, which is given there, we find, with slight deviations,
all the grandsons and great-grandsons of Jacob whose names
occur in this chapter, mentioned as the founders of the families,
into which the twelve tribes of Israel were subdivided in Moses'
days. The deviations are partly in form, partly in substance.
To the former belong the differences in particular names, which
are sometimes only different forms of the same name; *e.g.* Jemuel
and Zohar (ver. 10), for Nemuel and Zerah (Num. xxvi. 12, 13);
Ziphion and Arodi (ver. 16), for Zephon and Arod (Num. xxvi.

15 and 17); Huppim (ver. 21) for Hupham (Num. xxvi. 39); Ehi (ver. 21), an abbreviation of Ahiram (Num. xxvi. 38): sometimes different names of the same person; viz. Ezbon (ver. 16) and Ozni (Num. xxvi. 16); Muppim (ver. 21) and Shupham (Num. xxvi. 39); Hushim (ver. 23) and Shuham (Num. xxvi. 42). Among the differences in substance, the first to be noticed is the fact, that in Num. xxvi. Simeon's son Ohad, Asher's son Ishuah, and three of Benjamin's sons, Becher, Gera, and Rosh, are missing from the founders of families, probably for no other reason than that they either died childless, or did not leave a sufficient number of children to form independent families. With the exception of these, according to Num. xxvi., all the grandsons and great-grandsons of Jacob mentioned in this chapter were founders of families in existence in Moses' time. From this it is obvious that our list is intended to contain, not merely the sons and grandsons of Jacob, who were already born when he went down to Egypt, but in addition to the sons, who were the heads of the twelve tribes of the nation, *all* the grandsons and great-grandsons who became the founders of *mishpachoth, i.e.* of independent families, and who on that account took the place or were advanced into the position of the grandsons of Jacob, so far as the national organization was concerned.

On no other hypothesis can we explain the fact, that in the time of Moses there was not one of the twelve tribes, except the double tribe of Joseph, in which there were families existing, that had descended from either grandsons or great-grandsons of Jacob who are not already mentioned in this list. As it is quite inconceivable that no more sons should have been born to Jacob's sons after their removal into Egypt, so is it equally inconceivable, that all the sons born in Egypt either died childless, or founded no families. The rule by which the nation descending from the sons of Jacob was divided into tribes and families (*mishpachoth*) according to the order of birth was this, that as the twelve sons founded the twelve tribes, so their sons, *i.e.* Jacob's grandsons, were the founders of the families into which the tribes were subdivided, unless these grandsons died without leaving children, or did not leave a sufficient number of male descendants to form independent families, or the natural rule for the formation of tribes and families was set aside by other events or causes. On this hypothesis we can also explain the other real differences between this list and Num. xxvi.; viz. the fact that, according to Num. xxvi. 40, two of the sons of Benjamin mentioned in ver. 21, Naaman and Ard, were his grandsons, sons of Belah; and also the circumstance, that in ver. 20 only the two sons of Joseph, who were already born when Jacob arrived in Egypt, are mentioned, viz. Manasseh and Ephraim, and none of the sons who were born to him afterwards (xlviii. 6). The two grandsons of Benjamin could be reckoned among his sons in our list, because they founded independent families just like the sons. And of the sons of Joseph, Manasseh and Ephraim alone could be admitted into our list, because they were elevated above the sons born to Joseph afterwards, by the fact that shortly before Jacob's death he adopted them as his own sons and thus raised them to the rank of heads of tribes; so that wherever Joseph's descendants are reckoned as *one* tribe (*e.g.* Josh. xvi. 1, 4), Manasseh and Ephraim form the main divisions, or leading families of the tribe of Joseph, the subdivisions of which were founded partly by their brothers who were born afterwards, and partly by their sons and grandsons. Consequently the omission of the sons born afterwards, and the grandsons of Joseph, from whom the families of the two sons, Manasseh and Ephraim, who were elevated into tribes, descended, forms only an apparent and not a real exception to the general rule, that this list mentions all the grandsons of Jacob who founded the families of the twelve tribes, without regard to the question whether they were born before or after the removal of Jacob's house to Egypt, since this distinction was of no importance to the main purpose of our list. That this was the design of our list, is still further confirmed by a comparison of Ex. i. 5 and Deut. x. 22, where the seventy souls of the house of Jacob which went into Egypt are said to constitute the seed which, under the blessing of the Lord, had grown into the numerous people that Moses led out of Egypt, to take possession of the land of promise. From this point of view it was a natural thing to describe the seed of the nation, which grew up in tribes and families, in such a way as to give the germs and roots of all the tribes and families of the whole nation; *i.e.* not merely the grandsons who were born before the migration, but also the grandsons and great-grandsons who were born in Egypt, and became founders of independent families. By thus embracing all the founders of tribes and families, the significant number 70 was obtained, in which the number 7 (formed of the divine number 3, and the world number 4, as the seal of the covenant relation between God and Israel) is multiplied by the number 10, as the seal of completeness, so as to express the fact that these 70 souls comprehended the whole of the nation of God.[1]

Vers. 28–34. This list of the house of Jacob is followed by an account of the arrival in Egypt.—Ver. 28. Jacob sent his son Judah before him to Joseph, "to show (לְהוֹרֹת) before him to Goshen;" i.e. to obtain from Joseph the necessary instructions as to the place of their settlement, and then to act as guide to Goshen.—Ver. 29. As soon as they had arrived, Joseph had his chariot made ready to go up to Goshen and meet his father (וַיַּעַל applied to a journey from the interior to the desert or Canaan), and "showed himself to him there (lit. he appeared to him ; נִרְאָה, which is generally used only of the appearance of God, is selected here to indicate the glory in which Joseph came to meet his father) ; and fell upon his neck, continuing (עוֹד) upon his neck (i.e. in his embrace) weeping."—Ver. 30. Then Israel said to Joseph : "Now (הַפַּעַם lit. this time) will I die, after I have seen thy face, that thou (art) still alive."—Vers. 31, 32. But Joseph told his brethren and his father's house (his family) that he would go up to Pharaoh (עָלָה here used of going to the court, as an ideal ascent), to announce the arrival of his relations, who were אַנְשֵׁי מִקְנֶה "keepers of flocks," and had brought their sheep and oxen and all their possessions with them.—Vers. 33, 34. At the same time Joseph gave these instructions to his brethren, in case Pharaoh should send for them and inquire about their occupation : "Say, Thy servants have been keepers of cattle from our youth even until now, we like our fathers ; that ye may dwell in the land of Goshen ; for every shepherd is an abomination of the Egyptians." This last remark formed part of Joseph's words, and contained the reason why his brethren should describe themselves to Pharaoh as shepherds from of old, namely, that they might receive Goshen as their dwelling-place, and that their national and religious independence might

---

[1] This was the manner in which the earlier theologians solved the actual difficulties connected with our list ; and this solution has been adopted and defended against the objections offered to it by Hengstenberg (Dissertations) and Kurtz (History of the Old Covenant).

not be endangered by too close an intercourse with the Egyptians. The dislike of the Egyptians to shepherds arose from the fact, that the more completely the foundations of the Egyptian state rested upon agriculture with its perfect organization, the more did the Egyptians associate the idea of rudeness and barbarism with the very name of a shepherd. This is not only attested in various ways by the monuments, on which shepherds are constantly depicted as lanky, withered, distorted, emaciated, and sometimes almost ghostly figures (*Graul*, Reise 2, p. 171), but is confirmed by ancient testimony. According to *Herodotus* (2, 47), the swine-herds were the most despised; but they were associated with the cow-herds (βουκόλοι) in the seven castes of the Egyptians (Herod. 2, 164), so that *Diodorus Siculus* (1, 74) includes all herdsmen in one caste; according to which the word βουκόλοι in *Herodotus* not only denotes cow-herds, but *a potiori* all herdsmen, just as we find in the herds depicted upon the monuments, sheep, goats, and rams introduced by thousands, along with asses and horned cattle.

SETTLEMENT OF ISRAEL IN EGYPT; THEIR PROSPEROUS CONDITION DURING THE YEARS OF FAMINE.—CHAP. XLVII. 1–27.

Vers. 1–12. When Joseph had announced to Pharaoh the arrival of his relations in Goshen, he presented five out of the whole number of his brethren (מִקְצֵה אֶחָיו; on קָצֶה see chap. xix. 4) to the king.—Vers. 3 sqq. Pharaoh asked them about their occupation, and according to Joseph's instructions they replied that they were herdsmen (רֹעֵה צֹאן, the *singular* of the predicate, see *Ges.* § 147c), who had come to sojourn in the land (גּוּר, *i.e.* to stay for a time), because the pasture for their flocks had failed in the land of Canaan on account of the famine. The king then empowered Joseph to give his father and his brethren a dwelling (הוֹשִׁיב) in the best part of the land, in the land of Goshen, and, if he knew any brave men among them, to make them rulers over the royal herds, which were kept, as we may infer, in the land of Goshen, as being the best pasture-land.— Vers. 7–9. Joseph then presented his father to Pharaoh, but not till after the audience of his brothers had been followed by the royal permission to settle, for which the old man, who was bowed down with age, was not in a condition to sue. The patriarch saluted the king with a blessing, and replied to his inquiry as to his age, " *The days of the years of my pilgrimage are 130 years ; few and sorrowful are the days of my life's years, and have not reached* (the perfect in the presentiment of his approaching end) *the days of the life's years of my fathers in the days of their pilgrimage.*" Jacob called his own life and that of his fathers a pilgrimage (מְגוּרִים), because they had not come into actual possession of the promised land, but had been obliged all their life long to wander about, unsettled and homeless, in the land promised to them for an inheritance, as in a strange land. This pilgrimage was at the same time a figurative representation of the inconstancy and weariness of the earthly life, in which man does not attain to that true rest of peace with God and blessedness in His fellowship, for which he was created, and for which therefore his soul is continually longing (cf. Ps. xxxix. 13, cxix. 19, 54; 1 Chron. xxix. 15). The apostle, therefore, could justly regard these words as a declaration of the longing of the patriarchs for the eternal rest of their heavenly fatherland (Heb. xi. 13–16). So also Jacob's life was little (מְעַט) and evil (*i.e.* full of toil and trouble) in comparison with the life of his fathers. For Abraham lived to be 175 years old, and Isaac 180 ; and neither of them had led a life so agitated, so full of distress and dangers, of tribulation and anguish, as Jacob had from his first flight to Haran up to the time of his removal to Egypt.

Ver. 10. After this probably short interview, of which, however, only the leading incidents are given, Jacob left the king with a blessing.—Ver. 11. Joseph assigned to his father and his brethren, according to Pharaoh's command, a possession (אֲחֻזָּה) for a dwelling-place in the best part of Egypt, the land of *Raëmses,* and provided them with bread, " *according to the mouth of the little ones,*" *i.e.* according to the necessities of each family, answering to the larger or smaller number of their children. כִּלְכֵּל with a double accusative (*Ges.* § 139). The settlement of the Israelites is called the land of *Raëmses* (רַעְמְסֵס, in pause רַעְמְסֵס Ex. i. 11), instead of *Goshen,* either because the province of *Goshen* (Γεσέμ, LXX.) is indicated by the name of its former capital *Raëmses* (*i.e. Heroopolis,* on the site or in the immediate neighbourhood of the modern *Abu Keisheib,* in Wady Tumilat (*vid.* Ex. i. 11), or because Israel settled in the vicinity of *Raëmses.* The district of *Goshen* is to be sought in the modern

province of *el Sharkiyeh* (*i.e.* the eastern), on the east side of
the Nile, towards Arabia, still the most fertile and productive
province of Egypt (cf. *Robinson*, Pal. i. 78, 79). For Goshen
was bounded on the east by the desert of Arabia Petræa, which
stretches away to Philistia (Ex. xiii. 17, cf. 1 Chron. vii. 21)
and is called Γεσὲμ 'Αραβίας in the Septuagint in consequence
(chap. xlv. 10, xlvi. 34), and must have extended westwards to
the Nile, since the Israelites had an abundance of fish (Num.
xi. 5). It probably skirted the Tanitic arm of the Nile, as the
fields of *Zoan, i.e. Tanis*, are said to have been the scene of the
mighty acts of God in Egypt (Ps. lxxviii. 12, 43, cf. Num. xiii.
22). In this province Joseph assigned his relations settlements
near to himself (xlv. 10), from which they could quickly and
easily communicate with one another (xlvi. 28, xlviii. 1 sqq.).
Whether he lived at *Raëmses* or not, cannot be determined, just
because the residence of the Pharaoh of that time is not known,
and the notion that it was at Memphis is only based upon utterly
uncertain combinations relating to the Hyksos.

Vers. 13–27. To make the extent of the benefit conferred
by Joseph upon his family, in providing them with the necessary
supplies during the years of famine, all the more apparent, a
description is given of the distress into which the inhabitants of
Egypt and Canaan were plunged by the continuance of the
famine.—Ver. 13. The land of Egypt and the land of Canaan
were exhausted with hunger.—וַתֵּלַהּ: from לָהָהּ = לָאָה, to languish,
to be exhausted, only occurring again in Prov. xxvi. 18, *Hithp.*
in a secondary sense.—Ver. 14. All the money in both countries
was paid in to Joseph for the purchase of corn, and deposited by
him in Pharaoh's house, *i.e.* the royal treasury.—Vers. 15 sqq.
When the money was exhausted, the Egyptians all came to
Joseph with the petition: "*Give us bread, why should we die
before thee*" (*i.e.* so that thou shouldst see us die, when in reality
thou canst support us)? Joseph then offered to accept their
cattle in payment; and they brought him their herds, in return
for which he provided them that year with bread. נָהַל: *Piel* to
lead, with the secondary meaning, to care for (Ps. xxiii. 2; Isa.
xl. 11, etc.); hence the signification here, "to maintain."—Vers.
18, 19. When that year had passed (תֹּם, as in Ps. cii. 28, to
denote the termination of the year), they came again "the second
year" (*i.e.* after the money was gone, not the second of the seven

years of famine) and said : " *We cannot hide it from my lord*
(אֲדֹנִי, a title similar to *your majesty*), *but the money is all gone,
and the cattle have come to my lord ; we have nothing left to offer
to my lord but our bodies and our land.*" כִּי אִם is an intensified
כִּי following a negation (" but," as in chap. xxxii. 29, etc.), and
is to be understood elliptically ; *lit.* " for if," *sc.* we would speak
openly ; not " that because," for the causal signification of אִם is
not established. תַּם with אֶל is *constructio prægnans :* " completed
to my lord," *i.e.* completely handed over to my lord. נִשְׁאַר לִפְנֵי
is the same : " left before my lord," *i.e.* for us to lay before, or
offer to my lord. " *Why should we die before thine eyes, we and
our land ! Buy us and our land for bread, that we may be, we
and our land, servants* (subject) *to Pharaoh ; and give seed, that
we may live and not die, and the land become not desolate.*" In
the first clause נָמוּת is transferred *per zeugma* to the land ; in the
last, the word תֵּשַׁם is used to describe the destruction of the land.
The form תֵּשַׁם is the same as תֵּקַל in chap. xvi. 4.—Vers. 20, 21.
Thus Joseph secured the possession of the whole land to Pharaoh
by purchase, and " *the people he removed to cities, from one end of
the land of Egypt to the other.*" לֶעָרִים, not from one city to another,
but " according to (= κατά) the cities ;" so that he distributed
the population of the whole land according to the cities in which
the corn was housed, placing them partly in the cities themselves, and partly in the immediate neighbourhood.—Ver. 22.
The lands of the priests Joseph did not buy, " *for the priests
had an allowance from Pharaoh, and ate their allowance, which
Pharaoh gave them ; therefore they sold not their lands.*" חֹק a
fixed allowance of food, as in Prov. xxx. 8 ; Ezek. xvi. 27. This
allowance was granted by Pharaoh probably only during the
years of famine ; in any case it was an arrangement which
ceased when the possessions of the priests sufficed for their need,
since, according to *Diod. Sic.* i. 73, the priests provided the sacrifices and the support of both themselves and their servants from
the revenue of their lands ; and with this *Herodotus* also agrees
(2, 37).—Vers. 23 sqq. Then Joseph said to the people : " *Behold I have bought you this day and your land for Pharaoh ; there
have ye* (הֵא only found in Ezek. xvi. 43 and Dan. ii. 43) *seed, and
sow the land ; and of the produce ye shall give the fifth for Pharaoh,
and four parts* (יָדֹת, as in chap. xliii. 34) *shall belong to you for
seed, and for the support of yourselves, your families and children.*"

The people agreed to this; and the writer adds (ver. 26), it became a law, in existence to this day (his own time), " with regard to the land of Egypt for Pharaoh with reference to the fifth," *i.e.* that the fifth of the produce of the land should be paid to Pharaoh.

Profane writers have given at least an indirect support to the reality of this political reform of Joseph's. *Herodotus,* for example (2, 109), states that king Sesostris divided the land among the Egyptians, giving every one a square piece of the same size as his hereditary possession (κλῆρον), and derived his own revenue from a yearly tax upon them. *Diod. Sic.* (1, 73), again, says that all the land in Egypt belonged either to the priests, to the king, or to the warriors; and *Strabo* (xvii. p. 787), that the farmers and traders held rateable land, so that the peasants were not landowners. On the monuments, too, the kings, priests, and warriors only are represented as having landed property (cf. *Wilkinson,* Manners and Customs i. 263). The biblical account says nothing about the exemption of the warriors from taxation and their possession of land, for that was a later arrangement. According to *Herod.* 2, 168, every warrior had received from former kings, as an honourable payment, twelve choice fields (ἄρουραι) free from taxation, but they were taken away by the Hephæsto-priest *Sethos,* a contemporary of Hezekiah, when he ascended the throne (*Herod.* 2, 141). But when *Herodotus* and *Diodorus Sic.* attribute to *Sesostris* the division of the land into 36 νομοί, and the letting of these for a yearly payment; these comparatively recent accounts simply transfer the arrangement, which was actually made by Joseph, to a half-mythical king, to whom the later legends ascribed all the greater deeds and more important measures of the early Pharaohs. And so far as Joseph's arrangement itself was concerned, not only had he the good of the people and the interests of the king in view, but the people themselves accepted it as a favour, inasmuch as in a land where the produce was regularly thirty-fold, the cession of a fifth could not be an oppressive burden. And it is probable that Joseph not only turned the temporary distress to account by raising the king into the position of sole possessor of the land, with the exception of that of the priests, and bringing the people into a condition of feudal dependence upon him, but had also a still more comprehensive object in view; viz. to secure the population against the danger of starvation in case the crops should fail at any future time, not only by dividing the arable land in equal proportions among the people generally, but, as has been conjectured, by laying the foundation for a system of cultivation regulated by laws and watched over by the state, and possibly also by commencing a system of artificial irrigation by means of canals, for the purpose of conveying the fertilizing water of the Nile as uniformly as possible to all parts of the land. (An explanation of this system is given by *Hengstenberg* in his Dissertations, from the *Correspondance d'Orient par Michaud*, etc.) To mention either these or any other plans of a similar kind, did not come within the scope of the book of Genesis, which restricts itself, in accordance with its purely religious intention, to a description of the way in which, during the years of famine, Joseph proved himself to both the king and people of Egypt to be the true support of the land, so that in him Israel already became a saviour of the Gentiles. The measures taken by Joseph are thus circumstantially described, partly because the relation into which the Egyptians were brought to their visible king bore a typical resemblance to the relation in which the Israelites were placed by the Mosaic constitution to Jehovah, their God-King, since they also had to give a double tenth, *i.e.* the fifth of the produce of their lands, and were in reality only farmers of the soil which Jehovah had given them in Canaan for a possession, so that they could not part with their hereditary possessions in perpetuity (Lev. xxv. 23); and partly also because Joseph's conduct exhibited in type how God entrusts His servants with the good things of this earth, in order that they may use them not only for the preservation of the lives of individuals and nations, but also for the promotion of the purposes of His kingdom. For, as is stated in conclusion in ver. 27, not only did Joseph preserve the lives of the Egyptians, for which they expressed their acknowledgments (ver. 25), but under his administration the house of Israel was able, without suffering any privations, or being brought into a relation of dependence towards Pharaoh, to dwell in the land of Goshen, to establish itself there (נֵאָחֵז as in chap. xxxiv. 10), and to become fruitful and multiply.

JACOB'S LAST WISHES.—CHAP. XLVII. 28–31, AND XLVIII.

Vers. 28–31. Jacob lived in Egypt for 17 years. He then sent for Joseph, as he felt that his death was approaching; and having requested him, as a mark of love and faithfulness, not to bury him in Egypt, but near his fathers in Canaan, he made him assure him on oath (by putting his hand under his hip, *vid.* p. 257) that his wishes should be fulfilled. When Joseph had taken this oath, "*Israel bowed* (in worship) *upon the bed's head.*" He had talked with Joseph while sitting upon the bed; and when Joseph had promised to fulfil his wish, he turned towards the head of the bed, so as to lie with his face upon the bed, and thus worshipped God, thanking Him for granting his wish, which sprang from living faith in the promises of God; just as David also worshipped upon his bed (1 Kings i. 47, 48). The Vulgate rendering is correct: *adoravit Deum conversus ad lectuli caput.* That of the LXX., on the contrary, is προσεκύνησεν Ἰσραὴλ ἐπὶ τὸ ἄκρον τῆς ῥάβδου αὐτοῦ (*i.e.* הַמַּטֶּה); and the *Syriac* and *Itala* have the same (cf. Heb. xi. 21). But no fitting sense can be obtained from this rendering, unless we think of the staff with which Jacob had gone through life, and, taking αὐτοῦ therefore in the sense of αὑτοῦ, assume that Jacob made use of the staff to enable him to sit upright in bed, and so prayed, bent upon or over it, though even then the expression ראש המטה remains a strange one; so that unquestionably this rendering arose from a false reading of המטה, and is not proved to be correct by the quotation in Heb. xi. 21. "*Adduxit enim LXX. Interpr. versionem Apostolus, quod ea tum usitata esset, non quod lectionem illam præferendam judicaret (Calovii* Bibl. illustr. ad h. l.).

Chap. xlviii. 1–7. ADOPTION OF JOSEPH'S SONS.—Vers. 1, 2. After these events, *i.e.* not long after Jacob's arrangements for his burial, it was told to Joseph (וַיֹּאמֶר "one said," cf. ver. 2) that his father was taken ill; whereupon Joseph went to him with his two sons, Manasseh and Ephraim, who were then 18 or 20 years old. On his arrival being announced to Jacob, Israel made himself strong (collected his strength), and sat up on his bed. The change of names is as significant here as in chap. xlv. 27, 28. Jacob, enfeebled with age, gathered up his strength for a work, which he was about to perform as Israel, the bearer of the grace of the promise.—Vers. 3 sqq. Referring to the promise which the Almighty God had given him at Bethel (xxxv. 10 sqq. cf. xxviii. 13 sqq.), Israel said to Joseph (ver. 5): "*And now thy two sons, which were born to thee in the land of Egypt, until* (before) *I came to thee into Egypt . . . let them be mine; Ephraim and Manasseh, like Reuben and Simeon* (my first and second born), *let them be mine.*" The promise which Jacob had received empowered the patriarch to adopt the sons of Joseph in the place of children. Since the Almighty God had promised him the increase of his seed into a multitude of peoples, and Canaan as an eternal possession to that seed, he could so incorporate into the number of his descendants the two sons of Joseph who were born in Egypt before his arrival, and therefore outside the range of his house, that they should receive an equal share in the promised inheritance with his own eldest sons. But this privilege was to be restricted to the two first-born sons of Joseph. "*Thy descendants,*" he proceeds in ver. 6, "*which thou hast begotten since them, shall be thine; by the name of their brethren shall they be called in their inheritance;*" *i.e.* they shall not form tribes of their own with a separate inheritance, but shall be reckoned as belonging to Ephraim and Manasseh, and receive their possessions among these tribes, and in their inheritance. These other sons of Joseph are not mentioned anywhere; but their descendants are at any rate included in the families of Ephraim and Manasseh mentioned in Num. xxvi. 28–37; 1 Chron. vii. 14–29. By this adoption of his two eldest sons, Joseph was placed in the position of the first-born, so far as the inheritance was concerned (1 Chron v. 2). Joseph's mother, who had died so early, was also honoured thereby. And this explains the allusion made by Jacob in ver. 7 to his beloved Rachel, the wife of his affections, and to her death—how she died by his side (עָלַי), on his return from *Padan* (for *Padan-Aram*, the only place in which it is so called, cf. xxv. 20), without living to see her first-born exalted to the position of a saviour to the whole house of Israel.

Vers. 8–22. THE BLESSING OF EPHRAIM AND MANASSEH. —Vers. 8 sqq. Jacob now for the first time caught sight of Joseph's sons, who had come with him, and inquired who they were; for "*the eyes of Israel were heavy* (dim) *with age, so that he could not see well*" (ver. 10). The feeble old man, too, may not have seen the youths for some years, so that he did not recognise them again. On Joseph's answering, "*My sons whom God hath given me here*," he replied, "*Bring them to me then* (קָחֶם־נָא), *that I may bless them;*" and he kissed and embraced them, when Joseph had brought them near, expressing his joy, that whereas he never expected to see Joseph's face again, God had permitted him to see his seed. רָאֹה for רְאוֹת, like עָשׂוֹ (xxxi. 28). פִּלֵּל : to decide; here, to judge, to think.—Vers. 12, 13. Joseph then, in order to prepare his sons for the reception of the blessing, brought them from between the knees of Israel, who was sitting with the youths between his knees and embracing them, and having prostrated himself with his face to the earth, he came up to his father again, with Ephraim the younger on his right hand, and Manasseh the elder on the left, so that Ephraim stood at Jacob's right hand, and Manasseh at his left.—Vers. 14, 15. The patriarch then stretched out his right hand and laid it upon Ephraim's head, and placed his left upon the head of Manasseh (crossing his arms therefore), to bless Joseph in his sons. "*Guiding his hands wittingly;*" *i.e.* he placed his hands in this manner intentionally. Laying on the hand, which is mentioned here for the first time in the Scriptures, was a symbolical sign, by which the person acting transferred to another a spiritual good, a supersensual power or gift; it occurs elsewhere in connection with dedication to an office (Num. xxvii. 18, 23; Deut. xxxiv. 9; Matt. xix. 13; Acts vi. 6, viii. 17, etc.), with the sacrifices, and with the cures performed by Christ and the apostles. By the imposition of hands, Jacob transferred to Joseph in his sons the blessing which he implored for them from his own and his father's God: "*The God (Ha-Elohim) before whom my fathers Abraham and Isaac did walk, the God (Ha-Elohim) who hath fed me* (led and provided for me with a shepherd's faithfulness, Ps. xxiii. 1, xxviii. 9) *from my existence up to this day, the Angel which redeemed me from all evil, bless the lads.*" This triple reference to God, in which the Angel who is placed on an equality with *Ha-Elohim* cannot possibly be a created angel, but must be the "Angel of God," *i.e.* God manifested in the form of the Angel of Jehovah, or the "Angel of His face" (Isa. lxiii. 9), contains a foreshadowing of the Trinity, though only God and the Angel are distinguished, not three

persons of the divine nature. The God before whom Abraham
and Isaac walked, had proved Himself to Jacob to be "the God
which fed" and "the Angel which redeemed," *i.e.* according to
the more fully developed revelation of the New Testament, ὁ Θεός
and ὁ λόγος, Shepherd and Redeemer. By the singular יְבָרֵךְ
(bless, *benedicat*) the triple mention of God is resolved into the
unity of the divine nature. *Non dicit (Jakob) benedicant, plu-*
raliter, nec repetit sed conjungit in uno opere benedicendi tres per-
sonas, Deum Patrem, Deum pastorem et Angelum. Sunt igitur
hi tres unus Deus et unus benedictor. Idem opus facit Angelus
quod pastor et Deus Patrum (Luther). "Let my name be named
on them, and the names of my fathers Abraham and Isaac," *i.e.*
not, "they shall bear my name and my fathers'," "*dicantur filii*
mei et patrum meorum, licet ex te nati sint" (*Rosenm.*), which
would only be another way of acknowledging his adoption of
them, "*nota adoptionis*" (*Calvin*); for as the simple mention of
adoption is unsuitable to such a blessing, so the words appended,
"*and according to the name of my fathers Abraham and Isaac,*"
are still less suitable as a periphrasis for adoption. The thought
is rather: the true nature of the patriarchs shall be discerned
and acknowledged in Ephraim and Manasseh; in them shall
those blessings of grace and salvation be renewed, which Jacob
and his fathers Isaac and Abraham received from God. The
name expressed the nature, and "being called" is equivalent to
"being, and being recognised by what one is." The salvation
promised to the patriarchs related primarily to the multiplication
into a great nation, and the possession of Canaan. Hence
Jacob proceeds: "*and let them increase into a multitude in the*
midst of the land." דָּגָה: ἅπ. λεγ., "to increase," from which the
name דָּג, a fish, is derived, on account of the remarkable rapidity
with which they multiply.—Vers. 17-19. When Joseph observed
his father placing his right hand upon the head of Ephraim, the
younger son, he laid hold of it to put it upon Manasseh's head,
telling his father at the same time that he was the first-born;
but Jacob replied, "*I know, my son, I know: he also* (Manasseh)
will become a nation, and will become great, yet (וְאוּלָם as in xxviii.
19) *his younger brother will become greater than he, and his seed*
will become the fulness of nations." This blessing began to be
fulfilled from the time of the Judges, when the tribe of Ephraim
so increased in extent and power, that it took the lead of the

northern tribes and became the head of the ten tribes, and its name acquired equal importance with the name Israel, whereas under Moses, Manasseh had numbered 20,000 more than Ephraim (Num. xxvi. 34 and 37). As a result of the promises received from God, the blessing was not merely a pious wish, but the actual bestowal of a blessing of prophetic significance and force.—In ver. 20 the writer sums up the entire act of blessing in the words of the patriarch : "*In thee* (*i.e.* Joseph) *will Israel* (as a nation) *bless, saying : God make thee as Ephraim and Manasseh*" (*i.e.* Joseph shall be so blessed in his two sons, that their blessing will become a standing form of benediction in Israel) ; "*and thus he placed Ephraim before Manasseh,*" viz. in the position of his hands and the terms of the blessing. Lastly, (ver. 21) Israel expressed to Joseph his firm faith in the promise, that God would bring back his descendants after his death into the land of their fathers (Canaan), and assigned to him a double portion in the promised land, the conquest of which passed before his prophetic glance as already accomplished, in order to insure for the future the inheritance of the adopted sons of Joseph. "*I give thee one ridge of land above thy brethren*" (*i.e.* above what thy brethren receive, each as a single tribe), "*which I take from the hand of the Amorites with my sword and bow*" (*i.e.* by force of arms). As the perfect is used prophetically, transposing the future to the present as being already accomplished, so the words אֲשֶׁר לָקַחְתִּי must also be understood prophetically, as denoting that Jacob would wrest the land from the Amorites, not in his own person, but in that of his posterity.[1] The words cannot refer to the purchase of the piece of ground at Shechem (xxxiii. 19), for a purchase could not possibly be called a conquest by sword and bow ; and still less to the crime committed by the sons of Jacob against the inhabitants of Shechem, when they plundered the town (xxxiv. 25 sqq.), for Jacob could not

---

[1] There is no force in *Kurtz's* objection, that this gift did not apply to Joseph as the father of Ephraim and Manasseh, but to Joseph personally ; for it rests upon the erroneous assumption, that Jacob separated Joseph from his sons by their adoption. But there is not a word to that effect in ver. 6, and the very opposite in ver. 15, viz. that Jacob blessed Joseph *in* Ephraim and Manasseh. *Heim's* conjecture, which *Kurtz* approves, that by the land given to Joseph we are to understand the high land of Gilead, which Jacob had conquered from the Amorites, needs no refutation, for it is purely imaginary.

possibly have attributed to himself a deed for which he had pronounced a curse upon Simeon and Levi (xlix. 6, 7), not to mention the fact, that the plundering of Shechem was not followed in this instance by the possession of the city, but by the removal of Jacob from the neighbourhood. "Moreover, any conquest of territory would have been entirely at variance with the character of the patriarchal history, which consisted in the renunciation of all reliance upon human power, and a believing, devoted trust in the God of the promises" (*Delitzsch*). The land, which the patriarchs desired to obtain in Canaan, they procured not by force of arms, but by legal purchase (cf. chap. xxiv. and xxxiii. 19). It was to be very different in the future, when the iniquity of the Amorites was full (xv. 16). But Jacob called the inheritance, which Joseph was to have in excess of his brethren, שְׁכֶם (*lit.* shoulder, or more properly nape, neck; here figuratively a ridge, or tract of land), as a play upon the word *Shechem*, because he regarded the piece of land purchased at Shechem as a pledge of the future possession of the whole land. In the piece purchased there, the bones of Joseph were buried, after the conquest of Canaan (Josh. xxiv. 32); and this was understood in future times, as though Jacob had presented the piece of ground to Joseph (*vid.* John iv. 5).

JACOB'S BLESSING AND DEATH.—CHAP. XLIX.

Vers. 1–28. THE BLESSING.—Vers. 1, 2. When Jacob had adopted and blessed the two sons of Joseph, he called his twelve sons, to make known to them his spiritual bequest. In an elevated and solemn tone he said, " *Gather yourselves together, that I may tell you that which shall befall you* (יִקְרָא for יִקְרֶה, as in chap. xlii. 4, 38) *at the end of the days! Gather yourselves together and hear, ye sons of Jacob, and hearken unto Israel your father!*" The last address of Jacob-Israel to his twelve sons, which these words introduce, is designated by the historian (ver. 28) "the blessing," with which "their father blessed them, every one according to his blessing." This blessing is at the same time a prophecy. "Every superior and significant life becomes prophetic at its close" (*Ziegler*). But this was especially the case with the lives of the patriarchs, which were filled and sustained by the promises and revelations of God. As Isaac in his blessing (chap. xxvii.) pointed out prophetically to his two sons, by virtue of divine illumination, the future history of their families; " so Jacob, while blessing the twelve, pictured in grand outlines the *lineamenta* of the future history of the future nation " (*Ziegler*). The groundwork of his prophecy was supplied partly by the natural character of his twelve sons, and partly by the divine promise which had been given by the Lord to him and to his fathers Abraham and Isaac, and that not merely in these two points, the numerous increase of their seed and the possession of Canaan, but in its entire scope, by which Israel had been appointed to be the recipient and medium of salvation for all nations. On this foundation the Spirit of God revealed to the dying patriarch Israel the future history of his seed, so that he discerned in the characters of his sons the future development of the tribes proceeding from them, and with prophetic clearness assigned to each of them its position and importance in the nation into which they were to expand in the promised inheritance. Thus he predicted to the sons what would happen to them " in the last days," *lit.* " at the end of the days " (ἐπ' ἐσχάτων τῶν ἡμερῶν, LXX.), and not merely at some future time. אַחֲרִית, the opposite of רֵאשִׁית, signifies the end in contrast with the beginning (Deut. xi. 12; Isa. xlvi. 10); hence אחרית הימים in prophetic language denoted, not the future generally, but the last future (see *Hengstenberg's* History of Balaam, pp. 465-467, transl.), the Messianic age of consummation (Isa. ii, 2; Ezek. xxxviii. 8, 16; Jer. xxx. 24, xlviii. 47, xlix. 39, etc.: so also Num. xxiv. 14; Deut. iv. 30), like ἐπ' ἐσχάτου τῶν ἡμερῶν (2 Pet. iii. 3; Heb. i. 2), or ἐν ταῖς ἐσχάταις ἡμέραις (Acts ii. 17; 2 Tim. iii. 1). But we must not restrict " the end of the days" to the extreme point of the time of completion of the Messianic kingdom; it embraces " the whole history of the completion which underlies the present period of growth," or " the future as bringing the work of God to its ultimate completion, though modified according to the particular stage to which the work of God had advanced in any particular age, the range of vision opened to that age, and the consequent horizon of the prophet, which, though not absolutely dependent upon it, was to a certain extent regulated by it" (*Delitzsch*).

For the patriarch, who, with his pilgrim-life, had been obliged in the very evening of his days to leave the soil of the promised land and seek a refuge for himself and his house in Egypt, the final future, with its realization of the promises of God, commenced as soon as the promised land was in the possession of the twelve tribes descended from his sons.   He had already before his eyes, in his twelve sons with their children and children's children, the first beginnings of the multiplication of his seed into a great nation.   Moreover, on his departure from Canaan he had received the promise, that the God of his fathers would make him into a great nation, and lead him up again to Canaan (xlvi. 3, 4).   To the fulfilment of this promise his thoughts and hopes, his longings and wishes, were all directed.   This constituted the firm foundation, though by no means the sole and exclusive purport, of his words of blessing.   The fact was not, as *Baumgarten* and *Kurtz* suppose, that Jacob regarded the time of Joshua as that of the completion; that for him the end was nothing more than the possession of the promised land by his seed as the promised nation, so that all the promises pointed to this, and nothing beyond it was either affirmed or hinted at. Not a single utterance announces the capture of the promised land; not a single one points specially to the time of Joshua. On the contrary, Jacob presupposes not only the increase of his sons into powerful tribes, but also the conquest of Canaan, as already fulfilled ; foretells to his sons, whom he sees in spirit as populous tribes, growth and prosperity on the soil in their possession ; and dilates upon their relation to one another in Canaan and to the nations round about, even to the time of their final subjection to the peaceful sway of Him, from whom the sceptre of Judah shall never depart.   The ultimate future of the patriarchal blessing, therefore, extends to the ultimate fulfilment of the divine promises—that is to say, to the completion of the kingdom of God.   The enlightened seer's-eye of the patriarch surveyed, " as though upon a canvas painted without perspective," the entire development of Israel from its first foundation as the nation and kingdom of God till its completion under the rule of the Prince of Peace, whom the nations would serve in willing obedience ; and beheld the twelve tribes spreading themselves out, each in his inheritance, successfully resisting their enemies, and finding rest and full satisfaction in the enjoyment of the blessings of Canaan.

It is in this vision of the future condition of his sons as

grown into tribes that the prophetic character of the blessing consists; not in the prediction of particular historical events, all of which, on the contrary, with the exception of the prophecy of Shiloh, fall into the background behind the purely ideal portraiture of the peculiarities of the different tribes. The blessing gives, in short sayings full of bold and thoroughly original pictures, only general outlines of a prophetic character, which are to receive their definite concrete form from the historical development of the tribes in the future; and throughout it possesses both in form and substance a certain antique stamp, in which its genuineness is unmistakeably apparent. Every attack upon its genuineness has really proceeded from an *a priori* denial of all supernatural prophecies, and has been sustained by such misinterpretations as the introduction of special historical allusions, for the purpose of stamping it as a *vaticinia ex eventu*, and by other untenable assertions and assumptions; such, for example, as that people do not make poetry at so advanced an age or in the immediate prospect of death, or that the transmission of such an oration word for word down to the time of Moses is utterly inconceivable,—objections the emptiness of which has been demonstrated in *Hengstenberg's* Christology i. p. 76 (transl.) by copious citations from the history of the early Arabic poetry.

Vers. 3, 4. REUBEN, *my first-born thou, my might and first-fruit of my strength; pre-eminence in dignity and pre-eminence in power.*—As the first-born, the first sprout of the full virile power of Jacob, Reuben, according to natural right, was entitled to the first rank among his brethren, the leadership of the tribes, and a double share of the inheritance (xxvii. 29; Deut. xxi. 17). (שְׂאֵת: elevation, the dignity of the chieftainship; עָז, the earlier mode of pronouncing עֹז, the authority of the first-born.) But Reuben had forfeited this prerogative. "*Effervescence like water—thou shalt have no preference; for thou didst ascend thy father's marriage-bed: then hast thou desecrated; my couch has he ascended.*" פַּחַז: *lit.* the boiling over of water, figuratively, the excitement of lust; hence the verb is used in Judg. ix. 4, Zeph. iii. 4, for frivolity and insolent pride. With this predicate Jacob describes the moral character of Reuben; and the noun is stronger than the verb פחזת of the Samaritan, and אתרעת or ארתעת *efferbuisti, æstuasti* of the Sam. Vers., ἐξύβρισας of the LXX., and ὑπερζέσας of *Symm.* תּוֹתַר is to be explained by יֶתֶר: have no pre-eminence. His crime was, lying with Bilhah, his father's concubine (xxxv. 22). חִלַּלְתָּ is used absolutely : desecrated hast thou, *sc.* what should have been sacred to thee (cf. Lev. xviii. 8). From this wickedness the injured father turns away with indignation, and passes to the third person as he repeats the words, " my couch he has ascended." By the withdrawal of the rank belonging to the first-born, Reuben lost the leadership in Israel; so that his tribe attained to no position of influence in the nation (compare the blessing of Moses in Deut. xxxiii. 6). The leadership was transferred to Judah, the double portion to Joseph (1 Chron. v. 1, 2), by which, so far as the inheritance was concerned, the first-born of the beloved Rachel took the place of the first-born of the slighted Leah ; not, however, according to the subjective will of the father, which is condemned in Deut. xxi. 15 sqq., but according to the leading of God, by which Joseph had been raised above his brethren, but without the chieftainship being accorded to him.

Vers. 5-7. " SIMEON and LEVI *are brethren :*" emphatically *brethren* in the full sense of the word; not merely as having the same parents, but in their modes of thought and action. " *Weapons of wickedness are their swords.*" The ἅπαξ λεγ. מְכֵרֹת is rendered by *Luther,* etc., weapons or swords, from בָּרָה=כּוּר, to dig, dig through, pierce : not connected with μάχαιρα. *L. de Dieu* and others follow the Arabic and Æthiopic versions : " plans;" but בְּלֵי חָמָס, *utensils,* or instruments, of wickedness, does not accord with this. Such wickedness had the two brothers committed upon the inhabitants of Shechem (xxxiv. 25 sqq.), that Jacob would have no fellowship with it. " *Into their counsel come not, my soul; with their assembly let not my honour unite.*" סוֹד, a council, or deliberative *consessus.* תֵּחַד, *imperf.* of יָחַד; כְּבוֹדִי, like Ps. vii. 6, xvi. 9, etc., of the soul as the noblest part of man, the centre of his personality as the image of God. " *For in their wrath have they slain men, and in their wantonness houghed oxen.*" The singular nouns אִישׁ and שׁוֹר, in the sense of indefinite generality, are to be regarded as general rather than singular, especially as the plural form of both is rarely met with ; of אִישׁ, only in Ps. cxli. 4, Prov. viii. 4, and Isa. liii. 3 ; of שׁוֹר—שְׁוָרִים, only in Hos. xii. 12. רָצוֹן : inclination, here in a bad sense, wantonness. עָקַר : *νευροκοπεῖν*, to sever the houghs (tendons of the hind feet),—a process by which animals were not merely lamed, but rendered useless, since the tendon once severed could never be healed again, whilst as a rule the arteries were not cut so as to cause the animal to bleed to death (cf. Josh. xi. 6, 9; 2 Sam. viii. 4). In chap. xxxiv. 28 it is merely stated that the cattle of the Shechemites were carried off, not that they were lamed. But the one is so far from excluding the other, that it rather includes it in such a case as this, where the sons of Jacob were more concerned about revenge than booty. Jacob mentions the latter only, because it was this which most strikingly displayed their criminal wantonness. On this reckless revenge Jacob pronounces the curse, "*Cursed be their anger, for it was fierce; and their wrath, for it was cruel: I shall divide them in Jacob, and scatter them in Israel.*" They had joined together to commit this crime, and as a punishment they should be divided or scattered in the nation of Israel, should form no independent or compact tribes. This sentence of the patriarch was so fulfilled when Canaan was conquered, that on the second numbering under Moses, Simeon had become the weakest of all the tribes (Num. xxvi. 14); in Moses' blessing (Deut. xxxiii.) it was entirely passed over; and it received no separate assignment of territory as an inheritance, but merely a number of cities within the limits of Judah (Josh. xix. 1–9). Its possessions, therefore, became an insignificant appendage to those of Judah, into which they were eventually absorbed, as most of the families of Simeon increased but little (1 Chron. iv. 27); and those which increased the most emigrated in two detachments, and sought out settlements for themselves and pasture for their cattle outside the limits of the promised land (1 Chron. iv. 38–43). Levi also received no separate inheritance in the land, but merely a number of cities to dwell in, scattered throughout the possessions of his brethren (Josh. xxi. 1–40). But the scattering of Levi in Israel was changed into a blessing for the other tribes through its election to the priesthood. Of this transformation of the curse into a blessing, there is not the slightest intimation in Jacob's address; and in this we have a strong proof of its genuineness. After this honourable change had taken place under Moses, it would never have occurred to any one to cast such a reproach upon the forefather of the Levites. How different is the blessing pronounced by Moses upon Levi (Deut. xxxiii. 8 sqq.)! But though Jacob withdrew the rights of primogeniture from Reuben, and pronounced a curse upon the crime of Simeon and Levi, he deprived none of them of their share in the promised inheritance. They were merely put into the background because of their sins, but they were not excluded from the fellowship and call of Israel, and did not lose the blessing of Abraham, so that their father's utterances with regard to them might still be regarded as the bestowal of a blessing (ver. 28).

Vers. 8–12. JUDAH, the fourth son, was the first to receive a rich and unmixed blessing, the blessing of inalienable supremacy and power. *"Judah thou, thee will thy brethren praise! thy hand in the neck of thy foes! to thee will thy father's sons bow down!"* אתה, *thou,* is placed first as an absolute noun, like אֲנִי in chap. xvii. 4, xxiv. 27; יוֹדוּךָ is a play upon יְהוּדָה like אוֹדֶה in chap. xxix. 35. *Judah,* according to chap. xxix. 35, signifies: he for whom Jehovah is praised, not merely the praised one. "This *nomen,* the patriarch seized as an *omen,* and expounded it as a presage of the future history of Judah." Judah should be in truth all that his name implied (cf. xxvii. 36). Judah had already shown to a certain extent a strong and noble character, when he proposed to sell Joseph rather than shed his blood (xxxvii. 26 seq.); but still more in the manner in which he offered himself to his father as a pledge for Benjamin, and pleaded with Joseph on his behalf (xliii. 9, 10, xliv. 16 sqq.); and it was apparent even in his conduct towards Thamar. In this manliness and strength there slumbered the germs of the future development of strength in his tribe. Judah would put his enemies to flight, grasp them by the neck, and subdue them (Job xvi. 12, cf. Ex. xxiii. 27, Ps. xviii. 41). Therefore his *brethren* would do homage to him: not merely the sons of his mother, who are mentioned in other places (xxvii. 29; Judg. viii. 19), *i.e.* the tribes descended from Leah, but the sons of his father—all the tribes of Israel therefore; and this was really the case under David (2 Sam. v. 1, 2, cf. 1 Sam. xviii. 6, 7, and 16). This princely power Judah acquired through his lion-like nature.—Ver. 9. *"A young lion is Judah; from the prey, my son, art thou gone up: he has lain down; like a lion there he lieth,*

and like a lioness, who can rouse him up!" Jacob compares
Judah to a young, *i.e.* growing lion, ripening into its full
strength, as being the "ancestor of the lion-tribe." But he
quickly rises "to a vision of the tribe in the glory of its perfect
strength," and describes it as a lion which, after seizing prey,
ascends to the mountain forests (cf. Song of Sol. iv. 8), and
there lies in majestic quiet, no one daring to disturb it. To in
tensify the thought, the figure of a lion is followed by that of the
lioness, which is peculiarly fierce in defending its young. The
perfects are prophetic ; and עָלָה relates not to the growth or
gradual rise of the tribe, but to the ascent of the lion to its lair
upon the mountains. "The passage evidently indicates some
thing more than Judah's taking the lead in the desert, and in
the wars of the time of the Judges ; and points to the position
which Judah attained through the warlike successes of David"
(*Knobel*). The correctness of this remark is put beyond question by ver. 10, where the figure is carried out still further, but
in literal terms. "*The sceptre shall not depart from Judah, nor
the ruler's staff from between his feet, till* SHILOH *come and the
willing obedience of the nations be to him.*" The sceptre is the
symbol of regal command, and in its earliest form it was a long
staff, which the king held in his hand when speaking in public
assemblies (*e.g.* Agamemnon, Il. 2, 46, 101) ; and when he sat
upon his throne he rested it between his feet, inclining towards
himself (see the representation of a Persian king in the ruins of
Persepolis, *Niebuhr Reisebeschr.* ii. 145). מְחֹקֵק the determining
person or thing, hence a commander, legislator, and a commander's or ruler's staff (Num. xxi. 18); here in the latter sense,
as the parallels, "sceptre" and "from between his feet," require.
Judah—this is the idea—was to rule, to have the chieftainship,
till Shiloh came, *i.e.* for ever. It is evident that the coming of
Shiloh is not to be regarded as terminating the rule of Judah,
from the last clause of the verse, according to which it was only
then that it would attain to dominion over the nations. עַד כִּי
has not an exclusive signification here, but merely abstracts
what precedes from what follows the given *terminus ad quem*,
as in chap. xxvi. 13, or like עַד אֲשֶׁר chap. xxviii. 15, Ps. cxii. 8,
or עַד Ps. cx. 1, and ἕως Matt. v. 18.

But the more precise determination of the thought contained
in ver. 10 is dependent upon our explanation of the word *Shiloh*.

It cannot be traced, as the *Jerusalem Targum* and the *Rabbins* affirm, to the word שִׁיל *filius* with the suffix ה‏ = וֹ "*his son*," since such a noun as שִׁיל is never met with in Hebrew, and neither its existence nor the meaning attributed to it can be inferred from שִׁלְיָה, afterbirth, in Deut. xxviii. 57. Nor can the paraphrases of *Onkelos* (*donec veniat Messias cujus est regnum*), of the Greek versions (ἕως ἐὰν ἔλθη τὰ ἀποκείμενα αὐτῷ; or ᾧ ἀπόκειται, as *Aquila* and *Symmachus* appear to have rendered it), or of the *Syriac*, etc., afford any real proof, that the defective form שִׁלֹה, which occurs in 20 MSS., was the original form of the word, and is to be pointed שֶׁלֹּה for שֶׁלּוֹ = אֲשֶׁר לוֹ. For apart from the fact, that שׁ for אֲשֶׁר would be unmeaning here, and that no such abbreviation can be found in the Pentateuch, it ought in any case to read שֶׁלּוֹ הוּא " to whom it (the sceptre) is due," since שֶׁלּוֹ alone could not express this, and an ellipsis of הוּא in such a case would be unparalleled. It only remains therefore to follow *Luther*, and trace שִׁילֹה to שָׁלָה, to be quiet, to enjoy rest, security. But from this root *Shiloh* cannot be explained according to the analogy of such forms as קִימֹשׁ, בִּידוֹר. For these forms constitute no peculiar species, but are merely derived from the reduplicated forms, as קִמֹּשׂ, which occurs as well as קִימֹשׁ, clearly shows; moreover they are none of them formed from roots of ל"ה. שִׁילֹה points to שִׁילוֹן, to the formation of nouns with the termination *ôn*, in which the *liquids* are eliminated, and the remaining vowel וֹ is expressed by ה (*Ew.* § 84); as for example in the names of places, שִׁלֹה or שִׁלּוֹ, also שִׁילוֹ (Judg. xxi. 21; Jer. vii. 12) and גִּלֹה (Josh. xv. 51), with their derivatives שִׁילֹנִי (1 Kings xi. 29, xii. 15) and גִּלֹנִי (2 Sam. xv. 12), also אֲבַדֹּה (Prov. xxvii. 20) for אֲבַדֹּון (Prov. xv. 11, etc.), clearly prove. Hence שִׁילֹון either arose from שִׁילֹון (שָׁלָה), or was formed directly from שָׁלָה = שׁוּל, like גִּלֹון from גִּיל. But if שִׁילֹון is the original form of the word, שִׁילֹה cannot be an appellative noun in the sense of rest, or a place of rest, but must be a proper name. For the strong termination *ôn* loses its *n* after *o* only in proper names, like שְׁלֹמֹה, מְגִדֹּו by the side of מְגִדֹּון (Zech. xii. 11) and דֹּורֹו (Judg. x. 1). אֲבַדֹּה forms no exception to this; for when used in Prov. xxvii. 20 as a personification of hell, it is really a proper name. An appellative noun like שִׁילֹה, in the sense of rest, or place of rest, "would be unparalleled in the Hebrew *ihesaurus; the nouns used in this sense are שָׁלֹום, שַׁלְוָה, שֶׁלִי,

מְנֻחָה‏." For these reasons even *Delitzsch* pronounces the appellative rendering, "till rest comes," or till "he comes to a place
of rest," grammatically impossible. *Shiloh* or *Shilo* is a proper
name in every other instance in which it is used in the Old
Testament, and was in fact the name of a city belonging to the
tribe of Ephraim, which stood in the midst of the land of
Canaan, upon an eminence above the village of *Turmus Aya*,
in an elevated valley surrounded by hills, where ruins belonging both to ancient and modern times still bear the name of
Seilûn. In this city the tabernacle was pitched on the conquest
of Canaan by the Israelites under Joshua, and there it remained
till the time of Eli (Judg. xviii. 31; 1 Sam. i. 3, ii. 12 sqq.),
possibly till the early part of Saul's reign.

Some of the Rabbins supposed our *Shiloh* to refer to the city.
This opinion has met with the approval of most of the expositors,
from *Teller* and *Eichhorn* to *Tuch*, who regard the blessing as a
vaticinium ex eventu, and deny not only its prophetic character,
but for the most part its genuineness. *Delitzsch* has also decided
in its favour, because *Shiloh* or *Shilo* is the name of a town in
every other passage of the Old Testament; and in 1 Sam. iv.
12, where the name is written as an accusative of direction, the
words are written exactly as they are here. But even if we do
not go so far as *Hofmann*, and pronounce the rendering "till he
(Judah) come to Shiloh" the most impossible of all renderings,
we must pronounce it utterly irreconcilable with the prophetic
character of the blessing. Even if Shilo existed in Jacob's time
(which can neither be affirmed nor denied), it had acquired no
importance in relation to the lives of the patriarchs, and is not
once referred to in their history; so that Jacob could only have
pointed to it as the goal and turning point of Judah's supremacy
in consequence of a special revelation from God. But in that
case the special prediction would really have been fulfilled: not
only would Judah have come to Shiloh, but there he would
have found permanent rest, and there would the willing subjection of the nations to his sceptre have actually taken place.
Now none of these anticipations are confirmed by history. It is
true we read in Josh. xviii. 1, that after the promised land had
been conquered by the defeat of the Canaanites in the south and
north, and its distribution among the tribes of Israel had commenced, and was so far accomplished, that Judah and the double

tribe of Joseph had received their inheritance by lot, the congregation assembled at Shilo, and there erected the tabernacle, and it was not till after this had been done, that the partition of the land was proceeded with and brought to completion. But although this meeting of the whole congregation at Shilo, and the erection of the tabernacle there, was generally of significance as the turning point of the history, it was of equal importance to all the tribes, and not to Judah alone. If it were to this event that Jacob's words pointed, they should be rendered, " till they come to Shiloh," which would be grammatically allowable indeed, but very improbable with the existing context. And even then nothing would be gained. For, in the first place, up to the time of the arrival of the congregation at Shilo, Judah did not possess the promised rule over the tribes. The tribe of Judah took the first place in the camp and on the march (Num. ii. 3–9, x. 14)—formed in fact the van of the army; but it had no rule, did not hold the chief command. The sceptre or command was held by the Levite Moses during the journey through the desert, and by the Ephraimite Joshua at the conquest and division of Canaan. Moreover, Shilo itself was not the point at which the leadership of Judah among the tribes was changed into the command of nations. Even if the assembling of the congregation of Israel at Shiloh (Josh. xviii. 1) formed so far a turning point between two periods in the history of Israel, that the erection of the tabernacle for a permanent continuance at Shilo was a tangible pledge, that Israel had now gained a firm footing in the promised land, had come to rest and peace after a long period of wandering and war, had entered into quiet and peaceful possession of the land and its blessings, so that Shilo, as its name indicates, became the resting-place of Israel; Judah did not acquire the command over the twelve tribes at that time, nor so long as the house of God remained at Shilo, to say nothing of the submission of the nations. It was not till after the rejection of " the abode of Shiloh," at and after the removal of the ark of the covenant by the Philistines (1 Sam. iv.), with which the " tabernacle of Joseph" was also rejected, that God selected the tribe of Judah and chose David (Ps. lxxviii. 60–72). Hence it was not till after Shiloh had ceased to be the spiritual centre for the tribes of Israel, over whom Ephraim had exercised a kind of rule so long as the central sanctuary of the nation continued in its inheritance, that by David's election as prince (נָגִיד) over Israel the sceptre and the government over the tribes of Israel passed over to the tribe of Judah. Had Jacob, therefore, promised to his son Judah the sceptre or ruler's staff over the tribes until he came to Shiloh, he would have uttered no prophecy, but simply a pious wish, which would have remained entirely unfulfilled.

With this result we ought not to rest contented; unless, indeed, it could be maintained that because *Shiloh* was ordinarily the name of a city, it could have no other signification. But just as many other names of cities are also names of persons, *e.g.* Enoch (iv. 17), and Shechem (xxxiv. 2); so *Shiloh* might also be a personal name, and denote not merely the place of rest, but the man, or bearer, of rest. We regard *Shiloh*, therefore, as a title of the Messiah, in common with the entire Jewish synagogue and the whole Christian Church, in which, although there may be uncertainty as to the grammatical interpretation of the word, there is perfect agreement as to the fact that the patriarch is here proclaiming the coming of the Messiah. " For no objection can really be sustained against thus regarding it as a personal name, in closest analogy to שְׁלֹמֹה " (*Hofmann*). The assertion that *Shiloh* cannot be the subject, but must be the object in this sentence, is as unfounded as the historiological axiom, " that the expectation of a personal Messiah was perfectly foreign to the patriarchal age, and must have been foreign from the very nature of that age," with which *Kurtz* sets aside the only explanation of the word which is grammatically admissible as relating to the personal Messiah, thus deciding, by means of *a priori* assumptions which completely overthrow the supernaturally unfettered character of prophecy, and from a one-sided view of the patriarchal age and history, how much the patriarch Jacob ought to have been able to prophesy. The expectation of a personal Saviour did not arise for the first time with Moses, Joshua, and David, or first obtain its definite form after one man had risen up as the deliverer and redeemer, the leader and ruler of the whole nation, but was contained in the germ in the promise of the seed of the woman, and in the blessing of Noah upon Shem. It was then still further expanded in the promises of God to the patriarchs—" I will bless *thee;* be a blessing, and in *thee* shall all the families of the earth be blessed,"—by which Abraham,

Isaac, and Jacob (not merely the nation to descend from them) were chosen as the personal bearers of that salvation, which was to be conveyed by them through their seed to all nations. When the patriarchal monad was expanded into a dodekad, and Jacob had before him in his twelve sons the founders of the twelve-tribed nation, the question naturally arose, from which of the twelve tribes would the promised Saviour proceed? Reuben had forfeited the right of primogeniture by his incest, and it could not pass over to either Simeon or Levi on account of their crime against the Shechemites. Consequently the dying patriarch transferred, both by his blessing and prophecy, the chieftainship which belonged to the first-born and the blessing of the promise to his fourth son Judah, having already, by the adoption of Joseph's sons, transferred to Joseph the double inheritance associated with the birthright. Judah was to bear the sceptre with victorious lion-courage, until in the future *Shiloh* the obedience of the nations came to him, and his rule over the tribes was widened into the peaceful government of the world. It is true that it is not expressly stated that *Shiloh* was to descend from Judah; but this follows as a matter of course from the context, *i.e.* from the fact, that after the description of Judah as an invincible lion, the cessation of his rule, or the transference of it to another tribe, could not be imagined as possible, and the thought lies upon the surface, that the dominion of Judah was to be perfected in the appearance of *Shiloh*.

Thus the personal interpretation of *Shiloh* stands in the most beautiful harmony with the constant progress of the same revelation. To *Shiloh* will the nations belong. וְלוֹ refers back to שִׁילֹה. יְקָהַת, which only occurs again in Prov. xxx. 17, from יְקָהָה with *dagesh forte euphon.*, denotes the obedience of a son, willing obedience; and עַמִּים in this connection cannot refer to the associated tribes, for Judah bears the sceptre over the tribes of Israel before the coming of *Shiloh*, but to the nations universally. These will render willing obedience to *Shiloh*, because as a man of rest He brings them rest and peace.

As previous promises prepared the way for our prophecy, so was it still further unfolded by the Messianic prophecies which followed ; and this, together with the gradual advance towards fulfilment, places the personal meaning of *Shiloh* beyond all possible doubt.—In the order of time, the prophecy of Balaam stands next, where not only Jacob's proclamation of the lion-nature of Judah is transferred to Israel as a nation (Num. xxiii. 24, xxiv. 9), but the figure of the sceptre from Israel, *i.e.* the ruler or king proceeding from Israel, who will smite all his foes (xxiv. 17), is taken *verbatim* from vers. 9, 10 of this address. In the sayings of Balaam, the tribe of Judah recedes behind the unity of the nation. For although, both in the camp and on the march, Judah took the first place among the tribes (Num. ii. 2, 3, vii. 12, x. 14), this rank was no real fulfilment of Jacob's blessing, but a symbol and pledge of its destination to be the champion and ruler over the tribes. As champion, even after the death of Joshua, Judah opened the attack by divine direction upon the Canaanites who were still left in the land (Judg. i. 1 sqq.), and also the war against Benjamin (Judg. xx. 18). It was also a sign of the future supremacy of Judah, that the first judge and deliverer from the power of their oppressors was raised up to Israel from the tribe of Judah in the person of the Kenizzite Othniel (Judg. iii. 9 sqq.). From that time forward Judah took no lead among the tribes for several centuries, but rather fell back behind Ephraim, until by the election of David as king over all Israel, Judah was raised to the rank of ruling tribe, and received the sceptre over all the rest (1 Chron. xxviii. 4). In David, Judah grew strong (1 Chron. v. 2), and became a conquering lion, whom no one dared to excite. With the courage and strength of a lion, David brought under his sceptre all the enemies of Israel round about. But when God had given him rest, and he desired to build a house to the Lord, he received a promise through the prophet Nathan that Jehovah would raise up his seed after him, and establish the throne of his kingdom for ever (2 Sam. vii. 13 sqq.). " Behold, a son shall be born to thee, who shall be a man of rest; and I (Jehovah) will give him rest from all his enemies round about; for *Solomon* (*i.e. Friederich*, Frederick, the peaceful one) shall be his name, and I will give peace and rest unto Israel in his days . . . and I will establish the throne of his kingdom over Israel for ever." Just as Jacob's prophecy was so far fulfilled in David, that Judah had received the sceptre over the tribes of Israel, and had led them to victory over all their foes; and David upon the basis of this first fulfilment received through Nathan the divine promise, that the sceptre should not depart from his house, and therefore not from Judah; so the commencement of the coming of *Shiloh* received its first fulfilment in the peaceful sway of Solomon, even if David did not give his son the name *Solomon* with an allusion to the predicted Shiloh, which one might infer from the sameness in the meaning of שְׁלֹמֹה and שִׁילֹה when compared with the explanation given of the name Solomon in 1 Chron. xxii. 9, 10. But *Solomon* was not the true *Shiloh.* His peaceful sway was transitory, like the repose which Israel enjoyed under Joshua at the erection of the tabernacle at Shiloh (Josh. xi. 23, xiv. 15, xxi. 44); moreover it extended over Israel alone. The willing obedience of the nations he did not secure; Jehovah only gave rest from his enemies round about in his days, *i.e.* during his life.

But this first imperfect fulfilment furnished a pledge of the complete fulfilment in the future, so that Solomon himself, discerning in spirit the typical character of his peaceful reign, sang of the King's Son who should have dominion from sea to sea, and from the river to the ends of the earth, before whom all kings should bow, and whom all nations should serve (Ps. lxxii.); and the prophets after Solomon prophesied of the Prince of Peace, who should increase government and peace without end upon the throne of David, and of the sprout out of the rod of Jesse, whom the nations should seek (Isa. ix. 5, 6, xi. 1–10); and lastly, Ezekiel, when predicting the downfall of the Davidic kingdom, prophesied that this overthrow would last until He should come to whom the right belonged, and to whom Jehovah would give it (Ezek. xxi. 27). Since Ezekiel in his words, " till He come to whom the right belongs," takes up, as is generally admitted, our prophecy " till Shiloh come," and expands it still further in harmony with the purpose of his announcement, more especially from Ps. lxxii. 1–5, where righteousness and judgment are mentioned as the foundation of the peace which the King's Son would bring; he not only confirms the correctness of the personal and Messianic explanation of the word *Shiloh*, but shows that Jacob's prophecy of the sceptre not passing from Judah till Shiloh came, did not preclude a temporary loss of power. Thus all prophecies, and all the promises of God, in fact, are so fulfilled, as not to preclude the punishment of the sins of the elect, and yet, notwithstanding that punishment, assuredly and completely attain to their ultimate fulfilment. And thus did the kingdom of

Judah arise from its temporary overthrow to a new and imperishable glory in Jesus Christ (Heb. vii. 14), who conquers all foes as the Lion of the tribe of Judah (Rev. v. 5), and reigns as the true Prince of Peace, as "our peace" (Eph. ii. 14), for ever and ever.

In vers. 11 and 12 Jacob finishes his blessing on Judah by depicting the abundance of his possessions in the promised land. "*Binding his she-ass to the vine, and to the choice vine his ass's colt; he washes his garment in wine, and his cloak in the blood of the grape: dull are the eyes with wine, and white the teeth with milk.*" The participle אֹסְרִי has the old connecting vowel, *i*, before a word with a preposition (like Isa. xxii. 16; Mic. vii. 14, etc.); and בְּנִי in the construct state, as in chap. xxxi. 39. The subject is not Shiloh, but Judah, to whom the whole blessing applies. The former would only be possible, if the fathers and *Luther* were right in regarding the whole as an allegorical description of Christ, or if *Hofmann's* opinion were correct, that it would be quite unsuitable to describe Judah, the lion-like warrior and ruler, as binding his ass to a vine, coming so peacefully upon his ass, and remaining in his vineyard. But are lion-like courage and strength irreconcilable with a readiness for peace? Besides, the notion that riding upon an ass is an image of a peaceful disposition seems quite unwarranted; and the supposition that the ass is introduced as an animal of peace, in contrast with the war-horse, is founded upon Zech. ix. 9, and applied to the words of the patriarch in a most unhistorical manner. This contrast did not exist till a much later period, when the Israelites and Canaanites had introduced war-horses, and is not applicable at all to the age and circumstances of the patriarchs, since at that time the only animals there were to ride, beside camels, were asses and she-asses (xxii. 3 cf. Ex. iv. 20, Num. xxii. 21); and even in the time of the Judges, and down to David's time, riding upon asses was a distinction of nobility or superior rank (Judg. i. 14, x. 4, xii. 14; 2 Sam. xix. 27). Lastly, even in vers. 9 and 10 Judah is not depicted as a lion eager for prey, or as loving war and engaged in constant strife, but, according to *Hofmann's* own words, "as having attained, even before the coming of Shiloh, to a rest acquired by victory over surrounding foes, and as seated in his place with the insignia of his dominion." Now, when Judah's conflicts are

over, and he has come to rest, he also may bind his ass to the
vine and enjoy in peaceful repose the abundance of his inheritance. Of wine and milk, the most valuable productions of
his land, he will have such a superabundance, that, as Jacob
hyperbolically expresses it, he may wash his clothes in the blood
of the grape, and enjoy them so plentifully, that his eyes shall
be inflamed with wine, and his teeth become white with milk.[1]
The soil of Judah produced the best wine in Canaan, near
Hebron and Engedi (Num. xiii. 23, 24; Song of Sol. i. 14;
2 Chron. xxvi. 10 cf. Joel i. 7 sqq.), and had excellent pasture land in the desert by Tekoah and Carmel, to the south of
Hebron (1 Sam. xxv. 2; Amos i. 1; 2 Chron. xxvi. 10). סוּתֹה :
contracted from סְוּתֹה, from סָוָה to envelope, synonymous with
מַסְוֶה a veil (Ex. xxxiv. 33).

Ver. 13. ZEBULUN, *to the shore of the ocean will he dwell,
and indeed* (וְהוּא *isque*) *towards the coast of ships, and his side
towards Zidon* (directed up to Zidon)." This blessing on Leah's
sixth son interprets the name *Zebulun* (*i.e.* dwelling) as an *omen*,
not so much to show the tribe its dwelling-place in Canaan, as
to point out the blessing which it would receive from the situation of its inheritance (compare Deut. xxxiii. 19). So far as the
territory allotted to the tribe of Zebulun under Joshua can be
ascertained from the boundaries and towns mentioned in Josh.
xix. 10–16, it neither reached to the Mediterranean, nor touched
directly upon Zidon (see my Comm. on Joshua). It really lay
between the Sea of Galilee and the Mediterranean, near to both,
but separated from the former by Naphtali, from the latter by
Asher. So far was this announcement, therefore, from being a
vaticinium ex eventu taken from the geographical position of the
tribe, that it contains a decided testimony to the fact that
Jacob's blessing was not written after the time of Joshua.
יַמִּים denotes, not the two seas mentioned above, but, as Judg.

[1] *Jam de situ regionis loquitur, quæ sorte filiis Judæ obtigit. Significat
autem tantam illic fore vitium copiam, ut passim obviæ prostent non secus
atque alibi vepres vel infrugifera arbusta. Nam quum ad sepes ligari soleant
asini, vites ad hunc contemptibilem usum aeputat. Eodem pertinet quæ sequuntur hyperbolicæ loquendi formæ, quod Judas lavabit vestem suam in vino, et
oculis erit rubicundus. Tantam enim vini abundantiam fore intelligit, ut
promiscue ad lotiones, perinde ut aqua effundi queat sine magno dispendio;
assiduo autem largioreque illius potu rubedinem contracturi sint oculi.* CALVIN.

v. 17 proves, the Mediterranean, as a great ocean (chap. i. 10). "The coast of ships : " *i.e.* where ships are unloaded, and land the treasures of the distant parts of the world for the inhabitants of the maritime and inland provinces (Deut. xxxiii. 19). *Zidon,* as the old capital, stands for Phœnicia itself.

Vers. 14 and 15. " ISSACHAR *is a bony ass, lying between the hurdles. He saw that rest was a good* (טוֹב *subst.*), *and the land that it was pleasant ; and bowed his shoulder to bear, and became a servant unto tribute.*" The foundation of this award also lies in the name יִשָּׂא שָׂכָר, which is probably interpreted with reference to the character of Issachar, and with an allusion to the relation between שָׂכָר and שָׂכִיר, a daily labourer, as an indication of the character and fate of his tribe. " Ease at the cost of liberty will be the characteristic of the tribe of Issachar" (*Delitzsch*). The *simile* of a bony, *i.e.* strongly-built ass, particularly adapted for carrying burdens, pointed to the fact that this tribe would content itself with material good, devote itself to the labour and burden of agriculture, and not strive after political power and rule. The figure also indicated " that Issachar would become a robust, powerful race of men, and receive a pleasant inheritance which would invite to comfortable repose." (According to *Jos. de bell. jud.* iii. 3, 2, Lower Galilee, with the fruitful table land of Jezreel, was attractive even to τὸν ἥκιστα γῆς φιλόπονον). Hence, even if the simile of a bony ass contained nothing contemptible, it did not contribute to Issachar's glory. Like an idle beast of burden, he would rather submit to the yoke and be forced to do the work of a slave, than risk his possessions and his peace in the struggle for liberty. To bend the shoulder to the yoke, to come down to carrying burdens and become a mere serf, was unworthy of Israel, the nation of God that was called to rule, however it might befit its foes, especially the Canaanites upon whom the curse of slavery rested (Deut. xx. 11; Josh. xvi. 10; 1 Kings ix. 20, 21; Isa. x. 27). This was probably also the reason why Issachar was noticed last among the sons of Leah. In the time of the Judges, however, Issachar acquired renown for heroic bravery in connection with Zebulun (Judg. v. 14, 15, 18). The sons of Leah are followed by the four sons of the two maids, arranged, not according to their mothers or their ages, but accord ing to the blessing pronounced upon them, so that the two warlike tribes stand first.

Vers. 16 and 17. *" Dan will procure his people justice as one of the tribes of Israel. Let Dan become a serpent by the way, a horned adder in the path, that biteth the horse's heels, so that its rider falls back."* Although only the son of a maid-servant, Dan would not be behind the other tribes of Israel, but act according to his name (דָּן יָדִין), and as much as any other of the tribes procure justice to his people (*i.e.* to the people of Israel; not to his own tribe, as *Diestel* supposes). There is no allusion in these words to the office of judge which was held by Samson; they merely describe the character of the tribe, although this character came out in the expedition of a portion of the Danites to Laish in the north of Canaan, a description of which is given in Judg. xviii., as well as in the "romantic chivalry of the brave, gigantic Samson, when with the cunning of the serpent he overthrew the mightiest foes" (*Del.*). שְׁפִיפֹן : κεράστης, the very poisonous horned serpent, which is of the colour of the sand, and as it lies upon the ground, merely stretching out its feelers, inflicts a fatal wound upon any who may tread upon it unawares (*Diod. Sic.* 3, 49; Pliny, 8, 23).

Ver. 18. But this manifestation of strength, which Jacob expected from Dan and promised prophetically, presupposed that severe conflicts awaited the Israelites. For these conflicts Jacob furnished his sons with both shield and sword in the ejaculatory prayer, *"I wait for Thy salvation, O Jehovah!"* which was not a prayer for his own soul and its speedy redemption from all evil, but in which, as *Calvin* has strikingly shown, he expressed his confidence that his descendants would receive the help of his God. Accordingly, the later Targums (*Jerusalem* and *Jonathan*) interpret these words as Messianic, but with a special reference to Samson, and paraphrase ver. 18 thus: "Not for the deliverance of Gideon, the son of Joash, does my soul wait, for that is temporary; and not for the redemption of Samson, for that is transitory; but for the redemption of the Messiah, the Son of David, which Thou through Thy word hast promised to bring to Thy people the children of Israel: for this Thy redemption my soul waits." [1]

_____

[1] This is the reading according to the text of the Jerusalem Targum, in the London Polyglot as corrected from the extracts of *Fagius* in the *Critt.*

Ver. 19. " GAD—*a press presses him, but he presses the heel.*" The name *Gad* reminds the patriarch of גוּד to press, and גְּדוּד the pressing host, warlike host, which invades the land. The attacks of such hosts Gad will bravely withstand, and press their heel, *i.e.* put them to flight and bravely pursue them, not smite their rear-guard ; for עָקֵב does not signify the rear-guard even in Josh. viii. 13, but only the reserves (see my commentary on the passage). The blessing, which is formed from a triple alliteration of the name *Gad*, contains no such special allusions to historical events as to enable us to interpret it historically, although the account in 1 Chron. v. 18 sqq. proves that the Gadites displayed, wherever it was needed, the bravery promised them by Jacob. Compare with this 1 Chron. xii. 8—15, where the Gadites who come to David are compared to lions, and their swiftness to that of roes.

Ver. 20. " *Out of* ASHER (cometh) *fat, his bread, and he yieldeth royal dainties.*" לַחְמוֹ is in apposition to שְׁמֵנָה, and the suffix is to be emphasized : the fat, which comes from him, is his bread, his own food. The saying indicates a very fruitful soil. Asher received as his inheritance the lowlands of Carmel on the Mediterranean as far as the territory of Tyre, one of the most fertile parts of Canaan, abounding in wheat and oil, with which Solomon supplied the household of king Hiram (1 Kings v. 11).

Ver. 21. " NAPHTALI *is a hind let loose, who giveth goodly words.*" The hind or gazelle is a simile of a warrior who is skilful and swift in his movements (2 Sam. ii. 18 ; 1 Chron. xii. 8, cf. Ps. xviii. 33 ; Hab. iii. 19). שְׁלֻחָה here is neither hunted, nor stretched out or grown slim ; but let loose, running freely about (Job xxxix. 5). The meaning and allusion are obscure, since nothing further is known of the history of the tribe of Naphtali, than that Naphtali obtained a great victory under

Sacr., to which the Targum Jonathan also adds, " for Thy redemption, O Jehovah, is an everlasting redemption." But whilst the Targumists and several fathers connect the serpent in the way with Samson, by many others the serpent in the way is supposed to be Antichrist. On this interpretation *Luther* remarks : *Puto Diabolum hujus fabulæ auctorem fuisse et finxisse hanc glossam, ut nostras cogitationes a vero et præsente Antichristo abduceret.*

Barak in association with Zebulun over the Canaanitish king
Jabin, which the prophetess Deborah commemorated in her celebrated song (Judg. iv. and v.). If the first half of the verse be
understood as referring to the independent possession of a tract
of land, upon which Naphtali moved like a hind in perfect freedom, the interpretation of *Masius* (on Josh. xix.) is certainly the
correct one : "*Sicut cervus emissus et liber in herbosa et fertili
terra exultim ludit, ita et in sua fertili sorte ludet et excultabit
Nephtali.*" But the second half of the verse can hardly refer to
"beautiful sayings and songs, in which the beauty and fertility
of their home were displayed." It is far better to keep, as *Vatablius* does, to the general thought : *tribus Naphtali erit fortis-
sima, elegantissima et agillima et erit facundissima.*

Vers. 22–26. Turning to JOSEPH, the patriarch's heart
swelled with grateful love, and in the richest words and figures
he implored the greatest abundance of blessings upon his head.
—Ver. 22. "*Son of a fruit-tree is Joseph, son of a fruit-tree at
the well, daughters run over the wall.*" Joseph is compared to
the branch of a fruit-tree planted by a well (Ps. i. 3), which
sends its shoots over the wall, and by which, according to Ps.
lxxx., we are probably to understand a vine. בֵּן an unusual form
of the construct state for בֶּן, and פֹּרָת equivalent to פֹּרִיָה with the
old feminine termination *ath*, like זִמְרָת, Ex. xv. 2.—בָּנוֹת are the
twigs and branches, formed by the young fruit-tree. The singular צָעֲדָה is to be regarded as distributive, describing poetically
the moving forward, *i.e.* the rising up of the different branches
above the wall (*Ges.* § 146, 4). עֲלֵי, a poetical form, as in ver.
17.—Vers. 23, 24. "*Archers provoke him, and shoot and hate
him; but his bow abides in strength, and the arms of his hands
remain pliant, from the hands of the Mighty One of Jacob, from
thence, from the Shepherd, the Stone of Israel.*" From the simile
of the fruit-tree Jacob passed to a warlike figure, and described
the mighty and victorious unfolding of the tribe of Joseph in
conflict with all its foes, describing with prophetic intuition the
future as already come (*vid.* the *perf. consec.*). The words are
not to be referred to the personal history of Joseph himself, to
persecutions received by him from his brethren, or to his sufferings in Egypt; still less to any warlike deeds of his in Egypt
(*Diestel*) : they merely pointed to the conflicts awaiting his de-

scendants, in which they would constantly overcome all hostile attacks. מָרַר : *Piel*, to embitter, provoke, *lacessere*. רֹבּוּ : *perf.* o from רָבַב to shoot. בְּאֵיתָן : " in a strong, unyielding position " (*Del.*). פָּזַז : to be active, flexible ; only found here, and in 2 Sam. vi. 16 of a brisk movement, skipping or jumping. וְרֹעֵי : the arms, "without whose elasticity the hands could not hold or direct the arrow." The words which follow, " from the hands of the Mighty One of Jacob," are not to be linked to what follows, in opposition to the Masoretic division of the verses ; they rather form one sentence with what precedes : " pliant remain the arms of his hands from the hands of God," *i.e.* through the hands of God supporting them. " The Mighty One of Jacob," He who had proved Himself to be the Mighty One by the powerful defence afforded to Jacob ; a title which is copied from this passage in Isa. i. 24, etc. " From thence," an emphatic reference to Him, from whom all perfection comes— " from the Shepherd (xlviii. 15) and Stone of Israel." God is called " the Stone," and elsewhere " the Rock " (Deut. xxxii. 4, 18, etc.), as the immoveable foundation upon which Israel might trust, might stand firm and impregnably secure.

Vers. 25, 26. "*From the God of thy father, may He help thee, and with the help of the Almighty, may He bless thee,* (may there come) *blessings of heaven from above, blessings of the deep, that lieth beneath, blessings of the breast and of the womb. The blessing of thy father surpass the blessings of my progenitors to the border of the everlasting hills, may they come upon the head of Joseph, and upon the crown of the illustrious among his brethren.*" From the form of a description the blessing passes in ver. 25 into the form of a desire, in which the " from " of the previous clause is still retained. The words " and may He help thee," " may He bless thee," form parentheses, for " who will help and bless thee." וְאֵת is neither to be altered into וְאֵל (and from God), as *Ewald* suggests, in accordance with the LXX., *Sam.*, *Syr.*, and *Vulg.*, nor into מֵאֵת as *Knobel* proposes ; and even the supplying of מִן before אֵת from the parallel clause (*Ges.* § 154, 4) is scarcely allowable, since the repetition of מִן before another preposition cannot be supported by any analogous case ; but אֵת may be understood here, as in chap. iv. 1, v. 24, in the sense of helpful communion : " and with," *i.e.* with (in) the fellowship of, " the Almighty, may He bless thee,

let there be (or come) blessings," etc. The verb תִּהְיֶיןָ follows in
ver. 26 after the whole subject, which is formed of many parallel members. The blessings were to come from heaven above
and from the earth beneath. From the God of Jacob and by
the help of the Almighty should the rain and dew of heaven
(xxvii. 28), and fountains and brooks which spring from the great
deep or the abyss of the earth, pour their fertilizing waters over
Joseph's land, " so that everything that had womb and breast
should become pregnant, bring forth, and suckle." [1] הֹרִים from
הָרָה signifies *parentes* (*Chald.*, *Vulg.*); and תַּאֲוָה signifies not *desiderium* from אָוָה, but boundary from תָּאָה, Num. xxxiv. 7, 8,
= תָּוָה, 1 Sam. xxi. 14, Ezek. ix. 4, to mark or bound off, as most
of the Rabbins explain it. גָּבַר עַל to be strong above, *i.e.* to surpass. The blessings which the patriarch implored for Joseph
were to surpass the blessings which his parents transmitted to
him, to the boundary of the everlasting hills, *i.e.* surpass them
as far as the primary mountains tower above the earth, or so
that they should reach to the summits of the primeval mountains. There is no allusion to the lofty and magnificent
mountain-ranges of Ephraim, Bashan, and Gilead, which fell to
the house of Joseph, either here or in Deut. xxxiii. 15. These
blessings were to descend upon the head of Joseph, the נְזִיר
among his brethren, *i.e.* " the separated one," from נָזַר *separavit*.
Joseph is so designated, both here and Deut. xxxiii. 16, not on
account of his virtue and the preservation of his chastity and
piety in Egypt, but *propter dignitatem, qua excellit, ab omnibus
sit segregatus* (*Calv.*), on account of the eminence to which he
attained in Egypt. For this meaning see Lam. iv. 7 ; whereas
no example can be found of the transference of the idea of
Nasir to the sphere of morality.

Ver. 27. " BENJAMIN—*a wolf, which tears in pieces ; in the
morning he devours prey, and in the evening he divides spoil.*"
Morning and evening together suggest the idea of incessant
and victorious capture of booty (*Del.*). The warlike character
which the patriarch here attributes to Benjamin, was manifested

---

[1] " Thus is the whole composed in pictorial words. Whatever of man and
cattle can be fruitful shall multiply and have enough. Childbearing, and
the increase of cattle, and of the corn in the field, are not our affair, but
the mercy and blessing of God."—*Luther.*

by that tribe, not only in the war which he waged with all the tribes on account of their wickedness in Gibeah (Judg. xx.), but on other occasions also (Judg. v. 14), in its distinguished archers and slingers (Judg. xx. 16; 1 Chron. viii. 40, xii.; 2 Chron. xiv. 8, xvii. 17), and also in the fact that the judge Ehud (Judg. iii. 15 sqq.), and Saul, with his heroic son Jonathan, sprang from this tribe (1 Sam. xi. and xiii. sqq.; 2 Sam. i. 19 sqq.).

The concluding words in ver. 28, " *All these are the tribes of Israel, twelve,*" contain the thought, that in his twelve sons Jacob blessed the future tribes. "*Every one with that which was his blessing, he blessed them,*" *i.e.* every one with his appropriate blessing (אֲשֶׁר *accus.* dependent upon בֵּרַךְ which is construed with a double accusative) ; since, as has already been observed, even Reuben, Simeon, and Levi, though put down through their own fault, received a share in the promised blessing.

Vers. 29–33. DEATH OF JACOB.—After the blessing, Jacob again expressed to his twelve sons his desire to be buried in the sepulchre of his fathers (chap. xxiv.), where Isaac and Rebekah and his own wife Leah lay by the side of Abraham and Sarah, which Joseph had already promised on oath to perform (xlvii. 29–31). He then drew his feet into the bed to lie down, for he had been sitting upright while blessing his sons, and yielded up the ghost, and was gathered to his people (*vid.* xxv. 8). וַיִּגְוַע instead of וַיָּמֹת indicates that the patriarch departed from this earthly life without a struggle. His age is not given here, because that has already been done at chap. xlvii. 28.

BURIAL OF JACOB, AND DEATH OF JOSEPH—CHAP. L.

Vers. 1–14. BURIAL OF JACOB.—Vers. 1–3. When Jacob died, Joseph fell upon the face of his beloved father, wept over him, and kissed him. He then gave the body to the physicians to be embalmed, according to the usual custom in Egypt. The physicians are called his servants, because the reference is to the regular physicians in the service of Joseph, the eminent minister of state ; and according to Herod. 2, 84, there were special physicians in Egypt for every description of disease, among whom the *Taricheuta*, who superintended the embalming, were included,

as a special but subordinate class. The process of embalming
lasted 40 days, and the solemn mourning 70 (ver. 3). This is
in harmony with the statements of Herodotus and Diodorus
when rightly understood (see *Hengstenberg*, Egypt and the Books
of Moses, p. 67 sqq).—Vers. 4, 5. At the end of this period of
mourning, Joseph requested "the house of Pharaoh," *i.e.* the
attendants upon the king, to obtain Pharaoh's permission for him
to go to Canaan and bury his father, according to his last will,
in the cave prepared by him there. כָּרָה (ver. 5) signifies "to
dig" (used, as in 2 Chron. xvi. 14, for the preparation of a tomb),
not "to buy." In the expression כָּרִיתִי לִי Jacob attributes to
himself as patriarch what had really been done by Abraham
(chap. xxiv.). Joseph required the royal permission, because he
wished to go beyond the border with his family and a large procession. But he did not apply directly to Pharaoh, because his
deep mourning (unshaven and unadorned) prevented him from
appearing in the presence of the king.

Vers. 6–9. After the king's permission had been obtained,
the corpse was carried to Canaan, attended by a large company.
With Joseph there went up "*all the servants of Pharaoh, the
elders of his house, and all the elders of the land of Egypt*," *i.e.*
the leading officers of the court and state, "*and all the house of
Joseph, and his brethren, and his father's house*," *i.e.* all the
members of the families of Joseph, of his brethren, and of his
deceased father, "*excepting only their children and flocks; also
chariots and horsemen*," as an escort for the journey through the
desert, "*a very large army.*" The splendid retinue of Egyptian
officers may be explained, in part from the esteem in which
Joseph was held in Egypt, and in part from the fondness of the
Egyptians for such funeral processions (cf. *Hengst.* pp. 70, 71).—
Vers. 10 sqq. Thus they came to *Goren Atad* beyond the Jordan, as the procession did not take the shortest route by Gaza
through the country of the Philistines, probably because so large
a procession with a military escort was likely to meet with difficulties there, but went round by the Dead Sea. There, on the
border of Canaan, a great mourning and funeral ceremony was
kept up for seven days, from which the Canaanites, who watched
it from Canaan, gave the place the name of *Abel-Mizraim*, *i.e.*
meadow (אָבֵל with a play upon אֵבֶל mourning) of the Egyptians.
The situation of *Goren Atad* (the buck-thorn floor), or *Abel-*

Mizraim, has not been discovered. According to ver. 11, it was on the other side, *i.e.* the eastern side, of the Jordan. This is put beyond all doubt by ver. 12, where the sons of Jacob are said to have carried the corpse into the land of Canaan (the land on this side) after the mourning at Goren Atad.[1]—Vers. 12, 13. There the Egyptian procession probably stopped short; for in ver. 12 the sons of Jacob only are mentioned as having carried their father to Canaan according to his last request, and buried him in the cave of Machpelah.—Ver. 14. After performing this filial duty, Joseph returned to Egypt with his brethren and all their attendants.

Vers. 15–21. After their father's death, Joseph's brethren were filled with alarm, and said, *"If Joseph now should punish us and requite all the evil that we have done to him,"* sc. what would become of us! The sentence contains an *aposiopesis,* like Ps. xxvii. 13; and לֹא with the imperfect presupposes a condition, being used "in cases which are not desired, and for the present not real, though perhaps possible" (*Ew.* § 358). The brethren therefore deputed one of their number (possibly Benjamin) to Joseph, and instructed him to appeal to the wish expressed by their father before his death, and to implore forgiveness: " *O pardon the misdeed of thy brethren and their sin, that they have done thee evil; and now grant forgiveness to the misdeed of the servants of the God of thy father."* The ground of their plea is contained in וְעַתָּה " and now," sc. as we request it by the desire and direction of our father, and in the epithet applied to themselves, " servants of the God of thy father." There is no reason whatever for regarding the appeal to their father's wish as a mere pretence. The fact that no reference was made by Jacob

---

[1] Consequently the statement of *Jerome* in the *Onom. s. v. Area Atad—* "locus trans Jordanem, in quo planxerunt quondam Jacob, tertio ab Jerico lapide, duobus millibus ab Jordane, qui nunc vocatur Bethagla, quod interpretatur locus gyri, eo quod ibi more plangentium circumierint in funere Jacob"—is wrong. *Beth Agla* cannot be the same as *Goren Atad,* if only because of the distances given by *Jerome* from Jericho and the Jordan. They do not harmonize at all with his *trans Jordanem,* which is probably taken from this passage, but point to a place on this side of the Jordan; but still more, because *Beth Hagla* was on the frontier of Benjamin towards Judah (Josh. xv. 6, xviii. 19), and its name has been retained in the fountain and tower of *Hajla,* an hour and a quarter to the S.E. of *Riha* (Jericho), and three-quarters of an hour from the Jordan, by which the site of the ancient *Beth Hagla* is certainly determined. (*Vid. Robinson, Pa.. ii. p. 268 sqq.*)

in his blessing to their sin against Joseph, merely proved that
he as their father had forgiven the sin of his sons, since the
grace of God had made their misdeed the means of Israel's salvation; but it by no means proves that he could not have instructed his sons humbly to beg for forgiveness from Joseph,
even though Joseph had hitherto shown them only goodness and
love. How far Joseph was from thinking of ultimate retribution and revenge, is evident from the reception which he gave
to their request (ver. 17) : " *Joseph wept at their address to him,*"
viz. at the fact that they could impute anything so bad to him ;
and when they came themselves, and threw themselves as servants at his feet, he said to them (ver. 19), " *Fear not, for am I
in the place of God?*" *i.e.* am I in a position to interfere of my own
accord with the purposes of God, and not rather bound to submit to them myself? " *Ye had indeed evil against me in your
mind, but God had it in mind for good* (to turn this evil into
good), *to do* (עָשֹׂה like רְאֹה xlviii. 11), *as is now evident* (*lit.* as has
occurred this day, cf. Deut. ii. 30, iv. 20, etc.), *to preserve alive
a great nation* (cf. xlv. 7). *And now fear not, I shall provide for
you and your families.*" Thus he quieted them by his affectionate
words.

Vers. 22–26. DEATH OF JOSEPH.—Joseph lived to see the
commencement of the fulfilment of his father's blessing. Having
reached the age of 110, he saw Ephraim's בְּנֵי שִׁלֵּשִׁים " *sons of the
third link,*" *i.e.* of great-grandsons, consequently great-great-grand-
sons. שִׁלֵּשִׁים descendants in the third generation are expressly distinguished from "children's children" or grandsons in Ex. xxxiv.
7. There is no practical difficulty in the way of this explanation,
the only one which the language will allow. As Joseph's two sons
were born before he was 37 years old (chap. xli. 50), and Ephraim
therefore was born, at the latest, in his 36th year, and possibly
in his 34th, since Joseph was married in his 31st year, he might
have had grandsons by the time he was 56 or 60 years old, and
great-grandsons when he was from 78 to 85, so that great-great-
grandsons might have been born when he was 100 or 110 years
old. To regard the "sons of the third generation" as children
in the third generation (great-grandsons of Joseph and grandsons of Ephraim), as many commentators do, as though the
construct בְּנֵי stood for the absolute, is evidently opposed to the

context, since it is stated immediately afterwards, that sons of
Machir, the son of Manasseh, *i.e.* great-grandsons, were also born
upon his knees, *i.e.* so that he could take them also upon his
knees and show them his paternal love.   There is no reason for
thinking of adoption in connection with these words.   And if
Joseph lived to see only the great-grandsons of Ephraim as well
as of Manasseh, it is difficult to imagine why the same expression
should not be applied to the grandchildren of Manasseh, as to
the descendants of Ephraim.—Ver. 24. When Joseph saw his
death approaching, he expressed to his brethren his firm belief
in the fulfilment of the divine promise (xlvi. 4, 5, cf. xv. 16, 18
sqq.), and made them take an oath, that if God should bring
them into the promised land, they would carry his bones with
them from Egypt.   This last desire of his was carried out.
When he died, they embalmed him, and laid him (וַיִּישֶׂם from
שִׂים, like xxiv. 33 in the *chethib*) " in the coffin," *i.e.* the ordinary
coffin, constructed of sycamore-wood (see *Hengstenberg*, pp. 71,
72), which was then deposited in a room, according to Egyptian
custom (*Herod.* 2, 86), and remained in Egypt for 360 years,
until they carried it away with them at the time of the exodus,
when it was eventually buried in Shechem, in the piece of land
which had been bought by Jacob there (chap. xxxiii. 19 ; Josh.
xxiv. 32).

Thus the account of the pilgrim-life of the patriarchs terminates with an act of faith on the part of the dying Joseph ;
and after his death, in consequence of his instructions, the coffin
with his bones became a standing exhortation to Israel, to turn
its eyes away from Egypt to Canaan, the land promised to its
fathers, and to wait in the patience of faith for the fulfilment of
the promise.

CHRONOLOGICAL SURVEY OF THE LEADING EVENTS OF THE
PATRIARCHAL HISTORY,

*Arranged according to the Hebrew Text, as a continuation of the Chronological
Table at p.* 122, *with an additional calculation of the year before Christ.*

The Events.	Year of Migration to Egypt.	Year of Entrance into Canaan.	Year from the Creation.	Year before Christ.
Abram's entrance into Canaan, . .	...	1	2021	2137
Birth of Ishmael, ...	...	11	2032	2126
Institution of Circumcision, . . .	...	24	2045	2113
Birth of Isaac, ...	...	25	2046	2112
Death of Sarah, ...	...	62	2083	2075
Marriage of Isaac, ...	...	65	2086	2072
Birth of Esau and Jacob, ...	...	85	2106	2052
Death of Abraham, ...	...	100	2121	2037
Marriage of Esau, ...	...	125	2146	2012
Death of Ishmael, ...	...	148	2169	1989
Flight of Jacob to Padan Aram, . .	...	162	2183	1975
Jacob's Marriage, ...	...	169	2190	1968
Birth of Joseph, ...	...	176	2197	1961
Jacob's return from Padan Aram, . .	...	182	2203	1955
Jacob's arrival at Shechem in Canaan,	...	? 187	? 2208	? 1950
Jacob's return home to Hebron, . .	...	192	2213	1945
Sale of Joseph, ...	...	193	2214	1944
Death of Isaac, ...	...	205	2226	1932
Promotion of Joseph in Egypt, . .	...	206	2227	1931
Removal of Israel to Egypt, . . .	1	215	2236	1922
Death of Jacob, ...	17	232	2253	1905
Death of Joseph, ...	71	286	2307	1851
Birth of Moses, ...	350	565	2586	1572
Exodus of Israel from Egypt, . .	430	645	2666	1492

The calculation of the years B.C. is based upon the fact, that
the termination of the 70 years' captivity coincided with the first
year of the sole government of Cyrus, and fell in the year 536
B.C.; consequently the captivity commenced in the year 606 B.C.,
and, according to the chronological data of the books of Kings,
Judah was carried into captivity 406 years after the building
of Solomon's temple commenced, whilst the temple was built
480 years after the exodus from Egypt (1 Kings vi. 1).

THE SECOND BOOK OF MOSES

(EXODUS.)

INTRODUCTION

CONTENTS AND ARRANGEMENT OF THE BOOK OF EXODUS.

THE second book of Moses is called ואלה שמות in the Hebrew Codex from the opening words; but in the Septuagint and Vulgate it has received the name Ἔξοδος, *Exodus*, from the first half of its contents. It gives an account of the first stage in the fulfilment of the promises given to the patriarchs, with reference to the growth of the children of Israel into a numerous people, their deliverance from Egypt, and their adoption at Sinai as the people of God. It embraces a period of 360 years, extending from the death of Joseph, with which the book of Genesis closes, to the building of the tabernacle, at the commencement of the second year after the departure from Egypt. During this period the rapid increase of the children of Israel, which is described in chap. i., and which caused such anxiety to the new sovereigns of Egypt who had ascended the throne after the death of Joseph, that they adopted measures for the enslaving and suppression of the ever increasing nation, continued without interruption. With the exception of this fact, and the birth, preservation, and education of Moses, who was destined by God to be the deliverer of His people, which are circumstantially related in chap. ii., the entire book from chap. iii. to chap. xl. is occupied with an elaborate account of the events of two years, viz. the last year before the departure of the Israelites from Egypt, and the first year of

their journey. This mode of treating the long period in ques
tion, which seems out of all proportion when judged by a merely
outward standard, may be easily explained from the nature and
design of the sacred history. The 430 years of the sojourn of
the Israelites in Egypt were the period during which the immigrant family was to increase and multiply, under the blessing
and protection of God, in the way of natural development; until
it had grown into a nation, and was ripe for that covenant which
Jehovah had made with Abraham, to be completed with the
nation into which his seed had grown. During the whole of this
period the direct revelations from God to Israel were entirely
suspended; so that, with the exception of what is related in chap.
i and ii., no event occurred of any importance to the kingdom
of God. It was not till the expiration of these 400 years, that
the execution of the divine plan of salvation commenced with the
call of Moses (chap. iii.) accompanied by the founding of the
kingdom of God in Israel. To this end Israel was liberated
from the power of Egypt, and, as a nation rescued from human
bondage, was adopted by God, the Lord of the whole earth, as
the people of His possession.

These two great facts of far-reaching consequences in the
history of the world, as well as in the history of salvation, form
the kernel and essential substance of this book, which may be
divided accordingly into two distinct parts. In the *first* part,
chap. i.-xv. 21, we have seven sections, describing (1) the preparation for the saving work of God, through the multiplication of
Israel into a great people and their oppression in Egypt (chap.
i.), and through the birth and preservation of their liberator
(chap. ii.); (2) the call and training of Moses to be the deliverer and leader of Israel (chap. iii. and iv.); (3) the mission
of Moses to Pharaoh (chap. v.-vii. 7); (4) the negotiations
between Moses and Pharaoh concerning the emancipation of
Israel, which were carried on both in words and deeds or miraculous signs (chap. vii. 8-xi.); (5) the consecration of Israel
as the covenant nation through the institution of the feast of
Passover; (6) the exodus of Israel effected through the slaying
of the first-born of the Egyptians (chap. xii.-xiii. 16); and
(7) the passage of Israel through the Red Sea, and destruction
of Pharaoh and his host, with Israel's song of triumph at its
deliverance (xiii. 17-xv. 21).—In the *second* part, chap. xv.

22–xl., we have also seven sections, describing the adoption of Israel as the people of God; viz. (1) the march of Israel from the Red Sea to the mountain of God (chap. xv. 22–xvii. 7); (2) the attitude of the heathen towards Israel, as seen in the hostility of Amalek, and the friendly visit of Jethro the Midianite at Horeb (chap. xvii. 8–xviii.); (3) the establishment of the covenant at Sinai through the election of Israel as the people of Jehovah's possession, the promulgation of the fundamental law and of the fundamental ordinances of the Israelitish commonwealth, and the solemn conclusion of the covenant itself (chap. xix.–xxiv. 11); (4) the divine directions with regard to the erection and arrangement of the dwelling-place of Jehovah in Israel (chap. xxiv. 12–xxxi.); (5) the rebellion of the Israelites and their renewed acceptance on the part of God (chap. xxxii.–xxxiv.); (6) the building of the tabernacle and preparation of holy things for the worship of God (chap. xxxv.–xxxix.); and (7) the setting up of the tabernacle and its solemn consecration (chap. xl.).

These different sections are not marked off, it is true, like the ten parts of Genesis, by special headings, because the account simply follows the historical succession of the events described; but they may be distinguished with perfect ease, through the internal grouping and arrangement of the historical materials. The song of Moses at the Red Sea (chap. xv. 1–21) formed most unmistakeably the close of the first stage of the history, which commenced with the call of Moses, and for which the way was prepared, not only by the enslaving of Israel on the part of the Pharaohs, in the hope of destroying its national and religious independence, but also by the rescue and education of Moses, and by his eventful life. And the setting up of the tabernacle formed an equally significant close to the second stage of the history. By this, the covenant which Jehovah had made with the patriarch Abram (Gen. xv.) was established with the people Israel. By the filling of the dwelling-place, which had just been set up, with the cloud of the glory of Jehovah (Ex. xl. 34–38), the nation of Israel was raised into a congregation of the Lord and the establishment of the kingdom of God in Israel fully embodied in the tabernacle, with Jehovah dwelling in the Most Holy Place; so that all subsequent legislation, and the further progress of the history in the guidance of Israel from

Sinai to Canaan, only served to maintain and strengthen that fellowship of the Lord with His people, which had already been established by the conclusion of the covenant, and symbolically exhibited in the building of the tabernacle. By this marked conclusion, therefore, with a fact as significant in itself as it was important in the history of Israel, Exodus, which commences with a list of the names of the children of Israel who went down to Egypt, is rounded off into a complete and independent book among the five books of Moses.

INCREASE IN THE NUMBER OF THE ISRAELITES.   THEIR BONDAGE IN EGYPT.—CHAP. I.

The promise which God gave to Jacob on his departure from Canaan (Gen. xlvi. 3) was perfectly fulfilled. The children of Israel settled down in the most fruitful province of the fertile land of Egypt, and grew there into a great nation (vers. 1–7). But the words which the Lord had spoken to Abram (Gen. xv. 13) were also fulfilled in relation to his seed in Egypt. The children of Israel were oppressed in a strange land, were compelled to serve the Egyptians (vers. 8–14), and were in great danger of being entirely crushed by them (vers. 15–22).

Vers. 1–7. To place the multiplication of the children of Israel into a strong nation in its true light, as the commencement of the realization of the promises of God, the number of the souls that went down with Jacob to Egypt is repeated from Gen. xlvi. 27 (on the number 70, in which Jacob is included, see the notes on this passage); and the repetition of the names of the twelve sons of Jacob serves to give to the history which follows a character of completeness within itself. " *With Jacob they came, every one and his house,*" *i.e.* his sons, together with their families, their wives, and their children. The sons are arranged according to their mothers, as in Gen. xxxv. 23–26, and the sons of the two maid-servants stand last. Joseph, indeed, is not placed in the list, but brought into special prominence by the words, "*for Joseph was in Egypt*" (ver. 5), since he did not go down to Egypt along with the house of Jacob, and occupied an exalted position in relation to them there.— Vers. 6 sqq. After the death of Joseph and his brethren and the whole of the family that had first immigrated, there occurred that miraculous increase in the number of the children of Israel, by which the blessings of creation and promise were fully realized. The words פָּרוּ, יִשְׁרְצוּ (*swarmed*), and יִרְבּוּ point back to Gen. i. 28 and viii. 17, and יַעֲצְמוּ to גּוֹי עָצוּם in Gen. xviii. 18. " The land was filled with them," *i.e.* the land of Egypt, particularly Goshen, where they were settled (Gen. xlvii. 11). The extraordinary fruitfulness of Egypt in both men and cattle is attested not only by ancient writers, but by modern travellers also (*vid. Aristotelis hist. animal.* vii. 4, 5; *Columella de re rust.* iii. 8; *Plin. hist. n.* vii. 3; also *Rosenmüller a. und n. Morgenland* i. p. 252). This blessing of nature was heightened still further in the case of the Israelites by the grace of the promise, so that the increase became extraordinarily great (see the comm. on chap. xii. 37).

Vers. 8–14. The promised blessing was manifested chiefly in the fact, that all the measures adopted by the cunning of Pharaoh to weaken and diminish the Israelites, instead of checking, served rather to promote their continuous increase.—Ver. 8. " There arose a new king over Egypt, who knew not Joseph." וַיָּקָם signifies he came to the throne, קוּם denoting his appearance in history, as in Deut. xxxiv. 10. A " new king" (LXX.: βασιλεὺς ἕτερος; the other ancient versions, *rex novus*) is a king who follows different principles of government from his predecessors. Cf. אֱלֹהִים חֲדָשִׁים, " new gods," in distinction from the God that their fathers had worshipped, Judg. v. 8; Deut. xxxii. 17. That this king belonged to a new dynasty, as the majority of commentators follow *Josephus*[1] in assuming, cannot be inferred with certainty from the predicate *new;* but it is very probable, as furnishing the readiest explanation of the change in the principles of government. The question itself, however, is of no direct importance in relation to theology, though it has considerable interest in connection with Egyptological researches.[2] The

[1] Ant. ii. 9, 1. Τῆς βασιλείας εἰς ἄλλον οἶκον μεταληλυθυίας.

[2] The want of trustworthy accounts of the history of ancient. Egypt and its rulers precludes the possibility of bringing this question to a decision. It is true that attempts have been made to mix it up in various ways with the

new king did not acknowledge Joseph, *i.e.* his great merits in relation to Egypt. יָדַע לֹא signifies here, not to perceive, or acknowledge, in the sense of not wanting to know anything about him, as in 1 Sam. ii. 12, etc. In the natural course of things, the merits of Joseph might very well have been forgotten long before ; for the multiplication of the Israelites into a numerous people, which had taken place in the meantime, is a sufficient proof that a very long time had elapsed since Joseph's death. At the same time such forgetfulness does not usually take place all at once, unless the account handed down has been inten-

statements which Josephus has transmitted from *Manetho* with regard to the rule of the *Hyksos* in Egypt (*c. Ap.* i. 14 and 26), and the rising up of the "new king" has been identified sometimes with the commencement of the Hyksos rule, and at other times with the return of the native dynasty on the expulsion of the Hyksos. But just as the accounts of the ancients with regard to the Hyksos bear throughout the stamp of very distorted legends and exaggerations, so the attempts of modern inquirers to clear up the confusion of these legends, and to bring out the historical truth that lies at the foundation of them all, have led to nothing but confused and contradictory hypotheses ; so that the greatest Egyptologists of our own days,—viz. *Lepsius*, *Bunsen*, and *Brugsch*—differ throughout, and are even diametrically opposed to one another in their views respecting the dynasties of Egypt. Not a single trace of the Hyksos dynasty is to be found either in or upon the ancient monuments. The documental proofs of the existence of a dynasty of foreign kings, which the Vicomte *de Rougé* thought that he had discovered in the *Papyrus Sallier* No. 1 of the British Museum, and which *Brugsch* pronounced "an Egyptian document concerning the Hyksos period," have since then been declared untenable both by *Brugsch* and *Lepsius*, and therefore given up again. Neither *Herodotus* nor *Diodorus Siculus* heard anything at all about the Hyksos, though the former made very minute inquiry of the Egyptian priests of Memphis and Heliopolis. And lastly, the notices of Egypt and its kings, which we meet with in Genesis and Exodus, do not contain the slightest intimation that there were foreign kings ruling there either in Joseph's or Moses' days, or that the genuine Egyptian spirit which pervades these notices was nothing more than the "outward adoption" of Egyptian customs and modes of thought. If we add to this the unquestionably legendary character of the Manetho accounts, there is always the greatest probability in the views of those inquirers who regard the two accounts given by Manetho concerning the Hyksos as two different forms of one and the same legend, and the historical fact upon which this legend was founded as being the 430 years' sojourn of the Israelites, which had been thoroughly distorted in the national interests of Egypt.—For a further expansion and defence of this view see *Hävernick's Einleitung in d. A. T.* i. 2, pp. 338 sqq., Ed. 2 (Introduction to the Pentateuch, pp. 235 sqq. English translation).

tionally obscured or suppressed. If the new king, therefore, did not know Joseph, the reason must simply have been, that he did not trouble himself about the past, and did not want to know anything about the measures of his predecessors and the events of their reigns. The passage is correctly paraphrased by *Jonathan* thus : *non agnovit* (חַכִּים) *Josephum nec ambulavit in statutis ejus.* Forgetfulness of Joseph brought the favour shown to the Israelites by the kings of Egypt to a close. As they still continued foreigners both in religion and customs, their rapid increase excited distrust in the mind of the king, and induced him to take steps for staying their increase and reducing their strength. The statement that *"the people of the children of Israel"* (עַם בְּנֵי יִשְׂרָאֵל) lit. " nation, viz. the sons of Israel ;" for עַם with the dist. accent is not the construct state, and בני ישראל is in apposition, cf. *Ges. § 113*) were *"more and mightier"* than the Egyptians, is no doubt an exaggeration.—Ver. 10. *" Let us deal wisely with them,"* i.e. act craftily towards them. הִתְחַכֵּם, *sapiensem se gessit* (Eccl. vii. 16), is used here of political craftiness, or worldly wisdom combined with craft and cunning (κατασοφισώμεθα, LXX.), and therefore is altered into הִתְנַכֵּל in Ps. cv. 25 (cf. Gen. xxxvii. 18). The reason assigned by the king for the measures he was about to propose, was the fear that in case of war the Israelites might make common cause with his enemies, and then remove from Egypt. It was not the conquest of his kingdom that he was afraid of, but alliance with his enemies and emigration. עָלָה is used here, as in Gen. xiii. 1, etc., to denote removal from Egypt to Canaan. He was acquainted with the home of the Israelites therefore, and cannot have been entirely ignorant of the circumstances of their settlement in Egypt. But he regarded them as his subjects, and was unwilling that they should leave the country, and therefore was anxious to prevent the possibility of their emancipating themselves in the event of war.— In the form תִּקְרֶאנָה for תִּקְרֶינָה, according to the frequent interchange of the forms ל״ה and ל״א (*vid.* Gen. xlii. 4), נה is transferred from the feminine plural to the singular, to distinguish the 3d pers. fem. from the 2d pers., as in Judg. v. 26, Job xvii. 16 (*vid. Ewald, § 191c,* and *Ges. § 47,* 3, Anm. 3). Consequently there is no necessity either to understand מִלְחָמָה collectively as signifying soldiers, or to regard תִּקְרָאנוּ, the reading adopted by the LXX. (συμβῇ ἡμῖν), the Samaritan, Chaldee,

Syriac, and Vulgate, as " certainly the original," as *Knobel* has done.

The first measure adopted (ver. 11) consisted in the appointment of taskmasters over the Israelites, to bend them down by hard labour. שָׂרֵי מִסִּים bailiffs over the serfs. מִסִּים from מַס signifies, not feudal service, but feudal labourers, serfs (see my Commentary on 1 Kings iv. 6). עִנָּה to bend, to wear out any one's strength (Ps. cii. 24). By hard feudal labour (סִבְלוֹת burdens, burdensome toil) Pharaoh hoped, according to the ordinary maxims of tyrants (*Aristot. polit.* 5, 9 ; *Liv. hist.* i. 56, 59), to break down the physical strength of Israel and lessen its increase, —since a population always grows more slowly under oppression than in the midst of prosperous circumstances,—and also to crush their spirit so as to banish the very wish for liberty.—וַיִּבֶן, and so Israel built (was compelled to build) provision or magazine cities (*vid.* 2 Chron. xxxii. 28, cities for the storing of the harvest), in which the produce of the land was housed, partly for purposes of trade, and partly for provisioning the army in time of war ;—not fortresses, πόλεις ὀχυραί, as the LXX. have rendered it. *Pithom* was Πάτουμος ; it was situated, according to Herodotus (2, 158), upon the canal which commenced above Bybastus and connected the Nile with the Red Sea. This city is called *Thou* or *Thoum* in the *Itiner. Anton.*, the Egyptian article *pi* being dropped, and according to *Jomard* (*descript.* t. 9, p. 368) is to be sought for on the site of the modern *Abassieh* in the Wady Tumilat.—*Raemses* (cf. Gen. xlvii. 11) was the ancient *Heroopolis*, and is not to be looked for on the site of the modern *Belbeis.* In support of the latter supposition, *Stickel*, who agrees with *Kurtz* and *Knobel*, adduces chiefly the statement of the Egyptian geographer *Makrizi*, that in the (Jews') book of the law *Belbeis* is called the land of Goshen, in which Jacob dwelt when he came to his son Joseph, and that the capital of the province was *el Sharkiyeh.* This place is a day's journey (or as others affirm, 14 hours) to the north-east of Cairo on the Syrian and Egyptian road. It served as a meeting-place in the middle ages for the caravans from Egypt to Syria and Arabia (*Ritter, Erdkunde* 14, p. 59). It is said to have been in existence before the Mohammedan conquest of Egypt. But the clue cannot be traced any farther back; and it is too far from the Red Sea for the *Raemses* of the Bible (*vid.* chap. xii. 37). The authority of *Makrizi* is quite counterbalanced by the much older statement of the Septuagint, in which Jacob is made to meet his son Joseph in *Heroopolis;* the words of Gen. xlvi. 29, "and Joseph went up to meet Israel his father *to Goshen*," being rendered thus : εἰς συνάντησιν Ἰσραὴλ τῷ πατρὶ αὐτοῦ καθ' Ἡρώων πόλιν. *Hengstenberg* is not correct in saying that the later name *Heroopolis* is here substituted for the older name *Raemses;* and *Gesenius, Kurtz,* and *Knobel* are equally wrong in affirming that καθ' Ἡρώων πόλιν is supplied *ex ingenio suo ;* but the place of meeting, which is given indefinitely as *Goshen* in the original, is here distinctly named. Now if this more precise definition is not an arbitrary conjecture of the Alexandrian translators, but sprang out of their acquaintance with the country, and is really correct, as *Kurtz* has no doubt, it follows that *Heroopolis* belonged to the γῆ Ῥαμεσσῆ (Gen. xlvi. 28, LXX.), or was situated within it. But this district formed the centre of the Israelitish settlement in Goshen ; for according to Gen. xlvii. 11, Joseph gave his father and brethren "a possession in the best of the land, in the land of *Raemses*." Following this passage, the LXX. have also rendered אֶרֶץ גֹּשֶׁן in Gen. xlvi. 28 by εἰς γῆν Ῥαμεσσῆ, whereas in other places the land of Goshen is simply called γῆ Γεσέμ (Gen. xlv. 10, xlvi. 34, xlvii. 1, etc.). But if *Heroopolis* belonged to the γῆ Ῥαμεσσῆ, or the province of *Raemses*, which formed the centre of the land of Goshen that was assigned to the Israelites, this city must have stood in the immediate neighbourhood of *Raemses*, or have been identical with t. Now, since the researches of the scientific men attached to the great French expedition, it has been generally admitted that *Heroopolis* occupied the site of the modern *Abu Keisheib* in the Wady Tumilat, between *Thoum = Pithom* and the *Birket Temsah* or Crocodile Lake ; and according to the *Itiner.* p. 170, it was only 24 Roman miles to the east of *Pithom*,—a position that was admirably adapted not only for a magazine, but also for the gathering-place of Israel prior to their departure (chap. xii. 37).

But Pharaoh's first plan did not accomplish his purpose (ver. 12). The multiplication of Israel went on just in proportion to the amount of the oppression (כַּ =כַּאֲשֶׁר *prout, ita;* פָּרַץ as in Gen. xxx. 30, xxviii. 14), so that the Egyptians were dismayed at the Israelites (קוץ to feel dismay, or fear, Num. xxii. 3). In this in-

crease of their numbers, which surpassed all expectation, there
was the manifestation of a higher, supernatural, and to them
awful power. But instead of bowing before it, they still endeavoured to enslave Israel through hard servile labour. In
vers. 13, 14 we have not an account of any fresh oppression ;
but "the crushing by hard labour" is represented as enslaving
the Israelites and embittering their lives. פֶּרֶךְ hard oppression,
from the Chaldee פְּרַךְ to break or crush in pieces. "*They em-
bittered their life with hard labour in clay and bricks* (making
clay into bricks, and working with the bricks when made), *and
in all kinds of labour in the field* (this was very severe in Egypt
on account of the laborious process by which the ground was
watered, Deut. xi. 10), אֵת כָּל־עֲבֹדָתָם *with regard to all their labour,
which they worked* (*i.e.* performed) *through them* (viz. the Israelites) *with severe oppression.*" אֵת כל־ע' is also dependent upon
מֵרֲרוּ, as a second accusative (*Ewald,* § 277*d*). Bricks of clay
were the building materials most commonly used in Egypt. The
employment of foreigners in this kind of labour is to be seen
represented in a painting, discovered in the ruins of Thebes,
and given in the Egyptological works of *Rosellini* and *Wilkinson,*
in which workmen who are evidently not Egyptians are occupied
in making bricks, whilst two Egyptians with sticks are standing
as overlookers ;—even if the labourers are not intended for the
Israelites, as the Jewish physiognomies would lead us to suppose. (For fuller details, see *Hengstenberg's* Egypt and the
Books of Moses, p. 80 sqq. English translation).

Vers. 15–21. As the first plan miscarried, the king proceeded
to try a second, and that a bloody act of cruel despotism. He
commanded the midwives to destroy the male children in the
birth and to leave only the girls alive. The midwives named
in ver. 15, who are not Egyptian but Hebrew women, were no
doubt the heads of the whole profession, and were expected to
communicate their instructions to their associates. וַיֹּאמֶר in ver.
16 resumes the address introduced by ויאמר in ver. 15. The expression עַל־הָאָבְנָיִם, of which such various renderings have been
given, is used in Jer. xviii. 3 to denote the revolving table of a
potter, *i.e.* the two round discs between which a potter forms his
earthenware vessels by turning, and appears to be transferred
here to the vagina out of which the child twists itself, as it were
like the vessel about to be formed out of the potter's discs.

Knobel has at length decided in favour of this explanation, at which the Targumists hint with their מַתְבְּרָא. When the mid-wives were called in to assist at a birth, they were to look care-fully at the vagina; and if the child were a boy, they were to destroy it as it came out of the womb. וְחָיָה for חָיָיה from חָיַי, see Gen. iii. 22. The ו takes kametz before the major pause, as in Gen. xliv. 9 (cf. *Ewald*, § 243a).—Ver. 17. But the mid-wives feared God (*ha-Elohim*, the personal, true God), and did not execute the king's command.—Ver. 18. When questioned upon the matter, the explanation which they gave was, that the Hebrew women were not like the delicate women of Egypt, but were חָיוֹת "vigorous" (had much vital energy : *Abenezra*), so that they gave birth to their children before the midwives arrived. They succeeded in deceiving the king with this reply, as childbirth is remarkably rapid and easy in the case of Arabian women (see *Burckhardt, Beduinen,* p. 78 ; *Tischendorf, Reise* i. p. 108).—Vers. 20, 21. God rewarded them for their con-duct, and " made them houses," *i.e.* gave them families and pre-served their posterity. In this sense to " make a house" in 2 Sam. vii. 11 is interchanged with to "build a house" in ver. 27 (*vid.* Ruth iv. 11). לָהֶם for לָהֶן as in Gen. xxxi. 9, etc. Through not carrying out the ruthless command of the king, they had helped to build up the families of Israel, and their own families were therefore built up by God. Thus God rewarded them, " not, however, because they lied, but because they were merci-ful to the people of God ; it was not their falsehood therefore that was rewarded, but their kindness (more correctly, their fear of God), their benignity of mind, not the wickedness of their lying ; and for the sake of what was good, God forgave what was evil." (*Augustine,* contra mendac. c. 19.)

Ver. 22. The failure of his second plan drove the king to acts of open violence. He issued commands to all his subjects to throw every Hebrew boy that was born into the river (*i.e.* the Nile). The fact, that this command, if carried out, would necessarily have resulted in the extermination of Israel, did not in the least concern the tyrant ; and this cannot be adduced as forming any objection to the historical credibility of the narra-tive, since other cruelties of a similar kind are to be found recorded in the history of the world. *Clericus* has cited the conduct of the Spartans towards the helots. Nor can the numbers of the Israelites at the time of the exodus be adduced as a proof that no such murderous command can ever have been issued; for nothing more can be inferred from this, than that the command was neither fully executed nor long regarded, as the Egyptians were not all so hostile to the Israelites as to be very zealous in carrying it out, and the Israelites would certainly neglect no means of preventing its execution. Even Pharaoh's obstinate refusal to let the people go, though it certainly is inconsistent with the intention to destroy them, cannot shake the truth of the narrative, but may be accounted for on psychological grounds, from the very nature of pride and tyranny which often act in the most reckless manner without at all regarding the consequences, or on historical grounds, from the supposition not only that the king who refused the permission to depart was a different man from the one who issued the murderous edicts (cf. chap. ii. 23), but that when the oppression had continued for some time the Egyptian government generally discovered the advantage they derived from the slave labour of the Israelites, and hoped through a continuance of that oppression so to crush and break their spirits, as to remove all ground for fearing either rebellion, or alliance with their foes.

BIRTH AND EDUCATION OF MOSES; FLIGHT FROM EGYPT, AND LIFE IN MIDIAN.—CHAP. II.

Vers. 1–10. BIRTH AND EDUCATION OF MOSES.—Whilst Pharaoh was urging forward the extermination of the Israelites, God was preparing their emancipation. According to the divine purpose, the murderous edict of the king was to lead to the training and preparation of the human deliverer of Israel. —Vers. 1, 2. At the time when all the Hebrew boys were ordered to be thrown into the Nile, " *there went* (הָלַךְ contributes to the pictorial character of the account, and serves to bring out its importance, just as in Gen. xxxv. 22, Deut. xxxi. 1) *a man of the house of Levi*—according to chap. vi. 20 and Num. xxvi. 59, it was Amram, of the Levitical family of Kohath— *and married a daughter* (*i.e.* a descendant) *of Levi*," named Jochebed, who bore him a son, viz. MOSES. From chap. vi. 20 we learn that Moses was not the first child of this marriage, but his brother Aaron; and from ver. 7 of this chapter, it is evident that when Moses was born, his sister Miriam was by no means a child (Num. xxvi. 59). Both of these had been born before the murderous edict was issued (chap. i. 22). They are not mentioned here, because the only question in hand was the birth and deliverance of Moses, the future deliverer of Israel. " *When the mother saw that the child was beautiful*" (טוב as in Gen. vi. 2; LXX. ἀστεῖος), she began to think about his preservation. The very beauty of the child was to her " a peculiar token of divine approval, and a sign that God had some special design concerning him" (*Delitzsch* on Heb. xi. 23). The expression ἀστεῖος τῷ Θεῷ in Acts vii. 20 points to this. She therefore hid the new-born child for three months, in the hope of saving him alive. This hope, however, neither sprang from a revelation made to her husband before the birth of her child, that he was appointed to be the saviour of Israel, as *Josephus* affirms (Ant. ii. 9, 3), either from his own imagination or according to the belief of his age, nor from her faith in the patriarchal promises, but primarily from the natural love of parents for their offspring. And if the hiding of the child is praised in Heb. xi. 23 as an act of faith, that faith was manifested in their not obeying the king's commandment, but fulfilling without fear of man all that was required by that parental love, which God approved, and which was rendered all the stronger by the beauty of the child, and in their confident assurance, in spite of all apparent impossibility, that their effort would be successful (*vid. Delitzsch ut supra*). This confidence was shown in the means adopted by the mother to save the child, when she could hide it no longer. —Ver. 3. She placed the infant in an ark of bulrushes by the bank of the Nile, hoping that possibly it might be found by some compassionate hand, and still be delivered. The *dagesh dirim.* in הַצְּפִינוֹ serves to separate the consonant in which it stands from the syllable which follows (*vid. Ewald*, § 92c; Ges. § 20, 2b). תֵּבַת גֹּמֶא a little chest of rushes. The use of the word תֵּבָה (*ark*) is probably intended to call to mind the ark in which Noah was saved (*vid.* Gen. vi. 14). גֹּמֶא, *papyrus*, the paper reed : a kind of rush which was very common in ancient Egypt, but has almost entirely disappeared, or, as *Pruner* affirms (*ägypt. Naturgesch.* p. 55), is nowhere to be found. It had a triangular stalk about the thickness of a finger, which grew to the height of ten feet; and from this the lighter Nile boats were made, whilst the peeling of the plant was used for sails, mattresses, mats, sandals, and other articles, but chiefly for the preparation of paper (*vid. Celsii Hierobot.* ii. pp. 137 sqq.; *Hengstenberg*, Egypt and the Books of Moses, pp. 85, 86, transl.). וַתַּחְמְרָה, for תַּחְמְרָהּ with mappik omitted : *and cemented* (pitched) *it with* חֵמָר *bitumen,* the asphalt of the Dead Sea, to fasten the papyrus stalks, *and with pitch,* to make it water-tight, *and put it in the reeds by the bank of the Nile,* at a spot, as the sequel shows, where she knew that the king's daughter was accustomed to bathe.   For "the sagacity of the mother led her, no doubt, so to arrange the whole, that the issue might be just what is related in vers. 5–9" (*Baumgarten*).   The daughter stationed herself a little distance off, to see what happened to the child (ver. 4).   This sister of Moses was most probably the Miriam who is frequently mentioned afterwards (Num. xxvi. 59). תֵּתַצַּב for תְּתִיצַּב.   The infinitive form דֵּעָה as in Gen. xlvi. 3.—Ver. 5. Pharaoh's daughter is called *Thermouthis* or *Merris* in Jewish tradition, and by the Rabbins בתיה. עַל־הַיְאֹר is to be connected with תֵּרֶד, and the construction with עַל to be explained as referring to the descent into (upon) the river from the rising bank.   The fact that a king's daughter should bathe in the open river is certainly opposed to the customs of the modern, Mohammedan East, where this is only done by women of the lower orders, and that in remote places (*Lane*, Manners and Customs); but it is in harmony with the customs of ancient Egypt,[1] and in perfect agreement with the notions of the early Egyptians respecting the sanctity of the Nile, to which divine honours even were paid (*vid. Hengstenberg's* Egypt, etc. pp. 109, 110), and with the belief, which was common to both ancient and modern Egyptians, in the power of its waters to impart fruitfulness and prolong life (*vid. Strabo,* xv. p. 695, etc., and *Seetzen,* Travels iii. p. 204).

Vers. 6 sqq. The exposure of the child at once led the king's daughter to conclude that it was *one of the Hebrews' children.* The fact that she took compassion on the weeping child, and notwithstanding the king's command (i. 22) took it up and had it brought up (of course, without the knowledge of the king), may be accounted for from the love to children which is innate

---

[1] *Wilkinson* gives a picture of a bathing scene, in which an Egyptian woman of rank is introduced, attended by four female servants.

in the female sex, and the superior adroitness of a mother's heart, which co-operated in this case, though without knowing or intending it, in the realization of the divine plan of salvation. *Competens fuit divina vindicta, ut suis affectibus puniatur parricida et filiæ provisione pereat qui genitrices interdixerat parturire* (*August.* Sermo 89 de temp.).—Ver. 9. With the directions, " *Take this child away* (הֵילִיכִי for הוֹלִיכִי used here in the sense of leading, bringing, carrying away, as in Zech. v. 10, Eccl. x. 20) *and suckle it for me*," the king's daughter gave the child to its mother, who was unknown to her, and had been fetched as a nurse.—Ver. 10. When the child had grown large, *i.e.* had been weaned (יִגְדַּל as in Gen. xxi. 8), the mother, who acted as nurse, brought it back to the queen's daughter, who then adopted it as her own son, and called it *Moses* (מֹשֶׁה) : " *for*," she said, " *out of the water have I drawn him*" (מְשִׁיתִהוּ). As Pharaoh's daughter gave this name to the child as her adopted son, it must be an Egyptian name. The Greek form of the name, Μωϋσῆς (LXX.), also points to this, as *Josephus* affirms. " Thermuthis," he says, " imposed this name upon him, from what had happened when he was put into the river ; for the Egyptians call water MO, and those who are rescued from the water USES " (Ant. ii. 9, 6, Whiston's translation). The correctness of this statement is confirmed by the Coptic, which is derived from the old Egyptian.[1] Now, though we find the name explained in the text from the Hebrew מָשָׁה, this is not to be regarded as a philological or etymological explanation, but as a theological interpretation, referring to the importance of the person rescued from the water to the Israelitish nation. In the lips of an Israelite, the name *Mouje*, which was so little suited to the Hebrew organs of speech, might be involuntarily altered into *Moshe;* " and this transformation became an unintentional prophecy, for the person *drawn out* did become, in fact, the *drawer out*" (*Kurtz*). Consequently *Knobel's* supposition, that the writer regarded מֹשֶׁה as a participle *Poal* with the מ dropped, is to be rejected as inadmissible.—There can be no doubt that, as the adopted son of

---

[1] *Josephus* gives a somewhat different explanation in his book against Apion (i. 31), when he says, " His true name was Moüses, and signifies a person who is rescued from the water, for the Egyptians call water Moü." Other explanations, though less probable ones, are attempted by *Gesenius* in his *Thes.* p. 824, and *Knobel in loc.*

Pharaoh's daughter, Moses received a thoroughly Egyptian training, and was educated in all the wisdom of the Egyptians, as Stephen states in Acts vii. 22 in accordance with Jewish tradition.[1] Through such an education as this, he received just the training required for the performance of the work to which God had called him. Thus the wisdom of Egypt was employed by the wisdom of God for the establishment of the kingdom of God.

Vers. 11-20. FLIGHT OF MOSES FROM EGYPT TO MIDIAN. —The education of Moses at the Egyptian court could not extinguish the feeling that he belonged to the people of Israel. Our history does not inform us how this feeling, which was inherited from his parents and nourished in him when an infant by his mother's milk, was fostered still further after he had been handed over to Pharaoh's daughter, and grew into a firm, decided consciousness of will. All that is related is, how this consciousness broke forth at length in the full-grown man, in the slaying of the Egyptian who had injured a Hebrew (vers. 11, 12), and in the attempt to reconcile two Hebrew men who were quarrelling (vers. 13, 14). Both of these occurred " in those days," i.e. in the time of the Egyptian oppression, when Moses had become great (יִגְדַּל as in Gen. xxi. 20), i.e. had grown to be a man. According to tradition he was then forty years old (Acts vii. 23). What impelled him to this was not " a carnal ambition and longing for action," or a desire to attract the attention of his brethren, but fiery love to his brethren or fellow-countrymen, as is shown in the expression, " one of his brethren " (ver. 11), and deep sympathy with them in their oppression and sufferings ; whilst, at the same time, they undoubtedly displayed the fire of his impetuous nature, and the ground-work for his future calling. It was from this point of view that Stephen cited these facts (Acts vii. 25, 26), for the purpose of proving to the Jews of his own age, that they had been from time immemorial " stiff-necked and uncircumcised in heart and ears " (ver. 51). And this view is the correct one. Not only did Moses

---

[1] The tradition, on the other hand, that Moses was a priest of Heliopolis, named *Osarsiph* (*Jos. c. Ap.* i. 26, 28), is just as unhistorical as the legend of his expedition against the Ethiopians (Jos. Ant. ii. 10), and many others with which the later, glorifying Saga embellished his life in Egypt.

intend to help his brethren when he thus appeared among them, but this forcible interference on behalf of his brethren could and should have aroused the thought in their minds, that God would send them salvation through him. " But they understood not" (Acts vii. 25). At the same time Moses thereby declared that he would no longer " be called the son of Pharaoh's daughter ; and chose rather to suffer affliction with the people of God, than to enjoy the pleasures of sin for a season ; esteeming the reproach of Christ greater riches than the treasures of Egypt" (Heb. xi. 24–26 ; see *Delitzsch in loc.*). And this had its roots in faith ($\pi \iota \sigma \tau \epsilon \iota$). But his conduct presents another aspect also, which equally demands consideration. His zeal for the welfare of his brethren urged him forward to present himself as the umpire and judge of his brethren before God had called him to this, and drove him to the crime of murder, which cannot be excused as resulting from a sudden ebullition of wrath.[1] For he acted with evident deliberation. " *He looked this way and that way; and when he saw no one, he slew the Egyptian, and hid him in the sand*" (ver. 12). Through his life at the Egyptian court his own natural inclinations had been formed to rule, and they manifested themselves on this occasion in an ungodly way. This was thrown in his teeth by the man " in the wrong" (הָרָשָׁע, ver. 13), who was striving with his brother and doing him an

---

[1] The judgment of *Augustine* is really the true one. Thus, in his *c. Faustum Manich.* l. 22, c. 70, he says, " I affirm, that the man, though criminal and really the offender, ought not to have been put to death by one who had no legal authority to do so. But minds that are capable of virtues often produce vices also, and show thereby for what virtue they would have been best adapted, if they had but been properly trained. For just as farmers, when they see large herbs, however useless, at once conclude that the land is good for growing corn, so that very impulse of the mind which led Moses to avenge his brother when suffering wrong from a native, without regard to legal forms, was not unfitted to produce the fruits of virtue, but, though hitherto uncultivated, was at least a sign of great fertility." *Augustine* then compares this deed to that of Peter, when attempting to defend his Lord with a sword (Matt. xxvi. 51), and adds, " Both of them broke through the rules of justice, not through any base inhumanity, but through animosity that needed correction : both sinned through their hatred of another's wickedness, and their love, though carnal, in the one case towards a brother, in the other to the Lord. This fault needed pruning or rooting up ; but yet so great a heart could be as readily cultivated for bearing virtues, as land for bearing fruit."

injury: " Who made thee a ruler and judge over us " (ver. 14) ?
and so far he was right.   The murder of the Egyptian had also
become known ; and as soon as Pharaoh heard of it, he sought
to kill Moses, who fled into the land of Midian in fear for his
life (ver. 15).   Thus dread of Pharaoh's wrath drove Moses from
Egypt into the desert.   For all that, it is stated in Heb. xi. 27,
that " by faith ($\pi\iota\sigma\tau\epsilon\iota$) Moses forsook Egypt, not fearing the
wrath of the king."   This faith, however, he manifested not by
fleeing—his flight was rather a sign of timidity—but by leaving
Egypt ; in other words, by renouncing his position in Egypt,
where he might possibly have softened down the king's wrath,
and perhaps even have brought help and deliverance to his
brethren the Hebrews.   By the fact that he did not allow such
human hopes to lead him to remain in Egypt, and was not
afraid to increase the king's anger by his flight, he manifested
faith in the invisible One as though he saw Him, commending
not only himself, but his oppressed nation, to the care and protection of God (*vid. Delitzsch* on Heb. xi. 27).

   The situation of the land of MIDIAN, to which Moses fled,
cannot be determined with certainty.   The Midianites, who were
descended from Abraham through Keturah (Gen. xxv. 2, 4),
had their principal settlements on the eastern side of the Elanitic
Gulf, from which they spread northwards into the fields of
Moab (Gen. xxxvi. 35 ; Num. xxii. 4, 7, xxv. 6, 17, xxxi. 1 sqq. ;
Judg. vi. 1 sqq.), and carried on a caravan trade through Canaan
to Egypt (Gen. xxxvii. 28, 36 ; Isa. lx. 6).   On the eastern side
of the Elanitic Gulf, and five days' journey from Aela, there
stood the town of *Madian*, the ruins of which are mentioned
by *Edrisi* and *Abulfeda*, who also speak of a well there, from
which Moses watered the flocks of his father-in-law *Shoeib* (*i.e.*
Jethro).   But we are precluded from fixing upon this as the
home of Jethro by Ex. iii. 1, where Moses is said to have come
to Horeb, when he drove Jethro's sheep behind the desert.   The
Midianites on the eastern side of the Elanitic Gulf could not
possibly have led their flocks as far as Horeb for pasturage.   We
must assume, therefore, that one branch of the Midianites, to
whom Jethro was priest, had crossed the Elanitic Gulf, and
settled in the southern half of the peninsula of Sinai (cf. chap.
iii. 1).   There is nothing improbable in such a supposition.
There are several branches of the Towara Arabs occupying the

southern portion of Arabia, that have sprung from Hedjas in this way; and even in the most modern times considerable intercourse was carried on between the eastern side of the gulf and the peninsula, whilst there was formerly a ferry between *Szytta, Madian,* and *Nekba.*—The words " *and he sat down* (וַיֵּשֶׁב, *i.e.* settled) *in the land of Midian, and sat down by the well,*" are hardly to be understood as simply meaning that " when he was dwelling in Midian, he sat down one day by a well " (*Baumg.*), but that immediately upon his arrival in Midian, where he intended to dwell or stay, he sat down by the well. The definite article before בְּאֵר points to the well as the only one, or the principal well in that district. *Knobel* refers to " the well at *Sherm* ; " but at *Sherm el Moye* (*i.e.* water-bay) or *Sherm el Bir* (well-bay) there are " several deep wells finished off with stones," which are " evidently the work of an early age, and have cost great labour " (*Burckhardt,* Syr. p. 854) ; so that the expression " *the* well " would be quite unsuitable. Moreover there is but a very weak support for *Knobel's* attempt to determine the site of Midian, in the identification of the Μαρανῖται or Μαρανεῖς (of *Strabo* and *Artemidorus*) with *Madyan.*

Vers. 16. sqq. Here Moses secured for himself a hospitable reception from a priest of Midian, and a home at his house, by doing as Jacob had formerly done (Gen xxix. 10), viz. helping his daughters to water their father's sheep, and protecting them against the other shepherds.—On the form יוֹשִׁעֶן for יוֹשִׁעַן *vid.* Gen. xix. 19 ; and for the masculine suffixes to יְגָרְשׁוּם and צֹאנָם, Gen. xxxi. 9. תִּדְלֶנָה for תִּדְלֶינָה, as in Job v. 12, cf. *Ewald,* § 198a. —The flock of this priest consisted of nothing but צֹאן, *i.e.* sheep and goats (*vid.* chap. iii. 1). Even now there are no oxen reared upon the peninsula of Sinai, as there is not sufficient pasturage or water to be found. For the same reason there are no horses kept there, but only camels and asses (cf. *Seetzen,* R. iii. 100; *Wellsted,* R. in Arab. ii. p. 66). In ver. 18 the priest is called *Reguel,* in chap. iii. 1 *Jethro.* This title, " the priest of Midian," shows that he was the spiritual head of the branch of the Midianites located there, but hardly that he was the prince or temporal head as well, like Melchizedek, as the Targumists have indicated by רבא, and as *Artapanus* and the poet *Ezekiel* distinctly affirm. The other shepherds would hardly have treated the daughters of the Emir in the manner described in ver. 17.

The name רְעוּאֵל (*Reguel*, friend of God) indicates that this priest served the old Semitic God *El* (אֵל). This *Reguel*, who gave his daughter Zipporah to Moses, was unquestionably the same person as *Jethro* (יִתְרוֹ) the חֹתֵן of Moses and priest of Midian (chap. iii. 1). Now, as *Reguel's* son *Chobab* is called Moses' חֹתֵן in Num. x. 29 (cf. Judg. iv. 11), the Targumists and others supposed *Reguel* to be the grandfather of Zipporah, in which case אָב would mean the grandfather in ver. 18, and בַּת the granddaughter in ver. 21. This hypothesis would undoubtedly be admissible, if it were probable on other grounds. But as a comparison of Num. x. 29 with Ex. xviii. does not necessarily prove that *Chobab* and *Jethro* were the same persons, whilst Ex. xviii. 27 seems to lead to the very opposite conclusion, and חֹתֵן, like the Greek γαμβρός, may be used for both father-in-law and brother-in-law, it would probably be more correct to regard *Chobab* as Moses' brother-in-law, *Reguel* as the proper name of his father-in-law, and *Jethro*, for which *Jether* (*præstantia*) is substituted in chap. iv. 18, as either a title, or the surname which showed the rank of Reguel in his tribe, like the Arabic *Imam*, *i.e. præpositus*, *spec. sacrorum antistes*. *Ranke's* opinion, that *Jethro* and *Chobab* were both of them sons of Reguel and brothers-in-law of Moses, is obviously untenable, if only on the ground that according to the analogy of Num. x. 29 the epithet " son of Reguel " would not be omitted in chap. iii. 1.

Vers. 21-25. MOSES' LIFE IN MIDIAN.—As Reguel gave a hospitable welcome to Moses, in consequence of his daughters' report of the assistance that he had given them in watering their sheep; it pleased Moses (וַיּוֹאֶל) to dwell with him. The primary meaning of הוֹאִיל is *voluit* (*vid. Ges. thes.*). קְרָאֶן for קְרָאנָה: like שְׁמַעַן in Gen. iv. 23.—Although Moses received Reguel's daughter Zipporah as his wife, probably after a lengthened stay, his life in Midian was still a banishment and a school of bitter humiliation. He gave expression to this feeling at the birth of his first son in the name which he gave it, viz. *Gershom* (גֵּרְשֹׁם, *i.e.* banishment, from גָּרַשׁ to drive or thrust away); " *for*," he said, interpreting the name according to the sound, " *I have been a stranger* (גֵּר) *in a strange land.*" In a strange land he was obliged to live, far away from his brethren in Egypt, and far from his fathers' land of promise ; and in this strange land the longing for home seems to have been still further increased by his wife Zipporah, who, to judge from chap. iv. 24 sqq., neither understood nor cared for the feelings of his heart. By this he was urged on to perfect and unconditional submission to the will of his God. To this feeling of submission and confidence he gave expression at the birth of his second son, by calling him *Eliezer* (אֱלִיעֶזֶר, God is help) ; for he said, " *The God of my father* (Abraham or the three patriarchs, cf. iii. 6) *is my help, and has delivered me from the sword of Pharaoh* " (xviii. 4). The birth of this son is not mentioned in the Hebrew text, but his name is given in chap. xviii. 4, with this explanation.[1] In the names of his two sons, Moses expressed all that had affected his mind in the land of Midian. The pride and self-will with which he had offered himself in Egypt as the deliverer and judge of his oppressed brethren, had been broken down by the feeling of exile. This feeling, however, had not passed into despair, but had been purified and raised into firm confidence in the God of his fathers, who had shown himself as his helper by delivering him from the sword of Pharaoh. In this state of mind, not only did "his attachment to his people, and his longing to rejoin them, instead of cooling, grow stronger and stronger " (*Kurtz*), but the hope of the fulfilment of the promise given to the fathers was revived within him, and ripened into the firm confidence of faith.

Vers. 23–25 form the introduction to the next chapter. The cruel oppression of the Israelites in Egypt continued without intermission or amelioration. " *In those many days the king of Egypt died, and the children of Israel sighed by reason of the service*" (*i.e.* their hard slave labour). The "*many days*" are the years of oppression, or the time between the birth of Moses and the birth of his children in Midian. The king of Egypt who died, was in any case the king mentioned in ver. 15 ; but whether he was one and the same with the "*new king*" (i. 8), or a successor of his, cannot be decided. If the former were the case, we should have to assume, with *Baumgarten*, that the death of the king took place not very long after Moses' flight, seeing that

---

[1] In the Vulgate the account of his birth and name is interpolated here, and so also in some of the later codices of the LXX. But in the oldest and best of the Greek codices it is wanting here, so that there is no ground for the supposition that it has fallen out of the Hebrew text.

he was an old man at the time of Moses' birth, and had a grown-up daughter. But the greater part of the "many days" would then fall in his successor's reign, which is obviously opposed to the meaning of the words, "It came to pass in those many days, that the king of Egypt died." For this reason the other supposition, that the king mentioned here is a successor of the one mentioned in chap. i. 8, has far greater probability. At the same time, all that can be determined from a comparison of chap. vii. 7 is, that the Egyptian oppression lasted more than 80 years. This allusion to the complaints of the Israelites, in connection with the notice of the king's death, seems to imply that they hoped for some amelioration of their lot from the change of government; and that when they were disappointed, and groaned the more bitterly in consequence, they cried to God for help and deliverance. This is evident from the remark, "*Their cry came up unto God,*" and is stated distinctly in Deut. xxvi. 7.—Vers. 24, 25. *God heard their crying, and remembered His covenant with the fathers: "and God saw the children of Israel, and God noticed* (them)." "This seeing and noticing had regard to the innermost nature of Israel, namely, as the chosen seed of Abraham" (*Baumgarten*). God's notice has all the energy of love and pity. *Lyra* has aptly explained וַיֵּדַע thus: "*ad modum cognoscentis se habuit, ostendendo dilectionem circa eos;*" and *Luther* has paraphrased it correctly: "He accepted them."

CALL OF MOSES, AND HIS RETURN TO EGYPT.— CHAP. III. AND IV.

Chap. iii. 1-iv. 18. CALL OF MOSES.—Whilst the children of Israel were groaning under the oppression of Egypt, God had already prepared the way for their deliverance, and had not only chosen Moses to be the saviour of His people, but had trained him for the execution of His designs.—Ver. 1. When Moses was keeping the flock of Jethro, his father-in-law, he drove them on one occasion behind the desert, and came to the mountains of Horeb. הָיָה רֹעֶה, lit. "*he was feeding:*" the participle expresses the continuance of the occupation. אַחַר הַמִּדְבָּר does not mean *ad interiora deserti* (*Jerome*); but Moses drove the sheep from Jethro's home as far as Horeb, so that he passed through a desert with the flock before he reached the pasture land of Horeb. For "in this, the most elevated ground of the peninsula, you find the most fertile valleys, in which even fruit-trees grow. Water abounds in this district; consequently it is the resort of all the Bedouins when the lower countries are dried up" (*Rosenmüller*). Jethro's home was separated from Horeb, therefore, by a desert, and is to be sought to the south-east, and not to the north-east. For it is only a south-easterly situation that will explain these two facts : *First*, that when Moses returned from Midian to Egypt, he touched again at Horeb, where Aaron, who had come from Egypt, met him (iv. 27) ; and, *secondly*, that the Israelites never came upon any Midianites on their journey through the desert, whilst the road of Hobab the Midianite separated from theirs as soon as they departed from Sinai (Num. x. 30).[1] *Horeb* is called the Mount of God by anticipation, with reference to the consecration which it subsequently received through the revelation of God upon its summit. The supposition that it had been a holy locality even before the calling of Moses, cannot be sustained. Moreover, the name is not restricted to one single mountain, but applies to the central group of mountains in the southern part of the peninsula (*vid.* chap. xix. 1). Hence the spot where God appeared to Moses cannot be precisely determined, although tradition has very suitably given the name *Wady Shoeib, i.e.* Jethro's Valley, to the valley which bounds the *Jebel Musa* towards the east, and separates it from the *Jebel ed Deir*, because it is there that Moses is supposed to have fed the flock of Jethro. The monastery of Sinai, which is in this valley, is said to have been built upon the spot where the thorn-bush stood, according to the tradition in *Antonini Placent. Itinerar.* c. 37, and the annals of *Eutychius* (*vid. Robinson*, Palestine).

Vers. 2–5. Here, at Horeb, God appeared to Moses as the Angel of the Lord (*vid.* p. 185) "*in a flame of fire out of the midst of the thorn-bush*" (סְנֶה, βάτος, *rubus*), which burned in the fire and was not consumed. אָכַל, in combination with אֵינֶנּוּ, must be a participle for מְאֻכָּל. When Moses turned aside from the road

---

[1] The hypothesis, that, after the calling of Moses, this branch of the Midianites left the district they had hitherto occupied, and sought out fresh pasture ground, probably on the eastern side of the Elanitic Gulf, is as needless as it is without support.

or spot where he was standing, *" to look at this great sight"* (מַרְאֶה),
i.e. the miraculous vision of the bush that was burning and yet not
burned up, Jehovah called to him out of the midst of the thorn-
bush, *" Moses, Moses* (the reduplication as in Gen. xxii. 11),
*draw not nigh hither : put off thy shoes from off thy feet, for the
place whereon thou standest is holy ground"* (אֲדָמָה). The symbolical meaning of this miraculous vision,—that is to say, the
fact that it was a figurative representation of the nature and
contents of the ensuing message from God,—has long been admitted.   The thorn-bush in contrast with the more noble and
lofty trees (Judg. ix. 15) represented the people of Israel in their
humiliation, as a people despised by the world.   Fire and the
flame of fire were not " symbols of the holiness of God ;" for,
as the Holy One, " God is light, and in Him is no darkness at
all" (1 John i. 5), He " dwells in the light which no man can
approach unto" (1 Tim. vi. 16) ; and that not merely according
to the New Testament, but according to the Old Testament view
as well, as is evident from Isa. x. 17, where "the Light of Israel"
and "the Holy One of Israel" are synonymous.   But " the Light
of Israel became fire, and the Holy One a flame, and burned
and consumed its thorns and thistles."   Nor is " fire, from its
very nature, the source of light," according to the scriptural
view.   On the contrary, light, the condition of all life, is also
the source of fire.   The sun enlightens, warms, and burns (Job
xxx. 28 ; Sol. Song i. 6) ; the rays of the sun produce warmth,
heat, and fire ; and light was created before the sun.   Fire,
therefore, regarded as burning and consuming, is a figurative
representation of refining affliction and destroying punishment
(1 Cor. iii. 11 sqq.), or a symbol of the chastening and punitive
justice of the indignation and wrath of God.   It is in fire that
the Lord comes to judgment (Dan. vii. 9, 10 ; Ezek. i. 13, 14,
27, 28 ; Rev. i. 14, 15).   Fire sets forth the fiery indignation
which devours the adversaries (Heb. x. 27).   He who " judges
and makes war in righteousness" has eyes as a flame of fire
(Rev. xix. 11, 12).   Accordingly, the burning thorn-bush represented the people of Israel as they were burning in the fire of
affliction, the iron furnace of Egypt (Deut. iv. 20).   Yet, though
the thorn-bush was burning in the fire, it was not consumed ; for
in the flame was Jehovah, who chastens His people, but does
not give them over unto death (Ps. cxviii. 18).   The God of

Abraham, Isaac, and Jacob had come down to deliver His people out of the hand of the Egyptians (ver. 8). Although the affliction of Israel in Egypt proceeded from Pharaoh, yet was it also a fire which the Lord had kindled to purify His people and prepare it for its calling. In the flame of the burning bush the Lord manifested Himself as the "jealous God, who visits the sins of the fathers upon the children unto the third and fourth generations of them that hate Him, and showeth mercy unto thousands of them that love Him and keep His commandments' (chap. xx. 5; Deut. v. 9, 10), who cannot tolerate the worship of another god (xxxiv. 14), and whose anger burns against idolaters, to destroy them (Deut. vi. 15). The "jealous God" was a "consuming fire" in the midst of Israel (Deut. iv. 24). These passages show that the great sight which Moses saw not only had reference to the circumstances of Israel in Egypt, but was a prelude to the manifestation of God on Sinai for the establishment of the covenant (chap. xix. and xx.), and also a representation of the relation in which Jehovah would stand to Israel through the establishment of the covenant made with the fathers. For this reason it occurred upon the spot where Jehovah intended to set up His covenant with Israel. But, as a jealous God, He also "takes vengeance upon His adversaries" (Nahum i. 2 sqq.). Pharaoh, who would not let Israel go, He was about to smite with all His wonders (iii. 20), whilst He redeemed Israel with outstretched arm and great judgments (vi. 6).—The transition from the *Angel of Jehovah* (ver. 2) to *Jehovah* (ver. 4) proves the identity of the two; and the interchange of *Jehovah* and *Elohim*, in ver. 4, precludes the idea of Jehovah being merely a national God. The command of God to Moses to put off his shoes, may be accounted for from the custom in the East of wearing shoes or sandals merely as a protection from dirt. No Brahmin enters a pagoda, no Moslem a mosque, without first taking off at least his overshoes (*Rosenm.* Morgenl. i. 261; *Robinson*, Pal. ii. p. 373); and even in the Grecian temples the priests and priestesses performed the service barefooted (*Justin*, Apol. i. c. 62; *Bähr*, Symbol. ii. 96). When entering other holy places also, the Arabs and Samaritans, and even the Yezidis of Mesopotamia, take off their shoes, that the places may not be defiled by the dirt or dust upon them (*vid. Robinson*, Pal. iii. 100, and *Layard's* Nineveh and its Remains). The place of the burning bush was

holy because of the presence of the holy God, and putting off
the shoes was intended to express not merely respect for the
place itself, but that reverence which the inward man (Eph. iii.
16) owes to the holy God.

Ver. 6. Jehovah then made Himself known to Moses as the
God of his fathers, Abraham, Isaac, and Jacob, reminding him
through that name of the promises made to the patriarchs, which
He was about to fulfil to their seed, the children of Israel. In
the expression, " thy father," the three patriarchs are classed
together as one, just as in chap. xviii. 4 (" my father "), " because each of them stood out singly in distinction from the
nation, as having received the promise of seed directly from
God" (*Baumgarten*). "*And Moses hid his face, for he was afraid
to look upon God.*" The sight of the holy God no sinful man
can bear (cf. 1 Kings xix. 12).—Vers. 7–10. Jehovah had seen
the affliction of His people, had heard their cry under their taskmasters, and had come down (יָרַד, *vid.* Gen. xi. 5) to deliver them
out of the hand of the Egyptians, and to bring them up to a
good and broad land, to the place of the Canaanites ; and He
was about to send Moses to Pharaoh to bring them forth. The
land to which the Israelites were to be taken up is called a "*good*"
land, on account of its great fertility (Deut. viii. 7 sqq.), and a
"*broad*" land, in contrast with the confinement and oppression
of the Israelites in Egypt. The epithet "*good*" is then explained
by the expression, "*a land flowing with milk and honey* " (זָבַת,
a participle of זוב in the construct state ; *vid. Ges.* § 135) ; a proverbial description of the extraordinary fertility and loveliness
of the land of Canaan (cf. ver. 17, chap. xiii. 5, xvi. 14, etc.).
Milk and honey are the simplest and choicest productions of a
land abounding in grass and flowers, and were found in Palestine in great abundance even when it was in a desolate condition (Isa. vii. 15, 22 ; see my Comm. on Josh. v. 6). The
epithet broad is explained by an enumeration of the six tribes
inhabiting the country at that time (cf. Gen. x. 15 sqq. and xv.
20, 21).—Vers. 11, 12. To the divine commission Moses made
this reply : " *Who am I, that I should go to Pharaoh, and bring
forth the children of Israel out of Egypt?*" Some time before
he had offered himself of his own accord as a deliverer and
judge ; but now he had learned humility in the school of Midian,
and was filled in consequence with distrust of his own power and

fitness. The son of Pharaoh's daughter had become a shepherd, and felt himself too weak to go to Pharaoh. But God met this distrust by the promise, "*I will be with thee*," which He confirmed by a sign, namely, that when Israel was brought out of Egypt, they should serve (עָבַד, *i.e.* worship) God upon that mountain. This sign, which was to be a pledge to Moses of the success of his mission, was one indeed that required faith itself : but, at the same time, it was a sign adapted to inspire both courage and confidence. God pointed out to him the success of his mission, the certain result of his leading the people out: Israel should serve Him upon the very same mountain in which He had appeared to Moses. As surely as Jehovah had appeared to Moses as the God of his fathers, so surely should Israel serve Him there. The reality of the appearance of God formed the pledge of His announcement, that Israel would there serve its God ; and this truth was to fill Moses with confidence in the execution of the divine command. The expression "serve God" (λατρεύειν τῷ Θεῷ, LXX.) means something more than the *immolare* of the *Vulgate*, or the "sacrifice" of *Luther;* for even though sacrifice formed a leading element, or the most important part of the worship of the Israelites, the patriarchs before this had served Jehovah by calling upon His name as well as offering sacrifice. And the service of Israel at Mount Horeb consisted in their entering into covenant with Jehovah (chap. xxiv.) ; not only in their receiving the law as the covenant nation, but their manifesting obedience by presenting free-will offerings for the building of the tabernacle (chap. xxxvi. 1–7 ; Num. vii.).[1]

[1] *Kurtz* follows the Lutheran rendering "*sacrifice*," and understands by it the first national sacrifice ; and then, from the significance of the first, which included potentially all the rest, supposes the covenant sacrifice to be intended. But not only is the original text disregarded here, the fact is also overlooked, that *Luther* himself has translated עבד correctly, to " serve," in every other place. And it is not sufficient to say, that by the direction of God (iii. 18) Moses first of all asked Pharaoh for permission merely to go a three days' journey into the wilderness to sacrifice to their God (v. 1–3), in consequence of which Pharaoh afterwards offered to allow them to sacrifice (viii. 3) within the land, and at a still later period outside (viii. 21 sqq.). For the fact that Pharaoh merely spoke of sacrificing may be explained on the ground that at first nothing more was asked. But this first demand arose from the desire on the part of God to make known His purposes concerning Israel only step by step, that it might be all the easier for the hard heart of the king to grant what was required. But even if Pharaoh under-

Vers. 13–15. When Moses had been thus emboldened by the assurance of divine assistance to undertake the mission, he inquired what he was to say, in case the people asked him for the name of the God of their fathers. The supposition that the people might ask the name of their fathers' God is not to be attributed to the fact, that as the Egyptians had separate names for their numerous deities, the Israelites also would want to know the name of their own God. For, apart from the circumstance that the name by which God had revealed Himself to the fathers cannot have vanished entirely from the memory of the people, and more especially of Moses, the mere knowledge of the name would not have been of much use to them. The question, "What is His name?" presupposed that the name expressed the nature and operations of God, and that God would manifest in deeds the nature expressed in His name. God therefore told him His name, or, to speak more correctly, He explained the name יהוה, by which He had made Himself known to Abraham at the making of the covenant (Gen. xv. 7), in this way, אֶהְיֶה אֲשֶׁר אֶהְיֶה, "I am that I am," and designated Himself by this name as the absolute God of the fathers, acting with unfettered liberty and self-dependence (cf. pp. 74–6). This name precluded any comparison between the God of the Israelites and the deities of the Egyptians and other nations, and furnished Moses and his people with strong consolation in their affliction, and a powerful support to their confidence in the realization of His purposes of salvation as made known to the fathers. To establish them in this confidence, God added still further: "This is My name for ever, and My memorial unto all generations;" that is to say, God would even manifest Himself in the nature expressed by the name Jehovah, and by this He would have all generations both know and revere Him. שֵׁם, the name, expresses the objective manifestation of the divine nature; זֵכֶר, memorial, the subjective recognition of that nature on the part of men. דֹּר דֹּר, as in chap. xvii. 16 and Prov. xxvii. 24. The repetition of the same word suggests the idea of uninterrupted continuance and

stood nothing more by the expression "serve God" than the offering of sacrifice, this would not justify us in restricting the words which Jehovah addressed to Moses, " When thou hast brought forth the people out of Egypt, ye shall serve God upon this mountain," to the first national offering, or to the covenant sacrifice.

boundless duration (*Ewald*, § 313*a*). The more usual expression is דֹּר וָדֹר, Deut. xxxii. 7 ; Ps. x. 6, xxxiii. 11 ; or דֹּר דֹּרִים, Ps. lxxii. 5, cii. 25 ; Isa. li. 8.

Vers. 16–20. With the command, "*Go and gather the elders of Israel together*," God then gave Moses further instructions with reference to the execution of his mission. On his arrival in Egypt he was first of all to inform the elders, as the representatives of the nation (*i.e.* the heads of the families, households, and tribes), of the appearance of God to him, and the revelation of His design, to deliver His people out of Egypt and bring them to the land of the Canaanites. He was then to go with them to Pharaoh, and make known to him their resolution, in consequence of this appearance of God, to go a three days' journey into the wilderness and sacrifice to their God. The words, "*I have surely visited*," point to the fulfilment of the last words of the dying Joseph (Gen. l. 24). נִקְרָה עָלֵינוּ (ver. 18) does not mean "He is named upon us" (LXX., *Onk., Jon.*), nor "He has called us" (*Vulg., Luth.*). The latter is grammatically wrong, for the verb is *Niphal*, or passive ; and though the former has some support in the parallel passage in chap. v. 3, inasmuch as נִקְרָא is the verb used there, it is only in appearance, for if the meaning really were "His name is named upon (over) us," the word שְׁמוֹ (שֵׁם) would not be omitted (*vid.* Deut. xxviii. 10 ; 2 Chron. vii. 14). The real meaning is, "*He has met with us*," from נִקְרָה, *obruam fieri*, ordinarily construed with אֶל, but here with עַל, because God comes down from above to meet with man. The plural *us* is used, although it was only to Moses that God appeared, because His appearing had reference to the whole nation, which was represented before Pharaoh by Moses and the elders. In the words נֵלֲכָה־נָּא, "*we will go, then*," equivalent to "let us go," the request for Pharaoh's permission to go out is couched in such a form as to answer to the relation of Israel to Pharaoh. He had no right to detain them, but he had a right to consent to their departure, as his predecessor had formerly done to their settlement. Still less had he any good reason for refusing their request to go a three days' journey into the wilderness and sacrifice to their God, since their return at the close of the festival was then taken for granted. But the purpose of God was, that Israel should not return. Was it the case, then, that the delegates were "to deceive the king," as *Knobel* affirms ?

By no means. God knew the hard heart of Pharaoh, and therefore directed that no more should be asked at first than he must
either grant, or display the hardness of his heart. Had he consented, God would then have made known to him His whole
design, and demanded that His people should be allowed to
depart altogether. But when Pharaoh scornfully refused the
first and smaller request (chap. v.), Moses was instructed to
demand the entire departure of Israel from the land (vi. 10), and
to show the omnipotence of the God of the Hebrews before and
upon Pharaoh by miracles and heavy judgments (vii. 8 sqq.).
Accordingly, Moses persisted in demanding permission for the
people to go and serve their God (vii. 16, 26, viii. 16, ix. 1, 13,
x. 3) ; and it was not till Pharaoh offered to allow them to sacrifice in the land that Moses replied, " We will go three days'
journey into the wilderness, and sacrifice to Jehovah our God"
(viii. 27) ; but, observe, with this proviso, " as He shall command
us," which left, under the circumstances, no hope that they would
return. It was an act of mercy to Pharaoh, therefore, on the
one hand, that the entire departure of the Israelites was not demanded at the very first audience of Moses and the representatives of the nation ; for, had this been demanded, it would have
been far more difficult for him to bend his heart in obedience to
the divine will, than when the request presented was as trifling
as it was reasonable. And if he had rendered obedience to the
will of God in the smaller, God would have given him strength
to be faithful in the greater. On the other hand, as God foresaw his resistance (ver. 19), this condescension, which demanded
no more than the natural man could have performed, was also
to answer the purpose of clearly displaying the justice of God.
It was to prove alike to Egyptians and Israelites that Pharaoh
was " without excuse," and that his eventual destruction was
the well-merited punishment of his obduracy.[1] וְלֹא בְּיָד חֲזָקָה, " not
even by means of a strong hand;" " except through great power"
is not the true rendering, for וְלֹא does not mean ἐὰν μή, nisi.
What follows,—viz. the statement that God would so smite the

---

[1] "This moderate request was made only at the period of the earlier
plagues. It served to put Pharaoh to the proof. God did not come forth
with His whole plan and desire at first, that his obduracy might appear
so much the more glaring, and find no excuse in the greatness of the re-
quirement. Had Pharaoh granted this request, Israel would not have gone

Egyptians with miracles that Pharaoh would, after all, let Israel go (ver. 20),—is not really at variance with this, the only admissible rendering of the words. For the meaning is, that Pharaoh would not be willing to let Israel depart even when he should be smitten by the strong hand of God; but that he would be compelled to do so against his will, would be forced to do so by the plagues that were about to fall upon Egypt. Thus even after the ninth plague it is still stated (chap. x. 27), that "Pharaoh would (אבה) not let them go;" and when he had given permission, in consequence of the last plague, and in fact had driven them out (xii. 31), he speedily repented, and pursued them with his army to bring them back again (xiv. 5 sqq.); from which it is clearly to be seen that the strong hand of God had not broken his will, and yet Israel was brought out by the same strong hand of Jehovah.

Vers. 21, 22. Not only would God compel Pharaoh to let Israel go; He would not let His people go out empty, but, according to the promise in Gen. xv. 14, with great substance. "*I will give this people favour in the eyes of the Egyptians;*" that is to say, the Egyptians should be so favourably disposed towards them, that when they solicited of their neighbours clothes and ornaments of gold and silver, their request should be granted. "*So shall ye spoil the Egyptians.*" What is here foretold as a promise, the Israelites are directed to do in chap. xi. 2, 3; and according to chap. xii. 35, 36, it was really carried out. Immediately before their departure from Egypt, the Israelites asked (וִשְׁאֲלוּ) the Egyptians for gold and silver ornaments (כֵּלִים not vessels, either for sacrifice, the house, or the table, but jewels; cf. Gen. xxiv. 53; Ex. xxxv. 22; Num. xxxi. 50) and clothes; and God gave them favour in the eyes of the Egyptians, so that they gave them to them. For שְׁאֵלָה אִשָּׁה, "*Let every woman ask of her* (female) *neighbour and of her that sojourneth in her house*" (גָּרַת בֵּיתָהּ, from which it is evident that the Israelites did not live apart, but along with the Egyptians), we find in chap. xi. 2, "*Let every man ask of his neighbour, and every woman of her* (female) *neighbour.*"—וְשַׂמְתֶּם, "*and put them upon your sons and*

beyond it; but had not God foreseen, what He repeatedly says (compare, for instance, chap. iii. 18), that he would not comply with it, He would not thus have presented it; He would from the beginning have revealed His whole design. Thus *Augustine* remarks (*quæst.* 13 in Ex.)." *Hengstenberg,* Diss. on the Pentateuch, vol. ii. p. 427, Ryland's translation. Clark, 1847.

daughters." שׂוּם עַל, to put on, applied to clothes and ornaments in Lev. viii. 8 and Gen. xli. 42.   This command and its execution have frequently given occasion to the opponents of the Scriptures to throw contempt upon the word of God, the asking being regarded as borrowing, and the spoiling of the Egyptians as purloining.   At the same time, the attempts made to vindicate this purloining from the wickedness of stealing have been in many respects unsatisfactory.[1]   But the only meaning of שָׁאַל is to ask or beg,[2] and הִשְׁאִיל, which is only met with in chap. xii. 36 and 1 Sam. i. 28, does not mean to lend, but to suffer to ask, to hear and grant a request.   וַיַּשְׁאִלוּם (chap. xii. 36), *lit.* they allowed them to ask; *i.e.* "the Egyptians did not turn away the petitioners, as not wanting to listen to them, but received their petition with good-will, and granted their request.   No proof can be brought that הִשְׁאִיל means to *lend*, as is commonly supposed; the word occurs again in 1 Sam. i. 28, and there it means to grant or give" (*Knobel* on chap. xii. 36).   Moreover the circumstances under which the שָׁאַל and הִשְׁאִיל took place, were quite at variance with the idea of borrowing and lending.   For even if Moses had not spoken without reserve of the entire departure of the Israelites, the plagues which followed one after another, and with which the God of the Hebrews gave emphasis to His demand as addressed through Moses to Pharaoh, "Let My people go, that they may serve Me," must have made it evident to every Egyptian, that all this had reference to something greater than a three days' march to celebrate a festival.   And under these circumstances no Egyptian could have cherished the thought, that the Israelites were only borrowing the jewels they asked of them, and would return them after the festival.   What they gave under such circumstances, they could only give or present without the slightest prospect of restoration.   Still less could the Israelites have had merely the thought of borrowing in their mind, seeing that God had said to Moses, "I will give the Israelites favour in the eyes of the Egyptians; and it will come to pass, that when ye go out, ye shall not go out empty" (ver. 21).   If, therefore, it is "natural to suppose that these jewels

---

[1] For the different views as to the supposed borrowing of the gold and silver vessels, see *Hengstenberg*, Dissertations on the Pentateuch, vol. ii. pp. 419 sqq., and *Kurtz*, History of the Old Covenant, vol. ii. 319 sqq.

[2] Even in 2 Kings v. 6 ; see my commentary on the passage.

were festal vessels with which the Egyptians furnished the poor Israelites for the intended feast," and even if "the Israelites had their thoughts directed with all seriousness to the feast which they were about to celebrate to Jehovah in the desert" (*Baumgarten*); their request to the Egyptians cannot have referred to any borrowing, nor have presupposed any intention to restore what they received on their return. From the very first the Israelites asked without intending to restore, and the Egyptians granted their request without any hope of receiving back, because God had made their hearts favourably disposed to the Israelites. The expressions נִצְּלוּ אֶת־מִצְרַיִם in ver. 22, and וַיְנַצְּלוּ in chap. xii. 36, are not at variance with this, but rather require it. For נָצַל does not mean to purloin, to steal, to take away secretly by cunning and fraud, but *to plunder* (2 Chron. xx. 25), as both the *LXX.* (σκυλεύειν) and *Vulgate* (*spoliare*) have rendered it. *Rosenmüller*, therefore, is correct in his explanation: "*Et spoliabitis Ægyptios, ita ut ab Ægyptiis, qui vos tam dura servitute oppresserunt, spolia auferetis.*" So also is *Hengstenberg*, who says, "The author represents the Israelites as going forth, laden as it were with the spoils of their formidable enemy, trophies of the victory which God's power had bestowed on their weakness. While he represents the gifts of the Egyptians as spoils which God had distributed to His host (as Israel is called in chap. xii. 41), he leads us to observe that the bestowment of these gifts, which outwardly appeared to be the effect of the good-will of the Egyptians, if viewed more deeply, proceeded from another Giver; that the outwardly free act of the Egyptians was effected by an inward divine constraint which they could not withstand" (Dissertations, vol. ii. p. 431).— Egypt had spoiled Israel by the tributary labour so unjustly enforced, and now Israel carried off the spoil of Egypt—a prelude to the victory which the people of God will one day obtain in their conflict with the power of the world (cf. Zech. xiv. 14).

Chap. iv. 1-9. Moses now started a fresh difficulty: the Israelites would not believe that Jehovah had appeared to him. There was so far a reason for this difficulty, that from the time of Jacob—an interval, therefore, of 430 years—God had never appeared to any Israelite. God therefore removed it by giving him three signs by which he might attest his divine mission to his people. These three signs were intended indeed for the Israelites, to convince them of the reality of the appearance of Jehovah to Moses; at the same time, as even *Ephraem Syrus* observed, they also served to strengthen Moses' faith, and dissipate his fears as to the result of his mission. For it was apparent enough that Moses did not possess true and entire confidence in God, from the fact that he still raised this difficulty, and distrusted the divine assurance, "They will hearken to thy voice," chap. iii. 18). And finally, these signs were intended for Pharaoh, as is stated in ver. 21; and to him the אֹתֹת (σημεῖα) were to become מֹפְתִים (τέρατα). By these signs Moses was installed as the servant of Jehovah (xiv. 31), and furnished with divine power, with which he could and was to appear before the children of Israel and Pharaoh as the messenger of Jehovah. The character of the three signs corresponded to this intention.

Vers. 2–5. The first sign.—The turning of Moses' staff into a serpent, which became a staff again when Moses took it by the tail, had reference to the calling of Moses. The staff in his hand was his shepherd's crook (מַטֶּה ver. 2, for מַה־זֶּה, in this place alone), and represented his calling as a shepherd. At the bidding of God he threw it upon the ground, and the staff became a serpent, before which Moses fled. The giving up of his shepherd-life would expose him to dangers, from which he would desire to escape. At the same time, there was more implied in the figure of a serpent than danger which merely threatened his life. The serpent had been the constant enemy of the seed of the woman (Gen. iii.), and represented the power of the wicked one which prevailed in Egypt. The explanation in *Pirke Elieser*, c. 40, points to this : *ideo Deum hoc signum Mosi ostendisse, quia sicut serpens mordet et morte afficit homines, ita quoque Pharao et Ægyptii mordebant et necabant Israelitas.* But at the bidding of God, Moses seized the serpent by the tail, and received his staff again as " the rod of God," with which he smote Egypt with great plagues. From this sign the people of Israel would necessarily perceive, that Jehovah had not only called Moses to be the leader of Israel, but had endowed him with the power to overcome the serpent-like cunning and the might of Egypt; in other words, they would " believe that Jehovah, the God of the fathers, had appeared to him." (On the special meaning of this sign for Pharaoh, see chap. vii. 10 sqq.)

Vers. 6, 7. THE SECOND SIGN.—Moses' hand became leprous, and was afterwards cleansed again. The expression מְצֹרַעַת כַּשָּׁלֶג, *covered with leprosy like snow*, refers to the white leprosy (*vid.* Lev. xiii. 3).—"*Was turned again as his flesh;*" *i.e.* was restored, became healthy, or clean like the rest of his body. So far as the meaning of this sign is concerned, Moses' hand has been explained in a perfectly arbitrary manner as representing the Israelitish nation, and his bosom as representing first Egypt, and then Canaan, as the hiding-place of Israel. If the shepherd's staff represented Moses' calling, the hand was that which directed or ruled the calling. It is in the bosom that the nurse carries the sucking child (Num. xi. 12), the shepherd the lambs (Isa. xl. 11), and the sacred singer the many nations, from whom he has suffered reproach and injury (Ps. lxxxix. 50). So Moses also carried his people in his bosom, *i.e.* in his heart : of that his first appearance in Egypt was a proof (chap. ii. 11, 12). But now he was to set his hand to deliver them from the reproach and bondage of Egypt. He put (הֵבִיא) his hand into his bosom, and his hand was covered with leprosy. The nation was like a leper, who defiled every one that touched him. The leprosy represented not only "the servitude and contemptuous treatment of the Israelites in Egypt" (*Kurtz*), but the ἀσέβεια of the Egyptians also, as *Theodoret* expresses it, or rather the impurity of Egypt in which Israel was sunken. This Moses soon discovered (cf. chap. v. 17 sqq.), and on more than one occasion afterwards (cf. Num. xi.) ; so that he had to complain to Jehovah, "Wherefore hast Thou afflicted Thy servant, that Thou layest the burden of all this people upon me ? . . . Have I conceived all this people, that Thou shouldest say to me, Carry them in thy bosom ?" (Num. xi. 11, 12). But God had the power to purify the nation from this leprosy, and would endow His servant Moses with that power. At the command of God, Moses put his hand, now covered with leprosy, once more into his bosom, and drew it out quite cleansed. This was what Moses was to learn by the sign; whilst Israel also learned that God both could and would deliver it, through the cleansed hand of Moses, from all its bodily and spiritual misery. The object of the first miracle was to exhibit Moses as the man whom Jehovah had called to be the leader of His people ; that of the second, to show that, as the messenger of Jehovah, he was furnished with the necessary power for the execution of this calling. In this sense God says, in ver. 8, "*If they will not hearken to the voice of the first sign, they will believe the voice of the latter sign.*" A voice is ascribed to the sign, as being a clear witness to the divine mission of the person performing it (Ps. cv. 27).

Ver. 9. THE THIRD SIGN.—If the first two signs should not be sufficient to lead the people to believe in the divine mission of Moses, he was to give them one more practical demonstration of the power which he had received to overcome the might and gods of Egypt. He was to take of the water of the Nile (the river, Gen. xli. 1) and pour it upon the dry land, and it would become blood (the second וְהָיוּ is a resumption of the first, cf. chap. xii. 41). The Nile received divine honours as the source of every good and all prosperity in the natural life of Egypt, and was even identified with Osiris (cf. *Hengstenberg*, Egypt and the Books of Moses, p. 109 transl.). If Moses therefore had power to turn the life-distributing water of the Nile into blood, he must also have received power to destroy Pharaoh and his gods. Israel was to learn this from the sign, whilst Pharaoh and the Egyptians were afterwards to experience this might of Jehovah in the form of punishment (chap. vii. 15 sqq.). Thus Moses was not only entrusted with the word of God, but also endowed with the power of God; and as he was the first God-sent prophet, so was he also the first worker of miracles, and in this capacity a type of the Apostle of our profession (Heb. iii. 1), even the God-man, Christ Jesus.

Vers. 10–18. Moses raised another difficulty. "*I am not a man of words,*" he said (*i.e.* I do not possess the gift of speech), "*but am heavy in mouth and heavy in tongue*" (*i.e.* I find a difficulty in the use of mouth and tongue, not exactly "stammering"); and that "*both of yesterday and the day before*" (*i.e.* from the very first, Gen. xxxi. 2), "*and also since Thy speaking to Thy servant.*" Moses meant to say, "I neither possess the gift of speech by nature, nor have I received it since Thou hast spoken to me."— Vers. 11, 12. Jehovah both could and would provide for this defect. He had made man's mouth, and He made dumb or deaf, seeing or blind. He possessed unlimited power over all the senses, could give them or take them away; and He would be with Moses' mouth, and teach him what he was to say, *i.e.*

impart to him the necessary qualification both as to matter and mode.—Moses' difficulties were now all exhausted, and removed by the assurances of God. But this only brought to light the secret reason in his heart. He did not *wish* to undertake the divine mission.—Ver. 13. " *Send, I pray Thee*," he says, " *by whom Thou wilt send ;*" *i.e.* carry out Thy mission by whomsoever Thou wilt. שְׁלַח בְּיַד : to carry out a mission through any one, originally with *accus. rei* (1 Sam. xvi. 20; 2 Sam. xi. 14), then without the object, as here, " to send a person" (cf. 2 Sam. xii. 25; 1 Kings ii. 25). Before תִּשְׁלָח the word אֲשֶׁר is omitted, which stands with בְּיַד in the construct state (*vid.* Ges. § 123, 3). The anger of God was now excited by this groundless opposition. But as this unwillingness also arose from weakness of the flesh, the mercy of God came to the help of his weakness, and He referred Moses to his brother Aaron, who could speak well, and would address the people for him (vers. 14–17). Aaron is called הַלֵּוִי, the Levite, from his lineage, possibly with reference to the primary signification of לָוָה " to connect one's self " (*Baumgarten*), but not with any allusion to the future calling of the tribe of Levi (*Rashi* and *Calvin*). דַּבֵּר יְדַבֵּר הוּא *speak* will *he.* The inf. abs. gives emphasis to the verb, and the position of הוּא to the subject. He both can and will speak, if thou dost not know it.—Vers. 14, 15. And Aaron is quite ready to do so. He is already coming to meet thee, and is glad to see thee. The statement in ver. 27, where Jehovah directs Aaron to go and meet Moses, is not at variance with this. They can both be reconciled in the following simple manner : " As soon as Aaron heard that his brother had left Midian, he went to meet him of his own accord, and then God showed him by what road he must go to find him, viz. towards the desert" (*R. Mose ben Nachman*).—"*Put the words*" (*sc.* which I have told thee) " *into his mouth ;*" and I will support both thee and him in speaking. " *He will be mouth to thee, and thou shalt be God to him.*" Cf. vii. 1, " Thy brother Aaron shall be thy prophet." Aaron would stand in the same relation to Moses, as a prophet to God: the prophet only spoke what God inspired him with, and Moses should be the inspiring God to him. The Targum softens down the word " God" into " master, teacher." Moses was called *God*, as being the possessor and medium of the divine word. As *Luther* explains it, " Whoever possesses and believes the word of God, possesses the Spirit and power of God,

and also the divine wisdom, truth, heart, mind, and everything
that belongs to God." In ver. 17, the plural " *signs*" points to the
penal wonders that followed; for only one of the three signs given
to Moses was performed with the rod.—Ver. 18. In consequence
of this appearance of God, Moses took leave of his father-in-law
to return to his brethren in Egypt, though without telling him
the real object of his journey, no doubt because Jethro had not
the mind to understand such a divine revelation, though he subsequently recognised the miracles that God wrought for Israel
(chap. xviii.). By the " *brethren*" we are to understand not
merely the nearer relatives of Moses, or the family of Amram,
but the Israelites generally. Considering the oppression under
which they were suffering at the time of Moses' flight, the question might naturally arise, whether they were still living, and
had not been altogether exterminated.

Vers. 19–31. RETURN OF MOSES TO EGYPT.—Vers. 19–23.
On leaving Midian, Moses received another communication from
God with reference to his mission to Pharaoh. The word of
Jehovah, in ver. 19, is not to be regarded as a summary of the
previous revelation, in which case וַיֹּאמֶר would be a pluperfect,
nor as the account of another writer, who placed the summons
to return to Egypt not in Sinai but in Midian. It is not a fact
that the departure of Moses is given in ver. 18; all that is
stated there is, that Jethro consented to Moses' decision to return
to Egypt. It was not till after this consent that Moses was able
to prepare for the journey. During these preparations God
appeared to him in Midian, and encouraged him to return, by
informing him that all the men who had sought his life, *i.e.*
Pharaoh and the relatives of the Egyptian whom he had slain,
were now dead.—Ver. 20. Moses then set out upon his journey,
with his wife and sons. בָּנָיו is not to be altered into בְּנוֹ, as
Knobel supposes, notwithstanding the fact that the birth of only
one son has hitherto been mentioned (chap. ii. 22); for neither
there, nor in this passage (ver. 25), is he described as the only
son. The wife and sons, who were still young, he placed upon
the ass (the one taken for the purpose), whilst he himself went
on foot with " the staff of God"—as the staff was called with
which he was to perform the divine miracles (ver. 17)—in his
hand. Poor as his outward appearance might be, he had in his

hand the staff before which the pride of Pharaoh and all his might would have to bow.—Ver. 21. "*In thy going* (returning) *to Egypt, behold, all the wonders which I have put into thy hand, thou doest them before Pharaoh.*" מוֹפֵת, τὸ τέρας, *portentum*, is any object (natural event, thing, or person) of significance which surpasses expectation or the ordinary course of nature, and excites wonder in consequence. It is frequently connected with אוֹת, σημεῖον, a sign (Deut. iv. 34, vi. 22, vii. 19, etc.), and embraces the idea of אוֹת within itself, *i.e.* wonder-sign. The expression, "*all* those wonders," does not refer merely to the three signs mentioned in chap. iv. 2–9, but to all the miracles which were to be performed by Moses with the staff in the presence of Pharaoh, and which, though not named, were put into his hand potentially along with the staff.—But all the miracles would not induce Pharaoh to let Israel go, for Jehovah would harden his heart. אֲנִי אֲחַזֵּק אֶת־לִבּוֹ, *lit.* I will make his heart *firm*, so that it will not move, his feelings and attitude towards Israel will not change. For אֲנִי אֲחַזֵּק or וְחִזַּקְתִּי (xiv. 4) and אֲנִי מְחַזֵּק (xiv. 17), we find אֲנִי אַקְשֶׁה in chap. vii. 3, "I will make Pharaoh's heart *hard*, or unfeeling;" and in chap. x. 1, אֲנִי הִכְבַּדְתִּי "I have made his heart *heavy*," *i.e.* obtuse, or insensible to impressions or divine influences. These three words are expressive of the hardening of the heart.

The *hardening of Pharaoh* is ascribed to God, not only in the passages just quoted, but also in chap. ix. 12, x. 20, 27, xi. 10, xiv. 8; that is to say, ten times in all; and that not merely as foreknown or foretold by Jehovah, but as caused and effected by Him. In the last five passages it is invariably stated that " Jehovah hardened (וַיְחַזֵּק) Pharaoh's heart." But it is also stated just as often, viz. ten times, that Pharaoh hardened his own heart, or made it heavy or firm; *e.g.* in chap. vii. 13, 22, viii. 15, ix. 35, וַיֶּחֱזַק לֵב " and Pharaoh's heart was (or became) hard;" chap. vii. 14, כָּבֵד לֵב " Pharaoh's heart was heavy;" in chap. ix. 7, יִכְבַּד ל; in chap. viii. 11, 28, ix. 34, וְהִכְבֵּד or וַיַּכְבֵּד אֶת־לִבּוֹ; in chap. xiii. 15, כִּי הִקְשָׁה פ' " for Pharaoh made his heart hard." According to this, the hardening of Pharaoh was quite as much his own act as the decree of God. But if, in order to determine the precise relation of the divine to the human causality, we look more carefully at the two classes of expressions, we shall find that not only in connection with the first sign, by which Moses and Aaron were to show their credentials as the messengers of Jehovah, sent with the demand that he would let the people of Israel go (chap. vii. 13, 14), but after the first five penal miracles, the hardening is invariably represented as his own. After every one of these miracles, it is stated that Pharaoh's heart was firm, or dull, *i.e.* insensible to the voice of God, and unaffected by the miracles performed before his eyes, and the judgments of God suspended over him and his kingdom, and he did not listen to them (to Moses and Aaron with their demand), or let the people go (chap. vii. 22, viii. 8, 15, 28, ix. 7). It is not till after the sixth plague that it is stated that Jehovah made the heart of Pharaoh firm (ix. 12). At the seventh the statement is repeated, that "Pharaoh made his heart heavy" (ix. 34, 35); but the continued refusal on the part of Pharaoh after the eighth and ninth (x. 20, 27) and his resolution to follow the Israelites and bring them back again, are attributed to the hardening of his heart by Jehovah (chap. xiv. 8, cf. vers. 4 and 17). This hardening of his own heart was manifested first of all in the fact, that he paid no attention to the demand of Jehovah addressed to him through Moses, and *would* not let Israel go; and that not only at the commencement, so long as the Egyptian magicians imitated the signs performed by Moses and Aaron (though at the very first sign the rods of the magicians, when turned into serpents, were swallowed by Aaron's, vii. 12, 13), but even when the magicians themselves acknowledged, "This is the finger of God" (viii. 19). It was also continued after the fourth and fifth plagues, when a distinction was made between the Egyptians and the Israelites, and the latter were exempted from the plagues,—a fact of which the king took care to convince himself (ix. 7). And it was exhibited still further in his breaking his promise, that he would let Israel go if Moses and Aaron would obtain from Jehovah the removal of the plague, and in the fact, that even after he had been obliged to confess, "I have sinned, Jehovah is the righteous one, I and my people are unrighteous" (ix. 27), he sinned again, as soon as breathing-time was given him, and would not let the people go (ix. 34, 35). Thus Pharaoh would not bend his self-will to the will of God, even after he had discerned the finger of God and the omnipotence of Jehovah in the plagues suspended over him and his nation; he would not withdraw his haughty refusal, not withstanding the fact that he was obliged to acknowledge that it was sin against Jehovah. Looked at from this side, the hardening was a fruit of sin, a consequence of that self-will, high-mindedness, and pride which flow from sin, and a continuous and ever increasing abuse of that freedom of the will which is innate in man, and which involves the possibility of obstinate resistance to the word and chastisement of God even until death. As the freedom of the will has its fixed limits in the unconditional dependence of the creature upon the Creator, so the sinner may resist the will of God as long as he lives. But such resistance plunges him into destruction, and is followed inevitably by death and damnation. God never allows any man to scoff at Him. Whoever will not suffer himself to be led, by the kindness and earnestness of the divine admonitions, to repentance and humble submission to the will of God, must inevitably perish, and by his destruction subserve the glory of God, and the manifestation of the holiness, righteousness, and omnipotence of Jehovah.

But God not only permits a man to harden himself; He also produces obduracy, and suspends this sentence over the impenitent. Not as though God took pleasure in the death of the wicked! No; God desires that the wicked should repent of his evil way and live (Ezek. xxxiii. 11); and He desires this most earnestly, for " He will have all men to be saved and to come unto the knowledge of the truth" (1 Tim. ii. 4, cf. 2 Pet. iii. 9). As God causes His earthly sun to rise upon the evil and the good, and sendeth rain on the just and the unjust (Matt. v. 45), so He causes His sun of grace to shine upon all sinners, to lead them to life and salvation. But as the earthly sun produces different effects upon the earth, according to the nature of the soil upon which it shines, so the influence of the divine sun of grace manifests itself in different ways upon the human heart, according to its moral condition.[1] The penitent permit the proofs of divine goodness and grace to lead them to repentance and salvation; but the impenitent harden themselves more and more

---

[1] "The sun, by the force of its heat, moistens the wax and dries the clay, softening the one and hardening the other ; and as this produces opposite effects by the same power, so, through the long-suffering of God, which reaches to all, some receive good and others evil, some are softened and others hardened."—(*Theodoret, quæst.* 12 *in Ex.*)

against the grace of God, and so become ripe for the judgment of damnation. The very same manifestation of the mercy of God leads in the case of the one to salvation and life, and in that of the other to judgment and death, because he hardens himself against that mercy. In this increasing hardness on the part of the impenitent sinner against the mercy that is manifested towards him, there is accomplished the judgment of reprobation, first in God's furnishing the wicked with an opportunity of bringing fully to light the evil inclinations, desires, and thoughts that are in their hearts; and then, according to an invariable law of the moral government of the world, in His rendering the return of the impenitent sinner more and more difficult on account of his continued resistance, and eventually rendering it altogether impossible. It is the curse of sin, that it renders the hard heart harder, and less susceptible to the gracious manifestations of divine love, long-suffering, and patience. In this twofold manner God produces hardness, not only *permissive* but *effective; i.e.* not only by giving time and space for the manifestation of human opposition, even to the utmost limits of creaturely freedom, but still more by those continued manifestations of His will which drive the hard heart to such utter obduracy that it is no longer capable of returning, and so giving over the hardened sinner to the judgment of damnation. This is what we find in the case of Pharaoh. After he had hardened his heart against the revealed will of God during the first five plagues, the hardening commenced on the part of Jehovah with the sixth miracle (ix. 12), when the omnipotence of God was displayed with such energy that even the Egyptian magicians were covered with the boils, and could no longer stand before Moses (ix. 11). And yet, even after this hardening on the part of God, another opportunity was given to the wicked king to repent and change his mind, so that on two other occasions he acknowledged that his resistance was sin, and promised to submit to the will of Jehovah (ix. 27 sqq., x. 16 sqq.). But when at length, even after the seventh plague, he broke his promise to let Israel go, and hardened his heart again as soon as the plague was removed (ix. 34, 35), Jehovah so hardened Pharaoh's heart that he not only did not let Israel go, but threatened Moses with death if he ever came into his presence again (x. 20, 27, 28). The hardening was now completed so that he necessarily fell a

victim to judgment; though the very first stroke of judgment
in the slaying of the first-born was an admonition to consider
and return.   And it was not till after he had rejected the mercy
displayed in this judgment, and manifested a defiant spirit once
more, in spite of the words with which he had given Moses and
Aaron permission to depart, "Go, and bless me also" (xii. 31, 32),
that God completely hardened his heart, so that he pursued the
Israelites with an army, and was overtaken by the judgment of
utter destruction.

Now, although the hardening of Pharaoh on the part of
Jehovah was only the complement of Pharaoh's hardening of
his own heart, in the verse before us the former aspect alone is
presented, because the principal object was not only to prepare
Moses for the opposition which he would meet with from Pharaoh, but also to strengthen his weak faith, and remove at the
very outset every cause for questioning the omnipotence of
Jehovah.   If it was by Jehovah Himself that Pharaoh was
hardened, this hardening, which He not only foresaw and predicted by virtue of His omniscience, but produced and inflicted
through His omnipotence, could not possibly hinder the performance of His will concerning Israel, but must rather contribute
to the realization of His purposes of salvation and the manifestation of His glory (cf. chap. ix. 16, x. 2, xiv. 4, 17, 18).

Vers. 22, 23. In order that Pharaoh might form a true estimate of the solemnity of the divine command, Moses was to
make known to him not only the relation of Jehovah to Israel,
but also the judgment to which he would be exposed if he refused to let Israel go.   The relation in which Israel stood to
Jehovah was expressed by God in the words, "Israel is My first-
born son."   Israel was Jehovah's son by virtue of his election to
be the people of possession (Deut. xiv. 1, 2).   This election
began with the call of Abraham to be the father of the nation
in which all the families of the earth were to be blessed.   On
the ground of this promise, which was now to be realized in the
seed of Abraham by the deliverance of Israel out of Egypt, the
nation of Israel is already called Jehovah's "son," although it
was through the conclusion of the covenant at Sinai that it was
first exalted to be the people of Jehovah's possession out of all
the nations (xix. 5, 6).   The divine sonship of Israel was therefore spiritual in its nature: it neither sprang from the fact that

God, as the Creator of all nations, was also the Creator, or Begetter, and Father of Israel, nor was it founded, as *Baumgarten* supposes, upon "the physical generation of Isaac, as having its origin, not in the power of nature, but in the power of grace." The relation of God, as Creator, to man His creature, is never referred to in the Old Testament as that of a father to a son; to say nothing of the fact that the Creator of man is *Elohim*, and not *Jehovah*. Wherever Jehovah is called the Father, Begetter, or Creator of Israel (even in Deut. xxxii. 18; Jer. ii. 27; Isa. lxiv. 8; Mal. i. 6 and ii. 10), the fatherhood of God relates to the election of Israel as Jehovah's people of possession. But the election upon which the υἱοθεσία of Israel was founded, is not presented in the aspect of a "begetting through the Spirit;" it is spoken of rather as acquiring or buying (קָנָה), making (עָשָׂה), founding or establishing (כּוּן, Deut. xxxii. 6). Even the expressions, "the Rock that begat thee," "God that bare thee" (Deut. xxxii. 18), do not point to the idea of spiritual generation, but are to be understood as referring to the creation; just as in Ps. xc. 2, where Moses speaks of the mountains as "brought forth" and the earth as "born." The choosing of Israel as the son of God was an adoption flowing from the free grace of God, which involved the loving, fatherly treatment of the son, and demanded obedience, reverence, and confidence towards the Father (Mal. i. 6). It was this which constituted the very essence of the covenant made by Jehovah with Israel, that He treated it with mercy and love (Hos. xi. 1; Jer. xxxi. 9, 20), pitied it as a father pitieth his children (Ps. ciii. 13), chastened it on account of its sins, yet did not withdraw His mercy from it (2 Sam. vii. 14, 15; Ps. lxxxix. 31–35), and trained His son to be a holy nation by the love and severity of paternal discipline.—Still Israel was not only *a* son, but the "*first-born son*" of Jehovah. In this title the calling of the heathen is implied. Israel was not to be Jehovah's only son, but simply the first-born, who was peculiarly dear to his Father, and had certain privileges above the rest. Jehovah was about to exalt Israel above all the nations of the earth (Deut. xxviii. 1). Now, if Pharaoh would not let Jehovah's first-born son depart, he would pay the penalty in the life of his own first-born (cf. xii. 29). In this intense earnestness of the divine command, Moses had a strong support to his faith. If Israel was Jehovah's first-born son, Jehovah could not relinquish him, but must deliver His son from the bondage of Egypt.

Vers. 24–26. But if Moses was to carry out the divine commission with success, he must first of all prove himself to be a faithful servant of Jehovah in his own house. This he was to learn from the *occurrence at the inn :* an occurrence which has many obscurities on account of the brevity of the narrative, and has received many different interpretations. When Moses was on the way, Jehovah met him at the resting-place (מָלוֹן, see Gen. xlii. 27), and sought to kill him. In what manner, is not stated : whether by a sudden seizure with some fatal disease, or, what is more probable, by some act proceeding directly from Himself, which threatened Moses with death. This hostile attitude on the part of God was occasioned by his neglect to circumcise his son ; for, as soon as Zipporah cut off (circumcised) the foreskin of her son with a stone, Jehovah let him go. צוּר=צוֹר, a rock, or stone, here a stone knife, with which, according to hereditary custom, the circumcision commanded by Joshua was also performed ; not, however, because " stone knives were regarded as less dangerous than those of metal," nor because " for symbolical reasons preference was given to them, as a simple production of nature, over the metal knives that had been prepared by human hands and were applied to daily use." For if the Jews had detected any religious or symbolical meaning in stone, they would never have given it up for iron or steel, but would have retained it, like the Ethiopian tribe of the Alnaii, who used stone knives for that purpose as late as 150 years ago ; whereas, in the Talmud, the use of iron or steel knives for the purpose of circumcision is spoken of, as though they were universally employed. Stone knives belong to a time anterior to the manufacture of iron or steel ; and wherever they were employed at a later period, this arose from a devoted adherence to the older and simpler custom (see my Commentary on Josh. v. 2). From the word " her *son*," it is evident that Zipporah only circumcised one of the two sons of Moses (ver. 20) ; so that the other, no doubt the elder, had already been circumcised in accordance with the law. Circumcision had been enjoined upon Abraham by Jehovah as a covenant sign for all his descendants ; and the sentence of death was pronounced upon any neglect of it, as being a breach of the covenant (Gen. xvii. 14). Although in this passage it is the uncircumcised themselves who are threatened with death, yet in the case of children the punishment fell upon the parents, and first of all upon the father, who had neglected to keep the commandment of God. Now, though Moses had probably omitted circumcision simply from regard to his Midianitish wife, who disliked this operation, he had been guilty of a capital crime, which God could not pass over in the case of one whom He had chosen to be His messenger, to establish His covenant with Israel. Hence He threatened him with death, to bring him to a consciousness of his sin, either by the voice of conscience or by some word which accompanied His attack upon Moses; and also to show him with what earnestness God demanded the keeping of His commandments. Still He did not kill him; for his sin had sprung from weakness of the flesh, from a sinful yielding to his wife, which could both be explained and excused on account of his position in the Midianite's house. That Zipporah's dislike to circumcision had been the cause of the omission, has been justly inferred by commentators from the fact, that on Jehovah's attack upon Moses, she proceeded at once to perform what had been neglected, and, as it seems, with inward repugnance. The expression, "She threw (the foreskin of her son) at his (Moses') feet," points to this (הִגִּיעַ לְ, as in Isa. xxv. 12). The suffix in רַגְלָיו (his feet) cannot refer to the son, not only because such an allusion would give no reasonable sense, but also because the suffix refers to Moses in the immediate context, both before (in הֲמִיתוֹ, ver. 24) and after (in מִמֶּנּוּ, ver. 26); and therefore it is simpler to refer it to Moses here. From this it follows, then, that the words, "a blood-bridegroom art thou to me," were addressed to Moses, and not to the boy. Zipporah calls Moses a blood-bridegroom, "because she had been compelled, as it were, to acquire and purchase him anew as a husband by shedding the blood of her son" (*Glass*). "Moses had been as good as taken from her by the deadly attack which had been made upon him. She purchased his life by the blood of her son; she received him back, as it were, from the dead, and married him anew; he was, in fact, a bridegroom of blood to her" (*Kurtz*). This she said, as the historian adds, after God had let Moses go, לַמּוּלֹת, "with reference to the circumcisions." The plural is used quite generally and indefinitely, as Zipporah referred not merely to this one instance, but to circumcision generally. Moses was apparently induced by what had occurred to decide not to take his wife and children with him to Egypt, but to send them back to his father-in-law. We may infer this from the fact, that it was not till after Israel had arrived at Sinai that he brought them to him again (chap. xviii. 2).

Vers. 27–31. After the removal of the sin, which had excited the threatening wrath of Jehovah, Moses once more received a token of the divine favour in the arrival of Aaron, under the direction of God, to meet him at the Mount of God (chap. iii. 1). To Aaron he related all the words of Jehovah, with which He had sent (commissioned) him (שָׁלַח with a double accusative, as in 2 Sam. xi. 22; Jer. xlii. 5), and all the signs which He had commanded him (צִוָּה also with a double accusative, as in Gen. vi. 22). Another proof of the favour of God consisted of the believing reception of his mission on the part of the elders and the people of Israel. "*The people believed*" (וַיַּאֲמֵן) when Aaron communicated to them the words of Jehovah to Moses, and did the signs in their presence. "*And when they heard that Jehovah had visited the children of Israel, and had looked upon their affliction, they bowed and worshipped.*" (*Knobel* is wrong in proposing to alter יִשְׁמְעוּ into יִשְׂמְחוּ, according to the Sept. rendering, καὶ ἐχάρη). The faith of the people, and the worship by which their faith was expressed, proved that the promise of the fathers still lived in their hearts. And although this faith did not stand the subsequent test (chap. v.), yet, as the first expression of their feelings, it bore witness to the fact that Israel was willing to follow the call of God.

MOSES AND AARON ARE SENT TO PHARAOH.—CHAP. V.–VII. 7.

The two events which form the contents of this section,—viz. (1) the visit of Moses and Aaron to Pharaoh to make known the commands of their God, with the harsh refusal of their request on the part of Pharaoh, by an increase of the tributary labours of Israel (chap. v.); and (2) the further revelations of Jehovah to Moses, with the insertion of the genealogies of Moses and Aaron,—not only hang closely together so far as the subject-matter is concerned, inasmuch as the fresh declarations of Jehovah to Moses were occasioned by the complaint of Moses that his first attempt had so signally failed, but both of them belong to the complete equipment of Moses for his divine mission. Their visit to Pharaoh was only preliminary in its character. Moses and Aaron simply made known to the king the will of their God, without accrediting themselves by miraculous signs as the messengers of Jehovah, or laying any particular emphasis upon His demand. For this first step was only intended to enlighten Moses as to the attitude of Pharaoh and the people of Israel in relation to the work of God, which He was about to perform. Pharaoh answered the demand addressed to him, that he would let the people go for a few days to hold a sacrificial festival in the desert, by increasing their labours; and the Israelites complained in consequence that their good name had been made abhorrent to the king, and their situation made worse than it was. Moses might have despaired on this account; but he laid his trouble before the Lord, and the Lord filled his despondent heart with fresh courage through the renewed and strengthened promise that He would now for the first time display His name *Jehovah* perfectly—that He would redeem the children of Israel with outstretched arm and with great judgments—would harden Pharaoh's heart, and do many signs and wonders in the land of Egypt, that the Egyptians might learn through the deliverance of Israel that He was Jehovah, *i.e.* the absolute God, who works with unlimited freedom (cf. p. 75). At the same time God removed the difficulty which once more arose in the mind of Moses, namely, that Pharaoh would not listen to him because of his want of oratorical power, by the assurance, "*I make thee a god for Pharaoh, and Aaron shall be thy prophet*" (chap. vii. 1), which could not fail to remove all doubt as to his own incompetency for so great and severe a task. With this promise Pharaoh was completely given up into Moses' power, and Moses invested with all the plenipotentiary authority that was requisite for the performance of the work entrusted to him.

Chap. v. PHARAOH'S ANSWER TO THE REQUEST OF MOSES AND AARON.—Vers. 1–5. When the elders of Israel had listened with gladness and gratitude to the communications of Moses and Aaron respecting the revelation which Moses had received from Jehovah, that He was now about to deliver His people out of their bondage in Egypt; Moses and Aaron proceeded to Pharaoh, and requested in the name of the God of

Israel, that he would let the people of Israel go and celebrate a festival in the wilderness in honour of their God. When we consider that every nation presented sacrifices to its deities, and celebrated festivals in their honour, and that they had all their own modes of worship, which were supposed to be appointed by the gods themselves, so that a god could not be worshipped acceptably in every place; the demand presented to Pharaoh on the part of the God of the Israelites, that he would let His people go into the wilderness and sacrifice to Him, appears so natural and reasonable, that Pharaoh could not have refused their request, if there had been a single trace of the fear of God in his heart. But what was his answer? *"Who is Jehovah, that I should listen to His voice, to let Israel go? I know not Jehovah."* There was a certain truth in these last words. The God of Israel had not yet made Himself known to him. But this was no justification. Although as a heathen he might naturally measure the power of the God by the existing condition of His people, and infer from the impotence of the Israelites that their God must be also weak, he would not have dared to refuse the petition of the Israelites, to be allowed to sacrifice to their God or celebrate a sacrificial festival, if he had had any faith in gods at all.—Ver. 3. The messengers founded their request upon the fact that the God of the Hebrews had met them (נִקְרָא, *vid.* chap. iii. 18), and referred to the punishment which the neglect of the sacrificial festival demanded by God might bring upon the nation. פֶּן־יִפְגָּעֵנוּ: *"lest He strike us* (attack us) *with pestilence or sword."* פָּגַע: to strike, hit against any one, either by accident or with a hostile intent; ordinarily construed with בְּ, also with an accusative, 1 Sam. x. 5, and chosen here probably with reference to נִקְרָה = נִקְרָא. *"Pestilence or sword:"* these are mentioned as expressive of a violent death, and as the means employed by the deities, according to the ordinary belief of the nations, to punish the neglect of their worship. The expression "God of the Hebrews," for "God of Israel" (ver. 1), is not chosen as being "more intelligible to the king, because the Israelites were called Hebrews by foreigners, more especially by the Egyptians (i. 16, ii. 6)," as *Knobel* supposes, but to convince Pharaoh of the necessity for their going into the desert to keep the festival demanded by their God. In Egypt they might sacrifice to the gods of Egypt, but not to the God of the

Hebrews.—Vers. 4, 5. But Pharaoh would hear nothing of any worship. He believed that the wish was simply an excuse for procuring holidays for the people, or days of rest from their labours, and ordered the messengers off to their slave duties: " *Get you unto your burdens.*" For as the people were very numerous, he would necessarily lose by their keeping holiday. He called the Israelites " *the people of the land,*" not " as being his own property, because he was the lord of the land" (*Baumgarten*), but as the working class, "land-people," equivalent to "common people," in distinction from the ruling castes of the Egyptians (*vid.* Jer. lii. 25 ; Ezek. vii. 27).

Vers. 6–18. As Pharaoh possessed neither fear of God (εὐσέβεια) nor fear of the gods, but, in the proud security of his might, determined to keep the Israelites as slaves, and to use them as tools for the glorifying of his kingdom by the erection of magnificent buildings, he suspected that their wish to go into the desert was nothing but an excuse invented by idlers, and prompted by a thirst for freedom, which might become dangerous to his kingdom, on account of the numerical strength of the people. He therefore thought that he could best extinguish such desires and attempts by increasing the oppression and adding to their labours. For this reason he instructed his bailiffs to abstain from delivering straw to the Israelites who were engaged in making bricks, and to let them gather it for themselves ; but yet not to make the least abatement in the number (מַתְכֹּנֶת) to be delivered every day. הַנֹּגְשִׂים בָּעָם, " *those who urged the people on,*" were the bailiffs selected from the Egyptians and placed over the Israelitish workmen, the general managers of the work. Under them there were the שֹׁטְרִים (*lit.* writers, γραμματεῖς LXX., from שָׁטַר to write), who were chosen from the Israelites (*vid.* ver. 14), and had to distribute the work among the people, and hand it over, when finished, to the royal officers. לְבֹּן לְבֵנִים : to make bricks, not to burn them ; for the bricks in the ancient monuments of Egypt, and in many of the pyramids, are not burnt but dried in the sun (*Herod.* ii. 136 ; *Hengst.* Egypt and Books of Moses, pp. 2 and 79 sqq.). קֹשֵׁשׁ : a *denom.* verb from קַשׁ, to gather stubble, then to stubble, to gather (Num. xv. 32, 33). תֶּבֶן, of uncertain etymology, is chopped straw ; here, the stubble that was left standing when the corn was reaped, or the straw that lay upon the ground. This they chopped up and mixed with the clay, to give greater durability to the bricks, as may be seen in bricks found in the oldest monuments (cf. *Hgst.* p. 79).—Ver. 9. "*Let the work be heavy* (press heavily) *upon the people, and they shall make with it* (*i.e.* stick to their work), *and not look at lying words.*" By " lying words" the king meant the words of Moses, that the God of Israel had appeared to him, and demanded a sacrificial festival from His people. In ver. 11 special emphasis is laid upon אַתֶּם "*ye:*" "*Go, ye yourselves, fetch your straw,*" not others for you as heretofore ; "*for nothing is taken* (diminished) *from your work.*" The word כִּי *for* has been correctly explained by *Kimchi* as supposing a parenthetical thought, *et quidem alacriter vobis eundum est.*—Ver. 12. "לְקֹשֵׁשׁ ק : " to gather stubble for straw ;" not " stubble *for,* in the sense of *instead of* straw," for לְ is not equivalent to תַּחַת, but to gather the stubble left in the fields for the chopped straw required for the bricks.—Ver. 13. דְּבַר יוֹם בְּיוֹמוֹ, the quantity fixed for every day, "*just as when the straw was* (there)," *i.e.* was given out for the work.—Vers. 14 sqq. As the Israelites could not do the work appointed them, their overlookers were beaten by the Egyptian bailiffs ; and when they complained to the king of this treat-ment, they were repulsed with harshness, and told " *Ye are idle, idle; therefore ye say, Let us go and sacrifice to Jehovah.*" וְחָטָאת עַמֶּךָ : " *and thy people sin ;*" *i.e.* not " thy people (the Israelites) must be sinners," which might be the meaning of חָטָא accord-ing to Gen. xliii. 9, but " thy (Egyptian) people sin." "*Thy people*" must be understood as applying to the Egyptians, on account of the antithesis to " thy servants," which not only re-fers to the Israelitish overlookers, but includes all the Israelites, especially in the first clause. חָטָאת is an unusual feminine form, for חָטָאָה (*vid.* Gen. xxxiii. 11); and עַם is construed as a femi-nine, as in Judg. xviii. 7 and Jer. viii. 5.

Vers. 19—23. When the Israelitish overlookers saw that they were in evil (בְּרָע as in Ps. x. 6, *i.e.* in an evil condition), they came to meet Moses and Aaron, waiting for them as they came out from the king, and reproaching them with only making the circumstances of the people worse.—Ver. 21. " *Jehovah look upon you and judge*" (*i.e.* punish you, because) " *ye have made the smell of us to stink in the eyes of Pharaoh and his servants,*" *i.e.* destroyed our good name with the king and his servants, and turned it into hatred and disgust. רֵיחַ, a pleasant smell, is a figure employed for a good name or repute, and the figurative use of the word explains the connection with the eyes instead of the nose. " *To give a sword into their hand to kill us.*" Moses and Aaron, they imagined, through their appeal to Pharaoh had made the king and his counsellers suspect them of being restless people, and so had put a weapon into their hands for their oppression and destruction. What perversity of the natural heart! They call upon God to judge, whilst by their very complaining they show that they have no confidence in God and His power to save. Moses turned (וַיָּשָׁב ver. 22) to Jehovah with the question, " *Why hast Thou done evil to this people,*" —increased their oppression by my mission to Pharaoh, and yet not delivered them? " These are not words of contumacy or indignation, but of inquiry and prayer" (*Aug. quæst.* 14). The question and complaint proceeded from faith, which flies to God when it cannot understand the dealings of God, to point out to Him how incomprehensible are His ways, to appeal to Him to help in the time of need, and to remove what seems opposed to His nature and His will.

Chap. vi.-vii. 7. EQUIPMENT OF MOSES AND AARON AS MESSENGERS OF JEHOVAH.—Ver. 1. In reply to the complaining inquiry of Moses, Jehovah promised him the deliverance of Israel by a strong hand (cf. iii. 19), by which Pharaoh would be compelled to let Israel go, and even to drive them out of his land. Moses did not receive any direct answer to the question, " Why hast Thou so evil-entreated this people?" He was to gather this first of all from his own experience as the leader of Israel. For the words were strictly applicable here : " What I do thou knowest not now, but thou shalt know hereafter" (John xiii. 7). If, even after the miraculous deliverance of the Israelites from Egypt and their glorious march through the desert, in which they had received so many proofs of the omnipotence and mercy of their God, they repeatedly rebelled against the guidance of God, and were not content with the manna provided by the Lord, but lusted after the fishes, leeks, and onions of Egypt (Num. xi.) ; it is certain that in such a state of mind as this, they would never have been willing to leave Egypt and enter into a covenant with Jehovah, without a very great increase in the oppression they endured in Egypt.—The brief but comprehensive promise was still further explained by the Lord (vers. 2–9), and Moses was instructed and authorized to carry out the divine purposes in concert with Aaron (vers. 10–13, 28–30, chap. vii. 1–6). The genealogy of the two messengers is then introduced into the midst of these instructions (vi. 14–27); and the age of Moses is given at the close (vii. 7). This section does not contain a different account of the calling of Moses, taken from some other source than the previous one; it rather presupposes chap. iii.–v., and completes the account commenced in chap. iii. of the equipment of Moses and Aaron as the executors of the divine will with regard to Pharaoh and Israel. For the fact that the first visit paid by Moses and Aaron to Pharaoh was simply intended to bring out the attitude of Pharaoh towards the purposes of Jehovah, and to show the necessity for the great judgments of God, is distinctly expressed in the words, " Now shalt thou see what I will do to Pharaoh." But before these judgments commenced, Jehovah announced to Moses (ver. 2), and through him to the people, that henceforth He would manifest Himself to them in a much more glorious manner than to the patriarchs, namely, as JEHOVAH; whereas to Abraham, Isaac, and Jacob, He had only appeared as EL SHADDAI. The words, " By My name JEHOVAH was I not known to them," do not mean, however, that the patriarchs were altogether ignorant of the name Jehovah. This is obvious from the significant use of that name, which was not an unmeaning sound, but a real expression of the divine nature, and still more from the unmistakeable connection between the explanation given by God here and Gen. xvii. 1. When the establishment of the covenant commenced, as described in Gen. xv., with the institution of the covenant sign of circumcision and the promise of the birth of Isaac, Jehovah said to Abram, " I am EL SHADDAI, God Almighty," and from that time forward manifested Himself to Abram and his wife as the Almighty, in the birth of Isaac, which took place apart altogether from the powers of nature, and also in the preservation, guidance, and multiplication of his seed. It was in His attribute as El Shaddai that God had revealed His nature to the patriarchs; but now He was about to reveal Himself to Israel as JEHOVAH, as the absolute Being working with unbounded freedom in the performance of His promises. For not only had He established His covenant with the fathers

(ver. 4), but He had also heard the groaning of the children of
Israel, and remembered His covenant (ver. 5; וְנַם—וְנַם, not only
—but also). The divine promise not only commences in ver. 2,
but concludes at ver. 8, with the emphatic expression, " *I*
JEHOVAH*," to show that the work of Israel's redemption resided
in the power of the name Jehovah. In ver. 4 the covenant promises of Gen. xvii. 7, 8, xxvi. 3, xxxv. 11, 12, are all brought
together ; and in ver. 5 we have a repetition of chap. ii. 24, with
the emphatically repeated אֲנִי (*I*). On the ground of the erection of His covenant on the one hand, and, what was irreconcilable with that covenant, the bondage of Israel on the other,
Jehovah was now about to redeem Israel from its sufferings and
make it His own nation. This assurance, which God would carry
out by the manifestation of His nature as expressed in the name
Jehovah, contained three distinct elements : (*a*) the deliverance
of Israel from the bondage of Egypt, which, because so utterly
different from all outward appearances, is described in three
parallel clauses : bringing them out from under the burdens of
the Egyptians ; saving them from their bondage ; and redeeming
them with a stretched-out arm and with great judgments ;—
(*b*) the adoption of Israel as the nation of God ;—(*c*) the guidance of Israel into the land promised to the fathers (vers. 6–8).
זְרוֹעַ נְטוּיָה, a stretched-out arm, is most appropriately connected
with שְׁפָטִים גְּדֹלִים, great judgments ; for God raises, stretches out
His arm, when He proceeds in judgment to smite the rebellious.
These expressions repeat with greater emphasis the " strong
hand" of ver. 1, and are frequently connected with it in the
rhetorical language of Deuteronomy (*e.g.* chap. iv. 34, v. 15, vii.
19). The " great judgments " were the plagues, the judgments
of God, by which Pharaoh was to be compelled to let Israel go.
—Ver. 7. The adoption of Israel as the nation of God took place
at Sinai (xix. 5). אֲשֶׁר נָשָׂאתִי וגו', " *with regard to which I have
lifted up My hand to give it* " (ver. 8). Lifting up the hand (*sc.*
towards heaven) is the attitude of swearing (Deut. xxxii. 40
cf. Gen. xiv. 22) ; and these words point back to Gen. xxii. 16
sqq. and xxvi. 3 (cf. chap. xxiv. 7 and l. 24).

Vers. 9–13. When Moses communicated this solemn assur-
ance of God to the people, they did not listen to him מִקֹּצֶר רוּחַ, *lit.*
" *for shortness of breath ;*" not " from impatience" (like קְצַר־רוּחַ,
Prov. xiv. 29, in contrast to אֶרֶךְ אַפַּיִם), but from anguish, inward

pressure, which prevents a man from breathing properly. Thus the early belief of the Israelites was changed into the despondency of unbelief through the increase of their oppression. This result also produced despondency in Moses' mind, so that he once more declined the commission, which followed the promise, viz. to go to Pharaoh and demand that he would let Israel go out of his land (ver. 11). If the children of Israel would not listen to him, how should Pharaoh hear him, especially as he was uncircumcised in the lips (ver. 12)? עֲרַל שְׂפָתַיִם is one whose lips are, as it were, covered with a foreskin, so that he cannot easily bring out his words; in meaning the same as "heavy of mouth" in chap. iv. 10. The reply of God to this objection is given in chap. vii. 1-5. For, before the historian gives the decisive answer of Jehovah which removed all further hesitation on the part of Moses, and completed his mission and that of Aaron to Pharaoh, he considers it advisable to introduce the genealogy of the two men of God, for the purpose of showing clearly their genealogical relation to the people of Israel.—Ver. 13 forms a concluding summary, and prepares the way for the genealogy that follows, the heading of which is given in ver. 14.[1]

Vers. 14–27. THE GENEALOGY OF MOSES AND AARON.— " *These are their* (Moses' and Aaron's) *father's-houses.*" בֵּית־ אָבוֹת father's-houses (not fathers' house) is a composite noun, so formed that the two words not only denote one idea, but are treated grammatically as one word, like בֵּית־עֲצַבִּים idol-houses (1 Sam. xxxi. 9), and בֵּית־בָּמוֹת high-place-houses (cf. Ges. § 108, 3; *Ewald,* § 270c). *Father's-house* was a technical term applied to a collection of families, called by the name of a common ancestor. The father's-houses were the larger divisions into which the families (*mishpachoth*), the largest subdivisions of the tribes of Israel, were grouped. To show clearly the genealogical position of Levi, the tribe-father of Moses and Aaron, among the sons of Jacob, the genealogy commences with Reuben, the firstborn of Jacob, and gives the names of such of his sons and those of Simeon as were the founders of families (Gen. xlvi. 9, 10).

---

[1] The organic connection of this genealogy with the entire narrative has been so conclusively demonstrated by *Ranke,* in his *Unterss. ub. d. Pent.* i. p. 68 sqq. and ii. 19 sqq., that even *Knobel* has admitted it, and thrown away the fragmentary hypothesis.

Then follows Levi ; and not only are the names of his three sons given, but the length of his life is mentioned (ver. 16), also that of his son Kohath and his descendant Amram, because they were the tribe-fathers of Moses and Aaron. But the Amram mentioned in ver. 20 as the father of Moses, cannot be the same person as the Amram who was the son of Kohath (ver. 18), but must be a later descendant. For, however the sameness of names may seem to favour the identity of the persons, if we simply look at the genealogy before us, a comparison of this passage with Num. iii. 27, 28 will show the impossibility of such an assumption. "According to Num. iii. 27, 28, the Kohathites were divided (in Moses' time) into the four branches, Amramites, Izharites, Hebronites, and Uzzielites, who consisted together of 8600 men and boys (women and girls not being included). Of these, about a fourth, or 2150 men, would belong to the Amramites. Now, according to Ex. xviii. 3, 4, Moses himself had only two sons. Consequently, if Amram the son of Kohath, and tribe-father of the Amramites, was the same person as Amram the father of Moses, Moses must have had 2147 brothers and brothers' sons (the brothers' daughters, the sisters, and their daughters, not being reckoned at all). But as this is absolutely impossible, it must be granted that Amram the son of Kohath was not the father of Moses, and that an indefinitely long list of generations has been omitted between the former and his descendant of the same name" (*Tiele, Chron. des A. T.* p. 36).[1] The enumeration of only four generations, viz. Levi, Kohath, Amram, Moses, is unmistakeably related to Gen. xv. 16, where it is stated that the fourth generation would return to Canaan. Amram's wife *Jochebed*, who is merely spoken of in general terms as a daughter of Levi (a Levitess) in chap. ii. 1 and Num. xxvi. 59, is called here the דּוֹדָה " *aunt*" (father's sister) of Amram, a marriage which was prohibited in the Mosaic law (Lev. xviii. 12), but was allowed before the giving of the law ;

---

[1] The objections of *M. Baumgarten* to these correct remarks have been conclusively met by *Kurtz* (Hist. of O. C. vol. ii. p. 144). We find a similar case in the genealogy of Ezra in Ezra vii. 3, which passes over from Azariah the son of Meraioth to Azariah the son of Johanan, and omits five links between the two, as we may see from 1 Chron vi. 7–11. In the same way the genealogy before us skips over from Amram the son of Kohath to Amram the father of Moses without mentioning the generations between.

so that there is no reason for following the *LXX.* and *Vulgate,* and rendering the word, in direct opposition to the usage of the language, *patruelis,* the father's brother's daughter. Amram's sons are placed according to their age : Aaron, then Moses, as Aaron was three years older than his brother. Their sister Miriam was older still (*vid.* ii. 4). In the *LXX., Vulg.,* and one Hebrew MS., she is mentioned here ; but this is a later interpolation. In vers. 21 sqq. not only are the sons of Aaron mentioned (ver. 23), but those of two of Amram's brothers, Izhar and Uzziel (vers. 21, 22), and also Phinehas, the son of Aaron's son Eleazar (ver. 25) ; as the genealogy was intended to trace the descent of the principal priestly families, among which again special prominence is given to Aaron and Eleazar by the introduction of their wives. On the other hand, none of the sons of Moses are mentioned, because his dignity was limited to his own person, and his descendants fell behind those of Aaron, and were simply reckoned among the non-priestly families of Levi. The Korahites and Uzzielites are mentioned, but a superior rank was assigned to them in the subsequent history to that of other Levitical families (cf. Num. xvi., xvii., xxvi. 11, and iii. 30 with Lev. x. 4). Aaron's wife *Elisheba* was of the princely tribe of Judah, and her brother Naashon was a tribe-prince of Judah (cf. Num. ii. 3). רָאשֵׁי אָבוֹת (ver. 25), a frequent abbreviation for רָאשֵׁי בֵית־אָבוֹת, heads of the father's-houses of the Levites. In vers. 26 and 27, with which the genealogy closes, the object of introducing it is very clearly shown in the expression, " *These are that Aaron and Moses,*" at the beginning of ver. 26 ; and again, " *These are that Moses and Aaron,*" at the close of ver. 27. The reversal of the order of the names is also to be noticed. In the genealogy itself Aaron stands first, as the elder of the two ; in the conclusion, which leads over to the historical narrative that follows, Moses takes precedence of his elder brother, as being the divinely appointed redeemer of Israel. On the expression, " according to their armies," see chap. vii. 4.

Ver. 28–vii. 7. In vers. 28–30 the thread of the history, which was broken off at ver. 12, is again resumed. בְּיוֹם דִּבֶּר, on the day, *i.e.* at the time, when God spake. יוֹם is the construct state before an entire clause, which is governed by it without a relative particle, as in Lev. vii. 35, 1 Sam. xxv. 15 (*vid. Ewald,*

§ 286*i*). Moses' last difficulty (vi. 12, repeated in ver. 30) was removed by God with the words: " *See, I have made thee a god to Pharaoh, and Aaron thy brother shall be thy prophet*" (chap. vii. 1). According to chap. iv. 16, Moses was to be a god to Aaron; and in harmony with that, Aaron is here called the prophet of Moses, as being the person who would announce to Pharaoh the revelations of Moses. At the same time Moses was also made a god to Pharaoh; *i.e.* he was promised divine authority and power over Pharaoh, so that henceforth there was no more necessity for him to be afraid of the king of Egypt, but the latter, notwithstanding all resistance, would eventually bow before him. Moses was a god to Aaron as the revealer of the divine will, and to Pharaoh as the executor of that will.—In vers. 2–5 God repeats in a still more emphatic form His assurance, that notwithstanding the hardening of Pharaoh's heart, He would bring His people Israel out of Egypt. וְשִׁלַּח (ver. 2) does not mean *ut dimittat* or *mittat* (*Vulg. Ros.*; " *that he send,*" Eng. ver.); but ו is *vav consec. perf.*, " *and so he will send.*" On ver. 3 cf. chap. iv. 21.—Ver. 4. וְנָתַתִּי אֶת־יָדִי : " I will lay My hand on Egypt," *i.e.* smite Egypt, " and bring out My armies, My people, the children of Israel." צְבָאוֹת (armies) is used of Israel, with reference to its leaving Egypt equipped (chap. xiii. 18) and organized as an army according to the tribes (cf. vi. 26 and xii. 51 with Num. i. and ii.), to contend for the cause of the Lord, and fight the battles of Jehovah. In this respect the Israelites were called the hosts of Jehovah. The calling of Moses and Aaron was now concluded. Vers. 6 and 7 pave the way for the account of their performance of the duties consequent upon their call.

MOSES' NEGOTIATIONS WITH PHARAOH.—CHAP. VII. 8–XI. 10.

The negotiations of Moses and Aaron as messengers of Jehovah with the king of Egypt, concerning the departure of Israel from his land, commenced with a sign, by which the messengers of God attested their divine mission in the presence of Pharaoh (chap. vii. 8–13), and concluded with the announcement of the last blow that God would inflict upon the hardened king (chap. xi. 1–10). The centre of these negotiations, or rather the main point of this lengthened section, which is closely connected throughout, and formally rounded off by chap. xi. 9, 10 into an inward unity, is found in the *nine* plagues which the messengers of Jehovah brought upon Pharaoh and his kingdom at the command of Jehovah, to bend the defiant spirit of the king, and induce him to let Israel go out of the land and serve their God. If we carefully examine the account of these nine penal miracles, we shall find that they are arranged in three groups of three plagues each. For the first and second, the fourth and fifth, and the seventh and eighth were announced beforehand by Moses to the king (vii. 15, viii. 1, 20, ix. 1, 13, x. 1), whilst the third, sixth, and ninth were sent without any such announcement (viii. 16, ix. 8, x. 21). Again, the first, fourth, and seventh were announced to Pharaoh in the morning, and the first and fourth by the side of the Nile (vii. 15, viii. 20), both of them being connected with the overflowing of the river; whilst the place of announcement is not mentioned in the case of the seventh (the hail, chap. ix. 13), because hail, as coming from heaven, was not connected with any particular locality. This grouping is not a merely external arrangement, adopted by the writer for the sake of greater distinctness, but is founded in the facts themselves, and the effect which God intended the plagues to produce, as we may gather from these circumstances— that the Egyptian magicians, who had imitated the first plagues, were put to shame with their arts by the third, and were compelled to see in it the finger of God (viii. 19),—that they were smitten themselves by the sixth, and were unable to stand before Moses (ix. 11),—and that after the ninth, Pharaoh broke off all further negotiation with Moses and Aaron (x. 28, 29). The last plague, commonly known as the tenth, which Moses also announced to the king before his departure (xi. 4 sqq.), differed from the nine former ones both in purpose and form. It was the first beginning of the judgment that was coming upon the hardened king, and was inflicted directly by God Himself, for Jehovah "went out through the midst of Egypt, and smote the first-born of the Egyptians both of man and beast" (xi. 4, xii. 29); whereas seven of the previous plagues were brought by Moses and Aaron, and of the two that are not expressly said to have been brought by them, one, that of the dog-flies, was simply sent by Jehovah (viii. 21, 24), and the other, the murrain of beasts, simply came from His hand (ix. 3, 6). The last blow (נֶגַע xi. 1), which brought about the release of Israel, was also distinguished from the nine plagues, as the direct judgment of God, by the fact that it was not effected through the medium of any natural occurrence, as was the case with all the others, which were based upon the natural phenomena of Egypt, and became signs and wonders through their vast excess above the natural measure of such natural occurrences and their supernatural accumulation, blow after blow following one another in less than a year, and also through the peculiar circumstances under which they were brought about. In this respect also the triple division is unmistakeable. The first three plagues covered the whole land, and fell upon the Israelites as well as the Egyptians; with the fourth the separation commenced between Egyptians and Israelites, so that only the Egyptians suffered from the last six, the Israelites in Goshen being entirely exempted. The last three, again, were distinguished from the others by the fact, that they were far more dreadful than any of the previous ones, and bore visible marks of being the forerunners of the judgment which would inevitably fall upon Pharaoh, if he continued his opposition to the will of the Almighty God.

In this graduated series of plagues, the judgment of hardening was inflicted upon Pharaoh in the manner explained above. In the first three plagues God showed him, that He, the God of Israel, was Jehovah (vii. 17), *i.e.* that He ruled as Lord and King over the occurrences and powers of nature, which the Egyptians for the most part honoured as divine ; and before His power the magicians of Egypt with their secret arts were put to shame. These three wonders made no impression upon the king. The plague of frogs, indeed, became so troublesome to him, that he begged Moses and Aaron to intercede with their God to deliver him from them, and promised to let the people go (viii. 8). But as soon as they were taken away, he hardened his heart, and would not listen to the messengers of God. Of the three following plagues, the first (*i.e.* the fourth in the entire series), viz. the plague of swarming creatures or dog-flies, with which the distinction between the Egyptians and Israelites commenced, proving to Pharaoh that the God of Israel was Jehovah in the midst of the land (viii. 22), made such an impression upon the hardened king, that he promised to allow the Israelites to sacrifice to their God, first of all in the land, and when Moses refused this condition, even outside the land, if they would not go far away, and Moses and Aaron would pray to God for him, that this plague might be taken away by God from him and from his people (viii. 25 sqq.). But this concession was only forced out of him by suffering; so that as soon as the plague ceased he withdrew it again, and his hard heart was not changed by the two following plagues. Hence still heavier plagues were sent, and he had to learn from the last three that there was no god in the whole earth like Jehovah, the God of the Hebrews (ix. 14). The terrible character of these last plagues so affected the proud heart of Pharaoh, that twice he acknowledged he had sinned (ix. 27, x. 16), and gave a promise that he would let the Israelites go, restricting his promise first of all to the men, and then including their families also (x. 11, 24). But when this plague was withdrawn, he resumed his old sinful defiance once more (ix. 34, 35, x. 20), and finally was altogether hardened, and so enraged at Moses persisting in his demand that they should take their flocks as well, that he drove away the messengers of Jehovah and broke off all further negotiations, with the threat that he would kill them if ever they came into his presence again (x. 28, 29).

Chap. vii. 8–13. ATTESTATION OF THE DIVINE MISSION OF MOSES AND AARON.—By Jehovah's directions Moses and Aaron went to Pharaoh, and proved by a miracle (מוֹפֵת chap. iv. 21) that they were the messengers of the God of the Hebrews. Aaron threw down his staff before Pharaoh, and it became a serpent. Aaron's staff was no other than the wondrous staff of Moses (chap. iv. 2–4). This is perfectly obvious from a comparison of vers. 15 and 17 with vers. 19 and 20. If Moses was directed, according to vers. 15 sqq., to go before Pharaoh with his rod which had been turned into a serpent, and to announce to him that he would smite the water of the Nile with the staff in his hand and turn it into blood, and then, according to vers. 19 sqq., this miracle was carried out by Aaron taking his staff and stretching out his hand over the waters of Egypt, the staff which Aaron held over the water cannot have been any other than the staff of Moses which had been turned into a serpent. Consequently we must also understand by the staff of Aaron, which was thrown down before Pharaoh and became a serpent, the same wondrous staff of Moses, and attribute the expression " thy (*i.e.* Aaron's) staff" to the brevity of the account, *i.e.* to the fact that the writer restricted himself to the leading facts, and passed over such subordinate incidents as that Moses gave his staff to Aaron for him to work the miracle. For the same reason he has not even mentioned that Moses spoke to Pharaoh by Aaron, or what he said, although in ver. 13 he states that Pharaoh did not hearken unto them, *i.e.* to their message or their words. The serpent, into which the staff was changed, is not called נָחָשׁ here, as in ver. 15 and chap. iv. 3, but תַּנִּין (LXX. δράκων, dragon), a general term for snake-like animals. This difference does not show that there were two distinct records, but may be explained on the ground that the miracle performed before Pharaoh had a different signification from that which attested the divine mission of Moses in the presence of his people. The miraculous sign mentioned here is distinctly related to the art of snake-charming, which was carried to such an extent by the Psylli in ancient Egypt (cf. *Bochart*, and *Hengstenberg*, Egypt and Moses, pp. 98 sqq. transl.). It is probable that the Israelites in Egypt gave the name תַּנִּין (Eng. ver. *dragon*), which occurs in Deut. xxxii. 33 and Ps. xci. 13 as a parallel to פֶּתֶן (Eng. ver. *asp*), to the snake with which the Egyptian charmers generally performed their tricks, the *Hayeh* of the Arabs. What the magi and conjurers of Egypt boasted that they could perform by their secret or magical arts, Moses was to effect in reality in Pharaoh's presence, and thus manifest himself to the king as *Elohim* (ver. 1), *i.e.* as endowed with divine authority and power. All that is related of the Psylli of modern times is, that they understand the art of turning snakes into sticks, or of compelling them to become rigid and apparently dead (for examples see *Hengstenberg*); but who can tell what the ancient Psylli may have been able to effect, or may have pretended to effect, at a time when the demoniacal power of heathenism existed in its unbroken force? The magicians summoned by Pharaoh also turned their sticks into snakes (ver. 12); a fact which naturally excites the suspicion that the sticks themselves were only rigid snakes, though, with our very limited acquaintance with the dark domain of heathen conjuring, the possibility of their working " lying wonders after the working of Satan," *i.e.* supernatural things (2 Thess. ii. 9), cannot be absolutely denied. The words,

" They also, the *chartummim* of Egypt, did in like manner with their enchantments," are undoubtedly based upon the assumption, that the conjurers of Egypt not only pretended to possess the art of turning snakes into sticks, but of turning sticks into snakes as well, so that in the persons of the conjurers Pharaoh summoned the might of the gods of Egypt to oppose the might of Jehovah, the God of the Hebrews. For these magicians, whom the Apostle Paul calls *Jannes* and *Jambres*, according to the Jewish tradition (2 Tim. iii. 8), were not common jugglers, but חֲכָמִים " wise men," men educated in human and divine wisdom, and חַרְטֻמִּים, ἱερογραμματεῖς, belonging to the priestly caste (Gen. xli. 8) ; so that the power of their gods was manifested in their secret arts (לְהָטִים from לָהַט to conceal, to act secretly, like לְטִים in ver. 22 from לוּט), and in the defeat of their enchantments by Moses the gods of Egypt were overcome by Jehovah (chap. xii. 12). The supremacy of Jehovah over the demoniacal powers of Egypt manifested itself in the very first miraculous sign, in the fact that Aaron's staff swallowed those of the magicians ; though this miracle made no impression upon Pharaoh (ver. 13).

THE FIRST THREE PLAGUES.—CHAP. VII. 14—VIII. 15 (19).

When Pharaoh hardened his heart against the first sign, notwithstanding the fact that it displayed the supremacy of the messengers of Jehovah over the might of the Egyptian conjurers and their gods, and refused to let the people of Israel go ; Moses and Aaron were empowered by God to force the release of Israel from the obdurate king by a series of penal miracles. These מֹפְתִים were not purely supernatural wonders, or altogether unknown to the Egyptians, but were land-plagues with which Egypt was occasionally visited, and were raised into miraculous deeds of the Almighty God, by the fact that they burst upon the land one after another at an unusual time of the year, in unwonted force, and in close succession. These plagues were selected by God as miraculous signs, because He intended to prove thereby to the king and his servants, that He, Jehovah, was the Lord in the land, and ruled over the powers of nature with unrestricted freedom and omnipotence. For this reason God not only caused them to burst suddenly upon the land according to His word, and then as suddenly to disappear accord-

ing to His omnipotent will, but caused them to be produced by
Moses and Aaron and disappear again at their word and prayer,
that Pharaoh might learn that these men were appointed by Him
as His messengers, and were endowed by Him with divine power
for the accomplishment of His will.

Chap. vii. 14–25.—THE WATER OF THE NILE TURNED
INTO BLOOD.—In the morning, when Pharaoh went to the Nile,
Moses took his staff at the command of God; went up to him on
the bank of the river, with the demand of Jehovah that he would
let His people Israel go; and because hitherto (עַד־כֹּה) he had not
obeyed, announced this *first* plague, which Aaron immediately
brought to pass. Both time and place are of significance here.
Pharaoh went out in the morning to the Nile (ver. 15, chap.
viii. 20), not merely to take a refreshing walk, or to bathe in the
river, or to see how high the water had risen, but without doubt
to present his daily worship to the Nile, which was honoured by
the Egyptians as their supreme deity (*vid.* chap. ii. 5). At this
very moment the will of God with regard to Israel was declared
to him; and for his refusal to comply with the will of the Lord
as thus revealed to him, the smiting of the Nile with the staff
made known to him the fact, that the God of the Hebrews was
the true God, and possessed the power to turn the fertilizing
water of this object of their highest worship into blood. The
changing of the water into blood is to be interpreted in the same
sense as in Joel iii. 4, where the moon is said to be turned into
blood; that is to say, not as a chemical change into real blood,
but as a change in the colour, which caused it to assume the
appearance of blood (2 Kings iii. 22). According to the statements of many travellers, the Nile water changes its colour when
the water is lowest, assumes first of all a greenish hue and is
almost undrinkable, and then, while it is rising, becomes as red
as ochre, when it is more wholesome again. The causes of this
change have not been sufficiently investigated. The reddening
of the water is attributed by many to the red earth, which the
river brings down from Sennaar (cf. *Hengstenberg*, Egypt and the
Books of Moses, pp. 104 sqq. transl.; *Laborde, comment.* p. 28);
but *Ehrenberg* came to the conclusion, after microscopical exami-
nations, that it was caused by cryptogamic plants and infusoria.
This natural phenomenon was here intensified into a miracle, not

only by the fact that the change took place immediately in all the branches of the river at Moses' word and through the smiting of the Nile, but even more by a chemical change in the water, which caused the fishes to die, the stream to stink, and, what seems to indicate putrefaction, the water to become undrinkable; whereas, according to the accounts of travellers, which certainly do not quite agree with one another, and are not entirely trustworthy, the Nile water becomes more drinkable as soon as the natural reddening begins. The change in the water extended to " *the streams*," or different arms of the Nile; " *the rivers*," or Nile canals; " *the ponds*," or large standing lakes formed by the Nile; and all " *the pools of water*," lit. every collection of their waters, *i.e.* all the other standing lakes and ponds, left by the overflowings of the Nile, with the water of which those who lived at a distance from the river had to content themselves. " *So that there was blood in all the land of Egypt, both in the wood and in the stone;*" *i.e.* in the vessels of wood and stone, in which the water taken from the Nile and its branches was kept for daily use. The reference is not merely to the earthen vessels used for filtering and cleansing the water, but to every vessel into which water had been put. The " stone " vessels were the stone reservoirs built up at the corners of the streets and in other places, where fresh water was kept for the poor (cf. *Oedmann's verm. Samml.* p. 133). The meaning of this supplementary clause is not that even the water which was in these vessels previous to the smiting of the river was turned into blood, in which *Kurtz* perceives " the most miraculous part of the whole miracle;" for in that case the " wood and stone " would have been mentioned immediately after the "gatherings of the waters;" but simply that there was no more water to put into these vessels that was not changed into blood. The death of the fishes was a sign, that the smiting had taken away from the river its life-sustaining power, and that its red hue was intended to depict before the eyes of the Egyptians all the terrors of death; but we are not to suppose that there was any reference to the innocent blood which the Egyptians had poured into the river through the drowning of the Hebrew boys, or to their own guilty blood which was afterwards to be shed.—Ver. 22. This miracle was also imitated by the magicians. The question, where they got any water that was still unchanged, is not answered in the biblical text. *Kurtz* is of opinion that they took spring water for the purpose ; but he has overlooked the fact, that if spring water was still to be had, there would be no necessity for the Egyptians to dig wells for the purpose of finding drinkable water. The supposition that the magicians did not try their arts till the miracle wrought by Aaron had passed away, is hardly reconcilable with the text, which places the return of Pharaoh to his house after the work of the magicians. For it can neither be assumed, that the miracle wrought by the messengers of Jehovah lasted only a few hours, so that Pharaoh was able to wait by the Nile till it was over, since in that case the Egyptians would not have thought it necessary to dig wells ; nor can it be regarded as probable, that after the miracle was over, and the plague had ceased, the magicians began to imitate it for the purpose of showing the king that they could do the same, and that it was after this that the king went to his house without paying any heed to the miracle. We must therefore follow the analogy of chap. ix. 25 as compared with chap. x. 5, and not press the expression, "*every* collection of water" (ver. 19), so as to infer that there was no Nile water at all, not even what had been taken away before the smiting of the river, that was not changed, but rather conclude that the magicians tried their arts upon water that was already drawn, for the purpose of neutralizing the effect of the plague as soon as it had been produced. The fact that the clause, "Pharaoh's heart was hardened," is linked with the previous clause, "the magicians did so, etc.," by a *vav consecutive*, unquestionably implies that the imitation of the miracle by the magicians contributed to the hardening of Pharaoh's heart. The expression, "*to this also*," in ver. 23, points back to the first miraculous sign in vers. 10 sqq. This plague was keenly felt by the Egyptians ; for the Nile contains the only good drinking water, and its excellence is unanimously attested by both ancient and modern writers (*Hengstenberg ut sup.* pp. 108, 109, transl.). As they could not drink of the water of the river from their loathing at its stench (ver. 18), they were obliged to dig round about the river for water to drink (ver. 24). From this it is evident that the plague lasted a considerable time ; according to ver. 25, apparently seven days. At least this is the most natural interpretation of the words, "*and seven days were fulfilled after that Jehovah had smitten the river.*"

It is true, there is still the possibility that this verse may be connected with the following one, "*when seven days were fulfilled . . . Jehovah said to Moses.*" But this is not probable; for the time which intervened between the plagues is not stated anywhere else, nor is the expression, "Jehovah said," with which the plagues are introduced, connected in any other instance with what precedes. The narrative leaves it quite undecided how rapidly the plagues succeeded one another. On the supposition that the changing of the Nile water took place at the time when the river began to rise, and when the reddening generally occurs, many expositors fix upon the month of June or July for the commencement of the plague; in which case all the plagues down to the death of the first-born, which occurred in the night of the 14th Abib, *i.e.* about the middle of April, would be confined to the space of about nine months. But this conjecture is a very uncertain one, and all that is tolerably sure is, that the seventh plague (the hail) occurred in February (*vid.* chap. ix. 31, 32), and there were (not three weeks, but) eight weeks therefore, or about two months, between the seventh and tenth plagues; so that between each of the last three there would be an interval of fourteen or twenty days. And if we suppose that there was a similar interval in the case of all the others, the first plague would take place in September or October,—that is to say, after the yearly overflow of the Nile, which lasts from June to September.

Chap. viii. 1–15. The plague of FROGS, or the *second* plague, also proceeded from the Nile, and had its natural origin in the putridity of the slimy Nile water, whereby the marsh waters especially became filled with thousands of frogs. צְפַרְדֵּעַ is the small Nile frog, the *Dofda* of the Egyptians, called *rana Mosaica* or *Nilotica* by *Seetzen*, which appears in large numbers as soon as the waters recede. These frogs (הַצְפַרְדֵּעַ in chap. viii. 6, used collectively) became a penal miracle from the fact that they came out of the water in unparalleled numbers, in consequence of the stretching out of Aaron's staff over the waters of the Nile, as had been foretold to the king, and that they not only penetrated into the houses and inner rooms ("bed-chamber"), and crept into the domestic utensils, the beds (מִטָּה), the ovens, and the kneading-troughs (not the "dough" as *Luther* renders it), but even got upon the men themselves.—Ver. 7. This miracle was also imitated by the Egyptian augurs with their secret arts, and frogs were brought upon the land by them. But if they were able to bring the plague, they could not take it away. The latter is not expressly stated, it is true; but it is evident from the fact that Pharaoh was obliged to send for Moses and Aaron to intercede with Jehovah to take them away. The king would never have applied to Moses and Aaron for help if his charmers could have charmed the plague away. Moreover the fact that Pharaoh entreated them to intercede with Jehovah to take away the frogs, and promised to let the people go, that they might sacrifice to Jehovah (ver. 8), was a sign that he regarded the God of Israel as the author of the plague. To strengthen the impression made upon the king by this plague with reference to the might of Jehovah, Moses said to him (ver. 9), " *Glorify thyself over me, when I shall entreat for thee,*" *i.e.* take the glory upon thyself of determining the time when I shall remove the plague through my intercession. The expression is elliptical, and לֵאמֹר (saying) is to be supplied, as in Judg. vii. 2. To give Jehovah the glory, Moses placed himself below Pharaoh, and left him to fix the time for the frogs to be removed through his intercession.—Ver. 10. The king appointed the following day, probably because he hardly thought it possible for so great a work to be performed at once. Moses promised that it should be so: " *According to thy word* (sc. let it be), *that thou mayest know that there is not* (a God) *like Jehovah our God.*" He then went out and cried, *i.e.* called aloud and earnestly, to Jehovah concerning the matter (עַל דְּבַר) of the frogs, which he had set, *i.e.* prepared, for Pharaoh (שׂוּם as in Gen. xlv. 7). In consequence of his intercession God took the plague away. The frogs died off (מוּת מִן, to die away out of, from), out of the houses, and palaces, and fields, and were gathered together by bushels (חֳמָרִים from חֹמֶר, the *omer*, the largest measure used by the Hebrews), so that the land stank with the odour of their putrefaction. Though Jehovah had thus manifested Himself as the Almighty God and Lord of the creation, Pharaoh did not keep his promise; but when he saw that there was breathing-time (רְוָחָה, ἀνάψυξις, relief from an overpowering pressure), literally, as soon as he " *got air,*" he hardened his heart, so that he did not hearken to Moses and Aaron (וְהַכְבֵּד *inf. abs.* as in Gen. xli. 43).

Chap. viii. 16-19. The GNATS, or the *third* plague.—The כִּנָּם, or כִּנִּים (also כִּנָּם, probably an old singular form, *Ewald*, § 163*f*), were not "*lice*," but σκνῖφες, *sciniphes*, a species of gnats, so small as to be hardly visible to the eye, but with a sting which, according to *Philo* and *Origen*, causes a most painful irritation of the skin. They even creep into the eyes and nose, and after the harvest they rise in great swarms from the inundated rice-fields. This plague was caused by the fact that Aaron smote the dust of the ground with his staff, and all the dust throughout the land of Egypt turned into gnats, which were upon man and beast (ver. 17). "Just as the fertilizing water of Egypt had twice become a plague, so through the power of Jehovah the soil so richly blessed became a plague to the king and his people."—Ver. 18. "*The magicians did so with their enchantments (i.e.* smote the dust with rods), *to bring forth gnats, but could not.*" The cause of this inability is hardly to be sought for, as *Knobel* supposes, in the fact that "the thing to be done in this instance, was to call creatures into existence, and not merely to call forth and change creatures and things in existence already, as in the case of the staff, the water, and the frogs." For after this, they could neither call out the dog-flies, nor protect their own bodies from the boils; to say nothing of the fact, that as gnats proceed from the eggs laid in the dust or earth by the previous generation, their production is not to be regarded as a direct act of creation any more than that of the frogs. The miracle in both plagues was just the same, and consisted not in a direct creation, but simply in a sudden creative generation and supernatural multiplication, not of the gnats only, but also of the frogs, in accordance with a previous prediction. The reason why the arts of the Egyptian magicians were put to shame in this case, we have to seek in the omnipotence of God, restraining the demoniacal powers which the magicians had made subservient to their purposes before, in order that their inability to bring out these, the smallest of all creatures, which seemed to arise as it were from the dust itself, might display in the sight of every one the impotence of their secret arts by the side of the almighty creative power of the true God. This omnipotence the magicians were compelled to admit: they were compelled to acknowledge, "*This is the finger of God.*" "But they did not make this acknowledgment for the purpose of giving glory to

God Himself, but simply to protect their own honour, that Moses and Aaron might not be thought to be superior to them in virtue or knowledge. It was equivalent to saying, it is not by Moses and Aaron that we are restrained, but by a *divine power, which is greater than either*" (*Bochart*). The word *Elohim* is decisive in support of this view. If they had meant to refer to the God of Israel, they would have used the name *Jehovah.* The "finger of God" denotes creative omnipotence (Ps. viii. 3; Luke xi. 20, cf. Ex. xxxi. 18). Consequently this miracle also made no impression upon Pharaoh.

THE THREE FOLLOWING PLAGUES.—CHAP. VIII. 20–IX. 12.

As the Egyptian magicians saw nothing more than the finger of God in the miracle which they could not imitate, that is to say, the work of some deity, possibly one of the gods of the Egyptians, and not the hand of Jehovah the God of the Hebrews, who had demanded the release of Israel, a distinction was made in the plagues which followed between the Israelites and the Egyptians, and the former were exempted from the plagues : a fact which was sufficient to prove to any one that they came from the God of Israel. To make this the more obvious, the fourth and fifth plagues were merely announced by Moses to the king. They were not brought on through the mediation of either himself or Aaron, but were sent by Jehovah at the appointed time; no doubt for the simple purpose of precluding the king and his wise men from the excuse which unbelief might still suggest, viz. that they were produced by the powerful incantations of Moses and Aaron.

Chap. viii. 20–32. The *fourth* plague, the coming of which Moses foretold to Pharaoh, like the first, in the morning, and by the water (on the bank of the Nile), consisted in the sending of "*heavy vermin*," probably DOG-FLIES. עָרֹב, literally a mixture, is rendered κυνόμυια (dog-fly) by the LXX., πάμμυια (all-fly), a mixture of all kinds of flies, by *Symmachus.* These insects are described by *Philo* and many travellers as a very severe scourge (*vid. Hengstenberg ut sup.* p. 113). They are much more numerous and annoying than the gnats ; and when enraged, they fasten themselves upon the human body, especially upon the edges of the eyelids, and become a dreadful plague.

כָּבֵד : a *heavy* multitude, as in chap. x. 14, Gen. l. 9, etc. These
swarms were to fill "*the houses of the Egyptians, and even the
land upon which they* (the Egyptians) *were*," *i.e.* that part of the
land which was not occupied by houses; whilst the land of
Goshen, where the Israelites dwelt, would be entirely spared.
הִפְלָה (to separate, to distinguish in a miraculous way) is con-
jugated with an accusative, as in Ps. iv. 4. It is generally followed by בֵּין (chap. ix. 4, xi. 7), to distinguish between. עָמַד :
to stand upon a land, *i.e.* to inhabit, possess it; not to exist, or
live (chap. xxi. 21).—Ver. 23. "*And I will put a deliverance
between My people and thy people.*" פְּדֻת does not mean δια-
στολή, *divisio* (LXX., *Vulg.*), but redemption, deliverance.
Exemption from this plague was essentially a deliverance for
Israel, which manifested the distinction conferred upon Israel
above the Egyptians. By this plague, in which a separation
and deliverance was established between the people of God and
the Egyptians, Pharaoh was to be taught that the God who sent
this plague was not some deity of Egypt, *but* "*Jehovah in the
midst of the land*" (of Egypt); *i.e.* as *Knobel* correctly interprets
it, (*a*) that Israel's God was the author of the plague; (*b*) that
He had also authority over Egypt; and (*c*) that He possessed
supreme authority: or, to express it still more concisely, that
Israel's God was the Absolute God, who ruled both in and over
Egypt with free and boundless omnipotence.—Vers. 24 sqq. This
plague, by which the land was destroyed (תִּשָּׁחֵת), or desolated,
inasmuch as the flies not only tortured, "devoured" (Ps. lxxviii.
45) the men, and disfigured them by the swellings produced by
their sting, but also killed the plants in which they deposited
their eggs, so alarmed Pharaoh that he sent for Moses and
Aaron, and gave them permission to sacrifice to their God "*in
the land.*" But Moses could not consent to this restriction. "*It
is not appointed so to do*" נָכוֹן does not mean *aptum, conveniens,*
but *statutum, rectum*), for two reasons: (1) because sacrificing
in the land would be an abomination to the Egyptians, and
would provoke them most bitterly (ver. 26); and (2) because
they could only sacrifice to Jehovah their God as He had
directed them (ver. 27). The abomination referred to did not
consist in their sacrificing animals which the Egyptians regarded
as holy. For the word תּוֹעֵבָה (*abomination*) would not be applicable to the sacred animals. Moreover, the cow was the only

animal offered in sacrifice by the Israelites, which the Egyptian regarded as sacred. The abomination would rather be this, that the Israelites would not carry out the rigid regulations observed by the Egyptians with regard to the cleanness of the sacrificial animals (vid. Hengstenberg, p. 114), and in fact would not observe the sacrificial rites of the Egyptians at all. The Egyptians would be very likely to look upon this as an insult to their religion and their gods; "the violation of the recognised mode of sacrificing would be regarded as a manifestation of contempt for themselves and their gods" (Calvin), and this would so enrage them that they would stone the Israelites. The הֵן before מִזְבֵּחַ in ver. 26 is the interjection lo! but it stands before a conditional clause, introduced without a conditional particle, in the sense of if, which it has retained in the Chaldee, and in which it is used here and there in the Hebrew (e.g. Lev. xxv. 20).—Vers. 28–32. These reasons commended themselves to the heathen king from his own religious standpoint. He promised, therefore, to let the people go into the wilderness and sacrifice, provided they did not go far away, if Moses and Aaron would release him and his people from this plague through their intercession. Moses promised that the swarms should be removed the following day, but told the king not to deceive them again as he had done before (ver. 8). But Pharaoh hardened his heart as soon as the plague was taken away, just as he had done after the second plague (ver. 15), to which the word "also" refers (ver. 32).

Chap. ix. 1–7. The *fifth* plague consisted of a severe MUR-RAIN, which carried off the cattle (מִקְנֶה, the living property) of the Egyptians, that were in the field. To show how Pharaoh was accumulating guilt by his obstinate resistance, in the announcement of this plague the expression, "*If thou refuse to let them go*" (cf. viii. 2), is followed by the words, "*and wilt hold them* (the Israelites) *still*" (עוֹד still further, even after Jehovah has so emphatically declared His will).—Ver. 3. "*The hand of Jehovah will be* (הוֹיָה, which only occurs here, as the participle of הָיָה, generally takes its form from הֹוֶה, Neh. vi. 6; Eccl. ii. 22) *against thy cattle . . as a very severe plague* (דֶּבֶר that which sweeps away, a plague), *i.e.* will smite them with a severe plague. A distinction was again made between the Israelites and the Egyptians. "*Of all* (the cattle) *belonging to the children of Israel, not one* (דָּבָר ver. 4,=אֶחָד ver. 6) *shall die.*" A definite time was also fixed for the coming of the plague, as in the case of the previous one (viii. 23), in order that, whereas murrains occasionally occur in Egypt, Pharaoh might discern in his one the judgment of Jehovah.—Ver. 6. In the words *"all the cattle of the Egyptians died," all* is not to be taken in an absolute sense, but, according to popular usage, as denoting such a quantity, that what remained was nothing in comparison; and, according to ver. 3, it must be entirely restricted to the cattle *in the field.* For, according to vers. 9 and 19, much of the cattle of the Egyptians still remained even after this murrain, though it extended to all kinds of cattle, horses, asses, camels, oxen, and sheep, and differed in this respect from natural murrains.— Ver. 7. But Pharaoh's heart still continued hardened, though he convinced himself by direct inquiry that the cattle of the Israelites had been spared.

Vers. 8–12. The *sixth* plague smote man and beast with BOILS BREAKING FORTH IN BLISTERS.—שְׁחִין (a common disease in Egypt, Deut. xxviii. 27) from the unusual word שָׁחַן (*incaluit*) signifies inflammation, then an *abscess or boil* (Lev. xiii. 18 sqq.; 2 Kings xx. 7). אֲבַעְבֻּעֹת, from בּוּעַ, to spring up, swell up, signifies blisters, φλυκτίδες (LXX), *pustulæ.* The natural substratum of this plague is discovered by most commentators in the so-called Nile-blisters, which come out in innumerable little pimples upon the scarlet-coloured skin, and change in a short space of time into small, round, and thickly-crowded blisters. This is called by the Egyptians *Hamm el Nil,* or the heat of the inundation. According to Dr *Bilharz,* it is a rash, which occurs in summer, chiefly towards the close at the time of the overflowing of the Nile, and produces a burning and pricking sensation upon the skin; or, in *Seetzen's* words, " it consists of small, red, and slightly rounded elevations in the skin, which give strong twitches and slight stinging sensations, resembling those of scarlet fever" (p. 209). The cause of this eruption, which occurs only in men and not in animals, has not been determined; some attributing it to the water, and others to the heat. *Leyrer,* in *Herzog's* Cyclopædia, speaks of the " *Anthrax* which stood in a causal relation to the fifth plague ; a black, burning abscess, which frequently occurs after a murrain, especially the cattle distemper, and which might be called to mind by the name ἄνθραξ, coal, and the symbolical sprinkling of the soot of the furnace." In any case, the manner in which this plague was produced was significant, though it cannot be explained with positive certainty, especially as we are unable to decide exactly what was the natural disease which lay at the foundation of. the plague.   At the command of God, Moses and Aaron took *" handfuls of soot, and sprinkled it towards the heaven, so that it became dust over all the land of Egypt,"* i.e. flew like dust over the land, and became boils on man and beast.   פִּיחַ הַכִּבְשָׁן : soot or ashes of the smelting-furnace or lime-kiln.   כִּבְשָׁן is not an oven or cooking stove, but, as *Kimchi* supposes, a smelting-furnace or lime-kiln; not so called, however, *a metallis domandis*, but from כָּבַשׁ in its primary signification to press together, hence (*a*) to soften, or melt, (*b*) to tread down.   *Burder's* view seems inadmissible ; namely, that this symbolical act of Moses had some relation to the expiatory rites of the ancient Egyptians, in which the ashes of sacrifices, particularly human sacrifices, were scattered about.   For it rests upon the supposition that Moses took the ashes from a fire appropriated to the burning of sacrifices— a supposition to which neither כִּבְשָׁן nor פִּיחַ is appropriate.   For the former does not signify a fire-place, still less one set apart for the burning of sacrifices, and the ashes taken from the sacrifices for purifying purposes were called אֵפֶר, and not פִּיחַ (Num. xix. 10).   Moreover, such an interpretation as this, namely, that the ashes set apart for purifying purposes produced impurity in the hands of Moses, as a symbolical representation of the thought, that " the religious purification promised in the sacrificial worship of Egypt was really a defilement," does not answer at all to the effect produced.   The ashes scattered in the air by Moses did not produce defilement, but boils or blisters ; and we have no ground for supposing that they were regarded by the Egyptians as a religious defilement.   And, lastly, there was not one of the plagues in which the object was to pronounce condemnation upon the Egyptian worship or sacrifices ; since Pharaoh did not wish to force the Egyptian idolatry upon the Israelites, but simply to prevent them from leaving the country.

The ashes or soot of the smelting-furnace or lime-kiln bore, no doubt, the same relation to the plague arising therefrom, as the water of the Nile and the dust of the ground to the three plagues which proceeded from them.   As Pharaoh and his people owed their prosperity, wealth, and abundance of earthly goods to the fertilizing waters of the Nile and the fruitful soil, so it was from the lime-kilns, so to speak, that those splendid cities and pyramids proceeded, by which the early Pharaohs endeavoured to immortalize the power and glory of their reigns. And whilst in the first three plagues the natural sources of the land were changed by Jehovah, through His servants Moses and Aaron, into sources of evil, the sixth plague proved to the proud king that Jehovah also possessed the power to bring ruin upon him from the workshops of those splendid edifices, for the erection of which he had made use of the strength of the Israelites, and oppressed them so grievously with burdensome toil as to cause Egypt to become like a furnace for smelting iron (Deut. iv. 20), and that He could make the soot or ashes of the lime-kiln, the residuum of that fiery heat and emblem of the furnace in which Israel groaned, into a seed which, when carried through the air at His command, would produce burning boils on man and beast throughout all the land of Egypt. These boils were the first plague which attacked and endangered the lives of men; and in this respect it was the first foreboding of the death which Pharaoh would bring upon himself by his continued resistance. The priests were so far from being able to shelter the king from this plague by their secret arts, that they were attacked by them themselves, were unable to stand before Moses, and were obliged to give up all further resistance. But Pharaoh did not take this plague to heart, and was given up to the divine sentence of hardening.

THE LAST THREE PLAGUES.—CHAP. IX. 13–XI. 10.

As the plagues had thus far entirely failed to bend the unyielding heart of Pharaoh under the will of the Almighty God, the terrors of that judgment, which would infallibly come upon him, were set before him in three more plagues, which were far more terrible than any that had preceded them. That these were to be preparatory to the last decisive blow, is proved by the great solemnity with which they were announced to the hardened king (vers. 13–16). This time Jehovah was about to " send all His strokes at the heart of Pharaoh, and against his servants and his people" (ver. 14). אֶל־לִבְּךָ does not signify " against thy person," for לֵב is not used for נֶפֶשׁ, and even the latter is not a periphrasis for "person;" but the strokes were to go to the king's heart. "It announces that they will be plagues that will not only strike the head and arms, but penetrate the very heart, and inflict a mortal wound" (*Calvin*). From the plural "*strokes*," it is evident that this threat referred not only to the seventh plague, viz. the hail, but to all the other plagues, through which Jehovah was about to make known to the king that "there was none like Him in all the earth;" *i.e.* that not one of the gods whom the heathen worshipped was like Him, the only true God. For, in order to show this, Jehovah had not smitten Pharaoh and his people at once with pestilence and cut them off from the earth, but had set him up to make him see, *i.e.* discern or feel His power, and to glorify His name in all the earth (vers. 15, 16). In ver. 15 שָׁלַחְתִּי וגו׳ (I have stretched out, etc.) is to be taken as the conditional clause: "*If I had now stretched out My hand and smitten thee . . . thou wouldest have been cut off.*" הֶעֱמַדְתִּיךָ forms the antithesis to תִּכָּחֵד, and means to cause to stand or continue, as in 1 Kings xv. 4, 2 Chron. ix. 8 (διετηρήθης LXX.). Causing to stand presupposes setting up. In this first sense the Apostle Paul has rendered it ἐξήγειρα in Rom. ix. 17, in accordance with the purport of his argument, because "God thereby appeared still more decidedly as absolutely determining all that was done by Pharaoh" (*Philippi* on Rom. ix. 17). The reason why God had not destroyed Pharaoh at once was twofold: (1) that Pharaoh himself might experience (הַרְאֹת to cause to see, *i.e.* to experience) the might of Jehovah, by which he was compelled more than once to give glory to Jehovah (ver. 27, chap. x. 16, 17, xii. 31); and (2) that the name of Jehovah might be declared throughout all the earth. As both the rebellion of the natural man against the word and will of God, and the hostility of the world-power to the Lord and His people, were concentrated in Pharaoh, so there were manifested in the judgments suspended over him the patience and grace of the living God, quite as much as His holiness, justice, and omnipotence, as a warning to impenitent sinners, and a support to the faith of the godly, in a manner that should be typical for all times and circumstances of the kingdom of God in conflict with the ungodly world. The report of this glorious manifestation of Jehovah spread at once among all the surrounding nations (cf. xv. 14 sqq.), and travelled not only to the Arabians, but to the Greeks and Romans also, and eventually with the Gospel of Christ to all the nations of the earth (*vid. Tholuck* on Rom. ix. 17).

Chap. ix. 17–35. The *seventh plague*.—To break down Pharaoh's opposition, Jehovah determined to send such a HAIL as had not been heard of since the founding of Egypt, accompanied by thunder and masses of fire, and to destroy every man and beast that should be in the field. עוֹדְךָ מִסְתּוֹלֵל : "*thou still dammest thyself up against My people.*" הִסְתּוֹלֵל: to set one's self as a dam, *i.e.* to oppose; from סָלַל, to heap up earth as a dam or rampart. "*To-morrow about this time,*" to give Pharaoh time for reflection. Instead of "from the day that Egypt was founded until now," we find in ver. 24 "*since it became a nation,*" since its existence as a kingdom or nation.—Ver. 19. The good advice to be given by Moses to the king, to secure the men and cattle that were in the field, *i.e.* to put them under shelter, which was followed by the God-fearing Egyptians (ver. 21), was a sign of divine mercy, which would still rescue the hardened man and save him from destruction. Even in Pharaoh's case the possibility still existed of submission to the will of God; the hardening was not yet complete. But as he paid no heed to the word of the Lord, the predicted judgment was fulfilled (vers. 22–26). "*Jehovah gave voices*" (קֹלֹת); called "voices of God" in ver 28. This term is applied to the thunder (cf. xix. 16, xx. 18; Ps. xxix. 3–9), as being the mightiest manifestation of the omnipotence of God, which speaks therein to men (Rev. x. 3, 4), and warns them of the terrors of judgment. These terrors were heightened by masses of fire, which came down from the sky along with the hail that smote man and beast in the field, destroyed the vegetables, and shattered the trees. "*And fire ran along upon the ground :*" תִּהֲלַךְ is a Kal, though it sounds like Hithpael, and signifies *grassari*, as in Ps. lxxiii. 9.—Ver. 24. "*Fire mingled;*" lit. collected together, *i.e.* formed into balls (cf. Ezek. i. 4). "The lightning took the form of balls of fire, which came down like burning torches."—Ver. 25. The expressions, "*every herb,*" and "*every tree,*" are not to be taken absolutely, just as in ver. 6, as we may see from chap. x. 5. Storms are not common in Lower or Middle Egypt, but they occur most frequently between the months of December and April; and hail sometimes accompanies them, though not with great severity. In themselves, therefore, thunder, lightning, and hail were not unheard of. They also came at the time of year when they usually occur, namely, when the cattle were in the field, *i.e.* between January and April, the only period in which cattle are turned out for pasture (for proofs, see *Hengstenberg*, Egypt and the Books of Moses). The supernatural character of this plague was manifested, not only in its being predicted by Moses, and in the exemption of the land of Goshen, but more especially in the terrible fury of the hail-storm, which made a stronger impression upon Pharaoh than all the previous plagues. For he sent for Moses and Aaron, and confessed to them, " *I have sinned this time : Jehovah is righteous ; I and my people are the sinners*" (vers. 27 sqq.). But the very limitation "this time" showed that his repentance did not go very deep, and that his confession was far more the effect of terror caused by the majesty of God, which was manifested in the fearful thunder and lightning, than a genuine acknowledgment of his guilt. This is apparent also from the words which follow : " *Pray to Jehovah for me, and let it be enough* (רַב *satis*, as in Gen. xlv. 28) *of the being* (מִהְיֹת) *of the voices of God and of the hail ;*" *i.e.* there has been enough thunder and hail, they may cease now.—Ver. 29. Moses promised that his request should be granted, that he might know " *that the land belonged to Jehovah*," *i.e.* that Jehovah ruled as Lord over Egypt (cf. viii. 18) ; at the same time he told him that the fear manifested by himself and his servants was no true fear of God. יְרֵא מִפְּנֵי יי denotes the true fear of God, which includes a voluntary subjection to the divine will. Observe the expression, *Jehovah, Elohim* : Jehovah, who is Elohim, the Being to be honoured as supreme, the true God.

The account of the loss caused by the hail is introduced very appropriately in vers. 31 and 32, to show how much had been lost, and how much there was still to lose through continued refusal. " *The flax and the barley were smitten, for the barley was ear, and the flax was* גִּבְעֹל (*blossom*) ; *i.e.* they were neither of them quite ripe, but they were already in ear and blossom, so that they were broken and destroyed by the hail. " *The wheat*," on the other hand, " *and the spelt were not broken down, because they were tender, or late*" (אֲפִילֹת) ; *i.e.* they had no ears as yet, and therefore could not be broken by the hail. These accounts are in harmony with the natural history of Egypt. According to *Pliny*, the barley is reaped in the sixth month after the sowing-time, the wheat in the seventh. The barley is ripe about the end of February or beginning of March; the wheat, at the end of March or beginning of April. The flax is in flower at the end of January. In the neighbourhood of Alexandria, and therefore quite in the north of Egypt, the spelt is ripe at the end of April, and farther south it is probably somewhat earlier; for, according to other accounts, the wheat and spelt ripen at the same time (*vid. Hengstenberg*, p. 119). Consequently the plague of hail occurred at the end of January, or at the latest in the first half of February; so that there were at least eight weeks between the seventh and tenth plagues. The hail must have smitten the half, therefore, of the most important field-produce, viz. the barley, which was a valuable article of food both for men, especially the poorer classes, and for cattle, and the flax, which was also a very important part of the produce of Egypt; whereas the spelt, of which the Egyptians preferred to make their bread (*Herod.* 2, 36, 77), and the wheat were still spared.—Vers. 33–35. But even this plague did not lead Pharaoh to alter his mind. As soon as it had ceased on the intercession of Moses, he and his servants continued sinning and hardening their hearts.

Chap. x. 1–20. The eighth plague; the LOCUSTS.—Vers. 1–6. As Pharaoh's pride still refused to bend to the will of God, Moses was directed to announce another, and in some respects a more fearful, plague. At the same time God strengthened Moses' faith, by telling him that the hardening of Pharaoh and his servants was decreed by Him, that these signs might be done among them, and that Israel might perceive by this to all generations that He was Jehovah (cf. vii. 3–5). We may learn from Ps. lxxviii. and cv. in what manner the Israelites narrated these signs to their children and children's children. שִׁית אֹתֹת, to set or prepare signs (ver. 1), is interchanged with שֹׂים (ver. 2) in the same sense (*vid.* chap. viii. 12). The suffix in בְּקִרְבּוֹ (ver. 1) refers to Egypt as a country; and that in בָּם (ver. 2) to the Egyptians. In the expression, "*thou mayest tell,*" Moses is addressed as the representative of the nation. הִתְעַלֵּל : to have to do with a person, generally in a bad sense, to do him harm (1 Sam. xxxi. 4). "How I have put forth My might" (*De Wette*).—Ver. 3. As Pharaoh had acknowledged, when the previous plague was sent, that Jehovah was righteous (ix. 27), his crime was placed still more strongly before him: "*How long wilt thou refuse to humble*

thyself before Me?" (לְעֻנֹת for לְהֵעָנֹת, as in chap. xxxiv. 24).—
Vers. 4 sqq. To punish this obstinate refusal, Jehovah would
bring locusts in such dreadful swarms as Egypt had never known
before, which would eat up all the plants left by the hail, and
even fill the houses. *" They will cover the eye of the earth."*
This expression, which is peculiar to the Pentateuch, and only
occurs again in ver. 15 and Num. xxii. 5, 11, is based upon the
ancient and truly poetic idea, that the earth, with its covering of
plants, looks up to man. To substitute the rendering "surface"
for the "eye," is to destroy the real meaning of the figure;
"face" is better. It was in the swarms that actually hid the
ground that the fearful character of the plague consisted, as the
swarms of locusts consume everything green. "The residue of
the escape" is still further explained as "that which remaineth
unto you from the hail," viz. the spelt and wheat, and all the
vegetables that were left (vers. 12 and 15). For "all the trees
that sprout" (ver. 5), we find in ver. 15, "all the tree-fruits and
everything green upon the trees."

Vers. 7–11. The announcement of such a plague of locusts,
as their forefathers had never seen before since their existence
upon earth, *i.e.* since the creation of man (ver. 6), put the servants of Pharaoh in such fear, that they tried to persuade the
king to let the Israelites go. *" How long shall this* (Moses) *be a
snare to us? . . . Seest thou not yet, that Egypt is destroyed?"*
מוֹקֵשׁ, a snare or trap for catching animals, is a figurative expression for destruction. הָאֲנָשִׁים (ver. 7) does not mean the men,
but the people. The servants wished all the people to be allowed
to go as Moses had desired; but Pharaoh would only consent to
the departure of the men (הַגְּבָרִים, ver. 11).—Ver. 8. As Moses
had left Pharaoh after announcing the plague, he was fetched
back again along with Aaron, in consequence of the appeal made
to the king by his servants, and asked by the king, how many
wanted to go to the feast. מִי וָמִי, *" who and who still further
are the going ones;"* *i.e.* those who wish to go? Moses required
the whole nation to depart, without regard to age or sex, along
with all their flocks and herds. He mentioned *" young and old,
sons and daughters;"* the wives as belonging to the men being
included in the *" we."* Although he assigned a reason for this
demand, viz. that they were to hold a feast to Jehovah, Pharaoh
was so indignant, that he answered scornfully at first: *" Be it so;*

Jehovah be with you when I let you and your little ones go ;" i.e. may Jehovah help you in the same way in which I let you and your little ones go. This indicated contempt not only for Moses and Aaron, but also for Jehovah, who had nevertheless proved Himself, by His manifestations of mighty power, to be a God who would not suffer Himself to be trifled with. After this utterance of his ill-will, Pharaoh told the messengers of God that he could see through their intention. *"Evil is before your face ;"* i.e. you have evil in view. He called their purpose an evil one, because they wanted to withdraw the people from his service. *"Not so,"* i.e. let it not be as you desire. *"Go then, you men, and serve Jehovah."* But even this concession was not seriously meant. This is evident from the expression, *"Go then,"* in which the irony is unmistakeable ; and still more so from the fact, that with these words he broke off all negotiation with Moses and Aaron, and drove them from his presence. וַיְגָרֶשׁ : *"one drove them forth ;"* the subject is not expressed, because it is clear enough that the royal servants who were present were the persons who drove them away. *"For this are ye seeking :"* אַתֶּם relates simply to the words "serve Jehovah," by which the king understood the sacrificial festival, for which in his opinion only the men could be wanted ; not that "he supposed the people for whom Moses had asked permission to go, to mean only the men" (*Knobel*). The restriction of the permission to depart to the men alone was pure caprice ; for even the Egyptians, according to Herodotus (2, 60), held religious festivals at which the women were in the habit of accompanying the men.

Vers. 12–15. After His messengers had been thus scornfully treated, Jehovah directed Moses to bring the threatened plague upon the land. *"Stretch out thy hand over the land of Egypt with locusts ;"* i.e. so that the locusts may come. עָלָה, to go up : the word used for a hostile invasion. The locusts are represented as an army, as in Joel i. 6. Locusts were not an unknown scourge in Egypt ; and in the case before us they were brought, as usual, by the wind. The marvellous character of the phenomenon was, that when Moses stretched out his hand over Egypt with the staff, Jehovah caused an east wind to blow over the land, which blew a day and a night, and the next morning brought the locusts (*"brought :"* inasmuch as the swarms of locusts are really brought by the wind).—Ver. 13. *"An east*

wind : not νότος (LXX.), the south wind, as *Bochart* supposed.
Although the swarms of locusts are generally brought into Egypt
from Libya or Ethiopia, and therefore by a south or south-west
wind, they are sometimes brought by the east wind from Arabia,
as *Denon* and others have observed (Hgstb. p. 120). The fact
that the wind blew a day and a night before bringing the locusts,
showed that they came from a great distance, and therefore
proved to the Egyptians that the omnipotence of Jehovah reached
far beyond the borders of Egypt, and ruled over every land.
Another miraculous feature in this plague was its unparalleled
extent, viz. over the whole of the land of Egypt, whereas ordinary swarms are confined to particular districts. In this respect
the judgment had no equal either before or afterwards (ver. 14).
The words, " *Before them there were no such locusts as they, neither
after them shall be such,*" must not be diluted into "a hyperbolical and proverbial saying, implying that there was no recollection of such noxious locusts," as it is by *Rosenmüller.* This
passage is not at variance with Joel ii. 2, for the former relates
to Egypt, the latter to the land of Israel ; and Joel's description
unquestionably refers to the account before us, the meaning
being, that quite as terrible a judgment would fall upon Judah
and Israel as had formerly been inflicted upon Egypt and the
obdurate Pharaoh. In its dreadful character, this Egyptian
plague is a type of the plagues which will precede the last judgment, and forms the groundwork for the description in Rev. ix.
3–10 ; just as Joel discerned in the plagues which burst upon
Judah in his own day a presage of the day of the Lord (Joel i.
15, ii. 1), *i.e.* of the great day of judgment, which is advancing
step by step in all the great judgments of history or rather of
the conflict between the kingdom of God and the powers of this
world, and will be finally accomplished in the last general judgment.—Ver. 15. The darkening of the land, and the eating up
of all the green plants by swarms of locusts, have been described
by many eye-witnesses of such plagues. "*Locustarum plerumque
tanta conspicitur in Africa frequentia, ut volantes instar nebulæ
solis radios operiant*" (*Leo Afric.*). "*Solemque obumbrant*"
(*Pliny, h. n.* ii. 29).

Vers. 16–20. This plague, which even *Pliny* calls *Deorum
iræ pestis,* so terrified Pharaoh, that he sent for Moses and
Aaron in haste, confessed his sin against Jehovah and them,

and entreated them but this once more to procure, through their intercession with Jehovah their God, the forgiveness of his sin and the removal of " *this death.*" He called the locusts *death,* as bringing death and destruction, and ruining the country. *Mors etiam agrorum est et herbarum atque arborum,* as *Bochart* observes with references to Gen. xlvii. 19; Job xiv. 8; Ps. xlviii. 47.— Vers. 18, 19. To show the hardened king the greatness of the divine long-suffering, Moses prayed to the Lord, and the Lord cast the locusts into the Red Sea by a strong west wind. The expression "*Jehovah turned a very strong west wind*" is a concise form, for "Jehovah turned the wind into a very strong west wind." The fact that locusts do perish in the sea is attested by many authorities. *Gregatim sublatæ vento in maria aut stagna decidunt (Pliny);* many others are given by *Bochart* and *Volney.* וַיִּתְקָעֵהוּ : He thrust them, *i.e.* drove them with irresistible force, into the Red Sea. The Red Sea is called יַם סוּף, according to the ordinary supposition, on account of the quantity of sea-weed which floats upon the water and lies upon the shore; but *Knobel* traces the name to a town which formerly stood at the head of the gulf, and derived its name from the weed, and supports his opinion by the omission of the article before *Suph,* though without being able to prove that any such town really existed in the earlier times of the Pharaohs.

Vers. 21-29. Ninth plague: THE DARKNESS.—As Pharaoh's defiant spirit was not broken yet, a continuous darkness came over all the land of Egypt, with the exception of Goshen, without any previous announcement, and came in such force that the darkness could be felt. וְיָמֵשׁ חֹשֶׁךְ : " *and one shall feel, grasp darkness.*" הָמֵשׁ : as in Ps. cxv. 7, Judg. xvi. 26, ψηλαφη-τὸν σκότος (LXX.); not " feel in the dark," for מָשַׁשׁ has this meaning only in the Piel with בְּ (Deut. xxviii. 29). חֹשֶׁךְ אֲפֵלָה : *darkness of obscurity, i.e.* the deepest darkness. The combination of two words or synonyms gives the greatest intensity to the thought. The darkness was so great that they could not see one another, and no one rose up from his place. The Israelites alone " *had light in their dwelling-places.*" The reference here is not to the houses; so that we must not infer that the Egyptians were unable to kindle any lights even in their houses. The cause of this darkness is not given in the text; but the analogy of the other plagues, which had all of them a natural basis, warrants us in assuming, as most commentators have done, that there was the same here—that it was in fact the *Chamsin,* to which the LXX. evidently allude in their rendering: σκότος καὶ γνόφος καὶ θύελλα. This wind, which generally blows in Egypt before and after the vernal equinox and lasts two or three days, usually rises very suddenly, and fills the air with such a quantity of 'fine dust and coarse sand, that the sun loses its brightness, the sky is covered with a dense veil, and it becomes so dark that "the obscurity caused by the thickest fog in our autumn and winter days is nothing in comparison" (*Schubert*). Both men and animals hide themselves from this storm; and the inhabitants of the towns and villages shut themselves up in the innermost rooms and cellars of their houses till it is over, for the dust penetrates even through well-closed windows. For fuller accounts taken from travels, see *Hengstenberg* (pp. 120 sqq.) and *Robinson's* Palestine i. pp. 287–289. *Seetzen* attributes the rising of the dust to a quantity of electrical fluid contained in the air.—The fact that in this case the darkness alone is mentioned, may have arisen from its symbolical importance. "The darkness which covered the Egyptians, and the light which shone upon the Israelites, were types of the wrath and grace of God" (*Hengstenberg*). This occurrence, in which, according to Arabian chroniclers of the middle ages, the nations discerned a foreboding of the day of judgment or of the resurrection, filled the king with such alarm that he sent for Moses, and told him he would let the people and their children go, but the cattle must be left behind. יֻצָּג‎: *sistatur,* let it be placed, deposited in certain places under the guard of Egyptians, as a pledge of your return. *Maneat in pignus, quod reversuri sitis,* as *Chaskuni* correctly paraphrases it. But Moses insisted upon the cattle being taken for the sake of their sacrifices and burnt-offerings. "*Not a hoof shall be left behind.*" This was a proverbial expression for "not the smallest fraction." *Bochart* gives instances of a similar introduction of the "hoof" into proverbial sayings by both Arabians and Romans (Hieroz. i. p. 490). This firmness on the part of Moses he defended by saying, "*We know not with what we shall serve the Lord, till we come thither;*" *i.e.* we know not yet what kind of animals or how many we shall require for the sacrifices; our God will not make this known to us till we arrive at the place of sacrifice. עֲבֹד‎ ·

with a double accusative as in Gen. xxx. 29; to serve any one with a thing.—Vers. 27 sqq. At this demand, Pharaoh, with the hardness suspended over him by God, fell into such wrath, that he sent Moses away, and threatened him with death, if he ever appeared in his presence again. *"See my face,"* as in Gen. xliii. 3. Moses answered, *" Thou hast spoken rightly."* For as God had already told him that the last blow would be followed by the immediate release of the people, there was no further necessity for him to appear before Pharaoh.

Chap. xi. PROCLAMATION OF THE TENTH PLAGUE; OR THE DECISIVE BLOW.—Vers. 1–3. The announcement made by Jehovah to Moses, which is recorded here, occurred before the last interview between Moses and Pharaoh (x. 24–29); but it is introduced by the historian in this place, as serving to explain the confidence with which Moses answered Pharaoh (x. 29). This is evident from vers. 4–8, where Moses is said to have foretold to the king, before leaving his presence, the last plague and all its consequences. וַיֹּאמֶר therefore, in ver. 1, is to be taken in a pluperfect sense: *" had said;"* and may be grammatically accounted for from the old Semitic style of historical writing referred to at p. 87, as vers. 1 and 2 contain the foundation for the announcement in vers. 4–8. So far as the facts are concerned, vers. 1–3 point back to chap. iii. 19–22. One stroke more (נֶגַע) would Jehovah bring upon Pharaoh and Egypt, and then the king would let the Israelites go, or rather drive them out. כְּשַׁלְּחוֹ כָּלָה, *"when he lets you go altogether* (כָּלָה adverbial as in Gen. xviii. 21), *he will even drive you away."*—Vers. 2, 3 In this way Jehovah would overcome the resistance of Pharaoh; and even more than that, for Moses was to tell the people to ask the Egyptians for articles of silver and gold, for Jehovah would make them willing to give. The renown acquired by Moses through his miracles in Egypt would also contribute to this. (For the discussion of this subject, see chap. iii. 21, 22.) The communication of these instructions to the people is not expressly mentioned; but it is referred to in chap. xii. 35, 36, as having taken place.

Vers. 4–8. Moses' address to Pharaoh forms the continuation of his brief answer in chap. x. 29. At midnight Jehovah would go out through the midst of Egypt. This midnight could not be "the one following the day on which Moses was summoned to Pharaoh after the darkness," as *Baumgarten* supposes; for it was not till after this conversation with the king that Moses received the divine directions as to the Passover, and they must have been communicated to the people at least four days before the feast of the Passover and their departure from Egypt (chap. xii. 3). What midnight is meant, cannot be determined. So much is certain, however, that the last decisive blow did not take place in the night following the cessation of the ninth plague; but the institution of the Passover, the directions of Moses to the people respecting the things which they were to ask for from the Egyptians, and the preparations for the feast of the Passover and the exodus, all came between. The "*going out*" of Jehovah from His heavenly seat denotes His direct interposition in, and judicial action upon, the world of men. The last blow upon Pharaoh was to be carried out by Jehovah Himself, whereas the other plagues had been brought by Moses and Aaron. בְּתוֹךְ מִצְרָיִם "*in* (through) *the midst of Egypt:*" the judgment of God would pass from the centre of the kingdom, the king's throne, over the whole land. "*Every first-born shall die, from the first-born of Pharaoh, that sitteth upon his throne, even unto the first-born of the maid that is behind the mill,*" *i.e.* the meanest slave (cf. chap. xii. 29, where the captive in the dungeon is substituted for the maid, prisoners being often employed in this hard labour, Judg. xvi. 21; Isa. xlvii. 2), "*and all the first-born of cattle.*" This stroke was to fall upon both man and beast as a punishment for Pharaoh's conduct in detaining the Israelites and their cattle; but only upon the first-born, for God did not wish to destroy the Egyptians and their cattle altogether, but simply to show them that He had the power to do this. The first-born represented the whole race, of which it was the strength and bloom (Gen. xlix. 3). But against the whole of the people of Israel "*not a dog shall point its tongue*" (ver. 7). The dog points its tongue to growl and bite. The thought expressed in this proverb, which occurs again in Josh. x. 21 and Judith xi. 19, was that Israel would not suffer the slightest injury, either in the case of "man or beast." By this complete preservation, whilst Egypt was given up to death, Israel would discover that Jehovah had completed the separation between them and the Egyptians. The effect of this stroke upon the Egyptians would

be "*a great cry*," having no parallel before or after (cf. x. 14);
and the consequence of this cry would be, that the servants of
Pharaoh would come to Moses and entreat them to go out with
all the people. "*At thy feet*," *i.e.* in thy train (*vid.* Deut. xi. 6;
Judg. viii. 5). With this announcement Moses departed from
Pharaoh in great wrath. Moses' wrath was occasioned by the
king's threat (chap. x. 28), and pointed to the wrath of Jehovah, which Pharaoh would soon experience. As the more than
human patience which Moses had displayed towards Pharaoh
manifested to him the long-suffering and patience of his God,
in whose name and by whose authority he acted, so the wrath of
the departing servant of God was to show to the hardened king,
that the time of grace was at an end, and the wrath of God was
about to burst upon him.

In vers. 9 and 10 the account of Moses' negotiations with
Pharaoh, which commenced at chap. vii. 8, is brought to a close.
What God predicted to His messengers immediately before
sending them to Pharaoh (chap. vii. 3), and to Moses before
his call (iv. 21), had now come to pass. And this was the
pledge that the still further announcement of Jehovah in chap.
vii. 4 and iv. 23, which had already been made known to the
hardened king (vers. 4 sqq.), would be carried out. As these
verses have a terminal character, the *vav consecutive* in וַיֹּאמֶר denotes the order of thought and not of time, and the two verses
are to be rendered thus: "As Jehovah had said to Moses, Pharaoh will not hearken unto you, that My wonders may be multiplied in the land of Egypt, Moses and Aaron did all these
wonders before Pharaoh; and Jehovah hardened Pharaoh's
heart, so that he did not let the children of Israel go out of his
land."

END OF VOLUME I.

Commentary
on the
OLD TESTAMENT

BIBLICAL COMMENTARY

ON

THE OLD TESTAMENT

BY

C. F. KEIL, D.D., AND F. DELITZSCH, D.D.,
PROFESSORS OF THEOLOGY.

VOLUME II
THE PENTATEUCH

TRANSLATED FROM THE GERMAN

BY THE

REV. JAMES MARTIN, B.A.,

TABLE OF CONTENTS

THE SECOND BOOK OF MOSES (EXODUS).

THE THIRD BOOK OF MOSES (LEVITICUS).

INTRODUCTION.

EXPOSITION.

THE SECOND BOOK OF MOSES

(EXODUS.)

———◆———

CONSECRATION OF ISRAEL AS THE COVENANT NATION.
DELIVERANCE FROM EGYPT.—CHAP. XII.–XIII. 16.

HAP. xii. 1–28. INSTITUTION OF THE PASSOVER.—
The deliverance of Israel from the bondage of
Egypt was at hand; also their adoption as the nation
of Jehovah (chap. vi. 6, 7). But for this a divine
consecration was necessary, that their outward severance from
the land of Egypt might be accompanied by an inward severance from everything of an Egyptian or heathen nature. This
consecration was to be imparted by the Passover—a festival
which was to lay the foundation for Israel's birth (Hos. ii. 5)
into the new life of grace and fellowship with God, and to
renew it perpetually in time to come. This festival was therefore instituted and commemorated before the exodus from
Egypt. Vers. 1–28 contain the directions for the Passover:
viz. vers. 1–14 for the keeping of the feast of the Passover
before the departure from Egypt, and vers. 15–20 for the seven
days' feast of unleavened bread. In vers. 21–27 Moses communicates to the elders of the nation the leading instructions as
to the former feast, and the carrying out of those instructions
is mentioned in ver. 28.

Vers. 1 and 2. By the words, " *in the land of Egypt*," the
law of the Passover which follows is brought into connection
with the giving of the law at Sinai and in the fields of Moab,
and is distinguished in relation to the former as the first or foundation law for the congregation of Jehovah. The creation of

Israel as the people of Jehovah (Isa. xliii. 15) commenced with
the institution of the Passover. As a proof of this, it was preceded by the appointment of a new era, fixing the commencement of the congregation of Jehovah. " *This month*" (*i.e.* the
present in which ye stand) " *be to you the head* (*i.e.* the beginning) *of the months, the first let it be to you for the months of
the year;*" *i.e* let the numbering of the months, and therefore
the year also, begin with it. Consequently the Israelites had
hitherto had a different beginning to their year, probably only a
civil year, commencing with the sowing, and ending with the
termination of the harvest (cf. xxiii. 16); whereas the Egyptians
most likely commenced their year with the overflowing of the
Nile at the summer solstice (cf. *Lepsius, Chron.* 1, pp. 148 sqq.).
The month which was henceforth to be the first of the year, and
is frequently so designated (chap. xl. 2, 17; Lev. xxiii. 5, etc.),
is called *Abib* (the ear-month) in chap. xiii. 4, xxiii. 15, xxxiv.
18, Deut. xvi. 1, because the corn was then in ear; after the
captivity it was called *Nisan* (Neh. ii. 1; Esth. iii. 7). It corresponds very nearly to our April.

Vers. 3–14. *Arrangements for the Passover.*—"*All the congregation of Israel*" was the nation represented by its elders
(cf. ver. 21, and my bibl. Arch. ii. p. 221). " *On the tenth of this*
(*i.e.* the first) *month, let every one take to himself* שֶׂה (a lamb,
lit. a young one, either sheep or goats; ver. 5, and Deut. xiv. 4),
according to fathers' houses" (*vid.* vi. 14), *i.e.* according to the
natural distribution of the people into families, so that only the
members of one family or family circle should unite, and not an
indiscriminate company. In ver. 21 *mishpachoth* is used instead.
" *A lamb for the house,*" בַּיִת, *i.e.* the family forming a household.—Ver. 4. But if " *the house be too small for a lamb*" (*lit.*
" *small from the existence of a lamb,*" מִן comparative : הְיוֹת מִשֶּׂה
is an existence which receives its purpose from the lamb, which
answers to that purpose, viz. the consumption of the lamb, *i.e.* if
a family is not numerous enough to consume a lamb), " *let him*
(the house-father) *and his nearest neighbour against his house
take* (*sc.* a lamb) *according to the calculation of the persons.*"
מִכְסָה *computatio* (Lev. xxvii. 23), from כָּסַס *computare;* and מֶכֶס,
the calculated amount or number (Num. xxxi. 28): it only
occurs in the Pentateuch. " *Every one according to the measure
of his eating shall ye reckon for the lamb:*" *i.e.* in deciding whether

several families had to unite, in order to consume one lamb, they were to estimate how much each person would be likely to eat. Consequently more than two families might unite for this purpose, when they consisted simply of the father and mother and little children. A later custom fixed *ten* as the number of persons to each paschal lamb; and *Jonathan* has interpolated this number into the text of his Targum.—Ver. 5. The kind of lamb: תָּמִים *integer*, uninjured, without bodily fault, like all the sacrifices (Lev. xxii. 19, 20); a male like the burnt-offerings (Lev. i. 3, 11); בֶּן שָׁנָה one year old (ἐνιαύσιος, LXX). This does not mean " standing in the first year, viz. from the eighth day of its life to the termination of the first year" (*Rabb. Cler.*, etc.), a rule which applied to the other sacrifices only (chap. xxii. 29; Lev. xxii. 27). The opinion expressed by *Ewald* and others, that oxen were also admitted at a later period, is quite erroneous, and cannot be proved from Deut. xvi. 2, or 2 Chron. xxx. 24 and xxxv. 7 sqq. As the lamb was intended as a sacrifice (ver. 27), the characteristics were significant. Freedom from blemish and injury not only befitted the sacredness of the purpose to which they were devoted, but was a symbol of the moral integrity of the person represented by the sacrifice. It was to be a male, as taking the place of the male first-born of Israel; and a year old, because it was not till then that it reached the full, fresh vigour of its life. " *Ye shall take it out from the sheep or from the goats :*" i.e., as *Theodoret* explains it, " He who has a sheep, let him slay it ; and he who has no sheep, let him take a goat." Later custom restricted the choice to the lamb alone ; though even in the time of Josiah kids were still used as well (2 Chron. xxxv. 7).

Ver. 6. " *And it shall be to you for preservation* (ye shall keep it) *until the fourteenth day, and then . . . slay it at sunset.*" Among the reasons commonly assigned for the instruction to choose the lamb on the 10th, and keep it till the 14th, which *Jonathan* and *Rashi* supposed to refer to the Passover in Egypt alone, there is an element of truth in the one given most fully by *Fagius*, " that the sight of the lamb might furnish an occasion for conversation respecting their deliverance from Egypt, . . . and the mercy of God, who had so graciously looked upon them ;" but this hardly serves to explain the interval of exactly four days. *Hofmann* supposes it to refer to the four *doroth*

(Gen. xv. 16), which had elapsed since Israel was brought to Egypt, to grow into a nation. The probability of such an allusion, however, depends upon just what *Hofmann* denies without sufficient reason, viz. upon the lamb being regarded as a sacrifice, in which Israel consecrated itself to its God. It was to be slain by "*the whole assembly of the congregation of Israel:*" not by the whole assembled people, as though they gathered together for this purpose, for the slaughtering took place in every house (ver. 7); the meaning is simply, that the entire congregation, without any exception, was to slay it at the same time, viz. "*between the two evenings*" (Num. ix. 3, 5, 11), or "in the evening at sunset" (Deut. xvi. 6). Different opinions have prevailed among the Jews from a very early date as to the precise time intended. *Aben Ezra* agrees with the Caraites and Samaritans in taking the first evening to be the time when the sun sinks below the horizon, and the second the time of total darkness; in which case, "between the two evenings" would be from 6 o'clock to 7.20. *Kimchi* and *Rashi*, on the other hand, regard the moment of sunset as the boundary between the two evenings, and *Hitzig* has lately adopted their opinion. According to the rabbinical idea, the time when the sun began to descend, viz. from 3 to 5 o'clock, was the first evening, and sunset the second; so that "between the two evenings" was from 3 to 6 o'clock. Modern expositors have very properly decided in favour of the view held by *Aben Ezra* and the custom adopted by the Caraites and Samaritans, from which the explanation given by *Kimchi* and *Rashi* does not materially differ. It is true that this argument has been adduced in favour of the rabbinical practice, viz. that "only by supposing the afternoon to have been included, can we understand why the day of Passover is always called the 14th (Lev. xxiii. 5; Num. ix. 3, etc.);" and also, that "if the slaughtering took place after sunset, it fell on the 15th Nisan, and not the 14th." But both arguments are based upon an untenable assumption. For it is obvious from Lev. xxiii. 32, where the fast prescribed for the day of atonement, which fell upon the 10th of the 7th month, is ordered to commence on the evening of the 9th day, "from even to even," that although the Israelites reckoned the day of 24 hours from the evening sunset to sunset, in numbering the days they followed the natural day, and numbered each day according to the period between sunrise and sunset. Nevertheless there is no formal disagreement between the law and the rabbinical custom. The expression in Deut. xvi. 6, " at (towards) sunset," is sufficient to show that the boundary line between the two evenings is not to be fixed precisely at the moment of sunset, but only somewhere about that time. The daily evening sacrifice and the incense offering were also to be presented " between the two evenings" (chap. xxix. 39, 41, xxx. 8 ; Num. xxviii. 4). Now as this was not to take place exactly at the same time, but to precede it, they could not both occur at the time of sunset, but the former must have been offered before that. Moreover, in later times, when the paschal lamb was slain and offered at the sanctuary, it must have been slain and offered before sunset, if only to give sufficient time to prepare the paschal meal, which was to be over before midnight. It was from these circumstances that the rabbinical custom grew up in the course of time, and the lax use of the word evening, in Hebrew as well as in every other language, left space enough for this. For just as we do not confine the term morning to the time before sunset, but apply it generally to the early hours of the day, so the term evening is not restricted to the period after sunset. If the sacrifice prescribed for the morning could be offered after sunrise, the one appointed for the evening might in the same manner be offered before sunset.

Ver. 7. Some of the blood was to be put (נָתַן as in Lev. iv. 18, where יִתֵּן is distinguished from הִזָּה, to sprinkle, in ver. 17) upon the two posts and the lintel of the door of the house in which the lamb was eaten. This blood was to be to them a sign (ver. 13) ; for when Jehovah passed through Egypt to smite the first-born, He would see the blood, and would spare these houses, and not permit the destroyer to enter them (vers. 13, 23). The two posts with the lintel represented the door (ver. 23), which they surrounded ; and the doorway through which the house was entered stood for the house itself, as we may see from the frequent expression "in thy gates," for in thy towns (chap. xx. 10 ; Deut. v. 14, xii. 17, etc.). The threshold, which belonged to the door quite as much as the lintel, was not to be smeared with blood, in order that the blood might not be trodden under foot. By the smearing of the door-posts and lintel with blood, the house was expiated and consecrated on an altar. That the smearing with blood was to be regarded as an act of expiation, is evident from the simple fact, that a hyssop-bush was used for the purpose (ver. 22); for sprinkling with hyssop is never prescribed in the law, except in connection with purification in the sense of expiation (Lev. xiv. 49 sqq.; Num. xix. 18, 19). In Egypt the Israelites had no common altar; and for this reason, the houses in which they assembled for the Passover were consecrated as altars, and the persons found in them were thereby removed from the stroke of the destroyer. In this way the smearing of the door-posts and lintel became a sign to Israel of their deliverance from the destroyer. Jehovah made it so by His promise, that He would see the blood, and pass over the houses that were smeared with it. Through faith in this promise, Israel acquired in the sign a firm pledge of its deliverance. The smearing of the doorway was relinquished, after Moses (not Josiah, as *Vaihinger* supposes, cf. Deut. xvi. 5, 6) had transferred the slaying of the lambs to the court of the sanctuary, and the blood had been ordered to be sprinkled upon the altar there.

Vers. 8, 9. With regard to the preparation of the lamb for the meal, the following directions were given: " *They shall eat the lamb in that night* " (*i.e.* the night following the 14th), *and none of it* נָא (" *underdone*" or raw), *or* בָּשֵׁל (" *boiled*,"—lit. done, viz. מְבֻשָּׁל בַּמַּיִם, done in water, *i.e.* boiled, as בָּשֵׁל does not mean to be boiled, but to become ripe or done, Joel iii. 13); " *but roasted with fire, even its head on* (along with) *its thighs and entrails;*" *i.e.*, as *Rashi* correctly explains it, " undivided or whole, so that neither head nor thighs were cut off, and not a bone was broken (ver. 46), and the viscera were roasted in the belly along with the entrails," the latter, of course, being first of all cleansed. On כְּרָעַיִם and קֶרֶב see Lev. i. 9. These regulations are all to be regarded from one point of view. The first two, neither underdone nor boiled, were connected with the roasting of the animal whole. As the roasting no doubt took place on a spit, since the Israelites while in Egypt can hardly have possessed such ovens of their own, as are prescribed in the Talmud and are met with in Persia, the lamb would be very likely to be roasted imperfectly, or underdone, especially in the hurry that must have preceded the exodus (ver. 11). By boiling, again, the integrity of the animal would have been destroyed, partly through the fact that it could never have been got into a pot whole, as the Israel-

ites had no pots or kettles sufficiently large, and still more
through the fact that, in boiling, the substance of the flesh is
more or less dissolved. For it is very certain that the command
to roast was not founded upon the hurry of the whole procedure,
as a whole animal could be quite as quickly boiled as roasted, if
not even more quickly, and the Israelites must have possessed
the requisite cooking utensils. It was to be roasted, in order
that it might be placed upon the table undivided and essentially
unchanged. "Through the unity and integrity of the lamb
given them to eat, the participants were to be joined into an
undivided unity and fellowship with the Lord, who had provided
them with the meal" (cf. 1 Cor. x. 17).[1] They were to eat it
with מַצּוֹת (ἄζυμα, azymi panes; LXX., Vulg.), i.e. (not sweet, or
parched, but) pure loaves, not fermented with leaven; for leaven,
which sets the dough in fermentation, and so produces impurity,
was a natural symbol of moral corruption, and was excluded
from the sacrifices therefore as defiling (Lev. ii. 11). "Over
(upon) bitter herbs they shall eat it." מְרֹרִים, πικρίδες (LXX.),
lactucæ agrestes (Vulg.), probably refers to various kinds of
bitter herbs. Πικρίς, according to Aristot. Hist. an. 9, 6, and
Plin. h. n. 8, 41, is the same as lactuca silvestris, or wild lettuce;
but in Dioscor. 2, 160, it is referred to as the wild σέρις or
κιχώριον, i.e. wild endive, the intubus or intubum of the Romans.
As lettuce and endive are indigenous in Egypt, and endive is
also met with in Syria from the beginning of the winter months
to the end of March, and lettuce in April and May, it is to these
herbs of bitter flavor that the term merorim chiefly applies;

[1] See my Archäologie i. p. 386. Baehr (Symb. 2, 635) has given the
true explanation : "By avoiding the breaking of the bones, the animal was
preserved in complete integrity, undisturbed and entire (Ps. xxxiv. 20).
The sacrificial lamb to be eaten was to be thoroughly and perfectly whole,
and at the time of eating was to appear as a perfect whole, and therefore as
one; for it is not what is dissected, divided, broken in pieces, but only what
is whole, that is eo ipso one. There was no other reason for this, than that
all who took part in this one whole animal, i.e. all who ate of it, should look
upon themselves as one whole, one community, like those who eat the New
Testament Passover, the body of Christ (1 Cor. v. 7), of whom the apostle
says (1 Cor. x. 17), "There is one bread, and so we, being many, are one
body : for we are all partakers of one body." The preservation of Christ,
so that not a bone was broken, had the same signification; and God ordained
this that He might appear as the true paschal lamb, that was slain for the
sins of the world."

though others may also be included, as the Arabs apply the same term to *Scorzonera orient.*, *Picris scabra*, *Sonclus oler.*, *Hieracium uniflor.*, and others (*Forsk. flor.* cxviii. and 143); and in the *Mishnah*, Pes. 2, 6, five different varieties of bitter herbs are reckoned as *merorim*, though it is difficult to determine what they are (cf. *Bochart, Hieroz.* 1, pp. 691 sqq., and *Cels. Hierobot.* ii. p. 727). By עַל (upon) the bitter herbs are represented, both here and in Num. ix. 11, not as an accompaniment to the meat, but as the basis of the meal. עַל does not signify along with, or indicate accompaniment, not even in chap. xxxv. 22; but in this and other similar passages it still retains its primary signification, *upon* or *over*. It is only used to signify accompaniment in cases where the ideas of protection, meditation, or addition are prominent. If, then, the bitter herbs are represented in this passage as the basis of the meal, and the unleavened bread also in Num. ix. 11, it is evident that the bitter herbs were not intended to be regarded as a savoury accompaniment, by which more flavour was imparted to the sweeter food, but had a more profound signification. The bitter herbs were to call to mind the bitterness of life experienced by Israel in Egypt (i. 14), and this bitterness was to be overpowered by the sweet flesh of the lamb. In the same way the unleavened loaves are regarded as forming part of the substance of the meal in Num. ix. 11, in accordance with their significance in relation to it (*vid.* ver. 15). There is no discrepancy between this and Deut. xvi. 3, where the *mazzoth* are spoken of as an accompaniment to the flesh of the sacrifice; for the allusion there is not to the eating of the paschal lamb, but to sacrificial meals held during the seven days' festival.

Ver. 10. The lamb was to be all eaten wherever this was possible; but if any was left, it was to be burned with fire the following day,—a rule afterwards laid down for all the sacrificial meals, with one solitary exception (*vid.* Lev. vii. 15). They were to eat it בְּחִפָּזוֹן, "*in anxious flight*" (from חָפַז *trepidare*, Ps. xxxi. 23; to flee in terror, Deut. xx. 3, 2 Kings vii. 15); in travelling costume therefore,—with "*the loins girded*," that they might not be impeded in their walking by the long flowing dress (2 Kings iv. 29),—with "*shoes* (sandals) *on their feet*," that they might be ready to walk on hard, rough roads, instead of barefooted, as they generally went (cf. Josh. ix. 5, 13; *Bynæus de calceis* ii. 1, 7; and *Bochart, Hieroz.* i. pp. 686 sqq.), and *"staff in hand"* (Gen. xxxii. 11). The directions in ver. 11 had reference to the paschal meal in Egypt only, and had no other signification than to prepare the Israelites for their approaching departure. But though " this preparation was intended to give the paschal meal the appearance of a support for the journey, which the Israelites were about to take," this by no means exhausts its signification. The divine instructions close with the words, " *it is* פֶּסַח *to Jehovah;*" *i.e.* what is prescribed is a *pesach* appointed by Jehovah, and to be kept for Him (cf. chap. xx. 10, " Sabbath to Jehovah;" xxxii. 5, " feast to Jehovah"). The word פֶּסַח, *Aram.* פִּסְחָא, *Gr.* πάσχα, is derived from פָּסַח, lit. to leap or hop, from which these two meanings arise : (1) to limp (1 Kings xviii. 21; 2 Sam. iv. 4, etc.) ; and (2) to pass over, *transire* (hence *Tiphsah,* a passage over, 1 Kings iv. 24). It is for the most part used figuratively for ὑπερβαίνειν, to pass by or spare ; as in this case, where the destroying angel passed by the doors and houses of the Israelites that were smeared with blood. From this, *pesach* (ὑπέρβασις, *Aquil.* in ver. 11 ; ὑπερβασία, *Joseph.* Ant. ii. 14, 6) came afterwards to be used for the lamb, through which, according to divine appointment, the passing by or sparing had been effected (vers. 21, 27 ; 2 Chron. xxxv. 1, 13, etc.) ; then for the preparation of the lamb for a meal, in accordance with the divine instructions, or for the celebration of this meal (thus here, ver. 11 ; Lev. xxiii. 5 ; Num. ix. 7, etc.) ; and then, lastly, it was transferred to the whole seven days' observance of the feast of unleavened bread, which began with this meal (Deut. xvi. 1), and also to the sacrifices which were to be offered at that feast (Deut. xvi. 2 ; 2 Chron. xxxv. 1, 7, etc.). The killing of the lamb appointed for the *pesach* was a זֶבַח, *i.e.* a slain-offering, as Moses calls it when making known the command of God to the elders (ver. 27) ; consequently the eating of it was a sacrificial feast (" the sacrifice of the feast of the Passover," chap. xxxiv. 25). For זֶבַח is never applied to slaying alone, as שָׁחַט is. Even in Prov. xvii. 1 and 1 Sam. xxviii. 24, which *Hofmann* adduces in support of this meaning, it signifies " to sacrifice" only in a figurative or transferred sense. At the first Passover in Egypt, it is true, there was no presentation (הִקְרִיב), because Israel had no altar there. But the presentation took place at the very first repetition of the festival at Sinai (Num. ix. 7). The omission of this in Egypt, on account of the circumstances in which they were placed, constituted no essential difference between the first " sacrifice of the Passover" and the repetitions of it; for the choice of the lamb four days before it was slain, was a substitute for the presentation, and the sprinkling of the blood, which was essential to every sacrifice, was effected in the smearing of the door-posts and lintel. The other difference upon which *Hofmann* lays stress, viz. that at all subsequent Passovers the fat of the animal was burned upon the altar, is very questionable. For this custom cannot be proved from the Old Testament, though it is prescribed in the *Mishnah*.[1] But even if the burning of the fat of the paschal lamb had taken place shortly after the giving of the law, on the ground of the general command in Lev. iii. 17, vii. 23 sqq. (for this is not taken for granted in Ex. xxiii. 18, as we shall afterwards show), this difference could also be accounted for from the want of an altar in Egypt, and would not warrant us in refusing to admit the sacrificial character of the first Passover. For the appointment of the paschal meal by God does not preclude the idea that it was a religious service, nor the want of an altar the idea of sacrifice, as *Hofmann* supposes. All the sacrifices of the Jewish nation were minutely prescribed by God, so that the presentation of them was the consequence of divine instructions. And even though the Israelites, when holding the first Passover according to the command of God, merely gave expression to their desire to participate in the deliverance from destruction and the redemption from Egypt, and also to their faith in the word and promise of God, we must neither measure the signification of this divine institution by that fact, nor restrict it to

---

[1] In the elaborate account of the Passover under Josiah, in 2 Chron. xxxv., we have, it is true, an allusion to the presentation of the burnt-offering and fat (ver. 14) ; but the boiling of the offerings in pots, caldrons, and pans is also mentioned, along with the roasting of the Passover (ver.13) ; from which it is very obvious, that in this account the offering of burnt and slain-offerings is associated with the preparation of the paschal lamb, and the paschal meal is not specially separated from the sacrificial meals of the seven days' feast; just as we find that the king and the princes give the priests and Levites not only lambs and kids, but oxen also, for the sacrifices and sacrificial meals of this festival. (See my *Archäologie*, § 81, 8).

this alone, inasmuch as it is expressly described as a sacrificial meal.

In vers. 12 and 13 the name *pesach* is explained. In that night Jehovah would pass through Egypt, smite all the first-born of man and beast, execute judgment upon all the gods of Egypt, and *pass over* (פָּסַח) the Israelites. In what the judgment upon all the gods of Egypt consisted, it is hard to determine. The meaning of these words is not exhausted by Calvin's remark : " God declared that He would be a judge against the false gods, because it was most apparent then, how little help was to be found in them, and how vain and fallacious was their worship." The gods of Egypt were spiritual authorities and powers, δαι-μόνια, which governed the life and spirit of the Egyptians. Hence the judgment upon them could not consist of the destruction of idols, as *Ps. Jonathan's* paraphrase supposes : *idola fusa colliquescent, lapidea concidentur, testacea confringentur, lignea in cinerem redigentur.* For there is nothing said about this ; but in ver. 29 the death of the first-born of men and cattle alone is mentioned as the execution of the divine threat ; and in Num. xxxiii. 4 also the judgment upon the gods is connected with the burial of the first-born, without special reference to anything besides. From this it seems to follow pretty certainly, that the judgments upon the gods of Egypt consisted in the slaying of the first-born of man and beast. But the slaying of the first-born was a judgment upon the gods, not only because the impotence and worthlessness of the fancied gods were displayed in the consternation produced by this stroke, but still more directly in the fact, that in the slaying of the king's son and many of the first-born animals, the gods of Egypt, which were worshipped both in their kings and also in certain sacred animals, such as the bull Apis and the goat Nendes, were actually smitten themselves.—Ver. 13. To the Israelites, on the other hand, the blood upon the houses in which they were assembled would be a sign and pledge that Jehovah would spare them, and no plague should fall upon them to destroy (cf. Ezek. xxi. 36 ; not " for the destroyer," for there is no article with לְמַשְׁחִית).—Ver. 14. That day (the evening of the 14th) Israel was to keep " *for a commemoration as a feast to Jehovah,*" consecrated for all time, as an " *eternal ordinance,*" לְדֹרֹתֵיכֶם " *in your generations,*" *i.e.* for all ages, דֹרֹת denoting the succession of future generations (*vid.*

ver. 24). As the divine act of Israel's redemption was of eternal significance, so the commemoration of that act was to be an eternal ordinance, and to be upheld as long as Israel should exist as the redeemed people of the Lord, *i.e.* to all eternity, just as the new life of the redeemed was to endure for ever. For the Passover, the remembrance of which was to be revived by the constant repetition of the feast, was the celebration of their birth into the new life of fellowship with the Lord. The preservation from the stroke of the destroyer, from which the feast received its name, was the commencement of their redemption from the bondage of Egypt, and their elevation into the nation of Jehovah. The blood of the paschal lamb was atoning blood; for the Passover was a sacrifice, which combined in itself the signification of the future sin-offerings and peace-offerings; in other words, which shadowed forth both expiation and quickening fellowship with God. The smearing of the houses of the Israelites with the atoning blood of the sacrifice set forth the reconciliation of Israel and its God, through the forgiveness and expiation of its sins; and in the sacrificial meal which followed, their communion with the Lord, *i.e.* their adoption as children of God, was typically completed. In the meal the *sacrificium* became a *sacramentum*, the flesh of the sacrifice a means of grace, by which the Lord adopted His spared and redeemed people into the fellowship of His house, and gave them food for the refreshing of their souls.

Vers. 15-20. Judging from the words " *I brought out*" in ver. 17, Moses did not receive instructions respecting the *seven days' feast of Mazzoth* till after the exodus from Egypt; but on account of its internal and substantial connection with the Passover, it is placed here in immediate association with the institution of the paschal meal. " *Seven days shall ye eat unleavened bread, only* (אַךְ) *on the first day* (*i.e.* not later than the first day) *ye shall cause to cease* (*i.e.* put away) *leaven out of your houses.*" The first day was the 15th of the month (cf. Lev. xxiii. 6; Num. xxviii. 17). On the other hand, when בָּרִאשֹׁן is thus defined in ver. 18, " on the 14th day of the month at even," this may be accounted for from the close connection between the feast of Mazzoth and the feast of Passover, inasmuch as unleavened bread was to be eaten with the paschal lamb, so that the leaven had to be cleared away before this meal.

The significance of this feast was in the eating of the *mazzoth*, *i.e.* of pure unleavened bread (see ver. 8). As bread, which is the principal means of preserving life, might easily be regarded as the symbol of life itself, so far as the latter is set forth in the means employed for its own maintenance and invigoration, so the *mazzoth*, or unleavened loaves, were symbolical of the new life, as cleansed from the leaven of a sinful nature. But if the eating of mazzoth was to shadow forth the new life into which Israel was transferred, any one who ate leavened bread at the feast would renounce this new life, and was therefore to be cut off from Israel, *i.e.* " from the congregation of Israel" (ver. 19).— Ver. 16. On the first and seventh days, a holy meeting was to be held, and labour to be suspended. מִקְרָא־קֹדֶשׁ is not *indictio sancti, proclamatio sanctitatis* (*Vitringa*), but *a holy assembly*, *i.e.* a meeting of the people for the worship of Jehovah (Ezek. xlvi. 3, 9). מִקְרָא, from קָרָא to call, is that which is called, *i.e.* the assembly (Isa. iv. 5; Neh. viii. 8). No work was to be done upon these days, except what was necessary for the preparation of food; on the Sabbath, even this was prohibited (chap. xxxv. 2, 3). Hence in Lev. xxiii. 7, the " work" is called " servile work," ordinary handicraft.—Ver. 17. " *Observe the Mazzoth*" (*i.e.* the directions given in vers. 15 and 16 respecting the feast of Mazzoth), " *for on this very day I have brought your armies out of the land of Egypt.*" This was effected in the night of the 14th–15th, or rather at midnight, and therefore in the early morning of the 15th Abib. Because Jehovah had brought Israel out of Egypt on the 15th Abib, therefore Israel was to keep Mazzoth for seven days. Of course it was not merely a commemoration of this event, but the exodus formed the groundwork of the seven days' feast, because it was by this that Israel had been introduced into a new vital element. For this reason the Israelites were to put away all the leaven of their Egyptian nature, the leaven of malice and wickedness (1 Cor. v. 8), and by eating pure and holy bread, and meeting for the worship of God, to show that they were walking in newness of life. This aspect of the feast will serve to explain the repeated emphasis laid upon the instructions given concerning it, and the repeated threat of extermination against either native or foreigner, in case the law should be disobeyed (vers. 18–20). To eat leavened bread at this feast, would have been a denial of the divine act,

by which Israel was introduced into the new life of fellowship
with Jehovah. גֵּר, a stranger, was a non-Israelite who lived for
a time, or possibly for his whole life, in the midst of the Israelitish nation, but without being incorporated into it by circumcision. אֶזְרַח הָאָרֶץ, a tree that grows upon the soil in which it was
planted; hence *indigena*, the native of a country. This term
was applied to the Israelites, " because they had sprung from
Isaac and Jacob, who were born in the land of Canaan, and
had received it from God as a permanent settlement" (*Clericus*).
The feast of *Mazzoth*, the commemoration of Israel's creation
as the people of Jehovah (Isa. xliii. 15–17), was fixed for seven
days, to stamp upon it in the number seven the seal of the covenant relationship. This heptad of days was made holy through
the sanctification of the first and last days by the holding of a
holy assembly, and the entire suspension of work. The beginning and the end comprehended the whole. In the eating of
unleavened bread Israel laboured for meat for the new life
(John vi. 27), whilst the seal of worship was impressed upon
this new life in the holy convocation, and the suspension of
labour was the symbol of rest in the Lord.

Vers. 21–28. Of the directions given by Moses to the elders
of the nation, the leading points only are mentioned here, viz.
the slaying of the lamb and the application of the blood (vers.
21, 22). The reason for this is then explained in ver. 23, and
the rule laid down in vers. 24–27 for its observance in the
future.—Ver. 21. " *Withdraw and take:*" מִשְׁכוּ is intransitive
here, to draw away, withdraw, as in Judg. iv. 6, v. 14, xx. 37.
אֲגֻדַּת אֵזוֹב: a bunch or bundle of hyssop: according to *Maimonides*, " *quantum quis comprehendit manu sua.*" אֵזוֹב (ὕσσωπος)
was probably not the plant which we call hyssop, the *hyssopus
officinalis*, for it is uncertain whether this is to be found in Syria
and Arabia, but a species of *origanum* resembling hyssop, the
Arabian *zâter*, either wild marjoram or a kind of thyme,
Thymus serpyllum, mentioned in *Forsk. flora Aeg.* p. 107,
which is very common in Syria and Arabia, and is called *zâter*,
or *zatureya*, the pepper or bean plant. " *That is in the bason;*"
viz. the bason in which the blood had been caught when the
animal was killed. וְהִגַּעְתֶּם, " *and let it reach to, i.e.* strike, *the
lintel:*" in ordinary purifications the blood was *sprinkled* with
the bunch of hyssop (Lev. xiv. 51; Num. xix. 18). The reason

for the command not to go out of the door of the house was, that in this night of judgment there would be no safety any-where except behind the blood-stained door.—Ver. 23 (cf. ver. 13). " *He will not suffer* (יִתֵּן) *the destroyer to come into your houses :*" Jehovah effected the destruction of the first-born through הַמַּשְׁחִית, the destroyer, or destroying angel, ὁ ὀλοθρεύων (Heb. xi. 28), *i.e.* not a fallen angel, but the angel of Jehovah, in whom Jehovah revealed Himself to the patriarchs and Moses. This is not at variance with Ps. lxxviii. 49 ; for the writer of this psalm regards not only the slaying of the first-born, but also the pestilence (Ex. ix. 1–7), as effected through the medium of angels of evil : though, according to the analogy of 1 Sam. xiii. 17, הַמַּשְׁחִית might certainly be understood collectively as applying to a company of angels. Ver. 24. " *This word,*" *i.e.* the instruc-tions respecting the Passover, they were to regard as an institu-tion for themselves and their children for ever (עַד־עוֹלָם in the same sense as עוֹלָם, Gen. xvii. 7, 13) ; and when dwelling in the promised land, they were to explain the meaning of this service to their sons. The ceremony is called עֲבֹדָה, " service," inasmuch as it was the fulfilment of a divine command, a performance demanded by God, though it promoted the good of Israel.— Ver. 27. After hearing the divine instructions, the people, represented by their elders, bowed and worshipped ; not only to show their faith, but also to manifest their gratitude for the deliverance which they were to receive in the Passover.—Ver. 28. They then proceeded to execute the command, that through the obedience of faith they might appropriate the blessing of this " service."

Vers. 29–36. DEATH OF THE FIRST-BORN, AND RELEASE OF ISRAEL.—The last blow announced to Pharaoh took place in " the half of the night," *i.e.* at midnight, when all Egypt was lying in deep sleep (Matt. xxv. 5, 6), to startle the king and his people out of their sleep of sin. As all the previous plagues rested upon a natural basis, it might seem a probable supposition that this was also the case here, whilst the analogy of 2 Sam. xxiv. 15, 16 might lead us to think of a pestilence as the means employed by the destroying angel. In that case we should find the heightening of the natural occurrence into a miracle in the fact, that the first-born both of man and beast, and they alone, were all suddenly slain, whilst the Israelites remained uninjured in their houses. This view would be favoured, too, by the circumstance, that not only are pestilences of frequent occurrence in Egypt, but they are most fatal in the spring months. On a closer examination, however, the circumstances mentioned tell against rather than in favour of such a supposition. In 2 Sam. xxiv. 15, the pestilence is expressly alluded to; here it is not. The previous plagues were nearly all brought upon Egypt by Moses' staff, and with most of them the natural sources are distinctly mentioned; but the last plague came direct from Jehovah without the intervention of Moses, certainly for no other reason than to make it apparent that it was a purely supernatural punishment inflicted by His own omnipotence. The words, " *There was not a house where there was not one dead*," are to be taken literally, and not merely " as a general expression;" though, of course, they are to be limited, according to the context, to all the houses in which there were first-born of man or beast. The term " first-born" is not to be extended so far, however, as to include even heads of families who had children of their own, in which case there might be houses, as *Lapide* and others suppose, where the grandfather, the father, the son, and the wives were all lying dead, provided all of them were first-born. The words, " *From the son of Pharaoh, who will sit upon his throne, to the son of the prisoners in the prison*" (ver. 29 compared with chap. xiii. 15), point unquestionably to those first-born sons alone who were not yet fathers themselves. But even with this limitation the blow was so terrible, that the effect produced upon Pharaoh and his people is perfectly intelligible.

Ver. 30. The very same night Pharaoh sent for Moses and Aaron, and gave them permission to depart with their people, their children, and their cattle. The statement that Pharaoh sent for Moses and Aaron is not at variance with chap. x. 28, 29; and there is no necessity to resort to *Calvin*'s explanation, " Pharaoh himself is said to have sent for those whom he urged to depart through the medium of messengers from the palace." The command never to appear in his sight again did not preclude his sending for them under totally different circumstances. The permission to depart was given unconditionally, *i.e.* without involving an obligation to return. This is evident from the words, " Get you forth from among my people," com-

pared with chap. x. 8, 24, " Go ye, serve Jehovah," and viii. 25,
" Go ye, sacrifice to your God in the land." If in addition to
this we bear in mind, that although at first, and even after the
fourth plague (chap. viii. 27), Moses only asked for a three days'
journey to hold a festival, yet Pharaoh suspected that they
would depart altogether, and even gave utterance to this suspicion, without being contradicted by Moses (chap. viii. 28, and x.
10); the words " Get you forth from among my people" cannot mean anything else than " depart altogether." Moreover,
in chap. xi. 1 it was foretold to Moses that the result of the last
blow would be, that Pharaoh would let them go, or rather drive
them away; so that the effect of this blow, as here described,
cannot be understood in any other way. And this is really implied in Pharaoh's last words, " Go, and bless me also;" whereas
on former occasions he had only asked them to intercede for the
removal of the plagues (chap. viii. 8, 28, ix. 28, x. 17). בֵּרֵךְ, to
bless, indicates a final leave-taking, and was equivalent to a request that on their departure they would secure or leave behind
the blessing of their God, in order that henceforth no such
plague might ever befall him and his people. This view of the
words of the king is not at variance either with the expression
" as ye have said" in ver. 31, which refers to the words " serve
the Lord," or with the same words in ver. 32, for there they
refer to the flock and herds, or lastly, with the circumstance that
Pharaoh pursued the Israelites after they had gone, with the evident intention of bringing them back by force (chap. xiv. 5 sqq.),
because this resolution is expressly described as a change of
mind consequent upon renewed hardening (chap. xiv. 4, 5).

Ver. 33. " *And Egypt urged the people strongly* (חָזַק עַל to
press hard, κατεβιάζοντο, LXX.) *to make haste, to send them out
of the land;*" *i.e.* the Egyptians urged the Israelites to accelerate
their departure, " *for they said* (sc. to themselves), *We are all
dead,*" *i.e.* exposed to death. So great was their alarm at the death
of the first-born.—Ver. 34. This urgency of the Egyptians compelled the Israelites to take the dough, which they were probably
about to bake for their journey, before it was leavened, and also
their kneading-troughs bound up in their clothes (cloths) upon
their shoulders. שִׂמְלָה, ἱμάτιον, was a large square piece of stuff
or cloth, worn above the under-clothes, and could be easily used
for tying up different things together. The Israelites had in-

tended to leaven the dough, therefore, as the command to eat unleavened bread for seven days had not been given to them yet. But under the pressure of necessity they were obliged to content themselves with unleavened bread, or, as it is called in Deut. xvi. 3, "the bread of affliction," during the first days of their journey. But as the troubles connected with their departure from Egypt were merely the introduction to the new life of liberty and grace, so according to the counsel of God the bread of affliction was to become a holy food to Israel; the days of their exodus being exalted by the Lord into a seven days' feast, in which the people of Jehovah were to commemorate to all ages their deliverance from the oppression of Egypt. The long-continued eating of unleavened bread, on account of the pressure of circumstances, formed the historical preparation for the seven days' feast of Mazzoth, which was instituted afterwards. Hence this circumstance is mentioned both here and in ver. 39. On vers. 35 and 36, see chap. iii. 21, 22.

Vers. 37–42. *Departure of the children of Israel out of Egypt.* —The starting-point was *Raëmses*, from which they proceeded to *Succoth* (ver. 37), thence to *Etham* at the end of the desert (chap. xiii. 20), and from that by a curve to *Hachiroth*, opposite to the Red Sea, from which point they passed through the sea (chap. xiv. 2, 21 sqq.). Now, if we take these words simply as they stand, Israel touched the border of the desert of Arabia by the second day, and on the third day reached the plain of Suez and the Red Sea. But they could not possibly have gone so far, if *Raëmses* stood upon the site of the modern *Belbeis*. For though the distance from *Belbeis* to Suez by the direct road past *Rejûm el Khail* is only a little more than 15 geographical miles, and a caravan with camels could make the journey in two days, this would be quite impossible for a whole nation travelling with wives, children, cattle, and baggage. Such a procession could never have reached Etham, on the border of the desert, on their second day's march, and then on the third day, by a circuitous course " of about a day's march in extent," have arrived at the plain of Suez between *Ajirûd* and the sea. This is admitted by *Kurtz*, who therefore follows *v. Raumer* in making a distinction between a stage and a day's journey, on the ground that מַסַּע signifies the station or place of encampment, and not a day's journey. But the word neither means station nor place of encampment. It is derived from נָסַע to tear out (*sc.* the pegs of the tent), hence to take down the tent ; and denotes removal from the place of encampment, and the subsequent march (cf. Num. xxxiii. 1). Such a march might indeed embrace more than a day's journey; but whenever the Israelites travelled more than a day before pitching their tents, it is expressly mentioned (cf. Num. x. 33, and xxxiii. 8, with Ex. xv. 22). These passages show very clearly that the stages from Raëmses to Succoth, thence to Etham, and then again to Hachiroth, were a day's march each. The only question is, whether they only rested for one night at each of these places. The circumstances under which the Israelites took their departure favour the supposition, that they would get out of the Egyptian territory as quickly as possible, and rest no longer than was absolutely necessary; but the gathering of the whole nation, which was not collected together in one spot, as in a camp, at the time of their departure, and still more the confusion, and interruptions of various kinds, that would inevitably attend the migration of a whole nation, render it probable that they rested longer than one night at each of the places named. This would explain most simply, how Pharaoh was able to overtake them with his army at Hachiroth. But whatever our views on this point may be, so much is certain, that Israel could not have reached the plain of Suez in a three days' march from Belbeis with the circuitous route by Etham, and therefore that their starting-point cannot have been Belbeis, but must have been in the neighbourhood of Heröopolis; and there are other things that favour this conclusion. There is, first, the circumstance that Pharaoh sent for Moses the very same night after the slaying of the first-born, and told him to depart. Now the Pentateuch does not mention Pharaoh's place of abode, but according to Ps. lxxviii. 12 it was *Zoan, i.e. Tanis,* on the eastern bank of the Tanitic arm of the Nile. *Abu Keishib* (or *Heroopolis*) is only half as far from Tanis as Belbeis, and the possibility of Moses appearing before the king and returning to his own people between midnight and the morning is perfectly conceivable, on the supposition that Moses was not in Heroopolis itself, but was staying in a more northerly place, with the expectation that Pharaoh would send a message to him, or send for him, after the final blow. Again, *Abu Keishib* was on the way to Gaza; so that the Israelites might take the road towards the country of the Philistines, and then, as this was not the road they were to take, *turn round* at God's command by the road to the desert (chap. xiii. 17, 18). Lastly, Etham could be reached in two days from the starting-point named.[1] On the situation of *Succoth* and *Etham*, see chap. xiii. 20.

The Israelites departed, " *about* 600,000 *on foot that were men.*" רַגְלִי (as in Num. xi. 21, the infantry of an army) is added, because they went out as an army (ver. 41), and none are numbered but those who could bear arms, from 20 years old and upwards; and הַגְּבָרִים because of לְבַד מִטַּף, " *beside the little ones,*" which follows. טַף is used here in its broader sense, as in Gen. xlvii. 12, Num. xxxii. 16, 24, and applies to the entire family, including the wife and children, who did not travel on foot, but on beasts of burden and in carriages (Gen. xxxi. 17). The number given is an approximative one. The numbering at Sinai gave 603,550 males of 20 years old and upwards (Num. i. 46), and 22,000 male Levites of a month old and upwards (Num. iii. 39). Now if we add the wives and children, the total number of the people may have been about two million souls. The multiplication of the seventy souls, who went down with Jacob to Egypt, into this vast multitude, is not so disproportionate to the 430 years of their sojourn there, as to render it at all necessary to assume that the numbers given included not only the descendants of the seventy souls who went down with Jacob, but also those of " several thousand man-servants and maid-servants" who accompanied them. For, apart from the fact, that we are not warranted in concluding, that because Abraham had 318 fighting servants, the twelve sons of Jacob had several thousand, and took them with them into Egypt; even if the servants had been received into the religious fellowship of Israel by circumcision, they cannot have reckoned among the 600,000 who went out, for the simple reason that they are not included in the seventy souls who went down to Egypt; and in chap. i. 5 the number of those who came out is placed in unmistakeable connection with the number of those who went in. If we deduct from the 70 souls the patriarch Jacob, his 12 sons, Dinah, Asher's daughter Zerah, the three

---

[1] The different views as to the march of the Israelites from Raemses to their passage through the sea, are to be found in the *Studien und Kritiken*, 1850, pp. 328 sqq., and in *Kurtz*, ii. pp. 361 sqq.

sons of Levi, the four grandsons of Judah and Benjamin, and those grandsons of Jacob who probably died without leaving any male posterity, since their descendants are not mentioned among the families of Israel (cf. i. 372), there remain 41 grandsons of Jacob who founded families, in addition to the Levites. Now, if we follow 1 Chron. vii. 20 sqq., where ten or eleven generations are mentioned between Ephraim and Joshua, and reckon 40 years as a generation, the tenth generation of the 41 grandsons of Jacob would be born about the year 400 of the sojourn in Egypt, and therefore be over 20 years of age at the time of the exodus. Let us assume, that on an average there were three sons and three daughters to every married couple in the first six of these generations, two sons and two daughters in the last four, and we shall find, that in the tenth generation there would be 478,224 sons about the 400th year of the sojourn in Egypt, who would therefore be above 20 years of age at the time of the exodus, whilst 125,326 men of the ninth generation would be still living, so that there would be 478,224 + 125,326, or 603,550 men coming out of Egypt, who were more than 20 years old. But though our calculation is based upon no more than the ordinary number of births, a special blessing from God is to be discerned not only in this fruitfulness, which we suppose to have been uninterrupted, but still more in the fact, that the presumed number of children continued alive, and begot the same number of children themselves; and the divine grace was peculiarly manifest in the fact, that neither pestilence nor other evils, nor even the measures adopted by the Pharaohs for the suppression of Israel, could diminish their numbers or restrain their increase. If the question be asked, how the land of Goshen could sustain so large a number, especially as the Israelites were not the only inhabitants, but lived along with Egyptians there, it is a sufficient reply, that according to both ancient and modern testimony (cf. *Robinson*, Pal. i. p. 78), this is the most fertile province in all Egypt, and that we are not so well acquainted with the extent of the territory inhabited by the Israelites, as to be able to estimate the amount of its produce.

Ver. 38. In typical fulfilment of the promise in Gen. xii. 3, and no doubt induced by the signs and wonders of the Lord in Egypt to seek their good among the Israelites, a great crowd of mixed people (עֵרֶב רַב) attached themselves to them, whom Israel could not shake off, although they afterwards became a snare to them (Num. xi. 4). עֵרֶב: *lit.* a mixture, ἐπίμικτος *sc.* λαός (LXX.), a swarm of foreigners; called אֲסַפְסֻף in Num. xi. 4, a medley, or crowd of people of different nations. According to Deut. xxix. 10, they seem to have occupied a very low position among the Israelites, and to have furnished the nation of God with hewers of wood and drawers of water.—On ver. 39, see ver. 34.—Vers. 40, 41. The sojourn of the Israelites in Egypt had lasted 430 years. This number is not critically doubtful, nor are the 430 years to be reduced to 215 by an arbitrary interpolation, such as we find in the LXX., ἡ δὲ κατοίκησις τῶν υἱῶν Ἰσραὴλ, ἣν κατῴκησαν (*Cod. Alex.* αὐτοὶ καὶ οἱ πατέρες αὐτῶν) ἐν γῇ Αἰγύπτῳ καὶ ἐν γῇ Χαναὰν, κ.τ.λ. This chronological statement, the genuineness of which is placed beyond all doubt by *Onkelos*, the *Syriac, Vulgate*, and other versions, is not only in harmony with the prediction in Gen. xv. 13, where the round number 400 is employed in prophetic style, but may be reconciled with the different genealogical lists, if we only bear in mind that the genealogies do not always contain a complete enumeration of all the separate links, but very frequently intermediate links of little historical importance are omitted, as we have already seen in the genealogy of Moses and Aaron (chap. vi. 18–20). For example, the fact that there were more than the four generations mentioned in chap. vi. 16 sqq. between Levi and Moses, is placed beyond all doubt, not only by what has been adduced at chap. vi. 18–20, but by a comparison with other genealogies also. Thus, in Num. xxvi. 29 sqq., xxvii. 1, Josh. xvii. 3, we find six generations from Joseph to Zelophehad; in Ruth iv. 18 sqq., 1 Chron. ii. 5, 6, there are also six from Judah to Nahshon, the tribe prince in the time of Moses; in 1 Chron. ii. 18 there are seven from Judah to Bezaleel, the builder of the tabernacle; and in 1 Chron. vii. 20 sqq., nine or ten are given from Joseph to Joshua. This last genealogy shows most clearly the impossibility of the view founded upon the Alexandrian version, that the sojourn of the Israelites in Egypt lasted only 215 years; for ten generations, reckoned at 40 years each, harmonize very well with 430 years, but certainly not with 215.[1] The statement in ver. 41, "the self-same day,"

[1] The Alexandrian translators have arbitrarily altered the text to suit the genealogy of Moses in chap. vi. 16 sqq., just as in the genealogies of

is not to be understood as relating to the first day after the lapse of the 430 years, as though the writer supposed that it was on the 14th Abib that Jacob entered Egypt 430 years before, but points back to the day of the exodus, mentioned in ver. 14, as compared with vers. 11 sqq., *i.e.* the 15th Abib (cf. ver. 51 and chap. xiii. 4). On " the hosts of Jehovah," see chap. vii. 4.— Ver. 42. This day therefore was לֵיל שִׁמֻּרִים, " *a preservation-night of the Lord, to bring them out of the land of Egypt.*" The *apax legomenon* שִׁמֻּרִים does not mean " celebration, from שָׁמַר to observe, to honour" (*Knobel*), but " preservation," from שָׁמַר to keep, to preserve; and לַיהוָה is the same as in ver. 27. " *This same night is* (consecrated) *to the Lord as a preservation for all children of Israel in their families.*" Because Jehovah had preserved the children of Israel that night from the destroyer, it was to be holy to them, *i.e.* to be kept by them in all future ages to the glory of the Lord, as a preservation.

Vers. 43–50. Regulations concerning the Participants in the Passover.—These regulations, which were supplementary to the law of the Passover in vers. 3–11, were not communicated before the exodus; because it was only by the fact that a crowd of foreigners attached themselves to the Israelites, that Israel was brought into a connection with foreigners, which needed to be clearly defined, especially so far as the Passover was concerned, the festival of Israel's birth as the people of God. If the Passover was still to retain this signification, of course no foreigner could participate in it. This is the first regulation. But as it was by virtue of a divine call, and not through natural descent, that Israel had become the people of Jehovah, and as it was destined in that capacity to be a blessing to all nations, the attitude assumed towards foreigners was not to be an altogether repelling one. Hence the further directions in ver. 44: purchased servants, who had been politically incorporated as Israel's property, were to be entirely incorporated by circumcision, so as even to take part in the

the patriarchs in Gen. v. and xi. The view held by the Seventy became traditional in the synagogue, and the Apostle Paul followed it in Gal. iii. 17, where he reckoned the interval between the promise to Abraham and the giving of the law as 430 years, the question of chronological exactness having no bearing upon his subject at the time.

Passover. But settlers, and servants working for wages, were not to eat of it, for they stood in a purely external relation, which might be any day dissolved. בְּ אָכַל, *lit.* to eat *at* anything, to take part in the eating (Lev. xxii. 11). The deeper ground for this was, that in this meal Israel was to preserve and celebrate its unity and fellowship with Jehovah. This was the meaning of the regulations, which were repeated in vers. 46 and 47 from vers. 4, 9, and 10, where they had been already explained. If, therefore, a foreigner living among the Israelites wished to keep the Passover, he was first of all to be spiritually incorporated into the nation of Jehovah by circumcision (ver. 48). פֶּס וְעָשָׂה׳: " *And he has made* (*i.e.* made ready) *a passover to Jehovah, let every male be circumcised to him* (*i.e.* he himself, and the male members of his house), *and then he may draw near* (*sc.* to Jehovah) *to keep it.*" The first עָשָׂה denotes the wish or intention to do it, the second, the actual execution of the wish. The words תּוֹשָׁב, גֵּר, בֶּן־נֵכָר, and שָׂכִיר, are all indicative of non-Israelites. בֶּן־נֵכָר was applied quite generally to any foreigner springing from another nation; גֵּר was a foreigner living for a shorter or longer time in the midst of the Israelites; תּוֹשָׁב, *lit.* a dweller, settler, was one who settled permanently among the Israelites, without being received into their religious fellowship; שָׂכִיר was the non-Israelite, who worked for an Israelite for wages.—Ver. 49. There was one law with reference to the Passover which was applicable both to the native and the foreigner: no uncircumcised man was to be allowed to eat of it.—Ver. 50 closes the instructions concerning the Passover with the statement that the Israelites carried them out, viz. in after times (*e.g.* Num. ix. 5); and in ver. 51 the account of the exodus from Egypt is also brought to a close. All that Jehovah promised to Moses in chap. vi. 6 and 26 had now been fulfilled. But although ver. 51 is a concluding formula, and so belongs to the account just closed, *Abenezra* was so far right in wishing to connect this verse with the commencement of the following chapter, that such concluding formulæ generally serve to link together the different incidents, and therefore not only wind up what goes before, but introduce what has yet to come.

Chap. xiii. 1–16. SANCTIFICATION OF THE FIRST-BORN, AND PROMULGATION OF THE LAW FOR THE FEAST OF MAZZOTH.

—Vers. 1, 2. The sanctification of the first-born was closely connected with the Passover. By this the deliverance of the Israelitish first-born was effected, and the object of this deliverance was their sanctification. Because Jehovah had delivered the first-born of Israel, they were to be sanctified to Him. If the Israelites completed their communion with Jehovah in the Passover, and celebrated the commencement of their divine standing in the feast of unleavened bread, they gave uninterrupted effect to their divine sonship in the sanctification of the first-born. For this reason, probably, the sanctification of the first-born was commanded by Jehovah at Succoth, immediately after the exodus, and contemporaneously with the institution of the seven days' feast of Mazzoth (cf. chap. ii. 15), so that the place assigned it in the historical record is the correct one; whereas the divine appointment of the feast of Mazzoth had been mentioned before (chap. xii. 15 sqq.), and the communication of that appointment to the people was all that remained to be mentioned here.—Ver. 2. Every first-born of man and beast was to be sanctified to Jehovah, *i.e.* given up to Him for His service. As the expression, "all the first-born," applied to both man and beast, the explanation is added, "*everything that opens the womb among the Israelites, of man and beast.*" פֶּטֶר כָּל־רֶחֶם for כָּל־פֶּטֶר רֶחֶם (ver. 12): כֹּל is placed like an adjective after the noun, as in Num. viii. 16, בְּכוֹר כֹּל for כָּל־בְּכוֹר, διανοῖγον πᾶσαν μήτραν for πᾶν διανοῖγον μήτραν (ver. 12, LXX.). לִי הוּא: "*it is Mine,*" it belongs to Me. This right to the first-born was not founded upon the fact, that "Jehovah was the Lord and Creator of all things, and as every created object owed its life to Him, to Him should its life be entirely devoted," as *Kurtz* maintains, though without scriptural proof; but in Num. iii. 13 and viii. 17 the ground of the claim is expressly mentioned, viz. that on the day when Jehovah smote all the first-born of Egypt, He sanctified to Himself all the first-born of the Israelites, both of man and beast. Hence the sanctification of the first-born rested not upon the deliverance of the first-born sons from the stroke of the destroyer through the atoning blood of the paschal lamb, but upon the fact that God sanctified them for Himself at that time, and therefore delivered them. But Jehovah sanctified the first-born of Israel to Himself by adopting Israel as His first-born son (chap. iv. 22), or as His possession. Because Israel had been chosen as the nation of Jehovah, its first-born of man and beast were spared, and for that reason they were henceforth to be sanctified to Jehovah. In what way, is more clearly defined in vers. 12 sqq.

Vers. 3-10. The directions as to the seven days' feast of unleavened bread (chap. xii. 15-20) were made known by Moses to the people on the day of the exodus, at the first station, namely, Succoth; but in the account of this, only the most important points are repeated, and the yearly commemoration is enjoined. In ver. 3, Egypt is called a *" slave-house,"* inasmuch as Israel was employed in slave-labour there, and treated as a slave population (cf. chap. xx. 2; Deut. v. 6, vi. 12, etc.). חֹזֶק יָד *" strength of hand,"* in vers. 3, 14, and 16, is more emphatic than the more usual יָד חֲזָקָה (chap. iii. 19, etc.).—On ver. 5, see chap. iii. 8, and xii. 25. In ver. 6, the term *" feast to Jehovah"* points to the keeping of the seventh day by a holy convocation and the suspension of work (chap. xii. 16). It is only of the seventh day that this is expressly stated, because it was understood as a matter of course that the first was a feast of Jehovah. —Ver. 8. *" Because of that which Jehovah did to me"* (זֶה in a relative sense, *is qui,* for אֲשֶׁר, see *Ewald,* § 331): *sc.* "I eat unleavened bread," or, " I observe this service." This completion of the imperfect sentence follows readily from the context, and the whole verse may be explained from chap. xii. 26, 27.—Ver. 9. The festival prescribed was to be to Israel *" for a sign upon its hand, and for a memorial between the eyes."* These words presuppose the custom of wearing mnemonic signs upon the hand and forehead; but they are not to be traced to the heathen custom of branding soldiers and slaves with marks upon the hand and forehead. For the parallel passages in Deut. vi. 8 and xi. 18, " bind them for a sign upon your hand," are proofs that the allusion is neither to branding nor writing on the hand. Hence the sign upon the hand probably consisted of a bracelet round the wrist, and the *ziccaron* between the eyes, of a band worn upon the forehead. The words are then used figuratively, as a proverbial expression employed to give emphasis to the injunction to bear this precept continually in mind, to be always mindful to observe it. This is still more apparent from the reason assigned, *" that the law of Jehovah may be in thy mouth."* For it was not by mnemonic slips upon the hand and forehead that a law was so placed in the mouth as to be talked of continually (Deut. vi. 7,

xi. 19), but by the reception of it into the heart and its continual fulfilment. (See also ver. 16.) As the origin and meaning of the festival were to be talked of in connection with the eating of unleavened bread, so conversation about the law of Jehovah was introduced at the same time, and the obligation to keep it renewed and brought vividly to mind.—Ver. 10. This ordinance the Israelites were to keep לְמוֹעֲדָהּ, "at its appointed time" (i.e. from the 15th to the 21st Abib),—"from days to days," i.e. as often as the days returned, therefore from year to year (cf. Judg. xi. 40, xxi. 19; 1 Sam. i. 3, ii. 19).

In vers. 11–16, Moses communicated to the people the law briefly noticed in ver. 2, respecting the sanctification of the first-born. This law was to come into force when Israel had taken possession of the promised land. Then everything which opened the womb was to be given up to the Lord. הַעֲבִיר לַיהוָה: to cause to pass over to Jehovah, to consecrate or give up to Him as a sacrifice (cf. Lev. xviii. 21). In "all that openeth the womb" the first-born of both man and beast are included (ver. 2). This general expression is then particularized in three clauses, commencing with וְכֹל: (a) בְּהֵמָה cattle, i.e. oxen, sheep, and goats, as clean domestic animals, but only the males; (b) asses, as the most common of the unclean domestic animals, instead of the whole of these animals, Num. xviii. 15; (c) the first-born of the children of Israel. The female first-born of man and beast were exempted from consecration. Of the clean animals the first-born male (פֶּטֶר abbreviated from פֶּטֶר רֶחֶם, and שֶׁגֶר from the Chaldee שְׁגַר to throw, the dropped young one) was to belong to Jehovah, i.e. to be sacrificed to Him (ver. 15, and Num. xviii. 17). This law is still further explained in chap. xxii. 29, where it is stated that the sacrificing was not to take place till the eighth day after the birth; and in Deut. xv. 21, 22, it is still further modified by the command, that an animal which had any fault, and was either blind or lame, was not to be sacrificed, but to be slain and eaten at home, like other edible animals. These two rules sprang out of the general instructions concerning the sacrificial animals. The first-born of the ass was to be redeemed with a male lamb or kid (שֶׂה, as at chap. xii. 3); and if not redeemed, it was to be killed. עָרַף: from עֹרֶף the nape, to break the neck (Deut. xxi. 4, 6). The first-born sons of Israel were also to be consecrated to Jehovah as a sacrifice; not indeed in the manner of the heathen, by slaying and burning upon the altar, but by presenting them to the Lord as living sacrifices, devoting all their powers of body and mind to His service. Inasmuch as the first birth represented all the births, the whole nation was to consecrate itself to Jehovah, and present itself as a priestly nation in the consecration of the first-born. But since this consecration had its foundation, not in nature, but in the grace of its call, the sanctification of the first birth cannot be deduced from the separation of the first-born to the priesthood. This view, which was very prevalent among early writers, has been thoroughly overthrown by *Outram* (*de Sacrif.* 1, c. 4) and *Vitringa* (*observv.* ii. c. 2, pp. 272 sqq.). As the priestly character of the nation did not give a title in itself to the administration of the priesthood within the theocracy, so the first-born were not *eo ipso* chosen as priests through their consecration to Jehovah. In what way they were to consecrate their life to the Lord, depended upon the appointment of the Lord, which was, that they were to perform the non-priestly work of the sanctuary, to be servants of the priests in their holy service. Even this work was afterwards transferred to the Levites (Num. iii.). At the same time the obligation was imposed upon the people to redeem their first-born sons from the service which was binding upon them, but was now transferred to the Levites, who were substituted for them; in other words, to pay five shekels of silver *per* head to the priesthood (Num. iii. 47, xviii. 16). In anticipation of this arrangement, which was to be introduced afterwards, the *redemption* (פָּדָה) of the male first-born is already established here.—On ver. 14, see chap. xii. 26.   מָחָר: *to-morrow*, for the future generally, as in Gen. xxx. 33. מַה־זֹּאת: *what does this mean? quid sibi vult hoc præceptum ac primogenitura* (Jonathan). —Ver. 15. הִקְשָׁה לְשַׁלְּחֵנוּ: "*he made hard*" (*sc.* his heart, cf. chap. vii. 3) "*to let us go.*" The sanctification of the first-born is enforced in ver. 16 in the same terms as the keeping of the feast of Mazzoth in ver. 9, with this exception, that instead of לזכרון we have לְטוֹטָפֹת, as in Deut. vi. 8, and xi. 18. The word טוֹטָפֹת signifies neither amulet nor στίγματα, but "binding" or headbands, as is evident from the Chaldee טוֹטְפָא armlet (2 Sam. i. 10), טוֹטַפְתָּא *tiara* (Esth. viii. 15; Ezek. xxiv. 17, 23). This command was interpreted literally by the Talmudists, and the use of *tephillim*, phylacteries (Matt. xxiii. 5), founded upon it;[1] the Caraites, on the contrary, interpreted it figuratively, as a proverbial expression for constant reflection upon, and fulfilment of, the divine commands. The correctness of the latter is obvious from the words themselves, which do not say that the commands are to be written upon scrolls, but only that they are to be to the Israelites for signs upon the hand, and for bands between the eyes, *i.e.* they are to be kept in view like memorials upon the forehead and the hand. The expression in Deut. vi. 8, "Thou shalt bind them for a sign upon thine hand, and they shall be as frontlets between thine eyes," does not point at all to the symbolizing of the divine commands by an outward sign to be worn upon the hand, or to bands with passages of the law inscribed upon them, to be worn on the forehead between the eyes; nor does the "advance in Deut. vi. 8 from heart to word, and from word to hand or act," necessarily lead to the peculiar notion of *Schultz*, that "the sleeve and turban were to be used as reminders of the divine commands, the former by being fastened to the hand in a peculiar way, the latter by an end being brought down upon the forehead." The line of thought referred to merely expresses the idea, that the Israelites were not only to retain the commands of God in their hearts, and to confess them with the mouth, but to fulfil them with the hand, or in act and deed, and thus to show themselves in their whole bearing as the guardians and observers of the law. As the hand is the medium of action, and carrying in the hand represents handling, so the space between the eyes, or the forehead, is that part of the body which is generally visible, and what is worn there is worn to be seen. This figurative interpretation is confirmed and placed beyond doubt by such parallel passages as Prov. iii. 3, "Bind them (the commandments) about thy neck; write them upon the tables of thine heart" (cf. vers. 21, 22, iv. 21, vi. 21, 22, vii. 3).

---

[1] Possibly these scrolls were originally nothing more than a literal compliance with the figurative expression, or a change of the figure into a symbol, so that the custom did not arise from a pure misunderstanding; though at a later period the symbolical character gave place more and more to the casual misinterpretation. On the phylacteries generally, see my *Archäologie* and *Herzog's Cycl.*

Chap. xiii. 17–22. JOURNEY FROM SUCCOTH TO ETHAM.—
Succoth, Israel's first place of encampment after their departure,
was probably the rendezvous for the whole nation, so that it
was from this point that they first proceeded in an orderly
march. The shortest and most direct route from Egypt to
Canaan would have been by the road to Gaza, in the land of the
Philistines; but God did not lead them by this road, lest they
should repent of their movement as soon as the Philistines
opposed them, and so desire to return to Egypt. פֶּן: μή, after
אָמַר to say (to himself), i.e. to think, with the subordinate idea
of anxiety. The Philistines were very warlike, and would
hardly have failed to resist the entrance of the Israelites into
Canaan, of which they had taken possession of a very large
portion. But the Israelites were not prepared for such a conflict, as is sufficiently evident from their despair, in chap. xiv. 10
sqq. For this reason God made them turn round (יַסֵּב for יְסֵב,
see Ges. § 67) by the way of the desert of the Red Sea. Previous to the account of their onward march, it is still further
stated in vers. 18, 19, that they went out equipped, and took
Joseph's bones with them, according to his last request. חֲמֻשִׁים,
from חֹמֶשׁ lumbus, lit. lumbis accincti, signifies equipped, as a
comparison of this word as it is used in Josh. i. 14, iv. 12, with
חֲלוּצִים in Num. xxxii. 30, 32, Deut. iii. 18, places beyond all
doubt; that is to say, not "armed," καθωπλισμένοι (Sym.), but
prepared for the march, as contrasted with fleeing in disorder
like fugitives. For this reason they were able to fulfil Joseph's
request, from which fact Calvin draws the following conclusion:
"In the midst of their adversity the people had never lost sight
of the promised redemption. For unless the celebrated adjuration of Joseph had been a subject of common conversation
among them all, Moses would never have thought of it."—
Ver. 20. From Succoth they went to Etham. With regard to
the situation of Succoth (from סֻכֹּת huts, probably a shepherd
encampment), only so much can be determined, that this place
was to the south-east of Raëmses, on the way to Etham. Etham
was "at the end of the desert," which is called the desert of
Etham in Num. xxxiii. 8, and the desert of Shur (Jifar, see

Gen. xvi. 7) in Ex. xv. 22 ; so that it was where Egypt ends and the desert of Arabia begins, in a line which curves from the northern extremity of the Gulf of Arabia up to the *Birket Temseh*, or Crocodile Lake, and then on to Lake *Menzalet*. According to the more precise statements of travellers, this line is formed from the point of the gulf northwards, by a broad sandy tract of land to the east of *Ajrud*, which never rises more than about three feet above the water-mark (*Robinson*, Pal. i. p. 80). It takes in the banks of the old canal, which commence about an hour and a half to the north of *Suez*, and run northwards for a distance which *Seetzen* accomplished in 4 hours upon camels (*Rob. Pal.* i. p. 548; *Seetzen*, R. iii. pp. 151, 152). Then follow the so-called Bitter Lakes, a dry, sometimes swampy basin, or deep white salt plain, the surface of which, according to the measurements of French engineers, is 40 or 50 feet lower than the ordinary water-mark at Suez. On the north this basin is divided from the *Birket Temseh* by a still higher tract of land, the so-called Isthmus of *Arbek*. Hence " Etham at the end of the desert" is to be sought for either on the Isthmus of Arbek, in the neighbourhood of the later Serapeum, or at the southern end of the Bitter Lakes. The distance is a conclusive argument against the former, and in favour of the latter ; for although *Seetzen* travelled from Suez to Arbek in 8 hours, yet according to the accounts of the French *savan*, *du Bois Aymé*, who passed through this basin several times, from the northern extremity of the Bitter Lakes to Suez is 60,000 métres (16 hours' journey),—a distance so great, that the children of Israel could not possibly have gone from *Etham* to *Hachiroth* in a day's march. Hence we must look for *Etham* at the southern extremity of the basin of the Bitter Lake,[1] which Israel might reach in two days from *Abu Keishib*, and then on the third day arrive at the plain of Suez, between *Ajrud* and the sea. *Succoth*, therefore, must be sought on the

---

[1] There is no force in the objection to this situation, that according to different geognostic indications, the Gulf of Suez formerly stretched much farther north, and covered the basin of the Bitter Lake ; for there is no evidence that it reached as far as this in the time of Moses; and the statements of early writers as to the position of Heroopolis in the inner corner of the Arabian Gulf, and not far to the north of *Klysma*, furnish no clear evidence of this, as *Knobel* has already observed.

western border of the Bitter Lake.—Vers. 21, 22. From *Etham,* at the edge of the desert which separates Egypt from Asia, the Israelites were to enter the pathless desert, and leave the inhabited country. Jehovah then undertook to direct the march, and give them a safe-conduct, through a miraculous token of His presence. Whilst it is stated in vers. 17, 18, that *Elohim* led them and determined the direction of their road, to show that they did not take the course, which they pursued, upon their own judgment, but by the direction of God; in vers 21, 22, it is said that " JEHOVAH *went before them by day in a pillar of cloud, to lead them the way, and by night in a pillar of fire, to give them light, to go by day and night,*" *i.e.* that they might march at all hours.[1] To this sign of the divine presence and guidance there was a natural analogon in the caravan fire, which consisted of small iron vessels or grates, with wood fires burning in them, fastened at the end of long poles, and carried as a guide in front of caravans, and, according to *Curtius* (*de gestis Alex. M. V.* 2, 7), in trackless countries in the front of armies also, and by which the direction of the road was indicated in the day-time by the smoke, and at night by the light of the fire. There was a still closer analogy in the custom of the ancient Persians, as described by *Curtius* (iii. 3, 9), of carrying fire, " which they called sacred and eternal," in silver altars, in front of the army. But the pillar of cloud and fire must not be confounded with any such caravan and army fire, or set down as nothing more than a mythical conception, or a dressing up of this natural custom. The cloud was not produced by an ordinary caravan fire, nor was it " a mere symbol of the presence of God, which derived all its majesty from the belief of the Israelites, that Jehovah was there in the midst of them," according to *Köster's* attempt to idealize the rationalistic explanation ; but it had a miraculous origin and a supernatural character. We are not to regard the phenomenon as consisting of two different pillars, that appeared alternately, one of cloud, and the other of fire.

---

[1] *Knobel* is quite wrong in affirming, that according to the primary work, the cloud was first instituted after the erection of the tabernacle. For in the passages cited in proof of this (chap. xl. 34 sqq.; Num. ix. 15 sqq., x. 11, 12, cf. xvii. 7), *the* cloud is invariably referred to, with the definite article, as something already known, so that all these passages refer to ver. 21 of the present chapter.

There was but one pillar of both cloud *and* fire (chap. xiv. 24); for even when shining in the dark, it is still called the pillar of cloud (chap. xiv. 19), or the cloud (Num. ix. 21); so that it was a cloud with a dark side and a bright one, causing darkness and also lighting the night (xiv. 20), or " a cloud, and fire in it by night" (xl. 38). Consequently we have to imagine the cloud as the covering of the fire, so that by day it appeared as a dark cloud in contrast with the light of the sun, but by night as a fiery splendour, " a fire-look" (כְּמַרְאֵה־אֵשׁ, Num. ix. 15, 16). When this cloud went before the army of Israel, it assumed the form of a column; so that by day it resembled a dark column of smoke rising up towards heaven, and by night a column of fire, to show the whole army what direction to take. But when it stood still above the tabernacle, or came down upon it, it most probably took the form of a round globe of cloud; and when it separated the Israelites from the Egyptians at the Red Sea, we have to imagine it spread out like a bank of cloud, forming, as it were, a dividing wall. In this cloud Jehovah, or the Angel of God, the visible representative of the invisible God under the Old Testament, was really present with the people of Israel, so that He spoke to Moses and gave him His commandments out of the cloud. In this, too, appeared " the glory of the Lord" (chap. xvi. 10, xl. 34; Num. xvii. 7), the Shechinah of the later Jewish theology. The fire in the pillar of cloud was the same as that in which the Lord revealed Himself to Moses out of the bush, and afterwards descended upon Sinai amidst thunder and lightning in a thick cloud (chap. xix. 16, 18). It was a symbol of the " zeal of the Lord," and therefore was enveloped in a cloud, which protected Israel by day from heat, sunstroke, and pestilence (Isa. iv. 5, 6, xlix. 10; Ps. xci. 5, 6, cxxi. 6), and by night lighted up its path by its luminous splendour, and defended it from the terrors of the night and from all calamity (Ps. xxvii. 1 sqq., xci. 5, 6); but which also threatened sudden destruction to those who murmured against God (Num. xvii. 10), and sent out a devouring fire against the rebels and consumed them (Lev. x. 2; Num. xvi. 35). As *Sartorius* has aptly said, " We must by no means regard it as a mere appearance or a poetical figure, and just as little as a mere mechanical clothing of elementary forms, such, for example, as storm-clouds or natural fire. Just as little, too, must we sup-

pose the visible and material part of it to have been an element
of the divine nature, which is purely spiritual. We must rather
regard it as a dynamic conformation, or a higher corporeal form,
composed of the earthly sphere and atmosphere, through the
determining influence of the personal and specific (speciem
faciens) presence of God upon the earthly element, which corporeal form God assumed and pervaded, that He might manifest His own real presence therein."[1]—Ver. 22. This sign of the
presence of God did not depart from Israel so long as the people
continued in the wilderness.

Chap. xiv. PASSAGE OF THE ISRAELITES THROUGH THE
RED SEA; DESTRUCTION OF PHARAOH AND HIS ARMY.—
Vers. 1, 2. At Etham God commanded the Israelites to turn
(שׁוּב) and encamp by the sea, before *Pihachiroth*, between *Migdol* and the sea, before *Baalzephon*, opposite to it. In Num.
xxxiii. 7, the march is described thus: on leaving Etham they
turned up to (עַל) *Pihachiroth*, which is before (עַל־פְּנֵי in the
front of) *Baalzephon*, and encamped before *Migdol*. The only
one of these places that can be determined with any certainty is
Pihachiroth, or *Hachiroth* (Num. xxxiii. 8, *pi* being simply the
Egyptian article), which name has undoubtedly been preserved
in the *Ajrud* mentioned by *Edrisi* in the middle of the twelfth
century. At present this is simply a fort, with a well 250 feet
deep, the water of which is so bitter, however, that camels can
hardly drink it. It stands on the pilgrim road from Kahira to
Mecca, four hours' journey to the north-west of Suez (*vid.* Robinson, Pal. i. p. 65). A plain, nearly ten miles long and about
as many broad, stretches from *Ajrud* to the sea to the west of

---

[1] " This is done," *Sartorius* proceeds to say, " not by His making His
own invisible nature visible, nor yet merely figuratively or ideally, but by
His rendering it objectively perceptible through the energy it excites, and
the glorious effects it produces. The curtain (*velum*) of the natural which
surrounds the Deity is moved and lifted (*revelatur*) by the word of His will,
and the corresponding intention of His presence (*per dextram Dei*). But
this is effected not by His causing the light of His countenance, which is
unapproachable, to burst forth unveiled, but by His weaving out of the
natural element a holy, transparent veil, which, like the fiery cloud, both
shines and throws a shade, veils and unveils, so that it is equally true that
God dwells in light and that He dwells in darkness (2 Chron. vi. 1; 1 Tim.
vi. 16), as true that He can be found as that He must always be sought."

Suez, and from the foot of Atâkah to the arm of the sea on the north of Suez (*Robinson, Pal.* i. 65). This plain most probably served the Israelites as a place of encampment, so that they encamped before, *i.e.* to the east of, Ajrud towards the sea. The other places must also be sought in the neighbourhood of Hachiroth (Ajrud), though no traces of them have been discovered yet. *Migdol* cannot be the Migdol twelve Roman miles to the south of Pelusium, which formed the north-eastern boundary of Egypt (Ezek. xxix. 10), for according to Num. xxxiii. 7, Israel encamped *before* Migdol; nor is it to be sought for in the hill and mountain-pass called *Montala* by *Burckhardt, el Muntala* by *Robinson* (pp. 63, 64), two hours' journey to the north-west of *Ajrud*, as *Knobel* supposes, for this hill lies too far to the west, and when looked at from the sea is almost behind *Ajrud;* so that the expression " encamping before Migdol" does not suit this situation, not to mention the fact that a tower (מִגְדָּל) does not indicate a watch-tower (מִצְפֶּה). *Migdol* was probably to the south of *Ajrud*, on one of the heights of the Atâkah, and near it, though more to the south-east, *Baalzephon* (*locus Typhonis*), which *Michaelis* and *Forster* suppose to be *Heroopolis*, whilst *Knobel* places it on the eastern shore, and others to the south of Hachiroth. If Israel therefore did not go straight into the desert from Etham, on the border of the desert, but went southwards into the plain of Suez, to the west of the head of the Red Sea, they were obliged to bend round, *i.e.* " to turn" from the road they had taken first. The distance from Etham to the place of encampment at Hachiroth must be at least a six hours' journey (a tolerable day's journey, therefore, for a whole nation), as the road from Suez to Ajrud takes four hours (Robinson, i. p. 66).

Vers. 3-9. This turn in their route was not out of the way for the passage through the Red Sea; but apart from this, it was not only out of the way, but a very foolish way, according to human judgment. God commanded Moses to take this road, that He might be honoured upon Pharaoh, and show the Egyptians that He was Jehovah (cf. vers. 30, 31). Pharaoh would say of the Israelites, They have *lost their way;* they are wandering about in confusion; the desert has shut them in, as in a prison upon which the door is shut (סָגַר עַל as in Job xii. 14) ; and in his obduracy he would resolve to go after them with his army, and

bring them under his sway again.—Vers. 4 sqq. When it was
announced that Israel had fled, " *the heart of Pharaoh and his
servants turned against the people*," and they repented that they
had let them go.   When and whence the information came,
we are not told.   The common opinion, that it was brought after
the Israelites changed their route, has no foundation in the text.
For the change in Pharaoh's feelings towards the Israelites, and
his regret that he had let them go, were caused not by their
supposed mistake, but by their flight.   Now the king and his
servants regarded the exodus as a flight, as soon as they recovered
from the panic caused by the death of the first-born, and began to
consider the consequences of the permission given to the people to
leave his service.   This may have occurred as early as the second
day after the exodus.   In that case, Pharaoh would have had
time to collect chariots and horsemen, and overtake the Israelites
at Hachiroth, as they could easily perform the same journey in
two days, or one day and a half, to which the Israelites had
taken more than three.   "*He yoked his chariot* (had it yoked,
cf. 1 Kings vi. 14), *and took his people* (*i.e.* his warriors) *with
him*," viz. "*six hundred chosen war chariots* (ver. 7), and *all the
chariots of Egypt*" (*sc.* that he could get together in the time),
and "*royal guards upon them all.*"   שָׁלִשִׁים, τριστάται, tristatæ
qui et terni statores vocantur, nomen est secundi gradus post
regiam dignitatem (Jerome on Ezek. xxiii. 23), not charioteers
(see my Com. on 1 Kings ix. 22).   According to ver. 9, the army
raised by Pharaoh consisted of chariot horses (סוּס רֶכֶב), riding
horses (פָּרָשִׁים, lit. runners, 1 Kings v. 6), and חַיִל, the men belonging to them.   War chariots and cavalry were always the
leading force of the Egyptians (cf. Isa. xxxi. 1, xxxvi. 9).   Three
times (vers. 4, 8, and 17) it is stated that Jehovah hardened
Pharaoh's heart, so that he pursued the Israelites, to show that
God had decreed this hardening, to glorify Himself in the judgment and death of the proud king, who would not honour God,
the Holy One, in his life.   "*And the children of Israel were
going out with a high hand:*" ver. 8 is a conditional clause in the
sense of, " although they went out" (*Ewald*, § 341).   יָד רָמָה, the
high hand, is the high hand of Jehovah with the might which it
displayed (Isa. xxvi. 11), not the armed hand of the Israelites.
This is the meaning also in Num. xxxiii. 3 ; it is different in
Num. xv. 30.   The very fact that Pharaoh did not discern the

lifting up of Jehovah's hand in the exodus of Israel displayed the hardening of his heart. " *Beside Pihachiroth :*" see ver. 2.

Vers. 10–14. When the Israelites saw the advancing army of the Egyptians, they were greatly alarmed; for their situation to human eyes was a very unfortunate one. Shut in on the east by the sea, on the south and west by high mountains, and with the army of the Egyptians behind them, destruction seemed inevitable, since they were neither outwardly armed nor inwardly prepared for a successful battle. Although they cried unto the Lord, they had no confidence in His help, notwithstanding all the previous manifestations of the fidelity of the true God; they therefore gave vent to the despair of their natural heart in complaints against Moses, who had brought them out of the servitude of Egypt to give them up to die in the desert. " *Hast thou, because there were no graves at all* (אֵין מִבְּלִי, a double negation to give emphasis) *in Egypt, fetched us to die in the desert ?*" Their further words in ver. 12 exaggerated the true state of the case from cowardly despair. For it was only when the oppression increased, after Moses' first interview with Pharaoh, that they complained of what Moses had done (chap. v. 21), whereas at first they accepted his proposals most thankfully (chap. iv. 31), and even afterwards implicitly obeyed his directions.—Ver. 13. Moses met their unbelief and fear with the energy of strong faith, and promised them such help from the Lord, that they would never see again the Egyptians, whom they had seen that day. אֲשֶׁר רְאִיתֶם does not mean ὃν τρόπον ἑωράκατε (LXX.), *quemadmodum vidistis* (*Ros., Kn.*) ; but the sentence is inverted : " The Egyptians, whom ye have seen to-day, ye will never see again."—Ver. 14. " *Jehovah will fight for you* (לָכֶם, *dat comm.*), *but you will be silent,*" *i.e.* keep quiet, and not complain any more (cf. Gen. xxxiv. 5).

Vers. 15–29. The words of Jehovah to Moses, " *What criest thou to Me ?*" imply that Moses had appealed to God for help, or laid the complaints of the people before Him, and do not convey any reproof, but merely an admonition to resolute action. The people were to move forward, and Moses was to stretch out his hand with his staff over the sea and divide it, so that the people might go through the midst on dry ground. Vers. 17 and 18 repeat the promise in vers. 3, 4. The command and promise were followed by immediate help (vers. 19–29). Whilst Moses divided the water with his staff, and thus prepared the way, the angel of God removed from before the Israelites, and placed himself behind them as a defence against the Egyptians, who were following them. " *Upon his chariots, and upon his horsemen*" (ver. 17), is in apposition to " *all his host;*" as Pharaoh's army consisted entirely of chariots and horsemen (cf. ver. 18). —Ver. 20. "*And it was the cloud and the darkness* (sc. to the Egyptians), *and lighted up the night* (sc. to the Israelites)." *Fuit nubes partim lucida et partim tenebricosa, ex una parte tenebricosa fuit Ægyptiis, ex altera lucida Israelitis* (Jonathan). Although the article is striking in וְהַחֹשֶׁךְ, the difficulty is not to be removed, as *Ewald* proposes, by substituting וְהֶחְשִׁךְ, " and as for the cloud, it caused darkness;" for in that case the grammar would require the imperfect with ו *consec.* This alteration of the text is also rendered suspicious from the fact that both *Onkelos* and the LXX. read and render the word as a substantive.—Vers. 21, 22. When Moses stretched out his hand with the staff (ver. 16) over the sea, "*Jehovah made the water go* (flow away) *by a strong east wind the whole night, and made the sea into dry* (ground), *and the water split itself*" (*i.e.* divided by flowing northward and southward); " *and the Israelites went in the midst of the sea* (where the water had been driven away by the wind) *in the dry, and the water was a wall* (*i.e.* a protection formed by the damming up of the water) *on the right and on the left.*" קָדִים, the east wind, which may apply either to the south-east or north-east, as the Hebrew has special terms for the four quarters only. Whether the wind blew directly from the east, or somewhat from the south-east or north-east, cannot be determined, as we do not know the exact spot where the passage was made. In any case, the division of the water in both directions could only have been effected by an east wind; and although even now the ebb is strengthened by a north-east wind, as *Tischendorf* says, and the flood is driven so much to the south by a strong north-west wind that the gulf can be ridden through, and even forded on foot, to the north of Suez (*v. Schub.* Reise ii. p. 269), and " as a rule the rise and fall of the water in the Arabian Gulf is nowhere so dependent upon the wind as it is at Suez" (*Wellsted*, Arab. ii. 41, 42), the drying of the sea as here described cannot be accounted for by an ebb strengthened by the east wind, because the water is all driven southwards in the ebb, and not sent in two opposite directions. Such a division could only be produced by a wind sent by God, and working with omnipotent force, in connection with which the natural phenomenon of the ebb may no doubt have exerted a subordinate influence.[1] The passage was effected in the night, through the whole of which the wind was blowing, and in the morning watch (between three and six o'clock, ver. 24) it was finished.

As to the possibility of a whole nation crossing with their flocks, *Robinson* concludes that this might have been accomplished within the period of an extraordinary ebb, which lasted three, or at the most four hours, and was strengthened by the influence of a miraculous wind. "As the Israelites," he observes, "numbered more than two millions of persons, besides flocks and herds, they would of course be able to pass but slowly. If the part left dry were broad enough to enable them to cross in a body one thousand abreast, which would require a space of more than half a mile in breadth (and is perhaps the largest supposition admissible), still the column would be more than two thousand persons in depth, and in all probability could not have extended less than two miles. It would then have occupied at least an hour in passing over its own length, or in entering the sea; and deducting this from the largest time intervening, before the Egyptians also have entered the sea, there will remain only time enough, under the circumstances, for the body of the Israelites to have passed, at the most, over a space of three or four miles." (Researches in Palestine, vol. i. p. 84.)

But as the dividing of the water cannot be accounted for by an extraordinary ebb, even though miraculously strengthened, we have no occasion to limit the time allowed for the crossing to the ordinary period of an ebb. If God sent the wind, which divided the water and laid the bottom dry, as soon as night set in, the crossing might have begun at nine o'clock in the evening, if not before, and lasted till four or five o'clock in the morning

---

[1] But as the ebb at Suez leaves the shallow parts of the gulf so far dry, when a strong wind is blowing, that it is possible to cross over them, we may understand how the legend could have arisen among the Ichthyophagi of that neighbourhood (*Diod. Sic.* 3, 39) and even the inhabitants of Memphis (*Euseb. præp. ev.* 9, 27), that the Israelites took advantage of a strong ebb, and how modern writers like *Clericus* have tried to show that the passage through the sea may be so accounted for.

(see ver. 27).   By this extension of the time we gain enough for
the flocks, which *Robinson* has left out of his calculation.   The
Egyptians naturally followed close upon the Israelites, from
whom they were only divided by the pillar of cloud and fire;
and when the rear of the Israelites had reached the opposite
shore, they were in the midst of the sea.   And in the morning
watch Jehovah cast a look upon them in the pillar of cloud and
fire, and threw their army into confusion (ver. 24).   The breadth
of the gulf at the point in question cannot be precisely determined.   At the narrowest point above Suez, it is only two-thirds
of a mile in breadth, or, according to *Niebuhr*, 3450 feet; but
it was probably broader formerly, and even now is so farther up,
opposite to *Tell Kolzum* (*Rob.* i. pp. 84 and 70).   The place
where the Israelites crossed must have been broader, otherwise
the Egyptian army, with more than six hundred chariots and
many horsemen, could not have been in the sea and perished
there when the water returned.—"*And Jehovah looked at the
army of the Egyptians in* (with) *the pillar of cloud and fire, and
troubled it.*"   This look of Jehovah is to be regarded as the appearance of fire suddenly bursting forth from the pillar of cloud
that was turned towards the Egyptians, which threw the Egyptian army into alarm and confusion, and not as " a storm with
thunder and lightning," as *Josephus* and even *Rosenmüller* assume, on the ground of Ps. lxxviii. 18, 19, though without
noticing the fact that the psalmist has merely given a poetical
version of the event, and intends to show " how all the powers
of nature entered the service of the majestic revelation of Jehovah, when He judged Egypt and set Israel free" (*Delitzsch*).
The fiery look of Jehovah was a much more stupendous phenomenon than a storm; hence its effect was incomparably grander,
viz. a state of confusion in which the wheels of the chariots were
broken off from the axles, and the Egyptians were therefore
impeded in their efforts to escape.—Ver. 25.   " *And* (Jehovah)
made the wheels of his (the Egyptian's) *chariots give way, and
made, that he* (the Egyptian) *drove in difficulty.*"   נָהַג to drive a
chariot (2 Sam. vi. 3, cf. 2 Kings ix. 20).—Vers. 26, 27.   Then
God directed Moses to stretch out his staff again over the sea,
and the sea came back with the turning of the morning (when
the morning turned, or approached) to its position (אֵיתָן *peren-
nitas*, the lasting or permanent position), and the Egyptians were

flying to meet it. " When the east wind which divided the sea ceased to blow, the sea from the north and south began to flow together on the western side ;" whereupon, to judge from chap xv. 10, the wind began immediately to blow from the west, and drove the waves in the face of the flying Egyptians. " *And thus Jehovah shook the Egyptians* (*i.e.* plunged them into the greatest confusion) *in the midst of the sea*," so that Pharaoh's chariots and horsemen, to the very last man, were buried in the waves.

Vers. 30, 31. This miraculous deliverance of Israel from the power of Egypt, through the mighty hand of their God, produced so wholesome a fear of the Lord, that they believed in Jehovah, and His servant Moses.—Ver. 31. " The great hand :" *i.e.* the might which Jehovah had displayed upon Egypt. In addition to the glory of God through the judgment upon Pharaoh (vers. 4, 17), the guidance of Israel through the sea was also designed to establish Israel still more firmly in the fear of the Lord and in faith. But faith in the Lord was inseparably connected with faith in Moses as the servant of the Lord. Hence the miracle was wrought through the hand and staff of Moses. But this second design of the miraculous guidance of Israel did not exclude the first, viz. glory upon Pharaoh. From this manifestation of Jehovah's omnipotence, the Israelites were to discern not only the merciful Deliverer, but also the holy Judge of the ungodly, that they might grow in the fear of God, as well as in the faith which they had already shown, when, trusting in the omnipotence of Jehovah, they had gone, as though upon dry land (Heb. xi. 29), between the watery walls which might at any moment have overwhelmed them.

MOSES' SONG AT THE RED SEA.—CHAP. XV. 1–21.

In the song of praise which Moses and the children of Israel sang at the Red Sea, in celebration of the wonderful works of Jehovah, the congregation of Israel commemorated the fact of its deliverance and its exaltation into the nation of God. By their glorious deliverance from the slave-house of Egypt, Jehovah had practically exalted the seed of Abraham into His own nation ; and in the destruction of Pharaoh and his host, He had glorified Himself as God of the gods and King of the heathen, whom no power on earth could defy with impunity. As the fact of Israel's deliverance from the power of its oppressors is of everlasting importance to the Church of the Lord in its conflict with the ungodly powers of the world, in which the Lord con- tinually overthrows the enemies of His kingdom, as He over threw Pharaoh and his horsemen in the depths of the sea: so Moses' song at the Red Sea furnishes the Church of the Lord with the materials for its songs of praise in all the great con- flicts which it has to sustain, during its onward course, with the powers of the world. Hence not only does the key-note of this song resound through all Israel's songs, in praise of the glorious works of Jehovah for the good of His people (see especially Isa. xii.), but the song of Moses the servant of God will also be sung, along with the song of the Lamb, by the conquerors who stand upon the " sea of glass," and have gained the victory over the beast and his image (Rev. xv. 3).

The substance of this song, which is entirely devoted to the praise and adoration of Jehovah, is the judgment inflicted upon the heathen power of the world in the fall of Pharaoh, and the salvation which flowed from this judgment to Israel. Although Moses is not expressly mentioned as the author of the song, its authenticity, or Mosaic authorship, is placed beyond all doubt by both the contents and the form. The song is composed of three gradually increasing strophes, each of which commences with the praise of Jehovah, and ends with a description of the overthrow of the Egyptian host (vers. 2–5, 6–10, 11–18). The theme announced in the introduction in ver. 1 is thus treated in three different ways; and whilst the omnipotence of God, dis- played in the destruction of the enemy, is the prominent topic in the first two strophes, the third depicts with prophetic confi- dence the fruit of this glorious event in the establishment of Israel, as a kingdom of Jehovah, in the promised inheritance. Modern criticism, it is true, has taken offence at this prophetic insight into the future, and rejected the song of Moses, just be- cause the wonders of God are carried forward in vers. 16, 17, beyond the Mosaic times. But it was so natural a thing that, after the miraculous deliverance of the Israelites from Egypt, they should turn their eyes to Canaan, and, looking forward with certainty to the possession of the promised land, should an- ticipate with believing confidence the foundation of a sanctuary there, in which their God would dwell with them, that none but those who altogether reject the divine mission of Moses, and set down the mighty works of God in Egypt as myths, could ever deny to Moses this anticipation and prospect. Even *Ewald* admits that this grand song of praise " was probably the immediate effect of first enthusiasm in the Mosaic age," though he also ignores the prophetic character of the song, and denies the reality of any of the supernatural wonders of the Old Testament. There is nothing to prevent our understanding the words, " then sang Moses," as meaning that Moses not only sang this song with the Israelites, but composed it for the congregation to the praise of Jehovah.

Vers. 1b–5. *Introduction* and *first strophe*.—The introduction, which contains the theme of the song, " *Sing will I to the Lord, for highly exalted is He, horse and his rider He hath thrown into the sea,*" was repeated, when sung, as an anti-strophe by a chorus of women, with Miriam at their head (cf. vers. 20, 21); whether after every verse, or only at the close of the longer strophes, cannot be determined. גָּאָה to arise, to grow up, *trop.* to show oneself exalted; connected with an *inf. abs.* to give still further emphasis. Jehovah had displayed His superiority to all earthly power by casting horses and riders, the proud army of the haughty Pharaoh, into the sea. This had filled His people with rejoicing : (ver. 2), " *My strength and song is* JAH, *He became my salvation ; He is my God, whom I extol, my father's God, whom I exalt.*" עֹז strength, might, not praise or glory, even in Ps. viii. 2. זִמְרָת, an old poetic form for זִמְרָה, from זָמַר, primarily to hum ; thence זַמֵּר ψάλλειν, to play music, or sing with a musical accompaniment. JAH, the concentration of *Jehovah*, the God of salvation ruling the course of history with absolute freedom (cf. vol. i. p. 74), has passed from this song into the Psalms, but is restricted to the higher style of poetry. " *For He became salvation to me, granted me deliverance and salvation :*" on the use of *vav consec.* in explanatory clauses, see Gen. xxvi. 12. This clause is taken from our song, and introduced in Isa. xii. 2, Ps. cxviii. 14. זֶה אֵלִי : this *Jah*, such an one is my God. אַנְוֵהוּ : *Hiphil* of נָוָה, related to נאה, נאוה, to be lovely, delightful, *Hiph.* to extol, to praise, δοξάσω, *glorificabo* (*LXX., Vulg.*). " *The God of my father :*" *i.e.* of Abraham as the ancestor of Israel, or, as in chap. iii. 6, of the three patriarchs combined. What He promised them (Gen. xv. 14, xlvi. 3, 4) He had now fulfilled.—Ver. 3. *"Jehovah is a man of war :"* one who knows how to make war, and possesses the power to destroy His foes. *"Jehovah is His name :"* i.e. He has just proved Himself to be the God who rules with un- limited might. For (ver. 4) *"Pharaoh's chariots and his might* (his military force) *He cast into the sea, and the choice* (the chosen ones) *of his knights (shelishim,* see chap. xiv. 7) *were drowned in the Red Sea."*—Ver. 5. *"Floods cover them* (יְכַסְיֻמוּ, defectively written for יְכַסְיוּ = יְכַסְיוּ, and the suffix מוֹ for מוֹ, only used here) ; *they go down into the deep like stone,"* which never appears again.

Vers. 6-10. Jehovah had not only proved Himself to be a true man of war in destroying the Egyptians, but also as the glorious and strong one, who overthrows His enemies at the very moment when they think they are able to destroy His people.— Ver. 6. *"Thy right hand, Jehovah, glorified in power* (gloriously equipped with power : on the Yod in נָאְדָּרִי, see Gen. xxxi. 39 ; the form is masc., and יְמִין, which is of common gender, is first of all construed as a masculine, as in Prov. xxvii. 16, and then as a feminine), *Thy right hand dashes in pieces the enemy."* רָעַץ = רָצַץ : only used here, and in Judg. x. 8. The thought is quite a general one : the right hand of Jehovah smites every foe. This thought is deduced from the proof just seen of the power of God, and is still further expanded in ver 7, *" In the fulness of Thy majesty Thou pullest down Thine opponents."* הָרַס generally applied to the pulling down of buildings ; then used figuratively for the destruction of foes, who seek to de- stroy the building (the work) of God ; in this sense here and Ps. xxviii. 5. קָמִים : those that rise up in hostility against a man (Deut. xxxiii. 11 ; Ps. xviii. 40, etc.). *" Thou lettest out Thy burning heat, it devours them like stubble."* חָרֹן, the burning breath of the wrath of God, which Jehovah causes to stream out like fire (Ezek. vii. 3), was probably a play upon the fiery look cast upon the Egyptians from the pillar of cloud (cf. Isa. ix. 18, x. 17 ; and on the last words, Isa. v. 24, Nah. i. 10).— Vers. 8-10. Thus had Jehovah annihilated the Egyptians. *" And by the breath of Thy nostrils* (i.e. the strong east wind sent by God, which is described as the blast of the breath of His nostrils ; cf. Ps. xviii. 16) *the waters heaped themselves up* (piled themselves up, so that it was possible to go between them like walls); *the flowing ones stood like a heap*" (נֵד *cumulus;* it occurs in Josh. iii. 13, 16, and Ps. xxxiii. 7, lxxviii. 13, where it is borrowed from this passage. נֹזְלִים : the running, flowing ones; a poetic epithet applied to waves, rivers, or brooks, Ps. lxxviii. 16, 44; Isa. xliv. 3). "*The waves congealed in the heart of the sea :*" a poetical description of the piling up of the waves like solid masses.

Ver. 9. "*The enemy said : I pursue, overtake, divide spoil, my soul becomes full of them ; I draw my sword, my hand will root them out.*" By these short clauses following one another without any copula, the confidence of the Egyptian as he pursued them breathing vengeance is very strikingly depicted. נֶפֶשׁ : the soul as the seat of desire, *i.e.* of fury, which sought to take vengeance on the enemy, " to cool itself on them." הוֹרִישׁ : to drive from their possession, to exterminate (cf. Num. xiv. 12). —Ver. 10. "*Thou didst blow with Thy breath : the sea covered them, they sank as lead in the mighty waters.*" One breath of God was sufficient to sink the proud foe in the waves of the sea. The waters are called אַדִּירִים, because of the mighty proof of the Creator's glory which is furnished by the waves as they rush majestically along.

Vers. 11–18. *Third strophe.* On the ground of this glorious act of God, the song rises in the third strophe into firm assurance, that in His incomparable exaltation above all gods Jehovah will finish the work of salvation, already begun, fill all the enemies of Israel with terror at the greatness of His arm, bring His people to His holy dwelling-place, and plant them on the mountain of His inheritance. What the Lord had done thus far, the singer regarded as a pledge of the future.—Ver. 11. "*Who is like unto Thee among the gods, O Jehovah* (אֵלִים : not strong ones, but gods, *Elohim,* Ps. lxxxvi. 8, because none of the many so-called gods could perform such deeds), *who is like unto Thee, glorified in holiness ?*" God had glorified Himself in holiness through the redemption of His people and the destruction of His foes; so that Asaph could sing, " Thy way, O God, is in holiness" (Ps. lxxvii. 13). קֹדֶשׁ, holiness, is the sublime and incomparable majesty of God, exalted above all the imperfections and blemishes of the finite creature (*vid.* chap. xix. 6). "*Fearful for praises, doing wonders.*" The bold expression נוֹרָא תְהִלֹּת conveys more than *summe venerandus, s. colen-dus laudibus,* and signifies terrible to praise, *terribilis laudibus.* As His rule among men is fearful (Ps. lxvi. 5), because He performs fearful miracles, so it is only with fear and trembling that man can sing songs of praise worthy of His wondrous works. *Omnium enim laudantium vires, linguas et mentes superant ideoque magno cum timore et tremore eum laudant omnes angeli et sancti* (*C. a Lap.*). "*Thou stretchest out Thy hand, the earth swallows them.*" With these words the singer passes in survey all the mighty acts of the Lord, which were wrapt up in this miraculous overthrow of the Egyptians. The words no longer refer to the destruction of Pharaoh and his host. What Egypt had experienced would come upon all the enemies of the Lord and His people. Neither the idea of the earth swallowing them, nor the use of the imperfect, is applicable to the destruction of the Egyptians (see vers. 1, 4, 5, 10, 19, where the perfect is applied to it as already accomplished).—Ver. 13. "*Thou leadest through Thy mercy the people whom Thou redeemest; Thou guidest them through Thy might to Thy holy habitation.*" The deliverance from Egypt and guidance through the Red Sea were a pledge to the redeemed people of their entrance into the promised land. The holy habitation of God was Canaan (Ps. lxxviii. 54), which had been consecrated as a sacred abode for Jehovah in the midst of His people by the revelations made to the patriarchs there, and especially by the appearance of God at Bethel (Gen. xxviii. 16 sqq., xxxi. 13, xxxv. 7).—Ver. 14. "*People hear, they are afraid; trembling seizes the inhabitants of Philistia.*"—Ver. 15. "*Then are the princes (alluphim, see Gen. xxxvi. 15) of Edom confounded; the mighty men of Moab, trembling seizes them; all the inhabitants of Canaan despair.*" אֵילִים, like אוּלִים in 2 Kings xxiv. 15, *scriptio plena* for אֵלִים, strong, powerful ones. As soon as these nations should hear of the miraculous guidance of Israel through the Red Sea, and Pharaoh's destruction, they would be thrown into despair from anxiety and alarm, and would not oppose the march of Israel through their land.—Ver. 16. "*Fear and dread fall upon them; for the greatness of Thine arm* (the adjective גָּדוֹל placed as a substantive before the noun) *they are dumb* (יִדְּמוּ from דָּמַם) *as stones, till Thy people pass through, Jehovah, till the people which Thou hast purchased pass through.*" Israel was still on its march to Canaan, an evident proof that vers. 13–15 do not describe what was past, but that future events were foreseen in spirit, and are represented by the use of perfects as being quite as certain as if they had already happened. The singer mentions not only Edom and Moab, but Philistia also, and the inhabitants of Canaan, as enemies who are so paralyzed with terror, as to offer no resistance to the passage of Israel through their territory; whereas the history shows that Edom did oppose their passing through its land, and they were obliged to go round in consequence (Num. xx. 18 sqq.; Deut. ii. 3, 8), whilst Moab attempted to destroy them through the power of Balaam's curse (Num. xxii. 2 sqq.); and what the inhabitants of Philistia and Canaan had to fear, was not their passing through, but their conquest of the land.[1] We learn, however, from Josh. ii. 9, 10 and ix. 9, that the report of Israel's miraculous passage through the Red Sea had reached to Canaan, and filled its inhabitants with terror.—Ver. 17. " *Thou wilt bring and plant them in the mountain of Thine inheritance, the place which Thou hast made for Thy dwelling-place, Jehovah, for the sanctuary, Lord, which Thy hands prepared.*" On the *dagesh dirim.* in מִקְּדָשׁ, see chap. ii. 3. The futures are not to be taken as expressive of wishes, but as simple predictions, and are not to be twisted into preterites, as they have been by *Knobel.* The "*mountain of Jehovah's inheritance*" was not the hill country of Canaan (Deut. iii. 25), but the mountain which Jehovah had prepared for a sanctuary (Ps. lxxviii. 54), and chosen as a dwelling-place through the sacrifice of Isaac. The planting of Israel upon this mountain does not signify the introduction of the Israelites into the promised land, but the planting of the people of God in the house of the Lord (Ps. xcii. 14), in the future sanctuary, where Jehovah would perfect His fellowship with His people, and where the people would show themselves by their sacrifices to be the "people of possession," and would

---

[1] The fact that the inhabitants of Philistia and Canaan are described in the same terms as Edom and Moab, is an unquestionable proof that this song was composed at a time when the command to exterminate the Canaanites had not yet been given, and the boundary of the territory to be captured by the Israelites was not yet fixed; in other words, that it was sung by Moses and the Israelites after the passage through the Red Sea. In the words עַד יַעֲבֹר in ver. 16, there is by no means the allusion to, or play upon, the passage through the Jordan, which *Knobel* introduces.

serve Him for ever as their King. This was the goal, to which the redemption from Egypt pointed, and to which the prophetic foresight of Moses raised both himself and his people in this song, as he beholds in spirit and ardently desires the kingdom of Jehovah in its ultimate completion.[1] The song closes in ver. 18 with an inspiring prospect of the time, when "*Jehovah will be King* (of His people) *for ever and ever;*" and in ver. 19, it is dovetailed into the historical narrative by the repetition of the fact to which it owed its origin, and by the explanatory " for," which points back to the opening verse.

Vers. 19–21. In the words " *Pharaoh's horse, with his chariots and horsemen,*" Pharaoh, riding upon his horse as the leader of the army, is placed at the head of the enemies destroyed by Jehovah. In ver. 20, *Miriam* is called " *the prophetess,*" not *ob poeticam et musicam facultatem* (*Ros.*), but because of her prophetic gift, which may serve to explain her subsequent opposition to Moses (Num. xi. 1, 6) ; and " *the sister of Aaron,*" though she was Moses' sister as well, and had been his deliverer in his infancy, not " because Aaron had his own independent spiritual standing by the side of Moses" (*Baumg.*), but to point out the position which she was afterwards to occupy in the congregation of Israel, namely, as ranking, not with Moses, but with Aaron, and like him subordinate to Moses, who had been placed at the head of Israel as the mediator of the Old Covenant, and as such was Aaron's god (chap. iv. 16, *Kurtz*).

---

[1] *Auberlen's* remarks in the *Jahrb. f. d. Theol.* iii. p. 793, are quite to the point : " In spirit Moses already saw the people brought to Canaan, which Jehovah had described, in the promise given to the fathers and repeated to him, as His own dwelling-place where He would abide in the midst of His people in holy separation from the nations of the world. When the first stage had been so gloriously finished, he could already see the termination of the journey." . . . " The nation was so entirely devoted to Jehovah, that its own dwelling-place fell into the shade beside that of its God, and assumed the appearance of a sojourning around the sanctuary of Jehovah, for God went up before the people in the pillar of cloud and fire. The fact that a mountain is mentioned in ver. 17 as the dwelling-place of Jehovah is no proof of a *vaticinium post eventum*, but is a true prophecy, having its natural side, however, in the fact that mountains were generally the sites chosen for divine worship and for temples ; a fact with which Moses was already acquainted (Gen. xxii. 2; Ex. iii. 1, 12 ; compare such passages as Num. xxii. 41, xxxiii. 52, Micah iv. 1, 2). In the actual fulfilment it was Mount Zion upon which Jehovah was enthroned as King in the midst of His people.

As prophetess and sister of Aaron she led the chorus of women, who replied to the male chorus with timbrels and dancing, and by taking up the first strophe of the song, and in this way took part in the festival; a custom that was kept up in after times in the celebration of victories (Judg. xi. 34; 1 Sam. xviii. 6, 7, xxi. 12, xxix. 5), possibly in imitation of an Egyptian model (see my Archäologie, § 137, note 8).

ISRAEL CONDUCTED FROM THE RED SEA TO THE MOUNTAIN OF GOD.—CHAP. XV. 22—XVII. 7.

Chap. xv. 22-27. MARCH FROM THE RED SEA TO MARAH AND ELIM.—Being thus delivered from Egypt and led safely through the Red Sea, Israel was led into the desert to the sanctuary of Sinai, to be adopted and consecrated by Jehovah as His possession.—Ver. 22. Leaving the Red Sea, they went into the desert of *Shur*. This name is given to the tract of desert which separates Egypt from Palestine, and also from the more elevated parts of the desert of Arabia, and stretches from the Mediterranean to the head of the Arabian Gulf or Red Sea, and thence along the eastern shore of the sea to the neighbourhood of the Wady Gharandel. In Num. xxxiii. 8 it is called the desert of *Etham*, from the town of Etham, which stood upon the border (see chap. xiii. 20). The spot where the Israelites encamped after crossing the sea, and sang praises to the Lord for their gracious deliverance, is supposed to have been the present *Ayun Musa* (the springs of Moses), the only green spot in the northern part of this desolate tract of desert, where water could be obtained. At the present time there are several springs there, which yield a dark, brackish, though drinkable water, and a few stunted palms; and even till a very recent date country houses have been built and gardens laid out there by the richer inhabitants of Suez. From this point the Israelites went three days without finding water, till they came to *Marah*, where there was water, but so bitter that they could not drink it. The first spot on the road from *Ayun Musa* to Sinai where water can be found, is in the well of *Howâra*, 33 English miles from the former. It is now a basin of 6 or 8 feet in diameter, with two feet of water in it, but so disagreeably bitter and salt, that the Bedouins consider it the worst water in the whole neighbourhood (*Robinson*, i. 96). The distance from Ayun Musa and the quality of the water both favour the identity of *Howâra* and *Marah*. A whole people, travelling with children, cattle, and baggage, could not accomplish the distance in less than three days, and there is no other water on the road from Ayun Musa to Howâra. Hence, from the time of Burckhardt, who was the first to rediscover the well, *Howâra* has been regarded as the *Marah* of the Israelites. In the Wady *Amara*, a barren valley two hours to the north of Howâra, where *Ewald* looked for it, there is no water to be found ; and in the *Wady Gharandel*, two hours to the south, to which *Lepsius* assigned it, the quality of the water does not agree with our account.[1] It is true that no trace of the name has been preserved ; but it seems to have been given to the place by the Israelites simply on account of the bitterness of the water. This furnished the people with an inducement to murmur against Moses (ver. 24). They had probably taken a supply of water from Ayun Musa for the three days' march into the desert. But this store was now exhausted ; and, as *Luther* says, " when the supply fails, our faith is soon gone." Thus even Israel forgot the many proofs of the grace of God, which it had received already.—Ver. 25. When Moses cried to the Lord in consequence, He showed him some wood which, when thrown into the water, took away its bitterness. The Bedouins, who know the neighbourhood, are not acquainted with such a tree, or with any other means of making bitter water sweet ; and this power was hardly inherent in the tree itself, though it is ascribed to it in Ecclus. xxxviii. 5, but was imparted to it through the word and power of God. We cannot assign any reason for the choice of this particular earthly means, as the Scripture says nothing about any " evident and intentional contrast to the change in the Nile by which the sweet and pleasant water was rendered unfit for use " (*Kurtz*). The word עֵץ " *wood* " (see only Num. xix. 6), alone, without anything in the context to explain it, does not point to a " living tree " in con-

---

[1] The small quantity of water at *Howâra*, " which is hardly sufficient for a few hundred men, to say nothing of so large an army as the Israelites formed" (*Seetzen*), is no proof that *Howâra* and *Marah* are not identical. For the spring, which is now sanded up, may have flowed more copiously at one time, when it was kept in better order. Its present neglected state is the cause of the scarcity.

trast to the "dead stick." And if any contrast had been intended to be shown between the punishment of the Egyptians and the training of the Israelites, this intention would certainly have been more visibly and surely accomplished by using the staff with which Moses not only brought the plagues upon Egypt, but afterwards brought water out of the rock. If by עֵץ we understand a tree, with which וַיַּשְׁלֵךְ, however, hardly agrees, it would be much more natural to suppose that there was an allusion to the tree of life, especially if we compare Gen. ii. 9 and iii. 22 with Rev. xxii. 2, "the leaves of the tree of life were for the healing of the nations," though we cannot regard this reference as established. All that is clear and undoubted is, that by employing these means, Jehovah made Himself known to the people of Israel as their Physician, and for this purpose appointed the wood for the healing of the bitter water, which threatened Israel with disease and death (2 Kings iv. 40).

By this event Jehovah accomplished two things : (a) "*there He put* (made) *for it* (the nation) *an ordinance and a right*," and (b) "*there He proved it.*" The ordinance and right which Jehovah made for Israel did not consist in the words of God quoted in ver. 26, for they merely give an explanation of the law and right, but in the divine act itself. The leading of Israel to bitter water, which their nature could not drink, and then the sweetening or curing of this water, were to be a חֹק for Israel, *i.e.*, an institution or law by which God would always guide and govern His people, and a מִשְׁפָּט or right, inasmuch as Israel could always reckon upon the help of God, and deliverance from every trouble. But as Israel had not yet true confidence in the Lord, this was also a trial, serving to manifest its natural heart, and, through the relief of its distress on the part of God, to refine and strengthen its faith. The practical proof which was given of Jehovah's presence was intended to impress this truth upon the Israelites, that Jehovah as their Physician would save them from all the diseases which He had sent upon Egypt, if they would hear His voice, do what was right in His eyes, and keep all His commandments.

Ver. 27. *Elim*, the next place of encampment, has been sought from olden time in the Wady *Gharandel*, about six miles south of *Howâra ;* inasmuch as this spot, with its plentiful supply of comparatively good water, and its luxuriance of palms, tamarisks, acacias, and tall grass, which cause it to be selected even now as one of the principal halting-places between Suez and Sinai, quite answers to Elim, with its twelve wells of water and seventy palm-trees (cf. *Rob.* i. pp. 100, 101, 105). It is true the distance from Howâra is short, but the encampments of such a procession as that of the Israelites are always regulated by the supply of water. Both *Baumgarten* and *Kurtz* have found in Elim a place expressly prepared for Israel, from its bearing the stamp of the nation in the number of its wells and palms: a well for every tribe, and the shade of a palm-tree for the tent of each of the elders. But although the number of the wells corresponded to the twelve tribes of Israel, the number of the elders was much larger than that of the palms (chap. xxiv. 9). One fact alone is beyond all doubt, namely, that at Elim, this lovely oasis in the barren desert, Israel was to learn how the Lord could make His people lie down in green pastures, and lead them beside still waters, even in the barren desert of this life (Ps. xxiii. 2).

Chap. xvi. QUAILS AND MANNA IN THE DESERT OF SIN.— Ver. 1. From Elim the congregation of Israel proceeded into the desert of Sin. According to Num. xxxiii. 10, they encamped at the Red Sea between Elim and the desert of Sin; but this is passed over here, as nothing of importance happened there. Judging from the nature of the ground, the place of encampment *at the Red Sea* is to be found at the mouth of the Wady *Taiyibeh.* For the direct road from the W. Gharandel to Sinai, and the only practicable one for caravans, goes over the table-land between this wady and the Wady *Useit* to the upper end of the W. *Taiyibeh,* a beautiful valley, covered with tamarisks and shrubs, where good water may be found by digging, and which winds about between steep rocks, and opens to the sea at *Ras Zelimeh.* To the north of this the hills and rocks come close to the sea, but to the south they recede, and leave a sandy plain with numerous shrubs, which is bounded on the east by wild and rugged rocky formations, and stretches for three miles along the shore, furnishing quite space enough therefore for the Israelitish camp. It is about eight hours' journey from Wady Gharandel, so that by a forced march the Israelites might have accomplished it in one day. From this point they went "to the *desert of Sin,* which is between Elim and Sinai." The place of encampment here is doubtful. There are two roads that lead from W. Taiyibeh to Sinai : the *lower,* which enters the desert plain by the sea at the *Murkha* or *Morcha* well, not far from the mouth of the Wady *eth Thafary,* and from which you can either go as far as *Tûr* by the sea-coast, and then proceed in a north-easterly direction to Sinai, or take a more direct road through Wady *Shellâl* and *Badireh* into Wady *Mukatteb* and *Feirân,* and so on to the mountains of Horeb; and the *upper road,* first pointed out by *Burckhardt* and *Robinson,* which lies in a S.E. direction from W. Taiyibeh through W. *Shubeikeh,* across an elevated plain, then through Wady *Humr* to the broad sandy plain of *el Debbe* or *Debbet en Nasb,* thence through Wady *Nasb* to the plain of *Debbet er Ramleh,* which stretches far away to the east, and so on across the Wadys *Chamile* and *Seich* in almost a straight line to Horeb. One of these two roads the Israelites must have taken. The majority of modern writers have decided in favour of the lower road, and place the desert of *Sin* in the broad desert plain, which commences at the foot of the mountain that bounds the Wady Taiyibeh towards the south, and stretches along the sea-coast to *Ras Muhammed,* the southernmost point of the peninsula, the southern part of which is now called *el Kâa.* The encampment of the Israelites in the desert of *Sin* is then supposed to have been in the northern part of this desert plain, where the well *Murkha* still furnishes a resting-place plentifully supplied with drinkable water. *Ewald* has thus represented the Israelites as following the desert of *el Kâa* to the neighbourhood of *Tûr,* and then going in a north-easterly direction to Sinai. But apart from the fact that the distance is too great for the three places of encampment mentioned in Num. xxxiii. 12–14, and a whole nation could not possibly reach Rephidim in three stages by this route, it does not tally with the statement in Num. xxxiii. 12, that the Israelites left the desert of Sin and went to *Dofkah;* so that *Dofkah* and the places that follow were not in the desert of Sin at all. For these and other reasons, *De Laborde, v. Raumer,* and others suppose the Israelites to have gone from the fountain of *Murkha* to Sinai by the road which enters the mountains not far from this fountain through Wady Shellâl, and so continues through Wady Mukatteb to

Wady Feirân (*Robinson*, i. p. 105). But this view is hardly reconcilable with the encampment of the Israelites " in the desert of Sin, which is between Elim and Sinai." For instance, the direct road from W. Gharandel (Elim) to Sinai does not touch the desert plain of *el Kâa* at all, but turns away from it towards the north-east, so that it is difficult to understand how this desert could be said to lie between Elim and Sinai. For this reason, even *Kurtz* does not regard the clause "which is between Elim and Sinai" as pointing out the situation of the desert itself, but (contrary to the natural sense of the words) as a more exact definition of that part or point of the desert of Sin at which the road from Elim to Sinai crosses it. But nothing is gained by this explanation. There is no road from the place of encampment by the Red Sea in the Wady Taiyibeh by which a whole nation could pass along the coast to the upper end of this desert, so as to allow the Israelites to cross the desert on the way from Taiyibeh to the W. Shellâl. As the mountains to the south of the W. Taiyibeh come so close to the sea again, that it is only at low water that a narrow passage is left (*Burckhardt*, p. 985), the Israelites would have been obliged to turn eastwards from the encampment by the Red Sea, to which they had no doubt gone for the sake of the water, and to go all round the mountain to get to the Murkha spring. This spring (according to *Burckhardt*, p. 983, " a small lake in the sandstone rock, close at the foot of the mountain") is " the principal station on this road," next to Ayun Musa and Gharandel; but the water is " of the worst description, partly from the moss, the bog, and the dirt with which the well is filled, but chiefly no doubt from the salt of the soil by which it is surrounded," and men can hardly drink it; whereas in the Wady *Thafary*, a mile (? five English miles) to the north-east of Murkha, there is a spring that " yields the only sweet water between Tor and Suez" (p. 982). Now, even if we were to assume that the Israelites pitched their camp, not by this, the only sweet water in the neighbourhood, but by the bad water of Murkha, the Murkha spring is not situated in the desert of *el Kâa*, but only on the eastern border of it; so that if they proceeded thence into the Wady Shellâl, and so on to the Wady Feirân, they would not have crossed the desert at all. In addition to this, although the lower road through the valley of Mukatteb is described by *Burckhardt* as " much easier and more frequented," and by *Robinson* as "easier" than the upper road across Nasseb (Nasb), there are two places in which it runs through very narrow defiles, by which a large body of people like the Israelites could not possibly have forced their way through to Sinai. From the Murkha spring, the way into the valley of Mukatteb is through " a wild mountain road," which is shut out from the eyes of the wanderer by precipitous rocks. " We got off our dromedaries," says *Dieterici*, ii. p. 27, " and left them to their own instinct and sure tread to climb the dangerous pass. We looked back once more at the desolate road which we had threaded between the rocks, and saw our dromedaries, the only signs of life, following a serpentine path, and so climbing the pass in this rocky theatre Nakb el Butera." *Strauss* speaks of this road in the following terms : "We went eastwards through a large plain, overgrown with shrubs of all kinds, and reached a narrow pass, only broad enough for one camel to go through, so that our caravan emerged in a very pictorial serpentine fashion. The wild rocks frowned terribly on every side." Moreover, it is only through a " terribly wild pass" that you can descend from the valley Mukatteb into the glorious valley of Feiran (*Strauss*, p. 128).[1]

For these reasons we must adopt *Knobel's* conclusions, and seek the desert of Sin in the upper road which leads from

---

[1] This pass is also mentioned by *Graul* (*Reise* ii. p. 226) as " a wild romantic mountain pass," and he writes respecting it, " For five minutes the road down was so narrow and steep, that the camels stept in fear, and we ourselves preferred to follow on foot. If the Israelites came up here on their way from the sea at Ras Zelime, the immense procession must certainly have taken a long time to get through the narrow gateway." To this we may add, that if Moses had led the people to Sinai through one of these narrow passes, they could not possibly have reached Sinai in a month from the desert of Sin, to say nothing of eight days, which was all that was left for them, if, as is generally supposed, and as *Kurtz* maintains, their stay at the place of encampment in the desert of Sin, where they arrived on the 15th day of the second month (xvi. 1), lasted full seven days, and their arrival at Sinai took place on the first day of the third month. For if a pass is so narrow that only one camel can pass, not more than three men could walk abreast. Now if the people of Israel, consisting of two millions of men, had gone through such a pass, it would have taken at least twenty days for them all to pass through, as an army of 100,000 men, arranged three abreast, would reach 27 English miles ; so that, supposing the pass to be not more than five minutes walk long, 100,000 Israelites would hardly go through in a day, to say nothing at all about their flocks and herds.

Gharandel to Sinai, viz. in the broad sandy table-land *el Debbe* or *Debbet er Ramle*, which stretches from the Tih mountains over almost the whole of the peninsula from N.W. to S.E. (*vid. Robinson*, i. 112), and in its south-eastern part touches the northern walls of the Horeb or Sinai range, which helps to explain the connection between the names *Sin* and *Sinai*, though the meaning " thorn-covered" is not established, but is merely founded upon the idea that סִין has the same meaning as סְנֶה. This desert table-land, which is essentially distinguished from the limestone formations of the Tih mountains, and the granite mass of Horeb, by its soil of sand and sandstone, stretches as far as Jebel *Humr* to the north-west, and the Wady *Khamile* and *Barak* to the south-west (*vid. Robinson*, i. p. 101, 102). Now, if this sandy table-land is to be regarded as the desert of *Sin*, we must look for the place of Israel's encampment somewhere in this desert, most probably in the north-western portion, in a straight line between Elim (Gharandel) and Sinai, possibly in Wady *Nasb*, where there is a well surrounded by palm-trees about six miles to the north-west of *Sarbut el Khadin*, with a plentiful supply of excellent water, which *Robinson* says was better than he had found anywhere since leaving the Nile (i. 110). The distance from W. Taiyibeh to this spot is not greater than that from Gharandel to Taiyibeh, and might therefore be accomplished in a hard day's march.

Vers. 2–12. Here, in this arid sandy waste, the whole congregation murmured against Moses and Aaron on account of the want of food. What they brought with them from Egypt had been consumed in the 30 days that had elapsed since they came out (ver. 1). In their vexation the people expressed the wish that they had died in Egypt by the flesh-pot, in the midst of plenty, " *by the hand of Jehovah*," *i.e.* by the last plague which Jehovah sent upon Egypt, rather than here in the desert of slow starvation. The form וַיְלִּינוּ is a *Hiphil* according to the consonants, and should be pointed וַיַּלִּינוּ, from הִלְּין for הֵלִין (see *Ges.* § 72, Anm. 9, and *Ewald*, § 114c.). As the want really existed, Jehovah promised them help (ver. 4). He would rain bread from heaven, which the Israelites should gather every day for their daily need, to try the people, whether they would walk in His law or not. In what the trial was to consist, is briefly indicated in ver. 5 : " *And it will come to pass on the sixth day* (of the week), *that they will prepare what they have brought, and it will be double what they gather daily.*" The meaning is, that what they gathered and brought into their tents on the sixth day of the week, and made ready for eating, would be twice as much as what they gathered on every other day ; not that Jehovah would miraculously double what was brought home on the sixth day, as *Knobel* interprets the words in order to make out a discrepancy between ver. 5 and ver. 22. הֵכִין, *to prepare*, is to be understood as applying partly to the measuring of what had been gathered (ver. 18), and partly to the pounding and grinding of the grains of manna into meal (Num. xi. 8). In what respect this was a test for the people, is pointed out in vers. 16 sqq. Here, in vers. 4 and 5, the promise of God is only briefly noticed, and its leading points referred to ; it is described in detail afterwards, in the communications which Moses and Aaron make to the people. In vers. 6, 7, they first tell the people, " *At even, then shall ye know that Jehovah hath brought you out of Egypt ; and in the morning, then shall ye see the glory of the Lord.*" Bearing in mind the parallelism of the clauses, we obtain this meaning, that in the evening and in the morning the Israelites would perceive the glory of the Lord, who had brought them out of Egypt. " Seeing" is synonymous with " knowing." Seeing the glory of Jehovah did not consist in the sight of the glory of the Lord which appeared in the cloud, as mentioned in ver. 10, but in their perception or experience of that glory in the miraculous gift of flesh and bread (ver. 8, cf. Num. xiv. 22). " *By His hearing*" (בְּשָׁמְעוֹ), *i.e.* because He has heard, " *your murmuring against Jehovah* (" against Him" in ver. 8, as in Gen. xix. 24) ; *for what are we, that ye murmur against us ?*" The murmuring of the people against Moses and Aaron as their leaders really affected Jehovah as the actual guide, and not Moses and Aaron, who had only executed His will. Jehovah would therefore manifest His glory to the people, to prove to them that He had heard their murmuring. The announcement of this manifestation of God is more fully explained to the people by Moses in ver. 8, and the explanation is linked on to the leading clause in ver. 7 by the words, " when He giveth," etc. Ye shall see the glory of Jehovah, when Jehovah shall give you, etc.—Vers. 9, 10. But before Jehovah manifested Himself to the people in His glory, by relieving their distress, He gave them to behold His glory in the cloud, and by speaking out of the cloud, confirmed both the reproaches and promises of His servants. In the murmuring of the people, their unbelief in the actual presence of God had been clearly manifested. "It was a deep unbelief," says *Luther,* "that they had thus fallen back, letting go the word and promise of God, and forgetting His former miracles and aid." Even the pillar of cloud, this constant sign of the gracious guidance of God, had lost its meaning in the eyes of the people; so that it was needful to inspire the murmuring multitude with a salutary fear of the majesty of Jehovah, not only that their rebellion against the God who had watched them with a father's care might be brought to mind, but also that the fact might be deeply impressed upon their hearts, that the food about to be sent was a gift of His grace. "Coming near before Jehovah" (ver. 9), was coming out of the tents to the place where the cloud was standing. On thus coming out, "they turned towards the desert" (ver. 10), *i.e.* their faces were directed towards the desert of Sin; "and, behold, the glory of Jehovah appeared in the cloud," *i.e.* in a flash of light bursting forth from the cloud, and revealing the majesty of God. This extraordinary sign of the glory of God appeared in the desert, partly to show the estrangement of the murmuring nation from its God, but still more to show to the people, that God could glorify Himself by bestowing gifts upon His people even in the barren wilderness. For Jehovah spoke to Moses out of this sign, and confirmed to the people what Moses had promised them (vers. 11, 12).

Vers. 13–15. The same evening (according to ver. 12, "between the two evenings," *vid.* chap. xii. 6) quails came up and covered the camp. עָלָה: to advance, applied to great armies. הַשְּׂלָו, with the article indicating the generic word, and used in a collective sense, are quails, ὀρτυγομήτρα (LXX.); *i.e.* the quail-king, according to *Hesychius* ὄρτυξ ὑπερμεγέθης, and *Phot.* ὄρτυξ μέγας, hence a large species of quails, ὄρτυγες (*Josephus*), coturnices (*Vulg.*). Some suppose it to be the *Katà* of the Arabs, a kind of partridge which is found in great abundance in Arabia, Palestine, and Syria. These fly in such dense masses that the Arab boys often kill two or three at a time, by merely striking at them with a stick as they fly (*Burckhardt*, Syr. p. 681). But in spring the quails also come northwards in immense masses from the interior of Africa, and return in autumn, when they sometimes arrive so exhausted, that they can be caught with the hand (cf. *Diod. Sic.* i. 60; *v. Schubert, Reise* ii. p. 361). Such a flight of quails was now brought by God, who caused them to fall in the camp of the Israelites, so that it was completely covered by them. Then in the morning there came an "*effusion of dew round about the camp; and when the effusion of dew ascended (i.e.* when the mist that produced the dew had cleared away), *behold there* (it lay) *upon the surface of the desert, fine, congealed, fine as the hoar-frost upon the ground.*" The meaning of the ἁπ. λεγ. מְחֻסְפָּס is uncertain. The meaning, scaled off, scaly, *decorticatum,* which is founded upon the Chaldee rendering מְקַלֵּף, is neither suitable to the word nor to the thing. The rendering *volutatum, rotundum,* is better; and better still perhaps that of *Meier,* "run together, curdled." When the Israelites noticed this, which they had never seen before, they said to one another, מָן הוּא, τί ἐστι τοῦτο (LXX.), "*what is this?*" for they knew not what it was. מָן for מָה belongs to the popular phraseology, and has been retained in the Chaldee and Ethiopic, so that it is undoubtedly to be regarded as early Semitic. From the question, *man hu,* the divine bread received the name of *man* (ver. 31), or *manna. Kimchi,* however, explains it as meaning *donum et portio. Luther* follows him, and says, "*Mann* in Hebrew means ready money, a present or a gift;" whilst *Gesenius* and others trace the word to מָנָה, to divide, to apportion, and render מָן הוּא "what is apportioned, a gift or present." But the Arabic word to which appeal is made, is not early Arabic; and this explanation does not suit the connection. How could the people say "it is apportioned," when they did not know what it was, and Moses had to tell them, it is the bread which Jehovah has given you for food? If they had seen at once that it was food sent them by God, there would have been no necessity for Moses to tell them so.

Vers. 16–21. After explaining the object of the manna, Moses made known to them at once the directions of God about gathering it. *In the first place,* every one was to gather according to the necessities of his family, a bowl a head, which held, according to ver. 36, the tenth part of an ephah. Accordingly they gathered, "*he that made much, and he that made little*," *i.e.* he that gathered much, and he that gathered little, and measured it with the omer; and he who gathered much had no surplus, and he who gathered little had no lack: "*every one according to the measure of his eating had they gathered.*" These words are generally understood by the Rabbins as meaning, that whether they had gathered much or little, when they measured it in their tents, they had collected just as many omers as they needed for the number in their families, and therefore that no one had either superfluity or deficiency. *Calvin*, on the other hand, and other Christian commentators, suppose the meaning to be, that all that was gathered was placed in a heap, and then measured out in the quantity that each required. In the former case, the miraculous superintendence of God was manifested in this, that no one was able to gather either more or less than what he needed for the number in his family; in the second case, in the fact that the entire quantity gathered, amounted exactly to what the whole nation required. In both cases, the superintending care of God would be equally wonderful, but the words of the text decidedly favour the old Jewish view.—Vers. 19 sqq. *In the second place*, Moses commanded them, that no one was to leave any of what had been gathered till the next morning. Some of them disobeyed, but what was left went into worms (יָרֻם תּוֹלָעִים literally rose into worms) and stank. Israel was to take no care for the morrow (Matt. vi. 34), but to enjoy the daily bread received from God in obedience to the giver. The gathering was to take place in the morning (ver. 21); for when the sun shone brightly, it melted away.

Vers. 22–31. Moreover, God bestowed His gift in such a manner, that the Sabbath was sanctified by it, and the way was thereby opened for its sanctification by the law. On the sixth day of the week the quantity yielded was twice as much, viz. two omers for one (one person). When the princes of the congregation informed Moses of this, he said to them, "*Let to-morrow be rest* (שַׁבָּתוֹן), *a holy Sabbath to the Lord.*" They were to bake and boil as much as was needed for the day, and keep what was over for the morrow, for on the Sabbath they would find none in the field. They did this, and what was kept for the Sabbath neither stank nor bred worms. It is perfectly clear from this event, that the Israelites were not acquainted with any sabbatical observance at that time, but that, whilst the way was practically opened, it was through the decalogue that it was raised into a legal institution (see chap. xx. 8 sqq.). שַׁבָּתוֹן is an abstract noun denoting "rest," and שַׁבָּת a concrete, literally the observer, from which it came to be used as a technical term for the seventh day of the week, which was to be observed as a day of rest to the Lord.—Vers. 27 sqq. On the seventh day some of the people went out to gather manna, notwithstanding Moses' command, but they found nothing. Whereupon God reproved their resistance to His commands, and ordered them to remain quietly at home on the seventh day. Through the commandments which the Israelites were to keep in relation to the manna, this gift assumed the character of a temptation, or test of their obedience and faith (cf. ver. 4).—Ver. 31. The *manna* was "*like coriander-seed, white; and the taste of it like cake with honey.*" גַּד: Chald. גִּידָא; LXX. κόριον; *Vulg.* coriandrum; according to Dioscorid. 3, 64, it was called γοίδ by the Carthaginians. צַפִּיחִת is rendered ἔγκρις by the LXX.; according to *Athenæus* and the Greek Scholiasts, a sweet kind of confectionary made with oil. In Num. xi. 7, 8, the *manna* is said to have had the appearance of *bdellium*, a fragrant and transparent resin, resembling wax (Gen. ii. 12). It was ground in handmills or pounded in mortars, and either boiled in pots or baked on the ashes, and tasted like לְשַׁד הַשָּׁמֶן, "dainty of oil," *i.e.* sweet cakes boiled with oil.

This "bread of heaven" (Ps. lxxviii. 24, cv. 40) Jehovah gave to His people for the first time at a season of the year and also in a place in which natural manna is still found. It is ordinarily met with in the peninsula of Sinai in the months of June and July, and sometimes even in May. It is most abundant in the neighbourhood of Sinai, in Wady Feirân and es Sheikh, also in Wady Gharandel and Taiyibeh, and some of the valleys to the south-east of Sinai (*Ritter*, 14, p. 676; *Seetzen's* Reise iii. pp. 76, 129). In warm nights it exudes from the branches of the tarfah-tree, a kind of tamarisk, and falls down in the form of small globules upon the withered leaves and branches that lie under the trees; it is then gathered before sunrise, but melts in the heat of the sun. In very rainy seasons it continues in great abundance for six weeks long; but in many seasons it entirely fails. It has the appearance of gum, and has a sweet, honey-like taste; and when taken in large quantities, it is said to act as a mild aperient (*Burckhardt*, Syr. p. 954; *Wellsted* in *Ritter*, p. 674). There are striking points of resemblance, therefore, between the manna of the Bible and the tamarisk manna. Not only was the locality in which the Israelites first received the manna the same as that in which it is obtained now; but the time was also the same, inasmuch as the 15th day of the second month (ver. 1) falls in the middle of our May, if not somewhat later. The resemblance in colour, form, and appearance is also unmistakeable; for, though the tamarisk manna is described as a dirty yellow, it is also said to be white when it falls upon stones. Moreover, it falls upon the earth in grains, is gathered in the morning, melts in the heat of the sun, and has the flavour of honey. But if these points of agreement suggest a connection between the natural manna and that of the Scriptures, the differences, which are universally admitted, point with no less distinctness to the miraculous character of the bread of heaven. This is seen at once in the fact that the Israelites received the manna for 40 years, in all parts of the desert, at every season of the year, and in sufficient quantity to satisfy the wants of so numerous a people. According to ver. 35, they ate manna " until they came to a land inhabited, unto the borders of the land of Canaan;" and according to Josh. v. 11, 12, the manna ceased, when they kept the Passover after crossing the Jordan, and ate of the produce of the land of Canaan on the day after the Passover. Neither of these statements is to be so strained as to be made to signify that the Israelites ate no other bread than manna for the whole 40 years, even after crossing the Jordan : they merely affirm that the Israelites received no more manna after they had once entered the inhabited land of Canaan; that the period of manna or desert food entirely ceased, and that of bread baked from corn, or the ordinary food of the inhabited country, commenced when they kept the Passover in the steppes of Jericho, and ate unleavened bread and parched cakes of the produce of the land as soon as the new harvest had been consecrated by the presentation of the sheaf of first-fruits to God.

But even in the desert the Israelites had other provisions at command. In the first place, they had brought large flocks and herds with them out of Egypt (chap. xii. 38, xvii. 3) ; and these they continued in possession of, not only at Sinai (chap. xxxiv. 3), but also on the border of Edom and the country to the east of the Jordan (Num. xx. 19, xxxii. 1). Now, if the maintenance of these flocks necessitated, on the one hand, their seeking for grassy spots in the desert; on the other hand, the possession of cattle secured them by no means an insignificant supply of milk and flesh for food, and also of wool, hair, and skins for clothing. Moreover, there were different tribes in the desert at that very time, such as the Ishmaelites and Amalekites, who obtained a living for themselves from the very same sources which must necessarily have been within reach of the Israelites. Even now there are spots in the desert of Arabia where the Bedouins sow and reap ; and no doubt there was formerly a much larger number of such spots than there are now, since the charcoal trade carried on by the Arabs has interfered with the growth of trees, and considerably diminished both the fertility of the valleys and the number and extent of the green oases (cf. *Rüppell, Nubien,* pp. 190, 201, 256). For the Israelites were not always wandering about ; but after the sentence was pronounced, that they were to remain for 40 years in the desert, they may have remained not only for months, but in some cases even for years, in certain places of encampment, where, if the soil allowed, they could sow, plant, and reap. There were many of their wants, too, that they could supply by means of purchases made either from the trading caravans that travelled through the desert, or from tribes that were settled there ; and we find in one place an allusion made to their buying food and water from the Edomites (Deut. ii. 6, 7). It is also very obvious from Lev. viii. 2, xxvi. 31, 32, ix. 4, x. 12, xxiv. 5 sqq., and Num. vii. 13 sqq., that they were provided with wheaten meal during their stay at Sinai.[1] But notwithstanding all these resources, the desert was " great and terrible " (Deut. i. 19, viii. 15) ; so that, even though it is no doubt the fact that the want of food is very trifling in that region (cf. *Burckhardt,* Syria, p. 901), there must often have been districts to traverse, and seasons to endure, in which the natural resources were either insufficient for so numerous a people, or failed altogether. It was necessary, therefore, that God should

---

[1] *Vide Hengstenberg's Geschichte Bileam's,* p. 284 sqq. For the English translation, see " Hengstenberg on the Genuineness of Daniel, etc.," p. 566. Clark. 1847.

interpose miraculously, and give His people bread and water and flesh by supernatural means. So that it still remains true, that God fed Israel with manna for 40 years, until their entrance into an inhabited country rendered it possible to dispense with these miraculous supplies. We must by no means suppose that the supply of manna was restricted to the neighbourhood of Sinai; for it is expressly mentioned after the Israelites had left Sinai (Num. xi. 7 sqq.), and even when they had gone round the land of Edom (Num. xxi. 5). But whether it continued outside the true desert,—whether, that is to say, the Israelites were still fed with manna after they had reached the inhabited country, viz. in Gilead and Bashan, the Amoritish kingdoms of Sihon and Og, which extended to Edrei in the neighbourhood of Damascus, and where there was no lack of fields, and vineyards, and wells of water (Num. xxi. 22), that came into the possession of the Israelites on their conquest of the land,—or during their encampment in the fields of Moab opposite to Jericho, where they were invited by the Moabites and Edomites to join in their sacrificial meals (Num. xxv. 2), and where they took possession, after the defeat of the Midianites, of their cattle and all that they had, including 675,000 sheep and 72,000 beeves (Num. xxxi. 31 sqq.),—cannot be decided in the negative, as *Hengstenberg* supposes; still less can it be answered with confidence in the affirmative, as it has been by *C. v. Raumer* and *Kurtz*. For if, as even *Kurtz* admits, the manna was intended either to supply the want of bread altogether, or where there was bread to be obtained, though not in sufficient quantities, to make up the deficiency, it might be supposed that no such deficiency would occur in these inhabited and fertile districts, where, according to Josh. i. 11, there were sufficient supplies, at hand to furnish ample provision for the passage across the Jordan. It is possible too, that as there were more trees in the desert at that time than there are now, and, in fact, more vegetation generally, there may have been supplies of natural manna in different localities, in which it is not met with at present, and that this manna harvest, instead of yielding only 5 or 7 cwt., as is the case now, produced considerably more.[1] Nevertheless, the quantity which

---

[1] The natural manna was not exclusively confined to the tamarisk, which seems to be the only tree in the peninsula of Sinai that yields it now; but, according to both ancient and modern testimony, it has been found in Persia,

the Israelites gathered every day,—viz. an omer a head, or at least 2 lbs.,—still remains a divine miracle ; though this statement in vers. 16 sqq. is not to be understood as affirming, that for 40 years they collected that quantity every day, but only, that whenever and wherever other supplies failed, that quantity could be and was collected day by day.

Moreover, the divine manna differed both in origin and composition from the natural produce of the tamarisk. Though the tamarisk manna resembles the former in appearance, colour, and taste, yet according to the chemical analysis to which it has been submitted by *Mitscherlich,* it contains no farina, but simply saccharine matter, so that the grains have only the consistency of wax ; whereas those of the manna supplied to the Israelites were so hard that they could be ground in mills and pounded in mortars, and contained so much meal that it was made into cakes and baked, when it tasted like honey-cake, or sweet confectionary prepared with oil, and formed a good substitute for ordinary bread.   There is no less difference in the origin of the two. The manna of the Israelites fell upon the camp with the morning dew (vers. 13, 14 ; Num. xi. 9), therefore evidently out of the air, so that Jehovah might be said to have rained it from heaven (ver. 4) ; whereas the tamarisk manna drops upon the ground from the fine thin twigs of this shrub, and, in *Ehrenberg's* opinion, in consequence of the puncture of a small, yellow insect, called *coccus maniparus.*   But it may possibly be produced apart from this insect, as *Lepsius* and *Tischendorf* found branches with a considerable quantity of manna upon them, and saw it drop from trees in thick adhesive lumps, without being able to discover any *coccus* near (see *Ritter,* 14, pp. 675–6). Now, even though the manna of the Bible may be connected with the produce of the tamarisk, the supply was not so inseparably connected with these shrubs, as that it could only fall to the earth with the dew, as it was exuded from their branches. After all, therefore, we can neither deny that there was some connection between the two, nor explain the gift of the heavenly manna, as arising from an unrestricted multiplication and increase of this gift of nature.   We rather regard the bread of heaven as the production and gift of the grace of God, which fills all

Chorasan, and other parts of Asia, dropping from other trees. Cf. *Rosenmüller ubi supra,* and *Ritter,* 14, pp. 686 sqq.

nature with its powers and productions, and so applies them to its purposes of salvation, as to create out of that which is natural something altogether new, which surpasses the ordinary productions of nature, both in quality and quantity, as far as the kingdom of nature is surpassed by the kingdom of grace and glory.

Vers. 32–36. As a constant memorial of this bread of God for succeeding generations, Jehovah commanded Moses to keep a bowl full (מְלֹא הָעֹמֶר, the filling of a bowl) of the manna. Accordingly Aaron placed a jar of manna (as it is stated in vers. 34, 35, by way of anticipation, for the purpose of summing up everything of importance relating to the manna) "before Jehovah," or speaking still more exactly, "before the testimony," i.e. the tables of the law (see chap. xxv. 16), or according to Jewish tradition, in the ark of the covenant (Heb. ix. 4). צִנְצֶנֶת, from צָנַן to guard round, to preserve, signifies a jar or bottle, not a basket. According to the Jerusalem Targum, it was an earthenware jar; in the LXX. it is called στάμνος χρυσοῦς, a golden jar, but there is nothing of this kind in the original text.—Ver. 36. In conclusion, the quantity of the manna collected for the daily supply of each individual, which was preserved in the sanctuary, is given according to the ordinary measurement, viz. the ephah. The common opinion, that עֹמֶר was the name for a measure of capacity, which was evidently shared by the Seventy, who have rendered the word γομόρ, has no foundation so far as the Scriptures are concerned. Not only is it a fact, that the word omer is never used as a measure except in this chapter, but the tenth of an ephah is constantly indicated, even in the Pentateuch, by "the tenth part of an ephah" (Lev. v. 11, vi. 13; Num. v. 15, xxviii. 5), or "a tenth deal" (Ex. xxix. 40; Lev. xiv. 10, etc.; in all 30 times). The omer was a small vessel, cup, or bowl, which formed part of the furniture of every house, and being always of the same size, could be used as a measure in case of need.[1] The ephah is given by Bertheau as consisting of 1985·77 Parisian cubic inches, and

---

[1] *Omer proprie nomen poculi fuit, quale secum gestare solent Orientales, per deserta iter facientes, ad hauriendam si quam rivus vel fons offerret aquam. . . . Hoc in poculo, alia vasa non habentes, et mannam collegerunt Israelitæ* (Michaelis, Supplem. ad Lex. hebr., p. 1929). Cf. Hengstenberg, Dissertations on the Pentateuch, vol. ii. p. 172.

holding 739,800 Parisian grains of water; *Thenius,* however, gives only 1014·39 Parisian, or 1124·67 Rhenish inches. (See my Archäologie, ii. 141–2.)

Chap. xvii. 1–7. WANT OF WATER AT REPHIDIM.—Ver. 1. On leaving the desert of Sin, the Israelites came לְמַסְעֵיהֶם, "according to their journeys," *i.e.* in several marches performed with encampings and departures, to *Rephidim,* at Horeb, where they found no water. According to Num. xxxiii. 12–14, they encamped twice between the desert of Sin and Rephidim, viz. at *Dofkah* and *Alush.* The situation of *Rephidim* may be determined with tolerable certainty, partly from ver. 6 as compared with chap. xviii. 5, which shows that it is to be sought for at Horeb, and partly from the fact, that the Israelites reached the desert of Sinai, after leaving Rephidim, in a single day's march (chap. xix. 2). As the only way from *Debbet er Ramleh* to Horeb or Sinai, through which a whole nation could pass, lies through the large valley of *es-Sheikh,* Rephidim must be sought for at the point where this valley opens into the broad plain of *er Rahah;* and not in the defile with Moses' seat (*Mokad Seidna Musa*) in it, which is a day's journey from the foot of Sinai, or five hours from the point at which the Sheikh valley opens into the plain of er Rahah, or the plain of *Szueir* or *Suweiri,*[1] because this plain is so far from Sinai, that the Israelites could not possibly have travelled thence to the desert of Sinai in a single day; nor yet at the fountain of *Abu Suweirah,* which is three hours to the north of Sinai (*Strauss,* p. 131), for the Sheikh valley, which is only a quarter of a mile broad at this spot, and enclosed on both sides by tall cliffs (*Robinson,* i. 215), would not afford the requisite space for a whole nation; and the well found here, which though small is never dry (*Robinson,* i. 216), neither tallies with the want of water at Rephidim, nor stands "upon the rock at (in) Horeb," so that it could be taken to be the spring opened by Moses. The distance from Wady *Nasb* (in the desert of Sin) to the point at which the upper Sinai road reaches the Wady *es Sheikh* is about 15 hours (*Robinson,* vol. iii. app.), and the distance thence to the plain of

[1] *Burckhardt,* p. 799; *v. Raumer,* Zug der Israeliten, p. 29; *Robinson's* Palestine, pp. 178, 179; *De Laborde,* comment., p. 78; *Tischendorf,* Reise i. p. 244.

er Rahah through the Sheikh valley, which runs in a large semicircle to Horeb, 10 hours more (*Burckhardt,* pp. 797 sqq.), whereas the straight road across el Oerf, Wady Solaf, and Nukb Hawy to the convent of Sinai is only seven hours and a half (*Robinson,* vol. iii. appendix). The whole distance from Wady Nasb to the opening of the Sheikh valley into the plain of er Rahah, viz. 25 hours in all, the Israelites might have accomplished in three days, answering to the three stations, Dofkah, Alush, and Rephidim. A trace of Dofkah seems to have been retained in *el Tabbacha,* which *Seetzen* found in the narrow rocky valley of Wady *Gné, i.e. Kineh,* after his visit to Wady Mukatteb, on proceeding an hour and a half farther in a north-westerly (?) direction, and where he saw some Egyptian antiquities. *Knobel* supposes the station *Alush* to have been in the Wady *Oesch* or *Osh* (*Robinson,* i. 125; *Burckhardt,* p. 792), where sweet water may be met with at a little distance off. But apart from the improbability of *Alush* being identical with Osh, even if *al* were the Arabic article, the distance is against it, as it is at least twelve camel-hours from Horeb through the Sheikh valley. *Alush* is rather to be sought for at the entrance to the Sheikh valley; for in no other case could the Israelites have reached Rephidim in one day.

Vers. 2–7. As there was no water to drink in Rephidim, the people murmured against Moses, for having brought them out of Egypt to perish with thirst in the wilderness. This murmuring Moses called " tempting God," *i.e.* unbelieving doubt in the gracious presence of the Lord to help them (ver. 7). In this the people manifested not only their ingratitude to Jehovah, who had hitherto interposed so gloriously and miraculously in every time of distress or need, but their distrust in the guidance of Jehovah and the divine mission of Moses, and such impatience of unbelief as threatened to break out into open rebellion against Moses. " *Yet a little,*" he said to God (*i.e.* a very little more), " *and they stone me ;*" and the divine long-suffering and grace interposed in this case also, and provided for the want without punishing their murmuring. Moses was to pass on before the people, and, taking some of the elders with him, and his staff with which he smote the Nile, to go to the rock at Horeb, and 'smite upon the rock with the staff, at the place where God should stand before him, and water would come out of the rock. The elders were to be eye-witnesses of the miracle, that they might bear their testimony to it before the unbelieving people, " *ne dicere possint, jam ab antiquis temporibus fontes ibi fuisse*" (*Rashi*). Jehovah's standing before Moses upon the rock, signified the gracious assistance of God. עָמַד לִפְנֵי frequently denotes the attitude of a servant when standing before his master, to receive and execute his commands. Thus Jehovah condescended to come to the help of Moses, and assist His people with His almighty power. His gracious presence caused water to flow out of the hard dry rock, though not till Moses struck it with his staff, that the people might acknowledge him afresh as the possessor of supernatural and miraculous powers. The precise spot at which the water was smitten out of the rock cannot be determined; for there is no reason whatever for fixing upon the summit of the present Horeb, *Ras el Sufsafeh*, from which you can take in the whole of the plain of er Rahah (*Robinson*, i. p. 154).—Ver. 7. From this behaviour of the unbelieving nation the place received the names *Massah* and *Meribah*, " temptation and murmuring," that this sin of the people might never be forgotten (cf. Deut. vi. 16; Ps. lxxviii. 20, xcv. 8, cv. 41).

CONFLICT WITH AMALEK.—CHAP. XVII. 8–16.

Vers. 8–13. The want of water had only just been provided for, when Israel had to engage in a conflict with the Amalekites, who had fallen upon their rear and smitten it (Deut. xxv. 18). The expansion of this tribe, that was descended from a grandson of Esau (see Gen. xxxvi. 12), into so great a power even in the Mosaic times, is perfectly conceivable, if we imagine the process to have been analogous to that which we have already described in the case of the leading branches of the Edomites, who had grown into a powerful nation through the subjugation and incorporation of the earlier population of Mount Seir. The Amalekites had no doubt come to the neighbourhood of Sinai for the same reason for which, even in the present day, the Bedouin Arabs leave the lower districts at the beginning of summer, and congregate in the mountain regions of the Arabian peninsula, viz. because the grass is dried up in the former, whereas in the

latter the pasturage remains green much longer, on account of
the climate being comparatively cooler (*Burckhardt*, Syr. p. 789).
There they fell upon the Israelites, probably in the Sheikh valley, where the rear had remained behind the main body, not
merely for the purpose of plundering or of disputing the possession of this district and its pasture ground with the Israelites,
but to assail Israel as the nation of God, and if possible to destroy it.   The divine command to exterminate Amalek (ver. 14)
points to this; and still more the description given of the Amalekites in Balaam's utterances, as רֵאשִׁית גּוֹיִם, "the beginning," *i.e.*
the first and foremost of the heathen nations (Num. xxiv. 20).
In Amalek the heathen world commenced that conflict with the
people of God, which, while it aims at their destruction, can only
be terminated by the complete annihilation of the ungodly
powers of the world.   Earlier theologians pointed out quite correctly the deepest ground for the hostility of the Amalekites,
when they traced the *causa belli* to this fact, " *quod timebat Ama-
lec, qui erat de semine Esau, jam implendam benedictionem, quam
Jacob obtinuit et præripuit ipsi Esau, præsertim cum in magna
potentia venirent Israelitæ, ut promissam occuparent terram*"
Münster, C. a Lapide, etc.).   This peculiar significance in the
conflict is apparent, not only from the divine command to exterminate the Amalekites, and to carry on the war of Jehovah with
Amalek from generation to generation (vers. 14 and 16), but
also from the manner in which Moses led the Israelites to battle
and to victory.   Whereas he had performed all the miracles in
Egypt and on the journey by stretching out his staff, on this
occasion he directed his servant Joshua to choose men for the
war, and to fight the battle with the sword.   He himself went
with Aaron and Hur to the summit of a hill to hold up the
staff of God in his hands, that he might procure success to the
warriors through the spiritual weapons of prayer.

   The proper name of *Joshua*, who appears here for the first
time in the service of Moses, was Hosea (הוֹשֵׁעַ); he was a prince
of the tribe of Ephraim (Num. xiii. 8, 16; Deut. xxxii. 44).   The
name יְהוֹשֻׁעַ, " Jehovah is help" (or, God-help), he probably received at the time when he entered Moses' service, either before
or after the battle with the Amalekites (see Num. xiii. 16, and
Hengstenberg, Dissertations, vol. ii.).   *Hur*, who also held a prominent position in the nation, according to chap. xxiv. 14, in

connection with Aaron, was the son of Caleb, the son of Hezron, the grandson of Judah (1 Chron. ii. 18–20), and the grandfather of Bezaleel, the architect of the tabernacle (chap. xxxi. 2,
xxxv. 30, xxxviii. 22, cf. 1 Chron. ii. 19, 20). According to
Jewish tradition, he was the husband of Miriam.—The battle
was fought on the day after the first attack (ver. 9). The hill
(גִּבְעָה, not Mount Horeb), upon the summit of which Moses took
up his position during the battle, along with Aaron and Hur,
cannot be fixed upon with exact precision, but it was probably
situated in the table-land of *Fureia*, to the north of er Rahah
and the Sheikh valley, which is a fertile piece of pasture ground
(*Burckhardt*, p. 801; *Robinson*, i. pp. 139, 215), or else in the
plateau which runs to the north-east of the Horeb mountains
and to the east of the Sheikh valley, with the two peaks Umlanz
and Um Alawy; supposing, that is, that the Amalekites attacked
the Israelites from Wady Muklifeh or es Suweiriyeh. Moses
went to the top of the hill that he might see the battle from
thence. He took Aaron and Hur with him, not as adjutants to
convey his orders to Joshua and the army engaged, but to support him in his own part in connection with the conflict. This
was to hold up his hand with the staff of God in it. To understand the meaning of this sign, it must be borne in mind that,
although ver. 11 merely speaks of the raising and dropping of
the hand (in the singular), yet, according to ver. 12, both hands
were supported by Aaron and Hur, who stood one on either side,
so that Moses did not hold up his hands alternately, but grasped
the staff with both his hands, and held it up with the two. The
lifting up of the hands has been regarded almost with unvarying
unanimity by Targumists, Rabbins, Fathers, Reformers, and
nearly all the more modern commentators, as the sign or attitude of prayer. *Kurtz*, on the contrary, maintains, in direct
opposition to the custom observed throughout the whole of the
Old Testament by all pious and earnest worshippers, of lifting
up their hands to God in heaven, that this view attributes an
importance to the outward form of prayer which has no analogy
even in the Old Testament; he therefore agrees with *Lakemacher*, in *Rosenmüller's Scholien*, in regarding the attitude of
Moses with his hand lifted up as " the attitude of a commander
superintending and directing the battle," and the elevation of the
hand as only the means adopted for raising the staff, which was

elevated in the sight of the warriors of Israel as the banner of victory. But this meaning cannot be established from vers. 15 and 16. For the altar with the name "*Jehovah my banner*," and the watchword "*the hand on the banner of Jehovah, war of the Lord against Amalek*," can neither be proved to be connected with the staff which Moses held in his hand, nor be adduced as a proof that Moses held the staff in front of the Israelites as the banner of victory. The lifting up of the staff of God was, no doubt, a banner to the Israelites of victory over their foes, but not in this sense, that Moses directed the battle as commander-in-chief, for he had transferred the command to Joshua; nor yet in this sense, that he imparted divine powers to the warriors by means of the staff, and so secured the victory. To effect this, he would not have lifted it up, but have stretched it out, either over the combatants, or at all events towards them, as in the case of all the other miracles that were performed with the staff. The lifting up of the staff secured to the warriors the strength needed to obtain the victory, from the fact that by means of the staff Moses brought down this strength from above, *i.e.* from the Almighty God in heaven; not indeed by a merely spiritless and unthinking elevation of the staff, but by the power of his prayer, which was embodied in the lifting up of his hands with the staff, and was so far strengthened thereby, that God had chosen and already employed this staff as the medium of the saving manifestation of His almighty power. There is no other way in which we can explain the effect produced upon the battle by the raising and dropping (הֵנִיחַ) of the staff in his hands. As long as Moses held up the staff, he drew down from God victorious powers for the Israelites by means of his prayer; but when he let it fall through the exhaustion of the strength of his hands, he ceased to draw down the power of God, and Amalek gained the upper hand. The staff, therefore, as it was stretched out on high, was not a sign to the Israelites that were fighting, for it is by no means certain that they could see it in the heat of the battle; but it was a sign to Jehovah, carrying up, as it were, to God the wishes and prayers of Moses, and bringing down from God victorious powers for Israel. If the intention had been to hold it up before the Israelites as a banner of victory, Moses would not have withdrawn to a hill apart from the field of battle, but would either have carried it himself in front of the army, or have given it to Joshua as commander, to be borne by him in front of the combatants, or else have entrusted it to Aaron, who had performed the miracles in Egypt, that he might carry it at their head. The pure reason why Moses did not do this, but withdrew from the field of battle to lift up the staff of God upon the summit of a hill, and to secure the victory by so doing, is to be found in the important character of the battle itself. As the heathen world was now commencing its conflict with the people of God in the persons of the Amalekites, and the prototype of the heathen world, with its hostility to God, was opposing the nation of the Lord, that had been redeemed from the bondage of Egypt and was on its way to Canaan, to contest its entrance into the promised inheritance; so the battle which Israel fought with this foe possessed a typical significance in relation to all the future history of Israel. It could not conquer by the sword alone, but could only gain the victory by the power of God, coming down from on high, and obtained through prayer and those means of grace with which it had been entrusted. The means now possessed by Moses were the staff, which was, as it were, a channel through which the powers of omnipotence were conducted to him. In most cases he used it under the direction of God; but God had not promised him miraculous help for the conflict with the Amalekites, and for this reason he lifted up his hands with the staff in prayer to God, that he might thereby secure the assistance of Jehovah for His struggling people. At length he became exhausted, and with the falling of his hands and the staff he held, the flow of divine power ceased, so that it was necessary to support his arms, that they might be kept firmly directed upwards (אֱמוּנָה, *lit.* firmness) until the enemy was entirely subdued. And from this Israel was to learn the lesson, that in all its conflicts with the ungodly powers of the world, strength for victory could only be procured through the incessant lifting up of its hands in prayer. *"And Joshua discomfited Amalek and his people* (the Amalekites and their people) *with the edge of the sword"* (*i.e.* without quarter. See Gen. xxxiv. 26).

Vers. 14–16. As this battle and victory were of such significance, Moses was to write it for a memorial בַּסֵּפֶר, in *" the book"* appointed for a record of the wonderful works of God, and *" to put it into the ears of Joshua,"* i.e. to make known to him, and impress upon him, that Jehovah would utterly put out the remembrance of Amalek from under heaven; not "in order that he might carry out this decree of God on the conquest of Canaan, as *Knobel* supposes, but to strengthen his confidence in the help of the Lord against all the enemies of Israel. In Deut. xxv. 19 the Israelites are commanded to exterminate Amalek, when God should have given them rest in the land of Canaan from all their enemies round about.—Vers. 15, 16. To praise God for His help, Moses built an altar, which he called "*Jehovah my banner*," and said, when he did so, "*The hand on the throne* (or banner) *of Jah! War to the Lord from generation to generation!*" There is nothing said about sacrifices being offered upon this altar. It has been conjectured, therefore, that as a place of worship and thank-offering, the altar with its expressive name was merely to serve as a memorial to posterity of the gracious help of the Lord, and that the words which were spoken by Moses were to serve as a watchword for Israel, keeping this act of God in lively remembrance among the people in all succeeding generations. כִּי (ver. 16) merely introduces the words as in Gen. iv. 23, etc. The expression יָד עַל־כֵּס יָהּ is obscure, chiefly on account of the ἅπ. λεγ. כֵּס. In the ancient versions (with the exception of the Septuagint, in which כס יה is treated as one word, and rendered κρυφαία) כֵּס is taken to be equivalent to כִּסֵּה (1 Kings x. 19; Job xxvi. 9) for כִּסֵּא, and the clause is rendered "the hand upon the *throne* of the Lord." But whilst some understand the laying of the hand (*sc.* of God) upon the throne to be expressive of the attitude of swearing, others regard the hand as symbolical of power. There are others again, like *Clericus*, who suppose the hand to denote the hand laid by the Amalekites upon the throne of the Lord, *i.e.* on Israel. But if כֵּס signifies throne or *adytum arcanum*, the words can hardly be understood in any other sense than "the hand lifted up to the throne of Jehovah in heaven, war to the Lord," etc.; and thus understood, they can only contain an admonition to Israel to follow the example of Moses, and wage war against Amalek with the hands lifted up to the throne of Jehovah. Modern expositors, however, for the most part regard כֵּס as a corruption of נֵס, "the hand on the banner of the Lord." But even admitting this, though many objections may be offered to its correctness, we must not understand by "the banner of Jehovah'

the staff of Moses, but only the altar with the name Jehovah-
nissi, as the symbol or memorial of the victorious help afforded
by God in the battle with the Amalekites.

JETHRO THE MIDIANITE IN THE CAMP OF ISRAEL.—
CHAP. XVIII.

Vers. 1–12. The Amalekites had met Israel with hostility,
as the prototype of the heathen who would strive against the
people and kingdom of God. But Jethro, the Midianitish priest,
appeared immediately after in the camp of Israel, not only as
Moses' father-in-law, to bring back his wife and children, but
also with a joyful acknowledgment of all that Jehovah had done
to the Israelites in delivering them from Egypt, to offer burnt-
offerings to the God of Israel, and to celebrate a sacrificial meal
with Moses, Aaron, and all the elders of Israel; so that in the person of Jethro the first-fruits of the heathen, who would hereafter
seek the living God, entered into religious fellowship with the
people of God. As both the Amalekites and Midianites were descended from Abraham, and stood in blood-relationship to Israel,
the different attitudes which they assumed towards the Israelites
foreshadowed and typified the twofold attitude which the heathen
world would assume towards the kingdom of God. (On *Jethro*,
see chap. ii. 18; on Moses' wife and sons, see chap. ii. 21, 22;
and on the expression in ver. 2, "*after he had sent her back*,"
chap. iv. 26.)—Jethro came to Moses "*into the wilderness, where
he encamped at the mount of God.*" The mount of God is
Horeb (chap. iii. 1); and the place of encampment is Rephidim,
at Horeb, *i.e.* at the spot where the Sheikh valley opens into the
plain of er Rahah (chap. xvii. 1). This part is designated as a
wilderness; and according to *Robinson* (1, pp. 130, 131) the
district round this valley and plain is "naked desert," and
"wild and desolate." The occasion for Jethro the priest to
bring back to his son-in-law his wife and children was furnished
by the intelligence which had reached him, that Jehovah had
brought Israel out of Egypt (ver. 1), and, as we may obviously
supply, had led them to Horeb. When Moses sent his wife and
sons back to Jethro, he probably stipulated that they were to
return to him on the arrival of the Israelites at Horeb. For
when God first called Moses at Horeb, He foretold to him that

Israel would be brought to this mountain on its deliverance from
Egypt (chap. iii. 12).[1]

Vers. 6–12. When Jethro announced his arrival to Moses
("he said," *sc.* through a messenger), he received his father-in-
law with the honour due to his rank ; and when he had conducted
him to his tent, he related to him all the leading events connected
with the departure from Egypt, and all the troubles they had
met with on the way, and how Jehovah had delivered them out
of them all. Jethro rejoiced at this, and broke out in praise to
Jehovah, declaring that Jehovah was greater than all gods, *i.e.*
that He had shown Himself to be exalted above all gods, for
God is great in the eyes of men only when He makes known
His greatness through the display of His omnipotence. He then
gave a practical expression to his praise by a burnt-offering and
slain-offering, which he presented to God. The second כִּי in

---

[1] *Kurtz* (Hist. of O. C. iii. 46, 53) supposes that it was chiefly the report
of the glorious result of the battle with Amalek which led Jethro to resolve
to bring Moses' family back to him. There is no statement, however, to
this effect in the biblical text, but rather the opposite, namely, that what
Jethro had heard of all that God had done to Moses and Israel consisted of
the fact that Jehovah had brought Israel out of Egypt. Again, there are
not sufficient grounds for placing the arrival of Jethro at the camp of Israel,
in the desert of Sinai and after the giving of the law, as *Ranke* has done.
For the fact that the mount of God is mentioned as the place of encampment at the time, is an argument in favour of Rephidim, rather than against
it, as we have already shown. And we can see no force in the assertion that
the circumstances, in which we find the people, point rather to the longer
stay at Sinai, than to the passing halt at Rephidim. For how do we know
that the stay at Rephidim was such a passing one, that it would not afford
time enough for Jethro's visit? It is true that, according to the ordinary
assumption, only half a month intervened between the arrival of the Israelites in the desert of Sin and their arrival in the desert of Sinai; but within
this space of time everything might have taken place that is said to have
occurred on the march from the former to the latter place of encampment.
It is not stated in the biblical text that seven days were absorbed in the
desert of Sin alone, but only that the Israelites spent a Sabbath there, and
had received manna a few days before, so that three or four days (say from
Thursday to Saturday inclusive) would amply suffice for all that took place.
If the Israelites, therefore, encamped there in the evening of the 15th, they
might have moved farther on the morning of the 19th or 20th, and after a two
days' journey by Dofkah and Alush have reached Rephidim on the 21st or 22d.
They could then have fought the battle with the Amalekites the following
day, so that Jethro might have come to the camp on the 24th or 25th, and
held the sacrificial meal with the Israelites the next day. In that case there

ver. 11 is only an emphatic repetition of the first, and בִּדְבַר אֲשֶׁר is not dependent upon יָדַעְתִּי, but upon גָּדוֹל, or upon הִגְדִּיל understood, which is to be supplied in thought after the second כִּי: "*That He has proved Himself great by the affair in which they* (the Egyptians) *dealt proudly against them* (the Israelites)." Compare Neh. ix. 10, from which it is evident, that to refer these words to the destruction of Pharaoh and his army in the Red Sea as a punishment for their attempt to destroy the Israelites in the water (chap. i. 22) is too contracted an interpretation; and that they rather relate to all the measures adopted by the Egyptians for the oppression and detention of the Israelites, and signify that Jehovah had shown Himself great above all gods by all the plagues inflicted upon Egypt down to the destruction of Pharaoh and his army in the Red Sea.—Ver. 12. The sacrifices, which Jethro offered to God, were applied to a sacrificial meal, in which Moses joined, as well as Aaron and all the elders.

would still be four or five days left for him to see Moses sitting in judgment a whole day long (ver. 13), and for the introduction of the judicial arrangements proposed by Jethro;—amply sufficient time, inasmuch as one whole day would suffice for the sight of the judicial sitting, which is said to have taken place the day after the sacrificial meal (ver. 13). And the election of judges on the part of the people, for which Moses gave directions in accordance with Jethro's advice, might easily have been carried out in two days. For, on the one hand, it is most probable that after Jethro had watched this severe and exhausting occupation of Moses for a whole day, he spoke to Moses on the subject the very same evening, and laid his plan before him; and on the other hand, the execution of this plan did not require a very long time, as the people were not scattered over a whole country, but were collected together in one camp. Moreover, Moses carried on all his negotiations with the people through the elders as their representatives; and the judges were not elected in modern fashion by universal suffrage, but were nominated by the people, *i.e.* by the natural representatives of the nation, from the body of elders, according to their tribes, and then appointed by Moses himself.—Again, it is by no means certain that Israel arrived at the desert of Sinai on the *first* day of the third month, and that only half a month (15 or 16 days) elapsed between their arrival in the desert of Sin and their encamping at Sinai (cf. chap. xix. 1). And lastly, though *Kurtz* still affirms that Jethro lived on the other side of the Elanitic Gulf, and did not set out till he heard of the defeat of the Amalekites, in which case a whole month might easily intervene between the victory of Israel and the arrival of Jethro, the two premises upon which this conclusion is based, are assumptions without foundation, as we have already shown at chap. iii. 1 in relation to the former, and have just shown in relation to the latter.

Eating bread before God signified the holding of a sacrificial
meal, which was eating before God, because it was celebrated in
a holy place of sacrifice, where God was supposed to be present.

Vers. 13–24. The next day Jethro saw how Moses was occupied from morning till evening in judging the people, who
brought all their disputes to him, that he might settle them according to the statutes of God. עָמַד עַל‎: as in Gen. xviii. 8.
The people came to Moses "to seek or inquire of God" (ver.
15), i.e. to ask for a decision from God : in most cases, this
means to inquire through an oracle ; here it signifies to desire a
divine decision as to questions in dispute.   By judging or deciding the cases brought before him, Moses made known to the
people the ordinances and laws of God.   For every decision was
based upon some law, which, like all true justice here on earth,
emanated first of all from God.   This is the meaning of ver.
16, and not, as *Knobel* supposes, that Moses made use of the
questions in dispute, at the time they were decided, as good
opportunities for giving laws to the people.   Jethro condemned
this plan (vers. 18 sqq.) as exhausting, wearing out (נָבֵל *lit.* to
fade away, Ps. xxxvii. 2), both for Moses and the people : for
the latter, inasmuch as they not only got wearied out through
long waiting, but, judging from ver. 23, very often began to
take the law into their own hands on account of the delay in the
judicial decision, and so undermined the well-being of the community at large ; and for Moses, inasmuch as the work was
necessarily too great for him, and he could not continue for any
length of time to sustain such a burden alone (ver. 18).   The
obsolete form of the *inf. const.* עֲשׂהוּ for עֲשׂתוֹ is only used here,
but is not without analogies in the Pentateuch.   Jethro advised
him (vers. 19 sqq.) to appoint judges from the people for all the
smaller matters in dispute, so that in future only the more difficult cases, which really needed a superior or divine decision,
would be brought to him that he might lay them before God.
" *I will give thee counsel, and God be with thee* (*i.e.* help thee to
carry out this advice) : *Be thou to the people* מוּל הָאֱלֹהִים, *towards
God*," *i.e.* lay their affairs before God, take the place of God in
matters of judgment, or, as *Luther* expresses it, " take charge of
the people before God."   To this end, in the *first* place, he was to
instruct the people in the commandments of God, and their own
walk and conduct (הִזְהִיר) with a double accusative, to enlighten,

instruct; דֶּרֶךְ the walk, the whole behaviour; מַעֲשֶׂה particular actions); *secondly*, he was to select able men (אַנְשֵׁי חַיִל men of moral strength, 1 Kings i. 52) as judges, men who were God-fearing, sincere, and unselfish (gain-hating), and appoint them to administer justice to the people, by deciding the simpler matters themselves, and only referring the more difficult questions to him, and so to lighten his own duties by sharing the burden with these judges. הָקֵל מֵעָלֶיךָ (ver. 22) "*make light of* (that which lies) *upon thee.*" If he would do this, and God would command him, he would be able to stand, and the people would come to their place, *i.e.* to Canaan, in good condition (בְּשָׁלוֹם). The *apodosis* cannot begin with וְצִוְּךָ, "then God will *establish* thee," for צִוָּה never has this meaning; but the idea is this, "if God should preside over the execution of the plan proposed."—Ver. 24. Moses followed this sage advice, and, as he himself explains in Deut. i. 12—18, directed the people to nominate wise, intelligent, and well-known men from the heads of the tribes, whom he appointed as judges, instructing them to administer justice with impartiality and without respect of persons.

Vers. 25—27. The judges chosen were arranged as chiefs (שָׂרִים) over thousands, hundreds, fifties, and tens, after the analogy of the military organization of the people on their march (Num. xxxi. 14), in such a manner, however, that this arrangement was linked on to the natural division of the people into tribes, families, etc. (see my *Archäologie*, § 140). For it is evident that the decimal division was not made in an arbitrary manner according to the number of heads, from the fact that, on the one hand, the judges were chosen from the heads of the tribes and according to their tribes (Deut. i. 13); and on the other hand, the larger divisions of the tribes, viz. the families (*mishpachoth*), were also called thousands (Num. i. 16, x. 4; Josh. xxii. 14, etc.), just because the number of their heads of families would generally average about a thousand; so that in all probability the hundreds, fifties, and tens denote smaller divisions of the nation, in which there were about this number of fathers. Thus in Arabic, for example, "*the ten*" is a term used to signify a family (cf. *Hengstenberg*, Dissertations v. ii. 343, and my Arch. § 149). The difference between the harder or greater matters and the smaller matters consisted in this: questions which there was no definite law to decide were great or hard; whereas, on the other hand, those which could easily be decided from existing laws or general principles of equity were simple or small. (*Vide Joh. Selden de Synedriis* i. c. 16, in my *Arch.* § 149, Not. 3, where the different views are discussed respecting the relative positions and competency of the various judges, about which there is no precise information given in the law.) So far as the total number of judges is concerned, all that can be affirmed with certainty is, that the estimated number of 600 judges over thousands, 6000 over hundreds, 12,000 over fifties, and 60,000 over tens, in all 78,600 judges, which is given by *Grotius* and in the Talmud, and according to which there must have been a judge for every seven adults, is altogether erroneous (cf. *J. Selden l.c.* pp. 339 seq.). For if the thousands answered to the families (*mishpachoth*), there cannot have been a thousand males in every one; and in the same way the hundreds, etc., are not to be understood as consisting of precisely that number of persons, but as larger or smaller family groups, the numerical strength of which we do not know. And even if we did know it, or were able to estimate it, this would furnish no criterion by which to calculate the number of the judges, for the text does not affirm that every one of these larger or smaller family groups had a judge of its own ; in fact, the contrary may rather be inferred, from the fact that, according to Deut. i. 15, the judges were chosen out of the heads of the tribes, so that the number of judges must have been smaller than that of the heads, and can hardly therefore have amounted to many hundreds, to say nothing of many thousands.

ARRIVAL AT SINAI, AND PREPARATION FOR THE COVENANT.—CHAP. XIX.

Vers. 1, 2. In the third month after their departure from Egypt, the Israelites arrived at Sinai, proceeding from Rephidim into the desert of Sinai, and encamping there before the mountain. On what day of the month, the received text does not state. The striking expression בַּיּוֹם הַזֶּה (" the same day"), without any previous notice of the day, cannot signify the first day of the month ; nor can הַחֹדֶשׁ הַשְּׁלִישִׁי signify the third new moon in the year, and be understood as referring to the first day of the third month. For although, according to the etymology of חֹדֶשׁ (from חָדַשׁ to be new), it might denote the new moon, yet in chronological data it is never used in this sense; but the day of the month is invariably appended after the month itself has been given (e.g. אֶחָד לַחֹדֶשׁ chap. xl. 2, 17; Gen. viii. 5, 13; Num. i. 1, xxix. 1, xxxiii. 38, etc.). Moreover, in the Pentateuch the word חֹדֶשׁ never signifies new moon; but the new moons are called רָאשֵׁי חֳדָשִׁים (Num. x. 10, xxviii. 11, cf. *Hengstenberg*, Dissertations, vol. ii. 297). And even in such passages as 1 Sam. xx. 5, xviii. 24, 2 Kings iv. 23, Amos viii. 5, Isa. i. 13, etc., where חֹדֶשׁ is mentioned as a feast along with the Sabbaths and other feasts, the meaning new moon appears neither demonstrable nor necessary, as חֹדֶשׁ in this case denotes the feast of the month, the celebration of the beginning of the month. If, therefore, the text is genuine, and the date of the month has not dropt out (and the agreement of the ancient versions with the Masoretic text favours this conclusion), there is no other course open, than to understand יוֹם, as in Gen. ii. 4 and Num. iii. 1, and probably also in the unusual expression יוֹם הַחֹדֶשׁ, Ex. xl. 2, in the general sense of time; so that here, and also in Num. ix. 1, xx. 1, the month only is given, and not the day of the month, and it is altogether uncertain whether the arrival in the desert of Sinai took place on one of the first, one of the middle, or one of the last days of the month. The Jewish tradition, which assigns the giving of the law to the fiftieth day after the Passover, is of far too recent a date to pass for historical (see my *Archäologie*, § 83, 6).

The *desert of Sinai* is not the plain of er Rahah to the north of Horeb, but the desert in front (נֶגֶד) of the mountain, upon the summit of which Jehovah came down, whilst Moses ascended it to receive the law (ver. 20 and xxxiv. 2). This mountain is constantly called Sinai so long as Israel stayed there (vers. 18, 20, 23, xxiv. 16, xxxiv. 2, 4, 29, 32; Lev. vii. 38, xxv. 1, xxvi. 46, xxvii. 34; Num. iii. 1; see also Num. xxviii. 6 and Deut. xxxiii. 2); and the place of their encampment by the mountain is also called the " *desert of Sinai*," never the desert of Horeb (Lev. vii. 38; Num. i. 1, 19, iii. 14, ix. 1, x. 12, xxvi. 64, xxxiii. 15). But in Ex. xxxiii. 6 this spot is designated as "Mount Horeb," and in Deuteronomy, as a rule, it is spoken of briefly as "Horeb" (Deut. i. 2, 6, 19, iv. 10, 15, v. 2, ix. 8,

xviii. 16, xxviii. 69). And whilst the general identity of Sinai and Horeb may be inferred from this; the fact, that wherever the intention of the writer is to give a precise and geographical description of the place where the law was given, the name Sinai is employed, leads to the conclusion that the term Horeb was more general and comprehensive than that of Sinai; in other words, that Horeb was the range of which Sinai was one particular mountain, which only came prominently out to view when Israel had arrived at the mount of legislation. This distinction between the two names, which *Hengstenberg* was the first to point out and establish (in his Dissertations, vol. ii. p. 325), is now generally admitted; so that the only room that is left for any difference of opinion is with reference to the extent of the Horeb range. There is no ground for supposing that the name *Horeb* includes the whole of the mountains in the Arabian peninsula. Sufficient justice is done to all the statements in the Bible, if we restrict this name to the southern and highest range of the central mountains,—to the exclusion, therefore, of the Serbal group.[1] This southern range, which Arabian geographers and the Bedouins call *Jebel Tur* or *Jebel Tur Sina*, consists of three summits: (1) a central one, called by the Arabs *Jebel Musa* (Moses' Mountain), and by Christians either *Horeb* or else *Horeb-Sinai*, in which case the northern and lower peak, or *Ras es Sufsafeh*, is called Horeb, and the southern and loftier one Sinai; (2) a western one, called *Jebel Humr*, with *Mount Catherine* on the south, the loftiest point in the whole range; and (3) an eastern one, called *Jebel el Deir* (Convent Mountain) or *Episteme* (*vide Ritter*, 14, pp. 527 sqq.).—Near this range there are two plains, which furnish space enough for a large encampment. One of these is the plain of *er Rahah*, on the north and north-west of Horeb-Sinai, with a level space of an English square mile, which is considerably enlarged by the Sheikh valley that opens into it from the east. At its southern extremity Horeb, with its granite rocks, runs almost precipitously to the height of 1200 or 1500 feet; and towards the west it is also shut in as with a wall by the equally precipitous spurs of

---

[1] The hypothesis advocated by *Lepsius*, that Sinai or Horeb is to be sought for in *Serbal*, has very properly met with no favour. For the objections to this, see *Ritter*, Erdkunde 14, pp. 738 sqq.; and *Kurtz*, History of O. C., vol. iii. p. 94 sqq.

Jebel Humr. The other plain, which is called *Sebayeh*, lies to the south-east of Sinai, or Jebel Musa in the more restricted sense; it is from 1400 to 1800 feet broad, 12,000 feet long, and is shut in towards the south and east by mountains, which rise very gently, and do not reach any considerable height. There are three wadys leading to this plain from er Rahah and the Sheikh valley. The most westerly of these, which separates Horeb-Sinai from Jebel Humr with Mount Catherine on the south, is called *el Leja*, and is a narrow defile full of great blocks of stone, and shut in towards the south like a *cul de sac* by Mount Catherine. The central one, which separates Horeb from Jebel Deir, is Wady *Shoeib* (Jethro valley), with the convent of Sinai in it, which is also called the Convent Valley in consequence. This is less confined, and not so much strewed with stones; towards the south it is not quite shut in, and yet not quite open, but bounded by a steep pass and a grassy mountain-saddle, viz. the easily accessible *Jebel Sebayeh*. The third and most easterly is the Wady *es Sebayeh*, which is from 400 to 600 feet broad, and leads from the Sheikh valley, in a southern and south-westerly direction, to the plain of the same name, which stretches like an amphitheatre to the southern slope of Sinai, or Jebel Musa, in the more restricted sense. When seen from this plain, "Jebel Musa has the appearance of a lofty and splendid mountain cone, towering far above the lower gravelly hills by which it is surrounded" (*Ritter*, pp. 540, 541).

Since *Robinson*, who was the first to describe the plain of *er Rahah*, and its fitness for the encampment of Israel, visited Sinai, this plain has generally been regarded as the site where Israel encamped in the "desert of Sinai." *Robinson* supposed that he had discovered the Sinai of the Bible in the northern peak of Mount Horeb, viz. *Ras es Sufsafeh*. But *Ritter, Kurtz*, and others have followed *Laborde* and *F. A. Strauss*, who were the first to point out the suitableness of the plain of *Sebayeh* to receive a great number of people, in fixing upon *Jebel Musa* in the stricter sense, the southern peak of the central group, which tradition had already indicated as the scene of the giving of the law, as the true Mount Sinai, where Moses received the laws from God, and the plain of *Sebayeh* as the spot to which Moses led the people (*i.e.* the men) on the third day, out of the camp of God and through the *Sebayeh* valley (ver. 16). For this

plain is far better adapted to be the scene of such a display of
the nation, than the plain of er Rahah : first, because the hills
in the background slope gradually upwards in the form of an
amphitheatre, and could therefore hold a larger number of
people ; [1] whereas the mountains which surround the plain of
er Rahah are so steep and rugged, that they could not be made
use of in arranging the people;—and secondly, because the
gradual sloping of the plain upwards, both on the east and south,
would enable even the furthest rows to see Mount Sinai in all
its majestic grandeur ; whereas the plain of er Rahah slopes
downwards towards the north, so that persons standing in the
background would be completely prevented by those in front from
seeing Ras es Sufsafeh.—If, however, the plain of *es Sebayeh*
so entirely answers to all the topographical data of the Bible,
that we must undoubtedly regard it as the spot where the people
of God were led up to the foot of the mountain, we cannot
possibly fix upon the plain of er Rahah as the place of encampment in the desert of Sinai. The very expression "desert of
Sinai," which is applied to the place of encampment, is hardly
reconcilable with this opinion. For example, if the Sinai of
the Old Testament is identical with the present Jebel Musa,
and the whole group of mountains bore the name of Horeb, the
plain of er Rahah could not with propriety be called the desert
of Sinai, for Sinai cannot even be seen from it, but is completely
hidden by the Ras es Sufsafeh of Horeb. Moreover, the road
from the plain of er Rahah into the plain of es Sebayeh through
the Sebayeh valley is so long and so narrow, that the people of
Israel, who numbered more than 600,000 men, could not possibly have been conducted from the camp in er Rahah into
the Sebayeh plain, and so up to Mount Sinai, and then, after
being placed in order there, and listening to the promulgation
of the law, have returned to the camp again, all in a single day.
The Sebayeh valley, or the road from the Sheikh valley to the
commencement of the plain of Sebayeh, is, it is true, only an

[1] "Sinai falls towards the south for about 2000 feet into low granite
hills, and then into a large plain, which is about 1600 feet broad and nearly
five miles long, and rises like an amphitheatre opposite to the mountain
both on the south and east. It is a plain that seems made to accommodate a large number gathered round the foot of the mountain " (*Strauss*,
p. 135).

hour long. But we have to add to this the distance from the point at which the Sebayeh valley opens into the Sheikh valley to the western end of the plain of er Rahah, viz. two hours' journey, and the length of the plain of Sebayeh itself, which is more than five miles long; so that the Israelites, at least those who were encamped in the western part of the plain of er Rahah, would have to travel four or five hours before they could be posted at the foot of Sinai.[1] *Tischendorf* calls this a narrow, bad road, which the Israelites were obliged to pass through to Sinai, when they came out of the Sheikh valley. At any rate, this is true of the southern end of the valley of Sebayeh, from the point at which it enters the plain of Sebayeh, where we can hardly picture it to ourselves as broad enough for two hundred men to walk abreast in an orderly procession through the valley;[2] consequently, 600,000 men would have required two hours' time simply to pass through the narrow southern end of the valley of Sebayeh. Now, it is clear enough from the narrative itself that Moses did not take merely the elders, as the representatives of the nation, from the camp to the mountain to meet with God (ver. 17), but took the whole nation, that is to say, all the adult males of 20 years old and upwards; and this is especially evident from the command so emphatically and repeatedly given, that no one was to break through the hedge placed

[1] Some Englishmen who accompanied *F. A. Strauss* " had taken three-quarters of an hour for a fast walk from the Sebayeh plain to Wady es Sheikh ;" so that it is not too much to reckon an hour for ordinary walking. *Döbel* took quite six hours to go round Horeb-Sinai, which is only a little larger than Jebel Deir ; so that at least three hours must be reckoned as necessary to accomplish the walk from the eastern end of the plain of er Rahah through the Wady Sebayeh to the foot of Sinai. And *Robinson* took fifty minutes to go with camels from the commencement of the Sheikh valley, at the end of the Convent Valley, to the point at which it is joined by the valley of Sebayeh (Palestine i. p. 215).

[2] We are still in want of exact information from travellers as to the breadth of the southern end of the valley of Sebayeh. *Ritter* merely states, on the ground of MS. notes in Strauss' diary, that " at first it is somewhat contracted on account of projections in the heights by which it is bounded towards the south, but it still remains more than 500 feet broad." And " when it turns towards the north-west, the wady is considerably widened ; so that at the narrowest points it is more than 600 feet broad. And very frequently, at the different curves in the valley, large basins are formed, which would hold a considerable number of people."

round the mountain. It may also be inferred from the design of the revelation itself, which was intended to make the deepest impression upon the whole nation of that majesty of Jehovah and the holiness of His law.

Under these circumstances, if the people had been encamped in the plain of er Rahah and the Sheikh valley, they could not have been conducted to the foot of Sinai and stationed in the plain of Sebayeh in the course of six hours, and then, after hearing the revelation of the law, have returned to their tents on the same day; even assuming, as *Kurtz* does (iii. p. 117), that " the people were overpowered by the majesty of the promulgation of the law, and fled away in panic;" for flight through so narrow a valley would have caused inevitable confusion, and therefore would have prevented rather than facilitated rapidity of movement. There is not a word, however, in the original text about a panic, or about the people flying (see chap. xx. 18) : it is merely stated, that as soon as the people witnessed the alarming phenomena connected with the descent of God upon the mountain, they trembled in the camp (chap. xix. 16), and that when they were conducted to the foot of the mountain, and " saw the thunderings, and the lightnings, and the noise of the trumpet, and the mountain smoking," and heard the solemn promulgation of the decalogue, they trembled (יָנֻעוּ, chap. xx. 18), and said to Moses, through their elders and the heads of tribes, that they did not wish God to speak directly to them any more, but wished Moses to speak to God and listen to His words; whereupon, after God had expressed His approval of these words of the people, Moses directed the people to return to their tents (chap. xx. 18 sqq.; Deut. v. 23–30). If, again, we take into consideration, that after Moses had stationed the people at the foot of the mountain, he went up to God to the summit of Sinai, and came down again at the command of God to repeat the charge to the people, not to break through the hedge round the mountain (vers. 20–25), and it was not till after this, that God proclaimed the decalogue, and that this going up and down must also have taken up time, it cannot have been for so very short a time that the people continued standing round the bottom of the mountain. But if all these difficulties be regarded as trivial, and we include the evening and part of the night in order to afford time for the people to return to their tents; not only is there nothing in the biblical text to require the hypothesis which assigns the encampment to the plain of er Rahah, and the posting of the people at Sinai to the plain of Sebayeh, but there are various allusions which seem rather to show that such a hypothesis is inadmissible. It is very obvious from chap. xxiv. 17, that the glory of the Lord upon the top of the mountain could be seen from the camp; and from chap. xxxiv. 1–3, that the camp, with both the people and their cattle in it, was so immediately in the neighbourhood of Sinai, that the people could easily have ascended the mountain, and the cattle could have grazed upon it. Now this does not apply in the least to the plain of er Rahah, from which not even the top of Jebel Musa can be seen, and where the cattle could not possibly have grazed upon it, but only to the plain of Sebayeh; and therefore proves that the camp in "the desert of Sinai" is not to be sought for in the plain of er Rahah, but in the plain of Sebayeh, which reaches to the foot of Sinai. If it should be objected, on the other hand, that there is not room in this plain for the camp of the whole nation, this objection is quite as applicable to the plain of er Rahah, which is not large enough in itself to take in the entire camp, without including a large portion of the Sheikh valley; and it loses all its force from the fact, that the mountains by which the plain of Sebayeh is bounded, both on the south and east, rise so gently and gradually, that they could be made use of for the camp, and on these sides therefore the space is altogether unlimited, and would allow of the widest dispersion of the people and their flocks.

Vers. 3–6. Moses had known from the time of his call that Israel would serve God on this mountain (iii. 12); and as soon as the people were encamped opposite to it, he went up to God, i.e. up the mountain, to the top of which the cloud had probably withdrawn. There God gave him the necessary instructions for preparing for the covenant: first of all assuring him, that He had brought the Israelites to Himself to make them His own nation, and that He would speak to them from the mountain (vers. 4–9); and then ordering him to sanctify the people for this revelation of the Lord (vers. 10–15). The promise precedes the demand: for the grace of God always anticipates the wants of man, and does not demand before it has given. Jehovah spoke to Moses "from Mount Horeb." Moses had probably ascended one of the lower heights, whilst Jehovah is to be regarded as on the summit of the mountain. The words of God (vers. 4 sqq.) refer first of all to what He had done for the Egyptians, and how He had borne the Israelites on eagles' wings ; manifesting in this way not only the separation between Israel and the Egyptians, but the adoption of Israel as the nation of His especial grace and favour. The " eagles' wings" are figurative, and denote the strong and loving care of God. The eagle watches over its young in the most careful manner, flying under them when it leads them from the nest, lest they should fall upon the rocks, and be injured or destroyed (cf. Deut. xxxii. 11, and for proofs from profane literature, *Bochart*, Hieroz. ii. pp. 762, 765 sqq.). " *And brought you unto Myself :* " *i.e.* not " led you to the dwelling-place of God on Sinai," as *Knobel* supposes ; but took you into My protection and My especial care.—Ver. 5. This manifestation of the love of God to Israel formed only the prelude, however, to that gracious union which Jehovah was now about to establish between the Israelites and Himself. If they would hear His voice, and keep the covenant which was about to be established with them, they should be a costly possession to Him out of all nations (cf. Deut. vii. 6, xiv. 2, xxvi. 18). סְגֻלָּה does not signify property in general, but valuable property, that which is laid by, or put aside (סָגַל), hence a treasure of silver and gold (1 Chron. xxix. 3 ; Eccl. ii. 8). In the *Sept.* the expression is rendered λαὸς περιούσιος, which the Scholiast in *Octat.* interprets ἐξαίρετος, and in Mal. iii. 17 εἰς περιποίησιν : hence the two phrases in the New Testament, λαὸς περιούσιος in Tit. ii. 14, and λαὸς εἰς περιποίησιν in 1 Pet. ii. 9. Jehovah had chosen Israel as His costly possession out of all the nations of the earth, because the whole earth was His possession, and all nations belonged to Him as Creator and Preserver. The reason thus assigned for the selection of Israel precludes at the very outset the exclusiveness which would regard Jehovah as merely a national Deity. The idea of the *segullah* is explained in ver. 6 : " *Ye shall be unto Me a kingdom of priests.*" מַמְלָכָה signifies both *kingship*, as the embodiment of royal supremacy, exaltation, and dignity, and the *kingdom*, or the union of both king and subjects, *i.e.* the land and nation together with its king. In the passage before us, the word has been understood by most of the early commentators, both Jewish and Christian, and also in the ancient versions,[1] in the first or active sense, so that the expression contains the idea, " Ye shall be all priests and kings" (*Luther*) ; *præditos fore tam sacerdotali quam regio honore* (*Calvin*) ; *quod reges et sacerdotes sunt in republica, id vos eritis mihi* (*Drusius*). This explanation is required by both the passage itself and the context. For apart from the fact that kingship is the primary and most general meaning of the word מַמְלָכָה (cf. מַמְלֶכֶת דָּוִד, the kingship, or government of David), the other (passive) meaning would not be at all suitable here ; for a kingdom of priests could never denote the fellowship existing in a kingdom between the king and the priests, but only a kingdom or commonwealth consisting of priests, *i.e.* a kingdom the members and citizens of which were priests, and as priests constituted the מַמְלָכָה, in other words, were possessed of royal dignity and power ; for מַמְלָכָה, βασιλεία, always includes the idea of מֶלֶךְ or ruling (βασιλεύειν). The LXX. have quite hit the meaning in their rendering : βασίλειον ἱεράτευμα. Israel was to be a regal body of priests to Jehovah, and not merely a nation of priests governed by Jehovah. The idea of the theocracy, or government of God, as founded by the establishment of the Sinaitic covenant institution in Israel, is not at all involved in the term " kingdom of priests." The theocracy established by the conclusion of the covenant (chap. xxiv.) was only the means adopted by Jehovah for making His chosen people a royal body of priests ; and the maintenance of this covenant was the indispensable subjective condition, upon which their attainment of this divinely appointed destiny and glory depended. This promise of Jehovah expressed the design of the call of Israel, to which it was to be fully conducted by the covenant institution of the theocracy, if it maintained the covenant with Jehovah. The object of Israel's kingship and priesthood was to be found in the nations of the earth, out of which Jehovah had chosen Israel as a costly possession. This great and glorious promise, the fulfilment of which could not be attained till the completion

---

[1] LXX. : βασίλειον ἱεράτευμα, a royal priesthood, *i.e.* a priestly nation of royal power and glory. מַלְכִין כָּהֲנִין : Kings-priests (*Onkelos*).— " *Eritis coram me reges coronati* (קְטִירֵי כְלִילָא *vincti coronis*) *et sacerdotes ministrantes*" (*Jonathan*).—" *Eritis meo nomini reges et sacerdotes*" (*Jer. Targ.*).

of the kingdom of God, when the Israel of God, the Church of the Lord, which Jesus Christ, the first-begotten from the dead, and prince ($ἄρχων$, ruler) of the kings of the earth, has made a " kingdom," " priest· unto God and His Father" (Rev. i. 6 and v. 10, where the reading should be $βασιλεῖς$ $καὶ$ $ἱερεῖς$), is exalted to glory with Christ as the first-born among many brethren, and sits upon His throne and reigns, has not been introduced abruptly here. On the contrary, the way was already prepared by the promises made to the patriarchs, of the blessing which Abraham would become to all the nations of the earth, and of the kings who were to spring from him and come out of the loins of Israel (Gen. xii. 3, xvii. 6, xxxv. 11), and still more distinctly by Jacob's prophecy of the sceptre of Judah, to whom, through *Shiloh*, the willing submission of the nations should be made (Gen. xlix. 10). But these promises and prophecies are outshone by the clearness, with which kingship and priesthood over and for the nations are foretold of Israel here. This kingship, however, is not merely of a spiritual kind, consisting, as *Luther* supposes, in the fact, that believers " are lords over death, the devil, hell, and all evil," but culminates in the universal sway foretold by Balaam in Num. xxiv. 8 and 17 sqq., by Moses in his last words (Deut. xxxiii. 29), and still more distinctly in Dan. vii. 27, to the people of the saints of the Most High, as the ultimate end of their calling from God. The spiritual attitude of Israel towards the nations was the result of its priestly character. As the priest is a mediator between God and man, so Israel was called to be the vehicle of the knowledge and salvation of God to the nations of the earth. By this it unquestionably acquired an intellectual and spiritual character ; but this includes, rather than excludes, the government of the world. For spiritual and intellectual supremacy and rule must eventually ensure the government of the world, as certainly as spirit is the power that overcomes the world. And if the priesthood of Israel was the power which laid the foundation for its kingship,—in other words, if Israel obtained the מַמְלָכָה or government over the nations solely as a priestly nation,—the Apostle Peter, when taking up this promise (I. ii. 9), might without hesitation follow the Septuagint rendering ($βασί-$ $λειον$ $ἱεράτευμα$), and substitute in the place of the " priestly kingdom," a " royal priesthood ;" for there is no essential difference between the two, the kingship being founded upon the priesthood, and the priesthood completed by the kingship.

As a kingdom of priests, it was also necessary that Israel should be a "holy nation." *Gens sancta hic dicitur non respectu pietatis vel sanctimoniæ, sed quam Deus singulari privilegio ab aliis separavit. Verum ab hac sanctificatione pendet altera, nempe ut sanctitatem colant, qui Dei gratia eximii sunt, atque ita vicissim Deum sanctificent (Calvin).* This explanation is in general a correct one; for these words indicate the dignity to which Israel was to be elevated by Jehovah, the Holy One, through its separation from the nations of the earth. But it cannot be shown that קָרֹושׁ ever means "separated." Whether we suppose it to be related to חָדַשׁ, and חֹרֶשׁ the newly shining moonlight, or compare it with the Sanskrit *dhûsch*, to be splendid, or beautiful, in either case the primary meaning of the word is, "to be splendid, pure, untarnished." *Diestel* has correctly observed, that the holiness of God and Israel is most closely connected with the covenant relationship; but he is wrong in the conclusion which he draws from this, namely, that "holy" was originally only a "relative term," and that a thing was holy "so far as it was the property of God." For the whole earth is Jehovah's property (ver. 5), but it is not holy on that account. Jehovah is not holy only "so far as within the covenant He is both possession and possessor, absolute life and the source of life, and above all, both the chief good and the chief model for His people" (*Diestel*), or "as the truly separate One, enclosed within Himself, who is self-existent, in contrast with the world to which He does not belong" (*Hofmann*); but holiness pertains to God alone, and to those who participate in the divine holiness,—not, however, to God as the Creator and Preserver of the world, but to God as the Redeemer of man. Light is the earthly reflection of His holy nature: the Holy One of Israel is the light of Israel (Isa. x. 17, cf. 1 Tim. vi. 16). The light, with its purity and splendour, is the most suitable earthly element to represent the brilliant and spotless purity of the Holy One, in whom there is no interchange of light and darkness (Jas. i. 17). God is called the Holy One, because He is altogether pure, the clear and spotless light; so that in the idea of the holiness of God there are embodied the absolute moral purity and perfection of the divine nature, and His unclouded glory. Holiness and glory

are inseparable attributes in God; but in His relation to the
world they are so far distinguished, that the whole earth is full
of His glory, whilst it is to and in Israel that His holiness is
displayed (Isa. vi. 3); in other words, the glory of God is manifested in the creation and preservation of the world, and His
holy name in the election and guidance of Israel (compare
Ps. civ. with Ps. ciii.). God has displayed the glory of His
name in the creation of the heavens and the earth (Ps. viii.);
but His way in Israel (Ps. lxxvii. 14), *i.e.* the work of God in
His kingdom of grace, is holy; so that it might be said, that
the glory of God which streams forth in the material creation
is manifested as holiness in His saving work for a sinful world,
to rescue it from the φθόρα of sin and death and restore it to
the glory of eternal life, and that it was manifested here in the
fact, that by the counsels of His own spontaneous love (Deut.
iv. 37) He chose Israel as His possession, to make of it a holy
nation, if it hearkened to His voice and kept His covenant. It
was not made this, however, by being separated from the other
nations, for that was merely the means of attaining the divine
end, but by the fact, that God placed the chosen people in the
relation of covenant fellowship with Himself, founded His kingdom in Israel, established in the covenant relationship an institution of salvation, which furnished the covenant people with
the means of obtaining the expiation of their sins, and securing
righteousness before God and holiness of life with God, in order
that by the discipline of His holy commandments, under the
guidance of His holy arm, He might train and guide them to
the holiness and glory of the divine life. But as sin opposes
holiness, and the sinner resists sanctification, the work of the
holiness of God reveals itself in His kingdom of grace, not only
positively in the sanctification of those who suffer themselves to
be sanctified and raised to newness of life, but negatively also,
in the destruction of all those who obstinately refuse the guidance of His grace; so that the glory of the thrice Holy One (Isa.
vi. 3) will be fully manifested both in the glorification of His
chosen people and the deliverance of the whole creation from the
bondage of corruption into the glorious liberty of the children
of God (Rom. viii. 21), and also in the destruction of hardened
sinners, the annihilation of everything that is ungodly in this
world, the final overthrow of Satan and his kingdom, and the

founding of the new heaven and new earth. Hence not only is every person, whom God receives into the sphere of His sin-destroying grace, קָדוֹשׁ, or holy; but everything which is applied to the realization of the divine work of salvation, or consecrated by God to this object. The opposite of קָדוֹשׁ, holy, is חֹל, κοινός, *profanus* (from חָלַל to be loose, *lit.* the unbound), not devoted to holy purposes and uses (cf. Lev. x. 10); and this term was applied, not only to what was sinful and unclean (טָמֵא), but to everything earthly in its natural condition, because the whole earth, with all that is upon it, has been involved in the consequences of sin.

Vers. 7–15. When Moses communicated to the people through their elders this incomparable promise of the Lord, they promised unanimously (יַחְדָּו) to do all that Jehovah said; and when Moses reported to the Lord what the people had answered, He said to Moses, "*I will come to thee in the darkness of the cloud, that the people may listen to My speaking to thee* (שָׁמַע בְּ as in Gen. xxvii. 5, etc.), *and also believe thee for ever.*" As God knew the weakness of the sinful nation, and could not, as the Holy One, come into direct intercourse with it on account of its unholiness, but was about to conclude the covenant with it through the mediation of Moses, it was necessary, in order to accomplish the design of God, that the chosen mediator should receive special credentials; and these were to consist in the fact that Jehovah spoke to Moses in the sight and hearing of the people, that is to say, that He solemnly proclaimed the fundamental law of the covenant in the presence of the whole nation (chap. xix. 16–xx. 18), and showed by this fact that Moses was the recipient and mediator of the revelation of God, in order that the people might believe him "*for ever,*" as the law was to possess everlasting validity (Matt. v. 18).—Vers. 10–16. God then commanded Moses to prepare the people for His appearing or speaking to them: (1) by their sanctification, through the washing of the body and clothes (see Gen. xxxv. 2), and abstinence from conjugal intercourse (ver. 15) on account of the defilement connected therewith (Lev. xv. 18); and (2) by setting bounds round the people, that they might not ascend or touch the mountain. The hedging or bounding (הִגְבִּיל) of the people is spoken of in ver. 23 as setting bounds about the mountain, and consisted therefore in the erection of a barrier round the mountain, which was to prevent the people from ascending or touching it. Any one who touched it (קָצֵהוּ, "*its end*," *i.e.* the outermost or lowest part of the mountain) was to be put to death, whether man or beast. "*No hand shall touch him*" (the individual who passed the barrier and touched the mountain), *i.e.* no one was to follow him within the appointed boundaries, but he was to be killed from a distance either by stones or darts. (יָיָּרֶה for יִּוָּרֶה, see *Gesenius*, § 69.) Not till "*the drawing out of the trumpet blast*," or, as Luther renders it, "only when it sounded long," could they ascend the mountain (ver. 13). הַיּבֵל, from יָבַל to stream violently with noise, is synonymous with קֶרֶן הַיּבֵל (Josh. vi. 5), and was really the same thing as the שׁוֹפָר, *i.e.* a long wind instrument shaped like a horn. מָשַׁךְ הַיּבֵל is to draw the horn, *i.e.* to blow the horn with tones long drawn out. This was done either to give a signal to summon the people to war (Judg. iii. 27, vi. 34), or to call them to battle (Judg. vii. 18; Job xxxix. 24, 25, etc.), or for other public proclamations. No one (this is the idea) was to ascend the mountain on pain of death, or even to touch its outermost edge; but when the horn was blown with a long blast, and the signal to approach was given thereby, then they might ascend it (see ver. 21),—of course not 600,000 men, which would have been physically impossible, but the people in the persons of their representatives the elders. עֲלוֹת בָּהָר signifies to go up the mountain in ver. 13 as well as in ver. 12, and not merely to come to the foot of the mountain (see Deut. v. 5).

Vers. 16–25. After these preparations, on the morning of the third day (from the issuing of this divine command), Jehovah came down upon the top of Mount Sinai (ver. 20), manifesting His glory in fire as the mighty, jealous God, in the midst of thunders (קֹלֹת) and lightnings, so that the mountain burned with fire (Deut. iv. 11, v. 20), and the smoke of the burning mountain ascended as the smoke (עֶשֶׁן for עָשַׁן), and the whole mountain trembled (ver. 18), at the same time veiling in a thick cloud the fire of His wrath and jealousy, by which the unholy are consumed. Thunder and lightning bursting forth from the thick cloud, and fire with smoke, were the elementary substrata, which rendered the glory of the divine nature visible to men, though in such a way that the eye of mortals beheld no form of the spiritual and invisible Deity. These natural phenomena were accompanied by a loud trumpet blast, which "blew long and waxed louder and louder" (vers. 16 and 19; see Gen. viii. 3), and was, as it were, the herald's call, announcing to the people the appearance of the Lord, and summoning them to assemble before Him and listen to His words, as they sounded forth from the fire and cloudy darkness. The blast (קוֹל) of the *shophar* (ver. 19), *i.e.* the σάλπιγξ Θεοῦ, the trump of God, such a trumpet as is used in the service of God (in heaven, 1 Thess. iv. 16; see *Winer's* Grammar), is not "the voice of Jehovah," but a sound resembling a trumpet blast. Whether this sound was produced by natural means, or, as some of the earlier commentators supposed, by angels, of whom myriads surrounded Jehovah when He came down upon Sinai (Deut. xxxiii. 2), it is impossible to decide. At this alarming phenomenon, "*all the people that was in the camp trembled*" (ver. 16). For according to chap. xx. 20 (17), it was intended to inspire them with a salutary fear of the majesty of God. Then Moses conducted the people (*i.e.* the men) out of the camp of God, and stationed them at the foot of the mountain outside the barrier (ver. 17); and "*Moses spake*" (ver. 19), *i.e.* asked the Lord for His commands, "*and God answered loud*" (בְּקוֹל), and told him to come up to the top of the mountain. He then commanded him to go down again, and impress upon the people that no one was to break through to Jehovah to see, *i.e.* to break down the barriers that were erected around the mountain as the sacred place of God, and attempt to penetrate into the presence of Jehovah. Even the priests, who were allowed to approach God by virtue of their office, were to sanctify themselves, that Jehovah might not break forth upon them (יִפְרֹץ), *i.e.* dash them to pieces. (On the form הֶעֱלֹתָה for הֶעֱלֵיתָ, see *Ewald*, § 199 a). The *priests* were neither "the sons of Aaron," *i.e.* Levitical priests, nor the first-born or *principes populi*, but "those who had hitherto discharged the duties of the priestly office according to natural right and custom" (*Baumgarten*). Even these priests were too unholy to be able to come into the presence of the holy God. This repeated enforcement of the command not to touch the mountain, and the special extension of it even to the priests, were intended to awaken in the people a consciousness of their own unholiness quite as much as of the unapproachable holiness of Jehovah. But this separation from God, which arose from the unholiness of the nation, did not extend to Moses and Aaron, who were to act as mediators, and were permitted to ascend the mountain. Moreover, the prospect of ascending the holy mountain " at the drawing of the blast" was still before the people (ver. 13). And the strict prohibition against breaking through the barrier, to come of their own accord into the presence of Jehovah, is by no means at variance with this. When God gave the sign to ascend the mountain, the people might and were to draw near to Him. This sign, viz. the long-drawn trumpet blast, was not to be given in any case till after the promulgation of the ten words of the fundamental law. But it was not given even after this promulgation ; not, however, because " the development was altogether an abnormal one, and not in accordance with the divine appointment in ver. 13, inasmuch as at the thunder, the lightning, and the sound of the trumpet, with which the giving of the law was concluded, they lost all courage, and instead of waiting for the promised signal, were overcome with fear, and ran from the spot," for there is not a word in the text about running away ; but because the people were so terrified by the alarming phenomena which accompanied the coming down of Jehovah upon the mountain, that they gave up the right of speaking with God, and from a fear of death entreated Moses to undertake the intercourse with God on their behalf (chap. xx. 18–21). Moreover, we cannot speak of an " abnormal development" of the drama, for the simple reason, that God not only foresaw the course and issue of the affair, but at the very outset only promised that He would come to Moses in a thick cloud (ver. 9), and merely announced and carried out His own descent upon Mount Sinai before the eyes of the people in the terrible glory of His sacred majesty (ver. 11), for the purpose of proving the people, that His fear might be before their eyes (chap. xx. 20 ; cf. Deut. v. 28, 29). Consequently, apart from the physical impossibility of 600,000 ascending the mountain, it never was intended that all the people should do so.[1]   What God really intended, came to pass.

[1] The idea of the people fleeing and running away must have been got by *Kurtz* from either *Luther's* or *De Wette's* translation. They have both of them rendered וַיָּנֻעוּ וגו׳, " they *fled* and went far of," instead of " they trembled and stood far off." And not only the supposed flight, but his idea that " thunder, lightning, and the trumpet blast (which were silent in any case during the utterance of the ten commandments), concluded the pro-

After the people had been received into fellowship with Jehovah through the atoning blood of the sacrifice, they were permitted to ascend the mountain in the persons of their representatives, and there to see God (chap. xxiv. 9–11).

THE TEN WORDS OF JEHOVAH.—CHAP. XX. 1–21.

Ver. 1. The promulgation of the ten words of God, containing the fundamental law of the covenant, took place before Moses ascended the mountain again with Aaron (chap. xix. 24). "*All these words*" are the words of God contained in vers. 2–17, which are repeated again in Deut. v. 6–18, with slight variations that do not materially affect the sense,[1] and are called the " words

mulgation of the law, as they had already introduced it according to chap. xix. 16," also rests upon a misunderstanding of the text of the Bible. There is not a syllable in chap. xx. 18 about the thunder, lightning, and trumpet blast bursting forth afresh after the proclamation of the ten commandments. There is simply an account of the impression, which the alarming phenomena, mentioned in chap. xix. 16–19 as attending the descent of Jehovah upon the mountain (ver. 20), and preceding His speaking to Moses and the people, made upon the people, who had been brought out of the camp to meet with God.

[1] The discrepancies in the two texts are the following :—In Deut. v. 8 the cop. וְ ("*or*," Eng. Ver.), which stands before כָּל־תְּמוּנָה (any likeness), is omitted, to give greater clearness to the meaning; and on the other hand it is added before עַל שִׁלֵּשִׁים in ver. 9 for rhetorical reasons. In the fourth commandment (ver. 12) שָׁמוֹר is chosen instead of זָכוֹר in Ex. ver. 8, and זָכַר is reserved for the hortatory clause appended in ver. 15: "and remember that thou wast a servant," etc.; and with this is connected the still further fact, that instead of the fourth commandment being enforced on the ground of the creation of the world in six days and the resting of God on the seventh day, their deliverance from Egypt is adduced as the subjective reason for their observance of the command. In ver. 14, too, the clause "nor thy cattle" (Ex. ver. 10) is amplified rhetorically, and particularized in the words "thine ox, nor thine ass, nor any of thy cattle." So again, in ver. 16, the promise appended to the fifth commandment, " that thy days may be long in the land," etc., is amplified by the interpolation of the clause "and that it may go well with thee," and strengthened by the words "as Jehovah thy God hath commanded thee." In ver. 17, instead of עֵד שֶׁקֶר (Ex. ver. 16), the more comprehensive expression עֵד שָׁוְא is chosen. Again, in the tenth commandment (ver. 18), the "neighbour's wife" is placed first, and then, after the " house," the field is added before the "man-servant and maid-servant," whereas in Exodus the "neighbour's house" is

of the covenant, the ten words," in chap. xxxiv. 28, and Deut.
iv. 13, x. 4.   God spake these words directly to the people, and
not "through the medium of His finite spirits," as *v. Hofmann,
Kurtz,* and others suppose.   There is not a word in the Old Testament about any such mediation.   Not only was it *Elohim,* according to the chapter before us, who spake these words to the people,
and called Himself Jehovah, who had brought Israel out of
Egypt (ver. 2), but according to Deut. v. 4, Jehovah spake these
words to Israel "face to face, in the mount, out of the midst of
the fire."   Hence, according to *Buxtorf* (*Dissert. de Decalogo in
genere,* 1642), the Jewish commentators almost unanimously
affirm that God Himself spake the words of the decalogue, and
that words were formed in the air by the power of God, and not
by the intervention and ministry of angels.[1]   And even from the
New Testament this cannot be proved to be a doctrine of the
Scriptures.   For when Stephen says to the Jews, in Acts vii. 53,
"Ye have received the law" εἰς διαταγὰς ἀγγέλων (Eng. Ver.
"by the disposition of angels"), and Paul speaks of the law in
Gal. iii. 19 as διαταγεὶς δι' ἀγγέλων ("ordained by angels"),
these expressions leave it quite uncertain in what the διατάσσειν
of the angels consisted, or what part they took in connection

mentioned first, and then the "wife" along with the "man-servant and
maid-servant;" and instead of the repetition of תַחְמֹד, the synonym
תִתְאַוֶּה is employed.   Lastly, in Deuteronomy all the commandments from
לֹא תִרְצָח onwards are connected together by the repetition of the cop. וְ
before every one, whereas in Exodus it is not introduced at all.—Now if,
after what has been said, the rhetorical and hortatory intention is patent
in all the variations of the text of Deuteronomy, even down to the transposition of wife and house in the last commandment, this transposition
must also be attributed to the freedom with which the decalogue was reproduced, and the text of Exodus be accepted as the original, which is not
to be altered in the interests of any arbitrary exposition of the commandments.

[1] This also applies to the Targums.   *Onkelos* and *Jonathan* have וּמַלֵּל יְיָ
in ver. 1, and the Jerusalem Targum מַלִּיל מֵימְרָא דַיְיָ.   But in the popular
Jewish Midrash, the statement in Deut. xxxiii. 2 (cf. Ps. lxviii. 17), that
Jehovah came down upon Sinai "out of myriads of His holiness," *i.e.*
attended by myriads of holy angels, seems to have given rise to the notion
that God spake through angels.   Thus *Josephus* represents King Herod as
saying to the people, "For ourselves, we have learned from God the most
excellent of our doctrines, and the most holy part of our law *through angels*"
(Ant. 15, 5, 3, Whiston's translation).

with the giving of the law.[1] So again, in Heb. ii. 2, where the
law, "the word spoken by angels" (δι' ἀγγέλων), is placed in
contrast with the "salvation which at the first began to be
spoken by the Lord" (διὰ τοῦ Κυρίου), the antithesis is of so
indefinite a nature that 't is impossible to draw the conclusion
with any certainty, that the writer of this epistle supposed the
speaking of God at the promulgation of the decalogue to have
been effected through the medium of a number of finite spirits,
especially when we consider that in the Epistle to the Hebrews
speaking is the term applied to the divine revelation generally
(see chap. i. 1).   As his object was not to describe with precision the manner in which God spake to the Israelites from Sinai,
but only to show the superiority of the Gospel, as the revelation
of salvation, to the revelation of the law; he was at liberty to
select the indefinite expression δι' ἀγγέλων, and leave it to the
readers of his epistle to interpret it more fully for themselves
from the Old Testament.   According to the Old Testament,
however, the law was given through the medium of angels, only
so far as God appeared to Moses, as He had done to the patriarchs, in the form of the "Angel of the Lord," and Jehovah
came down upon Sinai, according to Deut. xxxiii. 2, surrounded
by myriads of holy angels as His escort.[2] The notion that God

[1] That Stephen cannot have meant to say that God spoke through a
number of finite angels, is evident from the fact, that in ver. 38 he had
spoken just before of *the* Angel (in the singular) who spoke to Moses upon
Mount Sinai, and had described him in vers. 35 and 30 as the Angel who appeared to Moses in the bush, *i.e.* as no other than the Angel of Jehovah who
was identical with Jehovah.   "The Angel of the Lord occupies the same
place in ver. 38 as Jehovah in Ex. xix.   The angels in ver. 53 and Gal.
iii. 19 are taken from Deut. xxxiii.   And there the angels do not come in
the place of the Lord, but the Lord comes attended by them" (*Hengstenberg*).

[2] *Lud. de Dieu*, in his commentary on Acts vii. 53, after citing the
parallel passages Gal. iii. 19 and Heb. ii. 2, correctly observes, that "horum
dictorum hæc videtur esse ratio et veritas.   S. Stephanus supra v. 39 dixit,
Angelum locutum esse cum Mose in monte Sina, eundem nempe qui in rubo
ipsa apparuerat, ver. 35 qui quamvis in se Deus hic tamen κατ' οἰκονομίαν
tanquam Angelus Dei cæterorumque angelorum præfectus consideratus e
medio angelorum, qui eum undique stipabant, legem in monte Mosi dedit.
. . .   Atque inde colligi potest causa, cur apostolus Heb. ii. 2, 3, Legi
Evangelium tantopere anteferat.   Etsi enim utriusque auctor et promul-
gator fuerit idem Dei filius, quia tamen legem tulit in forma angeli e
senatu angelico et velatus gloria angelorum, tandem vero caro factus et in

spake through the medium of "His finite spirits" can only be sustained in one of two ways: either by reducing the angels to personifications of natural phenomena, such as thunder, lightning, and the sound of a trumpet, a process against which the writer of the Epistle to the Hebrews enters his protest in chap. xii. 19, where he expressly distinguishes the "voice of words" from these phenomena of nature; or else by affirming, with *v. Hofmann*, that God, the supernatural, cannot be conceived of without a plurality of spirits collected under Him, or apart from His active operation in the world of bodies, in distinction from which these spirits are comprehended with Him and under Him, so that even the ordinary and regular phenomena of nature would have to be regarded as the workings of angels; in which case the existence of angels as created spirits would be called in question, and they would be reduced to mere personifications of divine powers.

The words of the covenant, or ten words, were written by God upon two tables of stone (chap. xxxi. 18), and are called the law and the commandment (הַתּוֹרָה וְהַמִּצְוָה) in chap. xxiv. 12, as being the kernel and essence of the law. But the Bible contains neither distinct statements, nor definite hints, with reference to the numbering and division of the commandments upon the two tables,—a clear proof that these points do not possess the importance which has frequently been attributed to them. Two different views have arisen in the course of time. Some divide the ten commandments into two pentads, one upon each table. Upon the first they place the commandments concerning (1) other gods, (2) images, (3) the name of God, (4) the Sabbath, and (5) parents; on the second, those concerning (1) murder, (2) adultery, (3) stealing, (4) false witness, and (5) coveting. Others, again, reckon only three to the first table, and seven to the second. In the first they include the commandments respecting (1) other gods, (2) the name of God, (3) the Sabbath, or those which concern the duties towards God; and in the second, those respecting (1) parents, (2) murder, (3) adultery, (4) stealing, (5) false witness, (6) coveting a neighbour's house, (7) coveting a neighbour's wife, servants, cattle, and other pos-

carne manifestatus, gloriam præ se ferens non angelorum sed unigeniti filii Dei, evangelium ipsemet, humana voce, habitans inter homines prædicavit, merito lex angelorum sermo, evangelium autem solius filii Dei dicitur."

sessions, or those which concern the duties towards one's neighbour. The *first* view, with the division into two fives, we find in *Josephus* (Ant. iii. 5, 5) and *Philo* (*quis rer. divin. hær.* § 35, *de Decal.* § 12, etc.); it is unanimously supported by the fathers of the first four centuries,[1] and has been retained to the present day by the Eastern and Reformed Churches. The later Jews agree so far with this view, that they only adopt *one* commandment against coveting; but they differ from it in combining the commandment against images with that against false gods, and taking the introductory words " I am the Lord thy God " to be the first commandment. This mode of numbering, of which we find the first traces in *Julian Apostata* (in *Cyrilli Alex. c. Julian l. V. init.*), and in an allusion made by *Jerome* (on Hos. x. 10), is at any rate of more recent origin, and probably arose simply from opposition to the Christians. It still prevails, however, among the modern Jews.[2]

The *second* view was brought forward by *Augustine,* and no one is known to have supported it previous to him. In his *Quæst.* 71 on Ex., when treating of the question how the commandments are to be divided (" *utrum* quatuor sint usque ad præceptum de Sabbatho, quæ ad ipsum Deum pertinent, sex autem reliqua, quorum primum : Honora patrem et matrem, quæ ad hominem pertinent: an potius illa tria sint et ipsa septem"), he explains the two different views, and adds, " Mihi tamen videntur congruentius accipi illa tria et ista septem, quoniam Trinitatem videntur illa, quæ ad Deum pertinent, insinuare diligentius intuentibus." He then proceeds still further to show that the commandment against images is only a fuller explanation of that against other gods, but that the commandment not to covet is divided into two commandments by the repetition of the words, " *Thou shalt not covet,*" although " concupiscentia

---

[1] They either speak of two tables with five commandments upon each (*Iren. adv. hær.* ii. 42), or mention only one commandment against coveting (*Constit. apost.* i. 1, vii. 3 ; *Theoph. ad Autol.* ii. 50 ; *Tertull. adv. Marc.* ii. 17 ; *Ephr. Syr. ad Ex.* 20 ; *Epiphan. hær.* ii. 2, etc.), or else they expressly distinguish the commandment against images from that against other gods (*Origen,* homil. 8 in Ex. ; *Hieron. ad Ephes.* vi. 2 ; *Greg. Naz. carm.* i. 1 ; *Sulpicius Sev. hist. sacr.* i. 17, etc.).

[2] It is adopted by *Gemar. Macc.* f. 24 a ; *Targ. Jon.* on Ex. and Deut.; *Mechilta* on Ex. xx. 16 ; *Pesikta* on Deut. v. 6 ; and the rabbinical commentators of the middle ages.

uxoris alienæ et concupiscentia domus alienæ tantum in peccando differant." In this division *Augustine* generally reckons the commandment against coveting the neighbour's wife as the *ninth*, according to the text of Deuteronomy; although in several instances he places it after the coveting of the house, according to the text of *Exodus*. Through the great respect that was felt for *Augustine*, this division became the usual one in the Western Church; and it was adopted even by *Luther* and the Lutheran Church, with this difference, however, that both the Catholic and Lutheran Churches regard the commandment not to covet a neighbour's house as the ninth, whilst only a few here and there give the preference, as *Augustine* does, to the order adopted in Deuteronomy.

Now if we inquire, which of these divisions of the ten commandments is the correct one, there is nothing to warrant either the assumption of the Talmud and the Rabbins, that the words, "I am Jehovah thy God," etc., form the first commandment, or the preference given by *Augustine* to the text of Deuteronomy. The words, "I am the Lord," etc., contain no independent member of the decalogue, but are merely the preface to the commandments which follow. "Hic sermo nondum sermo mandati est, sed quis sit, qui mandat, ostendit" (*Origen, homil.* 8 in Ex.). But, as we have already shown, the text of Deuteronomy, in all its deviations from the text of Exodus, can lay no claim to originality. As to the other two views which have obtained a footing in the Church, the historical credentials of priority and majority are not sufficient of themselves to settle the question in favour of the first, which is generally called the Philonian view, from its earliest supporter. It must be decided from the text of the Bible alone. Now in both substance and form this speaks against the Augustinian, Catholic, and Lutheran view, and in favour of the Philonian, or Oriental and Reformed. In *substance;* for whereas no essential difference can be pointed out in the two clauses which prohibit coveting, so that even *Luther* has made but one commandment of them in his smaller catechism, there was a very essential difference between the commandment against other gods and that against making an image of God, so far as the Israelites were concerned, as we may see not only from the account of the golden calf at Sinai, but also from the image worship of Gideon (Judg. viii. 27), Micah

(Judg. xvii.), and Jeroboam (1 Kings xii. 28 sqq.). In *form;* for the last five commandments differ from the first five, not only in the fact that no reasons are assigned for the former, whereas all the latter are enforced by reasons, in which the expression " Jehovah thy God" occurs every time; but still more in the fact, that in the text of Deuteronomy all the commandments after " Thou shalt do no murder" are connected together by the copula ו, which is repeated before every sentence, and from which we may see that Moses connected the commandments which treat of duties to one's neighbour more closely together, and by thus linking them together showed that they formed the second half of the decalogue.

The weight of this testimony is not counterbalanced by the division into *parashoth* and the double accentuation of the Masoretic text, viz. by accents both above and below, even if we assume that this was intended in any way to indicate a logical division of the commandments. In the Hebrew MSS. and editions of the Bible, the decalogue is divided into ten *parashoth*, with spaces between them marked either by ס (*Setuma*) or פ (*Phetucha*); and whilst the commandments against other gods and images, together with the threat and promise appended to them (vers. 3–6), form one *parashah*, the commandment against coveting (ver. 14) is divided by a *setuma* into two. But according to *Kennicott* (ad Ex. xx. 17, Deut. v. 18, and *diss. gener.* p. 59) this *setuma* was wanting in 234 of the 694 MSS. consulted by him, and in many exact editions of the Bible as well; so that the testimony is not unanimous here. It is no argument against this division into parashoth, that it does not agree either with the Philonian or the rabbinical division of the ten commandments, or with the Masoretic arrangement of the verses and the lower accents which correspond to this. For there can be no doubt that it is older than the Masoretic treatment of the text, though it is by no means original on that account. Even when the Targum on the Song of Sol. (v. 13) says that the tables of stone were written in ten שִׁטִּים or שִׁיטִים, *i.e.* rows or strophes, like the rows of a garden full of sweet odours, this Targum is much too recent to furnish any valid testimony to the original writing and plan of the decalogue. And the upper accentuation of the decalogue, which corresponds to the division into *parashoth*, has just as little claim to be received as a testimony in favour of "a division of the verses which was once evidently regarded as very significant" (*Ewald*); on the contrary, it was evidently added to the lower accentuation simply in order that the decalogue might be read in the synagogues on particular days after the parashoth.[1]   Hence the double accentuation was only so far of importance, as showing that the Masorites regarded the *parashoth* as sufficiently important, to be retained for reading in the synagogue by a system of accentuation which corresponded to them.   But if this division into *parashoth* had been regarded by the Jews from time immemorial as original, or Mosaic, in its origin; it would be impossible to understand either the rise of other divisions of the decalogue, or the difference between this division and the Masoretic accentuation and arrangement of the verses.   From all this so much at any rate is clear, that from a very early period there was a disposition to unite together the two commandments against other gods and images; but assuredly on no other ground than because of the threat and promise with which they are followed, and which must refer, as was correctly assumed, to both commandments.   But if these two commandments were classified as one, there was no other way of bringing out the number ten, than to divide the commandment against coveting into two.   But as the transposition of the wife and the house in the two texts could not well be reconciled with this, the *setuma* which separated them in ver 14 did not meet with universal reception.

Lastly, on the division of the ten covenant words upon the two tables of stone, the text of the Bible contains no other information, than that "the tables were written on both their sides" (chap. xxxii. 15), from which we may infer with tolerable certainty, what would otherwise have the greatest probability as being the most natural supposition, viz. that the entire contents of the "ten words" were engraved upon the tables, and not merely the

[1] See *Geiger* (wissensch. Ztschr. iii. 1, 151).   According to the testimony of a Rabbin who had embraced Christianity, the decalogue was read in one way, when it occurred as a Sabbath parashah, either in the middle of January or at the beginning of July, and in another way at the feast of Pentecost, as the feast of the giving of the law; the lower accentuation being followed in the former case, and the upper in the latter.   We may compare with this the account given in *En Israel*, fol. 103, col. 3, that one form of accentuation was intended for ordinary or private reading, the other for public reading in the synagogue.

ten commandments in the stricter sense, without the accompanying reasons.[1] But if neither the numbering of the ten commandments nor their arrangement on the two tables was indicated in the law as drawn up for the guidance of the people of Israel, so that it was possible for even the Israelites to come to different conclusions on the subject ; the Christian Church has all the more a perfect right to handle these matters with Christian liberty and prudence for the instruction of congregations in the law, from the fact that it is no longer bound to the ten commandments, as a part of the law of Moses, which has been abolished for them through the fulfilment of Christ, but has to receive them for the regulation of its own doctrine and life, simply as being the unchangeable norm of the holy will of God which was fulfilled through Christ.

Ver. 2. The TEN WORDS commenced with a declaration of Jehovah concerning Himself, which served as a practical basis for the obligation on the part of the people to keep the commandments : "*I am Jehovah* thy God, who brought thee," etc. By bringing them out of Egypt, the house of bondage, Jehovah had proved to the Israelites that He was their God. This glorious act, to which Israel owed its existence as an independent nation, was peculiarly fitted, as a distinct and practical manifestation of unmerited divine love, to kindle in the hearts of the people the warmest love in return, and to incite them to keep the commandments. These words are not to be regarded, as

[1] If the whole of the contents stood upon the table, the ten words cannot have been arranged either according to Philo's two pentads, or according to Augustine's division into three and seven ; for in either case there would have been far more words upon the first table than upon the second, and, according to Augustine's arrangement, there would have been 131 upon one table, and only 41 upon the other. We obtain a much more suitable result, if the words of vers. 2–7, *i.e.* the first three commandments according to Philo's reckoning, were engraved upon the one table, and the other seven from the Sabbath commandment onwards upon the other ; for in that case there would be 96 words upon the first table and 76 upon the second. If the reasons for the commandments were not written along with them upon the tables, the commandments respecting the name and nature of God, and the keeping of the Sabbath, together with the preamble, which could not possibly be left out, would amount to 73 words in all, the commandment to honour one's parents would contain 5 words, and the rest of the commandments 26.

Knobel supposes, as either a confession, or the foundation of the whole of the theocratical law, just as *Saleucus, Plato,* and other lawgivers placed a belief in the existence of the gods at the head of their laws. They were rather the preamble, as *Calvin* says, by which God prepared the minds of the people for obeying them, and in this sense they were frequently repeated to give emphasis to other laws, sometimes in full, as in chap. xxix. 46, Lev. xix. 36, xxiii. 43, xxv. 38, 55, xxvi. 13, etc., sometimes in the abridged form, " I am Jehovah your God," as in Lev. xi. 44, xviii. 2, 4, 30, xix. 4, 10, 25, 31, 34, xx. 7, etc., for which the simple expression, " I am Jehovah," is now and then substituted, as in Lev. xix. 12, 14, 16, 18, etc.

Ver. 3. The FIRST WORD.—" *Let there not be to thee* (thou shalt have no) *other gods* עַל פְּנֵי," *lit. beyond Me* (עַל as in Gen. xlviii. 22 ; Ps. xvi. 2), or in addition to Me (עַל as in Gen. xxxi. 50 ; Deut. xix. 9), equivalent to πλὴν ἐμοῦ (LXX.), " by the side of Me" (*Luther*). " Before Me," *coram me* (*Vulg.*, etc.), is incorrect ; also against Me, in opposition to Me. (On פְּנֵי see chap. xxxiii. 14). The singular יְהְיֶה does not require that we should regard *Elohim* as an abstract noun in the sense of Deity ; and the plural אֲחֵרִים would not suit this rendering (see Gen. i. 14). The sentence is quite a general one, and not only prohibits polytheism and idolatry, the worship of idols in thought, word, and deed (cf. Deut. viii. 11, 17, 19), but also commands the fear, love, and worship of God the Lord (cf. Deut. vi. 5, 13, 17, x. 12, 20). Nearly all the commandments are couched in the negative form of prohibition, because they presuppose the existence of sin and evil desires in the human heart.

Vers. 4–6. The SECOND WORD.—To the prohibition of idolatrous worship there is linked on, as a second word, the prohibition of the worship of images. " After declaring in the first commandment who was the true God, He commanded that He alone should be worshipped ; and now He defines what is His lawful worship" (*Calvin*). " *Thou shalt not make to thyself a likeness and any form of that which is in heaven above,*" etc. עָשָׂה is construed with a double accusative, so that the literal rendering would be " make, as a likeness and any form, that which is in heaven," etc. פֶּסֶל, from פָּסַל to carve wood or stone, is a figure made of wood or stone, and is used in Judg. xvii. 3 sqq. for a figure representing Jehovah, and in other places for figures of heathen deities—of Asherah, for example, in 2 Kings xxi. 7. תְּמוּנָה does not signify an image made by man, but a form which is seen by him (Num. xii. 8; Deut. iv. 12, 15 sqq. Job iv. 16; Ps. xvii. 15). In Deut. v. 8 (cf. iv. 16) we find פֶּסֶל כָּל־תְּמוּנָה "likeness of any form:" so that in this passage also וְכָל־תְּמוּנָה is to be taken as in apposition to פֶּסֶל, and the וְ as vav explic.: "and indeed any form," viz. of Jehovah, not of heathen gods. That the words should be so understood, is demanded by Deut. iv. 15 sqq., where Moses lays stress upon the command, not to make to themselves an image (פסל) in the form of any sculpture (סֶמֶל), and gives this as the reason: "For ye saw no form in the day when Jehovah spake to you at Horeb." This authoritative exposition of the divine prohibition on the part of Moses himself proves undeniably, that פסל and תמונה are to be understood as referring to symbolical representations of Jehovah. And the words which follow also receive their authoritative exposition from Deut. iv. 17 and 18. By "that which is in heaven" we are to understand the birds, not the angels, or at the most, according to Deut. iv. 19, the stars as well; by "that which is in earth," the cattle, reptiles, and the larger or smaller animals; and by "that which is in the water," fishes and water animals. "Under the earth" is appended to the "water," to express in a pictorial manner the idea of its being lower than the solid ground (cf. Deut. iv. 18). It is not only evident from the context that the allusion is not to the making of images generally, but to the construction of figures of God as objects of religious reverence or worship, but this is expressly stated in ver. 5; so that even Calvin observes, that "there is no necessity to refute what some have foolishly imagined, that sculpture and painting of every kind are condemned here." With the same aptness he has just before observed, that "although Moses only speaks of idols, there is no doubt that by implication he condemns all the forms of false worship, which men have invented for themselves."—Ver. 5. "Thou shalt not pray to them and serve them." (On the form תָּעָבְדֵם with the o-sound under the guttural, see Ewald, § 251d.). הִשְׁתַּחֲוָה signifies bending before God in prayer, and invoking His name; עָבַד, worship by means of sacrifice and religious ceremonies. The suffixes לָהֶם and ם־ (to them, and *them*) refer to the things in heaven, etc., which are made into *pesel*, symbols of Jehovah, as being the principal object of the previous clause, and not to פֶּסֶל וְכָל־תְּמוּנָה, although עָבַד פֶּסֶל is applied in Ps. xcvii. 7 and 2 Kings xvii. 41 to a rude idolatrous worship, which identifies the image as the symbol of deity with the deity itself.   Still less do they refer to אֱלֹהִים אֲחֵרִים in ver. 3.

The threat and promise, which follow in vers. 5*b* and 6, relate to the first two commandments, and not to the second alone; because both of them, although forbidding two forms of idolatry, viz. idolo-latry and ikono-latry, are combined in a higher unity, by the fact, that whenever Jehovah, the God who cannot be copied because He reveals His spiritual nature in no visible form, is worshipped under some visible image, the glory of the invisible God is changed, or Jehovah changed into a different God from what He really is.   Through either form of idolatry, therefore, Israel would break its covenant with Jehovah.   For this reason God enforces the two commandments with the solemn declaration: "I, Jehovah thy God, am אֵל קַנָּא a jealous God;" *i.e.* not only ζηλωτής, a zealous avenger of sinners, but ζηλό-τυπος, a jealous God, who will not transfer to another the honour that is due to Himself (Isa. xlii. 8, xlviii. 11), nor tolerate the worship of any other god (chap. xxxiv. 14), but who directs the warmth of His anger against those who hate Him (Deut. vi. 15), with the same energy with which the warmth of His love (Song of Sol. viii. 6) embraces those who love Him, except that love in the form of grace reaches much further than wrath.   The sin of the fathers He visits (punishes) on the children to the third and fourth generation.   שִׁלֵּשִׁים third (*sc.* children) are not grandchildren, but great-grandchildren, and רִבֵּעִים the fourth generation.   On the other hand He shows mercy to the thousandths, *i.e.* to the thousandth generation (cf. Deut. vii. 9, where לְאֶלֶף דּוֹר stands for לַאֲלָפִים).   The cardinal number is used here for the ordinal, for which there was no special form in the case of אֶלֶף.   The words לְשֹׂנְאַי and לְאֹהֲבַי, in which the punishment and grace are traced to their ultimate foundation, are of great importance to a correct understanding of this utterance of God.   The לְ before שֹׂנֵא does not take up the genitive with עֲוֺן again, as *Knobel* supposes, for no such use of לְ can be established from Gen. vii. 11, xvi. 3, xiv. 18, xli. 12, or in fact in any way whatever.   In this instance לְ signifies "at" or "in relation to;"

and לשנאי, from its very position, cannot refer to the fathers alone, but to the fathers and children to the third and fourth generation. If it referred to the fathers alone, it would necessarily stand after אָבֹת. לאהבי וגו׳ is to be taken in the same way. God punishes the sin of the fathers in the children to the third and fourth generation in relation to those who hate Him, and shows mercy to the thousandth generation in relation to those who love Him. The human race is a living organism, in which not only sin and wickedness are transmitted, but evil as the curse of the sin and the punishment of the wickedness. As children receive their nature from their parents, or those who beget them, so they have also to bear and atone for their fathers' guilt. This truth forced itself upon the minds even of thoughtful heathen from their own varied experience (cf. *Aeschyl. Sept.* 744 ; *Eurip.* according to *Plutarch de sera num. vind.* 12, 21 ; *Cicero de nat. deorum* 3, 38 ; and *Baumgarten-Crusius*, bibl. Theol. p. 208). Yet there is no *fate* in the divine government of the world, no irresistible necessity in the continuous results of good and evil ; but there reigns in the world a righteous and gracious God, who not only restrains the course of His penal judgments, as soon as the sinner is brought to reflection by the punishment and hearkens to the voice of God, but who also forgives the sin and iniquity of those who love Him, keeping mercy to the thousandth generation (chap. xxxiv. 7). The words neither affirm that sinning fathers remain unpunished, nor that the sins of fathers are punished in the children and grandchildren without any fault of their own : they simply say nothing about whether and how the fathers themselves are punished ; and, in order to show the dreadful severity of the penal righteousness of God, give prominence to the fact, that punishment is not omitted,—that even when, in the long-suffering of God, it is deferred, it is not therefore neglected, but that the children have to bear the sins of their fathers, whenever, for example (as naturally follows from the connection of children with their fathers, and, as *Onkelos* has added in his paraphrase of the words), "the children fill up the sins of their fathers," so that the descendants suffer punishment for both their own and their forefathers' misdeeds (Lev. xxvi. 39 ; Isa. lxv. 7 ; Amos vii. 17 ; Jer. xvi. 11 sqq. ; Dan. ix. 16). But when, on the other hand, the hating ceases, when the children forsake their fathers' evil ways, the warmth of the divine wrath is turned

into the warmth of love, and God becomes עֹשֶׂה חֶסֶד (" showing
mercy") to them; and this mercy endures not only to the third
and fourth generation, but to the thousandth generation, though
only in relation to those who love God, and manifest this love
by keeping His commandments. "If God continues for a long
time His visitation of sin, He continues to all eternity His manifestation of mercy, and we cannot have a better proof of this
than in the history of Israel itself" (*Schultz*).[1]

Ver. 7. The THIRD WORD, " *Thou shalt not take the name
of Jehovah thy God in vain,*" is closely connected with the former
two. Although there is no God beside Jehovah, the absolute
One, and His divine essence cannot be seen or conceived of
under any form, He had made known the glory of His nature
in His name (chap. iii. 14 sqq., vi. 2), and this was not to be
abused by His people. נָשָׂא שֵׁם does not mean to utter the name
(נָשָׂא never has this meaning), but in all the passages in which it
has been so rendered it retains its proper meaning, " to take up,
lift up, raise;" *e.g.* to take up or raise (begin) a proverb (Num.
xxiii. 7; Job xxvii. 1), to lift up a song (Ps. lxxxi. 3), or a prayer
(Isa. xxxvii. 4). And it is evident from the parallel in Ps.
xxiv. 4, " to lift up his soul to vanity," that it does not mean
" to utter" here. שָׁוְא does not signify *a lie* (שֶׁקֶר), but according
to its etymon שָׁאָה, to be waste, it denotes that which is waste
and in disorder, hence that which is empty, vain, and nugatory,
for which there is no occasion. This word prohibits all employment of the name of God for vain and unworthy objects, and
includes not only false swearing, which is condemned in Lev.
xix. 12 as a profanation of the name of Jehovah, but trivial
swearing in the ordinary intercourse of life, and every use of the
name of God in the service of untruth and lying, for imprecation, witchcraft, or conjuring; whereas the true employment of
the name of God is confined to " invocation, prayer, praise, and
thanksgiving," which proceeds from a pure, believing heart.
The natural heart is very liable to transgress this command, and
therefore it is solemnly enforced by the threat, " for Jehovah
will not hold him guiltless" (leave him unpunished), etc.

[1] On the visitation of the sins of the fathers upon the children, see also
Hengstenberg, Dissertations, vol. ii. p. 446 sqq.

Vers. 8–11. The FOURTH WORD, " *Remember the Sabbath-day, to keep it holy,*" presupposes an acquaintance with the Sabbath, as the expression " remember" is sufficient to show, but not that the Sabbath had been *kept* before this. From the history of the creation that had been handed down, Israel must have known, that after God had created the world in six days He rested the seventh day, and by His resting sanctified the day (Gen. ii. 3). But hitherto there had been no commandment given to man to sanctify the day. This was given for the first time to Israel at Sinai, after preparation had been made for it by the fact that the manna did not fall on the seventh day of the week (chap. xvi. 22). Here therefore the mode of sanctifying it was established for the first time. The seventh day was to be שַׁבָּת (a festival-keeper, see chap. xvi. 23), *i.e.* a day of rest belonging to the Lord, and to be consecrated to Him by the fact that no work was performed upon it. The command not to do any (בֹּל) work applied to both man and beast without exception. Those who were to rest are divided into two classes by the omission of the cop. ו before עַבְדְּךָ (ver. 10) : viz. *first*, free Israelites ("*thou*") and their children ("*thy son and thy daughter*"); and *secondly*, their slaves (*man-servant* and *maid-servant*), and cattle (beasts of draught and burden), and their strangers, *i.e.* foreign labourers who had settled among the Israelites. "*Within thy gates*" is equivalent to in the cities, towns, and villages of thy land, not in thy houses (cf. Deut. v. 14, xiv. 21, etc.). שַׁעַר (a gate) is only applied to the entrances to towns, or large enclosed courts and palaces, never to the entrances into ordinary houses, huts, and tents. מְלָאכָה *work* (cf. Gen. ii. 2), as distinguished from עֲבֹדָה *labour*, is not so much a term denoting a lighter kind of labour, as a general and comprehensive term applied to the performance of any task, whether easy or severe. עֲבֹדָה is the execution of a definite task, whether in field labour (Ps. civ. 23) and mechanical employment (chap. xxxix. 32) on the one hand, or priestly service and the duties connected with worship on the other (chap. xii. 25, 26; Num. iv. 47). On the Sabbath (and also on the day of atonement, Lev. xxiii. 28, 31) every occupation was to rest; on the other feast-days only laborious occupations (מְלֶאכֶת עֲבֹדָה, Lev. xxiii. 7 sqq.), *i.e.* such occupations as came under the denomination of labour, business, or industrial employment. Consequently, not only were ploughing

and reaping (xxxiv. 21), pressing wine and carrying goods
(Neh. xiii. 15), bearing burdens (Jer. xvii. 21), carrying on
trade (Amos viii. 5), and holding markets (Neh. xiii. 15 sqq.)
prohibited, but collecting manna (xvi. 26 sqq.), gathering wood
(Num. xv. 32 sqq.), and kindling fire for the purpose of boiling
or baking (chap. xxxv. 3). The intention of this resting from
every occupation on the Sabbath is evident from the foundation
upon which the commandment is based in ver. 11, viz. that at
the creation of the heaven and the earth Jehovah rested on the
seventh day, and therefore blessed the Sabbath-day and hallowed
it.   This does not imply, however, that " Israel was to follow
the Lord by keeping the Sabbath, and, in imitation of His
example, to be active where the Lord was active, and rest
where the Lord rested; to copy the Lord in accordance with
the lofty aim of man, who was created in His likeness, and make
the pulsation of the divine life in a certain sense his own"
(*Schultz*).   For although a parallel is drawn, between the creation
of the world by God in six days and His resting upon the seventh
day on the one hand, and the labour of man for six days
and his resting upon the seventh on the other; the reason for
the keeping of the Sabbath is not to be found in this parallel,
but in the fact that God blessed the seventh day and hallowed
it, because He rested upon it.   The significance of the Sabbath,
therefore, is to be found in God's blessing and sanctifying the
seventh day of the week at the creation, *i.e.* in the fact, that after
the work of creation was finished on the seventh day, God
blessed and hallowed the created world, filling it with the powers
of peace and good belonging to His own blessed rest, and raising it to a participation in the pure light of His holy nature (see
Gen. ii. 3).   For this reason His people Israel were to keep
the Sabbath now, not for the purpose of imitating what God
had done, and enjoying the blessing of God by thus following
God Himself, but that on this day they also might rest from their
work; and that all the more, because their work was no longer
the work appointed to man at the first, when he was created in the
likeness of God, work which did not interrupt his blessedness in
God (Gen. ii. 15), but that hard labour in the sweat of his brow
to which he had been condemned in consequence of the fall.   In
order therefore that His people might rest from toil so oppressive to both body and soul, and be refreshed, God prescribed the

keeping of the Sabbath, that they might thus possess a day for the repose and elevation of their spirits, and a foretaste of the blessedness into which the people of God are at last to enter, the blessedness of the eternal κατάπαυσις ἀπὸ τῶν ἔργων αὐτοῦ (Heb. iv. 10), the ἀνάπαυσις ἐκ τῶν κόπων (Rev. xiv. 13. See my Archæologie, § 77).

But instead of this objective ground for the sabbatical festival, which furnished the true idea of the Sabbath, when Moses recapitulated the decalogue, he adduced only the subjective aspect of rest or refreshing (Deut. v. 14, 15), reminding the people, just as in Ex. xxiii. 12, of their bondage in Egypt and their deliverance from it by the strong arm of Jehovah, and then adding, " therefore (that thou mightest remember this deliverance from bondage) Jehovah commanded thee to keep the Sabbath-day." This is not at variance with the reason given in the present verse, but simply gives prominence to a subjective aspect, which was peculiarly adapted to warm the hearts of the people towards the observance of the Sabbath, and to render the Sabbath rest dear to the people, since it served to keep the Israelites constantly in mind of the rest which Jehovah had procured for them from the slave labour of Egypt. For resting from every work is the basis of the observance of the Sabbath ; but this observance is an institution peculiar to the Old Testament, and not to be met with in any other nation, though there are many among whom the division of weeks occurs. The observance of the Sabbath, by being adopted into the decalogue, was made the foundation of all the festal times and observances of the Israelites, as they all culminated in the Sabbath rest. At the same time, as an ἐντολὴ τοῦ νόμου, an ingredient in the Sinaitic law, it belonged to the " shadow of (good) things to come" (Col. ii. 17, cf. Heb. x. 1), which was to be done away when the "body" in Christ had come. Christ is Lord of the Sabbath (Matt. xii. 8), and after the completion of His work, He also rested on the Sabbath. But He rose again on the Sunday ; and through His resurrection, which is the pledge to the world of the fruit of His redeeming work, He has made this day the κυριακὴ ἡμέρα (Lord's day) for His Church, to be observed by it till the Captain of its salvation shall return, and having finished the judgment upon all His foes to the very last shall lead it to the rest of that eternal Sabbath, which God prepared for the whole creation through His own resting after the completion of the heaven and the earth.

Ver. 12. The FIFTH WORD, " *Honour thy father and thy mother,*" does not refer to fellow-men, but to " those who are the representatives (*vicarii*) of God. Therefore, as God is to be served with honour and fear, His representatives are to be so too" (*Luther decem. præc.*). This is placed beyond all doubt by Lev. xix. 3, where reverence towards parents is placed on an equality with the observance of the Sabbath, and תִּירָא (*fear*) is substituted for כַּבֵּד (*honour*). It also follows from כַּבֵּד, which, as *Calvin* correctly observes, nihil aliud est quam Deo et hominibus, qui dignitate pollent, justum honorem deferre. Fellow-men or neighbours (רֵעַ) are to be loved (Lev. xix. 18) : parents, on the other hand, are to be honoured and feared ; reverence is to be shown to them with heart, mouth, and hand—in thought, word, and deed. But by father and mother we are not to understand merely the authors and preservers of our bodily life, but also the founders, protectors, and promoters of our spiritual life, such as prophets and teachers, to whom sometimes the name of father is given (2 Kings ii. 12, xiii. 14), whilst at other times paternity is ascribed to them by their scholars being called sons and daughters (Ps. xxxiv. 12, xlv. 11 ; Prov. i. 8, 10, 15, etc.) ; also the guardians of our bodily and spiritual life, the powers ordained of God, to whom the names of father and mother (Gen. xlv. 8 ; Judg. v. 7) may justly be applied, since all government has grown out of the relation of father and child, and draws its moral weight and stability, upon which the prosperity and well-being of a nation depends, from the reverence of children towards their parents.[1] And the promise, " *that thy days may be long* (thou mayest live long) *in the land which Jehovah thy God giveth thee,*" also points to this. There is a double promise here. So long as the nation rejoiced in the possession of obedient children, it was assured of a long life or existence in the land of Canaan ; but there is also included the promise

---

[1] " In this demand for reverence to parents, the fifth commandment lays the foundation for the sanctification of the whole social life, inasmuch as it thereby teaches us to acknowledge a divine authority in the same" (*Oehler,* Dekalog, p. 322).

of a long life, *i.e.* a great age, to individuals (cf. Deut. vi. 2, xxii. 7), just as we find in 1 Kings iii. 14 a good old age referred to as a special blessing from God. In Deut. v. 16, the promise of long life is followed by the words, " and that it may be well with thee," which do not alter the sense, but merely explain it more fully.

As the majesty of God was thus to be honoured and feared in parents, so the image of God was to be kept sacred in all men. This thought forms the transition to the rest of the commandments.

Vers. 13-17. The OTHER FIVE WORDS or commandments, which determine the duties to one's neighbour, are summed up in Lev. xix. 18 in the one word, " Love thy neighbour as thyself." The order in which they follow one another is the following: they first of all secure life, marriage, and property against active invasion or attack, and then, proceeding from deed to word and thought, they forbid false witness and coveting.[1] If, therefore, the first three commandments in this table refer primarily to deeds; the subsequent advance to the prohibition of desire is a proof that the deed is not to be separated from the disposition, and that " the fulfilment of the law is only complete when the heart itself is sanctified" (*Oehler*). Accordingly, in the command, " Thou shalt not *kill*," not only is the accomplished fact of murder condemned, whether it proceed from open violence or stratagem (chap. xxi. 12, 14, 18), but every act that endangers human life, whether it arise from carelessness (Deut. xxii. 8) or wantonness (Lev. xix. 14), or from hatred, anger, and revenge (Lev. xix. 17, 18). Life is placed at the head of these commandments, not as being the highest earthly possession, but because it is the basis of human existence, and in the life the personality is attacked, and in that the image of God (Gen. ix. 6). The omission of the object still remains to be

---

[1] *Luther* has pointed out this *mirum et aptum ordinem*, and expounds it thus : " Incipit prohibitio a majori usque ad minimum, nam maximum damnum est occisio hominis, deinde proximum violatio conjugis, tertium ablatio facultatis. Quod qui in iis nocere non possunt, saltem lingua nocent, ideo quartum est læsio famæ. Quodsi in iis non prævalent omnibus, saltem corde lædunt proximum, cupiendo quæ ejus sunt, in quo et invidia proprie consistit."

noticed, as showing that the prohibition includes not only the killing of a fellow-man, but the destruction of one's own life, or suicide.—The two following commandments are couched in equally general terms. *Adultery*, נָאַף, which is used in Lev. xx. 10 of both man and woman, signifies (as distinguished from זָנָה to commit fornication) the sexual intercourse of a husband with the wife of another, or of a wife with the husband of another. This prohibition is not only directed against any assault upon the husband's dearest possession, for the tenth commandment guards against that, but upholds the sacredness of marriage as the divine appointment for the propagation and multiplication of the human race ; and although addressed primarily to the man, like all the commandments that were given to the whole nation, applies quite as much to the woman as to the man, just as we find in Lev. xx. 10 that adultery was to be punished with death in the case of both the man *and* the woman.—Property was to be equally inviolable. The command, " Thou shalt not *steal*," prohibited not only the secret or open removal of another person's property, but injury done to it, or fraudulent retention of it, through carelessness or indifference (chap. xxi. 33, xxii. 13, xxiii. 4, 5 ; Deut. xxii. 1–4).—But lest these commandments should be understood as relating merely to the outward act as such, as they were by the Pharisees, in opposition to whom Christ set forth their true fulfilment (Matt. v. 21 sqq.), God added the further prohibition, " *Thou shalt not answer as a false witness against thy neighbour*," *i.e.* give false testimony against him. עָנָה with בְּ : to answer or give evidence against a person (Gen. xxx. 33). עֵד is not evidence, but a witness. Instead of עֵד שֶׁקֶר, a witness of a lie, who consciously gives utterance to falsehood, we find עֵד שָׁוְא in Deuteronomy, one who says what is vain, worthless, unfounded (שֵׁמַע שָׁוְא, chap. xxiii. 1 ; on שׁוֹא see ver. 7). From this it is evident, that not only is lying prohibited, but false and unfounded evidence in general ; and not only evidence before a judge, but false evidence of every kind, by which (according to the context) the life, married relation, or property of a neighbour might be endangered (cf. chap. xxiii. 1; Num. xxxv. 30 ; Deut. xvii. 6, xix. 15, xxii. 13 sqq.).—The last or tenth commandment is directed against desiring (coveting), as the root from which every sin against a neighbour springs, whether it be in word or deed. The חָמַד, ἐπιθυμεῖν

(LXX.), coveting, proceeds from the heart (Prov. vi. 25), and brings forth sin, which "is finished" in the act (Jas. i. 14, 15). The repetition of the words, "Thou shalt not covet," does not prove that there are two different commandments, any more than the substitution of תִּתְאַוֶּה in Deut. v. 18 for the second תַּחְמֹד. חָמַד and הִתְאַוָּה are synonyms,—the only difference between them being, that "the former denotes the desire as founded upon the perception of beauty, and therefore excited from without; the latter, desire originating at the very outset in the person himself, and arising from his own want or inclination" (*Schultz*). The repetition merely serves to strengthen and give the greater emphasis to that which constitutes the very kernel of the command, and is just as much in harmony with the simple and appropriate language of the law, as the employment of a synonym in the place of the repetition of the same word is with the rhetorical character of Deuteronomy. Moreover, the objects of desire do not point to two different commandments. This is evident at once from the transposition of the house and wife in Deuteronomy. בַּיִת (the house) is not merely the dwelling, but the entire household (as in Gen. xv. 2, Job viii. 15), either including the wife, or exclusive of her. In the text before us she is included; in Deuteronomy she is not, but is placed first as the crown of the man, and a possession more costly than pearls (Prov. xii. 4, xxxi. 10). In this case, the idea of the "house" is restricted to the other property belonging to the domestic economy, which is classified in Deuteronomy as fields, servants, cattle, and whatever else a man may have; whereas in Exodus the "house" is divided into wife, servants, cattle, and the rest of the possessions.

Vers. 18–21 (cf. Deut. v. 19–33). The terrible phenomena, amidst which the Lord displayed His majesty, made the intended impression upon the people who were stationed by the mountain below, so that they desired that God would not speak to them any more, and entreated Moses through their elders to act as mediator between them, promising at the same time that they would hear him (cf. chap. xix. 9, 16–19). רֹאִים, perceiving: רָאָה to see being frequently used for perceiving, as being the principle sense by which most of the impressions of the outer world are received (*e.g.* Gen. xlii. 1; Isa. xliv. 16; Jer. xxxiii. 24). לַפִּידִם, fire-torches, are the vivid flashes of lightning (chap.

xix. 16). " *They trembled and stood afar off:*" not daring to come nearer to the mountain, or to ascend it. "*And they said,*" viz. the heads of the tribes and elders: cf. Deut. v. 20, where the words of the people are more fully given. "*Lest we die:*" cf. Deut. v. 21–23. Though they had discovered that God speaks with man, and yet man lives; they felt so much that they were בָּשָׂר, *flesh, i.e.* powerless, frail, and alienated by sin from the holy God, that they were afraid lest they should be consumed by this great fire, if they listened any longer to the voice of God.—Ver. 20. To direct the sinner's holy awe in the presence of the holy God, which was expressed in these words of the people, into the proper course of healthy and enduring penitence, Moses first of all took away the false fear of death by the encouraging answer, " Fear not," and then immediately added, " for God is come to prove you." נַסּוֹת referred to the testing of the state of the heart in relation to God, as it is explained in the exegetical clause which follows: " *that His fear may be before your faces, that ye sin not.*" By this terrible display of His glory, God desired to inspire them with the true fear of Himself, that they might not sin through distrust, disobedience, or resistance to His guidance and commands.—Ver. 21. " *So the people stood afar off*" (as in ver 18), not " went far away," although, according to Deut. v. 30, Moses was directed by God to tell the people to return to their tents. This is passed over here, and it is merely observed, for the purpose of closing the first act in the giving the law, and preparing the way for the second, that the people remained afar off, whereas Moses (and Aaron, cf. xix. 24) drew near to the darkness where God was, to receive the further commands of the Lord.

THE LEADING FEATURES IN THE COVENANT CONSTITUTION.— CHAP. XX. 22–XXIV. 2.

These refer, *first* of all, to the general form of divine worship in Israel (xx. 22–26); *secondly*, to the rights of the Israelites, (*a*) in a civil or social point of view, *i.e.* so far as their relation to one another was concerned (xxi. 1–xxiii. 13), and (*b*) in their religious and theocratical relation to Jehovah (chap. xxiii. 14–19); and *thirdly*, to the attitude which Jehovah would maintain towards Israel (chap. xxiii. 20–33).

Chap. xx. 22–26. The General Form of Divine Worship in Israel.—As Jehovah had spoken to the Israelites from
heaven, they were not to make gods of earthly materials, such
as silver and gold, by the side of Him, but simply to construct
an altar of earth or unhewn stones without steps, for the offering up of His sacrifices at the place where He would reveal
Himself. "*From heaven*" Jehovah came down upon Sinai enveloped in the darkness of a cloud; and thereby He made known
to the people that His nature was heavenly, and could not be
imitated in any earthly material. "*Ye shall not make with Me*,"
place by the side of, or on a par with Me, "*gods of silver and
gold*,"—that is to say, idols primarily intended to represent the
nature of God, and therefore meant as symbols of Jehovah, but
which became false gods from the very fact that they were intended as representations of the purely spiritual God.—Ver. 24.
For the worship of Jehovah, the God of heaven, Israel needed
only an altar, on which to cause its sacrifices to ascend to God.
The altar, as an elevation built up of earth or rough stones, was
a symbol of the elevation of man to God, who is enthroned on
high in the heaven; and because man was to raise himself to
God in his sacrifices, Israel also was to make an altar, though
only of earth, or if of stones, not of hewn stones. "*For if thou
swingest thy tool* (חֶרֶב, *lit.* sharpness, then any edge tool) *over it*
(over the stone), *thou defilest it*" (ver. 25). "*Of earth:*" *i.e.*
not "of comparatively simple materials, such as befitted a representation of the creature" (*Schultz* on Deut. xii.); for the
altar was not to represent the creature, but to be the place to
which God came to receive man into His fellowship there. For
this reason the altar was to be made of the same material, which
formed the earthly soil for the kingdom of God, either of earth
or else of stones, just as they existed in their natural state; not,
however, "because unpolished stones, which retain their true
and native condition, appear to be endowed with a certain native
purity, and therefore to be most in harmony with the sanctity of
an altar" (*Spencer de legg. Hebr. rit. lib.* ii. c. 6), for the "native
purity" of the earth does not agree with Gen. iii. 17; but because
the altar was to set forth the nature of the simple earthly soil,
unaltered by the hand of man. The earth, which has been involved in the curse of sin, is to be renewed and glorified into the
kingdom of God, not by sinful men, but by the gracious hand

of God alone. Moreover, Israel was not to erect the altar for its sacrifices in any place that it might choose, but only in every place in which Jehovah should bring His name to remembrance. הַזְכִּיר שֵׁם וגו׳ does not mean "to make the name of the Lord remembered," *i.e.* to cause men to remember it; but to establish a memorial of His name, *i.e.* to make a glorious revelation of His divine nature, and thereby to consecrate the place into a holy soil (cf. iii. 5), upon which Jehovah would come to Israel and bless it. Lastly, the command not to go up to the altar by steps (ver. 26) is followed by the words, "that thy nakedness be not discovered thereon." It was in the feeling of shame that the consciousness of sin first manifested itself, and it was in the shame that the sin was chiefly apparent (Gen. iii. 7); hence the nakedness was a disclosure of sin, through which the altar of God would be desecrated, and for this reason it was forbidden to ascend to the altar by steps. These directions with reference to the altar to be built do not refer merely to the altar, which was built for the conclusion of the covenant, nor are they at variance with the later instructions respecting the one altar at the tabernacle, upon which all the sacrifices were to be presented (Lev. xvii. 8, 9; Deut. xii. 5 sqq.), nor are they merely "provisional;" but they lay the foundation for the future laws with reference to the places of worship, though without restricting them to one particular locality on the one hand, or allowing an unlimited number of altars on the other. Hence "several places and altars are referred to here, because, whilst the people were wandering in the desert, there could be no fixed place for the tabernacle" (*Riehm*). But the erection of the altar is unquestionably limited to every place which Jehovah appointed for the purpose by a revelation. We are not to understand the words, however, as referring merely to those places in which the tabernacle and its altar were erected, and to the site of the future temple (Sinai, Shiloh, and Jerusalem), but to all those places also where altars were built and sacrifices offered on extraordinary occasions, on account of God,—appearing there such, for example, as Ebal (Josh. viii. 30 compared with Deut. xxvii. 5), the rock in Ophrah (Judg. vi. 25, 26), and many other places besides.

Chap. xxi. 1–xxiii. 13. FUNDAMENTAL RIGHTS OF THE

ISRAELITES IN THEIR CIVIL OR SOCIAL RELATIONS.—Chap. xxi. 1–11. The *mishpatim* (ver. 1) are not the "laws, which were to be in force and serve as rules of action," as *Knobel* affirms, but the *rights*, by which the national life was formed into a civil commonwealth and the political order secured. These rights had reference first of all to the relation in which the individuals stood one towards another. The *personal rights* of dependants are placed at the head (vers. 2–11); and first those of *slaves* (vers. 2-6), which are still more minutely explained in Deut. xv. 12–18, where the observance of them is urged upon the hearts of the people on subjective grounds.— Ver. 2. The Hebrew servant was to obtain his freedom without paying compensation, after six years of service. According to Deut. xv. 12, this rule applied to the Hebrew maid-servant as well. The predicate עִבְרִי limits the rule to Israelitish servants, in distinction from slaves of foreign extraction, to whom this law did not apply (cf. Deut. xv. 12, "thy brother").[1] An Israelite might buy his own countryman, either when he was sold by a court of justice on account of theft (chap. xxii. 1), or when he was poor and sold himself (Lev. xxv. 39). The emancipation in the seventh year of service was intimately connected with the sabbatical year, though we are not to understand it as taking place in that particular year. "He shall go out free, *sc.* from his master's house, *i.e.* be set at liberty. חִנָּם : without compensation. In Deuteronomy the master is also commanded not to let him go out empty, but to load him (הַעֲנִיק to put upon his neck) from his flock, his threshing-floor, and his wine-press (*i.e.* with corn and wine); that is to say, to give him as much as he could carry away with him. The motive for this command is drawn from their recollection of their own deliverance by Jehovah from the bondage of Egypt. And in ver. 18 an additional reason is supplied, to incline the heart of the master to this emancipation, viz. that "he has served thee for six years the double of a labourer's wages,"—that is to say, "he has served and worked so much, that it would have cost twice as much, if it had been necessary to hire a labourer in his place" (*Schultz*),— and "Jehovah thy God hath blessed thee in all that thou doest,"

---

[1] *Saalschütz* is quite wrong in his supposition, that עִבְרִי relates not to Israelites, but to relations of the Israelites who had come over to them from their original native land. (See my *Archäologie*, § 112, Note 2.)

sc. through his service.—Vers. 3, 4. There were three different circumstances possible, under which emancipation might take place. The servant might have been unmarried and continued so (בְּגַפּוֹ : with his body, *i.e.* alone, single) : in that case, of course, there was no one else to set at liberty. Or he might have brought a wife with him ; and in that case his wife was to be set at liberty as well. Or his master might have given him a wife in his bondage, and she might have borne him children : in that case the wife and children were to continue the property of the master. This may appear oppressive, but it was an equitable consequence of the possession of property in slaves at all. At the same time, in order to modify the harshness of such a separation of husband and wife, the option was given to the servant to remain in his master's service, provided he was willing to renounce his liberty for ever (vers. 5, 6). This would very likely be the case as a general rule ; for there were various legal arrangements, which are mentioned in other places, by which the lot of Hebrew slaves was greatly softened and placed almost on an equality with that of hired labourers (cf. chap. xxiii. 12 ; Lev. xxv. 6, 39, 43, 53 ; Deut. xii. 18, xvi. 11). In this case the master was to take his servant אֶל הָאֱלֹהִים, *lit. to God, i.e.*, according to the correct rendering of the LXX., πρὸς τὸ κριτήριον, to the place where judgment was given in the name of God (Deut. i. 17 ; cf. chap. xxii. 7, 8, and Deut. xix. 17), in order that he might make a declaration there that he gave up his liberty. His ear was then to be bored with an awl against the door or lintel of the house, and by this sign, which was customary in many of the nations of antiquity, to be fastened as it were to the house for ever. That this was the meaning of the piercing of the ear against the door of the house, is evident from the unusual expression in Deut. xv. 17, " and put (the awl) into his ear and into the door, that he may be thy servant for ever," where the ear and the door are co-ordinates. *" For ever,"* i.e. as long as he lives. *Josephus* and the Rabbins would restrict the service to the time ending with the year of jubilee, but without sufficient reason, and contrary to the usage of the language, as לְעֹלָם is used in Lev. xxv. 46 to denote service which did not terminate with the year of jubilee. (See the remarks on Lev. xxv. 10 ; also my *Archäologie.*)

Vers. 7–11. The *daughter* of an Israelite, who had been *sold by her father as a maid-servant* (לְאָמָה), *i.e.*, as the sequel shows, as a housekeeper and concubine, stood in a different relation to her master's house. She was not to go out like the men-servants, *i.e.* not to be sent away as free at the end of six years of service ; but the three following regulations, which are introduced by אִם (ver. 8), וְאִם (ver. 9), and וְאִם (ver. 11), were to be observed with regard to her. In the *first* place (ver. 8), " *if she please not her master, who hath betrothed her to himself, then shall he let her be redeemed.*" The לֹא before יְעָדָהּ is one of the fifteen cases in which לֹא has been marked in the Masoretic text as standing for לוֹ ; and it cannot possibly signify *not* in the passage before us. For if it were to be taken as a negative, " that he do not appoint her," *sc.* as a concubine for himself, the pronoun לוֹ would certainly not be omitted. הֶפְדָּהּ (for הִפְדָּהּ, see Ges. § 53, Note 6), to let her be redeemed, *i.e.* to allow another Israelite to buy her as a concubine ; for there can hardly have been any thought of redemption on the part of the father, as it would no doubt be poverty alone that caused him to sell his daughter (Lev. xxv. 39). But " *to sell her unto a strange nation* (*i.e.* to any one but a Hebrew), *he shall have no power, if he acts unfaithfully towards her,*" *i.e.* if he do not grant her the promised marriage. In the *second* place (vers. 9, 10), " *if he appoint her as his son's wife, he shall act towards her according to the rights of daughters,*" *i.e.* treat her as a daughter ; " *and if he take him* (the son) *another* (wife),—whether because the son was no longer satisfied, or because the father gave the son another wife in addition to her,—" *her food* (שְׁאֵר flesh as the chief article of food, instead of לֶחֶם, bread, because the lawgiver had persons of property in his mind, who were in a position to keep concubines), *her raiment, and her duty of marriage he shall not diminish,*" *i.e.* the claims which she had as a daughter for support, and as his son's wife for conjugal rights, were not to be neglected ; he was not to allow his son, therefore, to put her away or treat her badly. With this explanation the difficulties connected with every other are avoided. For instance, if we refer the words of ver. 9 to the son, and understand them as meaning, " if the son should take another wife," we introduce a change of subject without anything to indicate it. If, on the other hand, we regard them as meaning, " if the father (the purchaser) should take to himself another wife," this ought to have come before ver. 9. In the *third* place (ver. 11), " *if he do not* (do not grant) *these three unto her, she shall go out for nothing, without money.*" "These three" are food, clothing, and conjugal rights, which are mentioned just before ; not " *si eam non desponderit sibi nec filio, nec redimi sit passus*" (*Rabbins* and others), nor "if he did not give her to his son as a concubine, but diminished her," as *Knobel* explains it.

Vers. 12–17. Still higher than personal liberty, however, is life itself, the right of existence and personality ; and the infliction of injury upon this was not only prohibited, but to be followed by punishment corresponding to the crime. The principle of retribution, *jus talionis*, which is the only one that embodies the idea of justice, lies at the foundation of these threats.—Vers. 12–14. A *death-blow* was to be punished with death (cf. Gen. ix. 6 ; Lev. xxiv. 17). " *He that smiteth a man and* (so that) *he die* (whether on the spot or directly afterwards did not matter), *he shall be put to death.*" This general rule is still further defined by a distinction being drawn between accidental and intentional killing. " *But whoever has not lain in wait* (for another's life), *and God has caused it to come to his hand*" (to kill the other) ; *i.e.* not only if he did not intend to kill him, but did not even cherish the intention of smiting him, or of doing him harm from hatred and enmity (Num. xxxv. 16–23 ; Deut. xix. 4, 5), and therefore did so quite unawares, according to a dispensation of God, which is generally called an accident because it is above our comprehension. For such a man God would appoint places of refuge, where he should be protected against the avenger of blood. (On this point, see Num. xxxv. 9 sqq.)—Ver. 14. " *But he who acts presumptuously against his neighbour, to slay him with guile, thou shalt take him from Mine altar that he may die.*" These words are not to be understood as meaning, that only intentional and treacherous killing was to be punished with death ; but, without restricting the general rule in ver. 12, they are to be interpreted from their antithesis to ver. 13, as signifying that even the altar of Jehovah was not to protect a man who had committed intentional murder, and carried out his purpose with treachery. (More on this point at Num. xxxv. 16 sqq.) By this regulation, the idea, which was common to the Hebrews and many other nations, that the altar as God's abode afforded protection to any life that was in danger from men, was brought back to the true measure of its validity, and the place of expiation for sins of weakness (cf. Lev. iv. 2, v. 15, 18; Num. xv. 27–31) was prevented from being abused by being made a place of refuge for criminals who were deserving of death. Maltreatment of a father and mother through striking (ver. 15), man-stealing (ver. 16), and cursing parents (ver. 17, cf. Lev. xx. 9), were all to be placed on a par with murder, and punished in the same way. By the " smiting " (הִכָּה) of parents we are not to understand smiting to death, for in that case וָמֵת would be added as in ver. 12, but any kind of maltreatment. The murder of parents is not mentioned at all, as not likely to occur and hardly conceivable. The cursing (קִלֵּל as in Gen. xii. 3) of parents is placed on a par with smiting, because it proceeds from the same disposition; and both were to be punished with death, because the majesty of God was violated in the persons of the parents (cf. chap. xx. 12). Man-stealing was also no less a crime, being a sin against the dignity of man, and a violation of the image of God. For אִישׁ " a man," we find in Deut. xxiv. 7, נֶפֶשׁ " a soul," by which both man and woman are intended, and the still more definite limitation, " of his brethren of the children of Israel." The crime remained the same whether he had sold him (the stolen man), or whether he was still found in his hand. (For וְ—וְ as a sign of an alternative in the linking together of short sentences, see Prov. xxix. 9, and Ewald, § 361.) This is the rendering adopted by most of the earlier translators, and we get no intelligent sense if we divide the clauses thus : " and sell him so that he is found in his hand."

Vers. 18–32. Fatal blows and the crimes placed on a par with them are now followed in simple order by the laws relating to *bodily injuries*.—Vers. 18, 19. If in the course of a quarrel one man should hit another with a stone or with his fist, so that, although he did not die, he " *lay upon his bed*," *i.e.* became bedridden ; if the person struck should get up again and walk out with his staff, the other would be innocent, he should " *only give him his sitting and have him cured*," *i.e.* compensate him for his loss of time and the cost of recovery. This certainly implies, on the one hand, that if the man died upon his bed, the injury was to be punished with death, according to ver. 12 ; and on the other hand, that if he died after getting up and going out, no further punishment was to be inflicted for the injury done.—

Vers. 20, 21. The case was different with regard to a slave. The master had always the right to punish or " chasten" him with a stick (Prov. x. 13, xiii. 24) ; this right was involved in the paternal authority of the master over the servants in his possession. The law was therefore confined to the abuse of this authority in outbursts of passion, in which case, " *if the servant or the maid should die under his hand* (*i.e.* under his blows), *he was to be punished*" (נָקֹם יִנָּקֵם : " vengeance shall surely be taken"). But in what the נָקֹם was to consist is not explained ; certainly not in slaying by the sword, as the Jewish commentators maintain. The lawgiver would have expressed this by מוֹת יוּמַת. No doubt it was left to the authorities to determine this according to the circumstances. The law in ver. 12 could hardly be applied to a case of this description, although it was afterwards extended to foreigners as well as natives (Lev. xxiv. 21, 22), for the simple reason, that it is hardly conceivable that a master would intentionally kill his slave, who was his possession and money. How far the lawgiver was from presupposing any such intention here, is evident from the law which follows in ver. 21, " Notwithstanding, if he continue a day or two (*i.e.* remain alive), it shall not be avenged, for he is his money." By the continuance of his life, if only for a day or two, it would become perfectly evident that the master did not wish to kill his servant ; and if nevertheless he died after this, the loss of the slave was punishment enough for the master. There is no ground whatever for restricting this regulation, as the Rabbins do, to slaves who were not of Hebrew extraction.—Vers. 22–25. If men strove and thrust against a woman with child, who had come near or between them for the purpose of making peace, so that her children come out (come into the world), and no injury was done either to the woman or the child that was born,[1] a pecuniary

---

[1] The words וְיָצְאוּ יְלָדֶיהָ are rendered by the LXX. καὶ ἐξέλθῃ τὸ παιδίον αὐτῆς μὴ ἐξεικονισμένον, and the corresponding clause וְאִם אָסוֹן יִהְיֶה by ἐὰν δὲ ἐξεικονισμένον ᾖ ; consequently the translators have understood the words as meaning that the fruit, the premature birth of which was caused by the blow, if not yet developed into a human form, was not to be regarded as in any sense a human being, so that the giver of the blow was only required to pay a pecuniary compensation,—as *Philo* expresses it, " on account of the injury done to the woman, and because he prevented nature, which forms and shapes a man into the most beautiful being, from bringing him forth alive." But the arbitrary character of this explanation is apparent at once ;

compensation was to be paid, such as the husband of the woman laid upon him, and he was to give it בִּפְלִלִים by (by an appeal to) arbitrators. A fine is imposed, because even if no injury had been done to the woman and the fruit of her womb, such a blow might have endangered life. (For יָצָא to go out of the womb, see Gen. xxv. 25, 26.) The plural יְלָדֶיהָ is employed for the purpose of speaking indefinitely, because there might possibly be more than one child in the womb. "*But if injury occur* (to the mother or the child), *thou shalt give soul for soul, eye for eye, . . . wound for wound:*" thus perfect retribution was to be made. —Vers. 26, 27. But the *lex talionis* applied to the free Israelite only, not to slaves. In the case of the latter, if the master struck out an eye and destroyed it, *i.e.* blinded him with the blow, or struck out a tooth, he was to let him go free, as a compensation for the loss of the member. Eye and tooth are individual examples selected to denote all the members, from the most important and indispensable down to the very least.— Vers. 28–32. The life of man is also protected against injury from cattle (cf. Gen. ix. 5). "*If an ox gore a man or a woman, that they die, the ox shall be stoned, and its flesh shall not be eaten;*" because, as the stoning already shows, it was laden with the guilt of murder, and therefore had become unclean (cf. Num. xxxv. 33). The master or owner of the ox was innocent, *sc.* if his ox had not been known to do so before. But if this were the case, "*if his master have been warned* (הוּעַד בִּבְעָלָיו, *lit.* testimony laid against its master), *and notwithstanding this he have not kept it in,*" then the master was to be put to death, because through his carelessness in keeping the ox he had caused the death, and therefore shared the guilt. As this guilt, however, had not been incurred through an intentional crime, but had arisen simply from carelessness, he was allowed to redeem

for יֶלֶד only denotes a child, as a fully developed human being, and not the fruit of the womb before it has assumed a human form. In a manner no less arbitrary אָסוֹן has been rendered by *Onkelos* and the *Rabbins* מוֹתָא, death, and the clause is made to refer to the death of the mother alone, in opposition to the penal sentence in vers. 23, 24, which not only demands life for life, but eye for eye, etc., and therefore presupposes not death alone, but injury done to particular members. The omission of לָהּ, also, apparently renders it impracticable to refer the words to injury done to the woman alone.

his forfeited life by the payment of expiation money (כֹּפֶר, *lit.* covering, expiation, cf. chap. xxx. 12), " *according to all that was laid upon him,*" *sc.* by the judge.—Vers. 31, 32. The death of a son or a daughter through the goring of an ox was also to be treated in the same way; but that of a slave (man-servant or maid-servant) was to be compensated by the payment of thirty shekels of silver (*i.e.* probably the ordinary price for the redemption of a slave, as the redemption price of a free Israelite was fifty shekels, Lev. xxvii. 3) on the part of the owner of the ox; but the ox was to be killed in this case also. There are other ancient nations in whose law books we find laws relating to the punishment of animals for killing or wounding a man, but not one of them had a law which made the owner of the animal responsible as well, for they none of them looked upon human life in its likeness of God.

Vers. 33–36. Passing from life to *property*, in connection with the foregoing, the life of the animal, the most important possession of the Israelites, is first of all secured against destruction through carelessness. If any one opened or dug a pit or cistern, and did not close it up again, and another man's ox or ass (mentioned, for the sake of example, as the most important animals among the live stock of the Israelites) fell in and was killed, the owner of the pit was to pay its full value, and the dead animal to belong to him. If an ox that was not known to be vicious gored another man's ox to death, the vicious animal was to be sold, and its money (what it fetched) to be divided; the dead animal was also to be divided, so that both parties bore an equal amount of damage. If, on the other hand, the ox had been known to be vicious before, and had not been kept in, carefully secured, by its possessor, he was to compensate the owner of the one that had been killed with the full value of an ox, but to receive the dead one instead.

Chap. xxii. 1–4 (or ver. 37–chap. xxii. 3). With regard to *cattle-stealing*, the law makes a distinction between what had been killed or sold, and what was still alive and in the thief's hand (or possession). In the latter case, the thief was to restore piece for piece twofold (ver. 4); in the former, he was to restore an ox fivefold and a small animal (a sheep or a goat) fourfold (ver. 1). The difference between the compensation for an ox and a small animal is to be accounted for from the comparative worth of the cattle to the possessor, which determined the magnitude of the theft and the amount of the compensation. But the other distinctions of twofold, fourfold, and fivefold restitution cannot be accounted for, either by supposing " that the animal slain or sold was lost to its master, and might have been of peculiar value to him" (*Knobel*), for such a consideration of personal feelings would have been quite foreign to the law,—not to mention the fact that an animal that had been sold might be recovered by purchase; or from the fact that " the thief in this case had carried his crime still further" (*Baumgarten*), for the main thing was still the theft, not the consumption or sale of the animal stolen. The reason can only have lain in the educational purpose of the law : viz. in the intention to lead the thief to repent of his crime, to acknowledge his guilt, and to restore what he had stolen. Now, as long as he still retained the stolen animal in his own possession, having neither consumed nor parted with it, this was always in his power ; but the possibility was gone as soon as it had either been consumed or sold (see my Archæologie, § 154, Note 3).[1]

Vers. 2, 3. Into the midst of the laws relating to theft, we have one introduced here, prescribing what was to be done with the thief. " *If the thief be found breaking in* (*i.e.* by night according to ver. 3), *and be smitten so that he die, there shall be no blood to him* (the person smiting him) ; *if the sun has risen upon him* (the thief breaking in), *there is blood to him:*" *i.e.* in the latter case the person killing him drew upon himself blood-guiltiness (דָּמִים *lit.* drops of blood, blood shed), in the former case he did not. " The reason for this disparity between a thief by night and one in the day is, that the power and intention of a nightly thief are uncertain, and whether he may not have come for the purpose of committing murder; and that by night, if thieves are resisted, they often proceed to murder in their rage; and also that they can neither be recognised, nor resisted and apprehended with safety" (*Calovius*). In the latter case the slayer contracted blood-guiltiness, because even the life of a thief was

---

[1] *Calvin* gives the same explanation : *Major in scelere obstinatio se prodit, ubi res furtiva in quæstum conversa est, nec spes est ulla resipiscentiæ, atque ita continuo progressu duplicatur malæ fidei crimen. Fieri potest ut fur statim post delictum contremisc : qui vero animal occidere ausus est, aut vendere, prorsus in maleficio obdt it.*

to be spared, as he could be punished for his crime, and what was stolen be restored according to the regulations laid down in vers. 1 and 4. But if he had not sufficient to make retribution, he was to be sold "*for his stolen,*" *i.e.* for the value of what he had stolen, that he might earn by his labour the compensation to be paid.

Vers. 5, 6. *Injury done to another man's field or corn* was also to be made good by compensation for the injury done. If any one should consume a field or a vineyard, and let loose his beast, so that it fed in another man's field, he was to give the best of his field and vineyard as restitution. These words do not refer to wilful injury, for שִׁלַּח does not mean to drive in, but simply to let loose, set at liberty; they refer to injury done from carelessness, when any one neglected to take proper care of a beast that was feeding in his field, and it strayed in consequence, and began grazing in another man's. Hence simple compensation was all that was demanded; though this was to be made "from the best of his field," *i.e. quicquid optimum habebit in agro vel vinea* (*Jerome*).[1]—Ver. 6 also relates to unintentional injury, arising from want of proper care: "*If fire break out and catch thorns*" (thorn-hedges surrounding a corn-field, Isa. v. 5; Sir. xxviii. 24), *and sheaves, or the standing seed* (הַקָּמָה the corn standing in the straw), *or the field be consumed, he that kindleth the fire shall make compensation* (for the damage done)."

Vers. 7–15. In cases of *dishonesty, or the loss of property entrusted*, the following was to be the recognised right: If money or articles (כֵּלִים, not merely tools and furniture, but clothes and ornaments, cf. Deut. xxii. 5; Isa. lxi. 10) given to a neighbour to keep should be stolen out of his house, the thief was to restore double if he could be found; but if he could not be discovered, the master of the house was to go before the judicial court (אֶל הָאֱלֹהִים, see chap. xxi. 6; נִקְרַב אֶל to draw near to), to see "*whether he has not stretched out his hand to his neighbour's goods.*" מְלָאכָה: *lit.* employment, then something earned by employment, a possession. Before the judicial court he was

---

[1] The LXX. have expanded this law by interpolating ἀποτίσει ἐκ τοῦ ἀγροῦ αὐτοῦ κατὰ τὸ γέννημα αὐτοῦ· ἐὰν δὲ πάντα τὸν ἀγρὸν καταβοσκήσῃ before מֵיטַב. And the Samaritan does the same. But this expansion is proved to be an arbitrary interpolation, by the simple fact that πάντα τὸν ἀγρόν forms no logical antithesis to ἀγρὸν ἕτερον.

to cleanse himself of the suspicion of having fraudulently appropriated what had been entrusted to him ; and in most cases this could probably be only done by an oath of purification. The Sept. and Vulg. both point to this by interpolating καὶ ὀμεῖται, *et jurabit* (" and he shall swear "), though we are not warranted in supplying וְנִשְׁבַּע in consequence. For, apart from the fact that אִם־לֹא is not to be regarded as a particle of adjuration here, as *Rosenmüller* supposes, since this particle signifies " truly " when employed in an oath, and therefore would make the declaration affirmative, whereas the oath was unquestionably to be taken as a release from the suspicion of fraudulent appropriation, and in case of confession an oath was not requisite at all ;—apart from all this, if the lawgiver had intended to prescribe an oath for such a case, he would have introduced it here, just as he has done in ver. 11. If the man could free himself before the court from the suspicion of unfaithfulness, he would of course not have to make compensation for what was lost, but the owner would have to bear the damage. This legal process is still further extended in ver. 9 : עַל־כָּל־דְּבַר־פֶּשַׁע, " *upon every matter of trespass*" (by which we are to understand, according to the context, unfaithfulness with regard to, or unjust appropriation of, the property of another man, not only when it had been entrusted, but also if it had been found), " *for ox, for ass*, etc., *or for any manner of lost thing, of which one says that it is this* ("*this*," viz. the matter of trespass), *the cause of both* (the parties contending about the right of possession) *shall come to the judicial court ; and he whom the court (Elohim) shall pronounce guilty* (of unjust appropriation) *shall give double compensation to his neighbour* : only double as in vers. 4 and 7, not four or fivefold as in ver. 1, because the object in dispute had not been consumed.—Vers. 10 sqq. If an animal entrusted to a neighbour to take care of had either died or hurt itself (נִשְׁבָּר, broken a limb), or been driven away by robbers when out at grass (1 Chron. v. 21 ; 2 Chron. xiv. 14, cf. Job i. 15, 17), without any one (else) seeing it, an oath was to be taken before Jehovah between both (the owner and the keeper of it), " whether he had not stretched out his hand to his neighbour's property," *i.e.* either killed, or mutilated, or disposed of the animal. This case differs from the previous one, not only in the fact that the animal had either become useless to the owner or was altogether lost, but also in the fact that the keeper, if his statement were true, had not been at all to blame in the matter. The only way in which this could be decided, if there was אֵין רֹאֶה, *i.e.* no other eye-witness present than the keeper him-self at the time when the fact occurred, was by the keeper taking an oath before Jehovah, that is to say, before the judicial court. And if he took the oath, the master (owner) of it (the animal that had perished, or been lost or injured) was to accept (*sc.* the oath), and he (the accused) was not to make reparation. "But if it had been stolen מֵעִמּוֹ from with him (*i.e.* from his house or stable), he was to make it good," because he might have prevented this with proper care (cf. Gen. xxxi. 39). On the other hand, if it had been torn in pieces (viz. by a beast of prey, while it was out at grass), he was not to make any com-pensation, but only to furnish a proof that he had not been wanting in proper care. יְבִאֵהוּ עֵד "*let him bring it as a witness*," viz. the animal that had been torn in pieces, or a por-tion of it, from which it might be seen that he had chased the wild beast to recover its prey (cf. 1 Sam. xvii. 34, 35 ; Amos iii. 12).—Vers. 14, 15. If any one borrowed an animal of his neighbour (to use it for some kind of work), and it got injured and died, he was to make compensation to the owner, unless the latter were present at the time ; but not if he were. "For either he would see that it could not have been averted by any human care; or if it could, seeing that he, the owner himself, was present, and did not avert it, it would only be right that he should suffer the consequence of his own neglect to afford assist-ance" (*Calovius*). The words which follow, אִם שָׂכִיר וגו', cannot have any other meaning than this, "*if it was hired, it has come upon his hire*," *i.e.* he has to bear the injury or loss for the money which he got for letting out the animal. The suggestion which *Knobel* makes with a "perhaps," that שָׂכִיר refers to a hired labourer, to whom the word is applied in other places, and that the meaning is this, "if it is a labourer for hire, he goes into his hire,—*i.e.* if the hirer is a daily labourer who has nothing with which to make compensation, he is to enter into the service of the person who let him the animal, for a sufficiently long time to make up for the loss,"—is not only opposed to the grammar (the perfect בָּא for which יָבֹא should be used), but is also at variance with the context, "not make it good."

Vers. 16, 17. The *seduction of a girl*, who belonged to her father as long as she was not betrothed (cf. chap. xxi. 7), was also to be regarded as an attack upon the family possession. Whoever persuaded a girl to let him lie with her, was to obtain her for a wife by the payment of a dowry (מֹהַר see Gen. xxxiv. 12) ; and if her father refused to give her to him, he was to weigh (pay) money equivalent to the dowry of maidens, *i.e.* to pay the father just as much for the disgrace brought upon him by the seduction of his daughter, as maidens would receive for a dowry upon their marriage. The seduction of a girl who was betrothed, was punished much more severely (see Deut. xxii. 23, 24).

Vers. 18–31. The laws which follow, from ver. 18 onwards, differ both in form and subject-matter from the determinations of right which we have been studying hitherto : in *form*, through the omission of the כִּי with which the others were almost invariably introduced; in subject-matter, inasmuch as they make demands upon Israel on the ground of its election to be the holy nation of Jehovah, which go beyond the sphere of natural right, not only prohibiting every inversion of the natural order of things, but requiring the manifestation of love to the infirm and needy out of regard to Jehovah. The transition from the former series to the present one is made by the command in ver. 18, " *Thou shalt not suffer a witch to live ;*" witchcraft being, on the one hand, "the vilest way of injuring a neighbour in his property, or even in his body and life" (*Ranke*), whilst, on the other hand, employment of powers of darkness for the purpose of injuring a neighbour was a practical denial of the divine vocation of Israel, as well as of Jehovah the Holy One of Israel. The witch is mentioned instead of the wizard, "not because witchcraft was not to be punished in the case of men, but because the female sex was more addicted to this crime" (*Calovius*). לֹא תְחַיֶּה (shalt not suffer to live) is chosen instead of the ordinary מוֹת יוּמַת (shall surely die), which is used in Lev. xx. 27 of wizards also, not " because the lawgiver intended that the Hebrew witch should be put to death in any case, and the foreigner only if she would not go when she was banished" (*Knobel*), but because *every* Hebrew witch was not to be put to death, but regard was to be had to the fact that witchcraft is often nothing but jugglery, and only those witches were to be put to death who would not give up their witchcraft when

it was forbidden. Witchcraft is followed in ver. 19 by the unnatural crime of lying with a beast; and this is also threatened
with the punishment of death (see Lev. xviii. 23, and xx. 15,
16).—Ver. 20. Whoever offered sacrifice to strange gods instead
of to Jehovah alone, was liable to death.   יָחֳרַם he shall be banned,
put under the ban (*cherem*), *i.e.* put to death, and by death devoted to the Lord, to whom he would not devote himself in life
(cf. Lev. xxvii. 29, and my *Archäologie*, § 70).—Ver. 21. The
Israelites were not to offer sacrifice to foreign deities; but a
foreigner himself they were not only to tolerate, but were not to
vex or oppress him, bearing in mind that they also had been
foreigners in Egypt (cf. chap. xxiii. 9, and Lev. xix. 33, 34).—
Whilst the foreigner, as having no rights, is thus commended to
the kindness of the people through their remembrance of what
they themselves had experienced in Egypt, those members of the
nation itself who were most in need of protection (viz. widows
and orphans) are secured from humiliation by an assurance of the
special care and watchfulness of Jehovah, under which such
forsaken ones stand, inasmuch as Jehovah Himself would take
their troubles upon Himself, and punish their oppressors with
just retribution.   עִנָּה to humiliate, includes not only unjust
oppression, but every kind of cold and contemptuous treatment.
The suffix in אֹתוֹ (ver. 23) refers to both אַלְמָנָה and יָתוֹם, according to the rule that when there are two or more subjects of
different genders, the masculine is employed (Ges. § 148, 2).
The כִּי before אִם expresses a strong assurance: "yea, if he cries
to Me, I will hearken to him" (see *Ewald*, § 330*b*). "Killing
with the sword" points to wars, in which men and fathers of
families perish, and their wives and children are made widows
and orphans.—Vers. 25–27. If a man should lend to one of the
poor of his own people, he was not to oppress him by demanding
interest; and if he gave his upper garment as a pledge, he was
to give it him back towards sunset, because it was his only
covering; as the poorer classes in the East use the upper garment, consisting of a large square piece of cloth, to sleep in.   "*It
is his clothing for his skin:*" *i.e.* it serves for a covering to his
body.   "*Wherein shall he lie ?*" *i.e.* in what shall he wrap himself
to sleep? (cf. Deut. xxiv. 6, 10–13).—With vers. 28 sqq. God
directs Himself at once to the hearts of the Israelites, and attacks the sins of selfishness and covetousness, against which the

precepts in vers. 21–27 were directed in their deepest root, for the purpose of opposing all inward resistance to the promotion of His commands.—Ver. 28. "*Thou shalt not despise God, and the prince among thy people thou shalt not curse.*" *Elohim* does not mean either the gods of other nations, as *Josephus, Philo,* and others, in their dead and work-holy monotheism, have rendered the word; or the rulers, as *Onkelos* and others suppose; but simply GOD, deity in general, whose majesty was despised in every breach of the commandments of Jehovah, and who was to be honoured in the persons of the rulers (cf. Prov. xxiv. 21; 1 Pet. ii. 17). Contempt of God consists not only in blasphemies of Jehovah openly expressed, which were to be punished with death (Lev. xxiv. 11 sqq.), but in disregard of His threats with reference to the oppression of the poorer members of His people (vers. 22–27), and in withholding from them what they ought to receive (vers. 29–31). Understood in this way, the command is closely connected not only with what precedes, but also with what follows. The prince (נָשִׂיא, *lit.* the elevated one) is mentioned by the side of God, because in his exalted position he has to administer the law of God among His people, and to put a stop to what is wrong.—Vers. 29, 30. "*Thy fulness and thy flowing thou shalt not delay* (to Me)." מְלֵאָה fulness, signifies the produce of corn (Deut. xxii. 9); and דֶּמַע (*lit.* tear, flowing, *liquor stillans*), which only occurs here, is a poetical epithet for the produce of the press, both wine and oil (cf. δάκρυον τῶν δένδρων, LXX.; *arborum lacrimæ*, Plin. xi. 6). The meaning is correctly given by the LXX.: ἀπαρχὰς ἅλωνος καὶ ληνοῦ σου. That the command not to delay and not to withhold the fulness, etc., relates to the offering of the first-fruits of the field and vineyard, as is more fully defined in chap. xxiii. 19 and Deut. xxvi. 2–11, is evident from what follows, in which the law given at the exodus from Egypt, with reference to the sanctification of the first-born of man and beast (xiii. 2, 12), is repeated and incorporated in the *rights* of Israel, inasmuch as the adoption of the first-born on the part of Jehovah was a perpetual guarantee to the whole nation of the right of covenant fellowship. (On the rule laid down in ver. 30, see Lev. xxii. 27.)—Ver. 31. As the whole nation sanctified itself to the Lord in the sanctification of the first-born, the Israelites were to show themselves to be holy men unto the Lord by not eating "flesh torn to pieces in the field," *i.e.* the flesh of an animal that had been torn to pieces by a wild beast in the field. Such flesh they were to throw to the dogs, because eating it would defile (cf. Lev. xvii. 15).

Chap. xxiii. 1–13.—Vers. 1–9. Lastly, no one was to violate another's rights.—Ver. 1. " *Thou shalt not raise* (bring out) *an empty report.*" שֵׁמַע שָׁוְא, a report that has no foundation, and, as the context shows, does injury to another, charges him with wrongdoing, and involves him in legal proceedings. " *Put not thine hand with a wicked man* (do not offer him thy hand, or render him assistance), *to be a witness of violence.*" This clause is unquestionably connected with the preceding one, and implies that raising a false report furnishes the wicked man with a pretext for bringing the man, who is suspected of crime on account of this false report, before a court of law; in consequence of which the originator or propagator of the empty report becomes a witness of injustice and violence.—Ver. 2. Just as little should a man follow a multitude to pervert justice. " *Thou shalt not be behind many* (follow the multitude) *to evil things, nor answer concerning a dispute to incline thyself after many* (*i.e.* thou shalt not give such testimony in connection with any dispute, in which thou takest part with the great majority), *so as to pervert*" (לְהַטּוֹת), *sc.* justice. But, on the other hand, "*neither shalt thou adorn the poor man in his dispute*" (ver. 3), *i.e.* show partiality to the poor or weak man in an unjust cause, out of weak compassion for him. (Compare Lev. xix. 15, a passage which, notwithstanding the fact that הָדַר is applied to favour shown to the great or mighty, overthrows *Knobel's* conjecture, that גָּדֹל should be read for דַּל, inasmuch as it prohibits the showing of favour to the one as much as to the other.)—Vers. 4, 5. Not only was their conduct not to be determined by public opinion, the direction taken by the multitude, or by weak compassion for a poor man; but personal antipathy, enmity, and hatred were not to lead them to injustice or churlish behaviour. On the contrary, if the Israelite saw his enemy's beast straying, he was to bring it back again; and if he saw it lying down under the weight of its burden, he was to help it up again (cf. Deut. xxii. 1–4). The words וְחָדַלְתָּ מֵעֲזֹב וגו׳, " *cease* (desist) *to leave it to him* (thine enemy); *thou shalt loosen it* (let it loose) *with him,*" which have been so variously explained, cannot have any other signification than this: " beware of leaving an ass which has sunk down beneath its burden in a helpless condition, even to thine enemy, to try whether he can help it up alone; rather help him to set it loose from its burden, that it may get up again." This is evident from Deut. xxii. 4, where לֹא הִתְעַלָּמְתָּ, "withdraw not thyself," is substituted for חָדַלְתָּ מֵעֲזֹב, and הָקֵם תָּקִים עִמּוֹ, "set up with him," for "עֹזֵב תַּעֲזֹב עִמּוֹ". From this it is obvious that עֹזֵב is used in the first instance in the sense of leaving it alone, leaving it in a helpless condition, and immediately afterwards in the sense of undoing or letting loose. The peculiar turn given to the expression, "thou shalt cease from leaving," is chosen because the ordinary course, which the natural man adopts, is to leave an enemy to take care of his own affairs, without troubling about either him or his difficulties. Such conduct as this the Israelite was to give up, if he ever found his enemy in need of help.— Vers. 6 sqq. The warning against unkindness towards an enemy is followed by still further prohibitions of injustice in questions of right: viz. in ver. 6, a warning against perverting the right of the poor in his cause; in ver. 7, a general command to keep far away from a false matter, and not to slay the innocent and righteous, i.e. not to be guilty of judicial murder, together with the threat that God would not justify the sinner; and in ver. 8, the command not to accept presents, i.e. to be bribed by gifts, because "the gift makes seeing men (פִּקְחִים open eyes) blind, and perverts the causes of the just." The rendering "words of the righteous" is not correct; for even if we are to understand the expression "seeing men" as referring to judges, the "righteous" can only refer to those who stand at the bar, and have right on their side, which judges who accept of bribes may turn into wrong.—Ver. 9. The warning against oppressing the foreigner, which is repeated from chap. xxii. 20, is not tautological, as Bertheau affirms for the purpose of throwing suspicion upon this verse, but refers to the oppression of a stranger in judicial matters by the refusal of justice, or by harsh and unjust treatment in court (Deut. xxiv. 17, xxvii. 19). "For ye know the soul (animus, the soul as the seat of feeling) of the stranger," i.e. ye know from your own experience in Egypt how a foreigner feels.

Vers. 10–12. Here follow directions respecting the year of rest and day of rest, the first of which lays the foundation for the keeping of the sabbatical and jubilee years, which are afterwards institutedin Lev. xxv., whilst the latter gives prominence to the element of rest and refreshment involved in the Sabbath, which had been already instituted (chap. xx. 9–11), and presses it in favour of beasts of burden, slaves, and foreigners. Neither of these instructions is to be regarded as laying down laws for the feasts; so that they are not to be included among the rights of Israel, which commence at ver. 14. On the contrary, as they are separated from these by ver. 13, they are to be reckoned as forming part of the laws relating to their mutual obligations one towards another. This is evident from the fact, that in both of them the care of the poor stands in the foreground. From this characteristic and design, which are common to both, we may explain the fact, that there is no allusion to the keeping of a Sabbath unto the Lord, as in chap. xx. 10 and Lev. xxv. 2, in connection with either the seventh year or seventh day : all that is mentioned being their sowing and reaping for six years, and working for six days, and then letting the land lie fallow in the seventh year, and their ceasing or resting from labour on the seventh day. "*The seventh year thou shalt let* (thy land) *loose* (שָׁמַט to leave unemployed), *and let it lie; and the poor of thy people shall eat* (the produce which grows of itself), *and their remainder* (what they leave) *shall the beast of the field eat.*" הִנָּפֵשׁ: *lit.* to breathe one's self, to draw breath, *i.e.* to refresh one's self (cf. chap. xxxi. 17; 2 Sam. xvi. 14).—With ver. 13*a* the laws relating to the rights of the people, in their relations to one another, are concluded with the formula enforcing their observance, "*And in all that I say to you, take heed,*" viz. that ye carefully maintain all the rights which I have given you. There is then attached to this, in ver. 13*b*, a warning, which forms the transition to the relation of Israel to Jehovah : "*Make no mention of the name of other gods, neither let it be heard out of thy mouth.*" This forms a very fitting boundary line between the two series of *mishpatim*, inasmuch as the observance and maintenance of both of them depended upon the attitude in which Israel stood towards Jehovah.

Chap. xxiii. 14–19. THE FUNDAMENTAL RIGHTS OF ISRAEL IN ITS RELIGIOUS AND THEOCRATICAL RELATION TO JEHOVAH. —As the observance of the Sabbath and sabbatical year is not instituted in vers. 10–12, so vers. 14–19 do not contain either the original or earliest appointment of the feasts, or a complete law concerning the yearly feasts. They simply command the observance of three feasts during the year, and the appearance of the people three times in the year before the Lord ; that is to say, the holding of three national assemblies to keep a feast before the Lord, or three annual pilgrimages to the sanctuary of Jehovah. The leading points are clearly set forth in vers. 14 and 17, to which the other verses are subordinate. These leading points are מִשְׁפָּטִים or *rights*, conferred upon the people of Israel in their relation to Jehovah ; for keeping a feast to the Lord, and appearing before Him, were both of them privileges bestowed by Jehovah upon His covenant people. Even in itself the festal rejoicing was a blessing in the midst of this life of labour, toil, and trouble ; but when accompanied with the right of appearing before the Lord their God and Redeemer, to whom they were indebted for everything they had and were, it was one that no other nation enjoyed. For though they had their joyous festivals, these festivals bore the same relation to those of Israel, as the dead and worthless gods of the heathen to the living and almighty God of Israel.

Of the three feasts at which Israel was to appear before Jehovah, the feast of *Mazzoth*, or unleavened bread, is referred to as already instituted, by the words " *as I have commanded thee,*" and " *at the appointed time of the earing month,*" which point back to chaps. xii. and xiii.; and all that is added here is, " *ye shall not appear before My face empty.*" " *Not empty :*" *i.e.* not with empty hands, but with sacrificial gifts, answering to the blessing given by the Lord (Deut. xvi. 16, 17). These gifts were devoted partly to the general sacrifices of the feast, and partly to the burnt and peace-offerings which were brought by different individuals to the feasts, and applied to the sacrificial meals (Num. xxviii. and xxix.). This command, which related to all the feasts, and therefore is mentioned at the very outset in connection with the feast of unleavened bread, did indeed impose a duty upon Israel, but such a duty as became a source of blessing to all who performed it. The gifts demanded by God were the tribute, it is true, which the Israelites paid to their God-King, just as all Eastern nations are required to bring presents when appearing in the presence of their kings ; but they were only gifts from God's own blessing, a portion of that which He had bestowed in rich abundance, and they were offered to

God in such a way that the offerer was thereby more and more confirmed in the rights of covenant fellowship. The other two festivals are mentioned here for the first time, and the details are more particularly determined afterwards in Lev. xxiii. 15 sqq., and Num. xxviii. 26 sqq. One was called the *feast of Harvest*, " of the first-fruits of thy labours which thou hast sown in the field," *i.e.* of thy field-labour. According to the subsequent arrangements, the first of the field-produce was to be offered to God, not the first grains of the ripe corn, but the first loaves of bread of white or wheaten flour made from the new corn (Lev. xxiii. 17 sqq.). In chap. xxxiv. 22 it is called the " feast of Weeks," because, according to Lev. xxiii. 15, 16, Deut. xvi. 9, it was to be kept seven weeks after the feast of *Mazzoth;* and the " feast of the first-fruits of wheat harvest," because the loaves of first-fruits to be offered were to be made of wheaten flour. The other of these feasts, *i.e.* the third in the year, is called " *the feast of Ingathering*, at the end of the year, in the gathering in of thy labours out of the field." This general and indefinite allusion to time was quite sufficient for the preliminary institution of the feast. In the more minute directions respecting the feasts given in Lev. xxiii. 34, Num. xxix. 12, it is fixed for the fifteenth day of the seventh month, and placed on an equality with the feast of Mazzoth as a seven days' festival. בְּצֵאת הַשָּׁנָה does not mean after the close of the year, *finito anno*, any more than the corresponding expression in chap. xxxiv. 22, תְּקוּפַת הַשָּׁנָה, signifies at the turning of the year. The year referred to here was the so-called civil year, which began with the preparation of the ground for the harvest-sowing, and ended when all the fruits of the field and garden had been gathered in. No particular day was fixed for its commencement, nor was there any new year's festival; and even after the beginning of the earing month had been fixed upon for the commencement of the year (chap. xii. 2), this still remained in force, so far as all civil matters connected with the sowing and harvest were concerned; though there is no evidence that a double reckoning was carried on at the same time, or that a civil reckoning existed side by side with the religious. בְּאָסְפְּךָ does not mean, " when thou hast gathered," *postquam collegisti;* for בְּ does not stand for אַחַר, nor has the infinitive the force of the preterite. On the contrary, the expression " *at thy gathering*

in," *i.e.* when thou gatherest in, is kept indefinite both here and
in Lev. xxiii. 39, where the month and days in which this feast
was to be kept are distinctly pointed out; and also in Deut.
xvi. 13, in order that the time for the feast might not be made
absolutely dependent upon the complete termination of the
gathering in, although as a rule it would be almost over. The
gathering in of "*thy labours out of the field*" is not to be restricted to the vintage and gathering of fruits: this is evident
not only from the expression "out of the field," which points
to field-produce, but also from the clause in Deut. xvi. 13,
"gathering of the floor and wine-press," which shows clearly
that the words refer to the gathering in of the whole of the
year's produce of corn, fruit, oil, and wine.—Ver. 17. "*Three
times in the year*" (*i.e.*, according to ver. 14 and Deut. xvi. 16,
at the three feasts just mentioned) "*all thy males shall appear
before the face of the Lord Jehovah.*" The command to appear,
i.e. to make a pilgrimage to the sanctuary, was restricted to the
male members of the nation, probably to those above 20 years
of age, who had been included in the census (Num. i. 3). But
this did not prohibit the inclusion of women and boys (cf. 1
Sam. i. 3 sqq., and Luke ii. 41 sqq.).

Vers. 18, 19. The blessing attending their appearing before
the Lord was dependent upon the feasts being kept in the proper
way, by the observance of the three rules laid down in vers. 18
and 19. "*Thou shalt not offer the blood of My sacrifice upon
leavened bread.*" עַל *upon,* as in chap. xii. 8, denoting the basis
upon which the sacrifice was offered. The meaning has been
correctly given by the early commentators, viz. "as long as there
is any leavened bread in your houses," or "until the leaven has
been entirely removed from your houses." The reference made
here to the removal of leaven, and the expression "blood of
My sacrifice," both point to the paschal lamb, which was regarded as *the* sacrifice of Jehovah κατ' ἐξοχήν, on account of its
great importance. *Onkelos* gives this explanation: "My Passover" for "My sacrifice."—"*Neither shall the fat of My feast
remain* (לִין to pass the night) *until the morning.*" "The fat of
My feast" does not mean the fat of My festal sacrifice, for חַג, a
feast, is not used for the sacrifice offered at the feast; it signifies rather the best of My feast, *i.e.* the paschal sacrifice, as we
may see from chap. xxxiv. 25, where "the sacrifice of the feast

of the Passover" is given as the explanation of "the fat of My feast." As the paschal sacrifice was the sacrifice of Jehovah *par excellence*, so the feast of the Passover was *the* feast of Jehovah *par excellence*. The expression " fat of My feast" is not to be understood as referring at all to the fat of the lamb, which was burned upon the altar in the case of the expiatory and whole offerings; for there could have been no necessity for the injunction not to keep this till the morning, inasmuch as those parts of every sacrifice which were set apart for the altar were burned immediately after the sprinkling of the blood. The allusion is to the flesh of the paschal lamb, which was eaten in the night before daybreak, after which anything that remained was to be burned. עַד־בֹּקֶר (without the article) *till morning*, has the same meaning as לַבֹּקֶר "for the (following) morning" in chap. xxxiv. 25.—The next command in ver. 19*a* nas reference to the feast of Harvest, or feast of Weeks. In " *the first-fruits of thy land* " there is an unmistakeable allusion to "the first-fruits of thy labours" in ver. 16. It is true the words, "the first of the first-fruits of thy land thou shalt bring into the house of the Lord thy God," are so general in their character, that we can hardly restrict them to the wave-loaves to be offered as first-fruits at the feast of Weeks, but must interpret them as referring to all the first-fruits, which they had already been commanded not to delay to offer (chap. xxii. 29), and the presentation of which is minutely prescribed in Num. xviii. 12, 13, and Deut. xxvi. 2–11,—including therefore the sheaf of barley to be offered in the second day of the feast of unleavened bread (Lev. xxiii. 9 sqq.). At the same time the reference to the feast of Weeks is certainly to be retained, inasmuch as this feast was an express admonition to Israel, to offer the first òf the fruits of the Lord. In the expression רֵאשִׁית בִּכּוּרֵי, the latter might be understood as explanatory of the former and in apposition to it, since they are both of them applied to the first-fruits of the soil (*vid.* Deut. xxvi. 2, 10, and Num. xviii. 13). But as רֵאשִׁית could hardly need any explanation in this connection, the partitive sense is to be preferred; though it is difficult to decide whether " the first of the first-fruits" signifies the first selection from the fruits that had grown, ripened, and been gathered first,—that is to say, not merely of the entire harvest, but of every separate production of the field and soil, according to the rendering of the LXX. ἀπαρχὰς τῶν πρωτογεννημάτον τῆς γῆς,—or whether the word רֵאשִׁית is used figuratively, and signifies the best of the first-fruits. There is no force in the objection offered to the former view, that "in no other case in which the offering of first-fruits generally is spoken of, is one particular portion represented as holy to Jehovah, but the first-fruits themselves are that portion of the entire harvest which was holy to Jehovah." For, apart from Num. xviii. 12, where a different rendering is sometimes given to ראשית, the expression מֵרֵאשִׁית in Deut. xxvi. 2 shows unmistakeably that only a portion of the first of all the fruit of the ground had to be offered to the Lord. On the other hand, this view is considerably strengthened by the fact, that whilst בִּכּוּר, בִּכּוּרִים signify those fruits which ripened first, i.e. earliest, רֵאשִׁית is used to denote the ἀπαρχή, the first portion or first selection from the whole, not only in Deut. xxvi. 2, 10, but also in Lev. xxiii. 10, and most probably in Num. xviii. 12 as well.—Now if these directions do not refer either exclusively or specially to the loaves of first-fruits of the feast of Weeks, the opinion which has prevailed from the time of *Abarbanel* to that of *Knobel*, that the following command, "Thou shalt not seethe a kid in his mother's milk," refers to the feast of Ingathering, is deprived of its principal support. And any such allusion is rendered very questionable by the fact, that in Deut. xiv. 21, where this command is repeated, it is appended to the prohibition against eating the flesh of an animal that had been torn to pieces. Very different explanations have been given to the command. In the *Targum, Mishnah*, etc., it is regarded as a general prohibition against eating flesh prepared with milk. *Luther* and others suppose it to refer to the cooking of the kid, before it has been weaned from its mother's milk. But the actual reference is to the cooking of a kid in the milk of its own mother, as indicating a contempt of the relation which God has established and sanctified between parent and young, and thus subverting the divine ordinances. As kids were a very favourite food (Gen. xxvii. 9, 14 ; Judg. vi. 19, xiii. 15 ; 1 Sam. xvi. 20), it is very likely that by way of improving the flavour they were sometimes cooked in milk. According to *Aben Ezra* and *Abarbanel*, this was a custom adopted by the *Ishmaelites;* and at the present day the Arabs are in the habit of cooking lamb in sour milk. A restriction is placed upon this custom in the prohibition before us, but there is no intention to prevent the introduction of a superstitious usage customary at the sacrificial meals of other nations, which *Spencer* and *Knobel* have sought to establish as at all events probable, though without any definite historical proofs, and for the most part on the strength of far-fetched analogies.

Chap. xxiii. 20–33. RELATION OF JEHOVAH TO ISRAEL. —The declaration of the rights conferred by Jehovah upon His people is closed by promises, through which, on the one hand, God insured to the nation the gifts and benefits involved in their rights, and, on the other hand, sought to promote that willing-ness and love which were indispensable to the fulfilment of the duties incumbent upon every individual in consequence of the rights conferred upon them. These promises secured to the people not only the protection and help of God during their journey through the desert, and in the conquest of Canaan, but also preservation and prosperity when they had taken possession of the land.—Ver. 20. Jehovah would send an angel before them, who should guard them on the way from injury and de-struction, and bring them to the place prepared for them, *i.e.* to Canaan. The name of Jehovah was in this angel (ver. 21), that is to say, Jehovah revealed Himself in him; and hence he is called in chap. xxxiii. 15, 16, the face of Jehovah, because the essential nature of Jehovah was manifested in him. This angel was not a created spirit, therefore, but the manifestation of Jehovah Himself, who went before them in the pillar of cloud and fire, to guide and to defend them (chap. xiii. 21). But because it was Jehovah who was guiding His people in the person of the angel, He demanded unconditional obedience (ver. 21), and if they provoked Him (תַּמֵּר for תָּמֶר, see chap. xiii. 18) by disobedience, He would not pardon their transgression; but if they followed Him and hearkened to His voice, He would be an enemy to their enemies, and an adversary to their adversa-ries (ver. 22). And when the angel of the Lord had brought them to the Canaanites and exterminated the latter, Israel was still to yield the same obedience, by not serving the gods of the Canaanites, or doing after their works, *i.e.* by not making any idolatrous images, but destroying them (these works), and smit-ing to pieces the pillars of their idolatrous worship (מַצֵּבֹת does not mean statues erected as idols, but memorial stones or columns

dedicated to idols : see my comm. on 1 Kings xiv. 23), and
serving Jehovah alone. Then would He bless them in the land
with bountiful provision, health, fruitfulness, and length of life
(vers. 23–26). " Bread and water" are named, as being the
provisions which are indispensable to the maintenance of life, as
in Isa. iii. 1, xxx. 20, xxxiii. 16. The taking away of " sickness" (cf. xv. 26) implied the removal of everything that could
endanger life. The absence of anything that miscarried, or was
barren, insured the continuance and increase of the nation ; and
the promise that their days should be fulfilled, *i.e.* that they
should not be liable to a premature death (cf. Isa. lxv. 20), was
a pledge of their well-being.—Vers. 27 sqq. But the most
important thing of all for Israel was the previous conquest of
the promised land. And in this God gave it a special promise
of His almighty aid. " *I will send My fear before thee.*" This
fear was to be the result of the terrible acts of God performed
on behalf of Israel, the rumour of which would spread before
them and fill their enemies with fear and trembling (cf. chap.
xv. 14 sqq. ; Deut. ii. 25 ; and Josh. ii. 11, where the beginning
of the fulfilment is described), throwing into confusion and
putting to flight every people against whom (אֲשֶׁר — בָּהֶם) Israel
came. נָתַן אֶת־אֹיֵב עֹרֶף to give the enemy to the neck, *i.e.* to
cause him to turn his back, or flee (cf. Ps. xviii. 41, xxi. 13 ;
Josh. vii. 8, 12). אֵלֶיךָ : in the direction towards thee.—Ver. 28.
In addition to the fear of God, hornets (הַצִּרְעָה construed as a
generic word with the collective article), a very large species
of wasp, that was greatly dreaded both by man and beast on
account of the acuteness of its sting, should come and drive out
the Canaanites, of whom three tribes are mentioned *instar
omnium*, from before the Israelites. Although it is true that
Ælian (*hist. anim.* 11, 28) relates that the Phaselians, who
dwelt near the Solymites, and therefore probably belonged to
the Canaanites, were driven out of their country by wasps, and
Bochart (*Hieroz.* iii. pp. 409 sqq.) has collected together accounts
of different tribes that have been frightened away from their
possessions by frogs, mice, and other vermin, " the sending of
hornets before the Israelites" is hardly to be taken literally, not
only because there is not a word in the book of Joshua about the
Canaanites being overcome and exterminated in any such way,
but chiefly on account of Josh. xxiv. 12, where Joshua says that

God sent the hornet before them, and drove out the two kings of the Amorites, referring thereby to their defeat and destruction by the Israelites through the miraculous interposition of God, and thus placing the figurative use of the term hornet beyond the possibility of doubt. These hornets, however, which are very aptly described in Wisdom xii. 8, on the basis of this passage, as πρόδρομους, the pioneers of the army of Jehovah, do not denote merely *varii generis mala,* as *Rosenmüller* supposes, but *acerrimos timoris aculeos, quibus quodammodo volantibus rumoribus pungebantur, ut fugerent (Augustine, quæst. 27 in Jos.).* If the fear of God which fell upon the Canaanites threw them into such confusion and helpless despair, that they could not stand before Israel, but turned their backs towards them, the stings of alarm which followed this fear would completely drive them away. Nevertheless God would not drive them away at once, " in one year," lest the land should become a desert for want of men to cultivate it, and the wild beasts should multiply against Israel; in other words, lest the beasts of prey should gain the upper hand and endanger the lives of man and beast (Lev. xxvi. 22 ; Ezek. xiv. 15, 21), which actually was the case after the carrying away of the ten tribes (2 Kings xvii. 25, 26). He would drive them out by degrees (מְעַט מְעַט, only used here and in Deut. vii. 22), until Israel was sufficiently increased to take possession of the land, *i.e.* to occupy the whole of the country. This promise was so far fulfilled, according to the books of Joshua and Judges, that after the subjugation of the Canaanites in the south and north of the land, when all the kings who fought against Israel had been smitten and slain and their cities captured, the entire land was divided among the tribes of Israel, in order that they might exterminate the remaining Canaanites, and take possession of those portions of the land that had not yet been conquered (Josh. xiii. 1-7). But the different tribes soon became weary of the task of exterminating the Canaanites, and began to enter into alliance with them, and were led astray by them to the worship of idols ; whereupon God punished them by withdrawing His assistance, and they were oppressed and humiliated by the Canaanites because of their apostasy from the Lord (Judg. i. and ii.).

Vers. 31 sqq. The divine promise closes with a general indication of the boundaries of the land, whose inhabitants Jehovah would give up to the Israelites to drive them out, and with a warning against forming alliances with them and their gods, lest they should lead Israel astray to sin, and thus become a snare to it. On the basis of the promise in Gen. xv. 18, certain grand and prominent points are mentioned, as constituting the boundaries towards both the east and west. On the west the boundary extended from the Red Sea (see chap. xiii. 18) to the sea of the Philistines, or Mediterranean Sea, the south-eastern shore of which was inhabited by the Philistines; and on the east from the desert, *i.e.*, according to Deut. xi. 24, the desert of Arabia, to the river (Euphrates). The poetic suffix מוֹ affixed to גֵּרַשְׁתָּ answers to the elevated oratorical style. Making a covenant with them and their gods would imply the recognition and toleration of them, and, with the sinful tendencies of Israel, would be inevitably followed by the worship of idols. The first כִּי in ver. 33 signifies *if*; the second, *imo*, verily, and serves as an energetic introduction to the apodosis. מוֹקֵשׁ, a snare (*vid.* chap. x. 7); here a cause of destruction, inasmuch as apostasy from God is invariably followed by punishment (Judg. ii. 3).

Chap. xxiv. 1, 2. These two verses form part of the address of God in chap. xx. 22–xxiii. 33; for וְאֶל מֹשֶׁה אָמַר (" *but to Moses He said*") cannot be the commencement of a fresh address, which would necessarily require וַיֹּאמֶר אֶל מ' (cf. ver. 12, chap. xix. 21, xx. 22). The turn given to the expression וְאֶל מ' presupposes that God had already spoken to others, or that what had been said before related not to Moses himself, but to other persons. But this cannot be affirmed of the decalogue, which applied to Moses quite as much as to the entire nation (a sufficient refutation of *Knobel's* assertion, that these verses are a continuation of chap. xix. 20–25, and are linked on to the decalogue), but only of the address concerning the *mishpatim*, or " rights," which commences with chap. xx. 22, and, according to chap. xx. 22 and xxi. 1, was intended for the nation, and addressed to it, even though it was through the medium of Moses. What God said to the people as establishing its rights, is here followed by what He said to Moses himself, namely, that he was to go up to Jehovah, along with Aaron, Nadab, Abihu, and seventy elders. At the same time, it is of course implied that Moses, who had ascended the mountain with Aaron alone (chap.

xx. 21), was first of all to go down again and repeat to the people
the " *rights*" which God had communicated to him, and only
when this had been done, to ascend again with the persons
named. According to vers. 3 and 12 (? 9), this is what Moses
really did. But Moses alone was to go near to Jehovah : the
others were to worship afar off, and the people were not to come
up at all.

CONCLUSION OF THE COVENANT.—CHAP. XXIV. 3–18.

The ceremony described in vers. 3–11 is called " the covenant which Jehovah made with Israel" (ver. 8). It was opened
by Moses, who recited to the people " *all the words of Jehovah*"
(*i.e.* not the decalogue, for the people had heard this directly
from the mouth of God Himself, but the words in chap. xx.
22–26), and " *all the rights*" (chap. xxi.–xxiii.) ; whereupon the
people answered unanimously (קוֹל אֶחָד), " *All the words which
Jehovah hath spoken will we do.*" This constituted the preparation for the conclusion of the covenant. It was necessary that
the people should not only know what the Lord imposed upon
them in the covenant about to be made with them, and what He
promised them, but that they should also declare their willingness to perform what was imposed upon them. The covenant
itself was commenced by Moses writing all the words of Jehovah
in " *the book of the covenant*" (vers. 4 and 7), for the purpose of
preserving them in an official record. The next day, early in
the morning, he built an altar at the foot of the mountain, and
erected twelve boundary-stones or pillars for the twelve tribes,
most likely round about the altar and at some distance from it,
so as to prepare the soil upon which Jehovah was about to enter
into union with the twelve tribes. As the altar indicated the
presence of Jehovah, being the place where the Lord would
come to His people to bless them (chap. xx. 24), so the twelve
pillars, or boundary-stones, did not serve as mere memorials of
the conclusion of the covenant, but were to indicate the place of
the twelve tribes, and represent their presence also.—Ver. 5.
After the foundation and soil had been thus prepared in the
place of sacrifice, for the fellowship which Jehovah was about
to establish with His people ; Moses sent young men of the children of Israel to prepare the sacrifices, and directed them to offer
burnt-offering and sacrifice slain-offerings, viz. שְׁלָמִים, " *peace-*

offerings (see at Lev. iii. 1) *for Jehovah,*" for which purpose פָּרִים,
bullocks, or young oxen, were used. The young men were not
first-born sons, who had officiated as priests previous to the
institution of the Levitical priesthood, according to the natural
right of primogeniture, as *Onkelos* supposes; nor were they the
sons of Aaron, as *Augustine* maintains: they simply acted as
servants of Moses; and the priestly duty of sprinkling the blood
was performed by him as the mediator of the covenant. It is
merely as *young* men, therefore, *i.e.* as strong and active, that
they are introduced in this place, and not as representatives of
the nation, " by whom the sacrifice was presented, and whose
attitude resembled that of a youth just ready to enter upon his
course" (*Kurtz*, O. C. iii. 143). For, as *Oehler* says, " this
was not a sacrifice presented by the nation on its own account.
The primary object was to establish that fellowship, by virtue of
which it could draw near to Jehovah in sacrifice. Moreover,
according to vers. 1 and 9, the nation possessed its proper representatives in the seventy elders" (*Herzog's* Cyclopædia). But
even though these sacrifices were not offered by the representatives of the nation, and for this very reason Moses selected
young men from among the people to act as servants at this
ceremony, they had so far a substitutionary position, that in
their persons the nation was received into fellowship with God
by means of the sprinkling of the blood, which was performed
in a peculiar manner, to suit the unique design of this sacrificial
ceremony.—Vers. 6–8. The blood was divided into two parts.
One half was swung by Moses upon the altar (זָרַק to swing,
shake, or pour out of the vessel, in distinction from הִזָּה to
sprinkle); the other half he put into basins, and after he had
read the book of the covenant to the people, and they had promised to do and follow all the words of Jehovah, he sprinkled
it upon the people with these words: " *Behold the blood of the
covenant, which Jehovah has made with you over all these words.*"
As several animals were slaughtered, and all of them young
oxen, there must have been a considerable quantity of blood
obtained, so that the one half would fill several basins, and many
persons might be sprinkled with it as it was being swung about.
The division of the blood had reference to the two parties to
the covenant, who were to be brought by the covenant into a
living unity; but it had no connection whatever with the heathen

customs adduced by *Bähr* and *Knobel*, in which the parties to a treaty mixed their own blood together. For this was not a mixture of different kinds of blood, but it was a division of one blood, and that *sacrificial* blood, in which animal life was offered instead of human life, making expiation as a pure life for sinful man, and by virtue of this expiation restoring the fellowship between God and man which had been destroyed by sin. But the sacrificial blood itself only acquired this signification through the sprinkling or swinging upon the altar, by virtue of which the human soul was received, in the soul of the animal sacrificed for man, into the fellowship of the divine grace manifested upon the altar, in order that, through the power of this sin-forgiving and sin-destroying grace, it might be sanctified to a new and holy life. In this way the sacrificial blood acquired the signification of a vital principle endued with the power of divine grace ; and this was communicated to the people by means of the sprinkling of the blood. As the only reason for dividing the sacrificial blood into two parts was, that the blood sprinkled upon the altar could not be taken off again and sprinkled upon the people ; the two halves of the blood are to be regarded as one blood, which was first of all sprinkled upon the altar, and then upon the people. In the blood sprinkled upon the altar, the natural life of the people was given up to God, as a life that had passed through death, to be pervaded by His grace ; and then through the sprinkling upon the people it was restored to them again, as a life renewed by the grace of God. In this way the blood not only became a bond of union between Jehovah and His people, but as the blood of the covenant, it became a vital power, holy and divine, uniting Israel and its God ; and the sprinkling of the people with this blood was an actual renewal of life, a transposition of Israel into the kingdom of God, in which it was filled with the powers of God's spirit of grace, and sanctified into a kingdom of priests, a holy nation of Jehovah (chap. xix. 6). And this covenant was made " upon all the words" which Jehovah had spoken, and the people had promised to observe. Consequently it had for its foundation the divine law and right, as the rule of life for Israel.

Vers. 9-11. Through their consecration with the blood of the covenant, the Israelites were qualified to ascend the mountain, and there behold the God of Israel and celebrate the covenant meal; of course, not the whole of the people, for that would have been impracticable on physical grounds, but the nation in the persons of its representatives, viz. the seventy elders, with Aaron and his two eldest sons. The fact that the latter were summoned along with the elders had reference to their future election to the priesthood, the bearers of which were to occupy the position of mediators between Jehovah and the nation, an office for which this was a preparation. The reason for choosing *seventy* out of the whole body of elders (ver. 3) is to be found in the historical and symbolical significance of this number (see vol. i. p. 374). " *They saw the God of Israel.*" This title is very appropriately given to Jehovah here, because He, the God of the fathers, had become in truth the God of Israel through the covenant just made. We must not go beyond the limits drawn in chap. xxxiii. 20-23 in our conceptions of what constituted the sight (חָזָה, ver. 11) of God; at the same time we must regard it as a vision of God in some form of manifestation which rendered the divine nature discernible to the human eye. Nothing is said as to the form in which God manifested Himself. This silence, however, is not intended " to indicate the imperfection of their sight of God," as *Baumgarten* affirms, nor is it to be explained, as *Hofmann* supposes, on the ground that " what they saw differed from what the people had constantly before their eyes simply in this respect, that after they had entered the darkness, which enveloped the mountain that burned as it were with fire at its summit, the fiery sign separated from the cloud, and assumed a shape, beneath which it was bright and clear, as an image of untroubled bliss." The words are evidently intended to affirm something more than, that they saw the fiery form in which God manifested Himself to the people, and that whilst the fire was ordinarily enveloped in a cloud, they saw it upon the mountain without the cloud. For, since Moses saw the form (תְּמוּנָה) of Jehovah (Num. xii. 8), we may fairly conclude, notwithstanding the fact that, according to ver. 2, the representatives of the nation were not to draw near to Jehovah, and without any danger of contradicting Deut. iv. 12 and 15, that they also saw a form of God. Only this form is not described, in order that no encouragement might be given to the inclination of the people to make likenesses of Jehovah. Thus we find that Isaiah gives no description of the form in which he saw the Lord sitting upon a high and lofty throne (Isa. vi. 1). Ezekiel is the first to describe the form of Jehovah which he saw in the vision, " as the appearance of a man" (Ezek. i. 26; compare Dan. vii. 9 and 13). " *And there was under His feet as it were work of clear sapphire* (לִבְנַת, from לְבֵנָה whiteness, clearness, not from לְבֵנָה a brick[1]), *and as the material* (עֶצֶם body, substance) *of heaven in brilliancy,*"—to indicate that the God of Israel was enthroned above the heaven in super-terrestrial glory and undisturbed blessedness. And God was willing that His people should share in this blessedness, for " *He laid not His hand upon the nobles of Israel,*" i.e. did not attack them. " *They saw God, and did eat and drink,*" i.e. they celebrated thus near to Him the sacrificial meal of the peace-offerings, which had been sacrificed at the conclusion of the covenant, and received in this covenant meal a foretaste of the precious and glorious gifts with which God would endow and refresh His redeemed people in His kingdom. As the promise in chap. xix. 5, 6, with which God opened the way for the covenant at Sinai, set clearly before the nation that had been rescued from Egypt the ultimate goal of its divine calling; so this termination of the ceremony was intended to give to the nation, in the persons of its representatives, a tangible pledge of the glory of the goal that was set before it. The sight of the God of Israel was a foretaste of the blessedness of the sight of God in eternity, and the covenant meal upon the mountain before the face of God was a type of the marriage supper of the Lamb, to which the Lord will call, and at which He will present His perfected Church in the day of the full revelation of His glory (Rev. xix. 7–9).

Vers. 12–18 prepare the way for the subsequent revelation recorded in chap. xxv.–xxxi., which Moses received concerning the erection of the sanctuary. At the conclusion of the covenant meal, the representatives of the nation left the mountain along with Moses. This is not expressly stated, indeed; since it followed as a matter of course that they returned to the camp, when the festival for which God had called them up was concluded. A command was then issued again to Moses to ascend the mountain, and remain there (וֶהְיֵה־שָׁם), for He was about to give him the tables of stone, with (וֹ as in Gen. iii. 24) the law and commandments, which He had written for their instruction

---

[1] This is the derivation adopted by the English translators in their rendering " *paved* work."—TR.

(cf. xxxi. 18).—Vers. 13, 14. When Moses was preparing to ascend the mountain with his servant Joshua (*vid.* xvii. 9), he ordered the elders to remain in the camp (בָּזֶה, *i.e.* where they were) till their return, and appcinted Aaron and Hur (*vid.* xvii. 10) as administrators of justice in case of any disputes occurring among the people. מִי־בַעַל דְּבָרִים : whoever has matters, matters of dispute (on this meaning of בַּעַל see Gen. xxxvii. 19). —Vers. 15–17. When he ascended the mountain, upon which the glory of Jehovah dwelt, it was covered for six days with the cloud, and the glory itself appeared to the Israelites in the camp below like devouring fire (cf. xix. 16); and on the seventh day He called Moses into the cloud. Whether Joshua followed him we are not told; but it is evident from chap. xxxii. 17 that he was with him on the mountain, though, judging from ver. 2 and chap. xxxiii. 11, he would not go into the immediate presence of God.—Ver. 18. "*And Moses was on the mountain forty days and forty nights,*" including the six days of waiting,—the whole time without eating and drinking (Deut. ix. 9). The number *forty* was certainly significant, since it was not only repeated on the occasion of his second protracted stay upon Mount Sinai (xxxiv. 28; Deut. ix. 18), but occurred again in the forty days of Elijah's journey to Horeb the mount of God in the strength of the food received from the angel (1 Kings xix. 8), and in the fasting of Jesus at the time of His temptation (Matt. iv. 2; Luke iv. 2), and even appears to have been significant in the forty years of Israel's wandering in the desert (Deut. viii. 2). In all these cases the number refers to a period of temptation, of the trial of faith, as well as to a period of the strengthening of faith through the miraculous support bestowed by God.

DIRECTIONS CONCERNING THE SANCTUARY AND PRIEST-HOOD.—CHAP. XXV.–XXXI.

To give a definite external form to the covenant concluded with His people, and construct a visible bond of fellowship in which He might manifest Himself to the people and they might draw near to Him as their God, Jehovah told Moses that the Israelites were to erect Him a sanctuary, that He might dwell in the midst of them (chap. xxv. 8). The construction and arrangement of this sanctuary were determined in all respects by

God Himself, who showed to Moses, when upon the mountain, a pattern of the dwelling and its furniture, and prescribed with great minuteness both the form and materials of all the different parts of the sanctuary and all the things required for the sacred service. If the sanctuary was to answer its purpose, the erection of it could not be left to the inventive faculty of any man whatever, but must proceed from Him, who was there to manifest Himself to the nation, as the Holy One, in righteousness and grace. The people could only carry out what God appointed, and could only fulfil their covenant duty, by the readiness with which they supplied the materials required for the erection of the sanctuary and completed the work with their own hands. The divine directions extended to all the details, because they were all of importance in relation to the design of God. The account therefore is so elaborate, that it contains a description not only of the directions of God with reference to the whole and every separate part (chap. xxv.–xxxi.), but also of the execution of the work in all its details (chap. xxxv.–xl.).

The following is the plan upon which this section is arranged. After the command of God to the people to offer gifts for the sanctuary about to be erected, which forms the introduction to the whole (chap. xxv. 1–9), the further directions commence with a description of the ark of the covenant, which Jehovah had appointed as His throne in the sanctuary, that is to say, as it were, with the sanctuary in the sanctuary (chap. xxv. 10–22). Then follow—(1) the table of shew-bread and the golden candlestick (vers. 23–40), as the two things by means of which the continual communion of Israel with Jehovah was to be maintained; (2) the construction of the dwelling, with an account of the position to be occupied by the three things already named (chap. xxvi.); (3) the altar of burnt-offering, together with the court which was to surround the holy dwelling (chap. xxvii. 1–19). This is immediately followed by the command respecting the management of the candlestick (vers. 20, 21), which prepares the way for an account of the institution of the priesthood, and the investiture and consecration of the priests (chap. xxviii. and xxix.), and by the directions as to the altar of incense, and the service to be performed at it (chap. xxx. 1–10); after which, there only remain a few subordinate instructions to complete the whole (chap. xxx. 11–xxxi. 17). "The description of the entire sanctuary commences, therefore," as *Ranke* has aptly observed, " with the ark of the law, the place of the manifestation of Jehovah, and terminates with the altar of incense, which stood immediately in front of it." The dwelling was erected round Jehovah's seat, and round this the court. The priests first of all presented the sacrifices upon the altar of burnt-offering, and then proceeded into the holy place and drew near to Jehovah. The highest act in the daily service of the priests was evidently this standing before Jehovah at the altar of incense, which was only separated by the curtain from the most holy place.

Chap. xxv. 1-9 (cf. chap. xxxv. 1-9). The Israelites were to bring to the Lord a heave-offering (תְּרוּמָה, from רוּם, a gift lifted, or heaved by a man from his own property to present to the Lord ; see at Lev. ii. 9), " *on the part of every one whom his heart drove,*" *i.e.* whose heart was willing (cf. נְדִיב לְבּוֹ chap. xxxv. 5, 22) : viz. gold, silver, brass, etc.—Ver. 4. תְּכֵלֶת, ὑάκινθος, purple of a dark blue shade, approaching black rather than bright blue. אַרְגָּמָן, πορφύρα (Chald. אַרְגְּוָן, 2 Chron. ii. 6 ; Dan. v. 7, 16;—Sanskrit, *râgaman* or *râgavan, colore rubro præditus*), true purple of a dark red colour. תּוֹלַעַת שָׁנִי, literally the crimson prepared from the dead bodies and nests of the glow-worm,[1] then the scarlet-red purple, or crimson. שֵׁשׁ, βύσσος, from שׁוּשׁ to be white, a fine white cotton fabric, not linen, muslin, or net. עִזִּים goats, here goats' hair (τρίχες αἰγείαι, LXX.).—Ver. 5. עֹרֹת אֵילִם מְאָדָּמִים rams' skins reddened, *i.e.* dyed red. תַּחַשׁ is either the seal, *phoca,* or else, as this is not known to exist in the Arabian Gulf, the φῶκος = φώκαινα of the ancients, as *Knobel* supposes, or κῆτος θαλάσσιον ὅμοιον δελφῖνι, the sea-cow (*Manati, Halicora*), which is found in the Red Sea, and has a skin that is admirably adapted for sandals. *Hesychius* supposes it to have been the latter, which is probably the same as the large fish *Tûn* or *Atûm,* that is caught in the Red Sea, and belongs to the same species as the *Halicora* (*Robinson,* Pal. i. p. 170) ; as its skin is also used by the Bedouin Arabs for making sandals (*Burckhardt,* Syr. p. 861). In the *Manati* the upper skin differs from the under ; the former being larger, thicker, and coarser than the latter, which is only two

[1] *Glanzwurm :* " the Linnean name is *coccus ilicis.* It frequents the boughs of a species of *ilex ;* on these it lays its eggs in groups, which become covered with a kind of down." *Smith's* Dictionary, Art. Colours.—TR.

lines in thickness and very tough, so that the skin would be well adapted either for the thick covering of tents or for the finer kinds of ornamental sandals (Ezek. xvi. 10). שִׁטִּים עֲצֵי acacia-wood. שִׁטָּה for שִׁנְטָה, the true acacia (*acacia vera*), which grows in Egypt and on the Arabian peninsula into a tree of the size of a nut-tree, or even larger;[1] the only tree in *Arabia deserta* from which planks could be cut, and the wood of which is very light and yet very durable.—Ver. 6. *Oil for the candlestick* (see at chap. xxvii. 20). בְּשָׂמִים perfumes, spices for the anointing oil (see at chap. xxx. 22 sqq.), and for the incense (הַפַּמִּים, *lit.* the scents, because the materials of which it was composed were not all of them fragrant; see at chap. xxx. 34 sqq.). —Ver. 7. Lastly, *precious stones*, אַבְנֵי שֹׁהַם probably beryls (see at Gen. ii. 12), for the ephod (chap. xxviii. 9), and אַבְנֵי מִלֻּאִים, *lit.* stones of filling, *i.e.* jewels that are set (see chap. xxviii. 16 sqq.). On *ephod* (אֵפֹד), see at chap. xxviii. 6; and on חֹשֶׁן, at chap. xxviii. 15. The precious stones were presented by the princes of the congregation (chap. xxxv. 27).

Vers. 8, 9. With these freewill-offerings they were to make the Lord a sanctuary, that He might dwell in the midst of them (see at ver. 22). "*According to all that I let thee see* (show thee), *the pattern of the dwelling and the pattern of all its furniture, so shall ye make it.*" The participle מַרְאֶה does not refer to the past; and there is nothing to indicate that it does, either in ver. 40,

---

[1] See *Abdallatif's* Merkwürdigkeiten Aegyptens, and *Rosenmüller, Althk.* iv. i. pp. 278-9. This genuine acacia, *Sont*, must not be confounded, according to *Robinson* (Pal. 2, 350), with the *Acacia gumnifera* (*Talh*). *Seetzen* also makes a distinction between the *Thollhh*, the *Szont* of the Egyptians, and the *Szeiâl*, and between an acacia which produces gum and one which does not; but he also observes that the same tree is called both *Thollhh* and *Szeiâl* in different places. He then goes on to say that he did not find a single tree large enough to furnish planks of ten cubits in length and one and a half in breadth for the construction of the ark (he means, of the tabernacle), and he therefore conjectures that the Israelites may have gone to Egypt for the materials with which to build the tabernacle. But he has overlooked the fact, that it is not stated in the text of the Bible that the boards of the tabernacle, which were a cubit and a half in breadth, were cut from one plank of the breadth named; and also that the trees in the valleys of the peninsula of Sinai are being more and more sacrificed to the charcoal trade of the Bedouin Arabs (see p. 71), and therefore that no conclusion can be drawn from the present condition of the trees as to what they were in the far distant antiquity.

where "in the mount" occurs, or in the use of the preterite in chap. xxvi. 30, xxvii. 8. It does not follow from the expression, "which is showed thee *in the mount*," that Moses had already left the mountain and returned to the camp; and the use of the preterite in the passages last named may be simply explained, either on the supposition that the sight of the pattern or model of the whole building and its component parts preceded the description of the different things required for the completion of the building, or that the instructions to make the different parts in such and such a way, pointed to a time when the sight of the model really belonged to the past. On the other hand, the model for the building could not well be shown to Moses, before he had been told that the gifts to be made by the people were to be devoted to the building of a sanctuary. תַּבְנִית, from בָּנָה to build, *lit.* a building, then a figure of anything, a copy or representation of different things, Deut. iv. 17 sqq.; a drawing or sketch, 2 Kings xvi. 10: it never means the original, not even in Ps. cxliv. 12, as *Delitzsch* supposes (see his Com. on Heb. viii. 5). In such passages as 1 Chron. xxviii. 11, 12, 19, where it may be rendered plan, it does not signify an original, but simply means a model or drawing, founded upon an idea, or taken from some existing object, according to which a building was to be constructed. Still less can the object connected with תבנית in the genitive be understood as referring to the original, from which the תבנית was taken; so that we cannot follow the Rabbins in their interpretation of this passage, as affirming that the heavenly originals of the tabernacle and its furniture had been shown to Moses in a vision upon the mountain. What was shown to him was simply a picture or model of the earthly tabernacle and its furniture, which were to be made by him. Both Acts vii. 44 and Heb. viii. 5 are perfectly reconcilable with this interpretation of our verse, which is the only one that can be grammatically sustained. The words of Stephen, that Moses was to make the tabernacle κατὰ τὸν τύπον ὃν ἑωράκει, "according to the fashion that he had seen," are so indefinite, that the text of Exodus must be adduced to explain them. And when the writer of the Epistle to the Hebrews cites the words, "See that thou make all things κατὰ τὸν τύπον τὸν δειχθέντα σοι ἐν τῷ ὄρει" (according to the pattern showed to thee in the mount), from ver. 40 of this chapter, as a proof the

Levitical priests only served the type and shadow of heavenly things (τῶν ἐπουρανίων); it is true, his words may be understood as showing that he regarded the earthly tabernacle with all its arrangements as only the counterpart and copy of a heavenly original. But this interpretation is neither necessary nor well founded. For although the author, by following the Sept., in which בְּתַבְנִיתָם is rendered κατὰ τὸν τύπον, the suffix being dropped, leaves it just a possible thing to understand the τύπος shown to Moses as denoting a heavenly tabernacle (or temple); yet he has shown very clearly that this was not his own view, when he explains the "patterns of things in the heavens" (ὑπο-δείγματα τῶν ἐν οὐρανοῖς) and "the true" things (τὰ ἀληθινά) of both the tabernacle and its furniture as denoting the "heaven" (οὐρανός) into which Christ had entered, and not any temple in heaven. If the ἐπουράνια are heaven itself, the τύπος showed to Moses cannot have been a temple in heaven, but either heaven itself, or, more probably still, as there could be no necessity for this to be shown to Moses in a pictorial representation, a picture of heavenly things or divine realities, which was shown to Moses that he might copy and embody it in the earthly tabernacle.[1] If we understand the verse before us in this sense, it merely expresses what is already implied in the fact itself. If God showed Moses a picture or model of the tabernacle, and in-

---

[1] The conclusion drawn by *Delitzsch* (Hebräerbrief, p. 337), that because the author does not refer to anything between the ἐπουράνια and their ἀντίτυπα (chap. ix. 24), the τύπος can only have consisted of the ἐπουράνια themselves, is a mistake. All that the premises preclude, is the intervention of any objective reality, or third material object, but not the introduction of a pictorial representation, through which Moses was shown how to copy the heavenly realities and embody them in an earthly form. The earthly tent would no more be a copy of the copy of a heavenly original in this case, than a palace built according to a model is a copy of that model. Moreover, *Delitzsch* himself thinks it is "not conceivable that, when Moses was favoured with a view of the heavenly world, it was left to him to embody what he saw in a material form, to bring it within the limits of space." He therefore assumes, both for the reason assigned, and because "no mortal has ever looked directly at heavenly things," that "inasmuch as what was seen could not be directly reflected in the mirror of his mind, not to mention the retina of his eye, it was set before him in a visible form, and according to the operation of God who showed it, in a manner adapted to serve as a model of the earthly sanctuary to be erected." Thus he admits that it is true that Moses did not see the heavenly world itself, but only a copy of it that was shown to him by God.

structed him to make everything exactly according to this pattern, we must assume that in the tabernacle and its furniture heavenly realities were to be expressed in earthly forms; or, to put it more clearly, that the thoughts of God concerning salvation and His kingdom, which the earthly building was to embody and display, were visibly set forth in the pattern shown. The symbolical and typical significance of the whole building necessarily follows from this, though without our being obliged to imitate the Rabbins, and seek in the tabernacle the counterpart or copy of a heavenly temple. What these divine thoughts were that were embodied in the tabernacle, can only be gathered from the arrangement and purpose of the whole building and its separate parts; and upon this point the description furnishes so much information, that when read in the light of the whole of the covenant revelation, it gives to all the leading points precisely the clearness that we require.

Vers. 10–22. THE ARK OF THE COVENANT (cf. chap. xxxvii. 1–9).—They were to make an ark (אָרוֹן) of acacia-wood, two cubits and a half long, one and a half broad, and one and a half high, and to plate it with pure gold both within and without. Round about it they were to construct a golden זֵר, *i.e.* probably a golden rim, encircling it like an ornamental wreath. They were also to cast four golden rings and fasten them to the four feet (פְּעָמֹת walking feet, feet bent as if for walking) of the ark, two on either side; and to cut four poles of acacia-wood and plate them with gold, and put them through the rings for carrying the ark. The poles were to remain in the rings, without moving from them, *i.e.* without being drawn out, that the bearers might not touch the ark itself (Num. iv. 15).—Ver. 16. Into this ark Moses was to put " the testimony" (הָעֵדֻת; cf. chap. xl. 20). This is the name given to the two tables of stone, upon which the ten words spoken by God to the whole nation were written, and which Moses was to receive from God (chap. xxiv. 12). Because these ten words were the declaration of God upon the basis of which the covenant was concluded (chap. xxxiv. 27, 28; Deut. iv. 13, x. 1, 2), these tables were called the tables of testimony (chap. xxxi. 18, xxxiv. 29), or tables of the covenant (Deut. ix. 9, xi. 15).—Vers. 17 sqq. In addition to this, Moses was to make a *capporeth* (ἱλαστήριον ἐπίθεμα,

LXX.; *propitiatorium, Vulg.*), an atoning covering. The meaning *operculum*, lid (*Ges.*), cannot be sustained, notwithstanding the fact that the *capporeth* was placed upon the ark (ver. 21) and covered the tables laid within it; for the verb כפר has not the literal signification of covering or covering up either in *Kal* or *Piel*. In *Kal* it only occurs in Gen. vi. 14, where it means to pitch or tar; in *Piel* it is only used in the figurative sense of covering up sin or guilt, *i.e.* of making atonement. 1 Chron. xxviii. 11 is decisive on this point, where the holy of holies, in which the *capporeth* was, is called בֵּית הַכַּפֹּרֶת, which cannot possibly mean the covering-house, but must signify the house of atonement. The force of this passage is not weakened by the remark made by *Delitzsch* and others, to the effect that it was only in the later usage of the language that the idea of covering gave place to that of the covering up or expiation of sin; for neither in the earlier nor earliest usage of the language can the supposed primary meaning of the word be anywhere discovered. *Knobel's* remark has still less force, viz. that the ark must have had a lid, and it must have been called a lid. For if from the very commencement this lid had a more important purpose than that of a simple covering, it might also have received its name from this special purpose, even though this was not fully explained to the Israelites till a later period in the giving of the law (Lev. xvi. 15, 16). It must, however, have been obvious to every one, that it was to be something more than the mere lid of the ark, from the simple fact that it was not to be made, like the ark, of wood plated with gold, but to be made of pure gold, and to have two golden cherubs upon the top. The *cherubim* (see vol. i. p. 107) were to be made of gold מִקְשָׁה (from קָשָׁה to turn), *i.e.*, literally, turned work (cf. Isa. iii. 24), here, according to *Onkelos*, נְגִיד *opus ductile*, work beaten with the hammer and rounded, so that the figures were not solid but hollow (see *Bähr*, i. p. 380).—Ver. 19. " Out of the *capporeth* shall ye make the cherubs at its two ends," *i.e.* so as to form one whole with the *capporeth* itself, and be inseparable from it.—Ver. 20. " *And let the cherubs be stretching out wings on high, screening* (סֹכְכִים, σνσκιάζοντες) *with their wings above the capporeth, and their faces* (turned) *one to the other; towards the capporeth let the faces of the cherubs be.*" That is to say, the cherubs were to spread out their wings in such a manner as to form a screen over the *capporeth*, with their faces turned towards one another, but inclining or stooping towards the *capporeth*. The reason for this is given in ver. 22. There—viz. above the capporeth that was placed upon the ark containing the testimony—Jehovah would present Himself to Moses (נוֹעַד, from יָעַד to appoint, to present one's self to a person at an appointed place, to meet with him), and talk with him "*from above the capporeth, out from between the two cherubs upon the ark of testimony, all that I shall command thee for the sons of Israel*" (cf. chap. xxix. 42). Through this divine promise and the fulfilment of it (chap. xl. 35; Lev. i. 1; Num. i. 1, xvii. 19), the ark of the covenant together with the capporeth became the throne of Jehovah in the midst of His chosen people, the footstool of the God of Israel (1 Chron. xxviii. 2, cf. Ps. cxxxii. 7, xcix. 5; Lam. ii. 1). The ark, with the tables of the covenant as the self-attestation of God, formed the foundation of this throne, to show that the kingdom of grace which was established in Israel through the medium of the covenant, was founded in justice and righteousness (Ps. lxxxix. 15, xcvii. 2). The gold plate upon the ark formed the footstool of the throne for Him, who caused His name, *i.e.* the real presence of His being, to dwell in a cloud between the two cherubim above their outspread wings; and there He not only made known His will to His people in laws and commandments, but revealed Himself as the jealous God who visited sin and showed mercy (chap. xx. 5, 6, xxxiv. 6, 7),—the latter more especially on the great day of atonement, when, through the medium of the blood of the sin-offering sprinkled upon and in front of the capporeth, He granted reconciliation to His people for all their transgressions in all their sins (Lev. xvi. 14 sqq.). Thus the footstool of God became a throne of grace (Heb. iv. 16, cf. ix. 5), which received its name *capporeth* or ἱλαστήριον from the fact that the highest and most perfect act of atonement under the Old Testament was performed upon it. Jehovah, who betrothed His people to Himself in grace and mercy for an everlasting covenant (Hos. ii. 2), was enthroned upon it, above the wings of the two cherubim, which stood on either side of His throne; and hence He is represented as " dwelling (between) the cherubim" יֹשֵׁב הַכְּרֻבִים (1 Sam. iv. 4; 2 Sam. vi. 2; Ps. lxxx. 2, etc.). The cherubs were not combinations of animal forms, taken from man, the lion, the ox, and the eagle, as many have inferred from Ezek.

i. and x., for even the composite beings which Ezekiel saw with
four faces had a human figure (Ezek. i. 5) ; but they are to be
regarded as figures made in a human form, and not in a kneel-
ing posture, but, according to the analogy of 2 Chron. iii. 13,
standing upright. Consequently, as the union of four faces in
one cherub is peculiar to Ezekiel, and the cherubs of the ark of
the covenant, like those of Solomon's temple, had but one face
each, not only did the human type form the general basis of
these figures, but in every respect, with the exception of the wings,
they were made in the likeness of men. And this is the only
form which would answer the purpose for which they were intended, viz. to represent the cherubim, or heavenly spirits, who
were stationed to prevent the return of the first man to the
garden of Eden after his expulsion thence, and keep the way to
the tree of life (see vol. i. p. 107). Standing upon the capporeth
of the ark of the covenant, the typical foundation of the throne
of Jehovah, which Ezekiel saw in the vision as דְּמוּת רָקִיעַ " the
likeness of a firmament" (Ezek. i. 22, 25), with their wings
outspread and faces lowered, they represented the spirits of
heaven, who surround Jehovah, the heavenly King, when seated
upon His throne, as His most exalted servants and the witnesses
of His sovereign and saving glory ; so that Jehovah enthroned
above the wings of the cherubim was set forth as the God of
Hosts who is exalted above all the angels, surrounded by the
assembly or council of the holy ones (Ps. lxxxix. 6–9), who bow
their faces towards the capporeth, studying the secrets of the
divine counsels of love (1 Pet. i. 12), and worshipping Him that
liveth for ever and ever (Rev. iv. 10).

Vers. 23–30. THE TABLE OF SHEW-BREAD (cf. chap. xxxvii.
10–16).—The table for the shew-bread (ver. 30) was to be made
of acacia-wood, two cubits long, one broad, and one and a half
high, and to be plated with pure gold, having a golden wreath
round, and a "*finish* (מִסְגֶּרֶת) *of a hand-breadth round about*,"
i.e. a border of a hand-breadth in depth surrounding and enclosing the four sides, upon which the top of the table was laid,
and into the four corners of which the feet of the table were
inserted. A golden wreath was to be placed round this rim.
As there is no article attached to זֵר־זָהָב in ver. 25 (cf. xxxvii. 12),
so as to connect it with the זֵר in ver. 24, we must conclude that

there were two such ornamental wreaths, one round the slab of the table, the other round the rim which was under the slab. At the four corners of the four feet, near the point at which they joined the rim, four rings were to be fastened for בָּתִּים, *i.e.* to hold the poles with which the table was carried, as in the case of the ark.—Ver. 29. Vessels of pure gold were also to be made, to stand upon the table (cf. xxxvii. 16). קְעָרֹת, τὰ τευβλία (LXX.), large deep plates, in which the shew-bread was not only brought to the table, but placed upon it. These plates cannot have been small, for the silver קְעָרָה, presented by Nahshon the tribe prince, weighed 130 shekels (Num. vii. 13). כַּפֹּת, from כַּף a hollow hand, small scoops, according to Num. vii. 14, only ten shekels in weight, used to put out the incense belonging to the shew-bread upon the table (cf. Lev. xxiv. 7 and Num. vii. 14) : LXX. θυΐσκη, *i.e.*, according to the *Etymol. Magn.*, σκάφη ἡ τὰ θύματα δεχομένη. There were also two vessels "to pour out," *sc.* the drink-offering, or libation of wine : viz. קְשׂוֹת, σπονδεῖα (LXX.), sacrificial spoons to make the libation of wine with, and מְנַקִּיֹת, κύαθοι (LXX.), goblets into which the wine was poured, and in which it was placed upon the table. (See chap. xxxvii. 16 and Num. iv. 7, where the goblets are mentioned before the sacrificial spoons.)—Ver. 30. Bread of the face (לֶחֶם פָּנִים), the mode of preparing and placing which is described in Lev. xxiv. 5 sqq., was to lie continually before (לְפָנַי) Jehovah. These loaves were called " bread of the face " (shew-bread), because they were to lie before the face of Jehovah as a meat-offering presented by the children of Israel (Lev. xxiv. 8), not as food for Jehovah, but as a symbol of the spiritual food which Israel was to prepare (John vi. 27, cf. iv. 32, 34), a figurative representation of the calling it had received from God; so that bread and wine, which stood upon the table by the side of the loaves, as the fruit of the labour bestowed by Israel upon the soil of its inheritance, were a symbol of its spiritual labour in the kingdom of God, the spiritual vineyard of its Lord.

Vers. 31–40 (cf. xxxvii. 17–24). THE CANDLESTICK was to be made of pure gold, "beaten work." מִקְשָׁה : see ver 18. For the form תֵּיעָשֶׂה instead of תֵּעָשֶׂה (which is probably the work of a copyist, who thought the reading should be תֵּעָשֶׂה in the *Niphal*, as the ' is wanting in many MSS.), see *Gesenius*, *Lehrgeb.* p. 52, and *Ewald*, § 83 *b*. " *Of it shall be* (*i.e.* there shall issue from it so as to form one complete whole) *its* יְרֵךְ " (*lit.* the loins, the upper part of the thigh, which is attached to the body, and from which the feet proceed,—in this case the base or pedestal, upon which the candelabrum stood); its קָנֶה, or reed, *i.e.* the hollow stem of the candelabrum rising up from the pedestal;—" *its* גְּבִיעִים," cups, resembling the calix of a flower;— כַּפְתֹּרִים, knobs, in a spherical shape (cf. Amos ix. 1, Zeph. ii. 14); —" *and* פְּרָחִים," flowers, ornaments in the form of buds just bursting.—Ver. 32. From the sides of the candlestick, *i.e.* of the upright stem in the middle, there were to be six branches, three on either side.—Vers. 33-34. On each of these branches (the repetition of the same words expresses the distributive sense) there were to be " *three cups in the form of an almond-flower*, (with) *knob and flower*," and on the shaft of the candlestick, or central stem, " *four cups in the form of almond-flowers, its knobs and its flowers*." As both כַּפְתֹּר וָפֶרַח (ver. 33) and כַּפְתֹּרֶיהָ וּפְרָחֶיהָ (ver. 34) are connected with the previous words without a copula, *Knobel* and *Thenius* regard these words as standing in explanatory apposition to the preceding ones, and suppose the meaning to be that the flower-cups were to consist of knobs with flowers issuing from them. But apart from the singular idea of calling a knob or bulb with a flower bursting from it a flower-cup, ver. 31 decidedly precludes any such explanation; for cups, knobs, and flowers are mentioned there in connection with the base and stem, as three separate things which were quite as distinct the one from the other as the base and the stem. The words in question are appended in both verses to גְּבִיעִים מְשֻׁקָּדִים in the sense of subordination; וְ is generally used in such cases, but it is omitted here before כפתר, probably to avoid ambiguity, as the two words to be subordinated are brought into closer association as one idea by the use of this copula. And if כפתר and פרח are to be distinguished from גביע, the objection made by *Thenius* to our rendering מְשֻׁקָּד " almond-blossom-shaped," namely, that neither the almond nor the almond-blossom has at all the shape of a basin, falls entirely to the ground; and there is all the less reason to question this rendering, on account of the unanimity with which it has been adopted in the ancient versions, whereas the rendering proposed by *Thenius*, " wakened up, *i.e.* a burst or opened calix," has neither foundation nor probability.—Ver. 35. *"And every pipe under the two branches shall be out from them* (be connected with them) *for the six* (side) *pipes going out from the candlestick;" i.e.* at the point where the three pairs of the six side pipes or arms branched off from the main pipe or stem of the candlestick, a knob should be so placed that the arms should proceed from the knob, or from the main stem immediately above the knob.—Ver. 36. *" Their knobs and their pipes (i.e.* the knobs and pipes of the three pairs of arms) *shall be of it* (the candlestick, *i.e.* combined with it so as to form one whole), *all one* (one kind of) *beaten work, pure gold."* From all this we get the following idea of the candlestick: Upon the base there rose an upright central pipe, from which three side pipes branched out one above another on either side, and curved upwards in the form of a quadrant to the level of the central stem. On this stem a calix and a knob and blossom were introduced four separate times, and in such a manner that there was a knob wherever the side pipes branched off from the main stem, evidently immediately below the branches; and the fourth knob, we may suppose, was higher up between the top branches and the end of the stem. As there were thus four calices with a knob and blossom in the main stem, so again there were three in each of the branches, which were no doubt placed at equal distances from one another. With regard to the relative position of the calix, the knob, and the blossom, we may suppose that the spherical knob was underneath the calix, and that the blossom sprang from the upper edge of the latter, as if bursting out of it. The candlestick had thus seven arms, and seven lights or lamps were to be made and placed upon them (הֶעֱלָה). *" And they* (all the lamps) *are to give light upon the opposite side of its front"* (ver. 37): *i.e.* the lamp was to throw its light upon the side that was opposite to the front of the candlestick. The פָּנִים of the candlestick (ver. 37 and Num. viii. 2) was the front shown by the seven arms, as they formed a straight line with their seven points; and עֵבֶר does not mean the side, but the opposite side, as is evident from Num. viii. 2, where we find אֶל מוּל instead. As the place assigned to the candlestick was on the south side of the dwelling-place, we are to understand by this opposite side the north, and imagine the lamp to be so placed that the line of lamps formed by the seven arms ran from front to back, by which arrangement the holy place would be better lighted, than if the candlestick had stood with the line of lamps from south to north, and so had turned all its seven lamps towards the person entering the holy place. The lamps were the receptacles for the wick and oil, which were placed on the top of the arms, and could be taken down to be cleaned. The hole from which the wick projected was not made in the middle, but at the edge, so that the light was thrown upon one side.— Ver. 38. The other things belonging to the candlestick were מֶלְקָחַיִם tongs (Isa. vi. 6), *i.e.* snuffers, and מַחְתּוֹת snuff-dishes, *i.e.* dishes to receive the snuff when taken from the wicks ; elsewhere the word signifies an ash-pan, or vessel used for taking away the coal from the fire (chap. xxvii. 3; Lev. xvi. 12; Num. xvii. 3 sqq.).—Ver. 39. " *Of a talent of pure gold* (*i.e.* 822,000 Parisian grains) *shall he make it* (the candlestick) *and all these vessels*," *i.e.*, according to chap. xxxvii. 24, all the vessels belonging to the candlestick. From this quantity of gold it was possible to make a candlestick of very considerable size. The size is not given anywhere in the Old Testament, but, according to *Bähr's* conjecture, it corresponded to the height of the table of shew-bread, namely, a cubit and a half in height and the same in breadth, or a cubit and a half between the two outside lamps.

The signification of the seven-armed candlestick is apparent from its purpose, viz. to carry seven lamps, which were trimmed and filled with oil every morning, and lighted every evening, and were to burn throughout the night (chap. xxvii. 20, 21, xxx. 7, 8 ; Lev. xxiv. 3, 4). As the Israelites were to prepare spiritual food in the shew-bread in the presence of Jehovah, and to offer continually the fruit of their labour in the field of the kingdom of God, as a spiritual offering to the Lord ; so also were they to present themselves continually to Jehovah in the burning lamps, as the vehicles and media of light, as a nation letting its light shine in the darkness of this world (cf. Matt. v. 14, 16; Luke xii. 35; Phil. ii. 15). The oil, through which the lamps burned and shone, was, according to its peculiar virtue in imparting strength to the body and restoring vital power, a representation of the Godlike spirit, the source of all the vital power of man ; whilst the oil, as offered by the congregation of Israel, and devoted to sacred purposes according to the command of God, is throughout the Scriptures a symbol of the

Spirit of God, by which the congregation of God was filled with higher light and life. By the power of this Spirit, Israel, in covenant with the Lord, was to let its light shine, the light of its knowledge of God and spiritual illumination, before all the nations of the earth. In its *seven* arms the stamp of the covenant relationship was impressed upon the candlestick; and the almond-blossom with which it was ornamented represented the seasonable offering of the flowers and fruits of the Spirit, the almond-tree deriving its name שָׁקֵד from the fact that it is the earliest of all the trees in both its blossom and its fruit (cf. Jer. i. 11, 12). The symbolical character of the candlestick is clearly indicated in the Scriptures. The prophet Zechariah (chap. iv.) sees a golden candlestick with seven lamps and two olive-trees, one on either side, from which the oil-vessel is supplied; and the angel who is talking with him informs him that the olive-trees are the two sons of oil, that is to say, the representatives of the kingdom and priesthood, the divinely appointed organs through which the Spirit of God was communicated to the covenant nation. And in Rev. i. 20, the seven churches, which represent the new people of God, *i.e.* the Christian Church, are shown to the holy seer in the form of seven candlesticks standing before the throne of God.—On ver. 40, see at ver. 9.

Chap. xxvi. (cf. xxxvi. 8–38). THE DWELLING-PLACE.— This was to be formed of a framework of wood, and of tapestry and curtains. The description commences with the tapestry or tent-cloth (vers. 1–14), which made the framework (vers. 15–30) into a dwelling. The inner lining is mentioned first (vers. 1–6), because this made the dwelling into a tent (tabernacle). This *inner tent-cloth* was to consist of ten curtains (יְרִיעֹת, αὐλαίαι), or, as *Luther* has more aptly rendered it, *Teppiche*, pieces of tapestry, *i.e.* of cloth composed of byssus yarn, hyacinth, purple, and scarlet. מָשְׁזָר twisted, signifies yarn composed of various colours twisted together, from which the finer kinds of byssus, for which the Egyptians were so celebrated, were made (*vid. Hengstenberg*, Egypt, pp. 139 sqq.). The byssus yarn was of a clear white, and this was woven into mixed cloth by combination with dark blue, and dark and fiery red. It was not to be in simple stripes or checks, however; but the variegated yarn was to be woven (embroidered) into the

white byssus, so as to form artistic figures of cherubim (" cherubim, work of the artistic weaver, shalt thou make it "). מַעֲשֵׂה
חֹשֵׁב (*lit.* work or labour of the thinker) is applied to artistic
weaving, in which either figures or gold threads (chap. xxviii.
6, 8, 15) are worked into the cloth, and which is to be distinguished from מַעֲשֵׂה רֹקֵם variegated weaving (ver. 36).—Vers.
2, 3. The length of each piece was to be 28 cubits, and the breadth
4 cubits, one measure for all ; and five of these pieces were to be
"joined together one to another," *i.e.* joined or sewed together into
a piece of 28 cubits in length and 20 in breadth, and the same
with the other five.—Vers. 4, 5. They were also to make 50
hyacinth loops *" on the border of the one piece of tapestry, from
the end in the join,"* *i.e.* on the extreme edge of the five pieces
that were sewed together; and the same *" on the border of the
last piece in the second joined tapestry."* Thus there were to be
fifty loops in each of the two large pieces, and these loops were
to be מַקְבִּילֹת *" taking up the loops one the other;"* that is to
say, they were to be so made that the loops in the two pieces
should exactly meet.—Ver. 6. Fifty golden clasps were also to
be made, to fasten the pieces of drapery (the two halves of the
tent-cloth) together, *" that it might be a dwelling-place."* This
necessarily leads to *Bähr's* conclusion, that the tent-cloth, which
consisted of two halves fastened together with the loops and
clasps, answering to the two compartments of the dwelling-
place (ver. 33), enclosed the whole of the interior, not only
covering the open framework above, but the side walls also, and
therefore that it hung down inside the walls, and that it was not
spread out upon the wooden framework so as to form the ceiling,
but hung down on the walls on the outside of the wooden beams,
so that the gilded beams were left uncovered in the inside.   For
if this splendid tent-cloth had been intended for the ceiling only,
and therefore only 30 cubits had been visible out of the 40 cubits
of its breadth, and only 10 out of the 28 of its length,—that is to
say, if not much more than a third of the whole had been seen
and used for the inner lining of the dwelling,—it would not have
been called " the dwelling " so constantly as it is (cf. chap.
xxxvi. 8, xl. 18), nor would the goats'-hair covering which was
placed above it have been just as constantly called the " tent
above the dwelling " (ver. 7, chap. xxxvi. 14, xl. 19).   This
inner tent-cloth was so spread out, that whilst it was fastened to

the upper ends of the beams in a way that is not explained in the text, it formed the ceiling of the whole, and the joining came just above the curtain which divided the dwelling into two compartments. One half therefore, viz. the front half, formed the ceiling of the holy place with its entire breadth of 20 cubits and 10 cubits of its length, and the remaining 18 cubits of its length hung down over the two side walls, 9 cubits down each wall,—the planks that formed the walls being left uncovered, therefore, to the height of 1 cubit from the ground. In a similar manner the other half covered the holy of holies, 10 cubits of both length and breadth forming the ceiling, and the 10 cubits that remained of the entire length covering the end wall; whilst the folds in the corners that arose from the 9 cubits that hung down on either side, were no doubt so adjusted that the walls appeared to be perfectly smooth. (For further remarks, see chap. xxxix. 33.)

Vers. 7–13. The *outer tent-cloth*, "for the tent over the dwelling," was to consist of eleven lengths of goats' hair, *i.e.* of cloth made of goats' hair;[1] each piece being thirty cubits long and four broad.—Ver. 9. Five of these were to be connected (sewed together) by themselves (לְבָד), and the other six in the same manner; and the sixth piece was to be made double, *i.e.* folded together, towards the front of the tent, so as to form a kind of gable, as *Josephus* has also explained the passage (Ant. iii. 6, 4).—Vers. 10, 11. Fifty loops and clasps were to be made to join the two halves together, as in the case of the inner tapestry, only the clasps were to be of brass or copper.—Vers. 12, 13. This tent-cloth was two cubits longer than the inner one, as each piece was 30 cubits long instead of 28; it was also two cubits broader, as it was composed of 11 pieces, the eleventh only reckoning as two cubits, as it was to be laid double. Consequently there was an excess (הָעֹדֵף that which is over) of two cubits each way; and according to vers. 12 and 13 this was to be disposed of in the following manner: "*As for the spreading out of the excess in the tent-cloths, the half of the cloth in excess shall spread out over the back of the dwelling; and the cubit from here and from there in the excess in the length of the tent-cloths (i.e. the*

[1] The coverings of the tents of the Bedouin Arabs are still made of cloth woven from black goats' hair, which the women spin and weave (see *Lynch's* Expedition of the United States to the Jordan and Dead Sea).

cubit over in the length in each of the cloths) *shall be spread out on the sides of the dwelling from here and from there to cover it.*" Now since, according to this, one half of the two cubits of the sixth piece which was laid double was to hang down the back of the tabernacle, there only remained one cubit for the gable of the front. It follows, therefore, that the joining of the two halves with loops and clasps would come a cubit farther back, than the place where the curtain of the holy of holies divided the dwelling. But in consequence of the cloth being a cubit longer in every direction, it nearly reached the ground on all three sides, the thickness of the wooden framework alone preventing it from reaching it altogether.

Ver. 14. *Two other coverings* were placed on the top of this tent : one made of rams' skins dyed red, " as a covering for the tent," and another upon the top of this, made of the skins of the sea-cow (תְּחָשִׁים, see at chap. xxv. 5).

Vers. 15–30. The *wooden framework.*—Vers. 15, 16. The boards for the dwelling were to be made " of acacia-wood standing," *i.e.* so that they could stand upright ; each ten cubits long and one and a half broad. The thickness is not given ; and if, on the one hand, we are not to imagine them too thin, as *Josephus* does, for example, who says they were only four fingers thick (Ant. iii. 6, 3), we have still less reason for following *Rashi, Lund, Bähr* and others, who suppose them to have been a cubit in thickness, thus making simple boards into colossal blocks, such as could neither have been cut from acacia-trees, nor carried upon desert roads.[1] To obtain boards of the required breadth, two or three planks were no doubt joined together according to the size of the trees.—Ver. 17. Every board was to have two יָדוֹת (*lit.* hands or holders) to hold them upright, pegs

---

[1] *Kamphausen* (*Stud. und Krit.* 1859, p. 117) appeals to *Bähr's Symbolik* 1, p. 261–2, and *Knobel, Exod.* p. 261, in support of the opinion, that at any rate formerly there were genuine acacias of such size and strength, that beams could have been cut from them a cubit and a half broad and a cubit thick ; but we look in vain to either of these writings for such authority as will establish this fact. Expressions like those of *Jerome* and *Hasselquist*, viz. *grandes arbores* and *arbor ingens ramosissima*, are far too indefinite. It is true that, according to *Abdullatif*, the *Sont* is " a very large tree," but he gives a quotation from *Dinuri*, in which it is merely spoken of as "a tree of the size of a nut-tree." See the passages cited in *Rosenmüller's bibl. Althk.* iv. 1, p. 278, Not. 7, where we find the following remark of *Wesling*

therefore; and they were to be "*bound to one another*" (מְשֻׁלָּב, from
שָׁלַב in Chald. to connect, hence שְׁלַבִּים in 1 Kings vii. 28, the
corner plates that hold together the four sides of a chest), not
"pegged into one another," but joined together by a fastening
dovetailed into the pegs, by which the latter were fastened still
more firmly to the boards, and therefore had greater holding
power than if each one had been simply sunk into the edge of
the board.—Vers. 18–21. Twenty of these boards were to be
prepared for the side of the dwelling that was turned towards
the south, and forty sockets (אֲדָנִים foundations, Job xxxviii. 6)
or bases for the pegs, *i.e.* to put the pegs of the boards into, that
the boards might stand upright; and the same number of boards
and sockets for the north side. תֵּימָנָה, "southward," is added to
לִפְאַת נֶגְבָּה in ver. 18, to give a clearer definition of *negeb*, which
primarily means the dry, and then the country to the south; an
evident proof that at that time *negeþ* was not established as a
geographical term for the south, and therefore that it was not
written here by a Palestinian, as *Knobel* supposes, but by Moses
in the desert. The form of the "sockets" is not explained, and
even in chap. xxxviii. 27, in the summing up of the gifts presented for the work, it is merely stated that a talent of silver
(about 93 lb.) was applied to every socket.—Vers. 22–24. Six
boards were to be made for the back of the dwelling westwards
(יָמָּה), and two boards "for the corners or angles of the dwelling
at the two outermost (hinder) sides." לִמְקֻצְעֹת (for cornered), from
מְקֻצָע, equivalent to מִקְצוֹעַ an angle (ver. 24; Ezek. xlvi. 21, 22),
from קָצַע to cut off, *lit.* a section, something cut off, hence an
angle, or corner-piece. These corner boards (ver. 24) were to
be "*doubled* (תֹּאֲמִם) *from below, and whole* (תַּמִּים, *integri*, forming a whole) *at its head* (or towards its head, cf. אֶל chap. xxxvi.

on *Prosper. Alpin. de plantis Æg.: Caudicem non raro ampliorem depre-
hendi, quam ut brachio meo circumdari possit.* Even the statement of *Theo-
phrast* (*hist. plant.* 4, 3), to the effect that rafters are cut from these trees 12
cubits long (δωδεκάπηχυς ἐρέψιμος ὕλη), is no proof that they were beams a
cubit and a half broad and a cubit thick. And even if there had been trees
of this size in the peninsula of Sinai in Moses' time, a beam of such dimensions, according to *Kamphausen's* calculation, which is by no means too high,
would have weighed more than twelve cwt. And certainly the Israelites
could never have carried beams of this weight with them through the
desert; for the waggons needed would have been such as could never be
used where there are no beaten roads.

29) *with regard to the one ring, so shall it be to both of them* (so shall they both be made); *to the two corners shall they be*" (*i.e.* designed for the two hinder corners). The meaning of these words, which are very obscure in some points, can only be the following : the two corner beams at the back were to consist of two pieces joined together at a right angle, so as to form as double boards one single whole from the bottom to the top. The expressions " from below" and " up to its head" are divided between the two predicates " doubled" (תֹּאֲמִים) and " whole" (תַּמִּים), but they belong to both of them. Each of the corner beams was to be double from the bottom to the top, and still to form one whole. There is more difficulty in the words אֶל־הַטַּבַּעַת הָאֶחָת in ver. 24. It is impossible to attach any intelligible meaning to the rendering " to the first ring," so that even *Knobel*, who proposed it, has left it unexplained. There is hardly any other way of explaining it, than to take the word אֶל in the sense of " having regard to a thing," and to understand the words as meaning, that the corner beams were to form one whole, from the fact that each received only one ring, probably at the corner, and not two, viz. one on each side. This one ring was placed half-way up the upright beam in the corner or angle, in such a manner that the central bolt, which stretched along the entire length of the walls (ver. 28), might fasten into it from both the side and back.—Ver. 25. Sixteen sockets were to be made for these eight boards, two for each.—Vers. 26–29. To fasten the boards, that they might not separate from one another, bars of acacia-wood were to be made and covered with gold, five for each of the three sides of the dwelling; and though it is not expressly stated, yet the reference to rings in ver. 29 as holders of the bars (בָּתִּים לַבְּרִיחִים) is a sufficient indication that they were passed through golden rings fastened into the boards.—Ver. 28. "*And the middle bar in the midst of the boards* (*i.e.* at an equal distance from both top and bottom) *shall be fastening* (מַבְרִיחַ) *from one end to the other.*" As it thus expressly stated with reference to the middle bar, that it was to fasten, *i.e.* to reach along the walls from one end to the other, we necessarily conclude, with *Rashi* and others, that the other four bars on every side were not to reach the whole length of the walls, and may therefore suppose that they were only half as long as the middle one, so that there were only three rows of bars on each wall, the upper and lower

being composed of two bars each.—Ver. 30. *"And set up the dwelling according to its right, as was shown thee upon the mountain"* (cf. chap. xxv. 9). Even the setting up and position of the dwelling were not left to human judgment, but were to be carried out כְּמִשְׁפָּטוֹ, *i.e.* according to the direction corresponding to its meaning and purpose. From the description which is given of the separate portions, it is evident that the dwelling was to be set up in the direction of the four quarters of the heavens, the back being towards the west, and the entrance to the east; whilst the whole of the dwelling formed an oblong of thirty cubits long, ten broad, and ten high. The length we obtain from the twenty boards of a cubit and a half in breadth ; and the breadth, by adding to the nine cubits covered by the six boards at the back, half a cubit as the inner thickness of each of the corner beams. The thickness of the corner beams is not given, but we may conjecture that on the outside which formed part of the back they were three-quarters of a cubit thick, and that half a cubit is to be taken as the thickness towards the side. In this case, on the supposition that the side beams were a quarter of a cubit thick, the inner space would be exactly ten cubits broad and thirty and a quarter long; but the surplus quarter would be taken up by the thickness of the pillars upon which the inner curtain was hung, so that the room at the back would form a perfect cube, and the one at the front an oblong of exactly twenty cubits in length, ten in breadth, and ten in height.

Vers. 31–37. To divide the *dwelling* into two rooms, a *curtain* was to be made, of the same material, and woven in the same artistic manner as the inner covering of the walls (ver. 1). This was called פָּרֹכֶת, *lit.* division, separation, from פָּרַךְ to divide, or פָּרֹכֶת מָסָךְ (chap. xxxv. 12, xxxix. 34, xl. 21) division of the covering, *i.e.* the covering separation, or veil. They were to put (נָתַן), *i.e.* to hang this *" upon four pillars of gilded acacia-wood and their golden hooks,* (standing) *upon four silver sockets,"* under the loops (קְרָסִים) which held the two halves of the inner covering together (ver. 6). Thus the curtain divided the dwelling into two compartments, the one occupying ten cubits and the other twenty of its entire length.—Ver. 33. " Thither (where the curtain hangs under the loops) within the curtain shalt thou bring the ark of testimony (chap. xxv. 16–22), and the curtain shall divide unto you between the holy place and the most holy"

(קֹרֶשׁ הַקֳּדָשִׁים the holy of holies). The inner compartment was made into the most holy place through the ark of the covenant with the throne of grace upon it.—Ver. 35. The two other things (already described) were to be placed outside the curtain, viz. in the holy place; the candlestick opposite to the table, the former on the south side of the dwelling, the latter towards the north.—Vers. 36, 37. For the entrance to the tent they were also to make a curtain (מָסָךְ, lit. a covering, from סָכַךְ to cover) of the same material as the inner curtain, but of work in mixed colours, i.e. not woven with figures upon it, but simply in stripes or checks. מַעֲשֵׂה רֹקֵם does not mean coloured needle-work, with figures or flowers embroidered with the needle upon the woven fabric (as I asserted in my *Archäologie*, in common with the Rabbins, *Gesenius*, *Bähr*, and others); for in the only other passage in which רקם occurs, viz. Ps. cxxxix. 15, it does not mean to embroider, but to weave, and in the Arabic it signifies to make points, stripes, or lines, to work in mixed colours (see *Hartmann die Hebräerinn am Putztisch* iii. 138 sqq.). This curtain was to hang on five gilded pillars of acacia-wood with golden hooks, and for these they were to cast sockets of brass. In the account of the execution of this work in chap. xxxvi. 38, it is still further stated, that the architect covered the heads (capitals) of the pillars and their girders (חֲשֻׁקִים, see chap. xxvii. 10) with gold. From this it follows, that the pillars were not entirely gilded, but only the capitals, and that they were fastened together with gilded girders. These girders were either placed upon the hooks that were fastened to the tops of the pillars, or, what I think more probable, formed a kind of architrave above the pillars, in which case the covering as well as the inner curtain merely hung upon the hooks of the columns. But if the pillars were not gilded all over, we must necessarily imagine the curtain as hung upon that side of the pillars which was turned towards the holy place, so that none of the white wood was to be seen inside the holy place; and the gilding of the capitals and architrave merely served to impress upon the forefront of the tabernacle the glory of a house of God.

If we endeavour to understand the reason for building the dwelling in this manner, there can be no doubt that the design of the wooden walls was simply to give stability to the tabernacle. Acacia-wood was chosen, because the acacia was the only tree to be found in the desert of Arabia from which planks and beams could be cut, whilst the lightness and durability of this wood rendered it peculiarly suitable for a portable temple. The wooden framework was covered both within and without with hangings of drapery and other coverings, to give it the character of a tent, which is the term really applied to it in chap. xxvii. 21, and in most instances afterwards. The sanctuary of Jehovah in the midst of His people was to be a tent, because, so long as the people were wandering about and dwelt in tents, the dwelling of their God in the midst of them must be a tent also. The division of the dwelling into two parts corresponded to the design of the tabernacle, where Jehovah desired not to dwell alone by Himself, but to come and meet with His people (chap. xxv. 22). The most holy place was the true dwelling of Jehovah, where He was enthroned in a cloud, the visible symbol of His presence, above the cherubim, upon the capporeth of the ark of the covenant (see p. 169). The holy place, on the other hand, was the place where His people were to appear before Him, and draw near to Him with their gifts, the fruits of their earthly vocation, and their prayers, and to rejoice before His face in the blessings of His covenant grace. By the establishment of the covenant of Jehovah with the people of Israel, the separation of man from God, of which the fall of the progenitors of our race had been the cause, was to be brought to an end; an institution was to be set up, pointing to the reunion of man and God, to true and full vital communion with Him; and by this the kingdom of God was to be founded on earth in a local and temporal form. This kingdom of God, which was founded in Israel, was to be embodied in the tabernacle, and shadowed forth in its earthly and visible form as confined within the limits of time and space. This meaning was indicated not only in the instructions to set up the dwelling according to the four quarters of the globe and heavens, with the entrance towards sunrise and the holy of holies towards the west, but also in the quadrangular form of the building, the dwelling as a whole assuming the form of an oblong of thirty cubits in length, and ten in breadth and height, whilst the most holy place was a cube of ten cubits in every direction. In the symbolism of antiquity, the square was a symbol of the universe or *cosmos*; and thus, too, in the symbolism of the Scriptures it is a type of the world as the scene of divine revelation, the sphere of the kingdom of God, for which the world from the very first had been intended by God, and to which, notwithstanding the fall of man, who was created lord of the earth, it was to be once more renewed and glorified. Hence the seal of the kingdom of God was impressed upon the sanctuary of God in Israel through the quadrangular form that was given to its separate rooms. And whilst the direction in which it was set up, towards the four quarters of the heavens, showed that the kingdom of God that was planted in Israel was intended to embrace the entire world, the oblong shape given to the whole building set forth the idea of the present incompleteness of the kingdom, and the cubic form of the most holy place its ideal and ultimate perfection.[1] Yet even in its temporal form, it was perfect of its kind, and therefore the component parts of the quadrangular building were regulated by the number ten, the stamp of completeness.

The splendour of the building, as the earthly reflection of the glory of the kingdom of God, was also in harmony with this explanation of its meaning. In the dwelling itself everything was either overlaid with gold or made of pure gold, with the exception of the foundations or sockets of the boards and inner pillars, for which silver was used. In the gold, with its glorious, yea, godlike splendour (Job xxxvii. 22), the glory of the dwelling-

---

[1] The significant character of these different quadrangular forms is placed beyond all doubt, when we compare the tabernacle and Solomon's temple, which was built according to the same proportions, with the prophetic description of the temple and holy city in Ezek. xl.–xlviii., and that of the heavenly Jerusalem in Rev. xxi. and xxii. Just as in both the tabernacle and Solomon's temple the most holy place was in the form of a perfect cube (of 10 and 20 cubits respectively), so John saw the city of God, which came down from God out of heaven, in the form of a perfect cube. "The length, and the breadth, and the height of it were equal," viz. 12,000 furlongs on every side (Rev. xxi. 16), a symbolical representation of the idea, that the holy of holies in the temple will be seen in its perfected form in the heavenly Jerusalem, and God will dwell in it for ever, along with the just made perfect. This city of God is "the tabernacle of God with men;" it has no longer a temple, but the Lord God of Hosts and the Lamb are the temple of it (ver. 22), and those who dwell therein see the face of God and the Lamb (chap. xxii. 4). The square comes next to the cube, and the regular oblong next to this. The tabernacle was in the form of an oblong: the dwelling was 30 cubits long and 10 broad, and the court 100 cubits long and 50 broad. Solomon's temple, when regarded as a whole, was in the same form; it was 60 cubits long and 20 cubits broad, apart from the

place of God was reflected; whilst the silver, as the symbol of moral purity, shadowed forth the holiness of the foundation of the house or kingdom of God. The four colours, and the figures upon the drapery and curtains of the temple, were equally significant. Whilst the *four* colours, like the same number of coverings, showed their general purpose as connected with the building of the kingdom of God, the brilliant white of the byssus stands prominently out among the rest of the colours as the ground of the woven fabrics, and the colour which is invariably mentioned first. The splendid white byssus represented the holiness of the building; the hyacinth, a dark blue approaching black rather than bright blue, but the true colour of the sky in southern countries, its heavenly origin and character; the purple, a dark rich red, its royal glory; whilst the crimson, a light brilliant red, the colour of blood and vigorous life, set forth the strength of imperishable life in the abode and kingdom of the holy and glorious God-King. Lastly, through the figures of cherubim woven into these fabrics the dwelling became a symbolical representation of the kingdom of glory, in which the heavenly spirits surround the throne of God, the heavenly Jerusalem with its myriads of angels, the city of the living God, to which the people of God will come when their heavenly calling is fulfilled (Heb. xii. 22, 23).

porch and side buildings. In Ezekiel's vision not only is the sanctuary a square of 500 reeds (Ezek. xlii. 15-20, xlv. 2), but the inner court (chap. xl. 23, 27, 47), the paved space in the outer court (xl. 19), and other parts also, are all in the form of squares. The city opposite to the temple was a square of 4500 reeds (chap. xlviii. 16), and the suburbs a square of 250 reeds on every side (ver. 17). The idea thus symbolically expressed is, that the temple and city, and in fact the whole of the holy ground, already approximate to the form of the most holy place. Both the city and temple are still distinct from one another, although they both stand upon holy ground in the midst of the land (chap. xlvii. and xlviii.); and in the temple itself the distinction between the holy place and the most holy is still maintained, although the most holy place is no longer separated by a curtain from the holy place; and in the same manner the distinction is still maintained between the temple-building and the courts, though the latter have acquired much greater importance than in Solomon's temple, and are very minutely described, whereas they are only very briefly referred to in the case of Solomon's temple. The sanctuary which Ezekiel saw, however, was only a symbol of the renewed and glorified kingdom of God, not of the perfected kingdom. This was first shown to the holy seer in Patmos, in the vision of the heavenly Jerusalem, as it appeared in a perfect cubical form.

Chap. xxvii. 1–8. THE ALTAR OF BURNT-OFFERING (cf. chap. xxxviii. 1–7).—" *Make the altar* (the altar of burnt-offering, according to chap. xxxviii. 1) *of acacia-wood, five cubits long, and five cubits broad* (רָבוּעַ " foured," *i.e.* four-sided or quadrangular), *and three cubits high. At its four corners shall its horns be from* (out of) *it*," *i.e.* not removable, but as if growing out of it. These horns were projections at the corners of the altar, formed to imitate in all probability the horns of oxen, and in these the whole force of the altar was concentrated. The blood of the sin-offering was therefore smeared upon them (Lev. iv. 7), and those who fled to the altar to save their lives laid hold of them (*vid.* chap. xxi. 14, and 1 Kings i. 50; also my commentary on the passage). The altar was to be covered with copper or brass, and all the things used in connection with it were to be made of brass. These were,—(1) the *pans*, to cleanse it of the ashes of the fat (ver. 3 : דִּשֵּׁן, a *denom.* verb from דֶּשֶׁן the ashes of fat, that is to say, the ashes that arose from burning the flesh of the sacrifice upon the altar, has a privative meaning, and signifies " to ash away," *i.e.* to cleanse from ashes); (2) יָעִים *shovels*, from יָעָה to take away (Isa. xxviii. 17); (3) מִזְרָקוֹת, things used for *sprinkling the blood*, from זָרַק to sprinkle; (4) מִזְלָגוֹת *forks*, flesh-hooks (cf. מַזְלֵג 1 Sam. ii. 13); (5) מַחְתּת *coal-scoops* (cf. xxv. 38). לְכָל־כֵּלָיו וגו׳ : either " for all the vessels thereof thou shalt make brass," or " as for all its vessels, thou shalt make (them) of brass."—Ver. 4. The altar was to have מִכְבָּר *a grating*, מַעֲשֵׂה רֶשֶׁת *net-work, i.e.* a covering of brass made in the form of a net, of larger dimensions than the sides of the altar, for this grating was to be under the " compass" (כַּרְכֹּב) of the altar from beneath, and to reach to the half of it (half-way up, ver. 5); and in it, *i.e.* at the four ends (or corners) of it, four brass rings were to be fastened, for the poles to carry it with. כַּרְכֹּב (from כִּרְכֵּב *circumdedit*) only occurs here and in chap. xxxviii. 4, and signifies a border (סֹבְבָא *Targums*), *i.e.* a projecting framework or bench running round the four sides of the altar, about half a cubit or a cubit broad, nailed to the walls (of the altar) on the outside, and fastened more firmly to them by the copper covering which was common to both. The copper grating was below this bench, and on the outside. The bench rested upon it, or rather it hung from the outer edge of the bench and rested upon the ground, like the inner chest, which it surrounded on all four sides, and in

which there were no perforations. It formed with the bench or
carcob a projecting footing, which caused the lower half of the
altar to look broader than the upper on every side. The priest
stood upon this *carcob* or bench when offering sacrifice, or when
placing the wood, or doing anything else upon the altar. This
explains Aaron's coming down (יֵרֶד) from the altar (Lev. ix. 22);
and there is no necessity to suppose that there were steps to the
altar, as *Knobel* does in opposition to chap. xx. 26. For even if
the height of the altar, viz. three cubits, would be so great
that a bench half-way up would be too high for any one
to step up to, the earth could be slightly raised on one side
so as to make the ascent perfectly easy; and when the priest
was standing upon the bench, he could perform all that was
necessary upon the top of the altar without any difficulty.—
Vers. 6, 7. The poles were to be made of acacia-wood, and
covered with brass, and to be placed in the rings that were fixed
in the two sides for the purpose of carrying the altar. The additional instructions in ver. 8, " hollow with tables shalt thou make
it, as it was showed thee in the mount" (cf. xxv. 9), refer apparently, if we judge from chap. xx. 24, 25, simply to the wooden
framework of the altar, which was covered with brass, and which
was filled with earth, or gravel and stones, when the altar was
about to be used, the whole being levelled so as to form a hearth.
The shape thus given to the altar of burnt-offering corresponded
to the other objects in the sanctuary. It could also be carried
about with ease, and fixed in any place, and could be used for
burning the sacrifices without the wooden walls being injured by
the fire.

Vers. 9–19 (cf. chap. xxxviii. 9–20). The COURT of the
dwelling was to consist of קְלָעִים " hangings" of spun byssus, and
pillars with brass (copper) sockets, and hooks and fastenings for
the pillars of silver. The pillars were of course made of acacia-
wood; they were five cubits high, with silvered capitals (chap.
xxxviii. 17, 19), and carried the hangings, which were fastened
to them by means of the hooks and fastenings. There were
twenty of them on both the southern and northern sides, and
the length of the drapery on each of these sides was 100 cubits
(מֵאָה בָאַמָּה, 100 (*sc.* measured) by the cubit), so that the court
was a hundred cubits long (ver. 18).—Vers. 12, 13. " *As for the*

breadth of the court on the west side, (there shall be) *curtains fifty cubits; their pillars twenty; and the breadth of the court towards the front, on the east side, fifty cubits."* The front is divided in vers. 14–16 into two כָּתֵף, *lit.* shoulders, *i.e.* sides or side-pieces, each consisting of 15 cubits of hangings and three pillars with their sockets, and a doorway (שַׁעַר), naturally in the middle, which was covered by a curtain (מָסָךְ) formed of the same material as the covering at the entrance to the dwelling, of 20 cubits in length, with four pillars and the same number of sockets. The pillars were therefore equidistant from one another, viz. 5 cubits apart. Their total number was 60 (not 56), which was the number required, at the distance mentioned, to surround a quadrangular space of 100 cubits long and 50 cubits broad.[1]— Ver. 17. *All the pillars of the court round about* (shall be) *bound with connecting rods of silver."* As the rods connecting the pillars of the court were of silver, and those connecting the pillars at the entrance to the dwelling were of wood overlaid with gold, the former must have been intended for a different purpose from the latter, simply serving as rods to which to fasten the hangings, whereas those at the door of the dwelling formed an architrave. The height of the hangings of the court and the covering of the door is given in chap. xxxviii. 18 as 5 cubits, corresponding to the height of the pillars given in ver. 18 of the chapter before

---

[1] Although any one may easily convince himself of the correctness of these numbers by drawing a figure, *Knobel* has revived *Philo's* erroneous statement about 56 pillars and the double reckoning of the pillars in the corner. And the statement in vers. 14–16, that three pillars were to be made in front to carry the hangings on either side of the door, and four to carry the curtain which covered the entrance, may be easily shown to be correct, notwithstanding the fact that, as every drawing shows, four pillars would be required, and not three only, to carry 15 cubits of hangings, and five (not four) to carry a curtain 20 cubits broad, if the pillars were to be placed 5 cubits apart; for the corner pillars, as belonging to both sides, and the pillars which stood between the hangings and the curtain on either side, could only be reckoned as halves in connection with each side or each post; and in reckoning the number of pillars according to the method adopted in every other case, the pillar from which you start would not be reckoned at all. Now, if you count the pillars of the eastern side upon this principle (starting from a corner pillar, which is not reckoned, because it is the starting-point and is the last pillar of the side wall), you have 1, 2, 3, then 1, 2, 3, 4, and then again 1, 2, 3; that is to say, 3 pillars for each wing and 4 for the curtain, although the hangings of each wing would really be supported by 4 pillars, and the curtain in the middle by 5.

us; but the expression in chap. xxxviii. 18, "the height in the breadth," is a singular one, and רֹחַב is probably to be understood in the sense of רְחֹב door-place or door-way,—the meaning of the passage being, "the height of the covering in the door-way." In ver. 18, "50 everywhere," πεντήκοντα ἐπὶ πεντήκοντα (LXX.), *lit.* 50 by 50, is to be understood as relating to the extent towards the north and south; and the reading of the Samaritan text, viz. בָּאַמָּה for בחמשׁים, is merely the result of an arbitrary attempt to bring the text into conformity with the previous מֵאָה בָאַמָּה, whilst the LXX., on the other hand, by an equally arbitrary change, have rendered the passage ἑκατὸν ἐφ᾽ ἑκατόν.—Ver. 19. "*All the vessels of the dwelling in all the work thereof* (*i.e.* all the tools needed for the tabernacle), *and all its pegs, and all the pegs of the court,* (shall be of) *brass or copper.*" The vessels of the dwelling are not the things required for the performance of worship, but the tools used in setting up the tabernacle and taking it down again.

If we inquire still further into the design and meaning of the court, the erection of a court surrounding the dwelling on all four sides is to be traced to the same circumstance as that which rendered it necessary to divide the dwelling itself into two parts, viz. to the fact, that on account of the unholiness of the nation, it could not come directly into the presence of Jehovah, until the sin which separates unholy man from the holy God had been atoned for. Although, by virtue of their election as the children of Jehovah, or their adoption as the nation of God, it was intended that the Israelites should be received by the Lord into His house, and dwell as a son in his father's house; yet under the economy of the law, which only produced the knowledge of sin, uncleanness, and unholiness, their fellowship with Jehovah, the Holy One, could only be sustained through mediators appointed and sanctified by God: viz. at the institution of the covenant, through His servant Moses; and during the existence of this covenant, through the chosen priests of the family of Aaron. It was through them that the Lord was to be approached, and the nation to be brought near to Him. Every day, therefore, they entered the holy place of the dwelling, to offer to the Lord the sacrifices of prayer and the fruits of the people's earthly vocation. But even they were not allowed to go into the immediate presence of the holy God. The most holy place, where God was enthroned, was hidden from them by the curtain, and only once a year was the high priest permitted, as the head of the whole congregation, which was called to be the holy nation of God, to lift this curtain and appear before God with the atoning blood of the sacrifice and the cloud of incense (Lev. xvi.). The access of the nation to its God was restricted to the court. There it could receive from the Lord, through the medium of the sacrifices which it offered upon the altar of burnt-offering, the expiation of its sins, His grace and blessing, and strength to live anew. Whilst the dwelling itself represented the house of God, the dwelling-place of Jehovah in the midst of His people (chap. xxiii. 19; Josh. vi. 24; 1 Sam. i. 7, 24, etc.), the palace of the God-King, in which the priestly nation drew near to Him (1 Sam. i. 9, iii. 3; Ps. v. 8, xxvii. 4, 6); the court which surrounded the dwelling represented the kingdom of the God-King, the covenant land or dwelling-place of Israel in the kingdom of its God. In accordance with this purpose, the court was in the form of an oblong, to exhibit its character as part of the kingdom of God. But its pillars and hangings were only five cubits high, i.e. half the height of the dwelling, to set forth the character of incompleteness, or of the threshold to the sanctuary of God. All its vessels were of copper-brass, which, being allied to the earth in both colour and material, was a symbolical representation of the earthly side of the kingdom of God; whereas the silver of the capitals of the pillars, and.of the hooks and rods which sustained the hangings, as well as the white colour of the byssus-hangings, might point to the holiness of this site for the kingdom of God. On the other hand, in the gilding of the capitals of the pillars at the entrance to the dwelling, and the brass of their sockets, we find gold and silver combined, to set forth the union of the court with the sanctuary, i.e. the union of the dwelling-place of Israel with the dwelling-place of its God, which is realized in the kingdom of God.

The design and significance of the court culminated in the altar of burnt-offering, the principal object in the court; and upon this the burnt-offerings and slain-offerings, in which the covenant nation consecrated itself as a possession to its God, were burnt. The heart of this altar was of earth or unhewn stones, having the character of earth, not only on account of its being appointed as the place of sacrifice and as the hearth for the offerings, but because the earth itself formed the real or material sphere for the kingdom of God in the Old Testament stage of its development. This heart of earth was elevated by the square copper covering into a vessel of the sanctuary, a place where Jehovah would record His name, and come to Israel and bless them (chap. xx. 24, cf. xxix. 42, 44), and was consecrated as a place of sacrifice, by means of which Israel could raise itself to the Lord, and ascend to Him in the sacrifice. And this significance of the altar culminated in its horns, upon which the blood of the sin-offering was smeared. Just as, in the case of the horned animals, their strength and beauty are concentrated in the horns, and the horn has become in consequence a symbol of strength, or of fulness of vital energy ; so the significance of the altar as a place of the saving and life-giving power of God, which the Lord bestows upon His people in His kingdom, was concentrated in the horns of the altar.

Vers. 20 and 21. The instructions concerning the OIL FOR THE CANDLESTICK, and the daily trimming of the lamps by the priests, form a transition from the fitting up of the sanctuary to the installation of its servants.—Ver. 20. The sons of Israel were to bring to Moses (*lit.* fetch to thee) olive oil, *pure* (*i.e.* prepared from olives " which had been cleansed from leaves, twigs, dust, etc., before they were crushed "), *beaten, i.e.,* obtained not by crushing in oil-presses, but by beating, when the oil which flows out by itself is of the finest quality and a white colour. This oil was to be " for the candlestick to set up a continual light."—Ver. 21. ·Aaron and his sons were to prepare this light in the tabernacle outside the curtain, which was over the testimony (*i.e.* which covered or concealed it), from evening to morning, before Jehovah. " The tabernacle of the congregation," *lit.* tent of assembly : this expression is applied to the sanctuary for the first time in the present passage, but it afterwards became the usual appellation, and accords both with its structure and design, as it was a tent in style, and was set apart as the place where Jehovah would meet with the Israelites and commune with them (chap. xxv. 22). The ordering of the light from evening to morning consisted, according to chap. xxx. 7, 8, and Lev. xxiv. 3, 4, in placing the lamps upon the candlestick in the evening and lighting them, that they might give light through the night, and then cleaning them in the morning and filling them with fresh oil. The words " a statute for ever unto their generations (see at chap. xii. 14) on the part of the children of Israel," are to be understood as referring not merely to the gift of oil to be made by the Israelites for all time, but to the preparation of the light, which was to be regarded as of perpetual obligation and worth. " For ever," in the same sense as in Gen. xvii. 7 and 13 (see vol. i. p. 227).

Chap. xxviii. (cf. xxxix. 1–31). APPOINTMENT AND CLOTHING OF THE PRIESTS.—Vers. 1, 5. " *Let Aaron thy brother draw near to thee from among the children of Israel, and his sons with him, that he may be a priest to Me.*" Moses is distinguished from the people as the mediator of the covenant. Hence he was to cause Aaron and his sons to come to him, *i.e.* to separate them from the people, and install them as priests, or perpetual mediators between Jehovah and His people. The primary meaning of *cohen*, the priest, has been retained in the Arabic, where it signifies *administrator alieni negotii*, viz. to act as a mediator for a person, or as his plenipotentiary, from which it came to be employed chiefly in connection with priestly acts. Among the heathen Arabs it is used " *maxime de hariolis vatibusque ;*" by the Hebrews it was mostly applied to the priests of Jehovah ; and there are only a few places in which it is used in connection with the higher officers of state, who stood next to the king, and acted as it were as mediators between the king and the nation (thus 2 Sam. viii. 18, xx. 26 ; 1 Kings iv. 5). For the duties of their office the priests were to receive " *holy garments for glory and for honour.*" Before they could draw near to Jehovah the Holy One (Lev. xi. 45), it was necessary that their unholiness should be covered over with holy clothes, which were to be made by men endowed with wisdom, whom Jehovah had filled with the spirit of wisdom. " *Wise-hearted,*" *i.e.* gifted with understanding and judgment ; the heart being regarded as the birth-place of the thoughts. In the Old Testament *wisdom* is constantly used for practical intelligence in the affairs of life ; here, for example, it is equivalent to artistic skill surpassing man's natural ability, which is therefore described as being filled with the divine spirit of wisdom. These clothes were to be used " *to sanctify him* (Aaron and his sons), *that he might be a priest to Jehovah.*" Sanctification, as the indispensable condition of priestly service, was not merely the removal of the uncleanness which flowed from sin, but, as it were, the transformation of the natural into the glory of the image of God. In this sense the holy clothing served the priest for glory and ornament. The different portions of the priest's state-dress mentioned in ver. 4 are described more fully afterwards. For making them, the skilled artists were to take *the* gold, *the* hyacinth, etc. The definite article is used before gold and the following words, because the particular materials, which would be presented by the people, are here referred to.

Vers. 6–14. The *first* part mentioned of Aaron's holy dress, *i.e.* of the official dress of the high priest, is the *ephod.* The etymology of this word is uncertain; the *Sept.* rendering is ἐπωμίς (*Vulg. superhumerale,* shoulder-dress; *Luther,* "body-coat"). It was to be made of gold, hyacinth, etc., artistically woven,—of the same material, therefore, as the inner drapery and curtain of the tabernacle; but instead of having the figures of cherubim woven into it, it was to be worked throughout with gold, *i.e.* with gold thread. According to chap. xxxix. 3, the gold plates used for the purpose were beaten out, and then threads were cut (from them), to be worked into the hyacinth, purple, scarlet, and byssus. It follows from this, that gold threads were taken for every one of these four yarns, and woven with them.[1]—Ver. 7. "Two connecting shoulder-pieces shall it have for its two ends, that it may be bound together." If we compare the statement in chap. xxxix. 4,—" shoulder-pieces they made for it, connecting; at its two ends was it connected,"—there can hardly be any doubt that the ephod consisted of two pieces, which were connected together at the top upon (over) the shoulders; and that *Knobel* is wrong in supposing that it consisted of a single piece, with a hole cut on each side for the arms to be put through. If it had been a compact garment, which had to be drawn over the head like the robe (vers. 31, 32), the

---

[1] The art of weaving fabrics with gold thread (cf. *Plin. h. n.* 33, c. 3, s. 19, " *aurum netur ac texitur lanæ modo et sine lana* "), was known in ancient Egypt. " Among the coloured Egyptian costumes which are represented upon the monuments, there are some that are probably woven with gold thread."— *Wilkinson* 3, 131. *Hengstenberg*, Egypt, etc., p. 140.

opening for the head would certainly have been mentioned, as it is in the case of the latter (ver. 32).   The words of the text point most decidedly to the rabbinical idea, that it consisted of two pieces reaching to about the hip, one hanging over the breast, the other down the back, and that it was constructed with two shoulder-pieces which joined the two together.   These shoulder-pieces were not made separate, however, and then sewed upon one of the pieces ; but they were woven along with the front piece, and that not merely at the top, so as to cover the shoulders when the ephod was worn, but according to ver. 25 (? 27), reaching down on both sides from the shoulders to the girdle (ver. 8).—Ver. 8. " *And the girdle of its putting on which* (is) *upon it, shall be of it, like its work, gold,* etc.''   There was to be a girdle upon the ephod, of the same material and the same artistic work as the ephod, and joined to it, not separated from it.   The חֵשֶׁב mentioned along with the ephod cannot mean ὕφασμα, *textura* (LXX., *Cler.*, etc.), but is to be traced to חָשַׁב = חָבַשׁ to bind, to fasten, and to be understood in the sense of *cingulum*, a girdle (compare chap. xxix. 5 with Lev. viii. 7, " he girded him with the girdle of the ephod ").   אֲפֻדָּה is no doubt to be derived from אֵפֹד, and signifies the putting on of the ephod. In Isa. xxx. 22 it is applied to the covering of a statue ; at the same time, this does not warrant us in attributing to the verb, as used in chap. ix. 5 and Lev. viii. 7, the meaning, to put on or clothe.   This girdle, by which the two parts of the ephod were fastened tightly to the body, so as not to hang loose, was attached to the lower part or extremity of the ephod, so that it was fastened round the body below the breastplate (cf. vers. 27, 28, chap. xxxix. 20, 21).—Vers. 9–12. Upon the shoulder-piece of the ephod two beryls (precious stones) were to be placed, one upon each shoulder ; and upon these the names of the sons of Israel were to be engraved, six names upon each " according to their generations," *i.e.* according to their respective ages, or, as *Josephus* has correctly explained it, so that the names of the six elder sons were engraved upon the precious stone on the right shoulder, and those of the six younger sons upon that on the left.—Ver. 11. " *Work of the engraver in stone, of seal-cutting shalt thou engrave the two stones according to the names of the sons of Israel.*"   The engraver in stone: *lit.* one who works stones ; here, one who cuts and polishes precious stones.

The meaning is, that just as precious stones are cut, and seals engraved upon them, so these two stones were to be engraved according to the names of the sons of Israel, *i.e.*, so that the engraving should answer to their names, or their names be cut into the stones. " *Surrounded by gold-twist shalt thou make it.*" מִשְׁבְּצוֹת זָהָב, from שָׁבַץ to twist, is used in ver. 39 (cf. Ps. xlv. 14) for a texture woven in checks; and here it denotes not merely a simple gold-setting, but, according to ver. 13, gold-twists or ornaments representing plaits, which surrounded the golden setting in which the stones were fixed, and not only served to fasten the stones upon the woven fabric, but formed at the same time clasps or brooches, by which the two parts of the ephod were fastened together. Thus Josephus says (Ant. iii. 7, 5) there were two sardonyxes upon the shoulders, to be used for clasps.—Ver. 12. The precious stones were to be upon the shoulder-pieces of the ephod, stones of memorial for the sons of Israel; and Aaron was to bear their names before Jehovah upon his two shoulders for a memorial, *i.e.* that Jehovah might remember the sons of Israel when Aaron appeared before Him clothed with the ephod (cf. ver. 29). As a shoulder-dress, the ephod was *par excellence* the official dress of the high priest. The burden of the office rested upon the shoulder, and the insignia of the office were also worn upon it (Isa. xxii. 22). The duty of the high priest was to enter into the presence of God and make atonement for the people as their mediator. To show that as mediator he brought the nation to God, the names of the twelve tribes were engraved upon precious stones on the shoulders of the ephod. The precious stones, with their richness and brilliancy, formed the most suitable earthly substratum to represent the glory into which Israel was to be transformed as the possession of Jehovah (xix. 5); whilst the colours and material of the ephod, answering to the colours and texture of the hangings of the sanctuary, indicated the service performed in the sanctuary by the person clothed with the ephod, and the gold with which the coloured fabric was worked, the glory of that service.—Vers. 13, 14. There were also to be made for the ephod two (see ver. 25) golden plaits, golden borders (probably small plaits in the form of rosettes), and two small chains of pure gold: " *close shalt thou make them, corded* " (*lit.* work of cords or strings), *i.e.* not formed of links, but of gold thread twisted into cords, which were to be placed upon the golden plaits or fastened to them. As these chains served to fasten the *choshen* to the ephod, a description of them forms a fitting introduction to the account of this most important ornament upon the state dress-of the high priest.

Vers. 15–30. The *second* ornament consisted of the *choshen* or *breastplate.* *Choshen mishpat,* λογεῖον τῶν κρίσεων (LXX.), *rationale judicii* (Vulg.). חֹשֶׁן probably signifies an ornament (*Arab. pulcher fuit; Ges.*); and the appended word *mishpat,* right, decision of right, points to its purpose (see at ver. 30). This breastplate was to be a woven fabric of the same material and the same kind of work as the ephod. "*Foured shall it be, doubled* (laid together), *a span* (half a cubit) *its length, and a span its breadth.*" The woven cloth was to be laid together double like a kind of pocket, of the length and breadth of half a cubit, *i.e.* the quarter of a square cubit.—Ver. 17. "*And fill thereon* (put on it) *a stone-setting, four rows of stones,*" *i.e.* fix four rows of set jewels upon it. The stones, so far as their names can be determined with the help of the ancient versions, the researches of *L. de Dieu* (*animadv.* ad Ex. xxviii.) and *Braun* (*vestit.* ii. c. 8–10), and other sources pointed out in *Winer's R. W.* (*s. v. Edelsteine*), were the following :—In the *first* or upper row, *odem* (σάρδιος), *i.e.* our cornelian, of a blood-red colour; *pitdah,* τοπάζιον, the golden topaz ; *bareketh, lit.* the flashing, σμάραγδος, the emerald, of a brilliant green. In the *second* row, *nophek,* ἄνθραξ, *carbunculus,* the ruby or carbuncle, a fire-coloured stone; *sappir,* the sapphire, of a sky-blue colour; *jahalom,* ἴασπις according to the LXX., but this is rather to be found in the *jaspeh,*—according to the *Græc., Ven.,* and *Pers.,* to *Aben Ezra,* etc., the diamond, and according to others the *onyx,* a kind of chalcedony, of the same colour as the nail upon the human finger through which the flesh is visible. In the *third* row, *leshem,* λιγύριον, *ligurius, i.e.,* according to *Braun* and others, a kind of hyacinth, a transparent stone chiefly of an orange colour, but running sometimes into a reddish brown, at other times into a brownish or pale red, and sometimes into an approach to a pistachio green ; *shevo,* ἀχάτης, a composite stone formed of quartz, chalcedony, cornelian, flint, jasper, etc., and therefore glittering with different colours ; and *achlamah,* ἀμέθυστος, amethyst, a stone for the most part of a violet colour.

In the *fourth* row, *tarshish*, χρυσόλιθος, chrysolite, a brilliant stone of a golden colour, not like what is now called a chrysolite, which is of a pale green with a double refraction ; *shoham*, beryl (see at Gen. ii. 12) ; and *jaspeh*, no doubt the jasper, an opaque stone, for the most part of a dull red, often with cloudy and flame-like shadings, but sometimes yellow, red, brown, or some other colour.—Ver. 20. " *Gold borders shall be on their settings* " (see at vers. 11 and 13). The golden capsules, in which the stones were " *filled*," *i.e.* set, were to be surrounded by golden orna-ments, which not only surrounded and ornamented the stones, but in all probability helped to fix them more firmly and yet more easily upon the woven fabric.—Ver. 21. " *And the stones shall be according to the names of the sons of Israel, twelve accord-ing to their names; seal-engraving according to each one's name shall be for the twelve tribes.*" (On שִׁישׁ before עַל־שְׁמֹו see at Gen. xv. 10.)—Vers. 22–25. To bind the *choshen* to the ephod there were to be two close, corded chains of pure gold, which are described here in precisely the same manner as in ver. 14; so that ver. 22 is to be regarded as a simple repetition of ver. 14, not merely because these chains are only mentioned once in the account of the execution of the work (chap. xxxix. 15), but be-cause, according to ver. 25, these chains were to be fastened upon the rosettes noticed in ver. 14, exactly like those described in ver. 13. These chains, which are called cords or strings at ver. 24, were to be attached to two golden rings at the two (upper) ends of the *choshen*, and the two ends of the chains were to be put, *i.e.* bound firmly to the golden settings of the shoulder-pieces of the ephod (ver. 13), upon the front of it (see at chap. xxvi. 9 and xxv. 37).—Ver. 26. Two other golden rings were to be " *put at the two ends of the choshen, at its edge, which is on the opposite side* (see at chap. xxv. 37) *of the ephod inwards,*" *i.e.* at the two ends or corners of the lower border of the choshen, upon the inner side—the side turned towards the ephod.—Vers. 27, 28. Two golden rings were also to be put " *upon the shoulder-pieces of the ephod underneath, toward the fore-part thereof, near the joining above the girdle of it,*" and to fasten the *choshen* from its (lower) rings to the (lower) rings of the ephod with threads of hyacinth, that it might be over the girdle (above it), and not move away (יִוַּח Niphal of זָחַח, in Arabic *removit*), *i.e.* that it might keep its place above the girdle and against the ephod

198   THE SECOND BOOK OF MOSES.

without shifting.—Ver. 29. In this way Aaron was to bear upon his breast the names of the sons of Israel engraved upon this breastplate, as a memorial before Jehovah, whenever he went into the sanctuary.—Ver. 30. Into this *choshen* Moses was to put the *Urim* and *Thummim*, that they might be upon his heart when he came before Jehovah, and that he might thus constantly bear the right (*mishpat*) of the children of Israel upon his heart before Jehovah. It is evident at once from this, that the Urim and Thummim were to bring the right of the children of Israel before the Lord, and that the breastplate was called *choshen mishpat* because the Urim and Thummim were in it. Moreover it also follows from the expression נָתַתָּ אֶל, both here and in Lev. viii. 8, that the Urim and Thummim were not only distinct from the *choshen*, but were placed in it, and not merely suspended upon it, as *Knobel* supposes. For although the LXX. have adopted the rendering ἐπιτιθέναι ἐπί, the phrase is constantly used to denote putting or laying one thing into another, and never (not even in 1 Sam. vi. 8 and 2 Sam. xi. 16) merely placing one thing upon or against another. For this, נָתַן עַל is the expression invariably used in the account before us (cf. vers. 14 and 23 sqq.).

What the *Urim* and *Thummim* really were, cannot be determined with certainty, either from the names themselves, or from any other circumstances connected with them.[1] The LXX. render the words δήλωσις (or δῆλος) καὶ ἀλήθεια, i.e. revelation and truth. This expresses with tolerable accuracy the meaning of *Urim* (אוּרִים light, illumination), but *Thummim* (תֻּמִּים) means *integritas*, inviolability, perfection, and not ἀλήθεια. The rendering given by *Symm.* and *Theod.*, viz. φωτισμοὶ καὶ τελειώσεις, illumination and completion, is much better; and there is no good ground for giving up this rendering in favour of that of the LXX., since the analogy between the Urim and Thummim and the ἄγαλμα of sapphire-stones, or the ζώδιον of precious stones, which was worn by the Egyptian high priest suspended by a golden chain, and called ἀλήθεια (*Aelian. var. hist.* 14, 34; *Diod. Sic.* i. 48, 75), sufficiently explains the rendering ἀλήθεια, which the LXX. have given to *Thummim*, but it by no means warrants *Knobel's* conclusion, that the Hebrews had adopted the Egyptian names along with the thing itself.

[1] The leading opinions and the most important writings upon the subject are given in my *Bib. Archæol.* § 39, note 9.

The words are therefore to be explained from the Coptic. The Urim and Thummim are analogous, it is true, to the εἰκὼν τῆς ἀληθείας, which the Egyptian ἀρχιδικαστής hung round his neck, but they are by no means identical with it, or to be regarded as two figures which were a symbolical representation of revelation and truth. If Aaron was to bring the right of the children of Israel before Jehovah in the breastplate that was placed upon his breast with the Urim and Thummim, the latter, if they were intended to represent anything, could only be symbolical of the right or rightful condition of Israel. But the words do not warrant any such conclusion. If the Urim and Thummim had been intended to represent any really existing thing, their nature, or the mode of preparing them, would certainly have been described. Now, if we refer to Num. xxvii. 21, where Joshua as the commander of the nation is instructed to go to the high priest Eleazar, that the latter may inquire before Jehovah, through the right of Urim, how the whole congregation should walk and act, we can draw no other conclusion, than that the Urim and Thummim are to be regarded as a certain medium, given by the Lord to His people, through which, whenever the congregation required divine illumination to guide its actions, that illumination was guaranteed, and by means of which the rights of Israel, when called in question or endangered, were to be restored, and that this medium was bound up with the official dress of the high priest, though its precise character can no longer be determined. Consequently the Urim and Thummim did not represent the illumination and right of Israel, but were merely a promise of these, a pledge that the Lord would maintain the rights of His people, and give them through the high priest the illumination requisite for their protection. Aaron was to bear the children of Israel upon his heart, in the precious stones to be worn upon his breast with the names of the twelve tribes. The heart, according to the biblical view, is the centre of the spiritual life,—not merely of the willing, desiring, thinking life, but of the emotional life, as the seat of the feelings and affections (see *Delitzsch bibl. Psychologie*, pp. 203 sqq.). Hence to bear upon the heart does not merely mean to bear in mind, but denotes " that personal intertwining with the life of another, by virtue of which the high priest, as *Philo* expresses it, was τοῦ σύμπαντος ἔθνους συγγενὴς καὶ ἀγχιστεὺς κοινός (*Spec. leg.* ii. 321),

and so stood in the deepest sympathy with those for whom he inter-
ceded" (*Oehler* in *Herzog's* Cycl.). As he entered the holy place
with this feeling, and in this attitude, of which the *choshen* was the
symbol, he brought Israel into remembrance before Jehovah that
the Lord might accept His people; and when furnished with the
Urim and Thummim, he appeared before Jehovah as the advocate
of the people's rights, that he might receive for the congregation
the illumination required to protect and uphold those rights.

Vers. 31–35. The *third* portion of Aaron's official dress was
the *robe*. To the ephod there also belonged a מְעִיל (from מָעַל to
cover or envelope), an upper garment, called the robe of the
ephod, the robe belonging to the ephod, "*all of dark-blue purple*"
(hyacinth), by which we are not to imagine a cloak or mantle,
but a long, closely-fitting coat; not reaching to the feet, however, as the Alex. rendering ποδήρης might lead us to suppose,
but only to the knees, so as to show the coat (ver. 39) which was
underneath.—Ver. 32. "*And the opening of the head thereof
shall be in the middle of it;*" *i.e.* there was to be an opening in
the middle of it to put the head through when it was put on;—
"*a hem shall be round the opening of it, weavers' work, like the
opening of the habergeon shall it* (the seam) *be to it; it shall not
be torn.*" By the habergeon (θώραξ), or coat-of-mail, we have
to understand the λινοθώρηξ, the linen coat, such as was worn by
Ajax for example (Il. 2, 529). Linen habergeons of this kind
were made in Egypt in a highly artistic style (see *Hengstenberg*,
Egypt, etc., pp. 141–2). In order that the *meïl* might not be torn
when it was put on, the opening for the head was to be made
with a strong hem, which was to be of weavers' work; from which
it follows as a matter of course that the robe was woven in one
piece, and not made in several pieces and then sewed together;
and this is expressly stated in chap. xxxix. 22. *Josephus* and
the Rabbins explain the words מַעֲשֵׂה אֹרֵג (ἔργον ὑφαντόν) in this
way, and observe at the same time that the *meïl* had no sleeves,
but only arm-holes.—Vers. 33, 34. On the lower hem (שׁוּלִים the
tail or skirt) there were to be pomegranates of dark-blue and
dark-red purple and crimson, made of twisted yarn of these
colours (chap. xxxix. 24), and little golden bells between them
round about, a bell and a pomegranate occurring alternately all
round. According to *Rashi* the pomegranates were "*globi
quidam rotundi instar malorum punicorum, quasi essent ova gal-*

linarum." פַּעֲמֹנִים (from פָּעַם to strike or knock, like the old High German *cloccon, clochon, i.e.* to smite) signifies a little bell, not a spherical ball.—Ver. 35. Aaron was to put on this coat, to minister, *i.e.* to perform the duties of his holy office, "*that his sound might be heard when he went into the holy place before Jehovah, and when he came out, and he might not die.*" These directions are referred to in Ecclus. xlv. 9, and explained as follows: "He compassed him with pomegranates and with many golden bells round about, that as he went there might be a sound, and a noise made, that might be heard in the temple, for a memorial to the children of his people." The probable meaning of these words is either that given by *Hiskuni* (in *Drusius*), *ut sciant tempus cultus divini atque ita præparent cor suum ad patrem suum, qui est in cœlis,* or that given by *Oehler,* viz. that the ringing of the bells might announce to the people in the court the entrance of the high priest and the rites he was performing, in order that they might accompany him with their thoughts and prayers. But this is hardly correct. For not only is the expression, "for a memorial to the children of Israel," evidently intended by the writer of Ecclesiasticus as a translation of the words זִכָּרוֹן לִבְנֵי יִשְׂרָאֵל in ver. 12 (cf. ver. 29), so that he has transferred to the bells of the *meïl* what really applies to the precious stones on the ephod, which contained the names of the twelve sons of Israel, but he has misunderstood the words themselves; for Aaron was to bear the names of the sons of Israel before Jehovah in these precious stones for a reminder, *i.e.* to remind Jehovah of His people. Moreover, the words "and he shall not die" are not in harmony with this interpretation. *Bähr, Oehler,* and others, regard the words as referring to the whole of the high priest's robes, and understand them as meaning, that he would be threatened with death if he appeared before Jehovah without his robes, inasmuch as he was merely a private individual without this holy dress, and could not in that case represent the nation. This is so far justifiable, no doubt, although not favoured by the position of the words in the context, that the bells were inseparably connected with the robe, which was indispensable to the ephod with the *choshen,* and consequently the bells had no apparent significance except in connection with the whole of the robes. But even if we do adopt this explanation of the words, we cannot suppose that Aaron's not dying depended upon the prayers of the congregation which accompanied his going in and out before Jehovah; for in that case the intercession of the high priest would have lost its objective meaning altogether, and his life would have been actually given up in a certain sense to the caprice of the people. All that remains, therefore, is to take the words as they occur: Aaron was not to appear before the Lord without the sound of the bells upon his robe being heard, in order that he might not die; so that to understand the reason for his not dying, we must inquire what the ringing of the bells signified, or rather, what was the signification of Aaron's robe, with its border of pomegranates and ringing bells. The trivial explanation given by *Abraham ben David*, viz. that the ringing was to take the place of knocking at the door of Jehovah's palace, as an abrupt entrance into the presence of a great king was punished with death, is no more deserving of a serious refutation than *Knobel's* idea, for which there is no foundation, that the sounding of the bells was to represent a reverential greeting, and a very musical offering of praise (!).

The special significance of the *meïl* cannot have resided in either its form or its colour; for the only feature connected with its form, that was at all peculiar to it, was its being woven in one piece, which set forth the idea of wholeness or spiritual integrity; and the dark-blue colour indicated nothing more than the heavenly origin and character of the office with which the robe was associated. It must be sought for, therefore, in the peculiar pendants, the meaning of which is to be gathered from the analogous instructions in Num. xv. 38, 39, where every Israelite is directed to make a fringe in the border of his garment, of dark-blue purple thread, and when he looks at the fringe to remember the commandments of God and do them. In accordance with this, we are also to seek for allusions to the word and testimony of God in the pendant of pomegranates and bells attached to the fringe of the high priest's robe. The simile in Prov. xxv. 11, where the word is compared to an apple, suggests the idea that the pomegranates, with their pleasant odour, their sweet and refreshing juice, and the richness of their delicious kernel, were symbols of the word and testimony of God as a sweet and pleasant spiritual food, that enlivens the soul and refreshes the heart (compare Ps. xix. 8–11, cxix. 25, 43, 50, with Deut. viii. 3, Prov. ix. 8, Ecclus. xv. 3), and that the bells were symbols of the sounding of this word, or the revelation and proclamation of the word. Through the robe, with this pendant attached, Aaron was represented as the recipient and medium of the word and testimony which came down from heaven; and this was the reason why he was not to appear before the Lord without that sound, lest he should forfeit his life. It was not because he would simply have appeared as a private person if he had gone without it, for he would always have the holy dress of a priest upon him, even when he was not clothed in the official decorations of the high priest; but because no mere priest was allowed to enter the immediate presence of the Lord. This privilege was restricted to the representative of the whole congregation, viz. the high priest; and even he could only do so when wearing the robe of the word of God, as the bearer of the divine testimony, upon which the covenant fellowship with the Lord was founded.

Vers. 36–38. The *fourth* article of the high priest's dress was the *diadem* upon his head-band. צִיץ, from צוּץ to shine, a plate of pure gold, on which the words קֹדֶשׁ לַיהוָֹה, " *holiness* (*i.e.* all holy) *to Jehovah*," were engraved, and which is called the " crown of holiness" in consequence, in chap. xxxix. 30. This gold plate was to be placed upon a riband of dark-blue purple, or, as it is expressed in chap. xxxix. 31, a riband of this kind was to be fastened to it, to attach it to the head-band, " *upon the fore-front* (as in chap. xxvi. 9) *of the head-band*," from above (chap. xxxix. 31); by which we are to understand that the gold plate was placed above the lower coil of the head-band and over Aaron's forehead. The word מִצְנֶפֶת, from צָנַף to twist or coil (Isa. xxii. 18), is only applied to the head-band or turban of the high priest, which was made of simple byssus (ver. 39), and, judging from the etymology, was in the shape of a turban. This is all that can be determined with reference to its form. The diadem was the only thing about it that had any special significance. This was to be placed above (upon) Aaron's forehead, that he " might bear the iniquity of the holy things, which the children of Israel sanctified, with regard to all their holy gifts, . . as an acceptableness for them before Jehovah." נָשָׂא עָוֹן: to bear iniquity (sin) and take it away; in other words, to exterminate it by taking it upon one's self. The high priest was exalted into an atoning mediator of the whole nation; and an atoning, sin-exterminating intercession was associated with his office. The qualification for this he received from the diadem upon his forehead with the inscription, " holiness to the Lord." Through this inscription, which was fastened upon his head-dress of brilliant white, the earthly reflection of holiness, he was crowned as the sanctified of the Lord (Ps. cvi. 16), and endowed with the power to exterminate the sin which clung to the holy offerings of the people on account of the unholiness of their nature, so that the gifts of the nation became well-pleasing to the Lord, and the good pleasure of God was manifested to the nation.[1]

Ver. 39. In addition to the distinguishing dress of the high priest, Aaron was also to wear, as the official costume of a priest, a *body-coat* (*cetoneth*) made of byssus, and woven in checks or cubes; the *head-band* (for the diadem), also made of simple byssus; and a *girdle* (*abnet*, of uncertain etymology, and only applied to the priest's girdle) of variegated work, *i.e.* made of yarn, of the same four colours as the holy things were to be made of (cf. chap. xxxix. 29).

Vers. 40–43. The *official dress of the sons of Aaron*, *i.e.* of the ordinary priests, was to consist of just the same articles as Aaron's priestly costume (ver. 39). But their *body-coat* is called weavers' work in chap. xxxix. 27, and was therefore quite a plain cloth, of white byssus or cotton yarn, though it was whole throughout, ἄρραφος without seam, like the robe of Christ (John xix. 23). It was worn close to the body, and, according to Jewish tradition, reached down to the ankles (cf. *Josephus*, iii. 7, 2). The *head-dress* of an ordinary priest is called מִגְבָּעָה, related to גָּבִיעַ a basin or cup, and therefore seems to have been in the form of an inverted cup, and to have been a plain white

---

[1] See my Archæology i. pp. 183-4. The following are *Calvin's* admirable remarks: Oblationum sanctarum iniquitas tollenda et purganda fuit per sacerdotem. Frigidum est illud commentum, si quid erroris admissum est in ceremoniis, remissum fuisse sacerdotis precibus. Longius enim respicere nos oportet: ideo oblationum iniquitatem deleri a sacerdote, quia nulla oblatio, quatenus est hominis, omni vitio caret. Dictu hoc asperum est et fere παράδοξον, sanctitates ipsas esse immundas, ut venia indigeant; sed tenendum est, nihil esse sane purum, quod non aliquid labis a nobis contrahat. . . . . Nihil Dei cultu præstantius: et tamen nihil offerre potuit populus, etiam a lege præscriptum, nisi intercedente venia, quam nonnisi per sacerdotem obtinuit.

cotton cap. The *girdle*, according to chap. xxxix. 29, was of the same material and work for Aaron and his sons. This dress was to be for glory and for beauty to the priests, just as Aaron's dress was to him (ver. 2). The glory consisted in the brilliant white colour, the symbol of holiness; whilst the girdle, which an oriental man puts on when preparing for the duties of an office, contained in the four colours of the sanctuary the indication that they were the officers of Jehovah in His earthly kingdom.— Ver. 41. But since the clothing prescribed was an official dress, Moses was to put it upon Aaron and his sons, to anoint them and fill their hands, *i.e.* to invest them with the requisite sacrificial gifts (see at Lev. vii. 37), and so to sanctify them that they should be priests of Jehovah. For although the holiness of their office was reflected in their dress, it was necessary, on account of the sinfulness of their nature, that they should be sanctified through a special consecration for the administration of their office; and this consecration is prescribed in chap. xxix. and carried out in Lev. viii.—Vers. 42, 43. The covering of their nakedness was an indispensable prerequisite. Aaron and his sons were therefore to receive מִכְנְסִים (from כָּנַס to cover or conceal, *lit.* concealers), short drawers, reaching from the hips to the thighs, and serving " to cover the flesh of the nakedness." For this reason the directions concerning them are separated from those concerning the different portions of the dress, which were for glory and beauty. The material of which these drawers were to be made is called בַּד. The meaning of this word is uncertain. According to chap. xxxix. 28, it was made of twined byssus or cotton yarn; and the rendering of the LXX., λίνα or λίνεος (Lev. vi. 3), is not at variance with this, as the ancients not only apply the term λίνον, *linum*, to flax, but frequently use it for fine white cotton as well. In all probability *bad* was a kind of white cloth, from בָּדַד to be white or clean, primarily to separate.—Ver. 43. These drawers the priests were to put on whenever they entered the sanctuary, that they might not " bear iniquity and die," *i.e.* incur guilt deserving of death, either through disobedience to these instructions, or, what was still more important, through such violation of the reverence due to the holiness of the dwelling of God as they would be guilty of, if they entered the sanctuary with their nakedness uncovered. For as the consciousness of sin and guilt made itself known first of all in the feeling of nakedness, so those members which sub-serve the natural secretions are especially *pudenda* or objects of shame, since the mortality and corruptibility of the body, which sin has brought into human nature, are chiefly manifested in these secretions. For this reason these members are also called the "flesh of nakedness." By this we are not to understand merely "the sexual member as the organ of generation or birth, because the existence and permanence of sinful, mortal human nature are associated with these," as *Bähr* supposes. For the frailty and nakedness of humanity are not manifested in the organ and act of generation, which rather serve to manifest the inherent capa-city and creation of man for imperishable life, but in the impu-rities which nature ejects through those organs, and which bear in themselves the character of corruptibility. If, therefore, the priest was to appear before Jehovah as holy, it was necessary that those parts of his body especially should be covered, in which the impurity of his nature and the nakedness of his flesh were most apparent. For this reason, even in ordinary life, they are most carefully concealed, though not, as *Baumgarten* supposes, "because the sin of nature has its principal seat in the flesh of nakedness."—"*A statute for ever :*" as in chap. xxvii. 31.

Chap. xxix. vers. 1–37. CONSECRATION OF AARON AND HIS SONS through the anointing of their persons and the offering of sacrifices, the directions for which form the subject of vers. 1–35. This can only be fully understood in connection with the sacrificial law contained in Lev. i.–vii. It will be more advis-able therefore to defer the examination of this ceremony till we come to Lev. viii., where the consecration itself is described. The same may also be said of the expiation and anointing of the altar, which are commanded in vers. 36 and 37, and carried out in Lev. viii. 11.

Vers. 38–46. The DAILY BURNT-OFFERING, MEAT-OFFER-ING, AND DRINK-OFFERING.—The directions concerning these are attached to the instructions for the consecration of the priests, because these sacrifices commenced immediately after the com-pletion of the tabernacle, and, like the shew-bread (xxv. 30), the daily trimming of the lamps (xxvii. 20, 21), and the daily in-cense-offering (xxx. 7 sqq.), were most intimately connected with the erection of the sanctuary.—Ver. 38. *"And this is what thou shalt make* (offer) *upon the altar; yearling lambs two a day continually,"* one in the morning, the other between the two evenings (see at chap. xii. 6); to every one a meat-offering (*minchah*) of a tenth of fine wheaten flour (*soleth*, see at Lev. ii. 1), mixed with a quarter of a hin of beaten oil (*cathith*, see at chap. xxvii. 20), and a drink-offering (*nesek*) of a quarter of a hin of wine. עִשָּׂרוֹן (a tenth) is equivalent to עֲשִׂירִת הָאֵיפָה, the tenth part of an ephah (Num. xxviii. 5), or 198·5 Parisian cubic inches according to *Bertheau's* measurement. *Thenius*, however, sets it down at 101·4 inches, whilst the Rabbins reckon it as equivalent to 43 hen's eggs of average size, *i.e.* somewhat more than 2¼ lbs. A *hin* (a word of Egyptian origin) is 330·9 inches according to *Bertheau*, 168·9 according to Thenius, or 72 eggs, so that a quarter of a hin would be 18 eggs.—Ver. 41. לָהּ is to be understood *ad sensum* as referring to עוֹלָה. The daily morning and evening sacrifices were to be "for a sweet savour, a firing unto Jehovah" (see at Lev. i. 9). In these Israel was to consecrate its life daily unto the Lord (see at Lev. i. and ii.). In order that the whole of the daily life might be included, it was to be offered continually every morning and evening for all future time ("throughout your generations" as at chap. xii. 14) at the door of the tabernacle, *i.e.* upon the altar erected there, before Jehovah, who would meet with the people and commune with them there (see chap. xxv. 22). This promise is carried out still further in vers. 43-46. First of all, for the purpose of elucidating and strengthening the words, "I will meet with you there" (ver. 42), the presence and communion of God, which are attached to the ark of the covenant in chap. xxv. 22, are ensured to the whole nation in the words, "And there I will meet with the children of Israel, and it (Israel) shall be sanctified through My glory." As the people were not allowed to approach the ark of the covenant, but only to draw near to the altar of burnt-offering in the sanctuary, it was important to declare that the Lord would manifest Himself to them even there, and sanctify them by His glory. Most of the commentators have taken the altar to be the subject of "shall be sanctified;" but this is certainly an error, not only because the altar is not mentioned in the previous clause, and only slightly hinted at in the לָהּ in ver. 41, but principally because the sanctification of the altar is noticed by itself afterwards in ver. 44. The correct exegesis is that adopted by *Baumgarten* and others, who supply the word *Israel* (viz. regarded as a nation), which they take from the expression " children of Israel" in the previous clause. In ver. 44, the sanctification of the tabernacle and altar on the part of God is promised, also that of His servants, and finally, in vers. 45, 46, the abode of God in the midst of the children of Israel, with an allusion to the blessings that would follow from Jehovah's dwelling in the midst of them as their God (Gen. xvii. 7).

Chap. xxx. 1–10. The ALTAR OF INCENSE AND INCENSE-OFFERING bring the directions concerning the sanctuary to a close. What follows, from xxx. 11–xxxi. 17, is shown to be merely supplementary to the larger whole by the formula " and Jehovah spake unto Moses," with which every separate command is introduced (cf. vers. 11, 17, 22, 34, xxxi. 1, 12).—Vers. 1–5 (cf. chap. xxxvii. 25–28). Moses was directed to make an *altar of burning of incense* (*lit.* incensing of incense), of acacia-wood, one cubit long and one broad, four-cornered, two cubits high, furnished with horns like the altar of burnt-offering (chap. xxvii. 1, 2), and to plate it with pure gold, the roof (גָּג) thereof (*i.e.* its upper side or surface, which was also made of wood), and its walls round about, and its horns; so that it was covered with gold quite down to the ground upon which it stood, and for this reason is often called the golden altar (chap. xxxix. 38, xl. 5, 26; Num. iv. 11). Moreover it was to be ornamented with a golden wreath, and furnished with golden rings at the corners for the carrying-poles, as the ark of the covenant and the table of shew-bread were (xxv. 11 sqq., 25 sqq.); and its place was to be in front of the curtain, which concealed the ark of the covenant (xxvi. 31), " before the capporeth" (xl. 5), so that, although it really stood in the holy place between the candlestick on the south side and the table on the north (xxvi. 35, xl. 22, 24), it was placed in the closest relation to the *capporeth*, and for this reason is not only connected with the most holy place in 1 Kings vi. 22, but is reckoned in Heb. ix. 4 as part of the furniture of the most holy place (see *Delitzsch* on Heb. ix. 4).—Vers. 7–9. Upon this altar Aaron was to burn fragrant incense, the preparation of which is described in vers. 34 sqq., every morning and evening before Jehovah, at the time when he trimmed the lamps. No "strange incense" was to be offered upon it,—*i.e.* incense which Jehovah had not appointed (cf. Lev. x. 1), that is to say, which had not been prepared according to His instructions, —nor burnt sacrifice, nor meat-offering; and no drink-offering was to be poured upon it. As the altar of incense was not only marked as a place of sacrifice by its name מִזְבֵּחַ, "place of slain-offering," but was put on a par with the altar of sacrifice by its square shape and its horns, it was important to describe minutely what sacrifices were to be offered upon it. For the burning of fragrant incense is shown to be a sacrifice, by the fact that it was offered upon a place of sacrifice, or altar. Moreover the word הִקְטִיר, to cause to ascend in smoke and steam, from קָטַר to smoke or steam, is not only applied to the lighting of incense, but also to the lighting and burning of the bleeding and bloodless sacrifices upon the altar of incense. Lastly, the connection between the incense-offering and the burnt-offering is indicated by the rule that they were to be offered at the same time. Both offerings shadowed forth the devotion of Israel to its God, whilst the fact that they were offered every day exhibited this devotion as constant and uninterrupted. But the distinction between them consisted in this, that in the burnt or whole offering Israel consecrated and sanctified its whole life and action in both body and soul to the Lord, whilst in the incense-offering its prayer was embodied as the exaltation of the spiritual man to God (cf. Ps. cxli. 2; Rev. v. 8, viii. 3, 4); and with this there was associated the still further distinction, that the devotion was completed in the burnt-offering solely upon the basis of the atoning sprinkling of blood, whereas the incense-offering presupposed reconciliation with God, and on the basis of this the soul rose to God in this embodiment of its prayer, and was thus absorbed into His Spirit. In this respect, the incense-offering was not only a spiritualizing and transfiguring of the burnt-offering, but a completion of that offering also.—Ver. 10. Once a year Aaron was to expiate the altar of incense with the blood of the sin-offering of atonement, because it was most holy to the Lord, that is to say, as is expressly observed in the directions concerning this expiatory act (Lev. xvi. 18, 19), to purify it from the uncleannesses of the children of Israel. כִּפֶּר, with עַל *objecti constr.*, signifies literally to cover over a thing, then to cover over sin, or make expiation. In the second clause we have "*upon it*" (the altar) instead of "upon the horns of it," because the altar itself was expiated in its horns. The use of מִן in מִדָּם is to be explained on the ground that only a part of the blood of the sin-offering was smeared with the finger upon the horns. (Far further remarks, see at Lev. xvi. 18, 19.) The term "most holy" is not only applied to this altar, in common with the inner division of the tabernacle (chap. xxvi. 33), but also to the altar of burnt-offering (chap. xxix. 37, xl. 10), and all the vessels of the sanctuary (chap. xxx. 29), which were anointed with holy oil; then to the whole of the tabernacle in its holiest aspect (Num. xviii. 10); and lastly, to all the sacrifices, which were given up entirely to Je-hovah (see at Lev. ii. 3);—consequently to everything which stood in so intimate a relation to Jehovah as to be altogether removed, not only from use and enjoyment on the part of man, but also from contact on the part of unsanctified men. Who-ever touched a most holy thing was sanctified thereby (compare ver. 29 with chap. xxix. 37).

Vers. 11–16. THE ATONEMENT-MONEY, which every Is-raelite had to pay at the numbering of the people, has the first place among the supplementary instructions concerning the erec-tion and furnishing of the sanctuary, and serves to complete the demand for freewill-offerings for the sanctuary (chap. xxv. 1–9). —Ver. 12. "*When thou takest the sum of the children of Israel according to them that are numbered, they shall give every one an expiation for his soul to the Lord at their numbering, that a plague may not strike them* (happen to them) *at their numbering.*" פָּקַד, lit. *adspexit*, then *inspexit explorandi causa*, hence to review, or number an army or a nation, for the purpose of enrolling for military service. לִפְקֻדֵיהֶם with reference to the numbered, *qui in censum veniunt.* כֹּפֶר (expiation, expiation-money, from כִּפֶּר to expiate) is to be traced to the idea that the object for which expiation was made was thereby withdrawn from the view of the person to be won or reconciled. It is applied in two ways: (1) on the supposition that the face of the person to be won was covered by the gift (Gen. xxxii. 21; 1 Sam. xii. 3); and (2) on the supposition that the guilt itself was covered up (Ps. xxxii. 1), or wiped away (Jer. xviii. 23), so far as the eye of God was concerned, as though it had no longer any existence, and that the sinful man was protected from the punishment of the judge in consequence of this covering. In this way כֹּפֶר has acquired the meaning λύτρον, a payment by which the guilty are redeemed (chap. xxi. 30; Num. xxxv. 31); and this is the meaning which it has in the passage before us, where the soul is said to be protected by the *copher*, so as to be able to come without danger into the presence of the holy God (Num. viii. 19. See *Oehler* in *Herzog's* Cycl.). Such an approach to God took place at the numbering of the people for the purpose of enrolling them in the army of Jehovah (Num. i. 3, cf. Ex. vii. 4, xii. 41). Hence " every one who passed over to those that were numbered," who was enrolled among them, *i.e.* in the army of Jehovah,—that is to say, every male Israelite of 20 years old and upwards (ver. 14),—was to pay half a shekel of the sanctuary as atonement-money; the rich no more, the poor no less (ver. 15), because all were equal in the sight of Jehovah; and this payment was to be a " heave" (*terumah*, see chap. xxv. 2) for Jehovah for the expiation of the souls. The shekel of the sanctuary, which contained 20 gerahs, was no doubt the original shekel of full weight, as distinguished from the lighter shekel which was current in ordinary use. In chap. xxxviii. 26 the half shekel is called בֶּקַע, *lit.* the split, *i.e.* half, from בָּקַע to split; and we find it mentioned as early as the time of the patriarchs as a weight in common use for valuing gold (Gen. xxiv. 22), so that, no doubt, even at that time there were distinct silver pieces of this weight, which were probably called shekels when employed for purposes of trade, since the word *shekel* itself does not denote any particular weight, as we may perceive at once from a comparison of 1 Kings x. 17 and 2 Chron. ix. 16, at least so far as later times are concerned. The sacred shekel, to judge from the weight of the Maccabean shekels, which are in existence still, and vary from 256 to 272 Parisian grains, weighed 274 grains, and therefore, according to present valuation, would be worth 26 groschen (about 2s. 7d.), so that the half-shekel or bekah would be 13 groschen (1s. 3½d.). —Ver. 16. This atonement-money Moses was to appropriate to the work of the sanctuary (cf. chap. xxxviii. 25–28, where the amount and appropriation are reported). Through this appropriation it became " a *memorial to the children of Israel before the Lord to expiate their souls*," *i.e.* a permanent reminder of their expiation before the Lord, who would henceforth treat them as reconciled because of this payment.   It was no ordinary tribute, therefore, which Israel was to pay to Jehovah as its King, but an act demanded by the holiness of the theocratic covenant.   As an expiation for souls, it pointed to the unholiness of Israel's nature, and reminded the people continually, that by nature it was alienated from God, and could only remain in covenant with the Lord and live in His kingdom on the ground of His grace, which covered its sin.   It was not till this sinful nature had been sanctified by a perfect atonement, and servitude under the law had been glorified and fully transformed into that sonship to which Israel was called as the first-born son of Jehovah, that as children of the kingdom they had no longer to pay this atonement-money for their souls (Matt. xvii. 25, 26).— According to Num. i. 1, 18, as compared with Ex. xl. 17, the census of the nation was not taken till a month after the building of the tabernacle was completed, and yet the atonement-money to be paid at the taking of the census was to be appropriated to the purpose of the building, and must therefore have been paid before.   This apparent discrepancy may be reconciled by the simple assumption, that immediately after the command of God had been issued respecting the building of the tabernacle and the contributions which the people were to make for that purpose, the numbering of the males was commenced and the atonement-money collected from the different individuals, that the tabernacle was then built and the whole ceremonial instituted, and that, after all this had been done, the whole nation was enrolled according to its tribes, fathers' houses, and families, on the basis of this provisional numbering, and thus the census was completed.   For this reason the census gave exactly the same number of males as the numbering (cf. chap. xxxviii. 26 and Num. i. 46), although the one had been carried out nine months before the other.

Vers. 17–21 (cf. chap. xxxviii. 8). The BRAZEN LAVER, and its use.—The making of this vessel is not only mentioned in a supplementary manner, but no description is given of it because of the subordinate position which it occupied, and from the fact that it was not directly connected with the sanctuary, but was only used by the priests to cleanse themselves for the performance of their duties.   כִּיּוֹר : a basin, a round, caldron-shaped vessel. כַּנּוֹ (its support) : by this we are not to understand the pedestal of the caldron, but something separate from the basin, which was no doubt used for drawing off as much water as was required for washing the officiating priests. For although כַּ belongs to כִּיּוֹר, the fact that it is always specially mentioned in connection with the basin necessarily leads to the conclusion, that it had a certain kind of independence (cf. chap. xxxi. 9, xxxv. 16, xxxix. 39, xl. 11; Lev. viii. 11). These two vessels were to be made of brass or copper, like the other things in the court; and, according to chap. xxxviii. 8, they were made of the brass of the mirrors of the women who served before the door of the tabernacle. בְּמַרְאֹת הַצֹּבְאֹת does not mean either " provided with mirrors of the women" (*Bähr*, i. pp. 485–6), or ornamented " with forms, figures of women, as they were accustomed to appear at the sanctuary" (*Knobel*). Both these views are overthrown by the fact, that בְּ never signifies *with* in the sense of an outward addition, but always denotes the means, " not an independent object, but something accompanying and contributing to the action referred to" (*Ewald*, § 217, f. 3). In this case בְּ can only apply to the material used, whether we connect it with וַיַּעַשׂ as in chap. xxxi. 4, or, what seems decidedly more correct, with נְחֹשֶׁת as a more precise definition; so that בְּ would denote that particular quality which distinguished the brass of which the basin was made (*Ewald*, § 217 f.),—apart altogether from the fact, that neither the mirrors of women, nor the figures of women, would form a fitting ornament for the basin, as the priests did not require to look at themselves when they washed their hands and feet; and there is still less ground for Knobel's fiction, that Levitical women went to the sanctuary at particular times, forming a certain procession, and taking things with them for the purpose of washing, cleaning, and polishing. The true meaning is given by the Septuagint, ἐκ τῶν κατόπτρων. According to 1 Sam. ii. 22, the צֹבְאֹת were women, though not washer-women, but women who dedicated their lives to the service of Jehovah, and spent them in religious exercises, in fasting and in prayer, like Anna, the daughter of Phanuel, mentioned in Luke ii. 37.[1] צְבָא denotes spiritual warfare, and is accordingly

---

[1] *Knobel's* objection to this explanation, viz. that " at a time when the sanctuary was not yet erected, the author could not speak of women as coming to the door of the sanctuary, or performing religious service there,"

rendered by the LXX. νηστεύειν, by *Onkelos, orare*, with which
the Rabbins agree. The mirrors of the women had been used
for the purpose of earthly adorning. But now the pious Israelites
renounced this earthly adorning, and offered it to the Lord as a
heave-offering to make the purifying laver in front of the sanctuary, in order that " what had hitherto served as a means of
procuring applause in the world might henceforth be the means
of procuring the approbation of God" (*Hengstenberg*, Dissert.
vol. ii.).—The laver was to be placed between the tabernacle,
i.e. the dwelling, and the altar in the court (ver. 18), probably
not in a straight line with the door of the dwelling and the altar
of burnt-offering, but more sideways, so as to be convenient for
the use of the priests, whether they were going into the tabernacle, or going up to the altar for service, to kindle a firing for
Jehovah, *i.e.* to offer sacrifice upon the altar. They were to
wash their hands, with which they touched the holy things, and
their feet, with which they trod the holy ground (see chap. iii.
5), " that they might not die," as is again emphatically stated
in vers. 20 and 21. For touching holy things with unclean
hands, and treading upon the floor of the sanctuary with dirty
feet, would have been a sin against Jehovah, the Holy One of
Israel, deserving of death. These directions do not imply "that,
notwithstanding all their consecration, they were regarded as
still defiled by natural uncleanness" (*Baumgarten*), but rather
that consecration did not stamp them with a *character indelebilis*,
or protect them from the impurities of the sinful nation in the
midst of which they lived, or of their own nature, which was
still affected with mortal corruption and sin.

Vers. 22–33. The HOLY ANOINTING OIL.—This was to be
prepared from the best perfumes (בְּשָׂמִים רֹאשׁ, where רֹאשׁ, *caput*,
the principal or chief, is subordinate to בְּשָׂמִים), viz. of four fragrant spices and olive-oil. The spices were, (1) *liquid myrrh*, as

would contain its own refutation, if there were any ground for it at all.
For before the sanctuary was erected, the author could not speak of Levitical
women as coming at particular times to the sanctuary, and bringing things
with them for the purpose of washing and cleaning. But the participle
צֹבְאֹת does not imply that they had served there before the erection of the
sanctuary, but only that from that time forward, they did perform service
there.

distinguished from the dry gum ;—(2) קִנְּמָן־בֶּשֶׂם, *cinnamon of fragrance*, the name having been introduced to the Semitic nations along with the thing itself, and then by the Phœnicians to the Greeks and Romans (*κινναμον, cinnamum*) : whether it came from Ceylon, the great mart of cinnamon, is very doubtful, as there is no word that can be discovered in the Indian dialects corresponding to *cinnamon;*—(3) *cane of fragrance*, the κάλαμος ἀρωματικός, *calamus odoratus*, of the Greeks and Romans, *i.e.* the scented calamus which is imported from India;—and (4) *kiddah*, probably *cassia*, and possibly the species called κιττώ in Dioscor. 1, 12, in which case קְצִיעָה (Ps. xlv. 9) is either the generic name for cassia, or else refers to a different species. The proportion in which these spices were to be taken was 500 shekels or 14½ lbs. of myrrh, half the quantity, *i.e.* 7 lbs., of cinnamon, and the same of calamus and cassia; in all, therefore, 21 lbs. of dry spices, which were to be mixed with one hin of oil (about 5 quarts) and 14 lbs. of liquid myrrh. These proportions preclude the supposition, that the spices were pulverized and mixed with the oil and myrrh in their natural condition, for the result in that case would have been a thick mess: they rather favour the statement of the Rabbins, that the dry spices were softened in water and boiled, to extract their essence, which was then mixed with oil and myrrh, and boiled again until all the watery part had evaporated. An artificial production of this kind is also indicated by the expressions רֹקַח מִרְקַחַת " *spice-work of spice-mixture*," and מַעֲשֵׂה רֹקֵחַ " *labour* (work) *of the perfumer or ointment-maker*."—Vers. 26 sqq. With this holy anointing oil the tabernacle and all its furniture were to be anointed and sanctified, that they might be most holy; also Aaron and his sons, that they might serve the Lord as priests (see at Lev. viii. 10 sqq.). This anointing oil was holy, either because it was made from the four fragrant substances according to the proportions commanded by Jehovah, or because God declared this kind of mixture and preparation holy (cf. ver. 32), and forbade for all time, on pain of death (ver. 31), not only the use of ointment so prepared for any ordinary anointings, but even an imitation of it. " *Upon man's flesh shall it not be poured*," *i.e.* it is not to be used for the ordinary practice of anointing the human body (ver. 32). " *Man*," *i.e.* the ordinary man in distinction from the priests. בְּמַתְכֻּנְתּוֹ according to its measure, *i.e.* according to the proportions prescribed for its manufacture. זָר (ver. 33), a stranger, is not only the non-Israelite, but laymen or non-priests in general. On the expression, " cut off from his people," see at Gen. xvii. 14.

Vers. 34-38. The HOLY INCENSE was also to be made of four ingredients, viz. (1) *nataph* (στακτή, *stacte*), *i.e.* not the resinous myrrh, or sap obtained from the fragrant myrrh and dried, but a kind of *storax* gum resembling myrrh, which was baked, and then used, like incense, for fumigating;—(2) *shecheleth* (ὄνυξ, *unguis odoratus*), the shell of a shell-fish resembling the *purpura*, of an agreeable odour;—(3) *chelbenah* (χαλβάνη), a resin of a pungent, bitter flavour, obtained, by means of an incision in the bark, from the *ferula*, a shrub which grows in Syria, Arabia, and Abyssinia, and then mixed with fragrant substances to give greater pungency to their odour;—and (4) *lebonah* (λίβανος or λιβανωτός), frankincense, a resin of a pleasant smell, obtained from a tree in Arabia Felix or India, but what tree has not been discovered. זַכָּה pure, *i.e.* unadulterated. The words בַּד בְּבַד יִהְיֶה " part for part shall it be," are explained by the LXX. as meaning ἴσον ἴσῳ ἔσται, *Vulg. æqualis ponderis erunt omnia, i.e.* with equal parts of all the different substances. But this is hardly correct, as בַּד literally means separation, and the use of בְּ in this sense would be very striking.   The explanation given by *Aben Ezra* is more correct, viz. " every part shall be for itself;" that is to say, each part was to be first of all prepared by itself, and then all the four to be mixed together afterwards.—Ver. 35. Of this Moses was to make incense, spicework, etc. (as in ver. 25), salted, seasoned with salt (מְמֻלָּח, a *denom.* from מֶלַח salt), like the meat-offering in Lev. ii. 13. The word does not mean μεμιγμένον, *mixtum* (LXX., *Vulg.*), or rubbed to powder, for the rubbing or pulverizing is expressed by שָׁחַקְתָּ־הֲדֵק in the following verse.—Ver. 36. Of this incense (a portion) was to be placed " *before the testimony in the tabernacle,*" *i.e.* not in the most holy place, but where the altar of incense stood (cf. xxx. 6 and Lev. xvi. 12). The remainder was of course to be kept elsewhere.—Vers 37, 38. There is the same prohibition against imitating or applying it to a strange use as in the case of the anointing oil (vers. 32, 33). " *To smell thereto,*" *i.e.* to enjoy the perfume of it.

Chap. xxxi. 1–11. The BUILDERS (cf. chap. xxxv. 30–xxxvi. 1).—After having given directions for the construction of the sanctuary, and all the things required for the worship, Jehovah pointed out the builders, whom He had called to carry out the work, and had filled with His Spirit for that purpose. To "*call by name*" is to choose or appoint by name for a particular work (cf. Isa. xlv. 3, 4). *Bezaleel* was a grandson of *Hur,* of the tribe of Judah, who is mentioned in chap. xvii. 10, xxiv. 14, and was called to be the master-builder, to superintend the whole of the building and carry out the artistic work; consequently he is not only invariably mentioned first (chap. xxxv. 30, xxxvi. 1, 2), but in the accounts of the execution of the separate portions he is mentioned alone (chap. xxxvii. 1, xxxviii. 22). Filling with the Spirit of God signifies the communication of an extraordinary and supernatural endowment and qualification, "in wisdom," etc., *i.e.* consisting of wisdom, understanding, knowledge, and every kind of workmanship, that is to say, for the performance of every kind of work. This did not preclude either natural capacity or acquired skill, but rather presupposed them; for in ver. 6 it is expressly stated in relation to his assistants, that God had put wisdom into all that were wise-hearted (see at chap. xxviii. 3). Being thus endowed with a supernaturally exalted gift, *Bezaleel* was qualified "*to think out inventions,*" *i.e.* ideas or artistic designs. Although everything had been minutely described by Jehovah, designs and plans were still needed in carrying out the work, so that the result should correspond to the divine instructions.—Ver. 6. There were associated with Bezaleel as assistants, *Oholiab,* the son of *Achisamach,* of the tribe of Dan, and other men endowed with understanding, whom God had filled with wisdom for the execution of His work. According to chap. xxxviii. 23, *Oholiab* was both *faber,* a master in metal, stone, and wood work, and also an artistic weaver of colours. In vers. 7–11, the works to be executed, which have been minutely described in chap. xxv.–xxx., are mentioned singly once more; and, in addition to these, we find in ver. 10 בִּגְדֵי הַשְּׂרָד mentioned, along with, or rather before, the holy dress of Aaron. This is the case also in chap. xxxv. 19 and xxxix. 41, where there is also the additional clause, "to serve (שָׁרֵת *ministrare*) in the sanctuary." They were composed, according to chap. xxxix. 1, of blue and red purple, and crimson. The meaning of the word *serad,* which only occurs in these passages, is quite uncertain. The Rabbins understand by the *bigde hasserad* the wrappers in which the vessels of the sanctuary were enclosed when the camp was broken up, as these are called *begadim* of blue and red purple, and crimson, in Num. iv. 6 sqq. But this rendering is opposed to the words which follow, and which indicate their use in the holy service, *i.e.* in the performance of worship, and therefore are quite inapplicable to the wrappers referred to. There is even less ground for referring them, as *Gesenius* and others do, to the inner curtains of the tabernacle, or the inner hangings of the dwelling-place. For, apart from the uncertainty of the rendering given to *serad,* viz. netted cloth, *filet,* it is overthrown by the fact that these curtains of the dwelling-place were not of net-work; and still more decisively by the order in which the *bigde hasserad* occur in chap. xxxix. 41, viz. not till the dwelling-place and tent, and everything belonging to them, have been mentioned, even down to the hangings of the court and the pegs of the tent, and all that remains to be noticed is the clothing of the priests. From the definition " to serve in the sanctuary," it is obvious that the *bigde serad* were clothes used in the worship, στολαὶ λειτουργικαί, as the LXX. have rendered it in agreement with the rest of the ancient versions,—that they were, in fact, the rich robes which constituted the official dress of the high priest, whilst " the holy garments for Aaron" were the holy clothes which were worn by him in common with the priests.

Vers. 12–17 (cf. chap. xxxv. 2, 3). God concludes by enforcing the observance of His Sabbaths in the most solemn manner, repeating the threat of death and extermination in the case of every transgressor. The repetition and further development of this command, which was included already in the decalogue, is quite in its proper place here, inasmuch as the thought might easily have occurred, that it was allowable to omit the keeping of the Sabbath, when the execution of so great a work in honour of Jehovah had been commanded. " *My Sabbaths:*" by these we are to understand the weekly Sabbaths, not the other sabbatical festivals, since the words which follow apply to the weekly Sabbath alone. This was " *a sign between Jehovah and Israel for all generations, to know* (*i.e.* by which Israel might learn) *that it was Jehovah who sanctified them,*" viz. by the sabbatical rest (see at chap. xx. 11). It was therefore a holy thing for Israel (ver. 14), the desecration of which would be followed by the punishment of death, as a breach of the covenant. The kernel of the Sabbath commandment is repeated in ver. 15; the seventh day of the week, however, is not simply designated a " Sabbath," but שַׁבָּת שַׁבָּתוֹן "a high Sabbath" (the repetition of the same word, or of an abstract form of the concrete noun, denoting the superlative; see *Ges.* § 113, 2), and "holy to Jehovah" (see at chap. xvi. 23). For this reason Israel was to keep it in all future generations, *i.e.* to observe it as an eternal covenant (ver. 16), as in the case of circumcision, since it was to be a sign for ever between Jehovah and the children of Israel (ver. 20). The eternal duration of this sign was involved in the signification of the sabbatical rest, which is pointed out in chap. xx. 11, and reaches forward into eternity.

Ver. 18. When Moses had received all the instructions respecting the sanctuary to be erected, Jehovah gave him the two tables of testimony,—tables of stone, upon which the decalogue was written with the finger of God. It was to receive these tables that he had been called up the mountain (chap. xxiv. 12). According to chap. xxxii. 16, the tables themselves, as well as the writing, were the work of God; and the writing was engraved upon them (חָרוּת from חָרַת =χαράττειν), and the tables were written on both their sides (chap. xxxii. 15). Both the choice of stone as the material for the tables, and the fact that the writing was engraved, were intended to indicate the imperishable duration of these words of God. The divine origin of the tables, as well as of the writing, corresponded to the direct proclamation of the ten words to the people from the summit of the mountain by the mouth of God. As this divine promulgation was a sufficient proof that they were the immediate word of God, unchanged by the mouth and speech of man, so the writing of God was intended to secure their preservation in Israel as a holy and inviolable thing. The writing itself was not a greater miracle than others, by which God has proved Himself to be the Lord of nature, to whom all things that He has created are subservient for the establishment and completion of His kingdom upon earth; and it can easily be conceived of without the anthropomorphic supposition of a material finger being possessed by God. Nothing is said about the dimensions of the tables: at the same time, we can hardly imagine them to have been as large as the inside of the ark ; for stone slabs $2\frac{1}{2}$ cubits long and $1\frac{1}{2}$ cubit broad, which must necessarily have been some inches in thickness to prevent their breaking in the hand, would have required the strength of Samson to enable Moses to carry them down the mountain "in his hand" (chap. xxxii. 15), or even "in his two hands" (Deut. ix. 15, 17). But if we suppose them to have been smaller than this, say at the most a cubit and a half long and one cubit broad, there would have been plenty of room on the four sides for the 172 words contained in the decalogue, with its threats and promises (chap. xx. 2–17), without the writing being excessively small.

THE COVENANT BROKEN AND RENEWED.—CHAP. XXXII.–XXXIV.

Chap. xxxii. 1–6. The long stay that Moses made upon the mountain rendered the people so impatient, that they desired another leader, and asked Aaron, to whom Moses had directed the people to go in all their difficulties during his absence (chap. xxiv. 14), to make them a god to go before them. The protecting and helping presence of God had vanished with Moses, of whom they said, " We know not what has become of him,' and whom they probably supposed to have perished on the mountain in the fire that was burning there. They came to Aaron, therefore, and asked him, not for a leader, but for a god to go before them ; no doubt with the intention of trusting the man as their leader who was able to make them a god. They were unwilling to continue longer without a God to go before them ; but the faith upon which their desire was founded was a very perverted one, not only as clinging to what was apparent to the eye, but as corrupted by the impatience and unbelief of a natural heart, which has not been pervaded by the power of the living God, and imagines itself forsaken by Him, whenever His help is not visibly and outwardly at hand.   The delay (בֹשֵׁשׁ, from בּוֹשׁ to act bashfully, or with reserve, then to hesitate, or delay) of Moses' return was a test for Israel, in which it was to prove its faith and confidence in Jehovah and His servant Moses (xix. 9), but in which it gave way to the temptation of flesh and blood.—Ver. 2. Aaron also succumbed to the temptation along with the people. Instead of courageously and decidedly opposing their proposal, and raising the despondency of the people into the strength of living faith, by pointing them to the great deeds through which Jehovah had proved Himself to be the faithful covenant God, he hoped to be able to divert them from their design by means of human craftiness. " *Tear off the golden ornaments in the ears of your wives, your sons, and your daughters, and bring them to me :*" this he said in the hope that, by a demand which pressed so heavily upon the vanity of the female sex and its love of display, he might arouse such opposition as would lead the people to desist from their desire. But his cleverness was put to shame. " All the people" tore off their golden ornaments and brought them to him (ver. 3) ; for their object was not merely " to accomplish an act of pure self-will, in which case there is no sacrifice that the human heart is not ready to make," but to secure a pledge of the protection of God through a visible image of the Deity. The weak-minded Aaron had no other course left than to make (*i.e.* to cause to be made) an image of God for the people.

Ver. 4. *He took* (the golden ear-rings) *from their hands, and formed it* (the gold) *with the graving-tool, or chisel, and made it a molten calf.*" Out of the many attempts that have been made at interpreting the words בַּחֶרֶט אֹתוֹ וַיָּצַר, there are only two that deserve any notice, viz. the one adopted by *Bochart* and *Schroeder*, " he bound it up in a bag," and the one given by the earlier translators, " he fashioned (יָצַר, as in 1 Kings vii. 15) the gold with the chisel." No doubt וַיָּצַר (from צוּר = צָרַר) does occur in the sense of binding in 2 Kings v. 23, and חֶרֶט may certainly be used for חָרִיט a bag ; but why should Aaron first tie up the golden ear-rings in a bag ? And if he did so, why this superfluous and incongruous allusion to the fact ? We give in our adhesion to the second, which is adopted by the LXX., *Onkelos*, the *Syriac*, and even *Jonathan*, though the other rendering is also interpolated into the text. Such objections, as that the calf is expressly spoken of as molten work, or that files are used, and not chisels, for giving a finer finish to casts, have no force whatever. The latter is not even correct. A graving-knife is quite as necessary as a file for chiselling, and giving a finer finish to things cast in a mould ; and *cheret* does not necessarily mean a chisel, but may signify any tool employed for carving, engraving, and shaping hard metals. The other objection rests upon the supposition that *massecah* means an image made entirely of metal (*e.g.* gold). But this cannot be sustained. Apart from the fact, that most of the larger idols worshipped by the ancients had a wooden centre, and were merely covered with gold plate, such passages as Isa. xl. 19 and xxx. 22 prove, not only that the casting of gold for idols consisted merely in casting the metal into a flat sheet, which the goldsmith hammered out and spread into a coating of gold plate, but also that a wooden image, when covered in this way with a coating of gold, was actually called *massecah*. And Aaron's molten calf was also made in this way : it was first of all formed of wood, and then covered with gold plate. This is evident from the way in which it was destroyed : the image was first of all burnt, and then beaten or crushed to pieces, and pounded or ground to powder (Deut. ix. 21) ; *i.e.* the wooden centre was first burnt into charcoal, and then the golden covering beaten or rubbed to pieces (ver. 20 compared with Deut. ix. 21).

The " golden calf " (עֵגֶל a young bull) was copied from the Egyptian *Apis* (*vid. Hengstenberg*, Dissertations) ; but for all that, it was not the image of an Egyptian deity,—it was no symbol of the generative or bearing power of nature, but an image of Jehovah. For when it was finished, those who had made the image, and handed it over to the people, said, " This is thy God (*pluralis majest.*), O Israel, who brought thee out of Egypt." This is the explanation adopted in Ps. cvi. 19, 20.— Vers. 5, 6. When Aaron saw it, he built an altar in front of the image, and called aloud to the people, " *To-morrow is a feast of Jehovah ;*" and the people celebrated this feast with burnt-offerings and thank-offerings, with eating and drinking, *i.e.* with sacrificial meals and sports (צָחַק), or with loud rejoicing, shouting, antiphonal songs, and dances (cf. vers. 17–19), in the same manner in which the Egyptians celebrated their feast of Apis (*Herod.* 2, 60, and 3, 27). But this intimation of an Egyptian custom is no proof that the feast was not intended for Jehovah ; for joyous sacrificial meals, and even sports and dances, are met with in connection with the legitimate worship of Jehovah (cf. chap. xv. 20, 21). Nevertheless the making of the calf, and the sacrificial meals and other ceremonies performed before it, were a shameful apostasy from Jehovah, a practical denial of the inimitable glory of the true God, and a culpable breach of the second commandment of the covenant words (chap. xx. 4), whereby Israel had broken the covenant with the Lord, and fallen back to the heathen customs of Egypt. Aaron also shared the guilt of this transgression, although it was merely out of sinful weakness that he had assented to the proposals of the people and gratified their wishes (cf. Deut. ix. 20). He also fell with the people, and denied the God who had chosen him, though he himself was unconscious of it, to be His priest, to bear the sins of the people, and to expiate them before Jehovah. The apostasy of the nation became a temptation to him, in which the unfitness of his nature for the office was to be made manifest, in order that he might ever remember this, and not excuse himself from the office, to which the Lord had not called him because of his own worthiness, but purely as an act of unmerited grace.

Vers. 7–14. Before Moses left the mountain, God told him of the apostasy of the people (vers. 7, 8). *" Thy people, which thou hast brought out of Egypt:"* God says this not in the sense of an *" obliqua exprobratio,"* or *" Mosen quodammodo vocare in partem criminis quo examinetur ejus tolerantia et plus etiam mœroris ex rei indignitate concipiat"* (*Calvin*), or even because the Israelites, who had broken the covenant, were no longer the people of Jehovah; but the transgression of the people concerned Moses as the mediator of the covenant.—Ver. 8. *" They have turned aside quickly (lit.* hurriedly)*:"* this had increased their guilt, and made their ingratitude to Jehovah, their Redeemer, all the more glaring.—Vers. 9, 10. *" Behold, it is a stiff-necked people* (a people with a hard neck, that will not bend to the commandment of God; cf. chap. xxxiii. 3, 5, xxxiv. 9; Deut. ix. 6, etc.): *now therefore suffer Me, that My wrath may burn against them, and I may consume them, and I will make of thee a great nation."* Jehovah, as the unchangeably true and faithful God, would not, and could not, retract the promises which He had given to the patriarchs, or leave them unfulfilled; and therefore if in His wrath He should destroy the nation, which had shown the obduracy of its nature in its speedy apostasy, He would still fulfil His promise in the person of Moses, and make of him a great nation, as He had promised Abraham in Gen. xii. 2. When God says to Moses, *" Leave Me, allow Me, that My wrath may burn,"* this is only done, as Gregory the Great expresses it, *deprecandi ansam præbere.* God puts the fate of the nation into the hand of Moses, that he may remember his mediatorial office, and show himself worthy of his calling. This condescension on the part of God, which placed the preservation or destruction of Israel in the hands of Moses, coupled with a promise, which left the fullest freedom to his decision, viz. that after the destruction of the people he should himself be made a great nation, constituted a great test for Moses, whether he would be willing to give up his own people, laden as they were with guilt, as the price of his own exaltation. And Moses stood the test. The preservation of Israel was dearer to him than the honour of becoming the head and founder of a new kingdom of God. True to his calling as mediator, he entered the breach before God, to turn away His wrath, that He might not destroy the sinful nation (Ps. cvi. 23).—But what if Moses had not stood the test, had not offered his soul for the preservation of his people, as he is said to have done in ver. 32? Would God in that case have thought him fit to make into a great nation? Unquestionably, if this had occurred, he would not have proved himself fit or worthy of such a call; but as God does not call those who are fit and worthy in themselves, for the accomplishment of His purposes of salvation, but chooses rather the unworthy, and makes them fit for His purposes (2 Cor. iii. 5, 6), He might have made even Moses into a great nation. The possibility of such a thing, however, is altogether an abstract thought: the case supposed could not possibly have occurred, since God knows the hearts of His servants, and foresees what they will do, though, notwithstanding His omniscience, He gives to human freedom room enough for self-determination, that He may test the fidelity of His servants. No human speculation, however, can fully explain the conflict between divine providence and human freedom. This promise is referred to by Moses in Deut. ix. 14, when he adds the words which God made use of on a subsequent occasion of a similar kind (Num. xiv. 12), "I will make of thee a nation stronger and more numerous than this."—Ver. 11. "*And Moses besought the Lord his God.*" חִלָּה אֶת־פְּנֵי יְיָ, *lit.* to stroke the face of Jehovah, for the purpose of appeasing His anger, *i.e.* to entreat His mercy, either by means of sacrifices (1 Sam. xiii. 12) or by intercession. He pleaded His acts towards Israel (ver. 11), His honour in the sight of the Egyptians (ver. 12), and the promises He had made to the patriarchs (ver. 13), and prayed that for His own sake, and the sake of His honour among the heathen, He would show mercy instead of justice. בְּרָעָה (ver. 12) does not mean μετὰ πονηρίας (LXX.), or *callide* (*Vulg.*), but "*for their hurt*,"—the preposition denoting the manner in which, or according to which, anything took place.—Ver. 14. "*And Jehovah repented of the evil*, etc."—On the repentance of God, see at Gen. vi. 6. *Augustine* is substantially correct in saying that "an unexpected change in the things which God has put in His own power is called repentance" (*contra adv. leg.* 1, 20), but he has failed to grasp the deep spiritual idea of the repentance of God, as an anthropopathic description of the pain which is caused to the love of God by the destruction of His creatures.—Ver. 14 contains a remark which anticipates the development of the history, and in which the historian mentions the result of the intercession of Moses, even before Moses had received the assurance of forgiveness, for the purpose of bringing the account of his first negotiations with Jehovah to a close. God let Moses depart without any such assurance, that He might display before the people the full severity of the divine wrath.

Vers. 15–24. When Moses departed from God with the two tables of the law in his hand (see at chap. xxxi. 18), and came to Joshua on the mountain (see at chap. xxiv. 13), the latter heard the shouting of the people (*lit.* the voice of the people in its noise, רֵעֹה for רֵעוֹ, from רֵעַ noise, tumult), and took it to be the noise of war; but Moses said (ver. 18), "*It is not the sound of the answering of power, nor the sound of the answering of weakness*," *i.e.* they are not such sounds as you hear in the heat of battle from the strong (the conquerors) and the weak (the conquered); "*the sound of antiphonal songs I hear*." (עַנּוֹת is to be understood, both here and in Ps. lxxxviii. 1, in the same sense as in chap. xv. 21.)—Ver. 19. But when he came nearer to the camp, and saw the calf and the dancing, his anger burned, and he threw down the tables of the covenant and broke them at the foot of the mountain, as a sign that Israel had broken the covenant.— Ver. 20. He then proceeded to the destruction of the idol. "*He burned it in* (with) *fire*," by which process the wooden centre was calcined, and the golden coating either entirely or partially melted; and what was left by the fire he ground till it was fine, or, as it is expressed in Deut. ix. 21, he beat it to pieces, grinding it well (*i.e.* crushing it with and between stones), till it was as fine as dust.[1] The dust, which consisted of particles of charcoal and gold, he then "*strewed upon the water*," or, according to Deuteronomy, "threw it into the brook which flowed down from the mountain, and made the children of Israel drink," *i.e.* compelled them to drink the dust that had been thrown in along with the water of the brook. The object of this was certainly not to make them ashamed, by showing them the worthlessness of their god, and humiliating them by such treatment as compelling them to swallow their own god (as *Knobel* supposes). It was intended rather to set forth in a visible manner both the sin and its consequences. The sin was poured as it were into their bowels along with the water, as a symbolical sign that they would have to bear it and atone for it, just as a woman who was suspected of adultery was obliged to drink the curse-water (Num. v. 24).—Ver. 21. After the calf had been destroyed, Moses called Aaron to account. "*What has this people done to thee* ("done" in a bad sense, as in Gen. xxvii. 45; Ex. xiv. 11), *that thou hast brought a great sin upon it?*" Even if Aaron had merely acted from weakness in carrying out the will of the people, he was the most to blame, for not having resisted the urgent entreaty of the people firmly and with strong faith, and even at the cost of his life. Consequently he could think of nothing better than the pitiful subterfuge, "*Be not angry, my lord* (he addresses Moses in this way on account of his office, and because of his anger, cf. Num. xii. 11): *thou knowest the people, that it is in wickedness*" (cf. 1 John v. 19), and the admission that he had been overcome by the urgency of the people, and had thrown the gold they handed him into the fire, and that this calf had come out (vers. 22–24), as if the image had come out of its own accord, without his intention or will. This excuse was so contemptible that Moses did not think it worthy of a reply, at the same time, as he told the people afterwards (Deut. ix. 20), he averted the great wrath of the Lord from him through his intercession.

Vers. 25–29. Moses then turned to the unbridled nation,

---

[1] There is no necessity to refer to the process of calcining gold, either here or in connection with the destruction of the *Asherah* by Josiah (2 Kings xxiii. 4, 12; 2 Chron. xxxiv. 4, 7), apart altogether from the question, whether this chemical mode of reducing the precious metals was known at all to Moses and the Israelites.

whom Aaron had set free from all restraint, "*for a reproach among their foes*," inasmuch as they would necessarily become an object of scorn and derision among the heathen on account of the punishment which their conduct would bring down upon them from God (compare ver. 12 and Deut. xxviii. 37), and sought to restrain their licentiousness and ward off the threatened destruction of the nation through the infliction of a terrible punishment. If the effect of this punishment should show that there were still some remains of obedience and faithfulness towards God left in the nation, Moses might then hope, that in accordance with the pleading of Abraham in Gen. xviii. 23 sqq., he should obtain mercy from God for the whole nation for the sake of those who were righteous. He therefore went into the gate of the camp (the entrance to the camp) and cried out : "*Whoever* (belongs) *to the Lord,* (come) *to me !*" and his hope was not disappointed. "*All the Levites gathered together to him.*" Why the Levites ? Certainly not merely, nor chiefly, "because the Levites for the most part had not assented to the people's sin and the worship of the calf, but had been displeased on account of it" (*C. a Lapide*); but partly because the Levites were more prompt in their determination to confess their crime, and return with penitence, and partly out of regard to Moses, who belonged to their tribe, in connection with which it must be borne in mind that the resolution and example of a few distinguished men was sure to be followed by all the rest of their tribe. The reason why no one came over to the side of Moses from any of the other tribes, must also be attributed, to some extent, to the bond that existed among members of the same tribe, and is not sufficiently explained by *Calvin's* hypothesis, that "they were held back, not by contempt or obstinacy, so much as by shame, and that they were all so paralyzed by their alarm, that they waited to see what Moses was about to do and to what length he would proceed."—Ver. 27. The Levites had to allow their obedience to God to be subjected to a severe test. Moses issued this command to them in the name of Jehovah the God of Israel : "*Let every one gird on his sword, and go to and fro through the camp from one gate* (end) *to the other, and put to death brothers, friends, and neighbours,*" *i.e.* all whom they met, without regard to relationship, friendship, or acquaintance. And they stood the test. About 3000 men fell by their sword on that day. There are several difficulties connected with this account, which have furnished occasion for doubts as to its historical credibility. The one of least importance is that which arises from the supposed severity and recklessness of Moses' proceedings. The severity of the punishment corresponded to the magnitude of the crime. The worship of an image, being a manifest transgression of one of the fundamental laws of the covenant, was a breach of the covenant, and as such a capital crime, bringing the punishment of death or extermination in its train. Now, although the whole nation had been guilty of this crime, yet in this, as in every other rebellion, the guilt of all would not be the same, but many would simply follow the example of others; so that, instead of punishing all alike, it was necessary that a separation should be made, if not between the innocent and guilty, yet between the penitent and the stiff-necked transgressors. To effect this separation, Moses called out into the camp: " Over to me, whoever is for the Lord!" All the Levites responded to his call, but not the other tribes; and it was necessary that the refractory should be punished. Even these, however, had not all sinned to the same extent, but might be divided into tempters and tempted; and as they were all mixed up together, nothing remained but to adopt that kind of punishment, which has been resorted to in all ages in such circumstances as these. "If at any time," as *Calvin* says, "mutiny has broken out in an army, and has led to violence, and even to bloodshed, by *universal law* a commander proceeds to *decimate* the guilty." He then adds, "How much milder, however, was the punishment here, when out of six hundred thousand only three thousand were put to death!" This decimation Moses committed to the Levites; and just as in every other decimation the selection must be determined by lot or accidental choice, so here Moses left it to be determined by chance, upon whom the sword of the Levites would fall, knowing very well that even the so-called chance would be under the direction of God.

There is apparently a greater difficulty in the fact, that not only did the Levites execute the command of Moses without reserve, but the people let them pass through the camp, and kill every one who came within reach of their sword, without offering the slightest resistance. To remove this difficulty, there is no necessity that we should either assume that the Levites knew who were the originators and ringleaders of the worship of the calf, and only used their swords against them, as *Calvin* does, or that we should follow *Kurtz*, and introduce into the text a "formal conflict between the two parties, in which some of Moses' party were also slain," since the history says nothing about "the men who sided with Moses gaining a complete victory," and merely states that in obedience to the word of Jehovah the God of Israel, as declared by Moses, they put 3000 men of the people to death with the sword. The obedience of the Levites was an act of faith, which knows neither the fear of man nor regard to person. The unresisting attitude of the people generally may be explained, partly from their reverence for Moses, whom God had so mightily and marvellously accredited as His servant in the sight of all the nation, and partly from the despondency and fear so natural to a guilty conscience, which took away all capacity for opposing the bold and determined course that was adopted by the divinely appointed rulers and their servants in obedience to the command of God. It must also be borne in mind, that in the present instance the sin of the people was not connected with any rebellion against Moses.

Very different explanations have been given of the words which were spoken by Moses to the Levites (ver. 29): "*Fill your hand to-day for Jehovah; for every one against his son and against his brother, and to bring a blessing upon you to-day.*" "To fill the hand for Jehovah" does not mean to offer a sacrifice to the Lord, but to provide something to offer to God (1 Chron. xxix. 5; 2 Chron. xxix. 31). Thus *Jonathan's* explanation, which *Kurtz* has revived in a modified form, viz. that Moses commanded the Levites to offer sacrifices as an expiation for the blood that they had shed, or for the rent made in the congregation by their reckless slaughter of their blood-relations, falls to the ground; though we cannot understand how the fulfilment of a divine command, or an act of obedience to the declared will of God, could be regarded as blood-guiltiness, or as a crime that needed expiation. As far as the clause which follows is concerned, so much is clear, viz. that the words can neither be rendered, "for every one is *in* his son," etc., nor "for every one *was* against his son," etc. To the former it is impossible to attach any sense; and the latter cannot be correct, because the preterite הָיָה could not be omitted after an imperative, if the explanatory clause referred to what was past. If כִּי were a causal particle in this case, the meaning could only be, "for every one shall be against his son," etc. But it is much better to understand it as indicating the object, "that every one may be against his son and against his brother;" *i.e.* that in the cause of the Lord every one may not spare even his nearest relative, but deny either son or brother for the Lord's sake (Deut. xxxiii. 9). "*And to give*" (or bring), *i.e.* so that ye may bring, "*a blessing upon yourselves to-day.*" The following, then, is the thought contained in the verse : Provide yourselves to-day with a gift for the Lord, consecrate yourselves to-day for the service of the Lord, by preserving the obedience you have just shown towards Him, by not knowing either son or brother in His service, and thus gain for yourselves a blessing. In the fulfilment of the command of God, with the denial of their own flesh and blood, Moses discerns such a disposition and act as would fit them for the service of the Lord. He there-fore points to the blessing which it would bring them, and ex-horts them by their election as the peculiar possession of Jeho-vah (Num. iii. iv.), which would be secured to them from this time forward, to persevere in this fidelity to the Lord. "The zeal of the tribe-father burned still in the Levites ; but this time it was for the glory of God, and not for their own. Their an-cestor had violated both truth and justice by his vengeance upon the Shechemites, from a false regard to blood-relationship, but now his descendants had saved truth, justice, and the covenant by avenging Jehovah upon their own relations" (*Kurtz*, and *Oehler* in *Herzog's* Cycl.), so that the curse which rested upon them (Gen. xlix. 7) could now be turned into a blessing (cf. Deut. xxxiii. 9).

Vers. 30–35. After Moses had thus avenged the honour of the Lord upon the sinful nation, he returned the next day to Jehovah as a mediator, who is not a mediator of one (Gal. iii. 20), that by the force of his intercession he might turn the divine wrath, which threatened destruction, into sparing grace and compassion, and that he might expiate the sin of the nation. He had received no assurance of mercy in reply to his first en-treaty (vers. 11–13). He therefore announced his intention to the people in these words : "*Peradventure I can make an atone-ment for your sin.*" But to the Lord he said (vers. 31, 32),

" *The sin of this people is a great sin ; they have made themselves a god of gold,*" in opposition to the clear commandment in chap. xx. 23 : " *and now, if Thou wilt forgive their sin, and if not, blot me out of the book that Thou hast written.*" The book which Jehovah has written is the book of life, or of the living (Ps. lxix. 29 ; Dan. xii. 1). This expression is founded upon the custom of writing the names of the burgesses of a town or country in a burgess-list, whereby they are recognised as natives of the country, or citizens of the city, and all the privileges of citizenship are secured to them. The book of life contains the list of the righteous (Ps. lxix. 29), and ensures to those whose names are written there, life before God, first in the earthly kingdom of God, and then eternal life also, according to the knowledge of salvation, which keeps pace with the progress of divine revelation, *e.g.* in the New Testament, where the heirs of eternal life are found written in the book of life (Phil. iv. 3 ; Rev. iii. 5, xiii. 8, etc.),—an advance for which the way was already prepared by Isa. iv. 3 and Dan. xii. 1. To blot out of Jehovah's book, therefore, is to cut off from fellowship with the living God, or from the kingdom of those who live before God, and to deliver over to death. As a true mediator of his people, Moses was ready to stake his own life for the deliverance of the nation, and not to live before God himself, if Jehovah did not forgive the people their sin. These words of Moses were the strongest expression of devoted, self-sacrificing love. And they were just as deep and true as the wish expressed by the Apostle Paul in Rom. ix. 3, that he might be accursed from Christ for the sake of his brethren according to the flesh. *Bengel* compares this wish of the apostle to the prayer of Moses, and says with regard to this unbounded fulness of love, " It is not easy to estimate the measure of love in a Moses and a Paul ; for the narrow boundary of our reasoning powers does not comprehend it, as the little child is unable to comprehend the courage of warlike heroes " (Eng. Tr.). The infinite love of God is unable to withstand the importunity of such love. God, who is holy love, cannot sacrifice the righteous and good for the unrighteous and guilty, nor can He refuse the mediatorial intercession of His faithful servant, so long as the sinful nation has not filled up the measure of its guilt, in which case even the intercession of a Moses and a Samuel would not be able to avert the judgment

(Jer. xv. 1, cf. Ezek. xiv. 16). Hence, although Jehovah puts back the wish and prayer of Moses with the words, " *Whoever* (מִי אֲשֶׁר, both here and in 2 Sam. xx. 11, is more emphatic than either one or the other alone) *has sinned, him will I blot out of My book,*" He yields to the entreaty that He will ensure to Moses the continuance of the nation under His guidance, and under the protection of His angel, which shall go before it (see at chap. xxxiii. 2, 3), and defer the punishment of their sin until the day of His visitation.—Ver. 35. " *Thus Jehovah smote the people because they had made the calf.*" With these words the historian closes the first act of Moses' negotiations with the Lord on account of this sin, from which it was apparent how God had repented of the evil with which He had threatened the nation (ver. 14). Moses had obtained the preservation of the people and their entrance into the promised land, under the protection of God, through his intercession, and averted from the nation the abrogation of the covenant ; but the covenant relation which had existed before was not restored in its integrity. Though grace may modify and soften wrath, it cannot mar the justice of the holy God. No doubt an atonement had been made to justice, through the punishment which the Levites had inflicted upon the nation, but only a passing and imperfect one. Only a small portion of the guilty nation had been punished, and that without the others showing themselves worthy of forgiving grace through sorrow and repentance. The punishment, therefore, was not remitted, but only postponed in the long-suffering of God, " until the day of retribution" or visitation. The day of visitation came at length, when the stiff-necked people had filled up the measure of their sin through repeated rebellion against Jehovah and 'His servant Moses, and were sentenced at Kadesh to die out in the wilderness (Num. xiv. 26 sqq.). The sorrow manifested by the people (chap. xxxiii. 4), when the answer of God was made known to them, was a proof that the measure was not yet full.

Chap. xxxiii. 1–6. Moses' negotiations with the people, for the purpose of bringing them to sorrow and repentance, commenced with the announcement of what Jehovah had said. The words of Jehovah in vers. 1–3, which are only a still further expansion of the assurance contained in chap. xxxii. 34, commence in a similar manner to the covenant promise in chap.

xxiii. 20, 23 ; but there is this great difference, that whereas the name, *i.e.* the presence of Jehovah Himself, was to have gone before the Israelites in the angel promised to the people as a leader in chap. xxiii. 20, now, though Jehovah would still send an angel before Moses and Israel, He Himself would not go up to Canaan (a land flowing, etc., see at iii. 8) in the midst of Israel, lest He should destroy the people by the way, because they were stiff-necked (אֲכֶלְךָ for אֲכַלְךָ, see *Ges.* § 27, 3, *Anm.* 2).—Ver. 4. The people were so overwhelmed with sorrow by this evil word, that they all put off their ornaments, and showed by this outward sign the trouble of their heart.—Ver. 5. That this good beginning of repentance might lead to a true and permanent change of heart, Jehovah repeated His threat in a most emphatic manner : " *Thou art a stiff-necked people ; if I go a moment in the midst of thee, I destroy thee :*" *i.e.* if I were to go up in the midst of thee for only a single moment, I should be compelled to destroy thee because of thine obduracy. He then issued this command : " *Throw thine ornament away from thee, and I shall know* (by that) *what to do to thee.*"—Ver. 6. And the people obeyed this commandment, renouncing all that pleased the eye. " *The children of Israel spoiled themselves* (see at chap. xii. 36) *of their ornament from Mount Horeb onwards.*" Thus they entered formally into a penitential condition. The expression, " from Mount Horeb onwards," can hardly be paraphrased as it is by *Seb. Schmidt*, viz. " going from Mount Horeb into the camp," but in all probability expresses this idea, that from that time forward, *i.e.* after the occurrence of this event at Horeb, they laid aside the ornaments which they had hitherto worn, and assumed the outward appearance of perpetual penitence.

Vers. 7–11. Moses then took a tent, and pitched it outside the camp, at some distance off, and called it " *tent of meeting.*" The " tent " is neither the sanctuary of the tabernacle described in chap. xxv. sqq., which was not made till after the perfect restoration of the covenant (chap. xxxv. sqq.), nor another sanctuary that had come down from their forefathers and was used before the tabernacle was built, as *Clericus, J. D. Michaelis, Rosenmüller*, and others suppose ; but a tent belonging to Moses, which was made into a temporary sanctuary by the fact that the pillar of cloud came down upon it, and Jehovah talked with Moses there, and which was called by the same name as the tabernacle, viz. אֹהֶל מוֹעֵד (see at chap. xxvii. 21), because Jehovah revealed Himself there, and every one who sought Him had to go to this tent outside the camp.   There were two reasons for this : in the first place, Moses desired thereby to lead the people to a fuller recognition of their separation from their God, that their penitence might be deepened in consequence ; and in the second place, he wished to provide such means of intercourse with Jehovah as would not only awaken in the minds of the people a longing for the renewal of the covenant, but render the restoration of the covenant possible.   And this end was answered. Not only did every one who sought Jehovah go out to the tent, but the whole nation looked with the deepest reverence when Moses went out to the tent, and bowed in adoration before the Lord, every one in front of his tent, when they saw the pillar of cloud come down upon the tent and stand before the door.   Out of this cloud Jehovah talked with Moses (vers. 7–10) "*face to face, as a man talks with his friend*" (ver. 11) ; that is to say, not from the distance of heaven, through any kind of medium whatever, but " mouth to mouth," as it is called in Num. xii. 8, as closely and directly as friends talk to one another.   " These words indicate, therefore, a familiar conversation, just as much as if it had been said, that God appeared to Moses in some peculiar form of manifestation. If any one objects to this, that it is at variance with the assertion which we shall come to presently, ' Thou canst not see My face,' the answer is a very simple one. Although Jehovah showed Himself to Moses in some peculiar form of manifestation, He never appeared in His own essential glory, but only in such a mode as human weakness could bear. This solution contains a tacit comparison, viz. that there never was any one equal to Moses, or who had attained to the same dignity as he" (*Calvin*). When Moses returned to the tent, his servant Joshua remained behind as guard.—This condescension on the part of Jehovah towards Moses could not fail to strengthen the people in their reliance upon their leader, as the confidant of Jehovah. And Moses himself was encouraged thereby to endeavour to effect a perfect restoration of the covenant bond that had been destroyed.

Vers. 12–23. Jehovah had commanded Moses to lead the

people to Canaan, and promised him the guidance of an angel; but He had expressly distinguished this angel from His own personal presence (vers. 1–3). Moreover, though it has not been mentioned before, Jehovah had said to Moses, " *I have known thee by name*,"—*i.e.* I have recognised thee as Mine, and chosen and called thee to execute My will (cf. Isa. xliii. 1, xlix. 1), or put thee into " a specifically personal relation to God, which was peculiar to Moses, and therefore was associated with his name" (*Oehler*) ;—" *and thou hast also found grace in My eyes*," inasmuch as God had granted a hearing to his former intercession. Moses now reminded the Lord of this divine assurance with such courage as can only be produced by faith, which wrestles with God and will not let Him go without a blessing (Gen. xxxii. 27); and upon the strength of this he presented the petition (ver. 13), " *Let me know Thy way* (the way which Thou wilt take with me and with this people), *that I may know Thee, in order that I may find grace in Thine eyes, and see that this people is Thy people.*" The meaning is this : If I have found grace in Thy sight, and Thou hast recognised me as Thy servant, and called me to be the leader of this people, do not leave me in uncertainty as to Thine intentions concerning the people, or as to the angel whom Thou wilt give as a guide to me and the nation, that I may know Thee, that is to say, that my finding grace in Thine eyes may become a reality ;[1] and if Thou wilt lead the people up to Canaan, consider that it is Thine own people, to whom Thou must acknowledge Thyself as its God. Such boldness of undoubting faith presses to the heart of God, and brings away the blessing. Jehovah replied (ver. 14), " *My face will go, and I shall give thee rest,*"—that is to say, shall bring thee and all this people into the land, where ye will find rest (Deut. iii. 20). The " face" of Jehovah is Jehovah in His own personal presence, and is identical with the " angel" in whom the name of Jehovah was (chap. xxiii. 20, 21), and who is therefore called in Isa. lxiii. 9 " the angel of His face."

With this assurance on the part of God, the covenant bond was completely restored. But to make more sure of it, Moses replied (vers. 15, 16), " *If Thy face is not going* (with us), *lead us not up hence And whereby shall it be known that I have found grace in thine eyes, I and Thy people, if not* (lit. is it not known)

[1] *Domine fac ut verbis tuis respondeat eventus* (*Calvin*).

in Thy going with us, that we, I and Thy people, are distinguished
(see at chap. viii. 18) *before every nation upon the face of the
earth ?*" These words do not express any doubt as to the truth of
the divine assurance, "but a certain feeling of the insufficiency
of the assurance," inasmuch as even with the restoration of the
former condition of things there still remained "the fear lest the
evil root of the people's rebellion, which had once manifested
itself, should break forth again at any moment" (*Baumgarten*).
For this reason Jehovah assured him that this request also should
be granted (ver. 17). "There was nothing extraordinary in the
fact that Moses desired for himself and his people that they might
be distinguished before every nation upon the face of the earth;
this was merely the firm hold of faith upon the calling and election of God (chap. xix. 5, 6)."—Ver. 18. Moses was emboldened
by this, and now prayed to the Lord, "*Let me see Thy glory.*"
What Moses desired to see, as the answer of God clearly shows,
must have been something surpassing all former revelations of
the glory of Jehovah (chap. xvi. 7, 10, xxiv. 16, 17), and even
going beyond Jehovah's talking with him face to face (ver. 11).
When God talked with him face to face, or mouth to mouth, he
merely saw a "similitude of Jehovah" (Num. xii. 8), a form
which rendered the invisible being of God visible to the human
eye, *i.e.* a manifestation of the divine glory in a certain form,
and not the direct or essential glory of Jehovah, whilst the people
saw this glory under the veil of a dark cloud, rendered luminous
by fire, that is to say, they only saw its splendour as it shone
through the cloud; and even the elders, at the time when the
covenant was made, only saw the God of Israel in a certain form
which hid from their eyes the essential being of God (xxiv. 10,
11). What Moses desired, therefore, was a sight of the glory
or essential being of God, without any figure, and without a veil.

Moses was urged to offer this prayer, as *Calvin* truly says,
not by "*stulta curiositas, quæ ut plurimum titillat hominum mentes,
ut audacter penetrare tentent usque ad ultima cœlorum arcana,*"
but by "a desire to cross the chasm which had been made by
the apostasy of the nation, that for the future he might have a
firmer footing than the previous history had given him. As so
great a stress had been laid upon his own person in his present
task of mediation between the offended Jehovah and the apostate
nation, he felt that the separation, which existed between himself

and Jehovah, introduced a disturbing element into his office.
For if his own personal fellowship with Jehovah was not fully
established, and raised above all possibility of disturbance, there
could be no eternal foundation for the perpetuity of his mediation" (*Baumgarten*).   As a man called by God to be His servant,
he was not yet the perfect mediator ; but although he was faithful
in all his house, it was only as a servant, called εἰς μαρτύριον
τῶν λαληθησομένων (Heb. iii. 5), *i.e.* as a herald of the saving
revelations of God, preparing the way for the coming of the
perfect Mediator.   Jehovah therefore granted his request, but
only so far as the limit existing between the infinite and holy
God and finite and sinful man allowed.   "*I will make all My
goodness pass before thy face, and proclaim the name of Jehovah
before thee* (קָרָא בְּשֵׁם see at Gen iv. 26), *and will be gracious to
whom I will be gracious, and will show mercy on whom I will show
mercy.   Thou canst not see My face, for man cannot see Me and
live.*"   The words וְחַנֹּתִי וגו׳, although only connected with the previous clause by the *cop.* וְ, are to be understood in a causative
sense, as expressing the reason why Moses' request was granted,
viz. that it was an act of unconditional grace and compassion on
the part of God, to which no man, not even Moses, could lay
any just claim.   The Apostle Paul uses the words in the same
sense in Rom. ix. 15, for the purpose of overthrowing the claims
of self-righteous Jews to participate in the Messianic salvation.
—No mortal man can see the face of God and remain alive ; for
not only is the holy God a consuming fire to unholy man, but a
limit has been set, in and with the σῶμα χοϊκον and ψυχικόν (the
earthly and psychical body) of man, between the infinite God, the
absolute Spirit, and the human spirit clothed in an earthly body,
which will only be removed by the " redemption of our body,"
and our being clothed in a " spiritual body," and which, so long
as it lasts, renders a direct sight of the glory of God impossible.
As our bodily eye is dazzled, and its power of vision destroyed,
by looking directly at the brightness of the sun, so would our
whole nature be destroyed by an unveiled sight of the brilliancy
of the glory of God.   So long as we are clothed with this body,
which was destined, indeed, from the very first to be transformed
into the glorified state of the immortality of the spirit, but has
become through the fall a prey to the corruption of death, we
can only walk in faith, and only see God with the eye of faith,

so far as He has revealed His glory to us in His works and His word. When we have become like God, and have been transformed into the "divine nature" (2 Pet. i. 4), then, and not till then, shall we see Him as He is; then we shall see His glory without a veil, and live before Him for ever. For this reason Moses had to content himself with the passing by of the glory of God before his face, and with the revelation of the name of Jehovah through the medium of the word, in which God discloses His inmost being, and, so to speak, His whole heart to faith. In ver. 22 "My glory" is used for "all My goodness," and in chap. xxxiv. 6 it is stated that *Jehovah* passed by before the face of Moses. טוב is not to be understood in the sense of beautiful, or beauty, but signifies goodness; not the brilliancy which strikes the senses, but the spiritual and ethical nature of the Divine Being. For the manifestation of Jehovah, which passed before Moses, was intended unquestionably to reveal nothing else than what Jehovah expressed in the proclamation of His name.

The manifested glory of the Lord would so surely be followed by the destruction of man, that even Moses needed to be protected before it (vers. 21, 22). Whilst Jehovah, therefore, allowed him to come to a place upon the rock near Him, *i.e.* upon the summit of Sinai (chap. xxxiv. 2), He said that He would put him in a cleft of the rock whilst He was passing by, and cover him with His hand, *i.e.* with His protecting power, and only take away His hand when He had gone by, that he might see His back, because His face could not be seen. The back, as contrasted with the face, signifies the reflection of the glory of God that had just passed by. The words are transferred anthropomorphically from man to God, because human language and human thought can only conceive of the nature of the absolute Spirit according to the analogy of the human form. As the inward nature of man manifests itself in his face, and the sight of his back gives only an imperfect and outward view of him, so Moses saw only the back and not the face of Jehovah. It is impossible to put more into human words concerning this unparalleled vision, which far surpasses all human thought and comprehension. According to chap. xxxiv. 2, the place where Moses stood by the Lord was at the top (the head) of Sinai, and no more can be determined with certainty concerning it. The cleft in the rock (ver. 22) has been supposed by some to be the same place as the "cave" in which Elijah lodged at Horeb, and where the Lord appeared to him in the still small voice (1 Kings xix. 9 sqq.). The real summit of the Jebel Musa consists of "a small area of huge rocks, about 80 feet in diameter," upon which there is now a chapel that has almost fallen down, and about 40 feet to the south-west a dilapidated mosque (*Robinson*, Palestine, vol. i. p. 153). Below this mosque, according to *Seetzen* (*Reise* iii. pp. 83, 84), there is a very small grotto, into which you descend by several steps, and to which a large block of granite, about a fathom and a half long and six spans in height, serves as a roof. According to the Mussulman tradition, which the Greek monks also accept, it was in this small grotto that Moses received the law; though other monks point out a "hole, just large enough for a man," near the altar of the Elijah chapel, on the small plain upon the ridge of Sinai, above which the loftier peak rises about 700 feet, as the cave in which Elijah lodged on Horeb (*Robinson*, Pal. *ut supra*).

Chap. xxxiv. 1–10. When Moses had restored the covenant bond through his intercession (chap. xxxiii. 14), he was directed by Jehovah to hew out two stones, like the former ones which he had broken, and to come with them the next morning up the mountain, and Jehovah would write upon them the same words as upon the first,[1] and thus restore the covenant record. It was also commanded, as in the former case (chap. xix. 12, 13), that no one should go up the mountain with him, or be seen upon it, and that not even cattle should feed against the mountain, *i.e.* in the immediate neighbourhood (ver. 3). The first tables of the covenant were called "tables of stone" (chap. xxiv. 12, xxxi. 18); the second, on the other hand, which were hewn by Moses, are called "tables of stones" (vers. 1 and 4); and the latter expression is applied indiscriminately to both of them in Deut. iv. 13, v. 19, ix. 9–11, x. 1–4. This difference does not indicate a diversity in the records, but may be explained very simply from the fact, that the tables prepared by Moses were hewn from two stones, and not both from the same block; whereas all that could be said of the former, which had been

---

[1] Namely, the ten words in chap. xx. 2–17, not the laws contained in vers. 12–26 of this chapter, as *Göthe* and *Hitzig* suppose. See *Hengstenberg*, Dissertations ii. p. 319, and *Kurtz* on the Old Covenant iii. 182 sqq.

made by God Himself, was that they were of stone, since no one knew whether God had used one stone or two for the purpose. There is apparently far more importance in the following distinction, that the second tables were delivered by Moses and only written upon by God, whereas in the case of the former both the writing and the materials came from God. This cannot have been intended either as a punishment for the nation (*Hengstenberg*), or as "the sign of a higher stage of the covenant, inasmuch as the further the reciprocity extended, the firmer was the covenant" (*Baumgarten*). It is much more natural to seek for the cause, as *Rashi* does, in the fact, that Moses had broken the first in pieces; only we must not regard it as a sign that God disapproved of the manifestation of anger on the part of Moses, but rather as a recognition of his zealous exertions for the restoration of the covenant which had been broken by the sin of the nation. As Moses had restored the covenant through his energetic intercession, he should also provide the materials for the renewal of the covenant record, and bring them to God, for Him to complete and confirm the record by writing the covenant words upon the tables.

On the following morning, when Moses ascended the mountain, Jehovah granted him the promised manifestation of His glory (vers. 5 sqq.). The description of this unparalleled occurrence is in perfect harmony with the mysterious and majestic character of the revelation. "*Jehovah descended* (from heaven) *in the cloud, and stood by him there, and proclaimed the name of Jehovah; and Jehovah passed by in his sight, and proclaimed Jehovah, Jehovah God, merciful and gracious,*" etc. What Moses saw we are not told, but simply the words in which Jehovah proclaimed all the glory of His being; whilst it is recorded of Moses, that he bowed his head toward the earth and worshipped. This "sermon on the name of the Lord," as *Luther* calls it, disclosed to Moses the most hidden nature of Jehovah. It proclaimed that God is love, but that kind of love in which mercy, grace, long-suffering, goodness, and truth are united with holiness and justice. As the merciful One, who is great in goodness and truth, Jehovah shows mercy to the thousandth, forgiving sin and iniquity in long-suffering and grace; but He does not leave sin altogether unpunished, and in His justice visits the sin of the fathers upon the children and the children's children even unto the fourth generation. The Lord had already revealed Himself to the whole nation from Mount Sinai as visiting sin and showing mercy (chap. xx. 5 sqq.). But whereas on that occasion the burning zeal of Jehovah which visits sin stood in the foreground, and mercy only followed afterwards, here grace, mercy, and goodness are placed in the front. And accordingly all the words which the language contained to express the idea of grace in its varied manifestations to the sinner, are crowded together here, to reveal the fact that in His inmost being God is love. But in order that grace may not be perverted by sinners into a ground of wantonness, justice is not wanting even here with its solemn threatenings, although it only follows mercy, to show that mercy is mightier than wrath, and that holy love does not punish till sinners despise the riches of the goodness, patience, and long-suffering of God. As Jehovah here proclaimed His name, so did He continue to bear witness of it to the Israelites, from their departure from Sinai till their entrance into Canaan, and from that time forward till their dispersion among the heathen, and even now in their exile showing mercy to the thousandth, when they turn to the Redeemer who has come out of Zion.—Ver. 9. On this manifestation of mercy, Moses repeated the prayer that Jehovah would go in the midst of Israel. It is true the Lord had already promised that His face should go with them (chap. xxxiii. 14); but as Moses had asked for a sight of the glory of the Lord as a seal to the promise, it was perfectly natural that, when this petition was granted, he should lay hold of the grace that had been revealed to him as it never had been before, and endeavour to give even greater stability to the covenant. To this end he repeated his former intercession on behalf of the nation, at the same time making this confession, " For it is a stiff-necked people; therefore forgive our iniquity and our sin, and make us the inheritance." Moses spoke collectively, including himself in the nation in the presence of God. The reason which he assigned pointed to the deep root of corruption that had broken out in the worship of the golden calf, and was appropriately pleaded as a motive for asking forgiveness, inasmuch as God Himself had assigned the natural corruption of the human race as a reason why He would not destroy it again with a flood (Gen. viii. 21). Wrath was mitigated by a regard to the natural condition.—נָחַל in the *Kal*, with an accusative of the person, does not mean to lead a person into the inheritance, but to make a person into an inheritance; here, therefore, to make Israel the possession of Jehovah (Deut. iv. 20, ix. 26, cf. Zech. ii. 16). Jehovah at once declared (ver. 10) that He would conclude a covenant, *i.e.* restore the broken covenant, and do marvels before the whole nation, such as had not been done in all the earth or in any nation, and thus by these His works distinguish Israel before all nations as His own property (chap. xxxiii. 16). The nation was to see this, because it would be terrible; terrible, namely, through the over-throw of the powers that resisted the kingdom of God, every one of whom would be laid prostrate and destroyed by the majesty of the Almighty.

Vers. 11–26. To recall the duties of the covenant once more to the minds of the people, the Lord repeats from among the rights of Israel, upon the basis of which the covenant had been established (chap. xxi.–xxiii.), two of the leading points which determined the attitude of the nation towards Him, and which constituted, as it were, the main pillars that were to support the covenant about to be renewed. These were, *first*, the warning against every kind of league with the Canaanites, who were to be driven out before the Israelites (vers. 11–16); and, *secondly*, the instructions concerning the true worship of Jehovah (vers. 17–26). The warning against friendship with the idolatrous Canaanites (vers. 11–16) is more fully developed and more strongly enforced than in chap. xxiii. 23 sqq. The Israelites, when received into the covenant with Jehovah, were not only to beware of forming any covenant with the inhabitants of Canaan (cf. xxiii. 32, 33), but were to destroy all the signs of their ido-latrous worship, such as altars, monuments (see chap. xxiii. 24), and *asherim*, the idols of Astarte, the Canaanitish goddess of nature, which consisted for the most part of wooden pillars (see my Comm. on 1 Kings xiv. 23), and to worship no other god, because Jehovah was called jealous, *i.e.* had revealed Himself as jealous (see at chap. xx. 5), and was a jealous God. This was commanded, that the Israelites might not suffer themselves to be led astray by such an alliance; to go a whoring after their gods, and sacrifice to them, to take part in their sacrificial festivals, or to marry their sons to the daughters of the Canaanites, by whom they would be persuaded to join in the worship of idols. The use of the expression " go a whoring" in a spiritual sense, in relation to idolatry, is to be accounted for on the ground, that the religious fellowship of Israel with Jehovah was a covenant resembling the marriage tie; and we meet with it for the first time here, immediately after the formation of this covenant between Israel and Jehovah. The phrase is all the more expressive on account of the literal prostitution that was frequently associated with the worship of Baal and Astarte (cf. Lev. xvii. 7, xx. 5, 6; Num. xiv. 33, etc.). We may see from Num. xxv. 1 sqq. how Israel was led astray by this temptation in the wilderness.—Vers. 17–26. The true way to worship Jehovah is then pointed out, first of all negatively, in the prohibition against making molten images, with an allusion to the worship of the golden calf, as evinced by the use of the expression אֱלֹהֵי מַסֵּכָה, which only occurs again in Lev. xix. 4, instead of the phrase "gods of silver and gold" (chap. xx. 23); and then positively, by a command to observe the feast of *Mazzoth* and the consecration of the first-born connected with the Passover (see at chap. xiii. 2, 11, and 12), also the Sabbath (ver. 21), the feasts of Weeks and Ingathering, the appearance of the male members of the nation three times a year before the Lord (ver. 22, see at chap. xxiii. 14–17), together with all the other instructions connected with them (vers. 25, 26). Before the last, however, the promise is introduced, that after the expulsion of the Canaanites, Jehovah would enlarge the borders of Israel (cf. xxiii. 31), and make their land so secure, that when they went up to the Lord three times in the year, no one should desire their land, *sc.* because of the universal dread of the might of their God (chap. xxiii. 27).

Vers. 27–35. Moses was to write down these words, like the covenant rights and laws that had been given before (chap. xxiv. 4, 7), because Jehovah had concluded the covenant with Moses and Israel according to the tenor of them. By the renewed adoption of the nation, the covenant in chap. xxiv. was *eo ipso* restored; so that no fresh conclusion of this covenant was necessary, and the writing down of the fundamental conditions of the covenant was merely intended as a proof of its restoration. It does not appear in the least degree "irreconcilable," therefore, with the writing down of the covenant rights before (*Knobel*).—Ver. 28. Moses remained upon the mountain forty days, just as on the former occasion (cf. xxiv. 18). "*And He* (Jehovah) *wrote upon the tables the ten covenant words*" (see at ver. 1).—

Vers. 29 sqq. The sight of the glory of Jehovah, though only of the back or reflection of it, produced such an effect upon Moses' face, that the skin of it shone, though without Moses observing it. When he came down from the mountain with the tables of the law in his hand, and the skin of his face shone בְּדַבְּרוֹ אִתּוֹ, i.e. on account of his talking with God, Aaron and the people were afraid to go near him when they saw the brightness of his face. But Moses called them to him,—viz. first of all Aaron and the princes of the congregation to speak to them, and then all the people to give them the commandments of Jehovah; but on doing this (ver. 33), he put a veil upon (before) his face, and only took it away when he went in before Jehovah to speak with Him, and then, when he came out (from the Lord out of the tabernacle, of course after the erection of the tabernacle), he made known His commands to the people. But while doing this, he put the veil upon his face again, and always wore it in his ordinary intercourse with the people (vers. 34, 35). This reflection of the splendour thrown back by the glory of God was henceforth to serve as the most striking proof of the confidential relation in which Moses stood to Jehovah, and to set forth the glory of the office which Moses filled. The Apostle Paul embraces this view in 2 Cor. iii. 7 sqq., and lays stress upon the fact that the glory was to be done away, which he was quite justified in doing, although nothing is said in the Old Testament about the glory being transient, from the simple fact that Moses died. The apostle refers to it for the purpose of contrasting the perishable glory of the law with the far higher and imperishable glory of the Gospel. At the same time he regards the veil which covered Moses' face as a symbol of the obscuring of the truth revealed in the Old Testament. But this does not exhaust the significance of this splendour. The office could only confer such glory upon the possessor by virtue of the glory of the blessings which it contained, and conveyed to those for whom it was established. Consequently, the brilliant light on Moses' face also set forth the glory of the Old Covenant, and was intended both for Moses and the people as a foresight and pledge of the glory to which Jehovah had called, and would eventually exalt, the people of His possession.

ERECTION OF THE TABERNACLE, AND PREPARATION OF THE
APPARATUS OF WORSHIP.—CHAP. XXXV.–XXXIX.

Chap. xxxv. 1-xxxvi. 7. PRELIMINARIES TO THE WORK.—
Chap. xxxv. 1–29. After the restoration of the covenant, Moses
announced to the people the divine commands with reference
to the holy place of the tabernacle which was to be built. He
repeated first of all (vers. 1–3) the law of the Sabbath according to chap. xxxi. 13–17, and strengthened it by the announcement, that on the Sabbath no fire was to be kindled in their
dwelling, because this rule was to be observed even in connection with the work to be done for the tabernacle. (For a fuller
comment, see at chap. xx. 9 sqq.) Then, in accordance with
the command of Jehovah, he first of all summoned the whole
nation to present freewill-offerings for the holy things to be prepared (vers. 4, 5), mentioning one by one all the materials that
would be required (vers. 5–9, as in chap. xxv. 3–7) ; and after
that he called upon those who were endowed with understanding to prepare the different articles, as prescribed in chap. xxv.–
xxx., mentioning these also one by one (vers. 11–19), even down
to the pegs of the dwelling and court (xxvii. 19), and " their
cords," *i.e.* the cords required to fasten the tent and the hangings round the court to the pegs that were driven into the
ground, which had not been mentioned before, being altogether
subordinate things. (On the " cloths of service," ver. 19, see
at chap. xxxi. 10.) In vers. 20–29 we have an account of the
fulfilment of this command. The people went from Moses, *i.e.*
from the place where they were assembled round Moses, away
to their tents, and willingly offered the things required as a
heave-offering for Jehovah ; every one " whom his heart lifted
up," *i.e.* who felt himself inclined and stirred up in his heart to
do this. The men along with (עַל as in Gen. xxxii. 12 ; see
Ewald, § 217) the women brought with a willing heart all
kinds of golden rings and jewellery : *chak*, *lit.* hook, here a
clasp or ring ; *nezem*, an ear or nose-ring (Gen. xxxv. 4, xxiv.
47) ; *tabbaath*, a finger-ring ; *cumaz*, *globulus aureus*, probably
little golden balls strung together like beads, which were worn
by the Israelites and Midianites (Num. xxxi. 50) as an ornament round the wrist and neck, as *Diod. Sic.* relates that they
were by the Arabians (3, 44). "*All kinds of golden jewellery,*

and every one who had waved (dedicated) *a wave* (offering) *of gold to Jehovah,*" *sc.* offered it for the work of the tabernacle. The meaning is, that in addition to the many varieties of golden ornaments, which were willingly offered for the work to be performed, every one brought whatever gold he had set apart as a wave-offering (a sacrificial gift) for Jehovah.   הֵנִיף to *wave, lit.* to swing or move to and fro, is used in connection with the sacrificial ritual to denote a peculiar ceremony, through which certain portions of a sacrifice, which were not intended for burning upon the altar, but for the maintenance of the priests (Num. xviii. 11), were consecrated to the Lord, or given up to Him in a symbolical manner (see at Lev. vii. 30).   *Tenuphah,* the wave-offering, accordingly denoted primarily those portions of the sacrificial animal which were allotted to the priests as their share of the sacrifices; and then, in a more general sense, every gift or offering that was consecrated to the Lord for the establishment and maintenance of the sanctuary and its worship.   In this wider sense the term *tenuphah* (wave-offering) is applied both here and in chap. xxxviii. 24, 29 to the gold and copper presented by the congregation for the building of the tabernacle.   So that it does not really differ from *terumah,* a *lift* or heave-offering, as every gift intended for the erection and maintenance of the sanctuary was called, inasmuch as the offerer lifted it off from his own property, to dedicate it to the Lord for the purposes of His worship.   Accordingly, in ver. 24 the freewill-offerings of the people in silver and gold for the erection of the tabernacle are called *terumah ;* and in chap. xxxvi. 6, all the gifts of metal, wood, leather, and woven materials, presented by the people for the erection of the tabernacle, are called תְּרוּמַת קֹדֶשׁ   (On heaving and the heave-offering, see at chap. xxv. 2 and Lev. ii. 9.)—Vers. 25, 26. All the women who understood it (were wise-hearted, as in chap. xxviii. 3) spun with their hands, and presented what they spun, viz. the yarn required for the blue and red purple cloth, the crimson and the byssus; from which it is evident that the coloured cloths were dyed in the yarn or in the wool, as was the case in Egypt according to different specimens of old Egyptian cloths (see *Hengstenberg,* Egypt and the Books of Moses, p. 144).   Other women spun goats' hair for the upper or outer covering of the tent (xxvi. 7 sqq.).   Spinning was done by the women in very early times (*Plin. hist. n.* 8, 48), particularly in Egypt, where women are represented on the monuments as busily engaged with the spindle (see *Wilkinson*, Manners ii. p. 60 ; iii. p. 133, 136), and at a later period among the Hebrews (Prov. xxxi. 19). At the present day the women in the peninsula of Sinai spin the materials for their tents from camels' and goats' hair, and prepare sheep's wool for their clothing (*Rüppell, Nubien*, p. 202) ; and at Neswa, in the province of *Omân*, the preparation of cotton yarn is the principal employment of the women (*Wellstedt*, i. p. 90). Weaving also was, and still is to a great extent, a woman's work (cf. 2 Kings xxiii. 7) ; it is so among the Arab tribes in the Wady Gharandel, for example (*Russegger*, iii. 24), and in Nubia (*Burckhardt*, Nub. p. 211) ; but at Neswa the weaving is done by the men (*Wellstedt*). The woven cloths for the tabernacle were prepared by men, partly perhaps because the weaving in Egypt was mostly done by the men (*Herod.* 2, 35 ; cf. Hengstenberg, p. 143), but chiefly for this reason, that the cloths for the hangings and curtains were artistic works, which the women did not understand, but which the men had learned in Egypt, where artistic weaving was carried out to a great extent (*Wilkinson*, iii. pp. 113 sqq.).[1]—Vers. 27, 28. The precious stones for the robes of the high priest, and the spices for the incense and anointing oil, were presented by the princes of the congregation, who had such costly things in their possession.

Ver. 30–chap. xxxvi. 7. Moses then informed the people that God had called *Bezaleel* and *Aholiab* as master-builders, to complete the building and all the work connected with it, and had not only endowed them with His Spirit, that they might draw the plans for the different works and carry them out, but " had put it into his (Bezaleel's) heart to teach " (ver. 34), that is to say, had qualified him to instruct labourers to prepare the different articles under his supervision and guidance. " *He and Aholiab* " (ver 34) are in apposition to " *his heart:* " into his and Aholiab's heart (see Ges. § 121, 3 ; Ewald, § 311 *a*). The concluding words in ver. 35 are in apposition to אֹתָם (*them*) : " *them* hath He filled with wisdom . . . . as performers of every kind of work and inventors of designs," *i.e.* that they may make

---

[1] For drawings of the Egyptian weaving-stool, see *Wilkinson*, iii. p. 135 ; also *Hartmann, die Hebräerinn am Putztisch* i. Taf. 1.

every kind of work and may invent designs. In chap. xxxvi. 1, וְעָשָׂה with *vav consec.* is dependent upon what precedes, and signifies either, "and so will make," or, so that he will make (see *Ewald*, § 342 *b*). The idea is this, "Bezaleel, Aholiab, and the other men who understand, into whom Jehovah has infused (נָתַן בְּ) wisdom and understanding, that they may know how to do, shall do every work for the holy service (worship) with regard to (לְ as in chap. xxviii. 38, etc.) all that Jehovah has commanded."—Vers. 2–7. Moses then summoned the master-builders named, and all who were skilled in art, "*every one whom his heart lifted up to come near to the work to do it*" (*i.e.* who felt himself stirred up in heart to take part in the work), and handed over to them the heave-offering presented by the people for that purpose, whilst the children of Israel still continued bringing freewill-offerings every morning.—Ver. 4. Then the wise workmen came, every one from his work that they were making, and said to Moses, "*Much make the people to bring, more than suffices for the labour* (the finishing, as in chap. xxvii. 19) *of the work*," *i.e.* they are bringing more than will be wanted for carrying out the work (the מִן in מִדֵּי is comparative); whereupon Moses let the cry go through the camp, *i.e.* had proclamation made, "No one is to make any more property (מְלָאכָה as in chap. xxii. 7, 10, cf. Gen. xxxiii. 14) for a holy heave-offering," *i.e.* to prepare anything more from his own property to offer for the building of the sanctuary; and with this he put a stop to any further offerings.—Ver. 7. "*And there was enough* (דַּיָּם their sufficiency, *i.e.* the requisite supply for the different things to be made) *of the property for every work to make it, and over*" (*lit.* and to leave some over). By this liberal contribution of freewill gifts, for the work commanded by the Lord, the people proved their willingness to uphold their covenant relationship with Jehovah their God.

Chap. xxxvi. 8–xxxviii. 20. EXECUTION OF THE WORK.— Preparation of the *dwelling-place:* viz. the hangings and coverings (chap. xxxvi. 8–19, as in chap. xxvi. 1–14); the wooden boards and bolts (vers. 20–34, as in chap. xxvi. 15–30); the two curtains, with the pillars, hooks, and rods that supported them (vers. 35–38, as in chap. xxvi. 31–37). As these have all been already explained, the only thing remaining to be noticed here is, that the verbs עָשָׂה in ver. 8, וַיַּחְבֵּר in ver. 10, etc., are in the third person singular with an indefinite subject, corresponding to the German *man* (the French *on*).—Preparation of the *vessels of the dwelling:* viz. the ark of the covenant (chap. xxxvii. 1–9, as in chap. xxv. 10–22); the table of shew-bread and its vessels (vers. 10–16, as in chap. xxv. 23–30); the candlestick (vers. 17–24, as in chap. xxv. 31–40); the altar of incense (vers. 25–28, as in chap. xxx. 1–10); the anointing oil and incense (ver. 29), directions for the preparation of which are given in chap. xxx. 22–38; the altar of burnt-offering (chap. xxxviii. 1–7, as in chap. xxvii. 1–8); the laver (ver. 8, as in chap. xxx. 17–21); and the court (vers. 9–20, as in chap. xxvii. 9–19). The order corresponds on the whole to the list of the separate articles in chap. xxxv. 11–19, and to the construction of the entire sanctuary; but the holy chest (the ark), as being the most holy thing of all, is distinguished above all the rest, by being expressly mentioned as the work of Bezaleel, the chief architect of the whole.

Chap. xxxviii. 21–31. ESTIMATE OF THE AMOUNT OF METAL USED.—Ver. 21. *" These are the numbered things of the dwelling, of the dwelling of the testimony, that were numbered at the command of Moses, through the service of the Levites, by the hand of Ithamar, the son of Aaron the priest."* פְּקוּדִים does not mean the numbering (equivalent to מִפְקָד 2 Sam. iv. 9, or פְּקֻדָּה 2 Chron. xvii. 14, xxvi. 11), as *Knobel* supposes, but here as elsewhere, even in Num. xxvi. 63, 64, it signifies " the numbered; " the only difference being, that in most cases it refers to persons, here to things, and that the reckoning consisted not merely in the counting and entering of the different things, but in ascertaining their weight and estimating their worth. *Lyra* has given the following correct rendering of this heading : " *hæc est summa numeri ponderis eorum, quæ facta sunt in tabernaculo ex auro, argento et ære."* It was apparently superfluous to enumerate the different articles again, as this had been repeatedly done before. The weight of the different metals, therefore, is all that is given. The " dwelling" is still further described as "the dwelling of the testimony," because the testimony, *i.e.* the decalogue written with the finger of God upon the tables of stone, was kept in the dwelling, and this testimony formed the base of the throne of Jehovah, and was the material pledge that Jehovah would cause His name, His manifested presence, to dwell there, and would thus show Himself to His people in grace and righteousness. "That which was numbered" is an explanatory apposition to the previous clause, "the numbering of the dwelling;" and the words עֲבֹדַת הַלְוִים, which follow, are an *accusative* construed freely to indicate more particularly the mode of numbering (*Ewald*, § 204 *a*), viz. "through the service," or "by means of the service of the Levites," not *for* their service. "By the hand of Ithamar:" who presided over the calculations which the Levites carried out under his superintendence.— Vers. 22, 23. The allusion to the service of the Levites under Ithamar leads the historian to mention once more the architects of the whole building, and the different works connected with it (cf. chap. xxxi. 2 sqq.).—Ver. 24. "(As for) *all the gold that was used* (הֶעָשׂוּי) *for the work in every kind of holy work, the gold of the wave-offering* (the gold that was offered as a wave-offering, see at chap. xxxv. 22) *was* (amounted to) 29 *talents and* 730 *shekels in holy shekel*," that is to say, 87,370 shekels or 877,300 thalers (L.131,595), if we accept *Thenius'* estimate, that the gold shekel was worth 10 thalers (L.1, 10s.), which is probably very near the truth.—Vers. 25 sqq. Of the silver, all that is mentioned is the amount of atonement-money raised from those who were numbered (see at chap. xxx. 12 sqq.) at the rate of half a shekel for every male, without including the freewill-offerings of silver (chap. xxxv. 24, cf. chap. xxv. 3), whether it was that they were too insignificant, or that they were not used for the work, but were placed with the excess mentioned in chap. xxxvi. 7. The result of the numbering gave 603,550 men, every one of whom paid half a shekel. This would yield 301,775 shekels, or 100 talents and 1775 shekels, which proves by the way that a talent contained 3000 shekels. A hundred talents of this were used for casting 96 sockets for the 48 boards, and 4 sockets for the 4 pillars of the inner court,—one talent therefore for each socket,—and the 1775 shekels for the hooks of the pillars that sustained the curtains, for silvering their capitals, and "for binding the pillars," *i.e.* for making the silver connecting rods for the pillars of the court (chap. xxvii. 10, 11, xxxviii. 10 sqq.).—Vers. 29 sqq. The copper of the wave-offering amounted to 70 talents and 2400 shekels; and of this the sockets of the pillars at the entrance of the tabernacle (chap. xxvi. 37), the altar of burnt-offering with its network and vessels, the supports of the pillars of the court, all the pegs of the dwelling and court, and, what is not expressly mentioned here, the laver with its support (xxx. 18), were made. עָשָׂה בְּ to work in (with) copper, *i.e.* to make of copper.

If this quantity of the precious metals may possibly strike some readers as very large, and was in fact brought forward years ago as a reason for questioning the historical credibility of our account of the building of the tabernacle, it has been frequently urged, on the other hand, that it looks quite small, in comparison with the quantities of gold and silver that have been found accumulated in the East, in both ancient and modern times. According to the account before us, the requisite amount of silver was raised by the comparatively small payment of half a shekel, about fifteen pence, for every male Israelite of 20 years old and upwards. Now no tenable objection can be raised against the payment of such a tribute, since we have no reason whatever for supposing the Israelites to have been paupers, notwithstanding the oppression which they endured during the closing period of their stay in Egypt. They were settled in the most fertile part of Egypt; and coined silver was current in western Asia even in the time of the patriarchs (Gen. xxiii. 16). But with reference to the quantities of gold and copper that were delivered, we need not point to the immense stores of gold and other metals that were kept in the capitals of the Asiatic kingdoms of antiquity,[1] but will merely call to mind the fact, that the kings of Egypt possessed many large gold mines on the frontiers of the country, and in the neighbouring lands of Arabia and Ethiopia, which were worked by criminals, prisoners of war, and others, under the harshest pressure, and the very earliest times copper mines were discovered on the

---

[1] Thus, to mention only one or two examples, the images in the temple of Belus, at Babylon, consisted of several thousand talents of gold, to say nothing of the golden tables, the bedsteads, and other articles of gold and silver (*Diod. Sic.* 2, 9 ; *Herod.* 1, 181, 183). In the siege of Nineveh, Sardanapalus erected a funeral pile, upon which he collected all his wealth, including 150 golden bedsteads, 150 golden tables, a million talents of gold, and ten times as much silver and other valuables, to prevent their falling into the hands of the foe (*Ctesias* in *Athen.* 12, 38, p. 529). According to a

Arabian peninsula, which were worked by a colony of labourers (*Lepsius*, Letters from Egypt, p. 336). Moreover, the love of the ancient Egyptians for valuable and elegant ornaments, gold rings, necklaces, etc., is sufficiently known from the monuments (see *Rosellini* in *Hengstenberg's* Egypt, p. 137). Is it not likely, then, that the Israelites should have acquired a taste for jewellery of this kind, and should have possessed or discovered the means of procuring all kinds of gold and silver decorations, not to mention the gold and silver jewellery which they received from the Egyptians on their departure? The liking for such things even among nomad tribes is very well known. Thus, for example, after the defeat of the Midianites, the Israelites carried off so much gold, silver, copper, and other metals as spoil, that their princes alone were able to offer 16,750 shekels of gold as a heave-offering to Jehovah from the booty that had been obtained in this kind of jewellery (Num. xxxi. 50 sqq.). *Diodorus Sic.* (3, 44) and *Strabo* (xvi. p. 778) bear witness to the great wealth of the Nabateans and other Arab tribes on the Elanitic Gulf, and mention not only a river, said to flow through the land, carrying gold dust with it, but also gold that was dug up, and which was found, " not in the form of sand, but of nuggets, which did not require much cleaning, and the smallest of which were of the size of a nut, the average size being that of a medlar, whilst the largest pieces were as big as a walnut. These they bored, and made necklaces or bracelets by stringing them together alternately with transparent stones. They also sold the gold very cheap to their neighbours, giving three times the quantity for copper, and double the quantity for iron, both on account of their inability to work these metals, and also because of the scarcity of the metals which were so much more necessary for daily use" (*Strabo*). The Sabæans and Gerrhæans are also mentioned as the richest of all the tribes of Arabia,

statement in *Pliny's Hist. Nat.* 33, 3, on the conquest of Asia by Cyrus, he carried off booty to the extent of 34,000 lbs. of gold, beside the golden vessels and 500,000 talents of silver, including the goblet of Semiramis, which alone weighed 15 talents. Alexander the Great found more than 40,000 talents of gold and silver and 9000 talents of coined gold in the royal treasury at Susa (*Diod. Sic.* 17, 66), and a treasure of 120,000 talents of gold in the citadel of Persepolis (*Diod. Sic.* 17, 71; *Curtius,* v. 6, 9). For further accounts of the enormous wealth of Asia in gold and silver, see *Bähr, Symbolik* i. pp. 258 sqq.

through their trade in incense and in cinnamon and other spices. From the Arabs, who carried on a very extensive caravan trade through the desert even at that time, the Israelites would be able to purchase such spices and materials for the building of the tabernacle as they had not brought with them from Egypt; and in Egypt itself, where all descriptions of art and handicraft were cultivated from the very earliest times (for proofs see *Hengst.* Egypt, pp. 133–139), they might so far have acquired all the mechanical and artistic ability required for the work, that skilled artisans could carry out all that was prescribed, under the superintendence of the two master-builders who had been specially inspired for the purpose.

Chap. xxxix. 1–31. *Preparation of the priests' clothes.*—Previous to the description of the dress itself, we have a statement in ver. 1 of the materials employed, and the purpose to which they were devoted (" cloths of service," see at chap. xxxi. 10). The robes consisted of the *ephod* (vers. 2–7, as in chap. xxviii. 6–12), the *choshen* or breastplate (vers. 8–21, as in chap. xxviii. 15–29), the *meïl* or over-coat (vers. 22–26, as in chap. xxviii. 31–34); the *body-coats, turbans, drawers,* and *girdles,* for Aaron and his sons (vers. 27–29, as in chap. xxviii. 39, 40, and 42). The Urim and Thummim are not mentioned (cf. chap. xxviii. 30). The head-dresses of the ordinary priests, which are simply called "bonnets" in chap. xxviii. 40, are called "goodly bonnets" or "ornamental caps" in ver. 28 of this chapter (פַּאֲרֵי מִגְבָּעֹת, from פְּאֵר an ornament, cf. פָּאַר *ornatus fuit*). The singular, "girdle," in ver. 29, with the definite article, "the girdle," might appear to refer simply to Aaron's girdle, *i.e.* the girdle of the high priest; but as there is no special description of the girdles of Aaron's sons (the ordinary priests) in chap. xxix. 40, where they are distinctly mentioned and called by the same name (*abnet*) as the girdle of Aaron himself, we can only conclude

---

[1] " They possess an immense quantity of gold and silver articles, such as beds, tripods, bowls, and cups, in addition to the decorations of their houses; for doors, walls, and ceilings are all wrought with ivory, gold, silver, and precious stones" (*Strabo* ut sup.). In accordance with this, *Pliny* (*h. n.* 6, 28) not only calls the Sabæans " *ditissimos silvarum fertilitate odorifera, auri metallis, etc.,*" but the tribes of Arabia in general, " *in universum gentes ditissimas, ut apud quas maximæ opes Romanorum Parthorum que subsistant, vendentibus quæ e mari aut silvis capiunt, nihil invicem redimentibus.*"

that they were of the same materials and the same form and
make as the latter, and that the singular, הָאַבְנֵט, is used here
either in the most general manner, or as a generic noun in a
collective sense (see *Ges.* § 109, 1). The last thing mentioned
is the diadem upon Aaron's turban (vers. 30, 31, as in chap.
xxviii. 36–38), so that the order in which the priests' robes are
given here is analogous to the position in which the ark of the
covenant and the golden altar stand to one another in the directions concerning the sacred things in chap. xxv.–xxx. "For just
as all the other things are there placed between the holy ark and
the golden altar as the two poles, so here all the rest of the
priests' robes are included between the shoulder-dress, the principal part of the official robes of the high priest, and the golden
frontlet, the inscription upon which rendered it the most striking sign of the dignity of his office" (*Baumgarten*).

Vers. 32–43. *Delivery of the work to Moses.*—The different
things are again mentioned one by one. By "the tent," in
ver. 33, we are to understand the two tent-cloths, the one of
purple and the other of goats' hair, by which the *dwelling* (מִשְׁכָּן,
generally rendered tabernacle) was made into *a tent* (אֹהֶל). From
this it is perfectly obvious, that the variegated cloth formed the
inner walls of the dwelling, or covered the boards on the inner
side, and that the goats' hair-cloth formed the other covering.
Moreover it is also obvious, that this is the way in which
הָאֹהֶל is to be understood, from the fact, that in the list of the
things belonging to the *ohel* the first to be mentioned are the
gold and copper hooks (xxvi. 6, 11) with which the two halves
of the drapery that formed the tent were joined together, and
then after that the boards, bolts, pillars, and sockets, as though
subordinate to the tent-cloths, and only intended to answer the
purpose of spreading them out into a tent or dwelling.—
Ver. 37. "*The lamps of the order,*" *i.e.* the lamps set in order
upon the candlestick. In addition to all the vessels of the sanctuary, shew-bread (ver. 36), holy oil for the candlestick and for
anointing, and fragrant incense (ver. 38), were also prepared
and delivered to Moses,—everything, therefore, that was required for the institution of the daily worship, as soon as the
tabernacle was set up.—Ver. 40. "*Vessels of service :*" see
chap. xxvii. 19.—Ver. 43. When Moses had received and examined all the different articles, and found that everything was

made according to the directions of Jehovah, he blessed the children of Israel. The readiness and liberality with which the people had presented the gifts required for this work, and the zeal which they had shown in executing the whole of the work in rather less than half a year (see at chap. xl. 17), were most cheering signs of the willingness of the Israelites to serve the Lord, for which they could not fail to receive the blessing of God.

ERECTION AND CONSECRATION OF THE TABERNACLE.—
CHAP. XL.

Vers. 1–16. After the completion of all the works, the command was given by God to Moses to set up the dwelling of the tabernacle on the first day of the first month (see at chap xix. 1), *sc.* in the second year of the Exodus (see ver. 17), and to put all the vessels, both of the dwelling and court, in the places appointed by God; also to furnish the table of shew-bread with its fitting out (עָרַךְ לֶחֶם = עֶרְכּוֹ ver. 23), *i.e.* to arrange the bread upon it in the manner prescribed (ver. 4 cf. Lev. xxiv. 6, 7), and to put water in the laver of the court (ver. 7). After that he was to anoint the dwelling and everything in it, also the altar of burnt-offering and laver, with the anointing oil, and to sanctify them (vers. 9–11); and to consecrate Aaron and his sons before the door of the tabernacle, and clothe them, anoint them, and sanctify them as priests (vers. 12–15). When we read here, however, that the dwelling and the vessels therein would be rendered "*holy*" through the anointing, but the altar of burnt-offering "*most holy*," we are not to understand this as attributing a higher degree of holiness to the altar of burnt-offering than to the dwelling and its furniture; but the former is called "most holy" merely in the sense ascribed to it in chap. xxx. 10, namely, that every one who touched it was to become holy; in other words, the distinction has reference to the fact, that, standing as it did in the court, it was more exposed to contact from the people than the vessels in the dwelling, which no layman was allowed to enter. In this relative sense we find the same statement in chap. xxx. 29, with reference to the tabernacle and all the vessels therein, the dwelling as well as the court, that they would become *most holy* in consequence of the anointing (see

the remarks on chap. xxx. 10). It is stated provisionally, in ver.
16, that this command was fulfilled by Moses. But from the
further history we find that the consecration of the priests did
not take place contemporaneously with the erection of the tabernacle, but somewhat later, or not till after the promulgation of
the laws of sacrifice (cf. Lev. viii. and Lev. i. 1 sqq.).

Vers. 17–33. On the day mentioned in ver. 2 the dwelling
and court were erected. As not quite nine months had elapsed
between the arrival of the Israelites at Sinai, in the third month
after the Exodus (chap. xix. 1), and the first day of the second
year, when the work was finished and handed over to Moses, the
building, and all the work connected with it, had not occupied
quite half a year; as we have to deduct from the nine months
(or somewhat less) not only the eighty days which Moses
spent upon Sinai (chap. xxiv. 18, xxxiv. 28), but the days of
preparation for the giving of the law and conclusion of the
covenant (chap. xix. 1–xxiv. 11), and the interval between the
first and second stay that Moses made upon the mountain (chap.
xxxii. and xxxiii.). The erection of the dwelling commenced
with the fixing of the sockets, into which the boards were placed
and fastened with their bolts, and the setting up of the pillars
for the curtains (ver. 18). *" He* (Moses) *then spread the tent over
the dwelling, and laid the covering of the tent upon the top."* By
the " covering of the tent" we are to understand the two coverings, made of red rams' skins and the skins of the sea-cow (chap.
xxvi. 14). In analogy with this, פָּרַשׂ אֶת־הָאֹהֶל denotes not only
the roofing with the goats' hair, but the spreading out of the
inner cloth of mixed colours upon the wooden frame-work.—
Vers. 20–21. *Arrangement of the ark.* " He took and put the
testimony into the ark." הָעֵדוּת does not mean " the revelation,
so far as it existed already, viz. with regard to the erection of
the sanctuary and institution of the priesthood (chap. xxv.–xxxi.),
and so forth," as *Knobel* arbitrarily supposes, but " the testimony," *i.e.* the decalogue written upon the two tables of stone,
or the tables of the covenant with the ten words; "the testimony," therefore, is an abbreviated expression for "the tables of
testimony" (chap. xxxi. 18, see at chap. xxv. 16). After the
ark had been brought into the dwelling, he " hung the curtain"
(vail, see at chap. xxvi. 31; *lit.* placed it upon the hooks of the
pillars), " and so covered over the ark of the testimony," since

the ark, when placed in the back part of the dwelling, was covered or concealed from persons entering the dwelling or the holy place. —Vers. 22–28. *Arrangement of the front room of the dwelling.* The table was placed on the right side, towards the north, and the shew-bread was laid upon it. עֶרֶךְ לֶחֶם does not signify " a row of bread," but the "position or placing of bread;" for, according to Lev. xxiv. 6, 7, the twelve loaves of shew-bread were placed upon the table in two rows, corresponding to the size of the tables (two cubits long and one cubit broad). The candlestick was placed upon the left side, opposite to the table, and the golden altar in front of the curtain, *i.e.* midway between the two sides, but near the curtain in front of the most holy place (see at chap. xxx. 6). After these things had been placed, the curtain was hung in the door of the dwelling.—Vers. 29–32. The altar of burnt-offering was then placed " *before the door of the dwelling of the tabernacle,*" and the laver " *between the tabernacle and the altar,*" from which it is evident that the altar was not placed close to the entrance to the dwelling, but at some distance off, though in a straight line with the door. The laver, which stood between the altar and the entrance to the dwelling, was probably placed more to the side ; so that when the priests washed their hands and feet, before entering the dwelling or approaching the altar, there was no necessity for them to go round the altar, or to pass close by it, in order to get to the laver. Last of all the court was erected round about the dwelling and the altar, by the setting up of the pillars, which enclosed the space round the dwelling and the altar with their drapery, and the hanging up of the curtain at the entrance to the court. There is no allusion to the anointing of these holy places and things, as commanded in vers. 9–11, in the account of their erection ; for this did not take place till afterwards, viz. at the consecration of Aaron and his sons as priests (Lev. viii. 10, 11). It is stated, however, on the other hand, that as the vessels were arranged, Moses laid out the shew-bread upon the table (ver. 23), burned sweet incense upon the golden altar (ver. 27), and offered " the burnt-offering and meat-offering," *i.e.* the daily morning and evening sacrifice, upon the altar of burnt-offering (chap. xxix. 38–42). Consequently the sacrificial service was performed upon them before they had been anointed. Although this may appear surprising, there is no ground for rejecting a conclusion, which follows so naturally from the words of the text. The tabernacle and its furniture were not made holy things for the first time by the anointing; this simply sanctified them for the use of the nation, *i.e.* for the service which the priests were to perform in connection with them on behalf of the congregation (see at Lev. viii. 10, 11). They were made holy things and holy vessels by the fact that they were built, prepared, and set up, according to the instructions given by Jehovah; and still more by the fact, that after the tabernacle had been erected as a dwelling, the "glory of the Lord filled the tabernacle" (ver. 34). But the glory of the Lord entered the dwelling before the consecration of the priests, and the accompanying anointing of the tabernacle and its vessels; for, according to Lev. i. 1 sqq., it was from the tabernacle that Jehovah spake to Moses, when He gave him the laws of sacrifice, which were promulgated before the consecration of the priests, and were carried out in connection with it. But when the glory of the Lord had found a dwelling-place in the tabernacle, Moses was not required to offer continually the sacrifice prescribed for every morning and evening, and by means of this sacrifice to place the congregation in spiritual fellowship with its God, until Aaron and his sons had been consecrated for this service.

Vers. 34–38. When the sanctuary, that had been built for the Lord for a dwelling in Israel, had been set up with all its apparatus, "*the cloud covered the tabernacle, and the glory of Jehovah filled the dwelling*," so that Moses was unable to enter. The cloud, in which Jehovah had hitherto been present with His people, and guided and protected them upon their journeying (see at chap. xiii. 21, 22), now came down upon the tabernacle and filled the dwelling with the gracious presence of the Lord. So long as this cloud rested upon the tabernacle the children of Israel remained encamped; but when it ascended, they broke up the encampment to proceed onwards. This sign was Jehovah's command for encamping or going forward "throughout all their journeys" (vers. 36–38). This statement is repeated still more elaborately in Num. ix. 15–23. The mode in which the glory of Jehovah filled the dwelling, or in which Jehovah manifested His presence within it, is not described; but the glory of Jehovah filling the dwelling is clearly distinguished from the cloud coming down upon the tabernacle. It is obvious, however, from

Lev. xvi. 2, and 1 Kings viii. 10, 11, that in the dwelling the glory of God was also manifested in a cloud. At the dedication of the temple (1 Kings viii. 10, 11) the expression "the cloud filled the house of Jehovah" is used interchangeably with "the glory of Jehovah filled the house of Jehovah." To consecrate the sanctuary, which had been finished and erected as His dwelling, and to give to the people a visible proof that He had chosen it for His dwelling, Jehovah filled the dwelling in both its parts with the cloud which shadowed forth His presence, so that Moses was unable to enter it. This cloud afterwards drew back into the most holy place, to dwell there, above the outspread wings of the cherubim of the ark of the covenant; so that Moses and (at a later period) the priests were able to enter the holy place and perform the required service there, without seeing the sign of the gracious presence of God, which was hidden by the curtain of the most holy place. So long as the Israelites were on their journey to Canaan, the presence of Jehovah was manifested outwardly and visibly by the cloud, which settled upon the ark, and rose up from it when they were to travel onward.

With the completion of this building and its divine consecration, Israel had now received a real pledge of the permanence of the covenant of grace, which Jehovah had concluded with it ; a sanctuary which perfectly corresponded to the existing circumstances of its religious development, and kept constantly before it the end of its calling from God. For although God dwelt in the tabernacle in the midst of His people, and the Israelites might appear before Him, to pray for and receive the covenant blessings that were promised them, they were still forbidden to go directly to God's throne of grace. The barrier, which sin had erected between the holy God and the unholy nation, was not yet taken away. To this end the law was given, which could only increase their consciousness of sin and unworthiness before God. But as this barrier had already been broken through by the promise of the Lord, that He would meet the people in His glory before the door of the tabernacle at the altar of burnt-offering (chap. xxix. 42, 43); so the entrance of the chosen people into the dwelling of God was effected mediatorially by the service of the sanctified priests in the holy place, which also prefigured their eventual reception into the house of the Lord. And even the curtain, which still hid the glory of God from the chosen priests and sanctified mediators of the nation, was to be lifted at least once a year by the anointed priest, who had been called by God to be the representative of the whole congregation. On the day of atonement the high priest was to sprinkle the blood of atonement in front of the throne of grace, to make expiation for the children of Israel because of all their sin (Lev. xvi.), and to prefigure the perfect atonement through the blood of the eternal Mediator, through which the way to the throne of grace is opened to all believers, that they may go into the house of God and abide there for ever, and for ever see God.

THE THIRD BOOK OF MOSES

(LEVITICUS.)

———◆———

INTRODUCTION.

CONTENTS AND PLAN OF LEVITICUS.

THE third book of Moses is headed ויקרא in the original text, from the opening word. In the Septuagint and Vulgate it is called Λευϊτικόν, sc. βίβλιον, *Leviticus*, from the leading character of its contents, and probably also with some reference to the titles which had obtained currency among the Rabbins, viz. " law of the priests," " law-book of sacrificial offerings." It carries on to its completion the giving of the law at Sinai, which commenced at Ex. xxv., and by which the covenant constitution was firmly established. It contains more particularly the laws regulating the relation of Israel to its God, including both the fundamental principles upon which its covenant fellowship with the Lord depended, and the directions for the sanctification of the covenant people in that communion. Consequently the laws contained in this book might justly be described as the " spiritual statute-book of Israel as the congregation of Jehovah." As every treaty establishes a reciprocal relation between those who are parties to it, so not only did Jehovah as Lord of the whole earth enter into a special relation to His chosen people Israel in the covenant made by Him with the seed of Abraham, which He had chosen as His own possession out of all the nations, but the nation of Israel was also to be brought into a real and living fellowship with Him as its God and Lord. And whereas Jehovah would be Israel's God, manifesting Himself to it in all the fulness of

His divine nature; so was it also His purpose to train Israel as His own nation, to sanctify it for the truest life in fellowship with Him, and to bless it with all the fulness of His salvation. To give effect to the former, or the first condition of the covenant, God had commanded the erection of a sanctuary for the dwelling-place of His name, or the true manifestation of His own essence; and on its erection, *i.e.* on the setting up of the tabernacle, He filled the most holy place with a visible sign of His divine glory (Ex. xl. 34), a proof that He would be ever near and present to His people with His almighty grace. When this was done, it was necessary that the other side of the covenant relation should be realized in a manner suited to the spiritual, religious, and moral condition of Israel, in order that Israel might become His people in truth. But as the nation of Israel was separated from God, the Holy One, by the sin and unholiness of its nature, the only way in which God could render access to His gracious presence possible, was by institutions and legal regulations, which served on the one hand to sharpen the consciousness of sin in the hearts of the people, and thereby to awaken the desire for mercy and for reconciliation with the holy God, and on the other hand furnished them with the means of expiating their sins and sanctifying their walk before God according to the standard of His holy commandments.

All the laws and regulations of Leviticus have this for their object, inasmuch as they, each and all, aim quite as much at the restoration of an inward fellowship on the part of the nation as a whole and the individual members with Jehovah their God, through the expiation or forgiveness of sin and the removal of all natural uncleanness, as at the strengthening and deepening of this fellowship by the sanctification of every relation of life. In accordance with this twofold object, the contents of the book are arranged in two larger series of laws and rules of life, the first extending from chap. i. to chap. xvi., the second from chap. xvii. to chap. xxv. The *first* of these, which occupies the earlier half of the book of Leviticus, opens with the laws of sacrifice in chap. i.–vii. As sacrifices had been from the very beginning the principal medium by which men entered into fellowship with God, the Creator, Preserver, and Governor of the world, to supplicate and appropriate His favour and grace, so Israel was not only permitted to draw near to its God with sacrificial gifts, but, by thus offering its sacrifices according to the precepts of the divine law, would have an ever open way of access to the throne of grace. The laws of sacrifice are followed in chap. viii.-x. by the consecration of Aaron and his sons, the divinely appointed priests, by their solemn entrance upon their official duties, and by the sanctification of their priesthood on the part of God, both in word and act. Then follow in chap. xi.-xv. the regulations concerning the clean and unclean animals, and various bodily impurities, with directions for the removal of all defilements; and these regulations culminate in the institution of a yearly day of atonement (chap. xvi.), inasmuch as this day, with its all-embracing expiation, foreshadowed typically and prefigured prophetically the ultimate and highest aim of the Old Testament economy, viz. perfect reconciliation. Whilst all these laws and institutions opened up to the people of Israel the way of access to the throne of grace, the *second* series of laws, contained in the later half of the book (chap. xvii.-xxv.), set forth the demands made by the holiness of God upon His people, that they might remain in fellowship with Him, and rejoice in the blessings of His grace. This series of laws commences with directions for the sanctification of life in food, marriage, and morals (chap. xvii.-xx.); it then advances to the holiness of the priests and the sacrifices (chaps. xxi. and xxii.), and from that to the sanctification of the feasts and the daily worship of God (chaps. xxiii. and xxiv.), and closes with the sanctification of the whole land by the appointment of the sabbatical and jubilee years (chap. xxv.). In these the sanctification of Israel as the congregation of Jehovah was to be glorified into the blessedness of the sabbatical rest in the full enjoyment of the blessings of the saving grace of its God; and in the keeping of the year of jubilee more especially, the land and kingdom of Israel were to be transformed into a kingdom of peace and liberty, which also foreshadowed typically and prefigured prophetically the time of the completion of the kingdom of God, the dawn of the glorious liberty of the children of God, when the bondage of sin and death shall be abolished for ever.

Whilst, therefore, the laws of sacrifice and purification, on the one hand, culminate in the institution of the *yearly day of atonement*, so, on the other, do those relating to the sanctification of life culminate in the appointment of the *sabbatical and jubilee years;* and thus the two series of laws in Leviticus are placed in unmistakeable correspondence to one another. In the ordinances, rights, and laws thus given to the covenant nation, not only was the way clearly indicated, by which the end of its divine calling was to be attained, but a constitution was given to it, fully adapted to all the conditions incident to this end, and this completed the establishment of the kingdom of God in Israel. To give a finish, however, to the covenant transaction at Sinai, it was still necessary to impress upon the hearts of the people, on the one hand, the blessings that would follow the faithful observance of the covenant of their God, and on the other hand, the evil of transgressing it (chap. xxvi.). To this there are also added, in the form of an appendix, the instructions concerning vows. The book of Leviticus is thus rounded off, and its unity and independence within the *Thorah* are established, not only by the internal unity of its laws and their organic connection, but also by the fact, so clearly proved by the closing formula in chap. xxvi. 46 and xxvii. 34, that it finishes with the conclusion of the giving of the law at Sinai.

EXPOSITION.

I. LAWS AND ORDINANCES DETERMINING THE COVENANT FELLOWSHIP BETWEEN THE LORD AND ISRAEL.

CHAP. I.–XVI.

THE LAWS OF SACRIFICE.—CHAP. I.–VII.

WHEN the glory of the Lord had entered the tabernacle in a cloud, God revealed Himself to Moses from this place of His gracious presence, according to His promise in Ex. xxv. 22, to make known His sacred will through him to the people (i. 1). The first of these revelations related to the sacrifices, in which the Israelites were to draw near to Him, that they might become partakers of His grace.[1]

[1] Works relating to the sacrifices : *Guil. Outram de sacrificiis libri duo,* Amst. 1688 ; *Bähr, Symbolik des mos. Cultus* ii. pp. 189 sqq.; *Kurtz* on the

The patriarchs, when sojourning in Canaan, had already worshipped the God who revealed Himself to them, with both burnt-offerings and slain-offerings. Whether their descendants, the children of Israel, had offered sacrifices to the God of their fathers during their stay in the foreign land of Egypt, we cannot tell, as there is no allusion whatever to the subject in the short account of these 430 years. So much, however, is certain, that they had not forgotten to regard the sacrifices as a leading part of the worship of God, and were ready to follow Moses into the desert, to serve the God of their fathers there by a solemn act of sacrificial worship (Ex. v. 1–3, compared with chap. iv. 31, viii. 4, etc.); and also, that after the exodus from Egypt, not only did Jethro offer burnt-offerings and slain-offerings to God in the camp of the Israelites, and prepare a sacrificial meal in which the elders of Israel took part along with Moses and Aaron (Ex. xviii. 12), but young men offered burnt-offerings and slain-offerings by the command of Moses at the conclusion of the covenant (Ex. xxiv. 5). Consequently the sacrificial laws of these chapters presuppose the presentation of burnt-offerings, meat-offerings, and slain-offerings as a custom well known to the people, and a necessity demanded by their religious feelings (chap. i. 2, 3, 10, 14, ii. 1, 4, 5, 14, iii. 1, 6, 11). They were not introduced among the Israelites for the first time by Moses, as *Knobel* affirms, who also maintains that the feast of the Passover was the first animal sacrifice, and in fact a very imperfect one. Even animal sacrifices date from the earliest period of our race. Not only did Noah offer burnt-offerings of all clean animals and birds (Gen. viii. 20), but Abel brought of the firstlings of his flock an offering to the Lord (Gen. iv. 4).[1] The object of the sacrificial laws in this book

Sacrificial Worship of the Old Testament (Clark, 1863); and *Oehler*, in *Herzog's* Cyclopædia. The rabbinical traditions are to be found in the two talmudical tractates *Sebachim* and *Menachoth*, and a brief summary of them is given in *Otho lex. rabbin. philol.* pp. 631 sqq.

[1] When *Knobel*, in his Commentary on Leviticus (p. 347), endeavours to set aside the validity of these proofs, by affirming that sacrificial worship in the earliest times is merely a fancy of the *Jehovist;* apart altogether from the untenable character of the Elohistic and Jehovistic hypothesis, there is a sufficient proof that this subterfuge is worthless, in the fact that the so-called *Elohist*, instead of pronouncing Moses the originator of the sacrificial worship of the Hebrews, introduces his laws of sacrifice with this

was neither to enforce sacrificial worship upon the Israelites, nor to apply " a theory concerning the Hebrew sacrifices" (*Knobel*), but simply to organize and expand the sacrificial worship of the Israelites into an institution in harmony with the covenant between the Lord and His people, and adapted to promote the end for which it was established.

But although sacrifice in general reaches up to the earliest times of man's history, and is met with in every nation, it was not enjoined upon the human race by any positive command of God, but sprang out of a religious necessity for fellowship with God, the author, protector, and preserver of life, which was as innate in man as the consciousness of God itself, though it assumed very different forms in different tribes and nations, in consequence of their estrangement from God, and their growing loss of all true knowledge of Him, inasmuch as their ideas of the Divine Being so completely regulated the nature, object, and signification of the sacrifices they offered, that they were quite as subservient to the worship of idols as to that of the one true God. To discover the fundamental idea, which was common to all the sacrifices, we must bear in mind, on the one hand, that the first sacrifices were presented after the fall, and on the other hand, that we never meet with any allusion to expiation in the pre-Mosaic sacrifices of the Old Testament. Before the fall, man lived in blessed unity with God. This unity was destroyed by sin, and the fellowship between God and man was disturbed, though not entirely abolished. In the punishment which God inflicted upon the sinners, He did not withdraw His mercy from men ; and before driving them out of paradise, He gave them clothes to cover the nakedness of their shame, by which they had first of all become conscious of their sin. Even after their expulsion He still manifested Himself to them, so

formula, " If any man of you bring an offering of cattle unto the Lord," and thus stamps the presentation of animal sacrifice as a traditional custom. *Knobel* cannot adduce any historical testimony in support of his assertion, that, according to the opinion of the ancients, there were no animal sacrifices offered to the gods in the earliest times, but only meal, honey, vegetables, and flowers, roots, leaves, and fruit ; all that he does is to quote a few passages from *Plato*, *Plutarch*, and *Porphyry*, in which these philosophers, who were much too young to answer the question, express their ideas and conjectures respecting the rise and progress of sacrificial worship among the nations.

that they were able once more to draw near to Him and enter into fellowship with Him. This fellowship they sought through the medium of sacrifices, in which they gave a visible expression not only to their gratitude towards God for His blessing and His grace, but also to their supplication for the further continuance of His divine favour. It was in this sense that both Cain and Abel offered sacrifice, though not with the same motives, or in the same state of heart towards God. In this sense Noah also offered sacrifice after his deliverance from the flood; the only apparent difference being this, that the sons of Adam offered their sacrifices to God from the fruit of their labour, in the tilling of the ground and the keeping of sheep, whereas Noah presented his burnt-offerings from the clean cattle and birds that had been shut up with him in the ark, *i.e.* from those animals which at any rate from that time forward were assigned to man as food (Gen. ix. 3). Noah was probably led to make this selection by the command of God to take with him into the ark not one or more pairs, but seven of every kind of clean beasts, as he may have discerned in this an indication of the divine will, that the seventh animal of every description of clean beast and bird should be offered in sacrifice to the Lord, for His gracious protection from destruction by the flood. Moses also received a still further intimation as to the meaning of the animal sacrifices, in the prohibition which God appended to the permission to make use of animals as well as green herbs for food; viz. "flesh with the life thereof, which is the blood thereof, shall ye not eat" (Gen. ix. 4, 5), that is to say, flesh which still contained the blood as the animal's soul. In this there was already an intimation, that in the bleeding sacrifice the soul of the animal was given up to God with the blood; and therefore, that by virtue of its blood, as the vehicle of the soul, animal sacrifice was the most fitting means of representing the surrender of the human soul to God. This truth may possibly have been only dimly surmised by Noah and his sons; but it must have been clearly revealed to the patriarch Abraham, when God demanded the sacrifice of his only son, with whom his whole heart was bound up, as a proof of his obedience of faith, and then, after he had attested his faith in his readiness to offer this sacrifice, supplied him with a ram to offer as a burnt-offering instead of his son (Gen. xxii.). In this the truth was practically revealed to him, that the true God did not require human sacrifice from His worshippers, but the surrender of the heart and the denial of the natural life, even though it should amount to a submission to death itself, and also that this act of surrender was to be perfected in the animal sacrifice; and that it was only when presented with these motives that sacrifice could be well-pleasing to God. Even before this, however, God had given His sanction to the choice of clean or edible beasts and birds for sacrifice, in the command to Abram to offer such animals, as the sacrificial substratum for the covenant to be concluded with him (Gen. xv.). Now, though nothing has been handed down concerning the sacrifices of the patriarchs, with the exception of Gen xlvi. 1 sqq., there can be no doubt that they offered burnt-offerings upon the altars which they built to the Lord, who appeared to them in different places in Canaan (Gen. xii. 7, xiii. 4, 18, xxvi. 25, xxxiii. 20, xxxv. 1-7), and embodied in these their solemn invocation of the name of God in prayer; since the close connection between sacrifice and prayer is clearly proved by such passages as Hos. xiv. 3, Heb. xiii. 15, and is universally admitted.[1] To the burnt-offering there was added, in the course of time, the slain-offering, which is mentioned for the first time in Gen. xxxi. 54, where Jacob seals the covenant, which has been concluded with Laban and sworn to by God, with a covenant meal. Whilst the burnt-offering, which was given wholly up to God and entirely consumed upon the altar, and which ascended to heaven in the smoke, set forth the self-surrender of man to God, the slain-offering, which culminated in the sacrificial meal, served as a seal of the covenant fellowship, and represented the living fellowship of man with God. Thus, when Jacob-Israel went down with his house to Egypt, he sacrificed at Beersheba, on the border of the promised land, to the God of his father Isaac, not burnt-offerings, but slain-offerings (Gen. xlvi. 1), through which he presented his prayer to the Lord for preservation in covenant fellowship even in a foreign land, and in consequence of which he received the promise from God in a nocturnal vision, that He, the God of his

---

[1] *Outram* (*l. c.* p. 213) draws the following conclusion from Hos. xiv. 3 : " Prayer was a certain kind of sacrifice, and sacrifice a certain kind of prayer. Prayers were, so to speak, spiritual sacrifices, and sacrifices *symbolical* prayers."

father, would go with him to Egypt and bring him up again to Canaan, and so maintain the covenant which He had made with his fathers, and assuredly fulfil it in due time. The expiatory offerings, properly so called, viz. the sin and trespass-offerings, were altogether unknown before the economy of the Sinaitic law; and even if an expiatory element was included in the burnt-offerings, so far as they embodied self-surrender to God, and thus involved the need of union and reconciliation with Him, so little prominence is given to this in the pre-Mosaic sacrifices, that, as we have already stated, no reference is made to expiation in connection with them.[1] The reason for this striking fact is to be found in the circumstance, that godly men of the primeval age offered their sacrifices to a God who had drawn near to them in revelations of love. It is true that in former times God had made known His holy justice in the destruction of the wicked and the deliverance of the righteous (Gen. vi. 13 sqq., xviii. 16 sqq.), and had commanded Abraham to walk blamelessly before Him (Gen. xvii. 1); but He had only manifested Himself to the patriarchs in His condescending love and mercy, whereas He had made known His holiness in His very first revelation to Moses in the words, "Draw not nigh hither; put off thy shoes," etc. (Ex. iii. 5), and unfolded it more and

---

[1] The notion, which is still very widely spread, that the burnt-offerings of Abel, Noah, and the patriarchs were expiatory sacrifices, in which the slaying of the sacrificial animals set forth the fact, that the sinner was deserving of death in the presence of the holy God, not only cannot be proved from the Scriptures, but is irreconcilable with the attitude of a Noah, an Abraham and other patriarchs, towards the Lord God. And even *Kahnis's* explanation, "The man felt that his own *ipse* must die, before it could enter into union with the Holy One, but he had also his surmises, that another life might possibly bear this death for him, and in this obscure feeling he took away the life of an animal that was physically clean," is only true and to the point so far as the deeper forms of the development of the heathen consciousness of God are concerned, and not in the sphere of revealed religion, in which the expiatory sacrifices did not originate in any dim consciousness on the part of the sinner that he was deserving of death, but were appointed for the first time by God at Sinai, for the purpose of awakening and sharpening this feeling. There is no historical foundation for the arguments adduced by *Hofmann* in support of the opinion, that there were sin-offerings before the Mosaic law; and the assertion, that sin-offerings and trespass-offerings were not really introduced by the law, but were presupposed as already well known, just as much as the burnt-offerings and thank-offerings, is obviously at variance with Lev. iv. and v.

more in all subsequent revelations, especially at Sinai. After Jehovah had there declared to the people of Israel, whom He had redeemed out of Egypt, that they were to be a holy nation to Him (Ex. xix. 6), He appeared upon the mountain in the terrible glory of His holy nature, to conclude His covenant of grace with them by the blood of burnt-offerings and slain-offerings, so that the people trembled and were afraid of death if the Lord should speak to them any more (Ex. xx. 18 sqq.). These facts preceded the laws of sacrifice, and not only prepared the way for them, but furnished the key to their true interpretation, by showing that it was only by sacrifice that the sinful nation could enter into fellowship with the holy God.

The laws of sacrifice in chap. i.–vii. are divisible into two groups. The first (chap. i.–v.) contains the general instructions, which were applicable both to the community as a whole and also to the individual Israelites. Chap. i.–iii. contain an account of the animals and vegetables which could be used for the three kinds of offerings that were already common among them, viz. the burnt-offerings, meat-offerings, and slain-offerings ; and precise rules are laid down for the mode in which they were to be offered. In chap. iv. and v. the occasions are described on which sin-offerings and trespass-offerings were to be presented ; and directions are given as to the sacrifices to be offered, and the mode of presentation on each separate occasion. The second group (chap. vi. and vii.) contains special rules for the priests, with reference to their duties in connection with the different sacrifices, and the portions they were to receive ; together with several supplementary laws, for example, with regard to the meat-offering of the priests, and the various kinds of slain or peace-offering. All these laws relate exclusively to the sacrifices to be offered spontaneously, either by individuals or by the whole community, the consciousness and confession of sin or debt being presupposed, even in the case of the sin and trespass-offerings, and their presentation being made to depend upon the free-will of those who had sinned. This is a sufficient explanation of the fact, that they contain no rules respecting either the time for presenting them, or the order in which they were to follow one another, when two or more were offered together. At the same time, the different rules laid down with regard to the ritual to be observed, applied not only to the private sacrifices, but also to those of the congregation, which were prescribed by special laws for every day, and for the annual festivals, as well as to the sacrifices of purification and consecration, for which no separate ritual is enjoined.

1. *General Rules for the Sacrifices.*—CHAP. I.–V.

The common term for sacrifices of every kind was CORBAN (presentation; see at chap. i. 2). It is not only applied to the burnt-offerings, meat-offerings, and slain or peace-offerings, in chap. i. 2, 3, 10, 14, ii. 1, 4 sqq., iii. 1, 6, etc., but also to the sin-offerings and trespass-offerings in chap. iv. 23, 28, 32, v. 11, Num. v. 15, etc., as being holy gifts (Ex. xxviii. 38 cf. Num. xviii. 9) with which Israel was to appear before the face of the Lord (Ex. xxiii. 15; Deut. xvi. 16, 17). These sacrificial gifts consisted partly of clean tame animals and birds, and partly of vegetable productions; and hence the division into the two classes of bleeding and bloodless (bloody and unbloody) sacrifices. The animals prescribed in the law are those of *the herd,* and *the flock,* the latter including both sheep and goats (chap. i. 2, 3, 10, xxii. 21; Num. xv. 3), two collective terms, for which ox and sheep, or goat (ox, sheep and goat) were the *nomina usitatis* (chap. vii. 23, xvii. 3, xxii. 19, 27; Num. xv. 11; Deut. xiv. 4), that is to say, none but tame animals whose flesh was eaten (chap. xi. 3; Deut. xiv. 4); whereas unclean animals, though tame, such as asses, camels, and swine, were inadmissible; and game; though edible, *e.g.* the hare, the stag, the roebuck, and gazelle (Deut. xiv. 5). Both male and female were offered in sacrifice, from the herd as well as the flock (chap. iii. 1), and young as well as old, though not under eight days old (chap. xxii. 27; Ex. xxii. 29); so that the ox was offered either as *calf* (chap. ix. 2; Gen. xv. 9; 1 Sam. xvi. 2) or as *bullock, i.e.* as young steer or heifer (chap. iv. 3), or as full-grown cattle. Every sacrificial animal was to be without blemish, *i.e.* free from bodily faults (chap. i. 3, 10, xxii. 19 sqq.). The only birds that were offered were turtle-doves and young pigeons (chap. i. 14), which were presented either by poor people as burnt-offerings, and as a substitute for the larger animals ordinarily required as sin-offerings and trespass-offerings (chap. v. 7, xii. 8, xiv. 22, 31), or as sin and burnt-offerings, for defilements of a less serious kind (chap. xii. 6, 7, xv. 14, 29, 30; Num. vi. 10, 11). The vegetable sacrifices consisted of meal, for the most part of fine flour (chap. ii. 1), of cakes of different kinds (chap. ii. 4–7), and of toasted ears or grains of corn (chap. ii. 14), to which there were generally added oil and incense, but never leaven or honey (chap. ii. 11) ; and also of wine for a drink-offering (Num. xv. 5 sqq.).

The *bleeding sacrifices* were divided into four classes : viz. (1) *burnt-offerings* (chap. i.), for which a male animal or pigeon only was admissible ; (2) *peace-offerings* (slain-offerings of peace, chap. iii.), which were divisible again into praise-offerings, vow-offerings, and freewill-offerings (chap. vii. 12, 16), and consisted of both male and female animals, but never of pigeons ; (3) *sin-offerings* (chap. iv. 1–v. 13) ; and (4) *trespass-offerings* (chap. v. 14–26).   Both male and female animals might be taken for the sin-offerings ; and doves also could be used, sometimes independently, sometimes as substitutes for larger animals ; and in cases of extreme poverty meal alone might be used (chap. v. 11) But for the trespass-offerings either a ram (chap. v. 15, 18, 25, xix. 21) or a lamb had to be sacrificed (chap. xiv. 12 ; Num. vi. 12).   All the sacrificial animals were to be brought " before Jehovah," *i.e.* before the altar of burnt-offering, in the court of the tabernacle (chap. i. 3, 5, 11, iii. 1, 7, 12, iv. 4).   There the offerer was to rest his hand upon the head of the animal (chap. i. 4), and then to slaughter it, flay it, cut it in pieces, and prepare it for a sacrificial offering ; after which the priest would attend to the sprinkling of the blood and the burning upon the altar fire (chap. i. 5–9, vi. 2 sqq., xxi. 6).   In the case of the burnt-offerings, peace-offerings, and trespass-offerings, the blood was swung all round against the walls of the altar (chap. i. 5, 11, iii. 2, 8, 13, vii. 2) ; in that of the sin-offerings a portion was placed upon the horns of the altar of burnt-offering, and in certain circumstances it was smeared upon the horns of the altar of incense, or sprinkled upon the ark of the covenant in the most holy place, and the remainder poured out at the foot of the altar of burnt-offering (iv. 5–7, 16–18, 25, 30).   In the case of the burnt-offering, the flesh was all burned upon the altar, together with the head and entrails, the latter having been previously cleansed (chap. i. 8, 13) ; in that of the peace-offerings, sin-offerings, and trespass-offerings, the fat portions only were burned upon the altar, viz. the larger and smaller caul, the fat upon the entrails and inner muscles of the loins, and the kidneys with their fat (chap. iii. 9–11, 14–16, iv. 8–10, 19, 26, 31, 35, vii. 3–5). When a peace-offering was presented, the breast piece and right leg were given to Jehovah for the priests, and the rest of the flesh was used and consumed by the offerer in a sacrificial meal (chap. vii. 15–17, 30–34). But the flesh of the trespass-offerings and sin-offerings of the laity was boiled and eaten by the priests in a holy place, *i.e.* in the court of the tabernacle (chap. vi. 19, 22, vii. 6). In the sin-offerings presented for the high priest and the whole congregation the animal was all burnt in a clean place outside the camp, including even the skin, the entrails, and the ordure (chap. iv. 11, 12, 21). When the sacrifice consisted of pigeons, the priest let the blood flow down the wall of the altar, or sprinkled it against it; and then, if the pigeon was brought as a burnt-offering, he burnt it upon the altar after taking away the crop and *fæces;* but if it was brought for a sin-offering, he probably followed the rule laid down in chap. i. 15 and v. 8.

The bloodless gifts were employed as meat and drink-offerings. The meat-offering (*minchah*) was presented sometimes by itself, at other times in connection with burnt-offerings and peace-offerings. The independence of the meat-offering, which has been denied by *Bähr* and *Kurtz* on insufficient grounds, is placed beyond all doubt, not only by the meat-offering of the priests (chap. vi. 13 sqq.) and the so-called jealousy-offering (Num. v. 15 sqq.), but also by the position in which it is placed in the laws of sacrifice, between the burnt and peace-offerings. From the instructions in Num. xv. 1–16, to offer a meat-offering mixed with oil and a drink-offering of wine with every burnt-offering and peace-offering, the quantity to be regulated by the size of the animal, it by no means follows that all the meat-offerings were simply accompaniments to the bleeding sacrifices, and were only to be offered in connection with them. On the contrary, inasmuch as these very instructions prescribe only a meat-offering of meal with oil, together with a drink-offering of wine, as the accompaniment to the burnt and peace-offerings, without mentioning incense at all, they rather prove that the meat-offerings mentioned in chap. ii., which might consist not only of meal and oil, with which incense had to be used, but also of cakes of different kinds and roasted corn, are to be distinguished from the mere accompaniments mentioned in Num. xv. In addition to this, it is to be observed that pastry, in the form of cakes of different kinds, was offered with the praise-offerings, according to chap. vii. 12 sqq., and probably with the two other species of peace-offerings as well; so that we should introduce an irreconcilable discrepancy between Num. xv. and Lev. ii., if we were to restrict all the meat-offerings to the accompaniments mentioned in Num. xv., or reduce them to merely dependent additions to the burnt and peace-offerings. Only a portion of the independent meat-offerings was burnt by the priest upon the altar (chap. ii. 2, 9, 16); the rest was to be baked without leaven, and eaten by the priests in the court, as being most holy (chap. vi. 8–11): it was only the meat-offering of the priests that was all burned upon the altar (chap. vi. 16).—The law contains no directions as to what was to be done with the drink-offering; but the wine was no doubt poured round the foot of the altar (Ecclus. l. 15. *Josephus, Ant.* iii. 9, 4).

The great importance of the sacrifices prescribed by the law may be inferred to a great extent, apart from the fact that sacrifice in general was founded upon the dependence of man upon God, and his desire for the restoration of that living fellowship with Him which had been disturbed by sin, from the circumstantiality and care with which both the choice of the sacrifices and the mode of presenting them are most minutely prescribed. But their special meaning and importance in relation to the economy of the Old Covenant are placed beyond all question by the position they assumed in the ritual of the Israelites, forming as they did the centre of all their worship, so that scarcely any sacred action was performed without sacrifice, whilst they were also the medium through which forgiveness of sin and reconciliation with the Lord were obtained, either by each individual Israelite, or by the congregation as a whole. This significance, which was deeply rooted in the spiritual life of Israel, is entirely destroyed by those who lay exclusive stress upon the notion of presentation or gift, and can see nothing more in the sacrifices than a " renunciation of one's own property," for the purpose of " expressing reverence and devotion, love and gratitude to God by such a surrender, and at the same time of earning and securing His favour." [1] The true significance of the legal sacri-

---

[1] This is the view expressed by *Knobel* in his Commentary on Leviticus, p. 346, where the idea is carried out in the following manner : in the dedication of animals they preferred to give the offering the form of a meal,

fices cannot be correctly and fully deduced from the term *corban*, which was common to them all, or from such names as were used to denote the different varieties of sacrifice, or even from the materials employed and the ritual observed, but only from all these combined, and from an examination of them in connection with the nature and design of the Old Testament economy.

Regarded as offerings or gifts, the sacrifices were only means by which Israel was to seek and sustain communion with its God. These gifts were to be brought by the Israelites from the blessing which God had bestowed upon the labour of their hands (Deut. xvi. 17), that is to say, from the fruit of their regular occupations, viz. agriculture and the rearing of cattle; in other words, from the cattle they had reared, or the produce of the land they had cultivated, which constituted their principal articles of food (viz. edible animals and pigeons, corn, oil, and wine), in order that in these sacrificial gifts they might consecrate to the Lord their God, not only their property and food, but also the fruit of their ordinary avocations. In this light the sacrifices are frequently called "food (bread) of firing for Jehovah" (chap. iii. 11, 16) and "bread of God" (chap. xxi. 6, 8, 17); by which we are not to suppose that food offered to God for His own nourishment is intended, but food produced by the labour of man, and then caused to ascend as a firing to his God, for an odour of satisfaction (*vid.* chap. iii. 11). In the clean animals, which he had obtained by his own training and care, and which constituted his ordinary live-stock, and in the produce obtained through the labour of his hands in the field and vineyard, from which he derived his ordinary support, the Israelite offered not his *victus* as a *symbolum vitæ*, but the food which he procured in which was provided for God, and of which flesh formed the principal part, though bread and wine could not be omitted. These meals of animal food were prepared every day in the daily burnt-offerings, just as the more respectable classes in the East eat animal food every day, and give the preference to food of this kind; and the daily offering of incense corresponded to the oriental custom of fumigating rooms, and burning perfumes in honour of a guest. At the same time *Knobel* also explains, that the Hebrews hardly attributed any wants of a sensual kind to Jehovah; or, at any rate, that the educated did not look upon the sacrifice as food for Jehovah, or regard the festal sacrifices as festal meals for Him, but may simply have thought of the fact that Jehovah was to be worshipped at all times, and more especially at the feasts, and that in this the prevailing and traditional custom was to be observed.

the exercise of his God-appointed calling, as a symbol of the spiritual food which endureth unto everlasting life (John vi. 27, cf. chap. iv. 34), and which nourishes both soul and body for imperishable life in fellowship with God, that in these sacrificial gifts he might give up to the Lord, who had adopted him as His own possession, not so much the substance of his life, or that which sustained and preserved it, as the *agens* of his life, or his labour and toil, and all the powers he possessed, and might receive sanctification from the Lord in return. In this way the sacrificial gifts acquire a representative character, and denote the self-surrender of a man, with all his labour and productions, to God. But the idea of representation received a distinct form and sacrificial character for the first time in the animal sacrifice, which was raised by the covenant revelation and the giving of the law into the very centre and soul of the whole institution of sacrifice, and primarily by the simple fact, that in the animal a life, a "living soul," was given up to death and offered to God, to be the medium of vital fellowship to the man who had been made a "living soul" by the inspiration of the breath of God; but still more by the fact, that God had appointed the blood of the sacrificial animal, as the vehicle of its soul, to be the medium of expiation for the souls of men (chap. xvii. 11).

The verb "*to expiate*" (כִּפֶּר, from כָּפַר to cover, construed with עַל *objecti*; see chap. i. 4) "does not signify to cause a sin not to have occurred, for that is impossible, nor to represent it as not existing, for that would be opposed to the stringency of the law, nor to pay or make compensation for it through the performance of any action; but to cover it over before God, *i.e.* to take away its power of coming in between God and ourselves" (*Kahnis, Dogmatik* i. p. 271). But whilst this is perfectly true, the object primarily expiated, or to be expiated, according to the laws of sacrifice, is not the sin, but rather the man, or the soul of the offerer. God gave the Israelites the blood of the sacrifices upon the altar to cover their souls (chap. xvii. 11). The end it answered was "to cover him" (the offerer, chap. i. 4); and even in the case of the sin-offering the only object was to cover him who had sinned, as concerning his sin (chap. iv. 26, 35, etc.). But the offerer of the sacrifice was covered, on account of his unholiness, from before the holy God, or, speaking more precisely, from the wrath of God and the manifestation of that wrath; that is to say, from the punishment which his sin had deserved, as we may clearly see from Gen. xxxii. 20, and still more clearly from Ex. xxxii. 30. In the former case Jacob's object is to reconcile (כִּפֶּר) the face of his brother Esau by means of a present, that is to say, to modify the wrath of his brother, which he has drawn upon himself by taking away the blessing of the first-born. In the latter, Moses endeavours by means of his intercession to expiate the sin of the people, over whom the wrath of God is about to burn to destroy them (Ex. xxxii. 9, 10); in other words, to protect the people from the destruction which threatens them in consequence of the wrath of God (see also Num. xvii. 11, 12, xxv. 11-13). The power to make expiation, *i.e.* to cover an unholy man from before the holy God, or to cover the sinner from the wrath of God, is attributed to the blood of the sacrificial animal, only so far as the soul lives in the blood, and the soul of the animal when sacrificed takes the place of the human soul. This substitution is no doubt incongruous, since the animal and man differ essentially the one from the other; inasmuch as the animal follows an involuntary instinct, and its soul being constrained by the necessities of its nature is not accountable, and it is only in this respect that it can be regarded as sinless; whilst man, on the contrary, is endowed with freedom of will, and his soul, by virtue of the indwelling of his spirit, is not only capable of accountability, but can contract both sin and guilt. When God, therefore, said, "I have given it to you upon the altar to make atonement for your souls" (chap. xvii. 11), and thus attributed to the blood of the sacrificial animals a significance which it could not naturally possess; this was done in anticipation of the true and perfect sacrifice which Christ, the Son of man and God, would offer in the fulness of time through the holy and eternal Spirit, for the reconciliation of the whole world (Heb. ix. 14). This secret of the unfathomable love of the triune God was hidden from the Israelites in the law, but it formed the real background for the divine sanction of the animal sacrifices, whereby they acquired a typical signification, so that they set forth in shadow that reconciliation, which God from all eternity had determined to effect by giving up His only-begotten Son to death, as a sacrifice for the sin of the whole world.

But however firmly the truth is established that the blood of the sacrifice intervened as a third object between the sinful man and the holy God, it was not the blood of the animal in itself which actually took the place of the man, nor was it the shedding of the blood in itself which was able to make expiation for the sinful man, in such a sense that the slaying of the animal had a judicial and penal character and the offering of sacrifice was an act of judgment instead of an ordinance of grace, as the juridical theory maintains. It was simply the blood as the vehicle of the soul, when sprinkled or poured out upon the altar, that is to say, it was the surrender of an innocent life to death, and through death to God, that was the medium of expiation. Even in the sacrifice of Christ it was not by the shedding of blood, or simply by the act of dying, that His death effected reconciliation, but by the surrender of His life to death, in which He not only shed His blood for us, but His body also was broken for us, to redeem us from sin and reconcile us to God. And even the suffering and death of Christ effect our reconciliation not simply by themselves, but as the completion of His sinless, holy life, in which, through doing and suffering, He was obedient even to the death of the cross, and through that obedience fulfilled the law as the holy will of God for us, and bore and suffered the punishment of our transgression. Through His *obedientia activa et passiva* in life and death Christ rendered to the holy justice of God that *satisfactio et pœna vicaria*, by virtue of which we receive forgiveness of sin, righteousness before God, reconciliation, grace, salvation, and eternal life. But these blessings of grace and salvation, which we owe to the sacrificial death of Christ, do not really become ours through the simple fact that Christ has procured them for man. We have still to appropriate them in faith, by dying spiritually with Christ, and rising with Him to a new life in God. This was also the case with the sacrifices of the Old Testament. They too only answered their end, when the Israelites, relying upon the word and promise of God, grasped and employed by faith the means of grace afforded them in the animal sacrifices; *i.e.* when in these sacrifices they offered themselves, or their personal life, as a sacrifice well-pleasing to God. The symbolical meaning of the sacrifices, which is involved in this, is not excluded or destroyed by the idea of representation, or representative mediation between sinful man and the holy

God, which was essential to them. It is rather demanded as their complement, inasmuch as, without this, the sacrificial worship would degenerate into a soulless *opus operatum*, and would even lose its typical character. This symbolical signifi- cance is strikingly expressed in the instructions relating to the nature of the sacrificial gifts, and the ritual connected with their presentation; and in the law it comes into the foreground just in proportion as the typical character of the sacrifices was concealed at the time in the wise economy of God, and was only unfolded to the spiritual vision of the prophets (Isa. liii.) with the progressive unfolding of the divine plan of salvation.

The leading features of the symbolical and typical meaning of the sacrifices are in their general outline the following. Every animal offered in sacrifice was to be תָּמִים, ἄμωμος, free from faults; not merely on the ground that only a faultless and perfect gift could be an offering fit for the Holy and Perfect One, but chiefly because moral faults were reflected in those of the body, and to prefigure the sinlessness and holiness of the true sacrifice, and warn the offerer that the sanctification of all his members was indispensable to a self-surrender to God, the Holy One, and to life in fellowship with Him. In connection with the act of sacrifice, it was required that the offerer should bring to the tabernacle the animal appointed for sacrifice, and there present it before Jehovah (chap. i. 3), because it was there that Jehovah dwelt among His people, and it was from His holy dwelling that He would reveal Himself to His people as their God. There the offerer was to lay his hand upon the head of the animal, that the sacrifice might be acceptable for him, to make expiation for him (chap. i. 4), and then to slay the animal and prepare it for a sacrificial gift. By the laying on of his hand he not only set apart the sacrificial animal for the purpose for which he had come to the sanctuary, but transferred the feelings of his heart, which impelled him to offer the sacrifice, or the intention with which he brought the gift, to the sacrificial animal, so that his own head passed, as it were, to the head of the animal, and the latter became his substitute (see my *Archä- ologie* i. 206; *Oehler*, p. 267; *Kahnis*, i. p. 270). By the slaughter of the animal he gave it up to death, not merely for the double purpose of procuring the blood, in which was the life of the animal, as an expiation for his own soul, and its flesh as fire-food for Jehovah,—for if the act of dying was profoundly significant in the case of the perfect sacrifice, it cannot have been without symbolical significance in the case of the typical sacrifice,—but to devote his own life to God in the death of the sacrificial animal which was appointed as his substitute, and to set forth not only his willingness to die, but the necessity for the old man to die, that he might attain to life in fellowship with God. After this self-surrender the priestly mediation commenced, the priest sprinkling the blood upon the altar, or its horns, and in one instance before Jehovah's throne of grace, and then burning the flesh or fat of the sacrifice upon the altar. The altar was the spot where God had promised to meet with His people (Ex. xxix. 42), to reconcile them to Himself, and bestow His grace upon them (see p. 207). Through this act of sprinkling the blood of the animal that had been given up to death upon the altar, the soul of the offerer was covered over before the holy God; and by virtue of this covering it was placed within the sphere of divine grace, which forgave the sin and filled the soul with power for new life. Fire was constantly burning upon the altar, which was prepared and kept up by the priest (chap. vi. 5). Fire, from its inherent power to annihilate what is perishable, ignoble, and corrupt, is a symbol in the Scriptures, sometimes of purification, and sometimes of torment and destruction. That which has an imperishable kernel within it is purified by the fire, the perishable materials which have adhered to it or penetrated within it being burned out and destroyed, and the imperishable and nobler substance being thereby purified from all dross; whilst, on the other hand, in cases where the imperishable is completely swallowed up in the perishable, no purification ensues, but total destruction by the fire (1 Cor. iii. 12, 13). Hence fire is employed as a symbol and vehicle of the Holy Spirit (Acts ii. 3, 4), and the fire burning upon the altar was a symbolical representation of the working of the purifying Spirit of God; so that the burning of the flesh of the sacrifice upon the altar "represented the purification of the man, who had been reconciled to God, through the fire of the Holy Spirit, which consumes what is flesh, to pervade what is spirit with light and life, and thus to transmute it into the blessedness of fellowship with God" (*Kahnis*, p. 272).—It follows from this, that the relation which the sprinkling of the blood and the burning of the flesh of the sacrifice upon the altar bore to one another was that of justification and sanctification, those two indispensable conditions, without which sinful man could not attain to reconciliation with God and life in God. But as the sinner could neither justify himself before God nor sanctify himself by his own power, the sprinkling of blood and the burning of the portions of the sacrifice upon the altar were to be effected, not by the offerer himself, but only by the priest, as the mediator whom God had chosen and sanctified, not only that the soul which had been covered by the sacrificial blood might thereby be brought to God and received into His favour, but also that the bodily members, of which the flesh of the sacrifice was a symbol, might be given up to the fire of the Holy Spirit, to be purified and sanctified from the dross of sin, and raised in a glorified state to God; just as the sacrificial gift was consumed in the altar fire, so that, whilst its earthly perishable elements were turned into ashes and left behind, its true essence ascended towards heaven, where God is enthroned, in the most ethereal and glorified of material forms, as a sweet-smelling savour, *i.e.* as an acceptable offering. These two priestly acts, however, were variously modified according to the different objects of the several kinds of sacrifice. In the *sin-offering* the expiation of the sinner is brought into the greatest prominence; in the *burnt-offering* this falls into the background behind the idea of the self-surrender of a man to God for the sanctification of all his members, through the grace of God; and lastly, the *peace-offering* culminated in the peace of living communion with the Lord. (See the explanation of the several laws.)

The materials and ritual of the bloodless sacrifices, and also their meaning and purpose, are much more simple. The meat and drink-offerings were not means of expiation, nor did they include the idea of representation. They were simply gifts, in which the Israelites offered bread, oil, and wine, as fruits of the labour of their hands in the field and vineyard of the inheritance they had received from the Lord, and embodied in these earthly gifts the fruits of their spiritual labour in the kingdom of God (see at chap. ii.).

Chap. i. THE BURNT-OFFERING.—Ver. 2. " *If any one of you present an offering to Jehovah of cattle, ye shall present your*

offering from the herd and from the flock." קָרְבָּן (*Corban*, from
הַקְרִיב to cause to draw near, to bring near, or present, an offering) is applied not only to the sacrifices, which were burned
either in whole or in part upon the altar (chap. vii. 38 ; Num.
xviii. 9, xxviii. 2, etc.), but to the first-fruits (chap. ii. 12), and
dedicatory offerings, which were presented to the Lord for His
sanctuary and His service without being laid upon the altar
(Num. vii. 3, 10 sqq., xxxi. 50). The word is only used in
Leviticus and Numbers, and two passages in Ezekiel (chap. xx.
28, xl. 43), where it is taken from the books of Moses, and is
invariably rendered δῶρον in the LXX. (cf. Mark vii. 11,
" *Corban,* that is to say *a gift*"). מִן הַבְּהֵמָה (*from the cattle*)
belongs to the first clause, though it is separated from it by the
Athnach ; and the apodosis begins with מִן הַבָּקָר (*from the herd*).
The actual antithesis to "the cattle" is "the fowl" in ver. 14 ;
though grammatically the latter is connected with ver. 10, rather
than ver. 2. The fowls (pigeons) cannot be included in the
behemah, for this is used to denote, not domesticated animals
generally, but the larger domesticated quadrupeds, or tame
cattle (cf. Gen. i. 25).—Vers. 3–9. *Ceremonial connected with
the offering of an ox as a burnt-offering.* עֹלָה (*vid.* Gen. viii. 20)
is generally rendered by the LXX. ὁλοκαύτωμα or ὁλοκαύτωσις,
sometimes ὁλοκάρπωμα or ὁλοκάρπωσις, in the *Vulgate holocaus-
tum,* because the animal was all consumed upon the altar. The
ox was to be a male without blemish (ἄμωμος, *integer; i.e.* free from
bodily faults, see chap. xxii. 19–25), and to be presented " *at the
door of the tabernacle,*"—*i.e.* near to the altar of burnt-offering
(Ex. xl. 6), where all the offerings were to be presented (chap.
xvii. 8, 9),—" *for good pleasure for him* (the offerer) *before Jehovah,*" *i.e.* that the sacrifice might secure to him the good
pleasure of God (Ex. xxviii. 38).—Ver. 4. " *He* (the offerer)
shall lay his hand upon the head of the burnt-offering." The
laying on of hands, by which, to judge from the verb סָמַךְ to
lean upon, we are to understand a forcible pressure of the hand
upon the head of the victim, took place in connection with all
the slain-offerings (the offering of pigeons perhaps excepted),
and is expressly enjoined in the laws for the burnt-offerings, the
peace-offerings (chap. iii. 2, 7, 13), and the sin-offerings (chap.
iv. 4, 15, 24, 29, 33), that is to say, in every case in which the
details of the ceremonial are minutely described. But if the

description is condensed, then no allusion is made to it : *e.g.* in
the burnt-offering of sheep and goats (ver. 11), the sin-offering
(chap. v. 6), and the trespass-offering (chap. v. 15, 18, 25).
This ceremony was not a sign of the removal of something
from his own power and possession, or the surrender and dedication of it to God, as *Rosenmüller* and *Knobel*[1] affirm ; nor
an indication of ownership and of a readiness to give up his
own to Jehovah, as *Bähr* maintains ; nor a symbol of the imputation of sin, as *Kurtz* supposes :[2] but the symbol of a transfer
of the feelings and intentions by which the offerer was actuated
in presenting his sacrifice, whereby he set apart the animal as a
sacrifice, representing his own person in one particular aspect
(see vol. i. p. 279). Now, so far as the burnt-offering expressed
the intention of the offerer to consecrate his life and labour to
the Lord, and his desire to obtain the expiation of the sin
which still clung to all his works and desires, in order that they
might become well-pleasing to God, he transferred the consciousness of his sinfulness to the victim by the laying on of
hands, even in the case of the burnt-offering. But this was not

---

[1] Hence *Knobel's* assertion (at Lev. vii. 2), that the laying on of the
hand upon the head of the animal, which is prescribed in the case of all
the other sacrifices, was omitted in that of the trespass-offering alone,
needs correction, and there is no foundation for the conclusion, that it did
not take place in connection with the trespass-offering.

[2] This was the view held by some of the Rabbins and of the earlier
theologians, *e.g. Calovius, bibl. ill. ad Lev.* i. 4, *Lundius* and others, but by
no means by "most of the Rabbins, some of the fathers, and most of the
earlier archæologists and doctrinal writers," as is affirmed by *Bähr* (ii. p.
336), who supports his assertion by passages from *Outram*, which refer to
the sin-offering only, but which *Bähr* transfers without reserve to all the
bleeding sacrifices, thus confounding substitution with the imputation of
sin, in his antipathy to the orthodox doctrine of satisfaction. *Outram's*
general view of this ceremony is expressed clearly enough in the following
passages : " *ritus erat ea notandi ac designandi, quæ vel morti devota erant,
vel Dei gratiæ commendata, vel denique gravi alicui muneri usuique sacro
destinata. Eique ritui semper adhiberi solebant verba aliqua explicata, quæ rei
susceptæ rationi maxime congruere viderentur*" (*l.c.* 8 and 9). With reference
to the words which explained the imposition of hands he observes : " *ita ut
sacris piacularibus culparum potissimum confessiones cum pœnæ deprecatione
junctas, voluntariis bonorum precationes, eucharisticis autem et votivis post res
prosperas impetratas periculave depulsa factis laudes et gratiarum actiones,
omnique denique victimarum generi ejusmodi preces adjunctas putem, quæ
cuique maxime conveniebant*" (*c.* 9).

all : he also transferred the desire to walk before God in holiness and righteousness, which he could not do without the grace of God. This, and no more than this, is contained in the words, "that it may become well-pleasing to him, to make atonement for him." כִּפֶּר with Seghol (Ges. § 52), to expiate (from the Kal כָּפַר, which is not met with in Hebrew, the word in Gen. vi. 14 being merely a *denom.* verb, but which signifies *texit* in Arabic), is generally construed with עַל like verbs of covering, and in the laws of sacrifice with the person as the object ("for *him*," chap. iv. 26, 31, 35, v. 6, 10 sqq., xiv. 20, 29, etc.; "for *them*," chap. iv. 20, x. 17; "for *her*," chap. xii. 7; for a *soul*, chap. xvii. 11; Ex. xxx. 15, cf. Num. viii. 12), and in the case of the sin-offerings with a second object governed either by עַל or מִן (עָלָיו עַל חַטָּאתוֹ chap. iv. 35, v. 13, 18, or עָלָיו מֵחַטָּאתוֹ chap. iv. 26, v. 6, etc., to expiate him over or on account of his sin); also, though not so frequently, with בְּעַד *pers.*, ἐξιλάζεσθαι περὶ αὐτοῦ (chap. xvi. 6, 24; 2 Chron. xxx. 18), and בְּעַד חַטָּאת, ἐξιλάζεσθαι περὶ τῆς ἁμαρτίας (Ex. xxxii. 30), and with לְ *pers.*, to permit expiation to be made (Deut. xxi. 8; Ezek. xvi. 63); also with the accusative of the object, though in prose only in connection with the expiation of inanimate objects defiled by sin (chap. xvi. 33). The expiation was always made or completed by the priest, as the sanctified mediator between Jehovah and the people, or, previous to the institution of the Aaronic priesthood, by Moses, the chosen mediator of the covenant, not by "Jehovah from whom the expiation proceeded," as *Bähr* supposes. For although all expiation has its ultimate foundation in the grace of God, which desires not the death of the sinner, but his redemption and salvation, and to this end has opened a way of salvation, and sanctified sacrifice as the means of expiation and mercy; it is not Jehovah who makes the expiation, but this is invariably the office or work of a mediator, who intervenes between the holy God and sinful man, and by means of expiation averts the wrath of God from the sinner, and brings the grace of God to bear upon him. It is only in cases where the word is used in the secondary sense of pardoning sin, or showing mercy, that God is mentioned as the subject (*e.g.* Deut. xxi. 8; Ps. lxv. 4, lxxviii. 38; Jer. xviii. 23).[1] The medium of

---

[1] The meaning "to make atonement" lies at the foundation in every passage in which the word is used metaphorically, such as Gen. xxxii. 21,

expiation in the case of the sacrifice was chiefly the blood of the sacrificial animal that was sprinkled upon the altar (chap. xvii. 11); in addition to which, the eating of the flesh of the sin-offering by the priests is also called bearing the iniquity of the congregation to make atonement for them (chap. x. 17). In other cases it was the intercession of Moses (Ex. xxxii. 30); also the fumigation with holy incense, which was a symbol of priestly intercession (Num. xvii. 11). On one occasion it was the zeal of Phinehas, when he stabbed the Israelite with a spear for committing fornication with a Midianite (Num. xxv. 8, 13). In the case of a murder committed by an unknown hand, it was the slaying of an animal in the place of the murderer who remained undiscovered (Deut. xxi. 1-9); whereas in other cases blood-guiltiness (murder) could not be expiated in any other way than by the blood of the person by whom it had been shed (Num. xxxv. 33). In Isa. xxvii. 9, a divine judgment, by

where Jacob seeks to *expiate* the face of his angry brother, *i.e.* to appease his wrath, with a present; or Prov. xvi. 14, "The wrath of a king is as messengers of death, but a wise man *expiates* it, *i.e.* softens, pacifies it;" Isa. xlvii. 11, "Mischief (destruction) will fall upon thee, thou wilt not be able to *expiate* it," that is to say, to avert the wrath of God, which has burst upon thee in the calamity, by means of an expiatory sacrifice. Even in Isa. xxviii. 18, "and your covenant with death is disannulled" (annihilated) (וְכֻפַּר), the use of the word כפר is to be explained from the fact that the guilt, which brought the judgment in its train, could be cancelled by a sacrificial expiation (cf. Isa. vi. 7 and xxii. 14); so that there is no necessity to resort to a meaning which is altogether foreign to the word, viz. that of covering up by blotting over. When *Hofmann* therefore maintains that there is no other way of explaining the use of the word in these passages, than by the supposition that, in addition to the verb כפר to cover, there was another denominative verb, founded upon the word כֹּפֶר a covering, or payment, the stumblingblock in the use of the word lies simply in this, that *Hofmann* has taken a one-sided view of the idea of expiation, through overlooking the fact, that the expiation had reference to the wrath of God which hung over the sinner and had to be averted from him by means of expiation, as is clearly proved by Ex. xxxii. 30 as compared with vers. 10 and 22. The meaning of expiation which properly belongs to the verb כֻּפַּר is not only retained in the nouns *cippurim* and *capporeth*, but lies at the root of the word *copher*, which is formed from the *Kal*, as we may clearly see from Ex. xxx. 12–16, where the Israelites are ordered to pay a *copher* at the census, to *expiate* their souls, *i.e.* to cover their souls from the death which threatens the unholy, when he draws near without expiation to a holy God. *Vid. Oehler* in Herzog's Cycl.

which the nation was punished, is so described, as serving to
avert the complete destruction which threatened it. And lastly,
it was in some cases a כֹּפֶר, such, for example, as the atonement-
money paid at the numbering of the people (Ex. xxx. 12 sqq.),
and the payment made in the case referred to in Ex. xxi. 30.

If, therefore, the idea of satisfaction unquestionably lay at
the foundation of the atonement that was made, in all those
cases in which it was effected by a penal judgment, or judicial
pœna; the intercession of the priest, or the fumigation which
embodied it, cannot possibly be regarded as a satisfaction rendered to the justice of God, so that we cannot attribute the idea
of satisfaction to every kind of sacrificial expiation. Still less
can it be discerned in the slaying of the animal, when simply
regarded as the shedding of blood. To this we may add, that
in the laws for the sin-offering there is no reference at all to
expiation; and in the case of the burnt-offering, the laying on
of hands is described as the act by which it was to become well-
pleasing to God, and to expiate the offerer. Now, if the laying
on of hands was accompanied with a prayer, as the Jewish tradition affirms, and as we may most certainly infer from Deut.
xxvi. 13, apart altogether from Lev. xvi. 21, although no prayer
is expressly enjoined; then in the case of the burnt-offerings and
peace-offerings, it is in this prayer, or the imposition of hands
which symbolized it, and by which the offerer substituted the
sacrifice for himself and penetrated it with his spirit, that we
must seek for the condition upon which the well-pleased acceptance of the sacrifice on the part of God depended, and in
consequence of which it became an atonement for him; in other
words, was fitted to cover him in the presence of the holiness
of God.

Vers. 5–9. The laying on of hands was followed by the
slaughtering (שָׁחַט, never הֵמִית to put to death), which was performed by the offerer himself in the case of the private sacrifices,
and by the priests and Levites in that of the national and festal
offerings (2 Chron. xxix. 22, 24, 34). The slaughtering took
place "*before Jehovah*" (see ver. 3), or, according to the more
precise account in ver. 11, on the side of the altar northward,
for which the expression "before the door of the tabernacle" is
sometimes used (chap. iii. 2, 8, 13, etc.). בֶּן בָּקָר (a young ox) is
applied to a calf (עֵגֶל) in chap. ix. 2, and a mature young bull

(פַּר) in chap. iv. 3, 14. But the animal of one year old is called
עֵגֶל in chap. ix. 2, and the mature ox of seven years old is called
פַּר in Judg. vi. 25. At the slaughtering the blood was caught
by the priests (2 Chron. xxix. 22), and sprinkled upon the altar.
When the sacrifices were very numerous, as at the yearly feasts,
the Levites helped to catch the blood (2 Chron. xxx. 16); but
the sprinkling upon the altar was always performed by the
priests alone. In the case of the burnt-offerings, the blood was
swung "against the altar round about," *i.e.* against all four sides
(walls) of the altar (not "over the surface of the altar"); *i.e.* it
was poured out of the vessel against the walls of the altar with
a swinging motion. This was also done when peace-offerings
(chap. iii. 2, 8, 13, ix. 18) and trespass-offerings (chap. vii. 2)
were sacrificed; but it was not so with the sin-offering (see at
chap. iv. 5).—Vers. 6 sqq. The offerer was then to flay the
slaughtered animal, to cut it (נִתַּח generally rendered μελίζειν in
the LXX.) into its pieces,—*i.e.* to cut it up into the different
pieces, into which an animal that has been killed is generally
divided, namely, according to the separate joints, or "according
to the bones" (Judg. xix. 29),—that he might boil its flesh in
pots (Ezek. xxiv. 4, 6). He was also to wash its intestines and
the lower part of its legs (ver. 9). קֶרֶב, the inner part of the
body, or the contents of the inner part of the body, signifies the
viscera; not including those of the breast, however, such as the
lungs, heart, and liver, to which the term is also applied in other
cases (for in the case of the peace-offerings, when the fat which
envelopes the intestines, the kidneys, and the liver-lobes was to be
placed upon the altar, there is no washing spoken of), but the
intestines of the abdomen or belly, such as the stomach and
bowels, which would necessarily have to be thoroughly cleansed,
even when they were about to be used as food. כְּרָעַיִם, which is
only found in the dual, and always in connection either with
oxen and sheep, or with the springing legs of locusts (chap. xi.
21), denotes the shin, or calf below the knee, or the leg from the
knee down to the foot.—Vers. 7, 8. It was the duty of the sons
of Aaron, *i.e.* of the priests, to offer the sacrifice upon the altar.
To this end they were to "*put fire upon the altar*" (of course
this only applies to the first burnt-offering presented after the
erection of the altar, as the fire was to be constantly burning
upon the altar after that, without being allowed to go out, vi. 6),

and to lay "*wood in order upon the fire*" (עָרַךְ to lay in regular order), and then to "*lay the parts, the head and the fat, in order upon the wood on the fire,*" and thus to cause the whole to ascend in smoke. פֶּדֶר, which is only used in connection with the burnt-offering (vers. 8, 12, and chap. viii. 20), signifies, according to the ancient versions (LXX. στέαρ) and the rabbinical writers, *the fat,* probably those portions of fat which were separated from the entrails and taken out to wash. *Bochart's* explanation is *adeps a carne sejunctus.* The head and fat are specially mentioned along with the pieces of flesh, partly because they are both separated from the flesh when animals are slaughtered, and partly also to point out distinctly that the whole of the animal ("*all,*" ver. 9) was to be burned upon the altar, with the exception of the skin, which was given to the officiating priest (chap. vii. 8), and the contents of the intestines. הִקְטִיר, to cause to ascend in smoke and steam (Ex. xxx. 7), which is frequently construed with הַמִּזְבֵּחָה towards the altar (ה local, so used as to include position in a place ; *vid.* vers. 13, 15, 17, chap ii. 2, 9, etc.), or with הַמִּזְבֵּחַ (chap. vi. 8), or עַל־הַמִּזְבֵּחַ (chap. ix. 13, 17), was the technical expression for burning the sacrifice upon the altar, and showed that the intention was not simply to burn those portions of the sacrifice which were placed in the fire, *i.e.* to destroy, or turn them into ashes, but by this process of burning to cause the odour which was eliminated to ascend to heaven as the ethereal essence of the sacrifice, for a "*firing of a sweet savour unto Jehovah.*" אִשֶּׁה, *firing* ("an offering made by fire," Eng. Ver.), is the general expression used to denote the sacrifices, which ascended in fire upon the altar, whether animal or vegetable (chap. ii. 2, 11, 16), and is also applied to the incense laid upon the shew-bread (chap. xxiv. 7) ; and hence the shew-bread itself (chap. xxiv. 7), and even those portions of the sacrifices which Jehovah assigned to the priests for them to eat (Deut. xviii. 1 cf. Josh. xiii. 14), came also to be included in the firings for Jehovah. The word does not occur out of the Pentateuch, except in Josh. xiii. 14 and 1 Sam. ii. 28. In the laws of sacrifice it is generally associated with the expression, "a sweet savour unto Jehovah" (ὀσμὴ εὐωδίας: LXX.): an anthropomorphic description of the divine satisfaction with the sacrifices offered, or the gracious acceptance of them on the part of God (see Gen. viii. 21), which is used in connection with all the sacrifices, even the expiatory or sin-offerings (chap. iv. 31), and with the drink-offering also (Num. xv. 7, 10).

Vers. 10–13. With regard to the mode of sacrificing, the instructions already given for the oxen applied to the flock (*i.e.* to the sheep and goats) as well, so that the leading points are repeated here, together with a more precise description of the place for slaughtering, viz. "*by the side of the altar towards the north,*" *i.e.* on the north side of the altar. This was the rule with all the slain-offerings; although it is only in connection with the burnt-offerings, sin-offerings, and trespass-offerings (chap. iv. 24, 29, 33, vi. 18, vii. 2, xiv. 13) that it is expressly mentioned, whilst the indefinite expression "*at the door* (in front) *of the tabernacle*" is applied to the peace-offerings in chap. iii. 2, 8, 13, as it is to the trespass-offerings in chap. iv. 4, from which the Rabbins have inferred, though hardly upon good ground, that the peace-offerings could be slaughtered in any part of the court. The northern side of the altar was appointed as the place of slaughtering, however, not from the idea that the Deity dwelt in the north (*Ewald*), for such an idea is altogether foreign to Mosaism, but, as *Knobel* supposes, probably because the table of shew-bread, with the continual meat-offering, stood on the north side in the holy place. Moreover, the eastern side of the altar in the court was the place for the refuse, or heap of ashes (ver. 16); the ascent to the altar was probably on the south side, as *Josephus* affirms that it was in the second temple (*J. de bell. jud.* v. 5, 6); and the western side, or the space between the altar and the entrance to the holy place, would unquestionably have been the most unsuitable of all for the slaughtering. In ver. 12 וְאֶת־רֹאשׁוֹ וּגוֹ׳ is to be connected *per zeugma* with לִנְתָחָיו, "*let him cut it up according to its parts, and* (sever) *its head and its fat.*"

Vers. 14–17. The burnt-offering of *fowls* was to consist of turtle-doves or young pigeons. The Israelites have reared pigeons and kept dovecots from time immemorial (Isa. lx. 8, cf. 2 Kings vi. 25); and the rearing of pigeons continued to be a favourite pursuit with the later Jews (*Josephus, de bell. jud.* v. 4, 4), so that they might very well be reckoned among the domesticated animals. There are also turtle-doves and wild pigeons in Palestine in such abundance, that they could easily furnish the ordinary animal food of the poorer classes, and serve as sacrifices in the place of the larger animals. The directions for sacrificing these, were that the priest was to bring the bird to the altar, to nip off its head, and cause it to ascend in smoke upon the altar. מָלַק, which only occurs in ver. 15 and chap. v. 8, signifies undoubtedly to pinch off, and not merely to pinch; for otherwise the words in chap. v. 8, "and shall not divide it asunder," would be superfluous. We have therefore to think of it as a severance of the head, as the LXX. (ἀποκνίζειν) and Rabbins have done, and not merely a wringing of the neck and incision in the skin by which the head was left hanging to the body; partly because the words, "and not divide it asunder," are wanting here, and partly also because of the words, "and burn it upon the altar," which immediately follow, and which must refer to the head, and can only mean that, after the head had been pinched off, it was to be put at once into the burning altar-fire. For it is obviously unnatural to regard these words as anticipatory, and refer them to the burning of the whole dove; not only from the construction itself, but still more on account of the clause which follows: "and the blood thereof shall be pressed out against the wall of the altar." The small quantity that there was of the blood prevented it from being caught in a vessel, and swung from it against the altar.—Vers. 16, 17. He then took out אֶת־מֻרְאָתוֹ בְּנֹצָתָהּ, i.e., according to the probable explanation of these obscure words, "*its crop in* (with) *the fœces thereof*," [1] and threw it "*at the side of the altar eastwards*," i.e. on the eastern side of the altar, "*on the ash-place*," where the ashes were thrown when taken from the altar (chap. vi. 3). He then made an incision in the wings of the pigeon, but with-

---

[1] This is the rendering adopted by *Onkelos*. The LXX., on the contrary, render it ἀφελεῖ τὸν πρόλοβον σὺν τοῖς πτεροῖς, and this rendering is followed by Luther (and the English Version, Tr.), "its crop with its feathers." But the Hebrew for this would have been וְנֹצָתוֹ. In *Mishnah, Sebach.* vi. 5, the instructions are the following: "*et removet ingluviem et pennas et viscera egredentia cum illa.*" This interpretation may be substantially correct, although the reference of בנוצתה to the feathers of the pigeon cannot be sustained on the ground assigned. For if the bird's crop was taken out, the intestines with their contents would unquestionably come out along with it. The plucking off of the feathers, however, follows from the analogy of the flaying of the animal. Only, in the text neither intestines nor feathers are mentioned; they are passed over as subordinate matters, that could readily be understood from the analogy of the other instructions.

out severing them, and burned them on the altar-fire (ver. 17, cf. ver. 9).

The burnt-offerings all culminated in the presentation of the whole sacrifice upon the altar, that it might ascend to heaven, transformed into smoke and fragrance. Hence it is not only called עֹלָה, the ascending (see Gen. viii. 20), but כָּלִיל, a whole-offering (Deut. xxxiii. 10; Ps. li. 21; 1 Sam. vii. 9). If the burning and sending up in the altar-fire shadowed forth the self-surrender of the offerer to the purifying fire of the Holy Ghost (p. 280); the burnt-offering was an embodiment of the idea of the consecration and self-surrender of the whole man to the Lord, to be pervaded by the refining and sanctifying power of divine grace. This self-surrender was to be vigorous and energetic in its character; and this was embodied in the instructions to choose male animals for the burnt-offering, the male sex being stronger and more vigorous than the female. To render the self-sacrifice perfect, it was necessary that the offerer should spiritually die, and that through the mediator of his salvation he should put his soul into a living fellowship with the Lord by sinking it as it were into the death of the sacrifice that had died for him, and should also bring his bodily members within the operations of the gracious Spirit of God, that thus he might be renewed and sanctified both body and soul, and enter into union with God.

Chap. ii. The MEAT-OFFERING.—The burnt-offerings are followed immediately by the meat-offerings, not only because they were offered along with them from the very first (Gen. iv. 3), but because they stood nearest to them in their general signification. The usual epithet applied to them is *minchah*, *lit.* a present with which any one sought to obtain the favour or good-will of a superior (Gen. xxxii. 21, 22, xliii. 11, 15, etc.), then the gift offered to God as a sign of grateful acknowledgment that the offerer owed everything to Him, as well as of a desire to secure His favour and blessing. This epithet was used at first for animal sacrifices as well as offerings of fruit (Gen. iv. 4, 5). But in the Mosaic law it was restricted to bloodless offerings, *i.e.* to the meat-offerings, whether presented independently, or in connection with the animal sacrifices (*zebachim*). The full term is *korban minchah*, offering of a gift: δῶρον θυσία or

προσφορά, also θυσία alone (LXX.).   The meat-offerings consisted of fine wheaten flour (vers. 1–3), or cakes of such flour
(vers. 4–6), or roasted grains as an offering of first-fruits (vers.
14–16). To all of them there were added oil (vers. 1, 4–7, 15) and
salt (ver. 13); and to those which consisted of flour and grains,
incense also (vers. 1 and 15).   Only a handful of each kind was
burnt upon the altar; the rest was handed over to the priests, as
" a thing most holy" (ver. 3).

Vers. 1–3. The *first* kind consisted of *soleth*, probably from
סָלָה = סָלַל to swing, swung flour, like πάλη from πάλλω, *i.e.*
fine flour ; and for this no doubt wheaten flour was always used,
even when חִטִּים is not added, as in Ex. xxix. 2, to distinguish
it from קֶמַח, or ordinary meal (σεμίδαλις : 1 Kings v. 2).   The
suffix in קָרְבָּנוֹ (his offering) refers to נֶפֶשׁ, which is frequently
construed as both masculine and feminine (chap. iv. 2, 27, 28,
v. 1, etc.), or as masculine only (Num. xxxi. 28) in the sense of
person, any one.   " *And let him pour oil upon it, and put incense thereon* (or add incense to it)."   This was not spread upon
the flour, on which oil had been poured, but added in such a
way, that it could be lifted from the *minchah* and burned upon
the altar (ver. 2). The priest was then to take a handful of the
gift that had been presented, and cause the *azcarah* of it to
evaporate above (together with) all the incense.   מְלֹא קֻמְצוֹ : the
filling of his closed hand, *i.e.* as much as he could hold with his
hand full, not merely with three fingers, as the Rabbins affirm.
Azcarah (from זָכַר, formed like אַשְׁמֻרָה from שָׁמַר) is only applied to Jehovah's portion, which was burned upon the altar in
the case of the meat-offering (vers. 9, 16, and chap. vi. 8), the
sin-offering of flour (chap. v. 12), and the jealousy-offering
(Num. v. 26), and to the incense added to the shew-bread
(chap. xxiv. 7).   It does not mean the prize portion, *i.e.* the
portion offered for the glory of God, as *De Dieu* and *Rosenmüller* maintain, still less the fragrance-offering (*Ewald*), but
the memorial, or remembrance-portion, μνημόσυννον or ἀνάμνη-
σις (chap. xxiv. 7, LXX.), *memoriale* (*Vulg.*), inasmuch as
that part of the *minchah* which was placed upon the altar
ascended in the smoke of the fire " on behalf of the giver, as a
practical *memento* (' remember me') to Jehovah ;" though there
is no necessity that we should trace the word to the *Hiphil* in
consequence.   The rest of the *minchah* was to belong to Aaron

and his sons, *i.e.* to the priesthood, as a most holy thing of the firings of Jehovah. The term " most holy" is applied to all the sacrificial gifts that were consecrated to Jehovah, in this sense, that such portions as were not burned upon the altar were to be eaten by the priests alone in a holy place; the laity, and even such of the Levites as were not priests, being prohibited from partaking of them (see at Ex. xxvi. 33 and xxx. 10). Thus the independent meat-offerings, which were not entirely consumed upon the altar (vers. 3, 10, vi. 10, x. 12), the sin-offerings and trespass-offerings, the flesh of which was not burned outside the camp (chap. vi. 18, 22, vii. 1, 6, x. 17, xiv. 13, Num. xviii. 9), the shew-bread (chap. xxiv. 9), and even objects put under the ban and devoted to the Lord, whether men, cattle, or property of other kinds (chap. xxvii. 28), as well as the holy incense (Ex. xxx. 36),—in fact, all the holy sacrificial gifts, in which there was any fear lest a portion should be perverted to other objects,—were called most holy; whereas the burnt-offerings, the priestly meat-offerings (chap. vi. 12–16) and other sacrifices, which were quite as holy, were not called most holy, because the command to burn them entirely precluded the possibility of their being devoted to any of the ordinary purposes of life.

Vers. 4–11. The *second* kind consisted of pastry of fine flour and oil prepared in different forms. The *first* was *maapheh tannur*, oven-baking: by תַּנּוּר we are not to understand a baker's oven (Hos. vii. 4, 6), but a large pot in the room, such as are used for baking cakes in the East even to the present day (see my Archäol. § 99, 4). The oven-baking might consist either of " *cakes of unleavened meal mixed* (made) *with oil*," or of " *pancakes of unleavened meal anointed* (smeared) *with oil.*" *Challoth :* probably from חָלַל to pierce, perforated cakes, of a thicker kind. *Rekikim :* from רָקַק to be beaten out thin; hence cakes or pancakes. As the latter were to be smeared with oil, we cannot understand בָּלוּל as signifying merely the pouring of oil upon the baked cakes, but must take it in the sense of mingled, mixed, *i.e.* kneaded with oil (πεφυραμένους (LXX.), or according to *Hesychius*, μεμιγμένους).—Vers. 5, 6. Secondly, if the *minchah* was an offering upon the pan, it was also to be made of fine flour mixed with oil and unleavened. *Machabath* is a pan, made, according to Ezek. iv. 3, of iron,—no doubt a

large iron plate, such as the Arabs still use for baking unleavened bread in large round cakes made flat and thin (*Robinson,*
Palestine i. 50, ii. 180).   These girdles or flat pans are still in use
among the Turcomans of Syria and the Armenians (see Burckhardt, Syr. p. 1003; *Tavernier, Reise* 1, p. 280), whilst the Ber-
bians and Cabyles of Africa use shallow iron frying-pans for
the purpose, and call them *tajen,*—the same name, no doubt, as
τήγανον, with which the LXX. have rendered *machabath.* These
cakes were to be broken in pieces for the *minchah,* and oil to be
poured upon them (the inf. abs. as in Ex. xiii. 3, xx. 8, *vid.* Ges.
§ 131, 4); just as the Bedouins break the cakes which they bake
in the hot ashes into small pieces, and prepare them for eating
by pouring butter or oil upon them.—Ver. 7. Thirdly, " *If thy
oblation be a tigel-minchah, it shall be made of fine flour with
oil.*" *Marchesheth* is not a gridiron (ἔσχαρα, LXX.); but, as it is
derived from חָרַשׁ, *ebullivit,* it must apply to a vessel in which food
was boiled. We have therefore to think of cakes boiled in oil.—
Vers. 8–10. The presentation of the *minchah* " made of these
things," *i.e.* of the different kinds of pastry mentioned in vers.
4–7, resembled in the main that described in vers. 1–3.   The
הֵרִים מִן in ver. 9 corresponds to the קָמַץ מִן in ver. 2, and does
not denote any special ceremony of heaving, as is supposed by
the Rabbins and many archæological writers, who understand
by it a solemn movement up and down.   This will be evident
from a comparison of chap. iii. 3 with chap. iv. 8, 31, 35, and
vii. 3.   In the place of יָרִים מִמֶּנּוּ in chap. iv. 8 we find הִקְרִיב מִזְבֵּחַ
in chap. iii. 3 (cf. chap. vii. 3), and instead of כַּאֲשֶׁר יוּרַם מִשּׁוֹר זֶבַח
in chap. iv. 10, כַּאֲשֶׁר הוּסַר חֵלֶב in chap. iv. 31 and 35 ; so that
הֵרִים מִן evidently denotes simply the lifting off or removal of
those parts which were to be burned upon the altar from the rest
of the sacrifice (cf. *Bähr,* ii. 357, and my *Archäologie* i. p. 244–
5).—In vers. 11–13 there follow two laws which were applicable
to all the meat-offerings : viz. to offer nothing leavened (ver. 11),
and to salt every meat-offering, and in fact every sacrifice, with
salt (ver. 13). Every *minchah* was to be prepared without leaven :
" *for all leaven, and all honey, ye shall not burn a firing of it for
Jehovah.   As an offering of first-fruits ye may offer them* (leaven
and honey, *i.e.* pastry made with them) *to Jehovah, but they shall
not come upon the altar.*"   Leaven and honey are mentioned
together as things which produce fermentation.   Honey has also

an acidifying or fermenting quality, and was even used for the preparation of vinegar (Plin. h. n. 11, 15 ; 21, 14). In rabbinical writings, therefore, הִדְבִּישׁ signifies not only *dulcedinem admittere,* but *corrumpsi, fermentari, fermentescere* (*vid. Buxtorf, lex. chald. talm. et rabb.* p. 500). By "honey" we are to understand not grape-honey, the *dibs* of the Arabs, as *Rashi* and *Bähr* do, but the honey of bees; for, according to 2 Chron. xxxi. 5, this alone was offered as an offering of first-fruits along with corn, new wine, and oil; and in fact, as a rule, this was the only honey used by the ancients in sacrifice (see *Bochart, Hieroz.* iii. pp. 393 sqq.). The loaves of first-fruits at the feast of Weeks were leavened; but they were assigned to the priests, and not burned upon the altar (chap. xxiii. 17, 20). So also were the cakes offered with the vow-offerings, which were applied to the sacrificial meal (chap. vii. 13); but not the shew-bread, as *Knobel* maintains (see at chap. xxiv. 5 sqq.). Whilst leaven and honey were forbidden to be used with any kind of *minchah,* because of their producing fermentation and corruption, salt on the other hand was not to be omitted from any sacrificial offering. *" Thou shalt not let the salt of the covenant of thy God cease from thy meat-offering,"* i.e. thou shalt never offer a meat-offering without salt. The meaning which the salt, with its power to strengthen food and preserve it from putrefaction and corruption, imparted to the sacrifice, was the unbending truthfulness of that self-surrender to the Lord embodied in the sacrifice, by which all impurity and hypocrisy were repelled. The salt of the sacrifice is called the salt of the covenant, because in common life salt was the symbol of covenant; treaties being concluded and rendered firm and inviolable, according to a well-known custom of the ancient Greeks (see *Eustathius ad Iliad.* i. 449) which is still retained among the Arabs, by the parties to an alliance eating bread and salt together, as a sign of the treaty which they had made. As a covenant of this kind was called a " covenant of salt," equivalent to an indissoluble covenant (Num. xviii. 19 ; 2 Chron. xiii. 5), so here the salt added to the sacrifice is designated as salt of the covenant of God, because of its imparting strength and purity to the sacrifice, by which Israel was strengthened and fortified in covenant fellowship with Jehovah. The following clause, " upon (with) every sacrificial gift of thine shalt thou offer salt," is not to be restricted to the

meat-offering, as *Knobel* supposes, nor to be understood as meaning that the salt was only to be added to the sacrifice externally,
to be offered with or beside it ; in which case the strewing of
salt upon the different portions of the sacrifice (Ezek. xliii. 24 ;
Mark ix. 49) would have been a departure from the ancient law.
For *korban* without any further definition denotes the sacrificial
offerings generally, the bleeding quite as much as the bloodless,
and the closer definition of הִקְרִיב עַל (offer upon) is contained in
the first clause of the verse, "season with salt." The words
contain a supplementary rule which was applicable to every
sacrifice (bleeding and bloodless), and was so understood from
time immemorial by the Jews themselves (cf. *Josephus, Ant.*
iii. 9, 1).[1]

Vers. 14–16. The *third* kind was the meat-offering of first-
fruits, *i.e.* of the first ripening corn. This was to be offered in
the form of " *ears parched or roasted by the fire;* in other words,
to be made from ears which had been roasted at the fire. To
this is added the further definition גֶּרֶשׂ כַּרְמֶל "rubbed out of field-
fruit." גֶּרֶשׂ, from גָּרַס=גָּרַשׂ, to rub to pieces, that which is rubbed
to pieces ; it only occurs here and in vers. 14 and 16. כַּרְמֶל is
applied generally to a corn-field, in Isa. xxix. 17 and xxxii. 16 to
cultivated ground, as distinguished from desert; here, and in
chap. xxiii. 14 and 2 Kings iv. 42, it is used metonymically for
field-fruit, and denotes early or the first-ripe corn. Corn roasted
by the fire, particularly grains of wheat, is still a very favourite
food in Palestine, Syria, and Egypt. The ears are either burnt
along with the stalks before they are quite ripe, and then rubbed
out in a sieve; or stalks of wheat are bound up in small bundles
and roasted at a bright fire, and then the grains are eaten
(*Seetzen*, i. p. 94, iii. p. 221 ; *Robinson*, Biblical Researches, p.
393). Corn roasted in this manner is not so agreeable as when
(as is frequently the case in harvest, Ruth ii. 14) the grains of
wheat are taken before they are quite dry and hard, and parched
in a pan or upon an iron plate, and then eaten either along with
or in the place of bread (*Robinson*, Pal. ii. 394). The *minchah*
mentioned here was prepared in the first way, viz. of roasted
ears of corn, which were afterwards rubbed to obtain the grains :

---

[1] The Greeks and Romans also regarded salt as indispensable to a sacrifice. *Maxime in sacris intelligitur auctoritas salis, quando nulla conficiuntur
sine mola salsa.   Plin. h. n.* 31, 7 (cf. 41).

it consisted, therefore, not of crushed corn or groats, but only of toasted grains. In the place of אָבִיב קָלוּי we find קָלִי (chap. xxiii. 14), or קָלוּי (Josh. v. 11), afterwards employed. Oil and incense were to be added, and the same course adopted with the offering as in the case of the offering of flour (vers. 2, 3).

If therefore, all the meat-offerings consisted either of flour and oil,—the most important ingredients in the vegetable food of the Israelites,—or of food already prepared for eating, there can be no doubt that in them the Israelite offered his daily bread to the Lord, though in a manner which made an essential difference between them and the merely dedicatory offerings of the first-fruits of corn and bread. For whilst the loaves of first-fruits were leavened, and, as in the case of the sheaf of first-fruits, no part of them was burnt upon the altar (chap. xxiii. 10, 11, xvii. 20), every independent meat-offering was to be prepared without leaven, and a portion given to the Lord as fire-food, for a savour of satisfaction upon the altar; and the rest was to be scrupulously kept from being used by the offerer, as *a most holy thing*, and to be eaten at the holy place by the sanctified priests alone, as the servants of Jehovah, and the mediators between Him and the nation. On account of this peculiarity, the meat-offerings cannot have denoted merely the sanctification of earthly food, but were symbols of the spiritual food prepared and enjoyed by the congregation of the Lord. If even the earthly life is not sustained and nourished merely by the daily bread which a man procures and enjoys, but by the power of divine grace, which strengthens and blesses the food as means of preserving life; much less can the spiritual life be nourished by earthly food, but only by the spiritual food which a man prepares and partakes of, by the power of the Spirit of God, from the true bread of life, or the word of God. Now, as oil in the Scriptures is invariably a symbol of the Spirit of God as the principle of all spiritual *vis vitæ* (see p. 174), so bread-flour and bread, procured from the seed of the field, are symbols of the word of God (Deut. viii. 3; Luke viii. 11). As God gives man corn and oil to feed and nourish his bodily life, so He gives His people His word and Spirit, that they may draw food from these for the spiritual life of the inner man. The work of sanctification consists in the operation of this spiritual food, through the right use of the means of grace for growth in pious conversation and good works (Matt. v. 16; 1 Pet. ii. 12). The enjoyment of this food fills the inner man with peace, joy, and blessedness in God. This fruit of the spiritual life is shadowed forth in the meat-offerings. They were to be kept free, therefore, both from the leaven of hypocrisy (Luke xii. 1) and of malice and wickedness (1 Cor. v. 8), and also from the honey of the *deliciæ carnis*, because both are destructive of spiritual life; whilst, on the other hand, the salt of the covenant of God (*i.e.* the purifying, strengthening, and quickening power of the covenant, by which moral corruption was averted) and the incense of prayer were both to be added, in order that the fruit of the spiritual life might become well-pleasing to the Lord. It was upon this signification that the most holy character of the meat-offerings was founded.

Chap. iii. THE PEACE-OFFERINGS.—The third kind of sacrifice is called זֶבַח שְׁלָמִים, commonly rendered thank-offering, but more correctly a saving-offering (*Heilsopfer: Angl.* peace-offering). Besides this fuller form, which is the one most commonly employed in Leviticus, we meet with the abbreviated forms זְבָחִים and שְׁלָמִים: *e.g.* זֶבַח in chap. vii. 16, 17, xxiii. 37, more especially in combination with עֹלָה, chap. xvii. 8 cf. Ex. x. 25, xviii. 12; Num. xv. 3, 5; Deut. xii. 27; Josh. xxii. 27; 1 Sam. vi. 15, xv. 22; 2 Kings v. 17, x. 24; Isa. lvi. 7; Jer. vi. 20, vii. 21, xvii. 26, etc.,—and שְׁלָמִים in chap. ix. 22; Ex. xx. 24, xxxii. 6; Deut. xxvii. 7; Josh. viii. 31; Judg. xx. 26, xxi. 4; 1 Sam. xiii. 9; 2 Sam. vi. 17, 18, xxiv. 25; 1 Kings iii. 15, etc. זֶבַח is derived from זָבַח, which is not applied to slaughtering generally (שָׁחַט), but, with the exception of Deut. xii. 15, where the use of זָבַח for slaughtering is occasioned by the retrospective reference to Lev. xvii. 3, 4, is always used for slaying as a sacrifice, or sacrificing; and even in 1 Sam. xxviii. 24, Ezek. xxxiv. 3 and xxxix. 17, it is only used in a figurative sense. The real meaning, therefore, is sacrificial slaughtering, or slaughtered sacrifice. It is sometimes used in a wider sense, and applied to every kind of bleeding sacrifice (1 Sam. i. 21, ii. 19), especially in connection with *minchah* (1 Sam. ii. 29; Ps. xl. 7; Isa. xix. 21; Dan. ix. 27, etc.); but it is mostly used in a more restricted sense, and applied to the peace-offerings, or slain-offerings, which culminated in a sacrificial meal, as distinguished from the burnt and sin-offerings, in which case it is synonymous with שְׁלָמִים or

זֶבַח שְׁלָמִים. The word *shelamim,* the singular of which (*shelem*) is only met with in Amos v. 22, is applied exclusively to these sacrifices, and is derived from שָׁלֵם to be whole, uninjured. It does not mean " compensation or restitution," for which we find the nouns שִׁלֻּם (Deut. xxxii. 35), שִׁלוּם (Hos. ix. 7), and שִׁלּוּמָה (Ps. xci. 8), formed from the *Piel* שִׁלֵּם, but *integritas completa, pacifica, beata,* answering to the *Sept.* rendering σωτήριον. The plural denotes the entire round of blessings and powers, by which the salvation or integrity of man in his relation to God is established and secured. The object of the *shelamim* was invariably salvation : sometimes they were offered as an embodiment of thanksgiving for salvation already received, sometimes as a prayer for the salvation desired ; so that they embraced both supplicatory offerings and thank-offerings, and were offered even in times of misfortune, or on the day on which supplication was offered for the help of God (Judg. xx. 26, xxi. 4; 1 Sam. xiii. 9; 2 Sam xxiv. 25).[1] The law distinguishes three different kinds : praise-offerings, vow-offerings, and freewill-offerings (chap. vii. 12, 16). They were all restricted to oxen, sheep, and goats, either male or female, pigeons not being allowed, as they were always accompanied with a common sacrificial meal, for which a pair of pigeons did not suffice.

Vers. 1—5. In the act of sacrificing, the presentation of the animal before Jehovah, the laying on of hands, the slaughtering, and the sprinkling of the blood were the same as in the case of the burnt-offering (chap. i. 3–5). It was in the application of the flesh that the difference first appeared.—Ver. 3. The person presenting the sacrifice was to offer as a firing for Jehovah, *first,* "the fat which covered the entrails" (chap. i. 9), *i.e.* the large net which stretches from the stomach over the bowels and completely envelopes the latter, and which is only met with in the case of men and the mammalia generally, and in the ruminant animals abounds with fat; *secondly,* "all the fat on the entrails," *i.e.* the fat attached to the intestines, which could easily be peeled off ; *thirdly,* "the two kidneys, and the fat upon them (and) that upon the loins (הַכְּסָלִים), *i.e.* upon the inner muscles of the loins, or in the region of the kidneys; and *fourthly,* "the net

[1] Cf. *Hengstenberg,* Dissertations. *Outram's* explanation is quite correct : *Sacrificia salutaria in sacris litteris shelamim dicta, ut quæ semper de rebus prosperis fieri solerent, impetratis utique aut impetrandis.*

upon the liver." The net (הַיֹּתֶרֶת) upon עַל vers. 4, 10, 15, chap.
iv. 9, vii. 4; Ex. xxix. 13), or from (מִן chap. ix. 10), or of the
liver (chap. viii. 16, 25, ix. 19; Ex. xxix. 22), cannot be the
large lobe of the liver, ὁ λοβὸς τοῦ ἥπατος (LXX.), because
this is part of the liver itself, and does not lie עַל־הַכָּבֵד over
(upon) the liver; nor is it simply a portion of fat, but the small
net (*omentum minus*), the liver-net, or stomach-net (*reticulum
jecoris; Vulg., Luth., De Wette,* and *Knobel*), which commences
at the division between the right and left lobes of the liver, and
stretches on the one side across the stomach, and on the other to
the region of the kidneys. Hence the clause, " on the kidneys
(*i.e.* by them, as far as it reaches) shall he take it away." This
smaller net is delicate, but not so fat as the larger net; though
it still forms part of the fat portions. The word יֹתֶרֶת, which only
occurs in the passages quoted, is to be explained from the Arabic
and Ethiopic (to stretch over, to stretch out), whence also the
words יֶתֶר a cord (Judg. xvi. 7; Ps. xi. 2), and מֵיתָר the bow-
string (Ps. xxi. 13) or extended tent-ropes (Ex. xxxv. 18), are
derived. The four portions mentioned comprehended all the
separable fat in the inside of the sacrificial animal. Hence they
were also designated "all the fat" of the sacrifice (ver. 16,
chap. iv. 8, 19, 26, 31, 35, vii. 3), or briefly "the fat" (הַחֵלֶב ver.
9, chap. vii. 33, xvi. 25, xvii. 6; Num. xviii. 17), "the fat portions" (הַחֲלָבִים chap. vi. 5, viii. 26, ix. 19, 20, 24, x. 15).—Ver. 5.
This fat the priests were to burn upon the altar, over the burnt
sacrifice, on the pieces of wood upon the fire. עַל־הָעֹלָה does not
mean "in the manner or style of the burnt-offering" (*Knobel*),
but "upon (over) the burnt-offering." For apart from the fact
that עַל cannot be shown to have this meaning, the peace-offering was preceded as a rule by the burnt-offering. At any rate it
was always preceded by the daily burnt-offering, which burned,
if not all day, at all events the whole of the forenoon, until it
was quite consumed; so that the fat portions of the peace-offerings were to be laid upon the burnt-offering which was burning
already. That this is the meaning of עַל־הָעֹלָה is placed beyond
all doubt, both by chap. vi. 5, where the priest is directed to burn
wood every morning upon the fire of the altar, and then to place
the burnt-offering upon it (עָלֶיהָ), and upon that to cause the fat
portions of the peace-offerings to evaporate in smoke, and also
by chap. ix. 14, where Aaron is said first of all to have burned

the flesh and head of the burnt-offering upon the altar, then to have washed the entrails and legs of the animal, and burned them on the altar, עַל הָעֹלָה, *i.e.* upon (over) the portions of the burnt-offering that were burning already.

Vers. 6–16. The same rules apply to the peace-offerings of sheep and goats, except that, in addition to the fat portions, which were to be burned upon the altar in the case of the oxen (vers. 3, 4) and goats (vers. 14, 15), the *fat tail* of the sheep was to be consumed as well. הָאַלְיָה תְמִימָה: "*the fat tail whole*" (ver. 9), *cauda ovilla vel arietina eaque crassa et adiposa;* the same in Arabic (*Ges. thes.* p. 102). The fat tails which the sheep have in Northern Africa and Egypt, also in Arabia, especially Southern Arabia, and Syria, often weigh 15 lbs. or more, and small carriages on wheels are sometimes placed under them to bear their weight (*Sonnini*, R. ii. p. 358 ; *Bochart, Hieroz.* i. pp. 556 sqq.). It consists of something between marrow and fat. Ordinary sheep are also found in Arabia and Syria; but in modern Palestine all the sheep are " of the broad-tailed species." The broad part of the tail is an excrescence of fat, from which the true tail hangs down (*Robinson,* Pal. ii. 166). "*Near the rump-bone shall he* (the offerer) *take it* (the fat tail) *away,*" *i.e.* separate it from the body. עָצֶה, *ἀπ. λεγ.*, is, according to *Saad.*, *os caudæ s. coccygis, i.e.* the rump or tail-bone, which passes over into the vertebræ of the tail (cf. *Bochart,* i. pp. 560–1). In vers. 11 and 16 the fat portions which were burned are called "food of the firing for Jehovah," or "food of the firing for a sweet savour," *i.e.* food which served as a firing for Jehovah, or reached Jehovah by being burned; cf. Num. xxviii. 24, "food of the firing of a sweet savour for Jehovah." Hence not only are the daily burnt-offerings and the burnt and sin-offerings of the different feasts called "food of Jehovah" ("My bread," Num. xxviii. 2); but the sacrifices generally are described as "the food of God" ("the bread of their God," chap. xxi. 6, 8, 17, 21, 22, and xxii. 25), as food, that is, which Israel produced and caused to ascend to its God in fire as a sweet smelling savour.— Nothing is determined here with regard to the appropriation of the flesh of the peace-offerings, as their destination for a sacrificial meal was already known from traditional custom. The more minute directions for the meal itself are given in chap. vii. 11–36, where the meaning of these sacrifices is more fully explained.—In ver. 17 (ver. 16) the general rule is added, "*all fat belongs to Jehovah*," and the law, "*eat neither fat nor blood*," is enforced as "*an eternal statute*" for the generations of Israel (see at Ex. xii. 14, 24) in all their dwelling-places (see Ex. x. 23 and xii. 20).

Chap. iv. and v. THE EXPIATORY SACRIFICES.—The sacrifices treated of in chap. i.–iii. are introduced by their names, as though already known, for the purpose of giving them a legal sanction. But in chap. iv. and v. sacrifices are appointed for different offences, which receive their names for the first time from the objects to which they apply, *i.e.* from the sin, or the trespass, or debt to be expiated by them : viz. חַטָּאת *sin, i.e. sin-offering* (chap. iv. 3, 8, 14, 19, etc.), and אָשָׁם *debt, i.e. debt-offering* (chap. v. 15, 16, 19, 25) ;—a clear proof that the sin and debt-offerings were introduced at the same time as the Mosaic law. The laws which follow are distinguished from the preceding ones by the new introductory formula in chap. iv. 1, 2, which is repeated in chap. v. 14. This repetition proves that chap. iv. 2– v. 13 treats of the sin-offerings, and chap. v. 14–26 of the trespass-offerings ; and this is confirmed by the substance of the two series of laws.

Chap. iv. 2–v. 13. The SIN-OFFERINGS.—The ritual prescribed for these differed, with regard to the animals sacrificed, the sprinkling of the blood, and the course adopted with the flesh, according to the position which the person presenting them happened to occupy in the kingdom of God. The classification of persons was as follows : (1) the anointed priest (chap. iv. 2–12) ; (2) the whole congregation of Israel (vers. 13–21) ; (3) the prince (vers. 22–26) ; (4) the common people (ver. 27–v. 13). In the case of the last, regard was also paid to their circumstances ; so that the sin-offerings could be regulated according to the ability of the offerer, especially for the lighter forms of sin (chap. v. 1–13).—Ver. 2. "*If a soul sin in wandering from any* (מִכֹּל in a partitive sense) *of the commandments of Jehovah, which ought not to be done, and do any one of them*" (מֵאַחַת with מִן partitive, cf. vers. 13, 22, 27, *lit.* anything of one). This sentence, which stands at the head of the laws for the sin-offerings, shows that the sin-offerings did not relate to sin or sinfulness in general, but to particular manifestations of sin, to certain distinct actions performed by individuals, or by the whole congregation. The distinguishing characteristic of the sin is expressed by the term בִּשְׁגָגָה (in error). No sins but those committed בִּשְׁגָגָה could be expiated by sin-offerings; whilst those committed with a high hand were to be punished by the extermination of the sinner (Num. xv. 27–31). שְׁגָגָה, from שָׁגָה = שָׁגַג to wander or go wrong, signifies mistake, error, oversight. But sinning "*in error*" is not merely sinning through ignorance (vers. 13, 22, 27, v. 18), hurry, want of consideration, or carelessness (chap. v. 1, 4, 15), but also sinning unintentionally (Num. xxxv. 11, 15, 22, 23); hence all such sins as spring from the weakness of flesh and blood, as distinguished from sins committed with a high (elevated) hand, or in haughty, defiant rebellion against God and His commandments.

Vers. 3–12. *The sin of the high priest.*—The high priest is here called the "anointed priest" (vers. 3, 5, 16, vi. 15) on account of the completeness of the anointing with which he was consecrated to his office (chap. viii. 12); in other places he is called the great (or high) priest (chap. xxi. 10; Num. xxxv. 25, etc.), and by later writers כֹּהֵן הָרֹאשׁ, the priest the head, or head priest (2 Kings xxv. 18; 2 Chron. xix. 11). If he sinned לְאַשְׁמַת הָעָם, "to the sinning of the nation," *i.e.* in his official position as representative of the nation before the Lord, and not merely in his own personal relation to God, he was to offer for a sin-offering because of his sin an ox without blemish, the largest of all the sacrificial animals, because he filled the highest post in Israel.—Ver. 4. The presentation, laying on of hands, and slaughtering, were the same as in the case of the other sacrifices (chap. i. 3–5). The first peculiarity occurs in connection with the blood (vers. 5–7). The anointed priest was to take (a part) of the blood and carry it into the tabernacle, and having dipped his finger in it, to sprinkle some of it seven times before Jehovah "*in the face of the vail of the Holy*" (Ex. xxvi. 31), *i.e.* in the direction towards the curtain; after that, he was to put (נָתַן) some of the blood upon the horns of the altar of incense, and then to pour out the great mass of the blood, of which only a small portion had been used for sprinkling and smearing upon the horns of the altar, at the bottom of the altar of burnt-offering. A sevenfold sprinkling "in the face of the vail" also took place in connection with the sin-offering for the whole

congregation, as well as with the ox and he-goat which the
high priest offered as sin-offerings on the day of atonement for
himself, the priesthood, and the congregation, when the blood
was sprinkled seven times before (לִפְנֵי) the capporeth (chap.
xvi. 14), and seven times upon the horns of the altar (chap. xvi.
18, 19). So too the blood of the red cow, that was slaughtered
as a sin-offering outside the camp, was sprinkled seven times in
the direction towards the tabernacle (Num. xix. 4). The sevenfold sprinkling at the feast of atonement had respect to the
purification of the sanctuary from the blemishes caused by the
sins of the people, with which they had been defiled in the
course of the year (see at chap. xvi.), and did not take place
till after the blood had been sprinkled once "against (? upon)
the capporeth in front" for the expiation of the sin of the
priesthood and people, and the horns of the altar had been
smeared with the blood (chap. xvi. 14, 18); whereas in the sin-
offerings mentioned in this chapter, the sevenfold sprinkling
preceded the application of the blood to the horns of the altar.
This difference in the order of succession of the two manipula-
tions with the blood leads to the conclusion, that in the case
before us the sevenfold sprinkling had a different signification
from that which it had on the day of atonement, and served as
a preliminary and introduction to the expiation. The blood
also was not sprinkled upon the altar of the holy place, but
only before Jehovah, against the curtain behind which Jehovah
was enthroned, that is to say, only into the neighbourhood of
the gracious presence of God; and this act was repeated seven
times, that in the number seven, as the stamp of the covenant,
the covenant relation, which sin had loosened, might be restored.
It was not till after this had been done, that the expiatory blood
of the sacrifice was put upon the horns of the altar,—not merely
sprinkled or swung against the wall of the altar, but smeared
upon the horns of the altar; not, however, that the blood might
thereby be brought more prominently before the eyes of God,
or lifted up into His more immediate presence, as *Hofmann* and
Knobel suppose, but because the significance of the altar, as the
scene of the manifestation of the divine grace and salvation,
culminated in the horns, as the symbols of power and might
(see p. 190). In the case of the sin-offerings for the high priest
and the congregation, the altar upon which this took place was

not the altar of burnt-offering in the court, but the altar of incense in the holy place; because both the anointed priest, by virtue of his calling and consecration as the mediator between the nation and the Lord, and the whole congregation, by virtue of its election as a kingdom of priests (Ex. xix. 6), were to maintain communion with the covenant God in the holy place, the front division of the dwelling-place of Jehovah, and were thus received into a closer relation of fellowship with Jehovah than the individual members of the nation, for whom the court with its altar was the divinely appointed place of communion with the covenant God. The remainder of the blood, which had not been used in the act of expiation, was poured out at the bottom of the altar of burnt-offering, as the holy place to which all the sacrificial blood was to be brought, that it might be received into the earth.—Vers. 8–10. The priest was to lift off *"all the fat"* from the sacrificial animal, *i.e.* the same fat portions as in the peace-offering (chap. iii. 3, 4, כָּל־חֵלֶב is the subject to יוּרם in ver. 10), and burn it upon the altar of burnt-offering. —Vers. 11, 12. The skin of the bullock, and all the flesh, together with the head and the shank and the entrails (chap. i. 9) and the fœces, in fact the whole bullock, was to be carried out by him (the sacrificing priest) to a clean place before the camp, to which the ashes of the sacrifices were carried from the ash-heap (chap. i. 16), and there burnt on the wood with fire. (On the construction of vers. 11 and 12 see *Ges.* § 145, 2).

The different course, adopted with the blood and flesh of the sin-offerings, from that prescribed in the ritual of the other sacrifices, was founded upon the special signification of these offerings. As they were presented to effect the expiation of sins, the offerer transferred the consciousness of sin and the desire for forgiveness to the head of the animal that had been brought in his stead, by the laying on of his hand; and after this the animal was slaughtered, and suffered death for him as the wages of sin. But as sin is not wiped out by the death of the sinner, unless it be forgiven by the grace of God, so devoting to death an animal laden with sin rendered neither a real nor symbolical satisfaction or payment for sin, by which the guilt of it could be wiped away; but the death which it endured in the sinner's stead represented merely the fruit and effect of sin. To cover the sinner from the holiness of God because of his sin, some of the blood of the sacrifice was sprinkled seven times before Jehovah in the holy place; and the covenant fellowship, which had been endangered, was thereby restored. After this, however, the soul, which was covered in the sacrificial blood, was given up to the grace of God that prevailed in the altar, by means of the sprinkling of the blood upon the horns of the altar of incense, that it might receive the forgiveness of sins and reconciliation with God, and the full enjoyment of the blessings of the covenant be ensured to it once more. But the sin, that had been laid upon the animal of the sin-offering, lay upon it still. The next thing done, therefore, was to burn the fat portions of its inside upon the altar of burnt-offering. Now, if the flesh of the victim represented the body of the offerer as the organ of his soul, the fat portions inside the body, together with the kidneys, which were regarded as the seat of the tenderest and deepest emotions, can only have set forth the better part or inmost kernel of the man, the ἔσω ἄνθρωπος (Rom. vii. 22; Eph. iii. 16). By burning the fat portions upon the altar, the better part of human nature was given up in symbol to the purifying fire of the Holy Spirit of God, that it might be purified from the dross of sin, and ascend in its glorified essence to heaven, for a sweet savour unto the Lord (ver. 31). The flesh of the sin-offering, however, or "the whole bullock," was then burned in a clean place outside the camp, though not merely that it might be thereby destroyed in a clean way, like the flesh provided for the sacrificial meals, which had not been consumed at the time fixed by the law (chap. vii. 17, viii. 32, xix. 6; Ex. xii. 10, xxix. 34), or the flesh of the sacrifices, which had been defiled by contact with unclean objects (chap. vii. 19); for if the disposal of the flesh formed an integral part of the sacrificial ceremony in the case of all the other sacrifices, and if, in the case of the sin-offerings, the blood of which was not brought into the interior of the sanctuary, the priests were to eat the flesh in a holy place, and that not "as a portion assigned to them by God as an honourable payment,' but, according to the express declaration of Moses, "to bear and take away (לָשֵׂאת) the iniquity of the congregation, to make atonement for them" (chap. x. 17), the burning of the flesh of the sin-offerings, i.e. of the animal itself, the blood of which was not brought into the holy place, cannot have been without significance, or simply the means adopted to dispose of it in a fitting manner, but must also have formed one factor in the ceremony of expiation. The burning outside the camp was rendered necessary, because the sacrifice had respect to the expiation of the priesthood, and the flesh or body of the bullock, which had been made חַטָּאת by the laying on of the hand, could not be eaten by the priests as the body of sin, that by the holiness of their official character they might bear and expiate the sin imputed to the sacrifice (see at chap. x. 17). In this case it was necessary that it should be given up to the effect of sin, viz. to death or destruction by fire, and that outside the camp; in other words, outside the kingdom of God, from which everything dead was removed. But, inasmuch as it was sacrificial flesh, and therefore most holy by virtue of its destination; in order that it might not be made an abomination, it was not to be burned in an unclean place, where carrion and other abominations were thrown (chap. xiv. 40, 45), but in the clean place, outside the camp, to which the ashes of the altar of burnt-offering were removed, as being the earthly sediment and remains of the sacrifices that had ascended to God in the purifying flames of the altar-fire.[1]

Vers. 13–21. *Sin of the whole congregation.*—This is still further defined, as consisting in the fact that the thing was hid (נֶעְלַם)[2] from the eyes of the congregation, *i.e.* that it was a sin

---

[1] The most holy character of the flesh of the sin-offering (chap. vi. 18 sqq.) furnishes no valid argument against the correctness of this explanation of the burning; for, in the first place, there is an essential difference between real or inherent sin, and sin imputed or merely transferred; and secondly, the flesh of the sin-offering was called most holy, not in a moral, but only in a liturgical or ritual sense, as subservient to the most holy purpose of wiping away sin; on which account it was to be entirely removed from all appropriation to earthly objects. Moreover, the idea that sin was imputed to the sin-offering, that it was made sin by the laying on of the hand, has a firm basis in the sacrifice of the red cow (Num. xix.), and also occurs among the Greeks (see *Oehler* in Herzog's Cycl.).

[2] In the correct editions נֶעְלַם has *dagesh* both here and in chap. v. 2, 4, as *Delitzsch* informs me, according to an old rule in pointing, which required that every consonant which followed a syllable terminating with a guttural should be pointed with *dagesh*, if the guttural was to be read with a quiescent *sheva* and not with *chateph*. This is the case in וַיֵּאָסֹר in Gen. xlvi. 29, Ex. xiv. 6, תֶּעְלִים in Ps. x. 1, and other words in the critical edition of the Psalter which has been carefully revised by *Bär* according to the Masora, and published with an introduction by *Delitzsch*. In other passages, such as בְּכָל־לִבִּי Ps. ix. 2, עַל־לְשֹׁנוֹ Ps. xv. 3, etc., the *dagesh* is introduced

which was not known to be such, an act which really violated a
commandment of God, though it was not looked upon as sin.
Every transgression of a divine command, whether it took place
consciously or unconsciously, brought guilt, and demanded a sin-
offering for its expiation; and this was to be presented as soon
as the sin was known. The sin-offering, which the elders had to
offer in the name of the congregation, was to consist of a young
ox, and was to be treated like that of the high priest (vers. 14–
23 compared with vers. 3–12), inasmuch as "the whole congregation" included the priesthood, or at any rate was on an equality with the priesthood by virtue of its calling in relation to the
Lord. חָטָא with עַל signifies to incur guilt upon (on the foundation of) sin (chap. v. 5, etc.); it is usually construed with an
accusative (vers. 3, 28, chap. v. 6, 10, etc.), or with בְּ, to sin with
a sin (ver. 23; Gen. xlii. 22). The subject of וְשָׁחַט (ver. 15) is
one of the elders. " The bullock for a sin-offering:" sc. the one
which the anointed priest offered for his sin, or as it is briefly
and clearly designated in ver. 21, "the former bullock" (ver. 12).
—Ver. 20. " And let the priest make an atonement for them, that it
may be forgiven them," or, "so will they be forgiven." This
formula recurs with all the sin-offerings (with the exception of
the one for the high priest), viz. vers. 26, 31, 35, v. 10, 13;
Num. xv. 25, 26, 28; also with the trespass-offerings, chap. v.
16, 18, 26, xix. 22,—the only difference being, that in the sin-
offerings presented for defilements cleansing is mentioned, instead
of forgiveness, as the effect of the atoning sacrifice (chap. xii. 7,
8, xiv. 20, 53; Num. viii. 21).

Vers. 22–26. The sin of a ruler.—Ver. 22. אֲשֶׁר: ὅτε, when.
נָשִׂיא is the head of a tribe, or of a division of a tribe (Num. iii.
24, 30, 35).—Ver. 23. " If (אוֹ, see Ges. § 155, 2) his sin is made
known to him," i.e. if any one called his attention to the fact
that he had transgressed a commandment of God, he was to
bring a he-goat without blemish, and, having laid his hand upon
it, to slay it at the place of burnt-offering; after which the
priest was to put some of the blood upon the horns of the altar
of burnt-offering, and pour out the rest of the blood at the foot

to prevent the second letter from being lost in the preceding one through the
rapidity of reading.—Ewald's conjectures and remarks about this " dagesh,
which is found in certain MSS.," is a proof that he was not acquainted with
this rule which the Masora recognises.

of the altar, and then to burn the whole of the fat upon the altar, as in the case of the peace-offering (see chap. iii. 3, 4), and thus to make atonement for the prince on account of his sin. עָזִים שָׂעִיר, or שָׂעִיר alone (*lit.* hairy, shaggy, Gen. xxvii. 11), is the buck-goat, which is frequently mentioned as the animal sacrificed as a sin-offering: *e.g.*, that of the tribe-princes (Num. vii. 16 sqq., xv. 24), and that of the nation at the yearly festivals (chap. xvi. 9, 15, xxiii. 19; Num. xxviii. 15, 22, 30, xxix. 5, 16 sqq.) and at the consecration of the tabernacle (chap. ix. 3, 15, x. 16). It is distinguished in Num. vii. 16 sqq. from the *attudim*, which were offered as peace-offerings, and frequently occur in connection with oxen, rams, and lambs as burnt-offerings and thank-offerings (Ps. l. 9, 13, lxvi. 15; Isa. i. 11, xxxiv. 6; Ezek. xxxix. 18). According to *Knobel*, שָׂעִיר עָזִים, or שָׂעִיר, was an old he-goat, the hair of which grew longer with age, particularly about the neck and back, and שְׂעִירַת עָזִים (ver. 28, chap. v. 16) an old she-goat; whilst עַתּוּד was the younger he-goat, which leaped upon the does (Gen. xxxi. 10, 12), and served for slaughtering like lambs, sheep, and goats (Deut. xxxii. 14; Jer. li. 40). But as the שָׂעִיר עָזִים was also slaughtered for food (Gen. xxxvii. 31), and the skins of quite young he-goats are called שְׂעִירֹת (Gen. xxvii. 23), the difference between שָׂעִיר and עַתּוּד is hardly to be sought in the age, but more probably, as *Bochart* supposes, in some variety of species, in which case *seir* and *seirah* might denote the rough-haired, shaggy kind of goat, and *attud* the buck-goat of stately appearance.

Vers. 27-35. In the case of the *sin of a common Israelite* ("of the people of the land," *i.e.* of the rural population, Gen. xxiii. 7), that is to say, of an Israelite belonging to the people, as distinguished from the chiefs who ruled over the people (2 Kings xi. 18, 19, xvi. 15), the sin-offering was to consist of a shaggy she-goat without blemish, or a ewe-sheep (ver. 32). The ceremonial in both cases was the same as with the he-goat (vers. 23 sqq.).—"*According to the offerings made by fire unto the Lord*" (ver. 35): see at chap. iii. 5.

Chap. v. 1-13. There follow here three special examples of sin on the part of the common Israelite, all sins of omission and rashness of a lighter kind than the cases mentioned in chap. iv. 27 sqq.; in which, therefore, if the person for whom expiation was to be made was in needy circumstances, instead of a goat

or ewe-sheep, a pair of doves could be received as a sacrificial
gift, or, in cases of still greater poverty, the tenth of an ephah
of fine flour. The following were the cases. The *first* (ver. 1),
when any one had heard the voice of an oath (an oath spoken
aloud) and was a witness, *i.e.* was in a condition to give evidence,
whether he had seen what took place or had learned it, that is
to say, had come to the knowledge of it in some other way. In
this case, if he did not make it known, he was to bear his offence,
i.e. to bear the guilt, which he had contracted by omitting to
make it known, with all its consequences. אָלָה does not mean a
curse in general, but an oath, as an imprecation upon one's self
(= the "oath of cursing" in Num. v. 21); and the sin referred
to did not consist in the fact that a person heard a curse, imprecation, or blasphemy, and gave no evidence of it (for neither the
expression "and is a witness," nor the words "hath seen or
known of it," are in harmony with this), but in the fact that one
who knew of another's crime, whether he had seen it, or had come
to the certain knowledge of it in any other way, and was therefore qualified to appear in court as a witness for the conviction
of the criminal, neglected to do so, and did not state what he
had seen or learned, when he heard the solemn adjuration of the
judge at the public investigation of the crime, by which all persons present, who knew anything of the matter, were urged to
come forward as witnesses (*vid. Oehler* in *Herzog's* Cycl.). נָשָׂא
עָוֹן, to bear the offence or sin, *i.e.* to take away and endure its consequences (see Gen. iv. 13), whether they consisted in chastise-
ments and judgments, by which God punished the sin (chap. vii.
18, xvii. 16, xix. 17), such as diseases or distress (Num. v. 31,
xiv. 33, 34), childlessness (chap. xx. 20), death (chap. xxii. 9),
or extermination (chap. xix. 8, xx. 17; Num. ix. 13), or in
punishment inflicted by men (chap. xxiv. 15), or whether they
could be expiated by sin-offerings (as in this passage and ver. 17)
and other kinds of atonement. In this sense נָשָׂא חֵטְא is also
sometimes used (see at chap. xix. 17).—Vers. 2, 3. The *second*
was, if any one had touched the carcase of an unclean beast, or
cattle, or creeping thing, or the uncleanness of a man of any
kind whatever ("with regard to all his uncleanness, with which
he defiles himself," *i.e.* any kind of defilement to which a man is
exposed), and "*it is hidden from him*," *sc.* the uncleanness or
defilement; that is to say, if he had unconsciously defiled him-

self by touching unclean objects, and had consequently neglected the purification prescribed for such cases. In this case, if he found it out afterwards, he had contracted guilt which needed expiation.—Ver. 4. The *third* was, if any one should " *swear to prate with the lips,*" *i.e.* swear in idle, empty words of the lips,— "*to do good or evil,*" *i.e.* that he would do anything whatever (Num. xxiv. 13 ; Isa. xli. 23),—"*with regard to all that he speaks idly with an oath,*" *i.e.* if it related to something which a man had affirmed with an oath in thoughtless conversation,—" *and it is hidden from him,*" *i.e.* if he did not reflect that he might commit sin by such thoughtless swearing, and if he perceived it afterwards and discovered his sin, and had incurred guilt with regard to one of the things which he had thoughtlessly sworn.—Vers. 5, 6. If any one therefore (the three cases enumerated are comprehended under the one expression וְהָיָה כִי, for the purpose of introducing the apodosis) had contracted guilt with reference to one of these (the things named in vers. 1–4), and confessed in what he had sinned, he was to offer as his guilt (trespass) to the Lord, for the sin which he had sinned, a female from the flock—for a sin-offering, that the priest might make atonement for him on account of his sin. אָשָׁם (ver. 6) does not mean either guilt-offering or *debitum* (*Knobel*), but *culpa, delictum, reatus*, as in ver. 7 : "as his guilt," *i.e.* for the expiation of his guilt, which he had brought upon himself.

Vers. 7–10. " *But if his hand does not reach what is sufficient for a sheep,*" *i.e.* if he could not afford enough to sacrifice a sheep ("his hand" is put for what his hand acquires), he was to bring two turtle-doves or two young pigeons, one for the sin-offering, the other for the burnt-offering. The pigeon intended for the sin, *i.e.* for the sin-offering, he was to bring first of all to the priest, who was to offer it in the following manner. The head was to be pinched off from opposite to its neck, *i.e.* in the nape just below the head, though without entirely severing it, that is to say, it was to be pinched off sufficiently to kill the bird and allow the blood to flow out. He was then to sprinkle of the blood upon the wall of the altar, which could be effected by swinging the bleeding pigeon, and to squeeze out the rest of the blood against the wall of the altar, because it was a sin-offering ; for in the burnt-offering he let all the blood flow out against the wall of the altar (chap. i. 15). What more was done with the pigeon is not stated. Hence it cannot be decided with certainty, whether, after the crop and its contents were removed and thrown upon the ash-heap, the whole of the bird was burned upon the altar, or whether it fell to the priest, as the *Mishnah* affirms (Seb. vi. 4), so that none of it was placed upon the altar. One circumstance which seems to favour the statement in the Talmud is the fact, that in the sin-offering of pigeons, a second pigeon was to be offered as a burnt-offering, and, according to ver. 10, for the purpose of making an atonement; probably for no other purpose than to burn it upon the altar, as the dove of the sin-offering was not burned, and the sacrifice was incomplete without some offering upon the altar. In the case of sin-offerings of quadrupeds, the fat portions were laid upon the altar, and the flesh could be eaten by the priest by virtue of his office; but in that of pigeons, it was not possible to separate fat portions from the flesh for the purpose of burning upon the altar by themselves, and it would not do to divide the bird in half, and let one half be burned and the other eaten by the priest, as this would have associated the idea of halfness or incompleteness with the sacrifice. A second pigeon was therefore to be sacrificed as a burnt-offering, כַּמִּשְׁפָּט, according to the right laid down in chap. i. 14 sqq., that the priest might make atonement for the offerer on account of his sin, whereas in the sin-offering of a quadruped one sacrificial animal was sufficient to complete the expiation.[1]

Vers. 11–13. But if any one could not afford even two pigeons, he was to offer the tenth of an ephah of fine flour as a sin-offering. תַּשִּׂיג יָדוֹ for תַּגִּיעַ יָדוֹ (ver. 7): his hand reaches to anything, is able to raise it, or with an accusative, obtains, gets anything (used in the same sense in chap. xiv. 30, 31), or else absolutely, acquires, or gets rich (chap. xxv. 26, 47). But it was to be offered without oil and incense, because it was a sin-offering, that is to say, " because it was not to have the character of a *minchah*" (*Oehler.*) But the reason why it was not to have this character was, that only those who were in a state

---

[1] From the instructions to offer two pigeons in order to obtain expiation, it is perfectly evident that the eating of the flesh of the sin-offering on the part of the priest formed an essential part of the act of expiation, and was not merely a kind of honourable tribute, which God awarded to His servants who officiated at the sacrifice.

of grace could offer a *minchah*, and not a man who had fallen from grace through sin. As such a man could not offer to the Lord the fruits of the Spirit of God and of prayer, he was not allowed to add oil and incense, as symbols of the Spirit and praise of God, to the sacrifice with which he sought the forgiveness of sin. The priest was to take a handful of the meal offered, and burn it upon the altar as a memorial, and thus make atonement for the sinner on account of his sin.—On *" his handful"* and *" a memorial" (azcarah),* see chap. ii. 2. *" In one of these"* (ver. 13 as in ver. 5) : cf. chap. iv. 2. *" And let it* (the remainder of the meal offered) *belong to the priest like the meatoffering :"* *i.e.* as being most holy (chap. ii. 3).

Chap. v. 14–26 (chap. v. 14–vi. 7).[1] The TRESPASS-OFFERINGS.—These were presented for special sins, by which a person had contracted guilt, and therefore they are not included in the general festal sacrifices. Three kinds of offences are mentioned in this section as requiring trespass-offerings. The *first* is, *" if a soul commit a breach of trust, and sin in going wrong in the holy gifts of Jehovah."* מָעַל, *lit.* to cover, hence מְעִיל the cloak, over-coat, signifies to act secretly, unfaithfully, especially against Jehovah, either by falling away from Him into idolatry, by which the fitting honour was withheld from Jehovah (chap. xxvi, 40 ; Deut. xxxii. 51 ; Josh. xxii. 16), or by infringing upon His rights, abstracting something that rightfully belonged to Him. Thus in Josh. vii. 1, xxii. 20, it is applied to fraud in relation to that which had been put under the ban; and in Num. v. 12, 27, it is also applied to a married woman's unfaithfulness to her husband : so that sin was called מַעַל, when regarded as a violation of existing rights. *" The holy things of Jehovah"* were the holy gifts, sacrifices, first-fruits, tithes, etc., which were to be offered to Jehovah, and were assigned by Him to the priests for their revenue (see chap. xxi. 22). חָטָא with מִן is *constructio prægnans :* to sin in anything by taking away from Jehovah that which belonged to Him. בִּשְׁגָגָה, *in error* (see chap. iv. 2) : *i.e.* in a forgetful or negligent way. Whoever sinned in this way was to offer to the Lord as his guilt (see ver.

---

[1] In the original the division of verses in the Hebrew text is followed ; but we have thought it better to keep to the arrangement adopted in our English version.—TR.

6) a ram from the flock without blemish for a trespass-offering (lit. *guilt-offering*), according to the estimate of Moses, whose place was afterwards taken by the officiating priest (chap. xxvii. 12 ; Num. xviii. 16). כֶּסֶף שְׁקָלִים " *money of shekels,*" *i.e.* several shekels in amount, which *Abenezra* and others have explained, no doubt correctly, as meaning that the ram was to be worth more than one shekel, two shekels at least.   The expression is probably kept indefinite, for the purpose of leaving some margin for the valuation, so that there might be a certain proportion between the value of the ram and the magnitude of the trespass committed (see *Oehler ut sup.* p. 645).   " *In the holy shekel:*" see Ex. xxx. 13.   At the same time, the culprit was to make compensation for the fraud committed in the holy thing, and add a fifth (of the value) over, as in the case of the redemption of the first-born, of the vegetable tithe, or of what had been vowed to God (chap. xxvii. 27, 31, and xxvii. 13, 15, 19).   The cere mony to be observed in the offering of the ram is described in chap. vii. 1 sqq.   It was the same as that of the sin-offerings, whose blood was not brought into the holy place, except with regard to the sprinkling of the blood, and in this the trespass-offering resembled the burnt-offerings and peace-offerings.

The *second* case (vers. 17–19), from its very position between the other two, which both refer to the violation of rights, must belong to the same category; although the sin is introduced with the formula used in chap. iv. 27 in connection with those sins which were to be expiated by a sin-offering.   But the violation of right can only have consisted in an invasion of Jehovah's rights with regard to Israel, and not, as *Knobel* supposes, in an invasion of the rights of private Israelites, as distinguished from the priests; an antithesis of which there is not the slightest indication.   This is evident from the fact, that the case before us is linked on to the previous one without anything intervening; whereas the next case, which treats of the violation of the rights of a neighbour, is separated by a special introductory formula. The expression, " *and wist it not,*" refers to ignorance of the sin, and not of the divine commands; as may be clearly seen from ver. 18 : " the priest shall make an atonement for him concerning his error, which he committed without knowing it."   The trespass-offering was the same as in the former case, and was also to be valued by the priest; but no compensation is mentioned, probably because the violation of right, which consisted in the transgression of one of the commands of God, was of such a kind as not to allow of material compensation.

The *third* case (chap. vi. 1–7, or vers. 20–26) is distinguished from the óther two by a new introductory formula. The sin and unfaithfulness to Jehovah are manifested in this case in a violation of the rights of a neighbour. "*If a man deny to his neighbour* (בְּחֵשׁ with a double בּ *obj.*, to deny a thing to a person) *a pikkadon* (*i.e.* a deposit, a thing entrusted to him to keep, Gen. xli. 36), *or* תְּשׂוּמֶת יָד, "*a thing placed in his hand*" (handed over to him as a pledge) "*or* גֵּזֶל, *a thing robbed*" (*i.e.* the property of a neighbour unjustly appropriated, whether a well, a field, or cattle, Gen. xxi. 25; Micah ii. 2; Job xxiv. 2), "*or if he have oppressed his neighbour*" (*i.e.* forced something from him or with-held it unjustly, chap. xix. 13; Deut. xxiv. 14; Hos. xii. 8; Mal. iii. 5), "*or have found a lost thing and denies it, and thereby swears to his lie*" (*i.e.* rests his oath upon a lie), "*on account of one of all that a man is accustomed to do to sin therewith:*" the false swearing here refers not merely to a denial of what is found, but to all the crimes mentioned, which originated in avarice and selfishness, but through the false swearing became frauds against Jehovah, adding guilt towards God to the injustice done to the neighbour, and requiring, therefore, not only that a material restitution should be made to the neighbour, but that compensation should be made to God as well. Whatever had been robbed, or taken by force, or entrusted or found, and anything about which a man had sworn falsely (vers. 23, 24), was to be restored "*according to its sum*" (cf. Ex. xxx. 12, Num. i. 2, etc.), *i.e.* in its full value; beside which, he was to "*add its fifths*" (on the plural, see *Ges.* § 87, 2; *Ew.* § 186 *e*), *i.e.* in every one of the things abstracted or withheld unjustly the fifth part of the value was to be added to the full amount (as in ver. 16). "*To him to whom it* (belongs), *shall he give it*" בְּיוֹם אַשְׁמָתוֹ : in the day when he makes atonement for his trespass, *i.e.* offers his trespass-offering. The trespass (guilt) against Jehovah was to be taken away by the trespass-offering according to the valuation of the priest, as in vers. 15, 16, and 18, that he might receive expiation and forgiveness on account of what he had done.

If now, in order to obtain a clear view of the much canvassed

difference between the sin-offerings and trespass-offerings,[1] we
look at once at the other cases, for which trespass-offerings were
commanded in the law; we find in Num. v. 5–8 not only a trespass against Jehovah, but an unjust withdrawal of the property
of a neighbour, clearly mentioned as a crime, for which material
compensation was to be made with the addition of a fifth of its
value, just as in vers. 2–7 of the present chapter. So also the
guilt of a man who had lain with the slave of another (Lev. xix.
20–22) did not come into the ordinary category of adultery, but
into that of an unjust invasion of the domain of another's property; though in this case, as the crime could not be estimated
in money, instead of material compensation being made, a civil
punishment (viz. bodily scourging) was to be inflicted; and for
the same reason nothing is said about the valuation of the sacrificial ram. Lastly, in the trespass-offerings for the cleansing of
a leper (chap. xiv. 12 sqq.), or of a Nazarite who had been defiled by a corpse (Num. vi. 12), it is true we cannot show in what
definite way the rights of Jehovah were violated (see the explanation of these passages), but the sacrifices themselves served
to procure the restoration of the persons in question to certain
covenant rights which they had lost; so that even here the trespass-offering, for which moreover only a male sheep was demanded, was to be regarded as a compensation or equivalent
for the rights to be restored. From all these cases it is perfectly
evident, that the idea of satisfaction for a right, which had been
violated but was about to be restored or recovered, lay at the
foundation of the trespass-offering,[2] and the ritual also points to
this. The animal sacrificed was always a ram, except in the
cases mentioned in chap. xiv. 12 sqq. and Num. vi. 12. This
fact alone clearly distinguishes the trespass-offerings from the
sin-offerings, for which all kinds of sacrifices were offered from

---

[1] For the different views, see *Bähr's* Symbolik ; *Winer's bibl. R. W.* ;
Kurtz on Sacrificial Worship ; *Riehm, theol. Stud. und Krit.* 1854, pp. 93 sqq. ;
Rinck, id. 1855, p. 369 ; *Oehler* in Herzog's Cycl.

[2] Even in the case of the trespass-offering, which those who had taken
heathen wives offered at Ezra's instigation (Ezra x. 18 sqq.), it had reference to a trespass (cf. vers. 2 and 10), an act of unfaithfulness to Jehovah,
which demanded satisfaction. And so again the Philistines (1 Sam. vi. 3
sqq.), when presenting gifts as a trespass-offering for Jehovah, rendered
satisfaction for the robbery committed upon Him by the removal of the ark
of the covenant.

an ox to a pigeon, the choice of the animal being regulated by the position of the sinner and the magnitude of his sin. But they are distinguished still more by the fact, that in the case of all the sin-offerings the blood was to be put upon the horns of the altar, or even taken into the sanctuary itself, whereas the blood of the trespass-offerings, like that of the burnt and peace-offerings, was merely swung against the wall of the altar (chap. vii. 2). Lastly, they were also distinguished by the fact, that in the trespass-offering the ram was in most instances to be valued by the priest, not for the purpose of determining its actual value, which could not vary very materially in rams of the same kind, but to fix upon it symbolically the value of the trespass for which compensation was required. Hence there can be no doubt, that as the idea of the expiation of sin, which was embodied in the sprinkling of the blood, was most prominent in the sin-offering; so the idea of satisfaction for the restoration of rights that had been violated or disturbed came into the fore-ground in the trespass-offering. This satisfaction was to be actually made, wherever the guilt admitted of a material valua-tion, by means of payment or penance; and in addition to this, the animal was raised by the priestly valuation into the authorized bearer of the satisfaction to be rendered to the rights of God, through the sacrifice of which the culprit could obtain the expiation of his guilt.

2. *Special Instructions concerning the Sacrifices for the Priests.* —CHAP. VI. and VII.

The instructions contained in these two chapters were made known to "*Aaron and his sons*" (chap. vi. 9, 20, 25), *i.e.* to the priests, and relate to the duties and rights which devolved upon, and pertained to, the priests in relation to the sacrifices. Although many of the instructions are necessarily repeated from the general regulations, as to the different kinds of sacrifice and the mode of presenting them; most of them are new, and of great importance in relation to the institution of sacrifice generally.

Chap. vi. 8–13 (Heb. vers. 1–6). THE LAW OF THE BURNT-OFFERING commences the series, and special reference is made to the daily burnt-offering (Ex. xxix. 38–42).—Ver. 2. "*It, the burnt-offering, shall* (burn) *upon the hearth upon the*

*altar the whole night till the morning, and the fire of the altar be
kept burning with it.*" The verb תּוּקַד is wanting in the first
clause, and only introduced in the second; but it belongs to the
first clause as well. The pronoun הוּא at the opening of the
sentence cannot stand for the verb *to be* in the imperative. The
passages, which *Knobel* adduces in support of this, are of a
totally different kind. The instructions apply primarily to the
burnt-offering, which was offered every evening, and furnished
the basis for all the burnt-offerings (Ex. xxix. 38, 39; Num.
xxxiii. 3, 4).—Vers. 3, 4. In the morning of every day the
priest was to put on his linen dress (see Ex. xxviii. 42) and the
white drawers, and lift off, *i.e.* clear away, the ashes to which
the fire had consumed the burnt-offering upon the altar (אָכַל is
construed with a double accusative, to consume the sacrifice to
ashes), and pour them down beside the altar (see chap. i. 16).
The ן in מְדוֹ is not to be regarded as the old form of the connecting vowel, as in Gen. i. 24 (*Ewald*, § 211 *b*; see *Ges.* §
90, 3*b*), but as the suffix, as in 2 Sam. xx. 8, although the use
of the suffix with the governing noun in the construct state can
only be found in other cases in the poetical writings (cf. *Ges.*
§ 121 *b*; *Ewald*, 291 *b*). He was then to take off his official
dress, and having put on other (ordinary) clothes, to take away
the ashes from the court, and carry them out of the camp to a
clean place. The priest was only allowed to approach the altar
in his official dress; but he could not go out of the camp with
this.—Ver. 12. The fire of the altar was also to be kept burning
"*with it*" (בּוֹ, viz. the burnt-offering) the whole day through
without going out. For this purpose the priest was to burn
wood upon it (the altar-fire), and lay the burnt-offering in order
upon it, and cause the fat portions of the peace-offerings to
ascend in smoke,—that is to say, whenever peace-offerings were
brought, for they were not prescribed for every day.—Ver. 13.
Fire was to be kept constantly burning upon the altar without
going out, not in order that the heavenly fire, which proceeded
from Jehovah when Aaron and his sons first entered upon the
service of the altar after their consecration, and consumed the
burnt-offerings and peace-offerings, might never be extinguished
(see at chap. ix. 24); but that the burnt-offering might never
go out, because this was the divinely appointed symbol and
visible sign of the uninterrupted worship of Jehovah, which the

covenant nation could never suspend either day or night, without being unfaithful to its calling. For the same reason other nations also kept perpetual fire burning upon the altars of their principal gods. (For proofs, see *Rosenmüller* and *Knobel ad h. l.*)

Vers. 14–18. THE LAW OF THE MEAT-OFFERING.—The regulations in vers. 14, 15, are merely a repetition of chap. ii. 2 and 3; but in vers. 16–18 the new instructions are introduced with regard to what was left and had not been burned upon the altar. The priests were to eat this as unleavened, *i.e.* to bake it without leaven, and to eat it in a holy place, viz. in the court of the tabernacle. מַצּוֹת תֵּאָכֵל in ver. 16 is explained by "*it shall not be baken with leaven*" in ver. 17. It was the priests' share of the firings of Jehovah (see chap. i. 9), and as such it was most holy (see chap. ii. 3), like the sin-offering and trespass-offering (vers. 25, 26, chap. vii. 6), and only to be eaten by the male members of the families of the priests. This was to be maintained as a statute for ever (see at chap. iii. 17). "*Every one that touches them* (the most holy offerings) *becomes holy.*" יִקְדָּשׁ does not mean he shall be holy, or shall sanctify himself (LXX., *Vulg., Luth., a Lap.,* etc.), nor he is consecrated to the sanctuary and is to perform service there (*Theodor., Knobel,* and others). In this provision, which was equally applicable to the sin-offering (ver. 27), to the altar of the burnt-offering (Ex. xxix. 37), and to the most holy vessels of the tabernacle (Ex. xxx. 29), the word is not to be interpreted by Num. xvii. 2, 3, or Deut xxii. 9, or by the expression "shall be holy" in chap. xxvii. 10, 21, and Num. xviii. 10, but by Isa. lxv. 5, "touch me not, for I am holy." The idea is this, every layman who touched these most holy things became holy through the contact, so that henceforth he had to guard against defilement in the same manner as the sanctified priests (chap. xxi. 1–8), though without sharing the priestly rights and prerogatives. This necessarily placed him in a position which would involve many inconveniences in connection with ordinary life.

Vers. 19–23. The MEAT-OFFERING OF THE PRIESTS is introduced, as a new law, with a special formula, and is inserted here in its proper place in the sacrificial instructions given for the priests, as it would have been altogether out of place among

the general laws for the laity. In *" the day of his anointing'*
(הִמָּשַׁח, construed as a passive with the accusative as in Gen.
iv. 18), Aaron and his sons were to offer a *corban* as *" a perpetual
meat-offering"* (*minchah*, in the absolute instead of the construct
state : cf. Ex. xxix. 42, Num. xxviii. 6 ; see *Ges.* § 116, 6,
Note *b*) ; and this was to be done in all future time by *" the
priest who was anointed of his sons in his stead,"* that is to say,
by every high priest at the time of his consecration. *" In the
day of his anointing :"* when the anointing was finished, the
seven were designated as *" the day,"* like the seven days of
creation in Gen. ii. 4. This *minchah* was not offered during
the seven days of the anointing itself, but after the consecration
was finished, *i.e.,* in all probability, as the Jewish tradition assumes, at the beginning of the eighth day, when the high priest
entered upon his office, viz. along with the daily morning sacrifices (Ex. xxix. 38, 39), and before the offering described in
chap. ix. It then continued to be offered, as *" a perpetual
minchah,"* every morning and evening during the whole term
of his office, according to the testimony of the Book of Wisdom
(chap. xlv. 14, where we cannot suppose the daily burnt-offering
to be intended) and also of *Josephus* (Ant. iii. 10, 7).[1] It was
to consist of the tenth of an ephah of fine flour, one half of
which was to be presented in the morning, the other in the
evening ;—not as flour, however, but made in a pan with oil,
" roasted " and תֻּפִינֵי מִנְחַת פִּתִּים (*" broken pieces of a minchah of
crumbs "*), *i.e.* in broken pieces, like a *minchah* composed of
crumbs. מֻרְבֶּכֶת (ver. 14 and 1 Chron. xxiii. 29) is no doubt
synonymous with סֹלֶת מֻרְבֶּכֶת, and to be understood as denoting
fine flour sufficiently burned or roasted in oil ; the meaning
mixed or mingled does not harmonise with chap. vii. 12, where

[1] *Vid. Lundius, jüd. Heiligthümer,* B. 3, c 9, § 17 and 19 ; *Thalhofer ut
supra,* p. 139 ; and *Delitzsch* on the Epistle to the Hebrews. The text evidently enjoins the offering of this *minchah* upon Aaron alone ; for though
Aaron and his sons are mentioned in ver. 13, as they were consecrated together, in ver. 15 the priest anointed of his sons in Aaron's stead, *i.e.* the
successor of Aaron in the high-priesthood, is commanded to offer it. Consequently the view maintained by *Maimonides, Abarbanel,* and others, which
did not become general even among the Rabbins, viz. that every ordinary
priest was required to offer this meat-offering when entering upon his office,
has no solid foundation in the law (see *Selden de success. in pontif.* ii. *c.* 9 ;
L' Empereur ad Middoth 1, 4, Not. 8 ; and *Thalhofer,* p. 150).

the mixing or kneading with oil is expressed by בְּלוּלֹת בַּשֶּׁמֶן. The
hapax legomenon תֻּפִינֵי signifies either broken or baked, according
as we suppose the word to be derived from the Arabic أَفَن
diminuit, or, as *Gesenius* and the Rabbins do, from אָפָה to bake,
a point which can hardly be decided with certainty. This
minchah, which was also instituted as a perpetual ordinance, was
to be burnt entirely upon the altar, like every meat-offering
presented by a priest, because it belonged to the category of the
burnt-offerings, and of these meat-offerings the offerer himself
had no share (chap. ii. 3, 10). *Origen* observes in his *homil.*
iv. in *Levit.*: *In cæteris quidem præceptis pontifex in offerendis
sacrificiis populo præbet officium, in hoc vero mandato quæ pro-
pria sunt curat et quod ad se spectat exequitur.* It is also to be
observed that the high priest was to offer only a bloodless
minchah for himself, and not a bleeding sacrifice, which would
have pointed to expiation. As the sanctified of the Lord, he
was to draw near to the Lord every day with a sacrificial gift,
which shadowed forth the fruits of sanctification.

Vers. 24–30. The LAW OF THE SIN-OFFERING, which is
introduced with a new introductory formula on account of the
interpolation of vers. 19–23, gives more precise instructions,
though chiefly with regard to the sin-offerings of the laity, first
as to the place of slaughtering, as in chap. iv. 24, and then as
to the most holy character of the flesh and blood of the sacrifices.
The flesh of these sin-offerings was to be eaten by the priest
who officiated at a holy place, in the fore-court (see ver. 16).
Whoever touched it became holy (see at ver. 18); and if
any one sprinkled any of the blood upon his clothes, whatever
the blood was sprinkled upon was to be washed in a holy
place, in order that the most holy blood might not be carried
out of the sanctuary into common life along with the sprinkled
clothes, and thereby be profaned. The words "*thou shalt
wash*" in ver. 20 are addressed to the priest.—Ver. 28. The
flesh was equally holy. The vessel, in which it was boiled for
the priests to eat, was to be broken in pieces if it were of earthenware, and scoured (מֹרַק *Pual*) and overflowed with water, *i.e.*
thoroughly rinsed out, if it were of copper, lest any of the most
holy flesh should adhere to the vessel, and be desecrated by its

being used in the preparation of common food, or for other earthly purposes. It was possible to prevent this desecration in the case of copper vessels by a thorough cleansing; but not so with earthen vessels, which absorb the fat, so that it cannot be removed by washing. The latter therefore were to be broken in pieces, *i.e.* thoroughly destroyed. On the other hand, earthen vessels that had been defiled were also ordered to be broken to pieces, though for the very opposite reason (see chap. xi. 33, 35).—Vers. 29, 30. The flesh of the sin-offering was to be eaten after it had been boiled, like the meat-offering (vers. 16 and 18), by the males among the priests alone. But this only applied to the sin-offerings of the laity (chap. iv. 22–v. 13). The flesh of the sin-offerings for the high priest and the whole congregation (chap. iv. 1–21), the blood of which was brought into the tabernacle "to make atonement in the sanctuary," *i.e.* that the expiation with the blood might be completed there, was not to be eaten, but to be burned with fire (chap. iv. 12, 21).—On the signification of this act of eating the flesh of the sin-offering, see at chap. x. 17.

Chap. vii. 1–10. The LAW OF THE TRESPASS-OFFERING embraces first of all the regulations as to the ceremonial connected with the presentation.—Ver. 2. The slaughtering and sprinkling of the blood were the same as in the case of the burnt-offering (chap. i. 5); and therefore, no doubt, the signification was the same.—Vers. 3–5. The fat portions only were to be burned upon the altar, viz. the same as in the sin and peace-offerings (see chap. iv. 8 and iii. 9); but the flesh was to be eaten by the priests, as in the sin-offering (chap. vi. 22), inasmuch as there was the same law in this respect for both the sin-offering and trespass-offering; and these parts of the sacrificial service must therefore have had the same meaning, every trespass being a sin (see chap. vi. 26).—Certain analogous instructions respecting the burnt-offering and meat-offering are appended in vers. 8–10 by way of supplement, as they ought properly to have been given in chap. vi., in the laws relating to the sacrifices in question.—Ver. 8. In the case of the burnt-offering, the skin of the animal was to fall to the lot of the officiating priest, viz. as payment for his services. הַכֹּהֵן is construed absolutely: " *as for the priest, who offereth—the skin of the burnt-offering which he offereth shall belong to the priest"* (for *" to him"*). This was probably the case also with the trespass-offerings and sin-offerings of the laity; whereas the skin of the peace-offerings belonged to the owner of the animal (see *Mishnah, Sebach.* 12, 3).—In vers. 9, 10, the following law is laid down with reference to the meat-offering, that everything baked in the oven, and everything prepared in a pot or pan, was to belong to the priest, who burned a portion of it upon the altar; and that everything mixed with oil and everything dry was to belong to all the sons of Aaron, *i.e.* to all the priests, to one as much as another, so that they were all to receive an equal share. The reason for this distinction is not very clear. That all the meat-offerings described in chap. ii. should fall to the sons of Aaron (*i.e.* to the priests), with the exception of that portion which was burned upon the altar as an *azcarah*, followed from the fact that they were most holy (see at chap. ii. 3). As the meat-offerings, which consisted of pastry, and were offered in the form of pre-pared food (ver. 9), are the same as those described in chap. ii. 4–8, it is evident that by those mentioned in ver. 10 we are to understand the kinds described in chap. ii. 1–3 and 14–16, and by the " dry," primarily the אָבִיב קָלוּי, which consisted of dried grains, to which oil was to be added (נָתַן chap. ii. 15), though not poured upon it, as in the case of the offering of flour (chap. ii. 1), and probably also in that of the sin-offerings and jealousy-offerings (chap. v. 11, and Num. v. 15), which consisted simply of flour (without oil). The reason therefore why those which consisted of cake and pastry fell to the lot of the officiating priest, and those which consisted of flour mixed with oil, of dry corn, or of simple flour, were divided among all the priests, was probably simply this, that the former were for the most part offered only under special circumstances, and then merely in small quantities, whereas the latter were the ordinary forms in which the meat-offerings were presented, and amounted to more than the officiating priests could possibly consume, or dispose of by themselves.

Vers. 11–36. The LAW OF THE PEACE-OFFERINGS, *" which he shall offer to Jehovah"* (the subject is to be supplied from the verb), contains instructions, (1) as to the bloodless accompani-ment to these sacrifices (vers. 12–14), (2) as to the eating of the flesh of the sacrifices (vers. 15–21), with the prohibition against eating fat and blood (vers. 22–27), and (3) as to Jehovah's share of these sacrifices (vers. 28–36).—In vers. 12 and 16 three classes of *shelamim* are mentioned, which differ according to their occasion and design, viz. whether they were brought עַל־תּוֹדָה, upon the ground of praise, *i.e.* to praise God for blessings received or desired, or as vow-offerings, or thirdly, as freewill-offerings (ver. 16). To (*lit.* upon, in addition to) the sacrifice of thanksgiving (ver. 12, "sacrifice of thanksgiving of his peace-offerings," vers. 13 and 15) they were to present "*unleavened cakes kneaded with oil, and flat cakes anointed with oil* (see at chap. ii. 4), *and roasted fine flour* (see vi. 14) *mixed as cakes with oil*," *i.e.* cakes made of fine flour roasted with oil, and thoroughly kneaded with oil (on the construction, see *Ges.* § 139, 2 ; *Ewald* § 284 *a*). This last kind of cakes kneaded with oil is also called oil-bread-cake (" a cake of oiled bread," chap. viii. 26 ; Ex. xxix. 23), or " cake unleavened, kneaded with oil " (Ex. xxix. 2), and probably differed from the former simply in the fact that it was more thoroughly saturated with oil, inasmuch as it was not only made of flour that had been mixed with oil in the kneading, but the flour itself was first of all roasted in oil, and then the dough was moistened still further with oil in the process of kneading. —Vers. 13, 14. This sacrificial gift the offerer was to present upon, or along with, cakes of leavened bread (round, leavened bread-cakes), and to offer " *thereof one out of the whole oblation*," namely, one cake of each of the three kinds mentioned in ver. 12, as a heave-offering for Jehovah, which was to fall to the priest who sprinkled the blood of the peace-offering. According to chap. ii. 9, an *azcarah* of the unleavened pastry was burned upon the altar, although this is not specially mentioned here any more than at vers. 9 and 10 ; whereas none of the leavened bread-cake was placed upon the altar (chap. ii. 12), but it was simply used as bread for the sacrificial meal. There is nothing here to suggest an allusion to the custom of offering unleavened sacrificial cakes upon a plate of leavened dough, as *J. D. Michaelis, Winer,* and others suppose.—Vers. 15–18. The flesh of the praise-offering was to be eaten on the day of presentation, and none of it was to be left till the next morning (cf. chap. xxii. 29, 30) ; but that of the vow and freewill-offerings might be eaten on both the first and second days. Whatever remained after that was to be burnt on the third day, *i.e.* to be destroyed by burning. If any was eaten on the third day, it was not well-pleasing (יֵרָצֶה "good pleasure," see chap. i. 4), and was "*not reckoned to the offerer,*" *sc.* as a sacrifice well-pleasing to God; it was "*an abomination.*" פִּגּוּל, an abomination, is only applied to the flesh of the sacrifices (chap. xix. 7 ; Ezek. iv. 14 ; Isa. lxv. 4), and signifies properly a stench ;—compare the talmudic word פִּגֵּל *fœtidum reddere.* Whoever ate thereof would bear his sin (see chap. v. 1). "*The soul that eateth*" is not to be restricted, as *Knobel* supposes, to the other participators in the sacrificial meal, but applies to the offerer also, in fact to every one who partook of such flesh. The burning on the third day was commanded, not to compel the offerer to invite the poor to share in the meal (*Theodoret, Clericus,* etc.), but to guard against the danger of a desecration of the meal. The sacrificial flesh was holy (Ex. xxix. 34) ; and in chap. xix. 8, where this command is repeated,[1] eating it on the third day is called a profanation of that which was holy to Jehovah, and ordered to be punished with extermination. It became a desecration of what was holy, through the fact that in warm countries, if flesh is not most carefully preserved by artificial means, it begins to putrefy, or becomes offensive (פִּגּוּל) on the third day. But to eat flesh that was putrid or stinking, would be like eating unclean carrion, or the נְבֵלָה with which putrid flesh is associated in Ezek. iv. 14. It was for this reason that burning was commanded, as *Philo* (*de vict.* p. 842) and *Maimonides* (*More Neboch* iii. 46) admit; though the former also associates with this the purpose mentioned above, which we decidedly reject (cf. *Outram* l.c. p. 185 seq., and *Bähr,* ii. pp. 375–6).

Vers. 19–21. In the same way all sacrificial flesh that had come into contact with what was unclean, and been defiled in consequence, was to be burned and not eaten. Ver. 19*b*, which is not found in the Septuagint and Vulgate, reads thus: "*and as*

---

[1] There is no foundation for *Knobel's* assertion, that in chap. xix. 5 sqq. another early lawgiver introduces a milder regulation with regard to the thank-offering, and allows all the thank-offerings to be eaten on the second day. For chap. xix. 5 sqq. does not profess to lay down a universal rule with regard to all the thank-offerings, but presupposes our law, and simply enforces its regulations with regard to the vow and freewill-offerings, and threatens transgressors with severe punishment.

for the flesh, every clean person shall eat flesh," i.e. take part in the sacrificial meal.—Ver. 20. On the other hand, " *the soul which eats flesh of the peace-offering, and his uncleanness is upon him* (for " whilst uncleanness is upon him ;" the suffix is to be understood as referring to נֶפֶשׁ construed as a masculine, see chap. ii. 1), " *shall be cut off* " (see Gen. xvii. 14). This was to be done, whether the uncleanness arose from contact with an unclean object (any unclean thing), or from the uncleanness of man (cf. chap. 12–15), or from an unclean beast (see at chap. xi. 4–8), or from any other unclean abomination. שֶׁקֶץ, abomination, includes the unclean fishes, birds, and smaller animals, to which this expression is applied in chap. xi. 10–42 (cf. Ezek. viii. 10, and Isa. lxvi. 17). Moreover contact with animals that were pronounced unclean so far as eating was concerned, did not produce uncleanness so long as they were alive, or if they had been put to death by man ; but contact with animals that had died a natural death, whether they belonged to the edible animals or not, that is to say, with carrion (see at chap. xi. 8).

There is appended to these regulations, as being substantially connected with them, the prohibition of fat and blood as articles of food (vers. 22–27). By " *the fat of ox, or of sheep, or of goat,*" i.e. the three kinds of animals used in sacrifice, or " *the fat of the beast of which men offer a firing to Jehovah* " (ver. 25), we are to understand only those portions of fat which are mentioned in chap. iii. 3, 4, 9 ; not fat which grows in with the flesh, nor the fat portions of other animals, which were clean but not allowed as sacrifices, such as the stag, the antelope, and other kinds of game.—Ver. 24. The fat of cattle that had fallen (נְבֵלָה), or been torn to pieces (viz. by beasts of prey), was not to be eaten, because it was unclean and defiled the eater (chap. xvii. 15, xxii. 8); but it might be applied " *to all kinds of uses,*" i.e. to the common purposes of ordinary life. *Knobel* observes on this, that " in the case of oxen, sheep, and goats slain in the regular way, this was evidently not allowable. But the law does not say what was to be done with the fat of these animals." Certainly it does not *disertis verbis ;* but indirectly it does so clearly enough. According to chap. xvii. 3 sqq., during the journey through the desert any one who wanted to slaughter an ox, sheep, or goat was to bring the animal to the tabernacle as a sacrificial gift, that the blood might be sprinkled against the altar, and the fat burned upon it. By this regulation every ordinary slaughtering was raised into a sacrifice, and the law determined what was to be done with the fat. Now if afterwards, when the people dwelt in Canaan, cattle were allowed to be slaughtered in any place, and the only prohibition repeated was that against eating blood (Deut. xii. 15, 16, 21 sqq.), whilst the law against eating fat was not renewed; it follows as a matter of course, that when the custom of slaughtering at the tabernacle was restricted to actual sacrifices, the prohibition against eating the fat portions came to an end, so far as those animals were concerned which were slain for consumption and not as sacrifices. The reason for prohibiting fat from being eaten was simply this, that so long as every slaughtering was a sacrifice, the fat portions, which were to be handed over to Jehovah and burned upon the altar, were not to be devoted to earthly purposes, because they were gifts sanctified to God. The eating of the fat, therefore, was neither prohibited on sanitary or social grounds, viz. because fat was injurious to health, as *Maimonides* and other Rabbins maintain, nor for the purpose of promoting the cultivation of olives, as *Michaelis* supposes, nor to prevent its being put into the unclean mouth of man, as *Knobel* imagines; but as being an illegal appropriation of what was sanctified to God, a wicked invasion of the rights of Jehovah, which was to be punished with extermination according to the analogy of Num. xv. 30, 31. The prohibition of blood in vers. 26, 27, extends to birds and cattle; fishes not being mentioned, because the little blood which they possess is not generally eaten. This prohibition Israel was to observe in all its dwelling-places (Ex. xii. 20, cf. chap. x. 23), not only so long as all the slaughterings had the character of sacrifices, but for all ages, because the blood was regarded as the soul of the animal, which God had sanctified as the medium of atonement for the soul of man (chap. xvii. 11), whereby the blood acquired a much higher degree of holiness than the fat.

Vers. 28–36. *Jehovah's share of the peace-offerings.*—Ver. 29. The offerer of the sacrifice was to bring his gift (*corban*) to Jehovah, *i.e.* to bring to the altar the portion which belonged to Jehovah.—Vers. 30, 31. His hands were to bring the firings of Jehovah, *i.e.* the portions to be burned upon the altar (chap. i. 9), viz. " *the fat* (the fat portions, chap. iii. 3, 4) *with the*

breast,"—the former to be burned upon the altar, the latter " *to
wave as a wave-offering before Jehovah.*" חָזֶה, τὸ στηθύνιον
(LXX.), *i.e.,* according to *Pollux,* τῶν στηθῶν τὸ μέσον, *pectus-
culum* or *pectus* (*Vulg.* cf. chap. ix. 20, 21, x. 15), signifies the
breast, the breast-piece of the sacrificial animals,[1] the brisket,
which consists for the most part of cartilaginous fat in the case
of oxen, sheep, and goats, and is one of the most savoury parts;
so that at the family festivities of the ancients, according to
Athen. Deipnos. ii. 70, ix. 10, στηθύνια παχέων ἀρνίων were
dainty bits. The breast-piece was presented to the Lord as a
wave-offering (*tenuphah*), and transferred by Him to Aaron and
his sons (the priests). תְּנוּפָה, from נוּף, הֵנִיף, to swing, to move to
and fro (see Ex. xxxv. 22), is the name applied to a ceremony
peculiar to the peace-offerings and the consecration-offerings : the
priest laid the object to be waved upon the hands of the offerer,
and then placed his own hands underneath, and moved the
hands of the offerer backwards and forwards in a horizontal
direction, to indicate by the movement forwards, *i.e.* in the direction towards the altar, the presentation of the sacrifice, or the
symbolical transference of it to God, and by the movement
backwards, the reception of it back again, as a present which
God handed over to His servants the priests.[2] In the peace-
offerings the waving was performed with the breast-piece, which
was called the " *wave-breast*" in consequence (ver. 34, chap. x.
14, 15 ; Num. vi. 20, xviii. 18 ; Ex. xxix. 27). At the consecration of the priests it was performed with the fat portions,
the right leg, and with some cakes, as well as with the breast of
the fill-offering (chap. viii. 25–29 ; Ex. xxix. 22–26). The ceremony of waving was also carried out with the sheaf of first-

---

[1] The etymology of the word is obscure. According to *Winer, Gesenius,*
and others, it signifies *adspectui patens;* whilst *Meier* and *Knobel* regard
it as meaning literally the division, or middle-piece; and *Dietrich* attributes
to it the fundamental signification, " to be moved," viz. the breast, as being
the part moved by the heart.

[2] In the Talmud (cf. *Gemar. Kiddush* 36, 2, *Gem. Succa* 37, 2, and
Tosaphta Menach. 7, 17), which *Maimonides* and *Rashi* follow, *tenuphah*
is correctly interpreted *ducebat et reducebat ;* but some of the later Rabbins
(*vid. Outram ut sup.*) make it out to have been a movement in the direction
of the four quarters of the heavens, and *Witsius* and others find an allusion in this to the omnipresence of God,—an allusion which is quite out of
character with the occasion.

fruits at the feast of Passover ; with the loaves of the first-
fruits, and thank-offering lambs, at the feast of Pentecost (chap.
xxiii. 11, 20); with the shoulder and meat-offering of the Nazarite (Num. vi. 20) ; with the trespass-offering of the leper (chap.
xiv. 12, 24); with the jealousy-offering (Num. v. 25) ; and lastly
with the Levites, at their consecration (Num. viii. 11 sqq.). In
the case of all these sacrifices, the object waved, after it had
been offered symbolically to the Lord by means of the waving,
became the property of the priests.   But of the lambs, which
were waved at the feast of Pentecost before they were slaughtered, and of the lamb which was brought as a trespass-offering
by the leper, the blood and fat were given up to the altar-fire ;
of the jealousy-offering, only an *azcarah ;* and of the fill-offering, for special reasons, the fat portions and leg, as well as the
cakes.   Even the Levites were given by Jehovah to the priests
to be their own (Num. viii. 19).   The *waving,* therefore, had
nothing in common with the *porricere* of the Romans, as the
portions of the sacrifices which were called *porriciæ* were precisely those which were not only given up to the gods, but burned
upon the altars.   In addition to the wave-breast, which the Lord
gave up to His servants as their share of the peace-offerings, the
officiating priest was also to receive for his portion the right leg
as a *terumah,* or heave-offering, or lifting off.   שׁוֹק is the thigh
in the case of a man (Isa. xlvii. 2 ; Song of Sol. v. 15), and therefore in the case of an animal it is not the fore-leg, or shoulder
(βραχίων, *armus*), which is called זְרֹעַ, or the arm (Num. vi. 19 ;
Deut. xviii. 3), but the hind-leg, or rather the upper part of it or
ham, which is mentioned in 1 Sam. ix. 24 as a peculiarly choice
portion (*Knobel*).   As a portion lifted off from the sacrificial
gifts, it is often called " the *heave-leg*" (ver. 34, chap. x. 14, 15 ;
Num. vi. 20 ; Ex. xxix. 27), because it was lifted or heaved off
from the sacrificial animal, as a gift of honour for the officiating priest, but without being waved like the breast-piece,—
though the more general phrase, " to wave a wave-offering before Jehovah" (chap. x. 15), includes the offering of the heave-
leg (see my *Archæologie* i. pp. 244–5).—Ver. 34. The wave-
breast and heave-leg Jehovah had taken of the children of Israel,
from off the sacrifices of their peace-offerings : *i.e.* had imposed
it upon them as tribute, and had given them to Aaron and his
sons, *i.e.* to the priests, " as a statute for ever,"—in other words, as

a right which they could claim of the Israelites for all ages (cf. Ex. xxvii. 21).—With vers. 35, 36, the instructions concerning the peace-offerings are brought to a close. " *This* (the wave-breast and heave-leg) *is the share of Aaron and his sons from the firings of Jehovah in the day* (*i.e.* which Jehovah assigned to them in the day) *when He caused them to draw near to become priests to Jehovah*," *i.e.*, according to the explanation in ver. 36, " *in the day of their anointing.*" The word מִשְׁחָה in ver. 35, like מָשְׁחָה in Num. xviii. 8, signifies not " *anointing*," but share, *portio*, literally a measuring off, as in Aramæan and Arabic, from מָשַׁח to stroke the hand over anything, to measure, or measure off.

The fulness with which every point in the sacrificial meal is laid down, helps to confirm the significance of the peace-offerings, as already implied in the name זֶבַח sacrificial slaughtering, slain-offering, viz. as indicating that they were intended for, and culminated in a liturgical meal. By placing his hand upon the head of the animal, which had been brought to the altar of Jehovah for the purpose, the offerer signified that with this gift, which served to nourish and strengthen his own life, he gave up the substance of his life to the Lord, that he might thereby be strengthened both body and soul for a holy walk and conversation. To this end he slaughtered the victim and had the blood sprinkled by the priest against the altar, and the fat portions burned upon it, that in these altar-gifts his soul and his inner man might be grounded afresh in the gracious fellowship of the Lord. He then handed over the breast-piece by the process of waving, also the right leg, and a sacrificial cake of each kind, as a heave-offering from the whole to the Lord, who transferred these portions to the priests as His servants, that they might take part as His representatives in the sacrificial meal. In consequence of this participation of the priests, the feast, which the offerer of the sacrifice prepared for himself and his family from the rest of the flesh, became a holy covenant meal, a meal of love and joy, which represented domestic fellowship with the Lord, and thus shadowed forth, on the one hand, rejoicing before the Lord (Deut. xii. 12, 18), and on the other, the blessedness of eating and drinking in the kingdom of God (Luke xiv. 15, xxii. 30). Through the fact that one portion was given up to the Lord, the earthly food was sanctified as a symbol of the true spiritual food, with which the Lord satisfies and refreshes the citizens of His kingdom. This religious aspect of the sacrificial meal will explain the instructions given, viz. that not only the flesh itself, but those who took part in the meal, were all to be clean, and that whatever remained of the flesh was to be burned, on the second or third day respectively, that it might not pass into a state of decomposition. The burning took place a day earlier in the case of the praise-offering than in that of the vow and freewill-offerings, of which the offerer was allowed a longer enjoyment, because they were the products of his own spontaneity, which covered any defect that might attach to the gift itself.

With vers. 37 and 38 the whole of the sacrificial law (chap. i.-vii.) is brought to a close. Among the sacrifices appointed, the fill-offering (הַמִּלֻּאִים) is also mentioned here; though it is not first instituted in these chapters, but in Ex. xxix. 19, 20 (vers. 22, 26, 27, 31). The name may be explained from the phrase to "*fill the hand*," which is not used in the sense of installing a man, or giving him authority, like נָתַן בְּיָד "commit into his hand" in Isa. xxii. 21 (*Knobel*), but was applied primarily to the ceremony of consecrating the priests, as described in chap. viii. 25 sqq., and was restricted to the idea of investiture with the *priesthood* (cf. chap. viii. 33, xvi. 32; Ex. xxviii. 41, xxix. 9, 29, 33, 35; Num. iii. 3; Judg. xvii. 5, 12). This gave rise to the expression "to fill the hand for Jehovah," *i.e.* to provide something to offer to Jehovah (1 Chron. xxix. 5; 2 Chron. xxix. 31, cf. Ex. xxxii. 29). Hence מִלֻּאִים denotes the filling of the hand with sacrificial gifts to be offered to Jehovah, and was used *primarily* of the particular sacrifice through which the priests were symbolically invested at their consecration with the gifts they were to offer, and were empowered, by virtue of this investiture, to officiate at the sacrifices; and *secondly*, in a less restricted sense, of priestly consecration generally (chap. viii. 33, "the days of your consecration"). The allusion to the place in ver. 38, viz. "*in the wilderness of Sinai*," points on the one hand back to Ex. xix. 1, and on the other hand forward to Num. xxvi. 63, 64, and xxxvi. 13, "*in the plains of Moab*" (cf. Num. i. 1, 19, etc.).

The sacrificial law, therefore, with the five species of sacrifices which it enjoins, embraces every aspect in which Israel was to manifest its true relation to the Lord its God. Whilst

the sanctification of the whole man in self-surrender to the Lord
was shadowed forth in the burnt-offerings, the fruits of this
sanctification in the meat-offerings, and the blessedness of the
possession and enjoyment of saving grace in the peace-offerings,
the expiatory sacrifices furnished the means of removing the
barrier which sins and trespasses had set up between the sinner
and the holy God, and procured the forgiveness of sin and guilt,
so that the sinner could attain once more to the unrestricted
enjoyment of the covenant grace. For, provided-only that the
people of God drew near to their God with sacrificial gifts, in
obedience to His commandments and in firm reliance upon His
word, which had connected the forgiveness of sin, strength for
sanctification, and the peace of fellowship with Him, with these
manifestations of their piety, the offerers would receive in truth
the blessings promised them by the Lord. Nevertheless these
sacrifices could not make those who drew near to God with them
and in them "perfect as pertaining to the conscience" (Heb. ix.
9, x. 1), because the blood of bulls and of goats could not
possibly take away sin (Heb. x. 4). The forgiveness of sin
which the atoning sacrifices procured, was only a πάρεσις of past
sins through the forbearance of God (Rom. iii. 25, 26), in anticipation of the true sacrifice of Christ, of which the animal
sacrifices were only a type, and by which the justice of God is
satisfied, and the way opened for the full forgiveness of sin and
complete reconciliation with God. So also the sanctification
and fellowship set forth by the burnt-offerings and peace-offerings, were simply a sanctification of the fellowship already
established by the covenant of the law between Israel and its
covenant God, which pointed forward to the true sanctification
and blessedness that grow out of the righteousness of faith, and
expand through the operation of the Holy Spirit into the true
righteousness and blessedness of the divine peace of reconciliation. The effect of the sacrifices was in harmony with the
nature of the old covenant. The fellowship with God, established by this covenant, was simply a faint copy of that true and
living fellowship with God, which consists in God's dwelling in
our hearts through His Spirit, transforming our spirit, soul, and
body more and more into His own image and His divine nature,
and making us partakers of the glory and blessedness of His
divine life. However intimately the infinite and holy God

connected Himself with His people in the earthly sanctuary of the tabernacle and the altar of burnt-offering, yet so long as this sanctuary stood, the God who was enthroned in the most holy place was separated by the veil from His people, who could only appear before Him in the fore-court, as a proof that the sin which separates unholy man from the holy God had not yet been taken out of the way. Just as the old covenant generally was not intended to secure redemption from sin, but the law was designed to produce the knowledge of sin; so the desire for reconciliation with God was not to be truly satisfied by its sacrificial ordinances, but a desire was to be awakened for that true sacrifice which cleanses from all sins, and the way to be prepared for the appearing of the Son of God, who would exalt the shadows of the Mosaic sacrifices into a substantial reality by giving up His own life as a propitiation for the sins of the whole world, and thus through the one offering of His own holy body would perfect all the manifold sacrifices of the Old Testament economy.

INDUCTION OF AARON AND HIS SONS INTO THE PRIESTLY OFFICE.—CHAP. VIII.-X.

To the law of sacrifice there is appended first of all an account of the fulfilment of the divine command to sanctify Aaron and his sons as priests, which Moses had received upon the mount along with the laws concerning the erection of the sanctuary of the tabernacle (Ex. xxviii. and xxix.). This command could not properly be carried out till after the appointment and regulation of the institution of sacrifice, because most of the laws of sacrifice had some bearing upon this act. The sanctification of the persons, whom God had called to be His priests, consisted in a solemn consecration of these persons to their office by investiture, anointing, and sacrifice (chap. viii.),—their solemn entrance upon their office by sacrifices for themselves and the people (chap. ix.),—the sanctification of their priesthood by the judgment of God upon the eldest sons of Aaron, when about to offer strange fire,—and certain instructions, occasioned by this occurrence, concerning the conduct of the priests in the performance of their service (chap. x.).

Chap. viii. CONSECRATION OF THE PRIESTS AND THE

SANCTUARY (cf. Ex. xxix. 1–37).—The consecration of Aaron and his sons as priests was carried out by Moses according to the instructions in Ex. xxix. 1–36, xl. 12–15; and the anointing of the tabernacle, with the altar and its furniture, as prescribed in Ex. xxix. 37, xxx. 26–29, and xl. 9–11, was connected with it (vers. 10, 11).—Vers. 1–5 contain an account of the preparations for this holy act, the performance of which was enjoined upon Moses by Jehovah after the publication of the laws of sacrifice (ver. 1). Moses brought the persons to be consecrated, the official costume that had been made for them (Ex. xxviii.), the anointing oil (Ex. xxx. 23 sqq.), and the requisite sacrificial offerings (Ex. xxix. 1–3), to the door of the tabernacle (*i.e.* into the court, near the altar of burnt-offering), and then gathered " the whole congregation"—that is to say, the nation in the persons of its elders—there also (see my *Archäologie* ii. p. 221). The definite article before the objects enumerated in ver. 2 may be explained on the ground that they had all been previously and more minutely described. The *" basket of the unleavened"* contained, according to Ex. xxix. 2, 3, (1) unleavened bread, which is called חַלָּה in ver. 26, *i.e.* round flat bread-cakes, and כִּכַּר לֶחֶם (loaf of bread) in Ex. xxix. 23, and was baked for the purpose of the consecration (see at vers. 31, 32); (2) unleavened oil-cakes; and (3) unleavened flat cakes covered with oil (see at chap. ii. 4 and vii. 12).—Ver. 5. When the congregation was assembled, Moses said, *" This is the word which Jehovah commanded you to do."* His meaning was, the substance or essential part of the instructions in Ex. xxviii. 1 and xxix. 1–37, which he had published to the assembled congregation before the commencement of the act of consecration, and which are not repeated here as being already known from those chapters. The congregation had been summoned to perform this act, because Aaron and his sons were to be consecrated as priests for them, as standing mediators between them and the Lord.—Vers. 6–9. After this the act of consecration commenced. It consisted of two parts: first, the consecration of the persons themselves to the office of the priesthood, by washing, clothing, and anointing (vers. 6–13); and secondly, the sacrificial rites, by which the persons appointed to the priestly office were inducted into the functions and prerogatives of priests (vers. 16–36).

Vers. 6–13. The *washing, clothing,* and *anointing.*—Ver. 6.

"*Moses brought Aaron and his sons, and washed them with water ;*"
i.e. directed them to wash themselves, no doubt all over, and not
merely their hands and feet. This cleansing from bodily uncleanness was a symbol of the putting away of the filth of sin ;
the washing of the body, therefore, was a symbol of spiritual
cleansing, without which no one could draw near to God, and
least of all those who were to perform the duties of reconciliation.
—Vers. 7–9. Then followed the clothing of Aaron. Moses put
upon him the body-coat (Ex. xxviii. 39) and girdle (Ex. xxviii.
39 and xxxix. 22), then clothed him with the *meïl* (Ex. xxviii.
31–35) and ephod (Ex. xxviii. 6–14), and the *choshen* with the
Urim and Thummim (Ex. xxviii. 15–30), and put the cap (Ex.
xxviii. 39) upon his head, with the golden diadem over his forehead (Ex. xxviii. 36–38). This investiture, regarded as the
putting on of an important official dress, was a symbol of his
endowment with the character required for the discharge of the
duties of his office, the official costume being the outward sign
of installation in the office which he was to fill.—Vers. 10–12.
According to the directions in Ex. xxx. 26–30 (cf. chap. xl. 9–
11), the anointing was performed first of all upon "*the tabernacle
and everything in it,*" *i.e.* the ark of the covenant, the altar of incense, the candlestick, and table of shew-bread, and their furniture ; and then upon the altar of burnt-offering and its furniture,
and upon the laver and Its pedestal ; and after this, upon Aaron
himself, by the pouring of the holy oil upon his head. This was
followed by the robing and anointing of Aaron's sons, the former
only of which is recorded in ver. 13 (according to Ex. xxviii. 40),
the anointing not being expressly mentioned, although it had not
only been commanded, in Ex. xxviii. 41 and xl. 15, but the performance of it is taken for granted in chap. vii. 36, x. 7, and
Num. iii. 3. According to the Jewish tradition, the anointing
of Aaron (the high priest) was different from that of the sons of
Aaron (the ordinary priests), the oil being *poured* upon the head
of the former, whilst it was merely smeared with the finger upon
the forehead in the case of the latter (cf. *Relandi Antiqq.* ss. ii.
1, 5, and 7, and *Selden, de succ. in pontif.* ii. 2). There appears
to be some foundation for this, as a distinction is assumed between the anointing of the high priest and that of the ordinary
priests, not only in the expression, "he poured of the anointing
oil upon Aaron's head" (ver. 12, cf. Ex. xxix. 7 ; Ps. cxxxiii. 2),

which is applied to Aaron only, but also in chap. xxi. 10, 12 ;
although the further statement of the later Talmudists and
Rabbins, that Aaron was also marked upon the forehead with the
sign of a Hebrew כ (the initial letter of כהן), has no support in
the law (vid. Selden, ii. 9; Vitringa, observv. ss. ii. c. 15, 9).—On
the mode in which the tabernacle and its furniture were anointed,
all that is stated is, that the altar of burnt-offering was anointed
by being sprinkled seven times with the anointing oil; from
which we may safely conclude, that the other portions and
vessels of the sanctuary were anointed in the same way, but that
the sprinkling was not performed more than once in their case.
The reason why the altar was sprinkled seven times with the
holy anointing oil, is to be sought for in its signification as the
place of worship.   The anointing, both of the sacred things and
also of the priests, is called קַדֵּשׁ "to sanctify," in vers. 10–12, as
well as in Ex. xl. 9–11 and 13 ; and in Ex. xl. 10 the following
stipulation is added with regard to the altar of burnt-offering:
" and it shall be most holy,"—a stipulation which is not extended
to the dwelling and its furniture, although those portions of the
sanctuary were most holy also, that the altar of burnt-offering,
which was the holiest object in the court by virtue of its appointment as the place of expiation, might be specially guarded from
being touched by unholy hands (see at Ex. xl. 16).   To impress upon it this highest grade of holiness, it was sprinkled
seven times with anointing oil; and in the number seven, the
covenant number, the seal of the holiness of the covenant of
reconciliation, to which it was to be subservient, was impressed
upon it.   To sanctify is not merely to separate to holy purposes,
but to endow or fill with the powers of the sanctifying Spirit of
God.   Oil was a fitting symbol of the Spirit, or spiritual principle of life, by virtue of its power to sustain and fortify the vital
energy; and the anointing oil, which was prepared according to
divine instructions, was therefore a symbol of the Spirit of God,
as the principle of spiritual life which proceeds from God and
fills the natural being of the creature with the powers of divine
life.   The anointing with oil, therefore, was a symbol of endowment with the Spirit of God (1 Sam. x. 1, 6, xvi. 13, 14; Isa.
lxi. 1) for the duties of the office to which a person was consecrated.   The holy vessels also were not only consecrated, through
the anointing, for the holy purposes to which they were to be

devoted (*Knobel*), but were also furnished in a symbolical sense
with powers of the divine Spirit, which were to pass from them
to the people who came to the sanctuary. The anointing was
not only to sanctify the priests as organs and mediators of the
Spirit of God, but the vessels of the sanctuary also, as channels
and vessels of the blessings of grace and salvation, which God
as the Holy One would bestow upon His people, through the
service of His priests, and in the holy vessels appointed by Him.
On these grounds the consecration of the holy things was associated with the consecration of the priests. The notion that
even vessels, and in fact inanimate things in general, can be endowed with divine and spiritual powers, was very widely spread
in antiquity. We meet with it in the anointing of memorial
stones (Gen. xxviii. 18, xxxv. 14), and it occurs again in the
instructions concerning the expiation of the sanctuary on the
annual day of atonement (chap. xvi.). It contains more truth
than some modern views of the universe, which refuse to admit
that any influence is exerted by the divine Spirit except upon
animated beings, and thus leave a hopeless abyss between spirit
and matter. According to Ex. xxix. 9, the clothing and anointing of Aaron and his sons were to be " *a priesthood to them for a
perpetual statute*," *i.e.* to secure the priesthood to them for all
ages; for the same thought is expressed thus in Ex. xl. 15:
" *their anointing shall surely be an everlasting priesthood throughout their generations.*" When the Talmudists refer these words
to the sons of Aaron or the ordinary priests, to the exclusion of
Aaron or the high priest, this is opposed to the distinct context,
according to which the sons of Aaron were to be anointed like
their father Aaron. The utter want of foundation for the rabbinical assumption, that the anointing of the sons of Aaron, performed by Moses, availed not only for themselves, but for their
successors also, and therefore for the priests of every age, is also
the more indisputable, because the Talmudists themselves infer
from chap. vi. 15 (cf. Ex. xxix. 29), where the installation of
Aaron's successor in his office is expressly designated an anointing, the necessity for every successor of Aaron in the high-priesthood to be anointed. The meaning of the words in question is
no doubt the following: the anointing of Aaron and his sons
was to stand as a perpetual statute for the priesthood, and to
guarantee it to the sons of Aaron for all time; it being assumed

as self-evident, according to chap. vi. 15, that as every fresh generation entered upon office, the anointing would be repeated or renewed.

Vers. 14–32. The *sacrificial ceremony* with which the consecration was concluded, consisted of a threefold sacrifice, the materials for which were not supplied by the persons about to be installed, but were no doubt provided by Moses at the expense of the congregation, for which the priesthood was instituted. Moses officiated as the mediator of the covenant, through whose service Aaron and his sons were to be consecrated as priests of Jehovah, and performed every part of the sacrificial rite,—the slaughtering, sprinkling of the blood, and burning of the altar gifts,—just as the priests afterwards did at the public daily and festal sacrifices, the persons to be consecrated simply laying their hands upon the sacrificial animals, to set them apart as their representatives.—Vers. 14–17. The first sacrifice was a sin-offering, for which a young ox was taken (Ex. xxix. 1), as in the case of the sin-offerings for the high priest and the whole congregation (chap. iv. 3, 14): the highest kind of sacrificial animal, which corresponded to the position to be occupied by the priests in the Israelitish kingdom of God, as the ἐκλογή of the covenant nation. Moses put some of the blood with his finger upon the horns of the altar of burnt-offering, and poured the rest at the foot of the altar. The fat portions (see chap. iii. 3, 4) he burned upon the altar; but the flesh of the ox, as well as the hide and dung, he burned outside the camp. According to the general rule of the sin-offerings, whose flesh was burnt outside the camp, the blood was brought into the sanctuary itself (chap. vi. 23); but here it was only put upon the altar of burnt-offering to make this sin-offering a consecration-sacrifice. Moses was to take the blood to "*purify* (יְחַטֵּא) *and sanctify the altar, to expiate it.*" As the altar had been sanctified immediately before by the anointing with holy oil (ver. 11), the object of the cleansing or sanctification of it through the blood of the sacrifice cannot have been to purify it a second time from uncleanness, that still adhered to it, or was inherent in it; but just as the purification or expiation of the vessels of worship generally applied only to the sins of the nation, by which these vessels had been defiled (chap. xvi. 16, 19), so here the purification of the altar with the blood of the sin-offering, upon which the priests had laid their hands, had reference simply to pollutions, with which the priests defiled the altar when officiating at it, through the uncleanness of their sinful nature. As the priests could not be installed in the functions of the priesthood, notwithstanding the holiness communicated to them through the anointing, without a sin-offering to awaken the consciousness in both themselves and the nation that the sinfulness which lay at the root of human nature was not removed by the anointing, but only covered in the presence of the holy God, and that sin still clung to man, and polluted all his doings and designs; so the altar, upon which they were henceforth to offer sacrifices, still required to be purified through the blood of the bullock, that had been slaughtered as a sin-offering for the expiation of their sins, to sanctify it for the service of the priests, *i.e.* to cover up the sins by which they would defile it when performing their service. For this sanctification the blood of the sin-offering, that had been slaughtered for them, was taken, to indicate the fellowship which was henceforth to exist between them and the altar, and to impress upon them the fact, that the blood, by which they were purified, was also to serve as the means of purifying the altar from the sins attaching to their service. Although none of the blood of this sin-offering was carried into the holy place, because only the anointed priests were to be thereby inducted into the fellowship of the altar, the flesh of the animal could only be burnt outside the camp, because the sacrifice served to purify the priesthood (see chap. iv. 11, 12). For the rest, the remarks made on p. 306 are also applicable to the symbolical meaning of this sacrifice.— Vers. 18-21. The sin-offering, through which the priests and the altar had been expiated, and every disturbance of the fellowship existing between the holy God and His servants at the altar, in consequence of the sin of those who were to be consecrated, had been taken away, was followed by a burnt-offering, consisting of a ram, which was offered according to the ordinary ritual of the burnt-offering (chap. i. 3-9), and served to set forth the priests, who had appointed it as their substitute through the laying on of hands, as a living, holy, and well-pleasing sacrifice to the Lord, and to sanctify them to the Lord with all the faculties of both body and soul.

Vers. 22-29. This was followed by the presentation of a peace-offering, which also consisted of a ram, called *"the ram of the*

filling," or "*of the fill-offering,*" from the peculiar ceremony performed with the flesh, by which this sacrifice became a consecration-offering, inducting the persons consecrated into the possession
and enjoyment of the privileges of the priesthood. A ram was
offered as a peace-offering, by the nation as a whole (chap. ix. 4,
18), the tribe-princes (Num. vii. 17 sqq.), and a Nazarite (Num. vi.
14, 17), who also occupied a higher position in the congregation
(Amos ii. 11, 12); but it was never brought by a private Israelite
for a peace-offering. The offering described here differed from
the rest of the peace-offerings, first of all, in the ceremony performed with the blood (vers. 23 and 24, cf. Ex. xxix. 20, 21).
Before sprinkling the blood upon the altar, Moses put some of it
upon the tip of the right ear, upon the right thumb, and upon
the great toe of the right foot of Aaron and his sons. Thus he
touched the extreme points, which represented the whole, of the
ear, hand, and foot on the right, or more important and principal
side : the *ear*, because the priest was always to hearken to the
word and commandment of God; the *hand*, because he was to
discharge the priestly functions properly; and the *foot*, because
he was to walk correctly in the sanctuary. Through this mani-
pulation the three organs employed in the priestly service were
placed, by means of their tips, *en rapport* with the sacrificial
blood; whilst through the subsequent sprinkling of the blood
upon the altar they were introduced symbolically within the
sphere of the divine grace, by virtue of the sacrificial blood, which
represented the soul as the principle of life, and covered it in the
presence of the holiness of God, to be sanctified by that grace to
the rendering of willing and righteous service to the Lord. The
sanctification was at length completed by Moses' taking some of
the anointing oil and some of the blood upon the altar, and
sprinkling Aaron and his sons, and also their clothes ; that is to
say, by his sprinkling the persons themselves, as bearers of the
priesthood, and their clothes, as the insignia of the priesthood,
with a mixture of holy anointing oil and sacrificial blood taken
from the altar (ver. 30). The blood taken from the altar shadowed forth the soul as united with God through the medium of
the atonement, and filled with powers of grace. The holy
anointing oil was a symbol of the Spirit of God. Consequently,
through this sprinkling the priests were endowed, both soul and
spirit, with the higher powers of the divine life. The sprinkling,

however, was performed, not upon the persons alone, but also upon their official dress. For it had reference to the priests, not in their personal or individual relation to the Lord, but in their official position, and with regard to their official work in the congregation of the Lord.[1]

In addition to this, the following appointment is contained in Ex. xxix. 29, 30 : "The holy garments of Aaron shall be his sons' after him," *i.e.* pass to his successors in the high-priesthood, " to anoint them therein and fill their hands therein. Seven days shall the priest of his sons in his stead put them on (לְבָשָׁם with the suffix ◌ָם‎ as in Gen. xix. 19), who shall go into the tabernacle to serve in the sanctuary." Accordingly, at Aaron's death his successor Eleazar was dressed in his robes (Num. xx. 26–28). It by no means follows from this, that a formal priestly consecration was repeated solely in the case of the high priest as the head of the priesthood, and that with the common priests the first anointing by Moses sufficed for all time. We have already observed at p. 337 that this is not involved in Ex. xl. 15 ; and the fact that it is only the official costume of the high priest which is expressly said to have passed to his successor, may be explained on the simple ground, that as his dress was only worn when he was discharging certain special functions before Jehovah, it would not be worn out so soon as the dress of the ordinary priests, which was worn in the daily service, and therefore would hardly last long enough to be handed down from father to son.[2]

The ceremony performed with the flesh of this sacrifice was also peculiarly significant (vers. 25–29). Moses took the fat portions, which were separated from the flesh in the case

---

[1] In the instructions in Ex. xxix. 21 this ceremony is connected with the sprinkling of the blood upon the altar ; but here, on the contrary, it is mentioned after the burning of the flesh. Whether because it was not performed till after this, or because it is merely recorded here in a supplementary form, it is difficult to decide. The latter is the more probable, because the blood upon the altar would soon run off ; so that if Moses wanted to take any of it off, it could not be long delayed.

[2] It no more follows from the omission of express instructions concerning the repetition of the ceremony in the case of every priest who had to be consecrated, that the future priests were not invested, anointed, and in all respects formally consecrated, than the fact that the anointing is not mentioned in ver. 13 proves that the priests were not anointed at all

of the ordinary peace-offerings and burned upon the altar, and the right leg, which was usually assigned to the officiating priest, and then laid by the pieces of flesh (or upon them) another cake of each of the three kinds of pastry, which fell to the portion of the priest in other cases, as a heave-offering for Jehovah, and put all this into the hands of Aaron and his sons, and waved it as a wave-offering for Jehovah, after which he took it from their hands and burned it upon the altar, " *as a filling* (מִלְאִים) *for a savour of satisfaction, as a firing for Jehovah.*" These last words, which are attached to the preceding without a conjunction, and, as the הֵם and הוּא show, form independent clauses (*lit. "filling are they . . . a firing is it for Jehovah"*), contain the reason for this unusual proceeding, so that *Luther's* explanation is quite correct, " for it is a fill-offering," etc. The ceremony of handing the portions mentioned to Aaron and his sons denoted the filling of their hands with the sacrificial gifts, which they were afterwards to offer to the Lord in the case of the peace-offerings, viz. the fat portions as a firing upon the altar, the right leg along with the bread-cake as a wave-offering, which the Lord then relinquished to them as His own servants. The filling of their hands with these sacrificial gifts, from which the offering received the name of fill-offering, signified on the one hand the communication of the right belonging to the priest to offer the fat portions to the Lord upon the altar, and on the other hand the enfeoffment of the priests with gifts, which they were to receive in future for their service. This symbolical signification of the act in question serves to explain the circumstance, that both the fat portions, which were to be burned upon the altar, and also the right leg with the bread-cakes which formed the priests' share of the peace-offerings, were merely placed in the priests' hands in this instance, and presented symbolically to the Lord by waving, and then burned by Moses upon the altar. For Aaron and his sons were not only to be enfeoffed with what they were to burn unto the Lord, but also with what they would receive for their service. And as even the latter was a prerogative bestowed upon them by the Lord, it was right that at their consecration they should offer it *symbolically* to the Lord by waving, and *actually* by burning upon the altar. But as the right leg was devoted to another purpose in this case, Moses received the breast-piece, which was presented to the Lord by waving (ver. 29), and which afterwards fell to the lot of the priests, as his portion for the sacrificial meal, which formed the conclusion of this dedicatory offering, as it did of all the peace-offerings. In Ex. xxix. 27, 28, we also find the command, that the wave-breast of the ram of the fill-offering, and the heave-leg which had been lifted off, should afterwards belong to Aaron and his sons on the part of the children of Israel, as a perpetual statute, *i.e.* as a law for all time; and the following reason is assigned: "*for it is a heave-offering (terumah, a lifting off), and shall be a heave-offering on the part of the children of Israel of their peace-offerings, their heave-offering for Jehovah,*" *i.e.* which they were to give to the Lord from their peace-offerings for the good of His servants. The application of the word *terumah* to both kinds of offering, the wave-breast and the heave-shoulder, may be explained on the simple ground, that the gift to be waved had to be lifted off from the sacrificial animal before the waving could be performed.—Vers. 31, 32. For the sacrificial meal, the priests were to boil the flesh in front of the door of the taber-nacle, or, according to Ex. xxix. 31, "at the holy place," *i.e.* in the court, and eat it with the bread in the fill-offering basket; and no stranger (*i.e.* layman or non-priest) was to take part in the meal, because the flesh and bread were holy (Ex. xxix. 33), that is to say, had served to make atonement for the priests, to fill their hands and sanctify them. Atoning virtue is attributed to this sacrifice in the same sense as to the burnt-offering in chap. i. 4. Whatever was left of the flesh and bread until the follow-ing day, that is to say, was not eaten on the day of sacrifice, was to be burned with fire, for the reason explained at chap. vii. 17. The exclusion of laymen from participating in this sacrificial meal is to be accounted for in the same way as the prohibition of unleavened bread, which was offered and eaten in the case of the ordinary peace-offerings along with the unleavened sacrificial cakes (see at chap. vii. 13). The meal brought the consecration of the priests to a close, as Aaron and his sons were thereby re-ceived into that special, priestly covenant with the Lord, the bless-ings and privileges of which were to be enjoyed by the consecrated priests alone. At this meal the priests were not allowed to eat leavened bread, any more than the nation generally at the feast of Passover (Ex. xii. 8 sqq.).

Vers. 33–36 (cf. Ex. xxix. 35–37). The consecration was to

last seven days, during which time the persons to be consecrated were not to go away from the door of the tabernacle, but to remain there day and night, and watch the watch of the Lord that they might not die. *"For the Lord will fill your hand seven days. As they have done on this* (the first) *day, so has Jehovah commanded to do to make atonement for you"* (ver. 34). That is to say, the rite of consecration which has been performed upon you to-day, Jehovah has commanded to be performed or repeated for seven days. These words clearly imply that the whole ceremony, in all its details, was to be repeated for seven days; and in Ex. xxix. 36, 37, besides the filling of the hands which was to be continued seven days, and which presupposes the daily repetition of the consecration-offering, the preparation of the sin-offering for reconciliation and the expiation or purification and anointing of the altar are expressly commanded for each of the seven days. This repetition of the act of consecration is to be regarded as intensifying the consecration itself; and the limitation of it to seven days is to be accounted for from the signification and holiness of the number seven as the sign of the completion of the works of God. The commandment not to leave the court of the tabernacle during the whole seven days, is of course not to be understood literally (as it is by some of the Rabbins), as meaning that the persons to be consecrated were not even to go away from the spot for the necessities of nature (cf. *Lund. jüd. Heiligth.* p. 448); but when taken in connection with the clause which follows, *" and keep the charge of the Lord,"* it can only be understood as signifying that during these days they were not to leave the sanctuary to attend to any earthly avocation whatever, but uninterruptedly to observe the charge of the Lord, *i.e.* the consecration commanded by the Lord. שָׁמַר מִשְׁמֶרֶת, *lit.* to watch the watch of a person or thing, *i.e.* to attend to them, to do whatever was required for noticing or attending to them (cf. Gen. xxvi. 5, and *Hengstenberg, Christology*).

Chap. ix. ENTRANCE OF AARON AND HIS SONS UPON THEIR OFFICE.—Vers. 1-7. On the eighth day, *i.e.* on the day after the seven days' consecration, Aaron and his sons entered upon their duties with a solemn sacrifice for themselves and the nation, to which the Lord had made Himself known by a special revelation of His glory, to bear solemn witness before the whole nation that their service at the altar was acceptable to Him, and to impress the divine seal of confirmation upon the consecration they had received. To this end Aaron and his sons were to bring to the front of the tabernacle a young calf as a sin-offering for themselves, and a ram for a burnt-offering; and the people were to bring through their elders a he-goat for a sin-offering, a yearling calf and yearling sheep for a burnt-offering, and an ox and ram for a peace-offering, together with a meat-offering of meal mixed with oil; and the congregation (in the persons of its elders) was to stand there before Jehovah, *i.e.* to assemble together at the sanctuary for the solemn transaction (vers. 1-5). If, according to this, even after the manifold expiation and consecration, which Aaron had received through Moses during the seven days, he had still to enter upon his service with a sin-offering and burnt-offering, this fact clearly showed that the offerings of the law could not ensure perfection (Heb. x. 1 sqq.). It is true that on this occasion a young calf was sufficient for a sin-offering for the priests, not a mature ox as in chap. viii. 14 and iv. 3; and so also for the burnt-offerings and peace-offerings of the people smaller sacrifices sufficed, either smaller in kind or fewer in number than at the leading feasts (Num. xxviii. 11 sqq.). Nevertheless, not one of the three sacrifices could be omitted; and if no special peace-offering was required of Aaron, this may be accounted for from the fact, that the whole of the sacrificial ceremony terminated with a national peace-offering, in which the priests took part, uniting in this instance with the rest of the nation in the celebration of a common sacrificial meal, to make known their oneness with them.—Vers. 6, 7. After everything had been prepared for the solemn ceremony, Moses made known to the assembled people what Jehovah had commanded them to do in order that His glory might appear (see at Ex. xvi. 10). Aaron was to offer the sacrifices that had been brought for the reconciliation of himself and the nation.

Vers. 8-21. Accordingly, he offered first of all the sin-offering and burnt-offering for himself, and then (vers. 15-21) the offerings of the people. The sin-offering always went first, because it served to remove the estrangement of man from the holy God arising from sin, by means of the expiation of the sinner, and to clear away the hindrances to his approach to

God. Then followed the burnt-offering, as an expression of the complete surrender of the person expiated to the Lord; and lastly the peace-offering, on the one hand as the utterance of thanksgiving for mercy received, and prayer for its further continuance, and on the other hand, as a seal of covenant fellowship with the Lord in the sacrificial meal. But when Moses says in ver. 7, that Aaron is to make atonement for himself and the nation with his sin-offering and burnt-offering, the atoning virtue which Aaron's sacrifice was to have for the nation also, referred not to sins which the people had committed, but to the guilt which the high priest, as the head of the whole congregation, had brought upon the nation by his sin (chap. iv. 3). In offering the sacrifices, Aaron was supported by his sons, who handed him the blood to sprinkle, and the sacrificial portions to burn upon the altar. The same course was adopted with Aaron's sin-offering (vers. 8-11) as Moses had pursued with the sin-offering at the consecration of the priests (chap. viii. 14-17). The blood was not taken into the sanctuary, but only applied to the horns of the altar of burnt-offering; because the object was not to expiate some particular sin of Aaron's, but to take away the sin which might make his service on behalf of the congregation displeasing to God; and the communion of the congregation with the Lord was carried on at the altar of burnt-offering. The flesh and skin of the animal were burnt outside the camp, as in the case of all the sin-offerings for the priesthood (chap. iv. 11, 12).—Vers. 12-14. The burnt-offering was presented according to the general rule (chap. i. 3-9), as in chap. viii. 18-21. הִמְצִיא (ver. 12): to cause to attain; here, and in ver. 18, to present, hand over. לִנְתָחֶיהָ, according to its pieces, into which the burnt-offering was divided (chap. i. 6), and which they offered to Aaron one by one. No meat-offering was connected with Aaron's burnt-offerings, partly because the law contained in Num. xv. 2 sqq. had not yet been given, but more especially because Aaron had to bring the special meat-offering commanded in chap. vi. 13, and had offered this in connection with the morning burnt-offering mentioned in ver. 17; though this offering, as being a constant one, and not connected with the offerings especially belonging to the consecration of the priests, is not expressly mentioned.—Vers. 15 sqq. Of the sacrifices of the nation, Aaron presented the sin-offering in the same manner as the first, *i.e.* the one offered for himself (vers. 8 sqq.). The blood of this sin-offering, which was presented for the congregation, was not brought into the holy place according to the rule laid down in chap. iv. 16 sqq., but only applied to the horns of the altar of burnt-offering; for the same reason as in the previous case (vers. 8 sqq.), viz. because the object was not to expiate any particular sin, or the sins of the congregation that had been committed in the course of time and remained unatoned for, but simply to place the sacrificial service of the congregation in its proper relation to the Lord. Aaron was reproved by Moses, however, for having burned the flesh (chap. x. 16 sqq.), but was able to justify it (see at chap. x. 16–20). The sin-offering (ver. 16) was also offered " *according to the right*" (as in chap. v. 10). Then followed the meat-offering (ver. 17), of which Aaron burned a handful upon the altar (according to the rule in chap. ii. 1, 2). He offered this in addition to the morning burnt-offering (Ex. xxix. 39), to which a meat-offering also belonged (Ex. xxix. 40), and with which, according to chap. vi. 12 sqq., the special meat-offering of the priests was associated. Last of all (vers. 18–21) there followed the peace-offering, which was also carried out according to the general rule. In הַמְכַסֶּה, " *the covering*" (ver. 19), the two fat portions mentioned in chap. iii. 3 are included. The fat portions were laid upon the breast-pieces by the sons of Aaron, and then handed by them to Aaron, the fat to be burned upon the altar, the breast to be waved along with the right leg, according to the instructions in chap. vii. 30–36. The meat-offering of pastry, which belonged to the peace-offering according to chap. vii. 12, 13, is not specially mentioned.

Vers. 22–24. When the sacrificial ceremony was over, Aaron blessed the people from the altar with uplifted hands (cf. Num. vi. 22 sqq.), and then came down : *sc.* from the bank surrounding the altar, upon which he had stood while offering the sacrifice (see at Ex. xxvii. 4, 5).—Ver. 23. After this Moses went with him into the tabernacle, to introduce him into the sanctuary, in which he was henceforth to serve the Lord, and to present him to the Lord : not to offer incense, which would undoubtedly have been mentioned; nor yet for the special purpose of praying for the manifestation of the glory of Jehovah, although there can be no doubt that they offered prayer in the sanctuary, and prayed for the blessing of the Lord for the right discharge of the office entrusted to them in a manner well-pleasing to Him.   On coming out again they united in bestowing that blessing upon the people which they had solicited for them in the sanctuary.   *" Then the glory of Jehovah appeared to all the people, and fire came out from before the face of Jehovah and consumed the burnt-offering and fat portions upon the altar"* (*i.e.* the sin and peace-offerings, not the thank-offerings merely, as *Knobel* supposes, according to his mistaken theory).   The appearance of the glory of Jehovah is probably to be regarded in this instance, and also in Num. xvi. 19, xvii. 7, and xx. 6, as the sudden flash of a miraculous light, which proceeded from the cloud that covered the tabernacle, probably also from the cloud in the most holy place, or as a sudden though very momentary change of the cloud, which enveloped the glory of the Lord, into a bright light, from which the fire proceeded in this instance in the form of lightning, and consumed the sacrifices upon the altar.   The fire issued " from before the face of Jehovah," *i.e.* from the visible manifestation of Jehovah.   It did not come down from heaven, like the fire of Jehovah, which consumed the sacrifices of David and Solomon (1 Chron. xxi. 26 ; 2 Chron. vii. 1).

The Rabbins believe that this divine fire was miraculously sustained upon the altar until the building of Solomon's temple, at the dedication of which it fell from heaven afresh, and then continued until the restoration of the temple-worship under Manasseh (2 Chron. xxxiii. 16 ; cf. *Buxtorf exercitatt. ad histor. ignis sacri*, c. 2) ; and the majority of them maintain still further, that it continued side by side with the ordinary altar-fire, which was kindled by the priests (chap. i. 7), and, according to chap. vi. 6, kept constantly burning by them.   The earlier Christian expositors are for the most part of opinion, that the heavenly fire, which proceeded miraculously from God and burned the first sacrifices of Aaron, was afterwards maintained by the priests by natural means (see *J. Marckii sylloge diss. philol. theol. ex.* vi. ad Lev. vi. 13).   But there is no foundation in the Scriptures for either of these views.   There is not a syllable about any miraculous preservation of the heavenly fire by the side of the fire which the priests kept burning by natural means.   And even the modified opinion of the Christian theologians, that the heavenly fire was preserved by natural means, rests upon the assumption, which there is nothing to justify, that the sacrifices offered by Aaron were first burned by the fire which issued from Jehovah, and therefore that the statements in the text, with reference to the burning of the fat portions and burnt-offerings, or causing them to ascend in smoke (vers. 10, 13, 17, and 20), are to be regarded as anticipations (*per anticipationem accipienda, C. a Lap.*), *i.e.* are to be understood as simply meaning, that when Aaron officiated at the different sacrifices, he merely laid upon the altar the pieces intended for it, but without setting them on fire. The fallacy of this is proved, not only by the verb הִקְטִיר, but by the fact implied in ver. 17, that the offering of these sacrifices, with which Aaron entered upon his office, was preceded by the daily morning burnt-offering, and consequently that at the time when Aaron began to carry out the special sacrifices of this day there was fire already burning upon the altar, and in fact a continual fire, that was never to be allowed to go out (chap. vi. 6). Even, therefore, if we left out of view the fire of the daily morning and evening sacrifice, which had been offered from the first day on which the tabernacle was erected (Ex. xl. 29), there were sacrifices presented every day during the seven days of the consecration of the priests (chap. viii.); and according to chap. i. 7, Moses must necessarily have prepared the fire for these. If it had been the intention of God, therefore, to originate the altar-fire by supernatural means, this would no doubt have taken place immediately after the erection of the tabernacle, or at least at the consecration of the altar, which was connected with that of the priests, and immediately after it had been anointed (chap. viii. 11). But as God did not do this, the burning of the altar-sacrifices by a fire which proceeded from Jehovah, as related in this verse, cannot have been intended to give a sanction to the altar-fire as having proceeded from God Himself, which was to be kept constantly burning, either by miraculous preservation, or by being fed in a natural way. The legends of the heathen, therefore, about altar-fires which had been kindled by the gods themselves present no analogy to the fact before us (cf. *Serv. ad Æn.* xii. 200; *Solin.* v. 23; *Pausan.* v. 27, 3; *Bochart, Hieroz.* lib. ii. c. 35, pp. 378 sqq.; *Dougtæi analect. ss.* pp. 79 sqq.).

The miracle recorded in this verse did not consist in the fact that the sacrificial offerings placed upon the altar were burned by fire which proceeded from Jehovah, but in the fact that the sacrifices, which were already on fire, were suddenly consumed by it. For although the verb תֹאכַל admits of both meanings, setting on fire and burning up (see Judg. vi. 21, and 1 Kings xviii. 38), the word literally denotes consuming or burning up, and must be taken in the stricter and more literal sense in the case before us, inasmuch as there was already fire upon the altar when the sacrifices were placed upon it. God caused this miracle, not to generate a supernatural altar-fire, but *ut ordinem sacerdotalem legis veteris a se institutum et suas de sacrificio leges hoc miraculo confirmaret et quasi obsignaret* (*C. a Lap.*), or to express it more briefly, to give a divine consecration to the altar, or sacrificial service of Aaron and his sons, through which a way was to be opened for the people to His throne of grace, and whereby, moreover, the altar-fire was consecrated *eo ipso* into a divine, *i.e.* divinely appointed, means of reconciliation to the community. The whole nation rejoiced at this glorious manifestation of the satisfaction of God with this the first sacrifice of the consecrated priests, and fell down upon their faces to give thanks to the Lord for His mercy.

Chap. x. The Sanctification of the Priesthood by both the Act and Word of God.—Vers. 1–3. The Lord had only just confirmed and sanctified the sacrificial service of Aaron and his sons by a miracle, when He was obliged to sanctify Himself by a judgment upon Nadab and Abihu, the eldest sons of Aaron (Ex. vi. 23), on account of their abusing the office they had received, and to vindicate Himself before the congregation, as one who would not suffer His commandments to be broken with impunity.—Ver. 1. Nadab and Abihu took their censers (*machtah*, Ex. xxv. 38), and having put fire in them, placed incense thereon, and brought strange fire before Jehovah, which He had not commanded them. It is not very clear what the offence of which they were guilty actually was. The majority of expositors suppose the sin to have consisted in the fact, that they did not take the fire for the incense from the altar-fire. But this had not yet been commanded by God; and in fact it is never commanded at all, except with regard to the incense-offering, with which the high priest entered the most holy place on the day of atonement (chap. xvi. 12), though we may certainly infer from this, that it was also the rule for the daily incense-offering. By the fire which they offered before Jehovah, we are no doubt to understand the firing of the incense-offering. This might be called "strange fire" if it was not offered in the manner prescribed in the law, just as in Ex. xxx. 9 incense not prepared according to the direction of God is called "strange incense." The supposition that they presented an incense-offering that was not commanded in the law, and apart from the time of the morning and evening sacrifice, and that this constituted their sin, is supported by the time at which their illegal act took place. It is perfectly obvious from vers. 12 sqq. and 16 sqq. that it occurred in the interval between the sacrificial transaction in chap. ix. and the sacrificial meal which followed it, and therefore upon the day of their inauguration. For in ver. 12 Moses commands Aaron and his remaining sons Eleazar and Ithamar to eat the meat-offering that was left from the firings of Jehovah, and inquires in ver. 16 for the goat of the sin-offering, which the priests were to have eaten in a holy place. *Knobel's* opinion is not an improbable one, therefore, that Nadab and Abihu intended to accompany the shouts of the people with an incense-offering to the praise and glory of God, and presented an incense-offering not only at an improper time, but not prepared from the altar-fire, and committed such a sin by this will-worship, that they were smitten by the fire which came forth from Jehovah, even before their entrance into the holy place, and so died "*before Jehovah*." The expression "before Jehovah" is applied to the presence of God, both in the dwelling (viz. the holy place and the holy of holies, *e.g.* chap. iv. 6, 7, xvi. 13) and also in the court (*e.g.* chap. i. 5, etc.). It is in the latter sense that it is to be taken here, as is evident from ver. 4, where the persons slain are said to have lain "before the sanctuary of the dwelling," *i.e.* in the court of the tabernacle. The fire of the holy God (Ex. xix. 18), which had just sanctified the service of Aaron as well-pleasing to God, brought destruction upon his two eldest sons, because they had not sanctified Jehovah in their hearts, but had taken upon themselves a self-willed service ; just as the same gospel is to one a savour of life unto life, and to another a savour of death unto death (2 Cor. ii. 16).—In ver. 3 Moses explains this judgment to Aaron : "*This is it that Jehovah spake, saying, I will sanctify Myself in him that is nigh to Me, and will glorify My-*

self in the face of all the people." אֶכָּבֵד is unquestionably to be taken in the same sense as in Ex. xiv. 4, 17; consequently אֶקָּדֵשׁ is to be taken in a reflective and not in a passive sense, as in Ezek. xxxviii. 16. The imperfects are used as aorists, in the sense of what God does at all times. But these words of Moses are no "reproof to Aaron, who had not restrained the untimely zeal of his sons" (*Knobel*), nor a reproach which made Aaron responsible for the conduct of his sons, but a simple explanation of the judgment of God, which should be taken to heart by every one, and involved an admonition to all who heard it, not to Aaron only but to the whole nation, to sanctify God continually in the proper way. Moreover Jehovah had not communicated to Moses by revelation the words which he spoke here, but had made the fact known by the position assigned to Aaron and his sons through their election to the priesthood. By this act Jehovah had brought them near to Himself (Num. xvi. 5), made them קְרֹבָי = קְרֹבִים לַיהוָה "*persons standing near to Jehovah*" (Ezek. xlii. 13, xliii. 19), and sanctified them to Himself by anointing (chap. viii. 10, 12; Ex. xxix. 1, 44, xl. 13, 15), that they might sanctify Him in their office and life. If they neglected this sanctification, He sanctified Himself in them by a penal judgment (Ezek. xxxviii. 16), and thereby glorified Himself as the Holy One, who is not to be mocked. "*And Aaron held his peace.*" He was obliged to acknowledge the righteousness of the holy God.

Vers. 4–7. Moses then commanded Mishael and Elzaphan, the sons of Uzziel Aaron's paternal uncle, Aaron's cousins therefore, to carry their brethren (relations) who had been slain from before the sanctuary out of the camp, and, as must naturally be supplied, to bury them there. The expression, " before the sanctuary" (equivalent to " before the tabernacle of the congregation" in chap. ix. 5), shows that they had been slain in front of the entrance to the holy place. They were carried out in their priests' body-coats, since they had also been defiled by the judgment. It follows from this, too, that the fire of Jehovah had not burned them up, but had simply killed them as with a flash of lightning.—Vers. 6 sqq. Moses prohibited Aaron and his remaining sons from showing any sign of mourning on account of this fatal calamity. " *Uncover not your heads,*" *i.e.* do not go about with your hair dishevelled, or flowing free and in disorder (chap. xiii. 45). פֶּרַע רֹאשׁ does not signify merely uncovering the head by taking off the head-band (LXX., *Vulg.*, *Kimchi*, etc.), or by shaving off the hair (*Ges.* and others; see on the other hand *Knobel* on chap. xxi. 10), but is to be taken in a similar sense to פֶּרַע שֵׂעַר רֹאשׁוֹ, the free growth of the hair, not cut short with scissors (Num. vi. 5; Ezek. xliv. 20). It is derived from פָּרַע, to let loose from anything (Prov. i. 25, iv. 5, etc.), to let a people loose, equivalent to giving them the reins (Ex. xxxii. 25), and signifies *solvere crines, capellos*, to leave the hair in disorder, which certainly implies the laying aside of the head-dress in the case of the priest, though without consisting in this alone. On this sign of mourning among the Roman and other nations, see *M. Geier de Ebræorum luctu* viii. 2. The Jews observe the same custom still, and in times of deep mourning neither wash themselves, nor cut their hair, nor pare their nails (see *Buxtorf, Synog. jud.* p. 706). They were also not to rend their clothes, *i.e.* not to make a rent in the clothes in front of the breast,—a very natural expression of grief, by which the sorrow of the heart was to be laid bare, and one which was not only common among the Israelites (Gen. xxxvii. 29, xliv. 13; 2 Sam. i. 11, iii. 31, xiii. 31), but was very widely spread among the other nations of antiquity (cf. *Geier* l.c. xxii. 9). פָּרַם, to rend, occurs, in addition to this passage, in chap. xiii. 45, xxi. 10; in other places קָרַע, to tear in pieces, is used. Aaron and his sons were to abstain from these expressions of sorrow, " lest they should die and wrath come upon all the people." Accordingly, we are not to seek the reason for this prohibition merely in the fact, that they would defile themselves by contact with the corpses, a reason which afterwards led to this prohibition being raised into a general law for the high priest (chap. xxi. 10, 11). The reason was simply this, that any manifestation of grief on account of the death that had occurred, would have indicated dissatisfaction with the judgment of God; and Aaron and his sons would thereby not only have fallen into mortal sin themselves, but have brought down upon the congregation the wrath of God, which fell upon it through every act of sin committed by the high priest in his official position (chap. iv. 3). " *Your brethren,* (namely) *the whole house of Israel, may bewail this burning*" (the burning of the wrath of Jehovah). Mourning was permitted to the nation, as an expression of sorrow on account of the calamity which had befallen the whole nation in the consecrated priests. For the nation generally did not stand in such close fellowship with Jehovah as the priests, who had been consecrated by anointing.—Ver. 7. The latter were not to go away from the door (the entrance or court of the tabernacle), *sc.* to take part in the burial of the dead, lest they should die, for the anointing oil of Jehovah was upon them. The anointing oil was the symbol of the Spirit of God, which is a Spirit of life, and therefore has nothing in common with death, but rather conquers death, and sin, which is the source of death (cf. chap. xxi. 12).

Vers. 8-11. Jehovah still further commanded Aaron and his sons not to drink wine and strong drink when they entered the tabernacle to perform service there, on pain of death, as a perpetual statute for their generations (Ex. xii. 17), that they might be able to distinguish between the holy and common, the clean and unclean, and also to instruct the children of Israel in all the laws which God had spoken to them through Moses (וֹ . . . וֹ, vers. 10 and 11, *et . . . et*, both . . . and also). *Shecar* was an intoxicating drink made of barley and dates or honey. הֹל, *profanus*, common, is a wider or more comprehensive notion than טָמֵא, unclean. Everything was common (profane) which was not fitted for the sanctuary, even what was allowable for daily use and enjoyment, and therefore was to be regarded as clean. The motive for laying down on this particular occasion a prohibition which was to hold good for all time, seems to lie in the event recorded in ver. 1, although we can hardly infer from this, as some commentators have done, that Nadab and Abihu offered the unlawful incense-offering in a state of intoxication. The connection between their act and this prohibition consisted simply in the rashness, which had lost the clear and calm reflection that is indispensable to right action.

Vers. 12-20. After the directions occasioned by this judgment of God, Moses reminded Aaron and his sons of the general laws concerning the consumption of the priests' portions of the sacrifices, and their relation to the existing circumstances: first of all (vers. 12, 13), of the law relating to the eating of the meat-offering, which belonged to the priests after the *azcarah* had been lifted off (chap. ii. 3, vi. 9-11), and then (vers. 14, 15) of that relating to the wave-breast and heave-leg (chap. vii.

32—34). By the *minchah* in ver. 12 we are to understand the
meal and oil, which were offered with the burnt-offering of the
nation (chap. ix. 4 and 7) ; and by the אִשִּׁים in vers. 12 and 15,
those portions of the burnt-offering, meat-offering, and peace-
offering of the nation which were burned upon the altar (chap.
ix. 13, 17, and 20). He then looked for " *the he-goat of the sin-
offering,*"—*i.e.* the flesh of the goat which had been brought for
a sin-offering (chap. ix. 15), and which was to have been eaten
by the priests in the holy place along with the sin-offerings,
whose blood was not taken into the sanctuary (chap. vi. 19,
22) ;—" *and, behold, it was burned*" (שֹׂרָף, 3 *perf. Pual*). Moses
was angry at this, and reproved Eleazar and Ithamar, who had
attended to the burning : " *Wherefore have ye not eaten the sin-
offering in a holy place ?*" he said ; " *for it is most holy, and He*
(Jehovah) *hath given it you to bear the iniquity of the congregation, to make atonement for it before Jehovah,*" as its blood had
not been brought into the holy place (הוּבָא construed as a passive with an accusative, as in Gen. iv. 18, etc.). " *To bear the
iniquity*" does not signify here, as in chap. v. 1, to bear and
atone for the sin in its consequences, but, as in Ex. xxviii. 38, to
take the sin of another upon one's self, for the purpose of can-
celling it, to make expiation for it. As, according to Ex. xxviii.
38, the high priest was to appear before the Lord with the
diadem upon his forehead, as the symbol of the holiness of his
office, to cancel, as the mediator of the nation and by virtue
of his official holiness, the sin which adhered to the holy
gifts of the nation (see the note on this passage), so here
it is stated with regard to the official eating of the most holy
flesh of the sin-offering, which had been enjoined upon the
priests, that they were thereby to bear the sin of the congregation, to make atonement for it. This effect or signification could only be ascribed to the eating, by its being
regarded as an incorporation of the victim laden with sin,
whereby the priests actually took away the sin by virtue of
the holiness and sanctifying power belonging to their office,
and not merely declared it removed, as *Oehler* explains the
words (*Herzog's* Cycl. x. p. 649). Ex. xxviii. 38 is decisive in
opposition to the declaratory view, which does not embrace
the meaning of the words, and is not applicable to the passage at all. " Incorporabant quasi peccatum populique reatum

in se recipiebant" (*Deyling observv. ss.* i. 45, 2).[1]—Vers. 19, 20. Aaron excused his sons, however, by saying, " *Behold, this day have they offered their sin-offering and their burnt-offering, and this has happened to me,*" *i.e.* the calamity recorded in vers. 1 sqq. has befallen me (קָרָא = קָרָה, as in Gen. xlii. 4) ; " *and if I had eaten the sin-offering to-day, would it have been well-pleasing to Jehovah ?*" וְאָכַלְתִּי וגו׳ is a conditional clause, as in Gen. xxxiii. 13, cf. *Ewald,* § 357. Moses rested satisfied with this answer. Aaron acknowledged that the flesh of the sin-offering ought to have been eaten by the priest in this instance (according to chap. vi. 19), and simply adduced, as the reason why this had not been done, the calamity which had befallen his two eldest sons. And this might really be a sufficient reason, as regarded both himself and his remaining sons, why the eating of the sin-offering should be omitted. For the judgment in question was so solemn a warning, as to the sin which still adhered to them even after the presentation of their sin-offering, that they might properly feel " that they had not so strong and overpowering a holiness as was required for eating the general sin-offering" (*M. Baumgarten*). This is the correct view, though others find the reason in their grief at the death of their sons or brethren, which rendered it impossible to observe a joyous sacrificial meal. But this is not for a moment to be thought of, simply because the eating of the flesh of the sin-offering was not a joyous meal at all (see at chap. vi. 19).[2]

[1] *C. a Lapide* has given this correct interpretation of the passage : " *ut scilicet cum hostiis populi pro peccato simul etiam populi peccata in vos quasi recipiatis, ut illa expietis.*" There is no foundation for the objection offered by *Oehler*, that the actual removal of guilt and the atonement itself were effected by the offering of the blood. For it by no means follows from Lev. xvii. 11, that the blood, as the soul of the sacrificial animal, covered or expiated the soul of the sinner, and that the removal and extinction of the sin had already taken place with the covering of the soul before the holy God, which involved the forgiveness of the sin and the reception of the sinner to mercy.

[2] Upon this mistaken view of the excuse furnished by Aaron, *Knobel* has founded his assertion, that " this section did not emanate from the Elohist, because he could not have written in this way," an assertion which falls to the ground when the words are correctly explained.

LAWS RELATING TO CLEAN AND UNCLEAN ANIMALS.—CHAP. XI.

(Cf. Deut. xiv. 3-20.)

The regulation of the sacrifices and institution of the priest-hood, by which Jehovah opened up to His people the way of access to His grace and the way to sanctification of life in fellowship with Him, were followed by instructions concerning the various things which hindered and disturbed this living fellowship with God the Holy One, as being manifestations and results of sin, and by certain rules for avoiding and removing these obstructions. For example, although sin has its origin and proper seat in the soul, it pervades the whole body as the organ of the soul, and shatters the life of the body, even to its complete dissolution in death and decomposition; whilst its effects have spread from man to the whole of the earthly creation, inasmuch as not only did man draw nature with him into the service of sin, in consequence of the dominion over it which was given him by God, but God Himself, according to a holy law of His wise and equitable government, made the irrational creature subject to "vanity" and "corruption" on account of the sin of man (Rom. viii. 20, 21), so that not only did the field bring forth thorns and thistles, and the earth produce injurious and poisonous plants (see at Gen. iii. 18), but the animal kingdom in many of its forms and creatures bears the image of sin and death, and is constantly reminding man of the evil fruit of his fall from God. It is in this penetration of sin into the material creation that we may find the explanation of the fact, that from the very earliest times men have neither used every kind of herb nor every kind of animal as food; but that, whilst they have, as it were, instinctively avoided certain plants as injurious to health or destructive to life, they have also had a *horror naturalis*, *i.e.* an inexplicable disgust, at many of the animals, and have avoided their flesh as unclean. A similar horror must have been produced upon man from the very first, before his heart was altogether hardened, by death as the wages of sin, or rather by the effects of death, viz. the decomposition of the body; and different diseases and states of the body, that were connected with symptoms of corruption and decomposition, may also have been regarded as rendering unclean. Hence in all the nations and all the religions of antiquity we find that contrast between clean and unclean, which was developed in a dualistic form, it is true, in many of the religious systems, but had its primary root in the corruption that had entered the world through sin. This contrast was limited in the Mosaic law to the animal food of the Israelites, to contact with dead animals and human corpses, and to certain bodily conditions and diseases that are associated with the decomposition, pointing out most minutely the unclean objects and various defilements within these spheres, and prescribing the means for avoiding or removing them.

The instructions in the chapter before us, concerning the clean and unclean animals, are introduced in the first place as laws of food (ver. 2) ; but they pass beyond these bounds by prohibiting at the same time all contact with animal carrion (vers. 8, 11, 24 sqq.), and show thereby that they are connected in principle and object with the subsequent laws of purification (chap. xii.–xv.), to which they are to be regarded as a preparatory introduction.

Vers. 1–8. The laws which follow were given to Moses and Aaron (ver. 1, chap. xiii. 1, xv. 1), as Aaron had been sanctified through the anointing to expiate the sins and uncleannesses of the children of Israel.—Vers. 2–8 (cf. Deut. xiv. 4–8). Of the larger quadrupeds, ·which are divided in Gen. i. 24, 25 into beasts of the earth (living wild) and tame cattle, only the cattle (*behemah*) are mentioned here, as denoting the larger land animals, some of which were reared by man as domesticated animals, and others used as food. Of these the Israelites might eat " *whatsoever parteth the hoof and is cloven-footed, and cheweth the cud among the cattle.*" שֹׁסַעַת שֶׁסַע פְּרָסֹת, literally " tearing (having) a rent in the hoofs," according to Deut. xiv. 5 into "two claws," *i.e.* with a hoof completely severed in two. גֵּרָה, rumination, μηρυκισμός (LXX.), from גָּרַר (cf. יַּר ver. 7), to draw (Hab. i. 15), to draw to and fro ; hence to bring up the food again, to ruminate. מַעֲלַת גֵּרָה is connected with the preceding words with *vav cop.* to indicate the close connection of the two regulations, viz. that there was to be the perfectly cloven foot as well as the rumination (cf. vers. 4 sqq.). These marks are combined in the oxen, sheep, and goats, and also in the stag and gazelle. The latter are expressly mentioned in Deut. xiv. 4, 5, where—in addition to the *common stag* (אַיָּל) and *gazelle* (צְבִי, δορκάς, LXX.), or *dorcas-antelope*, which is most frequently met with in Palestine, Syria, and Arabia, of the size of a roebuck, with a reddish brown back and white body, horns sixteen inches long, and fine dark eyes, and the flesh of which, according to *Avicenna*, is the best of all the wild game—the following five are also selected, viz. : (1) יַחְמוּר, not βούβαλος, the buffalo (LXX., and *Luther*), but *Damhirsch*, a stag which is still much more common in Asia than in Europe and Palestine (see *v. Schubert*, R. iii. p. 118) ; (2) אַקּוֹ, probably, according to the Chaldee, *Syriac*, etc., the *capricorn* (*Steinbock*), which is very common in Palestine, not τραγέλαφος (LXX., Vulg.), the buck-stag (*Bockhirsch*), an animal lately discovered in Nubia (cf. *Leyrer* in *Herzog's* Cycl. vi. p. 143) ; (3) דִּישׁוֹן, according to the *LXX*. and *Vulg.* πύραργος, a kind of *antelope* resembling the stag, which is met with in Africa (Herod. 4, 192),—according to the Chaldee and Syriac, the *buffalo-antelope*,—according to the Samar. and Arabic, the *mountain-stag* ; (4) תְּאוֹ, according to the Chaldee the *wild ox*, which is also met with in Egypt and Arabia, probably the *oryx* (LXX., *Vulg.*), a species of antelope as large as a stag ; and (5) זֶמֶר, according to the LXX. and most of the ancient versions, the *giraffe*, but this is only found in the deserts of Africa, and would hardly be met with even in Egypt,—it is more probably *capreæ sylvestris species*, according to the Chaldee.—Vers. 4, 5. Any animal which was wanting in either of these marks was to be unclean, or not to be eaten. This is the case with the *camel*, whose flesh is eaten by the Arabs ; it ruminates, but it has not cloven hoofs. Its foot is severed, it is true, but not thoroughly cloven, as there is a ball behind, upon which it treads. The *hare* and *hyrax* (*Klippdachs*) were also unclean, because, although they ruminate, they have not cloven hoofs. It is true that modern naturalists affirm that the two latter do not ruminate at all, as they have not the four stomachs that are common to ruminant animals ; but they move the jaw sometimes in a manner which looks like ruminating, so that even *Linnæus* affirmed that the hare chewed the cud, and Moses followed the popular opinion. According to *Bochart, Oedmann*, and others, the *shaphan* is the *jerboa*, and according to the Rabbins and Luther, the rabbit or coney. But the more correct view is, that it is the *wabr* of the Arabs, which is still called *tsofun* in Southern

Arabia (*hyrax Syriacus*), an animal which feeds on plants, a native of the countries of the Lebanon and Jordan, also of Arabia and Africa. They live in the natural caves and clefts of the rocks (Ps. civ. 18), are very gregarious, being often seen seated in troops before the openings to their caves, and extremely timid as they are quite defenceless (Prov. xxx. 26). They are about the size of rabbits, of a brownish grey or brownish yellow colour, but white under the belly; they have bright eyes, round ears, and no tail. The Arabs eat them, but do not place them before their guests.[1]—Ver. 7. The *swine* has cloven hoofs, but does not ruminate; and many of the tribes of antiquity abstained from eating it, partly on account of its uncleanliness, and partly from fear of skin-diseases.—Ver. 8. "*Of their flesh shall ye not eat* (*i.e.* not slay these animals as food), *and their carcase* (animals that had died) *shall ye not touch.*" The latter applied to the clean or edible animals also, when they had died a natural death (ver. 39).

Vers. 9-12 (cf. Deut. xiv. 9 and 10). Of *water animals*, everything in the water, in seas and brooks, that had fins and scales was edible. Everything else that swarmed in the water was to be an abomination, its flesh was not to be eaten, and its carrion was to be avoided with abhorrence. Consequently, not only were all water animals other than fishes, such as crabs, salamanders, etc., forbidden as unclean; but also fishes without scales, such as eels for example. Numa laid down this law for the Romans: *ut pisces qui squamosi non essent ni pollicerent* (sacrificed): *Plin. h. n.* 32, c. 2, s. 10. In Egypt fishes without scales are still regarded as unwholesome (*Lane*, Manners and Customs).

Vers. 13-19 (cf. Deut. xiv. 11-18). Of *birds*, twenty varieties are prohibited, including the *bat*, but without any common mark being given; though they consist almost exclusively of birds which live upon flesh or carrion, and are most of them natives of Western Asia.[2] The list commences with the *eagle*,

---

[1] See *Shaw*, iii. p. 301; Seetzen, ii. p. 228; *Robinson's* Biblical Researches, p. 387; and Roediger on Gesenius *thesaurus*, p. 1467.

[2] The list is "hardly intended to be exhaustive, but simply mentions those which were eaten by others, and in relation to which, therefore, it was necessary that the Israelites should receive a special prohibition against eating them" (*Knobel*). Hence in Deuteronomy Moses added the ראה and

as the king of the birds. *Nesher* embraces all the species of eagles proper. The idea that the eagle will not touch carrion is erroneous. According to the testimony of Arabian writers (*Damiri* in *Bochart*, ii. p. 577), and several naturalists who have travelled (*e.g. Forskal.* l.c. p. 12, and *Seetzen*, 1, p. 379), they will eat carrion if it is still fresh and not decomposed ; so that the eating of carrion could very properly be attributed to them in such passages as Job xxxix. 30, Prov. xxx. 17, and Matt. xxiv. 28. But the bald-headedness mentioned in Micah i. 16 applies, not to the true eagle, but to the carrion-kite, which is reckoned, however, among the different species of eagles, as well as the bearded or golden vulture. The next in the list is *peres*, from *paras = parash* to break, *ossifragus*, *i.e.* either the bearded or golden vulture, *gypaetos barbatus*, or more probably, as *Schultz* supposes, the *sea-eagle*, which may have been the species intended in the γρύψ = γρυπαίετος of the LXX. and *gryphus* of the Vulgate, and to which the ancients seem sometimes to have applied the name *ossifraga* (*Lucret.* v. 1079). By the next, עׇזְנִיׇה, we are very probably to understand the *bearded* or *golden vulture*. For this word is no doubt connected with the Arabic word for beard, and therefore points to the golden vulture, which has a tuft of hair or feathers on the lower beak, and which might very well be associated with the eagles so far as the size is concerned, having wings that measure 10 feet from tip to tip. As it really belongs to the family of vultures, it forms a very fitting link of transition to the other species of vulture and falcon (ver. 14). דׇּאׇה (*Deut.* דׇּיׇּה, according to a change which is by no means rare when the *aleph* stands between two vowels : cf. דׁואׇג in 1 Sam. xxi. 8, xxii. 9, and דׁוׁיׇג in 1 Sam. xxii. 18, 22), from דׇּאׇה to fly, is either the *kite*, or the *glede*, which is very common in Palestine (*v. Schubert, Reise* iii. p. 120), and lives on carrion. It is a gregarious bird (cf. Isa. xxxiv. 15), which other birds of prey are not, and is used by many different tribes as food (*Oedmann*, iii. p. 120). The conjecture that the black glede-kite is meant,—a bird which is particularly common in the East,—and that the name is derived from דׇּאׇה to be dark, is overthrown by the use of the word לְמִינׇהּ in Deuter-

enumerated twenty-one varieties; and no doubt, under other circumstances, he could have made the list still longer. In Deut. xiv. 11 צׅפּוֹר is used, as synonymous with עוֹף in ver. 20.

onomy, which shows that ראה is intended to denote the whole genus. אַיָּה, which is referred to in Job xxviii. 7 as sharp-sighted, is either the falcon, several species of which are natives of Syria and Arabia, and which is noted for its keen sight and the rapidity of its flight, or according to the *Vulgate, Schultz,* etc., *vultur,* the true vulture (the LXX. have ἰκτίν, the kite, here, and γρύψ, the griffin, in Deut. and Job), of which there are three species in Palestine (*Lynch,* p. 229). In Deut. xiv. 13 הָרָאָה is also mentioned, from רָאָה to see. Judging from the name, it was a keen-sighted bird, either a falcon or another species of vulture (*Vulg. ixion*).—Ver. 15. "*Every raven after his. kind,*" *i.e.* the whole genus of ravens, with the rest of the raven-like birds, such as crows, jackdaws, and jays, which are all of them natives of Syria and Palestine. The omission of ו before אֶת, which is found in several MSS. and editions, is probably to be regarded as the true reading, as it is not wanting before any of the other names.—Ver. 16. בַּת הַיַּעֲנָה, *i.e.* either daughter of screaming (*Bochart*), or daughter of greediness (*Gesenius,* etc.), is used according to all the ancient versions for the ostrich, which is more frequently described as the dweller in the desert (Isa. xiii. 21, xxxiv. 13, etc.), or as the mournful screamer (Micah i. 8; Job xxxix. 39), and is to be understood, not as denoting the female ostrich only, but as a noun of common gender denoting the ostrich generally. It does not devour carrion indeed, but it eats vege-table matter of the most various kinds, and swallows greedily stones, metals, and even glass. It is found in Arabia, and some-times in Hauran and Belka (*Seetzen* and *Burckhardt*), and has been used as food not only by the Struthiophagi of Ethiopia (*Diod. Sic.* 3, 27; *Strabo,* xvi. 772) and Numidia (*Leo Afric.* p. 766), but by some of the Arabs also (*Seetzen,* iii. p. 20; *Burck-hardt,* p. 178), whilst others only eat the eggs, and make use of the fat in the preparation of food. תַּחְמָס, according to *Bochart, Gesenius,* and others, is the *male ostrich;* but this is very impro-bable. According to the *LXX., Vulg.,* and others, it is the *owl* (*Oedmann,* iii. pp. 45 sqq.); but this is mentioned later under another name. According to *Saad. Ar. Erp.* it is the *swallow;* but this is called סִים in Jer. viii. 7. *Knobel* supposes it to be the *cuckoo,* which is met with in Palestine (*Seetzen,* 1, p. 78), and de-rives the name from חָמַס, *violenter egit,* supposing it to be so called from the violence with which it is said to turn out or devour the eggs and young of other birds, for the purpose of laying its own eggs in the nest (*Aristot. hist. an.* 6, 7; 9, 29; *Ael. nat. an.* 6, 7). שַׁחַף is the λάρος, or *slender gull*, according to the LXX. and *Vulg.* Knobel follows the Arabic, however, and supposes it to be a species of *hawk*, which is trained in Syria for hunting gazelles, hares, etc.; but this is certainly included in the genus נֵץ. נֵץ, from נָצַץ to fly, is the *hawk*, which soars very high, and spreads its wings towards the south (Job xxxix. 26). It stands in fact, as לְמִינֵהוּ shows, for the hawk-tribe generally, probably the ἱέραξ, *accipiter*, of which the ancients enumerate many different species. כּוֹס, which is mentioned in Ps. cii. 7 as dwelling in ruins, is an *owl* according to the ancient versions, although they differ as to the kind. In Knobel's opinion it is either the *screech-owl*, which inhabits ruined buildings, walls, and clefts in the rock, and the flesh of which is said to be very agreeable, or the *little screech-owl*, which also lives in old buildings and walls, and raises a mournful cry at night, and the flesh of which is said to be savoury. שָׁלָךְ, according to the ancient versions an aquatic bird, and therefore more in place by the side of the heron, where it stands in Deuteronomy, is called by the LXX. καταῤῥάκτης; in the *Targ.* and *Syr.* נוּנָא שָׁלֵי, *extrahens pisces*. It is not the *gull*, however (*larus catarractes*), which plunges with violence, for according to *Oken* this is only seen in the northern seas, but a species of *pelican*, to be found on the banks of the Nile and in the islands of the Red Sea, which swims well, and also dives, frequently dropping perpendicularly upon fishes in the water. The flesh has an oily taste, but it is eaten for all that. יַנְשׁוּף: from נָשַׁף to snort, according to Isa. xxxiv. 11, dwelling in ruins, no doubt a species of *owl*; according to the Chaldee and Syriac, the *uhu*, which dwells in old ruined towers and castles upon the mountains, and cries *uhupuhu*. תִּנְשֶׁמֶת, which occurs again in ver. 30 among the names of the lizards, is, according to *Damiri*, a bird resembling the uhu, but smaller. *Jonathan* calls it *uthya* = ὠτός, a *night-owl*. The primary meaning of the word נָשַׁם is essentially the same as that of נָשַׁף, to breathe or blow, so called because many of the owls have a mournful cry, and blow and snort in addition; though it cannot be decided whether the *strix otus* is intended, a bird by no means rare in Egypt, which utters a whistling blast, and rolls itself into a ball and then spreads itself out again, or the *strix flammea*, a native of Syria, which sometimes utters a mournful cry, and at other times snores like a sleeping man, and the flesh of which is said to be by no means unpleasant, or the hissing owl (*strix stridula*), which inhabits the ruins in Egypt and Syria, and is sometimes called *massusu*, at other times *bane*, a very voracious bird, which is said to fly in at open windows in the evening and kill children that are left unguarded, and which is very much dreaded in consequence. קָאַת, which also lived in desolate places (Isa. xxxiv. 11 ; Zeph. ii. 14), or in the desert itself (Ps. cii. 7), was not the *katà*, a species of partridge or heath-cock, which is found in Syria (*Robinson*, ii. p. 620), as this bird always flies in large flocks, and this is not in harmony with Isa. xxxiv. 11 and Zeph. ii. 14, but the *pelican* (πελεκάν, LXX.), as all the ancient versions render it, which *Ephraem* (on Num. xiv. 17) describes as a marsh-bird, very fond of its young, inhabiting desolate places, and uttering an incessant cry. It is the true pelican of the ancients (*pelecanus graculus*), the Hebrew name of which seems to have been derived from קִיא to spit, from its habit of spitting out the fishes it has caught, and which is found in Palestine and the reedy marshes of Egypt (Robinson, Palestine). רָחָם, in Deut. רָחָמָה, is κυκνός, the swan, according to the Septuagint *porphyrio*, the fish-heron, according to the Vulgate ; a marsh-bird therefore, possibly *vultur percnopterus* (*Saad. Ar. Erp.*), which is very common in Arabia, Palestine, and Syria, and was classed by the ancients among the different species of eagles (*Plin. h. n.* 10, 3), but which is said to resemble the vulture, and was also called ὀρειπέλαργος, the mountain-stork (*Arist. h. an.* 9, 32). It is a stinking and disgusting bird, of the raven kind, with black pinions ; but with this exception it is quite white. It is also bald-headed, and feeds on carrion and filth. But it is eaten notwithstanding by many of the Arabs (*Burckhardt, Syr.* p. 1046). It received its name of " *tenderly loving* " from the tenderness with which it watches over its young (*Bochart*, iii. pp. 56, 57). In this respect it resembles the stork, חֲסִידָה, *avis pia*, a bird of passage according to Jer. viii. 7, which builds its nest upon the cypresses (Ps. civ. 17, cf. *Bochart*, iii. pp. 85 sqq.). In the East the stork builds its nest not only upon high towers and the roofs of houses, but according to *Kazwini* and others mentioned by *Bochart* (iii. p. 60), upon lofty trees as well.[1] אֲנָפָה, according

---

[1] *Oedmann* (v. 58 sqq.), *Knobel*, and others follow the Greek translation

to the LXX. and *Vulgate* χαραδριός, a marsh-bird of the *snipe* kind, of which there are several species in Egypt (*Hasselquist*, p. 308). This is quite in accordance with the expression " after her kind," which points to a numerous genus. The omission of וְאֵת before הָאֲנָפָה, whereas it is found before the name of every other animal, is very striking; but as the name is preceded by the copulative *vav* in Deuteronomy, and stands for a particular bird, it may be accounted for either from a want of precision on the part of the author, or from an error of the copyist like the omission of the וְ before אֶת in ver. 15.[1] דּוּכִיפַת : according to the LXX., *Vulg.*, and others, the *lapwing*, which is found in Syria, Arabia, and still more commonly in Egypt (*Forsk, Russel, Sonnini*), and is eaten in some places, as its flesh is said to be fat and savoury in autumn (*Sonn.* 1, 204). But it has a disagreeable smell, as it frequents marshy districts seeking worms and insects for food, and according to a common belief among the ancients, builds its nest of human dung. Lastly, הָעֲטַלֵּף is the bat (Isa. ii. 20), which the Arabs also classified among the birds.

of Leviticus and the Psalms, and the *Vulgate* rendering of Leviticus, the Psalms, and Job, and suppose the reference to be to the ἐρωδιός, *herodius*, the heron : but the name *chasidah* points decidedly to the stork, which was generally regarded by the ancients as *pietatis cultrix* (*Petron.* 55, 6), whereas, with the exception of the somewhat indefinite passage in *Aelian* (*Nat. an.* 3, 23), καὶ τοὺς ἐρωδιοὺς ἀκούω ποιεῖν ταὐτόν (*i.e.* feed their young by spitting out their food) καὶ τοὺς πελεκᾶνας μέντοι, nothing is said about the parental affection of the heron. And the testimony of *Bellonius*, "*Ciconiæ quæ ætate in Europa sunt, magna hyemis parte ut in Aegypto sic etiam circa Antiochiam et juxta Amanum montem degunt*," is a sufficient answer to *Knobel's* assertion, that according to *Seetzen* there are no storks in Mount Lebanon.

[1] On account of the omission of וְאֵת *Knobel* would connect הָאֲנָפָה as an adjective with הַחֲסִידָה, and explain אֲנָף as derived from עָנָף *frons*, עָנֵף *frondens,* and signifying bushy. The herons were called " the bushy *chasidah*," he supposes, because they have a tuft of feathers at the back of their head, or long feathers hanging down from their neck, which are wanting in the other marsh-birds, such as the flamingo, crane, and ibis. But there is this important objection to the explanation, that the change of א for ע in such a word as עָנָף, *frons*, which occurs as early as chap. xxiii. 40, and has retained its ע even in the Aramæan dialects, is destitute of all probability. In addition to this, there is the improbability of the *chasidah* being the only bird to which a special epithet was applied, or of its being restricted by *anaphah* to the different species of heron, with three of which the ancients

Vers. 20-23 (cf. Deut. xiv. 19). To the birds there are appended flying animals of other kinds: "*all swarms of fowl that go upon fours,*" *i.e.* the smaller winged animals with four feet, which are called *sherez*, "swarms," on account of their multitude. These were not to be eaten, as they were all abominations, with the exception of those "*which have two shank-feet above their feet* (*i.e.* springing feet) *to leap with*" (אל for לו as in Ex. xxi. 8). Locusts are the animals referred to, four varieties being mentioned with their different species ("*after his kind*"); but these cannot be identified with exactness, as there is still a dearth of information as to the natural history of the oriental locust. It is well known that locusts were eaten by many of the nations of antiquity both in Asia and Africa, and even the ancient Greeks thought the *Cicades* very agreeable in flavour (*Arist. h. an.* 5, 30). In Arabia they are sold in the market, sometimes strung upon cords, sometimes by measure; and they are also dried, and kept in bags for winter use. For the most part, however, it is only by the poorer classes that they are eaten, and many of the tribes of Arabia abhor them (Robinson, ii. p. 628); and those who use them as food do not eat all the species indiscriminately. They are generally cooked over hot coals, or on a plate, or in an oven, or stewed in butter, and eaten either with salt or with spice and vinegar, the head, wings, and feet being thrown away. They are also boiled in salt and water, and eaten with salt or butter. Another process is to dry them thoroughly,

---

were acquainted (*Aristot. h. an.* 9, 2 ; *Plin. h. n.* 10, 60). If *chasidah* denoted the heron generally, or the white heron, the epithet *anaphah* would be superfluous. It would be necessary to assume, therefore, that *chasidah* denotes the whole tribe of marsh-birds, and that Moses simply intended to prohibit the heron or bushy marsh-bird. But either of these is very improbable : the former, because in every other passage of the Old Testament *chasidah* stands for one particular kind of bird ; the latter, because Moses could hardly have excluded storks, ibises, and other marsh-birds that live on worms, from his prohibition. All that remains, therefore, is to separate *ha-anaphah* from the preceding word, as in Deuteronomy, and to understand it as denoting the plover (?) or heron, as there were several species of both. Which is intended, it is impossible to decide, as there is nothing certain to be gathered from either the ancient versions or the etymology. *Bochart's* reference of the word to a fierce bird, viz. a species of eagle, which the Arabs call *Tummaj*, is not raised into a probability by a comparison with the similarly sounding ἀνοπαία of Od. 1, 320, by which *Aristarchus* understands a kind of eagle.

and then grind them into meal and make cakes of them. The Israelites were allowed to eat the *arbeh, i.e.*, according to Ex. x. 13, 19, Nahum iii. 17, etc., the flying migratory locust, *gryllus migratorius,* which still bears this name, according to *Niebuhr,* in Maskat and Bagdad, and is poetically designated in Ps. lxxviii. 46, cv. 34, as חָסִיל, *the devourer,* and יֶלֶק, *the eater-up;* but *Knobel* is mistaken in supposing that these names are applied to certain species of the *arbeh.* סָלְעָם, according to the Chaldee, *deglutivit, absorpsit,* is unquestionably a larger and peculiarly voracious species of locust. This is all that can be inferred from the *rashon* of the Targums and Talmud, whilst the ἀττάκης and *attacus* of the LXX. and Vulg. are altogether unexplained. חַרְגֹּל : according to the Arabic, a galloping, *i.e.* a hopping, not a flying species of locust. This is supported by the Samaritan, also by the LXX. and *Vulg.,* ὀφιομάχης, *ophiomachus.* According to *Hesychius* and *Suidas,* it was a species of locust without wings, probably a very large kind ; as it is stated in *Mishnah, Shabb.* vi. 10, that an egg of the *chargol* was sometimes suspended in the ear, as a remedy for earache. Among the different species of locusts in Mesopotamia, *Niebuhr* (Arab. p. 170) saw two of a very large size with springing feet, but without wings. חָגָב, a word of uncertain etymology, occurs in Num. xiii. 33, where the spies are described as being like *chagabim* by the side of the inhabitants of the country, and in 2 Chron. vii. 13, where the *chagab* devours the land. From these passages we may infer that it was a species of locust without wings, small but very numerous, probably the ἀττέλαβος, which is often mentioned along with the ἀκρίς, but as a distinct species, *locustarum minima sine pennis (Plin. h. n.* 29, *c.* 4, *s.* 29), or *parva locusta modicis pennis reptans potius quam volitans semperque subsiliens (Jerome* on Nahum iii. 17).[1]

---

[1] In Deut. xiv. 19 the edible kinds of locusts are passed over, because it was not the intention of Moses to repeat every particular of the earlier laws in these addresses. But when *Knobel* (on Lev. pp. 455 and 461) gives this explanation of the omission, that the eating of locusts is prohibited in Deuteronomy, and the Deuteronomist passes them over because in his more advanced age there was apparently no longer any necessity for the prohibition, this arbitrary interpretation is proved to be at variance with historical truth by the fact that locusts were eaten by John the Baptist, inasmuch as this proves at all events that a more advanced age had not given up the custom of eating locusts.

In vers. 24–28 there follow still further and more precise instructions, concerning defilement through contact with the carcases (*i.e.* the carrion) of the animals already mentioned. These instructions relate first of all (vers. 24 and 25) to aquatic and winged animals, which were not to be eaten because they were unclean (the expression "*for these*" in ver. 24 relates to them); and then (vers. 26–28) to quadrupeds, both cattle that have not the hoof thoroughly divided and do not ruminate (ver. 26), and animals that go upon their hands, *i.e.* upon paws, and have no hoofs, such as cats, dogs, bears, etc.—Vers. 27, 28. The same rule was applicable to all these animals : "*whoever toucheth the carcase of them shall be unclean until the even,*" *i.e.* for the rest of the day ; he was then of course to wash himself. Whoever carried their carrion, viz. to take it away, was also unclean till the evening, and being still more deeply affected by the defilement, he was to wash his clothes as well.

Vers. 29–38. To these there are attached analogous instructions concerning defilement through contact with the smaller creeping animals (*sherez*), which formed the fourth class of the animal kingdom ; though the prohibition against eating these animals is not introduced till vers. 41, 42, as none of these were usually eaten. *Sherez*, the swarm, refers to animals which swarm together in great numbers (see at Gen. i. 21), and is synonymous with *remes* (cf. Gen. vii. 14 and vii. 21), "the creeping ;" it denotes the smaller land animals which move without feet, or with feet that are hardly perceptible (see at Gen. i. 24). Eight of the creeping animals are named, as defiling not only the men with whom they might come in contact, but any domestic utensils and food upon which they might fall ; they were generally found in houses, therefore, or in the abodes of men. חֹלֶד is not the *mole* (according to *Saad. Ar. Abys.*, etc.), although the Arabs still call this *chuld*, but the *weasel* (LXX., *Onk.*, etc.), which is common in Syria and Palestine, and is frequently mentioned by the Talmudists in the feminine form חֻלְדָּה, as an animal which caught birds (*Mishn. Cholin* iii. 4), which would run over the wave-loaves with a *sherez* in its mouth (*Mishn. Tohor.* iv. 2), and which could drink water out of a vessel (*Mishn. Para* ix. 3). עַכְבָּר is the *mouse* (according to the ancient versions and the Talmud), and in 1 Sam. vi. 5 the *field-mouse*, the scourge of the fields, not the jerboa, as *Knobel* supposes; for this animal lives in holes in the ground, is very shy, and does not frequent houses as is assumed to be the case with the animals mentioned here. צָב is a kind of *lizard*, but whether the *thav* or *dsabb*, a harmless yellow lizard of 18 inches in length, which is described by *Seetzen*, iii. pp. 436 sqq., also by *Hasselquist* under the name of *lacerta Ægyptia*, or the *waral*, as *Knobel* supposes, a large land lizard reaching as much as four feet in length, which is also met with in Palestine (*Robinson*, ii. 160) and is called *el worran* by *Seetzen*, cannot be determined. —Ver. 30. The early translators tell us nothing certain as to the three following names, and it is still undecided how they should be rendered. אֲנָקָה is translated μυγάλη by the LXX., *i.e. shrew-mouse;* but the oriental versions render it by various names for a lizard. *Bochart* supposes it to be a species of lizard with a sharp groaning voice, because אָנַק signifies to breathe deeply, or groan. *Rosenmüller* refers it to the *lacerta Gecko*, which is common in Egypt, and utters a peculiar cry resembling the croaking of frogs, especially in the night. *Leyrer* imagines it to denote the whole family of *monitores;* and *Knobel*, the large and powerful river lizard, the water-waral of the Arabs, called *lacerta Nilotica* in *Hasselquist*, pp. 361 sqq., though he has failed to observe, that Moses could hardly have supposed it possible that an animal four feet long, resembling a crocodile, could drop down dead into either pots or dishes. כֹּחַ is not the chameleon (LXX.), for this is called *tinshemeth*, but the *chardaun* (*Arab.*), a lizard which is found in old walls in Natolia, Syria, and Palestine, *lacerta stellio*, or *lacerta coslordilos* (*Hasselquist*, pp. 351-2). *Knobel* supposes it to be the frog, because *coach* seems to point to the crying or croaking of frogs, to which the Arabs apply the term *kuk*, the Greeks κοάξ, the Romans *coaxare*. But this is very improbable, and the frog would be quite out of place in the midst of simple lizards. לְטָאָה, according to the ancient versions, is also a lizard. *Leyrer* supposes it to be the nocturnal, salamander-like family of *geckons;* *Knobel*, on the contrary, imagines it to be the tortoise, which creeps upon the earth (*terræ adhæret*), because the Arabic verb signifies *terræ adhæsit*. This is very improbable, however. חֹמֶט (LXX.), σαύρα, *Vulg. lacerta*, probably the *true lizard*, or, as *Leyrer* conjectures, the *anguis* (*Luth. Blindschleiche*, blindworm), or *zygnis*, which forms the link between lizards and snakes. The rendering "snail" (*Sam. Rashi*, etc.) is not so probable, as this is called שַׁבְּלוּל in Ps. lviii. 9; although the purple snail and all the marine species are eaten in Egypt and Palestine. Lastly, תִּנְשֶׁמֶת, the self-inflating animal (see at ver. 18), is no doubt the *chameleon*, which frequently inflates its belly, for example, when enraged, and remains in this state for several hours, when it gradually empties itself and becomes quite thin again. Its flesh was either cooked, or dried and reduced to powder, and used as a specific for corpulence, or a cure for fevers, or as a general medicine for sick children (*Plin. h. n.* 28, 29). The flesh of many of the lizards is also eaten by the Arabs (*Leyrer*, pp. 603, 604).—Ver. 31. The words, "*these are unclean to you among all swarming creatures,*" are neither to be understood as meaning, that the eight species mentioned were the only swarming animals that were unclean and not allowed to be eaten, nor that they possessed and communicated a larger amount of uncleanness; but when taken in connection with the instructions which follow, they can only mean, that such animals would even defile domestic utensils, clothes, etc., if they fell down dead upon them. Not that they were more unclean than others, since all the unclean animals would defile not only persons, but even the clothes of those who carried their dead bodies (vers. 25, 28); but there was more fear in their case than in that of others, of their falling dead upon objects in common use, and therefore domestic utensils, clothes, and so forth, could be much more easily defiled by them than by the larger quadrupeds, by water animals, or by birds. "*When they be dead,*" lit. "*in their dying;*" i.e. not only if they were already dead, but if they died at the time when they fell upon any object.—Ver. 32. In either case, anything upon which one of these animals fell became unclean, "*whether a vessel of wood, or raiment, or skin.*" Every vessel (כְּלִי in the widest sense, as in Ex. xxii. 6), "*wherein any work is done,*" i.e. that was an article of common use, was to be unclean till the evening, and then placed in water, that it might become clean again.—Ver. 33. Every earthen vessel, into which (*lit.* into the midst of which) one of them fell, became unclean, together with the whole of its contents, and was to be broken, *i.e.* destroyed, because the uncleanness was absorbed by the vessel, and could not be entirely removed by washing (see at chap. vi. 21). Of course the contents of such a vessel, supposing there were any, were not to be used.—Ver. 34. " *Every edible food* (מַיִם before כֹּל partitive, as in chap. iv. 2) *upon which water comes,*"—that is to say, which was prepared with water,—and " *every drink that is drunk . . . becomes unclean in every vessel,*" *sc.* if such an animal should fall dead upon the food, or into the drink. The traditional rendering of ver. 34*a*, " *every food upon which water out of such a vessel comes,*" is untenable ; because מַיִם without an article cannot mean such water, or this water. —Ver. 35. Every vessel also became unclean, upon which the body of such an animal fell : such as תַּנּוּר, the *earthen baking-pot* (see chap. ii. 4), and כִּירַיִם, the *covered pan* or *pot.* כִּיר, a *boiling* or *roasting vessel* (1 Sam. ii. 14), can only signify, when used in the dual, a vessel consisting of two parts, *i.e.* a pan or pot *with a lid.*—Ver. 36. Springs and wells were not defiled, because the uncleanness would be removed at once by the fresh supply of water. But whoever touched the body of the animal, to remove it, became unclean.—Vers. 37, 38. All seed-corn that was intended to be sown remained clean, namely, because the uncleanness attaching to it externally would be absorbed by the earth. But if water had been put upon the seed, *i.e.* if the grain had been softened by water, it was to be unclean, because in that case the uncleanness would penetrate the softened grains and defile the substance of the seed, which would therefore pro-duce uncleanness in the fruit.

Vers. 39–47. Lastly, contact with edible animals, if they had not been slaughtered, but had died a natural death, and had become carrion in consequence, is also said to defile (cf. vers. 39, 40 with vers. 24–28). This was the case, too, with the eating of the swarming land animals, whether they went upon the belly,[1] as snakes and worms, or upon four feet, as rats, mice, weasels, etc., or upon many feet, like the insects (vers. 41–43). Lastly (vers. 44, 45), the whole law is enforced by an appeal to the calling of the Israelites, as a holy nation, to be holy as Jehovah their God, who had brought them out of Egypt to be a God to them, was holy (Ex. vi. 7, xxix. 45, 46).—Vers. 46, 47, contain the concluding formula to the whole of this law.

If we take a survey, in closing, of the animals that are enu-

---

[1] The large ו in גָּחוֹן (ver. 42) shows that this *vav* is the middle letter of the Pentateuch.

merated as unclean and not suitable for food, we shall find that among the larger land animals they were chiefly beasts of prey, that seize upon other living creatures and devour them in their blood; among the water animals, all snake-like fishes and slimy shell-fish; among birds, the birds of prey, which watch for the life of other animals and kill them, the marsh-birds, which live on worms, carrion, and all kinds of impurities, and such mongrel creatures as the ostrich, which lives in the desert, and the bat, which flies about in the dark; and lastly, all the smaller animals, with the exception of a few graminivorous locusts, but more especially the snake-like lizards,—partly because they called to mind the old serpent, partly because they crawled in the dust, seeking their food in mire and filth, and suggested the thought of corruption by the slimy nature of their bodies. They comprised, in fact, all such animals as exhibited more or less the darker type of sin, death, and corruption; and it was on this ethical ground alone, and not for all kinds of sanitary reasons, or even from political motives, that the nation of Israel, which was called to sanctification, was forbidden to eat them. It is true there are several animals mentioned as unclean, *e.g.* the ass, the camel, and others, in which we can no longer recognise this type. But we must bear in mind, that the distinction between clean animals and unclean goes back to the very earliest times (Gen. vii. 2, 3), and that in relation to the large land animals, as well as to the fishes, the Mosaic law followed the marks laid down by tradition, which took its rise in the primeval age, whose childlike mind, acute perception, and deep intuitive insight into nature generally, discerned more truly and essentially the real nature of the animal creation than we shall ever be able to do, with thoughts and perceptions disturbed as ours are by the influences of unnatural and ungodly culture.[1]

LAWS OF PURIFICATION.—CHAP. XII.–XV.

The laws concerning defilement through eating unclean animals, or through contact with those that had died a natural death, are followed by rules relating to defilements proceeding from the

[1] "In its direct and deep insight into the entire *nexus* of the physical, psychical, and spiritual world, into the secret correspondences of the *cosmos* and *nomos*, this sense for nature anticipated discoveries which we shall never

human body, in consequence of which persons contaminated by them were excluded for a longer or shorter period from the fellowship of the sanctuary, and sometimes even from intercourse with their fellow-countrymen, and which had to be removed by washing, by significant lustrations, and by expiatory sacrifices. They comprised the uncleanness of a woman in consequence of child-bearing (chap. xii.), leprosy (chap. xiii. and xiv.), and both natural and diseased secretions from the sexual organs of either male or female (emissio seminis and gonorrhœa, also menses and flux: chap. xv.); and to these there is added in Num. xix. 11–22, defilement proceeding from a human corpse. Involuntary emission defiled the man; voluntary emission, in sexual intercourse, both the man and the woman and any clothes upon which it might come, for an entire day, and this defilement was to be removed in the evening by bathing the body, and by washing the clothes, etc. (chap. xv. 16–18). Secretions from the sexual organs, whether of a normal kind, such as the menses and those connected with child-birth, or the result of disease, rendered not only the persons affected with them unclean, but even their couches and seats, and any persons who might sit down upon them; and this uncleanness was even communicated to persons who touched those who were diseased, or to anything with which they had come in contact (chap. xv. 3–12, 19–27). In the case of the menses, the uncleanness lasted seven days (chap. xv. 19, 24); in that of child-birth, either seven or fourteen days, and then still further thirty-three or sixty-six, according to circumstances (chap. xii. 2, 4, 5); and in that of a diseased flux, as long as the disease itself lasted, and seven days afterwards (chap. xv. 13, 28); but the uncleanness communicated to others only lasted till the evening. In all these cases the purification consisted in the bathing of the body and washing of the clothes and other objects. But if the uncleanness lasted more than seven days, on the day after the purification with water a sin-offering and a burnt-offering were to be offered, that the priest might pronounce the person clean, or receive him once more into the fellowship of the holy God (chap. xii. 6, 8, xv. 14, 15, 29, 30). Leprosy made those who were affected with it so unclean, that they were ex-

make with our ways of thinking, but which a purified humanity, when looking back from the new earth, will fully understand, and will no longer only ' see through a glass darkly.'"—*Leyrer, Herzog's* Cycl.

cluded from all intercourse with the clean (chap. xiii. 45, 46) :
and on their recovery they were to be cleansed by a solemn lus-
tration, and received again with sacrifices into the congregation
of the Lord (chap. xiv. 1–32). There are no express instructions as to the communicability of leprosy; but this is implied
in the separation of the leper from the clean (chap. xiii. 45, 46),
as well as from the fact that a house affected by the leprosy
rendered all who entered it, or slept in it, unclean (chap. xiv.
46, 47). The defilement caused by a death was apparently
greater still. Not only the corpse of a person who had died a
natural death, as well as of one who had been killed by violence,
but a dead body or grave defiled, for a period of seven days, both
those who touched them, and (in the case of the corpse) the
house in which the man had died, all the persons who were in it
or might enter it, and all the open vessels that were there (Num.
xix. 11, 14–16). Uncleanness of this kind could only be removed
by sprinkling water prepared from running water and the ashes
of a sin-offering (Num. xix. 12, 17 sqq.), and would even spread
from the persons defiled to persons and things with which they
came in contact, so as to render them unclean till the evening
(Num. xix. 22) ; whereas the defilement caused by contact with
a dead animal lasted only a day, and then, like every other kind
of uncleanness that only lasted till the evening, could be removed
by bathing the persons or washing the things (chap. xi. 25 sqq.).

But whilst, according to this, generation and birth as well
as death were affected with uncleanness; generation and death,
the coming into being and the going out of being, were not
defiling in themselves, or regarded as the two poles which
bound, determine, and enclose the finite existence, so as to
warrant us in tracing the principle which lay at the foundation
of the laws of purification, as *Bähr* supposes, " to the antithesis
between the infinite and the finite being, which falls into the
sphere of the sinful when regarded ethically as the opposite to
the absolutely holy." Finite existence was created by God,
quite as much as the corporeality of man ; and both came forth
from His hand pure and good. Moreover it is not begetting, giving birth, and dying, that are said to defile; but the
secretions connected with generation and child-bearing, and the
corpses of those who had died. In the decomposition which
follows death, the effect of sin, of which death is the wages, is

made manifest in the body. Decomposition, as the embodiment of the unholy nature of sin, is uncleanness κατ' ἐξοχήν; and this the Israelite, who was called to sanctification in fellowship with God, was to avoid and abhor. Hence the human corpse produced the greatest amount of defilement; so great, in fact, that to remove it a sprinkling water was necessary, which had been strengthened by the ashes of a sin-offering into a kind of sacred alkali. Next to the corpse, there came on the one hand *leprosy*, that bodily image of death which produced all the symptoms of decomposition even in the living body, and on the other hand the offensive secretions from the organs of generation, which resemble the putrid secretions that are the signs in the corpse of the internal dissolution of the bodily organs and the commencement of decomposition. From the fact that the impurities, for which special rites of purification were enjoined, are restricted to these three forms of manifestation in the human body, it is very evident that the laws of purification laid down in the O. T. were not regulations for the promotion of cleanliness or of good morals and decency, that is to say, were not police regulations for the protection of the life of the body from contagious diseases and other things injurious to health; but that their simple object was " to impress upon the mind a deep horror of everything that is and is called death in the creature, and thereby to foster an utter abhorrence of everything that is or is called sin, and also, to the constant humiliation of fallen man, to remind him in all the leading processes of the natural life—generation, birth, eating, disease, death—how everything, even his own bodily nature, lies under the curse of sin (Gen. iii. 14–19), that so the law might become a ' schoolmaster to bring unto Christ,' and awaken and sustain the longing for a Redeemer from the curse which had fallen upon his body also (see Gal. iii. 24, Rom. vii. 24, viii. 19 sqq.; Phil. iii. 21)." *Leyrer.*

Chap. xii. UNCLEANNESS AND PURIFICATION AFTER CHILDBIRTH.—Vers. 2–4. " *If a woman bring forth* (תַזְרִיעַ) *seed and bear a boy, she shall be unclean seven days as in the days of the uncleanness of her* (monthly) *sickness.*" נִדָּה, from נָדַד to flow, *lit.* that which is to flow, is applied more especially to the uncleanness of a woman's secretions (chap. xv 19). דְוֹתָה, inf. of דָּוָה, to be sickly

or ill, is applied here and in chap. xv. 33, xx. 18, to the suffering
connected with an issue of blood.—Vers. 3, 4. After the expiration
of this period, on the eighth day, the boy was to be circumcised
(see at Gen. xvii.). She was then to sit, *i.e.* remain at home,
thirty-three days in the blood of purification, without touching
anything holy or coming to the sanctuary (she was not to take
any part, therefore, in the sacrificial meals, the Passover, etc.),
until the days of her purification were full, *i.e.* had expired.—
Ver. 5. But if she had given birth to a girl, she was to be unclean two weeks (14 days), as in her menstruation, and then
after that to remain at home 66 days. The distinction between
the seven (or fourteen) days of the "separation for her infirmity,"
and the thirty-three (or sixty-six) days of the "blood of her
purifying," had a natural ground in the bodily secretions connected with child-birth, which are stronger and have more blood
in them in the first week (*lochia rubra*) than the more watery
discharge of the *lochia alba*, which may last as much as five
weeks, so that the normal state may not be restored till about
six weeks after the birth of the child. The prolongation of the
period, in connection with the birth of a girl, was also founded
upon the notion, which was very common in antiquity, that the
bleeding and watery discharge continued longer after the birth
of a girl than after that of a boy (*Hippocr. Opp. ed. Kühn.* i.
p. 393; *Aristot. h. an.* 6, 22; 7, 3, cf. *Burdach, Physiologie* iii.
p. 34). But the extension of the period to 40 and 80 days can
only be accounted for from the significance of the numbers,
which we meet with repeatedly, more especially the number
forty (see at Ex. xxiv. 18).—Vers. 6, 7. After the expiration of
the days of her purification "*with regard to a son or a daughter*,"
i.e. according as she had given birth to a son or a daughter (not
for the son or daughter, for the woman needed purification for
herself, and not for the child to which she had given birth, and
it was the woman, not the child, that was unclean), she was to
bring to the priest a yearling lamb for a burnt-offering, and a
young pigeon or turtle-dove for a sin-offering, that he might
make atonement for her before Jehovah and she might become
clean from the source of her issue. בֶּן שְׁנָתוֹ, lit. *son of his year*,
which is a year old (cf. chap. xxiii. 12; Num. vi. 12, 14, vii.
15, 21, etc.), is used interchangeably with בֶּן שָׁנָה (Ex. xii. 5),
and with בְּנֵי שָׁנָה in the plural (chap. xxiii. 18, 19; Ex. xxix. 38;

Num. vii. 17, 23, 29). מְקוֹר דָּמִים, fountain of bleeding (see at Gen. iv. 10), equivalent to hemorrhage (cf. chap. xx. 18). The purification by bathing and washing is not specially mentioned, as being a matter of course; nor is anything stated with reference to the communication of her uncleanness to persons who touched either her or her couch, since the instructions with regard to the period of menstruation no doubt applied to the first seven and fourteen days respectively. For her restoration to the Lord and His sanctuary, she was to come and be cleansed with a sin-offering and a burnt-offering, on account of the uncleanness in which the sin of nature had manifested itself; because she had been obliged to absent herself in consequence for a whole week from the sanctuary and fellowship of the Lord. But as this purification had reference, not to any special moral guilt, but only to sin which had been indirectly manifested in her bodily condition, a pigeon was sufficient for the sin-offering, that is to say, the smallest of the bleeding sacrifices; whereas a yearling lamb was required for a burnt-offering, to express the importance and strength of her surrender of herself to the Lord after so long a separation from Him. But in cases of great poverty a pigeon might be substituted for the lamb (ver. 8, cf. chap. v. 7, 11).

Chap. xiii. and xiv. LEPROSY.—The law for leprosy, the observance of which is urged upon the people again in Deut. xxiv. 8, 9, treats, in the *first* place, of leprosy in men : (a) in its dangerous forms when appearing either on the skin (vers. 2–28), or on the head and beard (vers. 29-37); (b) in harmless forms (vers. 38 and 39); and (c) when appearing on a bald head (vers. 40-44). To this there are added instructions for the removal of the leper from the society of other men (vers. 45 and 46). It treats, *secondly*, of leprosy in linen, woollen, and leather articles, and the way to treat them (vers. 47–59); *thirdly*, of the purification of persons recovered from leprosy (chap. xiv. 1-32); and *fourthly*, of leprosy in houses and the way to remove it (vers. 33-53).—The laws for leprosy in man relate exclusively to the so-called white leprosy, λεύκη, λέπρα, *lepra*, which probably existed at that time in hither Asia alone, not only among the Israelites and Jews (Num. xii. 10 sqq.; 2 Sam. iii. 29; 2 Kings v. 27, vii. 3, xv. 5; Matt. viii. 2, 3, x. 8, xi. 5, xxvi. 6, etc.), but also among the Syrians (2 Kings v. 1 sqq.), and which is still found in that part of the world, most frequently in the countries of the Lebanon and Jordan and in the neighbourhood of Damascus, in which city there are three hospitals for lepers (*Seetzen,* pp. 277, 278), and occasionally in Arabia (*Niebuhr, Arab.* pp. 135 sqq.) and Egypt ; though at the present time the pimply leprosy, *lepra tuberosa s. articulorum* (the leprosy of the joints), is more prevalent in the East, and frequently occurs in Egypt in the lower extremities in the form of elephantiasis.   Of the white leprosy (called *Lepra Mosaica*), which is still met with in Arabia sometimes, where it is called *Baras, Trusen* gives the following description : "Very frequently, even for years before the actual outbreak of the disease itself, white, yellowish spots are seen lying deep in the skin, particularly on the genitals, in the face, on the forehead, or in the joints.   They are without feeling, and sometimes cause the hair to assume the same colour as the spots.   These spots afterwards pierce through the cellular tissue, and reach the muscles and bones.   The hair becomes white and woolly, and at length falls off ; hard gelatinous swellings are formed in the cellular tissue ; the skin gets hard, rough, and seamy, lymph exudes from it, and forms large scabs, which fall off from time to time, and under these there are often offensive running sores.   The nails then swell, curl up, and fall off : *entropium* is formed, with bleeding gums, the nose stopped up, and a considerable flow of saliva. . . . The senses become dull, the patient gets thin and weak, colliquative diarrhea sets in, and incessant thirst and burning fever terminate his sufferings" (*Krankheiten d. alten Hebr.* p. 165).

Chap. xiii. 2–28. *The symptoms of leprosy, whether proceeding directly from eruptions in the skin, or caused by a boil or burn.*— Vers. 2–8. *The first case :* "When a man shall have in the skin of his flesh (body) a raised spot or scab, or a bright spot." שְׂאֵת, a lifting up (Gen. iv. 7, etc.), signifies here an elevation of the skin in some part of the body, a raised spot like a pimple.   סַפַּחַת, an eruption, scurf, or scab, from סָפַח to pour out, " a pouring out as it were from the flesh or skin" (*Knobel*).   בַּהֶרֶת, from בָּהַר, in the Arabic and Chaldee to shine, is a bright swollen spot in the skin.   If either of these signs became " a spot of leprosy," the person affected was to be brought to the priest, that he might examine the complaint.   The term *zaraath*, from an Arabic word signifying to strike down or scourge, is applied to leprosy as a scourge of God, and in the case of men it always denotes the white leprosy, which the Arabs call *baras*. נֶגַע, a stroke (*lit.* " stroke of leprosy"), is applied not only to the spot attacked by the leprosy, the leprous mole (vers. 3, 29–32, 42, etc.), but to the persons and even to things affected with leprosy (vers. 4, 12, 13, 31, 50, 55).—Ver. 3. A person so diseased was to be pronounced unclean, (*a*) if the hair of his head had turned white on the mole, *i.e.* if the dark hair which distinguished the Israelites had become white ; and (*b*) if the appearance of the mole was deeper than the skin of the flesh, *i.e.* if the spot, where the mole was, appeared depressed in comparison with the rest of the skin. In that case it was leprosy.   These signs are recognised by modern observers (*e.g. Hensler*) ; and among the Arabs leprosy is regarded as curable if the hair remains black upon the white spots, but incurable if it becomes whitish in colour.—Vers. 4–6. But if the bright spot was white upon the skin, and its appearance was not deeper than the skin, and the place therefore was not sunken, nor the hair turned white, the priest was to shut up the leper, *i.e.* preclude him from intercourse with other men, for seven days, and on the seventh day examine him again.   If he then found that the mole still stood, *i.e.* remained unaltered, " in his eyes," or in his view, that it had not spread any further, he was to shut him up for seven days more.   And if, on further examination upon the seventh day, he found that the mole had become paler, had lost its brilliant whiteness, and had not spread, he was to declare him clean, for it was a scurf, *i.e.* a mere skin eruption, and not true leprosy.   The person who had been pronounced clean, however, was to wash his clothes, to change himself from even the appearance of leprosy, and then to be clean. —Vers. 7, 8. But if the scurf had spread upon the skin " after his (first) appearance before the priest with reference to his cleansing," *i.e.* to be examined concerning his purification ; and if the priest noticed this on his second appearance, he was to declare him unclean, for in that case it was leprosy.

The *second case* (vers. 9–17) : if the leprosy broke out without previous eruptions.—Vers. 9 sqq. "If a mole of leprosy is in a man, and the priest to whom he is brought sees that there is a white rising in the skin, and this has turned the hair white, and there is raw (proud) flesh upon the elevation, it is an old

leprosy." The apodosis to vers. 9 and 10 commences with ver.
11. בְּשָׂר חַי living, *i.e.* raw, proud flesh. מִחְיָה the preservation
of life (Gen xlv. 5), sustenance (Judg. vi. 4); here, in vers. 10
and 24, it signifies life in the sense of that which shows life, not
a blow or spot (נֶגַע, from מָחָה to strike), as it is only in a geographical sense that the verb has this signification, viz. to strike
against, or reach as far as (Num. xxxiv. 11). If the priest
found that the evil was an old, long-standing leprosy, he was to
pronounce the man unclean, and not first of all to shut him up,
as there was no longer any doubt about the matter.—Vers. 12,
13. If, on the other hand, the leprosy broke out blooming on the
skin, and covered the whole of the skin from head to foot " with
regard to the whole sight of the eyes of the priest," *i.e.* as far as
his eyes could see, the priest was to pronounce the person clean.
" He has turned quite white," *i.e.* his dark body has all become
white. The breaking out of the leprous matter in this complete
and rapid way upon the surface of the whole body was the crisis
of the disease; the diseased matter turned into a scurf, which
died away and then fell off.—Ver. 14. " But in the day when
proud flesh appears upon him, he is unclean, . . . the proud flesh is
unclean; it is leprosy." That is to say, if proud flesh appeared
after the body had been covered with a white scurf, with which
the diseased matter had apparently exhausted itself, the disease
was not removed, and the person affected with it was to be pronounced unclean.

The *third case:* if the leprosy proceeded from an abscess
which had been cured. In ver. 18 בָּשָׂר is first of all used absolutely, and then resumed with בּוֹ, and the latter again is more
closely defined in בְּעוֹרוֹ: " if there arises in the flesh, in him, in
his skin, an abscess, and (it) is healed, and there arises in the
place of the abscess a white elevation, or a spot of a reddish
white, he (the person so affected) shall appear at the priest's."—
Ver. 20. If the priest found the appearance of the diseased spot
lower than the surrounding skin, and the hair upon it turned
white, he was to pronounce the person unclean. " It is a mole
of leprosy: it has broken out upon the abscess."—Vers. 21 sqq.
But if the hair had not turned white upon the spot, and there
was no depression on the skin, and it (the spot) was pale, the
priest was to shut him up for seven days. If the mole spread
upon the skin during this period, it was leprosy; but if the spot

stood in its place, and had not spread, it was צָרֶבֶת הַשְּׁחִין, "the closing of the abscess:" literally "the burning;" here, that part of the skin or flesh which has been burnt up or killed by the inflammation or abscess, and gradually falls off as scurf (*Knobel*).

The *fourth case* (vers. 24-28) : if there was a burnt place upon the skin of the flesh (מִכְוַת אֵשׁ, a spot where he had burnt himself with fire, the scar of a burn), and the "life of the scar" —*i.e.* the skin growing or forming upon the scar (see ver. 10)— "becomes a whitish red, or white spot," *i.e.* if it formed itself into a bright swollen spot. This was to be treated exactly like the previous case. שְׂאֵת הַמִּכְוָה (ver. 28), rising of the scar of the burn, *i.e.* a rising of the flesh and skin growing out of the scar of the burn.

Vers. 29-37. *Leprosy upon the head or chin.*—If the priest saw a mole upon the head or chin of a man or woman, the appearance of which was deeper than the skin, and on which the hair was yellow (צָהֹב golden, reddish, fox-colour) and thin, he was to regard it as נֶתֶק. Leprosy on the head or chin is called נֶתֶק, probably from נָתַק to pluck or tear, from its plucking out the hair, or causing it to fall off; like κνήφη, the itch, from κνάω, to itch or scratch, and *scabies*, from *scabere*. But if he did not observe these two symptoms, if there was no depression of the skin, and the hair was black and not yellow, he was to shut up the person affected for seven days. In שָׁחֹר אֵין בּוֹ (ver. 31) there is certainly an error of the text : either שחר must be retained and אין dropped, or שָׁחֹר must be altered into צָהֹב, according to ver. 37. The latter is probably the better of the two.— Vers. 32 sqq. If the mole had not spread by that time, and the two signs mentioned were not discernible, the person affected was to shave himself, but not to shave the *nethek*, the eruption or scurfy place, and the priest was to shut him up for seven days more, and then to look whether any alteration had taken place; and if not, to pronounce him clean, whereupon he was to wash his clothes (see ver. 6).—Vers. 35, 36. But if the eruption spread even after his purification, the priest, on seeing this, was not to look for yellow hair. "He is unclean:" that is to say, he was to pronounce him unclean without searching for yellow hairs; the spread of the eruption was a sufficient proof of the leprosy.—Ver. 37. But if, on the contrary, the eruption stood (see ver. 5), and black hair grew out of it, he was healed, and the person affected was to be declared clean

Vers. 38 and 39. *Harmless leprosy.*—This broke out upon the skin of the body in בֶּהָרֹת plaits, "white rings." If these were dull or a pale white, it was the harmless *bohak*, ἀλφός (LXX.), which did not defile, and which even the Arabs, who still call it *bahak*, consider harmless. It is an eruption upon the skin, appearing in somewhat elevated spots or rings of unequal sizes and a pale white colour, which do not change the hair; it causes no inconvenience, and lasts from two months to two years.

Vers. 40–44. *The leprosy of bald heads.*—קֵרֵחַ is a head bald behind; גִּבֵּחַ, in front, "bald from the side, or edge of his face, *i.e.* from the forehead and temples." Bald heads of both kinds were naturally clean.—Vers. 42 sqq. But if a white reddish mole was formed upon the bald place before or behind, it was leprosy breaking out upon it, and was to be recognised by the fact that the rising of the mole had the appearance of leprosy on the skin of the body. In that case the person was unclean, and to be pronounced so by the priest. "On his head is his plague of leprosy," *i.e.* he has it in his head.

Vers. 45 and 46. With regard to *the treatment of lepers*, the lawgiver prescribed that they should wear mourning costume, rend their clothes, leave the hair of their head in disorder (see at chap. x. 6), keep the beard covered (Ezek. xxiv. 17, 22), and cry "Unclean, unclean," that every one might avoid them for fear of being defiled (Lam. iv. 15) ; and as long as the disease lasted they were to dwell apart outside the camp (Num. v. 2 sqq., xii. 10 sqq., cf. 2 Kings xv. 5, vii. 3),[1] a rule which implies that the leper rendered others unclean by contact. From this the Rabbins taught, that by merely entering a house, a leper polluted everything within it (*Mishnah*, Kelim i. 4; Negaim xiii. 11).

Vers. 47–59. *Leprosy in linen, woollen, and leather fabrics and clothes.*—The only wearing apparel mentioned in ver. 47 is either woollen or linen, as in Deut. xxii. 11, Hos. ii. 7, Prov. xxxi. 13; and among the ancient Egyptians and ancient Greeks these were the materials usually worn. In vers. 48 sqq. שְׁתִי and עֵרֶב, "the

---

[1] At the present day there are pest-houses specially set apart for lepers outside the towns. In Jerusalem they are situated against the Zion-gate (see *Robinson*, Pal. i. p. 364).

flax and the wool," *i.e.* for linen and woollen fabrics, are distinguished from clothes of wool or flax. The rendering given to these words by the early translators is στήμων and κρόκη, *stamen et subtegmen* (LXX., *Vulg.*), *i.e.* warp and weft. The objection offered to this rendering, that warp and weft could not be kept so separate from one another, that the one could be touched and rendered leprous without the other, has been met by *Gussetius* by the simple but correct remark, that the reference is to the yarn prepared for the warp and weft, and not to the woven fabrics themselves. So long as the yarn was not woven into a fabric, the warp-yarn and weft-yarn might very easily be separated and lie in different places, so that the one could be injured without the other. In this case the yarn intended for weaving is distinguished from the woven material, just as the leather is afterwards distinguished from leather-work (ver. 49). The signs of leprosy were, if the mole in the fabric was greenish or reddish. In that case the priest was to shut up the thing affected with leprosy for seven days, and then examine it. If the mole had spread in the meantime, it was a "grievous leprosy." מַמְאֶרֶת, from מאר *irritavit, recruduit (vulnus)*, is to be explained, as it is by *Bochart*, as signifying *lepra exasperata*. מַמְאֶרֶת הַנֶּגַע making the mole bad or angry; not, as *Gesenius* maintains, from מאר = מרר *acerbum faciens, i.e. dolorem acerbum excitans*, which would not apply to leprosy in fabrics and houses (chap. xiv. 44), and is not required by Ezek. xxviii. 24. All such fabrics were to be burned as unclean.—Vers. 53 sqq. If the mole had not spread during the seven days, the priest was to cause the fabric in which the mole appeared to be washed, and then shut it up for seven days more. If the mole did not alter its appearance after being washed, even though it had not spread, the fabric was unclean, and was therefore to be burned. "It is a corroding in the back and front" (of the fabric or leather). פְּחֶתֶת, from פָּחַת, in Syriac *fodit*, from which comes פַּחַת a pit, *lit.* a digging: here a corroding depression. קָרַחַת a bald place in the front or right side, גַּבַּחַת a bald place in the back or left side of the fabric or leather.—Ver. 56. But if the mole had turned pale by the seventh day after the washing, it (the place of the mole) was to be separated (torn off) from the clothes, leather or yarn, and then (as is added afterwards in ver. 58) the garment or fabric from which the mole had disappeared was to be washed

a second time, and would then be clean.—Ver. 57. But if the
mole appeared *again* in any such garment or cloth, *i.e.* if it appeared again after this, it was a leprosy bursting forth afresh,
and the thing affected with it was to be burned. Leprosy in
linen and woollen fabrics or clothes, and in leather, consisted in
all probability in nothing but so-called mildew, which commonly
arises from damp and want of air, and consists, in the case of
linen, of round, partially coloured spots, which spread, and
gradually eat up the fabric, until it falls to pieces like mould.
In leather the mildew consists most strictly of "holes eaten in,"
and is of a "greenish, reddish, or whitish colour, according to
the species of the delicate cryptogami by which it has been
formed."

Chap. xiv., vers. 1–32. *Purification of the leper*, after his
recovery from his disease. As leprosy, regarded as a decomposition of the vital juices, and as putrefaction in a living body,
was an image of death, and like this introduced the same dissolution and destruction of life into the corporeal sphere which
sin introduced into the spiritual ; and as the leper for this very
reason was not only excluded from the fellowship of the sanctuary, but cut off from intercourse with the covenant nation
which was called to sanctification : the man, when recovered from
leprosy, was first of all to be received into the fellowship of the
covenant nation by a significant rite of purification, and then
again to be still further inducted into living fellowship with
Jehovah in His sanctuary. Hence the purification prescribed
was divided into two acts, separated from one another by an
interval of seven days.

The first act (vers. 2–8) set forth the restoration of the man,
who had been regarded as dead, into the fellowship of the living
members of the covenant nation, and was therefore performed
by the priest outside the camp.—Vers. 2 sqq. On the day of his
purification the priest was to examine the leper outside the
camp; and if he found the leprosy cured and gone (נִרְפָּא מִן,
const. prægnans, healed away from, *i.e.* healed and gone away
from), he was to send for (*lit.* order them to fetch or bring) two
living (חַיּוֹת, with all the fulness of their vital power) birds (without any precise direction as to the kind, not merely sparrows),
and (a piece of) cedar-wood and coccus (probably scarlet wool,
or a little piece of scarlet cloth), and hyssop (see at Ex. xii. 22).

—Vers. 5 sqq. The priest was to have one of the birds killed *into* an earthen vessel upon fresh water (water drawn from a fountain or brook, chap. xv. 13, Gen. xxvi. 19), that is to say, slain in such a manner that its blood should flow into the fresh water which was in a vessel, and should mix with it. He was then to take the (other) live bird, together with the cedar-wood, scarlet, and hyssop, and dip them (these accompaniments) along with the bird into the blood of the one which had been killed over the water. With this the person cured of leprosy was to be sprinkled seven times (see chap. iv. 6) and purified; after which the living bird was to be " let loose upon the face of the field," *i.e.* to be allowed to fly away into the open country. The two birds were symbols of the person to be cleansed. The one let loose into the open country is regarded by all the commentators as a symbolical representation of the fact, that the former leper was now imbued with new vital energy, and released from the fetters of his disease, and could now return in liberty again into the fellowship of his countrymen. But if this is established, the other must also be a symbol of the leper; and just as in the second the essential point in the symbol was its escape to the open country, in the first the main point must have been its death. Not, however, in this sense, that it was a figurative representation of the previous condition of the leper; but that, although it was no true sacrifice, since there was no sprinkling of blood in connection with it, its bloody death was intended to show that the leper would necessarily have suffered death on account of his uncleanness, which reached to the very foundation of his life, if the mercy of God had not delivered him from this punishment of sin, and restored to him the full power and vigour of life again. The restitution of this full and vigorous life was secured to him symbolically, by his being sprinkled with the blood of the bird which was killed in his stead. But because his liability to death had assumed a bodily form in the uncleanness of leprosy, he was sprinkled not only with blood, but with the flowing water of purification into which the blood had flowed, and was thus purified from his mortal uncleanness. Whereas one of the birds, however, had to lay down its life, and shed its blood for the person to be cleansed, the other was made into a symbol of the person to be cleansed by being bathed in the mixture of blood and water; and its

release, to return to its fellows and into its nest, represented his
deliverance from the ban of death which rested upon leprosy,
and his return to the fellowship of his own nation.   This signification of the rite serves to explain not only the appointment of
birds for the purpose, since free unfettered movement in all
directions could not be more fittingly represented by anything
than by birds, which are distinguished from all other animals
by their freedom and rapidity of motion, but also the necessity
for their being alive and clean, viz. to set forth the renewal of
life and purification ; also the addition of cedar-wood, scarlet
wool, and hyssop, by which the life-giving power of the blood
mixed with living (spring) water was to be still further strengthened.   The cedar-wood, on account of its antiseptic qualities
(ἔχει ἄσηπτον ἡ κέδρος, *Theodor.* on Ezek. xvii. 22), was a
symbol of the continuance of life ; the coccus colour, a symbol of freshness of life, or fulness of vital energy ; and the
hyssop (βοτάνη ῥυπτική, *herba humilis, medicinalis, purgandis
pulmonibus apta : August.* on Ps. li.), a symbol of purification
from the corruption of death.   The sprinkling was performed
seven times, because it referred to a readmission into the covenant, the stamp of which was seven ; and it was made with a
mixture of blood and fresh water, the blood signifying life, the
water purification.—Ver. 8. After this symbolical purification
from the mortal ban of leprosy, the person cleansed had to
purify himself bodily, by washing his clothes, shaving off all
his hair—*i.e.* not merely the hair of his head and beard, but that
of his whole body (cf. ver. 9),—and bathing in water ; and he
could then enter into the camp.   But he had still to remain
outside his tent for seven days, not only because he did not yet
feel himself at home in the congregation, or because he was still
to retain the consciousness that something else was wanting
before he could be fully restored, but, as the Chaldee has explained it by adding the clause, *et non accedat ad latus uxoris
suæ,* that he might not defile himself again by conjugal rights,
and so interrupt his preparation for readmission into fellowship
with Jehovah.

The *second act* (vers. 9–20) effected his restoration to fellowship with Jehovah, and his admission to the sanctuary.   It
commenced on the seventh day after the first with a fresh
purification ; viz. shaving off all the hair from the head, the

beard, the eyebrows—in fact, the whole body,—washing the clothes, and bathing the body. On the eighth day there followed a sacrificial expiation; and for this the person to be expiated was to bring two sheep without blemish, a ewe-lamb of a year old, three-tenths of an ephah of fine flour mixed with oil as a meat-offering, and a log (or one-twelfth of a hin, i.e. as much as six hens' eggs, or 15·62 Rhenish cubic inches) of oil; and the priest was to present him, together with these gifts, before Jehovah, i.e. before the altar of burnt-offering. The one lamb was then offered by the priest as a trespass-offering, together with the log of oil; and both of these were waved by him. By the waving, which did not take place on other occasions in connection with sin-offerings and trespass-offerings, the lamb and oil were transferred symbolically to the Lord; and by the fact that these sacrificial gifts represented the offerer, the person to be consecrated to the Lord by means of them was dedicated to His service again, just as the Levites were dedicated to the Lord by the ceremony of waving (Num. viii. 11, 15). But a trespass-offering was required as the consecration-offering, because the consecration itself served as a restoration to all the rights of the priestly covenant nation, which had been lost by the mortal ban of leprosy.[1]—Vers. 13, 14. After the slaying of the lamb in the holy place, as the trespass-offering, like the sin-offering, was most holy and belonged to the priest (see at chap. vii. 6), the priest put some of its blood upon the tip of the right ear, the right thumb, and the great toe of the right foot of the person to be consecrated, in order that the organ of hearing, with which he hearkened to the word of the Lord, and those used in acting and walking according to His command-

---

[1] Others, e.g. Riehm and Oehler, regard this trespass-offering also as a kind of mulcta, or satisfaction rendered for the fact, that during the whole period of his sickness, and so long as he was excluded from the congregation, the leper had failed to perform his theocratical duties, and Jehovah had been injured in consequence. But if this was the idea upon which the trespass-offering was founded, the law would necessarily have required that trespass-offerings should be presented on the recovery of persons who had been affected with diseased secretions; for during the continuance of their disease, which often lasted a long time, even as much as 12 years (Luke viii. 43), they were precluded from visiting the sanctuary or serving the Lord with sacrifices, because they were unclean, and therefore could not perform their theocratical duties.

ments, might thereby be sanctified through the power of the atoning blood of the sacrifice; just as in the dedication of the priests (chap. viii. 24).—Vers. 15–18. The priest then poured some oil out of the log into the hollow of his left hand, and dipping the finger of his right hand in the oil, sprinkled it seven times before Jehovah, *i.e.* before the altar of burnt-offering, to consecrate the oil to God, and sanctify it for further use. With the rest of the oil he smeared the same organs of the person to be consecrated which he had already smeared with blood, placing it, in fact, *"upon the blood of the trespass-offering,"* *i.e.* upon the spots already touched with blood; he then poured the remainder upon the head of the person to be consecrated, and so made atonement for him before Jehovah. The priests were also anointed at their consecration, not only by the pouring of oil upon their head, but by the sprinkling of oil upon their garments (chap. viii. 12, 30). But in their case the anointing of their head preceded the consecration-offering, and holy anointing oil was used for the purpose. Here, on the contrary, it was ordinary oil, which the person to be consecrated had offered as a sacrificial gift; and this was first of all sanctified, therefore, by being sprinkled before Jehovah, after which the oil was sprinkled and poured upon the organs with which he was to serve the Lord, and then upon the head, which represented his personality. Just as the anointing oil, prepared according to divine directions, shadowed forth the power and gifts of the Spirit, with which God endowed the priests for their peculiar office in His kingdom; so the oil, which the leper about to be consecrated presented as a sacrifice out of his own resources, represented the spirit of life which he had received from God, and now possessed as his own. This property of his spirit was presented to the Lord by the priestly waving and sprinkling of the oil before Jehovah, to be pervaded and revived by His spirit of grace, and when so strengthened, to be not only applied to those organs of the person to be consecrated, with which he fulfilled the duties of his vocation as a member of the priestly nation of God, but also poured upon his head, to be fully appropriated to his person. And just as in the sacrifice the blood was the symbol of the soul, so in the anointing the oil was the symbol of the spirit. If, therefore, the soul was established in gracious fellowship with the Lord by being sprinkled with the atoning blood of sacrifice, the anointing with oil had reference to the spirit, which gives life to soul and body, and which was thereby endowed with the power of the Spirit of God. In this way the man cleansed from leprosy was reconciled to Jehovah, and reinstated in the covenant privileges and covenant grace.— Vers. 19, 20. It was not till all this had been done, that the priest could proceed to make expiation for him with the sin-offering, for which the ewe-lamb was brought, "on account of his uncleanness," *i.e.* on account of the sin which still adhered to him as well as to all the other members of the covenant nation, and which had come outwardly to light in the uncleanness of his leprosy; after which he presented his burnt-offering and meat-offering, which embodied the sanctification of all his members to the service of the Lord, and the performance of works well-pleasing to Him. The sin-offering, burnt-offering, and meat-offering were therefore presented according to the general instructions, with this exception, that, as a representation of diligence in good works, a larger quantity of meal and oil was brought than the later law in Num. xv. 4 prescribed for the burnt-offering.—Vers. 21–32. In cases of poverty on the part of the person to be consecrated, the burnt-offering and sin-offering were reduced to a pair of turtle-doves or young pigeons, and the meat-offering to a tenth of an ephah of meal and oil; but no diminution was allowed in the trespass-offering as the consecration-offering, since this was the *conditio sine qua non* of reinstatement in full covenant rights. On account of the importance of all the details of this law, every point is repeated a second time in vers. 21–32.

Vers. 33–53. *The law concerning the leprosy of houses* was made known to Moses and Aaron, as intended for the time when Israel should have taken possession of Canaan and dwell in houses. As it was Jehovah who gave His people the land for a possession, so "putting the plague of leprosy in a house of the land of their possession" is also ascribed to Him (ver. 34), inasmuch as He held it over them, to remind the inhabitants of the house that they owed not only their bodies but also their dwelling-places to the Lord, and that they were to sanctify these to Him. By this expression, "*I put*," the view which *Knobel* still regards as probable, viz. that the house-leprosy was only the transmission of human leprosy to the walls of the houses, is completely overthrown; not to mention the fact, that throughout the whole description there is not the slightest hint of any such transmission, but the inhabitants, on the contrary, are spoken of as clean, *i.e.* free from leprosy, and only those who went into the house, or slept in the house after it had been shut up as suspicious, are pronounced unclean (vers. 46, 47), though even they are not said to have been affected with leprosy. The only thing that can be gathered from the signs mentioned in ver. 37 is, that the house-leprosy was an evil which calls to mind " the vegetable formations and braid-like structures that are found on mouldering walls and decaying walls, and which eat into them so as to produce a slight depression in the surface."[1]—Vers. 35, 36. When the evil showed itself in a house, the owner was to send this message to the priest, "*A leprous evil has appeared in my house*," and the priest, before entering to examine it, was to have the house cleared, lest everything in it should become unclean. Consequently, as what was in the house became unclean only when the priest had declared the house affected with leprosy, the reason for the defilement is not to be sought for in physical infection, but must have been of an ideal or symbolical kind.— Vers. 37 sqq. If the leprous spot appeared in "*greenish or reddish depressions, which looked deeper than the wall*," the priest was to shut up the house for seven days. If after that time he found that the mole had spread on the walls, he was to break out the stones upon which it appeared, and remove them to an unclean place outside the town, and to scrape the house all round inside, and throw the dust that was scraped off into an unclean place outside the town. He was then to put other stones in their place, and plaster the house with fresh mortar.—Vers. 43 sqq. If the mole broke out again after this had taken place, it was a malicious leprosy, and the house was to be pulled down as unclean, whilst the stones, the wood, and the mortar were to be taken to an unclean place outside the town.—Vers. 46, 47. Whoever went into the house during the time that it was closed, became unclean till the evening and had to wash himself; but

[1] Cf. *Sommer* (p. 220), who says, " The crust of many of these lichens is so marvellously thin, that they simply appear as coloured spots, for the most part circular, which gradually spread in a concentric form, and can be rubbed off like dust. Some species have a striking resemblance to eruptions upon the skin. There is one genus called *spiloma* (spots) ; and another very numerous genus bears the name of *lepraria*."

whoever slept or ate therein during this time, was to wash his clothes, and of course was unclean till the evening. הִסְגִּיר אֹתוֹ (ver. 46) may be a perfect tense, and a relative clause dependent upon יְמֵי, or it may be an infinitive for הַסְגִּיר as in ver. 43.—Ver. 48. If the priest should find, however, that after the fresh plastering the mole had not appeared again, or spread (to other places), he was to pronounce the house clean, because the evil was cured, and (vers. 49–53) to perform the same rite of purification as was prescribed for the restoration of a man, who had been cured of leprosy, to the national community (vers. 4–7). The purpose was also the same, namely, to cleanse (חִטֵּא cleanse from sin) and make atonement for the house, i.e. to purify it from the uncleanness of sin which had appeared in the leprosy. For, although it is primarily in the human body that sin manifests itself, it spreads from man to the things which he touches, uses, inhabits, though without our being able to represent this spread as a physical contagion.—Vers. 54–57 contain the concluding formula to chap. xiii. and xiv. The law of leprosy was given " to teach in the day of the unclean and the clean," i.e. to give directions for the time when they would have to do with the clean and unclean.

Chap. xv. The UNCLEANNESS OF SECRETIONS.—These include (1) a running issue from a man (vers. 2–15) ; (2) involuntary emission of seed (vers. 16, 17), and the emission of seed in sexual intercourse (ver. 18) ; (3) the monthly period of a woman (vers. 19–24) ; (4) a diseased issue of blood from a woman (vers. 25–30). They consist, therefore, of two diseased and two natural secretions from the organs of generation.

Vers. 2–15. The *running issue from a man* is not described with sufficient clearness for us to be able to determine with certainty what disease is referred to : " if a man becomes flowing out of his flesh, he is unclean in his flux." That even here the term flesh is not a euphemism for the organ of generation, as is frequently assumed, is evident from ver. 13, " he shall wash his clothes and bathe his *flesh* in water," when compared with chap. xvi. 23, 24, 28, etc., where flesh cannot possibly have any such meaning. The "flesh" is the body as in ver. 7, " whoever touches the flesh of him that hath the issue," as compared with ver. 19, " whosoever toucheth her." At the same time, the agreement between the law relating to the man with an issue and that concerning the woman with an issue (ver. 19, "her issue in her flesh") points unmistakeably to a secretion from the sexual organs. Only the seat of the disease is not more closely defined. The issue of the man is not a hemorrhoidal disease, for nothing is said about a flow of blood; still less is it a syphilitic suppuration (*gonorrhœa virulenta*), for the occurrence of this at all in antiquity is very questionable; but it is either a diseased flow of *semen* (*gonorrhœa*), *i.e.* an involuntary flow drop by drop arising from weakness of the organ, as *Jerome* and the Rabbins assume, or more probably, simply *blenorrhœa urethræ*, a discharge of mucus arising from a catarrhal affection of the mucous membrane of the urethra (*urethritis*). The participle זָב יִהְיֶה is expressive of continued duration. In ver. 3 the uncleanness is still more closely defined: "whether his flesh run with his issue, or his flesh closes before his issue," *i.e.* whether the member lets the matter flow out or by closing retains it, "it is his uncleanness," *i.e.* in the latter case as well as the former it is uncleanness to him, he is unclean. For the "closing" is only a temporary obstruction, brought about by some particular circumstance.—Ver. 4. Every bed upon which he lay, and everything upon which he sat, was defiled in consequence; also every one who touched his bed (ver. 5), or sat upon it (ver. 6), or touched his flesh, *i.e.* his body (ver. 7), was unclean, and had to bathe himself and wash his clothes in consequence.—Vers. 9, 10. The conveyance in which such a man rode was also unclean, as well as everything under him; and whoever touched them was defiled till the evening, and the person who carried them was to wash his clothes and bathe himself.—Ver. 11. This also applied to every one whom the man with an issue might touch, without first rinsing his hands in water.—Vers. 12, 13. Vessels that he had touched were to be broken to pieces if they were of earthenware, and rinsed with water if they were of wood, for the reasons explained in chap. xi. 33 and vi. 21.—Vers. 13–15. When he was cleansed, *i.e.* recovered from his issue, he was to wait seven days with regard to his purification, and then wash his clothes and bathe his body in fresh water, and be clean. On the eighth day he was to bring two turtle-doves or young pigeons, in order that the priest might prepare one as a sin-offering and the other as a burnt-offering, and make an atonement for him before the Lord for his issue.

Vers. 16–18. *Involuntary emission of seed.*—This defiled for the whole of the day, not only the man himself, but any garment or skin upon which any of it had come, and required for purification that the whole body should be bathed, and the polluted things washed.—Ver. 18. *Sexual connection.* " If a man lie with a woman with the emission of seed, both shall be unclean till the evening, and bathe themselves in water." Consequently it was not the *concubitus* as such which defiled, as many erroneously suppose, but the emission of seed in the *coitus*. This explains the law and custom, of abstaining from conjugal intercourse during the preparation for acts of divine worship, or the performance of the same (Ex. xix. 5 ; 1 Sam. xxi. 5, 6 ; 2 Sam. xi. 4), in which many other nations resembled the Israelites. (For proofs see Leyrer's article in *Herzog's* Cyclopædia, and *Knobel in loco*, though the latter is wrong in supposing that conjugal intercourse itself defiled.)

Vers. 19–24. The *menses of a woman.*—"If a woman have an issue, (if) blood is her issue in her flesh, she shall be seven days in her uncleanness." As the discharge does not last as a rule more than four or five days, the period of seven days was fixed on account of the significance of the number seven. In this condition she rendered every one who touched her unclean (ver. 19), everything upon which she lay or sat (ver. 20), every one who touched her bed or whatever she sat upon (vers. 21, 22), also any one who touched the blood upon her bed or seat (ver. 23, where הוא and בּו are to be referred to דָּם) ; and they remained unclean till the evening, when they had to wash their clothes and bathe themselves.—Ver. 24. If a man lay with her and her uncleanness came upon him, he became unclean for seven days, and the bed upon which he lay became unclean as well. The meaning cannot be merely if he lie upon the same bed with her, but if he have conjugal intercourse, as is evident from chap. xx. 18 and Num. v. 13 (cf. Gen. xxvi. 10, xxxiv. 2, xxxv. 22 ; 1 Sam. ii. 22). It cannot be adduced as an objection to this explanation, which is the only admissible one, that according to chap. xviii. 19 and xx. 18 intercourse with a woman during her menses was an accursed crime, to be punished by extermination. For the law in chap. xx. 18 refers partly to conjugal intercourse during the hemorrhage of a woman after child-birth, as the similarity of the words in chap. xx. 18 and xii.

7 (מְקוֹר דָּמֶיהָ) clearly proves, and to the case of a man attempting cohabitation with a woman during her menstruation. The verse before us, on the contrary, refers simply to the possibility of menstruation commencing during the act of conjugal intercourse, when the man would be involuntarily defiled through the unexpected uncleanness of the woman.

Vers. 25–31. *Diseased issue from a woman.*—If an issue of blood in a woman flowed many days away from (not in) the time of her monthly uncleanness, or if it flowed beyond her monthly uncleanness, she was to be unclean as long as her unclean issue continued, just as in the days of her monthly uncleanness, and she defiled her couch as well as everything upon which she sat, as in the other case, also every one who touched either her or these things.—Vers. 28–30. After the issue had ceased, she was to purify herself like the man with an issue, as described in vers. 13–15.—Obedience to these commands is urged in ver. 31 : " Cause that the children of Israel free themselves from their uncleanness, that they die not through their uncleanness, by defiling My dwelling in the midst of them."   הִזִּיר, *Hiphil,* to cause that a person keeps aloof from anything, or loosens himself from it, from נָזַר, *Niphal* to separate one's self, signifies here deliverance from the state of uncleanness, purification from it. Continuance in it was followed by death, not merely in the particular instance in which an unclean man ventured to enter the sanctuary, but as a general fact, because uncleanness was irreconcilable with the calling of Israel to be a holy nation, in the midst of which Jehovah the Holy One had His dwelling-place (chap. xi. 44), and continuance in uncleanness without the prescribed purification was a disregard of the holiness of Jehovah, and involved rebellion against Him and His ordinances of grace.— Vers. 32, 33. *Concluding formula.*   The words, " *him that lieth with her that is unclean,*" are more general than the expression, "lie with her," in ver. 24, and involve not only intercourse with an unclean woman, but lying by her side upon one and the same bed.

THE DAY OF ATONEMENT.—CHAP. XVI.

The sacrifices and purifications enjoined thus far did not suffice to complete the reconciliation between the congregation of Israel, which was called to be a holy nation, but in its very nature was still altogether involved in sin and uncleanness, and Jehovah the Holy One,—that is to say, to restore the perfect reconciliation and true vital fellowship of the nation with its God, in accordance with the idea and object of the old covenant,—because, even with the most scrupulous observance of these directions, many sins and defilements would still remain unacknowledged, and therefore without expiation, and would necessarily produce in the congregation a feeling of separation from its God, so that it would be unable to attain to the true joyousness of access to the throne of grace, and to the place of reconciliation with God. This want was met by the appointment of a yearly general and perfect expiation of all the sins and uncleanness which had remained unatoned for and uncleansed in the course of the year. In this respect the laws of sacrifice and purification received their completion and finish in the institution of the festival of atonement, which provided for the congregation of Israel the highest and most comprehensive expiation that was possible under the Old Testament. Hence the law concerning the day of atonement formed a fitting close to the ordinances designed to place the Israelites in fellowship with their God, and raise the promise of Jehovah, "I will be your God," into a living truth. This law is described in the present chapter, and contains (1) the instructions as to the performance of the general expiation for the year (vers. 2–28), and (2) directions for the celebration of this festival every year (vers. 29–34). From the expiation effected upon this day it received the name of "*day of expiations*," *i.e.* of the highest expiation (chap. xxiii. 27). The Rabbins call it briefly יוֹמָא, the day κατ᾽ ἐξοχήν.

Vers. 1, 2. The chronological link connecting the following law with the death of the sons of Aaron (chap. x. 1–5) was intended, not only to point out the historical event which led to the appointment of the day of atonement, but also to show the importance and holiness attached to an entrance into the inmost sanctuary of God. The death of Aaron's sons, as a punishment for wilfully "drawing near before Jehovah," was to be a solemn warning to Aaron himself, "not to come at all times into the holy place within the vail, before the mercy-seat upon the ark," *i.e.* into the most holy place (see Ex. xxv. 10 sqq.), but only at the time to be appointed by Jehovah, and for the purposes instituted by Him, *i.e.*, according to vers. 29 sqq., only once a year, on the day of atonement, and only in the manner prescribed in vers. 3 sqq., that he might not die.—" For I will appear in the cloud above the capporeth." The cloud in which Jehovah appeared above the capporeth, between the cherubim (Ex. xxv. 22), was not the cloud of the incense, with which Aaron was to cover the capporeth on entering (ver. 13), as *Vitringa, Bähr,* and others follow the Sadducees in supposing, but the cloud of the divine glory, in which Jehovah manifested His essential presence in the most holy place above the ark of the covenant. Because Jehovah appeared in this cloud, not only could no unclean and sinful man go before the capporeth, *i.e.* approach the holiness of the all-holy God; but even the anointed and sanctified high priest, if he went before it at his own pleasure, or without the expiatory blood of sacrifice, would expose himself to certain death. The reason for this prohibition is to be found in the fact, that the holiness communicated to the priest did not cancel the sin of his nature, but only covered it over for the performance of his official duties, and so long as the law, which produced only the knowledge of sin and not its forgiveness and removal, was not abolished by the complete atonement, the holy God was and remained to mortal and sinful man a consuming fire, before which no one could stand.

Vers. 3–5. Only בְּזֹאת, " *with this,*" *i.e.* with the sacrifices, dress, purifications, and means of expiation mentioned afterwards, could he go into " the holy place," *i.e.,* according to the more precise description in ver. 2, into the inmost division of the tabernacle, which is called *Kodesh hakkadashim,* " the holy of holies," in Ex. xxvi. 33. He was to bring an ox (bullock) for a sin-offering and a ram for a burnt-offering, as a sacrifice for himself and his house (*i.e.* the priesthood, ver. 6), and two he-goats for a sin-offering and a ram for a burnt-offering, as a sacrifice for the congregation. For this purpose he was to put on, not the state-costume of the high priest, but a body-coat, drawers, girdle, and head-dress of white cloth (*bad :* see Ex. xxviii. 42), having first bathed his body, and not merely his hands and feet, as he did for the ordinary service, to appear before Jehovah as entirely cleansed from the defilement of sin (see at chap. viii. 6) and arrayed in clothes of holiness. The dress of white cloth was not the plain official dress of the ordinary priests, for the girdle of that dress was coloured (see at

Ex. xxviii. 39, 40) ; and in that case the high priest would not have appeared in the perfect purity of his divinely appointed office as chief of the priesthood, but simply as the priest appointed for this day (v. *Hofmann*). Nor did he officiate (as many of the Rabbins, and also *C. a Lapide, Grotius, Rosenmüller,* and *Knobel* suppose) as a penitent praying humbly for the forgiveness of sin. For where in all the world have clear white clothes been worn either in mourning or as a penitential garment ? The emphatic expression, " *these are holy garments,*" is a sufficient proof that the pure white colour of all the clothes, even of the girdle, was intended as a representation of holiness. Although in Ex. xxviii. 2, 4, etc., the official dress not only of Aaron, but of his sons also, that is to say, the priestly costume generally, is described as " holy garments," yet in the present chapter the word *kodesh,* " holy," is frequently used in an emphatic sense (for example, in vers. 2, 3, 16, of the most holy place of the dwelling), and by this predicate the dress is characterized as most holy. Moreover, it was in *baddim* (" linen") that the angel of Jehovah was clothed (Ezek. ix. 2, 3, 11, x. 2, 6, 7, and Dan. x. 5, xii. 6, 7), whose whole appearance, as described in Dan. x. 6, resembled the appearance of the glory of Jehovah, which Ezekiel saw in the vision of the four cherubim (chap. i.), and was almost exactly like the glory of Jesus Christ, which John saw in the Revelation (chap. i. 13–15). The white material, therefore, of the dress which Aaron wore, when performing the highest act of expiation under the Old Testament, was a symbolical shadowing forth of the holiness and glory of the one perfect Mediator between God and man, who, being the radiation of the glory of God and the image of His nature, effected by Himself the perfect cleansing away of our sin, and who, as the true High Priest, being holy, innocent, unspotted, and separate from sinners, entered once by His own blood into the holy place not made with hands, namely, into heaven itself, to appear before the face of God for us, and obtain everlasting redemption (Heb. i. 3, vii. 26, ix. 12, 24).

Vers. 6–10. With the bullock Aaron was to make atonement for himself and his house. The two he-goats he was to place before Jehovah (see chap. i. 5), and " *give lots over them,*" *i.e.* have lots cast upon them, one lot for Jehovah, the other for Azazel. The one upon which the lot for Jehovah fell (עָלָה, from the coming up of the lot out of the urn, Josh. xviii. 11, xix. 10), he was to prepare as a sin-offering for Jehovah, and to present the one upon which the lot for Azazel fell alive before Jehovah, לְכַפֵּר עָלָיו, " to expiate it," i.e. to make it the object of expiation (see at ver. 21), to send it (them) into the desert to Azazel. עֲזָאזֵל, which only occurs in this chapter, signifies neither " a remote solitude," nor any locality in the desert whatever (as Jonathan, Rashi, etc., suppose) ; nor the " he-goat" (from עֵז goat, and אָזַל to turn off, " the goat departing or sent away," as Symm., Theodot., the Vulgate, Luther, and others render it) ; nor " complete removal" (Bähr, Winer, Tholuck, etc.). The words, one lot for Jehovah and one for Azazel, require uncon-ditionally that Azazel should be regarded as a personal being, in opposition to Jehovah.   The word is a more intense form of אָזַל removit, dimovit, and comes from עֲזַלְזֵל by absorbing the liquid, like Babel from balbel (Gen. xi. 9), and Golgotha from gulgalta (Ewald, § 158c). The Septuagint rendering is correct, ὁ ἀπο-πομπαῖος ; although in ver. 10 the rendering ἀποπομπή is also adopted, i.e. " averruncus, a fiend, or demon whom one drives away" (Ewald). We have not to think, however, of any demon whatever, who seduces men to wickedness in the form of an evil spirit, as the fallen angel Azazel is represented as doing in the Jewish writings (Book of Enoch viii. 1, x. 12, xiii. 1 sqq.), like the terrible fiend Shibe, whom the Arabs of the peninsula of Sinai so much dread (Seetzen, i. pp. 273–4), but of the devil himself, the head of the fallen angels, who was afterwards called Satan ; for no subordinate evil spirit could have been placed in antithesis to Jehovah as Azazel is here, but only the ruler or head of the kingdom of demons.   The desert and deso-late places are mentioned elsewhere as the abode of evil spirits (Isa. xiii. 21, xxxiv. 14 ; Matt. xii. 43 ; Luke xi. 24 ; Rev. xviii. 2).   The desert, regarded as an image of death and desolation, corresponds to the nature of evil spirits, who fell away from the primary source of life, and in their hostility to God devastated the world, which was created good, and brought death and de-struction in their train.

Vers. 11–20. He was then to slay the bullock of the sin-offering, and make atonement for himself and his house (or family, i.e. for the priests, ver. 33). But before bringing the blood of the sin-offering into the most holy place, he was to take

" *the filling of the censer* (*machtah*, a coal-pan, Ex. xxv. 38) *with fire-coals*," *i.e.* as many burning coals as the censer would hold, from the altar of burnt-offering, and " *the filling of his hands*," *i.e.* two hands full of " *fragrant incense* " (Ex. xxx. 34), and go with this within the vail, *i.e.* into the most holy place, and there place the incense upon the fire before Jehovah, " *that the cloud of* (burning) *incense might cover the capporeth above the testimony, and he might not die*." The design of these instructions was not that the holiest place, the place of Jehovah's presence, might be hidden by the cloud of incense from the gaze of the unholy eye of man, and so he might separate himself reverentially from it, that the person approaching might not be seized with destruction. But as burning incense was a symbol of *prayer*, this covering of the capporeth with the cloud of incense was a symbolical covering of the glory of the Most Holy One with prayer to God, in order that He might not see the sin, nor suffer His holy wrath to break forth upon the sinner, but might graciously accept, in the blood of the sin-offering, the souls for which it was presented. Being thus protected by the incense from the wrath of the holy God, he was to sprinkle (once) some of the blood of the ox with his finger, first upon the capporeth *in front, i.e.* not upon the top of the capporeth, but merely upon or against the front of it, and then seven times *before* the capporeth, *i.e.* upon the ground in front of it. It is here assumed as a matter of course, that when the offering of incense was finished, he would necessarily come out of the most holy place again, and go to the altar of burnt-offering to fetch some of the blood of the ox which had been slaughtered there.—Ver. 15. After this he was to slay the he-goat as a sin-offering for the nation, for which purpose, of course, he must necessarily come back to the court again, and then take the blood of the goat into the most holy place, and do just the same with it as he had already done with that of the ox. A double sprinkling took place in both cases, first upon or against the capporeth, and then seven times in front of the capporeth. The first sprinkling, which was performed once only, was for the expiation of the sins, first of the high priest and his house, and then of the congregation of Israel (chap. iv. 7 and 18); the second, which was repeated seven times, was for the expiation of the sanctuary from the sins of the people. This is implied in the words of ver. 16*a*, " and so

shall he make expiation for the most holy place, on account of
the uncleanness of the children of Israel, and on account of their
transgressions with regard to all their sins," which refer to both
the sacrifices; since Aaron first of all expiated the sins of the
priesthood, and the uncleanness with which the priesthood had
stained the sanctuary through their sin, by the blood of the
bullock of the sin-offering; and then the sins of the nation, and
the uncleannesses with which it had defiled the sanctuary, by the
he-goat, which was also slain as a sin-offering.[1]—Vers. 16b and
17. "*And so shall he do to the tabernacle of the congregation that
dwelleth among them*" (*i.e.* has its place among them, Josh. xxii.
19) "*in the midst of their uncleanness.*" The holy things were
rendered unclean, not only by the sins of those who touched
them, but by the uncleanness, *i.e.* the bodily manifestations of
the sin of the nation; so that they also required a yearly expiation and cleansing through the expiatory blood of sacrifice. By
ohel moed, "the tabernacle of the congregation," in vers. 16 and
17, as well as vers. 20 and 33, we are to understand the holy
place of the tabernacle, to which the name of the whole is
applied on account of its occupying the principal space in the
dwelling, and in distinction from *kodesh* (the holy), which is
used in this chapter to designate the most holy place, or the
space at the back of the dwelling. It follows still further from
this, that by the altar in ver. 18, and also in vers. 20 and 33,
which is mentioned here as the third portion of the entire sanctuary, we are to understand the altar of burnt-offering in the
court, and not the altar of incense, as the Rabbins and most of
the commentators assume. This rabbinical view cannot be
sustained, either from Ex. xxx. 10 or from the context. Ex. xxx.
10 simply prescribes a yearly expiation of the altar of incense
on the day of atonement; and this is implied in the words "so
shall he do," in ver. 16b. For these words can only mean, that
in the same way in which he had expiated the most holy place
he was also to expiate the holy place of the tabernacle, in which
the altar of incense took the place of the ark of the covenant of

---

[1] *V. Hofmann's* objection to this rests upon the erroneous supposition
that a double act of expiation was required for the congregation, and only
a single one for the priesthood, whereas, according to the distinct words of
the text, a double sprinkling was performed with the blood of both the sin-
offerings, and therefore a double expiation effected.

the most holy place; so that the expiation was performed by his putting blood, in the first place, upon the horns of the altar, and then sprinkling it seven times upon the ground in front of it. The expression "go out" in ver. 18 refers, not to his going out of the most holy into the holy place, but to his going out of the *ohel moed* (or holy place) into the court.—Ver. 17. There was to be no one in the *ohel moed* when Aaron went into it to make expiation in the most holy place, until he came out (of the tabernacle) again; not because no one but the chief servant of Jehovah was worthy to be near or present either as spectator or assistant at this sacred act before Jehovah (*Knobel*), but because no unholy person was to defile by his presence the sanctuary, which had just been cleansed; just as no layman at all was allowed to enter the holy place, or could go with impunity into the presence of the holy God.—Vers. 18, 19. After he had made atonement for the dwelling, Aaron was to expiate the altar in the court, by first of all putting some of the blood of the bullock and he-goat upon the horns of the altar, and then sprinkling it seven times with his finger, and thus cleansing and sanctifying it from the uncleannesses of the children of Israel. The application of blood to the horns of the altar was intended to expiate the sins of the priests as well as those of the nation; just as in the case of ordinary sin-offerings it expiated the sins of individual members of the nation (chap. iv. 25, 30, 34), to which the priests also belonged; and the sevenfold sprinkling effected the purification of the place of sacrifice from the uncleannesses of the congregation.

The meaning of the sprinkling of blood upon the capporeth and the horns of the two altars was the same as in the case of every sin-offering (see pp. 280 and 304). The peculiar features in the expiatory ritual of the day of atonement were the following. In the first place, the blood of both sacrifices was taken not merely into the holy place, but into the most holy, and sprinkled directly upon the throne of God. This was done to show that the true atonement could only take place before the throne of God Himself, and that the sinner was only then truly reconciled to God, and placed in the full and living fellowship of peace with God, when he could come directly to the throne of God, and not merely to the place where, although the Lord did indeed manifest His grace to him, He was still separated from him by a curtain. In this respect, therefore, the bringing of the blood of atonement into the most holy place had a prophetic signification, and was a predictive sign that the curtain, which then separated Israel from its God, would one day be removed, and that with the entrance of the full and eternal atonement free access would be opened to the throne of the Lord. The *second* peculiarity in this act of atonement was the sprinkling of the blood seven times upon the holy places, the floor of the holy of holies and holy place, and the altar of the court; also the application of blood to the media of atonement in the three divisions of the tabernacle, for the cleansing of the holy places from the uncleanness of the children of Israel. As this uncleanness cannot be regarded as consisting of physical defilement, but simply as the ideal effluence of their sins, which had been transferred to the objects in question; so, on the other hand, the cleansing of the holy places can only be understood as consisting in an ideal transference of the influence of the atoning blood to the inanimate objects which had been defiled by sin. If the way in which the sacrificial blood, regarded as the expiation of souls, produced its cleansing effects was, that by virtue thereof the sin was covered over, whilst the sinner was reconciled to God and received forgiveness of sin and the means of sanctification, we must regard the sin-destroying virtue of the blood as working in the same way also upon the objects defiled by sin, namely, that powers were transferred to them which removed the effects proceeding from sin, and in this way wiped out the uncleanness of the children of Israel that was in them. This communication of purifying powers to the holy things was represented by the sprinkling of the atoning blood upon and against them, and indeed by their being sprinkled seven times, to set forth the communication as raised to an efficiency corresponding to its purpose, and to impress upon it the stamp of a divine act through the number seven, which was sanctified by the work of God in creation.

Vers. 20–22. After the completion of the expiation and cleansing of the holy things, Aaron was to bring up the live goat, *i.e.* to have it brought before the altar of burnt-offering, and placing both his hands upon its head, to confess all the sins and transgressions of the children of Israel upon it, and so put them upon its head. He was then to send the goat away into the desert by a man who was standing ready, that it might carry all its sins upon it into a land cut off; and there the man was to set the goat at liberty. עִתִּי, ἅπαξ λεγ. from עֵת an appointed time, signifies opportune, present at the right time, or ready. גְּזֵרָה, which is also met with in this passage alone, from גָּזַר to cut, or cut off, that which is severed, a country cut off from others, not connected by roads with any inhabited land. "The goat was not to find its way back" (Knobel). To understand clearly the meaning of this symbolical rite, we must start from the fact, that according to the distinct words of ver. 5, the two goats were to serve as a sin-offering (לְחַטָּאת). They were both of them devoted, therefore, to one and the same purpose, as was pointed out by the Talmudists, who laid down the law on that very account, that they were to be exactly alike, colore, statura, et valore. The living goat, therefore, is not to be regarded merely as the bearer of the sin to be taken away, but as quite as truly a sin-offering as the one that was slaughtered. It was appointed לְכַפֵּר עָלָיו (ver. 10), i.e. not that an expiatory rite might be performed over it, for עַל with כַּפֵּר always applies to the object of the expiation, but properly to expiate it, i.e. to make it the object of expiation, or make expiation with it. To this end the sins of the nation were confessed upon it with the laying on of hands, and thus symbolically laid upon its head, that it might bear them, and when sent into the desert carry them away thither. The sins, which were thus laid upon its head by confession, were the sins of Israel, which had already been expiated by the sacrifice of the other goat. To understand, however, how the sins already expiated could still be confessed and laid upon the living goat, it is not sufficient to say, with Bähr, that the expiation with blood represented merely a covering or covering up of the sin, and that in order to impress upon the expiation the stamp of the greatest possible completeness and perfection, a supplement was appended, which represented the carrying away and removal of the sin. For in the case of every sin-offering for the congregation, in addition to the covering or forgiveness of sin represented by the sprinkling of blood, the removal or abolition of it was also represented by the burning of the flesh of the sacrifice; and this took place in the present instance also. As both goats were intended for a sin-offering, the sins of the nation were confessed upon both, and placed upon the heads of both by the laying on of hands; though it is of the living goat only that this is expressly recorded, being omitted in the case of the other, because the rule laid down in chap. iv. 4 sqq. was followed.[1] By both Israel was delivered from all sins and transgressions; but by the one, upon which the lot " for Jehovah" fell, it was so with regard to Jehovah; by the other, upon which the lot "for Azazel" fell, with regard to Azazel. With regard to Jehovah, or in relation to Jehovah, the sins were wiped away by the sacrifice of the goat; the sprinkling of the blood setting forth their forgiveness, and the burning of the animal the blotting of them out; and with this the separation of the congregation from Jehovah because of its sin was removed, and living fellowship with God restored. But Israel had also been brought by its sin into a distinct relation to Azazel, the head of the evil spirits; and it was necessary that this should be brought to an end, if reconciliation with God was to be perfectly secured. This complete deliverance from sin and its author was symbolized in the leading away of the goat, which had been laden with the sins, into the desert. This goat was to take back the sins, which God had forgiven to His congregation, into the desert to Azazel, the father of all sin, on the one hand as a proof that his evil influences upon men would be of no avail in the case of those who had received expiation from God, and on the other hand as a proof to the congregation also that those who were laden with sin could not remain in the kingdom of God, but would be banished to the abode of evil spirits, unless they were redeemed therefrom. This last point, it is true, is not expressly mentioned in the text; but it is evident from the fate which necessarily awaited the goat, when driven into the wilderness in the " land cut off." It would be sure to perish out there in the desert, that is to say, to suffer just what a sinner would have to endure if his sins remained upon him; though probably it is only a later addition, not founded in the law, which we find in the *Mishnah, Joma* vi. 6, viz. that the goat was driven headlong from a rock in the desert, and dashed to pieces at the foot.

---

[1] The distinction, that in the case of all the other sacrifices *the* (one) *hand* is ordered to be laid upon the victim, whilst here *both hands* are ordered to be laid upon the goat, does not constitute an essential difference, as *Hofmann* supposes; but the laying on of both hands rendered the act more solemn and expressive, in harmony with the solemnity of the whole proceeding.

There is not the slightest idea of presenting a sacrifice to Azazel. This goat was a sin-offering, only so far as it was laden with the sins of the people to carry them away into the desert; and in this respect alone is there a resemblance between the two goats and the two birds used in the purification of the leper (chap. xiv. 4 sqq.), of which the one to be set free was bathed in the blood of the one that was killed. In both cases the reason for making use of two animals is to be found purely in the physical impossibility of combining all the features, that had to be set forth in the sin-offering, in one single animal.

Vers. 23-28. After the living goat had been sent away, Aaron was to go into the tabernacle, *i.e.* the holy place of the dwelling, and there take off his white clothes and lay them down, *i.e.* put them away, because they were only to be worn in the performance of the expiatory ritual of this day, and then bathe his body in the holy place, *i.e.* in the court, in the laver between the altar and the door of the dwelling, probably because the act of laying the sins upon the goat rendered him unclean. He was then to put on his clothes, *i.e.* the coloured state-dress of the high priest, and to offer in this the burnt-offerings, for an atonement for himself and the nation (see chap. i. 4), and to burn the fat portions of the sin-offerings upon the altar.—Vers. 26 sqq. The man who took the goat into the desert, and those who burned the two sin-offerings outside the camp (see at chap. iv. 11, 21), had also to wash their clothes and bathe their bodies before they returned to the camp, because they had been defiled by the animals laden with sin.

Vers. 29-34. *General directions for the yearly celebration of the day of atonement.*—It was to be kept on the tenth day of the seventh month, as an "everlasting statute" (see at Ex. xii. 14). On that day the Israelites were to "afflict their souls," *i.e.* to fast, according to chap. xxiii. 32, from the evening of the 9th till the evening of the 10th day. Every kind of work was to be suspended as on the Sabbath (Ex. xx. 10), by both natives and foreigners (see Ex. xii. 49), because this day was a high Sabbath (Ex. xxxi. 15). Both fasting and sabbatical rest are enjoined again in chap. xxiii. 27 sqq. and Num. xxix. 7, on pain of death. The fasting commanded for this day, the only fasting prescribed in the law, is most intimately connected with the signification of the feast of atonement. If the general atonement made on this day was not to pass into a dead formal service, the people must necessarily enter in spirit into the signification of the act of expiation, prepare their souls for it with penitential feelings, and manifest this penitential state by abstinence from the ordinary enjoyments of life. To "*afflict* (bow, humble) *the soul*," by restraining the earthly appetites, which have their seat in the soul, is the early Mosaic expression for *fasting* (ענה). The latter word came first of all into use in the time of the Judges (Judg. xx. 26; 1 Sam. vii. 6; cf. Ps. xxxv. 13: "I afflicted my soul with fasting"). "By bowing his soul the Israelite was to place himself in an inward relation to the sacrifice, whose soul was given for his soul; and by this state of mind, answering to the outward proceedings of the day, he was to appropriate the fruit of it to himself, namely, the reconciliation of his soul, which passed through the animal's death" (*Baumgarten*).—Vers. 32 sqq. In the future, the priest who was anointed and set apart for the duty of the priesthood in his father's stead, *i.e.* the existing high priest, was to perform the act of expiation in the manner prescribed, and that "once a year." The yearly repetition of the general atonement showed that the sacrifices of the law were not sufficient to make the servant of God perfect according to his own conscience. And this imperfection of the expiation, made with the blood of bullocks and goats, could not fail to awaken a longing for the perfect sacrifice of the eternal High Priest, who has obtained eternal redemption by entering once, through His own blood, into the holiest of all (Heb. ix. 7–12). And just as this was effected negatively, so by the fact that the high priest entered on this day into the holiest of all, as the representative of the whole congregation, and there, before the throne of God, completed its reconciliation with Him, was the necessity exhibited in a positive manner for the true reconciliation of man, and his introduction into a perfect and abiding fellowship with Him, and the eventual realization of this by the blood of the Son of God, our eternal High Priest and Mediator, prophetically foreshadowed. The closing words in ver. 34, "and he (*i.e.* Aaron, to whom Moses was to communicate the instructions of God concerning the feast of atonement, ver. 2) did as the Lord commanded Moses," are anticipatory in their character, like Ex. xii. 50. For the law in question could not be carried out till the seventh month of the current year, that is to say, as we find from a comparison of Num. x. 11 with Ex. xl. 17, not till after the departure of Israel from Sinai.

II.—LAWS FOR THE SANCTIFICATION OF ISRAEL IN THE COVENANT-FELLOWSHIP OF ITS GOD.

CHAP. XVII.–XXV.

HOLINESS OF CONDUCT ON THE PART OF THE ISRAELITES.— CHAP. XVII.–XX.

THE contents of these four chapters have been very fittingly summed up by *Baumgarten* in the following heading : " Israel is not to walk in the way of the heathen and of the Canaanites, but in the ordinances of Jehovah," as all the commandments contained in them relate to holiness of life.

Chap. xvii. HOLINESS OF FOOD.—The Israelites were not to slaughter domestic animals as food either within or outside the camp, but before the door of the tabernacle, and as slain-offerings, that the blood and fat might be offered to Jehovah. They were not to sacrifice any more to field-devils (vers. 3–7), and were to offer all their burnt-offerings or slain-offerings before the door of the tabernacle (vers. 8 and 9) ; and they were not to eat either blood or carrion (vers. 10–16). These laws are not intended simply as supplements to the food laws in chap. xi.; but they place the eating of food on the part of the Israelites in the closest relation with their calling as the holy nation of Jehovah, on the one hand to oppose an effectual barrier to the inclination of the people to idolatrous sacrificial meals, on the other hand to give a consecrated character to the food of the people in harmony with their calling, that it might be received with thanksgiving and sanctified with prayer (1 Tim. iv. 4, 5). —Vers. 1, 2. The directions are given to " Aaron and his sons, and all the children of Israel," because they were not only binding upon the nation generally, but upon the priesthood also ; whereas the instructions in chap. xviii.–xx. are addressed to " the children of Israel," or " the whole congregation" (chap.

xviii. 2, xix. 2, xx. 2), just as special laws are laid down for the priests in chap. xx. and xxi. with reference to the circumstances mentioned there.

Vers. 3–7. Whoever of the house of Israel slaughtered an ox, sheep, or goat, either within or outside the camp, without bringing the animal to the tabernacle, to offer a sacrifice therefrom to the Lord, " *blood was to be reckoned to him;*" that is to say, as the following expression, " he hath shed blood," shows, such slaughtering was to be reckoned as the shedding of blood, or blood-guiltiness, and punished with extermination (see Gen. xvii. 14). The severity of this prohibition required some explanation, and this is given in the reason assigned in vers. 5–7, viz. " that the Israelites may bring their slain-offerings, which they slay in the open field, before the door of the tabernacle, as peace-offerings to Jehovah," and " no more offer their sacrifices to the שְׂעִירִם, after whom they go a whoring" (ver. 7). This reason presupposes that the custom of dedicating the slain animals as sacrifices to some deity, to which a portion of them was offered, was then widely spread among the Israelites. It had probably been adopted from the Egyptians; though this is not expressly stated by ancient writers: *Herodotus* (i. 132) and *Strabo* (xv. 732) simply mentioning it as a Persian custom, whilst the law book of *Manu* ascribes it to the Indians. To root out this idolatrous custom from among the Israelites, they were commanded to slay every animal before the tabernacle, as a sacrificial gift to Jehovah, and to bring the slain-offerings, which they would have slain in the open field, to the priest at the tabernacle, as *shelamim* (praise-offerings and thank-offerings), that he might sprinkle the blood upon the altar, and burn the fat as a sweet-smelling savour for Jehovah (see chap. iii. 2–5). " *The face of the field*" (ver. 5, as in chap. xiv. 7, 53) : the open field, in distinction from the enclosed space of the court of Jehovah's dwelling. " *The altar of Jehovah*" is spoken of in ver. 6 instead of " *the altar*" only (chap. i. 5, xi. 15, etc.), on account of the contrast drawn between it and the altars upon which they offered sacrifice to *Seirim*. שְׂעִירִם, literally goats, is here used to signify *dæmones* (*Vulg.*), " field-devils" (*Luther*), demons, like the שֵׂדִים in Deut. xxxii. 17, who were supposed to inhabit the desert (Isa. xiii. 21, xxxiv. 14), and whose pernicious influence they sought to avert by sacrifices. The Israelites had brought this superstition, and the idolatry to which it gave rise, from Egypt. The *Seirim* were the gods whom the Israelites worshipped and went a whoring after in Egypt (Josh. xxiv. 14 ; Ezek. xx. 7, xxiii. 3, 8, 19, 21, 27). Both the thing and the name were derived from the Egyptians, who worshipped goats as gods (*Josephus c. Ap.* 2, 7), particularly *Pan*, who was represented in the form of a goat, a personification of the male and fertilizing principle in nature, whom they called *Mendes* and reckoned among the eight leading gods, and to whom they had built a splendid and celebrated temple in *Thmuis*, the capital of the Mendesian *Nomos* in Lower Egypt, and erected statues in the temples in all directions (cf. *Herod.* 2, 42, 46 ; *Strabo*, xvii. 802 ; *Diod. Sic.* i. 18). The expression " a statute for ever" refers to the principle of the law, that sacrifices were to be offered to Jehovah alone, and not to the law that every animal was to be slain before the tabernacle, which was afterwards repealed by Moses, when they were about to enter Canaan, where it could no longer be carried out (Deut. xii. 15).

Vers. 8–16. To this there are appended three laws, which are kindred in their nature, and which were binding not only upon the Israelites, but also upon the foreigners who dwelt in the midst of them.—Vers. 8, 9 contain the command, that whoever offered a burnt-offering or slain-offering, and did not bring it to the tabernacle to prepare it for Jehovah there, was to be exterminated ; a command which involved the prohibition of sacrifice in any other place whatever, and was given, as the further extension of this law in Deut. xii. clearly proves, for the purpose of suppressing the disposition to offer sacrifice to other gods, as well as in other places. In vers. 10–14 the prohibition of the eating of blood is repeated, and ordered to be observed on pain of extermination ; it is also extended to the strangers in Israel ; and after a more precise explanation of the reason for the law, is supplemented by instructions for the disposal of the blood of edible game. God threatens that He will inflict the punishment Himself, because the eating of blood was a transgression of the law which might easily escape the notice of the authorities. " To set one's face against :" *i.e.* to judge. The reason for the command in ver. 11, " For the soul of the flesh (the soul which gives life to the flesh) is in the blood, and I have given it to you upon the altar, to make an atonement for

your souls," is not a double one, viz. (1) because the blood contained the soul of the animal, and (2) because God had set
apart the blood, as the medium of expiation for the human soul,
for the altar, *i.e.* to be sprinkled upon the altar. The first reason
simply forms the foundation for the second : God appointed the
blood for the altar, as containing the soul of the animal, to be
the medium of expiation for the souls of men, and therefore
prohibited its being used as food. " For the blood it expiates
by virtue of the soul," not " the soul" itself. בְּ with כִּפֶּר has
only a local or instrumental signification (chap. vi. 23, xvi. 17,
27; also vii. 7; Ex. xxix. 33; Num. v. 8). Accordingly, it was
not the blood as such, but the blood as the vehicle of the soul,
which possessed expiatory virtue ; because the animal soul was
offered to God upon the altar as a substitute for the human
soul. Hence every bleeding sacrifice had an expiatory force,
though without being an expiatory sacrifice in the strict sense of
the word.—Ver. 13. The blood also of such hunted game as was
edible, whether bird or beast, was not to be eaten either by the
Israelite or stranger, but to be poured out and covered with
earth. In Deut. xii. 16 and 24, where the command to slay all
the domestic animals at the tabernacle as slain-offerings is repealed, this is extended to such domestic animals as were slaughtered for food ; their blood also was not to be eaten, but to be
poured upon the earth " like water," *i.e.* not *quasi rem profanam
et nullo ritu sacro* (*Rosenmüller*, etc.), but like water which is
poured upon the earth, sucked in by it, and thus given back to
the womb of the earth, from which God had caused the animals
to come forth at their creation (Gen. i. 24). Hence pouring it
out upon the earth like water was substantially the same as
pouring it out and covering it with earth (cf. Ezek. xxiv. 7, 8) ;
and the purpose of the command was to prevent the desecration of the vehicle of the soulish life, which was sanctified as the
medium of expiation.—Ver. 14. " *For as for the soul of all flesh
. . . its blood makes out its soul :*" *i.e.* " this is the case with the
soul of all flesh, that it is its blood which makes out its soul."
בְּנַפְשׁוֹ is to be taken as a predicate in its meaning, introduced
with *beth essentiale*. It is only as so understood, that the clause
supplies a reason at all in harmony with the context. Because
the distinguishing characteristic of the blood was, that it was
the soul of the being when living in the flesh ; therefore it was

not to be eaten in the case of any animal : and even in the case
of animals that were not proper for sacrifice, it was to be allowed
to run out upon the ground, and then covered with earth, or,
so to speak, buried.[1]—Lastly (vers. 15, 16), the prohibition
against eating " that which died" (xi. 39, 40), or " that which
was torn" (Ex. xxii. 30), is renewed and supplemented by the
law, that whoever, either of the natives or of foreigners, should
eat the flesh of that which had fallen (died a natural death), or
had been torn in pieces by wild beasts (sc. thoughtlessly or in
ignorance ; cf. chap. v. 2), and neglected the legal purification
afterwards, was to bear his iniquity (chap. v. 1). Of course the
flesh intended is that of animals which were clean, and therefore allowable as food, when properly slaughtered, and which
became unclean simply from the fact, that when they had died
a natural death, or had been torn to pieces by wild beasts, the
blood remained in the flesh, or did not flow out in a proper
manner. According to Ex. xxii. 30, the נְבֵלָה (that which
had fallen) was to be thrown to the dogs ; but in Deut. xiv. 21
permission is given either to sell it or give it to a stranger or
alien, to prevent the plea that it was a pity that such a thing
should be entirely wasted, and so the more effectually to secure
the observance of the command, that it was not to be eaten by
an Israelite.

Chap. xviii. HOLINESS OF THE MARRIAGE RELATION.—The
prohibition of incest and similar sensual abominations is introduced with a general warning as to the licentious customs of the
Egyptians and Canaanites, and an exhortation to walk in the

---

[1] On the truth which lay at the foundation of this idea of the unity of
the soul and blood, which others of the ancients shared with the Hebrews,
particularly the early Greek philosophers, see *Delitzsch's bibl. Psychol.* pp.
242 sqq. " It seems at first sight to be founded upon no other reason,
than that a sudden diminution of the quantity of the blood is sure to cause
death. But this phenomenon rests upon the still deeper ground, that all
the activity of the body, especially that of the nervous and muscular systems, is dependent upon the circulation of the blood ; for if the flow of
blood is stopped from any part of the body, all its activity ceases immediately ; a sensitive part loses all sensation in a very few minutes, and muscular action is entirely suspended. . . . The blood is really the basis of the
physical life ; and so far the soul, as the vital principle of the body, is pre-
eminently in the blood" (p. 245).

judgments and ordinances of Jehovah (vers. 2–5), and is brought to a close with a threatening allusion to the consequences of all such defilements (vers. 24–30).—Vers. 1–5. By the words, "I am Jehovah your God," which are placed at the head and repeated at the close (ver. 30), the observance of the command is enforced upon the people as a covenant obligation, and urged upon them most strongly by the promise, that through the observance of the ordinances and judgments of Jehovah they should live (ver. 5).—Ver. 5. "*The man who does them* (the ordinances of Jehovah) *shall live* (gain true life) *through them*" (see at Ex. i. 16 and Gen. iii. 22).

Vers. 6–18. The *laws against incest* are introduced in ver. 6 with the general prohibition, descriptive of the nature of this sin, "None of you shall approach אֶל־כָּל־שְׁאֵר בְּשָׂרוֹ to any flesh of his flesh, to uncover nakedness." The difference between שְׁאֵר flesh, and בָּשָׂר flesh, is involved in obscurity, as both words are used in connection with edible flesh (see the Lexicons). "Flesh of his flesh" is a flesh that is of his own flesh, belongs to the same flesh as himself (Gen. ii. 24), and is applied to a blood-relation, blood-relationship being called שְׁאֵרָה (or flesh-kindred) in Hebrew (ver. 17). Sexual intercourse is called uncovering the nakedness of another (Ezek. xvi. 36, xxiii. 18). The prohibition relates to both married and unmarried intercourse, though the reference is chiefly to the former (see ver. 18, chap. xx. 14, 17, 21). Intercourse is forbidden (1) with a mother, (2) with a step-mother, (3) with a sister or half-sister, (4) with a granddaughter, the daughter of either son or daughter, (5) with the daughter of a step-mother, (6) with an aunt, the sister of either father or mother, (7) with the wife of an uncle on the father's side, (8) with a daughter-in-law, (9) with a sister-in-law, or brother's wife, (10) with a woman and her daughter, or a woman and her granddaughter, and (11) with two sisters at the same time. No special reference is made to sexual intercourse with (*a*) a daughter, (*b*) a full sister, (*c*) a mother-in-law; the last, however, which is mentioned in Deut. xxvii. 23 as an accursed crime, is included here in No. 10, and the second in No. 3, whilst the first, like parricide in Ex. xxi. 15, is not expressly noticed, simply because the crime was regarded as one that never could occur. Those mentioned under Nos. 1, 2, 3, 8, and 10 were to be followed by the death or extermination of the criminals (chap.

xx. 11, 12, 14, 17), on account of their being accursed crimes (Deut. xxiii. 1, xxvii. 20, 22, 23). On the other hand, the only threat held out in the case of the connection mentioned under Nos. 6, 7, and 9, was that those who committed such crimes should bear their iniquity, or die childless (chap. xx. 19–21). The cases noticed under Nos. 4 and 5 are passed over in chap. xx., though they no doubt belonged to the crimes which were to be punished with death, and No. 11, for which no punishment was fixed, because the wrong had been already pointed out in ver. 18.[1]

The enumeration of the different cases commences in ver. 7 very appropriately with the prohibition of incest with a mother. Sexual connection with a mother is called "uncovering the nakedness of father and mother." As husband and wife are one flesh (Gen. ii. 24), the nakedness of the husband is uncovered in that of his wife, or, as it is described in Deut. xxii. 30, xxvii. 20, the wing, *i.e.* the edge, of the bedclothes of the father's bed, as the husband spreads his bedclothes over his wife as well as himself (Ruth iii. 9). For, strictly speaking, גִּלָּה עֶרְוָה is only used with reference to the wife; but in the dishonouring of his wife the honour of the husband is violated

[1] The marriage laws and customs were much more lax among the Gentiles. With the Egyptians it was lawful to marry sisters and half-sisters (*Diod. Sic.* i. 27), and the licentiousness of the women was very great among them (see at Gen. xxxix. 6 sqq.). With the Persians marriage was allowed with mother, daughter, and sister (*Clem. Al. strom.* iii. p. 431; *Eusebii præp. ev.* vi. 10); and this is also said to have been the case with the Medians, Indians, and Ethiopians, as well as with the Assyrians (*Jerome adv. Jovin.* ii. 7; *Lucian, Sacriff.* 5); whereas the Greeks and Romans abhorred such marriages, and the Athenians and Spartans only permitted marriages with half-sisters (cf. *Selden de jure nat. et gent.* v. 11, pp. 619 sqq.). The ancient Arabs, before the time of Mohammed, were very strict in this respect, and would not allow of marriage with a mother, daughter, or aunt on either the father's or mother's side, or with two sisters at the same time. The only cases on record of marriage between brothers and sisters are among the Arabs of Marbat (*Seetzen, Zach's Mon. Corresp.* Oct. 1809). This custom Mohammed raised into a law, and extended it to nieces, nurses, foster-sisters, etc. (*Koran, Sure* iv. 20 sqq.). Elaborate commentaries upon this chapter are to be found in *Michaelis Abhandl. über die Ehegesetze Mosis*, and his *Mos. Recht;* also in *Saalschütz Mos. Recht.* See also my *Archäologie* ii. p. 108. For the rabbinical laws and those of the Talmud, see *Selden uxor ebr.* lib. 1, c. 1 sqq., and *Saalschütz ut sup.*

also, and his bed defiled, Gen. xlix. 4. It is wrong, therefore, to interpret the verse, as *Jonathan* and *Clericus* do, as relating to carnal intercourse between a daughter and father. Not only is this at variance with the circumstance that all these laws are intended for the man alone, and addressed expressly to him, but also with ver. 8, where the nakedness of the father's wife is distinctly called the father's shame.—Ver. 8. Intercourse with a father's wife, *i.e.* with a step-mother, is forbidden as uncovering the father's nakedness; since a father's wife stood in blood-relationship only to the son whose mother she was. But for the father's sake her nakedness was to be inaccessible to the son, and uncovering it was to be punished with death as incest (chap. xx. 11; Deut. xxvii. 20). By the "father's wife" we are probably to understand not merely his full lawful wife, but his concubine also, since the father's bed was defiled in the latter case no less than in the former (Gen. xlix. 4), and an accursed crime was committed, the punishment of which was death. At all events, it cannot be inferred from chap. xix. 20–22 and Ex. xxi. 9, as *Knobel* supposes, that a milder punishment was inflicted in this case.—Ver. 9. By the sister, the daughter of father or mother, we are to understand only the step- or half-sister, who had either the same father or the same mother as the brother had. The clause, "*whether born at home or born abroad*," does not refer to legitimate or illegitimate birth, but is to be taken as a more precise definition of the words, daughter of thy father or of thy mother, and understood, as *Lud. de Dieu* supposes, as referring to the half-sister "of the first marriage, whether the father's daughter left by a deceased wife, or the mother's daughter left by a deceased husband," so that the person marrying her would be a son by a second marriage. Sexual intercourse with a half-sister is described as חֶסֶד in chap. xx. 17, and threatened with extermination. This word generally signifies sparing love, favour, grace; but here, as in Prov. xiv. 34, it means dishonour, shame, from the *Piel* חִפֵּד, to dishonour.—Ver. 10. The prohibition of marriage with a granddaughter, whether the daughter of a son or daughter, is explained in the words, "for they are thy nakedness," the meaning of which is, that as they were directly descended from the grandfather, carnal intercourse with them would be equivalent to dishonouring his own flesh and blood.—Ver. 11. "*The daughter of thy father's wife* (*i.e.* thy step-mother), *born to thy father*," is the half-sister by a second marriage; and the prohibition refers to the son by a first marriage, whereas ver. 9 treats of the son by a second marriage. The notion that the man's own mother is also included, and that the prohibition includes marriage with a full sister, is at variance with the usage of the expression "thy father's wife."—Vers. 12 and 13. Marriage or conjugal intercourse with the sister of either father or mother (*i.e.* with either the paternal or maternal aunt) was prohibited, because she was the blood-relation of the father or mother. שְׁאֵר בְּשָׂר=שְׁאֵר (ver. 6, as in chap. xx. 19, xxi. 2, Num. xxvii. 11), hence שַׁאֲרָה, blood-relationship (ver. 17).—Ver. 14. So, again, with the wife of the father's brother, because the nakedness of the uncle was thereby uncovered. The threat held out in chap. xx. 19 and 20 against the alliances prohibited in vers. 12–14, is that the persons concerned should bear their iniquity or sin, *i.e.* should suffer punishment in consequence (see at chap. v. 1); and in the last case it is stated that they should die childless. From this it is obvious that sexual connection with the sister of either father or mother was not to be punished with death by the magistrate, but would be punished with disease by God Himself.—Ver. 15. Sexual connection with a daughter-in-law, a son's wife, is called תֶּבֶל in chap. xx. 12, and threatened with death to both the parties concerned. תֶּבֶל, from בָּלַל to mix, to confuse, signifies a sinful mixing up or confusing of the divine ordinances by unnatural unchastity, like the lying of a woman with a beast, which is the only other connection in which the word occurs (ver. 23).—Ver. 16. Marriage with a brother's wife was a sin against the brother's nakedness, a sexual defilement, which God would punish with barrenness. This prohibition, however, only refers to cases in which the deceased brother had left children; for if he had died childless, the brother not only might, but was required to marry his sister-in-law (Deut. xxv. 5).—Ver. 17. Marriage with a woman and her daughter, whether both together or in succession, is described in Deut. xxvii. 20 as an accursed lying with the mother-in-law; whereas here it is the relation to the step-daughter which is primarily referred to, as we may see from the parallel prohibition, which is added, against taking the daughter of her son or daughter, *i.e.* the granddaughter-in-law. Both of these were crimes against blood-relationship which were to be punished with

death in the case of both parties (chap. xx. 14), because they
were "wickedness," זִמָּה, *lit.* invention, design, here applied to
the crime of licentiousness and whoredom (chap. xix. 29 ; Judg.
xx. 6 ; Job xxxi. 11.)—Ver. 18. Lastly, it was forbidden to
take a wife to her sister (עָלֶיהָ upon her, as in Gen. xxviii. 9,
xxxi. 50) in her life-time, that is to say, to marry two sisters at
the same time, לִצְרֹר " to pack together, to uncover their nakedness," *i.e.* to pack both together into one marriage bond, and so
place the sisters in carnal union through their common husband,
and disturb the sisterly relation, as the marriage with two sisters
that was forced upon Jacob had evidently done. No punishment is fixed for the marriage with two sisters ; and, of course,
after the death of the first wife a man was at liberty to marry
her sister.

Vers. 19–23. *Prohibition of other kinds of unchastity and of
unnatural crimes.*—Ver. 19 prohibits intercourse with a woman
during her uncleanness. נִדַּת טֻמְאָה signifies the uncleanness of
a woman's hemorrhage, whether menstruation or after child-
birth, which is called in chap. xii. 7, xx. 18, the fountain of
bleeding. The guilty persons were both of them to be cut off
from their nation according to chap. xx. 18, *i.e.* to be punished
with death.—Ver. 20. "To a neighbour's wife thou shalt not
give שְׁכָבְתְּךָ thy pouring as seed" (*i.e.* make her pregnant), "to
defile thyself with her," viz. by the *emissio seminis* (chap. xv.
16, 17), a defilement which was to be punished as adultery by
the stoning to death of both parties (chap. xx. 10 ; Deut. xxii.
22, cf. John ix. 5).—Ver. 21. To bodily unchastity there is
appended a prohibition of spiritual whoredom. " *Thou shalt not
give of thy seed to cause to pass through* (*sc.* the fire ; Deut. xviii.
10) *for Moloch.*" הַמֹּלֶךְ is constantly written with the article:
it is rendered by the LXX. ἄρχων both here and in chap. xx.
2 sqq., but ὁ Μολόχ βασιλεύς in other places (2 Kings xxiii.
10; Jer. xxxii. 35). *Moloch* was an old Canaanitish idol, called
by the Phœnicians and Carthaginians *Melkarth, Baal-melech,
Malcom,* and other such names, and related to Baal, a sun-god
worshipped, like *Kronos* and *Saturn,* by the sacrifice of children.
It was represented by a brazen statue, which was hollow and
capable of being heated, and formed with a bull's head, and
arms stretched out to receive the children to be sacrificed. From
the time of Ahaz children were slain at Jerusalem in the valley

of Ben-Hinnom, and then sacrificed by being laid in the heated arms and burned (Ezek. xvi. 20, 21, xx. 31; Jer. xxxii. 35; 2 Kings xxiii. 10, xvi. 3, xvii. 17, xxi. 6, cf. Ps. cvi. 37, 38). Now although this offering of children in the valley of Ben-Hinnom is called a "slaughtering" by Ezekiel (chap. xvi. 21), and a "burning through (in the) fire" by Jeremiah (chap. vii. 31), and although, in the times of the later kings, children were actually given up to Moloch and burned as slain-offerings, even among the Israelites; it by no means follows from this, that "passing through to Moloch," or "passing through the fire," or "passing through the fire to Moloch" (2 Kings xxiii. 10), signified slaughtering and burning with fire, though this has been almost unanimously assumed since the time of *Clericus*. But according to the unanimous explanation of the Rabbins, fathers, and earlier theologians, "causing to pass through the fire" denoted primarily going through the fire without burning, a februation, or purification through fire, by which the children were consecrated to Moloch; a kind of fire-baptism, which preceded the sacrificing, and was performed, particularly in olden time, without actual sacrificing, or slaying and burning. For februation was practised among the most different nations without being connected with human sacrifices; and, like most of the idolatrous rites of the heathen, no doubt the worship of Moloch assumed different forms at different times and among different nations. If the Israelites had really sacrificed their children to Moloch, *i.e.* had slain and burned them, before the time of Ahaz, the burning would certainly have been mentioned before; for Solomon had built a high place upon the mountain to the east of Jerusalem for Moloch, the abomination of the children of Ammon, to please his foreign wives (1 Kings xi. 7: see the Art. Moloch in *Herzog's* Cycl.). This idolatrous worship was to be punished with death by stoning, as a desecration of the name of Jehovah, and a defiling of His sanctuary (chap. xx. 3), *i.e.* as a practical contempt of the manifestations of the grace of the living God (chap. xx. 2, 3).—Vers. 22, 23. Lastly, it was forbidden to "lie with mankind as with womankind," *i.e.* to commit the crime of *pœderastia*, that sin of Sodom (Gen. xix. 5), to which the whole of the heathen were more or less addicted (Rom. i. 27), and from which even the Israelites did not keep themselves free (Judg. xix. 22 sqq.); or to "lie with any beast."

" Into no beast shalt thou give thine emission of seed, . . . and a woman shall not place herself before a beast to lie down thereto." רְבַע = רָבַע "to lie," is the term used particularly to denote a crime of this description (chap. xx. 13 and 15, 16, cf. Ex. xxii. 18). Lying with animals was connected in Egypt with the worship of the goat; at Mendes especially, where the women lay down before he-goats (*Herodotus*, 2, 46; *Strabo*, 17, p. 802). *Aelian* (*nat. an.* vii. 19) relates an account of the crime being also committed with a dog in Rome; and according to *Sonnini*, R̥. 11, p. 330, in modern Egypt men are said to lie even with female crocodiles.

Vers. 24–30. In the concluding exhortation God pointed expressly to the fact, that the nations which He was driving out before the Israelites (the participle מְשַׁלֵּחַ is used of that which is certainly and speedily coming to pass) had defiled the land by such abominations as those, that He had visited their iniquity and the land had spat out its inhabitants, and warned the Israelites to beware of these abominations, that the land might not spit them out as it had the Canaanites before them. The pret. וַתָּקִא (ver. 25) and קָאָה (ver. 28) are prophetic (cf. chap. xx. 22, 23), and the expression is poetical. The land is personified as a living creature, which violently rejects food that it dislikes. "*Hoc enim tropo vult significare Scriptura enormitatem criminum, quod scilicet ipsæ creaturæ irrationales suo creatori semper obedientes et pro illo pugnantes detestentur peccatores tales eosque terra quasi evomat, cum illi expelluntur ab ea*" (*C. a Lap.*).

Chap. xix. Holiness of Behaviour towards God and Man.—However manifold the commandments, which are grouped together rather according to a loose association of ideas than according to any logical arrangement, they are all linked together by the common purpose expressed in ver. 2 in the words, "*Ye shall be holy, for I am holy, Jehovah your God.*" The absence of any strictly logical arrangement is to be explained chiefly from the nature of the object, and the great variety of circumstances occurring in life which no casuistry can fully exhaust, so that any attempt to throw light upon these relations must consist more or less of the description of a series of concrete events.—Vers. 2–8. The commandment in ver. 2, "to be holy as God is holy," expresses on the one hand the principle upon which all the different commandments that follow were based, and on the other hand the goal which the Israelites were to keep before them as the nation of Jehovah.—Ver. 3. The first thing required is reverence towards parents and the observance of the Lord's Sabbaths,—the two leading pillars of the moral government, and of social well-being. To fear father and mother answers to the honour commanded in the decalogue to be paid to parents; and in the observance of the Sabbaths the labour connected with a social calling is sanctified to the Lord God.—Ver. 4 embraces the first two commandments of the decalogue: viz. not to turn to idols to worship them (Deut. xxxi. 18, 20), nor to make molten gods (see at Ex. xxxiv. 17). The gods beside Jehovah are called *elilim, i.e.* nothings, from their true nature.—Vers. 5-8. True fidelity to Jehovah was to be shown, so far as sacrifice, the leading form of divine worship, was concerned, in the fact, that the holiness of the sacrificial flesh was strictly preserved in the sacrificial meals, and none of the flesh of the peace-offerings eaten on the third day. To this end the command in chap. vii. 15-18 is emphatically repeated, and transgressors are threatened with extermination. On the singular יֵאָשֵׁ in ver. 8, see at Gen. xxvii. 29, and for the expression "shall be cut off," Gen. xvii. 14.

Vers. 9-18. Laws concerning the conduct towards one's neighbour, which should flow from unselfish love, especially with regard to the poor and distressed.—Vers. 9, 10. In reaping the field, " thou shalt not finish to reap the edge of thy field," *i.e.* not reap the field to the extreme edge; " neither shalt thou hold a gathering up (gleaning) of thy harvest," *i.e.* not gather together the ears left upon the field in the reaping. In the vineyard and olive-plantation, also, they were not to have any gleaning, or gather up what was strewn about (*peret* signifies the grapes and olives that had fallen off), but to leave them for the distressed and the foreigner, that he might also share in the harvest and gathering. כֶּרֶם, *lit.* a noble plantation, generally signifies a vineyard; but it is also applied to an olive-plantation (Judg. xv. 5), and here it is to be understood of both. For when this command is repeated in Deut. xxiv. 20, 21, both vineyards and olive-plantations are mentioned. When the olives had been gathered by being knocked off with sticks, the custom of shaking the boughs (פֵּאֵר) to get at those olives which could not be reached with the sticks was expressly forbidden, in the interest of the strangers, orphans, and widows, as well as gleaning after the vintage. The command with regard to the corn-harvest is repeated again in the law for the feast of Weeks or Harvest Feast (chap. xxiii. 20) ; and in Deut. xxiv. 19 it is extended, quite in the spirit of our law, so far as to forbid fetching a sheaf that had been overlooked in the field, and to order it to be left for the needy. (Compare with this Deut. xxiii. 25, 26.) —Vers. 11 sqq. The Israelites were not to steal (Ex. xx. 15) ; nor to deny, viz. anything entrusted to them or found (chap. v. 21 sqq.) ; nor to lie to a neighbour, *i.e.* with regard to property or goods, for the purpose of overreaching and cheating him ; nor to swear by the name of Jehovah to lie and defraud, and so profane the name of God (see Ex. xx. 7, 16) ; nor to oppress and rob a neighbour (cf. chap. v. 21), by the unjust abstraction or detention of what belonged to him or was due to him,—for example, they were not to keep the wages of a day-labourer over night, but to pay him every day before sunset (Deut. xxiv. 14, 15).—Ver. 14. They were not to do an injury to an infirm person : neither to ridicule or curse the deaf, who could not hear the ridicule or curse, and therefore could not defend himself (Ps. xxxviii. 15) ; nor " to put a stumblingblock before the blind," *i.e.* to put anything in his way over which he might stumble and fall (compare Deut. xxvii. 18, where a curse is pronounced upon the man who should lead the blind astray). But they were to " fear before God," who hears, and sees, and will punish every act of wrong (cf. ver. 32, xxv. 17, 36, 43).— Ver. 15. In judgment, *i.e.* in the administration of justice, they were to do no unrighteousness : neither to respect the person of the poor (πρόσωπον λαμβάνειν, to do anything out of regard to a person, used in a good sense in Gen. xix. 21, in a bad sense here, namely, to act partially from unmanly pity) ; nor to adorn the person of the great (*i.e.* powerful, distinguished, exalted), *i.e.* to favour him in a judicial decision (see at Ex. xxiii. 3).— Ver. 16. They were not to go about as calumniators among their countrymen, to bring their neighbour to destruction (Ezek. xxii. 9) ; nor to set themselves against the blood of a neighbour, *i.e.* to seek his life. רָכִיל does not mean calumny, but, according to its formation, a calumniator (*Ewald*, § 149*e*).—Ver. 17. They were not to cherish hatred in their hearts towards their brother, but to admonish a neighbour, *i.e.* to tell him openly what they had against him, and reprove him for his conduct, just as Christ teaches His disciples in Matt. xviii. 15–17, and " not to load a sin upon themselves." נָשָׂא עָלָיו חֵטְא does not mean to have to bear, or atone for a sin on his account (*Onkelos, Knobel*, etc.), but, as in chap. xxii. 9, Num. xviii. 32, to bring sin upon one's self, which one then has to bear, or atone for; so also in Num. xviii. 22, שְׂאֵת חֵטְא, from which the meaning " to bear," *i.e.* atone for sin, or suffer its consequences, was first derived.—Ver. 18. Lastly, they were not to avenge themselves, or bear malice against the sons of their nation (their countrymen), but to love their neighbour as themselves. נָטַר to watch for (Song of Sol. i. 6, viii. 11, 12), hence (= τηρεῖν) to cherish a design upon a person, or bear him malice (Ps. ciii. 9; Jer. iii. 5, 12; Nahum i. 2).

Vers. 19–32. The words, " Ye shall keep My statutes," open the second series of commandments, which make it a duty on the part of the people of God to keep the physical and moral order of the world sacred. This series begins in ver. 19 with the commandment not to mix the things which are separated in the creation of God. " Thou shalt not let thy cattle gender with a diverse kind : thou shalt not sow thy field with two kinds of seed, or put on a garment of mixed stuff." כִּלְאַיִם, from כָּלָא separation, signifies *duæ res diversi generis, heterogeneæ*, and is a substantive in the accusative, giving a more precise definition. שַׁעַטְנֵז is in apposition to בֶּגֶד כִּלְאַיִם, and according to Deut. xxii. 11 refers to cloth or a garment woven of wool and flax, to a mixed fabric therefore. The etymology is obscure, and the rendering given by the LXX., κίβδηλον, *i.e.* forged, not genuine, is probably merely a conjecture based upon the context. The word is probably derived from the Egyptian; although the attempt to explain it from the Coptic has not been so far satisfactory. In Deut. xxii. 9–11, instead of the field, the vineyard is mentioned, as that which they were not to sow with things of two kinds, *i.e.* so that a mixed produce should arise; and the threat is added, " that thy fulness (full fruit, Ex. xxii. 28), the seed, and the produce of the vineyard (*i.e.* the corn and wine grown upon the vineyard) may not become holy" (cf. chap. xxvii. 10, 21), *i.e.* fall to the sanctuary for its servants. It is also forbidden to plough with an ox and ass together, *i.e.* to yoke

them to the same plough. By these laws the observance of the
natural order and separation of things is made a duty binding
upon the Israelites, the people of Jehovah, as a divine ordinance founded in the creation itself (Gen. i. 11, 12, 21, 24, 25).
All the symbolical, mystical, moral, and utilitarian reasons that
have been supposed to lie at the foundation of these commands,
are foreign to the spirit of the law. And with regard to the
observance of them, the statement of *Josephus* and the Rabbins,
that the dress of the priests, as well as the tapestries and curtains of the tabernacle, consisted of wool and linen, is founded
upon the assumption, which cannot be established, that שֵׁשׁ,
βύσσος, is a term applied to linen. The mules frequently mentioned, *e.g.* in 2 Sam. xiii. 29, xviii. 9, 1 Kings i. 33, may have
been imported from abroad, as we may conclude from 1 Kings
x. 25.—Vers. 20–22. Even the personal rights of slaves were
to be upheld ; and a maid, though a slave, was not to be de-
graded to the condition of personal property. If any one lay
with a woman who was a slave and betrothed to a man, but
neither redeemed nor emancipated, the punishment of death was
not to be inflicted, as in the case of adultery (chap. xx. 10), or
the seduction of a free virgin who was betrothed (Deut. xxii.
23 sqq.), because she was not set free ; but scourging was to be
inflicted, and the guilty person was also to bring a trespass-
offering for the expiation of his sin against God (see at chap.
v. 15 sqq.). נֶחֱרֶפֶת, from חָרַף *carpere*, *lit.* plucked, *i.e.* set apart,
betrothed to a man, not abandoned or despised. הָפְדָּה redeemed,
חֻפְשָׁה emancipation without purchase,—the two ways in which a
slave could obtain her freedom. בִּקֹּרֶת, *ἀπ. λεγ.*, from בָּקַר to
examine (chap. xiii. 36), *lit.* investigation, then punishment,
chastisement. This referred to both parties, as is evident from
the expression, " they shall not be put to death ;" though it is
not more precisely defined. According to the *Mishnah, Kerith.*
ii. 4, the punishment of the woman consisted of forty stripes.—
Vers. 23–25. The garden-fruit was also to be sanctified to the
Lord. When the Israelites had planted all kinds of fruit-trees
in the land of Canaan, they were to treat the fruit of every tree
as uncircumcised for the first three years, *i.e.* not to eat it, as
being uncircumcised. The singular suffix in עָרְלָתוֹ refers to כֹּל,
and the verb עָרֵל is a *denom.* from עָרְלָה, to make into a foreskin,
to treat as uncircumcised, *i.e.* to throw away as unclean or un-

eatable. The reason for this command is not to be sought for in the fact, that in the first three years fruit-trees bear only a little fruit, and that somewhat insipid, and that if the blossom or fruit is broken off the first year, the trees will bear all the more plentifully afterwards (*Aben Esra, Clericus, J. D. Mich.*), though this end would no doubt be thereby attained; but it rests rather upon ethical grounds. Israel was to treat the fruits of horticulture with the most careful regard as a gift of God, and sanctify the enjoyment of them by a thank-offering. In the fourth year the whole of the fruit was to be a holiness of praise for Jehovah, *i.e.* to be offered to the Lord as a holy sacrificial gift, in praise and thanksgiving for the blessing which He had bestowed upon the fruit-trees. This offering falls into the category of first-fruits, and was no doubt given up entirely to the Lord for the servants of the altar; although the expression עָשָׂה הִלּוּלִים (Judg. ix. 27) seems to point to sacrificial meals of the first-fruits, that had already been reaped: and this is the way in which *Josephus* has explained the command (*Ant.* iv. 8, 19). For (ver. 25) they were not to eat the fruits till the fifth year, " to add (increase) its produce to you," viz. by the blessing of God, not by breaking off the fruits that might set in the first years.

Vers. 26–32. The Israelites were to abstain from all un-natural, idolatrous, and heathenish conduct.—Ver. 26. " Ye shall not eat upon blood " (עַל as in Ex. xii. 8, referring to the basis of the eating), *i.e.* no flesh of which blood still lay at the foundation, which was not entirely cleansed from blood (cf. 1 Sam. xiv. 32). These words were not a mere repetition of the law against eating blood (chap. xvii. 10), but a strengthening of the law. Not only were they to eat no blood, but no flesh to which any blood adhered. They were also " to practise no kind of incantations." נַחֵשׁ: from נַחַשׁ to whisper (see Gen. xliv. 5), or, according to some, a *denom.* verb from נָחָשׁ a serpent; literally, to prophesy from observing snakes, then to prophesy from auguries generally, *augurari.* עוֹנֵן a *denom.* verb, not from עָנָן a cloud, with the signification to prophesy from the motion of the clouds, of which there is not the slightest historical trace in Hebrew; but, as the Rabbins maintain, from עַיִן an eye, literally, to ogle, then to bewitch with an evil eye.—Ver. 27. " *Ye shall not round the border of your head:*" *i.e.* not cut the hair in a circle from one temple to the other, as some of the Arab tribes did, according to *Herodotus* (3, 8), in honour of their god 'Οροτάλ, whom he identifies with the *Dionysos* of the Greeks. In Jer. ix. 25, xxv. 23, xlix. 32, the persons who did this are called קְצוּצֵי פֵאָה, round-cropped, from their peculiar tonsure. "*Neither shalt thou mar the corners of thy beard,*" *sc.* by cutting it off (cf. chap. xxi. 5), which *Pliny* reports some of the Arabs to have done, *barba abraditur, præterquam in superiore labro, aliis et hæc intonsa,* whereas the modern Arabs either wear a short moustache, or shave off the beard altogether (*Niebuhr,* Arab. p. 68).—Ver. 28. "*Ye shall not make cuttings on your flesh* (body) *on account of a soul, i.e.* a dead person (נֶפֶשׁ = נֶפֶשׁ מֵת, chap. xxi. 11, Num. vi. 6, or מֵת, Deut. xiv. 1; so again in chap. xxii. 4, Num. v. 2, ix. 6, 7, 10), *nor make engraven* (or branded) *writing upon yourselves.*" Two prohibitions of an un-natural disfigurement of the body. The first refers to passionate outbursts of mourning, common among the excitable nations of the East, particularly in the southern parts, and to the custom of scratching the arms, hands, and face (Deut. xiv. 1), which is said to have prevailed among the Babylonians and Armenians (*Cyrop.* iii. 1, 13, iii. 3, 67), the Scythians (*Herod.* 4, 71), and even the ancient Romans (cf. *M. Geier de Ebræor. luctu,* c. 10), and to be still practised by the Arabs (*Arvieux Beduinen,* p. 153), the Persians (*Morier Zweite Reise,* p. 189), and the Abyssinians of the present day, and which apparently held its ground among the Israelites notwithstanding the prohibition (cf. Jer. xvi. 6, xli. 5, xlvii. 5),—as well as to the custom, which is also forbidden in chap. xxi. 5 and Deut. xiv. 1, of cutting off the hair of the head and beard (cf. Isa. iii. 24, xxii. 12 ; Micah i. 16 ; Amos viii. 10 ; Ezek. vii. 18). It cannot be inferred from the words of *Plutarch,* quoted by *Spencer,* δοκοῦντες χαρίζεσθαι τοῖς τετελευκη-κόσιν, that the heathen associated with this custom the idea of making an expiation to the dead. The prohibition of כְּתֹבֶת קַעֲקַע, *scriptio stigmatis,* writing corroded or branded (see *Ges. thes.* pp. 1207–8), *i.e.* of tattooing,—a custom not only very common among the savage tribes, but still met with in Arabia (*Arvieux Beduinen,* p. 155 ; *Burckhardt Beduinen,* pp. 40, 41) and in Egypt among both men and women of the lower orders (*Lane,* Manners and Customs i. pp. 25, 35, iii. p. 169),—had no reference to idolatrous usages, but was intended to inculcate upon the Israelites a proper reverence for God's creation.—Ver. 29. *"Do not prostitute thy daughter, to cause her to be a whore, lest the land fall to whoredom, and the land become full of vice"* (*zimmah:* see chap. xviii. 17). The reference is not to spiritual whoredom or idolatry (Ex. xxxiv. 16), but to fleshly whoredom, the word *zimmah* being only used in this connection. If a father caused his daughter to become a prostitute, immorality would soon become predominant, and the land (the population of the land) fall away to whoredom.—Ver. 30. The exhortation now returns to the chief point, the observance of the Lord's Sabbaths and reverence for His sanctuary, which embrace the true method of divine worship as laid down in the ritual commandments. When the Lord's day is kept holy, and a holy reverence for the Lord's sanctuary lives in the heart, not only are many sins avoided, but social and domestic life is pervaded by the fear of God and characterized by chasteness and propriety.—Ver. 31. True fear of God, however, awakens confidence in the Lord and His guidance, and excludes all superstitious and idolatrous ways and methods of discovering the future. This thought prepares the way for the warning against turning to familiar spirits, or seeking after wizards. אוֹב denotes a departed spirit, who was called up to make disclosures with regard to the future, hence a familiar spirit, *spiritum malum qui certis artibus eliciebatur ut evocaret mortuorum manes, qui prædicarent quæ ab eis petebantur* (*Cler.*). This is the meaning in Isa. xxix. 4, as well as here and in chap. xx. 6, as is evident from chap. xx. 27, "a man or woman in whom is an *ob*," and from 1 Sam. xxviii. 7, 8, *baalath ob*, "a woman with such a spirit." The name was then applied to the necromantist himself, by whom the departed were called up (1 Sam. xxviii. 3; 2 Kings xxiii. 24). The word is connected with *ob*, a skin. יִדְּעֹנִי, the knowing, so to speak, "clever man" (*Symm.* γνώστης, *Aq.* γνωριστής), is only found in connection with *ob*, and denotes unquestionably a person acquainted with necromancy, or a conjurer who devoted himself to the invocation of spirits. (For further remarks, see at 1 Sam. xxviii. 7 sqq.).—Ver. 32. This series concludes with the moral precept, *"Before a hoary head thou shalt rise up* (*sc.* with reverence, Job xxix. 8), *and the countenance* (the person) *of the old man thou shalt honour and fear before thy God."* God is honoured in the old man, and for this reason reverence for age is required. This virtue was cultivated even by the heathen, *e.g.* the Egyptians (*Herod.* 2, 80), the Spartans (*Plutarch*), and the ancient Romans (*Gellius*, ii. 15). It is still found in the East (*Lane, Sitten und Gebr.* ii. p. 121). Vers. 33–37. A few commandments are added of a judicial character.—Vers. 33, 34. The Israelite was not only not to oppress the foreigner in his land (as had already been commanded in Ex. xxii. 20 and xxiii. 9), but to treat him as a native, and love him as himself.—Vers. 35, 36. As a universal rule, they were to do no wrong in judgment (the administration of justice, ver. 15), or in social intercourse and trade with weights and measures of length and capacity; but to keep just scales, weights, and measures. On *ephah* and *hin*, see at Ex. xvi. 36 and xxix. 40. In the renewal of this command in Deut. xxv. 13–16, it is forbidden to carry "stone and stone" in the bag, *i.e.* two kinds of stones (namely, for weights), large and small; or to keep two kinds of measures, a large one for buying and a small one for selling; and full (unadulterated) and just weight and measure are laid down as an obligation. This was a command, the breach of which was frequently condemned (Prov. xvi. 11, xx. 10, 23; Amos viii. 5; Micah vi. 10, cf. Ezek. xlv. 10).—Ver. 37. Concluding exhortation, summing up all the rest.

Chap. xx. PUNISHMENTS FOR THE VICES AND CRIMES PROHIBITED IN CHAP. XVIII. AND XIX.—The list commences with idolatry and soothsaying, which were to be followed by extermination, as a practical apostasy from Jehovah, and a manifest breach of the covenant.—Ver. 2. Whoever, whether an Israelite or a foreigner in Israel, dedicated of his seed (children) to Moloch (see chap. xviii. 21), was to be put to death. The people of the land were to stone him. רָגַם בָּאֶבֶן, *lapide obruere,* is synonymous with סָקַל, *lit. lapidem jacere:* this was the usual punishment appointed in the law for cases in which death was inflicted, either as the result of a judicial sentence, or by the national community.—Ver. 3. By this punishment the nation only carried out the will of Jehovah; for He would cut off such a man (see at chap. xvii. 10 and xviii. 21) for having defiled the sanctuary of Jehovah and desecrated the name of Jehovah, not because he had brought the sacrifice to Moloch into the sanctuary of Jehovah, as *Movers* supposes, but in the same sense in which all the sins of Israel defiled the sanctuary in their midst (chap. xv. 31, xvi. 16).—Vers. 4, 5. If the people, however (the people of the land), should hide their eyes from him (on the *dagesh* in הַעְלֵם and יַעְלִימוּ see the note on p. 307), from an unscrupulous indifference or a secret approval of his sin, the Lord would direct His face against him and his family, and cut him off with all that went a whoring after him.—Ver. 6. He would also do the same to every soul that turned to familiar spirits and necromantists (chap. xix. 31, cf. Ex. xxii. 17), "to go a whoring after them," *i.e.* to make himself guilty of idolatry by so doing, such practices being always closely connected with idolatry.—Vers. 7, 8. For the Israelites were to sanctify themselves, *i.e.* to keep themselves pure from all idolatrous abominations, to be holy because Jehovah was holy (chap. xi. 44, xix. 2), and to keep the statutes of their God who sanctified them (Ex. xxxi. 13).

Vers. 9–18. Whoever cursed father or mother was to be punished with death (chap. xix. 3); "*his blood would be upon him.*" The cursing of parents was a capital crime (see at chap. xvii. 4, and for the plural דָּמָיו Ex. xxii. 1 and Gen. iv. 10), which was to return upon the doer of it, according to Gen. ix. 6. The same punishment was to be inflicted upon adultery (ver. 10, cf. chap. xviii. 20), carnal intercourse with a father's wife (ver. 11, cf. chap. xviii. 7, 8) or with a daughter-in-law (ver. 12, cf. chap. xviii. 17), sodomy (ver. 13, cf. chap. xviii. 22), sexual intercourse with a mother and her daughter, in which case the punishment was to be heightened by the burning of the criminals when put to death (ver. 14, cf. chap. xviii. 17), lying with a beast (vers. 15, 16, cf. chap. xviii. 23), sexual intercourse with a half-sister (ver. 17, cf. chap. xviii. 9 and 11), and lying with a menstruous woman (ver. 18, cf. chap. xviii. 19). The punishment of death, which was to be inflicted in all these cases upon both the criminals, and also upon the beast that had been abused (vers. 15, 16), was to be by stoning, according to vers. 2, 27, and Deut. xxii. 21 sqq.; and by the burning (ver. 14) we are not to understand death by fire, or burning alive, but, as we may clearly see from Josh. vii. 15 and 25, burning the corpse after death. This was also the case in chap. xxi. 9 and Gen. xxxviii. 24.

Vers. 19–21. No civil punishment, on the other hand, to be inflicted by the magistrate or by the community generally, was ordered to follow marriage with an aunt, the sister of father or mother (ver. 19, cf. chap. xviii. 12, 13), with an uncle's wife (ver. 20, cf. chap. xviii. 4), or with a sister-in-law, a brother's wife (ver. 21, cf. chap. xviii. 16). In all these cases the threat is simply held out, " they shall bear their iniquity," and (according to vers. 20, 21) " die childless ;" that is to say, God would reserve the punishment to Himself (see at chap. xviii. 14). In the list of punishments no reference is made to intercourse with a mother (chap. xviii. 7) or a granddaughter (chap. xviii. 10), as it was taken for granted that the punishment of death would be inflicted in such cases as these ; just as marriage with a daughter or a full sister is passed over in the prohibitions in chap. xviii.

Vers. 22–27. The list of punishments concludes, like the prohibitions in chap. xviii. 24 sqq., with exhortations to observe the commandments and judgments of the Lord, and to avoid such abominations (on ver. 22 cf. chap. xviii. 3–5, 26, 28, 30; and on ver. 23 cf. chap. xviii. 3 and 24). The reason assigned for the exhortations is, that Jehovah was about to give them for a possession the fruitful land, whose inhabitants He had driven out because of their abominations, and that Jehovah was their God, who had separated Israel from the nations. For this reason (ver. 25) they were also to sever (make distinctions) between clean and unclean cattle and birds, and not make their souls (*i.e.* their persons) abominable through unclean animals, with which the earth swarmed, and which God had " *separated to make unclean,*" *i.e.* had prohibited them from eating or touching when dead, because they defiled (see chap. xi.). For (ver. 26) they were to be holy, because Jehovah their God was holy, who had severed them from the nations, to belong to Him, *i.e.* to be the nation of His possession (see Ex. xix. 4–6).—Ver. 27. But because Israel was called to be the holy nation of Jehovah, every one, either man or woman, in whom there was a heathenish spirit of soothsaying, was to be put to death, viz. stoned (cf. chap. xix. 31), to prevent defilement by idolatrous abominations.

HOLINESS OF THE PRIESTS, OF THE HOLY GIFTS, AND OF SACRIFICES.—CHAP. XXI. AND XXII.

Chap. xxi. THE SANCTIFICATION OF THE PRIESTS.—As the whole nation was to strive after sanctification in all the duties of life, on account of its calling as a nation of God, the priests, whom Jehovah had chosen out of the whole nation to be the custodians of His sanctuary, and had sanctified to that end, were above all to prove themselves the sanctified servants of the Lord in their domestic life and the duties of their calling. (1) They were not to defile themselves by touching the dead or by signs of mourning (vers. 1–6 and 10–12); (2) they were to contract and maintain a spotless marriage (vers. 7–9 and 13–15); and (3) those members of the priesthood who had any bodily failings were to keep away from the duties of the priests' office (vers. 16–24).

Vers. 1–6. The priest was not to defile himself on account of a soul, *i.e.* a dead person (*nephesh*, as in chap. xix. 28), among his countrymen, unless it were of his kindred, who stood near to him (*i.e.* in the closest relation to him), formed part of the same family with him (cf. ver. 3), such as his mother, father, son, daughter, brother, or a sister who was still living with him as a virgin and was not betrothed to a husband (cf. Ezek. xliv. 25). As every corpse not only defiled the persons who touched it, but also the tent or dwelling in which the person had died (Num. xix. 11, 14); in the case of death among members of the family or household, defilement was not to be avoided on the part of the priest as the head of the family. It was therefore allowable for him to defile himself on account of such persons as these, and even to take part in their burial. The words of ver. 4 are obscure: "*He shall not defile himself* בְּעַמָּיו בַּעַל, *i.e.* as lord (pater-familias) among his countrymen, to desecrate himself;" and the early translators have wandered in uncertainty among different renderings. In all probability בַּעַל denotes the master of the house or husband. But, for all that, the explanation given by *Knobel* and others, "as a husband he shall not defile himself on the death of his wife, his mother-in-law and daughter-in-law, by taking part in their burial," is decidedly to be rejected. For, apart from the unwarrantable introduction of the mother-in-law and daughter-in-law, there is sufficient to prevent our thinking of defilement on the death of a wife, in the fact that the wife is included in the "kin that is near unto him" in ver. 2, though not in the way that many Rabbins suppose, who maintain that שְׁאֵר signifies wife, but *implicite*, the wife not being expressly mentioned, because man and wife form one flesh (Gen.

ii. 24), and the wife stands nearer to the husband than father and mother, son and daughter, or brother and sister. Nothing is proved by appealing to the statement made by *Plutarch*, that the priests of the Romans were not allowed to defile themselves by touching the corpses of their wives; inasmuch as there is no trace of this custom to be found among the Israelites, and the Rabbins, for this very reason, suppose the death of an illegitimate wife to be intended. The correct interpretation of the words can only be arrived at by considering the relation of the fourth verse to what precedes and follows. As vers. 1*b*–3 stand in a very close relation to vers. 5 and 6,—the defilement on account of a dead person being more particularly explained in the latter, or rather, strictly speaking, greater force being given to the prohibition,—it is natural to regard ver. 4 as standing in a similar relation to ver. 7, and to understand it as a general prohibition, which is still more clearly expounded in vers. 7 and 9. The priest was not to defile himself as a husband and the head of a household, either by marrying a wife of immoral or ambiguous reputation, or by training his children carelessly, so as to desecrate himself, *i.e.* profane the holiness of his rank and office by either one or the other (cf. vers. 9 and 15).—In ver. 5 desecration is forbidden in the event of a death occurring. He was not to shave a bald place upon his head. According to the *Chethib* יְקְרָחָה is to be pointed with הָ‑ attached, and the *Keri* יִקְרְחוּ is a grammatical alteration to suit the plural suffix in בְּרֹאשָׁם, which is obviously to be rejected on account of the parallel וּפְאַת זְקָנָם לֹא יְגַלֵּחוּ. In both of the clauses there is a *constructio ad sensum*, the prohibition which is addressed to individuals being applicable to the whole: upon their head shall no one shave a bald place, namely, in front above the forehead, "between the eyes" (Deut. xiv. 1). We may infer from the context that reference is made to a customary mode of mourning for the dead; and this is placed beyond all doubt by Deut. xiv. 1, where it is forbidden to all the Israelites "for the dead." According to *Herodotus*, 2, 36, the priests in Egypt were shaven, whereas in other places they wore their hair long. In other nations it was customary for those who were more immediately concerned to shave their heads as a sign of mourning; but the Egyptians let their hair grow both upon their head and chin when any of their relations were dead, whereas they shaved at other times. The two other outward signs of mourning mentioned, namely, cutting off the edge of the beard and making incisions in the body, have already been forbidden in chap. xix. 27, 28, and the latter is repeated in Deut. xiv. 1. The reason for the prohibition is given in ver. 6,—" *they shall be holy unto their God*," and therefore not disfigure their head and body by signs of passionate grief, and so profane the name of their God when they offer the firings of Jehovah; that is to say, when they serve and approach the God who has manifested Himself to His people as the Holy One. On the epithet applied to the sacrifices, " the food of God," see at chap. iii. 11 and 16.

Vers. 7–9. Their marriage and their domestic life were also to be in keeping with their holy calling. They were not to marry a whore (*i.e.* a public prostitute), or a fallen woman, or a woman put away (divorced) from her husband, that is to say, any person of notoriously immoral life, for this would be irreconcilable with the holiness of the priesthood, but (as may be seen from this in comparison with ver. 14) only a virgin or widow of irreproachable character. She need not be an Israelite, but might be the daughter of a stranger living among the Israelites; only she must not be an idolater or a Canaanite, for the Israelites were all forbidden to marry such a woman (Ex. xxxiv. 16; Deut. vii. 3).—Ver. 8. " *Thou shalt sanctify him therefore*," that is to say, not merely "respect his holy dignity" (*Knobel*), but take care that he did not desecrate his office by a marriage so polluted. The Israelites as a nation are addressed in the persons of their chiefs. The second clause of the verse, " *he shall be holy unto thee*," contains the same thought. The repetition strengthens the exhortation. The reason assigned for the first clause is the same as in ver. 6; and that for the second, the same as in chap. xx. 8, 26, Ex. xxxi. 13, etc.—Ver. 9. The priest's family was also to lead a blameless life. If a priest's daughter began to play the whore, she profaned her father, and was to be burned, *i.e.* to be stoned and then burned (see chap. xx. 14). אִישׁ כֹּהֵן, a man who is a priest, a priest-man.

Vers. 10–15. The high priest was to maintain a spotless purity in a higher degree still. He, whose head had been anointed with oil, and who had been sanctified to put on the holy clothes (see chap. viii. 7–12 and vii. 37), was not to go with his hair flying loose when a death had taken place, nor to

rend his clothes (see chap. x. 6), nor to go in to any dead body
(נַפְשֹׁת מֵת souls of a departed one, *i.e.* dead persons) ; he was not
to defile himself (cf. ver. 2) on account of his father and mother
(*i.e.* when they were dead), nor to go out of the sanctuary *funeris
nempe causa* (*Ros.*), to give way to his grief or attend the funeral.
We are not to understand by this, however, that the sanctuary
was to be his constant abode, as *Bähr* and *Baumgarten* maintain (cf. chap. x. 7). " *Neither shall he profane the sanctuary of
his God,*" sc. by any defilement of his person which he could
and ought to avoid ; " *for the consecration of the anointing oil of
his God is upon him*" (cf. chap. x. 7), and defilement was in-
compatible with this.   נֵזֶר does not mean the diadem of the
high priest here, as in Ex. xxix. 6, xxxix. 30, but *consecration*
(see at Num. vi. 7).—Vers. 13, 14. He was only to marry a
woman in her virginity, not a widow, a woman put away, or a
fallen woman, a whore (זֹנָה without a copulative is in apposition
to חֲלָלָה a fallen girl, who was to be the same to him as a whore),
but "a virgin of his own people," that is to say, only an Israelitish woman.—Ver. 15. " *Neither shall he profane his seed* (posterity) *among his people,*" sc. by contracting a marriage that was
not in keeping with the holiness of his rank.

Vers. 16–24. Directions for the sons (descendants) of Aaron
who were afflicted with bodily imperfections. As the spiritual
nature of a man is reflected in his bodily form, only a faultless
condition of body could correspond to the holiness of the priest ;
just as the Greeks and Romans required, for the very same
reason, that the priests should be ὁλόκληροι, *integri corporis*
(*Plato de legg.* 6, 759 ; *Seneca excerpt. controv.* 4, 2 ; *Plutarch
quœst. rom.* 73). Consequently none of the descendants of
Aaron, " according to their generations," *i.e.* in all future generations (see Ex. xii. 14), who had any blemish (*mum*, μῶμος,
bodily fault) were to approach the vail, *i.e.* enter the holy place,
or draw near to the altar (in the court) to offer the food of
Jehovah, viz. the sacrifices. No blind man, or lame man, or
charum, κολοβόριν (from κολοβός and ῥίν), *naso mutilus* (LXX.),
i.e. one who had sustained any mutilation, especially in the face,
on the nose, ears, lips, or eyes, not merely one who had a flat or
stunted nose ; or שָׂרוּעַ, *lit.* stretched out, *i.e.* one who had anything beyond what was normal, an ill-formed bodily member
therefore ; so that a man who had more than ten fingers and ten

toes might be so regarded (2 Sam. xxi. 20).—Ver. 19. Whoever
had a fracture in his foot or hand.—Ver. 20. גִּבֵּן a hump-backed
man. דַּק, *lit.* crushed to powder, fine: as distinguished from the
former, it signified one who had an unnaturally thin or withered
body or member, not merely consumptive or wasted away. תְּבַלֻּל
בְּעֵינוֹ mixed, *i.e.* spotted in his eye, one who had a white speck in
his eye (*Onk., Vulg., Saad.*), not blear-eyed (LXX.). גָּרָב, which
occurs nowhere else except in chap. xxii. 22 and Deut. xxviii.
27, signifies, according to the ancient versions, the itch; and
יַלֶּפֶת, which only occurs here and in chap. xxii. 22, the ring-
worm (LXX., *Targ.*, etc.). מְרוֹחַ אָשֶׁךְ, crushed in the stones,
one who had crushed or softened stones; for in Isa. xxxviii. 21,
the only other place where מָרַח occurs, it signifies, not to rub to
pieces, but to squeeze out, to lay in a squeezed or liquid form
upon the wound: the Sept. rendering is μόνορχις, having only
one stone. Others understand the word as signifying ruptured
(*Vulg., Saad.*), or with swollen testicles (*Juda ben Karish*). All
that is certain is, that we are not to think of castration of any
kind (cf. Deut. xxiii. 2), and that there is not sufficient ground
for altering the text into מְרוּחַ extension.—Ver. 22. Persons
afflicted in the manner described might eat the bread of their
God, however, the sacrificial gifts, the most holy and the holy, *i.e.*
the wave-offerings, the first-fruits, the firstlings, tithes and things
laid under a ban (Num. xviii. 11–19 and 26–29),—that is to say,
they might eat them like the rest of the priests; but they were
not allowed to perform any priestly duty, that they might not desecrate the sanctuary of the Lord (ver. 23, cf. ver. 12).—Ver. 24.
Moses communicated these instructions to Aaron and his sons.

Chap. xxii. Vers. 1–16. REVERENCE FOR THINGS SANCTI-
FIED.—The law on this matter was, (1) that no priest who had
become unclean was to touch or eat them (vers. 2–9), and
(2) that no one was to eat them who was not a member of a
priestly family (vers. 10–16).—Ver. 2. Aaron and his sons were
to keep away from the holy gifts of the children of Israel, which
they consecrated to Jehovah, that they might not profane the
holy name of Jehovah by defiling them. הִנָּזֵר with מִן to keep
away, separate one's self from anything, *i.e.* not to regard or
treat them as on a par with unconsecrated things. The words,
" *which they sanctify to Me,*" are a supplementary apposition,

added as a more precise definition of the "holy things of the
children of Israel;" as the expression "holy things" was applied
to the holy objects universally, including the furniture of the
tabernacle.   Here, however, the reference is solely to the holy
offerings or gifts, which were not placed upon the altar, but
presented to the Lord as heave-offerings and wave-offerings,
and assigned by Him to the priests as the servants of His house,
for their maintenance (Num. xviii. 11–19, 26–29).   None of the
descendants of Aaron were to approach these gifts, which were
set apart for them,—*i.e.* to touch them either for the purpose of
eating, or making them ready for eating,—whilst any uncleanness was upon them, on pain of extermination.—Vers. 4, 5.   No
leper was to touch them (see chap. xiii. 2), or person with
gonorrhœa (chap. xv. 2), until he was clean; no one who had
touched a person defiled by a corpse (chap. xix. 28; Num. xix.
22), or whose seed had gone from him (chap. xv. 16, 18); and
no one who had touched an unclean creeping animal, or an
unclean man.   לְכֹל טֻמְאָתוֹ, as in chap. v. 3, a closer definition of
אֲשֶׁר יִטְמָא לוֹ, "who is unclean to him with regard to (on account
of) any uncleanness which he may have."—Vers. 6, 7.   "*A soul
which touches it,*" *i.e.* any son of Aaron, who had touched either
an unclean person or thing, was to be unclean till the evening,
and then bathe his body; after sunset, *i.e.* when the day was over,
he became clean, and could eat of the sanctified things, for they
were his food.—Ver. 8.   In this connection the command given
to all the Israelites, not to eat anything that had fallen down
dead or been torn in pieces (chap. xvii. 15, 16), is repeated with
special reference to the priests.   (On ver. 9, see chap. viii. 35,
xviii. 30, and xix. 17.)   יְחַלְּלֻהוּ, "because they have defiled it (the
sanctified thing)."—Vers. 10–16.   No stranger was to eat a sanctified thing.   זָר is in general the non-priest, then any person who
was not fully incorporated into a priestly family, *e.g.* a visitor
or day-labourer (cf. Ex. xii. 49), who were neither of them
members of his family.—Ver. 11.   On the other hand, slaves
bought for money, or born in the house, became members of his
family and lived upon his bread; they were therefore allowed
to eat of that which was sanctified along with him, since the
slaves were, in fact, formally incorporated into the nation by
circumcision (Gen. xvii. 12, 13).—Vers. 12, 13.   So again the
daughter of a priest, if she became a widow, or was put away

by her husband, and returned childless to her father's house, and became a member of his family again, just as in the days of her youth, might eat of the holy things. But if she had any children, then after the death of her husband, or after her divorce, she formed with them a family of her own, which could not be incorporated into the priesthood, of course always sup- posing that her husband was not a priest.—Ver. 14. But if any one (*i.e.* any layman) should eat unawares of that which was sanctified, he was to bring it, *i.e.* an equivalent for it, with the addition of a fifth as a compensation for the priest; like a man who had sinned by unfaithfulness in relation to that which was sanctified (chap. v. 16).—In the concluding exhortation in vers. 15 and 16, the subject to יְחַלְּלוּ (profane) and הִשִּׂיאוּ (bear) is indefinite, and the passage to be rendered thus: "*They are not to profane the sanctified gifts of the children of Israel, what they heave for the Lord* (namely, by letting laymen eat of them), *and are to cause them* (the laymen) *who do this unawares to bear a trespass-sin* (by imposing the compensation mentioned in ver. 14), *if they eat their* (the priests') *sanctified gifts.*" Understood in this way, both verses furnish a fitting conclusion to the section vers. 10-14. On the other hand, according to the traditional interpretation of these verses, the priesthood is re- garded as the subject of the first verb, and a negative supplied before the second. Both of these are arbitrary and quite in- defensible, because vers. 10–14 do not refer to the priests but to laymen, and in the latter case we should expect וְלֹא יִשְׂאוּ אֲלֵיהֶם (cf. ver. 9) instead of the unusual הִשִּׂיאוּ אוֹתָם.

Vers. 17–33. ACCEPTABLE SACRIFICES. — Vers. 18–20. Every sacrifice offered to the Lord by an Israelite or foreigner, in consequence of a vow or as a freewill-offering (cf. chap. vii. 16), was to be faultless and a male, " for good pleasure to the offerer " (cf. i. 3), *i.e.* to secure for him the good pleasure of God. An animal with a fault would not be acceptable.—Vers. 21, 22. Every peace-offering was also to be faultless, whether brought " to fulfil a special (important) vow" (cf. Num. xv. 3, 8: פֶּלֶא, from פָּלָא to be great, distinguished, wonderful), or as a freewill gift; that is to say, it was to be free from such faults as blindness, or a broken limb (from lameness therefore: Deut. xv. 21), or cutting (*i.e.* mutilation, answering to חָרוּם chap. xxi.

18), or an abscess (יַבֶּלֶת, from יָבַל to flow, probably a flowing suppurating abscess).—Ver. 23. As a voluntary peace-offering they might indeed offer an ox or sheep that was שָׂרוּעַ וְקָלוּט, "stretched out and drawn together," *i.e.* with the whole body or certain limbs either too large or too small;[1] but such an animal could not be acceptable as a votive offering.—Ver. 24. Castrated animals were not to be sacrificed, nor in fact to be kept in the land at all. מָעוּךְ *compressus*, θλιβίας, an animal with the stones crushed; כָּתוּת *contusus*, θλασίας, with them beaten to pieces; נָתוּק *avulsus*, σπάδων, with them twisted off; כָּרוּת *excisus*, τομίας or ἐκτομίας, with them cut off. In all these different ways was the operation performed among the ancients (cf. *Aristot. hist. an.* ix. 37, 3; *Colum.* vi. 26, vii. 11; *Pallad.* vi. 7). "And in your land ye shall not make," *sc.* מָעוּךְ וגו, *i.e.* castrated animals, that is to say, "not castrate animals." This explanation, which is the one given by *Josephus* (Ant. iv. 8, 40) and all the Rabbins, is required by the expression "in your land," which does not at all suit the interpretation adopted by *Clericus* and *Knobel*, who understand by עָשָׂה the preparation of sacrifices, for sacrifices were never prepared outside the land. The castration of animals is a mutilation of God's creation, and the prohibition of it was based upon the same principle as that of mixing heterogeneous things in chap. xix. 19.—Ver. 25. Again, the Israelites were not to accept any one of all these, *i.e.* the faulty animals described, as sacrifice from a foreigner. "*For their corruption is in them,*" *i.e.* something corrupt, a fault, adheres to them; so that such offerings could not procure good pleasure towards them.—In vers. 26–30 three laws are given of a similar character.—Ver. 27. A young ox, sheep, or goat was to be seven days under its mother, and could only be sacrificed from the eighth day onwards, according to the rule laid down in Ex. xxii. 29 with regard to the first-born. The reason for this was, that the young animal had not attained to a mature and self-sustained life during the first week of its existence.[2]

---

[1] In explanation of these words *Knobel* very properly remarks, that with the Greeks the sacrificial animal was required to be ἀφελής (*Pollux* i. 1, 26), upon which *Hesychius* observes, μήτε πλεονάζων μήτε δέων τι τοῦ σώματος.

[2] For this reason the following rule was also laid down by the Romans: *Suis foetus sacrificio die quinto purus est, pecoris die octavo, bovis tricesimo* (*Plin.* h. n. 8, 51).

This maturity was not reached till after the lapse of a week, that period of time sanctified by the creation. There is no rule laid down in the law respecting the age up to which an animal was admissible in sacrifice. *Bullocks, i.e.* steers or young oxen of more than a year old, are frequently mentioned and pre-scribed for the festal sacrifices (for the young ox of less than a year old is called עֵגֶל; chap. ix. 3), viz. as *burnt-offerings* in chap. xxiii. 18, Num. vii. 15, 21, 27, 33, 39 sqq., viii. 8, xv. 24, xxviii. 11, 19, 27, xxix. 2, 8, and as *sin-offerings* in chap. iv. 3, 14, xvi. 3;—*sheep* (lambs) of one year old are also prescribed as *burnt-offerings* in chap. ix. 3, xii. 6, xxiii. 12, Ex. xxix. 38, Num. vi. 14, vii. 17, 21, 27, 33, 39 sqq., xxviii. 3, 9, 19, 27, xxix. 2, 8, 13, 17 sqq., as *peace-offerings* in Num. vii. 17, 23, xxix. 35 sqq., and as *trespass-offerings* in Num. vi. 12; also a yearling *ewe* as a sin-offering in chap. xiv. 10 and Num. vi. 14, and a yearling *goat* in Num. xv. 27. They generally brought older oxen or bullocks for peace-offerings (Num. vii. 17, xxiii. 29 sqq.), and sometimes as burnt-offerings. In Judg. vi. 25 an ox of seven years old is said to have been brought as a burnt-offering; and there can be no doubt that the goats and rams presented as sin-offerings and trespass-offerings were more than a year old.—Ver. 28. The command not to kill an ox or sheep at the same time as its young is related to the law in Ex. xxiii. 19 and Deut. xxii. 6, 7, and was intended to lay it down as a duty on the part of the Israelites to keep sacred the relation which God had established between parent and offspring.—In vers. 29, 30, the command to eat the flesh of the animal on the day on which it was offered (chap. vii. 15, xix. 5, 6) is repeated with special reference to the praise-offering.—Vers. 31–33. Concluding exhortation, as in chap. xviii. 29, xix. 37. (On ver. 32, cf. chap. xviii. 21 and xi. 44, 45.)

SANCTIFICATION OF THE SABBATH AND THE FEASTS OF JEHOVAH.—CHAP. XXIII.

This chapter does not contain a "calendar of feasts," or a summary and completion of the directions previously given in a scattered form concerning the festal times of Israel, but simply a list of those festal days and periods of the year at which holy meetings were to be held. This is most clearly stated in the heading (ver. 2): "*the festal times of Jehovah, which ye shall call out as holy meetings, these are they, My feasts,*" *i.e.* those which are to be regarded as My feasts, sanctified to Me. The festal seasons and days were called "feasts of Jehovah," times appointed and fixed by Jehovah (see Gen. i. 14), not because the feasts belonged to fixed times regulated by the course of the moon (*Knobel*), but because Jehovah had appointed them as days, or times, which were to be sanctified to Him. Hence the expression is not only used with reference to the Sabbath, the new moon, and the other yearly feasts ; but in Num. xxviii. 2 and xxix. 39 it is extended so as to include the times of the daily morning and evening sacrifice. (On the "holy convocation" see Ex. xii. 16.)

Ver. 3. At the head of these *moadim* stood the *Sabbath*, as the day which God had already sanctified as a day of rest for His people, by His own rest on the seventh creation-day (Gen. ii. 3, cf. Ex. xx. 8–11). On שַׁבַּת שַׁבָּתוֹן, see at Ex. xxxi. 15 and xvi. 33. As a weekly returning day of rest, the observance of which had its foundation in the creative work of God, the Sabbath was distinguished from the yearly feasts, in which Israel commemorated the facts connected with its elevation into a people of God, and which were generally called " feasts of Jehovah" in the stricter sense, and as such were distinguished from the Sabbath (vers. 37, 38 ; Isa. i. 13, 14 ; 1 Chron. xxiii. 31 ; 2 Chron. xxxi. 3 ; Neh. x. 34). This distinction is pointed out in the heading, " *these are the feasts of Jehovah*" (ver. 4).[1] In Num. xxviii. 11 the feast of new moon follows the Sabbath ; but this is passed over here, because the new moon was not to be observed either with sabbatical rest or a holy meeting.

Vers. 4–14. Ver. 4 contains the special heading for the yearly feasts. בְּמוֹעֲדָם at their appointed time.—Vers. 5–8. The leading directions for the *Passover* and *feast of Mazzoth* are

---

[1] Partly on account of this repetition, and partly because of the supposed discrepancy observable in the fact, that holy meetings are not prescribed for the Sabbath in the list of festal sacrifices in Num. xxviii. and xxix., *Hupfeld* and *Knobel* maintain that the words of vers. 2 and 3, from יְהֹוָה to מוֹשְׁבֹתֵיכֶם, notwithstanding their Elohistic expression, were not written by the Elohist, but are an interpolation of the later editor. The repetition of the heading, however, cannot prove anything at all with the constant repetitions that occur in the so-called Elohistic groundwork, especially as it can be fully explained by the reason mentioned in the text. And the pretended discrepancy rests upon the perfectly arbitrary assumption, that Num.

repeated from Ex. xii. 6, 11, 15–20. מְלֶאכֶת עֲבֹדָה, occupation of a work, signifies labour at some definite occupation, e.g. the building of the tabernacle, Ex. xxxv. 24, xxxvi. i. 3 ; hence occupation in connection with trade or one's social calling, such as agriculture, handicraft, and so forth ; whilst מְלָאכָה is the performance of any kind of work, e.g. kindling fire for cooking food (Ex. xxxv. 2, 3). On the Sabbath and the day of atonement every kind of civil work was prohibited, even to the kindling of fire for the purpose of cooking (vers. 3, 30, 31, cf. Ex. xx. 10, xxxi. 14, xxxv. 2, 3 ; Deut. v. 14 and Lev. xvi. 29 ; Num. xxix. 7) ; on the other feast-days with a holy convocation, only servile work (vers. 7, 8, 21, 25, 35, 36, cf. Ex. xii. 16, and the explanation in vol. i., and Num. xxviii. 18, 25, 26, xxix. 1, 12, 35). To this there is appended a fresh regulation in vers. 9–14, with the repetition of the introductory clause, " And the Lord spake," etc. When the Israelites had come into the land to be given them by the Lord, and had reaped the harvest, they were to bring a sheaf as first-fruits of their harvest to the priest, that he might wave it before Jehovah on the day after the Sabbath, i.e. after the first day of Mazzoth. According to Josephus and Philo, it was a sheaf of barley ; but this is not expressly commanded, because it would be taken for granted in Canaan, where the harvest began with the barley. In the warmer parts of Palestine the barley ripens about the middle of April, and is reaped in April or the beginning of May, whereas the wheat ripens two or three weeks later (Seetzen ; Robinson's Pal. ii. 263, 278). The priest was to wave the sheaf before Jehovah, i.e. to present it symbolically to Jehovah by the ceremony of waving, without burning any of it upon the altar. The rabbinical rule, viz. to dry a portion of the ears by the fire,

xxviii. and xxix. contain a complete codex of all the laws relating to all the feasts. How totally this assumption is at variance with the calendar of feasts, is clear enough from the fact, that no rule is laid down there for the observance of the Sabbath, with the exception of the sacrifices to be offered upon it, and that even rest from labour is not commanded. Moreover Knobel is wrong in identifying the " holy convocation" with a journey to the sanctuary, whereas appearance at the tabernacle to hold the holy convocations (for worship) was not regarded as necessary either in the law itself or according to the later orthodox custom, but, on the contrary, holy meetings for edification were held on the Sabbath in every place in the land, and it was out of this that the synagogues arose.

and then, after rubbing them out, to burn them on the altar, was
an ordinance of the later scribes, who knew not the law, and
was based upon chap. ii. 14. For the law in chap. ii. 14 refers
to the offerings of first-fruits made by private persons, which are
treated of in Num. xviii. 12, 13, and Deut. xxvi. 2 sqq. The
sheaf of first-fruits, on the other hand, which was to be offered
before Jehovah as a wave-offering in the name of the congregation, corresponded to the two wave-loaves which were leavened
and then baked, and were to be presented to the Lord as first-
fruits (ver. 17). As no portion of these wave-loaves was burned
upon the altar, because nothing leavened was to be placed upon
it (chap. ii. 11), but they were assigned entirely to the priests,
we have only to assume that the same application was intended
by the law in the case of the sheaf of first-fruits, since the text
only prescribes the waving, and does not contain a word about
roasting, rubbing, or burning the grains upon the altar. מָחֳרַת
הַשַּׁבָּת (the morrow after the Sabbath) signifies the next day after
the first day of the feast of Mazzoth, i.e. the 16th Abib (Nisan),
not the day of the Sabbath which fell in the seven days' feast
of Mazzoth, as the Bæthoseans supposed, still less the 22d of
Nisan, or the day after the conclusion of the seven days' feast,
which always closed with a Sabbath, as *Hitzig* imagines.[1] The

[1] The view advocated by the Bæthoseans, which has been lately supported by *W. Schultz*, is refuted not only by Josh. v. 11, but by the definite
article used, הַשַּׁבָּת, which points back to one of the feast-days already mentioned, and still more decisively by the circumstance, that according to
ver. 15 the seven weeks, at the close of which the feast of Pentecost was to
be kept, were to be reckoned from this Sabbath ; and if the Sabbath was
not fixed, but might fall upon any day of the seven days' feast of Mazzoth,
and therefore as much as five or six days after the Passover, the feast of
Passover itself would be forced out of the fundamental position which it
occupied in the series of annual festivals (cf. *Ranke*, Pentateuch ii. 108).
Hitzig's hypothesis has been revived by *Hupfeld* and *Knobel*, without any
notice of the conclusive refutation given to it by *Bähr* and *Wieseler ;* only
Knobel makes "the Sabbath" not the concluding but the opening Sabbath
of the feast of Passover, on the ground that " otherwise the festal sheaf
would not have been offered till the 22d of the month, and therefore would
have come *post festum.*" But this hypothesis, which renders it necessary
that the commencement of the ecclesiastical year should always be assigned
to a Saturday (Sabbath), in order to gain weekly Sabbaths for the 14th and
21st of the month, as the opening and close of the feast of Passover, gives
such a form to the Jewish year as would involve its invariably closing with
a broken week ; a hypothesis which is not only incapable of demonstration,

"Sabbath" does not mean the seventh day of the week, but the day of rest, although the weekly Sabbath was always the seventh or last day of the week; hence not only the seventh day of the week (Ex. xxxi. 15, etc.), but the day of atonement (the tenth of the seventh month), is called "Sabbath," and "Shabbath shabbathon" (ver. 32, chap. xvi. 31). As a day of rest, on which no laborious work was to be performed (ver. 8), the first day of the feast of *Mazzoth* is called "Sabbath," irrespectively of the day of the week upon which it fell; and "*the morrow after the Sabbath*" is equivalent to "the morrow after the Passover" mentioned in Josh. v. 11, where "Passover" signifies the day at the beginning of which the paschal meal was held, *i.e.* the first day of unleavened bread, which commenced on the evening of the 14th, in other words, the 15th Abib. By offering the sheaf of first-fruits of the harvest, the Israelites were to consecrate their daily bread to the Lord their God, and practically to acknowledge that they owed the blessing of the harvest to the grace of God. They were not to eat any bread or roasted grains of the new corn till they had presented the offering of their God (ver. 14). This offering was fixed for the second day of the feast of the Passover, that the connection between the harvest and the Passover might be kept in subordination to the leading idea of the Passover itself (see at Ex. xii. 15 sqq.). But

but, from the holiness attached to the Jewish division of weeks, is *a priori* improbable, and in fact inconceivable. The Mosaic law, which gave such sanctity to the division of time into weeks, as founded upon the history of creation, by the institution of the observance of the Sabbath, that it raised the Sabbath into the groundwork of a magnificent festal cycle, could not possibly have made such an arrangement with regard to the time for the observance of the Passover, as would involve almost invariably the mutilation of the last week of the year, and an interruption of the old and sacred weekly cycle with the Sabbath festival at its close. The arguments by which so forced a hypothesis is defended, must be very conclusive indeed, to meet with any acceptance. But neither *Hitzig* nor his followers have been able to adduce any such arguments as these. Besides the word "Sabbath" and Josh. v. 11, which prove nothing at all, the only other argument adduced by *Knobel* is, that "it is impossible to see why precisely the second day of the *azyma*, when the people went about their ordinary duties, and there was no meeting at the sanctuary, should have been distinguished by the sacrificial gift which was the peculiar characteristic of the feast,"—an argument based upon the fallacious principle, that anything for which I can see no reason, cannot possibly have occurred.

as the sheaf was not burned upon the altar, but only presented symbolically to the Lord by waving, and then handed over to the priests, an altar-gift had to be connected with it,—namely, a yearling sheep as a burnt-offering, a meat-offering of two-tenths of an ephah of fine flour mixed with oil, and a drink-offering of a quarter of a hin of wine,—to give expression to the obligation and willingness of the congregation not only to enjoy their earthly food, but to strengthen all the members of their body for growth in holiness and diligence in good works. The burnt-offering, for which a yearling lamb was prescribed, as in fact for all the regular festal sacrifices, was of course in addition to the burnt-offerings prescribed in Num. xxviii. 19, 20, for every feast-day. The meat-offering, however, was not to consist of one-tenth of an ephah of fine flour, as on other occasions (Ex. xxix. 40; Num. xxviii. 9, 13, etc.), but of two-tenths, that the offering of corn at the harvest-feast might be a more plentiful one than usual.

Vers. 15–22. The law for the special observance of the *feast of Harvest* (Ex. xxiii. 16) is added here without any fresh introductory formula, to show at the very outset the close connection between the two feasts. Seven whole weeks, or fifty days, were to be reckoned from the day of the offering of the sheaf, and then the *day of first-fruits* (Num. xxviii. 26) or *feast of Weeks* (Ex. xxxiv. 22; Deut. xvi. 10) was to be celebrated. From this reckoning the feast received the name of Pentecost (ἡ πεντηκοστή, Acts ii. 1). That שַׁבָּתוֹת (ver. 15) signifies weeks, like שָׁבֻעוֹת in Deut. xvi. 9, and τὰ σάββατα in the Gospels (*e.g.* Matt. xxviii. 1), is evident from the predicate תְּמִימֹת, "complete," which would be quite unsuitable if Sabbath-days were intended, as a long period might be reckoned by half weeks instead of whole, but certainly not by half Sabbath-days. Consequently "the morrow after the seventh Sabbath" (ver. 16) is the day after the seventh week, not after the seventh Sabbath. On this day, *i.e.* fifty days after the first day of *Mazzoth*, Israel was to offer a new meat-offering to the Lord, *i.e.* made of the fruit of the new harvest (chap. xxvi. 10), "wave-loaves" from its dwellings, two of two-tenths of an ephah of fine flour baked leavened, like the bread which served for their daily food, "as first-fruits unto the Lord," and of the wheat-harvest (Ex. xxxiv. 22), which fell in the second half of May and the first weeks of June (*Robinson, Palestine*), and therefore was finished as a whole by the feast of Weeks. The loaves differed from all the other meat-offerings, being made of leavened dough, because in them their daily bread was offered to the Lord, who had blessed the harvest, as a thank-offering for His blessing. They were therefore only given to the Lord symbolically by waving, and were then to belong to the priests (ver. 20). The injunction " out of your habitations" is not to be understood, as *Calvin* and others suppose, as signifying that every householder was to present two such loaves; it simply expresses the idea, that they were to be loaves made for the daily food of a household, and not prepared expressly for holy purposes.—Vers. 18, 19. In addition to the loaves, they were to offer seven yearling lambs, one young bullock, and two rams, as burnt-offerings, together with their (the appropriate) meat and drink-offerings, one he-goat as a sin-offering, and two yearling lambs as peace-offerings.—Ver. 20. " *The priest shall wave them* (the two lambs of the peace-offerings), *together with the loaves of the first-fruits, as a wave-offering before Jehovah ; with the two lambs* (the two just mentioned), *they* (the loaves) *shall be holy to Jehovah for the priest.*" In the case of the peace-offerings of private individuals, the flesh belonged for the most part to the offerer ; but here, in the case of a thank-offering presented by the congregation, it was set apart for the priest. The circumstance, that not only was a much more bountiful burnt-offering prescribed than in the offerings of the dedicatory sheaf at the commencement of harvest (ver. 12), but a sin-offering and peace-offering also, is to be attributed to the meaning of the festival itself, as a feast of thanksgiving for the rich blessing of God that had just been gathered in. The sin-offering was to excite the feeling and consciousness of sin on the part of the congregation of Israel, that whilst eating their daily leavened bread they might not serve the leaven of their old nature, but seek and implore from the Lord their God the forgiveness and cleansing away of their sin. Through the increased burnt-offering they were to give practical expression to their gratitude for the blessing of harvest, by a strengthened consecration and sanctification of all the members of the whole man to the service of the Lord; whilst through the peace-offering they entered into that fellowship of peace with the Lord to which they were called, and which they were eventually to enjoy through His blessing

in their promised inheritance. In this way the whole of the year's
harvest was placed under the gracious blessing of the Lord by
the sanctification of its commencement and its close; and the
enjoyment of their daily food was also sanctified thereby. For
the sake of this inward connection, the laws concerning the wave-
sheaf and wave-loaves are bound together into one whole ; and
by this connection, which was established by reckoning the time
for the feast of Weeks from the day of the dedication of the
sheaf, the two feasts were linked together into an internal unity.
The Jews recognised this unity from the very earliest times, and
called the feast of Pentecost *Azereth* (Greek, '*Ασαρθά*), because
it was the close of the seven weeks (see at ver. 36: *Josephus*,
Ant. iii. 10).[1]—Ver. 21. On this day a holy meeting was to be
held, and laborious work to be suspended, just as on the first and
seventh days of *Mazzoth*.   This was to be maintained as a statute
for ever (see ver. 14).   It was not sufficient, however, to thank
the Lord for the blessing of harvest by a feast of thanksgiving
to the Lord, but they were not to forget the poor and distressed
when gathering in their harvest.   To indicate this, the law laid
down in chap. xix. 9, 10 is repeated in ver. 22.

Vers. 23–25. On the first day of the seventh month there
was to be *shabbathon*, rest, *i.e.* a day of rest (see Ex. xvi. 23),
a *memorial of blowing of trumpets*, a holy convocation, the suspension of laborious work, and the offering of a firing for Jehovah, which are still more minutely described in the calendar of
festal sacrifices in Num. xxix. 2–6. תְּרוּעָה, a joyful noise, from
רוּע to make a noise, is used in ver. 24 for תְּרוּעַת שׁוֹפָר, a blast of
trumpets.   On this day the *shophar* was to be blown, a blast of
trumpets to be appointed for a memorial before Jehovah (Num.
x. 10), *i.e.* to call the congregation into remembrance before
Jehovah, that He might turn towards it His favour and grace
(see at Ex. xxviii. 12, 29, xxx. 16) ; and from this the feast-day
is called the day of the trumpet-blast (Num. xxix. 1). *Shophar*,
a trumpet, was a large horn which produced a dull, far-reaching
tone. *Buccina pastoralis est et cornu recurvo efficitur, unde et
proprie hebraice sophar, græce κερατίνη appellatur (Jerome on*

---

[1] A connection between the feast of Pentecost and the giving of the law,
which *Maimonides* (A.D. †1205) was the first to discover, is not only foreign
to the Mosaic law, but to the whole of the Jewish antiquity ; and even
Abarbanel expressly denies it.

Hos. **v.** 8).[1] The seventh month of the year, like the seventh day of the week, was consecrated as a Sabbath or sabbatical month, by a holy convocation and the suspension of labour, which were to distinguish the first day of the seventh month from the beginning of the other months or the other new moon days throughout the year. For the whole month was sanctified in the first day, as the beginning or head of the month; and by the sabbatical observance of the commencement, the whole course of the month was raised to a Sabbath. This was enjoined, not merely because it was the seventh month, but because the seventh month was to secure to the congregation the complete atonement for all its sins, and the wiping away of all the uncleannesses which separated it from its God, viz. on the day of atonement, which fell within this month, and to bring it a foretaste of the blessedness of life in fellowship with the Lord, viz. in the feast of Tabernacles, which commenced five days afterwards. This significant character of the seventh month was indicated by the trumpet-blast, by which the congregation presented the memorial of itself loudly and strongly before Jehovah on the first day of the month, that He might bestow upon them the promised blessings of His grace, for the realization of His covenant. The trumpet-blast on this day was a prelude of the trumpet-blast with which the commencement of the year of jubilee was proclaimed to the whole nation, on the day of atonement of every seventh sabbatical year, that great year of grace under the old covenant (chap. xxv. 9); just as the seventh month in general formed the link between the weekly Sabbath and the sabbatical and jubilee years, and corresponded as a Sabbath month to the year of jubilee rather than the sabbatical year, which had its prelude in the weekly Sabbath-day.

Vers. 26–32. On the tenth day of the seventh month the *day of atonement* was to be observed by a holy meeting, by fast-

---

[1] The word תְּרוּעָה is also used in Num. x. 5, 6 to denote the blowing with the silver trumpets; but there seems to be no ground for supposing these trumpets to be intended here, not only because of the analogy between the seventh day of the new moon as a jubilee day and the jubilee year (chap. xxv. 9, 10), but also because the silver trumpets are assigned to a different purpose in Num. x. 2-10, and their use is restricted to the blowing at the offering of the burnt-offerings on the feast-days and new moons. To this we have to add the Jewish tradition, which favours with perfect unanimity the practice of blowing with horns (the horns of animals).

ing from the evening of the ninth till the evening of the tenth, by resting from all work on pain of death, and with sacrifices, of which the great expiatory sacrifice peculiar to this day had already been appointed in chap. xvi., and the general festal sacrifices are described in Num. xxix. 8–11. (For fuller particulars, see at chap. xvi.) By the restrictive אַךְ, the observance of the day of atonement is represented *a priori* as a peculiar one. The אַךְ refers less to " the tenth day," than to the leading directions respecting this feast : " only on the tenth of this seventh month . . . there shall be a holy meeting to you, and ye shall afflict your souls," etc.—Ver. 32. " Ye shall rest your rest," *i.e.* observe the rest that is binding upon you from all laborious work.

Vers. 33–43. On the fifteenth of the same month the *feast of Tabernacles* was to be kept to the Lord for seven days : on the first day with a holy meeting and rest from all laborious work, and for seven days with sacrifices, as appointed for every day in Num. xxix. 13–33. Moreover, on the eighth day, *i.e.* the 22d of the month, the closing feast was to be observed in the same manner as on the first day (vers. 34–36). The name, " feast of Tabernacles" (booths), is to be explained from the fact, that the Israelites were to dwell in booths made of boughs for the seven days that this festival lasted (ver. 42). עֲצֶרֶת, which is used in ver. 36 and Num. xxix. 35 for the eighth day, which terminated the feast of Tabernacles, and in Deut. xvi. 8 for the seventh day of the feast of *Mazzoth*, signifies the solemn close of a feast of several days, *clausula festi*, from עָצַר to shut in, or close (Gen. xvi. 2; Deut. xi. 17, etc.), not *a coagendo, congregando populo ad festum,* nor *a cohibitione laboris, ab interdicto opere,* because the word is only applied to the last day of the feasts of *Mazzoth* and Tabernacles, and not to the first, although this was also kept with a national assembly and suspension of work. But as these *clausulæ festi* were holidays with a holy convocation and suspension of work, it was very natural that the word should be transferred at a later period to feasts generally, on which the people suspended work and met for worship and edification (Joel i. 14 ; Isa. i. 13 ; 2 Kings x. 20). The *azereth,* as the eighth day, did not strictly belong to the feast of Tabernacles, which was only to last seven days ; and it was distinguished, moreover, from these seven days by a smaller number of offer-

ings (Num. xxix. 35 sqq.). The eighth day was rather the
solemn close of the whole circle of yearly feasts, and therefore
was appended to the close of the last of these feasts as the
eighth day of the feast itself (see at Num. xxviii. seq.).—With
ver. 36 the enumeration of all the yearly feasts on which holy
meetings were to be convened is brought to an end. This is
stated in the concluding formula (vers. 37, 38), which answers
to the heading in ver. 4, in which the Sabbaths are excepted, as
they simply belonged to the *moadim* in the more general sense
of the word. In this concluding formula, therefore, there is no
indication that vers. 2 and 3 and vers. 39–43 are later additions
to the original list of feasts which were to be kept with a meeting for worship. וגו' לְהַקְרִיב (to offer, etc.) is not dependent upon
" holy convocations," but upon the main idea, " feasts of Jehovah." Jehovah had appointed *moadim*, fixed periods in the year,
for His congregation to offer sacrifices ; not as if no sacrifices
could be or were to be offered except at these feasts, but to remind His people, through these fixed days, of their duty to
approach the Lord with sacrifices. אִשֶּׁה is defined by the enumeration of four principal kinds of sacrifice,—burnt-offerings,
meat-offerings, slain (*i.e.* peace-) offerings, and drink-offerings.
דְּבַר יוֹם בּ' : " *every day those appointed for it*," as in Ex. v. 13.—
Ver. 38. "*Beside the Sabbaths :*" *i.e.* the Sabbath sacrifices (see
Num. xxviii. 9, 10), and the gifts and offerings, which formed
no integral part of the keeping of the feasts and Sabbaths, but
might be offered on those days. מַתָּנוֹת, gifts, include all the
dedicatory offerings, which were presented to the Lord without
being intended to be burned upon the altar ; such, for example,
as the dedicatory gifts of the tribe-princes (Num. vii.), the firstlings and tithes, and other so-called heave-offerings (Num. xviii.
11, 29). By the " *vows* " and נְדָבוֹת, " *freewill-offerings*," we are
to understand not only the votive and freewill slain or peace-
offerings, but burnt-offerings also, and meat-offerings, which
were offered in consequence of a vow, or from spontaneous
impulse (see Judg. xi. 31, where *Jephthah* vows a burnt-offering).—In vers. 39 sqq. there follows a fuller description of the
observance of the last feast of the year, for which the title,
" feast of Tabernacles" (ver. 34), had prepared the way, as the
feast had already been mentioned briefly in Ex. xxiii. 16 and
xxxiv. 22 as " feast of Ingathering," though hitherto no rule

had been laid down concerning the peculiar manner in which it was to be observed. In connection with this epithet in Exodus, it is described again in ver. 39, as in vers. 35, 36, as a seven days' feast, with sabbatical rest on the first and eighth day ; and in vers. 40 sqq. the following rule is given for its observance : " Take to you fruit of ornamental trees, palm-branches, and boughs of trees with thick foliage, and willows of the brook, and rejoice before the Lord your God seven days, every native in Israel." If we observe that there are only three kinds of boughs that are connected together by the copula (*vav*) in ver. 40, and that it is wanting before חֵמ׳ כַּפֹּת, there can hardly be any doubt that פְּרִי עֵץ הָדָר is the generic term, and that the three names which follow specify the particular kinds of boughs. By " the fruit," therefore, we understand the shoots and branches of the trees, as well as the blossom and fruit that grew out of them. עֵץ הָדָר, " *trees of ornament :*" we are not to understand by these only such trees as the orange and citron, which were placed in gardens for ornament rather than use, as the *Chald.* and *Syr.* indicate, although these trees grow in the gardens of Palestine (*Rob.*, Pal. i. 327, iii. 420). The expression is a more general one, and includes myrtles, which were great favourites with the ancients, on account of their beauty and the fragrant odour which they diffused, olive-trees, palms, and other trees, which were used as booths in Ezra's time (Neh. viii. 15). In the words, " Take fruit of ornamental trees," it is not expressly stated, it is true, that this fruit was to be used, like the palm-branches, for constructing booths ; but this is certainly implied in the context : " *Take . . . and rejoice . . . and keep a feast . . . in the booths shall ye dwell.*" בַּסֻּכֹּת with the article is equivalent to " in the booths which ye have constructed from the branches mentioned" (cf. *Ges.* § 109, 3). It was in this sense that the law was understood and carried out in the time of Ezra (Neh. viii. 15 sqq.).[1]

[1] Even in the time of the Maccabees, on the other hand (cf. 2 Macc. x. 6, 7), the feast of the Purification of the Temple was celebrated by the Jews after the manner of the Tabernacles (κατὰ σκηνωμάτων τρόπον) ; so that they offered songs of praise, holding (ἔχοντες, carrying ?) leafy poles (θύρσους, not branches of ivy, cf. *Grimm. ad l.c.*) and beautiful branches, also palms ; and in the time of Christ it was the custom to have sticks or poles (staves) of palm-trees and citron-trees (θύρσους ἐκ φοινίκων καὶ κιτρέων : *Josephus, Ant.* xiii. 13, 5), or to carry in the hand a branch of myrtle and willow bound round with wool, with palms at the top and an apple of the περσέα

The leading character of the feast of Tabernacles, which is indicated at the outset by the emphatic אַךְ (ver. 39, see at ver. 27), was to consist in "joy before the Lord." As a "feast," *i.e.* a feast of joy (חַג, from חָגַג = חוּג, denoting the circular motion of the dance, 1 Sam. xxx. 16), it was to be kept for seven days; so that Israel "should be only rejoicing," and give itself up entirely to joy (Deut. xvi. 15). Now, although the motive assigned in Deut. is this : "for God will bless thee (Israel) in all thine increase, and in all the work of thine hands ;" and although the feast, as a "feast of ingathering," was a feast of thanksgiving for the gathering in of the produce of the land, "the produce of the floor and wine-press ;" and the blessing they had received in the harvested fruits, the oil and wine, which contributed even more to the enjoyment of life than the bread that was needed for daily food, furnished in a very high degree the occasion and stimulus to the utterance of grateful joy : the origin and true signification of the feast of Tabernacles are not to be sought for in this natural allusion to the blessing of the harvest, but the dwelling in booths was the principal point in the feast ; and this was instituted as a law for all future time (ver. 41), that succeeding generations might know that Jehovah had caused the children of Israel to dwell in booths when He led them out of Egypt (ver. 43). סֻכָּה, a booth or hut, is not to be confounded with אֹהֶל a tent, but comes from סָכַךְ *texuit*, and signifies *casa, umbraculum ex frondibus ramisque consertum* (*Ges. thes. s. v.*), serving as a defence both against the heat of the sun, and also against wind and rain (Ps. xxxi. 21 ; Isa. iv. 6 ; Jonah iv. 5). Their dwelling in booths was by no means intended, as *Bähr* supposes, to bring before the minds of the people the unsettled wandering life of the desert, and remind

(peach or pomegranate ?) upon it (εἰρεσιώνην μυρσίνης καὶ ἰτέας σὺν κράδῃ Φοίνικος πεποιημένην, τοῦ μήλου τοῦ τῆς Περσέας προσόντος). This custom, which was still further developed in the Talmud, where a bunch made of palm, myrtle, and willow boughs is ordered to be carried in the right hand, and a citron or orange in the left, has no foundation in the law : it sprang rather out of an imitation of the Greek harvest-feast of the *Pyanepsia* and Bacchus festivals, from which the words θύρσοι and εἰρεσιώνη were borrowed by *Josephus*, and had been tacked on by the scribes to the text of the Bible (ver. 40) in the best way they could. See *Bähr, Symbol.* ii. p. 625, and the innumerable trivial laws in *Mishna Succa* and *Succa Codex talm. babyl. sive de tabernaculorum festo ed. Dachs. Utr.* 1726, 4.

them of the trouble endured there, for the recollection of privation and want can never be an occasion of joy; but it was to
place vividly before the eyes of the future generations of Israel
a memorial of the grace, care, and protection which God
afforded to His people in the great and terrible wilderness
(Deut. viii. 15). Whether the Israelites, in their journey
through the wilderness, not only used the tents which they had
taken with them (cf. chap. xiv. 8; Ex. xvi. 16, xviii. 7, xxxiii.
8 sqq.; Num. xvi. 26 sqq., xxiv. 5, etc.), but erected booths of
branches and bushes in those places of encampment where they
remained for a considerable time, as the Bedouins still do sometimes in the peninsula of Sinai (*Burckhardt, Syrien*, p. 858), or
not; at all events, the shielding and protecting presence of the
Lord in the pillar of cloud and fire was, in the words of the
prophet, " a booth (tabernacle) for a shadow in the day-time
from the heat, and for a place of refuge, and for a covert from
storm and from rain" (Isa. iv. 6) in the barren wilderness, to
those who had just been redeemed out of Egypt. Moreover,
the booths used at this feast were not made of miserable shrubs
of the desert, but of branches of fruit-trees, palms and thickly
covered trees, the produce of the good and glorious land into
which God had brought them (Deut. viii. 7 sqq.); and in this
respect they presented a living picture of the plenteous fulness
of blessing with which the Lord had enriched His people.
This fulness of blessing was to be called to mind by their
dwelling in booths; in order that, in the land " wherein they
ate bread without scarceness and lacked nothing, where they
built goodly houses and dwelt therein; where their herds and
flocks, their silver and their gold, and all that they had, multiplied" (Deut. viii. 9, 12, 13), they might not say in their
hearts, " My power, and the might of mine hand, hath gotten
me this wealth," but might remember that Jehovah was their
God, who gave them power to get wealth (vers. 17, 18), that so
their heart might not " be lifted up and forget Jehovah their
God, who had led them out of the land of Egypt, the house of
bondage." If, therefore, the foliage of the booths pointed to
the glorious possessions of the inheritance, which the Lord had
prepared for His redeemed people in Canaan, yet the natural
allusion of the feast, which was superadded to the historical, and
subordinate to it,—viz. to the plentiful harvest of rich and beau-

tiful fruits, which they had gathered in from this inheritance, and could now enjoy in peace after the toil of cultivating the land was over,—would necessarily raise their hearts to still higher joy through their gratitude to the Lord and Giver of all, and make this feast a striking figure of the blessedness of the people of God when resting from their labours.—Ver. 44. Communication of these laws to the people.

PREPARATION OF THE HOLY LAMPS AND SHEW-BREAD. PUNISHMENT OF A BLASPHEMER.—CHAP. XXIV.

Vers. 1–9. The directions concerning the *oil for the holy candlestick* (vers. 1–4) and the preparation of the *shew-bread* (vers. 5–9) lose the appearance of an interpolation, when we consider and rightly understand on the one hand the manner in which the two are introduced in ver. 2, and on the other their significance in relation to the worship of God. The introductory formula, "Command the children of Israel that they fetch (bring)," shows that the command relates to an offering on the part of the congregation, a sacrificial gift, with which Israel was to serve the Lord continually. This service consisted in the fact, that in the oil of the lamps of the seven-branched candlestick, which burned before Jehovah, the nation of Israel manifested itself as a congregation which caused its light to shine in the darkness of this world; and that in the shew-bread it offered the fruits of its labour in the field of the kingdom of God, as a spiritual sacrifice to Jehovah. The offering of oil, therefore, for the preparation of the candlestick, and that of fine flour for making the loaves to be placed before Jehovah, formed part of the service in which Israel sanctified its life and labour to the Lord its God, not only at the appointed festal periods, but every day; and the law is very appropriately appended to the sanctification of the Sabbaths and feast-days, prescribed in chap. xxiii. The first instructions in vers. 2–4 are a verbal repetition of Ex. xxvii. 20, 21, and have been explained already. Their execution by Aaron is recorded at Num. viii. 1–4; and the candlestick itself was set in order by Moses at the consecration of the tabernacle (Ex. xl. 25).—Vers. 5–9. The preparation of the shew-bread and the use to be made of it are described here for the first time; though it had already been offered by the congregation

at the consecration of the tabernacle, and placed by Moses
upon the table (Ex. xxxix. 36, xl. 23). Twelve cakes (*challoth*,
ii. 4) were to be made of fine flour, of two-tenths of an ephah
each, and placed in two rows, six in each row, upon the golden
table before Jehovah (Ex. xxv. 23 sqq.). Pure incense was
then to be added to each row, which was to be (to serve) as a
memorial (*azcarah*, see chap. ii. 2), as a firing for Jehovah.
נָתַן עַל to give upon, to add to, does not force us to the conclusion
that the incense was to be spread upon the cakes; but is easily
reconcilable with the Jewish tradition (*Josephus*, Ant. iii. 10, 7;
Mishnah, Menach. xi. 7, 8), that the incense was placed in golden
saucers with each row of bread. The number twelve corresponded to the number of the twelve tribes of Israel. The
arrangement of the loaves in rows of six each was in accordance
with the shape of the table, just like the division of the names
of the twelve tribes upon the two precious stones on Aaron's
shoulder-dress (Ex. xxviii. 10). By the presentation or preparation of them from the fine flour presented by the congregation,
and still more by the addition of incense, which was burned
upon the altar every Sabbath on the removal of the loaves as
azcarah, *i.e.* as a practical memento of the congregation before
God, the laying out of these loaves assumed the form of a bloodless sacrifice, in which the congregation brought the fruit of its
life and labour before the face of the Lord, and presented itself
to its God as a nation diligent in sanctification to good works.
If the shew-bread was a *minchah*, or meat-offering, and even a
most holy one, which only the priests were allowed to eat in the
holy place (ver. 9, cf. chap. ii. 3 and vi. 9, 10), it must naturally
have been unleavened, as the unanimous testimony of the
Jewish tradition affirms it to have been. And if as a rule no
meat-offering could be leavened, and of the loaves of first-fruits
prepared for the feast of Pentecost, which were actually leavened,
none was allowed to be placed upon the altar (chap. ii. 11, 12,
vi. 10); still less could leavened bread be brought into the
sanctuary before Jehovah. The only ground, therefore, on
which *Knobel* can maintain that those loaves were leavened, is
on the supposition that they were intended to represent the daily
bread, which could no more fail in the house of Jehovah than
in any other well-appointed house (see *Bähr, Symbolik* i. p.
410). The process of laying these loaves before Jehovah con-

tinually was to be "an everlasting covenant" (ver. 8), *i.e.* a
pledge or sign of the everlasting covenant, just as circumcision,
as the covenant in the flesh, was to be an everlasting covenant
(Gen. xvii. 13).

Vers. 10–23. The account of the PUNISHMENT OF A BLAS-
PHEMER is introduced in the midst of the laws, less because " it
brings out to view by a clear example the administration of the
divine law in Israel, and also introduces and furnishes the reason
for several important laws" (*Baumgarten*), than because the
historical occurrence itself took place at the time when the laws
relating to sanctification of life before the Lord were given,
whilst the punishment denounced against the blasphemer exhibited in a practical form, as a warning to the whole nation, the
sanctification of the Lord in the despisers of His name. The
circumstances were the following :—The son of an Israelitish
woman named Shelomith, the daughter of Dibri, of the tribe
of Dan, and of an Egyptian whom the Israelitish woman had
married, went out into the midst of the children of Israel, *i.e.*
went out of his tent or place of encampment among the Israelites. As the son of an Egyptian, he belonged to the foreigners
who had gone out with Israel (Ex. xii. 38), and who probably
had their tents somewhere apart from those of the Israelites,
who were encamped according to their tribes (Num. ii. 2).
Having got into a quarrel with an Israelite, this man scoffed at
the name (of Jehovah) and cursed. The cause of the quarrel
is not given, and cannot be determined. נָקַב : to bore, hollow
out, then to sting, metaphorically to separate, fix (Gen. xxx.
28), hence to designate (Num. i. 17, etc.), and to prick *in malam
partem*, to taunt, *i.e.* to *blaspheme, curse,* = קָבַב Num. xxiii. 11,
25, etc. That the word is used here in a bad sense, is evident
from the expression " and cursed," and from the whole context
of vers. 15 and 16. The Jews, on the other hand, have taken
the word נָקַב in this passage from time immemorial in the sense
of ἐπονομάζειν (LXX.), and founded upon it the well-known
law, against even uttering the name *Jehovah* (see particularly
ver. 16). " *The name*" κατ᾽ ἐξ. is the name " Jehovah " (cf. ver.
16), in which God manifested His nature. It was this passage
that gave rise to the custom, so prevalent among the Rabbins, of
using the expression " name," or " the name," for *Dominus*, or

Deus (see *Buxtorf, lex. talmud.* pp. 2432 sqq.). The blasphemer
was brought before Moses and then put into confinement, "*to
determine for them* (such blasphemers) *according to the mouth*
(command) *of Jehovah.*" פָּרַשׁ : to separate, distinguish, then to
determine exactly, which is the sense both here and in Num.
xv. 34, where it occurs in a similar connection.—Vers. 13–16.
Jehovah ordered the blasphemer to be taken out of the camp,
and the witnesses to lay their hands upon his head, and the
whole congregation to stone him ; and published at the same
time the general law, that whoever cursed his God should bear
(*i.e.* atone for) his sin (cf. Ex. xxii. 27), and whoever blasphemed
the name of Jehovah should be stoned, the native as well as the
foreigner. By laying (resting, cf. i. 4) their hands upon the
head of the blasphemer, the hearers or witnesses were to throw
off from themselves the blasphemy which they had heard, and
return it upon the head of the blasphemer, for him to expiate.
The washing of hands in Deut. xxi. 6 is analogous ; but the
reference made by *Knobel* to Deut. xvii. 7, where the witnesses
are commanded to turn their hand against an idolater who had
been condemned to death, *i.e.* to stone him, is out of place.—
Vers. 17–22. The decision asked for from God concerning the
crime of the blasphemer, who was the son of an Egyptian, and
therefore not a member of the congregation of Jehovah, furnished the occasion for God to repeat those laws respecting
murder or personal injury inflicted upon a man, which had
hitherto been given for the Israelites alone (Ex. xxi. 12 sqq.),
and to proclaim their validity in the case of the foreigner also
(vers. 17, 21, 22). To these there are appended the kindred
commandments concerning the killing of cattle (vers. 18, 21,
22), which had not been given, it is true, *expressis verbis*, but
were contained *implicite* in the rights of Israel (Ex. xxi. 33 sqq.),
and are also extended to foreigners. הִכָּה נֶפֶשׁ אָדָם, to smite the
soul of a man, *i.e.* to put him to death ;—the expression "soul
of a beast," in ver. 18, is to be understood in the same sense.—
Ver. 19. "*Cause a blemish,*" *i.e.* inflict a bodily injury. This is
still further defined in the cases mentioned (*breach, eye, tooth*),
in which punishment was to be inflicted according to the *jus
talionis* (see at Ex. xxi. 23 sqq.).—Ver. 23. After these laws
had been issued, the punishment was inflicted upon the blasphemer.

SANCTIFICATION OF THE POSSESSION OF LAND BY THE
SABBATICAL AND JUBILEE YEARS.—CHAP. XXV.

The law for the sabbatical and jubilee years brings to a close the laws given to Moses by Jehovah upon Mount Sinai. This is shown by the words of the heading (ver. 1), which point back to Ex. xxxiv. 32, and bind together into an inward unity the whole round of laws that Moses received from God upon the mountain, and then gradually announced to the people. The same words are repeated, not only in Lev. vii. 38 at the close of the laws of sacrifice, but also at chap. xxvi. 46, at the close of the promises and threats which follow the law for the sabbatical and jubilee years, and lastly, at chap. xxvii. 34, after the supplementary law concerning vows. The institution of the jubilee years corresponds to the institution of the day of atonement (chap. xvi.). Just as all the sins and uncleannesses of the whole congregation, which had remained unatoned for and uncleansed in the course of the year, were to be wiped away by the all-embracing expiation of the yearly recurring day of atonement, and an undisturbed relation to be restored between Jehovah and His people; so, by the appointment of the year of jubilee, the disturbance and confusion of the divinely appointed relations, which had been introduced in the course of time through the inconstancy of all human or earthly things, were to be removed by the appointment of the year of jubilee, and the kingdom of Israel to be brought back to its original condition. The next chapter (chap. xxvi.) bears the same relation to the giving of the law upon Sinai as Ex. xxiii. 20–33 to the covenant rights in Ex. xx. 22–xxiii. 19.

Vers. 2–7. The SABBATICAL YEAR.—When Israel had come into the land which the Lord gave to it, it was to sanctify it to the Lord by the observance of a Sabbath. As the nation at large, with its labourers and beasts of burden, was to keep a Sabbath or day of rest every seventh day of the week, so the land which they tilled was to rest (to keep, שָׁבַת שַׁבָּת as in chap. xxiii. 32) a Sabbath to the Lord. Six years they were to sow the field and cut the vineyard, i.e. cultivate the corn-fields, vineyards, and olive-yards (Ex. xxiii. 11 : see the remarks on *cerem* at chap. xix. 10), and gather in their produce; but in the seventh year the land was to keep a Sabbath of rest (*Sabbath sabbathon,* Ex. xxxi. 15), a Sabbath consecrated to the Lord (see Ex. xx. 10); and in this year the land was neither to be tilled nor reaped (cf. Ex. xxiii. 10, 11). זָמַר in *Kal* applies only to the cutting of grapes, and so also in *Niphal*, Isa. v. 6; hence *zemorah*, a vine-branch (Num. xiii. 23), and *mazmerah*, a pruning-knife (Isa. ii. 4, etc.).[1] The omission of sowing and reaping presupposed that the sabbatical year commenced with the civil year, in the autumn of the sixth year of labour, and not with the ecclesiastical year, on the first of Abib (Nisan), and that it lasted till the autumn of the seventh year, when the cultivation of the land would commence again with the preparation of the ground and the sowing of the seed for the eighth year; and with this the command to proclaim the jubilee year on "the tenth day of the seventh month" throughout all the land (ver. 9), and the calculation in vers. 21, 22, fully agree.—Ver. 5. "*That which has fallen out* (been shaken out) *of thy harvest* (*i.e.* the corn which had grown from the grains of the previous harvest that had fallen out) *thou shalt not reap, and the grapes of thine uncut thou shalt not gather.*" נָזִיר, the Nazarite, who let his hair grow freely without cutting it (Num. vi. 5), is used figuratively, both here and in ver. 11, to denote a vine not pruned, since by being left to put forth all its productive power it was consecrated to the Lord. The Roman poets employ a similar figure, and speak of the *viridis coma* of the vine (*Tibull.* i. 7, 34; *Propert.* ii. 15, 12).—Vers. 6, 7. "*And the Sabbath of the land* (*i.e.* the produce of the sabbatical year or year of rest, whatever grew that year without cultivation) *shall be to you for food, for thee and thy servant, . . . and for the beasts that are in thy land shall all its produce be for food.*" The meaning is, that what grew of itself was not to be reaped by the owner of the land, but that masters and servants, labourers and visitors, cattle and game, were to eat thereof away from the field (cf. ver. 12). The produce arising without tilling or sowing was to be a common good for man and beast. According to Ex. xxiii. 11, it was to belong to the poor and needy; but the owner was not forbidden to par-

---

[1] The meaning to sing and play, which is peculiar to the *Piel*, and is derived from *zamar*, to hum, has hardly anything to do with this. At all events the connection has not yet been shown to be a probable one. See *Hupfeld*, Ps. iv. pp. 421-2, note.

take of it also, so that there can be no discrepancy discovered between this passage and the verse before us. The produce referred to would be by no means inconsiderable, particularly if there had not been a careful gleaning after the harvest, or the corn had become over-ripe. In the fertile portions of Palestine, especially in the plain of Jezreel and on the table-land of Galilee, as well as in other parts, large quantities of wheat and other cereals are still self-sown from the ripe ears, the over-flowing of which is not gathered by any of the inhabitants of the land. *Strabo* gives a similar account of Albania, viz. that in many parts a field once sown will bear fruit twice and even three times, the first yield being as much as fifty-fold. The intention of this law was not so much to secure the physical re-creation of both the land and people, however useful and neces-sary this might be for men, animals, and land in this sublunary world; but the land was to keep Sabbath to the Lord in the seventh year. In the sabbatical year the land, which the Lord had given to His people, was to observe a period of holy rest and refreshment to its Lord and God, just as the congregation did on the Sabbath-day; and the hand of man was to be withheld from the fields and fruit-gardens from working them, that they might yield their produce for his use. The earth was to be saved from the hand of man exhausting its power for earthly purposes as his own property, and to enjoy the holy rest with which God had blessed the earth and all its productions after the creation. From this, Israel, as the nation of God, was to learn, on the one hand, that although the earth was created for man, it was not merely created for him to draw out its powers for his own use, but also to be holy to the Lord, and participate in His blessed rest; and on the other hand, that the great pur-pose for which the congregation of the Lord existed, did not consist in the uninterrupted tilling of the earth, connected with bitter labour in the sweat of his brow (Gen. iii. 17, 19), but in the peaceful enjoyment of the fruits of the earth, which the Lord their God had given them, and would give them still with-out the labour of their hands, if they strove to keep His covenant and satisfy themselves with His grace. This intention of the sabbatical year comes out still more plainly in the year of jubilee, in which the idea of the sanctification of the whole land as the Lord's property is still more strongly expressed, and whose inward connection with the sabbatical year is indicated by the fact that the time for observing it was regulated by the sabbatical years (ver. 8).

Vers. 8–55. The law for the YEAR OF JUBILEE refers first of all to its observance (vers. 8–12), and secondly to its effects (*a*) upon the possession of property (vers. 13–34), and (*b*) upon the personal freedom of the Israelites (vers. 35–55).—Vers. 8–12. *Keeping the year of jubilee.* Vers. 8, 9. Seven Sabbaths of years—*i.e.* year-Sabbaths or sabbatical years, or seven times seven years, the time of seven year-Sabbaths, that is to say, 49 years— they were to count, and then at the expiration of that time to cause the trumpet of jubilee to go (sound) through the whole land on the tenth of the seventh month, *i.e.* the day of atonement, to proclaim the entrance of the year of jubilee. This mode of announcement was closely connected with the idea of the year itself. The blowing of trumpets, or blast of the far-sounding horn (*shophar*, see at chap. xxiii. 24), was the signal of the descent of the Lord upon Sinai, to raise Israel to be His people, to receive them into His covenant, to unite them to Himself, and bless them through His covenant of grace (Ex. xix. 13, 16, 19, xx. 18). Just as the people were to come up to the mountain at the sounding of the יֹבֵל, or the voice of the *shophar*, to commemorate its union with the Lord, so at the expiration of the seventh sabbatical year the trumpet-blast was to announce to the covenant nation the gracious presence of its God, and the coming of the year which was to bring " liberty throughout the land to all that dwelt therein" (ver. 10),—deliverance from bondage (vers. 40 sqq.), return to their property and family (vers. 10, 13), and release from the bitter labour of cultivating the land (vers. 11, 12). This year of grace was proclaimed and began with the day of atonement of every seventh sabbatical year, to show that it was only with the full forgiveness of sins that the blessed liberty of the children of God could possibly commence. This grand year of grace was to return after seven times seven years; *i.e.*, as is expressly stated in ver. 10, every fiftieth year was to be sanctified as a year of jubilee. By this regulation of the time, the view held by *R. Jehuda*, and the chronologists and antiquarians who have followed him, that every seventh sabbatical year, *i.e.* the 49th

year, was to be kept as the year of jubilee, is proved to be at
variance with the text, and the fiftieth year is shown to be the
year of rest, in which the sabbatical idea attained its fullest
realization, and reached its earthly temporal close.—Ver. 10.
The words, "Ye shall proclaim liberty throughout all the land
unto all the inhabitants thereof," are more closely defined by the
two clauses commencing with יוֹבֵל הִיא in vers. 10 and 11. "A
trumpet-blast shall it be to you, that ye return every one to his
own possession, and every one to his family:".a still further
explanation is given in vers. 23–34 and 39–55. This was to be
the fruit or effect of the blast, *i.e.* of the year commencing with
the blast, and hence the year was called "the year of liberty,"
or free year, in Ezek. xlvi. 17. יוֹבֵל, from יָבַל to flow with a
rushing noise, does not mean jubilation or the time of jubilation
(*Ges., Kn.,* and others); but wherever it is not applied to the
year of jubilee, it signifies only the loud blast of a trumpet (Ex.
xix. 13; Josh. vi. 5). This meaning also applies here in vers.
10*b*, 11 and 12; whilst in vers. 15, 28, 30, 31, 33, xxvii. 18, and
Num. xxxvi. 4, it is used as an abbreviated expression for שְׁנַת
יוֹבֵל, the year of the trumpet-blast.—Vers. 11, 12. The other
effect of the fiftieth year proclaimed with the trumpet-blast
consisted in the fact that the Israelites were not to sow or reap,
just as in the sabbatical year (see vers. 4, 5). "For it is יוֹבֵל,"
i.e. not "jubilation or time of jubilation," but "the time or year
of the trumpet-blast, it shall be holy to you," *i.e.* a sabbatical
time, which is to be holy to you like the day of the trumpet-
blast (vers. 23, 24).

Vers. 13–34. One of the effects of the year of freedom is
mentioned here, viz. the *return of every man to his own possession;* and the way is prepared for it by a warning against overreaching in the sale of land, and the assignment of a reason for
this.—Vers. 14–17. In the purchase and sale of pieces of land
no one was to oppress another, *i.e.* to overreach him by false
statements as to its value and produce. הוֹנָה applies specially
to the oppression of foreigners (chap. xix. 33; Ex. xxii. 20), of
slaves (Deut. xxiii. 17), of the poor, widows, and orphans (Jer.
xxii. 3; Ezek. xviii. 8) in civil matters, by overreaching them
or taking their property away. The *inf. abs.* קָנֹה: as in Gen.
xli. 43. The singular suffix in עֲמִיתֶךָ is to be understood dis-
tributively of a particular Israelite.—Vers. 15, 16. The pur-

chase and sale were to be regulated by the number of years
that had elapsed since the year of jubilee, so that they were
only to sell the produce of the yearly revenues up to the next
jubilee year, and make the price higher or lower according to
the larger or smaller number of the years.—Vers. 17 sqq. Overreaching and oppression God would avenge ; they were therefore to fear before Him.   On the other hand, if they kept His
commandments and judgments, He would take care that they
should dwell in the land in safety (*secure*, free from anxiety),
and be satisfied with the abundance of its produce.   In this
way vers. 18–22 fit on exceedingly well to what precedes.[1]—
Vers. 20 sqq. Jehovah would preserve them from want, without
their sowing or reaping.   He would bestow His blessing upon
them in the sixth year, so that it should bear the produce of
three (עָשָׂת for עָשְׂתָה as in Gen. xxxiii. 11); and when they sowed
in the eighth year, they should eat the produce of the old year
up to the ninth year, that is to say, till the harvest of that year.
It is quite evident from vers. 21 and 22, according to which the
sixth year was to produce enough for three years, and the sowing for the ninth was to take place in the eighth, that not only
the year of jubilee, but the sabbatical year also, commenced in
the autumn, when they first began to sow for the coming year ;
so that the sowing was suspended from the autumn of the sixth
year till the autumn of the seventh, and even till the autumn of
the eighth, whenever the jubilee year came round, in which case
both sowing and reaping were omitted for two years in succession, and consequently the produce of the sixth year, which was
harvested in the seventh month of that year, must have sufficed
for three years, not merely till the sowing in the autumn of the

---

[1] To prove that this verse is an interpolation made by the Jehovist into
the Elohistic writings, *Knobel* is obliged to resort to two groundless assumptions : viz. (1) to regard vers. 23 and 24, which belong to what follows
(vers. 25 sqq.) and lay down the general rule respecting the possession and
redemption of land, as belonging to what precedes and connected with vers.
14–17 ; and (2) to explain vers. 18-22 in the most arbitrary manner, as a
supplementary clause relating to the *sabbatical year*, whereas the promise
that the sixth year should yield produce enough for three years (vers.
21, 22) shows as clearly as possible that they treat of the *year of jubilee*
together with the seventh sabbatical year which preceded it, and in ver.
20 the seventh year is mentioned simply as the beginning of the two years'
Sabbath which the land was to keep without either sowing or reaping.

eighth or fiftieth year, but,till the harvest of the ninth or fifty-first year, as the Talmud and Rabbins of every age have understood the law.

Vers. 23–28. What was already implied in the laws relating to the purchase and sale of the year's produce (vers. 15, 16), namely, that the land could not be alienated, is here clearly expressed ; and at the same time the rule is laid down, showing how a man, who had been compelled by poverty to sell his patrimony, was to recover possession of it by redemption. In the first place, ver. 23 contains the general rule, "the land shall not be sold לִצְמִיתֻת" (*lit.* to annihilation), *i.e.* so as to vanish away from, or be for ever lost to, the seller. For "*the land belongs to Jehovah :*" the Israelites, to whom He would give it (ver. 2), were not actual owners or full possessors, so that they could do what they pleased with it, but "strangers and sojourners with Jehovah" in His land. Consequently (ver. 24) throughout the whole of the land of their possession they were to grant גְּאֻלָּה release, redemption to the land. There were three ways in which this could be done. The first case (ver. 25) was this: if a brother became poor and sold his property, his nearest redeemer was to come and release what his brother had sold, *i.e.* buy it back from the purchaser and restore it to its former possessor. The nearest redeemer was the relative upon whom this obligation rested according to the series mentioned in vers. 48, 49.—The second case (vers. 26, 27) was this : if any one had no redeemer, either because there were no relatives upon whom the obligation rested, or because they were all too poor, and he had earned and acquired sufficient to redeem it, he was to calculate the years of purchase, and return the surplus to the man who had bought it, *i.e.* as much as he had paid for the years that still remained up to the next year of jubilee, that so he might come into possession of it again. As the purchaser had only paid the amount of the annual harvests till the next year of jubilee, all that he could demand back was as much as he had paid for the years that still remained.—Ver. 28. The third case was this : if a man had not earned as much as was required to make compensation for the recovery of the land, what he had sold was to remain in the possession of the buyer till the year of jubilee, and then it was to "go out," *i.e.* to become free again, so that the impoverished seller could enter into possession without compensation. The buyer lost nothing by this, for he had fully recovered all that he paid for the annual harvests up to the year of jubilee, from the amount which those harvests yielded. Through these legal regulations every purchase of land became simply a lease for a term of years.

Vers. 29-34. *Alienation and redemption of houses.*—Vers. 29, 30. On the sale of a dwelling-house in a wall-town (a town surrounded by a wall) there was to be redemption till the completion of the year of its purchase. יָמִים, " *days* (*i.e.* a definite period) *shall its redemption be;*" that is to say, the right of redemption or repurchase should be retained. If it was not redeemed within the year, it remained to the buyer for ever for his descendants, and did not go out free in the year of jubilee. קָם to arise for a possession, *i.e.* to become a fixed standing possession, as in Gen. xxiii. 17. אֲשֶׁר לֹא for אֲשֶׁר לֹו as in chap. xi. 21 (see at Ex. xxi. 8). This law is founded upon the assumption, that the houses in unwalled towns are not so closely connected with the ownership of the land, as that the alienation of the houses would alter the portion originally assigned to each family for a possession. Having been built by men, they belonged to their owners in full possession, whether they had received them just as they were at the conquest of the land, or had erected them for themselves. This last point of view, however, was altogether a subordinate one; for in the case of "the houses of the villages" (*i.e.* farm-buildings and villages, see Josh. xiii. 23, etc.), which had no walls round them, it was not taken into consideration at all.—Ver. 31. Such houses as these were to be reckoned as part of the land, and to be treated as landed property, with regard to redemption and restoration at the year of jubilee.—Ver. 32. On the other hand, so far as the Levitical towns, viz. the houses of the Levites in the towns belonging to them, were concerned, there was to be eternal redemption for the Levites; that is to say, when they were parted with, the right of repurchase was never lost. עוֹלָם (eternal) is to be understood as a contrast to the year allowed in the case of other houses (vers. 29, 30).—Ver. 33. "And whoever (if any one) redeems, *i.e.* buys, of the Levites, the house that is sold and (indeed in) the town of his possession is to go out free in the year of jubilee; for the houses of the Levitical towns are their (the Levites') possession among the children of Israel."

The meaning is this : If any one bought a Levite's house in one of the Levitical towns, the house he had bought was to revert to the Levite without compensation in the year of jubilee. The difficulty connected with the first clause is removed, if we understand the word יִגְאַל (to redeem, *i.e.* to buy back), as the Rabbins do, in the sense of קָנָה *to buy*, acquire. The use of גָּאַל for קָנָה may be explained from the fact, that when the land was divided, the Levites did not receive either an inheritance in the land, or even the towns appointed for them to dwell in as their own property. The Levitical towns were allotted to the different tribes in which they were situated, with the simple obligation to set apart a certain number of dwelling-houses for the Levites, together with pasture-ground for their cattle in the precincts of the towns (cf. Num. xxxv. 1 sqq. and my Commentary on Joshua, p. 453 translation). If a non-Levite, therefore, bought a Levite's house, it was in reality a repurchase of property belonging to his tribe, or the redemption of what the tribe had relinquished to the Levites as their dwelling and for their necessities.[1] The words וְעִיר אַחֻ are an explanatory apposition— "and that in the town of his possession,"—and do not mean "whatever he had sold of his house-property or anything else in his town," for the Levites had no other property in the town besides the houses, but "the house which he had sold, namely, in the town of his possession." This implies that the right of reversion was only to apply to the houses ceded to the Levites in their own towns, and not to houses which they had acquired in other towns either by purchase or inheritance. The singular הִיא is used after a subject in the plural, because the copula agrees with the object (see *Ewald*, § 319c). As the Levites were to have no hereditary property in the land except the

---

[1] This is the way in which it is correctly explained by *Hiskuni: Utitur scriptura verbo redimendi non emendi, quia quidquid Levitæ vendunt ex Israelitarum hæreditate est, non ex ipsorum hæreditate. Nam ecce non habent partes in terra, unde omnis qui accipit aut emit ab illis est acsi redimeret, quoniam ecce initio ipsius possessio fuit.* On the other hand, the proposal made by *Ewald, Knobel*, etc., after the example of the *Vulgate*, to supply לֹא before יִגְאַל is not only an unnecessary conjecture, but is utterly unsuitable, inasmuch as the words "if one of the Levites does not redeem it" would restrict the right to the Levites without any perceptible reason ; just as if a blood-relation on the female side, belonging to any other tribe, might not have done this.

houses in the towns appointed for them, it was necessary that
the possession of their houses should be secured to them for all
time, if they were not to fall behind the other tribes.—Ver. 34.
The field of the pasture-ground of the Levitical towns was not
to be sold.   Beside the houses, the Levites were also to receive
מִגְרָשׁ pasturage for their flocks (from גָּרַשׁ to drive, to drive out
the cattle) round about these cities (Num. xxxv. 2, 3).   These
meadows were not to be saleable, and not even to be let till the
year of jubilee; because, if they were sold, the Levites would
have nothing left upon which to feed their cattle.

Vers. 35–55. The *second* effect of the jubilee year, viz. *the
return of an Israelite, who had become a slave, to liberty and to
his family*, is also introduced with an exhortation to support an
impoverished brother (vers. 35–38), and preserve to him his
personal freedom.—Ver. 35. " If thy brother (countryman, or
member of the same tribe) becomes poor, and his hand trembles
by thee, thou shalt lay hold of him ;" *i.e.* if he is no longer able
to sustain himself alone, thou shalt take him by the arm to help
him out of his misfortune.   " Let him live with thee as a stranger
and sojourner." וָחַי introduces the apodosis (see *Ges.* § 126,
note 1).—Vers. 36 sqq. If he borrowed money, they were not
to demand interest ; or if food, they were not to demand any
addition, any larger quantity, when it was returned (cf. Ex. xxii.
24 ; Deut. xxiii. 20, 21), from fear of God, who had redeemed
Israel out of bondage, to give them the land of Canaan.   In
ver. 37 וְחֵי is an abbreviation of וְחַי, which only occurs here.—
From ver. 39 onwards there follow the laws relating to the bondage of the Israelite, who had been obliged to sell himself from
poverty.   Vers. 39–46 relate to his service in bondage to an
(other) Israelite.   The man to whom he had sold himself as
servant was not to have slave-labour performed by him (Ex. i.
14), but to keep him as a day-labourer and sojourner, and let
him serve with him till the year of jubilee.   He was then to go out
free with his children, and return to his family and the possession
of his fathers (his patrimony).   This regulation is a supplement
to the laws relating to the rights of Israel (Ex. xxi. 2–6), though
without a contradiction arising, as *Knobel* maintains, between
the different rules laid down.   In Ex. xxi. nothing at all is determined respecting the treatment of an Israelitish servant; it is
simply stated that in the seventh year of his service he was to

recover his liberty. This limit is not mentioned here, because
the chapter before us simply treats of the influence of the year
of jubilee upon the bondage of the Israelites. On this point
it is decided, that the year of jubilee was to bring freedom
even to the Israelite who had been brought into slavery by his
poverty,—of course only to the man who was still in slavery when
it commenced and had not served seven full years, provided,
that is to say, that he had not renounced his claim to be set free
at the end of his seven years' service, according to Ex. xxi. 5, 6.
We have no right to expect this exception to be expressly mentioned here, because it did not interfere with the idea of the
year of jubilee. For whoever voluntarily renounced the claim
to be set free, whether because the year of jubilee was still so
far off that he did not expect to live to see it, or because he had
found a better lot with his master than he could secure for himself in a state of freedom, had thereby made a voluntary renunciation of the liberty which the year of jubilee might have
brought to him (see *Oehler's* art. in *Herzog's Cycl.*, where the
different views on this subject are given).—Vers. 42, 43. Because the Israelites were servants of Jehovah, who had redeemed
them out of Pharaoh's bondage and adopted them as His people
(Ex. xix. 5, xviii. 10, etc.), they were not to be sold " a selling
of slaves," *i.e.* not to be sold into actual slavery, and no one of
them was to rule over another with severity (ver. 43, cf. Ex.
i. 13, 14). " Through this principle slavery was completely
abolished, so far as the people of the theocracy were concerned" (*Oehler*).—Vers. 44 sqq. As the Israelites could only
hold in slavery servants and maid-servants whom they had bought
of foreign nations, or foreigners who had settled in the land,
these they might leave as an inheritance to their children, and
" through them they might work," *i.e.* have slave-labour performed, but not through their brethren the children of Israel
(ver. 46, cf. ver. 43).—Vers. 47—55. The servitude of an
Israelite to a settler who had come to the possession of property, or a non-Israelite dwelling in the land, was to be redeem-
able at any time. If an Israelite had sold himself because of
poverty to a foreign settler (גֵּר תּוֹשָׁב, to distinguish the non-
Israelitish sojourner from the Israelitish, ver. 35), or to a stock
of a foreigner, then one of his brethren, or his uncle, or his
uncle's son or some one of his kindred, was to redeem him ; or

if he came into the possession of property, he was to redeem himself. When this was done, the time was to be calculated from the year of purchase to the year of jubilee, and " the money of his purchase was to be according to the number of the years," *i.e.* the price at which he had sold himself was to be distributed over the number of years that he would have to serve to the year of jubilee; and " according to the days of a day-labourer shall he be with him," *i.e.* the time that he had worked was to be estimated as that of a day-labourer, and be put to the credit of the man to be redeemed.—Vers. 51, 52. According as there were few or many years to the year of jubilee would the redemption-money to be paid be little or much. רַבּוֹת בַּשָּׁנִים much in years : רַבּוֹת neuter, and בְּ as in Gen. vii. 21, viii. 17 etc. לְפִיהֶן according to the measure of the same.—Ver. 53. During the time of service the buyer was to keep him as a day-labourer year by year, *i.e.* as a labourer engaged for a term of years, and not rule over him with severe oppression. " *In thine eyes,*" *i.e.* so that thou (the nation addressed) seest it.—Ver. 54. If he were not redeemed by these (the relations mentioned in vers. 48, 49), he was to go out free in the year of jubilee along with his children, *i.e.* to be liberated without compensation. For (ver. 55) he was not to remain in bondage, because the Israelites were the servants of Jehovah (cf. ver. 42).

But although, through these arrangements, the year of jubilee helped every Israelite, who had fallen into poverty and slavery, to the recovery of his property and personal freedom, and thus the whole community was restored to its original condition as appointed by God, through the return of all the landed property that had been alienated in the course of years to its original proprietor; the restoration of the theocratical state to its original condition was not the highest or ultimate object of the year of jubilee. The observance of sabbatical rest throughout the whole land, and by the whole nation, formed part of the liberty which it was to bring to the land and its inhabitants. In the year of jubilee, as in the sabbatical year, the land of Jehovah was to enjoy holy rest, and the nation of Jehovah to be set free from the bitter labour of cultivating the soil, and to live and refresh itself in blessed rest with the blessing which had been given to it by the Lord its God. In this way the year of jubilee became to the poor, oppressed, and suffering, in fact to the whole nation, a year of festivity and grace, which not only brought redemption to the captives and deliverance to the poor out of their distresses, but release to the whole congregation of the Lord from the bitter labour of this world; a time of refreshing, in which all oppression was to cease, and every member of the covenant nation find his redeemer in the Lord, who brought every one back to his own property and home. Because Jehovah had brought the children of Israel out of Egypt to give them the land of Canaan, where they were to live as His servants and serve Him, in the year of jubilee the nation and land of Jehovah were to celebrate a year of holy rest and refreshing before the Lord, and in this celebration to receive a foretaste of the times of refreshing from the presence of the Lord, which were to be brought to all men by One anointed with the Spirit of the Lord, who would come to preach the Gospel to the poor, to bind up the broken-hearted, to bring liberty to the captives and the opening of the prisons to them that were bound, to proclaim to all that mourn a year of grace from the Lord (Isa. lxi. 1–3; Luke iv. 17–21); and who will come again from heaven in the times of the restitution of all things to complete the ἀποκατά-στασις τῆς βασιλείας τοῦ Θεοῦ, to glorify the whole creation into a kingdom of God, to restore everything that has been destroyed by sin from the beginning of the world, to abolish all the slavery of sin, establish the true liberty of the children of God, emancipate every creature from the bondage of vanity, under which it sighs on account of the sin of man, and introduce all His chosen into the kingdom of peace and everlasting blessedness, which was prepared for their inheritance before the foundation of the world (Acts iii. 19, 20; Rom. viii. 19 sqq.; Matt. xxv. 34; Col. i. 12; 1 Pet. i. 4).

PROMISES AND THREATS.—CHAP. XXVI.

Just as the book of the covenant, the kernel containing the fundamental principles of the covenant fellowship, which the Lord established with the children of Israel whom He had adopted as His nation, and the rule of life for the covenant nation (Ex. xx. 22–xxiii. 19), concluded with promises and threats (Ex. xxiii. 20–33); so the giving of the law at Sinai, as the unfolding of the inner, spiritual side of the whole of the

covenant constitution, closes in this chapter with an elaborate
unfolding of the blessing which would be secured by a faithful
observance of the laws, and the curse which would follow the
transgression of them. But whilst the former promises and
threats (Ex. xxiii.) related to the conquest of the promised
land of Canaan, the promises in this chapter refer to the
blessings which were to be bestowed upon Israel when the land
was in their possession (vers. 3–13), and the threats to the judgments with which the Lord would visit His disobedient people
in their inheritance, and in fact drive them out and scatter them
among the heathen (vers. 14–39). When this had been done,
then, as is still further proclaimed with a prophetic look into the
distant future, would they feel remorse, acknowledge their sin
to the Lord, and be once more received into favour by Him, the
eternally faithful covenant God (vers. 40–45).[1] The blessing

---

[1] When modern critics, who are carried away by naturalism, maintain
that Moses was not the author of these exhortations and warnings, because
of their prophetic contents, and assign them to the times of the kings, the
end of the eighth, or beginning of the seventh century (see *Ewald*, Gesch.
i. 156), they have not considered, in their antipathy to any supernatural
revelations from God in the Old Testament, that even apart from any
higher illumination, the fundamental idea of these promises and threats
must have presented itself to the mind of the lawgiver Moses. It required
but a very little knowledge of the nature of the human heart, and a clear
insight into the spiritual and ethical character of the law, to enable him to
foresee that the earthly-minded, unholy nation would not fulfil the solemn
demand of the law that their whole life should be sanctified to the Lord God,
that they would transgress in many ways, and rebel against God and His holy
laws, and therefore that in any case times of fidelity and the corresponding
blessing would alternate with times of unfaithfulness and the corresponding
curse, but that, for all that, at the end the grace of God would obtain the
victory over the severely punished and deeply humbled nation, and bring
the work of salvation to a glorious close. It is true, the concrete character
of this chapter cannot be fully explained in this way, but it furnishes the
clue to the psychological interpretation of the conception of this prophetic
discourse, and shows us the subjective points of contact for the divine
revelation which Moses has announced to us here. For, as *Auberlen* observes, " there is a marvellous and grand display of the greatness of God in
the fact, that He holds out before the people, whom He has just delivered
from the hands of the heathen and gathered round Himself, the prospect of
being scattered again among the heathen, and that, even before the land is
taken by the Israelites, He predicts its return to desolation. These words
could only be spoken by One who has the future really before His mind,
who sees through the whole depth of sin, and who can destroy His own

and curse of the law were impressed upon the hearts of the people in a still more comprehensive manner at the close of the whole law (Deut. xxviii.–xxx.), and on the threshold of the promised land.

Vers. 1 and 2 form the *introduction ;* and the essence of the whole law, the observance of which will bring a rich blessing, and the transgression of it severe judgments, is summed up in two leading commandments, and placed at the head of the blessing and curse which were to be proclaimed. Ye shall not make to you *elilim,* nugatory gods, and set up carved images and standing images for worship, but worship Jehovah your God with the observance of His Sabbaths, and fear before His sanctuary. The prohibition of *elilim,* according to chap. xix. 4, calls to mind the fundamental law of the decalogue (Ex. xx. 3, 4, cf. chap. xxi. 23, Ex. xxiii. 24, 25). To *pesel* (cf. Ex. xx. 4) and *mazzebah* (cf. Ex. xxiii. 24), which were not to be set up, there is added the command not to put אֶבֶן מַשְׂכִּית, "figure-stones," in the land, to worship over (by) them. The "figure-stone" is a stone formed into a figure, and idol of stone, not merely a stone with an inscription or with hieroglyphical figures; it is synonymous with מַשְׂכִּית in Num. xxxiii. 52, and consequently we are to understand by *pesel* the wooden idol as in Isa. xliv. 15, etc. The construction of הִשְׁתַּחֲוָה with עַל may be explained on the ground that the worshipper of a stone image placed upon the ground rises above it (for עַל in this sense, see Gen. xviii. 2).— In ver. 3 the true way to serve God is urged upon the Israelites once more, in words copied verbally from chap. xix. 30.

Vers. 3–13. THE BLESSING OF FIDELITY TO THE LAW.— Vers. 3–5. If the Israelites walked in the commandments of the Lord (for the expression see chap. xviii. 3 sqq.), the Lord would give fruitfulness to their land, that they should have bread to the full. "*I will give you rain-showers in season.*" The allusion here is to the showers which fall at the two rainy seasons, and

work, and yet attain His end. But so much the more adorable and marvellous is the grace, which nevertheless begins its work among such sinners, and is certain of victory notwithstanding all retarding and opposing difficulties." The peculiar character of this revelation, which must deeply have affected Moses, will explain the peculiarities observable in the style, viz. the heaping up of unusual words and modes of expression, several of which never occur again in the Old Testament, whilst others are only used by the prophets who followed the Pentateuch in their style.

upon which the fruitfulness of Palestine depends, viz. the early and latter rain (Deut. xi. 14). The former of these occurs after the autumnal equinox, at the time of the winter-sowing of wheat and barley, in the latter half of October or beginning of November. It generally falls in heavy showers in November and December, and then after that only at long intervals, and not so heavily. The latter, or so-called latter rain, falls in March before the beginning of the harvest of the winter crops, at the time of sowing the summer seed, and lasts only a few days, in some years only a few hours (see *Robinson, Pal.* ii. pp. 97 sqq.). —On vers. 5, 6, see chap. xxv. 18, 19.—Vers. 6–8. The Lord would give peace in the land, and cause the beasts of prey which endanger life to vanish out of the land, and suffer no war to come over it, but would put to flight before the Israelites the enemies who attacked them, and cause them to fall into their sword. שָׁכַב, to lie without being frightened up by any one, is a figure used to denote the quiet and peaceable enjoyment of life, and taken from the resting of a flock in good pasture-ground (Isa. xiv. 30) exposed to no attacks from either wild beasts or men. מַחֲרִיד is generally applied to the frightening of men by a hostile attack (Micah iv. 4; Jer. xxx. 10; Ezek. xxxix. 26; Job xi. 19); but it is also applied to the frightening of flocks and animals (Isa. xvii. 2; Deut. xxviii. 26; Jer. vii. 33, etc.). חַיָּה רָעָה: an *evil animal*, for a beast of prey, as in Gen. xxxvii. 20. " *Sword*," as the principal weapon applied, is used for war. The pursuing of the enemy relates to neighbouring tribes, who would make war upon the Israelites. נָפַל לְחֶרֶב does not mean to be felled by the sword (*Knobel*), but to fall into the sword. The words, "five of you shall put a hundred to flight, and a hundred ten thousand," are a proverbial expression for the most victorious superiority of Israel over their enemies. It is repeated in the opposite sense and in an intensified form in Deut. xxxii. 30 and Isa. xxx. 17.—Ver. 9. Moreover the Lord would bestow His covenant blessing upon them without intermission. פָּנָה אֶל signifies a sympathizing and gracious regard (Ps. xxv. 16, lxix. 17). The multiplication and fruitfulness of the nation were a constant fulfilment of the covenant promise (Gen. xvii. 4–6) and an establishment of the covenant (Gen. xvii. 7); not merely the preservation of it, but the continual realization of the covenant grace, by which the covenant itself was carried on further and further towards its completion. This was the real purpose of the blessing, to which all earthly good, as the pledge of the constant abode of God in the midst of His people, simply served as the foundation.—Ver. 10. Notwithstanding their numerous increase, they would suffer no want of food. " Ye shall eat that which has become old, and bring out old for new." *Multiplicabo vos et multiplicabo simul annonam vestram, adeo ut illam præ multitudine et copia absumere non possitis, sed illam diutissime servare adeoque abjicere cogamini, novarum frugum suavitate et copia superveniente (C. a Lap.).* הוֹצִיא *vetustum triticum ex horreo et vinum ex cella promere* (*Calvin*).—Ver. 11. " I will make My dwelling among you, and My soul will not despise you." מִשְׁכָּן, applied to the dwelling of God among His people in the sanctuary, involves the idea of satisfied repose.—Ver. 12. God's walking in the midst of Israel does not refer to His accompanying and leading the people on their journeyings, but denotes the walking of God in the midst of His people in Canaan itself, whereby He would continually manifest Himself to the nation as its God and make them a people of possession, bringing them into closer and closer fellowship with Himself, and giving them all the saving blessings of His covenant of grace.—Ver. 13. For He was their God, who had brought them out of the land of the Egyptians, that they might no longer be servants to them, and had broken the bands of their yokes and made them go upright. מֹטֹת עֹל, *lit.* the poles of the yoke (cf. Ezek. xxxiv. 27), *i.e.* the poles which are laid upon the necks of beasts of burden (Jer. xxvii. 2) as a yoke, to bend their necks and harness them for work. It was with the burden of such a yoke that Egypt had pressed down the Israelites, so that they could no longer walk upright, till God by breaking the yoke helped them to walk upright again. As the yoke is a figurative description of severe oppression, so going upright is a figurative description of emancipation from bondage. קוֹמְמִיּוּת, *lit.* a substantive, an upright position; here it is an adverb (cf. *Ges.* § 100, 2).

Vers. 14–33. THE CURSE FOR CONTEMPT OF THE LAW.—The following judgments are threatened, not for single breaches of the law, but for contempt of all the laws, amounting to inward contempt of the divine commandments and a breach of the covenant (vers. 14, 15),—for presumptuous and obstinate rebellion, therefore, against God and His commandments. For this, severe judgments are announced, which were to be carried to their uttermost in a fourfold series, if the hardening were obstinately continued. If Israel acted in opposition to the Lord in the manner stated, He would act towards them as follows (vers. 16, 17) : He would appoint over them בֶּהָלָה terror—a general notion, which is afterwards particularized as consisting of diseases, sowing without enjoying the fruit, defeat in war, and flight before their enemies. Two kinds of disease are mentioned by which life is destroyed : consumption and burning, *i.e.* burning fever, πυρετός, *febris*, which cause the eyes (the light of this life) to disappear, and the soul (the life itself) to pine away ; whereas in Ex. xxiii. 25, xv. 26, preservation from diseases is promised for obedience to the law. Of these diseases, consumption is at present very rare in Palestine and Syria, though it occurs in more elevated regions ; but burning fever is one of the standing diseases. To these there would be added the invasion of the land by enemies, so that they would labour in vain and sow their seed to no purpose, for their enemies would consume the produce, as actually was the case (*e.g.* Judg. vi. 3, 4).—Ver. 17. Yea, the Lord would turn His face against them, so that they would be beaten by their enemies, and be so thoroughly humbled in consequence, that they would flee when no man pursued (cf. ver. 36).

But if these punishments did not answer their purpose, and bring Israel back to fidelity to its God, the Lord would punish the disobedient nation still more severely, and chasten the rebellious for their sin, not simply only, but sevenfold. This He would do, so long as Israel persevered in obstinate resistance, and to this end He would multiply His judgments by degrees. This graduated advance of the judgments of God is so depicted in the following passage, that four times in succession new and multiplied punishments are announced : (1) utter barrenness in their land,—that is to say, *one* heavier punishment (vers. 18–20) ; (2) the extermination of their cattle by beasts of prey, and childlessness,—*two* punishments (vers. 21, 22) ; (3) war, plague, and famine,—*three* punishments (vers. 23–26) ; (4) the destruction of all idolatrous abominations, the overthrow of their towns and holy places, the devastation of the land, and the dispersion of the people among the heathen,—*four* punishments which would bring the Israelites to the verge of destruction (vers. 27–33). In this way would the Lord punish the stiffneckedness of His people.—These divine threats embrace the whole of Israel's future. But the series of judgments mentioned is not to be understood historically, as a prediction of the temporal succession of the different punishments, but as an ideal account of the judgments of God, unfolding themselves with inward necessity in a manner answering to the progressive development of the sin. As the nation would not resist the Lord continually, but times of disobedience and apostasy would alternate with times of obedience and faithfulness, so the judgments of God would alternate with His blessings; and as the opposition would not increase in uniform progress, sometimes becoming weaker and then at other times gaining greater force again, so the punishments would not multiply continuously, but correspond in every case to the amount of the sin, and only burst in upon the incorrigible race in all the intensity foretold, when ungodliness gained the upper hand.

Vers. 18–20. *First* stage of the aggravated judgments.—If they did not hearken עַד־אֵלֶּה, "*up to these*" (the punishments named in vers. 16, 17), that is to say, if they persisted in their disobedience even when the judgments reached to this height, God would add a sevenfold chastisement on account of their sins, would punish them seven times more severely, and break down their strong pride by fearful drought. Seven, as the number of perfection in the works of God, denotes the strengthening of the chastisement, even to the height of its full measure (cf. Prov. xxiv. 16). גְּאוֹן עֹז, *lit.* the eminence or pride of strength, includes everything upon which a nation rests its might; then the pride and haughtiness which rely upon earthly might and its auxiliaries (Ex. xxx. 6, 18, xxxiii. 28); here it signifies the pride of a nation, puffed up by the fruitfulness and rich produce of its land. God would make their heaven (the sky of their land) like iron and their earth like brass, *i.e.* as hard and dry as metal, so that not a drop of rain and dew would fall from heaven to moisten the earth, and not a plant could grow out of the earth (cf. Deut. xxviii. 23); and when the land was cultivated, the people would exhaust their strength for nought. תָּמַם, *consumi.*

Vers 21, 22. The *second* stage.—But if the people's resist-

ance amounted to a hostile rebellion against God, He would
smite them sevenfold for their sin by sending beasts of prey and
childlessness.   By beasts of prey He would destroy their cattle,
and by barrenness He would make the nation so small that the
ways would be deserted, that high roads would cease because
there would be no traveller upon them on account of the de-
population of the land (Isa. xxxiii. 8; Zeph. iii. 6), and the few
inhabitants who still remained would be afraid to venture because of the wild beasts (Ezek. xiv. 15). הָלַךְ קֶרִי עִם ("*to go a
meeting with a person*," *i.e.* to meet a person in a hostile manner,
to fight against him) only occurs here in vers. 21 and 23, and
is strengthened in vers. 24, 27, 28, 40, 41 into הָלַךְ בְּקֶרִי עִם, to
engage in a hostile encounter with a person. מַכָּה שֶׁבַע, a sevenfold blow. "*According to your sins*," *i.e.* answering to them
sevenfold.   In ver. 22 the first clause corresponds to the third,
and the second to the fourth, so that Nos. 3 and 4 contain the
effects of Nos. 1 and 2.

Vers. 23–26. The *third* stage.—But if they would not be
chastened by these punishments, and still rose up in hostility to
the Lord, He would also engage in a hostile encounter with
them, and punish them sevenfold with war, plague, and hunger.
—Ver. 25. He would bring over them " the sword avenging
(*i.e.* executing) the covenant vengeance." The " *covenant vengeance*" was punishment inflicted for a breach of the covenant,
the severity of which corresponded to the greatness of the covenant blessings forfeited by a faithless apostasy. If they retreated
to their towns (fortified places) from the sword of the enemy,
the Lord would send a plague over them there, and give those
who were spared by the plague into the power of the foe.   He
would also " break in pieces the staff of bread," and compel
them by the force of famine to submit to the foe.   The means
of sustenance should become so scarce, that ten women could
bake their bread in a single oven, whereas in ordinary times
every woman would require an oven for herself; and they would
have to eat the bread which they brought home by weight, *i.e.*
not as much as every one pleased, but in rations weighed out
so scantily, that those who ate would not be satisfied, and would
only be able to sustain their life in the most miserable way.
Calamities such as these burst upon Israel and Judah more
than once when their fortified towns were besieged, particularly

in the later times of the kings, *e.g.* upon Samaria in the reign of Joram (2 Kings vi. 25 sqq.), and upon Jerusalem through the invasions of the Chaldeans (cf. Isa. iii. 1, Jer. xiv. 18, Ezek. iv. 16, v. 12).

Vers. 27-33. *Fourth* and severest stage.—If they should still persist in their opposition, God would chastise them with wrathful meeting, yea, punish them so severely in His wrath, that they would be compelled to eat the flesh of their sons and daughters, *i.e.* to slay their own children and eat them in the extremity of their hunger,—a fact which literally occurred in Samaria in the period of the Syrians (2 Kings vi. 28, 29), and in Jerusalem in that of the Chaldeans (Lam. ii. 20, iv. 10), and in the Roman war of extermination under Titus (*Josephus bell. jud.* v. 10, 3) in the most appalling manner. Eating the flesh of their own children is mentioned first, as indicating the extremity of the misery and wretchedness in which the people would perish; and after this, the judgment, by which the nation would be brought to this extremity, is more minutely described in its four principal features : viz. (1) the destruction of all idolatrous abominations (ver. 30); (2) the overthrow of the towns and sanctuaries (ver. 31); (3) the devastation of the land, to the amazement of the enemies who dwelt therein (ver. 32); and (4) the dispersion of the people among the heathen (ver. 33). The " high places" are altars erected upon heights and mountains in the land, upon which sacrifices were offered both to Jehovah in an unlawful way and also to heathen deities. חַמָּנִים, sun-pillars, are idols of the Canaanitish nature-worship, either simple pillars dedicated to Baal, or idolatrous statues of the sun-god (cf. *Movers Phönizier* i. pp. 343 sqq.). " *And I give your carcases upon the carcases of your idols.*" גִּלּוּלִים, *lit.* clods, from גָּלַל to roll, a contemptuous expression for idols. With the idols the idolaters also were to perish, and defile with their corpses the images, which had also become corpses as it were, through their overthrow and destruction. For the further execution of this threat, see Ezek. vi. 4 sqq. This will be your lot, for " My soul rejects you." By virtue of the inward character of His holy nature, Jehovah must abhor and reject the sinner.—Ver. 31. Their towns and their sanctuaries He would destroy, because He took no pleasure in their sacrificial worship. מִקְדָּשִׁים are the holy things of the worship of Jehovah, the tabernacle and temple,

with their altars and the rest of their holy furniture, as in Ps.
lxviii. 36, lxxiv. 7. רֵיחַ נִיחֹחַ (chap. i. 9) is the odour of the
sacrifice; and רִיחַ, to smell, an anthropomorphic designation of
divine satisfaction (cf. Amos v. 21, Isa. xi. 3).—Vers. 32, 33.
The land was to become a wilderness, so that even the enemies
who dwelt therein would be terrified in consequence (cf. Jer.
xviii. 16, xix. 8); and the Israelites would be scattered among
the heathen, because Jehovah would draw out His sword behind
them, *i.e.* drive them away with a drawn sword, and scatter
them to all the winds of heaven (cf. Ezek. v. 2, 12, xii. 14).

Vers. 34–45. OBJECT OF THE DIVINE JUDGMENTS IN
RELATION TO THE LAND AND NATION OF ISRAEL.—Vers. 34
and 35. The land would then enjoy and keep its Sabbaths, so
long as it was desolate, and Israel was in the land of its foes.
כֹּל יְמֵי הָשַּׁמָּה, during the whole period of its devastation. הָשַּׁמָּה,
inf. Hophal with the suffix, in which the *mappik* is wanting, as
in Ex. ii. 3 (cf. *Ewald*, § 131*e*). רָצָה to have satisfaction: with
בְ and an accusative it signifies to take delight, take pleasure, in
anything, *e.g.* in rest after the day's work is done (Job xiv. 6);
here also to enjoy rest (not "to pay its debt:" *Ges.*, *Kn.*). The
keeping of the Sabbath was not a performance binding upon
the land, nor had the land been in fault because the Sabbath
was not kept. As the earth groans under the pressure of the
sin of men, so does it rejoice in deliverance from this pressure,
and participation in the blessed rest of the whole creation.
תִּשְׁבַּת אֶת אֲשֶׁר וגו': the land "*will rest* (keep) *what it has not
rested on your Sabbaths and whilst you dwelt in it;*" *i.e.* it will
make up the rest which you did not give it on your Sabbaths
(daily and yearly). It is evident from this, that the keeping
of the Sabbaths and sabbatical years was suspended when the
apostasy of the nation increased,—a result which could be
clearly foreseen in consequence of the inward dislike of a sinner
to the commandments of the holy God, and which is described
in 2 Chron. xxvi. 31 as having actually occurred.—Vers.
36–38. So far as the *nation* was concerned, those who were
left when the kingdom was overthrown would find no rest in
the land of their enemies, but would perish among the heathen
for their own and their fathers' iniquities, till they confessed
their sins and bent their uncircumcised hearts under the right-

eousness of the divine punishments. הַנִּשְׁאָרִים בָּכֶם (nominative abs.): "as for those who are left in (as in chap. v. 9), *i.e.* of, you," who have not perished in the destruction of the kingdom and dispersion of the people, God will bring despair into their heart in the lands of your enemies, that the sound (" voice") of a moving leaf will hunt them to flee as before the sword, so that they will fall in their anxious flight, and stumble one over another, though no one is pursuing. The ἅπ. λεγ. מֹרֶךְ from מָרַךְ, related to מָרַח and מָרַק to rub, rub to pieces, signifies that inward anguish, fear, and despair, which rend the heart and destroy the life, δειλία, *pavor* (LXX., Vulg.), what is described in Deut. xxviii. 65 in even stronger terms as "a trembling heart, and failing of eyes, and sorrow of mind." There should not be to them תְּקוּמָה, *standi et resistendi facultas* (*Rosenmüller*), standing before the enemy; but they should perish among the nations. "The land of their enemies will eat them up," *sc.* by their falling under the pressure of the circumstances in which they were placed (cf. Num. xiii. 32; Ezek. xxxvi. 13).—Ver. 39. But those who still remained under this oppression would pine away in their iniquities (יִמַּקּוּ, *lit.* to rot, moulder away), and "also in the iniquities of their fathers with them." אִתָּם refers to עֲוֹנוֹת, "which are with them," which they carry with them and must atone for (see at Ex. xx. 5).—Vers. 40-43. In this state of pining away under their enemies, they would confess to themselves their own and their fathers' sins, *i.e.* would make the discovery that their sufferings were a punishment from God for their sins, and acknowledge that they were suffering what they had deserved, through their unfaithfulness to their God and rebellion against Him, for which He had been obliged to set Himself in hostility to them, and bring them into the land of their enemies; or rather their uncircumcised hearts would then humble themselves, and they would look with satisfaction upon this fruit of their sin. The construction is the following: וְזָכַרְתִּי (ver. 42) corresponds to הִתְוַדּוּ (ver. 40) as the apodosis; so that, according to the more strictly logical connection, which is customary in our language, we may unite vers. 40, 41 in one period with ver. 42. "If they shall confess their iniquity . . . or rather their uncircumcised heart shall humble itself . . . I will remember My covenant." With בְּמַעֲלָם a parenthetical clause is introduced into the main sentence explanatory of the iniquity, and reaches as far as "into the land of their enemies." With

אֲרָאֶ יְפָנַע, "or if, etc.," the main sentence is resumed. אֹ, "or rather" (as in 1 Sam. xxix. 3), bringing out the humiliation of the heart as the most important result to which the confession of sin ought to deepen itself. The heart is called "uncircumcised" as being unsanctified, and not susceptible to the manifestations of divine grace. יִרְצוּ אֶת־עֲוֹנָם εὐδοκήσουσι τὰς ἁμαρτίας αὐτῶν (LXX.), they will take pleasure, rejoice in their misdeeds, i.e. in the consequences and results of them—that their misdeeds have so deeply humbled them, and brought them to the knowledge of the corruption into which they have fallen : a bold and, so to speak, paradoxical expression for their complete change of heart, which we may render thus : "they will enjoy their misdeeds," as רָצָה may be rendered in the same way in ver. 43 also.[1] But where punishment bears such fruit, God looks upon the sinner with favour again. When Israel had gone so far, He would remember His covenant with the fathers ("My covenant with Jacob," בְּרִיתִי יַעֲקֹב : the suffix is attached to the governing noun, as in chap. vi. 3, because the noun governed, being a proper name, could not take the suffix), and remember the land (including its inhabitants), which, as is repeated again in ver. 43, would be left by them (become desolate) and enjoy its Sabbaths whilst it was waste (depopulated) from (i.e. away from, without) them ; and they would enjoy their iniquity, because they had despised the judgments of the Lord, and their soul had rejected His statutes.—Ver. 44. "And yet, even with regard to this, when they shall be in the land of their enemies, have I not despised them." That is to say, if it shall have come even so far as that they are in the land of their enemies (the words גַּם־זֹאת stand first in an absolute sense, and are strengthened or intensified by וְאַף and more fully explained by בִּהְיוֹתָם וגו'), I have not rejected them, to destroy them and break My covenant with them. For I am Jehovah their God, who, as the absolutely exist-

---

[1] *Luther* has translated עָוֹן in this sense, "punishment of iniquity," and observes in the marginal notes,—" (Pleasure), i.e. just as they had pleasure in their sins and felt disgust at My laws, so they would now take pleasure in their punishment and say, 'We have just what we deserve. This is what we have to thank our cursed sin for. It is just, O God, quite just.' And these are thoughts and words of earnest repentance, hating itself from the bottom of the heart, and crying out, Shame upon me, what have I done? This pleases God, so that He becomes gracious once more."

ing and unchangeably faithful One, keeps His promises and does not repent of His calling (Rom. xi. 29).—Ver. 45. He would therefore remember the covenant with the forefathers, whom He had brought out of Egypt before the eyes of the nations, to be a God to them; and He would renew the covenant with the fathers to them (the descendants), to gather them again out of the heathen, and adopt them again as His nation (cf. Deut. xxx. 3–5). In this way the judgment would eventually turn to a blessing, if they would bend in true repentance under the mighty hand of their God.

Ver. 46 contains the close of the entire book, or rather of the whole of the covenant legislation from Ex. xxv. onwards, although the expression "in Mount Sinai" points back primarily to Lev. xxv. 1.

OF VOWS.—CHAP. XXVII.

The directions concerning vows follow the express termination of the Sinaitic lawgiving (chap. xxvi. 46), as an appendix to it, because vows formed no integral part of the covenant laws, but were a freewill expression of piety common to almost all nations, and belonged to the modes of worship current in all religions, which were not demanded and might be omitted altogether, and which really lay outside the law, though it was necessary to bring them into harmony with the demands of the law upon Israel. Making a vow, therefore, or dedicating anything to the Lord by vowing, was not commanded, but was presupposed as a manifestation of reverence for God, sanctified by ancient tradition, and was simply regulated according to the principle laid down in Deut. xxiii. 22–24, that it was not a sin to refrain from vowing, but that every vow, when once it had been made, was to be conscientiously and inviolably kept (cf. Prov. xx. 25, Eccl. v. 3–5), and the neglect to keep it to be atoned for with a sin-offering (chap. v. 4).—The objects of a vow might be persons (vers. 2–8), cattle (vers. 9–13), houses (vers. 14, 15), and land (vers. 16–25), all of which might be redeemed with the exception of sacrificial animals; but not the first-born (ver. 26), nor persons and things dedicated to the Lord by the ban (vers. 28, 29), nor tithes (vers. 30–33), because all of these were to be handed over to the Lord according to the

law, and therefore could not be redeemed. This followed from
the very idea of the vow. For a vow was a promise made by
any one to dedicate and give his own person, or a portion of his
property, to the Lord for averting some danger and distress, or
for bringing to his possession some desired earthly good.—Besides ordinary vowing or promising to give, there was also vowing away, or the vow of renunciation, as is evident from Num.
xxx. The chapter before us treats only of ordinary vowing,
and gives directions for redeeming the thing vowed, in which it
is presupposed that everything vowed to the Lord would fall to
His sanctuary as *corban*, an offering (Mark vii. 11); and therefore, that when it was redeemed, the money would also be paid
to His sanctuary.—(On the vow, see my *Archæologie*, § 96;
Oehler in *Herzog's Cycl.*)

Vers. 2–8. The vowing of *persons*.—" If any one make a
special vow, souls shall be to the Lord according to thy valuation." הַפְלִא נֶדֶר does not mean to dedicate or set apart a vow,
but to make a special vow (see at chap. xxii. 21). The words
בְּעֶרְכְּךָ, " according to thy (Moses') valuation," it is more simple
to regard as an apodosis, so as to supply to לַיהֹוָה the substantive
verb תִּהְיֶינָה, than as a fuller description of the protasis, in which
case the apodosis would follow in ver. 3, and the verb יַקְדִּישׁ
would have to be supplied. But whatever may be the conclusion adopted, in any case this thought is expressed in the words,
that souls, *i.e.* persons, were to be vowed to the Lord according
to Moses' valuation, *i.e.* according to the price fixed by Moses.
This implies clearly enough, that whenever a person was vowed,
redemption was to follow according to the valuation. Otherwise
what was the object of valuing them? Valuation supposes
either redemption or purchase. But in the case of men (*i.e.*
Israelites) there could be no purchasing as slaves, and therefore
the object of the valuing could only have been for the purpose
of redeeming, buying off the person vowed to the Lord, and
the fulfilment of the vow could only have consisted in the payment into the sanctuary of the price fixed by the law.[1]—Vers.

---

[1] *Saalschütz* adopts this explanation in common with the *Mishnah*.
Oehler is wrong in citing 1 Sam. ii. 11, 22, 28 as a proof of the opposite.
For the dedication of Samuel did not consist of a simple vow, but was a
dedication as a Nazarite for the whole of his life, and Samuel was thereby
vowed to service at the sanctuary, whereas the law says nothing about.

3–7. This was to be, for persons between twenty and thirty years of age, 50 shekels for a man and 30 for a woman; for a boy between 5 and 20, 20 shekels, for a girl of the same age 10 shekels; for a male child from a month to five years 5 shekels, for a female of the same age 3 shekels; for an old man above sixty 15 shekels, for an old woman of that age 10; the whole to be in shekels of the sanctuary (see at Ex. xxx. 15). The valuation price was regulated, therefore, according to capacity and vigour of life, and the female sex, as the weaker vessel (1 Pet. iii. 7), was only appraised at half the amount of the male.—Ver. 8. But if the person making the vow was " poor before thy valuation," i.e. too poor to be able to pay the valuation price fixed by the law, he was to be brought before the priest, who would value him according to the measure of what his hand could raise (see chap. v. 11), i.e. what he was able to pay. This regulation, which made it possible for the poor man to vow his own person to the Lord, presupposed that the person vowed would have to be redeemed. For otherwise a person of this kind would only need to dedicate himself to the sanctuary, with all his power for work, to fulfil his vow completely.

Vers. 9–13. When *animals* were vowed, of the cattle that were usually offered in sacrifice, everything that was given to Jehovah of these (i.e. dedicated to Him by vowing) was to be holy and not changed, i.e. exchanged, a good animal for a bad, or a bad one for a good. But if such an exchange should be made, the animal first dedicated and the one substituted were both to be holy (vers. 9, 10). The expression " it shall be holy" unquestionably implies that an animal of this kind could not be redeemed; but if it was free from faults, it was offered in sacrifice: if, however, it was not fit for sacrifice on account of some blemish, it fell to the portion of the priests for their maintenance like the first-born of cattle (cf. ver. 33).—Vers. 11, 12. Every unclean beast, however,—an ass for example,—which could not be offered in sacrifice, was to be placed before the priest for him

attachment to the sanctuary in the case of the simple vowing of persons. But because redemption in the case of persons was not left to the pleasure or free-will of the person making the vow as in the case of material property, no addition is made to the valuation price as though for a merely possible circumstance.

to value it "between good and bad," *i.e.* neither very high as if it were good, nor very low as if it were bad, but at a medium price; and it was to be according to this valuation, *i.e.* to be worth the value placed upon it (כְּעֶרְכְּךָ הַכֹּהֵן according to thy, the priest's, valuation), namely, when sold for the good of the sanctuary and its servants.—Ver. 13. But if the person vowing wanted to redeem it, he was to add a fifth above the valuation price, as a kind of compensation for taking back the animal he had vowed (cf. chap. v. 16).

Vers. 14 and 15. When a *house* was vowed, the same rules applied as in the case of unclean cattle. *Knobel's* supposition, that the person making the vow was to pay the valuation price if he did not wish to redeem the house, is quite a groundless supposition. The house that was not redeemed was sold, of course, for the good of the sanctuary.

Vers. 16–25. With regard to the vowing of *land*, a difference was made between a field inherited and one that had been purchased.—Ver. 16. If any one sanctified to the Lord "of the field of his possession," *i.e.* a portion of his hereditary property, the valuation was to be made according to the measure of the seed sown; and an omer of barley was to be appraised at fifty shekels, so that a field sown with an omer of barley would be valued at fifty shekels. As an omer was equal to ten ephahs (Ezek. xlv. 11), and, according to the calculation made by *Thenius*, held about 225 lbs., the fifty shekels cannot have been the average value of the yearly produce of such a field, but must be understood, as it was by the Rabbins, as the value of the produce of a complete jubilee period of 49 or 50 years; so that whoever wished to redeem the field had to pay, according to *Mishnah, Erachin* vii. 1, a shekel and a fifth *per annum.*—Vers. 17, 18. If he sanctified his field from the year of jubilee, *i.e.* immediately after the expiration of that year, it was to "stand according to thy valuation," *i.e.* no alteration was to be made in the valuation. But if it took place after the year of jubilee, *i.e.* some time or some years after, the priest was to estimate the value according to the number of years to the next year of jubilee, and "*it shall be abated from thy valuation*," sc. *praeteritum tempus*, the time that has elapsed since the year of jubilee. Hence, for example, if the field was vowed ten years after the year of jubilee, the man who wished to redeem it had only forty shekels to pay for the forty years remaining up to the next year of jubilee, or, with the addition of the fifth, 48 shekels. The valuation was necessary in both cases, for the hereditary field was inalienable, and reverted to the original owner or his heirs in the year of jubilee without compensation (cf. ver. 21 and chap. xxv. 13, 23 sqq.); so that, strictly speaking, it was not the field itself, but the produce of its harvests up to the next year of jubilee, that was vowed, whether the person making the vow left it to the sanctuary *in natura* till the year of jubilee, or wished to redeem it again by paying the valuation price. In the latter case, however, he had to put a fifth over and above the valuation price (ver. 19, like vers. 13 and 15), that it might be left to him. —Vers. 20, 21. In case he did not redeem it, however, namely, before the commencement of the next year of jubilee, or sold it to another man, *i.e.* to a man not belonging to his family, he could no longer redeem it; but on its going out, *i.e.* becoming free in the year of jubilee (see chap. xxv. 28), it was to be hóly to the Lord, like a field under the ban (see ver. 28), and to fall to the priests as their property. *Hinc colligere est, redimendum fuisse ante Jubilæum consecratum agrum, nisi quis vellet eum plane abalienari (Clericus).* According to the distinct words of the text (observe the correspondence of אִם · · · אִם), the field, that had been vowed, fell to the sanctuary in the jubilee year not only when the owner had sold it in the meantime, but also when he had not previously redeemed it. The reason for selling the field at a time when he had vowed it to the sanctuary, need not be sought for in caprice and dishonesty, as it is by *Knobel.* If the field was vowed in this sense, that it was not handed over to the sanctuary (the priesthood) to be cultivated, but remained in the hands of the proprietor, so that every year he paid to the sanctuary simply the valuation price,—and this may have been the rule, as the priests whose duties lay at the sanctuary could not busy themselves about the cultivation of the field, but would be obliged either to sell the piece of land at once, or farm it,— the owner might sell the field up to the year of jubilee, to be saved the trouble of cultivating it, and the purchaser could not only live upon what it yielded over and above the price to be paid every year to the sanctuary, but might possibly realize something more. In such a case the fault of the seller, for which he had to make atonement by the forfeiture of his field to the sanctuary in the year of jubilee, consisted simply in the fact that he had looked upon the land which he vowed to the Lord as though it were his own property, still and entirely at his own disposal, and therefore had allowed himself to violate the rights of the Lord by the sale of his land. At any rate, it is quite inadmissible to supply a different subject to מָכַר from that of the parallel יִגְאַל, viz. the priest.—Vers. 22–24. If on the other hand any one dedicated to the Lord a "field of his purchase," *i.e.* a field that had been bought and did not belong to his patrimony, he was to give the amount of the valuation as estimated by the priest up to the year of jubilee "on that day," *i.e.* immediately, and all at once. This regulation warrants the conclusion, that on the dedication of hereditary fields, the amount was not paid all at once, but year by year. In the year of jubilee the field that had been vowed, if a field acquired by purchase, did not revert to the buyer, but to the hereditary owner from whom it had been bought, according to the law in chap. xxv. 23–28.— Ver. 25. All valuations were to be made according to the shekel of the sanctuary.

Vers. 26–29. What belonged to the Lord by law could not be dedicated to Him by a vow, especially the first-born of clean cattle (cf. Ex. xiii. 1, 2). The first-born of unclean animals were to be redeemed according to the valuation of the priest, with the addition of a fifth ; and if this was not done, it was to be sold at the estimated value. By this regulation the earlier law, which commanded that an ass should either be redeemed with a sheep or else be put to death (Ex. xiii. 13, xxxiv. 20), was modified in favour of the revenues of the sanctuary and its servants.— Vers. 28, 29. Moreover, nothing put under the ban, nothing that a man had devoted (banned) to the Lord of his property, of man, beast, or the field of his possession, was to be sold or redeemed, because it was most holy (see at chap. ii. 3). The man laid under the ban was to be put to death. According to the words of ver. 28, the individual Israelite was quite at liberty to ban, not only his cattle and field, but also men who belonged to him, that is to say, slaves and children. הֶחֱרִים signifies to dedicate something to the Lord in an unredeemable manner, as *cherem, i.e.* ban, or banned. חרם (to devote, or ban), judging from the cognate words in the Arabic, signifying *prohibere, vetare, illicitum facere, illicitum, sacrum,* has the primary signi-

fication " to cut off," and denotes that which is taken away
from use and abuse on the part of men, and surrendered to
God in an irrevocable and unredeemable manner, viz. human
beings by being put to death, cattle and inanimate objects by
being either given up to the sanctuary for ever or destroyed
for the glory of the Lord. The latter took place, no doubt,
only with the property of idolaters; at all events, it is commanded simply for the infliction of punishment on idolatrous
towns (Deut. xiii. 13 sqq.). It follows from this, however, that
the vow of banning could only be made in connection with
persons who obstinately resisted that sanctification of life which
was binding upon them; and that an individual was not at
liberty to devote a human being to the ban simply at his own
will and pleasure, otherwise the ban might have been abused to
purposes of ungodliness, and have amounted to a breach of the
law, which prohibited the killing of any man, even though he were
a slave (Ex. xxi. 20). In a manner analogous to this, too, the
owner of cattle and fields was only allowed to put them under
the ban when they had been either desecrated by idolatry or
abused to unholy purposes. For there can be no doubt that
the idea which lay at the foundation of the ban was that of a
compulsory dedication of something which resisted or impeded
sanctification; so that in all cases in which it was carried into
execution by the community or the magistracy, it was an act of
the judicial holiness of God manifesting itself in righteousness
and judgment.

Vers. 30–33. Lastly, the tenth of the land, both of the seed
of the land—*i.e.* not of what was sown, but of what was yielded,
the produce of the seed (Deut. xiv. 22), the harvest reaped, or
"corn of the threshing-floor," Num. xviii. 27—and also of the
fruit of the tree, *i.e.* "the fulness of the press" (Num. xviii. 27),
the wine and oil (Deut. xiv. 23), belonged to the Lord, were holy
to Him, and could not be dedicated to Him by a vow. At the
same time they could be redeemed by the addition of a fifth beyond the actual amount.—Ver. 32. With regard to all the tithes
of the flock and herd, of all that passed under the rod of the herds-
man, the tenth (animal) was to be holy to the Lord. No discrimi-
nation was to be made in this case between good and bad, and
no exchange to be made: if, however, this did take place, the
tenth animal was to be holy as well as the one for which it was

exchanged, and could not be redeemed. The words "whatsoever passeth under the rod" may be explained from the custom of numbering the flocks by driving the animals one by one past the shepherd, who counted them with a rod stretched out over them (cf. Jer. xxxiii. 13, Ezek. xx. 37). They mean everything that is submitted to the process of numbering, and are correctly explained by the Rabbins as referring to the fact that every year the additions to the flock and herd were tithed, and not the whole of the cattle. In these directions the tithe is referred to as something well known. In the laws published hitherto, it is true that no mention has been made of it; but, like the burnt-offerings, meat-offerings, and peace-offerings, it formed from time immemorial an essential part of the worship of God; so that not only did Jacob vow that he would tithe for the Lord all that He should give him in a foreign land (Gen. xxviii. 22), but Abraham gave a tenth of his booty to Melchizedek the priest (Gen. xiv. 20). Under these circumstances, it was really unnecessary to enjoin upon the Israelites for the first time the offering of tithe to Jehovah. All that was required was to incorporate this in the covenant legislation, and bring it into harmony with the spirit of the law. This is done here in connection with the holy consecrations; and in Num. xviii. 20–32 instructions are given in the proper place concerning their appropriation, and further directions are added in Deut. xii. 6, 11, xiv. 22 sqq. respecting a second tithe.—The laws contained in this chapter are brought to a close in ver. 34 with a new concluding formula (see chap. xxvi. 46), by which they are attached to the law given at Sinai.

Commentary
on the
OLD TESTAMENT

BIBLICAL COMMENTARY

ON

THE OLD TESTAMENT

BY

C. F. KEIL, D.D., AND F. DELITZSCH, D.D.,

PROFESSORS OF THEOLOGY.

VOLUME III

THE PENTATEUCH

TRANSLATED FROM THE GERMAN

BY THE

REV. JAMES MARTIN, B.A.,

TABLE OF CONTENTS

THE FOURTH BOOK OF MOSES (NUMBERS).

INTRODUCTION.

EXPOSITION.

THE FIFTH BOOK OF MOSES (DEUTERONOMY).

INTRODUCTION.

EXPOSITION.

THE FOURTH BOOK OF MOSES.

(NUMBERS.)

———◆———

INTRODUCTION.

THE fourth book of Moses, which the Jews call either *Vayedabber* (וידבר), from the opening word, מספרים ('Ἀριθ-μοί, *Numeri*, LXX., Vulg.), or פקודים *recensiones* (=*liber recensionum*), and to which the heading במדבר (*in the wilderness*) is given in the Masoretic texts with a more direct reference to its general contents, narrates the guidance of Israel through the desert, from Mount Sinai to the border of Canaan by the river Jordan, and embraces the whole period from the second month of the second year after the exodus from Egypt to the tenth month of the fortieth year.

As soon as their mode of life in a spiritual point of view had been fully regulated by the laws of Leviticus, the Israelites were to enter upon their journey to Canaan, and take possession of the inheritance promised to their fathers. But just as the way from Goshen to Sinai was a preparation of the chosen people for their reception into the covenant with God, so the way from Sinai to Canaan was also a preparation for the possession of the promised land. On their journey through the wilderness the Israelites were to experience on the one hand the faithful watchfulness and gracious deliverance of their God in every season of distress and danger, as well as the stern severity of the divine judgments upon the despisers of their God, that they might learn thereby to trust entirely in the Lord, and strive after His kingdom alone; and on the other hand they were to receive during their journey the laws and ordinances relating to their civil and political constitution, and thereby to be placed in a condition to form and maintain themselves as a consolidated nation by the side of and in opposition to the earthly kingdoms formed by the nations of the world, and to fulfil the task assigned them by God in the midst of the nations of the earth. These laws, which were given in part at Sinai, in relation to the external and internal organization of the tribes of Israel as the army and the congregation of Jehovah, and in part on various occasions during the march through the desert, as well as after their arrival in the steppes of Moab, on the other side of the Jordan opposite to Jericho, with especial reference to the conquest of Canaan and their settlement there, are not only attached externally to the history itself in the order in which they were given, but are so incorporated internally into the historical narrative, according to their peculiar character and contents, as to form a complete whole, which divides itself into three distinct parts corresponding to the chronological development of the history itself.

The FIRST part, which extends from chap. i.-x. 10, contains the preparations for departing from Sinai, arranged in four groups :—viz. (1) the outward arrangement and classification of the tribes in the camp and on their march, or the numbering and grouping of the twelve tribes around the sanctuary of their God (chap. i. and ii.), and the appointment of the Levites in the place of the first-born of the nation to act as servants of the priests in the sanctuary (chap. iii. and iv.) ; (2) the internal or moral and spiritual organization of the nation as the congregation of the Lord, by laws relating to the maintenance of the cleanliness of the camp, restitution for trespasses, conjugal fidelity, the fulfilment of the vow of the Nazarite, and the priestly blessing (chap. v. and vi.); (3) the closing events at Sinai, viz. the presentation of dedicatory offerings on the part of the tribe princes for the transport of the tabernacle and the altar service (chap. vii.), the consecration of the Levites (chap. viii.), and the feast of Passover, with an arrangement for a supplementary Passover (chap. ix. 1–14) ; (4) the appointment of signs and signals for the march in the desert (chap. ix. 5–x. 10). In the SECOND part (chap. x. 11–xxi.), the history of the journey is given in the three stages of its progress from Sinai to the heights of Pisgah, near to the Jordan, viz. (1) from their departure from the desert of Sinai (chap. x. 11–36) to their arrival at the desert of *Paran*, at Kadesh, including the occurrences at Tabeerah, at the graves of lust, and at Hazeroth (chap. xi. and xii.), and the events at Kadesh which led God to condemn the people who had revolted against Him to wander in the wilderness for forty years, until the older generation that came out of Egypt had all died (chap. xiii. and xiv.); (2) all that is related of the execution of this divine judgment, extending from the end of the second year to the reassembling of the congregation at Kadesh at the beginning of the fortieth year, is the history of the rebellion and destruction of Korah (chap. xvi.-xvii. 15), which is preceded by laws relating to the offering of sacrifices after entering Canaan, to the punishment of blasphemers, and to mementos upon the clothes (chap. xv.), and followed by the divine institution of the Aaronic priesthood (chap. xvii. 16-28), with directions as to the duties and rights of the priests and Levites (chap. xviii.), and the law concerning purification from uncleanness arising from contact with the dead (chap. xix.); (3) the journey of Israel in the fortieth year from Kadesh to Mount Hor, round Mount Seir, past Moab, and through the territory of the Amorites to the heights of Pisgah, with the defeat of the kings of the Amorites, Sihon and Og, and the conquest of their kingdoms in Gilead and Bashan (chap. xx. and xxi.). In the THIRD part (chap. xxii.-xxxvi.), the events which occurred in the steppes of Moab, on the eastern side of the plain of Jordan, are gathered into five groups, with the laws that were given there, viz. (1) the attempts of the Moabites and Midianites to destroy the people of Israel, first by the force of Balaam's curse, which was turned against his will into a blessing (chap. xxii.-xxiv.), and then by the seduction of the Israelites to idolatry (chap. xxv.); (2) the fresh numbering of the people according to their families (chap. xxvi.), together with a rule for the inheritance of landed property by daughters (chap. xxvii. 1-11), and the appointment of Joshua as the successor of Moses (chap. xxvii. 12-23); (3) laws relating to the sacrifices to be offered by the congregation on the Sabbath and feast days, and to the binding character of vows made by dependent persons (chap. xxviii.-xxx.); (4) the defeat of the Midianites (chap. xxxi.), the division of the land that had been conquered on the other side of the Jordan among the tribes of Reuben, Gad, and half Manasseh (chap. xxxii.), and the list of the halting-places (chap. xxxiii. 1-49); (5) directions as to the expulsion of the Canaanites, the conquest of Canaan and division of it among the tribes of Israel, the Levites and free cities, and the marriage of heiresses (chap. xxxiii. 50-xxxvi.).

EXPOSITION.

I. PREPARATIONS FOR THE DEPARTURE OF ISRAEL FROM SINAI.

CHAP. I. 1–X. 10.

NUMBERING OF THE PEOPLE OF ISRAEL AT SINAI.— CHAP. I.–IV.

FOUR weeks after the erection of the tabernacle (cf. chap. i. 1 and
Ex. xl. 17), Moses had the number of the whole congregation taken,
by the command of God, according to the families and fathers'
houses of the twelve tribes, and a list made of all the males above
twenty years of age for service in the army of Jehovah (chap. i.
1–3). Nine months before, the numbering of the people had taken
place for the purpose of collecting atonement-money from every
male of twenty years old and upwards (Ex. xxx. 11 sqq., compared
with chap. xxxviii. 25, 26), and the result was 603,550, the same
number as is given here as the sum of all that were mustered in the
twelve tribes (chap. i. 46). This correspondence in the number of
the male population after the lapse of a year is to be explained, as
we have already observed at Ex. xxx. 16, simply from the fact that
the result of the previous census, which was taken for the purpose
of raising head-money from every one who was fit for war, was
taken as the basis of the mustering of all who were fit for war,
which took place after the erection of the tabernacle ; so that,
strictly speaking, this mustering merely consisted in the registering
of those who had been numbered in the public records, according
to their families and fathers' houses. It is most probable, however,
that the numbering and registering took place according to the
classification adopted at Jethro's suggestion for the administration
of justice, viz. in thousands, hundreds, fifties, and tens (Ex. xviii.
25), and that the number of men in the different tribes was reckoned
in this way simply by thousands, hundreds, and tens,—a conclusion
which we may draw from the fact, that there are no units given in
the case of any of the tribes. On this plan the supernumerary
units might be used to balance the changes that had taken place in
the actual condition of the families and fathers' houses, between the
numbering and the preparation of the muster-rolls, so that the few

changes that had occurred in the course of nine months among those who were fit for war were not taken any further into consideration, on account of their being so inconsiderable in relation to the total result. A fresh census was taken 38 years later in the steppes of Moab (chap. xxvi.), for the division of the land of Canaan among the tribes according to the number of their families (chap. xxxiii. 54). The number which this gave was 601,730 men of twenty years old and upwards, not a single one of whom, with the exception of Joshua and Caleb, was included among those that were mustered at Sinai, because the whole of that generation had died in the wilderness (chap. xxvi. 63 sqq.). In the historical account, instead of these exact numbers, the number of adult males is given in a round sum of 600,000 (chap. xi. 21; Ex. xii. 37). To this the Levites had to be added, of whom there were 22,000 males at the first numbering and 23,000 at the second, reckoning the whole from a month old and upwards (chap. iii. 39, xxvi. 62). Accordingly, on the precarious supposition that the results obtained from the official registration of births and deaths in our own day furnish any approximative standard for the people of Israel, who had grown up under essentially different territorial and historical circumstances, the whole number of the Israelites in the time of Moses would have been about two millions.[1]

Modern critics have taken offence at these numbers, though without sufficient reason.[2] When David had the census taken by

[1] Statistics show that, out of 10,000 inhabitants in any country, about 5580 are over twenty years of age (cf. *Chr. Bernoulli, Hdb. der Populationistik*, 1841). This is the case in Belgium, where, out of 1000 inhabitants, 421 are under twenty years of age. According to the Danish census of 1840, out of 1000 inhabitants there were—

In Denmark, under twenty years of age, 432; above twenty, 568
Schleswig, „ „ 436; „ 564
Holstein, „ „ 460; „ 540
Lauenburg, „ „ 458; „ 542

According to this standard, if there were 600,000 males in Israel above twenty years of age, there would be in all 1,000,000 or 1,100,000 males, and therefore, including the females, more than two millions.

[2] *Knobel* has raised the following objections to the historical truth or validity of the numbers given above : (1.) So large a number could not possibly have lived for any considerable time in the peninsula of Sinai, as modern travellers estimate the present population at not more than from four to seven thousand, and state that the land could never have been capable of sustaining a population of 50,000. But the books of Moses do not affirm that the Israelites lived for forty years upon the natural produce of the desert, but that they were fed mira-

Joab, in the closing years of his reign, there were 800,000 men capable of bearing arms in Israel, and 500,000 in Judah (2 Sam. xxiv. 9). Now, if we suppose the entire population of a country to be about four times the number of its fighting men, there would be

culously with manna by God (see at Ex. xvi. 31). Moreover, the peninsula of Sinai yielded much more subsistence in ancient times than is to be found there at present, as is generally admitted, and only denied by *Knobel* in the interests of rationalism. The following are *Ritter's* remarks in his *Erdkunde*, 14, pp. 926–7: "We have repeatedly referred above to the earlier state of the country, which must have been vastly different from that of the present time. The abundant vegetation, for example; the larger number of trees, and their superiority in size, the destruction of which would be followed by a decrease in the quantity of smaller shrubs, etc.; also the greater abundance of the various kinds of food of which the children of Israel could avail themselves in their season; the more general cultivation of the land, as seen in the monumental period of the earliest Egyptians, viz. the period of their mines and cities, as well as in Christian times in the wide-spread remains of monasteries, hermitages, walls, gardens, fields, and wells; and, lastly, the possibility of a better employment of the temporary flow of water in the wadys, and of the rain, which falls by no means unfrequently, but which would need to be kept with diligence and by artificial means for the unfruitful periods of the year, as is the case in other districts of the same latitude. These circumstances, which are supported by the numerous inscriptions of Sinai and Serbal, together with those in the Wady Mokatteb and a hundred other valleys, as well as upon rocky and mountainous heights, which are now found scattered in wild solitude and utter neglect throughout the whole of the central group of mountains, prove that at one time a more numerous population both could and did exist there." (2.) "If the Israelites had been a nation of several millions in the Mosaic age, with their bravery at that time, they would have conquered the small land more easily and more rapidly than they seem to have done according to the accounts in the books of Joshua, Judges, and Samuel, which show that they were obliged to tolerate the Canaanites for a long time, that they were frequently oppressed by them, and that it was not till the time of David and Solomon that their supremacy was completely established." This objection of *Knobel's* is founded upon the supposition that the tribes of Canaan were very small and weak. But where has he learned that? As they had no less than 31 kings, according to Josh. xii., and dwelt in many hundreds of towns, they can hardly have been numerically weaker than the Israelites with their 600,000 men, but in all probability were considerably stronger in numbers, and by no means inferior in bravery; to say nothing of the fact that the Israelites neither conquered Canaan under Joshua by the strength of their hands, nor failed to exterminate them afterwards from want of physical strength. (3.) Of the remaining objections, viz. that so large a number could not have gone through the Arabian Gulf in a single night, or crossed the Jordan in a day, that Joshua could not have circumcised the whole of the males, etc., the first has been answered in vol. ii. (pp. 46, 47), by a proof that it was possible for the Red Sea to be crossed in the given time, and the others will be answered when we come to the particular events referred to.

about five millions of inhabitants in Palestine at that time. The area of this land, according to the boundaries given in chap. xxxiv. 2–12, the whole of which was occupied by Israel and Judah in the time of David, with the exception of a small strip of the Phœnician coast, was more than 500 square miles.[1] Accordingly there would be 10,000 inhabitants to each square mile (German); a dense though by no means unparalleled population;[2] so that it is certainly possible that in the time of Christ it may have been more numerous still, according to the accounts of *Josephus*, which are confirmed by *Dio Cassius* (cf. *C. v. Raumer, Palästina*, p. 93). And if Canaan could contain and support five millions of inhabitants in the flourishing period of the Israelitish kingdom, two millions or more could easily have settled and been sustained in the time of Joshua and the Judges, notwithstanding the fact that there still remained large tracts of land in the possession of the Canaanites and Philistines, and that the Israelites dwelt in the midst of the Canaanitish population which had not yet been entirely eradicated (Judg. iii. 1–5).

If we compare together the results of the two numberings in the second and fortieth years of their march, we shall find a considerable increase in some of the tribes, and a large decrease in others. The number of men of twenty years old and upwards in the different tribes was as follows :—

	First Numbering.	Second Numbering.
Reuben, ...	46,500	43,730
Simeon, ...	59,300	22,200
Gad, ...	45,650	40,500
Judah, ...	74,600	76,500
Issachar, ...	54,400	64,300
Zebulon, ...	57,400	60,500
Ephraim, ...	40,500	32,500
Manasseh, ...	32,200	52,700
Benjamin, ...	35,400	45,600
Dan, ...	62,700	64,400
Asher, ...	41,500	53,400
Naphtali, ...	53,400	45,400
Total, ...	603,550	601,730

Consequently by the second numbering Dan had increased 1700,

[1] The German mile being equal to about five English miles, this would give 12,500 square miles English.

[2] In the kingdom of Saxony (according to the census of the year 1855) there are 7501 persons to the square mile; in Belgium (according to the census of

Judah 1900, Zebulon 3100, Issachar 9900, Benjamin 10,200, Asher 11,900, Manasseh 20,900. This increase, which was about 19 per cent. in the case of Issachar, 29 per cent. in that of Benjamin and Asher, and 63 per cent. in that of Manasseh, is very large, no doubt; but even that of Manasseh is not unparalleled. The total population of Prussia increased from 10,349,031 to 17,139,288 between the end of 1816 and the end of 1855, that is to say, more than 65 per cent. in 39 years; whilst in England the population increased 47 per cent. between 1815 and 1849, *i.e.* in 34 years. On the other hand, there was a decrease in Reuben of 2770, in Gad of 5150, in Ephraim of 8000, in Naphtali of 8000, and in Simeon of 37,100. The cause of this diminution of 6 per cent. in the case of Reuben, 12 per cent. in Gad, 15 per cent. in Naphtali, 20 per cent. in Ephraim, and nearly 63 per cent. in Simeon, it is most natural to seek for in the different judgments which fell upon the nation. If it be true, as the earlier commentators conjectured, with great plausibility, on account of the part taken by Zimri, a prince of the tribe (chap. xxv. 6, 14), that the Simeonites were the worst of those who joined in the idolatrous worship of Baal Peor, the plague, in which 24,000 men were destroyed (chap. xxv. 9), would fall upon them with greater severity than upon the other tribes; and this would serve as the principal explanation of the circumstance, that in the census which was taken immediately afterwards, the number of men in that tribe who were capable of bearing arms had melted away to 22,200. But for all that, the total number included in the census had only been reduced by 1820 men during the forty years of their journeying through the wilderness.

The tribe of Levi appears very small in comparison with the rest of the tribes. In the second year of their journey, when the first census was taken, it only numbered 22,000 males of a month old and upwards; and in the fortieth year, when the second was taken, only 23,000 (chap. iii. 39, xxvi. 62). " Reckoning," says

1856) 8462; and in the district of Düsseldorf there are 98·32 square miles and (according to the census of 1855) 1,007,570 inhabitants, so that there must be 10,248 persons to the square mile. Consequently, not only could more than five millions have lived in Palestine, but, if we take into account on the one hand what is confirmed by both biblical and other testimonies, viz. the extraordinary fertility of the land in ancient times (cf. *v. Raumer, Pal.* pp. 92 sqq.), and on the other hand the well-known fact that the inhabitants of warm countries require less food than Europeans living in colder climates, they could also have found a sufficient supply of food.

Knobel, " that in Belgium, for example, in the rural districts, out of 10,000 males, 1074 die in the first month after their birth, and 3684 between the first month and the twentieth year, so that only 5242 are then alive, the tribe of Levi would only number about 13,000 men of 20 years old and upwards, and consequently would not be half as numerous as the smallest of the other tribes, whilst it would be hardly a sixth part the size of Judah, which was the strongest of the tribes." But notwithstanding this, the correctness of the numbers given is not to be called in question. It is not only supported by the fact, that the number of the Levites capable of service between the ages of 30 and 50 amounted to 8580 (chap. iv. 48),— a number which bears the most perfect proportion to that of 22,000 of a month old and upwards,—but is also confirmed by the fact, that in the time of David the tribe of Levi only numbered 38,000 of thirty years old and upwards (1 Chron. xxiii. 3); so that in the interval between Moses and David their rate of increase was still below that of the other tribes, which had grown from 600,000 to 1,300,000 in the same time. Now, if we cannot discover any reason for this smaller rate of increase in the tribe of Levi, we see, at any rate, that it was not uniform in the other tribes. If Levi was not half as strong as Manasseh in the first numbering, neither Manasseh nor Benjamin was half as strong as Judah ; and in the second numbering, even Ephraim had not half the number of men that Judah had.

A much greater difficulty appears to lie in the fact, that the number of all the male first-born of the twelve tribes, which was only 22,273 according to the census taken for the purpose of their redemption by the Levites (chap. iii. 43), bore no kind of proportion to the total number of men capable of bearing arms in the whole of the male population, as calculated from these. If the 603,550 men of twenty years old and upwards presuppose, according to what has been stated above, a population of more than a million males ; then, on the assumption that 22,273 was the sum total of the first-born sons throughout the entire nation, there would be only one first-born to 40 or 45 males, and consequently every father of a family must have begotten, or still have had, from 39 to 44 sons ; whereas the ordinary proportion of first-born sons to the whole male population is one to four. But the calculation which yields this enormous disproportion, or rather this inconceivable proportion, is founded upon the supposition that the law, which commanded the sanctification of the male first-born, had a retrospective force, and was to be understood as requiring that not only the first-born sons, who were born from the time when the law was given, but all the first-born sons throughout the entire nation, should be offered to the Lord and redeemed with five shekels each, even though they were fathers or grandfathers, or even great-grand-fathers, at that time. Now if the law is to be interpreted in this sense, as having a retrospective force, and applying to those who were born before it was issued, as it has been from the time of *J. D. Michaelis* down to that of *Knobel*, it is an unwarrantable liberty to restrict its application to the first-born sons, who had not yet become fathers themselves,—a mere subterfuge, in fact, invented for the purpose of getting rid of the disproportion, but without answering the desired end.[1] If we look more closely at the law, we cannot find in the words themselves " all the first-born, whatsoever

---

[1] This is evident from the different attempts which have been made to get rid of the difficulty, in accordance with this hypothesis. *J. D. Michaelis* thought that he could explain the disproportion from the prevalence of poly-gamy among the Israelites ; but he has overlooked the fact, that polygamy never prevailed among the Israelites, or any other people, with anything like the universality which this would suppose. *Hävernick* adopted this view, but differed so far from *Michaelis*, that he understood by *first-born* only those who were so on both the father's and mother's side,—a supposition which does not remove the difficulty, but only renders it perfectly incredible. Others ima-gined, that only those first-born were counted who had been born as the result of marriages contracted within the last six years. *Baumgarten* supports this on the ground that, according to Lev. xxvii. 6, the redemption-fee for boys of this age was five shekels (chap. iii. 47) ; but this applies to vows, and proves nothing in relation to first-born, who could not have been the object of a vow (Lev. xxvii. 26). *Bunsen* comes to the same conclusion, on the ground that it was at this age that children were generally dedicated to Moloch (*sic!*). Lastly, *Kurtz* endeavours to solve the difficulty, first, by referring to the great fruitful-ness of the Israelitish women ; secondly, by excluding, (*a*) the first-born of the father, unless at the same time the first-born of the mother ; (*b*) all the first-born who were fathers of families themselves ; and thirdly, by observing, that in a population of 600,000 males above 20 years of age, we may assume that there would be about 200,000 under the age of fifteen. Now, if we deduct these 200,000 who were not yet fifteen, from the 600,000 who were above twenty, there would remain 400,000 married men. " In that case the total number of 22,273 first-born would yield this proportion, that there would be one first-born to nine male births. And on the ground assigned under No. 2 (*a*), this proportion would have to be reduced one-half. So that for every family we should have, on an average, four or five sons, or nine children,—a result by no means surprising, considering the fruitfulness of Hebrew marriages." This would be undoubtedly true, and the *facit* of the calculation quite correct, as $9 \times 22,273 = 200,457$, if only the subtraction upon which it is based were recon-cilable with the rules of arithmetic, or if the reduction of 600,000 men to 400,000 could in any way be justified.

openeth the womb" (Ex. xiii. 2, cf. Num. iii. 12), or in the *ratio legis*, or in the circumstances under which the law was given, either a necessity or warrant for any such explanation or extension. According to Ex. xiii. 2, after the institution of the Passover and its first commemoration, God gave the command, " Sanctify unto Me all the first-born both of man and of beast ;" and added, according to vers. 11 sqq., the further explanation, that when the Israelites came into the land of Canaan, they were to set apart every first-born unto the Lord, but to redeem their first-born sons. This further definition places it beyond all doubt, that what God prescribed to His people was not a supplementary sanctification of all the male first-born who were then to be found in Israel, but simply the sanctification of all that should be born from that time forward. A confirmation of this is to be found in the explanation given in Num. iii. 13 and viii. 17: " All the first-born are Mine ; for on the day that I smote all the first-born in the land of Egypt, I hallowed unto Me all the first-born in Israel, both man and beast." According to this distinct explanation, God had actually sanctified to Himself all the first-born of Israel by the fact, that through the blood of the paschal lamb He granted protection to His people from the stroke of the destroyer (Ex. xii. 22, 23), and had instituted the Passover, in order that He might therein adopt the whole nation of Israel, with all its sons, as the people of *His* possession, or induct the nation which He had chosen as His first-born son (Ex. iv. 22) into the condition of a child of God. This condition of sonship was henceforth to be practically manifested by the Israelites, not only by the yearly repetition of the feast of Passover, but also by the presentation of all the male first-born of their sons and their cattle to the Lord, the first-born of the cattle being sacrificed to Him upon the altar, and the first-born sons being redeemed from the obligation resting upon them to serve at the sanctuary of their God. Of course the reference was only to the first-born of men and cattle that should come into the world from that time forward, and not to those whom God had already sanctified to Himself, by sparing the Israelites and their cattle.[1]

---

[1] *Vitringa* drew the correct conclusion from Ex. xiii. 11, 12, in combination with the fact that this law was not carried out previous to the adoption of the Levites in the place of the first-born for service at the sanctuary—that the law was intended chiefly for the future : " This law," he observes (in his *Obs. ss.* L. ii. c. 2, § 13), " relates to the tabernacle to be afterwards erected, and to the regular priests to be solemnly appointed ; when this law, with many others of a

This being established, it follows that the 22,273 first-born, who were exchanged for the Levites (ch. iii. 45 sqq.), consisted only of the first-born sons who had been born between the time of the exodus from Egypt and the numbering of the twelve tribes, which took place thirteen months afterwards. Now, if, in order to form an idea of the proportion which this number would bear to the whole of the male population of the twelve tribes of Israel, we avail ourselves of the results furnished by modern statistics, we may fairly assume, according to these, that in a nation comprising 603,550 males above 20 years of age, there would be 190,000 to 195,100 between the ages of 20 and 30.[1] And, supposing that this was the age at which the Israelites married, there would be from 19,000 to 19,500 marriages contracted upon an average every year ; and in a nation which had grown up in a land so celebrated as Egypt was in antiquity for the extraordinary fruitfulness of its inhabitants, almost as many first-born, say at least 19,000, might be expected to come into the world. This average number would be greater if we fixed the age for marrying between 18 and 28, or reduced it to the seven years between 18 and 25.[2] But even without doing this, we must take into consideration the important fact that such averages, based upon a considerable length of time, only give an approximative idea of the actual state of things in any single year ; and that, as a matter of fact, in years of oppression and distress the numbers may sink to half the average, whilst in other

similar kind, would have to be observed. The first-born were set apart by God to be consecrated to Him, as servants of the priests and of the sacred things, either in their own persons, or in that of others who were afterwards substituted in the goodness of God. This command therefore presupposed the erection of the tabernacle, the ordination of priests, the building of an altar, and the ceremonial of the sacred service, and showed from the very nature of the case, that there could not be any application of this law of the first-born before that time."

[1] According to the census of the town of Basle, given by *Bernoulli* in his *Populationistik*, p. 42, and classified by age, out of 1000 inhabitants in the year 1837, there were 326 under 20 years of age, 224 between 20 and 30, and 450 of 30 years old and upwards. Now, if we apply this ratio to the people of Israel, out of 603,550 males of 20 years old and upwards, there would be 197,653 between the ages of 20 and 30. The statistics of the city of Vienna and its suburbs, as given by *Brachelli* (*Geographie und Statistik*, 1861), yield very nearly the same results. At the end of the year 1856 there were 88,973 male inhabitants under 20 years of age, 44,000 between 20 and 30, and 97,853 of 30 years old and upwards, not including the military and those who were in hospitals. According to this ratio, out of the 603,550 Israelites above 20 years of age, 187,209 would be between 20 and 30.

[2] From a comparison with the betrothals which take place every year in

years, under peculiarly favourable circumstances, they may rise again to double the amount.[1] When the Israelites were groaning under the hard lash of the Egyptian taskmasters, and then under the inhuman and cruel edict of Pharaoh, which commanded all the Hebrew boys that were born to be immediately put to death, the number of marriages no doubt diminished from year to year. But the longer this oppression continued, the greater would be the number of marriages concluded at once (especially in a nation rejoicing in the promise of numerous increase which it had received from its God), when Moses had risen up and proved himself, by the mighty signs and wonders with which he smote Egypt and its haughty king, to be the man whom the God of the fathers had sent and endowed with power to redeem His nation out of the bondage of Egypt, and lead it into Canaan, the good land that He had promised to the fathers. At that time, when the spirits of the nation revived, and the hope of a glorious future filled every heart, there might very well have been about 38,000 marriages contracted in a year, say from the time of the seventh plague, three months before the exodus, and about 37,600 children born by the second month of the second year after the exodus, 22,273 of them being boys, as the proportion of male births to female varies very remarkably, and may be shown to have risen even as high as 157 to 100, whilst among the Jews of modern times it has frequently been as high as 6 to 5, and has even risen to 3 to 2 (or more exactly 29 to 20).[2]

the Prussian state, it is evident that the number given in the text as the average number of marriages contracted every year is not too high, but most assuredly too low. In the year 1858 there were 167,387 betrothals in a population of 17,793,900; in 1816, on the other hand, there were 117,448 in a population of 10,402,600 (vid. Brachelli, Geog. und Statistik von Preussen, 1861). The first ratio, if applied to Israel with its two millions, would yield 19,000 marriages annually; the second, 22,580; whilst we have, in addition, to bear in mind how many men there are in the European states who would gladly marry, if they were not prevented from doing so by inability to find the means of supporting a house of their own.

[1] How great the variations are in the number of marriages contracted year by year, even in large states embracing different tribes, and when no unusual circumstances have disturbed the ordinary course of things, is evident from the statistics of the Austrian empire as given by Brachelli, from which we may see that in the year 1851, with a total population of 36½ millions, there were 361,249 betrothals, and in the year 1854, when the population had increased by half a million, only 279,802. The variations in particular districts are, as might be supposed, considerably larger.

[2] According to Bernoulli (p. 143), in the city of Geneva, there were 157 boys born to every 100 girls in the year 1832. He also observes, at p. 153: "It is

In this way the problem before us may be solved altogether independently of the question, whether the law relates to all the first-born sons on the father's side, or only to those who were first-born on both father's and mother's side, and without there having been a daughter born before. This latter view we regard as quite unfounded, as a mere subterfuge resorted to for the purpose of removing the supposed disproportion, and in support of which the expression " opening the womb" (*fissura uteri*, i.e. *qui findit uterum*) is pressed in a most unwarrantable manner. On this point, *J. D. Michaelis* has correctly observed, that "the etymology ought not to be too strongly pressed, inasmuch as it is not upon this, but upon usage chiefly, that the force of words depends." It is a fact common to all languages, that in many words the original literal signification falls more and more into the background in the course of years, and at length is gradually lost sight of altogether. Moreover, the expression " openeth the womb" is generally employed in cases in which a common term is required to designate the first-born of both man and beast (Ex. xiii. 2, 12–15, xxxiv. 19, 20 ; Num. iii. 12, 13, viii. 16, 17, xviii. 15 ; Ezek. xx. 16) ; but even then, wherever the two are distinguished, the term בְּכוֹר is applied as a rule to the first-born sons, and פֶּטֶר to the first-born of animals (comp. Ex. xiii. 13*b* with vers. 12 and 13*a* ; and chap. xxxiv. 20*b* with vers. 19 and 20*a*). On the other hand, where only first-born sons are referred to, as in Deut. xxi. 15–17, we look in vain for the expression *peter rechem*, " openeth the womb." Again, the Old Testament, like modern law, recognises only first-born *sons*, and does not apply the term first-born to daughters at all ; and in relation to the inheritance, even in the case of two wives, both of whom had born sons to their husband, it recognises only *one* first-born son, so that the fact of its being the first birth on the mother's side is not taken into consideration at all (cf. Gen. xlvi. 8, xlix. 3 ; Deut. xxi. 15–17). And the established rule in relation to the birth-right,—namely, that the first son of the father was called the first-born, and possessed all the rights of the first-born, independently

remarkable that, according to a very frequent observation, there are an unusual number of boys born among the Jews ; " and as a proof, he cites the fact that, according to *Burdach*, the lists of births in Leghorn show 120 male children born among the Jews to 100 female, whilst, according to *Hufeland*, there were 528 male Jews and 365 female born in Berlin in the course of 16 years, the proportion therefore being 145 to 100. And, according to this same proportion, we have calculated above, that there would be 15,327 girls to 22,273 boys.

altogether of the question whether there had been daughters born before,—would no doubt be equally applicable to the sanctification of the first-born sons. Or are we really to believe, that inasmuch as the child first born is quite as often a girl as a boy, God exempted every father in Israel whose eldest child was a daughter from the obligation to manifest his own sonship by consecrating his first-born son to God, and so demanded the performance of this duty from half the nation only? We cannot for a moment believe that such an interpretation of the law as this would really be in accordance with the spirit of the Old Testament economy.

Chap. i. MUSTER OF THE TWELVE TRIBES, WITH THE EXCEPTION OF THAT OF LEVI.—Vers. 1–3. Before the departure of Israel from Sinai, God commanded Moses, on the first of the second month in the second year after the exodus from Egypt, to take the number of the whole congregation of the children of Israel, *" according to their families, according to their fathers' houses* (see Ex. vi. 14), *in* (according to) *the number of their names,"* i.e. each one counted singly and entered, but only *" every male according to their heads of twenty years old and upwards"* (see Ex. xxx. 14), viz. only כָּל־יֹצֵא צָבָא *" all who go forth of the army,"* i.e. all the men capable of bearing arms, because by means of this numbering the tribes and their subdivisions were to be organized as hosts of Jehovah, that the whole congregation might fight as an army for the cause of their Lord (see at Ex. vii. 4).

Vers. 4–16. Moses and Aaron, who were commanded to number, or rather to muster, the people, were to have with them *" a man of every tribe, who was head-man of his fathers' houses,"* i.e. a tribe-prince, viz. to help them to carry out the mustering. *Beth aboth* ("fathers' houses"), in ver. 2, is a technical expression for the subdivisions in which the *mishpachoth*, or families of the tribes, were arranged, and is applied in ver. 4 according to its original usage, based upon the natural division of the tribes into *mishpachoth* and families, to the fathers' houses which every tribe possessed in the family of its first-born. In vers. 5–15, these heads of tribes are mentioned by name, as in chap. ii. 3 sqq., vii. 12 sqq., x. 14 sqq. In ver. 16 they are designated as *" called men of the congregation,"* because they were called to diets of the congregation, as representatives of the tribes, to regulate the affairs of the nation ; also *" princes of the tribes of their fathers,"* and *" heads of the thousands of Israel:" " princes,"* from the nobility of their birth ; and "*heads*," as chiefs of the *alaphim* composing the tribes. *Alaphim* is equivalent to *mishpachoth* (cf. chap. x. 4; Josh. xxii. 14); because the number of heads of families in the *mishpachoth* of a tribe might easily amount to a *thousand* (see at Ex. xviii. 25). In a similar manner, the term "*hundred*" in the old German came to be used in several different senses (see *Grimm, deutsche Rechts-alter-thümer*, p. 532).

Vers. 17–47. This command was carried out by Moses and Aaron. They took for this purpose the twelve heads of tribes who are pointed out (see at Lev. xxiv. 11) by name, and had the whole congregation gathered together by them and enrolled in genealogical tables. הִתְיַלֵּד, to *announce themselves as born, i.e.* to have themselves entered in genealogical registers (books of generations). This entry is called a פָּקַד, *mustering*, in ver. 19, etc. In vers. 20–43 the number is given of those who were mustered of all the different tribes, and in vers. 44–47 the total of the whole nation, with the exception of the tribe of Levi. "*Their generations*" (vers. 20, 22, 24, etc.), *i.e.* those who were begotten by them, so that "*the sons of Reuben, Simeon*," etc., are mentioned as the fathers from whom the *mishpachoth* and fathers' houses had sprung. The לְ before בְּנֵי שִׁמְעוֹן in ver. 22, and the following names (in vers. 24, 26, etc.), signifies "*with regard to*" (as in Isa. xxxii. 1; Ps. xvii. 4, etc.).

Vers. 48–54. Moses was not to muster the tribe of Levi along with the children of Israel, *i.e.* with the other tribes, or take their number, but to appoint the Levites for the service of the dwelling of the testimony (Ex. xxxviii. 21), *i.e.* of the tabernacle, that they might encamp around it, might take it down when the camp was broken up, and set it up when Israel encamped again, and that no stranger (*zar*, non-Levite, as in Lev. xxii. 10) might come near it and be put to death (see chap. iii.). The rest of the tribes were to encamp every man in his place of encampment, and by his banner (see at chap. ii. 2), in their hosts (see chap. ii.), that wrath might not come upon the congregation, viz. through the approach of a stranger. קֶצֶף, the wrath of Jehovah, breaking in judgment upon the unholy who approached His sanctuary in opposition to His command (chap. viii. 19, xviii. 5, 22). On the expression "*keep the charge*" (*shamar mishmereth*), see at Gen. xxvi. 5 and Lev. viii. 35.

Chap. ii. ORDER OF THE TWELVE TRIBES IN THE CAMP AND ON THE MARCH.—Vers. 1, 2. The twelve tribes were to encamp each one by his standard, by the signs of their fathers' houses, opposite to the tabernacle (at some distance) round about, and, according to the more precise directions given afterwards, in such order that on every side of the tabernacle three tribes were encamped side by side and united under one banner, so that the twelve tribes formed four large camps or divisions of an army. Between these camps and the court surrounding the tabernacle, the three leading *mishpachoth* of the Levites were to be encamped on three sides, and Moses and Aaron with the sons of Aaron (*i.e.* the priests) upon the fourth, *i.e.* the front or eastern side, before the entrance (chap. iii. 21–38). דֶּגֶל, a standard, banner, or flag, denotes primarily the larger *field sign*, possessed by every division composed of three tribes, which was also the banner of the tribe at the head of each division; and secondarily, in a derivative signification, it denotes the *army* united under one standard, like σημεία, or *vexillum*. It is used thus, for example, in vers. 17, 31, 34, and in combination with מַחֲנֶה in vers. 3, 10, 18, and 25, where " standard of the camp of Judah, Reuben, Ephraim, and Dan" signifies the hosts of the tribes arranged under these banners. אֹתֹת, the *signs* (ensigns), were the smaller flags or banners which were carried at the head of the different tribes and subdivisions of the tribes (the fathers' houses). Neither the Mosaic law, nor the Old Testament generally, gives us any intimation as to the form or character of the standard (*degel*). According to rabbinical tradition, the standard of Judah bore the figure of a lion, that of Reuben the likeness of a man or of a man's head, that of Ephraim the figure of an ox, and that of Dan the figure of an eagle; so that the four living creatures united in the cherubic forms described by Ezekiel were represented upon these four standards.[1]

[1] Jerome Prado, in his commentary upon Ezekiel (chap. i. p. 44), gives the following minute description according to rabbinical tradition : " The different leaders of the tribes had their own standards, with the crests of their ancestors depicted upon them. On the east, above the tent of *Naasson* the first-born of *Judah*, there shone a standard of a green colour, this colour having been adopted by him because it was in a green stone, viz. an emerald, that the name of his forefather Judah was engraved on the breastplate of the high priest (Ex. xxv. 15 sqq.), and on this standard there was depicted a lion, the crest and hieroglyphic of his ancestor Judah, whom Jacob had compared to a lion, saying, ' Judah is a lion's whelp.' Towards the south, above the tent of *Elisur* the son of *Reuben*, there floated a red standard, having the colour of the sardus, on which the name of his father, viz. Reuben, was engraved upon the breastplate of the high priest. The symbol depicted upon this standard was a human head, because Reuben was the first-born, and head of the family. On the west, above the tent of *Elishamah* the son of *Ephraim*, there was a golden flag, on which the

Vers. 3–31. *Order of the tribes in the camp and on the march.*— Vers. 3–9. The standard of the tribe of Judah was to encamp in front, namely towards the east, according to its hosts; and by its side the tribes of Issachar and Zebulun, the descendants of Leah, under the command and banner of Judah: an army of 186,400 men, which was to march out first when the camp was broken up (ver. 9), so that Judah led the way as the champion of his brethren (Gen. xlix. 10).—Ver. 4. "*His host, and those that were numbered of them*" (cf. vers. 6, 8, 11, etc.), *i.e.* the army according to its numbered men.—Vers. 10–16. On the south side was the standard of Reuben, with which Simeon and Gad, descendants of Leah and her maid Zilpah, were associated, and to which they were subordinated. In ver. 14, *Reuel* is a mistake for *Deuel* (chap. i. 14, vii. 42, x. 20), which is the reading given here in 118 MSS. cited by *Kennicott* and *De Rossi*, in several of the ancient editions, and in the *Samaritan, Vulgate,* and *Jon. Saad.*, whereas the LXX., *Onk.*, *Syr.*, and *Pers.* read *Reuel.* This army of 151,450 men was to break up and march as the second division.—Ver. 17. The tabernacle, the camp of the Levites, was to break up after this in the midst of the camps (*i.e.* of the other tribes). "*As they encamp, so shall they break up,*" that is to say, with Levi in the midst of the tribes, "*every man in his place, according to his banner.*" רַד, *place,* as in Deut. xxiii. 13, Isa. lvii. 8.—Vers. 18–24. On the west the standard of Ephraim, with the tribes of Manasseh and Benjamin, that is to say, the whole of the descendants of Rachel, 108,100 men, as the third division of the army.—Vers. 25–31. Lastly, towards the north was the standard of Gad, with Asher and Naphtali, the descendants of the maids Bilhah and Zilpah, 157,600 men, who were

head of a calf was depicted, because it was through the vision of the calves or oxen that his ancestor Joseph had predicted and provided for the famine in Egypt (Gen. xli.); and hence Moses, when blessing the tribe of Joseph, *i.e.* Ephraim (Deut. xxxiii. 17), said, 'his glory is that of the first-born of a bull.' The golden splendour of the standard of Ephraim resembled that of the chrysolite, in which the name of Ephraim was engraved upon the breastplate. Towards the north, above the tent of *Ahiezer* the son of *Dan,* there floated a motley standard of white and red, like the jaspis (or, as some say, a carbuncle), in which the name of Dan was engraved upon the breastplate. The crest upon this was an eagle, the great foe to serpents, which had been chosen by the leader in the place of a serpent, because his forefather Jacob had compared Dan to a serpent, saying, 'Dan is a serpent in the way, an adder (*cerastes*, a horned snake) in the path;' but Ahiezer substituted the eagle, the destroyer of serpents, as he shrank from carrying an adder upon his flag."

to be the last to break up, and formed the rear on the march.—Ver. 31. לְדִגְלֵיהֶם (*according to their standards*) is equivalent to לְצִבְאֹתָם (*according to their hosts*) in vers. 9, 16, and 24, *i.e.* according to the hosts of which they consisted.

Vers. 32–34. In ver. 32 we have the whole number given, 603,550 men, not including the Levites (ver. 33, see at chap. i. 49); and in ver. 34 the concluding remark as to the subsequent execution of the divine command,—an anticipatory notice, as in Ex. xii. 50, xl. 16, etc.

Chap. iii. MUSTER OF THE TRIBE OF LEVI.—As Jacob had adopted the two sons of Joseph as his own sons, and thus promoted them to the rank of heads of tribes, the tribe of Levi formed, strictly speaking, the thirteenth tribe of the whole nation, and was excepted from the muster of the twelve tribes who were destined to form the army of Jehovah, because God had chosen it for the service of the sanctuary. Out of this tribe God had not only called Moses to be the deliverer, lawgiver, and leader of His people, but Moses' brother Aaron, with the sons of the latter, to be the custodians of the sanctuary. And now, lastly, the whole tribe was chosen, in the place of the first-born of all the tribes, to assist the priests in performing the duties of the sanctuary, and was numbered and mustered for this its special calling.

Vers. 1–4. In order to indicate at the very outset the position which the Levites were to occupy in relation to the priests (viz. Aaron and his descendants), the account of their muster commences not only with the enumeration of the sons of Aaron who were chosen as priests (vers. 2–4), but with the heading: " *These are the generations of Aaron and Moses in the day* (*i.e.* at the time) *when Jehovah spake with Moses in Mount Sinai* (ver. 1). The *toledoth* (see at Gen. ii. 4) of Moses and Aaron are not only the families which sprang from Aaron and Moses, but the Levitical families generally, which were named after Aaron and Moses, because they were both of them raised into the position of heads or spiritual fathers of the whole tribe, namely, at the time when God spoke to Moses upon Sinai. Understood in this way, the notice as to the time is neither a superfluous repetition, nor introduced with reference to the subsequent numbering of the people in the steppes of Moab (chap. xxvi. 57 sqq.). Aaron is placed before Moses here (see at Ex. vi. 26 sqq.), not merely as being the elder of the two, but because his sons received the priesthood, whilst the sons of

Moses, on the contrary, were classed among the rest of the Levitical families (cf. 1 Chron. xxiii. 14).—Vers. 2 sqq. Names of the sons of Aaron, the " *anointed priests* (see Lev. viii. 12), *whose hand they filled to be priests,*" *i.e.* who were appointed to the priesthood (see at Lev. vii. 37). On Nadab and Abihu, see Lev. x. 1, 2. As they had neither of them any children when they were put to death, Eleazar and Ithamar were the only priests " *in the sight of Aaron their father,*" *i.e.* during his lifetime. "*In the sight of :*" as in Gen. xi. 28.

Vers. 5–10. The Levites are placed before Aaron the priest, to be his servants.—Ver. 6. "*Bring near :*" as in Ex. xxviii. 1. The expression עָמַד לִפְנֵי is frequently met with in connection with the position of a servant, as standing before his master to receive his commands.—Ver. 7. They were to keep the charge of Aaron and the whole congregation before the tabernacle, to attend to the service of the dwelling, *i.e.* to observe what Aaron (the priest) and the whole congregation were bound to perform in relation to the service at the dwelling-place of Jehovah. "*To keep the charge :*" see chap. i. 53 and Gen. xxvi. 5. In ver. 8 this is more fully explained : they were to keep the vessels of the tabernacle, and to attend to all that was binding upon the children of Israel in relation to them, *i.e.* to take the oversight of the furniture, to keep it safe and clean.—Ver. 9. Moses was also to give the Levites to Aaron and his sons. "*They are wholly given to him out of the children of Israel :*" the repetition of נְתוּנִם here and in chap. viii. 16 is emphatic, and expressive of complete surrender (*Ewald,* § 313). The Levites, however, as *nethunim,* must be distinguished from the *nethinim* of non-Israelitish descent, who were given to the Levites at a later period as temple slaves, to perform the lowest duties connected with the sanctuary (see at Josh. ix. 27).—Ver. 10. Aaron and his sons were to be appointed by Moses to take charge of the priesthood ; as no stranger, no one who was not a son of Aaron, could approach the sanctuary without being put to death (cf. chap. i. 53 and Lev. xxii. 10).

Vers. 11–13. God appointed the Levites for this service, because He had decided to adopt them as His own in the place of all the first-born of Egypt. When He slew the first-born of Egypt, He sanctified to Himself all the first-born of Israel, of man and beast, for His own possession (see Ex. xiii. 1, 2). By virtue of this sanctification, which was founded upon the adoption of the whole nation as His first-born son (see vol. ii. p. 33), the nation was required to dedicate to Him its first-born sons for service at the sanctuary, and sacrifice all the first-born of its cattle to Him. But now the Levites and their cattle were to be adopted in their place, and the first-born sons of Israel to be released in return (vers. 40 sqq.). By this arrangement, through which the care of the service at the sanctuary was transferred to one tribe, which would and should henceforth devote itself with undivided interest to this vocation, not only was a more orderly performance of this service secured, than could have been effected through the first-born of all the tribes; but so far as the whole nation was concerned, the fulfilment of its obligations in relation to this service was undoubtedly facilitated. Moreover, the Levites had proved themselves to be the most suitable of all the tribes for this post, through their firm and faithful defence of the honour of the Lord at the worship of the golden calf (Ex. xxxii. 26 sqq.). It is in this spirit, which distinguished the tribe of Levi, that we may undoubtedly discover the reason why they were chosen by God for the service of the sanctuary, and not in the fact that Moses and Aaron belonged to the tribe, and desired to form a hierarchical caste of the members of their own tribe, such as was to be found among other nations : the magi, for example, among the Medes, the Chaldeans among the Persians, and the Brahmins among the Indians. לִי אֲנִי יְהֹוָה, "to Me, to Me, Jehovah" (vers. 13, 41, and 45; cf. Ges. § 121, 3).

Vers. 14–20. The muster of the Levites included all the males from a month old and upwards, because they were to be sanctified to Jehovah in the place of the first-born; and it was at the age of a month that the latter were either to be given up or redeemed (comp. vers. 40 and 43 with chap. xviii. 16). In vers. 17–20 the sons of Levi and their sons are enumerated, who were the founders of the *mishpachoth* among the Levites, as in Ex. vi. 16–19.

Vers. 21–26. The Gershonites were divided into two families, containing 7500 males. They were to encamp under their chief Eliasaph, behind the tabernacle, *i.e.* on the western side (vers. 23, 24), and were to take charge of the dwelling-place and the tent, the covering, the curtain at the entrance, the hangings round the court with the curtains at the door, and the cords of the tent, " *in relation to all the service thereof*" (vers. 25 sqq.) ; that is to say, according to the more precise injunctions in chap. iv. 25–27, they were to carry the tapestry of the dwelling (the inner covering, Ex. xxvi. 1 sqq.), and of the tent (*i.e.* the covering made of goats' hair, Ex. xxvi. 7 sqq.), the covering thereof (*i.e.* the covering of rams' skins dyed red, and the covering of sea-cow skin upon the top of

it, Ex. xxvii. 16), the hangings of the court and the curtain at the
entrance (Ex. xxvii. 9, 16), which surrounded the altar (of burnt-
offering) and the dwelling round about, and their cords, *i.e.* the
cords of the tapestry, coverings, and curtains (Ex. xxvii. 14), and
all the instruments of their service, *i.e.* the things used in connection with their service (Ex. xxvii. 19), and were to attend to everything that had to be done to them; in other words, to perform
whatever was usually done with those portions of the sanctuary that
are mentioned here, especially in setting up the tabernacle or taking
it down.   The suffix in מֵיתָרָיו (ver. 26) does not refer to the court
mentioned immediately before; for, according to ver. 37, the Merarites were to carry the cords of the hangings of the court, but to
the "dwelling and tent," which stand farther off. In the same way
the words, "*for all the service thereof*," refer to all those portions of
the sanctuary that are mentioned, and mean "everything that had
to be done or attended to in connection with these things."

Vers. 27–32. The *Kohathites*, who were divided into four families, and numbered 8600, were to encamp on the south side of the
tabernacle, and more especially to keep the charge of the sanctuary
(ver. 28), viz. to take care of the ark of the covenant, the table
(of shew-bread), the candlestick, the altars (of incense and burnt-
offering), with the holy things required for the service performed
in connection therewith, and the curtain (the veil before the most
holy place), and to perform whatever had to be done ("all the
service thereof," see at ver. 26), *i.e.* to carry the said holy things
after they had been rolled up in covers by the priests (see chap. iv.
5 sqq.).—Ver. 32. As the priests also formed part of the Kohathites,
their chief is mentioned as well, viz. *Eleazar* the eldest son of Aaron
the high priest, who was placed over the chiefs of the three Levitical
families, and called פְּקֻדַּה, *oversight of the keepers of the charge of the
sanctuary*," *i.e.* authority, superior, of the servants of the sanctuary.

Vers. 33–37. The *Merarites*, who formed two families, comprising 6200 males, were to encamp on the north side of the tabernacle, under their prince *Zuriel*, and to observe the boards, bolts,
pillars, and sockets of the dwelling-place (Ex. xxvi. 15, 26, 32, 37),
together with all the vessels thereof (the plugs and tools), and all
that had to be done in connection therewith, also the pillars of the
court with their sockets, the plugs and the cords (Ex. xxvii. 10, 19,
xxxv. 18); that is to say, they were to take charge of these when
the tabernacle was taken down, to carry them on the march, and to
fix them when the tabernacle was set up again (chap. iv. 31, 32).

Vers. 38, 39. Moses and Aaron, with the sons of the latter (the priests), were to encamp in front, before the tabernacle, viz. on the eastern side, " *as keepers of the charge of the sanctuary for the charge of the children of Israel*," *i.e.* to attend to everything that was binding upon the children of Israel in relation to the care of the sanctuary, as no stranger was allowed to approach it on pain of death (see chap. i. 51).—Ver. 39. The number of the Levites mustered, 22,000, does not agree with the numbers assigned to the three families, as 7500 + 8600 + 6200 = 22,300. But the total is correct; for, according to ver. 46, the number of the first-born, 22,273, exceeded the total number of the Levites by 273. The attempt made by the Rabbins and others to reconcile the two, by supposing the 300 Levites in excess to be themselves first-born, who were omitted in the general muster, because they were not qualified to represent the first-born of the other tribes, is evidently forced and unsatisfactory. The whole account is so circumstantial, that such a fact as this would never have been omitted. We must rather assume that there is a copyist's error in the number of one of the Levitical families; possibly in ver. 28 we should read שלש for שש (8300 for 8600). The *puncta extraordinaria* above וְאַהֲרֹן are intended to indicate that this word is either suspicious or spurious (see at Gen. xxxiii. 5) ; and it is actually omitted in *Sam.*, *Syr.*, and 12 MSS., but without sufficient reason : for although the divine command to muster the Levites (vers. 5 and 14) was addressed to Moses alone, yet if we compare chap. iv. 1, 34, 37, 41, 45, where the Levites qualified for service are said to have been mustered by Moses and Aaron, and still more chap. iv. 46, where the elders of Israel are said to have taken part in the numbering of the Levites as well as in that of the twelve tribes (chap. i. 3, 4), there can be no reason to doubt that Aaron also took part in the mustering of the whole of the Levites, for the purpose of adoption in the place of the first-born of Israel; and no suspicion attaches to this introduction of his name in ver. 39, although it is not mentioned in vers. 5, 11, 14, 40, and 44.

Vers. 40-51. After this, Moses numbered the first-born of the children of Israel, to exchange them for the Levites according to the command of God, which is repeated in vers. 41 and 44-45 from vers. 11-13, and to adopt the latter in their stead for the service at the sanctuary (on vers. 41 and 45, cf. vers. 11–13). The number of the first-born of the twelve tribes amounted to 22,273 of a month old and upwards (ver. 43). Of this number 22,000 were exchanged for the 22,000 Levites, and the cattle of the Levites were also set against the first-born of the cattle of the tribes of Israel, though without their being numbered and exchanged head for head. In vers. 44 and 45 the command of God concerning the adoption of the Levites is repeated, for the purpose of adding the further instructions with regard to the 273, the number by which the first-born of the tribes exceeded those of the Levites. " And as for the redemption of the 273 (lit. the 273 to be redeemed) of the first-born of the children of Israel which are more than the Levites, thou shalt take five shekels a head," etc. This was the general price established by the law for the redemption of the first-born of men (see chap. xviii. 16). On the sacred shekel, see at Ex. xxx. 13. The redemption money for 273 first-born, in all 1365 shekels, was to be paid to Aaron and his sons as compensation for the persons who properly belonged to Jehovah, and had been appointed as first-born for the service of the priests.—Ver. 49. " The redeemed of the Levites " are the 22,000 who were redeemed by means of the Levites. In ver. 50, the Chethibh הַפְּדֻים is the correct reading, and the Keri הַפְּדֻיִם an unnecessary emendation. The number of the first-born and that of the Levites has already been noticed at pp. 8, 9.

Chap. iv. RULES OF SERVICE, AND NUMBERING OF THE LEVITES QUALIFIED FOR SERVICE.—After the adoption of the Levites for service at the sanctuary, in the place of the first-born of Israel, Moses and Aaron mustered the three families of the Levites by the command of God for the service to be performed by those who were between the ages of 30 and 50. The particulars of the service are first of all described in detail (vers. 4–33); and then the men in each family are taken, of the specified age for service (vers. 34–49). The three families are not arranged according to the relative ages of their founders, but according to the importance or sacredness of their service. The Kohathites take the lead, because the holiest parts of the tabernacle were to be carried and kept by this family, which included the priests, Aaron and his sons. The service to be performed by each of the three Levitical families is introduced in every case by a command from God to take the sum of the men from 30 years old to 50 (see vers. 1–3, 21–23, 29 and 30).

Vers. 2–20. Service of the Kohathites, and the number qualified for service.—Vers. 2, 3. " Take the sum of the sons of Kohath from among the sons of Levi :" i.e. by raising them out of the sum total

of the Levites, by numbering them first and specially, viz. the
men from 30 to 50 years of age, " *every one who comes to the service,*"
i.e. who has to enter upon service " *to do work at the tabernacle.*"
צָבָא (*Angl.* '*host*') signifies military service, and is used here with
special reference to the service of the Levites as the *militia sacra* of
Jehovah.—Ver. 4. The service of the Kohathites at the tabernacle
is (relates to) " *the most holy* " (see at Ex. xxx. 10). This term
includes, as is afterwards explained, the most holy things in the
tabernacle, viz. the ark of the covenant, the table of shew-bread,
the candlestick, the altar of incense and altar of burnt-offering,
together with all the other things belonging to these. When the
camp was broken up, the priests were to roll them up in wrappers,
and hand them ŏver in this state to the Kohathites, for them to
carry (vers. 5–15). First of all (vers. 5, 6), Aaron and his sons
were to take down the curtain between the holy place and the most
holy (see Ex. xxvi. 31), and to cover the ark of testimony with it
(Ex. xxv. 10). Over this they were to place a wrapper of sea-cow
skin (*tachash*, see Ex. xxv. 5), and over this again another covering
of cloth made entirely of hyacinth-coloured purple (as in Ex. xxviii.
31). The sea-cow skin was to protect the inner curtain, which was
covered over the ark, from storm and rain ; the hyacinth purple, to
distinguish the ark of the covenant as the throne of the glory of
Jehovah. Lastly, they were to place the staves into the rings again,
that is to say, the bearing poles, which were always left in their
places on the ark (Ex. xxv. 15), but had necessarily to be taken
out while it was being covered and wrapped up.—Vers. 7, 8. Over
the table of shew-bread (Ex. xxv. 23) they were to spread a hyacinth
cloth, to place the plates, bowls, wine-pitchers, and drink-offering
bowls (Ex. xxv. 29) upon the top of this, and to lay shew-bread
thereon ; and then to spread a crimson cloth over these vessels and
the shew-bread, and cover this with a sea-cow skin, and lastly to put
the bearing poles in their places.—Vers. 9, 10. The candlestick,
with its lamps, snuffers, extinguishers (Ex. xxv. 31–37), and all its
oil-vessels (oil-cans), " *wherewith they serve it,*" *i.e.* prepare it for the
holy service, were to be covered with a hyacinth cloth, and then with
a wrapper of sea-cow skin, and laid upon the carriage. מוֹט (vers.
10 and 12), bearing frame, in chap. xiii. 23 bearing poles.—Vers.
11, 12. So again they were to wrap up the altar of incense (Ex.
xxx. 1), to adjust its bearing poles ; and having wrapped it up in
such coverings, along with the vessels belonging to it, to lay it upon
the frame.—Vers. 13, 14. The altar of burnt-offering was first of

all to be cleansed from the ashes; a crimson cloth was then to be covered over it, and the whole of the furniture belonging to it to be placed upon the top; and lastly, the whole was to be covered with a sea-cow skin. The only thing not mentioned is the copper laver (Ex. xxx. 18), probably because it was carried without any cover at all. The statement in the Septuagint and the Samaritan text, which follows ver. 14, respecting its covering and conveyance upon a frame, is no doubt a spurious interpolation.—Ver. 15. After the priests had completed the wrapping up of all these things, the Kohathites were to come up to carry them; but they were not to touch "the holy" (the holy things), lest they should die (see chap. i. 53, xviii. 3, and comp. 2 Sam. vi. 6, 7).—Ver. 16. The oversight of the oil for the candlestick (Ex. xxvii. 20), the incense (Ex. xxx. 34), the continual meat-offering (Ex. xxix. 40), and the anointing oil (Ex. xxx. 23), belonged to Eleazar as the head of all the Levites (chap. iii. 32). He had also the oversight of the dwelling' and all the holy things and furniture belonging to it; and, as a comparison of vers. 28 and 33 clearly shows, of the services of the Kohathites also.—Vers. 17-20. In order to prevent as far as possible any calamity from befalling the Levites while carrying the most holy things, the priests are again urged by the command of God to do what has already been described in detail in vers. 5–15, lest through any carelessness on their part they should cut off the tribe of the families of the Kohathites, i.e. should cause their destruction; viz. if they should approach the holy things before they had been wrapped up by Aaron and his sons in the manner prescribed and handed over to them to carry. If the Kohathites should come for only a single moment to look at the holy things, they would die. אַל־תַּכְרִיתוּ, "cut ye not off," i.e. "take care that the Kohathites are not cut off through your mistake and negligence" (Ros.). "The tribe of the families of the Kohathites:" shebet, the tribe, is not used here, as it frequently is, in its derivative sense of tribe (tribus), but in the original literal sense of stirps.—Ver. 19. "This do to them:" sc. what is prescribed in vers. 5–15 with reference to their service.—Ver. 20. כְּבַלַּע, "like a swallow, a gulp," is probably a proverbial expression, according to the analogy of Job vii. 19, for "a single instant," of which the Arabic also furnishes examples (see A. Schultens on Job vii. 19). The Sept. rendering, ἐξάπινα, conveys the actual sense. A historical illustration of ver. 20 is furnished by 1 Sam. vi. 19.[1]

[1] According to Knobel, vers. 17-20 have been interpolated by the Jehovist into the Elohistic text. But the reasons for this assumption are weak through-

Vers. 21–28. *The service of the Gershonites* is introduced in vers. 21–23 in the same manner as that of the Kohathites in vers. 1–3; and in vers. 24–26 it is described in accordance with the brief notice and explanation already given in chap. iii. 24–26.—Ver. 27. Their service was to be performed "*according to the mouth (i.e.* according to the appointment) *of Aaron and his sons, with regard to all their carrying* (all that they were to carry), *and all their doing.*"—"*And ye* (the priests) *shall appoint to them for attendance* (in charge) *all their carrying,*" *i.e.* all the things they were to carry. פָּקַד בְּמִשְׁמֶרֶת, to give into keeping. The combination of פָּקַד with בְּ and the accusative of the object is analogous to נָתַן בְּ, to give into a person's hand, in Gen. xxvii. 17; and there is no satisfactory reason for any such emendations of the text as *Knobel* proposes. —Ver. 28. "*Their charge (mishmereth) is in the hand of Ithamar,*" *i.e.* is to be carried out under his superintendence (cf. Ex. xxxviii. 21).

Vers. 29–33. *Service of the Merarites.*—Vers. 29 and 30, like vers. 22 and 23. פָּקַד, to muster, *i.e.* to number, equivalent to נָשָׂא רֹאשׁ, to take the number.—Vers. 31 and 32, like chap. iii. 36 and 37. "*The charge of their burden*" (their carrying), *i.e.* the things which it was their duty to carry.—Ver. 32. לְכָל-כְּלֵיהֶם: with regard to all their instruments, *i.e.* all the things used for setting up, fastening, or undoing the beams, bolts, etc.; see chap. iii. 36, and Ex. xxvii. 19.

Vers. 34–49. Completion of the prescribed mustering, and statement of the number of men qualified for service in the three Levitical families: viz. 2750 Kohathites, 2630 Gershonites, and 3200 Merarites—in all, 8580 Levites fit for service: a number which bears a just proportion to the total number of male Levites of a month old and upwards, viz. 22,000 (see above, p. 9).—Ver. 49. "*According to the commandment of Jehovah, they appointed them through the hand of Moses (i.e.* under his direction), *each one*

out. Neither the peculiar use of the word *shebet*, to which there is no corresponding parallel in the whole of the Old Testament, nor the construction of נָשָׂא with אֵת, which is only met with in 1 Sam. ix. 18 and xxx. 21, nor the *Hiphil* הִכְרִית, can be regarded as criteria of a Jehovistic usage. And the assertion, that the Elohist lays the emphasis upon approaching and touching the holy things (ver. 15, chap. viii. 19, xviii. 3, 22), and not upon seeing or looking at them, rests upon an antithesis which is arbitrarily forced upon the text, since not only seeing (ver. 20), but touching also (ver. 19), is described as causing death; so that seeing and touching form no antithesis at all.

to his service, and his burden, and his mustered things (פְּקֻדָיו), *i.e.* the things assigned to him at the time of the mustering as his special charge (see Ex. xxxviii. 21).

SPIRITUAL ORGANIZATION OF THE CONGREGATION OF ISRAEL.— CHAP. V. AND VI.

From the outward organization of the tribes of Israel as the army of Jehovah, the law proceeds to their internal moral and spiritual order, for the purpose of giving an inward support, both moral and religious, to their outward or social and political unity. This is the object of the directions concerning the removal of unclean persons from the camp (chap. v. 1-4), the restitution of anything unjustly appropriated (vers. 5-10), the course to be pursued with a wife suspected of adultery (vers. 11-31), and also of the laws relating to the Nazarite (chap. vi. 1-21), and to the priestly blessing (vers. 22-27).

Chap. v. 1-4. Removal of Unclean Persons out of the Camp.—As Jehovah, the Holy One, dwelt in the midst of the camp of His people, those who were affected with the uncleanness of leprosy (Lev. xiii.), of a diseased flux, or of menstruation (Lev. xv. 2 sqq., 19 sqq.), and those who had become unclean through touching a corpse (chap. xix. 11 sqq., cf. Lev. xxi. 1, xxii. 4), whether male or female, were to be removed out of the camp, that they might not defile it by their uncleanness. The command of God, to remove these persons out of the camp, was carried out at once by the nation ; and even in Canaan it was so far observed, that lepers at any rate were placed in special pest-houses outside the cities (see at Lev. xiii. 45, 46).

Vers. 5-10. Restitution in case of a Trespass.—No crime against the property of a neighbour was to remain without expiation in the congregation of Israel, which was encamped or dwelt around the sanctuary of Jehovah ; and the wrong committed was not to remain without restitution, because such crimes involved unfaithfulness (מַעַל, see Lev. v. 15) towards Jehovah. *"If a man or a woman do one of the sins of men, to commit unfaithfulness against Jehovah, and the same soul has incurred guilt, they shall confess their sin which they have done, and (the doer) shall recom-*

pense his debt according to its sum" (בְּרֹאשׁוֹ, as in Lev. v. 24), etc.
מִכָּל־חַטֹּאת הָאָדָם, one of the sins occurring among men, not "a sin
against a man" (*Luther, Ros.,* etc). The meaning is a sin, with which
a מַעַל was committed against Jehovah, *i.e.* one of the acts described
in Lev. v. 21, 22, by which injury was done to the property of
a neighbour, whereby a man brought a debt upon himself, for the
wiping out of which a material restitution of the other's property
was prescribed, together with the addition of a fifth of its value,
and also the presentation of a sin-offering (Lev. v. 23–26). To
guard against that disturbance of fellowship and peace in the congregation, which would arise from such trespasses as these, the law
already given in Lev. v. 20 is here renewed and supplemented by
the additional stipulation, that if the man who had been unjustly
deprived of some of his property had no *Goël*, to whom restitution
could be made for the debt, the compensation should be paid to
Jehovah for the priests. The *Goël* was the nearest relative, upon
whom the obligation rested to redeem a person who had fallen into
slavery through poverty (Lev. xxv. 25). The allusion to the *Goël*
in this connection presupposes that the injured person was no
longer alive. To this there are appended, in vers. 9 and 10, the
directions which are substantially connected with this, viz. that
every heave-offering (*terumah,* see at Lev. ii. 9) in the holy gifts of
the children of Israel, which they presented to the priest, was to
belong to him (the priest), and also all the holy gifts which were
brought by different individuals. The reference is not to literal
sacrifices, *i.e.* gifts intended for the altar, but to dedicatory offerings, first-fruits, and such like. אִישׁ אֶת־קֳדָשָׁיו, "*with regard to every
man's, his holy gifts . . . to him* (the priest) *shall they be; what
any man gives to the priest shall belong to him.*" The second clause
serves to explain and confirm the first. אֵת: *as far,* with regard to,
quoad (see *Ewald,* § 277, *d*; Ges. § 117, 2, note).

Vers. 11–31. SENTENCE OF GOD UPON WIVES SUSPECTED
OF ADULTERY.—As any suspicion cherished by a man against his
wife, that she either is or has been guilty of adultery, whether well-
founded or not, is sufficient to shake the marriage connection to its
very roots, and to undermine, along with marriage, the foundation
of the civil commonwealth, it was of the greatest importance to
guard against this moral evil, which was so utterly irreconcilable
with the holiness of the people of God, by appointing a process
in harmony with the spirit of the theocratical law, and adapted

to bring to light the guilt or innocence of any wife who had fallen
into such suspicion, and at the same time to warn fickle wives
against unfaithfulness.   This serves to explain not only the introduction of the law respecting the *jealousy-offering* in this place,
but also the general importance of the subject, and the reason for
its being so elaborately described.

Vers. 12–15. If a man's wife went aside, and was guilty of
unfaithfulness towards him (ver. 13 is an explanatory clause),
through a (another) man having lain with her with emissio seminis,
and it was hidden from the eyes of her husband, on account of her
having defiled herself secretly, and there being no witness against
her, and her not having been taken (in the act); but if, for all that,
a spirit of jealousy came upon him, and he was jealous of his wife,
and she was defiled, . . . or she was not defiled : the man was to
take his wife to the priest, and bring as her sacrificial gift, on her
account, the tenth of an ephah of barley meal, without putting oil
or incense, " *for it is a meat-offering of jealousy, a meat-offering of
memory, to bring iniquity to remembrance.*"   As the woman's crime,
of which her husband accused her, was naturally denied by herself,
and was neither to be supported by witnesses nor proved by her
being taken in the very act, the only way left to determine whether
there was any foundation or not for the spirit of jealousy excited in
her husband, and to prevent an unrighteous severance of the divinely
appointed marriage, was to let the thing be decided by the verdict
of God Himself.   To this end the man was to bring his wife to the
priest with a sacrificial gift, which is expressly called קָרְבָּנָה, *her*
offering, brought עָלֶיהָ " on *her* account," that is to say, with a meat-
offering, the symbol of the fruit of her walk and conduct before
God.   Being the sacrificial gift of a wife who had gone aside and
was suspected of adultery, this meat-offering could not possess the
character of the ordinary meat-offerings, which shadowed forth the
fruit of the sanctification of life in good works (vol. ii. p. 207); could
not consist, that is to say, of fine wheaten flour, but only of barley
meal.   Barley was worth only half as much as wheat (2 Kings vii.
1, 16, 18), so that only the poorer classes, or the people generally in
times of great distress, used barley meal as their daily food (Judg.
vii. 13 ; 2 Kings iv. 42 ; Ezek. iv. 12 ; John vi. 9, 13), whilst those
who were better off used it for fodder (1 Kings v. 8).   Barley meal
was prescribed for this sacrifice, neither as a sign that the adulteress
had conducted herself like an irrational animal (*Philo, Jonathan,
Talm.,* the *Rabb.,* etc.), nor " because the persons presenting the

offering were invoking the punishment of a crime, and not the favour of God" (*Cler.*, *Ros.*) : for the guilt of the woman was not yet established ; nor even, taking a milder view of the matter, to indicate that the offerer might be innocent, and in that case no offering at all was required (*Knobel*), but to represent the questionable repute in which the woman stood, or the ambiguous, suspicious character of her conduct. Because such conduct as hers did not proceed from the Spirit of God, and was not carried out in prayer ; oil and incense, the symbols of the Spirit of God and prayer (see vol. ii. pp. 174 and 209), were not to be added to her offering. It was an offering of jealousy (קְנָאֹת, an intensive plural), and the object was to bring the ground of that jealousy to light ; and in this respect it is called the " *meat-offering of remembrance,*" sc. of the woman, before Jehovah (cf. chap. x. 10, xxxi. 54 ; Ex. xxviii. 12, 29, xxx. 16 ; Lev. xxiii. 24), namely, " *the remembrance of iniquity,*" bringing her crime to remembrance before the Lord, that it might be judged by Him.

Vers. 16–22. The priest was to bring her near to the altar at which he stood, and place her before Jehovah, who had declared Himself to be present at the altar, and then to take holy water, probably water out of the basin before the sanctuary, which served for holy purposes (Ex. xxx. 18), in an earthen vessel, and put dust in it from the floor of the dwelling. He was then to loosen the hair of the woman who was standing before Jehovah, and place the jealousy-offering in her hands, and holding the water in his own hand, to pronounce a solemn oath of purification before her, which she had to appropriate to herself by a confirmatory Amen, Amen. The water, which the priest had prepared for the woman to drink, was taken from the sanctuary, and the dust to be put into it from the floor of the dwelling, to impregnate this drink with the power of the Holy Spirit that dwelt in the sanctuary. The dust was strewed upon the water, not to indicate that man was formed from dust and must return to dust again, but as an allusion to the fact, that dust was eaten by the serpent (Gen. iii. 14) as the curse of sin, and therefore as the symbol of a state deserving a curse, a state of the deepest humiliation and disgrace (Micah vii. 17 ; Isa. xlix. 23 ; Ps. lxxii. 9). On the very same ground, an earthen vessel was chosen ; that is to say, one quite worthless in comparison with the copper one. The loosening of the hair of the head (see Lev. xiii. 45), in other cases a sign of mourning, is to be regarded here as a removal or loosening of the female head-dress, and a symbol of the

loss of the proper ornament of female morality and conjugal
fidelity. During the administration of the oath, the offering was
placed in her hands, that she might bring the fruit of her own
conduct before God, and give it up to His holy judgment. The
priest, as the representative of God, held the vessel in his hand,
with the water in it, which was called the " *water of bitterness, the
curse-bringing*," inasmuch as, if the crime imputed to her was well-
founded, it would bring upon the woman bitter suffering as the
curse of God.—Ver. 19. The oath which the priest required her to
take is called, in ver. 21, שְׁבֻעַת הָאָלָה, " *oath of cursing*" (see Gen.
xxvi. 28) ; but it first of all presupposes the possibility of the woman
being innocent, and contains the assurance, that in that case the
curse-water would do her no harm.   " *If no* (other) *man has lain
with thee, and thou hast not gone aside to union* (טִמְאָה, accus. of more
precise definition, as in Lev. xv. 2, 18), *under thy husband*," *i.e.* as
a wife subject to thy husband (Ezek. xxiii. 5 ; Hos. iv. 12), " *then
remain free from the water of bitterness, this curse-bringing*," *i.e.* from
the effects of this curse-water.   The imperative is a sign of certain
assurance (see Gen. xii. 2, xx. 7 ; cf. *Ges.* § 130, 1).   " *But if
thou hast gone aside under thy husband, if thou hast defiled thyself,
and a man has given thee his seed beside thy husband*," . . . (the
priest shall proceed to say ; this is the meaning of the repetition of
לְאִשָּׁה . . . וְהִשְׁבִּיעַ, ver. 21), " *Jehovah shall make thee a curse and an
oath among thy people, by making thy hip to fall and thy belly to swell ;
and this curse-bringing water shall come into thy bowels, to make the
belly to vanish and the hip to fall*."   To this oath that was spoken
before her the woman was to reply, " *true, true*," or " *truly, truly*,"
and thus confirm it as taken by herself (cf. Deut. xxvii. 15 sqq. ;
Neh. v. 13).   It cannot be determined with any certainty what
was the nature of the disease threatened in this curse.   *Michaelis*
supposes it to be dropsy of the ovary (*hydrops ovarii*), in which a
tumour is formed in the place of the *ovarium*, which may even
swell so as to contain 100 lbs. of fluid, and with which the patient
becomes dreadfully emaciated.   *Josephus* says it is ordinary dropsy
(*hydrops ascites : Ant.* iii. 11, 6).   At any rate, the idea of the
curse is this : Δι' ὧν γὰρ ἡ ἁμαρτία, διὰ τούτων ἡ τιμωρία (" the
punishment shall come from the same source as the sin," *Theodoret*).
The punishment was to answer exactly to the crime, and to fall
upon those bodily organs which had been the instruments of the
woman's sin, viz. the organs of child-bearing.

Vers. 23–28. After the woman's *Amen*, the priest was to write

" *these curses*," those contained in the oath, in a book-roll, and wash them in the bitter water, *i.e.* wash the writing in the vessel with water, so that the words of the curse should pass into the water, and be imparted to it; a symbolical act, to set forth the truth, that God imparted to the water the power to act injuriously upon a guilty body, though it would do no harm to an innocent one. The remark in ver. 24, that the priest was to give her this water to drink, is anticipatory; for according to ver. 26 this did not take place till after the presentation of the sacrifice and the burning of the memorial of it upon the altar. The woman's offering, however, was not presented to God till after the oath of purification, because it was by the oath that she first of all purified herself from the suspicion of adultery, so that the fruit of her conduct could be given up to the fire of the holiness of God. As a known adulteress, she could not have offered a meat-offering at all. But as the suspicion which rested upon her was not entirely removed by her oath, since she might have taken a false oath, the priest was to give her the curse-water to drink after the offering, that her guilt or innocence might be brought to light in the effects produced by the drink. This is given in ver. 27 as the design of the course prescribed: " *When he hath made her to drink the water, then it shall come to pass, that if she be defiled, and have done trespass against her husband, the water that causeth the curse shall come* (enter) *into her as bitterness* (*i.e.* producing bitter sufferings), *namely, her belly shall swell and her hip vanish : and so the woman shall become a curse in the midst of her people.*"—Ver. 28. " *But if she have not defiled herself, and is clean* (from the crime of which she was suspected), *she will remain free* (from the threatened punishment of God), *and will conceive seed,*" *i.e.* be blessed with the capacity and power to conceive and bring forth children.

Vers. 29–31 bring the law of jealousy to a formal close, with the additional remark, that the man who adopted this course with a wife suspected of adultery was free from sin, but the woman would bear her guilt (see Lev. v. 1), *i.e.* in case she were guilty, would bear the punishment threatened by God. Nothing is said about what was to be done in case the woman refused to take the oath prescribed, because that would amount to a confession of her guilt, when she would have to be put to death as an adulteress, according to the law in Lev. xx. 10; and not she alone, but the adulterer also. In the law just mentioned the man is placed on an equality with the woman with reference to the sin of adultery ; and thus the apparent partiality, that a man could sue his wife for adultery, but not the wife her husband, is removed. But the law before us applied to the woman only, because the man was at liberty to marry more than one wife, or to take concubines to his own wife; so that he only violated the marriage tie, and was guilty of adultery, when he formed an illicit connection with another man's wife. In that case, the man whose marriage had been violated could proceed against his adulterous wife, and in most instances convict the adulterer also, in order that he might receive his punishment too. For a really guilty wife would not have made up her mind so easily to take the required oath of purification, as the curse of God under which she came was no easier to bear than the punishment of death. For this law prescribed no ordeal whose effects were uncertain, like the ordeals of other nations, but¹ a judgment of God, from which the guilty could not escape, because it had been appointed by the living God.

Chap. vi. 1–21. THE NAZARITE.—The legal regulations concerning the vow of the Nazarite are appended quite appropriately to the laws intended to promote the spiritual order of the congregation of Israel. For the Nazarite brought to light the priestly character of the covenant nation in a peculiar form, which had necessarily to be incorporated into the spiritual organization of the community, so that it might become a means of furthering the sanctification of the people in covenant with the Lord.¹

Vers. 1 and 2. The words, "*if a man or woman make a separate vow, a Nazarite vow, to live consecrated to the Lord,*" with which the law is introduced, show not only that the vow of the Nazarite was a matter of free choice, but that it was a mode of practising godliness and piety already customary among the people. *Nazir*, from נזר to separate, *lit.* the separated, is applied to the man who vowed that he would make a separation to (for) Jehovah, *i.e.* lead a separate life for the Lord and His service. The origin of this custom is involved in obscurity. There is no certain clue to indicate that it was derived from Egypt, for the so-called hair-offering vows are met with among several ancient tribes (see the proofs in *Spencer, de legg. Hebr. rit.* iv. 16, and *Knobel in loc.*), and have no special rela-

¹ The rules of the Talmud are found in the *tract. Nasir* in the *Mishnah.*
See also *Lundius, jüd. Heiligthümer*, B. iii. p. 53. *Bähr, Symbolik*, ii. pp. 430 sqq.;
Hengstenberg, Egypt and the Books of Moses, pp. 190 sqq. My Archæologie, i. §
67; and *Herzog's* Cyclopædia.

tionship to the Nazarite, whilst vows of abstinence were common to all the religions of antiquity. The Nazarite vow was taken at first for a particular time, at the close of which the separation terminated with release from the vow. This is the only form in which it is taken into consideration, or rules are laid down for it in the law before us. In after times, however, we find life-long Nazarites among the Israelites, *e.g.* Samson, Samuel, and John the Baptist, who were vowed or dedicated to the Lord by their parents even before they were born (Judg. xiii. 5, 14; 1 Sam. i. 11; Luke i. 15).[1]

Vers. 3-8. The vow consisted of the three following points, vers. 1-4 : In the *first* place, he was to abstain from wine and intoxicating drink (*shecar*, see Lev. x. 9); and neither to drink vinegar of wine, strong drink, nor any juice of the grape (*lit.* dissolving of grapes, *i.e.* fresh must pressed out), nor to eat fresh grapes, or dried (raisins). In fact, during the whole period of his vow, he was not to eat of anything prepared from the vine, *" from the kernels even to the husk,"* *i.e.* not the smallest quantity of the fruit of the vine. The design of this prohibition can hardly have been, merely that, by abstaining from intoxicating drink, the Nazarite might preserve perfect clearness and temperance of mind, like the priests when engaged in their duties, and so conduct himself as one sanctified to the Lord (*Bähr*); but it goes much further, and embraces entire abstinence from all the *deliciæ carnis* by which holiness could be impaired. Vinegar, fresh and dried grapes, and food prepared from grapes and raisins, *e.g.* raisin-cakes, are not intoxicating; but grape-cakes, as being the dainties sought after by epicures and debauchees, are cited in Hos. iii. 1 as a symbol of the sensual attractions of idolatry, a luxurious kind of food, that was not in harmony with the solemnity of the worship of Jehovah. The Nazarite was to avoid everything that proceeded from the vine, because its fruit was regarded as the sum and substance of all sensual enjoyments.—Ver. 5. *Secondly*, during the whole term of his vow of consecration, no razor was to come upon his head. Till the days were fulfilled which he had consecrated to the Lord, he was to be holy, *" to make great the free growth* (see Lev. x. 6) *of the hair of his head."* The free growth of the hair is called, in

---

[1] This is also related by *Hegesippus* (in *Euseb. hist. eccl.* ii. 23) of James the Just, the first bishop of Jerusalem. On other cases of this kind in the Talmud, and particularly on the later form of the Nazarite vow,—for example, that of the Apostle Paul (Acts xviii. 18),—see *Winer, bibl. R. W.* ii. pp. 138-9, and *Oehler* in *Herzog's* Cycl.

ver. 7, " *the diadem of his God upon his head,*" like the golden diadem upon the turban of the high priest (Ex. xxix. 6), and the anointing oil upon the high priest's head (Lev. xxi. 12). By this he sanctified his head (ver. 11) to the Lord, so that the consecration of the Nazarite culminated in his uncut hair, and expressed in the most perfect way the meaning of his vow (*Oehler*). Letting the hair grow, therefore, was not a sign of separation, because it was the Israelitish custom to go about with the hair cut; nor a practical profession of a renunciation of the world, and separation from human society (*Hengstenberg,* pp. 190–1); nor a sign of abstinence from every appearance of self-gratification (*Baur* on Amos ii. 11); nor even a kind of humiliation and self-denial (*Lightfoot, Carpzov. appar.* p. 154); still less a " sign of dependence upon *some other present power*" (*M. Baumgarten*), or " the symbol of a state of perfect liberty" (*Vitringa, obss. ss.* 1, c. 6, § 9; cf. vi. 22, 8). The free growth of the hair, unhindered by the hand of man, was rather " the symbol of strength and abundant vitality" (cf. 2 Sam. xiv. 25, 26). It was not regarded by the Hebrews as a sign of sanctity, as *Bähr* supposes, but simply as an ornament, in which the whole strength and fulness of vitality were exhibited, and which the Nazarite wore in honour of the Lord, as a sign that he " belonged to the Lord, and dedicated himself to His service," with all his vital powers.[1]—Vers. 6–8. Because the Nazarite wore the diadem of his God upon his head in the growth of his hair, and was holy to the Lord during the whole period of his consecration, he was to approach no dead person during that time, not even to defile himself for his parents, or his brothers and sisters, when they died, according to the law laid down for the high priest in Lev. xxi. 11. Consequently, as a matter of course, he was to guard most scrupulously against other defilements, not only like ordinary Israelites, but also like the priests. Samson's mother, too, was not allowed to eat anything unclean during the period of her pregnancy (Judg. xiii. 4, 7, 14).

Vers. 9–12. But if any one died suddenly in a moment " by him" (עָלָיו, in his neighbourhood), and he therefore involuntarily

---

[1] In support of this explanation, *Oehler* calls to mind those heathen hair-offerings of the Athenian youths, for example (*Plut. Thes.* c. 5), which were founded upon the idea, that the hair in general was a symbol of vital power, and the hair of the beard a sign of virility; and also more especially the example of Samson, whose hair was not only the symbol, but the vehicle, of the power which fitted him to be the deliverer of his people

defiled his consecrated head, he was to shave his head on the day of his purification, *i.e.* on the seventh day (see chap. xix. 11, 14, 16, and 19), not "because such uncleanness was more especially caught and retained by the hair," as *Knobel* fancies, but because it was the diadem of his God (ver. 7), the ornament of his condition, which was sanctified to God. On the eighth day, that is to say, on the day after the legal purification, he was to bring to the priest at the tabernacle two turtle-doves or young pigeons, that he might make atonement for him (see at Lev. xv. 14, 15, 29 sqq., xiv. 30, 31, and xii. 8), on account of his having been defiled by a corpse, by preparing the one as a sin-offering, and the other as a burnt-offering; he was also " *to sanctify his head that same day*," *i.e.* to consecrate it to God afresh, by the unimpeded growth of his hair.—Ver. 12. He was then " *to consecrate to Jehovah the days of his consecration*," *i.e.* to commence afresh the time of dedication that he had vowed, and " *to bring a yearling sheep as a trespass-offering;*" and the days that were before were " *to fall*," *i.e.* the days of consecration that had already elapsed were not to be reckoned on account of their having fallen, " *because his consecration had become unclean.*" He was therefore to commence the whole time of his consecration entirely afresh, and to observe it as required by the vow. To this end he was to bring a trespass-offering, as a payment or recompense for being reinstated in the former state of consecration, from which he had fallen through his defilement, but not as compensation " for having prolonged the days of separation through his carelessness with regard to the defilement; that is to say, for having extended the time during which he led a separate, retired, and inactive life, and suspended his duties to his own family and the congregation, thus doing an injury to them, and incurring a debt in relation to them through his neglect" (*Knobel*). For the time that the Nazarite vow lasted was not a lazy life, involving a withdrawal from the duties of citizenship, by which the congregation might be injured, but was perfectly reconcilable with the performance of all domestic and social duties, the burial of the dead alone excepted; and no harm could result from this, either to his own relations or the community generally, of sufficient importance to require that the omission should be repaired by a trespass-offering, from which neither his relatives nor the congregation derived any actual advantage. Nor was it a species of fine, for having deprived Jehovah of the time dedicated to Him through the breach of the vow, or for withholding the payment of his vow for so much longer a time

(*Oehler* in *Herzog*). For the position of a Nazarite was only assumed for a definite period, according to the vow; and after this had been interrupted, it had to be commenced again from the very beginning: so that the time dedicated to God was not shortened in any way by the interruption of the period of dedication, and nothing whatever was withheld from God of what had been vowed to Him, so as to need the presentation of a trespass-offering as a compensation or fine. And there is no more reason for saying that the payment of the vow was withheld, inasmuch as the vow was fulfilled or paid by the punctual observance of the three things of which it was composed; and the sacrifices to be presented after the time of consecration was over, had not in the least the character of a payment, but simply constituted a solemn conclusion, corresponding to the idea of the consecration itself, and were the means by which the Nazarite came out of his state of consecration, without involving the least allusion to satisfaction, or reparation for any wrong that had been done.

The position of the Nazarite, therefore, as *Philo, Maimonides,* and others clearly saw, was a condition of life consecrated to the Lord, resembling the sanctified relation in which the priests stood to Jehovah, and differing from the priesthood solely in the fact that it involved no official service at the sanctuary, and was not based upon a divine calling and institution, but was undertaken spontaneously for a certain time and through a special vow. The object was simply the realization of the idea of a priestly life, with its purity and freedom from all contamination from everything connected with death and corruption, a self-surrender to God stretching beyond the deepest earthly ties, "a spontaneous appropriation of what was imposed upon the priest by virtue of the calling connected with his descent, namely, the obligation to conduct himself as a person betrothed to God, and therefore to avoid everything that would be opposed to such surrender" (*Oehler*). In this respect the Nazarite's sanctification of life was a step towards the realization of the priestly character, which had been set before the whole nation as its goal at the time of its first calling (Ex. xix. 5); and although it was simply the performance of a vow, and therefore a work of perfect spontaneity, it was also a work of the Spirit of God which dwelt in the congregation of Israel, so that Amos could describe the raising up of Nazarites along with prophets as a special manifestation of divine grace. The offerings, with which the vow was brought to a close after the time of consecration had expired, and the Nazarite was released from his consecration, also corresponded to the character we have described.

Vers. 13–21. The directions as to the release from consecration are called " *the law of the Nazarite* " (ver. 13), because the idea of the Nazarite's vows culminated in the sacrificial festival which terminated the consecration, and it was in this that it attained to its fullest manifestation. " *On the day of the completion of the days of his consecration,*" *i.e.* on the day when the time of consecration expired, the Nazarite was to bring to the tabernacle, or offer as his gifts to the Lord, a sheep of a year old as a burnt-offering, and an ewe of a year old as a sin-offering ; the latter as an expiation for the sins committed involuntarily during the period of consecration, the former as an embodiment of that surrender of himself, body and soul, to the Lord, upon which every act of worship should rest. In addition to this he was to bring a ram without blemish as a peace-offering, together with a basket of unleavened cakes and wafers baked, which were required, according to Lev. vii. 12, for every praise-offering, " *and their meat and drink-offerings,*" *i.e.* the gifts of meal, oil, and wine, which belonged, according to chap. xv. 3 sqq., to the burnt-offerings and peace-offerings.—Ver. 16. The sin-offering and burnt-offering were carried out according to the general instructions.—Ver. 17. The completion of the consecration vow was concentrated in the preparation of the ram and the basket of un-leavened bread for the peace-offering, along with the appropriate meat-offering and drink-offering.—Ver. 18. The Nazarite had also to shave his consecrated head, and put the hair into the altar-fire under the peace-offering that was burning, and thus hand over and sacrifice to the Lord the hair of his head which had been worn in honour of Him.—Vers. 19, 20. When this had been done, the priest took the boiled shoulder of the ram, with an unleavened cake and wafer out of the basket, and placed these pieces in the hands of the Nazarite, and waved them before Jehovah. They then became the portion of the priest, in addition to the wave-breast and heave-leg which fell to the priest in the case of every peace-offering (Lev. vii. 32–34), to set forth the participation of the Lord in the sacrificial meal (see vol. ii. pp. 329, 330). But the fact that, in addition to these, the boiled shoulder was given up symbolically to the Lord through the process of waving, together with a cake and wafer, was intended to indicate that the table-fellowship with the Lord, shadowed forth in the sacri-ficial meal of the peace-offering, took place here in a higher degree; inasmuch as the Lord directed a portion of the Nazarite's meal to be handed over to His representatives and servants for them to eat, that he might thus enjoy the blessedness of having fellowship with his God, in accordance with that condition of priestly sanctity into which the Nazarite had entered through the vow that he had made. —Ver. 20. "*After that the Nazarite may drink wine*" (again), probably at the sacrificial meal, after the Lord had received His share of the sacrifice, and his release from consecration had thus been completed.—Ver. 21. "*This is the law of the Nazarite, who vowed his sacrificial gifts to the Lord on the ground of his consecration*," *i.e.* who offered his sacrifice in accordance with the state of a Nazarite into which he had entered. For the sacrifices mentioned in vers. 14 sqq. were not the object of a special vow, but contained in the vow of the Nazarite, and therefore already vowed (*Knobel*). "*Beside what his hand grasps*," *i.e.* what he is otherwise able to perform (Lev. v. 11), "*according to the measure of his vow, which he vowed, so must he do according to the law of his consecration*," *i.e.* he had to offer the sacrifices previously mentioned on the ground of his consecration vow. Beyond that he was free to vow anything else according to his ability, to present other sacrificial gifts to the Lord for His sanctuary and His servants, which did not necessarily belong to the vow of the Nazarite, but were frequently added. From this the custom afterwards grew up, that when poor persons took the Nazarite's vow upon them, those who were better off defrayed the expenses of the sacrifices (Acts xxi. 24; *Josephus, Ant.* xix. 6, 1; *Mishnah Nasir*, ii. 5 sqq.).

Vers. 22–27. THE PRIESTLY OR AARONIC BLESSING.—The spiritual character of the congregation of Israel culminated in the blessing with which the priests were to bless the people. The directions as to this blessing, therefore, impressed the seal of perfection upon the whole order and organization of the people of God, inasmuch as Israel was first truly formed into a congregation of Jehovah by the fact that God not only bestowed His blessing upon it, but placed the communication of this blessing in the hands of the priests, the chosen and constant mediators of the blessings of His grace, and imposed it upon them as one portion of their official duty. The blessing which the priests were to impart to the people, consisted of a triple blessing of two members each, which stood related to each other thus: The second in each case contained a special application of the first to the people, and the three gradations unfolded the substance of the blessing step by step with ever increasing emphasis.—The *first* (ver. 24), "*Jehovah bless thee and keep thee*," conveyed the blessing in the most general form, merely describing it as coming from Jehovah, and setting forth preservation from the evil of the world as His work. "The blessing of God is the goodness of God in action, by which a supply of all good pours down to us from His good favour as from their only fountain ; then follows, secondly, the prayer that He would keep the people, which signifies that He alone is the defender of the Church, and that it is He who preserves it with His guardian care" (*Calvin*). —The *second* (ver. 25), "*Jehovah make His face shine upon thee, and be gracious unto thee*," defined the blessing more closely as the manifestation of the favour and grace of God. The face of God is the personality of God as turned towards man. Fire goes out from Jehovah's face, and consumes the enemy and the rebellious (Lev. x. 2, cf. xvii. 10, xx. 3 ; Ex. xiv. 24 ; Ps. xxxiv. 17), and also a sunlight shining with love and full of life and good (Deut. xxx. 30 ; Ps. xxvii. 1, xliii. 3, xliv. 4). If "the light of the sun is sweet, and pleasant for the eyes to behold" (Eccl. xi. 7), "the light of the divine countenance, the everlasting light (Ps. xxxvi. 10), is the sum of all delight" (*Baumg.*). This light sends rays of mercy into a heart in need of salvation, and makes it the recipient of grace.—The *third* (ver. 26), "*Jehovah lift up His face to thee, and set* (or give) *thee peace*" (good, salvation), set forth the blessing of God as a manifestation of power, or a work of power upon man, the end of which is peace (*shalom*), the sum of all the good which God sets, prepares, or establishes for His people. נָשָׂא פָּנִים אֶל, to lift up the face to any one, is equivalent to looking at him, and does not differ from נָשָׂא עֵינַיִם or שִׂים (Gen. xliii. 29, xliv. 21). When affirmed of God, it denotes His providential work upon man. When God looks at a man, He saves him out of his distresses (Ps. iv. 7, xxxiii. 18, xxxiv. 16).—In these three blessings most of the fathers and earlier theologians saw an allusion to the mystery of the Trinity, and rested their conclusion, (*a*) upon the triple repetition of the name *Jehovah ;* (*b*) upon the *ratio prædicati*, that Jehovah, by whom the blessing is desired and imparted, is the Father, Son, and Holy Ghost ; and (*c*) upon the *distinctorum benedictionis membrorum consideratio*, according to which *bis trina beneficia* are mentioned (cf. *Calovii Bibl. illustr. ad h. l.*). There is truth in this, though the grounds assigned seem faulty. As the threefold repetition of a word or sentence serves to express the thought as strongly as possible (cf. Jer. vii. 4, xxii. 29), the triple blessing expressed in the most unconditional manner the thought, that God would bestow upon His congregation the whole fulness of the blessing enfolded in His Divine Being which was manifested as Jehovah. But not only does the name Jehovah denote God as the absolute Being, who revealed Himself as Father, Son, and Spirit in the historical development of His purpose of salvation for the redemption of fallen man ; but the substance of this blessing, which He caused to be pronounced upon His congregation, unfolded the grace of God in the threefold way in which it is communicated to us through the Father, Son, and Spirit.[1]—Ver. 27. This blessing was not to remain merely a pious wish, however, but to be manifested in the people with all the power of a blessing from God. This assurance closes the divine command : " *They shall put My name upon the children of Israel, and I will bless them.*"

CLOSING EVENTS AT SINAI.—CHAP. VII.–IX. 14.

Chap. vii. Presentation of Dedicatory Gifts by the Princes of the Tribes.—Ver. 1. This presentation took place at the time (םוֹי) when Moses, after having completed the erection of the tabernacle, anointed and sanctified the dwelling and the altar, together with their furniture (Lev. viii. 10, 11). Chronologically considered, this ought to have been noticed after Lev. viii. 10. But in order to avoid interrupting the connection of the Sinaitic laws, it is introduced for the first time at this point, and placed at the

---

[1] See the admirable elaboration of these points in *Luther's* exposition of the blessing. *Luther* refers the first blessing to " bodily life and good." The blessing, he says, desired for the people " that God would give them prosperity and every good, and also guard and preserve them." This is carried out still further, in a manner corresponding to his exposition of the first article. The second blessing he refers to " the spiritual nature and the soul," and observes, " Just as the sun, when it rises and diffuses its rich glory and soft light over all the world, merely lifts up its face upon all the world ; . . . so when God gives His word, He causes His face to shine clearly and joyously upon all minds, and makes them joyful and light, and as it were new hearts and new men. For it brings forgiveness of sins, and shows God as a gracious and merciful Father, who pities and sympathizes with our grief and sorrow. The third also relates to the spiritual nature and the soul, and is a desire for consolation and final victory over the cross, death, the devil, and all the gates of hell, together with the world and the evil desires of the flesh. The desire of this blessing is, that the Lord God will lift up the light of His word upon us, and so keep it over us, that it may shine in our hearts with strength enough to overcome all the opposition of the devil, death, and sin, and all adversity, terror, or despair."

head of the events which immediately preceded the departure of the people from Sinai, because these gifts consisted in part of materials that were indispensably necessary for the transport of the tabernacle during the march through the desert. Moreover, there was only an interval of at the most forty days between the anointing of the tabernacle, which commenced after the first day of the first month (cf. Ex. xl. 16 and Lev. viii. 10), and lasted eight days, and the departure from Sinai, on the twentieth day of the second month (chap. x. 11), and from this we have to deduct six days for the Passover, which took place before their departure (chap. ix. 1 sqq.); and it was within this period that the laws and ordinances from Lev. xi. to Num. vi. had to be published, and the dedicatory offerings to be presented. Now, as the presentation itself was distributed, according to vers. 11 sqq., over twelve or thirteen days, we may very well assume that it did not entirely precede the publication of the laws referred to, but was carried on in part contemporaneously with it. The presentation of the dedicatory gifts of one tribe-prince might possibly occupy only a few hours of the day appointed for the purpose; and the rest of the day, therefore, might very conveniently be made use of by Moses for publishing the laws. In this case the short space of a month and a few days would be amply sufficient for everything that took place.

Vers. 2-9. *The presentation of six waggons and twelve oxen* for the carriage of the materials of the tabernacle is mentioned first, and was no doubt the first thing that took place. The princes of Israel, viz. the heads of the tribe-houses (fathers' houses), or princes of the tribes (see chap. i. 4 sqq.), " *those who stood over those that were numbered,*" *i.e.* who were their leaders or rulers, offered as their sacrificial gift six covered waggons and twelve oxen, one ox for each prince, and a waggon for every two. עֶגְלֹת צָב, ἁμάξας λαμπηνίκας (LXX.), *i.e.* according to *Euseb. Emis.*, two-wheeled vehicles, though the Greek scholiasts explain λαμπήνη as signifying ἅμαξα περιφανής, βασιλικὴ and ῥέδιον περιφανὲς ὅ ἐστιν ἅρμα σκεπαστόν (cf. *Schleussner, Lex. in* LXX. *s. v.*), and *Aquila*, ἅμαξαι σκεπασταί, *i.e. plaustra tecta* (*Vulg.* and *Rabb.*). The meaning " litters," which *Gesenius* and *De Wette* support, can neither be defended etymologically, nor based upon צַבִּים in Isa. lxvi. 20.—Vers. 4-6. At the command of God, Moses received them to apply them to the purposes of the tabernacle, and handed them over to the Levites, " *to every one according to the measure of his service,*" *i.e.* to the different classes of Levites, according to the requirements of their respective

duties.—Vers. 7–9. He gave two waggons and four oxen to the
Gershonites, and four waggons and eight oxen to the Merarites, as
the former had less weight to carry, in the coverings and curtains
of the dwelling and the hangings of the court, than the latter, who
had to take charge of the beams and pillars (chap. iv. 24 sqq., 31
sqq.). *"Under the hand of Ithamar"* (ver. 8); as in chap. iv. 28,
33. The Kohathites received no waggon, because it was their
place to attend to *"* the sanctuary" (the holy), *i.e.* the holy things,
which had to be conveyed upon their shoulders, and were provided
with poles for the purpose (chap. iv. 4 sqq.).

Vers. 10–88. *Presentation of dedicatory gifts for the altar.*—
Ver. 10. Every prince offered *"the dedication of the altar,"* i.e. what
served for the dedication of the altar, equivalent to his sacrificial
gift for the consecration of the altar, *"on the day,"* i.e. at the time,
" that they anointed it." " Day:" as in Gen. ii. 4. Moses was
directed by God to receive the gifts from the princes on separate
days, one after another; so that the presentation extended over
twelve days. The reason for this regulation was not to make a
greater display, as *Knobel* supposes, or to avoid cutting short the
important ceremony of consecration, but was involved in the very
nature of the gifts presented. Each prince, for example, offered,
(1) a *silver dish* (*kearah*, Ex. xxv. 29) of 130 sacred shekels weight,
i.e. about 4½ lbs.; (2) a *silver bowl* (*mizrak*, a sacrificial bowl, not
a sacrificial can, or wine-can, as in Ex. xxvii. 3) of 70 shekels
weight, both filled with fine flour mixed with oil for a meat-offering;
(3) a *golden spoon* (*caph*, as in Ex. xxv. 29) filled with incense for
an incense-offering; (4) *a bullock, a ram, and a sheep* of a year old
for a burnt-offering; (5) a *shaggy goat* for a sin-offering; (6) *two
oxen, five rams, five he-goats,* and *five sheep* of a year old for a peace-
offering. Out of these gifts the fine flour, the incense, and the
sacrificial animals were intended for sacrificing upon the altar, and
that not as a provision for a lengthened period, but for immediate
use in the way prescribed. This could not have been carried out
if more than one prince had presented his gifts, and brought them
to be sacrificed on any one day. For the limited space in the court
of the tabernacle would not have allowed of 252 animals being
received, slaughtered, and prepared for sacrificing all at once, or on
the same day; and it would have been also impossible to burn 36
whole animals (oxen, rams, and sheep), and the fat portions of 216
animals, upon the altar.—Vers. 12–83. All the princes brought the
same gifts. The order in which the twelve princes, whose names

have already been given at chap. i. 5–15, made their presentation, corresponded to the order of the 'tribes in the camp (chap. ii.), the tribe-prince of Judah taking the lead, and the prince of Naphtali coming last. In the statements as to the weight of the silver *kearoth* and the golden *cappoth*, the word *shekel* is invariably omitted, as in Gen. xx. 16, etc.—In vers. 84–86, the dedication gifts are summed up, and the total weight given, viz. twelve silver dishes and twelve silver bowls, weighing together 2400 shekels, and twelve golden spoons, weighing 120 shekels in all. On the sacred shekel, see at Ex. xxx. 13; and on the probable value of the shekel of gold, at Ex. xxxviii. 24, 25. The sacrificial animals are added together in the same way in vers. 87, 88.

Ver. 89. Whilst the tribe-princes had thus given to the altar the consecration of a sanctuary of their God, through their sacrificial gifts, Jehovah acknowledged it as His sanctuary, by causing Moses, when he went into the tabernacle to speak to Him, and to present his own entreaties and those of the people, to hear the voice of Him that spake to him from between the two cherubim upon the ark of the covenant. The suffix in אִתּוֹ points back to the name *Jehovah*, which, though not expressly mentioned before, is contained *implicite* in *ohel moëd*, " *the tent of meeting*." For the holy tent became an *ohel moëd* first of all, from the fact that it was there that Jehovah appeared to Moses, or met with him (נוֹעַד, Ex. xxv. 22). מִדַּבֵּר, *part. Hithpael*, to hold conversation. On the fact itself, see the explanation in Ex. xxv. 20, 22. " This voice from the inmost sanctuary to Moses, the representative of Israel, was Jehovah's reply to the joyfulness and readiness with which the princes of Israel responded to Him, and made the tent, so far as they were concerned, a place of holy meeting" (*Baumg.*). This was the reason for connecting the remark in ver. 89 with the account of the dedicatory gifts.

Chap. viii. CONSECRATION OF THE LEVITES.—The command of God to consecrate the Levites for their service, is introduced in vers. 1–4 by directions issued to Aaron with regard to the *lighting of the candlestick* in the dwelling of the tabernacle. Aaron was to place the seven lamps upon the candlestick in such a manner that they would shine אֶל־מוּל פְּנֵי. These directions are not a mere repetition, but also a more precise definition, of the general instructions given in Ex. xxv. 37, when the candlestick was made, to place the seven lamps upon the candlestick in such a manner that each should give light over against its front, *i.e.* should throw its light upon the side opposite to the front of the candlestick (see vol. ii. p. 173). In itself, therefore, there is nothing at all striking in the renewal and explanation of those directions, which committed the task of lighting the lamps to Aaron ; for this had not been done before, as Ex. xxvii. 21 merely assigns the daily preparation of the candlestick to Aaron and his sons ; and their being placed in the connection in which we find them may be explained from the signification of the seven lamps in relation to the dwelling of God, viz. as indicating that Israel was thereby to be represented perpetually before the Lord as a people causing its light to shine in the darkness of this world (vol. ii. p. 174). And when Aaron is commanded to attend to the lighting of the candlestick, so that it may light up the dwelling, in these special instructions the entire fulfilment of his service in the dwelling is enforced upon him as a duty. In this respect the instructions themselves, coupled with the statement of the fact that Aaron had fulfilled them, stand quite appropriately between the account of what the tribe-princes had done for the consecration of the altar service as representatives of the congregation, and the account of the solemn inauguration of the Levites in their service in the sanctuary. The repetition on this occasion (ver. 4) of an allusion to the artistic character of the candlestick, which had been made according to the pattern seen by Moses in the mount (Ex. xxv. 31 sqq.), is quite in keeping with the antiquated style of narrative adopted in these books.

Vers. 5-22. *Consecration of the Levites* for their service in the sanctuary.—The choice of the Levites for service in the sanctuary, in the place of the first-born of the people generally, has been already noticed in chap. iii. 5 sqq., and the duties binding upon them in chap. iv. 4 sqq. But before entering upon their duties they were to be consecrated to the work, and then formally handed over to the priests. This consecration is commanded in vers. 7 sqq., and is not called קַדֵּשׁ, like the consecration of the priests (Ex. xxix. 1 ; Lev. viii. 11), but טַהֵר, *to cleanse.* It consisted in sprinkling them with sin-water, shaving off the whole of the hair from their bodies, and washing their clothes, accompanied by a sacrificial ceremony, by which they were presented symbolically to the Lord as a sacrifice for His service. The first part of this ceremony had reference to outward purification, and represented cleansing from the defilement of sin ; hence the performance of it is called הִתְחַטָּא (to cleanse from sin) in ver. 21. "*Sprinkle sin-water upon them.*" The words are addressed to Moses, who had to officiate at the inauguration of the Levites, as he had already done at that of the priests. " *Water of sin*" is water having reference to sin, designed to remove it, just as the sacrifice offered for the expiation of sin is called חַטָּאת (sin) in Lev. iv. 14, etc.; whilst the " water of uncleanness" in chap. xix. 9, 13, signifies water by which uncleanness was removed or wiped away. The nature of this purifying water is not explained, and cannot be determined with any certainty. We find directions for preparing sprinkling water in a peculiar manner, for the purpose of cleansing persons who were cured of leprosy, in Lev. xiv. 5 sqq., 50 sqq.; and also for cleansing both persons and houses that had been defiled by a corpse, in chap. xix. 9 sqq. Neither of these, however, was applicable to the cleansing of the Levites, as they were both of them composed of significant ingredients, which stood in the closest relation to the special cleansing to be effected by them, and had evidently no adaptation to the purification of the Levites. At the same time, the expression " sin-water" precludes our understanding it to mean simply clean water. So that nothing remains but to regard it as referring to the water in the laver of the sanctuary, which was provided for the purpose of cleansing the priests for the performance of their duties (Ex. xxx. 18 sqq.), and might therefore be regarded by virtue of this as cleansing from sin, and be called " sin-water" in consequence. " *And they shall cause the razor to pass over their whole body*," *i.e.* shave off all the hair upon their body, "*and wash their clothes, and so cleanse themselves.*" הֶעֱבִיר תַּעַר is to be distinguished from גִּלַּח. The latter signifies to make bald or shave the hair entirely off, which was required of the leper when he was cleansed (Lev. xiv. 8, 9); the former signifies merely cutting the hair, which was part of the regular mode of adorning the body. The Levites also were not required to bathe their bodies, as lepers were (Lev. xiv. 8, 9), and also the priests at their consecration (Lev. viii. 6), because they were not affected with any special uncleanness, and their duties did not require them to touch the most holy instruments of worship. The washing of the clothes, on the other hand, was a thing generally required as a preparation for acts of worship (Gen. xxxv. 2; Ex. xix. 10), and was omitted in the case of the consecration of the priests, simply because they received a holy official dress. הִפְּטַהֲרוּ for הִטַּהֲרוּ, as in 2 Chron. xxx. 18. —Ver. 8. After this purification the Levites were to bring two young bullocks, one with the corresponding meat-offering for a burnt-sacrifice, the other for a sin-offering.—Ver. 9. Moses was then to cause them to draw near before the tabernacle, *i.e.* to enter the court, and to gather together the whole congregation of Israel, viz. in the persons of their heads and representatives.—Ver. 10. After this the Levites were to come before Jehovah, *i.e.* in front of the altar; and the children of Israel, *i.e.* the tribe-princes in the name of the Israelites, were to lay their hands upon them, not merely "as a sign that they released them from the possession of the nation, and assigned them and handed them over to Jehovah" (*Knobel*), but in order that by this symbolical act they might transfer to the Levites the obligation resting upon the whole nation to serve the Lord in the persons of its first-born sons, and might present them to the Lord as representatives of the first-born of Israel, to serve Him as living sacrifices.—Ver. 11. This transfer was to be completed by Aaron's waving the Levites as a wave-offering before Jehovah on behalf of the children of Israel, *i.e.* by his offering them symbolically to the Lord as a sacrifice presented on the part of the Israelites. The ceremony of waving consisted no doubt in his conducting the Levites solemnly up to the altar, and then back again. On the signification of the verb, see at Lev. vii. 30. The design of the waving is given in ver. 11, viz. "*that they might be to perform the service of Jehovah*" (vers. 24–26 compared with chap. iv. 4–33).—Ver. 12. The Levites were then to close this transfer of themselves to the Lord with a sin-offering and burnt-offering, in which they laid their hands upon the sacrificial animals. By this imposition of hands they made the sacrificial animals their representatives, in which they presented their own bodies to the Lord as a living sacrifice well-pleasing to Him (see vol. ii. pp. 279, 280). The signification of the dedication of the Levites, as here enjoined, is still further explained in vers. 13–19. The meaning of vers. 13 sqq. is this: According to the command already given (in vers. 6–12), thou shalt place the Levites before Aaron and his sons, and wave them as a wave-offering before the Lord, and so separate them from the midst of the children of Israel, that they may be Mine. They shall then come to serve the tabernacle. So shalt thou cleanse them and wave them. The same reason is assigned for this in vers. 16, 17, as in chap. iii. 11–13 (בְּכוֹר בֹּל for כָּל־בְּכוֹר, cf. chap. iii. 13); and in vers. 18 and 19, what was commanded in chap. iii. 6–9 is described as having been carried out. On ver. 19*b* see chap. i. 53. —Vers. 20–22 contain an account of the execution of the divine command.

Vers. 23–26. *The Levitical period of service* is fixed here at twenty-five years of age and upwards to the fiftieth year. " *This is what concerns the Levites,*" *i.e.* what follows applies to the Levites. " *From the age of twenty-five years shall he* (the Levite) *come to do service at the work of the tabernacle; and at fifty years of age shall he return from the service of the work, and not work any further, but only serve his brethren at the tabernacle in keeping charge,*" *i.e.* help them to look after the furniture of the tabernacle. " Charge" (*mishmereth*), as distinguished from " work," signified the oversight of all the furniture of the tabernacle (see chap. iii. 8); " work" (service) applied to laborious service, *e.g.* the taking down and setting up of the tabernacle and cleaning it, carrying wood and water for the sacrificial worship, slaying the animals for the daily and festal sacrifices of the congregation, etc.—Ver. 26*b*. " *So shalt thou do to the Levites* (*i.e.* proceed with them) *in their services.*" מִשְׁמֶרֶת from מִשְׁמֶרֶת, attendance upon an official post. Both the heading and final clause, by which this law relating to the Levites' period of service is bounded, and its position immediately after the induction of the Levites into their office, show unmistakeably that this law was binding for all time, and was intended to apply to the standing service of the Levites at the sanctuary; and consequently that it was not at variance with the instructions in chap. iv., to muster the Levites between thirty and fifty years of age, and organize them for the transport of the tabernacle on the journey through the wilderness (chap. iv. 3–49). The transport of the tabernacle required the strength of a full-grown man, and therefore the more advanced age of thirty years; whereas the duties connected with the tabernacle when standing were of a lighter description, and could easily be performed from the twenty-fifth year (see *Hengstenberg's* Dissertations, vol. ii. pp. 321 sqq.). At a later period, when the sanctuary was permanently established on Mount Zion, David employed the Levites from their twentieth year (1 Chron. xxiii. 24, 25), and expressly stated that he did so because the Levites had no longer to carry the dwelling and its furniture; and this regulation continued in force from that time forward (cf. 2 Chron. xxxi. 17 ; Ezra iii. 8). But if the supposed discrepancy between the verses before us and chap. iv. 3, 47, is removed by this distinction, which is gathered in the most simple manner from the context, there is no ground whatever for critics to deny that the regulation before us could have proceeded from the pen of the Elohist.

Chap. ix. 1–14. THE PASSOVER AT SINAI, and INSTRUCTIONS

FOR A SUPPLEMENTARY PASSOVER.—Vers. 1–5. On the first institution of the Passover, before the exodus from Egypt, God had
appointed the observance of this feast as an everlasting statute for
all future generations (Ex. xii. 14, 24, 25). In the first month of
the second year after the exodus, that is to say, immediately after
the erection of the tabernacle (Ex. xl. 2, 17), this command was
renewed, and the people were commanded " to keep the Passover
in its appointed season, according to all its statutes and rights ;" not
to postpone it, that is, according to an interpretation that might
possibly have been put upon Ex. xii. 24, 25, until they came to
Canaan, but to keep it there at Sinai. And Israel kept it in the
wilderness of Sinai, in exact accordance with the commands which
God had given before (Ex. xii.). There is no express command,
it is true, that the blood of the paschal lambs, instead of being
smeared upon the lintel and posts of the house-doors (or the entrances to the tents), was to be sprinkled upon the altar of burnt-
offering ; nor is it recorded that this was actually done ; but it
followed of itself from the altered circumstances, inasmuch as there
was no destroying angel to pass through the camp at Sinai and
smite the enemies of Israel, whilst there was an altar in existence
now upon which all the sacrificial blood was to be poured out, and
therefore the blood of the paschal sacrifice also.[1]

[1] If we take into consideration still further, the fact that the law had
already been issued that the blood of all the animals slain for food, whether
inside or outside the camp, was to be sprinkled upon the altar (Lev. xvii. 3–6),
there can be no doubt that the blood of the paschal lambs would also have to be
sprinkled upon the altar, notwithstanding the difficulties referred to by *Kurtz*,
arising from the small number of priests to perform the task, viz. Aaron,
Eleazar, and Ithamar, as Nadab and Abihu were now dead. But (1) *Kurtz*
estimates the number of paschal lambs much too high, viz. at 100,000 to
140,000 ; for when he reckons the whole number of the people at about two
millions, and gives one lamb upon an average to every fifteen or twenty persons,
he includes infants and sucklings among those who partook of the Passover.
But as there were only 603,550 males of twenty years old and upwards in the
twelve tribes, we cannot reckon more than about 700,000 males as participants
in the paschal meal, since the children under ten or twelve years of age would
not come into the calculation, even if those who were between eight and twelve
partook of the meal, since there would be many adults who could not eat the
Passover, because they were unclean. Now if, as *Josephus* affirms (*de bell. jud.*
vi. 9, 3), there were never less than ten, and often as many as twenty, who
joined together in the time of Christ (οὐκ ἔλασσον ἀνδρῶν δέκα . . . πολλοὶ δὲ
καὶ σὺν εἴκοσιν ἀθροίζονται), we need not assume that there were more than
50,000 lambs required for the feast of Passover at Sinai ; because even if all
the women who were clean took part in the feast, they would confine them-

Vers. 6–14. There were certain men who were defiled by human corpses (see Lev. xix. 28), and could not eat the Passover on the day appointed. These men came to Moses, and asked, " *Why are we diminished* (prevented) *from offering the sacrificial gift of Jehovah at its season in the midst of the children of Israel* (*i.e.* in common with the rest of the Israelites) ?" The exclusion of persons defiled from offering the Passover followed from the law, that only clean persons were to participate in a sacrificial meal (Lev. vii. 21), and that no one could offer any sacrifice in an unclean state.—Ver. 8. Moses told them to wait (stand), and he would hear what the Lord, of whom he would inquire, would command.—Vers. 9 sqq. Jehovah gave these general instructions : "*Every one who is defiled by a corpse or upon a distant*[1] *journey, of you and your future families, shall keep the Passover in the second month on the fourteenth, between the two evenings,*" and that in all respects according to the statute of this feast, the three leading points of which—viz. eating the lamb with unleavened bread and bitter herbs, leaving nothing till the next day, and not breaking a bone (Ex. xii. 8, 10, 46)—are repeated

selves as much as possible to the quantity actually needed, and one whole sheep of a year old would furnish flesh enough for one supper for fifteen males and fifteen females. (2) The slaughtering of all these lambs need not have taken place in the narrow space afforded by the court, even if it was afterwards performed in the more roomy courts of the later temple, as has been inferred from 2 Chron. xxx. 16 and xxxv. 11. Lastly, the sprinkling of the blood was no doubt the business of the priests. But the Levites assisted them, so that they sprinkled the blood upon the altar " out of the hand of the Levites" (2 Chron. xxx. 16). Moreover, we are by no means in a condition to pronounce positively whether three priests were sufficient or not at Sinai, because we have no precise information respecting the course pursued. The altar, no doubt, would appear too small for the performance of the whole within the short time of hardly three hours (from the ninth hour of the day to the eleventh). But if it was possible, in the time of the Emperor Nero, to sprinkle the blood of 256,500 paschal lambs (for that number was actually counted under *Cestius;* see *Josephus, l. c.*) upon the altar of the temple of that time, which was six, or eight, or even ten times larger, it must have been also possible, in Moses' time, for the blood of 50,000 lambs to be sprinkled upon the altar of the tabernacle, which was five cubits in length, and the same in breadth.

[1] The רְחֹקָה is marked as suspicious by *puncta extraordinaria*, probably first of all simply on the ground that the more exact definition is not found in ver. 13. The Rabbins suppose the marks to indicate that *rechokah* is not to be taken here in its literal sense, but denotes merely distance from Jerusalem, or from the threshold of the outer court of the temple. See *Mishnah Pesach* ix. 2, with the commentaries of *Bartenora* and *Maimonides,* and the conjectures of the *Pesikta* on the ten passages in the Pentateuch with *punctis extraordinariis,* in *Drusii notæ uberiores ad h. v.*

here. But lest any one should pervert this permission, to celebrate the Passover a month later in case of insuperable difficulties, which had only been given for the purpose of enforcing the obligation to keep the covenant meal upon every member of the nation, into an excuse for postponing it without any necessity and merely from indifference, on the ground that he could make it up afterwards, the threat is held out in ver. 13, that whoever should omit to keep the feast at the legal time, if he was neither unclean nor upon a journey, should be cut off; and in ver. 14 the command is repeated with reference to foreigners, that they were also to keep the law and ordinance with the greatest minuteness when they observed the Passover: cf. Ex. xii. 48, 49, according to which the stranger was required first of all to let himself be circumcised. In ver. 14*b*, יִהְיֶה stands for תִּהְיֶה, as in Ex. xii. 49; cf. *Ewald*, § 295, *d.* וֹ . . . ן *et . . . et*, both . . . and.

SIGNS AND SIGNALS FOR THE MARCH.—CHAP. IX. 15–X. 10.

With the mustering of the people and the internal organization of the congregation, the preparations for the march from the desert of Sinai to the promised land of Canaan were completed; and when the feast of the Passover was ended, the time for leaving Sinai had arrived. Nothing now remained to be noticed except the required instructions respecting the guidance of the people in their journey through the wilderness, to which the account of the actual departure and march is appended. The account before us describes first of all the manner in which God Himself conducted the march (chap. ix. 15–23); and secondly, instructions are given respecting the signals to be used for regulating the order of the march (chap. x. 1–10).

Chap. ix. 15–23. SIGNS FOR REMOVING AND ENCAMPING.—On their way through the desert from the border of Egypt to Sinai, Jehovah Himself had undertaken to guide His people by a cloud, as the visible sign and vehicle of His gracious presence (Ex. xiii. 21, 22). This cloud had come down upon the dwelling when the tabernacle was erected, whilst the glory of the Lord filled the holy of holies (Ex. xl. 34–38). In ver. 15 the historian refers to this fact, and then describes more fully what had been already briefly alluded to in Ex. xl. 36, 37, namely, that when the cloud rose up from the dwelling of the tabernacle it was a sign for removing, and

when it came down upon the dwelling, a sign for encamping. In
ver. 15a, "on the day of the setting up of the dwelling," Ex. xl.
34, 35, is resumed; and in ver. 15b the appearance of the cloud
during the night, from evening till morning, is described in accordance with Ex. xl. 38. (On the fact itself, see the exposition of Ex.
xiii. 21, 22.)　מִשְׁכָּן לְאֹהֶל הָעֵדֻת, "the dwelling of the tent of witness"
(לְ used for the genitive to avoid a double construct state: Ewald, §
292, a). In the place of ohel moëd, "tent of the meeting of Jehovah
with His people," we have here "tent of witness" (or "testimony"),
i.e. of the tables with the decalogue which were laid up in the ark
of the covenant (Ex. xxv. 16), because the decalogue formed the
basis of the covenant of Jehovah with Israel, and the pledge of the
gracious presence of the Lord in the tabernacle. In the place of
"dwellings of the tent of witness," we have "dwelling of witness"
(testimony) in chap. x. 11, and "tent of witness" in chap. xviii. 2,
xvii. 22, to denote the whole dwelling, as divided into the holy place
and the holy of holies, and not the holy of holies alone. This is
unmistakeably evident from a comparison of the verse before us
with Ex. xl. 34, according to which the cloud covered not merely
one portion of the tabernacle, but the whole of the tent of meeting
(ohel moëd). The rendering, "the cloud covered the dwelling at
the tent of witness," i.e. at that part of it in which the witness (or
"testimony") was kept, viz. the holy of holies, which Rosenmüller
and Knobel adopt, cannot be sustained, inasmuch as לְ has no such
meaning, but simply conveys the idea of motion and passage into a
place or condition (cf. Ewald, § 217, d); and the dwelling or tabernacle was not first made into the tent of witness through the cloud
which covered it.—Ver. 16. The covering of the dwelling, with the
cloud which shone by night as a fiery look, was constant, and not
merely a phenomenon which appeared when the tabernacle was
first erected, and then vanished away again.—Ver. 17. "In accordance with the rising of the cloud from the tent, then afterwards the
children of Israel broke up," i.e. whenever the cloud ascended up
from the tent, they always broke up immediately afterwards; "and
at the place where the cloud came down, there they encamped." The
שָׁכַן, or settling down of the cloud, sc. upon the tabernacle, we can
only understand in the following manner, as the tabernacle was
all taken to pieces during the march: viz. that the cloud visibly
descended from the height at which it ordinarily soared above the
ark of the covenant, as it was carried in front of the army, for a
signal that the tabernacle was to be set up there; and when this

had been done, it settled down upon it.—Ver. 18. As Jehovah was
with His people in the cloud, the rising and falling of the cloud
was "the command of the Lord" to the Israelites to break up or
to pitch the camp. As long, therefore, as the cloud rested upon
the dwelling, *i.e.* remained stationary, they continued their encampment.—Vers. 19 sqq. Whether it might rest many days long (הַאֲרִיךְ,
to lengthen out the resting), or only a few days (Gen. xxxiv. 30),
or only from evening till morning, and then rise up again in the
morning, or for a day and a night, or for two days, or for a month,
or for days (*yamim*), *i.e.* a space of time not precisely determined
(cf. Gen. iv. 3, xl. 4), they encamped without departing. "*Kept
the charge of the Lord*" (vers. 19 and 23), *i.e.* observed what was
to be observed towards Jehovah (see Lev. viii. 35). With וְיֵשׁ אֲשֶׁר,
"was it that," or "did it happen that," two other possible cases are
introduced. After ver. 20*a*, the apodosis, "*they kept the charge of
the Lord*," is to be repeated in thought from ver. 19. The elaboration of the account (vers. 15–23), which abounds with repetitions,
is intended to bring out the importance of the fact, and to awaken
the consciousness not only of the absolute dependence of Israel
upon the guidance of Jehovah, but also of the gracious care of
their God, which was thereby displayed to the Israelites throughout
all their journeyings.

Chap. x. 1–10. The Silver Signal-Trumpets.—Although
God Himself appointed the time for removal and encampment by
the movement of the cloud of His presence, signals were also requisite for ordering and conducting the march of so numerous a body,
by means of which Moses, as commander-in-chief, might make
known his commands to the different divisions of the camp. To
this end God directed him to prepare two silver trumpets of beaten
work (*mikshah*, see Ex. xxv. 18), which should serve "for the
calling of the assembly, and for the breaking up of the camps,"
i.e. which were to be used for this purpose. The form of these
trumpets is not further described. No doubt they were straight,
not curved, as we may infer both from the representation of these
trumpets on the triumphal arch of Titus at Rome, and also from
the fact, that none but straight trumpets occur on the old Egyptian
monuments (see my *Arch.* ii. p. 187). With regard to the use of
them for calling the congregation, the following directions are given
in vers. 3, 4 : "*When they shall blow with them* (*i.e.* with both), *the
whole congregation* (in all its representatives) *shall assemble at the*

door of the tabernacle; if they blow with only one, the princes or heads of the families of Israel shall assemble together."—Vers. 5, 6. To give the signal for breaking up the camp, they were to blow תְּרוּעָה, *i.e.* a noise or alarm. At the first blast the tribes on the east, *i.e.* those who were encamped in the front of the tabernacle, were to break up; at the second, those who were encamped on the south; and so on in the order prescribed in chap. ii., though this is not expressly mentioned here. The alarm was to be blown לְמַסְעֵיהֶם, with regard to their breaking up or marching.—Ver. 7. But to call the congregation together they were to *blow*, not to sound an alarm. תָּקַע signifies blowing in short, sharp tones. תָּקַע תְּרוּעָה = הָרִיעַ, blowing in a continued peal.—Vers. 8–10. These trumpets were to be used for the holy purposes of the congregation generally, and therefore not only the making, but the manner of using them was prescribed by God Himself. They were to be blown by the priests alone, and *" to be for an eternal ordinance to the families of Israel,"* *i.e.* to be preserved and used by them in all future times, according to the appointment of God. The blast of these trumpets was to call Israel to remembrance before Jehovah in time of war and on their feast-days.—Ver. 9. *" If ye go to war in your land against the enemy who oppresses you, and ye blow the trumpets, ye shall bring yourselves to remembrance before Jehovah, and shall be saved* (by Him) *from your enemies."* בּוֹא מִלְחָמָה, to come into war, or go to war, is to be distinguished from בּוֹא לַמִּלְחָמָה, to make ready for war, go out to battle (chap. xxxi. 21, xxxii. 6).—Ver. 10. *" And on your joyous day, and your feasts and new moons, ye shall blow the trumpets over your burnt-offerings and peace-offerings, that they may be to you for a memorial* (remembrance) *before your God."*— יוֹם הַשִּׂמְחָה is any day on which a practical expression was given to their joy, in the form of a sacrifice. The מוֹעֲדִים are the feasts enumerated in chaps. xxviii. and xxix. and Lev. xxiii. The " beginnings of the months," or new-moon days, were not, strictly speaking, feast-days, with the exception of the seventh new moon of the year (see at chap. xxviii. 11). On the object, viz. *" for a memorial,"* see Ex. xxviii. 29, and the explanation, vol. ii. p. 199. In accordance with this divine appointment, so full of promise, we find that in after times the trumpets were blown by the priests in war (chap. xxxi. 6; 2 Chron. xiii. 12, 14, xx. 21, 22, 28) as well as on joyful occasions, such as at the removal of the ark (1 Chron. xv. 24, xvi. 6), at the consecration of Solomon's temple (2 Chron. v. 12, vii. 6), the laying of the foundation of the second temple

(Ezra iii. 10), the consecration of the walls of Jerusalem (Neh. xii. 35, 41), and other festivities (2 Chron. xxix. 27).

II.—JOURNEY FROM SINAI TO THE STEPPES OF MOAB.

CHAP. X. 11–XXI.

THE straight and shortest way from Sinai to Kadesh, on the southern border of Canaan, was only a journey of eleven days (Deut. i. 2). By this road God led His people, whom He had received into the covenant of His grace at Sinai, and placed under the discipline of the law, to the ultimate object of their journey through the desert; so that, a few months after leaving Horeb or Sinai, the Israelites had already arrived at Kadesh, in the desert of Zin, on the southern border of the promised land, and were able to send out men as spies, to survey the inheritance of which they were to take possession. The way from Sinai to the desert of Zin forms the *first* stage in the history of the guidance of Israel through the wilderness to Canaan.

FROM SINAI TO KADESH.—CHAP. X. 11–XIV. 45.

Removal of the Camp from the Desert of Sinai.—Chap. x. 11–36.

Vers. 11, 12. After all the preparations were completed for the journey of the Israelites from Sinai to Canaan, on the 20th day of the second month, in the second year, the cloud rose up from the tent of witness, and the children of Israel broke up out of the desert of Sinai, לְמַסְעֵיהֶם, " according to their journeys" (*lit.* breakings up; see at Gen. xiii. 3 and Ex.   37), *i.e.* in the order prescribed in chap. ii. 9, 16, 24, 31, and described in vers. 14 sqq. of this chapter. "*And the cloud rested in the desert of Paran.*" In these words, the whole journey from the desert of Sinai to the desert of Paran is given summarily, or as a heading; and the more minute description follows from ver. 14 to chap. xii. 16. The "*desert of Paran*" was not the first station, but the third; and the Israelites did not arrive at it till after they had left Hazeroth (chap. xii. 16). The desert of Sinai is mentioned as the starting-point of the journey through the desert, in contrast with the desert of Paran, in the neighbourhood of Kadesh, whence the spies were sent out to Canaan (chap. xiii. 2, 21), the goal and termination of their journey through the desert. That the words, "the cloud rested in the desert of Paran" (ver. 12b), contain a preliminary statement (like Gen. xxvii. 23, xxxvii. 5, as compared with ver. 8, and 1 Kings vi. 9 as compared with ver. 14, etc.), is unmistakeably apparent, from the fact that Moses' negotiations with Hobab, respecting his accompanying the Israelites to Canaan, as a guide who knew the road, are noticed for the first time in vers. 29 sqq., although they took place before the departure from Sinai, and that after this the account of the breaking-up is resumed in ver. 33, and the journey itself described. Hence, although *Kurtz* (iii. 220) rejects this explanation of ver. 12b as "forced," and regards the desert of Paran as a place of encampment between Tabeerah and Kibroth-hattaavah, even he cannot help identifying the breaking-up described in ver. 33 with that mentioned in ver. 12 ; that is to say, regarding ver. 12 as a summary of the events which are afterwards more fully described.

The desert of Paran is the large desert plateau which is bounded on the east by the Arabah, the deep valley running from the southern point of the Dead Sea to the Elanitic Gulf, and stretches westwards to the desert of Shur (*Jifar*; see Gen. xvi. 7 ; Ex. xv. 22), that separates Egypt from Philistia : it reaches southwards to Jebel et Tih, the foremost spur of the Horeb mountains, and northwards to the mountains of the Amorites, the southern border of Canaan. The origin and etymology of the name are obscure. The opinion that it was derived from פער, to open wide, and originally denoted the broad valley of Wady Murreh, between the Hebrew Negeb and the desert of Tih, and was then transferred to the whole district, has very little probability in it (*Knobel*). All that can be regarded as certain is, that the *El-Paran* of Gen. xiv. 6 is a proof that in the very earliest times the name was applied to the whole of the desert of Tih down to the Elanitic Gulf, and that the *Paran* of the Bible had no historical connection either with the κώμη Φαρὰν and tribe of Φαρανῖται mentioned by *Ptol.* (v. 17, i. 3), or with the town of Φαράν, of which the remains are still to be seen in the Wady *Feiran* at Serbal, or with the tower of *Faran Ahrun* of *Edrisi*, the modern *Hammân Faraun*, on the Red Sea, to the south of the Wady Gharandel. By the Arabian geographers, *Isztachri, Kazwini,* and others, and also by the Bedouins, it is called *et Tih*, *i.e.* the wandering of the children of Israel, as being the ground upon which the children of Israel wandered about in the wilderness for forty years (or more accurately, thirty-eight). This desert plateau, which is thirty German miles (150 English) long from south to north, and almost as broad, consists, according to Arabian geographers, partly of sand and partly of firm soil, and is intersected through almost its entire length by the *Wady el Arish*, which commences at a short distance from the northern extremity of the southern border mountains of *et Tih*, and runs in nearly a straight line from south to north, only turning in a north-westerly direction towards the Mediterranean Sea, on the north-east of the *Jebel el Helal*. This wady divides the desert of Paran into a western and an eastern half. The western half lies lower than the eastern, and slopes off gradually, without any perceptible natural boundary, into the flat desert of Shur (*Jifar*), on the shore of the Mediterranean Sea. The eastern half (between the Arabah and the Wady *el Arish*) consists throughout of a lofty mountainous country, intersected by larger and smaller wadys, and with extensive table-land between the loftier ranges, which slopes off somewhat in a northerly direction, its southern edge being formed by the eastern spurs of the Jebel et Tih. It is intersected by the Wady *el Jerafeh*, which commences at the foot of the northern slope of the mountains of *Tih*, and after proceeding at first in a northerly direction, turns higher up in a north-easterly direction towards the Arabah, but rises in its northern portion to a strong mountain fortress, which is called, from its present inhabitants, the highlands of the *Azazimeh*, and is bounded on both south and north by steep and lofty mountain ranges. The southern boundary is formed by the range which connects the *Araif en Nakba* with the *Jebel el Mukrah* on the east; the northern boundary, by the mountain barrier which stretches along the Wady *Murreh* from west to east, and rises precipitously from it, and of which the following description has been given by *Rowland* and *Williams*, the first of modern travellers to visit this district, who entered the *terra incognita* by proceeding directly south from Hebron, past *Arara* or Aroër, and surveyed it from the border of the *Rachmah* plateau, *i.e.* of the mountains of the Amorites (Deut. i. 7, 20, 44), or the southernmost plateau of the mountains of Judah (see at chap. xiv. 45) :—" A gigantic mountain towered above us in savage grandeur, with masses of naked rock, resembling the bastions of some Cyclopean architecture, the end of which it was impossible for the eye to reach, towards either the west or the east. It extended also a long way towards the south ; and with its rugged, broken, and dazzling masses of chalk, which reflected the burning rays of the sun, it looked like an unapproachable furnace, a most fearful desert, without the slightest trace of vegetation. A broad defile, called Wady *Murreh*, ran at the foot of this bulwark, towards the east; and after a course of several miles, on reaching the strangely formed mountain of Moddera (Madurah), it is divided into two parts, the southern branch still retaining the same name, and running eastwards to the Arabah, whilst the other was called Wady Fikreh, and ran in a north-easterly direction to the Dead Sea. This mountain barrier proved to us beyond a doubt that we were now standing on the southern boundary of the promised land; and we were confirmed in this opinion by the statement of the guide, that *Kadesh* was only a few hours distant from the point where we were standing" (*Ritter*, xiv. p. 1084). The place of encampment in the desert of Paran is to be sought for at the north-west corner of this lofty mountain range (see at chap. xii. 16).

In vers. 13–28 the removal of the different camps is more fully described, according to the order of march established in chap. ii., the order in which the different sections of the Levites drew out and marched being particularly described in this place alone (cf. vers. 17 and 21 with chap. ii. 17). First of all (*lit.* "*at the beginning*") the banner of Judah drew out, with Issachar and Zebulun (vers. 14–16; cf. chap. ii. 3–9). The tabernacle was then taken down, and the Gershonites and Merarites broke up, carrying those portions of it which were assigned to them (ver. 17; cf. chap. iv. 24 sqq., and 31 sqq.), that they might set up the dwelling at the place to be chosen for the next encampment, before the Kohathites arrived with the sacred things (ver. 21). The banner of Reuben followed next with Simeon and Gad (vers. 18–21; cf. chap. ii. 10–16), and the Kohathites joined them bearing the sacred things (ver. 21). הַמִּקְדָּשׁ (= הַקֹּדֶשׁ, chap. vii. 9, and קֹדֶשׁ הַקֳּדָשִׁים, chap. iv. 4) signifies the sacred things mentioned in chap. iii. 31. In ver. 21*b* the subject is the Gershonites and Merarites, who had broken up before with the component parts of the dwelling, and set up the dwelling, עַד־בֹּאָם, against their (the Kohathites') arrival, so that they might place the holy things at once within it.—Vers. 22–28. Behind the sacred things came the banners of Ephraim, with Manasseh and Benjamin (see chap. ii. 18–24), and Dan with Asher and Naphtali (chap. ii. 25–31); so that the camp of Dan was the "*collector of all the camps according to their hosts,*" *i.e.* formed that division of the army which kept the hosts together.

Vers. 29–32. The conversation in which Moses persuaded *Hobab* the Midianite, the son of Reguel (see at Ex. ii. 16), and his brother-in-law, to go with the Israelites, and being well acquainted with the desert to act as their leader, preceded the departure in order of time ; but it is placed between the setting out and the march itself, as being subordinate to the main events. When and why Hobab came into the camp of the Israelites,—whether he came with his father Reguel (or Jethro) when Israel first arrived at Horeb, and so remained behind when Jethro left (Ex. xviii. 27), or whether he did not come till afterwards,—was left uncertain, because it was a matter of no consequence in relation to what is narrated here.[1] The request addressed to Hobab, that he would go with them to the place which Jehovah had promised to give them, *i.e.* to Canaan, was supported by the promise that he would do good to them (Hobab and his company), as Jehovah had spoken good concerning Israel, *i.e.* had promised it prosperity in Canaan. And when Hobab declined the request, and said that he should return into his own land, *i.e.* to Midian at the south-east of Sinai (see at Ex. ii. 15 and iii. 1), and to his kindred, Moses repeated the request, *"Leave us not, forasmuch as thou knowest our encamping in the desert,"* *i.e.* knowest where we can pitch our tents; *"therefore be to us as eyes,"* *i.e.* be our leader and guide,—and promised at the same time to do him the good that Jehovah would do to them. Although Jehovah led the march of the Israelites in the pillar of cloud, not only giving the sign for them to break up and to encamp, but showing generally the direction they were to take; yet Hobab, who was well acquainted with the desert, would be able to render very important service to the Israelites, if he only pointed out, in those places where the sign to encamp was given by the cloud, the

---

[1] The grounds upon which *Knobel* affirms that the "Elohist" is not the author of the account in vers. 29–36, and pronounces it a Jehovistic interpolation, are perfectly futile. The assertion that the Elohist had already given a full description of the departure in vers. 11–28, rests upon an oversight of the peculiarities of the Semitic historians. The expression "they set forward" in ver. 28 is an anticipatory remark, as *Knobel* himself admits in other places (*e.g.* Gen. vii. 12, viii. 3 ; Ex. vii. 6, xii. 50, xvi. 34). The other argument, that Moses' brother-in-law is not mentioned anywhere else, involves a *petitio principii*, and is just as powerless a proof, as such peculiarities of style as "mount of the Lord," "ark of the covenant of the Lord," הֵיטִיב to do good (ver. 29), and others of a similar kind, of which the critics have not even attempted to prove that they are at variance with the style of the Elohist, to say nothing of their having actually done so.

springs, oases, and plots of pasture which are often buried quite out of sight in the mountains and valleys that overspread the desert. What Hobab ultimately decided to do, we are not told; but " as no further refusal is mentioned, and the departure of Israel is related immediately afterwards, he probably consented" (*Knobel*). This is raised to a certainty by the fact that, at the commencement of the period of the Judges, the sons of the brother-in-law of Moses went into the desert of Judah to the south of Arad along with the sons of Judah (Judg. i. 16), and therefore had entered Canaan with the Israelites, and that they were still living in that neighbourhood in the time of Saul (1 Sam. xv. 6, xxvii. 10, xxx. 29).

Vers. 33–36. "*And they* (the Israelites) *departed from the mount of Jehovah* (Ex. iii. 1) *three days' journey ; the ark of the covenant of Jehovah going before them, to search out a resting-place for them. And the cloud of Jehovah was over them by day, when they broke up from the camp.*" Jehovah still did as He had already done on the way to Sinai (Ex. xiii. 21, 22): He went before them in the pillar of cloud, according to His promise (Ex. xxxiii. 13), on their journey from Sinai to Canaan ; with this simple difference, however, that henceforth the cloud that embodied the presence of Jehovah was connected with the ark of the covenant, as the visible throne of His gracious presence which had been appointed by Jehovah Himself. To this end the ark of the covenant was carried separately from the rest of the sacred things, in front of the whole army ; so that the cloud which went before them floated above the ark, leading the procession, and regulating its movements and the direction it took in such a manner that the permanent connection between the cloud and the sanctuary might be visibly manifested even during their march. It is true that, in the order observed in the camp and on the march, no mention is made of the ark of the covenant going in front of the whole army ; but this omission is no more a proof of any discrepancy between this verse and chap. ii. 17, or of a difference of authorship, than the separation of the different divisions of the Levites upon the march, which is also not mentioned in chap. ii. 17, although the Gershonites and Merarites actually marched between the banners of Judah and Reuben, and the Kohathites with the holy things between the banners of Reuben and Ephraim (vers. 17 and 21).[1] The words, "the cloud was above them" (the Israelites), and so forth, can be reconciled with this supposition

---

[1] As the critics do not deny that vers. 11-28 are written by the " Elohist" notwithstanding this difference, they have no right to bring forward the account

without any difficulty, whether we understand them as signifying
that the cloud, which appeared as a guiding column floating above
the ark and moved forward along with it, also extended itself along
the whole procession, and spread out as a protecting shade over the
whole army (as *O. v. Gerlach* and *Baumgarten* suppose), or that
"above them" (upon them) is to be regarded as expressive of the
fact that it accompanied them as a protection and shade.   Nor is
Ps. cv. 39, which seems, so far as the words are concerned, rather to
favour the first explanation, really at variance with this view; for
the Psalmist's intention is not so much to give a physical description
of the phenomenon, as to describe the sheltering protection of God
in poetical words as a spreading out of the cloud above the wandering people of God, in the form of a protection against both heat and
rain (cf. Isa. iv. 5, 6).   Moreover, vers. 33b and 34 have a poetical
character, answering to the elevated nature of their subject, and
are to be interpreted as follows according to the laws of a poetical
parallelism: The one thought that the ark of the covenant, with
the cloud soaring above it, led the way and sheltered those who
were marching, is divided into two clauses; in ver. 33b only the
ark of the covenant is mentioned as going in front of the Israelites,
and in ver. 34 only the cloud as a shelter over them: whereas
the carrying of the ark in front of the army could only accomplish
the end proposed, viz. to search out a resting-place for them, by
Jehovah going above them in the cloud, and showing the bearers
of the ark both the way they were to take, and the place where
they were to rest.   The ark with the tables of the law is not called
"the ark of testimony" here, according to its contents, as in Ex.
xxv. 22, xxvi. 33, 34, xxx. 6, etc., but the ark of the covenant of
Jehovah, according to its design and signification for Israel, which
was the only point, or at any rate the principal point, in consideration here.   The resting-place which the ark of the covenant found
at the end of three days, is not mentioned in ver. 34; it was not
Tabeerah, however (chap. xi. 3), but Kibroth-hattaavah (chap. xi.
34, 35; cf. chap. xxxiii. 16).

In vers. 35 and 36, the words which Moses was in the habit of
uttering, both when the ark removed and when it came to rest
again, are given not only as a proof of the joyous confidence of
Moses, but as an encouragement to the congregation to cherish the
same believing confidence.   When breaking up, he said, "*Rise up,*

of the ark going first as a contradiction to chap. ii., and therefore a proof that
vers. 33 sqq. are not of Elohistic origin.

Jehovah! that Thine enemies may be scattered, and they tnat hate Thee may flee before Thy face;" and when it rested, *" Return, Jehovah, to the ten thousand thousands of Israel!"* Moses could speak in this way, because he knew that Jehovah and the ark of the covenant were inseparably connected, and saw in the ark of the covenant, as the throne of Jehovah, a material pledge of the gracious presence of the Almighty God. He said this, however, not merely with reference to enemies who might encounter the Israelites in the desert, but with a confident anticipation of the calling of Israel, to strive for the cause of the Lord in this hostile world, and rear His kingdom upon earth. Human power was not sufficient for this; but to accomplish this end, it was necessary that the Almighty God should go before His people, and scatter their foes. The prayer addressed to God to do this, is an expression of bold believing confidence,—a prayer sure of its answer; and to Israel it was the word with which the congregation of God was to carry on the conflict at all times against the powers and authorities of a whole hostile world. It is in this sense that in Ps. lxviii. 2, the words are held up by David before himself and his generation as a banner of victory, *"to arm the Church with confidence, and fortify it against the violent attacks of its foes"* (*Calvin*). שׁוּבָה is construed with an accusative : return to the ten thousands of the hosts of Israel, *i.e.* after having scattered Thine enemies, turn back again to Thy people to dwell among them. The *" thousands of Israel,"* as in chap. i. 16.[1]

[1] The inverted *nuns*, ׆, at the beginning and close of vers. 35, 36, which are found, according to *R. Menachem's de Lonzano Or Torah* (f. 17), in all the Spanish and German MSS., and are sanctioned by the Masorah, are said by the Talmud (*tract de sabbatho*) to be merely *signa parentheseos, quæ monerent præter historiæ seriem versum 35 et 36 ad capitis finem inseri* (cf. *Matt. Hilleri de Arcano Kethib et Keri libri duo*, pp. 158, 159). The Cabbalists, on the other hand, according to *R. Menach.* l. c., find an allusion in it to the *Shechinah*, *" quæ velut obversa ad tergum facie sequentes Israelitas ex impenso amore respiceret"* (see the note in *J. H. Michaelis' Bibl. hebr.*). In other MSS., however, which are supported by the *Masora Erffurt*, the inverted *nun* is found in the words בִּנְסֹעַ (ver. 35) and וַיְהִי הָעָם כְּמִתְאֹנְנִים (chap. xi. 1) : the first, *ad innuendum ut sic retrorsum agantur omnes hostes Israelitarum;* the second, *ut esset symbolum perpetuum perversitatis populi, inter tot illustria signa liberationis et maximorum beneficiorum Dei acerbe quiritantium, ad declarandam ingratitudinem et contumaciam suam* (cf. *J. Buxtorf, Tiberias*, p. 169).

OCCURRENCES AT TABEERAH AND KIBROTH-HATTAAVAH.—
CHAP. XI.

Vers. 1–3. After a three days' march the Israelites arrived at a resting-place; but the people began at once to be discontented with their situation.[1] *The people were like those who complain in the ears of Jehovah of something bad;* i.e. they behaved like persons who groan and murmur because of some misfortune that has happened to them. No special occasion is mentioned for the complaint. The words are expressive, no doubt, of the general dissatisfaction and discontent of the people at the difficulties and privations connected with the journey through the wilderness, to which they gave utterance so loudly, that their complaining reached the ears of Jehovah. At this His wrath burned, inasmuch as the complaint was directed against Him and His guidance, " *so that fire of Jehovah burned against them, and ate at the end of the camp.*" בָּעַר בְּ signifies here, not to burn a person (Job i. 16), but to burn against. " *Fire of Jehovah:*" a fire sent by Jehovah, but not proceeding directly from Him, or bursting forth from the cloud, as in Lev. x. 2. Whether it was kindled through a flash of lightning, or in some other such way, cannot be more exactly determined. There is not sufficient ground for the supposition that the fire merely seized upon the bushes about the camp and the tents of the people, but not upon human beings (*Ros., Knobel*). All that is plainly taught in the words is, that the fire did not extend over the whole camp, but merely broke out at one end of it, and sank down again, i.e. was extinguished very quickly, at the intercession of Moses; so that in this judgment the Lord merely manifested His power to destroy the murmurers, that He might infuse into the whole nation a wholesome dread of His holy majesty.—Ver. 3. From this judgment the place where the fire had burned received the name of " *Tabeerah,*" i.e. burning, or place of burning. Now, as this spot is distinctly described as the end or outermost edge of the camp, this " place

---

[1] The arguments by which *Knobel* undertakes to prove, that in chaps. xi. and xii. of the original work different foreign accounts respecting the first encampments after leaving Sinai have been woven together by the " Jehovist," are founded upon misinterpretations and arbitrary assumptions and conclusions, such as the assertion that the tabernacle stood outside the camp (chaps. xi. 25, xii. 5); that Miriam entered the tabernacle (chap. xii. 4, 5); that the original work had already reported the arrival of Israel in *Paran* in chap. x. 12; and that no reference is ever made to a camping-place called Tabeerah, and others of the same kind. For the proof, see the explanation of the verses referred to.

of burning" must not be regarded, as it is by *Knobel* and others, as a different station from the "graves of lust." *Tabeerah* was simply the local name given to a distant part of the whole camp, which received soon after the name of *Kibroth-Hattaavah*, on account of the greater judgment which the people brought upon themselves through their rebellion. This explains not only the omission of the name Tabeerah from the list of encampments in chap. xxxiii. 16, but also the circumstance, that nothing is said about any removal from Tabeerah to Kibroth-Hattaavah, and that the account of the murmuring of the people, because of the want of those supplies of food to which they had been accustomed in Egypt, is attached, without anything further, to the preceding narrative. There is nothing very surprising either, in the fact that the people should have given utterance to their wish for the luxuries of Egypt, which they had been deprived of so long, immediately after this judgment of God, if we only understand the whole affair as taking place in exact accordance with the words of the texts, viz. that the unbelieving and discontented mass did not discern the chastising hand of God at all in the conflagration which broke out at the end of the camp, because it was not declared to be a punishment from God, and was not preceded by a previous announcement; and therefore that they gave utterance in loud murmurings to the discontent of their hearts respecting the want of flesh, without any regard to what had just befallen them.

Vers. 4–9. The first impulse to this came from the mob that had come out of Egypt along with the Israelites. "*The mixed multitude:*" see at Ex. xii. 38. They felt and expressed a longing for the better food which they had enjoyed in Egypt, and which was not to be had in the desert, and urged on the Israelites to cry out for flesh again, especially for the flesh and the savoury vegetables in which Egypt abounded. The words "*they wept again*" (שׁוּב used adverbially, as in Gen. xxvi. 18, etc.) point back to the former complaints of the people respecting the absence of flesh in the desert of Sin (Ex. xvi. 2 sqq.), although there is nothing said about their weeping there. By the flesh which they missed, we are not to understand either the fish which they expressly mention in the following verse (as in Lev. xi. 11), or merely oxen, sheep, and goats; but the word בָּשָׂר signifies flesh generally, as being a better kind of food than the bread-like manna. It is true they possessed herds of cattle, but these would not have been sufficient to supply their wants, as cattle could not be bought for slaughtering, and it was necessary to spare what they had. The greedy people also longed for other flesh, and said, " *We remember the fish which we ate in Egypt for nothing.*" Even if fish could not be had for nothing in Egypt, according to the extravagant assertions of the murmurers, it is certain that it could be procured for such nominal prices that even the poorest of the people could eat it. The abundance of the fish in the Nile and the neighbouring waters is attested unanimously by both classical writers (*e.g. Diod. Sic.* i. 36, 52 ; *Herod.* ii. 93 ; *Strabo*, xvii. p. 829) and modern travellers (cf. *Hengstenberg*, Egypt, etc., p. 211 Eng. tr.). This also applies to the vegetables for which the Israelites longed in the desert. The קִשֻּׁאִים, or cucumbers, which are still called *katteh* or *chate* in the present day, are a species differing from the ordinary cucumbers in size and colour, and distinguished for softness and sweet flavour, and are described by *Forskal* (*Flor. Aeg.* p. 168), as *fructus in Ægypto omnium vulgatissimus, totis plantatus agris.* אֲבַטִּחִים : water-melons, which are still called *battieh* in modern Egypt, and are both cultivated in immense quantities and sold so cheaply in the market, that the poor as well as the rich can enjoy their refreshing flesh and cooling juice (see *Sonnini* in *Hengstenberg, ut sup.* p. 212). חָצִיר does not signify grass here, but, according to the ancient versions, *chives*, from their grass-like appearance ; *laudatissimus porrus in Ægypto* (Plin. h. n. 19, 33). בְּצָלִים : onions, which flourish better in Egypt than elsewhere, and have a mild and pleasant taste. According to *Herod.* ii. 125, they were the ordinary food of the workmen at the pyramids ; and, according to *Hasselquist, Sonnini,* and others, they still form almost the only food of the poor, and are also a favourite dish with all classes, either roasted, or boiled as a vegetable, and eaten with animal food. שׁוּמִים : garlic, which is still called *tum, tom* in the East (*Seetzen*, iii. p. 234), and is mentioned by *Herodotus* in connection with onions, as forming a leading article of food with the Egyptian workmen. Of all these things, which had been cheap as well as refreshing, not one was to be had in the desert. Hence the people complained still further, " *and now our soul is dried away,*" *i.e.* faint for want of strong and refreshing food, and wanting in fresh vital power (cf. Ps. xxii. 16, cii. 5) : " *we have nothing* (אֵין כֹּל, there is nothing in existence, equivalent to nothing to be had) *except that our eye (falls) upon this manna,*" *i.e.* we see nothing else before us but the manna, *sc.* which has no juice, and supplies no vital force. Greediness longs for juicy and savoury food, and in fact, as a rule, for change of food and stimulating flavour. " This is the perverted nature of man, which cannot continue in the quiet enjoyment of what is clean and unmixed, but, from its own inward discord, desires a stimulating admixture of what is sharp and sour" (*Baumgarten*). To point out this inward perversion on the part of the murmuring people, Moses once more described the nature, form, and taste of the manna, and its mode of preparation, as a pleasant food which God sent down to His people with the dew of heaven (see at Ex. xvi. 14, 15, and 31). But this sweet bread of heaven wanted "the sharp and sour, which are required to give a stimulating flavour to the food of man, on account of his sinful, restless desires, and the incessant changes of his earthly life." In this respect the manna resembled the spiritual food supplied by the word of God, of which the sinful heart of man may also speedily become weary, and turn to the more piquant productions of the spirit of the world.

Vers. 10–15. When Moses heard the people weep, "*according to their families, every one before the door of his tent,*" *i.e.* heard complaining in all the families in front of every tent, so that the weeping had become universal throughout the whole nation (cf. Zech. xii. 12 sqq.), and the wrath of the Lord burned on account of it, and the thing displeased Moses also, he brought his complaint to the Lord. The words "*Moses also was displeased,*" are introduced as a circumstantial clause, to explain the matter more clearly, and show the reason for the complaint which Moses poured out before the Lord, and do not refer exclusively either to the murmuring of the people or to the wrath of Jehovah, but to both together. This follows evidently from the position in which the clause stands between the two antecedent clauses in ver. 10 and the apodosis in ver. 11, and still more evidently from the complaint of Moses which follows. For "the whole attitude of Moses shows that his displeasure was excited not merely by the unrestrained rebellion of the people against Jehovah, but also by the unrestrained wrath of Jehovah against the nation" (*Kurtz*). But in what was the wrath of Jehovah manifested? It broke out against the people first of all when they had been satiated with flesh (ver. 33). There is no mention of any earlier manifestation. Hence Moses can only have discovered a sign of the burning wrath of Jehovah in the fact that, although the discontent of the people burst forth in loud cries, God did not help, but withdrew with His help, and let the whole storm of the infuriated people burst upon him.—Vers. 11 sqq. In Moses' complaint there is an unmistakeable discontent arising from the excessive burden of his office. "*Why hast Thou done evil to Thy servant? and why have I not found favour in Thy sight, to lay upon me the burden of all this people?"* The "burden of all this people" is the expression which he uses to denote "the care of governing the people, and providing everything for it" (*C. a. Lap.*). This burden, which God imposed upon him in connection with his office, appeared to him a bad and ungracious treatment on the part of God. This is the language of the discontent of despair, which differs from the murmuring of unbelief, in the fact that it is addressed to God, for the purpose of entreating help and deliverance from Him; whereas unbelief complains of the ways of God, but while complaining of its troubles, does not pray to the Lord its God. *"Have I conceived all this people,"* Moses continues, *"or have I brought it forth, that Thou requirest me to carry it in my bosom, as a nursing father carries the suckling, into the promised land?"* He does not intend by these words to throw off entirely all care for the people, but simply to plead with God that the duty of carrying and providing for Israel rests with Him, the Creator and Father of Israel (Ex. iv. 22; Isa. lxiii. 16). Moses, a weak man, was wanting in the omnipotent power which alone could satisfy the crying of the people for flesh. יִבְכּוּ עָלַי, *"they weep unto me,"* i.e. they come weeping to ask me to relieve their distress. *"I am not able to carry this burden alone; it is too heavy for me."*—Ver. 15. *"If Thou deal thus with me, then kill me quite* (הָרֹג *inf. abs.*, expressive of the uninterrupted process of killing; see *Ewald*, § 280, *b.*), *if I have found favour in Thine eyes* (i.e. if Thou wilt show me favour), *and let me not see my misfortune."* "My misfortune:" i.e. the calamity to which I must eventually succumb.

Vers. 16–23. There was good ground for his complaint. The burden of the office laid upon the shoulders of Moses was really too heavy for one man; and even the discontent which broke out in the complaint was nothing more than an outpouring of zeal for the office assigned him by God, under the burden of which his strength would eventually break down, unless he received some support. He was not tired of the office, but would stake his life for it if God did not relieve him in some way, as office and life were really one in him. Jehovah therefore relieved him in the distress of which he complained, without blaming the words of His servant, which bordered on despair. *"Gather unto Me,"* He said to Moses (vers. 16, 17), *"seventy men of the elders of Israel, whom thou knowest as elders and officers (shoterim, see Ex. v. 6) of the people, and bring them unto the tabernacle, that they may place themselves there with thee. I will come down* (see at ver. 25) *and speak with thee there, and will take of the spirit which is upon thee, and will put it upon them, that they may bear the burden of the people with thee.*"—Vers. 18 sqq. Jehovah would also relieve the complaining of the people, and that in such a way that the murmurers should experience at the same time the holiness of His judgments. The people were to sanctify themselves for the next day, and·were then to eat flesh (receive flesh to eat). הִתְקַדֵּשׁ (as in Ex. xix. 10), to prepare themselves by purifications for the revelation of the glory of God in the miraculous gift of flesh. Jehovah would give them flesh, so that they should eat it not one day, or two, or five, or ten, or twenty, but a whole month long (of " days," as in Gen. xxix. 14, xli. 1), " *till* it come out of your nostrils, and become loathsome unto you," as a punishment for having despised Jehovah in the midst of them, in their contempt of the manna given by God, and for having shown their regret at leaving the land of Egypt in their longing for the provisions of that land.—Vers. 21 sqq. When Moses thereupon expressed his amazement at the promise of God to provide flesh for 600,000 men for a whole month long even to satiety, and said, " *Shall flocks and herds be slain for them, to suffice them? or shall all the fish of the sea be gathered together for them, to suffice them?*" he was answered by the words, " *Is the arm of Jehovah too short* (*i.e.* does it not reach far enough; is it too weak and powerless)? *Thou shalt see now whether My word shall come to pass unto thee or not.*"

Vers. 24–30. After receiving from the Lord this reply to his complaint, Moses went out (*sc.* " of the tabernacle," where he had laid his complaint before the Lord) into the camp; and having made known to the people the will of God, gathered together seventy men of the elders of the people, and directed them to station themselves around the tabernacle. " *Around the tabernacle*," does not signify in this passage on all four sides, but in a semicircle around the front of the tabernacle; the verb is used in this sense in chap. xxi. 4, when it is applied to the march round Edom.— Ver. 25. Jehovah then came down in the cloud, which soared on high above the tabernacle, and now came down to the door of it (chap. xii. 5; Ex. xxxiii. 9; Deut. xxxi. 15). The statement in chap. ix. 18 sqq., and Ex. xl. 37, 38, that the cloud dwelt (שָׁכַן) above the dwelling of the tabernacle during the time of encampment, can be reconciled with this without any difficulty; since the only idea that we can form of this " dwelling upon it" is, that the cloud stood still, soaring in quietness above the tabernacle, without

moving to and fro like a cloud driven by the wind. There is no
such discrepancy, therefore, as *Knobel* finds in these statements.
When Jehovah had come down, He spoke to Moses, *sc.* to explain
to him and to the elders what was about to be done, and then laid
upon the seventy elders of the Spirit which was upon him. We
are not to understand this as implying, that the fulness of the Spirit
possessed by Moses was diminished in consequence; still less to
regard it, with *Calvin*, as *signum indignationis*, or *nota ignominiæ*,
which God intended to stamp upon him. For the Spirit of God is
not something material, which is diminished by being divided, but
resembles a flame of fire, which does not decrease in intensity, but
increases rather by extension. As *Theodoret* observed, " Just as a
person who kindles a thousand flames from one, does not lessen the
first, whilst he communicates light to the others, so God did not
diminish the grace imparted to Moses by the fact that He communicated of it to the seventy." God did this to show to Moses,
as well as to the whole nation, that the Spirit which Moses had
received was perfectly sufficient for the performance of the duties
of his office, and that no supernatural increase of that Spirit was
needed, but simply a strengthening of the natural powers of Moses
by the support of men who, when endowed with the power of the
Spirit that was taken from him, would help him to bear the burden
of his office. We have no description of the way in which this
transference took place; it is therefore impossible to determine
whether it was effected by a sign which would strike the outward
senses, or passed altogether within the sphere of the Spirit's life, in
a manner which corresponded to the nature of the Spirit itself. In
any case, however, it must have been effected in such a way, that
Moses and the elders received a convincing proof of the reality of
the affair. When the Spirit descended upon the elders, " *they
prophesied, and did not add ;*" *i.e.* they did not repeat the prophesyings any further. וְלֹא יָסָפוּ is rendered correctly by the LXX.,
καὶ οὐκ ἔτι προσέθεντο; the rendering supported by the *Vulgate*
and *Onkelos, nec ultro cessaverunt* (" and ceased not"), is incorrect.
הִתְנַבֵּא, " *to prophesy*," is to be understood generally, and especially
here, not as the foretelling of future things, but as speaking in an
ecstatic and elevated state of mind, under the impulse and inspiration of the Spirit of God, just like the " speaking with tongues,"
which frequently followed the gift of the Holy Ghost in the days
of the apostles. But we are not to infer from the fact, that the
prophesying was not repeated, that the Spirit therefore departed

from them after this one extraordinary manifestation. This mira-culous manifestation of the Spirit was intended simply to give to the whole nation the visible proof that God had endowed them with His Spirit, as helpers of Moses, and had given them the authority required for the exercise of their calling.—Ver. 26. But in order to prove to the whole congregation that the Spirit of the Lord was working there, the Spirit came not only upon the elders assembled round Moses, and in front of the tabernacle, but also upon two of the persons who had been chosen, viz. Eldad and Medad, who had remained behind in the camp, for some reason that is not reported, so that they also prophesied. " *Them that were written*," *conscripti*, for " called," because the calling of the elders generally took place in writing, from which we may see how thoroughly the Israelites had acquired the art of writing in Egypt.—Vers. 27, 28. This phenomenon in the camp itself produced such excitement, that a boy (הַנַּעַר, with the article like הַפָּלִיט in Gen. xiv. 13) reported the thing to Moses, whereupon Joshua requested Moses to prohibit the two from prophesying. Joshua felt himself warranted in doing this, because he had been Moses' servant from his youth up (see at Ex. xvii. 9), and in this capacity he regarded the prophesying of these men in the camp as detracting from the authority of his lord, since they had not received this gift from Moses, at least not through his mediation. Joshua was jealous for the honour of Moses, just as the disciples of Jesus, in Mark ix. 38, 39, were for the honour of their Lord ; and he was reproved by Moses, as the latter afterwards were by Christ.—Ver. 29. Moses replied, " *Art thou jealous for me ? Would that all the Lord's people were prophets, that Jehovah would put His Spirit upon them !*" As a true servant of God, who sought not his own glory, but the glory of his God, and the spread of His kingdom, Moses rejoiced in this manifesta-tion of the Spirit of God in the midst of the nation, and desired that all might become partakers of this grace.—Ver. 30. Moses returned with the elders into the camp, *sc.* from the tabernacle, which stood upon an open space in the midst of the camp, at some distance from the tents of the Levites and the rest of the tribes of Israel, which were pitched around it, so that whoever wished to go to it, had first of all to go out of his tent.[1]

[1] For the purpose of overthrowing the historical character of this marvellous event, the critics, from *Vater* to *Knobel*, have identified the appointment of the seventy elders to support Moses with the judicial institute established at Sinai by the advice of Jethro (Ex. xviii.), and adduce the obvious differences

No account has been handed down of the further action of this committee of elders. It is impossible to determine, therefore, in what way they assisted Moses in bearing the burden of governing the people. All that can be regarded as following unquestionably from the purpose given here is, that they did not form a permanent body, which continued from the time of Moses to the Captivity, and after the Captivity was revived again in the Sanhedrim, as Talmudists, Rabbins, and many of the earlier theologians suppose (see *Selden de Synedriis, l. i. c.* 14, ii. *c.* 4; *Jo. Marckii sylloge dissertatt. phil. theol. ad V. T. exercit.* 12, pp. 343 sqq.). On the opposite side *vid. Relandi Antiquitates*, ss. ii. 7, 3; *Carpz. apparat.* pp. 573 sq., etc.

Vers. 31–34. As soon as Moses had returned with the elders into the camp, God fulfilled His second promise. *" A wind arose from Jehovah, and brought quails (salvim,* see Ex. xvi. 13) *over from the sea, and threw them over the camp about a day's journey wide from here and there (i.e.* on both sides), *in the neighbourhood of the camp, and about two cubits above the surface."* The wind was a south-east wind (Ps. lxxviii. 26), which blew from the Arabian Gulf and brought the quails—which fly northwards in the spring from the interior of Africa in very great numbers (see vol. ii. p. 67)—from the sea to the Israelites. גּוּז, which only occurs here and in the Psalm of Moses (Ps. xc. 10), signifies to drive over, in

between these two entirely different institutions as arguments for the supposed diversity of documents and legends. But what ground is there for identifying things so totally different from one another? The assertion of *Knobel*, that in Deut. i. 9–18, Moses " evidently" refers to both events (Ex. xviii. and Num. xi.), is unfounded and untrue. Or are the same official duties and rank assigned to the elders who were chosen as judges in Ex. xviii., as to the seventy elders who were called by God, and endowed with His Spirit. that they might help Moses to govern the people who had rebelled against him and against Jehovah on account of the want of flesh, and to restore and uphold the authority of Moses as the divinely chosen leader of Israel, which had been shaken thereby? Can the judges of a land be identified without reserve with the executive of the land? The mere fact, that this executive court was chosen, like the judges, from the whole body of elders, does not warrant us in identifying the two institutions. Nor does it follow from the fact, that at Sinai seventy of the elders of Israel ascended the mountain with Moses, Aaron, and his sons, and there saw God (Ex. xxiv. 9 sqq.), that the seventy persons chosen here were the same as the seventy mentioned there. The sameness of the numbers does not prove that the persons were the same, but simply that the number seventy was the most suitable, on account of its historical and symbolical significance, to form a representation of the whole body of the people. For a further refutation of this futile objection, see *Ranke, Unterss. üb. d. Pent. II.* pp. 183 sqq.

Arabic and Syriac to pass over, not " to cut off," as the Rabbins suppose: the wind cut off the quails from the sea. נָטַשׁ, to throw them scattered about (Ex. xxix. 5, xxxi. 12, xxxii. 4). The idea is not that the wind caused the flock of quails to spread itself out as much as two days' journey over the camp, and to fly about two cubits above the surface of the ground; so that, being exhausted with their flight across the sea, they fell partly into the hands of the Israelites and partly upon the ground, as *Knobel* follows the *Vulgate* (*volabant in aëre duobus cubitis altitudine super terram*) and many of the Rabbins in supposing: for נָטַשׁ עַל הַמַּחֲנֶה does not mean to cause to fly or spread out over the camp, but to throw over or upon the camp. The words cannot therefore be understood in any other way than they are in Ps. lxxviii. 27, 28, viz. that the wind threw them about over the camp, so that they fell upon the ground a day's journey on either side of it, and that in such numbers that they lay, of course not for the whole distance mentioned, but in places about the camp, as much as two cubits deep. It is only in this sense of the words, that the people could possibly gather quails the whole of that day, the whole night, and the whole of the next day, in such quantities that he who had gathered but little had collected ten homers. A *homer*, the largest measure of capacity among the Hebrews, which contained ten ephahs, held, according to the lower reckoning of *Thenius*, 10,143 Parisian inches, or about two bushels Dresden measure. By this enormous quantity, which so immensely surpassed the natural size of the flocks of quails, God purposed to show the people His power, to give them flesh not for one day or several days, but for a whole month, both to put to shame their unbelief, and also to punish their greediness. As they could not eat this quantity all at once, they spread them round the camp to dry in the sun, in the same manner in which the Egyptians are in the habit of drying fish (*Herod*. ii. 77).—Ver. 33. But while the flesh was still between their teeth, and before it was ground, *i.e.* masticated, the wrath of the Lord burned against them, and produced among the people a very great destruction. This catastrophe is not to be regarded as "the effect of the excessive quantity of quails that they had eaten, on account of the quails feeding upon things which are injurious to man, so that eating the flesh of quails produces convulsions and giddiness (for proofs, see *Bochart, Hieroz.* ii. pp. 657 sqq.)," as *Knobel* supposes, but as an extraordinary judgment inflicted by God upon the greedy people, by which a great multitude of people were suddenly swept away.

—Ver. 34. From this judgment the place of encampment received the name *Kibroth-hattaavah, i.e.* graves of greediness, because there the people found their graves while giving vent to their greedy desires.

Ver. 35. From the graves of greediness the people removed to *Hazeroth*, and there they remained (הָיָה as in Ex. xxiv. 12). The situation of these two places of encampment is altogether unknown. *Hazeroth*, it is true, has been regarded by many since *Burckhardt* (Syr. p. 808) as identical with the modern *Hadhra* (in *Robinson's* Pal. *Ain el Hudhera*), eighteen hours to the north-east of Sinai, partly because of the resemblance in the name, and partly because there are not only low palm-trees and bushes there, but also a spring, of which *Robinson* says (Pal. i. p. 223) that it is the only spring in the neighbourhood, and yields tolerably good water, though somewhat brackish, the whole year round. But *Hadhra* does not answer to the Hebrew חָצֵר, to shut in, from which *Hazeroth* (enclosures) is derived; and there are springs in many other places in the desert of *et Tih* with both drinkable and brackish water. Moreover, the situation of this well does not point to *Hadhra*, which is only two days' journey from Sinai, so that the Israelites might at any rate have pitched their tents by this well after their first journey of three days (chap. x. 33), whereas they took three days to reach the graves of lust, and then marched from thence to Hazeroth. Consequently they would only have come to Hadhra on the supposition that they had been about to take the road to the sea, and intended to march along the coast to the Arabah, and so on through the Arabah to the Dead Sea (*Robinson*, p. 223); in which case, however, they would not have arrived at Kadesh. The conjecture that *Kibroth-hattaavah* is the same as *Di-Sahab* (Deut. i. 1), the modern *Dahab* (*Mersa Dahab, Minna el Dahab*), to the east of Sinai, on the Elanitic Gulf, is still more untenable. For what end could be answered by such a circuitous route, which, instead of bringing the Israelites nearer to the end of their journey, would have taken them to Mecca rather than to Canaan? As the Israelites proceeded from Hazeroth to Kadesh in the desert of Paran (chap. xiii. 3 and 26), they must have marched from Sinai to Canaan by the most direct route, through the midst of the great desert of et Tih, most probably by the desert road which leads from the *Wady es Sheikh* into the *Wady ez-Zuranuk*, which breaks through the southern border mountains of et Tih, and passes on through the *Wady ez-Zalakah* over *el Ain* to *Bir-et-*

Themmed, and then due north past *Jebel Araif* to the Hebron road. By this route they could go from Horeb to Kadesh Barnea in eleven days (Deut. i. 2), and it is here that we are to seek for the two stations in question. *Hazeroth* is probably to be found, as *Fries* and *Kurtz* suppose, in *Bir-et-Themmed*, and *Kibroth-hatta-avah* in the neighbourhood of the southern border mountains of *et Tih*.

REBELLION OF MIRIAM AND AARON AGAINST MOSES.—CHAP. XII.

Vers. 1-3. All the rebellions of the people hitherto had arisen from dissatisfaction with the privations of the desert march, and had been directed against Jehovah rather than against Moses. And if, in the case of the last one, at Kibroth-hattaavah, even Moses was about to lose heart under the heavy burden of his office; the faithful covenant God had given the whole nation a practical proof, in the manner in which He provided him support in the seventy elders, that He had not only laid the burden of the whole nation upon His servant Moses, but had also communicated to him the power of His Spirit, which was requisite to enable him to carry this burden. Thus not only was his heart filled with new courage when about to despair, but his official position in relation to all the Israelites was greatly exalted. This elevation of Moses excited envy on the part of his brother and sister, whom God had also richly endowed and placed so high, that Miriam was distinguished as a prophetess above all the women of Israel, whilst Aaron had been raised by his investiture with the high-priesthood into the spiritual head of the whole nation. But the pride of the natural heart was not satisfied with this. They would dispute with their brother Moses the pre-eminence of his special calling and his exclusive position, which they might possibly regard themselves as entitled to contest with him not only as his brother and sister, but also as the nearest supporters of his vocation. Miriam was the instigator of the open rebellion, as we may see both from the fact that her name stands before that of Aaron, and also from the use of the feminine verb תְּדַבֵּר in ver. 1. Aaron followed her, being no more able to resist the suggestions of his sister, than he had formerly been to resist the desire of the people for a golden idol (Ex. xxxii.). Miriam found an occasion for the manifestation of her discontent in the Cushite wife whom Moses had taken. This wife cannot have been Zip-porah the Midianite: for even though Miriam might possibly

have called her a Cushite, whether because the Cushite tribes
dwelt in Arabia, or in a contemptuous sense as a Moor or Hamite,
the author would certainly not have confirmed this at all events
inaccurate, if not contemptuous epithet, by adding, "*for he had
taken a Cushite wife;*" to say nothing of the improbability of
Miriam having made the marriage which her brother had contracted when he was a fugitive in a foreign land, long before he
was called by God, the occasion of reproach so many years afterwards. It would be quite different if, a short time before, probably
after the death of Zipporah, he had contracted a second marriage
with a Cushite woman, who either sprang from the Cushites dwelling in Arabia, or from the foreigners who had come out of Egypt
along with the Israelites. This marriage would not have been wrong
in itself, as God had merely forbidden the Israelites to marry the
daughters of Canaan (Ex. xxxiv. 16), even if Moses had not contracted it " with the deliberate intention of setting forth through this
marriage with a Hamite woman the fellowship between Israel and
the heathen, so far as it could exist under the law ; and thus practically exemplifying in his own person that equality between the
foreigners and Israel which the law demanded in various ways"
(*Baumgarten*), or of "prefiguring by this example the future union
of Israel with the most remote of the heathen," as *O. v. Gerlach*
and many of the fathers suppose.   In the taunt of the brother
and sister, however, we meet with that carnal exaggeration of the
Israelitish nationality which forms so all-pervading a characteristic
of this nation, and is the more reprehensible the more it rests upon
the ground of nature rather than upon the spiritual calling of Israel
(*Kurtz*).—Ver. 2. Miriam and Aaron said, " *Hath Jehovah then
spoken only by Moses, and not also by us?*"   Are not we—the high
priest Aaron, who brings the rights of the congregation before
Jehovah in the Urim and Thummim (Ex. xxviii. 30), and the
prophetess Miriam (Ex. xv. 20)—also organs and mediators of
divine revelation?   " They are proud of the prophetic gift, which
ought rather to have fostered modesty in them.   But such is the
depravity of human nature, that they not only abuse the gifts of
God towards the brother whom they despise, but by an ungodly
and sacrilegious glorification extol the gifts themselves in such a
manner as to hide the Author of the gifts" (*Calvin*).—" *And Jehovah heard.*"   This is stated for the purpose of preparing the way
for the judicial interposition of God.   When God hears what is
wrong, He must proceed to stop it by punishment.   Moses might

also have heard what they said, but "*the man Moses was very meek*
(πραΰς, LXX., *mitis,* Vulg.; not 'plagued,' *geplagt,* as *Luther* renders
it), *more than all men upon the earth.*" No one approached Moses
in meekness, because no one was raised so high by God as he was.
The higher the position which a man occupies among his fellow-
men, the harder is it for the natural man to bear attacks upon himself with meekness, especially if they are directed against his official
rank and honour. This remark as to the character of Moses serves
to bring out to view the position of the person attacked, and points
out the reason why Moses not only abstained from all self-defence,
but did not even cry to God for vengeance on account of the injury
that had been done to him. Because he was the meekest of all
men, he could calmly leave this attack upon himself to the all-wise
and righteous Judge, who had both called and qualified him for his
office. "For this is the idea of the eulogium of his meekness. It
is as if Moses had said that he had swallowed the injury in silence,
inasmuch as he had imposed a law of patience upon himself because
of his meekness" (*Calvin*).

The self-praise on the part of Moses, which many have discovered in this description of his character, and on account of
which some even of the earlier expositors regarded this verse as a
later gloss, whilst more recent critics have used it as an argument
against the Mosaic authorship of the Pentateuch, is not an expression of vain self-display, or a glorification of his own gifts
and excellences, which he prided himself upon possessing above all
others. It is simply a statement, which was indispensable to a full
and correct interpretation of all the circumstances, and which was
made quite objectively, with reference to the character which
Moses had not given to himself but had acquired through the
grace of God, and which he never falsified from the very time of
his calling until the day of his death, either at the rebellion of the
people at Kibroth-hattaavah (chap. xi.), or at the water of strife
at Kadesh (chap. xx.). His despondency under the heavy burden
of his office in the former case (chap. xi.) speaks rather for than
against the meekness of his character; and the sin at Kadesh
(chap. xx.) consisted simply in the fact, that he suffered himself to
be brought to doubt either the omnipotence of God, or the possibility of divine help, on account of the unbelief of the people.[1]

[1] There is not a word in Num. xx. 10 or Ps. cvi. 32 to the effect, that
"his dissatisfaction broke out into evident passion" (*Kurtz*). And it is quite a
mistake to observe, that in the case before us there was nothing at all to pro-

No doubt it was only such a man as Moses who could speak of himself in such a way,—a man who had so entirely sacrificed his own personality to the office assigned him by the Lord, that he was ready at any moment to stake his life for the cause and glory of the Lord (cf. chap. xi. 15, and Ex. xxxii. 32), and of whom *Calmet* observes with as much truth as force, " As he praises himself here without pride, so he will blame himself elsewhere with humility," —a man of God whose character is not to be measured by the standard of ordinary men (cf. *Hengstenberg, Dissertations,* vol. ii. pp. 141 sqq.).

Vers. 4–10. Jehovah summoned the opponents of His servant to come at once before His judgment-seat. He commanded Moses, Aaron, and Miriam suddenly to come out of the camp (see at chap. xi. 30) to the tabernacle. Then He Himself came down in a pillar of cloud to the door of the tabernacle, *i.e.* to the entrance to the court, not to the dwelling itself, and called Aaron and Miriam out, *i.e.* commanded them to come out of the court,[1] and said to them (vers. 6 sqq.): " *If there is a prophet of Jehovah to you (i.e. if you have one), I make Myself known to him in a vision; I speak to him in a dream* (בּוֹ, *lit. "in him,"* inasmuch as a revelation in a dream fell within the inner sphere of the soul-life). *Not so My servant Moses: he is approved in My whole house; mouth to mouth I speak to him, and as an appearance, and that not in enigmas; and he sees the form of Jehovah. Why are ye not afraid to speak against My servant, against Moses?* " נְבִיאֲכֶם=נָבִיא לָכֶם, the suffix used with the noun instead of the separate pronoun in the dative, as in Gen. xxxix. 21, Lev. xv. 3, etc. The noun *Jehovah* is in all probability to be taken as a genitive, in connection with the word

voke Moses to appeal to his meekness, since it was not his meekness that Miriam had disputed, but only his prophetic call. If such grounds as these are interpolated into the words of Moses, and it is to be held that an attack upon the prophetic calling does not involve such an attack upon the person as might have excited anger, it is certainly impossible to maintain the Mosaic authorship of this statement as to the character of Moses ; for the vanity of wishing to procure the recognition of his meekness by praising it, cannot certainly be imputed to Moses the man of God.

[1] The discrepancy discovered by *Knobel*, in the fact that, according to the so-called Elohist, no one but Moses, Aaron, and the sons of Aaron were allowed to enter the sanctuary, whereas, according to the Jehovist, others did so,— *e.g.* Miriam here, and Joshua in Ex. xxxiii. 11,—rests entirely upon a groundless fancy, arising from a misinterpretation, as there is not a word about entering the sanctuary, *i.e.* the dwelling itself, either in the verse before us or in Ex. xxxiii. 11.

נְבִיאֲכֶם ("a prophet to you"), as it is in the LXX. and Vulg., and not to be construed with the words which follow ("I Jehovah will make Myself known"). The position of Jehovah at the head of the clause without a preceding אָנֹכִי (I) would be much more remarkable than the separation of the dependent noun from the governing noun by the suffix, which occurs in other cases also (e.g. Lev. vi. 3, xxvi. 42, etc.); moreover, it would be by no means suited to the sense, as no such emphasis is laid upon the fact that it was Jehovah who made Himself known, as to require or even justify such a construction. The "whole house of Jehovah" (ver. 7) is not "primarily His dwelling, the holy tent" (Baumgarten),—for, in that case, the word "whole" would be quite superfluous,—but the whole house of Israel, or the covenant nation regarded as a kingdom, to the administration and government of which Moses had been called : as a matter of fact, therefore, the whole economy of the Old Testament, having its central point in the holy tent, which Jehovah had caused to be built as the dwelling-place of His name. It did not terminate, however, in the service of the sanctuary, as we may see from the fact that God did not make the priests who were entrusted with the duties of the sanctuary the organs of His saving revelation, but raised up and called prophets after Moses for that purpose. Compare the expression in Heb. iii. 6, "Whose house we are." נֶאֱמָן with בְּ does not mean to be, or become, entrusted with anything (Baumgarten, Knobel), but simply to be lasting, firm, constant, in a local or temporal sense (Deut. xxviii. 59 ; 1 Sam. ii. 35 ; 2 Sam. vii. 16, etc.) ; in a historical sense, to prove or attest one's self (Gen. xlii. 20) ; and in an ethical sense, to be found proof, trustworthy, true (Ps. lxxviii. 8 ; 1 Sam. iii. 20, xxii. 14 : see Delitzsch on Heb. iii. 2). In the participle, therefore, it signifies proved, faithful, πιστός (LXX.). "Mouth to mouth" answers to the "face to face" in Ex. xxxiii. 11 (cf. Deut. xxxiv. 10), i.e. without any mediation or reserve, but with the same closeness and freedom with which friends converse together (Ex. xxxiii. 11). This is still further strengthened and elucidated by the words in apposition, "in the form of seeing (appearance), and not in riddles," i.e. visibly, and not in a dark, hidden, enigmatical way. מַרְאֶה is an accusative defining the mode, and signifies here not vision, as in ver. 6, but adspectus, view, sight; for it forms an antithesis to בְּמַרְאָה in ver. 6. "The form (Eng. similitude) of Jehovah" was not the essential nature of God, His unveiled glory,—for this no mortal man can see (vid. Ex. xxxiii. 18 sqq.),—but a form which manifested the invisible God to the eye of man in a clearly discernible mode, and which was essentially different, not only from the visionary sight of God in the form of a man (Ezek. i. 26 ; Dan. vii. 9 and 13), but also from the appearances of God in the outward world of the senses, in the person and form of the angel of Jehovah, and stood in the same relation to these two forms of revelation, so far as directness and clearness were concerned, as the sight of a person in a dream to that of the actual figure of the person himself. God talked with Moses without figure, in the clear distinctness of a spiritual communication, whereas to the prophets He only revealed Himself through the medium of ecstasy or dream.

Through this utterance on the part of Jehovah, Moses is placed above all the prophets, in relation to God and also to the whole nation. The divine revelation to the prophets is thereby restricted to the two forms of inward intuition (vision and dream). It follows from this, that it had always a visionary character, though it might vary in intensity; and therefore that it had always more or less obscurity about it, because the clearness of self-consciousness and the distinct perception of an external world, both receded before the inward intuition, in a dream as well as in a vision. The prophets were consequently simply organs, through whom Jehovah made known His counsel and will at certain times, and in relation to special circumstances and features in the development of His kingdom. It was not so with Moses. Jehovah had placed him over all His house, had called him to be the founder and organizer of the kingdom established in Israel through his mediatorial service, and had found him faithful in His service. With this servant ($\theta\epsilon\rho\acute{a}\pi\omega\nu$, LXX.) of His, He spake mouth to mouth, without a figure or figurative cloak, with the distinctness of a human interchange of thought; so that at any time he could inquire of God and wait for the divine reply. Hence Moses was not a prophet of Jehovah, like many others, not even merely the first and highest prophet, *primus inter pares*, but stood above all the prophets, as the founder of the theocracy, and mediator of the Old Covenant. Upon this unparalleled relation of Moses to God and the theocracy, so clearly expressed in the verses before us, the Rabbins have justly founded their view as to the higher grade of inspiration in the *Thorah*. This view is fully confirmed through the history of the Old Testament kingdom of God, and the relation in which the writings of the prophets stand to those of Moses. The prophets subsequent to Moses simply continued to build upon the foundation which Moses laid. And if Moses stood in this unparalleled relation to the Lord, Miriam and Aaron sinned grievously against him, when speaking as they did. Ver. 9. After this address, " *the wrath of Jehovah burned against them, and He went.*" As a judge, withdrawing from the judgment-seat when he has pronounced his sentence, so Jehovah went, by the cloud in which He had come down withdrawing from the tabernacle, and ascending up on high. And at the same moment, Miriam, the instigator of the rebellion against her brother Moses, was covered with leprosy, and became white as snow.

Vers. 11–16. When Aaron saw his sister smitten in this way, he said to Moses, " *Alas! my lord, I beseech thee, lay not this sin upon us, for we have done foolishly ;*" *i.e.* let us not bear its punishment. " *Let her* (Miriam) *not be as the dead thing, on whose coming out of its mother's womb half its flesh is consumed ;*" *i.e.* like a stillborn child, which comes into the world half decomposed. His reason for making this comparison was, that leprosy produces decomposition in the living body.—Ver. 13. Moses, with his mildness, took compassion upon his sister, upon whom this punishment had fallen, and cried to the Lord, " *O God, I beseech Thee, heal her.*" The connection of the particle נָא with אֵל is certainly unusual, but yet it is analogous to the construction with such exclamations as אוֹי (Jer. iv. 31, xlv. 3) and הִנֵּה (Gen. xii. 11, xvi. 2, etc.) ; since אֵל in the vocative is to be regarded as equivalent to an exclamation ; whereas the alteration into אַל, as proposed by *J. D. Michaelis* and *Knobel*, does not even give a fitting sense, apart altogether from the fact, that the repetition of נָא after the verb, with אֵל נָא before it, would be altogether unexampled.—Vers. 14, 15. Jehovah hearkened to His servant's prayer, though not without inflicting deep humiliation upon Miriam. " *If her father had but spit in her face, would she not be ashamed seven days?*" *i.e.* keep herself hidden from Me out of pure shame. She was to be shut outside the camp, to be excluded from the congregation as a leprous person for seven days, and then to be received in again. Thus restoration and purification from her leprosy were promised to her after the endurance of seven days' punishment. Leprosy was the just punishment for her sin. In her haughty exaggeration of the worth of her own prophetic gift, she had placed herself on a par with Moses, the divinely appointed head of the whole nation, and exalted herself above the congregation of the Lord. For this she was afflicted with a disease which shut her out of the number of the members of the people of

God, and thus actually excluded from the camp; so that she could only be received back again after she had been healed, and by a formal purification. The latter followed as a matter of course, from Lev. xiii. and xiv., and did not need to be specially referred to here. —Vers. 15*b*, 16. The people did not proceed any farther till the restoration of Miriam. After this they departed from Hazeroth, and encamped in the desert of *Paran*, namely at Kadesh, on the southern boundary of Canaan. This is evident from chap. xiii., more especially ver. 26, as compared with Deut. i. 19 sqq., where it is stated not merely that the spies, who were sent out from this place of encampment to Canaan, returned to the congregation at Kadesh, but that they set out from Kadesh-Barnea for Canaan, because there the Israelites had come to the mountains of the Amorites, which God had promised them for an inheritance.

With regard to the situation of *Kadesh*, it has already been observed at Gen. xiv. 7, that it is probably to be sought for in the neighbourhood of the fountain of *Ain Kades*, which was discovered by *Rowland*, to the south of *Bir Seba* and *Khalasa*, on the heights of Jebel *Helal*, *i.e.* at the north-west corner of the mountain land of *Azazimeh*, which is more closely described at chap. x. 12 (see pp. 57, 58), where the western slopes of this highland region sink gently down into the undulating surface of the desert, which stretches thence to *El Arish*, with a breadth of about six hours' journey, and keeps the way open between Arabia Petræa and the south of Palestine. " In the northern third of this western slope, the mountains recede so as to leave a free space for a plain of about an hour's journey in breadth, which comes towards the east, and to which access is obtained through one or more of the larger wadys that are to be seen here (such as Retemat, Kusaimeh, el Ain, Muweileh)." At the north-eastern background of this plain, which forms almost a rectangular figure of nine miles by five, or ten by six, stretching from west to east, large enough to receive the camp of a wandering people, and about twelve miles to the E.S.E. of Muweileh, there rises, like a large solitary mass, at the edge of the mountains which run on towards the north, a bare rock, at the foot of which there is a copious spring, falling in ornamental cascades into the bed of a brook, which is lost in the sand about 300 or 400 yards to the west. This place still bears the ancient name of *Kudēs*. There can be no doubt as to the identity of this *Kudēs* and the biblical Kadesh. The situation agrees with all the statements in the Bible concerning Kadesh : for example, that Israel had then reached the border of the promised land ; also that the spies who were sent out from Kadesh returned thither by coming from Hebron to the wilderness of Paran (chap. xiii. 26) ; and lastly, according to the assertions of the Bedouins, as quoted by *Rowland,* this Kudes was ten or eleven days' journey from Sinai (in perfect harmony with Deut. i. 2), and was connected by passable wadys with Mount Hor. The Israelites proceeded, no doubt, through the wady *Retemat, i.e. Rithmah* (see at chap. xxxiii. 18), into the plain of Kadesh. (On the town of Kadesh, see at chap. xx. 16.)[1]

SPIES SENT OUT. MURMURING OF THE PEOPLE, AND THEIR PUNISHMENT.—CHAP. XIII. AND XIV.

When they had arrived at Kadesh, in the desert of Paran (chap. xiii. 26), Moses sent out spies by the command of God, and according to the wishes of the people, to explore the way by which they could enter into Canaan, and also the nature of the land, of its cities, and of its population (chap. xiii. 1–20). The men who were sent out passed through the land, from the south to the northern frontier, and on their return reported that the land was no doubt one of pre-eminent goodness, but that it was inhabited by a strong people, who had giants among them, and were in possession of very large fortified towns (vers. 21–29) ; whereupon Caleb declared that it was quite possible to conquer it, whilst the others despaired of overcoming the Canaanites, and spread an evil report among the people concerning the land (vers. 30–33). The congregation then raised a loud lamentation, and went so far in their murmuring against Moses and Aaron, as to speak without reserve or secrecy of deposing Moses, and returning to Egypt under another leader : they even wanted to stone Joshua and Caleb, who tried to calm the excited multitude, and urged them to trust in the Lord. But suddenly the glory of the Lord interposed with a special manifestation of judgment (chap. xiv. 1–10). Jehovah made known to Moses His resolution to destroy the rebellious nation, but suffered Himself to be moved by the intercession of Moses so far as to promise that He would preserve the nation, though He would exclude the murmuring multitude from the promised land (vers. 11–25). He then directed Moses and Aaron to proclaim to the people the following

---

[1] See *Kurtz,* History of the Old Covenent, vol. iii. p. 225, where the current notion, that Kadesh was situated on the western border of the Arabah, below the Dead Sea, by either Ain Hasb or Ain el Weibeh, is successfully refuted.

punishment for their repeated rebellion: that they should bear their iniquity for forty years in the wilderness; that the whole nation that had come out of Egypt should die there, with the exception of Caleb and Joshua; and that only their children should enter the promised land (vers. 26–39). The people were shocked at this announcement, and resolved to force a way into Canaan; but, as Moses predicted, they were beaten by the Canaanites and Amalekites, and driven back to Hormah (vers. 40–45).[1]

These events form a grand turning-point in the history of Israel, in which the whole of the future history of the covenant nation is typically reflected. The constantly repeated unfaithfulness of the nation could not destroy the faithfulness of God, or alter His purposes of salvation. In wrath Jehovah remembered mercy; through judgment He carried out His plan of salvation, that all the world might know that no flesh was righteous before Him, and that the unbelief and unfaithfulness of men could not overturn the truth of God.

Chap. xiii. 1–20. DESPATCH OF THE SPIES TO CANAAN.— Vers. 1 sqq. The command of Jehovah, to send out men to spy out the land of Canaan, was occasioned, according to the account given by Moses in Deut. i. 22 sqq., by a proposal of the congregation, which pleased Moses, so that he laid the matter before the Lord, who then commanded him to send out for this purpose, "*of every tribe of their fathers a man, every one a ruler among them,* i.e. none

---

[1] According to *Knobel*, the account of these events arose from two or three documents interwoven with one another in the following manner: chap. xiii. 1–17a, 21, 25, 26, 32, and xiv. 2a, 5–7, 10b, 36–38, was written by the Elohist, the remainder by the Jehovist,—chap. xiii. 22–24, 27–31, xiv. 1b, 11–25, 39–45, being taken from his first document, and chap. xiii. 17b–20, xiv. 2b–4, 8–10a, 26–33, 35, from his second; whilst, lastly, chap. xiii. 33, and the commencement of chap. xiv. 1, were added from his own resources, because it contains contradictory statements. " According to the Elohist," says this critic, " the spies went through the whole land (chap. xiii. 32, xiv. 7), and penetrated even to the north of the country (chap. xiii. 21): they took forty days to this (chap. xiii. 25, xiv. 34); they had among them Joshua, whose name was altered at that time (chap. xiii. 16), and who behaved as bravely as Caleb (chap. xiii. 8, xiv. 6, 38). According to the Jehovistic completion, the spies did not go through the whole land, but only entered into it (chap. xiii. 27), merely going into the neighbourhood of Hebron, in the south country (chap. xiii. 22, 23); there they saw the gigantic Anakites (chap. xiii. 22, 28, 33), cut off the large bunch of grapes in the valley of Eshcol (chap. xiii. 23, 24), and then came back to Moses. Caleb was the only one who showed himself courageous, and Joshua was not with them at all (chap. xiii. 30, xiv. 24)." But these discre-

but men who were princes in their tribes, who held the prominent
position of princes, *i.e.* distinguished persons of rank; or, as it is
stated in ver. 3, " *heads of the children of Israel,*" *i.e.* not the tribe-
princes of the twelve tribes, but those men, out of the total number
of the heads of the tribes and families of Israel, who were the most
suitable for such a mission, though the selection was to be made in
such a manner that every tribe should be represented by one of its
own chiefs.   That there were none of the twelve tribe-princes
among them is apparent from a comparison of their names (vers.
4–15) with the (totally different) names of the tribe-princes (chap.
i. 3 sqq., vii. 12 sqq.).   Caleb and Joshua are the only spies that
are known.   The order, in which the tribes are placed in the list of
the names in vers. 4–15, differs from that in chap. i. 5–15 only in
the fact that in ver. 10 Zebulun is separated from the other sons of
Leah, and in ver. 11 Manasseh is separated from Ephraim.   The
expression " *of the tribe of Joseph,*" in ver. 11, stands for " of the
children of Joseph," in chap. i. 10, xxxiv. 23.   At the close of the
list it is still further stated, that Moses called *Hoshea* (*i.e.* help), the
son of Nun, *Jehoshua,* contracted into *Joshua* (*i.e.* Jehovah-help,
equivalent to, whose help is Jehovah).   This statement does not
present any such discrepancy, when compared with Ex. xvii. 9, 13,
xxiv. 13, xxxii. 17, xxxiii. 11, and Num. xi. 28, where Joshua bears
this name as the servant of Moses at a still earlier period, as to point
to any diversity of authorship.   As there is nothing of a genea-

pancies do not exist in the biblical narrative; on the contrary, they have been
introduced by the critic himself, by the forcible separation of passages from
their context, and by arbitrary interpolations.   The words of the spies in chap.
xiii. 27, "We came into the land whither thou sentest us, and surely it floweth
with milk and honey," do not imply that they *only* came into the southern
portion of the land, any more than the fact that they brought a bunch of
grapes from the neighbourhood of Hebron is a proof that they did not go
beyond the valley of Eshcol.   Moreover, it is not stated in chap. xiii. 30 that
Joshua was not found among the tribes.   Again, the circumstance that in chap.
xiv. 11–25 and 26–35 the same thing is said twice over,—the special instructions
as to the survey of the land in chap. xiii. 17*b*–20, which were quite unnecessary
for intelligent leaders,—the swearing of God (chap. xiv. 16, 21, 23),—the forced
explanation of the name *Eshcol,* in chap. xiii. 24, and other things of the same
kind,—are said to furnish further proofs of the interpolation of Jehovistic clauses
into the Elohistic narrative; and lastly, a number of the words employed are
supposed to place this beyond all doubt.   Of these proofs, however, the first rests
upon a simple misinterpretation of the passage in question, and a disregard of
the peculiarities of Hebrew history; whilst the rest are either subjective conclusions, dictated by the taste of vulgar rationalism, or inferences and assumptions, of which the tenability and force need first of all to be established.

logical character in any of these passages, so as to warrant us in
expecting to find the family name of Joshua in them, the name
Joshua, by which Hosea had become best known in history, could
be used proleptically in them all. On the other hand, however, it
is not distinctly stated in the verse before us, that this was the
occasion on which Moses gave Hosea the new name of Joshua. As
the *Vav consec.* frequently points out merely the order of thought,
the words may be understood without hesitation in the following
sense : These are the names borne by the heads of the tribes to be
sent out as spies, as they stand in the family registers according to
their descent; Hosea, however, was named Joshua by Moses; which
would not by any means imply that the alteration in the name had
not been made till then. It is very probable that Moses may have
given him the new name either before or after the defeat of the
Amalekites (Ex. xvii. 9 sqq.), or when he took him into his service,
though it has not been mentioned before ; whilst here the circumstances themselves required that it should be stated that Hosea, as
he was called in the list prepared and entered in the documentary
record according to the genealogical tables of the tribes, had received from Moses the name of Joshua. In vers. 17–20 Moses
gives them the necessary instructions, defining more clearly the
motive which the congregation had assigned for sending them out,
namely, that they might search out the way into the land and to its
towns (Deut. i. 22). " *Get you up there* (זֶה) *in the south country,
and go up to the mountain.*" *Negeb, i.e.* south country, *lit.* dryness,
aridity, from נגב, to be dry or arid (in *Syr., Chald.,* and *Samar.*).
Hence the dry, parched land, in contrast to the well-watered country
(Josh. xv. 19 ; Judg. i. 15), was the name given to the southern
district of Canaan, which forms the transition from the desert to
the strictly cultivated land, and bears for the most part the character
of a steppe, in which tracts of sand and heath are intermixed with
shrubs, grass, and vegetables, whilst here and there corn is also
cultivated ; a district therefore which was better fitted for grazing
than for agriculture, though it contained a number of towns and
villages (see at Josh. xv. 21–32). " *The mountain*" is the mountainous part of Palestine, which was inhabited by Hittites, Jebusites,
and Amorites (ver. 29), and was called the mountains of the Amorites, on account of their being the strongest of the Canaanitish
tribes (Deut. i. 7, 19 sqq.). It is not to be restricted, as *Knobel*
supposes, to the limits of the so-called mountains of Judah (Josh.
xv. 48-62), but included the mountains of Israel or Ephraim also

(Josh. xi. 21, xx. 7), and formed, according to Deut. i. 7, the back-bone of the whole land of Canaan up to Lebanon.—Ver. 18. They were to see the land, " what it was," *i.e.* what was its character, and the people that dwelt in it, whether they were strong, *i.e.* courage-ous and brave, or weak, *i.e.* spiritless and timid, and whether they were little or great, *i.e.* numerically ; (ver. 19) what the land was, whether good or bad, *sc.* with regard to climate and cultivation, and whether the towns were camps, *i.e.* open villages and hamlets, or fortified places ; also (ver. 20) whether the land was fat or lean, *i.e.* whether it had a fertile soil or not, and whether there were trees in it or not.   All this they were to search out courageously (הִתְחַזַּק, to show one's self courageous in any occupation), and to fetch (some) of the fruits of the land, as it was the time of the first-ripe grapes. In Palestine the first grapes ripen as early as August, and sometimes even in July (*vid. Robinson,* ii. 100, ii. 611), whilst the vintage takes place in September and October.

Vers. 21-33. JOURNEY OF THE SPIES ; THEIR RETURN, AND REPORT.—Ver. 21. In accordance with the instructions they had received, the men who had been sent out passed through the land, from the desert of Zin to Rehob, in the neighbourhood of Hamath, *i.e.* in its entire extent from south to north.   The *" Desert of Zin"* (which occurs not only here, but in chap. xx. 1, xxvii. 14, xxxiii. 36, xxxiv. 3, 4 ; Deut. xxxii. 51, and Josh. xv. 1, 3) was the name given to the northern edge of the great desert of Paran, viz. the broad ravine of Wady *Murreh* (see p. 59), which separates the lofty and precipitous northern border of the table-land of the Azazimeh from the southern border of the Rakhma plateau, *i.e.* of the southernmost plateau of the mountains of the Amorites (or the mountains of Judah), and runs from Jebel *Madarah* (*Moddera*) on the east, to the plain of Kadesh, which forms part of the desert of Zin (cf. chap. xxvii. 14, xxxiii. 36 ; Deut. xxxii. 51), on the west. The south frontier of Canaan passed through this from the southern end of the Dead Sea, along the Wady *el Murreh* to the Wady *el Arish* (chap. xxxiv. 3).—*" Rehob, to come* (coming) *to Hamath,"* *i.e.* where you enter the province of Hamath, on the northern boundary of Canaan, is hardly one of the two Rehobs in the tribe of Asher (Josh. xix. 28 and 30), but most likely *Beth-Rehob* in the tribe of Naphtali, which was in the neighbourhood of *Dan Lais,* the modern *Tell el Kadhy* (Judg. xviii. 28), and which *Robinson* imagined that he had identified in the ruins of the castle of *Hunin* or *Honin,* in the village of the same name, to the south-west of *Tell el Kadhy*, on the range of mountains which bound the plain towards the west above Lake *Huleh* (Bibl. Researches, p. 371). In support of this conjecture, he laid the principal stress upon the fact that the direct road to Hamath through the Wady *et Teim* and the *Bekaa* commences here. The only circumstance which it is hard to reconcile with this conjecture is, that Beth-Rehob is never mentioned in the Old Testament, with the exception of Judg. xviii. 28, either among the fortified towns of the Canaanites or in the wars of the Israelites with the Syrians and Assyrians, and therefore does not appear to have been a place of such importance as we should naturally be led to suppose from the character of this castle, the very situation of which points to a bold, commanding fortress (see Lynch's Expedition), and where there are still remains of its original foundations built of large square stones, hewn and grooved, and reminding one of the antique and ornamental edifices of Solomon's times (cf. *Ritter, Erdkunde*, xv. pp. 242 sqq.).—*Hamath* is *Epiphania* on the *Orontes*, now *Hamah* (see at Gen. x. 18).

After the general statement, that the spies went through the whole land from the southern to the northern frontier, two facts are mentioned in vers. 22–24, which occurred in connection with their mission, and were of great importance to the whole congregation. These single incidents are linked on, however, in a truly Hebrew style, to what precedes, viz. by an *imperfect* with *Vav consec.*, just in the same manner in which, in 1 Kings vi. 9, 15, the detailed account of the building of the temple is linked on to the previous statement, that Solomon built the temple and finished it; [1] so that the true rendering would be, "now they ascended in the south country and came to Hebron (וַיָּבֹא is apparently an error in writing for וַיָּבֹאוּ), and there were יְלִידֵי הָעֲנָק, the children of Anak," three of whom are mentioned by name. These three, who were afterwards expelled by Caleb, when the land was divided and the city of Hebron was given to him for an inheritance (Josh. xv. 14;

---

[1] A comparison of 1 Kings vi., where we cannot possibly suppose that two accounts have been linked together or interwoven, is specially adapted to give us a clear view of the peculiar custom adopted by the Hebrew historians, of placing the end and ultimate result of the events they narrate as much as possible at the head of their narrative, and then proceeding with a minute account of the more important of the attendant circumstances, without paying any regard to the chronological order of the different incidents, or being at all afraid of repetitions, and so to prove how unwarrantable and false are the conclusions of those critics who press such passages into the support of their

Judg. i. 20), were descendants of *Arbah*, the lord of Hebron, from whom the city received its name of *Kirjath-Arbah*, or city of Arbah, and who is described in Josh. xiv. 15 as "the great (*i.e.* the greatest) man among the Anakim," and in Josh. xv. 13 as the "father of Anak," *i.e.* the founder of the Anakite family there. For it is evident enough that הָעֲנָק (*Anak*) is not the proper name of a man in these passages, but the name of a family or tribe, from the fact that in ver. 33, where Anak's sons are spoken of in a general and indefinite manner, בְּנֵי עֲנָק has not the article; also from the fact that the three Anakites who lived in Hebron are almost always called יְלִידֵי הָעֲנָק, Anak's born (vers. 22, 28), and that בְּנֵי הָעֲנָק (sons of Anak), in Josh. xv. 14, is still further defined by the phrase יְלִידֵי הָעֲנָק (children of Anak); and lastly, from the fact that in the place of "sons of Anak," we find "sons of the Anakim" in Deut. i. 28 and ix. 2, and the "Anakim" in Deut. ii. 10, xi. 21; Josh. xiv. 12, etc. *Anak* is supposed to signify long-necked; but this does not preclude the possibility of the founder of the tribe having borne this name. The origin of the *Anakites* is involved in obscurity. In Deut. ii. 10, 11, they are classed with the *Emim* and *Rephaim* on account of their gigantic stature, and probably reckoned as belonging to the pre-Canaanitish inhabitants of the land, of whom it is impossible to decide whether they were of Semitic origin or descendants of Ham (see vol. i. p. 203). It is also doubtful, whether the names found here in vers. 21, 28, and in Josh. xv. 14, are the names of individuals, *i.e.* of chiefs of the Anakites, or the names of Anakite tribes. The latter supposition is favoured by the circumstance, that the same names occur even after the capture of Hebron by Caleb, or at least fifty years after the event referred to here. With regard to Hebron, it is still further observed in ver. 22*b*, that it was built seven years before *Zoan* in Egypt. *Zoan*—the Tanis of the Greeks and Romans, the *San* of the Arabs, which is called *Jani, Jane* in Coptic writings—was situated upon the eastern side of the Tanitic arm of the Nile, not

hypotheses. We have a similar passage in Josh. iv. 11 sqq., where, after relating that when *all* the people had gone through the Jordan the priests also passed through with the ark of the covenant (ver. 11), the historian proceeds in vers. 12, 13, to describe the crossing of the two tribes and a half; and another in Judg. xx., where, at the very commencement (ver. 35), the issue of the whole is related, viz. the defeat of the Benjamites; and then after that there is a minute description in vers. 36—46 of the manner in which it was effected. This style of narrative is also common in the historical works of the Arabs.

far from its mouth (see *Ges. Thes.* p. 1177), and was the residence of Pharaoh in the time of Moses (see vol. ii. p. 27). The date of its erection is unknown ; but Hebron was in existence as early as Abraham's time (Gen. xiii. 18, xxiii. 2 sqq.).—Ver. 23. The spies also came into the valley of *Eshcol*, where they gathered pomegranates and figs, and also cut down a vine-branch with grapes upon it, which two persons carried upon a pole, most likely on account of its extraordinary size. Bunches of grapes are still met with in Palestine, weighing as much as eight, ten, or twelve pounds, the grapes themselves being as large as our smaller plums (cf. *Tobler Denkblätter*, pp. 111, 112). The grapes of Hebron are especially celebrated. To the north of this city, on the way to Jerusalem, you pass through a valley with vineyards on the hills on both sides, containing the largest and finest grapes in the land, and with pomegranates, figs, and other fruits in great profusion (*Robinson*, Palestine, i. 316, compared with i. 314 and ii. 442). This valley is supposed, and not without good ground, to be the *Eshcol* of this chapter, which received its name of *Eshcol* (cluster of grapes), according to ver. 24, from the bunch of grapes which was cut down there by the spies. This statement, of course, applies to the Israelites, and would therefore still hold good, even if the conjecture were a well-founded one, that this valley received its name originally from the *Eshcol* mentioned in Gen. xiv. 13, 24, as the terebinth grove did from *Mamre* the brother of Eshcol.

Vers. 25 sqq. In forty days the spies returned to the camp at Kadesh (see at chap. xvi. 6), and reported the great fertility of the land (" *it floweth with milk and honey*," see at Ex. iii. 8), pointing, at the same time, to the fruit they had brought with them ; " *nevertheless*," they added (אֶפֶס כִּי, " only that "), " *the people be strong that dwell in the land, and the cities are fortified, very large : and, moreover, we saw the children of Anak there.*" Amalekites dwelt in the south (see at Gen. xxxvi. 12) ; Hittites, Jebusites, and Amorites in the mountains (see at Gen. x. 15, 16) ; and Canaanites by the (Mediterranean) Sea and on the side of the Jordan, *i.e.* in the Arabah or Ghor (see at Gen. xiii. 7 and x. 15–18).—Ver. 30. As these tidings respecting the towns and inhabitants of Canaan were of a character to excite the people, Caleb calmed them before Moses by saying, " *We will go up and take it ; for we shall overcome it.*" The fact that Caleb only is mentioned, though, according to chap. xiv. 6, Joshua also stood by his side, may be explained on the simple ground, that at first Caleb was the only one to speak and maintain the possibility of conquering Canaan.—Ver. 31. But his companions were of an opposite opinion, and declared that the people in Canaan were stronger than the Israelites, and therefore it was impossible to go up to it.—Ver. 32. Thus they spread an evil report of the land among the Israelites, by exaggerating the difficulties of the conquest in their unbelieving despair, and describing Canaan as a land which *" ate up its inhabitants."* Their meaning certainly was not " that the wretched inhabitants were worn out by the laborious task of cultivating it, or that the land was pestilential on account of the inclemency of the weather, or that the cultivation of the land was difficult, and attended with many evils," as *Calvin* maintains. Their only wish was to lay stress upon the difficulties and dangers connected with the conquest and maintenance of the land, on account of the tribes inhabiting and surrounding it: the land was an apple of discord, because of its fruitfulness and situation ; and as the different nations strove for its possession, its inhabitants wasted away (*Cler., Ros., O. v. Gerlach*). The people, they added, are אַנְשֵׁי מִדּוֹת, " *men of measures,*" *i.e.* of tall stature (cf. Isa. xlv. 14), *" and there we saw the Nephilim, i.e.* primeval tyrants (see at Gen. vi. 4), *Anak's sons, giants of Nephilim, and we seemed to ourselves and to them as small as grasshoppers."*

Chap. xiv. 1–10. UPROAR AMONG THE PEOPLE.—Vers. 1–4. This appalling description of Canaan had so depressing an influence upon the whole congregation (cf. Deut. i. 28 : they "made their heart melt," *i.e.* threw them into utter despair), that they raised a loud cry, and wept in the night in consequence. The whole nation murmured against Moses and Aaron their two leaders, saying *" Would that we had died in Egypt or in this wilderness ! Why will Jehovah bring us into this land, to fall by the sword, that our wives and our children should become a prey* (be made slaves by the enemy; cf. Deut. i. 27, 28)? *Let us rather return into Egypt ! We will appoint a captain, they said one to another, and go back to Egypt."*—Vers. 5–9. At this murmuring, which was growing into open rebellion, Moses and Aaron fell upon their faces before the whole of the assembled congregation, namely, to pour out their distress before the Lord, and move Him to interpose ; that is to say, after they had made an unsuccessful attempt, as we may supply from Deut. i. 29–31, to cheer up the people, by pointing them to the help they had thus far received from God. " In such distress, nothing remained but to pour out their desires before God; offering their prayer in public, however, and in the sight of all the people, in the hope of turning their minds" (*Calvin*). Joshua and Caleb, who had gone with the others to explore the land, also rent their clothes, as a sign of their deep distress at the rebellious attitude of the people (see at Lev. x. 6), and tried to convince them of the goodness and glory of the land they had travelled through, and to incite them to trust in the Lord. "*If Jehovah take pleasure in us,*" they said, "*He will bring us into this land. Only rebel not ye against Jehovah, neither fear ye the people of the land; for they are our food;*" *i.e.* we can and shall swallow them up, or easily destroy them (cf. chap. xxii. 4, xxiv. 8; Deut. vii. 16; Ps. xiv. 4). "*Their shadow is departed from them, and Jehovah is with us: fear them not!*" "*Their shadow*" is the shelter and protection of God (cf. Ps. xci., cxxi. 5). The shadow, which defends from the burning heat of the sun, was a very natural figure in the sultry East, to describe defence from injury, a refuge from danger and destruction (Isa. xxx. 2). The protection of God had departed from the Canaanites, because God had determined to destroy them when the measure of their iniquity was full (Gen. xv. 16; cf. Ex. xxxiv. 24; Lev. xviii. 25, xx. 23). But the excited people resolved to stone them, when Jehovah interposed with His judgment, and His glory appeared in the tabernacle to all the Israelites; that is to say, the majesty of God flashed out before the eyes of the people in a light which suddenly burst forth from the tabernacle (see at Ex. xvi. 10).

Vers. 11–25. INTERCESSION OF MOSES.—Vers. 11, 12. Jehovah resented the conduct of the people as base contempt of His deity, and as utter mistrust of Him, notwithstanding all the signs which He had wrought in the midst of the nation; and declared that He would smite the rebellious people with pestilence, and destroy them, and make of Moses a greater and still mightier people. This was just what He had done before, when the rebellion took place at Sinai (Ex. xxxii. 10). But Moses, as a servant who was faithful over the whole house of God, and therefore sought not his own honour, but the honour of his God alone, stood in the breach on this occasion also (Ps. cvi. 23), with a similar intercessory prayer to that which he had presented at Horeb, except that on this occasion he pleaded the honour of God among the heathen, and the glorious revelation of the divine nature with which he had been favoured at Sinai, as a motive for sparing the rebellious nation (vers. 13–19;

cf. Ex. xxxii. 11–13, and xxxiv. 6, 7). The first he expressed in these words (vers. 13 sqq.): "*Not only have the Egyptians heard that Thou hast brought out this people from among them with Thy might; they have also told it to the inhabitants of this land. They* (the Egyptians and the other nations) *have heard that Thou, Jehovah, art in the midst of this people; that Thou, Jehovah, appearest eye to eye, and Thy cloud stands over them, and Thou goest before them in a pillar of cloud by day and a pillar of fire by night. Now, if Thou shouldst slay this people as one man, the nations which have heard the tidings of Thee would say, Because Jehovah was not able to bring this people into the land which He sware to them, He has slain them in the desert.*" In that case God would be regarded by the heathen as powerless, and His honour would be impaired (cf. Deut. xxxii. 27; Josh. vii. 9). It was for the sake of His own honour that God, at a later time, did not allow the Israelites to perish in exile (cf. Isa. xlviii. 9, 11, lii. 5; Ezek. xxxvi. 22, 23).— וְאָמְרוּ . . . וְשָׁמְעוּ (vers. 13, 14), *et audierunt et dixerunt;* וְ — וְ = *et— et,* both—and. The inhabitants of this land (ver. 13) were not merely the Arabians, but, according to Ex. xv. 14 sqq., the tribes dwelling in and round Arabia, the Philistines, Edomites, Moabites, and Canaanites, to whom the tidings had been brought of the miracles of God in Egypt and at the Dead Sea. שָׁמְעוּ, in ver. 14, can neither stand for כִּי שָׁמְעוּ (*dixerunt*) *se audivisse,* nor for אֲשֶׁר שָׁמְעוּ, *qui audierunt.* They are neither of them grammatically admissible, as the relative pronoun cannot be readily omitted in prose; and neither of them would give a really suitable meaning. It is rather a rhetorical resumption of the שָׁמְעוּ in ver. 13, and the subject of the verb is not only "*the Egyptians,*" but also "*the inhabitants of this land*" who held communication with the Egyptians, or "*the nations*" who had heard the report of Jehovah (ver. 15), *i.e.* all that God had hitherto done for and among the Israelites in Egypt, and on the journey through the desert. "*Eye to eye:*" *i.e.* Thou hast appeared to them in the closest proximity. On the pillar of cloud and fire, see at Ex. xiii. 21, 22. "*As one man,*" equivalent to "with a stroke" (Judg. vi. 16).—In vers. 17, 18, Moses adduces a second argument, viz. the word in which God Himself had revealed His inmost being to him at Sinai (Ex. xxxiv. 6, 7). The words, "*Let the power be great,*" equivalent to "show Thyself great in power," are not to be connected with what precedes, but with what follows; viz. "*show Thyself mighty by verifying Thy word, 'Jehovah, long-suffering and great in mercy,' etc.; forgive, I beseech*

Thee, this people according to the greatness of Thy mercy, and as Thou hast forgiven this people from Egypt even until now." נָשָׂא (ver. 19) = עָוֹן נָשָׂא (ver. 18).—Ver. 20. In answer to this importunate prayer, the Lord promised forgiveness, namely, the preservation of the nation, but not the remission of the well-merited punishment. At the rebellion at Sinai, He had postponed the punishment "till the day of His visitation" (Ex. xxxii. 34). And that day had now arrived, as the people had carried their continued rebellion against the Lord to the furthest extreme, even to an open declaration of their intention to depose Moses, and return to Egypt under another leader, and thus had filled up the measure of their sins. " *Nevertheless,*" added the Lord (vers. 21, 22), " *as truly as I live, and the glory of Jehovah will fill the whole earth, all the men who have seen My glory and My miracles . . . shall not see the land which I sware unto their fathers.*" The clause, " all the earth," etc., forms an apposition to " as I live." Jehovah proves Himself to be living, by the fact that His glory fills the whole earth. But this was to take place, not, as *Knobel,* who mistakes the true connection of the different clauses, erroneously supposes, by the destruction of the whole of that generation, which would be talked of by all the world, but rather by the fact that, notwithstanding the sin and opposition of these men, He would still carry out His work of salvation to a glorious victory. The כִּי in ver. 22 introduces the substance of the oath, as in Isa. xlix. 18 ; 1 Sam. xiv. 39, xx. 3 ; and according to the ordinary form of an oath, אִם in ver. 23 signifies " *not.*"—" They have tempted Me now ten times." Ten is used as the number of completeness and full measure; and this answered to the actual fact, if we follow the Rabbins, and add to the murmuring (1) at the Red Sea, Ex. xiv. 11, 12 ; (2) at Marah, Ex. xv. 23 ; (3) in the wilderness of Sin, Ex. xvi. 2 ; (4) at Rephidim, Ex. xvii. 1 ; (5) at Horeb, Ex. xxxii. ; (6) at Tabeerah, Num. xi. 1 ; (7) at the graves of lust, Num. xi. 4 sqq. ; and (8) here again at Kadesh, the *twofold* rebellion of certain individuals against the commandments of God at the giving of the manna (Ex. xvi. 20 and 27). The despisers of God should none of them see the promised land.—Ver. 24. But because there was another spirit in Caleb,—*i.e.* not the unbelieving, despairing, yet proud and rebellious spirit of the great mass of the people, but the spirit of obedience and believing trust, so that " he followed Jehovah fully" (*lit.* "fulfilled to walk behind Jehovah"), followed Him with unwavering fidelity,—God would bring him into the land into which he had gone, and his seed should possess it. (מֵלֵא אַחֲרַי here, and at chap. xxxii. 11, 12 ; Deut. i. 36 ; Josh. xiv. 8, 9 ; 1 Kings xi. 6, is a *constructio prægnans* for מֵלֵא לָלֶכֶת אַחֲרַי; cf. 2 Chron. xxxiv. 31.) According to the context, the reference is not to Hebron particularly, but to Canaan generally, which God had sworn unto the fathers (ver. 23, and Deut. i. 36, comp. with ver. 35) ; although, when the land was divided, Caleb received Hebron for his possession, because, according to his own statement in Josh. xiv. 6 sqq., Moses had sworn that he would give it to him. But this is not mentioned here ; just as Joshua also is not mentioned in this place, as he is at vers. 30 and 38, but Caleb only, who opposed the exaggerated accounts of the other spies at the very first, and endeavoured to quiet the excitement of the people by declaring that they were well able to overcome the Canaanites (chap. xiii. 30). This first revelation of God to Moses is restricted to the main fact ; the particulars are given afterwards in the sentence of God, as intended for communication to the people (vers. 26–38).—Ver. 25. The divine reply to the intercession of Moses terminated with a command to the people to turn on the morrow, and go to the wilderness to the Red Sea, as the Amalekites and Canaanites dwelt in the valley. " *The Amalekites,*" etc. : this clause furnishes the reason for the command which follows. On the Amalekites, see at Gen. xxxvi. 12, and Ex. xvii. 8 sqq. The term Canaanite is a general epithet applied to all the inhabitants of Canaan, instead of the Amorites mentioned in Deut. i. 44, who held the southern mountains of Canaan. "The valley" is no doubt the broad *Wady Murreh* (see at chap. xiii. 21), including a portion of the *Negeb*, in which the Amalekites led a nomad life, whilst the Canaanites really dwelt upon the mountains (ver. 45), close up to the *Wady Murreh.*

Vers. 26–38. SENTENCE UPON THE MURMURING CONGREGATION.—After the Lord had thus declared to Moses in general terms His resolution to punish the incorrigible people, and not suffer them to come to Canaan, He proceeded to tell him what announcement he was to make to the people.—Ver. 27. This announcement commences in a tone of anger, with an *aposiopesis,* " *How long this evil congregation*" (sc. " shall I forgive it," the simplest plan being to supply אֶשָּׂא, as *Rosenmüller* suggests, from ver. 18), " *that they murmur against Me ?*"—Vers. 28–31. Jehovah swore that it should happen to the murmurers as they had spoken. Their corpses should fall in the desert, even all who had been numbered, from

twenty years old and upwards: they should not see the land into
which Jehovah had lifted up His hand (see at Ex. vi. 8) to lead them,
with the sole exception of Caleb and Joshua. But their children,
who, as they said, would be a prey (ver. 3), them Jehovah would
bring, and they should learn to know the land which the others had
despised.—Vers. 32, 33. *" As for you, your carcases will fall in this
wilderness. But your sons will be pasturing (i.e.* will lead a restless
shepherd life) *in the desert forty years, and bear your whoredom (i.e.*
endure the consequences of your faithless apostasy ; see Ex. xxxiv.
16), *until your corpses are finished in the desert,"* i.e. till you have all
passed away.—Ver. 34. *" After the number of the forty days that ye
have searched the land, shall ye bear your iniquity,* (reckoning) *a day
for a year, and know My turning away from you,"* or תְּנוּאָה, *abalienatio,*
from נוא (chap. xxxii. 7).—Ver. 35. As surely as Jehovah had
spoken this, would He do it to that evil congregation, to those who
had allied themselves against Him (נוֹעַד, to bind themselves together,
to conspire ; chap. xvi. 11, xxvii. 3). There is no ground whatever
for questioning the correctness of the statement, that the spies had
travelled through Canaan for forty days, or regarding this as a so-
called round number—that is to say, as unhistorical. And if this
number is firmly established, there is also no ground for disputing
the forty years' sojourn of the people in the wilderness, although
the period during which the rebellious generation, consisting of
those who were numbered at Sinai, died out, was actually thirty-
eight years, reaching from the autumn of the second year after
their departure from Egypt to the middle of the fortieth year of
their wanderings, and terminating with the fresh numbering (chap.
xxvi.) that was undertaken after the death of Aaron, and took place
on the first of the fifth month of the fortieth year (chap. xx. 23
sqq., compared with chap. xxxiii. 38). Instead of these thirty-eight
years, the forty years of the sojourn in the desert are placed in
connection with the forty days of the spies, because the people had
frequently fallen away from God, and been punished in consequence, even during the year and a half before their rejection ;
and in this respect the year and a half could be combined with the
thirty-eight years which followed into one continuous period, during
which they bore their iniquity, to set distinctly before the minds of
the disobedient people the contrast between that peaceful dwelling
in the promised land which they had forfeited, and the restless
wandering in the desert, which had been imposed upon them as a
punishment, and to impress upon them the causal connection be-

tween sin and suffering. " Every year that passed, and was deducted from the forty years of punishment, was a new and solemn
exhortation to repent, as it called to mind the occasion of their
rejection" (*Kurtz*). When *Knobel* observes, on the other hand,
that " it is utterly improbable that all who came out of Egypt
(that is to say, all who were twenty years old and upward when
they came out) should have fallen in the desert, with the exception
of two, and that there should have been no men found among the
Israelites when they entered Canaan who were more than sixty
years of age," the express statement, that on the second numbering
there was not a man among those that were numbered who had
been included in the numbering at Sinai, except Joshua and Caleb
(chap. xxvi. 64 sqq.), is amply sufficient to overthrow this " improbability" as an unfounded fancy. Nor is this statement rendered
at all questionable by the fact, that " Aaron's son Eleazar, who
entered Canaan with Joshua" (Josh. xiv. 1, etc.), was most likely
more than twenty years old at the time of his consecration at Sinai,
as the Levites were not qualified for service till their thirtieth or
twenty-fifth year. For, in the first place, the regulation concerning
the Levites' age of service is not to be applied without reserve to
the priests also, so that we could infer from this that the sons of
Aaron must have been at least twenty-five or thirty years old when
they were consecrated; and besides this, the priests do not enter
into the question at all, for the tribe of Levi was excepted from
the numbering in chap. i., and therefore Aaron's sons were not
included among the persons numbered, who were sentenced to die
in the wilderness. Still less does it follow from Josh. xxiv. 7 and
Judg. ii. 7, where it is stated that, after the conquest of Canaan,
there were many still alive who had been eye-witnesses of the
wonders of God in Egypt, that they must have been more than
twenty years old when they came out of Egypt; for youths from
ten to nineteen years of age would certainly have been able to
remember such miracles as these, even after the lapse of forty or
fifty years.—Vers. 36—38. But for the purpose of giving to the
whole congregation a practical proof of the solemnity of the divine
threatening of punishment, the spies who had induced the congregation to revolt, through their evil report concerning the inhabitants
of Canaan, were smitten by a " stroke before Jehovah," *i.e.* by a
sudden death, which proceeded in a visible manner from Jehovah
Himself, whilst Joshua and Caleb remained alive.

Vers. 39-45 (cf. Deut. i. 41-44). The announcement of the

sentence plunged the people into deep mourning. But instead of bending penitentially under the judgment of God, they resolved to atone for their error, by preparing the next morning to go to the top of the mountain and press forward into Canaan. And they would not even suffer themselves to be dissuaded from their enterprise by the entreaties of Moses, who denounced it as a transgression of the word of God which could not succeed, and predicted their overthrow before their enemies, but went presumptuously (יַעְפִּלוּ לַעֲלוֹת) up without the ark of the covenant and without Moses, who did not depart out of the midst of the camp, and were smitten by the Amalekites and Canaanites, who drove them back as far as Hormah. Whereas at first they had refused to enter upon the conflict with the Canaanites, through their unbelief in the might of the promise of God, now, through unbelief in the severity of the judgment of God, they resolved to engage in this conflict by their own power, and without the help of God, and to cancel the old sin of unbelieving despair through the new sin of presumptuous self-confidence,—an attempt which could never succeed, but was sure to plunge deeper and deeper into misery. Where " *the top* (or height) *of the mountain*" to which the Israelites advanced was, cannot be precisely determined, as we have no minute information concerning the nature of the ground in the neighbourhood of Kadesh. No doubt the allusion is to some plateau on the northern border of the valley mentioned in ver. 25, viz. the Wady *Murreh*, which formed the southernmost spur of the mountains of the Amorites, from which the Canaanites and Amalekites came against them, and drove them back. In Deut. i. 44, Moses mentions the Amorites instead of the Amalekites and Canaanites, using the name in a broader sense for all the Canaanites, and contenting himself with naming the leading foes with whom the Amalekites who wandered about in the *Negeb* had allied themselves, as Bedouins thirsting for booty. These tribes came down (ver. 45) from the height of the mountain to the lower plateau or saddle, which the Israelites had ascended, and smote them and יַכְּתוּם (from כָּתַת, with the reduplication of the second radical anticipated in the first : see *Ewald*, § 193, *c.*), " discomfited them, as far as Hormah," or as Moses expresses it in Deut. i. 44, They " chased you, as bees do" (which pursue with great ferocity any one who attacks or disturbs them), "and destroyed you in Seir, even unto Hormah." There is not sufficient ground for altering " in Seir" into " from Seir," as the LXX., *Syriac*, and *Vulgate* have done. But בְּשֵׂעִיר might signify " into Seir, as far as Hormah." As the

Edomites had extended their territory at that time across the Arabah towards the west, and taken possession of a portion of the mountainous country which bounded the desert of Paran towards the north (see at chap. xxxiv. 3), the Israelites, when driven back by them, might easily be chased into the territory of the Edomites. *Hormah* (*i.e.* the ban-place) is used here proleptically (see at chap. xxi. 3).

OCCURRENCES DURING THE THIRTY-SEVEN YEARS OF WANDERING IN THE WILDERNESS.—CHAP. XV.–XIX.

After the unhappy issue of the attempt to penetrate into Canaan, in opposition to the will of God and the advice of Moses, the Israelites remained " many days" in Kadesh, as the Lord did not hearken to their lamentations concerning the defeat which they had suffered at the hands of the Canaanites and Amalekites. Then they turned, and took their journey, as the Lord had commanded (chap. xiv. 25), into the wilderness, in the direction towards the Red Sea (Deut. i. 45, ii. 1) ; and in the first month of the fortieth year they came again into the desert of Zin, to Kadesh (chap. xx. 1). All that we know respecting this journeying from Kadesh into the wilderness in the direction towards the Red Sea, and up to the time of their return to the desert of Zin, is limited to a number of names of places of encampment given in the list of journeying stages in chap. xxxiii. 19–30, out of which, as the situation of the majority of them is altogether unknown, or at all events has not yet been determined, no connected account of the journeys of Israel during this interval of thirty-seven years can possibly be drawn. The most important event related in connection with this period is the rebellion of the company of Korah against Moses and Aaron, and the re-establishment of the Aaronic priesthood and confirmation of their rights, which this occasioned (chaps. xvi.–xviii.). This rebellion probably occurred in the first portion of the period in question. In addition to this there are only a few laws recorded, which were issued during this long time of punishment, and furnished a practical proof of the continuance of the covenant which the Lord had made with the nation of Israel at Sinai. There was nothing more to record in connection with these thirty-seven years, which formed the *second* stage in the guidance of Israel through the desert. For, as *Baumgarten* has well observed, " the fighting men of Israel had fallen under the judgment of Jehovah, and the sacred history, therefore, was no longer concerned with them ; whilst the youth, in whom the life and hope of Israel were preserved, had as yet no history at all." Consequently we have no reason to complain, as *Ewald* does (*Gesch.* ii. pp. 241, 242), that "the great interval of forty years remains a perfect void ;" and still less occasion to dispose of the gap, as this scholar has done, by supposing that the last historian left out a great deal from the history of the forty years' wanderings. The supposed "void" was completely filled up by the gradual dying out of the generation which had been rejected by God.

Various Laws of Sacrifice. Punishment of a Sabbath-breaker. Command to wear Tassels upon the Clothes.—Chap. xv.

Vers. 1–31. REGULATIONS CONCERNING SACRIFICES.—Vers. 1–16. For the purpose of reviving the hopes of the new generation that was growing up, and directing their minds to the promised land, during the mournful and barren time when judgment was being executed upon the race that had been condemned, Jehovah communicated various laws through Moses concerning the presentation of sacrifices in the land that He would give them (vers. 1 and 2), whereby the former laws of sacrifice were supplemented and completed. The *first* of these laws had reference to the connection between meat-offerings and drink-offerings on the one hand, and burnt-offerings. and slain-offerings on the other.—Vers. 3 sqq. In the land of Canaan, every burnt and slain-offering, whether prepared in fulfilment of a vow, or spontaneously, or on feast-days (cf. Lev. vii. 16, xxii. 18, and xxiii. 38), was to be associated with a meat-offering of fine flour mixed with oil, and a drink-offering of wine,— the quantity to be regulated according to the kind of animal that was slain in sacrifice. (See Lev. xxiii. 18, where this connection is already mentioned in the case of the festal sacrifices.) For a lamb (כֶּבֶשׂ, *i.e.* either sheep or goat, cf. ver. 11), they were to take the tenth of an ephah of fine flour, mixed with the quarter of a hin of oil and the quarter of a hin of wine, as a drink-offering. In ver. 5, the construction changes from the third to the second person. עָשָׂה, to prepare, as in Ex. xxix. 38.—Vers. 6, 7. For a ram, they were to take two tenths of fine flour, with the third of a hin of oil and the third of a hin of wine.—Vers. 8 sqq. For an ox, three tenths of fine flour, with half a hin of oil and half a hin of wine. The הִקְרִיב (3d person) in ver. 9, between תַּעֲשֶׂה in ver. 8,. and תַּקְרִיב in ver. 10, is certainly striking and unusual, but not so offensive as to render it necessary to alter it into וְתַקְרִיב.—Vers. 11, 12. The quantities mentioned were to be offered with every ox, or ram, or lamb, of either sheep or goat, and therefore the number of the appointed quantities of meat and drink-offerings was to correspond to the number of sacrificial animals.—Vers. 13–16. These rules were to apply not only to the sacrifices of those that were born in Israel, but also to those of the strangers living among them. By " these things," in ver. 13, we are to understand the meat and drink-offerings already appointed.—Ver. 15. " *As for the assembly, there shall be one law for the Israelite and the stranger, . . . an eternal ordinance . . . before Jehovah.*" הַקָּהָל, which is construed absolutely, refers to the assembling of the nation before Jehovah, or to the congregation viewed in its attitude with regard to God.

A *second* law (vers. 17–21) appoints, on the ground of the general regulations in Ex. xxii. 28 and xxiii. 19, the presentation of a heave-offering from the bread which they would eat in the land of Canaan, viz. a first-fruit of groat-meal (רֵאשִׁית עֲרִיסֹת) baked as cake (חַלָּה). *Arisoth*, which is only used in connection with the gift of first-fruits, in Ezek. xliv. 30, Neh. x. 38, and the passage before us, signifies most probably groats, or meal coarsely bruised, like the talmudical עֲרַסָן, *contusum, mola, far*, and indeed *far hordei*. This cake of the groats of first-fruits they were to offer " *as a heave-offering of the threshing-floor*," i.e. as a heave-offering of the bruised corn, in the same manner as this (therefore, in addition to it, and along with it); and that " *according to your generations* " (see Ex. xii. 14), that is to say, for all time, to consecrate a gift of first-fruits to the Lord, not only of the grains of corn, but also of the bread made from the corn, and " *to cause a blessing to rest upon his house*" (Ezek. xliv. 30). Like all the gifts of first-fruits, this cake also fell to the portion of the priests (see Ezek. and Neh. *ut sup.*).

To these there are added, in vers. 22, 31, laws relating to *sin-offerings*, the first of which, in vers. 22–26, is distinguished from the case referred to in Lev. iv. 13–21, by the fact that the sin is not described here, as it is there, as " doing one of the commandments of Jehovah which ought not to be done," but as " not doing all that Jehovah had spoken through Moses." Consequently, the allusion here is not to sins of commission, but to sins of omission, not following the law of God, " *even* (as is afterwards explained in ver. 23) *all that the Lord hath commanded you by the hand of Moses from the day that the Lord hath commanded, and thenceforward according to your generations*," i.e. since the first beginning of the giving of the law, and during the whole of the time following (*Knobel*). These words apparently point to a complete falling away of the congregation from the whole of the law. Only the further stipulation in ver. 24, " *if it occur away from the eyes of the congregation through error* " (in oversight), cannot be easily reconciled with this, as it seems hardly conceivable that an apostasy from the entire law should have remained hidden from the congregation. This " not doing all the commandments of Jehovah," of which the congregation is supposed to incur the guilt without perceiving it, might consist either in the fact that, in particular instances, whether from oversight or negligence, the whole congregation omitted to fulfil the commandments of God, *i.e.* certain precepts of the law, *sc.* in the fact that they neglected the true and proper fulfilment of the whole law, either, as *Outram* supposes, " by retaining to a certain extent the national rites, and following the worship of the true God, and yet at the same time acting unconsciously in opposition to the law, through having been led astray by some common errors ; " or by allowing the evil example of godless rulers to seduce them to neglect their religious duties, or to adopt and join in certain customs and usages of the heathen, which appeared to be reconcilable with the law of Jehovah, though they really led to contempt and neglect of the commandments of the Lord.[1] But as a disregard or neglect of the commandments of God had to be expiated, a burnt-offering was to be added to the sin-offering, that the separation of the congregation from the Lord, which had arisen from the sin of omission, might be entirely removed. The apodosis commences with וְהָיָה in ver. 24, but is interrupted by אִם מֵעֵינֵי, and resumed again with וְעָשׂוּ, " *it shall be, if . . . . the whole congregation shall prepare*," etc. The burnt-offering, being the principal sacrifice, is mentioned as usual before the sin-offering, although, when presented, it followed the latter, on account of its being necessary that

---

[1] *Maimonides* (see *Outram, ex veterum sententia*) understands this law as relating to extraneous worship ; and *Outram* himself refers to the times of the wicked kings, " when the people neglected their hereditary rites, and, forgetting the sacred laws, fell by a common sin into the observance of the religious rites of other nations." Undoubtedly, we have historical ground in 2 Chron. xxix. 21 sqq., and Ezra viii. 35, for this interpretation of our law, but further allusions are not excluded in consequence. We cannot agree with *Baumgarten*, therefore, in restricting the difference between Lev. iv. 13 sqq. and the passage before us to the fact, that the former supposes the transgression of one particular commandment on the part of the whole congregation, whilst the latter (vers. 22, 23) refers to a continued lawless condition on the part of Israel.

the sin should be expiated before the congregation could sanctify its life and efforts afresh to the Lord in the burnt-offering. *" One kid of the goats :"* see Lev. iv. 23. כַּמִּשְׁפָּט (as in Lev. v. 10, ix. 16, etc.) refers to the right established in vers. 8, 9, concerning the combination of the meat and drink-offering with the burnt-offering. The sin-offering was to be treated according to the rule laid down in Lev. iv. 14 sqq.—Ver. 26. This law was to apply not only to the children of Israel, but also to the stranger among them, *"for* (*sc.* it has happened) *to the whole nation in mistake."* As the sin extended to the whole nation, in which the foreigners were also included, the atonement was also to apply to the whole.—Vers. 27–31. In the same way, again, there was one law for the native and the stranger, in relation to sins of omission on the part of single individuals. The law laid down in Lev. v. 6 (cf. Lev. iv. 27 sqq.) for the Israelites, is repeated here in vers. 27, 28, and in ver. 28 it is raised into general validity for foreigners also. In ver. 29, הָאֶזְרָח is written absolutely for לָאֶזְרָח.—Vers. 30, 31. But it was only sins committed by mistake (see at Lev. iv. 2) that could be expiated by sin-offerings. Whoever, on the other hand, whether a native or a foreigner, committed a sin *" with a high hand,"*—*i.e.* so that he raised his hand, as it were, against Jehovah, or acted in open rebellion against Him,—blasphemed God, and was to be cut off (see Gen. xvii. 14) ; for he had despised the word of Jehovah, and broken His commandment, and was to atone for it with his life. עֲוֹנָה בָהּ, *" its crime upon it ;"* *i.e.* it shall come upon such a soul in the punishment which it shall endure.

Vers. 32–36. The HISTORY OF THE SABBATH-BREAKER is no doubt inserted here as a practical illustration of sinning " with a high hand." It shows, too, at the same time, how the nation, as a whole, was impressed with the inviolable sanctity of the Lord's day. From the words with which it is introduced, *" and the children of Israel were in the wilderness,"* all that can be gathered is, that the occurrence took place at the time when Israel was condemned to wander about in the wilderness for forty years. They found a man gathering sticks in the desert on the Sabbath, and brought him as an open transgressor of the law of the Sabbath before Moses and Aaron and the whole congregation, *i.e.* the college of elders, as the judicial authorities of the congregation (Ex. xviii. 25 sqq.). They kept him in custody, like the blasphemer in Lev. xxiv. 12, because it had not yet been determined what was to be done to him. It

is true that it had already been laid down in Ex. xxxi. 14, 15, and
xxxv. 2, that any breach of the law of the Sabbath should be
punished by death and extermination, but the mode had not yet
been prescribed. This was done now, and Jehovah commanded
stoning (see Lev. xx. 2), which was executed upon the criminal
without delay.

Vers. 37–41 (cf. Deut. xxii. 12). The command to wear
TASSELS ON THE EDGE OF THE UPPER GARMENT appears to have
been occasioned by the incident just described. The Israelites
were to wear צִיצִת, tassels, on the wings of their upper garments,
or, according to Deut. xxii. 12, at the four corners of the upper
garment. כְּסוּת, the covering in which a man wraps himself, synonymous with בֶּגֶד, was the upper garment, consisting of a four-cornered cloth or piece of stuff, which was thrown over the body-coat
(see my *Bibl. Archäol.* ii. pp. 36, 37), and is not to be referred, as
Schultz supposes, to the bed-coverings also, although this garment
was actually used as a counterpane by the poor (see Ex. xxii. 25,
26). "*And upon the tassel of the wing they shall put a string of
hyacinth-blue,*" namely, to fasten the tassel to the edge of the garment. צִיצִת (*fem.*, from צִיץ, the glittering, the bloom or flower)
signifies something flowery or bloom-like, and is used in Ezek. viii. 3
for a lock of hair; here it is applied to a tassel, as being made of
twisted threads: LXX. κράσπεδα; Matt. xxiii. 5, "borders." The
size of these tassels is not prescribed. The Pharisees liked to make
them large, to exhibit openly their punctilious fulfilment of the law.
For the Rabbinical directions how to make them, see *Carpzov.
apparat.* pp. 197 sqq.; and *Bodenschatz, kirchliche Verfassung der
heutigen Juden,* iv. pp. 11 sqq.—Ver. 39. "*And it shall be to you for a
tassel,*" *i.e.* the fastening of the tassel with the dark blue thread to the
corners of your garments shall be to you a tassel, "*that ye, when ye
see it, may remember all the commandments of Jehovah, and do them;
and ye shall not stray after your hearts and your eyes, after which ye
go a whoring.*" The *zizith* on the sky-blue thread was to serve as
a memorial sign to the Israelites, to remind them of the commandments of God, that they might have them constantly before their
eyes and follow them, and not direct their heart and eyes to the
things of this world, which turn away from the word of God, and
lead astray to idolatry (cf. Prov. iv. 25, 26). Another reason for
these instructions, as is afterwards added in ver. 40, was to remind
Israel of all the commandments of the Lord, that they might do

them and be holy to their God, and sanctify their daily life to Him
who had brought them out of Egypt, to be their God, *i.e.* to show
Himself as God to them.

Rebellion of Korah's Company.—Chap. xvi.-xvii. 5.

The sedition of Korah and his company, with the renewed
sanction of the Aaronic priesthood on the part of God which it
occasioned, is the only important occurrence recorded in connection
with the thirty-seven years' wandering in the wilderness. The
time and place are not recorded. The fact that the departure from
Kadesh is not mentioned in chap. xiv., whilst, according to Deut.
i. 46, Israel remained there many days, is not sufficient to warrant
the conclusion that it took place in Kadesh. The departure from
Kadesh is not mentioned even after the rebellion of Korah; and
yet we read, in chap. xx. 1, that the whole congregation came again
into the desert of Zin to Kadesh at the beginning of the fortieth
year, and therefore must previously have gone away. All that can
be laid down as probable is, that it occurred in one of the earliest
of the thirty-seven years of punishment, though we have no firm
ground even for this conjecture.

Vers. 1–3. The authors of the rebellion were *Korah* the Levite,
a descendant of the Kohathite Izhar, who was a brother of Amram,
an ancestor (not the father) of Aaron and Moses (see at Ex. vi. 18),
and three Reubenites, viz. *Dathan* and *Abiram*, sons of Eliab, of
the Reubenitish family of Pallu (chap. xxvi. 8, 9), and *On*, the son
of Peleth, a Reubenite, not mentioned again. The last of these
(*On*) is not referred to again in the further course of this event,
either because he played altogether a subordinate part in the affair,
or because he had drawn back before the conspiracy came to a
head. The persons named took (יִּקַּח), *i.e.* gained over to their plan,
or persuaded to join them, 250 distinguished men of the other
tribes, and rose up with them against Moses and Aaron. On the
construction וַיָּקֻמוּ . . . וַיִּקַּח (vers. 1 and 2), *Gesenius* correctly
observes in his *Thesaurus* (p. 760), " There is an *anakolouthon*
rather than an ellipsis, and not merely a copyist's error, in these
words, ' *and Korah, . . . and Dathan and Abiram, took and rose up
against Moses with* 250 *men,*' for they took 250 men, and rose up
with them against Moses," etc. He also points to the analogous
construction in 2 Sam. xviii. 18. Consequently there is no necessity either to force a meaning upon לָקַח, which is altogether foreign
to it, or to attempt an emendation of the text. " *They rose up*

before Moses :" this does not mean, " they stood up in front of his tent," as *Knobel* explains it, for the purpose of bringing ver. 2 into contradiction with ver. 3, but they created an uproar before his eyes ; and with this the expression in ver. 3, *" and they gathered themselves together against Moses and Aaron,"* may be very simply and easily combined. The 250 men of the children of Israel who joined the rebels no doubt belonged to the other tribes, as is in-directly implied in the statement in chap. xxvii. 3, that Zelophehad the Manassite was not in the company of Korah. These men were *"princes of the congregation," i.e.* heads of the tribes, or of large divisions of the tribes, *" called men of the congregation," i.e.* mem-bers of the council of the nation which administered the affairs of the congregation (cf. i. 16), *" men of name"* (אַנְשֵׁי שֵׁם, see Gen. vi. 4). The leader was Korah ; and the rebels are called in conse-quence *" Korah's company"* (vers. 5, 6, chap. xxvi. 9, xxvii. 3). He laid claim to the high-priesthood, or at least to an equality with Aaron (ver. 17). Among his associates were the Reubenites, Dathan and Abiram, who, no doubt, were unable to get over the fact that the birthright had been taken away from their ancestor, and with it the headship of the house of Israel (*i.e.* of the whole nation). Apparently their present intention was to seize upon the government of the nation under a self-elected high priest, and to force Moses and Aaron out of the post assigned to them by God,— that is to say, to overthrow the constitution which God had given to His people.—Ver. 3. רַב־לָכֶם, *" enough for you !"* (רַב, as in Gen. xlv. 28), they said to Moses and Aaron, *i.e.* " let the past suffice you" (*Knobel*) ; ye have held the priesthood and the government quite long enough. It must now come to an end; *" for the whole congregation, all of them* (*i.e.* all the members of the nation), *are holy, and Jehovah is in the midst of them. Wherefore lift ye your-selves above the congregation of Jehovah ?"* The distinction between עֵדָה and קָהָל is the following: עֵדָה signifies *conventus,* the congrega-tion according to its natural organization ; קהל signifies *convocatio,* the congregation according to its divine calling and theocratic purpose. The use of the two words in the same verse upsets the theory that עֲדַת יְהוָֹה belongs to the style of the original work, and קְהַל יְהוָֹה to that of the Jehovist. The rebels appeal to the calling of all Israel to be the holy nation of Jehovah (Ex. xix. 5, 6), and infer from this the equal right of all to hold the priesthood, " leav-ing entirely out of sight, as blind selfishness is accustomed to do, the transition of the universal priesthood into the special mediatorial

office and priesthood of Moses and Aaron, which had their foundation in fact" (*Baumgarten*) ; or altogether overlooking the fact that
God Himself had chosen Moses and Aaron, and appointed them as
mediators between Himself and the congregation, to educate the
sinful nation into a holy nation, and train it to the fulfilment of its
proper vocation. The rebels, on the contrary, thought that they
were holy already, because God had called them to be a holy nation,
and in their carnal self-righteousness forgot the condition attached
to their calling, "If ye will obey My voice indeed, and keep My
covenant" (Ex. xix. 5).

Vers. 4–17. When Moses heard these words of the rebels, he
fell upon his face, to complain of the matter to the Lord, as in
chap. xiv. 5. He then said to Korah and his company, " *To-morrow Jehovah will show who is His and holy, and will let him come
near to Him, and he whom He chooseth will draw near to Him.*"
The meaning of אֲשֶׁר לֹו is evident from אֲשֶׁר יִבְחַר בּוֹ. He is Jehovah's, whom He chooses, so that He belongs to Him with his
whole life. The reference is to the priestly rank, to which God had
chosen Aaron and his sons out of the whole nation, and sanctified
them by a special consecration (Ex. xxviii. 1, xxix. 1 ; Lev. viii. 12,
30), and by which they became the persons "standing near to Him"
(Lev. x. 3), and were qualified to appear before Him in the sanctuary, and present to Him the sacrifices of the nation.—Ver. 6. To
leave the decision of this to the Lord, Korah and his company, who
laid claim to this prerogative, were to take censers, and bring lighted
incense before Jehovah. He whom the Lord should choose was to
be the sanctified one. This was to satisfy them. With the expression רַב־לָכֶם in ver. 7, Moses gives the rebels back their own
words in ver. 3. The divine decision was connected with the offering of incense, because this was the holiest function of the priestly
service, which brought the priest into the immediate presence of
God, and in connection with which Jehovah had already shown to
the whole congregation how He sanctified Himself, by a penal
judgment on those who took this office upon themselves without a
divine call (Lev. x. 1–3). Vers. 8 sqq. He then set before them
the wickedness of their enterprise, to lead them to search themselves, and avert the judgment which threatened them. In doing
this, he made a distinction between Korah the Levite, and Dathan
and Abiram the Reubenites, according to the difference in the
motives which prompted their rebellion, and the claims which they
asserted. He first of all (vers. 8–11) reminded Korah the Levite

of the way in which God had distinguished his tribe, by separating
the Levites from the rest of the congregation, to attend to the service of the sanctuary (chap. iii. 5 sqq., viii. 6 sqq.), and asked him,
" *Is this too little for you?   The God of Israel* (this epithet is used
emphatically for Jehovah) *has brought thee near to Himself, and all
thy brethren the sons of Levi with thee, and ye strive after the priesthood also.   Therefore . . . thou and thy company, who have leagued
themselves against Jehovah: . . . and Aaron, what is he, that ye murmur
against him?*"   These last words, as an expression of wrath, are
elliptical, or rather an *aposiopesis*, and are to be filled up in the
following manner : " Therefore, . . . as Jehovah has distinguished
you in this manner, . . . what do ye want ?   Ye rebel against Jehovah ! why do ye murmur against Aaron ?   He has not seized upon
the priesthood of his own accord, but Jehovah has called him to it,
and he is only a feeble servant of God" (cf. Ex. xvi. 7).   Moses
then (vers. 12–14) sent for Dathan and Abiram, who, as is tacitly
assumed, had gone back to their tents during the warning given to
Korah.   But they replied, " *We shall not come up.*"   עָלָה, to go up,
is used either with reference to the tabernacle, as being in a spiritual
sense the culminating point of the entire camp, or with reference
to appearance before Moses, the head and ruler of the nation.
" *Is it too little that thou hast brought us out of a land flowing with
milk and honey* (they apply this expression in bitter irony to Egypt),
to kill us in the wilderness (deliver us up to death), *that thou wilt be
always playing the lord over us ?*"   The idea of continuance, which
is implied in the *inf. abs.*, הִשְׂתָּרֵר, from שָׂרַר, to exalt one's self as
ruler (*Ges.* § 131, 36), is here still further intensified by גַּם.   " *Moreover, thou hast not brought us into a land flowing with milk and
honey, or given us fields and vineyards for an inheritance* (*i.e.* thou
hast not kept thy promise, Ex. iv. 30 compared with chap. iii. 7
sqq.).   *Wilt thou put out the eyes of these people ?*" *i.e.* wilt thou
blind them as to thy doings and designs ?—Ver. 15. Moses was so
disturbed by these scornful reproaches, that he entreated the Lord,
with an asertion of his own unselfishness, not to have respect to their
gift, *i.e.* not to accept the sacrifice which they should bring (cf.
Gen. iv. 4).   " *I have not taken one ass from them, nor done harm to
one of ·them,*" *i.e.* I have not treated them as a ruler, who demands
tribute of his subjects, and oppresses them (cf. 1 Sam. xii. 3).—
Vers. 16, 17. In conclusion, he summoned Korah and his associates
once more, to present themselves the following day before Jehovah
with censers and incense.

Vers. 18–35. The next day the rebels presented themselves with censers before the tabernacle, along with Moses and Aaron ; and the whole congregation also assembled there at the instigation of Korah. The Lord then interposed in judgment. Appearing in His glory to the whole congregation (just as in chap. xiv. 10), He said to Moses and Aaron, " *Separate yourselves from this congregation ; I will destroy them in a moment.*" By assembling in front of the tabernacle, the whole congregation had made common cause with the rebels. God threatened them, therefore, with sudden destruction. But the two men of God, who were so despised by the rebellious faction, fell on their faces, interceding with God, and praying, " *God, Thou God of the spirits of all flesh ! this one man* (*i.e.* Korah, the author of the conspiracy) *hath sinned, and wilt Thou be wrathful with all the congregation ?*" *i.e.* let Thine anger fall upon the whole congregation. The Creator and Preserver of all beings, who has given and still gives life and breath to all flesh, is God of the spirits of all flesh. As the author of the spirit of life in all perishable flesh, God cannot destroy His own creatures in wrath ; this would be opposed to His own paternal love and mercy. In this epithet, as applied to God, therefore, Moses appeals " to the universal blessing of creation. It is of little consequence whether these words are to be understood as relating to all the animal kingdom, or to the human race alone ; because Moses simply prayed, that as God was the creator and architect of the world, He would not destroy the men whom He had created, but rather have mercy upon the works of His own hands" (*Calvin*). The intercession of the prophet Isaiah, in Isa. lxiv. 8, is similar to this, though that is founded upon the special relation in which God stood to Israel.—Vers. 23 sqq. Jehovah then instructed Moses, that the congregation was to remove away (עָלָה, to get up and away) from about the dwelling-place of Korah, Dathan, and Abiram ; and, as we may supply from the context, the congregation fell back from Korah's tent, whilst Dathan and Abiram, possibly at the very first appearance of the divine glory, drew back into their tents. Moses therefore betook himself to the tents of Dathan and Abiram, with the elders following him, and there also commanded the congregation to depart from the tents of these wicked men, and not touch anything they possessed, that they might not be swept away in all their sins.—Ver. 27. The congregation obeyed ; but Dathan and Abiram came and placed themselves in front of the tents, along with their wives and children, to see what Moses would do. Moses then announced the sentence : " *By this shall ye know that Jehovah hath sent me to do all these works, that not out of my own heart* (*i.e.* that I do not act of my own accord). *If these men die like all men* (*i.e.* if these wicked men die a natural death like other men), *and the oversight of all men take place over them* (*i.e.* if the same providence watches over them as over all other men, and preserves them from sudden death), *Jehovah hath not sent me. But if Jehovah create a creation* (בָּרָא בְּרִיאָה, *i.e.* work an extraordinary miracle), *and the earth open its mouth and swallow them up, with all that belongs to them, so that they go down alive into hell, ye shall perceive that these men have despised Jehovah."*—Vers. 31–33. And immediately the earth clave asunder, and swallowed them up, with their families and all their possessions, and closed above them, so that they perished without a trace from the congregation. אֹתָם refers to the three ringleaders. *" Their houses ;"* i.e. their families, not their tents, as in chap. xviii. 31, Ex. xii. 3. *" All the men belonging to Korah"* were his servants ; for, according to chap. xxvi. 11, his sons did not perish with him, but perpetuated his family (chap. xxvi. 58), to which the celebrated Korahite singers of David's time belonged (1 Chron. vi. 18-22, ix. 19).—Ver. 34. This fearful destruction of the ringleaders, through which Jehovah glorified Moses afresh as His servant in a miraculous way, filled all the Israelites round about with such terror, that they fled לְקֹלָם, *" at their noise,"* i.e. at the commotion with which the wicked men went down into the abyss which opened beneath their feet, *lest*, as they said, *the earth should swallow them up also.*— Ver. 35. The other 250 rebels, who were probably still in front of the tabernacle, were then destroyed by fire which proceeded from Jehovah, as Nadab and Abihu had been before (Lev. x. 2).

Vers. 36–40 (or xvii. 1-5). After the destruction of the sinners, the Lord commanded that Eleazar should take up the censers *" from between the burning,"* i.e. from the midst of the men that had been burned, and scatter the fire (the burning coals in the pans) far away, that it might not be used any more. *" For they* (the censers) *are holy ;"* that is to say, they had become holy through being brought before Jehovah (ver. 39) ; and therefore, when the men who brought them were slain, they fell as banned articles to the Lord (Lev. xxvii. 28). *" The censers of these sinners against their souls"* (*i.e.* the men who have forfeited their lives through their sin : cf. Prov. xx. 2, Hab. ii. 10), *" let them make into broad plates for a covering to the altar"* (of burnt-offering). Through this application of them they became a sign, or, according to ver. 39, a memorial 'to all who drew near to the sanctuary, which was to remind them continually of this judgment of God, and warn the congregation of grasping at the priestly prerogatives. The words, וְלֹא יְהְיֶה, in ver. 40, introduce the predicate in the form of an apodosis to the subject, which is written absolutely, and consists of an entire sentence. הָיָה with כְּ signifies, " to experience the same fate as" another.

Punishment of the murmuring Congregation, and Confirmation of the High-priesthood of Aaron.—Chap. xvi. 41–xvii. 13 (or chap. xvii. 6–28).

Vers. 41–50. PUNISHMENT OF THE MURMURING CONGREGATION.—The judgment upon the company of Korah had filled the people round about with terror and dismay, but it had produced no change of heart in the congregation that had risen up against its leaders. The next morning the whole congregation began to murmur against Moses and Aaron, and to charge them with having slain the people of Jehovah. They referred to Korah and his company, but especially to the 250 chiefs of renown, whom they regarded as the kernel of the nation, and called " the people of Jehovah." They would have made Moses and Aaron responsible for their death, because in their opinion it was they who had brought the judgment upon their leaders ; whereas it was through the intercession of Moses (chap. xvi. 22) that the whole congregation was saved from the destruction which threatened it. To such an extent does the folly of the proud heart of man proceed, and the obduracy of a race already exposed to the judgment of God.— Ver. 7. When the congregation assembled together, Moses and Aaron turned to the tabernacle, and saw how the cloud covered it, and the glory of the Lord appeared. As the cloud rested continually above the tabernacle during the time of encampment (chap. ix. 18 sqq.; Ex. xl. 38), we must suppose that at this time the cloud covered it in a fuller and much more conspicuous sense, just as it had done when the tabernacle was first erected (chap. ix. 15; Ex. xl. 34), and that at the same time the glory of God burst forth from the dark cloud in a miraculous splendour.—Vers. 8 sqq. Thereupon they both went into the court of (אֶל פְּנֵי, as in Lev. ix. 5) the tabernacle, and God commanded them to rise up (הֵרֹמּוּ, Niphal of רָמַם = רוּם ; see *Ges.* § 65, Anm. 5) out of this congregation, which He would immediately destroy. But they fell upon their faces in prayer, as in chap. xvi. 21, 22. This time, however, they could not avert the bursting forth of the wrathful judgment, as they had done the day before (chap. xvi. 22). The plague had already commenced, when Moses told Aaron to take the censer quickly into the midst of the congregation, with coals and incense (הוֹלֵךְ, imper. Hiph.), to make expiation for it with an incense-offering. And when this was done, and Aaron placed himself between the dead and the living, the plague, which had already destroyed 14,700 men, was stayed. The plague consisted apparently of a sudden death, as in the case of a pestilence raging with extreme violence, though we cannot regard it as an actual pestilence.

The means resorted to by Moses to stay the plague showed afresh how the faithful servant of God bore the rescue of his people upon his heart. All the motives which he had hitherto pleaded, in his repeated intercession that this evil congregation might be spared, were now exhausted. He could not stake his life for the nation, as at Horeb (Ex. xxxii. 32), for the nation had rejected him. He could no longer appeal to the honour of Jehovah among the heathen, seeing that the Lord, even when sentencing the rebellious race to fall in the desert, had assured him that the whole earth should be filled with His glory (chap. xiv. 20 sqq.). Still less could he pray to God that He would not be wrathful with all for the sake of one or a few sinners, as in chap. xvi. 22, seeing that the whole congregation had taken part with the rebels. In this condition of things there was but one way left of averting the threatened destruction of the whole nation, namely, to adopt the means which the Lord Himself had given to His congregation, in the high-priestly office, to wipe away their sins, and recover the divine grace which they had forfeited through sin,—viz. the offering of incense which embodied the high-priestly prayer, and the strength and operation of which were not dependent upon the sincerity and earnestness of subjective faith, but had a firm and immovable foundation in the objective force of the divine appointment. This was the means adopted by the faithful servant of the Lord, and the judgment of wrath was averted in its course; the plague was averted.—The effectual operation of the incense-offering of the high priest also served to furnish the people with a practical proof of the power and operation of the true and divinely appointed priesthood. " The priesthood which the company of Korah had so wickedly usurped, had brought down death and destruction upon himself, through his offering of incense; but the divinely appointed priesthood of Aaron averted death and destruction from the whole congregation when incense was offered by him, and stayed the well-merited judgment, which had broken forth upon it" (*Kurtz*).

Chap. xvii. 1–13 (or chap. xvii. 16–28). CONFIRMATION OF THE HIGH-PRIESTHOOD OF AARON.—Whilst the Lord had thus given a practical proof to the people, that Aaron was the high priest appointed by Him for His congregation, by allowing the high-priestly incense offered by Aaron to expiate His wrath, and by removing the plague; He also gave them a still further confirmation of His priesthood, by a miracle which was well adapted to put to silence all the murmuring of the congregation.—Vers. 16–20. He commanded Moses to take twelve rods of the tribe-princes of Israel, one for the fathers' house of each of their tribes, and to write upon each the name of the tribe; but upon that of the tribe of Levi he was to write Aaron's name, because each rod was to stand for the head of their fathers' houses, *i.e.* for the existing head of the tribe; and in the case of Levi, the tribe-head was Aaron. As only twelve rods were taken for all the tribes of Israel, and Levi was included among them, Ephraim and Manasseh must have been reckoned as the one tribe of Joseph, as in Deut. xxvii. 12. These rods were to be laid by Moses in the tabernacle before the testimony, or ark of the covenant (Ex. xxv. 21, xxix. 42). And there the rod of the man whom Jehovah chose, *i.e.* entrusted with the priesthood (see chap. xvi. 5), would put forth shoots, to quiet the murmuring of the people. שָׁכַךְ, *Hiph.*, to cause to sink, to bring to rest, construed with מֵעַל in a pregnant signification, to quiet in such a way that it will not rise again.—Vers. 6–9. Moses carried out this command. And when he went into the tabernacle the following morning, behold Aaron's rod of the house of Levi had sprouted, and put forth shoots, and had borne blossoms and matured almonds. And Moses brought all the rods out of the sanctuary, and gave every man his own; the rest, as we may gather from the context, being all unchanged, so that the whole nation could satisfy itself that God had chosen Aaron. Thus was the word fulfilled which Moses had spoken at the commencement of the rebellion of the company of Korah (chap. xvi. 5), and that in a way which could not fail to accredit him before the whole congregation as sent of God.

So far as the occurrence itself is concerned, there can hardly be any need to remark, that the natural interpretation which has lately been attempted by *Ewald*, viz. that Moses had laid several

almond rods in the holy place, which had just been freshly cut
off, that he might see the next day which of them would flower
the best during the night, is directly at variance with the words of
the text, and also with the fact, that a rod even freshly cut off,
when laid in a dry place, would not bear ripe fruit in a single
night. The miracle which God wrought here as the Creator of
nature, was at the same time a significant symbol of the nature and
meaning of the priesthood. The choice of the rods had also a bearing upon the object in question. A man's rod was the sign of his
position as ruler in the house and congregation ; with a prince the
rod becomes a sceptre, the insignia of rule (Gen. xlix. 10). As a
severed branch, the rod could not put forth shoots and blossom in
a natural way. But God could impart new vital powers even to
the dry rod. And so Aaron had naturally no pre-eminence above
the heads of the other tribes. But the priesthood was founded not
upon natural qualifications and gifts, but upon the power of the
Spirit, which God communicates according to the choice of His
wisdom, and which He had imparted to Aaron through his consecration with holy anointing oil. It was this which the Lord intended
to show to the people, by causing Aaron's rod to put forth branches,
blossom, and fruit, through a miracle of His omnipotence ; whereas
the rods of the other heads of the tribes remained as barren as
before. In this way, therefore, it was not without deep significance that Aaron's rod not only put forth shoots, by which the
divine election might be recognised, but bore even blossom and ripe
fruit. This showed that Aaron was not only qualified for his calling, but administered his office in the full power of the Spirit, and
bore the fruit expected of him. The almond rod was especially
adapted to exhibit this, as an almond-tree flowers and bears fruit
the earliest of all the trees, and has received its name of שָׁקֵד,
" awake," from this very fact (cf. Jer. i. 11).

God then commanded (vers. 10, 11) that Aaron's rod should be
taken back into the sanctuary, and preserved before the testimony,
" for a sign for the rebellious, that thou puttest an end to their murmuring, and they die not." The preservation of the rod before the ark
of the covenant, in the immediate presence of the Lord, was a pledge
to Aaron of the continuance of his election, and the permanent
duration of his priesthood ; though we have no need to assume, that
through a perpetual miracle the staff continued green and blossoming. In this way the staff became a sign to the rebellious, which
could not fail to stop their murmuring.—Vers. 12, 13. This miracle

awakened a salutary terror in all the people, so that they cried out
to Moses in mortal anguish, *"Behold, we die, we perish, we all
perish! Every one who comes near to the dwelling of Jehovah dies;
are we all to die?"* Even if this fear of death was no fruit of
faith, it was fitted for all that to prevent any fresh outbreaks of
rebellion on the part of the rejected generation.

Service and Revenues of the Priests and Levites.—Chap. xviii.

The practical confirmation of the priesthood of Aaron and his
family, on the part of God, is very appropriately followed by the
legal regulations concerning the official duties of the priests and
Levites (vers. 1–7), and the revenues to be assigned them for their
services (vers. 8–32), as the laws hitherto given upon this subject,
although they contain many isolated stipulations, have not laid
down any complete and comprehensive arrangement. The instructions relating to this subject were addressed by Jehovah directly to
Aaron (see vers. 1 and 8), up to the law, that out of the tenths
which the Levites were to collect from the people, they were to
pay a tenth again to the priests; and this was addressed to Moses
(ver. 25), as the head of all Israel.

Vers. 1–7. THE OFFICIAL DUTIES AND RIGHTS OF THE PRIESTS
AND LEVITES.—Ver. 1. To impress upon the minds of the priests
and Levites the holiness and responsibility of their office, the service
of Aaron, of his sons, and of his father's house, *i.e.* of the family of
the Kohathites, is described as "bearing the iniquity of the sanctuary," and the service which was peculiar to the Aaronides, as "bearing the iniquity of their priesthood." *"To bear the iniquity of the
sanctuary"* signifies not only "to have to make expiation for all
that offended against the laws of the priests and the holy things, *i.e.*
the desecration of these" (*Knobel*), but "iniquity or transgression
at the sanctuary," *i.e.* the defilement of it by the sin of those who
drew near to the sanctuary; not only of the priests and Levites, but
of the whole people who defiled the sanctuary in the midst of them
with its holy vessels, not only by their sins (Lev. xvi. 6), but even
by their holy gifts (Ex. xxviii. 38), and thus brought guilt upon
the whole congregation, which the priests were to bear, *i.e.* to take
upon themselves and expunge, by virtue of the holiness and sanctifying power communicated to their office (see at Ex. xxviii. 38).
The "iniquity of the priesthood," however, not only embraced
every offence against the priesthood, every neglect of the most

scrupulous and conscientious fulfilment of duty in connection with their office, but extended to all the sin which attached to the official acts of the priests, on account of the sinfulness of their nature. It was to wipe out these sins and defilements, that the annual expiation of the holy things on the day of atonement had been appointed (Lev. xvi. 16 sqq.). The father's house of Aaron, *i.e.* the Levitical family of Kohath, was also to join in bearing the iniquity of the sanctuary, because the oversight of the holy vessels of the sanctuary devolved upon it (chap. iv. 4 sqq.).—Vers. 2-4. Aaron was also to bring his (other) brethren (*sc.* to the sanctuary), viz. the tribe of Levi, that is to say, the Gershonites and Merarites, that they might attach themselves to him and serve him, both him (וְאִתְּה) and his sons, before the tent of testimony, and discharge the duties that were binding upon them, according to chap. iv. 24 sqq., 31 sqq. (cf. chap. iii. 6, 7, viii. 26). Only they were not to come near to the holy vessels and the altar, for that would bring death both upon them and the priests (see at chap. iv. 15). On ver. 4, cf. chap. i. 53 and iii. 7.—Vers. 5-7. The charge of the sanctuary (*i.e.* the dwelling) and the altar (of burnt-offering) devolved upon Aaron and his sons, that the wrath of God might not come again upon the children of Israel (see chap. viii. 19),—namely, through such illegal acts as Nadab and Abihu (Lev. x. 2), and the company of Korah (chap. xvi. 35), had committed. To this end God had handed over the Levites to them as a gift, to be their assistants (see at chap. iii. 9 and viii. 16, 19). But Aaron and his sons were to attend to the priesthood "*with regard to everything of the altar and within the vail*" (*i.e.* of the most holy place, see Lev. xvi. 12). The allusion is to all the priestly duties from the altar of burnt-offering to the most holy place, including the holy place which lay between. This office, which brought them into the closest fellowship with the Lord, was a favour accorded to them by the grace of God. This is expressed in the words, "*as a service of gift* (a service with which I present you) *I give you the priesthood.*" The last words in ver. 7 are the same as in chap. i. 51; and "*stranger*" (*zar*), as in Lev. xxii. 10.

Vers. 8-20. THE REVENUES OF THE PRIESTS.—These are summed up in ver. 8 in these words, "*I give thee the keeping of My heave-offerings in all holy gifts for a portion, as an eternal statute.*" The notion of מִשְׁמֶרֶת, keeping, as in Ex. xii. 6, xvi. 23, 32, is defined in the second parallel clause as מָשְׁחָה, a portion (see at Lev. vii. 35).

The priests were to keep all the heave-offerings, as the portion which belonged to them, out of the sacrificial gifts that the children of Israel offered to the Lord. תְּרוּמֹת, heave-offerings (see at Ex. xxv. 2, and Lev. ii. 9), is used here in the broadest sense, as including all the holy gifts (*kodashim*, see Lev. xxi. 22) which the Israelites lifted off from their possessions and presented to the Lord (as in chap. v. 9). Among these, for example, were, *first* of all, the most holy gifts in the meat-offerings, sin-offerings, and trespass-offerings (vers. 9, 10; see at Lev. ii. 3). The burnt-offerings are not mentioned, because the whole of the flesh of these was burned upon the altar, and the skin alone fell to the portion of the priest (Lev. vii. 8). "*From the fire*," sc. of the altar. אֵשׁ, fire, is equivalent to אִשֶּׁה, firing (see Lev. i. 9). These gifts they were to eat, as most holy, in a most holy place, *i.e.* in the court of the tabernacle (see Lev. vi. 9, 19, vii. 6), which is called "*most holy*" here, to lay a stronger emphasis upon the precept. In the *second* place, these gifts included also "*the holy gifts;*" viz. (*a*) (ver. 11) the heave-offering of their gifts in all wave-offerings (*tenuphoth*), *i.e.* the wave-breast and heave-leg of the peace-offerings, and whatever else was waved in connection with the sacrifices (see at Lev. vii. 33): these might be eaten by both the male and female members of the priestly families, provided they were legally clean (Lev. xxii. 3 sqq.); (*b*) (ver. 12) the gifts of first-fruits: "*all the fat* (*i.e.* the best, as in Gen. xlv. 18) *of oil, new wine, and corn*," viz. רֵאשִׁיתָם, "*the first of them*," the בִּכּוּרִים, "*the first-grown fruits*" of the land, and that of all the fruit of the ground (Deut. xxvi. 2, 10; Prov. iii. 9; Ezek. xliv. 30), corn, wine, oil, honey, and tree-fruit (Deut. viii. 8, compared with Lev. xix. 23, 24), which were offered, according to 2 Chron. xxxi. 5, Neh. x. 36, 38, Tob. i. 6, as first-fruits every year (see *Mishnah, Bikkur,* i. 3, 10, where the first-fruits are specified according to the productions mentioned in Deut. viii. 8; the law prescribed nothing in relation to the quantity of the different first-fruits, but left this entirely to the offerer himself); (*c*) (ver. 14) everything placed under a ban (see at Lev. xxvii. 28); and (*d*) (vers. 15–18) the first-born of man and beast. The first-born of men and of unclean beasts were redeemed according to chap. iii. 47, Ex. xiii. 12, 13, and Lev. xxvii. 6, 27; but such as were fit for sacrifice were actually offered, the blood being swung against the altar, and the fat portions burned upon it, whilst the whole of the flesh fell to the portion of the priests. So far as the redemption of human beings was concerned (ver. 16), they were

" *to redeem from the monthly child,*" *i.e.* the first-born child as soon as it was a month old.—Ver. 19. " *All the holy heave-offerings*" are not the thank-offerings (*Knobel*), but, as in ver. 8, all the holy gifts enumerated in vers. 9–18. Jehovah gives these to the priests as an eternal claim. " *An eternal covenant of salt is this before Jehovah,*" for Aaron and his descendants. A " covenant of salt ;" equivalent to an indissoluble covenant, or inviolable contract (see at Lev. ii. 13).—Ver. 20. For this reason, Aaron was to receive no inheritance in the land among the children of Israel. Aaron, as the head of the priests, represents the whole priesthood ; and with regard to the possession, the whole tribe of Levi is placed, in ver. 23, on an equality with the priests. The Levites were to receive no portion of the land as an inheritance in Canaan (cf. chap. xxvi. 62 ; Deut. xii. 12, xiv. 27 ; Josh. xiv. 3). Jehovah was the portion and inheritance, not only of Aaron and his sons, but of the whole tribe of Levi (cf. Deut. x. 9, xviii. 2 ; Josh. xiii. 33) ; or, as it is expressed in Josh. xviii. 7, " the priesthood of Jehovah was their inheritance," though not in the sense that *Knobel* supposes, viz. " the priesthood with its revenues," which would make the expression " Jehovah, the God of Israel" (Josh. xiii. 33), to be metonymical for " sacrificial gifts, first-fruits, and tenths." The possession of the priests and Levites did not consist in the revenues assigned to them by God, but in the possession of Jehovah, the God of Israel. In the same sense in which the tribe of Levi was the peculiar possession of Jehovah out of the whole of the people of possession, was Jehovah also the peculiar possession of Levi ; and just as the other tribes were to live upon what was afforded by the land assigned them as a possession, Levi was to live upon what Jehovah bestowed upon it. And inasmuch as not only the whole land of the twelve tribes, with which Jehovah had enfeoffed them, but the whole earth, belonged to Jehovah (Ex. xix. 5), He was necessarily to be regarded as the greatest possession of all, beyond which nothing greater is conceivable, and in comparison with which every other possession is to be regarded as nothing. Hence it was evidently the greatest privilege and highest honour to have Him for a portion and possession (*Bähr, Symbolik*, ii. p. 44). " For truly," as *Masius* writes (Com. on Josh.), " he who possesses God possesses all things ; and the worship (*cultus*) of Him is infinitely fuller of delight, and far more productive, than the cultivation (*cultus*) of any soil."

Vers. 21–24. REVENUES OF THE LEVITES.—For (חֵלֶף, instead

of, for) their service at the tabernacle God assigns them " *every tenth in Israel as an inheritance.*" On the tenth, see at Lev. xxvii. 30–33. The institution and description of their service in vers. 22 and 23 is the same as that in chap. i. 53 and viii. 19. " Lest they *bear sin :*" see at Lev. xix. 17.

Vers. 25–32. *Appropriation of the Tithe.*—Vers. 26 sqq. When the Levites took (received) from the people the tithe assigned them by Jehovah, they were to lift off from it a heave-offering for Jehovah, a tithe of the tithe for Aaron the priest (*i.e.* for the priesthood ; see at ver. 20). " *Your heave-offering shall be reckoned to you as the corn of the threshing-floor, and the fulness* (see Ex. xxii. 28) *of the wine-press,*" *i.e.* according to ver. 30, as the revenue of the threshing-floor and wine-press ; that is to say, as corn and wine which they had reaped themselves.—Ver. 29. The whole of this heave-offering of Jehovah, *i.e.* the tithe of the tithe, they were to lift off from all their gifts, from all the tithes of the people which they received ; " *of all the fat of it,*" *i.e.* of all the best of the heave-offering they received, they were to lift off אֶת־מִקְדְּשׁוֹ, " *its holy,*" *i.e.* the holy part, which was to be dedicated to Jehovah.—Ver. 30. They might eat it (the tithe they had received, after taking off the priests' tithe) in any place with their families, as it was the reward for their service at the tabernacle.—Ver. 32. They would load no sin upon themselves by so doing (see Lev. xix. 17), if they only lifted off the best as tithe (for the priest), and did not desecrate the holy gifts, *sc.* by eating in all kinds of places, which was not allowed, according to ver. 10, with regard to the most holy gifts.

These regulations concerning the revenues of the priests and Levites were in perfect accordance with the true idea of the Israelitish kingdom of God. Whereas in heathen states, where there was an hereditary priestly caste, that caste was generally a rich one, and held a firm possession in the soil (in Egypt, for example ; see at Gen. xlvii. 22), the Levites received no hereditary landed property in the land of Israel, but only towns to dwell in among the other tribes, with pasturage for their cattle (chap. xxxv.), because Jehovah, the God of Israel, would be their inheritance. In this way their earthly existence was based upon the spiritual ground and soil of faith, in accordance with the calling assigned them, to be the guardians and promoters of the commandments, statutes, and rights of Jehovah ; and their authority and influence among the people were bound up with their unreserved surrender of themselves to the Lord, and their firm reliance upon the possession of their God Now, whilst this position was to be a constant incitement to the Levites to surrender themselves entirely to the Lord and His service, it was also to become to the whole nation a constant admonition, inasmuch as it was a prerogative conferred upon them by the Lord, to seek the highest of all good in the possession of the Lord, as its portion and inheritance.—The revenue itself, however, which the Lord assigned to the Levites and priests, as His servants, consisting of the tenths and first-fruits, as well as certain portions of the different sacrificial gifts that were offered to Him, appears to have been a very considerable one, especially if we adopt the computation of *J. D. Michaelis* (*Mos. Recht.* i. § 52) with reference to the tithes. "A tribe," he says, " which had only 22,000 males in it (23,000 afterwards), and therefore could hardly have numbered more than 12,000 grown-up men, received the tithes of 600,000 Israelites; consequently one single Levite, without the slightest necessity for sowing, and without any of the expenses of agriculture, reaped or received from the produce of the flocks and herds as much as five of the other Israelites." But this leaves out of sight the fact that tithes are never paid so exactly as this, and that no doubt there was as little conscientiousness in the matter then as there is at the present day, when those who are entitled to receive a tenth often receive even less than a twentieth. Moreover, the revenue of the tribe, which the Lord had chosen as His own peculiar possession, was not intended to be a miserable and beggarly one; but it was hardly equal, at any time, to the revenues which the priestly castes of other nations derived from their endowments. Again, the Levites had to give up the tenth of all the tithes they received to the priests; and the priests were to offer to Jehovah upon the altar a portion of the first-fruits, heave-offerings, and wave-offerings that were assigned to them. Consequently, as the whole nation was to make a practical acknowledgment, in the presentation of the tithe and first-fruits, that it had received its hereditary property as a fief from the Lord its God, so the Levites, by their payment of the tenth to the priests, and the priests, by presenting a portion of their revenues upon the altar, were to make a practical confession that they had received all their revenues from the Lord their God, and owed Him praise and adoration in return (see *Bähr, Symbolik,* ii. pp. 43 sqq.).

The Law concerning Purification from the Uncleanness of Death.— Chap. xix.

In order that a consciousness of the continuance of the covenant relation might be kept alive during the dying out of the race that had fallen under the judgment of God, after the severe stroke with which the Lord had visited the whole nation in consequence of the rebellion of the company of Korah, He gave the law concerning purification from the uncleanness of death, in which first of all the preparation of a sprinkling water is commanded for the removal of this uncleanness (vers. 1–10a) ; and then, secondly, the use of this purifying water enjoined as an eternal statute (vers. 10b–22). The thought that death, and the putrefaction of death, as being the embodiment of sin, defiled and excluded from fellowship with the holy God, was a view of the fall and its consequences which had been handed down from the primeval age (see vol. ii. p. 357), and which was not only shared by the Israelites with many of the nations of antiquity,[1] but presupposed by the laws given on Sinai as a truth well known in Israel ; and at the same time confirmed, both in the prohibition of the priests from defiling themselves with the dead, except in the case of their nearest blood-relations (Lev. xxi. 1–6, 10–12), and in the command, that every one who was defiled by a corpse should be removed out of the camp (chap. v. 2–4). Now, so long as the mortality within the congregation did not exceed the natural limits, the traditional modes of purification would be quite sufficient. But when it prevailed to a hitherto unheard-of extent, in consequence of the sentence pronounced by God, the defilements would necessarily be so crowded together, that the whole congregation would be in danger of being infected with the defilement of death, and of forfeiting its vocation to be the holy nation of Jehovah, unless God provided it with the means of cleansing itself from this uncleanness, without losing the fellowship of His covenant of grace. The law which follows furnished the means. In ver. 2 this law is called חֻקַּת הַתּוֹרָה, a " *statute of instruction*," or law-statute. This combination of the two words commonly used for law and statute, which is only met with again in chap. xxxi. 21, and there, as here, in connection with a rule relating to purification from the uncleanness of death, is probably intended to give emphasis to the design of the law about to be given, to point it out as one of great importance, but not as *decretum absque ulla ratione*, a decree without any reason, as the Rabbins suppose.

Vers. 2–10a. *Preparation of the Purifying Water.*—As water is the ordinary means by which all kinds of uncleanness are removed,

---

[1] Vid. *Bähr, Symbolik*, ii. pp. 466 sqq. ; *Sommer, bibl. Abhdll.* pp. 271 sqq. ; *Knobel* on this chapter, and *Leyrer* in *Herzog's* Cyclopædia.

it was also to be employed in the removal of the uncleanness of death. But as this uncleanness was the strongest of all religious defilements, fresh water alone was not sufficient to remove it; and consequently a certain kind of sprinkling-water was appointed, which was strengthened by the ashes of a sin-offering, and thus formed into a holy alkali. The main point in the law which follows, therefore, was the preparation of the ashes, and these had to be obtained by the *sacrifice of a red heifer*.[1]—Vers. 2 sqq. The sons of Israel were to bring to Moses a red heifer, entirely without blemish, and to give it to Eleazar the priest, that he might have it slaughtered in his presence outside the camp. פָּרָה is not a cow generally, but a young cow, a heifer, δάμαλις (LXX.), *juvenca*, between the calf and the full-grown cow. אֲדֻמָּה, of a red colour, is not to be connected with תְּמִימָה in the sense of " quite red," as the Rabbins interpret it; but תְּמִימָה, *integra*, is to be taken by itself, and the words which follow, " *wherein is no blemish*," to be regarded as defining it still more precisely (see Lev. xxii. 19, 20). The slaying of this heifer is called חַטָּאת, a sin-offering, in vers. 9 and 17. To remind the congregation that death was the wages of sin, the antidote to the defilement of death was to be taken from a sin-offering. But as the object was not to remove and wipe away sin as such, but simply to cleanse the congregation from the uncleanness which proceeded from death, the curse of sin, it was necessary that the sin-offering should be modified in a peculiar manner to accord with this special design. The sacrificial animal was not to be a bullock, as in the case of the ordinary sin-offerings of the congregation (Lev. iv. 14), but a female, because the female sex is the bearer of life (Gen. iii. 20), a פָּרָה, *i.e. lit.* the fruit-bringing; and of a red colour, not because the blood-red colour points to sin (as *Hengstenberg* follows the Rabbins and earlier theologians in supposing), but as the colour of the most " intensive life," which has its seat in the blood, and shows itself in the red colour of the face (the cheeks and lips); and one " upon which no yoke had ever come," *i.e.* whose vital energy had not yet been crippled by labour under the yoke. Lastly,

[1] On this sacrifice, which is so rich in symbolical allusions, but the details of which are so difficult to explain, compare the rabbinical statutes in the talmudical tractate *Para* (*Mishnah*, *v. Surenh.* vi. pp. 269 sqq.); *Maimonides de vacca rufa;* and *Lundius jüd. Heiligth.* pp. 680 sqq. Among modern treatises on this subject, are *Bähr's Symbolik*, ii. pp. 493 sqq.; *Hengstenberg*, Egypt and the Books of Moses, pp. 173 sqq.; *Leyrer* in *Herzog's Cycl.; Kurtz* in the *Theol. Studien und Kritiken*, 1846, pp. 629 sqq. (also *Sacrificial Worship of the Old Testament*, pp. 422 sqq., Eng. transl., Tr.); and my *Archäologie*, i. p. 58.

like all the sacrificial animals, it was to be uninjured, and free from faults, inasmuch as the idea of representation, which lay at the foundation of all the sacrifices, but more especially of the sin-offerings, demanded natural sinlessness and original purity, quite as much as imputed sin and transferred uncleanness. Whilst the last-mentioned prerequisite showed that the victim was well fitted for bearing sin, the other attributes indicated the fulness of life and power in their highest forms, and qualified it to form a powerful antidote to death. As thus appointed to furnish a reagent against death and mortal corruption, the sacrificial animal was to possess throughout, viz. in colour, in sex, and in the character of its body, the fulness of life in its greatest freshness and vigour.—Ver. 3. The sacrifice itself was to be superintended by Eleazar the priest, the eldest son of the high priest, and his presumptive successor in office; because Aaron, or the high priest, whose duty it was to present the sin-offerings for the congregation (Lev. iv. 16), could not, according to his official position, which required him to avoid all uncleanness of death (Lev. xxi. 11, 12), perform such an act as this, which stood in the closest relation to death and the uncleanness of death, and for that very reason had to be performed outside the camp. The subject, to " *bring her forth*" and " *slay her*," is indefinite; since it was not the duty of the priest to slay the sacrificial animal, but of the offerer himself, or in the case before us, of the congregation, which would appoint one of its own number for the purpose. All that the priest had to do was to sprinkle the blood; at the same time the slaying was to take place לְפָנָיו, before him, *i.e.* before his eyes. Eleazar was to sprinkle some of the blood seven times " towards the opposite," *i.e.* towards the front of the tabernacle (*seven times*, as in Lev. iv. 17). Through this sprinkling of the blood the slaying became a sacrifice, being brought thereby into relation to Jehovah and the sanctuary; whilst the life, which was sacrificed for the sin of the congregation, was given up to the Lord, and offered up in the only way in which a sacrifice, prepared like this, outside the sanctuary, could possibly be offered.

After this (vers. 5, 6), they were to burn the cow, with the skin, flesh, blood, and dung, before his (Eleazar's) eyes, and he was to throw cedar-wood, hyssop, and scarlet wool into the fire. The burning of the sacrificial animal outside the camp took place in the case of every sin-offering for the whole congregation, for the reasons expounded in vol. ii. p. 307. But in the case before us, the whole of the sacrificial act had to be performed outside the camp, *i.e.* outside the sphere of the theocracy; because the design of this sin-offering was not that the congregation might thereby be received through the expiation of its sin into the fellowship of the God and Lord who was present at the altar and in the sanctuary, but simply that an antidote to the infection of death might be provided for the congregation, which had become infected through fellowship with death; and consequently, the victim was to represent, not the living congregation as still associated with the God who was present in His earthly kingdom, but those members of the congregation who had fallen victims to temporal death as the wages of sin, and, as such, were separated from the earthly theocracy (see my *Archæology*, i. p. 283). In this sacrifice, the blood, which was generally poured out at the foot of the altar, was burned along with the rest, and the ashes to be obtained were impregnated with the substance thereof. But in order still further to increase the strength of these ashes, which were already well fitted to serve as a powerful antidote to the corruption of death, as being the incorruptible residuum of the sin-offering which had not been destroyed by the fire, cedar-wood was thrown into the fire, as the symbol of the incorruptible continuance of life; and hyssop, as the symbol of purification from the corruption of death; and scarlet wool, the deep red of which shadowed forth the strongest vital energy (see at Lev. xiv. 6),—so that the ashes might be regarded " as the quintessence of all that purified and strengthened life, refined and sublimated by the fire " (*Leyrer*). —Vers. 7-10*a*, etc. The persons who took part in this—viz. the priest, the man who attended to the burning, and the clean man who gathered the ashes together, and deposited them in a clean place for subsequent use—became unclean till the evening in consequence; not from the fact that they had officiated for unclean persons, and, in a certain sense, had participated in their uncleanness (*Knobel*), but through the uncleanness of sin and death, which had passed over to the sin-offering; just as the man who led into the wilderness the goat which had been rendered unclean through the imposition of sin, became himself unclean in consequence (Lev. xvi. 26). Even the sprinkling water prepared from the ashes defiled every one who touched it (ver. 21). But when the ashes were regarded in relation to their appointment as the means of purification, they were to be treated as clean. Not only were they to be collected together by a clean man; but they were to be kept for use in a clean place, just as the ashes of the sacrifices that were taken away from the altar were to be carried to a clean place outside the camp (Lev. vi. 4). These defilements, like every other which only lasted till the evening, were to be removed by washing (see vol. ii. pp. 373–4). The ashes thus collected were to serve the congregation לְמֵי נִדָּה, *i.e.* literally as water of uncleanness; in other words, as water by which uncleanness was to be removed. "*Water of uncleanness*" is analogous to "water of sin" in chap. viii. 7.

Vers. 10*b*–22. *Use of the Water of Purification.*—The words in ver. 10*b*, "*And it shall be to the children of Israel, and to the stranger in the midst of them, for an everlasting statute,*" relate to the preparation and application of the sprinkling water, and connect the foregoing instructions with those which follow.—Vers. 11–13 contain the general rules for the use of the water; vers. 14–22 a more detailed description of the execution of those rules.—Vers. 11 sqq. Whoever touched a corpse, "*with regard to all the souls of men,*" *i.e.* the corpse of a person, of whatever age or sex, was unclean for seven days, and on the third and seventh day he was to cleanse himself (הִתְחַטֵּא, as in chap. viii. 21) with the water (בּוֹ refers, so far as the sense is concerned, to the water of purification). If he neglected this cleansing, he did not become clean, and he defiled the dwelling of Jehovah (see at Lev. xv. 31). Such a man was to be cut off from Israel (*vid.* at Gen. xvii. 14).—Vers. 14–16. Special instructions concerning the defilement. If a man died in a tent, every one who entered it, or who was there at the time, became unclean for seven days. So also did every "*open vessel upon which there was not a covering, a string,*" *i.e.* that had not a covering fastened by a string, to prevent the smell of the corpse from penetrating it. פָּתִיל, a string, is in apposition to צָמִיד, a band. or binding (see *Ges.* § 113; *Ewald*, § 287, *e.*). This also applied to any one in the open field, who touched a man who had either been slain by the sword or had died a natural death, or even a bone (skeleton), or a grave.—Vers. 17–19. *Ceremony of purification.* They were to take for the unclean person some of the dust of the burning of the cow, *i.e.* some of the ashes obtained by burning the cow, and put living, *i.e.* fresh water (see Lev. xiv. 5), upon it in a vessel. A clean man was then to take a bunch of hyssop (see Ex. xii. 22), on account of its inherent purifying power, and dip it in the water, on the third and seventh day after the defilement had taken place, and to sprinkle the tent, with the vessels and persons in it, as well as every one who had touched a corpse, whether a person slain, or one who had died a natural death, or a grave; after which the persons were to wash their clothes and bathe, that they might be clean in the evening. As the uncleanness in question is held up as the highest grade of uncleanness, by its duration being fixed at seven days, *i.e.* an entire week, so the appointment of a double purification with the sprinkling water shows the force of the uncleanness to be removed; whilst the selection of the third and seventh days was simply determined by the significance of the numbers themselves. In ver. 20, the threat of punishment for the neglect of purification is repeated from ver. 13, for the purpose of making it most emphatic.—Vers. 21, 22. This also was to be an everlasting statute, that he who sprinkled the water of purification, or even touched it (see at vers. 7 sqq.), and he who was touched by a person defiled (by a corpse), and also the person who touched him, should be unclean till the evening,—a rule which also applied to other forms of uncleanness.

ISRAEL'S LAST JOURNEY FROM KADESH TO THE HEIGHTS OF PISGAH IN THE FIELDS OF MOAB.—CHAP. XX. AND XXI.

In the first month of the fortieth year, the whole congregation of Israel assembled again at Kadesh, in the desert of Zin, to commence the march to Canaan. In Kadesh, Miriam died (chap. xx. 1), and the people murmured against Moses and Aaron on account of the want of water. The Lord relieved this want, by pouring water from the rock; but Moses sinned on this occasion, so that he was not allowed to enter Canaan (vers. 2–13). From Kadesh, Moses sent messengers to the king of Edom, to ask permission for the Israelites to pass peaceably through his land; but this was refused by the king of Edom (vers. 14–21). In the meantime, the Israelites marched from Kadesh to Mount Hor, on the borders of the land of Edom; and there Aaron died, and Eleazar was invested with the high-priesthood in his stead (vers. 22–29). On this march they were attacked by the Canaanitish king of Arad; but they gained a complete victory, and laid his cities under the ban (chap. xix. 1–3). As the king of Edom opposed their passing through his land, they were compelled to go from Mount Hor to the Red Sea, and round the land of Edom. On the way the murmuring people were bitten by poisonous serpents; but the penitent among them were healed of the bite of the serpent, by looking at the brazen serpent which Moses set up at the command of God (vers. 4–9). After going round the Moabitish mountains, they

turned to the north, and went along the eastern side of the Edomitish and Moabitish territory, as far as the Arnon, on the border
of the Amoritish kingdom of Sihon, with the intention of going
through to the Jordan, and so entering Canaan (vers. 10–20).
But as Sihon would not allow the Israelites to pass through his
land, and made a hostile demonstration against them, they smote
him and conquered his land, and also the northern Amoritish kingdom of Og, king of Bashan (vers. 21–35), and forced their way
through the Amoritish territory to the heights of Pisgah, for the
purpose of going forward thence into the steppes of Moab by the
Jordan (chap. xxii. 1). These marches formed the *third* stage in
the guidance of Israel through the desert to Canaan.

*Death of Miriam.   Water out of the Rock.   Refusal of a Passage
through Edom.   Aaron's Death.   Conquest over the King of
Arad.*—Chap. xx.–xxi. 3.

The events mentioned in the heading, which took place either
in Kadesh or on the march thence to the mountain of Hor, are
grouped together in chap. xx. 1–xxi. 3, rather in a classified order
than in one that is strictly chronological. The death of Miriam
took place during the time when the people were collected at Kadesh-
Barnea in the desert of Zin (ver. 21). But when the whole nation
assembled together in this desert there was a deficiency of water,
which caused the people to murmur against Moses, until God relieved the want by a miracle (vers. 2–13). It was from Kadesh
that messengers were sent to the king of Edom (vers. 14 sqq.) ;
but instead of waiting at Kadesh till the messengers returned,
Moses appears to have proceeded with the people in the meantime
into the Arabah. When and where the messengers returned to
Moses, we are not informed. So much is certain, however, that the
Edomites did not come with an army against the Israelites (vers.
20, 21), until they approached their land with the intention of
passing through. For it was in the Arabah, at Mount Hor, that
Israel first turned to go round the land of Edom (chap. xxi. 4).
The attack of the Canaanites of Arad (chap. xxi. 1–3), who attempted to prevent the Israelites from advancing into the desert of
Zin, occurred in the interval between the departure from Kadesh
and the arrival in the Arabah at Mount Hor ; so that if a chronological arrangement were adopted, this event would be placed in
chap. xx. 22, between the first and second clauses of this verse.
The words " *and came to Mount Hor*" (ver. 22*b*) are anticipatory,

and introduce the most important event of all that period, viz. the death of Aaron at Mount Hor (vers. 23–29).[1]

Ver. 1. ASSEMBLING OF THE CONGREGATION AT KADESH.— In the first month the children of Israel came into the desert of Zin, *i.e.* in the fortieth year of their wanderings, at the commencement of which "the whole congregation" assembled together once more in the very same place where the sentence had been passed thirty-seven years and a half before, that they should remain in the desert for forty years, until the rebellious generation had died out. The year is not mentioned in ver. 1, but, according to chap. xiv. 32 sqq., it can only be the year with which the forty years of the sentence that they should die out in the wilderness came to an end, that is to say, the fortieth year of their wandering. This is put

---

[1] Even *Fries* (pp. 53, 54) has admitted that the account in Num. xxi. 1, xxxiii. 40, is to be regarded as a rehearsal of an event which took place before the arrival of the Israelites at Mount Hor, and that the conflict with the king of Arad must have occurred immediately upon the advance of Israel into the desert of Zin ; and he correctly observes, that the sacred writer has arranged what stood in practical connection with the sin of Moses and Aaron, and the refusal of Edom, in the closest juxtaposition to those events : whereas, after he had once commenced his account of the tragical occurrences in chap. xx., there was no place throughout the whole of that chapter for mentioning the conflict with Arad ; and consequently this battle could only find a place in the second line, after the record of the most memorable events which occurred between the death of Miriam and that of Aaron, and to which it was subordinate in actual significance. On the other hand, *Fries* objects to the arrangement we have adopted above, and supposes that Israel did not go straight from Kadesh through the Wady *Murreh* into the Arabah, and to the border of the (actual) land of Edom, and then turn back to the Red Sea ; but that after the failure of the negotiations with the king of Edom, Moses turned at once from the desert of Zin and plain of Kadesh, and went back in a south-westerly direction to the Hebron road ; and having followed this road to Jebel Araif, the south-western corner-pillar of the western Edom, turned at right angles and went by the side of Jebel Mukrah to the Arabah, where he was compelled to alter his course again through meeting with Mount Hor, the border-pillar of Edom at that point, and to go southwards to the Red Sea (pp. 88–9). But although this combination steers clear of the difficulty connected with our assumption,—viz. that when Israel advanced into the Arabah to encamp at Mount Hor, they had actually trodden upon the Edomitish territory in that part of the Arabah which connected the mountain land of Azazimeh, of which the Edomites had taken forcible possession, with their hereditary country, the mountains of Seir,—we cannot regard this view as in harmony with the biblical account. For, apart from the improbability of Moses going a second time to Mount Hor on the border of Edom, after he had been compelled to desist from his advance through the desert of Zin (Wady *Murreh*), and take a circuitous route, or rather make a

beyond all doubt by what follows. For the whole congregation proceeds from Kadesh in the desert of Zin to Mount Hor, where Aaron died, and that, according to chap. xxxiii. 38, in the fifth month of the fortieth year after the exodus from Egypt. Miriam died during the time that the people were staying (יֵשֶׁב) in Kadesh, and there she was buried.

Vers. 2–13. SIN OF MOSES AND AARON AT THE WATER OF STRIFE AT KADESH.—In the arid desert the congregation was in want of water, and the people quarrelled with Moses in consequence. In connection with the first stay in Kadesh there is nothing said about any deficiency of water. But as the name Kadesh embraces a large district of the desert of Zin, and is not confined to one particular spot, there might easily be a want of water in this place or

retrograde movement, on the western side of the Edomitish territory of the land of Azazimeh, only to be driven back a second time, the account of the contest with the king of Arad is hard to reconcile with this combination. In that case the king of Arad must have attacked or overtaken the Israelites when they were collected together in the desert of Zin at Kadesh. But this does not tally with the words of chap. xxi. 1, " When the Canaanite heard that Israel came (was approaching) by the way of the spies ; " for if Moses turned round in Kadesh to go down the Hebron road as far as Jebel Araif, in consequence of the refusal of Edom, the Israelites did not take the way of the spies at all, for their way went northwards from Kadesh to Canaan. The supposition of *Fries* (p. 54), that the words in chap. xxi. 1, "came by the way of the spies," are a permutation of those in chap. xx. 1, " came into the desert of Zin," and that the two perfectly coincide as to time, is forced ; as the Israelites are described in chap. xx. 1 not only as coming into the desert of Zin in general, but as assembling together there at Kadesh.

Modern critics (*Knobel* and others) have also mutilated these chapters, and left only chap. xx. 1 (in part), 2, 6, 22–29, xxi. 10, 11, xxii. 1, as parts of the original work, whilst all the rest is described as a Jehovistic addition, partly from ancient sources and partly from the invention of the Jehovist himself. But the supposed contradiction—viz. that whilst the original work describes the Israelites as going through northern Edom, and going round the Moabitish territory in the more restricted sense, the Jehovist represents them as going round the land of Edom upon the west, south, and east (chap. xx. 21, xxi. 4), and also as going round the land of the Arnon in a still larger circle, and past other places as well (chap. xxi. 12, 16, 18)—rests upon a false interpretation of the passages in question. The other arguments adduced—viz. the fact that the Jehovist gives great prominence to the hatred of the Edomites (chap. xx. 18, 20) and interweaves poetical sentences (chap. xxi. 14, 15, 17, 18, 27, 28), the miraculous rod in Moses' hand (chap. xx. 8), and the etymology (chap. xxi. 3) —are all just arguing in a circle, since the supposition that all these things are foreign to the original work, is not a fact demonstrated, but a simple *petitio principii.*

the other. In their faithless discontent, the people wished that they had died when their brethren died before Jehovah. The allusion is not to Korah's company, as *Knobel* supposes, and the word יוע, " to expire," would be altogether inapplicable to their destruction; but the reference is to those who had died one by one during the thirty-seven years. " *Why*," they murmured once more against Moses and Aaron, " *have ye brought the congregation of God into this desert, to perish there with their cattle? Why have ye brought it out of Egypt into this evil land, where there is no seed, no fig-trees and pomegranates, no vines, and no water to drink?*"—Ver. 6. Moses and Aaron then turned to the tabernacle, to ask for the help of the Lord; and the glory of the Lord immediately appeared (see at chap. xvii. 7 and xiv. 10).—Vers. 7, 8. The Lord relieved the want of water. Moses was to take the staff, and with Aaron to gather together the congregation, and speak to the rock before their eyes, when it would give forth water for the congregation and their cattle to drink.—Vers. 9–11. Moses then took the rod " from before Jehovah,"—*i.e.* the rod with which he had performed miracles in Egypt (Ex. xvii. 5), and which was laid up in the sanctuary, not Aaron's rod which blossomed (chap. xvii. 25),—and collected the congregation together before the rock, and said to them, " *Hear, ye rebels, shall we fetch you water out of this rock?*" He then smote the rock twice with his rod, whereupon much water came out, so that the congregation and their cattle had water to drink.—Ver. 12. The Lord then said to both of them, both Moses and Aaron, " *Because ye have not trusted firmly in Me, to sanctify Me before the eyes of the children of Israel, therefore ye shall not bring this congregation into the land which I have given them.*" The want of belief or firm confidence in the Lord, through which both of them had sinned, was not actual unbelief or distrust in the omnipotence and grace of God, as if God could not relieve the want of water or extend His help to the murmuring people ; for the Lord had promised His help to Moses, and Moses did what the Lord had commanded him. It was simply the want of full believing confidence, a momentary wavering of that immovable assurance, which the two heads of the nation ought to have shown to the congregation, but did not show. Moses did even more than God had commanded him. Instead of speaking to the rock with the rod of God in his hand, as God directed him, he spoke to the congregation, and in these inconsiderate words, " Shall we fetch you water out of the rock?" words which, if they did not express any doubt in the help of the Lord, were certainly fitted to strengthen the people in their unbelief, and are therefore described in Ps. cvi. 33 as prating (speaking unadvisedly) with the lips (cf. Lev. v. 4). He then struck the rock twice with the rod, " as if it depended upon human exertion, and not upon the power of God alone," or as if the promise of God " would not have been fulfilled without all the smiting on his part" (*Knobel*). In the ill-will expressed in these words the weakness of faith was manifested, by which the faithful servant of God, worn out with the numerous temptations, allowed himself to be overcome, so that he stumbled, and did not sanctify the Lord before the eyes of the people, as he ought to have done. Aaron also wavered along with Moses, inasmuch as he did nothing to prevent Moses' fall. But their sin became a grievous one, from the fact that they acted unworthily of their office. God punished them, therefore, by withdrawing their office from them before they had finished the work entrusted to them. They were not to conduct the congregation into the promised land, and therefore were not to enter in themselves (cf. chap. xxvii. 12–14 ; Deut. xxxii. 48 sqq.). The rock, from which water issued, is distinguished by the article הַסֶּלַע, not as being already known, or mentioned before, but simply as a particular rock in that neighbourhood ; though the situation is not described, so as to render it possible to search for it now.[1]— Ver. 13. The account closes with the words, " *This is the water of strife, about which the children of Israel strove with Jehovah, and He sanctified Himself on them.*" This does not imply that the scene of

[1] *Moses Nachmanides* has given a correct interpretation of the words, " Speak to the rock before their eyes " (ver. 8) : viz. " to the first rock in front of them, and standing in their sight." The fable attributed to the Rabbins, viz. that the rock of *Rephidim* followed the Israelites all about in the desert, and supplied them with water, cannot be proved from the talmudical and rabbinical passages given by *Buxtorf* (*historia Petræ in deserto*) in his *exercitatt. c. v.*, but is simply founded upon a literal interpretation of certain rabbinical statements concerning the identity of the well at Rephidim with that at Kadesh, which were evidently intended to be figurative, as *Abarbanel* expressly affirms (*Buxtorf, l. c.* pp. 422 seq.). " Their true meaning,": he says, " was, that those waters which flowed out in Horeb were the gift of God granted to the Israelites, and continued all through the desert, just like the manna. For wherever they went, fountains of living waters were opened to them as the occasion required. And for this reason, the rock in Kadesh was the same rock as that in Horeb. Still less ground is there for supposing that the Apostle Paul alluded to any such rabbinical fable when he said, " They drank of that spiritual rock that followed them" (1 Cor. x. 4), and gave it a spiritual interpretation in the words, " and that rock was Christ."

this occurrence received the name of "strife-water," but simply that the water which God brought out of the rock for the Israelites received that name. But God sanctified Himself on them, by the fact that, on the one hand, He put their unbelief to shame by the miraculous gift of water, and on the other hand punished Moses and Aaron for the weakness of their faith.[1]

Vers. 14–21. MESSAGE OF THE ISRAELITES TO THE KING OF EDOM.—As Israel was about to start from Kadesh upon its march to Canaan, but wished to enter it from the east across the Jordan, and not from the south, where the steep and lofty mountain ranges presented obstacles which would have been difficult to overcome, if not quite insuperable, Moses sent messengers from Kadesh to the king of Edom, to solicit from the kindred nation a friendly and unimpeded passage through their land. He reminded the king of the relationship of Israel, of their being brought down to Egypt, of the oppression they had endured there, and their deliverance out of the land, and promised him that they would not pass through fields and vineyards, nor drink the water of their wells, but keep to the king's way, without turning to the right hand or the left, and thus would do no injury whatever to the land (vers. 14–16).[2] By the "angel" who led Israel out of Egypt we are naturally to understand not the pillar of cloud and fire (*Knobel*), but the angel of the Lord, the visible revealer of the invisible God, whom the messengers

---

[1] The assumption of neological critics, that this occurrence is identical with the similar one at Rephidim (Ex. xvii.), and that this is only another saga based upon the same event, has no firm ground whatever. The want of water in the arid desert is a fact so constantly attested by travellers, that it would be a matter of great surprise if Israel had only experienced this want, and quarrelled with its God and its leaders, once in the course of forty years. As early as Ex. xv. 22 sqq. the people murmured because of the want of drinkable water, and the bitter water was turned into sweet ; and immediately after the event before us, it gave utterance to the complaint again, " We have no bread and no water" (chap. xxi. 4, 5). But if the want remained the same, the relief of that want would necessarily be repeated in the same or a similar manner. Moreover, the occurrences at Rephidim (or Massah-Meribah) and at Kadesh are altogether different from each other. In Rephidim, God gave the people water out of the rock, and the murmuring of the people was stayed. In Kadesh, God no doubt relieved the distress in the same way ; but the mediators of His mercy, Moses and Aaron, sinned at the time, so that God sanctified Himself upon them by a judgment, because they had not sanctified Him before the congregation. (See *Hengstenberg*, Dissertations, vol. ii.)

[2] We learn from Judg. xi. 17, that Israel sent messengers from Kadesh to the king of Moab also, and with a similar commission, and that he also refused

describe indefinitely as " an angel," when addressing the Edomites. *Kadesh* is represented in ver. 16 as a city on the border of the Edomitish territory. The reference is to *Kadesh-Barnea* (chap. xxxii. 8, xxxiv. 4; Deut. i. 2, 19, ii. 14, ix. 23; Josh. x. 41, xiv. 6, 7, xv. 3). This city was no doubt situated quite in the neighbourhood of *Ain Kudes,* the well of Kadesh, discovered by *Rowland.* This well was called *En-Mishpat,* the fountain of judgment, in Abraham's time (Gen. xiv. 7); and the name *Kadesh* occurs first of all on the first arrival of the Israelites in that region, in the account of the events which took place there, as being the central point of the place of encampment, the " desert of Paran," or " desert of Zin" (cf. chap. xiii. 26 with ver. 21, and chap. xii. 16). And even on the second arrival of the congregation in that locality, it is not mentioned till after the desert of Zin (chap. xx. 1); whilst the full name *Kadesh-Barnea* is used by Moses for the first time in chap. xxxii. 8, when reminding the people of those mournful occurrences in Kadesh in chap. xiii. and xiv. The conjecture is therefore a very natural one, that the place in question received the name of *Kadesh* first of all from that tragical occurrence (chap. xiv.), or possibly from the murmuring of the congregation on account of the want of water, which led Moses and Aaron to sin, so that the Lord sanctified (יִקָּדֵשׁ) Himself upon them by a judgment, because they had not sanctified Him before the children of Israel (vers. 12 and 13); that *Barnea* was the older or original name of the town, which was situated in the neighbourhood of the " water of strife," and that this name was afterwards united with *Kadesh,* and formed into a composite noun. If this conjecture is a correct one, the name *Kadesh* is used proleptically, not only in Gen. xiv. 7, as a more precise definition of *En-Mishpat,* but also in Gen. xvi. 14, xx. 1; and Num. xiii. 26, and xx. 1; and there is no lack of analogies for this. It is in this too that we are probably to seek for an explanation of the fact, that in the list of stations in chap. xxxiii. the name Kadesh does not occur in connection with the first arrival of the congregation in the desert of Zin, but only in connection with their second arrival (ver. 36), and that the place of encampment on their first arrival is called *Rithmah,* and not *Barnea,* because

to grant the request for an unimpeded passage through his land. This message is passed over in silence here, because the refusal of the Moabites had no influence upon the further progress of the Israelites. " For if they could not pass through Edom, the permission of the Moabites would not help them at all. It was only *eventualiter* that they sought this permission."—*Hengstenberg,* Diss.

the headquarters of the camp were in the Wady *Retemath*, not at the town of *Barnea*, which was farther on in the desert of Zin. The expression " *town of the end of thy territory* " is not to be understood as signifying that the town belonged to the Edomites, but simply affirms that it was situated on the border of the Edomitish territory. The supposition that Barnea was an Edomitish town is opposed by the circumstance that, in chap. xxxiv. 4, and Josh xv. 3, it is reckoned as part of the land of Canaan ; that in Josh. x. 41 it is mentioned as the southernmost town, where Joshua smote the Canaanites and conquered their land ; and lastly, that in Josh. xv. 23 it is probably classed among the towns allotted to the tribe of Judah, from which it seems to follow that it must have belonged to the Amorites. " The end of the territory" of the king of Edom is to be distinguished from " the territory of the land of Edom" in ver. 23. The land of Edom extended westwards only as far as the Arabah, the low-lying plain, which runs from the southern point of the Dead Sea to the head of the Elanitic Gulf. At that time, however, the Edomites had spread out beyond the Arabah, and taken possession of a portion of the desert of Paran belonging to the peninsula of Sinai, which was bounded on the north by the desert of Zin (see at chap. xxxiv. 3). By their not drinking of the water of the wells (ver. 17), we are to understand, according to ver. 19, their not making use of the wells of the Edomites either by violence or without compensation. The " king's way" is the public high road, which was probably made at the cost of the state, and kept up for the king and his armies to travel upon, and is synonymous with the " sultan-road" (*Derb es Sultan*) or " emperor road," as the open, broad, old military roads are still called in the East (cf. *Robinson*, Pal. ii. 340 ; *Seetzen*, i. pp. 61, 132, ii. pp. 336, etc.).

This military road led, no doubt, as *Leake* has conjectured (*Burckhardt*, Syr. pp. 21, 22), through the broad Wady *el Ghuweir*, which not only forms a direct and easy passage to the level country through the very steep mountains that fall down into the Arabah, but also a convenient road through the land of Edom (*Robinson*, ii. pp. 552, 583, 610), and is celebrated for its splendid meadows, which are traceable to its many springs (*Burckhardt*, pp. 688, 689) ; for the broad Wady *Murreh* runs from the northern border of the mountain-land of Azazimeh, not only as far as the mountain of Moddera (Madurah), where it is divided, but in its southern half as far as the Arabah (see p. 59). This is very likely the " great route through broad wadys," which the Bedouins who accompanied *Rowland* assured him " was very good, and led direct to Mount Hor, but with which no European traveller was acquainted " (*Ritter's* Erdk. xiv. p. 1088). It probably opens into the Arabah at the Wady *el Weibeh*, opposite to the Wady *Ghuweir.* —Vers. 18, 19. The Edomites refused the visit of the Israelites in a most unbrotherly manner, and threatened to come out against them with the sword, without paying the least attention to the repeated assurance of the Israelitish messengers, that they would only march upon the high road, and would pay for water for themselves and their cattle.   רַק אֵין־דָּבָר, lit. " *it is nothing at all; I will go through with my feet:*" i.e. we want no great thing; we will only make use of the high road.—Ver. 20. To give emphasis to his refusal, Edom went against Israel " *with much people and with a strong hand,*" sc. when they approached its borders. This statement, as well as the one in ver. 21, that Israel turned away before Edom, anticipates the historical order ; for, as a matter of course, the Edomites cannot have come at once with an army on the track of the messengers, for the purpose of blocking up the road through the Wady Murreh, which runs along the border of its territory to the west of the Arabah.

Vers. 22–29. DEATH OF AARON AT MOUNT HOR.—The Israelites left Kadesh, and passed along the road just mentioned to Mount *Hor.* This mountain, which was situated, according to chap. xxxiii. 37, on the border of the land of Edom, is placed by *Josephus* (Ant. iv. 4, 7) in the neighbourhood of *Petra ;* so also by *Eusebius* and *Jerome :* " *Or mons, in quo mortuus est Aaron, juxta civitatem Petram.*" According to modern travellers, it is Mount *Harun,* on the north-western side of Wady *Musa* (*Petra*), which is described by *Robinson* (vol. ii. p. 508) as " a cone irregularly truncated, having three ragged points or peaks, of which that upon the north-east is the highest, and has upon it the Muhammedan Wely, or tomb of Aaron," from which the mountain has received its name " *Harun,*" i.e. *Aaron* (vid. *Burckhardt,* Syr. pp. 715, 716 ; v. *Schubert, Reise,* ii. pp. 419 sqq. ; *Ritter, Erdkunde,* xiv. pp. 1127 sqq.). There can be no doubt as to the general correctness of this tradition ;[1] for even if the Mohammedan tradition concerning Aaron's grave is not well accredited, the situation of this mountain

[1] There is no force whatever in the arguments by which *Knobel* has endeavoured to prove that it is incorrect. The *first* objection, viz. that the Hebrews reached Mount Hor from Kadesh in a single march, has no foundation

is in perfect harmony with the statement in ver. 23 and chap. xxxiii. 37, viz. that the Israelites had then reached the border of the land of Edom. The place where the people encamped is called *Mosera* in Deut. x. 6, and *Moseroth* in the list of stations in chap. xxxiii. 30, and is at all events to be sought for in the Arabah, in the neighbourhood of Mount *Hor*, though it is altogether unknown to us. The camp of 600,000 men, with their wives, children, and flocks, would certainly require a space miles wide, and might therefore easily stretch from the mouths of the Wady el Weibeh and Wady Ghuweir, in the Arabah, to the neighbourhood of Mount *Harun*. The place of encampment is called after this mountain, *Hor*, both here and in chap. xxxiii. 37 sqq., because it was there that Aaron died and was buried. The Lord foretold his death to Moses, and directed him to take off Aaron's priestly robes, and put them upon Eleazar his son, as Aaron was not to enter the promised land, because they (Aaron and Moses) had opposed the command of Jehovah at the water of strife (see at ver. 12). "Gathered to his people," like the patriarchs (Gen. xxv. 8, 17, xxxv. 29, xlix. 33).—Vers. 27, 28. Moses executed this command, and Aaron died upon the top of the mountain, according to chap. xxxiii. 37, 38, on the first day of the fifth month, in the fortieth year after the exodus from Egypt, at the age of 123 years (which agrees with Ex. vii. 7), and was mourned by all Israel for thirty days.

in the biblical text, and cannot be inferred from the circumstance that there is no place of encampment mentioned between Kadesh and Mount Hor ; for, on the one hand, we may clearly see, not only from chap. xxi. 10, but even from Ex. xvii. 1, as compared with Num. xxxiii. 41 sqq. and 12 sqq., that only those places of encampment are mentioned in the historical account where events occurred that were worthy of narrating ; and, on the other hand, it is evident from chap. x. 33, that the Israelites sometimes continued marching for several days before they formed an encampment again. The *second* objection— viz. that if Hor was near Petra, it is impossible to see how the advance of the Hebrews from Kadesh to Hor could be regarded by the king of Arad, who lived more than thirty hours' journey to the north, as coming (chap. xxxiii. 40), not to mention " coming by the way of the spies " (chap. xxi. 1), and how this king could come into conflict with the Hebrews when posted at Petra—rests upon the erroneous assumption, that the attack of the king of Arad did not take place till after the death of Aaron, because it is not mentioned till afterwards. Lastly, the *third* objection—viz. that a march from Kadesh in a south-westerly direction to Wady Musa, and then northwards past Zalmona to Phunon (chap. xxxiii. 41), is much too adventurous—is overthrown by chap. xxi. 4, where the Israelites are said to have gone from Mount Hor by the way of the Red Sea. (See the notes on chap. xxi. 10.)

Chap. xxi. 1–3. VICTORY OF ISRAEL OVER THE CANAANITISH KING OF ARAD.—When this Canaanitish king, who dwelt in the Negeb, *i.e.* the south of Palestine (*vid.* chap. xiii. 17), heard that Israel was coming the way of the spies, he made war upon the Israelites, and took some of them prisoners. *Arad* is mentioned both here and in the parallel passage, chap. xxxiii. 40, and also by the side of *Hormah,* in Josh. xii. 14, as the seat of a Canaanitish king (cf. Judg. i. 16, 17). According to *Eusebius* and *Jerome* in the *Onomast.,* it was twenty Roman miles to the south of Hebron, and has been preserved in the ruins of *Tell Arad,* which v. *Schubert* (ii. pp. 457 sqq.) and *Robinson* (ii. pp. 473, 620, and 624) saw in the distance ; and, according to *Roth* in *Petermann's* geographische Mittheilungen (1858, p. 269), it was situated to the south-east of Kurmul (Carmel), in an undulating plain, without trees or shrubs, with isolated hills and ranges of hills in all directions, among which was *Tell Arad.* The meaning of דֶּרֶךְ הָאֲתָרִים is uncertain. The LXX., *Saad.,* and others, take the word *Atharim* as the proper name of a place not mentioned again ; but the *Chaldee, Samar.,* and *Syr.* render it with much greater probability as an appellative noun formed from תּוּר with א *prosthet.,* and synonymous with הַתָּרִים, the spies (chap. xiv. 6). The way of the spies was the way through the desert of Zin, which the Israelitish spies had previously taken to Canaan (chap. xiii. 21). The territory of the king of Arad extended to the southern frontier of Canaan, to the desert of Zin, through which the Israelites went from Kadesh to Mount Hor. The Canaanites attacked them when upon their march, and made some of them prisoners.—Vers. 2, 3. The Israelites then vowed to the Lord, that if He would give this people into their hands, they would "ban" their cities ; and the Lord hearkened to the request, and delivered up the Canaanites, so that they put them and their cities under the ban. (On the ban, see at Lev. xxvii. 28.) "*And they called the place Hormah,*" *i.e.* banning, ban-place. "The place" can only mean the spot where the Canaanites were defeated by the Israelites. If the town of Zephath, or the capital of Arad, had been specially intended, it would no doubt have been also mentioned, as in Judg. i. 17. As it was not the intention of Moses to press into Canaan from the south, across the steep and difficult mountains, for the purpose of effecting its conquest, the Israelites could very well content themselves for the present with the defeat inflicted upon the Canaanites, and defer the complete execution of their vow until the time when they had gained a firm footing in

Canaan. The banning of the Canaanites of Arad and its cities necessarily presupposed the immediate conquest of the whole territory, and the laying of all its cities in ashes. And so, again, the introduction of a king of *Hormah*, *i.e.* *Zephath*, among the kings defeated by Joshua (Josh. xii. 14), is no proof that Zephath was conquered and called Hormah in the time of Moses. Zephath may be called Hormah proleptically both there and in Josh. xix. 4, as being the southernmost border town of the kingdom of Arad, in consequence of the ban suspended by Moses over the territory of the king of Arad, and may not have received this name till after its conquest by the Judæans and Simeonites. At the same time, it is quite conceivable that Zephath may have been captured in the time of Joshua, along with the other towns of the south, and called Hormah at that time, but that the Israelites could not hold it then ; and therefore, after the departure of the Israelitish army, the old name was restored by the Canaanites, or rather only retained, until the city was retaken and permanently held by the Israelites after Joshua's death (Judg. i. 16, 17), and received the new name once for all. The allusion to Hormah here, and in chap. xiv. 45, does not warrant the opinion in any case, that it was subsequently to the death of Moses and the conquest of Canaan under Joshua that the war with the Canaanites of Arad and their overthrow occurred.

March round the land of Edom and Moab. Conquest of Sihon and Og, kings of the Amorites.—Chap. xxi. 4–35.

Vers. 4–9. March of Israel through the Arabah. Plague of Serpents, and Brazen Serpent.—Ver. 4. As the Edomites refused a passage through their land when the Israelites left Mount Hor, they were obliged to take the way to the Red Sea, in order to go round the land of Edom, that is to say, to go down the Arabah to the head of the Elanitic Gulf.—Vers. 5, 6. As they went along this road the people became impatient ("the soul of the people was much discouraged," see Ex. vi. 9), and they began once more to murmur against God and Moses, because they had neither bread nor water (cf. chap. xx. 4 sqq.), and were tired of the loose, *i.e.* poor, food of manna (קְלֹקֵל from קָלַל). The low-lying plain of the Arabah, which runs between steep mountain walls from the Dead Sea to the Red Sea, would be most likely to furnish the Israelites with very little food, except the manna which God gave them ; for although it is not altogether destitute of vegetation, especially at the mouths of the wadys and winter torrents from the hills, yet on the whole it is a horrible desert, with a loose sandy soil, and drifts of granite and other stones, where terrible sandstorms sometimes arise from the neighbourhood of the Red Sea (see *v. Schubert*, R. ii. pp. 396 sqq., and *Ritter, Erdk.* xiv. pp. 1013 sqq.) ; and the want of food might very frequently be accompanied by the absence of drinkable water. The people rebelled in consequence, and were punished by the Lord with fiery serpents, the bite of which caused many to die. נְחָשִׁים שְׂרָפִים, *lit.* burning snakes, so called from their burning, *i.e.* inflammatory bite, which filled with heat and poison, just as many of the snakes were called by the Greeks, *e.g.* the διψάς, πρηστῆρες, and καύσωνες (*Dioscor.* vii. 13 : *Aelian. nat. anim.* vi. 51), not from the skin of these snakes with fiery red spots, which are frequently found in the Arabah, and are very poisonous.[1]—Ver. 7. This punishment brought the people to reflection. They confessed their sin to Moses, and entreated him to deliver them from the plague through his intercession with the Lord. And the Lord helped them ; in such a way, however, that the reception of help was made to depend upon the faith of the people.—Vers. 8, 9. At the command of God, Moses made a *brazen serpent,* and put it upon a standard.[2] Whoever then of the persons bitten by the poisonous serpents looked at the brazen serpent with faith in the promise of God, lived, *i.e.* recovered from the serpent's bite. The serpent was to be made of brass or copper, because the colour of this metal, when the sun was shining upon it, was most like the appearance of the fiery serpents ; and thus the symbol would be more like the thing itself.

Even in the book of Wisdom (chap. xvi. 6, 7), the brazen serpent is called " a symbol of salvation ; for he that turned himself toward it was not saved by the thing that he saw, but by Thee,

---

[1] This is the account given by *v. Schubert*, R. ii. p. 406 : " In the afternoon they brought us a very mottled snake of a large size, marked with fiery red spots and wavy stripes, which belonged to the most poisonous species, as the formation of its teeth clearly showed. According to the assertion of the Bedouins, these snakes, which they greatly dreaded, were very common in that neighbourhood."

[2] For the different views held by early writers concerning the brazen serpent, see *Buxtorf, historia serp. aen.*, in his Exercitt. pp. 458 sqq. ; *Deyling, observatt. ss.* ii. obs. 15, pp. 156 sqq. ; *Vitringa, observ. ss.* 1, pp. 403 sqq. ; *Jo. Marck, Scripturariæ Exercitt. exerc.* 8, pp. 465 sqq. ; *Iluth, Serpens exaltatus non contritoris sed conterendi imago*, Erl. 1758 ; *Gottfr. Menken* on the brazen serpent ; *Sack, Apologetik,* 2 Ausg. pp. 355 sqq. *Hofmann, Weissagung u. Erfüllung,* ii. pp. 142, 143 ; *Kurtz,* History of the Old Covenant, iii. 345 sqq. ; and the commentators on John iii. 14 and 15.

that art the Saviour of all." It was not merely intended, however, as *Ewald* supposes (*Gesch.* ii. p. 228), as a "sign that just as this serpent hung suspended in the air, bound and rendered harmless by the command of Jehovah, so every one who looked at this with faith in the redeeming power of Jehovah, was secured against the evil,—a figurative sign, therefore, like that of St George and the Dragon among ourselves;" for, according to this, there would be no internal causal link between the fiery serpents and the brazen image of a serpent. It was rather intended as a figurative representation of the poisonous serpents, rendered harmless by the mercy of God. For God did not cause a real serpent to be taken, but the image of a serpent, in which the fiery serpent was stiffened, as it were, into dead brass, as a sign that the deadly poison of the fiery serpents was overcome in this brazen serpent. This is not to be regarded as a symbol of the divine healing power; nor is the selection of such a symbol to be deduced and explained, as it is by *Winer*, *Kurtz*, *Knobel*, and others, from the symbolical view that was common to all the heathen religions of antiquity, that the serpent was a beneficent and health-bringing power, which led to its being exalted into a symbol of the healing power, and a representation of the gods of healing. This heathen view is not only foreign to the Old Testament, and without any foundation in the fact that, in the time of Hezekiah, the people paid a superstitious worship to the brazen serpent erected by Moses (2 Kings xviii. 4); but it is irreconcilably opposed to the biblical view of the serpent, as the representative of evil, which was founded upon Gen. iii. 15, and is only traceable to the magical art of serpent-charming, which the Old Testament abhorred as an idolatrous abomination. To this we may add, that the thought which lies at the foundation of this explanation, viz. that poison is to be cured by poison, has no support in Hos. xiii. 4, but is altogether foreign to the Scriptures. God punishes sin, it is true, by sin; but He neither cures sin by sin, nor death by death. On the contrary, to conquer sin it was necessary that the Redeemer should be without sin; and to take away its power from death, it was requisite that Christ, the Prince of life, who had life in Himself, should rise again from death and the grave (John v. 26, xi. 25; Acts iii. 15; 2 Tim. i. 10).

The brazen serpent became a symbol of salvation on the three grounds which *Luther* pointed out. In the *first* place, the serpent which Moses was to make by the command of God was to be of brass or copper, that is to say, of a reddish colour, and (although

without poison) altogether like the persons who were red and burning with heat because of the bite of the fiery serpents. In the
second place, the brazen serpent was to be set up upon a pole for a
sign. And in the *third* place, those who desired to recover from
the fiery serpent's bite and live, were to look at the brazen serpent
upon the pole, otherwise they could not recover or live (*Luther's*
Sermon on John iii. 1–15). It was in these three points, as *Luther*
has also clearly shown, that the typical character of this symbol
lay, to which Christ referred in His conversation with Nicodemus
(John iii. 14). The brazen serpent had the form of a real serpent,
but was "without poison, and altogether harmless." So God sent
His Son in the form of sinful flesh, and yet without sin (Rom.
viii. 3; 2 Cor. v. 21; 1 Pet. ii. 22–24).—2. In the lifting up of
the serpent as a standard. This was a δειγματίζειν ἐν παρρησίᾳ,
a θριαμβεύειν (a "showing openly," or "triumphing"), a triumphal
exhibition of the poisonous serpents as put to death in the brazen
image, just as the lifting up of Christ upon the cross was a public
triumph over the evil principalities and powers below the sky (Col.
ii. 14, 15).—3. In the cure effected through looking at the image
of the serpent. Just as the Israelites had to turn their eyes to the
brazen serpent in believing obedience to the word of the Lord, in
order to be cured of the bite of the poisonous serpents, so must we
look with faith at the Son of man lifted up upon the cross, if we
would be delivered from the bite of the old serpent, from sin, death,
the devil, and hell. "Christ is the antitype of the serpent, inasmuch as He took upon Himself the most pernicious of all pernicious
potencies, viz. sin, and made a vicarious atonement for it" (*Hengstenberg* on John iii. 14). The brazen image of the serpent was
taken by the Israelites to Canaan, and preserved till the time of
Hezekiah, who had it broken in pieces, because the idolatrous
people had presented incense-offerings to this holy relic (2 Kings
xviii. 4).

Vers. 10–20. MARCH OF ISRAEL ROUND EDOM AND MOAB,
TO THE HEIGHTS OF PISGAH IN THE FIELD OF MOAB (cf. chap.
xxxiii. 41–47).—Ver. 10. From the camp in the Arabah, which is
not more particularly described, where the murmuring people were
punished by fiery serpents, Israel removed to *Oboth*. According to
the list of stations in chap. xxxiii. 41 sqq., they went from Hor to
Zalmonah, the situation of which has not been determined; for *C. v.
Raumer's* conjecture (*der Zug der Israeliten*, p. 45), that it was the

same place as the modern *Maan*, has no firm basis in the fact that
Maan is a station of the Syrian pilgrim caravans. From Zalmonah
they went to *Phunon*, and only then to *Oboth*. The name *Phunon*
is no doubt the same as *Phinon*, a tribe-seat of the Edomitish Phy-
larch (Gen. xxxvi. 41); and according to *Jerome* (*Onom. s. v. Fenon*),
it was " a little village in the desert, where copper was dug up by
condemned criminals (see at Gen. xxxvi. 41), between Petra and
Zoar." This statement suits very well, provided we imagine the
situation of Phunon to have been not in a straight line between Petra
and Zoar, but more to the east, between the mountains on the edge
of the desert. For the Israelites unquestionably went from the
southern end of the Arabah to the eastern side of Idumæa, through
the Wady *el Ithm* (*Getum*), which opens into the Arabah from the
east, a few hours to the north of Akaba and the ancient Ezion-geber.
They had then gone round the mountains of Edom, and begun to
" turn to the north" (Deut. ii. 3), so that they now proceeded
farther northwards, on the eastern side of the mountains of Edom,
" through the territory of the sons of Esau," no doubt by the same
road which is taken in the present day by the caravans which go
from Gaza to Maan, through the Ghor. "This runs upon a grassy
ridge, forming the western border of the coast of Arabia, and the
eastern border of the cultivated land, which stretches from the land
of Edom to the sources of the Jordan, on the eastern side of the
Ghor" (*v. Raumer*, Zug, p. 45). On the western side of their mountains the Edomites had refused permission to the Israelites to pass
through their land (chap. xx. 18 sqq.), as the mountains of Seir
terminate towards the Ghor (the Arabah) in steep and lofty preci-
pices, and there are only two or three narrow wadys which intersect
them from west to east; and of these the Wady Ghuweir is the only
one which is practicable for an army, and even this could be held
so securely by a moderate army, that no enemy could force its way
into the heart of the country (see *Leake* in *Burckhardt*, pp. 21, 22;
and *Robinson*, ii. p. 583). It was different on the eastern side,
where the mountains slope off into a wide extent of table-land,
which is only slightly elevated above the desert of Arabia. Here,
on the weaker side of their frontier, the Edomites lost the heart to
make any attack upon the Israelites, who would now have been able
to requite their hostilities. But the Lord had commanded Israel
not to make war upon the sons of Esau; but when passing through
their territory, to purchase food and water from them for money
(Deut. ii. 4–6). The Edomites submitted to the necessity, and

endeavoured to take advantage of it, by selling provisions, "in the same way in which, at the present day, the caravan from Mecca is supplied with provisions by the inhabitants of the mountains along the pilgrim road" (*Leake* in *Burckhardt*, p. 24). The situation of *Oboth* cannot be determined.

Ver. 11. The next encampment was "*Ije-Abarim* in the desert, which lies before Moab towards the sun-rising," *i.e.* on the eastern border of Moabitis (chap. xxxiii. 44). As the Wady *el Ahsy*, which runs into the Dead Sea, in a deep and narrow rocky bed, from the south-east, and is called *el Kerahy* in its lower part (*Burckhardt*, Syr. pp. 673–4), separates Idumæa from Moabitis; *Ije-Abarim* (*i.e.* ruins of the crossings over) must be sought for on the border of Moab to the north of this wady, but is hardly to be found, as *Knobel* supposes, on the range of hills called *el Tarfuye*, which is known by the name of *Orokaraye*, still farther to the south, and terminates on the south-west of *Kerek*, whilst towards the north it is continued in the range of hills called *el Ghoweithe* and the mountain range of *el Zoble;* even supposing that the term *Abarim*, "the passages or sides," is to be understood as referring to these ranges of hills and mountains which skirt the land of the Amorites and Moabites, and form the enclosing sides. For the boundary line between the hills of *el-Tarfuye* and those of *el-Ghoweithe* is so near to the Arnon, that there is not the necessary space between it and the Arnon for the encampment at the brook Zared (ver. 12). *Ije-Abarim* or *Jim* cannot have been far from the northern shore of the *el Ahsy*, and was probably in the neighbourhood of *Kalaat el Hassa* (Ahsa), the source of the *Ahsy*, and a station for the pilgrim caravans (*Burckhardt*, p. 1035). As the Moabites were also not to be attacked by the Israelites (Deut. ii. 9 sqq.), they passed along the eastern border of Moabitis as far as the brook *Zared* (ver. 12). This can hardly have been the Wady *el-Ahsy* (*Robinson*, ii. p. 555; *Ewald, Gesch.* ii. p. 259; *Ritter, Erdk.* xv. p. 689); for that must already have been crossed when they came to the border of Moab (ver. 11). Nor can it well have been "the brook *Zaide*, which runs from the south-east, passes between the mountain ranges of *Ghoweithe* and *Tarfuye*, and enters the Arnon, of which it forms the leading source,"—the view adopted by *Knobel*, on the very questionable ground that the name is a corruption of *Zared*. In all probability it was the Wady *Kerek*, in the upper part of its course, not far from *Katrane*, on the pilgrim road (*v. Raumer*, Zug, p. 47; *Kurtz*, and others).—Ver. 13. The next encampment was "*beyond* (*i.e.* by the side of) *the Arnon, which is in the desert, and that cometh out of the territory of the Amorites.*" The *Arnon, i.e.* the present Wady *Mojeb*, is formed by the union of the *Seyl* (*i.e.* brook or river) *Saïde*, which comes from the south-east, not far from Katrane, on the pilgrim road, and the *Lejum* from the north-east, which receives the small rivers *el Mekhreys* and *Balua*, the latter flowing from the pilgrim station *Kalaat Balua*, and then continues its course to the Dead Sea, through a deep and narrow valley, shut in by very steep and lofty cliffs, and covered with blocks of stone, that have been brought down from the loftier ground (*Burckhardt*, pp. 633 sqq.), so that there are only a few places where it is passable; and consequently a wandering people like the Israelites could not have crossed the *Mojeb* itself to force an entrance into the territory of the hostile Amorites.[1] For the Arnon formed the boundary between Moab and the country of the Amorites. The spot where Israel encamped on the Arnon must be sought for in the upper part of its course, where it is still flowing " in the desert;" not at Wady *Zaïde*, however, although *Burckhardt* calls this the main source of the Mojeb, but at the *Balua*, which flows into the Lejum. In all probability these streams, of which the *Lejum* came from the north, already bore the name of *Arnon;* as we may gather from the expression, " that cometh out of the coasts of the Amorites." The place of Israel's encampment, " *beyond the Arnon in the desert*," is to be sought for, therefore, in the neighbourhood of *Kalaat Balua*, and on the south side of the *Arnon* (*Balua*). This is evident enough from Deut. ii. 24, 26 sqq., where the Israelites are represented as entering the territory of the Amoritish king Sihon, when they crossed the Arnon, having first of all sent a deputation, with a peaceable request for permission to pass through his land (cf. vers. 21 sqq.). Although this took place, according to Deut. ii. 26, " out of the wilderness of *Kedemoth*," an Amoritish town, it by no means follows that the Israelites had already crossed the Arnon and entered the territory of the Amorites, but only that they were standing on the border of it, and in the desert which took its name from Kedemoth, and ran up to this, the most easterly town, as the name seems to imply, of the country of the Amorites. After the conquest of the country, *Kedemoth* was

---

[1] It is utterly inconceivable that a whole people, travelling with all their possessions as well as with their flocks, should have been exposed without necessity to the dangers and enormous difficulties that would attend the crossing of so dreadfully wild and so deep a valley, and that merely for the purpose of forcing an entrance into an enemy's country.—*Ritter, Erdk.* xv. p. 1207.

allotted to the *Reubenites* (Josh. xiii. 18), and made into a Levitical city (Josh. xxi. 37 ; 1 Chron. vi. 64).

The Israelites now received instructions from the Lord, to cross the river Arnon, and make war upon the Amoritish king Sihon of Heshbon, and take possession of his land, with the assurance that the Lord had given Sihon into the hand of Israel, and would fill all nations before them with fear and trembling (Deut. ii. 24, 25). This summons, with its attendant promises, not only filled the Israelites with courage and strength to enter upon the conflict with the mightiest of all the tribes of the Canaanites, but inspired poets in the midst of them to commemorate in odes the wars of Jehovah, and His victories over His foes. A few verses are given here out of one of these odes (vers. 14 sqq.), not for the purpose of verifying the geographical statement, that the Arnon touches the border of Moabitis, or that the Israelites had only arrived at the border of the Moabite and Amorite territory, but as an evidence that there, on the borders of Moab, the Israelites had been inspired through the divine promises with the firm assurance that they should be able to conquer the land of the Amorites which lay before them.—Vers. 14, 15. *" Therefore,"* sc. because the Lord had thus given king Sihon, with all his land, into the hand of Israel, *" it is written in the book of the wars of the Lord: Vaheb* (Jehovah takes) *in storm, and the brooks of Arnon and the valley of the brooks, which turns to the dwelling of Ar, and leans upon the border of Moab."* The book of the wars of Jehovah is neither an Amoritish book of the conflicts of Baal, in which the warlike feats performed by Sihon and other Amoritish heroes with the help of Baal were celebrated in verse, as *G. Unruh* fabulously asserts in his *Zug der Isr. aus Æg. nach Canaan* (p. 130), nor a work " dating from the time of Jehoshaphat, containing the early history of the Israelites, from the Hebrew patriarchs till past the time of Joshua, with the law interwoven," which is the character that *Knobel's* critical fancy would stamp upon it, but a collection of odes of the time of Moses himself, in celebration of the glorious acts of the Lord to and for the Israelites ; and " the quotation bears the same relation to the history itself, as the verses of *Körner* would bear to the writings of any historian of the wars of freedom, who had himself taken part in these wars, and introduced the verses into his own historical work" (*Hengstenberg*).[1] The strophe selected

[1] " That such a book should arise in the last days of Moses, when the youthful generation began for the first time to regard and manifest itself, both vigorously and generally, as the army of Jehovah, is so far from being a surprising fact,

from the ode has neither subject nor verb in it, as the ode was well known to the contemporaries, and what had to be supplied could easily be gathered from the title, " Wars of Jehovah." *Vaheb* is no doubt the proper name of an Amoritish fortress ; and בְּסוּפָה, " in storm," is to be explained according to Nah. i. 3, " The Lord, in the storm is His way." " Advancing in storm, He took Vaheb and the brooks of Arnon," *i.e.* the different wadys, valleys cut by brooks, which open into the Arnon. אֲשֵׁר הַנְּחָלִים, *lit.* pouring of the brooks, from אָשֵׁד, *effusio*, the pouring, then the place where brooks pour down, the slope of mountains or hills, for which the term אֲשֵׁדָה is generally used in the plural, particularly to denote the slopes of the mountains of Pisgah (Deut. iii. 17, iv. 49 ; Josh. xii. 3, xiii. 20), and the hilly region of Palestine, which formed the transition from the mountains to the plain (Josh. x. 40 and xii. 8). שֶׁבֶת, the dwelling, used poetically for the dwelling-place, as in 2 Sam. xxiii. 7 and Obad. 3. עָר (*Ar*), the antiquated form for עִיר, a city, is the same as *Ar Moab* in ver. 28 and Isa. xv. 1, " the city of Moab, on the border of the Arnon, which is at the end of the (Moabitish) territory" (chap. xxii. 36). It was called Areopolis by the Greeks, and was near to Aroër (Deut. ii. 36 and Josh. xiii. 9), probably standing at the confluence of the Lejum and Mojeb, in the " fine green pasture land, in the midst of which there is a hill with some ruins," and not far away the ruin of a small castle, with a heap of broken columns (*Burckhardt*, Syr. p. 636). This *Ar* is not to be identified with the modern *Rabba*, in the midst of the land of the Moabites, six hours to the south of Lejum, to which the name *Areopolis* was transferred in the patristic age, probably after the destruction of *Ar*, the ancient Areopolis, by an earthquake, of which *Jerome* gives an account in connection with his own childhood (see his Com. on Isa. xv.), possibly the earthquake which occurred in the year A.D. 342, and by which many cities of the East were destroyed, and among others Nicomedia (cf. *Hengstenberg, Balaam,* pp. 525–528 ; *Ritter, Erdkunde,* xv. pp. 1212 sqq. ; and *v. Raumer, Palästina,* pp. 270, 271, Ed. 4).

that we can scarcely imagine a more suitable time for the commencement of such a work" (*Baumgarten*). And if this is the case, the allusion to this collection of odes cannot be adduced as an argument against the Mosaic authorship of the Pentateuch, since Moses certainly did not write out the history of the journey from Kadesh to the Arboth Moab until after the two kings of the Amorites had been defeated, and the land to the east of the Jordan conquered, or till the Israelites had encamped in the steppes of Moab, opposite to Jericho.

Vers. 16–18. They proceeded thence to *Beer* (*a well*), a place of encampment which received its name from the fact that here God gave the people water, not as before by a miraculous supply from a rock, but by commanding wells to be dug. This is evident from the ode with which the congregation commemorated this divine gift of grace. " *Then Israel sang this song: Spring up, O well! Sing ye to it! Well which princes dug, which the nobles of the people hollowed out, with the sceptre, with their staves.*" עָנָה, as in Ex. xv. 21 and xxxii. 18. מְחֹקֵק, ruler's staff, cf. Gen. xlix. 10. *Beer*, probably the same as *Beer Elim* (Isa. xv. 8), on the north-east of Moab, was in the desert ; for the Israelites proceeded thence " *from the desert to Mattanah* " (ver. 18), thence to Nahaliel, and thence to Bamoth. According to *Eusebius* (cf. *Reland, Pal. ill.* p. 495), *Mattanah* (Μαθθανέμ) was by the valley of the Arnon, twelve Roman miles to the east (or more properly south-east or south) of *Medabah*, and is probably to be seen in *Tedun*, a place now lying in ruins, near the source of the *Lejum* (*Burckhardt*, pp. 635, 636 ; *Hengstenberg, Balaam*, p. 530 ; *Knobel*, and others). The name of *Nahaliel* is still retained in the form *Encheileh*. This is the name given to the Lejum, after it has been joined by the Balua, until its junction with the Saide (*Burckhardt*, p. 635). Consequently the Israelites went from *Beer* in the desert, in a north-westerly direction to *Tedun*, then westwards to the northern bank of the *Encheileh*, and then still farther in a north-westerly and northerly direction to *Bamoth*. There can be no doubt that *Bamoth* is identical with *Bamoth Baal*, i.e. heights of Baal (chap. xxii. 4). According to Josh. xiii. 17 (cf. Isa. xv. 2), *Bamoth* was near to *Dibon* (*Dibân*), between the Wady Wale and Wady Mojeb, and also to *Beth-Baal Meon*, i.e. *Myun*, half a German mile (2½ English) to the south of Heshbon ; and, according to chap. xxii. 41, you could see *Bamoth Baal* from the extremity of the Israelitish camp in the steppes of Moab. Consequently *Bamoth* cannot be the mountain to the south of Wady Wale, upon the top of which *Burckhardt* says there is a very beautiful plain (p. 632 ; see *Hengstenberg, Balaam*, p. 532) ; because the steppes of Moab cannot be seen at all from this plain, as they are covered by the Jebel Attarus. It is rather a height upon the long mountain *Attarus*, which runs along the southern shore of the Zerka Maein, and may possibly be a spot upon the summit of the Jebel Attarus, " the highest point in the neighbourhood," upon which, according to *Burckhardt* (p. 630), there is " a heap of stones overshadowed by a very large pistachio-tree." A little farther down to the south-west of this lies the fallen town *Kereijat* (called *Körriat* by *Seetzen*, ii. p. 342), *i.e. Kerioth*, Jer. xlviii. 24; Amos ii. 2.—Ver. 20. From *Bamoth* they proceeded "*to the valley, which* (is) *in the field of Moab, upon the top of Pisgah, and looks across the face of the desert.*" ראֹשׁ הַפִּסְגָּה, head, or height of the *Pisgah*, is in apposition to the field of Moab. The "*field of Moab*" was a portion of the table-land which stretches from Rabbath Ammân to the Arnon, which "is perfectly treeless for an immense distance in one part (viz. the neighbourhood of *Eleale*), but covered over with the ruins of towns that have been destroyed," and which "extends to the desert of Arabia towards the east, and slopes off to the Jordan and the Dead Sea towards the west" (*v. Raumer*, Pal. p. 71). It is identical with "the whole plain from *Medeba* to *Dibon*" (Josh. xiii. 9), and "the whole plain by *Medeba*" (ver. 16), in which Heshbon and its cities were situated (ver. 17; cf. ver. 21 and Deut. iii. 10). The valley in this table-land was upon the height of *Pisgah, i.e.* the northern part of the mountains of Abarim, and looked across the surface of the desert. *Jeshimon*, the desert, is the plain of *Ghor el Belka, i.e.* the valley of desolation on the north-eastern border of the Dead Sea, which stretches from the Wady *Menshalla* or Wady *Ghuweir* (*el Guer*) to the small brook *el Szuême* (*Wady es Suweimeh* on *Van de Velde's* map) at the Dead Sea, and narrows it more and more at the north-ern extremity on this side. "*Ghor el Belka* consists in part of a barren, salt, and stony soil; though there are some portions which can be cultivated. To the north of the brook *el Szuême*, the great plain of the Jordan begins, which is utterly without fertility till you reach the *Nahr Hesbân*, about two hours distant, and produces nothing but bitter, salt herbs for camels" (*Seetzen*, ii. pp. 373, 374), and which was probably reckoned as part of *Jeshimon*, since *Beth-Jeshimoth* was situated within it (see at chap. xxiii. 28). The valley in which the Israelites were encamped in the field of Moab upon the top of Pisgah, is therefore to be sought for to the west of Heshbon, on the mountain range of Abarim, which slopes off into the Ghor el Belka. From this the Israelites advanced into the *Arboth Moab* (see chap. xxii. 1).

If we compare the places of encampment named in vers. 11–20 with the list of stations in chap. xxxiii. 41–49, we find, instead of the seven places mentioned here between *Ijje Abarim* and the *Arboth Moab*,—viz. Brook Zared, on the other side of the Arnon in the desert, Beer, Mattana, Nahaliel, Bamoth, and the valley in the field of

Moab upon the top of Pisgah,—only three places given, viz. *Dibon* of Gad, *Almon Diblathaim*, and Mount *Abarim* before *Nebo*. That the last of these is only another name for the valley in the field of Moab upon the top of Pisgah, is undoubtedly proved by the fact that, according to Deut. xxxiv. 1 (cf. chap. iii. 27), Mount Nebo was a peak of *Pisgah*, and that it was situated, according to Deut. xxxii. 49, upon the mountains of *Abarim*, from which it is evident at once that the *Pisgah* was a portion of the mountains of *Abarim*, and in fact the northern portion opposite to Jericho (see at chap. xxvii. 12). The two other differences in the names may be explained from the circumstance that the space occupied by the encampment of the Israelites, an army of 600,000 men, with their wives, children, and cattle, when once they reached the inhabited country with its towns and villages, where every spot had its own fixed name, must have extended over several places, so that the very same encampment might be called by one or other of the places upon which it touched. If *Dibon Gad* (chap. xxxiii. 45) was the Dibon built (*i.e.* rebuilt or fortified) by the Gadites after the conquest of the land (chap. xxxii. 3, 34), and allotted to the Reubenites (Josh. xiii. 9, 17), which is still traceable in the ruins of *Dibân*, an hour to the north of the Arnon (*v. Raumer, Pal.* p. 261), (and there is no reason to doubt it), then the place of encampment, *Nahaliel* (*Encheile*), was identical with *Dibon* of Gad, and was placed after this town in chap. xxxiii. 45, because the camp of the Israelites extended as far as *Dibon* along the northern bank of that river. *Almon Diblathaim* also stands in the same relation to *Bamoth*. The two places do not appear to have been far from one another ; for *Almon Diblathaim* is probably identical with *Beth Diblathaim*, which is mentioned in Jer. xlviii. 22 along with *Dibon*, *Nebo*, and other Moabite towns, and is to be sought for to the north or north-west of Dibon. For, according to *Jerome* (*Onom. s. v. Jassa*), *Jahza* was between *Medaba* and *Deblatai*, for which *Eusebius* has written $\Delta\eta\beta o\acute{v}\varsigma$ by mistake for $\Delta\iota\beta\acute{\omega}\nu$; *Eusebius* having determined the relative position of Jahza according to a more southerly place, Jerome according to one farther north. The camp of the Israelites therefore may easily have extended from Almon or Beth-Diblathaim to Bamoth, and might very well take its name from either place.[1]

[1] Neither this difference in the names of the places of encampment, nor the material diversity,—viz. that in the chapter before us there are four places more introduced than in chap. xxxiii., whereas in every other case the list in chap.

Vers. 21–35. DEFEAT OF THE AMORITE KINGS, SIHON OF
HESHBON AND OG OF BASHAN, AND CONQUEST OF THEIR
KINGDOMS.—Vers. 21–23. When the Israelites reached the eastern
border of the kingdom of the Amorite king *Sihon* (see at ver. 13),
they sent messengers to him, as they had previously done to the
king of Edom, to ask permission to pass peaceably through his
territory upon the high road (cf. ver. 22 and chap. xx. 17); and
Sihon refused this request, just as the king of Edom had done, and
marched with all his people against the Israelites. But whereas
the Lord forbade the Israelites to make war upon their kinsmen
the Edomites, He now commanded them to make war upon the
Amorite king, and take possession of his land (Deut. ii. 24, 25);
for the Amorites belonged to the Canaanitish tribes which were
ripe for the judgment of extermination (Gen. xv. 16). And if,
notwithstanding this, the Israelites sent to him with words of peace
(Deut. ii. 26), this was simply done to leave the decision of his fate
in his own hand (see at Deut. ii. 24). Sihon came out against the
Israelites into the desert as far as *Jahza*, where a battle was fought,
in which he was defeated. The accounts of the *Onom.* concerning
Jahza, which was situated, according to *Eusebius*, between *Medamon*
(*Medaba*) and *Debous* (*Dibon*, see above), and according to Jerome,
between *Medaba* and *Deblatai*, may be reconciled with the statement that it was in the desert, provided we assume that it was not
in a straight line between the places named, but in a more easterly
direction on the edge of the desert, near to the commencement of
the Wady *Wale*, a conclusion to which the juxtaposition of *Jahza*

xxxiii. contains a larger number of stations than we read of in the historical
account,—at all warrants the hypothesis, that the present chapter is founded upon
a different document from chap. xxxiii. For they may be explained in a very
simple manner, as *Kurtz* has most conclusively demonstrated (vol. iii. pp. 383–5),
from the diversity in the character of the two chapters. Chap. xxxiii. is purely
statistical. The catalogue given there " contains a complete list in regular order
of all the stations properly so called, that is to say, of those places of encampment where Israel made a longer stay than at other times, and therefore not
only constructed an organized camp, but also set up the tabernacle." In the
historical account, on the other hand, the places mentioned are simply those
which were of historical importance. For this reason there are fewer stations
introduced between Mount Hor and Ijje Abarim than in chap. xxxiii., stations
where nothing of importance occurred being passed over; but, on the other
hand, there are a larger number mentioned between Ijje Abarim and Arboth
Moab, and some of them places where no complete camp was constructed with
the tabernacle set up, probably because they were memorable as starting-points
for the expeditions into the two Amorite kingdoms.

and *Mephaot* in Josh. xiii. 18, xxi. 37, and Jer. xlviii. 21, also points (see at Josh. xiii. 18).—Ver. 24. Israel smote him with the edge of the sword, *i.e.* without quarter (see Gen. xxxiv. 26), and took possession of his land "*from Arnon* (Mojeb) *to the Jabbok, unto the children of Ammon,*" *i.e.* to the upper Jabbok, the modern *Nahr* or *Moiet Ammân.* The *Jabbok,* now called *Zerka,* *i.e.* the blue, does not take its rise, as *Seetzen* supposed, on the pilgrim-road by the castle of *Zerka;* but its source, according to *Abulfeda (tab. Syr.* p. 91) and *Buckingham,* is the *Nahr Ammân,* which flowed down from the ancient capital of the Ammonites, and was called the *upper Jabbok,* and formed the western border of the Ammonites towards the kingdom of Sihon, and subsequently towards Gad (Deut. ii. 37, iii. 16; Josh. xii. 2). "*For the border of the Ammonites was strong*" (firm), *i.e.* strongly fortified; "for which reason Sihon had only been able to push his conquests to the upper Jabbok, not into the territory of the Ammonites." This explanation of *Knobel's* is perfectly correct; since the reason why the Israelites did not press forward into the country of the Ammonites, was not the strength of their frontier, but the word of the Lord, "Make not war upon them, for I shall give thee no possession of the land of the children of Ammon" (Deut. ii. 19). God had only promised the patriarchs, on behalf of their posterity, that He would give them the land of Canaan, which was bounded towards the east by the Jordan (chap. xxxiv. 2–12; compared with Gen. x. 19 and xv. 19–21); and the Israelites would have received no settlement at all on the eastern side of the Jordan, had not the Canaanitish branch of the Amorites extended itself to that side in the time of Moses, and conquered a large portion of the possessions of the Moabites, and also (according to Josh. xiii. 25, as compared with Judg. xi. 13) of the Ammonites, driving back the Moabites as far as the Arnon, and the Ammonites behind the Nahr *Ammân.* With the defeat of the Amorites, all the land that they had conquered passed into the possession of the Israelites, who took possession of these towns (cf. Deut. ii. 34–36). The statement in ver. 25, that Israel settled in all the towns of the Amorites, is somewhat anticipatory of the history itself, as the settlement did not occur till Moses gave the conquered land to the tribes of Reuben and Gad for a possession (chap. xxxii.). The only places mentioned here are *Heshbon* and her daughters, *i.e.* the smaller towns belonging to it (cf. Josh. xiii. 17), which are enumerated singly in chap. xxxii. 34–38, and Josh. xiii. 15–28. In explanation of the expression, "Heshbon and her

daughters," it is added in ver. 26, that Heshbon was the city, *i.e.*
the capital of the Amorite king Sihon, who had made war upon
the former king of Moab, and taken away all his land as far as the
Arnon. Consequently, even down to the time of the predecessor
of Balak, the king of the Moabites at that time, the land to the
north of the Arnon, and probably even as far as the lower Jabbok,
to which point the kingdom of Sihon extended (see Deut. iii. 12,
13; Josh. xii. 5), belonged to the Moabites. And in accordance
with this, the country where the Israelites encamped opposite to
Jericho, before crossing the Jordan, is reckoned as part of the land
of Moab (Deut. i. 5, xxviii. 69, xxxii. 49, xxxiv. 5, 6), and called
Arboth Moab (see chap. xxii. 1); whilst the women who seduced
the Israelites to join in the idolatrous worship of Baal Peor are
called daughters of Moab (chap. xxv. 1).

Vers. 27–30. The glorious conquest and destruction of the
capital of the powerful king of the Amorites, in the might of the
Lord their God, inspired certain composers of proverbs (מֹשְׁלִים
denom. from מָשָׁל) to write songs in commemoration of the victory.
Three strophes are given from a song of this kind, and introduced
with the words "*therefore*," sc. because Heshbon had fallen in this
manner, "*the composers of proverbs say.*" The first strophe (vers.
27b and 28) runs thus: "*Come to Heshbon: Built and restored
be the city of Sihon! For fire went out of Heshbon; flames from
the city of Sihon. It devoured Ar Moab, the lords of the heights
of Arnon.*" The summons to come to Heshbon and build this
ruined city up again, was not addressed to the Israelites, but to
the conquered Amorites, and is to be interpreted as ironical (*F. v.
Meyer; Ewald, Gesch.* ii. pp. 267, 268): "*Come to Heshbon, ye
victorious Amorites, and build your royal city up again, which
we have laid in ruins! A fire has gone out of it, and burned up
Ar Moab, and the lords of the heights of the Arnon.*" The reference is to the war-fire, which the victorious Amorites kindled
from Heshbon in the land of Moab under the former king of
Moab; that is to say, the war in which they subjugated Ar Moab
and the possessors of the heights of Arnon. *Ar Moab* (see at
ver. 15) appears to have been formerly the capital of all Moabitis,
or at least of that portion of it which was situated upon the northern side of the Arnon; and the prominence given to it in Deut.
ii. 9, 18, 29, is in harmony with this. The heights of Arnon are
mentioned as the limits to which Sihon had carried his victorious
supremacy over Moab. The "*lords*" of these heights are the Moab-

ites.—Ver. 29. *Second strophe:* "*Woe to thee, Moab! Thou art lost, people of Chemosh! He has given up his sons as fugitives, and his daughters into captivity—to Sihon, king of the Amorites.*" The poet here turns to Moab, and announces its overthrow. *Chemosh* (כְּמוֹשׁ, from כָּמַשׁ = כָּבַשׁ, *subactor, domitor*) was the leading deity of the Moabites (Jer. xlviii. 7) as well as of the Ammonites (Judg. xi. 24), and related not only to *Milcom*, a god of the Ammonites, but also to the early Canaanitish deity *Baal* and *Moloch*. According to a statement of *Jerome* (on Isa. xv.), it was only another name for *Baal Peor*, probably a god of the sun, which was worshipped as the king of his nation and the god of war. He is found in this character upon the coins of *Areopolis*, standing upon a column, with a sword in his right hand and a lance and shield in the left, and with two fire-torches by his side (cf. *Ekhel doctr. numm. vet.* iii. p. 504), and was appeased by the sacrifice of children in times of great distress (2 Kings iii. 27). Further information, and to some extent a different view, are found in the article by *J. G. Müller* in *Herzog's* Cyclopædia. The subject to נָתַן is neither Moab nor Jehovah, but Chemosh. The thought is this: as Chemosh, the god of Moab, could not deliver his people from the Amorite king; so now that Israel has conquered the latter, Moab is utterly lost. In the triumph which Israel celebrated over Moab through conquering its conquerors, there is a forewarning expressed of the ultimate subjection of Moab under the sceptre of Israel.—Ver. 30. *Third strophe*, in which the woe evoked upon Moab is justified: "*We cast them down: Heshbon is lost even to Dibon; and we laid it waste even to Nophah, with fire to Medeba.*" וַנִּירָם is the first pers. pl. imperf. Kal of יָרָה with the suffix ־ם for ־ם (as in Ex. xxix. 30). יָרָה, to cast arrows, to shoot down (Ex. xix. 13): figuratively to throw to the ground (Ex. xv. 4). נַשִּׁים for נַשֵּׁם, first *pers. pl. imperf. Hiph.* of נָשָׁה, synonymous with נָצָה, Jer. iv. 7. The suffixes of both verbs refer to the Moabites as the inhabitants of the cities named. Accordingly *Heshbon* also is construed as a masculine, because it was not the town as such, but the inhabitants, that were referred to. *Heshbon,* the residence of king Sihon, stood pretty nearly in the centre between the Arnon and the Jabbok (according to the *Onom.* twenty Roman miles from the Jordan, opposite to Jericho), and still exists in extensive ruins with deep bricked wells, under the old name of *Hesbân* (cf. *v. Raumer, Pal.* p. 262). On *Dibon* in the south, not more than an hour from Arnon, see p. 288. *Nophach* is probably the same as *Nobach*, Judg. viii. 11, but not the same as

Kenath, which was altered into *Nobach* (chap. xxxii. 42). According-ing to Judg. viii. 11, it was near Jogbeha, not far from the eastern desert; and in all probability it still exists in the ruined place called *Nowakis* (*Burckhardt,* p. 619 ; *Buckingham,* ii. p. 46 ; *Robinson,* App. p. 188), to the north-west of *Ammán* (*Rabbath-Ammon*). *Nophach,* therefore, is referred to as a north-eastern town or for-tress, and contrasted with *Dibon,* which was in the south. The words which follow, 'מ עד אֲשֶׁר, "*which to Medeba,*" yield no intel-ligible meaning. The Seventy give πῦρ ἐπὶ M. (fire upon Medeba), and seem to have adopted the reading אֵשׁ עַד. In the Masoretic punctuation also, the ר in אשׁר is marked as suspicious by a *punct. extraord.* Apparently, therefore, אֲשׁר was a copyist's error of old standing for אֵשׁ, and is to be construed as governed by the verb נְשִׁים, " with fire to *Medeba.*" This city was about two hours to the south-east of Heshbon, and is still to be seen in ruins bearing the name of *Medaba,* upon the top of a hill of about half-an-hour's journey in circumference (*Burckhardt,* p. 625 ; *v. Raumer,* Pal. pp. 264–5).[1]

Vers. 31, 32. When Israel was sitting, *i.e.* encamped, in the land of the Amorites, Moses reconnoitred *Jaezer,* after which the Israel-ites took " its daughters," *i.e.* the smaller places dependent upon Jaezer, and destroyed the Amorites who dwelt in them. It is evident from chap. xxxii. 35, that Jaezer was not only conquered, but destroyed. This city, which was situated, according to the *Onom.* (*s. v. Jazer*), ten Roman miles to the west of *Philadelphia* (*Rabbath-Ammon*), and fifteen Roman miles to the north of Hesh-bon, is most probably to be sought for (as *Seetzen* supposes, i. pp. 397, 406, iv. p. 216) in the ruins of *es Szir,* at the source of the *Nahr Szir,* in the neighbourhood of which *Seetzen* found some pools, which are probably the remains of " the sea of Jazer," mentioned in Jer. xlviii. 32. There is less probability in *Burckhardt's* con-jecture (p. 609), that it is to be found in the ruins of *Ain Hazir,*

---

[1] *Ewald* and *Bleek* (*Einleitung* in d. A. T. p. 200) are both agreed that this ode was composed on the occasion of the defeat of the Amorites by the Israel-ites, and particularly on the capture of the capital Heshbon, as it depicts the fall of Heshbon in the most striking way ; and this city was rebuilt shortly afterwards by the Reubenites, and remained ever afterwards a city of some importance. *Knobel,* on the other hand, has completely misunderstood the meaning and substance of the verses quoted, and follows some of the earliest commentators, such as *Clericus* and others, in regarding the ode as an Amoritish production, and interpreting it as relating to the conquest and fortification of Heshbon by Sihon.

near *Kherbet el Suk*, to the south-west of *es Salt*; though *v. Raumer* (Pal. p. 262) decides in its favour (see my Commentary on Josh. xiii. 25).—Vers. 33–35. The Israelites then turned towards the north, and took the road to Bashan, where king Og came against them with his people, to battle at *Edrei*. From what point it was that the Israelites entered upon the expedition against Bashan, is not stated either here or in Deut. iii. 1 sqq., where Moses recapitulates these events, and gives a more detailed account of the conquests than he does here, simply because it was of no importance in relation to the main object of the history. We have probably to picture the conquest of the kingdoms of Sihon and Og as taking place in the following manner : namely, that after Sihon had been defeated at Jahza, and his capital had been speedily taken in consequence of this victory, Moses sent detachments of his army from the places of encampment mentioned in vers. 16, 18–20, into the different divisions of his kingdom, for the purpose of taking possession of their towns. After the conquest of the whole of the territory of Sihon, the main army advanced to Bashan and defeated king Og in a great battle at Edrei, whereupon certain detachments of the army were again despatched, under courageous generals, to secure the conquest of the different parts of his kingdom (cf. chap. xxxii. 39, 41, 42). The kingdom of Og embraced the northern half of Gilead, *i.e.* the country between the Jabbok and the Mandhur (Deut. iii. 13 ; Josh. xii. 5), the modern Jebel *Ajlun*, and " all Bashan," or " all the region of *Argob*" (Deut. iii. 4, 13, 14), the modern plain of *Jaulan* and *Hauran*, which extended eastwards to *Salcha*, north-eastwards to *Edrei* (Deut. iii. 10), and northwards to *Geshur* and *Maacha* (Josh. xii. 5). For further remarks, see Deut. iii. 10. There were two towns in Bashan of the name of *Edrei*. One of them, which is mentioned in Deut. i. 4 and Josh. xii. 4, along with *Ashtaroth*, as a second residence of king Og, is described in the *Onom.* (*s. v. Ashtaroth* and *Edrei*) as six Roman miles, *i.e.* fully two hours, from Ashtaroth, and twenty-four or twenty-five miles from Bostra, and called *Adraa* or *Adara*. This is the modern *Derà* or *Draà* (in *Burckhardt*, p. 385 ; *Seetzen*, i. pp. 363, 364), and *Draah, Idderat* (in *Buckingham, Syr.* ii. p. 146), a place which still exists, consisting of a number of miserable houses, built for the most part of basalt, and standing upon a small elevation in a treeless, hilly region, with the ruins of an old church and other smaller buildings, supposed to belong to the time when *Draa, Adraa* (as *urbs Arabiae*), was an episcopal see, on the east of the pilgrim-road between *Remtha* and *Mezareib*, by the side of a small wady (see *Ritter, Erdk.* xv. pp. 838 sqq.). The other *Edrei*, which is mentioned in Deut. iii. 10 as the north-western frontier of Bashan, was farther towards the north, and is still to be seen in the ruins of *Zorah* or *Ethra* (see at Deut. iii. 10). In the present instance the southern town is intended, which was not far from the south-west frontier of Bashan, as Og certainly did not allow the Israelites to advance to the northern frontier of his kingdom before he gave them battle.—Vers. 34, 35. Just as in the case of Sihon, the Lord had also promised the Israelites a victory over Og, and had given him into their power, so that they smote him, with his sons and all his people, without leaving any remnant, and executed the ban, according to Deut. ii. 34, upon both the kings. (See the notes on Deut. iii.)

III.—OCCURRENCES IN THE STEPPES OF MOAB, WITH INSTRUCTIONS RELATING TO THE CONQUEST AND DISTRIBUTION OF THE LAND OF CANAAN.

CHAP. XXII.–XXXVI.

Chap. xxii. 1. After the defeat of the two Amorite kings, Sihon and Og, and the conquest of their kingdoms in Gilead and Bashan, the Israelites removed from the height of Pisgah, on the mountains of Abarim before Nebo (see at chap. xxi. 20), and encamped in the *"Arboth Moab* (the steppes of Moab), on the other side of the Jordan of Jericho," *i.e.* that part of the Jordan which skirted the province of Jericho. *Arboth Moab* was the name given to that portion of the Arabah, or large plain of the Jordan, the present *Ghor* (see at Deut. i. 1), which belonged to the territory of the Moabites previous to the spread of the Amorites under Sihon in the land to the east of the Jordan, and which probably reached from the Dead Sea to the mouth of the Jabbok. The site of the Israelitish camp is therefore defined with greater minuteness by the clause " beyond the Jordan of Jericho." This place of encampment, which is frequently alluded to (chap. xxvi. 3, 63, xxxi. 12, xxxiii. 48, 50, xxxv. 1, xxxvi. 13; Josh. xiii. 32), extended, according to chap. xxxiii. 49, from *Beth-Jeshimoth* to *Abel-Shittim. Beth-Jeshimoth* (*i.e.* house of wastes), on the north-eastern desert border (*Jeshimon*, chap. xxi. 20) of the Dead Sea, a town allotted to the tribe of Reuben (Josh. xii. 3, xiii. 20), was situated, according to the *Onom.* (*s. v. Βηθασιμούθ, Bethsimuth*), ten Roman miles, or four hours, to the south (S.E.) of Jericho, on the Dead Sea; according to *Josephus* (*bell. jud.* iv. 7, 6), it was to the south of *Julias* (*Livias*), *i.e. Beth-Haram*, or *Rameh*, on the northern edge of the Wady Hesban (see at chap. xxxii. 36), or in the *Ghor el Seisabân*, on the northern coast of the Dead Sea, and the southern end of the plain of the Jordan. *Abel Shittim* (אָבֵל הַשִּׁטִּים), *i.e.* the acacia-meadow, or, in its briefer form, *Shittim* (chap. xxv. 1), was situated, according to Josephus (*Ant.* iv. 8, 1), on the same spot as the later town of *Abila*, in a locality rich in date-palms, sixty stadia from the Jordan, probably by the Wady *Eshtah* to the north of the Wady Hesban; even if *Knobel's* supposition that the name is connected with אִשְׁטָה =שָׁטָה with א *prost.* should not be a tenable one. From *Shittim* or *Sittim* the Israelites advanced, under Joshua, to the Jordan, to effect the conquest of Canaan (Josh. iii. 1).

In the steppes of Moab the Israelites encamped upon the border of the promised land, from which they were only separated by the Jordan. But before this boundary line could be passed, there were many preparations that had to be made. In the first place, the whole congregation was to pass through a trial of great importance to all future generations, as bearing upon the relation in which it stood to the heathen world; and in the second place, it was here that Moses, who was not to enter Canaan because of his sin at the water of strife, was to bring the work of legislation to a close before his death, and not only to issue the requisite instructions concerning the conquest of the promised inheritance, and the division of it among the tribes of Israel, but to impress once more upon the hearts of the whole congregation the essential contents of the whole law, with all that the Lord had done for Israel, that they might be confirmed in their fidelity to the Lord, and preserved from the danger of apostasy. This last work of the faithful servant of God, with which he brought his mediatorial work to a close, is described in the book of Deuteronomy; whilst the laws relating to the conquest and partition of Canaan, with the experience of Israel in the steppes of Moab, fill up the latter portion of the present book.

BALAAM AND HIS PROPHECIES.—CHAP. XXII. 2—XXIV. 25.

The rapid defeat of the two mighty kings of the Amorites filled the Moabites with such alarm at the irresistible might of Israel, that Balak their king, with the princes of Midian, sought to bring the powers of heathen magic to bear against the nation of God; and to this end he sent messengers with presents to BALAAM, the celebrated soothsayer, in Mesopotamia, who had the reputation of being able both to bless and curse with great success, to entreat him to come, and so to weaken the Israelites with his magical curses, that he might be able to smite them, and drive them out of his land (chap. xxii. 1–7). At first Balaam declined this invitation, in consequence of divine instructions (vers. 8–14); but when a second and still more imposing embassy of Moabite princes appeared before him, God gave him permission to go with them, but on this condition, that he should do nothing but what Jehovah should tell him (vers. 15–21). When on the way, he was warned again by the miraculous opposition of the angel of the Lord, to say nothing but what God should say to him (vers. 22–35). When Balak, therefore, came to meet him, on his arrival at the border of his kingdom, to give him a grand reception, Balaam explained to him, that he could only speak the word which Jehovah would put into his mouth (vers. 36–40), and then proclaimed, in *four* different utterances, what God inspired him to declare. First of all, as he stood upon the height of Bamoth-Baal, from which he could see the end of the Israelitish camp, he declared that it was impossible for him to curse this matchless, numerous, and righteous people, because they had not been cursed by their God (chap. xxii. 41–xxiii. 10). He then went to the head of Pisgah, where he could see all Israel, and announced that Jehovah would bless this people, because He saw no unrighteousness in them, and that He would dwell among them as their King, making known His word to them, and endowing them with activity and lion-like power (chap. xxiii. 11–24). And lastly, upon the top of Peor, where he could see Israel encamped according to its tribes, he predicted, in two more utterances, the spread and powerful development of Israel in its inheritance, under the blessing of God (chap. xxiii. 25–xxiv. 9), the rise of a star out of Jacob in the far distant future, and the appearance of a ruler in Israel, who would break to pieces all its foes (chap. xxiv. 10–24); and upon this Balak sent him away (ver. 25).

From the very earliest times opinions have been divided as to the character of Balaam.[1] Some (*e.g. Philo, Ambrose*, and *Augus-*

---

[1] On Balaam and his prophecies see *G. Moebius Prophetæ Bileami historia*, Lips. 1676; *Lüderwald, die Geschichte Bileams deutlich u. begreiflich erklärt* (*Helmst.* 1787); *B. R. de Geer, Diss. de Bileamo, ejus historia et vaticiniis; Tholuck's vermischte Schriften* (i. pp. 406 sqq.); *Hengstenberg*, History of

tine) have regarded him as a wizard and false prophet, devoted to the worship of idols, who was destitute of any susceptibility for the true religion, and was compelled by God, against his will, to give utterance to blessings upon Israel instead of curses. Others (*e.g. Tertullian* and *Jerome*) have supposed him to be a genuine and true prophet, who simply fell through covetousness and ambition. But these views are both of them untenable in this exclusive form. *Witsius* (*Miscell. ss.* i. lib. i. c. 16, § 33 sqq.), *Hengstenberg* (Balaam and his Prophecies), and *Kurtz* (History of the Old Covenant), have all of them clearly demonstrated this. The name בִּלְעָם (LXX. Βαλαάμ) is not to be derived, as *Gesenius* suggests, from בַּל and עָם, *non populus*, not a people, but either from בְּלַע and עָם (dropping one ע), devourer of the people (*Simonis* and *Hengstenberg*), or more probably from בָּלַע, with the terminal syllable ‑ם, devourer, destroyer (*Fürst, Dietrich*), which would lead to the conclusion, that " he bore the name as a dreaded wizard and conjurer; whether he received it at his birth, as a member of a family in which this occupation was hereditary, and then afterwards actually became in public opinion what the giving of the name expressed as an expectation and desire; or whether the name was given to him at a later period, according to Oriental custom, when the fact indicated by the name had actually made its appearance" (Hengstenberg). In its true meaning, the name is related to that of his father, Beor.[1] בְּעוֹר, from בָּעַר, to burn, eat off, destroy: so called on account of the destructive power attributed to his curses (*Hengstenberg*). It is very probable, therefore, that Balaam belonged to a family in which the mantic character, or magical art, was hereditary. These names at once warrant the conjecture that Balaam was a heathen conjurer or soothsayer. Moreover, he is never called נָבִיא, a prophet, or חֹזֶה, a seer, but הַקּוֹסֵם, the soothsayer (Josh. xiii. 22), a title which

---

Balaam, etc. (Berlin, 1842, and English translation by Ryland: Clark, 1847); *Kurtz*, History of the Old Covenant (English translation: Clark, 1859); and *Gust. Baur*, Gesch. der alttestl. Weissagung, Giessen, 1861, where the literature is given more fully still.

[1] The form *Bosor*, which we find instead of *Beor* in 2 Pet. ii. 15, appears to have arisen from a peculiar mode of pronouncing the guttural ע (see *Loescher de causis ling. ebr.* p. 246); whereas *Vitringa* maintains (in his *obss. ss.* l. iv. c. 9), that Peter himself invented this form, " that by this sound of the word he might play upon the Hebrew בָּשָׂר, which signifies flesh, and thus delicately hint that *Balaam*, the false prophet, deserved to be called the son of Bosor, *i.e.* בָּשָׂר, or flesh, on account of his persuading to the indulgence of carnal lusts."

is never used in connection with the true prophets. For קֶסֶם, sooth-saying, is forbidden to the Israelites in Deut. xviii. 10 sqq., as an abomination in the sight of Jehovah, and is spoken of everywhere not only as a grievous sin (1 Sam. xv. 23; Ezek. xiii. 23; 2 Kings xvii. 17), but as the mark of a false prophet (Ezek. xiii. 9, xxii. 28, Jer. xiv. 14, and even in Isa. iii. 2, where קֹסֵם forms the antithesis to נָבִיא). Again, Balaam resorts to auguries, just like a heathen soothsayer (chap. xxiv. 1, compared with chap. xxiii. 3, 5), for the purpose of obtaining revelations; from which we may see that he was accustomed to adopt this as his ordinary mode of soothsaying.[1] On the other hand, Balaam was not without a certain measure of the true knowledge of God, and not without susceptibility for such revelations of the true God as he actually received; so that, without being really a prophet, he was able to give utterance to true pro-phecies from Jehovah. He not only knew Jehovah, but he con-fessed Jehovah, even in the presence of Balak, as well as of the Moabitish messengers. He asked His will, and followed it (chap. xxii. 8, 13, 18, 19, 38, xxiii. 12), and would not go with the messengers of Balak, therefore, till God had given him permission (chap. xxii. 20). If he had been altogether destitute of the fear of God, he would have complied at once with Balak's request. And again, although at the outset it is only *Elohim* who makes known His will (chap. xxii. 9, 20), and even when he first of all goes out in search of oracles, it is *Elohim* who comes to him (chap. xxiii. 4); yet not only does the angel of *Jehovah* meet him by the way (chap. xxii. 22 sqq.), but *Jehovah* also puts words into his mouth, which he an-nounces to the king of the Moabites (chap. xxiii. 5, 12, 16), so that all his prophecies are actually uttered from a mind moved and governed by the Spirit of God, and that not from any physical constraint exerted upon him by God, but in such a manner that he enters into them with all his heart and soul, and heartily desires to die the death of these righteous, *i.e.* of the people of Israel (chap. xxiii. 10); and when he finds that it pleases Jehovah to bless Israel, he leaves off resorting any longer to auguries (chap. xxiv. 1), and eventually declares to the enraged monarch, that he cannot trans-

[1] " The fact that he made use of so extremely uncertain a method as augury, the insufficiency of which was admitted even by the heathen themselves (*vid.* *Nägelsbach, homer. Theol.* pp. 154 sqq.), and which no true prophet among the Israelites ever employed, is to be attributed to the weakness of the influence exerted upon him by the Spirit of God. When the Spirit worked with power, there was no need to look round at nature for the purpose of ascertaining the will of God" (*Hengstenberg*).

gress the command of Jehovah, even if the king should give him his house full of silver and gold (chap. xxiv. 13).[1]

This double-sidedness and ambiguity of the religious and prophetic character of Balaam may be explained on the supposition that, being endowed with a predisposition to divination and prophecy, he practised soothsaying and divination as a trade; and for the purpose of bringing this art to the greatest possible perfection, brought not only the traditions of the different nations, but all the phenomena of his own times, within the range of his observations. In this way he may have derived the first elements of the true knowledge of God from different echoes of the tradition of the primeval age, which was then not quite extinct, and may possibly have heard in his own native land some notes of the patriarchal revelations out of the home of the tribe-fathers of Israel. But these traditions are not sufficient of themselves to explain his attitude towards Jehovah, and his utterances concerning Israel. Balaam's peculiar knowledge of Jehovah, the God of Israel, and of all that He had done to His people, and his intimate acquaintance with the promises made to the patriarchs, which strike us in his prophecies (comp. chap. xxiii. 10 with Gen. xiii. 16, xxiii. 24; chap. xxiv. 9 with Gen. xlix. 9; and chap. xxiv. 17 with Gen. xlix. 10), can only be explained from the fact that the report of the great things which God had done to and for Israel in Egypt and at the Dead Sea, had not only spread among all the neighbouring tribes, as was foretold in Ex. xv. 14, and is attested by Jethro, Ex. xviii. 1 sqq., and Rahab the Canaanite, Josh. ii. 9 sqq., but had even penetrated into Mesopotamia, as the countries of the Euphrates had maintained a steady commercial intercourse from the very earliest times with Hither Asia and the land of Egypt. Through these tidings Balaam

---

[1] The significant interchange in the use of the names of God, which is seen in the fact, that from the very outset Balaam always speaks of Jehovah (chap. xxii. 8, 13, 18, 19),—whereas, according to the historian, it is only *Elohim* who reveals Himself to him (chap. xxii. 9, 10, 12),—has been pointed out by *Hengstenberg* in his Dissertations; and even *Baur*, in his *Geschichte der alttestl. Weissagung* (i. p. 334), describes it as a "fine distinction;" but neither of them satisfactorily explains this diversity. For the assumption that Balaam is thereby tacitly accused of hypocrisy (*Hengstenberg*), or that the intention of the writer is to intimate that "the heathen seer did not stand at first in any connection whatever with the true God of Israel" (*Baur*), sets up a chasm between *Elohim* and *Jehovah*, with which the fact that, according to chap. xxii. 22, the wrath of *Elohim* on account of Balaam's journey was manifested in the appearance of the angel of *Jehovah*, is irreconcilable. The manifestation of God in the form of

was no doubt induced not only to procure more exact information concerning the events themselves, that he might make a profitable use of it in connection with his own occupation, but also to dedicate himself to the service of Jehovah, "in the hope of being able to participate in the new powers conferred upon the human race; so that henceforth he called Jehovah his God, and appeared as a prophet in His name" (*Hengstenberg*). In this respect Balaam resembles the Jewish exorcists, who cast out demons in the name of Jesus without following Christ (Mark ix. 38, 39; Luke ix. 49), but more especially Simon Magus, his "New Testament antitype," who was also so powerfully attracted by the new divine powers of Christianity that he became a believer, and submitted to baptism, because he saw the signs and great miracles that were done (Acts viii. 13). And from the very time when Balaam sought Jehovah, the fame of his prophetical art appears to have spread. It was no doubt the report that he stood in close connection with the God of Israel, which induced Balak, according to chap. xxii. 6, to hire him to oppose the Israelites; as the heathen king shared the belief, which was common to all the heathen, that Balaam was able to work upon the God he served, and to determine and regulate His will. God had probably given to the soothsayer a few isolated but memorable glimpses of the unseen, to prepare him for the service of His kingdom. But "Balaam's heart was not right with God," and "he loved the wages of unrighteousness" (Acts viii. 21; 2 Pet. ii. 15). His thirst for honour and wealth was not so overcome by the revelations of the true God, that he could bring himself to give up his soothsaying, and serve the living God with an undivided heart. Thus it came to pass, that through the appeal addressed to him by Balak, he was brought into a situation in which, although he did not venture to attempt anything in opposition to the will of Jehovah,

the angel of *Jehovah*, was only a higher stage of the previous manifestations of *Elohim*. And all that follows from this is, that Balaam's original attitude towards Jehovah was a very imperfect one, and not yet in harmony with the true nature of the God of Israel. In his *Jehovah* Balaam worshipped only *Elohim*, *i.e.* only a divine being, but not the God of Israel, who was first of all revealed to him according to His true essence, in the appearance of the angel of Jehovah, and still more clearly in the words which He put into his mouth. This is indicated by the use of *Elohim*, in chap. xxii. 9, 10, 12. In the other passages, where this name of God still occurs, it is required by the thought, viz. in chap. xxii. 22, to express the essential identity of *Elohim* and the *Maleach Jehovah*; and in chap. xxii. 38, xxiii. 27, and xxiv. 2, to show that Balaam did not speak out of his *own* mind, but from the inspiration of the Spirit of *God*.

his heart was never thoroughly changed ; so that, whilst he refused the honours and rewards that were promised him by Balak, and pronounced blessings upon Israel in the strength of the Spirit of God that came upon him, he was overcome immediately afterwards by the might of the sin of his own unbroken heart, fell back into the old heathen spirit, and advised the Midianites to entice the Israelites to join in the licentious worship of Baal Peor (chap. xxxi. 16), and was eventually put to death by the Israelites when they conquered these their foes (chap. xxxi. 8).[1]

Chap. xxii. 2–21. BALAAM HIRED BY BALAK TO CURSE ISRAEL. —Vers. 2–4. As the Israelites passed by the eastern border of the land of Moab, the Moabites did not venture to make any attack upon them ; on the contrary, they supplied them with bread and water for money (Deut. ii. 29). At that time they no doubt cherished the hope that Sihon, their own terrible conqueror, would be able with perfect ease either to annihilate this new foe, or to drive them back into the desert from which they had come. But when they saw this hope frustrated, and the Israelites had overthrown the two kings of the Amorites with victorious power, and had conquered their kingdoms, and pressed forward through what was formerly Moabitish territory, even to the banks of the Jordan, the close proximity of so powerful a people filled Balak, their king, with terror and dismay, so that he began to think of the best means of destroying them. There was no ground for such alarm, as the Israelites, in consequence of divine instructions (Deut. ii. 9), had offered no hostilities to the Moabites, but had conscientiously spared their territory and property ; and even after the defeat of the

---

[1] When modern critics, such as *Knobel*, *Baur*, etc., affirm that the tradition in chap. xxxi. 8, 16, Josh. xiii. 22—viz. that Balaam was a *kosem*, or soothsayer, who advised the Midianites to seduce the Israelites to join in the worship of Baal—is irreconcilable with the account in chap. xxii.–xxiv. concerning Balaam himself, his attitude towards Jehovah, and his prophecies with regard to Israel, they simply display their own incapacity to comprehend, or form any psychological appreciation of, a religious character such as Balaam ; but they by no means prove that the account in chap. xxii.–xxiv. is interpolated by the Jehovist into the Elohistic original. And all that they adduce as a still further confirmation of this hypothesis (namely, that the weaving of prophetic announcements into the historical narrative, the interchange of the names of God, Jehovah, and Elohim, the appearance of the angel of the Lord, the talking of the ass, etc., are foreign to the Elohistic original), are simply assertions and assumptions, which do not become any more conclusive from the fact that they are invariably adduced when no better arguments can be hunted up.

Amorites, had not turned their arms against them, but had advanced
to the Jordan to take possession of the land of Canaan.   But the
supernatural might of the people of God was a source of such dis-
comfort to the king of the Moabites, that a horror of the Israelites
came upon him.   Feeling too weak to attack them with force of
arms, he took counsel with the elders of Midian.   With these words,
" *This crowd will now lick up all our environs, as the ox licketh up the
green of the field*," *i.e.* entirely consume all our possessions, he called
their attention to the danger which the proximity of Israel would
bring upon him and his territory, to induce them to unite with him
in some common measures against this dangerous foe.   This intention is implied in his words, and clearly follows from the sequel
of the history.   According to ver. 7, the elders of Midian went to
Balaam with the elders of Moab; and there is no doubt that the
Midianitish elders advised Balak to send for Balaam, with whom
they had become acquainted upon their trading journeys (cf. Gen.
xxxvii.), to come and curse the Israelites.   Another circumstance
also points to an intimate connection between Balaam and the
Midianites, namely, the fact that, after he had been obliged to bless
the Israelites in spite of the inclination of his own natural heart,
he went to the Midianites and advised them to make the Israelites
harmless, by seducing them to idolatry (chap. xxxi. 16).   The
Midianites, who are referred to here, must be distinguished from
the branch of the same tribe which dwelt in the peninsula of Sinai
(chap. x. 29, 30 ; Ex. ii. 15, 16, iii. 1).   They had been settled for
a long time (cf. Gen. xxxvi. 35) on the eastern border of the
Moabitish and Amoritish territory, in a grassy but treeless steppe-
land, where many ruins and wells are still to be found belonging to
very ancient times (*Buckingham, Syr.* ii. pp. 79 sqq., 95 sqq.), and
lived by grazing (chap. xxxi. 32 sqq.) and the caravan trade.   They
were not very warlike, and were not only defeated by the Edomites
(Gen. xxxvi. 35), but were also subdued and rendered tributary by
Sihon, king of the Amorites (see at chap. xxxi. 8).   In the time of
the Judges, indeed, they once invaded the land of Israel in company
with the Amalekites and the sons of the East, but they were beaten
by Gideon, and entirely repulsed (Judg. vi. and vii.), and from that
time forth they disappear entirely from history.   The " *elders of
Midian* " are heads of tribes, who administered the general affairs
of the people, who, like the Israelites, lived under a patriarchal
constitution.   The most powerful of them bore the title of " kings "
(chap. xxxi. 8) or " princes " (Josh. xiii. 21).   The clause, " and

Balak, the son of Zippor, was king of the Moabites at that time,"
is added as a supplementary note to explain the relation of Balak
to the Moabites.

Vers. 5 and 6. Balak sent messengers to Balaam to *Pethor* in
Mesopotamia.   The town of *Pethor,* or *Pethora* (Φαθούρα, LXX.),
is unknown.   There is something very uncertain in *Knobel's* supposition, that it is connected with Φαθούσαι, a place to the south of
Circessium (*Zozim.* iii. 14), and with the Βέθαννα mentioned by
Ptolemy, v. 18, 6, and that these are the same as *Anah,* 'Αναθώ,
Anatha (*Ammian. Marcell.* xxiv. 1, 6).   And the conjecture that
the name is derived from פָּתַר, to interpret dreams (Gen. xli. 8),
and marks the place as a seat of the possessors of secret arts, is also
more than doubtful, since פְּשַׁר corresponds to פְּתַר in Aramæan;
although there can be no doubt that *Pethor* may have been a noted
seat of Babylonian magi, since these wise men were accustomed to
congregate in particular localities (cf. *Strabo,* xvi. 1, § 6, and *Mün-
ter Relig. der Babyl.* p. 86).   Balak desired Balaam to come and
curse the people of Israel, who had come out of Egypt, and were
so numerous that they covered the eye of the earth (see Ex. x. 5),
i.e. the whole face of the land, and sat down (were encamped)
opposite to him ; that he might then perhaps be able to smite them
and drive them out of the land.   On אָרָה for אֹר, the imperative of
אָרַר, see *Ewald,* § 228, *b.*—" *For I know that he whom thou blessest
is blessed, and he whom thou cursest is cursed.*"   Balak believed, in
common with the whole of the ancient world, in the real power and
operation of the curses, anathemas, and incantations pronounced by
priests, soothsayers, and *goetæ.*   And there was a truth at the
foundation of this belief, however it may have been perverted by
heathenism into phantasy and superstition.   When God endows a
man with supernatural powers of His word and Spirit, he also confers upon him the power of working upon others in a supernatural
way.   Man, in fact, by virtue of the real connection between his spirit
and the higher spiritual world, is able to appropriate to himself
supernatural powers, and make them subservient to the purposes of
sin and wickedness, so as to practise magic and witchcraft with them,
arts which we cannot pronounce either mere delusion or pure superstition, since the scriptures of both the Old and New Testaments
speak of witchcraft, and condemn it as a real power of evil and of
the kingdom of darkness (see vol. i. p. 476).   Even in the narrative
itself, the power of Balaam to bless and to curse is admitted ; and,
in addition to this, it is frequently celebrated as a great favour dis-

played towards Israel, that the Lord did not hearken to Balaam, but turned the curse into a blessing (Deut. xxiii. 5 ; Josh. xxiv. 10 ; Micah vi. 3 ; Neh. xiii. 2). This power of Balaam is not therefore traced, it is true, to the might of heathen deities, but to the might of Jehovah, whose name Balaam confessed ; but yet the possibility is assumed of his curse doing actual, and not merely imaginary, harm to the Israelites. Moreover, the course of the history shows that in his heart Balaam was very much inclined to fulfil the desire of the king of the Moabites, and that this subjective inclination of his was overpowered by the objective might of the Spirit of Jehovah.

Vers. 7–14. When the elders of Moab and Midian came to him with wages of divination in their hand, he did not send them away, but told them to spend the night at his house, that he might bring them word what Jehovah would say to him. קְסָמִים, from קֶסֶם, soothsaying, signifies here that which has been wrought or won by soothsaying—the soothsayer's wages ; just as בְּשׂרָה, which signifies literally glad tidings, is used in 2 Sam. iv. 10 for the wages of glad tidings ; and פֹּעַל, פְּעֻלָּה, which signifies work, is frequently used for that which is wrought, the thing acquired, or the wages. If Balaam had been a true prophet and a faithful servant of Jehovah, he would at once have sent the messengers away and refused their request, as he must then have known that God would not curse His chosen people. But Balaam loved the wages of unrighteousness. This corruptness of his heart obscured his mind, so that he turned to God not as a mere form, but with the intention and in the hope of obtaining the consent of God to his undertaking. And God came to him in the night, and made known His will. Whether it was through the medium of a dream or of a vision, is not recorded, as this was of no moment in relation to the subject in hand. The question of God in ver. 9, " Who are these men with thee ?" not only served to introduce the conversation (Knobel), but was intended to awaken "the slumbering conscience of Balaam, to lead him to reflect upon the proposal which the men had made, and to break the force of his sinful inclination" (Hengstenberg).—Ver. 12. God then expressly forbade him to go with the messengers to curse the Israelites, as the people was blessed ; and Balaam was compelled to send back the messengers without attaining their object, because Jehovah had refused him permission to go with them. קׇבָה־לִּי, ver. 11, imper. of קׇבַב = נָקַב (see at Lev. xxiv. 11).

Vers. 15-21. The answer with which Balaam had sent the Moabitish messengers away, encouraged Balak to cherish the hope of gaining over the celebrated soothsayer to his purpose notwithstanding, and to send an embassy " of princes more numerous and more honourable than those," and to make the attempt to overcome his former resistance by more splendid promises ; whether he regarded it, as is very probable, " as the remains of a weakly fear of God, or simply as a *ruse* adopted for the purpose of obtaining better conditions" (*Hengstenberg*). As a genuine heathen, who saw nothing more in the God of Israel than a national god of that people, he thought that it would be possible to render not only men, but gods also, favourable to his purpose, by means of splendid honours and rich rewards.[1]—Vers. 18, 19. But Balaam replied to the proposals of these ambassadors : " *If Balak gave me his house full of silver and gold, I cannot transgress the mouth* (command) *of Jehovah, my God, to do little or great,*" *i.e.* to attempt anything in opposition to the will of the Lord (cf. 1 Sam. xx. 2, xxii. 15, xxv. 36). The inability flowed from moral awe of God and dread of His punishment. "From beginning to end this fact was firmly established in Balaam's mind, viz. that in the work to which Balak summoned him he could do nothing at all except through Jehovah. This knowledge he had acquired by virtue of his natural gifts as seer, and his previous experience. But this clear knowledge of Jehovah was completely obscured again by the love for the wages which ruled in his heart. Because he loved Balak, the enemy of Israel, for the sake of the wages, whereas Jehovah loved Israel for His own name's sake ; Balaam was opposed to Jehovah in his inmost nature and will, though he knew himself to be in unison with Him by virtue of his natural gift. Consequently he fell into the same blindness of contradiction to which Balak was in bondage" (*Baumgarten*). And in this blindness he hoped to be able to turn Jehovah round to oppose Israel, and favour the wishes of his own and Balak's heart. He therefore told the messengers to wait again, that he might ask Jehovah a second time (ver. 19). And this

[1] Compare the following remarks of *Pliny* (*h. n.* xxviii. 4) concerning this belief among the Romans : " *Verrius Flaccus auctores ponit, quibus credat, in oppugnationibus ante omnia solitum a Romanis sacerdotibus evocari Deum, cujus in tutela id oppidum esset, promittique illi eundem aut ampliorem apud Romanos cultum. Et durat in Pontificum disciplina id sacrum, constatque ideo occultatum, in cujus Dei tutela Roma esset, ne qui hostium simili modo agerent ;*"—and the further explanations of this heathen notion in *Hengstenberg's* Balaam and his Prophecies.

time (ver. 20) God allowed him to go with them, but only on the condition that he should do nothing but what He said to him. The apparent contradiction in His first of all prohibiting Balaam from going (ver. 12), then permitting it (ver. 20), and then again, when Balaam set out in consequence of this permission, burning with anger against him (ver. 22), does not indicate any variableness in the counsels of God, but vanishes at once when we take into account the pedagogical purpose of the divine consent. When the first messengers came and Balaam asked God whether he might go with them and curse Israel, God forbade him to go and curse. But since Balaam obeyed this command with inward repugnance, when he asked a second time on the arrival of the second embassy, God permitted him to go, but on the condition already mentioned, namely, that he was forbidden to curse. God did this not merely because it was His own intention to put blessings instead of curses into the prophet's mouth,—and "the blessings of the celebrated prophet might serve as means of encouraging Israel and discouraging their foes, even though He did not actually stand in need of them" (*Knobel*),—but primarily and principally for the sake of Balaam himself, viz. to manifest to this soothsayer, who had so little susceptibility for higher influences, both His own omnipotence and true deity, and also the divine election of Israel, in a manner so powerful as to compel him to decide either for or against the God of Israel and his salvation. To this end God permitted him to go to Balak, though not without once more warning him most powerfully by the way of the danger to which his avarice and ambition would expose him. This immediate intention in the guidance of Balaam, by which God would have rescued him if possible from the way of destruction, into which he had been led by the sin which ruled in his heart, does not at all preclude the much further-reaching design of God, which was manifested in Balaam's blessings, namely, to glorify His own name among the heathen and in Israel, through the medium of this far-famed soothsayer.

Vers. 22–35. BALAAM'S SPEAKING ASS.—Ver. 22. "*And the anger of God burned, that he was going* (הוֹלֵךְ הוּא): *and the angel of Jehovah placed himself in the way, as an adversary to him.*" From the use of the participle הוֹלֵךְ instead of the imperfect, with which it is not interchangeable, it is evident, on the one hand, that the anger of God was not excited by the fact that Balaam went with the elders of Moab, but by his behaviour either on setting out or upon the journey ;[1] and, on the other hand, that the occurrence which followed did not take place at the commencement, but rather towards the close of, the journey. As it was a longing for wages and honour that had induced the soothsayer to undertake the journey, the nearer he came to his destination, under the guidance of the distinguished Moabitish ambassadors, the more was his mind occupied with the honours and riches in prospect ; and so completely did they take possession of his heart, that he was in danger of casting to the winds the condition which had been imposed upon him by God. The wrath of God was kindled against this dangerous enemy of his soul ; and as he was riding upon his ass with two attendants, the angel of the Lord stood in his way לוֹ לְשָׂטָן, " as an adversary to him," i.e. to restrain him from advancing farther on a road that would inevitably lead him headlong into destruction (cf. ver. 32). This visible manifestation of God (on the angel of the Lord, see vol. i. pp. 185 sqq.) was seen by the ass ; but Balaam the seer was so blinded, that it was entirely hidden from his eye, darkened as it was by sinful lust ; and this happened three times before Jehovah brought him to his senses by the speaking of the dumb animal, and thus opened his eyes.[2] The " drawn sword " in the angel's hand was a manifestation of the wrath of God. The

[1] From a failure to observe the use of the participle in distinction from the preterite, and from a misinterpretation of the words of the angel of the Lord (ver. 32), " I have come out as an adversary, for the way leads headlong to destruction," which have been understood as implying that the angel meant to prohibit the seer from going, whereas he only intended to warn him of the destruction towards which he was going, the critics have invented a contradiction between the account of the speaking ass (vers. 22–35) and the preceding part of the history. And in consequence of this, A. G. Hoffmann and others have pronounced the section from ver. 22 to ver. 35 to be a later interpolation ; whilst Baur, on the other hand (in his Geschichte d. alttestl. Weissagung), regards the account of the ass as the original form of the narrative, and the preceding portion as a composition of the Jehovist. But there is no " contradiction " or " evident incongruity," unless we suppose that the only reason for the appearance of the angel of the Lord was, that he might once more forbid the seer to go, and then give him permission, with a certain limitation. The other differences, which E. v. Ortenberg adduces, are involved in the very nature of the case. The manifestation of God, in the form of the Angel of Jehovah, was necessarily different in its character from a direct spiritual revelation of the divine will. And lastly, the difference in the expressions used to signify " three times," in chap. xxii. 28, 32, 33, and chap. xxiv. 10, etc., prove nothing more than that king Balak did not mould his style of speaking according to that of the ass.

[2] " To the great disgrace of the prophet, the glory of the angel was first of all apparent to the ass. . . . He had been boasting before this of extraordinary

ass turned from the road into the field before the threatening sight, and was smitten by Balaam in consequence to turn her or guide her back into the road.—Vers. 24, 25. The angel then stationed himself in a pass of the vineyards where walls (גְּדֵר, vineyard walls, Isa. v. 5) were on both sides, so that the animal, terrified by the angel, pressed against the wall, and squeezed Balaam's foot against the wall, for which Balaam smote her again.—Vers. 26, 27. The angel moved still farther, and stationed himself in front of him, in so narrow a pass, that there was no room to move either to the right or to the left. As the ass could neither turn aside nor go past this time, she threw herself down. Balaam was still more enraged at this, and smote her with the stick (בַּמַּקֵּל, which he carried; see Gen. xxxviii. 18).—Vers. 28 sqq. " *Then Jehovah opened the mouth of the ass, and she said to Balaam, What have I done to thee, that thou hast smitten me now three times?* " But Balaam, enraged at the refractoriness of his ass, replied, " *Because thou hast played me ill* (הִתְעַלַּל, see Ex. x. 2): *if there were only a sword in my hand, verily I should now have killed thee.*" But the ass replied, that she had been ridden by him from a long time back, and had never been accustomed to act in this way towards him. These words of the irrational beast, the truth of which Balaam was obliged to admit, made an impression upon him, and awakened him out of his blindness, so that God could now open his eyes, and he saw the angel of the Lord.

In this miraculous occurrence, which scoffers at the Bible constantly bring forward as a weapon of attack upon the truth of the word of God, the circumstance that the ass perceived the appearance of the angel of the Lord sooner than Balaam did, does not present the slightest difficulty; for it is a well-known fact, that irrational animals have a much keener instinctive presentiment of many natural phenomena, such as earthquakes, storms, etc., than man has with the five senses of his mind. And the fact is equally undeniable, that many animals, *e.g.* horses and cows, see the so-called second sight, and are terrified in consequence.[1] The rock of offence in this narrative is to be found in the rational words of an

visions, and now what was visible to the eyes of a beast was invisible to him. Whence came this blindness, but from the avarice by which he had been so stupefied, that he preferred filthy lucre to the holy calling of God?" (*Calvin.*)

[1] In support of this we will simply cite the following from the remarks made by *Martin* upon this subject, and quoted by *Hengstenberg* in his Balaam (p. 385), from *Passavant's* work on animal magnetism and clairvoyance: " That horses see it (the second sight), is also evident from their violent and rapid snorting,

irrational and speechless ass. It is true, that in the actual meaning of the words there is nothing beyond the sensations and feelings to which animals constantly give utterance in gestures and inarticulate sounds, when subjected to cruel treatment. But in this instance the feelings were expressed in the rational words of human language, which an animal does not possess; and hence the question arises, Are we to understand this miracle as being a purely internal fact of an ecstatic nature, or a fact that actually came under the cognizance of the senses? If we examine the arguments which *Hengstenberg* has adduced in favour of the former, and *Kurtz* in support of the latter, there is nothing at all in the circumstance, that the narrative itself says nothing about Balaam being in an ecstasy, nor in the statement that " Jehovah opened the mouth of the ass," nor lastly, in the words of 2 Pet. ii. 16, " The dumb ass, speaking with man's voice, forbade the madness of the prophet," to furnish conclusive, not to say irresistible, proofs of the assertion, that " as the ass was corporeally and externally visible, its speaking must have been externally and corporeally audible" (*Kurtz*). All that is contained in the two scriptural testimonies is, that the ass spoke in a way that was perceptible to Balaam, and that this speaking was effected by Jehovah as something altogether extraordinary. But whether Balaam heard the words of the animal with the outward, *i.e.* the bodily ear, or with an inward spiritual ear, is not decided by them. On the other hand, neither the fact that Balaam expressed no astonishment at the ass speaking, nor the circumstance that Balaam's companions—viz. his two servants (ver. 22) and the Moabitish messengers, who were also present, according to ver. 35— did not see the angel or hear the ass speaking, leads with certainty to the conclusion, that the whole affair must have been a purely internal one, which Balaam alone experienced in a state of ecstasy, since *argumenta e silentio* confessedly prove but very little. With regard to Balaam, we may say with *Augustine* (*quæst.* 50 in Num.), " he was so carried away by his cupidity, that he was not terrified by this marvellous miracle, and replied just as if he had been speaking to a man, when God, although He did not change the nature of the ass into that of a rational being, made it give utterance to whatever He pleased, for the purpose of restraining his

when their rider has had a vision of any kind either by day or night. And in the case of the horse it may also be observed, that it will refuse to go any farther in the same road until a circuitous course has been taken, and even then it is quite in a sweat."

madness." But with regard to the Moabitish messengers, it is very doubtful whether they were eye-witnesses and auditors of the affair. It is quite possible that they had gone some distance in advance, or were some distance behind, when Balaam had the vision. On the other hand, there was no necessity to mention particularly that they saw the appearance of the angel, and heard the speaking of the animal, as this circumstance was not of the least importance in connection with the main purpose of the narrative. And still less can it be said that " the ass's speaking, if transferred to the sphere of outward reality, would obviously break through the eternal boundary-line which has been drawn in Gen. i. between the human and the animal world." The only thing that would have broken through this boundary, would have been for the words of the ass to have surpassed the feelings and sensations of an animal; that is to say, for the ass to have given utterance to truths that were essentially human, and only comprehensible by human reason. Now that was not the case. All that the ass said was quite within the sphere of the psychical life of an animal.

The true explanation lies between the notion that the whole occurrence was purely internal, and consisted exclusively in ecstasy brought by God upon Balaam, and the grossly realistic reduction of the whole affair into the sphere of the senses and the outward material world. The angel who met the soothsayer in the road, as he was riding upon his ass, and who was seen at once by the ass, though he was not seen by Balaam till Jehovah had opened his eyes, did really appear upon the road, in the outward world of the senses. But the form in which he appeared was not a grossly sensuous or material form, like the bodily frame of an ordinary visible being; for in that case Balaam would inevitably have seen him, when his beast became alarmed and restive again and again and refused to go forward, since it is not stated anywhere that God had smitten him with blindness, like the men of Sodom (Gen. xix. 11), or the people in 2 Kings vi. 18. It rather resembled the appearance of a spirit, which cannot be seen by every one who has healthy bodily eyes, but only by those who have their senses awakened for visions from the spirit-world. Thus, for example, the men who went to Damascus with Paul, saw no one, when the Lord appeared to him in a miraculous light from heaven, and spoke to him, although they also heard the voice[1] (Acts ix. 7). Balaam

[1] Or, strictly speaking, they saw the *light* (Acts xxii. 9), but saw *no man* (Acts ix. 7); and they heard the *sound* (τῆς φωνῆς, the voice or noise generally,

wanted the spiritual sense to discern the angel of the Lord, because
his spirit's eye was blinded by his thirst for wealth and honour.
This blindness increased to such an extent, with the inward excitement caused by the repeated insubordination of his beast, that he
lost all self-control. As the ass had never been so restive before,
if he had only been calm and thoughtful himself, he would have
looked about to discover the cause of this remarkable change, and
would then, no doubt, have discovered the presence of the angel.
But as he lost all his thoughtfulness, God was obliged to open the
mouth of the dumb and irrational animal, to show a seer by profession his own blindness. " He might have reproved him by the
words of the angel; but because the rebuke would not have been
sufficiently severe without some deep humiliation, He made the
beast his teacher" (*Calvin*). The ass's speaking was produced by
the omnipotence of God; but it is impossible to decide whether the
modulation was miraculously communicated to the animal's voice,
so that it actually gave utterance to the human words which fell
upon Balaam's ears (*Kurtz*), or whether the cries of the animal
were formed into rational discourse in Balaam's soul, by the direct
operation of God, so that he alone heard and understood the speech
of the animal, whereas the servants who were present heard nothing
more than unintelligible cries.[1] In either case Balaam received a
deeply humiliating admonition from the mouth of the irrational beast,
and that not only to put him to shame, but also to call him to his
senses, and render him capable of hearing the voice of God. The
seer, who prided himself upon having eyes for divine revelations,
was so blind, that he could not discern the appearance of the angel,
which even the irrational beast had been able to see.[2] By this he
was taught, that even a beast is more capable of discerning things
from the higher world, than a man blinded by sinful desires. It
was not till after this humiliation that God opened his eyes, so that

Acts ix. 7), but not the words (τὴν φωνὴν τοῦ λαλοῦντός μοι, the voice or articulate words of the person speaking, Acts xxii. 9). The construction of ἀκούω,
with the genitive in the one case and the accusative in the other, is evidently
intended to convey this distinct and distinctive meaning.—Tr.

[1] See the analogous case mentioned in John xii. 28; 29, of the voice which
came to Jesus from the skies, when some of the people who were standing by
said that it only thundered, whilst others said an angel spoke to Him.

[2] God made use of the voice of an ass, both because it was fitting that a
brutish mind should be taught by a brute, and also, as *Nyssenus* says, to instruct
and chastise the vanity of the augur (Balaam), who was accustomed to observe
the meaning of the braying of the ass and the chirping of birds (*C. a. Lap.*).

he saw the angel of the Lord with a drawn sword standing in his
road, and fell upon his face before this fearful sight.

Vers. 32–34. To humble him deeply and inwardly, the Lord
held up before him the injustice of his cruel treatment of the ass,
and told him at the same time that it had saved his life by turning
out of the way. " *I have come out*," said the angel of the Lord,
" *as an adversary; for the way leads headlong into destruction before
me;*" *i.e.* the way which thou art going is leading thee, in my eyes,
in my view, into destruction. יָרַט, to plunge, *sc.* into destruction,
both here, and also in Job xvi. 11, the only other passage in which
it occurs.—Ver. 33. The angel of the Lord sought to preserve
Balaam from the destruction which threatened him, by standing
in his way; but he did not see him, though his ass did. אוּלַי
נָטְתָה וגו׳, " *perhaps it turned out before me; for otherwise I should
surely have killed thee, and let her live.*" The first clause is to be
regarded, as *Hengstenberg* supposes, as an aposiopesis. The angel
does not state positively what was the reason why perhaps the ass
had turned out of the way: he merely hints at it lightly, and leaves
it to Balaam to gather from the hint, that the faithful animal had
turned away from affection to its master, with a dim foreboding of
the danger which threatened him, and yet for that very reason, as
it were as a reward for its service of love, had been ill-treated by
him. The traditional rendering, " if the ass had not turned aside,
surely," etc., cannot be defended according to the rules of the language; and there is not sufficient ground for any such alteration of
the text as *Knobel* suggests, viz. into לוּלֵי. These words made an
impression, and Balaam made this acknowledgment (ver. 34) : " *I
have sinned, for I knew not that thou stoodest in the way against me;
and now, if it displease thee, I will get me back again.*" The angel
of the Lord replied, however (ver. 35) : " *Go with the men; but
only the word that I shall speak unto thee, that shalt thou speak.*"
This was sufficient to show him, that it was not the journey in itself
that was displeasing to God, but the feelings and intentions with
which he had entered upon it. The whole procedure was intended
to sharpen his conscience and sober his mind, that he might pay
attention to the word which the Lord would speak to him. At the
same time the impression which the appearance and words of the
angel of the Lord made upon his heart, enveloped in mist as it was
by the thirst for gold and honour, was not a deep one, nor one that
led him to a thorough knowledge of his own heart; otherwise,
after such a warning, he would never have continued his journey.

Vers. 36-41. RECEPTION OF BALAAM BY THE KING OF THE MOABITES.—Vers. 36, 37. As soon as Balak heard of Balaam's coming, he went to meet him at a city on the border of the Arnon, which flowed at the extreme (north) boundary (of the Moabitish territory), viz. at *Areopolis* (see at chap. xxi. 15), probably the capital of the kingdom at one time, but now reduced to a frontier town, since Sihon the Amorite had taken all the land as far as the Arnon; whilst *Rabbah*, which was farther south, had been selected as the residence of the king. By coming as far as the frontier of his kingdom to meet the celebrated soothsayer, Balak intended to do him special honour. But he could not help receiving him with a gentle reproof for not having come at his first invitation, as if he, the king, had not been in a condition to honour him according to his merits.—Ver. 38. But Balaam, being still mindful of the warning which he had just received from God, replied, " *Lo, I am come unto thee now : have I then any power to speak anything* (sc. of my own accord) ? *The word which God puts into my mouth, that will I speak.*" With this reply he sought, at the very outset, to soften down the expectations of Balak, inasmuch as he concluded at once that his coming was a proof of his willingness to curse (*Hengstenberg*). As a matter of fact, Balaam did not say anything different to the king from what he had explained to his messengers at the very first (cf. ver. 18). But just as he had not told them the whole truth, but had concealed the fact that Jehovah, his God, had forbidden the journey at first, on the ground that he was not to curse the nation that was blessed (ver. 12), so he could not address the king in open, unambiguous words.—Vers. 39, 40. He then went with Balak to *Kirjath-Chuzoth*, where the king had oxen and sheep slaughtered in sacrifice, and sent flesh to Balaam as well as to the princes that were with him for a sacrificial meal, to do honour to the soothsayer thereby. The sacrifices were not so much thank-offerings for Balaam's happy arrival, as supplicatory offerings for the success of the undertaking before them. " This is evident," as *Hengstenberg* correctly observes, " from the place and time of their presentation ; for the place was not that where Balak first met with Balaam, and they were only presented on the eve of the great event." Moreover, they were offered unquestionably not to the Moabitish idols, from which Balak expected no help, but to Jehovah, whom Balak wished to draw away, in connection with Balaam, from His own people (Israel), that he might secure His favour to the Moabites. The situation of *Kirjath-Chuzoth*, which is only men-

tioned here, cannot be determined with absolute certainty. As
Balak went with Balaam to Bamoth-Baal on the morning following
the sacrificial meal, which was celebrated there, Kirjath-Chuzoth
cannot have been very far distant. *Knobel* conjectures, with some
probability, that it may have been the same as *Kerioth* (Jer. xlviii.
24), *i.e. Kereïjat* or *Körriat*, at the foot of Jebel Attarus, at the
top of which Bamoth-Baal was situated (see at chap. xxi. 19).—
Ver. 41. But Balak conducted the soothsayer to *Bamoth-Baal*, not
because it was consecrated to Baal, but because it was the first
height on the way to the steppes of Moab, from which they could
see the camp of Israel, or at all events, " the end of the people,"
i.e. the outermost portion of the camp. For " Balak started with
the supposition, that Balaam must necessarily have the Israelites in
view if his curse was to take effect" (*Hengstenberg*).

Chap. xxiii. 1–24. BALAAM'S FIRST WORDS.—Vers. 1–3. *Preparations* for the first act, which was performed at Bamoth-Baal.
At Balaam's command Balak built seven altars, and then selected
seven bullocks and seven rams, which they immediately sacrificed,
namely, one bullock and one ram upon each altar. The nations of
antiquity generally accompanied all their more important undertakings with sacrifices, to make sure of the protection and help of
the gods ; but this was especially the case with their ceremonies of
adjuration. According to *Diod. Sic.* ii. 29, the Chaldeans sought to
avert calamity and secure prosperity by sacrifices and adjurations.
The same thing is also related of other nations (see *Hengstenberg*,
Balaam, p. 392). Accordingly, Balaam also did everything that
appeared necessary, according to his own religious notions, to ensure
the success of Balak's undertaking, and bring about the desired
result. The erection of *seven* altars, and the sacrifice of *seven*
animals of each kind, are to be explained from the sacredness acquired by this number, through the creation of the world in seven
days, as being the stamp of work that was well-pleasing to God.
The sacrifices were burnt-offerings, and were offered by themselves
to Jehovah, whom Balaam acknowledged as his God.—Vers. 3, 4.
After the offering of the sacrifices, Balaam directed the king to
stand by his burnt-offering, *i.e.* by the sacrifices that had been
offered for him upon the seven altars, that he might go out for
auguries. The meaning of the words, " *I will go, peradventure
Jehovah will come to meet me,*" is apparent from chap. xxiv. 1 : and
" *he went no more to meet with the auguries*" (נְחָשִׁים, see at Lev. xix.

26). Balaam went out to look for a manifestation of Jehovah in the significant phenomena of nature. The word which Jehovah should show to him, he would report to Balak. We have here what is just as characteristic in relation to Balaam's religious stand-point, as it is significant in its bearing upon the genuine historical character of the narrative, namely, an admixture of the religious ideas of both the Israelites and the heathen, inasmuch as Balaam hoped to receive or discover, in the phenomena of nature, a revelation from Jehovah. Because heathenism had no " sure word of prophecy," it sought to discover the will and counsel of God, which are displayed in the events of human history, through various signs that were discernible in natural phenomena, or, as *Chrysippus* the Stoic expresses it in *Cicero de divin.* ii. 63, " *Signa quæ a Diis hominibus portendantur.*"[1] To look for a word of Jehovah in this way, Balaam betook himself to a " *bald height.*" This is the only meaning of שְׁפִי, from שָׁפָה, to rub, to scrape, to make bare, which is supported by the usage of the language ; it is also in perfect harmony with the context, as the heathen augurs were always accustomed to select elevated places for their auspices, with an extensive prospect, especially the towering and barren summits of mountains that were rarely visited by men (see *Hengstenberg, ut sup.*). *Ewald,* however, proposes the meaning " alone," or " to spy," for which there is not the slightest grammatical foundation.—Ver. 4. " *And God came to meet Balaam,*" who thought it necessary, as a true *hariolus,* to call the attention of God to the altars which had been built for Him, and the sacrifices that had been offered upon them. And God made known His will to him, though not in a natural sign of doubtful signification. He put a very distinct and unmistakeable word into his mouth, and commanded him to make it known to the king.

---

[1] See the remarks of *Nägelsbach* and *Hartung* on the nature of the heathen auspices, in *Hengstenberg's* Balaam and his Prophecies (pp. 396–7). *Hartung* observes, for example : " As the gods did not live outside the world, or separated from it, but the things of time and space were filled with their essence, it followed, as a matter of course, that the signs of their presence were sought and seen in all the visible and audible occurrences of nature, whether animate or inanimate. Hence all the phenomena which affected the senses, either in the elements or in the various creatures, whether sounds or movements, natural productions or events, of a mechanical or physical, or voluntary or involuntary kind, might serve as the media of revelation." And again (p. 397) : " The sign in itself is useless, if it be not observed. It was therefore necessary that man and God should come to meet one another, and that the sign should not merely be given, but should also be received."

Vers. 7–10. Balaam's *first* saying.—Having come back to the burnt-offering, Balaam commenced his utterance before the king and the assembled princes. מָשָׁל, *lit.* a simile, then a proverb, because the latter consists of comparisons and figures, and lastly a sentence or saying. The application of this term to the announcements made by Balaam (vers. 7, 18, xxiv. 3, 15, 20), whereas it is never used of the prophecies of the true prophets of Jehovah, but only of certain songs and similes inserted in them (cf. Isa. xiv. 4; Ezek. xvii. 2, xxiv. 3; Micah ii. 4), is to be accounted for not merely from the poetic form of Balaam's utterances, the predominance of poetical imagery, the sustained *parallelism*, the construction of the whole discourse in brief pointed sentences, and other peculiarities of poetic language (*e.g.* בְּנוֹ, chap. xxiv. 3, 15), but it points at the same time to the difference which actually exists between these utterances and the predictions of the true prophets. The latter are orations addressed to the congregation, which deduce from the general and peculiar relation of Israel to the Lord and to His law, the conduct of the Lord towards His people either in their own or in future times, proclaiming judgment upon the ungodly and salvation to the righteous. "Balaam's mental eye," on the contrary, as *Hengstenberg* correctly observes, "was simply fixed upon what he saw; and this he reproduced without any regard to the impression that it was intended to make upon those who heard it." But the very first utterance was of such a character as to deprive Balak of all hope that his wishes would be fulfilled.—Ver. 7. "*Balak, the king of Moab, fetches me from Aram, from the mountains of the East*," *i.e.* of Mesopotamia, which was described, as far back as Gen. xxix. 1, as the land of the sons of the East (cf. chap. xxii. 5). Balaam mentions the mountains of his home in contradistinction to the mountains of the land of the Moabites upon which he was then standing. "*Come, curse me Jacob, and come threaten Israel.*" Balak had sent for him for this purpose (see chap. xxii. 11, 17). זָעֲמָה, for זַעֲמָה, imperative (see *Ewald*, § 228, *b.*). זָעַם, to be angry, here to give utterance to the wrath of God, synonymous with נָקַב or קָבַב, to curse. *Jacob :* a poetical name for the nation, equivalent to *Israel.*—Ver. 8. "*How shall I curse whom God does not curse, and how threaten whom Jehovah does not threaten?*" Balak imagined, like all the heathen, that Balaam, as a *goetes* and magician, could distribute blessings and curses according to his own will, and put such constraint upon his God as to make Him subservient to his own will (see at chap. xxii. 6). The seer opposes this delusion:

The God of Israel does not curse His people, and therefore His servant cannot curse them. The following verses (vers. 9 and 10) give the reason why : " *For from the top of the rocks I see him, and from the hills I behold him. Lo, it is a people that dwelleth apart, and is not numbered among the heathen. Who determines the dust of Jacob, and in number the fourth part of Israel ? Let my soul die the death of the righteous, and my end be like his !* " There were two reasons which rendered it impossible for Balaam to curse Israel : (1) Because they were a people both outwardly and inwardly different from other nations, and (2) because they were a people richly blessed and highly favoured by God. From the top of the mountains Balaam looked down upon the people of Israel. The outward and earthly height upon which he stood was the substratum of the spiritual height upon which the Spirit of God had placed him, and had so enlightened his mental sight, that he was able to discern all the peculiarities and the true nature of Israel. In this respect the first thing that met his view was the fact that this people dwelt alone. Dwelling alone does not denote a quiet and safe retirement, as many commentators have inferred from Deut. xxxiii. 28, Jer. xlix. 31, and Micah vii. 14 ; but, according to the parallel clause, " it is not reckoned among the nations," it expresses the separation of Israel from the rest of the nations. This separation was manifested outwardly to the seer's eye in the fact that " the host of Israel dwelt by itself in a separate encampment upon the plain. In this his spirit discerned the inward and essential separation of Israel from all the heathen" (*Baumgarten*). This outward "dwelling alone" was a symbol of their inward separation from the heathen world, by virtue of which Israel was not only saved from the fate of the heathen world, but could not be overcome by the heathen ; of course only so long as they themselves should inwardly maintain this separation from the heathen, and faithfully continue in covenant with the Lord their God, who had separated them from among the nations to be His own possession. As soon as Israel lost itself in heathen ways, it also lost its own external independence. This rule applies to the Israel of the New Testament as well as the Israel of the Old, to the congregation or Church of God of all ages. לֹא יִתְחַשָּׁב, " *it does not reckon itself among the heathen nations,*" *i.e.* it does not share the lot of the other nations, because it has a different God and protector from the heathen (cf. Deut. iv. 8, xxxiii. 29). The truth of this has been so marvellously realized in the history of the Israelites, notwithstanding their

falling short of the idea of their divine calling, " that whereas all the
mightier kingdoms of the ancient world, Egypt, Assyria, Babel,
etc., have perished without a trace, Israel, after being rescued from
so many dangers which threatened utter destruction under the Old
Testament, still flourishes in the Church of the New Testament,
and continues also to exist in that part which, though rejected
now, is destined one day to be restored" (*Hengstenberg*).

In this state of separation from the other nations, Israel rejoiced
in the blessing of its God, which was already visible in the innumerable multitude into which it had grown. " *Who has ever determined
the dust of Jacob?*" As the dust cannot be numbered, so is the
multitude of Israel innumerable. These words point back to the
promise in Gen. xiii. 16, and applied quite as much to the existing
state as to the future of Israel. The beginning of the miraculous
fulfilment of the promise given to the patriarchs of an innumerable
posterity, was already before their eyes (cf. Deut. x. 22). Even
now the fourth part of Israel is not to be reckoned. Balaam speaks
of the fourth part with reference to the division of the nation into
four camps (chap. ii.), of which he could see only one from his
point of view (chap. xxii. 41), and therefore only the fourth part
of the nation. מִסְפָּר is an accusative of definition, and the subject
and verb are to be repeated from the first clause ; so that there is no
necessity to alter מִסְפָּר into מִי סָפַר.—But Israel was not only visibly
blessed by God with an innumerable increase ; it was also inwardly
exalted into a people of יְשָׁרִים, righteous or honourable men. The
predicate יְשָׁרִים is applied to Israel on account of its divine calling,
because it had a God who was just and right, a God of truth and
without iniquity (Deut. xxxii. 4), or because the God of Israel was
holy, and sanctified His people (Lev. xx. 7, 8 ; Ex. xxxi. 13) and
made them into a *Jeshurun* (Deut. xxxii. 15, xxxiii. 5, 26). Righteousness, probity, is the idea and destination of this people, which
has never entirely lost it, though it has never fully realized it.
Even in times of general apostasy from the Lord, there was always
an ἐκλογή in the nation, of which probity and righteousness could
truly be predicated (cf. 1 Kings xix. 18). The righteousness of
the Israelites was " a product of the institutions which God had
established among them, of the revelation of His holy will which
He had given them in His law, of the forgiveness of sins which He
had linked on to the offering of sacrifices, and of the communication of His Spirit, which was ever living and at work in His Church,
and in it alone" (*Hengstenberg*). Such a people Balaam could not

curse; he could only wish that the end of his own life might resemble the end of these righteous men. Death is introduced here
as the end and completion of life. "Balaam desires for himself
the entire, full, indestructible, and inalienable blessedness of the
Israelite, of which death is both the close and completion, and also
the seal and attestation" (*Kurtz*). This desire did not involve the
certain hope of a blessed life beyond the grave, which the Israelites
themselves did not then possess; it simply expressed the thought
that the death of a pious Israelite was a desirable good. And this
it was, whether viewed in the light of the past, the present, or the
future. In the hour of death the pious Israelite could look back
with blessed satisfaction to a long life, rich "in traces of the beneficent, forgiving, delivering, and saving grace of God;" he could
comfort himself with the delightful hope of living on in his children
and his children's children, and in them of participating in the
future fulfilment of the divine promises of grace; and lastly, when
dying in possession of the love and grace of God, he could depart
hence with the joyful confidence of being gathered to his fathers
in Sheol (Gen. xxv. 8).

Vers. 11–17. Balak reproached Balaam for this utterance, which
announced blessings to the Israelites instead of curses. But he met
his reproaches with the remark, that he was bound by the command
of Jehovah. The infinitive absolute, בָּרֵךְ, after the finite verb, expresses the fact that Balaam had continued to give utterance to nothing but blessings. שָׁמַר לְדַבֵּר, to observe to speak; שָׁמַר, to notice
carefully, as in Deut. v. 1, 29, etc. But Balak thought that the reason
might be found in the unfavourable locality; he therefore led the
seer to "*the field of the watchers, upon the top of Pisgah,*" whence he
could see the whole of the people of Israel. The words אֲשֶׁר תִּרְאֶנּוּ וגו׳
(ver. 13) are to be rendered, "*whence thou wilt see it* (Israel); *thou
seest only the end of it, but not the whole of it*" (*sc.* here upon Bamoth-
Baal). This is required by a comparison of the verse before us with
chap. xxii. 41, where it is most unquestionably stated, that upon the
top of Bamoth-Baal Balaam only saw "the end of the people." For
this reason Balak regarded that place as unfavourable, and wished
to lead the seer to a place from which he could see the people,
without any limitation whatever. Consequently, notwithstanding
the omission of כִּי (for), the words אֶפֶס קָצֵהוּ can only be intended
to assign the reason why Balak supposed the first utterances of
Balaam to have been unfavourable. קְצֵה הָעָם = קָצֵהוּ, the end of the
people (chap. xxii. 41), cannot possibly signify the whole nation,

or, as *Marck, de Geer, Gesenius,* and *Kurtz* suppose, " the people from one end to the other," in which case קְצֵה הָעָם (the end of the people) would signify the very opposite of קָצֵהוּ (the end of it) ; for קְצֵה הָעָם is not interchangeable, or to be identified, with כָּל־הָעָם מִקָּצֶה (Gen. xix. 4), " the whole people, from the end or extremity of it," or from its last man ; in other words, " to the very last man." Still less does אֶפֶס קְצֵה הָעָם signify " the uttermost end of the whole people, the end of the entire people," notwithstanding the fact that *Kurtz* regards the expression, " the end of the end of the people," as an intolerable tautology. קָבְנוֹ, imperative with *nun epenth.,* from קָבַב. The " field of the watchers," or " spies (*zophim*), upon the top of *Pisgah*," corresponds, no doubt, to " the field of Moab, upon the top of *Pisgah*," on the west of Heshbon (see at chap. xxi. 20). Mount *Nebo,* from which Moses surveyed the land of Canaan in all its length and breadth, was one summit, and possibly *the* summit of Pisgah (see Deut. iii. 27, xxxiv. 1). The field of the spies was very probably a tract of table-land upon Nebo ; and so called either because watchers were stationed there in times of disturbance, to keep a look-out all round, or possibly because it was a place where augurs made their observations of the heavens and of birds (*Knobel*). The locality has not been thoroughly explored by travellers ; but from the spot alluded to, it must have been possible to overlook a very large portion of the *Arboth Moab.* Still farther to the north, and nearer to the camp of the Israelites in these Arboth, was the summit of *Peor,* to which Balak afterwards conducted Balaam (ver. 28), and where he not only saw the whole of the people, but could see distinctly the camps of the different tribes (chap. xxiv. 2). —Vers. 14*b*–17. Upon Pisgah, Balak and Balaam made the same preparations for a fresh revelation from God as upon Bamoth-Baal (vers. 1–6). כֹּה in ver. 15 does not mean " here" or " yonder," but " so" or " thus," as in every other case. The thought is this : " Do thou stay (*sc.* as thou art), and I will go and meet thus" (*sc.* in the manner required). אִקָּרֶה ' (I will go and meet) is a technical term here for going out for auguries (chap. xxiv. 1), or for a divine revelation.

Vers. 18–24. The *second* saying.—" *Up, Balak, and hear ! Hearken to me, son of Zippor !* " קוּם, " stand up," is a call to mental elevation, to the perception of the word of God ; for Balak was standing by his sacrifice (ver. 17). הַאֲזִין with עַד, as in Job xxxii. 11, signifies a hearing which presses forward to the speaker, *i.e.* in keen and minute attention (*Hengstenberg*). בְּנוֹ, with the antiquated union vowel for בֵּן ; see at Gen. i. 24.—Ver. 19. " *God is not a man, that He should lie ; nor a son of man, that He should repent : hath He said, and should He not do it? and spoken, and should not carry it out ?"*—Ver. 20. *" Behold, I have received to bless : and He hath blessed ; and I cannot turn it."* Balaam meets Balak's expectation that he will take back the blessing that he has uttered, with the declaration, that God does not alter His purposes like changeable and fickle men, but keeps His word unalterably, and carries it into execution. The unchangeableness of the divine purposes is a necessary consequence of the unchangeableness of the divine nature. With regard to His own counsels, God repents of nothing ; but this does not prevent the repentance of God, understood as an anthropopathic expression, denoting the pain experienced by the love of God, on account of the destruction of its creatures (see at Gen. vi. 6, and Ex. xxxii. 14). The ה before הוא (ver. 19) is the interrogative ה (see Ges. § 100, 4). The two clauses of ver. 19*b*, " Hath He spoken," etc., taken by themselves, are no doubt of universal application ; but taken in connection with the context, they relate specially to what God had spoken through Balaam, in his first utterance with reference to Israel, as we may see from the more precise explanation in ver. 20, " Behold, I have received to bless" (לָקַח, taken, accepted), etc. הֵשִׁיב, to lead back, to make a thing retrograde (Isa. xliii. 13). Samuel afterwards refused Saul's request in these words of Balaam (ver. 19*a*), when he entreated him to revoke his rejection on the part of God (1 Sam. xv. 29).—Ver. 21. After this decided reversal of Balak's expectations, Balaam carried out still more fully the blessing which had been only briefly indicated in his first utterance. *" He beholds not wickedness in Jacob, and sees not suffering in Israel : Jehovah his God is with him, and the shout* (jubilation) *of a king in the midst of him."* The subject in the first sentence is God (see Hab. i. 3, 13). God sees not אָוֶן, worthlessness, wickedness, and עָמָל, tribulation, misery, as the consequence of sin, and therefore discovers no reason for cursing the nation. That this applied to the people solely by virtue of their calling as the holy nation of Jehovah, and consequently that there is no denial of the sin of individuals, is evident from the second hemistich, which expresses the thought of the first in a positive form : so that the words, " Jehovah his God is with him," correspond to the words, " He beholds not wickedness ;" and " the shout of a king in the midst of it," to His not seeing suffering. Israel therefore rejoiced in the blessing of God only so long as it remained faithful to the idea of its divine calling, and continued in

covenant fellowship with the Lord. So long the power of the world
could do it no harm.   The " shout of a king" in Israel is the rejoicing of Israel at the fact that Jehovah dwells and rules as King
in the midst of it (cf. Ex. xv. 18 ; Deut. xxxiii. 5).   Jehovah had
manifested Himself as King, by leading them out of Egypt.—
Ver. 22. " *God brings them out of Egypt ; his strength is like that of
a buffalo.*" אֵל is God as the strong, or mighty one. The participle
מוֹצִיאָם is not used for the preterite, but designates the leading out
as still going on, and lasting till the introduction into Canaan.
The plural suffix, ◌ָ֫ם, is used *ad sensum*, with reference to Israel
as a people.   Because God leads them, they go forward with the
strength of a buffalo. תּוֹעֲפֹת, from יָעֵף, to weary, signifies that
which causes weariness, exertion, the putting forth of power; hence
the fulness of strength, ability to make or bear exertions.   רְאֵם is
the buffalo or wild ox, an indomitable animal, which is especially
fearful on account of its horns (Job xxxix. 9–11; Deut. xxxiii. 17;
Ps. xxii. 22).—Ver. 23. The fellowship of its God, in which Israel
rejoiced, and to which it owed its strength, was an actual truth.
" *For there is no augury in Jacob, and no divination in Israel.   At
the time it is spoken to Jacob, and to Israel what God doeth.*" כִּי does
not mean, " so that, as an introduction to the sequel," as *Knobel*
supposes, but " *for*," as a causal particle.   The fact that Israel was
not directed, like other nations, to the uncertain and deceitful in-
strumentality of augury and divination, but enjoyed in all its concerns the immediate revelation of its God, furnished the proof that
it had its God in the midst of it, and was guided and endowed with
power by God Himself. נַחַשׁ and קֶסֶם, οἰωνισμός and μαντεία,
augurium et divinatio (LXX., *Vulg.*), were the two means employed
by the heathen for looking into futurity.   The former (see at Lev.
xix. 26) was the unfolding of the future from signs in the phenomena of nature, and inexplicable occurrences in animal and human
life ; the latter, prophesying from a pretended or supposed revelation of the Deity within the human mind.   כָּעֵת, " according to the
time," *i.e.* at the right time, God revealed His acts, His counsel, and
His will to Israel in His word, which He had spoken at first to the
patriarchs, and afterwards through Moses and the prophets.   In
this He revealed to His people in truth, and in a way that could
not deceive, what the heathen attempted in vain to discover through
augury and divination (cf. Deut. xviii. 14–19).[1]—Ver. 24. Through

---

[1] " What is here affirmed of Israel, applies to the Church of all ages, and also
to every individual believer.   The Church of God knows from His word what

the power of its God, Israel was invincible, and would crush all its foes. *" Behold, it rises up, a people like the lioness, and lifts itself up like the lion. It lies not down till it eats dust, and drinks the blood of the slain."* What the patriarch Jacob prophesied of Judah, the ruler among his brethren, in Gen. xlix. 9, Balaam here transfers to the whole nation, to put to shame all the hopes indulged by the Moabitish king of the conquest and destruction of Israel.

Chap. xxiii. 25–xxiv. 25. BALAAM'S LAST WORDS.—Vers. 25–30. Balak was not deterred, however, from making another attempt. At first, indeed, he exclaimed in indignation at these second sayings of Balaam : *" Thou shalt neither curse it, nor even bless."* The double ‎גַּם‎ with ‎לֹא‎ signifies "neither—nor ;" and the rendering, " if thou do not curse it, thou shalt not bless it," must be rejected as untenable. In his vexation at the second failure, he did not want to hear anything more from Balaam. But when he replied again, that he had told him at the very outset that he could do nothing but what God should say to him (cf. chap. xxii. 38), he altered his mind, and resolved to conduct Balaam to another place with this hope : *" peradventure it will please God that thou mayest curse me them from thence."* *Clericus* observes upon this passage, " It was the opinion of the heathen, that what was not obtained through the first, second, or third victim, might nevertheless be secured through a fourth ;" and he adduces proofs from *Suetonius, Curtius, Gellius,* and others.—Ver. 29. He takes the seer *" to the top of Peor, which looks over the face of the desert"* (*Jeshimon :* see at chap. xxi. 20), and therefore was nearer to the camp of the Israelites. Mount *Peor* was one peak of the northern part of the mountains of Abarim by the town of *Beth-peor,* which afterwards belonged to the Reubenites (Josh. xiii. 20), and opposite to which the Israelites were encamped in the steppes of Moab (Deut. iii. 29, iv. 46). According to *Eusebius* (*Onom. s. v. Φογώρ*), *Peor* was above *Libias* (*i.e. Bethharam*),[1] which was situated in the valley of the Jordan ; and according to the account given under

God does, and what it has to do in consequence. The wisdom of this world resembles augury and divination. The Church of God, which is in possession of His word, has no need of it, and it only leads its followers to destruction, from inability to discern the will of God. To discover this with certainty, is the great privilege of the Church of God" (*Hengstenberg*).

[1] Ὑπέρκειται δὲ τῆς νῦν Λιβιάδος καλουμένης. *Jerome* has *" in supercilio Libiados."*

Araboth Moab,[1] it was close by the Arboth Moab, opposite to Jericho, on the way from Libias to Heshbon. *Peor* was about seven Roman miles from Heshbon, according to the account given *s. v. Danaba;* and *Beth-peor* (*s. v. Bethphozor*) was near Mount *Peor*, opposite to Jericho, six Roman miles higher than Libias, *i.e.* to the east of it (see *Hengstenberg*, Balaam, p. 538).—Vers. 29, 30. The sacrifices offered in preparation for this fresh transaction were the same as in the former cases (ver. 14, and vers. 1, 2).

Chap. xxiv. 1–9. The *third* saying.—Vers. 1 and 2. From the two revelations which he had received before, Balaam saw, *i.e.* perceived, that it pleased Jehovah to bless Israel. This induced him not to go out for auguries, as on the previous occasions. כְּפַעַם־בְּפַעַם, " as time after time," *i.e.* as at former times (chap. xxiii. 3 and 15). He therefore turned his face to the desert, *i.e.* to the steppes of Moab, where Israel was encamped (chap. xxii. 1). And when he lifted up his eyes, " *he saw Israel encamping according to its tribes; and the Spirit of God came over him.*" The impression made upon him by the sight of the tribes of Israel, served as the subjective preparation for the reception of the Spirit of God to inspire him. Of both the earlier utterances it is stated that " Jehovah put a word into his mouth" (chap. xxiii. 5 and 16); but of this third it is affirmed that "the Spirit of God came over him." The former were communicated to him, when he went out for a divine revelation, without his being thrown into an ecstatic state; he heard the voice of God within him telling him what he was to say. But this time, like the prophets in their prophesyings, he was placed by the Spirit of God in a state of ecstatic sight; so that, with his eyes closed as in clairvoyance, he saw the substance of the revelation from God with his inward mental eye, which had been opened by the Spirit of God. Thus not only does he himself describe his own condition in vers. 3 and 4, but his description is in harmony with the announcement itself, which is manifestly the result both in form and substance of the intuition effected within him by the Spirit of God.—Vers. 3 and 4 contain the preface to the prophecy : " *The divine saying of Balaam the son of Beor, the divine saying of the man with closed eye, the divine saying of the hearer of divine words, who sees the vision of the Almighty, falling down and with opened eyes.*" For the participial noun נְאֻם the meaning divine saying (*effatum*, not *inspiratum, Domini*) is undoubtedly established

---

[1] Καὶ ἔστι τόπος εἰς δεῦρο δεικνύμενος παρὰ τῷ ὄρει Φογὼρ, ὁ παράκειται ἀνιόντων ἀπὸ Λιβιάδος ἐπὶ Ἐσσεβοὺς (*i.e. Heshbon*) τῆς Ἀραβίας ἀντικρὺ Ἱεριχώ.

by the expression נְאֻם יְהֹוָה, which recurs in chap. xiv. 28 and Gen. xxii. 16, and is of constant use in the predictions of the prophets; and this applies even to the few passages where a human author is mentioned instead of Jehovah, such as vers. 3, 4, and 15, 16; also 2 Sam. xxiii. 1; Prov. xxx. 1; and Ps. xxxvi. 2, where a נְאֻם is ascribed to the personified wickedness. Hence, when Balaam calls the following prophecy a נְאֻם, this is done for the purpose of designating it as a divine revelation received from the Spirit of God. He had received it, and now proclaimed it as a man שְׁתֻם הָעָיִן, with closed eye. שְׁתַם does not mean to open, a meaning in support of which only one passage of the *Mishnah* can be adduced, but to close, like סְתַם in Dan. viii. 26, and שָׂתַם in Lam. iii. 8, with the שׁ softened into ס or שׂ (see *Roediger* in *Ges. thes.*, and *Dietrich's* Hebrew Lexicon). " Balaam describes himself as the man with closed eye with reference to his state of ecstasy, in which the closing of the outer senses went hand in hand with the opening of the inner" (*Hengstenberg*). The cessation of all perception by means of the outer senses, so far as self-conscious reflection is concerned, was a feature that was so common to both the vision and the dream, the two forms in which the prophetic gift manifested itself (chap. xii. 6), and followed from the very nature of the inward intuition. In the case of prophets whose spiritual life was far advanced, inspiration might take place without any closing of the outward senses. But upon men like Balaam, whose inner religious life was still very impure and undeveloped, the Spirit of God could only operate by closing their outward senses to impressions from the lower earthly world, and raising them up to visions of the higher and spiritual world.[1] What Balaam heard in this ecstatic condition was אִמְרֵי אֵל, the sayings of God, and what he saw מַחֲזֵה שַׁדַּי, the vision of the Almighty. The Spirit of God came upon him with such power that he fell down (נֹפֵל), like Saul in 1 Sam. xix. 24; not merely " prostrating himself with reverential awe at seeing and hearing the things of God" (*Knobel*), but thrown to the ground by the Spirit of God, who " came like an armed man upon the seer," and that in such a way that as he fell his (spirit's)

---

[1] Hence, as *Hengstenberg* observes (Balaam, p. 449), we have to picture Balaam as giving utterance to his prophecies with the eyes of his body closed; though we cannot argue from the fact of his being in this condition, that an Isaiah would be in precisely the same. Compare the instructive information concerning analogous phenomena in the sphere of natural *mantik* and ecstasy in *Hengstenberg* (pp. 449 sqq.), and *Tholuck's Propheten*, pp. 49 sqq.

eyes were opened. This introduction to his prophecy is not an utterance of boasting vanity; but, as *Calvin* correctly observes, "the whole preface has no other tendency than to prove that he was a true prophet of God, and had received the blessing which he uttered from a celestial oracle."

The blessing itself in vers. 5 sqq. contains two thoughts: (1) the glorious prosperity of Israel, and the exaltation of its kingdom (vers. 5–7); (2) the terrible power, so fatal to all its foes, of the people which was set to be a curse or a blessing to all the nations (vers. 8, 9).—Vers. 5–7. "*How beautiful are thy tents, O Jacob! thy dwellings, O Israel! Like valleys are they spread out, like gardens by the stream, like aloes which Jehovah has planted, like cedars by the waters. Water will flow out of his buckets, and his seed is by many waters. And loftier than Agag be his king, and his kingdom will be exalted.*" What Balaam had seen before his ecstasy with his bodily eyes, formed the substratum for his inward vision, in which the dwellings of Israel came before his mental eye adorned with the richest blessing from the Lord. The description starts, it is true, from the time then present, but it embraces the whole future of Israel. In the blessed land of Canaan the dwellings of Israel will spread out like valleys. נְחָלִים does not mean brooks here, but valleys watered by brooks. נָטָה, to extend oneself, to stretch or spread out far and wide. Yea, "like gardens by the stream," which are still more lovely than the grassy and flowery valleys with brooks. This thought is carried out still further in the two following figures. אֲהָלִים are aloe-trees, which grow in the East Indies, in Siam, in Cochin China, and upon the Moluccas, and from which the aloe-wood was obtained, that was so highly valued in the preparation of incense, on account of its fragrance. As the aloes were valued for their fragrant smell, so the cedars were valued on account of their lofty and luxuriant growth, and the durability of their wood. The predicate, "which Jehovah hath planted," corresponds, so far as the actual meaning is concerned, to עֲלֵי מַיִם, "by water;" for this was "an expression used to designate trees that, on account of their peculiar excellence, were superior to ordinary trees" (*Calvin;* cf. Ps. civ. 16).—Ver. 7. And not only its dwellings, but Israel itself would also prosper abundantly. It would have an abundance of water, that leading source of all blessing and prosperity in the burning East. The nation is personified as a man carrying two pails overflowing with water. דָּלְיָו is the dual דָּלְיַיִם. The dual is generally used in connection with objects

which are arranged in pairs, either naturally or artificially (Ges. §
88, 2). " *His seed* " (*i.e.* his posterity, not his sowing corn, the
introduction of which, in this connection, would, to say the least,
be very feeble here) " *is*," *i.e.* grows up, " *by many waters*," that is
to say, enjoys the richest blessings (comp. Deut. viii. 7 and xi. 10
with Isa. xliv. 4, lxv. 23). יָרֹם (optative), " *his king be high before*
(higher than) *Agag*." *Agag* (אֲגַג, the fiery) is not the proper name
of the Amalekite king defeated by Saul (1 Sam. xv. 8), but the
title (*nomen dignitatis*) of the Amalekite kings in general, just as
all the Egyptian kings had the common name of *Pharaoh*, and the
Philistine kings the name of *Abimelech*.[1]   The reason for mentioning the king of the Amalekites was, that he was selected as the im-
personation of the enmity of the world against the kingdom of God,
which culminated in the kings of the heathen; the Amalekites
having been the first heathen tribe that attacked the Israelites on
their journey to Canaan (Ex. xvii. 8).   The introduction of one
particular king would have been neither in keeping with the context, nor reconcilable with the general character of Balaam's utterances.   Both before and afterward, Balaam predicts in great general
outlines the good that would come to Israel; and how is it likely
that he would suddenly break off in the midst to compare the kingdom of Israel with the greatness of one particular king of the
Amalekites?   Even his fourth and last prophecy merely announces
in great general terms the destruction of the different nations that
rose up in hostility against Israel, without entering into special
details, which, like the conquest of the Amalekites by Saul, had no
material or permanent influence upon the attitude of the heathen
towards the people of God; for after the defeat inflicted upon this
tribe by Saul, they very speedily invaded the Israelitish territory
again, and proceeded to plunder and lay it waste in just the same

---

[1] See *Hengstenberg* (Dissertations, ii. 250; and Balaam, p. 458).   Even
Gesenius could not help expressing some doubt about there being any reference
in this prophecy to the event described in 1 Sam. xv. 8 sqq., " unless," he says,
" you suppose the name *Agag* to have been a name that was common to the
kings of the Amalekites " (*thes.* p. 19).   He also points to the name *Abimelech*,
of which he says (p. 9) : " It was the name of several kings in the land of the
Philistines, as of the king of Gerar in the times of Abraham (Gen. xx. 2, 3,
xxi. 22, 23), and of Isaac (Gen. xxvi. 1, 2), and also of the king of Gath in the
time of David (Ps. xxxiv. 1; coll. 1 Sam. xxi. 10, where the same king is
called *Achish*).   It seems to have been the common name and title of those
kings, as Pharaoh was of the early kings of Egypt, and Cæsar and Augustus of
the emperors of Rome."

manner as before (cf. 1 Sam. xxvii. 8, xxx. 1 sqq.; 2 Sam. viii. 12).[1] מַלְכּוֹ, his king, is not any one particular king of Israel, but quite generally the king whom the Israelites would afterwards receive. For מַלְכּוֹ is substantially the same as the parallel מַלְכֻתוֹ, the kingdom of Israel, which had already been promised to the patriarchs (Gen. xvii. 6, xxxv. 11), and in which the Israelites were first of all to obtain that full development of power which corresponded to its divine appointment; just as, in fact, the development of any people generally culminates in an organized kingdom.—The king of Israel, whose greatness was celebrated by Balaam, was therefore neither the Messiah exclusively, nor the earthly kingdom without the Messiah, but the kingdom of Israel that was established by David, and was exalted in the Messiah into an everlasting kingdom, the enemies of which would all be made its footstool (Ps. ii. and cx.).

In vers. 8 and 9, Balaam proclaims still further: " *God leads him out of Egypt ; his strength is as that of a buffalo : he will devour nations his enemies, and crush their bones, and dash them in pieces with his arrows. He has encamped, he lies down like a lion, and like a lioness : who can drive him up? Blessed be they who bless thee, and cursed they who curse thee!* " The fulness of power that dwelt in the people of Israel was apparent in the force and prowess with which their God brought them out of Egypt. This fact Balaam repeats from the previous saying (chap. xxiii. 22), for the purpose of linking on to it the still further announcement of the manner in which the power of the nation would show itself upon its foes in time to come. The words, " he will devour nations," call up the image of a lion, which is employed in ver. 9 to depict the indomitable heroic power of Israel, in words taken from Jacob's blessing in Gen. xlix. 9. The *Piel* גֵּרֵם is a *denom.* verb from גֶּרֶם, with the meaning to destroy, crush the bones, like שֵׁרֵשׁ, to root out (cf. *Ges.* § 52, 2; *Ewald,* § 120, *e.*). חִצָּיו is not the object to יִמְחַץ; for מָחַץ, to dash to pieces, does not apply to arrows, which may be broken in pieces, but not dashed to pieces ; and the singular suffix in חִצָּיו can only apply to the singular idea in the verse, *i.e.* to Israel, and not to

[1] Even on the supposition (which is quite at variance with the character of all the prophecies of Balaam) that in the name of Agag, the contemporary of Saul, we have a *vaticinium ex eventu,* the allusion to this particular king would be exceedingly strange, as the Amalekites did not perform any prominent part among the enemies of Israel in the time of Saul ; and the command to exterminate them was given to Saul, not because of any special harm that they had done to Israel at that time, but on account of what they had done to Israel on their way out of Egypt (comp. 1 Sam. xv. 2 with Ex. xvii. 8).

its enemies, who are spoken of in the plural. *Arrows* are singled out as representing weapons in general.[1] Balaam closes this utterance, as he had done the previous one, with a quotation from Jacob's blessing, which he introduces to show to Balak, that, according to words addressed by Jehovah to the Israelites through their own tribe-father, they were to overcome their foes so thoroughly, that none of them should venture to rise up against them again. To this he also links on the word with which Isaac had transferred to Jacob in Gen. xxvii. 29 the blessing of Abraham in Gen. xii. 3, for the purpose of warning Balak to desist from his enmity against the chosen people of God.

Vers. 10–14. This repeated blessing of Israel threw Balak into such a violent rage, that he smote his hands together, and advised Balaam to fly to his house: adding, " *I said, I will honour thee greatly* (cf. xxii. 17 and 37); *but, behold, Jehovah has kept thee back from honour.*" " Smiting the hands together" was either a sign of horror (Lam. ii. 15) or of violent rage; it is in the latter sense that it occurs both here and in Job xxvii. 33. In the words, " Jehovah hath kept thee back from honour," the irony with which Balak scoffs at Balaam's confidence in Jehovah is unmistakeable. —Ver. 12. But Balaam reminds him, on the other hand, of the declaration which he made to the messengers at the very outset (chap. xxii. 18), that he could not on any account speak in opposition to the command of Jehovah, and then adds, " *And now, behold, I go to my people. Come, I will tell thee advisedly what this people will do to thy people at the end of the days.*" יָעַץ, to advise; here it denotes an announcement, which includes advice. The announcement of what Israel would do to the Moabites in the future, contains the advice to Balak, what attitude he should assume towards Israel, if this people was to bring a blessing upon his own people and not a curse. On " *the end of the days*," see at Gen. xlix. 1.

Vers. 15–24. Balaam's *fourth* and last prophecy is distinguished from the previous ones by the fact that, according to the announcement in ver. 14, it is occupied exclusively with the future, and foretells the victorious supremacy of Israel over all its foes, and the

[1] The difficulty which many feel in connection with the word חִצָּיו cannot be removed by alterations of the text. The only possible conjecture חֲלָצָיו (his loins) is wrecked upon the singular suffix, for the dashing to pieces of the loins of Israel is not for a moment to be thought of. *Knobel's* proposal, viz. to read קָמָיו, has no support in Deut. xxxiii. 11, and is much too violent to reckon upon any approval.

destruction of all the powers of the world. This prophecy is divided
into four different prophecies by the fourfold repetition of the
words, " he took up his parable" (vers. 15, 20, 21, and 23).   The
first of these refers to the two nations that were related to Israel,
viz. Edom and Moab (vers. 17–19) ; the *second* to Amalek, the
arch-enemy of Israel (ver. 20) ; the *third* to the Kenites, who were
allied to Israel (vers. 21 and 22); and the *fourth* proclaims the
overthrow of the great powers of the world (vers. 23 and 24).—The
introduction in vers. 15 and 16 is the same as that of the previous
prophecy in vers. 3 and 4, except that the words, " *he which knew
the knowledge of the Most High,*" are added to the expression, " *he
that heard the words of God,*" to show that Balaam possessed the
knowledge of the Most High, *i.e.* that the word of God about to be
announced had already been communicated to him, and was not
made known to him now for the first time ; though without implying that he had received the divine revelation about to be uttered
at the same time as those which he had uttered before.—Ver. 17.
The prophecy itself commences with a picture from the " end of
the days," which rises up before the mental eye of the seer.   " *I
see Him, yet not now; I behold Him, but not nigh.   A star appears
out of Jacob, and a sceptre rises out of Israel, and dashes Moab in
pieces on both sides, and destroys all the sons of confusion.*"   The
suffixes to אֶרְאֶנּוּ and אֲשׁוּרֶנּוּ refer to the star which is mentioned
afterwards, and which Balaam sees in spirit, but " not now," *i.e.*
not as having already appeared, and " not nigh," *i.e.* not to appear
immediately, but to come forth out of Israel in the far distant
future.   " A star is so natural an image and symbol of imperial
greatness and splendour, that it has been employed in this sense in
almost every nation.   And the fact that this figure and symbol are
so natural, may serve to explain the belief of the ancient world, that
the birth and accession of great kings was announced by the appearance of stars" (*Hengstenberg*, who cites *Justini hist.* xxxvii. 2 ;
Plinii h. n. ii. 23 ; *Sueton. Jul. Cæs.* c. 78 ; and *Dio Cass.* xlv. p.
273).   If, however, there could be any doubt that the rising star
represented the appearance of a glorious ruler or king, it would be
entirely removed by the parallel, " a sceptre arises out of Israel."
The sceptre, which was introduced as a symbol of dominion even
in Jacob's blessing (Gen. xlix. 10), is employed here as the figurative representation and symbol of the future ruler in Israel.   This
ruler would destroy all the enemies of Israel.   *Moab* and (ver. 18)
Edom are the first of these that are mentioned, viz. the two nations

that were related to Israel by descent, but had risen up in hostility against it at that time. Moab stands in the foremost rank, not merely because Balaam was about to announce to the king of Moab what Israel would do to his people in the future, but also because the hostility of the heathen to the people of God had appeared most strongly in Balak's desire to curse the Israelites. פַּאֲתֵי מוֹאָב, "*the two corners or sides of Moab*," equivalent to Moab on both sides, from one end to the other. For קַרְקַר, the *inf. Pilp.* of קוּר or קִיר, the meaning to destroy is fully established by the parallel מָחַץ, and by Isa. xxii. 5, whatever may be thought of its etymology and primary meaning. And neither the Samaritan text nor the passage in Isaiah (xlviii. 45), which is based upon this prophecy, at all warrants an alteration of the reading קַרְקַר into קָדְקֹד (the crown of the head), since Jeremiah almost invariably uses earlier writings in this free manner, viz. by altering the expressions employed, and substituting in the place of unusual words either more common ones, or such as are similar in sound (cf. *Küper, Jerem. libror. ss. interpres atque vindex*, pp. xiii. sqq. and p. 43).—כָּל־בְּנֵי־שֵׁת does not mean "*all the sons of Seth*," *i.e.* all mankind, as the human race is never called by the name of Seth; and the idea that the ruler to arise out of Israel would destroy all men, would be altogether unsuitable. It signifies rather "*all the sons of confusion*," by which, according to the analogy of Jacob and Israel (ver. 17), Edom and Seir (ver. 18), the Moabites are to be understood as being men of wild, warlike confusion. שֵׁת is a contraction of שְׁאֵת (Lam. iii. 47), and derived from שָׁאָה; and in Jer. xlviii. 45 it is correctly rendered בְּנֵי שָׁאוֹן.[1]

In the announcement of destruction which is to fall upon the enemies of Israel through the star and sceptre out of the midst of

[1] On the other hand, the rendering, "all the sons of the drinker, *i.e.* of Lot," which *Hiller* proposed, and *v. Hofmann* and *Kurtz* have renewed, is evidently untenable. For, in the first place, the fact related in Gen. xix. 32 sqq. does not warrant the assumption that Lot ever received the name of the "drinker," especially as the word used in Gen. xix. is not שָׁתָה, but שָׁקָה. Moreover, the allusion to "all the sons of Lot," *i.e.* the Moabites and Ammonites, neither suits the thoroughly synonymous parallelism in the saying of Balaam, nor corresponds to the general character of his prophecies, which announced destruction primarily only to those nations that rose up in hostility against Israel, viz. Moab, Edom, and Amalek, whereas hitherto the Ammonites had not assumed either a hostile or friendly attitude towards them. And lastly, all the nations doomed to destruction are mentioned by name. Now the Ammonites were not a branch of the Moabites by descent, nor was their territory enclosed within the Moabitish territory, so that it could be included, as *Hofmann* supposes, within the "four corners of Moab."

it, Moab is followed by "its southern neighbour Edom."—Ver. 18.
"*And Edom becomes a possession, and Seir becomes a possession, its
enemies ; but Israel acquires power.*" Whose possession Edom and
Seir are to become, is not expressly stated ; but it is evident from the
context, and from אֹיְבָיו (its enemies), which is not a genitive dependent upon *Seir*, but is in apposition to *Edom* and *Seir*, just as צָרָיו
in ver. 8 is in apposition to גּוֹיִם. Edom and Seir were his, *i.e.*
Israel's enemies ; therefore they were to be taken by the ruler who
was to arise out of Israel. *Edom* is the name of the people, *Seir*
of the country, just as in Gen. xxxii. 4 ; so that Seir is not to be
understood as relating to the præ-Edomitish population of the land,
which had been subjugated by the descendants of Esau, and had
lost all its independence a long time before. In Moses' days the
Israelites were not allowed to fight with the Edomites, even when
they refused to allow them to pass peaceably through their territory
(see chap. xx. 21), but were commanded to leave them in their
possessions as a brother nation (Deut. ii. 4, 5). In the future, however, their relation to one another was to be a very different one ;
because the hostility of Edom, already in existence, grew more and
more into obstinate and daring enmity, which broke up all the ties
of affection that Israel was to regard as holy, and thus brought
about the destruction of the Edomites.—The fulfilment of this
prophecy commenced with the subjugation of the Edomites by
David (2 Sam. viii. 14 ; 1 Kings xi. 15, 16 ; 1 Chron. xviii. 12, 13),
but it will not be completed till "the end of the days," when all
the enemies of God and His Church will be made the footstool of
Christ (Ps. cx. 1 sqq.). That David did not complete the subjugation of Edom is evident, on the one hand, from the fact that the
Edomites revolted again under Solomon, though without success
(1 Kings xi. 14 sqq.) ; that they shook off the yoke imposed upon
them under Joram (2 Kings viii. 20) ; and notwithstanding their
defeat by Amaziah (2 Kings xiv. 7 ; 2 Chron. xxv. 11) and Uzziah
(2 Kings xiv. 22 ; 2 Chron. xxvi. 2), invaded Judah a second time
under Ahaz (2 Chron. xxviii. 17), and afterwards availed themselves of every opportunity to manifest their hostility to the kingdom of Judah and the Jews generally,—as for example at the
conquest of Jerusalem by the Chaldeans (Ezek. xxxv. 15, xxxvi. 5 ;
Obad. 10 and 13), and in the wars between the Maccabees and
the Syrians (1 Macc. v. 3, 65 ; 2 Macc. x. 15, xii. 38 sqq.),—until
they were eventually conquered by John Hyrcanus in the year B.C.
129, and compelled to submit to circumcision, and incorporated in

the Jewish state (*Josephus, Ant.* xiii. 9, 1, xv. 7, 9 ; Wars of the Jews, iv. 5, 5).   But notwithstanding this, they got the government over the Jews into their own hands through *Antipater* and *Herod* (*Josephus, Ant.* xiv. 8, 5), and only disappeared from the stage of history with the destruction of the Jewish state by the Romans. On the other hand, the declarations of the prophets (Amos ix. 12 ; Obad. 17 sqq.), which foretell, with an unmistakeable allusion to this prophecy, the possession of the remnant of Edom by the kingdom of Israel, and the announcements in Isa. xxxiv. and lxiii. 1–6, Jer. xlix. 7 sqq., Ezek. xxv. 12 sqq. and 35, comp. with Ps. cxxxvii. 7 and Lam. iv. 21, 22, prove still more clearly that Edom, as the leading foe of the kingdom of God, will only be utterly destroyed when the victory of the latter over the hostile power of the world has been fully and finally secured.—Whilst Edom falls, Israel will acquire power. עָשָׂה חַיִל, to acquire ability or power (Deut. viii. 17, 18 ; Ruth iv. 11), not merely to show itself brave or strong.   It is rendered correctly by *Onkelos,* "*prosperabitur in opibus ;*" and *Jonathan,* "*prævalebunt in opibus et possidebunt eos.*"—Ver. 19. "*And a ruler shall come out of Jacob, and destroy what is left out of cities.*"   The subject to יֵרְדְּ is indefinite, and to be supplied from the verb itself.   We have to think of the ruler foretold as star and sceptre.   The abbreviated form וְיֵרְדְּ is not used for the future יִרְדֶּה, but is jussive in its force.   One out of Jacob shall rule. מֵעִיר is employed in a collected and general sense, as in Ps. lxxii. 16.   Out of every city in which there is a remnant of Edom, it shall be destroyed. שָׂרִיד is equivalent to שְׁאֵרִית אֱדוֹם (Amos ix. 12).   The explanation, " destroy the remnant out of the city, namely, out of the holy city of Jerusalem" (*Ewald* and *Baur*), is forced, and cannot be sustained from the parallelism.

Ver. 20. The *second* saying in this prophecy relates to the *Amalekites.*   Balaam sees them, not with the eyes of his body, but in a state of ecstasy, like the star out of Jacob.   " *Beginning of the heathen is Amalek, and its end is destruction.*"   Amalek is called the beginning of the nations, not "as belonging to the most distinguished and foremost of the nations in age, power, and celebrity " (*Knobel*), —for in all these respects this Bedouin tribe, which descended from a grandson of Esau, was surpassed by many other nations,—but as the first heathen nation which opened the conflict of the heathen nations against Israel as the people of God (see at Ex. xvii. 8 sqq.). As its beginning had been enmity against Israel, its end would be " even to the perishing " (עֲדֵי אֹבֵד), *i.e.* reaching the position of one who was perishing, falling into destruction, which commenced under Saul and was completed under Hezekiah (see vol. i. p. 324).

Vers. 21 and 22. The third *saying* relates to the *Kenites*, whose origin is involved in obscurity (see at Gen. xv. 19), as there are no other Kenites mentioned in the whole of the Old Testament, with the exception of Gen. xv. 19, than the Kenites who went to Canaan with Hobab the brother-in-law of Moses (chap. x. 29 sqq.: see Judg. i. 16, iv. 11; 1 Sam. xv. 6, xxvii. 10, xxx. 29); so that there are not sufficient grounds for the distinction between Canaanitish and Midianitish Kenites, as *Michælis*, *Hengstenberg*, and others suppose. The hypothesis that Balaam is speaking of Canaanitish Kenites, or of the Kenites as representatives of the Canaanites, is as unfounded as the hypothesis that by the Kenites we are to understand the Midianites, or that the Kenites mentioned here and in Gen. xv. 19 are a branch of the supposed aboriginal Amalekites (*Ewald*). The saying concerning the Kenites runs thus: " *Durable is thy dwelling-place, and thy nest laid upon the rock; for should Kain be destroyed until Asshur shall carry thee captive?* " This saying " applies to friends and not to foes of Israel " (*v. Hofmann*), so that it is perfectly applicable to the Kenites, who were friendly with Israel. The antithetical association of the Amalekites and Kenites answers perfectly to the attitude assumed at Horeb towards Israel, on the one hand by the Amalekites, and on the other hand by the Kenites, in the person of Jethro the leader of their tribe (see Ex. xvii. 8 sqq., xviii., and vol. ii. p. 83). The dwelling-place of the Kenites was of lasting duration, because its nest was laid upon a rock (שׂים is a passive participle, as in 2 Sam. xiii. 32, and Obad. 4). This description of the dwelling-place of the Kenites cannot be taken literally, because it cannot be shown that either the Kenites or the Midianites dwelt in inaccessible mountains, as the Edomites are said to have done in Obad. 3, 4; Jer. xlix. 16. The words are to be interpreted figuratively, and in all probability the figure is taken from the rocky mountains of Horeb, in the neighbourhood of which the Kenites led a nomade life before their association with Israel (see at Ex. iii. 1). As *v. Hofmann* correctly observes: " Kain, which had left its inaccessible mountain home in Horeb, enclosed as it was by the desert, to join a people who were only wandering in search of a home, by that very act really placed its rest upon a still safer rock." This is sustained in ver. 22 by the statement that Kain would not be given up to destruction till Asshur carried it away into captivity. כִּי אִם does not mean " nevertheless."

It signifies "*unless*" after a negative clause, whether the negation be expressed directly by לֹא, or indirectly by a question; and
"*only*" where it is not preceded by either a direct or an indirect
negation, as in Gen. xl. 14; Job xlii. 8. The latter meaning,
however, is not applicable here, because it is unsuitable to the עַד־מָה
(until) which follows. Consequently אִם can only be understood in
the sense of "is it that," as in 1 Kings i. 27, Isa. xxix. 16, Job
xxxi. 16, etc., and as introducing an indirect query in a negative
sense: "For is it (the case) that Kain shall fall into destruction
until . . . ?"—equivalent to "Kain shall not be exterminated until
Asshur shall carry him away into captivity;" Kain will only be
overthrown by the Assyrian imperial power. *Kain*, the tribe-father,
is used poetically for *the Kenite*, the tribe of which he was the
founder. בָּעֵר, to exterminate, the sense in which it frequently
occurs, as in Deut. xiii. 6, xvii. 7, etc. (cf. 2 Sam. iv. 11; 1 Kings
xxii. 47).—For the fulfilment of this prophecy we are not to look
merely to the fact that one branch of the Kenites, which separated
itself, according to Judg. iv. 11, from its comrades in the south of
Judah, and settled in Naphtali near Kadesh, was probably carried
away into captivity by Tiglath-Pileser along with the population of
Galilee (2 Kings xv. 29); but the name Asshur, as the name of
the first great kingdom of the world, which rose up from the east
against the theocracy, is employed, as we may clearly see from ver.
24, to designate all the powers of the world which took their rise
in Asshur, and proceeded forth from it (see also Ezra vi. 22, where
the Persian king is still called king of *Asshur* or Assyria). Balaam
did not foretell that this worldly power would oppress Israel also,
and lead it into captivity, because the oppression of the Israelites
was simply a transitory judgment, which served to refine the nation
of God and not to destroy it, and which was even appointed according to the counsel of God to open and prepare the way for the
conquest of the kingdoms of the world by the kingdom of God.
To the Kenites only did the captivity become a judgment of
destruction; because, although on terms of friendship with the
people of Israel, and outwardly associated with them, yet, as is
clearly shown by 1 Sam. xv. 6, they never entered inwardly into
fellowship with Israel and Jehovah's covenant of grace, but sought
to maintain their own independence side by side with Israel, and
thus forfeited the blessing of God which rested upon Israel.[1]

[1] This simple but historically established interpretation completely removes
the objection, "that Balaam could no more foretell destruction to the friends of

Vers. 23, 24. The *fourth* saying applies to *Asshur*, and is introduced by an exclamation of woe : " *Woe! who will live, when God sets this! And ships* (come) *from the side of Chittim, and press Asshur, and press Eber, and he also perishes.*" The words " Woe, who will live," point to the fearfulness of the following judgment, which went deep to the heart of the seer, because it would fall upon the sons of his own people (see at chap. xxii. 5). The meaning is, " Who will preserve his life in the universal catastrophe that is coming?" (*Hengstenberg.*) מִשֻּׂמוֹ, either " since the setting of it," equivalent to " from the time when God sets (determines) this " (ὅταν θῇ ταῦτα ὁ Θεός, *quando faciet ista Deus;* LXX., *Vulg.*), or " on account of the setting of it," *i.e.* because God determines this. שׂוּם, to set, applied to that which God establishes, ordains, or brings to pass, as in Isa. xliv. 7 ; Hab. i. 12. The suffix in שׂוּמוֹ is not to be referred to *Asshur*, as *Knobel* supposes, because the prophecy relates not to Asshur " as the mighty power by which everything was crushed and overthrown," but to a power that would come from the far west and crush Asshur itself. The suffix refers rather to the substance of the prophecy that follows, and is to be understood in a neuter sense. אֵל is " GOD," and not an abbreviation of אֵלֶּה, which is always written with the article in the Pentateuch (הָאֵל, Gen. xix. 8, 25, xxvi. 3, 4 ; Lev. xviii. 27 ; Deut. iv. 42, vii. 22, xix. 11), and only occurs once without the article, viz. in 1 Chron. xx. 8. צִים, from צִי (Isa. xxxiii. 21), signifies ships, like צִיִּים in the passage in Dan. xi. 30, which is founded upon the prophecy before us. מִיַּד, from the side, as in Ex. ii. 5, Deut. ii. 37, etc. כִּתִּים is Cyprus with the capital *Citium* (see at Gen. x. 4), which is mentioned as intervening between Greece and Phœnicia, and the principal station for the maritime commerce of Phœnicia, so that all the fleets passing from the west to the east necessarily took Cyprus in their way (Isa. xxiii. 1). The nations that would come across the sea from the side of Cyprus to humble Asshur, are not mentioned by name, because this lay beyond the range of Balaam's vision. He simply gives utterance to the thought, " A power comes from Chittim over the sea, to which Asshur and Eber, the eastern and the western Shem, will both succumb " (*v. Hofmann*). *Eber* neither refers to the Israelites merely as Hebrews (LXX.,

Israel than to Israel itself," by which *Kurtz* would preclude the attempt to refer this prophecy to the Kenites, who were in alliance with Israel. His further objections to *v. Hofmann's* view are either inconclusive, or at any rate do not affect the explanation that we have given.

Vulg.), nor to the races beyond the Euphrates, as *Onkelos* and others suppose, but, like "all the sons of Eber" in Gen. x. 21, to the posterity of Abraham who descended from Eber through Peleg, and also to the descendants of Eber through Joktan: so that *Asshur*, as the representative of the Shemites who dwelt in the far east, included Elam within itself; whilst *Eber*, on the other hand, represented the western Shemites, the peoples that sprang from Arphaxad, Lud, and Aram (Gen. x. 21). "*And he also shall perish for ever:*" these words cannot relate to Asshur and Eber, for their fate is already announced in the word עִנָּה (afflict, press), but only to the new western power that was to come over the sea, and to which the others were to succumb. "Whatever powers might rise up in the world of peoples, the heathen prophet of Jehovah sees them all fall, one through another, and one after another; for at last he loses in the distance the power to discern whence it is that the last which he sees rise up is to receive its fatal blow" (*v. Hofmann*, p. 520). The overthrow of this last power of the world, concerning which the prophet Daniel was the first to receive and proclaim new revelations, belongs to "the end of the days," in which the star out of Jacob is to rise upon Israel as a "bright morning star" (Rev. xxii. 16).

Now if according to this the fact is firmly established, that in this last prophecy of Balaam, "the judgment of history even upon the imperial powers of the *West*, and the final victory of the King of the kingdom of God were proclaimed, though in fading outlines, more than a thousand years before the events themselves," as *Tholuck* has expressed it in his *Propheten und ihre Weissagung;* the announcement of the star out of Jacob, and the sceptre out of Israel, *i.e.* of the King and Ruler of the kingdom of God, who was to dash Moab to pieces and take possession of Edom, cannot have received its complete fulfilment in the victories of David over these enemies of Israel; but will only be fully accomplished in the future overthrow of all the enemies of the kingdom of God. By the "end of days," both here and everywhere else, we are to understand the Messianic era, and that not merely at its commencement, but in its entire development, until the final completion of the kingdom of God at the return of our Lord to judgment. In the "star out of Jacob," Balaam beholds not David as the cne king of Israel, but the Messiah, in whom the royalty of Israel promised to the patriarchs (Gen. xvii. 6, 16, xxxv. 11) attains its fullest realization. The star and sceptre are symbols not of "Israel's royalty personified"

(*Hengstenberg*), but of the real King in a concrete form, as He was to arise out of Israel at a future day. It is true that Israel received the promised King in David, who conquered and subjugated the Moabites, Edomites, and other neighbouring nations that were hostile to Israel. But in the person of David and his rule the kingly government of Israel was only realized in its first and imperfect beginnings. Its completion was not attained till the coming of the second David (Hos. iii. 5; Jer. xxx. 9; Ezek. xxxiv. 24, xxxvii. 24, 25), the Messiah Himself, who breaks in pieces all the enemies of Israel, and founds an everlasting kingdom, to which all the kingdoms and powers of this world are to be brought into subjection (2 Sam vii. 12–16; Ps. ii., lxxii., and cx.).[1]

If, however, the star out of Jacob first rose upon the world in Christ, the star which showed the wise men from the east the way to the new-born " King of the Jews," and went before them, till it stood above the manger at Bethlehem (Matt. ii. 1–11), is intimately related to our prophecy. Only we must not understand the allusion as being so direct, that Balaam beheld the very star which appeared to the wise men, and made known to them the birth of the Saviour of the world. The star of the wise men was rather an embodiment of the star seen by Balaam, which announced to them the fulfilment of Balaam's prophecy,—a visible sign by which God revealed to them the fact, that the appearance of the star which

---

[1] The application of the star out of Jacob to the Messiah is to be found even in *Onkelos;* and this interpretation was so widely spread among the Jews, that the pseudo-Messiah who arose under Hadrian, and whom even *R. Akiba* acknowledged, took the name of *Bar Cochba* (son of a star), in consequence of this prophecy, from which the nickname of *Bar Coziba* (son of a lie) was afterwards formed, when he had submitted to the Romans, with all his followers. In the Christian Church also the Messianic explanation was the prevalent one, from the time of *Justin* and *Irenæus* onwards (see the proofs in *Calovii Bibl. ad h. l.*), although, according to a remark of *Theodoret* (*qu.* 44 *ad Num.*), there were some who did not adopt it. The exclusive application of the passage to David was so warmly defended, first of all by *Grotius*, and still more by *Verschuir*, that even *Hengstenberg* and *Tholuck* gave up the Messianic interpretation. But they both of them came back to it afterwards, the former in his " Balaam " and the second edition of his Christology, and the latter in his treatise on "the Prophets." At the present time the Messianic character of the prophecy is denied by none but the supporters of the more vulgar rationalism, such as *Knobel* and others; whereas *G. Baur* (in his History of Old Testament Prophecy) has no doubt that the prediction of the star out of Jacob points to the exalted and glorious King, filled with the Holy Spirit, whom Isaiah (ch. ix. 5, xi. 1 sqq.) and Micah (v. 2) expected as the royal founder of the theocracy. *Reinke* gives a complete history of the interpretation of this passage in his *Beiträge*, iv. 186 sqq.

Balaam beheld in the far distant future had been realized at Bethlehem in the birth of Christ, the King of the Jews.—The " wise men from the east," who had been made acquainted with the revelations of God to Israel by the Jews of the *diaspora*, might feel themselves specially attracted in their search for the salvation of the world by the predictions of Balaam, from the fact that this seer belonged to their own country, and came " out of the mountains of the east" (ch. xxiii. 7) ; so that they made his sayings the centre of their expectations of salvation, and were also conducted through them to the Saviour of all nations by means of supernatural illumination. " God unfolded to their minds, which were already filled with a longing for the ' star out of Jacob' foretold by Balaam, the meaning of the star which proclaimed the fulfilment of Balaam's prophecy ; He revealed to them, that is to say, the fact that it announced the birth of the ' King of the Jews.' And just as Balaam had joyously exclaimed, ' I see Him,' and ' I behold Him,' they also could say, ' We have seen His star'" (*Hengstenberg*).

If, in conclusion, we compare Balaam's prophecy of the star that would come out of Jacob, and the sceptre that would rise out of Israel, with the prediction of the patriarch Jacob, of the sceptre that should not depart from Judah, till the *Shiloh* came whom the nations would obey (Gen. xlix. 10), it is easy to observe that Balaam not only foretold more clearly the attitude of Israel to the nations of the world, and the victory of the kingdom of God over every hostile kingdom of the world ; but that he also proclaimed the Bringer of Peace expected by Jacob at the end of the days to be a mighty ruler, whose sceptre would break in pieces and destroy all the enemies of the nation of God. The tribes of Israel stood before the mental eye of the patriarch in their full development into the nation in which all the families of the earth were to be blessed. From this point of view, the salvation that was to blossom in the future for the children of Israel culminated in the peaceful kingdom of the *Shiloh*, in whom the dominion of the victorious lion out of Judah was to attain its fullest perfection. But the eye of Balaam, the seer, which had been opened by the Spirit of God, beheld the nation of Israel encamped, according to its tribes, in the face of its foes, the nations of this world. They were endeavouring to destroy Israel ; but according to the counsel of the Almighty God and Lord of the whole world, in their warfare against the nation that was blessed of Jehovah, they were to succumb one after

the other, and be destroyed by the king that was to arise out of
Israel. This determinate counsel of the living God was to be
proclaimed by Balaam, the heathen seer out of Mesopotamia the
centre of the national development of the ancient world : and, first
of all, to the existing representatives of the nations of the world
that were hostile to Israel, that they might see what would at all
times tend to their peace—might see, that is to say, that in their
hostility to Israel they were rebelling against the Almighty God of
heaven and earth, and that they would assuredly perish in the conflict, since life and salvation were only to be found with the people
of Israel, whom God had blessed.   And even though Balaam had
to make known the purpose of the Lord concerning His people
primarily, and in fact solely, to the Moabites and their neighbours,
who were like-minded with them, his announcement was also intended for Israel itself, and was to be a pledge to the congregation
of Israel for all time of the certain fulfilment of the promises of
God ; and so to fill them with strength and courage, that in all their
conflicts with the powers of this world, they should rely upon the
Lord their God with the firmest confidence of faith, should strive
with unswerving fidelity after the end of their divine calling, and
should build up the kingdom of God on earth, which is to outlast
all the kingdoms of the world.—In what manner the Israelites became acquainted with the prophecies of Balaam, so that Moses
could incorporate them into the *Thorah*, we are nowhere told, but
we can infer it with tolerable certainty from the subsequent fate of
Balaam himself.

Ver. 25. At the close of this announcement Balaam and Balak
departed from one another. "*Balaam rose up, and went and turned
towards his place*" (*i.e.* set out on the way to his house) ; "*and king
Balak also went his way.*"   יָשָׁב לִמְקֹמוֹ does not mean, " he returned
to his place," into his home beyond the Euphrates (equivalent to
יָשָׁב אֶל־מְקֹמוֹ), but merely "he turned towards his place" (both here
and in Gen. xviii. 33). That he really returned home, is not implied
in the words themselves ; and the question, whether he did so, must
be determined from other circumstances. In the further course of
the history, we learn that Balaam went to the Midianites, and advised them to seduce the Israelites to unfaithfulness to Jehovah,
by tempting them to join in the worship of Peor (chap. xxxi. 16).
He was still with them at the time when the Israelites engaged in
the war of vengeance against that people, and was slain by the
Israelites along with the five princes of Midian (chap. xxxi. 8 ;

Josh. xiii. 22). At the time when he fell into the hands of the Israelites, he no doubt made a full communication to the Israelitish general, or to Phinehas, who accompanied the army as priest, concerning his blessings and prophecies, probably in the hope of saving his life; though he failed to accomplish his end.[1]

WHOREDOM OF ISRAEL, AND ZEAL OF PHINEHAS.—CHAP. XXV.

Vers. 1–5. The Lord had defended His people Israel from Balaam's curse; but the Israelites themselves, instead of keeping the covenant of their God, fell into the snares of heathen seduction (vers. 1, 2). Whilst encamped at Shittim, in the steppes of Moab, the people began to commit whoredom with the daughters of Moab: they accepted the invitations of the latter to a sacrificial festival of their gods, took part in their sacrificial meals, and even worshipped the gods of the Moabites, and indulged in the licentious worship of *Baal-Peor*. As the princes of Midian, who were allied to Moab, had been the advisers and assistants of the Moabitish king in the attempt to destroy the Israelites by a curse of God; so now, after the failure of that plan, they were the soul of the new undertaking to weaken Israel and render it harmless, by seducing it to idolatry, and thus leading it into apostasy from its God. But it was Balaam, as is afterwards casually observed in chap. xxxi. 16, who first of all gave this advice. This is passed over here, because the point of chief importance in relation to the object of the narrative, was not Balaam's share in the proposal, but the carrying out of the proposal itself. The daughters of Moab, however, also took part in carrying it out, by forming friendly associations with the Israelites, and then inviting them to their sacrificial festival. They only are mentioned in vers. 1, 2, as being the daughters of the land. The participation of the Midianites appears first of all in the shameless licentiousness of *Cozbi*, the daughter of the Midianitish prince, from which we not only see that the princes of Midian performed their

---

[1] It is possible, however, as *Hengstenberg* imagines, that after Balaam's departure from Balak, he took his way into the camp of the Israelites, and there made known his prophecies to Moses or to the elders of Israel, in the hope of obtaining from them the reward which Balak had withheld, and that it was not till after his failure to obtain full satisfaction to his ambition and covetousness here, that he went to the Midianites, to avenge himself upon the Israelites, by the proposals that he made to them. The objections made by *Kurtz* to this conjecture are not strong enough to prove that it is inadmissible, though the possibility of the thing does not involve either its probability or its certainty.

part, but obtain an explanation of the reason why the judgment upon the crafty destroyers of Israel was to be executed upon the Midianites.[1] *Shittim*, an abbreviation of *Abel-Shittim* (see at chap. xxii. 1), to which the camp of the Israelites in the steppes of Moab reached (chap. xxxiii. 49), is mentioned here instead of *Arboth-Moab*, because it was at this northern point of the camp that the Israelites came into contact with the Moabites, and that the latter invited them to take part in their sacrificial meals; and in Josh. ii. 1 and iii. 1, because it was from this spot that the Israelites commenced the journey to Canaan, as being the nearest to the place where they were to pass through the Jordan. זָנָה, construed with אֶל, as in Ezek. xvi. 28, signifies to incline to a person, to attach one's self to him, so as to commit fornication. The word applies to carnal and spiritual whoredom. The lust of the flesh induced the Israelites to approach the daughters of Moab, and form acquaintances and friendships with them, in consequence of which they were invited by them " to the slain-offerings of their gods," *i.e.* to the sacrificial festivals and sacrificial meals, in connection with which they also "adored their gods," *i.e.* took part in the idolatrous worship connected with the sacrificial festival. These sacrificial meals were celebrated in honour of the Moabitish god *Baal-Peor*, so that the Israelites joined themselves to him. צָמַד, in the *Niphal*, to bind one's self to a person. *Baal-Peor* is the *Baal* of *Peor*, who was worshipped in the city of *Beth-Peor* (Deut. iii. 29, iv. 46; see at chap. xxiii. 28), a Moabitish *Priapus*, in honour of whom women and virgins prostituted themselves. As the god of war, he was called *Chemosh* (see at chap. xxi. 29).—Vers. 3–5. And the anger of the Lord burned against the people, so that Jehovah commanded Moses to fetch the heads of the people, *i.e.* to assemble them together, and to " hang up" the men who had joined themselves to Baal-Peor " before the Lord against the sun," that the anger of God might turn away from Israel. The burning of the wrath of God, which was to be turned away from the people by the punishment of the

[1] Consequently there is no discrepancy between vers. 1–5 and 6–18, to warrant the violent hypothesis of *Knobel*, that there are two different accounts mixed together in this chapter,—an Elohistic account in vers. 6–18, of which the commencement has been dropped, and a Jehovistic account in vers. 1–5, of which the latter part has been cut off. The particular points adduced in proof of this fall to the ground, when the history is correctly explained; and such assertions as these, that the name Shittim and the allusion to the judges in ver. 5, and to the wrath of Jehovah in vers. 3 and 4, are foreign to the Elohist, are not proofs, but empty assumptions.

guilty, as enjoined upon Moses, consisted, as we may see from vers. 8, 9, in a plague inflicted upon the nation, which carried off a great number of the people, a sudden death, as in chap. xiv. 37, xvii. 11. הוֹקִיעַ, from יָקַע, to be torn apart or torn away (*Ges.*, *Winer*), refers to the punishment of crucifixion, a mode of capital punishment which was adopted by most of the nations of antiquity (see *Winer*, *bibl. R. W.* i. p. 680), and was carried out sometimes by driving a stake into the body, and so impaling them (ἀνασκολοπίζειν), the mode practised by the Assyrians and Persians (*Herod.* iii. 159, and *Layard's* Nineveh and its Remains, vol. ii. p. 374, and plate on p. 369), at other times by fastening them to a stake or nailing them to a cross (ἀνασταυροῦν). In the instance before us, however, the idolaters were not impaled or crucified alive, but, as we may see from the word הַרְגוּ in ver. 5, and in accordance with the custom frequently adopted by other nations (see *Herzog's* Encyclopædia), they were first of all put to death, and then impaled upon a stake or fastened upon a cross, so that the impaling or crucifixion was only an aggravation of the capital punishment, like the burning in Lev. xx. 14, and the hanging (תָּלָה) in Deut. xxi. 22. The rendering adopted by the LXX. and *Vulgate* is παραδειγματίζειν, *suspendere*, in this passage, and in 2 Sam. xxi. 6, 9, ἐξηλιάζειν (to expose to the sun), and *crucifigere*. לַיהוָה, for Jehovah, as satisfaction for Him, *i.e.* to appease His wrath. אוֹתָם (*them*) does not refer to the heads of the nation, but to the guilty persons, upon whom the heads of the nation were to pronounce sentence.—Ver. 5. The judges were to put to death every one his men, *i.e.* such of the evil-doers as belonged to his forum, according to the judicial arrangements instituted in Ex. xviii. This command of Moses to the judges was not carried out, however, because the matter took a different turn.

Vers. 6-9. Whilst the heads of the people were deliberating on the subject, and the whole congregation was assembled before the tabernacle, weeping on account of the divine wrath, there came an Israelite, a prince of the tribe of Simeon, who brought a Midianitish woman, the daughter of a Midianitish chief (ver. 14), to his brethren, *i.e.* into the camp of the Israelites, before the eyes of Moses and all the congregation, to commit adultery with her in his tent. This shameless wickedness, in which the depth of the corruption that had penetrated into the congregation came to light, inflamed the zeal of *Phinehas*, the son of Eleazar the high priest, to such an extent, that he seized a spear, and rushing into the tent of

the adulterer, pierced both of them through in the very act. הַקֻּבָּה,
lit. the arched, or arch, is applied here to the inner or hinder division
of the tent, the sleeping-room and women's room in the larger tents
of the upper classes.—Vers. 8, 9. Through this judgment, which
was executed by Phinehas with holy zeal upon the daring sinners,
the plague was restrained, so that it came to an end. The example
which Phinehas had made of these sinners was an act of intercession, by which the high priest appeased the wrath of God, and
averted the judgment of destruction from the whole congregation
(" he was zealous for his God," וַיְכַפֵּר, ver. 13). The thought upon
which this expression is founded is, that the punishment which
was inflicted as a purifying chastisement served as a *" covering "*
against the exterminating judgment (see *Herzog's* Cyclopædia).[1]—
Ver. 9. Twenty-four thousand men were killed by this plague.
The Apostle Paul deviates from this statement in 1 Cor. x. 8, and
gives the number of those that fell as twenty-three thousand, probably from a traditional interpretation of the schools of the scribes,
according to which a thousand were deducted from the twenty-four
thousand who perished, as being the number of those who were
hanged by the judges, so that only twenty-three thousand would be
killed by the plague; and it is to these alone that Paul refers.

Vers. 10–15. For this act of divine zeal the eternal possession
of the priesthood was promised to Phinehas and his posterity as
Jehovah's covenant of peace. בְּקַנְאוֹ, by displaying my zeal in the
midst of them (viz. the Israelites). קִנְאָתִי is not " zeal for me," but
" my zeal," the zeal of Jehovah with which Phinehas was filled,
and impelled to put the daring sinners to death. By doing this
he had averted destruction from the Israelites, and restrained the
working of Jehovah's zeal, which had manifested itself in the
plague. *" I gave him my covenant of peace "* (the suffix is attached
to the governing noun, as in Lev. vi. 3). נָתַן בְּרִית, as in Gen. xvii.
2, to give, *i.e.* to fulfil the covenant, to grant what was promised in
the covenant. The covenant granted to Phinehas consisted in the
fact, that an " eternal priesthood " (*i.e.* the eternal possession of the

---

[1] Upon this act of Phinehas, and the similar examples of Samuel (1 Sam. xv.
33) and Mattathias (1 Macc. ii. 24), the later Jews erected the so-called " zealot
right," *jus zelotarum*, according to which any one, even though not qualified by
his official position, possessed the right, in cases of any daring contempt of the
theocratic institutions, or any daring violation of the honour of God, to proceed
with vengeance against the criminals. (See *Salden, otia theol.* pp. 609 sqq., and
Buddeus, de jure zelotarum apud Hebr. 1699, and in *Oelrich's collect.* T. i. Diss.
5.) The stoning of Stephen furnishes an example of this.

priesthood) was secured to him, not for himself alone, but for his descendants also, as a covenant, *i.e.* in a covenant, or irrevocable form, since God never breaks a covenant that He has made. In accordance with this promise, the high-priesthood which passed from Eleazar to Phinehas (Judg. xx. 28) continued in his family, with the exception of a brief interruption in Eli's days (see at 1 Sam. i.–iii. and xiv. 3), until the time of the last gradual dissolution of the Jewish state through the tyranny of Herod and his successors (see my *Archäologie*, § 38).—In vers. 14, 15, the names of the two daring sinners are given. The father of Cozbi, the Midianitish princess, was named *Zur*, and is described here as "head of the tribes (אֻמּוֹת, see at Gen. xxv. 16) of a father's house in Midian," *i.e.* as the head of several of the Midianitish tribes that were descended from one tribe-father; in chap. xxxi. 8, however, he is described as a king, and classed among the five kings of Midian who were slain by the Israelites.

Vers. 16–18. The Lord now commanded Moses to show hostility (צָרַר) to the Midianites, and smite them, on account of the stratagem which they had practised upon the Israelites by tempting them to idolatry, "in order that the practical zeal of Phinehas against sin, by which expiation had been made for the guilt, might be adopted by all the nation" (*Baumgarten*). The *inf. abs.* צָרוֹר, instead of the *imperative*, as in Ex. xx. 8, etc. עַל־דְּבַר פ׳, in consideration of *Peor*, and indeed, or especially, in consideration of *Cozbi*. The repetition is emphatic. The wickedness of the Midianites culminated in the shameless wantonness of Cozbi the Midianitish princess. "*Their sister*," *i.e.* one of the members of their tribe.—The 19th verse belongs to the following chapter, and forms the introduction to chap. xxvi. 1.[1]

MUSTERING OF ISRAEL IN THE STEPPES OF MOAB.—CHAP. XXVI.

Before taking vengeance upon the Midianites, as they had been commanded, the Israelites were to be mustered as the army of Jehovah, by means of a fresh numbering, since the generation that was mustered at Sinai (chap. i.–iv.) had died out in the wilderness, with the sole exception of Caleb and Joshua (vers. 64, 65). On this ground the command of God was issued, "after the plague," for a fresh census and muster. For with the plague the last of those who came out of Egypt, and were not to enter Canaan, had

[1] In the English version this division is adopted.—TR.

been swept away, and thus the sentence had been completely executed.—The object of the fresh numbering, however, was not
merely to muster Israel for the war with the Midianites, and in the
approaching conquest of the promised land with the Canaanites
also, but was intended to serve at the same time as a preparation for
their settlement in Canaan, viz. for the division of the conquered
land among the tribes and families of Israel. For this reason
(chap. xxvi.) the families of the different tribes are enumerated
here, which was not the case in chap. i.; and general instructions
are also given in vers. 52–56, with reference to the division of
Canaan.—The numbering was simply extended, as before, to the
male population of the age of 20 years and upwards, and was no
doubt carried out, like the previous census at Sinai, by Moses and
the high priest (Eleazar), with the assistance of the heads of the
tribes, although the latter are not expressly mentioned here.—The
names of the families correspond—with very few exceptions, which
have been already noticed in vol. i. pp. 372–3—to the grandsons and
great-grandsons of Jacob mentioned in Gen. xlvi.—With regard to
the total number of the people, and the number of the different
tribes, compare the remarks at pp. 4 sqq.

Vers. 1–51. MUSTERING OF THE TWELVE TRIBES.—Vers. 1–4.
The command of God to Moses and Eleazar is the same as in chap.
i., ii., and iii., except that it does not enter so much into details.
—Ver. 3. "And Moses and Eleazar the priest spake with them"
(דִּבֶּר with the accusative, as in Gen. xxxvii. 4). The pronoun
refers to "the children of Israel," or more correctly, to the heads
of the nation as the representatives of the congregation, who were
to carry out the numbering. On the Arboth-Moab, see at chap.
xxii. 1. Only the leading point in their words is mentioned, viz.
"from twenty years old and upwards" (sc. shall ye take the number of the children of Israel), since it was very simple to supply
the words "take the sum" from ver. 2.[1]—The words from "the

---

[1] This is, at all events, easier and simpler than the alterations of the text
which have been suggested for the purpose of removing the difficulty. Knobel
proposes to alter וַיְדַבֵּר into וַיַּדְבֵּר, and לֵאמֹר into לִפְקֹד: "Moses and Eleazar
arranged the children of Israel when they mustered them." But הִדְבִּיר does
not mean to arrange, but simply to drive in pairs, to subjugate (Ps. xviii. 48,
and xlvii. 4),—an expression which, as must be immediately apparent, is altogether inapplicable to the arrangement of the people in families for the purpose
of taking a census.

children of Israel" in ver. 4 onwards form the introduction to the enumeration of the different tribes (vers. 5 sqq.), and the verb יְהִי (were) must be supplied. "*And the children of Israel, who went forth out of Egypt, were Reuben,*" etc.—Vers. 5–11. The families of *Reuben* tally with Gen. xlvi. 9, Ex. vi. 14, and 1 Chron. v. 3. The plural בְּנֵי (sons), in ver. 8, where only one son is mentioned, is to be explained from the fact, that several sons of this particular son (*i.e.* grandsons) are mentioned afterwards. On *Dathan* and *Abiram,* see at chap. xvi. 1 and 32 sqq. See also the remark made here in vers. 10*b* and 11, viz. that those who were destroyed with the company of Korah were for a sign (נֵס, here a warning); but that the sons of Korah were not destroyed along with their father. —Vers. 12–14. The *Simeonites* counted only five families, as *Ohad* (Gen. xlvi. 10) left no family. *Nemuel* is called *Jemuel* there, as *yod* and *nun* are often interchanged (cf. *Ges. thes.* pp. 833 and 557); and *Zerach* is another name of the same signification for *Zohar* (*Zerach,* the rising of the sun; *Zohar, candor,* splendour).— Vers. 15–18. The *Gadites* are the same as in Gen. xlvi. 16, except that *Ozni* is called *Ezbon* there.—Vers. 19–22. The sons and families of Judah agree with Gen. xlvi. 12 (cf. Gen. xxxviii. 6 sqq.); also with 1 Chron. ii. 3–5.—Vers. 23–25. The families of *Issachar* correspond to the sons mentioned in Gen. xlvi. 13, except that the name *Job* occurs there instead of *Jashub.* The two names have the same signification, as *Job* is derived from an Arabic word which signifies to return.—Vers. 26 and 27. The families of *Zebulun* correspond to the sons named in Gen. xlvi. 14.—Vers. 28–37. The descendants of *Joseph* were classified in two leading families, according to his two sons *Manasseh* and *Ephraim,* who were born before the removal of Israel to Egypt, and were raised into founders of tribes in consequence of the patriarch Israel having adopted them as his own sons (Gen. xlviii.).—Vers. 29–34. *Eight families descended from Manasseh*: viz. one from his son *Machir,* the second from Machir's son or Manasseh's grandson *Gilead,* and the other six from the *six sons of Gilead.* The genealogical accounts in chap. xxvii. 1, xxxvi. 1, and Josh. xvii. 1 sqq., fully harmonize with this, except that *Iezer* (ver. 30) is called *Abiezer* in Josh. xvii. 2; whereas only a part of the names mentioned here occur in the genealogical fragments in 1 Chron. ii. 21–24, and vii. 14–29. In ver. 33, a son of *Hepher,* named *Zelophehad,* is mentioned. He had no sons, but only daughters, whose names are given here to prepare the way for the legal regulations mentioned in chap. xxvii. and xxxvi., to which this fact gave rise. —Vers. 35–37. There were four families descended from *Ephraim*; three from his sons, and one from his grandson. Of the descendants of *Sutelah* several successive links are given in 1 Chron. vii. 20 sqq.—Vers. 38–41. The children of *Benjamin* formed *seven* families, five of whom were founded by his sons, and two by grandsons. (On the differences which occur between the names given here and those in Gen. xlvi. 21, see vol. i. pp. 372, 373.) Some of the sons and grandsons of Benjamin mentioned here are also found in the genealogical fragments in 1 Chron. vii. 6–18, and viii. 1 sqq.—Vers. 42 and 43. The descendants of *Dan* formed only *one* family, named from a son of Dan, who is called *Shuham* here, but *Hushim* in Gen. xlvi. 23; though this family no doubt branched out into several smaller families, which are not named here, simply because this list contains only the leading families into which the tribes were divided.—Vers. 44–47. The families of *Asher* agree with the sons of Asher mentioned in Gen. xlvi. 17 and 1 Chron. vii. 30, except that *Ishuah* is omitted here, because he founded no family.—Vers. 48–50. The families of *Naphtali* tally with the sons of Naphtali in Gen. xlvi. 24 and 1 Chron. vii. 30.—Ver. 51. The total number of the persons mustered was 601,730.

Vers. 52–56. INSTRUCTIONS CONCERNING THE DISTRIBUTION OF THE LAND.—In vers. 53, 54, the command is given to distribute the land as an inheritance among the twelve tribes ("unto these"), according to the number of the names (chap. i. 2–18), *i.e.* of the persons counted by name in each of their families. To a numerous tribe they were to make the inheritance great; to the littleness, *i.e.* to the tribes and families that contained only a few persons, they were to make it small; to every one according to the measure of its mustered persons (ל must be repeated before אִישׁ). In vers. 55, 56, it is said further commanded that the distribution should take place by lot. "*According to the names of their paternal tribes shall they* (the children of Israel) *receive it* (the land) *for an inheritance.*" The meaning of these words can only be, that every tribe was to receive a province of its own for an inheritance, which should be called by its name for ever. The other regulation in ver. 56, "*according to the measure of the lot shall its inheritance* (the inheritance of every tribe) *be divided between the numerous and the small* (tribe)," is no doubt to be understood as signifying, that in the division of the tribe territories, according to the comparative sizes of the different tribes, they were to adhere to that portion of land which fell to every tribe in the casting of the lots. The magnitude and limits of the possessions of the different tribes could not be determined by the lot according to the magnitude of the tribes themselves: all that could possibly be determined was the situation to be occupied by the tribe; so that *R. Bechai* is quite correct in observing that "the casting of the lot took place for the more convenient distribution of the different portions, whether of better or inferior condition, that there might be no occasion for strife and covetousness," though the motive assigned is too partial in its character. The lot was to determine the portion of every tribe, not merely to prevent all occasion for dissatisfaction and complaining, but in order that every tribe might receive with gratitude the possession that fell to its lot as the inheritance assigned it by God, the result of the lot being regarded by almost all nations as determined by God Himself (cf. Prov. xvi. 33, xviii. 18). On this ground not only was the lot resorted to by the Greeks and Romans in the distribution of conquered lands (see the proofs in *Clericus, Rosenmüller,* and *Knobel*), but it is still employed in the division of lands. (For further remarks, see at Josh. xiv. 1 sqq.)

Vers. 57–62. MUSTERING OF THE LEVITES.—The enumeration of the different Levitical families into which the three leading families of Levi, that were founded by his three sons Gershon, Kohath, and Merari, were divided, is not complete, but is broken off in ver. 58 after the notice of five different families, for the purpose of tracing once more the descent of Moses and Aaron, the heads not of this tribe only, but of the whole nation, and also of giving the names of the sons of the latter (vers. 59–61). And after this the whole is concluded with a notice of the total number of those who were mustered of the tribe of Levi (ver. 62).—Of the different families mentioned, *Libni* belonged to Gershon (cf. chap. iii. 21), *Hebroni* to Kohath (chap. iii. 27), *Machli* and *Mushi* to Merari (chap. iii. 33), and *Korchi, i.e.* the family of Korah (according to chap. xvi. 1; cf. Ex. vi. 21 and 24), to Kohath. Moses and Aaron were descendants of Kohath (see at Ex. vi. 20 and ii. 1). Some difficulty is caused by the relative clause, "*whom* (one) *had born to Levi in Egypt*" (ver. 59), on account of the subject being left indefinite. It cannot be Levi's wife, as *Jarchi, Abenezra,* and

others suppose; for *Jochebed*, the mother of Moses, was not a
daughter of Levi in the strict sense of the word, but only a Levitess
or descendant of Levi, who lived about 300 years after Levi; just
as her husband *Amram* was not actually the son of Amram, who
bore that name (Ex. vi. 18), but a later descendant of this older
Amram (see vol. i. pp. 469 sqq.). The missing subject must be
derived from the verb itself, viz. either הִלֶּדֶת or אִמָּהּ (her mother),
as in 1 Kings i. 6, another passage in which "his mother" is to be
supplied (cf. *Ewald*, § 294, *b*.).—Vers. 60, 61. *Sons of Aaron:* cf.
chap. iii. 2 and 4; Ex. vi. 23; Lev. x. 1, 2.—Ver. 62. The Levites
were not mustered along with the rest of the tribes of Israel,
because the mustering took place with especial reference to the
conquest of Canaan, and the Levites were not to receive any territory as a tribe (see at chap. xviii. 20).—Vers. 63–65. Concluding
formula with the remark in ver. 65, that the penal sentence which
God had pronounced in chap. xiv. 29 and 38 upon the generation
which came out of Egypt, had been completely carried out.

THE DAUGHTERS OF ZELOPHEHAD CLAIM TO INHERIT. THE
DEATH OF MOSES FORETOLD: CONSECRATION OF JOSHUA AS
HIS SUCCESSOR.—CHAP. XXVII.

Vers. 1–11. CLAIMS OF ZELOPHEHAD'S DAUGHTERS TO AN
INHERITANCE IN THE PROMISED LAND.—Vers. 1–4. The divine
instructions which were given at the mustering of the tribes, to the
effect that the land was to be divided among the tribes in proportion to the larger or smaller number of their families (chap. xxvi.
52–56), induced the daughters of *Zelophehad* the Manassite of the
family of Gilead, the son of Machir, to appear before the princes of
the congregation, who were assembled with Moses and Eleazar at
the tabernacle, with a request that they would assign them an
inheritance in the family of the father, as he had died in the desert
without leaving any sons, and had not taken part in the rebellion
of the company of Korah, which might have occasioned his exclusion from any participation in the promised land, but had simply
died "through his (own) sin," *i.e.* on account of such a sin as every
one commits, and such as all who died in the wilderness had committed as well as he. " *Why should the name of our father be cut
off* (cease) *from the midst of his family?*" This would have been
the case, for example, if no inheritance had been assigned him in
the land, because he left no son. In that case his family would have

become extinct, if his daughters had married into other families or tribes. On the other hand, if his daughters received a possession of their own among the brethren of their father, the name of their father would be preserved by it, since they could then marry husbands who would enter upon their landed property, and their father's name and possession would be perpetuated through their children. This wish on the part of the daughters was founded upon an assumption which rested no doubt upon an ancient custom, namely, that in the case of marriages where the wives had brought landed property as their dowry, the sons who inherited the maternal property were received through this inheritance into the family of their mother, *i.e.* of their grandfather on the mother's side. We have an example of this in the case of *Jarha,* who belonged to the pre-Mosaic times (1 Chron. ii. 34, 35). In all probability this took place in every instance in which daughters received a portion of the paternal possessions as their dowry, even though there might be sons alive. This would explain the introduction of *Jair* among the Manassites in chap. xxxii. 41, Deut. iii. 14. His father *Segub* was the son of *Hezron* of the tribe of Judah, but his mother was the daughter of *Machir* the Manassite (1 Chron. ii. 21, 22). We find another similar instance in Ezra ii. 61 and Neh. vii. 63, where the sons of a priest who had married one of the daughters of *Barzillai* the rich Gileadite, are called sons of *Barzillai.*—Vers. 5-7. This question of right (*mishpat*) Moses brought before God, and received instructions in reply to give the daughters of Zelophehad an inheritance among the brethren of their father, as they had spoken right. Further instructions were added afterwards in chap. xxxvi. in relation to the marriage of heiresses.—Vers. 8-11. On this occasion God issued a general law of inheritance, which was to apply to all cases as "a statute of judgment" (or right), *i.e.* a statute determining right. If any one died without leaving a son, his landed property was to pass to his daughter (or daughters); in default of daughters, to his brothers; in the absence of brothers, to his paternal uncles; and if there were none of them, to his next of kin.—On the intention of this law, see my Archæol. § 142 (ii. pp. 212, 213); and on the law of inheritance generally, see *J. Selden, de success. ad leges Hebr. in bona defunctorum, Fkft. a. O.* 1695.

Vers. 12–14. THE DEATH OF MOSES FORETOLD.—After these instructions concerning the division of the land, the Lord announced to Moses his approaching end. From the mountains of Abarim he was to see the land which the Israelites would receive, and then like Aaron to be gathered to his people, because like him he also had sinned at the water of strife at Kadesh.   This announcement was made, "that he might go forward to his death with the fullest consciousness, and might set his house in order, that is to say, might finish as much as he could while still alive, and provide as much as possible what would make up after his death for the absence of his own person, upon which the whole house of Israel was now so dependent" (*Baumgarten*).   The fulfilment of this announcement is described in Deut. xxxii. 48–52.   The particular spot upon the mountains of Abarim from which Moses saw the land of Canaan, is also minutely described there.   It was Mount *Nebo*, upon which he also died.   The mountains of *Abarim* (cf. chap. xxxiii. 47) are the mountain range forming the Moabitish table-land, which slope off into the steppes of Moab.   It is upon this range, the northern portion of which opposite to Jericho bore the name of Pisgah, that we are to look for Mount *Nebo*, which is sometimes described as one of the mountains of *Abarim* (Deut. xxxii. 49), and at other times as the top of *Pisgah* (Deut. iii. 27, xxxiv. 1 ; see at chap. xxi. 20). *Nebo* is not to be identified with Jebel *Attarus*, but to be sought for much farther to the north, since, according to *Eusebius* (*s. v.* 'Aβαρείμ), it was opposite to Jericho, between *Livias*, which was in the valley of the Jordan nearly opposite to Jericho, and *Heshbon ;* consequently very near to the point which is marked as the "*Heights of Nebo*" on *Van de Velde's* map.   The prospect from the heights of Nebo must have been a very extensive one.   According to *Burck-hardt* (*Syr.* ii. pp. 106–7), "even the city of *Heshbon* (*Hhuzban*) itself stood upon so commanding an eminence, that the view extended at least thirty English miles in all directions, and towards the south probably as far as sixty miles."   On the expression, "gathered unto thy people," see at Gen. xxv. 8, and on Aaron's death see Num. xx. 28.   כַּאֲשֶׁר מְרִיתֶם : "*as ye transgressed My commandment.*"   By the double use of כַּאֲשֶׁר (*quomodo*, "as"), the death of Aaron, and also that of Moses, are placed in a definite relation to the sin of these two heads of Israel.   As they both sinned at Kadesh· against the commandment of the Lord, so they were both of them to die without entering the land of Canaan.   On the sin, see at chap. xx. 12, 13, and on the desert of Zin, at chap. xiii. 21.

Vers. 15–23. Consecration of Joshua as the Successor of Moses. — Vers. 15–17.   The announcement thus made to

Moses led him to entreat the Lord to appoint a leader of His people, that the congregation might not be like a flock without a shepherd. As " God of the spirits of all flesh," *i.e.* as the giver of life and breath to all creatures (see at chap. xvi. 22), he asks Jehovah to appoint a man over the congregation, who should go out and in before them, and should lead them out and in, *i.e.* preside over and direct them in all their affairs. צֵאת וָבוֹא (" go out," and " go in ") is a description of the conduct of men in every-day life (Deut. xxviii. 6, xxxi. 2 ; Josh. xiv. 11). הוֹצִיא וְהֵבִיא (" lead out," and " bring in ") signifies the superintendence of the affairs of the nation, and is founded upon the figure of a shepherd.—Vers. 18–21. The Lord then appointed Joshua to this office as a man " who had spirit." רוּחַ (*spirit*) does not mean " insight and wisdom" (*Knobel*), but the higher power inspired by God into the soul, which quickens the moral and religious life, and determines its development ; in this case, therefore, it was the spiritual endowment requisite for the office he was called to fill. Moses was to consecrate him for entering upon this office by the laying on of hands, or, as is more fully explained in vers. 19 and 20, he was to set him before Eleazar the high priest and the congregation, to command (צִוָּה) him, *i.e.* instruct him with regard to his office before their eyes, and to lay·of his eminence (הוֹד) upon him, *i.e.* to transfer a portion of his own dignity and majesty to him by the imposition of hands, that the whole congregation might hearken to him, or trust to his guidance. The object to יִשְׁמְעוּ (hearken) must be supplied from the context, viz. אֵלָיו (to him), as Deut. xxxiv. 9 clearly shows. The מִן (of) in ver. 20 is partitive, as in Gen. iv. 4, etc. The eminence and authority of Moses were not to be entirely transferred to Joshua, for they were bound up with his own person alone (cf. chap. xii. 6–8), but only so much of it as he needed for the discharge of the duties of his office. Joshua was to be neither the lawgiver nor the absolute governor of Israel, but to be placed under the judgment of the *Urim*, with which Eleazar was entrusted, so far as the supreme decision of the affairs of Israel was concerned. This is the meaning of ver. 21 : " *Eleazar shall ask to him* (for him) *the judgment of the Urim before Jehovah.*" *Urim* is an abbreviation for *Urim and Thummim* (Ex. xxviii. 30), and denotes the means with which the high priest was entrusted of ascertaining the divine will and counsel in all the important business of the congregation. " *After his mouth*" (*i.e.* according to the decision of the high priest, by virtue of the right of Urim and Thummim entrusted to him), Joshua and the whole congregation were to go out and in, *i.e.* to regulate their conduct and decide upon their undertakings. " All the congregation," in distinction from " all the children of Israel," denotes the whole body of heads of the people, or the college of elders, which represented the congregation and administered its affairs.—Vers. 22, 23. Execution of the divine command.

ORDER OF THE DAILY AND FESTAL OFFERINGS OF THE CONGREGATION.—CHAP. XXVIII. AND XXIX.

When Israel was prepared for the conquest of the promised land by the fresh numbering and mustering of its men, and by the appointment of Joshua as commander, its relation to the Lord was regulated by a law which determined the sacrifices through which it was to maintain its fellowship with its God from day to day, and serve Him as His people (chap. xxviii. and xxix.). . Through this order of sacrifice, the object of which was to form and sanctify the whole life of the congregation into a continuous worship, the sacrificial and festal laws already given in Ex. xxiii. 14–17, xxix. 38–42, xxxi. 12–17, Lev. xxiii., and Num. xxv. 1–12, were completed and arranged into a united and well-ordered whole. " It was very fitting that this law should be issued a short time before the advance into Canaan ; for it was there first that the Israelites were in a position to carry out the sacrificial worship in all its full extent, and to observe all the sacrificial and festal laws " (*Knobel*). The law commences with the daily morning and evening burnt-offering (vers. 3–8), which was instituted at Sinai at the dedication of the altar. It is not merely for the sake of completeness that it is introduced here, or for the purpose of including all the national sacrifices that were to be offered during the whole year in one general survey ; but also for an internal reason, viz. that the daily sacrifice was also to be offered on the Sabbaths and feast-days, to accompany the general and special festal sacrifices, and to form the common substratum for the whole of these. Then follow in vers. 9–15 the sacrifices to be offered on the Sabbath and at the new moon ; and in ver. 16—chap. xxix. 38 the general sacrifices for the different yearly feasts, which were to be added to the sacrifices that were peculiar to each particular festival, having been appointed at the time of its first institution, and being specially adapted to give expression to its specific character, so that, at the yearly feasts, the congregation had to offer their different kinds of sacrifices : (*a*) the daily morning and evening sacrifice ; (*b*) the general sacrifices that were offered on every feast-day ; and (*c*) the festal sacrifices that were peculiar to each particular feast. This cumulative arrangement is to be explained from the significance of the daily and of the festal sacrifices. In the daily burnt-offering the congregation of Israel, as a congregation of Jehovah, was to sanctify its life, body, soul, and spirit, to the Lord its God ; and on the Lord's feast-days it was to give expression to this sanctification in an intensified form. This stronger practical exhibition of the sanctification of the life was embodied in the worship by the elevation and graduation of the daily sacrifice, through the addition of a second and much more considerable burnt-offering, meat-offering, and drink-offering. The graduation was regulated by the significance of the festivals. On the Sabbaths the daily sacrifice was doubled, by the presentation of a burnt-offering consisting of two lambs. On the other feast-days it was increased by a burnt-offering composed of oxen, rams, and yearling lambs, which was always preceded by a sin-offering.—As the seventh day of the week, being a Sabbath, was distinguished above the other days of the week, as a day that was sanctified to the Lord in a higher degree than the rest, by an enlarged burnt-offering, meat-offering, and drink-offering ; so the seventh month, being a Sabbath-month, was raised above the other months of the year, and sanctified as a festal month, by the fact that, in addition to the ordinary new moon sacrifices of two bullocks, one ram, and seven yearling lambs, a special festal sacrifice was also offered, consisting of one bullock, one ram, and seven yearling lambs (chap. xxix. 2), which was also repeated on the day of atonement, and at the close of the feast of Tabernacles (chap. xxix. 8, 36) ; and also that the feast of Tabernacles, which fell in this month, was to be celebrated by a much larger number of burnt-offerings, as the largest and holiest feast of the congregation of Israel.[1]

---

[1] *Knobel's* remarks as to the difference in the sacrifices are not only erroneous, but likely to mislead, and tending to obscure and distort the actual facts. " On those feast-days," he says, " which were intended as a general festival to Jehovah, viz. the sabbatical portion of the seventh new moon, the day of atonement, and the closing day of the yearly feasts, the sacrifices consisted of one bullock, one ram, and seven yearling lambs (chap. xxix. 2, 8, 36) ; whereas at the older festivals which had a reference to nature, such as the new moons, the days of unleavened bread, and the feast of Weeks, they consisted of two bullocks, one ram, and seven yearling lambs (chap. xxviii. 11, 19, 24, 27 ; xxix. 6), and at the feast of Tabernacles of even a larger number, especially of bullocks (chap. xxix. 12 sqq.). In the last, Jehovah was especially honoured, as having poured

All the feasts of the whole year, for example, formed a cycle of feast-days, arranged according to the number seven, which had its starting-point and centre in the Sabbath, and was regulated according to the division of time established at the creation, into weeks, months, years, and periods of years, ascending from the weekly Sabbath to the monthly Sabbath, the sabbatical year, and the year of jubilee.   In this cycle of holy periods, regulated as it was by the number seven, and ever expanding into larger and larger circles, there was embodied the whole revolution of annually recurring festivals, established to commemorate the mighty works of the Lord for the preservation and inspiration of His people. And this was done in the following manner : in the *first* place, the number of yearly feasts amounted to exactly *seven,* of which the two leading feasts (*Mazzoth* and the feast of *Tabernacles*) lasted *seven* days ; in the *second* place, in all the feasts, some of which were of only one day's duration, whilst others lasted seven days, there were only *seven* days that were to be observed with sabbatical rest and a holy meeting ; and in the *third* place, the seven feasts were formed into two large festal circles, each of which consisted of an introductory feast, the main feast of *seven* days, and a closing feast of one day.   The *first* of these festal circles was commemorative of the elevation of Israel into the nation of God, and its subsequent preservation.   It commenced on the 14th Abib (Nisan) with the Passover, which was appointed to commemorate the deliverance of Israel from the destroying angel who smote the firstborn of Egypt, as the introductory festival.   It culminated in the *seven* days' feast of unleavened bread, as the feast of the deliverance of Israel from bondage, and its elevation into the nation of

out His blessing upon nature, and granted a plentiful harvest to the cultivation of the soil.   The ox was the beast of agriculture." It was not the so-called " older festivals which had reference to nature " that were distinguished by a larger number of sacrificial animals, above those feast-days which were intended as general festivals to Jehovah, but the feasts of the seventh month alone. Thus the seventh new moon's day was celebrated by a double new moon's sacrifice, viz. with three bullocks, two rams, and fourteen yearling lambs ; the feast of atonement, as the introductory festival of the feast of Tabernacles, by a special festal sacrifice, whilst the day of Passover, which corresponded to it in the first festal cycle, as the introductory festival of the feast of unleavened bread, had no general festal sacrifices ; and, lastly, the feast of Tabernacles, not only by a very considerable increase in the number of the festal sacrifices on every one of the seven days, but also by the addition of an eighth day, as the octave of the feast, and a festal sacrifice answering to those of the first and seventh days of this month.

God; and closed with the feast of Weeks, Pentecost, or the feast of Harvest, which was kept *seven* weeks after the offering of the sheaf of first-fruits, on the second day of Mazzoth. This festal circle contained only three days that were to be kept with sabbatical rest and a holy meeting (viz. the first and seventh days of Mazzoth and the day of Pentecost). The *second* festal circle fell entirely in the seventh month, and its main object was to inspire the Israelites in their enjoyment of the blessings of their God : for this reason it was celebrated by the presentation of a large number of burnt-offerings. This festal circle opened with the day of atonement, which was appointed for the tenth day of the seventh month, as the intro-ductory feast, culminated in the *seven days'* feast of Tabernacles, and closed with the eighth day, which was added to the seven feast-days as the octave of this festive circle, or the solemn close of all the feasts of the year. This also included only three days that were to be commemorated with sabbatical rest and a holy meeting (the 10th, 15th, and 22d of the month) ; but to these we have to add the day of trumpets, with which the month commenced, which was also a Sabbath of rest with a holy meeting; and this completes the seven days of rest (see my *Archæologie*, i. § 76).

Chap. xxviii. Ver. 2 contains the general instruction to offer to the Lord His sacrificial gift " at the time appointed by Him." On *corban*, see at Lev. i. 2 (vol. ii. p. 282, comp. with p. 271); on " *the bread of Jehovah*," at Lev. iii. 11; on the " *sacrifice made by fire*," and " *a sweet savour*," at Lev. i. 9 ; and on " *moed*," at Lev. xxiii. 2, 4.— Vers. 3–8. *The daily sacrifice* : as it had already been instituted at Sinai (Ex. xxix. 38–42).—Ver. 7. " *In the sanctuary*," *i.e.* περὶ τὸν βωμόν (round about the altar), as *Josephus* paraphrases it (Ant. iii. 10); not " with (in) holy vessels," as *Jonathan* and others interpret it. " *Pour out a drink-offering, as* שֵׁכָר *for Jehovah*." *Shecar* does not mean intoxicating drink here (see at Lev. x. 9), but *strong drink*, in distinction from water as simple drink. The drink-offering con-sisted of wine only (see at chap. xv. 5 sqq.) ; and hence *Onkelos* paraphrases it, " of old wine."—Vers. 9, 10. The *Sabbath-offering*, which was to be added to the daily sacrifice (עָלָיו, upon it), consisted of two yearling lambs as a burnt-offering, with the corresponding meat-offering and drink-offering, according to the general rule laid down in chap. xv. 3 sqq., and is appointed here for the first time; whereas the sabbatical feast had already been instituted at Ex. xx. 8–11 and Lev. xxiii. 3. " *The burnt-offering of the Sabbath on its Sabbath*," *i.e.* as often as the Sabbath occurred, every Sabbath.—

Vers. 11–15. At the beginnings of the month, *i.e.* at the *new moons*, a larger burnt-offering was to be added to the daily or continual burnt-offering, consisting of two bullocks (young oxen), one ram, and seven yearling lambs, with the corresponding meat and drink-offerings, as the " month's burnt-offering in its (*i.e.* every) month with regard to the months of the year," *i.e.* corresponding to them. To this there was also to be added a sin-offering of a shaggy goat (see at Lev. iv. 23). The custom of distinguishing the beginnings of the months or new moon's days by a peculiar festal sacrifice, without their being, strictly speaking, festal days, with sabbatical rest and a holy meeting,[1] arose from the relation in which the month stood to the single day. " If the congregation was to sanctify its life and labour to the Lord every day by a burnt-offering, it could not well be omitted at the commencement of the larger division of time formed by the month; on the contrary, it was only right that the commencement of a new month should be sanctified by a special sacrifice. Whilst, then, a burnt-offering, in which the idea of expiation was subordinate to that of consecrating surrender to the Lord, was sufficient for the single day; for the whole month it was necessary that, in consideration of the sins that had been committed in the course of the past month, and had remained without expiation, a special sin-offering should be offered for their expiation, in order that, upon the ground of the forgiveness and reconciliation with God which had been thereby obtained, the lives of the people might be sanctified afresh to the Lord in the burnt-offering. This significance of the new moon sacrifice was still further intensified by the fact, that during the presentation of the sacrifice the priests sounded the silver trumpets, in order that it might be to the congregation for a memorial before God (chap. x. 10). The trumpet blast was intended to bring before God the prayers of the congregation embodied in the sacrifice, that God might remember them in mercy, granting them the forgiveness of their sins and power for sanctification, and quickening them again in the fellowship of His saving grace" (see my *Archæologie*, i.

---

[1] In later times, however, the new moon grew more and more into a feast-day, trade was suspended (Amos viii. 5), the pious Israelite sought instruction from the prophets (2 Kings iv. 23), many families and households presented yearly thank-offerings (1 Sam. xx. 6, 29), and at a still later period the most devout abstained from fasting (Judith viii. 6) ; consequently it is frequently referred to by the prophets as a feast resembling the Sabbath (Isa. i. 13 ; Hos. ii. 13 ; Ezek. xlvi. 1).

p. 369).—Vers. 16–25. The same number of sacrifices as at the new moon were to be offered on every one of the seven days of the feast of unleavened bread (*Mazzoth*), from the 15th to the 21st of the month, whereas there was no general festal offering on the day of the Passover, or the 14th of the month (Ex. xii. 3–14). With regard to the feast of *Mazzoth*, the rule is repeated from Ex. xii. 15–20 and Lev. xxiii. 6–8, that on the first and seventh day there was to be a Sabbath rest and holy meeting.—Vers. 23, 24. The festal sacrifices of the seven days were to be prepared " in addition to the morning burnt-offering, which served as the continual burnt-offering." This implies that the festal sacrifices commanded were to be prepared and offered every day after the morning sacrifice.— Vers. 26–31. The same number of sacrifices is appointed for the day of the first-fruits, *i.e.* for the *feast of Weeks* or *Harvest feast* (cf. Lev. xxiii. 15–22). The festal burnt-offering and sin-offering of this one day was independent of the supplementary burnt-offering and sin-offering of the wave-loaves appointed in Lev. xxiii. 18, and was to be offered before these and after the daily morning sacrifice.

Chap. xxix. 1–6. The festal sacrifice for the *new moon of the seventh month* consisted of a burnt-offering of one bullock, one ram, and seven yearling lambs, with the corresponding meat-offerings and drink-offerings, and a sin-offering of a he-goat, "besides" (*i.e.* in addition to) the monthly and daily burnt-offering, meat-offering, and drink-offering. Consequently the sacrifices presented on the seventh new moon's day were, (1) a yearling lamb in the morning and evening, with their meat-offering and drink-offering; (2) in the morning, after the daily sacrifice, the ordinary new moon's sacrifice, consisting of two bullocks, one ram, and seven yearling lambs, with their corresponding meat-offerings and drink-offerings (see at ver. 11); (3) the sin-offering of the he-goat, together with the burnt-offering of one bullock, one ram, and seven yearling lambs, with their proper meat-offerings and drink-offerings, the meaning of which has been pointed out at Lev. xxiii. 23 sqq.—Vers. 7–11. On the *day of atonement*, on the tenth of the seventh month, a similar festal sacrifice was to be offered to the one presented on the seventh new moon's day (a burnt-offering and sin-offering), in addition to the sin-offering of atonement prescribed at Lev. xvi., and the daily burnt-offerings. For a more minute description of this festival, see at Lev. xvi. and xxiii. 26–32.—Vers. 12–34. The *feast of Tabernacles*, the special regulations for the celebration of which are contained in Lev. xxiii. 34–36 and 39–43, was distin-

guished above all the other feasts of the year by the great number
of burnt-offerings, which raised it into the greatest festival of joy.
On the seven feast-days, the first of which was to be celebrated
with sabbatical rest and a holy meeting, there were to be offered, in
addition to the daily burnt-offering, every day a he-goat for a sin-
offering, and seventy oxen in all for a burnt-offering during the
seven days, as well as every day two rams and fourteen yearling
lambs, with the requisite meat-offerings and drink-offerings. Whilst,
therefore, the number of rams and lambs was double the number
offered at the Passover and feast of Pentecost, the number of oxen
was fivefold; for, instead of fourteen, there were seventy offered
during the seven days. This multiplication of the oxen was distributed in such a way, that instead of there being ten offered every
day, there were thirteen on the first day, twelve on the second, and
so on, deducting one every day, so that on the seventh day there
were exactly seven offered; the arrangement being probably made
for the purpose of securing the holy number seven for this last day,
and indicating at the same time, through the gradual diminution in
the number of sacrificial oxen, the gradual decrease in the festal
character of the seven festal days. The reason for this multiplication
in the number of burnt-offerings is to be sought for in the nature
of the feast itself. Their living in booths had already visibly represented to the people the defence and blessing of their God; and
the foliage of these booths pointed out the glorious advantages of
the inheritance received from the Lord. But this festival followed
the completion of the ingathering of the fruits of the orchard and
vineyard, and therefore was still more adapted, on account of the
rich harvest of splendid and costly fruits which their inheritance
had yielded, and which they were about to enjoy in peace now that
the labour of agriculture was over, to fill their hearts with the
greatest joy and gratitude towards the Lord and Giver of them all,
and to make this festival a speaking representation of the blessedness of the people of God when resting from their labours. This
blessedness which the Lord had prepared for His people, was also
expressed in the numerous burnt-offerings that were sacrificed on
every one of the seven days, and in which the congregation presented
itself soul and body to the Lord, upon the basis of a sin-offering, as
a living and holy sacrifice, to be more and more sanctified, transformed, and perfected by the fire of His holy love (see my *Archäol.*
i. p. 416).—Vers. 35-38. The *eighth* day was to be *azereth*, a closing
feast, and only belonged to the feast of Tabernacles so far as the

Sabbath rest and holy meeting of the seventh feast-day were transferred to it; whilst, so far as its sacrifices were concerned, it resembled
the seventh new moon's day and the day of atonement, and was
thus shown to be the octave or close of the second festal circle (see
at Lev. xxiii. 36).—Ver. 39. The sacrifices already mentioned were
to be presented to the Lord on the part of the congregation, in
addition to the burnt-offerings, meat-offerings, drink-offerings, and
peace-offerings which individuals or families might desire to offer
either spontaneously or in consequence of vows. On the vowing of
burnt-offerings and peace-offerings, see chap. xv. 3, 8 ; Lev. xxii.
18, 21.—Ver. 40 forms the conclusion of the list of sacrifices in
chap. xxviii. and xxix.

INSTRUCTIONS AS TO THE FORCE OF VOWS.—CHAP. XXX.

The rules by which vows were to be legally regulated, so far as
their objects and their discharge were concerned, has been already
laid down in Lev. xxvii. ; but the chapter before us contains instructions with reference to the force of vows and renunciations.
These are so far in place in connection with the general rules of
sacrifice, that vows related for the most part to the presentation
of sacrifices ; and even vows of renunciation partook of the character
of worship. The instructions in question were addressed (ver. 1) to
" the heads of the tribes," because they entered into the sphere of
civil rights, namely, into that of family life.—Ver. 2. At the head
there stands the general rule, " *If any one vow a vow to Jehovah, or
swear an oath, to bind his soul to abstinence, he shall not break his
word ; he shall do according to all that has gone out of his mouth:*"
i.e. he shall keep or fulfil the vow, and the promise of abstinence, in
perfect accordance with his word. נֶדֶר is a positive vow, or promise
to give or sanctify any part of one's property to the Lord. אִסָּר,
from אָסַר, to bind or fetter, the negative vow, or vow of abstinence.
אֱסֹר אִסָּר עַל־נַפְשׁוֹ, to take an abstinence upon his soul. In what
such abstinence consisted is not explained, because it was well
understood from traditional customs ; in all probability it consisted
chiefly in fasting and other similar abstinence from lawful things.
The Nazarite's vow, which is generally reckoned among the vows of
abstinence, is called *neder* in chap. vi. 2 sqq., not *issar*, because it
consisted not merely in abstinence from the fruit of the vine, but
also in the positive act of permitting the hair to grow freely in
honour of the Lord. The expression " swear an oath" (ver. 2 ; cf.

ver. 13) shows that, as a rule, they bound themselves to abstinence by an oath. The *inf. constr.*, הִשָּׁבַע, is used here, as in other places, for the *inf. abs.* (cf. *Ges.* § 131, 4, note 2). יָחֵל, from חָלַל, for יְחֵל, as in Ezek. xxxix. 7 (cf. *Ges.* § 67, note 8), to desecrate (his word), *i.e.* to leave it unfulfilled or break it.—Vers. 3–15 contain the rules relating to positive and negative vows made by a woman, and four different examples are given. The first case (vers. 3–5) is that of a woman in her youth, while still unmarried, and living in her father's house. If she made a vow of performance or abstinence, and her father heard of it and remained silent, it was to stand, *i.e.* to remain in force. But if her father held her back when he heard of it, *i.e.* forbade her fulfilling it, it was not to stand or remain in force, and Jehovah would forgive her because of her father's refusal. Obedience to a father stood higher than a self-imposed religious service.—The *second* case (vers. 6–8) was that of a vow of performance or abstinence, made by a woman before her marriage, and brought along with her (עָלֶיהָ, " upon herself") into her marriage. In such a case the husband had to decide as to its validity, in the same way as the father before her marriage. In the day when he heard of it he could hold back his wife, *i.e.* dissolve her vow ; but if he did not do this at once, he could not hinder its fulfilment afterwards. מִבְטָא שְׂפָתֶיהָ, gossip of her lips, that which is uttered thoughtlessly or without reflection (cf. Lev. v. 4). This expression implies that vows of abstinence were often made by unmarried women without thought or reflection.—The *third* case (ver. 9) was that of a vow made by a widow or divorced woman. Such a vow had full force, because the woman was not dependent upon a husband.—The *fourth* case (vers. 10–12) was that of a vow made by a wife in her married state. Such a vow was to remain in force if her husband remained silent when he heard of it, and did not restrain her. On the other hand, it was to have no force if her husband dissolved it at once. After this there follows the general statement (vers. 13–16), that a husband could establish or dissolve every vow of performance or abstinence made by his wife. If, however, he remained silent " from day to day," he confirmed it by his silence; and if afterwards he should declare it void, he was to bear his wife's iniquity. עֲוֹנָהּ, the sin which the wife would have had to bear if she had broken the vow of her own accord. This consisted either in a sin-offering to expiate her sin (Lev. v. 4 sqq.); or if this was omitted, in the punishment which God suspended over the sin (Lev. v. 1).—Ver. 16, concluding formula.

ROUND

WAR OF REVENGE AGAINST THE MIDIANITES.—CHAP. XXXI.

Vers. 1-12. The *Campaign.*—After the people of Israel had been mustered as the army of Jehovah, and their future relation to the Lord had been firmly established by the order of sacrifice that was given to them immediately afterwards, the Lord commanded Moses to carry out that hostility to the Midianites which had already been commanded in chap. xxv. 16-18. Moses was to revenge (*i.e.* to execute) the revenge of the children of Israel upon the Midianites, and then to be gathered to his people, *i.e.* to die, as had already been revealed to him (chap. xxvii. 13). "The revenge of the children of Israel" was revenge for the wickedness which the tribes of the Midianites who dwelt on the east of Moab (see at chap. xxii. 4) had practised upon the Israelites, by seducing them to the idolatrous worship of Baal Peor. This revenge is called the "revenge of Jehovah" in ver. 3, because the seduction had violated the divinity and honour of Jehovah. The daughters of Moab had also taken part in the seduction (chap. xxv. 1, 2); but they had done so at the instigation of the Midianites (see p. 203), and not of their own accord, and therefore the Midianites only were to atone for the wickedness.—Vers. 3-6. To carry out this revenge, Moses had 1000 men of each tribe delivered (יִמָּסְרוּ, see at ver. 16) from the families (*alaphim*, see chap. i. 16) of the tribes, and equipped for war; and these he sent to the army (into the war) along with Phinehas the son of Eleazar the high priest, who carried the holy vessels, viz. the alarm-trumpets, in his hand. *Phinehas* was attached to the army, not as the leader of the soldiers, but as the high priest with the holy trumpets (chap. x. 9), because the war was a holy war of the congregation against the enemies of themselves and their God. *Phinehas* had so distinguished himself by the zeal which he had displayed against the idolaters (chap. xxv. 7), that it was impossible to find any other man in all the priesthood to attach to the army, who would equal him in holy zeal, or be equally qualified to inspire the army with zeal for the holy conflict. "The holy vessels" cannot mean the ark of the covenant on account of the plural, which would be inapplicable to it; nor the Urim and Thummim, because Phinehas was not yet high priest, and the expression כְּלִי would also be unsuitable to these. The allusion can only be to the trumpets mentioned immediately afterwards, the וְ before חֲצֹצְרוֹת being the וְ *explic.*, "and in fact." Phinehas took these in his hand, because the Lord had assigned them to His congregation, to bring them into remembrance before Him in time of war, and to ensure His aid (chap. x. 9).—Vers. 7-10. Of the campaign itself, the results are all that is recorded. No doubt it terminated with a great battle, in which the Midianites were taken unawares and completely routed. As it was a war of vengeance of Jehovah, the victors slew all the males, *i.e.* all the adult males, as the sequel shows, without quarter; and "upon those that were slain," *i.e.* in addition to them, the five Midianitish kings and Balaam, who first advised the Midianites, according to ver. 16, to tempt the Israelites to idolatry. The five kings were chiefs of the larger or more powerful of the Midianitish tribes, as *Zur* is expressly said to have been in chap. xxv. 15. In Josh. xiii. 21 they are called "vassals of Sihon," because Sihon had subjugated them and made them tributary when he first conquered the land. The women and children of the Midianites were led away prisoners; and their cattle (*behemah*, beasts of draft and burden, as in Ex. xx. 10), their flocks, and their goods taken away as spoil. The towns in their dwellings, and all their villages (*tiroth*, tent-villages, as in Gen. xxv. 16), were burnt down. The expression "*towns in their dwellings*" leads to the conclusion that the towns were not the property of the Midianites themselves, who were a nomad people, but that they originally belonged in all probability to the Moabites, and had been taken possession of by the Amorites under Sihon. This is confirmed by Josh. xiii. 21, according to which these five Midianitish vassals of Sihon dwelt in the land, *i.e.* in the kingdom of Sihon. This also serves to explain why the conquest of their country is not mentioned in the account before us, although it is stated in Joshua (*l.c.*), that it was allotted to the Reubenites with the kingdom of Sihon.—Vers. 11, 12. All this booty (*shalal*, booty in goods), and all the prey in man and beast (*malkoach*), was brought by the conquerors to Moses and Eleazar and the congregation, into the camp in the steppes of Moab. In ver. 12, שְׁבִי applies to the women and children who were taken prisoners, מַלְקוֹחַ to the cattle taken as booty, and שָׁלָל to the rest of the prey.

Vers. 13-18. *Treatment of the Prisoners.*—When Moses went out to the front of the camp with Eleazar and the princes of the congregation to meet the returning warriors, he was angry with the commanders, because they had left all the women alive, since it was they who had been the cause, at Balaam's instigation, of the falling away of the Israelites from Jehovah to worship Peor; and he commanded all the male children to be slain, and every woman who had lain with a man, and only the young girls who had hitherto had no connection with a man to be left alive. פְּקוּדֵי הֶחָיִל, *lit.* the appointed persons, *i.e.* the officers of the army, who were then divided into princes (captains) over thousands and hundreds. —" *Which came from the battle*," *i.e.* who had returned. The question in ver. 15, " *Have ye left all the women alive?*" is an expression of dissatisfaction, and reproof for their having done this. הָיוּ . . . לִמְסָר־מַעַל, " *they have become to the Israelites to work unfaithfulness towards Jehovah*," *i.e.* they have induced them to commit an act of unfaithfulness towards Jehovah. The word מָסַר, which only occurs in this chapter, viz. in vers. 5 and 16, appears to be used in the sense of giving, delivering, and then, like נָתַן, doing, making, effecting. On the fact itself, see chap. xxv. 6 sqq. The object of the command to put all the male children to death, was to exterminate the whole nation, as it could not be perpetuated in the women. Of the female sex, all were to be put to death who had known the lying with a man, and therefore might possibly have been engaged in the licentious worship of Peor (chap. xxv. 2), to preserve the congregation from all contamination from that abominable idolatry.

Vers. 19–24. *Purification of the Warriors, the Prisoners, and the Booty.*—Moses commanded the men of war to remain for seven days outside the camp of the congregation, to carry out upon the third and seventh day the legal purification of such persons and things as had been rendered unclean through contact with dead bodies. Every one who had slain a soul (person), or touched one who had been slain, was to be purified, whether he were a warrior or a prisoner. And so also were all the clothes, articles of leather, materials of goats' hair, and all wooden things.—Vers. 21–24. To this end Eleazar, whose duty it was as high priest to see that the laws of purification were properly observed, issued fuller instructions with reference to the purification of the different articles, in accordance with the law in chap. xix. הַבָּאִים לַמִּלְחָמָה, those who came to the war, *i.e.* who went into the battle (see at chap. x. 9). " The ordinance of the law :" as in chap. xix. 2. The metal (gold, silver, copper, tin, lead), all that usually comes into the fire, *i.e.* that will bear the fire, was to be drawn through the fire, that it might become clean, and was then to be sprinkled with water of purification (chap. xix. 9); but everything that would not bear the fire was to be drawn through water.—The washing of clothes on the seventh day was according to the rule laid down in chap. xix. 19.

Vers. 25–47. *Distribution of the Booty.*—God directed Moses, with Eleazar and the heads of the fathers' houses ("fathers" for "fathers' houses:" see at Ex. vi. 14) of the congregation, to take the whole of the booty in men and cattle, and divide it into two halves: one for the men of war (תֹּפְשֵׂי הַמִּלְחָמָה, those who grasped at war, who engaged in war), the other for the congregation, and to levy a tribute upon it (מֶכֶם = מִכְסָה, *computatio*, a certain amount: see Ex. xii. 4) for Jehovah. Of the half that came to the warriors, one person and one head of cattle were to be handed over to Eleazar the priest out of every 500 (*i.e.* one-fifth per cent.), as a heave-offering for Jehovah; and of the other half that was set apart for the children of Israel, *i.e.* for the congregation, one out of every fifty (*i.e.* 2 per cent.) was to be taken for the Levites. אָחַז, laid hold of, *i.e.* snatched out of the whole number during the process of counting; not seized or touched by the lot, as in 1 Chron. xxiv. 6, as there was no reason for resorting to the lot in this instance. The division of the booty into two equal halves, one of which was given to the warriors, and the other to the congregation that had taken no part in the war, was perfectly reasonable and just. As the 12,000 warriors had been chosen out of the whole congregation to carry on the war on their behalf, the congregation itself could properly lay claim to its share of the booty. But as the 12,000 had had all the trouble, hardships, and dangers of the war, they could very properly reckon upon some reward for their service; and this was granted them by their receiving quite as much as the whole of the congregation which had taken no part in the war,—in fact, more, because the warriors only gave one-fifth per cent. of their share as a thank-offering for the victory that had been granted them, whilst those who remained at home had to give 2 per cent. of their share to Jehovah for the benefit of the priests and Levites. The arrangement, however, was only made for this particular case, and not as a law for all times, although it was a general rule that those who remained at home received a share of the booty brought back by the warriors (cf. Josh. xxii. 8; 1 Sam. xxx. 24, 25; 2 Macc. viii. 28, 30).— Vers. 31 sqq. The booty, viz. "the rest of the booty, which the men of war had taken," *i.e.* all the persons taken prisoners that had not been put to death, and all the cattle taken as booty that had not been consumed during the march home, amounted to 675,000 head of small cattle, 72,000 oxen, 61,000 asses, and 32,000 maidens.

Each half, therefore, consisted of 337,500 head of small cattle, 36,000 oxen, 30,500 asses, and 16,000 maidens (vers. 36 and 43–46). Of the one half the priests received 675 head of small cattle, 72 oxen, 61 asses, and 32 maidens for Jehovah; and these Moses handed over to Eleazar, in all probability for the maintenance of the priests, in the same manner as the tithes (chap. xviii. 26–28, and Lev. xxvii. 30–33), so that they might put the cattle into their own flocks (chap. xxxv. 3), and slay oxen or sheep as they required them, whilst they sold the asses, and made slaves of the girls; and not in the character of a vow, in which case the clean animals would have had to be sacrificed, and the unclean animals, as well as the human beings, to be redeemed (Lev. xxvii. 2–13). Of the other half, the Levites received the fiftieth part (vers. 43–47), that is to say, 6750 head of small cattle, 720 oxen, 610 asses, and 320 girls. The מַחֲצִית וגו׳ ("the half," etc.), in ver. 42, is resumed in ver. 47, and the enumeration of the component parts of this half in vers. 43–46 is to be regarded as parenthetical.

Vers. 48–54. *Sacred Oblations of the Officers.*—When the officers reviewed the men of war who were "in their hand," *i.e.* who had fought the battle under their command, and found not a single man missing, they felt constrained to give a practical expression to their gratitude for this miraculous preservation of the whole of the men, by presenting a sacrificial gift to Jehovah; they therefore brought all the golden articles that they had received as booty, and offered them to the Lord "for the expiation of their souls" (see at Lev. i. 4), namely, with the feeling that they were not worthy of any such grace, and not "because they had done wrong in failing to destroy all the enemies of Jehovah" (*Knobel*). This gift, which was offered as a heave-offering for Jehovah, consisted of the following articles of gold: אֶצְעָדָה, "*arm-rings*," according to 2 Sam. i. 10 (LXX. χελιδῶνα; *Suidas: χελιδόναι κοσμοὶ περὶ τοὺς βραχίονας, καλοῦνται δὲ βραχιάλια*); צָמִיד, *bands*, generally *armlets* (Gen. xxiv. 22, etc.); טַבַּעַת, *signet-rings;* עָגִיל, *hoops,*—according to Ezek. xvi. 12, *ear-rings;* and כּוּמָז, *gold balls* (Ex. xxxv. 22). They amounted in all to 16,750 shekels; and the men of war had received their own booty in addition to this. This gift, presented on the part of the officers, was brought into the tabernacle "as a memorial of the children of Israel before Jehovah" (cf. Ex. xxx. 16); that is to say, it was placed in the treasury of the sanctuary.

The fact that the Israelites did not lose a single man in the battle, is certainly a striking proof of the protection of God; but it is not so marvellous as to furnish any good ground for calling in question the correctness of the narrative.[1] The Midianites were a nomad tribe, who lived by rearing flocks and herds, and therefore were not a warlike people. Moreover, they were probably attacked quite unawares, and being unprepared, were completely routed and cut down without quarter. The quantity of booty brought home is also not so great as to appear incredible. Judging from the 32,000 females who had never lain with a man, the tribes governed by the five kings may have numbered about 130,000 or 150,000, and therefore not have contained much more than 35,000 fighting men, who might easily have been surprised by 12,000 brave warriors, and entirely destroyed. And again, there is nothing in the statement that 675,000 sheep and goats, 72,000 oxen, and 61,000 asses were taken as booty from these tribes, to astonish any one who has formed correct notions of the wealth of nomad tribes in flocks and herds. The only thing that could appear surprising is, that there are no camels mentioned. But it is questionable, in the first place, whether the Midianites were in the habit of rearing camels; and, in the second place, if they did possess them, it is still questionable whether the Israelitish army took them away, and did not rather put to death all that they found, as being of no value to the Israelites in their existing circumstances. Lastly, the quantity of jewellery seized as booty is quite in harmony with the well-known love of nomads, and even of barbarous tribes, for ornaments of this kind; and the peculiar liking of the Midianites for such things is confirmed by the account in Judg. viii. 26, according to which Gideon took as much as 1700 shekels in weight of golden rings from the Midianites alone, beside ornaments of other kinds. If we take the golden shekel at 10 thalers (30 shillings : see vol. ii. p. 250), the value of the ornaments taken by the officers under Moses would be about 167,500 thalers (L.25,125). It is quite possible that the kings and other chiefs, together with their wives, may have possessed as much as this.

[1] *Rosenmüller* has cited an example from *Tacitus* (Ann. xiii. 39), of the Romans having slaughtered all the foe without losing a single man on the capture of a Parthian castle; and another from *Strabo* (xvi. 1128), of a battle in which 1000 Arabs were slain, and only 2 Romans. And *Hävernick* mentions a similar account from the life of Saladin in his Introduction (i. 2, p. 452).

DIVISION OF THE CONQUERED LAND BEYOND THE JORDAN AMONG
THE TRIBES OF REUBEN, GAD, AND HALF-MANASSEH.—CHAP.
XXXII.[1]

Vers. 1–5. The Reubenites and Gadites, who had very large
flocks and herds, petitioned Moses, Eleazar, and the princes of the
congregation, to give them the conquered land of Gilead for a possession, as a land that was peculiarly adapted for flocks, and not to
make them pass over the Jordan. עָצוּם מְאֹד, "very strong," is an
apposition introduced at the close of the sentence to give emphasis
to the רַב. The land which they wished for, they called the "land
of *Jaëzer* (see chap. xxi. 32), and the land of *Gilead.*" They put
Jaëzer first, probably because this district was especially rich in
excellent pasture land. *Gilead* was the land to the south and north
of the Jabbok (see at Deut. iii. 10), the modern provinces of *Belka*
in the south between the Jabbok and the Arnon, and *Jebel Ajlun*
to the north of the Jabbok, as far as the Mandhur. Ancient Gilead
still shows numerous traces of great fertility even in its present
desolation, covered over as it is with hundreds of ruins of old towns
and hamlets. *Belka* is mountainous towards the north, but in the
south as far as the Arnon it is for the most part table-land; and in
the mountains, as *Buckingham* says, "we find on every hand a
pleasant shade from fine oaks and wild pistachio-trees, whilst the
whole landscape has more of a European character. The pasturage

---

[1] This chapter is also cut in pieces by *Knobel*: vers. 1, 2, 16–19, 24, 28–30,
and 33–38, being assigned to the Elohist; and the remainder, viz. vers. 3–5,
6–15, 20-23, 25–27, 31, 32, and 39–42, to the Jehovist. But as the supposed
Elohistic portions are fragmentary, inasmuch as it is assumed, for example, in
ver. 19, that the tribes of Reuben and Gad had already asked for the land of
the Jordan and been promised it by Moses, whereas there is nothing of the kind
stated in vers. 1 and 2, the Elohistic account is said to have been handed down
in a fragmentary state. The main ground for this violent hypothesis is the fancy
of the critic, that the tribes mentioned could not have been so shameless as to
wish to remain on the eastern side of the Jordan, and leave the conquest of
Canaan to the other tribes, and that the willingness to help their brethren to
conquer Canaan which they afterwards express in vers. 16 sqq., is irreconcilable
with their previous refusal to do this,—arguments which need no refutation
for an unprejudiced reader of the Bible who is acquainted with the selfishness
of the natural heart. The arguments founded upon the language employed are
also all weak. Because there are words in vers. 1 and 29, which the critics
pronounce to be Jehovistic, they must proceed, both here and elsewhere, to
remove all that offends them with their critical scissors, in order that they may
uphold the full force of their *dicta !*

in *Belka* is much better than it is anywhere else throughout the whole of southern Syria, so that the Bedouins say, 'You can find no country like Belka.' The oxen and sheep of this district are considered the very best" (see *v. Raumer*, Pal. p. 82). The mountains of Gilead on both sides of the Jabbok are covered for the most part with glorious forests of oak. " *Jebel Ajlun*," says *Robinson* (Pal. App. 162), "presents the most charming rural scenery that I have seen in Syria. A continued forest of noble trees, chiefly the evergreen oak (Sindiân), covers a large part of it, while the ground beneath is covered with luxuriant grass, which we found a foot or more in height, and decked with a rich variety of flowers" (see *v. Raumer, ut sup.*). This also applies to the ancient *Basan*, which included the modern plains of *Jaulan* and *Hauran*, that were also covered over with ruins of former towns and hamlets. The plain of *Hauran*, though perfectly treeless, is for all that very fertile, rich in corn, and covered in some places with such luxuriant grass that horses have great difficulty in making their way through it; for which reason it is a favourite resort of the Bedouins (*Burckhardt*, p. 393). "The whole of Hauran," says *Ritter* (*Erdkunde*, xv. pp. 988, 989), "stretches out as a splendid, boundless plain, between Hermon on the west, Jebel Hauran on the east, and Jebel Ajlun to the south; but there is not a single river in which there is water throughout the whole of the summer. It is covered, however, with a large number of villages, every one of which has its cisterns, its ponds, or its *birket*; and these are filled in the rainy season, and by the winter torrents from the snowy Jebel Hauran. Wherever the soil, which is everywhere black, deep, dark brown, or ochre-coloured, and remarkably fertile, is properly cultivated, you find illimitable corn-fields, and chiefly golden fields of wheat, which furnish Syria in all directions with its principal food. By far the larger part of this plain, which was a luxuriant garden in the time of the Romans, is now uncultivated, waste, and without inhabitants, and therefore furnishes the Bedouins of the neighbourhood with the desired paradise for themselves and their flocks." On its western slope *Jebel Hauran* is covered with splendid forests of oak, and rich in meadow land for flocks (*Burckhardt*, pp. 152, 169, 170, 173, 358; *Wetstein, Reiseber.* pp. 39 sqq. and 88). On the nature of the soil of *Hauran*, see at Deut. iii. 4. The plain of *Jaulan* appears in the distance like the continuation of Hauran (*Robinson*, App. 162); it has much bush-land in it, but the climate is not so healthy as in Hauran (*Seetzen*, i. pp. 353, 130, 131). "In general, Hauran, Jaulan, el

Botthin, el Belka, and Ejlun, are the paradise of nomads, and in all their wanderings eastwards they find no pasture like it" (*Seetzen*, i. p. 364). מָקוֹם, a locality, or district. אֶרֶץ מִקְנֶה = מְקוֹם מִקְנֶה (ver. 4), a district adapted for grazing. In ver. 3 the country is more distinctly defined by the introduction of the names of a number of important towns, whilst the clause " the country which the Lord smote before the congregation of Israel," in which the defeat of Sihon is referred to, describes it as one that was without a ruler, and therefore could easily be taken possession of. For more minute remarks as to the towns themselves, see at vers. 34 sqq. On the construction יִתַּן אֶת, see at Gen. iv. 18.—The words, " *let us not go over the Jordan*," may be understood as expressing nothing more than the desire of the speakers not to receive their inheritance on the western side of the Jordan, without their having any intention of withdrawing their help from the other tribes in connection with the conquest of Canaan, according to their subsequent declaration (vers. 16 sqq.) ; but they may also be understood as expressing a wish to settle at once in the land to the east of the Jordan, and leave the other tribes to conquer Canaan alone. Moses understood them in the latter sense (vers. 6 sqq.), and it is probable that this was their meaning, as, when Moses reproved them, the speakers did not reply that they had not cherished the intention attributed to them, but simply restricted themselves to the promise of co-opera-tion in the conquest of Canaan. But even in this sense their request did not manifest " a shamelessness that would hardly be historically true" (*Knobel*). It may very well be explained from the opinion which they cherished, and which is perfectly intelligible after the rapid and easy defeat of the two mighty kings of the Amorites, Sihon and Og, that the remaining tribes were quite strong enough to conquer the land of Canaan on the west of the Jordan. But for all that, the request of the Reubenites and Gadites did indicate an utter want of brotherly feeling, and complete in-difference to the common interests of the whole nation, so that they thoroughly deserved the reproof which they received from Moses.

Vers. 6–15. Moses first of all blames their want of brotherly feeling: " *Shall your brethren go into the war, and ye sit here?*" He then calls their attention to the fact, that by their disinclina-tion they would take away the courage and inclination of the other tribes to cross over the Jordan and conquer the land, and would bring the wrath of God upon Israel even more than their fathers who were sent from Kadesh to spy out the land, and who led away the heart of the people into rebellion through their unfavourable account of the inhabitants of Canaan, and brought so severe a judgment upon the congregation. הֵנִיא אֶת־לֵב מִן, to hold away the heart, i.e. render a person averse to anything. The Keri תְּנִיאוּן, as in ver. 9, is unquestionably to be preferred to the Kal תְּנוּאוּן, in the *Kethib* of ver. 7.—In vers. 8–13, Moses reminds them of the occurrences described in chap. xiii. and xiv. On the expression, "*wholly followed Jehovah,*" cf. chap. xiv. 24. The words, "*He drove them about in the desert,*" caused them to wander backwards and forwards in it for forty years, point back to chap. xiv. 33–35.—Ver. 14. "*Behold, ye rise up instead of your fathers,*" i.e. ye take their place, "*an increase* (תַּרְבּוּת, from רָבָה; equivalent to a brood) *of sinners, to augment yet the burning of the wrath of Jehovah against Israel.*" סָפָה עַל, to add to, or increase.—Ver. 15. "*If ye draw back behind Him,*" i.e. resist the fulfilment of the will of God, to bring Israel to Canaan, "*He will leave it* (Israel) *still longer in the desert, and ye prepare destruction for all this nation.*"

Vers. 16–27. The persons thus reproved came near to Moses, and replied, "*We will build sheep-folds here for our flocks, and towns for our children; but we will equip ourselves hastily* (חֻשִׁים, part. pass. hasting) *before the children of Israel, till we bring them to their place*" (*i.e.* to Canaan). גִּדְרֹת צֹאן, folds or pens for flocks, that were built of stones piled up one upon another (1 Sam. xxiv. 4).[1] By the building of towns, we are to understand the rebuilding and fortification of them. טַף, the children, including the women, and such other defenceless members of the family as were in need of protection (see at Ex. xii. 37). When their families were secured in fortified towns against the inhabitants of the land, the men who could bear arms would not return to their houses till the children of Israel, *i.e.* the rest of the tribes, had all received their inheritance: for they did not wish for an inheritance on the other side of Jordan and farther on, if (כִּי) their inheritance was assigned them on this side Jordan towards the east. The application of the expression מֵעֵבֶר הַיַּרְדֵּן to the land on the east of the Jordan, as well as to that on the west, points to a time when the Israelites had not

---

[1] According to *Wetstein* (*Reiseber.* p. 29), it is a regular custom with the nomads in *Leja,* to surround every place, where they pitch their tents, with a *Sira,* i.e. with an enclosure of stones about the height of a man, that the flocks may not be scattered in the night, and that they may know at once, from the noise made by the falling of the smaller stones which are laid at the top, if a wolf attempts to enter the enclosure during the night.

yet obtained a firm footing in Canaan. At that time the land to the west of the river could very naturally be spoken of as "*beyond the Jordan*," from the subjective stand-point of the historian, who was then on the east of the river; whereas, according to the objective and geographical usage, the land "beyond Jordan" signifies the country to the east of the river. But in order to prevent misunderstanding, in this particular instance the expression עֵבֶר הַיַּרְדֵּן is defined more precisely as מִזְרָחָה, "*towards the east*," when it is intended to apply to the land on the east of the Jordan.—Vers. 20–24. Upon this declaration Moses absolves them from all guilt, and promises them the desired land for a possession, on condition that they fulfil their promise; but he reminds them again of the sin that they will commit, and will have to atone for, if their promise is not fulfilled, and closes with the admonition to build towns for their families and pens for their flocks, and to do what they have promised. Upon this they promise again (vers. 25–27), through their spokesman (as the singular וַיֹּאמֶר in ver. 25, and the suffix in אֲדֹנִי in ver. 27, clearly show), that they will fulfil his command. The use of the expression "*before Jehovah*," in the words, "go armed before Jehovah to war," in vers. 20 and 21, may be explained from the fact, that in the war which they waged at the command of their God, the Israelites were the army of Jehovah, with Jehovah in the midst. Hence the ark of the covenant was taken into the war, as the vehicle and substratum of the presence of Jehovah; whereas it remained behind in the camp, when the people wanted to press forward into Canaan of their own accord (chap. xiv. 44). But if this is the meaning of the expression "before Jehovah," we may easily understand why the Reubenites and Gadites do not make use of it in ver. 17, namely, because they only promise to go equipped "before the children of Israel," *i.e.* to help their brethren to conquer Canaan. In ver. 32 they also adopt the expression, after hearing it from the mouth of Moses (ver. 20).[1] נְקִיִּם, innocent, "free from guilt before Jehovah and before Israel." By drawing back from participation in the war against the Canaanites, they would not only sin against Jehovah, who had promised Canaan to all Israel, and commanded them to take it, but also against Israel

---

[1] This completely sets aside the supposed discrepancy which *Knobel* adduces in support of his fragmentary hypothesis, viz. that the Elohist writes " before Israel" in vers. 17 and 29, when the Jehovist would write "before Jehovah,"—a statement which is not even correct; since we find " before Jehovah" in ver. 29, which *Knobel* is obliged to erase from the text in order to establish his assertion.

itself, *i.e.* against the rest of the tribes, as is more fully stated in vers. 7–15. In ver. 22*b*, " before Jehovah" signifies according to the judgment of Jehovah, with divine approval. וִדַעְתֶּם חַטַּאתְכֶם, " *ye will know your sin*," which will overtake (מָצָא) or smite you, *i.e.* ye will have to make atonement for them.

Vers. 28–33. Moses thereupon commanded Eleazar, Joshua, and the heads of the tribes of Israel, *i.e.* the persons entrusted in chap. xxxiv. 17 sqq. with the division of the land of Canaan, to give the Gadites and Reubenites the land of Gilead for a possession, after the conquest of Canaan, if they should go along with them across the Jordan equipped for battle. But if they should not do this, they were to be made possessors (*i.e.* to be settled; נֹאחֲזוּ in a passive sense, whereas in Gen. xxxiv. 10, xlvii. 27, it is reflective, to fix oneself firmly, to settle) in the land of Canaan along with the other tribes. In the latter case, therefore, they were not only to receive no possession in the land to the east of the Jordan, but were to be compelled to go over the Jordan with their wives and children, and to receive an inheritance there for the purpose of preventing a schism of the nation.—Ver. 31. The Gadites and Reubenites repeated their promise once more (ver. 25), and added still further (ver. 32) : " *We will pass over armed before Jehovah into the land of Canaan, and let our inheritance be with us* (*i.e.* remain to us) *beyond the Jordan.*"—Ver. 33. Moses then gave to the sons of Gad and Reuben, and the half-tribe of Manasseh, the kingdom of Sihon king of the Amorites, and Og king of Bashan, namely, " *the land according to its towns, in* (its) *districts,* (namely) *the towns of the land round about,*" *i.e.* the whole of the land with its towns and the districts belonging to them, or surrounding the towns. It appears strange that the half-tribe of Manasseh is included here for the first time at the close of the negotiations, whereas it is not mentioned at all in connection with the negotiations themselves. This striking fact may easily be explained, however, on the supposition that it was by the two tribes of Reuben and Gad alone that the request was made for the land of Gilead as a possession; but that when Moses granted this request, he did not overlook the fact, that some of the families of Manasseh had conquered various portions of Gilead and Bashan (ver. 39), and therefore gave these families, at the same time, the districts which they had conquered, for their inheritance, that the whole of the conquered land might be distributed at once. As *O. v. Gerlach* observes, " the participation of this half-tribe in the possession is accounted for in ver. 39." Moses restricted himself, however, to a general conveyance of the land that had been taken on the east of the Jordan to these two and a half tribes for their inheritance, without sharing it amongst them, or fixing the boundaries of the territory of each particular tribe. That was left to the representatives of the nation mentioned in ver. 28, and was probably not carried out till the return of the fighting men belonging to these tribes, who went with the others over the Jordan. In the verses which follow, we find only those towns mentioned which were fortified by the tribes of Gad and Reuben, and in which they constructed sheep-folds (vers. 34–38), and the districts which the families of Manasseh had taken and received as their possession (vers. 39–42).

Vers. 34–36. The *Gadites* built, *i.e.* restored and fortified, the following places. *Dibon*, also called Dibon Gad, an hour's journey to the north of the central Arnon (see p. 149). *Ataroth*, probably preserved in the extensive ruins of *Attarus*, on Jebel Attarus, between el Körriath (Kureyat) and Mkaur, *i.e.* Machaerus (see *Seetzen*, ii. p. 342). *Aroer*, not the Aroer before Rabbah, which was allotted to the Gadites (Josh. xiii. 25), as *v.* Raumer supposes ; but the *Aroer of Reuben* in the centre of the valley of the Arnon (Josh. xii. 2, xiii. 9, 16), which is still to be seen in the ruins of *Araayr*, on the edge of the lofty rocky wall which bounds the Modjeb (*Burckhardt*, p. 633). *Atroth Shophan :* only mentioned here ; situation unknown. *Jaezer :* probably to be sought for in the ruins of *es Szir*, to the west of Ammân (see at chap. xxi. 32). *Jogbehah :* only mentioned again in Judg. viii. 11, and preserved in the ruins of *Jebeiha*, about two hours to the north-west of Ammân (*Burckhardt*, p. 618 ; *Robinson*, App. p. 168). *Beth-Nimrah*, contracted into Nimrah (ver. 3), according to Josh. xiii. 27, in the valley of the Jordan, and according to the *Onomast.* (*s. v.* Βηθναβράν) *Bethamnaram*, five Roman miles to the north of *Libias* (*Bethharam*), now to be seen in the ruins of *Nimrein* or *Nemrin*, where the Wady *Shaib* enters the Jordan (*Burckhardt*, pp. 609, 661 ; *Robinson*, ii. p. 279), in a site abounding in water and pasturage (*Seetzen*, ii. pp. 318, 716). *Beth-Haran*, or *Beth-Haram* (Josh. xiii. 27) : *Bethramphtha*, according to *Josephus*, Ant. xviii. 2, 1, which was called *Julias*, in honour of the wife of Augustus. According to the *Onomast.* it was called *Beth-Ramtha* by the Syrians (בֵּית רַמְתָא, the form of the Aramæan *stat. emphat.*), and was named *Livias* by Herod Antipas, in honour of *Livia*, the wife of Augustus. It has been preserved in the ruins of *Rameh*, not far from the mouth of the

Wady Hesbân (*Burckhardt*, p. 661, and *Robinson*, ii. 305). The words 'עֲרֵי מִבְצָר וגו in ver. 36 are governed by וַיִּבְנוּ in ver. 34 : " they built them as fortified cities and folds for flocks," *i.e.* they fortified them, and built folds in them.

Vers. 37 and 38. The *Reubenites* built *Heshbon*, the capital of king Sihon (see chap. xxi. 16), which was allotted to the tribe of Reuben (Josh. xiii. 17), but relinquished to the Gadites, because it was situated upon the border of their territory, and given up by them to the Levites (Josh. xxi. 39 ; 1 Chron. vi. 66). It stood almost in the centre between the Arnon and Jabbok, opposite to Jericho, and, according to the Onomast., twenty Roman miles from the Jordan, where the ruins of a large town of about a mile in circumference are still to be seen, with deep bricked wells, and a large reservoir, bearing the ancient name of *Hesban* or *Hüsban* (*Seetzen ; Burckhardt*, p. 623 ; *Robinson*, Pal. ii. 278 ; cf. *v. Raumer*, Pal. p. 262 ; and *Ritter's Erdkunde*, xv. p. 1176).—*Elealeh :* half-an-hour's journey to the north-east of Heshbon, now called *el Aal*, *i.e.* the height, upon the top of a hill, from which you can see the whole of southern Belka ; it is now in ruins with many cisterns, pieces of wall, and foundations of houses (*Burckhardt*, p. 623).—*Kirjathaim*, probably to the south-west of Medeba, where the ruins of *el Teym* are now to be found (see at Gen. xiv. 5). *Nebo*, on Mount Nebo (see at chap. xxvii. 12). The *Onomast.* places the town eight Roman miles to the south of Heshbon, whilst the mountain is six Roman miles to the west of that town. *Baal-Meon*, called *Beon* in ver. 3, *Beth-Meon* in Jer. xlviii. 23, and more fully *Beth-Baal-Meon* in Josh. xiii. 17, is probably to be found, not in the ruins of *Maein* discovered by *Seetzen* and *Legh*, an hour's journey to the south-west of *Tueme* (*Teim*), and the same distance to the north of *Habbis*, on the north-east of Jebel Attarus, and nine Roman miles to the south of Heshbon, as most of the modern commentators from *Rosenmüller* to *Knobel* suppose ; but in the ruins of *Myun*, mentioned by *Burckhardt* (p. 624), three-quarters of an hour to the south-east of Heshbon, where we find it marked upon *Kiepert's* and *Van de Velde's* maps.[1] *Shibmah* (ver. 3, *Shebam*), which was only 500 paces from Heshbon, according to Jerome (on Isa. xiv. 8),

---

[1] Although *Baal-Meon* is unquestionably identified with *Maein* in the *Onom.* (see *v. Raumer*, Pal. p. 259), 1 Chron. v. 8 is decidedly at variance with this. It is stated there that " *Bela* dwelt in *Aroer*, and even unto *Nebo* and *Baal-Meon*," a statement which places *Baal-Meon* in the neighbourhood of *Nebo*, like the passage before us, and is irreconcilable with the supposition that it was

has apparently disappeared, without leaving a trace behind.[1] Thus all the places built by the Reubenites were but a short distance from Heshbon, and surrounded this capital ; whereas those built by the Gadites were some of them to the south of it, on the Arnon, and others to the north, towards Rabbath-Ammon. It is perfectly obvious from this, that the restoration of these towns took place before the distribution of the land among these tribes, without any regard to their possession afterwards. In the distribution, therefore, the southernmost of the towns built by the Gadites, viz. Aroer, Dibon, and Ataroth, fell to the tribe of Reuben ; and Heshbon, which was built by the Reubenites, fell to the tribe of Gad. The words שֵׁם מוּסַבֹּת, " changed of name," are governed by בָּנוּ: " they built the towns with an alteration of their names," *mutatis nominibus* (for סָבַב, in the sense of changing, see Zech. xiv. 10). There is not sufficient ground for altering the text, שֵׁם into שׁוּר (*Knobel*), according to the περικυκλωμένας of the LXX., or the περιτετευχισμένας of *Symmachus*. The Masoretic text is to be found not only in the Chaldee, the Syriac, the Vulgate, and the Saadic versions, but also in the Samaritan. The expression itself, too, cannot be justly described as " awkward," nor is it a valid objection that the naming is mentioned afterwards ; for altering the name of a town and giving it a new name are not tautological. The insertion of the words, " their names being changed," before Shibmah, is an indication that the latter place did not receive any other name. Moreover, the new names which the builders gave to these towns did not continue in use long, but were soon pressed out by the old ones again. " And they called by names the names of the towns :" this is a

identical with *Maein* in the neighbourhood of *Attarus*. In the case of *Seetzen*, however, the identification of *Maein* with *Baal-Meon* is connected with the supposition, which is now generally regarded as erroneous, namely, that *Nebo* is the same as the Jebel *Attarus*. (See, on the other hand, *Hengstenberg*, Balaam ; and *Ritter's Erdkunde*, xv. pp. 1187 sqq.)

[1] The difference in the forms *Shibmah*, *Baal-Meon* (ver. 38), and *Beth-Nimrah* (ver. 36), instead of *Shebam*, *Beon*, and *Nimrah* (ver. 3), is rendered useless as a proof that ver. 3 is Jehovistic, and vers. 36–38 Elohistic, from the simple fact that *Baal-Meon* itself is a contraction of Beth-Baal-Meon (Josh. xiii. 17). If the Elohist could write this name fully in one place and abbreviated in another, he could just as well contract it still further, and by exchanging the labials call it *Beon ;* and so also he could no doubt omit the *Beth* in the case of *Nimrah*, and use the masculine form *Shebam* in the place of *Shibmah*. The contraction of the names in ver. 3 is especially connected with the fact, that diplomatic exactness was not required for an historical account, but that the abbreviated forms in common use were quite sufficient.

roundabout way of saying, they called the towns by (other, or new) names : cf. 1 Chron. vi. 50.

Vers. 39–42. Moses gave the *Manassites* the land which was conquered by them ; in fact, the whole of the kingdom of *Bashan*, including not only the province of *Bashan*, but the northern half of Gilead (see at chap. xxi. 33, 34). Of this the *sons of Machir* received Gilead, the modern *Jebel Ajlun*, between the *Jabbok* (*Zerka*) and the *Mandhur* (Hieromax, *Jarmuk*), because they had taken it and driven out the Amorites and destroyed them (see Deut. iii. 13). The imperfects in ver. 39 are to be understood in the sense of pluperfects, the different parts being linked together by וֹ *consec.* according to the simple style of the Semitic historical writings explained in the note on Gen. ii. 19, and the leading thought being preceded by the clauses which explain it, instead of their being logically subordinated to it. " *The sons of Machir went to Gilead and took it . . . . and Moses gave,*" etc., instead of " Moses gave Gilead to the sons of Machir, who had gone thither and taken it . . . ." The words וַיֵּשֶׁב בָּהּ, " Machir dwelt therein (in Gilead)," do not point to a later period than the time of Moses, but simply state that the Machirites took possession of Gilead. As soon as Moses had given them the conquered land for their possession, they no doubt brought their families, like the Gadites and Reubenites, and settled them in fortified towns, that they might dwell there in safety, whilst the fighting men helped the other tribes to conquer Canaan. יָשַׁב signifies not merely " to dwell," but literally to place oneself, or settle down (*e.g.* Gen. xxxvi. 8, etc.), and is even applied to the temporary sojourn of the Israelites in particular encampments (chap. xx. 1). —*Machir* (ver. 40) : for the sons of Machir, or Machirites (chap. xxvi. 29). But as *Gilead* does not mean the whole of the land with this name, but only the northern half, so the sons of Machir are not the whole of his posterity, but simply those who formed the family of Machirites which bore its father's name (chap. xxvi. 29), *i.e.* the seven fathers' houses or divisions of the family, the heads of which are named in 1 Chron. v. 24. The other descendants of *Machir* through Gilead, who formed the six families of Gilead mentioned in chap. xxvi. 29–33, and Josh. xvii. 2, received their inheritance in Canaan proper (Josh. xvii.).—Ver. 41. The family of Manasseh named after Machir included " *Jair* the son (*i.e.* descendant) of Manasseh." Jair, that is to say, was the grandson of a daughter of Machir the son of Manasseh, and therefore a great-grandson of Manasseh on the mother's side. His father Segub was the son of

Hezron of the tribe of Judah, who had married a daughter of Manasseh (1 Chron. ii. 21, 22) ; so that Jair, or rather Segub, had gone over with his descendants into the maternal tribe, contrary to the ordinary rule, and probably because Machir had portioned his daughter with a rich dowry like an heiress. *Jair* took possession of the whole of the province of *Argob* in Bashan, *i.e.* in the plain of Jaulan and Hauran (Deut. iii. 4 and 14), and gave the conquered towns the name of *Havvoth Jair, i.e.* Jair's-lives (see at Deut. iii. 14). —Ver. 42. *Nobah,* whose family is never referred to, but who probably belonged, like Jair, to one of the families of Machirites, took the town of *Kenath* and its daughters, *i.e.* the smaller towns dependent upon it (see chap. xxi. 25), and gave it his own name *Nobah.* The name has not been preserved, and is not to be sought, as *Kurtz* supposes, in the village of *Nowa (Newe),* in Jotan, which is mentioned by *Burckhardt* (p. 443), and was once a town of half an hour's journey in circumference. For *Kenath,* which is only mentioned again in 1 Chron. ii. 23 as having been taken from the Israelites by Gesur and Aram, is Κάναθα, which *Josephus (de bell. Jud.* i. 19, 2) and *Ptolemy* speak of as belonging to Cœlesyria, and *Pliny* (h. n. 5, 16) to Decapolis, and which was situated, according to *Jerome,* "in the region of Trachonitis, near to Bostra." The ruins are very extensive even now, being no less than 2½ or 3 miles in circumference, and containing magnificent remains of palaces from the times of Trajan and Hadrian. It is on the western slope of Jebel Hauran, and is only inhabited by a few families of Druses. The present name is *Kanuat.* (For descriptions, see *Seetzen,* i. pp. 78 sqq.; *Burckhardt,* pp. 157 sqq. ; cf. *Ritter, Erdk.*)

LIST OF ISRAEL'S ENCAMPMENTS.—CHAP. XXXIII. 1–49.

As the Israelites had ended their wanderings through the desert, when they arrived in the steppes of Moab by the Jordan opposite to Jericho (chap. xxii. 1), and as they began to take possession when the conquered land beyond Jordan was portioned out (chap. xxxii.), the history of the desert wandering closes with a list of the stations which they had left behind them. This list was written out by Moses " at the command of Jehovah " (ver. 2), as a permanent memorial for after ages, as every station which Israel left behind on the journey from Egypt to Canaan " through the great and terrible desert," was a memorial of the grace and faithfulness with which the Lord led His people safely " in the

desert land and in the waste howling wilderness, and kept him
as the apple of His eye, as an eagle fluttereth over her young,
spreadeth abroad her wings, taketh them, beareth them on her
wings" (Ex. xix. 4; Deut. xxxii. 10 sqq.).

Vers. 1–15. The first and second verses form the heading:
"*These are the marches of the children of Israel, which they marched
out,*" *i.e.* the marches which they made from one place to another,
on going out of Egypt. מַסַּע does not mean a station, but the
breaking up of a camp, and then a train, or march (see at Ex.
xii. 37, and Gen. xiii. 3). לְצִבְאֹתָם (see Ex. vii. 4). בְּיַד, under the
guidance, as in chap. iv. 28, and Ex. xxxviii. 21. מוֹצָאֵיהֶם לְמַסְעֵיהֶם,
" *their goings out* (properly, their places of departure) *according to
their marches,*" is really equivalent to the clause which follows:
" *their marches according to their places of departure.*" The march
of the people is not described by the stations, or places of encampment, but by the particular spots from which they set out.
Hence the constant repetition of the word וַיִּסְעוּ, " *and they broke
up.*" In vers. 3–5, the departure is described according to Ex.
xii. 17, 37–41. On the judgments of Jehovah upon the gods of
Egypt, see at Ex. xii. 12. " With an high hand:" as in Ex.
xiv. 8.—The places of encampment from *Succoth* to the *desert
of Sinai* (vers. 5–15) agree with those in the historical account,
except that the stations at the *Red Sea* (ver. 10) and those at
Dophkah and *Alush* (vers. 13 and 14) are passed over there. For
Raemses, see at Ex. xii. 37. *Succoth* and *Etham* (Ex. xiii. 20).
Pihahiroth (Ex. xiv. 2). " *The wilderness* " (ver. 8) is the desert
of *Shur,* according to Ex. xv. 22. *Marah,* see Ex. xv. 23. *Elim*
(Ex. xv. 27). For the *Red Sea* and the *wilderness of Sin,* see Ex.
xvi. 1. For *Dophkah, Alush,* and *Rephidim,* see Ex. xvii. 1; and
for the wilderness of *Sinai,* Ex. xix. 2.

In vers. 16–36 there follow twenty-one names of places where
the Israelites encamped from the time that they left the *wilderness
of Sinai* till they encamped in the *wilderness of Zin, i.e. Kadesh.*
The description of the latter as "the wilderness of Zin, which is
Kadesh," which agrees almost word for word with Num. xx. 1,
and still more the agreement of the places mentioned in vers.
37–49, as the encampments of Israel after leaving Kadesh till their
arrival in the steppes of Moab, with the march of the people in the
fortieth year as described in chap. xx. 22–xxii. 1, put it beyond all
doubt that the encampment in the wilderness of Zin, *i.e.* Kadesh
(ver. 36), is to be understood as referring to the second arrival in

Kadesh after the expiration of the thirty-eight years of wandering in the desert to which the congregation had been condemned. Consequently the twenty-one names in vers. 16–36 contain not only the places of encampment at which the Israelites encamped in the second year of their march from Sinai to the desert of *Paran* at Kadesh, whence the spies were despatched into Canaan, but also those in which they encamped for a longer period during the thirty-eight years of punishment in the wilderness. This view is still further confirmed by the fact that the two first of the stations named after the departure from the wilderness of Sinai, viz. *Kibroth-hattaavah* and *Hazeroth*, agree with those named in the historical account in chap. xi. 34 and 35. Now if, according to chap. xii. 16, when the people left *Hazeroth*, they encamped in the desert of *Paran*, and despatched the spies thence out of the desert of *Zin* (chap. xiii. 21), who returned to the congregation after forty days "into the desert of Paran to *Kadesh*" (chap. xiii. 26), it is as natural as it well can be to seek for this place of encampment in the desert of Paran or Zin at Kadesh under the name of *Rithmah*, which follows Hazeroth in the present list (ver. 18). This natural supposition reaches the highest degree of probability, from the fact that, in the historical account, the place of encampment, from which the sending out of the spies took place, is described in so indefinite a manner as the " desert of *Paran*," since this name does not belong to a small desert, just capable of holding the camp of the Israelites, but embraces the whole of the large desert plateau which stretches from the central mountains of Horeb in the south to the mountains of the Amorites, which really form part of Canaan, and contains no less than 400 (? 10,000 English) square miles (see pp. 57–8). In this desert the Israelites could only pitch their camp in one particular spot, which is called *Rithmah* in the list before us ; whereas in the historical account the passage is described, according to what the Israelites performed and experienced in this encampment, as near to the southern border of Canaan, and is thus pointed out with sufficient clearness for the purpose of the historical account. To this we may add the coincidence of the name *Rithmah* with the Wady *Abu Retemat*, which is not very far to the south of Kadesh, " a wide plain with shrubs and *retem*," *i.e.* broom (*Robinson*, i. p. 279), in the neighbourhood of which, and behind the chalk formation which bounds it towards the east, there is a copious spring of sweet water called *Ain el Kudeirât*. This spot was well adapted for a place of en-

campment for Israel, which was so numerous that it might easily
stretch into the desert of Zin, and as far as Kadesh.

The seventeen places of encampment, therefore, that are mentioned in vers. 19-36 between *Rithmah* and *Kadesh*, are the places
at which Israel set up camps during the thirty-seven years of their
wandering about in the desert, from their return from Kadesh into
the " desert of the way to the Red Sea " (chap. xiv. 25), till the
reassembling of the whole congregation in the desert of Zin at
Kadesh (chap. xx. 1).[1] Of all the seventeen places not a single
one is known, or can be pointed out with certainty, except *Eziongeber*. Only the four mentioned in vers. 30-33, *Moseroth, Bene-
Jaakan, Hor-hagidgad*, and *Jotbathah*, are referred to again, viz. in
Deut. x. 6, 7, where Moses refers to the divine protection enjoyed
by the Israelites in their wandering in the desert, in these words :
" And the children of Israel took their journey from *Beeroth-bene-
Jaakan* to *Mosera;* there Aaron died, and there he was buried. . . .
From thence they journeyed unto *Gudgodah*, and from *Gudgodah*
to *Jotbathah*, a land of water-brooks." Of the identity of the places
mentioned in the two passages there can be no doubt whatever.
Bene Jaakan is simply an abbreviation of *Beeroth-bene-Jaakan*,
wells of the children of Jaakan. Now if the children of *Jaakan*
were the same as the Horite family of *Jakan* mentioned in Gen.

---

[1] The different hypotheses for reducing the journey of the Israelites to a
few years, have been refuted by *Kurtz* (iii. § 41) in the most conclusive manner
possible, and in some respects more elaborately than was actually necessary.
Nevertheless *Knobel* has made a fresh attempt, in the interest of his fragmentary
hypothesis, to explain the twenty-one places of encampment given in vers.
16-37 as twenty-one marches made by Israel from Sinai till their first arrival
at Kadesh. As the whole distance from Sinai to Kadesh by the straight road
through the desert consists of only an eleven days' journey, *Knobel* endeavours
to bring his twenty-one marches into harmony with this statement, by reckoning only five hours to each march, and postulating a few detours in addition,
in which the people occupied about a hundred hours or more. The objection
which might be raised to this, namely, that the Israelites made much longer
marches than these on their way from Egypt to Sinai, he tries to set aside by
supposing that the Israelites left their flocks behind them in Egypt, and procured fresh ones from the Bedouins at Sinai. But this assertion is so arbitrary
and baseless an idea, that it is not worth while to waste a single word upon the
subject (see Ex. xii. 38). The reduction of the places of encampment to simple
marches is proved to be at variance with the text by the express statement in
chap. x. 33, that when the Israelites left the wilderness of Sinai they went a
three days' journey, until the cloud showed them a resting-place. For it is perfectly evident from this, that the march from one place to another cannot be
understood without further ground as being simply a day's march of five hours.

xxxvi. 27,—and the reading יַעֲקָן for וַעֲקָן in 1 Chron. i. 42 seems to favour this,—the wells of *Jaakan* would have to be sought for on the mountains that bound the *Arabah* on either the east or west. *Gudgodah* is only a slightly altered and abbreviated form of *Hor-hagidgad*, the cave of *Gidgad* or *Gudgodah;* and lastly, *Moseroth* is simply the plural form of *Mosera.* But notwithstanding the identity of these four places, the two passages relate to different journeys. Deut. x. 6 and 7 refers to the march in the fortieth year, when the Israelites went from Kadesh through the Wady *Murreh* into the Arabah to Mount *Hor*, and encamped in the Arabah first of all at the wells of the children, and then at *Mosera*, where Aaron died upon Mount *Hor*, which was in the neighbourhood, and whence they travelled still farther southwards to *Gudgodah* and *Jotbathah.* In the historical account in chap. xx. and xxi. the three places of encampment, *Bene-Jaakan*, *Gudgodah*, and *Jotbathah*, are not mentioned, because nothing worthy of note occurred there. *Gudgodah* was perhaps the place of encampment mentioned in chap. xxi. 4, the name of which is not given, where the people were punished with fiery serpents; and *Jotbathah* is probably to be placed before *Zalmonah* (ver. 41). The clause, "a land of water-brooks" (Deut. x. 7), points to a spot in or near the southern part of the Arabah, where some wady, or valley with a stream flowing through it, opened into the Arabah from either the eastern or western mountains, and formed a green oasis through its copious supply of water in the midst of the arid steppe. But the Israelites had encamped at the very same places once before, namely, during their thirty-seven years of wandering, in which the people, after returning from Kadesh to the Red Sea through the centre of the great desert of *et Tih*, after wandering about for some time in the broad desert plateau, went through the Wady *el Jerafeh* into the Arabah as far as the eastern border of it on the slopes of Mount *Hor*, and there encamped at *Mosera* (*Moseroth*) somewhere near *Ain et Taiyibeh* (on *Robinson's* map), and then crossed over to *Bene-Jaakan*, which was probably on the western border of the Arabah, somewhere near *Ain el Ghamr* (*Robinson*), and then turning southwards passed along the Wady *el Jeib* by *Hor-gidgad* (*Gudgodah*), *Jotbathah*, and *Abronah* to *Eziongeber* on the Red Sea; for there can be no doubt whatever that the *Eziongeber* in vers. 35, 36, and that in Deut. ii. 8, are one and the same town, viz. the well-known port at the northern extremity of the Elanitic Gulf, where the Israelites in the time of Solomon and

Jehoshaphat built a fleet to sail to *Ophir* (1 Kings ix. 26, xxii. 49). It was not far from *Elath* (*i.e. Akaba*), and is supposed to have been " the large and beautiful town of *Asziun*," which formerly stood, according to *Makrizi*, near to *Aila*, where there were many dates, fields, and fruit-trees, though it has now long since entirely disappeared.

Consequently the Israelites passed twice through a portion of the Arabah in a southerly direction towards the Red Sea, the second time from Wady Murreh by Mount Hor, to go round the land of Edom, not quite to the head of the gulf, but only to the Wady *el Ithm*, through which they crossed to the eastern side of Edomitis (p. 142) ; the first time during the thirty-seven years of wandering from Wady el Jerafeh to Moseroth and Bene Jaakan, and thence to Eziongeber.—Ver. 36. "*And they removed from Eziongeber, and encamped in the desert of Zin, that is Kadesh :*" the return to Kadesh towards the end of the thirty-ninth year is referred to here. The fact that no places of encampment are given between Eziongeber and Kadesh, is not to be attributed to the " plan of the author, to avoid mentioning the same places of encampment a second time," for any such plan is a mere conjecture ; but it may be simply and perfectly explained from the fact, that on this return route —which the whole of the people, with their wives, children, and flocks, could accomplish without any very great exertion in ten or fourteen days, as the distance from Aila to Kadesh through the desert of Paran is only about a forty hours' journey upon camels, and *Robinson* travelled from Akabah to the Wady Retemath, near Kadesh, in four days and a half—no formal camp was pitched at all, probably because the time of penal wandering came to an end at Eziongeber, and the time had arrived when the congregation was to assemble again at Kadesh, and set out thence upon its journey to Canaan.—Hence the eleven names given in vers. 19–30, between *Rithmah* and *Moseroth*, can only refer to those stations at which the congregation pitched their camp for a longer or shorter period during the thirty-seven years of punishment, on their slow return from Kadesh to the Red Sea, and previous to their entering the Arabah and encamping at Moseroth.

This number of stations, which is very small for thirty-seven years (only seventeen from Rithmah or Kadesh to Eziongeber), is a sufficient proof that the congregation of Israel was not constantly wandering about during the whole of that time, but may have remained in many of the places of encampment, probably those which furnished an abundant supply of water and pasturage, not only for weeks and months, but even for years, the people scattering themselves in all directions round about the place where the tabernacle was set up, and making use of such means of support as the desert afforded, and assembling together again when this was all gone, for the purpose of travelling farther and seeking somewhere else a suitable spot for a fresh encampment. Moreover, the words of Deut. i. 46, " ye abode in Kadesh many days," when compared with chap. ii. 1, " then we turned, and took our journey into the wilderness of the way to the Red Sea," show most distinctly, that after the sentence passed upon the people in Kadesh (chap. xiv.), they did not begin to travel back at once, but remained for a considerable time in Kadesh before going southwards into the desert. With regard to the direction which they took, all that can be said, so long as none of the places of encampment mentioned in vers. 19–29 are discovered, is that they made their way by a very circuitous route, and with many a wide detour, to Eziongeber, on the Red Sea.[1]

Vers. 37–49. The places of encampment on the journey of the fortieth year from Kadesh to Mount Hor, and round Edom and Moab into the steppes of Moab, have been discussed at chap. xx. and xxi. On Mount Hor, and Aaron's death there, see at chap. xx. 22. For the remark in ver. 40 concerning the Canaanites of Arad,

---

[1] We agree so far, therefore, with the view adopted by *Fries*, and followed by *Kurtz* (History of Old Covenant, iii. 306–7) and *Schultz* (Deut. pp. 153–4), that we regard the stations given in vers. 19–35, between *Rithmah* and *Eziongeber*, as referring to the journeys of Israel, after its condemnation in Kadesh, during the thirty-seven years of its wandering about in the desert. But we do not regard the view which these writers have formed of the marches themselves as being well founded, or in accordance with the text,—namely, that the people of Israel did not really come a second time in full procession from the south to Kadesh, but that they had never left Kadesh entirely, inasmuch as when the nation was rejected in Kadesh, the people divided themselves into larger and smaller groups, and that portion which was estranged from Moses, or rather from the Lord, remained in Kadesh even after the rest were scattered about ; so that, in a certain sense, Kadesh formed the standing encampment and meeting-place of the congregation even during the thirty-seven years. According to this view, the removals and encampments mentioned in vers. 19–36 do not describe the marches of the whole nation, but are to be understood as the circuit made by the headquarters during the thirty-seven years, with Moses at the head and the sanctuary in the midst (*Kurtz*), or else as showing " that Moses and Aaron, with the sanctuary and the tribe of Levi, altered their resting-place, say from year to year, thus securing to every part of the nation in turn the nearness of the sanctuary, in accordance with the signals appointed by God (Num. x. 11, 12), and thus passed over the space between Kadesh and Eziongeber within the first eighteen years, and then, by a similar change of place,

see at chap. xxi. 1. On *Zalmonah, Phunon, and Oboth*, see at chap.
xxi. 10 ; on *Ijje Abarim*, at chap. xxi. 11 ; on *Dibon Gad, Almon
Diblathaim*, and the mountains of *Abarim*, before *Nebo*, chap. xxi.
16–20 (see p. 149). On *Arboth Moab*, see at chap. xxii. 1.

INSTRUCTIONS CONCERNING THE CONQUEST AND DISTRIBUTION OF CANAAN.—CHAP. XXXIII. 50–CHAP. XXXVI. 13.

These instructions, with which the eyes of the Israelites were
directed to the end of all their wandering, viz. the possession of the
promised land, are arranged in two sections by longer introductory formulas (chap. xxxiii. 50 and xxxv. 1). The *former* contains
the divine commands (*a*) with regard to the extermination of the
Canaanites and their idolatry, and the division of the land among
the tribes of Israel (chap. xxxiii. 50–56) ; (*b*) concerning the boundaries of Canaan (chap. xxxiv. 1–15) ; (*c*) concerning the men who
were to divide the land (chap. xxxiv. 16–29). The second contains
commands (*a*) respecting the towns to be given up to the Levites
(chap. xxxv. 1–8) ; (*b*) as to the setting apart of cities of refuge

gradually drew near to Kadesh during the remaining eighteen or nineteen years,
and at length in the last year summoned the whole nation (all the congregation) to assemble together at this meeting-place." Now we cannot admit that
in this view "we find all the different and scattered statements of the Pentateuch explained and rendered intelligible." In the first place, it does not do
justice even to the list of stations ; for if the constantly repeated expression,
" and they (the children of Israel, ver. 1) removed . . . and encamped," denotes
the removal and encamping of the whole congregation in vers. 3–18 and 37–49,
it is certainly at variance with the text to explain the same words in vers. 19–36
as signifying the removal and encamping of the headquarters only, or of Moses,
with Aaron and the Levites, and the tabernacle. Again, in all the laws that
were given and the events that are described as occurring between the first halt
of the congregation in Kadesh (chap. xiii. and xiv.) and their return thither at
the commencement of the fortieth year (chap. xx.), the presence of the whole
congregation is taken for granted. The sacrificial laws in chap. xv., which
Moses was to address to the children of Israel (ver. 1), were given to "the whole
congregation" (cf. vers. 24, 25, 26). The man who gathered wood on the
Sabbath was taken out of the camp and stoned by "all the congregation"
(chap. xv. 36). "All the congregation" took part in the rebellion of the
company of Korah (chap. xvi. 19, xvii. 6, 21 sqq.). It is true this occurrence
is supposed by *Kurtz* to have taken place "during the halt in Kadesh," but the
reasons given are by no means conclusive (p. 105). Besides, if we assign everything that is related in chap. xv.–xix. to the time when the whole congregation
abode in Kadesh, this deprives the hypothesis of its chief support in Deut. i. 46,
"and ye abode in Kadesh a long time, according to the days that ye abode."
For in that case the long abode in Kadesh would include the period of the laws

for unintentional manslayers, and the course to be adopted in relation to such manslayers (chap. xxxv. 9–34); and (c) a law concerning the marrying of heiresses within their own tribes (chap. xxxvi.). —The careful dovetailing of all these legal regulations by separate introductory formulas, is a distinct proof that the section chap. xxxiii. 50–56 is not to be regarded, as *Baumgarten, Knobel,* and others suppose, in accordance with the traditional division of the chapters, as an appendix or admonitory conclusion to the list of stations, but as the general legal foundation for the more minute instructions in chap. xxxiv.–xxxvi.

Chap. xxxiii. 50–56. COMMAND TO EXTERMINATE THE CANAANITES, AND DIVIDE THEIR LAND AMONG THE FAMILIES OF ISRAEL.—Vers. 51–53. When the Israelites passed through the Jordan into the land of Canaan, they were to exterminate all the inhabitants of the land, and to destroy all the memorials of their idolatry; to take possession of the land and dwell therein, for Jehovah had given it to them for a possession. הוֹרִישׁ, to take possession of (vers. 53, etc.), then to drive out of their possession, to

and incidents recorded in chap. xv.–xix., and yet, after all, " the whole congregation " went away. In no case, in fact, can the words be understood as signifying that a portion of the nation remained there during the thirty-seven years. Nor can this be inferred in any way from the fact that their departure is not expressly mentioned ; for, at all events, the statement in chap. xx. 1, " and the children of Israel, the whole congregation, came into the desert of Zin," presupposes that they had gone away. And the " inconceivable idea, that in the last year of their wanderings, when it was their express intention to cross the Jordan and enter Canaan from the east, they should have gone up from Eziongeber to the southern boundary of Canaan, which they had left thirty-seven years before, merely to come back again to the neighbourhood of Eziongeber, after failing in their negotiations with the king of Edom, which they might have carried on from some place much farther south, and to take the road from that point to the country on the east of the Jordan after all" (*Fries*), loses all the surprising character which it apparently has, if we only give up the assumption upon which it is founded, but which has no support whatever in the biblical history, viz. that during the thirty-seven years of their wandering in the desert, Moses was acquainted with the fact that the Israelites were to enter Canaan from the east, or at any rate that he had formed this plan for some time. If, on the contrary, when the Lord rejected the murmuring nation (chap. xiv. 26), He decided nothing with reference to the way by which the generation that would grow up in the desert was to enter Canaan,—and it was not till after the return to Kadesh that Moses was informed by God that they were to advance into Canaan from the east and not from the south,—it was perfectly natural that when the time of punishment had expired, the Israelites should assemble in Kadesh again, and start from that point upon their journey onward.

exterminate (ver. 52 ; cf. chap. xiv. 12, etc.).   On ver. 52, see Ex.
xxxiv. 13. מַשְׂכִּית, an idol of stone (cf. Lev. xxvi. 1). צַלְמֵי מַסֵּכֹת,
idols cast from brass. *Massecah,* see at Ex. xxxii. 4. *Bamoth,* altars
of the Canaanites upon high places (see Lev. xxvi. 30).—Ver.
54. The command to divide the land by lot among the families is
partly a verbal repetition of chap. xxvi. 53–56. אֶל־אֲשֶׁר יֵצֵא לוֹ וגו׳ :
literally, " into that, whither the lot comes out to him, shall be
to him" (*i.e.* to each family) ; in other words, it is to receive that
portion of land to which the lot that comes out of the urn shall
point it.   " According to the tribes of your fathers :" see at chap.
xxvi. 55.—The command closes in vers. 55, 56, with the threat,
that if they did not exterminate the Canaanites, not only would
such as were left become "thorns in their eyes and stings in their
sides," *i.e.* inflict the most painful injuries upon them, and make
war upon them in the land ; but Jehovah would also do the very
same things to the Israelites that He had intended to do to the
Canaanites, *i.e.* drive them out of the land and destroy them. This
threat is repeated by Joshua in his last address to the assembled
congregation (Josh. xxiii. 13).

Chap. xxxiv. 1–15. BOUNDARIES OF THE LAND OF CANAAN.
—Ver. 2. " *When ye come into the land of Canaan, this shall be the
land which will fall to you as an inheritance, the land of Canaan
according to its boundaries :*" *i.e.* ye shall receive the land of Canaan
for an inheritance, within the following limits.—Vers. 3–5. The
southern boundary is the same as that given in Josh. xv. 2–4 as the
boundary of the territory of the tribe of Judah. We have first the
general description, " *The south side shall be to you from the desert
of Zin on the sides of Edom onwards,*" *i.e.* the land was to extend
towards the south as far as the desert of Zin on the sides of Edom.
עַל־יְדֵי, " on the sides," differs in this respect from עַל־יַד, " on the
side" (Ex. ii. 5 ; Josh. xv. 46 ; 2 Sam. xv. 2), that the latter is
used to designate contact at a single point or along a short line ; the
former, contact for a long distance or throughout the whole extent
(= כָּל־יַד, Deut. ii. 37).   " *On the sides of Edom*" signifies, therefore, that the desert of Zin stretched along the side of Edom, and
Canaan was separated from Edom by the desert of Zin.   From
this it follows still further, that Edom in this passage is not the
mountains of Edom, which had their western boundary on the
Arabah, but the country to the south of the desert of *Zin* or Wady
Murreh (see p. 87), viz. the mountain land of the Azazimeh, which

still bears the name of *Seir* or *Serr* among the Arabs (see *Seetzen* and *Rowland* in *Ritter's* Erdk. xiv. pp. 840 and 1087). The statement in Josh. xv. 1 also agrees with this, viz. that Judah's inheritance was " to the territory of Edom, the desert of Zin towards the south," according to which the desert of Zin was also to divide the territory of Edom from that of the tribe of Judah (see the remarks on chap. xiv. 45). With ver. 3*b* the more minute description of the southern boundary line commences : " *The south border shall be from the end of the Salt Sea eastward,*" *i.e.* start from " the tongue which turns to the south" (Josh. xv. 2), from the southern point of the Dead Sea, where there is now a salt marsh with the salt mountain at the south-west border of the lake. " *And turn to the south side* (מִנֶּגֶב) *of the ascent of Akrabbim*" (*ascensus scorpionum*), *i.e.* hardly " the steep pass of *es Sufah*, 1434 feet in height, which leads in a south-westerly direction from the Dead Sea along the northern side of Wady *Fikreh*, a wady three-quarters of an hour's journey in breadth, and over which the road from Petra to Heshbon passes,"[1] as *Knobel* maintains ; for the expression נָסַב (turn), in ver. 4, according to which the southern border turned at the height of Akrabbim, that is to say, did not go any farther in the direction from N.E. to S.W. than from the southern extremity of the Salt Sea to this point, and was then continued in a straight line from east to west, is not at all applicable to the position of this pass, since there would be no bend whatever in the boundary line at the pass of *es Sufah*, if it ran from the Arabah through Wady Fikreh, and so across to Kadesh. The " height of *Akrabbim*," from which the country round was afterwards called *Akrabattine*, *Akrabatene* (1 Macc. v. 3 ; *Josephus*, Ant. xii. 8, 1),[2] is most probably the lofty row of " white cliffs" of sixty or eighty feet in height, which run obliquely across the Arabah at a distance of about eight miles below the Dead Sea and, as seen from the south-west point of the Dead Sea, appear to shut in the Ghor, and which form the dividing line between the two sides of the great valley, which is called *el Ghor* on one side, and *el Araba* on the other (*Robinson*, ii. 489, 494, 502). Consequently it was not the Wady Fikreh, but a wady

---

[1] See *Robinson*, vol. ii. pp. 587, 591 ; and *v. Schubert*, ii. pp. 443, 447 sqq.

[2] It must be distinguished, however, from the *Akrabatta* mentioned by *Josephus* in his Wars of the Jews (iii. 3, 5), the modern *Akrabeh* in central Palestine (*Rob. Bibl. Res.* p. 296), and from the toparchy *Akrabattene* mentioned in *Josephus* (Wars of the Jews, ii. 12, 4 ; 20, 4 ; 22, 2), which was named after this place.

which opened into the Arabah somewhat farther to the south, possibly the southern branch of the Wady *Murreh* itself, which formed the actual boundary. "*And shall pass over to Zin*" (*i.e.* the desert of Zin, the great Wady *Murreh*, see at chap. xiv. 21), "*and its going forth shall be to the south of Kadesh-Barnea*," at the western extremity of the desert of Zin (see at chap. xx. 16). From this point the boundary went farther out (יָצָא) "*to Hazar-Addar, and over* (עָבַר) *to Azmon.*" According to Josh. xv. 3, 4, it went to the south of Kadesh-Barnea over (עָבַר) to *Hezron*, and ascended (עָלָה) to *Addar*, and then turned to *Karkaa*, and went over to *Azmon*. Consequently *Hazar-Addar* corresponds to *Hezron* and *Addar* (in Josh́ua) ; probably the two places were so close to each other that they could be joined together. Neither of them has been discovered yet. This also applies to *Karkaa* and *Azmon*. The latter name reminds us of the Bedouin tribe *Azazimeh*, inhabiting the mountains in the southern part of the desert of Zin (*Robinson*, i. pp. 274, 283, 287 ; *Seetzen*, iii. pp. 45, 47). *Azmon* is probably to be sought for near the Wady *el Ain*, to the west of the Hebron road, and not far from its entrance into the Wady *el Arish ;* for this is "*the river* (brook) *of Egypt*," to which the boundary turned from Azmon, and through which it had "its outgoings at the sea," *i.e.* terminated at the Mediterranean Sea. The "brook of Egypt," therefore, is frequently spoken of as the southern boundary of the land of Israel (1 Kings viii. 65, 2 Kings xxiv. 7, 2 Chron. vii. 8, and Isa. xxvii. 12, where the LXX. express the name by Ῥινοκορούρα). Hence the southern boundary ran, throughout its whole length, from the Arabah on the east to the Mediterranean on the west, along valleys which form a natural division, and constitute more or less the boundary line between the desert and the cultivated land.[1]

Ver. 6. The *western boundary* was to be "the great sea and its territory," *i.e.* the Mediterranean Sea with its territory or coast (cf Deut. iii. 16, 17 ; Josh. xiii. 23, 27, xv. 47).

[1] On the lofty mountains of *Madara*, where the Wady *Murreh* is divided into two wadys (*Fikreh* and *Murreh*) which run to the Arabah, *v. Schubert* observed "some mimosen-trees," with which, as he expresses it, "the vegetation of Arabia took leave of us, as it were, as they were the last that we saw on our road." And *Dieterici* (*Reisebilder*, ii. pp. 156–7) describes the mountain ridge at *Nakb es Sufah* as "the boundary line between the yellow desert and green steppes," and observes still further, that on the other side of the mountain (*i.e.* northwards) the plain spread out before him in its fresh green dress. "The desert journey was over, the empire of death now lay behind us, and a new life blew towards us from fields covered with green."—In the same way the

Vers. 7–9. The *northern boundary* cannot be determined with certainty. " *From the great sea, mark out to you* (תְּתָאוּ, from תָּאָה = תָּוָה, to mark or point out), *i.e.* fix, *Mount Hor as the boundary*"— from thence " *to come to Hamath; and let the goings forth of the boundary be to Zedad. And the boundary shall go out to Ziphron, and its goings out be at Hazar-enan.*" Of all these places, *Hamath*, the modern *Hamah*, or the *Epiphania* of the Greeks and Romans on the Orontes (see at chap. xiii. 21, and Gen. x. 18), is the only one whose situation is well known; but the geographical description of the northern boundary of the land of Israel לְבֹא חֲמָת (chap. xiii. 21; Josh. xiii. 5; Judg. iii. 3; 1 Kings viii. 65; 2 Kings xiv. 25; 1 Chron. xiii. 5; 2 Chron. vii. 8; Amos vi. 14; Ezek. xlvii. 15, 20, xlviii. 1) is so indefinite, that the boundary line cannot be determined with exactness. For no proof can be needed in the present day that לְבֹא חֲמָת cannot mean "to Hamath" (*Ges. thes.* i. p. 185; *Studer* on Judg. iii. 3, and *Baur* on Amos vi. 2), in such a sense as would make the town of Hamath the border town, and בֹּא a

country between Kadesh and the Hebron road, which has become better known to us through the descriptions of travellers, is described as a natural boundary. *Seetzen*, in his account of his journey from Hebron to Sinai (iii. p. 47), observes that the mountains of *Tih* commence at the Wady *el Ain* (fountain-valley), which takes its name from a fountain that waters thirty date-palms and a few small corn-fields (*i.e. Ain el Kuderat*, in *Robinson*, i. p. 280), and describes the country to the south of the small flat Wady *el Kdeis* (*el Kideise*), in which many tamarisks grew (*i.e.* no doubt a wady that comes from Kadesh, from which it derives its name), as a "most dreadful wilderness, which spreads out to an immeasurable extent in all directions, without trees, shrubs, or a single spot of green" (p. 50), although the next day he "found as an unexpected rarity another small field of barley, which might have been an acre in extent" (pp. 52, 53). *Robinson* (i. pp. 280 sqq.) also found, upon the route from Sinai to Hebron, more vegetation in the desert between the Wady *el Kusaimeh* and *el Ain* than anywhere else before throughout his entire journey; and after passing the Wady *el Ain* to the west of Kadesh, he "came upon a broad tract of tolerably fertile soil, capable of tillage, and apparently once tilled." Across the whole of this tract of land there were long ranges of low stone walls visible (called "*el Muzeiriât*," "little plantations," by the Arabs), which had probably served at some former time as boundary walls between the cultivated fields. A little farther to the north the Wady *es Serâm* opens into an extended plain, which looked almost like a meadow with its bushes, grass, and small patches of wheat and barley. A few Azazimeh Arabs fed their camels and flocks here. The land all round became more open, and showed broad valleys that were capable of cultivation, and were separated by low and gradually sloping hills. The grass became more frequent in the valleys, and herbs were found upon the hills. "We heard (he says at p. 283) this morning for the first time the songs of many birds, and among them the lark."

perfectly superfluous pleonasm. In all the passages mentioned, *Hamath* refers, not to the town of that name (*Epiphania* on the Orontes), but to the kingdom of *Hamath*, which was named after its capital, as is proved beyond all doubt by 2 Chron. viii. 4, where Solomon is said to have built store cities " in Hamath." The city of Hamath never belonged to the kingdom of Israel, not even under David and Solomon, and was not reconquered by Jeroboam II., as *Baur* supposes (see my Commentary on the Books of Kings, and *Thenius* on 2 Kings xiv. 25). How far the territory of the kingdom of Hamath extended towards the south in the time of Moses, and how much of it was conquered by Solomon (2 Chron. viii. 4), we are nowhere informed. We simply learn from 2 Kings xxv. 21, that Riblah (whether the same Riblah as is mentioned in ver. 11 as a town upon the eastern boundary, is very doubtful) was situated in the land of Hamath in the time of the Chaldeans. Now if this Riblah has·been preserved in the modern *Ribleh*, a miserable village on the Orontes, in the northern part of the *Bekaa*, ten or twelve hours' journey to the south-west of *Hums*, and fourteen hours to the north of *Baalbek* (*Robinson*, iii. p. 461, App. 176, and Bibl. Researches, p. 544), the land of Canaan would have reached a little farther northwards, and almost to *Hums* (*Emesa*). *Knobel* moves the boundary still farther to the north. He supposes Mount *Hor* to be *Mons Casius*, to the south-west of Antioch, on the Orontes, and agrees with *Robinson* (iii. 461) in identifying *Zedad*, in the large village of *Zadad* (*Sudud* in *Rob.*), which is inhabited exclusively by Syriac Christians, who still speak Syriac according to *Seetzen* (i. 32 and 279), a town containing about 3000 inhabitants (*Wetstein, Reiseber.* p. 88), to the south-east of *Hums*, on the east of the road from Damascus to Hunes, a short day's journey to the north of *Nebk*, and four (or, according to *Van de Velde's* memoir, from ten to twelve) hours' journey to the south of *Hasya* (*Robinson*, iii. p. 461; *Ritter, Erdk.* xvii. pp. 1443–4). *Ziphron*, which was situated upon the border of the territory of Hamath and Damascus, if it is the same as the one mentioned in Ezek. xlvii. 16, is supposed by *Knobel* and *Wetstein* (p. 88) to be preserved in the ruins of *Zifran*, which in all probability have never been visited by any European, fourteen hours to the north-east of Damascus, near to the road from Palmyra. Lastly, *Hazar-enan* (equivalent to fountain-court) is supposed to be the station called *Centum Putea* (Πούτεα in *Ptol.* v. 15, 24), mentioned in the *Tabul. Peuting.* x. 3, on the road from *Apamia* to *Palmyra*, twenty-seven miles, or about eleven hours, to the north-west of Palmyra.—But we may say with certainty that all these conclusions are incorrect, because they are irreconcilable with the eastern boundary described in vers. 10, 11. For example, according to vers. 10, 11, the Israelites were to draw (fix) the eastern boundary "from *Hazar-enan* to *Shepham*," which, as *Knobel* observes, " cannot be determined with exactness, but was farther south than *Hazar-enan*, as it was a point on the eastern boundary which is traced here from north to south, and also farther west, as we may infer from the allusion to Riblah, probably at the northern end of Antilibanus" (?). From *Shepham* the boundary was " *to go down to Riblah*," which *Knobel* finds in the *Ribleh* mentioned above. Now, if we endeavour to fix the situation of these places according to the latest and most trustworthy maps, the incorrectness of the conclusions referred to becomes at once apparent. From *Zadad* (*Sudad*) to *Zifran*, the line of the northern boundary would not have gone from west to east, but from north to south, or rather towards the south-west, and from *Zifran* to *Centum Putea* still more decidedly in a south-westerly direction. Consequently the northern boundary would have described a complete semicircle, commencing in the north-west and terminating in the south-east. But if even in itself this appears very incredible, it becomes perfectly impossible when we take the eastern boundary into consideration. For if this went down to the south-west from *Hazar-enan* to *Shepham* according to *Knobel's* conclusions, instead of going down (ver. 11) from *Shepham* to *Riblah*, it would have gone *up* six or seven geographical miles from south to north, and then have gone down again from north to south along the eastern coast of the Lake of Gennesareth. Now it is impossible that Moses should have fixed such a boundary to the land of Israel on the north-east, and equally impossible that a later Hebrew, acquainted with the geography of his country, should have described it in this way.

If, in order to obtain a more accurate view of the extent of the land towards the north and north-east, we compare the statements of the book of Joshua concerning the conquered land with the districts which still remained to be taken at the time of the distribution; Joshua had taken the land " from the bald mountain which ascends towards Seir," *i.e.* probably the northern ridge of the *Azazimeh* mountains, with its white masses of chalk (*Fries, ut sup.* p. 76 ; see also at Josh. xi. 17), " to *Baal-Gad*, in the valley of Lebanon, below Mount *Hermon*" (Josh. xi. 17 ; cf. chap. xii. 7). But *Baal-Gad* in the valley (בִּקְעָה) of Lebanon is not *Heliopolis* (now *Baal-*

bek in the *Bekaa*, or *Cœlesyria*), as many, from *Iken* and *J. D. Michaelis* down to *Knobel*, suppose; for " the *Bekaa* is not under the *Hermon*," and " there is no proof, or even probability, that Joshua's conquests reached so far, or that Baalbek was ever regarded as the northern boundary of Palestine, nor even that the adjoining portion of Anti-Lebanon was ever called Hermon" (*Robinson*, Biblical Researches, p. 409). *Baal-Gad*, which is called *Baal-Hermon* in Judg. iii. 3 and 1 Chron. v. 23, was the later *Paneas* or *Cæsarea Philippi*, the modern *Banias*, at the foot of the Hermon (cf. *v. Raumer*, Pal. p. 245; *Rob.* Bibl. Res. pp. 408-9, Pal. iii. pp. 347 sqq.). This is placed beyond all doubt by 1 Chron. v. 23, according to which the Manassites, who were increasing in numbers, dwelt " from Bashan to Baal-Hermon, and Senir, and the mountains of Hermon," since this statement proves that Baal-Hermon was between Bashan and the mountains of Hermon. In harmony with this, the following places in the north of Canaan are mentioned in Josh. xiii. 4, 5, and Judg. iii. 3, as being left unconquered by Joshua :—(1.) " All the land of the Canaanites (*i.e.* of the Phœnicians who dwelt on the coast), and the cave of the Sidonians to Aphek ;" מְעָרָה, probably the *spelunca inexpugnabilis in territorio Sidoniensi, quæ vulgo dicitur cavea de Tyrum* (*Wilh. Tyr.* xix. 11), the present *Mughr Jezzin, i.e.* caves of *Jezzin*, to the east of Sidon upon Lebanon (*Ritter, Erdk.* xvii. pp. 99, 100); and *Aphek*, probably the modern *Afka*, to the north-east of Beirut (*Robinson*, Bibl. Res.). (2.) " The land of the *Giblites*," *i.e.* the territory of *Byblos*, and " all Lebanon towards the east, from Baal-Gad below Hermon, till you come to Hamath," *i.e.* not Antilibanus, but Lebanon, which lies to the east of the land of the Giblites. The land of the Giblites, or territory of *Gebal*, which is cited here as the northernmost district of the unconquered land, so that its northern boundary must have coincided with the northern boundary of Canaan, can hardly have extended to the latitude of Tripoli, but probably only reached to the cedar grove at *Bjerreh*, in the neighbourhood of which the highest peaks of the Lebanon are found. The territory of the tribes of Asher and Naphtali (Josh. xix. 24—39) did not reach farther up than this. From all these accounts, we must not push the northern boundary of Canaan as far as the *Eleutherus*, *Nahr el Kebir*, but must draw it farther to the south, across the northern portion of the Lebanon; so that we may look for *Hazar-enan* (fountain-court), which is mentioned as the end of the northern boundary, and the starting-point of the eastern, near the fountain of *Lebweh*. This fountain forms the water-shed in the Bekaa, between the Orontes, which flows to the north, and the Leontes, which flows to the south (cf. *Robinson*, Bibl. Res. p. 531), and is not only a very large fountain of the finest clear water, springing at different points from underneath a broad piece of coarse gravel, which lies to the west of a vein of limestone, but the whole of the soil is of such a character, that " you have only to dig in the gravel, to get as many springs as you please." The quantity of water which is found here is probably even greater than that at the *Anjar*. In addition to the four principal streams, there are three or four smaller ones (*Robinson*, Bibl. Res. p. 532), so that this place might be called, with perfect justice, by the name of *fountain-court*. The probability of this conjecture is also considerably increased by the fact, that the *Ain*, mentioned in ver. 11 as a point upon the eastern boundary, can also be identified without any difficulty (see at ver. 11).

Vers. 10–12. The *Eastern Boundary.*—If we endeavour to trace the upper line of the eastern boundary from the fountain-place just mentioned, it ran from *Hazar-enan* to *Shepham*, the site of which is unknown, and " from *Shepham* it was to go down to *Riblah*, on the east of *Ain*" (the fountain). The article הָרִבְלָה, and still more the precise description, " to the east of Ain, the fountain, or fountain locality" (*Knobel*), show plainly that this *Riblah* is to be distinguished from the *Riblah* in the land of Hamath (2 Kings xxiii. 33, xxv. 21 ; Jer. xxxix. 9, lii. 27), with which it is mostly identified. *Ain* is supposed to be " the great fountain of *Neba Anjar*, at the foot of Antilibanus, which is often called *Birket Anjar*, on account of its taking its rise in a small reservoir or pool" (*Robinson*, Bibl. Res. p. 498), and near to which *Mej-del-Anjar* is to be seen, consisting of " the ruins of the walls and towers of a fortified town, or rather of a large citadel" (*Robinson*, p. 496; cf. *Ritter*, xvii. pp. 181 sqq.).[1] From this point the boundary went farther down, and pressed (מָחָה) " upon the shoulder of the lake of *Chinnereth* towards the east," *i.e.* upon the north-east shore of the Sea of Galilee (see Josh. xix. 35). Hence it ran down along the Jordan to the Salt Sea (Dead Sea). According to these statements, therefore, the eastern boundary went from Bekaa along the western slopes of

---

[1] *Knobel* regards *Ain* as the source of the Orontes, *i.e. Neba Lebweh*, and yet, notwithstanding this, identifies *Riblah* with the village of *Ribleh* mentioned above. But can this *Ribleh*, which is at least eight hours to the north of *Neba Lebweh*, be described as on the east of *Ain*, *i.e. Neba Lebweh* ?

Antilibanus, over or past *Rasbeya* and *Banyas*, at the foot of Hermon, along the edge of the mountains which bound the *Huleh* basin towards the east, down to the north-east corner of the Sea of Galilee; so that *Hermon* itself (*Jebel es Sheikh*) did not belong to the land of Israel.—Vers. 13–15. This land, according to the boundaries thus described, the Israelites were to distribute by lot (chap. xxvi. 56), to give it to the nine tribes and a half, as the tribes of Reuben, Gad, and half Manasseh had already received their inheritance on the other side of the Jordan (chap. xxxii. 33 sqq.).

Vers. 16–29. List of the Men appointed to distribute the Land.—In addition to Eleazar and Joshua, the former of whom was to stand at the head as high priest, in accordance with the divine appointment in chap. xxvii. 21, and the latter to occupy the second place as commander of the army, a prince was selected from each of the ten tribes who were interested in the distribution, as Reuben and Gad had nothing to do with it. Of these princes, namely heads of fathers' houses of the tribes (Josh. xiv. 1), not heads of tribes (see at chap. xiii. 2), Caleb, who is well known from chap. xiii., is the only one whose name is known. The others are not mentioned anywhere else. The list of tribes, in the enumeration of their princes, corresponds, with some exceptions, to the situation of the territory which the tribes received in Canaan, reckoning from south to north, and deviates considerably from the order in which the lots came out for the different tribes, as described in Josh. 15–19. נָחַל in the *Kal*, in vers. 17 and 18, signifies to give for an inheritance, just as in Ex. xxxiv. 8, to put into possession. There is not sufficient ground for altering the *Kal* into *Piel*, especially as the *Piel* in ver. 29 is construed with the accusative of the person, and with the thing governed by בְּ; whereas in ver. 17 the *Kal* is construed with the person governed by לְ, and the accusative of the thing.

Chap. xxxv. 1–8. Appointment of Towns for the Levites. —As the Levites were to receive no inheritance of their own, *i.e.* no separate tribe-territory, in the land of Canaan (chap. xviii. 20 and 23), Moses commanded the children of Israel, *i.e.* the rest of the tribes, in accordance with the divine instructions, to give (vacate) towns to the Levites to dwell in of the inheritance that fell to them for a possession, with pasturage by the cities round about them for their cattle. "Towns to dwell in," *i.e.* not the whole of the towns as their own property, but as many houses in the towns as sufficed for the necessities of the Levites as their hereditary possession, which could be redeemed, if sold at any time, and which reverted to them without compensation in the year of jubilee, even if not redeemed before (Lev. xxv. 32, 33) ; but any portion of the towns which was not taken possession of by them, together with the fields and villages, continued the property of those tribes to which they had been assigned by lot (cf. Josh: xxi. 12, and my commentary on this passage : also *Bähr, Symbolik*, ii. p. 50 ; *Ewald, Gesch.* ii. p. 403). They were also to give them מִגְרָשׁ (from גָּרַשׁ, to drive, drive out), pasturage or fields, to feed their flocks upon, all round the cities ; and according to Lev. xxv. 34, this was not to be sold, but to remain the eternal possession of the Levites. לִבְהֶמְתָּם, for their oxen and beasts of burden, and לִרְכֻשָׁם, for their (remaining) possessions in flocks (sheep and goats), which are generally described in other cases as *mikneh*, in distinction from *behemah* (*e.g.* chap. xxxii. 26 ; Gen. xxxiv. 23, xxxvi. 6). לְכָל־חַיָּתָם, and for all their animals, is merely a generalizing summary signifying all the animals which they possessed.—Ver. 4. The pasture lands of the different towns were to measure "*from the town wall outwards a thousand cubits round about,*" *i.e.* on each of the four sides. "*And measure from without the city, the east side 2000 cubits, and the south side 2000 cubits, and the west side 2000 cubits, and the north side 2000 cubits, and the city in the middle,*" *i.e.* so that the town stood in the middle of the measured lines, and the space which they occupied was not included in the 2000 cubits. The meaning of these instructions, which have caused great perplexity to commentators, and have latterly been explained by *Saalschütz* (*Mos. R.* pp. 100, 101) in a

Fig. *a.*   Fig. *b.*

marvellously erroneous manner, was correctly expounded by *J. D. Michaelis* in the notes to his translation. We must picture the towns

and the surrounding fields as squares, the pasturage as stretching
1000 cubits from the city wall in every direction, as the accompanying figures show, and the length of each outer side as 2000 cubits,
apart from the length of the city wall: so that, if the town itself
occupied a square of 1000 cubits (see fig. *a*), the outer side of the
town fields would measure 2000 + 1000 cubits in every direction;
but if each side of the city wall was only 500 cubits long (see
fig. *b*), the outer side of the town fields would measure 2000 + 500
cubits in every direction.—Vers. 6–8. Of these cities which were
given up to the Levites, *six* were to serve as cities of refuge (see at
ver. 12) for manslayers, and in addition to these (עֲלֵיהֶם, over upon
them) the Israelites were to give of their possessions forty-two others,
that is to say, forty-eight in all; and they were to do this, giving
much from every tribe that had much, and little from the one
which had little (chap. xxvi. 54). With the accusatives אֵת הֶעָרִים
and אֵת שֵׁשׁ עָרֵי (ver. 6), the writer has already in his mind the verbs
תִּרְבּוּ and תַּמְעִיטוּ of ver. 8, where he takes up the object again in the
word וְהֶעָרִים. According to Josh. xxi., the Levites received nine
cities in the territory of Judah and Simeon, four in the territory of
each of the other tribes, with the exception of Naphtali, in which
there were only three, that is to say, ten in the land to the east of
the Jordan, and thirty-eight in Canaan proper, of which the thirteen
given up by Judah, Simeon, and Benjamin were assigned to the
families of the priests, and the other thirty-five to the three Levitical families. This distribution of the Levites among all the tribes
—by which the curse of division and dispersion in Israel, which
had been pronounced upon Levi in Jacob's blessing (Gen. xlix. 7),
was changed into a blessing both for the Levites themselves and
also for all Israel—was in perfect accordance with the election and
destination of this tribe. Called out of the whole nation to be the
peculiar possession of Jehovah, to watch over His covenant, and
teach Israel His rights and His law (Deut. xxxiii. 9, 10; Lev. x. 11;
Deut. xxxi. 9–13), the Levites were to form and set forth among
all the tribes the ἐκλογή of the nation of Jehovah's possession, and
by their walk as well as by their calling to remind the Israelites
continually of their own divine calling; to foster and preserve the
law and testimony of the Lord in Israel, and to awaken and spread
the fear of God and piety among all the tribes. Whilst their
distribution among all the tribes corresponded to this appointment,
the fact that they were not scattered in all the towns and villages
of the other tribes, but were congregated together in separate towns

among the different tribes, preserved them from the disadvantages of standing alone, and defended them from the danger of moral and spiritual declension. Lastly, in the number forty-eight, the quadrupling of the number of the tribes (twelve) is unmistakeable. Now, as the number four is the seal of the kingdom of God in the world, the idea of the kingdom of God is also represented in the four times twelve towns (cf. *Bähr, Symbolik*, ii. pp. 50, 51).

Vers. 9-34. SELECTION AND APPOINTMENT OF CITIES OF REFUGE FOR UNPREMEDITATED MANSLAYERS. — Vers. 10, 11. When the Israelites had come into the land of Canaan, they were to choose towns conveniently situated as cities of refuge, to which the manslayer, who had slain a person (*nephesh*) by accident (בִּשְׁגָגָה : see at Lev. iv. 2), might flee. הִקְרָה, from קָרָה, to hit, *occurrit*, as well as *accidit*; signifies here to give or make, *i.e.* to choose something suitable (*Dietrich*), but not " to build or complete" (*Knobel*), in the sense of קָרָה, as the only meaning which this word has is *contignare*, to join with beams or rafters; and this is obviously unsuitable here. Through these directions, which are repeated and still further expanded in Deut. xix. 1–13, God fulfilled the promise which He gave in Ex. xxi. 13 : that He would appoint a place for the man who should unintentionally slay his neighbour, to which he might flee from the avenger of blood.—Vers. 12-15. These towns were to serve for a refuge from the avenger of blood, that the manslayer might not die before he had taken his trial in the presence of the congregation. The number of cities was fixed at six, three on the other side of the Jordan, and three on this side in the land of Canaan, to which both the children of Israel, and also the foreigners and settlers who were dwelling among them, might flee. In Deut. xix. 3 sqq., Moses advises the congregation to prepare (הֵכִין) the way to these cities, and to divide the territory of the land which Jehovah would give them into three parts (שִׁלֵּשׁ), *i.e.* to set apart a free city in every third of the land, that every manslayer might flee thither, *i.e.* might be able to reach the free city without being detained by length of distance or badness of road, lest, as is added in ver. 6, the avenger of blood pursue the slayer while his heart is hot (יֵחַם, *imperf. Kal* of חָמַם), and overtake him because the way is long, and slay him (הִכָּה נֶפֶשׁ, as in Gen. xxxvii. 21), whereas he was not worthy of death (*i.e.* there was no just ground for putting him to death), " because he had not done it out of hatred." The three cities of refuge on the other side were selected, by Moses himself (Deut. iv. 41-43); the three in Canaan were not appointed till the land was distributed among the nine tribes and a half (Josh. xx. 7). Levitical or priests' towns were selected for all six, not only because it was to the priests and Levites that they would first of all look for an administration of justice (*Schultz* on Deut. xix. 3), but also on the ground that these cities were the property of Jehovah, in a higher sense than the rest of the land, and for this reason answered the idea of cities of refuge, where the manslayer, when once received, was placed under the protection of divine grace, better than any other places possibly could.

The establishment of cities of refuge presupposed the custom and right of revenge. The custom itself goes back to the very earliest times of the human race (Gen. iv. 15, 24, xxvii. 45); it prevailed among the Israelites, as well as the other nations of antiquity, and still continues among the Arabs in unlimited force (cf. *Niebuhr*, Arab. pp. 32 sqq.; *Burckhardt*, Beduinen, 119, 251 sqq.). " Revenge of blood prevailed almost everywhere, so long as there was no national life generated, or it was still in the first stages of its development; and consequently the expiation of any personal violation of justice was left to private revenge, and more especially to family zeal " (*Oehler* in *Herzog's* B. Cycl., where the proofs may be seen). The warrant for this was the principle of retribution, the *jus talionis*, which lay at the foundation of the divine order of the world in general, and the Mosaic law in particular, and which was sanctioned by God, so far as murder was concerned, even in the time of Noah, by the command, " Whoso sheddeth man's-blood," etc. (Gen. ix. 5, 6). This warrant, however, or rather obligation to avenge murder, was subordinated to the essential principle of the theocracy, under the Mosaic law. Whilst God Himself would avenge the blood that was shed, not only upon men, but upon animals also (Gen. ix. 5), and commanded blood-revenge, He withdrew the execution of it from subjective caprice, and restricted it to cases of premeditated slaying or murder, by appointing cities of refuge, which were to protect the manslayer from the avenger, until he took his trial before the congregation. גֹּאֵל, redeemer, is " that particular relative whose special duty it was to restore the violated family integrity, who had to redeem not only landed property that had been alienated from the family (Lev. xxv. 25 sqq.), or a member of the family that had fallen into slavery (Lev. xxv. 47 sqq.), but also the blood that had been taken away from the family by murder " (*Oehler*). In the latter respect he was called גֹּאֵל הַדָּם,

(vers. 19, 21, 24 sqq.; Deut. xix. 6, 12). From 2 Sam. xiv. 7, we may see that it was the duty of the whole family to take care that blood-revenge was carried out. The performance of the duty itself, however, was probably regulated by the closeness of the relationship, and corresponded to the duty of redeeming from bondage (Lev. xxv. 49), and to the right of inheritance (chap. xxvii. 8 sqq.). What standing before the congregation was to consist of, is defined more fully in what follows (vers. 24, 25). If we compare with this Josh. xx. 4 sqq., the manslayer, who fled from the avenger of blood into a free city, was to stand before the gates of the city, and state his cause before the elders. They were then to receive him into the city, and give him a place that he might dwell among them, and were not to deliver him up to the avenger of blood till he had stood before the congregation for judgment. Consequently, if the slayer of a man presented himself with the request to be received, the elders of the free city had to make a provisional inquiry into his case, to decide whether they should grant him protection in the city; and then if the avenger of blood appeared, they were not to deliver up the person whom they had received, but to hand him over, on the charge of the avenger of blood, to the congregation to whom he belonged, or among whom the act had taken place, that they might investigate the case, and judge whether the deed itself was wilful or accidental.

Special instructions are given in vers. 16–28, with reference to the judicial procedure. First of all (vers. 16–21), with regard to qualified slaying or murder. If any person has struck another with an *iron instrument* (an axe, hatchet, hammer, etc.), or *" with a stone of the hand, from which one dies,"* i.e. with a stone which filled the hand,—a large stone, therefore, with which it was possible to kill,—or *" with a wooden instrument of the hand, from which one dies,"* i.e. with a thick club, or a large, strong wooden instrument, and he then died (so that he died in consequence), he was a murderer, who was to be put to death. "For the suspicion would rest upon any one who had used an instrument, that endangered life and therefore was not generally used in striking, that he had intended to take life away" (*Knobel*).—Ver. 19. The avenger of blood could put him to death, when he hit upon him, i.e. whenever and wherever he met with him.—Ver. 20. And so also the man who hit another in hatred, or threw at him by lying in wait, or struck him with the hand in enmity, so that he died. And if a murderer of this kind fled into a free city, the elders of his city were to have him fetched

out and delivered up to the avenger of blood (Deut. xix. 11, 12).
Then follow, in vers. 22–28, the proceedings to be taken with an
unintentional manslayer, viz. if any one hit another "in the moment," *i.e.* suddenly, unawares (chap. vi. 9), without enmity, or by
throwing anything upon him, without lying in wait, or by letting a
stone, by which a man might be killed, fall upon him without seeing
him, so that he died in consequence, but without being his enemy,
or watching to ao him harm. In using the expression בְּבְל־אֶבֶן, the
writer had probably הִשְׁלִיךְ still in his mind; but he dropped this
word, and wrote וַיַּפֵּל in the form of a fresh sentence. The thing
intended is explained still more clearly in Deut. xix. 4, 5. Instead
of בְּפֶתַע, we find there בִּבְלִי דַעַת, without knowing, unintentionally.
The words, "without being his enemy," are paraphrased there by,
"without hating him from yesterday and the day before yesterday"
(*i.e.* previously), and are explained by an example taken from the
life: "*When a man goeth into the wood with his neighbour to hew
wood, and his hand fetcheth a stroke with the axe to cut down the tree,
and the iron slippeth* (נָשַׁל Niphal of שָׁלַל) *from the wood* (handle), *and
lighteth upon his neighbour.*"—Vers. 24, 25. In such a case as this,
the congregation was to judge between the slayer and the avenger
of blood, according to the judgments before them. They were to
rescue the innocent man from the avenger of blood, to bring him
back to his (*i.e.* the nearest) city of refuge to which he had fled,
that he might dwell there till the death of the high priest, who had
been anointed with the holy oil.—Vers. 26–28. If he left the city
of refuge before this, and the avenger of blood got hold of him, and
slew him outside the borders (precincts) of the city, it was not to be
reckoned to him as blood (אֵין לוֹ דָם, like אֵין לוֹ דָּמִים, Ex. xxii. 1). But
after the death of the high priest he might return "into the land of his
possession," *i.e.* his hereditary possession (cf. Lev. xxvii. 22), *sc.* without the avenger of blood being allowed to pursue him any longer.

In these regulations "all the rigour of the divine justice is manifested in the most beautiful concord with His compassionate mercy.
Through the destruction of life, even when not wilful, human
blood had been shed, and demanded expiation. Yet this expiation
did not consist in the death of the offender himself, because he had
not sinned wilfully." Hence an asylum was provided for him in
the free city, to which he might escape, and where he would lie
concealed. This sojourn in the free city was not to be regarded as
banishment, although separation from house, home, and family was
certainly a punishment; but it was a concealment under "the pro-

tection of the mercy of God, which opened places of escape in the cities of refuge from the carnal ardour of the avenger of blood, where the slayer remained concealed until his sin was expiated by the death of the high priest." For the fact, that the death of the high priest was hereby regarded as expiatory, as many of the Rabbins, fathers, and earlier commentators maintain (see my Comm. on Joshua, p. 448), is unmistakeably evident from the addition of the clause, "who has been anointed with the holy oil," which would appear unmeaning and superfluous on any other view. This clause points to the inward connection between the return of the slayer and the death of the high priest. "The anointing with the holy oil was a symbol of the communication of the Holy Ghost, by which the high priest was empowered to act as mediator and representative of the nation before God, so that he alone could carry out the yearly and general expiation for the whole nation, on the great day of atonement. But as his life and work acquired a representative signification through this anointing with the Holy Ghost, his death might also be regarded as a death for the sins of the people, by virtue of the Holy Ghost imparted to him, through which the unintentional manslayer received the benefits of the propitiation for his sin before God, so that he could return cleansed to his native town, without further exposure to the vengeance of the avenger of blood" (Comm. on Joshua, p. 448). But inasmuch as, according to this view, the death of the high priest had the same result in a certain sense, in relation to his time of office, as his function on the day of atonement had had every year, "the death of the earthly high priest became thereby a type of that of the heavenly One, who, through the eternal (holy) Spirit, offered Himself without spot to God, that we might be redeemed from our transgressions, and receive the promised eternal inheritance (Heb. ix. 14, 15). Just as the blood of Christ wrought out eternal redemption, only because through the eternal Spirit He offered Himself without spot to God, so the death of the high priest of the Old Testament secured the complete deliverance of the manslayer from his sin, only because he had been anointed with the holy oil, the symbol of the Holy Ghost" (p. 449).

If, therefore, the confinement of the unintentional manslayer in the city of refuge was neither an ordinary exile nor merely a means of rescuing him from the revenge of the enraged *goel*, but an appointment of the just and merciful God for the expiation of human blood even though not wilfully shed, that, whilst there was no vio-

lation of judicial righteousness, a barrier might be set to the unrighteousness of family revenge; it was necessary to guard against
any such abuse of this gracious provision of the righteous God, as
that into which the heathen right of asylum had degenerated.[1]
The instructions which follow in vers. 29–34 were intended to
secure this object. In ver. 29, there is first of all the general
law, that these instructions (those given in vers. 11–28) were to be
for a statute of judgment (see chap. xxvii. 11) for all future ages
("throughout your generations," see Ex. xii. 14, 20). Then, in
ver. 30, a just judgment is enforced in the treatment of murder.
" *Whoso killeth any person* (these words are construed absolutely),
at the mouth (the testimony) *of witnesses shall the murderer be put to
death; and one witness shall not answer* (give evidence) *against a person to die;*" *i.e.* if the taking of life were in question, capital punishment was not to be inflicted upon the testimony of one person only,
but upon that of a plurality of witnesses. One witness could not
only be more easily mistaken than several, but would be more likely
to be partial than several persons who were unanimous in bearing
witness to one and the same thing. The number of witnesses was
afterwards fixed at two witnesses, at least, in the case of capital
crimes (Deut. xvii. 6), and two or three in the case of every crime
(Deut. xix. 15; cf. John viii. 17, 2 Cor. xiii. 1, Heb. x. 28).—
Lastly (vers. 31 sqq.), the command is given not to take redemption
money, either for the life of the murderer, who was a wicked man
to die, *i.e.* deserving of death (such a man was to be put to death);
nor " *for fleeing into the city of refuge, to return to dwell in the land
till the death of the high priest:* " that is to say, they were neither to
allow the wilful murderer to come to terms with the relative of the
man who had been put to death, by the payment of a redemption
fee, and so to save his life, as is not unfrequently the case in the
East at the present day (cf. *Robinson,* Pal. i. p. 209, and *Lane's*
Manners and Customs)'; nor even to allow the unintentional murderer to purchase permission to return home from the city of refuge

---

[1] On the *asyla,* in general, see *Winer's Real-Wörterbuch,* art. *Freistatt;
Pauly,* Real-encykl. der class. Alterthums-wissenschaft, Bd. i. *s. v. Asylum;* but
more especially *K. Dann,* " *über den Ursprung des Asylrechts und dessen Schicksale
und Ueberreste* in Europa," in his *Ztschr. für deutsches Recht,* Lpz. 1840. " The
asyla of the *Greeks, Romans,* and *Germans* differed altogether from those of the
Hebrews; for whilst the latter were never intended to save the wilful criminal
from the punishment he deserved, but were simply established for the purpose
of securing a just sentence, the former actually answered the purpose of rescuing the criminal from the punishment which he legally deserved."

before the death of the high priest, by the payment of a money compensation.—Ver. 33. The Israelites were not to desecrate their land by sparing the murderer; as blood, *i.e.* bloodshed or murder, desecrated the land, and there was no expiation (יְכֻפַּר) to the land for the blood that was shed in it, except through the blood of the man who had shed it, *i.e.* through the execution of the murderer, by which justice would be satisfied.—Ver. 34. And they were not to desecrate the land in which they dwelt by tolerating murderers, because Jehovah, the Holy One, dwelt in it, among the children of Israel (cf. Lev. xviii. 25 sqq.).

LAW CONCERNING THE MARRIAGE OF HEIRESSES.—CHAP. XXXVI.

Vers. 1-4. The occasion for this law was a representation made to Moses and the princes of the congregation by the heads of the fathers' houses (הָאָבוֹת for בֵּית־הָאָבוֹת, as in Ex. vi. 25, etc.) of the family of Gilead the Manassite, to which *Zelophehad* (chap. xxvi. 33) belonged, to the effect that, by allotting an hereditary possession to the daughters of Zelophehad, the tribe-territory assigned to the Manassites would be diminished if they should marry into another tribe. They founded their appeal upon the command of Jehovah, that the land was to be distributed by lot among the Israelites for an inheritance (ver. 2 compared with chap. xxvi. 55, 56, and xxxiii. 54); and although it is not expressly stated, yet on the ground of the promise of the everlasting possession of Canaan (Gen. xvii. 8), and the provision made by the law, that an inheritance was not to be alienated (Lev. xxv. 10, 13, 23 sqq.), they understood it as signifying that the portion assigned to each tribe was to continue unchanged to all generations. (The singular pronoun, *my* Lord, in ver. 2, refers to the speaker, as in chap. xxxii. 27.) Now, as the inheritance of their brother, *i.e.* their tribe-mate Zelophehad, had been given to his daughters (chap. xxvii. 1), if they should be chosen as wives by any of the children of the (other) tribes of Israel, *i.e.* should marry into another tribe, their inheritance would be taken away from the tribe-territory of Manasseh, and would be added to that of the tribe into which they were received. The suffix לָהֶם (ver. 3) refers *ad sensum* to מַטֶּה, the tribe regarded according to its members.—Ver. 4. And when the year of jubilee came round (see Lev. xxv. 10), their inheritance would be entirely withdrawn from the tribe of Manasseh. Strictly speaking, the hereditary property would pass at once, when the marriage took place, to the tribe into which an heiress married, and not merely at the year of jubilee. But up to the year of jubilee it was always possible that the hereditary property might revert to the tribe of Manasseh, either through the marriage being childless, or through the purchase of the inheritance. But in the year of jubilee all landed property that had been alienated was to return to its original proprietor or his heir (Lev. xxv. 33 sqq.). In this way the transfer of an inheritance from one tribe to another, which took place in consequence of a marriage, would be established in perpetuity. And it was in this sense that the elders of the tribe of Manasseh meant that a portion of the inheritance which had fallen to them by lot would be taken away from their tribe at the year of jubilee.— Vers. 5–9. Moses declared that what they had affirmed was right (כֵּן), and then, by command of Jehovah, he told the daughters of Zelophehad that they might marry whoever pleased them (the suffix הֶם, attached to בְּעֵינֵי, for הֵן, as in Ex. i. 21, Gen. xxxi. 9, etc.), but that he must belong to the family of their father's tribe, that is to say, must be a Manassite. For (ver. 7) the inheritance was not to turn away the Israelites from one tribe to another (not to be transferred from one to another), but every Israelite was to keep to the inheritance of his father's tribe, and no one was to enter upon the possession of another tribe by marrying an heiress belonging to that tribe. This is afterwards extended, in vers. 8 and 9, into a general law for every heiress in Israel.

In vers. 10–12 it is related that, in accordance with these instructions, the five daughters of Zelophehad, whose names are repeated from chap. xxvi. 33 and xxvii. 1 (see also Josh. xvii. 3), married husbands from the families of the Manassites, namely, sons of their cousins (? uncles), and thus their inheritance remained in their father's tribe (הָיָה עַל, to be and remain upon anything).—Ver. 13. The conclusion refers not merely to the laws and rights contained in chap. xxxiii. 50–xxxvi. 13, but includes the rest of the laws given in the steppes of Moab (chap. xxv.–xxx.), and forms the conclusion to the whole book, which places the lawgiving in the steppes of Moab by the side of the lawgiving at Mount Sinai (Lev. xxvi. 46, xlvii. 34) and brings it to a close, though without in any way implying that the explanation (בֵּאַר, Deut. i. 5), further development, and hortatory enforcement of the law and its testimonies, statutes, and judgments (Deut. i. 5, iv. 44 sqq., xii. 1 sqq.), which follow in *Deuteronomy*, are not of Mosaic origin.

THE FIFTH BOOK OF MOSES

(DEUTERONOMY.)

·

INTRODUCTION.

CONTENTS, ARRANGEMENT, AND CHARACTER OF DEUTERONOMY.

THE fifth book of Moses, which is headed אלה הדברים, or briefly דברים, in the Hebrew Bibles, from the opening words of the book, is called מִשְׁנֵה הַתּוֹרָה (*repetitio legis*), or merely מִשְׁנֶה by the Hellenistic Jews and some of the Rabbins, with special reference to its contents as described in chap. xvii. 18. The rabbinical explanation of the latter given in *Münster* and *Fagius* is זכרן דראשונים, "*memoria rerum priorum, quæ in aliis scribuntur libris.*" By some of the Rabbins the book is also called סֵפֶר תּוֹכָחוֹת, *liber redargutionum.* The first of these titles has become current in the Christian Church through the rendering given by the LXX. and Vulgate, Δευτερονόμιον, *Deuteronomium;* and although it has arisen from an incorrect rendering of chap. xvii. 18 (see the exposition of the passage), it is so far a suitable one, that it describes quite correctly the leading contents of the book itself. The book of Deuteronomy contains not so much "a recapitulation of the things commanded and done, as related in Exodus, Leviticus, and Numbers" (*Theod.*), as "a compendium and summary of the whole law and wisdom of the people of Israel, wherein those things which related to the priests and Levites are omitted, and only such things included as the people generally required to know" (*Luther*). Consequently it is not merely a repetition and summary of the most important laws and events contained in the previous books, still less a mere "summons to the law and testimony," or a "fresh and independent lawgiving standing side by side with the earlier one," a "transformation of the old law to suit the altered circumstances," or "merely a second book of the law, intended for the people that knew not the law" (*Ewald, Riehm*, etc.); but *a hortatory description, explanation, and enforcement of the most essential contents of the covenant revelation and covenant laws, with emphatic prominence given to the spiritual principle of the law and its fulfilment, and with a further development of the ecclesiastical, judicial, political, and civil organization, which was intended as a permanent foundation for the life and well-being of the people in the land of Canaan.* There is not the slightest trace, throughout the whole book, of any intention whatever to give a new or second law. Whilst the laws as well as the divine promises and threatenings in the three middle books of the Pentateuch are all introduced as words of Jehovah to Moses, which he was to make known to the people, and even where the announcement passes over into the form of an address,—as, for example, in Ex. xxiii. 20 sqq., Lev. xxvi.,—are not spoken by Moses in his own name, but spoken by Jehovah to Israel through Moses; the book of Deuteronomy, with the exception of chap. xxxi.-xxxiv., contains nothing but words addressed by Moses to the people, with the intention, as he expressly affirms in chap. i. 5, of explaining (בֵּאֵר) the law to the people. Accordingly he does not quote those laws, which were given before and are merely repeated here, nor the further precepts and arrangements that were added to them, such as those concerning the one site for the worship of God, the prophetic and regal qualifications, the administration of justice and carrying on of war, in the categorical language of law; but clothes them, as well as the other commandments, in the hortatory form of a paternal address, full of solemn and affectionate admonition, with the addition of such reminiscences and motives as seemed best adapted to impress their observance upon the hearts of the people. As the repetition not only of the decalogue, which God addressed to the people directly from Sinai, but also of many other laws, which He gave through Moses at Sinai and during the journey through the desert, had no other object than this, to make the contents of the covenant legislation intelligible to all the people, and to impress them upon their hearts; so those laws which are peculiar to our book are not additions made to this legislation for the purpose of completing it, but simply furnish such explanations and illustrations of its meaning as were rendered necessary by the peculiar relations and forms of the religious, social, and political life of the nation in the promised land of Canaan. Throughout the whole book, the law, with its commandments, statutes, and judgments, which Moses laid "this day" before the people, is never described as either new or altered; on the contrary, it is only the law of the covenant, which Jehovah had concluded with His people at Horeb (chap. v. 1 sqq.); and the commandments, statutes, and judgments of this law Moses had received from the Lord upon the Mount (Sinai), that he might teach Israel to keep them (chap. v. 31 sqq.; comp. chap. vi. 20–25). The details of the book also bear this out.

The *first* part of the book, which embraces by far the greater portion of it, viz. chap. i.–xxx., consists of three long addresses, which Moses delivered to all Israel, according to the heading of chap. i. 1–4, in the land of Moab, on the first of the eleventh month, in the fortieth year after the exodus from Egypt. The *first* of these addresses (chap. i. 6–iv. 40) is intended to prepare the way for the exposition and enforcement of the law, which follow afterwards. Moses calls to their recollection the most important facts connected with the history of their forty years' wandering in the desert, under the protection and merciful guidance of the Lord (chap. i. 6–iii. 29); and to this he attaches the exhortation not to forget the revelation of the Lord, which they had seen at Horeb, or the words of the covenant which they had heard, but to bear in mind at all times, that Jehovah alone was God in heaven and on earth, and to keep His commandments and rights, that they might enjoy long life and prosperity in the land of Canaan (chap. iv. 1–40). This is followed by the statement in chap. iv. 41–43, that Moses set apart three cities of refuge in the land to the east of the Jordan for unintentional manslayers. The *second* address (chap. v.–xxvi.) is described in the heading in chap. iv. 44–49 as the law, which Moses set before the children of Israel, and consists of two parts, the one general and the other particular. In the *general* part (chap. v.–xi.), Moses repeats the ten words of the covenant, which Jehovah spoke to Israel from Sinai out of the midst of the fire, together with the circumstances which attended their promulgation (chap. v.), and then expounds the contents of the first two commandments of the decalogue, that Jehovah alone is the true and absolute God, and requires love from His people with all their heart and all their soul, and therefore will not tolerate the worship of any other god beside Himself (chap. vi.). For this reason the Israelites were not only to form no alliance with the Canaanites after conquering them, and taking possession of the promised land, but to exterminate them without quarter, and destroy their altars and idols, because the Lord had chosen them to be His holy nation from love to their forefathers, and would keep the covenant of His grace, and bestow the richest blessings upon them, if they observed His commandments (chap. vii.) ; but when in possession and enjoyment of the riches of this blessed land, they were to remain for ever mindful of the temptation, humiliation, and fatherly chastisement which they had experienced at the hand of their God in the wilderness, that they might not forget the Lord and His manifestations of mercy in their self-exaltation (chap. viii.), but might constantly remember that they owed their conquest and possession of Canaan not to their own righteousness, but solely to the compassion and covenant faithfulness of the Lord, whom they had repeatedly provoked to anger in the wilderness, (chap. ix. 1–x. 11), and might earnestly strive to serve the Lord in true fear and love, and to keep His commandments, that they might inherit the promised blessing, and not be exposed to the curse which would fall upon transgressors and the worshippers of idols (chap. x. 12–xi. 32). To this there is added in the more *special* part (chap. xii.–xxvi.), an account of the most important laws which all Israel was to observe in the land of its inheritance, viz. : (1.) Directions for the behaviour of Israel towards the Lord God, *e.g.* as to the presentation of sacrificial offerings and celebration of sacrificial meals at no other place than the one chosen by God for the revelation of His name (chap. xii.) ; as to the destruction of all seducers to idolatry, whether prophets who rose up with signs and wonders, or the closest blood-relations, and such towns in the land as should fall away to idolatry (chap. xiii.) ; as to abstinence from the mourning ceremonies of the heathen, and from unclean food, and the setting apart of tithes for sacrificial meals and for the poor (chap. xiv.) ; as to the observance of the year of remission, the emancipation of Hebrew slaves in the seventh year, and the dedication of the first-born of oxen and sheep (chap. xv.), and as to the celebration of the feast of Passover, of Weeks, and of Tabernacles, by sacrificial meals at the sanctuary (chap. xvi. 1–17). (2.) Laws concerning the organization of the theocratic state, and especially as to the appointment of judges and official persons in every town, and the trial of idolaters and evil-doers in both the lower and higher forms (chap. xvi. 18–xvii. 13) ; concerning the choice of a king in the future, and his duties (chap. xvii. 14–20) ; concerning the rights of priests and Levites (chap. xviii. 1–8) ; and concerning false and true prophets (vers. 9–22). (3.) Regulations bearing upon the sanctification of human life : viz. legal instructions as to the establishment of cities of refuge for unintentional man-slayers (chap. xix. 1-13) ; as to the maintenance of the sanctity of the boundaries of landed property, and abstinence from false charges against a neighbour (vers. 14-21) ; as to the conduct of war, with special reference to the duty of sparing their own fighting men, and also defenceless enemies and their towns (chap. xx.) ; as to the expiation of inexplicable murders (chap. xxi. 1-9) ; as to the mild treatment of women taken in war (vers. 10-14) ; the just use of paternal authority (vers. 15-21) ; and the burial of criminals that had been executed (vers. 22, 23). (4.) The duty of paying affectionate regard to the property of a neighbour, and cherishing a sacred dread of violating the moral and natural order of the world (chap. xxii. 1-12), with various precepts for the sanctification of the marriage bond (chap. xxii. 13-xxiii. 1), of the theocratic union as a congregation (chap. xxiii. 2-26), and also of domestic and social life, in all its manifold relations (chaps. xxiv. and xxv.) ; and lastly, the appointment of prayers of thanksgiving on the presenta-tion of the first-fruits and tenths of the fruits of the field (chap. xxvi. 1-15) ; together with a closing admonition (vers. 16-19) to observe all these laws and rights with all the heart. The *third* address (chap. xxvii.-xxx.) has reference to the renewal of the cove-nant. This solemn act is introduced with a command to write the law upon large stones when Canaan should be conquered, and to set up these stones upon Mount Ebal, to build an altar there ; and after presenting burnt-offerings and slain-offerings, to proclaim in the most solemn manner both the blessing and curse of the law, the former upon Gerizim, and the latter upon Ebal (chap. xxvii.). Moses takes occasion from this command to declare most fully what blessings and curses would come upon the people, according as they should or should not hearken to the voice of the Lord (chap. xxviii.). Then follows the renewal of the covenant, which consisted in the fact that Moses recited once more, in a solemn address to the whole of the national assembly, all that the Lord had done for them and to them ; and after pointing again to the blessings and curses of the law, called upon them and adjured them to enter into the covenant of Jehovah their God, which He had that day concluded with them, and having before them blessing and cursing, life and death, to make the choice of life.—The *second* and much shorter portion of the book (chap. xxxi.-xxxiv.) contains the close of Moses' life and labours : (*a*) the appointment of Joshua to be the leader of Israel into Canaan, and the handing over of the book of the law, when completed, to the priests, for them to keep and read to the people at the feast of Tabernacles in the year of jubilee (chap. xxxi.); (b) the song of Moses (chap. xxxii. 1–47), and the announcement of his death (vers. 48–52); (c) the blessing of Moses (chap. xxxiii.); and (d) the account of his death (chap. xxxiv.).

From this general survey of the contents, it is sufficiently evident that the exposition of the commandments, statutes, and rights of the law had no other object than this, to pledge the nation in the most solemn manner to an inviolable observance, in the land of Canaan, of the covenant which Jehovah had made with Israel at Horeb (chap. xxviii. 69). To this end Moses not only repeats the fundamental law of this covenant, the decalogue, but many of the separate commandments, statutes, and rights of the more expanded Sinaitic law. These are rarely given *in extenso* (*e.g.* the laws of food in chap. xiv.), but for the most part simply in brief hints, bringing out by way of example a few of the more important rules, for the purpose of linking on some further explanations of the law in its application to the peculiar circumstances of the land of Canaan. And throughout, as *F. W. Schultz* correctly observes, the intention of the book is, "by means of certain supplementary and auxiliary rules, to ensure the realization of the laws or institutions of the earlier books, the full validity of which it presupposes; and that not merely in some fashion or other, but in its true essence, and according to its higher object and idea, notwithstanding all the difficulties that might present themselves in Canaan or elsewhere." Not only are the instructions relating to the building of the sanctuary, the service of the priests and Levites, and the laws of sacrifice and purification, passed over without mention as being already known; but of the festivals and festive celebrations, only the three annual feasts of Passover, Pentecost, and Tabernacles are referred to, and that but briefly, for the purpose of commanding the observance of the sacrificial meals which were to be held at the sanctuary in connection with these feasts (chap. xvi.). The tithes and first-fruits are noticed several times, but only so far as they were to be applied to common sacrificial meals before the Lord. The appointment of judges is commanded in all the towns of the land, and rules are given by which the judicial form of procedure is determined more minutely; but no rule is laid down as to the election of the judges, simply because this had been done before. On the other hand, instructions are given concerning the king whom the people would one day desire to set over themselves; concerning the prophets whom the Lord would raise up; and also concerning any wars that might be waged with other nations than the Canaanites, the extermination of the latter being enforced once more; and several things besides. —And if this selection of materials indicates an intention, not so much to complete the legislation of the earlier books by the addition of new laws, as to promote its observance and introduction into the national life, and secure its permanent force; this intention becomes still more apparent when we consider how Moses, after repeating the decalogue, not only sums up the essential contents of all the commandments, statutes, and rights which Jehovah has commanded, in the one command to love God with all the heart, etc., and sets forth this commandment as the sum of the whole law, but in all his expositions of the law, all his exhortations to obedience, and all threats and promises, aims ever at this one object, to awaken in the hearts of the people a proper state of mind for the observance of the commandments of God, viz. a feeling of humility and love and willing obedience, and to destroy that love for merely outward legality and pharisaic self-righteousness which is inherent in the natural man, that the people may circumcise the foreskin of their heart, and enter heartily into the covenant of their God, and maintain that covenant with true fidelity.

It is in this peculiar characteristic and design of the legislative addresses which the book contains, and not in the purpose attributed to it, of appending a general law for the nation to the legislation of the previous books, which had reference chiefly to the priests and Levites,[1] that we are to seek for that completion of the law which the book of *Deuteronomy* supplies. And in this we may find the strongest proof of the Mosaic origin of this concluding part of the Thorah. What the heading distinctly states (chap. i. 1–4),—viz.

---

[1] In opposition to this view of *Ed. Riehm, Schultz* justly argues that the book of Deuteronomy is very far from containing everything that concerned the people and was of great importance to them. It does not even repeat those laws of the first book of the covenant in Ex. xx.-xxiii., which affected most closely the social every-day life of the people. It contains nothing about circumcision, which certainly could not have been omitted from the national law-book; no further details as to the Passover, Pentecost, and the feast of Tabernacles; it does not even mention the great day of atonement, on which every Israelite had to fast on pain of death, nor the feast of trumpets and year of jubilee; and the Sabbath command is simply introduced quite briefly in and with the decalogue. Of all the defilements and washings, which were of the greatest moment, according to the Old Testament view, to every individual, there is not a single word.

that Moses delivered this address to all Israel a short time before his death in the land of Moab, on the other side of the Jordan, and therefore on the threshold of the promised land,—is confirmed by both the form and contents of the book. As *Hengstenberg* has well observed (*Ev. K. Z.* 1862, No. 5, pp. 49 sqq.), "the address of Moses is in perfect harmony with his situation. He speaks like a dying father to his children. The words are earnest, inspired, impressive. He looks back over the whole of the forty years of their wandering in the desert, reminds the people of all the blessings they have received, of the ingratitude with which they have so often repaid them, and of the judgments of God, and the love that continually broke forth behind them; he explains the laws again and again, and adds what is necessary to complete them, and is never weary of urging obedience to them in the warmest and most emphatic words, because the very life of the nation was bound up with this; he surveys all the storms and conflicts which they have passed through, and, beholding the future in the past, takes a survey also of the future history of the nation, and sees, with mingled sorrow and joy, how the three great features of the past—viz. apostasy, punishment, and pardon—continue to repeat themselves in the future also.—The situation throughout is the time when Israel was standing on the border of the promised land, and preparing to cross the Jordan; and there is never any allusion to what formed the centre of the national life in future times—to Jerusalem and its temple, or to the Davidic monarchy. The approaching conquest of the land is merely taken for granted as a whole; the land is dressed throughout in all the charms of a desired good, and no reference is ever made to the special circumstances of Israel in the land about to be conquered." To this there is to be added what makes its appearance on every hand—the most lively remembrance of Egypt, and the condition of the people when living there (cf. chap. v. 15, vii. 15, xi. 10, xv. 15, xvi. 12, xxiv. 18, xxviii. 27, 35, 60), and an accurate acquaintance with the very earliest circumstances of the different nations with which the Israelites came into either friendly or hostile contact in the Mosaic age (chap. ii.); together with many other things that were entirely changed a short time after the conquest of Canaan by the Israelites.

And just as these addresses, which complete the giving of the law and bring it to a close, form an integral part of the *Thorah*, so the historical account of the finishing of the book of the law, and its being handed over to the priests, together with the song and blessing of Moses (chap. xxxi.–xxxiii.), form a fitting conclusion to the work of Moses, the lawgiver and mediator of the old covenant; and to this the account of his death, with which the Pentateuch closes (chap. xxxiv.), is very appropriately appended.

EXPOSITION.

HEADING AND INTRODUCTION.

CHAP. I. 1–5.

VERS. 1–4 contain the heading to the whole book; and to this the introduction to the first address is appended in ver. 5. By the expression, " *These be the words,*" etc., Deuteronomy is attached to the previous books; the word " *these,*" which refers to the addresses that follow, connects what follows with what goes before, just as in Gen. ii. 4, vi. 9, etc. The geographical data in ver. 1 present no little difficulty; for whilst the general statement as to the place where Moses delivered the addresses in this book, viz. *beyond Jordan,* is particularized in the introduction to the second address (chap. iv. 46), as " *in the valley over against Beth-Peor,*" here it is described as " *in the wilderness, in the Arabah,*" etc. This contrast between the verse before us and chap. iv. 45, 46, and still more the introduction of the very general and loose expression, " *in the desert,*" which is so little adapted for a geographical definition of the locality, that it has to be defined itself by the additional words " *in the Arabah,*" suggest the conclusion that the particular names introduced are not intended to furnish as exact a geographical account as possible of the spot where Moses explained the law to all Israel, but to call up to view the scene of the addresses which follow, and point out the situation of all Israel at that time. Israel was " *in the desert,*" not yet in Canaan the promised inheritance, and in fact " *in the Arabah.*" This is the name given to the deep low-lying plain on both sides of the Jordan, which runs from the Lake of Gennesaret to the Dead Sea, and stretches southwards from the Dead Sea to *Aila,* at the northern extremity of the Red Sea, as we may see very clearly from chap. ii. 8, where the way which the Israelites took past Edom to *Aila* is called the " way of the *Arabah,*" and also from the fact that the Dead Sea is called " the sea of the

Arabah" in chap. iii. 17 and iv. 49. At present the name *Arabah* is simply attached to the southern half of this valley, between the Dead Sea and the Red Sea; whilst the northern part, between the Dead Sea and the Sea of Galilee, is called *el Ghor;* though *Abulfeda, Ibn Haukal,* and other Arabic geographers, extend the name *Ghor* from the Lake of Gennesaret to Aila (cf. *Ges. thes.* p. 1166; *Hengstenberg,* Balaam, p. 520; *Robinson,* Pal. ii. p. 596).— מוֹל סוּף, "*over against Suph*" (מוֹל for מוּל, chap. ii. 19, iii. 29, etc., for the sake of euphony, to avoid the close connection of the two *u*-sounds). *Suph* is probably a contraction of יַם־סוּף, "the Red Sea" (see at Ex. x. 19). This name is given not only to the Gulf of *Suez* (Ex. xiii. 18, xv. 4, 22, etc.), but to that of *Akabah* also (Num. xiv. 25, xxi. 4, etc.). There is no other *Suph* that would be at all suitable here. The LXX. have rendered it πλήσιον τῆς ἐρυθρᾶς θαλάσσης; and *Onkelos* and others adopt the same rendering. This description cannot serve as a more precise definition of the *Arabah,* in which case אֲשֶׁר (which) would have to be supplied before מוֹל, since "the Arabah actually touches the Red Sea." Nor does it point out the particular spot in the Arabah where the addresses were delivered, as *Knobel* supposes; or indicate the connection between the Arboth Moab and the continuation of the Arabah on the other side of the Dead Sea, and point out the Arabah in all this extent as the heart of the country over which the Israelites had moved during the whole of their forty years' wandering (*Hengstenberg*). For although the Israelites passed twice through the Arabah (see p. 246), it formed by no means the heart of the country in which they continued for forty years. The words "opposite to *Suph,*" when taken in connection with the following names, cannot have any other object than to define with greater exactness the desert in which the Israelites had moved during the forty years. Moses spoke to all Israel on the other side of the Jordan, when it was still in the desert, in the Arabah, still opposite to the Red Sea, after crossing which it had entered the wilderness (Ex. xv. 22), "between *Paran,* and *Tophel,* and *Laban,* and *Hazeroth,* and *Di-Sahab.*" *Paran* is at all events not the desert of this name in all its extent (see vol. ii. pp. 58, 59), but the place of encampment in the "desert of *Paran*" (Num. x. 12, xii. 16), *i.e.* the district of *Kadesh* in the desert of *Zin* (Num. xiii. 21, 26); and *Hazeroth* is most probably the place of encampment of that name mentioned in Num. xi. 35, xii. 16, from which Israel entered the desert of *Paran.* Both places had been very eventful to the Israelites. At *Hazeroth,* Miriam the prophetess and Aaron the high priest had stumbled through rebellion against Moses (Num. xii.). In the desert of *Paran* by *Kadesh* the older generation had been rejected, and sentenced to die in the wilderness on account of its repeated rebellion against the Lord (Num. xiv.) ; and when the younger generation that had grown up in the wilderness assembled once more in *Kadesh* to set out for Canaan, even Moses and Aaron, the two heads of the nation, sinned there at the water of strife, so that they two were not permitted to enter Canaan, whilst Miriam died there at that time (Num. xx.). But if Paran and Hazeroth are mentioned on account of the tragical events connected with these places, it is natural to conclude that there were similar reasons for mentioning the other three names as well. *Tophel* is supposed by *Hengstenberg* (*Balaam*, p. 517) and *Robinson* (Pal. ii. p. 570) and all the more modern writers, to be the large village of *Tafyleh*, with six hundred inhabitants, the chief place in *Jebal*, on the western side of the Edomitish mountains, in a well-watered valley of the wady of the same name, with large plantations of fruit-trees (*Burckhardt, Syr.* pp. 677, 678). The Israelites may have come upon this place in the neighbourhood of *Oboth* (Num. xxi. 10, 11) ; and as its inhabitants, according to *Burckhardt,* p. 680, supply the Syrian caravans with a considerable quantity of provisions, which they sell to them in the castle of *el Ahsa, Schultz* conjectures that it may have been here that the people of Israel purchased food and drink of the Edomites for money (chap. ii. 29), and that *Tafyleh* is mentioned as a place of refreshment, where the Israelites partook for the first time of different food from the desert supply. There is a great deal to be said in favour of this conjecture : for even if the Israelites did not obtain different food for the first time at this place, the situation of *Tophel* does warrant the supposition that it was here that they passed for the first time from the wilderness to an inhabited land ; on which account the place was so memorable for them, that it might very well be mentioned as being the extreme east of their wanderings in the desert, as the opposite point to the encampment at *Paran*, where they first arrived on the western side of their wandering, at the southern border of Canaan. *Laban* is generally identified with *Libnah*, the second place of encampment on the return journey from Kadesh (Num. xxxiii. 22), and may perhaps have been the place referred to in Num. xvi., but not more precisely defined, where the rebellion of the company of Korah occurred. Lastly, *Di-Sahab* has been identified by modern commentators with *Mersa Dahab* or *Mina Dahab, i.e.* gold-harbour, a place upon a tongue of land in the Elanitic Gulf, about the same latitude as Sinai, where there is nothing to be seen now except a quantity of date-trees, a few sand-hills, and about a dozen heaps of stones piled up irregularly, but all showing signs of having once been joined together (cf. *Burckhardt*, pp. 847–8 ; and *Ritter, Erdk.* xiv. pp. 226 sqq.). But this is hardly correct. As *Roediger* has observed (on *Wellsted's Reisen,* ii. p. 127), " the conjecture has been based exclusively upon the similarity of name, and there is not the slightest exegetical tradition to favour it." But similarity of names cannot prove anything by itself, as the number of places of the same name, but in different localities, that we meet with in the Bible, is very considerable. Moreover, the further assumption which is founded upon this conjecture, namely, that the Israelites went from Sinai past *Dahab,* not only appears untenable for the reasons given above (p. 230), but is actually rendered impossible by the locality itself. The approach to this tongue of land, which projects between two steep lines of coast, with lofty mountain ranges of from 800 to 2000 feet in height on both north and south, leads from Sinai through far too narrow and impracticable a valley for the Israelites to be able to march thither and fix an encampment there.[1] And if Israel cannot have touched *Dahab* on its march, every probability vanishes that Moses should have mentioned this place here, and the name *Di-Sahab* remains at present undeterminable. But in spite of our ignorance of this place, and notwithstanding the fact that even the conjecture expressed with regard to *Laban* is very uncertain, there can be no well-founded doubt that the words " *between Paran and Tophel*" are to be understood as embracing the whole period of the thirty-seven years of mourning, at the commencement of which Israel was in Paran, whilst at the end they sought to enter Canaan by *Tophel* (the Edomitish *Tafyleh*), and that the expression " *opposite to Suph*" points back to their first entrance into the desert.—Looking from the steppes of Moab over the ground that the Israelites had traversed, *Suph,* where they first entered the desert of Arabia, would lie between *Paran,* where the congregation arrived at the borders of Canaan towards the west, and *Tophel,* where they first ended their desert wanderings thirty-seven years later on the east.

[1] From the mouth of the valley through the masses of the primary mountains to the sea-coast, there is a fan-like surface of drifts of primary rock, the radius of which is thirty-five minutes long, the progressive work of the inundations of an indefinable course of thousands of years " (*Rüppell*, Nubien, p. 206).

In ver. 2 also the retrospective glance at the guidance through the desert is unmistakeable. "*Eleven days is the way from Horeb to the mountains of Seir as far as Kadesh-Barnea.*" With these words, which were unquestionably intended to be something more than a geographical notice of the distance of Horeb from Kadesh-Barnea, Moses reminded the people that they had completed the journey from Horeb, the scene of the establishment of the covenant, to Kadesh, the border of the promised land, in eleven days (see pp. 246–7), that he might lead them to lay to heart the events which took place at Kadesh itself. The "way of the mountains of Seir" is not the way along the side of these mountains, *i.e.* the way through the Arabah, which is bounded by the mountains of Seir on the east, but the way which leads to the mountains of Seir, just as in chap. ii. 1 the way of the Red Sea is the way that leads to this sea. From these words, therefore, it by no means follows that *Kadesh-Barnea* is to be sought for in the Arabah, and that Israel passed through the Arabah from Horeb to Kadesh. According to ver. 19, they departed from Horeb, went through the great and terrible wilderness by the way to the mountains of the Amorites, and came to Kadesh-Barnea. Hence the way to the mountains of the Amorites, *i.e.* the southern part of what were afterwards the mountains of Judah (see at Num. xiii. 17), is the same as the way to the mountains of Seir; consequently the *Seir* referred to here is not the range on the eastern side of the Arabah, but *Seir* by *Hormah* (ver. 44), *i.e.* the border plateau by Wady *Murreh,* opposite to the mountains of the Amorites (Josh xi. 17, xii. 7 : see at Num. xxxiv. 3).

Vers. 3, 4. To the description of the ground to which the following addresses refer, there is appended an allusion to the not less significant time when Moses delivered them, viz. "*on the first of the eleventh month in the fortieth year,*" consequently towards the end of his life, after the conclusion of the divine lawgiving; so that he was able to speak "*according to all that Jehovah had given him in commandment unto them*" (the Israelites), namely, in the legislation of the former books, which is always referred to in this way (chap. iv. 5, 23, v. 29, 30, vi. 1). The time was also significant, from the fact that Sihon and Og, the kings of the Amorites, had then been slain. By giving a victory over these mighty kings, the Lord had begun to fulfil His promises (see chap. ii. 25), and had thereby laid Israel under the obligation to love, gratitude, and obedience (see Num. xxi. 21–35). The suffix in הַכֹּתוֹ refers to

Moses, who had smitten the Amorites at the command and by the power of Jehovah. According to Josh. xii. 4, xiii. 12, 31, *Edrei* was the second capital of Og, and it is as such that it is mentioned, and not as the place where Og was defeated (chap. iii. 1; Num. xxi. 33). The omission of the copula וְ before בְּאֶדְרֶעִי is to be accounted for from the oratorical character of the introduction to the addresses which follow. *Edrei* is the present *Draà* (see at Num. xxi. 33).—In ver. 5, the description of the locality is again resumed in the words "*beyond the Jordan*," and still further defined by the expression "*in the land of Moab;*" and the address itself is introduced by the clause, "*Moses took in hand to expound this law,*" which explains more fully the דִּבֶּר (spake) of ver. 3. "In the land of Moab" is a rhetorical and general expression for "in the Arboth Moab." הוֹאִיל does not mean to begin, but to undertake, to take in hand, with the subordinate idea sometimes of venturing, or daring (Gen. xviii. 27), sometimes of a bold resolution : here it denotes an undertaking prompted by internal impulse. Instead of being construed with the infinitive, it is construed rhetorically here with the finite verb without the copula (cf. *Ges.* § 143, 3, *b.*). בְּאֵר probably signified to dig in the *Kal;* but this is not used. In the *Piel* it means to *explain* (διασαφῆσαι, *explanare,* LXX. *Vulg.*), never to engrave, or stamp, not even here nor in chap. xxvii. 8 and Hab. ii. 2. Here it signifies "to expound this law clearly," although the exposition was connected with an earnest admonition to preserve and obey it. "This" no doubt refers to the law expounded in what follows; but substantially it is no other than the law already given in the earlier books. "Substantially there is throughout but one law" (*Schultz*). That the book of Deuteronomy was not intended to furnish a new or second law, is as evident as possible from the word בְּאֵר.

I.—THE FIRST PREPARATORY ADDRESS.

CHAP. I. 6–IV. 40.

FOR the purpose of enforcing upon the people the obligation to true fidelity to the covenant, Moses commenced his address with a retrospective glance at the events that had taken place during the forty years of their journey from Sinai to the steppes of Moab, and showed in striking outlines how, when the Lord had called upon the Israelites in Horeb to arise and take possession of the land of Canaan, that had been promised to the patriarchs for their descendants (chap. i. 6–8), they had greatly increased, and were well organized by chiefs and judges (vers. 9–18); how they had proceeded to Kadesh-Barnea on the border of this land (ver. 19), and there refused to enter in, notwithstanding the report of the spies who were sent out as to the goodness of the land (vers. 20–25), but were alarmed at the might and strength of the Canaanites from a want of confidence in the assistance of the Lord, and had rebelled against their God, and been shut out in consequence from the promised land (vers. 26–46). It was true that at the expiration of this period of punishment the Lord had not permitted them to make war upon Edom and Moab, and drive out these nations from the possessions which they had received from God; but after they had gone round the mountains of Edom and the land of Moab (chap. ii. 1–23), He had given Sihon and Og, the kings of the Amorites, into the power of the Israelites, that they might take possession of their kingdoms in Gilead and Bashan (chap. ii. 24–iii. 17); and after the conquest of these, He had imposed upon the tribes of Reuben, Gad, and half Manasseh, who received the conquered land for their inheritance, the obligation to go with their brethren across the Jordan and help them to conquer Canaan, and had also appointed Joshua as their commander, who would divide the land among them, since he (Moses) himself was not to be allowed to cross the Jordan with them because of the anger of God which he had drawn upon himself on their account (chap. iii. 18–29). He therefore appealed to Israel to hearken to the commandments of the Lord, to preserve and fulfil them without addition or diminution; to continue mindful of the covenant which the Lord had made with them; to make themselves no image or likeness of Jehovah, that they might not draw His wrath upon themselves and be scattered among the heathen, but might ever remain in the land, of which they were now about to take possession (chap. iv.).—In this address, therefore, Moses reminded the whole congregation how the Lord had fulfilled His promise from Horeb to the steppes of Moab, but how they had sinned against their God through unbelief and rebellion, and had brought upon themselves their long wanderings in the desert, that he might append to this the pressing warning not to forfeit the permanent possession of the land they were about to conquer, through a continued and fresh transgression of the covenant.—Certainly a very fitting preparation for the exposition of the law which follows.

REVIEW OF THE DIVINE GUIDANCE OF ISRAEL FROM HOREB TO KADESH.—CHAP. I. 6–46.

Vers. 6–18. Moses commenced with the summons issued by the Lord to Israel at Horeb, to rise and go to Canaan.—Ver. 6. As the epithet applied to God, " *Jehovah our God,*" presupposes the reception of Israel into covenant with Jehovah, which took place at Sinai, so the words, " *ye have dwelt long enough at this mountain,*" imply that the purpose for which Israel was taken to Horeb had been answered, *i.e.* that they had been furnished with the laws and ordinances requisite for the fulfilment of the covenant, and could now remove to Canaan to take possession of the promised land. The word of Jehovah mentioned here is not found in this form in the previous history; but as a matter of fact it is contained in the divine instructions that were preparatory to their removal (Num. i.–iv. and ix. 15–x. 10), and the rising of the cloud from the tabernacle, which followed immediately afterwards (Num. x. 11). The fixed use of the name *Horeb* to designate the mountain group in general, instead of the special name *Sinai*, which is given to the particular mountain upon which the law was given (see vol. ii. p. 90), is in keeping with the rhetorical style of the book.—Ver. 7. " *Go to the mount of the Amorites, and to all who dwell near.*" The mount of the Amorites is the mountainous country inhabited by this tribe, the leading feature in the land of Canaan, and is synonymous with the "land of the Canaanites" which follows; the Amorites being mentioned *instar omnium* as being the most powerful of all the tribes in Canaan, just as in Gen. xv. 16 (see at Gen. x. 16). שְׁכֵנָיו, " *those who dwell by it,*" are the inhabitants of the whole of Canaan, as is shown by the enumeration of the different parts of the land, which follows immediately afterwards. Canaan was naturally divided, according to the character of the ground, into the *Arabah*, the modern *Ghor* (see at ver. 1); the *mountain*, the subsequent mountains of Judah and Ephraim (see at Num. xiii. 17); the *lowland (shephelah), i.e.* the low flat country lying between the mountains of Judah and the Mediterranean Sea, and stretching from the promontory of Carmel down to Gaza, which is intersected by only small undulations and ranges of hills, and generally includes the hill country which formed the transition from the mountains to the plain, though the two are distinguished in Josh. x. 40 and xii. 8 (see at Josh. xv. 33 sqq.); the *south land* (*negeb*: see at Num. xiii. 17); and the *sea-shore, i.e.* the generally narrow strip of coast running along by the Mediterranean Sea from Joppa to the Tyrian ladder, or *Rás el Abiad,* just below Tyre (*vid. v. Raumer,* Pal. p. 49).—The special mention of *Lebanon* in connection with the land of the Canaanites, and the enumeration of the separate parts of the land, as well as the extension of the eastern frontier as far as the Euphrates (see at Gen. xv. 18), are to be attributed to the rhetorical fulness of the style. The reference, however, is not to Antilibanus, but to Lebanon proper, which was within the northern border of the land of Israel, as fixed in Num. xxxiv. 7–9.—Ver. 8. This land the Lord had placed at the disposal of the Israelites for them to take possession of, as He had sworn to the fathers (patriarchs) that He would give it to their posterity (cf. Gen. xii. 7, xiii. 15, xv. 18 sqq., etc.). The "swearing" on the part of God points back to Gen. xxii. 16. The expression "*to them and to their seed*" is the same as "to thee and to thy seed" in Gen. xiii. 15, xvii. 8, and is not to be understood as signifying that the patriarchs themselves ought to have taken actual possession of Canaan; but "*to their seed*" is in apposition, and also a more precise definition (comp. Gen. xv. 7 with ver. 18, where the simple statement "to thee" is explained by the fuller statement "to thy seed"). רְאֵה has grown into an interjection = הִנֵּה. נָתַן לִפְנֵי: to give before a person, equivalent to give up to a person, or place at his free disposal (for the use of the word in this sense, see Gen. xiii. 9, xxxiv. 10). Jehovah (this is the idea of vers. 6–8), when He concluded the covenant with the Israelites at Horeb, had intended to fulfil at once the promise which He gave to the patriarchs, and to put them into possession of the promised land; and Moses had also done what was required on his part, as he explained in vers. 9–18, to bring the people safely to Canaan (cf. Ex. xviii. 23). As the nation had multiplied as the stars of heaven, in accordance with the promise of the Lord, and he felt unable to bear the burden alone and settle all disputes, he had placed over them at that time wise and intelligent men from the heads of the tribes to act as judges, and had instructed them to adjudicate upon the smaller matters of dispute righteously and without respect of person. For further particulars concerning the appointment of the judges, see at Ex. xviii. 13–26, where it is related how Moses adopted this plan at the advice of Jethro, even before the giving of the law at Sinai. The expression "*at that time,*" in ver. 9, is not at variance with this. The imperfect

וַיֹּאמֶר with *vav rel.*, expresses the order of thought and not of time. For Moses did not intend to recall the different circumstances to the recollection of the people in their chronological order, but arranged them according to their relative importance in connection with the main object of his address. And this required that he should begin with what God had done for the fulfilment of His promise, and then proceed afterwards to notice what he, the servant of God, had done in his office, as an altogether subordinate matter. So far as this object was concerned, it was also perfectly indifferent who had advised him to adopt this plan, whilst it was very important to allude to the fact that it was the great increase in the number of the Israelites which had rendered it necessary, that he might remind the congregation how the Lord, even at that time, had fulfilled the promise which He gave to the patriarchs, and in that fulfilment had given a practical guarantee of the certain fulfilment of the other promises as well. Moses accomplished this by describing the increase of the nation in such a way that his hearers would be involuntarily reminded of the covenant promise in Gen. xv. 5 sqq. (cf. Gen. xii. 2, xviii. 18, xxii. 17, xxvi. 4).—Ver. 11. But in order to guard against any misinterpretation of his words, "I cannot bear you myself alone," Moses added, "May the Lord fulfil the promise of numerous increase to the nation a thousand-fold." "*Jehovah, the God of your fathers* (*i.e.* who manifested Himself as God to your fathers), *add to you a thousand times,* כָּכֶם, *as many as ye are, and bless you as He has said.*" The "blessing" after "multiplying" points back to Gen. xii. 2. Consequently, it is not to be restricted to "strengthening, rendering fruitful, and multiplying," but must be understood as including the spiritual blessing promised to Abraham.—Ver. 12. "*How can I myself alone bear your cumbrance, and your burden, and your strife?*" The burden and cumbrance of the nation are the nation itself, with all its affairs and transactions, which pressed upon the shoulders of Moses.—Vers. 13 sqq. הָבוּ לָכֶם, give here, provide for yourselves. The congregation was to nominate, according to its tribes, wise, intelligent, and well-known men, whom Moses would appoint as heads, *i.e.* as judges, over the nation. At their installation he gave them the requisite instructions (ver. 16): "*Ye shall hear between your brethren,*" *i.e.* hear both parties as mediators, "*and judge righteously, without respect of person.*" הִכִּיר פָּנִים, to look at the face, equivalent to נָשָׂא פָנִים (Lev. xix. 15), *i.e.* to act partially (cf. Ex. xxiii. 2, 3). "*The judgment is God's,*" *i.e.* appointed by God, and to be administered in the name of God, or in accordance with His justice; hence the expression "to bring before God" (Ex. xxi. 6, xxii. 7, etc.). On the difficult cases which the judges were to bring before Moses, see at Ex. xviii. 26.

Vers. 19–46. Everything had been done on the part of God and Moses to bring Israel speedily and safely to Canaan. The reason for their being compelled to remain in the desert for forty years was to be found exclusively in their resistance to the commandments of God. The discontent of the people with the guidance of God was manifested at the very first places of encampment in the desert (Num. xi. and xii.); but Moses passed over this, and simply reminded them of the rebellion at Kadesh (Num. xiii. and xiv.), because it was this which was followed by the condemnation of the rebellious generation to die out in the wilderness.—Ver. 19. *"When we departed from Horeb, we passed through the great and dreadful wilderness, which ye have seen,"* i.e. become acquainted with, viz. the desert of *et Tih* (see p. 57), *" of the way to the mountains of the Amorites, and came to Kadesh-Barnea"* (see at Num. xii. 16). הָלַךְ, with an accusative, to pass through a country (cf. chap. ii. 7; Isa. l. 10, etc.). Moses had there explained to the Israelites, that they had reached the mountainous country of the Amorites, which Jehovah was about to give them; that the land lay before them, and they might take possession of it without fear (vers. 20, 21). But they proposed to send out men to survey the land, with its towns, and the way into it. Moses approved of this proposal, and sent out twelve men, one from each tribe, who went through the land, etc. (as is more fully related in Num. xiii., and has been expounded in connection with that passage, vers. 22–25). Moses' summons to them to take the land (vers. 20, 21) is not expressly mentioned there, but it is contained *implicite* in the fact that spies were sent out; as the only possible reason for doing this must have been, that they might force a way into the land, and take possession of it. In ver. 25, Moses simply mentions so much of the report of the spies as had reference to the nature of the land, viz. that it was good, that he may place in immediate contrast with this the refusal of the people to enter in.—Vers. 26, 27. *" But ye would not go up, and were rebellious against the mouth (i.e.* the express will) *of Jehovah your God, and murmured in your tents, and said, Because Jehovah hated us, He hath brought us forth out of the land of Egypt, to give us into the hand of the Amorites to destroy us."* שִׂנְאָה, either an infinitive with a feminine termination, or a verbal noun construed with an accusative (see *Ges.* § 133; *Ewald,* § 238, a.).—By the allusion to the murmuring in the tents, Moses points them to Num. xiv. 1, and then proceeds to describe the rebellion of the congregation related there (vers. 2–4), in such a manner that the state of mind manifested on that occasion presents the appearance of the basest ingratitude, inasmuch as the people declared the greatest blessing conferred upon them by God, viz. their deliverance from Egypt, to have been an act of hatred on His part. At the same time, by addressing the existing members of the nation, as if they themselves had spoken so, whereas the whole congregation that rebelled at Kadesh had fallen in the desert, and a fresh generation was now gathered round him, Moses points to the fact, that the sinful corruption which broke out at that time, and bore such bitter fruit, had not died out with the older generation, but was germinating still in the existing Israel, and even though it might be deeply hidden in their hearts, would be sure to break forth again.—Ver. 28. " *Whither shall we go up ? Our brethren* (the spies) *have quite discouraged our heart*" (הֵמַסּוּ, *lit.* to cause to flow away ; cf. Josh. ii. 9), viz. through their report (Num. xiii. 28, 29, 31–33), the substance of which is repeated here. The expression בַּשָּׁמַיִם, " *in heaven*," towering up into heaven, which is added to " *towns great and fortified*," is not an exaggeration, but, as Moses also uses it in chap. ix. 1, a rhetorical description of the impression actually received with regard to the size of the towns.[1] " *The sons of the Anakims :*" see at Num. xiii. 22.—Vers. 29–31. The attempt made by Moses to inspire the despondent people with courage, when they were ready to despair of ever conquering the Canaanites, by pointing them to the help of the Lord, which they had experienced in so mighty and visible a manner in Egypt and the desert, and to urge them to renewed confidence in this their almighty Helper and Guide, was altogether without success. And just because the appeal of Moses was unsuccessful, it is passed over in the historical account in Num. xiv. ; all that is mentioned there (vers. 6–9) being the effort made by Joshua and Caleb to stir up the people, and that on account of the effects which followed the courageous bearing of these two men, so far as their own future history was concerned. The words " *goeth before you*," in ver. 30, are resumed in ver. 33, and carried out still further. "*Jehovah, . . .*

---

[1] " The eyes of weak faith or unbelief saw the towns really towering up to heaven. Nor did the height appear less, even to the eyes of faith, in relation, that is to say, to its own power. Faith does not hide the difficulties from itself, that it may not rob the Lord, who helps it over them, of any of the praise that is justly His due" (*Schultz*).

He shall fight for you according to all (בְּכֹל) *that,"* i.e. in exactly the same manner as, " *He did for you in Egypt,"* especially at the crossing of the Red Sea (Ex. xiv.), " *and in the wilderness, which thou hast seen* (רָאִיתָ, as in ver. 19), *where* (אֲשֶׁר) without בּוֹ in a loose connection ; see *Ewald,* § 331, c. and 333, a.) *Jehovah thy God bore thee as a man beareth his son ;"* i.e. supported, tended, and provided for thee in the most fatherly way (see the similar figure in Num. xi. 12, and expanded still more fully in Ps. xxiii.).—Vers. 32, 33. " *And even at this word ye remained unbelieving towards the Lord ;"* i.e. notwithstanding the fact that I reminded you of all the gracious help that ye had experienced from your God, ye persisted in your unbelief. The participle אֵינְכֶם מַאֲמִינִם, " *ye were not believing,"* is intended to describe their unbelief as a permanent condition. This unbelief was all the more grievous a sin, because the Lord their God went before them all the way in the pillar of cloud and fire, to guide and to defend them. On the fact itself, comp. Num. ix. 15 sqq., x. 33, with Ex. xiii. 21, 22.—Vers. 34–36. Jehovah was angry, therefore, when He heard these loud words, and swore that He would not let any one of those men, that evil generation, enter the promised land, with the exception of Caleb, because he had followed the Lord faithfully (cf. Num. xiv. 21–24). The *yod* in זוּלָתִי is the antiquated connecting vowel of the construct state.

But in order that he might impress upon the people the judgment of the holy God in all its stern severity, Moses added in ver. 37 : " *also Jehovah was angry with me for your sakes, saying, Thou also shalt not go in thither ;"* and he did this before mentioning Joshua, who was excepted from the judgment as well as Caleb, because his ultimate intention was to impress also upon the minds of the people the fact, that even in wrath the Lord had been mindful of His covenant, and when pronouncing the sentence upon His servant Moses, had given the people a leader in the person of Joshua, who was to bring them into the promised inheritance. We are not to infer from the close connection in which this event, which did not take place according to Num. xx. 1–13 till the second arrival of the congregation at Kadesh, is placed with the earlier judgment of God at Kadesh, that the two were contemporaneous, and so supply, after " the Lord was angry with me," the words " on that occasion." For Moses did not intend to teach the people history and chronology, but to set before them the holiness of the judgments of the Lord. By using the expression " for your sakes," Moses did not wish to free himself from guilt. Even in this book his sin at the water of strife is not passed over in silence (cf. chap. xxxii. 51). But on the present occasion, if he had given prominence to his own fault, he would have weakened the object for which he referred to this event, viz. to stimulate the consciences of the people, and instil into them a wholesome dread of sin, by holding up before them the magnitude of their guilt. But in order that he might give no encouragement to false security respecting their own sin, on the ground that even highly gifted men of God fall into sin as well, Moses simply pointed out the fact, that the quarrelling of the people with him occasioned the wrath of God to fall upon him also.—Ver. 38. " *Who standeth before thee*," equivalent to " in thy service" (Ex. xxiv. 13, xxxiii. 11 : for this meaning, see chap. x. 8, xviii. 7 ; 1 Kings i. 28). " *Strengthen him :*" comp. chap. xxxi. 7 ; and with regard to the installation of Joshua as the leader of Israel, see Num. xxvii. 18, 19. The suffix in יַנְחִלֶנָּה points back to הָאָרֶץ in ver. 35. Joshua would divide the land among the Israelites for an inheritance, viz. (ver. 39) among the young Israelites, the children of the condemned generation, whom Moses, when making a further communication of the judicial sentence of God (Num. xiv. 31), had described as having no share in the sins of their parents, by adding, " who know not to-day what is good and evil." This expression is used to denote a condition of spiritual infancy and moral responsibility (Isa. vii. 15, 16). It is different in 2 Sam. xix. 36.—In vers. 40–45 he proceeds to describe still further, according to Num. xiv. 39–45, how the people, by resisting the command of God to go back into the desert (ver. 41, compared with Num. xiv. 25), had simply brought still greater calamities upon themselves, and had had to atone for the presumptuous attempt to force a way into Canaan, in opposition to the express will of the Lord, by enduring a miserable defeat. Instead of " they acted presumptuously to go up" (Num. xiv. 44), Moses says here, in ver. 41, " *ye acted frivolously to go up ;*" and in ver. 43, " *ye acted rashly, and went up.*" הֵזִיד, from זוּד, to boil, or boil over (Gen. xxv. 29), signifies to act thoughtlessly, haughtily, or rashly. On the particular fact mentioned in ver. 44, see at Num. 14, 45.—Vers. 45, 46. " *Then ye returned and wept before Jehovah,*" *i.e.* before the sanctuary ; " *but Jehovah did not hearken to your voice.*" שׁוּב does not refer to the return to Kadesh, but to an inward turning, not indeed true conversion to repentance, but simply the giving up of their rash enterprise, which they had undertaken in opposition to the commandment of God,—the return from a defiant attitude to unbelieving complaining on account of the misfortune that had come upon them. Such complaining God never hears. " *And ye sat* (remained) *in Kadesh many days, that ye remained,*" *i.e.* not " as many days as ye had been there already before the return of the spies," or " as long as ye remained in all the other stations together, viz. the half of thirty-eight years" (as *Seder Olam* and many of the Rabbins interpret); but " just as long as ye did remain there," as we may see from a comparison of chap. ix. 25. It seemed superfluous to mention more precisely the time they spent in Kadesh, because that was well known to the people, whom Moses was addressing. He therefore contented himself with fixing it by simply referring to its duration, which was known to them all. It is no doubt impossible for us to determine the time they remained in Kadesh, because the expression " many days " is simply a relative one, and may signify many years, just as well as many months or weeks. But it by no means warrants the assumption of *Fries* and others, that no absolute departure of the whole of the people from Kadesh ever took place. Such an assumption is at variance with chap. ii. 1. The change of subjects, " *ye* sat," etc. (ver. 46), and " *we* turned and removed" (chap. ii. 1), by no means proves that Moses only went away with that part of the congregation which attached itself to him, whilst the other portion, which was most thoroughly estranged from him, or rather from the Lord, remained there still. The change of subject is rather to be explained from the fact that Moses was passing from the consideration of the events in Kadesh, which he held up before the people as a warning, to a description of the further guidance of Israel. The reference to those events had led him involuntarily, from ver. 22 onwards, to distinguish between himself and the people, and to address his words to them for the purpose of bringing out their rebellion against God. And now that he had finished with this, he returned to the communicative mode of address with which he set out in ver. 6, but which he had suspended again until ver. 19.

REVIEW OF THE DIVINE GUIDANCE OF ISRAEL ROUND EDOM AND MOAB TO THE FRONTIER OF THE AMORITES, AND OF THE GRACIOUS ASSISTANCE AFFORDED BY THE LORD IN THE CONQUEST OF THE KINGDOMS OF SIHON AND OG.—CHAP. II. AND III.

Vers. 1–23. MARCH FROM KADESH TO THE FRONTIER OF THE AMORITES.—Ver. 1. After a long stay in Kadesh, they commenced their return into the desert. The words, " *We departed . . . by the way to the Red Sea,*" point back to Num. xiv. 25. This departure is expressly designated as an act of obedience to the divine command recorded there, by the expression "*as Jehovah spake to me.*" Consequently Moses is not speaking here of the second departure of the congregation from Kadesh to go to Mount Hor (Num. xx. 22), but of the first departure after the condemnation of the generation that came out of Egypt. "*And we went round Mount Seir many days.*" This going round Mount Seir includes the thirty-eight years' wanderings, though we are not therefore to picture it as " going backwards and forwards, and then entering the Arabah again" (*Schultz*). Just as Moses passed over the reassembling of the congregation at Kadesh (Num. xx. 1), so he also overlooked the going to and fro in the desert, and fixed his eye more closely upon the last journey from Kadesh to Mount Hor, that he might recall to the memory of the congregation how the Lord had led them to the end of all their wandering.—Vers. 2 sqq. When they had gone through the Arabah to the southern extremity, the Lord commanded them to turn northwards, *i.e.* to go round the southern end of Mount Seir, and proceed northwards on the eastern side of it (see at Num. xxi. 10), without going to war with the Edomites (הִתְגָּרָה, to stir oneself up against a person to conflict, מִלְחָמָה), as He would not give them a foot-breadth of their land ; for He had given Esau (the Edomites) Mount Seir for a possession. For this reason they were to buy victuals and water of them for money (כָּרָה, to dig, to dig water, *i.e.* procure water, as it was often necessary to dig wells, and not merely to draw it, Gen. xxvi. 25. The verb כָּרָה does not signify to buy).—Ver. 7. And this they were able to do, because the Lord had blessed them in all the work of their hand, *i.e.* not merely in the rearing of flocks and herds, which they had carried on in the desert (Ex. xix. 13, xxxiv. 3; Num. xx. 19, xxxii. 1 sqq.), but in all that they did for a living ; whether, for example, when stopping for a long time in the same place of encampment, they sowed in suitable spots and reaped, or whether they sold the produce of their toil and skill to the Arabs of the desert. "*He hath observed thy going through this great desert*" (יָדַע, to know, then to trouble oneself, Gen. xxxix. 6 ; to observe carefully, Prov. xxvii. 23, Ps. i. 6) ; and He has not suffered thee to want anything for forty years, but as often as want has occurred, He has miraculously provided for every necessity.—Ver. 8. In accordance with this divine command, they went past the Edomites by the side of their mountains, "*from the way of the Arabah, from Elath* (see at Gen. xiv. 6) *and Eziongeber*" (see at Num. xxxiii. 35), *sc.* into the steppes of Moab, where they were encamped at that time.

God commanded them to behave in the same manner towards the Moabites, when they approached their frontier (ver. 9). They were not to touch their land, because the Lord had given *Ar* to the descendants of Lot for a possession. In ver. 9 the Moabites are mentioned, and in ver. 19 the Amorites also. The Moabites are designated as "sons of Lot," for the same reason for which the Edomites are called "brethren of Israel" in ver. 4. The Israelites were to uphold the bond of blood-relationship with these tribes in the most sacred manner. *Ar*, the capital of Moabitis (see at Num. xxi. 15), is used here for the land itself, which was named after the capital, and governed by it.—Vers. 11, 12. To confirm the fact that the Moabites and also the Edomites had received from God the land which they inhabited as a possession, Moses interpolates into the words of Jehovah certain ethnographical notices concerning the earlier inhabitants of these lands, from which it is obvious that Edom and Moab had not destroyed them by their own power, but that Jehovah had destroyed them before them, as is expressly stated in vers. 21, 22. "*The Emim dwelt formerly therein*," *sc.* in Ar and its territory, in Moabitis, "*a high* (*i.e.* strong) *and numerous people, of gigantic stature, which were also reckoned among the Rephaites, like the Enakites (Anakim).*" *Emim, i.e.* frightful, terrible, was the name given to them by the Moabites. Whether this earlier or original population of Moabitis was of Hamitic or Semitic descent cannot be determined, any more than the connection between the *Emim* and the *Rephaim* can be ascertained. On the *Rephaim*, see vol. i. p. 203 ; and on the Anakites, at Num. xiii. 22.—Ver. 12. The origin of the *Horites* (*i.e.* the dwellers in caves) of Mount *Seir*, who were driven out of their possessions by the descendants of Esau, and completely exterminated (see at Gen. xiv. 6, and xxxvi. 20), is altogether involved in obscurity. The words, "*as Israel has done to the land of his possession, which Jehovah has given them,*" do not presuppose the conquest of the land of Canaan or a post-Mosaic authorship ; but "*the land of his possession*" is the land to the east of the Jordan (Gilead and Bashan), which was conquered by the Israelites under Moses, and divided among the two tribes and a half, and which is also described in chap. iii. 20 as the "possession" which Jehovah had given to these tribes.—Vers. 13–15. For this reason Israel was to remove from the desert of Moab (*i.e.* the desert

which bounded Moabitis on the east), and to cross over the brook
Zered, to advance against the country of the Amorites (see at Num.
xxi. 12, 13). This occurred thirty-eight years after the condemnation of the people at Kadesh (Num. xiv. 23, 29), when the
generation rejected by God had entirely died out (תָּמַם, to be all
gone, to disappear), so that not one of them saw the promised land.
They did not all die a natural death, however, but *" the hand of the
Lord was against them to destroy them"* (הָמַם, *lit.* to throw into confusion, then used with special reference to the terrors with which
Jehovah destroyed His enemies; Ex. xiv. 24, xxiii. 27, etc.), *sc.* by
extraordinary judgments (as in Num. xvi. 35, xvii. 14, xxi. 6, xxv.
9).—Vers. 16–19. When this generation had quite died out, the
Lord made known to Moses, and through him to the people, that
they were to cross over the boundary of Moab (*i.e.* the Arnon, ver.
24; see at Num. xxi. 13), *the land of Ar* (see at ver. 9), *" to come
nigh over against the children of Ammon,"* *i.e.* to advance into the
neighbourhood of the Ammonites, who lived to the east of Moab;
but they were not to meddle with these descendants of Lot, because
He would give them nothing of the land that was given them for a
possession (ver. 19, as at vers. 5 and 9).—To confirm this, ethnographical notices are introduced again in vers. 20–22 into the words
of God (as in vers. 10, 11), concerning the earlier population of
the country of the Ammonites. Ammonitis was also regarded as
a land of the Rephaites, because Rephaites dwelt therein, whom
the Ammonites called *Zamzummim.* *" Zamzummim,"* from זָמַם, to
hum, then to muse, equivalent to the humming or roaring people,
probably the same people as the *Zuzim* mentioned in Gen. xiv. 5.
This giant tribe Jehovah had destroyed before the Ammonites
(ver. 22), just as He had done for the sons of Esau dwelling upon
Mount Seir, namely, destroyed the Horites before them, so that the
Edomites " dwelt in their stead, even unto this day."—Ver. 23.
As the Horites had been exterminated by the Edomites, so were the
Avvœans (Avvim), who dwelt in farms (villages) at the south-west
corner of Canaan, as far as Gaza, driven out of their possessions
and exterminated by the *Caphtorites,* who sprang from *Caphtor* (see
at Gen. x. 14), although, according to Josh. xiii. 3, some remnants
of them were to be found among the Philistines even at that time.
This notice appears to be attached to the foregoing remarks simply
on account of the substantial analogy between them, without there
being any intention to imply that the Israelites were to assume the
same attitude towards the Caphtorites, who afterwards rose up in

the persons of the Philistines, as towards the descendants of Esau and Lot.

Vers. 24–37. THE HELP OF GOD IN THE CONQUEST OF THE KINGDOM OF SIHON.—Vers. 24 sqq. Whereas the Israelites were not to make war upon the kindred tribes of Edomites, Moabites, and Ammonites, or drive them out of the possessions given to them by God; the Lord had given the Amorites, who had forced a way into Gilead and Bashan, into their hands.—Vers. 24, 25. While they were encamped on the Arnon, the border of the Amoritish king of Sihon, He directed them to cross this frontier and take possession of the land of Sihon, and promised that He would give this king with all his territory into their hands, and that henceforward ("*this day*," the day on which Israel crossed the Arnon) He would put fear and terror of Israel upon all nations under the whole heaven, so that as soon as they heard the report of Israel they would tremble and writhe before them. הָחֵל רָשׁ, "*begin, take*," an oratorical expression for "begin to take" (רָשׁ in pause for רֵשׁ, chap. i. 21). The expression, "*all nations under the whole heaven*," is hyperbolical; it is not to be restricted, however, to the Canaanites and other neighbouring tribes, but, according to what follows, to be understood as referring to all nations to whom the report of the great deeds of the Lord upon and on behalf of Israel should reach (cf. chap. xi. 25 and Ex. xxiii. 27). אֲשֶׁר, *so that* (as in Gen. xi. 7, xiii. 16, xxii. 14). וְחָלוּ, with the accent upon the last syllable, on account of the ו consec. (*Ewald*, § 234, *a.*), from חוּל, to twist, or writhe with pain, here with anxiety.—Vers. 26–29. If Moses, notwithstanding this, sent messengers to king Sihon with words of peace (vers. 26 sqq.; cf. Num. xxi. 21 sqq.), this was done to show the king of the Amorites, that it was through his own fault that his kingdom and lands and life were lost. The wish to pass through his land in a peaceable manner was quite seriously expressed; although Moses foresaw, in consequence of the divine communication, that he would reject his proposal, and meet Israel with hostilities. For Sihon's kingdom did not form part of the land of Canaan, which God had promised to the patriarchs for their descendants; and the divine foreknowledge of the hardness of Sihon no more destroyed the freedom of his will to resolve, or the freedom of his actions, than the circumstance that in ver. 30 the unwillingness of Sihon is described as the effect of his being hardened by God Himself. The hardening was quite as much the production of human freedom and guilt, as the consequence of the divine decree; just as in the case of Pharaoh (see the discussion in vol. i. pp. 453 sqq.). On *Kedemoth*, see p. 144. בְּדֶרֶךְ בַּדֶּרֶךְ, equivalent to "upon the way, and always upon the way," *i.e.* upon the high road alone, as in Num. xx. 19. On the behaviour of the Edomites towards Israel, mentioned in ver. 29, see p. 142. In the same way the Moabites also supplied Israel with provisions for money. This statement is not at variance with the unbrotherly conduct for which the Moabites are blamed in chap. xxiii. 4, viz. that they did not meet the Israelites with bread and water. For קִדֵּם, to meet and anticipate, signifies a hospitable reception, the offering of food and drink without reward, which is essentially different from selling for money. "*In Ar*" (ver. 29), as in ver. 18. The suffix in בּוֹ (ver. 30) refers to the king, who is mentioned as the lord of the land, in the place of the land itself, just as in Num. xx. 18.—Ver. 31. The refusal of Sihon was suspended over him by God as a judgment of hardening, which led to his destruction. "*As this day*," an abbreviation of "as it has happened this day," *i.e.* as experience has now shown (cf. chap. iv. 20, etc.).—Vers. 32–37. Defeat of Sihon, as already described in the main in Num. xxi. 23–26. The war was a war of extermination, in which all the towns were laid under the ban (see Lev. xxvii. 29), *i.e.* the whole of the population of men, women, and children were put to death, and only the flocks and herds and material possessions were taken by the conquerors as prey.—Ver. 34. עִיר מְתִם (city of men) is the town population of men.—Ver. 36. They proceeded this way with the whole of the kingdom of Sihon. "*From Aroër on the edge of the Arnon valley* (see at Num. xxxii. 34), *and, in fact, from the city which is in the valley*," *i.e. Ar*, or *Areopolis* (see at Num. xxi. 15),—Aroër being mentioned as the inclusive *terminus a quo* of the land that was taken, and the Moabitish capital Ar as the exclusive *terminus*, as in Josh. xiii. 9 and 16; "*and as far as Gilead*," which rises on the north, near the Jabbok (or Zerka, see at chap. iii. 4), "*there was no town too high for us*," *i.e.* so strong that we could not take it.—Ver. 37. Only along the land of the Ammonites the Israelites did not come, namely, along the whole of the side of the brook Jabbok, or the country of the Ammonites, which was situated upon the eastern side of the upper Jabbok, and the towns of the mountain, *i.e.* of the Ammonitish highlands, and "*to all that the Lord had commanded*," *sc.* commanded them not to remove. The statement, in Josh xiii. 25, that the half of the country of the Ammonites was given to the

tribe of Gad, is not at variance with this; for the allusion there is
to that portion of the land of the Ammonites which was between the
Arnon and the Jabbok, and which had already been taken from the
Ammonites by the Amorites under Sihon (cf. Judg. xi. 13 sqq.).

Chap. iii. 1–11. THE HELP OF GOD IN THE CONQUEST OF
THE KINGDOM OF OG OF BASHAN.—Vers. 1 sqq. After the defeat
of king Sihon and the conquest of his land, the Israelites were able
to advance to the Jordan. But as the powerful Amoritish king
Og still held the northern half of Gilead and all Bashan, they
proceeded northwards at once and took the road to Bashan, that
they might also defeat this king, whom the Lord had likewise
given into their hand, and conquer his country (cf. Num. xxi.
33, 34). They smote him at *Edrei*, the modern *Draà* (see p. 155),
without leaving him even a remnant; and took all his towns,
i.e., as is here more fully stated in vers. 4 sqq., "*sixty towns,
the whole region of Argob, the kingdom of Og in Bashan.*" These
three definitions refer to one and the same country. The whole
region of *Argob* included the sixty towns which formed the kingdom of Og in Bashan, *i.e.* all the towns of the land of Bashan, viz.
(according to ver. 5) all the fortified towns, besides the unfortified
and open country towns of Bashan. חֶבֶל, the chain for measuring,
then the land or country measured with the chain. The name
"*region of Argob*," which is given to the country of Bashan here,
and in vers. 4, 13, 14, and also in 1 Kings iv. 13, is probably derived
from רְגוֹב, stone-heaps, related to רֶגֶב, a clump or clod of earth (Job
xxi. 33, xxxviii. 38). The Targumists have rendered it correctly
מְרְכוֹנָא (*Trachona*), from τραχών, a rough, uneven, stony district, so
called from the basaltic hills of Hauran; just as the plain to the
east of Jebel Hauran, which resembles Hauran itself, is sometimes
called *Tellul*, from its tells or hills (*Burckhardt*, Syr. p. 173).[1] This
district has also received the name of *Bashan*, from the character
of its soil; for בָּשָׁן signifies a soft and level soil. From the name
given to it by the Arabic translators, the Greek name Βαταναία,
Batanœa, and possibly also the modern name of the country on the
north-eastern slope of Hauran at the back of Mount Hauran,
viz. *Bethenije*, are derived.—The name *Argob* probably originated
in the north-eastern part of the country of Bashan, viz. the modern

---

[1] The derivation is a much more improbable one, " from the town of *Argob*,
πρὸς Γέρασαν πόλιν Ἀραβίας, according to the *Onomast.*, fifteen Roman miles to
the west of *Gerasa*, which is called Ῥαγαβᾶ by *Josephus* (Ant. xiii. 15, 5)."

Leja, with its stony soil covered with heaps of large blocks of stone (*Burckhardt,* p. 196), or rather in the extensive volcanic region to the east of Hauran, which was first of all brought to distinct notice in *Wetzstein's* travels, and of which he says that the "southern portion, bearing the name *Harra,* is thickly covered with loose volcanic stones, with a few conical hills among them, that have been evidently caused by eruptions" (*Wetzstein,* p. 6). The central point of the whole is *Safa,* "a mountain nearly seven hours' journey in length and about the same in breadth," in which "the black mass streaming from the craters piled itself up wave upon wave, so that the centre attained to the height of a mountain, without acquiring the smoothness of form observable in mountains generally,"—"the black flood of lava being full of innumerable streams of stony waves, often of a bright red colour, bridged over with thin arches, which rolled down the slopes out of the craters and across the high plateau" (*Wetzstein,* pp. 6 and 7). At a later period this name was transferred to the whole of the district of Hauran (= Bashan), because not only is the Jebel Hauran entirely of volcanic formation, but the plain consists throughout of a reddish brown soil produced by the action of the weather upon volcanic stones, and even "the *Leja* plain has been poured out from the craters of the Hauran mountains" (*Wetzstein,* p. 23). Through this volcanic character of the soil, Hauran differs essentially from Belka, Jebel *Ajlun,* and the plain of *Jaulan,* which is situated between the Sea of Galilee and the upper Jordan on the one side, and the plain of Hauran on the other, and reaches up to the southern slope of the Hermon. In these districts the limestone and chalk formations prevail, which present the same contrast to the basaltic formation of the Hauran as white does to black (cf. *v. Raumer,* Pal. pp. 75 sqq.).—The land of the limestone and chalk formation abounds in caves, which are not altogether wanting indeed in Hauran (as *v. Raumer* supposes), though they are only found in eastern and south-eastern Hauran, where most of the volcanic elevations have been perforated by troglodytes (see *Wetzstein,* pp. 92 and 44 sqq.). But the true land of caves on the east of the Jordan is northern Gilead, viz. *Erbed* and *Suêt* (*Wetzst.* p. 92). Here the troglodyte dwellings predominate, whereas in Hauran you find for the most part towns and villages with houses of one or more stories built above the surface of the ground, although even on the eastern slope of the Hauran mountains there are hamlets to be seen, in which the style of building forms a transition from actual caves to dwellings built upon the ground. An excavation is first of all made in the rocky plateau, of the breadth and depth of a room, and this is afterwards arched over with a solid stone roof. The dwellings made in this manner have all the appearance of cellars or tunnels. This style of building, such as *Wetzstein* found in *Hibbike* for example, belongs to the most remote antiquity. In some cases, hamlets of this kind were even surrounded by a wall. Those villages of Hauran which are built above the surface of the ground, attract the eye and stimulate the imagination, when seen from a distance, in various ways. " In the first place, the black colour of the building materials presents the greatest contrast to the green around them, and to the transparent atmosphere also. In the second place, the height of the walls and the compactness of the houses, which always form a connected whole, are very imposing. In the third place, they are surmounted by strong towers. And in the fourth place, they are in such a good state of preservation, that you involuntarily yield to the delusion that they must of necessity be inhabited, and expect to see people going out and in " (*Wetzstein*, p. 49). The larger towns are surrounded by walls ; but the smaller ones as a rule have none : "the backs of the houses might serve as walls." The material of which the houses are built is a grey dolerite, impregnated with glittering particles of olivine. "The stones are rarely cemented, but the fine and for the most part large squares lie one upon another as if they were fused together." "Most of the doors of the houses which lead into the streets or open fields are so low, that it is impossible to enter them without stooping ; but the large buildings and the ends of the streets have lofty gateways, which are always tastefully constructed, and often decorated with sculptures and Greek inscriptions." The "larger gates have either simple or (what are most common) double doors. They consist of a slab of dolerite. There are certainly no doors of any other kind." These stone doors turn upon pegs, deeply inserted into the threshold and lintel. "Even a man can only shut and open doors of this kind, by pressing with the back or feet against the wall, and pushing the door with both hands " (*Wetzstein*, pp. 50 sqq. ; compare with this the testimony of *Buckingham, Burckhardt, Seetzen*, and others, in *v. Raumer's* Palestine, pp. 78 sqq.).

Now, even if the existing ruins of Hauran date for the most part from a later period, and are probably of a Nabatæan origin belonging to the times of Trajan and the Antonines, yet consider-

ing the stability of the East, and the peculiar nature of the soil of
Hauran, they give a tolerably correct idea of the sixty towns of the
kingdom of Og of Bashan, all of which were fortified with high
walls, gates, and bars, or, as it is stated in 1 Kings iv. 13, " with
walls and brazen bars." [1] The brazen bars were no doubt, like the
gates themselves, of basalt or dolerite, which might easily be mistaken for brass. Besides the sixty fortified towns, the Israelites took
a very large number of עָרֵי הַפְּרָזִי, " towns of the inhabitants of the flat
country," i.e. unfortified open hamlets and villages in Bashan, and put
them under the ban, like the towns of king Sihon (vers. 6, 7 ; cf.
chap. ii. 34, 35). The infinitive, הַחֲרֵם, is to be construed as a gerund
(cf. Ges. § 131, 2 ; Ewald, § 280, a.). The expression, " kingdom of
Og in Bashan," implies that the kingdom of Og was not limited to
the land of Bashan, but included the northern half of Gilead as well.

In vers. 8–11, Moses takes a retrospective view of the whole of
the land that had been taken on the other side of the Jordan ; first
of all (ver. 9) in its whole extent from the Arnon to Hermon, then
(ver. 10) in its separate parts, to bring out in all its grandeur what
the Lord had done for Israel. The notices of the different names
of Hermon (ver. 9), and of the bed of king Og (ver. 11), are also
subservient to this end. Hermon is the southernmost spur of Antilibanus, the present Jebel es Sheikh, or Jebel et Telj. The Hebrew
name is not connected with חֵרֶם, anathema, as Hengstenberg supposes
(Diss. pp. 197–8); nor was it first given by the Israelites to this mountain, which formed part of the northern boundary of the land which
they had taken ; but it is to be traced to an Arabic word signifying
prominens montis vertex, and was a name which had long been current
at that time, for which the Israelites used the Hebrew name שִׂיאֹן
(Sion = שִׂיאֹן, the high, eminent : chap. iv. 48), though this name
did not supplant the traditional name of Hermon. The Sidonians
called it Sirion, a modified form of שִׂרְיֹן (1 Sam. xvii. 5), or סִרְיֹן
(Jer. xlvi. 4), a " coat of mail ;" the Amorites called it Senir, probably a word with the same meaning. In Ps. xxix. 6, Sirion is used

---

[1] It is also by no means impossible, that many of the oldest dwellings in the
ruined towers of Hauran date from a time anterior to the conquest of the land
by the Israelites. " Simple, built of heavy blocks of basalt roughly hewn, and
as hard as iron, with very thick walls, very strong stone gates and doors, many
of which were about eighteen inches thick, and were formerly fastened with
immense bolts, and of which traces still remain ; such houses as these may have
been the work of the old giant tribe of Rephaim, whose king, Og, was defeated
by the Israelites 3000 years ago" (C. v. Raumer, Pal. p. 80, after Porter's Five
Years in Damascus).

poetically for *Hermon;* and Ezekiel (xxvii. 4) uses *Senir,* in a mournful dirge over Tyre, as synonymous with *Lebanon;* whilst *Senir* is mentioned in 1 Chron. v. 23, and *Shenir* in Cant. iv. 8, in connection with Hermon, as a part of Antilibanus, as it might very naturally happen that the Amoritish name continued attached to one or other of the peaks of the mountain, just as we find that even Arabian geographers, such as *Abulfeda* and *Maraszid,* call that portion of Antilibanus which stretches from Baalbek to Emesa (Homs, Heliopolis) by the name of *Sanir.*—Ver. 10. The different portions of the conquered land were the following: הַמִּישֹׁר, *the plain,* *i.e.* the Amoritish table-land, stretching from the Arnon to Heshbon, and in a north-easterly direction nearly as far as Rabbath-Ammon, with the towns of *Heshbon, Bezer, Medeba, Jahza,* and *Dibon* (chap. iv. 43; Josh. xiii. 9, 16, 17, 21, xx. 8; Jer. xlviii. 21 sqq.), which originally belonged to the Moabites, and is therefore called " the field of Moab" in Num. xxi. 20 (see p. 148). *" The whole of Gilead,"* *i.e.* the mountainous region on the southern and northern sides of the Jabbok, which was divided into two halves by this river. The southern half, which reached to Heshbon, belonged to the kingdom of Sihon (Josh. xii. 2), and was assigned by Moses to the Reubenites and Gadites (ver. 12); whilst the northern half, which is called " the rest of Gilead" in ver. 13, the modern Jebel *Ajlun,* extending as far as the land of Bashan (Hauran and Jaulan), belonged to the kingdom of Og (Josh. xii. 5), and was assigned to the Manassite family of Machir (ver. 15, and Josh. xiii. 31; cf. *v. Raumer,* Pal. pp. 229, 230). *" And all Bashan unto Salcah and Edrei."* All Bashan included not only the country of Hauran (the plain and mountain), but unquestionably also the district of *Jedur* and *Jaulan,* to the west of the sea of Galilee and the upper Jordan, or the ancient *Gaulonitis* (*Jos. Ant.* xviii. 4, 6, etc.), as the kingdom of Og extended to the coasts of Geshuri and Maachathi (see at ver. 14). Og had not conquered the whole of the land of Hauran, however, but only the greater part of it. His territory extended eastwards to *Salcah, i.e.* the present *Szalchat* or *Szarchad,* about six hours to the east of *Bozrah,* south of Jebel Hauran, a town with 800 houses, and a castle upon a basaltic rock, but uninhabited (cf. *v. Raumer,* Pal. p. 255); and northwards to *Edrei, i.e.* the northern *Edrei* (see at Num. xxi. 33), a considerable ruin on the north-west of *Bozrah,* three or four English miles in extent, in the old buildings of which there are 200 families living at present (Turks, Druses, and Christians). By the Arabian geographers (*Abulfeda,*

Ibn Batuta) it is called *Sora,* by modern travellers *Adra* or *Edra* (*v. Richter*), or *Oezraa* (*Seetzen*), or *Ezra* (*Burckhardt*), and *Edhra* (*Robinson,* App. 155). Consequently nearly the whole of Jebel Hauran, and the northern portion of the plain, viz. the *Leja,* were outside the kingdom of Og and the land of Bashan, of which the Israelites took possession, although *Burckhardt* reckons Ezra as part of the Leja.—Ver. 11. Even in Abraham's time, the giant tribe of *Rephaim* was living in Bashan (Gen. xiv. 5). But out of the remnant of these, king Og, whom the Israelites defeated and slew, was the only one left. For the purpose of recalling the greatness of the grace of God that had been manifested in that victory, and not merely to establish the credibility of the statements concerning the size of Og (" just as things belonging to an age that has long passed away are shown to be credible by their remains," *Spinoza,* etc.), Moses points to the iron bed of this king, which was still in Rabbath-Ammon, and was nine cubits long and four broad, " after the cubit of a man," *i.e.* the ordinary cubit in common use (see the analogous expression, " a man's pen," Isa. viii. 1). הַלֹּה, for הֲלֹא, synonymous with הִנֵּה. There is nothing to amaze us in the size of the bed or bedstead given here. The ordinary Hebrew cubit was only a foot and a half, probably only eighteen Dresden inches (see my *Archäologie,* ii. p. 126, Anm. 4). Now a bed is always larger than the man who sleeps in it. But in this case *Clericus* fancies that Og " intentionally exceeded the necessary size, in order that posterity might be led to draw more magnificent conclusions from the size of the bed, as to the stature of the man who was accustomed to sleep in it." He also refers to the analogous case of Alexander the Great, of whom *Diod. Sic.* (xvii. 95) affirms, that whenever he was obliged to halt on his march to India, he made colossal arrangements of all kinds, causing, among other things, two couches to be prepared in the tents for every foot-soldier, each five cubits long, and two stalls for every horseman, twice as large as the ordinary size, " to represent a camp of heroes, and leave striking memorials behind for the inhabitants of the land, of gigantic men and their supernatural strength." With a similar intention Og may also have left behind him a gigantic bed as a memorial of his superhuman greatness, on the occasion of some expedition of his against the Ammonites ; and this bed may have been preserved in their capital as a proof of the greatness of their foe.[1] Moses might then refer

---

[1] " It will often be found, that very tall people are disposed to make themselves appear even taller than they actually are" (*Hengstenberg,* Diss. ii. p. 201).

to this gigantic bed of Og, which was known to the Israelites; and there is no reason for resorting to the improbable conjecture, that the Ammonites had taken possession of a bed of king Og upon some expedition against the Amorites, and had carried it off as a trophy into their capital.[1] " *Rabbath* of the sons of Ammon," or briefly *Rabbah*, *i.e.* the great (Josh. xiii. 25; 2 Sam. xi. 1), was the capital of the Ammonites, afterwards called *Philadelphia*, probably from Ptolemæus Philadelphus; by *Polybius*, 'Ραββατάμαυα; by *Abulfeda*, *Ammân*, which is the name still given to the uninhabited ruins on the *Nahr Ammân*, *i.e.* the upper Jabbok (see *Burckhardt*, pp. 612 sqq., and *v. Raumer*, Pal. p. 268).

Vers. 12–20. Review of the Distribution of the Conquered Land.—The land which the Israelites had taken belonging to these two kingdoms was given by Moses to the two tribes and a half for their possession, viz. the southern portion from Aroer in the Arnon valley (see at Num. xxxii. 34), and half Gilead (as far as the Jabbok: see at ver. 10) with its towns, which are enumerated in Josh. xiii. 15–20 and 24–28, to the Reubenites and Gadites; and the northern half of Gilead, with the whole of Bashan (*i.e.* all the region of Argob: see at ver. 4, and Num. xxxii. 33), to the half-tribe of Manasseh. לְכָל־הַבָּשָׁן, "*as for all Bashan*," is in apposition to "*all the region of Argob*," and the לְ simply serves to connect it; for "all the region of Argob" was not merely one portion of Bashan, but was identical with "all Bashan," so far as it belonged to the kingdom of Og (see at ver. 4). All this region passed for a land of giants. הִקָּרֵא, to be called, *i.e.* to be, and to be recognised as being.—Ver. 14. The region of Argob, or the country of Bashan, was given to *Jair* (see Num. xxxii. 41), as far as the territory of the Geshurites and Maachathites (cf. Josh. xii. 5, xiii. 11). " *Unto*," as far as, is to be understood as inclusive. This is evident from

Moreover, there are still giants who are eight feet high and upwards. " According to the *N. Preuss. Zeit.* of 1857, there came a man to Berlin 8 feet 4 inches high, and possibly still growing, as he was only twenty years old; and he was said to have a great-uncle who was nine inches taller" (*Schultz*).

[1] There is still less probability in the conjecture of *J. D. Michaelis, Vater, Winer*, and others, that Og's iron bed was a sarcophagus of basalt, such as are still frequently met with in those regions, as much as 9 feet long and 3½ feet broad, or even as much as 12 feet long and 6 feet in breadth and height (*vid. Burckhardt*, pp. 220, 246; *Robinson*, iii. p. 385; *Seetzen*, i. pp. 355, 360); and the still further assumption, that the corpse of the fallen king was taken to Rabbah, and there interred in a royal way, is altogether improbable.

the statement in Josh. xiii. 13: "*The children of Israel expelled not the Geshurites nor the Maachathites; but the Geshurites and the Maachathites dwell among the Israelites until this day.*" Consequently Moses allotted the territory of these two tribes to the Manassites, because it formed part of the kingdom of Og. "*Geshuri and Maachathi*" are the inhabitants of *Geshur* and *Maachah*, two provinces which formed small independent kingdoms even in David's time (2 Sam. iii. 3, xiii. 37, and x. 6). *Geshur* bordered on Aram. The Geshurites and Aramæans afterwards took from the Israelites the *Jair*-towns and *Kenath*, with their daughter towns (1 Chron. ii. 23). In David's time *Geshur* had a king *Thalmai*, whose daughter David married. This daughter was the mother of Absalom; and it was in Geshur that Absalom lived for a time in exile (2 Sam. iii. 3, xiii. 37, xiv. 23, xv. 8). The exact situation of *Geshur* has not yet been determined. It was certainly somewhere near Hermon, on the eastern side of the upper Jordan, and by a *bridge* over the Jordan, as *Geshur* signifies bridge in all the Semitic dialects. *Maachah*, which is referred to in 1 Chron. xix. 6 as a kingdom under the name of *Aram-Maachah* (Eng. V. Syria-Maachah), is probably to be sought for to the north-east of *Geshur*. According to the *Onomast.* (*s. v.* Μαχαθί), it was in the neighbourhood of the Hermon. "*And he called them* (the towns of the region of Argob) *after his own name; Bashan* (*sc.* he called) *Havvoth Jair unto this day*" (cf. Num. xxxii. 41). The word חַוֺּת (*Havvoth*), which only occurs in connection with the *Jair*-towns, does not mean towns or camps of a particular kind, viz. tent villages, as some suppose, but is the plural of חַוָּה, life (*Leben,* a common German termination, *e.g. Eisleben*), for which afterwards the word חַיָּה was used (comp. 2 Sam. xxiii. 13 with 1 Chron. xi. 15). It applies to any kind of dwelling-place, being used in the passages just mentioned to denote even a warlike encampment. The *Jair's-lives* (*Jairsleben*) were not a particular class of towns, therefore, in the district of Argob, but *Jair* gave this collective name to all the sixty fortified towns, as is perfectly evident from the verse before us when compared with ver. 5 and Num. xxxii. 41, and expressly confirmed by Josh. xiii. 30 and 1 Kings iv. 13, where the sixty fortified towns of the district of Argob are called *Havvoth Jair.*—The statement in 1 Chron. ii. 22, 23, that "*Jair had twenty-three towns in Gilead* (which is used here as in chap. xxxiv. 1, Josh. xxii. 9, xiii. 15, Judg. v. 17, xx. 1, to denote the whole of Palestine to the east of the Jordan), *and Geshur and Aram took the Havvoth Jair from them,* (and) *Kenath and its daughters, sixty towns* (*sc.* in all)," is by no means at variance with this, but, on the contrary, in the most perfect harmony with it. For it is evident from this passage, that the twenty-three *Havvoth Jair*, with *Kenath* and its daughters, formed sixty towns altogether. The distinction between the twenty-three *Havvoth Jair* and the other thirty-seven towns, viz. *Kenath* and its daughters, is to be explained from the simple fact that, according to Num. xxxii. 42, *Nobah*, no doubt a family of sons of Machir related to Jair, conquered Kenath and its daughters, and called the conquered towns by his name, namely, when they had been allotted to him by Moses. Consequently Bashan, or the region of Argob, with its sixty fortified towns, was divided between two of the leading families of Machir the Manassite, viz. the families of *Jair* and *Nobah*, each family receiving the districts which it had conquered, together with their towns; namely, the family of *Nobah*, Kenath and its daughter towns, or the eastern portion of Bashan; and the family of *Jair*, twenty-three towns in the west, which are called *Havvoth Jair* in 1 Chron. ii. 23, in harmony with Num. xxxii. 41, where Jair is said to have given this name to the towns which were conquered by him. In the address before us, however, in which Moses had no intention to enter into historical details, all the (sixty) towns of the whole district of Argob, or the whole of Bashan, are comprehended under the name of *Havvoth Jair*, probably because *Nobah* was a subordinate branch of the family of *Jair*, and the towns conquered by him were under the supremacy of Jair. The expression " unto this day " certainly does not point to a later period than the Mosaic age. This definition of time is simply a relative one. It does not necessarily presuppose a very long duration, and here it merely serves to bring out the marvellous change which was due to the divine grace, viz. that the sixty fortified towns of the giant king Og of Bashan had now become Jair's lives.[1]—Ver. 15. Machir received Gilead (see Num. xxxii. 40).—In vers. 16 and 17 the possession of the tribes of Reuben and Gad is described more fully according to its boundaries. They received the land of Gilead (to the south of the Jabbok) as far as the brook Arnon, the middle of the valley and its territory. תּוֹךְ הַנַּחַל is a more precise definition of נַחַל אַרְנֹן, ex-

---

[1] The conquest of these towns, in fact, does not seem to have been of long duration, and the possession of them by the Israelites was a very disputed one (cf. 1 Chron. ii. 22, 23). In the time of the judges we find thirty in the possession of the judge *Jair* (Judg. x. 4), which caused the old name *Havvoth Jair* to be revived.

pressive of the fact that the territory of these tribes was not to reach
merely to the northern edge of the Arnon valley, but into the
middle of it, viz. to the river Arnon, which flowed through the
middle of the valley; and וּגְבֻל (and the border) is an explanatory
apposition to what goes before, as in Num. xxxiv. 6, signifying,
"*viz. the border of the Arnon valley as far as the river.*" On the east,
"*even unto Jabbok the brook, the* (western) *border of the Ammonites*"
(*i.e.* as far as the upper Jabbok, the *Nahr Ammân :* see at Num.
xxi. 24); and on the west "*the Arabah* (the Ghor: see chap. i. 1)
and the Jordan with territory" (*i.e.* with its eastern bank), "*from
Chinnereth*" (*i.e.* the town from which the Sea of Galilee received
the name of Sea of Chinnereth: Num. xxxiv. 11; see at Josh.
xix. 35) "*to the sea of the Arabah, the Salt Sea under the slopes of
Pisgah* (see at Num. xxi. 15 and xxvii. 12) *eastward*" (*i.e.* merely
the eastern side of the Arabah and Jordan).—In vers. 18–20 Moses
reminds them of the conditions upon which he had given the two
tribes and a half the land referred to for their inheritance (cf.
Num. xxxii. 20–32).

Vers. 21–29. NOMINATION OF JOSHUA AS HIS SUCCESSOR.—
This reminiscence also recalls the goodness of God in the appointment of Joshua (Num. xxvii. 12 sqq.), which took place "*at that
time,*" *i.e.* after the conquest of the land on the east of the Jordan.
In accordance with the object of his address, which was to hold up to
view what the Lord had done for Israel, he here relates how, at the
very outset, he pointed Joshua to the things which he had seen with
his eyes (עֵינֶיךָ הָרֹאֹת, thine eyes were seeing; cf. *Ewald*, § 335, *b.*),
namely, to the defeat of the two kings of the Amorites, in which
the pledge was contained, that the faithful covenant God would
complete the work He had begun, and would do the same to all
kingdoms whither Joshua would go over (*i.e.* across the Jordan).—
Ver. 22. For this reason they were not to be afraid; for Jehovah
Himself would fight for them. "*He*" is emphatic, and adds force
to the subject.—Vers. 23 sqq. Moses then describes how, notwithstanding his prayer, the Lord had refused him permission to cross
over into Canaan and see the glorious land. This prayer is not
mentioned in the historical account given in the fourth book; but
it must have preceded the prayer for the appointment of a shepherd
over the congregation in Num. xxvii. 16, as the Lord directs him
in His reply (ver. 28) to appoint Joshua as the leader of the people.
In his prayer, Moses appealed to the manifestations of divine grace

which he had already received.   As the Lord had already begun to
show him His greatness and His mighty hand, so might He also show
him the completion of His work.   The expression, " begun to show
Thy greatness," relates not so much to the mighty acts of the Lord
in Egypt and at the Red Sea (as in Ex. xxxii. 11, 12, and Num.
xiv. 13 sqq.), as to the manifestation of the divine omnipotence in
the defeat of the Amorites, by which the Lord had begun to bring
His people into the possession of the promised land, and had made
Himself known as God, to whom there was no equal in heaven or
on earth.   אֲשֶׁר before מִי אֵל (ver. 24) is an explanatory and causal relative : because (quod, quia), or for.   " For what God is there in heaven
and on earth," etc.   These words recall Ex. xv. 11, and are echoed
in many of the Psalms—in Ps. lxxxvi. 8 almost verbatim.   The contrast drawn between Jehovah and other gods does not involve the
reality of the heathen deities, but simply presupposes a belief in the
existence of other gods, without deciding as to the truth of that
belief.   נְּבוּרֹת, manifestations of נְּבוּרָה, mighty deeds.—Ver. 25. " I
pray Thee, let me go over."   אֶעְבְּרָה־נָּא, a form of desire, used as a
petition, as in chap. ii. 27, Num. xxi. 22, etc.   " That goodly mountain" is not one particular portion of the land of Canaan, such
as the mountains of Judah, or the temple mountain (according to
Ex. xv. 17), but the whole of Canaan regarded as a mountainous
country, Lebanon being specially mentioned as the boundary wall
towards the north.   As Moses stood on the lower level of the
Arabah, the promised land presented itself not only to his eyes, but
also to his soul, as a long mountain range ; and that not merely as
suggestive of the lower contrast, that " whereas the plains in the
East are for the most part sterile, on account of the want of springs
or rain, the mountainous regions, which are well watered by springs
and streams, are very fertile and pleasant" (Rosenmüller), but also
on a much higher ground, viz. as a high and lofty land, which would
stand by the side of Horeb, "where he had spent the best and
holiest days of his life, and where he had seen the commencement
of the covenant between God and His people" (Schultz).—Ver. 26.
But the Lord would not grant his request.   " Let it suffice thee"
(satis sit tibi, as in chap. i. 6), substantially equivalent to 2 Cor.
xii. 8, " My grace is sufficient for thee" (Schultz).   דִּבֵּר בְּ, to speak
about a thing (as in chap. vi. 7, xi. 19, etc.).—Ver. 27 is a rhetorical paraphrase of Num. xxvii. 12, where the mountains of Abarim
are mentioned in the place of Pisgah, which was the northern portion of Abarim.   (On ver. 28, cf. chap. i. 38 and Num. xxvii. 23.)

—Ver. 29. " *So we abode in the valley over against Beth-Peor*," *i.e.* in the Arboth Moab (Num. xxii. 1), *sc.* where we still are. The pret. וַיֵּשֶׁב is used, because Moses fixes his eye upon the past, and looks back upon the events already described in Num. xxviii.– xxxiv. as having taken place there. On *Beth-Peor*, see at Num. xxiii. 28.

EXHORTATION TO A FAITHFUL OBSERVANCE OF THE LAW.—
CHAP. IV. 1–40.

With the word וְעַתָּה, " *and now*," Moses passes from a contemplation of what the Lord had done for Israel, to an exhortation to keep the law of the Lord.   The divine manifestations of grace laid Israel under the obligation to a conscientious observance of the law, that they might continue to enjoy the blessings of the covenant.   The exhortation commences with the appeal, to hear and keep the commandments and rights of the Lord, without adding to them or taking from them ; for not only were life and death suspended upon their observance, but it was in this that the wisdom and greatness of Israel before all the nations consisted (vers. 1–8). It then proceeds to a warning, not to forget the events at Horeb (vers. 9–14) and so fall into idolatry, the worship of images or idol deities (vers. 15–24) ; and it closes with a threat of dispersion among the heathen as the punishment of apostasy, and with a promise of restoration as the consequence of repentance and sincere conversion (vers. 25–31), and also with a reason for this threat and promise drawn from the history of the immediate past (vers. 32–34), for the purpose of fortifying the nation in its fidelity to its God, the sole author of its salvation (vers. 35–40).

Vers. 1–8. The Israelites were to hearken to the laws and rights which Moses taught to do (that they were to do), that they might live and attain to the possession of the land which the Lord would give them. " Hearkening " involves laying to heart and observing.   The words " *statutes and judgments* " (as in Lev. xix. 37) denote the whole of the law of the covenant in its two leading features. חֻקִּים, *statutes*, includes the moral commandments and statutory covenant laws, for which חֹק and חֻקָּה are mostly used in the earlier books; that is to say, all that the people were bound to observe ; מִשְׁפָּטִים, *rights*, all that was due to them, whether in relation to God or to their fellow-men (cf. chap. xxvi. 17).   Sometimes הַמִּצְוָה, the *commandment*, is connected with it, either placed first in the singular, as a general comprehensive notion (chap. v. 28, vi. 1, vii. 11), or in the plural (chap. viii. 11, xi. 1, xxx. 16) ; or הָעֵדֹת, the *testimonies*, the commandments as a manifestation of the will of God (ver. 45, vi. 17, 20).—Life itself depended upon the fulfilment, or long life in the promised land (Ex. xx. 12), as Moses repeatedly impressed upon them (cf. ver. 40, chap. v. 30, vi. 2, viii. 1, xi. 21, xvi. 20, xxv. 15, xxx. 6, 15 sqq., xxxii. 47). יְרִשְׁתֶּם, for יְרַשְׁתֶּם (as in ver. 22, Josh. i. 16 ; cf. Ges. § 44, 2, *Anm.* 2).—Ver. 2. The observance of the law, however, required that it should be kept as it was given, that nothing should be added to it or taken from it, but that men should submit to it as to the inviolable word of God. Not by omissions only, but by additions also, was the commandment weakened, and the word of God turned into ordinances of men, as Pharisaism sufficiently proved. This precept is repeated in chap. xiii. 1 ; it is then revived by the prophets (Jer. xxvi. 2 ; Prov. xxx. 6), and enforced again at the close of the whole revelation (Rev. xxii. 18, 19). In the same sense Christ also said that He had not come to destroy the law or the prophets, but to fulfil (Matt. v. 17) ; and the old covenant was not abrogated, but only glorified and perfected, by the new.—Vers. 3, 4. The Israelites had just experienced how a faithful observance of the law gave life, in what the Lord had done on account of Baal-Peor, when He destroyed those who worshipped this idol (Num. xxv. 3, 9), whereas the faithful followers of the Lord still remained alive. דָּבַק בְּ, to cleave to any one, to hold fast to him. This example was adduced by Moses, because the congregation had passed through all this only a very short time before ; and the results of faithfulness towards the Lord on the one hand, and of the unfaithfulness of apostasy from Him on the other, had been made thoroughly apparent to it. " *Your eyes the seeing*," as in chap. iii. 21.—Vers. 5, 6. But the laws which Moses taught were commandments of the Lord. Keeping and doing them were to be the wisdom and understanding of Israel in the eyes of the nations, who, when they heard all these laws, would say, " *Certainly* (רַק, only, no other than) *a wise and understanding people is this great nation.*" History has confirmed this. Not only did the wisdom of a Solomon astonish the queen of Sheba (1 Kings x. 4 sqq.), but the divine truth which Israel possessed in the law of Moses attracted all the more earnest minds of the heathen world to seek the satisfaction of the inmost necessities of their heart and the salvation of their souls in Israel's knowledge of God, when, after a short period of bloom, the inward self-dis-

solution of the heathen religions had set in; and at last, in Christianity, it has brought one heathen nation after another to the
knowledge of the true God, and to eternal salvation, notwithstanding the fact that the divine truth was and still is regarded as
folly by the proud philosophers and self-righteous Epicureans and
Stoics of ancient and modern times.—Vers. 7, 8. This mighty and
attractive force of the wisdom of Israel consisted in the fact, that
in Jehovah they possessed a God who was at hand with His help
when they called upon Him (cf. chap. xxxiii. 29; Ps. xxxiv. 19,
cxlv. 18; 1 Kings ii. 7), as none of the gods of the other nations
had ever been; and that in the law of God they possessed such
statutes and rights as the heathen never had. True right has its
roots in God; and with the obscuration of the knowledge of God,
law and right, with their divinely established foundations, are also
shaken and obscured (cf. Rom. i. 26–32).

Vers. 9–14. Israel was therefore not to forget the things which
it had seen at Horeb with its own eyes.—Ver. 9. " *Only beware and
take care of thyself.*" To "keep the soul," *i.e.* to take care of the
soul as the seat of life, to defend one's life from danger and injury
(Prov. xiii. 3, xix. 16). " *That thou do not forget* אֶת־הַדְּבָרִים (the
facts described in Ex. xix.–xxiv.), *and that they do not depart from
thy heart all the days of thy life,*" *i.e.* are not forgotten as long as
thou livest, " *and thou makest them known to thy children and thy
children's children.*" These acts of God formed the foundation of the
true religion, the real basis of the covenant legislation, and the firm
guarantee of the objective truth and divinity of all the laws and
ordinances which Moses gave to the people. And it was this which
constituted the essential distinction between the religion of the Old
Testament and all heathen religions, whose founders, it is true,
professed to derive their doctrines and statutes from divine inspiration, but without giving any practical guarantee that their origin
was truly divine.—Vers. 10–12. In the words, " *The day* (הַיּוֹם, adverbial accusative) " *that thou stoodest before Jehovah thy God at
Horeb,*" etc., Moses reminds the people of the leading features of
those grand events: first of all of the fact that God directed him to
gather the people together, that He might make known His words
to them (Ex. xix. 9 sqq.), that they were to learn to fear Him
all their life long, and to teach their children also (יִרְאָה, inf., like
שְׂנֵאָה, chap. i. 27); and secondly (ver. 11), that they came near to
the mountain which burned in fire (cf. Ex. xix. 17 sqq.). The expression, burning in fire " *even to the heart of heaven,*" *i.e.* quite into

the sky, is a rhetorical description of the awful majesty of the pillar of fire, in which the glory of the Lord appeared upon Sinai, intended to impress deeply upon the minds of the people the remembrance of this manifestation of God. And the expression, "*darkness, clouds, and thick darkness,*" which is equivalent to the smoking of the great mountain (Ex. xix. 18), is employed with the same object. And lastly (vers. 12, 13), he reminds them that the Lord spoke out of the midst of the fire, and adds this important remark, to prepare the way for what is to follow, " *Ye heard the sound of the words, but ye did not see a shape,*" which not only agrees most fully with Ex. xxiv., where it is stated that the sight of the glory of Jehovah upon the mountain appeared to the people as they stood at the foot of the mountain " like devouring fire" (ver. 17), and that even the elders who " saw God" upon the mountain at the conclusion of the cove- nant saw no form of God (ver. 11), but also with Ex. xxxiii. 20, 23, according to which no man can see the face (פָּנִים) of God. Even the similitude (*temunah*) of Jehovah, which Moses saw when the Lord spoke to him mouth to mouth (Num. xii. 8), was not the form of the essential being of God which was visible to his bodily eyes, but simply a manifestation of the glory of God answering to his own intuition and perceptive faculty, which is not to be regarded as a form of God which was an adequate representation of the divine nature. The true God has no such form which is visible to the human eye.—Ver. 13. The Israelites, therefore, could not see a form of God, but could only hear the voice of His words, when the Lord proclaimed His covenant to them, and gave utterance to the ten words, which He afterwards gave to Moses written upon two tables of stone (Ex. xx. 1–14 (17), and xxxi. 18, compared with chap. xxiv. 12). On the " tables of stone," see at Ex. xxxiv. 1.— Ver. 14. When the Lord Himself had made known to the people in the ten words the covenant which He commanded them to do, He directed Moses to teach them laws and rights which they were to observe in Canaan, viz. the rights and statutes of the Sinaitic legislation, from Ex. xxi. onwards.

Vers. 15–24. As the Israelites had seen no shape of God at Horeb, they were to beware for their souls' sake (for their lives) of acting corruptly, and making to themselves any kind of image of Jehovah their God, namely, as the context shows, to worship God in it. (On *pesel*, see at Ex. xx. 4.) The words which follow, viz. " *a form of any kind of sculpture,*" and " *a representation of male or female*" (for *tabnith*, see at Ex. xxv. 9), are in apposition to " graven

image," and serve to explain and emphasize the prohibition.—Vers.
17, 18. They were also not to make an image of any kind of beast;
a caution against imitating the animal worship of Egypt.—Ver. 19.
They were not to allow themselves to be torn away (נִדַּח) to worship
the stars of heaven, namely, by the seductive influence exerted upon
the senses by the sight of the heavenly bodies as they shone in their
glorious splendour. The reason for this prohibition is given in the
relative clause, " *which Jehovah thy God hath allotted to all nations
under the whole heaven.*" The thought is not, " God has given the
heathen the sun, moon, and stars for service, *i.e.* to serve them with
their light," as *Onkelos,* the *Rabbins, Jerome,* and others, suppose,
but He has allotted them to them for worship, *i.e.* permitted them
to choose them as the objects of their worship, which is the view
adopted by *Justin Martyr, Clemens Alex.,* and others. According
to the scriptural view, even the idolatry of the heathen existed by
divine permission and arrangement. God gave up the heathen
to idolatry and shameful lusts, because, although they knew Him
from His works, they did not praise Him as God (Rom. i. 21, 24,
26).—Ver. 20. The Israelites were not to imitate the heathen in
this respect, because Jehovah, who brought them out of the iron
furnace of Egypt, had taken them (לָקַח) to Himself, *i.e.* had drawn
them out or separated them from the rest of the nations, to be a
people of inheritance. They were therefore not to seek God and
pray to Him in any kind of creature, but to worship Him without
image and form, in a manner corresponding to His own nature,
which had been manifested in no form, and therefore could not be
imitated. כּוּר בַּרְזֶל, an iron furnace, or furnace for smelting iron,
is a significant figure descriptive of the terrible sufferings endured
by Israel in Egypt. עַם נַחֲלָה (a people of inheritance) is synonymous with עַם סְגֻלָּה (a special people, chap. vii. 6 : see at Ex. xix.
5, " a peculiar treasure"). " *This day :*" as in chap. ii. 30.—Vers.
21 sqq. The bringing of Israel out of Egypt reminds Moses of the
end, viz. Canaan, and leads him to mention again how the Lord
had refused him permission to enter into this good land ; and to
this he adds the renewed warning not to forget the covenant or
make any image of God, since Jehovah, as a jealous God, would
never tolerate this. The swearing attributed to God in ver. 21 is
neither mentioned in Num. xx. nor at the announcement of Moses'
death in Num. xxvii. 12 sqq. ; but it is not to be called in question
on that account, as *Knobel* supposes. It is perfectly obvious from
chap. iii. 23 sqq. that all the details are not given in the historical

account of the event referred to. פֶּסֶל תְּמוּנַת כֹּל, "*image of a form of all that Jehovah has commanded*," sc. not to be made (vers. 16–18). "*A consuming fire*" (ver. 24): this epithet is applied to God with special reference to the manifestation of His glory in burning fire (Ex. xxiv. 17). On the symbolical meaning of this mode of revelation, see at Ex. iii. 2 (vol. i. pp. 438–9). "*A jealous God:*" see at Ex. xx. 5.

Vers. 25–31. To give emphasis to this warning, Moses holds up the future dispersion of the nation among the heathen as the punishment of apostasy from the Lord.—Vers. 25, 26. If the Israelites should beget children and children's children, and grow old in the land, and then should make images of God, and do that which was displeasing to God to provoke Him; in that case Moses called upon heaven and earth as witnesses against them, that they should be quickly destroyed out of the land. "*Growing old in the land*" involved forgetfulness of the former manifestations of grace on the part of the Lord, but not necessarily becoming voluptuous through the enjoyment of the riches of the land, although this might also lead to forgetfulness of God and the manifestations of His grace (cf. chap. vi. 10 sqq., xxxii. 15). The apodosis commences with ver. 26. הֵעִיד, with בְּ and the accusative, to take or summon as a witness against a person. Heaven and earth do not stand here for the rational beings dwelling in them, but are personified, represented as living, and capable of sensation and speech, and mentioned as witnesses who would rise up against Israel, not to proclaim its guilt, but to bear witness that God, the Lord of heaven and earth, had warned the people, and, as it is described in the parallel passage in chap. xxx. 19, had set before them the choice of life and death, and therefore was just in punishing them for their unfaithfulness (cf. Ps. l. 6, li. 6). "Prolong days," as in Ex. xx. 12.—Ver. 27. Jehovah would scatter them among the nations, where they would perish through want and suffering, and only a few (מְתֵי מִסְפָּר, Gen. xxxiv. 30) would be left. "*Whither*" refers to the nations whose land is thought of (cf. chap. xii. 29, xxx. 3). For the thing intended, see Lev. xxvi. 33, 36, 38, 39, and Deut. xxviii. 64 sqq., from which it is evident that the author had not "the fate of the nation in the time of the Assyrians in his mind" (*Knobel*), but rather all the dispersions which would come upon the rebellious nation in future times, even down to the dispersion under the Romans, which continues still; so that Moses contemplated the punishment in its fullest extent.—Ver. 28. There among the heathen they would be obliged to serve gods that were the work of men's hands, gods of wood and stone, that could neither hear, nor eat, nor smell, *i.e.* possessed no senses, showed no sign of life. What Moses threatens here, follows from the eternal laws of the divine government. The more refined idolatry of image-worship leads to coarser and coarser forms, in which the whole nature of idol-worship is manifested in all its pitiableness. "When once the God of revelation is forsaken, the God of reason and imagination must also soon be given up and make way for still lower powers, that perfectly accord with the *I* exalted upon the throne, and in the time of pretended 'illumination' to atheism and materialism also" (*Schultz*).—Ver. 29. From thence Israel would come to itself again in the time of deepest misery, like the prodigal son in the gospel (Luke xv. 17), would seek the Lord its God, and would also find Him if it sought with all its heart and soul (cf. chap. vi. 5, x. 12).—Ver. 30. "*In tribulation to thee* (in thy trouble), *all these things* (the threatened punishments and sufferings) *will befall thee; at the end of the days* (see at Gen. xlix. 1) *thou wilt turn to Jehovah thy God, and hearken to His voice.*" With this comprehensive thought Moses brings his picture of the future to a close. (On the subject-matter, *vid.* Lev. xxvi. 39, 40.) Returning to the Lord and hearkening to His voice presuppose that the Lord will be found by those who earnestly seek Him; "*for* (ver. 31) *He is a merciful God, who does not let His people go, nor destroy them, and who does not forget the covenant with the fathers*" (cf. Lev. xxvi. 42 and 45). הִרְפָּה, to let loose, to withdraw the hand from a person (Josh. x. 6).

Vers. 32–40. But in order to accomplish something more than merely preserving the people from apostasy by the threat of punishment, namely, to secure a more faithful attachment and continued obedience to His commands by awakening the feeling of cordial love, Moses reminds them again of the glorious miracles of divine grace performed in connection with the election and deliverance of Israel, such as had never been heard of from the beginning of the world; and with this strong practical proof of the love of the true God, he brings his first address to a close. This closing thought in ver. 32 is connected by כִּי (*for*) with the leading idea in ver. 31, "Jehovah thy God is a merciful God," to show that the sole ground for the election and redemption of Israel was the compassion of God towards the human race. "*For·ask now of the days that are past, from the day that God created man upon the*

*earth, and from one end of the heaven unto the other, whether so great
a thing has ever happened, or anything of the kind has been heard of:"*
i.e. the history of all times since the creation of man, and of all
places under the whole heaven, can relate no such events as those
which have happened to Israel, viz. at Sinai (ver. 33; cf. ver. 12).
From this awfully glorious manifestation of God, Moses goes back
in ver. 34 to the miracles with which God effected the deliverance
of Israel out of Egypt. *" Or has a god attempted* (made the attempt) *to come and take to himself people from people* (*i.e.* to fetch
the people of Israel out of the midst of the Egyptian nation), *with
temptations* (the events in Egypt by which Pharaoh's relation to
the Lord was put to the test; cf. chap. vi. 22 and vii. 18, 19), *with
signs and wonders* (the Egyptian plagues, see Ex. vii. 3), *and with
conflict* (at the Red Sea : Ex. xiv. 14, xv. 3), *and with a strong
hand and outstretched arm* (see Ex. vi. 6), *and with great terrors?"*
In the three points mentioned last, all the acts of God in Egypt
are comprehended, according to both cause and effect. They were
revelations of the omnipotence of the Lord, and produced great
terrors (cf. Ex. xii. 30-36).—Ver. 35. Israel was made to see all
this, that it might know that Jehovah was God (הָאֱלֹהִים, *the* God,
to whom the name of *Elohim* rightfully belonged), and there was
none else beside Him (cf. ver. 39, xxxii. 39 ; Isa. xlv. 5, 6).—Ver.
36. But the Lord had spoken to Israel chiefly down from heaven
(cf. Ex. xx. 19 (22)), and that out of the great fire, in which He
had come down upon Sinai, to chastise it. יִסֵּר does not mean "to
instruct the people with regard to His truth and sovereignty," as
Schultz thinks, but " to take them under holy discipline" (*Knobel*),
to inspire them with a salutary fear of the holiness of His ways
and of His judgments by the awful phenomena which accompanied
His descent, and shadowed forth the sublime and holy majesty of
His nature.—Vers. 37-40. All this He did from love to the fathers
of Israel (the patriarchs): *"and indeed because He loved thy fathers,
He chose his seed* (the seed of Abraham, the first of the patriarchs)
after him, and brought thee (Israel) *out of Egypt by His face with
great power, to drive out . . . and to bring thee, to give thee their
land . . . so that thou mightest know and take to heart . . . and keep
His laws,"* etc. With regard to the construction of these verses,
the clause וְתַחַת כִּי (and because) in ver. 37 is not to be regarded as
dependent upon what precedes, as *Schultz* supposes ; nor are vers.
37 and 38 to be taken as the protasis, and vers. 39, 40 as the
apodosis (as *Knobel* maintains). Both forms of construction are

forced and unnatural. The verses form an independent thought;
and the most important point, which was to bind Israel to faithfulness towards Jehovah, is given as the sum and substance of the
whole address, and placed as a protasis at the head of the period.
The only thing that admits of dispute, is whether the apodosis
commences with וַיִּבְחַר (" *He chose*," ver. 37), or only with וַיּוֹצִאֲךָ
("*brought thee out*"). Either is possible; and it makes no difference,
so far as the main thought is concerned, whether we regard the
choice of Israel, or simply the deliverance from Egypt, in which
that choice was carried into practical effect, as the consequence of
the love of Jehovah to the patriarchs.—The copula וְ before תַּחַת is
specially emphatic, " *and truly*," and indicates that the sum and
substance of the whole discourse is about to follow, or the one
thought in which the whole appeal culminates. It was the love of
God to the fathers, not the righteousness of Israel (chap. ix. 5),
which lay at the foundation of the election of their posterity to be
the nation of Jehovah's possession, and also of all the miracles of
grace which were performed in connection with their deliverance out
of Egypt. Moses returns to this thought again at chap. x. 15, for
the purpose of impressing it upon the minds of the people as the
one motive which laid them under the strongest obligation to circumcise the foreskin of their heart, and walk in the fear and love
of the Lord their God (chap. x. 12 sqq.).—The singular suffixes in
זַרְעוֹ (his seed) and אַחֲרָיו (after him) refer to Abraham, whom Moses
had especially in his mind when speaking of "thy fathers," because
he was pre-eminently the lover of God (Isa. xli. 8 ; 2 Chron. xx. 7),
and also the beloved or friend of God (Jas. ii. 23 ; cf. Gen. xviii.
17 sqq.). " *By His face*" points back to Ex. xxxiii. 14. The face
of Jehovah was Jehovah in His personal presence, in His own
person, who brought Israel out of Egypt, to root out great and
mighty nations before it, and give it their land for an inheritance.
" *As this day*" (clearly shows), viz. by the destruction of Sihon
and Og, which gave to the Israelites a practical pledge that the
Canaanites in like manner would be rooted out before them. The
expression " as this day " does not imply, therefore, that the Canaanites were already rooted out from their land.—Vers. 39, 40. By
this the Israelites were to know and lay it to heart, that Jehovah
alone was God in heaven and on earth, and were to keep His
commandments, in order that (אֲשֶׁר) it might be well with them
and their descendants, and they might have long life in Canaan.
כָּל־הַיָּמִים, " all time," for all the future (cf. Ex. xx. 12).

of the fulfilment of the further promises of God, led Moses to mention again, though briefly, the defeat of the two kings of the Amorites, together with the conquest of their land, just as he had done before in chap. ii. 32–36 and iii. 1–17. On ver. 48, cf. chap. iii. 9, 12–17. *Sion*, for Hermon (see at chap. iii. 9).

A. THE TRUE ESSENCE OF THE LAW AND ITS FULFILMENT.

Exposition of the Decalogue, and its Promulgation.—Chap. v.

The exposition of the law commences with a repetition of the ten words of the covenant, which were spoken to all Israel directly by the Lord Himself.—Vers. 1–5 form the introduction, and point out the importance and great significance of the exposition which follows. Hence, instead of the simple sentence "*And Moses said*," we have the more formal statement "*And Moses called all Israel, and said to them.*" The great significance of the laws and rights about to be set before them, consisted in the fact that they contained the covenant of Jehovah with Israel.—Vers. 2, 3. "*Jehovah our God made a covenant with us in Horeb; not with our fathers, but with ourselves, who are all of us here alive this day.*" The "fathers" are neither those who died in the wilderness, as *Augustine* supposed, nor the forefathers in Egypt, as *Calvin* imagined; but the patriarchs, as in chap. iv. 37. Moses refers to the conclusion of the covenant at Sinai, which was essentially distinct from the covenant made with Abraham (Gen. xv. 18), though the latter laid the foundation for the Sinaitic covenant. But Moses passed over this, as it was not his intention to trace the historical development of the covenant relation, but simply to impress upon the hearts of the existing generation the significance of its entrance into covenant with the Lord. The generation, it is true, with which God made the covenant at Horeb, had all died out by that time, with the exception of Moses, Joshua, and Caleb, and only lived in the children, who, though in part born in Egypt, were all under twenty years of age at the conclusion of the covenant at Sinai, and therefore were not among the persons with whom the Lord concluded the covenant. But the covenant was made not with the particular individuals who were then alive, but rather with the nation as an organic whole. Hence Moses could with perfect justice identify those who constituted the nation at that time, with those who had entered into covenant with the Lord at Sinai. The separate pronoun (*we*) is added to the pronominal suffix for the sake of emphasis, just as in Gen. iv. 26, etc.; and אֵלֶּה again is so connected with אֲנַחְנוּ, as to include the relative in itself.—Ver. 4. "*Jehovah talked with you face to face in the mount out of the midst of the fire,*" *i.e.* He came as near to you as one person to another. פָּנִים בְּפָנִים is not perfectly synonymous with פָּנִים אֶל פָּנִים, which is used in Ex. xxxiii. 11 with reference to God's speaking to Moses (cf. chap. xxxiv. 10, and Gen. xxxii. 31), and expresses the very confidential relation in which the Lord spoke to Moses as one friend to another; whereas the former simply denotes the directness with which Jehovah spoke to the people.—Before repeating the ten words which the Lord addressed directly to the people, Moses introduces the following remark in ver. 5—"*I stood between Jehovah and you at that time, to announce to you the word of Jehovah; because ye were afraid of the fire, and went not up into the mount*"—for the purpose of showing the mediatorial position which he occupied between the Lord and the people, not so much at the proclamation of the ten words of the covenant, as in connection with the conclusion of the covenant generally, which alone in fact rendered the conclusion of the covenant possible at all, on account of the alarm of the people at the awful manifestation of the majesty of the Lord. The word of Jehovah, which Moses as mediator had to announce to the people, had reference not to the instructions which preceded the promulgation of the decalogue (Ex. xix. 11 sqq.), but, as is evident from vers. 22–31, primarily to the further communications which the Lord was about to address to the nation in connection with the conclusion of the covenant, besides the ten words (viz. Ex. xx. 18, 22–xxiii. 33), to which in fact the whole of the Sinaitic legislation really belongs, as being the further development of the covenant laws. The alarm of the people at the fire is more fully described in vers. 25 sqq. The word "*saying*" at the end of ver. 5 is dependent upon the word "*talked*" in ver. 4; ver. 5 simply containing a parenthetical remark.

In vers. 6–21, the ten covenant words are repeated from Ex. xx., with only a few variations, which have already been discussed in connection with the exposition of the decalogue at Ex. xx. 1–14.— In vers. 22–33, Moses expounds still further the short account in Ex. xx. 18–21, viz. that after the people had heard the ten covenant words, in their alarm at the awful phenomena in which the Lord revealed His glory, they entreated him to stand between as mediator, that God Himself might not speak to them any further, and that

they might not die, and then promised that they would hearken to
all that the Lord should speak to him (vers. 23–31). His purpose
in doing so was to link on the exhortation in vers. 32, 33, to keep
all the commandments of the Lord and do them, which paves the
way for passing to the exposition of the law which follows. " *A great
voice*" (ver. 22) is an adverbial accusative, signifying " *with* a great
voice" (cf. *Ges.* § 118, 3). " *And He added no more :*" as in Num.
xi. 25. God spoke the ten words directly to the people, and then
no more; *i.e.* everything further He addressed to Moses alone, and
through his mediation to the people. As mediator He gave him
the two tables of stone, upon which He had written the decalogue
·(cf. Ex. xxxi. 18). This statement somewhat forestalls the historical
course ; and in chap. ix. 10, 11, it is repeated again in its proper
historical connection.—Vers. 24–27 contain a rhetorical, and at the
same time really a more exact, account of the events described in
Ex. xx. 18–20 (15–17), and already expounded in vol. ii. p. 125.
וְאַתְּ (ver. 24), a contraction of וְאַתָּה, as in Num. xi. 15 (cf. *Ewald,*
§ 184, *a.*). Jehovah's reply to the words of the people (vers. 28–31)
is passed over in Ex. xx. God approved of what the people said,
because it sprang from a consciousness of the unworthiness of any
sinner to come into the presence of the holy God ; and He added,
" Would that there were always this heart in them to fear Me,"
i.e. would that they were always of the same mind to fear Me and
keep all My commandments, that it might be well with them and
their children for ever. He then directed the people to return to
their tents, and appointed Moses as the mediator, to whom He would
address all the law, that he might teach it to the people (cf. chap.
iv. 5). Having been thus entreated by the people to take the office
of mediator, and appointed to that office by the Lord, Moses could
very well bring his account of these events to a close (vers. 32, 33),
by exhorting them to observe carefully all the commandments of
the Lord, and not to turn aside to the right hand or to the left,
i.e. not to depart in any way from the mode of life pointed out in
the commandments (cf. chap. xvii. 11, 20, xxviii. 14 ; Josh. i. 7,
etc.), that it might be well with them, etc. (cf. chap. iv. 40). וְטוֹב,
perfect with ו rel. instead of the imperfect.

On loving Jehovah, the one God, with all the Heart.—Chap. vi.

Vers. 1–3. Announcement of the commandments which follow,
with a statement of the reason for communicating them, and the
beneficent results of their observance. הַמִּצְוָה, that which is com-

manded, *i.e.* the substance of all that Jehovah had commanded, synonymous therefore with the *Thorah* (chap. iv. 44). The words, " *the statutes and the rights*," are explanatory of and in apposition to " *the commandment.*" These commandments Moses was to teach the Israelites to keep in the land which they were preparing to possess (cf. chap. iv. 1).—Ver. 2. The reason for communicating the law was to awaken the fear of God (cf. chap. iv. 10, v. 26), and, in fact, such fear of Jehovah as would show itself at all times in the observ-ance of every commandment. " *Thou and thy son :*" this forms the subject to " *thou mightest fear,*" and is placed at the end for the sake of emphasis. The *Hiphil* הַאֲרִיךְ has not the transitive meaning, " to make long," as in chap. v. 30, but the intransitive, to *last long*, as in chap. v. 16, Ex. xx. 12, etc.—Ver. 3. The maintenance of the fear of God would bring prosperity, and the increase of the nation promised to the fathers. In form this thought is not con-nected with ver. 3 as the apodosis, but it is appended to the leading thought in ver. 1 by the words, " *Hear therefore, O Israel!*" which correspond to the expression " *to teach you*" in ver. 1. אֲשֶׁר, *that, in order that* (as in chap. ii. 25, iv. 10, etc.). The increase of the nation had been promised to the patriarchs from the very first (Gen. xii. 1 ; see vol. i. p. 193 ; cf. Lev. xxvi. 9).—On " *milk and honey,*" see at Ex. iii. 8.

Vers. 4–9. With ver. 4 the burden of the law commences, which is not a new law added to the ten commandments, but simply the development and unfolding of the covenant laws and rights enclosed as a germ in the decalogue, simply an exposition of the law, as had already been announced in chap. i. 5. The exposition com-mences with an explanation and enforcing of the first commandment. There are two things contained in it : (1) that Jehovah is the one absolute God ; (2) that He requires love with all the heart, all the soul, and all the strength. " *Jehovah our God is one Jehovah.*"[1] This does not mean Jehovah is one God, Jehovah alone (*Abenezra*), for in that case יְהֹוָה לְבַדּוֹ would be used instead of יְהֹוָה אֶחָד ; still less Jehovah our God, namely, Jehovah is one (*J. H. Michaelis*).

---

[1] On the *majuscula* ע and ד in שְׁמַע and אֶחָד, *R. Bochin* has this remark : " It is possible to confess one God with the mouth, although the heart is far from Him. For this reason ע and ד are *majuscula*, from which with *tsere* sub-scribed the word עֵד, 'a witness,' is formed, that every one may know, when he professes the unity of God, that his heart ought to be engaged, and free from every other thought, because God is a *witness* and knows all things" (*J. H. Mich. Bibl. Hebr.*).

יְהוָֹה אֶחָד together form the predicate of the sentence. The idea is not, Jehovah our God is one (the only) God, but " *one* (or the only) *Jehovah* :" not in this sense, however, that " He has not adopted one mode of revelation or appearance here and another there, but one mode only, viz. the revelation which Israel had received" (*Schultz*) ; for *Jehovah* never denotes merely a mode in which the true God is revealed or appears, but God as the absolute, unconditioned, or God according to the absolute independence and constancy of His actions (see vol. i. pp. 72–5). Hence what is predicated here of Jehovah (*Jehovah one*) does not relate to the unity of God, but simply states that it is to Him alone that the name *Jehovah* rightfully belongs, that He is the one absolute God, to whom no other *Elohim* can be compared. This is also the meaning of the same expression in Zech. xiv. 9, where the words added, " and His name one," can only signify that in the future Jehovah would be acknowledged as the one absolute God, as King over all the earth. This clause not merely precludes polytheism, but also syncretism, which reduces the one absolute God to a national deity, a Baal (Hos. ii. 18), and in fact every form of theism and deism, which creates for itself a supreme God according to philosophical abstractions and ideas. For Jehovah, although the absolute One, is not an abstract notion like "absolute being" or "the absolute idea," but the absolutely living God, as He made Himself known in His deeds in Israel for the salvation of the whole world.—Ver. 5. As the one God, therefore, Israel was to love Jehovah its God with all its heart, with all its soul, and with all its strength. The motive for this is to be found in the words " thy God," in the fact that Jehovah was Israel's God, and had manifested Himself to it as one God. The demand "with all the heart" excludes all half-heartedness, all division of the heart in its love. The heart is mentioned first, as the seat of the emotions generally and of love in particular ; then follows the soul (*nephesh*) as the centre of personality in man, to depict the love as pervading the entire self-consciousness ; and to this is added, "with all the strength," *sc.* of body and soul. Loving the Lord with all the heart and soul and strength is placed at the head, as the spiritual principle from which the observance of the commandments was to flow (see also chap. xi. 1, xxx. 6). It was in love that the fear of the Lord (chap. x. 12), hearkening to His commandments (chap. xi. 13), and the observance of the whole law (chap. xi. 22), were to be manifested ; but love itself was to be shown by walking in all the ways of the Lord (chap. xi. 22, xix.

9, xxx. 16). Christ therefore calls the command to love God with all the heart "the first and great commandment," and places on a par with this the commandment contained in Lev. xix. 8 to love one's neighbour as oneself, and then observes that on these two commandments hang all the law and the prophets (Matt. xxii. 37-40; Mark xii. 29–31; Luke x. 27).[1] Even the gospel knows no higher commandment than this. The distinction between the new covenant and the old consists simply in this, that the love of God which the gospel demands of its professors, is more intensive and cordial than that which the law of Moses demanded of the Israelites, according to the gradual unfolding of the love of God Himself, which was displayed in a much grander and more glorious form in the gift of His only begotten Son for our redemption, than in the redemption of Israel out of the bondage of Egypt.—Vers. 6 sqq. But for the love of God to be of the right kind, the commandments of God must be laid to heart, and be the constant subject of thought and conversation. " *Upon thine heart:*" *i.e.* the commandments of God were to be an affair of the heart, and not merely of the memory (cf. chap. xi. 18). They were to be enforced upon the children, talked of at home and by the way, in the evening on lying down and in the morning on rising up, *i.e.* everywhere and at all times ; they were to be bound upon the hand for a sign, and worn as bands (frontlets) between the eyes (see at Ex. xiii. 16). As these words are figurative, and denote an undeviating observance of the divine commands, so also the commandment which follows, viz. to write the words upon the door-posts of the house, and also upon the gates, are to be understood spiritually ; and the literal fulfilment of such a command could only be a praiseworthy custom or well-pleasing to God when resorted to as the means of keeping the commandments of God constantly before the eye. The precept itself, however, presupposes the existence of this custom, which is not only met with in the Mahometan countries of the East at the

---

[1] In quoting this commandment, Matthew (xxii. 37) has substituted διάνοια, " thy mind," for " thy strength," as being of especial importance to spiritual love, whereas in the LXX. the mind (διάνοια) is substituted for the heart. Mark (xii. 30) gives the triad of Deuteronomy (*heart, soul,* and *strength*) ; but he has inserted " *mind*" (διάνοια) before strength (ἰσχύς), whilst in ver. 33 the *understanding* (σύνεσις) is mentioned between the heart and the soul. Lastly, Luke has given the three ideas of the original passage quite correctly, but has added at the end, " and with all thy mind" (διάνοια). Although the term διάνοια (mind) originated with the Septuagint, not one of the Evangelists has adhered strictly to this version.

present day (cf. *A. Russell, Naturgesch. v. Aleppo*, i. p. 36 ; *Lane, Sitten u. Gebr.* i. pp. 6, 13, ii. p. 71), but was also a common custom in ancient Egypt (cf. *Wilkinson*, Manners and Customs, vol. ii. p. 102).[1]

Vers. 10–19. To the positive statement of the command there is attached, in the next place, the negative side, or a warning against the danger to which prosperity and an abundance of earthly goods so certainly expose, viz. of forgetting the Lord and His manifestations of mercy. The Israelites were all the more exposed to this danger, as their entrance into Canaan brought them into the possession of all the things conducive to well-being, in which the land abounded, without being under the necessity of procuring these things by the labour of their own hands;—into the possession, namely, of great and beautiful towns which they had not built, of houses full of all kinds of good things which they had not filled, of wells ready made which they had not dug, of vineyards and olive-plantations which they had not planted.—The nouns עָרִים, etc. are formally dependent upon לָתֶת לָךְ, and serve as a detailed description of the land into which the Lord was about to lead His people.— Ver. 12. *"House of bondage,"* as in Ex. xiii. 3. *"Not forgetting"* is described from a positive point of view, as fearing God, *serving Him,* and *swearing by His name.* Fear is placed first, as the fundamental characteristic of the Israelitish worship of God ; it was no slavish fear, but simply the holy awe of a sinner before the holy God, which includes love rather than excludes it. "Fearing" is a matter of the heart ; "serving," a matter of working and striving ; and "swearing in His name," the practical manifestation of the worship of God in word and conversation. It refers not merely to a solemn oath before a judicial court, but rather to asseverations on oath in the ordinary intercourse of life, by which the religious attitude of a man involuntarily reveals itself.—Vers. 14 sqq. The worship of Jehovah not only precludes all idolatry, which the Lord, as a jealous God, will not endure (see at Ex. xx. 5), but will punish with destruction from the earth ("the face of the ground," as in Ex. xxxii. 12) ; but it also excludes tempting the Lord by an

---

[1] The Jewish custom of the *Medusah* is nothing but a formal and outward observance founded upon this command. It consists in writing the words of Deut. vi. 4–9 and xi. 13–20 upon a piece of parchment, which is then placed upon the top of the doorway of houses and rooms, enclosed in a wooden box : this box they touch with the finger and then kiss the finger on going either out or in. *S. Buxtorf, Synag. Jud.* pp. 582 sqq. ; and *Bodenschatz, Kirchl. Verfassung der Juden*, iv. pp. 19 sqq.

unbelieving murmuring against God, if He does not remove any
kind of distress immediately, as the people had already sinned at
Massah, *i.e.* at Rephidim (Ex. xvii. 1–7).—Vers. 17–19. They
were rather to observe all His commandments diligently, and do
what was right and good in His eyes. The infinitive לַהֲדֹף וגו contains the further development of לְמַעַן יִיטַב וגו': "*so that He* (Jehovah)
thrust out all thine enemies before thee, as He hath spoken" (viz. Ex.
xxiii. 27 sqq., xxxiv. 11).

In vers. 20–25, the teaching to the children, which is only
briefly hinted at in ver. 7, is more fully explained. The Israelites
were to instruct their children and descendants as to the nature,
meaning, and object of the commandments of the Lord; and in
reply to the inquiries of their sons, to teach them what the Lord had
done for the redemption of Israel out of the bondage of Egypt,
and how He had brought them into the promised land, and thus
to awaken in the younger generation love to the Lord and to His
commandments. The "*great and sore miracles*" (ver. 22) were the
Egyptian plagues, like מֹפְתִים, in chap. iv. 34.—"*To fear*," etc., *i.e.*
that we might fear the Lord.—Ver. 25. "*And righteousness will be
to us, if we observe to do:*" *i.e.* our righteousness will consist in the
observance of the law; we shall be regarded and treated by God as
righteous, if we are diligent in the observance of the law. "*Before
Jehovah*" refers primarily, no doubt, to the expression, "to do all
these commandments;" but, as we may see from chap. xxiv. 13, this
does not prevent the further reference to the "righteousness" also.
This righteousness before Jehovah, it is true, is not really the
gospel "righteousness of faith;" but there is no opposition between
the two, as the righteousness mentioned here is not founded upon
the outward (pharisaic) righteousness of works, but upon an earnest
striving after the fulfilment of the law, to love God with all the
heart; and this love is altogether impossible without living faith.

Command to destroy the Canaanites and their Idolatry.—Chap. vii.

Vers. 1–11. As the Israelites were warned against idolatry in
chap. vi. 14, so here are they exhorted to beware of the false tolerance of sparing the Canaanites and enduring their idolatry.—Vers.
1 5. When the Lord drove out the tribes of Canaan before the
Israelites, and gave them up to them and smote them, they were to
put them under the ban (see at Lev. xxvii. 28), to make no treaty
with them, and to contract no marriage with them. נָשַׁל, to draw
out, to cast away, *e.g.* the sandals (Ex. iii. 5); here and ver. 22 it

signifies to draw out, or drive out a nation from its country and possessions : it occurs in this sense in the *Piel* in 2 Kings xvi. 6. On the Canaanitish tribes, see at Gen. x. 15 sqq. and xv. 20, 21. There are seven of them mentioned here, as in Josh. iii. 10 and xxiv. 11 ; on the other hand, there are only six in chap. xx. 17, as in Ex. iii. 8, 17, xxiii. 23, and xxxiii. 2, the Girgashites being omitted. The prohibition against making a covenant, as in Ex. xxiii. 32 and xxxiv. 12, and that against marrying, as in Ex. xxxiv. 16, where the danger of the Israelites being drawn away to idolatry is mentioned as a still further reason for these commands. כִּי יָסִיר, "*for he* (the Canaanite) *will cause thy son to turn away from behind me,*" *i.e.* tempt him away from following me, "*to serve other gods.*" Moses says "from following *me,*" because he is speaking in the name of Jehovah. The consequences of idolatry, as in chap. vi. 15, iv. 26, etc.—Ver. 5. The Israelites were rather to destroy the altars and idols of the Canaanites, according to the command in Ex. xxxiv. 13, xxiii. 24.—Vers. 6–8. They were bound to do this by virtue of their election as a holy nation, the nation of possession, which Jehovah had singled out from all other nations, and brought out of the bondage of Egypt, not because of its greatness, but from love to them, and for the sake of the oath given to the fathers. This exalted honour Israel was not to cast away by apostasy from the Lord. It was founded upon the word of the Lord in Ex. xix. 5, 6, which Moses brought to the recollection of the people, and expressly and emphatically developed. "*Not because of your multitude before all nations* (because ye were more numerous than all other nations) *hath Jehovah turned to you in love* (חָשַׁק, to bind oneself with, to hang upon a person, out of love), *for ye are the littleness of all nations*" (the least numerous). Moses could say this to Israel with reference to its descent from Abraham, whom God chose as the one man out of all the world, whilst nations, states, and kingdoms had already been formed all around (*Baumgarten*). "*But because Jehovah loved you, and kept His oath which He had sworn to the fathers, He hath brought you out,*" etc. Instead of saying, He hath chosen you out of love to your fathers, as in chap. iv. 37, Moses brings out in this place love to the people of Israel as the divine motive, not for choosing Israel, but for leading it out and delivering it from the slave-house of Egypt, by which God had practically carried out the election of the people, that He might thereby allure the Israelites to a reciprocity of love.—Vers. 9–11. By this was Israel to know that Jehovah their God was the true

God, the faithful God, who keeps His covenant, showing mercy to those who love Him, even to the thousandth generation, but repaying those who hate Him to the face. This development of the nature of God Moses introduces from Ex. xx. 5, 6, as a light warning not to forfeit the mercy of God, or draw upon themselves His holy wrath by falling into idolatry. To this end He emphatically carries out still further the thought of retribution, by adding לְהַאֲבִידוֹ, " to destroy him" (the hater), and לֹא יְאַחֵר וגו', " He delays not to His hater (sc. to repay him); He will repay him to his face." " To the face of every one of them," i.e. that they may see and feel that they are smitten by God (Rosenmüller).—Ver. 11. This energy of the grace and holiness of the faithful covenant God was a powerful admonition to keep the divine commandments.

Vers. 12–26. The observance of these commandments would also bring great blessings (vers. 12–16). " If ye hearken to these demands of right" (mishpatim) of the covenant Lord upon His covenant people, and keep them and do them, " Jehovah will keep unto thee the covenant and the mercy which He hath sworn to thy fathers." In עֵקֶב, for עֵקֶב אֲשֶׁר (Gen. xxii. 18), there is involved not only the idea of reciprocity, but everywhere also an allusion to reward or punishment (cf. chap. viii. 20; Num. xiv. 24). חֶסֶד was the favour displayed in the promises given to the patriarchs on oath (Gen. xxii. 16).—Ver. 13. This mercy flowed from the love of God to Israel, and the love was manifested in blessing and multiplying the people. The blessing is then particularized, by a further expansion of Ex. xxiii. 25–27, as a blessing upon the fruit of the body, the fruits of the field and soil, and the rearing of cattle. שֶׁגֶר, see Ex. xiii. 12. עַשְׁתְּרֹת צֹאן only occurs again in Deut. xxviii. 4, 18, 51, and certainly signifies the young increase of the flocks. It is probably a Canaanitish word, derived from Ashtoreth (Astharte), the female deity of the Canaanites, which was regarded as the conceiving and birth-giving principle of nature, literally Veneres, i.e. amores gregis, hence soboles (Ges.); just as the Latin poets employ the name Ceres to signify the corn, Venus for love and sexual intercourse, and Lucina for birth. On vers. 14 and 15, see Ex. xxiii. 26. In ver. 15, the promise of the preservation of Israel from all diseases (Ex. xv. 26, and xxiii. 25) is strengthened by the addition of the clause, " all the evil diseases of Egypt," by which, according to chap. xxviii. 27, we are probably to understand chiefly the malignant species of leprosy called elephantiasis, and possibly also the plague and other malignant forms of disease. In Egypt, diseases for the most part readily assume a very dangerous character. *Pliny* (*h. n.* xxvi. 1) calls Egypt the *genitrix* of contagious pestilence, and modern naturalists have confirmed this (see *Hengstenberg*, Egypt and the Books of Moses, p. 215; and *Pruner, Krankheiten des Orients*, pp. 460 sqq.). Diseases of this kind the Lord would rather bring upon the enemies of Israel. The Israelites, on the other hand, should be so strong and vigorous, that they would devour, *i.e.* exterminate, all the nations which their God would give into their hands (cf. Num. xiv. 9). With this thought Moses reverts with emphasis to the command to root out the Canaanites without reserve, and not to serve their gods, because they would become a snare to them (see Ex. x. 7); and then in vers. 17–26 he carries out still further the promise in Ex. xxiii. 27–30 of the successful subjugation of the Canaanites through the assistance of the Lord, and sweeps away all the objections that a weak faith might raise to the execution of the divine command.—Vers. 17–26. To suppress the thought that was rising up in their heart, how could it be possible for them to destroy these nations which were more numerous than they, the Israelites were to remember what the Lord had done in Egypt and to Pharaoh, namely, the great temptations, signs, and wonders connected with their deliverance from Egypt (cf. chap. iv. 34 and vi. 22). He would do just the same to the Canaanites.—Ver. 20. He would also send hornets against them, as He had already promised in Ex. xxiii. 28 (see the passage), until all that were left and had hidden themselves should have utterly perished.—Vers. 21 sqq. Israel had no need to be afraid of them, as Jehovah was in the midst of it a mighty God and terrible. He would drive out the nations, but only gradually, as He had already declared to Moses in Ex. xxiii. 30, 31, and would smite them with great confusion, till they were destroyed, as was the case for example at Gibeon (Josh. x. 10; cf. Ex. xxiii. 27, where the form הָמַם is used instead of הוּם), and would also deliver their kings into the hand of Israel, so that their names should vanish under the heaven (cf. chap. ix. 14, xxv. 19; and for the fulfilment, Josh. x. 22 sqq., xi. 12, xii. 7–24). No one would be able to stand before Israel.—Ver. 24. "*To stand before thee:*" *lit.* to put oneself in the face of a person, so as to withstand him. הִשְׁמִיד for הַשְׁמִיד, as in Lev. xiv. 43, etc.—Vers. 25, 26. Trusting to this promise, the Israelites were to burn up the idols of the Canaanites, and not to desire the silver and gold upon them (with which the statues were overlaid: see vol. ii. p. 222), or take it to themselves, lest they should be snared in it, *i.e.* lest the silver and gold should become a snare to them. It would become so, not from any danger lest they should practise idolatry with it, but because silver and gold which had been used in connection with idolatrous worship was an abomination to Jehovah, which the Israelites were not to bring into their houses, lest they themselves should fall under the ban, to which all the objects connected with idolatry were devoted, as the history of Achan in Josh. vii. clearly proves. For this reason, any such abomination was to be abhorred, and destroyed by burning or grinding to powder (cf. Ex. xxxii. 20; 2 Kings xxiii. 4, 5; 2 Chron. xv. 16).

Review of the Guidance of God, and their Humiliation in the Desert, as a Warning against Highmindedness and Forgetfulness of God. —Chap. viii.

Vers. 1–6. In addition to the danger of being drawn aside to transgress the covenant, by sparing the Canaanites and their idols out of pusillanimous compassion and false tolerance, the Israelites would be especially in danger, after their settlement in Canaan, of falling into pride and forgetfulness of God, when enjoying the abundant productions of that land. To guard against this danger, Moses set before them how the Lord had sought to lead and train them to obedience by temptations and humiliations during their journey through the desert. In order that his purpose in doing this might be clearly seen, he commenced (ver. 1) with the renewed admonition to keep the whole law which he commanded them that day, that they might live and multiply and attain to the possession of the promised land (cf. chap. iv. 1, vi. 3).—Ver. 2. To this end they were to remember the forty years' guidance through the wilderness (chap. i. 31, ii. 7), by which God desired to humble them, and to prove the state of their heart and their obedience. Humiliation was the way to prove their attitude towards God. עִנָּה, to *humble, i.e.* to bring them by means of distress and privations to feel their need of help and their dependence upon God. נִסָּה, to *prove,* by placing them in such positions in life as would drive them to reveal what was in their heart, viz. whether they believed in the omnipotence, love, and righteousness of God, or not.—Ver. 3. The humiliation in the desert consisted not merely in the fact that God let the people hunger, *i.e.* be in want of bread and their ordinary food, but also in the fact that He fed them with manna, which was unknown to them and their fathers (cf. Ex. xvi. 16 sqq.). Feeding with manna is called a humiliation, inasmuch as God intended to show to the people through this food, which had previously been altogether unknown to them, that man does not live by bread alone, that the power to sustain life does not rest upon bread only (Isa. xxxviii. 16; Gen. xxvii. 40), or belong simply to it, but to all that goeth forth out of the mouth of Jehovah. That which "*proceedeth out of the mouth of Jehovah*" is not the word of the law, as the Rabbins suppose, but, as the word כֹּל (all, every) shows, "*the word*" generally, the revealed will of God to preserve the life of man in whatever way (*Schultz*): hence all means designed and appointed by the Lord for the sustenance of life. In this sense Christ quotes these words in reply to the tempter (Matt. iv. 4), not to say to him, The Messiah lives not by (material) bread only, but by the fulfilment of the will of God (*Usteri, Ullmann*), or by trusting in the sustaining word of God (*Olshausen*); but that He left it to God to care for the sustenance of His life, as God could sustain His life in extraordinary ways, even without the common supplies of food, by the power of His almighty word and will.— Ver. 4. As the Lord provided for their nourishment, so did He also in a marvellous way for the clothing of His people during these forty years. "*Thy garment did not fall off thee through age, and thy foot did not swell.*" בָּלָה with מִן, to fall off from age. בָּצֵק only occurs again in Neh. ix. 21, where this passage is repeated. The meaning is doubtful. The word is certainly connected with בָּצֵק (dough), and probably signifies to become soft or to swell, although בָּצֵק is also used for unleavened dough. The Septuagint rendering here is ἐτυλώθησαν, to get hard skin; on the other hand, in Neh. ix. 21, we find the rendering ὑποδήματα αὐτῶν οὐ διερράγησαν, "their sandals were not worn out," from the parallel passage in Deut. xxix. 5. These words affirm something more than "clothes and shoes never failed you," inasmuch as ye always had wool, hides, leather, and other kinds of material in sufficient quantities for clothes and shoes, as not only *J. D. Michaelis* and others suppose, but *Calmet,* and even *Kurtz. Knobel* is quite correct in observing, that "this would be altogether too trivial a matter by the side of the miraculous supply of manna, and moreover that it is not involved in the expression itself, which rather affirms that their clothes did not wear out upon them, or fall in tatters from their backs, because God gave them a miraculous durability" (*Luther, Calvin, Baumgarten, Schultz,* etc.). At the same time, there is no necessity to follow some of the *Rabbins* and *Justin Martyr (dial. c. Tryph. c.* 131), who so magnify the miracle of divine providence,

as to maintain not only that the clothes of the Israelites did not
get old, but that as the younger generation grew up their clothes
also grew upon their backs, like the shells of snails. Nor is it necessary to shut out the different natural resources which the people
had at their command for providing clothes and sandals, any more
than the gift of manna precluded the use of such ordinary provisions as they were able to procure.—Ver. 5. In this way Jehovah
humbled and tempted His people, that they might learn in their
heart, *i.e.* convince themselves by experience, that their God was
educating them as a father does his son. יִסַּר, to admonish, chasten,
educate; like παιδεύειν. "It includes everything belonging to a
proper education" (*Calvin*).—Ver. 6. The design of this education
was to train them to keep His commandments, that they might
walk in His ways and fear Him (chap. vi. 24).

Vers. 7–20. The Israelites were to continue mindful of this
paternal discipline on the part of their God, when the Lord should
bring them into the good land of Canaan. This land Moses describes in vers. 8, 9, in contrast with the dry unfruitful desert, as a
well-watered and very fruitful land, which yielded abundance of
support to its inhabitants; a land of water-brooks, fountains, and
floods (תְּהוֹמוֹת, see Gen. i. 2), which had their source (took their
rise) in valleys and on mountains; a land of wheat and barley, of
the vine, fig, and pomegranate, and full of oil and honey (see at
Ex. iii. 8); lastly, a land "*in which thou shalt not eat* (support thyself) *in scarcity, and shalt not be in want of anything; a land whose
stones are iron, and out of whose mountains thou hewest brass.*" The
stones are iron, *i.e.* ferruginous. This statement is confirmed by
modern travellers, although the Israelites did not carry on mining,
and do not appear to have obtained either iron or brass from their
own land. The iron and brass which David collected such quantities for the building of the temple (1 Chron. xxii. 3, 14), he procured from *Betach* and *Berotai* (2 Sam. viii. 8), or *Tibchat* and
Kun (1 Chron. xviii. 8), towns of Hadadezer, that is to say, from
Syria. According to Ezek. xxvii. 19, however, the Danites brought
iron-work to the market of Tyre. Not only do the springs near
Tiberias contain iron (*v. Schubert,* R. iii. p. 239), whilst the soil at
Hasbeya and the springs in the neighbourhood are also strongly
impregnated with iron (*Burckhardt, Syrien,* p. 83), but in the
southern mountains as well there are probably strata of iron be-
tween Jerusalem and Jericho (*Russegger,* R. iii. p. 250). But
Lebanon especially abounds in iron-stone; iron mines and smelting

furnaces being found there in many places (*Volney*, Travels; *Burckhardt*, p. 73; *Seetzen*, i. pp. 145, 187 sqq., 237 sqq.). The basalt also, which occurs in great masses in northern Canaan by the side of the limestone, from the plain of Jezreel onwards (*Robinson*, iii. p. 313), and is very predominant in Bashan, is a ferruginous stone. Traces of extinct copper-works are also found upon Lebanon (*Volney*, Travels; *Ritter's Erdkunde*, xvii. p. 1063).—Vers. 10–18. But if the Israelites were to eat there and be satisfied, *i.e.* to live in the midst of plenty, they were to beware of forgetting their God; that when their prosperity—their possessions, in the form of lofty houses, cattle, gold and silver, and other good things—increased, their heart might not be lifted up, *i.e.* they might not become proud, and, forgetting their deliverance from Egypt and their miraculous preservation and guidance in the desert, ascribe the property they had acquired to their own strength and the work of their own hands. To keep the people from this danger of forgetting God, which follows so easily from the pride of wealth, Moses once more enumerates in vers. 14*b*–16 the manifestations of divine grace, their deliverance from Egypt the slave-house, their being led through the great and terrible desert, whose terrors he depicts by mentioning a series of noxious and even fatal things, such as snakes, burning snakes (*saraph*, see at Num. xxi. 6), scorpions, and the thirsty land where there was no water. The words from נָחָשׁ, onwards, are attached rhetorically to what precedes by simple apposition, without any logically connecting particle; though it will not do to overlook entirely the rhetorical form of the enumeration, and supply the preposition בְּ before נָחָשׁ and the words which follow, to say nothing of the fact that it would be quite out of character before these nouns in the singular, as a whole people could not go through one serpent, etc. In this parched land the Lord brought the people water out of the flinty rock, the hardest stone, and fed them with manna, to humble them and tempt them (cf. ver. 2), in order (this was the ultimate intention of all the humiliation and trial) "*to do thee good at thy latter end.*" The "latter end" of any one is "the time which follows some distinct point in his life, particularly an important epoch-making point, and which may be regarded as the end by contrast, the time before that epoch being considered as the beginning" (*Schultz*). In this instance Moses refers to the period of their life in Canaan, in contrast with which the period of their sojourn in Egypt and their wandering in the desert is regarded as the beginning; consequently the expression does not relate to death as the end of life, as in Num. xxiii. 10, although this allusion is not to be altogether excluded, as a blessed death is only the completion of a blessed life.—Like all the guidance of Israel by the Lord, what is stated here is applicable to all believers. It is through humiliations and trials that the Lord leads His people to blessedness. Through the desert of tribulation, anxiety, distress, and merciful interposition, He conducts them to Canaan, into the land of rest, where they are refreshed and satisfied in the full enjoyment of the blessings of His grace and salvation ; but those alone who continue humble, not attributing the good fortune and prosperity to which they attain at last, to their own exertion, strength, perseverance, and wisdom, but gratefully enjoying this good as a gift of the grace of God. עָשָׂה חַיִל, to create property, to prosper in wealth (as in Num. xxiv. 18). God gave strength for this (ver. 18), not because of Israel's merit and worthiness, but to fulfil His promises which He had made on oath to the patriarchs. " As this day," as was quite evident then, when the establishment of the covenant had already commenced, and Israel had come through the desert to the border of Canaan (see chap. iv. 20).—Vers. 19, 20. To strengthen his admonition, Moses pointed again in conclusion, as he had already done in chap. vi. 14 (cf. chap. iv. 25 sqq.), to the destruction which would come upon Israel through apostasy from its God.

Warning against Self-righteousness, founded upon the recital of their previous Sins.—Chap. ix.-x. 11.

Besides the more vulgar pride which entirely forgets God, and attributes success and prosperity to its own power and exertion, there is one of a more refined character, which very easily spreads—namely, pride which acknowledges the blessings of God ; but instead of receiving them gratefully, as unmerited gifts of the grace of the Lord, sees in them nothing but proofs of its own righteousness and virtue. Moses therefore warned the Israelites more particularly of this dangerous enemy of the soul, by first of all declaring without reserve, that the Lord was not about to give them Canaan because of their own righteousness, but that He would exterminate the Canaanites for their own wickedness (vers. 1–6) ; and then showing them for their humiliation, by proofs drawn from the immediate past, how they had brought upon themselves the anger of the Lord, by their apostasy and rebellion against their God, directly after the conclusion of the covenant at Sinai ; and that in such a way, that it was only by his earnest intercession that he had been able to prevent

the destruction of the people (vers. 7–24), and to secure a further
renewal of the pledges of the covenant (ver. 25–chap. x. 11).

Vers. 1–6. Warning against a conceit of righteousness, with
the occasion for the warning. As the Israelites were now about to
cross over the Jordan (" this day," to indicate that the time was
close at hand), to take possession of nations that were superior to
them in size and strength (the tribes of Canaan mentioned in chap.
vii. 1), and great fortified cities reaching to the heavens (cf. chap.
i. 28), namely, the great and tall nation of the Enakites (chap. i. 28),
before which, as was well known, no one could stand (הִתְיַצֵּב, as in
chap. vii. 24) ; and as they also knew that Jehovah their God was
going before them to destroy and humble these nations, they were
not to say in their heart, when this was done, For my righteousness
Jehovah hath brought me in to possess this land. In ver. 3, וְיָדַעְתָּ
הַיּוֹם is not to be taken in an imperative sense, but as expressive of
the actual fact, and corresponding to ver. 1, " thou art to pass."
Israel now knew for certain—namely, by the fact, which spoke so
powerfully, of its having been successful against foes which it could
never have conquered by itself, especially against Sihon and Og—
that the Lord was going before it, as the leader and captain of His
people (Schultz : see chap. i. 30). The threefold repetition of הוּא
in ver. 3. is peculiarly emphatic. " A consuming fire :" as in chap.
iv. 24. הוּא יַשְׁמִידֵם is more particularly defined by וְהוּא יַכְנִיעֵם וגו',
which follows : not, however, as implying that הִשְׁמִיד does not signify complete destruction in this passage, but rather as explaining
how the destruction would take place. Jehovah would destroy the
Canaanites, by bringing them down, humbling them before Israel,
so that they would be able to drive them out and destroy them
quickly. " מַהֵר, quickly, is no more opposed to chap. vii. 22, ' thou
mayest not destroy them quickly,' than God's not delaying to
requite (chap. vii. 10) is opposed to His long-suffering" (Schultz).
So far as the almighty assistance of God was concerned, the Israelites would quickly overthrow the Canaanites ; but for the sake of
the well-being of Israel, the destruction would only take place by
degrees. " As Jehovah hath said unto thee :" viz. Ex. xxiii. 23, 27
sqq., and at the beginning of the conflict, chap. ii. 24 sqq.—Ver. 4.
When therefore Jehovah thrust out these nations before them (הָדַף,
as in chap. vi. 19), the Israelites were not to say within themselves,
" By (for, on account of) my righteousness Jehovah hath brought me
(led me hither) to possess this land." The following word, וּבְרִשְׁעַת,
is adversative : " but because of the wickedness of these nations," etc.

—To impress this truth deeply upon the people, Moses repeats the thought once more in ver. 5. At the same time he mentions, in addition to righteousness, straightness or uprightness of heart, to indicate briefly that outward works do not constitute true righteousness, but that an upright state of heart is indispensable, and then enters more fully into the positive reasons. The wickedness of the Canaanites was no doubt a sufficient reason for destroying *them*, but not for giving their land to the people of Israel, since they could lay no claim to it on account of their own righteousness. The reason for giving Canaan to the Israelites was simply the promise of God, the word which the Lord had spoken to the patriarchs on oath (cf. chap. vii. 8), and therefore nothing but the free grace of God,—not any merit on the part of the Israelites who were then living, for they were a people " of a hard neck," *i.e.* a stubborn, untractable generation. With these words, which the Lord Himself had applied to Israel in Ex. xxxii. 9, xxxiii. 3, 5, Moses prepares the way for passing to the reasons for his warning against self-righteous pride, namely, the grievous sins of the Israelites against the Lord.

Vers. 7–24. He reminded the people how they had provoked the Lord in the desert, and had shown themselves rebellious against God, from the day of their departure from Egypt till their arrival in the steppes of Moab. אֶת־אֲשֶׁר, for אֲשֶׁר, is the object to תִּשְׁכַּח (*Ewald*, § 333, *a.*) : " *how* thou hast provoked." הִמְרָה, generally with אֶת־פִּי (cf. chap. i. 26), to be rebellious against the commandment of the Lord : here with עִם, construed with a person, to deal rebelliously *with God*, to act rebelliously in relation to Him (cf. chap. xxxi. 27). The words, " *from the day that thou camest out*," etc., are not to be pressed. It is to be observed, however, that the rebellion against the guidance of God commenced before they passed through the Red Sea (Ex. xiv. 11). This general statement Moses then followed up with facts, first of all describing the worship of the calf at Horeb, according to its leading features (vers. 8–21), and then briefly pointing to the other rebellions of the people in the desert (vers. 22, 23).—Ver. 8. " *And indeed even in Horeb ye provoked Jehovah to wrath.*" By the *vav explic.* this sin is brought into prominence, as having been a specially grievous one. It was so because of the circumstances under which it was committed.— Vers. 9–12. When Moses went up the mountain, and stayed there forty days, entirely occupied with the holiest things, so that he neither ate nor drank, having gone up to receive the tables of the law, upon which the words were written with the finger of God, just as the Lord had spoken them directly to the people out of the midst of the fire,—at a time, therefore, when the Israelites should also have been meditating deeply upon the words of the Lord which they had but just heard,—they acted so corruptly, as to depart at once from the way that had been pointed out, and make themselves a molten image (comp. Ex. xxxi. 18–xxxii. 6, with chaps. xxiv. 12–xxxi. 17). " *The day of the assembly*," *i.e.* the day on which Moses gathered the people together before God (chap. iv. 10), calling them out of the camp, and bringing them to the Lord to the foot of Sinai (Ex. xix. 17). The construction of the sentence is this : the apodosis to " *when I was gone up*" commences with " *the Lord delivered unto me*," in ver. 10; and the clause, " *then I abode*," etc., in ver. 9, is a parenthesis.—The words of God in vers. 12–14 are taken almost word for word from Ex. xxxii. 7–10. הֶרֶף (ver. 14), the imperative Hiphil of רָפָה, desist from me, that I may destroy them, for הַנִּיחָה לִּי, in Ex. xxxii. 10. But notwithstanding the apostasy of the people, the Lord gave Moses the tables of the covenant, not only that they might be a testimony of His holiness before the faithless nation, but still more as a testimony that, in spite of His resolution to destroy the rebellious nation, without leaving a trace behind, He would still uphold His covenant, and make of Moses a greater people. There is nothing at all to favour the opinion, that handing over the tables (ver. 11) was the first beginning of the manifestations of divine wrath (*Schultz*); and this is also at variance with the preterite, נָתַן, in ver. 11, from which it is very evident that the Lord had already given the tables to Moses, when He commanded him to go down quickly, not only to declare to the people the holiness of God, but to stop the apostasy, and by his mediatorial intervention to avert from the people the execution of the divine purpose. It is true, that when Moses came down and saw the idolatrous conduct of the people, he threw the two tables from his hands, and broke them in pieces before the eyes of the people (vers. 15–17; comp. with Ex. xxxii. 15–19), as a practical declaration that the covenant of the Lord was broken by their apostasy. But this act of Moses furnishes no proof that the Lord had given him the tables to declare His holy wrath in the sight of the people. And even if the tables of the covenant were " in a certain sense the indictments in Moses' hands, accusing them of a capital crime" (*Schultz*), this was not the purpose for which God had given them to him. For if it had been, Moses would not have broken them in pieces, destroying, as it were, the indictments themselves, before the people had been tried. Moses passed over the fact, that even before coming down from the mountain he endeavoured to mitigate the wrath of the Lord by his intercession (Ex. xxxii. 11–14), and simply mentioned (in vers. 15–17) how, as soon as he came down, he charged the people with their great sin ; and then, in vers. 18, 19, how he spent another forty days upon the mountain fasting before God, on account of this sin, until he had averted the destructive wrath of the Lord from Israel, through his earnest intercession. The forty days that Moses spent upon the mountain, " *as at the first,*" in prayer before the Lord, are the days mentioned in Ex. xxxiv. 28 as having been passed upon Sinai for the perfect restoration of the covenant, and for the purpose of procuring the second tables (cf. chap. x. 1 sqq.).—Ver. 20. It was not from the people only, but from Aaron also, that Moses averted the wrath of God through his intercession, when it was about to destroy him. In the historical account in Ex. xxxii., there is no special reference to this intercession, as it is included in the intercession for the whole nation. On the present occasion, however, Moses gave especial prominence to this particular feature, not only that he might make the people thoroughly aware that at that time Israel could not even boast of the righteousness of its eminent men (cf. Isa. xliii. 27), but also to bring out the fact, which is described still more fully in chap. x. 6 sqq., that Aaron's investiture with the priesthood, and the maintenance of this institution, was purely a work of divine grace. It is true that at that time Aaron was not yet high priest; but he had been placed at the head of the nation in connection with *Hur*, as the representative of Moses (Ex. xxiv. 14), and was already designated by God for the high-priesthood (Ex. xxviii. 1). The fact, however, that Aaron had drawn upon himself the wrath of God in a very high degree, was intimated plainly enough in what Moses told him in Ex. xxxii. 21.—In ver. 21, Moses mentions again how he destroyed that manifested sin of the nation, namely, the molten calf (see at Ex. xxxii. 20).—Vers. 22–24. And it was not on this occasion only, viz. at Horeb, that Israel aroused the anger of the Lord its God by its sin, but it did so again and again at other places : at Tabeerah, by discontent at the guidance of God (Num. xi. 1–3) ; at Massah, by murmuring on account of the want of water (Ex. xvii. 1 sqq.) ; at the graves of lust, by longing for flesh (Num. xi. 4 sqq.) ; and at Kadesh-Barnea by unbelief, of which they had already been reminded at chap. i. 26 sqq. The list is not arranged chronologically, but advances gradually from the smaller to the more serious forms of guilt. For Moses was seeking to sharpen the consciences of the people, and to impress upon them the fact that they had been rebellious against the Lord (see at ver. 7) from the very beginning, " from the day that I knew you."

Vers. 25–29. After vindicating in this way the thought expressed in ver. 7, by enumerating the principal rebellions of the people against their God, Moses returns in vers. 25 sqq. to the apostasy at Sinai, for the purpose of showing still further how Israel had no righteousness or ground for boasting before God, and owed its preservation, with all the saving blessings of the covenant, solely to the mercy of God and His covenant faithfulness. To this end he repeats in vers. 26–29 the essential points in his intercession for the people after their sin at Sinai, and then proceeds to explain still further, in chap. x. 1–11, how the Lord had not only renewed the tables of the covenant in consequence of this intercession (vers. 1–5), but had also established the gracious institution of the priesthood for the time to come by appointing Eleazar in Aaron's stead as soon as his father died, and setting apart the tribe of Levi to carry the ark of the covenant and attend to the holy service, and had commanded them to continue their march to Canaan, and take possession of the land promised to the fathers (vers. 6–11). With the words "thus I fell down," in ver. 25, Moses returns to the intercession already briefly mentioned in ver. 18, and recalls to the recollection of the people the essential features of his plea at that time. For the words " *the forty days and nights that I fell down*," see at chap. i. 46. The substance of the intercession in vers. 26–29 is essentially the same as that in Ex. xxxii. 11–13; but given with such freedom as any other than Moses would hardly have allowed himself (*Schultz*), and in such a manner as to bring it into the most obvious relation to the words of God in vers. 12, 13. אַל־תַּשְׁחֵת, " *Destroy not Thy people and Thine inheritance*," says Moses, with reference to the words of the Lord to him : " *thy people have corrupted themselves* " (ver. 12). Israel was not Moses' nation, but the nation and inheritance of Jehovah ; it was not Moses, but Jehovah, who had brought it out of Egypt. True, the people were stiffnecked (cf. ver. 13) ; but let the Lord remember the fathers, the oath given to Abraham, which is expressly mentioned in Ex. xxxii. 13 (see at chap. vii. 8), and not turn to the stiffneckedness of the people (קְשִׁי equivalent to קְשֵׁה עֹרֶף, vers. 13 and 6), and to their wickedness and sin (*i.e.* not regard them and punish them). The honour of the Lord before the nations was concerned in this (ver. 28). The land whence Israel came out ("the land" = the people of the land, as in Gen. x. 25, etc., viz. the Egyptians : the word is construed as a collective with a plural verb) must not have occasion to say, that Jehovah had not led His people into the promised land from incapacity or hatred. מִבְּלִי יְכֹלֶת recalls Num. xiv. 16. Just as "inability" would be opposed to the nature of the absolute God, so "hatred" would be opposed to the choice of Israel as the inheritance of Jehovah, which He had brought out of Egypt by His divine and almighty power (cf. Ex. vi. 6).

Chap. x. 1–11. In vers. 1–5 Moses briefly relates the success of his earnest intercession. "*At that time*," of his intercession, God commanded him to hew out new tables, and prepare an ark in which to keep them (cf. Ex. xxxiv. 1 sqq.). Here again Moses links together such things as were substantially connected, without strictly confining himself to the chronological order, which was already well known from the historical account, inasmuch as this was not required by the general object of his address. God had already given directions for the preparation of the ark of the covenant, before the apostasy of the nation (Ex. xxv. 10 sqq.); but it was not made till after the tabernacle had been built, and the tables were only deposited in the ark when the tabernacle was consecrated (Ex. xl. 20).—Vers. 6 and 7. And the Israelites owed to the grace of their God, which was turned towards them once more, through the intercession of Moses, not only the restoration of the tables of the covenant as a pledge that the covenant itself was restored, but also the institution and maintenance of the high-priesthood and priesthood generally for the purpose of mediation between them and the Lord.[1] Moses reminds the people of this

---

[1] Even *Clericus* pointed out this connection, and paraphrased vers. 6 and 7 as follows : "But when, as I have said, God forgave the Hebrew people, He pardoned my brother Aaron also, who did not die till the fortieth year after we had come out of Egypt, and when we were coming round the borders of the Edomites to come hither. God also showed that He was reconciled towards him by conferring the priesthood upon him, which is now borne by his son Eleazar according to the will of God." *Clericus* has also correctly brought out the fact that Moses referred to what he had stated in chap. ix. 20 as to the wrath of God against Aaron and his intercession on his behalf, or rather that he mentioned his intercession on behalf of Aaron in that passage, because he intended to call more particular attention to the successful result of it in this. *Hengstenberg* (Dissertations, vol. ii. pp. 351-2) has since pointed out briefly, but very conclusively, the connection of thought between vers. 6, 7, and what goes before and follows after. "Moses," he says, " points out to the people how the Lord had continued unchangeable in His mercy notwithstanding all their sins.

gracious gift on the part of their God, by recalling to their memory the time when Aaron died and his son Eleazar was invested with the high-priesthood in his stead. That he may transport his hearers the more distinctly to the period in question, he lets the history itself speak, and quotes from the account of their journeys the passage which supplied the practical proof of what he desires to say. Instead of saying: And the high-priesthood also, with which Aaron was invested by the grace of God notwithstanding his sin at Sinai, the Lord has still preserved to you; for when Aaron died, He invested his son with the same honour,[1] and also directed you to continue your journey,—he proceeds in the following historical style : "*And the children of Israel took their journey from the wells of the sons of Jaakan to Mosera: there Aaron died, and there he was buried; and Eleazar his son became priest in his stead. And from thence they journeyed unto Gudgodah, and from Gudgodah to Jotbath, a land of water-brooks.*" The allusion to these marches, together with the events which had taken place at Mosera, taught in very few words " not only that Aaron was forgiven at the intercession of Moses, and even honoured with the high-priesthood, the medium of grace and blessing to the people of God (*e.g.* at the wells of Bene-Jaakan) until the time of his death; but also that through this same intercession the high-priesthood was maintained in perpetuity, so that when Aaron had to die in the wilderness in consequence of a fresh sin (Num. xx. 12), it continued notwith-

Although they had rendered themselves unworthy of such goodness by their worship of the calf, He gave them the ark of the covenant with the new tables of the law in it (chap. x. 1-5). He followed up this gift of His grace by instituting the high-priesthood, and when Aaron died He caused it to be transferred to his son Eleazar (vers. 6, 7). He set apart the tribe of Levi to serve Him and bless the people in His name, and thus to be the mediators of His mercy (vers. 8, 9). In short, He omitted nothing that was requisite to place Israel in full possession of the dignity of a people of God." There is no ground for regarding vers. 6, 7, as a gloss, as *Capellus, Dathe,* and *Rosenmüller* do, or vers. 6–9 as " an interpolation of a historical statement concerning the bearers of the ark of the covenant and the holy persons generally, which has no connection with Moses' address," as *Knobel* maintains. The want of any formal connection is quite in keeping with the spirit of simplicity which characterizes the early Hebrew diction and historical writings. " The style of the Hebrews is not to be tried by the rules of rhetoricians " (*Clericus*).

[1] " In the death of Aaron they might discern the punishment of their rebellion. But the fact that Eleazar was appointed in his place, was a sign of the paternal grace of God, who did not suffer them to be forsaken on that account " (*Calvin*).

standing, and by no means diminished in strength, as might have been feared, since it led the way from the wells to water-brooks, helped on the journey to Canaan, which was now the object of their immediate aim, and still sustained their courage and their faith" (*Schultz*). The earlier commentators observed the inward connection between the continuation of the high-priesthood and the water-brooks. *J. Gerhard*, for example, observes : " God generally associates material blessings with spiritual ; as long as the ministry of the word and the observance of divine worship flourish among us, God will also provide for our temporal necessities." On the places mentioned, see pp. 244–5.

In ver. 8, Moses returns to the form of an address again, and refers to the separation of the tribe of Levi for the holy service, as a manifestation of mercy on the part of the Lord towards Israel. The expression "*at that time*" is not to be understood as relating to the time of Aaron's death in the fortieth year of the march, in which *Knobel* finds a contradiction to the other books. It refers quite generally, as in chap. ix. 20 and x. 1, to the time of which Moses is speaking here, viz. the time when the covenant was re-stored at Sinai. The appointment of the tribe of Levi for service at the sanctuary took place in connection with the election of Aaron and his sons to the priesthood (Ex. xxviii. and xxix.), although their call to this service, instead of the first-born of Israel, was not carried out till the numbering and mustering of the people (Num. i. 49 sqq., iv. 17 sqq., viii. 6 sqq.). Moses is speaking here of the election of the whole of the tribe of Levi, including the priests (Aaron and his sons), as is very evident from the account of their service. It is true that the carrying of the ark upon the march through the desert was the business of the (non-priestly) Levites, viz. the Kohathites (Num. iv. 4 sqq.) ; but on solemn occasions the priests had to carry it (cf. Josh. iii. 3, 6, 8, vi. 6 ; 1 Kings viii. 3 sqq.). "Standing before the Lord, to serve Him, and to bless in His name," was exclusively the business of the priests (cf. chap. xviii. 5, xxi. 5, and Num. vi. 23 sqq.), whereas the Levites were only assistants of the priests in their service (see at chap. xviii. 7). This tribe therefore received no share and possession with the other tribes, as was already laid down in Num. xviii. 20 with reference to the priests, and in ver. 24 with regard to all the Levites ; to which passages the words "as the Lord thy God promised him" refer.—Lastly, in vers. 10, 11, Moses sums up the result of his intercession in the words, "*And I stood upon the mount as the first days, forty days* (a resumption of chap. ix. 18 and 25) ; *and the Lord hearkened to me this time also* (word for word, as in chap. ix. 19). *Jehovah would not destroy thee* (Israel)." Therefore He commanded Moses to arise to depart before the people, *i.e.* as leader of the people to command and superintend their removal and march. In form, this command is connected with Ex. xxxiv. 1 ; but Moses refers here not only to that word of the Lord with the limitation added there in ver. 2, but to the ultimate, full, and unconditional assurance of God, in which the Lord Himself promised to go with His people and bring them to Canaan (Ex. xxxiv. 14 sqq.).

Admonition to fear and love God. The Blessing or Curse conse-quent upon the Fulfilment or Transgression of the Law.—Chap. x. 12–xi. 32.

Vers. 12–15. The proof that Israel had no righteousness before God is followed on the positive side by an expansion of the main law laid down in chap. vi. 4 sqq., to love God with all the heart, which is introduced by the words, " and now Israel," *sc.* now that thou hast everything without desert or worthiness, purely from for-giving grace. " *What doth the Lord thy God require of thee?*" Nothing further than that thou fearest Him, " to walk in all His ways, and to love Him, and to serve Him with all the heart and all the soul." כִּי אִם, *unless*, or *except that*, presupposes a negative clause (cf. Gen. xxxix. 9), which is implied here in the previous question, or else to be supplied as the answer. The demand for fear, love, and reverence towards the Lord, is no doubt very hard for the natural man to fulfil, and all the harder the deeper it goes into the heart ; but after such manifestations of the love and grace of God, it only follows as a matter of course. "Fear, love, and obedience would naturally have taken root of themselves within the heart, if man had not corrupted his own heart." Love, which is the only thing demanded in chap. vi. 5, is here preceded by fear, which is the only thing mentioned in chap. v. 26 and vi. 24.[1] The fear of the Lord, which springs from the knowledge of one's own unholiness in the presence of the holy God, ought to form the one leading emotion in the heart prompting to walk in all the ways of the Lord, and to maintain morality of conduct in its strictest form.

[1] The fear of God is to be united with the love of God ; for love without fear makes men remiss, and fear without love makes them servile and desperate (*J. Gerhard*).

This fear, which first enables us to comprehend the mercy of God, awakens love, the fruit of which is manifested in serving God with all the heart and all the soul (see chap. vi. 5). *"For thy good,"* as in chap. v. 30 and vi. 24.—Vers. 14, 15. This obligation the Lord had laid upon Israel by the love with which He, to whom all the heavens and the earth, with everything upon it, belong, had chosen the patriarchs and their seed out of all nations. By "the heavens of the heavens," the idea of heaven is perfectly exhausted. This God, who might have chosen any other nation as well as Israel, or in fact all nations together, had directed His special love to Israel alone.

Vers. 16–22. Above all, therefore, they were to circumcise the foreskin of their hearts, *i.e.* to lay aside all insensibility of heart to impressions from the love of God (cf. Lev. xxvi. 41; and on the spiritual signification of circumcision, see vol. i. p. 227), and not stiffen their necks any more, *i.e.* not persist in their obstinacy, or obstinate resistance to God (cf. chap. ix. 6, 13). Without circumcision of heart, true fear of God and true love of God are both impossible. As a reason for this admonition, Moses adduces in vers. 17 sqq. the nature and acts of God. Jehovah as the absolute God and Lord is mighty and terrible towards all, without respect of person, and at the same time a just Judge and loving Protector of the helpless and oppressed. From this it follows that the true God will not tolerate haughtiness and stiffness of neck either towards Himself or towards other men, but will punish it without reserve. To set forth emphatically the infinite greatness and might of God, Moses describes Jehovah the God of Israel as the *"God of gods,"* *i.e.* the supreme God, the essence of all that is divine, of all divine power and might (cf. Ps. cxxxvi. 2),—and as the *"Lord of lords,"* *i.e.* the supreme, unrestricted Ruler ("the only Potentate," 1 Tim. vi. 15), above all powers in heaven and on earth, *"a great King above all gods"* (Ps. xcv. 3). Compare Rev. xvii. 14 and xix. 16, where these predicates are transferred to the exalted Son of God, as the Judge and Conqueror of all dominions and powers that are hostile to God. The predicates which follow describe the unfolding of the omnipotence of God in the government of the world, in which Jehovah manifests Himself as the great, mighty, and terrible God (Ps. lxxxix. 8), who does not regard the person (cf. Lev. xix. 15), or accept presents (cf. chap. xvi. 19), like a human judge. —Vers. 18, 19. As such, Jehovah does justice to the defenceless (orphan and widow), and exercises a loving care towards the stranger in his oppression. For this reason the Israelites were not to close their hearts egotistically against the stranger (cf. Ex. xxii. 20). This would show whether they possessed any love to God, and had circumcised their hearts (cf. 1 John iii. 10, 17).—Vers. 20 sqq. After laying down the fundamental condition of a proper relation towards God, Moses describes the fear of God, i.e. true reverence of God, in its threefold manifestation, in deed (serving God), in heart (cleaving to Him; cf. chap. iv. 4), and with the mouth (swearing by His name; cf. chap. vi. 13). Such reverence as this Israel owed to its God; for " *He is thy praise, and He is thy God* " (ver. 21). He has given thee strong inducements to praise. By the great and terrible things which thine eyes have seen, He has manifested Himself as God to thee. " *Terrible things* " are those acts of divine omnipotence, which fill men with fear and trembling at the majesty of the Almighty (cf. Ex. xv. 11). עָשָׂה אִתְּךָ, " done with thee," i.e. shown to thee (אֶת in the sense of practical help).—Ver. 22. One marvel among these great and terrible acts of the Lord was to be seen in Israel itself, which had gone down to Egypt in the persons of its fathers as a family consisting of seventy souls, and now, notwithstanding the oppression it suffered there, had grown into an innumerable nation. So marvellously had the Lord fulfilled His promise in Gen. xv. 5. By referring to this promise, Moses intended no doubt to recall to the recollection of the people the fact that the bondage of Israel in a foreign land for 400 years had also been foretold (Gen. xv. 13 sqq.). On the seventy souls, see at Gen. xlvi. 26, 27.

Chap. xi. In vers. 1–12 the other feature in the divine requirements (chap. x. 12), viz. love to the Lord their God, is still more fully developed. Love was to show itself in the distinct perception of what had to be observed towards Jehovah (to " *keep His charge,*" see at Lev. viii. 35), i.e. in the perpetual observance of His commandments and rights. The words, " *and His statutes,*" etc., serve to explain the general notion, "His charge." " *All days,*" as in chap. iv. 10.—Vers. 2 sqq. To awaken this love they were now to know, i.e. to ponder and lay to heart, the discipline of the Lord their God. The words from " *for* (I speak) *not*" to " *have not seen*" are a parenthetical clause, by which Moses would impress his words most strongly upon the hearts of the older generation, which had witnessed the acts of the Lord. The clause is without any verb or predicate, but this can easily be supplied from the sense. The best suggestion is that of *Schultz*, viz. הַדִּבֵּר הַהוּא, " for it is not with your

children that I have to do," not to them that this admonition applies.
Moses refers to the children who had been born in the desert, as
distinguished from those who, though not twenty years old when
the Israelites came out of Egypt, had nevertheless seen with their
own eyes the plagues inflicted upon Egypt, and who were now of
mature age, viz. between forty and sixty years old, and formed, as
the older and more experienced generation, the stock and kernel of
the congregation assembled round him now. To the words, " *which
have not known and have not seen*," it is easy to supply from the
context, " what ye have known and seen." The accusatives from
" the chastisement" onwards belong to the verb of the principal
sentence, " know ye this day." The accusatives which follow show
what we are to understand by " the chastisement of the Lord," viz.
the mighty acts of the Lord to Egypt and to Israel in the desert.
The object of them all was to *educate* Israel in the fear and love of
God. In this sense Moses calls them מוּסָר (*Eng. Ver. chastisement*),
παιδεία, *i.e.* not punishment only, but education by the manifestation of love as well as punishment (like יַסֵּר in chap. iv. 36; cf.
Prov. i. 2, 8, iv. 1, etc.). " *His greatness*," etc., as in chap. iii. 24
and iv. 34. On the signs and acts in Egypt, see at chap. iv. 34,
vi. 22; and on those at the Red Sea, at Ex. xiv. אֲשֶׁר הֵצִיף—עַל־פְּנֵיהֶם,
" *over whose face He made the waters of the Red Sea to flow;*" cf.
Ex. xiv. 26 sqq.—By the acts of God in the desert (ver. 5) we are
not to understand the chastenings in Num. xi.–xv. either solely or
pre-eminently, but all the manifestations of the omnipotence of
God in the guidance of Israel, proofs of love as well as the penal
wonders. Of the latter, the miraculous destruction of the company
of Korah is specially mentioned in ver. 6 (cf. Num. xvi. 31–33).
Here Moses only mentions Dathan and Abiram, the followers of
Korah, and not Korah himself, probably from regard to his sons,
who were not swallowed up by the earth along with their father, but
had lived to perpetuate the family of Korah. " *Everything existing,
which was in their following*" (see Ex. xi. 8), does not mean their
possessions, but their servants, and corresponds to " all the men who
belonged to Korah" in Num. xvi. 32, whereas the possessions mentioned there are included here in the "tents." הַיְקוּם is only applied
to living beings, as in Gen. vii. 4 and 23.—In ver. 7 the reason is
given for the admonition in ver. 2: the elders were to know (discern) the educational purpose of God in those mighty acts of the
Lord, because they had seen them with their own eyes.—Vers. 8, 9.
And this knowledge was to impel them to keep the law, that they

might be strong, *i.e.* spiritually strong (chap. i. 38), and not only go into the promised land, but also live long therein (cf. chap. iv. 26, vi. 3).—In vers. 10–12 Moses adduces a fresh motive for his admonition to keep the law with fidelity, founded upon the peculiar nature of the land. Canaan was a land the fertility of which was not dependent, like that of Egypt, upon its being watered by the hand of man, but was kept up by the rain of heaven which was sent down by God the Lord, so that it depended entirely upon the Lord how long its inhabitants should live therein. Egypt is described by Moses as a land which Israel sowed with seed, and watered with its foot like a garden of herbs. In Egypt there is hardly any rain at all (cf. *Herod.* ii. 4, *Diod. Sic.* i. 41, and other evidence in *Hengstenberg's* Egypt and the Books of Moses, pp. 217 sqq.). The watering of the land, which produces its fertility, is dependent upon the annual overflowing of the Nile, and, as this only lasts for about 100 days, upon the way in which this is made available for the whole year, namely, by the construction of canals and ponds throughout the land, to which the water is conducted from the Nile by forcing machines, or by actually carrying it in vessels up to the fields and plantations.[1] The expression, " with thy foot," probably refers to the large pumping wheels still in use there, which are worked by the feet, and over which a long endless rope passes with pails attached, for drawing up the water (cf. *Niebuhr, Reise,* i. 149), the identity of which with the ἕλιξ described by *Philo* as ὑδρηλὸν ὄργανον (*de confus. ling.* i. 410) cannot possibly be called in question ; provided, that is to say, we do not confound this ἕλιξ with the Archimedean water-screw mentioned by *Diod. Sic.* i. 34, and described more minutely at v. 37, the construction of which was entirely different (see my Archæology, ii. pp. 111–2).—The Egyptians, as genuine heathen, were so thoroughly conscious of this peculiar characteristic of their land, which made its fertility far more dependent upon the labour of human hands than upon the rain of heaven or divine providence, that *Herodotus* (ii. 13) represents them as saying, " The Greeks, with their dependence upon the gods, might be disappointed in their brightest hopes and

---

[1] Upon the ancient monuments we find not only the draw-well with the long rope, which is now called *Shaduf,* depicted in various ways (see *Wilkinson,* i. p. 35, ii. 4) ; but at *Beni-Hassan* there is a representation of two men carrying a water-vessel upon a pole on their shoulders, which they fill from a draw-well or pond, and then carry to the field (cf. *Hengstenberg,* Egypt and the Books of Moses, pp. 220–1).

suffer dreadfully from famine." The land of Canaan yielded no
support to such godless self-exaltation, for it was "a land of mountains and valleys, and drank water of the rain of heaven" (לְ before
מָטָר, to denote the external cause ; see *Ewald*, § 217, *d.*) ; *i.e.* it
received its watering, the main condition of all fertility, from the
rain, by the way of the rain, and therefore through the providential care of God.—Ver. 12. It was a land which Jehovah inquired
after, *i.e.* for which He cared (דָּרַשׁ, as in Prov. xxxi. 13, Job iii.
4) ; His eyes were always directed towards it from the beginning
of the year to the end ; a land, therefore, which was dependent
upon God, and in this dependence upon God peculiarly adapted
to Israel, which was to live entirely to its God, and upon His
grace alone.

Vers. 13-32. This peculiarity in the land of Canaan led Moses
to close the first part of his discourse on the law, his exhortation to
fear and love the Lord, with a reference to the blessing that would
follow the faithful fulfilment of the law, and a threat of the curse
which would attend apostasy to idolatry.—Vers. 13-15. If Israel
would serve its God in love and faithfulness, He would give the
land early and latter rain in its season, and therewith a plentiful
supply of food for man and beast (see Lev. xxvi. 3 and 5; and for
the further expansion of this blessing, chap. xxviii. 1-12).—Vers. 16
and 17. But if, on the other hand, their heart was foolish to turn
away from the Lord and serve other gods, the wrath of the Lord
would burn against them, and God would shut up the heaven, that
no rain should fall and the earth should yield no produce, and they
would speedily perish (cf. Lev. xxvi. 19, 20, and Deut. xxviii.
23, 24). Let them therefore impress the words now set before
them very deeply upon themselves and their children (vers. 18-21,
in which there is in part a verbal repetition of chap. vi. 6-9). The
words, "*as the days of the heaven above the earth,*" *i.e.* as long as the
heaven continues above the earth,—in other words, to all eternity
(cf. Ps. lxxxix. 30; Job xiv. 12),—belong to the main sentence,
" *that your days may be multiplied,*" etc. (ver. 21). " The promise
to give the land to Israel for ever was not made unconditionally; an
unconditional promise is precluded by the words, 'that your days
may be multiplied'" (*Schultz*). (For further remarks, see at chap.
xxx. 3-5.) For (vers. 22-25) if they adhered faithfully to the
Lord, He would drive out before them all the nations that dwelt in
the land, and would give them the land upon which they trod in
all its length and breadth, and so fill the Canaanites with fear and

terror before them, that no one should be able to stand against them. (On ver. 23, cf. chap. vii. 1, 2, ix. 1, and i. 28.) The words, "every place whereon the soles of your feet shall tread shall be yours," are defined more precisely, and restricted to the land of Canaan on both sides of the Jordan by the boundaries which follow: "*from the desert* (of Arabia on the south), *and Lebanon* (on the north), *and from the river Euphrates* (on the east) *to the hinder sea*" (the Mediterranean on the west; see Num. xxxiv. 6). The Euphrates is given as the eastern boundary, as in chap. i. 7, according to the promise in Gen. xv. 18. (On ver. 25, cf. chap. vii. 24, ii. 25, and Ex. xxiii. 27.)—Vers. 26–28. Concluding summary. "*I set before you this day the blessing and the curse.*" The blessing, if (אֲשֶׁר, ὅτε, as in Lev. iv. 22) ye hearken to the commandments of your God; the curse, if ye do not give heed to them, but turn aside from the way pointed out to you, to go after other gods. To this there are added instructions in vers. 29 and 30, that when they took possession of the land they should *give* the blessing upon Mount Gerizim and the curse upon Mount Ebal, *i.e.* should give utterance to them there, and as it were transfer them to the land to be apportioned to its inhabitants according to their attitude towards the Lord their God. (For further comment, see at chap. xxvii. 14.) The two mountains mentioned were selected for this act, no doubt because they were opposite to one another, and stood, each about 2500 feet high, in the very centre of the land not only from west to east, but also from north to south. Ebal stands upon the north side, Gerizim upon the south; between the two is *Sichem*, the present *Nabulus*, in a tolerably elevated valley, fertile, attractive, and watered by many springs, which runs from the south-east to the north-west from the foot of Gerizim to that of Ebal, and is about 1600 feet in breadth. The blessing was to be uttered upon Gerizim, and the curse upon Ebal; though not, as the earlier commentators supposed, because the peculiarities of these mountains, viz. the fertility of Gerizim and the barrenness of Ebal, appeared to accord with this arrangement: for when seen from the valley between, "the sides of both these mountains are equally naked and sterile;" and "the only exception in favour of the former is a small ravine coming down, opposite the west end of the town, which is indeed full of fountains and trees" (*Rob. Pal.* iii. 96, 97). The reason for selecting Gerizim for the blessings was probably, as *Schultz* supposes, the fact that it was situated on the south, towards the region of the light. "Light and blessing are essentially one. From the light-giving face of God there come blessing and life (Ps. xvi. 11)."—In ver. 30 the situation of these mountains is more clearly defined: they were "*on the other side of the Jordan*," *i.e.* in the land to the west of the Jordan, "*behind the way of the sunset*," *i.e.* on the other side of the road of the west, which runs through the land on the west of the Jordan, just as another such road runs through the land on the east (*Knobel*). The reference is to the main road which ran from Upper Asia through Canaan to Egypt, as was shown by the journeys of Abraham and Jacob (Gen. xii. 6, xxxiii. 17, 18). Even at the present day the main road leads from Beisan to Jerusalem round the east side of Ebal into the valley of Sichem, and then again eastwards from Gerizim through the Mukra valley on towards the south (cf. *Rob.* iii. 94; *Ritter, Erdkunde,* xvi. pp. 658–9). "*In the land of the Canaanite who dwells in the Arabah.*" By the *Arabah, Knobel* understands the plain of *Nabulus,* which is not much less than four hours' journey long, and on an average from a half to three-quarters broad, "the largest of all upon the elevated tract of land between the western plain and the valley of the Jordan" (*Rob.* iii. p. 101). This is decidedly wrong, however, as it is opposed to the fixed use of the word, and irreconcilable with the character of this plain, which, *Robinson* says, "is cultivated throughout and covered with the rich green of millet intermingled with the yellow of the ripe corn, which the country people were just reaping" (Pal. iii. 93). The *Arabah* is the western portion of the *Ghor* (see at chap. i. 1), and is mentioned here as that portion of the land on the west of the Jordan which lay stretched out before the eyes of the Israelites who were encamped in the steppes of Moab. "*Over against Gilgal,*" *i.e.* not the southern *Gilgal* between Jericho and the Jordan, which received its name for the first time in Josh. iv. 20 and v. 9; but probably the Gilgal mentioned in Josh. ix. 6, x. 6 sqq., and very frequently in the history of Samuel, Elijah, and Elisha, which is only about twelve and a half miles from Gerizim in a southern direction, and has been preserved in the large village of *Jiljilia* to the south-west of Sinjil, and which stands in such an elevated position, "close to the western brow of the high mountain tract," that you "have here a very extensive prospect over the great lower plain, and also over the sea, whilst the mountains of Gilead are seen in the east" (*Rob.* Pal. iii. 81). Judging from this description of the situation, Mount Gerizim must be visible from this Gilgal, so that Gerizim and Ebal might very well be described as over against

Gilgal.[1] The last definition, "*beside the terebinths of Moreh*," is intended no doubt to call to mind the consecration of that locality even from the times of the patriarchs (*Schultz:* see at Gen. xii. 6, and xxxv. 4).—Vers. 31–2 contain the reason for these instructions, founded upon the assurance that the Israelites were going over the Jordan and would take possession of the promised land, and should therefore take care to keep the commandments of the Lord (cf. chap. iv. 5, 6).

B. EXPOSITION OF THE PRINCIPAL LAWS.—CHAP. XII.–XXVI.

The statutes and rights which follow in the second or special half of this address, and which consist in part of rules having regard to circumstances not contemplated by the Sinaitic laws, and partly of repetitions of laws already given, were designed as a whole to regulate the ecclesiastical, civil, and domestic life of Israel in the land of Canaan, in harmony with its calling to be the holy nation of the Lord. Moses first of all describes the religious and ecclesiastical life of the nation, in its various relations to the Lord (chap. xii.–xvi. 17); and then the political organization of the congregation, or the rights and duties of the civil and spiritual leaders of the nation (chap. xvi. 18–xviii. 22); and lastly, seeks to establish upon a permanent basis the civil and domestic well-being of the whole congregation and its individual members, by a multiplicity of precepts, intended to set before the people, as a conscientious obligation on their part, reverence and holy awe in relation to human life, to property, and to personal rights; a pious regard for the fundamental laws of the world; sanctification of domestic life and of the social bond; practical brotherly love towards the poor, the oppressed, and the needy; and righteousness of walk and conversation (chap. xix.–xxvi.).—So far as the arrangement of this address is concerned, the first two series of these laws may be easily regarded

---

[1] There is much less ground for the opinion of *Winer, Knobel,* and *Schultz,* that *Gilgal* is the *Jiljule* mentioned by *Robinson* (*Pal.* iii. 47; and *Bibl. Researches,* p. 138), which evidently corresponds to the *Galgula* placed by *Eusebius* and *Jerome* six Roman miles from *Antipatris,* and is situated to the south-east of *Kefr Saba* (*Antipatris*), on the road from Egypt to Damascus. For this place is not only farther from Gerizim and Ebal, viz. about seventeen miles, but from its position in the lowland by the sea-shore it presents no salient point for determining the situation of the mountains of Gerizim and Ebal. Still less can we agree with *Knobel,* who speaks of the village of *Kilkilia,* to the north-east of *Kefr Saba,* as the name itself has nothing in common with Gilgal.

as expositions, expansions, and completions of the commandments in the decalogue in relation to the Sabbath, and to the duty of honouring parents; and in the third series also there are unquestionably many allusions to the commandments in the second table of the decalogue. But the order in which the different laws and precepts in this last series are arranged, does not follow the order of the decalogue, so as to warrant us in looking there for the leading principle of the arrangement, as *Schultz* has done. Moses allows himself to be guided much more by analogies and the free association of ideas than by any strict regard to the decalogue; although, no doubt, the whole of the book of Deuteronomy may be described, as *Luther* says, as " a very copious and lucid explanation of the decalogue, an acquaintance with which will supply all that is requisite to a full understanding of the ten commandments."

The one Place for the Worship of God, and the right Mode of worshipping Him.—Chap. xii.

The laws relating to the worship of the Israelites commence with a command to destroy and annihilate all places and memorials of the Canaanitish worship (vers. 2-4), and then lay it down as an established rule, that the Israelites were to worship the Lord their God with sacrifices and gifts, only in the place which He Himself should choose (vers. 5–14). On the other hand, in the land of Canaan cattle might be slain for eating and the flesh itself be consumed in any place; though sacrificial meals could only be celebrated in the place of the sanctuary appointed by the Lord (vers. 15–19). Moreover, on the extension of the borders of the land, oxen, and sheep, and goats could be slaughtered for food in any place; but the blood was not to be eaten, and consecrated gifts and votive sacrifices were not to be prepared as meals anywhere, except at the altar of the Lord (vers. 20–28). Lastly, the Israelites were not to be drawn aside by the Canaanites, to imitate them in their worship (vers. 29–31).

Vers. 1–14. On the heading in ver. 1, see chaps. vi. 1 and iv. 1. " *All the days that ye live*" relates to the more distant clause, " which ye shall observe," etc. (cf. chap. iv. 10).—Vers. 2, 3. Ye shall destroy all the places where the Canaanites worship their gods, upon the high mountains, upon the hills, and under every green tree (cf. Jer. ii. 20, iii. 6, xvii. 2; 2 Kings xvi. 4, xvii. 10). The choice of mountains and hills for places of worship by most of the heathen nations, had its origin in the wide-spread belief, that men were

nearer to the Deity and to heaven there. The green trees are connected with the holy groves, of which the heathen nations were so
fond, and the shady gloom of which filled the soul with holy awe at
the nearness of the Deity. In the absence of groves, they chose green
trees with thick foliage (Ezek. vi. 13, xx. 28), such as the vigorous
oak, which attains a great age, the evergreen terebinth (Isa. i. 29,
30, lvii. 5), and the poplar or osier, which continues green even in
the heat of summer (Hos. iv. 13), and whose deep shade is adapted
to dispose the mind to devotion.—Ver. 3. Beside the places of
worship, they were also to destroy all the idols of the Canaanitish
worship, as had already been commanded in chap. vii. 5, and to blot
out even their names, *i.e.* every trace of their existence. (cf. chap.
vii. 24).—Ver. 4. " *Ye shall not do so to Jehovah your God,*" *i.e.* not
build altars and offer sacrifices to Him in any place you choose, but
(vers. 5 sqq.) shall only keep yourselves (אֶל תִּדְרְשׁוּ) to the place " *which
He shall choose out of all the tribes to put His name there for His
dwelling.*" Whereas the heathen seeks and worships his nature-
gods, wherever he thinks he can discern in nature any trace of
Divinity, the true God has not only revealed His eternal power and
Godhead in the works of creation, but His personal being, which
unfolds itself to the world in love and holiness, in grace and righteousness, He has made known to man, who was created in His image,
in the words and works of salvation ; and in these testimonies of
His saving presence He has fixed for Himself a name, in which He
dwells among His people. This name presents His personality, as
comprehended in the word *Jehovah,* in a visible sign, the tangible
pledge of His essential presence. During the journeying of the
Israelites this was effected by the pillar of cloud and fire; and after
the erection of the tabernacle, by the cloud in the most holy place,
above the ark of the covenant, with the cherubim upon it, in which
Jehovah had promised to appear to the high priest as the representative of the covenant nation. Through this, the tabernacle,
and afterwards Solomon's temple, which took its place, became the
dwelling-place of the name of the Lord. But if the knowledge of
the true God rested upon direct manifestations of the divine nature,—and the Lord God had for that very reason made Himself
known to His people in words and deeds as their God,—then as a
matter of course the mode of His worship could not be dependent
upon any appointment of men, but must be determined exclusively
by God Himself. The place of His worship depended upon the
choice which God Himself should make, and which would be made

known by the fact that He " put His name," *i.e.* actually manifested His own immediate presence, in one definite spot. By the
building of the tabernacle, which the Lord Himself prescribed as
the true spot for the revelation of His presence among His people,
the place where His name was to dwell among the Israelites was
already so far determined, that only the particular town or locality
among the tribes of Israel where the tabernacle was to be set up
after the conquest of Canaan remained to be decided. At the same
time, Moses not only speaks of the Lord choosing the place among
all the tribes for the erection of His sanctuary, but also of His
choosing the place where He would put His name, that He might
dwell there (לְשִׁכְנוֹ from שָׁכֵן, for שָׁכְנוֹ from שֹׁכֵן). For the presence of
the Lord was not, and was not intended, to be exclusively confined to
the tabernacle (or the temple). As God of the whole earth, wherever it might be necessary, for the preservation and promotion of His
kingdom, He could make known His presence, and accept the sacrifices of His people in other places, independently of this sanctuary;
and there were times when this was really done. The unity of the
worship, therefore, which Moses here enjoined, was not to consist in
the fact that the people of Israel brought all their sacrificial offerings
to the tabernacle, but in their offering them only in the spot where
the Lord made His name (that is to say, His presence) known.

What Moses commanded here, was only an explanation and
more emphatic repetition of the divine command in Ex. xx. 23, 24
(21 and 22); and to understand "the place which Jehovah would
choose" as relating exclusively to Jerusalem or the temple-hill, is a
perfectly arbitrary assumption. Shiloh, the place where the tabernacle was set up after the conquest of the land (Josh. xviii. 1), and
where it stood during the whole of the times of the judges, was also
chosen by the Lord (cf. Jer. vii. 12). It was not till after David
had set up a tent for the ark of the covenant upon Zion, in the city
of Jerusalem, which he had chosen as the capital of his kingdom,
and had erected an altar for sacrifice there (2 Sam. vi. 17; 1 Chron.
xvi.), that the will of the Lord was made known to him by the
prophet Gad, that he should build an altar upon the threshing-floor
of Araunah, where the angel of the Lord had appeared to him; and
through this command the place was fixed for the future temple
(2 Sam. xxiv. 18; 1 Chron. xxi. 18). דָּרַשׁ with אֶל, to turn in a
certain direction, to inquire or to seek. שׂוּם אֶת־שְׁמוֹ, "to put His
name," *i.e.* to make known His presence, is still further defined by
the following word לְשִׁכְנוֹ, as signifying that His presence was to be

of permanent duration. It is true that this word is separated by an *athnach* from the previous clause; but it certainly cannot be connected with תִּדְרְשׁוּ (*ye shall seek*), not only because of the standing phrase, שְׁמוֹ שָׁם לְשַׁכֵּן ("*to cause His name to dwell there*," ver. 11, chap. xiv. 23, xvi. 2, 6, etc.), but also because this connection would give no fitting sense, as the infinitive שָׁכֵן does not mean "a dwelling-place."—Vers. 6, 7. Thither they were to take all their sacrificial gifts, and there they were to celebrate their sacrificial meals. The gifts are classified in four pairs: (1) the sacrifices intended for the altar, burnt-offerings and slain-offerings being particularly mentioned as the two principal kinds, with which, according to Num. xv. 4 sqq., meat-offerings and drink-offerings were to be associated; (2) "your tithes and every heave-offering of your hand." By the tithes we are to understand the tithes of field-produce and cattle, commanded in Lev. xxvii. 30–33 and Num. xviii. 21–24, which were to be brought to the sanctuary because they were to be offered to the Lord, as was the case under Hezekiah (2 Chron. xxxi. 5–7). That the tithes mentioned here should be restricted to vegetable tithes (of corn, new wine, and oil), is neither allowed by the general character of the expression, nor required by the context. For instance, although, according to vers. 7 and 11, 12, as compared with ver. 17, a portion of the vegetable tithe was to be applied to the sacrificial meals, there is no ground whatever for supposing that all the sacrifices and consecrated gifts mentioned in ver. 6 were offerings of this kind, and either served as sacrificial meals, or had such meals connected with them. Burnt-offerings, for example, were not associated in any way with the sacrificial meals. The difficulty, or as some suppose "the impossibility," of delivering all the tithes from every part of the land at the place of the sanctuary, does not warrant us in departing from the simple meaning of Moses' words in the verse before us. The arrangement permitted in chap. xiv. 24, 25, with reference to the so-called second tithe,—viz. that if the sanctuary was too far off, the tithe might be sold at home, and whatever was required for the sacrificial meals might be bought at the place of the sanctuary with the money so obtained,—might possibly have been also adopted in the case of the other tithe. At all events, the fact that no reference is made to such cases as these does not warrant us in assuming the opposite. As the institution of tithes generally did not originate with the law of Moses, but is presupposed as a traditional and well-known custom, —all that is done being to define them more precisely, and regulate the way in which they should be applied (cf. vol. ii. p. 485),—Moses does not enter here into any details as to the course to be adopted in delivering them, but merely lays down the law that all the gifts intended for the Lord were to be brought to Him at His sanctuary, and connects with this the further injunction that the Israelites were to rejoice there before the Lord, that is to say, were to celebrate their sacrificial meals at the place of His presence which He had chosen.—The gifts, from which the sacrificial meals were prepared, are not particularized here, but are supposed to be already known either from the earlier laws or from tradition. From the earlier laws we learn that the whole of the flesh of the burnt-offerings was to be consumed upon the altar, but that the flesh of the slain-offerings, except in the case of the peace-offerings, was to be applied to the sacrificial meals, with the exception of the fat pieces, and the wave-breast and heave-shoulder. With regard to the tithes, it is stated in Num. xviii. 21-24 that Jehovah had given them to the Levites as their inheritance, and that they were to give the tenth part of them to the priests. In the laws contained in the earlier books, nothing is said about the appropriation of any portion of the tithes to sacrificial meals. Yet in Deuteronomy this is simply assumed as a customary thing, and not introduced as a new commandment, when the law is laid down (in ver. 17, chap. xiv. 22 sqq., xxvi. 12 sqq.), that they were not to eat the tithe of corn, new wine, and oil within their gates (in the towns of the land), any more than the first-born of oxen and sheep, but only at the place of the sanctuary chosen by the Lord ; and that if the distance was too great for the whole to be transported thither, they were to sell the tithes and firstlings at home, and then purchase at the sanctuary whatever might be required for the sacrificial meals. From these instructions it is very apparent that sacrificial meals were associated with the delivery of the tithes and firstlings to the Lord, to which a tenth part of the corn, must, and oil was applied, as well as the flesh of the first-born of edible cattle. This tenth formed the so-called second tithe (δευτέραν δεκάτην, Tob. i. 7), which is mentioned here for the first time, but not introduced as a new rule or an appendix to the former laws. It is rather taken for granted as a custom founded upon tradition, and brought into harmony with the law relating to the oneness of the sanctuary and worship.[1] " *The heave-offerings of your hand*," which are mentioned

---

[1] The arguments employed by *De Wette* and *Vater* against this arrangement with regard to the vegetable tithe, which is established beyond all question by

again in Mal. iii. 8 along with the tithes, are not to be restricted to the first-fruits, as we may see from Ezek. xx. 40, where the *terumoth* are mentioned along with the first-fruits. We should rather understand them as being free gifts of love, which were consecrated to the Lord in addition to the legal first-fruits and tithes without being actual sacrifices, and which were then applied to sacrificial meals.— The other gifts were (3) נְדָרִים and נְדָבוֹת, sacrifices which were offered partly in consequence of vows and partly of their own free will (see at Lev. xxiii. 38, compared with Lev. vii. 16, xxii. 21, and Num. xv. 3, xxix. 39) ; and lastly (4), " firstlings of your herds and of your flocks," viz. those commanded in Ex. xiii. 2, 12 sqq., and Num. xviii. 15 sqq.

According to Ex. xiii. 15, the Israelites were to sacrifice the firstlings to the Lord ; and according to Num. xviii. 8 sqq. they belonged to the holy gifts, which the Lord assigned to the priests for their maintenance, with the more precise instructions in vers. 17, 18, that the first-born of oxen, sheep, and goats were not to be redeemed, but being holy were to be burned upon the altar in the same manner as the *shelamim*, and that the flesh was to belong to the priests, like the wave-breast and right leg of the shelamim. These last words, it is true, are not to be understood as signifying that the only portions of the flesh of the firstlings which were to be given to the priest were the wave-breast and heave-leg, and that the remainder of the flesh was to be left to the offerer to be applied

the custom of the Jews themselves, have been so fully met by *Hengstenberg* (Dissertations, ii. 334 sqq.), that *Riehm* has nothing to adduce in reply, except the assertion that in Deut. xviii., where the revenues of the priests and Levites are given, there is nothing said about the tithe, and the tithe of the tithe, and also that the people would have been overburdened by a second tithe. But, apart from the fact that *argumenta e silentio* generally do not prove much, the first assertion rests upon the erroneous assumption that in Deut. xviii. all the revenues of the priests are given separately ; whereas Moses confines himself to this general summary of the revenues of the priests and Levites enumerated singly in Num. xviii., " The firings of Jehovah shall be the inheritance of the tribe of Levi, these they shall eat," and then urges upon the people in vers. 3–5 an addition to the revenues already established. The second objection is refuted by history. For if in later times, when the people of Israel had to pay very considerable taxes to the foreign kings under whose rule they were living, they could give a second tenth of the fruits of the ground in addition to the priests' tithe, as we may see from Tobit i. 7, such a tax could not have been too grievous a burden for the nation in the time of its independence ; to say nothing of the fact that this second tenth belonged in great part to the donors themselves, since it was consumed in sacrificial meals, to which only poor and needy persons were invited, and therefore could not be regarded as an actual tax.

to a sacrificial meal (*Hengstenberg*) ; but they state most unequi-
vocally that the priest was to apply the flesh to a sacrificial meal,
like the wave-breast and heave-leg of all the peace-offerings, which
the priest was not even allowed to consume with his own family at
home, like ordinary flesh, but to which the instructions given for all
the sacrificial meals were applicable, namely, that " whoever was
clean in the priest's family" might eat of it (Num. xviii. 11), and
that the flesh was to be eaten on the day when the sacrifice was
offered (Lev. vii. 15), or at the latest on the following morning, as
in the case of the votive offering (Lev. vii. 16), and that whatever
was left was to be burnt. These instructions concerning the flesh
of the firstlings to be offered to the Lord no more prohibit the
priest from allowing the persons who presented the firstlings to take
part in the sacrificial meals, or handing over to them some portion
of the flesh which belonged to himself to hold a sacrificial meal,
than any other law does ; on the contrary, the duty of doing this
was made very plain by the fact that the presentation of firstlings is
described as זֶבַח לַיהֹוָה in Ex. xiii. 15, in the very first of the general
instructions for their sanctification, since even in the patriarchal
times the זֶבַח was always connected with a sacrificial meal in which
the offerer participated. Consequently it cannot be shown that
there is any contradiction between Deuteronomy and the earlier
laws with regard to the appropriation of the first-born. The command to bring the firstlings of the sacrificial animal, like all the
rest of the sacrifices, to the place of His sanctuary which the Lord
would choose, and to hold sacrificial meals there with the tithes of
corn, new wine, and oil, and also with the firstlings of the flocks
and herds, is given not merely to the laity of Israel, but to the
whole of the people, including the priests and Levites, without the
distinction between the tribe of Levi and the other tribes, established in the earlier laws, being even altered, much less abrogated.
The Israelites were to bring all their sacrificial gifts to the place of
the sanctuary to be chosen by the Lord, and there, not in all their
towns, they were to eat their votive and free-will offerings in sacrificial meals. This, and only this, is what Moses commands the
people both here in vers. 7 and 17, 18, and also in chap. xiv. 22
sqq. and xv. 19 sqq.[1] " *Rejoice in all that your hand has acquired.*"

[1] If, therefore, the supposed discrepancies between the law of Deuteronomy
and that of Exodus and Leviticus concerning the tithes and firstlings vanish
into mere appearance when the passages in Deuteronomy are correctly explained,
the conclusions to which *Riehm* comes (pp. 43 sqq.)—viz. that in Deuteronomy

The phrase מִשְׁלַח יָד (cf. ver. 18, chap. xv. 10, xxiii. 21, xxviii. 8, 20) signifies that to which the hand is stretched out, that which a man undertakes (synonymous with מַעֲשֶׂה), and also what a man acquires by his activity : hence Isa. xi. 14, מִשְׁלוֹחַ יָד, what a man appropriates to himself with his hand, or takes possession of. אֲשֶׁר before בֵּרַכְךָ is dependent upon מִשְׁלַח יָדֶכֶם, and בֵּרֵךְ is construed with a double accusative, as in Gen. xlix. 25. The reason for these instructions is given in vers. 8, 9, namely, that this had not hitherto taken place, but that up to this day every one had done what he thought right, because they had not yet come to the rest and to the inheritance which the Lord was about to give them. The phrase, " whatsoever is right in his own eyes," is applied to actions performed according to a man's own judgment, rather than according to the standard of objective right and the law of God (cf. Judg. xvii. 6, xxi. 25). The reference is probably not so much to open idolatry, which was actually practised, according to Lev. xvii. 7, Num. xxv., Ezek. xx. 16, 17, Amos v. 25, 26, as to acts of illegality, for which some excuse might be found in the circumstances in which they were placed when wandering through the desert,—such, for example, as the omission of the daily sacrifice when the tabernacle was not set up, and others of a similar kind.—Vers. 10–14. But when the Israelites had crossed over the Jordan, and dwelt peaceably in Canaan, secured against their enemies round about, these irregularities were not to occur any more ; but all the sacrifices were to be offered at the place chosen by the Lord for the dwelling-place of His name, and there the sacrificial meals were to be held with joy before the Lord. "The choice of your vows," equivalent to your chosen vows, inasmuch as every vow was something special, as the standing phrase פִּלֵּא נֶדֶר (Lev. xxii. 21, and Num. xv. 3, 8) distinctly shows.—"Rejoicing before the Lord," which is the phrase applied in Lev. xxiii. 40 to the celebration of the feast of Tabernacles, was to be the distinctive feature of all the sacrificial meals held by the people at the sanctuary, as is repeatedly affirmed (chap. xiv. 26, xvi. 11, xxvi. 11, xxvii. 7). This holy joy in the participation of the blessing bestowed by the Lord was to be shared not only by sons and daughters, but also by slaves (men-

the tithes and firstlings are no longer the property of the priests and Levites, and that all the laws concerning the redemption and sale of them are abrogated there—are groundless assertions, founded upon the unproved and unfounded assumption, that Deuteronomy was intended to contain a repetition of the whole of the earlier law.

servants and maid-servants), that they too might taste the friendliness of their God, and also by " *the Levite that is in your gates*" (*i.e.* your towns and hamlets; see at Ex. xx. 10). This frequently recurring description of the Levites (cf. ver. 18, chap. xiv. 27, xvi. 11, 14, xviii. 6, xxvi. 12) does not assume that they were homeless, which would be at variance with the allotment of towns for them to dwell in (Num. xxxv.); but simply implies what is frequently added in explanation, that the Levites had "no part nor inheritance," no share of the land as their hereditary property, and in this respect resembled strangers (chap. xiv. 21, 29, xvi. 11, etc.).[1] And the repeated injunction to invite the Levites to the sacrificial meals is not at variance with Num. xviii. 21, where the tithes are assigned to the tribe of Levi for their maintenance. For however ample this revenue may have been according to the law, it was so entirely dependent, as we have observed at p. 120, upon the honesty and conscientiousness of the people, that the Levites might very easily be brought into a straitened condition, if indifference towards the Lord and His servants should prevail throughout the nation.—In vers. 13, 14, Moses concludes by once more summing up these instructions in the admonition to beware of offering sacrifices in every place that they might choose, the burnt-offering, as the leading sacrifice, being mentioned *instar omnium*.

Vers. 15–19. But if these instructions were really to be observed by the people in Canaan, it was necessary that the law which had been given with reference to the journey through the wilderness, viz. that no animal should be slain anywhere else than at the tabernacle in the same manner as a slain-offering (Lev. xvii. 3–6), should be abolished. This is done in ver. 15, where Moses, in direct connection with what goes before, allows the people, as an exception (רק, only) to the rules laid down in vers. 4–14, to kill and eat flesh for their own food according to all their soul's desire. Flesh that was slaughtered for food could be eaten by both clean and unclean, such for example as the roebuck and the hart, animals which could not be offered in sacrifice, and in which, therefore, the distinction between clean and unclean on the part of the eaters did not come into consideration at all.—Ver. 16. But blood was forbidden to be

---

[1] The explanation given by *De Wette*, and adopted by *Riehm*, of the expression, " the Levite that is within thy gates," is perfectly arbitrary and unfounded: viz. that " the Levites did not live any longer in the towns assigned them by the earlier laws, but were *scattered about* in the different towns of the other tribes."

eaten (see at Lev. xvii. 10 sqq.). The blood was to be poured out upon the earth like water, that it might suck it in, receive it into its bosom (see vol. ii. p. 410).—Vers. 17 sqq. Sacrificial meals could only be held at the sanctuary; and the Levite was not to be forgotten or neglected in connection with them (see at vers. 6, 7, and 12). לֹא תוּכַל, "*thou must not*," as in chap. vii. 22.

Vers. 20–31. These rules were still to remain in force, even when God should extend the borders of the land in accordance with His promise. This extension relates partly to the gradual but complete extermination of the Canaanites (chap. vii. 22, comp. with Ex. xxiii. 27–33), and partly to the extension of the territory of the Israelites beyond the limits of Canaan Proper, in accordance with the divine promise in Gen. xv. 18. The words "as He hath spoken to thee" refer primarily to Ex. xxiii. 27–33. (On ver. 20*b*, see ver. 15.)—In ver. 21*a*, "*if the place . . . be too far from thee*," supplies the reason for the repeal of the law in Lev. xvii. 3, which restricted all slaughtering to the place of the sanctuary. The words "*kill . . . as I have commanded thee*" refer back to ver. 15.— Ver. 22. Only the flesh that was slaughtered was to be eaten as the hart and the roebuck (cf. ver. 15), *i.e.* was not to be made into a sacrifice. יַחְדָּו, together, *i.e.* the one just the same as the other, as in Isa. x. 8, without the clean necessarily eating along with the unclean.—Vers. 23, 24. The law relating to the blood, as in ver. 16.—"*Be strong not to eat the blood*," *i.e.* stedfastly resist the temptation to eat it.—Ver. 25. On the promise for doing what was right in the eyes of the Lord, see chap. vi. 18.—In vers. 26, 27, the command to offer all the holy gifts at the place chosen by the Lord is enforced once more, as in vers. 6, 11, 17, 18; also to prepare the sacrifices at His altar. קָדָשִׁים, the holy offerings prescribed in the law, as in Num. xviii. 8; see at Lev. xxi. 22. The "votive offerings" are mentioned in connection with these, because vows proceeded from a spontaneous impulse. אֲשֶׁר יִהְיוּ לְךָ, "*which are to thee*," are binding upon thee. In ver. 27, "the flesh and the blood" are in opposition to "thy burnt-offerings:" "thy burnt-offerings, namely the flesh and blood of them," thou shalt prepare at the altar of Jehovah; *i.e.* the flesh and blood of the burnt-offerings were to be placed upon and against the altar (see at Lev. i. 5–9). Of the slain-offerings, *i.e.* the *shelamim*, the blood was to be poured out against the altar (Lev. iii. 2, 8, 13); "the flesh thou canst eat" (cf. Lev. vii. 11 sqq.). There is no ground for seeking an antithesis in יְשָׁפֵּךְ, as *Knobel* does, to the יָרַק in the sacrificial ritual.

The indefinite expression may be explained from the retrospective allusion to ver. 24 and the purely suggestive character of the whole passage, the thing itself being supposed to be sufficiently known from the previous laws.—Ver. 28. The closing admonition is a further expansion of ver. 25 (see at ch. xi. 21).—In vers. 29–31, the exhortation goes back to the beginning again, viz. to a warning against the Canaanitish idolatry (cf. vers. 2 sqq.). When the Lord had cut off the nations of Canaan from before the Israelites, they were to take heed that they did not get into the snare behind them, *i.e.* into the sin of idolatry, which had plunged the Canaanites into destruction (cf. chap. vii. 16, 25). The clause " *after they be destroyed from before thee* " is not mere tautology, but serves to depict the danger of the snare most vividly before their eyes. The second clause, " *that thou inquire not after them* " (their gods), etc., explains more fully to the Israelites the danger which threatened them. This danger was so far a pressing one, that the whole of the heathen world was animated with the conviction, that to neglect the gods of a land would be sure to bring misfortune (cf. 2 Kings xvii. 26).—Ver. 31*a*, like ver. 4, with the reason assigned in ver. 31*b* : " for the Canaanites prepare (עָשׂה, as in ver. 27) all kinds of abominations for their gods," *i.e.* present offerings to these, which Jehovah hates and abhors ; they even burn their children to their idols—for example, to Moloch (see at Lev. xviii. 21).

Punishment of Idolaters, and Tempters to Idolatry.—Chap. xiii.

Ver. 1. (chap. xii. 32). The admonition to observe the whole law, without adding to it or taking from it (cf. chap. iv. 2), is regarded by many commentators as the conclusion of the previous chapter. But it is more correct to understand it as an intermediate link, closing what goes before, and introductory to what follows. Strictly speaking, the warning against inclining to the idolatry of the Canaanites (chap. xii. 29–31) forms a transition from the enforcement of the true mode of worshipping Jehovah to the laws relating to tempters to idolatry and worshippers of idols (chap. xiii.). The Israelites were to cut off not only the tempters to idolatry, but those who had been led astray to idolatry also. Three different cases are mentioned.

Vers. 2–6 (1–5). The *first* case. If a prophet, or one who had dreams, should rise up to summon to the worship of other gods, with signs and wonders which came to pass, the Israelites were not to hearken to his words, but to put him to death. The introduction of חֹלֵם חֲלוֹם, " *a dreamer of dreams*," along with the prophet, answers to the two media of divine revelation, the vision and the dream, by which, according to Num. xii. 6, God made known His will. With regard to the signs and wonders (*mopheth*, see at Ex. iv. 21) with which such a prophet might seek to accredit his higher mission, it is taken for granted that they come to pass (בּוֹא) ; yet for all that, the Israelites were to give no heed to such a prophet, to walk after other gods. It follows from this, that the person had not been sent by God, but was a false prophet, and that the signs and wonders which he gave were not wonders effected by God, but σημεῖα καὶ τέρατα ψεύδους (" lying signs and wonders," 2 Thess. ii. 9) ; *i.e.* not merely seeming miracles, but miracles wrought in the power of the wicked one, Satan, the possibility and reality of which even Christ attests (Matt. xxiv. 24).—The word לֵאמֹר, *saying*, is dependent upon the principal verb of the sentence : " if a prophet rise up . . . . saying, We will go after other gods."—Ver. 4. God permitted false prophets to rise up with such wonders, to try the Israelites, whether they loved Him, the Lord their God, with all their heart. (נִסָּה as in Gen. xxii. 1.) הֲיִשְׁכֶם אֹהֲבִים, whether ye are loving, *i.e.* faithfully maintain your love to the Lord. It is evident from this, " that however great the importance attached to signs and wonders, they were not to be regarded among the Israelites, either as the highest test, or as absolutely decisive, but that there was a certainty in Israel, which was so much the more certain and firm than any proof from miracles could be, that it might be most decidedly opposed to it " (*Baumgarten*). This certainty, however, was not " the knowledge of Jehovah," as *B.* supposes ; but as *Luther* correctly observes, " the word of God, which had already been received, and confirmed by its own signs," and which the Israelites were to preserve and hold fast, without adding or subtracting anything. " In opposition to such a word, no prophets were to be received, although they rained signs and wonders ; not even an angel from heaven, as Paul says in Gal. i. 8." The command to hearken to the prophets whom the Lord would send at a future time (chap. xviii. 18 sqq.), is not at variance with this : for even their announcements were to be judged according to the standard of the fixed word of God that had been already given ; and so far as they proclaimed anything new, the fact that what they announced did not occur was to be the criterion that they had not spoken in the name of the Lord, but in that of other gods (chap. xviii. 21, 22), so that even there the signs and wonders of the prophets are not made the criteria of their divine mission.—Vers. 5, 6. Israel was to adhere firmly to the Lord its God (cf. chap. iv. 4), and to put to death the prophet who preached apostasy from Jehovah, the Redeemer of Israel out of the slave-house of Egypt. לְהַדִּיחֲךָ, " to force thee from the way in which Jehovah hath commanded thee to walk." The execution of seducers to idolatry is enjoined upon the *people*, *i.e.* the whole community, not upon single individuals, but upon the authorities who had to maintain and administer justice. *" So shalt thou put the evil away from the midst of thee."* הָרָע is neuter, as we may see from chap. xvii. 7, as comp. with ver. 2. The formula, " so shalt thou put the evil away from the midst of thee," which occurs again in chap. xvii. 7, 12, xix. 19, xxi. 21, xxii. 21, 22, 24, and xxiv. 7 (cf. chap. xix. 13 and xxi. 9), belongs to the hortatory character of Deuteronomy, in accordance with which a reason is given for all the command-ments, and the observance of them is urged upon the congregation as a holy affair of the heart, which could not be expected in the objective legislation of the earlier books.

Vers. 7–12 (6–11). The *second* case was when the temptation to idolatry proceeded from the nearest blood-relations and friends. The clause, " son of thy mother," is not intended to describe the brother as a step-brother, but simply to bring out the closeness of the fraternal relation ; like the description of the wife as the wife of thy bosom, who lies in thy bosom, rests upon thy breast (as in chap. xxviii. 54 ; Micah vii. 5), and of the friend as " thy friend which is as thine own soul," *i.e.* whom thou lovest as much as thy life (cf. 1 Sam. xviii. 1, 3). בַּסֵּתֶר belongs to יָסִית : if the temptation occurred in secret, and therefore the fact might be hidden from others. The power of love and relationship, which flesh and blood find it hard to resist, is placed here in contrast with the supposed higher or divine authority of the seducers. As the persuasion was already very seductive, from the fact that it proceeded from the nearest blood-relations and most intimate friends, and was offered in secret, it might become still more so from the fact that it recom-mended the worship of a deity that had nothing in common with the forbidden idols of Canaan, and the worship of which, therefore, might appear of less consequence, or commend itself by the charm of peculiarity and novelty. To prevent this deceptive influence of sin, it is expressly added in ver. 8 (7), *" of the gods nigh unto thee or far off from thee, from the one end of the earth even unto the other end of the earth,"* *i.e.* whatever gods there might be upon the whole circuit of the earth.—Vers. 9 (8) sqq. To such persuasion Israel was not to yield, nor were they to spare the tempters. The accumulation of synonyms (pity, spare, conceal) serves to make the passage more emphatic. כִּפָּה, to cover, *i.e.* to keep secret, conceal. They were to put him to death without pity, viz. to stone him (cf. Lev. xx. 2). That the execution even in this case was to be carried out by the regular authorities, is evident from the words, "thy hand shall be first against him to put him to death, and the hand of all the people afterwards," which presuppose the judicial procedure prescribed in chap. xvii. 7, that the witnesses were to cast the first stones at the person condemned.—Ver. 12. This was to be done, and all Israel was to hear it and fear, that no such wickedness should be performed any more in the congregation. The fear of punishment, which is given here as the ultimate end of the punishment itself, is not to be regarded as the principle lying at the foundation of the law, but simply, as *Calvin* expresses it, as "the utility and fruit of severity," one reason for carrying out the law, which is not to be confounded with the so-called deterrent theory, *i.e.* the attempt to deter from crime by the mode of punishing (see my *Archäologie*, ii. p. 262).

Vers. 13–19 (12–18). The *third* case is that of a town that had been led away to idolatry. "*If thou shalt hear in one of thy cities.*" בְּאַחַת, not *de una*, of one, which שָׁמַע with בְּ never can mean, and does not mean even in Job xxvi. 14. The thought is not that they would hear in one city about another, as though one city had the oversight over another; but there is an inversion in the sentence, "*if thou hear, that in one of thy cities . . . worthless men have risen up, and led the inhabitants astray to serve strange gods.*" לֵאמֹר introduces the substance of what is heard, which follows in ver. 14. יָצְא merely signifies to rise up, to go forth. מִקִּרְבֶּךָ, out of the midst of the people.—Ver. 15 (14). Upon this report the people as a whole, of course through their rulers, were to examine closely into the affair (הֵיטֵב, an adverb, as in chap. ix. 21), whether the word was established as truth, *i.e.* the thing was founded in truth (cf. chap. xvii. 4, xxii. 20); and if it really were so, they were to smite the inhabitants of that town with the edge of the sword (cf. Gen. xxxiv. 26), putting the town and all that was in it under the ban. "*All that is in it*" relates to men, cattle, and the material property of the town, and not to men alone (*Schultz*). The clause from "destroying" to "therein" is a more minute definition of the punishment introduced as a parenthesis; for "the cattle thereof," which follows, is also governed by "thou shalt smite." The ban was to be executed in all its severity as upon an idolatrous city: man and beast were to be put to death without reserve ; and its booty, *i.e.* whatever was to be found in it as booty—all material goods, therefore—were to be heaped together in the market, and burned along with the city itself. כָּלִיל לַיהוָה (*Eng. Ver.* " every whit, for the Lord thy God") signifies " *as a whole offering for the Lord* " (see Lev. vi. 15, 16), *i.e.* it was to be sanctified to Him entirely by being destroyed. The town was to continue an eternal hill (or heap of ruins), never to be built up again.—Ver. 18 (17). To enforce this command still more strongly, it is expressly stated, that of all that was burned, nothing whatever was to cleave or remain hanging to the hand of Israel, that the Lord might turn from His wrath and have compassion upon the nation, *i.e.* not punish the sin of one town upon the nation as a whole, but have mercy upon it and multiply it,—make up the diminution consequent upon the destruction of the inhabitants of that town, and so fulfil the promise given to the fathers of the multiplication of their seed.— Ver. 19 (18). Jehovah would do this if Israel hearkened to His voice, to do what was right in His eyes. In what way the appropriation of property laid under the ban brought the wrath of God upon the whole congregation, is shown by the example of Achan (Josh. vii.).

Avoidance of the Mourning Customs of the Heathen, and Unclean Food. Application of the Tithe of Fruits.—Chap. xiv.

Vers. 1–21. The Israelites were not only to suffer no idolatry to rise up in their midst, but in all their walk of life to show themselves as a holy nation of the Lord ; and neither to disfigure their bodies by passionate expressions of sorrow for the dead (vers. 1 and 2), nor to defile themselves by unclean food (vers. 3–21). Both of these were opposed to their calling. To bring this to their mind, Moses introduces the laws which follow with the words, " ye are children to the Lord your God." The divine sonship of Israel was founded upon its election and calling as the holy nation of Jehovah, which is regarded in the Old Testament not as generation by the Spirit of God, but simply as an adoption springing out of the free love of God, as the manifestation of paternal love on the part of Jehovah to Israel, which binds the son to obedience, reverence, and childlike trust towards a Creator and Father, who would train it up into a holy people (see vol. i. p. 457). The laws in ver. 1*b* are simply a repetition of Lev. xix. 28 and xxi. 5. לְמֵת, with reference to, or on account of, a dead person, is more expressive than לְנֶפֶשׁ (for a soul) in Lev. xix. 28. The reason assigned for this command in ver. 2 (as in chap. vii. 6) is simply an emphatic elucidation of the first clause of ver. 1. (On the substance of the verse, see Ex. xix. 5, 6.) — Vers. 3–20. With reference to food, the Israelites were to eat nothing whatever that was abominable. In explanation of this prohibition, the laws of Lev. xi. relating to clean and unclean animals are repeated in all essential points in vers. 4–20 (for the exposition, see at Lev. xi.); also in ver. 21 the prohibition against eating any animal that had fallen down dead (as in Ex. xxxii. 30 and Lev. xvii. 15), and against boiling a kid in its mother's milk (as in Ex. xxiii. 19).

Vers. 22–29. As the Israelites were to sanctify their food, on the one hand, positively by abstinence from everything unclean, so were they, on the other hand, to do so negatively by delivering the tithes and firstlings at the place where the Lord would cause His name to dwell, and by holding festal meals on the occasion, and rejoicing there before Jehovah their God. This law is introduced with the general precept, " *Thou shalt tithe all the produce of thy seed which groweth out of the field* (יָצָא construes with an accusative, as in Gen. ix. 10, etc.) *year by year*" (שָׁנָה שָׁנָה, *i.e.* every year; cf. *Ewald*, § 313, *a*.), which recalls the earlier laws concerning the tithe (Lev. xxvii. 30, and Num. xviii. 21, 26 sqq.), without repeating them one by one, for the purpose of linking on the injunction to celebrate sacrificial meals at the sanctuary from the tithes and firstlings. Moses had already directed (chap. xii. 6 sqq.) that all the sacrificial meals should take place at the sanctuary, and had then alluded to the sacrificial meals to be prepared from the tithes, though only casually, because he intended to speak of them more fully afterwards. This he does here, and includes the firstlings also, inasmuch as the presentation of them was generally associated with that of the tithes, though only casually, as he intends to revert to the firstlings again, which he does in chap. xv. 19 sqq. The connection between the tithes of the fruits of the ground and the firstlings of the cattle which were devoted to the sacrificial meals, and the tithes and first-fruits which were to be delivered to the Levites and priests, we have already discussed at chap. xii. (p. 356). The sacrificial meals were to be held before the Lord, in the place where He caused His name to dwell (see at chap. xii. 5), that Israel might learn to fear Jehovah its God always; not, however, as *Schultz* supposes, that by the confession of its dependence upon Him it might accustom itself more and more to the feeling of dependence. For the fear of the Lord is not merely a feeling of dependence upon Him, but also includes the notion of divine blessedness, which is the predominant idea here, as the sacrificial meals were to furnish the occasion and object of the rejoicing before the Lord. The true meaning therefore is, that Israel might rejoice with holy reverence in the fellowship of its God.—Vers. 24 sqq. In the land of Canaan, however, where the people would be scattered over a great extent of country, there would be many for whom the fulfilment of this command would be very difficult—would, in fact, appear almost impossible. To meet this difficulty, permission was given for those who lived at a great distance from the sanctuary to sell the tithes at home, provided they could not convey them in kind, and then to spend the money so obtained in the purchase of the things required for the sacrificial meals at the place of the sanctuary. כִּי־יִרְבֶּה מִמְּךְ, "*if the way be too great* (too far) *for thee*," etc., *sc.* for the delivery of the tithe. The parenthetical clause, "if Jehovah thy God shall bless thee," hardly means "if He shall extend thy territory" (*Knobel*), but if He shall bless thee by plentiful produce from the field and the cattle.—Ver. 25. "*Turn it into money*," *lit.* "give it up for silver," *sc.* the produce of the tithe; "and bind the silver in thy hand," *const. prægnans* for "bind it in a purse and take it in thy hand . . . . and give the silver for all that thy soul desireth, for oxen and small cattle, for wine and strong drink," to hold a joyous meal, to which the Levite was also to be invited (as in chap. xii. 12, 18, and 19).—Vers. 28 and 29. Every third year, on the other hand, they were to separate the whole of the tithe from the year's produce ("bring forth," *sc.* from the granary), and leave it in their gates (*i.e.* their towns), and feed the Levites, the strangers, and the widows and orphans with it. They were not to take it to the sanctuary, therefore; but according to chap. xxvi. 12 sqq., after bringing it out, were to make confession to the Lord of what they had done, and pray for His blessing. "*At the end of three years:*" *i.e.* when the third year, namely the civil year, which closed with the harvest (see at Ex. xxiii. 16), had come to an end. This regulation as to the time was founded upon the observance of the sabbatical year, as we may see from chap. xv. 1, where the seventh year is no other than the sabbatical year. Twice, therefore, within the period of a sabbatical year, namely in the third and sixth years, the tithe set apart for a sacrificial meal was not to be eaten at the sanctuary, but to be used in the different towns of the land in providing festal meals for those who had no possessions, viz. the Levites, strangers, widows, and orphans. Consequently this tithe cannot properly be called the "third tithe," as it is by many of the Rabbins, but rather the "poor tithe," as it was simply in the way of applying it that it differed from the "second" (see *Hottinger, de decimis, exerc.* viii. pp. 182 sqq., and my *Archäol.* i. p. 339). As an encouragement to carry out these instructions, Moses closes in ver. 29 with an allusion to the divine blessing which would follow their observance.

On the Year of Release, the Emancipation of Hebrew Slaves, and the Sanctification of the First-born of Cattle.—Chap. xv.

Vers. 1-11. ON THE YEAR OF RELEASE.—The first two regulations in this chapter, viz. vers. 1-11 and 12-18, follow simply upon the law concerning the poor tithe in chap. xiv. 28, 29. The Israelites were not only to cause those who had no possessions (Levites, strangers, widows, and orphans) to refresh themselves with the produce of their inheritance, but they were not to force and oppress the poor. Debtors especially were not to be deprived of the blessings of the sabbatical year (vers. 1-6). "*At the end of seven years thou shalt make a release.*" The expression, " at the end of seven years," is to be understood in the same way as the corresponding phrase, " at the end of three years," in chap. xiv. 28. The end of seven years, *i.e.* of the seven years' cycle formed by the sabbatical year, is mentioned as the time when debts that had been contracted were usually wiped off or demanded, after the year's harvest had been gathered in (cf. chap. xxxi. 10, acccording to which the feast of Tabernacles occurred at the end of the year). שְׁמִטָּה, from שָׁמַט, to let lie, to let go (cf. Ex. xxiii. 11), does not signify a remission of the debt, the relinquishing of all claim for payment, as *Philo* and the Talmudists affirm, but simply lengthening the term, not pressing for payment. This is the explanation in ver. 2 : " *This is the manner of the release*" (*shemittah*) : cf. chap. xix. 4 ; 1 Kings ix. 15. " *Every owner of a loan of his hand shall release* (leave) *what he has lent to his neighbour ; he shall not press his neighbour, and indeed his brother ; for they have proclaimed release for Jehovah.*" As שָׁמוֹט (release) points unmistakeably back to Ex. xxiii. 11, it must be interpreted in the same manner here as there. And as it is not used there to denote the entire renunciation of a field or possession, so here it cannot mean the entire renunciation of what had been lent, but simply leaving it, *i.e.* not pressing for it during the seventh year. This is favoured by what follows, " *thou shalt not press thy neighbour,*" which simply forbids an unreserved demand, but does not require that the debt should be remitted or presented to the debtor (see also *Bähr, Symbolik*, ii. pp. 570–1). " The loan of the hand :" what the hand has lent to another. " The master of the loan of the hand :" *i.e.* the owner of a loan, the lender. " His brother" defines with greater precision the idea of " a neighbour." Calling a release, presupposes that the sabbatical year was publicly proclaimed, like the year of jubilee (Lev. xxv. 9). קָרָא is impersonal (" they call"), as in Gen. xi. 9 and xvi. 14. " *For Jehovah :*" *i.e.* in honour of Jehovah, sanctified to Him, as in Ex. xii. 42.—This law points back to the institution of the sabbatical year in Ex. xxiii. 10, Lev. xxv. 2–7, though it is not to be regarded as an appendix to the law of the sabbatical year, or an expansion of it, but simply as an exposition of what was already implied in the main provision of that law, viz. that the cultivation of the land should be suspended in the sabbatical year. If no harvest was gathered in, and even such produce as had grown without sowing was to be left to the poor and the beasts of the field, the landowner could have no income from which to pay his debts. The fact that the " *sabbatical year*" is not expressly mentioned, may be accounted for on the ground, that even in the principal law itself this name does not occur ; and it is simply commanded that every seventh year there was to be a sabbath of rest to the land (Lev. xxv. 4). In the subsequent passages in which it is referred to (ver. 9 and chap. xxxi. 10), it is still not called a sabbatical year, but simply the " year of release," and that not merely with reference to debtors, but also with reference to the release (*shemittah*) to be allowed to the field (Ex. xxiii. 11).—Ver. 3. The foreigner thou mayest press, but what thou hast with thy brother shall thy hand let go. נָכְרִי is a stranger of another nation, standing in no inward relation to Israel at all, and is to be distinguished from גֵּר, the foreigner who lived among the Israelites, who had a claim upon their protection and pity. This rule breathes no hatred of foreigners, but simply allows the Israelites the right of every creditor to demand his debts, and enforce the demand upon foreigners, even in the sabbatical year. There was no severity in this, because foreigners could get their ordinary income in the seventh year as well as in any other.—Ver. 4. " *Only that there shall be no poor with thee.*" יִהְיֶה is jussive, like the foregoing imperfects. The meaning in this connection is, " Thou needest not to remit a debt to foreigners in the seventh year; thou hast only to take care that there is no poor man with or among thee, that thou dost not cause or increase their poverty, by oppressing the brethren who have borrowed of thee." Understood in this way, the sentence is not at all at variance with ver. 11, where it is stated that the poor would never cease out of the land. The following clause, " for Jehovah will bless thee," etc., gives a reason for the main thought, that they were not to press the Israelitish debtor. The creditor, therefore, had no need to fear that he would suffer want, if he refrained from exacting his debt from his brother in the seventh year.—Vers. 5, 6. This blessing would not fail, if the Israelites would only hearken to the voice of the Lord; " *for Jehovah blesseth thee*" (by the perfect בֵּרַכְךָ, the blessing is represented not as a possible and future one only, but as one already bestowed according to the counsel of God, and, so far as the commencement was concerned, already fulfilled), " *as He hath spoken*" (see at chap. i. 11). " *And thou wilt lend on pledge to many nations, but thou thyself wilt not borrow upon pledge.*" עָבַט, a *denom.* verb, from עֲבוֹט, a pledge, signifies in *Kal* to give a pledge for the purpose of borrowing; in *Hiphil*, to cause a person to give a pledge, or furnish occasion for giving a pledge, *i.e.* to lend upon pledge. " *And thou wilt rule over many nations,*" etc. Ruling is mentioned here as the result of superiority in wealth (cf. chap. xxviii. 1: *Schultz*).—Vers. 7–11. And in general Israel was to be ready to lend to the poor among its brethren, not to harden its heart, to be hard-hearted, but to lend to the poor brother דֵּי מַחְסֹרוֹ, " the sufficiency of his need," whatever he might need to relieve his wants.—Vers. 9, 10. Thus they were also to beware " *that there was not a word in the heart, worthlessness,*" *i.e.* that a worthless thought did not arise in their hearts (בְּלִיַּעַל is the predicate of the sentence, as the more precise definition of the word that was in the heart); so that one should say, " *The seventh year is at hand, the year of release,*" *sc.* when I shall not be able to demand what I have lent, and " *that thine eye be evil towards thy poor brother,*" *i.e.* that thou cherishest ill-will towards him (cf. chap. xxviii. 54, 56), " *and givest him not, and he appeals to Jehovah against thee, and it becomes sin to thee,*" *sc.* which brings down upon thee the wrath of God.—Ver. 10. Thou shalt give him, and thy heart shall not become evil, *i.e.* discontented thereat (cf. 2 Cor. ix. 7), for Jehovah will bless thee for it (cf. Prov. xxii. 9, xxviii. 27; Ps. xli. 2; Matt. vi. 4).—Ver. 11. For the poor will never cease in the land, even the land that is richly blessed, because poverty is not only the penalty of sin, but is ordained by God for punishment and discipline.

Vers. 12–18. These provisions in favour of the poor are followed very naturally by the rules which the Israelites were to be urged to observe with reference to the *manumission of Hebrew slaves.* It is not the reference to the sabbatical year in the foregoing precepts which forms the introduction to the laws which follow respecting the manumission of Hebrews who had become slaves, but the poverty and want which compelled Hebrew men and women to sell themselves as slaves. The seventh year, in which they were to be set free, is not the same as the sabbatical year, therefore, but the seventh year of bondage. Manumission in the seventh year of service had already been commanded in Ex. xxi. 2–6, in the rights laid down for the nation, with special reference to the conclusion of the covenant. This command is not repeated here for the purpose of extending the law to Hebrew women, who are not expressly mentioned in Ex. xxi.; for that would follow as a matter of course, in the case of a law which was quite as applicable to women as to men, and was given without any reserve to the whole congregation. It is rather repeated here as a law which already existed as a right, for the purpose of explaining the true mode of fulfilling it, viz. that it was not sufficient to give a man-servant and maid-servant their liberty after six years of service, which would not be sufficient relief to those who had been obliged to enter into slavery on account of poverty, if they had nothing with which to set up a home of their own; but love to the poor was required to do more than this, namely, to make some provision for the continued prosperity of those who were set at liberty. " *If thou let him go free from thee, thou shalt not let him go* (send him away) *empty :*" this was the new feature which Moses added here to the previous law. " *Thou shalt load* (הַעֲנִיק, *lit.* put upon the neck) *of thy flock, and of thy floor* (corn), *and of thy press* (oil and wine); *wherewith thy God hath blessed thee, of that thou shalt give to him.*"—Ver. 15. They were to be induced to do this by the recollection of their own redemption out of the bondage of Egypt,—the same motive that is urged for the laws and exhortations enjoining compassion towards foreigners, servants, maids, widows, orphans, and the poor, not only in chap. v. 15, x. 19, xvi. 12, xxiv. 18, 22, but also in Ex. xxii. 20, xxiii. 9, and Lev. xix. 34.—Vers. 16, 17. But if the man-servant and the maid-servant should not wish for liberty in the sixth year, because it was well with them in the house of their master, they were not to be compelled to go, but were to be bound to eternal, *i.e.* lifelong bondage, in the manner prescribed in Ex. xxi. 5, 6.[1] This is repeated from

---

[1] *Knobel's* assertion, that the judicial process enjoined in Ex. xxi. 6 does not seem to have been usual in the author's own time, is a worthless *argumentum e silentio.*

Ex. xxi., to guard against such an application of the law as might be really cruelty under the circumstances rather than love. Manumission was only an act of love, when the person to be set free had some hope of success and of getting a living for himself; and where there was no such prospect, compelling him to accept of freedom might be equivalent to thrusting him away.—Ver. 18. If, on the other hand, the servant (or maid) wished to be set free, the master was not to think it hard; "*for the double of the wages of a day-labourer he has earned for thee for six years*," *i.e.* not "twice the time of a day-labourer, so that he had really deserved twice the wages" (*Vatablius, Ad. Osiander, J. Gerhard*), for it cannot be proved from Isa. xvi. 14, that a day-labourer generally hired himself out for three years; nor yet, "he has been obliged to work much harder than a day-labourer, very often by night as well as day" (*Clericus, J. H. Michaelis, Rosenmüller, Baumgarten*); but simply, "he has earned and produced so much, that if you had been obliged to keep a day-labourer in his place, it would have cost you twice as much" (*Schultz, Knobel*).

Vers. 19–23. APPLICATION OF THE FIRST-BORN OF CATTLE. —From the laws respecting the poor and slaves, to which the instructions concerning the tithes (chap. xiv. 22-29) had given occasion, Moses returns to appropriation of the first-born of the herd and flock to sacrificial meals, which he had already touched upon in chap. xii. 6, 17, and xiv. 23, and concludes by an explanation upon this point. The command, which the Lord had given when first they came out of Egypt (Ex. xiii. 2, 12), that all the first-born of the herd and flock should be sanctified to Him, is repeated here by Moses, with the express injunction that they were not to work with the first-born of cattle (by yoking them to the plough or waggon), and not to shear the first-born of sheep; that is to say, they were not to use the first-born animals which were sanctified to the Lord for their own earthly purposes, but to offer them year by year as sacrifices to the Lord, and consume them in sacrificial meals, in the manner explained at p. 357. To this he adds (vers. 21, 22) the further provision, that first-born animals, which were blind or lame, or had any other bad fault, were not to be offered in sacrifice to the Lord, but, like ordinary animals used for food, could be eaten in all the towns of the land. Although the first part of this law was involved in the general laws as to the kind of animal that could be offered in sacrifice (Lev. xxii. 19 sqq.), it was by no means unimportant to point out distinctly their applicability to the first-born, and add some instructions with regard to the way in which they were to be applied. (On vers. 22 and 23, see chap. xii. 15 and 16.)

On the Celebration of the Feasts of Passover, of Pentecost, and of Tabernacles.—Chap. xvi. 1–17.

The annual feasts appointed by the law were to be celebrated, like the sacrificial meals, at the place which the Lord would choose for the revelation of His name; and there Israel was to rejoice before the Lord with the presentation of sacrifices. From this point of view Moses discusses the feasts of Passover, Pentecost, and Tabernacles, assuming the laws previously given concerning these festivals (Ex. xii., Lev. xxiii., and Num. xxviii. and xxix.) as already known, and simply repeating those points which related to the sacrificial meals held at these festivals. This serves to explain the reason why only those three festivals are mentioned, at which Israel had already been commanded to appear before the Lord in Ex. xxiii. 14–17, and xxxiv. 18, 24, 25, and not the feast of trumpets or day of atonement: viz. because the people were not required to assemble at the sanctuary out of the whole land on the occasion of these two festivals.[1]

Vers. 1–8. Israel was to make ready the Passover to the Lord in the earing month (see at Ex. xii. 2). The precise day is supposed to be known from Ex. xii., as in Ex. xxiii. 15. עָשָׂה פֶּסַח (*to prepare the Passover*), which is used primarily to denote the preparation of the paschal lamb for a festal meal, is employed here in a wider signification, viz. "*to keep the Passover.*" At this feast they were to slay sheep and oxen to the Lord for a Passover, at the place, etc. In ver. 2, as in ver. 1, the word "Passover" is employed in a broader sense, and includes not only the paschal lamb, but the paschal sacrifices generally, which the Rabbins embrace under the

---

[1] That the assembling of the people at the central sanctuary is the leading point of view under which the feasts are regarded here, has been already pointed out by *Bachmann* (*die Feste*, p. 143), who has called attention to the fact that "the place which Jehovah thy God will choose" occurs six times (vers. 2, 6, 7, 11, 15, 16); and "before the face of Jehovah" three times (vers. 11 and 16 twice) ; and that the celebration of the feast at any other place is expressly declared to be null and void. At the same time, he has once more thoroughly exploded the contradictions which are said to exist between this chapter and the earlier festal laws, and which *Hupfeld* has revived in his comments upon the feasts, without troubling himself to notice the careful discussion of the subject by *Hävernick* in his Introduction, and *Hengstenberg* in his Dissertations.

common name of *chagiga;* not the burnt-offerings and sin-offerings, however, prescribed in Num. xxviii. 19–26, but all the sacrifices that were slain at the feast of the Passover (*i.e.* during the seven days of the *Mazzoth,* which are included under the name of *pascha*) for the purpose of holding sacrificial meals. This is evident from the expression "*of the flock and the herd;*" as it was expressly laid down, that only a שֶׂה, *i.e.* a yearling animal of the sheep or goats, was to be slain for the paschal meal on the fourteenth of the month in the evening, and an ox was never slaughtered in the place of the lamb. But if any doubt could exist upon this point, it would be completely set aside by ver. 3: "*Thou shalt eat no leavened bread with it: seven days shalt thou eat unleavened bread therewith.*" As the word "*therewith*" cannot possibly refer to anything else than the "Passover" in ver. 2, it is distinctly stated that the slaughtering and eating of the Passover was to last seven days, whereas the Passover lamb was to be slain and consumed in the evening of the fourteenth Abib (Ex. xii. 10). Moses called the unleavened bread "*the bread of affliction,*" because the Israelites had to leave Egypt in anxious flight (Ex. xii. 11) and were therefore unable to leaven the dough (Ex. xii. 39), for the purpose of reminding the congregation of the oppression endured in Egypt, and to stir them up to gratitude towards the Lord their deliverer, that they might remember that day as long as they lived. (On the meaning of the *Mazzoth,* see at Ex. xii. 8 and 15.)—On account of the importance of the unleavened bread as a symbolical shadowing forth of the significance of the Passover, as the feast of the renewal and sanctification of the life of Israel (see vol. ii. p. 21), Moses repeats in ver. 4 two of the points in the law of the feast: first of all the one laid down in Ex. xiii. 7, that no leaven was to be seen in the land during the seven days; and secondly, the one in Ex. xxiii. 18 and xxxiv. 25, that none of the flesh of the paschal lamb was to be left till the next morning, in order that all corruption might be kept at a distance from the paschal food. Leaven, for example, sets the dough in fermentation, from which putrefaction ensues (see vol. ii. p. 15); and in the East, if flesh is kept, it very quickly decomposes. He then once more fixes the time and place for keeping the Passover (the former according to Ex. xii. 6 and Lev. xxiii. 5, etc.), and adds in ver. 7 the express regulation, that not only the slaughtering and sacrificing, but the roasting (see at Ex. xii. 9) and eating of the paschal lamb were to take place at the sanctuary, and that the next morning they could turn and go back home.

This rule contains a new feature, which Moses prescribes with reference to the keeping of the Passover in the land of Canaan, and by which he modifies the instructions for the first Passover in Egypt, to suit the altered circumstances. In Egypt, when Israel was not yet raised into the nation of Jehovah, and had as yet no sanctuary and no common altar, the different houses necessarily served as altars. But when this necessity was at an end, the slaying and eating of the Passover in the different houses were to cease, and they were both to take place at the sanctuary before the Lord, as was the case with the feast of Passover at Sinai (Num. ix. 1–5). Thus the smearing of the door-posts with the blood was tacitly abolished, since the blood was to be sprinkled upon the altar as sacrificial blood, as it had already been at Sinai (see vol. ii. p. 50). —The expression "*to thy tents*," for going "home," points to the time when Israel was still dwelling in tents, and had not as yet secured any fixed abodes and houses in Canaan, although this expression was retained at a still later time (*e.g.* 1 Sam. xiii. 2 ; 2 Sam. xix. 9, etc.). The going home in the morning after the paschal meal, is not to be understood as signifying a return to their homes in the different towns of the land, but simply, as even *Riehm* admits, to their homes or lodgings at the place of the sanctuary. How very far Moses was from intending to release the Israelites from the duty of keeping the feast for seven days, is evident from the fact that in ver. 8 he once more enforces the observance of the seven days' feast. The two clauses, "six days thou shalt eat *mazzoth*," and "on the seventh day shall be *azereth* (Eng. Ver. 'a solemn assembly') to the Lord thy God," are not placed in antithesis to each other, so as to imply (in contradiction to vers. 3 and 4 ; Ex. xii. 18, 19, xiii. 6, 7, Lev. xxiii. 6; Num. xxviii. 17) that the feast of Mazzoth was to last only six days instead of seven; but the seventh day is brought into especial prominence as the *azereth* of the feast (see at Lev. xxiii. 36), simply because, in addition to the eating of *mazzoth*, there was to be an entire abstinence from work, and this particular feature might easily have fallen into neglect at the close of the feast. But just as the eating of *mazzoth* for seven days is not abolished by the first clause, so the suspension of work on the first day is not abolished by the second clause, any more than in Ex. xiii. 6 the first day is represented as a working day by the fact that the seventh day is called "a feast to Jehovah."

Vers. 9–12. With regard to the FEAST OF WEEKS (see at Ex. xxiii. 16), it is stated that the time for its observance was to be reckoned from the Passover. Seven weeks shall they count "*from the beginning of the sickle to the corn*," *i.e.* from the time when the sickle began to be applied to the corn, or from the commencement of the corn-harvest. As the corn-harvest was opened with the presentation of the sheaf of first-fruits on the second day of the Passover, this regulation as to time coincides with the rule laid down in Lev. xxiii. 15. "*Thou shalt keep the feast to the Lord thy God according to the measure of the free gift of thy hand, which thou givest as Jehovah thy God blesseth thee.*" The ἁπ. λεγ. מִסַּת is the standing rendering in the Chaldee for דַּי, sufficiency, need ; it probably signifies abundance, from מָסָה = מָסַס, to flow, to overflow, to derive. The idea is this : Israel was to keep this feast with sacrificial gifts, which every one was able to bring, according to the extent to which the Lord had blessed him, and (ver. 11) to rejoice before the Lord at the place where His name dwelt with sacrificial meals, to which the needy were to be invited (cf. xiv. 29), in remembrance of the fact that they also were bondmen in Egypt (cf. xv. 15). The "*free-will offering of the hand*," which the Israelites were to bring with them to this feast, and with which they were to rejoice before the Lord, belonged to the free-will gifts of burnt-offerings, meat-offerings, drink-offerings, and thank-offerings, which might be offered, according to Num. xxix. 39 (cf. Lev. xxiii. 38), at every feast, along with the festal sacrifices enjoined upon the congregation. The latter were binding upon the priests and congregation, and are fully described in Num. xxviii. and xxix., so that there was no necessity for Moses to say anything further with reference to them.

Vers. 13–17. In connection with the FEAST OF TABERNACLES also, he simply enforces the observance of it at the central sanctuary, and exhorts the people to rejoice at this festival, and not only to allow their sons and daughters to participate in this joy, but also the man-servant and maid-servant, and the portionless Levites, strangers, widows, and orphans. After what had already been stated, Moses did not consider it necessary to mention expressly that this festal rejoicing was also to be manifested in joyous sacrificial meals ; it was enough for him to point to the blessing which God had bestowed upon their cultivation of the corn, the olive, and the vine, and upon all the works of their hands, *i.e.* upon their labour generally (vers. 13–15), as there was nothing further to remark after the instructions which had already been given with reference to this feast also (Lev. xxiii. 34–36, 39–43 ; Num. xxix. 12–38).—Vers. 16, 17. In conclusion, the law is repeated, that the men were to appear before the Lord three times a year at the three feasts just mentioned (compare Ex. xxiii. 17 with ver. 15, and chap. xxxiv. 23), with the additional clause, " *at the place which the Lord shall choose*," and the following explanation of the words " not empty :" " *every man according to the gift of his hand, according to the blessing of Jehovah his God, which He hath given thee*," *i.e.* with sacrificial gifts, as much as every one could offer, according to the blessing which he had received from God.

On the Administration of Justice and the Choice of a King.— Chap. xvi. 18–xvii. 20.

Just as in its religious worship the Israelitish nation was to show itself to be the holy nation of Jehovah, so was it in its political relations also. This thought forms the link between the laws already given and those which follow. Civil order—that indispensable condition of the stability and prosperity of nations and states—rests upon a conscientious maintenance of right by means of a well-ordered judicial constitution and an impartial administration of justice.—For the purpose of settling the disputes of the people, Moses had already provided them with judges at Sinai, and had given the judges themselves the necessary instructions for the fulfilment of their duties (Ex. xviii.). This arrangement might suffice as long as the people were united in one camp and had Moses for a leader, who could lay before God any difficult cases that were brought to him, and give an absolute decision with divine authority. But for future times, when Israel would no longer possess a prophet and mediator like Moses, and after the conquest of Canaan would live scattered about in the towns and villages of the whole land, certain modifications and supplementary additions were necessary to adapt this judicial constitution to the altered circumstances of the people. Moses anticipates this want in the following provisions, in which he *first* of all commands the appointment of judges and officials in every town, and gives certain precise injunctions as to their judicial proceedings (chap. xvi. 18–xvii. 7); and *secondly*, appoints a higher judicial court at the place of the sanctuary for the more difficult cases (chap. xvii. 8–13); and *thirdly*, gives them a law for the future with reference to the choice of a king (vers. 14–20).

Chap. xvi. 18–xvii. 7. APPOINTMENT AND INSTRUCTION OF THE JUDGES.—Ver. 18. " *Judges and officers thou shalt appoint thee in all thy gates* (places, see at Ex. xx. 10), *which Jehovah thy God shall give thee, according to thy tribes."* The nation is addressed as a whole, and directed to appoint for itself judges and officers, *i.e.* to choose them, and have them appointed by its rulers, just as was done at Sinai, where the people chose the judges, and Moses inducted into office the persons so chosen (cf. chap. i. 12—18). That the same course was to be adopted in future, is evident from the expression, " throughout thy tribes," *i.e.* according to thy tribes, which points back to chap. i. 13. Election by majorities was unknown to the Mosaic law. The *shoterim*, officers (*lit.* writers, see at Ex. v. 6), who were associated with the judges, according to chap. i. 15, even under the previous arrangement, were not merely messengers and servants of the courts, but secretaries and advisers of the judges, who derived their title from the fact that they had to draw up and keep the genealogical lists, and who are mentioned as already existing in Egypt as overseers of the people and of their work (see at Ex. v. 6 ; and for the different opinions concerning their official position, see *Selden, de Synedriis,* i. pp. 342–3). The new features, which Moses introduces here, consist simply in the fact that every place was to have its own judges and officers, whereas hitherto they had only been appointed for the larger and smaller divisions of the nation, according to their genealogical organization. Moses lays down no rule as to the number of judges and *shoterim* to be appointed in each place, because this would depend upon the number of the inhabitants; and the existing arrangement of judges over tens, hundreds, etc. (Ex. xviii. 21), would still furnish the necessary standard. The statements made by *Josephus* and the *Rabbins* with regard to the number of judges in each place are contradictory, or at all events are founded upon the circumstances of much later times (see my *Archäologie,* ii. pp. 257-8).—These judges were to judge the people with just judgment. The admonition in ver. 19 corresponds to the instructions in Ex. xxiii. 6 and 8. " Respect persons :" as in chap. i. 17. To this there is added, in ver. 20, an emphatic admonition to strive zealously to maintain justice. The repetition of the word justice is emphatic : justice, and nothing but justice, as in Gen. xiv. 10, etc. But in order to give the people and the judges appointed by them a brief practical admonition, as to the things they were more especially to observe in their administration of justice, Moses notices by way of example a few crimes that were deserving of punishment (vers. 21, 22, and chap. xvii. 1), and then proceeds in chap. xvii. 2-7 to describe more fully the judicial proceedings in the case of idolaters. — Ver. 21. *" Thou shalt not plant thee as asherah any wood beside the altar of Jehovah."* נָטַע, to plant, used figuratively, to plant up or erect, as in Eccles. xii. 11, Dan. xi. 25 ; cf. Isa. li. 16. *Asherah,* the symbol of *Astarte* (see at Ex. xxxiv. 13), cannot mean either a green tree or a grove (as *Movers, Relig. der Phönizier,* p. 572, supposes), for the simple reason that in other passages we find the words עָשָׂה, make (1 Kings xiv. 15, xvi. 33 ; 2 Kings xvii. 16, xxi. 3 ; 2 Chron. xxxiii. 3), or הִצִּיב, set up (2 Kings xvii. 10), הֶעֱמִיד, stand up (2 Chron. xxxiii. 19), and בָּנָה, build (1 Kings xiv. 23), used to denote the erection of an *asherah,* not one of which is at all suitable to a tree or grove.　But what is quite decisive is the fact that in 1 Kings xiv. 23, 2 Kings xvii. 10, Jer. xvii. 2, the *asherah* is spoken of as being set up under, or by the side of, the green tree. This idol generally consisted of a wooden column ; and a favourite place for setting it up was by the side of the altars of Baal.—Ver. 22. They were also to abstain from setting up any *mazzebah, i.e.* any memorial stone, or stone pillar dedicated to Baal (see at Ex. xxiii. 24).

Chap. xvii. 1. Not only did the inclination to nature-worship, such as the setting up of the idols of *Ashera* and *Baal,* belong to the crimes which merited punishment, but also a manifest transgression of the laws concerning the worship of Jehovah, such as the offering of an ox or sheep that had some fault, which was an abomination in the sight of Jehovah (see at Lev. xxii. 20 sqq.). *" Any evil thing,"* i.e. any of the faults enumerated in Lev. xxii. 22-24.—Vers. 2–7. If such a case should occur, as that a man or woman transgressed the covenant of the Lord and went after other gods and worshipped them ; when it was made known, the facts were to be carefully inquired into ; and if the charge were substantiated, the criminal was to be led out to the gate and stoned.　On the testimony of two or three witnesses, not of one only, he was to be put to death (see at Num. xxxv. 30) ; and the hand of the witnesses was to be against him first to put him to death, *i.e.* to throw the first stones at him, and all the people were to follow.　With regard to the different kinds of idolatry in ver. 3, see chap. iv. 19. (On ver. 4, see chap. xiii. 15.)　*" Bring him out to thy gates,"* i.e. to one of the gates of the town in which the crime was committed. By the gates we are to understand the open space near the gates, where the judicial proceedings took place (cf. Neh. viii. 1, 3 ; Job xxix. 7), the sentence itself being executed outside the town (cf. chap. xxii. 24 ; Acts vii. 58 ; Heb. xiii. 12), just as it had been outside the camp during the journey through the wilderness (Lev. xxiv. 14; Num. xv. 36), to indicate the exclusion of the criminal from the congregation, and from fellowship with God. The infliction of punishment in vers. 5 sqq. is like that prescribed in chap. xiii. 10, 11, for those who tempted others to idolatry; with this exception, that the testimony of more than one witness was required before the sentence could be executed, and the witnesses were to be the first to lift up their hands against the criminal to stone him, that they might thereby give a practical proof of the truth of their statement, and their own firm conviction that the condemned was deserving of death,—" a rule which would naturally lead to the supposition that no man would come forward as a witness without the fullest certainty or the greatest depravity" (*Schnell, das isr. Recht*).[1] הַמֵּת (ver. 6), the man exposed to death, who was therefore really *ipso facto* already dead. " *So shalt thou put the evil away*," etc. : cf. chap. xiii. 6.

Vers. 8–13. THE HIGHER JUDICIAL COURT AT THE PLACE OF THE SANCTUARY.—Just as the judges appointed at Sinai were to bring to Moses whatever cases were too difficult for them to decide, that he might judge them according to the decision of God (Ex. xviii. 26 and 19); so in the future the judges of the different towns were to bring all difficult cases, which they were unable to decide, before the Levitical priests and judges at the place of the sanctuary, that a final decision might be given there.—Vers. 8 sqq. " *If there is to thee a matter too marvellous for judgment* (נִפְלָא with מִן, too wonderful, incomprehensible, or beyond carrying out, Gen. xviii. 14, *i.e.* too difficult to give a judicial decision upon), *between blood and blood, plea and plea, stroke and stroke* (i.e. too hard for you to decide according to what legal provisions a fatal blow, or dispute on some civil matter, or a bodily injury, is to be settled), *disputes in thy gates* (a loosely arranged apposition in this sense, disputes of different kinds, such as shall arise in thy towns); *arise, and get thee to the place which Jehovah thy God shall choose; and go to the Levitical priests and the judge that shall be in those days, and in-*

---

[1] " He assigned this part to the witnesses, chiefly because there are so many whose tongue is so slippery, not to say good for nothing, that they would boldly strangle a man with their words, when they would not dare to touch him with one of their fingers. It was the best remedy, therefore, that could be tried for restraining such levity, to refuse to admit the testimony of any man who was not ready to execute judgment with his own hand" (*Calvin*).

quire." Israel is addressed here as a nation, but the words are not
to be supposed to be directed " first of all to the local courts
(chap. xvi. 18), and lastly to the contending parties" (*Knobel*), nor
" directly to the parties to the suit" (*Schultz*), but simply to the persons whose duty it was to administer justice in the nation, *i.e.* to
the regular judges in the different towns and districts of the land.
This is evident from the general fact, that the Mosaic law never
recognises any appeal to higher courts by the different parties to a
lawsuit, and that in this case also it is not assumed, since all that is
enjoined is, that if the matter should be too difficult for the local
judges to decide, they themselves were to carry it to the superior
court. As *Oehler* has quite correctly observed in *Herzog's* Cyclopædia, " this superior court was not a court of appeal ; for it did
not adjudicate after the local court had already given a verdict, but
in cases in which the latter would not trust itself to give a verdict
at all." And this is more especially evident from what is stated in
ver. 10, with regard to the decisions of the superior court, namely,
that they were to do whatever the superior judges taught, without
deviating to the right hand or to the left. This is unquestionably
far more applicable to the judges of the different towns, who were
to carry out exactly the sentence of the higher tribunal, than to the
parties to the suit, inasmuch as the latter, at all events those who
were condemned for blood (*i.e.* for murder), could not possibly be
in a position to alter the decision of the court at pleasure, since it
did not rest with them, but with the authorities of their town, to
carry out the sentence.

Moses did not directly institute a superior tribunal at the place
of the sanctuary on this occasion, but rather assumed its existence ;
not however its existence at that time (as *Riehm* and other modern
critics suppose), but its establishment and existence in the future.
Just as he gives no minute directions concerning the organization
of the different local courts, but leaves this to the natural development of the judicial institutions already in existence, so he also
restricts himself, so far as the higher court is concerned, to general
allusions, which might serve as a guide to the national rulers of a
future day, to organize it according to the existing models. He had
no disorganized mob before him, but a well-ordered nation, already
in possession of civil institutions, with fruitful germs for further
expansion and organization. In addition to its civil classification
into tribes, families, fathers' houses, and family groups, which possessed at once their rulers in their own heads, the nation had

received in the priesthood, with the high priest at the head, and the Levites as their assistants, a spiritual class, which mediated between the congregation and the Lord, and not only kept up the knowledge of right in the people as the guardian of the law, but by virtue of the high priest's office was able to lay the rights of the people before God, and in difficult cases could ask for His decision. Moreover, a leader had already been appointed for the nation, for the time immediately succeeding Moses' death ; and in this nomination of Joshua, a pledge had been given that the Lord would never leave it without a supreme ruler of its civil affairs, but, along with the high priest, would also appoint a judge at the place of the central sanctuary, who would administer justice in the highest court in association with the priests. On the ground of these facts, it was enough for the future to mention the Levitical priests and the judge who would be at the place of the sanctuary, as constituting the court by which the difficult questions were to be decided.[1] For instance, the words themselves show distinctly enough, that by " the judge " we are not to understand the high priest, but the temporal judge or president of the superior court ; and it is evident from the singular, " *the priest that standeth to minister there before the Lord*" (ver. 12), that the high priest is included among the priests. The expression " *the priests the Levites* " (Levitical priests), which also occurs in ver. 18, chap. xviii. 1, xxi. 5, xxiv. 8, xxvii. 9, xxxi. 9, instead of " sons of Aaron," which we find in the middle books, is quite in harmony with the time and character of the book before us. As long as Aaron was living with his sons, the priesthood consisted only of himself and his sons, that is to say, of one family. Hence all the instructions in the middle books are addressed to them, and for the most part to Aaron personally (*vid.* Ex. xxviii. and xxix. ; Lev. viii.–x. ; Num. xviii., etc.). This was all changed when Aaron died ; henceforth the priesthood consisted simply of the descendants of Aaron and his sons, who were no longer one family, but formed a distinct class in the nation, the legitimacy of which arose from its connection with the tribe of Levi, to which Aaron himself had belonged. It was evidently more appropriate, therefore, to describe them as sons of

---

The simple fact, that the judicial court at the place of the national sanctuary is described in such general terms, furnishes a convincing proof that we have here the words of Moses, and not those of some later prophetic writer who had copied the superior court at Jerusalem of the times of the kings, as *Riehm* and the critics assume.

Levi than as sons of Aaron, which had been the title formerly given to the priests, with the exception of the high priest, viz. Aaron himself.—In connection with the superior court, however, the priests are introduced rather as knowing and teaching the law (Lev. x. 11), than as actual judges. For this reason appeal was to be made not only to them, but also to the judge, whose duty it was in any case to make the judicial inquiry and pronounce the sentence.—The object of the verb "*inquire*" (ver. 9) follows after "they shall show thee," viz. "*the word of right*," the judicial sentence which is sought (2 Chron. xix. 6).—Vers. 10, 11. They shall do "*according to the sound of the word which they utter*" (follow their decision exactly), and that "*according to the sound of the law which they teach*," and "*according to the right which they shall speak*." The sentence was to be founded upon the *Thorah*, upon the law which the priests had to teach.—Ver. 12. No one was to resist in pride, to refuse to listen to the priest or to the judge. Resistance to the priest took place when any one was dissatisfied with his interpretation of the law ; to the judge, when any one was discontented with the sentence that was passed on the basis of the law. Such refractory conduct was to be punished with death, as rebellion against God, in whose name the right had been spoken (chap. i. 17). (On ver. 13, see chap. xiii. 12.)

Vers. 14–20. Choice and Right of the King.—Vers. 14, 15. If Israel, when dwelling in the land which was given it by the Lord for a possession, should wish to appoint a king, like all the nations round about, it was to appoint the man whom Jehovah its God should choose, and that from among its brethren, *i.e.* from its own people, not a foreigner or non-Israelite. The earthly kingdom in Israel was not opposed to the theocracy, *i.e.* to the rule of Jehovah as king over the people of His possession, provided no one was made king but the person whom Jehovah should choose. The appointment of a king is not *commanded*, like the institution of judges (chap. xvi. 18), because Israel could exist under the government of Jehovah, even without an earthly king ; it is simply *permitted*, in case the need should arise for a regal government. There was no necessity to describe more minutely the course to be adopted, as the people possessed the natural provision for the administration of their national affairs in their well-organized tribes, by whom this point could be decided. Moses also omits to state more particularly in what way Jehovah would make known the choice of the king to be appointed. The congregation, no doubt, possessed one means of asking the will of the Lord in the Urim and Thummim of the high priest, provided the Lord did not reveal His will in a different manner, namely through a prophet, as He did in the election of Saul and David (1 Sam. viii., ix., and xvi.). The command not to choose a foreigner, acknowledged the right of the nation to choose. Consequently the choice on the part of the Lord may have consisted simply in His pointing out to the people, in a very evident manner, the person they were to elect, or in His confirming the choice by word and act, as in accordance with His will.—Three rules are laid down for the king himself in vers. 16-20. In the *first* place, he was not to keep many horses, or lead back the people to Egypt, to multiply horses, because Jehovah had forbidden the people to return thither by that way. The notion of modern critics, that there is an allusion in this prohibition to the constitution of the kingdom under Solomon, is so far from having any foundation, that the reason assigned—namely, the fear lest the king should lead back the people to Egypt from his love of horses, " to the end that he should multiply horses"—really precludes the time of Solomon, inasmuch as the time had then long gone by when any thought could have been entertained of leading back the people to Egypt. But such a reason would be quite in its place in Moses' time, and only then, " when it would not seem impossible to reunite the broken band, and when the people were ready to express their longing, and even their intention, to return to Egypt on the very slightest occasion; whereas the reason assigned for the prohibition might have furnished Solomon with an excuse for regarding the prohibition itself as merely a temporary one, which was no longer binding" (*Oehler* in *Herzog's Cyclopædia: vid.* Hengstenberg's Dissertations).[1]

The *second* admonition also, that the king was not to take to himself many wives, and turn away his heart (*sc.* from the Lord), nor

[1] When *Riehm* objects to this, that if such a prohibition had been unnecessary in a future age, in which the people had reached the full consciousness of its national independence, and every thought of the possibility of a reunion with the Egyptians had disappeared, Moses would never have issued it, since he must have foreseen the national independence of the people ; the force of this objection rests simply upon his confounding foreseeing with assuming, and upon a thoroughly mistaken view of the prophet's vision of the future. Even if Moses, as " a great prophet," did foresee the future national independence of Israel, he had also such experience of the fickle character of the people, that he could not regard the thought of returning to Egypt as absolutely an impossible one, even after the conquest of Canaan, or reject it as inconceivable. Moreover, the

greatly multiply to himself silver and gold, can be explained without the hypothesis that there is an allusion to Solomon's reign, although this king did transgress both commands (1 Kings x. 14 sqq., xi. 1 sqq.). A richly furnished harem, and the accumulation of silver and gold, were inseparably connected with the luxury of Oriental monarchs generally; so that the fear was a very natural one, that the future king of Israel might follow the general customs of the heathen in these respects.—Vers. 18 sqq. And *thirdly*, Instead of hanging his heart upon these earthly things, when he sat upon his royal throne he was to have a copy of the law written out by the Levitical priests, that he might keep the law by him, and read therein all the days of his life. כָּתַב does not involve writing with his own hand (*Philo*), but simply having it written. מִשְׁנֵה הַתּוֹרָה הַזֹּאת does not mean τὸ δευτερονόμιον τοῦτο (LXX.), " this repetition of the law," as הַזֹּאת cannot stand for הַזֶּה ; but a copy of this law, as most of the Rabbins correctly explain it in accordance with the Chaldee version, though they make *mishneh* to signify *duplum*, two copies (see *Hävernick*, Introduction).—Every copy of a book is really a repetition of it. " *From before the priests*," *i.e.* of the law which lies before the priests or is kept by them. The object of the daily reading in the law (vers. 19b and 20) was " *to learn the fear of the Lord, and to keep His commandments*" (cf. v. 25, vi. 2, xiv. 23),

prophetic foresight of Moses was not, as *Riehm* imagines it, a foreknowledge of all the separate points in the historical development of the nation, much less a foreknowledge of the thoughts and desires of the heart, which might arise in the course of time amidst the changes that would take place in the nation. A foresight of the development of Israel into national independence, so far as we may attribute it to Moses as a prophet, was founded not upon the character of the people, but upon the divine choice and destination of Israel, which by no means precluded the possibility of their desiring to return to Egypt, even at some future time, since God Himself had threatened the people with dispersion among the heathen as the punishment for continued transgression of His covenant, and yet, notwithstanding this dispersion, had predicted the ultimate realization of His covenant of grace. And when *Riehm* still further observes, that the taste for horses, which lay at the foundation of this fear, evidently points to a later time, when the old repugnance to cavalry which existed in the nation in the days of the judges, and even under David, had disappeared ; this supposed repugnance to cavalry is a fiction of the critic himself, without any historical foundation. For nothing more is related in the history, than that before the time of Solomon the Israelites had not cultivated the rearing of horses, and that David only kept 100 of the war-horses taken from the Syrians for himself, and had the others put to death (2 Sam. viii. 4). And so long as horses were neither reared nor possessed by the Israelites, there can be no ground for speaking of the old repugnance to cavalry. On the other hand, the impossibility of tracing this that his heart might not be lifted up above his brethren, that he might not become proud (chap. viii. 14), and might not turn aside from the commandments to the right hand or to the left, that he and his descendants might live long upon the throne.

Rights of the Priests, the Levites, and the Prophets.—Chap. xviii.

In addition to the judicial order and the future king, it was necessary that the position of the priests and Levites, whose duties and rights had been regulated by previous laws, should at least be mentioned briefly and finally established (vers. 1–8), and also that the prophetic order should be fully accredited by the side of the other state authorities, and its operations regulated by a definite law (vers. 9–22).

Vers. 1–8. The Rights of the Priests and Levites.— With reference to these, Moses repeats *verbatim* from Num. xviii. 20, 23, 24, the essential part of the rule laid down in Num. xviii. : " *The priests the Levites, the whole tribe of Levi, shall have no part nor inheritance with Israel.*" " All the tribe of Levi " includes the priests and Levites. They were to eat the " firings of Jehovah and His inheritance," as described in detail in Num. xviii. The inherit- ance of Jehovah consisted of the holy gifts as well as the sacrifices,

prohibition to the historical circumstances of the time of Solomon, or even a later age, is manifest in the desperate subterfuge to which *Riehm* has recourse, when he connects this passage with the threat in chap. xxviii. 68, that if all the punishments suspended over them should be ineffectual, God would carry them back in ships to Egypt, and that they should there be sold to their enemies as men-servants and maid-servants, and then discovers a proof in this, that the Egyptian king Psammetichus, who sought out foreign soldiers and employed them, had left king Manasseh some horses, solely on the condition that he sent him some Israelitish infantry, and placed them at his disposal. But this is not expounding Scripture ; it is putting hypotheses into it. As *Oehler* has already observed, this hypothesis has no foundation whatever in the Old Testament, nor (we may add) in the accounts of Herodotus and Diodorus Siculus concerning Psammetichus. According to *Diod.* (i. 66), Psammetichus hired soldiers from Arabia, Caria, and Ionia ; and according to *Herodotus* (i. 152), he hired Ionians and Carians armed with brass, that he might conquer his rival kings with their assistance. But neither of these historians says anything at all about Israelitish infantry. And even if it were conceivable that any king of Israel or Judah could carry on such traffic in men, as to sell his own subjects to the Egyptians for horses, it is very certain that the prophets, who condemned every alliance with foreign kings, and were not silent with regard to Manasseh's idolatry, would not have passed over such an abomination as this without remark or without reproof.

i.e. the tithes, firstlings, and first-fruits. Moses felt it to be superfluous to enumerate these gifts one by one from the previous laws, and
also to describe the mode of their application, or define how much
belonged to the priests and how much to the Levites. However
true it may be that the author assigns all these gifts to the Levites
generally, the conclusion drawn from this, viz. that he was not
acquainted with any distinction between priests and Levites, but
placed the Levites entirely on a par with the priests, is quite a false
one. For, apart from the evident distinction between the priests and
Levites in ver. 1, where there would be no meaning in the clause,
" all the tribe of Levi," if the Levites were identical with the
priests, the distinction is recognised and asserted as clearly as possible in what follows, when a portion of the slain-offerings is allotted
to the priests in vers. 3–5, whilst in vers. 6–8 the Levite is allowed
to join in eating the altar gifts, if he come to the place of the sanctuary and perform service there. The repetition in ver. 2 is an
emphatic confirmation : " *As He hath said unto them:*" as in chap.
x. 9.—Vers. 3–5. " *This shall be the right of the priests on the part
of the people, on the part of those who slaughter slain-offerings, whether
ox or sheep ; he* (the offerer) *shall give the priest the shoulder, the
cheek, and the stomach.*" הַזְּרֹעַ, the shoulder, *i.e.* the front leg; see
Num. vi. 19. הַקֵּבָה, the rough stomach, τὸ ἤνυστρον (LXX.), *i.e.*
the fourth stomach of ruminant animals, in which the digestion of
the food is completed ; Lat. *omasus* or *abomasus*, though the Vulgate has *ventriculus* here. On the choice of these three pieces in
particular, *Münster* and *Fagius* observe that " the sheep possesses
three principal parts, the head, the feet, and the trunk ; and of each
of these some portion was to be given to the priest who officiated" (?).
" Of each of these three principal parts of the animal," says *Schultz*,
" some valuable piece was to be presented : the shoulder at least,
and the stomach, which was regarded as particularly fat, are seen at
once to have been especially good." That this arrangement is not at
variance with the command in Lev. vii. 32 sqq., to give the wave-
breast and heave-leg of the peace-offerings to the Lord for the
priests, but simply enjoins a further gift to the priests on the part
of the people, in addition to those portions which were to be given
to the Lord for His servants, is sufficiently evident from the context, since the heave-leg and wave-breast belonged to the firings of
Jehovah mentioned in ver. 1, which the priests had received as an
inheritance from the Lord, that is to say, to the *tenuphoth* of the
children of Israel, which the priests might eat with their sons and

daughters, though only with such members of their house as were levitically clean (Num. xviii. 11); and also from the words of the present command, viz. that the portions mentioned were to be a right of the priests *on the part of the people*, on the part of those who slaughtered slain-offerings, *i.e.* to be paid to the priest as a right that was due to him on the part of the people. מִשְׁפָּט was what the priest could justly claim. This right was probably accorded to the priests as a compensation for the falling off which would take place in their incomes in consequence of the repeal of the law that every animal was to be slaughtered at the sanctuary as a sacrifice (Lev. xvii.; *vid.* chap. xii. 15 sqq.).

The only thing that admits of dispute is, whether this gift was to be presented from every animal that was slaughtered at home for private use, or only from those which were slaughtered for sacrificial meals, and therefore at the place of the sanctuary. Against the former view, for which appeal is made to *Philo, Josephus* (Ant. iv. 4, 4), and the Talmud, we may adduce not only " the difficulty of carrying out such a plan" (was every Israelite who slaughtered an ox, a sheep, or a goat to carry the pieces mentioned to the priests' town, which might be many miles away, or were the priests to appoint persons to collect them?), but the general use of the words זֶבַח זָבַח. The noun זֶבַח always signifies either slaughtering for a sacrificial meal or a slain sacrifice, and the verb זָבַח is never applied to ordinary slaughtering (for which שָׁחַט is the verb used), except in chap. xii. 15 and 21 in connection with the repeal of the law that every slaughtering was to be a זֶבַח שְׁלָמִים (Lev. xvii. 5); and there the use of the word זֶבַח, instead of שָׁחַט, may be accounted for from the allusion to this particular law. At the same time, the Jewish tradition is probably right, when it understands by the זִבְחֵי הַזֶּבַח in this verse, κατ' οἶκον θύειν εὐωχίας ἕνεκα (*Josephus*), or ἔξω τοῦ βωμοῦ θυομένοις ἕνεκα κρεωφαγίας (*Philo*), or, as in the *Mishnah Chol.* (x. 1), refers the gift prescribed in this passage to the חולין, *profana*, and not to the מוקדשין, *consecrata*, that is to say, places it in the same category with the first-fruits, the tithe of tithes, and other less holy gifts, which might be consumed outside the court of the temple and the holy city (compare *Reland, Antiqq. ss.* P. ii. c. 4, § 11, with P. ii. c. 8, § 10). In all probability, the reference is to the slaughtering of oxen, sheep, or goats which were not intended for *shelamim* in the more limited sense, *i.e.* for one of the three species of peace-offerings (Lev. vii. 15, 16), but for festal meals in the broader sense, which were held in connection with the sacrificial meals prepared from the *shelamim*. For it is evident that the meals held by the people at the annual feasts when they had to appear before the Lord were not all *shelamin* meals, but that other festal meals were held in connection with these, in which the priests and Levites were to share, from the laws laid down with reference to the so-called second tithe, which could not only be turned into money by those who lived at a great distance from the sanctuary, such money to be applied to the purchase of the things required for the sacrificial meals at the place of the sanctuary, but which might also be appropriated every third year to the preparation of love-feasts for the poor in the different towns of the land (chap. xiv. 22–29). For in this case the animals were not slaughtered or sacrificed as *shelamim*, at all events not in the latter instance, because the slaughtering did not take place at the sanctuary. If therefore we restrict the gift prescribed here to the slaughtering of oxen and sheep or goats for such sacrificial meals in the wider sense, not only are the difficulties connected with the execution of this command removed, but also the objection, which arises out of the general use of the expression זֶבַח זָבַח, to the application of this expression to every slaughtering that took place for domestic use. And beside this, the passage in 1 Sam. ii. 13–16, to which *Calvin* calls attention, furnishes a historical proof that the priests could claim a portion of the flesh of the slain-offerings in addition to the heave-leg and wave-breast, since it is there charged as a sin on the part of the sons of Eli, not only that they took out of the cauldrons as much of the flesh which was boiling as they could take up with three-pronged forks, but that before the fat was burned upon the altar they asked for the pieces which belonged to the priest, to be given to them not cooked, but raw. From this *Michaelis* has drawn the correct conclusion, that even at that time the priests had a right to claim that, in addition to the portions of the sacrifices appointed by Moses in Lev. vii. 34, a further portion of the thank-offerings should be given to them; though he does not regard the passage as referring to the law before us, since he supposes this to relate to every slaughtered animal which was not placed upon the altar.

In ver. 4, Moses repeats the law concerning the first-fruits in Num. xviii. 12, 13 (cf. Ex. xxii. 28), for the purpose of extending it to the first produce of the sheep-shearing.—Ver. 5. The reason for the right accorded to the priests was the choice of them for the office of standing " to minister in the name of Jehovah," *sc.* for all the tribes. " *In the name of Jehovah*," not merely by the appointment, but also in the power of the Lord, as mediators of His grace. The words " *he and his sons* " point back quite to the Mosaic times, in which Aaron and his sons held the priest's office.—Vers. 6-8. As the priests were to be remembered for their service on the part of the people (vers. 3–5), so the Levite also, who came from one of the towns of the land with all the desire of his soul to the place of the sanctuary, to minister there in the name of the Lord, was to eat a similar portion to all his Levitical brethren who stood there in service before the Lord. The verb גּוּר (sojourned) does not pre-suppose that the Levites were houseless, but simply that they had no hereditary possession in the land as the other tribes had, and merely lived like sojourners among the Israelites in the towns which were given up to them by the other tribes (see at chap. xii. 12). " *All his brethren the Levites* " are the priests and those Levites who officiated at the sanctuary as assistants to the priests. It is assumed, therefore, that only a part of the Levites were engaged at the sanctuary, and the others lived in their towns. The apodosis follows in ver. 8, " *part like part shall they eat,* " *sc.* the new-comer and those already there. The former was to have the same share to eat as the latter, and to be maintained from the revenues of the sanctuary. These revenues are supposed to be already apportioned by the previous laws, so that they by no means abolish the distinc-tion between priests and Levites. We are not to think of those portions of the sacrifices and first-fruits only which fell to the lot of the priests, nor of the tithe alone, or of the property which flowed into the sanctuary through vows or free-will offerings, or in any other way, and was kept in the treasury and storehouse, but of tithes, sacrificial portions, and free-will offerings generally, which were not set apart exclusively for the priests. לְבַד מִמְכָּרָיו וגו', " *beside his sold with the fathers,* " *i.e.* independently of what he receives from the sale of his patrimony. מִמְכָּר, the sale, then the thing sold, and the price or produce of what is sold, like מֶכֶר in Num. xx. 19. לְבַד is unusual without מִן, and *Knobel* would read מִמְּכָרָיו, from מְכָרָיו and מִן, in consequence. עַל הָאָבוֹת stands for עַל בֵּית־אָבוֹת (see at Ex. vi. 25; κατὰ τὴν πατρίαν, LXX.), according to or with the fathers' houses, *i.e.* the produce of the property which he possesses according to his family descent, or which is with his kindred. Whether עַל in this passage signifies " according to the measure of," or " with," in the sense of keeping or administering, cannot be decided. As the law in Lev. xxv. 33, 34, simply forbids the sale of the pasture grounds belonging to the Levites, but permits the sale

of their houses, a Levite who went to the sanctuary might either
let his property in the Levitical town, and draw the yearly rent, or
sell the house which belonged to him there. In any case, these
words furnish a convincing proof that there is no foundation for
the assertion that the book of Deuteronomy assumes or affirms that
the Levites were absolutely without possessions.

Vers. 9–22. THE GIFT OF PROPHECY.—The Levitical priests,
as the stated guardians and promoters of the law, had to conduct
all the affairs of Israel with the Lord, not only instructing the
people out of the law concerning the will of God, but sustaining
and promoting the living fellowship with the Lord both of individuals and of the whole congregation, by the offering of sacrifices
and service at the altar. But if the covenant fellowship with
Himself and His grace, in which Jehovah had placed Israel as His
people of possession, was to be manifested and preserved as a living
reality amidst all changes in the political development of the nation
and in the circumstances of private life, it would not do for the
revelations from God to cease with the giving of the law and the
death of Moses. For, as *Schultz* observes, " however the revelation
of the law might aim at completeness, and even have regard to the
more remote circumstances of the future, as, for example, where the
king is referred to ; yet in the transition from extraordinary circumstances into a more settled condition, which it foretells in chap. xvii.
14, and which actually took place under Samuel when the nation
grew older (chap. iv. 25), and in the decline and apostasy which
certainly awaited it according to chap. xxxi. 16–29, when false
prophets should arise, by whom they were in danger of being led
astray (chap. xiii. 2 and xviii. 20), as well as in the restoration
which would follow after the infliction of punishment (chap. iv.
29, 30, xxx. 1 sqq) ; in all these great changes which awaited Israel
from inward necessity, the revelation of the will of the Lord which
they possessed in the law would nevertheless be insufficient." The
priesthood, with its ordinances, would not suffice for that. As the
promise of direct communications from God through the Urim and
Thummim of the high priest was restricted to the single circumstance of the right of the whole congregation being endangered,
and did not extend to the satisfaction of the religious necessities
of individuals, it could afford no godly satisfaction to that desire
for supernatural knowledge which arose at times in the hearts of
individuals, and for which the heathen oracles made such ample

provision in ungodly ways. If Israel therefore was to be preserved in faithfulness towards God, and attain the end of its calling as the congregation of the Lord, it was necessary that the Lord should make known His counsel and will at the proper time through the medium of prophets, and bestow upon it in sure prophetic words what the heathen nations endeavoured to discover and secure by means of augury and soothsaying. This is the point of view from which Moses promises the sending of prophets in vers. 15–18, and lays down in vers. 19–22 the criteria for distinguishing between true and false prophets, as we may clearly see from the fact that in vers. 9–14 he introduces this promise with a warning against resorting to heathen augury, soothsaying, and witchcraft.

Vers. 9 sqq. When Israel came into the land of Canaan, it was "*not to learn to do like the abominations of these nations*" (the Canaanites or heathen). There was not to be found in it any who caused his son or his daughter to pass through the fire, *i.e.* any worshipper of Moloch (see at Lev. xviii. 21), or one who practised soothsaying (see at Num. xxiii. 23), or a wizard (see at Lev. xix. 26), or a snake-charmer (see at Lev. xix. 26), or a conjurer, or one who pronounced a ban (חֹבֵר חֶבֶר, probably referring to the custom of binding or banning by magical knots), a necromancer and wise man (see at Lev. xix. 31), or one who asked the dead, *i.e.* who sought oracles from the dead. Moses groups together all the words which the language contained for the different modes of exploring the future and discovering the will of God, for the purpose of forbidding every description of soothsaying, and places the prohibition of Moloch-worship at the head, to show the inward connection between soothsaying and idolatry, possibly because februation, or passing children through the fire in the worship of Moloch, was more intimately connected with soothsaying and magic than any other description of idolatry.—Ver. 12. Whoever did this was an abomination to the Lord, and it was because of this abomination that He rooted out the Canaanites before Israel (cf. Lev. xviii. 24 sqq.).—Vers. 13 and 14. Israel, on the other hand, was to be *blameless* with Jehovah (עָם, in its intercourse with the Lord). Though the heathen whom they exterminated before them hearkened to conjurers and soothsayers, Jehovah their God had not allowed anything of the kind to them. וְאַתָּה is placed first as a nominative absolute, for the sake of emphasis: "*but thou, so far as thou art concerned, not so.*" כֵּן, *thus*, just so, such things (cf. Ex. x. 14). נָתַן, to grant, to allow (as in Gen. xx. 6, etc.).—Ver. 15. "*A*

*prophet out of the midst of thee, out of thy brethren, as I am, will
Jehovah thy God raise up to thee; to him shall ye hearken.*" When
Moses thus attaches to the prohibition against hearkening to soothsayers and practising soothsaying, the promise that Jehovah would
raise up a prophet, etc., and contrasts what the Lord would do for
His people with what He did not allow, it is perfectly evident from
this simple connection alone, apart from the further context of the
passage, in which Moses treats of the temporal and spiritual rulers
of Israel (chap. xvii. and xviii.), that the promise neither relates to
one particular prophet, nor directly and exclusively to the Messiah,
but treats of the sending of prophets generally. And this is also
confirmed by what follows with reference to true and false prophets,
which presupposes the rise of a plurality of prophets, and shows
most incontrovertibly that it is not one prophet only, nor the Messiah
exclusively, who is promised here. It by no means follows from the
use of the singular, " a prophet," that Moses is speaking of one
particular prophet only ; but the idea expressed is this, that at any
time when the people stood in need of a mediator with God like
Moses, God would invariably send a prophet. The words, " out of
the midst of thee, of thy brethren," imply that there would be no
necessity for Israel to turn to heathen soothsayers or prophets, but
that it would find the men within itself who would make known the
word of the Lord. The expression, " like unto me," is explained by
what follows in vers. 16–18 with regard to the circumstances, under
which the Lord had given the promise that He would send a
prophet. It was at Sinai ; when the people were filled with mortal
alarm, after hearing the ten words which God addressed to them out
of the fire, and entreated Moses to act as mediator between the Lord
and themselves, that God might not speak directly to them any more.
At that time the Lord gave the promise that He would raise up a
prophet, and put His words into his mouth, that he might speak to
the people all that the Lord commanded (cf. chap. v. 20 sqq.).
The promised prophet, therefore, was to resemble Moses in this
respect, that he would act as mediator between Jehovah and the
people, and make known the words or the will of the Lord. Consequently the meaning contained in the expression " like unto me" was
not that the future prophet would resemble Moses in all respects,—
a meaning which has been introduced into it through an unwarrantable use of Num. xii. 6–8, Deut. xxxiv. 10, and Heb. iii. 2, 5, for
the purpose of proving the direct application of the promise to the
Messiah alone, to the exclusion of the prophets of the Old Testament.

If the resemblance of the future prophet to Moses, expressed in the words " like unto me," be understood as indicating the precise form in which God revealed Himself to Moses, speaking with him mouth to mouth, and not in a dream or vision, a discrepancy is introduced between this expression and the words which follow in ver. 18, " I will put My words in his mouth ; " since this expresses not the particular mode in which Moses received the revelations from God, in contrast with the rest of the prophets, but simply that form of divine communication or inspiration which was common to all the prophets (*vid.* Jer. i. 9, v. 14).

But whilst we are obliged to give up the direct and exclusive reference of this promise to the Messiah, which was the prevailing opinion in the early Church, and has been revived by *Kurtz, Auberlen,* and *Tholuck,* as not in accordance with the context or the words themselves, we cannot, on the other hand, agree with *v. Hofmann, Baur,* and *Knobel,* in restricting the passage to the Old Testament prophets, to the exclusion of the Messiah. There is no warrant for this limitation of the word " prophet," since the expectation of the Messiah was not unknown to Moses and the Israel of his time, but was actually expressed in the promise of the seed of the woman, and Jacob's prophecy concerning *Shiloh ;* so that *O. v. Gerlach* is perfectly right in observing, that " this is a prediction of Christ as the true Prophet, precisely like that of the seed of the woman in Gen. iii. 15." The occasion, also, on which Moses received the promise of the " prophet" from the Lord, which he here communicated to the people,—namely, when the people desired a mediator between themselves and the Lord at Sinai, and this desire on their part was pleasing to the Lord,—shows that the promise should be understood in the full sense of the words, without any limitation whatever ; that is to say, that Christ, in whom the prophetic character culminated and was completed, is to be included. Even *Ewald* admits, that " the prophet like unto Moses, whom God would raise up out of Israel and for Israel, can only be the true prophet generally ;" and *Baur* also allows, that " historical exposition will not mistake the anticipatory reference of this expression to Christ, which is involved in the expectation that, in the future completion of the plan of salvation, the prophetic gift would form an essential element." And lastly, the comparison instituted between the promised prophet and Moses, compels us to regard the words as referring to the Messiah. The words, " like unto me," " like unto thee," no more warrant us in excluding the Messiah on the one hand, than in excluding the Old Testament prophets on the other, since it is unquestionably affirmed that the prophet of the future would be as perfectly equal to his calling as Moses was to his,[1]—that He would carry out the mediation between the Lord and the people in the manner and the power of Moses. In this respect not one of the Old Testament prophets was fully equal to Moses, as is distinctly stated in chap. xxxiv. 10. All the prophets of the Old Testament stood within the sphere of the economy of the law, which was founded through the mediatorial office of Moses ; and even in their predictions of the future, they simply continued to build upon the foundation which was laid by Moses, and therefore prophesied of the coming of the servant of the Lord, who, as the Prophet of all prophets, would restore Jacob, and carry out the law and right of the Lord to the nations, even to the end of the world (Isa. xlii., xlix., l., lxi.). This prophecy, therefore, is very properly referred to Jesus Christ in the New Testament, as having been fulfilled in Him. Not only had Philip this passage in his mind when he said to Nathanael, "We have found Him of whom Moses in the law did write, Jesus of Nazareth," whilst Stephen saw the promise of the prophet like unto Moses fulfilled in Christ (Acts vii. 37) ; but Peter also expressly quotes it in Acts iii. 22, 23, as referring to Christ ; and even the Lord applies it to Himself in John v. 45–47, when He says to the Jews, " Moses, in whom ye trust, will accuse you; for if ye believed Moses, ye would also believe Me : for Moses wrote of Me." In John xii. 48–50, again, the reference to vers. 18 and 19 of this chapter is quite unmistakeable ; and in the words, " hear ye Him," which were uttered from the cloud at the transfiguration of Jesus (Matt. xvii. 5), the expression in ver. 15, " unto Him shall ye hearken," is used *verbatim* with reference to Christ. Even the Samaritans founded their expectation of the Messiah (John iv. 25) upon these words of Moses.[2]

Vers. 16–22. With this assurance the Lord had fully granted the request of the people, " *according to all that thou desiredst of the Lord thy God ;*" and Israel, therefore, was all the more bound to hearken to the prophets, whom God would raise up from the midst of itself, and not to resort to heathen soothsayers. (On the

---

[1] Let any one paraphrase the passage thus : " A prophet inferior indeed to me, but yet the channel of divine revelations," and he will soon feel how unsuitable it is" (*Hengstenberg*).

[2] On the history of the exposition of this passage, see *Hengstenberg's* Christology.

fact itself, comp. chap. v. 20 sqq. with Ex. xx. 15-17.) *" In the day of the assembly,"* as in chap. ix. 10, x. 4.—The instructions as to their behaviour towards the prophets are given by Moses (vers. 19, 20) in the name of the Lord, for the purpose of enforcing obedience with all the greater emphasis. Whoever did not hearken to the words of the prophet who spoke in the name of the Lord, of him the Lord would require it, *i.e.* visit the disobedience with punishment (cf. Ps. x. 4, 13). On the other hand, the prophet who spoke in the name of the Lord what the Lord had not commanded him, *i.e.* proclaimed the thoughts of his own heart as divine revelations (cf. Num. xvi. 28), should die, like the prophet who spoke in the name of other gods. With וּמֵת, the predicate is introduced in the form of an apodosis.—Vers. 21, 22. The false prophet was to be discovered by the fact, that the word proclaimed by him did not follow or come to pass, *i.e.* that his prophecy was not fulfilled. Of him they were not to be afraid. By this injunction the occurrence of what had been predicted is made the criterion of true prophecy, and not signs and wonders, which false prophets could also perform (cf. chap. xiii. 2 sqq.).

Laws concerning the Cities of Refuge, the Sacredness of Landmarks, and the Punishment of False Witnesses.—Chap. xix.

After laying down the most important features in the national constitution, Moses glances at the manifold circumstances of civil and family life, and notices in this and the two following chapters the different ways in which the lives of individuals might be endangered, for the purpose of awakening in the minds of the people a holy reverence for human life.

Vers. 1-13. The laws concerning the CITIES OF REFUGE FOR UNINTENTIONAL MANSLAYERS are not a mere repetition of the laws given in Num. xxxv. 9-34, but rather an admonition to carry out those laws, with special reference to the future extension of the boundaries of the land.—Vers. 1-7. As Moses had already set apart the cities of refuge for the land on the east of the Jordan (chap. iv. 41 sqq.), he is speaking here simply of the land on the west, which Israel was to take possession of before long; and supplements the instructions in Num. xxxv. 14, with directions to maintain the roads to the cities of refuge which were to be set apart in Canaan itself, and to divide the land into three parts, viz. for the purpose of setting apart these cities, so that one city might be chosen for the purpose in every third of the land. For further remarks upon this point, as well as with regard to the use of these cities (vers. 4-7), see at Num. xxxv. 11 sqq.—In vers. 8-10 there follow the fresh instructions, that if the Lord should extend the borders of Israel, according to His promise given to the patriarchs, and should give them the whole land from the Nile to the Euphrates, according to Gen. xv. 18, they were to add three other cities of refuge to these three, for the purpose of preventing the shedding of innocent blood. The three new cities of refuge cannot be the three appointed in Num. xxxv. 14 for the land on this side of the Jordan, nor the three mentioned in ver. 7 on the other side of Jordan, as *Knobel* and others suppose. Nor can we adopt *Hengstenberg's* view, that the three new ones are the same as the three mentioned in vers. 2 and 7, since they are expressly distinguished from "these three." The meaning is altogether a different one. The circumstances supposed by Moses never existed, since the Israelites did not fulfil the conditions laid down in ver. 9, viz. that they should keep the law faithfully, and love the Lord their God (cf. chap. iv. 6, vi. 5, etc.). The extension of the power of Israel to the Euphrates under David and Solomon, did not bring the land as far as this river into their actual possession, since the conquered kingdoms of Aram were still inhabited by the Aramæans, who, though conquered, were only rendered tributary. And the Tyrians and Phœnicians, who belonged to the Canaanitish population, were not even attacked by David.—Ver. 10. Innocent blood would be shed if the unintentional manslayer was not protected against the avenger of blood, by the erection of cities of refuge in every part of the land. If Israel neglected this duty, it would bring blood-guiltiness upon itself (" *and so blood be upon thee*"), because it had not done what was requisite to prevent the shedding of innocent blood.—Vers. 11-13. But whatever care was to be taken by means of free cities to prevent the shedding of blood, the cities of refuge were not to be asyla for criminals who were deserving of death, nor to afford protection to those who had slain a neighbour out of hatred. If such murderers should flee to the free city, the elders (magistrates) of his own town were to fetch him out, and deliver him up to the avenger of blood, that he might die. The law laid down in Num. xxxv. 16-21 is here still more minutely defined; but this does not transfer to the elders the duty of instituting a judicial inquiry, and deciding the matter, as *Riehm* follows *Vater* and *De Wette* in maintaining, for the purpose of proving that there is a discrepancy between Deuteronomy and the previous legislation. They are simply commanded to perform the duty devolving upon them as magistrates and administrators of local affairs. (On ver. 13, see chap. xiii. 8 and 5.)

Ver. 14. The prohibition against REMOVING A NEIGHBOUR'S LANDMARK, which his ancestors had placed, is inserted here, not because landmarks were of special importance in relation to the free cities, and the removal of them might possibly be fatal to the unintentional manslayer (as *Clericus* and *Rosenmüller* assume), for the general terms of the prohibition are at variance with this, viz. " thy neighbour's landmark," and " in thine inheritance which thou shalt inherit in the land;" but on account of the close connection in which a man's possession as the means of his support stood to the life of the man himself, " because property by which life is supported participates in the sacredness of life itself, just as in chap. xx. 19, 20, sparing the fruit-trees is mentioned in connection with the men who were to be spared" (*Schultz*). A curse was to be pronounced upon the remover of landmarks, according to chap. xxvii. 17, just as upon one who cursed his father, who led a blind man astray, or perverted the rights of orphans and widows (cf. Hos. v. 10; Prov. xxii. 28, xxiii. 10). Landmarks were regarded as sacred among other nations also; by the Romans, for example, they were held to be so sacred, that whoever removed them was to be put to death.

Vers. 15–21. THE PUNISHMENT OF A FALSE WITNESS.—To secure life and property against false accusations, Moses lays down the law in ver. 15, that one witness only was not " to rise up against any one with reference to any crime or sin, with every sin that one commits" (*i.e.* to appear before a court of justice, or be accepted as sufficient), but everything was to be established upon the testimony of two or three witnesses. The rule laid down in chap. xvii. 6 and Num. xxxv. 30 for capital crimes, is raised hereby into a law of general application (see at Num. xxxv. 30). קוּם (in ver. 15*b*), to stand, *i.e.* to acquire legal force.—But as it was not always possible to bring forward two or three witnesses, and the statement of one witness could not well be disregarded, in vers. 16–18 Moses refers accusations of this kind to the higher tribunal at the sanctuary for investigation and decision, and appoints the same punishment for a false witness, which would have fallen upon the person accused, if he had been convicted of the crime with which he was charged. לַעֲנוֹת בּוֹ סָרָה, " to testify against his departure," sc. from the law of God, not merely falling away into idolatry (chap. xiii. 6), but any

kind of crime, as we may gather from ver. 19, which would be
visited with capital punishment.—Ver. 17. The two men between
whom the dispute lay, the accused and the witness, were to come
before Jehovah, viz. before the priests and judges who should be in
those days,—namely, at the place of the sanctuary, where Jehovah
dwelt among His people (cf. chap. xvii. 9), and not before the local
courts, as *Knobel* supposes. These judges were to investigate the
case most thoroughly (cf. chap. xiii. 15); and if the witness had
spoken lies, they were to do to him as he thought to do to his
brother. The words from " *behold* " to " *his brother* " are parenthetical circumstantial clauses : " *And, behold, is the witness a false
witness, has he spoken a lie against his brother?   Ye shall do,*" etc.
זָמַם, generally to meditate evil. On ver. 20, see chap. xiii. 12.—
Ver. 21. The *lex talionis* was to be applied without reserve (see at
Ex. xxi. 23; Lev. xxiv. 20). According to *Diod. Sic.* (i. 77), the
same law existed in Egypt with reference to false accusers.

Instructions for future Wars.—Chap. xx.

The instructions in this chapter have reference to the wars
which Israel might wage in future against non-Canaanitish nations
(vers. 15 sqq.), and enjoin it as a duty upon the people of God to
spare as much as possible the lives of their own soldiers and also of
their enemies. All wars against their enemies, even though they
were superior to them in resources, were to be entered upon by them
without fear in reliance upon the might of their God; and they were
therefore to exempt from military service not only those who had
just entered into new social relations, and had not enjoyed the
pleasures of them, but also the timid and fainthearted (vers. 1-9).
Moreover, whenever they besieged hostile towns, they were to offer
peace to their enemies, excepting only the Canaanites; and even if
it were not accepted, they were to let the defenceless (viz. women
and children) live, and not to destroy the fruit-trees before the
fortifications (vers. 10-20).

Vers. 1-9. INSTRUCTIONS RELATING TO MILITARY SERVICE.
—If the Israelites went out to battle against their foes, and saw
horses and chariots, a people more numerous than they were, they
were not to be afraid, because Jehovah their God was with them.
Horses and chariots constituted the principal strength of the enemies round about Israel; not of the Egyptians only (Ex. xiv. 7),
and of the Canaanites and Philistines (Josh. xvii. 16; Judg. iv. 3,

1 Sam. xiii. 5), but of the Syrians also (2 Sam. viii. 4; 1 Chron. xviii. 4, xix. 18; cf. Ps. xx. 8).—Vers. 2-4. If they were thus drawing near to war, *i.e.* arranging themselves for war for the purpose of being mustered and marching in order into the battle (not just as the battle was commencing), the priest was to address the warriors, and infuse courage into them by pointing to the help of the Lord. " *The priest* " is not the high priest, but the priest who accompanied the army, like Phinehas in the war against the Midianites (Num. xxxi. 6; cf. 1 Sam. iv. 4, 11, 2 Chron. xiii. 12), whom the Rabbins call מְשִׁיחַ הַמִּלְחָמָה (the anointed of the battle), and raise to the highest dignity next to the high priest, no doubt simply upon the ground of Num. xxxi. 6 (see *Lundius, jüd. Heiligth.* p. 523).—Vers. 5-9. Moreover, the *shoterim*, whose duty it was, as the keepers of the genealogical tables, to appoint the men who were bound to serve, were to release such of the men who had been summoned to the war as had entered into domestic relations, which would make it a harder thing for them to be exposed to death than for any of the others: for example, any man who had built a new house and had not yet consecrated it, or had planted a vineyard and not yet eaten any of the fruit of it, or was betrothed to a wife and had not yet married her,—that such persons might not die before they had enjoyed the fruits of what they had done. " *Who is the man, who,*" *i.e.* whoever, every man who. " *Consecrated the house,*" viz. by taking possession and dwelling in it; entrance into the house was probably connected with a hospitable entertainment. According to *Josephus* (Ant. iv. 8, 41), the enjoyment of them was to last a year (according to the analogy of chap. xxiv. 5). The Rabbins elaborated special ceremonies, among which *Jonathan* in his Targum describes the fastening of slips with sentences out of the law written upon them to the door-posts, as being the most important (see at chap. vi. 9: for further details, see *Selden, de Synedriis* l. iii. c. 14, 15). *Cerem* is hardly to be restricted to vineyards, but applied to olive-plantations as well (see at Lev. xix. 10). חִלֵּל, to make common, is to be explained from the fact, that when fruit-trees were planted (Lev. xix. 23 sqq.), or vines set (Judg. xix. 24), the fruit was not to be eaten for the first three years, and that of the fourth year was to be consecrated to the Lord; and it was only the fruit that was gathered in the fifth year which could be applied by the owner to his own use,—in other words, could be made common. The command to send away from the army to his own home a man who was betrothed but had not yet

taken his wife, is extended still further in chap. xxiv. 5, where it is stated that a newly married man was to be exempt for a whole year from military service and other public burdens. The intention of these instructions was neither to send away all persons who were unwilling to go into the war, and thus avoid the danger of their interfering with the readiness and courage of the rest of the army in prospect of the battle, nor to spare the lives of those persons to whom life was especially dear; but rather to avoid depriving any member of the covenant nation of his enjoyment of the good things of this life bestowed upon him by the Lord.—Ver. 8. The first intention only existed in the case of the timid (the soft-hearted or despondent). וְלֹא יִמַּס, that the heart of thy brethren " *may not flow away*," *i.e.* may not become despondent (as in Gen. xvii. 15, etc.). —Ver. 9. When this was finished, the *shoterim* were to appoint captains at the head of the people (of war). פָּקַד, to inspect, to muster, then to give the oversight, to set a person over anything (Num. iii. 10, iv. 27). The meaning "to lead the command" (*Schultz*) cannot be sustained; and if "captains of the armies" were the subject, and reference were made to the commanders in the war, the article would not be omitted. If the *shoterim* had to raise men for the war and organize the army, the division of the men into hosts (*zebaoth*) and the appointment of the leaders would also form part of the duties of their office.

Vers. 10–20. Instructions concerning Sieges.—Vers. 10, 11. On advancing against a town to attack it, they were " *to call to it for peace*," *i.e.* to summon it to make a peaceable surrender and submission (cf. Judg. xxi. 13). " *If it answered peace*," *i.e.* returned an answer conducing to peace, and " *opened*" (*sc.* its gates), the whole of its inhabitants were to become tributary to Israel, and serve it; consequently even those who were armed were not to be put to death, for Israel was not to shed blood unnecessarily. מַס does not mean feudal *service*, but a feudal slave (see at Ex. i. 11).—Vers. 12, 13. If the hostile town, however, did not make peace, but prepared for war, the Israelites were to besiege it; and if Jehovah gave it into their hands, they were to slay all the men in it without reserve ("with the edge of the sword," see at Gen. xxxiv. 26); but the women and children and all that was in the city, all its spoil, they were to take as prey for themselves, and to consume (eat) the spoil, *i.e.* to make use of it for their own maintenance.—Vers. 15–18. It was in this way that Israel was to act with towns that were far off; but not with the towns of the Canaanites ("*these nations*"), which Jehovah gave them for an inheritance. In these no soul was to be left alive; but these nations were to be laid under the ban, *i.e.* altogether exterminated, that they might not teach the Israelites their abominations and sins (cf. chap. vii. 1–4, xii. 31). כָּל־נְשָׁמָה, *lit.* every breath, *i.e.* everything living, by which, however, human beings alone are to be understood (comp. Josh. x. 40, xi. 11, with chap. xi. 14).—Vers. 19, 20. When they besieged a town a long time to conquer it, they were not to destroy its trees, to swing the axe upon them. That we are to understand by עֵצָהּ the fruit-trees in the environs and gardens of the town, is evident from the motive appended: "*for of them* (מִמֶּנּוּ refers to עֵץ as a collective) *thou eatest, and thou shalt not hew them down.*" The meaning is: thou mayest suppress and destroy the men, but not the trees which supply thee with food. "*For is the tree of the field a man, that it should come into siege before thee?*" This is evidently the only suitable interpretation of the difficult words כִּי הָאָדָם עֵץ הַשָּׂדֶה, and the one which has been expressed by all the older commentators, though in different ways. But it is one which can only be sustained grammatically by adopting the view propounded by *Clericus* and others: viz. by pointing the noun הָאָדָם with ה *interrog.*, instead of הָאָדָם, and taking אָדָם as the object, which its position in the sentence fully warrants (cf. *Ewald*, § 324, *b.* and 306, *b.*). The Masoretic punctuation is founded upon the explanation given by *Aben Ezra*, "Man is a tree of the field, *i.e.* lives upon and is fed by the fruits of the trees," which *Schultz* expresses in this way, "Man is bound up with the tree of the field, *i.e.* has his life in, or from, the tree of the field,"—an explanation, however, which cannot be defended by appealing to chap. xxiv. 6, Eccl. xii. 13, Ezek. xii. 10, as these three passages are of a different kind. In no way whatever can הָאָדָם be taken as the subject of the sentence, as this would not give any rational meaning. And if it were rendered as the object, in such sense as this, The tree of the field is a thing or affair of man, it would hardly have the article. —Ver. 20. "*Only the trees which thou knowest that they are not trees of eating* (*i.e.* do not bear edible fruits), *mayest thou hew down, and build a rampart against the town till it come down,*" *i.e.* fall down from its eminence. For יָרַד as applied to the falling or sinking of lofty fortifications, see chap. xxviii. 52, Isa. xxxii. 19. מָצוֹר, compressing or forcing down; hence, as applied to towns, בֹּא בַמָצוֹר, to come into siege, *i.e.* to be besieged (ver. 19; 2 Kings

xxiv. 10, xxv. 2). In ver. 20 it is used to denote the object, viz. the means of hemming in a town, *i.e.* the besieging rampart (cf. Ezek. iv. 2).

Expiation of an uncertain Murder. Treatment of a Wife who had been taken captive. Right of the First-born. Punishment of a refractory Son. Burial of a Man who had been hanged.—Chap. xxi.

The reason for grouping together these five laws, which are apparently so different from one another, as well as for attaching them to the previous regulations, is to be found in the desire to bring out distinctly the sacredness of life and of personal rights from every point of view, and impress it upon the covenant nation.

Vers. 1-9. EXPIATION OF A MURDER COMMITTED BY AN UNKNOWN HAND.—Vers. 1 and 2. If any one was found lying in a field in the land of Israel (נֹפֵל fallen, then lying, Judg. iii. 25, iv. 22), having been put to death without its being known who had killed him (לֹא נוֹדַע וגו', a circumstantial clause, attached without a copula, see *Ewald*, § 341, *b*. 3), the elders and judges, *sc.* of the neighbouring towns,—the former as representatives of the communities, the latter as administrators of right,—were to go out and measure to the towns which lay round about the slain man, *i.e.* measure the distance of the body from the towns that were lying round about, to ascertain first of all which was the nearest town.— Vers. 3, 4. This nearest town was then required to expiate the blood-guiltiness, not only because the suspicion of the crime or of participation in the crime fell soonest upon it, but because the guilt connected with the shedding of innocent blood rested as a burden upon it before all others. To this end the elders were to take a heifer (young cow), with which no work had ever been done, and which had not yet drawn in the yoke, *i.e.* whose vital force had not been diminished by labour (see at Num. xix. 2), and bring it down into a brook-valley with water constantly flowing, and there break its neck. The expression, *"it shall be that the city,"* is more fully defined by *"the elders of the city shall take."* The elders were to perform the act of expiation in the name of the city. As the murderer was not to be found, an animal was to be put to death in his stead, and suffer the punishment of the murderer. The slaying of the animal was not an expiatory sacrifice, and consequently there was no slaughtering and sprinkling of the blood; but, as the mode of death, viz. breaking the neck (*vid.* Ex. xiii. 13), clearly shows, it was a symbolical infliction of the punishment that should have been borne by the murderer, upon the animal which was substituted for him. To be able to take the guilt upon itself and bear it, the animal was to be in the full and undiminished possession of its vital powers. The slaying was to take place in a נַחַל אֵיתָן, a valley with water constantly flowing through it, which was not worked (cultivated) and sown. This regulation as to the locality in which the act of expiation was to be performed was probably founded upon the idea, that the water of the brook-valley would suck in the blood and clean it away, and that the blood sucked in by the earth would not be brought to light again by the ploughing and working of the soil.—Ver. 5. The priests were to come near during this transaction; i.e. some priests from the nearest Levitical town were to be present at it, not to conduct the affair, but as those whom Jehovah had chosen to serve Him and to bless in His name (cf. chap. xviii. 5), and according to whose mouth (words) every dispute and every stroke happened (cf. chap. xvii. 8), i.e. simply as those who were authorized by the Lord, and as the representatives of the divine right, to receive the explanation and petition of the elders, and acknowledge the legal validity of the act.—Vers. 6-8. The elders of the town were to wash their hands over the slain heifer, i.e. to cleanse themselves by this symbolical act from the suspicion of any guilt on the part of the inhabitants of the town in the murder that had been committed (cf. Ps. xxvi. 6, lxxiii. 13; Matt. xxvii. 24), and then answer (to the charge involved in what had taken place), and say, "Our hands have not shed this blood (on the singular שָׁפְכָה, see Ewald, § 317, a.), and our eyes have not seen" (sc. the shedding of blood), i.e. we have neither any part in the crime nor any knowledge of it: "grant forgiveness (lit. 'cover up,' viz. the blood-guiltiness) to Thy people . . . and give not innocent blood in the midst of Thy people Israel," i.e. lay not upon us the innocent blood that has been shed by imputation and punishment. "And the blood shall be forgiven them," i.e. the bloodshed or murder shall not be imputed to them. On נִכַּפֵּר, a mixed form from the Niphal and Hithpael, see Ges. § 55, and Ewald, § 132, c.—Ver. 9. In this way Israel was to wipe away the innocent blood (the bloodshed) from its midst (cf. Num. xxxv. 33). If the murderer were discovered afterwards, of course the punishment of death which had been inflicted vicariously upon the animal, simply because the criminal himself could not be found, would still fall upon him.

Vers. 10-14. Treatment of a Wife who had been a
Prisoner of War.—If an Israelite saw among the captives, who
had been brought away in a war against foreign nations, a woman
of beautiful figure, and loved her, and took her as his wife, he was
to allow her a month's time in his house, to bewail her separation
from her home and kindred, and accustom herself to her new condition of life, before he married her. What is said here does not
apply to the wars with the·Canaanites, who were to be cut off (vid.
chap. vii. 3), but, as a comparison of the introductory words in ver.
1 with chap. xx. 1 clearly shows, to the wars which Israel would
carry on with surrounding nations after the conquest of Canaan.
שְׁבִי and שִׁבְיָה, the captivity, for the captives.—Vers. 12, 13. When
the woman was taken home to the house of the man who had loved
her, she was to shave her head, and make, i.e. cut, her nails (cf. 2
Sam. xix. 25),—both customary signs of purification (on this signification of the cutting of the hair, see Lev. xiv. 8 and Num. viii. 7),
—as symbols of her passing out of the state of a slave, and of her
reception into the fellowship of the covenant nation. This is perfectly obvious in her laying aside her prisoner's clothes. After
putting off the signs of captivity, she was to sit (dwell) in the
house, and bewail her father and mother for a month, i.e. console
herself for her separation from her parents, whom she had lost, that
she might be able to forget her people and her father's house (Ps.
xlv. 11), and give herself up henceforth in love to her husband
with an undivided heart. The intention of these laws was not to
protect the woman against any outbreak of rude passion on the
part of the man, but rather to give her time and leisure to loosen
herself inwardly from the natural fellowship of her nation and
kindred, and to acquire affection towards the fellowship of the
people of God, into which she had entered against her will, that
her heart might cherish love to the God of Israel, who had given
her favour in the eyes of her master, and had taken from her
the misery and reproach of slavery. By her master becoming her
husband, she entered into the rights of a daughter of Israel,
who had been sold by her father to a man to be his wife (Ex.
xxi. 7 sqq.). If after this her husband should find no pleasure in
her, he was to let her go לְנַפְשָׁהּ, i.e. at her free will, and not sell
her for money (cf. Ex. xxi. 8). "Thou shalt not put constraint
upon her, because thou hast humbled her." הִתְעַמֵּר, which only occurs
again in chap. xxiv. 7, probably signifies to throw oneself upon a
person, to practise violence towards him (cf. Ges. thes. p. 1046).

Vers. 15–17. THE RIGHT OF THE FIRST-BORN.—Whilst the previous law was intended to protect the slave taken in war against the caprice of her Israelitish master, the law which follows is directed against the abuse of paternal authority in favour of a favourite wife. If a man had two wives, of whom one was beloved and the other hated, —as was the case, for example, with Jacob,—and had sons by both his wives, but the first-born by the wife he hated, he was not, when dividing his property as their inheritance, to make the son of the wife he loved the first-born, *i.e.* was not to give him the inheritance of the first-born, but was to treat the son of the hated wife, who was really the first-born son, as such, and to give him a double share of all his possession. בִּכֵּר, to make or institute as first-born. עַל־פְּנֵי בֶּן וגו׳, over (by) the face of, *i.e.* opposite to the first-born son of the hated, when he was present; in other words, "during his lifetime" (cf. Gen. xi. 28). יַכִּיר, to regard as that which he is, the rightful first-born. The inheritance of the first-born consisted in "*a mouth of two*" (*i.e.* a mouthful, portion, share of two) of all that was by him, all that he possessed. Consequently the first-born inherited twice as much as any of the other sons. "*Beginning of his strength*" (as in Gen. xlix. 3). This right of primogeniture did not originate with Moses, but was simply secured by him against arbitrary invasion. It was founded, no doubt, upon hereditary tradition; just as we find in many other nations, that certain privileges are secured to the first-born sons above those born afterwards.

Vers. 18–21. PUNISHMENT OF A REFRACTORY SON.—The laws upon this point aim not only at the defence, but also at the limitation, of parental authority. If any one's son was unmanageable and refractory, not hearkening to the voice of his parents, even when they chastised him, his father and mother were to take him and lead him out to the elders of the town into the gate of the place. The elders are not regarded here as judges in the strict sense of the word, but as magistrates, who had to uphold the parental authority, and administer the local police. The gate of the town was the forum, where the public affairs of the place were discussed (cf. chap. xxii. 15, xxv. 7); as it is in the present day in Syria (*Seetzen*, R. ii. p. 88), and among the Moors (*Höst*, Nachrichten v. Marokkos, p. 239). —Ver. 20. Here they were to accuse the son as being unmanageable, refractory, disobedient, as "a glutton and a drunkard." These last accusations show the reason for the unmanageableness and refractoriness.—Ver. 21. In consequence of this accusation, all the men of the town were to stone him, so that he died. By this the right was taken away from the parents of putting an incorrigible son to death (cf. Prov. xix. 18), whilst at the same time the parental authority was fully preserved. Nothing is said about any evidence of the charge brought by the parents, or about any judicial inquiry generally. " In such a case the charge was a proof in itself. For if the heart of a father and mother could be brought to such a point as to give up their child to the judge before the community of the nation, everything would have been done that a judge would need to know " (*Schnell, d. isr. Recht*, p. 11).—On ver. 21*b*, cf. chap. xiii. 6 and 12.

Vers. 22 and 23. Burial of those who had been hanged. —If there was a sin upon a man, מִשְׁפַּט מָוֶת, *lit.* a right of death, *i.e.* a capital crime (cf. chap. xix. 6 and xxii. 26), and he was put to death, and they hanged him upon a tree (wood), his body was not to remain upon the wood over night, but they were to bury him on the same day upon which he was hanged; "*for the hanged man is a curse of God*," and they were not to defile the land which Jehovah gave for an inheritance. The hanging, not of criminals who were to be put to death, but of those who had been executed with the sword, was an intensification of the punishment of death (see at Num. xxv. 4), inasmuch as the body was thereby exposed to peculiar kinds of abominations. Moses commanded the burial of those who had been hanged upon the day of their execution,—that is to say, as we may see from the application of this law in Josh. viii. 29, x. 26, 27, before sunset,—because the hanged man, being a curse of God, defiled the land. The land was defiled not only by vices and crimes (cf. Lev. xviii. 24, 28; Num. xxxv. 34), but also by the exposure to view of criminals who had been punished with death, and thus had been smitten by the curse of God, inasmuch as their shameful deeds were thereby publicly exposed to view. We are not to think of any bodily defilement of the land through the de- composition consequent upon death, as *J. D. Mich.* and *Sommer* suppose ; so that there is no ground for speaking of any discre- pancy between this and the old law.—(On the application of this law to Christ, see Gal. iii. 13.)—This regulation is appended very loosely to what precedes. The link of connection is contained in the thought, that with the punishment of the wicked the recollec- tion of their crimes was also to be removed.

The Duty to love one's Neighbour ; and Warning against a Violation of the Natural Order of Things. Instructions to sanctify the Marriage State.—Chap. xxii.

Going deeper and deeper into the manifold relations of the national life, Moses first of all explains in vers. 1–12 the attitude of an Israelite, on the one hand, towards a neighbour ; and, on the other hand, towards the natural classification and arrangement of things, and shows how love should rule in the midst of all these relations. The different relations brought under consideration are selected rather by way of examples, and therefore follow one another without any link of connection, for the purpose of exhibiting the truth in certain concrete cases, and showing how the covenant people were to hold all the arrangements of God sacred, whether in nature or in social life.

Vers. 1–12. In vers. 1–4 Moses shows, by a still further expansion of Ex. xxiii. 4, 5, how the property of a neighbour was to be regarded and preserved. If any man saw an ox or a sheep of his brother's (fellow-countryman) going astray, he was not to draw back from it, but to bring it back to his brother ; and if the owner lived at a distance, or was unknown, he was to take it into his own house or farm, till he came to seek it. He was also to do the same with an ass or any other property that another had lost.—Ver. 4. A fallen animal belonging to another he was also to help up (as in Ex. xxiii. 5 : except that in this case, instead of a brother generally, an enemy or hater is mentioned).—Ver. 5. As the property of a neighbour was to be sacred in the estimation of an Israelite, so also the divine distinction of the sexes, which was kept sacred in civil life by the clothing peculiar to each sex, was to be not less but even more sacredly observed. " *There shall not be man's things upon a woman, and a man shall not put on a woman's clothes.*" כְּלִי does not signify clothing merely, nor arms only, but includes every kind of domestic and other utensils (as in Ex. xxii. 6 ; Lev. xi. 32, xiii. 49). The immediate design of this prohibition was not to prevent licentiousness, or to oppose idolatrous practices (the proofs which *Spencer* has adduced of the existence of such usages among heathen nations are very far-fetched) ; but to maintain the sanctity of that distinction of the sexes which was established by the creation of man and woman, and in relation to which Israel was not to sin. Every violation or wiping out of this distinction—such even, for example, as the emancipation of a woman—was unnatural, and therefore an abomination in the sight of God.—Vers. 6, 7. The affectionate relation of parents to their young, which God had established even in the animal world, was also to be kept just as sacred. If any one found a bird's nest by the road upon a tree, or upon the ground, with young ones or eggs, and the mother sitting upon them, he was not to take the mother with the young ones, but to let the mother fly, and only take the young. נִקְרָא for נִקְרָה, as in Ex. v. 3. The command is related to the one in Lev. xxii. 28 and Ex. xxiii. 19, and is placed upon a par with the commandment relating to parents, by the fact that obedience is urged upon the people by the same promise in both instances (*vid.* chap. v. 16 ; Ex. xx. 12).—Ver. 8. Still less were they to expose human life to danger through carelessness. " *If thou build a new house, make a rim (maakeh)—i.e.* a balustrade—*to thy roof, that thou bring not blood-guiltiness upon thy house, if any one fall from it.*" The roofs of the Israelitish houses were flat, as they mostly are in the East, so that the inhabitants often lived upon them (Josh. ii. 6 ; 2 Sam. xi. 2 ; Matt. x. 27).—In vers. 9–11, there follow several prohibitions against mixing together the things which are separated in God's creation, consisting partly of a verbal repetition of Lev. xix. 19 (see the explanation of this passage).—To this there is appended in ver. 12 the law concerning the tassels upon the hem of the upper garment (Num. xv. 37 sqq.), which were to remind the Israelites of their calling, to walk before the Lord in faithful fulfilment of the commandments of God (see the commentary upon this passage).

Vers. 13–29. LAWS OF CHASTITY AND MARRIAGE.—Higher and still holier than the order of nature stands the moral order of marriage, upon which the well-being not only of domestic life, but also of the civil commonwealth of nations, depends. Marriage must be founded upon fidelity and chastity on the part of those who are married. To foster this, and secure it against outbreaks of malice and evil lust, was the design and object of the laws which follow. The first (vers. 13–21) relates to the chastity of a woman on entering into the married state, which might be called in question by her husband, either from malice or with justice. The former case is that which Moses treats of first of all. If a man took a wife, and came to her, and hated her, *i.e.* turned against her after gratifying his carnal desires (like Amnon, for example, 2 Sam. xiii. 15), and in order to get rid of her again, attributed " deeds or things of words " to her, *i.e.* things which give occasion for words or talk, and so brought an evil name upon her, saying, that on coming to her he did not find virginity in her. בְּתוּלִים, virginity, here the signs of it, viz., according to ver. 17, the marks of a first intercourse upon the bed-clothes or dress.—Vers. 15 sqq. In such a case the parents of the young woman (הַנַּעַר for הַנַּעֲרָה, as in Gen. xxiv. 14, 28, according to the earliest usage of the books of Moses, a virgin, then also a young woman, e.g. Ruth ii. 6, iv. 12) were to bring the matter before the elders of the town into the gate (the judicial forum; see chap. xxi. 19), and establish the chastity and innocence of their daughter by spreading the bed-clothes before them. It was not necessary to this end that the parents should have taken possession of the spotted bed-clothes directly after the marriage night, as is customarily done by the Bedouins and the lower classes of the Moslem in Egypt and Syria (cf. *Niebuhr, Beschr. v. Arab.* pp. 35 sqq.; *Arvieux, merkw. Nachr.* iii. p. 258; *Burckhardt, Beduinen,* p. 214, etc.). It was sufficient that the cloth should be kept, in case such a proof might be required.—Vers. 18 sqq. The elders, as the magistrates of the place, were then to send for the man who had so calumniated his young wife, and to chastise him (יִסַּר, as in chap. xxi. 18, used to denote bodily chastisement, though the limitation of the number of strokes to forty save one, may have been a later institution of the schools); and in addition to this they were to impose a fine upon him of 100 shekels of silver, which he was to pay to the father of the young wife for his malicious calumniation of an Israelitish maiden,—twice as much as the seducer of a virgin was to pay to her father for the reproach brought upon him by the humiliation of his daughter (ver. 29); and lastly, they were to deprive the man of the right of divorce from his wife.—Vers. 20, 21. In the other case, however, if the man's words were true, and the girl had not been found to be a virgin, the elders were to bring her out before the door of her father's house, and the men of the town were to stone her to death, because she had committed a folly in Israel (cf. Gen. xxxiv. 7), to commit fornication in her father's house. The punishment of death was to be inflicted upon her, not so much because she had committed fornication, as because notwithstanding this she had allowed a man to marry her as a spotless virgin, and possibly even after her betrothal had gone with another man (cf. vers. 23, 24). There is no ground for thinking of unnatural wantonness, as *Knobel* does.—Ver. 22. If any one lay with a married woman, they were both of them to be put to death as adulterers (cf. Lev. xx. 10).

Vers. 23–29. In connection with the seduction of a virgin (נַעֲרָ, *puella*, a marriageable girl ; בְּתוּלָה, *virgo immaculata*, a virgin), two, or really three, cases are distinguished ; viz. (1) whether she was betrothed (vers. 23–27), or not betrothed (vers. 28, 29) ; (2) if she were betrothed, whether it was (*a*) in the town (vers. 23, 24) or (*b*) in the open field (vers. 25–27) that she had been violated by a man.—Vers. 23, 24. If a betrothed virgin had allowed a man to have intercourse with her (*i.e.* one who was not her bridegroom), they were both of them, the man and the girl, to be led out to the gate of the town, and stoned that they might die : the girl, because she had not cried in the city, *i.e.* had not called for help, and consequently was to be regarded as consenting to the deed ; the man, because he had humbled his neighbour's wife.   The betrothed woman was placed in this respect upon a par with a married woman, and in fact is expressly called a wife in ver. 24.   Betrothal was the first step towards marriage, even if it was not a solemn act attested by witnesses.   Written agreements of marriage were not introduced till a later period (Tobit vii. 14 ; *Tr. Ketuboth* i. 2).— Vers. 25–27. If, on the other hand, a man met a betrothed girl in the field, and laid hold of her and lay with her, the man alone was to die, and nothing was to be done to the girl.   "*There is in the damsel no death-sin* (*i.e.* no sin to be punished with death) ; *but as when a man riseth against his neighbour and slayeth him, even so is this matter.*"   In the open field the girl had called for help, but no one had helped her.   It was therefore a forcible rape.—Vers. 28, 29. The last case : if a virgin was not betrothed, and a man seized her and lay with her, and they were found, *i.e.* discovered or convicted of their deed, the man was to pay the father of the girl fifty shekels of silver, for the reproach brought upon him and his house, and to marry the girl whom he had humbled, without ever being able to divorce her.   This case is similar to the one mentioned in Ex. xxii. 15, 16.   The omission to mention the possibility of the father refusing to give him his daughter for a wife, makes no essential difference.   It is assumed as self-evident here, that such a right was possessed by the father.

Ver. 30 (or chap. xxiii. 1). This verse, in which the prohibition of incest is renewed by a repetition of the first provision in the earlier law (Lev. xviii. 7, 8), is no doubt much better adapted to form the close of the laws of chastity and marriage, than the introduction to the laws which follow concerning the right of citizenship in the congregation of the Lord.

Regulations as to the Right of Citizenship in the Congregation of the Lord.—Chap. xxiii.

From the sanctification of the house and the domestic relation, to which the laws of marriage and chastity in the previous chapter pointed, Moses proceeds to instructions concerning the sanctification of their union as a congregation : he gives directions as to the exclusion of certain persons from the congregation of the Lord, and the reception of others into it (vers. 1–8) ; as to the preservation of the purity of the camp in time of war (vers. 9–14) ; as to the reception of foreign slaves into the land, and the removal of licentious persons out of it (vers. 15–18) ; and lastly, as to certain duties of citizenship (19–25).

Vers. 1–8. The Right of Citizenship in the Congregation of the Lord.—Ver. 1. Into the congregation of the Lord there was not to come, *i.e.* not to be received, any person who was mutilated in his sexual member. פְּצוּעַ־דַּכָּה, literally wounded by crushing, *i.e.* mutilated in this way; *Vulg. eunuchus attritis vel amputatis testiculis.* Not only animals (see at Lev. xxii. 24), but men also, were castrated in this way. כְּרוּת שָׁפְכָה was one whose sexual member was cut off; *Vulg. abscisso veretro.* According to *Mishnah Jebam.* vi. 2, "*contusus* דַּכָּה *est omnis, cujus testiculi vulnerati sunt, vel certe unus eorum; exsectus* (כְּרוּת)*, cujus membrum virile praecisum est.*". In the modern East, emasculation is generally performed in this way (see *Tournefort, Reise.* ii. p. 259, and *Burckhardt, Nubien,* pp. 450, 451). The reason for the exclusion of emasculated persons from the congregation of Jehovah, *i.e.* not merely from office (*officio et publico magistratu,* Luth.) and from marriage with an Israelitish woman (*Fag., C. a Lap.,* and others), but from admission into the covenant fellowship of Israel with the Lord, is to be found in the mutilation of the nature of man as created by God, which was irreconcilable with the character of the people of God. Nature is not destroyed by grace, but sanctified and transformed. This law, however, was one of the ordinances intended for the period of infancy, and has lost its significance with the spread of the kingdom of God over all the nations of the earth (Isa. lvi. 4).—Ver. 2. So also with the מַמְזֵר, *i.e.* not persons begotten out of wedlock, illegitimate children generally (LXX., *Vulg.*), but, according to the *Talmud* and the *Rabbins,* those who were begotten in incest or adultery (cf. *Ges. thes.* p. 781). The etymology of the word is obscure. The only other place in which it occurs is Zech. ix. 6 ; and it is neither contracted from מוּם and זָר (according to the *Talmud*, and *Hitzig* on Zech. ix. 6), nor from מֵעַם זָר (*Geiger Urschr.* p. 52), but in all probability is to be derived from a root מָזַר, synonymous with the Arabic word " to be corrupt, or foul." The additional clause, " *not even in the tenth generation,*" precludes all possibility of their ever being received. Ten is the number of com- plete exclusion. In ver. 3, therefore, " *for ever*" is added. The reason is the same as in the case of mutilated persons, namely, their springing from a connection opposed to the divine order of the crea- tion.—Vers. 3–6. Also no Ammonite or Moabite was to be received, not even in the tenth generation ; not, however, because their fore- fathers were begotten in incest (Gen. xix. 30 sqq.), as *Knobel* sup- poses, but on account of the hostility they had manifested to the establishment of the kingdom of God. Not only had they failed to give Israel a hospitable reception on its journey (see at chap. ii. 29), but they (viz. the king of the Moabites) had even hired Balaam to curse Israel. In this way they had brought upon themselves the curse which falls upon all those who curse Israel, according to the infallible word of God (Gen. xii. 3), the truth of which even Balaam was obliged to attest in the presence of Balak (Num. xxiv. 9) ; although out of love to Israel the Lord turned the curse of Balaam into a blessing (cf. Num. xxii.–xxiv.). For this reason Israel was never to seek their welfare and prosperity, *i.e.* to make this an object of its care (" to seek," as in Jer. xxix. 7) ; not indeed from personal hatred, for the purpose of repaying evil with evil, since this neither induced Moses to publish the prohibition, nor in- stigated Ezra when he put the law in force, by compelling the sepa- ration of all Ammonitish, Moabitish, and Canaanitish wives from the newly established congregation in Jerusalem (Ezra ix. 12). How far Moses was from being influenced by such motives of personal or national revenge is evident, apart from the prohibition in chap. ii. 9 and 19 against making war upon the Moabites and Am- monites, from the command which follows in vers. 8 and 9 with reference to the Edomites and Egyptians. These nations had also manifested hostility to the Israelites. Edom had come against them when they desired to march peaceably through his land (Num. xx. 18 sqq.), and the Pharaohs of Egypt had heavily oppressed them. Nevertheless, Israel was to keep the bond of kindred sacred (" he is thy brother"), and not to forget in the case of the Egyptians the benefits derived from their sojourn in their land. Their children might come into the congregation of the Lord in the third generation, *i.e.* the great-grandchildren of Edomites or Egyptians, who had lived as strangers in Israel (see at Ex. xx. 5). Such persons might be incorporated into the covenant nation by circumcision.

Vers. 9–14. PRESERVATION OF THE PURITY OF THE CAMP IN TIME OF WAR.—The bodily appearance of the people was also to correspond to the sacredness of Israel as the congregation of the Lord, especially when they gathered in hosts around their God. *"When thou marchest out as a camp against thine enemies, beware of every evil thing."* What is meant by an "evil thing" is stated in vers. 10–13, viz. uncleanness, and uncleanliness of the body.—Vers. 10, 11. The person who had become unclean through a nightly occurrence, was to go out of the camp and remain there till he had cleansed himself in the evening. On the journey through the desert, none but those who were affected with uncleanness of a longer duration were to be removed from the camp (Num. v. 2); but when they were encamped, this law was to apply to even lighter defilements.—Vers. 12, 13. The camp of war was also not to be defiled with the dirt of excrements. Outside the camp there was to be a space or place (יָד, as in Num. ii. 17) for the necessities of nature, and among their implements they were to have a spade, with which they were to dig when they sate down, and then cover it up again. יָתֵד, generally a plug, here a tool for sticking in, *i.e.* for digging into the ground.—Ver. 14. For the camp was to be (to be kept) holy, because Jehovah walked in the midst of it, in order that He might not see "*nakedness of a thing*," *i.e.* anything to be ashamed of (see at chap. xxiv. 1) in the people, "*and turn away from thee.*" There was nothing shameful in the excrement itself; but the want of reverence, which the people would display through not removing it, would offend the Lord and drive Him out of the camp of Israel.

Vers. 15–18. TOLERATION AND NON-TOLERATION IN THE CONGREGATION OF THE LORD.—Vers. 15, 16. A slave who had escaped from his master to Israel was not to be given up, but to be allowed to dwell in the land, wherever he might choose, and not to be oppressed. The reference is to a slave who had fled to them from a foreign country, on account of the harsh treatment which he had received from his heathen master. The plural אֲדֹנִים denotes the rule.—Vers. 17, 18. On the other hand, male and female prostitutes of Israelitish descent were not to be tolerated; *i.e.* it was not to be allowed, that either a male or female among the Israelites should give himself up to prostitution as an act of religious worship. The exclusion of foreign prostitutes was involved in the command to root out the Canaanites. קָדֵשׁ and קְדֵשָׁה were persons who prostituted themselves in the worship of the Canaanitish Astarte (see at Gen. xxxviii. 21).—" *The wages of a prostitute and the money of dogs shall not come into the house of the Lord on account of* (לְ, for the more remote cause, *Ewald*, § 217) *any vow; for even both these* (viz. even the prostitute and dog, not merely their dishonourable gains) *are abomination unto the Lord thy God.*" "The hire of a whore" is what the *kedeshah* was paid for giving herself up. "The price of a dog" is not the price paid for the sale of a dog (*Bochart, Spencer, Iken, Baumgarten*, etc.), but is a figurative expression used to denote the gains of the *kadesh*, who was called κίναιδος by the Greeks, and received his name from the dog-like manner in which the male *kadesh* debased himself (see Rev. xxii. 15, where the unclean are distinctly called "dogs").

Vers. 19–25. DIFFERENT THEOCRATIC RIGHTS OF CITIZENSHIP. — Vers. 19, 20. Of his brother (*i.e.* his countryman), the Israelite was not to take interest for money, food, or anything else that he lent to him; but only of strangers (non-Israelites: cf. Ex. xxii. 24 and Lev. xxv. 36, 37).—Vers. 21–23. Vows vowed to the Lord were to be fulfilled without delay; but omitting to vow was not a sin. (On vows themselves, see at Lev. xxvii. and Num. xxx. 2 sqq.) נְדָבָה is an accusative defining the meaning more fully : in free will, spontaneously.—Vers. 24, 25. In the vineyard and corn-field of a neighbour they might eat at pleasure to still their hunger, but they were not to put anything into a vessel, or swing a sickle upon another's corn, that is to say, carry away any store of grapes or ears of corn. כְּנַפְשֶׁךָ, according to thy desire, or appetite (cf. chap. xiv. 26). "*Pluck the ears:*" cf. Matt. xii. 1 ; Luke vi. 1.— The right of hungry persons, when passing through a field, to pluck ears of corn, and rub out the grains and eat, is still recognised among the Arabs (*vid. Rob. Pal.* ii. 192).

On Divorce.   Warnings against want of Affection or Injustice.— Chap. xxiv.

Vers. 1–5 contain two laws concerning the relation of a man to his wife. The first (vers. 1–4) has reference to divorce. In these verses, however, divorce is not established as a right; all that is done is, that in case of a divorce a reunion with the divorced wife is forbidden, if in the meantime she had married another man, even though the second husband had also put her away, or had died. The four verses form a period, in which vers. 1–3 are the clauses of the protasis, which describe the matter treated about; and ver. 4 contains the apodosis, with the law concerning the point in question. If a man married a wife, and he put her away with a letter of divorce, because she did not please him any longer, and the divorced woman married another man, and he either put her away in the same manner or died, the first husband could not take her as his wife again. The putting away (divorce) of a wife with a letter of divorce, which the husband gave to the wife whom he put away, is assumed as a custom founded upon tradition. This tradition left the question of divorce entirely at the will of the husband : " *if the wife does not find favour in his eyes* (*i.e.* does not please him), *because he has found in her something shameful*" (chap. xxiii. 15). עֶרְוָה, nakedness, shame, disgrace (Isa. xx. 4; 1 Sam. xx. 30); in connection with דָּבָר, the shame of a thing, *i.e.* a shameful thing (LXX. ἄσχημον πρᾶγμα; *Vulg. aliquam fœtiditatem*). The meaning of this expression as a ground of divorce was disputed even among the Rabbins. *Hillel's* school interpret it in the widest and most lax manner possible, according to the explanation of the Pharisees in Matt. xix. 3, "for every cause." They no doubt followed the rendering of *Onkelos*, עֲבֵירַת פִּתְגָם, the transgression of a thing ; but this is contrary to the use of the word עֶרְוָה, to which the interpretation given by *Shammai* adhered more strictly. His explanation of עֶרְוַת דָּבָר is "*rem impudicam, libidinem, lasciviam, impudicitiam.*" Adultery, to which some of the Rabbins would restrict the expression, is certainly not to be thought of, because this was to be punished with death.[1] סֵפֶר כְּרִיתֻת, βιβλίον ἀπο-στασίου, a letter of divorce ; כְּרִיתֻת, hewing off, cutting off, *sc.* from the man, with whom the wife was to be one flesh (Gen. ii. 24). The custom of giving letters of divorce was probably adopted by the Israelites in Egypt, where the practice of writing had already found its way into all the relations of life.[2] The law that the first husband could not take his divorced wife back again, if she had

---

[1] For the different views of the Rabbins upon this subject, see *Mishnah tract. Gittin* ix. 10; *Buxtorf, de sponsal. et divort.* pp. 88 sqq.; *Selden, uxor ebr.* l. iii. c. 18 and 20 ; and *Lightfoot, horæ ebr. et talm. ad Matth.* v. 31 sq.

[2] The rabbinical rules on the grounds of divorce and the letter of divorce, according to *Maimonides*, have been collected by *Surenhusius, ad Mishn. tr.*

married another husband in the meantime, even supposing that the second husband was dead, would necessarily put a check upon frivolous divorces. Moses could not entirely abolish the traditional custom, if only " because of the hardness of the people's hearts" (Matt. xix. 8). The thought, therefore, of the impossibility of reunion with the first husband, after the wife had contracted a second marriage, would put some restraint upon a frivolous rupture of the marriage tie : it would have this effect, that whilst, on the one hand, the man would reflect when inducements to divorce his wife presented themselves, and would recall a rash act if it had been performed, before the wife he had put away had married another husband; on the other hand, the wife would yield more readily to the will of her husband, and seek to avoid furnishing him with an inducement for divorce. But this effect would be still more readily produced by the reason assigned by Moses, namely, that the divorced woman was defiled (הֻטַּמָּאָה, *Hothpael*, as in Num. i. 47) by her marriage with a second husband. The second marriage of a woman who had been divorced is designated by Moses a defilement of the woman, primarily no doubt with reference to the fact that the *emissio seminis* in sexual intercourse rendered unclean, though not merely in the sense of such a defilement as was removed in the evening by simple washing, but as a moral defilement, *i.e.* blemishing, desecration of the sexual communion which was sanctified by marriage, in the same sense in which adultery is called a defilement in Lev. xviii. 20 and Num. v. 13, 14. Thus the second marriage of a divorced woman was placed *implicite* upon a par with adultery, and some approach made towards the teaching of Christ concerning marriage : " Whosoever shall marry her that is divorced, committeth adultery" (Matt. v. 32).—But if the second marriage of a divorced woman was a moral defilement, of course the wife could not marry the first again even after the death of her second husband, not only because such a reunion would lower the dignity of the woman, and the woman would appear too much like property, which could be disposed of at one time and reclaimed at another (*Schultz*), but because the defilement of the wife would be thereby repeated, and even increased, as the moral defilement which the divorced wife acquired through the second marriage was not removed by a divorce from the second husband, nor yet by his death. Such defilement was

Gittin, c. 1 (T. iii. pp. 322 sq. of the *Mishnah of Sur.*), where different specimens of letters of divorce are given ; the latter also in *Lightfoot*, *l.c.*

an abomination before Jehovah, by which they would cause the land to sin, *i.e.* stain it with sin, as much as by the sins of incest and unnatural licentiousness (Lev. xviii. 25).

Attached to this law, which is intended to prevent a frivolous severance of the marriage tie, there is another in ver. 5, which was of a more positive character, and adapted to fortify the marriage bond. The newly married man was not required to perform military service for a whole year; "*and there shall not come* (anything) *upon him with regard to any matter.*" The meaning of this last clause is to be found in what follows : "*Free shall he be for his house for a year,*" *i.e.* they shall put no public burdens upon him, that he may devote himself entirely to his newly established domestic relations, and be able to gladden his wife (compare chap. xx. 7).

Vers. 6–9. *Various Prohibitions.*—Ver. 6. "*No man shall take in pledge the handmill and millstone, for he* (who does this) *is pawning life.*" רֵחַיִם, the handmill; רֶכֶב, *lit.* the runner, *i.e.* the upper millstone. Neither the whole mill nor the upper millstone was to be asked for as a pledge, by which the mill would be rendered useless, since the handmill was indispensable for preparing the daily food for the house; so that whoever took them away injured life itself, by withdrawing what was indispensable to the preservation of life. The mill is mentioned as one specimen of articles of this kind, like the clothing in Ex. xxii. 25, 26, which served the poor man as bed-clothes also. Breaches of this commandment are reproved in Amos ii. 8 ; Job xxii. 6 ; Prov. xx. 16, xxii. 27, xxvii. 13.—Ver. 7. Repetition of the law against man-stealing (Ex. xxi. 16).—Vers. 8, 9. The command, "*Take heed by the plague of leprosy to observe diligently and to do according to all that the priests teach thee,*" etc., does not mean, that when they saw signs of leprosy they were to be upon their guard, to observe everything that the priests directed them, as *Knobel* and many others suppose. For, in the first place, the reference to the punishment of Miriam with leprosy is by no means appropriate to such a thought as this, since Miriam did not act in opposition to the priests after she had been smitten with leprosy, but brought leprosy upon herself as a punishment, by her rebellion against Moses (Num. xii. 10 sqq.). And in the second place, this view cannot be reconciled with הִשָּׁמֶר בְּנֶגַע, since הִשָּׁמֶר with בְּ, either to be upon one's guard against (before) anything (2 Sam. xx. 10), or when taken in connection with בְּנֶפֶשׁ, to beware by the soul, *i.e.* for the sake of the worth of the soul (Jer. xvii. 21). The thought here, therefore, is, " Be on thy guard because of the plague of leprosy," *i.e.* that thou dost not get it, have to bear it, as the reward for thy rebellion against what the priests teach according to the commandment of the Lord. " Watch diligently, that thou do not incur the plague of leprosy" (*Vulgate*); or, " that thou do not sin, so as to be punished with leprosy" (*J. H. Michaelis*).

Vers. 10–15. *Warning against oppressing the Poor.*—Vers. 10, 11. If a loan of any kind was lent to a neighbour, the lender was not to go into his house to pledge (take) a pledge, but was to let the borrower bring the pledge out. The meaning is, that they were to leave it to the borrower to give a pledge, and not compel him to give up something as a pledge that might be indispensable to him. —Vers. 12, 13. And if the man was in distress (עָנִי), the lender was not to lie (sleep) upon his pledge, since the poor man had very often nothing but his upper garment, in which he slept, to give as a pledge. This was to be returned to him in the evening. (A repetition of Ex. xxii. 25, 26.) On the expression, " it shall be righteousness unto thee," see chap. vi. 25.—Vers. 14, 15. They were not to oppress a poor and distressed labourer, by withholding his wages. This command is repeated here from Lev. xix. 13, with special reference to the distress of the poor man. "*And to it* (his wages) *he lifts up his soul:*" *i.e.* he feels a longing for it. " Lifts up his soul:" as in Ps. xxiv. 4; Hos. iv. 8; Jer. xxii. 27. On ver. 15*b*, see chap. xv. 9 and Jas. v. 4.

Vers. 16–18. *Warning against Injustice.*—Ver. 16. Fathers were not to be put to death upon (along with) their sons, nor sons upon (along with) their fathers, *i.e.* they were not to suffer the punishment of death with them for crimes in which they had no share; but every one was to be punished simply for his own sin. This command was important, to prevent an unwarrantable and abusive application of the law which is manifest in the movements of divine justice to the criminal jurisprudence of the land (Ex. xx. 5), since it was a common thing among heathen nations—*e.g.* the Persians, Macedonians, and others—for the children and families of criminals to be also put to death (cf. Esther ix. 13, 14; *Herod.* iii. 19; *Ammian Marcell.* xxiii. 6; *Curtius*, vi. 11, 20, etc.). An example of the carrying out of this law is to be found in 2 Kings xiv. 6, 2 Chron. xxv. 4. In vers. 17, 18, the law against perverting the right of strangers, orphans, and widows, is repeated from Ex. xxii. 20, 21, and xxiii. 9; and an addition is made, namely, that they were not to take a widow's raiment in pledge (cf. Lev. xix. 33, 34).—Vers. 19–22. Directions to allow strangers, widows, and orphans to glean in time of harvest (as in Lev. xix. 9, 10, and xxiii. 22). The reason is given in ver. 22, viz. the same as in ver. 18 and chap. xv. 15.

Laws relating to Corporal Punishment; Levirate Marriages; and Just Weights and Measures.—Chap. xxv.

Vers. 1–3. Corporal Punishment.—The rule respecting the corporal punishment to be inflicted upon a guilty man is introduced in ver. 1 with the general law, that in a dispute between two men the court was to give right to the man who was right, and to pronounce the guilty man guilty (cf. Ex. xxii. 8 and xxiii. 7).—Ver. 2. If the guilty man was sentenced to stripes, he was to receive his punishment in the presence of the judge, and not more than forty stripes, that he might not become contemptible in the eyes of the people. בֶּן הַכּוֹת, son of stripes, *i.e.* a man liable to stripes, like son (child) of death, in 1 Sam. xx. 31. " *According to the need of his crime in number,*" *i.e.* as many stripes as his crime deserved.—Ver. 3. " *Forty shall ye beat him, and not add,*" *i.e.* at most forty stripes, and not more. The strokes were administered with a stick upon the back (Prov. x. 13, xix. 29, xxvi. 3, etc.). This was the Egyptian mode of whipping, as we may see depicted upon the monuments, when the culprits lie flat upon the ground, and being held fast by the hands and feet, receive their strokes in the presence of the judge (*vid. Wilkinson,* ii. p. 11, and *Rosellini,* ii. 3, p. 274, 78). The number forty was not to be exceeded, because a larger number of strokes with a stick would not only endanger health and life, but disgrace the man : " *that thy brother do not become contemptible in thine eyes.*" If he had deserved a severer punishment, he was to be executed. In Turkey the punishments inflicted are much more severe, viz. from fifty to a hundred lashes with a whip; and they are at the same time inhuman (see *v. Tornauw, Moslem. Recht,* p. 234). The number, forty, was probably chosen with reference to its symbolical significance, which it had derived from Gen. vii. 12 onwards, as the full measure of judgment. The Rabbins fixed the number at forty save one (*vid.* 2 Cor. xi. 24), from a scrupulous fear of transgressing the letter of the law, in case a mistake should be made in the counting; yet they felt no conscientious scruples about using a whip of twisted thongs instead of a stick (*vid. tract. Macc.* iii. 12 ; *Buxtorf, Synag. Jud.* pp. 522–3; and *Lundius, Jüd. Heiligth.* p. 472).—Ver. 4. The command not to put a muzzle upon the ox when threshing, is

no doubt proverbial in its nature, and even in the context before us
is not intended to apply merely literally to an ox employed in threshing, but to be understood in the general sense in which the Apostle
Paul uses it in 1 Cor. ix. 9 and 1 Tim. v. 18, viz. that a labourer
was not to be deprived of his wages. As the mode of threshing
presupposed here—namely, with oxen yoked together, and driven
to and fro over the corn that had been strewn upon the floor, that
they might kick out the grains with their hoofs—has been retained
to the present day in the East, so has also the custom of leaving
the animals employed in threshing without a muzzle (*vid. Hoest,
Marokos*, p. 129 ; *Wellst. Arabien,* i. p. 194 ; *Robinson,* Pal. ii.
pp. 206–7, iii. p. 6), although the Mosaic injunctions are not so
strictly observed by the Christians as by the Mohammedans (Robinson, ii. p. 207).

Vers. 5–10. On Levirate Marriages. — Vers. 5, 6. If
brothers lived together, and one of them died childless, the wife
of the deceased was not to be married outside (*i.e.* away from the
family) to a strange man (one not belonging to her kindred) ; her
brother-in-law was to come to her and take her for his wife, and
perform the duty of a brother-in-law to her.   יַבֵּם, *denom.* from
יָבָם, a brother-in-law, husband's brother, *lit.* to act the brother-in-
law, *i.e.* perform the duty of a brother-in-law, which consisted in
his marrying his deceased brother's widow, and begetting a son or
children with her, the first-born of whom was " to stand upon the
name of his deceased brother," *i.e.* be placed in the family of the
deceased, and be recognised as the heir of his property, that his
name (the name of the man who had died childless) might not be
wiped out or vanish out of Israel.   The provision, " without having
a son" (*ben*), has been correctly interpreted by the LXX., *Vulg.,
Josephus* (Ant. iv. 8, 23), and the *Rabbins,* as signifying childless
(having no seed, Matt. xxii. 25) ; for if the deceased had simply a
daughter, according to Num. xxvii. 4 sqq., the perpetuation of his
house and name was to be ensured through her.   The obligation
of a brother-in-law's marriage only existed in cases where the
brothers had lived together, *i.e.* in one and the same place, not
necessarily in one house or with a common domestic establishment
and home (*vid.* Gen. xiii. 6, xxxvi. 7).—This custom of a brother-
in-law's (Levirate) marriage, which is met with in different nations,
and was an old traditional custom among the Israelites (see at Gen.
xxxviii. 8 sqq.), had its natural roots in the desire inherent in man,

who is formed for immortality, and connected with the hitherto undeveloped belief in an eternal life, to secure a continued personal existence for himself and immortality for his name, through the perpetuation of his family and in the life of the son who took his place. This desire was not suppressed in Israel by divine revelation, but rather increased, inasmuch as the promises given to the patriarchs were bound up with the preservation and propagation of their seed and name. The promise given to Abraham for his seed would of necessity not only raise the begetting of children in the religious views of the Israelites into a work desired by God and well-pleasing to Him, but would also give this significance to the traditional custom of preserving the name and family by the substitution of a marriage of duty, that they would thereby secure to themselves and their family a share in the blessing of promise. Moses therefore recognised this custom as perfectly justifiable; but he sought to restrain it within such limits, that it should not present any impediment to the sanctification of marriage aimed at by the law. He took away the compulsory character, which it hitherto possessed, by prescribing in vers. 7 sqq., that if the surviving brother refused to marry his widowed sister-in-law, she was to bring the matter into the gate before the elders of the town (*vid.* chap. xxi. 19), *i.e.* before the magistrates; and if the brother-in-law still persisted in his refusal, she was to take his shoe from off his foot and spit in his face, with these words: " *So let it be done to the man who does not build up his brother's house.*" The taking off of the shoe was an ancient custom in Israel, adopted, according to Ruth iv. 7, in cases of redemption and exchange, for the purpose of confirming commercial transactions. The usage arose from the fact, that when any one took possession of landed property he did so by treading upon the soil, and asserting his right of possession by standing upon it in his shoes. In this way the taking off of the shoe and handing it to another became a symbol of the renunciation of a man's position and property,—a symbol which was also common among the Indians and the ancient Germans (see my *Archäologie,* ii. p. 66). But the custom was an ignominious one in such a case as this, when the shoe was publicly taken off the foot of the brother-in-law by the widow whom he refused to marry. He was thus deprived of the position which he ought to have occupied in relation to her and to his deceased brother, or to his paternal house; and the disgrace involved in this was still further heightened by the fact that his sister-in-law spat in his face. This is the meaning of the words (cf. Num. xii. 14), and not merely spit on the ground before his eyes, as *Saalschütz* and others as well as the Talmudists (*tr. Jebam.* xii. 6) render it, for the purpose of diminishing the disgrace. "*Build up his brother's house,*" *i.e.* lay the foundation of a family or posterity for him (cf. Gen. xvi. 2).—In addition to this, the unwilling brother-in-law was to receive a name of ridicule in Israel: "*House of the shoe taken off*" (חֲלוּץ הַנַּעַל, taken off as to his shoe; cf. *Ewald*, § 288, b.), *i.e.* of the barefooted man, equivalent to "the miserable fellow;" for it was only in miserable circumstances that the Hebrews went barefoot (*vid.* Isa. xx. 2, 3; Micah i. 8; 2 Sam. xv. 30). If the brother-in-law bore this reproach upon himself and his house, he was released from his duty as a brother-in-law. By these regulations the brother-in-law's marriage was no doubt recognised as a duty of affection towards his deceased brother, but it was not made a command, the neglect of which would involve guilt and punishment. Within these limits the brother-in-law's marriage might co-exist with the prohibition of marriage with a brother's wife; "whereas, if the deceased brother had a son or children, such a marriage was forbidden as prejudicial to the fraternal relation. In cases where the deceased was childless, it was commanded as a duty of affection for the building up of the brother's house, and the preservation of his family and name. By the former prohibition, the house (family) of the brother was kept in its integrity, whilst by the latter command its permanent duration was secured. In both cases the deceased brother was honoured, and the fraternal affection preserved as the moral foundation of his house" (*vid.* my *Archäologie*, pp. 64, 65).

Vers. 11 and 12. "But in order that the great independence which is here accorded to a childless widow in relation to her brother-in-law, might not be interpreted as a false freedom granted to the female sex" (*Baumgarten*), the law is added immediately afterwards, that a woman whose husband was quarrelling with another, and who should come to his assistance by laying hold of the secret parts of the man who was striking her husband, should have her hand cut off.

Vers. 13–19. The duty of integrity in trade is once more enforced in vers. 13–16 (as in Lev. xix. 35, 36). "*Stone and stone,*" *i.e.* two kinds of stones for weighing (cf. Ps. xii. 3), viz. large ones for buying and small ones for selling. On the promise in ver. 15b, see chap. iv. 26, v. 16; ver. 16a, as in chap. xxii. 5, xviii. 12, etc. In the concluding words, ver. 16b, "*all that do unrighteously,*" Moses sums up all breaches of the law.—Vers. 17–19. But whilst the Israelites were to make love the guiding principle of their conduct in their dealings with a neighbour, and even with strangers and foes, this love was not to degenerate into weakness or indifference towards open ungodliness. To impress this truth upon the people, Moses concludes the discourse on the law by reminding them of the crafty enmity manifested towards them by Amalek on their march out of Egypt, and with the command to root out the Amalekites (cf. Ex. xvii. 9–16). This heathen nation had come against Israel on its journey, viz. at Rephidim in Horeb, and had attacked its rear : " *All the enfeebled behind thee, whilst thou wast faint and weary, without fearing God.*" זָנַב, *lit.* to tail, hence to attack or destroy the rear of an army or of a travelling people (cf. Josh. x. 19). For this reason, when the Lord should have given Israel rest in the land of its inheritance, it was to root out the remembrance of Amalek under heaven. (On the execution of this command, see 1 Sam. xv.) " *Thou shalt not forget it :*" an emphatic enforcement of the " remember" in ver. 17.

Thanksgiving and Prayer at the Presentation of First-fruits and Tithes.—Chap. xxvi.

To the exposition of the commandments and rights of Israel Moses adds, in closing, another ordinance respecting those gifts, which were most intimately connected with social and domestic life, viz. the first-fruits and second tithes, for the purpose of giving the proper consecration to the attitude of the nation towards its Lord and God.

Vers. 1–11. Of the first of the fruit of the ground, which was presented from the land received from the Lord, the Israelite was to take a portion (מֵרֵאשִׁית with מִן partitive), and bring it in a basket to the place of the sanctuary, and give it to the priest who should be there, with the words, " *I have made known to-day to the Lord thy God, that I have come into the land which the Lord swore to our fathers to give us,*" upon which the priest should take the basket and put it down before the altar of Jehovah (vers. 1–4). From the partitive מֵרֵאשִׁית we cannot infer, as *Schultz* supposes, that the first-fruits were not to be all delivered at the sanctuary, any more than this can be inferred from Ex. xxiii. 19 (see the explanation of this passage). All that is implied is, that, for the purpose described afterwards, it was not necessary to put all the offerings of first-fruits into a basket and set them down before the altar. טָנָא

(vers. 2, 4, and chap. xxviii. 5, 17) is a basket of wicker-work, and not, as *Knobel* maintains, the Deuteronomist's word for צִנְצֶנֶת (Ex. xvi. 33). "*The priest*" is not the high priest, but the priest who had to attend to the altar-service and receive the sacrificial gifts.— The words, "I have to-day made known to the Lord thy God," refer to the practical confession which was made by the presentation of the first-fruits. The fruit was the tangible proof that they were in possession of the land, and the presentation of the first of this fruit the practical confession that they were indebted to the Lord for the land. This confession the offerer was also to embody in a prayer of thanksgiving, after the basket had been received by the priest, in which he confessed that he and his people owed their existence and welfare to the grace of God, manifested in the miraculous redemption of Israel out of the oppression of Egypt and their guidance into Canaan.—Ver. 5. אֲרַמִּי אֹבֵד אָבִי, "*a lost* (perishing) *Aramœan was my father*" (not the Aramæan, *Laban*, wanted to destroy my father, *Jacob*, as the *Chald.*, *Arab.*, *Luther*, and others render it). אֹבֵד signifies not only going astray, wandering, but perishing, in danger of perishing, as in Job xxix. 13, Prov. xxxi. 6, etc. Jacob is referred to, for it was he who went down to Egypt in few men. He is mentioned as the tribe-father of the nation, because the nation was directly descended from his sons, and also derived its name of *Israel* from him. Jacob is called an Aramæan, not only because of his long sojourn in Aramæa (Gen. xxix.–xxxi.), but also because he got his wives and children there (cf. Hos. xii. 13); and the relatives of the patriarchs had accompanied Abraham from Chaldæa to Mesopotamia (Aram; see Gen. xi. 30). בִּמְתֵי מְעָט, consisting of few men (בְּ, the so-called *beth essent.*, as in chap. x. 22, Ex. vi. 3, etc.; *vid. Ewald*, § 299, *q.*). Compare Gen. xxxiv. 30, where Jacob himself describes his family as "few in number." On the number in the family that migrated into Egypt, reckoned at seventy souls, see the explanation at Gen. xlvi. 27. On the multiplication in Egypt into a great and strong people, see Ex. i. 7, 9; and on the oppression endured there, Ex. i. 11–22, and ii. 23 sqq.—The guidance out of Egypt amidst great signs (ver. 8), as in chap. iv. 34.—Ver. 10. "*So shalt thou set it down* (the basket with the first-fruits) *befqre Jehovah.*" These words are not to be understood, as *Clericus, Knobel,* and others suppose, in direct opposition to vers. 4 and 5, as implying that the offerer had held the basket in his hand during the prayer, but simply as a remark which closes the instructions.—Ver. 11. Rejoicing in all the good, etc., points to the joy connected with the sacrificial meal, which followed the act of worship (as in chap. xii. 12). The presentation of the first-fruits took place, no doubt, on their pilgrimages to the sanctuary at the three yearly festivals (chap. xvi.) ; but it is quite without ground that *Riehm* restricts these words to the sacrificial meals to be prepared from the tithes, as if they had been the only sacrificial meals (see at chap. xviii. 3).

Vers. 12–15. The delivery of the tithes, like the presentation of the first-fruits, was also to be sanctified by prayer before the Lord. It is true that only a prayer after taking the second tithe in the third year is commanded here ; but that is simply because this tithe was appropriated everywhere throughout the land to festal meals for the poor and destitute (chap. xiv. 28), when prayer before the Lord would not follow *per analogiam* from the previous injunction concerning the presentation of first-fruits, as it would in the case of the tithes with which sacrificial meals were prepared at the sanctuary (chap. xiv. 22 sqq.). לְעַשֵּׂר is the infinitive Hiphil for לְהַעֲשֵׂר, as in Neh. x. 39 (on this form, *vid. Ges.* § 53, 3 Anm. 2 and 7, and *Ew.* § 131, *b.* and 244, *b.*). "Saying before the Lord" does not denote prayer in the sanctuary (at the tabernacle), but, as in Gen. xxvii. 7, simply prayer before God the omnipresent One, who is enthroned in heaven (ver. 15), and blesses His people from above from His holy habitation. The declaration of having fulfilled the commandments of God refers primarily to the directions concerning the tithes, and was such a rendering of an account as springs from the consciousness that a man very easily transgresses the commandments of God, and has nothing in common with the blindness of pharisaic self-righteousness. " *I have cleaned out the holy out of my house :*" the holy is that which is sanctified to God, that which belongs to the Lord and His servants, as in Lev. xxi. 22. בִּעֵר signifies not only to remove, but to clean out, wipe out. That which was sanctified to God appeared as a debt, which was to be wiped out of a man's house (*Schultz*).—Ver. 14. " *I have not eaten thereof in my sorrow.*" אֹנִי, from אָן, tribulation, distress, signifies here in all probability mourning, and judging from what follows, mourning for the dead, equivalent to " in a mourning condition," *i.e.* in a state of legal (Levitical) uncleanness ; so that בְּאֹנִי really corresponded to the בְּטָמֵא which follows, except that טָמֵא includes every kind of legal uncleanness. " *I have removed nothing thereof as unclean,*" *i.e.* while in the state of an unclean person. Not only not eaten of any, but not removed any of it from the house, carried it away in an unclean state, in which they were forbidden to touch the holy gifts (Lev. xxii. 3). "*And not given (any) of it on account of the dead.*" This most probably refers to the custom of sending provisions into a house of mourning, to prepare meals for the mourners (2 Sam. iii. 25; Jer. xvi. 7; Hos. ix. 4; Tobit iv. 17). A house of mourning, with its inhabitants, was regarded as unclean; consequently nothing could be carried into it of that which was sanctified. There is no good ground for thinking of idolatrous customs, or of any special superstition attached to the bread of mourning; nor is there any ground for understanding the words as referring to the later Jewish custom of putting provisions into the grave along with the corpse, to which the Septuagint rendering, οὐκ ἔδωκα ἀπ' αὐτῶν τῷ τεθνηκότι, points. (On ver. 15, see Isa. lxiii. 15.)

Vers. 16–19. At the close of his discourse, Moses sums up the whole in the earnest admonition that Israel would give the Lord its God occasion to fulfil the promised glorification of His people, by keeping His commandments with all their heart and soul.—Ver. 16. On this day the Lord commanded Israel to keep these laws and rights with all the heart and all the soul (cf. chap. vi. 5, x. 12 sqq.). There are two important points contained in this (vers. 17 sqq.). The acceptance of the laws laid before them on the part of the Israelites involved a practical declaration that the nation would accept Jehovah as its God, and walk in His way (ver. 17); and the giving of the law on the part of the Lord was a practical confirmation of His promise that Israel should be His people of possession, which He would glorify above all nations (vers. 18, 19). "*Thou hast let the Lord say to-day to be thy God,*" *i.e.* hast given Him occasion to say to thee that He will be thy God, manifest Himself to thee as thy God. "*And to walk in His ways, and to keep His laws,*" etc., for "and that thou wouldst walk in His ways, and keep His laws." The acceptance of Jehovah as its God involved *eo ipso* a willingness to walk in His ways.—Vers. 18, 19. At the same time, Jehovah had caused the people to be told that they were His treasured people of possession, as He had said in Ex. xix. 5, 6; and that if they kept all His commandments, He would set them highest above all nations whom He had created, "for praise, and for a name, and for glory," *i.e.* make them an object of praise, and renown, and glorification of God, the Lord and Creator of Israel, among all nations (*vid.* Jer. xxxiii. 9 and xiii. 11; Zeph. iii. 19, 20). "*And that it should become a holy people unto the Lord,*" as He had already said in Ex. xix. 6. The sanctification of Israel was the

design and end of its divine election, and would be accomplished in
the glory to which the people of God were to be exalted (see the
commentary on Ex. xix. 5, 6). The *Hiphil* הֶאֱמִיר, which is only
found here, has no other meaning than this, " to cause a person to
say," or " give him occasion to say ;" and this is perfectly appropriate here, whereas the other meaning suggested, " to exalt," has
no tenable support either in the paraphrastic rendering of these
verses in the ancient versions, or in the Hithpael in Ps. xciv. 4, and
moreover is altogether unsuitable in ver. 17.

III.—THIRD DISCOURSE, OR RENEWAL OF THE COVENANT.

CHAP. XXVII.–XXX.

THE conclusion of the covenant in the land of Moab, as the last
address in this section (chap. xxix. and xxx.) is called in the heading
(chap. xxviii. 69) and in the introduction (chap. xxix. 9 sqq.), *i.e.*
the renewal of the covenant concluded at Horeb, commences with
instructions to set up the law in a solemn manner in the land of
Canaan after crossing over the Jordan (chap. xxvii.). After this
there follows an elaborate exposition of the blessings and curses
which would come upon the people according to their attitude
towards the law (chap. xxviii.). And lastly, Moses places the
whole nation with a solemn address before the face of the Lord,
and sets before it once more the blessing and the curse in powerful
and alarming words, with the exhortation to choose the blessing and
life (chap. xxix. and xxx.).

ON THE SETTING UP OF THE LAW IN THE LAND OF CANAAN.— CHAP. XXVII.

The instructions upon this point are divisible into two : viz. (*a*)
to set up large stones covered with lime upon Mount Ebal, after
crossing into Canaan, and to build an altar there for the presentation of burnt-offerings and slain-offerings, and to write the law upon
these stones (vers. 1–8) ; and (*b*) to proclaim the blessing and curse
of the law upon Mount Gerizim and Mount Ebal (vers. 11–26).
These two instructions are bound together by the command to
observe the law (vers. 9 and 10), in which the internal or essential
connection of the two is manifested externally also. The fulfilment

of these directions after the entrance of Israel into Canaan is described in Josh. viii. 30–35. The act itself had a symbolical meaning. The writing of the law upon stones, which were erected on a mountain in the midst of the land, with the solemn proclamation of blessings and curses, was a practical acknowledgment of the law of the Lord on the part of Israel,—a substantial declaration that they would make the law the rule and standard of their life and conduct in the land which the Lord had given them for an inheritance.

Vers. 1–10. The command in ver. 1 to keep the whole law (שָׁמוֹר, *inf. abs.* for the imperative, as in Ex. xiii. 3, etc.), with which the instructions that follow are introduced, indicates at the very outset the purpose for which the law written upon stones was to be set up in Canaan, namely, as a public testimony that the Israelites who were entering into Canaan possessed in the law their rule and source of life. The command itself is given by Moses, together with the elders, because the latter had to see to the execution of it after Moses' death ; on the other hand, the priests are mentioned along with Moses in ver. 9, because it was their special duty to superintend the fulfilment of the commands of God.—Vers. 2 and 3 contain the general instructions ; vers. 4–8, more minute details. In the appointment of the time, " *on the day when ye shall pass over Jordan into the land,*" etc., the word " *day* " must not be pressed, but is to be understood in a broader sense, as signifying the time when Israel should have entered the land and taken possession of it. The stones to be set up were to be covered with lime, or gypsum (whether *sid* signifies lime or gypsum cannot be determined), and all the words of the law were to be written upon them. The writing, therefore, was not to be· cut into the stones and then covered with lime (as *J. D. Mich., Ros.*), but to be inscribed upon the plaistered stones, as was the custom in Egypt, where the walls of buildings, and even monumental stones, which they were about to paint with figures and hieroglyphics, were first of all covered with a coating of lime or gypsum, and then the figures painted upon this (see the testimonies of *Minutoli, Heeren, Prokesch* in *Hengstenberg's* Dissertations, i. 433, and Egypt and the· Books of Moses, p. 90). The object of this writing was not to hand down the law in this manner to posterity without alteration, but, as has already been stated, simply to set forth a public acknowledgment of the law on the part of the people, first of all for the sake of the generation which took possession of the land, and for posterity, only so far as this act was recorded in the book of Joshua and thus transmitted to future generations.—Ver. 3. Upon the stones there were to be written " *all the words of this law :* " obviously, therefore, not only the blessings and curses in vers. 15–26 (as *Josephus, Ant.* iv. 8, 44, *Masius, Clericus,* and others maintain), nor only Deuteronomy (*J. Gerhard, A. Osiander, Vater,* etc.), since this contained no independent " second law," but the whole of the Mosaic law ; not, indeed, the entire Pentateuch, with its historical narratives, its geographical, ethnographical, and other notices, but simply the legal part of it,—the commandments, statutes, and rights of the *Thorah.* But whether all the 613 commandments contained in the Pentateuch, according to the Jewish reckoning (vid. *Bertheau, die* 7 *Gruppen Mos. Ges.* p. 12), or only the quintessence of them, with the omission of the numerous repetitions of different commands, cannot be decided, and is of no importance to the matter in hand. The object aimed at would be attained by writing the essential kernel of the whole law ; though the possibility of all the commandments being written, of course without the reasons and exhortations connected with them, cannot be denied, since it is not stated how many stones were set up, but simply that large stones were to be taken, which would therefore contain a great deal.   In the clause, " *that thou mayest come into the land which Jehovah thy God giveth thee,*" etc., the coming involves the permanent possession of the land.   Not only the treading or conquest of Canaan, but the maintenance of the conquered land as a permanent hereditary possession, was promised to Israel ; but it would only permanently rejoice in the fulfilment of this promise, if it set up the law of its God in the land, and observed it.—Vers. 4–8. In the further expansion of this command, Moses first of all fixes the place where the stones were to be set up, namely, upon Mount Ebal (see at chap. xi. 29),—not upon Gerizim, according to the reading of the Samaritan Pentateuch ; for since the discussion of the question by *Verschuir (dissertt. phil. exeg. diss.* 3) and *Gesenius (de Pent. Samar.* p. 61), it may be regarded as an established fact, that this reading is an arbitrary alteration. The following clause, " *thou shalt plaister,*" etc., is a repetition in the earliest form of historical writing among the Hebrews.   To this there are appended in vers. 5–7 the new and further instructions, that an altar was to be built upon Ebal, and burnt-offerings and slain-offerings to be sacrificed upon it.   The notion that this altar was to be built of the stones with the law written upon them, or even with a portion of them, needs no refutation, as it has not the slightest support in the words

of the text.   For according to these the altar was to be built of
unhewn stones (therefore not of the stones covered with cement),
in obedience to the law in Ex. xx. 22 (see the exposition of this
passage, where the reason for this is discussed).   The spot selected
for the setting up of the stones with the law written upon it, as
well as for the altar and the offering of sacrifice, was Ebal, the
mountain upon which the curses were to be proclaimed; not Gerizim, which was appointed for the publication of the blessings, for
the very same reason for which only the curses to be proclaimed are
given in vers. 14 sqq. and not the blessings,—not, as *Schultz* supposes, because the law in connection with the curse speaks more
forcibly to sinful man than in connection with the blessing, or
because the curse, which manifests itself on every hand in human
life, sounds more credible than the promise; but, as the *Berleburger
Bible* expresses it, " to show how the law and economy of the Old
Testament would denounce the curse which rests upon the whole
human race because of sin, to awaken a desire for the Messiah, who
was to take away the curse and bring the true blessing instead."   For
however remote the allusion to the Messiah may be here, the truth
is unquestionably pointed out in these instructions, that the law primarily and chiefly brings a curse upon man because of the sinfulness
of his nature, as Moses himself announces to the people in chap.
xxxi. 16, 17.   And for this very reason the book of the law was to
be laid by the side of the ark of the covenant as a " testimony
against Israel" (chap. xxxi. 26).   But the altar was built for the
offering of sacrifices, to mould and consecrate the setting up of the
law upon the stones into a renewal of the covenant.   In the burnt-
offerings Israel gave itself up to the Lord with all its life and labour,
and in the sacrificial meal it entered into the enjoyment of the blessings of divine grace, to taste of the blessedness of vital communion
with its God.   By connecting the sacrificial ceremony with the
setting up of the law, Israel gave a practical testimony to the fact
that its life and blessedness were founded upon its observance of
the law.   The sacrifices and the sacrificial meal have the same signification here as at the conclusion of the covenant at Sinai (Ex.
xxiv. 11).—In ver. 8 the writing of the law upon the stones is commanded once more, and the further injunction is added, "*very
plainly*."—The writing of the law is mentioned last, as being the
most important, and not because it was to take place after the sacrificial ceremony.   The different instructions are arranged according
to their character, and not in chronological order.

The words of Moses which follow in vers. 9 and 10, *"Be silent, and hearken, O Israel; To-day thou hast become the people of the Lord thy God,"* show the significance of the act enjoined; although primarily they simply summon the Israelites to listen attentively to the still further commands. When Israel renewed the covenant with the Lord, by solemnly setting up the law in Canaan, it became thereby the nation of God, and bound itself, at the same time, to hearken to the voice of the Lord and keep His commandments, as it had already done (cf. chap. xxvi. 17, 18).

Vers. 11–26. With the solemn erection of the stones with the law written upon them, Israel was to transfer to the land the blessing and curse of the law, as was already commanded in chap. xi. 29; that is to say, according to the more minute explanation of the command which is given here, the people themselves were solemnly to give expression to the blessing and the curse: to the former upon Mount Gerizim, and to the latter upon Ebal. On the situation of these mountains, see at chap. xi. 29. To this end six tribes were to station themselves upon the top or side of. Gerizim, and six upon the top or side of Ebal. The blessing was to be uttered by the tribes of Simeon, Levi, Judah, Issachar, Joseph, and Benjamin, who sprang from the two wives of Jacob; and the curse by Reuben, with the two sons of Leah's maid Zilpah, and by Zebulun, with Dan and Naphtali, the sons of Rachel's maid Bilhah. It was natural that the utterance of the blessing should be assigned to the tribes which sprang from Jacob's proper wives, since the sons of the wives occupied a higher position than the sons of the maids,— just as the blessing had pre-eminence over the curse. But in order to secure the division into two sixes, it was necessary that two of the eight sons of the wives should be associated with those who pronounced the curses. The choice fell upon Reuben, because he had forfeited his right of primogeniture by his incest (Gen. xlix. 4), and upon Zebulun, as the youngest son of Leah. *" They shall stand there upon the curse:"* i.e. to pronounce the curse.—Ver. 14. *" And the Levites shall lift up and speak to all the men of Israel with a high* (loud) *voice:"* i.e. they shall pronounce the different formularies of blessing and cursing, turning towards the tribes to whom these utterances apply; and all the men of Israel shall answer *" Amen,"* to take to themselves the blessing and the curse, as uttered by them; just as in the case of the priestly blessing in Num. v. 22, and in connection with every oath, in which the person swearing took upon himself the oath that was pronounced, by replying "Amen." "*The Levites*" are not all the members of the tribe of Levi, but those " in whom the spiritual character of Levi was most decidedly manifested" (*Baumgarten*), *i.e.* the Levitical priests, as the guardians and teachers of the law, and those who carried the ark of the covenant (Josh. viii. 33). From the passage in Joshua, where the fulfilment of the Mosaic injunctions is recorded, we learn that the Levitical priests stationed themselves in the centre between the two mountains, with the ark of the covenant, and that the people took up their position, on both sides, opposite to the ark, viz. six tribes on Gerizim, and six on Ebal. The priests, who stood in the midst, by the ark of the covenant, then pronounced the different formularies of blessing and cursing, to which the six tribes answered "Amen." From the expression " all the men of Israel," it is perfectly evident that in this particular ceremony the people were not represented by their elders or heads, but were present in the persons of all their adult men who were over twenty years of age; and with this Josh. viii. 33, when rightly interpreted, fully harmonizes.

In vers. 15–26 there follow *twelve* curses, answering to the number of the tribes of Israel. The *first* is directed against those who make graven or molten images of Jehovah, and set them up in secret, that is to say, against secret breaches of the second commandment (Ex. xx. 4); the *second* against contempt of, or want of reverence towards, parents (Ex. xxi. 17); the *third* against those who remove boundaries (chap. xix. 14); the *fourth* against the man who leads the blind astray (Lev. xix. 14); the *fifth* against those who pervert the right of orphans and widows (chap. xxiv. 17); the *sixth* against incest with a mother (chap. xxiii. 1; Lev. xviii. 8); the *seventh* against unnatural vices (Lev. xviii. 23); the *eighth* and *ninth* against incest with a sister or a mother-in-law (Lev. xviii. 9 and 17); the *tenth* against secret murder (Ex. xx. 13; Num. xxxv. 16 sqq.); the *eleventh* against judicial murder (" he that taketh reward to slay a soul, *namely*, innocent blood :" Ex. xxiii. 7, 8); the *twelfth* against the man who does not set up the words of this law to do them, who does not make the laws the model and standard of his life and conduct. From this last curse, which applied to every breach of the law, it evidently follows, that the different sins and transgressions already mentioned were only selected by way of example, and for the most part were such as could easily be concealed from the judicial authorities. At the same time, " the office of the law is shown in this last utterance, the summing up of all the rest, to have been pre-eminently to proclaim condemnation. Every conscious act of transgression subjects the sinner to the curse of God, from which none but He who has become a curse for us can possibly deliver us" (Gal. iii. 10, 13. *O. v. Gerlach*).—On the reason why the blessings are not given, see the remarks on ver. 4. As the curses against particular transgressions of the law simply mention some peculiarly grievous sins by way of example, it would be easy to single out corresponding blessings from the general contents of the law : *e.g.* " Blessed be he who faithfully follows the Lord his God, or loves Him with the heart, who honours his father and his mother," etc. ; and lastly, all the blessings of the law could be summed up in the words, " Blessed be he who setteth up the words of this law, to do them."

BLESSING AND CURSE.—CHAP. XXVIII. 1-68.

For the purpose of impressing upon the hearts of all the people in the most emphatic manner both the blessing which Israel was to proclaim upon Gerizim, and the curse which it was to proclaim upon Ebal, Moses now unfolds the blessing of fidelity to the law and the curse of transgression in a longer address, in which he once more resumes, sums up, and expands still further the promises and threats of the law in Ex. xxiii. 20–33, and Lev. xxvi.

Vers. 1–14. THE BLESSING.—Ver. 1. If Israel would hearken to the voice of the Lord its God, the Lord would make it the highest of all the nations of the earth. This thought, with which the discourse on the law in chap. xxvi. 19 terminated, forms the theme, and in a certain sense the heading, of the following description of the blessing, through which the Lord, according to the more distinct declaration in ver. 2, would glorify His people above all the nations of the earth. The indispensable condition for obtaining this blessing, was obedience to the word of the Lord, or keeping His commandments. To impress this *conditio sine qua non* thoroughly upon the people, Moses not only repeats it at the commencement (ver. 2), and in the middle (ver. 9), but also at the close (vers. 13, 14), in both a positive and a negative form. In ver. 2, " the way in which Israel was to be exalted is pointed out" (*Schultz*) ; and thus the theme is more precisely indicated, and the elaboration of it is introduced. " All these blessings (those mentioned singly in what follows) will come upon thee and reach thee." The blessings are represented as actual powers, which follow the footsteps of the nation, and overtake it. In vers. 3–6, the fulness of the blessing of God in all the relations of life is depicted in a sixfold repetition of the word "blessed." Israel will be blessed in the town and in the field, the two spheres in which its life moves (ver. 3); blessed will be the fruit of the body, of the earth, and of the cattle, *i.e.* in all its productions (ver. 4; for each one, see chap. vii. 13, 14); blessed will be the basket (chap. xxvi. 2) in which the fruits are kept, and the kneading-trough (Ex. xii. 34) in which the daily bread is prepared (ver. 5); blessed will the nation be in all its undertakings ("coming in and going out;" *vid.* Num. xxvii. 17).—Vers. 7–14 describe the influence and effect of the blessing upon all the circumstances and situations in which the nation might be placed: in vers. 7–10, with reference (*a*) to the attitude of Israel towards its enemies (ver. 7); (*b*) to its trade and handicraft (ver. 8); (*c*) to its attitude towards all the nations of the earth (vers. 9, 10). The optative forms, יְהִי and יְצַו (in vers. 7 and 8), are worthy of notice. They show that Moses not only proclaimed the blessing to the people, but desired it for them, because he knew that Israel would not always or perfectly fulfil the condition upon which it was to be bestowed. " *May the Lord be pleased to give thine enemies . . . smitten before thee,*" *i.e.* give them up to thee as smitten (נָתַן לִפְנֵי, to give up before a person, to deliver up to him: cf. chap. i. 8), so that they shall come out against thee by one way, and flee from thee by seven ways, *i.e.* in wild dispersion (cf. Lev. xxvi. 7, 8).—Ver. 8. " *May the Lord command the blessing with thee* (put it at thy disposal) *in thy barns* (granaries, store-rooms) *and in all thy business*" (" to set the hand;" see chap. xii. 7).—Vers. 9, 10. " *The Lord will exalt thee for a holy nation to Himself, . . . so that all the nations of the earth shall see that the name of Jehovah is named upon thee, and shall fear before thee.*" The Lord had called Israel as a holy nation, when He concluded the covenant with it (Ex. xix. 5, 6). This promise, to which the words " as He hath sworn unto thee" point back, and which is called an oath, because it was founded upon the promises given to the patriarchs on oath (Gen. xxii. 16), and was given *implicite* in them, the Lord would fulfil to His people, and cause the holiness and glory of Israel to be so clearly manifested, that all nations should perceive or see " *that the name of the Lord is named upon Israel.*" The name of the Lord is the revelation of His glorious nature. It is named upon Israel, when Israel is transformed into the glory of the divine nature (cf. Isa. lxiii. 19; Jer. xiv. 9). It was only in feeble commencements that this blessing was fulfilled upon Israel under the Old Tes-

tament ; and it is not till the restoration of Israel, which is to take
place in the future according to Rom. xi. 25 sqq., that its complete
fulfilment will be attained. In vers. 11 and 12, Moses returns to
the earthly blessing, for the purpose of unfolding this still further.
" *Superabundance will the Lord give thee for good* (*i.e.* for happiness
and prosperity ; *vid.* chap. xxx. 9), *in fruit of thy body,*" etc. (cf.
ver. 4). He would open His good treasure-house, the heaven, to
give rain to the land in its season (cf. chap. xi. 14 ; Lev. xxvi. 4, 5),
and bless the work of the hands, *i.e.* the cultivation of the soil, so
that Israel would be able to lend to many, according to the prospect
already set before it in chap. xv. 6.—Vers. 13, 14. By such blessings
He would " *make Israel the head, and not the tail,*"—a figure taken
from life (*vid.* Isa. ix. 13), the meaning of which is obvious, and is
given literally in the next sentence, " *thou wilt be above only, and not
beneath,*" *i.e.* thou wilt rise more and more, and increase in wealth,
power, and dignity. With this the discourse returns to its commencement ; and the promise of blessing closes with another emphatic repetition of the condition on which the fulfilment depended
(vers. 13*b* and 14. On ver. 14, see chap. v. 29, xi. 28).

Vers. 15–68. THE CURSE, in case Israel should not hearken to
the voice of its God, to keep His commandments. After the announcement that all these (the following) curses would come upon
the disobedient nation (ver. 15), the curse is proclaimed in all its
extent, as covering all the relations of life, in a sixfold repetition
of the word " cursed" (vers. 16–19, as above in vers. 3–6) ; and the
fulfilment of this threat in plagues and diseases, drought and famine,
war, devastation of the land, and captivity of the people, is so depicted, that the infliction of these punishments stands out to view
in ever increasing extent and fearfulness. We are not to record
this, however, as a gradual heightening of the judgments of God,
in proportion to the increasing rebellion of Israel, as in Lev. xxvi.
14 sqq., although it is obvious that the punishments threatened did
not fall upon the nation all at once.—Vers. 16–19 correspond precisely to vers. 3–6, so as to set forth the curse as the counterpart of
the blessing, except that the basket and kneading-trough are mentioned before the fruit of the body.

Vers. 20–26. The *first* view, in which the bursting of the threatened curse upon the disobedient people is proclaimed in all its forms.
First of all, quite generally in ver. 20. " *The Lord will send the
curse against thee, consternation and threatening in every undertaking*

of thy hand which thou carriest out (see chap. xii. 7), *till thou be destroyed, till thou perish quickly, because of the wickedness of thy doings, because thou hast forsaken Me.*" The three words, מְאֵרָה, מְהוּמָה, and מִגְעֶרֶת, are synonymous, and are connected together to strengthen the thought. מְאֵרָה, curse or malediction ; הַמְּהוּמָה, the consternation produced by the curse of God, namely, the confusion with which God smites His foes (see at chap. vii. 23) ; הַמִּגְעֶרֶת is the threatening word of the divine wrath.—Then vers. 21 sqq. in detail. "*The Lord will make the pestilence fasten upon* (cleave to) *thee, till He hath destroyed thee out of the land . . . to smite thee with giddiness and fever* (cf. Lev. xxvi. 16), *inflammation, burning, and sword, blasting of corn, and mildew* (of the seed) ;" seven diseases therefore (seven as the stamp of the works of God), whilst pestilence in particular is mentioned first, as the most terrible enemy of life. דַּלֶּקֶת, from דָּלַק to burn, and חַרְחֻר, from חָרַר to glow, signify inflammatory diseases, burning fevers ; the distinction between these and קַדַּחַת cannot be determined. Instead of חֶרֶב, the sword as the instrument of death, used to designate slaughter and death, the *Vulgate, Arabic,* and *Samaritan* have adopted the reading חֹרֶב, *æstus,* heat (Gen. xxxi. 40), or drought, according to which there would be four evils mentioned by which human life is attacked, and three which are injurious to the corn. But as the LXX., *Jon., Syr.,* and others read חֶרֶב, this alteration is very questionable, especially as the reading can be fully defended in this connection ; and one objection to the alteration is, that drought is threatened for the first time in vers. 23, 24. שִׁדָּפוֹן, from שָׁדַף to singe or blacken, and יֵרָקוֹן, from יָרַק to be yellowish, refer to two diseases which attack the corn : the former to the withering or burning of the ears, caused by the east wind (Gen. xli. 23) ; the other to the effect produced by a warm wind in Arabia, by which the green ears are turned yellow, so that they bear no grains of corn.—Vers. 23, 24. To this should be added terrible drought, without a drop of rain from heaven (cf. Lev. xxvi. 19). Instead of rain, dust and ashes should fall from heaven. נָתַן construed with a double accusative : to make the rain of the land into dust and ashes, to give it in the form of dust and ashes. When the heat is very great, the air in Palestine is often full of dust and sand, the wind assuming the form of a burning sirocco, so that the air resembles the glowing heat at the mouth of a furnace (*Robinson,* ii. 504).—Vers. 25, 26. Defeat in battle, the very opposite of the blessing promised in ver. 7. Israel should become לְזַעֲוָה, "*a moving to and fro,*" *i.e.* so to speak, " a ball for all the kingdoms of the earth to play with" (*Schultz*). זַעֲוָה, here and at Ezek. xxiii. 46, is not a transposed and later form of זְוָעָה, which has a different meaning in Isa. xxviii. 19, but the original, uncontracted form, which was afterwards condensed into זוֹעָה ; for this, and not זְוָעָה, is the way in which the *Chethib* should be read in Jer. xv. 4, xxiv. 9, xxix. 18, xxxiv. 17, and 2 Chron. xxix. 8, where this threat is repeated (*vid. Ewald*, § 53, *b.*). The corpses of those who were slain by the foe should serve as food for the birds of prey and wild beasts—the greatest ignominy that could fall upon the dead, and therefore frequently held out as a threat against the ungodly (Jer. vii. 33, xvi. 4 ; 1 Kings xiv. 11, etc.).

Vers. 27–34. The *second* view depicts still further the visitation of God both by diseases of body and soul, and also by plunder and oppression on the part of their enemies.—In ver. 27 four incurable diseases of the body are threatened : the ulcer of Egypt (see at Ex. ix. 9), *i.e.* the form of leprosy peculiar to Egypt, *elephantiasis* (*Aegypti peculiare malum: Plin.* xxvi. c. 1, s. 5), which differed from *lepra tuberosa*, however, or tubercular leprosy (ver. 35 ; cf. Job ii. 7), in degree only, and not in its essential characteristics (see *Tobler, mediz. Topogr. v. Jerus.* p. 51). עֳפָלִים, from עֹפֶל, a swelling, rising, signifies a tumour, and according to the Rabbins a disease of the anus : in men, *tumor in posticis partibus ;* in women, *durius quoddam* οἴδημα *in utero.* It was with this disease that the Philistines were smitten (1 Sam. v.). גָּרָב (see Lev. xxi. 20) and חֶרֶס, from חָרַס, to scrape or scratch, also a kind of itch, of which there are several forms in Syria and Egypt.—Vers. 28, 29. In addition to this, there would come idiocy, blindness, and confusion of mind,—three psychical maladies ; for although עִוָּרוֹן signifies primarily bodily blindness, the position of the word between idiocy and confusion of heart, *i.e.* of the understanding, points to mental blindness here.—Ver. 29 leads to the same conclusion, where it is stated that Israel would grope in the bright noon-day, like a blind man in the dark, and not make his ways prosper, *i.e.* not hit upon the right road which led to the goal and to salvation, would have no good fortune or success in its undertakings (cf. Ps. xxxvii. 7). Being thus smitten in body and soul, it would be *only* (אַךְ as in chap. xvi. 15), *i.e.* utterly, oppressed and spoiled evermore. These words introduce the picture of the other calamity, viz. the plundering of the nation and the land by enemies (vers. 30–33). Wife, house, vineyard, ox, ass, and sheep would be taken away by the foe ; sons and daughters would be carried away into captivity before the eyes of the people, who would see it and pine after the children, *i.e.* with sorrow and longing after them; " *and thy hand shall not be to thee towards God,*" *i.e.* all power and help will fail thee. (On this proverbial expression, see Gen. xxxi. 29; and on חֵל, in ver. 30, see at chap. xx. 6.)—In vers. 33, 34, this threat is summed up in the following manner: the fruit of the field and all their productions would be devoured by a strange nation, and Israel would be only oppressed and crushed to pieces all its days, and become mad on account of what its eyes would be compelled to see.

Vers. 35–46. The *third* view.—With the words, "*the Lord will smite thee,*" Moses resumes in ver. 35 the threat of ver. 27, to set forth the calamities already threatened under a new aspect, namely, as signs of the rejection of Israel from covenant fellowship with the Lord.—Ver. 35. The Lord would smite the people with grievous abscesses in the knees and thighs, that should be incurable, even from the sole of the foot to the crown of the head. שְׁחִין רָע is the so-called joint-leprosy, a form of the *lepra tuberosa* (*vid.* Pruner, p. 167). From the clause, however, "*from the sole of thy foot unto the top of thy head,*" it is evident that the threat is not to be restricted to this species of leprosy, since " the upper parts of the body often remain in a perfectly normal state in cases of leprosy in the joints; and after the diseased parts have fallen off, the patients recover their previous health to a certain degree" (*Pruner*). Moses mentions this as being a disease of such a nature, that it would render it utterly impossible for those who were afflicted with it either to stand or walk, and then heightens the threat by adding the words, " from the sole of the foot to the top of the head." Leprosy excluded from fellowship with the Lord, and deprived the nation of the character of a nation of God.—Vers. 36, 37. The loss of their spiritual character would be followed by the dissolution of the covenant fellowship. This thought connects ver. 36 with ver. 35, and not the thought that Israel being afflicted with leprosy would be obliged to go into captivity, and in this state would become an object of abhorrence to the heathen (*Schultz*). The Lord would bring the nation and its king to a foreign nation that it did not know, and thrust them into bondage, so that it would be obliged to serve other gods,—wood and stone (*vid.* chap. iv. 28),—and would become an object of disgust, a proverb, and a byword to all nations whither God should drive it (*vid.* 1 Kings ix. 7; Jer. xxiv. 9).—Vers. 38 sqq. Even in their own land the curse would fall upon every kind of labour and enterprise. Much

seed would give little to reap, because the locust would devour the
seed; the planting and dressing of the vineyard would furnish no
wine to drink, because the worm would devour the vine. תּוֹלֵעַ is
probably the ἴψ or ἴξ of the Greeks, the *convolvulus* of the Romans,
our vine-weevil.—Ver. 40. They would have many olive-trees in
the land, but not anoint themselves with oil, because the olive-tree
would be rooted out or plundered (יִשַּׁל, Niphal of שָׁלַל, as in chap.
xix. 5, not the Kal of נָשַׁל, which cannot be shown to have the intransitive meaning *elabi*).—Ver. 41. Sons and daughters would they
beget, but not keep, because they would have to go into captivity.—
Ver. 42. All the trees and fruits of the land would the buzzer take
possession of. צְלָצַל, from צָלַל to *buzz*, a rhetorical epithet applied to
locusts, not the grasshopper, which does not injure the fruits of the
tree or ground sufficiently for the term יָרַשׁ, "to take possession
of," to be applicable to it.—Ver. 43. Israel would be utterly impoverished, and would sink lower and lower, whilst the stranger in
the midst of it would, on the contrary, get above it very high; not
indeed " because he had no possession, but was dependent upon
resources of other kinds" (*Schultz*), but rather because he would
be exempted with all his possessions from the curse of God, just as
the Israelites had been exempted from the plagues which came
upon the Egyptians (Ex. ix. 6, 7, 26).—Ver. 44. The opposite of
vers. 12 and 13 would come to pass.—In ver. 46 the address
returns to its commencement in ver. 15, with the terrible threat,
" *These curses shall be upon thee for a sign and for a wonder, and
upon thy seed for ever*," for the purpose of making a pause, if not of
bringing the whole to a close. The curses were for a sign and
wonder (מוֹפֵת, that which excites astonishment and terror), inasmuch as their magnitude and terrible character manifested most
clearly the supernatural interposition of God (*vid.* chap. xxix. 23).
" *For ever* " applies to the generation smitten by the curse, which
would remain for ever rejected, though without involving the perpetual rejection of the whole nation, or the impossibility of the conversion and restoration of a remnant, or of a holy seed (Isa. x. 22,
vi. 13 ; Rom. ix. 27, xi. 5).

Vers. 47–57. The *fourth* view.—Although in what precedes
every side of the national life has been brought under the curse,
yet love to his people, and the desire to preserve them from the
curse, by holding up before them the dreadful severity of the wrath
of God, impel the faithful servant of the Lord to go still further,
and depict more minutely still the dreadful horrors consequent upon

Israel being given up to the power of the heathen, and first of all
in vers. 47–57 the horrible calamities which would burst upon Israel
on the conquest of the land and its fortresses by its foes.—Vers.
47, 48. Because it had not served the Lord its God with joy and
gladness of heart, " *for the abundance of all*," *i.e.* for the abundance
of all the blessings bestowed upon it by its God, it would serve its
enemies in hunger, and thirst, and nakedness, and want of everything, and wear an iron yoke, *i.e.* be obliged to perform the hardest
tributary service till it was destroyed (הִשְׁמִיד for הַשְׁמִיד, as in chap.
vii. 24).—Vers. 49, 50. The Lord would bring against it from afar
a barbarous, hardhearted nation, which knew no pity. " *From
afar*" is still further strengthened by the addition of the words,
" *from the end of the earth.*" The greater the distance off, the more
terrible does the foe appear. He flies thence like an eagle, which
plunges with violence upon its prey, and carries it off with its
claws ; and Israel does not understand its language, so as to be able
to soften its barbarity, or come to any terms. A people " *firm,
hard of face,*" *i.e.* upon whom nothing makes an impression (*vid.*
Isa. l. 7),—a description of the audacity and shamelessness of its
appearance (Dan. viii. 23 ; cf. Prov. vii. 13, xxi. 29), which spares
neither old men nor boys. This description no doubt applies to
the Chaldeans, who are described as flying eagles in Hab. i. 6 sqq.,
Jer. xlviii. 40, xlix. 22, Ezek. xvii. 3, 7, as in the verses before us ;
but it applies to other enemies of Israel beside these, namely to the
great imperial powers generally, the Assyrians, Chaldeans, and
Romans, whom the Lord raised up as the executors of His curse
upon His rebellious people. Isaiah therefore depicts the Assyrians
in a similar manner, namely, as a people with an unintelligible language (chap. v. 26, xxviii. 11, xxxiii. 19), and describes the cruelty
of the Medes in chap. xiii. 17, 18, with an unmistakeable allusion
to ver. 50 of the present threat.—Vers. 51 sqq. This foe would
consume all the fruit of the cattle and the land, *i.e.* everything
which the nation had acquired through agriculture and the breeding of stock, without leaving it anything, until it was utterly destroyed (see chap. vii. 13), and would oppress, *i.e.* besiege it in all
its gates (towns, *vid.* chap. xii. 12), till the lofty and strong walls
upon which they relied should fall (יָרַד, as in chap. xx. 20).—Ver.
53. It would so distress Israel, that in their distress and siege they
would be driven to eat the fruit of their body, and the flesh of their
own children (with regard to the fulfilment of this, see the remarks
on Lev. xxvi. 29).—This horrible distress is depicted still more fully

in vers. 54–57, where the words, " *in the siege and in the straitness,*" etc. (ver. 53*b*), are repeated as a *refrain,* with their appalling sound, in vers. 55 and 57.—Vers. 54, 55. The effeminate and luxurious man would look with ill-favour upon his brother, the wife of his bosom, and his remaining children, " *to give*" (so that he would not give) to one of them of the flesh of his children which he was consuming, because there was nothing left to him in the siege. " *His eye shall be evil,*" *i.e.* look with envy or ill-favour (cf. chap. xv. 9). מִבְּלִי הִשְׁאִיר, on account of there not being anything left for himself. בֹּל with בְּלִי signifies literally " *all not,*" *i.e.* nothing at all. הִשְׁאִיר, an infinitive, as in chap. iii. 3 (see at ver. 48).—Vers. 56, 57. The delicate and luxurious woman, who had not attempted to put her feet to the ground (had always been carried therefore either upon a litter or an ass: cf. Judg. v. 10, and *Arvieux, Sitten der Beduinen Ar.* p. 143), from tenderness and delicacy—her eye would look with envy upon the husband of her bosom and her children, and that (*vav expl.*) because of (for) her after-birth, which cometh out from between her feet, and because of her children which she bears (*sc.* during the siege) ; " *for she will eat them secretly in the want of everything,*" that is to say, first of all attempt to appease her hunger with the after-birth, and then, when there was no more left, with her own children. To such an awful height would the famine rise !

Vers. 58–68. The *fifth* and last view.—And yet these horrible calamities would not be the end of the distress. The full measure of the divine curse would be poured out upon Israel, when its disobedience had become hardened into disregard of the glorious and fearful name of the Lord its God. To point this out, Moses describes the resistance of the people in ver. 58 ; not, as in vers. 15 and 45, as not hearkening to the voice of the Lord to keep all His commandments, which he (Moses) had commanded this day, or which Jehovah had commanded (ver. 45), but as " not observing to do all the words which are written in this book, to fear the glorified and fearful name," (viz.) Jehovah its God. " *This book*" is not Deuteronomy, even if we should assume that Moses had not first of all delivered the discourses in this book to the people and then written them down, but had first of all written them down and then read them to the people (see at chap. xxxi. 9), but the book of the law, *i.e.* the Pentateuch, so far as it was already written. This is evident from vers. 60, 61, according to which the grievous diseases of Egypt were written in this book of the law, which points to the book of Exodus, where grievous diseases occur among the Egyptian plagues. In fact, Moses could not have thought of merely laying the people under the obligation to keep the laws of the book of Deuteronomy, since this book does not contain all the essential laws of the covenant, and was never intended to form an independent book of the law. The infinitive clause, " to fear," etc., serves to explain the previous clause, " to do," etc., whether we regard the two clauses as co-ordinate, or the second as subordinate to the first. Doing all the commandments of the law must show and prove itself in fearing the revealed name of the Lord. Where this fear is wanting, the outward observance of the commandments can only be a pharisaic work-righteousness, which is equivalent to a transgression of the law. But the object of this fear was not to be a God, according to human ideas of the nature and working of God; it was to be " this glorified and fearful name," i.e. Jehovah the absolute God, as He glorifies Himself and shows Himself to be fearful in His doings upon earth. " The name," as in Lev. xxiv. 11. נִכְבָּד in a reflective sense, as in Ex. xiv. 4, 17, 18; Lev. x. 3.—Ver. 59. If Israel should not do this, the Lord would make its strokes and the strokes of its seed wonderful, i.e. would visit the people and their descendants with extraordinary strokes, with great and lasting strokes, and with evil and lasting diseases (ver. 60), and would bring all the pestilences of Egypt upon it. הֵשִׁיב, to turn back, inasmuch as Israel was set free from them by the deliverance out of Egypt. מַדְוֶה is construed with the plural as a collective noun. —Ver. 61. Also every disease and every stroke that was not written in this book of the law,—not only those that were written in the book of the law, but those also that did not stand therein. The diseases of Egypt that were written in the book of the law include the murrain of cattle, the boils and blains, and the death of the first-born (Ex. ix. 1–10, xii. 29); and the strokes (מַכָּה) the rest of the plagues, viz. the frogs, gnats, dog-flies, hail, locusts, and darkness (Ex. viii.–x.). יַעְלֵם, an uncommon and harder form of יַעְלֵם (Judg. xvi. 3; cf. Ewald, § 138, a.).—Ver. 62. Israel would be almost annihilated thereby. " Ye will be left in few people (a small number; cf. chap. xxvi. 5), whereas ye were as numerous as the stars of heaven."

Vers. 63 sqq. Yea, the Lord would find His pleasure in the destruction and annihilation of Israel, as He had previously rejoiced in blessing and multiplying it. With this bold anthropomorphic expression Moses seeks to remove from the nation the last prop of false confidence in the mercy of God. Greatly as the sin of man troubles God, and little as the pleasure may be which He has in the death of the wicked, yet the holiness of His love demands the punishment and destruction of those who despise the riches of His goodness and long-suffering; so that He displays His glory in the judgment and destruction of the wicked no less than in blessing and prospering the righteous.—Vers. 63*b* and 64. Those who had not succumbed to the plagues and strokes of God, would be torn from the land of their inheritance, and scattered among all nations to the end of the earth, and there be compelled to serve other gods, which are wood and stone, which have no life and no sensation, and therefore can hear no prayer, and cannot deliver out of any distress (cf. chap. iv. 27 sqq.).—Vers. 65, 66. When banished thus among all nations, Israel would find no ease or rest, not even rest for the sole of its foot, *i.e.* no place where it could quietly set its foot, and remain and have peace in its heart. To this extreme distress of homeless banishment there would be added " *a trembling heart, failing of the eyes* (the light of life), *and despair of soul*" (*vid.* Lev. xxvi. 36 sqq.).—Ver. 66. " *Thy life will be hung up before thee,*" *i.e.* will be like some valued object, hanging by a thin thread before thine eyes, which any moment might tear down (*Knobel*), that is to say, will be ever hanging in the greatest danger. " *Thou wilt not believe in thy life,*" *i.e.* thou wilt despair of its preservation (cf. Job xxiv. 22).[1]—Ver. 67. In the morning they would wish it were evening, and in the evening would wish it were morning, from perpetual dread of what each day or night would bring.—Ver. 68. Last of all, Moses mentions the worst, namely, their being taken back to Egypt into ignominious slavery. " If the exodus was the birth of the nation of God as such, return would be its death" (*Schultz*). " *In ships :*" *i.e.* in a way which would cut off every possibility of escape. The clause, " *by the way whereof I spake unto thee, thou shalt see it no more again,*" is not a more precise explanation of the expression " in ships," for it was not in ships that Israel came out of Egypt, but by land, through the desert; on the contrary, it simply serves to strengthen the announcement, " The Lord shall bring thee into Egypt again," namely, in the sense that God would cause them to take a road which they would never have seen again if they had continued in faithful dependence upon the Lord.

---

[1] " I have never seen a passage which describes more clearly the misery of a guilty conscience, in words and thoughts so fitting and appropriate. For this is just the way in which a man is affected, who knows that God is offended, *i.e.* who is harassed with the consciousness of sin " (*Luther*).

This was the way to Egypt, in reality such a return to this land as Israel ought never to have experienced, namely, a return to slavery. *" There shall ye be sold to your enemies as servants and maids, and there shall be no buyer,"* i.e. no one will buy you as slaves. This clause, which indicates the utmost contempt, is quite sufficient to overthrow the opinion of *Ewald, Riehm,* and others, already referred to at pp. 385–6, namely, that this verse refers to Psammetichus, who procured some Israelitish infantry from Manasseh. Egypt is simply mentioned as a land where Israel had lived in ignominious bondage. " As a fulfilment of a certain kind, we might no doubt adduce the fact that Titus sent 17,000 adult Jews to Egypt to perform hard labour there, and had those who were under 17 years of age publicly sold (*Josephus, de bell. Jud.* vi. 9, 2), and also that under Hadrian Jews without number were sold at Rachel's grave (*Jerome, ad* Jer. 31). But the word of God is not so contracted, that it can be limited to one single fact. The curses were fulfilled in the time of the Romans in Egypt (*vid. Philo in Flacc.,* and *leg. ad Caium*), but they were also fulfilled in a horrible manner during the middle ages (*vid. Depping, die Juden im Mittelalter*) ; and they are still in course of fulfilment, even though they are frequently less sensibly felt " (*Schultz*).—Ver. 69 (or chap. xxix. 1) is not the close of the address in chap. v.–xxviii., as *Schultz, Knobel,* and others suppose; but the heading to chap. xxix. xxx., which relate to the making of the covenant mentioned in this verse (*vid.* chap. xxix. 12, 14).

CONCLUSION OF THE COVENANT IN THE LAND OF MOAB.— CHAP. XXIX. AND XXX.

The addresses which follow in chap. xxix. and xxx. are announced in the heading in chap. xxix. 1 as " *words* (addresses) *of the covenant which Jehovah commanded Moses to make with the children of Israel, beside the covenant which He made with them in Horeb,*" and consist, according to vers. 10 sqq., in a solemn appeal to all the people to enter into the covenant which the Lord made with them that day ; that is to say, it consisted literally in a renewed declaration of the covenant which the Lord had concluded with the nation at Horeb, or in a fresh obligation imposed upon the nation to keep the covenant which had been concluded at Horeb, by the offering of sacrifices and the sprinkling of the people with the sacrificial blood (Ex. xxiv.). There was no necessity for any repetition of this act, because, notwithstanding the frequent transgressions on the part of the nation, it had not been abrogated on the part of God, but still remained in full validity and force. The obligation binding upon the people to fulfil the covenant is introduced by Moses with an appeal to all that the Lord had done for Israel (chap. xxix. 2–9); and this is followed by a summons to enter into the covenant which the Lord was concluding with them now, that He might be their God, and fulfil His promises concerning them (vers. 10–15), with a repeated allusion to the punishment which threatened them in case of apostasy (vers. 16–29), and the eventual restoration on the ground of sincere repentance and return to the Lord (chap. xxx. 1–14), and finally another solemn adjuration, with a blessing and a curse before them, to make choice of the blessing (vers. 15–20).

Chap. xxix. 2–9. The introduction in ver. 2a resembles that in chap. v. 1. " *All Israel* " is the nation in all its members (see vers. 10, 11).—Israel had no doubt seen the mighty acts of the Lord in Egypt (vers. 2b and 3; cf. chap. iv. 34, vii. 19), but Jehovah had not given them a heart, *i.e.* understanding, to perceive, eyes to see, and ears to hear, until this day. With this complaint, Moses does not intend to excuse the previous want of susceptibility on the part of the nation to the manifestations of grace on the part of the Lord, but simply to explain the necessity for the repeated allusion to the gracious acts of God, and to urge the people to lay them truly to heart. " By reproving the dulness of the past, he would stimulate them to a desire to understand: just as if he had said, that for a long time they had been insensible to so many miracles, and therefore they ought not to delay any longer, but to arouse themselves to hearken better unto God" (*Calvin*). The Lord had not yet given the people an understanding heart, because the people had not yet asked for it, simply because the need of it was not felt (cf. chap. v. 26).—Vers. 5 sqq. With the appeal to the gracious guidance of Israel by God through the desert, the address of Moses passes imperceptibly into an address from the Lord, just as in chap. xi. 14. (On vers. 5, 6, *vid.* chap. viii. 3, 4; on ver. 7, *vid.* chap. ii. 26 sqq., and chap. iii. 1 sqq. and 12 sqq.).—Ver. 9. These benefits from the Lord demanded obedience and fidelity. " *Keep the words of this covenant*," etc. (cf. chap. viii. 18). הַשְׂכִּיל, to act wisely (as in chap. xxxii. 29), bearing in mind, however, that Jehovah Himself is the wisdom of Israel (chap. iv. 6), and the search for this wisdom brings prosperity and salvation (cf. Josh. i. 7, 8).

Vers. 10–15. Summons to enter into the covenant of the Lord, namely, to enter inwardly, to make the covenant an affair of the heart and life.—Vers. 10 sqq. " *To-day*," when the covenant-law and covenant-right were laid before them, the whole nation stood before the Lord without a single exception—the heads and the tribes, the elders and the officers, all the men of Israel. The two members are parallel. The heads of the people are the elders and officers, and the tribes consist of all the men. The rendering given by the LXX. and Syriac (also in the English version : *Tr.*), " *heads* (captains) *of your tribes*," is at variance with the language. —Ver. 11. The covenant of the Lord embraced, however, not only the men of Israel, but also the wives and children, and the stranger who had attached himself to Israel, such as the Egyptians who came out with Israel (Ex. xii. 38 ; Num. xi. 4), and the Midianites who joined the Israelites with Hobab (Num. x. 29), down to the very lowest servant, " *from thy hewer of wood to thy drawer of water* " (cf. Josh. ix. 21, 27).—Ver. 12. " *That thou shouldest enter into the covenant of the Lord thy God, and the engagement on oath, which the Lord thy God concludeth with thee to-day.*" עָבַר with בְּ, as in Job xxxiii. 28, " to enter into," expresses entire entrance, which goes completely through the territory entered, and is more emphatic than בּוֹא בִבְרִית (2 Chron. xv. 12). " Into the oath :" the covenant confirmed with an oath, covenants being always accompanied with oaths (*vid.* Gen. xxvi. 28).—Ver. 13. " *That He may set thee up* (exalt thee) *to-day into a people for Himself, and that He may be* (become) *unto thee a God*" (*vid.* chap. xxviii. 9, xxvii. 9 ; Ex. xix. 5, 6).—Vers. 14, 15. This covenant Moses made not only with those who are present, but with all whether present or not ; for it was to embrace not only those who were living then, but their descendants also, to become a covenant of blessing for all nations (cf. Acts ii. 39, and the intercession of Christ in John xvii. 20).

Vers. 16–29. The summons to enter into the covenant of the Lord is explained by Moses first of all by an exposition of the evil results which would follow from apostasy from the Lord, or the breach of His covenant. This exposition he introduces with an allusion to the experience of the people with reference to the worthlessness of idols, both in Egypt itself, and upon their march through the nations, whose territory they passed through (vers. 16, 17). The words, " *for ye have learned how we dwelt in Egypt, and passed through the nations . . . . and have seen their abominations and their idols*" (*gillulim :* lit. clods, see Lev. xxvi. 30), have this signification : In our abode in Egypt, and upon our march through different lands, ye have become acquainted with the idols of these nations, that they are not gods, but only wood and stone (see at chap. iv. 28), silver and gold. אֶת־אֲשֶׁר, as in chap. ix. 7 literally "ye know that which we dwelt," *i.e.* know what our dwelling there showed, what experience we gained there of the nature of heathen idols. —Ver. 18. " *That there may not be among you,*" etc. : this sentence may be easily explained by introducing a thought which may be easily supplied, such as " consider this," or " do not forget what ye have seen, that no one, either man or woman, family or tribe, may turn away from Jehovah our God."—" *That there may not be a root among you which bears poison and wormwood as fruit.*" A striking image of the destructive fruit borne by idolatry (cf. Heb. xii. 15). *Rosh* stands for a plant of a very bitter taste, as we may see from the frequency with which it is combined with לַעֲנָה, wormwood : it is not, strictly speaking, a poisonous plant, although the word is used in Job xx. 16 to denote the poison of serpents, because, in the estimation of a Hebrew, bitterness and poison were kindred terms. There is no other passage in which it can be shown to have the meaning " poison." The sense of the figure is given in plain terms in ver. 19, " *that no one when he hears the words of this oath may bless himself in his heart, saying, It will prosper with me, for I walk in the firmness of my heart.*" To bless himself in his heart is to congratulate himself. שְׁרִירוּת, firmness, a *vox media ;* in Syriac, firmness, in a good sense, equivalent to truth ; in Hebrew, generally in a bad sense, denoting hardness of heart ; and this is the sense in which Moses uses it here.—" *To sweep away that which is saturated with the thirsty :* " a proverbial expression, of which very different interpretations have been given (see *Rosenmüller ad h. l.*), taken no doubt from the land and transferred to persons or souls ; so that we might supply *Nephesh* in this sense, " to destroy all, both those who have drunk its poison, and those also who are still thirsting for it " (*Knobel*). But even if we were to supply אֶרֶץ (the land), we should not have to think of the land itself, but simply of its inhabitants, so that the thought would still remain the same.—Vers. 20, 21. " *For the Lord will not forgive him* (who thinks or speaks in this way) ; *but then will His anger smoke* (break forth in fire ; *vid.* Ps. lxxiv. 1), *and His jealousy against that man, and the whole curse of the law will lie upon him, that his name may be blotted out under heaven* (*vid.* chap. xxv. 19 ; Ex. xvii. 14). *The Lord will separate him unto evil from all the tribes,*—so that he will be shut out from the covenant nation, and from its salvation, and be exposed to destruction,—*according to all the curses of the covenant.*" Although the pronominal suffix refers primarily to the man, it also applies, according to ver. 18, to the woman, the family, and the tribe. "That is written," etc., as in chap. xxviii. 58, 61.—Vers. 22–24. How thoroughly Moses was filled with the thought, that not only individuals, but whole families, and in fact the greater portion of the nation, would fall into idolatry, is evident from the further expansion of the threat which follows, and in which he foresees in the Spirit, and foretells, the extermination of whole families, and the devastation of the land by distant nations; as in Lev. xxvi. 31, 32. Future generations of Israel, and the stranger from a distant land, when they saw the strokes of the Lord which burst upon the land, and the utter desolation of the land, would ask whence this devastation, and receive the reply, The Lord had smitten the land thus in His anger, because its inhabitants (the Israelites) had forsaken His covenant. With regard to the construction, observe that וְאָמַר, in ver. 22, is resumed in וְאָמְרוּ, in ver. 24, the subject of ver. 22 being expanded into the general notion, "all nations" (ver. 24). With וְרָאוּ, in ver. 22*b*, a parenthetical clause is inserted, giving the reason for the main thought, in the form of a circumstantial clause; and to this there is attached, by a loose apposition in ver. 23, a still further picture of the divine strokes according to their effect upon the land. The nouns in ver. 23, "*brimstone and salt burning,*" are in apposition to the strokes (plagues), and so far depend upon "they see." The description is borrowed from the character of the Dead Sea and its vicinity, to which there is an express allusion in the words, "*like the overthrow of Sodom,*" etc., *i.e.* of the towns of the vale of Siddim (see at Gen. xiv. 2), which resembled paradise, the garden of Jehovah, before their destruction (*vid.* Gen. xiii. 10 and xix. 24 sqq.).—Ver. 24. "*What is this great burning of wrath?*" *i.e.* what does it mean—whence does it come? The reply to such a question would be (vers. 25–29): The inhabitants of the land have forsaken the covenant of the Lord, the God of their fathers; therefore has the wrath of the Lord burned over the land.—Ver. 26. "*Gods which God had not assigned them*" (*vid.* chap. iv. 19). "All the curses," etc., are the curses contained in chap. xxviii. 15–68, Lev. xxvi. 14–38.—Those who give the answer close their address in ver. 29 with an expression of pious submission and solemn admonition. "*That which is hidden belongs to the Lord our God* (is His affair), *and that which is revealed belongs to us and our chil-*

dren for ever, to do (that we may do) *all the words of this law.*"
That which is revealed includes the law with its promises and threats;
consequently that which is hidden can only refer to the mode in
which God will carry out in the future His counsel and will, which
He has revealed in the law, and complete His work of salvation
notwithstanding the apostasy of the people.[1]

Chap. xxx. 1-10. Nevertheless the rejection of Israel and its
dispersion among the heathen were not to be the close. If the
people should return to the Lord their God in their exile, He would
turn His favour towards them again, and gather them again out of
their dispersion, as had already been proclaimed in chap. iv. 29 sqq.
and Lev. xxvi. 40 sqq., where it was also observed that the extremity of their distress would bring the people to reflection and induce
them to return.—Vers. 1–3. "*When all these words, the blessing and
the curse which I have set before thee, shall come.*" The allusion to
the blessing in this connection may be explained on the ground that
Moses was surveying the future generally, in which not only a curse
but a blessing also would come upon the nation, according to its
attitude towards the Lord as a whole and in its several members,
since even in times of the greatest apostasy on the part of the
nation there would always be a holy seed which could not die out;
because otherwise the nation would necessarily have been utterly
and for ever rejected, whereby the promises of God would have
been brought to nought,—a result which was absolutely impossible.
"*And thou takest to heart among all nations,*" etc., *sc.* what has befallen thee,—not only the curse which presses upon thee, but also
the blessing which accompanies obedience to the commands of
God,—"*and returnest to the Lord thy God, and hearkenest to His
voice with all the heart,*" etc. (cf. chap. iv. 29) ; "*the Lord will turn
thy captivity, and have compassion upon thee, and gather thee again.*"
שׁוּב אֶת־שְׁבוּת does not mean to bring back the prisoners, as the
more modern lexicographers erroneously suppose (the *Kal* שׁוּב never
has the force of the *Hiphil*), but to turn the imprisonment, and that

---

[1] What the *puncta extraordinaria* above (ר)עַ וּלְבָנֵינוּ לָנוּ mean, is uncertain.
Hiller's conjecture is the most probable, " that they are intended to indicate a
various reading, formed by the omission of eleven consonants, and the transposition of the rest עָם וְהַנִּגְלֹת (*at magnalia sæculi sunt*) ; " whereas there is no
foundation for *Lightfoot's* notion, that " they served as a warning, that we
should not wish to pry with curiosity into the secret things of God, but should
be content with His revealed will,"—a notion which rests upon the supposition
that the points are inspired.

in a figurative sense, viz. to put an end to the distress (Job xlii. 10; Jer. xxx. 8; Ezek. xvi. 53; Ps. xiv. 7; also Ps. lxxxv. 2, cxxvi. 2, 4), except that in many passages the misery of exile in which the people pined is represented as imprisonment. The passage before us is fully decisive against the meaning to bring back the prisoners, since the gathering out of the heathen is spoken of as being itself the consequence of the " turning of the captivity; " so also is Jer. xxix. 14, where the bringing back (הֵשִׁיב) is expressly distinguished from it. But especially is this the case with Jer. xxx. 18, where "turning the captivity of Jacob's tents" is synonymous with having mercy on his dwelling-places, and building up the city again, so that the city lying in ruins is represented as שְׁבוּת, an imprisonment.[1] —Vers. 4, 5. The gathering of Israel out of all the countries of the earth would then follow. Even though the rejected people should be at the end of heaven, the Lord would fetch them thence, and bring them back into the land of their fathers, and do good to the nation, and multiply them above their fathers. These last words show that the promise neither points directly to the gathering of Israel from dispersion on its ultimate conversion to Christ, nor furnishes any proof that the Jews will then be brought back to Palestine. It is true that even these words have some reference to the final redemption of Israel. This is evident from the curse of dispersion, which cannot be restricted to the Assyrian and Babylonian captivities, but includes the Roman dispersion also, in which the nation continues still; and it is still more apparent from the renewal of this promise in Jer. xxxii. 37 and other prophetic passages. But this application is to be found in the spirit, and not in the letter. For if there is to be an increase in the number of the Jews, when gathered out of their dispersion into all the world, above the number of their fathers, and therefore above the number of the Israelites in the time of Solomon and the first monarchs of the two kingdoms, Palestine will never furnish room enough for a nation multiplied like this. The multiplication promised here, so far as it falls within the Messianic age, will consist in the realiza-

---

[1] *Hupfeld* (on Ps. xiv. 7) has endeavoured to sustain the assertion that שְׁבוּת is a later form for the older and simpler forms, שְׁבִי, שְׁבִיה, by citing one single passage of the Old Testament. The abstract form of שְׁבִי is שְׁבִית, imprisonment (Num. xxi. 29), then prisoners. This form has been substituted by Jeremiah for שְׁבוּת in one passage, viz. chap. xxxii. 44; and the Masoretic punctuators were the first to overlook the difference in the two words, and point them promiscuously.

tion of the promise given to Abraham, that his seed should grow into nations (Gen. xvii. 6 and 16), *i.e.* in the innumerable multiplication, not of the "Israel according to the flesh," but of the "Israel according to the spirit," whose land is not restricted to the boundaries of the earthly Canaan or Palestine (see vol. i. p. 226). The possession of the earthly Canaan for all time is nowhere promised to the Israelitish nation in the law (see at chap. xi. 21).—Ver. 6. The Lord will then circumcise their heart, and the heart of their children (see chap. x. 16), so that they will love Him with all their heart. When Israel should turn with true humility to the Lord, He would be found of them,—would lead them to true repentance, and sanctify them through the power of His grace,—would take away the stony heart out of their flesh, and give them a heart of flesh, a new heart and a new spirit,—so that they should truly know Him and keep His commandments (*vid.* Ezek. xi. 19, xxxvi. 26; Jer. xxxi. 33 sqq. and xxxii. 39 sqq.). "*Because of thy life*," *i.e.* that thou mayest live, *sc.* attain to true life. The fulfilment of this promise does not take place all at once. It commenced with small beginnings at the deliverance from the Babylonian exile, and in a still higher degree at the appearance of Christ in the case of all the Israelites who received Him as their Saviour. Since then it has been carried on through all ages in the conversion of individual children of Abraham to Christ; and it will be realized in the future in a still more glorious manner in the nation at large (Rom. xi. 25 sqq.). The words of Moses do not relate to any particular age, but comprehend all times. For Israel has never been hardened and rejected in all its members, although the mass of the nation lives under the curse even to the present day.—Ver. 7. But after its conversion, the curses, which had hitherto rested upon it, would fall upon its enemies and haters, according to the promise in Gen. xii. 3.—Vers. 8 sqq. Israel would then hearken again to the voice of the Lord and keep His commandments, and would rejoice in consequence in the richest blessing of its God. In the expression, אַתָּה תָשׁוּב וְשָׁמַעְתָּ ("*thou shalt return and hearken*"), תָּשׁוּב ("*thou shalt return*") has an adverbial signification. This is evident from the corresponding expression in ver. 9*b*, "for Jehovah will again rejoice over thee" (*lit.* "will return and rejoice"), in which the adverbial signification is placed beyond all doubt.—Vers. 8–10 contain the general thought, that Israel would then come again into its normal relation to its God, would enter into true and perfect covenant fellowship with the Lord, and enjoy all the blessings of the

covenant.—Ver. 9*a* is a repetition of chap. xxviii. 11. The Lord
will rejoice again over Israel, to do them good (*vid.* chap. xxviii. 63),
as He had rejoiced over their fathers. The fathers are not the
patriarchs alone, but all the pious ancestors of the people.—Ver. 10.
A renewed enforcement of the indispensable condition of salvation.
Vers. 11–20. The fulfilment of this condition is not impossible,
nor really very difficult. This natural thought leads to the motive,
which Moses impresses upon the hearts of the people in vers. 11–14,
viz. that He might turn the blessing to them. God had done everything to render the observance of His commandments possible to
Israel. " *This commandment* " (used as in chap. vi. 1 to denote the
whole law) is " *not too wonderful for thee*," *i.e.* is not too hard to
grasp, or unintelligible (*vid.* chap. xvii. 8), nor is it too far off : it is
neither *in heaven*, *i.e.* at an inaccessible height; nor *beyond the sea*,
i.e. at an unattainable distance, at the end of the world, so that any
one could say, Who is able to fetch it thence? but it is *very near
thee, in thy mouth and in thy heart to do it.* It not only lay before
the people in writing, but it was also preached to them by word of
mouth, and thus brought to their knowledge, so that it had become
a subject of conversation as well as of reflection and careful examination. But however near the law had thus been brought to man,
sin had so estranged the human heart from the word of God, that
doing and keeping the law had become invariably difficult, and in
fact impossible ; so that the declaration, " the word is in thy heart,"
only attains its full realization through the preaching of the gospel
of the grace of God, and the righteousness that is by faith ; and
to this the Apostle Paul applies the passage in Rom. x. 25 sqq.
—Vers. 15–20. In conclusion, Moses sums up the contents of the
whole of this preaching of the law in the words, " life and good,
and death and evil," as he had already done at chap. xi. 26, 27, in
the first part of this address, to lay the people by a solemn adjuration under the obligation to be faithful to the Lord, and through
this obligation to conclude the covenant afresh. He had set before
them this day life and good ("*good*" = prosperity and salvation), as
well as death and evil (רע, adversity and destruction), by commanding them to love the Lord and walk in His ways. Love is placed
first, as in chap. vi. 5, as being the essential principle of the fulfilment of the commandments. Expounding the law was setting
before them life and death, salvation and destruction, because the
law, as the word of God, was living and powerful, and proved itself
in every man a power of life or of death, according to the attitude

which he assumed towards it (*vid.* chap. xxxii. 47). נִדַּח, to permit oneself to be torn away to idolatry (as in chap. iv. 19).—Ver. 18, as chap. iv. 26, viii. 19. He calls upon heaven and earth as witnesses (ver. 19, as in chap. iv. 26), namely, that he had set before them life and death. וּבָחַרְתָּ, in ver. 19, is the apodosis : " *therefore choose life.*"—Ver. 20. כִּי הוּא חַיֶּיךָ, *for that* (namely, to love the Lord) *is thy life*, that is, the condition of life, and of long life, in the promised land (*vid.* chap. iv. 40).

IV.—MOSES' FAREWELL AND DEATH.

CHAP. XXXI.–XXXIV.

WITH the renewal of the covenant, by the choice set before the people between blessing and curse, life and death, Moses had finished the interpretation and enforcement of the law (chap. i. 5), and brought the work of legislation to a close. But in order that the work to which the Lord had called him might be thoroughly completed, it still remained for him, before his approaching death, to hand over the task of leading the people into Canaan to Joshua, who had been appointed as his successor, to finish writing out the laws, and to hand over the book of the law to the priests. The Lord also directed him to write an ode, as a witness against the people, on account of their obstinacy, and teach it to the Israelites. To these last arrangements and acts of Moses, which are narrated in chap. xxxi. and xxxii., there are added in chap. xxxiii. the blessing with which this man of God bade farewell to the tribes of Israel, and in chap. xxxiv. the account of his death, with which the Pentateuch closes.

MOSES' FINAL ARRANGEMENTS. COMPLETION AND HANDING OVER OF THE BOOK OF THE LAW.—CHAP. XXXI.

The final arrangements which Moses made before his departure, partly of his own accord, and partly by the command of God, relate to the introduction of the Israelites into the promised land, and the confirmation of their fidelity towards the Lord their God.—Vers. 1-13 describe how Moses promised the help of the Lord in the conquest of the land, both to the people generally, and also to Joshua, their leader into Canaan (vers. 2-8), and commanded the priests to keep the book of the law, and read it publicly every seventh year (vers. 9-13) ; and vers. 14-23, how the Lord appeared to Moses before the tabernacle, and directed him to compose an ode as a testimony against the apostasy of the people, and promised Joshua His assistance. And lastly, vers. 24-27 relate how the book of the law, when brought to completion, was handed over to the Levites ; and vers. 28-30 describe the reading of the ode to the people.

Vers. 1-8. In ver. 1 Moses' final arrangements are announced. וַיֵּלֶךְ does not mean " he went away" (into his tent), which does not tally with what follows (" and spake") ; nor is it merely equivalent to *porro, amplius*. It serves, as in Ex. ii. 1 and Gen. xxxv. 22, as a pictorial description of what he was about to do, in the sense of " he prepared himself," or rose up. After closing the exposition of the law, Moses had either withdrawn, or at any rate made a pause, before he proceeded to make his final arrangements for laying down his office, and taking leave of the people.—Ver. 2. These last arrangements he commences with the declaration, that he must now bid them farewell, as he is 120 years old (which agrees with Ex. vii. 7), and can no more go out and in, *i.e.* no longer work in the nation and for it (see at Num. xxvii. 17) ; and the Lord has forbidden him to cross over the Jordan and enter Canaan (see Num. xx. 24). The first of these reasons is not at variance with the statement in chap. xxxiv. 7, that up to the time of his death his eyes were not dim, nor his strength abated. For this is merely an affirmation, that he retained the ability to see and to work to the last moment of his life, which by no means precludes his noticing the decline of his strength, and feeling the approach of his death.—Vers. 3-5. But although Moses could not, and was not to lead his people into Canaan, the Lord would fulfil His promise, to go before Israel and destroy the Canaanites, like the two kings of the Amorites ; only they (the Israelites) were to do to them as the Lord had commanded them, *i.e.* to root out the Canaanites (*vid.* chap. vii. 2 sqq. ; Num. xxxiii. 51 sqq. ; Ex. xxxiv. 11 sqq.).—Ver. 6. Israel was therefore to be of good courage, and not to be afraid of them (*vid.* chap. i. 21, xx. 3).—Vers. 7, 8. Moses then encourages Joshua in the same way in the presence of all the people, on the strength of the promise of God in chap. i. 38 and Num. xxvii. 18 sqq. תָּבוֹא אֶת־הָעָם, " *thou wilt come with this people into the land.*" These words are quite appropriate ; and the alteration of תָּבוֹא into תָּבִיא, according to ver. 23 (*Samar., Syr., Vulg.*), is a perfectly unnecessary conjecture ; for

Joshua was not appointed leader of the people here, but simply promised an entrance with all the people into Canaan.

Vers. 9–13. Moses then handed over the law which- he had written to the Levitical priests who carried the ark of the covenant, and to all the elders of Israel, with instructions to read it to the people at the end of every seven years, during the festal season of the year of release (" at the end," as in chap. xv. 1), viz. at the feast of Tabernacles (see Lev. xxiii. 34), when they appeared before the Lord. It is evident from the context and contents of these verses, apart from ver. 24, that the ninth verse is to be understood in the way described, *i.e.* that the two clauses, which are connected together by *vav. relat.* (" *and Moses wrote this law*," " *and delivered it*"), are not logically co-ordinate, but that the handing over of the written law was the main thing to be recorded here. With regard to the handing over of the law, the fact that Moses not only gave the written law to the priests, that they might place it by the ark of the covenant, but also " *to all the elders of Israel*," proves clearly enough that Moses did not intend at this time to give the law-book entirely out of his own hands, but that this handing over was merely an assignment of the law to the persons who were to take care, that in the future the written law should be kept before the people, as the rule of their life and conduct, and publicly read to them. The explanation which *J. H. Mich.* gives is perfectly correct, " He gave it for them to teach and keep." The law-book would only have been given to the priests, if the object had been simply that it should be placed by the ark of the covenant, or at the most, in the presence of the elders, but certainly not *to* all the elders, since they were not allowed to touch the ark. The correctness of this view is placed beyond all doubt by the contents of vers. 10 sqq. The main point in hand was not the writing out of the law, or the transfer of it to the priests and elders of the nation, but the command to read the law in the presence of the people at the feast of Tabernacles of the year of release. The writing out and handing over simply formed the substratum for this command, so that we cannot infer from them, that by this act Moses formally gave the law out of his own hands. He entrusted the reading to the priesthood and the college of elders, as the spiritual and secular rulers of the congregation ; and hence the singular, " Thou shalt read this law to all Israel." The regulations as to the persons who were to undertake the reading, and also as to the particular time during the seven days' feast, and the portions that were to be read, he left to the rulers of the congregation. We learn from Neh. viii. 18, that in Ezra's time they read *in* the book of the law every day from the first to the last day of the feast, from which we may see on the one hand, that the whole of the *Thorah* (or Pentateuch), from beginning to end, was not read ; and on the other hand, by comparing the expression in ver. 18, " the book of the law of God," with " the law," in ver. 14, that the reading was not restricted to Deuteronomy : for, according to ver. 14, they had already been reading in Leviticus (chap. xxiii.) before the feast was held,—an evident proof that Ezra the scribe did not regard the book of Deuteronomy like the critics of our day, as the true national law-book, an acquaintance with which was all that the people required. Moses did not fix upon the feast of Tabernacles of the sabbatical year as the time for reading the law, because it fell at the beginning of the year,[1] as *Schultz* wrongly supposes, that the people might thereby be incited to occupy this year of entire rest in holy employment with the word and works of God. And the reading itself was neither intended to promote a more general acquaintance with the law on the part of the people,— an object which could not possibly have been secured by reading it once in seven years ; nor was it merely to be a solemn promulgation and restoration of the law as the rule for the national life, for the purpose of removing any irregularities that might have found their way in the course of time into either the religious or the political life of the nation (*Bähr*, Symbol. ii. p. 603). To answer this end, it should have been connected with the Passover, the festival of Israel's birth. The reading stood rather in close connection with the idea of the festival itself ; it was intended to quicken the soul with the law of the Lord, to refresh the heart, to enlighten the eyes,—in short, to offer the congregation the blessing of the law, which David celebrated from his own experience in Ps. xix. 8–15,

---

[1] It by no means follows, that because the sabbatical year commenced with the omission of the usual sowing, *i.e.* began in the autumn with the civil year, it therefore commenced with the feast of Tabernacles, and the order of the feasts was reversed in the sabbatical year. According to Ex. xxiii. 16, the feast of Tabernacles did not fall at the beginning, but at the end of the civil year. The commencement of the year with the first of *Tisri* was an arrangement introduced after the captivity, which the Jews had probably adopted from the Syrians (see my *bibl. Archæol.* i. § 74, note 15). Nor does it follow, that be- cause the year of jubilee was to be proclaimed on the day of atonement in the sabbatical year with a blast of trumpets (Lev. xxv. 9), therefore the year of jubilee must have begun with the feast of Tabernacles. The proclamation of festivals is generally made some time before they commence.

to make the law beloved and prized by the whole nation, as a precious gift of the grace of God. Consequently (vers. 12, 13), not only the men, but the women and children also, were to be gathered together for this purpose, that they might hear the word of God, and learn to fear the Lord their God, as long as they should live in the land which He gave them for a possession. On ver. 11, see Ex. xxiii. 17, and xxxiv. 23, 24, where we also find לִרְאוֹת for לֵרָאוֹת (ver. 24).

Vers. 14–23. After handing over the office to Joshua, and the law to the priests and elders, Moses was called by the Lord to come to the tabernacle with Joshua, to command him (צָוָּה), *i.e.* to appoint him, confirm him in his office. To this end the Lord appeared in the tabernacle (ver. 15), in a pillar of cloud, which remained standing before it, as in Num. xii. 5 (see the exposition of Num. xi. 25). But before appointing Joshua, He announced to Moses that after his death the nation would go a whoring after other gods, and would break the covenant, for which it would be visited with severe afflictions, and directed him to write an ode and teach it to the children of Israel, that when the apostasy should take place, and punishment from God be felt in consequence, it might speak as a witness against the people, as it would not vanish from their memory. The Lord communicated this commission to Moses in the presence of Joshua, that he also might hear from the mouth of God that the Lord foreknew the future apostasy of the people, and yet nevertheless would bring them into the promised land. In this there was also implied an admonition to Joshua, not only to take care that the Israelites learned the ode and kept it in their memories, but also to strive with all his might to prevent the apostasy, so long as he was leader of Israel; which Joshua did most faithfully to the very end of his life (*vid.* Josh. xxiii. and xxiv.).— The announcement of the falling away of the Israelites from the Lord into idolatry, and the burning of the wrath of God in consequence (vers. 16–18), serves as a basis for the command in vers. 19 sqq. In this announcement the different points are simply linked together with "and," whereas in their actual signification they are subordinate to one another: When thou shalt lie with thy fathers, and the people shall rise up, and go a whoring after other gods: My anger will burn against them, etc. קוּם, to rise up, to prepare, serves to bring out distinctly the course which the thing would take. The expression, "*foreign gods of the land,*" indicates that in the land which Jehovah gave His people, He (Jehovah) alone was God and Lord, and that He alone was to be worshipped there. בְּקִרְבּוֹ is in apposition to שָׁמָּה, "whither thou comest, in the midst of it." The punishment announced in ver. 17 corresponds most closely to the sin of the nation. For going a whoring after strange gods, the anger of the Lord would burn against them; for forsaking Him, He would forsake them; and for breaking His covenant, He would hide His face from them, i.e. withdraw His favour from them, so that they would be destroyed. הָיָה לֶאֱכֹל, it (the nation) will be for devouring, i.e. will be devoured or destroyed (see Ewald, § 237, c.; and on אָכַל in this sense, see chap. vii. 16, and Num. xiv. 9). "And many evils and troubles will befall it; and it will say in that day, Do not these evils befall me, because my God is not in the midst of me?" When the evils and troubles broke in upon the nation, the people would inquire the cause, and would find it in the fact that they were forsaken by their God; but the Lord ("but I" in ver. 18 forms the antithesis to "they" in ver. 17) would still hide His face, namely, because simply missing God is not true repentance.—Ver. 19. "And now," sc. because what was announced in vers. 16–18 would take place, "write you this song." "This" refers to the song which follows in chap. xxxii. Moses and Joshua were to write the song, because they were both of them to strive to prevent the apostasy of the people; and Moses, as the author, was to teach it to the children of Israel, to make them learn it, that it might be a witness for the Lord (for Me) against the children of Israel. "This" is defined still further in vers. 20, 21: if Israel, through growing satisfied and fat in its land, which was so rich in costly good, should turn to other gods, and the Lord should visit it in consequence with grievous evils and troubles, the song was to answer before Israel as a witness; i.e. not only serve the Lord as a witness to the people that He had foretold all the evil consequences of apostasy, and had given Israel proper warning (Knobel), but to serve, as we may see from vers. 20, 21, and from the contents of the song, as a witness, on the one hand, that the Lord had conferred upon the people so many benefits and bestowed upon them such abundant blessings of His grace, that apostasy from Him was the basest ingratitude, for which they would justly be punished; and, on the other hand, that the Lord had not rejected His people in spite of the punishments inflicted upon them, but would once more have compassion upon them and requite their foes, and thus would sanctify and glorify Himself as the only true God by His judgments upon Israel and the nations.

The law, with its commandments, promises, and threats, was already a witness of this kind against Israel (cf. ver. 26); but just as in every other instance the appearance of a plurality of unanimous witnesses raises the matter into an indisputable truth, so the Lord would set up another witness against the Israelites besides the law, in the form of this song, which was adapted to give all the louder warning, "because the song would not be forgotten out of the mouths of their seed" (ver. 21). The song, when once it had passed into the mouths of the people, would not very readily vanish from their memory, but would be transmitted from generation to generation, and be heard from the mouths of their descendants, as a perpetual warning voice, as it would be used by Israel; for God knew the invention of the people, *i.e.* the thoughts and purposes of their heart, which they cherished (עָשָׂה used to denote the doing of the heart, as in Isa. xxxii. 6) even then before He had brought them into Canaan. (On ver. 20a, *vid.* chap. vii. 5, ix. 5, and Ex. iii. 8.)—In ver. 22 the result is anticipated, and the command of God is followed immediately by an account of its completion by Moses (just as in Ex. xii. 50; Lev. xvi. 34, etc.).—After this command with reference to the song, the Lord appointed Joshua to the office which he had been commanded to take, urging him at the same time to be courageous, and promising him His help in the conquest of Canaan. That the subject to וַיְצַו is not Moses, but Jehovah, is evident partly from the context, the retrospective glance at ver. 14, and partly from the words themselves, "I will be with thee" (*vid.* Ex. iii. 12).[1]

Vers. 24–27. With the installation of Joshua on the part of God, the official life of Moses was brought to a close. Having returned from the tabernacle, he finished the writing out of the laws, and then gave the book of the law to the Levites, with a command to put it by the side of the ark of the covenant, that it might be there for a witness against the people, as He knew its rebellion and stiffneckedness (vers. 24–27). כָּתַב עַל־סֵפֶר, to write upon a book, equivalent to write down, commit to writing. עַד תֻּמָּם, till their being finished, *i.e.* complete. By the "*Levites who bare the ark of the covenant*" we are not to understand ordinary Levites, but the

---

[1] *Knobel's* assertion (on Num. xxvii. 23) that the appointment of Joshua on the part of Moses by the imposition of hands, as described in that passage, is at variance with this verse, scarcely needs any refutation. Or is it really the case, that the installation of Joshua on the part of God is irreconcilable with his ordination by Moses?

Levitical priests, who were entrusted with the ark. "The Levites" is simply a contraction for the full expression, " the priests the sons of Levi " (ver. 9). It is true that, according to Num. iv. 4 sqq., the Kohathites were appointed to carry the holy vessels, which included the ark of the covenant, on the journey through the desert; but it was the priests, and not they, who were the true bearers and guardians of the holy things, as we may see from the fact that the priests had first of all to wrap up these holy things in a careful manner, before they handed them over to the Kohathites, that they might not touch the holy things and die (Num. iv. 15). Hence we find that on solemn occasions, when the ark was to be brought out in all its full significance and glory,—as, for example, in the crossing of the Jordan (Josh. iii. 3 sqq., iv. 9, 10), when encompassing Jericho (Josh. vi. 6, 12), at the setting up of the law on Ebal and Gerizim (Josh. viii. 33), and at the consecration of Solomon's temple (1 Kings viii. 3),—it was not by the Levites, but by the priests, that the ark of the covenant was borne. In fact the Levites were, strictly speaking, only their (the priests') servants, who relieved them of this and the other labour, so that what they did was done in a certain sense through them. If the (non-priestly) Levites were not to touch the ark of the covenant, and not even to put in the poles (Num. iv. 6), Moses would not have handed over the law-book, to be kept by the ark of the covenant, to them, but to the priests. מִצַּד אֲרֹן, at the side of the ark, or, according to the paraphrase of *Jonathan*, "in a case on the right side of the ark of the covenant," which may be correct, although we must not think of this case, as many of the early theologians do, as a secondary ark attached to the ark of the covenant (see *Lundius, Jüd. Heiligth.* pp. 73, 74). The tables of the law were deposited in the ark (Ex. xxv. 16, xl. 20), and the book of the law was to be kept by its side. As it formed, from its very nature, simply an elaborate commentary upon the decalogue, it was also to have its place outwardly as an accompaniment to the tables of the law, for a witness against the people, in the same manner as the song in the mouth of the people (ver. 21). For, as Moses adds in ver. 27, in explanation of his instructions, "*I know thy rebelliousness, and thy stiff neck : behold, while I am yet alive with you this day, ye have been rebellious against the Lord (vid.* chap. ix. 7) ; *and how much more after my death.*"

With these words Moses handed over the complete book of the law to the Levitical priests. For although the handing over is not expressly mentioned, it is unquestionably implied in the words, "Take this book, and put it by the side of the ark of the covenant," as the finishing of the writing of the laws is mentioned immediately before. But if Moses finished the writing of the law after he had received instructions from the Lord to compose the ode, what he wrote will reach to ver. 23 ; and what follows from ver. 24 onwards will form the appendix to his work by a different hand.[1] The supposition that Moses himself inserted his instructions concerning the preservation of the book of the law, and the ode which follows, is certainly possible, but not probable. The decision as to the place where it should be kept was not of such importance as to need insertion in the book of the law, since sufficient provision for its safe keeping had been made by the directions in vers. 9 sqq. ; and although God had commanded him to write the ode, it was not for the purpose of inserting it in the *Thorah* as an essential portion of it, but to let the people learn it, to put it in the mouth of the people. The allusion to this ode in vers. 19 sqq. furnishes no conclusive evidence, either that Moses himself included it in the law-book which he had written with the account of his oration in vers. 28–30 and chap. xxxii. 1–43, or that the appendix which Moses did not write commences at ver. 14 of this chapter. For all that follows with certainty from the expression "this song" (vers. 19 and 22), which certainly points to the song in chap. xxxii., is that Moses himself handed over the ode to the priests with the complete book of the law, as a supplement to the law, and that this ode was then inserted by the writer of the appendix in the appendix itself.

Vers. 28–30. Directly after handing over the book of the law, Moses directed the elders of all the tribes, together with the official persons, to gather round him, that he might rehearse to them the ode which he had written for the people. The summons, "gather unto me," was addressed to the persons to whom he had given the book of the law. The elders and officers, as the civil authorities of the congregation, were collected together by him to hear the ode, because they were to put it in the mouth of the people, *i.e.* to take care that

---

[1] The objection brought against this view by *Riehm*, namely, that "it founders on the fact that the style and language in chap. xxxi. 24–30 and xxxii. 44–47 are just the same as in the earlier portion of the book," simply shows that he has not taken into consideration that, with the simple style adopted in Hebrew narrative, we could hardly expect in eleven verses, which contain for the most part simply words and sayings of Moses, to find any very striking difference of language or of style. This objection, therefore, merely proves that no valid arguments can be adduced against the view in question.

all the nation should learn it. The words, " *I will call heaven and earth as witnesses against you*," refer to the substance of the ode about to be rehearsed, which begins with an appeal to the heaven and the earth (chap. xxxii. 1). The reason assigned for this in ver. 29 is a brief summary of what the Lord had said to Moses in vers. 16–21, and Moses thought it necessary to communicate to the representatives of the nation. " *The work of your hands* " refers to the idols (*vid.* chap. iv. 28).—Ver. 30 forms the introduction to the rehearsal of the ode.

SONG OF MOSES, AND ANNOUNCEMENT OF HIS DEATH.— CHAP. XXXII.

Vers. 1–43. THE SONG OF MOSES.—In accordance with the object announced in chap. xxxi. 19, this song contrasts the unchangeable fidelity of the Lord with the perversity of His faithless people. After a solemn introduction pointing out the importance of the instruction about to be given (vers. 1–3), this thought is placed in the foreground as the theme of the whole : the Lord is blameless and righteous in His doings, but Israel acts corruptly and perversely ; and this is carried out in the first place by showing the folly of the Israelites in rebelling against the Lord (vers. 6–18) ; secondly, by unfolding the purpose of God to reject and punish the rebellious generation (vers. 19–23) ; and lastly, by announcing and depicting the fulfilment of this purpose, and the judgment in which the Lord would have mercy upon His servants and annihilate His foes (vers. 34–43).

The song embraces the whole of the future history of Israel, and bears all the marks of a prophetic testimony from the mouth of Moses, in the perfectly ideal picture which it draws, on the one hand, of the benefits and blessings conferred by the Lord upon His people ; and on the other hand, of the ingratitude with which Israel repaid its God for them all. " This song, soaring as it does to the loftiest heights, moving amidst the richest abundance of pictures of both present and future, with its concise, compressed, and pictorial style, rough, penetrating, and sharp, but full of the holiest solemnity, a witness against the disobedient nation, a celebration of the covenant God, sets before us in miniature a picture of the whole life and conduct of the great man of God, whose office it pre-eminently was to preach condemnation" (*O. v. Gerlach*).—It is true that the persons addressed in this ode are not the contemporaries of

Moses, but the Israelites in Canaan, when they had grown haughty in the midst of the rich abundance of its blessings, and had fallen away from the Lord, so that the times when God led the people through the wilderness to Canaan are represented as days long past away. But this, the stand-point of the ode, is not to be identified with the poet's own time. It is rather a prophetic anticipation of the future, which has an *analogon* in a poet's absorption in an ideal future, and differs from this merely in the certainty and distinctness with which the future is foreseen and proclaimed. The assertion that the entire ode moves within the epoch of the kings who lived many centuries after the time of Moses, rests upon a total misapprehension of the nature of prophecy, and a mistaken attempt to turn figurative language into prosaic history. In the whole of the song there is not a single word to indicate that the persons addressed were " already sighing under the oppression of a wild and hostile people, the barbarous hordes of Assyrians or Chaldeans" (*Ewald, Kamphausen,* etc.).[1] The Lord had indeed determined to reject the idolatrous nation, and excite it to jealousy through those that were "no people," and to heap up all evils upon it, famine, pestilence, and sword ; but the execution of this purpose had not yet taken place, and, although absolutely certain, was in the future still. Moreover, the benefits which God had conferred upon His people, were not of such a character as to render it impossible that they should have been alluded to by Moses. All that the Lord had done for Israel, by delivering it from bondage and guiding it miraculously through the wilderness, had been already witnessed by Moses himself ; and the description in vers. 13 and 14, which goes beyond that time, is in reality nothing more than a pictorial expansion of the thought that Israel was most bountifully provided with the

---

[1] How little firm ground there is for this assertion in the contents of the ode, is indirectly admitted even by *Kamphausen* himself in the following remarks : " The words of the ode leave us quite in the dark as to the author ;" and " if it were really certain that Deuteronomy was composed by Moses himself, the question as to the authenticity of the ode would naturally be decided in the traditional way." Consequently, the solution of the whole is to be found in the *dictum*, that " the circumstances which are assumed in any prophecy as already existing, and to which the prophetic utterances are appended as to something well known (?), really determine the time of the prophet himself ;" and, according to this canon, which is held up as " certain and infallible," but which is really thoroughly uncritical, and founded upon the purely dogmatic assumption that any actual foreknowledge of the future is impossible, the ode before us is to be assigned to a date somewhere about 700 years before Christ.

richest productions of the land of Canaan, which flowed with milk
and honey. It is true, the satisfaction of Israel with these blessings
had not actually taken place in the time of Moses, but was still only
an object of hope; but it was hope of such a kind, that Moses could
not cherish a moment's doubt concerning it. Throughout the whole
we find no allusions to peculiar circumstances or historical events
belonging to a later age.—On the other hand, the whole circle of
ideas, figures, and words in the ode points decidedly to Moses as the
author.   Even if we leave out of sight the number of peculiarities
of style (ἄπ. λεγόμενα), which is by no means inconsiderable, and
such bold original composite words as לֹא־אֵל (not-God, ver. 21;
cf. ver. 17) and לֹא־עָם (not-people, ver. 21), which point to a very
remote antiquity, and furnish evidence of the vigour of the earliest
poetry,—the figure of the *eagle* in ver. 11 points back to Ex. xix. 4;
the description of God as a *rock* in vers. 4, 15, 18, 30, 31, 37, recalls
Gen. xlix. 24; the *fire* of the wrath of God, burning even to the
world beneath (ver. 22), points to the representation of God in chap.
iv. 24 as a consuming fire; the expression "to move to *jealousy*,"
in vers. 16 and 21, recalls the "jealous God" in chap. iv. 24, vi.
15, Ex. xx. 5, xxxiv. 14; the description of Israel as *children* (sons)
in ver. 5, and "children without faithfulness" in ver. 20, suggests
chap. xiv. 1; and the words, "O that they were *wise*," in ver. 29,
recall chap. iv. 6, "a wise people."   Again, it is only in the Pentateuch that the word גֹּדֶל (*greatness*, ver. 3) is used to denote the
greatness of God (*vid.* Deut. iii. 24, v. 21, ix. 26, xi. 2; Num. xiv.
19); the name of honour given to Israel in ver. 15, viz. *Jeshurun*,
only occurs again in chap. xxxiii. 5 and 26, with the exception of
Isa. xliv. 2, where it is borrowed from these passages; and the
plural form יְמוֹת, in ver. 7, is only met with again in the prayer of
Moses, viz. Ps. xc. 15.

Vers. 1–5. *Introduction and Theme.*—In the introduction (vers.
1–3),—"*Give ear, O ye heavens, I will speak; and let the earth hear the
words of my mouth.   Let my doctrine drop as the rain, let my speech
fall as the dew; as showers upon green, and rain-drops upon herb .
for I will publish the name of the Lord; give ye greatness to our
God,*"—Moses summons heaven and earth to hearken to his words,
because the instruction which he was about to proclaim concerned
both heaven and earth, *i.e.* the whole universe.   It did so, however,
not merely as treating of the honour of its Creator, which was disregarded by the murmuring people (*Kamphausen*), or to justify God,
as the witness of the righteousness of His doings, in opposition to

the faithless nation, when He punished it for its apostasy (just as in chap. iv. 26, xxx. 19, xxxi. 28, 29, heaven and earth are appealed to as witnesses against rebellious Israel), but also inasmuch as heaven and earth would be affected by the judgment which God poured out upon faithless Israel and the nations, to avenge the blood of His servants (ver. 43) ; since the faithfulness and righteousness of God would thus become manifest in heaven and on earth, and the universe be sanctified and glorified thereby. The *vav consec.* before אֲדַבְּרָה expresses the desired or intended sequel : so that I may then speak, or "so will I then speak" (*vid. Köhler* on *Hagg.* p. 44, note). —Ver. 2. But because what was about to be announced was of such importance throughout, he desired that the words should trickle down like rain and dew upon grass and herb. The point of comparison lies in the refreshing, fertilizing, and enlivening power of the dew and rain. Might the song exert the same upon the hearts of the hearers. לֶקַח, accepting, then, in a passive sense, that which is accepted, *instruction* (doctrine, Prov. xvi. 21, 23 ; Isa. xxix. 24). To "*publish the name of the Lord :*" lit. call, *i.e.* proclaim (not "call upon"), or *praise*. It was not by himself alone that Moses desired to praise the name of the Lord ; the hearers of his song were also to join in this praise. The second clause requires this : "*give ye* (*i.e.* ascribe by word and conduct) *greatness to our God.*" גֹּדֶל, applied here to God (as in chap. iii. 24, v. 21, ix. 26, xi. 2), which is only repeated again in Ps. cl. 2, is the greatness manifested by God in His acts of omnipotence ; it is similar in meaning to the term "glory" in Ps. xxix. 1, 2, xcvi. 7, 8.

Vers. 4, 5. "*The Rock—blameless is His work ; for all His ways are right : a God of faithfulness, and without injustice ; just and righteous is He. Corruptly acts towards Him, not His children ; their spot, a perverse and crooked generation.*" הַצּוּר is placed first absolutely, to give it the greater prominence. God is called "the rock," as the unchangeable refuge, who grants a firm defence and secure resort to His people, by virtue of His unchangeableness or impregnable firmness (see the synonym, "the Stone of Israel," in Gen. xlix. 24). This epithet points to the Mosaic age ; and this is clearly shown by the use made of this title of God (*Zur*) in the construction of surnames in the Mosaic era ; such, for example, as *Pedahzur* (Num. i. 10), which is equivalent to *Pedahel* ("God-redeemed," Num. xxxiv. 28), *Elizur* (Num. i. 5), *Zuriel* (Num. iii. 35), and *Zurishaddai* (Num. i. 6, ii. 12). David, who had so often experienced the rock-like protection of his God, adopted it in his

Psalms (2 Sam. xxii. 3, 32 = Ps. xviii. 3, 32 ; also Ps. xix. 15, xxxi. 3, 4, lxxi. 3). *Perfect* (*i.e.* blameless, without fault or blemish) is His work ; for His ways, which He adopts in His government of the world, are right.   As the rock, He is " a God of faithfulness," upon which men may rely and build in all the storms of life, and " without iniquity," *i.e.* anything crooked or false in His nature.— Ver. 5. His people Israel, on the contrary, had acted corruptly towards Him.   The subject of " acted corruptly" is the rebellious generation of the people ; but before this subject there is introduced parenthetically, and in apposition, " not his children, but their spot." *Spot* (*mum*) is used here in a moral sense, as in Prov. ix. 7, Job xi. 15, xxxi. 7, equivalent to stain.   The rebellious and ungodly were not children of the Lord, but a stain upon them.   If these words had stood after the actual subject, instead of before them, they would have presented no difficulty.   This verse is the original of the expression, " children that are corrupters," in Isa. i. 4.

Vers. 6–18. Expansion of the theme according to the thought expressed in ver. 5.   The perversity of the rebellious generation manifested itself in the fact, that it repaid the Lord, to whom it owed existence and well-being, for all His benefits, with a foolish apostasy from its Creator and Father.   This thought is expressed in ver. 6, in a reproachful question addressed to the people, and then supported in vers. 7–14 by an enumeration of the benefits conferred by God, and in vers. 15–18 by a description of the ingratitude of the people.—Ver. 6.   " *Will ye thus repay the Lord? thou foolish people and unwise!   Is He not thy Father, who hath founded thee, who hath made thee and prepared thee?*"   גָּמַל, the primary idea of which is doubtful, signifies properly *to show*, or *do*, for the most part *good*, but sometimes *evil* (*vid.* Ps. vii. 5).   For the purpose of painting the folly of their apostasy distinctly before the eyes of the people, Moses crowds words together to describe what God was to the nation,—" *thy Father*," to whose love Israel was indebted for its elevation into an independent people : comp. Isa. lxiii. 16, where Father and Redeemer are synonymous terms, with Isa. lxiv. 7, God the Father, Israel the clay which He had formed, and Mal. ii. 10, where God as Father is said to have created Israel ; see also the remarks at chap. xiv. 1 on the notion of Israel's sonship.—קָנֶךָ, *He has acquired thee* ; קָנָה, κτᾶσθαι, to get, acquire (Gen. iv. 1), then so as to involve the idea of κτίζειν (Gen. xiv. 9), though without being identical with בָּרָא.   It denotes here the founding of Israel as a nation, by its deliverance out of the power of Pharaoh.   The verbs which

follow (*made* and *established*) refer to the elevation and preparation of the redeemed nation, as the nation of the Lord, by the conclusion of a covenant, the giving of the law, and their guidance
through the desert.—Ver. 7. " *Remember the days of old, consider
the years of the past generations : ask thy father, that he may make
known to thee ; thine old men, that they may tell it to thee !*" With
these words Moses summons the people to reflect upon what the
Lord had done to them. The days of old (עוֹלָם), and years of generation and generation, *i.e.* years through which one generation after
another had lived, are the times of the deliverance of Israel out
of Egypt, including the pre-Mosaic times, and also the immediate
post-Mosaic, when Israel had entered into the possession of Canaan.
These times are described by Moses as a far distant past, because
he transported himself in spirit to the " latter days" (chap. xxxi.
29), when the nation would have fallen away from its God, and
would have been forsaken and punished by God in consequence.
" *Days of eternity*" are times which lie an eternity behind the
speaker, not necessarily, however, before all time, but simply at a
period very far removed from the present, and of which even the
fathers and old men could only relate what had been handed down
by tradition to them.

Vers. 8 and 9. " *When the Most High portioned out inheritance
to the nations, when He divided the children of men; He fixed the
boundaries of the nations according to the number of the sons of
Israel : for the Lord's portion is His people ; Jacob the cord of His
inheritance.*" Moses commences his enumeration of the manifestations of divine mercy with the thought, that from the very commencement of the forming of nations God had cared for His people
Israel. The meaning of ver. 8 is given in general correctly by
Calvin: " In the whole arrangement of the world God had kept
this before Him as the end : to consult the interests of His chosen
people." The words, " when the Most High portioned out inheritance to the nations," etc., are not to be restricted to the one fact of
the confusion of tongues and division of the nations as described in
Gen. xi., but embrace the whole period of the development of the
one human family in separate tribes and nations, together with their
settlement in different lands ; for it is no doctrine of the Israelitish
legend, as *Kamphausen* supposes, that the division of the nations was
completed once for all. The book of Genesis simply teaches, that
after the confusion of tongues at the building of the tower of Babel,
God scattered men over the entire surface of the earth (chap. xi.

9), and that the nations were divided, *i.e.* separate nations were formed from the families of the sons of Noah (Gen. x. 32); that is to say, the nations were formed in the divinely-appointed way of generation and multiplication, and so spread over the earth. And the Scriptures say nothing about a division of the countries among the different nations at one particular time; they simply show, that, like the formation of the nations from families and tribes, the possession of the lands by the nations so formed was to be traced to God, —was the work of divine providence and government,—whereby God so determined the boundaries of the nations ("the nations" are neither the tribes of Israel, nor simply the nations round about Canaan, but the nations generally), that Israel might receive as its inheritance a land proportioned to its numbers.[1]—Ver. 9. God did this, because He had chosen Israel as His own nation, even before it came into existence. As the Lord's people of possession (cf. chap. vii. 6, x. 15, and Ex. xix. 5), Israel was Jehovah's portion, and the inheritance assigned to Him. חֶבֶל, a *cord*, or measure, then a piece of land measured off; here it is figuratively applied to the nation.—Vers. 10 sqq. He had manifested His fatherly care and love to Israel as His own property.

Ver. 10. "*He found him in the land of the desert, and in the wilderness, the howling of the steppe; He surrounded him, took care of him, protected him as the apple of His eye.*" These words do not "relate more especially to the conclusion of the covenant at Sinai" (*Luther*), nor merely to all the proofs of the paternal care with which God visited His people in the desert, to lead them to Sinai, there to adopt them as His covenant nation, and then to guide them to Canaan, to the exclusion of their deliverance from the bondage of Egypt. The reason why Moses does not mention this fact, or the passage through the Red Sea, is not to be sought for, either solely or even in part, in the fact that "the song does not rest upon the stand-point of the Mosaic times;" for we may see clearly that distance of time would furnish no adequate ground for "singling out and elaborating certain points only from the re-nowned stories of old," say from the 105th Psalm, which no one would think of pronouncing an earlier production than this song.

---

[1] The Septuagint rendering, "according to the number of the angels of God," is of no critical value,—in fact, is nothing more than an arbitrary interpretation founded upon the later Jewish notion of guardian angels of the different nations (Sir. xvii. 14), which probably originated in a misunderstanding of chap. iv. 19, as compared with Dan. x. 13, 20, 21, and xii. 1.

Nor is it because the gracious help of God, which the people experienced up to the time of the exodus from Egypt, was inferior in importance to the divine care exercised over it during the march through the desert (a fact which would need to be proved), or because the solemn conclusion of the covenant, whereby Israel first became the people of God, took place during the sojourn at Sinai, that Moses speaks of God as finding the people in the desert and adopting them there ; but simply because it was not his intention to give a historical account of the acts performed by God upon and towards Israel, but to describe how Israel was in the most helpless condition when the Lord had compassion upon it, to take it out of that most miserable state in which it must have perished, and bring it into the possession of the richly-blessed land of Canaan. The whole description of what the Lord did for Israel (vers. 10–14) is figurative. Israel is represented as a man in the horrible desert, and in danger of perishing in the desolate waste, where not only bread and water had failed, but where ravenous beasts lay howling in wait for human life, when the Lord took him up and delivered him out of all distress. The expression "found him" is also to be explained from this figure. Finding presupposes seeking, and in the seeking the love which goes in search of the loved one is manifested. Also the expression "land of the desert"—a land which is a desert, without the article defining the desert more precisely—shows that the reference is not to the finding of Israel in the desert of Arabia, and that these words are not to be understood as relating to the fact, that when His people entered the desert the Lord appeared to them in the pillar of cloud and fire (Ex. xiii. 20, Schultz). For although the figure of the desert is chosen, because in reality the Lord had led Israel through the Arabian desert to Canaan, we must not so overlook the figurative character of the whole description as to refer the expression "in a desert land" directly and exclusively to the desert of Arabia. The measures adopted by the Pharaohs, the object of which was the extermination or complete suppression of Israel, made even Egypt a land of desert to the Israelites, where they would inevitably have perished if the Lord had not sought, found, and surrounded them there. To depict still further the helpless and irremediable situation of Israel, the idea of the desert is heightened still further by the addition of וּבְתֹהוּ וגו׳, "and in fact (וּ is explanatory) in a waste," or wilderness (tohu recalls Gen. i. 2). "Howling of the desert" is in apposition to tohu (waste), and not a genitive dependent upon it, viz. "waste of the howling of the desert, or of the desert in which wild beasts howl" (*Ewald*), as if יְלֵל stood after יְשִׁימֹן. "Howling of the desert" does not mean the desert in which wild beasts howl, but the howling which is heard in the desert of wild beasts. The meaning of the passage, therefore, is "in the midst of the howling of the wild beasts of the desert." This clause serves to strengthen the idea of *tohu* (waste), and describes the waste as a place of the most horrible howling of wild beasts. It was in this situation that the Lord surrounded His people. סוֹבֵב, to surround with love and care, not merely to protect (*vid.* Ps. xxvi. 6; Jer. xxxi. 22). בּוֹנֵן, from בִּין or הֵבִין, to pay attention, in the sense of "not to lose sight of them." "To keep as the apple of the eye" is a figurative description of the tenderest care. The apple of the eye is most carefully preserved (*vid.* Ps. xvii. 8; Prov. vii. 2).

Ver. 11. "*As an eagle, which stirreth up its nest and soars over its young, He spread out His wings, took him up, carried him upon His wings.*" Under the figure of an eagle, which teaches its young to fly, and in doing so protects them from injury with watchful affection, Moses describes the care with which the Lord came to the relief of His people in their helplessness, and assisted them to develop their strength. This figure no doubt refers more especially to the protection and assistance of God experienced by Israel in its journey through the Arabian desert; but it must not be restricted to this. It embraces both the deliverance of Israel out of Egypt by the outstretched arm of the Lord, as we may see from a comparison with Ex. xix. 4, where the Lord is said to have brought His people out of Egypt upon eagles' wings, and also the introduction into Canaan, when the Lord drove the Canaanites out from before them and destroyed them. This verse contains an independent thought; the first half is the protasis, the second the apodosis. The nominative to "spreadeth abroad" is Jehovah; and the suffixes in יִקָּחֵהוּ and יִשָּׂאֵהוּ ("taketh" and "beareth") refer to Israel or Jacob (ver. 9), like the suffixes in ver. 10. As כְּ cannot open a sentence like כַּאֲשֶׁר, we must supply the relative אֲשֶׁר after נֶשֶׁר. יָעִיר קִנּוֹ, to waken up, rouse up its nest, *i.e.* to encourage the young ones to fly. It is rendered correctly by the Vulgate, *provocans ad volandum pullos suos*; and freely by *Luther*, "bringeth out its young.' " *Soareth over its young*:" namely, in order that, when they were attempting to fly, if any were in danger of falling through exhaustion, it might take them at once upon its powerful wings, and preserve them from harm. Examples of this, according to the popular belief, are given by *Bochart* (*Hieroz.* ii. p. 762). רָחַף, from רָחַף to be loose or slack (Jer. xxiii. 9): in the *Piel* it is applied to a bird in the sense of loosening its wings, as distinguished from binding its wings to its body; hence (1) to sit upon eggs with loosened wings, and (2) to fly with loosened wings. Here it is used in the latter sense, because the young are referred to. The point of comparison between the conduct of God towards Jacob and the acts of an eagle towards its young, is the loving care with which He trained Israel to independence. The carrying of Israel upon the eagle's wings of divine love and omnipotence was manifested in the most glorious way in the guidance of it by the pillar of cloud and fire, though it was not so exclusively in this visible vehicle of the gracious presence of God as that the comparison can be restricted to this phenomenon alone. *Luther's* interpretation is more correct than this,—"Moses points out in these words, how He fostered them in the desert, bore with their manners, tried them and blessed them that they might learn to fly, *i.e.* to trust in Him,"—except that the explanation of the expression " to fly " is narrowed too much.

Vers. 12–14. " *The Lord alone did lead him, and with Him was no strange god. He made him drive over the high places of the earth, and eat the productions of the field; and made him suck honey out of the rock, and oil out of the flint-stone. Cream of cattle, and milk of the flock, with the fat of lambs, and rams of Bashan's kind, and bucks, with the kidney-fat of wheat: and grape-blood thou drankest as fiery wine.*" Moses gives prominence to the fact that Jehovah alone conducted Israel, to deprive the people of every excuse for their apostasy from the Lord, and put their ingratitude in all the stronger light. If no other god stood by the Lord to help Him, He had thereby laid Israel under the obligation to serve Him alone as its God. " *With Him*" refers to Jehovah, and not to Israel.—Vers. 13, 14. The Lord caused the Israelites to take possession of Canaan with victorious power, and enter upon the enjoyment of its abundant blessings. The phrase, " to cause to drive over the high places of the earth," is a figurative expression for the victorious subjugation of a land; it is not taken from Ps. xviii. 34, as *Ewald* assumes, but is original both here and in chap. xxxiii. 29. " *Drive*" (ride) is only a more majestic expression for " advance." The reference to this passage in Isa. lviii. 14 is unmistakeable. Whoever has obtained possession of the high places of a country is lord of the land. The " high places of the earth " do not mean the high places of Canaan only, although the expression in this instance relates to the possession of Canaan. "*And he* (Jacob) *ate :*" for, so that he could now eat, the productions of the field, and in fact all the riches of the fruitful land, which are then described in superabundant terms. Honey out of the rock and oil out of the flint-stone, *i.e.* the most valuable productions out of the most unproductive places, since God so blessed the land that even the rocks and stones were productive. The figure is derived from the fact that Canaan abounds in wild bees, which make their hives in clefts of the rock, and in olive-trees which grow in a rocky soil. "Rock-flints," *i.e.* rocky flints. The nouns in ver. 14 are dependent upon "to suck" in ver. 13, as the expression is not used literally. "Things which are sweet and pleasant to eat, people are in the habit of sucking" (*Ges. thes.* p. 601). חֶמְאָה and חָלָב (though חֵלֶב seems to require a form חָלָב; *vid. Ewald*, § 213, *b.*) denote the two forms in which the milk yielded by the cattle was used; the latter, milk in general, and the former thick curdled milk, cream, and possibly also butter. The two are divided poetically here, the cream being assigned to the cattle, and the milk to the sheep and goats. "*The fat of lambs,*" *i.e.* "lambs of the best description laden with fat" (*Vitringa*). Fat is a figurative expression for the best (*vid.* Num. xviii. 12). "*And rams :*" grammatically, no doubt, this might also be connected with "the fat," but it is improbable from a poetical point of view, since the enumeration would thereby drag prosaically; and it is also hardly reconcilable with the apposition בְּנֵי בָשָׁן, *i.e.* reared in Bashan (*vid.* Ezek. xxxix. 18), which implies that Bashan was celebrated for its rams, and not merely for its oxen. This epithet, which *Kamphausen* renders "of Bashan's kind," is unquestionably used for the best description of rams. The list becomes poetical, if we take "rams" as an accusative governed by the verb "to suck" (ver. 13). "*Kidney-fat (i.e.* the best fat) *of wheat,*" the finest and most nutritious wheat. Wine is mentioned last, and in this case the list passes with poetic freedom into the form of an address. "*Grape-blood*" for red wine (as in Gen. xlix. 11). חֶמֶר, from חָמַר to ferment, froth, foam, *lit.* the foaming, *i.e.* fiery wine, serves as a more precise definition of the "blood of the grape."

Vers. 15-18. Israel had repaid its God for all these benefits by a base apostasy.—Ver. 15. "*But Righteous-nation became fat, and struck out—thou becamest fat, thick, gross—and let go God who made him, and despised the rock of his salvation.*" So much is certain concerning *Jeshurun*, that it was an honourable surname given to Israel; that it is derived from יָשַׁר, and describes Israel as a nation of just or right men (a similar description to that given by Balaam in Num. xxiii. 10), because Jehovah, who is just and right (ver. 4), had called it to uprightness, to walk in His righteousness, and chosen it as His servant (Isa. xliv. 2). The prevalent opinion, that *Jeshurun* is a diminutive, and signifies *rectalus*, or "little pious" (*Ges.* and others), has no more foundation than the derivation from Israel, and the explanation, "little Israel," since there is no philological proof that the termination *un* ever had a diminutive signification in Hebrew (see *Hengstenberg*, Balaam, p. 415); and an *appellatio blanda et charitativa* is by no means suitable to this passage, much less to chap. xxxiii. 5. The epithet *Righteous-nation*, as we may render *Jeshurun*, was intended to remind Israel of its calling, and involved the severest reproof of its apostasy. "By placing the name of *righteous* before Israel, he censured ironically those who had fallen away from righteousness; and by thus reminding them with what dignity they had been endowed, he upbraided them with the more severity for their guilt of perfidy. For in other places (*sc.* chap. xxxiii. 5, 26) Israel is honoured with an eulogium of the same kind, without any such sinister meaning, but with simple regard to its calling; whilst here Moses shows reproachfully how far they had departed from that pursuit of piety, to the cultivation of which they had been called" (*Calvin*). The words, "became fat, and struck out," are founded upon the figure of an ox that had become fat, and intractable in consequence (*vid.* Isa. x. 27, Hos. iv. 16; and for the fact itself, Deut. vi. 11, viii. 10, xxxi. 20). To sharpen this reproof, Moses repeats the thought in the form of a direct address to the people: "Thou hast become fat, stout, gross." Becoming fat led to forsaking God, the Creator and ground of its salvation. "A full stomach does not promote piety, for it stands secure, and neglects God" (*Luther*). נִבֵּל is no doubt a *denom.* verb from נָבָל, *lit.* to treat as a fool, *i.e.* to despise (*vid.* Micah vii. 6).

Vers. 16–18. "*They excited His jealousy through strange (gods), they provoked Him by abominations. They sacrificed to devils, which (were) not-God; to gods whom they knew not, to new (ones) that had lately come up, whom your fathers feared not. The rock which begat thee thou forsookest, and hast forgotten the God that bare thee.*" These three verses are only a further expansion of ver. 15b. Forsaking the rock of its salvation, Israel gave itself up to the service of worthless idols. The expression "excite to jealousy" is founded upon the figure of a marriage covenant, under which the relation of the Lord to Israel is represented (*vid.* chap. xxxi. 16, and the com. on Ex. xxxiv. 15). "This jealousy rests¹ upon the sacred and spiritual marriage tie, by which God had bound the people to Himself" (*Calvin*). "Strange gods," with which Israel committed adultery, as in Jer. ii. 25, iii. 13. The idols are called "abominations" because Jehovah abhorred them (chap. vii. 25, xxvii. 15; cf. 2 Kings xxiii. 13). שֵׁדִים signifies *demons* in Syriac, as it has been rendered by the LXX. and Vulgate here; *lit.* lords, like Baalim. It is also used in Ps. cvi. 37.— "*Not-God*," a composite noun, in apposition to *Shedim* (devils), like the other expressions which follow : "gods whom they knew not," *i.e.* who had not made themselves known to them as gods by any benefit or blessing (*vid.* chap. xi. 28) ; "new (ones), who had come from near," *i.e.* had but lately risen up and been adopted by the Israelites. "Near," not in a local but in a temporal sense, in contrast to *Jehovah*, who had manifested and attested Himself as God from of old (ver. 7). שָׂעַר, to shudder, construed here with an accusative, to experience a holy shuddering before a person, to revere with holy awe.—In ver. 18 Moses returns to the thought of ver. 15, for the purpose of expressing it emphatically once more, and paving the way for a transition to the description of the acts of the Lord towards His rebellious nation. To bring out still more prominently the base ingratitude of the people, he represents the creation of Israel by Jehovah, the rock of its salvation, under the figure of generation and birth, in which the paternal and maternal love of the Lord to His people had manifested itself. חוֹלֵל, to twist round, then applied to the pains of childbirth. The ἁπ. λεγ. תְּשִׁי is to be traced to שָׁיָה, and is a pausal form like יְחִי in chap. iv. 33. שָׁיָה = שָׁהָה, to forget, to neglect.

Vers. 19–33. For this foolish apostasy the Lord would severely visit His people. This visitation is represented indeed in ver. 19, as the consequence of apostasy that had taken place,—not, however, as a punishment already inflicted, but simply as a resolution which God had formed and would carry out,—an evident proof that we have no song here belonging to the time when God visited with severe punishments the Israelites who had fallen into idolatry. In ver. 19 the determination to reject the degenerate children is announced, and in vers. 20–22 this is still further defined and explained.—Ver. 19. "*And the Lord saw it, and rejected—from indignation at His sons and daughters.*" The object to "saw" may easily be supplied from the context : He saw the idolatry of the people, and rejected those who followed idols, and that because of indignation that His sons and daughters practised such abominations. The expression "he saw" simply serves to bring out the causal link between the apostasy and the punishment. וַיַּרְא has been very well rendered by *Kamphausen*, "He resolved upon rejection," since vers. 20 sqq. clearly show that the rejection had only been resolved upon by God, and was not yet carried out. In what follows, Moses puts this resolution into the mouth of the Lord Himself.—Vers. 20–22. *"And He said, I will hide My face from them, I will see what their end will be: for they are a generation full of perversities, children in whom is no faithfulness. They excited My jealousy by a no-god, provoked Me by their vanities: and I also will excite their jealousy by a no-people, provoke them by a foolish nation. For a fire blazes up in My nose, and burns to the lowest hell, and consumes the earth with its increase, and sets on fire the foundations of the mountains."* The divine purpose contains two things:—*first* of all (ver. 20) the negative side, to hide the face, *i.e.* to withdraw His favour and see what their end would be, *i.e.* that their apostasy would bring nothing but evil and destruction; for they were "a nation of perversities" (*tahpuchoth* is moral perversity, Prov. ii. 14, vi. 14), *i.e.* "a thoroughly perverse and faithless generation" (*Knobel*);—and then, *secondly* (ver. 21), the positive side, viz. chastisement according to the right of complete retaliation. The Israelites had excited the jealousy and vexation of God by a *no-god* and vanities; therefore God would excite their jealousy and vexation by a *no-people* and a foolish nation. How this retaliation would manifest itself is not fully defined however here, but is to be gathered from the conduct of Israel towards the Lord. Israel had excited the jealousy of God by preferring a no-god, or הֲבָלִים, nothingnesses, *i.e.* gods that were vanities or nothings (*Elilim*, Lev. xix. 4), to the true and living God, its Father and Creator. God would therefore excite them to jealousy and ill-will by a no-people, a foolish nation, *i.e.* by preferring a no-people to the Israelites, transferring His favour to them, and giving the blessing which Israel had despised to a foolish nation. It is only with this explanation of the words that full justice is done to the idea of retribution; and it was in this sense that Paul understood this passage as referring to the adoption of the Gentiles as the people of God (Rom. x. 19), and that not merely by adaptation, or by connecting another meaning with the words, as *Umbreit* supposes, but by interpreting it in exact accordance with the

true sense of the words.[1] The adoption of the Gentile world
into covenant with the Lord involved the rejection of the disobedient Israel; and this rejection would be consummated in severe
judgments, in which the ungodly would perish. In this way the
retribution inflicted by the Lord upon the faithless and perverse
generation of His sons and daughters becomes a judgment upon
the whole world. The jealousy of the Lord blazes up into a fire
of wrath, which burns down to sheol. This aspect of the divine
retribution comes into the foreground in what follows, from ver. 23
onwards; whilst the adoption of the Gentile world, which the
Apostle Paul singles out as the leading thought of this verse, in
accordance with the special purpose of the song, falls back behind
the thought, that the Lord would not utterly destroy Israel, but
when all its strength had disappeared would have compassion upon
His servants, and avenge their blood upon His foes. The idea
of a *no-people* is to be gathered from the antithesis *no-god*. As

---

[1] But when *Kamphausen*, on the other hand, maintains that this thought,
which the apostle finds in the passage before us, would be " quite erroneous if
taken as an exposition of the words," the assertion is supported by utterly
worthless arguments: for example, (1) that throughout this song the exalted
heathen are never spoken of as the bride of God, but simply as a rod of discipline used against Israel; (2) that this verse refers to the whole nation of
Israel, and there is no trace of any distinction between the righteous and the
wicked; and (3) that the idea that God would choose another people as the
covenant nation would have been the very opposite of that Messianic hope with
which the author of this song was inspired. To begin with the last, the Messianic hope of the song consisted unquestionably in the thought that the Lord
would do justice to His people, His servants, and would avenge their blood,
even when the strength of the nation should have disappeared (vers. 36 and
43). But this thought, that the Lord would have compassion upon Israel at
last, by no means excludes the reception of the heathen into the kingdom of
God, as is sufficiently apparent from Rom. ix.–xi. The assertion that this verse
refers to the whole nation is quite incorrect. The plural suffixes used throughout in vers. 20 and 21 show clearly that both verses simply refer to those who
had fallen away from the Lord; and nowhere throughout the whole song is it
assumed, that the whole nation would fall away to the very last man, so that
there would be no further remnant of faithful servants of the Lord, to whom
the Lord would manifest His favour again. And lastly, it is nowhere affirmed
that God would simply use the heathen as a rod against Israel. The reference
is solely to enemies and oppressors of Israel; and the chastisement of Israel by
foes holds the second, and therefore a subordinate, place among the evils with
which God would punish the rebellious. It is true that the heathen are not
described as the bride of God in this song, but that is for no other reason than
because the idea of moving them to jealousy with a not-people is not more
fully expanded.

Schultz justly observes, " the expression *no-people* can no more
denote a people of monsters, than the *no-god* was a monster, by
which Israel had excited the Lord to jealousy." This remark is
quite sufficient to show that the opinion of *Ewald* and others is
untenable and false, namely, that " the expression *no-people* signifies a truly inhuman people, terrible and repulsive." No-god
is a god to whom the predicate of godhead cannot properly be
applied ; and so also *no-people* is a people that does not deserve the
name of a people or nation at all. The further definition of *no-
god* is to be found in the word *" vanities."* *No-god* are the idols,
who are called vanities or nothingnesses, because they deceive the
confidence of men in their divinity ; because, as Jeremiah says
(Jer. xiv. 22), they can give no showers of rain or drops of water
from heaven. *No-people* is explained by a " foolish nation." A
" foolish nation " is the opposite of a wise and understanding
people, as Israel is called in chap. iv. 6, because it possessed
righteous statutes and rights in the law of the Lord. The foolish
nation therefore is not " an ungodly nation, which despises all laws
both *human* and divine " (*Ros., Maur.*), but a people whose laws
and rights are not founded upon divine revelation. Consequently
the *no-people* is not " a barbarous and inhuman people " (*Ros.*); or
" a horde of men that does not deserve to be called a people "
(*Maurer*), but a people to which the name of a people or nation is
to be refused, because its political and judicial constitution is the
work of man, and because it has not the true God for its head and
king ; or, as *Vitringa* explains, " a people not chosen by the true
God, passed by when a people was chosen, shut out from the
fellowship and grace of God, alienated from the commonwealth
of Israel, and a stranger from the covenant of promise (Eph. ii.
12)." In this respect every heathen nation was a " no-people,"
even though it might not be behind the Israelites so far as its outward organization was concerned. This explanation cannot be set
aside, either by the objection that at that time Israel had brought
itself down to the level of the heathen, by its apostasy from the
Eternal,—for the notion of people and no-people is not taken from
the outward appearance of Israel at any particular time, but is
derived from its divine idea and calling,—or by an appeal to the
singular, " a foolish nation," whereas we should expect " foolish
nations " to correspond to the " vanities," if we were to understand
by the *no-people* not one particular heathen nation, but the heathen
nations generally. The singular, " a foolish nation," was required

by the antithesis, upon which it is rounded, the "wise nation," from which the expression *no-people* first receives its precise definition, which would be altogether obliterated by the plural. Moreover, Moses did not intend to give expression to the thought that God would excite Israel to jealousy by either few, or many, or all the Gentile nations.

In ver. 22, the determination of the Lord with regard to the faithless generation is explained by the threat, that the wrath of the Lord which was kindled against this faithlessness would set the whole world in flames down to the lowest hell. We may see how far the contents of this verse are from favouring the conclusion that "no-people" means a barbarous and inhuman horde, from the difficulty which the supporters of this view have found in dealing with the word כִּי. *Ewald* renders it *doch* (yet), in total disregard of the usages of the language; and *Venema, certe, profecto* (surely); whilst *Kamphausen* supposes it to be used in a somewhat careless manner. The contents of ver. 22, which are introduced with כִּי, by no means harmonize with the thought, "I will send a barbarous and inhuman horde;" whilst the announcement of a judgment setting the whole world in flames may form a very suitable explanation of the thought, that the Lord would excite faithless Israel to jealousy by a "no-people." This judgment, for example, would make the worthlessness of idols and the omnipotence of the God of Israel manifest in all the earth, and would lead the nations to seek refuge and salvation with the living God; and, as we learn from the history of the kingdom of God, and the allusions of the Apostle Paul to this mystery of the divine counsels, the heathen themselves would be the first to do so when they saw all their power and glory falling into ruins, and then the Israelites, when they saw that God had taken the kingdom from them and raised up the heathen who were converted to Him to be His people. The fire in the nose of the Lord is a figurative description of burning wrath and jealousy (*vid.* chap. xxix. 19). The fire signifies really nothing else than His jealousy, His vital energy, and in a certain sense His breath; it therefore naturally burns in the nose (*vid.* Ps. xviii. 9). In this sense the Lord as "a jealous God" is a consuming fire (*vid.* chap. iv. 24, and the exposition of Ex. iii. 2). This fire burns down even to the lower hell. The lower hell, *i.e.* the lowest region of sheol, or the lower regions, forms the strongest contrast to heaven; though we cannot deduce any definite doctrinal conclusions from the expression as to the existence of more hells than one. This fire "consumes the earth with its increase," *i.e.* all its vegetable productions, and sets on fire the foundations of the mountains. This description is not a hyperbolical picture of the judgment which was to fall upon the children of Israel alone (*Kamphausen, Aben-Ezra,* etc.); for it is a mistake to suppose that the judgment foretold affected the Israelitish nation only. The thought is weakened by the assumption that the language is hyperbolical. The words are not intended to foretell one particular penal judgment, but refer to judgment in its totality and universality, as realized in the course of centuries in different judgments upon the nations, and only to be completely fulfilled at the end of the world. *Calvin* is right therefore when he says, "As the indignation and anger of God follow His enemies to hell, to eternal flames and infernal tortures, so they devour their land with its produce, and burn the foundations of the mountains ; ... there is no necessity therefore to imagine that there is any hyperbole in the words, ' to the lower hell.'" This judgment is then depicted in vers. 23–33 as it would discharge itself upon rebellious Israel.

Ver. 23. "*I will heap up evils upon them, use up My arrows against them.*" The evils threatened against the despisers of the Lord and His commandments would be poured out in great abundance by the Lord upon the foolish generation. סָפָה, to add one upon the other (*vid.* Num. xxxii. 14); hence in *Hiphil* to heap up, sweep together. These evils are represented in the second clause of the verse as arrows, which the Lord as a warrior would shoot away at His foes (as in ver. 42 ; cf. Ps. xxxviii. 3, xci. 5 ; Job vi. 4). כִּלָּה, to bring to an end, to use up to the very last.—Ver. 24. "*Have they wasted away with hunger, are they consumed with pestilential heat and bitter plague: I will let loose the tooth of beasts upon them, with the poison of things that crawl in the dust.*"—Ver. 25. "*If the sword without shall sweep them away, and in the chambers of terrors, the young man as the maiden, the suckling with the grey-haired man.*" The evils mentioned are hunger, pestilence, plague, wild beasts, poisonous serpents, and war. The first hemistich in ver. 24 contains simply nouns construed absolutely, which may be regarded as a kind of circumstantial clause. The literal meaning is, "With regard to those who are starved with hunger, etc., I will send against them ;" *i.e.* when hunger, pestilence, plague, have brought them to the verge of destruction, I will send, etc. מְזֵי, construct state of מָזֶה, *ἀπ. λεγ.*, with which *Cocceius* compares מָצָה and מָצַץ, to suck out, and for which *Schultens* has cited analogies from the Arabic. "Sucked out by hunger," *i.e.* wasted away.

"Tooth of beasts and poison of serpents:" poetical for beasts of prey and poisonous animals. See Lev. xxvi. 22, where wild beasts are mentioned as a plague along with pestilence, famine, and sword. —Ver. 25. These are accompanied by the evils of war, which sweeps away the men outside in the slaughter itself by the sword, and the defenceless—viz. youths and maidens, sucklings and old men—in the chambers by alarm. אֵימָה is a sudden mortal terror, and *Knobel* is wrong in applying it to hunger and plague. The use of the verb שִׁכֵּל, to make childless, is to be explained on the supposition that the nation or land is personified as a mother, whose children are the members of the nation, old and young together. Ezekiel has taken the four grievous judgments out of these two verses : sword, famine, wild beasts, and pestilence (Ezek. xiv. 21 : see also v. 17, and Jer. xv. 2, 3).

Vers. 26 and 27. "*I should say, I will blow them away, I will blot out the remembrance of them among men ; if I did not fear wrath upon the enemy, that their enemies might mistake it, that they might say, Our hand was high, and Jehovah has not done all this.*" The meaning is, that the people would have deserved to be utterly destroyed, and it was only for His own name's sake that God abstained from utter destruction. אָמַרְתִּי to be construed conditionally requires לוּלֵי : if I did not fear (as actually was the case) I should resolve to destroy them, without leaving a trace behind. "*I should say,*" used to denote the purpose of God, like "he said" in ver. 20. The ἅπ. λεγ. אַפְאֵיהֶם, which has been rendered in very different ways, cannot be regarded, as it is by the Rabbins, as a *denom.* verb from פֵּאָה, a corner ; and *Calvin's* rendering, "to scatter through corners," does not suit the context ; whilst the meaning, "to cast or scare out of all corners," cannot be deduced from this derivation. The context requires the signification to annihilate, as the remembrance of them was to vanish from the earth. We get this meaning if we trace it to פָּאָה, to blow,—related to פָּעָה (Isa. xlii. 14) and פָּהָה, from which comes פֶּה,—in the Hiphil "to blow away," not to blow asunder. הִשְׁבִּית, not "to cause to rest," but to cause to cease, *delere* (as in Amos viii. 4). "*Wrath upon the enemy,*" *i.e.* "displeasure on the part of God at the arrogant boasting of the enemy, which was opposed to the glory of God" (*Vitringa*). פֶּן, *lest*, after גוּר, to fear. On this reason for sparing Israel, see chap. ix. 28 ; Ex. xxxii. 12 ; Num. xiv. 13 sqq. ; Isa. x. 5 sqq. *Enemy* is a generic term, hence it is followed by the plural. נָכַר, Piel, to find strange, *sc.* the destruction of Israel, *i.e.* to mistake the reason for it, or, as is shown by what follows, to ascribe the destruction of Israel to themselves and their own power, whereas it had been the work of God. "*Our hand was high,*" *i.e.* has lifted itself up or shown itself mighty, an intentional play upon the "high hand" of the Lord (Ex. xiv. 8 ; cf. Isa. xxvi. 11).—The reason why Israel did not deserve to be spared is given in ver. 28 : "*For a people forsaken of counsel are they, and there is not understanding in them.*" "Forsaken of counsel," *i.e.* utterly destitute of counsel.

This want of understanding on the part of Israel is still further expounded in vers. 29–32, where the words of God pass imperceptibly into the words of Moses, who feels impelled once more to impress the word which the Lord had spoken upon the hearts of the people.—Vers. 29–31. "*If they were wise, they would understand this, would consider their end. Ah, how could one pursue a thousand, and two put ten thousand to flight, were it not that their Rock had sold them, and Jehovah had given them up! For their rock is not as our rock ; of that our enemies are judges.*" לֹּא presupposes a case, which is either known not to exist, or of which this is assumed ; " if they were wise," which they are not. " *This*" refers to the leading thought of the whole, viz. that apostasy from God the Lord is sure to be followed by the severest judgment. " *Their end,*" as in ver. 20, the end towards which the people were going through obstinate perseverance in their sin, *i.e.* utter destruction, if the Lord did not avert it for His name's sake.—Ver. 30. If Israel were wise, it could easily conquer all its foes in the power of its God (*vid.* Lev. xxvi. 8) ; but as it had forsaken the Lord its rock, He, their (Israel's) rock, had given them up into the power of the foe. אִם לֹא כִּי is more emphatic or distinct than אִם לֹא only, and introduces an exception which does not permit the desired event to take place. Israel could have put all its enemies to flight were it not that its God had given it entirely up to them (sold them as slaves). The supposition that this had already occurred by no means proves, as *Kamphausen* believes, "that the poet was speaking of the existing state of the nation," but merely that Moses thinks of the circumstances as certain to occur when the people should have forsaken their God. The past implied in the verbs " sold " and " given up " is a prophetically ideal past or present, but not a real and historical one. The assertion of *Hupfeld* and *Kamphausen*, that מָכַר, as used with special reference to the giving up of a nation into the power of the heathen, " belongs to a somewhat later usage of the language," is equally groundless.—Ver. 31. The giving up of Israel into the power of the heathen arose, not from the superior power of the heathen and their gods, but solely from the apostasy of Israel from its own God. " Our rock," as Moses calls the Lord, identifying himself with the nation, is not as their rock, *i.e.* the gods in whom the heathen trust. That the pronoun in "*their* rock" refers to the heathen, is so perfectly obvious from the antithesis "*our* rock," that there cannot possibly be any doubt about it. The second hemistich in ver. 30 contains a circumstantial clause, introduced to strengthen the thought which precedes it. The heathen themselves could be arbitrators (*vid.* Ex. xxi. 22), and decide whether the gods of the heathen were not powerless before the God of Israel. " Having experienced so often the formidable might of God, they knew for a certainty that the God of Israel was very different from their own idols" (*Calvin*). The objection offered by *Schultz*, namely, that " the heathen would not admit that their idols were inferior to Jehovah, and actually denied this at the time when they had the upper hand (Isa. x. 10, 11)," has been quite anticipated by *Calvin*, when he observes that Moses " leaves the decision to the unbelievers, not as if they would speak the truth, but because he knew that they must be convinced by experience." As a confirmation of this, *Luther* and others refer not only to the testimony of Balaam (Num. xxiii. and xxiv.), but also to the Egyptians (Ex. xiv. 25) and Philistines (1 Sam. v. 7 sqq.), to which we may add Josh. ii. 9, 10.

Vers. 32 and 33. " *For their vine is of the vine of Sodom, and of the fields of Gomorrah : their grapes are poisonous grapes, bitter clusters have they. Dragon-poison is their wine, and dreadful venom of asps.*" The connection is pointed out by *Calovius* thus : " Moses returns to the Jews, showing why, although the rock of the Jews was very different from the gods of the Gentiles, even according to the testimony of the heathen themselves, who were their foes, they were nevertheless to be put to flight by their enemies and sold ; and why Jehovah sold them, namely, *because their vine* was of the vine of Sodom, *i.e.* of the very worst kind, resembling the inhabitants of Sodom and Gomorrah, as if they were descended from them, and not from their holy patriarchs." The " *for*" in ver. 32 is neither co-ordinate nor subordinate to that in ver. 31. To render it as subordinate would give no intelligible meaning ; and the supposition that it is co-ordinate is precluded by the fact, that in that case vers. 32 and 33 would contain a description of the corruptions of the heathen. The objections to this view have been thus expressed

by *Schultz* with perfect justice : " It is *à priori* inconceivable, that
in so short an ode there should be so elaborate a digression on the
subject of the heathen, seeing that their folly is altogether foreign
to the theme of the whole." To this we may add, that throughout
the Old Testament it is the moral corruption and ungodliness of
the Israelites, and never the vices of the heathen, that are compar .
to the sins of Sodom and Gomorrah. The Israelites who wer forsaken by the Lord, were designated by Isaiah (i. 10) as a people
of Gomorrah, and their rulers as rulers of Sodom (cf. Isa. iii. 9) ;
the inhabitants of Jerusalem were all of them like Sodom and
Gomorrah (Jer. xxiii. 14) ; and the sin of Jerusalem was greater
than that of Sodom (Ezek. xvi. 46 sqq.). The only sense in which
the " for " in ver. 32 can be regarded as co-ordinate to that in
ver. 31; is on the supposition that the former gives the reason for
the thought in ver. 30*b*, whilst the latter serves to support the idea
in ver. 30*a*. The order of thought is the following : Israel would
have been able to smite its foes with very little difficulty, because
the gods of the heathen are not a rock like Jehovah ; but Jehovah
had given up His people to the heathen, because it had brought
forth fruits like Sodom, *i.e.* had resembled Sodom in its wickedness.
The vine and its fruits are figurative terms, applied to the nation
and its productions. " The nation was not only a degenerate, but
also a poisonous vine, producing nothing but what was deadly"
(*Calvin*). This figure is expanded still further by Isa. v. 2 sqq.
Israel was a vineyard planted by Jehovah, that it might bring
forth good fruits, instead of which it brought forth wild grapes
(*vid.* Jer. ii. 21 ; Ps. lxxx. 9 sqq. ; Hos. x. 1). " Their vine " is
the Israelites themselves, their nature being compared to a vine
which had degenerated as much as if it had been an offshoot of a
Sodomitish vine. שַׁדְמֹת, the construct state of שְׁדֵמֹת, floors, fields.
The grapes of this vine are worse than wild grapes, they are bitter,
poisonous grapes.—Ver. 33. The wine of these grapes is snakepoison. *Tannin :* see Ex. vii. 9, 10. *Pethen :* the asp or adder, one
of the most poisonous kinds of snake, whose bite was immediately
fatal (*vid. Rosenmüller, bibl. Althk.* iv. 2, pp. 364 sqq.). These
figures express the thought, that " nothing could be imagined worse,
or more to be abhorred, than that nation " (*Calvin*). Now although
this comparison simply refers to the badness of Israel, the thought
of the penal judgment that fell upon Sodom lies behind. " They
imitate the Sodomites, they bring forth the worst fruits of all impiety, they deserve to perish like Sodom " (*J. H. Michaelis*).

The description of this judgment commences in ver. 34. Israel had deserved for its corruption to be destroyed from the earth (ver. 26); yet for His name's sake the Lord would have compassion upon it, when it was so humiliated with its heavy punishments that its strength was coming to an end.—Ver. 34. " *Is not this hidden with Me, sealed up in My treasuries ?*" The allusion in this verse has been disputed ; many refer it to what goes before, others to what follows after. There is some truth in both. The verse forms the transition, closing what precedes, and introducing what follows. The assertion that the figure of preserving in the treasuries precludes the supposition that " *this* " refers to what follows, cannot be sustained. For although in Hos. xiii. 12, and Job xiv. 17, the binding and sealing of sins in a bundle are spoken of, yet it is very evident from Ps. cxxxix. 16, Mal. iii. 16, and Dan. vii. 10, that not only the evil doings of men, but their days generally, *i.e.* not only their deeds, but the things which happen to them, are written in a book before God. *O. v. Gerlach* has explained it correctly : " All these things have been decreed long ago ; their coming is infallibly certain." " *This* " includes not only the sins of the nation, but also the judgments of God. The apostasy of Israel, as well as the consequent punishment, is laid up with God—sealed up in His treasuries—and therefore they have not yet actually occurred : an evident proof that we have prophecy before us, and not the description of an apostasy that had already taken place, and of the punishment inflicted in consequence. The ἀπ. λεγ. כָּמֻס in this connection signifies to lay up, preserve, conceal, although the etymology is disputed. The figure in the second hemistich is not taken from secret archives, but from treasuries or stores, in which whatever was to be preserved was to be laid up, to be taken out in due time.

Vers. 35 and 36. " *Vengeance is Mine, and retribution for the time when their foot shall shake: for the day of their destruction is near, and that which is determined for them cometh hastily. For the Lord will judge His people, and have compassion upon His servants, when He seeth that every hold has disappeared, and the fettered and the free are gone.*"—The Lord will punish the sins of His people in due time. " Vengeance is Mine :" it belongs to Me, it is My part to inflict. שִׁלֵּם is a *noun* here for the usual שִׁלּוּם, retribution (*vid. Ewald*, § 156, *b.*). The shaking of the foot is a figure representing the commencement of a fall, or of stumbling (*vid.* Ps. xxxviii. 17, xciv. 18). The thought in this clause is not, " At or

towards the time when their misfortune begins, I will plunge them
into the greatest calamity," as *Kamphausen* infers from the fact
that the shaking denotes the beginning of the calamity ; and yet
the vengeance can only be completed by plunging them into
calamity,—a thought which he justly regards as unsuitable, though
he resorts to emendations of the text in consequence. But the
supposed unsuitability vanishes, if we simply regard the words,
" Vengeance is Mine, and retribution," not as the mere announcement of a quality founded in the nature of God, and residing in
God Himself, but as an expression of the divine energy, with this
signification, I will manifest Myself as an avenger and recompenser,
when their foot shall shake. Then what had hitherto been hidden
with God, lay sealed up as it were in His treasuries, should come
to light, and be made manifest to the sinful nation. God would
not delay in this ; for the day of their destruction was near. אֵיד
signifies misfortune, and sometimes utter destruction. The primary
meaning of the word cannot be determined with certainty. That
it does not mean utter destruction, we may see from the parallel
clause. " The things that shall come upon them," await them, or
are prepared for them, are, according to the context, both in ver.
26 and also in vers. 36 sqq., not destruction, but simply a calamity
or penal judgment that would bring them near to utter destruction.
Again, these words do not relate to the punishment of " the wicked
deeds of the inhuman horde," or the vengeance of God upon the
enemies of Israel (*Ewald, Kamphausen*), but to the vengeance or
retribution which God would inflict upon Israel. This is evident,
apart from what has been said above against the application of vers.
33, 34, to the heathen, simply from ver. 36*b*, which unquestionably
refers to Israel, and has been so interpreted by every commentator.
—The first clause is quoted in Rom. xii. 19 and Heb. x. 30, in
the former to warn against self-revenge, in the latter to show the
energy with which God will punish those who fall away from the
faith, in connection with ver. 36*a*, " the Lord will judge His
people."—In ver. 36 the reason is given for the thought in ver. 35.
דִּין is mostly taken here in the sense of " procure right," help to
right, which it certainly often has (*e.g.* Ps. liv. 3), and which is not
to be excluded here ; but this by no means exhausts the idea of the
word. The parallel יִתְנֶחָם does not compel us to drop the idea of
punishment, which is involved in the judging ; for it is a question
whether the two clauses are perfectly synonymous. " Judging His
people" did not consist merely in the fact that Jehovah punished

the heathen who oppressed Israel, but also in the fact that He punished the wicked in Israel who oppressed the righteous. " His people " is no doubt Israel as a whole (as, for example, in Isa. i. 3), but this whole was composed of righteous and wicked, and God could only help the righteous to justice by punishing and destroying the wicked. In this way the judging of His people became compassion towards His servants. " His servants" are the righteous, or, speaking more correctly, all who in the time of judgment are found to be the servants of God, and are saved. Because Israel was His nation, the Lord judged it in such a manner as not to destroy it, but simply to punish it for its sins, and to have compassion upon His servants, when He saw that the strength of the nation was gone. יָד, the hand, with which one grasps and works, is a figure employed to denote power and might (vid. Isa. xxviii. 2). אָזַל, to run out, or come to an end (1 Sam. ix. 7 ; Job xiv. 11). The meaning is, " when every support is gone," when all the rotten props of its might, upon which it has rested, are broken (Ewald). The noun אֶפֶס, cessation, disappearance, takes the place of a verb. The words עָצוּר וְעָזוּב are a proverbial phrase used to denote all men, as we may clearly see from 1 Kings xiv. 10, xxi. 21 ; 2 Kings iv. 8, xiv. 6. The literal meaning of this form, however, cannot be decided with certainty. The explanation given by L. de Dieu is the most plausible one, viz. the man who is fettered, restrained, i.e. married, and the single or free. For עָזוּב the meaning caelebs is established by the Arabic, though the Arabic can hardly be appealed to as proving that עָצוּר means paterfamilias, as this meaning, which Roediger assigns to the Arabic word, is founded upon a mistaken interpretation of a passage in Kamus.

Vers. 37-39. The Lord would then convince His people of the worthlessness of idols and the folly of idolatry, and bring it to admit the fact that He was God alone. " Then will He say, Where are their gods, the rock in whom they trusted; who consumed the fat of their burnt-offerings, the wine of their libations ? Let them rise up and help you, that there may be a shelter over you ! See now that I, I am it, and there is no God beside Me : I kill, and make alive ; I smite in pieces, and I heal ; and there is no one who delivers out of My hand." וְאָמַר might be taken impersonally, as it has been by Luther and others, " men will say ;" but as it is certainly Jehovah who is speaking in ver. 39, and what Jehovah says there is simply a deduction from what is addressed to the people in vers. 37 and 38, there can hardly be any doubt that Jehovah is speaking in vers.

37, 38, as well as in vers. 34, 35, and therefore that Moses simply distinguishes himself from Jehovah in ver. 36, when explaining the reason for the judgment foretold by the Lord. The expression, " *their* gods," relates, not to the heathen, but to the Israelites, upon whom the judgment had fallen. The worthlessness of their gods had become manifest, namely, of the strange gods or idols, which the Israelites had preferred to the living God (*vid.* vers. 16, 17), and to which they had brought their sacrifices and drink-offerings. In ver. 38, אֲשֶׁר is the subject,—the gods, who consumed the fat of the sacrifices offered to them by their worshippers (the foolish Israelites),—and is not to be taken as the relative with זִבְחֵימוֹ, as the LXX., *Vulg.*, and *Luther* have rendered it, viz. " whose sacrifices they (the Israelites) ate," which neither suits the context nor the word חֵלֶב (fat), which denotes the fat portions of the sacrificial animals that were burned upon the altar, and therefore presented to God. The wine of the drink-offerings was also poured out upon the altar, and thus given up to the deity worshipped. The handing over of the sacrificial portions to the deity is described here with holy irony, as though the gods themselves consumed the fat of the slain offerings, and drank the wine poured out for them, for the purpose of expressing this thought: "The gods, whom ye entertained so well, and provided so abundantly with sacrifices, let them now arise and help you, and thus make themselves clearly known to you." The address here takes the form of a direct appeal to the idolaters themselves; and in the last clause the imperative is introduced instead of the optative, to express the thought as sharply as possible, that men need the protection of God, and are warranted in expecting it from the gods they worship : " let there be a shelter over you." *Sithrah* for *sether,* a shelter or defence.—Ver. 39. The appeal to their own experience of the worthlessness of idols is followed by a demand that they should acknowledge Jehovah as the only true God. The repetition of " *I*" is emphatic : " *I, I only it,*" as an expression of being; I *am* it, ἐγώ εἰμι, John viii. 24, xviii. 5. The predicate *Elohim* (*vid.* 2 Sam. vii. 28 ; Isa. xxxvii. 16) is omitted, because it is contained in the thought itself, and moreover is clearly expressed in the parallel clause which follows, " there is not a God beside Me." Jehovah manifests Himself in His doings, which Israel had experienced already, and still continued to experience. He kills and makes alive, etc., *i.e.* He has the power of life and death. These words do not refer to the immortality of the soul, but to the restoration to life of the people of Israel, which

God had delivered up to death (so 1 Sam. ii. 6 ; 2 Kings v. 7 ; cf. Isa. xxvi. 19 ; Hos. xiii. 10 ; Wisd. xvi. 13 ; Tobit xiii. 2). This thought, and the following one, which is equally consolatory, that God smites and heals again, are frequently repeated by the prophets (*vid.* Hos. vi. 1 ; Isa. xxx. 26, lvii. 17, 18 ; Jer. xvii. 14). None can deliver out of His hand (*vid.* Isa. xliii. 13 ; Hos. v. 14, ii. 12).

Vers. 40–43. The Lord will show Himself as the only true God, who slays and makes alive, etc. He will take vengeance upon His enemies, avenge the blood of His servants, and expiate His land, His people. With this promise, which is full of comfort for all the servants of the Lord, the ode concludes. "*For I lift up My hand to heaven, and say, As truly as I live for ever, if I have sharpened My flashing sword, and My hand grasps for judgment, I will repay vengeance to My adversaries, and requite My haters. I will make My arrows drunk with blood, and My sword will eat flesh ; with the blood of the slain and prisoners, with the hairy head of the foe.*" Lifting up the hand to heaven was a gesture by which a person taking an oath invoked God, who is enthroned in heaven, as a witness of the truth and an avenger of falsehood (Gen. xiv. 22). Here, as in Ex. vi. 8 and Num. xiv. 30, it is used anthropomorphically of God, who is in heaven, and can swear by no greater than Himself (*vid.* Isa. xlv. 23 ; Jer. xxii. 5 ; Heb. vi. 17). The oath follows in vers. 41 and 42. אִם, however, is not the particle employed in swearing, which has a negative meaning (*vid.* Gen. xiv. 23), but is conditional, and introduces the protasis. As the avenger of His people upon their foes, the Lord is represented as a warlike hero, who whets His sword, and has a quiver filled with arrows (as in Ps. vii. 13). "As long as the Church has to make war upon the world, the flesh, and the devil, it needs a warlike head" (*Schultz*). בְּרַק חֶרֶב, the flash of the sword, *i.e.* the flashing sword (*vid.* Gen. iii. 24 ; Nahum iii. 3 ; Hab. iii. 11). In the next clause, "and My hand grasps judgment," *mishpat* (judgment) does not mean punishment or destruction hurled by God upon His foes, nor the weapons employed in the execution of judgment, but judgment is introduced poetically as the thing which God takes in hand for the purpose of carrying it out. הֵשִׁיב נָקָם, to lead back vengeance, *i.e.* to repay it. Punishment is retribution for evil done. By the enemies and haters of Jehovah, we need not understand simply the heathen enemies of the Israelites, for the ungodly in Israel were enemies of God quite as much as the ungodly heathen. If it is evident from vers. 25–27, where God is spoken of as punishing Israel to the utmost when it had fallen

into idolatry, but not utterly destroying it, that the punishment
which God would inflict would also fall upon the heathen, who
would have made an end of Israel; it is no less apparent from vers.
37 and 38, especially from the appeal in ver. 38, Let your idols arise
and help you (ver. 38), which is addressed, as all admit, to the
idolatrous Israelites, and not to the heathen, that those Israelites
who had made worthless idols their rock would be exposed to the
vengeance and retribution of the Lord. In ver. 42 the figure of
the warrior is revived, and the judgment of God is carried out still
further under this figure. Of the four different clauses in this
verse, the third is related to the first, and the fourth to the second.
God would make His arrows drunk with the blood not only of the
slain, but also of the captives, whose lives are generally spared, but
were not to be spared in this judgment. This sword would eat flesh
of the hairy head of the foe. The edge of the sword is represented
poetically as the mouth with which it eats (2 Sam. ii. 26, xviii. 8,
etc.); "the sword is said to devour bodies when it slays them by
piercing" (*Ges. thes.* p. 1088). פְּרָעוֹת, from פְּרַע, a luxuriant, uncut
growth of hair (Num. vi. 5; see at Lev. x. 6). The hairy head is
not a figure used to denote the "wild and cruel foe" (*Knobel*), but
a luxuriant abundance of strength, and the indomitable pride of the
foe, who had grown fat and forgotten his Creator (ver. 15). This
explanation is confirmed by Ps. lxviii. 22; whereas the rendering
ἄρχοντες, princes, leaders, which is given in the Septuagint, has no
foundation in the language itself, and no tenable support in Judg.
v. 2.—Ver. 43. For this retribution which God accomplishes upon
His enemies, the nations were to praise the people of the Lord. As
this song commenced with an appeal to heaven and earth to give
glory to the Lord (vers. 1–3), so it very suitably closes with an
appeal to the heathen to rejoice with His people on account of the acts
of the Lord. " Rejoice, nations, over His people; for He avenges
the blood of His servants, and repays vengeance to His adversaries,
and so expiates His land, His people." " His people" is an accusative, and not in apposition to nations in the sense of " nations
which are His people." For, apart from the fact that such a
combination would be unnatural, the thought that the heathen had
become the people of God is nowhere distinctly expressed in the
song (not even in ver. 21); nor is the way even so prepared for it
as that we could expect it here, although the appeal to the nations
to rejoice with His people on account of what God had done involves
the Messianic idea, that all nations will come to the knowledge of

the Lord (*vid.* Ps. xlvii. 2, lxvi. 8, lxvii. 4).—The reason for this
rejoicing is the judgment through which the Lord avenges the
blood of His servants and repays His foes.   As the enemies of God
are not the heathen as such (see at ver. 41), so the servants of
Jehovah are not the nation of Israel as a whole, but the faithful
servants whom the Lord had at all times among His people, and
who were persecuted, oppressed, and put to death by the ungodly.
By this the land was defiled, covered with blood-guiltiness, so that
the Lord was obliged to interpose as a judge, to put an end to the
ways of the wicked, and to expiate His land, His people, *i.e.* to
wipe out the guilt which rested upon the land and people, by the
punishment of the wicked, and the extermination of idolatry and
ungodliness, and to sanctify and glorify the land and nation (*vid.*
Isa. i. 27, iv. 4, 5).

In vers. 44–47 it is stated that Moses, with Joshua, spake the
song to the people ; and on finishing this rehearsal, once more
impressed upon the hearts of the people the importance of observing
all the commandments of God.   This account proceeds from the
author of the supplement to the *Thorah* of Moses, who inserted
the song in the book of the law.   This explains the name Hoshea,
instead of *Jehoshuah* (Joshua), which Moses had given to his servant
(Num. xiii. 8, 16), and invariably uses (compare chap. xxxi. 3, 7,
14, 23, with chap. i. 38, iii. 21, 28, and the exposition of Num. xiii.
16).—On ver. 46, *vid.* chap. vi. 7 and xi. 19 ; and on ver. 47, *vid.*
chap. xxx. 20.

Vers. 48–52. "*That self-same day*," viz. the day upon which
Moses had rehearsed the song to the children of Israel, the Lord
renewed the announcement of his death, by repeating the command
already given to him (Num. xxvii. 12–14) to ascend Mount Nebo,
there to survey the land of Canaan, and then to be gathered unto
his people.   In form, this repetition differs from the previous
announcement, partly in the fact that the situation of Mount Nebo
is more fully described (in the land of Moab, etc., as in chap. i. 5,
xxviii. 69), and partly in the continual use of the imperative, and a
few other trifling points.   These differences may all be explained from
the fact that the account here was not written by Moses himself.

MOSES' BLESSING.—CHAP. XXXIII.

Before ascending Mount Nebo to depart this life, Moses took
leave of his people, the tribes of Israel, in the blessing which is

very nttingly inserted in the book of the law between the divine
announcement of his approaching death and the account of the
death itself, as being the last words of the departing man of God.
The blessing opens with an allusion to the solemn conclusion of the
covenant and giving of the law at Sinai, by which the Lord became
King of Israel, to indicate at the outset the source from which all
blessings must flow to Israel (vers. 2–5). Then follow the separate
blessings upon the different tribes (vers. 6–25). And the whole
concludes with an utterance of praise to the Lord, as the mighty
support and refuge of His people in their conflicts with all their
foes (vers. 26–29). This blessing was not written down by Moses
himself, like the song in chap. xxxii., but simply pronounced in the
presence of the assembled tribes. This is evident, not only from
the fact that there is nothing said about its being committed to
writing, but also from the heading in ver. 1, where the editor
clearly distinguishes himself from Moses, by speaking of Moses as
"the man of God," like Caleb in Josh. xiv. 6, and the author of the
heading to the prayer of Moses in Ps. xc. 1. In later times, "man
of God" was the title usually given to a prophet (*vid.* 1 Sam. ix. 6;
1 Kings xii. 22, xiii. 14, etc.), as a man who enjoyed direct intercourse with God, and received supernatural revelations from Him.
Nevertheless, we have Moses' own words, not only in the blessings
upon the several tribes (vers. 6–25), but also in the introduction
and conclusion of the blessing (vers. 2–5 and 26–29). The introductory words before the blessings, such as " and this for Judah "
in ver. 7, " and to Levi he said " (ver. 8), and the similar formulas
in vers. 12, 13, 18, 20, 22, 23, and 24, are the only additions made
by the editor who inserted the blessing in the Pentateuch. The
arrangement of the blessings in their present order is probably also
his work. It neither accords with the respective order of the sons
of Jacob, nor with the distribution of the tribes in the camp, nor
with the situation of their possessions in the land of Canaan. It is
true that Reuben stands first as the eldest son of Jacob; but Simeon
is then passed over, and Judah, to whom the dying patriarch be-
queathed the birthright which he withdrew from Reuben, stands
next; and then Levi, the priestly tribe. Then follow Benjamin
and Joseph, the sons of Rachel; Zebulun and Issachar, the last
sons of Leah (in both cases the younger before the elder); and
lastly, the tribes descended from the sons of the maids: Gad, the
son of Zilpah; Dan and Naphtali, the sons of Bilhah; and finally,
Asher, the second son of Zilpah. To discover the guiding prin-

ciple in this arrangement, we must look to the blessings themselves, which indicate partly the position already obtained by each tribe, as a member of the whole nation, in the earthly kingdom of God, and partly the place which it was to reach and occupy in the further development of Israel in the future, not only in relation to the Lord, but also in relation to the other nations. The only exception to this is the position assigned to Reuben, who occupies the foremost place as the first-born, notwithstanding his loss of the birthright. In accordance with this principle, the first place properly belonged to the tribe of Judah, who was raised into the position of lord over his brethren, and the second to the tribe of Levi, which had been set apart to take charge of the sacred things; whilst Benjamin is associated with Levi as the " beloved of the Lord." Then follow Joseph, as the representative of the might which Israel would manifest in conflict with the nations; Zebulun and Issachar, as the tribes which would become the channels of blessings to the nations through their wealth in earthly good; and lastly, the tribes descended from the sons of the maids, Asher being separated from his brother Gad, and placed at the end, in all probability simply because it was in the blessing promised to him that the earthly blessedness of the people of God was to receive its fullest manifestation.

On comparing the blessing of Moses with that of Jacob, we should expect at the very outset, that if the blessings of these two men of God have really been preserved to us, and they are not later inventions, their contents would be essentially the same, so that the blessing of Moses would contain simply a confirmation of that of the dying patriarch, and would be founded upon it in various ways. This is most conspicuous in the blessing upon Joseph; but there are also several other blessings in which it is unmistakeable, although Moses' blessing is not surpassed in independence and originality by that of Jacob, either in its figures, its similes, or its thoughts. But the resemblance goes much deeper. It is manifest, for example, in the fact, that in the case of several of the tribes, Moses, like Jacob, does nothing more than expound their names, and on the ground of the peculiar characters expressed in the names, foretell to the tribes themselves their peculiar calling and future development within the covenant nation. Consequently we have nowhere any special predictions, but simply prophetic glances at the future, depicted in a purely ideal manner, whilst in the case of most of the tribes the utter want of precise information concerning their future history prevents us from showing in what way they were fulfilled. The difference in the times at which the two blessings were uttered is also very apparent. The existing circumstances from which Moses surveyed the future history of the tribes of Israel in the light of divine revelation, were greatly altered from the time when Jacob blessed the heads of the twelve tribes before his death, in the persons of his twelve sons. These tribes had now grown into a numerous people, with which the Lord had established the covenant that He had made with the patriarchs. The curse of dispersion in Israel, which the patriarch had pronounced upon Simeon and Levi (Gen. xlix. 5–7), had been changed into a blessing so far as Levi was concerned. The tribe of Levi had been entrusted with the "light and right" of the Lord, had been called to be the teacher of the rights and law of God in Israel, because it had preserved the covenant of the Lord, after the conclusion of the covenant at Sinai, even though it involved the denial of flesh and blood. Reuben, Gad, and half Manasseh had already received their inheritance, and the other tribes were to take possession of Canaan immediately. These circumstances formed the starting-point for the blessings of Moses, not only in the case of Levi and Gad, where they are expressly mentioned, but in that of the other tribes also, where they do not stand prominently forward, because for the most part Moses simply repeats the leading features of their future development in their promised inheritance, as already indicated in the blessing of Jacob, and "thus bore his testimony to the patriarch who anticipated him, that the spirit of his prophecy was truth" (*Ziegler*, p. 159).

In this peculiar characteristic of the blessing of Moses, we have the strongest proof of its authenticity, particularly in the fact that there is not the slightest trace of the historical circumstances of the nation at large and the separate tribes which were peculiar to the post-Mosaic times. The little ground that there is for the assertion which *Knobel* repeats, that the blessing betrays a closer acquaintance with the post-Mosaic times, such as Moses himself could not possibly have possessed, is sufficiently evident from the totally different expositions which have been given by the different commentators of the saying concerning Judah in ver. 7, which is adduced in proof of this. Whilst *Knobel* finds the desire expressed in this verse on behalf of Judah, that David, who had fled from Saul, might return, obtain possession of the government, and raise his tribe into the royal tribe, *Graf* imagines that it expresses the longing of the kingdom of Judah for reunion with that of Israel;

and *Hofmann* and *Maurer* even trace an allusion to the inhabitants of Judea who were led into captivity along with Jehoiachin : one assumption being just as arbitrary and as much opposed to the text as the other.—All the objections brought against the genuineness of this blessing are founded upon an oversight or denial of its prophetic character, and upon untenable interpretations of particular expressions abstracted from it. Not only is there no such thing in the whole blessing as a distinct reference to the peculiar historical circumstances of Israel which arose after Moses' death, but there are some points in the picture which Moses has drawn of the tribes that it is impossible to recognise in these circumstances. Even *Knobel* from his naturalistic stand-point is obliged to admit, that no traces can be found in the song of any allusion to the calamities which fell upon the nation in the Syrian, Assyrian, and Chaldæan periods. And hitherto it has proved equally impossible to point out any distinct allusion to the circumstances of the nation in the period of the judges. On the contrary, as *Schultz* observes, the speaker rises throughout to a height of ideality which it would have been no longer possible for any sacred author to reach, when the confusions and divisions of a later age had actually taken place. He sees nothing of the calamities from without, which fell upon the nation again and again with destructive fury, nothing of the Canaanites who still remained in the midst of the Israelites, and nothing of the hostility of the different tribes towards one another; he simply sees how they work together in the most perfect harmony, each contributing his part to realize the lofty ideal of Israel. And again he grasps this ideal and the realization of it in so elementary a way, and so thoroughly from the outer side, without regard to any inward transformation and glorification, that he must have lived in a time preceding the prophetic age, and before the moral conflicts had taken place.

Vers. 2–5. In the introduction Moses depicts the elevation of Israel into the nation of God, in its origin (ver. 2), its nature (ver. 3), its intention and its goal (vers. 4, 5).—Ver. 2. " *Jehovah came from Sinai, and rose up from Seir unto them ; He shone from the mountains of Paran, and came out of holy myriads, at His right rays of fire to them.*" To set forth the glory of the covenant which God made with Israel, Moses depicts the majesty and glory in which the Lord appeared to the Israelites at Sinai, to give them the law, and become their king. The three clauses, " Jehovah came from Sinai . . . from Seir . . . from the mountains of Paran," do not refer to different manifestations of God (*Knobel*), but to the one appearance of God at Sinai. Like the sun when it rises, and fills the whole of the broad horizon with its beams, the glory of the Lord, when He appeared, was not confined to one single point, but shone upon the people of Israel from Sinai, and Seir, and the mountains of Paran, as they came from the west to Sinai. The Lord appeared to the people from the summit of Sinai, as they lay encamped at the foot of the mountain. This appearance rose like a streaming light from Seir, and shone at the same time from the mountains of Paran. *Seir* is the mountain land of the Edomites to the east of Sinai; and the mountains of Paran are in all probability not the mountains of *et-Tih*, which form the southern boundary of the desert of Paran, but rather the mountains of the Azazimeh, which ascend to a great height above Kadesh, and form the boundary wall of Canaan towards the south. The glory of the Lord, who appeared upon Sinai, sent its beams even to the eastern and northern extremities of the desert. This manifestation of God formed the basis for all subsequent manifestations of the omnipotence and grace of the Lord for the salvation of His people. This explains the allusions to the description before us in the song of Deborah (Judg. v. 4) and in Hab. iii. 3.—The Lord came not only from Sinai, but from heaven, " out of holy myriads," *i.e.* out of the midst of the thousands of holy angels who surround His throne (1 Kings xxii. 19; Job i. 6; Dan. vii. 10), and who are introduced in Gen. xxviii. 12 as His holy servants, and in Gen. xxxii. 2, 3, as the hosts of God, and form the assembly of holy ones around His throne (Ps. lxxxix. 6, 8; cf. Ps. lxviii. 18; Zech. xiv. 5; Matt. xxvi. 53; Heb. xii. 22; Rev. v. 11, vii. 11).—The last clause is a difficult one. The writing אֵשׁ דָּת in two words, " fire of the law," not only fails to give a suitable sense, but has against it the fact that דָּת, law, *edictum*, is not even a Semitic word, but was adopted from the Persian into the Chaldee, and that it is only by Gentiles that it is ever applied to the law of God (Ezra vii. 12, 21, 25, 26; Dan. vi. 6). It must be read as one word, אשׁדת, as it is in many MSS. and editions,—not, however, as connected with אֲשֵׁדוֹת אֲשֶׁר, the pouring out of the brooks, slopes of the mountains (Num. xxi. 15), but in the form אֶשְׁדָּת, composed, according to the probable conjecture of *Böttcher*, of אֵשׁ, fire, and שָׁדָה (in the Chaldee and Syriac), to throw, to shoot arrows, in the sense of " fire of throwing," shooting fire, a figurative description of the flashes of lightning. *Gesenius* adopts this explanation, except that he derives דת from יָדָה, to throw. It is favoured by the

fact that, according to Ex. xix. 16, the appearance of God upon
Sinai was accompanied by thunder and lightning; and flashes of
lightning are often called the arrows of God, whilst שָׂרָה, in Hebrew,
is established by the name שְׁדִיאוּר (Num. i. 5, ii. 10). To this we
may add the parallel passage, Hab. iii. 4, "rays out of His hand,"
which renders this explanation a very probable one. By " them,"
in the second and fifth clauses, the Israelites are intended, to
whom this fearful theophany referred. On the signification of the
manifestation of God in fire, see chap. iv. 11, and the exposition of
Ex. iii. 2.

Ver. 3. " *Yea, nations He loves ; all His holy ones are in Thy
hand : and they lie down at Thy feet ; they rise up at Thy words.*"
חֹבֵב עַמִּים is the subject placed first absolutely : " nations loving,"
sc. is he ; or " as loving nations—all Thy holy ones are in Thy
hand." The nations or peoples are not the tribes of Israel here,
any more than in chap. xxxii. 8, or Gen. xxviii. 3, xxxv. 11, and
xlviii. 4 ; whilst Judg. v. 14 and Hos. x. 14 cannot come into
consideration at all, for there the word is defined by a suffix. The
meaning of the words depends upon whether " all His holy ones"
are the godly in Israel, or the Israelites generally, or the angels.
There is nothing to favour the first explanation, as the distinction
between the godly and the wicked would be out of place in the
introduction to a blessing upon all the tribes. The second has only
a seeming support in Dan. vii. 21 sqq. and Ex. xix. 6. It does not
follow at once from the calling of Israel to be the holy nation of
Jehovah, that all the Israelites were or could be called " holy ones
of the Lord." Least of all should Num. xvi. 3 be adduced in
support of this. Even in Dan. vii. the holy ones of the Most High
are not the Jews generally, but simply the godly, or believers, in the
nation of God. The third view, on the other hand, is a perfectly
natural one, on account of the previous reference to the holy
myriads.
The meaning, therefore, would be this : The Lord embraces all
nations with His love, He who, so to speak, has all His holy angels
in His hand, *i.e.* His power, so that they serve Him as their Lord.
They lie down at His feet. The ἅπ. λεγ. תֻּכּוּ is explained by
Kimchi and *Saad.* as signifying *adjuncti sequuntur vestigia sua ;* and
by the Syriac, They follow thy foot, from conjecture rather than any
certain etymology. The derivation proposed by modern linguists,
from the verb תָּכָה, according to an Arabic word signifying *recubuit,
innixus est,* has apparently more to support it. יִשָּׂא, it rises up : intransitive, as in Hab. i. 3, Nah. i. 5, Hos. xiii. 1, and Ps. lxxxix. 10.

מִדַּבְּרֹתֶיךָ is not a Hithpael participle (that which is spoken) ; for מִדַּבֵּר has not a passive, but an active signification, to converse (Num. vii. 89 ; Ezek. ii. 2, etc.). It is rather a noun, דַּבְּרֹת, from דַּבְּרָה, words, utterances. The singular, יִשָּׂא, is distributive : every one (of them) rises on account of thine utterances, *i.e.* at thy words. The suffixes relate to God, and the discourse passes from the third to the second person. In our own language, such a change in a sentence like this, " all His (God's) holy ones are in Thy (God's) hand," would be intolerably harsh, but in Hebrew poetry it is by no means rare (see, for example, Ps. xlix. 19).

Vers. 4, 5. " *Moses appointed us a law, a possession of the congregation of Jacob. And He became King in righteous-nation* (Jeshurun); *there the heads of the people assembled, in crowds the tribes of Israel.*" The God who met Israel at Sinai in terrible majesty, out of the myriads of holy angels, who embraces all nations in love, and has all the holy angels in His power, so that they lie at His feet and rise up at His word, gave the law through Moses to the congregation of Jacob as a precious possession, and became King in Israel. This was the object of the glorious manifestation of His holy majesty upon Sinai. Instead of saying, " He gave the law to the tribes of Israel through my mediation," Moses personates the listening nation, and not only speaks of himself in the third person, but does so by identifying his own person with the nation, because he wished the people to repeat his words from thorough conviction, and because the law which he gave in the name of the Lord was given to himself as well, and was as binding upon him as upon every other member of the congregation. In a similar manner the prophet Habakkuk identifies himself with the nation in chap. iii., and says in ver. 19, out of the heart of the nation, " The Lord is my strength, . . . who maketh me to walk upon mine high places,"—an expression which did not apply to himself, but to the nation as a whole. So again in the 20th and 21st Psalms, which David composed as the prayers of the nation for its king, he not only speaks of himself as the anointed of the Lord, but addresses such prayers to the Lord for himself as could only be offered by the nation for its king. " A possession for the congregation of Jacob." " Israel was distinguished above all other nations by the possession of the divinely revealed law (chap. iv. 5–8) ; that was its most glorious possession, and therefore is called its true κειμήλιον" (*Knobel*). The subject in ver. 5 is not Moses but Jehovah, who became King in Jeshurun (see at chap. xxxii. 15 and Ex. xv. 18).

" Were gathered together ;" this refers to the assembling of the nation around Sinai (chap. iv. 10 sqq.; cf. Ex. xix. 17 sqq.), to the day of assembly (chap. ix. 10, x. 4, xviii. 16).

Ver. 6. The blessings upon the tribes commence with this verse. "*Let* REUBEN *live and not die, and there be a* (small) *number of his men.*" The rights of the first-born had been withheld from Reuben in the blessing of Jacob (Gen. xlix. 3); Moses, however, promises this tribe continuance and prosperity. The words, "and let his men become a number," have been explained in very different ways. מִסְפָּר in this connection cannot mean a large number (πολὺς ἐν ἀριθμῷ, LXX.), but, like מְתֵי מִסְפָּר (chap. iv. 27; Gen. xxxiv. 30; Jer. xliv. 28), simply a *small* number, that could easily be counted (cf. chap. xxviii. 62). The negation must be carried on to the last clause. This the language will allow, as the rule that a negation can only be carried forward when it stands with emphatic force at the very beginning (*Ewald,* § 351) is not without exceptions; see for example Prov. xxx. 2, 3, where three negative clauses follow a positive one, and in the last the לֹא is omitted, without the particle of negation having been placed in any significant manner at the beginning.—*Simeon* was the next in age to Reuben; but he is passed over entirely, because according to Jacob's blessing (Gen. xlix. 7) he was to be scattered abroad in Israel, and lost his individuality as a tribe in consequence of this dispersion, in accordance with which the Simeonites simply received a number of towns within the territory of Judah (Josh. xix. 2–9), and, "having no peculiar object of its own, took part, as far as possible, in the fate and objects of the other tribes, more especially of Judah" (*Schultz*). Although, therefore, it is by no means to be regarded as left without a blessing, but rather as included in the general blessings in vers. 1 and 29, and still more in the blessing upon Judah, yet it could not receive a special blessing like the tribe of Reuben, because, as *Ephraem Syrus* observes, the Simeonites had not endeavoured to wipe out the stain of the crime which Jacob cursed, but had added to it by fresh crimes (more especially the audacious prostitution of Zimri, Num. xxv.). Even the Simeonites did not become extinct, but continued to live in the midst of the tribe of Judah, so that as late as the eighth century, in the reign of Hezekiah, thirteen princes are enumerated with their families, whose fathers' houses had increased greatly (1 Chron. iv. 34 sqq.); and these families effected conquests in the south, even penetrating into the mountains of Seir, for the purpose of seeking fresh pasture (1 Chron. iv. 39–43). Hence the assertion that the omission of Simeon is only conceivable from the circumstances of a later age, is as mistaken as the attempt made in some of the MSS. of the Septuagint to interpolate the name of Simeon in the second clause of ver. 6.

Ver. 7. The blessing upon JUDAH is introduced with the formula, "*And this for Judah, and he said:*" "*Hear, Jehovah, the voice of Judah, and bring him to his people; with his hands he fights for him; and help against his adversaries wilt Thou be.*" Judah, from whom the sceptre was not to depart (Gen. xlix. 10), is mentioned before Levi as the royal tribe. The prayer, May Jehovah bring Judah to his people, can hardly be understood in any other way than it is by *Onkelos* and *Hengstenberg* (Christol. i. 80), viz. as founded upon the blessing of Jacob, and expressing the desire, that as Judah was to lead the way as the champion of his brethren in the wars of Israel against the nations, he might have a prosperous return to his people; for the thought, "introduce him to the kingdom of Israel and Judah" (*Luther*), or "give up to him the people which belongs to him according to Thine appointment" (*Schultz*), is hardly implied in the words, "bring to his people." Other explanations are not worth mentioning. What follows points to strife and war: "With his hands (יָדָיו accusative of the instrument, *vid. Ges.* § 138, 1, note 3; *Ewald*, § 283, *a.*) is he fighting (רָב participle of רִיב) for it (the nation); Thou wilt grant him help, deliverance before his foes."

Vers. 8–11. LEVI.—Vers. 8, 9. "*Thy right and Thy light is to Thy godly man, whom Thou didst prove in Massah, and didst strive with him at the water of strife; who says to his father and his mother, I see him not; and does not regard his brethren, and does not know his sons: for they observed Thy word, and kept Thy covenant.*" This blessing is also addressed to God as a prayer. The *Urim* and *Thummim*—that pledge, which the high priest wore upon his breast-plate, that the Lord would always give His people light to preserve His endangered right (*vid.* Ex. xxviii. 29, 30)—are here regarded as a prerogative of the whole of the tribe of Levi. *Thummim* is placed before *Urim*, to indicate at the outset that Levi had defended the right of the Lord, and that for that very reason the right of the Urim and Thummim had been given to him by the Lord. "Thy holy one" is not Aaron, but Levi the tribe-father, who represents the whole tribe to which the blessing applies; hence in vers. 9*b* and 10 the verb passes into the plural. To define more

precisely the expression "Thy holy one," reference is made to the
trials at Massah and at the water of strife, on the principle that the
Lord humbles His servants before He exalts them, and confirms
those that are His by trying and proving them. The proving
at Massah refers to the murmuring of the people on account of
the want of water at *Rephidim* (Ex. xvii. 1-7, as in chap. vi. 16
and ix. 22), from which the place received the name of *Massah*
and *Meribah*; the striving at the water of strife, to the rebellion of
the people against Moses and Aaron on account of the want of
water at *Kadesh* (Num. xx. 1-13). At both places it was primarily
the people who strove with Moses and Aaron, and thereby tempted
God. For it is evident that even at Massah the people murmured
not only against Moses, but against their leaders generally, from
the use of the plural verb, " *Give ye* us water to drink" (Ex. xvii.
2). This proving of the people, however, was at the same time a
proof, to which the Lord subjected the heads and leaders of the
nation, for the purpose of trying their faith. And thus also, in
chap. viii. 2 sqq., the whole of the guidance of Israel through the
desert is described as a trial and humiliation of the people by the
Lord. But in Moses and Aaron, the heads of the tribe of Levi,
the whole of the tribe of Levi was proved. The two provings by
means of water are selected, as *Schultz* observes, "because in their
correlation they were the best adapted to represent the beginning
and end, and therefore the whole of the temptations."—Ver. 9. In
these temptations Levi had proved itself "a holy one," although in
the latter Moses and Aaron stumbled, since the Levites had risen
up in defence of the honour of the Lord and had kept His covenant, even with the denial of father, mother, brethren, and children
(Matt. x. 37, xix. 29). The words, "who says to his father," etc.,
relate to the event narrated in Ex. xxxii. 26-29, where the Levites
draw their swords against the Israelites their brethren, at the command of Moses, after the worship of the golden calf, and execute
judgment upon the nation without respect of person. To this we
may add Num. xxv. 8, where Phinehas interposes with his sword in
defence of the honour of the Lord against the shameless prostitution with the daughters of Moab. On these occasions the Levites
manifested the spirit which Moses predicates here of all the tribe.
By the interposition at Sinai especially, they devoted themselves
with such self-denial to the service of the Lord, that the dignity of
the priesthood was conferred upon their tribe in consequence.—In
vers. 10 and 11, Moses celebrates this vocation : " *They will teach*

Jacob Thy rights, and Israel Thy law; bring incense to Thy nose, and whole-offering upon Thine altar. Bless, Lord, his strength, and let the work of his hands be well-pleasing to Thee: smite his adversaries and his haters upon the hips, that they may not rise!" The tribe of Levi had received the high and glorious calling to instruct Israel in the rights and commandments of God (Lev. x. 11), and to present the sacrifices of the people to the Lord, viz. incense in the holy place, whole-offering in the court. " Whole-offering," a term applied to the burnt-offering (see vol. ii. p. 291), which is mentioned *instar omnium* as being the leading sacrifice. The priests alone were actually entrusted with the instruction of the people in the law and the sacrificial worship; but as the rest of the Levites were given them as assistants in their service, this service might very properly be ascribed to the whole tribe; and no greater blessing could be desired for it than that the Lord should give them power to discharge the duties of their office, should accept their service with favour, and make their opponents powerless. The enemies and haters of Levi were not only envious persons, like Korah and his company (Num. xvi. 1), but all opponents of the priests and Levites. The *loins* are the seat of strength (Ps. lxix. 24; Job xl. 16; Prov. xxxi. 17). This is the only place in which מִן is used before a finite verb, whereas it often stands before the infinitive (*e.g.* Gen. xxvii. 1, xxxi. 29).

Ver. 12. BENJAMIN.—" *The beloved of the Lord will dwell safely with Him; He shelters him at all times, and he dwells between His shoulders.*" Benjamin, the son of prosperity, and beloved of his father (Gen. xxxv. 18, xliv. 20), should bear his name with right. He would be the beloved of the Lord, and as such would dwell in safety with the Lord (עָלָיו, *lit.* founded upon Him). The Lord would shelter him continually. The participle expresses the permanence of the relation: is his shelterer. In the third clause Benjamin is the subject once more; he dwells between the shoulders of Jehovah. " Between the shoulders" is equivalent to " upon the back" (*vid.* 1 Sam. xvii. 6). The expression is founded upon the figure of a father carrying his son (chap. i. 29). This figure is by no means so bold as that of the eagle's wings, upon which the Lord had carried His people, and brought them to Himself (Ex. xix. 4; *vid.* Deut. xxxii. 11). There is nothing strange in the change of subject in all three clauses, since it is met with repeatedly even in plain prose (*e.g.* 2 Sam. xi. 13); and here it follows simply enough from the thoughts contained in the different clauses, whilst the suffix in all three clauses refers to the same noun, *i.e.* to Jehovah.[1] There are some who regard Jehovah as the subject in the third clause, and explain the unheard-of figure which they thus obtain, viz. that of Jehovah dwelling between the shoulders of Benjamin, as referring to the historical fact that God dwelt in the temple at Jerusalem, which was situated upon the border of the tribes of Benjamin and Judah. To this application of the words *Knobel* has properly objected, that God did not dwell between ridges (= shoulders) of mountains there, but upon the top of Moriah; but, on the other hand, he has set up the much more untenable hypothesis, that the expression refers to Gibeon, where the tabernacle stood after the destruction of Nob by Saul.—Moreover, the whole nation participated in the blessing which Moses desired for Benjamin; and this applies to the blessings of the other tribes also. All Israel was, like Benjamin, the beloved of the Lord (*vid.* Jer. xi. 15; Ps. lx. 7), and dwelt with Him in safety (*vid.* ver. 28).

Vers. 13–17. JOSEPH.—Ver. 13. "*Blessed of the Lord be his land, of* (in) *the most precious things of heaven, the dew, and of the flood which lies beneath,* (ver. 14) *and of the most precious of the produce of the sun, and of the most precious of the growth of the moons,* (ver. 15) *and of the head of the mountains of olden time, and of the most precious thing of the everlasting hills,* (ver. 16) *and of the most precious thing of the earth, and of its fulness, and the good-will of Him that dwelt in the bush: let it come upon the head of Joseph, and upon the crown of him that is illustrious among his brethren.*" What Jacob desired and solicited for his son Joseph, Moses also desires for this tribe, namely, the greatest possible abundance of earthly blessing, and a vigorous manifestation of power in conflict with the nations. But however unmistakeable may be the connection between these words and the blessing of Jacob (Gen. xlix. 22 sqq.), not only in the things desired, but even in particular expressions, there is an important difference which equally strikes us, namely, that in the case of Jacob the main point of the blessing is the growth of Joseph into a powerful tribe, whereas with Moses it is the development of power on the part of this tribe in the land of its inheritance, in perfect harmony with the different times at which the blessings were pronounced. Jacob described the growth of Joseph under the figure of the luxuriant branch of a fruit-tree

---

[1] "To dwell upon God and between His shoulders is the same as to repose upon Him: the simile being taken from fathers who carry their sons while delicate and young" (*Calvin*).

planted by the water; whilst Moses fixes his eye primarily upon the land of Joseph, and desires for him the richest productions. " May his land be blessed by Jehovah from (מִן of the cause of the blessing, whose author was Jehovah; vid. Ps. xxviii. 7, civ. 3) the most precious thing of the heaven." מֶגֶד, which only occurs again in the Song of Sol. iv. 13, 16, and vii. 14, is applied to precious fruits. The most precious fruit which the heaven yields to the land is the dew. The " productions of the sun," and גֶּרֶשׁ, ἅπ. λεγ. from גָּרַשׁ, " the produce of the moons," are the fruits of the earth, which are matured by the influence of the sun and moon, by their light, their warmth. At the same time, we can hardly so distinguish the one from the other as to understand by the former the fruits which ripen only once a year, and by the latter those which grow several times and in different months; and Ezek. xlvii. 12 and Rev. xxii. 2 cannot be adduced as proofs of this. The plural " moons" in parallelism with the sun does not mean months, as in Ex. ii. 2, but the different phases which the moon shows in its revolution round the earth. מֵרֹאשׁ (from the head), in ver. 15, is a contracted expression signifying " from the most precious things of the head." The most precious things of the head of the mountains of old and the eternal hills, are the crops and forests with which the tops of the mountains and hills are covered. Moses sums up the whole in the words, " the earth, and the fulness thereof:" everything in the form of costly good that the earth and its productions can supply.—To the blessings of the heaven and earth there are to be added the good-will of the Lord, who appeared to Moses in the thorn-bush to redeem His people out of the bondage and oppression of Egypt and bring it into the land of Canaan, the land flowing with milk and honey (Ex. iii. 2 sqq.). The expression " that dwells in the bush" is to be explained from the significance of this manifestation of God as shown at Ex. iii., which shadowed forth a permanent relation between the Lord and His people. The spiritual blessing of the covenant grace is very suitably added to the blessings of nature; and there is something no less suitable in the way in which the construction commencing with וּרְצוֹן is dropped, so that an anakolouthon ensues. This word cannot be taken as an accusative of more precise definition, as Schultz supposes; nor is מִן to be supplied before it, as Knobel suggests. Grammatically considered, it is a nominative to which the verb תְּבוֹאתָה properly belongs, although, as a matter of fact, not only the good-will, but the natural blessings, of the Lord were also to come

upon the head of Joseph. Consequently we have not יָבֹא (*masc.*),
which רָצוֹן would require, but the lengthened poetical feminine form
תְּבוֹאתָה (*vid. Ewald*, § 191, *c.*), used in a neuter sense. It, *i.e.*
everything mentioned before, shall come upon Joseph. On the
expression, "illustrious among his brethren," see at Gen. xlix. 26.
In the strength of this blessing, the tribe of Joseph would attain to
such a development of power, that it would be able to tread down
all nations.—Ver. 17. "*The first-born of his ox, majesty is to him,
and buffalo-horns his horns : with them he thrusts down nations, all at
once the ends of the earth. These are the myriads of Ephraim, and
these the thousands of Manasseh.*" The "first-born of his (Joseph's)
oxen" (*shor*, a collective noun, as in chap. xv. 19) is not Joshua
(*Rabb., Schultz*); still less is it Joseph (*Bleek, Diestel*), in which
case the pronoun *his* ox would be quite out of place ; nor is it King
Jeroboam II., as *Graf* supposes. It is rather Ephraim, whom the
patriarch Jacob raised into the position of the first-born of Joseph
(Gen. xlviii. 8 sqq.). All the sons of Joseph resembled oxen, but
Ephraim was the most powerful of them all. He was endowed
with majesty ; his horns, the strong weapon of oxen, in which all
their strength is concentrated, were not the horns of common oxen,
but horns of the wild buffalo (*reem*, Num. xxiii. 22), that strong
indomitable beast (cf. Job xxxix. 9 sqq.; Ps. xxii. 22). With them
he would thrust down nations, the ends of the earth, *i.e.* the most
distant nations (*vid.* Ps. ii. 8, vii. 9, xxii. 28). "*Together*," *i.e.* all
at once, belongs rhythmically to "the ends of the earth." Such are
the myriads of Ephraim, *i.e.* in such might will the myriads of
Ephraim arise. To the tribe of Ephraim, as the more numerous,
the ten thousands are assigned ; to the tribe of Manasseh, the
thousands.

Vers. 18 and 19. ZEBULUN and ISSACHAR.—"*Rejoice, Zebulun,
at thy going out; and, Issachar, at thy tents. Nations will they invite
to the mountain ; there offer the sacrifices of righteousness : for they
suck the affluence of the seas, and the hidden treasures of the sand.*"
The tribes of the last two sons of Leah Moses unites together, and,
like Jacob in Gen. xlix. 13, places Zebulun the younger first. He
first of all confirms the blessing which Jacob pronounced through
simply interpreting their names as *omina*, by calling upon them to
rejoice in their undertakings abroad and at home. "At thy tents"
corresponds to "at thy going out" (tents being used poetically for
dwellings, as in chap. xvi. 7) ; like "sitting" to "going out and
coming in" in 2 Kings xix. 27, Isa. xxxvii. 28, Ps. cxxxix. 2 ; and

describes life in its two aspects of work and production, rest and recreation. Although "going out" (enterprise and labour) is attributed to Zebulun, and "remaining in tents" (the comfortable enjoyment of life) to Issachar, in accordance with the delineation of their respective characters in the blessing of Jacob, this is to be attributed to the poetical parallelism of the clauses, and the whole is to be understood as applying to both in the sense suggested by *Graf*, "Rejoice, Zebulun and Issachar, in your labour and your rest." This peculiarity, which is founded in the very nature of poetical parallelism, which is to individualize the thought by distributing it into parallel members, has been entirely overlooked by all the commentators who have given a historical interpretation to each, referring the "going out" to the shipping trade and commercial pursuits of the Zebulunites, and the expression "in thy tents" either to the spending of a nomad life in tents, for the purpose of performing a subordinate part in connection with trade (*Schultz*), or to the quiet pursuits of agriculture and grazing (*Knobel*). They were to rejoice in their undertakings at home and abroad; for they would be successful. The good things of life would flow to them in rich abundance; they would not make them into mammon, however, but would invite nations to the mountain, and there offer sacrifices of righteousness. "The peoples" are nations generally, not the tribes of Israel, still less the members of their own tribes. By the "*mountain*," without any more precise definition, we are not to understand Tabor or Carmel any more than the mountain land of Canaan. It is rather "the mountain of the Lord's inheritance" (Ex. xv. 17), upon which the Lord was about to plant His people, the mountain which the Lord had chosen for His sanctuary, and in which His people were to dwell with Him, and rejoice in sacrificial meals of fellowship with Him (see vol. ii. p. 55). To this end the Lord had sanctified Moriah through the sacrifice of Isaac which He required of Abraham, though it had not been revealed to Moses that it was there that the temple, in which the name of the Lord in Israel would dwell, was afterwards to be built. There is no distinct or direct allusion to Moriah or Zion, as the temple-mountain, involved in the words of Moses. It was only by later revelations and appointments on the part of God that this was to be made known. The words simply contain the Messianic thought that Zebulun and Issachar would offer rich praise-offerings and thank-offerings to the Lord, from the abundant supply of earthly good that would flow to them, upon the mountain which He would make

ready as the seat of His gracious presence, and would call, *i.e.* invite
the nations to the sacrificial meals connected with them, to delight
themselves with them in the rich gifts of the Lord, and worship
the Lord who blessed His people thus. For the explanation of this
thought, see Ps. xxii. 28–31. Sacrifice is mentioned here as an
expression of divine worship, which culminated in sacrifice; and
slain-offerings are mentioned, not burnt-offerings, to set forth the
worship of God under the aspect of blessedness in fellowship with
the Lord. "Slain-offerings of righteousness" are not merely outwardly legal sacrifices, in conformity with the ritual of the law, but
such as were offered in a right spirit, which was well-pleasing to God
(as in Ps. iv. 6, li. 21). It follows as a matter of course, therefore,
that by the abundance of the seas we are not merely to understand the profits of trade upon the Mediterranean Sea; and that
we are still less to understand by the hidden treasures of the sand
"the fish, the purple snails, and sponges" (*Knobel*), or "tunny-fish,
purple shells, and glass" (*Ps. Jon.*); but that the words receive their
best exposition from Isa. lx. 5, 6, 16, and lxvi. 11, 12, *i.e.* that the
thought expressed is, that the riches and treasures of both sea and
land would flow to the tribes of Israel.

Vers. 20 and 21. GAD.—"*Blessed be He that enlargeth Gad: like
a lioness he lieth down, and teareth the arm, yea, the crown of the head.
And he chose his first-fruit territory, for there was the leader's portion
kept; and he came to the heads of the people, he executed the justice of
the Lord, and his rights with Israel.*" Just as in the blessing of Noah
(Gen. ix. 26) the God of Shem is praised, to point out the salvation
appointed by God for Shem, so here Moses praises the Lord, who
enlarged Gad, *i.e.* who not only gave him a broad territory in the
conquered kingdom of Sihon, but furnished generally an unlimited
space for his development (*vid.* Gen. xxvi. 22), so that he might
unfold his lion-like nature in conflict with his foes. On the figure
of a lioness, see Gen. xlix. 9; and on the warlike character of the
Gadites, the remarks on the blessing of Jacob upon Gad (Gen.
xlix. 19). The second part of the blessing treats of the inheritance
which Gad obtained from Moses at his own request beyond Jordan.
רָאָה, with an accusative and לְ, signifies to look out something for
oneself (Gen. xxii. 8; 1 Sam. xvi. 17). The "first-fruit" refers
here to the first portion of the land which Israel received for a possession; this is evident from the reason assigned, כִּי שָׁם חֶלְקַת, whilst
the statement that Gad chose the hereditary possession is in harmony with Num. xxxii. 2, 6, 25 sqq., where the children of Gad are

described as being at the head of the tribes, who came before Moses
to ask for the conquered land as their possession. The meaning of
the next clause, of which very different explanations have been
given, can only be, that Gad chose such a territory for its inheritance as became a leader of the tribes. מְחֹקֵק, he who determines,
commands, organizes; hence both a commander and also a leader in
war. It is in the latter sense that it occurs both here and in Judg.
v. 14. חֶלְקַת מְחֹקֵק, the field, or territory of the leader, may either
be the territory appointed or assigned by the lawgiver, or the territory falling to the lot of the leader. According to the former view,
Moses would be the *mechokek.* But the thought, that Moses appointed or assigned him his inheritance, could be no reason why
Gad should choose it for himself. Consequently חֶלְקַת מְחֹקֵק can only
mean the possession which the *mechokek* chose for himself, as befit-
ting him, or specially adapted for him. Consequently the *mechokek*
was not Moses, but the tribe of Gad, which was so called because
it unfolded such activity and bravery at the head of the tribes in
connection with the conquest of the land, that it could be regarded
as their leader. This peculiar prominence on the part of the Gadites
may be inferred from the fact, that they distinguished themselves
above the Reubenites in the fortification of the conquered land
(Num. xxxii. 34 sqq.). סָפוּן, from סָפַן, to cover, hide, preserve, is a
predicate, and construed as a noun, " a thing preserved."—On the
other hand, the opinion has been very widely spread, from the time
of *Onkelos* down to *Baumgarten* and *Ewald,* that this hemistich refers
to Moses : " there is the portion of the lawgiver hidden," or " the
field of the hidden leader," and that it contains an allusion to the
fact that the grave of Moses was hidden in the inheritance of Gad.
But this is not only at variance with the circumstance, that a prophetic allusion to the grave of Moses such as *Baumgarten* assumes
is apparently inconceivable, from the simple fact that we cannot
imagine the Gadites to have foreseen the situation of Moses' grave
at the time when they selected their territory, but also with the fact
that, according to Josh. xiii. 20, the spot where this grave was situated (chap. xxxiv. 5) was not allotted to the tribe of Gad, but to
that of Reuben; and lastly, with the use of the word *chelkah,* which
does not signify a burial-ground or grave.—But although Gad chose
out an inheritance for himself, he still went before his brethren, *i.e.*
along with the rest of the tribes, into Canaan, to perform, in connection with them, what the Lord demanded of His people as a right.
This is the meaning of the second half of the verse. The clause,

" he came to the heads of the people," does not refer to the fact that the Gadites came to Moses and the heads of the congregation, to ask for the conquered land as a possession (Num. xxxii. 2), but expresses the thought that Gad joined the heads of the people to go at the head of the tribes of Israel (comp. Josh. i. 14, iv. 12, with Num. xxxii. 17, 21, 32), to conquer Canaan with the whole nation, and root out the Canaanites. The Gadites had promised this to Moses and the heads of the people ; and this promise Moses regarded as an accomplished act, and praised in these words with prophetic foresight as having been already performed, and that not merely as one single manifestation of their obedience towards the word of the Lord, but rather as a pledge that Gad would always manifest the same disposition. " To do the righteousness of Jehovah," *i.e.* to do what Jehovah requires of His people as righteousness,—namely, to fulfil the commandments of God, in which the righteousness of Israel was to consist (chap. vi. 25). יֵתֵא, imperfect Kal for יֶאֱתֶה or יֶאְתֶה ; see *Ges.* § 76, 2, *c.*, and *Ewald,* § 142, *c.* " *With Israel :*" in fellowship with (the rest of) Israel.

Ver. 22. DAN is " *a young lion which springs out of Bashan.*" Whilst Jacob compared him to a serpent by the way, which suddenly bites a horse's feet, so that its rider falls backward, Moses gives greater prominence to the strength which Dan would display in conflict with foes, by calling him a young lion which suddenly springs out of its ambush. The reference to Bashan has nothing to do with the expedition of the Danites against Laish, in the valley of Rehoboth (Judg. xviii. 28), as this valley did not belong to Bashan. It is to be explained from the simple fact, that in the regions of eastern Bashan, which abound with caves, and more especially in the woody western slopes of Jebel Hauran, many lions harboured, which rushed forth from the thicket, and were very dangerous enemies to the herds of Bashan. Even if no other express testimonies to this fact are to be found, it may be inferred from the description given of the eastern spurs of Antilibanus in the Song of Sol. (iv. 8), as the abodes of lions and leopards. The meaning leap forth, spring out, is confirmed by both the context and dialects, though the word only occurs here.

Ver. 23. NAPHTALI.—" *O Naphtali, satisfied with favour, and full of the blessing of Jehovah ; of sea and south shall he take possession.*" If the gracefulness of Naphtali is set forth in the blessing of Jacob, by comparing it to a gazelle, here Moses assures the same tribe of satisfaction with the favour and blessing of God, and promises it the possession of the sea and of the south, *i.e.* an inherit-ance which should combine the advantages of the sea—a healthy sea-breeze—with the grateful warmth of the south. This blessing is expressed in far too general terms for it to be possible to interpret it historically, as relating to the natural characteristics of the in-heritance of the Naphtalites in Canaan, or to regard it as based upon them, apart altogether from the fact, that the territory of Naphtali was situated in the north-east of Canaan, and reached as far as the sea of Galilee, and that it was for the most part moun-tainous, though it was a very fertile hill-country (Josh. xviii. 32–39). יְרָשָׁה is a very unique form of the imperative, though this does not warrant an alteration of the text.

Vers. 24 and 25. ASHER.—"*Blessed before the sons be Asher; let him be the favoured among his brethren, and dipping his foot in oil. Iron and brass be thy castle; and as the days of thy life let thy rest continue.*" Asher, the prosperous (see at Gen. xxx. 15), was justly to bear the name. He was to be a child of prosperity; blessed with earthly good, he was to enjoy rest all his life long in strong for-tresses. It is evident enough that this blessing is simply an expo-sition of the name *Asher*, and that Moses here promises the tribe à verification of the *omen* contained in its name. בָּרוּךְ מִבָּנִים does not mean "blessed with children," or "praised because of his children," in which case we should have בָּנָיו; but "blessed before the sons" (cf. Judg. v. 24), *i.e.* blessed before the sons of Jacob, who were peculiarly blessed, equivalent to the most blessed of all the sons of Israel. רְצוּי אֶחָיו does not mean the beloved among his brethren, acceptable to his brethren, but the one who enjoyed the favour of the Lord, *i.e.* the one peculiarly favoured by the Lord. Dipping the foot in oil points to a land flowing with oil (Job xxix. 6), *i.e.* fat or fertile throughout, which Jacob had already promised to Asher (see Gen. xlix. 20). To complete the prosperity, however, security and rest were required for the enjoyment of the blessings bestowed by God; and these are promised in ver. 25. מִנְעָל (ἅπ. λεγ.) does not mean a shoe, but is derived from נָעַל, to bolt (Judg. iii. 23), and signifies either a bolt, or that which is shut fast; a poetical expres-sion for a castle or fortress. Asher's dwellings were to be castles, fortresses of iron and brass; *i.e.* as strong and impregnable as if they were built of iron and brass. The pursuit of mining is not to be thought of as referred to here, even though the territory of Asher, which reached to Lebanon, may have contained brass and iron (see at chap. viii. 9). *Luther* follows the LXX. and Vulgate, and renders this clause, " iron and brass be upon his shoes ;" but this is undoubtedly wrong, as the custom of fastening the shoes or sandals with brass or iron was quite unknown to the Israelites; and even Goliath, who was clothed in brass from head to foot, and wore iron greaves, had no iron sandals, though the military shoes of the ancient Romans had nails in the soles. Moreover, the context contains no reference to war, so as to suggest the idea that the treading down and crushing of the foe are intended. "As thy days," *i.e.* as long as the days of thy life last, let thy rest be (continue). *Luther's* rendering, " let thine old age be as thy youth," which follows the *Vulgate*, cannot be sustained ; for although דֹּבֶא, derived from דָּאַב, to vanish away, certainly might signify old age, the expression " thy days" cannot possibly be understood as signifying youth.

Vers. 26–29. The conclusion of the blessing corresponds to the introduction. As Moses commenced with the glorious fact of the founding of the kingdom of Jehovah in Israel, as the firm foundation of the salvation of His people, so he also concludes with a reference to the Lord their eternal refuge, and with a congratulation of Israel which could find refuge in such a God.—Vers. 26, 27. *" Who is as God, a righteous nation, who rides in heaven to thy help, and in His exaltation upon the clouds. Abiding is the God of olden time, and beneath are everlasting arms : and He drives the enemy before thee, and says, Destroy."* The meaning is : No other nation has a God who rules in heaven with almighty power, and is a refuge and help to his people against every foe. *Jeshurun* is a vocative, and the alteration of כָּאֵל into כְּאֵל, " as the God of Jeshurun," according to the ancient versions, is to be rejected on the simple ground that the expression " in thy help," which follows immediately afterwards, is an address to Israel. Riding upon the heaven and the clouds is a figure used to denote the unlimited omnipotence with which God rules the world out of heaven, and is the helper of His people. " In thy help," *i.e.* as thy helper. This God is a dwelling to His people. מְעֹנָה, like the masculine מָעוֹן in Ps. xc. 1, and xci. 9, signifies " dwelling,"—a genuine Mosaic figure, to which, in all probability, the houseless wandering of the people in the desert, which made them feel the full worth of a dwelling, first gave rise. The figure not only implies that God grants protection and a refuge to His people in the storms of life (Ps. xci. 1, 2, cf. Isa. iv. 6), but also that He supplies His people with everything that can afford a safe abode. " The God of old," *i.e.* who has proved Himself to be God from the very beginning of the world (*vid.* Ps. xc. 1 ; Hab. i. 12). The expression " underneath" is to be explained from the antithesis to the heaven where God is enthroned above mankind. He who is enthroned in heaven above is also the God who is with His people upon the earth below, and holds and bears them in His arms. " Everlasting arms" are arms whose strength is never exhausted. There is no need to supply " thee" after " underneath ;" the expression should rather be left in its general form, " upon the earth beneath." The reference to Israel is obvious from the context. The driving of the enemy before Israel is not to be restricted to the rooting out of the Canaanites, but applies to every enemy of the congregation of the Lord.—Ver. 28. " *And Israel dwells safely, alone the fountain of Jacob, in a land full of corn and wine ; his heavens also drop down dew.*" Because the God of old was the dwelling and help of Israel, it dwelt safely and separate from the other nations, in a land abounding with corn and wine. " The fountain of Jacob" is parallel to " Israel ;" " *alone* (separate) *dwells the fountain of Jacob.*" This title is given to Israel as having sprung from the patriarch Jacob, in whom it had its source. A similar expression occurs in Ps. lxviii. 27. It completely destroys the symmetry of the clauses of the verse to connect the words, as *Luther* does, with what follows, in the sense of " the eye of Jacob is directed upon a land." The construction of שָׁכֵן with אֶל, to dwell into a land, may be explained on the ground that the dwelling involves the idea of spreading out over the land. On the " land of corn," etc., see chap. viii. 7 and 8. אַף is emphatic : yea his heaven, *i.e.* the heaven of this land drops down dew (*vid.* Gen. xxvii. 28). Israel was to be congratulated upon this.—Ver. 29. " *Hail to thee, O Israel! who is like thee, a people saved in the Lord, the shield of thy help, and who* (is) *the sword of thine eminence. Thine enemies will deny themselves to thee, and thou ridest upon their heights.*" " Saved ;" not merely delivered from danger and distress, but in general endowed with salvation (like Zech. ix. 9 ; see also Isa. xlv. 17). The salvation of Israel rested in the Lord, as the ground out of which it grew, from which it descended, because the Lord was its help and shield, as He had already promised Abraham (Gen. xv. 1), and " the sword of his eminence," *i.e.* the sword which had fought for the eminence of Israel. But because the Lord was Israel's shield and sword, or, so to speak, both an offensive and defensive weapon, his enemies denied themselves to him, *i.e.* feigned friendship, did not venture to appear openly as enemies (for the meaning " feign," act the hypocrite, see

Ps. xviii. 45, lxxxi. 16). But Israel would ride upon their heights, the high places of their land, *i.e.* would triumph over all its foes (see at chap. xxxii. 13).

DEATH AND BURIAL OF MOSES.—CHAP. XXXIV.

Vers. 1–8. After blessing the people, Moses ascended Mount Nebo, according to the command of God (chap. xxxii. 48–51), and there the Lord showed him, in all its length and breadth, that promised land into which he was not to enter. From Nebo, a peak of Pisgah, which affords a very extensive prospect on all sides (see p. 214), he saw the land of Gilead, the land to the east of the Jordan as far as Dan, *i.e.* not Laish-Dan near the central source of the Jordan (Judg. xviii. 27), which did not belong to Gilead, but a Dan in northern Peræa, which has not yet been discovered (see at Gen. xiv. 14); and the whole of the land on the west of the Jordan, Canaan proper, in all its different districts, namely, " *the whole of Naphtali,*" *i.e.* the later Galilee on the north, " *the land of Ephraim and Manasseh*" in the centre, and " *the whole of the land of Judah,*" the southern portion of Canaan, in all its breadth, " *to the hinder* (Mediterranean) *sea*" (see chap. xi. 24); also " *the south land*" (*Negeb*: see at Num. xiii. 17), the southern land of steppe towards the Arabian desert, and " *the valley of the Jordan*" (see Gen. xiii. 10), *i.e.* the deep valley from Jericho the palm-city (so called from the palms which grew there, in the valley of the Jordan: Judg. i. 16, iii. 43; 2 Chron. xxviii. 15) " *to Zoar*" at the southern extremity of the Dead Sea (see at Gen. xix. 22). This sight of every part of the land on the east and west was not an ecstatic vision, but a sight with the bodily eyes, whose natural power of vision was miraculously increased by God, to give Moses a glimpse at least of the glorious land which he was not to tread, and delight his eye with a view of the inheritance intended for his people.—Vers. 5, 6. After this favour had been granted him, the aged servant of the Lord was to taste death as the wages of sin. There, *i.e.* upon Mount Nebo, he died, " *at the mouth,*" *i.e.* according to the commandment, " *of the Lord*" (not " by a kiss of the Lord," as the Rabbins interpret it), in the land of Moab, not in Canaan (see at Num. xxvii. 12–14). " *And He buried him in the land of Moab, over against Beth Peor.*" The subject in this sentence is Jehovah. Though the third person singular would allow of the verb being taken as impersonal (ἔθαψαν αὐτόν, LXX.: they buried him), such a rendering is precluded by the statement which follows, " *no man knoweth of his sepulchre unto this day*." "The valley" where the Lord buried Moses was certainly not the Jordan valley, as in chap. iii. 29, but most probably "the valley in the field of Moab, upon the top of Pisgah," mentioned in Num. xxi. 20, near to Nebo (see p. 148); in any case, a valley on the mountain, not far from the top of Nebo.—The Israelites inferred what is related in vers. 1–6 respecting the end of Moses' life, from the promise of God in chap. xxxii. 49, and Num. xxvii. 12, 13, which was communicated to them by Moses himself (chap. iii. 27), and from the fact that Moses went up Mount Nebo, from which he never returned. On his ascending the mountain, the eyes of the people would certainly follow him as far as they possibly could. It is also very possible that there were many parts of the Israelitish camp from which the top of Nebo was visible, so that the eyes of his people could not only accompany him thither, but could also see that when the Lord had shown him the promised land, He went down with him into the neighbouring valley, where Moses was taken for ever out of their sight. There is not a word in the text about God having brought the body of Moses down from the mountain and buried it in the valley. This "romantic idea" is invented by *Knobel*, for the purpose of throwing suspicion upon the historical truth of a fact which is offensive to him. The fact itself that the Lord buried His servant Moses, and no man knows of his sepulchre, is in perfect keeping with the relation in which Moses stood to the Lord while he was alive. Even if his sin at the water of strife rendered it necessary that he should suffer the punishment of death, as a memorable example of the terrible severity of the holy God against sin, even in the case of His faithful servant; yet after the justice of God had been satisfied by this punishment, he was to be distinguished in death before all the people, and glorified as the servant who had been found faithful in all the house of God, whom the Lord had known face to face (ver. 10), and to whom He had spoken mouth to mouth (Num. xii. 7, 8). The burial of Moses by the hand of Jehovah was not intended to conceal his grave, for the purpose of guarding against a superstitious and idolatrous reverence for his grave; for with the opinion held by the Israelites, that corpses and graves defiled, there was but little fear of this; but, as we may infer from the account of the transfiguration of Jesus, the intention was to place him in the same category with Enoch and Elijah. As *Kurtz* observes, "The purpose of God was to prepare for him a condition, both of body and soul, resembling that of these two men of God. Men bury a corpse that it may pass into corruption. If Jehovah, therefore, would not suffer the body of Moses to be buried by men, it is but natural to seek for the reason in the fact that He did not intend to leave him to corruption, but, when burying it with His own hand, imparted a power to it which preserved it from corruption, and prepared the way for it to pass into the same form of existence to which Enoch and Elijah were taken, without either death or burial."—There can be no doubt that this truth lies at the foundation of the Jewish theologoumenon mentioned in the Epistle of Jude, concerning the contest between Michael the archangel and the devil for the body of Moses.—Vers. 7, 8. Though he died at the age of one hundred and twenty (see at chap. xxxi. 2), Moses' eyes had not become dim, and his freshness had not abated (לֵחַ ἄπ λεγ., connected with לַח in Gen. xxx. 37, signifies freshness). Thus had the Lord preserved the full vital energy of His servant, even till the time of his death. The mourning of the people lasted thirty days, as in the case of Aaron (Num. xx. 29).

Vers. 9–12. Joshua now took Moses' place as the leader of the people, filled with the spirit of wisdom (practical wisdom, manifesting itself in action), because Moses had ordained him to his office by the laying on of hands (Num. xxvii. 18). And the people obeyed him; but he was not like Moses. "*There arose no more a prophet in Israel like unto Moses, whom the Lord knew face to face,*" *i.e.* so far as the miracles and signs were concerned which Moses did, by virtue of his divine mission, upon Pharaoh, his servants, and his land, and the terrible acts which he performed before the eyes of Israel (vers. 11 and 12 ; *vid.* chap. xxvi. 8, and iv. 34). "*Whom Jehovah knew :*" not who knew Him, the Lord. "To know," like γινώσκειν in 1 Cor. viii. 3, relates to the divine knowledge, which not only involves a careful observance (chap. ii. 7), but is also a manifestation of Himself to man, a penetration of man with the spiritual power of God. Because he was thus known by the Lord, Moses was able to perform signs and wonders, and mighty, terrible acts, such as no other performed either before or after him. In this respect Joshua stood far below Moses, and no prophet arose in Israel like unto Moses.—This remark concerning Moses does not presuppose that a long series of prophets had already risen up since the time of Moses. When Joshua had defeated the Canaanites, and conquered their land with the powerful help of the Lord, which was still manifested in signs and wonders, and had divided it among the children of Israel, and when the tribes had settled down in their inheritance, so that the different portions of the land began to be called by the names of Naphtali, Ephraim, Manasseh, and Judah, as is the case in ver. 2 ; the conviction might already have become established in Israel, that no other prophet would arise like Moses, to whom the Lord had manifested Himself with such signs and wonders before the Egyptians and the eyes of Israel. The position occupied by Joshua in relation to this his predecessor, as the continuer of his work, would necessarily awaken and confirm this conviction, in connection with what the Lord had said as to the superiority of Moses to all the prophets (Num. xii. 6 sqq.). Moses was the founder and mediator of the old covenant. As long as this covenant was to last, no prophet could arise in Israel like unto Moses. There is but One who is worthy of greater honour than Moses, namely, the Apostle and High Priest of our profession, who is placed as the Son over all the house of God, in which Moses was found faithful as a servant (compare Heb. iii. 2–6 with Num. xii. 7), Jesus Christ, the founder and mediator of the new and ever-lasting covenant.

CONCLUDING REMARKS ON THE COMPOSITION OF THE PENTATEUCH.

IF we close our commentary with another survey of tne entire work, viz. the five books of Moses, we may sum up the result of our detailed exposition, so far as critical opinions respecting its origin are concerned, in these words : We have found the decision which we pronounced in our General Introduction, as to the internal unity and system of the whole *Thorah*, as well as its Mosaic origin, thoroughly confirmed. With the exception of the last chapters of the fifth book, which are distinctly shown to be an appendix to the Mosaic *Thorah*, added by a different hand, by the statement in Deut. xxxi. 24 sqq., that when the book of the law was finished Moses handed it over to the Levites to keep, there is nothing in the whole of the five books which Moses might not have written. There are no historical circumstances or events either mentioned or assumed, which occurred for the first time after Moses was dead. Neither the allusion to the place called Dan in Gen. xiv. 14 (cf. Deut. xxxiv. 1) ; nor the remark in Gen. xxxvi. 1, that there were kings in the land of Edom before the children of Israel had a king over them; nor the statement that the monument which Jacob erected over Rachel's grave remained "to this day" (Gen. xxxv. 20); nor even the assertion in Deut. iii. 14, that Jair called Bashan "Chavvoth Jair" after his own name, furnishes any definite and unmistakeable indication of a post-Mosaic time.[1] And the account in Ex. xvi. 35, that the Israelites ate the manna forty years, till they came to an inhabited land, "to the end," *i.e.* the extreme boundary, of the land of Canaan, could only be adduced by *Bleek* (*Einl.* p. 204) as an evident proof that "this could not have been written before the arrival of the Israelites in the land of Canaan," through a παρερμηνεία, or misinterpretation of the words, "into the land of their dwelling." For were not the Israelites on the border of the land when they were encamped in the steppes of Moab by the Jordan opposite to Jericho? Or are we to suppose that the kingdoms of Sihon and Og with their cities, which the Israelites had already conquered under Moses, were an uninhabited land? The passage mentioned last simply proves, that in the middle books of the Pentateuch we have not simple diaries before us containing the historical occurrences of the Mosaic times, but a work drawn up according to a definite plan, and written in the last year of Moses' life. This is apparent from the remarks about the shining face of Moses (Ex. xxxiv. 33–35), and the guidance of Israel in all its journeys by the pillar of cloud (Ex. xl. 38, cf. Num. x. 34), as well as from the systematic arrangement and distribution of the materials according to certain well-defined and obvious points of view, as we have already endeavoured to show in the introductions to the different books, and in the exposition itself.

If, however, the composition of the whole *Thorah* by Moses is thus firmly established, in accordance with the statements in Deut. xxxi. 9 and 24, it by no means follows that Moses wrote the whole

---

[1] But even if the remarks in Gen. xxxv. 20 and Deut. iii. 14 concerning the preservation of the monument over Rachel's grave, and the retention of the names which Jair gave to the towns of Bashan, should really point to a post-Mosaic time, no modest critic would ever think of adducing two such gloss-like notices as a proof of the later origin of the whole Pentateuch, but would regard these notices as nothing more than a gloss interpolated by a later hand. In the case of the monument upon Rachel's grave, however, if it continued in existence for centuries, it is not only conceivable, but by no means improbable, that the spies sent into Canaan from Kadesh, who passed through the land from Hebron to Hamath, saw it by the high road where the grave was situated, and brought the intelligence of its preservation to Moses and the people.

work from Gen. i. to Deut. xxxi. *uno tenore*, and in the closing days of his life. Even in this case it may have been written step by step; and not only Genesis, but the three middle books, may have been composed before the discourses in the fifth book, so that the whole work was simply finished and closed after the renewal of the covenant recorded in Deut. xxix. and xxx. Again, such statements as that Moses wrote this law, and made an end of writing the words of this law in a book till they were finished (Deut. xxxi. 9 and 24), by no means require us to assume that Moses wrote it all with his own hand. The epistles which the Apostle Paul sent to the different churches were rarely written with his own hand, but were dictated to one of his assistants; yet their Pauline origin is not called in question in consequence. And so Moses may have employed some assistant, either a priest or scribe (*shoter*), in the composition of the book of the law, without its therefore failing to be his own work. Still less is the Mosaic authorship of the Pentateuch rendered doubtful by the fact that he availed himself of written documents from earlier times in writing the primeval history, and incorporated them to some extent in the book of Genesis without alteration; and that in the history of his own time, and when introducing the laws into his work, he inserted documents in the middle books which had been prepared by the priests and *shoterim* at his own command,—such, for example, as the lists of the numbering of the people (Num. i.-iii. and xxvi.), the account of the dedicatory offerings of the tribe-princes (Num. vii.), and of the committee of heads of tribes appointed for the purpose of dividing the land of Canaan (Num. xxxiv. 16 sqq.),—in the exact form in which they had been drawn up for public use. This conjecture is rendered very natural by the contents and form of the Pentateuch.

The Pentateuch contains historical narrative and law, answering to the character of the divine revelation, which consisted in historical facts, and received a development in accordance with the times. And on closer inspection we find that several different elements may be distinguished in each of these. The historical contents are divisible into an annalistic or monumental portion, and into prophetico-historical accounts. The former includes the simple notices of the most important events from the creation of the world to the death of Moses, with their exact chronological, ethnographical, and geographical data; also the numerous genealogical documents introduced into the history. To the latter belong statements, whether shorter or longer, respecting those revelations and promises of God, by which the Creator of the heaven and the earth prepared the way from the very earliest time for the redemption of the fallen human race, and which, after laying the foundation for the Old Testament kingdom of God by the guidance of the patriarchs and the redemption of Israel out of the bondage of Egypt, He eventually carried out at Sinai by the conclusion of a covenant and the giving of a law. In the same way, we may distinguish a twofold element in the legal portion of the Pentateuch. The kernel of the Sinaitic legislation is to be found in the decalogue, with the moral and rightful conditions upon the basis of which the Lord concluded the covenant with Israel. The religious and moral truths and commandments, which, as being the absolute demands of the holiness and justice, the love and mercy of God, constitute the very essence of true religion, are surrounded in the covenant economy of the Old Testament by certain religious statutes and institutions, which were imposed upon the people of God simply for the time of its infancy, and constituted that "shadow of things to come" which was to pass away when the "body" appeared. This "shadow" embraces all the special theocratic ordinances and precepts of the so-called Levitical law (whether ecclesiastical, disciplinary, or magisterial), in which religious and ethical ideas were symbolically incorporated; so that they contained within them eternal truths, whilst their earthly form was to pass away. These covenant statutes are so intimately bound up with the general religious doctrines and the purely moral commands, by virtue of their symbolical significance, that in many respects they interlace one another, the moral commands being enclosed and pervaded by the covenant statutes, and the latter again being sanctified and transformed by the former, so that the entire law assumes the form of a complete organic whole. A similar organic connection is also apparent between the historical and legal constituents of the Pentateuch. The historical narrative not only supplied the framework or outward setting for the covenant legislation, but it also prepared the way for that legislation, just as God Himself prepared the way for concluding the covenant with Israel by His guidance of the human race and the patriarchs of Israel; and it so pervades every portion of it also, that, on the one hand, the historical circumstances form the groundwork for the legal institutions, and on the other hand a light is thrown by the historical occurrences upon the covenant ordinances and laws. Just as nature and spirit interpenetrate each other in the world around us and in human life, and the spirit not only comes to view in the life of nature, but transforms it at the same time; so has God planted His kingdom of grace in the natural order of the world, that nature may be sanctified by grace. But, notwithstanding this organic connection between the various constituents of the Pentateuch, from the very nature of the case not only are the historical and legal portions kept quite distinct from one another in many passages, but the distinctions between these two constituents are here and there brought very clearly out to view.

The material differences necessarily determined in various ways the form of the narrative, the phraseology, and even the words employed. In the historical portions many words and expressions occur which are never met with in the legal sections, and *vice versa*. The same remark also applies to the different portions in which we have either historical narrative, or the promulgation of laws. In addition to this, we might reasonably expect to find whole sections also, in which the ideas and verbal peculiarities of the different constituents are combined. And this is really the case. The differences stand out very sharply in the earliest chapters of Genesis, where the account of paradise and the fall, together with the promise of the victory of the seed of the woman over the serpent, which contains the germ of all future revelations of God (chap. ii. 4 sqq.), is appended immediately to the history of the creation of the world (chap. i. 1–ii. 3); whilst in the mode of narration it differs considerably from the style of the first chapter. Whereas in chap. i. the Creator of the heaven and the earth is called *Elohim* simply; in the history of paradise and the fall, not to mention other differences, we meet with the composite name *Jehovah Elohim*; and, after this, the two names *Elohim* and *Jehovah* are used interchangeably, so that in many chapters the former only occurs, and in others again only the latter, until the statement in Ex. vi., that God appeared to Moses and commissioned him to bring the people of Israel out of Egypt, after which the name *Jehovah* predominates, so that henceforth, with but few exceptions, *Elohim* is only used in an appellative sense.

Upon this interchange in the names of God in the book of Genesis, modern critics have built up their hypothesis as to the composition of Genesis, and in fact of the entire Pentateuch, either from different documents, or from repeated supplementary additions, in accordance with which they discover an outward cause for the change of names, viz. the variety of editors, instead of deducing it from the different meanings of the names themselves ; whilst they also adduce, in support of their view, the fact that certain ideas and expressions change in connection with the name of God. The fact is obvious enough. But the change in the use of the different names of God is associated with the gradual development of the saving purposes of God; and as we have already shown in vol. i. pp. 73 sqq., the names *Elohim* and *Jehovah* are expressive of different relations on the part of God to the world. Now, as God did not reveal Himself in the full significance of His name *Jehovah* till the time of the exodus of Israel out of Egypt, and the conclusion of the covenant at Sinai, we could expect nothing else than what we actually find in Genesis, namely, that this name is not used by the author of the book of Genesis before the call of Abraham, except in connection with such facts as were directly preparatory to the call of Abraham to be the father of the covenant nation ; and that even in the history of the patriarchs, in which it predominates from Gen. xii.–xvi., it is used less frequently again after Jehovah revealed Himself to Abraham as *El Shaddai*, and other titles of God sprang out of the continued manifestations of God to the patriarchs, which could take the place of that name. (For more detailed remarks, see vol. i. pp. 330 sqq.). It would not have been by any means strange, therefore, if the name *Jehovah* had not occurred at all in the account of the creation of the world, in the genealogies of the patriarchs of the primeval and preparatory age (Gen. v. and xi.), in the table of nations (Gen. x.), in the account of the negotiations of Abraham with the Hittites concerning the purchase of the cave of Machpelah for a family sepulchre (Gen. xxiii.), in the notices respecting Esau and the Edomitish tribe-princes and kings (Gen. xxxvi.), and other narratives of similar import. Nevertheless we find it in the genealogy in Gen. v. 29, and in the table of nations in Gen. x. 9, where the critics, in order to save their hypothesis, are obliged to have recourse to an assumption of glosses, or editorial revisions. They have dealt still more violently with Gen. xvii. 1. There Jehovah appears to Abram, and manifests Himself to him as *El Shaddai*, from which it is very evident that the name *El Shaddai* simply expresses one particular feature in the manifestation of Jehovah, and describes a preliminary stage, anticipatory of the full development of the nature of the absolute God, as expressed in the name *Jehovah*. This is put beyond all doubt by the declaration of God to Moses in Ex. vi. 3, " I appeared to Abraham, Isaac, and Jacob, as *El Shaddai*, and by My name *Jehovah* was I not known to them."

Even *Astruc* observes, with reference to these words, " The passage in Exodus, when properly understood, does not prove that the name of Jehovah was a name of God unknown to the patriarchs, and revealed for the first time to Moses ; it simply proves that God had not shown the patriarchs the full extent of the meaning of this name, as He had made it known to Moses." The modern critics, on the other hand, have erased *Jehovah* from the text in Gen. xvii. 1, and substituted *Elohim* in its place, and then declare *El Shaddai* synonymous with *Elohim*, whilst they have so perverted Ex. vi. 3 as to make the name *Jehovah* utterly unknown to the patriarchs. By similar acts of violence they have mangled the text in very many other passages, for the purpose of carrying out the distinction between the Elohim and Jehovah documents ; and yet for all that they cannot escape the admission, that there are certain portions or sections of the book of Genesis in which the separation is impossible.

It is just the same with the supposed " favourite expressions" of the Elohistic and Jehovistic sections, as with the names of God. " There are certain favourite expressions, it is said, which are common to the Elohistic portions ; and the same things are frequently called by different names in the Elohistic and Jehovistic sections. Among the Elohistic expressions are : אֲחֻזָּה (possession), אֶרֶץ מְגוּרִים (land of the stranger's sojourn), בְּעֶצֶם הַיּוֹם הַזֶּה, לְמִינוֹ, לְדֹרֹתֵיכֶם (the self-same day), *Padan-Aram* (the Jehovistic for this is always (?) *Aram-Naharaim*, or simply *Aram*),[1] הֵקִים בְּרִית, פָּרָה וְרָבָה (the Jehovistic is כָּרַת בְּרִית) ; wherever the name Elohim occurs, these expressions also appear as its inseparable satellites." This statement is in part incorrect, and not in accordance with fact ; and even where there is any foundation for it, it really proves nothing. In the first place, it is not correct that אֲחֻזָּה and אֶרֶץ מְגוּרִים are only to be met with in Elohistic portions. In the very first passage in which we meet with this word in the Pentateuch (Gen. xvii. 8), it is not *Elohim*, but Jehovah, who appears as *El Shaddai*, and promises Abraham and his seed the land of his pilgrimage, the land of Canaan, לַאֲחֻזַּת עוֹלָם.

---

[1] The actual fact is, that *Aram-Naharaim* only occurs twice in the Pentateuch, viz. Gen. xxiv. 10 and Deut. xxiii. 5, for which *Aram* alone occurs in Num. xxiii. 7, which is well known to apply not merely to Mesopotamia, but to Syria as well, and is used here simply as a poetical term for *Aram-Naharaim*. Moreover, *Padan-Aram* and *Aram-Naharaim* are not identical ; but the former merely denotes one particular district of " Aram of the two rivers," or Mesopotamia.

This passage is clearly pointed to in Gen. xlviii. 4. In addition to this, the word *achuzzah* occurs in Gen. xxiii. 4, 9, 20, xlix. 30, l. 13, in connection with the family sepulchre which Abraham had acquired as a possession by purchase; also in the laws concerning the sale and redemption of landed property (Lev. xxv. and xxvii. very frequently), and in those concerning the division of the land as a possession among the tribes and families of Israel (Num. xxvii. 7, xxxii. 5 sqq., xxxv. 2, 8); also in Lev. xxv. 34 and Gen. xxxvi. 43,—in both passages with reference to property or a fixed landed possession, for which there was no other word in the Hebrew language that could be used in these passages; not to mention the fact, that *Stähelin, Knobel,* and others, pronounce Num. xxxii. 32 a Jehovistic passage. So again the expressions הֵקִים בְּרִית (to set up a covenant) and לְדֹרֹתָם (in their generations) occur in Gen. xvii. 7 in a Jehovistic framework; for it was not *Elohim,* but Jehovah, who appeared to Abram (see ver. 1), to set up (not conclude) His covenant with him and his posterity as an everlasting covenant, according to their generations. To set up (*i.e.* realize, carry out) a covenant, and to conclude a covenant, are certainly two distinct ideas.—In Gen. xlvii. 27, again, and Lev. xxvi. 9, we meet with פָּרָה וְרָבָה in two sections, which are pronounced Jehovistic. The other three, no doubt, occur in Genesis in connection with *Elohim;* but the expression, " in the self-same day," could not be expected in Jehovistic sections, for the simple reason, that the time of the revelations and promises of God is not generally reckoned by day and hour. " After his kind" is only met with in four sections in the whole of the Pentateuch,—in the accounts of the creation and that of the flood (Gen. i. and vi. vii.), and in the laws concerning clean and unclean beasts (Lev. xi. and Deut. xiv.), where it is simply the species of animals that are referred to. Can this word then be called a favourite Elohistic expression, which constantly appears like an inseparable satellite, wherever the name *Elohim* occurs? The same remarks apply to other words and phrases described as Elohistic: *e.g. tholedoth* (which stands at the head of a Jehovistic account, however, in Gen. ii. 4), " *father's house,*" " in their families" (*mishpachoth*), and many others. But just as such expressions as these are not to be expected in the prophetico-historical sections, for the simple reason that the ideas which they express belong to a totally different sphere, so, on the other hand, a considerable number of notions and words, which are associated with the visible manifestations of God, the promises to the patriarchs,

their worship, etc., are found in the book of Genesis always in connection with the name *Jehovah :* see, for example, קָרָא בְּשֵׁם יְהֹוָה,
רֵיחַ הַנִּחֹחַ, הֶעֱלָה עֹלָה (עֹלוֹת), and others of the same kind. And yet
the last two occur in the laws of the middle books, which the critics
attribute to the Elohist much more frequently than many of the
so-called Elohistic expressions and formulas of the book of Genesis.
This fact clearly shows, that there are no such things as favourite
expressions of the Elohist and Jehovist, but that the words are
always adapted to the subject. In the covenant statutes of the
middle books, we find Elohistic and Jehovistic expressions combined,
because the economy of the Sinaitic covenant was anticipated on
the one hand by the patriarchal revelations of Jehovah the covenant God, and established on the other hand upon the natural
foundations of the Israelitish commonwealth. The covenant which
Jehovah concluded with the people of Israel at Sinai (Ex. xxiv.)
was simply the setting up and full realization of the covenant which
He made with Abram (Gen. xv.), and had already begun to set up
with him by the promise of a son, and the institution of circumcision as the covenant sign (Gen. xvii.). The indispensable condition of membership in the covenant was circumcision, which Jehovah
commanded to Abraham when He made Himself known to him as
El Shaddai (Gen. xvii.), and in connection with which we meet
for the first time with the legal formulas, " a statute for ever," " in
your generations," and " that soul shall be cut off," which recur so
constantly in the covenant statutes of the middle books, but so
arranged, that the expression " a statute for ever " is never used
in connection with general religious precepts or purely moral commandments, the eternal significance of which did not need to be
enjoined, since it naturally followed from the unchangeable holiness
and justice of the eternal God, whilst this could not be assumed
without further ground of the statutory laws and ordinances of the
covenant. But these covenant ordinances also had their roots in
the natural order of the world and of the national life. The nation
of Israel which sprang from the twelve sons of Israel by natural
generation, received its division into tribes, and the constitution
founded upon this, as a covenant nation and congregation of Jehovah. The numbering of the people was taken in tribes, according to the families and fathers' houses of the different tribes ; and
the land of Canaan, which was promised them for an inheritance,
was to be divided among the tribes, with special reference to the
number and magnitude of their families. It is perfectly natural,

therefore, that in the laws and statements concerning these things, words and formularies should be repeated which already occur in the book of Genesis in connection with the genealogical notices.

Modern critics, as is well known, regard the whole of the Sinaitic legislation, from Ex. xxv. to Num. x. 28, as an essential part of the original work, with the exception of Ex. xx.-xxiii., Lev. xvii.-xx. and xxvi., and a few verses in Lev. x., xxiii., xxiv., xxv., and Num. iv. and viii. Now, as a great variety of things are noticed in this law—such as the building and setting up of the tabernacle, the description of the priests' clothes, the order of sacrifice—which are not mentioned again in the other parts of the Pentateuch, it was very easy for *Knobel* to fill several pages with expressions from the original Elohistic work, which are neither to be found in the Jehovistic historical narratives, nor in the general commands of a religious and moral character, by simply collecting together all the names of these particular things. But what does such a collection prove? Nothing further than that the contents of the Pentateuch are very varied, and the same things are not repeated throughout. Could we expect to find beams, pillars, coverings, tapestries, and the vessels of the sanctuary, or priests' dresses and sacrificial objects, mentioned in the ten commandments, or among the rights of Israel (Ex. xx.-xxiii.), or in the laws of marriage and chastity and the moral commandments (Lev. xvii.-xx.)? With the exception of the absence of certain expressions and formulas, which are of frequent occurrence in the covenant statutes, the critics are unable to adduce any other ground for excluding the general religious and moral commandments from the legislation of the so-called original work, than the *a priori* axiom, "The Elohist had respect simply to the theocratic law; and such laws as are introduced in Ex. xxi.-xxiii., in connection with moral and civil life, lay altogether outside his plan." These are assertions, not proofs. The use of words in the Pentateuch could only furnish conclusive evidence that it had been composed by various authors, if the assertion were a well founded one, that different expressions are employed for the same thing in different parts of the work. But all that has hitherto been adduced in proof of this amounts to nothing more than a few words, chiefly in the early chapters of Genesis; whilst it is assumed at the same time that Gen. ii. 4 sqq. contains a second account of the creation, whereas it simply gives a description of paradise, and a more minute account of the creation of man than is to be found in Gen. i., the difference in the point of view requiring different words.

To this we have to add the fact, that by no means a small number of sections exhibit, so far as the language is concerned, the peculiarities of the two original documents or main sources, and render a division utterly impossible. The critics have therefore found themselves compelled to assume that there was a third or even a fourth source, to which they refer whatever cannot be assigned to the other two. This assumption is a pure offshoot of critical difficulty, whilst the fact itself is a proof that the Pentateuch is founded upon unity of language, and that the differences which occur here and there arise for the most part from the variety and diversity of the actual contents; whilst in a very few instances they may be attributable to the fact that Moses availed himself. of existing writings in the composition of the book of Genesis, and in the middle books inserted public documents without alteration in his historical account.

The other proofs adduced, for the purpose of supporting the evidence from language, viz. the frequent *repetitions* of the same thing and the actual *discrepancies*, are even weaker still. No doubt the Pentateuch abounds in repetitions. The longest and most important is the description of the tabernacle, where we have, first of all, the command to prepare this sanctuary given in Ex. xxv.– xxxi., with a detailed description of all the different parts, and all the articles of furniture, as well as of the priests' clothing and the consecration of the priests and the altar; and then again, in Ex. xxxv.-xxxix. and Lev. viii., a detailed account of the fulfilment of these instructions in almost the same words. The holy candlestick is mentioned five times (Ex. xxv. 31–40, xxvii. 20, 21, xxx. 7, 8, Lev. xxiv. 1–4, and Num. viii. 1–4); the command not to eat blood occurs as many as eight times (Gen. ix. 4; Lev. iii. 17, vii. 26, 27, xvii. 10–14; Deut. xii. 16, 23, 24, and xv. 23), and on the first three occasions, at all events, in passages belonging to the so-called original work. Now, if these repetitions have not been regarded by any of the critics, with the exception of *J. Popper*, as furnishing proofs of difference of authorship, what right can we have to adduce other repetitions of a similar kind as possessing any such significance ?—But lastly, the critics have involved *themselves* in almost incomprehensible contradictions, through the supposed contradictions in the Pentateuch. Some of them, *e.g. Stähelin* and *Bertheau*, think these discrepancies only apparent, or at least as of such a character that the last editor saw no discrepancies in them, otherwise he would have expunged them. Others, such as *Knobel* and *Hupfeld*, place them in the foreground, as the main proofs of a plurality of authors; whilst *Hupfeld* especially, by a truly inquisitorial process, has made even the smallest differences into irreconcilable contradictions. Yet, for all that, he maintains that the Pentateuch, in its present form, is a work characterized by unity, arranged and carried out according to a definite plan, in which the different portions are so arranged and connected together, " with an intelligent regard to connection and unity or plan," yea, " dovetailed together in so harmonious a way, that they have the deceptive appearance of a united whole " (*Hupfeld, die Quellen der Genes.* p. 196). In working up the different sources, the editor, it is said, " did not hesitate to make systematic corrections of the one to bring it into harmony with the other," as, for example, in the names Abram and Sarai, which he copied from the original document into the Jehovistic portions before Gen. xvii., because " he would not allow of any discrepancy between his sources in these points, and in fact could not have allowed it without a manifest contradiction, and the consequent confusion of his readers" (p. 198). How then does it square with so intelligent a procedure, to assume that there are irreconcilable contradictions in the work ? An editor who worked with so much intelligence and reflection would never have left actual contradictions standing; and modern critics have been able to discover them simply because they judge the biblical writings according to modern notions, and start in their operations from a fundamental opinion which is directly at variance with the revelation of the Bible.

The strength of the opposition to the unity and Mosaic authorship of the Pentateuch arises much less from the peculiarities of form, which the critics have placed in the foreground, than from the offence which they take at the contents of the books of Moses, which are irreconcilable with the naturalism of the modern views of the world. To the leaders of modern criticism, not only is the spuriousness, or post-Mosaic origin of the Pentateuch, an established fact, but the gradual rise of the Mosaic laws in connection with the natural development of the Hebrew people, without any direct or supernatural interposition on the part of God, is also firmly established *a priori* on dogmatical grounds. This is openly expressed by *De Wette* in the three first editions of his Introduction, in which he opens the critical inquiry concerning the Pentateuch with this observation (§ 145): "Many occurrences are opposed to the laws of nature, and presuppose a direct interposition on the part of

God;" and then proceeds to say, that " if to an educated mind it is a *decided* fact that such miracles have never really occurred, the question arises whether, perhaps, they may have *appeared* to do so to the eye-witnesses and persons immediately concerned ; but to this also we must give a negative reply. And *thus* we are brought to the conclusion that the narrative is not contemporaneous, or derived from contemporaneous sources." *Ewald* has expressed his naturalistic views, which acknowledge no supernatural revelation from God, in his " History of the People of Israel," and developed the gradual formation of the Pentateuch from the principles involved in these fundamental views. But just as *De Wette* expressed this candid confession in a much more cautious and disguised manner in the later editions of his Introduction, so have his successors endeavoured more and more to conceal the naturalistic background of their critical operations, and restricted themselves to arguments, the weakness and worthlessness of which they themselves admit in connection with critical questions which do not affect their naturalistic views. So long as biblical criticism is fettered by naturalism, it will never rise to a recognition of the genuineness and internal unity of the Pentateuch. For if the miraculous acts of the living God recorded in it are not true, and did not actually occur, the account of them cannot have come down from eye-witnesses, but can only be myths, which grew up in the popular belief long after the events referred to. And if there is no prophetic foresight of the future produced by the Spirit of God, Moses cannot have foretold the rejection of Israel and their dispersion among the heathen even before their entrance into Canaan, whereas they did not take place till many centuries afterwards.

If, on the other hand, the reality of the supernatural revelations of God, together with miracles and prophecies, be admitted, not only are the contents of the Pentateuch in harmony with its Mosaic authorship, but even its formal arrangement can be understood and scientifically vindicated, provided only we suppose the work to have originated in the following manner. After the exodus of the tribes of Israel from Egypt, and their adoption as the people of Jehovah through the conclusion of the covenant at Sinai, when Moses had been commanded by God to write down the covenant rights (Ex. xxiv. 4, and xxxiv. 27), and then formed the resolution not only to ensure the laws which the Lord had given to the people through his mediation against alteration and distortion, and hand them down to futurity by committing them to writing, but to write down all the great and glorious things that the Lord had done for His people, for the instruction of his own and succeeding generations, and set himself to carry out this resolution; he collected together the traditions of the olden time, which had been handed down in Israel from the days of the patriarchs, partly orally, and partly in writings and records, for the purpose of combining them into a preliminary history of the kingdom of God, which was founded by the conclusion of the covenant at Sinai. Accordingly, in all probability during the stay at Sinai, in the five or six months which were occupied in building the tabernacle, he wrote not only the book of Genesis, but the history of the deliverance of Israel out of Egypt and the march to Sinai (Ex. xix.), to which the decalogue, with the book of the covenant (Ex. xx.–xxiii.), is attached, according to that plan of the kingdom of God which had then been fully revealed, or, in other words, from a theocratic point of view. As he had written the covenant rights in a book by the command of God, as a preliminary to the conclusion of the covenant itself (Ex. xxiv. 4), there can be no doubt whatever that he did not merely publish to the people by word of mouth the very elaborate revelation and directions of God concerning the construction of the tabernacle and the apparatus of worship, which he had received upon the mountain (Ex. xxv.–xxxi.), as well as all the rest of the laws, but either committed them to writing himself directly after he had received them from the Lord, or had them written out by one of his assistants, and collected together for the purpose of forming them eventually into a complete work. We may make the same assumption with reference to the most important events which occurred during the forty years' journey through the desert, so that, on the arrival of the camp in the steppes of Moab, the whole of the historical and legal materials for the three middle books of the Pentateuch were already collected together, and all that remained to be done was to form them into a united whole, and give them a final revision. The collection, arrangement, and final working up of these materials would be accomplished in a very short time, since Moses had, at all events, the priests and *shoterim* by his side.—All this had probably taken place before the last addresses of Moses, which compose the book of Deuteronomy, so that nothing further remained to be done but to write down these addresses, and append them as a fifth book to the four already in existence. With this the writing of "all the words of this book of the law" was finished, so that the whole book of the law could be handed over in a complete state to the priests, to be properly taken care of by them (Deut. xxxi. 24 sqq.).

A copy of the song of Moses was added to this written work, in all probability immediately after it had been deposited by the side of the ark of the covenant; and, after his death, the blessing pronounced upon the tribes before his departure was also committed to writing. Finally, after the conquest of Canaan, possibly on the renewal of the covenant under Joshua, an account of the death of Moses was added to these last two testimonies of the man of God, and adopted along with them, in the form of an appendix, into his book of the law.

END OF VOL. III.